THE EU GENERAL DATA PROTECTION REGULATION (GDPR)

The EU General Data Protection Regulation (GDPR)

A Commentary

Edited by

CHRISTOPHER KUNER
LEE A. BYGRAVE
CHRISTOPHER DOCKSEY

Assistant Editor
LAURA DRECHSLER

OXFORD
UNIVERSITY PRESS

Great Clarendon Street, Oxford, OX2 6DP,
United Kingdom

Oxford University Press is a department of the University of Oxford.
It furthers the University's objective of excellence in research, scholarship,
and education by publishing worldwide. Oxford is a registered trade mark of
Oxford University Press in the UK and in certain other countries

© Oxford University Press 2020

The moral rights of the authors have been asserted

First Edition published in 2020

Impression: 3

All rights reserved. No part of this publication may be reproduced, stored in
a retrieval system, or transmitted, in any form or by any means, without the
prior permission in writing of Oxford University Press, or as expressly permitted
by law, by licence or under terms agreed with the appropriate reprographics
rights organization. Enquiries concerning reproduction outside the scope of the
above should be sent to the Rights Department, Oxford University Press, at the
address above

You must not circulate this work in any other form
and you must impose this same condition on any acquirer

Crown copyright material is reproduced under Class Licence
Number C01P0000148 with the permission of OPSI
and the Queen's Printer for Scotland

Published in the United States of America by Oxford University Press
198 Madison Avenue, New York, NY 10016, United States of America

British Library Cataloguing in Publication Data

Data available

Library of Congress Control Number: 2019942848

ISBN 978-0-19-882649-1

Printed and bound by
CPI Group (UK) Ltd, Croydon, CR0 4YY

Links to third party websites are provided by Oxford in good faith and
for information only. Oxford disclaims any responsibility for the materials
contained in any third party website referenced in this work.

Foreword

It is a truism that the law lags behind technology. The British Statute of Anne enacted in 1710, considered to be the world's first legislation to grant copyright under public law, appeared over 250 years after Gutenberg introduced the movable type printing press. By that reckoning, data protection law has reacted with nimble vigour to the digitalisation of society and the economy. The EU's General Data Protection Regulation ('GDPR') must be viewed in the context of the worldwide trend to adopt similar laws, a trend inspired by the EU itself. On the adoption of the GDPR's predecessor, Directive 95/46/EC, around 30 countries had similar rules, and the bulk of these were within Western Europe; now there are almost 130, across all continents.

The EU remains, however, wholly unique in one sense—it is the only jurisdiction whose own constitution, in the form of Article 8 of the Charter of Fundamental Rights and Article 16 of the Treaty on the Functioning of the European Union, obliges the adoption of comprehensive rules for the protection of personal data. The GDPR is indeed comprehensive: its material and territorial scope matches the depth and breadth of digital technologies' encroachment (welcome or not) into our lives; updated or brand new rights and obligations with regards to profiling, automated decision-making, portability, erasure and other areas take aim at standard practices which potentially harm the individual; and the powers of independent supervisory authorities are expanded at the same time as the requirements for them to cooperate and apply the law consistently are set down in remarkable detail.

This towering new Commentary unfolds, in thoughtful and erudite detail, the context, significance and interplay of each of the GDPR's 173 recitals and 99 articles. It will become indispensable to anyone expected to engage actively with the Regulation and its counterparts beyond the EU.

By implication the Commentary also illustrates the massive scale of the challenge facing all of us in the data protection and human rights community. The GDPR is an extraordinary legislative achievement, and yet it is only one piece of a much bigger puzzle. Enforcement will be contested and loopholes explored. On the one hand, it has already had an enormous impact on the perception of privacy by individuals, companies and governments, and its influence—combined with the Charter—can be seen in the increasingly positive and expert jurisprudence of the CJEU and national courts. On the other hand, its limits will inevitably be challenged as machine learning, ubiquitous and covert surveillance, genetic engineering and other techniques expand against a backdrop of ever starker global inequalities. These technologies will have a profound impact—one that is already being felt—on the dignity not only of individuals but also of groups and whole societies. That is why I expect the next generation will see the GDPR as a staging post, important but incomplete, in humanity's endless grappling with what is possible, what is lawful and what is right—in other words, with the legal and ethical challenges that we are confronted with in our digitised world.

Nonetheless, the GDPR is an enormous achievement, it is with us now, and it will provide the legal bedrock for protecting privacy and personal data in many years to come.

This Commentary makes a valuable contribution to promoting understanding of this extraordinary piece of legislation and to implementing the legal, ethical and social values of the European Union.

GIOVANNI BUTTARELLI
European Data Protection Supervisor
Brussels, February 2019

Editors' Preface

The General Data Protection Regulation ('GDPR') adopted by the European Union ('EU') in May 2016 is a landmark in both data protection law and EU law. European legislation on data protection has exercised unparalleled influence around the world, and the GDPR is likely to set the global standard for data protection legislation. The GDPR also reflects a number of momentous changes to EU law that have occurred in recent years, such as the enactment of the Treaty of Lisbon and the elevation of the Charter of Fundamental Rights to primary law.

Preparation of this Commentary has not been easy. Worldwide interest in the GDPR grew into a near frenzy as 25 May 2018 (its date of application) approached. Our contributors, all of whom are in great demand as recognised experts in the field of data protection, understandably had little time for writing their parts of the Commentary until this interest had calmed down somewhat. In addition, data protection law has become an exceptionally fast-paced area of the law, with court judgments, guidelines and opinions of data protection authorities, and scholarly publications being issued at a rate that left us struggling to keep up. As a result, we had to push the delivery date for this Commentary further into the future than we had originally hoped. This has, however, had the advantage of allowing us to take into account legal processes up to 1 August 2019, and thus to cover a large number of important developments that occurred after the GDPR began to be applied, including judgments of the Court of Justice of the EU, guidelines and opinions of the European Data Protection Board, and corrigenda to the text of the GDPR.

The sheer length of the GDPR means that an exhaustive analysis of all the issues it raises would span many volumes. We have thus tried to strike a balance between providing a full exposition of the relevant issues and keeping the book to a manageable length. To this end, we plan to place additional materials and updates online on the Oxford University Press website, and to update this volume in the future. We considered including the full text of the GDPR, including the recitals, in an appendix, but decided not to, as this would have made a long book even longer. The corrected text of the GDPR can be easily found on the Europa web site of the European Union. We can also assure the reader that all the recitals of the GDPR are reproduced together with the various articles to which they relate.

We view the creation of an extensively harmonised, pan-European framework for data protection as one of the GDPR's most important innovations. The book thus focuses on the GDPR as an instrument of EU law and does not cover the many Member State laws that have accompanied its application. However, we do discuss Member State developments on a selective basis, in order to illustrate how the GDPR has been received in national legal systems. Similarly, we do not cover in detail other important instruments of EU data protection law, such as the Law Enforcement Directive, the e-Privacy Directive and the EU Regulation on Data Processing by the EU Institutions, except when this is particularly relevant to understanding the GDPR.

Between us, we three editors have written the commentaries on 21 articles of the GDPR. For the remaining 78 articles, we have been fortunate to assemble an outstanding team of contributors from different Member States and legal systems across Europe and from outside the EU. We hope that this gives our Commentary a breadth of outlook that reflects the pan-European view of data protection that both the EU legislator and the Court of Justice of the EU have taken. We also believe that it was crucial to include contributors from different sectors and with a variety of expertise and outlooks. Thus, we are pleased that our Commentary includes authors from academia, EU institutions, data protection authorities, national governments, law firms and the private sector.

While there is still a lack of precedent and practice for many provisions of the GDPR, we believe that readers will be looking for guidance as to what particular provisions mean and how courts and regulators may interpret them. We have thus encouraged authors to go beyond mere description of the articles assigned to them and to indicate, where appropriate, their opinion as to what the best interpretation of a provision might be. We have also made enormous efforts to review the commentaries carefully for quality and consistency. We hope that this has resulted in a book which is of consistently high quality and provides substantial insight into the many questions raised by the GDPR. Because of the global interest in the GDPR and its international impact, we have also tried to keep in mind the needs of readers outside of Europe.

A project of such immense scope can only succeed as a team effort, and we could never have hoped to finish it without the assistance and contributions of many people.

In the first place, we would like to thank our assistant editor, Laura Drechsler. This book would never have come to fruition without her untiring assistance, particularly in her meticulous review of all the commentaries. She has been a true partner in this project, and we owe her our deep gratitude.

Other contributors have also gone far beyond the call of duty. In particular, Hielke Hijmans and Luca Tosoni have not only written several commentaries but have also provided invaluable input on a number of difficult legal issues related to some of the other ones. They were always available to help when needed, and their expertise was crucial in allowing us to bring this project to a successful conclusion.

We are proud to have assembled such an outstanding group of contributors, and we would like to express our sincere gratitude to all of them for their hard work and for giving us the benefit of their expertise. We may not always have been easy in the demands we made on them, but all have been receptive to our requests and willing to take our comments into account.

We are deeply saddened by the passing away of Giovanni Buttarelli, who kindly wrote the preface to this volume, and who left us just a few months before it was published. He was a visionary, an indefatigable champion for data protection, and a good friend to the nascent GDPR in which he invested so much. We are much poorer for his loss, but his work will live on. Si monumentum requiris, circumspice.

Others also played an important role in the success of this Commentary and deserve our thanks. Joseph Williams performed sterling duty as our language editor. Anna Ciesielska, Rossana Fol, Bastiaan Suurmond, Valda Beizitere and Pilar Cordoba Fernandez provided invaluable research assistance. The Brussels office of Wilson Sonsini Goodrich & Rosati provided both logistical and moral support. Various data protection officials who shall remain anonymous gave of their time to discuss our questions and provided valuable insights.

We also express our sincere gratitude to Oxford University Press, in particular to our editor Alex Flach and his colleagues Clare Jones, Emma Taylor, Natalie Patey, Rachel Mullaly, Gemma Parsons and Ruth Anderson. They have been willing to do everything possible to make the book a success, and were unfailingly patient every time we explained why we had to delay it further because of some new development.

Last but not least, we are very grateful to our families for their patience and understanding in tolerating our obsession with the GDPR, and we apologise for the many hours that this project took us away from them.

We will be happy if this book makes some small contribution to help the GDPR realise its potential as the bedrock of the European Union's system of data protection, and to promote understanding of it around the world.

CHRISTOPHER KUNER   LEE A. BYGRAVE   CHRISTOPHER DOCKSEY
Brussels and Oslo, October 2019

Is a Éléonore Kessy, we are very grateful to our families for their patience and understanding in tolerating our obsession with the COLPR, and we apologise for the many hours that this project took us away from them.

We will be happy if this book makes even a small contribution to help the COLPR centre its potential as the bedrock of the European Union's system of data protection, and to promote modern thinking on it around the world.

CHRISTOPHER KUNER, LEE A. BYGRAVE, CHRISTOPHER DOCKSEY
Brussels and Oslo, October 2019

Contents

Table of Cases — xvii
Table of Instruments — xxxix
List of Abbreviations — lxxxvii
List of Contributors — lxxxix

Background and Evolution of the EU General Data Protection Regulation (GDPR) (Christopher Kuner, Lee A. Bygrave and Christopher Docksey) — 1

Chapter I: General Provisions (Articles 1–4) — 48
Article 1 **Subject-matter and objectives** (Hielke Hijmans) — 48
Article 2 **Material scope** (Herke Kranenborg) — 60
Article 3 **Territorial scope** (Dan Jerker B. Svantesson) — 74
Article 4 **Definitions** (Luca Tosoni and Lee A. Bygrave) — 100
Article 4(1) **Personal data** (Lee A. Bygrave and Luca Tosoni) — 103
Article 4(2) **Processing** (Luca Tosoni and Lee A. Bygrave) — 116
Article 4(3) **Restriction of processing** (Luca Tosoni) — 123
Article 4(4) **Profiling** (Lee A. Bygrave) — 127
Article 4(5) **Pseudonymisation** (Luca Tosoni) — 132
Article 4(6) **Filing system** (Luca Tosoni) — 138
Article 4(7) **Controller** (Lee A. Bygrave and Luca Tosoni) — 145
Article 4(8) **Processor** (Lee A. Bygrave and Luca Tosoni) — 157
Article 4(9) **Recipient** (Luca Tosoni) — 163
Article 4(10) **Third party** (Luca Tosoni) — 170
Article 4(11) **Consent** (Lee A. Bygrave and Luca Tosoni) — 174
Article 4(12) **Personal data breach** (Luca Tosoni) — 188
Article 4(13) **Genetic data** (Lee A. Bygrave and Luca Tosoni) — 196
Article 4(14) **Biometric data** (Lee A. Bygrave and Luca Tosoni) — 207
Article 4(15) **Data concerning health** (Lee A. Bygrave and Luca Tosoni) — 217
Article 4(16) **Main establishment** (Luca Tosoni) — 225
Article 4(17) **Representative** (Luca Tosoni) — 238
Article 4(18) **Enterprise** (Lee A. Bygrave and Luca Tosoni) — 246
Article 4(19) **Group of undertakings** (Luca Tosoni) — 253
Article 4(20) **Binding corporate rules** (Luca Tosoni) — 257
Article 4(21) **Supervisory authority** (Lee A. Bygrave) — 265
Article 4(22) **Supervisory authority concerned** (Luca Tosoni) — 272
Article 4(23) **Cross-border processing** (Luca Tosoni) — 279

Article 4(24) **Relevant and reasoned objection** (Luca Tosoni) 288
Article 4(25) **Information society service** (Luca Tosoni) 292
Article 4(26) **International organisation** (Lee A. Bygrave and Luca Tosoni) 303

Chapter II: Principles (Articles 5–11) 309

Article 5 **Principles relating to processing of personal data** (Cécile de Terwangne) 309
Article 6 **Lawfulness of processing** (Waltraut Kotschy) 321
Article 7 **Conditions for consent** (Eleni Kosta) 345
Article 8 **Conditions applicable to child's consent in relation to information society services** (Eleni Kosta) 355
Article 9 **Processing of special categories of personal data** (Ludmila Georgieva and Christopher Kuner) 365
Article 10 **Processing of personal data relating to criminal convictions and offences** (Ludmila Georgieva) 385
Article 11 **Processing which does not require identification** (Ludmila Georgieva) 391

Chapter III: Rights of the Data Subject (Articles 12–23) 398

Section 1 Transparency and modalities
Article 12 **Transparent information, communication and modalities for the exercise of the rights of the data subject** (Radim Polčák) 398

Section 2 Information and access to personal data
Article 13 **Information to be provided where personal data are collected from the data subject** (Gabriela Zanfir-Fortuna) 413
Article 14 **Information to be provided where personal data have not been obtained from the data subject** (Gabriela Zanfir-Fortuna) 434
Article 15 **Right of access by the data subject** (Gabriela Zanfir-Fortuna) 449

Section 3 Rectification and erasure
Article 16 **Right to rectification** (Cécile de Terwangne) 469
Article 17 **Right to erasure ('right to be forgotten')** (Herke Kranenborg) 475
Article 18 **Right to restriction of processing** (Gloria González Fuster) 485
Article 19 **Notification obligation regarding rectification or erasure of personal data or restriction of processing** (Gloria González Fuster) 492
Article 20 **Right to data portability** (Orla Lynskey) 497

Section 4 Right to object and automated individual decision-making
Article 21 **Right to object** (Gabriela Zanfir-Fortuna) 508
Article 22 **Automated individual decision-making, including profiling** (Lee A. Bygrave) 522

Section 5 Restrictions
Article 23 **Restrictions** (Dominique Moore) 543

Chapter IV: Controller and Processor (Articles 24–43) ... 555

Section 1 General obligations
Article 24 Responsibility of the controller (Christopher Docksey) ... 555
Article 25 Data protection by design and by default (Lee A. Bygrave) ... 571
Article 26 Joint controllers (Christopher Millard and Dimitra Kamarinou) ... 582
Article 27 Representatives of controllers or processors not established in the Union (Christopher Millard and Dimitra Kamarinou) ... 589
Article 28 Processor (Christopher Millard and Dimitra Kamarinou) ... 599
Article 29 Processing under the authority of the controller or processor (Christopher Millard and Dimitra Kamarinou) ... 612
Article 30 Records of processing activities (Waltraut Kotschy) ... 616
Article 31 Cooperation with the supervisory authority (Waltraut Kotschy) ... 625

Section 2 Security of personal data
Article 32 Security of processing (Cédric Burton) ... 630
Article 33 Notification of a personal data breach to the supervisory authority (Cédric Burton) ... 640
Article 34 Communication of a personal data breach to the data subject (Cédric Burton) ... 654

Section 3 Data protection impact assessment and prior consultation
Article 35 Data protection impact assessment (Eleni Kosta) ... 665
Article 36 Prior consultation (Cecilia Alvarez Rigaudias and Alessandro Spina) ... 680

Section 4 Data protection officer
Article 37 Designation of the data protection officer (Cecilia Alvarez Rigaudias and Alessandro Spina) ... 688
Article 38 Position of the data protection officer (Cecilia Alvarez Rigaudias and Alessandro Spina) ... 700
Article 39 Tasks of the data protection officer (Cecilia Alvarez Rigaudias and Alessandro Spina) ... 709

Section 5 Codes of conduct and certification
Article 40 Codes of conduct (Irene Kamara) ... 716
Article 41 Monitoring of approved codes of conduct (Irene Kamara) ... 725
Article 42 Certification (Ronald Leenes) ... 732
Article 43 Certification bodies (Ronald Leenes) ... 744

Chapter V: Transfers of Personal Data to Third Countries or International Organisations (Articles 44–50) ... 755
Article 44 General principle for transfers (Christopher Kuner) ... 755
Article 45 Transfers on the basis of an adequacy decision (Christopher Kuner) ... 771
Article 46 Transfers subject to appropriate safeguards (Christopher Kuner) ... 797

Article 47 Binding corporate rules (Christopher Kuner) — 813
Article 48 Transfers or disclosures not authorised by Union law (Christopher Kuner) — 825
Article 49 Derogations for specific situations (Christopher Kuner) — 841
Article 50 International cooperation for the protection of personal data (Christopher Kuner) — 857

Chapter VI: Independent Supervisory Authorities (Articles 51–59) — 863

Section 1 Independent status
Article 51 Supervisory authority (Hielke Hijmans) — 863
Article 52 Independence (Thomas Zerdick) — 873
Article 53 General conditions for the members of the supervisory authority (Hielke Hijmans) — 884
Article 54 Rules on the establishment of the supervisory authority (Hielke Hijmans) — 893

Section 2 Competence, tasks and powers
Article 55 Competence (Hielke Hijmans) — 902
Article 56 Competence of the lead supervisory authority (Hielke Hijmans) — 913
Article 57 Tasks (Hielke Hijmans) — 927
Article 58 Powers (Ludmila Georgieva and Matthias Schmidl) — 939
Article 59 Activity reports (Hielke Hijmans) — 949

Chapter VII: Cooperation and Consistency (Articles 60–76) — 953

Section 1 Cooperation
Article 60 Cooperation between the lead supervisory authority and the other supervisory authorities concerned (Luca Tosoni) — 953
Article 61 Mutual assistance (Peter Blume) — 973
Article 62 Joint operations of supervisory authorities (Peter Blume) — 986

Section 2 Consistency
Article 63 Consistency mechanism (Patrick Van Eecke and Anrijs Šimkus) — 995
Article 64 Opinion of the Board (Patrick Van Eecke and Anrijs Šimkus) — 1005
Article 65 Dispute resolution by the Board (Hielke Hijmans) — 1014
Article 66 Urgency procedure (Ludmila Georgieva) — 1027
Article 67 Exchange of information (Patrick Van Eecke and Anrijs Šimkus) — 1032

Section 3 European Data Protection Board
Article 68 European Data Protection Board (Christopher Docksey) — 1041
Article 69 Independence (Christopher Docksey) — 1055
Article 70 Tasks of the Board (Christopher Docksey) — 1069
Article 71 Reports (Christopher Docksey) — 1085
Article 72 Procedure (Christopher Docksey) — 1090

Article 73 Chair (Christopher Docksey) ... 1095
Article 74 Tasks of the Chair (Christopher Docksey) ... 1098
Article 75 Secretariat (Christopher Docksey) ... 1102
Article 76 Confidentiality (Christopher Docksey) ... 1111

Chapter VIII: Remedies, Liability and Penalties (Articles 77–84) ... 1117
Article 77 **Right to lodge a complaint with a supervisory authority** (Waltraut Kotschy) ... 1117
Article 78 **Right to an effective judicial remedy against a supervisory authority** (Waltraut Kotschy) ... 1125
Article 79 **Right to an effective judicial remedy against a controller or processor** (Waltraut Kotschy) ... 1133
Article 80 **Representation of data subjects** (Gloria González Fuster) ... 1142
Article 81 **Suspension of proceedings** (Waltraut Kotschy) ... 1153
Article 82 **Right to compensation and liability** (Gabriela Zanfir-Fortuna) ... 1160
Article 83 **General conditions for imposing administrative fines** (Waltraut Kotschy) ... 1180
Article 84 **Penalties** (Orla Lynskey) ... 1194

Chapter IX: Provisions Relating to Specific Processing Situations (Articles 85–91) ... 1202
Article 85 **Processing and freedom of expression and information** (Herke Kranenborg) ... 1202
Article 86 **Processing and public access to official documents** (Herke Kranenborg) ... 1213
Article 87 **Processing of the national identification number** (Patrick Van Eecke and Anrijs Šimkus) ... 1223
Article 88 **Processing in the context of employment** (Patrick Van Eecke and Anrijs Šimkus) ... 1229
Article 89 **Safeguards and derogations relating to processing for archiving purposes in the public interest, scientific or historical research purposes or statistical purposes** (Christian Wiese Svanberg) ... 1240
Article 90 **Obligations of secrecy** (Christian Wiese Svanberg) ... 1252
Article 91 **Existing data protection rules of churches and religious associations** (Luca Tosoni) ... 1257

Chapter X: Delegated Acts and Implementing Acts (Articles 92–93) ... 1268
Article 92 **Exercise of the delegation** (Luca Tosoni) ... 1268
Article 93 **Committee procedure** (Luca Tosoni) ... 1278

Chapter XI: Final Provisions (Articles 94–99) ... 1291
Article 94 **Repeal of Directive 95/46/EC** (Dominique Moore) ... 1291
Article 95 **Relationship with Directive 2002/58/EC** (Piedade Costa de Oliveira) ... 1294

Article 96 Relationship with previously concluded Agreements
  (Dominique Moore) 1302
Article 97 Commission reports (Thomas Zerdick) 1308
Article 98 Review of other Union legal acts on data protection
  (Luca Tosoni) 1312
Article 99 Entry into force and application (Dominique Moore) 1320

Index 1323

Table of Cases

For the benefit of digital users, table entries that span two pages (e.g., 52–3) may, on occasion, appear on only one of those pages.

EUROPEAN UNION
Numerical

Case C-505/19, *Bundesrepublik Deutschland* (pending) 764n56
Case C-272/19, *V.Q. v Land Hessen* (pending) 149n16, 458n40
Case C-61/19, *Orange Romania SA v Autoritatea Națională de Supraveghere a Prelucrării
    Datelor cu Caracter Personal* (pending) 180
Case C-708/18, *TK v Asociația de Proprietari bloc M5A Scara-A* (pending)..................... 313
Case C-687/18, *SY v Associated Newspapers Ltd* (pending) 1139, 1163n7, 1207–8
Case C-621/18, *Andy Wightman and Others v Secretary of State for Exiting the European Union*,
    judgment of 10 December 2018 (Full Court) (ECLI:EU:C:2018:999) 83–84
Case C-390/18, Opinion of Advocate General Szpunar in *AIRBNB Ireland*, delivered on
    30 April 2019 (ECLI:EU:C:2019:336) 295n8, 295n10, 297n21, 298,
                                                                     298n25, 299–300n38
Case C-311/18, *Data Protection Commissioner v Facebook Ireland Limited,
    Maximillian Schrems* (pending) 791, 802, 1280n6
Case C-142/18, *Skype Communications Sàrl v Institut belge des services postaux et
    des télécommunications (IBPT)*, judgment of 5 June 2019 (ECLI:EU:C:2019:460)......... 298n29
Case C-673/17, *Planet49 GmbH v Bundesverband der Verbraucherzentralen und
    Verbraucherverbände – Verbraucherzentrale Bundesverband e.V.* (pending) 349
Case C-673/17, Opinion of Advocate General Szpunar in *Planet49 GmbH v Bundesverband
    der Verbraucherzentralen und Verbraucherverbände – Verbraucherzentrale Bundesverband e.V.*,
    delivered on 21 March 2019 (ECLI:EU:C:2019:246) 10, 177n10, 177–78n12–13, 180n24,
                            180n25, 181n35, 181n37, 182–83, 184, 184–85n56, 232–33n32, 242–43n25
Case C-623/17, *Privacy International v Secretary of State for Foreign and Commonwealth
    Affairs and Others* (pending) 69n31
Case T-612/17, *Google v Commission* (pending) 1186n21
Case C-507/17, *Google Inc. v Commission nationale de l'informatique et des libertés
    (CNIL)* (pending) 478n2
Case C-507/17, Opinion of Advocate General Szpunar in *Google Inc. v Commission nationale de
    l'informatique et des libertés (CNIL)*, delivered on 10 January 2019 (ECLI:EU:C:2019:15) 81,
                                                                                    478n2, 481
Case T-458/17, *Harry Shindler and Others v Council of the European Union*, GC,
    judgment 26 November 2018 (ECLI:EU:T:2018:838)..................... 1129, 1129–30n18
Case C-378/17, *The Minister for Justice and Equality and The Commissioner of the Garda Síochána
    v Workplace Relations Commission*, judgment of 4 December 2018 (Grand Chamber)
    (ECLI:EU:C:2018:979)... 1175n92
Case C-345/17, *Proceedings brought by Sergejs Buivids*, judgment of 14 February 2019
    (ECLI:EU:C:2019:122)................. 109–10n29, 120n21, 120n25, 1205, 1207, 1208, 1209
Case C-193/17, Opinion of Advocate General Bobek in *Cresco Investigation GmbH v
    Markus Achatzi*, delivered on 25 July 2018 (ECLI:EU:C:2018:614)..................... 1263
Joined Cases C-183/17 P and C-184/17 P, *International Management Group v
    European Commission*, judgment of 31 January 2019 (ECLI:EU:C:2019:78) 306n21, 307n26
Case C-136/17, *G.C., A.F., B.H., E.D. v Commission nationale de l'informatique
    et des libertés (CNIL)* (pending) 377n62, 478n2
Case C-136/17, Opinion of Advocate General Szpunar in *G.C., A.F., B.H., E.D. v
    Commission nationale de l'informatique et des libertés (CNIL)*, delivered on
    10 January 2019 (ECLI:EU:C:2019:14)...................................... 478n2, 1208n25
Joined Cases C-61/17, C-62/17 and C-72/17, *Miriam Bichat and Others v APSB - Aviation Passage
    Service Berlin GmbH & Co. KG*, judgment of 7 August 2018 (ECLI:EU:C:2018:653) 256n11

Case C-40/17, *Fashion ID GmbH & Co.KG v Verbraucherzentrale NRW e.V.*, judgment
of 29 July 2019 (ECLI:EU:C:2019:629) 119, 120n26, 148n7, 148n9, 150n27, 150n28,
151–52n38–39, 152n43, 152–53n51, 153, 154, 183–84n52,
328, 337–38, 424, 426–27n78, 566n58, 585–86, 1151
Case C-40/17, Opinion of Advocate General Bobek in *Fashion ID GmbH & Co. KG v
Verbraucherzentrale NRW e.V.*, delivered on 19 December 2018 (ECLI:EU:C:2018:1039) 108n16,
118–19n6–7, 120n26–27, 136n20, 140n7, 142n15, 142n18, 148n7, 153
Case C-25/17, *Jehovan todistajat — uskonnollinen yhdyskunta*, judgment of
10 July 2018 (Grand Chamber) (ECLI:EU:C:2018:551) 65–66n7, 68–69, 140n5, 141n12,
142n13, 142n14, 142–43n19–22, 143n23–25, 148n11, 148, 149n14,
150n27–29, 151–52n38, 585, 1259n5, 1261, 1262, 1263, 1265n52
Case C-25/17, Opinion of Advocate General Mengozzi in *Jehovan todistajat —
uskonnollinen yhdyskunta*, delivered on 1 February 2018 (ECLI:EU:C:2018:57) 1258–59, 1263
Case T-738/16, *La Quadrature du Net and Others v Commission* (pending) 1280n6
Case T-670/16, *Digital Rights Ireland Ltd v European Commission*, GC, order of
22 November 2017 (ECLI:EU:T:2017:838)..111n40, 791n145
Joined Cases C-596/16 and C-597/16, *Enzo Di Puma v Commissione Nazionale per le Società
e la Borsa (Consob) and Commissione Nazionale per le Società e la Borsa (Consob) v
Antonio Zecca*, judgment of 20 March 2018 (Grand Chamber) (ECLI:EU:C:2018:192) 1200
Case C-537/16, *Garlsson Real Estate SA and Others v Commissione Nazionale per le Società e la Borsa
(Consob)*, judgment of 20 March 2018 (Grand Chamber) (ECLI:EU:C:2018:193) 1200
Case C-528/16, Opinion of Advocate General Bobek in *Confédération paysanne and Others v
Premier ministre and Ministre de l'agriculture, de l'agroalimentaire et de la forêt*, delivered
on 18 January 2018 (ECLI:EU:C:2018:20) 1314–16
Case C-498/16, *Maximilian Schrems v Facebook Ireland Limited*, judgment of
25 January 2018 (ECLI:EU:C:2018:37) 1145
Case C-498/16, Opinion of Advocate General Bobek in *Maximilian Schrems v Facebook
Ireland Limited*, delivered on 14 November 2017 (ECLI:EU:C:2017:863)................. 1143
Case C-434/16, *Peter Nowak v Data Protection Commissioner*, judgment of 20 December 2017
(ECLI:EU:C:2017:994)............ 9–10, 109, 109–10n30, 110, 142n14, 143, 458, 473, 513–14
Case C-434/16, Opinion of Advocate General Kokott in *Peter Nowak v Data Protection
Commissioner*, delivered on 20 July 2017 (ECLI:EU:C:2017:58) 514
Case C-426/16, *Liga van Moskeeën en Islamitische Organisaties Provincie Antwerpen, VZW
and Others v Vlaams Gewest*, judgment of 29 May 2018 (Grand Chamber)
(ECLI:EU:C:2018:335)... 1262
Case C-320/16, *Criminal proceedings against Uber France*, judgment of 10 April 2018
(Grand Chamber) (ECLI:EU:C:2018:221) 299
Case C-265/16, *VCAST Limited v RTI SpA*, judgment of 29 November 2017
(ECLI:EU:C:2017:913)... 300n40
Case C-265/16, Opinion of Advocate General Szpunar in *VCAST Limited v RTI SpA*, delivered
on 7 September 2017 (ECLI:EU:C:2017:649)..................................... 300n40
Case C-255/16, *Criminal proceedings against Bent Falbert and Others*, judgment of
20 December 2017 (ECLI:EU:C:2017:983).. 298n30
Case C-210/16, *Unabhängiges Landeszentrum für Datenschutz Schleswig-Holstein v
Wirtschaftsakademie Schleswig-Holstein GmbH*, judgment of 5 June 2018
(Grand Chamber) (ECLI:EU:C:2018:388) 241n13, 261n27, 275n11, 282n15,
566n58, 585, 592–93, 958, 959, 979, 1021
Case C-210/16, Opinion of Advocate General Bot in *Unabhängiges Landeszentrum für
Datenschutz Schleswig-Holstein v Wirtschaftsakademie Schleswig-Holstein GmbH*, delivered
on 24 October 2017 (ECLI:EU:C:2017:796)....... 9–10, 76n2, 78n9, 80, 84, 85, 148n9, 150n28,
152–53, 154n61, 227n2, 229n13, 232n29, 959n25, 1021
Case C-207/16, *Ministerio Fiscal*, judgment of 2 October 2018 (Grand Chamber)
(ECLI:EU:C:2018:788)..65–66n6, 549–50
Case C-183/16 P, *Tilly-Sabco SAS v European Commission*, judgment of
20 September 2017 (ECLI:EU:C:2017:704) 1280n5, 1280n8–9
Case C-74/16, *Congregación de Escuelas Pías Provincia Betania v Ayuntamiento de Getafe*,
judgment of 27 June 2017 (Grand Chamber) (ECLI:EU:C:2017:496).... 250n12, 255n6, 262–63n38

Table of Cases xix

Case C-73/16, *Peter Puškár v Finančné riaditeľstvo Slovenskej republiky and Kriminálny úrad finančnej správy*, judgment of 27 September 2017 (ECLI:EU:C:2017:725) ... 65–66, 120n24, 1063–64, 1136, 1137–38, 1184–85n14

Case C-73/16, Opinion of Advocate General Kokott in *Peter Puškár v Finančné riaditeľstvo Slovenskej republiky and Kriminálny úrad finančnej správy*, delivered on 30 March 2017 (ECLI:EU:C:2017:253) 65–66n6

Case T-758/15, *EDF Toruń SA v European Chemicals Agency*, GC, judgment of 18 July 2017 (ECLI:EU:T:2017:519) 251–52n18

Case C-617/15, *Hummel Holding A/S v Nike Inc. and Nike Retail B.V.*, judgment of 18 May 2017 (ECLI:EU:C:2017:390) 230n18, 250n9, 255n3, 277n19

Case C-617/15, Opinion of Advocate General Tanchev in *Hummel Holding A/S v Nike Inc. and Nike Retail B.V.*, delivered on 12 January 2017 (ECLI:EU:C:2017:13) 230n19

Case T-540/15, *Emilio De Capitani v European Parliament*, GC, judgment of 22 March 2018 (ECLI:EU:T:2018:167) 1113n5

Case C-516/15 P, *Akzo Nobel NV and Others v European Commission*, judgment of 27 April 2017 (ECLI:EU:C:2017:314) 250n10, 255n4

Case C-434/15, *Asociación Profesional Elite Taxi v Uber Systems Spain, SL*, judgment of 20 December 2017 (Grand Chamber) (ECLI:EU:C:2017:981) 299, 299n32, 299n34

Case C-434/15, Opinion of Advocate General Szpunar in *Asociación Profesional Elite Taxi v Uber Systems Spain, SL*, delivered on 11 May 2017 (ECLI:EU:C:2017:364) 299, 299n32, 299n34

Case C-429/15, *Evelyn Danqua v Minister for Justice and Equality and Others*, judgment of 20 October 2016 (ECLI:EU:C:2016:789) 1138n20

Case C-424/15, *Xabier Ormaetxea Garai and Bernardo Lorenzo Almendros v Administración del Estado*, judgment of 19 October 2016 (ECLI:EU:C:2016:780) 885n1, 887, 891, 1058–59

Case C-424/15, Opinion of Advocate General Bot in *Xabier Ormaetxea Garai and Bernardo Lorenzo Almendros v Administración del Estado*, delivered on 30 June 2016 (ECLI:EU:C:2016:503) 1058–59

Case C-413/15, Opinion of Advocate General Sharpston in *Elaine Farrell v Alan Whitty and Others*, delivered on 22 June 2017 (ECLI:EU:C:2017:492) 1162–63

Case C-398/15, *Camera di Commercio, Industria, Artigianato e Agricoltura di Lecce v Salvatore Manni*, judgment of 9 March 2017 (ECLI:EU:C:2017:197) 478, 482–83, 494, 514–15

Case C-398/15, Opinion of Advocate General Bot in *Camera di Commercio, Industria, Artigianato e Agricoltura di Lecce v Salvatore Manni*, delivered on 8 September 2016 (ECLI:EU:C:2016:652) 9–10, 120n23

Case C-339/15, *Criminal proceedings against Luc Vanderborght*, judgment of 4 May 2017 (ECLI:EU:C:2017:335) 298n30

Case C-337/15 P, *European Ombudsman v Claire Staelen*, judgment of 4 April 2017 (Grand Chamber) (ECLI:EU:C:2017:256) 1121n19, 1123

Case C-327/15, *TDC A/S v Teleklagenævnet and Erhvervs- og Vækstministeriet*, judgment of 21 December 2016 (ECLI:EU:C:2016:974) 1138n20

Joined Cases C-203/15 and C-698/15, *Tele2 Sverige AB v Post-och telestyrelsen and Secretary of State for Home Department v Tom Watson and Others*, judgment of 21 December 2016 (Grand Chamber) (ECLI:EU:C:2016:970) 53n13, 65–66, 69, 313, 546n3, 546n5, 548–49, 550, 552, 791, 878n25, 1254, 1296–97, 1306n13

Case C-192/15, *T. D. Rease, P. Wullems v College bescherming persoonsgegevens*, order of 9 December 2015 (ECLI:EU:C:2015:861) 936

Case C-191/15, *Verein für Konsumenteninformation v Amazon EU Sàrl*, judgment of 28 July 2016 (ECLI:EU:C:2016:612) 79, 229n13, 241n12, 261n27, 275n11, 275n12, 282n15, 283n20, 592–93, 905n11, 906, 1021n21

Case C-191/15, Opinion of Advocate General Saugmandsgaard Øe in *Verein für Konsumenteninformation v Amazon EU Sàrl*, delivered on 2 June 2016 (ECLI:EU:C:2016:388) 80, 229n13, 241n12, 1021n21

Case C-134/15, Opinion of Advocate General Bobek in *Lidl GmbH & Co. KG v Freistaat Sachsen*, delivered on 16 March 2016 (EU:C:2016:169) 1314–15n18

Opinion 2/15, Opinion of 16 May 2017 (Full Court) (ECLI:EU:C:2017:376) 1306n15

Opinion 1/15, Opinion of 26 July 2017 (Grand Chamber) (ECLI:EU:C:2017:592) 52, 372, 380–81n88, 423–24, 532–33n38, 548, 553n33, 757–58n5, 759n16, 761, 763, 777, 779, 782–84, 829, 834–35, 878n26, 1061n25, 1304–5n10, 1305n12

Opinion 1/15, Opinion of Advocate General Mengozzi in *Opinion 1/15*, delivered on
  8 September 2016 (ECLI:EU:C:2016:656) 782–83, 791
Case C-582/14, *Patrick Breyer v Bundesrepublik Deutschland*, judgment of 26 October 2016
  (ECLI:EU:C:2016:779)....... 53n8, 109–10n31, 110–11, 328n5, 340n81, 394, 395, 494, 868n24
Case C-566/14 P, *Jean-Charles Marchiani v European Parliament*, judgment of 14 June 2016
  (Grand Chamber) (ECLI:EU:C:2016:437) 965n53
Case C-484/14, *Tobias Mc Fadden v Sony Music Entertainment Germany GmbH*, judgment
  of 15 September 2016 (ECLI:EU:C:2016:689) 297n21
Case C-419/14, *WebMindLicenses kft v Nemzeti Adó- és Vámhivatal Kiemelt Adó- és Vám
  Főigazgatóság*, judgment of 17 December 2015 (ECLI:EU:C:2015:832) 111n40, 1297n14
Case C-419/14, Opinion of Advocate General Wathelet in *WebMindLicenses Kft. v Nemzeti
  Adó- és Vámhivatal Kiemelt Adó- és Vám Főigazgatóság*, delivered on 16 September 2015
  (ECLI:EU:C:2015:606) 111n41
Case C-362/14, *Maximillian Schrems v Data Protection Commissioner*, judgment of 6 October 2015
  (Grand Chamber) (ECLI:EU:C:2015:650) 9, 33, 53, 120n22, 266n1, 473, 548–49,
         553n31–32, 562n24, 757–58, 760, 761, 763, 775–76, 777, 779–82, 784, 785, 786n93,
         788, 790, 791, 800, 809, 815n2, 829, 846n17, 867n14, 867, 875n1, 878n25, 879n33, 896n12,
         907–8, 932, 933n18, 935–36, 945, 978–79, 1025n38, 1062–63, 1063n36, 1065n46, 1066n51,
                1115n15, 1121, 1123, 1129, 1130–31n26, 1137, 1164n18–19, 1265n51, 1280, 1310
Case C-362/14, Opinion of Advocate General Bot in *Maximilian Schrems v Data Protection
  Commissioner*, delivered on 23 September 2015 (ECLI:EU:C:2015:650) 779
Case C-286/14, *European Parliament v European Commission*, judgment of 17 March 2016
  (ECLI:EU:C:2016:183).................................. 1270n7, 1270n9
Case C-230/14, *Weltimmo s.r.o. v Nemzeti Adatvédelmi és Információszabadság Hatóság*, judgment
  of 1 October 2015 (ECLI:EU:C:2015:639) 80–81, 120n14, 240, 241, 242, 261n26–27,
         275n10, 282n14, 282–83n15–16, 282–83n18, 283n21, 283n23, 592–93, 905–6,
         906n15, 906n19, 907, 908, 943n3, 945, 946n25, 957n10, 958–59, 978, 1063n38, 1122–23
Case C-230/14, Opinion of Advocate General Cruz Villalón in *Weltimmo s.r.o. v Nemzeti
  Adatvédelmi és Információszabadság Hatóság*, delivered on 25 June 2015
  (ECLI:EU:C:2015:426) 84, 85, 229n12–13, 235n42, 903–4n3
Case C-201/14, *Smaranda Bara and Others v Casa Națională de Asigurări de Sănătate and Others*,
  judgment of 1 October 2015 (ECLI:EU:C:2015:638) 109–10n26, 313, 422–23, 442, 447, 548
Case C-185/14, *'EasyPay' AD and 'Finance Engineering' AD v Ministerski savet na
  Republika Bulgaria and Natsionalen osiguritelen institut*, judgment of
  22 October 2015 (ECLI:EU:C:2015:716) 250n11, 255n5
Case C-88/14, *European Commission v European Parliament and Council of the European Union*,
  judgment of 16 July 2015 (Grand Chamber) (ECLI:EU:C:2015:499) 1270n7, 1280n5
Case C-615/13 P, *ClientEarth and Pesticide Action Network Europe (PAN Europe) v European
  Food Safety Authority*, judgment of 16 July 2015 (ECLI:EU:C:2015:489) 1220
Case C-583/13 P, *Deutsche Bahn AG and Others v European Commission*, judgment of 18 June 2015
  (ECLI:EU:C:2015:404).................................. 1187
Case T-483/13, *Athanassios Oikonomopoulos v European Commission*, GC, judgment of
  20 July 2016 (ECLI:EU:T:2016:421).................................. 691n12, 712
Case T-392/13, *Leone La Ferla SpA v Commission and European Chemicals Agency*, GC,
  judgment of 15 September 2016 (ECLI:EU:T:2016:478).................................. 251n18
Case T-343/13, *CN v European Parliament*, GC, judgment of 3 December 2015
  (ECLI:EU:T:2015:926).................................. 1171
Case C-291/13, *Sotiris Papasavvas v O Fileleftheros Dimosia Etaireia Ltd and Others*, judgment
  of 11 September 2014 (ECLI:EU:C:2014:2209) 296–97n17, 297n22
Case C-212/13, *František Ryneš v Úřad pro ochranu osobních údajů*, judgment of
  11 December 2014 (ECLI:EU:C:2014:2428) 68, 109–10n29, 120n21, 149n17, 442–43, 1265n51
Case C-201/13, *Johan Deckmyn and Vrijheidsfonds VZW v Helena Vandersteen and Others*,
  judgment of 3 September 2014 (Grand Chamber) (ECLI:EU:C:2014:2132).......... 242–43n25
Case C-140/13, *Annett Altmann and Others v Bundesanstalt für Finanzdienstleistungsaufsicht*,
  judgment of 12 November 2014 (ECLI:EU:C:2014:2362) 896n13, 899n27
Case T-115/13, *Gert-Jan Dennekamp v European Parliament*, GC, judgment of 15 July 2015
  (ECLI:EU:T:2015:497).................................. 452n5, 1220
Case C-110/13, *HaTeFo GmbH v Finanzamt Haldensleben*, judgment of 27 February 2014
  (ECLI:EU:C:2014:114).................................. 251n19

Table of Cases

Case C-67/13 P, *Groupement des cartes bancaires (CB) v European Commission*, judgment
of 11 September 2014 (ECLI:EU:C:2014:2204) 1185n16, 1187
Case C-65/13, *European Parliament v European Commission*, judgment of 15 October 2014
(ECLI:EU:C:2014:2289) 1280n5
Case C-486/12, *X*, judgment of 12 December 2013 (ECLI:EU:C:2013:836) 404, 458
Case C-473/12, *Institut professionnel des agents immobiliers (IPI) v Geoffrey Englebert and
Others*, judgment of 7 November 2013 (ECLI:EU:C:2013:715) 423, 441–42
Joined Cases C-446/12 to C-449/12, *W. P. Willems and Others v Burgemeester van Nuth and
Others*, judgment of 16 April 2015 (ECLI:EU:C:2015:238) 211n15
Case C-427/12, *European Commission v European Parliament and Council of the European Union*,
judgment of 18 March 2014 (Grand Chamber) (ECLI:EU:C:2014:170) 1270n7, 1280n5
Case C-342-12, *Worten — Equipamentos para o Lar SA v Autoridade para as Condições de
Trabalho (ACT)*, judgment of 30 May 2013 (ECLI:EU:C:2013:355) 1232
Joined Cases C-293/12 and C-594/12, *Digital Rights Ireland Ltd v Minister for Communications,
Marine and Natural Resources and Others and Kärntner Landesregierung, Michael Seitlinger,
Christof Tschohl and Others*, judgment of 8 April 2014 (Grand Chamber)
(ECLI:EU:C:2014:238) 9, 53n13, 58n30, 109–10n31, 120n20, 313, 548–49, 550,
553n29–30, 575n7, 791, 846n17, 878n25, 907, 1121, 1144–45, 1254, 1296
Case C-291/12, *Michael Schwarz v Stadt Bochum*, judgment of 17 October 2013
(ECLI:EU:C:2013:670) 109–10n28, 120n19, 211
Case C-291/12, Opinion of Advocate General Mengozzi in *Michael Schwarz v Stadt Bochum*,
delivered on 13 June 2013 (ECLI:EU:C:2013:401) 369–70n10, 372
Case C-288/12, *European Commission v Hungary*, judgment of 8 April 2014 (Grand Chamber)
(ECLI:EU:C:2014:237) 35–36, 268–69n11, 867n12, 878, 879n29, 879n31,
880–81n39–40, 887, 890–91, 896n12, 932n9, 1058, 1121n16, 1122n28, 1254–55n9
Case C-288/12, Opinion of Advocate General Wathelet in *European Commission v Hungary*,
delivered on 10 December 2013 (ECLI:EU:C:2013:816) 891n25
Case C-279/12, *Fish Legal, Emily Shirley v Information Commissioner, United Utilities Water plc,
Yorkshire Water Services Ltd, Southern Water Services Ltd*, judgment of 19 December 2013
(ECLI:EU:C:2013:853) 149n16, 250n14, 255n8, 262–63n37, 269n17
Case C-270/12, *United Kingdom of Great Britain and Northern Ireland v European Parliament and
Council of the European Union ('ESMA')*, judgment of 22 January 2014 (Grand Chamber)
(ECLI:EU:C:2014:18) 1044n9, 1045n15–16
Case T-242/12, *Société nationale des chemins de fer français (SNCF) v European Commission*, GC,
judgment of 17 December 2015 (ECLI:EU:T:2015:1003) 965n53
Joined Cases C-141/12 and C-372/12, *YS v Minister voor Immigratie, Integratie en Asiel and
Minister voor Immigratie, Integratie en Asiel v M and S*, judgment of 17 July 2014
(ECLI:EU:C:2014:2081) 404, 457–58
Joined Cases C-141/12 and C-372/12, Opinion of Advocate General Sharpston in
*YS v Minister voor Immigratie, Integratie en Asiel and Minister voor Immigratie,
Integratie en Asiel v M and S*, delivered on 12 December 2013
(ECLI:EU:C:2013:838) 109, 110, 120n13, 120–21
Case C-131/12, *Google Spain SL v Agencia Española de Protección de Datos (AEPD) and Mario
Costeja González*, judgment of 13 May 2014 (Grand Chamber) (ECLI:EU:C:2014:317) 9, 79, 85,
148n9, 151, 154n61, 229n11, 235n43–44, 275n9, 282n13, 283n21, 283n23,
283n24, 283n26, 394, 404, 478, 479, 480, 488, 515–16, 575, 584–85,
592–93, 906–7, 919, 922n50, 1077–78, 1205, 1208, 1209, 1244
Case C-131/12, *Opinion of Advocate General Jääskinen in Google Spain SL v Agencia Española
de Protección de Datos (AEPD) and Mario Costeja González*, delivered on 25 June 2013
(ECLI:EU:C:2013:424) 9–10, 229n11, 235n43–44, 297n22, 1244
Joined Cases C-103/12 and C-165/12, *European Parliament and European Commission v Council
of the European Union*, judgment of 26 November 2014 (Grand Chamber)
(ECLI:EU:C:2014:2400) 305n18
Case C-617/10, *Åkerberg Fransson*, judgment of 26 February 2013 (ECLI:EU:C:2013:105) 757n1,
802n25, 827n14, 846–47n19, 945, 946–47n27, 1199
Case C-614/10, *European Commission v Republic of Austria*, judgment of 16 October 2012
(Grand Chamber) (ECLI:EU:C:2012:631) ... 35–36, 268–69n11, 867n12, 878, 879n28, 880n38,
882n46, 882n48, 887n7, 896n12, 897n17, 910n41, 932n9, 1044n10,
1046n30, 1061n24, 1064–65, 1104, 1106n22, 1108, 1254–55n9

Case C-489/10, *Łukasz Marcin Bonda*, judgment of 5 June 2012 (Grand Chamber)
 (ECLI:EU:C:2012:319) 388n8
Joined Cases C-468/10 and C-469/10, *Asociación Nacional de Establecimientos Financieros
 de Crédito (ASNEF) and Federación de Comercio Electrónico y Marketing Directo
 (FECEMD) v Administración des Estados*, judgment of 24 November 2011
 (ECLI:EU:C:2011:777) 53, 328, 340n81
Case C-461/10, *Bonnier Audio AB and Others v Perfect Communication Sweden AB*, judgment
 of 19 April 2012 (ECLI:EU:C:2012:219) 120n17
Case C-406/10, *SAS Institute Inc. v World Programming Ltd*, judgment of 2 May 2012
 (Grand Chamber) (ECLI:EU:C:2012:259) 407n28
Case C-400/10 PPU, *J. McB v L. E.*, judgment of 5 October 2010 (ECLI:EU:C:2010:582) 576n11
Case C-386/10 P, *Chalkor AE Epexergasias Metallon v European Commission*, judgment of
 8 December 2011 (ECLI:EU:C:2011:815) 1185n16, 1187
Case C-366/10, *Air Transport Association of America and Others v Secretary of State for Energy
 and Climate Change*, judgment of 21 December 2011 (Grand Chamber)
 (ECLI:EU:C:2011:864) 77n4, 95–96n85, 764n53
Case C-355/10, *European Parliament v Council of the European Union*, judgment of
 5 September 2012 (Grand Chamber) (ECLI:EU:C:2012:516) 1270n7, 1271n15, 17
Case T-190/10, *Kathleen Egan and Margaret Hackett v European Parliament*, GC, judgment
 of 28 March 2012 (ECLI:EU:T:2012:165) 373
Case C-109/10 P, *Solvay SA v Commission*, judgment of 25 October 2011
 (ECLI:EU:C:2011:686) 1188n41
Case C-70/10, *Scarlet Extended SA v Société belge des auteurs, compositeurs et éditeurs SCRL (SABAM)*,
 judgment of 24 November 2011 (EU:C:2011:771) 8
Case C-543/09, *Deutsche Telekom AG v Bundesrepublik Deutschland*, judgment of 5 May 2011
 (ECLI:EU:C:2011:279) 179
Case C-324/09, *L'Oréal and Others v eBay International AG and Others*, judgment of
 12 July 2011 (Grand Chamber) (ECLI:EU:C:2011:474) 298n30
Case C-108/09, *Ker-Optika bt v ÀNTSZ Dél-dunántúli Regionális Intézete*, judgment of
 2 December 2010 (ECLI:EU:C:2010:725) 297n23, 298n30, 300–1n42
Joined Cases C-92/09 and 93/09, *Volker and Markus Schecke GbR and Hartmut Eifert v
 Land Hessen*, judgment of 9 November 2010 (Grand Chamber)
 (ECLI:EU:C:2010:662) 24–25n115, 111n40, 313, 545n1, 843–44n2, 1216
Case C-90/09 P, *General Química SA and Others v European Commission*, judgment of
 20 January 2011 (ECLI:EU:C:2011:21) 250n10, 250n16, 255n4
Case T-82/09, *Gert-Jan Dennekamp v European Parliament*, GC, judgment of
 23 November 2011 (ECLI:EU:T:2011:688) 1214
Case F-46/09, *V v European Parliament*, CST, judgment of 5 July 2011
 (ECLI:EU:F:2011:101) 373, 1166–67, 1170–71, 1188n37, 1233
Joined Cases C-585/08 and C-144/09, *Peter Pammer v Reederei Karl Schlüter GmbH & Co.
 KG and Hotel Alpenhof GmbH v Oliver Heller*, judgment of 7 December 2010
 (Grand Chamber) (ECLI:EU:C:2010:740) 12, 89–90
Case T-461/08, *Evropaïki Dynamiki - Proigmena Systimata Tilepikoinonion Pliroforikis kai
 Tilematikis AE v European Investment Bank*, GC, judgment of 20 September 2011
 (ECLI:EU:T:2011:494) 1134–35n3
Case C-386/08, *Firma Brita GmbH v Hauptzollamt Hamburg-Hafen*, judgment of
 25 February 2010 (ECLI:EU:C:2010:91) 305n17
Case T-380/08, *Kingdom of the Netherlands v European Commission*, GC, judgment of
 13 September 2013 (ECLI:EU:T:2013:480) 896n13, 899n26
Joined Cases C-317/08, C-318/08, C-319/08 and C-320/08 *Rosalba Alassini v Telecom
 Italia SpA, Filomena Califano v Wind SpA, Lucia Anna Giorgia Iacono v Telecom Italia SpA
 and Multiservice Srl v Telecom Italia SpA*, judgment of 18 March 2010
 (ECLI:EU:C:2010:146) 1063n34, 1063–64n39
Joined Cases C-236/08 to C-238/08, *Google France SARL and Google Inc. v Louis
 Vuitton Malletier SA, Google France SARL v Viaticum SA and Luteciel SARL and Google
 France SARL v Centre national de recherche en relations humaines (CNRRH) SARL and
 Others*, judgment of 23 March 2010 (Grand Chamber) (ECLI:EU:C:2010:159) 297n22
Case C-28/08 P, *European Commission v Bavarian Lager*, judgment of 29 June 2010 (Grand Chamber)
 (ECLI:EU:C:2010:378) 57n25, 66–67, 120n16, 142n14, 452n5, 1114, 1216, 1219–20

Case C-553/07, *College van burgemeester en wethouders van Rotterdam v M. E. E. Rijkeboer*,
    judgment of 7 May 2009 (ECLI:EU:C:2009:293) 394, 404–5, 457, 471n1, 494, 561n20
Case C-553/07, Opinion of Advocate General Ruiz-Jarabo Colomer in *College van burgemeester
    en wethouders van Rotterdam v M.E.E. Rijkeboer*, delivered on 22 December 2008
    (ECLI:EU:C:2008:773) 488, 489
Case C-518/07, *European Commission v Federal Republic of Germany*, judgment of
    9 March 2010 (Grand Chamber) (ECLI:EU:C:2010:125) 35–36, 53, 266n1, 268–69n11–12,
        691n8, 711n5, 865n1, 865n2, 867n12, 867n13, 867n16, 868, 875n1, 875, 877–78,
        879n27, 879n30, 880, 887n7, 896n12, 897n17, 898n19, 932n9–10, 933n21,
        950n7, 998n8, 1008n11, 1018n8, 1022n32, 1044n9, 1044n10, 1045n18,
        1046n29, 1060n21, 1061n24, 1063, 1065–66n47, 1087n8, 1254–55n9
Case C-118/07, *Commission of the European Communities v Republic of Finland*, judgment
    of 19 November 2009 (ECLI:EU:C:2009:715) 1304n9, 1306n14
Case C-113/07 P, *SELEX Sistemi Integrati SpA v Commission of the European Communities and
    Organisation européenne pour la sécurité de la navigation aérienne (Eurocontrol)*, judgment
    of 26 March 2009 (ECLI:EU:C:2009:191) 250n14, 255n8, 262–63n37, 307n28
Case C-73/07, *Tietosuojavaltuutettu v Satakunnan Markkinapörssi Oy and Satamedia Oy*, judgment
    of 16 December 2008 (Grand Chamber) (ECLI:EU:C:2008:727) 11n55, 40–41, 67n15,
        67–68n17, 109–10n26, 120n15, 142n14, 1205–7, 1208, 1210, 1253n1
Case C-73/07, Opinion of Advocate General Kokott in *Tietosuojavaltuutettu v Satakunnan
    Markkinapörssi Oy and Satamedia Oy*, delivered on 8 May 2008 (ECLI:EU:C:2008:266)... 1206–7n12–13
Case C-42/07, Opinion of Advocate General Bot in *Liga Portuguesa de Futebol Profissional and
    Bwin International Ltd v Departamento de Jogos da Santa Casa da Misericórdia de Lisboa*,
    delivered on 14 October 2008 (ECLI:EU:C:2008:560)............................ 296–97n17
Case C-524/06, *Heinz Huber v Bundesrepublik Deutschland*, judgment of 16 December 2008
    (Grand Chamber) (ECLI:EU:C:2008:724).................... 109–10n27, 328, 336, 1244
Case C-450/06, *Varec SA v Belgian State*, judgment of 14 February 2008
    (ECLI:EU:C:2008:91) 1297n15
Case C-281/06, *Hans-Dieter Jundt, Hedwig Jundt v Finanzamt Offenburg*, judgment of
    18 December 2007 (ECLI:EU:C:2007:816) 296–97n18–19
Case C-275/06, *Productores de Música de España (Promusicae) v Telefónica de España SAU*,
    judgment of 29 January 2008 (Grand Chamber) (ECLI:EU:C:2008:54) 548, 1253n2
Case C-275/06, Opinion of Advocate General Kokott in *Productores de Música de España
    (Promusicae) v Telefónica de España SAU*, delivered on 18 July 2007 (ECLI:EU:C:2008:54) ... 8, 69
Case C-249/06, *Commission of the European Communities v Kingdom of Sweden*, judgment
    of 3 March 2009 (Grand Chamber) (ECLI:EU:C:2009:119)................. 1304n9, 1306n14
Case C-210/06, *Cartesio Oktató és Szolgáltató bt*, judgment of 16 December 2008 (Grand Chamber)
    (ECLI:EU:C:2008:723) 231
Case C-205/06, *Commission of the European Communities v Republic of Austria*, judgment of
    3 March 2009 (Grand Chamber) (ECLI:EU:C:2009:118) 1304n9, 1306n14
Case T-452/05, *Belgian Sewing Thread (BST) NV v European Commission*, GC, judgment
    of 28 April 2010 (ECLI:EU:T:2010:167) 1166–67n32
Joined Cases C-402 and 415/05 P, *Yassin Abdullah Kadi and Al Barakaat International
    Foundation v Council of the European Union and Commission of the European Communities*,
    judgment of 3 September 2008 (Grand Chamber) (ECLI:EU:C:2008:461) 764n54, 829n31
Case C-328/05 P, *SGL Carbon AG v Commission of the European Communities*, judgment of
    10 May 2007 (ECLI:EU:C:2007:277)... 1187
Case C-217/05, *Confederación Española de Empresarios de Estaciones de Servicio v Compañía
    Española de Petróleos SA*, judgment of 14 December 2006 (ECLI:EU:C:2006:784)....... 1187n31
Case C-504/04, *Agrarproduktion Staebelow GmbH v Landrat des Landkreises Bad Doberan*,
    judgment of 12 January 2006 (ECLI:EU:C:2006:30) 1314–15n20
Joined Cases C-317/04 and C-318/04, *European Parliament v Council and Commission of the European
    Communities*, judgment 30 May 2006 (ECLI:EU:C:2006:346) 64n4, 759–60n17, 775–76n8
Case C-317/04, *European Parliament v Council of the European Union ('PNR')*, order of
    17 March 2005 (Grand Chamber) (ECLI:EU:C:2005:189).................. 1044n9, 1045n17
Case T-201/04, *Microsoft Corp. v Commission of the European Communities*, CFI, judgment
    of 17 September 2007 (ECLI:T:2007:289) 502n25
Case C-196/04, *Cadbury Schweppes plc and Cadbury Schweppes Overseas Ltd v Commissioners of Inland
    Revenue*, judgment of 12 September 2006 (Grand Chamber) (ECLI:EU:C:2006:544)........ 241n16

Case T-194/04, *The Bavarian Lager Co. Ltd v Commission of the European Communities*, CFI,
 judgment of 8 November 2007 (ECLI:EU:T:2007:334) 1219n30
Case C-89/04, *Mediakabel BV v Commissariaat voor de Media*, judgment of 2 June 2005
 (ECLI:EU:C:2005:348) 299–300
Case C-503/03, *Commission of the European Communities v Kingdom of Spain*, judgment
 of 31 January 2006 (Grand Chamber) (ECLI:EU:C:2006:74) 978
Joined Cases C-346/03 and C-529/03, *Giuseppe Atzeni and Others and Marco Scalas and Renato
 Lilliu v Regione autonoma della Sardegna*, judgment of 23 February 2006
 (ECLI:EU:C:2006:130) 1131
Joined Cases C-346/03 and C-529/03, Opinion of Advocate General Ruiz-Jarabo Colomer in
 *Giuseppe Atzeni and Others and Marco Scalas and Renato Lilliu v Regione autonoma della
 Sardegna*, delivered on 28 April 2005 (ECLI:EU:C:2005:256) 1131
Case T-259/03, *Kalliopi Nikolaou v Commission of the European Communities*, CFI, judgment
 of 12 September 2007 (ECLI:EU:T:2007:254) 1170
Case T-198/03, *Bank Austria Creditanstalt AG v Commission of the European Communities*,
 CFI, judgment of 30 May 2006 (ECLI:EU:T:2006:136) 111n42
Case C-176/03, *Commission of the European Communities v Council of the European Union
 ('Environmental Sanctions')*, judgment of 13 September 2005 (Grand Chamber)
 (ECLI:EU:C:2005:542) 1196–97n11
Case T-105/03, *Triantafyllia Dionyssopoulou v Council of the European Union*, CFI, judgment
 of 31 May 2005 (ECLI:EU:T:2005:189) 221–22
Case T-320/02, *Monika Esch-Leonhardt, Tillmann Frommhold and Emmanuel Larue v
 European Central Bank*, CFI, judgment of 18 February 2004 (ECLI:EU:T:2004:45) 372–73
Case C-278/02, *Herbert Handlbauer GmbH*, judgment of 24 June 2004 (ECLI:EU:C:2004:388)... 1163
Case C-201/02, *The Queen, on the application of Delena Wells v Secretary of State for Transport,
 Local Government and the Regions*, judgment of 7 January 2004 (ECLI:EU:C:2004:12) ... 1138n20
Joined Cases C-397/01 to C-403/01, *Bernhard Pfeiffer, Wilhelm Roith, Albert Süß, Michael
 Winter, Klaus Nestvogel, Roswitha Zeller and Matthias Döbele v Deutsches Rotes Kreuz,
 Kreisverband Waldshut e.V.*, judgment of 5 October 2004 (Grand Chamber)
 (ECLI:EU:C:2004:584) 180n30, 182n42, 183–84n52
Case C-241/01, *National Farmers' Union v Secrétariat général du gouvernement*, judgment
 of 22 October 2002 (ECLI:EU:C:2002:604) 1025n39, 1131n28
Case C-241/01, Opinion of Advocate General Misho in *National Farmers' Union v Secrétariat
 général du gouvernement*, delivered on 2 July 2002 (ECLI:EU:C:2002:415).......... 1314–15n18
Case C-207/01, *Altair Chimica SpA v ENEL Distribuzione SpA*, judgment of
 11 September 2003 (ECLI:EU:C:2003:451) 1063n34
Case C-101/01, *Criminal proceedings against Bodil Lindqvist*, judgment of 6 November 2003
 (ECLI:EU:C:2003:596) 11, 67–68, 109–10n25, 120n14, 149n17, 203n40, 221, 260–61,
                              372, 761, 762–63, 779, 1205, 1206, 1259n6, 1261–62
Case C-101/01, Opinion of Advocate General Tizzano in *Criminal proceedings against Bodil
 Lindqvist*, delivered on 19 September 2002 (ECLI:EU:C:2002:513) 1257
Joined Cases C-465/00, C-138/01 and C-139/01, *Rechnungshof v Österreichischer Rundfunk and
 Others and Christa Neukomm and Joseph Lauermann*, judgment of 20 May 2003
 (ECLI:EU:C:2003:294) 53, 67, 109–10n26, 373–74n47, 516n47, 547–48, 1232
Case C-355/00, *Freskot AE v Elliniko Dimosio*, judgment of 22 May 2003
 (ECLI:EU:C:2003:298) 296–97n20
Case C-50/00 P, *Unión de Pequeños Agricultores v Council of the European Union*, judgment
 of 25 July 2002 (ECLI:EU:C:2002:462) 1134–35n3
Case C-62/99, *Betriebsrat der bofrost* Josef H. Boquoi Deutschland West GmbH & Co. KG v
 Bofrost* Josef H. Boquoi Deutschland West GmbH & Co. KG.*, judgment of 29 March
 2001(ECLI:EU:C:2001:188)..255–56n9
Case C-403/98, *Azienda Agricola Monte Arcosu Srl v Regione Autonoma della Sardegna,
 Organismo Comprensoriale n° 24 della Sardegna and Ente Regionale per l'Assistenza Tecnica in
 Agricoltura (ERSAT)*, judgment of 11 January 2001 (ECLI:EU:C:2001:6) 1163
Case C-223/98, *Adidas AG*, judgment of 14 October 1999 (ECLI:EU:C:1999:500) 1257
Case C-223/98, Opinion of Advocate General Cosmas in *Adidas AG*, delivered on
 10 June 1998 (ECLI:EU:C:1999:300) 1263

Case C-78/98, *Shirley Preston and Others v Wolverhampton Healthcare NHS Trust and Others and Dorothy Fletcher and Others v Midland Bank plc*, judgment of 16 May 2000 (ECLI:EU:C:2000:247) 1198–99n22
Case C-54/96, *Dorsch Consult Ingenieurgesellschaft mbH v Bundesbaugesellschaft Berlin mbH*, judgment of 17 September 1997 (ECLI:EU:C:1997:413)........................ 910n41
Case C-343/95, *Diego Calì & Figli Srl v Servizi ecologici porto di Genova SpA (SEPG)*, judgment of 18 March 1997 (ECLI:EU:C:1997:160)..................................... 250n14, 255n8
Case C-312/93, *Peterbroeck, Van Campenhout & Cie SCS v Belgian State*, judgment of 14 December 1995 (ECLI:EU:C:1995:437) 1138n20
Case C-406/92, *The owners of the cargo lately laden on board the ship 'Tatry' v the owners of the ship 'Maciej Rataj'*, judgment of 6 December 1994 (ECLI:EU:C:1994:400) 1156n8
Case C-364/92, *SAT Fluggesellschaft v Eurocontrol*, judgment of 19 January 1994 (ECLI:EU:C:1994:7)................................... 250n14, 255n8, 262–63n37, 307n28
Case C-275/92, *Her Majesty's Customs and Excise v Gerhart Schindler and Jörg Schindler*, judgment of 24 March 1994 (ECLI:EU:C:1994:119)................................ 296–97n19
Case C-188/92, *TWD Textilwerke Deggendorf GmbH v Bundesrepublik Deutschland*, judgment of 9 March 1994 (ECLI:EU:C:1994:90) 1025n39, 1129, 1131–32
Case C-327/91, *French Republic v Commission*, judgment of 9 August 1994 (ECLI:EU:C:1994:305)... 834n73
Case C-62/90, *Commission of the European Communities v Federal Republic of Germany*, judgment of 8 April 1992 (ECLI:EU:C:1992:169)................................... 221n17
Case C-41/90, *Klaus Höfner and Fritz Elser v Macrotron GmbH*, judgment of 23 April 1991 (ECLI:EU:C:1991:161) 250n10, 255n4, 1187n31
Case C-246/89, *Commission of the European Communities v United Kingdom of Great Britain and Northern Ireland*, judgment of 4 October 1991 (ECLI:EU:C:1991:375) 241n15
Case C-221/89, *The Queen v Secretary of State for Transport, ex parte Factortame Ltd and others*, judgment of 25 July 1991 (ECLI:EU:C:1991:320)..................................... 241n15
Case C-188/89, *A. Foster and others v British Gas plc*, judgment of 12 July 1990 (ECLI:EU:C:1990:313)... 269n18
Case C-112/89, *Upjohn Company and Upjohn NV v Farzoo Inc. and J. Kortmann*, judgment of 16 April 1991 (ECLI:EU:C:1991:147) 203n39
Case T-11/89, *Shell International Chemical Company Ltd v Commission of the European Communities*, CFI, judgment of 10 March 1992 (ECLI:EU:T:1992:33).......... 250n15, 250–51
Case C-322/88, *Salvatore Grimaldi v Fonds des maladies professionnelles*, judgment of 13 December 1989 (ECLI:EU:C:1989:646) 1021–22n26, 1063n34
Case C-68/88, *Commission of the European Communities v Hellenic Republic ('Greek Maize')*, judgment of 21 September 1989 (ECLI:EU:C:1989:339) 1198
Case C-81/87, *The Queen v Treasury and Commissioners of Inland Revenue, ex parte Daily Mail and General Trust plc*, judgment of 27 September 1988 (ECLI:EU:C:1988:456)... 230–31n27
Case C-81/87, Opinion of Advocate General Darmon in *The Queen v Treasury and Commissioners of Inland Revenue, ex parte Daily Mail and General Trust plc*, delivered on 7 June 1988 (ECLI:EU:C:1988:286)... 230–31n27
Case C-30/87, *Bodson v Pompes funèbres des régions libérées*, judgment of 4 May 1988 (ECLI:EU:C:1988:225)... 250n14, 255n8, 262–63n37
Case C-144/86, *Gubisch Maschinenfabrik KG v Giulio Palumbo*, judgment of 8 December 1987 (ECLI:EU:C:1987:528)... 1156n7
Case C-199/82, *Amministrazione delle Finanze dello Stato v SpA San Giorgio*, judgment of 9 November 1983 (ECLI:EU:C:1983:318) 1138n20
Case C-33/76, *Rewe-Zentralfinanz eG and Rewe-Zentral AG v Landwirtschaftskammer für das Saarland*, judgment of 16 December 1976 (ECLI:EU:C:1976:188) 1138n20, 1198–99n21
Case C-22/70, *Commission of the European Communities v Council of the European Communities (AETR/ERTA)*, judgment of 31 March 1971 (ECLI:EU:C:1971:32) 760–61n31
Case C-52/69, *J. R. Geigy AG v Commission of the European Communities*, judgment of 14 July 1972 (ECLI:EU:C:1972:73)... 76–77n3
Case C-9/56, *Meroni & Co., Industrie Metallurgiche, SpA v High Authority of the European Coal and Steel Community*, judgment of 13 June 1958 (ECLI:EU:C:1958:7) 1044, 1045

Alphabetical

Adidas AG, Case C-223/98, judgment of 14 October 1999 (ECLI:EU:C:1999:500) 1257
Adidas AG, Case C-223/98, Opinion of Advocate General Cosmas, delivered on
    10 June 1998 (ECLI:EU:C:1999:300) 1263
Agrarproduktion Staebelow GmbH v Landrat des Landkreises Bad Doberan, Case C-504/04,
    judgment of 12 January 2006 (ECLI:EU:C:2006:30) 1314–15n20
Air Transport Association of America and Others v Secretary of State for Energy and Climate Change,
    Case C-366/10, judgment of 21 December 2011 (Grand Chamber)
    (ECLI:EU:C:2011:864)..................................... 77n4, 95–96n85, 764n53
AIRBNB Ireland, Case C-390/18, Opinion of Advocate General Szpunar, delivered on
    30 April 2019 (ECLI:EU:C:2019:336) 295n8, 295n10, 297n21, 298,
                                               298n25, 299, 299n33, 299n37, 299–300n38
Akzo Nobel NV, and Others v European Commission, Case C-516/15 P, judgment of
    27 April 2017 (ECLI:EU:C:2017:314)................................ 250n10, 255n4
*Alassini (Rosalba) v Telecom Italia SpA, Filomena Califano v Wind SpA, Lucia Anna Giorgia Iacono v
    Telecom Italia SpA and Multiservice Srl v Telecom Italia SpA*, Joined Cases C-317/08, C-318/08,
    C-319/08 and C-320/08 judgment of 18 March 2010 (ECLI:EU:C:2010:146).... 1063n34, 1063–64n39
Altair Chimica SpA v ENEL Distribuzione SpA, Case C-207/01, judgment of 11 September 2003
    (ECLI:EU:C:2003:451)..1063n34
Altmann (Annett) and Others v Bundesanstalt für Finanzdienstleistungsaufsicht,
    Case C-140/13, judgment of 12 November 2014 (ECLI:EU:C:2014:2362)........ 896n13, 899n27
Amministrazione delle Finanze dello Stato v SpA San Giorgio, Case C-199/82, judgment of
    9 November 1983 (ECLI:EU:C:1983:318) 1138n20
Athanassios Oikonomopoulos v European Commission, GC, Case T-483/13, judgment of
    20 July 2016 (ECLI:EU:T:2016:421)....................................... 691n12, 712
*Asociación Nacional de Establecimientos Financieros de Crédito (ASNEF) and Federación de
    Comercio Electrónico y Marketing Directo (FECEMD) v Administración des Estados*,
    Joined Cases C-468/10 and C-469/10, judgment of 24 November 2011
    (ECLI:EU:C:2011:777).. 53, 328, 340n81
Asociación Profesional Elite Taxi v Uber Systems Spain, SL, Case C-434/15, judgment of
    20 December 2017 (Grand Chamber) (ECLI:EU:C:2017:981) 299
Asociación Profesional Elite Taxi v Uber Systems Spain, SL, Case C-434/15, Opinion of Advocate
    General Szpunar, delivered on 11 May 2017 (ECLI:EU:C:2017:364) 299
*Atzeni (Giuseppe) and Others and Marco Scalas and Renato Lilliu v Regione autonoma della
    Sardegna*, Joined Cases C-346/03 and C-529/03, judgment of 23 February 2006
    (ECLI:EU:C:2006:130) 1131
Atzeni (Giuseppe) and Others and Marco Scalas and Renato Lilliu v Regione autonoma della Sardegna,
    Joined Cases C-346/03 and C-529/03, Opinion of Advocate General Ruiz-Jarabo Colomer,
    delivered on 28 April 2005 (ECLI:EU:C:2005:256) 1131
*Azienda Agricola Monte Arcosu Srl v Regione Autonoma della Sardegna, Organismo
    Comprensoriale n° 24 della Sardegna and Ente Regionale per l'Assistenza Tecnica in Agricoltura
    (ERSAT)*, Case C-403/98, judgment of 11 January 2001 (ECLI:EU:C:2001:6) 1163

Bank Austria Creditanstalt AG v Commission of the European Communities, CFI, Case T-198/03,
    judgment of 30 May 2006 (ECLI:EU:T:2006:136)................................ 111n42
Bavarian Lager Co. Ltd (The) v Commission of the European Communities, CFI, Case T-194/04,
    judgment of 8 November 2007 (ECLI:EU:T:2007:334) 1219n30
Belgian Sewing Thread (BST) NV v European Commission, GC, Case T-452/05, judgment
    of 28 April 2010 (ECLI:EU:T:2010:167) 1166–67n32
Betriebsrat der bofrost Josef H. Boquoi Deutschland West GmbH & Co. KG v Bofrost*
    Josef H. Boquoi Deutschland West GmbH & Co. KG.*, Case C-62/99, judgment of
    29 March 2001 (ECLI:EU:C:2001:188) 255–56n9
Bichat (Miriam) and Others v APSB - Aviation Passage Service Berlin GmbH & Co. KG,
    Joined Cases C-61/17, C-62/17 and C-72/17, judgment of 7 August 2018
    (ECLI:EU:C:2018:653).. 256n11
Bodson v Pompes funèbres des régions libérées, Case C-30/87, judgment of 4 May 1988
    (ECLI:EU:C:1988:225)................................... 250n14, 255n8, 262–63n37

Bonda (Łukasz Marcin), Case C-489/10, judgment of 5 June 2012 (Grand Chamber)
(ECLI:EU:C:2012:319) 388n8
Bonnier Audio AB and Others v Perfect Communication Sweden AB, Case C-461/10, judgment
of 19 April 2012 (ECLI:EU:C:2012:219) 120n17
Breyer (Patrick) v Bundesrepublik Deutschland, Case C-582/14, judgment of 26 October 2016
(ECLI:EU:C:2016:779) 53n8, 109–10n31, 110–11, 328n5,
340n81, 394, 395, 494, 868n24
Buivids (Sergejs) Proceedings brought by, Case C-345/17, judgment of 14 February 2019
(ECLI:EU:C:2019:122) 109–10n29, 120n21, 1205, 1207, 1208, 1209
Bundesrepublik Deutschland, Case C-505/19 (pending) 764n56

Cadbury Schweppes plc and Cadbury Schweppes Overseas Ltd v Commissioners of Inland Revenue,
Case C-196/04, judgment of 12 September 2006 (Grand Chamber) (ECLI:EU:C:2006:544) ... 241n16
Camera di Commercio, Industria, Artigianato e Agricoltura di Lecce v Salvatore Manni,
Case C-398/15, judgment of 9 March 2017 (ECLI:EU:C:2017:197) 478, 482–83, 514–15
Camera di Commercio, Industria, Artigianato e Agricoltura di Lecce v Salvatore Manni,
Case C-398/15, Opinion of Advocate General Bot, delivered on 8 September 2016
(ECLI:EU:C:2016:652) 9–10, 120n23
Cartesio Oktató és Szolgáltató bt, Case C-210/06, judgment of 16 December 2008
(Grand Chamber) (ECLI:EU:C:2008:723) 231, 494
Chalkor AE Epexergasias Metallon v European Commission, Case C-386/10 P, judgment of
8 December 2011 (ECLI:EU:C:2011:815) 1185n16, 1187
ClientEarth and Pesticide Action Network Europe (PAN Europe) v European Food Safety Authority,
Case C-615/13 P, judgment of 16 July 2015 (ECLI:EU:C:2015:489) 1220
CN v European Parliament, GC, Case T-343/13, judgment of 3 December 2015
(ECLI:EU:T:2015:926) 1171
College van burgemeester en wethouders van Rotterdam v M. E. E. Rijkeboer, Case C-553/07,
judgment of 7 May 2009 (ECLI:EU:C:2009:293) 394, 404–5, 457, 471n1, 494, 561n20
College van burgemeester en wethouders van Rotterdam v M. E. E. Rijkeboer, Case C-553/07,
Opinion of Advocate General Ruiz-Jarabo Colomer, delivered on 22 December 2008
(ECLI:EU:C:2008:773) 488, 489
*Commission of the European Communities v Council of the European Communities
(AETR/ERTA)*, Case C-22/70, judgment of 31 March 1971 (ECLI:EU:C:1971:32) 760–61n31
*Commission of the European Communities v Council of the European Union
('Environmental Sanctions')*, Case C-176/03, judgment of 13 September 2005
(Grand Chamber) (ECLI:EU:C:2005:542) 1196–97n11
Commission of the European Communities v Federal Republic of Germany, Case C-62/90,
judgment of 8 April 1992 (ECLI:EU:C:1992:169) 221n17
Commission of the European Communities v Hellenic Republic ('Greek Maize'), Case C-68/88,
judgment of 21 September 1989 (ECLI:EU:C:1989:339) 1198
Commission of the European Communities v Kingdom of Spain, Case C-503/03, judgment of
31 January 2006 (Grand Chamber) (ECLI:EU:C:2006:74) 978
Commission of the European Communities v Kingdom of Sweden, Case C-249/06, judgment
of 3 March 2009 (Grand Chamber) (ECLI:EU:C:2009:119) 1304n9, 1306n14
Commission of the European Communities v Republic of Austria, Case C-205/06, judgment of
3 March 2009 (Grand Chamber) (ECLI:EU:C:2009:118) 1304n9, 1306n14
Commission of the European Communities v Republic of Finland, Case C-118/07, judgment of
19 November 2009 (ECLI:EU:C:2009:715) 1304n9, 1306n14
Commission of the European Communities v United Kingdom of Great Britain and Northern Ireland,
Case C-246/89, judgment of 4 October 1991 (ECLI:EU:C:1991:375) 241n15
*Confederación Española de Empresarios de Estaciones de Servicio v Compañía Española de
Petróleos SA*, Case C-217/05, judgment of 14 December 2006 (ECLI:EU:C:2006:784) ... 1187n31
*Confédération paysanne and Others v Premier ministre and Ministre de l'agriculture,
de l'agroalimentaire et de la forêt*, Case C-528/16, Opinion of Advocate General Bobek,
delivered on 18 January 2018 (ECLI:EU:C:2018:20) 1314–16
Congregación de Escuelas Pías Provincia Betania v Ayuntamiento de Getafe, Case C-74/16, judgment
of 27 June 2017 (Grand Chamber) (ECLI:EU:C:2017:496) 250n12, 255n6, 262–63n38

Cresco Investigation GmbH v Markus Achatzi, Case C-193/17, Opinion of Advocate General
  Bobek, delivered on 25 July 2018 (ECLI:EU:C:2018:614) 1263
Criminal proceedings against Bodil Lindqvist, Case C-101/01, judgment of 6 November 2003
  (ECLI:EU:C:2003:596) 11, 67–68, 110n25, 120n14, 149n17, 204n40, 221,
                                                 260–61, 372, 761, 762–63, 779, 1205, 1206, 1259n6, 1261–62
Criminal proceedings against Bodil Lindqvist, Case C-101/01, Opinion of Advocate
  General Tizzano, delivered on 19 September 2002 (ECLI:EU:C:2002:513) 1257

Danqua (Evelyn) v Minister for Justice and Equality and Others, Case C-429/15, judgment of
  20 October 2016 (ECLI:EU:C:2016:789) 1138n20
Data Protection Commissioner v Facebook Ireland Limited, Maximillian Schrems,
  Case C-311/18 (pending) 791, 802, 1280n6
De Capitani (Emilio) v European Parliament, GC, Case T-540/15, judgment of 22 March 2018
  (ECLI:EU:T:2018:167) 1113n5
Deckmyn (Johan) and Vrijheidsfonds VZW v Helena Vandersteen and Others, Case C-201/13,
  judgment of 3 September 2014 (Grand Chamber) (ECLI:EU:C:2014:2132) 242–43n25
Dennekamp (Gert-Jan) v European Parliament, GC, Case T-115/13, judgment of 15 July 2015
  (ECLI:EU:T:2015:497) 452n5, 1220
Dennekamp (Gert-Jan) v European Parliament, GC, Case T-82/09, judgment of
  23 November 2011 (ECLI:EU:T:2011:688) 1214
Deutsche Bahn AG and Others v European Commission, Case C-583/13 P, judgment of
  18 June 2015 (ECLI:EU:C:2015:404) 1187
Deutsche Telekom AG v Bundesrepublik Deutschland, Case C-543/09, judgment of
  5 May 2011 (ECLI:EU:C:2011:279) 179
*Di Puma (Enzo) v Commissione Nazionale per le Società e la Borsa (Consob) and Commissione
  Nazionale per le Società e la Borsa (Consob) v Antonio Zecca*, Joined Cases C-596/16 and
  C-597/16, judgment of 20 March 2018 (Grand Chamber) (ECLI:EU:C:2018:192) 1200n28
Diego Calì & Figli Srl v Servizi ecologici porto di Genova SpA (SEPG), Case C-343/95, judgment
  of 18 March 1997 (ECLI:EU:C:1997:160) 250n14, 255n8
Digital Rights Ireland Ltd v European Commission, GC, Case T-670/16, order of
  22 November 2017 (ECLI:EU:T:2017:838) 111n40, 791n145
*Digital Rights Ireland Ltd v Minister for Communications, Marine and Natural Resources and
  Others and Kärntner Landesregierung, Michael Seitlinger, Christof Tschohl and Others*,
  Joined Cases C-293/12 and C-594/12, judgment of 8 April 2014 (Grand Chamber)
  (ECLI:EU:C:2014:238) 9, 53n13, 58n30, 109–10n31, 120n20, 313, 548–49, 550,
                                                 553n29–30, 575n7, 791, 846n17, 878n25, 907, 1121, 1144–45, 1254, 1296
Dionyssopoulou (Triantafyllia) v Council of the European Union, Case T-105/03, CFI judgment
  of 31 May 2005 (ECLI:EU:T:2005:189) 221–22
Dorsch Consult Ingenieurgesellschaft mbH v Bundesbaugesellschaft Berlin mbH, Case C-54/96,
  judgment of 17 September 1997 (ECLI:EU:C:1997:413) 910n41

*'EasyPay' AD and 'Finance Engineering' AD v Ministerski savet na Republika Bulgaria and
  Natsionalen osiguritelen institut*, Case C-185/14, judgment of 22 October 2015
  (ECLI:EU:C:2015:716) 250n11, 255n5
EDF Toruń SA v European Chemicals Agency, GC, Case T-758/15, judgment of 18 July 2017
  (ECLI:EU:T:2017:519) 251n18
Egan (Kathleen) and Margaret Hackett v European Parliament, GC, Case T-190/10, judgment
  of 28 March 2012 (ECLI:EU:T:2012:165) 373
Esch-Leonhardt (Monika), Tillmann Frommhold and Emmanuel Larue v European Central Bank,
  CFI, Case T-320/02, judgment of 18 February 2004 (ECLI:EU:T:2004:45) 372–73
European Commission v Bavarian Lager, Case C-28/08 P, judgment of 29 June 2010
  (Grand Chamber) (ECLI:EU:C:2010:378) 57n25, 66–67, 120n16, 142n14,
                                                                      452n5, 1114, 1216, 1219–20
European Commission v European Parliament and Council of the European Union,
  Case C-88/14, judgment of 16 July 2015 (Grand Chamber) (ECLI:EU:C:2015:499) 1270n7, 1280n5
European Commission v European Parliament and Council of the European Union, Case C-427/12,
  judgment of 18 March 2014 (Grand Chamber) (ECLI:EU:C:2014:170) 1270n7, 1280n5

European Commission v Federal Republic of Germany, Case C-518/07, judgment of
  9 March 2010 (Grand Chamber) (ECLI:EU:C:2010:125) 35–36, 53, 266n1, 268–69n11–12,
                  691n8, 711n5, 864–65n1, 865n2, 867n12–13, 867n16, 868, 875, 877–78,
                  879n27, 879n30, 880, 887n7, 896n12, 897n17, 898n19, 932n9–10, 933n21,
                            951n7, 998n8, 1008n11, 1018n8, 1022n32, 1044n9–10, 1045n18,
                                   1046n29, 1060–61, 1063, 1065n47, 1087n8, 1254–55n9
European Commission v Hungary, Case C-288/12, judgment of 8 April 2014
  (Grand Chamber) (ECLI:EU:C:2014:237) 35–36, 268n11, 867n12, 878, 879n29,
                                    879n31, 880–81n39–40, 887, 890–91, 896n12,
                                    932n9, 1058, 1121n16, 1122n28, 1254–55n9
European Commission v Hungary, Case C-288/12, Opinion of Advocate General Wathelet,
  delivered on 10 December 2013 (ECLI:EU:C:2013:816) 891n29
European Commission v Republic of Austria, Case C-614/10, judgment of
  16 October 2012 (Grand Chamber) (ECLI:EU:C:2012:631) 35–36, 268n11, 867n12,
          878, 879n28, 880n38, 882n46, 882n48, 887n7, 896n12, 897n17, 910n41,
          932n9, 1044n10, 1046n30, 1061n24, 1064–65, 1104, 1106n22, 1108, 1254–55n9
European Ombudsman v Claire Staelen, Case C-337/15 P, judgment of 4 April 2017
  (Grand Chamber) (ECLI:EU:C:2017:256) 1121n19, 1123
European Parliament v Council of the European Union, Case C-355/10, judgment of
  5 September 2012 (Grand Chamber) (ECLI:EU:C:2012:516)..........1270n7, 1271n15–17
European Parliament v Council and Commission of the European Communities,
  Joined Cases C-317/04 and C-318/04, judgment 30 May 2006
  (ECLI:EU:C:2006:346) 64n4, 759n17, 776n8
European Parliament v Council of the European Union ('PNR'), Case C-317/04, order of
  17 March 2005 (Grand Chamber) (ECLI:EU:C:2005:189)................ 1044n9, 1045n17
European Parliament v European Commission, Case C-286/14, judgment of 17 March 2016
  (ECLI:EU:C:2016:183)... 1270n7, 1270n9
European Parliament v European Commission, Case C-65/13, judgment of 15 October 2014
  (ECLI:EU:C:2014:2289)..1280n5
European Parliament and European Commission v Council of the European Union,
  Joined Cases C-103/12 and C-165/12, judgment of 26 November 2014 (Grand Chamber)
  (ECLI:EU:C:2014:2400) 305n18
*Evropaïki Dynamiki - Proigmena Systimata Tilepikoinonion Pliroforikis kai Tilematikis AE v
  European Investment Bank*, GC, Case T-461/08, judgment of 20 September 2011
  (ECLI:EU:T:2011:494) 1134–35n3

Falbert (Bent) and Others, Case C-255/16, *Criminal proceedings against* judgment of
  20 December 2017 (ECLI:EU:C:2017:983).................................298n30
Farrell (Elaine) v Alan Whitty and Others, Case C-413/15, Opinion of Advocate General
  Sharpston, delivered on 22 June 2017 (ECLI:EU:C:2017:492) 1162–63
Fashion ID GmbH & Co. KG v Verbraucherzentrale NRW e.V., Case C-40/17, judgment of
  29 July 2019 (ECLI:EU:C:2019:629)................. 119, 120n26–27, 148n7, 148n9, 150n27–28,
                       151–52n43, 152–53n51, 153–54, 183–84n52, 328,
                       337–38, 424, 426–27n78, 566n58, 585–86, 1151
Fashion ID GmbH & Co. KG v Verbraucherzentrale NRW e.V., Case C-40/17, Opinion of
  Advocate General Bobek, delivered on 19 December 2018 (ECLI:EU:C:2018:1039) 108n16,
                              118–19n6, 119n7, 120n27, 136n20, 140n7,
                              142n15, 142n18, 148n7, 153, 159n8
Firma Brita GmbH v Hauptzollamt Hamburg-Hafen, Case C-386/08, judgment of
  25 February 2010 (ECLI:EU:C:2010:91) 305n17
*Fish Legal, Emily Shirley v Information Commissioner, United Utilities Water plc,
  Yorkshire Water Services Ltd, Southern Water Services Ltd*, Case C-279/12, judgment of
  19 December 2013 (ECLI:EU:C:2013:853) 149n16, 250n14, 255n8, 262n37, 263, 269n17
Foster (A.) and others v British Gas plc, Case C-188/89, judgment of 12 July 1990
  (ECLI:EU:C:1990:313)...269n18
Fransson (Åkerberg), Case C-617/10, judgment of 26 February 2013
  (ECLI:EU:C:2013:105)............... 757n1, 802n25, 827n14, 846–47n19, 945, 946n27, 1199

French Republic v Commission, Case C-327/91, judgment of 9 August 1994 (ECLI:EU:C:1994:305) 834n73
Freskot AE v Elliniko Dimosio, Case C-355/00, judgment of 22 May 2003 (ECLI:EU:C:2003:298). . . . 296–97n20

Garlsson Real Estate SA and Others v Commissione Nazionale per le Società e la Borsa (Consob),
    Case C-537/16, judgment of 20 March 2018 (Grand Chamber) (ECLI:EU:C:2018:193) 1200
G.C., A.F., B.H., E.D. v Commission nationale de l'informatique et des libertés (CNIL)
    Case C-136/17 (pending) 376–77, 478n2, 480n11
G.C., A.F., B.H., E.D. v Commission nationale de l'informatique et des libertés (CNIL)
    Case C-136/17, Opinion of Advocate General Szpunar, delivered on 10 January 2019
    (ECLI:EU:C:2019:14). 478n2, 1208n25
Geigy (J.R.) AG v Commission of the European Communities, Case C-52/69 judgment
    of 14 July 1972 (ECLI:EU:C:1972:73). 76–77n3
General Química SA and Others v European Commission, Case C-90/09 P, judgment of
    20 January 2011 (ECLI:EU:C:2011:21). 250n10, 250n16, 255n4
Google v Commission, Case T-612/17 (pending) 1186n21
*Google France SARL and Google Inc. v Louis Vuitton Malletier SA, Google France SARL v
    Viaticum SA and Luteciel SARL* and *Google France SARL v Centre national de recherche
    en relations humaines (CNRRH) SARL and Others*, Joined Cases C-236/08 to C-238/08,
    judgment of 23 March 2010 (Grand Chamber) (ECLI:EU:C:2010:159). 297n22, 300n38
Google Inc. v Commission nationale de l'informatique et des libertés (CNIL),
    Case C-507/17 (pending) 478n2
Google Inc. v Commission nationale de l'informatique et des libertés (CNIL), Case C-507/17, Opinion
    of Advocate General Szpunar, delivered on 10 January 2019 (ECLI:EU:C:2019:15) 81, 478n2, 481
Google Spain SL v Agencia Española de Protección de Datos (AEPD) and Mario Costeja González,
    Case C-131/12, judgment of 13 May 2014 (Grand Chamber)
    (ECLI:EU:C:2014:317). 9, 85, 120n14, 148n9, 151, 154n61, 275n9, 282n13, 283n13,
            283n21, 283n24, 283n26, 394, 404, 478, 479, 480, 483n30, 575,
        584–85, 592–93, 906–7, 919, 922n50, 1077–78, 1205, 1208, 1209, 1244
Google Spain SL v Agencia Española de Protección de Datos (AEPD) and Mario Costeja González,
    Case C-131/12, Opinion of Advocate General Jääskinen, delivered on 25 June 2013
    (ECLI:EU:C:2013:424) 9–10, 120n14, 297n22, 1244
Groupement des cartes bancaires (CB) v European Commission, Case C-67/13 P, judgment of
    11 September 2014 (ECLI:EU:C:2014:2204) 1185n16, 1187
Gubisch Maschinenfabrik KG v Giulio Palumbo, Case 144/86, judgment of 8 December 1987
    (ECLI:EU:C:1987:528). 1156n7

HaTeFo GmbH v Finanzamt Haldensleben, Case C-110/13, judgment of 27 February 2014
    (ECLI:EU:C:2014:114) 251n19, 252
Her Majesty's Customs and Excise v Gerhart Schindler and Jörg Schindler, Case C-275/92,
    judgment of 24 March 1994 (ECLI:EU:C:1994:119). 297n19
Herbert Handlbauer GmbH, Case C-278/02, judgment of 24 June 2004 (ECLI:EU:C:2004:388) 1163
Höfner (Klaus) and Fritz Elser v Macrotron GmbH, Case C-41/90, judgment of 23 April 1991
    (ECLI:EU:C:1991:161) 250n10, 255n4, 1187n31
Huber (Heinz) v Bundesrepublik Deutschland, Case C-524/06, judgment of 16 December 2008
    (Grand Chamber) (ECLI:EU:C:2008:724). 109–10n27, 328, 336, 1244
Hummel Holding A/S v Nike Inc. and Nike Retail B.V., Case C-617/15, judgment of
    18 May 2017 (ECLI:EU:C:2017:390) 230n18, 250n9, 255n3, 277n19
Hummel Holding A/S v Nike Inc. and Nike Retail B.V., Case C-617/15, Opinion of Advocate
    General Tanchev, delivered on 12 January 2017 (ECLI:EU:C:2017:13). 230n19, 250n9

International Management Group v European Commission, Joined Cases C-183/17 P and
    C-184/17 P, judgment of 31 January 2019 (ECLI:EU:C:2019:78) 306n21, 307n26
IPI (Institut professionnel des agents immobiliers) v Geoffrey Englebert and Others,
    Case C-473/12, judgment of 7 November 2013 (ECLI:EU:C:2013:715). 423, 441–42

Jehovan todistajat — uskonnollinen yhdyskunta, Case C-25/17, judgment of 10 July 2018
    (Grand Chamber) (ECLI:EU:C:2018:551) 65–66n7, 68–69, 140n5, 141n12, 142n13,
            142n14, 142n19, 143n21–22, 143n25–26, 149n14,
        150n27–29, 150–51, 585, 1259n6, 1261, 1262, 1263, 1265n52

Jehovan todistajat — uskonnollinen yhdyskunta, Case C-25/17, Opinion of Advocate
General Mengozzi, delivered on 1 February 2018 (ECLI:EU:C:2018:57) 1258–59, 1263
Jundt (Hans-Dieter), Hedwig Jundt v Finanzamt Offenburg, Case C-281/06, judgment
of 18 December 2007 (ECLI:EU:C:2007:816) 296n18, 297n19

*Kadi (Yassin Abdullah) and Al Barakaat International Foundation v Council of the European Union
and Commission of the European Communities*, Joined Cases C-402 and 415/05 P, judgment
of 3 September 2008 (Grand Chamber) (ECLI:EU:C:2008:461) 764n54, 829n31
Ker-Optika bt v ÀNTSZ Dél-dunántúli Regionális Intézete, Case C-108/09, judgment of
2 December 2010 (ECLI:EU:C:2010:725) 297n23, 298n30, 300–1n42
Kingdom of the Netherlands v European Commission, Case T-380/08, GC, judgment of
13 September 2013 (ECLI:EU:T:2013:480) 896n13, 899n26

La Quadrature du Net and Others v Commission, Case T-738/16 (pending) 1280n6
Leone La Ferla SpA v Commission and European Chemicals Agency, GC, Case T-392/13,
judgment of 15 September 2016 (ECLI:EU:T:2016:478) 251n18
Lidl GmbH & Co. KG v Freistaat Sachsen, Case C-134/15, Opinion of Advocate General
Bobek, delivered on 16 March 2016 (EU:C:2016:169)....................... 1314–15n18
*Liga Portuguesa de Futebol Profissional and Bwin International Ltd v Departamento de Jogos da
Santa Casa da Misericórdia de Lisboa*, Case C-42/07, Opinion of Advocate General Bot,
delivered on 14 October 2008 (ECLI:EU:C:2008:560)............................... 296n17
Liga van Moskeeën en Islamitische Organisaties Provincie Antwerpen, VZW and Others v Vlaams Gewest,
Case C-426/16, judgment of 29 May 2018 (Grand Chamber) (ECLI:EU:C:2018:335) 1262
L'Oréal and Others v eBay International AG and Others, Case C-324/09, judgment of
12 July 2011 (Grand Chamber) (ECLI:EU:C:2011:474) 298n30

Marchiani (Jean-Charles) v European Parliament, Case C-566/14 P, judgment of
14 June 2016 (Grand Chamber) (ECLI:EU:C:2016:437) 965n53
McB (J) v L. E., Case C-400/10 PPU, judgment of 5 October 2010 (ECLI:EU:C:2010:582) 576n11
McFadden (Tobias) v Sony Music Entertainment Germany GmbH, Case C-484/14, judgment
of 15 September 2016 (ECLI:EU:C:2016:689) 297n21
Mediakabel BV v Commissariaat voor de Media, Case C-89/04, judgment of 2 June 2005
(ECLI:EU:C:2005:348) 299–300
*Meroni & Co., Industrie Metallurgiche, SpA v High Authority of the European Coal and Steel
Community*, Case C-9/56, judgment of 13 June 1958 (ECLI:EU:C:1958:7) 1044, 1045
Microsoft Corp. v Commission of the European Communities, CFI, Case T-201/04, judgment
of 17 September 2007 (ECLI:EU:T:2007:289) 502n25
*Minister (The) for Justice and Equality and The Commissioner of the Garda Síochána v Workplace
Relations Commission*, Case C-378/17, judgment of 4 December 2018 (Grand Chamber)
(ECLI:EU:C:2018:979)... 1175n92
Ministerio Fiscal, Case C-207/16, judgment of 2 October 2018 (Grand Chamber)
(ECLI:EU:C:2018:788)...65–66n6, 549–50

National Farmers' Union v Secrétariat général du gouvernement, Case C-241/01, judgment of
22 October 2002 (ECLI:EU:C:2002:604) 1025n39, 1131n28
National Farmers' Union v Secrétariat général du gouvernement, Case C-241/01, Opinion of
Advocate General Misho, delivered on 2 July 2002 (ECLI:EU:C:2002:415) 1314–15n18
Nikolaou (Kalliopi) v Commission of the European Communities, CFI, Case T-259/03, judgment
of 12 September 2007 (ECLI:EU:T:2007:254) 1170
Nowak (Peter) v Data Protection Commissioner, Case C-434/16, judgment of 20 December 2017
(ECLI:EU:C:2017:994)................. 9–10, 109, 109–10n30, 142n14, 143, 458, 473, 513–14
Nowak (Peter) v Data Protection Commissioner, Case C-434/16, Opinion of Advocate
General Kokott, delivered on 20 July 2017 (ECLI:EU:C:2017:58) 514

Opinion 1/15, Opinion of 26 July 2017 (Grand Chamber) (ECLI:EU:C:2017:592) 52, 372,
380–81n88, 423–24, 548, 553n33, 757–58n5, 759n16, 761, 763, 777, 779,
782–84, 829, 834–35, 878n26, 1061n25, 1304–5n10, 1305n12
Opinion 1/15, Opinion of Advocate General Mengozzi, delivered on 8 September 2016
(ECLI:EU:C:2016:656) 782–83, 791

Opinion 2/15, Opinion of 16 May 2017 (Full Court) (ECLI:EU:C:2017:376) 1306n15
Orange Romania SA v Autoritatea Națională de Supraveghere a Prelucrării Datelor cu Caracter Personal, Case C-61/19 (pending) 180

Pammer (Peter) v Reederei Karl Schlüter GmbH & Co. KG and Hotel Alpenhof GmbH v Oliver Heller, Joined Cases C-585/08 and C-144/09, judgment of 7 December 2010 (Grand Chamber) (ECLI:EU:C:2010:740) 12, 89–90
Papasavvas (Sotiris) v O Fileleftheros Dimosia Etaireia Ltd and Others, Case C-291/13, judgment of 11 September 2014 (ECLI:EU:C:2014:2209) 296n17, 297n22
Peterbroeck, Van Campenhout & Cie SCS v Belgian State, Case C-312/93, judgment of 14 December 1995 (ECLI:EU:C:1995:437) 1138n20
Pfeiffer (Bernhard), Wilhelm Roith, Albert Süß, Michael Winter, Klaus Nestvogel, Roswitha Zeller and Matthias Döbele v Deutsches Rotes Kreuz, Kreisverband Waldshut e.V., Joined Cases C-397/01 to C-403/01, judgment of 5 October 2004 (Grand Chamber) (ECLI:EU:C:2004:584) 180n30, 182n42, 183–84n52
Planet49 GmbH v Bundesverband der Verbraucherzentralen und Verbraucherverbände – Verbraucherzentrale Bundesverband e.V., Case C-673/17 (pending) 349
Planet49 GmbH v Bundesverband der Verbraucherzentralen und Verbraucherverbände – Verbraucherzentrale Bundesverband e.V., Case C-673/17, Opinion of Advocate General Szpunar, delivered on 21 March 2019 (ECLI:EU:C:2019:246) 10, 177n10, 177–78n12–13, 180, 181n35, 181n37, 182–83, 184, 184n56, 233n32, 242–43n25
Preston (Shirley) and Others v Wolverhampton Healthcare NHS Trust and Others and Dorothy Fletcher and Others v Midland Bank plc, Case C-78/98, judgment of 16 May 2000 (ECLI:EU:C:2000:247) 1198n22
Privacy International v Secretary of State for Foreign and Commonwealth Affairs and Others, Case C-623/17 (pending) 69
Productores de Música de España (Promusicae) v Telefónica de España SAU, Case C-275/06, judgment of 29 January 2008 (Grand Chamber) (ECLI:EU:C:2008:54) 548, 1253n2
Productores de Música de España (Promusicae) v Telefónica de España SAU, Case C-275/06, Opinion of Advocate General Kokott, delivered on 18 July 2007 (ECLI:EU:C:2008:54) 8
Puškár (Peter) v Finančné riaditeľstvo Slovenskej republiky and Kriminálny úrad finančnej správy, Case C-73/16, judgment of 27 September 2017 (ECLI:EU:C:2017:725) 65–66, 120n24, 1063–64, 1136, 1137–38, 1184–85n14
Puškár (Peter) v Finančné riaditeľstvo Slovenskej republiky and Kriminálny úrad finančnej správy, Case C-73/16, Opinion of Advocate General Kokott, delivered on 30 March 2017 (ECLI:EU:C:2017:253) 65–66n7

Queen (The), on the application of Delena Wells v Secretary of State for Transport, Local Government and the Regions, Case C-201/02, judgment of 7 January 2004 (ECLI:EU:C:2004:12) 1138n20
Queen (The) v Secretary of State for Transport, ex parte Factortame Ltd and others, Case C-221/89, Case C-221/89, judgment of 25 July 1991 (ECLI:EU:C:1991:320) 241n15
Queen (The) v Treasury and Commissioners of Inland Revenue, ex parte Daily Mail and General Trust plc, Case C-81/87, judgment of 27 September 1988 (ECLI:EU:C:1988:456) 231n23
Queen (The) v Treasury and Commissioners of Inland Revenue, ex parteDaily Mail and General Trust plc, Case C-81/87, Opinion of Advocate General Darmon, delivered on 7 June 1988 (ECLI:EU:C:1988:286) 230–31, 231n22

Rease (T. D.), P. Wullems v College bescherming persoonsgegevens, Case C-192/15, order of 9 December 2015 (ECLI:EU:C:2015:861) 936
Rechnungshof v Österreichischer Rundfunk and Others and Christa Neukomm and Joseph Lauermann, Joined Cases C-465/00, C-138/01 and C-139/01, judgment of 20 May 2003 (ECLI:EU:C:2003:294) 53, 67, 109n23, 373n46, 516n47, 547–48, 1232
Rewe-Zentralfinanz eG and Rewe-Zentral AG v Landwirtschaftskammer für das Saarland, Case C-33/76, judgment of 16 December 1976 (ECLI:EU:C:1976:188) 1138n20, 1198n21
Ryneš (František) v Úřad pro ochranu osobních údajů, Case C-212/13, judgment of 11 December 2014 (ECLI:EU:C:2014:2428) 68, 109–10n29, 120n21, 149n17, 442–43, 1265n51

Salvatore Grimaldi v Fonds des maladies professionnelles, Case C-322/88, judgment of 13 December 1989 (ECLI:EU:C:1989:646) 1021–22n26, 1063n34

SAS Institute Inc. v World Programming Ltd, Case C-406/10, judgment of 2 May 2012
  (Grand Chamber) (ECLI:EU:C:2012:259) 407n28
SAT Fluggesellschaft v Eurocontrol, Case C-364/92, judgment of 19 January 1994
  (ECLI:EU:C:1994:7)... 250n14, 255n8, 262n37, 307n28
Satamedia see *Tietosuojavaltuutettu v Satakunnan Markkinapörssi Oy*
Scarlet Extended SA v Société belge des auteurs, compositeurs et éditeurs SCRL (SABAM),
  Case C-70/10, judgment of 24 November 2011 (EU:C:2011:771) 8
Schecke (Volker and Markus) GbR and Hartmut Eifert v Land Hessen, Joined9, judgment of
  9 November 2010 (Grand Chamber) (ECLI:EU:C:2010:662).......... 24–25n115, 111n40, 313,
                                                       545n1, 843–44n2, 1216
Schrems (Maximillian) v Data Protection Commissioner, Case C-362/14, judgment of
  6 October 2015 (Grand Chamber) (ECLI:EU:C:2015:650)..................9, 33, 53, 120n22,
              266n1, 473, 548–49, 553n31–32, 562n24, 757–58, 760–61, 763, 775–76,
              777, 779–82, 784–85, 786n93, 787–88, 790–91, 800, 809, 815n2, 829, 846n17,
              867n14, 875n1, 878n25, 879n33, 896n12, 907–8, 932, 933n18, 935–36, 945,
              978–79, 1025n38, 1062–63, 1065n46, 1066n51, 1115n15, 1121,
              1123, 1128n9, 1129, 1130–31n26, 1137, 1164, 1265n51, 1280, 1310
Schrems (Maximillian) v Data Protection Commissioner, Case C-362/14, Opinion of
  Advocate General Bot, delivered on 23 September 2015 (ECLI:EU:C:2015:650) 779
Schrems (Maximilian) v Facebook Ireland Limited, Case C-498/16, judgment of
  25 January 2018 (ECLI:EU:C:2018:37) 1145–46
Schrems (Maximillian) v Facebook Ireland Limited, Case C-498/16, Opinion of Advocate
  General Bobek, delivered on 14 November 2017 (ECLI:EU:C:2017:863) 1143
Schwarz (Michael) v Stadt Bochum, Case C-291/12, judgment of 17 October 2013
  (ECLI:EU:C:2013:670)... 109–10n28, 120n19, 211
Schwarz (Michael) v Stadt Bochum, Case C-291/12, Opinion of Advocate General Mengozzi,
  delivered on 13 June 2013 (ECLI:EU:C:2013:401) 369–70n10, 372
*SELEX Sistemi Integrati SpA v Commission of the European Communities and Organisation
  européenne pour la sécurité de la navigation aérienne (Eurocontrol)*, Case C-113/07 P,
  judgment of 26 March 2009 (ECLI:EU:C:2009:191) 250n14, 255n8, 262n37, 307n28
SGL Carbon AG v Commission of the European Communities, Case C-328/05 P, judgment of
  10 May 2007 (ECLI:EU:C:2007:277)... 1187
Shell International Chemical Company Ltd v Commission of the European Communities, CFI,
  Case T-11/89, judgment of 10 March 1992 (ECLI:EU:T:1992:33)................. 250–51
Shindler (Harry) and Others v Council of the European Union, Case T-458/17 GC, judgment
  26 November 2018 (ECLI:EU:T:2018:838)............................. 1129, 1129–30n18
Skype Communications Sàrl v Institut belge des services postaux et des télécommunications (IBPT),
  Case C-142/18, judgment of 5 June 2019 (ECLI:EU:C:2019:460) 298n29
Smaranda Bara and Others v Casa Naţională de Asigurări de Sănătate and Others,
  Case C-201/14, judgment of 1 October 2015 (ECLI:EU:C:2015:638)........... 109–10n26, 313,
                                                       422–23, 442, 447, 548
Société nationale des chemins de fer français (SNCF) v European Commission, GC,
  Case T-242/12, judgment of 17 December 2015 (ECLI:EU:T:2015:1003)............... 965n53
Solvay SA v Commission, Case C-109/10 P, judgment of 25 October 2011 (ECLI:EU:C:2011:686).... 1188n41
SY v Associated Newspapers Ltd, Case C-687/18 (pending) 1139, 1163n7, 1207–8

TDC A/S v Teleklagenævnet and Erhvervs- og Vækstministeriet, Case C-327/15, judgment of
  21 December 2016 (ECLI:EU:C:2016:974) 1138n20
*Tele2 Sverige AB v Post-och telestyrelsen and Secretary of State for Home Department v Tom
  Watson and Others*, Joined Cases C-203/15 and C-698/15, judgment of 21 December 2016
  (Grand Chamber) (ECLI:EU:C:2016:970) 53n13, 65–66, 313, 546n3, 546n5,
                                                       548–50, 552, 791, 878n25, 1254, 1296–97, 1306n13
The owners of the cargo lately laden on board the ship 'Tatry' v the owners of the ship 'Maciej Rataj',
  Case C-406/92, judgment of 6 December 1994 (ECLI:EU:C:1994:400) 1156n8
Tietosuojavaltuutettu v Satakunnan Markkinapörssi Oy and Satamedia Oy, Case C-73/07,
  judgment of 16 December 2008 (Grand Chamber) (ECLI:EU:C:2008:727) 11n55, 40–41,
              67n15, 67n17, 109–10n26, 120n15, 142n14, 1205, 1206–7, 1208, 1210, 1253n1
Tietosuojavaltuutettu v Satakunnan Markkinapörssi Oy and Satamedia Oy, Case C-73/07, Opinion
  of Advocate General Kokott, delivered on 8 May 2008 (ECLI:EU:C:2008:266) 1206n13

Tilly-Sabco SAS v European Commission, Case C-183/16 P, judgment of 20 September 2017
  (ECLI:EU:C:2017:704) 1280n5, 1280n8–9
TK v Asociaţia de Proprietari bloc M5A Scara-A, Case C-708/18 (pending) 313
TWD Textilwerke Deggendorf GmbH v Bundesrepublik Deutschland, Case C-188/92,
  judgment of 9 March 1994 (ECLI:EU:C:1994:90) 1025n39, 1129, 1131–32

Uber France, Criminal proceedings against, Case C-320/16, judgment of 10 April 2018
  (Grand Chamber) (ECLI:EU:C:2018:221) 299
*Unabhängiges Landeszentrum für Datenschutz Schleswig-Holstein v Wirtschaftsakademie
  Schleswig-Holstein GmbH*, Case C-210/16, judgment of 5 June 2018 (Grand Chamber)
  (ECLI:EU:C:2018:388) 241n13, 261n27, 275n11, 282n15, 566n58, 585,
                                                    592–93, 870–71n40, 958, 959, 979, 1021
*Unabhängiges Landeszentrum für Datenschutz Schleswig-Holstein v Wirtschaftsakademie
  Schleswig-Holstein GmbH*, Case C-210/16, Opinion of Advocate General Bot, delivered
  on 24 October 2017 (ECLI:EU:C:2017:796). 9–10, 76n2, 78n9, 80, 84, 85,
                          152–53, 154n63, 227n2, 229n12–13, 232n29, 870–71n40, 959n25, 979, 1021
Unión de Pequeños Agricultores v Council of the European Union, Case C-50/00 P, judgment
  of 25 July 2002 (ECLI:EU:C:2002:462) 1134–35n3
*United Kingdom of Great Britain and Northern Ireland v European Parliament and Council
  of the European Union ('ESMA')*, Case C-270/12, judgment of 22 January 2014
  (Grand Chamber) (ECLI:EU:C:2014:18) 1044n9, 1045n15–16
Upjohn Company and Upjohn NV v Farzoo Inc. and J. Kortmann, Case C-112/89, judgment
  of 16 April 1991 (ECLI:EU:C:1991:147) 204n39

V v European Parliament, CST, Case F-46/09, judgment of 5 July 2011
  (ECLI:EU:F:2011:101) 373, 1166–67, 1170–71, 1188n37, 1233
V.Q. v Land Hessen, Case C-272/19 (pending) 149n16, 458
Vanderborght (Luc) Criminal proceedings against, Case C-339/15, judgment of 4 May 2017
  (ECLI:EU:C:2017:335) 298n30
Varec SA v Belgian State, Case C-450/06, judgment of 14 February 2008
  (ECLI:EU:C:2008:91) 1297n15
VCAST Limited v RTI SpA, Case C-265/16, judgment of 29 November 2017
  (ECLI:EU:C:2017:913) 300n40
VCAST Limited v RTI SpA, Case C-265/16, Opinion of Advocate General Szpunar, delivered
  on 7 September 2017 (ECLI:EU:C:2017:649) 300n40
Verein für Konsumenteninformation v Amazon EU Sàrl, Case C-191/15, judgment of
  28 July 2016 (ECLI:EU:C:2016:612) 79, 229n13, 241n12, 261n27, 275n12, 282n15,
                                                       283n20, 592–93, 905n11, 906
Verein für Konsumenteninformation v Amazon EU Sàrl, Case C-191/15, Opinion of Advocate
  General Saugmandsgaard, delivered on 2 June 2016 (ECLI:EU:C:2016:388) ... 80, 229n13, 241n13

WebMindLicenses kft v Nemzeti Adó- és Vámhivatal Kiemelt Adó- és Vám Főigazgatóság, Case
  C-419/14, judgment of 17 December 2015 (ECLI:EU:C:2015:832) 111n41, 1297n14
WebMindLicenses Kft.v Nemzeti Adó- és Vámhivatal Kiemelt Adó- és Vám Főigazgatóság,
  Case C-419/14, Opinion of Advocate General Wathelet, delivered on 16 September 2015
  (ECLI:EU:C:2015:606) 111n41
Weltimmo s.r.o. v Nemzeti Adatvédelmi és Információszabadság Hatóság, Case C-230/14, judgment
  of 1 October 2015 (ECLI:EU:C:2015:639) 80–81, 120n14, 240–42, 261n26–27,
                        275n10, 282n14–18, 283n21, 283n23, 592–93, 905–6, 906n19,
                        907–8, 943n3, 945, 946n25, 957n10, 958–59, 978, 1063n38, 1122–23
Weltimmo s.r.o. v Nemzeti Adatvédelmi és Információszabadság Hatóság, Case C-230/14,
  Opinion of Advocate General Cruz Villalón, delivered on 25 June 2015
  (ECLI:EU:C:2015:426) 84, 85, 120n14, 229n13–14, 235n43, 903–4n3
Wightman (Andy) and Others v Secretary of State for Exiting the European Union, Case C-621/18,
  judgment of 10 December 2018 (Full Court) (ECLI:EU:C:2018:999) 83–84
Willems (W.P.) and Others v Burgemeester van Nuth and Others, Joined Cases C-446/12 to
  C-449/12, judgment of 16 April 2015 (ECLI:EU:C:2015:238) 211
Worten — Equipamentos para o Lar SA v Autoridade para as Condições de Trabalho (ACT), Case
  C-342-12, judgment of 30 May 2013 (ECLI:EU:C:2013:355) 1232

X, Case C-486/12, judgment of 12 December 2013 (ECLI:EU:C:2013:836) 404, 458
Xabier Ormaetxea Garai and Bernardo Lorenzo Almendros v Administración del Estado, Case C-424/15,
    judgment of 19 October 2016 (ECLI:EU:C:2016:780)............ 885n1, 887, 891, 895n4, 1058–59
Xabier Ormaetxea Garai and Bernardo Lorenzo Almendros v Administración del Estado, Case C-424/15,
    Opinion of Advocate General Bot, delivered on 30 June 2016 (ECLI:EU:C:2016:503) 1058–59

*YS v Minister voor Immigratie, Integratie en Asiel and Minister voor Immigratie, Integratie en Asiel v
    M and S*, Joined Cases C-141/12 and C-372/12, judgment of 17 July 2014
    (ECLI:EU:C:2014:2081) 404, 457–58
*YS v Minister voor Immigratie, Integratie en Asiel and Minister voor Immigratie, Integratie en
    Asiel v M and S*, Joined Cases C-141/12 and C-372/12, Opinion of Advocate General
    Sharpston, delivered on 12 December 2013 (ECLI:EU:C:2013:838)........... 109, 110, 120–21

EUROPEAN COURT OF HUMAN RIGHTS

Adolf v Austria, Appl. No. 8269/78, judgment of 26 March 1982......................... 1184n8
Antoneta Tudor v Romania see *Tudor (Antoneta) v Romania*
Antović and Mirković v Montenegro, Appl. No. 70838/13, judgment of 28 November 2017 1233–34
Armoniene v Lithuania, Appl. No. 36919/02, judgment of 25 November 2008 1172
Association for European Integration and Human Rights and Ekimdzhiev v Bulgaria, Appl.
    No. 62540/00, judgment of 30 January 2008 406
Aycaguer v France, Appl. No. 8806/12, judgment of 22 June 2017 201
Bărbulescu v Romania, Appl. No. 61496/08, judgment of 5 September 2017 .... 424, 1233, 1295n3
Biriuk v Lithuania, Appl. No. 23373/03, judgment of 25 November 2008.................... 1172
Brunet v France, Appl. No. 21010/10, judgment of 18 September 2014 .... 388n9
Campbell and Fell v United Kingdom, Appl. Nos. 7819/77 and 7878/77, judgment of
    28 June 1984 .... 1184–85n10
Cemalettin Canli v Turkey, Appl. No. 22427/04, judgment of 18 November 2008............. 472–73
Centrum För Rättvisa v Sweden, Appl. No. 35252/08, 19 June 2018 .... 945n23
Ciubotaru v Moldova, Appl. No. 27138/04, judgment of 27 July 2010 472–73
Copland v United Kingdom, Appl. No. 62617/00, judgment of 3 April 2007 .... 313n11,
                                                                              424–25, 1233n17
Couderc and Hackette Filipacchi Associés v France, Appl. No. 40454/07, judgment of
    10 November 2015 ....34, 1209n30, 1209n32
Dalea v France, Appl. No. 964/07, judgment of 2 February 2010 470
Delfi AS v Estonia, Appl. No. 64569/09, judgment of 16 June 2015 .... 479n6, 1210n37
Demicoli v Malta, Appl. No. 13057/87, judgment of 27 August 1991....................... 1184n8
Dumitru Popescu v Romania No. 2 see *Popescu (Dumitru) v Romania No. 2*
Engel and Others v The Netherlands, Appl. Nos. 5100/71, 5101/71, 5102/71, 5354/72
    and 5370/72, judgment of 8 June 1976 .... 1184–85n9, 1199
Gabriele Weber and Cesar Richard Saravia v Germany see *Weber (Gabrielle) and Cesar Richard
    Saravia v Germany*
Gaskin v United Kingdom, Appl. No. 10454/83, judgment of 7 July 1989....313n12, 406, 459, 1217–18n18
Gheorghe (Nicoleta) v Romania, Appl. No. 23470/05, judgment of 3 April 2012............. 1184–85n9
Godelli v Italy, Appl. No. 33783/09, judgment of 25 September 2012 .... 406, 459n42
Guerra v Italy, Appl. No. 14967/89, judgment of 19 February 1998 1218
Haralambie v Romania, Appl. No. 21737, judgment of 27 October 2009... 313n12, 406, 452n6, 459n47
I v Finland, Appl. No. 20511/03, judgment of 17 July 2008 .... 218n1, 221n18, 329–30n16,
                                                                      358–59, 373n44, 575–76, 1171–72
Jäggi v Switzerland, Appl. No. 58757/00, judgment of 13 July 2006 .... 1225–26n13
Jarnea v Romania, Appl. No. 41838/05, judgment of 19 July 2011 .... 452n6, 459n47
Joanna Szulc v Poland see *Szulc (Joanna) v Poland*
Kennedy v United Kingdom, Appl. No. 26839/05, judgment of 18 May 2010 406
K.H. and Others v Slovakia, Appl. No. 32881/04, judgment of 28 April 2009 .... 314n19, 406, 459
Khelili v Switzerland, Appl. No. 16188/07, judgment of 18 October 2011 .... 388–89n9
Klass and Others v Germany, Appl. No. 5029/71, judgment of 6 September 1978.................. 406
K.U. v Finland, Appl. No. 2872/02, judgment of 2 December 2008 358–59
Leander v Sweden, Appl. No. 9248/81, judgment of 26 March 1987..................... 268–69n15,
                                                                      458–59, 472n9, 1217–18n18
L.H. v Latvia, Appl. No. 52019/07, judgment of 29 April 2014 .... 373n44

Libert v France, Appl. No. 588/13, judgment of 22 February 2018 1233
L.L. v France, Appl. No. 7508/02, judgment of 10 October 2006 .... 373n44
Lopez Ribalda and Others v Spain see *Ribalda (Lopez) and Others v Spain*
Lutz v Germany, Appl. No. 9912/82, judgment of 25 August 1987 .... 1184–85n9
Magyar Helsinki Bizottság v Hungary, Appl. No. 18030/11, judgment of
   8 November 2016 1216–20
Menarini Diagnostics (A), S.R.L. v Italy, Appl. No. 43509/08, judgment of
   27 September 2011 .... 1184n8, 1199n26
M.K. v France, Appl. No. 19522/09, judgment of 18 April 2013 .... 211n18
M.L. and W.W. v Germany, Appl. Nos. 60798/10 and 65599/10, judgment of 28 June 2018 ..... 480n8
M.M. v United Kingdom, Appl. No. 24029/07, judgment of 13 November 2012 388
Mosley v United Kingdom, Appl. No. 48009/08, judgment of 10 May 2011 .... 516n47
MS v Sweden, Appl. No. 20837/92, judgment of 27 August 1997 .... 221n18, 313
Nicoleta Gheorghe v Romania see *Gheorghe (Nicoleta) v Romania*
Niemietz v Germany, Appl. No. 13710/88, judgment of 16 December 1992 .... 1297n16
Odièvre v France, Appl. No. 42326/98, judgment of 13 February 2003 ...... 406, 459n42, 1225–26n13
Öztürk v Germany, Appl. No. 8544/79, judgment of 21 February 1984 .... 1184–85n9
Peck v United Kingdom, Appl. No. 44647/98, judgment of 28 January 2003 .... 1297n16
Popescu (Dumitru) v Romania No. 2, Appl. No. 71525/01, judgment of 26 April 2007 406
Pruteanu v Romania, Appl. No. 30181/05, judgment of 3 February 2015 1172–73
Rees v the United Kingdom, Appl. No. 9532/91, judgment of 17 October 1986 405
Ribalda (Lopez) and Others v Spain, Appl. Nos. 1774/13 and 8567/13, judgment of
   9 January 2018 .... 425, 1234, 1236n27
Roche v United Kingdom, Appl. No. 32555/96, judgment of 19 October 2005 406
Roman Zakharov v Russia see *Zakharov (Roman) v Russia*
Rotaru v Romania [GC], Appl. No. 28341/95, judgment of 4 May 2000 .... 313, 472n9
S and Marper v United Kingdom, Appl. Nos. 30562/04, 30566/04, judgment of
   4 December 2008 .... 107–8n15, 109–10n28, 201, 211, 313, 373n44
Satakunnan Markkinapörssi Oy and Satamedia Oy v Finland, Appl. No. 931/13, judgment
   of 27 June 2017 1210
Satakunnan Markkinapörssi Oy and Satamedia Oy v Finland, Appl. No. 931/13, judgment
   of 21 July 2015 1210
Sdružení Jihočeské Matky v Czech Republic, Appl. No. 19101/03 (decision on admissibility),
   judgment of 10 July 2006 1218
Segerstedt-Wiberg and Others v Sweden, Appl. No. 62332/00, judgment of 6 June 2006 .... 406, 459
Société Colas Est and Others v France, Appl. No. 37971/97, judgment of 16 April 2002 .... 1297n16
Sporrong and Lönnroth v Sweden, Appl. No. 7151/75, judgment of 23 September 1982 .... 404n13
Sunday Times (The) v United Kingdom, Appl. No. 6538/74, judgment of 26 April 1979 .... 1217n17
Szabo and Vissy v Hungary, Appl. No. 37138/14, judgment of
   12 January 2016 .... 313n13, 548–49, 550
Szulc (Joanna) v Poland, Appl. No. 43932/08, judgment of 13 November 2012 .... 452n6
Társaság a Szabadságjogokért v Hungary, Appl. No. 37374/05, judgment of 14 April 2009 1218
Times Newspapers Ltd v United Kingdom (nos. 1 and 2), Appl. Nos. 3002/03 and 23676/03,
   judgment of 10 March 2009 1244
Tudor (Antoneta) v Romania, Appl. No. 23445/04, judgment of September 24 2013 .... 452n6
Verlagsgruppe News GmbH v Austria (no. 2), Appl. No. 10/520/02, judgment of 14 December 2006. ... 516n47
Vinci Construction and GTM Génie Civil et Services v France, Appl. Nos. 63629/10 and
   60567/10, judgment of 2 April 2015 .... 1297n16
Von Hannover v Germany (No. 3), Appl. No. 8772/10, judgment of 19 September 2013 .... 516n47
Von Hannover v Germany (No. 2), Appl. Nos. 40660/08 and 60641/08, judgment of
   7 February 2012 .... 1205n7, 1209–10, 1210n38
Von Hannover v Germany, Appl. No. 59320/00, judgment of 24 September 2004 ...... 325n1, 1209–10
Vučković and Others v Serbia [GC], Appl. Nos. 17153/11, 17157/11, 17160/11, 17163/11,
   17168/11, 17173/11, 17178/11, 17181/11, 17182/11, 17186/11, 17343/11, 17344/11,
   17362/11, 17364/11, 17367/11, 17370/11, 17372/11, 17377/11, 17380/11, 17382/11,
   17386/11, 17421/11, 17424/11, 17428/11, 17431/11, 17435/11, 17438/11, 17439/11,
   17440/11 and 17443/11, judgment of 25 March 2014 .... 1134–35n2
Vukota-Bojic v Switzerland, Appl. No. 61838/10, judgment of 18 October 2016 .... 373n44

Weber (Gabrielle) and Cesar Richard Saravia v Germany, Appl. No. 54934/00, Decision of
 29 June 2006..406
Węgrzynowski and Smolczewski v Poland, Appl. No. 33846/07, judgment of
 16 July 2013..478–80, 516n46, 1264–65n48
Z v Finland, Appl. No. 22009/93, judgment of 25 February 1997...................218n1, 221n18,
 329–30n16, 358–59, 373n44
Zakharov (Roman) v Russia, Appl. No. 47143/06, judgment of 4 December 2015..........406, 548–50, 760

NATIONAL CASES

Austria
Verfassungsgerichtshof, 27.06.2014, G47/2012 ua (ECLI:AT:VFGH:2014:G47.2012)....1145, 1185n15
Verfassungsgerichtshof, 28.11.2003, KR1/00 (ECLI:AT:VFGH:2003:KR1.2000)..............1232n9

Belgium
Court of Cassation, *D.J-M. v Belfius Banque sa*, judgment of 22 February 2017...................142
Court of Appeal of Brussels, judgment of 8 May 2019 (18N – 2018/AR/410).................958n18
Court of Appeal of Liège, judgment of 6 February 2006 142

France
Cour de Cassation, Chambre Civile 1, 94-14.798, 5 November 1996 ....1175–76n95
Cour de Cassation, Chambre criminelle, audience publique du 24 septembre 1998, No.
 de pourvoi 97-81.748, Publié au bulletin...529n18
Tribunal de Grand Instance de Paris, ¼ social, jugement du 9 avril 2019, *UFC - Que choisir /
 Société Facebook Ireland Limited*, N° RG: 14/07298......................................1146n22
Tribunal de Grand Instance de Paris, ¼ social, jugement du 12 février 2019, *UFC - Que choisir /
 Société Google Inc.*, N° RG: 14/07224..1146n22
Tribunal de Grand Instance de Paris, ¼ social, jugement du 7 août 2018, *UFC - Que choisir /
 Société Twitter Inc. et Société Twitter International Company*, N° RG 14/07300 ....1146n22

Germany
German Federal Court of Justice
Bundesgerichtshof, Urteil vom 28. 1. 2014, VI ZR 156/13....................................529
Bundesgerichtshof, Urteil vom 16. 07. 2008, VIII ZR 348/06..............................349n7–8
Bundesgerichtshof, Urteil vom 27.06.2007, XII ZB 114/06................................231n25

German Federal Constitutional Court
Bundesverfassungsgerichtshof, Urteil vom 15.12.1983, VZG 83 1 BVerfGE 65
 ('Volkzählungsurteil')...877

Ireland
Collins v FBD Insurance plc [2013] IEHC 137, 14 March 2013.......................1164–65n21
Data Protection Commissioner and Facebook Ireland Limited and Maximilian Schrems,
 Irish High Court, 2016 No. 4809 P, 3 October 2017..........................791n146, 802
Digital Rights Ireland Ltd v Minister for Communication and Others [2010] IEHC 221,
 judgment by J. McKechnie delivered on 5 May 2010..................................1145n8
Judgment of Mr Justice Clark, Irish Supreme Court, 2018 No. 2018/68, 31 July 2018............802

Italy
Balducci Romano v Azienda per l'Assistenza Sanitaria n. 3 Alto Friuli Collinare Medio Friuli,
 Tribunale Amministrativo Regionale- Friuli Venezia Giulia Reg. Ric. 00135/2018...........692
Italian Supreme Court, judgment No. 10280 of 20 May 2015............................221–22
Italian Supreme Court, judgment No. 18980 of 8 August 2013..........................221–22
Judgment of the Court of Padua of 26 May 2000 (case No. 3531/99)...........1260n16, 1260n18–19

Netherlands
Hoge Raad, judgment of 23 March 2010 (ECLI:NL:HR:2010:BK6331)........................208

Romania

Court of Appeal, Cluj, Decision No. 88/A of 25 September 2012 . . . . 1175–76n95
Court of First Instance (Judecătoria Sectorului 1), Bucharest, Sector 1, Case No. 19326/299/2008,
    judgment of 16 March 2009 1174

Spain

Spanish Supreme Court (Tribunal Supremo), judgment No. 383/2011 of 4 February 2011 142

United Kingdom

B v The General Medical Council [2018] EWCA Civ 1497 . . . . 221n19
Durant v Financial Services Authority [2003] EWCA Civ 1746. 107–8n15, 142
Google Inc. v Vidal-Hall, Hann and Bradshaw [2015] EWCA Civ 311 (CA) 1173
Ittihadieh v Cheyne Gardens joined with Deer v University of Oxford [2017] EWCA Civ 121 459–60
R v Department of Health; ex parte Source Informatics Ltd [2000] 1 All ER 786. 121
Stunt v Associated Newspapers Ltd [2018] EWCA Civ 1780. 1207–8
Young v Anglo American South Africa Limited [2014] EWCA Civ 1130. 231

United States

*In the matter of a warrant to search a certain e-mail account controlled and maintained by
    Microsoft Corporation*, 829 F3d 197 (2nd Cir. 2016), cert. granted, 16 October 2017,
    dismissed per curiam, 584 US ___ (2018) 829
Société Nationale Industrielle Aérospatiale v United States, 482 US 522 (1987) 826n1
United States v Microsoft Corporation, 584 US ___ (2018) (per curiam). 829
Volkswagen v Valdez, 909 SW2d 900 (Tex. 1995). 829–30

Table of Instruments

For the benefit of digital users, table entries that span two pages (e.g., 52–3) may, on occasion, appear on only one of those pages.

EUROPEAN UNION INSTRUMENTS

The GDPR

General Data Protection Regulation 2016: Regulation (EU) 2016/679 of the European Parliament and of the Council of 27 April 2016 on the protection of natural persons with regard to the processing of personal data and on the free movement of such data, and repealing Directive 95/46/EC ('GDPR') 2, 10, 200
Recital 2 .... 50, 57, 869n30
Recital 3 .... 869n29
Recital 4 .... 57, 381n94, 522, 526, 1202, 1257–59
Recital 6 .... 756–57, 773, 798, 814, 843, 857–58
Recital 7 .... 53–54, 1028, 1092n9
Recital 8 .... 340n80
Recital 9 ... 119, 141–42, 166n7, 283n22, 1250
Recital 10 ... 119, 141–42, 166n7, 283n22, 366, 369n1, 590, 757, 1250
Recital 11 .... 104, 571–72
Recital 13 ... 75, 246–47, 249, 601, 954–55, 1181
Recital 14 .... 60, 65, 75, 88
Recital 15 .... 51, 60, 66–67, 75, 116, 138
Recital 16 .... 51, 60, 69, 75
Recital 17 ..... 51, 61, 75, 1264, 1312, 1313–14, 1315n24
Recital 18 .... 51, 61, 67–68, 70, 75
Recital 19 .... 51, 61, 75, 385, 387–90
Recital 20 .... 51, 61, 70–71, 75, 692, 902, 904, 909–10
Recital 21 .... 51, 62, 75, 292
Recital 22 ... 51, 62, 74, 87, 225, 229, 235n43, 261, 272, 275, 279, 282, 903–4, 907n24, 991n19
Recital 23 .... 51, 62, 74, 89, 590
Recital 24 .... 51, 62, 74–75, 89–90, 127, 522, 590
Recital 25 .... 51, 62, 75, 92–95
Recital 26 ..... 62, 103, 105–6n2, 106, 108–9, 110–11, 132, 196, 202, 207, 214–15, 217, 222, 391, 392–93n6, 395, 1242
Recital 27 .... 62, 75, 103, 112, 142, 537n61, 1247n29, 1248n30
Recital 28 .... 132, 571–72
Recital 29 132
Recital 30 .... 8, 14, 103, 127
Recital 31 .... 138, 163
Recital 32 .... 174, 183–85, 292, 324, 345–46
Recital 33 .... 174–75, 183, 345–46, 1249n41–42
Recital 34 .... 103, 104, 112, 196, 201, 202, 207, 217, 368
Recital 35 .... 103–4, 112, 196, 202, 207, 215, 217, 222–23, 368
Recital 36 .... 225–26, 230, 233, 235, 272, 276, 954–55, 1016
Recital 37 .... 225–26, 235n45, 246–47, 255–56, 262n29
Recital 38 .... 127, 175, 292, 357, 359, 522–23, 527, 534–36
Recital 39 ...... 175, 183n48, 309–10, 314–15, 317–18, 324, 391–92, 427n79, 450, 469–70, 525, 556, 582
Recital 40 .... 175, 310, 322, 345–46
Recital 41 .... 310, 322, 544
Recital 42 .... 174–75, 182n39, 183–85, 310, 329–30, 345–46, 348, 350, 1229
Recital 43 ...... 19, 174–75, 181–82, 310, 322, 330, 345–46, 348, 352–53, 537, 1229, 1236
Recital 44 .... 303, 310, 322
Recital 45 .... 303, 310, 322, 341n83, 341n85, 544
Recital 46 .... 303, 310, 323, 333–35, 368, 379
Recital 47 .... 170, 303, 310, 323, 336n57, 337–38, 343n99, 388n6
Recital 48 .... 303, 310, 323, 337, 756, 843
Recital 49 .... 303, 310, 323, 337
Recital 50 .... 175, 303, 310, 315–16n29, 323–24, 341n86, 342, 345–46, 386, 544, 1242
Recital 51 .... 104, 175, 196, 207, 212–13, 217, 324, 366, 369–70, 374–75, 376n58, 378, 590
Recital 52 .... 367, 379n74, 590, 1229, 1242
Recital 53 .... 196, 217, 367, 372n33, 380–81, 391, 590, 1242
Recital 54 .... 367, 380, 590
Recital 55 367
Recital 56 .... 367, 379n77
Recital 57 .... 392–94, 450

Recital 58.........310, 355, 399, 449–50, 461,
           463, 525
Recital 59...... 24–25n116, 399, 410, 450, 470,
           473–74, 508–9
Recital 60...... 127, 175, 310, 399–400, 410,
           414, 435, 450, 523, 525, 590,
           700–1, 1071, 1268
Recital 61........163, 175, 310, 400, 414, 435,
           498, 590, 700–1
Recital 62..............175, 400, 414, 435–36,
           446–47, 498, 590
Recital 63....127, 163–64, 399–400, 407, 410,
           450, 464–65, 500n11, 523
Recital 64................. 391–92, 450, 460
Recital 65.......... 175, 292, 294n4, 345–46,
           469–70, 475–76, 481–82,
           508–9, 516–17, 1203
Recital 66 ....476, 1203
Recital 67............123, 125, 138, 485, 488,
           490–91, 508–9
Recital 68............. 175, 345–46, 497–98,
           504n35, 504–5
Recital 69.......... 170, 292, 476, 508, 516–17
Recital 70................ 127, 292, 476, 508, 525
Recital 71.....127, 175, 196, 207, 217, 345–46,
           355, 523, 526–27, 534,
           535–36, 538, 571–72
Corrigenda to Recital 71..........524, 526n5
Recital 72...........................127, 524
Recital 73........127, 188, 324, 450, 470, 489,
           497–98, 508–9, 524, 543–44, 545
Recital 74........ 145, 310, 555, 564n40, 564,
           582, 681, 718, 726
Recital 75........133, 310, 386, 555, 565, 718,
           726, 922, 1252, 1255
Recital 76..................310, 555, 718, 726
Recital 77....... 310, 556, 562–63, 681, 689,
           700–1, 709, 717–18, 725–26, 733, 745
Recital 78......26, 133, 391–92, 556, 564n44,
           565n53, 571, 577–78
Recital 79..........................145, 582
Recital 80........... 238, 242–43, 244, 386,
           589, 590, 595–96, 597
Recital 81............... 157, 160n18, 571–72,
           578, 582, 600, 717, 726, 733, 995
Recital 82..............556, 590, 601, 681,
           689, 700–1, 710
Recital 83.................310, 391–92, 556,
           571–72, 718, 726
Recital 84........ 525, 556, 566n61, 571–72,
           680–81, 684–85, 718, 726, 929
Recital 85..............133, 188, 564n49, 689,
           700–1, 710, 1252
Recital 86................ 188–89, 564n49
Recital 87 ....189, 571–72, 578
Recital 88 ....189, 571–72, 578
Recital 89....................556, 590, 681
Recital 90.... 556, 566n61, 590, 689, 700–1, 710

Recital 91......... 127, 196, 207, 217, 284n32,
           368, 386, 388, 524–25, 556,
           590, 595, 689, 693, 700–1, 710
Recital 92 ....556, 590
Recital 93..........................341, 590
Recital 94........... 590, 681, 684–85, 689,
           700–1, 710, 929, 941
Recital 95...............................681
Recital 96 ....681, 686
Recital 97 ......243–44, 368, 386, 388, 556,
           563n35, 590, 681, 688–89,
           695, 700–1, 703, 706, 709–10
Recital 98 .....246–47, 556, 717–18, 726, 929
Recital 99 ....556, 718
Recital 100........ 556, 564n46, 732, 733n2,
           736n24, 745, 929, 1071,
           1085, 1088n14, 1268
Recital 101.................75, 164, 303, 304,
           755, 757, 762, 763
Recital 102... 75, 303, 756, 760–61, 773, 777,
           825, 834–35, 857, 954–55, 1303–4n8
Recital 103............... 75, 303, 756, 772
Recital 104............... 9, 33, 75, 756, 772,
           859n12, 874, 929
Recital 105.............75, 303, 756, 772–73,
           785n90, 788n117
Recital 106........75, 303, 756, 773, 790n133
Recital 107........... 75, 257, 303, 756, 773
Recital 108.........75, 257, 556, 700–1, 710,
           718, 726, 756, 797–98,
           802, 803, 808n48, 929
Recital 109............75, 718, 726, 756, 798,
           802–3, 805–6, 929
Recital 110.....75, 246–47, 258, 556, 756, 814
Recital 111....75, 164, 175, 345–46, 756, 842,
           848, 851, 851n50, 853n61
Recital 112..............75, 175, 303, 377–78,
           756, 842, 850, 852
Recital 113..........75, 756, 802–3n26, 842,
           853n65, 854n68
Recital 114..............75, 756, 798, 802–3, 843
Recital 115.............. 75, 756, 825, 833–34
Recital 116.............. 75, 756, 857, 859n11,
           929, 941, 954–55, 974, 986–87
Recital 117........ 265, 266, 269, 270, 700–1,
           863, 864–65, 868, 873, 875n2, 884,
           893, 903, 941, 1055, 1063
Recital 118....265, 269, 700–1, 864, 873, 884,
           894, 903, 1041, 1055, 1102, 1106
Recital 119...........265, 863, 884, 894, 903
Recital 120....... 265, 269, 700–1, 864, 873,
           881n42, 884, 894, 903, 1055
Recital 121..... 265, 269, 700–1, 864, 873–74,
           882n47, 884, 888, 890, 893–94,
           897–98, 903, 1055
Recital 122.........75, 265, 269, 700–1, 710,
           863–64, 868–69, 902–3, 914,
           928, 933, 941, 946n25, 954–55, 1118

Table of Instruments

Recital 123 .... 75, 234n40, 265, 269, 864,
868–69, 903, 914, 928, 933,
954–55, 973–74, 980, 987,
1006, 1016, 1028n1, 1032
Recital 124 ... 75, 226, 265, 272–73, 278, 279,
285–86, 288, 290n8, 864, 903, 906–7n22,
913–14, 954–55, 974, 987, 995, 1006, 1016,
1070–71, 1122n34
Recital 125 .... 226, 265, 864, 903, 914,
954–55, 960, 966, 974, 987
Recital 126 .... 226, 265, 864, 903, 914,
954–55, 962, 963, 974, 987
Recital 127 .... 75, 226, 265, 288–89, 864, 903,
914, 921, 922, 923n53, 954–55, 974, 987
Recital 128 ...... 75, 226, 265, 864, 902, 903,
914, 941, 954–55, 960n29, 974, 987
Recital 129 ....75, 265, 681, 864, 903, 914,
928–29, 932, 940–41, 943n4, 949,
954–55, 962, 965–66n54, 966n57,
1041, 1126, 1130, 1182, 1252
Recital 130 ..... 226, 265, 864, 903, 914, 941,
954, 962, 963, 974, 979–80n22,
987, 991n18, 995
Recital 131........... 75, 226, 265, 864, 903,
914, 941, 954, 974, 987
Recital 132 .... 247–48n2, 265, 864,
903, 914, 929
Recital 133 ....75, 265, 864, 903, 914,
929, 941, 954–55, 974, 980,
987, 1006, 1027–28n1
Recital 134 ...... 265, 864, 914, 941, 954–55,
974, 987, 991, 1006
Recital 135...... 265, 273, 279, 284, 864, 914,
922, 954–55, 995, 999–1000, 1006,
1007n5, 1016, 1028n1, 1055, 1071, 1098
Recital 136 ....265, 864, 914, 954–55,
964–65, 974, 999–1000, 1006,
1015, 1019, 1020, 1021, 1022,
1027–28, 1055, 1071, 1090, 1098
Recital 137 .... 75, 265, 864, 914, 954–55,
969, 1016, 1027, 1030, 1090
Recital 138 ...... 265, 273, 864, 914, 954–55,
974, 983, 987, 993, 995,
999, 1000, 1006, 1016, 1027
Recital 139 ...... 265, 700–1, 864, 874, 1041,
1044, 1045–46, 1055, 1059, 1071, 1074,
1080, 1085, 1090, 1095, 1098, 1102, 1291
Recital 140 .... 1016, 1041, 1090,
1098, 1102, 1107
Recital 141...........75, 929, 941, 1117, 1118,
1123, 1125, 1126, 1130n21,
1133, 1153, 1161, 1182
Recital 142 .... 1118, 1126, 1133,
1142, 1148–49n35, 1161
Recital 143 .....954–55, 964–65n49, 966–67,
967n60, 1015, 1017–18, 1024,
1025, 1125–26, 1129–31,
1130n19–20, 1132

Recital 144 .... 1126, 1133, 1153, 1156,
1156n9, 1161
Recital 145..... 75, 590, 601, 1017, 1118, 1126,
1133, 1153, 1160, 1161, 1182
Recital 146 .....582, 601, 1126, 1133, 1139n23,
1160, 1175n94, 1176–77n97–98
Recital 147........75, 82n27, 601, 1126, 1133,
1137, 1140, 1161, 1177n99
Recital 148....556, 929, 946–47, 1133, 1181–82,
1189n43, 1189, 1223, 1229
Recital 149.............1182, 1188, 1194, 1198
Recital 150...............246–47, 249, 254–55,
262–63, 307, 556, 718, 726, 941,
1016, 1126, 1182, 1187, 1189, 1194, 1198
Recital 151.... 556, 718, 726, 1182, 1194, 1198
Recital 152............. 1126, 1182, 1194–95
Recital 153....... 773, 814, 843, 874, 1202–3,
1204, 1209, 1210–11, 1213
Recital 154..................1203, 1213, 1217
Recital 155................ 345–46, 1229
Recital 156....132–33, 324, 470, 485–86, 498,
1240–41, 1246n23, 1246–47, 1249n39
Recital 157................ 324, 1241, 1248n32
Recital 158..........310, 324, 1241, 1247n28,
1247n29, 31, 1248n36–37
Recital 159.... 310, 324, 1241, 1248, 1248n33,
1249n38, 1249n40
Recital 160 ....310, 324, 1241, 1247n29,
1248n34–35
Recital 161.......... 324, 419, 1241, 1246n24
Recital 162.....310, 324, 1241–42, 1249, 1250
Recital 163...................310, 324, 1242
Recital 164 .... 941, 1111, 1116, 1252
Recital 165............ 1257, 1258–59, 1263
Recital 166 ..... 400, 733, 745, 752n37, 1268,
1271, 1272
Recital 167.... 247–48n1, 752n36, 1032, 1278
Recital 168 ....303, 718, 726, 733,
745, 1032, 1278
Recital 169............ 303, 1278, 1286
Recital 171........ 345–46, 847–48, 1291–92
Recital 173.............71, 1291, 1292, 1294,
1295n1, 1299, 1312, 1313–14
Arts 1–4................................ 11–16
Arts 1–10...................................6n24
Arts 1–40....................................6n25
Art 1...................... 48–58, 62, 943
Art 1(1)......... 50, 52–53, 54–56, 868, 1309
Art 1(2) 50–51, 53
Art 1(3) 50, 51, 53, 57, 908
Art 1(5) 1309
Art 2 .... 11–12, 51, 55–56, 60–72, 75,
116, 139–40, 832
Art 2(1) 63, 66n9, 119, 138, 139–40n2,
141–42, 1250n47
Art 2(2) 11–12, 1261, 1265
Art 2(2)(a) 69, 834n72
Art 2(2)(b)........................... 70

Art 2(2)(c) 11, 67–68
Art 2(2)(d) . . . 11–12, 70, 386–87, 389n13, 406,
    792n149, 809n52, 834n75
Art 2(3) 12, 64, 71, 1264, 1312,
    1313n4, 1314, 1315, 1316
Art 2(4) 72, 292
Art 3 . . . . 12–13, 51, 62, 63, 74–96,
    488, 590, 758, 832, 906
Art 3(1) 9, 79, 83, 84, 85, 86, 87,
    88, 92, 594, 903–4
Art 3(2) 83, 86, 88, 89, 91, 95, 242n17,
    395, 428, 590–91, 858, 918–19
Art 3(2)(a) 89, 90, 91
Art 3(2)(b) 89, 90–91, 127, 525
Art 3(3) 13, 83, 92–95
Art 4 . . . . 13–16, 100–2, 374, 395,
    728, 1229, 1242
Art 4(1) . . . 8, 13–14, 62, 66, 103–112, 113–14,
    170, 196, 202, 207, 214–15, 217,
    222, 324, 368, 391–92, 394, 1250
Art 4(1)(a) 906–7n22
Art 4(2) 62, 66, 116–21, 247–48, 273,
    279, 368, 518, 765n57, 1292
Art 4(3) 123–25, 486, 490
Art 4(4) 24, 90n69, 127–31, 525,
    526, 533–34
Art 4(5) 15–16, 104, 112,
    132–36, 394, 571–72
Art 4(6) 62, 66, 119, 135, 138–43, 1016
Art 4(7) 145–55, 159, 170, 226, 244, 258,
    578, 582
Art 4(8) 146, 157–61, 170, 226,
    244, 258, 601
Art 4(9) 160, 163–68, 170, 335n46,
    492, 495n14
Art 4(10) 166, 170–72
Art 4(11) 174–86, 329, 345–46, 348, 351,
    368, 415n3, 439n17, 537, 847, 1235
Art 4(12) 188–93, 460n54, 876, 1298n21
Art 4(13) 104, 112, 196–203, 207, 213,
    217, 222, 368, 369n2, 374n54
Art 4(14) 104, 112, 202–3, 207–14, 222,
    368, 369n2, 374n55
Art 4(15) 104, 112, 196, 202–3, 207, 213,
    217–23, 368, 374n56
Art 4(16) 14–15, 196, 217, 225–36, 260, 261,
    262–63, 914, 920, 954–55, 960–61
Art 4 (16)(a) 232, 234
Art 4 (16)(b) 234–35
Art 4(17) 238–44, 590, 595–96
Art 4(18) 246–52, 253, 820
Art 4(19) 226, 246–47,
    253–56, 258, 262, 820
Art 4(20) 246–47, 253, 256n10,
    257–63, 756, 814–15, 820n15
Art 4(21) 265–70, 273, 864, 874, 884,
    894, 903, 929, 941, 1027–28, 1029
Art 4(22) 265, 272–78, 914, 954–55,
    962–63n41, 1027–28, 1029

Art 4(22)(a) 275, 276, 285–86
Art 4(22)(b) 275, 276–77, 286, 1030
Art 4(22)(c) 275, 278, 1030
Art 4(23) 273, 279–86, 762, 914, 918,
    954–55, 991, 1123n40
Art 4(23)(a) 281–82
Art 4(23)(b) 281–82, 284–85
Art 4(24) 288–91, 954–55, 962n38,
    1016, 1019n12, 1020
Art 4(25) 292–301, 359
Art 4(26) 303–7, 786–87
Arts 5–7 1191
Arts 5–11 16–20
Art 5 . . . . 127, 175, 309–19, 324, 325, 327, 343,
    386, 388, 390, 393, 395, 476, 544,
    550–51, 556, 577, 582, 738,
    803, 1242, 1244–45n18
Art 5(b) 551
Art 5(e) 551
Art 5(1) 325, 386–87, 391–92, 395, 414,
    436, 450, 566, 722
Art 5(1)(a) 314–15, 415n2, 416n11,
    486, 525, 538
Art 5(1)(b) 16–17, 181, 183–84, 315–17,
    326–27, 341–43, 392n1,
    430–31, 446n63, 1245
Art 5(1)(c) 317, 381–82n95, 392n1, 395–96,
    486, 490, 577, 1227n17, 1246–47
Art 5(1)(d) 317, 470, 471, 486, 489
Art 5(1)(e) 318, 392n1, 395–96
Art 5(1)(f) 318, 765n58
Art 5(2) 145, 318–19, 352, 525, 538,
    561–62, 566, 571–72, 573, 576, 707,
    719, 733, 736, 745, 757, 936, 1176n96
Art 6 . . . . 95–96, 127, 314, 321–43, 376–77,
    378, 386, 390, 391–92, 395, 396,
    498, 509, 525, 738, 1217, 1220,
    1235n21, 1242, 1245, 1300
Art 6(1) 310, 325–26, 329–40, 343,
    386–87, 388, 396, 490
Art 6(1)(a) 175, 176–77, 180, 181, 183, 329,
    331–32, 334, 339, 345–46, 349,
    359, 377, 1249n41–43
Art 6(1)(b) 329, 330–32, 335, 335n50
Art 6(1)(c) 84, 326, 329, 330–31,
    332–33, 334, 335–36, 337–38,
    337n65, 339, 340, 482, 904
Art 6(1)(d) 329, 334, 337–38
Art 6(1)(e) 84, 326, 329, 330, 333, 334,
    335–36, 339, 340, 351, 379, 481–82,
    490, 509n1, 513, 516–17, 519, 904
Art 6(1)(f) 17–18, 170, 326, 329,
    330–32, 333, 334, 335, 335n50,
    336, 337–38, 338n60, 339, 339n79,
    340, 343, 351, 379, 428, 481–82, 490,
    509n2, 512n13, 513, 516–17, 519,
    722, 853–54, 1208, 1245
Art 6(2) 326, 329n11, 335–36, 340, 341,
    341n84, 909–10

Table of Instruments

Art 6(3) 326, 329n11, 335–36, 339–41, 849n33, 1245n22
Art 6(3)(a) 827
Art 6(4) 16–17, 310, 315–16, 326–327, 337–38n68, 338n75, 341–43, 376–77, 394, 396, 430–31, 1300
Art 6(4)(a) 341
Art 6(4)(b) 341
Art 6(4)(c) 341–43, 368, 382n101
Art 6(4)(d) 341–42
Art 6(4)(e) 133, 341–43, 571–72, 578
Art 6(f) 1236
Art 7 . . . . 18–19, 175, 181, 324, 329, 345–53, 355, 1229
Art 7(1) 185, 349–50, 352
Art 7(2) 350
Art 7(3) 183–84, 351, 439n17, 516, 538
Art 7(4) 182, 332n33, 349, 351–52, 537
Art 8 . . . . 14, 19, 127, 175, 181, 292, 294n3, 324, 329, 345–46, 355–62, 525, 1189, 1190
Art 8(1) 14, 57–58, 360–61
Art 8(2) 361
Art 8(7) 1223
Arts 9–10 19–20
Art 9 . . . . 183, 214, 332, 334, 342n95, 342–43, 365–82, 386, 387, 388, 429–30, 482, 498, 539–40, 590, 693–94, 908, 1191, 1229, 1242, 1244–45n18, 1245
Art 9(1) 196, 198, 207, 209, 213–14, 217, 373–74, 375, 526, 527, 530, 539
Art 9(2) 324, 332, 345–46, 369n7, 375, 376–81, 1230
Art 9(2)(a) 175, 176–77, 185, 349, 372, 377n63, 382, 537, 539, 847
Art 9(2)(b) 372, 377n66, 381n90
Art 9(2)(c) 334, 377n67
Art 9(2)(d) 378n68, 381n91, 1257, 1258, 1259
Art 9(2)(e) 378n71
Art 9(2)(f) 369n3, 379n73
Art 9(2)(g) 332n34, 369n6, 372, 379n75, 379, 381n90, 382, 539, 849n34
Art 9(2)(h) 369n4, 372, 379, 379n78
Art 9(2)(i) 369n5, 372, 379–80
Art 9(2)(j) 133, 372, 379–80, 380n85, 381n90, 1245
Art 9(3) 369n7, 372, 379–80, 1252
Art 9(4) 200, 213, 220–21, 222, 369n7, 372
Art 10 . . . . 342n95, 342–43, 375, 385–90, 590, 693–94
Art 11 . . . . 21, 104, 391–97, 400, 406–7, 409–10, 450, 466–67, 1190
Art 11(1) 394, 395–96
Art 11(2) 392, 393, 394, 395, 396–97, 409–10, 466–67, 502–3, 505, 1243n5
Arts 12–14 . . . . 21– 22, 183–84, 315
Arts 12–22 . . . . 550–51, 1191
Arts 12–23 . . . . 20–25, 738

Art 12 . . . . . . .310, 311, 355, 391–92, 398–411, 414, 416n11, 436, 450, 465, 470, 492, 496, 508–9, 520, 525, 544, 1071, 1189
Art 12(1) 19, 406–7, 408, 410–11, 465
Art 12(2) 393, 406–7, 409–11, 466–67, 473–74
Art 12(3) 408–9, 465
Art 12(4) 409, 466
Art 12(5) 403, 406–7, 408–9, 466, 520n60
Art 12(5)(a) 408–9
Art 12(5)(b) 408, 409
Art 12(6) 409–10, 460, 505
Art 12(7) 22, 410–11, 1075, 1268, 1269, 1270–71, 1272–73
Art 12(8) 22, 410–11, 1268, 1269, 1270–72
Arts 13–15 165
Arts 13–22 . . . . 406–7, 408
Art 13 . . . . . . .75, 175, 181, 315, 395, 400, 407, 410–11, 413–31, 436–37, 438, 441, 443–44, 445, 446, 450, 452, 462, 498, 503, 519, 531, 544, 587, 590, 596, 722, 853
Art 13(1) 427–28, 431
Art 13(1)(a) 238, 244, 594n24
Art 13(1)(b) 351, 697, 700–1, 714
Art 13(1)(d) 170
Art 13(1)(e) 164, 757, 804
Art 13(1)(f) 757, 773, 804, 814, 843
Art 13(2) 427–31
Art 13(2)(c) 345–46, 351, 368, 377n65
Art 13(2)(e) 443–44n50
Art 13(2)(f) 127, 525, 531, 538
Art 13(3) 430–31
Art 13(4) 351, 431
Art 14 . . . . 175, 181, 315, 395, 400, 407, 410–11, 414, 415n1, 416n11, 434–47, 450, 452, 462, 498, 519, 531, 544, 587, 590, 596, 722, 853, 1244–45n18
Art 14(1) 445
Art 14(1)(a) 238, 244, 594n24
Art 14(1)(b) 697, 700–1, 714
Art 14 (1)(c) 444n52
Art 14 (1)(d) 444n51
Art 14 (1)(e) 164, 757, 804
Art 14 (1)(f) 164, 757, 773, 804, 814, 843
Art 14(2) 445
Art 14(2)(b) 170
Art 14 (2)(d) 345–46, 351, 377n65
Art 14 (2)(f) 444n53
Art 14(2)(g) 127, 525, 538
Art 14 (3)(a) 445
Art 14 (3)(b) 445
Art 14 (3)(c) 164, 445
Art 14(4) 446
Art 14(5) 446–47
Art 14(5)(a) 351, 438n7, 446n64
Art 14(5)(b) 446n65, 446–47
Art 14(5)(c) 440n20, 447n71
Art 14(5)(d) 440n21, 447n72
Arts 15–20 . . . . 392, 393, 395, 396, 409

Arts 15–22 ...... 112, 393, 407, 408, 409, 410
Art 15 .... 391–92, 414, 416n11, 436, 449–67,
    500, 544, 596, 722, 1247, 1249–50
Art 15(1) 461–62, 464
Art 15(1)(a)–(h) 462n56
Art 15(1)(c) 164, 757, 773, 804, 814,
    843, 857–58
Art 15(1)(h) 127, 462n56, 462–63, 525, 538
Art 15(2) 462, 757, 798, 804
Art 15(3) 461–62, 464
Art 15(4) 9–10, 460n53, 464, 466
Art 16 ..... 391–92, 452, 469–74, 486, 489, 492,
    494–95, 544, 596, 722, 1247, 1249–50
Art 17 .... 22–23, 175, 391–92, 471,
    475–83, 508–9, 516–17, 544,
    596, 722, 1203, 1244–45n18
Art 17(1) 481, 492, 494–95
Art 17(1)(a) 481, 482
Art 17(1)(b) 345–46, 351, 368, 379–80,
    481, 482, 517, 518
Art 17(1)(c) 481–82, 517, 518
Art 17(1)(d) 481, 486, 489–90
Art 17(1)(e) 481–82
Art 17(1)(f) 292, 294n4
Art 17(2) 483, 495, 495n13
Art 17(3) 495n11, 504
Art 17(3)(a) 481
Art 17(3)(b) 9–10, 482–83
Art 17(3)(c) 368, 379–80
Art 17(3)(d) 9–10
Art 17(3)(e) 486
Art 17(9) 489n10
Art 18 .... 123, 124, 391–92, 471, 490–91,
    492, 494–95, 508–9, 544, 596,
    722, 1247, 1249–50
Art 18(1) 490
Art 18(1)(a) 489, 491
Art 18(1)(b) 491
Art 18(1)(c) 491
Art 18(1)(d) 491, 517
Art 18(2) 345–46, 485–91, 518n52
Art 18(3) 491, 495n15
Art 19 ...... 123, 164, 391–92, 470, 471, 474,
    476, 486, 491, 492–96, 596, 1247
Art 20 .... 22, 175, 391–92, 497–506,
    544, 596, 722, 943n9, 1247
Art 20(1) 504
Art 20(1)(a) 345–46, 368, 379–80
Art 20(2) 504
Art 20(3) 504n35
Art 20(4) 505
Art 21 .... 23–24, 124, 127, 336, 339,
    409–10, 476, 481–82, 486,
    508–20, 525, 544, 596, 722,
    1244–45n18, 1247, 1249–50
Art 21(1) 331n31, 333, 351, 481–82, 490,
    509, 512n11, 513, 517, 518
Art 21(2) 351, 509, 517, 518

Art 21(3) 516n49, 518
Art 21(4) 428–29, 519
Art 21(5) 292, 294, 519
Art 21(6) 519
Art 22 .... 24, 127, 175, 355, 407, 410,
    421–22, 522–41, 544, 571–72, 722
Art 22(1) 130, 284, 429–30, 462–63,
    530–36, 538, 539–40
Art 22(2) 176–77, 530–31,
    536–37, 538, 539, 565
Art 22(2)(a) 536, 537
Art 22(2)(b) 537, 538
Art 22(2)(c) 345–46, 349, 530–31, 537,
    538, 539
Art 22(3) 441, 530–31, 536, 537, 538, 539
Art 22(4) 196, 207, 217, 368, 382n98, 429–30,
    462–63, 530, 531, 536, 537, 539
Art 23 .... 24–25, 69, 127, 324, 327, 343,
    414, 436, 440, 450, 452–53, 456,
    466, 470, 493, 498, 508–9, 513,
    517, 525, 543–53, 685, 909–10
Art 23(1) 553, 684
Art 23(1)(a)–(d) 421n30
Art 23(1)(e) 9–10, 421n30
Art 23(2) 552–53
Art 23(2)(d) 773, 814, 843
Arts 24–43 25–32
Art 24 .... 25–26, 145, 310, 311, 318–19,
    391–92, 394, 394n13, 395–96, 538,
    555–68, 571–72, 573, 576, 582, 681,
    682, 718, 722, 726, 757, 936
Art 24(1) 562, 707
Art 24(2) 562
Art 24(3) 25, 562, 565, 566, 733, 738–39
Arts 25–39 1190
Art 25 .... 26, 136, 318, 338n74, 391–92,
    394, 395–96, 410, 556, 565, 567,
    571–79, 722, 738, 1252, 1255
Art 25(1) 133, 136, 445n59,
    566n61, 576, 577, 578
Art 25(2) 136, 575–76, 577
Art 25(3) 562, 577, 733, 738–39
Art 26 .... 27, 145, 152, 582–87, 1021
Art 27 .... 238, 239, 244, 386,
    589–97, 706, 946
Art 27(1) 242n17, 243n27, 595
Art 27(2) 595
Art 27(2)(a) 368, 382n102
Art 27(4) 239, 243n26, 596, 706n23, 1169
Art 27(5) 597
Art 28 ..... 27–28, 157, 160, 426–27, 571–72,
    582, 599–610, 721, 739
Art 28(1) 160, 578
Arts 28(2)–(6) 86
Art 28(3) 804
Art 28(3)(a) 757, 773, 804, 814, 843
Art 28(3)(e) 455n19, 461
Art 28(3)(h) 562

Art 28(5)	733, 738–39
Art 28(6)	27–28
Art 28(7)	27–28, 1278, 1281
Art 28(8)	27–28, 929, 995, 1008n15
Art 28(10)	160, 587
Art 29	86, 157, 160, 170, 601
Art 30	26, 28, 238, 243n26, 244, 386, 556, 560, 565, 587, 590, 594–95, 596, 601, 681, 682, 689, 700–1, 710, 853, 1077
Art 30(1)	713*fn*14
Art 30(1)(a)	594n22
Art 30(1)(d)	164, 495n12, 757, 804
Art 30(1)(e)	757, 773, 804, 814, 843
Art 30(2)	86, 157–58, 713*f*
Art 30(2)(a)	594n22
Art 30(2)(c)	757, 773, 804, 814, 843
Art 30(4)	596
Art 30(5)	20n96, 246–47, 247–48n1, 368, 382n103
Art 31	86, 238, 243n26, 244, 590, 594–95, 596
Art 32	28, 86, 191–92, 310, 311, 391–92, 394, 395–96, 556, 560, 566n61, 567, 571–72, 576, 712–14, 722, 738, 739, 765n59, 1298n21
Art 32(1)	136, 738–39
Art 32(1)(a)	133, 136
Art 32(2)	1092n10
Art 32(3)	562, 733, 738–39
Art 32(4)	86
Arts 33–34	29, 1298n21
Art 33	86–87, 189, 190, 192, 689, 700–1, 710, 722, 738, 933–34, 1252
Art 33(1)	133
Art 33(2)	157–58
Art 33(b)	697
Art 34	189, 190, 192, 406–7, 408, 414, 436, 544, 550–51, 578, 722
Art 34(2)	406–7
Art 34(3)(a)	571–72, 578
Arts 35–36	29–30
Art 35	26, 355, 386, 388, 556, 565, 571–72, 576, 590, 595, 681, 682, 689, 700–1, 710, 718, 726, 765n60, 1237
Art 35(1)	30, 531–32, 540n75, 576
Art 35(2)	713*fn*12
Art 35(3)(a)	127, 284, 463n59, 525, 531–32, 540
Art 35(3)(b)	196, 207, 217, 284n32, 368, 382n99, 388
Arts 35(3)(c)	284n32
Art 35(4)	935, 1008n12
Art 35(6)	995
Art 35(7)(d)	738
Art 35(9)	244
Art 35(11)	684
Art 36	590, 680–687, 689, 700–1, 710, 941, 946n26, 947
Art 36(1)	531–32, 684, 686
Art 36(2)	685–86, 929
Art 36(3)	686
Art 36(3)(a)	253
Art 36(4)	683, 686–87
Art 36(5)	683, 687, 944–45
Arts 37–39	26, 30–31
Art 37	86, 95–96, 157–58, 386, 556, 565, 688–98, 700–1, 710, 738
Art 37(1)	692–94
Art 37(1)(a)	690
Art 37(1)(b)	692
Art 37(1)(c)	368, 382n100, 388, 692, 693
Corrigenda to Art 37(1)(c)	688n1, 1055n1
Art 37(2)	253, 694
Art 37(3)	694
Art 37(4)	693–94, 695
Art 37(5)	695
Art 37(6)	696
Art 37(7)	594n23, 697–98, 714
Art 38	86, 556, 565, 596, 689, 691, 694–95, 700–7, 710, 722, 894
Art 38(1)	706
Art 38(2)	563n37, 706–7
Art 38(3)	243–44, 563n36, 703, 704, 706
Art 38(4)	564n48
Art 38(5)	704, 899
Art 38(6)	243–44, 705, 898
Art 39	556, 565, 596, 681, 689, 694–95, 700–1, 702, 709–14, 735
Art 39(1)(b)	712–13
Art 39(1)(d)	705–6n20
Art 39(1)(e)	683, 686, 705–6n21, 714
Art 39(2)	713*fn*13
Art 39(4)	714
Art 39(b)	562
Art 40	25, 31, 258–59, 556, 562, 571–72, 716–723, 726, 730n15, 806, 807, 936n36, 1190n51
Art 40(1)	246–47, 247–48n1, 722, 929, 1078
Art 40(2)	722, 728
Art 40(2)(d)	133
Art 40(2)(g)	355, 361
Art 40(2)(h)	577
Art 40(2)(i)	189
Art 40(2)(j)	773, 807n45, 814, 843
Art 40(3)	721, 722, 722n19, 807
Art 40(4)	723n22, 1190n51
Art 40(5)	721, 807, 929
Art 40(6)	723n23
Art 40(7)	995, 1008n13, 1078n32
Art 40(8)	1078n33
Art 40(9)	721, 807, 1078n34, 1278, 1281
Art 40(10)	723n23
Art 40(11)	723n22, 1078n35
Art 41	556, 718, 721, 722, 725–30, 936n36, 1190n51
Corrigenda to Art 41	727, 1190n51

Art 41(1) 729, 737
Art 41(2) 728, 729
Art 41(3) 725n1, 727, 929, 995, 1008n14
Corrigenda to Art 41(3) 725n1, 727
Art 41(4) 1190
Art 41(5) 727
Corrigenda to Art 41(5) 725n2, 727
Art 42 . . . . 31–32, 258, 556, 562,
577, 732–741, 734, 745, 747, 806,
807–8, 936n36, 1071, 1085, 1190
Corrigenda to Art 42 734
Art 42(1) 25, 246–47, 562, 736, 737,
738, 752, 807–8, 929, 1078, 1268
Art 42(2) 739, 808
Art 41(2)(a) 728n11
Art 41(2)(c) 729n12
Art 41(2)(d) 728n11
Art 41(4) 1190
Art 42(2) 1283–84
Art 42(3) 741, 1283–84
Art 42(4) 562n27, 736, 1283–84
Art 42(5) 739, 739n40, 750, 807–8,
929, 995, 1008n14, 1078
Art 42(6) 738, 739, 1190
Art 42(7) 732n1, 734, 738, 739–40,
929, 946, 1078
Corrigenda to Art 42(7) 732n1, 734
Art 42(8) 1088n11
Art 43 . . . . 556, 725, 729–30, 733,
735, 736, 737, 738, 739, 744–53,
807–8, 936n36, 1071, 1190
Corrigenda to Art 43 746
Art 43(1) 747–48, 748n11, 749n20, 929
Art 43(1)(a) 748
Art 43(1)(b) 748, 749
Art 43(2)(b) 749
Art 43(2) 729–30, 750–51
Art 43(3) 744n1, 746, 749n20, 995, 1008n14
Corrigenda to Art 43(3) 744n1, 746
Art 43(4) 730, 749
Art 43(6) 745n2
Corrigenda to Art 43(6) 745n2, 746
Art 43(7) 749
Art 43(8) 736, 747, 752, 1075, 1268, 1269,
1270–73, 1288
Art 43(9) 736, 747, 752, 753,
1278, 1281, 1288
Arts 44–49 1191
Arts 44–50 . . . . 32–35, 75, 304n3
Art 44 . . . . . . 755–66, 773, 777, 792, 798, 804,
846n18, 854, 1302
Art 45 . . . . 32–33, 258–59, 756, 757, 759,
761–62, 766, 771–91, 792,
799, 853, 874, 879, 1302
Art 45(1) 778, 786n94
Art 45(2) 775, 788, 802
Art 45(2)(a) 763, 765, 789
Art 45(2)(b) 785, 876

Art 45(2)(c) 788
Art 45(3) 785, 790n129, 791, 799, 945,
1270, 1278, 1280, 1281, 1309–10
Art 45(4) 1270
Art 45(5) 775, 789, 1270, 1278, 1280,
1281, 1286
Art 45(8) 785n87
Art 45(9) 33, 791, 1309–10
Art 46 . . . . 33–34, 258–59, 428, 462, 718,
722, 726, 756, 766, 789–90,
792, 797–809, 853, 995
Art 46(1) 721, 799n1, 803n27, 807, 808
Art 46(2) 721, 800–1, 804–5, 806,
807–8, 1270, 1280
Art 46(2)(a) 806, 808
Art 46(2)(b) 258, 815n3, 821n22
Art 46(2)(c) 801, 803, 1278, 1281
Art 46(2)(d) 801, 803, 929, 1008n15,
1278, 1281
Art 46(2)(e) 806, 807
Art 46(2)(f) 800–1, 806, 807–8
Art 46(2)(f) 733
Art 46(3) 801, 804, 808, 929
Art 46(3)(a) 164, 803, 1008n16
Art 46(3)(b) 806, 808, 809
Art 46(4) 801, 929
Art 46(5) 33, 804–5, 816
Art 47 . . . . . 26, 34, 246–47, 253, 256n10, 258,
260, 428, 556, 562, 565, 700–1,
710, 756, 766, 789–90, 792,
813–23, 929, 995, 1008n17
Art 47(1) 816, 821
Art 47(1)(a) 816
Art 47(1)(b) 816
Art 47(1)(c) 816
Art 47(2) 817
Art 47(2)(d) 763, 765
Art 47(2)(e) 127, 525, 539
Art 47(2)(f) 822–23
Art 47(3) 816, 1278, 1281
Art 48 . . . . 34–35, 756, 766, 789–90, 792,
825–36, 849–50n35
Art 49 . . . . 35, 258, 258–59n2, 756, 766,
789–90, 792, 831–32, 841–55
Art 49(1) 35, 428, 621–22, 831–32,
846, 853
Art 49(1)(a) . . . 175, 176–77, 184, 185, 345–46,
377, 831–32, 847
Art 49(1)(b) 846n14, 848, 849
Art 49(1)(c) 846n14, 849
Art 49(1)(d) 827, 831–32, 849, 854–55
Art 49(1)(e) 831–32, 851
Art 49(1)(f) 831–32, 852
Art 49(1)(g) 846, 852
Art 49(1)(1) 853
Art 49(1)(2) 847
Art 49(2) 164, 846n16, 847, 853
Art 49(3) 846n16, 847–48, 849, 853–54

Art 49(4) 827, 836, 846n14, 846n16, 847, 849–50	Art 55(3) 70–71, 692, 904–5, 909–10, 1119n3, 1127n5, 1135, 1184
Art 49(5) 35, 836, 847, 854	Art 56 ..... 36–37, 75, 85, 226, 227, 265, 273, 279, 288–89, 594, 733, 738, 745, 748, 762, 821, 864, 903, 904, 907, 909, 913–24, 945, 954–55, 956–57, 960n29, 974, 987, 1020–21, 1030, 1123, 1257, 1265–66
Art 49(6) 846n15, 847, 853	
Art 50 .... 756, 766, 857–61, 929, 941, 954–55, 960, 969–70, 974, 987, 1000–01	
Art 50(1)(b)........................979, 990	
Art 50(a) 860	Art 56(1) 273n2, 276, 280, 871, 917, 918–19, 921, 922, 958, 960–61, 962, 992
Art 50(b) 860	
Art 50(c) 860	Art 56(2) 286, 915, 921–23, 924
Art 50(d) 860	Art 56(3) 915, 921n48, 923
Arts 51–62...........................35–37	Art 56(4) 915, 922, 923, 924
Art 51 .... 181, 265, 738, 863–871, 875, 884, 894, 896, 897, 903, 1028n1, 1257, 1265–66	Art 56(5) 915, 923, 924
	Art 56(6) 697–98, 918n22, 923–24, 962
	Art 57 .... 75, 265, 700–1, 710, 718, 726, 738, 864, 869, 879–80, 887, 903, 914, 927–37, 941, 943, 946, 949, 951–52, 1029, 1041, 1060–61, 1074, 1118, 1120, 1127n4, 1257, 1265–66
Art 51(1)............... 865, 868, 951n14, 1121	
Art 51(2) 865, 866, 868–70, 933–34, 937, 974, 1032, 1062–63	
Art 51(3) 270, 865, 870–71	
Art 52 ......265, 268–69, 273, 278, 691, 738, 864, 873–82, 884, 894, 896, 897, 903, 941, 1061, 1102, 1127n2, 1184n5, 1257, 1265–66	Art 57(1) 908
	Art 57(1)(a) 934
	Art 57(1)(b) 19, 935
	Art 57(1)(c) 935, 947n28
Art 52(1) 700–1, 879, 880, 1055, 1056	Art 57(1)(d) 935
Art 52(2) 880, 1056	Art 57(1)(e) 935, 937
Art 52(3) 880, 881	Art 57(1)(f) 935, 1121, 1142
Art 52(4) 880, 881, 896	Art 57(1)(g) 859–60n13, 869, 932, 937, 954–55, 974, 979, 983, 987, 990, 993
Art 52(5) 278, 880, 882n47, 1108	
Art 52(5)(g)........................... 164	
Art 52(5)(j) 164	Art 57(1(h).............................. 934
Art 52(6) 880, 882	Art 57(1)(i)............................ 935
Art 53 ....265, 738, 864, 884–91, 894, 895–96, 897, 903, 1048, 1127n3, 1257, 1265–66	Art 57(1)(l) 935
	Art 57(1)(m)–(n)....................... 935
	Art 57(1)(n)–(q)....................... 733
Art 53(1) 879, 885–86, 887, 888–89	Art 57(1)(p)–(q) 745
Art 53(2) 887, 889	Art 57(1)(o) 739–40, 748–49
Art 53(3) 887, 890	Art 57(1)(p) 749
Art 53(4) 887, 890–91	Corrigenda to Art 57(1)(p).............. 928n1
Art 52(5) 887, 933	Art 57(1)(q) 749n21, 936n36
Art 54 .... 265, 738, 864, 880n34, 884, 885, 893–900, 903, 1127n3, 1257, 1265–66	Art 57(1)(s) 258
	Art 57(1)(u) 949, 951n9
	Art 57(1)(v) 932
Art 54(1) 890, 895–96, 897	Art 57(2)–(4)......................935–36
Art 54(1)(a) 896, 897	Art 57(e)............................. 1076
Art 54(1)(b).......................896, 897	Art 57(f)............................. 1076
Art 54(1)(c) 889, 896, 897	Art 57(g) 1062–63
Art 54(1)(d)............890–91n24, 896, 897	Art 58 ..... 75, 265, 531–32, 596, 681, 726, 738, 864, 869, 879–80, 903, 907, 914, 929, 932, 934, 936, 939–47, 949, 951–52, 954–55, 1029, 1041, 1060–61, 1077–78, 1120, 1123, 1126, 1127n4, 1182, 1187, 1191, 1195, 1254–56, 1257, 1265–66
Art 54(1)(e) 896, 897	
Art 54(1)(f) 881, 890, 896, 897, 898	
Art 54(2) 895, 896, 897, 899, 1111, 1115–16, 1252, 1253, 1254–55	
Art 55 .... 75, 265, 733, 738, 739n39, 745, 748, 801, 807, 821, 864, 902–910, 941, 954–55, 1020–21, 1029, 1257, 1265–66	
	Art 58(1) 943, 944, 946, 947, 1191, 1252
	Art 58(1)(a) 238, 244, 594n25
	Art 58(1)(b)........................712–13
Art 55(1) 903–4, 905, 906, 963, 979–80n22, 981, 991n18, 1021, 1122n31	Art 58(1)(e) 167, 1254–55, 1256
	Art 58(1)(f)... 944n14, 944–45, 1254–55, 1256
Art 55(2) 904, 909, 918, 918n25, 960n29, 1122n32, 1154n4	Art 58(1)(g)........................486, 488

Art 58(2) 943, 944, 946–47, 949, 951–52, 1119n4, 1135, 1188, 1191	Art 61(8) 980, 981, 992–93, 1030, 1031
Art 58(2)(a) 946	Art 61(9) 980, 1278, 1281
Art 58(2)(e) 189	Art 62 . . . . . 265, 864, 907, 909, 914, 924, 929, 941, 946, 947, 954–55, 960, 963, 974, 979, 986–93, 1006, 1008–9, 1012, 1019, 1027–28
Art 58(2)(f) 531–32	
Art 58(2)(g) 123, 492	
Art 58(2)(h) 739–40n42, 748–49	
Art 58(2)(j) 791, 809	Art 62(1) 991, 993
Art 58(3) 943, 944, 946, 947	Art 62(2) 991
Art 58(3)(a) 686	Art 62(3) 991–92
Art 58(3)(b) 686–87, 944–45	Art 62(4) 992
Art 58(3)(c) 936, 944–45	Art 62(5) 992
Art 58(3)(d) 936n36	Art 62(6) 992
Art 58(3)(e) 745, 749n21	Art 62(7) 992, 1030, 1031
Art 58(3)(f) 936n36	Art 63 . . . . 37–39, 265, 273, 279, 284, 288, 722, 733, 745, 750, 801, 804, 821, 864, 907, 914, 954–55, 964–65, 995–1002, 1006, 1016, 1019n9, 1027–28, 1030, 1050, 1058, 1064, 1071, 1073–74, 1078, 1091–92, 1098, 1099
Art 58(3)(g) 798	
Art 58(3)(h) 798, 936	
Art 58(3)(i) 936	
Art 58(3)(j) 258, 814, 936	
Art 58(4) 943, 944, 945, 947, 1255–56	
Art 58(5) 791, 809, 947	Art 63(1) 870–71
Art 58(6) 943, 944n15, 944, 946, 947	Art 63(2) 870–71
Art 58(h) 733	Arts 64–66 . . . . 274n4
Arts 59–61 9–10	Art 64 . . . . . 265, 273, 718, 726, 864, 907, 914, 954–55, 996–97, 999–1000, 1005–12, 1016, 1017, 1021–22, 1027–28, 1029, 1030, 1033, 1036–37, 1061, 1062, 1071, 1074, 1078, 1090, 1095, 1098, 1099
Art 59 . . . . 265, 738, 864, 879–80, 903, 914, 929, 932, 949–52, 1085, 1087, 1257, 1265–66	
Arts 60–76 37–39	
Art 60 . . . . 226, 265, 273, 274n4, 276n13, 288–89, 290, 864, 907, 909, 914, 915, 918, 922, 923, 929, 945, 946, 947n29, 953–70, 974, 975, 979, 981–82, 987, 988, 990, 1027–28, 1029, 1030, 1122n33–34, 1123, 1157n10	
	Art 64(1) 999–1000n17, 1007, 1008, 1009, 1078, 1099
	Art 64(1)(a) 1008n12, 1021
	Art 64(1)(b) 1008n13
	Art 64(1)(c) 733, 745, 750, 1008n14
Art 60(1)–(9), (12) 962–67	Corrigenda to Art 64(1)(c) 1005n1
Art 60(1) 918n21, 963, 981	Art 64(1)(d) 798, 801, 1008n15
Art 60(2) 941, 963, 975, 979–80, 988, 991	Art 64(1)(e) 798, 801, 1008n16
Art 60(3) 288–89, 963, 964, 979–80, 991	Art 64(1)(f) 258, 814, 821n21, 1008n17
Art 60(4) 289, 290–91, 918n20, 964, 995, 1016	Art 64(2) 921–22, 963, 974, 981, 993, 999–1000n19, 1007–9, 1009n18, 1011, 1012, 1022, 1050, 1055, 1058, 1064, 1065, 1073–74, 1078, 1099
Art 60(5) 290, 964	
Art 60(6) 966, 967n60	
Art 60(7) 966, 967–69, 1016, 1130	Art 64(3) 1007, 1009, 1028n2, 1031, 1091–92, 1099
Art 60(8) 966, 969, 1016, 1130	
Art 60(9) 963, 966, 969, 1016, 1130	Art 64(4) 980, 1006, 1007, 1010, 1032, 1033
Art 60(10) 967–69, 1130	Art 64(5) 1007, 1010, 1099
Art 60(11) 968–69	Art 64(5)(a)–(b) 1050, 1058, 1064, 1104
Art 60(12) 963, 980	Art 64(6) 1005n2, 1007, 1008, 1011
Art 61 . . . . 265, 864, 907, 909, 914, 924, 929, 941, 946, 954–55, 960, 969n67, 973–83, 987, 988, 990, 991, 1006, 1008–9, 1012, 1027–28	Corrigenda to Art 64(6) 1005n2
	Art 64(7) 999–1000, 1007, 1008, 1011, 1021–22n25, 1061, 1099
	Corrigenda to Art 64(7) 1006n3
	Art 64(8) 981, 993, 1007, 1011, 1061, 1078n40, 1099
Art 61(1) 980, 981	
Art 61(2) 980	Corrigenda to Art 64(8) 1006n4
Art 61(3) 980	Art 65 . . . . . 226, 265, 273, 288, 822, 864, 907, 914, 954–55, 964–65, 996–97, 999–1000, 1006, 1011, 1012, 1014–25, 1027–28, 1029, 1030, 1036–37, 1049, 1061, 1062, 1071, 1074, 1078, 1087, 1090, 1098, 1099, 1131–32, 1310
Art 61(4) 980	
Art 61(4)(b) 982	
Art 61(5) 980, 981	
Art 61(6) 980	
Art 61(7) 980, 982	

Art 65(1) 921–22, 1000n20, 1012, 1017	Art 70(1)(i) 258, 1076n22, 1076–77
Art 65(1)(a) 290, 964–65, 1016–17, 1019, 1020, 1023, 1023–24n36	Art 70(1)(j) 843, 1076n23, 1076–77, 1080
	Art 70(1)(k) 1077–78, 1080
Corrigenda to Art 65(1)(a). 1014n1	Art 70(1)(l) 1069n1, 1076n24, 1076–77, 1087, 1310
Art 65(1)(b) 919n36, 1017, 1019, 1020–21, 1023, 1023	
	Corrigenda to Art 70(1)(l). . . . 1069n1, 1076–77
Art 65(1)(c) 981, 993, 1016, 1017, 1018, 1019, 1021–22, 1023, 1050, 1058, 1064, 1073–74	Art 70(1)(m) 1076n24, 1076–77, 1080
	Art 70(1)(n) 733, 1078, 1080
	Art 70(1)(o) 733, 745, 1070n2, 1078n36, 1078n39, 1080, 1088n12
Art 65(2) 964–65, 1017, 1022–23, 1024, 1028n2, 1031, 1091–92	
	Corrigenda to Art 70(1)(o). 1070n2
Art 65(3) 964–65, 1017, 1022, 1091–92, 1099	Art 70(1)(p) 733, 745, 749n22, 1070n3, 1078n37, 1080
Art 65(4) 1017, 1022–23	Corrigenda to Art 70(1)(p) 1070n3
Art 65(5) 1017, 1022, 1023, 1050, 1058, 1064, 1099, 1104, 1131–32	Art 70(1)(q) 733, 745, 1075n14, 1078n38, 1080, 1268, 1272–73
Art 65(6) 965, 966, 1017–18, 1024n37, 1024, 1062	Art 70(1)(r) 1075n15, 1080, 1268, 1272–73
	Art 70(1)(s). 773, 785n90, 1075n17, 1283–84
Art 66 . . . . 265, 273, 276, 864, 907, 914, 954–55, 969, 996–97, 1027–31, 1036–37, 1071, 1078, 1090	Art 70(1)(t) 1078, 1080
	Art 70(1)(u) 1079n46
	Art 70(1)(v) 857–58, 860, 1079n47
Art 66(1) 981, 992–93, 1029, 1030, 1031	Art 70(1)(w). 857–58, 860, 1079n48
Art 66(2) 279, 285–86, 981, 992–93, 1029, 1030, 1031	Art 70(1)(x) 1078n34, 1283n29
	Art 70(1)(y) 1079, 1088n13
Art 66(3) 1029, 1031	Art 70(2) 1076, 1283–84
Art 66(4) 1016, 1031, 1091–92	Art 70(3) 1074n9, 1278, 1283–84
Art 67 . . . . . . 265, 864, 907, 914, 980, 996–97, 1006, 1010, 1032–39, 1278, 1281	Art 70(4) 1023, 1077
	Art 71 . . . . 949, 952, 1041, 1047, 1085–88, 1090, 1092, 1102
Arts 68–76. 39	
Art 68 . . . . 265, 864, 1041–52, 1064, 1071, 1085, 1090, 1092, 1095, 1098, 1102, 1105–6, 1291	Art 71(1) 1087
	Art 71(2) 1023, 1086, 1087, 1088, 1310
	Art 72 . . . . 1041, 1047, 1090–93, 1095, 1098, 1102
Art 68(1) 869, 924, 1045–46, 1131	
Art 68(2) 1047, 1099	Art 72(1) 1091
Art 68(3) 244, 1047–48	Art 72(2) 1108
Art 68(4) 244, 290, 865, 1047–48	Art 73 . . . . .1041, 1047, 1090, 1092, 1095–97, 1098, 1102
Art 68(5) 1022, 1049–50, 1055, 1065, 1099	
Art 68(6) 1049	Art 73(1) 1095–96
Art 69(5) 869n31	Art 73(2) 897
Art 69 . . . . . 691, 700–1, 874, 876, 1001, 1041, 1045–46, 1047, 1055–66, 1071, 1090, 1092, 1102	Art 74 . . . . .273, 1041, 1047, 1090, 1091–92, 1095, 1098–100, 1102
	Art 74(1) 1099
Art 69(1) 1076	Art 74(1)(b) 274n4, 1016
Art 69(2) 1064, 1065, 1066, 1076	Art 74(1)(c) 1016
Art 70 . . . . . 718, 726, 929, 1027–28, 1036–37, 1041, 1047, 1060–61, 1069–81, 1085, 1090, 1092, 1102	Art 74(2) .1092, 1099–100
	Art 75 . . . . 1041, 1047, 1090, 1092, 1098, 1102–9
Art 70(1) 1006, 1074, 1075, 1080, 1278	Art 75(1) 1104–5
Art 70(1)(a) 1019, 1080	Art 75(2) 1099, 1100, 1107
Art 70(1)(b) 1074–75, 1076, 1283–84, 1310	Art 75(3) 1107
Art 70(1)(c) 258, 814, 1075n16, 1080, 1283n29	Art 75(4) 1092, 1103, 1108
	Art 75(5) 1108–9
Art 70(1)(d) 1076n19, 1076–77, 1080	Art 75(6) 1109
Art 70(1)(e) 933–34n23, 1012, 1050, 1058, 1064, 1073–74, 1076–77	Art 75(6)(b). 1050, 1058, 1064, 1104
	Art 75(6)(g). 1016
Art 70(1)(f). . . . 127, 525, 536, 1076n20, 1076–77	Art 76 . . . . .894, 1023, 1041, 1090, 1092, 1111–16
Art 70(1)(g) 189, 1076n21, 1076–77	
Art 70(1)(h) 189, 1076n21, 1076–77	Art 76(1) 1016, 1113, 1114

Art 76(2) 244, 1046–47, 1114–15	Art 83(2)(g) 1189
Arts 77–84 39–40	Art 83(2)(h) 1189
Art 77 . . . . 273, 278, 382, 397, 791, 809, 822–23, 907n28, 929, 936, 1117–23, 1126, 1128, 1133, 1135, 1136, 1142, 1147, 1148, 1149, 1161, 1299	Art 83(2)(i) 1189
	Art 83(2)(j) 718–19n3
	Art 83(2)(k) 1189
	Art 83(3) 192–93n25, 947n29, 1189n47
Art 77(1) 1121, 1122–23	Art 83(4) 246–47, 248, 249n8, 307n29, 571–72, 1189–90, 1191
Art 77(2) 947n29, 1123	
Art 77(3) 27	Art 83(4)(a) 361–62, 397, 597, 702, 707
Art 78 . . . . .397, 686, 751n32, 791, 809, 822, 879, 947, 1029, 1118, 1119, 1122, 1123, 1125–32, 1133, 1135, 1136, 1139–40, 1142, 1147, 1148, 1149, 1149n37, 1153, 1161, 1182, 1185, 1299	Art 83(5) 246–47, 248, 249n8, 307n29, 1189–91
	Art 83(5)(a) 368, 382, 390
	Art 83(5)(c) 164, 756, 766, 773, 809, 814, 822–23, 825, 843, 1250
	Art 83(5)(e) 1191
Art 78(2) 947n29, 1123, 1130n22, 1154n4	Art 83(6) 246–47, 248, 249n8, 307n29, 1191
Art 78(3) 966–67, 967n60, 1123, 1130, 1139–40	Art 83(7) 943n5, 1188
	Art 83(8) 1133, 1188
Art 78(4) 1130n25	Art 83(9) 1184n3
Art 79 . . . . .75, 157–58, 382, 397, 590, 601, 822–23, 907n28, 936, 1118, 1119, 1122, 1126, 1128, 1133–40, 1142, 1147, 1148, 1149, 1149n37, 1153, 1161, 1163n6, 1168, 1182, 1184, 1195, 1299	Art 84 . . . . .947n30, 1182, 1188, 1194–201
	Arts 85–91. . . . . 40–41, 1001n25
	Art 85 . . . . .456, 478, 481, 874, 1202–11, 1213, 1216–17, 1220
	Art 85(2) 1210–11
Art 79(1) 1119, 1136, 1138, 1157	Art 85(3) 1210–11
Art 79(2) 1138, 1139–40, 1157	Art 85(3)(c) 792, 855
Art 80 . . . . . .1024, 1118, 1126, 1133, 1142–50, 1161, 1169	Art 86 . . . . .1203, 1213–21
	Art 87 . . . . 375, 1223–27
Art 80(1) 1147	Art 88 . . . . 84–85n42, 253, 1229–38
Art 80(2) 1149	Art 88(1) 1234
Art 81(1). 1158n13	Art 88(2) 246–47, 256n10
Art 81(3) 1157, 1158–59	Art 88(3) 1235
Art 80(a) 6n24	Art 89 . . . . . 324, 456, 470, 486, 487, 1240–50
Art 81 . . . . .1024, 1126, 1130, 1133, 1140, 1153–59, 1161	Art 89(1) 133, 136, 310, 316n33, 342–43, 380–81, 446–47, 487, 519, 571–72, 578–79, 1245, 1246–47, 1249–50
Art 81(2) 1154, 1155, 1156, 1158	
Art 81(3) 1155	
Art 82 . . . . 157–58, 390, 582, 601, 1126, 1133, 1135, 1135n6, 1142, 1148–49, 1160–77, 1182, 1195, 1299	Art 89(1)(d) 482–83
	Art 89(2) 495n16, 1246, 1249–50
	Art 89(3) 492, 493, 495n16, 1246, 1247
Art 82(1) 1175, 1176	Art 89(4) 1246n26, 1246
Art 82(2) 1176	Art 90 . . . . .941, 1252–56
Art 82(3) 1176	Art 90(1) 1254–55
Art 82(4) 583, 1176–77	Art 91 1257–66
Art 82(5) 1176–77	Art 91(1). 1264–66
Art 82(6) 1177	Art 91(2) .270, 870, 1254
Art 83 . . . . 6n24, 40, 249, 254–55, 307, 345–46, 556, 566, 718, 726, 929, 934, 946–47, 951–52, 1126, 1127n5, 1135n6, 1180–91, 1195, 1197, 1198, 1199, 1200, 1223, 1229	Art 92 . . . . 41–43, 400, 1268–75, 1278
	Art 92(2) 1272
	Art 92(3) 1271–72
	Art 92(4) 1273
	Art 92(5) 1273
	Art 93 . . . . .41–43, 718, 726, 790, 1074, 1268, 1270, 1278–1289
Art 83(1) 1188–89	Art 93(1) 1282
Art 83(2) 947n29, 1189n45, 1197	Art 93(2) . . . 784–85n83, 785n92, 789, 800–1, 804–5, 808, 816, 1032, 1033, 1282
Art 83(2)(a) 1189	
Art 83(2)(b). 192–93n25, 567, 1189	
Art 83(2)(c) 567, 1189	Art 93(3) 789, 1286n53
Art 83(2)(d). 567, 571–72, 578, 1189	Art 93(4)(b). 733
Art 83(2)(e) 1189	Arts 94–99 43
Art 83(2)(f) 1189	

Art 94	348, 1166, 1291–92, 1294, 1320	Recital 21	2, 4(25)
Art 94(1)	1309–10	Recital 22	3, 4(16), 4(22), 4(23)
Art 94(2)	177–78, 1298	Recital 23	3
Art 95	71, 348, 1294–300	Recital 24	3, 4(4), 22
Art 96	756, 760–61, 773, 777, 857–58, 1302–6	Recital 25	3
		Recital 26	4(1), 4(5), 11
Art 97	949, 952, 1087, 1308–10	Recital 27	4(1)
Art 97(1)	1309–10	Recital 28	4(5)
Art 97(2)	1309–10	Recital 29	4(5)
Art 97(3)	1309, 1310	Recital 30	4(1), 4(4)
Art 97(4)	1309, 1310	Recital 31	4(6), 4(9)
Art 97(5)	1309, 1310, 1312, 1317	Recital 32	4(11), 4(25)
Art 98	62, 64, 71, 1264, 1291, 1292, 1312–1317	Recital 33	4(11)
		Recital 34	4(1), 4(13)
Art 99	1257, 1291, 1291–92n1, 1320–21	Recital 35	4(1), 4(15)
Art 99(1)	1320	Recital 36	4(16), 4(22)
Art 99(2)	1291–92, 1320	Recital 37	4(19)
Ch I	1210	Recital 38	8, 22
Ch II	551	Recital 39	5, 16
Ch III	440	Recital 40	6
Ch V	756, 757, 758, 761–62, 764–65, 766, 774, 777, 799, 815, 827, 835, 846, 846n18, 853, 858, 1087, 1308, 1309–10	Recital 41	6
		Recital 42	4(11), 7
		Recital 43	4(11), 6, 7
		Recital 44	6
		Recital 45	6
Ch VI	270, 866, 867, 876, 932, 942–43, 947, 1028–29, 1121, 1308	Recital 46	6
		Recital 47	4(10), 6
s 1	876, 896, 897	Recital 48	6
Ch VII	867, 932, 937, 942–43, 944, 975–76, 979, 988, 1028–29, 1036, 1042, 1309–10	Recital 49	6
		Recital 50	6
		Recital 51	4(11), 4(14), 9
s 1	871, 979, 981, 982, 990, 992, 1028	Recital 52	9
s 2	981, 992, 1028	Recital 53	9
s 3	1028, 1044, 1072	Recital 54	9
Ch VIII	867, 1119, 1122, 1128, 1135, 1210	Recital 55	9
Ch IX	326, 340, 1001, 1191, 1242–43	Recital 56	9
Explanatory Memorandum	563	Recital 57	11
		Recital 58	12, 15

Articles where GDPR recitals are reproduced

Recital 1	1	Recital 59	12, 15
Recital 2	1	Recital 60	12, 13, 14, 22
Recital 3	1	Recital 61	4(9), 13, 14
Recital 4	1, 22, 85, 91	Recital 62	13, 14
Recital 5	1	Recital 63	4(9), 12, 15, 22
Recital 6	1, 44	Recital 64	15
Recital 7	1	Recital 65	16, 17
Recital 8	1	Recital 66	17
Recital 9	1	Recital 67	4(3), 4(6), 18
Recital 10	9	Recital 68	20
Recital 11	12	Recital 69	4(10), 21
Recital 12	1	Recital 70	21
Recital 13	4(18), 83	Recital 71	22
Recital 14	2	Recital 72	4(4), 22
Recital 15	2, 4(2), 4(6)	Recital 73	4(12), 20, 22, 23
Recital 16	2	Recital 74	24
Recital 17	2, 98	Recital 75	24, 35
Recital 18	2	Recital 76	24
Recital 19	2, 10	Recital 77	24, 39, 40, 41
Recital 20	2, 55	Recital 78	25

Recital 79	26
Recital 80	4(17), 27
Recital 81	28, 29, 40, 41
Recital 82	30, 31
Recital 83	32
Recital 84	35, 36
Recital 85	4(12), 33
Recital 86	4(12), 34
Recital 87	4(12), 33, 34
Recital 88	4(12), 34
Recital 89	30, 35, 36
Recital 90	35
Recital 91	22, 35
Recital 92	35
Recital 93	35
Recital 94	36
Recital 95	36
Recital 96	36
Recital 97	37, 38, 39
Recital 98	4(18), 40, 41
Recital 99	40
Recital 100	42, 43
Recital 101	4(9), 44
Recital 102	44, 45, 48, 50
Recital 103	45
Recital 104	45
Recital 105	45
Recital 106	45
Recital 107	4(20), 45
Recital 108	4(20), 46
Recital 109	46
Recital 110	4(18), 4(20), 47
Recital 111	4(9), 4(9)
Recital 112	49
Recital 113	49
Recital 114	46, 49
Recital 115	48
Recital 116	50, 62
Recital 117	4(21), 51, 52, 54
Recital 118	52, 75
Recital 119	51
Recital 120	52
Recital 121	52, 53, 54
Recital 122	4(21), 51, 55, 57
Recital 123	4(21), 51, 57, 61
Recital 124	4(22), 4(23), 4(24), 56, 70
Recital 125	56
Recital 126	56
Recital 127	56
Recital 128	55, 56
Recital 129	57, 58
Recital 130	60
Recital 131	60
Recital 132	57
Recital 133	57, 61
Recital 134	62
Recital 135	63, 64
Recital 136	64, 65, 70
Recital 137	66
Recital 138	61, 62, 63, 64, 66
Recital 139	68, 69, 70
Recital 140	75
Recital 141	77, 78
Recital 142	80
Recital 143	65, 78
Recital 144	81
Recital 145	79, 82
Recital 146	77, 82
Recital 147	78, 79, 82
Recital 148	58, 83
Recital 149	83, 84
Recital 150	58, 83, 84
Recital 151	83, 84
Recital 152	83, 84
Recital 153	85
Recital 154	86
Recital 155	88
Recital 156	4(5), 18, 20, 89
Recital 157	89
Recital 158	89
Recital 159	89
Recital 160	89
Recital 161	89
Recital 162	89
Recital 163	89
Recital 164	90
Recital 165	91
Recital 166	12, 92
Recital 167	93
Recital 168	40, 41, 67, 93
Recital 169	93
Recital 170	1
Recital 171	94
Recital 172	70
Recital 173	95, 98
Corrigendum to General Data Protection Regulation 2016 (May 2018)	7, 752
Recital 71	524, 526
Art 37(1)(c)	688, 1055
Art 41	727
Art 41(3)	725, 727
Art 41(5)	725, 727
Art 42	734
Art 42(7)	732, 734
Art 43	746
Art 43(3)	744, 746
Art 43(6)	745, 746
Art 57(1)(p)	928
Art 64(1)(c)	1005
Art 64(6)	1005
Art 64(7)	1006
Art 64(8)	1006
Art 65(1)(a)	1014
Art 70(1)(l)	1069
Art 70(1)(o)	1170
Art 70(1)(p)	1070

EU Treaties

Charter of Fundamental Rights of the European Union 2009 ('CFR') ... 3, 9, 48, 57, 85, 211, 325–26, 337, 389–90, 418–19, 757–58, 775, 777, 779, 780, 782–83, 802, 827, 846–47, 868, 945, 950, 965–66, 1064, 1135, 1304–5
- Art 2 .... 333n41
- Art 7 .... 53, 56, 57, 106, 111, 130, 176, 211, 372, 375, 418n18, 423–24, 482–83, 488, 545, 547, 548–49, 550, 551–52, 553, 576, 781, 782, 783, 802n22, 1174, 1295, 1297, 1304–5n10, 1305
- Art 8 .... v, 50–51, 52, 53, 88, 106, 111, 130, 211, 347, 372, 418n18, 423–24, 452–53, 456, 482–83, 488, 545, 547, 548–49, 550, 551–52, 552–53n27, 553, 575, 576, 782, 783, 802n22, 909, 1059–60, 1118, 1174, 1176–77, 1295, 1297, 1304–5n10, 1305, 1313–14
- Art 8(1) 48, 56, 267, 1121
- Art 8(2) 16–17, 176–77, 267, 327, 329–30n16, 348, 452–53, 454, 456, 458, 465, 473, 545, 783, 866, 933, 1047, 1049, 1121
- Art 8(3) 78, 267, 784, 864–65, 868, 875, 878, 879, 910, 931, 934, 1011, 1056, 1057, 1058, 1059, 1061–62, 1066, 1121, 1254–55
- Art 10 .... 57, 369–70n11, 375, 1262
- Art 10(1) 68–69
- Art 11 ..... 50–51, 57, 375, 480n11, 1204, 1297
- Art 12 .... 369–70n11
- Art 16 57
- Art 17 548
- Art 18(3) 1045
- Art 20 .... 1264n43
- Art 21 .... 50–51, 199, 199–200n14
- Art 21(1) 374–75
- Art 22 .... 57, 375, 1134
- Art 24 356
- Art 27 1297
- Art 28 375
- Art 41 .... 924, 950n1, 951–52, 1011, 1023, 1024, 1046–47, 1079, 1086
- Art 41(2) 924, 965, 1022n34
- Art 41(2)(c) 1011
- Art 42 .... 57, 452n4, 888, 1023, 1046–47, 1111–12, 1115, 1214
- Art 47 ..... 53, 57, 379, 473, 548, 553, 781, 879, 936, 1017–18, 1119, 1121, 1122, 1125, 1129, 1135, 1136, 1137–38, 1164, 1168, 1174, 1176–77, 1184–85, 1184n7, 1184–85n13, 1188, 1304–5n10, 1305
- Art 47(1) 1143–44
- Art 47(2) 1122n27
- Art 50 .... 1188, 1199, 1200
- Art 51 .... 55–56, 1023n35
- Art 51(1) 1199, 1296–97
- Art 52 .... 545, 548–49, 550, 552, 552–53n27, 1188
- Art 52(1) 314, 325–26, 339–40, 418n18, 452–53n7, 454, 545, 547, 548, 782, 783, 1297
- Art 52(3) 325n2, 545, 576, 1184n7, 1297

Maastricht Treaty *see* Treaty on European Union 1992 ('TEU')

Treaty Establishing the European Community ('EC Treaty')
- Art 95 51
- Art 100a 1314n7
- Art 286 876

Treaty of Lisbon 2009 ...... 3, 6, 51, 53, 54, 63–64, 868, 1106n20, 1270, 1304
- declaration 21 63–64

Treaty of Rome 1957
- Art 58 230

Treaty on European Union 1992 ('TEU') 3
- Art 2 886
- Art 3(3) 356
- Art 4(2) 55–56n23, 69
- Art 4(3) 865, 869, 1022–23, 1062–63, 1306
- Art 6(1) 763n47
- Art 13 1046
- Art 16 .... 1284n34
- Art 17 869
- Art 17(3) 879n32
- Art 39 .... 63–64, 70, 875
- Art 42(1) 71n35
- Art 43 .... 71n35
- Art 44 .... 71n35
- Art 50 .... 83–84, 762, 787, 803, 822, 836, 847
- Art 71 .... 787, 822n25
- Title V, Ch 2 63–64

Protocol to the TEU on the Statute of the Court of Justice
- Art 6 890

Treaty on the Functioning of the European Union ('TFEU') 1304–5
- Art 2 .... 1305n11
- Art 2(2) 760–61n32, 1303–4n7
- Art 6(2) 3n5
- Art 10(3) 888
- Art 15 .... 888, 891, 950, 951–52, 1023, 1046, 1086, 1214
- Art 15(1) 888
- Art 15(3) 888, 1111–12, 1115
- Art 16 ..... 3, 50, 54, 55, 63–64, 67, 70, 423–24, 552, 552–53n27, 576, 782, 876, 1059–60, 1121n20, 1304–5n10, 1305, 1313–14
- Art 16(1) 48, 56, 267, 909
- Art 16(2) ... 4, 49, 50, 52, 54–56, 70, 267, 372, 552, 782–83, 864–65, 866, 868, 875, 879, 931, 933, 934, 1011, 1056, 1057, 1058, 1061–62, 1254–55

Art 17 .... 1258–59, 1262, 1263
Art 17(1). 1258n3
Art 17(2) 1263n36
Art 19 374–75
Art 54 ....228, 230
Art 57 296
Art 81(1). 917n17
Art 82(1) 917n17
Art 82(1)(d) 782–83
Art 87(2)(a) 782–83
Art 101. ....249n5, 249, 307, 1187
Art 102.......... 249n5, 249, 307, 502, 1187
Art 106(1) 909
Art 114. .... 51, 63–64, 1314n7
Art 169(1) 1146
Art 179........................ 1242–43n1
Art 216(1) 1303–4n7
Art 238 ....1284n34
Art 238(3)(a) 1284n34
Art 247. 890
Art 253. 889
Art 254. 889
Art 258. ....867, 1000, 1062–63, 1065
Art 263 ....42n183, 791, 822, 964–65n49,
   1015, 1021n22, 1024, 1046–47,
   1092, 1125–26, 1129–30, 1131
Art 267. ....1015, 1025, 1062–63, 1126,
   1130–31, 1158
Art 267(3) 1158
Art 287 1046–47
Art 288 .... 10n52, 51, 791,
   1163n9, 1281–82
Art 289 ....1316n28
Art 290 .... 41, 42n178, 1269, 1270n8–9,
   1271, 1272
Art 290(2) 42n180
Art 291. .... 41, 42n179, 1279, 1281
Art 291(1) 1279n1
Art 291(3) 1279n3
Art 294. 4
Art 297(1) 1320n1
Art 297(2) 1273n39, 1286n52
Art 314(1) 1106n20
Art 314(2) 1106n21
Art 338(2) 1249
Art 339. .... 899, 1112
Art 340(2) 1166–67, 1170n49
Art 351. .... 1304, 1306, 1306n15
Art 355. ....786n99
Art 355(1) 83n29, 786n100
Art 355(4) 83n30
Title V 834
Ch 4 and 5. .... 71, 540
Annex II. 83n31, 786n98
Pt III 552
Protocol 21 836

EU Regulations

Accreditation Regulation 2008: Regulation (EC) No. 765/2008 of the European Parliament and of the Council of 9 July 2008 setting out the requirements for accreditation and market surveillance relating to the marketing of products and repealing Regulation (EEC) No. 339/93, OJ 2008 L 218/30. .... 729–30, 737, 746, 748, 749, 750, 751
Art 2(10) 747
Art 4(5) 751–52n33
Art 4(7) 751–52n33
Art 5(1) 749n23
Art 5(3) 749n24
Art 5(4) 749n25
Art 5(5) 751–52
Art 7 .... 748n11
Antitrust Regulation: Council Regulation 1/2003: Council Regulation (EC) No. 1/2003 of 16 December 2002 on the implementation of the rules on competition laid down in Articles 81 and 82 of the Treaty, OJ 2003 L 1/1 .... 889, 916, 997
BEREC Regulation: Regulation (EC) No. 1211/2009 of the European Parliament and of the Council of 25 November 2009 establishing the Body of European Regulators for Electronic Communications (BEREC) and the Office, OJ 2009 L 337/1 ....997, 1057
Recital 6. .... 1045–46n20
Art 1(3) 1057
Art 3 .... 997n2, 1007
Art 3(1) 1007n7
Art 3(3) 916n7, 1007n8
Brussels I Regulation (recast): Regulation (EU) No. 1215/2012 of the European Parliament and of the Council of 12 December 2012 on jurisdiction and the recognition and enforcement of judgments in civil and commercial matters (recast), OJ 2012 L 351/1 ......82, 1126, 1133, 1137, 1140, 1177
Art 7(1). 1140n28
Art 7(2) 1139, 1140n28
Art 29(1) 1154
Art 29(2) 1156
Art 60(1)(b). 228n7, 231
Art 63(1)(b). 228n7
CIS Regulation: Council Regulation (EC) No. 515/97 of 13 March 1997 on mutual Assistance between the Administrative Authorities of the Member States and cooperation between the latter and the Commission to ensure the correct Application of the law on customs and

Agricultural matters, OJ L 82, 22.3.1997, p. 1, As Amended by Regulation (EC) No. 766/2008 of 9 July 2008, OJ L 218, 13.8.2008
Art 37............................1080n50
Clinical Trials Regulation: Regulation (EU) 563/2014 of the European Parliament and of the Council of 16 April 2014 on clinical trials on medicinal products for human use, OJ 2014 L 158/1 419
Art 28(1)(d).......................... 419
Art 28(3) 419n21
Art 29 419
Art 29(2) 419n20
Art 81 419
Commission Implementing Regulation August 2018: Commission Implementing Regulation (EU) 2018/1101 of 3 August 2018 laying down the criteria for the Application of the second paragraph of Article 5 of Council Regulation (EC) No. 2271/96 protecting Against the effects of the extra-territorial Application of legislation Adopted by a third country, and Actions based thereon or resulting therefrom, 2018 OJ LI 199/7 828
Commission Regulation 773/2004: Commission Regulation (EC) No. 773/2004 of 7 April 2004 relating to the conduct of proceedings by the Commission pursuant to Articles 81 and 82 of the EC Treaty, OJ 2004 L 123/18
Art 12......................... 965–66n56
Comitology Regulation 182/2011: Regulation (EU) No. 182/2011 of the European Parliament and of the Council of 16 February 2011 laying down the rules and general principles concerning mechanisms for control by Member States of the Commission's exercise of implementing powers, OJ 2011 L 55/13 .... 1279, 1280
Art 3(2) 1282n15
Art 3(4) 1284n31
Art 3(5) 1283n20
Art 3(7) 1285n42, 1285n47–48
Art 5 .... 784–85, 804, 1282
Art 5(1) 1284n33
Art 5(2) 1284n37
Art 5(3) 1285n38–39
Art 5(4) 1285n40–41
Art 6 ....1285n42
Art 6(3) 1286n49–50
Art 8 1286
Art 8(2) 1286n54
Art 8(3) 1286n56
Art 8(4) 1286n57
Art 10(5) 1283n23
Art 11 .... 1283n27–28
Council Regulation (EC) No. 168/2007 see FRA Council Regulation
Council Regulation (EC) No. 139/2004 see Merger Regulation
Council Regulation 1/2003 see Antitrust Regulation
Council Regulation 44/2001: Council Regulation (EC) No. 44/2001 of 22 December 2000 on jurisdiction and the recognition and enforcement of judgments in civil and commercial matters, OJ 2001 L 12/1 .... 1145, 1146
Council Regulation (EC) No. 515/97 see CIS Regulation
Council Regulation 2271/96: Council Regulation (EC) No. 2271/96 of 22 November 1996 protecting against the effects of the extra-territorial application of legislation adopted by a third country, and Actions based thereon or resulting therefrom, OJ 1996 L 309/1, Amended by Commission Delegated Regulation (EU) 2018/1100 of 6 June 2018 amending the Annex to Council Regulation (EC) No. 2271/96 protecting against the effects of extra-territorial Application of legislation adopted by a third country, and Actions based thereon or resulting therefrom, OJ LI 199/1 828
Council Regulation 2328/91: Council Regulation (EEC) No. 2328/91 of 15 July 1991 on improving the efficiency of Agricultural structures, OJ 1991 L 218/91 .... 1163n14
Council Regulation 797/85: Council Regulation (EEC) No. 797/85 of 12 March 1985 on improving the efficiency of Agricultural structures, OJ 1985 L 93/1............. 1163n14
Cybersecurity Act: Regulation (EU) 2019/881 of the European Parliament and of the Council of 17 April 2019 on ENISA (the European Union Agency for Cybersecurity) and on information and communications technology cybersecurity certification and repealing Regulation (EU) No. 526/2013 (Cybersecurity Act), OJ 2019 L 151/15 ....633, 643, 657
Rec 41 ....579n21
Title III 734–35n16
eIDAS Regulation: Regulation (EU) No. 910/2014 of the European Parliament and of the Council of 23 July 2014 on electronic identification and trust services for electronic transactions in the internal

market and repealing Directive 1999/93/EC,
   2014 OJ L 257/73 . . . . 656–57, 1227
Art 3(25) 737n31
Art 6(1) 1227
Art 19 642–43
Art 19(2) 656n7
EPPO Regulation 2017: Council Regulation (EU) 2017/1939 of 12 October 2017 implementing enhanced cooperation on the establishment of the European Public Prosecutor's Office ('EPPO Regulation'), OJ 2017 L 238/1 199
   Recital 108 306–7
Art 2(19) 199
Art 2(21) 219
Art 2(23) 304, 306–7n24
Art 85 . . . . .1049n39
Art 87 . . . . 1080–81n53
Ch VIII 71n34
EU Staff Regulations: Regulation No. 31 (EEC), 11 (EAEC) of 14 June 1962 laying down the Staff Regulations of Officials and the Conditions of Employment of Other Servants of the European Economic Community and the European Atomic Energy Community as amended, OJ 1962 L 45/1385 . . . . .898, 1107
Art 1b. 1046n27, 1105n14
Art 11. . . . . .895, 898
Art 11a. 895
Art 16. 895
Art 17. . . . . .895, 899
EUDPR Regulation 2019: Regulation (EU) 2018/1725 of The European Parliament and of The Council of 23 October 2018 on the protection of natural persons with regard to the processing of personal data by the Union institutions, bodies, offices and Agencies and on the free movement of such data, and repealing Regulation (EC) No 45/2001 and Decision No 1247/2002/EC ('EUDPR') 55, 71, 357, 454, 471, 511–12, 537, 687, 690, 691, 702, 711, 875, 895, 904–5, 951, 969, 976, 1049, 1075, 1080, 1264, 1316–17
Recital 2. . . . . 874, 1042
Recital 5. . . . . 120, 125, 131, 140, 161, 168, 193, 210n7, 219, 219n4, 294n6, 304, 348, 370, 393, 579, 1316–17
Recital 7. . . . . 116, 139
Recital 8. . . . . 62, 116, 139
Recitals 7–15 62
Recital 13. .1312, 1317n31
Recital 16. . . . . . . 104, 196–97, 208, 217–18, 392
Recital 17. 572
Recital 18. . . . . . 104, 128, 196–97, 208, 217–18
Recital 19. . . . . . 176, 292–93, 346, 348, 355–56
Recital 20 . . . . 176, 392
Recital 22 176

Recital 26 . . . . 176, 346, 348, 355–56
Recital 27 . . . . 128, 176, 292–93, 357, 525
Recital 29. . . . . . . 176, 196–97, 208, 217–18, 346
Recital 33. 572
Recital 34 . . . . 451, 470
Recital 35. . . . . 128, 176, 525, 1269
Recital 36 . . . . 176, 525
Recital 37. . . . . 128, 525
Recital 38 . . . . 176, 292–93, 346
Recital 40 123
Recital 41. . . . . 176, 346
Recital 42 292–93
Recital 43 . . . . 128, 176, 346, 355–56, 525, 572
Recital 45. . . . . 556, 572
Recital 46 355–56
Recital 48 . . . . .392, 556, 572
Recital 51. 572
Recital 53. . . . . .392, 572, 886
Recital 55. 189, 572, 879
Recital 56 . . . . 189, 572
Recital 57. . . . . 128, 525
Recital 58. . . . . 128, 525, 572, 682
Recital 59. 682
Recital 60 . . . . 682, 687, 1042, 1072, 1075, 1076, 1269, 1272–73, 1279, 1283–84, 1316
Recital 61. . . . . 1072, 1103
Recital 62. . . . . 689, 701, 710, 1118
Recitals 63–67 303
Recital 68 . . . . 176, 303, 346, 1183
Recital 69. 303
Recital 70. 303
Recital 71. . . . . 303, 955, 974, 987, 1072
Recital 72 . . . 266, 874, 885, 1042, 1059–60n18
Recital 74. 62
Recital 75. 949
Recital 76. 1111, 1112n3
Recital 77 266
Recital 78 . . . 266, 955, 974, 977, 1072, 1080–81
Recital 79. . . . . 1127, 1134
Recital 83. 1111
Recital 84 1279
Recital 87 . . . . 874, 885
Recital 88 346
Art 2 62
Art 2(1) 116
Art 2(3) 71n35, 1312, 1315n23
Art 2(4) 71n35
Art 3(1) 104, 196–97, 208, 217–18, 368, 392
Art 3(2) 120, 1317n31
Art 3(3) 116, 368
Art 3(4) 123
Art 3(5) 123, 128, 131, 525
Art 3(6) 104, 133
Art 3(7) .139, 140, 154–55
Art 3(8) 145
Art 3(9) 154–55
Art 3(12) 157, 161
Art 3(13) 164, 168
Art 3(14) 171

Art 3(15) 176, 346, 348, 355–56, 368	Art 30 157
Art 3(16) 189, 193	Art 32(3) 1119–20n7
Art 3(17) 104, 196–97, 199, 208, 217–18, 368	Art 33 .... 392, 572
Art 3(18) 104, 196–97, 208, 210, 217–18, 368	Art 34 189
Art 3(19) 104, 196–97, 208, 217–18, 219, 368	Art 35 189
Art 3(20) 292–93, 294	Art 35(3)(a) 572
Art 3(22) 266	Art 36 572
Art 4 .... 176, 392	Art 37 572
Art 4(1)(a) 525	Art 38 511–12
Art 4(2) 525, 556, 572	Art 39 .... 355–56, 572
Art 5 .... 128, 392, 525	Art 39(3)(a) 128, 525, 540
Art 5(1)(d) 176, 355–56	Art 39(3)(b) 196–97, 208, 217–18, 368
Art 6 .... 128, 368, 525	Art 39(6) 1072, 1076
Art 6(e) 572	Art 40 572
Art 7 .... 176, 346, 348, 355–56	Art 40(2) 540
Art 7(3) 511–12	Art 40(4) 1279, 1281n10
Art 8 .... 128, 176, 292–93, 294n5, 346, 348, 357, 525	Art 41(1) 1075–76
Art 10 .... 368, 370	Art 41(2) 1075–76
Art 10(1) 196–97, 208, 217–18	Art 41(3) 1076
Art 10(2)(a) 176, 346, 348	Art 41(4) 1075
Art 10(2)(i) 1254n6	Art 42 .... 1072, 1269, 1279, 1312
Art 10(3) 1254n6	Art 42(1) 682, 687n11, 1075, 1273, 1283–84, 1316
Art 12 .... 392, 393	Art 42(2) 1283–84
Art 13 572	Art 42(3) 1283–84, 1316
Art 14 .... 392, 525	Art 42(4) 1273
Art 14(8) 1269	Art 43 .... 689, 690, 701, 710
Art 15 176	Art 44 .... 689, 701, 710
Art 15(2)(c) 346, 368	Art 44(1) 690–91
Art 15(2)(f) 128, 525	Art 44(7) 704
Art 16 176	Art 44(8) 690
Art 16(2)(c) 346	Art 44(9) 690
Art 16(2)(f) 128, 525	Art 45 .... 689, 701, 710
Art 16(5)(d) 1254n6	Art 45(1)(d) 189
Art 17 .... 392, 451, 454	Art 47 .... 1119–20n7
Art 17(1)(h) 128, 525	Art 48(2)(b)–(c) 1279, 1281n10
Art 18 .... 392, 470, 471, 511–12	Art 50(1)(a) 176, 346, 348
Art 19 .... 176, 392	Art 51 .... 955, 970, 974, 977, 987, 1072
Art 19(1)(b) 346, 368	Art 52(1) 1057
Art 19(1)(f) 292–93, 294n5	Art 52(4) 1111, 1112
Art 19(3)(c) 368	Art 53 .... 885, 894
Art 20 392	Art 53(2) 889
Art 20(2) 346	Art 54 894
Art 21 392	Art 54(1) 1095, 1096n11
Art 22 .... 176, 392	Art 54(2) 1072
Art 22(1)(a) 346, 368	Art 54(4) 1103
Art 23 511–12	Art 54(5) 1111
Art 23(1) 128, 525	Art 55 .... 874, 876, 894, 1042
Art 23(3) 292–93, 294n5	Art 55(1) 267, 876, 1057
Art 24 .... 128, 176, 355–56, 525, 540, 572	Art 55(1)(k) 1042
Art 24(2)(c) 346	Art 55(2) 267, 876, 880, 1056
Art 24(4) 196–97, 208, 217–18, 368	Art 56 .... 894, 899, 1111, 1112–13
Art 25(1) 511–12	Art 57 .... 931, 1118
Art 26 .... 392, 556, 572	Art 57(1) 904–5n6
Art 27 .... 392, 572, 579	Art 57(1)(a) 62
Art 29 .... 157, 572	Art 57(1)(g) 682, 687n11, 1072, 1075
Art 29(7) 1279, 1281n10	Art 57(1)(k) 1072, 1075–76
	Art 57(1)(l) 1072, 1103

Art 58	1118, 1119–20n7, 1128n11
Art 58(2)(f)	189
Art 58(2)(g)	540
Art 58(3)(c)	682, 687n11
Art 60	949, 950n3
Art 61	955, 970, 974, 977, 987
Art 62	977n8, 1072, 1080–81
Art 62(1)	1080
Art 62(2)	1080
Art 62(3)	1080–81
Art 63(2)	1119–20n7, 1127, 1128n11, 1134
Art 64	1119–20n7, 1127, 1128n11, 1134
Art 65	1166–67
Art 66	346, 1183
Art 66(1)(c)	572
Art 66(2)	572, 1188n36
Art 66(3)	1188n36
Art 66(3)(a)	368
Art 76	196–97, 208, 217–18
Art 77	128, 525, 540
Art 77(2)	196–97, 208, 217–18
Art 77(3)	196–97, 208, 217–18
Art 90	139
Art 91(1)	196–97, 208, 217–18
Art 92	189
Art 93	189
Art 96	1279, 1280
Art 96(1)	1282n18
Art 97	1312
Art 98	71n36, 1081, 1312, 1315n23, 1317
Art 98(2)	62
Art 100	891
Art 100(1)	891n30
Art 101(2)	1049n40
Ch IX	540

Eurodac Regulation: Regulation (EU) No. 603/2013 of the European Parliament and of the Council of 26 June 2013 on the establishment of 'Eurodac' for the comparison of fingerprints for the effective Application of Regulation (EU) No. 604/2013 establishing the criteria and mechanisms for determining the Member State responsible for examining an Application for international protection lodged in one of the Member States by a third-country national or a stateless person and on requests for the comparison with Eurodac data by Member States' law enforcement authorities and Europol for law enforcement purposes, and Amending Regulation (EU) No. 1077/2011 establishing a European agency for the operational management of large scale IT systems in the Area of freedom, security and justice (recast), OJ L 180, 29.6.2013 1314

Art 32	1080n50

Eurojust Regulation 2018: Regulation (EU) 2018/1727 of the European Parliament and of the Council of 14 November 2018 on the European Union Agency for Criminal Justice Cooperation (Eurojust), and replacing and repealing Council Decision 2002/187/JHA, OJ 2018 L 295/138 ('Eurojust Regulation') 71n34, 71, 904–5n7, 1057n6–7

Recital 29	1080n49
Art 26(1)	71
Art 42	1080n54

Europol Regulation 2016: Regulation (EU) 2016/794 of the European Parliament and of the Council of 11 May 2016 on the European Agency for Law Enforcement Cooperation (Europol), OJ 2016 L 135/53 .... 71n34, 304, 1057, 1060, 1314, 1315

Recital 32	306–7
Recital 52	1057, 1060, 1080n52
Art 2(e)	304
Art 2(j)	199
Art 25	304n8
Arts 28–46	1315n23
Art 30(2)	219
Art 42	1060
Art 43	1049n38
Art 45	1057n7, 1060, 1080n52
Art 45(2)	1058
Art 45(3)	1060
Art 45(4)	1060
Ch VI	71n34

FRA Council Regulation: Council Regulation (EC) No. 168/2007 of 15 February 2007 establishing a European Union Agency for Fundamental Rights, OJ 2007 L 53/1

Art 16(1)	1057

Free Flow of Non-Personal Data Regulation: Regulation (EU) 2018/1807 of the European Parliament and of the Council of 14 November 2018 on a framework for the free flow of non-personal data in the European Union, OJ 2018 L 303/59

Art 2(1)	759
Art 2(2)	113n50
Art 4	759
Art 4(1)	105–6

IMI Regulation: Regulation (EU) No. 1024/2012 of the European Parliament and of the Council of 25 October 2012 on Administrative cooperation through the Internal Market Information System and repealing Commission Decision 2008/49/EC ('IMI Regulation'), OJ 2012 L 316/1 1038

Art 5(g)	1038
Art 21	1080n50

Merger Regulation: Council Regulation
(EC) No. 139/2004 of 20 January
2004 on the control of concentrations
between undertakings (the EC Merger
Regulation), OJ 2004 L 24/1
   Recital 8. . . . . .956–57n7
Public Access to Documents Regulation:
   Regulation (EC) No. 1049/2001 of the
   European Parliament and of the Council
   of 30 May 2001 regarding public access
   to European Parliament, Council and
   Commission documents, OJ 2001
   L 145/43 . . . . .373, 452n4, 891, 1046–47,
                  1100, 1111, 1112, 1114–15, 1216
   Recital 11. 1115
   Art 2(3) 1112, 1114–15
   Art 4. 1115
   Art 4(1)(a) 1114
   Art 4(1)(b) 1114, 1216, 1219
   Art 4(2) 1114, 1115
   Art 4(3) 1115
   Art 7. . . . . 1100, 1115
   Art 8. . . . . 1100, 1115
Public Health Regulation: Regulation
   (EC) No. 1338/2008 of the European
   Parliament and of the Council of 16
   December 2008 on Community statistics
   on public health and health and
   safety at work, OJ 2008 L354/70. 380
   Art 3(c). 380n81
Regulation (EU) 2018/1724 see Single Digital
   Gateway Regulation
Regulation (EU) 2017/2226 of the European
   Parliament and of the Council of 30
   November 2017 establishing an Entry/
   Exit System (EES) to register entry and
   exit data and refusal of entry data of
   third-country nationals crossing the external
   borders of the Member States and
   determining the conditions for access
   to the EES for law enforcement purposes,
   and Amending the Convention
   implementing the Schengen Agreement
   and Regulations (EC) No. 767/2008 and
   (EU) No. 1077/2011, OJ 2017 L 327/20 . . . 210
Regulation (EU) 2017/746: Regulation (EU)
   2017/746 of the European Parliament
   and of the Council of 5 April 2017 on
   in vitro diagnostic medical devices
   and repealing Directive 98/79/EC and
   Commission Decision 2010/227/EU,
   OJ 2017 L 117/176
   Art 6(1) 295n12
   Art 11 592
   Art 11(4) 592n5
   Art 11(5) 592
Regulation 2017/745: Regulation (EU) 2017/
   745 of the European Parliament and of

the Council of 5 April 2017 on medical
devices, Amending Directive 2001/83/
EC, Regulation (EC) No. 178/2002 and
Regulation (EC) No. 1223/2009 and
repealing Council Directives 90/385/EEC
and 93/42/EEC (OJ L 117/1, 5 May 2017)
   Art 11 592
   Art 11(4) 592n5
   Art 11(5) 592
Regulation 2016/796: Regulation (EU)
   2016/796 of the European Parliament
   and of the Council of 11 May 2016 on
   the European Union agency for Railways
   and repealing Regulation (EC)
   No. 881/2004, OJ 2016 L 138/1
   Art 12. . . . . .956–57n7
Regulation 2016/794: Regulation (EU) 2016/
   794 of the European Parliament and of the
   Council of 11 May 2016 on the European
   Union agency for Law Enforcement
   Cooperation (Europol) and replacing and
   repealing Council Decisions 2009/371/
   JHA, 2009/934/JHA, 2009/935/JHA,
   2009/936/JHA and 2009/968/JHA,
   OJ 2016 L 135/53 . . . . 977n9
Regulation 910/2014 see eIDAS Regulation
Regulation (EU) 563/2014 see Clinical Trials
   Regulation
Regulation 952/2013: Regulation (EU)
   No. 952/2013 of the European
   Parliament and of the Council of 9
   October 2013 laying down the Union
   Customs Code, OJ 2013 L 269/1. . . . . . 532n32
   Art 47(1) 956–57n7
Regulation (EU) No. 603/2013 see Eurodac
   Regulation: Regulation (EU) No.
   1024/2012 see IMI Regulation
Regulation 966/2012: Regulation (EU,
   EURATOM) No. 966/2012 of the European
   Parliament and of the Council of 25 October
   2012 on the financial rules applicable to the
   general budget of the Union and repealing
   Council Regulation (EC, Euratom) No.
   1605/2002 as Amended by Regulation (EU,
   Euratom) No. 547/2014 of the European
   Parliament and of the Council of 15 May
   2014 and Regulation (EU, Euratom) 2015/
   1929 of the European Parliament and of the
   Council of 28 October 2015, OJ 2012 L 298/1
   Art 2(b) 1046n26, 1105n13, 1106n19
Regulation (EU) No. 182/2011 see
   Comitology Regulation 182/2011
Regulation 913/2010: Regulation (EU) No.
   913/2010 of the European Parliament
   and of the Council of 22 September 2010
   concerning a European rail network for
   competitive freight, OJ 2010 L 276/22
   Art 13. . . . . .956–57n7

Regulation (EC) No. 1211/2009 see BEREC Regulation
Regulation 223/2009: Regulation (EC) No. 223/2009 of the European Parliament and of the Council of 11 March 2009 on European statistics and repealing Regulation (EC, Euratom) No. 1101/2008 of the European Parliament and of the Council on the transmission of data subject to statistical confidentiality to the Statistical Office of the European Communities, Council Regulation (EC) No. 322/97 on Community Statistics, and Council Decision 89/382/EEC, Euratom establishing a Committee on the Statistical Programmes of the European Communities, OJ 2009 L 87/164 1249
Regulation (EC) No. 1338/2008 see Public Health Regulation
Regulation (EC) No. 767/2008 see VIS Regulation
Regulation (EC) No. 765/2008 see Accreditation Regulation
Regulation (EC) No. 593/2008 see Rome I Regulation
Regulation (EC) No. 864/2007 see Rome II Regulation
Regulation (EC) No. 168/2007 see FRA Council Regulation
Regulation (EC) No. 1987/2006 see SIS II Regulation
Regulation (EC) No. 2252/2004 of the European Parliament and of the Council of 13 December 2004 on standards for security features and biometrics in passports and travel documents issued by Member States, OJ 2004 L 385/1 .... 210, 211, 372
   Art 3 .... 209–10, 211–12
Regulation 773/2004 see Commission Regulation (EC) No. 773/2004
Regulation (EC) No. 139/2004 see Merger Regulation
Regulation 1/2003 see Antitrust Regulation
Regulation 1049/2001 see Public Access to Documents Regulation
Regulation (EC) No 45/2001 of the European Parliament and of the Council of 18 December 2000 on the protection of individuals with regard to the processing of personal data by the Community institutions and bodies and on the free movement of such data 8, 12, 55, 66n9, 71, 348, 454, 471, 687, 690, 691, 702, 711, 876, 895, 904–5, 951, 1112, 1113n4, 1166–67, 1170–71, 1216, 1219–20, 1233, 1313n4, 1314, 1315, 1316, 1317
   Art 3(1) 66n9
   Art 5 1170
   Art 5(d) 347–48
   Art 8(b) 1219–20
   Art 9(1) 347–48
   Art 9(2) 347–48
   Art 9(6)(a) 347–48
   Art 10 .... 347–48, 370
   Art 10(1) 372–73
   Art 10(2)(d) 372–73, 373n40
   Art 13 454
   Art 14 471
   Art 15 124
   Art 24 690
   Art 24(1) 690–91
   Art 24(4) 690
   Art 24(5) 690
   Art 25(1) 691, 712
   Art 28(2) 686–87
   Art 32(3) 1128n11
   Art 41(1) 1057n4
   Art 41(2) 686–87
   Art 42 .... 886, 895
   Art 42(2) 889
   Art 42(3) 876
   Art 43 895
   Art 44 .... 875, 876, 877–78, 879, 895
   Art 44(1) 267, 880, 1057n5
   Art 44(2) 267, 876, 889, 1056
   Art 44(4) 895
   Art 45 1116
   Art 46 .... 931, 950
   Art 46(c) 904–5n5
   Art 46(d) 686–87
   Art 47 .... 943, 1128n11
   Annex, s 3 704
Regulation 44/2001 see Council Regulation (EC) No. 44/2001
Regulation (EC) No. 515/97 see CIS Regulation
Regulation 2271/96 see Council Regulation 2271/96
Regulation 2328/91 see Council Regulation (EEC) No. 2328/91 improving the efficiency of Agricultural structures, OJ 1991 L 218/Regulation 797/85 see Council Regulation (EEC) No. 797/85
Regulation No. 31 (EEC), 11 (EAEC) of 14 June 1962 see EU Staff Regulations
Rome I Regulation: Regulation (EC) No. 593/2008 of the European Parliament and of the Council of 17 June 2008 on the law applicable to contractual obligations OJ 2008 L 177/6 ('Rome I')
   Art 9(1) 82n24
   Art 19(1) 228n7
Rome II Regulation: Regulation (EC) No. 864/2007 of the European Parliament and of the Council of 11 July 2007 on the law applicable to non-contractual obligations, OJ 2007 L 199/40 ('Rome II') 85
   Art 1(2)(g) 85n45

Single Digital Gateway Regulation:
Regulation (EU) 2018/1724 of the
European Parliament and the Council
of 2 October 2018 establishing a single
digital gateway to provide access to
information, to procedures and to assistance and problem-solving services and
Amending Regulation (EU) No. 1024/
2012, OJ 2018 L 295/1. . . . . 1038n32
Art 38. . . . . 1038n31
SIS II Regulation: Regulation (EC) No. 1987/
2006 of the European Parliament and
of the Council of 20 December 2006
on the establishment, operation and
use of the second generation Schengen
Information System (SIS II), OJ L 381,
28.12.2006 1314
Art 46. . . . . 1080n50
VIS Regulation: Regulation (EC) No. 767/
2008 of the European Parliament and of
the Council of 9 July 2008 concerning
the Visa Information System (VIS) and
the exchange of data between Member
States on short-stay visas
(VIS Regulation), OJ L 218, 13.8.2008
Art 43. . . . . 1080n50

EU Directives

Consumer Rights Directive 2011: Directive
2011/83/EU of the European Parliament
and of the Council of 25 October 2011
on consumer rights, amending Council
Directive 93/13/EEC and Directive
1999/44/EC of the European Parliament
and of the Council and repealing
Council Directive 85/577/EEC and
Directive 97/7/EC of the European
Parliament and of the Council, OJ
2011 L 304/64 . . . . 10n53
Art 6(1) 402
Council Directive 93/42/EEC see Directive
93/42/EEC
Data Protection Directive 1995: Directive 95/
46/EC on the protection of individuals
with regard to the processing of personal
data and on the free movement of such
data ('DPD') 2, 3, 4, 9–11, 13, 14,
15, 20–22, 23–24, 25, 31, 33, 35, 39, 43,
51, 52–54, 55, 63–64, 65–66, 67, 71, 76,
92, 108–9, 113, 124–25, 127, 134, 141,
146–47, 148, 151–52, 165, 177–78, 199,
200, 210, 220, 228, 241, 259, 260–61, 267,
274, 280–81, 289, 295, 304, 314, 317,
318–19, 327, 328, 329, 335, 343n98, 347–48,
356–57, 358, 360, 371, 372, 393, 404, 417,
419, 437, 442–43, 453, 456, 457, 459–60,
462–63, 464, 473, 487, 488, 489, 502,
510–11, 513–14, 516, 550–51, 573, 583,
587, 593, 691, 702, 710, 712, 718, 719,
720, 727, 734, 736, 746, 747, 757–58, 762,
763, 779, 780, 782, 785, 786, 791, 799–800,
801, 803, 806, 815, 817, 821, 843–44, 858,
859, 865, 866, 867, 868, 870, 876, 877,
882, 896, 904–5, 906, 907–8, 931,
935, 943, 956, 957, 957n9, 958, 959,
975–76, 978, 988, 996, 998, 1001–2,
1007, 1021, 1028–29, 1035, 1047–48,
1064, 1085, 1119–20, 1129, 1136–37,
1144, 1154, 1166, 1196–97, 1200–1, 1204,
1214, 1215, 1220–21, 1224, 1230, 1231,
1232, 1235, 1236, 1244–45, 1253, 1258,
1270, 1280, 1291–92, 1296, 1298,
1303–4, 1305, 1309–10, 1314, 1320
Preamble 1314n7
Recital 2. 526
Recitals 3 and 4. 51
Recital 5. 248
Recital 19. . . . . 228, 261, 275, 282
Recital 25. 248
Recital 26 . . . . 106, 108, 109, 719
Recital 27 141
Recital 29. 1243
Recital 33. 1253–54
Recital 37. 402
Recital 40 . . . . 1243n2
Recital 41. 402
Recital 46 573
Recital 47. 146
Recital 49. 690
Recital 54 711
Recital 62. . . . . 266, 267, 866,
875n2, 1028–29, 1057
Recital 63. . . . . 865–66n5, 932, 1028–29,
1119n5
Recital 64 . . . . 975–76, 988, 1028–29
Recital 65. . . . . 869n25, 1043, 1057,
1061n23, 1073
Recital 72. 1215
Art 1 . . . . 51, 56
Art 1(1). 1196n8
Art 1(2) 53, 758–59n12
Art 2(a). 13, 106, 107
Art 2(b) 118, 119n11, 120–21, 124, 211
Art 2(c). 139–40, 143n28
Art 2(d) 146, 148, 583–84, 585
Art 2(e). 158
Art 2(f) 166, 171, 172n10
Art 2(g) 165
Art 2(h) 177, 180, 347
Art 3 64
Art 3(1) 141
Art 3(2) 11, 11n54–56,
65–66, 1259, 1261, 1262
Art 3(2)(b). 1259
Art 4 . . . . 12, 77, 79, 81, 83
Art 4(1) 9, 84, 593, 957

Art 4(1)(a)	79, 80, 84, 85, 86, 87, 228, 242, 908
Art 4(1)(b)	13, 92, 905n11
Art 4(1)(c)	88
Art 4(2)	239–41, 591, 592, 593–94
Art 6	16, 211, 311, 312
Art 6(1)	312, 546, 547–48, 550–51, 561–62
Art 6(1)(a)	551
Art 6(1)(b)	551, 1243n2
Art 6(1)(c)	551
Art 6(1)(d)	551
Art 6(1)(e)	551, 1243n2, 1243n5
Art 6(2)	312, 557, 558, 566
Art 7	16, 210n10, 211, 327, 328, 329n10, 330–31, 334
Art 7(a)	177, 329, 347
Art 7(c)	332, 332n35, 333
Art 7(d)	333
Art 7(e)	328, 335n45
Art 7(f)	328, 334, 337, 338, 515, 1208, 1243, 1245n20
Art 7(1)	53
Art 8	369, 370, 371, 372, 373–74n45, 375, 381, 387, 1224, 1253–54, 1259n10
Art 8(1)	219, 372, 387, 530, 1259
Art 8(2)	375
Art 8(2)(a)	347
Art 8(2)(b)	1230
Art 8(2)(d)	1259–61
Art 8(3)	1253–54
Art 8(4)	379, 1243
Art 8(5)	375, 387
Art 8(7)	375, 1223n1, 1224, 1225
Art 9	40–41, 1204, 1205, 1206–7, 1208, 1209
Arts 10–12	165
Art 10	417, 422–23, 437, 441–42, 443, 546, 550–51, 596
Art 10 (a)	417n15
Art 10 (b)	417n15
Art 10 (c)	417n16, 417n17
Art 11	417n13, 422–23, 437, 438, 441–43, 596
Art 11(1)	437n5, 546, 550–51
Art 11(2)	438, 442, 443
Art 12	402, 404, 454, 477, 493, 546, 550–51
Art 12(a)	129, 402, 404, 405, 406–7, 453, 458, 462–63, 527
Art 12(b)	124, 402, 471, 477, 487n2, 515
Art 12(c)	471, 477, 493n2
Art 13	24–25, 65–66, 417, 422–23, 441–42, 546, 547–48, 550–51, 551n23, 552, 1165
Art 13(e) and (f)	547–48
Art 13(1)	423
Art 13(1)(a)–(g)	546
Art 13(1)(d)	423, 443
Art 14	510, 514
Art 14(a)	510, 515
Art 14(b)	510–11
Art 14(1)(a)	510
Art 15	129, 130, 526, 527, 528, 529, 529n18, 530, 532–33n37, 537
Art 15(1)	24, 129, 130, 526, 527, 527n8, 529, 530–31, 532, 532n33–34, 534–35, 539–40n74
Art 15(2)(a)	536, 538
Art 15(2)(b)	537
Art 16	312
Art 17	27, 312, 318, 557, 564, 573, 1298n21
Art 17(1)	558
Art 18	560, 690, 711
Art 18(2)	690, 702n5, 712n8
Art 18(4)	1259–60
Art 19	560
Art 20	711
Art 20(1)	682
Art 20(2)	682
Art 21	546, 550–51
Art 22	1137
Art 23	1164–65, 1170, 1173–74
Art 23(2)	1164–65
Art 24	40, 1185, 1195–96, 1197–98
Art 25	259, 260, 548, 756, 757, 758, 761–62, 775, 815, 1303–4
Art 25(1)	758–59, 761–62
Art 25(2)	347, 787–88
Art 25(4)	775, 1270, 1280
Art 25(5)	1270, 1280
Art 25(6)	33, 779, 945, 1270, 1280, 1309–10
Art 26	259, 756, 799, 804
Art 26(1)	177, 347, 844, 847
Art 26(1)(a)	844
Art 26(1)(b)	844, 848
Art 26(1)(c)	844, 849
Art 26(1)(d)	844
Art 26(1)(e)	844
Art 26(1)(f)	844
Art 26(2)	33, 259–60, 799, 804–5, 815
Art 26(3)	1270, 1280
Art 26(4)	804–5, 1270, 1280
Art 27	259n5, 719, 720–21, 727n4, 727, 734, 756
Art 28	267, 268, 865–66, 877–78, 904, 905, 906, 931, 945, 1028–29, 1057, 1128, 1186
Art 28(1)	228, 267, 865–66, 875, 876, 877–78, 879, 945, 1058, 1061
Art 28(2)	267
Art 28(3)	487n2, 931, 943, 945, 978–79, 1119–20, 1128, 1129, 1136, 1137, 1186, 1253n3
Art 28(4)	907–8, 931, 945, 957, 1119n5, 1122–23, 1144

Art 28(5) 950, 1086
Art 28(6) 906, 945, 957, 959, 975–76,
    978, 979, 988, 1033–34, 1063
Art 28(7) 1253
Art 29 ....869n25, 1043, 1090–91
Art 29(1) 1059
Art 29(2) 1043, 1047, 1048, 1065
Art 29(3) 1043, 1065n44, 1090–91
Art 29(4) 1043, 1095
Art 29(5) 1104
Art 29(6) 1090–91, 1104
Art 29(7) 1098
Art 30 ....1072, 1073
Art 30(1)(a) 869n25
Art 30(1)(c) 1074–75
Art 30(2) 997, 1074–75
Art 30(3) 1074–75
Art 30(4) 1074–75
Art 30(6) 1086, 1087
Art 31 ....42, 785, 1280
Art 33 ....1086, 1309
Art 33(2) 1309–10, 1314
Ch II 761, 1204
Ch III 550–51
Ch IV 318, 756, 1204
Ch VI 1204
Data Retention Directive: Directive 2006/24/
    EC of the European Parliament and of
    the Council of 15 March 2006 on the re-
    tention of data generated or processed in
    connection with the provision of publicly
    available electronic communications ser-
    vices or of public communications
    networks and Amending Directive
    2002/58/EC, OJ 2006 L 105/54
    (no longer in force) 1144, 1145, 1296
Directive (EU) 2018/1972 see EECC Directive
Directive (EU) 2016/1148 see NIS Directive 2016
Directive (EU) 2016/681 see PNR Directive
Directive (EU) 2016/680 see Law
    Enforcement Directive 2016
Directive 2016/343/EU: Directive (EU)
    2016/343 of the European Parliament
    and of the Council of 9 March 2016 on
    the strengthening of certain aspects of
    the presumption of innocence and of the
    right to be present at the trial in criminal
    proceedings, OJ 2016 L 65/1..........1188n41
Directive 2015/2366/EU see PSD2 Directive
Directive (EU) 2015/1535: Directive (EU)
    2015/1535 of the European Parliament
    and of the Council of 9 September
    2015 laying down a procedure for the
    provision of information in the field of
    technical regulations and of rules on
    Information Society services,
    OJ 2015 L 241/1 295
Art 1(1)(b) 294, 295, 296, 359

Art 1(1)(b)(i) 297
Art 1(1)(b)(ii).......................... 298
Art 1(1)(b)(iii) 299–300
Annex 1 ....294n1, 298n24, 298n27–29,
    299–300n39
Directive (EU) 2015/849 see Fourth Anti-Money
    Laundering Directive
Directive 2014/53/EU see Radio Equipment
    Directive
Directive 2014/40/EU of the European
    Parliament and of the Council of 3 April
    2014 on the Approximation of the laws,
    regulations and Administrative provi-
    sions of the Member States concerning
    the manufacture, presentation and sale
    of tobacco and related products and
    repealing Directive 2001/37/EC,
    OJ 2014 L 127/1
Art 18(1)(b) 295n12
Directive 2013/48/EU: Directive 2013/48/EU
    of the European Parliament and of the
    Council of 22 October 2013 on the right
    of Access to a lawyer in criminal
    proceedings and in European arrest
    warrant proceedings, and on the right
    to have a third Party informed upon
    deprivation of liberty and to communicate
    with third persons and with consular
    authorities while deprived of
    liberty, OJ 2013 L 294/1 ....1188n41
Directive 2013/37/EU see PSI Directive
Directive 2012/13/EU: Directive 2012/13/EU
    of the European Parliament and of the
    Council of 22 May 2012 on the right to
    information in criminal proceedings,
    OJ 2012 L 142/1 ....1188n41
Directive 2011/95/EU: Directive 2011/95/
    EU of the European Parliament and of
    the Council of 13 December 2011 on
    standards for the qualification of third-
    country nationals or stateless persons as
    beneficiaries of international protection,
    for a uniform status for refugees or for
    persons eligible for subsidiary protection,
    and for the content of the protection
    granted, OJ 2011 L 337/9
Art 10(1)(b) 1262–63
Directive 2011/83/EU see Consumer Rights
    Directive 2011
Directive 2010/64/EU: Directive 2010/64/EU
    of the European Parliament and of the
    Council of 20 October 2010 on the right
    to interpretation and translation in
    criminal proceedings, OJ 2010
    L 289/1 ....1188n41
Directive 2009/38/EC see European Works
    Council Directive 2009
Directive 2006/24/EC see Data Retention Directive

Table of Instruments

Directive 2005/60/EC *see* Third Anti-Money Laundering Directive
Directive 2005/29/EC *see* Unfair Commercial Practices Directive
Directive 2003/98/EC on the re-use of public sector information, OJ 2003 L 345/90
   Recital 1220–21
   Art 1(4) 1220–21
see also PSI Directive
Directive 2003/4/EC of the European Parliament and of the Council of 28 January 2003 on public access to environmental information and repealing Council Directive 90/313/EEC, OJ 2003 L 41/26 .... 403, 1214n1
Directive 2002/65/EC of the European Parliament and of the Council of 23 September 2002 concerning the distance marketing of consumer financial services and Amending Council Directive 90/619/EEC and Directives 97/7/EC and 98/27/EC, OJ 2002 L 271/16
   Art 3 402–3
Directive 2002/58/EC *see* Privacy and Electronic Communications Directive 2002
Directive 2002/22/EC *see* Universal Service Directive
Directive 2002/21/EC of the European Parliament and of the Council of 7 March 2002 on a common regulatory framework for electronic communications networks and services, OJ 2002 L 108/33
   Recital 10 .... 295n12
   Art 2(c) 295n12
Directive 2001/83/EC of the European Parliament and of the Council of 6 November 2001 on the Community code relating to medicinal products for human use, OJ 2001 L 311/67 289
   Art 29 .... 289n5
Directive 2000/31/EC *see* E-Commerce Directive 2000
Directive 98/84/EC of the European Parliament and of the Council of 20 November 1998 on the legal protection of services based on, or consisting of, conditional Access, OJ 1998 L 320/54 .... 295n12
Directive 98/79/EC (repealed) on in vitro diagnostic medical devices
   Art 10(3) 592
Directive 98/48/EC of the European Parliament and of the Council of 20 July 1998 Amending Directive 98/34/EC laying down a procedure for the provision of information in the field of technical standards and regulations, OJ 1998 L 217/18 295
   Art 1(2) 295n7

Directive 98/34/EC of the European Parliament and of the Council of 22 June 1998 laying down a procedure for the provision of information in the field of technical standards and regulations, OJ 1998 L 204/37 .... 294, 295, 296
   Art 1(2) 295, 296n17
Directive 97/67/EC: Directive 97/66/EC of the European Parliament and of the Council of 15 December 1997 on common rules for the development of the internal market for Community postal services and the improvement of quality of service, OJ 1997 L 15/14 ... 1295–96
   Art 2(19) 1295–96
Directive 97/66/EC: Directive 97/66/EC of the European Parliament and of the Council of 15 December 1997 concerning the processing of personal data and the protection of privacy in the telecommunications sector, OJ 1998 L 24/1 1295–96
   Art 2(1) 1296n7
Directive 95/46/EC *see* Data Protection Directive 1995
Directive 93/42/EEC of 14 June 1993 concerning medical devices, OJ 1993 L 169/1 .... 240n6, 242n22
Directive 93/13/EEC *see* Unfair Contract Terms Directive
Directive 68/151/EEC: First Council Directive 68/151/EEC of 9 March 1968 on co-ordination of safeguards which, for the protection of the interests of members and others, are required by Member States of companies within the meaning of the second paragraph of Article 58 of the Treaty, with a view to making such safeguards equivalent throughout the Community, OJ 1968 L 65/8 514
Directive 65/65: Council Directive 65/65/EEC of 26 January 1965 on the Approximation of provisions laid down by Law, Regulation or Administrative Action relating to proprietary medicinal products, OJ 1965 L 22/369
   Art 1(2) 204n39
E-Commerce Directive 2000: Directive 2000/31/EC of the European Parliament and of the Council of 8 June 2000 on certain legal aspects of information society services, in Particular electronic commerce, in the Internal Market, OJ 2000 L 178/1 ('E-commerce Directive') 64, 72, 296
   Recital 18 .... 297n21
   Art 2(a) 295n11
   Arts 12–15 72

EECC Directive: Directive (EU) 2018/
   1972 of the European Parliament and
   of the Council of 11 December 2018
   establishing the European Electronic
   Communications Code (Recast),
   OJ 2018 L 321/36 .... 1299n24
   Art 40(1) 632–33n8, 642–43n12
   Art 40(2) 656–57n12
Electronic Privacy Directive *see* Privacy and
   Electronic Communications
   Directive 2002
European Works Council Directive 2009:
   Directive 2009/38/EC of the European
   Parliament and of the Council of 6
   May 2009 on the establishment of A
   European Works Council or A pro-
   cedure in Community-scale under-
   takings and Community-scale groups
   of undertakings for the purposes of
   informing and consulting employees,
   OJ 2009 L 122/28
   Art 2(1)(b) 254
   Art 3 .... 256n11
   Art 3(1) 254, 256
   Art 3(2) 256
Fourth Anti-Money Laundering Directive:
   Directive (EU) 2015/849 of the
   European Parliament and of the Council
   of 20 May 2015 on the prevention of
   the use of the financial system for the
   purposes of money laundering or ter-
   rorist financing, Amending Regulation
   (EU) No. 648/2012 of the European
   Parliament and of the Council, and
   repealing Directive 2005/60/EC of the
   European Parliament and of the Council
   and Commission Directive 2006/70/
   EC, OJ 2015 L 141/73 .... 1314n11, 1315
   Arts 40–44 .... 1314n11
Law Enforcement Directive 2016: Directive
   (EU) 2016/680 of the European
   Parliament and of the Council of 27
   April 2016 on the protection of natural
   persons with regard to the processing of
   personal data by competent Authorities
   for the purposes of the prevention,
   investigation, detection or prosecution
   of criminal offences or the execution
   of criminal penalties, and on the free
   movement of such data, and repealing
   Council Framework Decision 2008/
   977/JHA ('LED') 4, 7, 8, 63, 64, 70,
         167, 219, 304, 317, 357, 386–87, 389, 393,
         418–19, 438, 487, 493, 511, 537, 777, 792,
         834–35n75, 843–44, 910, 969–70, 976,
               1080, 1165–66, 1272, 1281n10,
               1282n16, 1303, 1306, 1315, 1317
   Recitals 1–2 51

Recital 4 756
Recitals 8–9 51
Recitals 10–14 .... 51, 62
Recital 11 .... 70, 601
Recital 13 .... 70, 386, 388n7
Recital 16 1213
Recital 18 .... 116, 138
Recital 19 .... 1312, 1313n4
Recital 21 .... 104, 196, 207–8, 217
Recital 22 138
Recital 25 .... 306–7, 756, 858, 955
Recital 26 .... 310, 418–19, 1242
Recital 27 310
Recital 28 310
Recital 30 470
Recital 39 324
Recital 33 324
Recital 34 .... 310, 324
Recital 35 .... 175, 178, 178n16, 182n40,
                            324, 346, 773
Recital 36 .... 324, 756, 798, 843
Recital 37 .... 175, 178, 346, 368
Recital 38 .... 128, 368, 400, 525
Recital 39 .... 310, 355, 400
Recital 40 .... 123, 310, 400, 450, 470, 498–99
Recital 41 400
Recital 42 .... 310, 419, 498–99
Recital 43 .... 128, 400, 450, 498–99,
                                525, 929–30
Recital 44 .... 400, 450, 498–99, 544
Recital 45 .... 400, 498–99
Recital 46 .... 400, 498–99, 544
Recital 47 .... 400, 470, 471–72, 476, 486,
                                498–99, 509
Recital 48 .... 400, 470, 476, 498–99
Recital 49 .... 400, 470, 476, 498–99
Recital 50 .... 310, 355, 368, 556, 572, 582
Recital 51 .... 128, 196, 207–8, 217, 310,
                     355, 525, 540n75, 556 681
Recital 52 .... 128, 525, 540n75, 556, 681
Recital 53 .... 556, 572, 579, 681
Recital 54 582
Recital 55 .... 572, 601
Recital 56 .... 556, 601
Recital 57 .... 556, 572
Recital 58 .... 128, 368, 525, 556, 572, 681
Recital 59 .... 601, 929–30
Recital 60 .... 310, 368, 556, 572, 601
Recital 61 189
Recital 62 .... 189, 400
Recital 63 .... 556, 582, 689, 701, 710
Recitals 64–72 303
Recital 64 756
Recital 65 756
Recital 66 773
Recital 67 .... 773, 955, 974, 987
Recital 68 .... 773, 1072
Recital 69 773

Recital 70	773
Recital 71	798, 955
Recital 72	843
Recital 73	858, 955
Recital 74	858, 929–30, 955, 974, 987
Recital 75	265, 864, 874, 884–85, 894, 929–30, 942
Recital 76	265, 864, 874, 884–85, 894, 929–30, 942
Recital 77	265, 864, 874, 884–85, 894, 955, 974, 987
Recital 78	874, 884–85, 894
Recital 79	874, 884–85, 894, 929–30, 942
Recital 80	903, 910
Recital 81	929–30, 955, 974, 987
Recital 82	929–30, 942, 974, 987
Recital 83	929–30, 955, 974, 987
Recital 84	929–30, 955, 974, 987, 1041, 1072, 1074, 1080
Recital 85	400, 929–30, 955, 974, 987, 1118, 1133, 1161
Recital 86	942, 1126, 1161, 1183
Recital 87	1142, 1161
Recital 88	1161
Recital 90	955, 974, 987, 1032, 1278
Recital 91	1032, 1278
Recital 92	1278
Recital 94	1308
Recital 95	1302, 1303
Recital 96	1320
Recital 98	1291
Art 1	51, 62, 386
Art 1(1)	4n10, 386n81, 386–87, 389n13
Art 2	51, 62, 386
Art 2(2)	70
Art 2(2)(d)	386–87
Art 2(3)	70
Art 3	386, 582, 601
Art 3(1)	62, 70, 104, 196, 207–8, 217
Art 3(2)	62, 70, 116, 120
Art 3(3)	123, 125, 210, 486
Art 3(4)	128, 131, 540
Art 3(5)	104, 133
Art 3(6)	62, 70, 138, 140
Art 3(7)	62, 70, 154–55, 386–87, 389n12
Art 3(8)	145, 154–55, 1165n27
Art 3(9)	157, 161
Art 3(10)	164, 168, 170, 171n2
Art 3(11)	189, 193
Art 3(12)	104, 196, 199, 207–8, 217
Art 3(13)	104, 196, 207–8, 217
Art 3(14)	104, 196, 207–8, 217, 219
Art 3(15)	265, 884–85, 894, 929–30, 942
Art 3(16)	303, 306–7n25
Art 4	310, 324, 511, 1242
Art 4(1)(c)	317
Art 4(1)(d)	470
Art 4(1)(e)	318
Art 4(1)(f)	318
Art 4(2)	316
Art 4(3)	317
Art 4(4)	572
Art 5	318, 324
Art 7(2)	317
Art 8	178n14, 314, 324, 511
Art 9	324, 1242
Art 9(1)	310
Art 9(2)	310
Art 10	196, 207–8, 217, 368, 511, 539–40
Art 11	128, 368, 400, 539–40
Art 11(1)	453–54, 531, 539–40
Art 11(2)	196, 207–8, 217, 539–40
Art 11(3)	539–40
Art 12	128, 400, 419, 450, 498–99
Art 12(1)	419n19
Art 13	310, 315n22, 355, 400, 414, 436, 438, 498–99
Art 13(1)(e)	470
Art 13(3)	418–19, 544
Art 14	315n21, 400, 450, 453–54, 498–99
Art 15	400, 450, 498–99, 544, 1165
Art 15(1)	454
Art 16	400, 476, 486, 487n1, 498–99, 509
Art 16(1)	470, 471–72
Art 16(4)	470, 544
Art 16(5)	470, 472n4
Art 16(6)	470, 471–72n5, 492, 493n1
Art 17	400, 470, 498–99, 929–30
Art 18	400, 498–99
Art 19	310, 368, 556, 572, 582, 681
Art 20	318, 556, 572, 577, 579
Art 21	582
Art 22	157, 355, 572, 601
Art 23	157
Art 24	128, 368, 556, 601
Art 24(1)(e)	539
Art 24(1)(i)	572
Art 25	556, 572
Art 26	601
Art 27	128, 368, 540, 556, 572, 681
Art 28	601, 681, 929–30
Art 27(1)	540n75
Art 28	942
Arts 29–31	318
Art 29	310, 368, 556, 572, 601
Art 29(1)	196, 207–8, 217
Art 30	189, 601
Art 31	189, 400
Art 31(3)(a)	572
Art 32	556, 689
Art 33	556, 701
Art 34	556, 710
Art 35–40	303
Art 35	766, 773
Art 36	766, 773, 777n20, 792
Art 36(2)(b)	792

Table of Instruments

Art 36(3)–(5) 1278, 1281n10
Art 37 .... 766, 798
Art 37(1) 809
Art 38 .... 766, 843, 843–44n6
Art 39 .... 766, 843
Art 39(1)(c) 766n61
Art 40 .... 766, 858, 929–30, 955, 969–70, 974, 987
Art 41 .... 265, 864, 884–85, 894, 929–30, 942
Art 41(2) 996
Art 42 .... 884–85, 894
Art 42(1) 929–30
Art 43 .... 884–85, 894, 942
Art 44 .... 884–85, 894
Art 44(2) 1111
Art 45 .... 903, 929–30, 942
Art 45(2) 70n32, 910n43
Art 46 929–30
Art 46(1)(h) 955, 974, 987
Art 46(1)(i) 955, 974, 987
Art 47 .... 929–30, 942
Art 47(1) 974, 987
Art 49 .... 949, 1085
Art 50 ..... 929–30, 955, 969–70, 974, 976, 987
Art 50(8) 1032, 1278, 1281n10
Art 51 .... 929–30, 996, 1041, 1072, 1080
Art 51(1) 1278
Art 51(1)(d) 189
Art 51(1)(e) 189
Art 51(1)(g) 773
Art 51(1)(i)–(j) 858
Art 51(3) 1278, 1283–84
Art 52 .... 511, 929–30, 1118, 1142, 1161
Art 53 .... 942, 1126, 1142, 1161, 1183
Art 54 ... 511, 601, 1133, 1142, 1161, 1165–66
Art 55 .... 1142, 1161
Art 56 .... 1161, 1165–66
Art 57 .... 1183, 1195
Art 58 .... 1278, 1280
Art 58(1) 4n12, 1282n17
Art 59 1291
Art 61 .... 1302, 1303, 1304
Art 62 .... 949, 1308
Art 62(6) 1312, 1317
Art 63 .... 55, 1320
Art 64 1320
Ch V 766
NIS Directive 2016: Directive (EU) 2016/1148 of the European Parliament and of the Council of 6 July 2016 concerning measures for a high common level of security of network and information systems across the Union, OJ 2016 L 194/1 .... 192, 633, 643, 889
Art 1(3) 643n14, 657n15
Art 8 .... 889n22
Art 14 .... 633n10, 642–43n9

Art 14(3) 192n22
Art 14(6) 656n9
Art 16 .... 633n10, 642n9
Art 16(7) 656n9
Payment Services Directive 2015/2366/EU 633
PNR Directive: Directive (EU) 2016/681 of the European Parliament and of the Council of 27 April 2016 on the use of passenger name record (PNR) data for the prevention, detection, investigation and prosecution of terrorist offences and serious crime, OJ 2016 L 119/132.... 909, 1314
Art 6(5) 540
Art 8 909
Privacy and Electronic Communications Directive 2002: Directive 2002/58/EC of the European Parliament and of the Council of 12 July 2002 concerning the processing of personal data and the protection of privacy in the electronic communications sector ('EPD') 8, 10, 71, 111n43, 199, 348, 357, 393, 417–18, 438, 511, 591, 734, 916n6, 969, 976, 1166, 1292n2, 1295–96, 1297, 1298, 1299, 1299n24, 1314, 1315, 1316, 1317
Recital 2 1297
Recital 3....................... 368, 450, 582
Recital 4............................. 582
Recital 9............................. 133
Recital 10...... 62, 582, 590, 1291, 1294, 1296
Recital 11.............. 62, 544, 546, 1291
Recital 12............................ 62, 1294
Recital 14............................. 450
Recital 17.................. 175, 177n11, 346
Recital 20 ...... 189, 400, 556, 582, 601, 1072
Recital 21............................. 450
Recital 22....................... 346, 450
Recital 23............................. 450
Recital 24....................... 128, 400
Recital 25............ 128, 292, 346, 368, 400
Recital 26............................. 400
Recital 30............................. 346
Recital 31....................... 346, 574
Recital 32............ 346, 400, 582, 601
Recital 33............................. 572
Recital 35............ 346, 368, 400, 450
Recital 38............................. 400
Recital 39............................. 346
Recital 40....................... 346, 509
Recital 42............................. 346
Recital 45............................. 292
Recital 47...................... 1161, 1195
Recital 48............................. 1072
Art 1 .... 62, 75
Art 1(2) 71, 1294, 1296, 1297, 1298, 1298n22, 1299
Art 1(3) 65–66, 1296–97
Art 2 .... 116, 292, 346

Art 2(1) 190, 193
Art 2(c)................................ 368
Art 2(f) 175, 177–78, 180, 348
Art 2(i) 189, 1298n21
Art 3 .... 75, 1296–97
Art 4 .... 189, 400, 414, 436, 558, 582,
             601, 1072, 1298, 1298n21, 1299
Art 4(1) 556, 574, 1298
Art 4(1)(a) 556, 1298
Art 4(2) 418, 438
Art 4(3) 190, 191, 942, 1298, 1298n21
Art 4(4) 942
Art 4(5) 996
Art 5 .... 128, 324, 346, 368, 400, 414,
                     436, 450, 551–52, 582
Art 5(3) 180, 348, 417, 438
Art 6 ....324, 346, 348, 400, 414, 436,
                              450, 551–52
Art 6(1) 476
Art 6(4) 418, 438
Art 6(5) 601
Art 8(1)–(4)......................... 551–52
Art 9 .... 324, 346, 348, 368, 400,
                   414, 436, 450, 551–52, 601
Art 9(1) 418
Art 12 ....346, 400
Art 12(1) 179
Art 12(2) 179
Art 13 .... 341–42n94, 346, 348, 509
Arts 13(a) and 13(b)................ 643, 657
Art 13(2) 511
Art 14 ....292, 572
Art 14(3) 574
Art 14(a)......................... 1279, 1280
Art 15 ....62, 386, 544, 546, 547, 548–49,
              550, 551n24, 551–52, 930, 1118,
              1126, 1133, 1161, 1291, 1292, 1296
Art 15(1).............. 65–66, 548, 1296–97
Art 15(1b) 942
Art 15(2) 1166
Art 15(3) 1072, 1292
Art 15a 885, 894, 930, 942, 1072,
                          1118, 1126, 1133, 1183
Art 15a(4) 955, 970, 974, 976, 987, 996
Art 17 1320
Art 18 ....949, 1086, 1087, 1312, 1315n22
Art 20 1320
PSD2 Directive: Directive 2015/2366/EU
   of the European Parliament and of
   the Council of 25 November 2015 on
   payment services in the internal market,
   Amending Directives 2002/65/EC,
   2009/110/EC and 2013/36/EU and
   Regulation (EU) No. 1093/2010, and
   repealing Directive 2007/64/EC,
   OJ 2015 L 337/35 .... 633, 656–57
Art 96............................642n11
PSI Directive: Directive 2013/37/EU of the
   European Parliament and of the Council
   of 26 June 2013 Amending Directive
   2003/98/EC on the re-use of
   public sector information,
   OJ 2013 L 175/1 .... 403, 656n11
Radio Equipment Directive: Directive 2014/
   53/EU of the European Parliament
   and of the Council of 16 April 2014 on
   the harmonisation of the laws of the
   Member States relating to the making
   Available on the market of radio equip-
   ment and repealing Directive 1999/5/
   EC, OJ 2014 L 153/62 591
Art 2(13) 591
Art 3(3)(e) 574
Art 11(2) 591
Third Anti-Money Laundering Directive:
   Directive 2005/60/EC of the
   European Parliament and of the
   Council of 26 October 2005 on the
   prevention of the use of the finan-
   cial system for the purpose of money
   laundering and terrorist financing,
   OJ 2005 L 309/15 1314
Unfair Commercial Practices Directive
   (UCPD): Directive 2005/29/EC of
   the European Parliament and of the
   Council of 11 May 2005 concerning
   unfair business-to-consumer commer-
   cial practices in the internal market and
   Amending Council Directive 84/450/
   EEC, Directives 97/7/EC, 98/27/EC and
   2002/65/EC of the European Parliament
   and of the Council and Regulation
   (EC) No. 2006/2004 of the European
   Parliament and of the Council, OJ 2005
   L 149/22............................. 720
Art 2(f)............................720n10
Art 6(2)(b) 720n11
Art 10................................ 720
Unfair Contract Terms Directive: Council
   Directive 93/13/EEC of 5 April 1993
   on unfair terms in consumer contracts,
   OJ 1993 L 95/29 ('UCTD') 350
Universal Service Directive: Directive 2002/
   22/EC of the European Parliament
   and of the Council of 7 March 2002
   on universal service and users' rights
   relating to electronic communications
   networks and services (Universal Service
   Directive), OJ 2002 L 108/51
Art 11(3) 402–3
Art 30 ....500n13

EU Decisions

Commission Decision 2016/2295:
   Commission Implementing Decision
   (EU) 2016/2295 of 16 December 2016
   Amending Decisions 2000/518/EC,

2002/2/EC, 2003/490/EC, 2003/821/
EC, 2004/411/EC, 2008/393/EC, 2010/
146/EU, 2010/625/EU, 2011/61/EU and
Implementing Decisions 2012/484/EU,
2013/65/EU on the adequate protection
of personal data by certain countries, pursuant to Article 25(6) of Directive
95/46/EC of the European Parliament
and of the Council (notified under document C(2016) 8353), OJ 2016 L 344/ 83 ... 776
Commission Decision Andorra: Commission
Decision of 19 October 2010 pursuant
to Directive 95/46/EC of the European
Parliament and of the Council on the
Adequate protection of personal data in
Andorra, OJ 2010 L 277/27........ 775n6, 776
Commission Decision Argentina 2003:
Commission Decision 2003/1731 of 30
June 2003 pursuant to Directive (EC)
95/46 of the European Parliament and
of the Council on the Adequate protection of personal data in Argentina,
OJ 2003 L 168/19...............775n6, 776,
790n136, 832–33n56
Commission Decision Canada 2006:
Commission Decision of 6 September
2005 on the Adequate protection of
personal data contained in the Passenger
Name Record of Air passengers transferred
to the Canada Border Services Agency,
OJ 2006 L 91/49 (expired) 759n16
Commission Decision Faroe Islands 2010:
Commission Decision of 5 March 2010
pursuant to Directive 95/46/EC of the
European Parliament and of the Council
on the Adequate protection provided
by the Faeroese Act on the processing of
personal data, OJ 2010 L 58/17 ....775n6
Commission Decision Guernsey 2003:
Commission Decision 2003/821 of 21
November 2003 on the Adequate
protection of personal data in Guernsey,
OJ 2003 L 308/27........775n6, 776, 790n136
Commission Decision Isle of Man 2004:
Commission Decision 2004/411 of 28
April 2004 on the Adequate protection
of personal data in the Isle of Man,
OJ 2004 L 151/1................. 775n6, 776
Commission Decision Israel 2011:
Commission Decision 2011/61/EU of 31
January 2011 pursuant to Directive 95/
46/EC of the European Parliament and
of the Council on the Adequate protection of personal data by the State of Israel
with regard to Automated processing of
personal data, OJ 2011 L 27/39 .... 775n6,
776, 785n84, 790n136
Commission Decision Japan 2019:
Commission Implementing Decision
(EU) 2019/419 of 23 January 2019
pursuant to Regulation (EU) 2016/679
of the European Parliament and of the
Council on the Adequate protection of
personal data by Japan under the Act on
the Protection of Personal Information,
OJ 2019 L 76/1 .... 775n6, 777, 785n91,
786, 1289
Commission Decision Jersey 2008:
Commission Decision of 8 May 2008
pursuant to Directive 95/46/EC of the
European Parliament and of the Council
on the Adequate protection
of personal data in Jersey,
OJ 2008 L 138/21 .... 775n6, 776
Commission Decision New Zealand 2012:
Commission Implementing Decision
of 19 December 2012 pursuant to
Directive 95/46/EC of the European
Parliament and of the Council on the
Adequate protection of personal
data by New Zealand, OJ 2013
L 28/12 .... 775n6, 776
Commission Decision PIPEDA 2002:
Commission Decision (EC) 2002/
2 of 20 December 2001 pursuant to
Directive (EC) 95/46 of the European
Parliament and of the Council on the
Adequate protection of personal data
provided by the Canadian Personal
Information Protection and Electronic
Documents Act, OJ 2002 L 2/13....... 775n6,
776, 786
Commission Decision Privacy Shield 2016:
Commission Implementing Decision
(EU) 2016/1250 of 12 July 2016 pursuant to Directive 95/46/EC of the
European Parliament and of the Council
on the Adequacy of the protection provided by the EU-U.S. Privacy Shield,
OJ 2016 L 207/1 .... 775n6, 786, 790,
791, 832–33, 1120, 1280
Commission Decision Switzerland 2000:
Commission Decision of 26 July 2000
pursuant to Directive 95/46/EC of the
European Parliament and of the Council
on the Adequate protection of personal
data provided in Switzerland, OJ 2000
L215/1 .... 775n6, 776
Commission Decision Uruguay 2012:
Commission Implementing Decision
of 21 August 2012 pursuant to
Directive 95/46/EC of the European
Parliament and of the Council on the
Adequate protection of personal data
by the Eastern Republic of Uruguay
with regard to Automated
processing of personal data,
OJ 2012 L 227/11..............775n6, 776

Commission Decision US 2004: Commission Decision of 14 May 2004 on the Adequate protection of personal data contained in the Passenger Name Record of Air passengers transferred to the United States' Bureau of Customs and Border Protection, OJ 2004 L 235/11 .... 759n17, 775–76

Council Decision Australia 2008: Council Decision of 30 June 2008 on the signing, on behalf of the European Union, of an Agreement between the European Union and Australia on the processing and transfer of European Union-sourced passenger name record (PNR) data by Air carriers to the Australian Customs Service, OJ 2008 L 213/47 .... 759n15

Council Decision Canada 2006: Council Decision of 18 July 2005 on the conclusion of an Agreement between the European Community and the Government of Canada on the processing of API/PNR data, OJ 2006 L 82/14 .... 759n16

Council Decision TFTP US 2010: Council Decision of 13 July 2010 on the conclusion of the Agreement between the European Union and the United States of America on the processing and transfer of Financial Messaging Data from the European Union to the United States for the purposes of the Terrorist Finance Tracking Program, OJ 2010 L 195/3 .... 759–60n19

Council Decision US 2007: Council Decision 2007/551/CFSP/JHA of 23 July 2007 on the signing, on behalf of the European Union, of an Agreement between the European Union and the United States of America on the processing and transfer of Passenger Name Record (PNR) data by Air carriers to the United States Department of Homeland Security (DHS) (2007 PNR Agreement), OJ 2007 L 204/16. .... 759n17

Council Decision US 2006: Council Decision 2 of 16 October 2006 on the signing, on behalf of the European Union, of an Agreement between the European Union and the United States of America on the processing and transfer of passenger name record (PNR) data by Air carriers to the United States Department of Homeland Security, OJ 2006 L 298/27 .... 759n16

Council Decision US 2004: Council Decision of 17 May 2004 on the conclusion of an Agreement between the European Community and the United States of America on the processing and transfer of PNR data by Air Carriers to the United States Department of Homeland Security, Bureau of Customs and Border Protection, OJ 2004 L 183/83 .... 759n17

Safe Harbour 2000: Commission Decision 2000/520 of 26 July 2000 pursuant to Directive 95/46 of the European Parliament and of the Council on the Adequacy of the protection provided by the safe harbor privacy principles and related frequently asked questions issued by the US Department of Commerce, OJ 2000 L 215/7 (annulled) 473, 779–82

INTERNATIONAL INSTRUMENTS

International Treaties, Conventions, and Agreements involving the EU

Agreement between the United States of America and the European Union on the protection of personal information relating to the prevention, investigation, detection, and prosecution of criminal offences, OJ 2016 L 336/3 (Umbrella Agreement US) 777–78, 834–35n77
Art 1(3) ...759–60n21, 777–78n23, 834–35n77
Art 5(3) 777–78n24
Art 16, 16(3) and 17 .... 403, 759–60

Agreement EU Switzerland 2008: Agreement between the European Union, the European Community and the Swiss Confederation of 27 February 2008 on the Swiss Confederation's Association with the implementation, Application and development of the Schengen Acquis, OJ 2008 L 53/77. 1051

Joint Declaration EU Switzerland 2008: Joint Declaration of the Contracting Parties of 27 February 2008 on Directive 95/46/EC of the European Parliament and the Council on data protection, annexed to the Agreement between the European Community and the Swiss Confederation concerning the criteria and mechanisms for establishing the State responsible for examining a request for Asylum lodged in a Member State or in Switzerland, OJ 2008 L 53/15 ..... 1051n50

PNR Agreement Australia 2012: Agreement between the European Union and Australia on the processing and transfer of Passenger Name Record (PNR) data by air carriers to the Australian Customs and Border Protection Service, OJ 2012 L 186/4. .... 759n15, 834
Art 5. .... 759n18

Table of Instruments

PNR Agreement Australia 2008: Agreement between the European Union and Australia on the processing and transfer of European Union-sourced passenger name record (PNR) data by air carriers to the Australian customs service, OJ 2008 L 213/49 (never entered into force).......................... 759n13

PNR Agreement Canada 2006: Agreement between the European Community and the Government of Canada on the processing of Advance Passenger Information and Passenger Name Record data, OJ 2006 L 82/15 (expired)........................... 759n16

PNR Agreement US 2012: Agreement between the United States of America and the European Union on the use and transfer of passenger name records to the United States Department of Homeland Security, OJ 2012 L 215/5 .... 759n17, 834

Agreement US 2007: Agreement between the European Union and the United States of America on the processing and transfer of Passenger Name Record (PNR) data by air carriers to the United States Department of Homeland Security (DHS) (2007 PNR Agreement), OJ 2007 L 204/18.................... 759n17

PNR Agreement US 2006: Agreement between the European Community and the United States of America on the processing and transfer of PNR data by air carriers to the United States Department of Homeland Security, OJ 2006 L 298/29.................... 759n17

TFTP US 2010: Agreement between the European Union and the United States of America on the processing and transfer of Financial Messaging Data from the European Union to the United States for purposes of the Terrorist Finance Tracking Program, OJ 2010 L 8/11 .... 759–60n19

Umbrella Agreement US *see* Agreement between the United States of America and the European Union on the protection of personal information 759–60n20

Withdrawal Agreement: Agreement on the withdrawal of the United Kingdom of Great Britain and Northern Ireland from the European Union and the European Atomic Energy Community, As endorsed by leaders at a special meeting of the European Council on 25 November 2018 (25 November 2018).... 83–84, 787, 822
Art 71.......... 83n35, 787n109, 822n25, 822

Other International Treaties, Conventions, and Agreements

Aarhus Convention: Convention on Access to Information, Public Participation in Decision-Making and Access to Justice in Environmental Matters, 25 June 1998... 1214n1

Additional Protocol Convention 108 *see under* Council of Europe Convention for the Protection of Individuals with regard to Automatic Processing of Personal Data ('Convention 108')

Additional Protocol Biomedicine Convention *see under* Convention for the Protection of Human Rights and Dignity of the Human Being with regard to the Application of Biology and Medicine ('Biomedicine Convention')

Agreement on the European Economic Area *see* EEA Agreement Convention for the Protection of Human Rights and Dignity of the Human Being with regard to the Application of Biology and Medicine, 4 April 1997 ('Biomedicine Convention').................... 199–200
Art 10(1) 220
Art 10(2) 220
Art 11 199–200
Art 12............................... 199
Ch IV 199–200

Additional Protocol to Convention for the Protection of Human Rights and Dignity of the Human Being with regard to the Application of Biology and Medicine, concerning Genetic Testing for Health Purposes, 27 November 2008
Art 2(1) 199n12
Art 4 .... 203n35

Council of Europe Convention on Access to Official Documents, CETS No. 205..... 1215
Art 3(1)(f) 1215

Convention on Civil Aviation 1944, 15 U.N.T.S. 295 (Chicago Convention/Aviation Convention)
Art 13................................ 784

Council of Europe Convention for the Protection of Individuals with regard to Automatic Processing of Personal Data ('Convention 108')..........2–3, 52, 106, 107, 124, 127, 134, 140–41, 158, 165, 171, 178, 190, 199, 210, 228, 240, 267, 281, 289–90, 295, 304–5, 311, 317, 327, 348, 357, 370, 387, 393, 438, 487, 493, 512, 516, 528, 557, 574, 584, 592, 683, 691, 702, 711–12, 727, 760, 775, 788, 845, 858–59, 866, 876, 905, 1034, 1120n9, 1144, 1204, 1215, 1224, 1231, 1254, 1260
Art 1 78

Art 2(a) 106, 107
Art 2(b) 140–41
Art 2(c) 118
Art 2(d) 146–47
Art 3 140–41
Art 5 . . . . 311, 312, 327, 546
Art 5(a) 420
Art 6 . . . . 219, 327, 371, 372, 387, 546
Art 7 312
Art 8 . . . . 420, 546
Art 8(a) 420
Art 8(b) 420n22, 455, 501
Art 8(c) 472, 478
Art 9 . . . . 546, 547, 550
Art 9(2)(b) 1204, 1205
Art 9(3) 1243–44
Art 10 . . . . 1120, 1186
Art 12 845
Arts 13–17 957
Art 13 977
Art 13(3) 1034n6
Art 13(3)(b) 977, 982, 989, 1043n4
Additional Protocol Convention 108:
    Additional Protocol to the Convention
    for the Protection of Individuals with re-
    gard to Automatic Processing of Personal
    Data, regarding supervisory Authorities
    and transborder data flows [ETS 181]
    (2001) 760, 845, 866, 886, 905,
                        931, 957, 1086, 1120
    Art 1 . . . . 866, 905
    Art 1(1) 944
    Art 1(2)(a) 944
    Art 1(2)(b) 944
    Art 1(3) 876, 886, 895–96
    Art 1(4) 1128
    Art 1(5) 916, 957, 977, 1043n5
    Art 2(1) 845
    Art 2(2) 845n9
    Explanatory Report 107n7, 146–47, 371,
                        472, 563, 720, 845, 880n34,
                        881n45, 1205, 1224n2
Council of Europe Modernised Convention
    108 on Data Protection 2018
    ('Modernised Convention 108') . . . 2–3, 52, 65,
    106, 107, 124, 129, 134, 140–41, 146–47, 165,
    171, 178, 190, 199–200, 210, 228, 304–5,
    312, 327, 357, 393, 403, 420, 438, 455, 487,
    493, 501, 512, 516, 547, 561, 592, 683, 691,
            702, 711–12, 720, 760n24, 845, 877,
            895–96, 931, 950, 977, 1029, 1034, 1144,
            1167, 1168, 1204, 1224, 1231, 1254, 1260
    Preamble 52, 1215
    Art 1 . . . . 52n3
    Art 2 584
    Art 2(a) 106, 107
    Art 2(b) 118
    Art 2(c) 140–41

Art 2(d) 146–47, 584
Art 2(e) 165
Art 2(f) 158
Art 3 . . . . 65n5, 78
Art 5(2) 178, 179, 327, 348, 512n12
Art 5(4) 327, 547
Art 5(4)(b) 1243–44
Art 6 371
Art 6(1) 199, 210, 214, 387
Art 6(2) 369n9, 387
Art 7(1) 312
Art 7(2) 190, 312, 547, 643n16
Art 8 . . . . 438, 455, 472, 547
Art 8(1) 438, 547
Art 8(1)(b) 403
Art 8(2) 439n12
Art 8(3) 439n13, 1243–44
Art 9 . . . . 547, 1167
Art 9(1) 528–528
Art 9(1)(a) 528
Art 9(1)(d) 124, 512
Art 9(2) 528, 1243–44
Art 9(b) 455
Art 9(e) 472, 478
Art 9(f) 1167
Art 10 559
Art 10(1) 312
Art 10(2) 574, 683n3
Art 10(3) 501, 574
Art 10(4) 574
Art 11 . . . . 65, 547, 1243–44
Art 11(1) 327, 547, 684
Art 11(1)(b) 1204, 1205
Art 11(2) 547
Art 11(3) 547
Art 12 . . . . 760, 1120, 1167, 1186, 1198
Art 14(2) 304–5, 304n10
Art 14(4)(a) 179, 348
Arts 15–21 . . . . 267, 866
Art 15 . . . . 357, 886, 895–96n9,
                        931n7, 1120, 1128
Art 15(2) 944
Art 15(2)(c) 1120n12
Art 15(5) 877
Art 15(6) 877
Art 15(7) 950n4, 1086
Art 15(8) 896
Art 15(10) 905
Arts 16–21 957
Art 17 916
Art 17(1)(a) 977, 1034n7
Art 17(1)(b) 916, 989
Art 17(2) 179, 348, 977, 982
Art 17(3) 916, 977, 1034n8, 1043, 1073,
                        1098–99
Art 27(1) 304–5, 304n11
Ch IV 866
Ch V 977, 989

Explanatory report 107n7, 146–47, 158,
165, 178, 199, 210, 214n29, 219–20,
304–5, 316n35, 438–39, 439n14,
455, 472, 501, 512, 895–96, 1167–68
Art 143. . . . . .1043, 1073
Cybercrime Convention: Council of Europe
Convention on Cybercrime 2001, ETS
No. 185. . . . . .829n27
EEA Agreement: Agreement on the European
Economic Area, OJ 1994 L 1/3 . . . .421, 439–40,
777–78, 800–1, 803, 916, 944, 950,
998, 1007–8, 1018, 1043–44, 1047–48,
1049, 1050, 1058, 1064, 1073–74,
1087, 1091, 1095–96, 1104
Art 109. . . . . 998, 1007–8, 1018, 1073–74
Protocol I. 229n9, 239n1, 281n12
s 8 . . . . .83n33, 229n9, 239n1, 281n12
Decision of the EEA Joint Committee:
Decision of the EEA Joint Committee,
No 154/2018 of 6 July 2018 Amending
Annex XI (Electronic communication,
Audiovisual services and information
society) and Protocol 37 (containing the
list provided for in Article 101) to the
EEA Agreement [2018/1022], OJ 2018
L183/2 . . . . 778n27, 786n97, 800–1n17,
916, 950n5, 998n6, 1018n5, 1043, 1058,
1073n4, 1087, 1091, 1095–96, 1104
EEA Decision 1999: Decision of the EEA
Joint Committee No. 83/1999 of
25 June 1999 Amending Protocol 37
and Annex XI (Telecommunication
services) to the EEA Agreement,
OJ 2000 L 296/41. . . . . 758–59n11
European Convention on Human Rights
('ECHR') 3, 56, 85, 325–26, 389–90,
472–73, 760, 1120, 1167–68
Art 6 . . . . . . .379, 1120n10, 1121, 1127n1, 1128,
1184–85, 1188n41, 1255–56
Art 6(1) 1128, 1184–85n9
Art 8 . . . . . 56, 106, 111n41, 176, 201, 211, 221,
313, 329n14, 358–59, 373, 375,
388, 388n9, 403, 406, 418–19,
423–25, 458–59, 478–79, 480, 516,
545, 546, 547–48, 550, 551–52,
575–76, 945, 1165, 1167–68,
1171–73, 1205, 1216, 1217–19, 1231,
1232, 1233–34, 1295–96, 1297
Art 8(1) 269, 576, 1297
Art 8(2) 314, 325–26, 329–30n16,
418n18, 458–59, 546, 546n4, 845
Art 9 375
Art 10 . . . . 478–79, 480, 516, 1204,
1205, 1216, 1217–19
Art 10(2) 1217–18
Art 11 375
Art 13 78
Art 14 374–75

Art 41 .1167–68, 1171–72
Protocol No. VII, Art 4 1188
Hague Evidence Convention: Hague
Convention on the Taking of Evidence
Abroad in Civil or Commercial Matters,
18 March 1970, 847 UNTS 231 759–60,
826, 829, 834
Art 1. 834
International Covenant on Civil and
Political Rights ('ICCPR')
Art 2(1) 78–79
Art 19(2) 843–44n3
United Nations Convention on the Rights
of the Child ('UNCRC'). 357
Art 5. 357
Universal Declaration of Human
Rights 1948, GA res. 217A (III),
UN Doc. A/810
Art 19. . . . . 843–44n3
Vienna Convention on Consular
Relations 1963 93
Vienna Convention on Diplomatic
Relations 1961 93
Art 22 . . . . 92n73
Art 29 . . . . 92n72
Art 41 92
Vienna Convention on the Law of
Treaties 1969 305
Art 2(1)(i). 305n18

TABLE OF EUROPEAN DATA PROTECTION BOARD, EUROPEAN DATA PROTECTION SUPERVISOR AND ARTICLE 29 WORKING PARTY DOCUMENTS

European Data Protection Board ('EDPB') Documents

Draft Administrative Arrangements 2019:
'Draft Administrative Arrangement for
the transfer of personal data between
each of the European Economic
Area ("EEA") Authorities set out in
Appendix A and each of the non-EEA
Authorities set out in Appendix B'
(7 January 2019) 809n50
EDPB EDPS Response Cloud Act: 'EPDB-
EDPS Joint Response to the LIBE
Committee on the impact of the US
Cloud Act on the European legal
framework for personal data protection
(annex)' (10 July 2019). 333n40,
334n44, 336n59, 339n76, 761–62n40,
826–27n10, 830n41, 831n44, 831n46,
831–32n51–52, 832–33n61, 833n63,
833n65, 834n70, 835n80, 839n81,
850n42, 851n52, 852n59, 854n71

EDPB 2019, 'Guidelines 3/2019 on the processing of personal data through video devices (version for public consultation)' (10 July 2019) 69n28, 69, 69n29, 181n32, 212n21–22, 338n69, 339n76, 370–71n20, 374n50, 376–77n61, 378n72, 408n30, 426n73, 464n64, 467n70, 482n23, 633n12, 674n37

EDPB 2019, 'Opinion 8/2019 on the competence of a supervisory authority in case of a change in circumstances relating to the main or single establishment' (9 July 2019)................... 234n39, 920n41, 962n40

EDPB 2019, 'Opinion 14/2019 on the draft Standard Contractual Clauses submitted by the DK SA (Article 28(8) GDPR)' (9 July 2019) 606n15, 804n39

EDPB 2019, 'Guidelines 1/2019 on Codes of Conduct and Monitoring Bodies under Regulation 2016/679' (4 June 2019) 807n46

EDPB 2019, 'Guidelines 4/2018 on the Accreditation of Certification. Bodies under Article 43 of the General Data Protection Regulation (2016/679)' (4 June 2019). 747n9, 748n14, 749n20, 750n26, 750n28, 751n31

EDPB 2019, 'Guidelines 1/2018 on Certification and Identifying Certification Criteria in Accordance with Article 42 and 43 of the Regulation 2016/679' (4 June 2019) 737n32, 738n33, 738n35, 739n41, 740n43, 741n47–48, 748n15, 748–49n16, 749n20, 750n26, 750–51n29

EDPB 2019, '1 year GDPR – tacking stock' (22 May 2019). 956n4, 1038n36

EDPB 2019, 'Guidelines 2/2019 on the processing of personal data under Article 6(1)(b) GDPR in the context of the provision of online services to data subjects' (9 April 2019) 330n20, 330n22, 331n28–29, 331–32n32

EDPB 2019, 'First overview on the implementation of the GDPR and the roles and means of the national supervisory Authorities' (26 February 2019)...... 921n45, 962n39, 962n40, 963n44, 983n33, 992n23, 1009n20, 1019n14, 1038n37, 1078–79n41

EDPB 2019, 'Information Note on Data Transfers under the GDPR in the Event of a No-Deal Brexit' (12 February 2019) 758, 787, 803, 822n28, 847, 918–19n27

EDPB 2019, 'Information Note on BCRs for Companies which Have ICO as BCR Lead Supervisory Authority' (12 February 2019). 822n28

EDPB 2019, 'Opinion 4/2019 on the draft Administrative Arrangement for the transfer of personal data between European Economic Area ("EEA") Financial Supervisory Authorities and non-EEA Financial Supervisory Authorities' (12 February 2019). 809n51

EDPB 2019, 'Opinion 3/2019 Concerning the Questions and Answers on the Interplay between the Clinical Trials Regulation (CTR) and the General Data Protection regulation (GDPR) (Art. 70.1.b)' (23 January 2019).............. 181n32, 182

EDPB 2018, 'Opinion 28/2018 Regarding the European Commission Draft Implementing Decision on the Adequate Protection of Personal Data in Japan' (5 December 2018).......... 777n15, 785n91

EDPB 2018, 'Guidelines 4/2018 on the Accreditation of Certification Bodies under Article 43 of the General Data Protection Regulation (2016/679)' (4 December 2018).... 748n15, 749n20, 751n30

EDPB Rules of Procedure: European Data Protection Board 'Rules of Procedure' Version 2 (Adopted on 25 May 2018, as last modified and Adopted on 23 November 2018) 1049

EDPB 2018, Guidelines 3/2018 on the Territorial scope of the GDPR (Article 3) — Version for Public Consultation' (16 November 2018) 82, 84, 86–91, 93, 160, 239n2–3, 240–41, 242n22, 243n26, 243n28, 244n30, 275n12, 282n17, 282n19, 283n25–26, 428n85–87, 593–94n19, 594–95n26, 595–96n30, 596–97, 706, 903–4n2, 918–19n27, 919

EDPB 2018, European Data Protection Board, 'Opinion 2/2018 on the Draft List of the Competent Supervisory Authority of Belgium Regarding the Processing Operations Subject to the Requirement of a Data Protection Impact Assessment (Article 35.4 GDPR)' (25 September 2018) 1011n32

EDPB 2018, 'Guidelines 2/2018 on Derogations of Article 49 under Regulation 2016/679' (25 May 2018) 184n55, 185n63, 718–19n3, 834, 846n13, 846n16, 847n24, 848, 849n32, 849–50n36, 851n46, 851, 852, 852n57, 853n66, 853–54, 854n72

EDPB 2018, 'Guidelines 1/2018 on Certification and Identifying Certification Criteria in Accordance with Articles 42 and 43 the Regulation 2016/679' (25 May 2018) 737 739, 741, 750–51n29, 1077n25, 1077

Table of Instruments lxxv

EDPB 2018, 'Endorsement 1/2018'
(25 May 2018) 259–60n11, 632n3,
788, 816, 1077

European Data Protection Supervisor ('EDPS') Documents

EDPS 2019, 'Opinion 2/2019: EDPS Opinion on the negotiating mandate of an EU-US agreement on cross-border access to electronic evidence' (2 April 2019) 828n22

EDPS 2018, 'Guidance on Article 25 of the New Regulation and Internal Rules' (20 December 2018) 511–12

EDPS Annual Report 2017, European Data Protection Supervisor, 'Annual Report 2017' (19 March 2018) 1106n24, 1107n32, 1107n37

EDPS Annual Report 2016, European Data Protection Supervisor, 'Annual Report 2016' (4 May 2017) 1106n27, 1107n31

EDPS 2017, European Data Protection Supervisor, 'Upgrading Data Protection Rules for EU Institutions and Bodies', EDPS Opinion 5/2017 on the proposal for a Regulation on the protection of individuals with regard to the processing of personal data by the Union institutions, bodies, offices and Agencies and on the free movement of such data, and repealing Regulation (EC) No. 45/2001 and Decision No. 1247/2002/EC,
(15 March 2017) 1075, 1080n49, 1313–14, 1316

EDPS Annual Report 2015, European Data Protection Supervisor, 'Annual Report 2015' (24 May 2016) 1106n26, 1107n29–30

EDPS 2016, 'Opinion 1/2016, Preliminary Opinion on the Agreement between the United States of America and the European Union on the Protection of Personal Information Relating to the Prevention, Investigation, Detection and Prosecution of Criminal Offences'
(12 February 2016) 777–78n23

EDPS 2015, 'Opinion 2/2015 (with Addendum) Europe's Big Opportunity—EDPS Recommendations on the EU's Options for Data Protection Reform
(9 October 2015) 7

EDPS 2015, European Data Protection Supervisor, 'Annex to Opinion 3/2015 Comparative Table of GDPR Texts with EDPS Recommendations' (27 July 2015) 417n14

EDPS Annual Report 2014, European Data Protection Supervisor, 'Annual Report 2014' (2 July 2015) 1107n28

EDPS 2014, European Data Protection Supervisor, 'The EDPS as an advisor to EU Institutions on Policy and Legislation: Building on Ten Years of Experience'
(4 June 2014) 686–87n10

EDPS Annual Report 2013, European Data Protection Supervisor, 'Annual Report 2013' (1 April 2014) 1106

EDPS 2014, 'Preliminary Opinion Privacy and Competitiveness in the Age of Big Data: The Interplay between Data Protection, Competition Law and Consumer Protection in the Digital Economy'
(March 2014) 500

EDPS 2014, 'Guidelines on the Rights of Individuals with Regard to Processing of Personal Data'
(25 February 2014) 415–16n5, 454

EDPS 2012, 'Monitoring Compliance of EU Institutions and Bodies with Article 24 of Regulation (EC) 45/2001—Report on the Status of Data Protection Officers'
(17 December 2012) 694n24, 703–4, 705, 710n1

EDPS 2012, 'Policy on Consultations in the Field of Supervision and Enforcement'
(23 November 2012) 565n55

EDPS 2012, 'Opinion of the European Data Protection Supervisor on the Data Protection Reform Package'
(7 March 2012) 52n5, 349n10, 357n12, 869–70n32, 917n16, 932, 969n68, 997n5, 1022n30, 1065–66, 1075, 1270–71n12, 1281–82n12, 1314n16, 1314n17

EDPS 2011, 'Public access to Documents Containing Personal Data After the Bavarian Lager Ruling'
(24 March 2011) 1114n11, 1219n29

EDPS 2011, 'Opinion of 14 January 2011 on the Commission's Communication on the reform of 4 November 2010' 8, 12n58

EDPS 2011, 'Opinion of the European Data Protection Supervisor on the Communication from the Commission to the European Parliament, the Council, the Economic and Social Committee and the Committee of the Regions—A Comprehensive approach on Personal Data Protection in the European Union' (14 January 2011) 1314

EDPS 2010, 'Monitoring and Ensuring Compliance with Regulation (EC) 45/2001—Policy Paper'
(13 December 2010) 1120n8

EDPS 2009, 'Second Opinion of the European Data Protection Supervisor on the Review of Directive 2002/58/EC Concerning the Processing of Personal Data and the Protection of Privacy in the Electronic Communications Sector (Directive on Privacy and Electronic Communications)' (6 June 2009) 193

EDPS 2009, 'Opinion of the European Data Protection Supervisor on the Proposal for a Directive of the European Parliament and of the Council on the Application of Patients' Rights in Cross-Border Healthcare', OJ 2009 C 128/03 ...... 222n24

EDPS 2005, 'Position Paper on the Role of Data Protection Officers in Ensuring Effective Compliance with Regulation (EC) 45/2001' (28 November 2005) 690, 691n6, 705, 711, 713fn11, 714

EDPS 2005, 'Public access to Documents and Data Protection' (July 2005) 1219n29

EDPS 2005, 'Opinion on the Proposal for a Regulation of the European Parliament and of the Council Concerning the Visa Information System (VIS) and the Exchange of Data between Member States on Short-Stay Visas' (23 March 2005) 369–70n10

EDPS 2004, 'Annual Report 2004' (18 March 2005) 691n6

Art 29 (WP29) Working Party Documents

WP29, 'EU General Data Protection Regulation: General Information Document' 81–82

WP29 2018, 'Working Party 29 Position Paper on the Derogations from the Obligation to Maintain Records of Processing Activities Pursuant to Article 30(5) GDPR' (19 April 2018) 1077n29

WP29 2018, 'Recommendation on the Standard Application form for Approval of Processor Binding Corporate Rules for the Transfer of Personal Data' (WP 265, 11 April 2018) 259–60n11, 1077n29

WP29 2018, 'Recommendation on the Standard Application for Approval of Controller Binding Corporate Rules for the Transfer of Personal Data (WP 264, 11 April 2018) 258–59n2, 259–60n11, 1077n29

WP29 2018, 'Guidelines on Transparency under Regulation 2016/269' (WP260 rev.01, 11 April 2018) 427, 428n88, 443–47, 622n16, 1077n29

WP29 2018, 'Working Document Setting Forth a Co-Operation Procedure for the Approval of "Binding Corporate Rules" for Controllers and Processors under the GDPR' (WP 263 rev.01, 11 April 2018) 259n5, 259–60n11, 1077n29

WP29 2016, 'Guidelines on Consent under Regulation 2016/679' (WP 259 rev.01, as last revised and Adopted on 10 April 2018) 330n17

WP29 2018, 'Guidelines on Consent under Regulation 2016/679' (WP 259 rev.01, 10 April 2018) 177–78, 181–2, 182n38, 182n41, 182n44, 183, 183–84n54, 185–86, 349n10, 350n11–12, 351n14, 351n16, 352–53, 352n17, 360–61n35, 361n39–40, 361–62n42, 1077n29

WP29 2018, 'Letter to Alban Schmutz' (23 February 2018) 718–19n3, 719

WP29 2018, 'Guidelines on the Application and Setting of Administrative Fines for the Purposes of the Regulation 2016/679' (WP 253, 13 February 2018) 719n7

WP29 2018, 'Draft Guidelines on the Accreditation of Certification Bodies under Regulation (EU) 2016/679' (WP 261, 6 February 2018) ... 747n9, 748n14, 750n26

WP29 2018, 'Working Document Setting Forth a Table with the Elements and Principles to Be Found in Processor Binding Corporate Rules' (WP 257 rev.01, as last revised and Adopted on 6 February 2018) 259–60n11, 820n12, 1077n29

WP29 2018, 'Draft Guidelines on the Accreditation of Certification Bodies under Regulation (EU) 2016/679' (WP 261, 6 February 2018) 747n9, 748n14

WP29 2018, 'Working Document Setting Up a Table with the Elements and Principles to Be Found in Binding Corporate Rules' (WP 256 rev.01, as last revised and Adopted on 6 February 2018) 1077n29

WP29 2018, 'Adequacy Referential' (WP 254 rev.01, as last revised and Adopted on 6 February 2018) 1077n29, 1283n29

WP29 2018, 'Guidelines on Automated Individual Decision Making and Profiling for the Purposes of Regulation 2016/679' (WP 251 rev.01, as last revised and Adopted on 6 February 2018) 130n13, 130n16, 284n30, 429–30n96, 430–31, 463, 530n20, 530–31, 531n28–29, 532–33, 533n42, 534, 534–35n49–51, 535n53, 535–36n56–57, 537n62, 1077n29

WP29 2018, 'Guidelines on Personal data Breach Notification under Regulation 2016/679' (WP 250 rev.01 as last revised and adopted on 6 February 2018) 192n15–20, 518n53, 1077n29

WP29 2017, 'Opinion on Some Key Issues of the Law Enforcement Directive (EU 2016/680)' (WP 258, 29 November 2017) 537n62, 538n68–69, 540n75, 577, 579

WP29 2017, 'Working Document Setting Up a Table with the Elements and Principles to Be Found in Binding Corporate Rules' (WP 256, 29 November 2017)............ 259–60n11, 815n5, 820n11

WP29 2017, 'Statement of the Article 29 Working Party on Data Protection and Privacy Aspects of Cross-Border access to Electronic Evidence' (29 November 2017) 87

WP29 2017, 'Guidelines on Consent under Regulation 2016/679' (WP 259, 28 November 2017) 298–99, 299n34, 352, 847n23

WP29 2017, 'Adequacy Referential (updated)' (WP 254, 28 November 2017)...... 763, 775, 785n88, 788–89, 790n130, 790n135

WP29 Letter 2017, 'Letter to Jan Koom Regarding WhatsApp' (24 October 2017) 989n7

WP29 2017, 'Opinion 03/2017 on Processing Personal Data in the Context of Cooperative Intelligent Transport Systems (C-ITS)' (WP 252, 4 October 2017) 388–89n9, 393, 395–97

WP29 2017, 'Guidelines on Data Protection Impact Assessment (DPIA) and Determining whether Processing Is "Likely to Result in a High Risk" for the Purposes of Regulation 2016/679' (WP 248 rev.01, as last revised and Adopted on 4 October 2017) 564n42, 565n54, 1077n29

WP29 2017, 'Guidelines on the Application and Setting of Administrative Fines for the Purpose of the Regulation 2016/679' (WP 253, 3 October 2017) 1020n17, 1077n29, 1187, 1187n31, 1187–88n32, 1189n43–44, 1189n48, 1200–1n40

WP29 2017, 'Opinion 2/2017 On Data Processing at Work' (WP 249, 8 June 2017) 182n42, 1235–36n23, 1236n26, 1236n28, 1237n29

WP29 2017, 'Guidelines for Identifying a Controller or Processor's Lead Supervisory Authority' (WP 244 rev.01, as last revised and Adopted on 5 April 2017)......227, 227n2, 232n28, 232, 233n33, 233–34, 234n41, 235, 236, 243–44, 276n15, 277n18, 284–85, 594n21, 917, 918–19n27, 919, 920, 922, 960–61, 991n19, 1017n2, 1020–21, 1021n23, 1077n29

WP29 2017, 'Guidelines on Data Protection Officers ('DPOs')' (WP 243 rev.01, as last revised and Adopted 5 April 2017) 242n18, 565n55, 595, 689–90, 692, 693, 694–95, 696, 697, 703, 704, 705–6, 707, 710–11n1, 712, 713fn12, 713fn14, 714, 1077n29

WP29 2017, 'Guidelines on the Right to Data Portability' (WP 242 rev.01, as last revised and Adopted on 5 April 2017) 499, 500, 502–3, 504–6, 1077n29

WP29 2017, 'Guidelines on Data Protection Impact Assessment (DPIA) and Determining whether Processing Is "Likely to Result in a High Risk" for the Purposes of Regulation 2016/679' (WP 248, 4 April 2017).......... 684, 685n7

WP29 2018, 'Article 29 Working Party, "Fablab GDPR/from Concepts to Operational Toolbox, DIY—Results of the Discussion'" (26 July 2016) 722n17

WP29 2016, 'Opinion 02/2016 on the Publication of Personal Data for Transparency Purposes in the Public Sector' (WP 239, 8 June 2016)........853n62

WP29 2016: Article 29 Working Party, 'Working Document 01/2016 on the Justification of Interferences with the Fundamental Rights to Privacy and Data Protection through Surveillance Measures when Transferring Personal Data (European Essential Guarantees)' (WP 237, 13 April 2016)................ 775

WP29 2016, 'Statement on the 2016 Action Plan for the Implementation of the General Data Protection Regulation (GDPR)' (WP 236, 2 February 2016) 1042–43

WP29 2015, 'Update of Opinion 8/2010 on Applicable Law in Light of the CJEU Judgement in Google Spain' (WP 179 update 16 December 2015)...... 235n44, 592

WP29 2015, 'Propositions Regarding the European Data Protection Board Internal Structure' (25 September 2015) 1096n11, 1099n4

WP29 2015, 'Opinion 2/2015 on C-SIG Code of Conduct on Cloud Computing' (WP 232, 22 September 2015).........719n7

WP29 2015, 'Letter to DG FISMA on Possible Delegated Acts for the Implementation of EU Legislation on Both Markets in Financial Instruments (MIFID II) and on Market Abuse Regulation (MAR)' (7 July 2015)................... 1272–73n32

WP29 2015, 'Opinion 1/2015 on Privacy and Data Protection Issues Relating to the Utilisation of Drones' (WP 231, 16 June 2015)................... 119, 119n10

WP29 2015, 'Explanatory Document on the Processor Binding Corporate Rules' (WP 204 rev. 01, 22 May 2015) 259n5, 259–60n11, 815n5, 832–33n58

WP29 2015, 'Press Release on Chapter II of the Draft Regulation for the March JHA Council' (17 March 2015).........16–17n81, 316n31

WP29 2015, 'Letter from the Art 29 WP to the European Commission, DG CONNECT on mHealth' (with Annex) (5 February 2015) 1245
WP29 2015, 'Annex—Health Data in Apps and Devices' (5 February 2015) 222
WP29 Letter Google Spain, 'Letter of 6 January 2015 to Google on the Right to Be Delisted' (6 January 2015) 481
WP29 2014, 'Guidelines on the Implementation of the Court of Justice of the European Union Judgment on "Google Spain and Inc. v Agencia Española de Protección de Datos (AEPD) and Mario Costeja González C-131/12"' (WP 225, 26 November 2014) 481, 1077–78
WP29 2014, 'Opinion 8/2014 on Recent Developments on the Internet of Things' (WP 223, 16 September 2014) 573
WP29 2014, 'Statement on the Role of a Risk-Based Approach in Data Protection Legal Frameworks' (WP 218, 30 May 2014) 564
WP29 2014, 'Opinion 06/2014 on the Notion of Legitimate Interests of the Data Controller under Article 7 of Directive 95/46/EC' (WP 217, 9 April 2014) ... 329n13, 330n21, 331n28, 332n35, 333, 336n58, 337n62, 337–38, 339n79, 1243n6
WP29 2014, 'Opinion 05/2014 on Anonymisation Techniques' (WP 216, 10 April 2014) 105–6n2, 119, 121, 133–34n3, 135n11, 135n15, 135–36, 1250
WP29 2014, 'Working Document 01/2014 on Draft Ad Hoc Contractual Clauses "EU Data Processor to Non-EU Sub-processor"' (WP 214, 21 March 2014) 805–6
WP29 2014, 'Opinion 02/2014 on a Referential for Requirements for Binding Corporate Rules Submitted to National Data Protection Authorities in the EU and Cross Border Privacy Rules Submitted to APEC CBPR Accountability Agents' (WP 212, 27 February 2014) 254n5, 259–60n11, 558, 815n5, 860–61
WP29 Annual Report 2013: Report of the Article 29 Working Party on Data Protection, covering the year 2013, European Commission (2016) 1051n49, 1051n51, 1086n4
WP29 2013, 'Opinion 06/2013 on Open Data and Public Sector Information ('PSI') Reuse' (WP 207, 5 June 2013) ... 853n62, 1250
WP29 2013, 'Advice Paper on Essential Elements of a Definition and A Provision on Profiling within the EU General Data Protection Regulation' (13 May 2013) ... 129n7

WP29 2013: Article 29 Working Party, 'Opinion 04/2013 on the Data Protection Impact Assessment Template for Smart Grid and Smart Metering Systems ("DPIA Template") Prepared by Expert Group 2 of the Commission's Smart Grid Task Force' (WP 205, 22 April 2013) 976n6
WP29 2013, 'Opinion 3/2013 on Purpose Limitation' (WP 203, 2 April 2013) ... 183n49, 315n23–25, 315–16n28, 316n31, 327, 341n87, 341–42n88, 341–42n92, 342n96, 343n98, 551n24, 564n39
WP29 2013, 'Opinion 02/2013 on Apps on SmArt Devices)' (WP 202, 27 February 2013) 356–57n8
WP29 2013, 'Working Document 01/2013 Input on the Proposed Implementing Acts' (WP 200, 22 January 2013) 1281–82n12
WP29 2012, 'Opinion 08/2012 Providing Further Input on the Data Protection Reform Discussions' (WP 199, 5 October 2012) 108–9, 338n73, 1269n3, 1270–71n12–13, 1272–73n32, 1281–82n12–13
WP29 2012, 'Opinion on the level of protection of personal data in the Principality of Monaco' (WP 198, 19 July 2012) 795
WP29 2012, 'Recommendation 1/2012 on the Standard Application form for Approval of Binding Corporate Rules for the Transfer of Personal Data for Processing Activities' (WP 195a, 17 September 2012) 259n5, 259–60n11, 815n5
WP29 2012, 'Opinion 05/2012 on Cloud Computing' (WP 196, 1 July 2012) 157–58n2, 587
WP29 2012, 'Working Document 02/2012 Setting Up a Table with the Elements and Principles to Be Found in Processor Binding Corporate Rules' (WP 195, 6 June 2012) 259n5, 259–60n11, 260n14, 815n5
WP29 2012, 'Opinion 3/2012 on Developments in Biometric Technologies' (WP 193, 27 April 2012) .. 202n32, 209, 209n4, 213, 223n28, 370–71n18
WP29 2012, 'Opinion 01/2012 on the Data Protection Reform Proposals' (WP 191 Adopted on 23 March 2012) 227n1, 227n4, 356, 997n5, 1001n24, 1065–66, 1075, 1105n16, 1264–65, 1270–71n13, 1272–73n32, 1281–82n12
WP29 2011, 'Opinion 15/2011 on the Definition of Consent' (WP 187, 13 July 2011) 181, 181n31, 181n33, 329–30, 360

WP29 2011, 'Advice Paper on the Practical
    Implementation of the Article 28(6)
    of the Directive 95/46/EC' (20 April
    2011) 957n9, 976n2, 988n3
WP29 2011: Article 29 Working Party,
    'Advice Paper on Special Categories of
    Data' (4 April 2011) 369–70n12, 370n17,
            373n45, 374n48, 374–75,
            379, 381, 382, 387–88n4
WP29 2010, 'Opinion 8/2010 on Applicable
    Law' (WP 179, 16 December 2010). 92,
            240–41n9
WP29 2010, 'Opinion 3/2010 on the
    Principle of Accountability' (WP 173,
    13 July 2010) 318n42, 557–58, 561–63,
        562n26, 564, 565, 566–67, 733–34, 746
WP29 2010, 'Opinion 2/2010 on Online
    Behavioural Advertising' (WP 171,
    22 June 2010) 356–57n8
WP29 2010, 'Opinion 01/2010 on the
    Concepts of "Controller" and
    "Processor"' (WP 169, 16 February
    2010) 146, 148, 148n10, 149, 149n15,
            150, 152, 152n41, 159n9, 160, 583,
            586–7, 587n35, 1255n10
WP29 Rules of Procedure 'Rules of
    Procedure' (15 February 2010) 1050n48,
            1086, 1090–91, 1091n5, 1095,
            1099n4, 1104–5, 1111n1, 1112
WP29 2009, 'The Future of Privacy: Joint
    Contribution to the Consultation of the
    European Commission on the Legal
    Framework for the Fundamental Right
    to Protection of Personal Data' (WP 168,
    1 December 2009) 8, 11n54, 67–68,
            557, 563, 734, 1314n6, 1314n8–9
WP29 2009, 'Opinion 5/2009 on Online
    Social Networking' (WP 163, 12 June
    2009) 356–57n9, 586n23
WP29 2009, 'Second Opinion 4/2009 on the
    World Anti-Doping agency (WADA)
    International Standard for the Protection
    of Privacy and Personal Information, on
    Related Provisions of the WADA Code
    and on Other Privacy Issues in the Context
    of the Fight Against Doping in Sport by
    WADA and (National) Anti-Doping
    Organisations' (WP 162, 6 April 2009) . . . 719n7
WP29 2009, 'Opinion 2/2009 on the
    Protection of Children's Personal Data
    (General Guidelines and the Special
    Case of Schools)' (WP 160, 11 February
    2009) 356–57
WP29 2009, 'Working Document 1/2009
    on Pre-Trial Discovery for Cross Border
    Civil Litigation' (WP 158, 11 February
    2009) 826
WP29 2008, 'Working Document Setting
    Up a Framework for the Structure of
    Binding Corporate Rules' (WP 154, 25
    June 2008) 259n5, 259–60n11,
            763, 815n5
WP29 2008, 'Working Document on
    Frequently Asked Questions (FAQs)
    related to Binding Corporate Rules'
    (WP 155 rev. 4, 24 June 2008) 259n5,
            259–60n11, 815n5
WP29 2008, 'Working Document Setting Up
    a Table with the Elements and Principles
    to Be Found in Binding Corporate
    Rules' (WP 153, 24 June 2008) 259n5,
            259–60n11, 815n5
WP29 2008: Article 29 Data Protection
    Working Party, 'Opinion 1/2008
    on Data Protection Issues Related to
    Search Engines' (WP 148, 04 April
    2008) 356–57n8, 481n16
WP29 2007, 'Opinion 04/2007 on the
    Concept of Personal Data' (WP 136,
    20 June 2007) 109, 110n32,
            112, 133–34n1, 134n4, 135n13–14,
            139–40n4, 196, 211–12, 215n34
WP29 2007, 'Working Document on the
    Processing of Personal Data Relating
    to Health in Electronic Health
    Records (EHR)' (WP 131,
    15 February 2007) 222n23, 223n28
WP29 2007, 'Recommendation 1/2007 on
    the Standard Application for Approval
    of Binding Corporate Rules for the
    Transfer of Personal Data' (WP133,
    10 January 2007) 259–60n11, 815n5
WP29 2006, 'Opinion 1/2006 on the
    Application of EU Data Protection Rules
    to Internal Whistleblowing Schemes
    in the Fields of Accounting, Internal
    Accounting Controls, Auditing Matters,
    Fight Against Bribery, Banking and
    Financial Crime' (WP 117, 1 February
    2006) 826
WP29 2005, 'Working Document on a
    Common Interpretation of Article 26(1)
    of Directive 95/46/EC of October 24, 1995'
    (WP 114, 25 November 2005) 843–44n5,
            848, 851n48, 852n56
WP29 2005: Article 29 Working Party,
    'Opinion 3/2005 on Implementing
    Council Resolution (EC) No. 2252/
    2004 of 13 December 2004 on
    Standards for Security Features and
    Biometrics in Passports and Travel
    Documents Issued by Member States'
    (WP 112, 30 September 2005) 370–71n18
WP29 2005, 'Working Document
    Establishing a Model Checklist
    Application for Approval of Binding
    Corporate Rules' (WP 108,
    14 April 2005) 259n5, 259–60n11, 815n5

WP29 2005, 'Working Document Setting
 Forth a Co-Operation Procedure for
 Issuing Common Opinions on Adequate
 Safeguards Resulting From "Binding
 Corporate Rules"' (WP 107, 14 April
 2005) 259n5, 259–60n11, 815–16n5
WP29 2004, 'Model Checklist, Application
 for Approval of Binding Corporate
 Rules' (WP 102, 25 November
 2004) 259n5, 259–60n11, 815–16n5
WP29 2004, 'Opinion No. 7/2004 on the
 Inclusion of Biometric Elements in
 Residence Permits and Visas Taking
 Account of the Establishment of
 the European Information System
 on visas (VIS)' (WP 96,
 11 August 2004)................370–71n18
WP29 2004, 'Working Document on Genetic
 Data' (WP 91, 17 March 2004)....... 197–98,
 200, 202, 370–71n19
WP29 2003, 'Working Document on
 Biometrics' (WP 80,
 1 August 2003) 209n4, 210n9, 213–14n27,
 214–15n31–32, 370–71n18
WP29 2003, 'Opinion 3/2003 on the
 European Code of Conduct of FEDMA
 for the Use of Personal Data in Direct
 Marketing' (WP 77, 13 June 2003)....... 719
WP29 2003, 'Working Document on
 Transfers of Personal Data to Third
 Countries: Applying WP29 Article
 26(2) of the EU Data Protection
 Directive to Binding Corporate Rules for
 International Data Transfers' (WP 74,
 3 June 2003) 259, 259–60n11–12,
 260n19, 815n5
WP29 2002: Article 29 Working Party,
 'Opinion 6/2002 on Transmission of
 Passenger Manifest Information and
 Other Data from Airlines to the United
 States' (WP 66, 24 October 2002).....850n40
WP29 2002: Article 29 Working Party,
 'Working Document on the Surveillance
 of Electronic Communications in the
 Workplace' (WP 55, 29 May 2002).....1236n28
WP29 2001, 'Opinion 8/2001 on the
 Processing of Personal Data in the
 Employment Context' (WP 48,
 13 September 2001) ... 143n28, 1235–36n23,
 1236n27–28
WP29 2001, 'Opinion 5/2001 on the European
 Ombudsman Special Report to the
 European Parliament Following the
 Draft Recommendation to the European
 Commission in Complaint 713/98/IJH'
 (WP 44, 17 May 2001) 1217n13

WP29 2000, 'Opinion 6/2000 on the Human
 Genome and Privacy' (WP 34, 13 July
 2000) 197
WP29 1998: Article 29 Working Party,
 'Future Work on Codes of Conduct:
 Working Document on the Procedure
 for the Consideration by the Working
 Party of Community Codes of Conduct'
 (WP 13, 10 September 1998) 719
WP29 1998, 'Transfers of Personal Data to
 Third Countries: Applying Articles
 25 and 26 of the EU Data Protection
 Directive' (WP 12, 24 July 1998).........528,
 787–88, 843–44
WP29 1997, 'Recommendation 3/97:
 Anonymity on the Internet'
 (WP 6, 3 December 1997) 134n4
WP29 1997, 'First Orientations on
 Transfers of Personal Data to Third
 Countries—Possible Ways Forward
 in Assessing Adequacy' (WP 4,
 26 June 1997) 787n114

NATIONAL INSTRUMENTS
Australia
Privacy Act 1988 (No. 199, 1988) Sch 1........ 560

Austria
Federal Data Protection Act: Bundesgesetz
 zum Schutz natürlicher Personen bei der
 Verarbeitung personenbezogener Daten
 (Datenschutzgesetz—DSG), BGBl.
 I Nr. 165/1999 zuletzt geändert durch
 BGBl. I Nr. 24/2018
 s 21(3)............................748n10
 s 22................................. 945
 s 24 945
 s 25................................. 945
 s 55........................ 644n31, 658n28
Federal Data Protection Act 2000:
 Bundesgesetz über den Schutz
 personenbezogener Daten
 (Datenschutzgesetz 2000 – DSG
 2000), BGBl. I Nr 165/1999 zuletzt
 geändert durch BGBl. I
 Nr. 132/2015 (repealed)............... 135
Art 2, Part 1, § 4(1)..................... 135
Art 2, Part 2, § 13(3)(2)................. 135
Arts 26–28 ....404n9
Regulation on Equivalence 1980:
 Verordnung des Bundeskanzlers
 vom 18. Dezember 1980 über die
 Gleichwertigkeit Ausländischer
 Datenschutzbestimmungen, BGBl II
 Nr. 612/3403........................758n8

Belgium

AML Law: Loi relative à la prévention
du blanchiment de capitaux et du
financement du terrorisme et à la limita-
tion de l'utilisation des espèces, Moniteur
Belge 6 October 2017, p. 90839
Art 28.................................. 1227
Civil Code: Burgerlijk Wetboek van 21 ma
Art 1804; Code civil du 21 mars 1804
Art 1382 ....1168n43
Data Protection Law 2017: 7: Loi portant création
de l'Autorité de protection des données, du
3 decembre 2017; Wet tot oprichting van de
Gegevensbeschermingsautoriteit,
van 3 december 2017
Art 38............................898n20
Data Protection Law 1992: Wet tot
bescherming van de persoonlijke
levenssfeer ten opzichte van de
verwerking van persoonsgegevens,
van 8 december 1992; Loi relative à la
protection de la vie privée à l'égard des
traitements de données à caractère personnel, du 8 décembre 1992) (repealed)
Art 1(2) 118n1
Art 1(6) 171n4
Art 1(7) 166n8
Art 10 ....404n10
Art 12*bis* 529n16
Arts 16(1)(3) 603n5
Art 16(4) 603n5, 632n5
Explanatory Memorandum Belgian Act
1998: PROJET DE LOI transposant la
Directive 95/46/CE du 24 octobre 1995
du Parlement européen et du Conseil
relative à la protection des personnes
physiques à l'égard du traitement des
données à caractère personnel et à la libre
circulation de ces données— Expose des
Motifs (20 May 1998) 166n12
GDPR Implementation Law: Wet betreffende
de bescherming van natuurlijke personen
met betrekking tot de verwerking van
persoonsgegevens, van 30 juli 2018; Loi
relative à la protection des personnes
physiques à l'égard des traitements de
données à caractère personnel, du
30 juillet 2018. ....870n37
Art 4(1) 58n27

Canada

Personal Information Protection and Electronic
Documents Act, S.C. 2000 c. 5, S.C.
2000, last Amended on November 1, 2018.
(PIPEDA 2018)................ 775n6, 786

Sch 1 559–60
Annex 720

Denmark

Data Protection Act 2018: Lov nr. 502 av 23.
mai 2018 om supplerende bestemmelser
til forordning om beskyttelse af fysiske
personer i forbindelse med behandling
af personoplysninger og om fri
udveksling af sådanne oplysninger
(databeskyttelsesloven)
Art 2(5) 112
s 10 ....1244n8

Finland

Law on Personal Data 1999: (Henkilötietolaki
No. 523/1999) (repealed) 158
Art 3(3) 141
s 3(6) 158n5, 171n4

France

Access to Evidence for Foreigners Act
1980: Loi n° 80–538 du 16 juillet
1980 relative à la communication de
documents ou renseignements d'ordre
économique, commercial ou technique
à des personnes physiques ou morales
étrangères 829
Access to Evidence for Foreigners Act 1968:
Loi n° 68–678 du 26 juillet 1968 relative
à la communication de documents et
renseignements d'ordre économique,
commercial 829
Civil Code: Code civil, version consolidée au
1 octobre 2018
Art 9.........................1175–76n95
Art 1240 (Former
Art 1382).......................1168n43
Data Protection Act 1978: Act No. 78–17
of 6 January 1978 on Data Processing,
Files and Individual Liberties (Loi
n° 78–17 du 6 janvier 1978 relative
à l'informatique, aux fichiers et aux
libertés), as last Amended by Law
No. 2014–334 of 17 March 2014.... 158, 437,
456, 510, 735–36, 866, 898
Art 2 .... 118n4, 529, 529n14, 529n18
Art 3 ....416, 437, 456, 462–63, 529n14
Art 3(2) 158n6, 166
Art 5(2) 240n7
Art 10 ....529n14, 529n18
Art 26 510
Art 27 437
Art 34 .... 456, 472
Art 35 456

Art 36 472
Art 39(1) 529n14
Art 44 (et seq) 945
Arts 70(1)(g) 644
Ch I 171n3
GDPR Implementation Law: Ordonnance n°
    2018–1125 du 12 décembre 2018 prise en application de l'Article 32 de la loi n° 2018–493 du 20 juin 2018 relative à la protection des données personnelles et portant modification de la loi n° 78–17 du 6 janvier 1978 relative à l'informatique, aux fichiers et aux libertés et diverses dispositions concernant la protection des données à caractère personnel
    Art 3(II) 58n28
    Art 9 . . . . 888n18
Tax Procedure Code: French Tax Procedure Code (Livre des procédures fiscales) 167

Germany

Civil Code: Bürgerliches Gesetzbuch, in der Fassung der Bekanntmachung vom 02.01.2002, BGBl. 2003 Teil I Nr. 42
    Art 823. . . . . 1168n43
Code of Civil Procedure
    s 184 1169
Federal Data Protection Act 2017:
    Bundesdatenschutzgesetz vom 30. Juni 2017, BGBl. 2017 Teil I Nr. 2097 871
    s 26 .1231–32, 1235
    s 42a 643n17
    Art 64 633
    Ch 5 . . . . .871n41
Federal Data Protection Act 2009:
    Bundesdatenschutzgesetz (BDSG) vom 20. Dezember 1990 (BGBl. I S. 2954), neugefasst durch Bekanntmachung vom 14. Januar 2003 (BGBl. I S. 66), zuletzt geändert durch Gesetz vom 29.07.2009 (BGBl. I, S. 2254), durch Artikel 5 des Gesetzes vom 29.07.2009 (BGBl. I, S. 2355 [2384] und durch Gesetz vom 14.08.2009 (BGBl. I, S. 2814), BGBl 2009 Teil I Nr. 54 (repealed). 1186
    Arts 11(2)(1) and 11(2)(10). 603n6
    Art 42a 191n9
Federal Data Protection Act 1990: Gesetz zur Fortentwicklung der Datenverarbeitung und des Datenschutzes (Bundesdatenschutzgesetz), BGBl 1990 Teil 1 Nr. 2954 (repealed) 125n7
    s 3a 575
    s 3(4)(4) 124–25
    s 3(6a) 134
    s 4(a) 349
Federal Data Protection Act 1977:
    Gesetz zum Schutz vor Mißbrauch personenbezogener Daten bei der Datenverarbeitung (Bundesdatenschutzgesetz), BGBl. 1977 Teil I Nr. 7 (repealed) 455
    Art 4(1) 455
Federal Registry Act 2017:
    Bundeszentralregistergesetz in der Fassung der Bekanntmachung vom 21. September 1984 (BGBl. I S. 1229, 1985 I S. 195), das zuletzt durch Artikel 1 des Gesetzes vom 18. Juli 2017 (BGBl. I S. 2732) geändert worden ist 387
GDPR Implementation Law: Gesetz zur Anpassung des Datenschutzrechts an die Verordnung (EU) 2016/679 und zur Umsetzung der Richtlinie (EU) 2016/680 (DatenschutzAnpassungs- und Umsetzungsgesetz EU—DsAnpUG-EU), BGBl 2017 Teil 1 Nr. 44. . . . . . 136, 421, 440, 456, 513, 917, 958, 1018
    s 16 945
    s 18 . . . . 917n13, 958n16, 1018n7
    s 19 . . . . 228, 917n13, 958n16
    s 29(1) 440n23
    s 32 421
    s 32(1)(1) 421n29
    s 32(1)(2) 421n30
    s 32(1)(3) 421n31
    s 32(1)(5) 421n32–33
    s 32(2) 421n34
    s 33(1) 440n24–25
    s 33(2) 440n26
    s 34 456
    s 36 . . . . .513n20
    s 44(1) 1169
    s 44(3) 243n27, 1169
    s 71 575
    s 71(1) 134, 136, 575
Schleswig-Holstein Regulation 2013:
    Landesverordnung über ein Datenschutzgütesiegel, (Datenschutzgütesiegelverordnung – DSGSVO) vom 30. November 2013, GVOBl. 2013 S. 536. . . . . 735–36n23, 746–47n8

Greece

Data Protection Law: Law 2472/1997 on the Protection of Individuals with regard to the Processing of Personal Data (as amended)
    Art 2(g) 148
    Art 10 . . . . .614n4
    Art 12 . . . . .404n10

Hungary

Information Act 2011: Hungarian Act CXII of 2011 on the Right of Informational Self-Determination and on Freedom of Information
    Art 3(1) 118
    Art 3(25) 260

Ireland

Data Protection Act 2018: Data Protection
　Act 2018 (Number 7 of 2018) 513, 537
　　s 35 . . . . 748n11
　　Art 59 . . . . 513n21
Data Protection Act 2003: Data Protection
　Act 2003 (Number 6 of 2003)
　　s 2 . . . . 537n61
　　s 6B(2)(b) 537n63
Data Protection Act 1988: Data Protection
　Act (Number 25 of 1988)
　　s 4(1) 404n9

Italy

Constitution of the Italian Republic 1260–61
　Art 7 . . . . 1258n2, 1260–61
　Art 8 . . . . 1258n2
Data Protection Code 2018: Decreto
　Legislativo 10 Agosto 2018 n. 101:
　Disposizioni per l'adeguamento della
　normativa nazionale Alle disposizioni
　del regolamento (UE) 2016/679 del
　Parlamento europeo e del Consiglio, del
　27 Aprile 2016, relative alla protezione
　delle persone fisiche con riguardo al
　trattamento dei dati personali, nonche'
   alla libera circolazione di tali dati e che
　abroga la direttiva 95/46/CE
　(regolamento generale sulla
　protezione dei dati) (n. 101) . . .112n44, 159n10,
　　　166n4, 172, 693–94n20, 1263–64n41
Data Protection Code 2003: Decreto
　legislativo 30 giugno 2003, n. 196:
　Codice in Materia di Protezione dei
　Dati Personali 1260–61
　Art 2 . . . . 112n44, 537n61
　Art 4 . . . . 141n11, 166n4
　Art 4(1)(b) 124–25
　Art 4(1)(h) 159n10, 172
　Art 6 . . . . 141n10
　Art 9 . . . . 407n28
　Art 14 . . . . 529n17
　Art 26(3)(a) 1260–61
　Art 30 172
　Art 181(6) 1260–61
Data Protection Law 1996: Legge n. 675
　del 31 dicembre 1996 - Tutela delle
　persone e di altri soggetti rispetto al
　trattamento dei dati personali 1260–61
e-Commerce Law 2003: Decreto legislativo
　9 Aprile 2003, n. 70: Attuazione
　della direttiva 2000/31/CE relativa
　a taluni Aspetti giuridici dei servizi
　della società dell'informazione, in
　Particolare il commercio elettronico,
　nel mercato interno
　Art 2(1)(a) 295n14
Episcopal Decree 2018: Decreto Generale:
　Disposizioni per la Tutela del Diritto
　Alla Buona Fama e Alla Riservatezza del
　25 maggio 2018 . . . . 1264n46
　Art 8(8) 1264–65
Episcopal Decree 1999: Decreto Generale:
　Disposizioni per la Tutela del Diritto
　Alla Buona Fama e Alla Riservatezza
　del 30 ottobre 1999 1260–61
Legislative Decree 2015: Decreto Legislativo
　14 settembre 2015, n. 151: Disposizioni
　di razionalizzazione e semplificazione
　delle procedure e degli Adempimenti
　a carico di cittadini e imprese e Altre
　disposizioni in materia di rapporto
　di lavoro e pari opportunità, in
　Attuazione della legge 10 dicembre
　2014, n. 183 . . . . 124–25n6, 141n10,
　　　　　　　　　　　　　159n10, 166n4, 172n8

Netherlands

Data Protection Act Law 2006: Kaderwet
　zelfstandige bestuursorganen van 2
　november 2006 898
GDPR Implementation Law:
　Uitvoeringswet Algemene verordening
　gegevensbescherming, versie van 25 mei
　2018 643
　Art 4(1) 58n26
Personal Data Protection Act 2015: Wet
　bescherming persoonsgegevens (WBP),
　versie van 1 januari 2015 (repealed) 358
　Art 25 . . . . 727n9
　Art 34(a) 191n7

Norway

Personal Data Act 2000: Act of 14 April 2000
　No. 31 relating to the processing of
　personal data (Personal Data Act) (lov
　14. april 2000 nr. 31 om behandling av
　personopplysninger) (repealed)
　　s 2 . . . . 166n4, 171n3
　　s 4 . . . . 240n7

Philippines

Data Privacy Act 2012: Act Protecting Individual
　Personal Information in Information
　and Communications Systems in the
　Government and the Private Sector,
　Creating for this Purpose a National Privacy
　Commission, and for Other Purposes,
　Republic Act No. 10173 501
　　s 18 . . . . 501n19
　　s 36 . . . . 501n20

Poland

Constitution of the Republic of Poland
　Art 25 . . . . 1258n2
Data Protection Act 1997: USTAWA z dnia 29
　sierpnia 1997 r.o ochronie danych osobowych
　Art 27(2)(4) 1261

Art 41(1)(3) 1261
Art 43(2) 1261
Episcopal Decree 2018: Dekret ogólny w sprawie ochrony osób fizycznych w związku z przetwarzaniem danych osobowych w Kościele katolickim wydany przez Konferencję Episkopatu Polski, w dniu 13 marca 2018 r., podczas 378 .... 1261, 1264n46
Arts 13 and 14(4) 1264–65n47
Arts 35–40 1266

Portugal
Civil Code: Código Civil, DL n.º 47344/66, de 25 de Novembr
Arts 70–81 .... 1174–75n91

Romania
Civil Code: Noul Cod Civil Actualizat 2018 – Legea 287/2009
Arts 58–81 .... 1174–75n91
Art 73(a) 1175–76n95
Arts 252–57 .... 1174–75n91
Art 253(4) 1168n43
Art 998 1174
Art 999 1174
Art 1357 .... 1168n43

Spain
Civil Code: Real Decreto de 24 de julio de 1889 por el que se publica el Código Civil
Art 1902 .... 1168n43
Data Protection Act 2018: Ley Orgánica 3/2018, de 5 de diciembre, de Protección de Datos y de Garantía de los Derechos Digitales 421–22
Art 11 .... 421–22n35–37
Art 30(1) 597
Art 30(2) 597, 1169
Data Protection Law 2007: Real Decreto 1720/2007, de 21 de diciembre, por el que se Aprueba el Reglamento de desarrollo de la Ley Orgánica 15/1999, de 13 de diciembre, de protección de datos de carácter personal 643
Data Protection Act 1999: Ley Orgánica 15/1999, de protección de datos de carácter personal (repealed) 685n8
GDPR Implementation Law: Spanish GDPR Implementation Law 3/2018, de 27 de julio, de medidas urgentes para la Adaptación del Derecho español a la normativa de la Unión Europea en materia de protección de datos Arts 61, 64, 66, 68 and 75 .... 958n17

Information Society Law 2002: Ley 34/2002, de 11 de julio, de la Sociedad de la Información y de Comercio Electrónico
Annex, (a) 295n12

Sweden
Personal Data Act 1998: Personal Data Act 1998 (Personuppgiftslagen (SFS1998:204)) (repealed)
s 4 79
s 29 .... 529n15
Personal Data Act 1973 (Datalagen, SFS 298:73) ... 220
s 4 220

Switzerland
Federal Law on Data Protection 1992: Bundesgesetz vom 19 Juni 1992 über den Datenschutz/Loi fédérale du 19 juin 1992 sur la protection des données.
Art 3(d) 129

United Kingdom
Data Protection Act 2018 (Chapter 12) ... 441, 456, 513, 584, 836, 1173
s 14(4) 440–41
s 14(4)(a) 440–41n27
s 14(4)(b) 440–41n28
s 182(1) 1169
s 182(3) 1169
Sch 2 .... 456, 513
Art 2(1)(c) 513n23
Art 4(1)(1) 513n24
Sch 3 .... 513, 513n27
Art 5(1) 513n25
Art 5(3)(a) 513n26
Data Protection Act 1998 (Chapter 29) 121, 148
s 1(1) 148, 584
s 13 1173
s 13(1) 1174
s 13(2) 1174
Data Protection Act 1984 (Chapter 35)
s 21 456
Enterprise and Regulatory Reform Act 2013 (Chapter 24) 502
Statute of Anne 1710 v

United States
CCPA 2018: California Consumer Privacy Act of 2018, AB375, Title 1.81.5 (coming into force 1/1/20) 1164
Children's Online Privacy Protection Act of 1998, 15 U.S.C. 6501–6505 (COPPA) 360–61
CLOUD Act 2018: Clarifying Lawful Overseas Use of Data Act (CLOUD Act), HR 1625, Division V, 115th Congress, 23 March 2018 .... 826–27n9, 829n36, 850–51n39

Federal Trade Commission Act 1914
   s 5 560
Health Insurance Portability and
   Accountability Act, Public
   Law 104–191 (104th) (HIPAA 1996)
   Congress 501

Preamble 501
Helms-Burton Act 828
Sarbanes-Oxley Act 2002:
   Sarbanes-Oxley Act of 2002,
   Pub. L. No. 107–204 826
   § 301(4)(A), (B) 826n4

List of Abbreviations

Additional Protocol Convention 108	Additional Protocol to the Convention for the Protection of Individuals with regard to Automatic Processing of Personal Data, regarding supervisory authorities and transborder data flows [ETS 181]
APEC	Asia-Pacific Economic Cooperation
Charter/CFR	Charter of Fundamental Rights of the European Union
CFI	Court of First Instance, now the General Court (GC)
CJEU	Court of Justice of the European Union
CNIL	Commission Nationale de l'Informatique et des Libertés (France)
CoE	Council of Europe
Commission	European Commission
Convention 108	Convention for the Protection of Individuals with regard to Automatic Processing of Personal Data [ETS 108]
Council	European Council
CST	Civil Service Tribunal
DPA	data protection authority (also called 'supervisory authority')
DPD	Data Protection Directive—Directive 95/46/EC
EC	European Commission
ECHR	European Convention for the Protection of Human Rights and Fundamental Freedoms
ECtHR	European Court of Human Rights
EDPS	European Data Protection Supervisor
EEA	European Economic Area
EFTA	European Free Trade Association
EPD	Electronic Privacy Directive—Directive 2002/58/EC, as revised
EDPB	European Data Protection Board
EPR Proposal	Proposal for Electronic Privacy Regulation
ESA	EFTA Surveillance Authority
EU	European Union
EUDPR Proposal	Proposal for successor to Regulation 45/2001
EUDPR	Successor to Regulation 45/2001—Regulation (EU) 2018/1725 on the protection of natural persons with regard to the processing of personal data by the EU institutions, bodies, offices and agencies
FRA	Fundamental Rights Agency (EU)
FTC	Federal Trade Commission (US)
GC	General Court of the European Union
GDPR	General Data Protection Regulation—Regulation (EU) 2016/679
GDPR Proposal	Proposal for the General Data Protection Regulation
ICO	Information Commissioner's Office (UK)
LED	Law Enforcement Directive—Directive (EU) 2016/680
LED Proposal	Proposal for the Law Enforcement Directive

Modernised Convention 108	Modernised Convention for the Protection of Individuals with Regard to the Processing of Personal Data, CM/Inf(2018)15-final (also called 'Convention 108+').
OECD	Organisation for Economic Cooperation and Development
Parliament	European Parliament
Regulation 45/2001	Regulation on the protection of individuals with regard to the processing of personal data by the Community institutions and bodies
TEU	Treaty on European Union
TFEU	Treaty on the Functioning of the European Union
UK	United Kingdom
US	United States
WP29	Article 29 Working Party

List of Contributors

Cecilia Alvarez Rigaudias is the former Chairwoman of the Spanish Association of Privacy Professionals (APEP).

Peter Blume is Professor of Data Protection Law and Legal Method at the Faculty of Law, University of Copenhagen.

Cédric Burton is partner in the Brussels office of Wilson Sonsini Goodrich & Rosati, where he heads the firm's EU data protection and cyber security practice.

Giovanni Buttarelli, who sadly passed away in August 2019, was the European Data Protection Supervisor (EDPS), and former Secretary General of the Italian Data Protection Authority.

Lee A. Bygrave is Professor of Law at the Norwegian Research Center for Computers and Law (NRCCL), University of Oslo.

Piedade Costa de Oliveira is a Member of the Legal Service of the European Commission and a Visiting Professor at the University of São Paulo, Brazil.

Cécile de Terwangne is Professor at the Faculty of Law of the University of Namur (Belgium) and Research Director at the CRIDS (Research Centre for Information, Law and Society), University of Namur.

Christopher Docksey is Honorary Director General at the EDPS, member of the Guernsey Data Protection Authority, and Visiting Fellow and member of the Advisory Board of the European Centre on Privacy and Cybersecurity (ECPC) at Maastricht University Faculty of Law.

Laura Drechsler is a Ph.D. researcher (FWO aspirant) at the Brussels Privacy Hub (BPH) at the Law, Science, Technology and Society (LSTS) Research Group of the Vrije Universiteit Brussel (VUB).

Ludmila Georgieva holds a doctoral degree in law from the University of Vienna, was formerly Attaché at the Austrian Permanent Representation to the EU for Cybersecurity, Data Protection and Media Policy where she negotiated a number of EU data protection and cybersecurity instruments (such as the GDPR and the EU Cybersecurity Act), and is now at Google in Brussels.

Gloria González Fuster is a Research Professor at the Faculty of Law and Criminology of the Vrije Universiteit Brussel (VUB), where she is also co-director of the Law, Science, Technology and Society (LSTS) Research Group and member of the Brussels Privacy Hub (BPH).

Hielke Hijmans is Member of the Executive Committee and President of the Litigation Chamber of the Belgian Data Protection Authority, has a standing affiliation with the Vrije Universiteit Brussel (VUB)/Brussels Privacy Hub, and is a member of the Meijers Committee in The Netherlands.

Irene Kamara is researcher at the Tilburg Institute for Law, Technology and Society (TILT) of Tilburg University, affiliate researcher at the Law, Science, Technology and Society (LSTS) Research Group of the Vrije Universiteit Brussel (VUB) and attorney-at-law admitted to the Athens Bar Association.

Dimitra Kamarinou is a Researcher at the Cloud Legal Project, Centre for Commercial Law Studies, Queen Mary, University of London and a qualified Greek attorney-at-law.

Eleni Kosta is Full Professor of Technology Law and Human Rights at the Tilburg Institute for Law, Technology and Society (TILT) of Tilburg University and a part time associate at the Brussels-based law firm time.lex.

Waltraut Kotschy is Senior Of Counsel for the Ludwig Boltzmann Institute of Human Rights (Vienna), CEO of DPCC e.U. and dsgvo-help.gmbh. and a former Austrian Data Protection Commissioner.

Herke Kranenborg is a member of the Legal Service of the European Commission and affiliated senior researcher at the Institute for European Law of KU Leuven.

Christopher Kuner is Professor of Law and Co-Director of the Brussels Privacy Hub at the Vrije Universiteit Brussel (VUB), Visiting Professor in the Faculty of Law at Maastricht University, Senior Privacy Counsel in the Brussels office of Wilson Sonsini Goodrich & Rosati, editor-in-chief of the journal *International Data Privacy Law*, and a member of the European Commission's multistakeholder expert group to support the application of the GDPR.

Ronald Leenes is Professor in Regulation by Technology and Director of the Tilburg Institute for Law, Technology and Society (TILT), Tilburg University.

Orla Lynskey is an Associate Professor of Law at the London School of Economics and Political Science and an editor of *International Data Privacy Law*.

Christopher Millard is Professor of Privacy and Information Law and Head of the Cloud Legal Project at Queen Mary University of London, Senior Counsel at the law firm Bristows and an Editor of the *International Journal of Law and Information Technology* and of *International Data Privacy Law*.

Dominique Moore is a member of the Legal Service of the European Parliament.

Radim Polčák is the head of the Institute of Law and Technology, Faculty of Law, Masaryk University, Brno.

Matthias Schmidl is the Deputy Director of the Austrian Data Protection Authority and Co-Editor of a Commentary on the GDPR and on the Austrian Data Protection Act.

Anrijs Šimkus is a paralegal at DLA Piper's Brussels office and holds a master's degree in law from the University of Latvia and a master's degree in IP & ICT law from KU Leuven.

Alessandro Spina is a member of the Legal Service of the European Commission and former data protection officer of the European Medicines Agency (EMA).

Dan Jerker B. Svantesson is Professor and Co-Director of the Centre for Commercial Law at the Faculty of Law of Bond University (Australia) and a Researcher at the Swedish Law & Informatics Research Institute of Stockholm University.

Luca Tosoni is a Belgian and Italian qualified lawyer and a Doctoral Research Fellow at the Norwegian Research Center for Computers and Law (NRCCL), University of Oslo.

Patrick Van Eecke is global co-chair of DLA Piper's Data Protection, Privacy and Information Security Practice and a professor at the University of Antwerp teaching European Cyberlaw.

Christian Wiese Svanberg is the Chief Privacy Officer and Data Protection Officer of the Danish Police and External Lecturer in European Data Protection Law at the University of Copenhagen.

Gabriela Zanfir-Fortuna is an independent expert on EU data protection law, with affiliations at the Future of Privacy Forum (Washington DC), Ankura Consulting, and the Vrije Universiteit Brussel, and was formerly legal officer at the European Data Protection Supervisor.

Thomas Zerdick is Head of Unit in the Secretariat of the European Data Protection Supervisor and was formerly an official specialising in data protection in the European Commission.

Background and Evolution of the EU General Data Protection Regulation (GDPR)

CHRISTOPHER KUNER   LEE A. BYGRAVE   CHRISTOPHER DOCKSEY

Table of Contents

I. Introduction — 2
II. The legislative history — 3
  1. The Commission's GDPR Proposal — 3
  2. The legislative procedure — 5
    2.1 The European Parliament — 5
    2.2 The Council of the European Union — 6
    2.3 The trilogue — 7
  3. The role of the supervisory authorities — 8
  4. The role of the Court of Justice of the European Union — 8
III. The evolution of the text — 10
  1. Chapter I: General Provisions (Articles 1–4) — 11
    1.1 Article 2—Material scope — 11
      1.1.1 Purely personal activity (Article 2(2)(c)) — 11
      1.1.2 Law enforcement (Article 2(2)(d)) — 11
      1.1.3 Processing by EU institutions (Article 2(3)) — 12
    1.2 Article 3—Territorial scope — 12
    1.3 Article 4—Definitions — 13
      1.3.1 Personal data (Article 4(1)) — 13
      1.3.2 Definition of 'child' — 14
      1.3.3 Main establishment (Article 4(16)) — 14
      1.3.4 'Producer' of a data filing system — 15
      1.3.5 Pseudonymous data (Article 4(5)) and anonymous data — 15
  2. Chapter II: Principles (Articles 5–11) — 16
    2.1 Purpose limitation (Articles 5(1)(b) and 6(4)) — 16
    2.2 Legitimate interest (Article 6(1)(f)) — 17
    2.3 Consent (Article 7) — 18
    2.4 Consent from children (Article 8) — 19
    2.5 Sensitive data (Articles 9–10) — 19
    2.6 Small and medium-sized enterprises — 20
  3. Chapter III: Rights of the Data Subject (Articles 12–23) — 20
    3.1 Processing not requiring identification (Article 11) — 21
    3.2 Notice obligations and privacy policies (Articles 12–14) — 21
    3.3 Data portability (Article 20) — 22
    3.4 The right to erasure ('right to be forgotten') (Article 17) — 22
    3.5 The right to object (Article 21) — 23
    3.6 Automated decision-making, including profiling (Article 22) — 24
    3.7 Restrictions (Article 23) — 24
  4. Chapter IV: Controller and Processor (Articles 24–43) — 25
    4.1 Accountability (Article 24) — 25
    4.2 Risk-based approach — 26
    4.3 Data protection by design and by default (Article 25) — 26

Kuner/Bygrave/Docksey

4.4	Joint controllers (Article 26)	27
4.5	Processing and sub-processing (Article 28)	27
4.6	Records of processing activities (Article 30)	28
4.7	Security of processing (Article 32)	28
4.8	Data breach notification (Articles 33–34)	29
4.9	Data protection impact assessment and consultation of the DPA (Articles 35–36)	29
4.10	Data Protection Officers (Articles 37–39)	30
4.11	Codes of conduct (Article 40)	31
4.12	Certification, seals and marks (Article 42)	31
5. Chapter V: Transfers of Personal Data to Third Countries or International Organisations (Articles 44–50)		32
5.1	Adequacy (Article 45)	32
5.2	Appropriate safeguards (Article 46)	33
5.3	Binding corporate rules (BCRs) (Article 47)	34
5.4	Transfers or disclosures not authorised by Union law (Article 48)	34
5.5	Derogations for specific situations (Article 49)	35
6. Chapter VI: Independent Supervisory Authorities (Articles 51–59)		35
6.1	Overview	35
6.2	The one-stop-shop mechanism (Article 56)	36
7. Chapter VII: Cooperation and Consistency (Articles 60–76)		37
7.1	Consistency mechanism (Article 63)	37
7.2	The EDPB (Articles 68–76)	39
8. Chapter VIII: Remedies, Liability and Penalties (Articles 77–84)		39
9. Chapter IX: Provisions Relating to Specific Processing Situations (Articles 85–91)		40
10. Chapter X: Delegated Acts and Implementing Acts (Articles 92–93)		41
11. Chapter XI: Final Provisions (Articles 94–99)		43

I. INTRODUCTION

This book provides an article-by-article commentary on the EU General Data Protection Regulation ('GDPR'). Adopted in April 2016 and applicable from May 2018, the GDPR is the centrepiece of the reform of the EU regulatory framework for protection of personal data. While retaining the conceptual framework of the Data Protection Directive 95/46 ('DPD') that it replaced, the GDPR represents a major shift in the way that data protection is regulated in EU law. In addition, the GDPR has already become a global benchmark in the field.

The GDPR is a huge text. Although many of its provisions replicate the DPD or reflect pre-existing jurisprudence and administrative practice, much of its text is new, with very limited authoritative guidance on how it is to be understood. Interpreting the GDPR is accordingly very much a journey into uncharted territory. This book is a systematic attempt to chart this territory by a relatively large and diversely constituted group of experts in the field.

It is important to note that the reform of the EU regulatory framework on data protection occurred against the backdrop of similar reform processes undertaken by other international organisations that have been influential in the field. In particular, the Council of Europe modernised its 1981 Convention on data protection ('Convention 108') in parallel with the EU's work on drafting the GDPR.[1] Both reform processes helped shape each other.

The story of the GDPR's birth is long, intricate and often difficult to follow. At the same time, it is both fascinating and instructive, not just in terms of showing how data protection has developed within the EU but also in terms of the insights it provides on the mechanics of the EU legislative process more generally. It demonstrates the complexities of that process, as well as the growing significance of data protection in economic, social and political terms and the strengthening of the fundamental right to data protection in the EU legal order. The GDPR's route through the EU legislative procedure and the way its text evolved further illustrates its major concepts and the changes that it made to EU data protection law.[2]

II. THE LEGISLATIVE HISTORY

The legislative history of the GDPR illustrates how EU legislation is proposed and enacted by the Commission, Parliament and Council. In addition, the supervisory authorities, both formally and informally, and the Court of Justice of the EU ('CJEU') all had considerable influence on the process, as discussed below.

1. The Commission's GDPR Proposal

On 15 May 2003, the Directorate General of the Commission for the Internal Market ('DG MARKT'), which had jurisdiction over data protection policy making in the Commission at that time, published its 'First report on the implementation of the Data Protection Directive (95/46/EC)'.[3] Despite identifying numerous difficulties with the Directive—not least significant shortfalls in achieving its objective of harmonising Member States' data protection regimes—the Commission took the view that amending the Directive would be premature. On 7 March 2007, the Commission adopted a Communication concluding that the DPD should not be revised.[4]

In 2009, the Treaty of Lisbon brought about major constitutional changes in the legal structure of the European Union. The changes included: introducing the right to data protection and a specific legal basis for data protection legislation in Article 16 of the Treaty on the Functioning of the European Union ('TFEU'); elimination of most aspects of the Maastricht Treaty's 'pillar' structure (meaning essentially that the same basic legal protections should apply to all types of data processing); increased oversight of and participation in data protection policy-making by the European Parliament; the elevation of the Charter of Fundamental Rights of the EU ('CFR'), which includes a specific right to data protection (Article 8 CFR), to constitutional status; and the obligation of the EU to accede to the European Convention on Human Rights ('ECHR').[5]

---

[1] Modernised Convention 108 was adopted on 18 May 2018, one week before the GDPR became applicable.
[2] This discussion draws from the following articles: Burton et al. 2013; Burton et al. 2014; Burton et al. 2015; Burton et al. 2016; and Kuner 2012.
[3] EC Report DPD 2003.   [4] EC Communication 2007, p. 9.   [5] Art. 6(2) TFEU.

On 4 November 2010, the Commission released a further Communication[6] concluding that, while the core principles of the DPD were still valid, it could no longer meet the challenges of rapid technological developments and globalisation, and required revision. The Commission then proceeded to engage in consultations, both public and private, with citizens' groups, businesses, data protection authorities, national governments, technical experts, NGOs and other actors.

The Commission assessed three policy options of different degrees of intervention: (1) minimal legislative amendments and the use of interpretative Communications and policy support measures such as funding programmes and technical tools; (2) a set of legislative provisions addressing each of the issues identified in the analysis; and (3) the centralisation of data protection at EU level through precise and detailed rules for all sectors and the establishment of an EU agency for monitoring and enforcement of the provisions. The Commission ultimately decided on the second option, consisting essentially of a thorough modernisation of the legal framework. On 29 November 2011, the Directorate General for Justice, DG JUST, circulated among the Commission services an internal consultative draft of the GDPR Proposal (the 'GDPR Interservice Draft'),[7] which nonetheless was widely leaked and provoked intensive lobbying. The draft also proved controversial inside the Commission, which led to several of the Commission services issuing negative opinions during the Commission interservice consultation procedure. Following agreement on numerous changes and improvements to the texts, the final GDPR Proposal was adopted on 25 January 2012,[8] on the basis of Article 16(2) TFEU, meaning that it was adopted by the so-called 'ordinary legislative procedure' under Article 294 TFEU.

The GDPR Proposal was part of a package of instruments issued on 25 January 2012 that also included a Communication outlining the Commission's strategy (the 'Communication'),[9] the Proposal for a directive covering personal data processed to prevent, investigate or prosecute criminal offences or enforce criminal penalties (the 'Law Enforcement Directive' or 'LED'),[10] and various other documents.[11] The LED, which was intended to replace the Council Framework Decision in the same area,[12] is not discussed further in this chapter, with a few exceptions. However, it is worth noting that Parliament insisted that the institutions work on the GDPR Proposal and the LED Proposal in tandem, so as not to neglect the law enforcement element of the reform package. In the end, the LED was adopted and entered into force on 5 May 2016, and Member States had to implement it into national law by 6 May 2018.

The political reaction to the GDPR Proposal was contentious, particularly at national level. For example, concerns about it were voiced in Germany, where Johannes Masing, a judge on the German Federal Constitutional Court (*Bundesverfassungsgericht*), published an article in a leading German newspaper on 9 January 2012 arguing that a data protection regulation would reduce the level of data protection compared to that under German constitutional law.[13]

---

[6] EC Communication 2010.   [7] GDPR Interservice Draft.
[8] GDPR Proposal. The term 'GDPR Proposal' is used throughout to refer to the text originally proposed by the Commission. Unless otherwise indicated, throughout this chapter the relevant provisions of the Proposal are indicated in parentheses after the text to which they refer.
[9] EC Communication 2012.   [10] Art. 1(1) LED Proposal.
[11] The following other documents were included in the package: EC Report 2012; EC Impact Assessment GDPR 2012, EC Staff Working Paper 2012.
[12] Council Framework Decision 2008/977/JHA. See Art. 58(1) LED Proposal, repealing the Council Framework Decision.
[13] Masing 2012.

2. The legislative procedure

Once adopted, the GDPR Proposal entered into the EU ordinary legislative procedure, which requires agreement on the final text between the European Parliament and the Council of the EU.

2.1 The European Parliament

The European Parliament began preparing its response to the GDPR Proposal by appointing German Green MEP Jan Philipp Albrecht as the main rapporteur for the Proposal. On 8 January 2013, he issued his draft report (the Albrecht Report)[14] on the GDPR Proposal for the Parliament's Committee on Civil Liberties, Justice and Home Affairs (the 'LIBE' Committee).[15] The Albrecht Report included 350 draft amendments.

Other committees in the EU Parliament besides the LIBE Committee also issued draft opinions on the GDPR Proposal. These bodies included the Employment and Social Affairs Committee ('EMPL'), the Industry, Research and Energy Committee ('ITRE'), the Internal Market and Consumer Protection Committee ('IMCO') and the Legal Affairs Committee ('JURI'). However, the Albrecht Report was particularly significant since Mr Albrecht was Parliament's lead rapporteur.

The Albrecht Report generally supported the objectives of the Commission's proposed reform and its aim to establish a 'coherent, harmonious and robust framework with a high level of protection of all data processing activities in the EU'.[16] In particular, the Report strongly supported the decision in the GDPR Proposal to choose a regulation (rather than a directive) as the legal basis for the data protection framework, the objective being to reduce the fragmented and often divergent approach to data protection in the EU.

The Report further supported the Commission's ambition of 'reducing the administrative burden, strengthening individuals' rights, further advancing the internal market dimension and ensuring better enforcement of data protection rules, and strengthening the global dimension'.[17] The Commission reacted positively to the Albrecht Report, and the EU Council (via the Irish Council Presidency) committed to make the GDPR Proposal a major priority, and to work on it in cooperation with the EU Parliament.[18]

After publication of the Albrecht Report in January 2013, all MEPs were invited to submit amendments. The European Parliament was flooded with one of the largest lobbying offensives in its political history, and a record 3,999 amendments were tabled. To help the rapporteur deal with the sheer number of these amendments, the EDPS set up a task force to analyse and group them by theme, setting forth the results in a report furnished to the Chair of the LIBE.[19]

In the meantime, a major event that played a role in the Parliament's deliberations was the revelation in the spring of 2013 of widespread government intelligence surveillance, particularly by the US (the 'Snowden revelations').[20] This event gave new energy to the Parliament and helped to prevent the legislative effort on the GDPR from stalling under the weight of the large number of tabled amendments.

---

[14] EP Draft Report LIBE 2012. An erratum to the Albrecht Report was issued on 9 January 2013. See EP Draft Report LIBE Erratum 2013.
[15] The Report was officially presented during a LIBE Committee meeting on 10 January 2013.
[16] See EP Draft Report LIBE 2012, p. 209.   [17] Ibid., pp. 211–215.
[18] See Press Release Irish Presidency 2013.
[19] See EDPS Letter 2013; EDPS 2013.   [20] See Greenwald 2014; Milanovic 2015.

On 21 October 2013, consolidated amendments were adopted by the LIBE Committee. While many of the compromise amendments were similar to those presented in the Albrecht Report, the text also made some significant changes. The consolidated draft was adopted by 49 votes in favour, with one against and three abstentions.

The LIBE Committee's compromise amendments were heavily debated in Parliament and triggered numerous comments from stakeholders. After lengthy discussions in different committees, the Parliament adopted its amendments to the GDPR Proposal on 12 March 2014.[21] The Parliament voted in plenary to endorse the LIBE Committee's amendments, with 621 votes in favour, 10 against and 22 abstentions.[22] The formal 'first reading' was adopted by the Parliament in order to consolidate the work done so far before the then forthcoming European elections. As a result, the newly elected Parliament of May 2014 did not have to restart work on the proposed legislation from scratch but was able to build its position on the basis of the first reading.

2.2 The Council of the European Union

The work of the Council is led by the Presidency which rotates among Member States every six months. The Council's work led to adoption of its General Approach. This is different from the Council's formal 'position at first reading' (which was also known as the Council's 'Common Position' prior to adoption of the Lisbon Treaty). The latter formally concludes the first reading of the ordinary legislative procedure and is binding, whereas a General Approach is a political agreement on the text by which the Council indicates its informal position. The adoption of a General Approach by the Council forms the basis for informal negotiations ('trilogue') with the Parliament, with the help of the Commission. To respect the ordinary legislative procedure, once the agreement on a joint text is informally reached between the Parliament and the Council, the joint text has to be formally adopted by the Council ('first reading procedure'). As a final step, the informal joint text has to be formally adopted also by the Parliament ('second reading procedure') after which the draft measure is finally adopted.[23]

When the GDPR Proposal was adopted in February 2012, the Danish government held the presidency of the Council. It began work in a series of meetings with representatives of Member State governments (meeting under the auspices of the EU Council's Working Party on Information Exchange and Data Protection, known as 'DAPIX'). The approach of the Danish Presidency was methodical, and involved processing the GDPR Proposal article by article.[24] This approach continued in the following Council Presidency held by Cyprus which additionally decided to follow a horizontal approach focusing on three main issues: (1) delegated and implementing acts; (2) administrative burdens and compliance costs; and (3) more flexibility for the public sector.[25]

Due to the length of the GDPR Proposal, the Danish and Cypriot Presidencies resulted in the Council reviewing less than half of it by the end of 2012. In addition, many of the tentative conclusions reached in the DAPIX meetings were made subject to reservations on behalf of various Member States, indicating that there was substantial disagreement among them on individual points (one of the most contentious points

---

[21] EP Resolution GDPR 2014. [22] EP Website Vote 12 March 2014.
[23] For more information on the EU's ordinary legislative procedure, see EP Website Legislative Powers.
[24] The Danish presidency reviewed Arts. 1–10 as well as Arts. 80(a) and 83 GDPR and proposed amendments: see Council Report 2012A.
[25] The Cyprus presidency reviewed up to Art. 40 of the Regulation: see Council Report 2012B.

being the insistence of Germany that public authorities be exempted from the scope of the Regulation). Work on the Proposal was also subjected to a barrage of lobbying, particularly by US-based companies and the US government.

From 2013 onwards, the Council continued to work on its own amendments to the GDPR Proposal in parallel to the negotiations in the Parliament. Its work was spread over a relatively large number of successive Council Presidencies, including those of Ireland (first half of 2013), Lithuania (second half of 2013), Greece (first half of 2014), Italy (second half of 2014) and Latvia (first half of 2015). After lengthy debates, the Council finally arrived at a General Approach, including hundreds of amendments relating to all the topics and articles of the GDPR Proposal,[26] on 15 June 2015 under the Latvian Presidency.[27]

2.3 The trilogue

Once the Council had adopted its General Approach, the three EU institutions were able to begin the final stage of the legislative process, the 'trilogue'. This is the negotiation between representatives of the Council, the Commission and the Parliament which takes place behind closed doors, in which the three institutions attempt to reach an agreement. The GDPR trilogue began with a meeting in Brussels on 24 June 2015. In tandem, the Council adopted its General Approach on the LED on 9 October 2015, permitting the LED trilogue to begin on 27 October.

In order to increase the transparency of the process, the texts of the three institutions discussed in the trilogue were published by the EDPS, together with its own comments and textual recommendations.[28] There were 13 GDPR trilogue meetings between 24 June and 15 December, which discussed outstanding issues, such as Data Protection Officers ('DPOs'), data breach notifications and administrative fines.[29] The GDPR was finally agreed at 9.30 p.m. on 15 December 2015.

On 18 December 2015, the Permanent Representatives Committee ('Coreper') of the Council confirmed that the two legislative package texts had been agreed with Parliament on 15 December.[30] This was the last major step in agreeing the texts of the GDPR and the LED.

After review by the legal services of the EU institutions and lawyer-linguists, the GDPR was submitted for adoption by the Parliament (in plenary session) and Council, and jointly signed by the Presidents and Secretaries General of both institutions. Following review by lawyer-linguists, the text of the GDPR was published in the EU's Official Journal on 4 May 2016 and entered into force on 25 May 2016. Unusually, the institutions later published a Corrigendum to the GDPR text on 4 May 2018 which applied from 25 May 2018 and contained both linguistic and substantive changes.[31] The initial failure of the institutions to publicise the Corrigendum widely was unfortunate as it potentially exacerbated public confusion around the GDPR's requirements (e.g. the old version of the GDPR text was still available on the Commission website for several months after the corrigendum was issued).

---

[26] Council Report 2015A. This text was approved as a General Approach on 15 June 2015.
[27] See Council Press Release 2015A. [28] EDPS 2015.
[29] See e.g. the Council's preparation for the trilogue of 27 November 2015 in Council Report 2015C. The trilogue calendar and agendas are set out at the end of the EDRi GDPR Document Pool.
[30] See Council Press Release 2015B. [31] See Table of Legislation.

Following adoption of the GDPR and the LED, the EU began work on other data protection legislative initiatives. In particular, in January 2017, the Commission adopted its EPR Proposal to replace the EPD,[32] and its EUDPR Proposal to replace Regulation 45/2001.[33]

3. The role of the supervisory authorities

The supervisory authorities (i.e. the data protection authorities or 'DPAs') devoted significant time and resources to supporting the data protection reform. At EU level the WP29 and the EDPS were active at every step of the reform, beginning with the WP29 Opinion on the Future of Privacy of 1 December 2009,[34] commenting on the Commission's initial consultation of July 9 that year, and the EDPS Opinion of 14 January 2011 on the Commission's Communication on the reform of 4 November 2010.[35] Both bodies adopted Opinions on the GDPR Proposal in early 2012 and then at the various stages of the legislative process. The EDPS took two specific actions worthy of note when assessing influence: it issued a report to the LIBE Committee in 2013 analysing the thousands of amendments to facilitate the work of the Committee and its rapporteur, and released an app in 2015 containing all the trilogue texts in a comparative table, together with a compromise text recommended by the EDPS. As noted elsewhere, the relationship between the advisory work by the EDPS and the EDPB is now addressed by the EUDPR that regulates data protection in the EU institutions, bodies and agencies.

The main objectives successfully achieved by the data protection authorities with regard to controllers were the inclusion of the principle of accountability, rules on privacy by design, certification and the role of the DPO, and the consolidation of binding corporate rules with regard to international transfers. The use of a regulation rather than a directive to ensure greater harmonisation was also a major objective, together with the substantial reinforcement of individual rights, including more stringent provisions on consent and profiling, and the strengthening of the role and powers of national supervisory authorities. Attempts to water down existing safeguards, such as the definition of personal data and the purpose limitation principle, were successfully resisted.

4. The role of the Court of Justice of the European Union

The judgments of the CJEU had a significant impact on the development of the GDPR. The first and most venerable influence was the case law establishing that dynamic internet protocol ('IP') addresses can be used to identify individuals. IP addresses were first discussed by Advocate General Kokott in *Promusicae*,[36] and the CJEU specifically confirmed that IP addresses are personal data 'because they allow those users to be precisely identified' in *Scarlet Extended*.[37] This approach can now be found in the reference to an 'online identifier' in Article 4(1) GDPR on the definition of personal data and in Recital 30 GDPR which explains that individuals 'may be associated with online identifiers provided by their devices, applications, tools and protocols, such as internet protocol addresses, cookie identifiers or other identifiers such as radio frequency identification tags'.

---

[32] EPR Proposal. [33] EUDPR Proposal. For Regulation 45/2001, see Table of Legislation. [34] WP29 2009. [35] EDPS 2011. [36] Case C-275/06, *Promusicae* (AG Opinion), paras. 30–31. [37] Case C-70/10, *Scarlet Extended*, para. 51.

Between the adoption of the GDPR Proposal on 25 January 2012 and agreement on the final compromise GDPR text on 15 December 2015, the CJEU issued several landmark data protection judgments which influenced, directly or indirectly, the final text of the GDPR.

On 8 April 2014, the CJEU invalidated the Data Retention Directive in *Digital Rights Ireland*[38] on the grounds of serious interference with fundamental rights under the Charter. This proved to be a ground-breaking judgment that helped pave the way for the Court's affirmation of the fundamental right to data protection in other cases as well.

A month later, on 13 May 2014, the CJEU ruled in *Google Spain* on two matters relevant to the GDPR.[39] First, it followed the Opinion of Advocate General Jääskinen[40] and ruled that the processing of personal data by the Google search engine was carried out 'in the context of the activities' of Google's establishment in Spain. This confirmed the approach to territorial scope in Article 4(1) DPD that was carried over into Article 3(1) GDPR. Secondly, it ruled that individuals have a qualified right not to figure in a public index of internet search results when the data in question are inaccurate, incomplete or irrelevant. Advocate General Jääskinen had concluded that there was no such right under the DPD. However, the Court took a different view, which may be considered to have been influenced by the GDPR Proposal, albeit without any reference to it.

The final judgment the Court handed down during the legislative process was its influential ruling in *Schrems v Data Protection Commissioner*.[41] In this case the Court invalidated the EU–US Safe Harbour data transfer mechanism between the EU and the US. The judgment was delivered on 6 October 2015, shortly before the compromise GDPR text was agreed on 15 December 2015. As a result, recital 104 GDPR further refined the criteria that the Commission should consider when assessing the level of protection of a third country, territory or specified sector therein, or international organisation. For example, the Commission must assess any national security laws in the third country and how public authorities can access personal data. Recital 104 GDPR also clarifies that adequacy decisions can only be granted when the level of data protection is 'essentially equivalent' to that guaranteed in the EU, as stipulated in *Schrems*.

Schrems also indicates the Court's 'dynamic assessment' of the fundamental right to data protection.[42] As President of the CJEU Koen Lenaerts has stated, 'the preliminary reference for controlling the validity of an act of the Union is not only without limit in time ... but also may be reviewed in terms of the legal framework existing at the date of the Court's judgment ... '[43] Thus, the CJEU will make a 'dynamic assessment' in data protection cases and evaluate whether they meet the legal standards in force at the time that it makes its judgment and not just those that applied when the case was brought.

The GDPR Proposal was first mentioned in the case law of the CJEU in the Opinion of Advocate General Jääskinen in *Google Spain*, where he observed however that 'the dispute to hand has to be decided on the basis of existing law'.[44] With regard to the question of DPA jurisdiction, in his Opinion in *Wirtschaftsakademie* Advocate General Bot

---

[38] Joined Cases C-293/12 and C-594/12, *Digital Rights Ireland*.
[39] Case C-131/12, *Google Spain*.   [40] Case C-131/12, *Google Spain* (AG Opinion).
[41] Case C-362/14, *Maximillian Schrems v Data Protection Commissioner*, judgment of 6 October 2015 (Grand Chamber) (ECLI:EU:C:2015:650).
[42] See the commentary on Art. 45 in this volume for further discussion of this point.
[43] Lenaerts speech 2018, between 27'07" and 30'35".
[44] Case C-131/12, *Google Spain* (AG Opinion), para. 9.

invited the Court to decide the case exclusively on the basis of the enforcement model of the DPD, without pre-empting the 'sophisticated cooperation mechanism' in the GDPR Proposal, because it was not yet applicable.[45] Following the adoption of the GDPR, the same Advocate General observed in *Manni*[46] that his analysis under the DPD was also 'in step' with Article 17(3)(b) and (d) of the GDPR. In *Nowak*,[47] the GDPR is mentioned in the list of legislative instruments under 'European Law',[48] and is then described in paragraphs 59–61 with regard to the observations of the Court *obiter* on the broader reasons which may be used for restrictions of rights under Articles 23(1)(e) and 15(4) GDPR, in the future.

The first ruling by the Court directly based on the GDPR will be in *Planet49*, dealing with a question on valid consent under the GDPR by the national referring court (the Court had not yet handed down its judgment when this text was finalised). In his Opinion,[49] Advocate General Szpunar noted that the GDPR has been applicable since 25 May 2018, repealing the DPD with effect from the same date. He advised that the applicable law was the EPD, in combination with the DPD for situations before 25 May 2018, and in combination with the GDPR for situations as from 25 May 2018. Since the applicant in that case was seeking an injunction to restrain future unlawful behaviour, the Advocate General found that the GDPR was applicable to that part of the case, and the questions referred had to be answered having regard to both the DPD and the GDPR.[50]

III. THE EVOLUTION OF THE TEXT

The following analysis traces the evolution of the GDPR's text in light of some of the main topics that were discussed between the EU institutions during the legislative process. The chief points of comparison are the original GDPR Proposal, the texts of the Parliament and the Council's General Approach. In a few cases, the final text of the GDPR Proposal is compared to the earlier interservice draft, to show how it evolved internally within the Commission.[51]

One of the most significant changes wrought by the GDPR concerns its legal nature. There had been a great deal of discussion as to whether the new instrument should take the form of a directive or a regulation. A regulation has general application and is directly applicable (i.e. it does not require implementation by Member States), whereas a directive sets forth the results to be achieved, but leaves the means for achieving them largely up to implementation into national law by the Member States.[52]

One of the major complaints about the DPD had been the lack of harmonisation made possible by its status as a directive. In theory, the type of legal instrument used is not in itself determinative with regard to harmonisation; for example, it is possible for a directive to leave little margin for Member State implementation.[53] However, in practice

---

[45] C-210/16, *Wirtschaftsakademie* (AG Opinion), para. 103.
[46] Case C-398/15, *Manni* (AG Opinion).   [47] Case C-434/16, *Nowak*.
[48] Ibid., paras. 11–13.   [49] Case C-673/17, *Planet49* (AG Opinion).
[50] Ibid., paras. 45–49.
[51] The chapter numbers and article numbers in the headings are those of the final text of the GDPR. The numbers of the articles and recitals in the text refer to the version being discussed on the basis of the GDPR Proposal, and so will differ between the various legislative proposed texts and the final text of the GDPR (e.g. the provision on responsibility (accountability) is referred to as Art. 22 GDPR Proposal and as Art. 24 GDPR).
[52] Art. 288 TFEU.   [53] An example is the Consumer Rights Directive.

a regulation generally leads to a greater degree of harmonisation, since it immediately becomes part of a national legal system, without the need for adoption of separate national legislation; has legal effect independent of national law; and overrides contrary national laws. As a result, the GDPR is directly applicable in all EU Member States. In principle, Member States do not need to adopt national legislation to transpose the new rules into their legal system. This means that most national data protection acts will either be repealed or severely reduced in scope (so that they regulate matters that the GDPR does not cover or specifically leaves to national law). At the same time, the GDPR contains many 'opening clauses' (i.e. clauses that allow derogation under Union or Member State law), so that it will not lead to complete harmonisation.

1. Chapter I: General Provisions (Articles 1–4)

1.1 Article 2—Material scope

1.1.1 Purely personal activity (Article 2(2)(c))

The GDPR excludes from its scope the processing of personal data 'by a natural person in the course of a purely personal or household activity' (Article 2(2)(c)), thus replicating the exemption under Article 3(2) DPD. The GDPR Proposal formulated this exclusion in terms of data processing by a natural person 'without any gainful interest in the course of its own exclusively personal or natural or household activity' (Article 2(2)(d) GDPR Proposal). The rationale for this formulation was concern among European data protection authorities and the Commission that the scope of the exemption under Article 3(2) DPD was too broad, since it could be construed to exempt from EU data protection law activities such as the processing of personal data by online social networks.[54] The GDPR Interservice Draft originally contained a further restriction stating that data processed for a personal or household activity were not covered by the exemption if they were 'made accessible to an indefinite number of individuals', reflecting the judgment of the CJEU in the *Lindqvist* case,[55] but this was deleted in the final version of the GDPR Proposal.

1.1.2 Law enforcement (Article 2(2)(d))

Data processing under the former 'third pillar' of EU law (i.e. for matters involving law enforcement) was outside the scope of the DPD,[56] which made such processing subject to a variety of different rules on a national level. The easiest way of dealing with this situation would have been to subject law enforcement issues to the GDPR Proposal as well, especially since it generally covered data processing by public authorities,[57] but this proved politically impossible. Thus, data processing by 'competent authorities' (i.e. public authorities) for the purpose of preventing, investigating, detecting or prosecuting criminal offenses, or for executing criminal penalties was exempted from the scope of

---

[54] See WP29 2009, para. 71, stating that the exemption under Art. 3(2) DPD leads to 'a lack of safeguards which may need to be addressed'. Art. 3(2) DPD exempted data processing 'by a natural person in the course of a purely personal or household activity'.

[55] Case C-101/01, *Lindqvist*, para. 47, where the Court found that the exemption contained in Art. 3(2) DPD for personal or household processing only relates to 'activities which are carried out in the course of private or family life of individuals', and thus did not apply to activities that were intended to make the data collected accessible to an indefinite number of people. See too Case C-73/07, *Satamedia*, para. 44.

[56] See Art. 3(2) DPD.

[57] See Art. 4(5)–(6) GDPR Proposal, defining both 'controller' and 'processor' to include public authorities and agencies.

the GDPR Proposal, as was data processing by Member States that falls within the EU Common Foreign and Security Policy (Article 2(2)). Instead, data protection in law enforcement is now regulated at the level of EU law under the LED.

1.1.3 Processing by EU institutions (Article 2(3))

The GDPR Proposal also did not cover data processing by the EU institutions, which would have allowed for an updating of Regulation 45/2001 covering data processing by the EU institutions.[58] That update, though, was eventually done with the adoption of the EUDPR.

1.2 Article 3—Territorial scope

Article 3 of the GDPR Proposal set forth the rules governing its territorial scope. It retained from Article 4 DPD the concept of 'the processing of personal data in the context of the activities of an establishment' in the EU as the basic test for determining when EU data protection law applies (Article 3(1)). However, it went on to make several significant changes with regard to jurisdiction. Under Article 3(2), controllers not established in the EU were subject to EU law when their processing activities related to (a) 'the offering of goods or services' to data subjects residing in the EU, or (b) the monitoring of the behaviour of such EU residents. The effect of these changes was to bring more non-EU-based controllers offering services over the internet within the reach of EU law.

The interservice draft of these provisions based jurisdiction over non-EU controllers on 'directing activities' to EU residents or monitoring their behaviour, using criteria articulated in the 2010 CJEU judgment in *Pammer*.[59] However, the final version of the GDPR Proposal abandoned the criteria listed therein and substituted 'the offering of goods or services' for 'directing activities'.

The Albrecht Report broadened the criteria for the application of EU data protection law. As stated in the Report, non-EU controllers that collect data of EU individuals with the aim of offering goods or services (even without any payment) or monitoring such individuals (not just their behaviour) would be subject to EU data protection law.[60]

Whilst the GDPR Proposal and the Albrecht Report applied the Regulation only to non-EU controllers, the LIBE Committee's compromise text extended the GDPR to apply to processors not established in the EU as well as non-EU controllers when: (a) offering services to individuals in the EU, irrespective of whether payment is required; or (b) monitoring such individuals ('monitoring' involving tracking and the creation of profiles) (Article 3 and recital 21 EP Resolution GDPR 2014). The GDPR was thus applied to a variety of online service providers located outside of the EU.

The Council's General Approach limited the extraterritorial scope of application of the GDPR to non-EU controllers and clarified that offering of goods and services does not require a payment from individuals (Article 3(2) Council Report 2015A). Consequently, non-EU processors were not directly subject to the Regulation under the Council's text. Monitoring of behaviour was covered as far as such behaviour took place within the EU.

---

[58] See EDPS 2011, para. 8, urging inclusion of data processing by EU institutions and bodies in the Commission's proposal.

[59] Joined Cases C-585/08 and C-144/09, *Pammer*. Rec. 15 GDPR Interservice Draft contained criteria to determine when targeting occurs that were taken from conclusions of the judgment.

[60] According to the Albrecht Report, the 'Regulation should cover not only the monitoring of the behavior of Union residents by data controllers outside of the Union, such as through internet tracking, but all collection and processing of personal data about Union residents': see EP Draft Report LIBE 2012, p. 63.

Non-EU controllers subject to EU data protection law had to appoint in writing a representative in the EU (Article 25). The final text of Article 3 applies the GDPR to non-EU controllers and processors that carry out processing activities related to 'the offering of goods or services, irrespective of whether a payment of the data subject is required, to such data subjects in the Union' or to 'the monitoring of their behaviour as far as their behaviour takes place within the Union'.[61]

The GDPR retains in Article 3(3) the unfortunate formulation contained in Article 4(1)(b) DPD stating that it applies to non-EU controllers 'in a place where Member State law applies by virtue of public international law'. As explained in the commentary to Article 3 in this volume, this suggests that the EU legislator did not fully understand the jurisdictional rules of public international law.

1.3 Article 4—Definitions

Article 4 of the GDPR Proposal made changes to some of the definitions contained in the DPD, such as the definition of 'personal data', and introduced new definitions, including those of 'child', 'personal data breach', 'genetic data', 'data concerning health', 'binding corporate rules' (BCRs) and 'main establishment'.[62]

1.3.1 Personal data (Article 4(1))

Article 4(1) of the GDPR Proposal moved the elements of the definition of 'personal data' in Article 2(a) DPD into the definition of 'data subject' as a natural person who is identified or identifiable, per recital 23 of the Proposal. It added to that definition examples of identifiers such as location data or online identifiers. It implied that 'online identifiers' (e.g. internet protocol ('IP') addresses and cookies) were generally to be considered as personal data, but a sentence was added to recital 24 after the interservice version clarifying that '[i]dentification numbers, location data, online identifiers or other specific factors as such need not necessarily be considered as personal data in all circumstances'. Article 10 specified that controllers did not need to identify a person just to comply with the provisions of the GDPR Proposal, and recital 23 stated that 'the principles of data protection should not apply to data rendered anonymous in such a way that the data subject is no longer identifiable'.

The Albrecht Report added new definitional elements to the mix by providing that data subjects included natural persons who can be identified or 'singled out' directly or indirectly, 'alone or in combination with associated data'.[63] According to the Report, IP addresses, cookies and other unique identifiers would in most cases be considered to be personal data, since they leave traces and can be used to single out natural persons, unless it can be shown that they do not allow for the singling out of a natural person. In the latter respect, the Report stated that IP addresses used by companies can in theory not be considered as personal data.[64]

In contrast, the LIBE Committee's compromise text explicitly stated that cookies and IP addresses constituted personal data, unless they did not relate to an identified or identifiable individual (recital 24), and the reference in the Albrecht Report that IP addresses used by companies would in theory not qualify as personal data was deleted.

---

[61] See further the commentary on Art. 3 in this volume for the regulation of territorial scope in the final version of the GDPR.
[62] See the commentary on Art. 4 in this volume, for details on all GDPR definitions.
[63] See EP Draft Report LIBE 2012, amendment 84.   [64] Ibid., p. 16.

The Council's General Approach took a more flexible position by adding that identification numbers, location data, online identifiers or other specific factors as such should not be considered as personal data if they did not identify an individual or make an individual identifiable (recital 24).[65]

The GDPR as finally adopted specifies that online identifiers, provided by devices, applications, tools and protocols, including IP addresses, cookie identifiers, as well as other identifiers such as Radio Frequency Identification tags ('RFID'), may leave 'traces' that can be used to identify individuals, in particular when combined with 'unique identifiers and other information received by the servers' (recital 30).

1.3.2 Definition of 'child'

The DPD did not contain any specific provisions dealing with the processing of children's data. This situation was often criticised, and resulted in such rules being incorporated in Article 8 GDPR.[66] The GDPR Proposal introduced a new definition of a 'child' as any person below 18 years (Article 4(18)), to complement a number of protections when data on children are processed (e.g. Articles 8, 33(2)(d) and 52(2)). However, in the subsequent legislative process, the definition of 'child' ended up being removed from Article 4, and the age at which personal data of a child may not be processed online without consent of the parent or custodian was lowered to a minimum of 13 years (Article 8(1) GDPR).[67] The differences between the definition of a child in the respective Member States' laws proved particularly controversial during the legislative process.[68]

1.3.3 Main establishment (Article 4(16))

The 'one-stop-shop' mechanism introduced by the GDPR hinges upon the new concept of the 'main establishment' of a company, which is important to determine which DPA is competent for a company's data processing activities in the EU.[69] This determination is crucial for both companies and for DPAs themselves. Article 4(13) of the GDPR Proposal provided different criteria for determining the main establishment of the controller: either the place where the main decisions are taken; the place of the processor; or the place of the processor's central administration. Despite lobbying efforts and other parliamentary committee opinions proposing amendments to the main establishment concept, the Albrecht Report did not include any amendments related to this specific issue.

Article 4(13) of the LIBE Committee's compromise text suggested harmonising the concept of 'main establishment' for both controllers and processors, contrary to the GDPR Proposal. The decisive criterion for both was the location where the main decisions are taken with regard to the conditions and means of the processing. In addition, the compromise text provided three criteria to take into account in deciding where such main decisions are taken: an organisation's headquarters; the location of management functions and administrative responsibilities that can enforce the data protection rules; and the location of effective and real management activities.[70]

The Council's General Approach proposed that the main establishment for both controllers and processors should be the place of their central administration in the EU. The Council provided the following exceptions to this rule: (1) for controllers, if decisions on

---

[65] See Council Report 2015A. [66] See further the commentary on Art. 8 in this volume.
[67] Ibid. [68] Ibid.
[69] See further the commentaries on Arts. 4(16), 56 and 60 in this volume.
[70] EP Resolution GDPR 2014.

the purposes and means of the data processing are taken in another establishment of the controller in the EU, which has the power to have such decisions implemented, then that other establishment would be the main establishment; (2) for processors with no central administration in the EU, the main establishment would be the location in the EU where the main processing activities in the context of the activities of an establishment of the processor take place.[71] This approach is followed in Article 4(16) GDPR.

1.3.4 'Producer' of a data filing system

In addition to the definition of controller and processor in the GDPR Proposal, the Albrecht Report introduced the concept of 'producer' of a data filing system (i.e. the entity that creates automated data processing or filing systems to be used by controllers or processors). This was intended to cover software and hardware developers. The producer would have to comply with the principles of data protection by design and by default. The idea was not taken further in the legislative process. Nonetheless, the enhanced duties that the GDPR imposes on controllers and processors, together with the Regulation's provisions on data protection by design and by default, create pressure, if only indirectly, on software and hardware developers to 'raise the bar' in terms of producing products and systems that are GDPR-compliant.

1.3.5 Pseudonymous data (Article 4(5)) and anonymous data

The Albrecht Report created a new category of 'pseudonymous data' that did not exist under the DPD. According to the Report, a pseudonym is a 'unique identifier which is specific to one given context and which does not permit the direct identification of a natural person, but allows the singling out of a data subject'.[72] The intent behind the insertion of the concept of pseudonymisation was to provide for some flexibility, with the processing of pseudonymous data being subject to lighter data protection obligations.[73]

The Albrecht Report also introduced a definition of anonymous data as:

> any data that cannot be related, directly or indirectly, alone or in combination with associated data, to a natural person or where establishing such a relation would require a disproportionate amount of time, expense and effort, taking into account the state of the art in technology at the time of the processing and the possibilities for development during the period for which the data would be processed.[74]

The processing of anonymous data was not made subject to the GDPR.[75]

The LIBE Committee's compromise text modified the concept of pseudonymous data and introduced a new concept of encrypted data. It defined 'pseudonymous data' as personal data that 'cannot be attributed to a specific individual without the use of additional information', as long as such information was kept separately and secure. 'Encrypted data' were defined as personal data that are 'rendered unintelligible' to unauthorised access due to security measures (Article 4(2a) and (2b)). The compromise amendments clarified that such types of data were considered personal data under the GDPR, but added that they would be subject to less stringent requirements.[76]

The Council's General Approach did not adopt the Parliament's concepts of pseudonymous and encrypted data, but it did add the concept of 'pseudonymisation' to its text. Pseudonymisation was defined as 'the processing of personal data in such a way that

---

[71] Council Report 2015A.　[72] See EP Draft Report LIBE, amendment 85.　[73] Ibid.
[74] Ibid., amendment 14.　[75] Ibid.　[76] EP Resolution GDPR 2014.

the data can no longer be attributed to a specific data subject without the use of additional information, as long as such additional information is kept separately and subject to technical and organisational measures to ensure non-attribution to an identified or identifiable person' (Article 4(3b)). Whilst the initial intent behind the insertion of the concept of pseudonymisation was to provide for some flexibility, the Council's version removed this flexibility by providing that although 'pseudonymisation' reduced the risks of the processing it was not intended to preclude any other measures of data protection (recital 23a).[77]

The GDPR treats pseudonymisation as a privacy-enhancing measure that aims to reduce the risk of singling out one individual in a data pool. It is also a tool for compliance, helping controllers and processors meet their data protection obligations (recital 28).[78] The Parliament's proposals for considering encrypted data as a separate category of personal data and defining anonymous data did not make it into the GDPR.

2. Chapter II: Principles (Articles 5–11)

The GDPR Proposal foresaw a strengthening of the general conditions for data processing. This was reflected first of all in Article 5, which was an amended version of Article 6 DPD. Article 5(c) provided a more explicit expression of the 'data minimisation' principle than was contained in the DPD. Article 5(f) also strengthened the accountability of controllers by requiring that personal data be processed under the responsibility and liability of the controller, who was also responsible for compliance.

Article 6 of the GDPR Proposal (corresponding to Article 7 DPD) contained several important changes to the legal bases for data processing. Article 6(3) stated that any data processing could only be based on EU law or Member State law. A requirement that sending direct marketing required the consent (i.e. opt-in consent) of the recipient, which was contained in the Draft GDPR Interservice Draft, was deleted from the final version of the proposal—Article 19 only provided for a right to object for the sending of direct marketing.

2.1 Purpose limitation (Articles 5(1)(b) and 6(4))

Article 6(4) of the GDPR Proposal permitted subsequent incompatible processing so long as it had a legal basis on one of the grounds of lawful processing in Article 6(1). This was initially deleted by the Parliament, but the Council's General Approach was similar to the GDPR Proposal.

The Council also added a set of criteria to determine whether or not the purpose of further data processing is compatible with the purpose for which the data were initially collected (Article 6(3a)). In addition, the Council proposed a new paragraph that permitted further processing by the same controller for incompatible purposes on the ground of legitimate interests of that controller or a third party, if those interests overrode the interests of the data subject (Article 6(4)), presumably to facilitate the use of 'big data' applications.[79] This proposal did not make it into the GDPR, as already during the vote on the Council's General Approach on 15 June 2015, 11 Member States expressed reservations.[80] The Council's Legal Service stated that it considered this provision

---

[77] Council Report 2015A. [78] See further the commentary on Art. 4(5) in this volume.
[79] Council Report 2015A.
[80] Austria, Belgium, Bulgaria, Cyprus, Estonia, France, Hungary, Italy, Lithuania, Malta and Poland.

to be incompatible with Article 8(2) CFR. The WP29 also raised concerns regarding this point.[81]

The concept of 'subsequent incompatible processing' was perhaps the most striking element of the GDPR Proposal that was not retained in the GDPR. In the end the institutions agreed on a compromise which does not permit subsequent incompatible processing per se but which included in Article 6(4) GDPR the criteria suggested by the Council for determining whether or not a new purpose of further data processing is compatible with the purpose for which the data were initially collected. These criteria include any links between the original purpose and the new purpose, the context in which the personal data were originally collected and, interestingly in view of the debate on pseudonymisation, the existence of appropriate safeguards, which may include encryption or pseudonymisation.

2.2 Legitimate interest (Article 6(1)(f))

The Albrecht Report restricted the legal bases for the processing of personal data. In particular, it stated that processing data for the purpose of the legitimate interest pursued by the controller that was not overridden by the interest of the data subject ('balancing of interests test') should be only used 'in exceptional circumstances'.[82] Therefore, controllers relying on this legal basis would have to comply with additional requirements, such as providing information about why their legitimate interest should prevail.

The Report also specified situations where the legitimate interests of the controller should and should not prevail. For example, the legitimate interest of the controller would override that of the data subject's where the controller could rely on the right to freedom of expression, or processed data for the direct marketing of its own similar products or services to existing customers.[83] However, the legitimate interest of the controller would not prevail if the processing involved sensitive data, location data and biometric data, or included profiling and large-scale data combinations.[84] Finally, controllers would not be able to rely on the balancing of interests to process personal data for a purpose different than that of data collection.

The LIBE Committee's compromise text retained but further restricted the use of a company's legitimate interest as a legal basis. Whilst the Albrecht Report had limited the use of legitimate interest to 'exceptional cases', the compromise text allowed controllers to rely on their legitimate interest to process data when it met individuals' 'reasonable expectations' (Article 6). What this would mean in practice was unclear, but it could be used to restrict the processing of personal data. In addition, controllers would be allowed to rely on their legitimate interest to process pseudonymous data (recital 38), which was not contemplated in the Albrecht Report.[85]

The Council's General Approach extended the provision to cover the legitimate interests of a third party as well as the controller, and clarified that a legitimate interest exists 'when there is a relevant and appropriate connection between the data subject and the controller in situations such as the data subject being a client or in the service of the controller' (recital 38). The Council also specified situations where controllers should be able to rely on their

---

[81] The WP29 issued a statement that it was 'very much concerned' about this aspect of the Council's proposal: see WP29 Press Release 2015. For details on the final result, see the commentaries on Arts. 5–6 in this volume.

[82] EP Draft Report LIBE 2012, amendment 22. [83] Ibid., amendment 101.

[84] Ibid., amendment 102. [85] EP Resolution GDPR 2014.

legitimate interest to process personal data: intra-group communication of data for internal administrative purposes (without prejudice to restrictions on data transfers) (recital 38a); ensuring network and information security; fraud prevention; certain marketing activities (recital 39); and communicating possible criminal acts or threats to public security to a competent authority (subject to an obligation of secrecy) (recital 40).[86]

2.3 Consent (Article 7)

Article 7(1) of the GDPR Proposal shifted the burden of proof onto controllers to show that the data subject had consented to the processing of their personal data. Article 7(2) required that if individuals' consent is obtained in the context of a written declaration which also concerns other matters, the request for consent must be clearly distinguishable from the other matters. Under Article 7(3), the data subject had the right to withdraw consent at any time. Under Article 7(4), the use of consent was also not allowed 'where there is a significant imbalance between the position of the data subject and the controller'. In addition, Article 4(8) of the Proposal tightened the definition of consent so that it had always to be 'explicit' (i.e. opt-in). At the same time, certain changes were introduced to recital 25 to soften the consent requirements of the interservice version in the online context, such as stating that the giving of electronic consent should not be 'unnecessarily disruptive', and that consent could be given by a 'statement or a clear affirmative action'.

The Albrecht Report considered consent as the cornerstone of EU data protection law and as the best way for individuals to control data processing activities. As indicated by MEP Albrecht during a press conference on 9 January 2013, the Report supported the idea of 'if you want my data, ask for consent'.[87] Accordingly, the importance of consent was increased compared to the GDPR Proposal. The Report required consent to be freely given, specific, informed and explicit, consequently impeding controllers from relying on implicit consent and on pre-ticked boxes.[88] In addition, the processing of data for the execution of a contract could not be made conditional on consent for uses of personal data that are not necessary for the execution of the contract or to provide the service. This meant, for example, that consent would not be a valid legal basis where the company 'is in a dominant market position with respect to the products or services offered to the data subject, or where a unilateral and nonessential change in terms of service gives a data subject no option other than to accept the change or abandon an online resource in which they have invested significant time'.[89]

The LIBE Committee's compromise text imposed additional requirements in order for consent to be valid. In particular, it required controllers to obtain 'free' consent (preticked boxes would not suffice), to limit consent to specific purposes and not to make consent conditional for processing that was not necessary for the requested services (Article 7 and recitals 32–33). In addition, the compromise text clarified that consent requires an affirmative action (e.g. ticking a box), that mere use of a service should not constitute consent (recital 25) and that consent cannot be given for the processing of personal data of third persons (recital 32).[90]

---

[86] Council Report 2015A. For the final decision regarding legitimate interests, see the commentary on Art. 6 in this volume.
[87] Albrecht Press Conference 2013.
[88] See EP Draft Report LIBE 2012, amendments 17 and 19.
[89] Ibid., amendment 20.   [90] EP Resolution GDPR 2014.

The Council's General Approach removed the requirement that consent must always be explicit (Article 4(8)). Under the Council's text, consent would only have to be unambiguous (Article 7(1)), with a few exceptions for which it must be explicit, namely sensitive data (Article 7(1a)) and international data transfers (Article 44(1)(a)). The Council also provided examples of consent that would be acceptable, such as the data subject's conduct in a particular context, or through the data subject's browser setting (recital 25). Finally, the Council clarified that when there are various purposes, the request for consent must be presented in plain and easily accessible language (Article 7(2)) and consent should be given for all purposes (recital 25). It also included some unbundling requirements for consent to be valid (recital 34). This latter approach is followed in the GDPR.[91]

The basic criteria for consent in the GDPR have thus remained the same, that it must be 'freely given, specific, informed and unambiguous'. However, the criteria have been strengthened in a number of significant respects through the introduction of a new specific clause on consent (Article 7), which requires the following: (1) the burden of proof is placed on the controller to show that consent has been given; (2) if individuals' consent is obtained in the context of a written declaration which also concerns other matters, the request for consent must be clearly and understandably distinguishable from the other matters; (3) the data subject has the right to withdraw consent at any time; and (4) consent cannot be 'bundled' to cover a service which is not necessary for the performance of a contract. Recital 43 GDPR explains that consent is not freely given where there is a clear imbalance between the data subject and the controller. However, the Commission proposal to tighten 'unambiguous' consent so that it had to be 'explicit' was not finally adopted.

2.4 Consent from children (Article 8)

The GDPR Proposal introduced new conditions for children's consent to the processing of their personal data in relation to information society services. Article 8(1) provided that when processing personal data of a child below the age of 13, the controller had to obtain the parent's consent. The Parliament and the Council added that the data processing activity is not lawful without parental consent or authorisation by the legal guardian (Parliament) or holder of parental responsibility (Council). The Council's General Approach removed the threshold of 13 years and required the controller to take reasonable efforts and use available technology to verify that consent has been obtained in the prescribed fashion (Article 8(1a)). Other provisions of the GDPR also contain special protections for the processing of the personal data of children (e.g. Articles 12(1) and 57(1)(b)).

2.5 Sensitive data (Articles 9–10)

Article 9(1) of the GDPR Proposal expanded the definition of sensitive data to include genetic data and data concerning 'criminal convictions or related security measures'. The concept of genetic data was further developed by the Parliament, with a broad definition that did not require that such data provide unique information about the physiology or health of an individual. Biometric data were added to the category of sensitive data.[92]

---

[91] See Council Report 2015A. For more details on consent in the GDPR, see the commentaries on Arts. 4(11) and 7 in this volume.
[92] EP Resolution GDPR 2014.

The Council's General Approach defined genetic data more narrowly as 'all personal data relating to the genetic characteristics of an individual that have been inherited or acquired, which give unique information about the physiology or the health of that individual, resulting in particular from an analysis of a biological sample from the individual in question' (Article 4 (10)). The Council's text confirmed that genetic data are sensitive data, and allowed Member States to adopt specific conditions for the processing of genetic or health data (Article 9(5)).

Biometric data remained a defined concept in the text of the Council, covering 'any personal data resulting from specific technical processing relating to the physical, physiological or behavioural characteristics of an individual which allows or confirms the unique identification of that individual, such as facial images, or dactyloscopic data' (Article 4(11)). Although biometric data were not considered to be a type of sensitive data according to the Council, the latter took the view that processing of such data may trigger some specific obligations such as the requirement to conduct data protection impact assessments (Article 33(2)(b)).[93]

Whilst the GDPR Proposal restricted the processing of data relating to criminal 'convictions', the Council's General Approach also captured criminal 'offences' and moved this topic to a separate section (Article 9a). This approach was taken in the final version of the GDPR.[94]

2.6 Small and medium-sized enterprises

The situation of small and medium-sized enterprises ('SMEs') presented special challenges during the legislative process. Many of them were concerned about the burdens that compliance with the GDPR could bring. At the same time, the fact that in some Member States the vast majority of enterprises are SMEs raised concerns about granting them broad exemptions. The GDPR Proposal subjected several of the specific accountability tools to a threshold of 250 employees so as to protect SMEs. The Albrecht Report modified some of the SME exemptions in order to increase the reach of the GDPR. In particular, reference to the threshold of 250 employees was replaced by a criterion based on the number of data subjects involved in the processing activities, and as soon as data from 500 data subjects were processed per year, the exceptions would not apply. According to the Report, the rationale of this change was to cover areas like cloud computing where small companies 'can process large amounts of data through online services'.[95] The end result is that SMEs are subject to the GDPR, but with exemptions from certain requirements.[96]

3. Chapter III: Rights of the Data Subject (Articles 12–23)

The GDPR Proposal was generally aimed at strengthening individuals' pre-existing rights and protections under the DPD (i.e. notice obligation, rights of access, rectification and erasure, the right to object and the right not to be subject to automated decision-making,

---

[93] Council Report 2015A. For details on the final versions of these provisions, see the commentaries on Arts. 4(14) and 9 in this volume.

[94] For more details on the treatment of data on criminal convictions, see the commentary on Art. 10 in this volume.

[95] See EP Draft Report LIBE 2012, amendment 223.

[96] E.g. most companies with fewer than 250 employees do not need to keep records of their processing activities (Art. 30(5) GDPR).

including profiling), but also included a number of new rights (restriction of processing and data portability). The aim of strengthening rights was also set out in a new clause proposed by the Parliament, Article 10(a), which did not make it into the GDPR.[97]

Another basic aim of the GDPR Proposal was to increase the transparency of data processing, and to this end the Proposal imposed stricter informational and transparency obligations on controllers than under the DPD. Some of these requirements were phrased in broad terms (e.g. Article 11, mandating that controllers have 'transparent and easily accessible policies with regard to the processing of personal data and for the exercise of data subjects' rights'), and others in quite detailed form (e.g. the procedures for allowing individuals to exercise their rights in Article 12 and the list of the types of information that controllers must provide to data subjects in Article 14).

The Albrecht Report shared these aims, though it tended to reinforce existing rights and tried also to simplify the legal framework for individuals by merging some of them (e.g. combining information and documentation requirements). It broadened the right of access under Article 15 to include new elements such as the right to obtain information regarding profiling in clear and plain language, and the right to obtain confirmation as to whether public authorities have requested personal data, together with information about whether or not the relevant authority had complied with such request and an overview of the disclosed data.[98]

3.1 Processing not requiring identification (Article 11)

Article 10 of the GPDR Proposal introduced some flexibility for controllers in situations where they are not in a position to identify the data subject. In such situations, a controller was not obliged to acquire additional information in order to identify the individual for the sole purpose of complying with the Regulation.

The Council's General Approach provided that, in the situation where the purposes for which a controller processes personal data do not or no longer require the identification of an individual, the controller will not be obliged to maintain, acquire or process additional information in order to identify the individual for the sole purpose of complying with the Regulation (Article 10(1)). Additionally, the right to restriction of processing, the notification obligation regarding rectification, erasure or restriction, and the right to data portability would not apply, unless the individual provides additional information enabling his or her identification for exercising his or her rights (Article 10(2)). Controllers were thus not obliged to engage in new or additional data processing to comply with individuals' rights. However, controllers could not refuse to accept additional information provided by an individual in order to support the exercise of his or her rights. In addition, the controller bore the burden of proof under Article 12(1a) to demonstrate that it was not in a position to identify the individual concerned.[99]

3.2 Notice obligations and privacy policies (Articles 12–14)

Article 11 of the GDPR Proposal contained stricter requirements for controllers' privacy policies compared to the DPD, requiring these policies to be transparent and easily accessible. The Albrecht Report strengthened notice obligations on controllers in a number

---

[97] EP Resolution GDPR 2014.   [98] EP Draft Report LIBE 2012.
[99] Council Report 2015A. For details on the final version of Art. 11, see the commentary on Art. 11 in this volume.

of circumstances. Joint controllers would also be subject to increased notice obligations as they would have to describe the allocation of roles and responsibilities among them. However, the Report encouraged the use of multilayered privacy notices together with the use of symbols.[100]

Article 13a of the LIBE Committee's compromise text required controllers to complement privacy policies with icons that would describe in a graphical way a number of elements, such as how personal data are collected, retained and shared with third parties, and how encryption is used. In addition, the compromise text stipulated that privacy policies should be as clear and transparent as possible, and should not contain hidden or disadvantageous clauses (recital 32).[101]

The Council's General Approach referred to the possibility to use visualisation (recital 46), but generally remained closer to the Commission's text and required many more elements to be included in a privacy policy than under the DPD, such as references to legitimate interest where relevant, data transfers, the right to withdraw consent and the right to data portability (Article 14).[102]

Articles 12–14 GDPR require the controller to provide the individual with information describing the purpose of the data collection in a concise, transparent, intelligible and easily accessible form, using clear and plain language. The Parliament's suggestion to include the use of standardised icons to enhance transparency is included in Article 12(7) GDPR, but is to be further specified by the Commission via a delegated act under Article 12(8).[103]

3.3 Data portability (Article 20)

Article 18(1) of the GDPR Proposal further strengthened individuals' control over their personal data by creating a new 'right to data portability'. This right was designed to allow individuals to change online services more easily by giving them the right to obtain a copy of their data from their service provider in an electronic and structured format which is commonly used. Article 18(2) added the right to export their data from one controller to another, without hindrance from the first controller. In contrast, the Albrecht Report considered the right to data portability as a 'mere specification' of the right of access and merged it into a new Article 15(2a).[104]

The Council's General Approach narrowed the right to receive personal data which the individual had provided to the controller, so that it applied where the data processing is based on consent or the performance of a contract and carried out by automated means (Article 18(2)(a)–(b)). However, controllers were required to make the data available in a machine-readable format that allows the individual to transfer the data to another controller (Article 18(2) and recital 55).[105]

3.4 The right to erasure ('right to be forgotten') (Article 17)

Article 17 of the GDPR Proposal provided for the 'right to be forgotten and to erasure'. The provision had been amended during the interservice consultation to limit it somewhat.

---

[100] EP Draft Report LIBE 2012.   [101] EP Resolution GDPR 2014.   [102] Council Report 2015A.
[103] For more information regarding the transparency obligations of the GDPR, see the commentaries on Arts. 12–14 in this volume.
[104] EP Draft Report LIBE 2012.
[105] Council Report 2015A. For details on the final version of data portability in the GDPR, see the commentary on Art. 20 in this volume.

In particular, in the original version, controllers who made data public had a duty to ensure the erasure of any internet link to or copy of the data.[106] This duty was subsequently limited to informing third parties processing the data that the data subject requested that the data be erased (Article 17(2)), and such duty was limited to what is possible and does not involve a disproportionate effort (Article 13). Article 17(3) provided for a number of situations in which the right to be forgotten does not apply, namely when the processing of personal data is necessary for exercising the right of freedom of expression, reasons of public interest in the area of public health and for historical, statistical and scientific research purposes.

The Albrecht Report viewed the right to be forgotten as an extension of the right to erasure and rectification. The Report restricted the scope of the right by providing that it was 'neither legitimate or realistic' in situations where the individual has agreed to make his/her personal data public.[107] Therefore, if the initial publication of the data by the controller was conducted with the data subject's consent or based on another lawful legal basis, the controller would no longer have to take reasonable steps to contact third parties and request them to erase copies of data. However, in cases where data are transferred or published without a proper legal basis, the original controller would be obliged to inform such third parties and ensure the erasure of the data. The Report maintained freedom of expression as a potential exception to the right to be forgotten, underlying the importance of balancing these two rights against each other for 'any measures for erasure of published personal data'.[108]

Following criticism that the name 'right to be forgotten' was a misnomer, Article 17 of the LIBE Committee's compromise text renamed the provision and merged it with the right to erasure. In addition, individuals could request third parties to erase any links to or copies of data or otherwise request restriction of the processing based on a court order or if the particular type of storage technology no longer allowed for erasure.[109]

The Council's General Approach followed a similar approach to the Parliament's text, and required controllers under Article 17 to erase personal data without undue delay where: (1) the data are no longer necessary in relation to the purposes for which they were collected or otherwise processed; (2) individuals withdraw their consent to the processing; (3) individuals object to the processing; (4) the data were unlawfully processed; or (5) a law requires the controller to erase the data. The Council added compliance with a legal obligation, archiving purposes and the establishment, exercise or defence of legal claims to the situations in which the right to be forgotten does not apply. Concerning data made public by the controller, the Council provided that the controller should take reasonable steps to notify the request for erasure to the controller who received the data (Article 17(2)(a) and recital 54). As the Council's text did not offer any substantial deviation from the Parliament's approach, it was adopted in Article 17 GDPR.[110]

3.5 The right to object (Article 21)

The DPD already provided for a general right to object, but it was weakened by the wide latitude that Member States had in implementing it. Article 19 of the GDPR Proposal thus

---

[106] GDPR Interservice Draft. [107] EP Draft Report LIBE 2012, p. 212.
[108] Ibid., amendment 148. [109] EP Resolution GDPR 2014.
[110] Council Report 2015A. For more information on the right to be forgotten, see the commentary on Art. 17 in this volume.

contained enhancements to the right. The Albrecht Report broadened and strengthened the right further, and also no longer allowed the continued processing of data in case of a compelling legitimate ground under Article 19(1).

3.6 Automated decision-making, including profiling (Article 22)

Profiling was not defined in the GDPR Proposal or the Council's General Approach. However, Parliament introduced a definition in Article 4(3a) which was the basis of the definition in Article 4(4) GDPR as 'any form of automated processing of personal data consisting of the use of personal data to evaluate certain personal aspects relating to a natural person, in particular to analyse or predict aspects concerning that natural person's performance at work, economic situation, health, personal preferences, interests, reliability, behaviour, location or movements'.

Article 20 of the GDPR Proposal regulated the use of 'profiling', and was based both on Article 15(1) DPD and on the Council of Europe Recommendation on profiling.[111] It provided that measures based solely on automated processing which produce legal effects or significantly affect individuals are only allowed in certain limited situations—e.g. with the individuals' consent or when profiling was explicitly permitted by legislation.

The Albrecht Report tightened the legal regime applicable to profiling, and stricter rules were applied. For example, profiling had to be 'necessary' for entering into or the performance of a contract, subject to certain restrictions (rather than merely carried out in the course of the contract), and profiling that involved sensitive data or children was prohibited.[112]

The LIBE Committee's compromise text similarly restricted profiling activities. However, the LIBE Committee's compromise text provided some flexibility in cases where profiling is based on pseudonymous data, which was presumed not to affect significantly the interests of the data subject, provided that it was impossible for the controller to attribute the data to a specific individual based on a single source of pseudonymous data or on aggregated pseudonymous data (recital 58a).[113] This flexibility allowed for some leeway concerning online data analytics (Article 20 and recital 58).

The Council's General Approach did not include Parliament's flexibility for profiling based on pseudonymous data. However, the Council text clarified the meaning of processing 'significantly affecting the interests, rights and freedoms of individuals' by giving a few examples: 'automatic refusal of an on-line credit application or e-recruiting practices without any human intervention' (recital 58). Whilst Parliament had simply prohibited profiling activity based on sensitive data, the Council text permitted it if individuals' explicit consent was obtained.[114]

3.7 Restrictions (Article 23)

Article 13 DPD provided that Member States could adopt 'legislative measures' to restrict the scope of the obligations and rights provided for in certain articles. The GDPR Proposal stated that data protection is not an absolute right, but must be considered in relation to its function in society, and must be balanced with other fundamental rights

---

[111] COM Recommendation 2010.
[112] EP Draft Report LIBE 2012, amendments 38, 158 and 160.
[113] EP Resolution GDPR 2014.
[114] Council Report 2015A. For details on the final implementation of rules concerning automated decision-making in the GDPR, see the commentary on Art. 22 in this volume.

(recital 139).[115] Under Article 21, a number of rights and obligations (including the rights of information, access, rectification, erasure, data portability and the right to object; protections against profiling; and the communication of a data breach to individuals) could be limited to safeguard certain public interests (such as public security, important economic or financial interests, various regulatory functions and others).[116] The final version of Article 23 GDPR applies to all the various obligations and rights which fall under the heading of 'Rights of the data subject' in Chapter III.

4. Chapter IV: Controller and Processor (Articles 24–43)

4.1 Accountability (Article 24)

One of the main novelties of the GDPR Proposal was a shift in regulatory focus from notifying data processing to DPAs to practical mechanisms inspired by the accountability principle and implemented by data protection officers ('DPOs'). Under the principle of accountability, controllers were obliged to implement appropriate and effective measures and to demonstrate the compliance of processing activities, including the effectiveness of the measures (Article 22 and recital 60 GDPR Proposal). In addition, the GDPR Proposal replaced the obligation to register data processing activities with national DPAs with the requirement to keep internal privacy documentation. Article 22(3) mandated that compliance measures be independently verified, though the use of 'independent internal or external auditors' was only required if 'proportionate'. An earlier provision requiring that data protection compliance be mentioned in annual corporate reports and other documents that companies are required to file by law was deleted following the interservice consultation.

The Albrecht Report welcomed the shift in regulatory focus in the GDPR Proposal. In consequence, obligations resulting from the accountability principle were maintained, reinforced and to some extent simplified.[117]

Article 22(1a) of the LIBE Committee's compromise text proposed to add a mandatory biannual review and update of compliance policies and procedures. This did not make it into the GDPR.[118]

The Council's General Approach took a more lenient approach towards demonstrating compliance. For instance, its Article 22(b) provided that approved codes of conduct and certification mechanisms could be used.[119]

The principle of accountability enshrined in Article 24 GDPR is now one of the central pillars of the GDPR as well as being one of its most significant innovations. Instead of the specific obligation of notification to DPAs under the former DPD, the principle of accountability places responsibility firmly on the controller to take proactive action to ensure compliance and to be ready to demonstrate how it has done so. The GDPR does not define what is necessary to demonstrate compliance, but Article 24(3) notes that adherence to approved codes of conduct under Article 40 or approved certification mechanisms, as well as data protection seals and marks under Article 42(1) may be used as elements to demonstrate compliance.

---

[115] See Joined Cases C-29/09 and C-93/09, *Schecke and Eifert*. [116] See rec. 59 GDPR.
[117] EP Draft Report LIBE 2012. [118] EP Resolution GDPR 2014.
[119] Council Report 2015A. For details on the implementation of accountability into the GDPR, see the commentary on Art. 24 in this volume.

The GDPR accompanies the principle of accountability with a suite of practical tools for controllers to implement effective data protection. As well as codes of conduct and certification, the GDPR implements a number of other significant mechanisms such as the requirements of data protection by design and by default under Article 25, the keeping of records under Article 30, data protection impact assessments ('DPIA') under Article 35, the Data Protection Officer ('DPO') under Articles 37–39 and BCRs under Article 47.

4.2 Risk-based approach

One of the principal novelties of the Council's General Approach was that it emphasised a risk-based approach to data protection. At a high level, the risk-based approach consists in adjusting some of the data protection obligations to the risks presented by a data processing activity. For this assessment, the nature, scope, context and purpose of the processing, as well as the likelihood and severity of the risks for the rights and freedoms of individuals posed by the data processing activities are taken into account. This approach was applied to accountability under Article 22(1) and to other provisions such as those on data protection by design and by default (Article 23), appointment of a representative in the EU by a non-EU controller or processor (recital 63 and Article 25(2)(b)), documentation requirements (Article 28(4), DPOs (Article 37(2a)) and security requirements (Article 30). A two-level risk approach was used (i.e. 'risk' or 'high risk'). High risk was defined as a 'particular risk of prejudice to the rights and freedoms of individuals' (recital 60b). The obligations relevant for processing of high risk included: (1) when to conduct a data protection impact assessment (Article 33); (2) when to notify data breaches (Articles 31, 32); and (3) when to launch a prior consultation with DPAs (Article 34(2)).[120]

4.3 Data protection by design and by default (Article 25)

Article 23(1) of the GDPR Proposal required that data controllers implement 'appropriate technical and organisational measures and procedures in such a way that the processing will meet the requirements of this Regulation and ensure the protection of the rights of the data subject' ('data protection by design'). In addition, Article 23(2) required that measures be implemented 'by default' so that 'only those personal data are processed which are necessary for each specific purpose of the processing' ('data protection by default').

The Albrecht Report welcomed these two requirements in the GDPR Proposal as core innovations of the reform. As noted earlier in this chapter, the Report also provided for a new obligation on producers of data filing systems to comply with the requirements of data protection by design and by default.[121] This obligation did not make it into the final version of the GDPR, although the preamble to the Regulation provides that producers of applications, services and products that are based on the processing of personal data or process personal data to fulfil their task, 'should be encouraged to take into account the right to data protection when developing and designing such products, services and applications' (recital 78 GDPR). The final version of the GDPR otherwise contains fairly lengthy provisions on data protection by design and by default in Article 25.[122]

---

[120] Council Report 2015A.   [121] EP Draft Report LIBE 2012.
[122] See further the commentary on Art. 25 in this volume.

4.4 Joint controllers (Article 26)

Article 24 of the GDPR Proposal contained a provision dealing with joint data controllers which required them to determine their respective responsibilities by concluding an 'arrangement' allocating data protection responsibility between them. Article 25 obliged non-EU-based controllers processing the data of EU citizens related to the offering of goods or services to them or to the monitoring of their behaviour to appoint a representative established in an EU Member State, with some important exceptions as stated in Article 25(2).

The Albrecht Report reinforced the obligations applicable to joint controllers and required them to allocate clearly their roles and responsibilities among themselves by means of a 'written arrangement' and to describe such allocation in their privacy policies.[123] The LIBE Committee's compromise text replaced these requirements by requiring that such an arrangement should duly reflect the roles and relationships vis-à-vis individuals, and that its essence should be made available for individuals. Where the allocation of liability between joint controllers was unclear, the Albrecht Report had limited their joint liability to cases related to individuals exercising their rights, but the compromise text stated that they should be jointly and severally liable (Article 24).[124]

The Council's General Approach substantially adopted the Parliament's amendment, but added an obligation for joint controllers to determine how they would comply with the notice obligation. The Council also added that the arrangement should designate which of the joint controllers acts as single point of contact for data subjects to exercise their rights. If the data subject has been properly informed of which joint controller is responsible, the data subject should exercise his/her rights with that controller (Article 24). Absent such information, or if the arrangement is unfair to the data subject, he or she could exercise their rights against any of the data controllers. Another key aspect of the Council's text was that it removed the joint and several liability between joint controllers provided by the Parliament's text. Article 82(3) GDPR follows this approach.[125]

4.5 Processing and sub-processing (Article 28)

The responsibilities of data processors set forth in Article 26 of the GDPR Proposal were more extensive than those contained in Article 17 DPD. Under Article 26(4), processors that exceeded the data processing instructions given them by controllers would be subject to all the obligations of joint controllers contained in Article 24.

The Council's General Approach added a number of obligations on processors. In particular, the data processing agreement between the controller and the processor had to include an obligation for the processor to allow for and contribute to audits conducted by the controller, an obligation to inform the controller of a legal requirement that might impede it to comply with the controller's instructions and a commitment to respect the controller's conditions for enlisting sub-processors. Processors were also prohibited from outsourcing sub-processing to third parties except with the general or specific authorisation of the controller. If the controller gave a general authorisation, the processor had to inform the controller of its intent to use a sub-processor and the controller had to have

---

[123] Ibid. [124] EP Resolution GDPR 2014.
[125] Council Report 2015A. For more details on joint controllers, see the commentaries on Arts. 26 and 82 in this volume.

the opportunity to object to the sub-processing. In addition, the contract between the processor and the sub-processor had to include similar obligations as those between the controller and the processor. Finally, the initial processor had to remain liable to the controller for the performance of the sub-processor's obligations (Article 26). Article 26(2ab) of the Council's text allowed for the use of model contracts for data processing agreements, adopted either by the Commission using implementing acts under Article 26(2b) or by a DPA in accordance with the consistency mechanism under Article 26(2c). Article 28 paragraphs 6–8 GDPR follow this approach.[126]

4.6 Records of processing activities (Article 30)

The GDPR Proposal replaced the requirement to register data processing activities with the national DPA by a requirement to put in place internal documentation. It made both controllers and processors (except for individuals processing data without a commercial interest) responsible for keeping detailed documentation of all data processing operations, and this documentation had to be produced upon request to DPAs (Article 28). A late addition to the text in the interservice consultation exempted companies with fewer than 250 employees from this requirement (Article 28(4)).

The Albrecht Report regarded the documentation requirement and notice obligation as two sides of the same coin, and controllers were required to prepare only one set of documentation on their data processing activities that would allow them to comply with both the documentation and notice requirements and thus reduce administrative burdens.[127]

4.7 Security of processing (Article 32)

The GDPR Proposal contained a number of important provisions concerning data security. Article 30 imposed wide-ranging security obligations on both controllers and processors, the details of which were to be specified by the Commission.

Article 30(1a) of the Parliament's text added a number of elements for a security policy. These included the ability to ensure the integrity of the personal data is validated; the ability to ensure the ongoing confidentiality, integrity, availability and resilience of systems and services processing personal data; the ability to restore the availability and access to personal data in a timely manner in the event of a physical or technical incident; and a process for regularly testing, assessing and evaluating the effectiveness of security policies, procedures and plans put in place to ensure ongoing effectiveness.[128]

Article 30(1) of the Council's General Approach required controllers and processors to implement appropriate technical and organisational measures, such as pseudonymisation of personal data, so as to ensure a level of security appropriate to the security risks presented by the data processing. Such measures had to take into account the nature, scope, context and purposes of the processing as well as the likelihood and severity of the risk for the rights and freedoms of individuals.[129]

---

[126] Council Report 2015A. For more details on the obligations for processors, see the commentary on Art. 28 in this volume.

[127] EP Draft Report LIBE 2012, amendment 126, moving the content of Art. 28 on documentation requirements to Art. 14 on information rights. For more details on requirements relating to records of processing activities in the GDPR, see the commentary on Art. 30 in this volume.

[128] EP Resolution GDPR 2014.

[129] Council Report 2015A. For more details on data security, see the commentary on Art. 32 in this volume.

4.8 Data breach notification (Articles 33–34)

The GDPR Proposal introduced a general data breach notification requirement applicable horizontally to all types of data controllers. Article 4(9) defined a personal data breach as 'a breach of security leading to accidental or unlawful destruction, loss, alteration, unauthorised disclosure of, or access to, personal data transmitted, stored or otherwise processed'. Notification of a breach was to be given by a controller to its lead DPA under Article 31 and, 'when the personal data breach is likely to adversely affect the protection of the personal data or privacy of the data subject', to the data subjects concerned under Article 32. Notification to the data subject was to be made after notification to the DPA, and then 'without undue delay' (Article 32(1)). Notification to the data subject was not required if the controller had implemented 'appropriate technological protection measures' prior to the data breach (Article 32(3)). Article 31(2) of the Proposal also required processors to notify any data breach to controllers, irrespective of the risks the data breach entailed.

The Albrecht Report extended the deadline within which data breaches must be notified to the DPA from 24 hours to 72 hours, but DPAs were required to keep a public register of the types of breaches notified. Furthermore, to prevent notification fatigue, data subjects were only to be notified where a breach was likely to affect adversely the protection of their personal data, their privacy, their rights or their legitimate interests (e.g. in cases of identity theft or fraud, financial loss, physical harm, significant humiliation or damage to reputation).[130] The LIBE Committee's compromise text withdrew the 24 or 72 hour deadline to notify data breaches to DPAs contained respectively in the initial GDPR Proposal and in the Albrecht Report. Instead, controllers were required to notify 'without undue delay' (Article 31).[131]

The Council's General Approach provided for a 72-hour deadline after having become aware of a breach, where feasible, and notification to the affected individuals without undue delay. In line with its risk-based approach, the Council limited notification to both DPAs and individuals to breaches that are likely to result in a high risk for the rights and freedoms of individuals, such as discrimination, identity theft or fraud, financial loss, unauthorised reversal of pseudonymisation, damage to reputation, loss of confidentiality of data protected by professional secrecy, or any other significant economic or social disadvantage (Article 31). The Council also provided a number of exceptions for notification to individuals such as the use of encryption and the implementation of mitigating measures (Article 32(3)). This considerably reduced the number of instances where breach notification to individuals would be required.[132]

4.9 Data protection impact assessment and consultation of the DPA (Articles 35–36)

Article 33 of the GDPR Proposal required controllers and processors to carry out data protection impact assessments ('DPIAs') where processing operations presented specific risks. During the interservice consultation, recital 71 was added indicating that the requirement to conduct them should apply in particular 'to newly established large scale filing systems, which aim at processing a considerable amount of personal data at regional,

---

[130] EP Draft Report LIBE 2012.   [131] EP Resolution GDPR 2014.
[132] Council Report 2015A. For more details on data breach notifications, see the commentaries on Arts. 33–34 in this volume.

national or supranational level and which could affect a large number of data subjects'. In addition, provisions that would have required DPIAs in most routine situations under which employee data are processed were deleted during the interservice process. Prior authorisation of data processing by the DPA, or consultation with it, was required in some cases, as provided in Article 34.

The Albrecht Report welcomed DPIAs as another core innovation of the reform and increased the number of instances in which such an assessment was required (e.g. where personal data are made accessible to a large number of persons or where high volumes of personal data are processed or combined with other data). The Report suggested that the DPO be consulted where a DPIA indicates that processing operations involve high risks.[133] The Parliament added a requirement in Article 32a to perform first a risk analysis after which, in certain situations, controllers and processors would have to conduct a DPIA.[134]

The Council's General Approach did not maintain the risk analysis obligation but further developed the requirement to carry out a DPIA for processing that presents a high risk. However, it limited this obligation to controllers. In addition, the Council required a DPIA for profiling activities, the processing of sensitive data, biometric data and data relating to criminal convictions or offences. It proposed that DPAs establish a list of types of processing operations subject to the requirement for a DPIA (Article 33(2a)) and those for which no DPIA was required (Article 33(2b)). In the event the DPIA indicated that the risk of the processing was high, and the controller did not (or could not) take measures to mitigate the risk, the controller should consult a DPA prior to the processing (Article 34(2)), which would have to reply in writing within a maximum period of six weeks.[135]

The final overarching result is contained in Article 35(1) GDPR which requires controllers to carry out a DPIA in cases when their data processing activities are likely to result in a high risk for the rights and freedoms of individuals.[136]

4.10 Data Protection Officers (Articles 37–39)

The GDPR Proposal made the appointment of DPOs mandatory for all public authorities and for all companies with more than 250 permanent employees (Article 35(1)). A group of undertakings could appoint a single DPO for the group. Articles 35–37 regulated in detail the designation, role, position and tasks of DPOs, including requirements that they must exercise their duties in complete independence (Article 36(2)), and must be employed for at least two years (Article 35(7)). The threshold of 250 employees was derived from the Commission definition of SMEs,[137] but the duty to appoint a DPO was required also for companies with fewer than 250 employees if their core activities 'consist of processing operations which, by virtue of their nature, their scope and/or their purposes, require regular and systematic monitoring of data subjects' (Article 35(1)(c)).

---

[133] EP Draft Report LIBE 2012.   [134] EP Resolution GDPR 2014.
[135] Council Report 2015A. The text was unclear and contradictory, as Art. 34(2) required consulting the DPA when the processing would result in a high risk 'in the absence of measures' to be taken by the controller to mitigate the risk, while rec. 74 provided that the controller should consult the DPA when the processing would result in a high risk 'despite the envisaged safeguards, security measures and mechanisms' to mitigate the risk.
[136] For more details on DPIAs, see the commentaries on Arts. 35–36 in this volume.
[137] See rec. 11 GDPR Proposal.

The Albrecht Report strengthened the role of DPOs, inspired to a large extent by the German legal framework. One of the major changes concerned the criterion for the designation of a DPO. The Report provided that mandatory designation of a DPO was no longer based on the size of the enterprise (i.e. 250 employees or more), but rather on the magnitude and character of the data processing (i.e. a DPO would have to be appointed as soon as a controller or processor processes data about more than 500 individuals per year). The Report also required controllers with a core activity consisting in processing sensitive data or conducting profiling activities to appoint a DPO. The minimum period of appointment for DPOs was extended from two to four years, and DPOs would have to be direct subordinates of the head of the company's management. In addition, DPOs would be bound by strict confidentiality requirements and subject to an obligation to report suspected violations to DPAs.[138]

The LIBE Committee's compromise text required controllers to designate a DPO when the processing affected more than 5,000 individuals in a consecutive 12-month period (Article 35). A group of undertakings could appoint a main DPO for the group, as long as the DPO was easily accessible for each undertaking.[139]

The Council's General Approach abolished the mandatory requirement to appoint a DPO, made it optional and left it to the Member States to impose this obligation via national law (Article 35).[140]

4.11 Codes of conduct (Article 40)

The GDPR Proposal envisaged the possibility for associations and other bodies representing controllers or processors to draw up codes of conduct covering various data protection sectors, and allowed them to be submitted to DPAs, which could give an opinion as to whether they are 'in compliance with this Regulation' (Article 38(2)), and to the Commission, which could adopt implementing acts determining that codes 'have general validity' (Article 38(4)). A code of conduct was regarded as contributing to the proper application of the GDPR.

This option was taken over by the Council with some variations. The Council's General Approach included a possibility for DPAs to approve codes of conduct that do not relate to processing activities in several Member States (Article 38(2a)). However, codes of conduct relating to processing activities in several Member States should be submitted to the EDPB via the consistency mechanism (Article 38(2b)), and, in case of a positive EDPB opinion, to the Commission for approval. Accredited bodies had to monitor compliance with codes of conduct (Article 38a).

4.12 Certification, seals and marks (Article 42)

The GDPR Proposal encouraged the establishment of 'data protection certification mechanisms and of data protection seals and marks', and the Commission was given the power to recognise them (Article 39). These mechanisms are another novelty of the GDPR compared to the DPD.

The LIBE Committee's compromise text introduced the 'European Data Protection Seal', a standardised data protection mark to be issued by DPAs to certify a controller's or processor's compliance with the Regulation (recital 77 and Article 39). The seal would limit administrative liability to cases of intentional or negligent non-compliance (Article 79).

---

[138] EP Draft Report LIBE 2012.   [139] EP Resolution GDPR 2014.
[140] Council Report 2015A. For more details on DPOs, see the commentaries on Arts. 37–39 in this volume.

Further, like BCRs or standard contractual clauses, the seal would exempt controllers from having to obtain authorisation before transferring data to third countries or international organisations (Article 42).[141]

The Council's General Approach elaborated on these data protection certification mechanisms. Independent certification bodies were to certify controllers and monitor proper compliance with the certification. Certifications would be issued for a maximum period of three years with a possibility of renewal (Article 39(4)). Certification bodies had to be accredited by either the DPA or the National Accreditation Body (Article 39a). In the same way as for codes of conduct, the Council recognised certification, seals and marks as a valid mechanism for data transfers to third countries or international organisations (Article 39(1a)).[142]

5. Chapter V: Transfers of Personal Data to Third Countries or International Organisations (Articles 44–50)

The provisions of the GDPR Proposal concerning the transfer of personal data outside the EU received a great deal of attention during the legislative process. Article 40 of the Proposal abandoned the presumption under the DPD that personal data could not be transferred absent an 'adequate level of protection' in the recipient country, and instead set forth general principles that must be fulfilled for international data transfers. There were three categories of mechanisms that could legalise international data transfers: a Commission adequacy decision under Article 41; the use of 'appropriate safeguards' under Article 42, which included BCRs under Article 43; or the application of a derogation under Article 44. Articles 41(8) and 42(5) of the GDPR Proposal, together with recital 134, confirmed that despite the repeal of the DPD, existing Commission decisions (such as adequacy decisions, and those approving standard contractual clauses) and those of DPAs remained in force. This language was not in the interservice version.

5.1 Adequacy (Article 45)

The GDPR Proposal expanded the scope of Commission adequacy decisions by explicitly providing that they could cover not only an entire country, but also a territory within a third country, a processing sector or an international organisation (Article 41(1) and (3)). The Proposal also gave the Commission increased power to decide that a territory, processing sector or international organisation did not provide adequate protection, and to enforce such decision by prohibiting data transfers to it (Article 41(5)–(6)). Article 41(8) provided that adequacy decisions would remain in force until amended, replaced or repealed by the Commission.

The Albrecht Report rejected the option under the GDPR Proposal of recognising specific sectors in third countries as providing an adequate level of data protection. This option was rejected because it 'would increase legal uncertainty and undermine the Union's goal of a harmonised and coherent international data protection framework'. The criteria for assessing the adequacy of third countries were strengthened, and the Commission was given an obligation to monitor the effectiveness of its adequacy findings.[143]

---

[141] EP Draft Report LIBE 2012.
[142] Council Report 2015A. For more details on the certification mechanism, see the commentaries on Arts. 41–42 in this volume.
[143] EP Draft Report LIBE 2012, amendment 241.

Article 41(8) of the LIBE Committee's compromise text provided that Commission adequacy decisions would remain in force for five years after the Regulation went into effect, unless they were amended, replaced or repealed by the Commission, contrary to the Albrecht Report that provided for a two-year period regarding the same matter.[144]

The Council's General Approach added a number of criteria that the Commission had to take into account when assessing the level of protection of a country or sector, including the rules for onward transfers, the existence of effective and enforceable rights for individuals and the existence of an independent authority which is responsible for ensuring and enforcing compliance with data protection rules (Article 41(2)(a)–(b)). In addition, the Council text required that the Commission take into account the third country's general and sectoral law, including laws relating to public security, defence and national security, as well as public order and criminal law (recital 81).[145]

In October 2015, shortly before the compromise GDPR text was agreed, the CJEU handed down its judgment in *Schrems*, which invalidated the Safe Harbour adequacy decision. In consequence, recital 104 GDPR further refined the criteria that the Commission should consider when assessing the level of protection of a third country, territory or specified sector therein.[146]

Article 41(8) of the GDPR Proposal provided that the decisions on adequacy and standard contractual clauses adopted by the Commission under the DPD would remain in force until amended, replaced or repealed by the Commission. However, like the Albrecht Report, Article 42(5) of the LIBE Committee's compromise text contained a sunset clause for data transfer authorisations based on Article 26(2) DPD, meaning, for example, that authorisations for BCRs or standard contractual clauses would have to be reissued by DPAs within two years of the entry into force of the Regulation.[147]

Articles 41(4a) and 42(5b) of the Council's General Approach allowed for an easier transition from the existing DPD to the Regulation as concerns Commission adequacy decisions and authorisations for international data transfers, removing the sunset clauses introduced by Parliament for adequacy decisions under Article 25(6) DPD (five years) and data transfer authorisations based on Article 26(2) of the DPD (two years).[148] This approach was followed in Articles 45(9) and 46(5) GDPR, which should ensure continuity.

5.2 *Appropriate safeguards (Article 46)*

The GDPR Proposal also made international data transfers possible if 'appropriate safeguards' were in place (Article 42(2)), meaning one of the following mechanisms: BCRs; standard data protection clauses approved by the Commission; standard data protection clauses adopted by a DPA in accordance with the consistency mechanism; 'ad hoc' contractual clauses authorised by a DPA; or other appropriate safeguards 'not provided for in a legally binding instrument'. Of these, transfers based on ad hoc contractual clauses and those using other appropriate safeguards not provided for in a legally binding instrument required further authorisation by the DPA (Article 34(1)).

---

[144] EP Resolution GDPR 2014.   [145] Council Report 2015A.
[146] Case C-362/14, *Schrems*. For more details on GDPR adequacy requirements related to international data transfers, see the commentaries on Arts. 44–45 in this volume.
[147] EP Draft Report LIBE 2012; EP Resolution GDPR 2014.
[148] Council Report 2015A.

The Albrecht Report modified the general approach of the GDPR Proposal regarding international data transfers by way of appropriate safeguards, providing for a general prohibition of data transfers that applied unless adequate safeguards were implemented.[149]

Article 42(2)(b)–(c) of the Council's General Approach explicitly provided for the use of clauses adopted by the Commission, contrary to the Parliament's text that seemed to allow only clauses adopted through the consistency mechanism. In addition, Article 42(2)(d)–(e) introduced two new important grounds for international data transfers: adherence to a code of conduct or to a certification mechanism. Both mechanisms were required to consist of binding and enforceable commitments from the controller or processor in the third country to apply the appropriate safeguards and to include a third party beneficiary right for individuals or its equivalent.[150]

5.3 Binding corporate rules (BCRs) (Article 47)

Article 43 of the GDPR Proposal gave explicit legal recognition to BCRs for both controllers and processors. Use of BCRs was limited to companies in 'the same corporate group of undertakings' (recital 85). The requirements for BCRs contained in Article 43 were generally similar to those developed by the WP29. BCRs were to be approved by the DPAs using the consistency mechanism (Article 43(1)). Article 43(2) listed the type of provisions that should be, at a minimum, included in BCRs. The Commission also retained important powers to adopt delegated and implementing acts with regard to the format, procedures and requirements for approval of BCRs (Article 43(3)–(4)).

The Council's General Approach specified that the controller or the processor could adduce appropriate safeguards for data transfers, which included BCRs. This removed the concern that was created by the Parliament's amendments, which took away the reference to BCRs for processors from the Commission's text, but kept the reference to BCRs for controllers. In addition, Article 43(1)(a) of the Council's text referred to BCRs for a 'group of undertakings or group of enterprises engaged in a joint economic activity'. This new text also opened the door to BCRs for companies that were not part of the same group but engaged in a joint economic activity. Article 43(2)(l) of the Council's text included the obligation to report to the DPA any legal requirements that could conflict or affect the guarantees provided by the BCRs.[151]

5.4 Transfers or disclosures not authorised by Union law (Article 48)

A provision in the interservice version of the GDPR Proposal prohibited the transfer of personal data based on orders or requests from non-EU courts, tribunals, administrative authorities and other governmental entities, unless mutual legal assistance treaties or procedures under international agreements were followed, or unless the relevant DPA had approved the transfer. This prohibition was deleted in the final version of the GDPR Proposal.

Both the Albrecht Report and the LIBE Committee's compromise text provided for a specific legal regime regarding data transfers to non-EU public authorities that required controllers and processors to notify DPAs about requests to disclose personal data in response to a court or other legal order issued outside of the EU, and to obtain formal

---

[149] EP Draft Report LIBE 2012.
[150] Council Report 2015A. For more details on appropriate safeguards, see the commentary on Art. 46 in this volume.
[151] Council Report 2015A. For more details on BCRs, see the commentary on Art. 47 in this volume.

approval from DPAs before turning over, for law enforcement purposes, data originating in Europe (Article 43a). Driven by concern about the Snowden revelations, recital 82 of the Parliament's text also provided that 'any legislation which provides for extra-territorial access to personal data processed in the Union without authorisation under Union or Member State law should be considered as an indication of a lack of adequacy'.[152] This approach by Parliament was not included in the Council's General Approach.[153] The final version of Article 48 GDPR makes visible the compromise between the Parliament and the Council.[154]

5.5 Derogations for specific situations (Article 49)

The GDPR Proposal made the use of derogations to transfer personal data possible under Article 44 in the same limited number of circumstances as under Article 26 DPD, though their scope was changed somewhat in comparison with the DPD. Article 44(1)(a) introduced new restrictions on the use of consent to transfer personal data. A major change was introduced in Article 44(1)(h), which provided that 'a data transfer may, under limited circumstances, be justified on a legitimate interest of the controller or processor, but only after having assessed and documented the circumstances of that transfer operation'.[155]

The derogation from the prohibition on international data transfers for transfers based on the compelling legitimate interest of the controller was deleted from the Parliament's text. The Council's General Approach retained the derogation but added two conditions: (1) the transfers are not large scale or frequent; and (2) the controller's interests are not overridden by the interests or rights and freedom of individuals. The controller also needed to 'adduce suitable safeguards' to protect the personal data, taking into account the circumstances surrounding the data transfer, though the text does not specify how the 'suitable safeguards' should be adduced.[156] Article 49(1) GDPR follows this approach and adds the requirements to inform the DPA and the data subject about the transfer and the compelling legitimate interests that the controller pursues.

Article 44(5a) of the Council's General Approach also introduced a provision according to which Member States could invoke 'important reasons of public interest' to 'expressly set limits' to the transfer of certain types of data to a third country or international organisation that has not received an adequacy decision. If Member States enact such limits, they must notify them to the Commission.[157] This provision, which was finally adopted in Article 49(5) GDPR, seems out of place in Article 49.[158]

6. Chapter VI: Independent Supervisory Authorities (Articles 51–59)

6.1 Overview

Article 47 of the GDPR Proposal contained enhanced protections for the independence of DPAs, and provisions designed to ensure their effective functioning, which was important following the CJEU decisions in the cases *Commission v Germany, Commission v*

---

[152] EP Draft Report LIBE 2012; EP Resolution GDPR 2014. [153] Council Report 2015A.
[154] For more details on transfers or disclosures not authorised by Union law, see the commentary on Art. 48 in this volume.
[155] GDPR Proposal, explanatory memorandum, 12. [156] Council Report 2015A.
[157] For more details on transfers based on derogations, see the commentary on Art. 49 in this volume.
[158] For further discussion of this point, see the commentary on Art. 49 in this volume.

Austria and *Commission v Hungary*.[159] The DPAs had been hoping that specific standards for funding of their operations would be included, but the GDPR Proposal adopted a vague requirement that each Member State shall ensure that a DPA is provided with 'adequate human, technical and financial resources, premises and infrastructure necessary for the effective performance of its duties and powers' (Article 47(5)), without specifying a formula for determining the adequacy of such support. The duties and powers of DPAs were also harmonised at a high level of abstraction (Articles 52 and 53).

The Albrecht Report required Member States to comply with certain minimum requirements regarding the staffing and resourcing of DPAs, and welcomed their empowerment under the GDPR Proposal to impose strong fines on controllers violating EU data protection rules. Article 51 of the Report confirmed that each DPA had jurisdiction on the territory of its own Member State. Article 54a established a 'lead DPA' for controllers with operations in more than one Member State. The DPAs of the Member States where a controller had operations were supposed to work together under the so-called mutual assistance and cooperation procedures pursuant to Articles 55–56. Article 75(2) empowered individuals to bring suit against a controller or processor either before the courts of the Member State where the controller or processor has an establishment, or before those of the individual's habitual residence except in the case of suits against a public authority of a Member State. Generally speaking, the Albrecht Report gave more power to DPAs, either directly or through the EDPB, the role of which was also significantly increased.[160]

6.2 The one-stop-shop mechanism (Article 56)

The GDPR Proposal sought to advance the internal market by introducing a 'one-stop-shop' for controllers that are established in multiple EU Member States and creating a co-operation and consistency procedure between DPAs, the EDPB and the Commission. This was intended both to facilitate compliance with EU data protection law for multinational companies and to ensure a consistent approach to EU data protection law. Article 51(2) provided that controllers and processors doing business in multiple EU Member States would only be subject to the jurisdiction of the DPA of the Member State in which they had their main establishment (as defined in Article 4). To further the consistent application of the GDPR in the EU and to resolve disagreements between DPAs, Articles 57–58 created a consistency mechanism under the authority of the EDPB, together with special intervention powers for the Commission under Articles 59–60.

The Albrecht Report weakened the one-stop-shop approach by adding that the 'lead' authority would still need to cooperate with other DPAs. Each DPA was to be competent to supervise all data processing operations on the territory of its Member State or where the data of its residents were processed, and individuals were to be able to lodge a complaint before the DPA of their home jurisdiction. Under the Albrecht Report, the lead DPA would only serve as a single contact point to ensure cooperation among DPAs for cross-border issues (i.e. when a controller or processor was established in more than one Member State or where personal data of the residents in several Member States are

---

[159] Case C-518/07, *Commission v Germany*; Case C-614/10, *Commission v Austria*; Case C-288/12, *Commission v Hungary*. Further on these decisions, see the commentaries on Arts. 4(21) and 51–52 in this volume.

[160] EP Draft Report LIBE 2012. For more details on supervisory authorities, see the commentaries on Arts. 4(21), 51–59 and 69 in this volume.

processed). In other words, instead of having a single DPA competent for data protection law throughout the EU, the lead DPA would in effect become a central contact point for controllers, but they would still have to deal indirectly with other DPAs. In situations where there was a disagreement over which DPA is the lead DPA, the EDPB had to be notified of such disagreement and could ultimately adopt a binding opinion determining the lead DPA (Article 58a(7)).[161]

The LIBE Committee's compromise text further amended the one-stop-shop mechanism. In contrast to the Albrecht Report, that considered the lead DPA to be a mere contact and coordination point, and to the GDPR Proposal, that provided for a comprehensive one-stop-shop approach, the compromise text took an intermediary position and created a system where the lead DPA would be the sole authority empowered to take legal decisions with regard to a controller, but would have complex cooperation obligations with other relevant DPAs (Article 54a). Furthermore, individuals could lodge a complaint before the DPA of their home jurisdiction, and the lead DPA would be required to coordinate its work with that DPA.[162]

The Council's General Approach followed an approach similar to the Parliament, but weakened the one-stop-shop mechanism by, among other things, giving the DPAs of all Member States concerned the right to intervene in the decision-making process and by opening the door to complaints, investigations and litigation in every Member State.[163] The 'one-stop-shop' survived the trilogue negotiations, but the end result is quite different from how the Commission had originally conceived the concept.[164]

7. Chapter VII: Cooperation and Consistency (Articles 60–76)

The GDPR Proposal contained several provisions designed to oblige DPAs to cooperate more closely, including a duty for DPAs to take action on request of another DPA within one month (Article 55(2)), and a provision empowering DPAs to conduct joint enforcement actions (Article 56). It also provided that when, in certain circumstances, a DPA did not act within one month of being requested to by other DPAs, those other DPAs could take provisional enforcement or compliance actions in the Member State of the first DPA (Articles 55(8) and 56(5)).

7.1 Consistency mechanism (Article 63)

A major innovation of the GDPR Proposal was the creation of a 'consistency mechanism', designed to ensure that the DPAs take a more consistent line on data protection issues of common interest. This involved a DPA communicating certain enforcement and compliance measures it intended to take in advance to the Commission and the EDPB. The Board was then supposed to vote by a simple majority on the measure, and the DPA was to 'take account' of the opinion of the Board and communicate to it within two weeks whether it would take the measure or not (Article 58). The Commission was also supposed to adopt an opinion in relation to such measures, of which the DPAs were to take the 'utmost account' (Article 59). The Commission gained substantial powers to force the DPAs to take a more harmonised approach: under Article 58(4), it could request that any matter be dealt with via the consistency mechanism; and under Article 60(1), it could

---

[161] EP Draft Report LIBE 2012.   [162] EP Resolution GDPR 2014.
[163] Council Report 2015A.
[164] For details on the one-stop-shop, see the commentaries on Arts. 56 and 60–62 in this volume.

also adopt a reasoned decision requiring a DPA to suspend the adoption of a measure when it had 'serious doubts as to whether the draft measure would ensure the correct application of the Regulation or would otherwise result in its inconsistent application'. Article 63(2) provided that DPA decisions and measures were made enforceable in all Member States, except when the DPA did not notify them to the Commission and the Board under the consistency mechanism.

The Albrecht Report heavily modified the consistency mechanism. The Report created an alternative consistency mechanism based on the lead DPA principle that turned the EDPB into an appellate body that could take legally binding decisions in case of disagreement between DPAs about a matter or on the determination of the lead DPA. The Report required the lead DPA to ensure coordination among the various DPAs involved and to consult with them before adopting a measure. If a DPA disagreed with the draft measure proposed by the lead DPA, the EDPB would have the right to intervene and to issue an opinion. If the lead DPA did not intend to follow this opinion, it would be required to provide a reasoned opinion to the EDPB. The EDPB could then adopt a final decision, by a qualified majority, which would be legally binding upon the lead DPA. This decision could be subject to judicial review and be suspended or challenged by the Commission or before the CJEU.[165]

The LIBE Committee's compromise text further developed the approach taken in the Albrecht Report, where the EDPB would act as an appeal mechanism in case of disagreement between DPAs, and could take decisions that would be legally binding upon DPAs. The compromise text created a system where 'matters of general application' (e.g. adoption of standard contractual clauses and approval of BCRs) and 'individual cases' (i.e. measures adopted by the lead DPA where the one-stop-shop was triggered) were treated differently. While matters of general application would trigger an opinion of the EDPB taken by a simple majority, all measures to be adopted by the lead DPA would be subject to a complex two-step process, including veto rights of other DPAs. In the latter respect, if other DPAs had serious objections to a draft measure submitted by the lead DPA, the measure could not be adopted, but would be submitted to the EDPB, the opinion of which was supposed to be given the 'utmost account' by the lead DPA. If the lead DPA did not follow the opinion of the EDPB, the EDPB could adopt a measure by a two-thirds majority that would be binding upon the DPAs involved (Articles 57–58a).

Like the Parliament, the Council's General Approach proposed amendments to turn the EDPB into an appellate body that could take legally binding decisions in case of disagreement between DPAs about a matter or on the determination of the lead DPA (Article 57(3)). According to the Council, the EDPB could take binding decisions in three cases: (1) if there was disagreement between DPAs with regard to a draft decision (e.g. a local DPA objected to a draft decision of the lead DPA); (2) if there was disagreement between DPAs over what DPA is competent for the main establishment; and (3) if a DPA did not request an opinion of the EDPB while this was required by the Regulation, or when a DPA did not follow an EDPB opinion. Moreover, the EDPB could issue non-binding opinions in a variety of matters concerning DPIAs, codes of conduct, certification, standard contractual clauses, ad hoc contracts or BCRs (Article 57(2)). Furthermore, any DPA, the Chair of the EDPB or the Commission could request that any matter of general application or producing effects in more than one Member State be examined

---

[165] EP Draft Report LIBE 2012.

by the EDPB with a view to obtaining an opinion, in particular where a DPA does not comply with the obligations for mutual or joint operations (Article 57(4)).[166]

7.2 The EDPB (Articles 68–76)

The GDPR Proposal renamed the WP29 as the 'European Data Protection Board', and its functioning was set out in more detail than in the DPD. The secretariat of the Board was moved from the Commission to the EDPS (Article 71), though the Commission remained an observer (Article 64(4)). The Board was to be independent (Article 65), and its tasks (Article 66) and decision-making procedures (to be taken by a simple majority of members: Article 68(1)) were also set forth. Article 69(1) provided that one deputy chairperson should be the EDPS.

Parliament and the Council agreed that the Board should have legal personality and that the EDPS should not automatically be one of the two deputy chairpersons (Article 69(1)). However a number of other proposals were not retained: Article 64(4) of the Council's General Approach had provided that the EDPS should not have a voting right in the Board; Article 69(2a) of the Parliament's text had proposed that the position of the Chair of the Board should be full-time; and Article 71(1) of the Council's text had provided that the EDPB Secretariat should be provided by the secretariat of the EDPS.[167]

8. Chapter VIII: Remedies, Liability and Penalties (Articles 77–84)

An important change from the DPD is that the GDPR Proposal harmonised data protection enforcement in the EU. There had been frequent complaints during the life of the DPD that supervisory authorities lacked uniform enforcement powers and sufficient mechanisms to sanction data protection violations. Article 73 of the GDPR Proposal addressed these complaints. Paragraph 1 of that Article provided that an individual in any Member State could lodge a complaint with any DPA, not just the one where they reside. The Proposal also gave organisations and associations the right to bring representative claims before the DPAs, both on behalf of individuals (paragraph 2) and on their own behalf (paragraph 3). Article 74 of the Proposal provided both natural and legal persons with the right to launch a judicial action against DPAs (paragraph 1). Elements of Article 74 which were not retained included the possibility for an individual to request a DPA to bring suit against another DPA (paragraph 4) and the obligation on Member States to enforce final court decisions against DPAs (paragraph 5) or against a data controller or processor (Article 75(4)) in any Member State, just as they were with regard to decisions of DPAs (Article 63(1)).

The Albrecht Report further strengthened the possibilities for individuals and associations to seek effective redress. For example, the right to lodge a complaint before DPAs, to go before the courts, and to seek redress for non-pecuniary loss would be extended to any associations acting in the public interest, not just associations specialised in data protection.[168]

---

[166] Council Report 2015A. For more details on the consistency mechanism, see the commentary on Art. 63 in this volume.
[167] EP Resolution GDPR 2014. Council Report 2015A. For more details on the EDPB, see the commentaries on Arts. 68–76 in this volume.
[168] EP Draft Report LIBE 2012.

The amount of administrative sanctions was left to implementation by the Member States under Article 24 DPD, with the result that they varied widely. Article 79 of the GDPR Proposal determined and greatly increased the sanctions that could be imposed on data controllers over what was previously possible. Article 79(2) provided that fines were to be imposed mandatorily for any intentional or negligent violation of certain provisions of the GDPR Proposal, and provided that the amount of fines imposed depended on various criteria, including the severity and duration of the breach, the intentional or negligent character of the violation, any mitigation measures, the categories of personal data affected, the degree of cooperation with DPAs and previous violations by the same controller or processor. Fines were divided under Article 79 paras. 4–6 into three categories, ranging from up to € 250,000 or 0.5 per cent, € 500,000 or 1 per cent, or € 1 million or 2 per cent of a company's annual worldwide turnover (i.e. its worldwide revenues) respectively (whichever was greater). The text gave no discretion to DPAs, which only had the power under Article 79(3) to abstain from a fine in cases of a first and non-intentional violation committed by a natural person processing data without a commercial interest, or by an organisation with fewer than 250 employees that processed personal data 'only as an activity ancillary to its main activities'.

The Albrecht Report largely followed the sanctions regime under the GDPR Proposal. The tiered fine system was retained, but the Report provided that the highest level of fine applied when the violation was not explicitly mentioned in one of the lower categories of fines. Consequently, this increased the number of instances in which the highest level of fines would apply. Nevertheless, the Report introduced some proportionality and flexibility regarding the actual level of sanctions. In particular, DPAs and the EDPB would have more flexibility to determine the amount of the applicable fine by taking into account various criteria in their assessment. Such criteria included an assessment of whether accountability measures were implemented, and whether the company actively cooperated with DPAs to remedy the infringement and mitigate possible adverse effects.[169]

The LIBE Committee's compromise text significantly increased fines compared to the GDPR Proposal and the Albrecht Report (i.e. fines of up to € 1 million or up to 2 per cent of a company's annual worldwide turnover), which could now amount to € 100 million or up to 5 per cent of a company's annual worldwide turnover, whichever was greater (Article 79).[170] The Council's General Approach returned to the maximum fine provided in the GDPR Proposal (i.e. fines of up to € 1 million or up to 2 per cent of a company's annual worldwide turnover) (Article 79a(3)).[171] The final compromise contained in Article 83 GDPR is that fines can extend to € 20 million or 4 per cent of global annual turnover. It is accordingly fair to say that the Parliament won this particular battle.[172]

9. Chapter IX: Provisions Relating to Specific Processing Situations (Articles 85–91)

The GDPR Proposal contained articles dealing with a number of specific data processing situations where Member States were required to take action. Article 80 required Member

---

[169] Ibid.   [170] EP Resolution GDPR 2014.   [171] Council Report 2015A.
[172] For more details on remedies, liability and sanctions, see the commentaries on Arts. 77–84 in this volume.

States to provide exemptions or derogations for the processing of personal data for journalistic purposes or for artistic and literary expression, and was an elaboration of Article 9 DPD. The definition of 'journalistic activities' as explained in recital 121 reflected the broad interpretation of that term by the CJEU in *Satamedia*.[173] Articles 81–82 encouraged Member States to enact legislation covering the subjects of data processing for health purposes and data processing in the employment context respectively. Article 83 contained rules for historical, statistical and scientific research. Article 84 contained enhanced obligations of secrecy for investigations by DPAs of controllers or processors who were themselves subject to obligations of professional secrecy (such as doctors and lawyers). Article 85, added during the interservice procedure, provided that data processing rules used by churches and religious associations could continue to be used, provided they were brought into line with the GDPR Proposal.

Limited amendments in the Albrecht Report gave leeway to Member States to regulate the employment sector.[174] However the LIBE Committee's compromise text added specific restrictions that had to be respected in all Member States. These included limitations on profiling performed on employees, the exclusion of consent as a legal basis for the processing if it was not freely given and a number of minimum standards such as: prohibiting any data processing without employees' knowledge; respecting a number of requirements before collecting employee data based on suspicion of 'crime or serious dereliction of duty' (including having concrete suspicion, respecting proportionality and defining data deletion periods); prohibiting the use of covert CCTV measures at all times, and limiting the use of open CCTV measures so that they would not be used in areas such as bathrooms, changing rooms etc.; setting out rules for the processing of medical examinations and aptitude tests by the employer, including prohibiting the use of employee data for the purpose of genetic testing and analyses; regulating the monitoring of IT systems (such as telephone, email and internet) at the workplace; where the private use of IT systems was allowed, limiting the monitoring of IT traffic data solely for security, operational and billing purposes (unless there was a concrete suspicion of illegal activity in the employment context); and prohibiting the use of employees' sensitive data for blacklisting employees. In addition, the LIBE Committee's compromise text aimed to facilitate the transmission of employee data within a group of undertakings and to service providers providing legal and tax advice, but clarified that the GDPR's data transfer restrictions would continue to apply for the transfer of employee data to third countries (Article 82).[175]

10. Chapter X: Delegated Acts and Implementing Acts (Articles 92–93)

The GDPR Proposal provided that the Commission could determine certain technical details via secondary legislation, either delegated acts (Article 290 TFEU) or implementing acts (Article 291 TFEU). It contained 26 instances in which the Commission had the power to adopt delegated acts and 22 instances where it had the power to adopt implementing acts.[176]

---

[173] Case C-73/07, *Satamedia*.   [174] EP Draft Report LIBE 2012.
[175] EP Resolution GDPR 2014. For more details on specific data processing situations, see the commentaries on Art. 85–91 in this volume.
[176] See Council Report 2015B.

Delegated and implementing acts may take the form of a regulation, a directive or a decision,[177] though they are adopted under specific procedures that differ from the co-decision procedure for the normal legislative instruments. Delegated acts are designed to supplement or amend non-essential elements of EU legislative acts,[178] while implementing acts are designed simply to implement them.[179] The distinction is important, since the procedures for review and scrutiny of these two types of acts differ substantially: under the procedure laid down in Article 86 of the Proposal, Parliament and the Council would exercise extensive scrutiny over delegated acts, including the right to reject the Commission's proposed measure in certain cases,[180] whereas the adoption of implementing acts is subject to a complex series of committee procedures laid down in a separate EU regulation[181] and is largely under the control of the Commission, with input from the Council (but not the Parliament).[182]

In most cases, implementing acts, the legal basis for which was specified in Article 62 of the GDPR Proposal, were to be adopted under the so-called 'examination procedure' under Article 87 of the Proposal, whereas in a few cases of particular urgency (such as under Article 41(5)) an expedited procedure could be used under Article 87(3). In adopting implementing acts, the Commission was to be assisted by a committee comprised of Member State representatives, which would in effect play the role that the Article 31 Committee played under the DPD. The legality of both delegated and implementing acts is subject to review by the CJEU.[183]

Article 62(1)(a) of the GDPR Proposal also gave the Commission the power to issue as many additional implementing acts as it felt necessary in order to decide:

> on the correct application of this Regulation in accordance with its objectives and requirements in relation to matters communicated by supervisory authorities pursuant to Article 58 or 61, concerning a matter in relation to which a reasoned decision has been adopted pursuant to Article 60(1), or concerning a matter in relation to which a supervisory authority does not submit a draft measure and that supervisory authority has indicated that it does not intend to follow the opinion of the Commission adopted pursuant to Article 59.

The Albrecht Report considerably reduced the number of Commission delegated and implementing acts, and the GDPR itself only retains two delegated acts and 11 implementing acts. Most of the provisions that the Commission initially proposed to regulate via secondary legislation are now either incorporated into the GDPR or left to be set out by the EDPB or codes of conduct.[184] Since the Commission is subject to more scrutiny with regard to delegated acts than implementing acts, Parliament asked for certain important issues to be worked out via delegated acts but finally accepted that some issues (e.g. adequacy decisions, procedures around BCRs and codes of conduct) could be handled via implementing acts. Nevertheless, the use of icons in privacy notices will be worked out by delegated acts.

The Commission is now expected to start preparing this secondary legislation. In this respect, the 'Legislative Financial Statement' attached to the GDPR Proposal estimated

---

[177] Craig 2010, pp. 254–255.
[178] See Art. 290 TFEU.
[179] Ibid., Art. 291.
[180] Ibid., Art. 290(2).
[181] Regulation 182/2011.
[182] Craig 2010, p. 275.
[183] See Art. 263 TFEU, referring to review of 'acts ... of the Commission'.
[184] EP Draft Report LIBE 2012.

that 'up to three implementing measures may be handled per year, while the process may take up to 24 months'.[185]

11. Chapter XI: Final Provisions (Articles 94–99)

The GDPR Proposal included standard final provisions on matters such as the repeal of the DPD, the relationship to the EPD, the evaluation report to be prepared by the Commission in due course, and the GDPR's entry into force and into application. Article 94 GDPR Proposal repealed the DPD and references to it were to be construed as references to the GDPR. Article 95, a provision incorporated in the Proposal following the interservice consultation, clarified the relationship between the GDPR Proposal and the EPD, stating in effect that the EPD (as the more specialised instrument) took precedence over the GDPR on points with which both of them deal—i.e. the GDPR Proposal did not impose extra obligations in areas already covered in the EPD (Article 89).[186]

Select Bibliography

CJEU case law

Case C-73/07, *Tietosuojavaltuutettu v Satakunnan Markkinapörssi Oy and Satamedia Oy*, judgment of 16 December 2009 (Grand Chamber) (ECLI:EU:C:2008:727).

Case C-518/07, *European Commission v Federal Republic of Germany*, judgment of 9 March 2010 (Grand Chamber) (ECLI:EU:C:2010:125).

Joined Cases C-29/09 and C-93/09, *Volker und Markus Schecke GbR* and *Hartmut Eifert v Land Hessen*, judgment of 9 November 2010 (Grand Chamber) (ECLI:EU:C:2010:662).

Joined Cases C-585/08 and C-144/09, *Peter Pammer v Reederei Karl Schlüter GmbH & Co. KG* and *Hotel Alpenhof GmbH v Oliver Heller*, judgment of 7 December 2010 (Grand Chamber) (ECLI:EU:C:2010:740).

Case C-70/10, *Scarlet Extended SA v Société belge des auteurs, compositeurs et éditeurs SCRL (SABAM)*, judgment of 24 November 2011 (EU:C:2011:771).

Case C-614/10, *European Commission v Republic of Austria*, judgment of 16 October 2012 (Grand Chamber) (ECLI:EU:C:2012:631).

Case C-131/12, *Google Spain SL v Agencia Española de Protección de Datos (AEPD) and Mario Costeja González*, judgment of 13 May 2014 (Grand Chamber) (ECLI:EU:C:2014:317).

Opinion of Advocate General Jääskinen in Case C-131/12, *Google Spain SL v Agencia Española de Protección de Datos (AEPD) and Mario Costeja González*, delivered on 25 June 2013 (ECLI:EU:C:2013:424).

Case C-288/12, *European Commission v Hungary*, judgment of 8 April 2014 (Grand Chamber) (ECLI:EU:C:2014:237).

Joined Cases C-293/12 and C-594/12, *Digital Rights Ireland Ltd v Minister for Communications, Marine and Natural Resources and Others* and *Kärntner Landesregierung, Michael Seitlinger, Christof Tschohl and Others*, judgment of 8 April 2014 (Grand Chamber) (ECLI:EU:C:2014:238).

Case C-362/14, *Maximillian Schrems v Data Protection Commissioner*, judgment of 6 October 2015 (Grand Chamber) (ECLI:EU:C:2015:650).

---

[185] GDPR Proposal, p. 114. For more details regarding delegated and implemented acts under the GDPR, see the commentary on Arts. 92–93 in this volume.

[186] On 10 January 2017 the Commission proposed the EPR to replace the EPD (see EPR Proposal). For more details on the final provisions of the GDPR, see the commentaries on Arts. 94–99 in this volume.

Case C-434/16, *Peter Nowak v Data Protection Commissioner*, judgment of 20 December 2017 (ECLI:EU:C:2017:994).

Case C-275/06, *Productores de Música de España (Promusicae) v Telefónica de España SAU*, judgment of 29 January 2008 (Grand Chamber) (ECLI:EU:C:2008:54).

Opinion of Advocate General Kokott in Case C-275/06, *Productores de Música de España (Promusicae) v Telefónica de España SAU*, delivered on 18 July 2007 (ECLI:EU:C:2008:54).

Case C-398/15, *Camera di Commercio, Industria, Artigianato e Agricoltura di Lecce v Salvatore Manni*, judgment of 9 March 2017 (ECLI:EU:C:2017:197).

Opinion of Advocate General Bot in Case C-398/15, *Camera di Commercio, Industria, Artigianato e Agricoltura di Lecce v Salvatore Manni*, delivered on 8 September 2016 (ECLI:EU:C:2016:652).

C-210/16, *Unabhängiges Landeszentrum für Datenschutz Schleswig-Holstein v Wirtschaftsakademie Schleswig-Holstein GmbH*, judgment of 5 June 2018 (Grand Chamber) (ECLI:EU:C:2018:388).

Opinion of Advocate General Bot in C-210/16, *Unabhängiges Landeszentrum für Datenschutz Schleswig-Holstein v Wirtschaftsakademie Schleswig-Holstein GmbH*, delivered on 24 October 2017 (ECLI:EU:C:2017:796).

Case C-673/17, *Planet49 GmbH v Bundesverband der Verbraucherzentralen und Verbraucherverbände – Verbraucherzentrale Bundesverband e.V.* (pending).

Opinion of Advocate General Szpunar in Case C-673/17, *Planet49 GmbH v Bundesverband der Verbraucherzentralen und Verbraucherverbände – Verbraucherzentrale Bundesverband e.V.*, delivered on 21 March 2019 (ECLI:EU:C:2019:246).

EU legislation

Consumer Rights Directive: Directive 2011/83/EU of the European Parliament and of the Council of 25 October 2011 on consumer rights, amending Council Directive 93/13/EEC and Directive 1999/44/EC of the European Parliament and of the Council and repealing Council Directive 85/577/EEC and Directive 97/7/EC of the European Parliament and of the Council, OJ 2011 L 304/64.

Council Framework Decision 2008/977/JHA: Council Framework Decision 2008/977/JHA of 27 November 2008 on the protection of personal data processed in the framework of police and judicial cooperation in criminal matters, OJ 2008 L 350/60.

EPR Proposal: Proposal for a Regulation of the European Parliament and of the Council concerning the respect for private life and the protection of personal data in electronic communications and repealing Directive 2002/58/EC (Regulation on Privacy and Electronic Communications), COM(2017)10 final, 10 January 2017.

EUDPR Proposal: Proposal for a Regulation of the European Parliament and of the Council on the protection of individuals with regard to the processing of personal data by the Union institutions, bodies, offices and agencies and on the free movement of such data, and repealing Regulation (EC) No. 45/2001 and Decision No. 1247/2002/EC, COM(2017) 8 final, 10 January 2017.

GDPR Proposal: Proposal for a Regulation of the European Parliament and of the Council on the protection of individuals with regard to the processing of personal data and on the free movement of such data (General Data Protection Regulation), COM(2012) 11 final, 25 January 2012.

LED Proposal: Proposal for a Directive of The European Parliament and of the Council on the protection of individuals with regard to the processing of personal data by competent authorities for the purposes of prevention, investigation, detection or prosecution of criminal offences or the execution of criminal penalties, and the free movement of such data, COM(2012) 10 final, 25 January 2012.

Regulation 182/2011: Regulation (EU) No. 182/2011 of the European Parliament and of the Council of 16 February 2011 laying down the rules and general principles concerning mechanisms for control by Member States of the Commission's exercise of implementing powers, OJ 2011 L 55/13.

Academic writings

Burton et al. 2013: Burton, Kuner and Pateraki, 'The Proposed EU Data Protection Regulation One Year Later: The Albrecht Report', *Bloomberg BNA Privacy and Security Law Report* (2013), 1.

Burton et al. 2014: Burton, Kuner and Pateraki, 'The Proposed EU Data Protection Regulation Two Years Later', *Bloomberg BNA Privacy and Security Law Report* (2014), 1.

Burton et al. 2015: Burton, de Boel, Kuner and Pateraki, 'The Proposed EU Data Protection Regulation Three Years Later: The Council Position', *Bloomberg BNA Privacy and Security Law Report* (2015), 1.

Burton et al. 2016: Burton, de Boel, Hoffman, Kuner and Pateraki, 'The Final European Union General Data Protection Regulation', *Bloomberg BNA Privacy and Security Law Report* (2016), 1.

Craig 2010: Craig, *The Lisbon Treaty* (OUP 2010).

Greenwald 2014: Greenwald, *No Place to Hide: Edward Snowden, the NSA, and the US Surveillance State* (MacMillan 2014).

Kuner 2012: Kuner, 'The European Commission's Proposed Data Protection Regulation: A Copernican Revolution in European Data Protection Law', *Bloomberg BNA Privacy and Security Law Report* (2012), 1.

Kuner 2019: Kuner, 'The Internet and the Global Reach of EU Law', in Cremona and Scott (eds.), *EU Law Beyond EU Borders: The Extraterritorial Reach of EU Law* (OUP 2019), 112.

Milanovic 2015: Milanovic, 'Human Rights Treaties and Foreign Surveillance: Privacy in the Digital Age', 56(1) *Harvard International Law Journal* (2015), 81.

Papers of data protection authorities

EDPS 2011: European Data Protection Supervisor, 'Opinion of the European Data Protection Supervisor on the Communication from the Commission to the European Parliament, the Council, the Economic and Social Committee and the Committee of the Regions—A Comprehensive Approach on Personal Data Protection in the European Union' (14 January 2011).

EDPS 2013: European Data Protection Supervisor, 'Additional EDPS Comments on the Data Protection Reform Package' (15 March 2013).

EDPS 2015: European Data Protection Supervisor: 'Opinion 2/2015 (with addendum) Europe's Big Opportunity—EDPS Recommendations on the EU's Options for Data Protection Reform (9 October 2015).

WP29 2009: Article 29 Working Party and Working Party on Police and Justice, 'The Future of Privacy: Joint Contribution to the Consultation of the European Commission on the Legal Framework for the Fundamental Right to Protection of Personal Data' (WP 168, 1 December 2009).

Reports and recommendations

COM Recommendation 2010: Committee of Ministers of the Council of Europe, 'Recommendation on the Protection of Individuals with Regard to Automatic Processing of Personal Data in the Context of Profiling' (Rec(2010)13, 23 November 2010).

Council Report 2012A: Proposal for a regulation of the European Parliament and of the Council on the protection of individuals with regard to the processing of personal data and on the free movement of such data (General Data Protection Regulation), 11326/12, 22 June 2012.

Council Report 2012B: Data protection package—Report on progress achieved under the Cyprus Presidency, 16525/12, 26 November 2012.

Council Report 2015A: Preparation of a general approach, 9565/15, 11 June 2015.

Council Report 2015B: Delegated and implementing acts, 8833/15, 13 May 2015.

Council Report 2015C: Preparation for trilogue, 14605/15, 27 November 2015.

EC Communication 2007: Communication from the Commission to the European Parliament and the Council on the follow-up of the Work Programme for better implementation of the Data Protection Directive, COM(2007) 87 final, 7 March 2007.

EC Communication 2010: Communication from the Commission to the European Parliament, the Council, the Economic and Social Committee and the Committee of Regions 'A Comprehensive Approach on Personal Data Protection in the European Union', COM(2010) 609 final, 4 November 2010.

EC Communication 2012: Communication from the Commission to the European Parliament, the Council, the European Economic and Social Committee and the Committee of the Regions, 'Safeguarding Privacy in a Connected World—A European Data Protection Framework for the 21st Century', COM(2012) 09 final, 25 January 2012.

EC Impact Assessment GDPR 2012: Commission Staff Working Paper, 'Impact Assessment', SEC(2012) 72 final, 25 January 2012.

EC Report DPD 2003: Report from the Commission—First report on the implementation of the Data Protection Directive (95/46/EC), COM(2003) 265 final, 15 May 2003.

EC Report 2012: Report from the Commission to the European Parliament, the Council, the European Economic and Social Committee and the Committee of the Regions based on Article 29(2) of the Council Framework Decision of 27 November 2008 on the protection of personal data processed in the framework of police and judicial cooperation in criminal matters (including annex), COM(2012) 12 final, 25 January 2012.

EC Staff Working Paper 2012: Commission Staff Working Paper, 'Executive Summary of the Impact Assessment', SEC(2012) 73 final, 25 January 2012.

EP Draft Report LIBE 2012: Draft report on the proposal for a regulation of the European Parliament and of the Council on the protection of individual with regard to the processing of personal data and on the free movement of such data (General Data Protection Regulation), 2012/0011 (COD), 17 December 2012.

EP Draft Report LIBE Erratum 2013: Erratum to the draft report on the proposal for a regulation of the European Parliament and of the Council on the protection of individual with regard to the processing of personal data and on the free movement of such data (General Data Protection Regulation), 2012/011(COD), 9 January 2013.

EP Resolution GDPR 2014: European Parliament legislative resolution of 12 March 2014 on the proposal for a regulation of the European Parliament and of the Council on the protection of individuals with regard to the processing of personal data and on the free movement of such data (General Data Protection Regulation), P7_TA(2014)0212, 12 March 2014.

GDPR Interservice Draft: Proposal for a Regulation of the European Parliament and of the Council on the protection of individuals with regard to the processing of personal data and on the free movement of such data (General Data Protection Regulation), Version 56, 29 November 2011.

Others

Albrecht Press Conference 2013: European Parliament, 'Jan Philipp Albrecht—LIBE rapporteur' (9 January 2013), available at http://www.europarl.europa.eu/ep-live/en/other-events/video?event=20130109-1000-SPECIAL-UNKN.

Council Press Release 2015A: Council, 'Data Protection: Council Agrees on a General Approach' (15 June 2015), available at https://www.consilium.europa.eu/en/press/press-releases/2015/06/15/jha-data-protection/.

Council Press Release 2015B: Council, 'EU Data Protection Reform: Council Confirms Agreement with the European Parliament' (18 December 2015), available at https://www.consilium.europa.eu/en/press/press-releases/2015/12/18/data-protection/.

EDPS Letter 2013: European Data Protection Supervisor, 'Letter to Mr. Juan Fernando López Aguilar' (25 March 2013), available at https://edps.europa.eu/sites/edp/files/publication/13-03-15_letter_lopez_aguilar_libe_en.pdf.

EDRi GDPR Document Pool: European Digital Rights, 'General Data Protection Regulation: Document Pool' (25 June 2015), available at https://edri.org/gdpr-document-pool/.

EP Website Legislative Powers: European Parliament, 'Legislative Powers', available at http://www.europarl.europa.eu/about-parliament/en/powers-and-procedures/legislative-powers.

EP Website Vote 12 March 2014: European Parliament, 'Results of Vote in Parliament—Statistics—2012/0011(COD)' (12 March 2014), available at https://oeil.secure.europarl.europa.eu/oeil/popups/sda.do?id=23714&l=en.

Lenaerts speech 2018: Lenaerts, 'The EU General Data Protection Regulation Five Months On', speech by CJEU President Koen Lenaerts at the 40th International Conference of Data Protection and Privacy Commissioners (25 October 2018), available at https://www.youtube.com/watch?v=fZaKPaGbXNg.

Masing 2012: Johannes Masing, 'Ein Abschied von den Grundrechten', *Süddeutsche Zeitung* (9 January 2012), 10.

Press Release Irish Presidency 2013: Irish Presidency, 'Minister for Justice, Equality and Defence Publishes Agenda for Justice and Home Affairs Informal' (11 January 2013), available at http://www.eu2013.ie/news/news-items/20130111jhaagenda/.

WP29 Press Release 2015: Article 29 Working Party, 'Press Release on Chapter II of the Draft Regulation for the March JHA Council' (17 March 2015), available at https://ec.europa.eu/justice/article-29/press-material/press-release/art29_press_material/2015/20150317__wp29_press_release_on_on_chapter_ii_of_the_draft_regulation_for_the_march_jha_council.pdf.

Chapter I General Provisions (Articles 1–4)

Article 1. Subject-matter and objectives

HIELKE HIJMANS[*]

1. This Regulation lays down rules relating to the protection of natural persons with regard to the processing of personal data and rules relating to the free movement of personal data.
2. This Regulation protects fundamental rights and freedoms of natural persons and in particular their right to the protection of personal data.
3. The free movement of personal data within the Union shall be neither restricted nor prohibited for reasons connected with the protection of natural persons with regard to the processing of personal data.

Relevant Recitals

(1) The protection of natural persons in relation to the processing of personal data is a fundamental right. Article 8(1) of the Charter of Fundamental Rights of the European Union (the 'Charter') and Article 16(1) of the Treaty on the Functioning of the European Union (TFEU) provide that everyone has the right to the protection of personal data concerning him or her.

(2) The principles of, and rules on the protection of natural persons with regard to the processing of their personal data should, whatever their nationality or residence, respect their fundamental rights and freedoms, in particular their right to the protection of personal data. This Regulation is intended to contribute to the accomplishment of an area of freedom, security and justice and of an economic union, to economic and social progress, to the strengthening and the convergence of the economies within the internal market, and to the well-being of natural persons.

(3) Directive 95/46/EC of the European Parliament and of the Council seeks to harmonise the protection of fundamental rights and freedoms of natural persons in respect of processing activities and to ensure the free flow of personal data between Member States.

(4) The processing of personal data should be designed to serve mankind. The right to the protection of personal data is not an absolute right; it must be considered in relation to its function in society and be balanced against other fundamental rights, in accordance with the principle of proportionality. This Regulation respects all fundamental rights and observes the freedoms and principles recognised in the Charter as enshrined in the Treaties, in particular the respect for private and family life, home and communications, the protection of personal data, freedom of thought, conscience and religion, freedom of expression and information, freedom to conduct a business, the right to an effective remedy and to a fair trial, and cultural, religious and linguistic diversity.

(5) The economic and social integration resulting from the functioning of the internal market has led to a substantial increase in cross-border flows of personal data. The exchange of personal data between public and private actors, including natural persons, associations and undertakings across the Union has increased. National authorities in the Member States are being called upon by Union

---

[*] The views expressed are solely those of the author and do not necessarily reflect those of the Belgian Data Protection Authority.

law to cooperate and exchange personal data so as to be able to perform their duties or carry out tasks on behalf of an authority in another Member State.

(6) Rapid technological developments and globalisation have brought new challenges for the protection of personal data. The scale of the collection and sharing of personal data has increased significantly. Technology allows both private companies and public authorities to make use of personal data on an unprecedented scale in order to pursue their activities. Natural persons increasingly make personal information available publicly and globally. Technology has transformed both the economy and social life, and should further facilitate the free flow of personal data within the Union and the transfer to third countries and international organisations, while ensuring a high level of the protection of personal data.

(7) Those developments require a strong and more coherent data protection framework in the Union, backed by strong enforcement, given the importance of creating the trust that will allow the digital economy to develop across the internal market. Natural persons should have control of their own personal data. Legal and practical certainty for natural persons, economic operators and public authorities should be enhanced.

(8) Where this Regulation provides for specifications or restrictions of its rules by Member State law, Member States may, as far as necessary for coherence and for making the national provisions comprehensible to the persons to whom they apply, incorporate elements of this Regulation into their national law.

(9) The objectives and principles of Directive 95/46/EC remain sound, but it has not prevented fragmentation in the implementation of data protection across the Union, legal uncertainty or a widespread public perception that there are significant risks to the protection of natural persons, in particular with regard to online activity. Differences in the level of protection of the rights and freedoms of natural persons, in particular the right to the protection of personal data, with regard to the processing of personal data in the Member States may prevent the free flow of personal data throughout the Union. Those differences may therefore constitute an obstacle to the pursuit of economic activities at the level of the Union, distort competition and impede authorities in the discharge of their responsibilities under Union law. Such a difference in levels of protection is due to the existence of differences in the implementation and application of Directive 95/46/EC.

(12) Article 16(2) TFEU mandates the European Parliament and the Council to lay down the rules relating to the protection of natural persons with regard to the processing of personal data and the rules relating to the free movement of personal data.

(170) Since the objective of this Regulation, namely to ensure an equivalent level of protection of natural persons and the free flow of personal data throughout the Union, cannot be sufficiently achieved by the Member States and can rather, by reason of the scale or effects of the action, be better achieved at Union level, the Union may adopt measures, in accordance with the principle of subsidiarity as set out in Article 5 of the Treaty on European Union (TEU). In accordance with the principle of proportionality as set out in that Article, this Regulation does not go beyond what is necessary in order to achieve that objective.

Closely Related Provisions

Article 2 (Material scope) (see too recitals 15–21); Article 3 (Territorial scope) (see too recitals 22–25)

Related Provisions in LED [Directive (EU) 2016/680]

Article 1 (Subject-matter and objectives) (see too recitals 1–2 and 8–9); Article 2 (Scope) (see too recitals 10–14)

Relevant Case Law

CJEU

Joined Cases C-465/00, C-138/01 and C-139/01, *Rechnungshof v Österreichischer Rundfunk and Others* and *Christa Neukomm* and *Joseph Lauermann*, judgment of 20 May 2003 (ECLI:EU:C:2003:294).

Case C-518/07, *Commission v Federal Republic of Germany*, judgment of 9 March 2010 (Grand Chamber) (ECLI:EU:C:2010:125).

Case C-28/08 P, *European Commission v Bavarian Lager*, judgment of 29 June 2010 (Grand Chamber) (ECLI:EU:C:2010:378).

Joined Cases C-468/10 and C-469/10, *Asociación Nacional de Establecimientos Financieros de Crédito (ASNEF) and Federación de Comercio Electrónico y Marketing Directo (FECEMD) v Administración des Estados*, judgment of 24 November 2011 (ECLI:EU:C:2011:777).

Joined Cases C-293/12 and C-594/12, *Digital Rights Ireland Ltd v Minister for Communications, Marine and Natural Resources and Others and Kärntner Landesregierung and Others*, judgment of 8 April 2014 (Grand Chamber) (ECLI:EU:C:2014:238).

Case C-362/14, *Maximillian Schrems v Data Protection Commissioner*, judgment of 6 October 2015 (Grand Chamber) (ECLI:EU:C:2015:650).

Case C-582/14, *Patrick Breyer v Bundesrepublik Deutschland*, judgment of 26 October 2016 (ECLI:EU:C:2016:779).

Joined Cases C-203/15 and C-698/15, *Tele2 Sverige AB v Post-och telestyrelsen* and *Secretary of State for Home Department v Tom Watson and Others*, judgment of 21 December 2016 (Grand Chamber) (ECLI:EU:C:2016:970).

Case C-536/15, *Tele2 (Netherlands) BV and Others v Autoriteit Consument en Markt (ACM)*, judgment of 15 March 2017 (ECLI:EU:C:2017:214).

Opinion 1/15, Opinion of 26 July 2017 (Grand Chamber) (ECLI:EU:C:2017:592).

A. Rationale and Policy Underpinnings

Article 1 defines the subject-matter of the GDPR. It gives effect to Article 16 of the Treaty on the Functioning of the European Union ('TFEU'), particularly its second paragraph. Article 16(2) TFEU provides that the European Parliament and the Council shall lay down the rules relating to the protection of individuals with regard to the processing of personal data and the rules relating to the free movement of such data. Article 1(1) clarifies that the GDPR lays down these rules.

The second and the third paragraph of Article 1 distinguish the two rationales that are traditionally linked to rules on data protection: protecting the fundamental rights of individuals as well as the free flow of personal data within the internal market. This dual rationale is also made explicit in recital 2 GDPR, which mentions the accomplishment of the area of freedom, security and justice and also the economic union and the strengthening and the convergence of the economies within the internal market.

Article 1(2) consolidates the view that data protection is not only a fundamental right in itself and, as such, included in Article 8 of the Charter of Fundamental Rights of the European Union ('CFR'), but also has a wider goal in that it serves to protect as a general matter the fundamental rights of individuals. The right to privacy—which is not explicitly mentioned in Article 1(2)—has special value in this context. However, the right to data protection also serves to enhance the effective protection of other fundamental rights. The freedom of expression and information (Article 11 CFR) and the right not to be discriminated against (Article 21 CFR) are examples of rights that can be reinforced by effective data protection.

Article 1(3) aims to give effect to the economic underpinning of data protection and, more specifically, the rationale of the internal market, where data—including personal data—should flow freely. As the Commission states, '[b]uilding a Digital Single Market is a key part of the EU's strategy to prepare itself for the future and to continue to deliver high living standards for its population'.[1] It is against this background that Article 1(3) provides that reasons of data protection should not serve as the basis for restrictions or prohibitions on the free flow of personal data between the Member States.

B. Legal Background

1. EU legislation

Article 1 is the sequel of Article 1 DPD, which specified the subject-matter of the DPD. Article 1 DPD emphasised, on the one hand, the need for protection of individuals' fundamental rights and, on the other hand, the requirement of not restricting nor prohibiting the free flow of personal data between Member States for reasons connected with the fundamental rights protection. This double rationale was well explained in recitals 3 and 4 of the DPD.

The differences between Article 1 GDPR and Article 1 DPD can largely be explained by the changed context. First, differences follow from the different types of legal instrument. Since under EU law directives are addressed to the Member States (Article 288 TFEU), Article 1 DPD placed obligations on them. The Member States were to protect fundamental rights and at the same time abstain from restricting or protecting data flows. The GDPR, however, is a regulation and applies directly in the national jurisdictions. Therefore, the Member States are not mentioned, notwithstanding the fact that they have an important role to play in ensuring data protection. At the same time, they must abstain from creating legal or administrative borders that would hamper the functioning of the internal market.

Secondly, the DPD dates from before the adoption of the Charter, which recognises data protection as a separate fundamental right next to the right to privacy. Article 1 DPD included the obligation for Member States to ensure the privacy of individuals. The fact that privacy is no longer mentioned in Article 1 GDPR can be explained by the fact that there was no longer a need to mention it, precisely because of the recognition in EU law of the fundamental right to data protection.

Thirdly, the DPD was enacted before the adoption of the Lisbon Treaty recognising data protection as a subject requiring EU legislation. The DPD was legally grounded on Article 95 of the EC Treaty (currently Article 114 TFEU) concerning realisation of the internal market. There was no incentive for the EU legislator to specify in a first article that the Regulation gives effect to a specific mandate. The DPD was one of the many EU rules aimed at facilitating the functioning of the internal market.

[1] EC Communication 2015.

2. International instruments

Convention 108 of the Council of Europe was the first binding international instrument with data protection as its main subject and is considered to be the chief inspiration for the involvement of the EU in this policy area, which started with the DPD.[2] In its modernised form, which came into effect in 2018, the Convention defines its purpose as 'to protect every individual, whatever his or her nationality or residence, with regard to the processing of their personal data, thereby contributing to respect for his or her human rights and fundamental freedoms, and in particular the right to privacy'.[3]

Convention 108 and its successor, the Modernised Convention 108, do not have a dual purpose, that is to say they do not have as primary aims the facilitating of the free flow of personal data, although the preamble to the Modernised Convention 108 reaffirms the Council of Europe's commitment to freedom of information regardless of frontiers. This is not the same as the free flow of information as a precondition for economic growth in the internal market, but it is related.

3. National developments

At national level, data protection laws existed within the European Economic Area ('EEA') resulting from transposition of the DPD. Moreover, while Convention 108 inspired the EU to act in this domain, the Convention itself was inspired by pre-existing national laws. The laws adopted in the 1970s in the German State of Hessen, in Sweden and in France are examples.

As far as the fundamental right to data protection, as included in Article 8 CFR, is concerned, there is a link with the German legal concept of 'informational self-determination' ('informationelle Selbstbestimmung'). This concept was developed pursuant to German constitutional law, and aims to give the individual full control over his personal information. Arguably, the right to data protection is not the same as the right to informational self-determination. Its main aim is not to give the individual full control, but to ensure that data are processed in a fair manner.[4]

Under the GDPR, the role of national laws is limited to those topics where the Member States are empowered or mandated to exercise competence.[5]

4. Case law

In *Opinion 1/15*, the CJEU dealt with the mandate of the EU legislator under Article 16(2) TFEU, although in a limited way. It states that an EU legal instrument containing detailed rules concerning the use of personal data should be based on Article 16(2) TFEU. Unfortunately, there is no further case law interpreting this mandate of the EU legislator.[6] A close reading of Article 16(2) TFEU raises questions in relation to the nature and scope of the mandate.

The CJEU has opined on several occasions on the dual purpose of the DPD, which is also emphasised in Article 1(1) GDPR. According to this provision, the GDPR sets out

---

[2] See González Fuster 2014, para. 4.2, and Hijmans 2016, para. 2.10.
[3] Art. 1 Modernised Convention 108.
[4] As argued by the author in: Hijmans 2016, para. 2.11; based on Hustinx 2017 and Kranenborg 2014.
[5] See EDPS 2012, para. II.2.a.   [6] *Opinion 1/15*, paras. 80–94.

rules both on data protection and on the free movement of data. However, as the case law underlines, these are not two separate sets of rules.

In *Commission v Germany*, the CJEU found that the role of the independent supervisory authorities consists 'of establishing a fair balance between the protection of the right to private life and the free movement of personal data'.[7] The ruling in *Breyer* further explained that the margin of discretion enjoyed by Member States can be 'used only in accordance with the objective pursued by that directive [95/46] of maintaining a balance between the free movement of personal data and the protection of private life'.[8] In short, the Court clarified that application of data protection law requires the balancing of its two underlying purposes.

Initially, the purpose of the free movement of personal data on the internal market seemed predominant in the Court's case law. In the *Österreichischer Rundfunk and Others* case,[9] the Court ruled that the DPD 'is intended to ensure the free movement of personal data between Member States through the harmonisation of national provisions on the protection of individuals with regard to the processing of such data'.

The digital single market also played a significant role in the *ASNEF* case,[10] when the Court precluded the Member States from adjusting a core norm of data protection in national law. This ruling concerned one of the legal grounds for data processing, namely the legitimate interests pursued by the controller (Article 7(f) DPD).

The Court has since shifted its emphasis towards the effectiveness of the protection of the individual's fundamental rights.[11] After the entry into force of the Lisbon Treaty, the Court has (more or less)[12] systematically interpreted the DPD in the light of the fundamental rights to privacy and data protection that should be respected under Articles 7 and 8 CFR.[13] Sometimes, it also mentions other fundamental rights in the same context, such as, in the *Schrems* ruling, the right to an effective remedy and to a fair trial (Article 47 CFR).[14] The free movement of data seems to play a less prominent role, but is sometimes still mentioned by the CJEU.[15]

Hence, Article 1(2) and (3) GDPR affirms the case law of the CJEU. The main objective of the GDPR—the protection of fundamental rights—is laid down in Article 1(2) GDPR, whereas Article 1(3) ensures that the achievement of this objective does not adversely affect the free movement of personal data. Article 1(2) DPD, the predecessor of Article 1(3) GDPR, was also mentioned in *Österreichischer Rundfunk*.[16]

C. Analysis

1. The GDPR as a continuation of the DPD

Article 1 GDPR illustrates that the GDPR is a continuation of the DPD. Recital 7 declares that rapid technological changes and globalisation 'require a strong and more

---

[7] Case C-518/07, *Commission v Germany*, para. 30.   [8] Case C-582/14, *Breyer*, para. 58.
[9] Case C-465/00, *Österreichischer Rundfunk*, para. 39.
[10] Joined Cases C-468/10 and C-469/10, *ASNEF*.
[11] See on this shift also Lynskey 2015, chapter 3.
[12] The Court is not always consistent in its approach: see Hijmans 2016, para. 2.13.
[13] See e.g. Joined Cases C-293/12 and C-594/12, *Digital Rights Ireland*; Case C-362/14, *Schrems*; Joined Cases C-203/15 and C-698/15, *Tele2*.
[14] Case C-362/14, *Schrems*, para. 95.   [15] Ibid., para. 42.
[16] Case C-465/00, *Österreichischer Rundfunk*, para. 39.

coherent data protection framework in the Union, backed by strong enforcement', yet the underlying reasons and principles for EU involvement in data protection remain the same, including the double purpose.[17]

This double purpose also results from the starting points for the new rules, namely the new challenges for data protection that—according to the Commission—needed to be met. Those challenges are: addressing the impact of new technologies; enhancing the internal market dimension of data protection; addressing globalisation and improving international data transfers; providing a stronger institutional arrangement for the effective enforcement of data protection rules; and improving the coherence of the data protection legal framework.[18]

The double purpose was not evident after the entry into force of the Lisbon Treaty in 2009, which included both the enactment of a binding fundamental rights charter and the recognition of data protection as a fundamental right. The Lisbon Treaty also brought in Article 16 TFEU as a specific legal basis for data protection rules, which aimed to make this fundamental right effective. It can be noted that the CJEU takes a strong position in defence of the right to data protection, which also exists in Article 16 TFEU.

Emphasis has shifted from data protection as an internal market instrument towards its role in protecting fundamental rights. This shift is logical in view of the changes explained above. However, it has a gradual nature, and the dual purpose of data protection has been retained.

2. Article 1(1) GDPR in light of Article 16(2) TFEU

Article 1(1) GDPR has a close link with Article 16(2) TFEU, first sentence. At first glance, Article 1(1) GDPR transposes the mandate of Article 16(2) TFEU, first sentence, into a more operational wording. This is not easy because of the ambiguities of Article 16 itself.

The analysis therefore starts with Article 16(2) TFEU, which reads as follows:

The European Parliament and the Council, acting in accordance with the ordinary legislative procedure, shall lay down the rules relating to the protection of individuals with regard to the processing of personal data by Union institutions, bodies, offices and agencies, and by the Member States when carrying out activities which fall within the scope of Union law, and the rules relating to the free movement of such data.

This mandate raises a number of questions:[19]

1. What does it mean that the EU legislator (the European Parliament and the Council) shall lay down the rules? Does this leave scope for Member State rules?
2. The rules on data protection apply to processing by the Union institutions, bodies, offices and agencies and by the Member States. Does this contain any limitation, as far as personal data are processed by the private sector?
3. What does the limitation—in relation to processing by the Member States—'within the scope of Union law' mean?
4. Does the addition of the rules relating to the free movement of such data mean that those rules may be outside the scope of Article 16(1) which defines the individual's

---

[17] As Lynskey puts it, data protection rules reflect aspects of economic regulation: see Lynskey 2015, p. 76.
[18] EC Communication 2010.   [19] See also Hijmans 2016, para. 6.2.

right to data protection? Could the rules relating to the protection of individuals be different from those on the free movement of data? Could the legislator make a distinction?

Arguably, some of these questions are of a purely academic nature, in view of the solutions found by the EU legislator, but examining them nevertheless reveal essentials of the system.

First, the EU legislator shall lay down the rules. This implies that the thrust of Article 16 TFEU, first sentence, has a mandatory nature and that there is no room left any more for intervention by the national legislator. As Article 1 GDPR specifies, the GDPR lays down rules and, by doing so, fulfils—within its scope of application—the obligation under Article 16. The Member States are only entitled to adopt or maintain national law on data protection or on the free flow of personal data in so far as this is explicitly provided for in the GDPR. A further remark can be made on the remaining competence of the Member States within the scope of Article 16 TFEU, but outside the scope of the GDPR. Article 16 TFEU seems also to preclude national laws which are not foreseen in an EU legal instrument. The obvious example of an EU legal instrument which requires national legislation is the LED. Article 63 LED on transposition requires the Member States to publish and adopt the laws, regulations and administrative provisions to comply with that directive by 6 May 2018.

Secondly, according to Article 16 TFEU, the rules on data protection should cover the processing of personal data by Union institutions, bodies, offices and agencies and by the Member States. The rules covering the processing of personal data by the EU institutions remain outside the scope of the GDPR and were—as far as the former first pillar of the EU Treaty was concerned—included in Regulation 45/2001.[20] This regulation was replaced by the EUDPR which took effect on 11 December 2018 and also covers police and judicial cooperation in criminal matters.

The reference to processing by the Member States is less straightforward, since this seems to imply that only public authorities of the Member States would be covered. If this would indeed be the case, the private sector would not be covered. This is obviously not the reading followed by the GDPR. Such reading would also be incompatible with the legal history—the DPD does not distinguish between the public and the private sector—and with the Court's case law which aims at ensuring respect of the fundamental right to data protection in both sectors. The common understanding seems to be that data protection in the private sector is fully covered, through the reference to the free movement of personal data.[21]

Thirdly, the limitation to Member States' activities within the scope of EU law is elaborated in Article 2 GDPR. The limitation to 'within the scope of Union law' is comparable to a similar limitation in Article 51 CFR. The latter article limits the scope of the CFR to 'Member States only when they are implementing Union law', but this is in the Court's case law understood as covering activities that are within the scope of EU law. When EU law applies, the Charter applies.[22] Moreover, the limitation in Article 16(2) TFEU does not have autonomous value, since as a result of the wide mandate of Article 16 itself data protection falls by definition within the scope of EU

---

[20] See Table of Legislation.   [21] Hijmans 2016, para. 6.2.2.   [22] See also Hancox 2013.

law. Hence, it only refers to areas where Union law does not apply, such as the area of national security.[23]

Fourthly, one could question whether the separate notion of rules on the free movement of personal data in Article 16(2) TFEU has added value, other than ensuring that processing by the private sector is covered by Article 16(2) or, possibly, clarifying the double purpose of the data protection rules. On the one hand, the argument could be made that this separate notion is mainly a remnant of the past, where the link to the internal market had to be made to establish EU competence. One could develop this argument further by contending that Article 16(2) is the result of poor draftsmanship and that the provision does not intend to set forth two different sets of rules, but aims to ensure that the rules should have a dual objective. On the other hand, one could argue that the notion of free movement widens the possible scope of data protection rules. This obviously does not mean that two different sets of rules are needed, but it would mean that not all the rules adopted under Article 16(2) aim at respecting an individual's right to data protection; they could also relate to the free movement of personal data.

This latter option would mean that the GDPR could include rules that facilitate the free movement of data, but do not necessarily deliver data protection. Possibly, some of the provisions of Chapter V GDPR on the transfer of personal data could be read in this perspective. In any event, Article 1(1) GDPR repeats the ambiguity of Article 16(2) TFEU, first sentence.

3. Article 1(2) GDPR: A shift of balance

While Article 1(1) GDPR gives effect to Article 16(2) TFEU, first sentence, Article 1(2) GDPR can be considered as implementing Article 16(1) TFEU and the identical text of Article 8(1) CFR. Article 1(2) introduces as a main objective of the GDPR that it must give meaning to the individual's right to the protection of personal data.

This must be seen in the light of the nature of the right to data protection. This right entails a positive obligation for governments to ensure such protection. The right to data protection, as a right to fair processing, cannot work by itself, contrary to fundamental rights of the first generation that in essence require governments to abstain, or, in other words that contain a negative obligation. A number of these so-called fundamental rights of the first generation were included in the European Convention on Human Rights ('ECHR'), giving protection against governments, as a reaction to the atrocities of the Second World War. Article 8 ECHR and the corresponding Article 7 CFR include such rights, although they can now also be invoked against actors in the private sector.

By adopting the GDPR, the EU legislator aims—again, within its scope of application which excludes authorities of police and criminal justice—to give meaning to the fundamental right to data protection. At the same time, Article 1(2) is a reflection of the shift of balance. A similar provision is not included in Article 1 DPD. Article 1(2) GDPR does not state that the GDPR protects (or ensures) the free movement of personal data. However, it must be admitted that this assessment of the shift of balance is not shared by all scholars. For example, Lynskey argues that the two objectives of EU data protection law have equal importance.[24]

---

[23] As specified in Art. 4(2) Treaty on European Union ('TEU'). See the commentary on Art. 2 in this volume.

[24] Lynskey 2015, chapter 3.

4. Data protection and other fundamental rights

Article 1(2) GDPR not only refers to the right to data protection, but states, in general, that the Regulation protects the fundamental rights and freedoms of natural persons. This is a quite ambitious wording, supported by recitals 2 and 4, which state that the GDPR 'respects' the fundamental rights and freedoms of individuals. The wording 'respects' is an indication that as concerns other fundamental rights, the GDPR should not have an adverse effect, and reflects a negative obligation of the legislator not to interfere with other fundamental rights and freedoms.

Recital 4 also lists the other fundamental rights in the CFR that are considered relevant in this context. These are: the right to privacy (Article 7); freedom of thought, conscience and religion (Article 10); freedom of expression and information (Article 11); freedom to conduct a business (Article 16); the right to an effective remedy and to a fair trial (Article 47); and cultural, religious and linguistic diversity (Article 22).

This list is not exhaustive and possibly not even the result of in-depth analysis. It is remarkable that the right not to be discriminated against (Article 21) is not mentioned. Equally, there is no mention of the right of access to documents (Article 42), although the balancing between data protection and access to public documents has led to extensive case law of the CJEU.[25] At the same time, the link between data protection and cultural, religious and linguistic diversity is not obvious.

More important, the list in recital 4 GDPR seems to indicate the need for balancing between data protection and these other fundamental rights. There is, however, another essential perspective: data protection as a prerequisite for the effective exercise of other fundamental rights. A key example is that data protection is essential for freedom of expression: effective data protection— in particular, freedom from being monitored— allows individuals to develop their thoughts, often in communication with others. These individuals can subsequently express their views at a stage where their thoughts are developed and at a time of their choosing.

It is in that sense that Article 1(2) mentions that the GDPR protects fundamental rights in general. The rules on data protection should reinforce the protection of fundamental rights, whereas, on the other hand, sometimes a balancing between fundamental rights is needed.

5. Article 1(3) GDPR: the free flow of personal data

Article 1(3) GDPR is formulated in a negative manner (i.e. data protection should not restrict the free movement of personal data). This provision mainly reproduces a guiding principle of internal market law, and can also be explained by the fact that the GDPR is meant to ensure the free flow of personal data within the EU.

Article 1(3) does not mention the addressees of this negative obligation. Arguably, this provision is addressed to the Member States and is meant to prevent them from adopting national laws restricting the free movement of data.

However, Article 1(3) GDPR may have important practical meaning for the scope of national data protection laws implementing the GDPR, in situations where the GDPR allows a different level of protection. For example, assume that Member State A applies

---

[25] The leading case being Case C-28/08 P, *Bavarian Lager*. See also the commentary on Art. 86 in this volume.

the minimum age of 16 years for consent of minors according to Article 8(1) GDPR. Would Article 1(3) GDPR prohibit Member State A from applying this minimum age vis-à-vis a service provider offering a service from Member State B where the minimum age is set at 13 years in accordance with the same Article?

This all relates closely to the territorial scope of national data protection laws. Notably, the practice of the Member States is not uniform in this regard. In a number of them, the law applies to processing of personal data in the context of the activities of a controller or processor on the territory of that Member State. This is, for instance, the case in the Netherlands[26] and in Belgium.[27] In France, however, the national law applies where the person concerned resides in France, including where the controller is not established in France.[28] Coming back to the minimum age mentioned above, the same French national law provides that the minimum age for minors to give consent without parental authorisation is 15.[29] What if an internet provider offers a service to minors of 13 and 14 years of age without asking for parental authorisation, a service that is legal in the country where the provider is established?

The solution to this hypothetical case is not evident. On the one hand, one can argue that France would not be allowed to invoke its minimum age vis-à-vis this service, because this would not be in conformity with Article 1(3) GDPR. On the other hand, France could argue that its law can be applied, because the opposite would render the minimum age of 15 years ineffective in the digital world, whereas setting this age limit is explicitly allowed under the GDPR.

Article 1(3) GDPR could also play a role in the case of a Member State's national law providing for an obligation to store personal data on servers within that Member State. However, it can be questioned whether such a provision would normally fall within the scope of Article 1(3) GDPR. The latter only refers to restrictions or prohibitions that are adopted for reasons of data protection. A provision requiring service providers to store data within the Member State could be justified by other public interests, such as to facilitate police access to a data base for reasons connected with law enforcement[30] or for reasons of public health.

Select Bibliography

National legislation

Belgian GDPR Implementation Law: Wet betreffende de bescherming van natuurlijke personen met betrekking tot de verwerking van persoonsgegevens, van 30 juli 2018; Loi relative à la protection des personnes physiques à l'égard des traitements de données à caractère personnel, du 30 juillet 2018.
Dutch GDPR Implementation Law: Uitvoeringswet Algemene verordening gegevensbescherming, versie van 25 mei 2018.
French GDPR Implementation Law: Ordonnance n° 2018-1125 du 12 décembre 2018 prise en application de l'article 32 de la loi n° 2018-493 du 20 juin 2018 relative à la protection des

---

[26] Art. 4(1) Dutch GDPR Implementation Law.
[27] Art. 4 (1) Belgian GDPR Implementation Law.
[28] Art. 3(II) French GDPR Implementation Law.
[29] Ibid., Art. 45.
[30] This example is taken from Joined Cases C-293/12 and C-594/12, *Digital Rights Ireland*, para. 68, where the CJEU found that the storage of data outside EU territory interfered with control by independent supervisory authorities as required by the Charter.

données personnelles et portant modification de la loi n° 78-17 du 6 janvier 1978 relative à l'informatique, aux fichiers et aux libertés et diverses dispositions concernant la protection des données à caractère personnel.

Academic writings

Gonzaléz Fuster 2014: González Fuster, *The Emergence of Personal Data Protection as a Fundamental Right of the EU* (Springer 2014).
Hancox 2013: Hancox, 'The Meaning of "Implementing" EU law under Article 51(1) of the Charter: *Åkerberg Fransson*', 50(5) *Common Market Law Review* (2013), 1411.
Hijmans 2016: Hijmans, *The European Union as Guardian of Internet Privacy* (Springer 2016).
Hustinx 2017: Hustinx, 'EU Data Protection Law: The Review of Directive 95/46/EC and the General Data Protection Regulation', in Cremona (ed.), *New Technologies and EU Law* (OUP 2017), 123.
Kranenborg 2014: Kranenborg, 'Article 8', in Peers, Hervey, Kenner and Ward (eds.), *The EU Charter of Fundamental Rights—A Commentary* (Hart Publishing 2014), 222.
Lynskey 2015: Lynskey, *The Foundations of EU Data Protection Law* (OUP 2015).

Papers of data protection authorities

EDPS 2012: European Data Protection Supervisor, 'Opinion on the Data Protection Reform Package' (7 March 2012).
Article 29 Working Party, 'Opinion 01/2012 on the Data Protection Reform Proposals' (WP 191, 23 March 2012).

Reports and recommendations

EC Communication 2010: Communication from the Commission to the European Parliament, the Council, the European Economic and Social Committee and the Committee of the Regions, 'A Comprehensive Approach on Personal Data Protection in the European Union', COM (2010) 609 final, 4 November 2010.
EC Communication 2015: Communication from the Commission to the European Parliament, the Council, the European Economic and Social Committee and the Committee of the Regions, 'A Digital Single Market Strategy for Europe', COM(2015) 192 final, 6 May 2015.

Article 2. Material scope

HERKE KRANENBORG[*]

1. This Regulation applies to the processing of personal data wholly or partly by automated means and to the processing other than by automated means of personal data which form part of a filing system or are intended to form part of a filing system.
2. This Regulation does not apply to the processing of personal data:
   (a) in the course of an activity which falls outside the scope of Union law;
   (b) by the Member States when carrying out activities which fall within the scope of Chapter 2 of Title V of the TEU;
   (c) by a natural person in the course of a purely personal or household activity;
   (d) by competent authorities for the purposes of the prevention, investigation, detection or prosecution of criminal offences or the execution of criminal penalties, including the safeguarding against and the prevention of threats to public security.
3. For the processing of personal data by the Union institutions, bodies, offices and agencies, Regulation (EC) No 45/2001 applies. Regulation (EC) No 45/2001 and other Union legal acts applicable to such processing of personal data shall be adapted to the principles and rules of this Regulation in accordance with Article 98.
4. This Regulation shall be without prejudice to the application of Directive 2000/31/EC, in particular of the liability rules of intermediary service providers in Articles 12 to 15 of that Directive.

Relevant Recitals

(14) The protection afforded by this Regulation should apply to natural persons, whatever their nationality or place of residence, in relation to the processing of their personal data. This Regulation does not cover the processing of personal data which concerns legal persons and in particular undertakings established as legal persons, including the name and the form of the legal person and the contact details of the legal person.

(15) In order to prevent creating a serious risk of circumvention, the protection of natural persons should be technologically neutral and should not depend on the techniques used. The protection of natural persons should apply to the processing of personal data by automated means, as well as to manual processing, if the personal data are contained or are intended to be contained in a filing system. Files or sets of files, as well as their cover pages, which are not structured according to specific criteria should not fall within the scope of this Regulation.

(16) This Regulation does not apply to issues of protection of fundamental rights and freedoms or the free flow of personal data related to activities which fall outside the scope of Union law, such as activities concerning national security. This Regulation does not apply to the processing of personal data by the Member States when carrying out activities in relation to the common foreign and security policy of the Union.

---

[*] The views expressed are solely those of the author and do not necessarily reflect those of the European Commission. The author would like to thank Daniele Nardi for his comments on previous versions of this and other contributions in this volume by the present author.

(17) Regulation (EC) No 45/2001 of the European Parliament and of the Council applies to the processing of personal data by the Union institutions, bodies, offices and agencies. Regulation (EC) No 45/2001 and other Union legal acts applicable to such processing of personal data should be adapted to the principles and rules established in this Regulation and applied in the light of this Regulation. In order to provide a strong and coherent data protection framework in the Union, the necessary adaptations of Regulation (EC) No 45/2001 should follow after the adoption of this Regulation, in order to allow application at the same time as this Regulation.

(18) This Regulation does not apply to the processing of personal data by a natural person in the course of a purely personal or household activity and thus with no connection to a professional or commercial activity. Personal or household activities could include correspondence and the holding of addresses, or social networking and online activity undertaken within the context of such activities. However, this Regulation applies to controllers or processors which provide the means for processing personal data for such personal or household activities.

(19) The protection of natural persons with regard to the processing of personal data by competent authorities for the purposes of the prevention, investigation, detection or prosecution of criminal offences or the execution of criminal penalties, including the safeguarding against and the prevention of threats to public security and the free movement of such data, is the subject of a specific Union legal act. This Regulation should not, therefore, apply to processing activities for those purposes. However, personal data processed by public authorities under this Regulation should, when used for those purposes, be governed by a more specific Union legal act, namely Directive (EU) 2016/680 of the European Parliament and of the Council. Member States may entrust competent authorities within the meaning of Directive (EU) 2016/680 with tasks which are not necessarily carried out for the purposes of the prevention, investigation, detection or prosecution of criminal offences or the execution of criminal penalties, including the safeguarding against and prevention of threats to public security, so that the processing of personal data for those other purposes, in so far as it is within the scope of Union law, falls within the scope of this Regulation.

With regard to the processing of personal data by those competent authorities for purposes falling within scope of this Regulation, Member States should be able to maintain or introduce more specific provisions to adapt the application of the rules of this Regulation. Such provisions may determine more precisely specific requirements for the processing of personal data by those competent authorities for those other purposes, taking into account the constitutional, organisational and administrative structure of the respective Member State. When the processing of personal data by private bodies falls within the scope of this Regulation, this Regulation should provide for the possibility for Member States under specific conditions to restrict by law certain obligations and rights when such a restriction constitutes a necessary and proportionate measure in a democratic society to safeguard specific important interests including public security and the prevention, investigation, detection or prosecution of criminal offences or the execution of criminal penalties, including the safeguarding against and the prevention of threats to public security. This is relevant for instance in the framework of anti-money laundering or the activities of forensic laboratories.

(20) While this Regulation applies, inter alia, to the activities of courts and other judicial authorities, Union or Member State law could specify the processing operations and processing procedures in relation to the processing of personal data by courts and other judicial authorities. The competence of the supervisory authorities should not cover the processing of personal data when courts are acting in their judicial capacity, in order to safeguard the independence of the judiciary in the performance of its judicial tasks, including decision-making. It should be possible to entrust supervision of such data processing operations to specific bodies within the judicial system of the Member State, which should, in particular ensure compliance with the rules of this Regulation, enhance awareness among members of the judiciary of their obligations under this Regulation and handle complaints in relation to such data processing operations.

(21) This Regulation is without prejudice to the application of Directive 2000/31/EC of the European Parliament and of the Council, in particular of the liability rules of intermediary service providers in Articles 12 to 15 of that Directive. That Directive seeks to contribute to the proper functioning of the internal market by ensuring the free movement of information society services between Member States.

Closely Related Provisions

Article 1 (Subject-matter and objectives); Article 3 (Territorial scope) (see also recitals 22–25); Article 4(1), (2) and (6) (Definitions of 'personal data', 'processing' and 'filing system') (see also recitals 26–27); Article 98 (Review of other Union legal acts on data protection)

Related Provisions in LED [Directive (EU) 2016/680]

Article 1 (Subject-matter and objectives); Article 2 (Scope) (see also recitals 10–14); Article 3(1), (2), (6) and (7) (Definitions of 'personal data', 'processing' and 'filing system')

Related Provisions in EPD [Directive 2002/58/EC]

Article 1 (Scope and aim) (see also recitals 10 and 12); Article 15 (Restrictions) (see also recital 11)

Related Provisions in EUDPR [Regulation 2018/1725]

Article 2 (Scope) (see too recitals 8–15); Article 57(1)(a) (Exception of processing of personal data by the Court of Justice acting in its judicial capacity) (see too recital 74); Article 98(2) (Proposals to apply EUDPR to Europol and EPPO) (see too recital 13)

Relevant Case Law

CJEU

Joined Cases C-465/00, C-138/01 and C-139/01, *Rechnungshof v Österreichischer Rundfunk and Others* and *Christa Neukomm* and *Joseph Lauermann*, judgment of 20 May 2003 (ECLI:EU:C:2003:294).

Case C-101/01, *Bodil Lindqvist*, judgment of 6 November 2003 (ECLI:EU:C:2003:596).

Joined Cases C-317/04 and C-318/04, *European Parliament v Council* and *Commission of the European Communities*, judgment of 30 May 2006 (ECLI:EU:C:2006:346).

Case C-73/07, *Tietosuojavaltuutettu v Satakunnan Markkinapörssi Oy and Satamedia Oy*, judgment of 16 December 2009 (Grand Chamber) (ECLI:EU:C:2008:727).

Opinion of Advocate General Kokott in Case C-73/07, *Tietosuojavaltuutettu v Satakunnan Markkinapörssi Oy and Satamedia Oy*, delivered on 8 May 2008 (ECLI:EU:C:2008:266).

Case C-28/08P, *European Commission v Bavarian Lager*, judgment of 29 June 2010 (Grand Chamber) (EU:C:2010:378).

Opinion of Advocate General Sharpston in Case C-28/08P, *European Commission v Bavarian Lager*, delivered on 15 October 2009 (ECLI:EU:C:2009:624).

Case C-212/13, *František Ryneš v Úřad pro ochranu osobních údajů*, judgment of 11 December 2014 (ECLI:EU:C:2014:2428).

Opinion of Advocate General Jääskinen in Case C-212/13, *František Ryneš v Úřad pro ochranu osobních údajů*, delivered on 10 July 2014 (ECLI:EU:C:2014:2072).

Joined Cases C-203/15 and C-698/15, *Tele2 Sverige AB v Post-och telestyrelsen* and *Secretary of State for Home Department v Tom Watson and Others*, judgment of 21 December 2016 (Grand Chamber) (ECLI:EU:C:2016:970).

Case C-73/16, *Peter Puškár v Finančné riaditeľstvo Slovenskej republiky and Kriminálny úrad finančnej správy*, judgment of 27 September 2017 (ECLI:EU:C:2017:725).

Opinion of Advocate General Kokott in Case C-73/16, *Peter Puškár v Finančné riaditeľstvo Slovenskej republiky and Kriminálny úrad finančnej správy*, delivered on 30 March 2017 (ECLI:EU:C:2017:253).

Case C-25/17, *Proceedings brought by Tietosuojavaltuutettu (Jehovan todistajat)*, judgment of 10 July 2018 (Grand Chamber) (ECLI:EU:C:2018:551).

Case C-207/16, *Ministerio Fiscal*, judgment of 2 October 2018 (Grand Chamber) (ECLI:EU:C:2018:788).

Case C-623/17, *Privacy International v Secretary of State for Foreign and Commonwealth Affairs and Others* (still pending).

A. Rationale and Policy Underpinnings

Article 2 determines the *material* scope of the GDPR, whereas Article 3 defines its *territorial* scope.

The first paragraph of Article 2 positively formulates what is covered by the GDPR: the processing of personal data wholly or partly by automated means and other than by automated means when the personal data form part of a filing system or are intended to form part of such a system. Article 2 does not differentiate between the public and private sectors, and thus covers both of them.[1] The scope formulated in the first paragraph is limited by the second paragraph, which excludes certain processing activities from the scope of the GDPR. Generally excluded is the processing of data for purely personal or household activities.

The other exclusions in paragraph 2 are linked to policy areas for which the EU has no, or only limited competence, or for which specific Union rules apply. This includes the processing of personal data by competent authorities in the law enforcement area, which is covered by the LED. These exclusions reflect the former EU pillar structure which was in principle abolished with the entry into force of the Lisbon Treaty in 2009.

The Lisbon Treaty introduced a separate legal basis for rules on data protection: Article 16 Treaty on the Functioning of the European Union ('TFEU').[2] The former DPD was based on the general legal basis for setting rules to establish the internal market (now: Article 114 TFEU). The DPD being an internal market instrument excluded from its scope the area covered by the former second and third pillar of the Union.[3] The new legal basis in principle allowed the Union to adopt a single set of rules potentially applying to the processing of personal data by competent authorities for criminal investigation and also to the Union institutions and bodies. However, the European Commission, on the basis of Article 16 TFEU, decided to still propose a general regulation on data protection and a specific directive on data protection in the law enforcement sector. This was due to the political sensitivity of harmonizing rules in this area (before, the rules were laid down in a Framework Decision (2008/977/JHA) which only

---

[1] For criticism of the GDPR based on the contention that it would have been better to have tailor-made rules for the public sector, see Blume and Svanberg 2013.

[2] See on Art. 16 TFEU Hijmans 2016.   [3] See further also Hijmans and Scirocco 2009.

applied to cross-border data processing operations), as reflected in declaration 21 of the Lisbon Treaty in which the Intergovernmental Conference acknowledged that specific rules on the basis of Article 16 TFEU in this area 'may prove necessary'. The exclusion from the scope of the GDPR of Member State activities under the former second pillar of the Union (the common foreign and security policy, Chapter 2 of Title V of the Treaty on European Union ('TEU')) follows from Article 16 TFEU itself, which states that it is without prejudice to the specific rules laid down in Article 39 TEU. That provision constitutes a separate legal basis for rules on data protection for Member State activities in that area.

In a separate paragraph 3 of Article 2, it is indicated that the processing of personal data by the Union institutions and bodies, offices and agencies is subject to separate rules which are adapted to the principles and rules of the GDPR in accordance with Article 98. During the legislative process, the European Parliament tried to include the Union institutions and bodies in the scope of the GDPR (the European Commission had proposed not to), but in the final negotiations it was agreed to leave them out, with the clear obligation on the Union legislator to bring the then existing specific rules in line with the GDPR. This led to the adoption of the EUDPR in October 2018.

B. Legal Background

1. EU legislation

Article 2 GDPR follows to a large extent the equivalent provision in the DPD, namely Article 3. The positive formulation of the material scope is the same.

In the exclusions, the main difference is that Article 2 GDPR includes a specific reference to the special rules of the law enforcement sector. The GDPR no longer refers to 'activities of the state in areas of criminal law', but aligns the exclusion with the scope of the LED. This creates clarity as to whether private entities are covered by the GDPR when they are providing information they collected for commercial purposes to law enforcement authorities. In the so-called 'PNR cases', the CJEU considered the activities of the airline companies, namely providing their Passenger Name Records ('PNR') to US law enforcement authorities, as falling within a framework established by the public authorities that relates to public security. As a consequence, with reference to the cited phrase in Article 3 DPD, the CJEU concluded that EU measures aiming at such activities fell outside the scope of the DPD and could not be based on the internal market legal basis, but had to be based on a legal basis in the former third pillar of the Union.[4] The transmission of PNR data by airline companies to law enforcement authorities would seem to be covered by the provisions of the GDPR, since the exclusion for the law enforcement sector refers explicitly only to the processing of personal data 'by competent authorities' (Article 2(2)(d)).

New in Article 2 compared to Article 3 DPD is that the rules for Union institutions and bodies are explicitly mentioned (they did not exist at the time the DPD was adopted). Also new is the paragraph on Directive 2000/31/EC (which also did not exist at the time).

---

[4] Joined Cases C-317/04 and C-318/04, *EP v Council*, para. 58. See generally Docksey 2014, p. 97

2. International instruments

The present Convention 108 only contains a positive description of its material scope, leaving it to the parties to notify, by a declaration to the Secretary General of the Council of Europe, the exclusion of certain categories of automated personal data files.

The material scope of Convention 108 is restricted to automated personal data files. However, parties could decide, by declaration, to apply the Convention to personal data files which were not processed automatically. In the same way, parties could also apply the Convention to information relating to groups of persons, associations, foundations, companies, corporations and any other bodies consisting directly or indirectly of individuals, whether or not such bodies possess legal personality. The application of the GDPR to such data is excluded (see recital 14).

In Modernised Convention 108, material scope is defined as data processing in the public and private sectors, without any reference to the automated nature of the processing.[5] An exception to processing carried out by an individual in the course of purely personal or household activities is added. The possibilities to notify by declaration certain exclusions or extensions are deleted. Instead, on the basis of the exceptions and restrictions clause (Article 11), parties can, by law, make exceptions to certain provisions to safeguard certain interests.

3. National developments

Although the GDPR in several instances leaves room for implementing Member State legislation, this is not the case with regard to the scope of the GDPR. That being said, the scope of the exclusion for competent authorities for the purposes of the prevention, investigation, detection or prosecution of criminal offences or the execution of criminal penalties, including the safeguarding against and the prevention of threats to public security, depends to a certain extent on national legislation.

4. Case law

The CJEU has expressed itself on the scope of the DPD in several cases. In particular, the relation between Article 3(2), first indent, and Article 13 (the general restrictions clause) of the DPD has been subject of consideration. This relationship triggered debate since both provisions contained similar grounds: processing operations concerning public security, defence, state security and the activities of the state in areas of criminal law were excluded from the scope of the DPD, while on the other hand Article 13 DPD allowed Member States to adopt legislative measures to restrict the scope of certain obligations and rights provided for in the DPD when such a restriction constitutes a necessary measure to safeguard national security; defence; public security; or the prevention, investigation, detection and prosecution of criminal offences or of breaches of ethics for regulated professions. In the *Tele2* case, which concerned the equivalent provisions of the EPD (Articles 1(3) and 15(1)), the CJEU concluded that there was a substantial overlap between the respective objectives and concluded, with regard to national legislative measures on data retention for law enforcement purposes, that excluding those national measures from the

---

[5] Art. 3 Modernised Convention 108.

scope of the EPD would deprive Article 15(1) EPD of any purpose.[6] In the *Puškár* case, the CJEU concluded that the exception provided for in the first indent of Article 3(2) DPD (which covers activities falling outside the scope of Community law) had to be interpreted strictly.[7]

C. Analysis

1. Introduction

The first paragraph of Article 2 is the point of departure as regards the material scope of the GDPR: it applies to processing of personal data wholly or partly by automated means and other than by automated means when the personal data form part of a filing system or are intended to form part of such a system. In order to fully understand the material scope, one needs to look at the definitions of 'personal data', 'processing' and 'filing system' in Article 4(1), (2) and (6) GDPR.

2. Key terms

It follows from recital 15 GDPR that, as regards manual processing, files or sets of files, as well as their cover pages, which are not structured according to specific criteria should not fall within the scope of that Regulation. Excluding the purely manual and unstructured processing of personal data reflects the initial reason for specific rules on data protection: the introduction of computers, which made it possible to easily structure and search personal data.[8] In the case *Bavarian Lager*, which concerned the rights of public access to documents concerning a request for access to a document containing personal data, Advocate General Sharpston used the idea of the filing system to justify the disclosure of the document.[9] The Advocate General argued that the situation fell outside the material scope of the applicable data protection rules since it did not constitute processing by automatic means, even though the Union institution used automated search functions to locate a document (containing personal data) requested under the public access to document rules. According to the Advocate General, minutes of a meeting (even if they are structured according to certain criteria) only containing 'incidental' personal data were not part of a 'structured set of personal data which are accessible according to specific criteria' (this is the definition of 'filing system').[10] The use of automated means to locate the requested document, according to the Advocate General, just replicated something that could be done manually.[11] Although the Advocate General provided an original way out of the complicated reconciliation of data protection and public access rules, the Court did

---

[6] See Joined Cases C-203/15 and C-698/15, *Tele2*, paras. 72 and 73. This position was confirmed in Case C-207/16, *Ministerio Fiscal*, paras. 29–39. See on the relationship between Art. 3(2), first indent, and Art. 13 DPD the CJEU in Case C-73/16, *Puškár*, paras. 35–44. See also the Opinion in Case C-73/16, *Puškár* (AG Opinion), paras. 26–30.

[7] See Case C-73/16, *Puškár*, para. 38. See also Case C-25/17, *Jehovan todistajat*, para. 37.

[8] Kranenborg 2014, pp. 243–247.

[9] The case concerned the data protection rules applicable to the Union institutions and bodies (Regulation 45/2001), which had to be reconciled with the rules on public access to documents (Regulation 1049/2001). The text of Art. 3(1) Regulation 45/2001 (on scope) was similar to Art. 2(1) GDPR. For Regulation 45/2001, see Table of Legislation.

[10] Case C-28/08 P, *Bavarian Lager* (AG Opinion), para. 137.   [11] Ibid., paras. 137 and 144.

not follow her in this respect, and applied the data protection rules without going into the suggested limitation of the material scope.[12]

In its first two rulings on the DPD in 2003, the CJEU was confronted with questions about the scope of the data protection rules. The DPD was based on an internal market legal basis aiming at the approximation of laws, and the referring national courts queried whether the situations at hand could actually be qualified as falling under the internal market rules. In *Österreichischer Rundfunk*, there was a conflict between local and regional authorities and the Austrian Court of Auditors (the Rechnungshof) as to whether the authorities were obliged to provide certain income data about their employees to the Rechnungshof in order for the latter to perform its audit function and whether this was in conformity with the data protection rules of the DPD. According to the Austrian government the DPD was not applicable as the control activity of the Rechnungshof pursued an objective in the public interest in the field of public accounts which did not fall with the scope of Union law.[13] The second case, *Lindqvist*, concerned the publication on a Swedish internet site of certain personal information by Mrs Lindqvist about colleague volunteers in the Swedish church. Mrs Lindqvist argued that the DPD did not apply, since her activities were essentially not economic but charitable and religious.

In both cases the CJEU concluded that the DPD did apply. The CJEU considered that the recourse to an internal market legal basis does not presuppose the existence of an actual link with the free movement between Member States in every situation referred to by the measure founded on that basis. A contrary interpretation, according to the Court, could make the limits of the field of application of the DPD particularly unsure and uncertain.[14] It led Advocate General Kokott to conclude, in a later case, that the broad scope of the DPD 'reaches almost beyond the establishment of the internal market'.[15] Article 16 TFEU, the new single legal basis for data protection rules, refers to the free movement of personal data. It may be assumed that the broad material scope of the GDPR has not changed in this respect.[16]

3. Personal or household activities

Another question in *Lindqvist* was whether the activities of Mrs Lindqvist should not be considered as activities in the course of purely personal or household activities under Article 3 DPD (the exclusion of Article 2(2)(c) GDPR). Examples of such activities given in recital 18 of the GDPR are correspondence and the holding of addresses, or social networking and online activity undertaken within the context of such activities. In *Lindqvist*, the CJEU was firm on this. It considered that the processing of personal data consisting in publication on the internet so that the data are made accessible to an indefinite number of people clearly cannot be qualified as purely personal or household activities.[17] In its Opinion on social networks, the WP29 concluded that, in principle, data processing by users in the context of such networks (Facebook, LinkedIn) falls within the

---

[12] Case C-28/08 P, *Bavarian Lager*.
[13] Joined Cases C-465/00, C-138/01 and C-139/01, *Österreichischer Rundfunk*, para. 36.
[14] Case C-101/01, *Lindqvist*, paras. 40–41; Joined Cases C-465/00, C-138/01 and C-139/01, *Österreichischer Rundfunk*, paras. 41–42.
[15] Case C-73/07, *Satamedia* (AG Opinion), para. 53.
[16] See on Art. 16 TFEU also Hijmans 2016, chapters 4–6.
[17] Case C-101/01, *Lindqvist*, para. 47. See also Case C-73/07, *Satamedia*, para. 44.

scope of the household exemption.[18] However, under certain circumstances the activities of a user could extend beyond a purely personal or household activity, for instance if the social network is used as a collaboration platform for an association or a company. Also, according to the WP29, a high number of contacts could be an indication that the household exception does not apply.[19] Probably because it is difficult to draw a line, the GDPR has not yet ruled on this point. Recital 18 only underlines that the GDPR applies to controllers or processors which provide the means for processing personal data for such personal or household activities.

The exclusion of purely personal or household activities was also considered in *Ryneš*. A surveillance camera installed by a private individual (Mr Ryneš) on his private premises for security reasons did not qualify as processing of personal data in the course of purely personal or household activities, since it covered a public space (a public footpath in front of the house) and was accordingly directed outwards from the private setting of the person processing the data.[20] In its analysis, the CJEU referred to the examples of correspondence and the keeping of address books, and added that these may qualify as purely personal or household activities, 'even if they incidentally concern or may concern the private life of other persons'.[21] The CJEU seemed to be inspired by the Opinion of Advocate General Jääskinen in the case, although it did not as such adopt his elaborate reasoning on this point. The Advocate General had defined *personal* activities as 'activities which are closely and objectively linked to the private life of an individual and which do not significantly impinge upon the personal sphere of others'.[22] According to the Advocate General these activities could take place also outside the home, whereas *household* activities are linked to family life and normally take place at a person's home or in other places shared with family members, such as second homes, hotel rooms or private cars. In the end the Advocate General took the view that the data processed by Mr Ryneš through his camera fell within the scope of the data protection rules as they could not be seen as *purely* personal or household activities.[23] The CJEU followed this position, stressing that the exception, like all derogations from fundamental rights, had to be narrowly construed and that the processing carried out was a 'purely' personal or household activity and not 'simply' a personal or household activity.[24]

It follows from both *Lindqvist* and *Ryneš* that the exclusion of purely personal or household activities must be interpreted as covering only activities that are carried out in the context of the private or family life of individuals. In that connection, an activity cannot be regarded as being purely personal or domestic where its purpose is to make the data collected accessible to an unrestricted number of people or where that activity extends, even partially, to a public space and is accordingly directed outwards from the private setting of the person processing the data in that manner.

The CJEU applied this test in *Jehovah's Witnesses*, in which a Finnish court had asked, relating to the DPD, whether the taking of notes by Jehovah's Witnesses of persons they did or did not speak to during their door-to-door preaching, could be considered as a collection of personal data in the course of a purely personal activity.[25] The CJEU considered the data collection by the Jehovah's Witnesses could not be qualified as taking place in the course of a purely personal activity. According to the Court the

---

[18] See WP29 2009, p. 5.   [19] Ibid., p. 6.   [20] Case C-212/13, *Ryneš*, para. 33.
[21] Ibid., para. 32.   [22] Case C-212/13, *Ryneš* (AG Opinion), para. 51.   [23] Ibid., para. 56.
[24] Case C-212/13, *Ryneš*, paras. 28–31.   [25] Case C-25/17, *Jehovan todistajat*, para. 42.

door-to-door preaching, by its very nature, was intended to spread the faith of the Jehovah's Witnesses community among people who do not belong to the faith of the members who engage in preaching. Therefore, that activity was directed outwards from the private setting of the members who engage in preaching. Furthermore, some of the data collected by the members of that community were sent by them to the congregations of that community which compiled lists from that data of persons who no longer wish to receive visits from those members. Thus, in the course of their preaching, those members made at least some of the data collected accessible to a potentially unlimited number of persons.[26] The Court also considered that although the door-to-door preaching activities of the member of a religious community are protected by the freedom of religion enshrined in Article 10(1) of the Charter as an expression of the faith of those preachers, that fact did not confer an exclusively personal or household character on that activity.[27]

The EDBP has opined on the scope of personal and household activities in the scope of video surveillance. In its guidelines on video surveillance, the EDPB stated that whether video surveillance falls under the household exemption depends on several factors,[28] and gives the following examples:

'Example: A tourist is recording videos both through his mobile phone and through a camcorder to document his holidays. He shows the footage to friends and family but does not make it accessible for an indefinite number of people. This would fall under the household exemption.

Example: A downhill mountainbiker wants to record her descent with an actioncam. She is riding in a remote area and only plans to use the recordings for her personal entertainment at home. This would fall under the household exemption.

Example: Somebody is monitoring and recording his own garden. The property is fenced and only the controller himself and his family are entering the garden on a regular basis. This would fall under the household exemption, provided that the video surveillance does not extend even partially to a public space or neighbouring property'.[29]

4. Activities outside the scope of Union law

Processing of personal data in the course of an activity that falls outside the scope of Union law is also excluded from the material scope of the GDPR (Article 2(2)(a)). The main example is activities concerning national security (see recital 16). According to Article 4(2) TEU 'national security remains the sole responsibility of each Member State'.[30] However, since the objective of national security also appears in Article 23 GDPR, the general restrictions clause, it could be questioned whether certain activities in the context of national security can be assessed against the requirements in the GDPR, read in the light of the Charter, in particular if it involves use of data initially collected by private entities, such as telecommunications providers, for their business purposes. This could follow from the *Tele2* ruling, which was already referred to above. It is precisely this question which was put to the CJEU in *Privacy International*, in which the CJEU was asked whether the same reasoning of the CJEU in the *Tele2* case applied in case the measures at stake do not concern law enforcement but national security. The case was still pending when this text was finalised.[31]

---

[26] Ibid., paras. 44–45.   [27] Ibid., para. 49.   [28] EDPB 2019, p. 6.   [29] Ibid., p. 7.
[30] See on this also Timmermans 2017, chapter 2.   [31] Case C-623/17, *Privacy International*.

5. Activities in relation to the common foreign and security policy

As said, the exclusion from the scope of the GDPR of Member State activities in relation to the common foreign and security policy (Article 2(2)(b) GDPR) follows from Article 16 TFEU, which states that it is without prejudice to the specific rules laid down in Article 39 TEU. According to Article 39 TEU the Council shall adopt a decision laying down the data protection rules with regard to the processing of personal data by the Member States when carrying out activities which fall within the scope of the common foreign and security policy. Article 39 TEU derogates from Article 16(2) TFEU in terms of decision-making procedure: whereas under Article 16 TFEU the ordinary legislative procedure applies, under Article 39 TEU the Council decides alone, acting unanimously. No specific rules had yet been adopted when this text was finalised.

6. Law enforcement activities

The processing of personal data by competent authorities for the purposes of the prevention, investigation, detection or prosecution of criminal offences or the execution of criminal penalties, including the safeguarding against and the prevention of threats to public security (Article 2(2)d) GDPR), refers to the LED. The scope of this exclusion is similar to the actual scope of the LED. Article 2(2) LED repeats the positively formulated material scope of the GDPR and has the same definitions of 'personal data', 'processing' and 'filing system' (see Article 3(1), (2) and (6) LED). It excludes from its scope processing of personal data in the course of an activity that falls outside the scope of the Union law, and by the Union institutions, bodies, offices and agencies (Article 2(3) LED). However, the specific material scope of the LED depends on the notions of 'competent authority' and 'criminal offences'. The first is defined in Article 3(7) LED, however, the second is not defined in the LED, despite the statement in recital 13 that the notion of 'criminal offence' is an autonomous concept of Union law. The competent authority is defined as 'any public authority competent for the prevention, investigation, detection or prosecution of criminal offences or the execution of criminal penalties, including the safeguarding against and the prevention of threats to public security' or 'any other body or entity entrusted by Member State law to exercise public authority and public powers' for such purposes. It follows that to a certain extent, the precise delimitation between GDPR and LED depends on the law of the Member States. As follows from recital 18 of the GDPR (and recital 11 LED) a single public authority can be subject to both the GDPR and the LED depending on the purposes of its activities.

7. Data processing by courts and judicial authorities

Although not set forth in Article 2 or in any other provisions of the GDPR, recital 20 states that, when the GDPR applies, Union or Member State law may specify the processing operations and processing procedures in relation to the processing of personal data by courts and other judicial authorities. The competence of the supervisory authorities does not cover the processing of personal data when courts act in their judicial capacity. The latter limitation is laid down in Article 55(3) GDPR.[32] According to recital

---

[32] See also Art. 45(2) LED.

20, it should also be possible to entrust supervision of such data processing operations to specific bodies within the judicial system of the Member State.

8. EU institutions

The rules for processing of personal data by Union institutions and bodies were laid down in Regulation 45/2001. This Regulation also established the EDPS, who started work in 2004.

Following Article 2(3) and Article 98 of the GDPR, the European Commission tabled a proposal to revise Regulation 45/2001 in order to align it with the GDPR.[33] This led to the adoption of the EUDPR in October 2018. Although in principle covering all EU institutions and bodies, the EUDPR proposal made clear that where the founding act of a Union agency carrying out activities which fall within the scope of Chapters 4 and 5 of Title V TFEU (judicial cooperation in criminal matter and police cooperation) contains a stand-alone data protection regime for data protection, these regimes should be unaffected. This referred to Europol, Eurojust and the European Public Prosecutor's Office ('EPPO').[34] The proposal of the Commission did not contain any specific rules for the area of criminal law enforcement.

However, during the legislative process the European Parliament insisted on having a chapter dedicated to protection of personal data in the context of EU law enforcement activities which would contain the general, overarching rules on data protection for the Union bodies active in this area. The co-legislators finally agreed to include such a chapter in the EUDPR, but also laid down that the chapter would not apply to Europol and the EPPO until their founding regulations were adapted.[35] A review of these acts has to be performed by the European Commission by 30 April 2022.[36] The then pending legislative procedure on the revision of the founding act of Eurojust was used to adjust the Eurojust Regulation in such a way that the specific law enforcement chapter in the EUDPR would apply to Eurojust.[37]

9. EPD

Nothing can be found in Article 2 GDPR about its relationship with the EPD, although Article 95 states that the GDPR may not impose additional obligations on natural or legal persons in relation to processing for which they are subject to specific obligations with the same objectives set out in the EPD (see the commentary on Article 95 in this volume). The EPD itself determines in Article 1(2) that the provisions of the EPD 'particularise and complement' the DPD. The same wording has been included in the proposal for a new EPR.[38] The proposal to revise the EPD follows from the instruction in recital 173 GDPR to amend and review the EPD in order to clarify its relationship with the GDPR and to ensure consistency with the GDPR. The legislative procedure on the EPR was still pending when this text was finalised.

---

[33] EUDPR Proposal.
[34] See Europol Regulation 2016, in particular Chapter VI; Council Decision 2002/187/JHA; and EPPO Regulation 2017, Chapter VIII. Chapter VIII of the EPPO Regulation more or less constitutes a 'transposition' of the LED. The Eurojust Regulation was adopted on 14 November 2018.
[35] See Art. 2(3) EUDPR. Art. 2(4) EUDPR provides that it does not apply to the processing of personal data by missions referred to in Arts. 42(1), 43 and 44 TEU.
[36] See Art. 98 EUDPR.   [37] See Art. 26(1) Eurojust Regulation 2018.   [38] EPR Proposal.

10. e-Commerce Directive

The fourth paragraph of Article 2 states that the GDPR is without prejudice to the e-Commerce Directive (Directive 2000/31/EC). Reference is made in particular to Articles 12–15 of that Directive which contain rules on the liability of intermediary service providers. These rules establish the liability of such providers for situations in which they (1) merely transmit information, (2) 'cache' information for the sole purpose of making the transmission of information more efficient or (3) only store information.

Select Bibliography

EU legislation

Council Decision 2002/187/JHA: Council Decision 2002/187/JHA of 28 February 2002 setting up Eurojust with a view to reinforcing the fight against serious crime (as amended), OJ 2002 L 63/1.

Directive 2000/31/EC of the European Parliament and of the Council of 8 June 2000 on certain legal aspects of information society services, in particular electronic commerce, in the Internal Market ('Directive on electronic commerce'), OJ 2000 L 178/1.

EPPO Regulation 2017: Council Regulation (EU) 2017/1939 of 12 October 2017 implementing enhanced cooperation on the establishment of the European Public Prosecutor's Office ('the EPPO'), OJ 2017 L 238/1.

EPR Proposal: Proposal for a Regulation of the European Parliament and the Council concerning the respect for private life and the protection of personal data in electronic communications and repealing Directive 2002/58/EC (Regulation on Privacy and Electronic Communications), COM(2017) 10 final.

EUDPR Proposal: Proposal for a Regulation of the European Parliament and the Council on the protection of individuals with regard to the processing of personal data by the Union institutions, bodies, offices and agencies and on the free movement of such data, and repealing Regulation (EC) No. 45/2001 and Decision No. 1247/2002/EC, COM(2017) 8 final.

Eurojust Regulation 2018: Regulation (EU) 2018/1727 of the European Parliament and of the Council of 14 November 2018 on the European Union Agency for Criminal Justice Cooperation (Eurojust), and replacing and repealing Council Decision 2002/187/JHA, OJ 2018 L 295/138.

Europol Regulation 2016: Regulation (EU) 2016/794 of the European Parliament and of the Council of 11 May 2016 on the European Agency for Law Enforcement Cooperation (Europol), OJ 2016 L 135/53.

Regulation 1049/2001: Regulation (EC) No. 1049/2001 of the European Parliament and of the Council of 30 May 2001 regarding public access to European Parliament, Council and Commission documents, OJ 2001 L 145/43.

Academic writings

Blume and Svanberg 2013: Blume and Svanberg, 'The Proposed Data Protection Regulation: The Illusion of Harmonisation, the Private/Public Sector Divide and the Bureaucratic Apparatus', 15 *Cambridge Yearbook of European Legal Studies* (2013), 27.

Docksey 2014: Docksey, 'The European Court of Justice and the Decade of Surveillance', in Hijmans and Kranenborg (eds.), *Data Protection Anno 2014: How to Restore Trust?* (Intersentia 2014), 97.

Hijmans 2016: Hijmans, *The European Union as a Constitutional Guardian of Internet Privacy and Data Protection* (Springer 2016).

Hijmans and Scirocco 2009: Hijmans and Scirocco, 'Shortcomings in EU Data Protection in the Third and Second Pillars: Can the Lisbon Treaty Be Expected to Help?', 46(5) *Common Market Law Review* (2009), 1485.

Kranenborg 2014: Kranenborg, 'Article 8', in Peers, Hervey, Kenner and Ward (eds.), *The EU Charter of Fundamental Rights—A Commentary* (Hart Publishing 2014).

Timmermans 2017: Timmermans, 'The Competence Divide of the Lisbon Treaty Six Years After', in Garben and Govaere (eds.), *The Division of Competences between the EU and the Member States: Reflections on the Past, the Present and the Future* (Bloomsbury Publishing plc 2017), 19.

Papers of data protection authorities

EDPB 2019: European Data Protection Board, 'Guidelines 3/2019 on the processing of personal data through video devices (version for public consultation)' (10 July 2019).

WP29 2009: Article 29 Working Party, 'Opinion 5/2009 on Online Social Networking' (WP 163, 12 June 2009).

Article 29 Working Party, 'Opinion 4/2007 on the Concept of Personal Data' (WP 136, 20 June 2007).

Article 3. Territorial scope

DAN JERKER B. SVANTESSON

1. This Regulation applies to the processing of personal data in the context of the activities of an establishment of a controller or a processor in the Union, regardless of whether the processing takes place in the Union or not.
2. This Regulation applies to the processing of personal data of data subjects who are in the Union by a controller or processor not established in the Union, where the processing activities are related to:
   (a) the offering of goods or services, irrespective of whether a payment of the data subject is required, to such data subjects in the Union; or
   (b) the monitoring of their behaviour as far as their behaviour takes place within the Union.
3. This Regulation applies to the processing of personal data by a controller not established in the Union, but in a place where Member State law applies by virtue of public international law.

Relevant Recitals

(22) Any processing of personal data in the context of the activities of an establishment of a controller or a processor in the Union should be carried out in accordance with this Regulation, regardless of whether the processing itself takes place within the Union. Establishment implies the effective and real exercise of activity through stable arrangements. The legal form of such arrangements, whether through a branch or a subsidiary with a legal personality, is not the determining factor in that respect.

(23) In order to ensure that natural persons are not deprived of the protection to which they are entitled under this Regulation, the processing of personal data of data subjects who are in the Union by a controller or a processor not established in the Union should be subject to this Regulation where the processing activities are related to offering goods or services to such data subjects irrespective of whether connected to a payment. In order to determine whether such a controller or processor is offering goods or services to data subjects who are in the Union, it should be ascertained whether it is apparent that the controller or processor envisages offering services to data subjects in one or more Member States in the Union. Whereas the mere accessibility of the controller's, processor's or an intermediary's website in the Union, of an email address or of other contact details, or the use of a language generally used in the third country where the controller is established, is insufficient to ascertain such intention, factors such as the use of a language or a currency generally used in one or more Member States with the possibility of ordering goods and services in that other language, or the mentioning of customers or users who are in the Union, may make it apparent that the controller envisages offering goods or services to data subjects in the Union.

(24) The processing of personal data of data subjects who are in the Union by a controller or processor not established in the Union should also be subject to this Regulation when it is related to the monitoring of the behaviour of such data subjects in so far as their behaviour takes place within the Union. In order to determine whether a processing activity can be considered to monitor the behaviour of data subjects, it should be ascertained whether natural persons are tracked on the internet including potential subsequent use of personal data processing techniques which consist

of profiling a natural person, particularly in order to take decisions concerning her or him or for analysing or predicting her or his personal preferences, behaviours and attitudes.

(25) Where Member State law applies by virtue of public international law, this Regulation should also apply to a controller not established in the Union, such as in a Member State's diplomatic mission or consular post.

Closely Related Provisions

Article 2 (Material scope) (see too recitals 13–21 and 27); Articles 44–50 (Transfer of personal data to third countries or international organisations) (see too recitals 101–116); Articles 55–58 (Competence, tasks and powers) (see too recitals 122–124, 127–129, 131–133 and 137); Article 79 (Right to an effective judicial remedy against a controller or processor) (see too recitals 141, 145 and 147)

Related Provisions in EPD [Directive 2002/58/EC]

Articles 1 (Scope and aim) and 3 (Services concerned)

Relevant Case Law

CJEU

Case 52/69, *J. R. Geigy AG v Commission of the European Communities*, judgment of 14 July 1972 (ECLI:EU:C:1972:73).
Case C-366/10, *Air Transport Association of America and Others v Secretary of State for Energy and Climate Change*, judgment of 21 December 2011 (Grand Chamber) (ECLI:EU:C:2011:864).
Joined Cases C-585/08 and C-144/09, *Peter Pammer v Reederei Karl Schlüter GmbH & Co. KG and Hotel Alpenhof GesmbH v Oliver Heller*, judgment of 7 December 2010 (Grand Chamber) (ECLI:EU:C:2010:740).
Case C-131/12, *Google Spain SL and Google Inc. v Agencia Española de Protección de Datos (AEPD) and Mario Costeja González*, judgment of 13 May 2014 (Grand Chamber) (ECLI:EU:C:2014:317).
Case C-230/14, *Weltimmo s.r.o. v Nemzeti Adatvédelmi és Információszabadság Hatóság*, judgment of 1 October 2015 (ECLI:EU:C:2015:639).
Opinion of Advocate General Cruz Villalón in C-230/14, *Weltimmo s.r.o. v Nemzeti Adatvédelmi és Információszabadság Hatóság*, delivered on 25 June 2015 (ECLI:EU:C:2015:426).
Case C-191/15, *Verein für Konsumenteninformation v Amazon EU Sàrl*, judgment of 28 July 2016 (ECLI:EU:C:2016:612).
Opinion of Advocate General Saugmandsgaard Øe in C-191/15, *Verein für Konsumenteninformation v Amazon EU Sàrl*, delivered on 2 June 2016 (ECLI:EU:C:2016:388).
Case C-210/16, *Unabhängiges Landeszentrum für Datenschutz Schleswig-Holstein v Wirtschaftsakademie Schleswig-Holstein GmbH*, judgment of 5 June 2018 (Grand Chamber) (ECLI:EU:C:2018:388).
Opinion of Advocate General Bot in C-210/16, *Unabhängiges Landeszentrum für Datenschutz Schleswig-Holstein v Wirtschaftsakademie Schleswig-Holstein GmbH*, delivered on 24 October 2017 (ECLI:EU:C:2017:796).
Case C-621/18, *Andy Wightman and Others v Secretary of State for Exiting the European Union*, judgment of 10 December 2018 (Full Court) (ECLI:EU:C:2018:999).
Opinion of Advocate General Szpunar in Case C-507/17, *Google Inc. v Commission nationale de l'informatique et des libertés (CNIL)*, delivered on 10 January 2019 (ECLI:EU:C:2019:15).

United States

Amicus Brief of Amici Curiae Jan Philipp Albrecht, Sophie in t'Veld, Viviane Reding, Birgit Sippel, and Axel Voss, Members of the European Parliament in support of respondent Microsoft Corporation in: *United States v Microsoft Corporation*, US 584 (2018), available at https://blogs.microsoft.com/datalaw/wp-content/uploads/sites/149/2018/01/Brief-of-EU-Parliament-Members.pdf.

Amicus Brief of the European Commission on behalf of the European Union as *Amicus Curiae* in support of neither party in: *United States v Microsoft Corporation*, US 584 (2018), available at https://www.supremecourt.gov/DocketPDF/17/17-2/23655/20171213123137791_17-2%20ac%20European%20Commission%20for%20filing.pdf.

A. Rationale and Policy Underpinnings

Article 3 delineates the GDPR's scope of application, purportedly in a spatial sense. Yet, to understand the rationale underpinning Article 3, we must start by recognising that the Article's rubric 'Territorial scope' should not be taken literally. Disregarding occasional expansions, and events such as 'Brexit', the EU's territory is stable, (largely) undisputed and measurable in square metres. However, it is not *that* territorial scope to which the Article relates. Rather, Article 3 outlines what types of contact with the EU's territory will activate the application of the GDPR, and it does so in a manner that is partly territoriality-dependent and partly territoriality-independent.

Already from the outset, it was clear that a key policy driving, as well as justifying, the data protection reform that resulted in the GDPR was a perceived need to expand the scope of application of the EU's data protection law. Such an expansion was argued to ensure a 'level playing-field' between businesses based in the EU and businesses based outside the EU, but doing business on the European market. This, it was suggested, would lead to fair competition in a globalised world.[1] This thinking may be criticised as unrealistic, and lacking nuance, in that compliance with the GDPR as a whole is likely to be prohibitively expensive for many controllers and processors not established in the Union. Thus, some may see the GDPR's broad scope of application as anti-competitive in a globalised world. Nevertheless, the policy approach expressed in this thinking must be noted as it potentially will impact the practical application of Article 3. Put somewhat simplistically, this policy aim points to a likelihood of Article 3 being interpreted in a manner giving it a broad reach.

Further, it is here worth recalling the frequency with which the CJEU's interpretation of various aspects of the DPD have been guided by the fact that 'the directive aims to ensure a high level of protection of the fundamental rights and freedoms of natural persons, in particular their right to privacy, with respect to the processing of personal data'.[2] This suggests that courts and DPAs will give Article 3 a broad reach.

However, it must be emphasised that a key purpose of Article 3 is to position the GDPR within the international system. And in this context, clear guidance is provided by the Commission, in the form of its amicus brief filed in relation to the matter between the United States of America and Microsoft Corporation (the *Microsoft Warrant* case) heard in the United States Supreme Court on 27 February 2018. There, the Commission refers

---

[1] See Reding 2014; a similar sentiment is expressed by Albrecht 2016, p. 476.
[2] See e.g. Case C-210/16, *Wirtschaftsakademie Schleswig-Holstein*, para. 26.

to Articles 3(5) and 21(1) Treaty on European Union ('TEU'), and the cases *Geigy*[3] and *Air Transport*[4] and notes:

Any domestic law that creates cross-border obligations—whether enacted by the United States, the European Union, or another state—should be applied and interpreted in a manner that is mindful of the restrictions of international law and considerations of international comity. The European Union's foundational treaties and case law enshrine the principles of 'mutual regard to the spheres of jurisdiction' of sovereign states and of the need to interpret and apply EU legislation in a manner that is consistent with international law.[5]

This proclamation may no doubt be seen as the key to understanding the proper application of Article 3, and clearly calls for a degree of restraint in recognition of the interests of foreign states and the international order. Indeed, this proclamation draws attention to the fact that a provision such as Article 3 is designed, not only to maximise the implementation of the policy goals pursued in the GDPR, but also to ensure the harmonious coexistence between different legal systems.

Finally, it is worth emphasising the importance of the very fact that a provision like Article 3 is included in the GDPR. Not all data protection schemes, or even all EU instruments, include a provision aimed at clarifying their scope of application. The inclusion of an Article like Article 3 is useful and, as noted by Jääskinen and Ward, it is good practice for the 'EU legislature to address the external reach of measures of EU private law in the individual measures themselves, whether that be a regulation or a directive'.[6]

B. Legal Background

1. EU legislation

Article 3's predecessor in the DPD is Article 4. It reads as follows:

Article 4—National law applicable

1. Each Member State shall apply the national provisions it adopts pursuant to this Directive to the processing of personal data where:
   (a) the processing is carried out in the context of the activities of an establishment of the controller on the territory of the Member State; when the same controller is established on the territory of several Member States, he must take the necessary measures to ensure that each of these establishments complies with the obligations laid down by the national law applicable;
   (b) the controller is not established on the Member State's territory, but in a place where its national law applies by virtue of international public law;
   (c) the controller is not established on Community territory and, for purposes of processing personal data makes use of equipment, automated or otherwise, situated on the territory of the said Member State, unless such equipment is used only for purposes of transit through the territory of the Community.
2. In the circumstances referred to in paragraph 1 (c), the controller must designate a representative established in the territory of that Member State, without prejudice to legal actions which could be initiated against the controller himself.

---

[3] Case C-52/69, *Geigy*, para. 11.   [4] Case C-366/10, *Air Transport*, para. 123.
[5] EC amicus brief, *United States v Microsoft Corporation*, p. 7.
[6] Jääskinen and Ward 2016, p. 128.

2. International instruments

There are no international treaties that specifically and expressly regulate the scope of application of data protection laws. However, it should be noted that: 'EU data protection law is based largely on fundamental rights law so that the permissibility of extraterritoriality in data protection depends largely on the extraterritorial scope of EU fundamental rights instruments'.[7] As a consequence, several international treaties impact Article 3 indirectly. For example, according to Article 13 European Convention of Human Rights ('ECHR'): 'Everyone whose rights and freedoms as set forth in this Convention are violated shall have an effective remedy before a national authority notwithstanding that the violation has been committed by persons acting in an official capacity'.

Furthermore, the Council of Europe's Convention 108 is relevant. Article 1 of the current version reads as follows: 'The purpose of this convention is to secure in the territory of each Party for every individual, whatever his nationality or residence, respect for his rights and fundamental freedoms, and in particular his right to privacy, with regard to automatic processing of personal data relating to him ("data protection")'. In May 2018 the Convention was modernised, though the new version of the Convention has not yet entered into force. Article 3 of the Modernised Convention reads as follows:

Article 3—Scope

1. Each Party undertakes to apply this Convention to data processing subject to its jurisdiction in the public and private sectors, thereby securing every individual's right to protection of his or her personal data.
2. This Convention shall not apply to data processing carried out by an individual in the course of purely personal or household activities. [8]

Mention should also be made of how Article 8(3) of the Charter of Fundamental Rights of the European Union ('CFR') points to the fact that 'the national supervisory authorities are responsible ... for monitoring compliance with the EU rules concerning the protection of individuals with regard to the processing of personal data'.[9]

Finally, the fact that the application of the GDPR will impact the human rights of non-EU individuals is of great significance; it means that in assessing the human rights implications of the GDPR account must be taken of human rights law beyond Europe's human rights law.

Article 2(1) of the International Covenant on Civil and Political Rights ('ICCPR') states:

Each State Party to the present Covenant undertakes to respect and to ensure to all individuals within its territory and subject to its jurisdiction the rights recognized in the present Covenant, without distinction of any kind, such as race, colour, sex, language, religion, political or other opinion, national or social origin, property, birth or other status.

Arguably, the phrase 'to respect and to ensure to all individuals within its territory and subject to its jurisdiction the rights recognised in the present Covenant' expresses two separate requirements rather than a double requirement.[10] From that vantage point, each signatory state has an obligation to provide legal protection against unlawful infringements

---

[7] Kuner 2015, p. 243. [8] Art. 3 Modernised Convention 108.
[9] Case C-210/16, *Wirtschaftsakademie Schleswig-Holstein*, para. 71. [10] Svantesson 2014, p. 78.

of the rights of people subject to its jurisdiction and those present within its territory, regardless of the origins of such infringements.

3. National developments

Being of central importance, provisions delineating the territorial scope of application are commonly found in national data protection legislation. An example of the national implementation of Article 3's predecessor in the DPD (Article 4) can be found in section 4 of the former Swedish Personal Data Act:

This Act applies to those controllers of personal data who are established in Sweden. The Act is also applicable when the controller of personal data is established in a third country but for the processing of the personal data uses equipment that is situated in Sweden.

However, this does not apply if the equipment is only used to transfer information between a third country and another such country.

In the case referred to in the second paragraph, first sentence, the controller of personal data shall appoint a representative for himself who is established in Sweden. The provisions of this Act concerning the controller of personal data shall also apply to the representative.[11]

The Swedish Act has since been replaced by the GDPR.

4. Case law

The CJEU has ruled directly on the subject matter of Article 3 on a number of occasions, but thus far only in the context of Article 4 DPD. One example is its judgment in the *Google Spain* case. The reason the *Google Spain* case gave rise to Article 4 considerations is because Google argued that the local branch of Google (in this case, Google Spain) being within the reach of the local law did not automatically mean that the US-based Google Inc. (now Google LLC), that operates the company's well-known search engine, would be. The CJEU concluded that 'the activities of the operator of the search engine and those of its establishment situated in the Member State concerned are inextricably linked'[12] meaning that Google Inc. also falls within the ambit of Article 4(1)(a) DPD (and presumably Article 3(1) GDPR). This conclusion was justified by reference to the objective of the DPD and of the wording of Article 4(1)(a) thereof, as well as the fact that Google Spain is intended to promote and sell, in Spain, advertising space to make the service offered by Google Inc. profitable—thus, meeting the test of the processing being carried out in the context of the activities of an establishment of the controller on the territory of the Member State (in this case, Spain), articulated in Article 4(1)(a) DPD.

The wider impact of the *Google Spain* case—as far as the territorial scope is concerned—should be read in conjunction with two other CJEU decisions. In *Verein für Konsumenteninformation*, the CJEU concluded that Article 4(1)(a) DPD must be interpreted as meaning that the processing of personal data carried out by an undertaking engaged in electronic commerce is governed by the law of the Member State to which that undertaking directs its activities, if it is shown that the undertaking carries out the data processing in question in the context of the activities of an establishment situated in that Member State. The CJEU also emphasised that it is for the national court to ascertain whether that is so.[13]

---

[11] Swedish Personal Data Act 1998, s. 4.   [12] Case C-131/12, *Google Spain*, paras. 55–56.
[13] Case C-191/15, *Verein für Konsumenteninformation*, para. 82.

In his Opinion in *Verein für Konsumenteninformation*, Advocate General Saugmandsgaard Øe emphasised that the reason the CJEU in *Google Spain* gave such a broad interpretation to Article 4(1)(a) DPD was to avoid the processing in question escaping the obligations laid down in the DPD.[14] Thus, such a broad interpretation might not be legitimate where such a risk is not present. On the other hand, in *Wirtschaftsakademie Schleswig-Holstein*, Advocate General Bot expressed the view that: 'The fact that, by contrast with the situation in the case which gave rise to the judgment of 13 May 2014, *Google Spain*, ... the Facebook group has a European head office, in Ireland, does not mean that the interpretation of Article 4(1)(a) of Directive 95/46 which the Court adopted in that judgment cannot be applied in the present case'.[15] Consequently, this matter remained to be adequately clarified. While the CJEU did not engage with this distinction in its decision in *Wirtschaftsakademie Schleswig-Holstein*, it clearly sided with the view expressed by Advocate General Bot in holding that:

[W]here an undertaking established outside the European Union has several establishments in different Member States, the supervisory authority of a Member State is entitled to exercise the powers conferred on it by Article 28(3) of that directive with respect to an establishment of that undertaking situated in the territory of that Member State even if, as a result of the division of tasks within the group, first, that establishment is responsible solely for the sale of advertising space and other marketing activities in the territory of that Member State and, second, exclusive responsibility for collecting and processing personal data belongs, for the entire territory of the European Union, to an establishment situated in another Member State.[16]

Weltimmo involved a blatant instance of a business in one Member State (Slovakia) being set up to engage only in business in another Member State (Hungary). In discussing the meaning of the term 'establishment', the CJEU noted that, while the owner resided in Hungary, Weltimmo was registered in Slovakia and was, therefore, established there within the meaning of company law. However, Weltimmo carried out no activity in Slovakia but had representatives in Hungary. Weltimmo had opened a bank account in Hungary and had a letter box there for its everyday business affairs. The property website which constituted its main business was written exclusively in Hungarian and dealt only with properties in Hungary. All this suggests that Weltimmo had a substantial connection to Hungary and that Hungary had a legitimate interest in the matter. It also suggests that the actual link to Slovakia—the place of registration—was comparatively weak.

In the light of this, the CJEU held that Weltimmo pursued a real and effective activity in Hungary, and the Court stressed the need for a flexible definition of the concept of 'establishment', rather than a formalistic approach whereby undertakings are established solely in the place where they are registered:

Article 4(1)(a) ... must be interpreted as permitting the application of the law on the protection of personal data of a Member State other than the Member State in which the controller with respect to the processing of those data is registered, in so far as that controller exercises, through stable arrangements in the territory of that Member State, a real and effective activity—even a minimal one—in the context of which that processing is carried out ... [17]

---

[14] Case C-191/15, *Verein für Konsumenteninformation* (AG Opinion), paras. 124–125.
[15] Case C-210/16, *Unabhängiges Landeszentrum* (AG Opinion), para. 95.
[16] Case C-210/16, *Unabhängiges Landeszentrum*, para. 75.
[17] Case C-230/14, *Weltimmo*, para. 41.

Expanding upon this point, the CJEU also noted:

[I]n order to ascertain, in circumstances such as those at issue in the main proceedings, whether that is the case, the referring court may, in particular, take account of the fact (i) that the activity of the controller in respect of that processing, in the context of which that processing takes place, consists of the running of property dealing websites concerning properties situated in the territory of that Member State and written in that Member State's language and that it is, as a consequence, mainly or entirely directed at that Member State, and (ii) that controller has a representative in that Member State, who is responsible for recovering the debts resulting from that activity and for representing the controller in the administrative and judicial proceedings relating to the processing of the data concerned ... [18]

The Court added that, by contrast, the issue of the nationality of the persons concerned by such data processing is irrelevant.[19]

Further clarification of the territorial scope of the GDPR under Article 3 is expected by the CJEU. In *Google Inc. v CNIL*,[20] Advocate General Szpunar proposed on 10 January 2019 that the scope of the de-referencing that search engine operators are required to carry out should be limited to the EU.[21] The Court had not issued its judgment at the time this commentary was finalised.

C. Analysis

1. Introduction

Article 3 outlining the GDPR's territorial scope is one of its most important provisions; after all, unless the criteria set out in Article 3 are met, the GDPR does not apply and none of the other Articles are of relevance. Especially for data controllers, processors and subjects outside of the EU, Article 3 ought to be the first provision of the GDPR that they consult. To this may be added that delineating the territorial reach of an instrument such as the GDPR is a complex task, and while it seems clear that Article 3 represents an expansion of the reach of EU's data protection law (compared to how Article 4 DPD was applied), the actual scope of application catered for under Article 3 is far from clear. At the time the GDPR came into effect, the EDPB had not yet issued any guidance on the territorial scope of the GDPR. However, the WP29 had published the following brief statement as part of a general factsheet aimed at helping Asia-Pacific privacy authorities understand the basic requirements included in the GDPR:

The GDPR applies to data controllers and data processors with an establishment in the EU, or with an establishment outside the EU that target individuals in the EU by offering goods and services (irrespective of whether a payment is required) or that monitor the behaviour of individuals in the EU (where that behaviour takes place in the EU). Factors such as the use of a language or a currency generally used in one or more Member States with the possibility of ordering goods and services in that other language, or the mentioning of customers or users who are in the Union, may make it apparent that the controller envisages offering goods or services to data subjects in the Union.

Data controllers and/or data processors not established in the EU, but whose activities fall within the scope of the GDPR, will generally (some exceptions apply) have to appoint a representative

---

[18] Ibid., para. 41.   [19] Ibid., para. 41.
[20] Case C-507/17, *Google Inc. v Commission nationale de l'informatique et des libertés (CNIL)* (AG Opinion).
[21] See the commentary on Art. 17 in this volume.

established in an EU member state. The representative is the point of contact for all Data Protection Authorities (DPAs) and individuals in the EU on all issues related to data processing (Article 27).[22]

Thus, only very limited guidance as to the operation of Article 3 was available at the time the GDPR became binding law. The EDPB only published the public consultation version of its Guidelines on the territorial scope of the GDPR on 16 November 2018, i.e. almost half a year after the GDPR fully entered into application (they are referred to here as the 'Guidelines', even though the final version had not been published when this text was finalised). The delay in providing guidance on Article 3 is made even more remarkable given that the EDPB specifically acknowledges that clarification of the criteria for determining the application of the territorial scope of the GDPR is 'essential for controllers and processors, both within and outside the EU, so that they may assess whether they need to comply with the GDPR'.[23]

2. Mandatory nature of Article 3 and relation to other jurisdictional rules

The rules of Article 3 are mandatory in nature and non-derogable.[24] This means that a court or DPA will regard any attempt to change them (for example, by specifying different rules on jurisdiction or choice of law in an online privacy policy or in a contract) as null and void.[25] Furthermore, the jurisdictional rules of the GDPR are not prejudiced by general jurisdictional rules contained in other EU legislation, in particular the recast Brussels I Regulation,[26] and so can be viewed as coexisting with them.[27]

3. Targeting

The inclusion of the phrase 'target individuals in the EU' in its General Information Document quoted above was the WP29's first express acknowledgement that the GDPR adopts the 'targeting' test. In the WP29's general factsheet aimed at assisting Asia-Pacific privacy authorities we also find the following example illustrating the practical application of Article 3: 'A Japanese web shop, offering products, available online in English with payments to be made in Euros, processing multiple orders a day from individuals within the EU and shipping these products to them, should be compliant with the GDPR'.[28]

Unfortunately, this example raises more questions than it answers. We may, for example, wonder whether the Japanese web shop in question would avoid the GDPR by only accepting payment in non-EU currencies? And what if the Japanese web shop, rather than 'processing multiple orders a day from individuals within the EU', merely accept such orders occasionally, or once a day? What are the actual thresholds that will be applied? While the EDPB Guidelines provide more guidance, many of these questions remain unanswered, contributing to an unhealthy legal uncertainty for many non-EU businesses.

---

[22] WP29, General Information Document, p. 2.   [23] EDPB 2018, p. 3.
[24] See Kohler 2016, p. 661, also stating that the rules of the GDPR can be regarded as overriding mandatory provisions in the sense of Art. 9(1) of the Rome I Regulation on the law applicable to contractual obligations.
[25] See Kohler 2016, p. 662.   [26] Brussels I Regulation (recast).
[27] See rec. 147 GDPR. See also the commentary on Art. 79 in this volume.
[28] WP29, General Information Document, p. 2.

At any rate, given the combination of Article 3's complexity and resulting uncertainty on the one hand, and its central importance on the other hand, it is only natural if litigation arises in relation to Article 3 over the GDPR's early years of operation.

From an analytical perspective, Article 3 may be broken down into three parts. The first (Article 3(1)), ensures that the GDPR applies to the processing of personal data by a controller or a processor with an establishment in the Union. The second (Article 3(2)), extends the GDPR's application to a controller or a processor that lacks an establishment in the Union, under certain defined circumstances. The third (Article 3(3)), addresses specific situations where Member State law applies by virtue of public international law. However, before considering these three parts, some overarching issues need to be noted.

4. Application of the GDPR outside the EU

While Article 3 focuses on events and persons 'in the Union' in contrast to Article 4's DPD focus on events and persons 'on the territory of the Member State', it may perhaps be presumed that this is not intended to change anything. In this context, it should be noted that under provisions of the EU treaties dealing with the application of EU law, the GDPR also applies in Guadeloupe, French Guiana, Martinique, Réunion, Saint-Barthélemy, Saint-Martin, the Azores, Madeira and the Canary Islands,[29] as well as in the Åland Islands.[30] However, as noted by Jääskinen and Ward:

> The special arrangement of association with the EU, as prescribed by Article 355(2) Treaty on the Functioning of the European Union ('TFEU'), has spawned a complex body of case law on the circumstances in which EU law extends to the associated countries, given that they inevitably entail assessment of conduct and legal relations that have occurred outside of EU territory.[31]

In addition, the GDPR has been implemented in the three non-EU states—Norway, Iceland and Liechtenstein—that are part of the European Economic Area ('EEA') Agreement but are not Member States of the EU,[32] so that it is applicable in those three states as well. It should be noted that pursuant to Protocol 1 to the EEA Agreement, whenever the acts incorporated in the Annexes to the Agreement (like the GDPR) refer to the territory of the 'Community' (now, 'Union'), such references should be understood also as references to the territories of the other EEA countries (i.e. Iceland, the Liechtenstein and Norway).[33]

On 29 March 2017, the UK invoked Article 50 TEU and indicated its intention to leave the EU, at which time it will become a third country by operation of law ('Brexit') and all Union primary and secondary law will cease to apply to the UK.[34] On 14 November 2018, the parties agreed on a Withdrawal Agreement that sets forth the terms of the UK's withdrawal. The Withdrawal Agreement includes a 21-month implementation period during which the GDPR would continue to apply to all personal data which has been collected and processed in the UK until 31 December 2020.[35] However, during this period, the UK will have exited the EU and will no longer be an EU Member State. The Withdrawal Agreement will only come into effect if it is approved by the UK House of Commons and then by the Parliament. If the Withdrawal Agreement is not approved

---

[29] Art. 355(1) TFEU. [30] Ibid., Art. 355(4).
[31] Jääskinen and Ward 2016, p. 129. For all different territories see Annex II TFEU.
[32] Decision of the EEA Joint Committee.   [33] See s. 8 of Protocol 1 to the EEA Agreement.
[34] Commission Brexit Preparedness Notice, p. 1.   [35] Art. 71 Withdrawal Agreement.

and adopted, then EU law will cease to apply with immediate effect. At the same time, the CJEU found on 10 December 2018 that the UK could unilaterally revoke its invocation of the withdrawal procedure if it wanted to.[36] Since Brexit is subject to political factors that were unresolved at the time this text was finalised, it is uncertain whether and to what extent the GDPR will continue to apply to the UK in the future.

5. Applicable law

In Advocate General Cruz Villalón's discussion in *Weltimmo*, he seeks to clarify the complex operation of Article 4(1) DPD and points to the Article's dual function:

On the one hand, it [Article 4(1)(a)] enables the application of EU law through the law of one of the Member States where data processing is carried out solely 'in the context' of the activities of an establishment situated in that Member State, even though, strictly speaking, the processing is carried out in a non-member country (as was the case in *Google Spain and Google*). On the other hand, that provision operates as a rule for determining the applicable law as between Member States (which is the question at issue in the present case). In the latter situation, Article 4(1)(a) of the directive is the provision which determines the applicable law in so far as it is a rule governing conflict between the laws of the different Member States.[37] (internal footnote omitted)

The second of these functions—that of operating as a rule for determining the applicable law as between Member States—was re-emphasised by the CJEU in *Wirtschaftsakademie Schleswig-Holstein*, where it expressly noted that: 'The question of which national law applies to the processing of personal data is governed by Article 4 of Directive 95/46'.[38] However, it may be argued that this role is called into question as far as Article 3(1) is concerned. After all, with a regulation, as opposed to a directive, the question of applicable law should, generally, not matter. As is strongly emphasised in the EDPB's Guidelines: 'the main objective of Article 4 of the Directive was to define which Member State's national law is applicable, whereas Article 3 of the GDPR defines the territorial scope of a directly applicable text'.[39]

Having said that, there are a number of Articles in the GDPR that allow derogations under national law (so-called 'opening clauses'); an example is Article 6(1)(c) and (e), which allows Member States to set more specific requirements for some of the legal bases for data processing.[40] Indeed, the EDPB's Guidelines observes that: 'Several provisions of the GDPR indeed allow Member States to introduce additional conditions and to define a specific data protection framework at national level in certain areas or in relation to specific processing situations'.[41] Thus, there can be no doubt that the question of applicable law remains of relevance also under the GDPR. Indeed, it may be that the move to a Regulation does less than what may have been assumed to limit the importance of which Member States' law is applicable.

Determining the applicable law in conflicts situations involving opening clauses (i.e. where the implementation by multiple Member States of such a clause may have a connection to the matter at issue) will require examining the particular provision of the

---

[36] Case C-621/18, *Wightman*.　[37] Case C-230/14, *Weltimmo* (AG Opinion), para. 23.
[38] Case C-210/16, *Wirtschaftsakademie Schleswig-Holstein*, para. 51.　[39] EDPB 2018, p. 3.
[40] For an exhaustive analysis of the relationship between the GDPR and national law, see Kühling et al. 2016. Regarding tensions between the GDPR and national law with regard to data protection in the public sector, see Blume and Svanberg 2013.
[41] EDPB 2018, p. 12.

GDPR involved as well as the relevant Member State law. The GDPR does not regulate which Member State implementation of an opening clause should apply, so difficult issues are bound to arise in this regard. It has been suggested that when private law relationships are involved, then the Member State law of the *lex causae* should apply.[42] However, complexities will arise and great care must be taken so as to avoid one Member State imposing its position on others. In enforcement actions Member State law will also be relevant to the extent that it relates to rules that stand outside the GDPR, such as those dealing with abuse of rights.[43]

While the CFR and the ECHR have led to increased harmonisation of fundamental human rights within the Member States, the reality is that, on a practical level, they merely establish the parameters within which the Member States may apply their particular balance between competing human rights. Thus, there is still significant scope for differences amongst how the various Member States balance competing human rights. In fact, the differences are such that the Member States decided that the Rome II Regulation[44]—which determines the applicable law in non-contractual matters—must not govern 'non-contractual obligations arising out of violations of privacy and rights relating to personality, including defamation'.[45] This exclusion is a direct result of the considerable differences that exists in the balancing between competing fundamental rights amongst the Member States of the European Union. Thus, the question of choice of law in non-contractual obligations arising out of violations of privacy and rights relating to personality is left to the domestic law of the Member State that claims jurisdiction.

The recognition that differences exist in the balancing between competing fundamental rights amongst the Member States must carry over to the application of the GDPR in any instance where its application involves such a balancing. And in that context, it may be emphasised that, in fact, any situation where the courts or authorities of one Member State are empowered to make a determination—on a matter involving the balancing of fundamental rights—for the entire European Union, results in fairness, accuracy and the values of the individual Member States being sacrificed on the altar of procedural efficiency.

6. Processing in the context of the activities of an establishment of a controller or a processor in the EU

Article 3(1) adopts largely the same focus on processing of personal data in the context of the activities of an establishment of a controller in the Union as did Article 4(1)(a) DPD. Consequently, the CJEU's decisions in *Weltimmo*, *Google Spain*, *Verein für Konsumenteninformation* and *Wirtschaftsakademie Schleswig-Holstein* (discussed above) likely set important precedents for the operation of the GDPR. Yet, while the similarities between Article 4(1)(a) DPD and Article 3(1) GDPR are obvious, so too are the differences. For example, while Article 4(1)(a) DPD specifically addressed situations where the same controller is established on the territory of several Member States, Article 3(1) GDPR does not do so. Under the GDPR, such situations are instead addressed in other provisions (see in particular Article 56).

---

[42] See Kohler 2016, pp. 657–658 note 14, who mentions as an example Article 88 GDPR referring to 'performance of the contract of employment', in which case the law governing the employment contract should apply.
[43] Ibid., p. 671.   [44] Rome II Regulation.   [45] Art. 1(2)(g) Rome II Regulation.

Furthermore, while Article 4(1)(a) DPD only referred to the activities of an establishment of the *controller*, GDPR Article 3(1) deals with the processing of personal data in the context of the activities of an establishment of a *controller or a processor*. In that context it should be noted that the EDPB's Guidelines emphasise the importance of considering the establishment of the controller and processor separately,[46] and state that:

> The GDPR envisages different and dedicated provisions or obligations applying to data controllers and processors, and as such, should a data controller or processor be subject to the GDPR as per Article 3(1), the related obligations would apply to them respectively and separately. In this context, the EDPB notably deems that a processor in the EU should not be considered to be an establishment of a data controller within the meaning of Article 3(1) merely by virtue of its status as processor. The existence of a relationship between a controller and a processor does not necessarily trigger the application of the GDPR to both, should one of these two entities not be established in the Union.[47]

Particular complications may arise where a non-EU controller, not caught by Article 3, uses a processor in the EU. The EDPB's Guidelines emphasise that the controller in such a scenario 'will not become subject to the GDPR simply because it chooses to use a processor in the Union'.[48] The processor will be caught by Article 3(1), but processors are subject to more limited obligations than are controllers. The EDPB notes:

> When it comes to a data processor carrying out processing on behalf of a data controller established outside the Union and which does not fall under the territorial scope of the GDPR as per Article 3(2), the processor will be subject to the following relevant GDPR provisions directly applicable to data processors:
>
> — The obligations imposed on processors under Article 28 (2), (3), (4), (5) and (6), on the duty to enter into a data processing agreement, with the exception of those relating to the assistance to the data controller in complying with its (the controller's) own obligations under the GDPR.
> — The processor and any person acting under the authority of the controller or of the processor, who has access to personal data, shall not process those data except on instructions from the controller, unless required to do so by Union or Member State law, as per Article 29 and Article 32(4).
> — Where applicable, the processor shall maintain a record of all categories of processing carried out on behalf of a controller, as per Article 30(2).
> — Where applicable, the processor shall, upon request, cooperate with the supervisory authority in the performance of its tasks, as per Article 31.
> — The processor shall implement technical and organisational measures to ensure a level of security appropriate to the risk, as per Article 32.
> — The processor shall notify the controller without undue delay after becoming aware of a personal data breach, as per Article 33.
> — Where applicable, the processor shall designate a data protection officer as per Articles 37 and 38.
> — The provisions on transfers of personal data to third countries or international organisations, as per Chapter V.[49]

However, despite the EDPB taking 'the view that the Union territory cannot be used as a "data haven"',[50] this structure may nevertheless be seen to lead to a potential gap in the coverage of the GDPR. For example, while the processor shall notify the controller without undue delay after becoming aware of a personal data breach, as per Article 33,

---

[46] EDPB 2018, p. 10.   [47] Ibid., p. 9.   [48] Ibid., p. 10.   [49] Ibid., p. 11.
[50] Ibid., p. 12.

the non-EU controller does not have a corresponding duty to act upon being notified of the personal data breach.

A further difference between the GDPR and the DPD can be found in how Article 3(1), unlike Article 4(1)(a) DPD, expressly states that the GDPR applies to the processing of personal data in the context of the activities of an establishment of a controller or a processor in the Union, *regardless of whether the processing takes place in the Union or not*. And in this context, it is prudent to recall that it is not the location of the data that is the criterion used under EU data protection law to define its territorial scope: 'The WP29 stresses that the location of the data is not the criterion used under the GDPR to define its territorial scope'.[51]

In its Guidelines, the EDPB advocates a three-pronged approach to working with Article 3(1). The first step involves assessing whether we are dealing with 'an establishment in the Union'. In this context, guidance can be gained from the cases discussed above, as well as from recital 22's observation that: 'Establishment implies the effective and real exercise of activity through stable arrangements. The legal form of such arrangements, whether through a branch or a subsidiary with a legal personality, is not the determining factor in that respect'.

The second step involves ascertaining whether the processing of personal data is carried out 'in the context of the activities of' an establishment. In this context, the EDPB recommends that 'determining whether an entity based in the EU is to be considered as an establishment of the controller or processor for the purposes of Article 3(1) is made on a case-by-case basis and based on an analysis *in concreto*. Each scenario must be assessed on its own merits, taking into account the specific facts of the case'.[52]

This type of reference to the need for a case-by-case analysis *in concreto* is common throughout the EDPB's Guidelines. While it may be seen as a natural consequence of the limits of the text of Article 3, and the complexity of the subject matter, it must be admitted that it has little or no value in Guidelines meant to clarify the relevant criteria and 'to ensure a consistent application of the GDPR'.[53]

Furthermore, an observation such as that '[t]he EDPB considers that, for the purpose of Article 3(1), the meaning of "processing in the context of the activities of an establishment of a controller or processor" is to be understood in light of the relevant case law'[54] is of little value. Surely it goes without saying that 'relevant' case law must be taken into account? As is made clear in the case law discussion above, guidance on the issue of whether the processing of personal data is carried out 'in the context of the activities of' an establishment has been provided by the CJEU over the past years.

The third, and last, step proposed by the EDPB aims to bring attention to the fact that it is 'the presence, through an establishment, of a data controller or processor in the EU and the fact that a processing takes place in the context of the activities of this establishment that trigger the application of the GDPR to its processing activities',[55] and that, thus, 'the place of processing is not relevant in determining whether or not the processing,

---

[51] WP29 2017, p. 5. The WP29 is clearly correct and it is unfortunate that several MEPs who have worked closely on the GDPR have sought to focus on the location of data in their amicus brief filed in relation to the *Microsoft Warrant* case, claiming that the EU data protection regime was 'specifically intended and designed to cover data stored in an EU Member State', and that 'Personal data located in EU territory is subject to strict rules designed to maintain the autonomy of the affected individual (the "data subject")'. See Albrecht amicus brief, *United States v Microsoft Corporation*, pp. 14 and 5.
[52] EDPB 2018, p. 6.   [53] Ibid., p. 3.   [54] Ibid., p. 6.   [55] Ibid., p. 8.

carried out in the context of the activities of an EU establishment, falls within the scope of the GDPR'.[56]

Finally, in the context of Article 3(1), it should be noted that the EDPB stresses that:

> The text of Article 3(1) does not restrict the application of the GDPR to the processing of personal data of individuals who are in the Union. The EDPB therefore considers that any personal data processing in the context of the activities of an establishment of a controller or processor in the Union would fall under the scope of the GDPR, regardless of the location or the nationality of the data subject whose personal data are being processed.[57]

7. Controllers and processors not established in the Union

Turning to Article 3(2), this provision is fundamentally different from its predecessor in the DPD (Article 4(1)(c)). Instead of focusing on the use of equipment situated in the EU (as did Article 4(1)(c) DPD), Article 3(2) describes two circumstances under which the GDPR applies to a controller or processor not established in the Union. A requirement shared by both those circumstances is that the processing must be of personal data of data subjects who are in the Union. Application of the GDPR under Article 3(2) means that the non-EU controller or processor must appoint a representative in the Union.[58]

When it comes to the application of Article 3(2), the EDPB favours a two-pronged approach, in which the first steps aims to determine whether the processing relates to personal data of data subjects who are in the Union, while the second steps ascertains whether it relates to the offering of goods or services or to the monitoring of data subjects' behaviour in the Union.[59]

7.1 Data subjects in the Union

As to the first step, the fact that Article 3(2) refers to 'personal data of data subjects who are in the Union' highlights that Article 3(2) applies regardless of 'the citizenship, residence or other type of legal status of the data subject whose personal data are being processed'.[60] This interpretation is consistent with Article 8 of the Charter of Fundamental Rights (which provides that the right to the protection of personal data is applicable to 'everyone') and further support may be found in recital 14. Thus, also the temporary physical presence of a foreign citizen and residence in the EU may trigger the application of the GDPR. As noted in the EDPB's Guidelines:

> The requirement that the data subject be located in the Union must be assessed at the moment when the relevant trigger activity takes place, i.e. at the moment of offering of goods or services or the moment when the behaviour is being monitored, regardless of the duration of the offer made or monitoring undertaken.[61]

At the same time, the EDPB underlines that, absent the element of 'targeting' individuals in the EU, 'the fact of processing personal data of an individual in the Union alone is not sufficient to trigger the application of the GDPR to processing activities of a controller or processor not established in the Union'.[62] To illustrate this point, the Guidelines includes the following example:

---

[56] Ibid., p. 8. [57] Ibid., p. 9 [58] See the commentary on Art. 27 in this volume.
[59] EDPB 2018, p. 13. [60] Ibid., p. 13. [61] Ibid., p. 13. [62] Ibid., p. 14.

A U.S. citizen is travelling through Europe during his holidays. While in Europe, he downloads and uses a news app that is offered by a U.S. company. The app is exclusively directed at the U.S. market. The collection of the U.S. tourist's personal data via the app by the U.S. company is not subject to the GDPR.[63]

This is an odd conclusion indeed. It may of course be argued that the US company in question does not offer goods or services to data subjects in the Union. However, it seems impossible to avoid the conclusion that it is monitoring the behaviour of the US citizen travelling through Europe during his holidays, and that the US citizen is a data subject in the Union whose behaviour takes place within the Union during the holiday. As the criteria of Article 3(2)(a) and of Article 3(2)(b) are independent rather than cumulative, it would seem that GDPR is applicable in this scenario due to Article 3(2)(b). Thus, in this respect, the EDPB's Guidelines unfortunately add to the confusion, rather than provide clarification.

7.2 Targeting

Article 3(2)(a) ensures that the GDPR applies to a controller or processor not established in the Union where it is offering goods or services to data subjects in the Union. Importantly, application of the GDPR does not depend on whether a payment of the data subject is required. Thus, its application extends to 'free' goods or services, which is a particularly important matter in the online context. Article 3(2)(b) ensures that the GDPR applies to a controller or processor not established in the Union where it is monitoring the behaviour of data subjects in the Union, as far as their behaviour takes place within the Union. Thus, Article 3(2)(b) is even broader in scope than is Article 3(2)(a) and is likely to capture a diverse range of both online and offline activities.

Some guidance as to the likely application of Article 3(2) can be discerned from recitals 23 and 24. The recitals make clear that the drafters of Article 3 are seeking to leverage the 'targeting' test that has started to play an increasing role in EU consumer protection law, predominantly via the joined CJEU decisions in *Pammer*.[64] This is confirmed in the EDPB's Guidelines.[65]

Drawing upon legal solutions from other fields is sensible, and consumer protection law shares several key features with data privacy law. In addition, the targeting test is frequently trumpeted as a solution to internet jurisdiction issues. Yet, while targeting is attractive in theory, on a practical level, applying this test in the context of Article 3(2) will not be easy and will not necessarily lead to a high degree of predictability for data subjects, controllers, processors or, indeed, data protection authorities.

A key challenge here is the limited number of what we may call 'indicators of targeting'. In *Pammer*, the CJEU discussed a non-exhaustive list of indicators such as the mention of telephone numbers with the international dialling code, the use of a certain language and/or currency and the use of a certain top-level domain name as potentially indicating that the party in question had targeted the relevant Member State. However, these indicators of targeting may be missing or irrelevant, for example, in the context of assessing whether a controller or processor not established in the Union is offering free services to data subjects in the Union. Thus, there is a clear risk that, for a large number of controllers and processors, courts will have to conclude either that they 'target' nearly every

---

[63] Ibid., p. 14. [64] Joined Cases C-585/08 and C-144/09, *Pammer*.
[65] EDPB 2018, p. 15.

country in the world or no countries at all. Both of these options are serious impediments for the practical usefulness of the targeting approach adopted in Article 3.

The EDPB's Guidelines seek to summarise the 'indicators of targeting' and state that:

When taking into account the specific facts of the case, the following factors could therefore inter alia be taken into consideration, possibly in combination with one another:

- The EU or at least one Member State is designated by name with reference to the good or service offered;
- The data controller or processor pays a search engine operator for an internet referencing service in order to facilitate access to its site by consumers in the Union; or the controller or processor has launched marketing and advertisement campaigns directed at an EU country audience[;]
- The international nature of the activity at issue, such as certain tourist activities;
- The mention of dedicated addresses or phone numbers to be reached from an EU country;
- The use of a top-level domain name other than that of the third country in which the controller or processor is established, for example '.de', or the use of neutral top-level domain names such as '.eu';
- The description of travel instructions from one or more other EU Member States to the place where the service is provided;
- The mention of an international clientele composed of customers domiciled in various EU Member States, in particular by presentation of accounts written by such customers;
- The use of a language or a currency other than that generally used in the trader's country, especially a language or currency of one or more EU Member states;
- The data controller offers the delivery of goods in EU Member States.[66]

Importantly, the EDPB goes on to emphasise that 'several of the elements listed above, if taken alone may not amount to a clear indication of the intention of a data controller to offer goods or services to data subjects in the Union'.[67] Rather these indicators of targeting 'should each be taken into account in any *in concreto* analysis in order to determine whether the combination of factors relating to the data controller's commercial activities can together be considered as an offer of goods or services directed at data subjects in the Union'.[68]

A potential complication arises from the focus on *subjective targeting*, as opposed to *objective targeting*. Recital 23 refers to it being 'apparent that the controller or processor *envisages offering* services to data subjects in one or more Member States in the Union' (emphasis added). This suggests that it is what is in the mind of the controller or processor that matters, rather than whether targeting occurs from an objective perspective.

7.3 Monitoring

While, as discussed above, recital 23 clearly imposes an expressed intention requirement in relation to Article 3(2)(a), no such requirement is included in Article 3(2)(b). Based on this difference, it may be argued that unintentional monitoring may also be caught by Article 3(2)(b).

At the same time, recital 24 makes clear that, when seeking to ascertain whether certain conduct amounts to monitoring, we must take account of the potential subsequent use of personal data processing techniques which consist of 'profiling'[69] a natural person.

---

[66] Ibid., pp. 15–16. [67] Ibid., p. 16. [68] Ibid., p. 16.
[69] Defined in Art. 4(4) GDPR.

Thus, it may, for example, be argued that, where the monitoring is unintentional and is carried by an entity that does not associate the collected data with any potential data processing techniques which consist of profiling a natural person, that entity is not caught by Article 3(2)(b).

On this topic, the EDPB's Guidelines take the view that:

However, the use of the word 'monitoring' implies that the controller has a specific purpose in mind for the collection and subsequent reuse of the relevant data about an individual's behaviour within the EU. The EDPB does not consider that any online collection or analysis of personal data of individuals in the EU would automatically count as 'monitoring'. It will be necessary to consider the controller's purpose for processing the data and, in particular, any subsequent behavioural analysis or profiling techniques involving that data. The EDPB takes into account the wording of recital 24, which indicates that to determine whether processing involves monitoring of a data subject behaviour, the tracking of natural persons on the Internet, including the potential subsequent use of profiling techniques, is a key consideration.[70]

In relation to Article 3(2)(b), the EDPB also emphasises that a broad range of monitoring activities are covered, including in particular the following:

– behavioural advertisement
– geo-localisation activities, in particular for marketing purposes
– online tracking through the use of cookies or other tracking techniques, such as fingerprinting, personalised diet and health analytics services online
– CCTV
– market surveys and other behavioural studies based on individual profiles
– monitoring or regular reporting on an individual's health status.[71]

To conclude the discussion of Article 3(2), it may be noted that it is unclear whether only business-to-consumer ('B2C') scenarios are covered, or whether also business-to-business ('B2B') scenarios may trigger the application of the GDPR based on Article 3(2). Imagine, for example, that a non-EU company is selling industrial products online that are clearly only meant for companies.

In such a scenario we may of course encounter specific difficulties in drawing sharp lines where the company that acquires the product is a small and medium-sized enterprise ('SME') or a one-man company. However, more broadly it would seem that in such a scenario, the 'offering of goods or services' is not to a 'data subject in the Union' as is required to trigger Article 3(2)(a). The product is only on direct offer to a legal person, and may only indirectly reach relevant natural persons (e.g. employees of the company that acquires the product).

However, when it comes to Art 3(2)(b) it is possible to reach a different conclusion. If, as per the example, a non-EU company is selling industrial products online that are clearly only meant for companies, and the product allows the non-EU company to monitor the behaviour of the employees of the company that bought the product, the non-EU company would seem to be caught by Art 3(2)(b) assuming the employee behaviour takes place within the Union. This matter, while clearly of practical importance, is not considered in the EDPB's Guidelines.

---

[70] EDPB 2018, p. 18.   [71] Ibid., p. 18.

8. Application of the GDPR by virtue of public international law

Turning to Article 3(3), three observations can be made: first, it largely mirrors Article 4(1)(b) of the DPD, and secondly, recital 25 suggests that it is aimed at data processing such as that as occurs in the context of a Member State's diplomatic mission or consular post. Thirdly, while the text of the relevant recital (25) indicates that Article 3(3) will have a limited scope of application, the text itself gives it the potential for an expansive reach.

Given that Article 3(3) is nearly identical to Article 4(1)(b) DPD, it may perhaps be assumed that it was included without much thought or analysis. This is unfortunate since neither Article 3(3) GDPR, nor Article 4(1)(b) DPD before it, actually cater for the GDPR/DPD applying to a Member State's diplomatic mission or consular post as anticipated in the recital.

The DPD assumed, and the GDPR now assumes, that public international law results in Member State law applying to data processing in its diplomatic missions and consular posts. However, this is assumption is incorrect.

It is true that diplomatic staff enjoy certain privileges and immunities.[72] It is also true that diplomatic premises are protected in various ways.[73] However, while Grotius and his contemporaries argued that ambassadors were deemed to be outside the territory of the host state, 'it is now widely acknowledged that diplomatic premises are not part of foreign territory'.[74] To this may be added that, Article 41 of the Vienna Convention on Diplomatic Relations states: 'Without prejudice to their privileges and immunities, it is the duty of all persons enjoying such privileges and immunities to respect the laws and regulations of the receiving State'. Given the above, the majority view in contemporary public international law does not support the assumption that Member State law automatically applies to data processing in its diplomatic missions and consular posts as an obligation of public international law.

Of course, diplomatic agents and diplomatic missions are inviolable, so the receiving state has little, or no, practical means to compel compliance with its local law. In practice, such agents and missions may also tend to apply their own national data protection law. However, they must still comply with local law. Thus, the WP29's assumption that, for example, French data protection law automatically applies in the French embassy in Washington as a matter of public international law is incorrect.[75]

The other side of this coin potentially has even greater implications. Foreign states may, based on recital 25, have believed that the GDPR would not extend to their diplomatic missions and consular posts in the EU. However, in the light of the above, it would seem that such bodies may indeed be caught by Article 3(1), and in that context, the assertion that the GDPR applies regardless of whether the processing takes place in the Union or not may be a particularly controversial matter.

It may seem desirable for the GDPR to apply to Member States' diplomatic missions or consular posts as is anticipated in recital 25. However, it seems that the only way in which we can reconcile the wording of Article 3(3) with that ambition is to argue that, since public international law allows nationality-based prescriptive jurisdiction, the EU has the right to extend the application of the GDPR to the Member States' diplomatic missions or consular posts, and that it does so via recital 25. The fact that the Member

---

[72] See Art. 29 Vienna Convention on Diplomatic Relations. [73] Ibid., Art. 22.
[74] D'Aspremont 2009, para. 3.   [75] WP29 2010, p. 18.

States' diplomatic missions or consular posts *also* have to respect local law does not necessarily stand in the way of such an argument. This far-fetched approach would, however, require an extraordinarily broad reading of the phrase 'where Member State law applies by virtue of public international law' by assuming this to refer to any place where public international law allows Member State law to apply. In other words, the phrase 'applies by virtue of public international law' would have to be read to mean 'is permitted to be applied under public international law'. We strongly caution against such an interpretation, and conclude that neither Article 3(3) nor the other subsections of Article 3 extend the GDPR to operate in a Member State's diplomatic mission or consular post. In this respect, Article 3 is then too limited and fails to give the GDPR its intended reach of operation.

The important complications discussed directly abroad are oddly brushed aside in the EDPB's Guidelines. Having noted, without any attempt at analysis, that the 'definitions and status of diplomatic missions and consular posts are laid down in international law, respectively in the Vienna Convention on Diplomatic Relations of 1961 and the Vienna Convention on Consular Relations of 1963',[76] the EDPB goes on to conclude that:

The EDPB considers that the GDPR applies to personal data processing carried out by EU Member States' embassies and consulates, insofar as such processing falls within the material scope of the GDPR, as defined in its Article 2. A Member State's diplomatic or consular post, as a data controller or processor, would then be subject to all relevant provisions of the GDPR, including when it comes to the rights of the data subject, the general obligations related to controller and processor and the transfers of personal data to third countries or international organisations.[77]

As a result, it is clear that the EDPB here fails to apply the relevant international law it notes is applicable, and misguidedly gives the text of the recital priority over the text of Article 3(3).

To understand the potential reach of Article 3(3)'s claim that the GDPR applies to controllers (but apparently not processors) not established in the Union but in 'a place where Member State law applies by virtue of public international law', we must understand the extent to which public international law places restrictions on the reach of so-called prescriptive (or legislative) jurisdiction. The wording of Article 3(3), and of the recital, seems to assume that public international law provides a clear delineation in this respect. However, such an assumption is erroneous. Public international law does not provide clear guidance as to the exact reach of prescriptive jurisdiction.[78] This gives rise to a structural issue. Public international law provides for a wide discretion as to where states claim prescriptive jurisdiction, but through Article 3(3) the EU asserts that the scope of the GDPR is determined by public international law. This circularity means that the GDPR tells us to consult public international law, while public international law—due to the discretions it affords—tells us to primarily seek guidance in the GDPR.

Furthermore, even if we were to settle for a superficial assessment and accept the principles advanced through the influential 1935 'Harvard Draft'[79] (possibly accompanied by the so-called 'effects doctrine') as representing the view of public international law on the matter, we would have to conclude that Article 3(3) entitles the EU to apply the

---

[76] Vienna Convention on Consular Relations.   [77] EDPB 2018, p. 19.
[78] Svantesson 2017, p. 43.   [79] 'Introductory Comment' 1935.

GDPR broadly indeed. And, as is well known, not all the 'Harvard Draft' principles are focused on territoriality, which adds to the sense that the heading of Article 3—territorial scope—is somewhat misguided.

We can, however, get out of this quagmire and regain firm ground if it is accepted that, in referring to 'a place where Member State law applies by virtue of public international law', Article 3(3) includes only those places where public international law causes Member State law to apply, at that place, on a permanent basis, as opposed to Member State law being applicable merely as a result of the public international law principles commonly used specifically to allocate prescriptive jurisdiction. Where this is accepted, we avoid the risk of Article 3(3) being given an overly expansive meaning so as to make the GDPR applicable based e.g. on nothing but the fact that some effect was felt in a Member State or based on the nationality of the controller.

At any rate, it seems clear that Article 3(3) gives the GDPR a broader scope of application than the examples mentioned in recital 25. For instance, the EDPB's Guidelines include the following example:

> A German cruise ship travelling in international waters is processing data of the guests on board for the purpose of tailoring the in-cruise entertainment offer.
>
> While the ship is located outside the Union, in international waters, the fact that it is German registered cruise ship means that by virtue of public international law the GDPR shall be applicable to its processing of personal data, as per Article 3(3).[80]

To this may be added that the ship, in the example, obviously remains a German registered cruise ship also as it enters the territorial waters of non-EU states. Presumably the GDPR will then continue to apply.

Furthermore, under the same reasoning, the GDPR will apply to onboard aircraft registered in EU Member States. However, interpreting exactly how Article 3(3) applies, e.g. in the context of onboard internet access for passengers, is made more difficult by the fact that recital 25 instructs us as follows: 'Where Member State law applies by virtue of public international law, this Regulation should also apply to a controller not established in the Union, such as in a Member State's diplomatic mission or consular post'.[81]

Thus, while Article 3(3) clearly is focused on the location of the controller's establishment ('This Regulation applies to the processing of personal data by a controller not established in the Union, but in a place where Member State law applies by virtue of public international law'), the recital—meant to clarify the application of the Regulation text—points to the question of whether Member State law applies by virtue of public international law at the particular locality at issue. The difference is obvious if we seek to apply this to a practical scenario.

Imagine, for example, that a passenger connects to the internet onboard a flight outside the EU. Imagine further that the airline is established neither in the EU, nor in a place where Member State law applies by virtue of public international law. Now imagine that the aircraft in question is registered in an EU Member State. Under these circumstances, the data collection associated with the onboard internet connection is presumably not caught by Article 3(3) as the airline (i.e. the controller) is established neither in the EU,

---

[80] EDPB 2018, p. 19. [81] Rec. 25 GDPR.

nor in a place where Member State law applies by virtue of public international law. Yet, the recital suggests this data processing should fall within Article 3(3) as the aircraft is a place where Member State law applies by virtue of public international law (given the nationality focus based on registration).

9. International organisations

The GDPR does not directly address its application to international organisations (i.e. organisations established under public international law), and this must be determined based on relevant principles of EU law and international law.[82] Discussion are ongoing between the United Nations and the Commission regarding the GDPR's impact on the UN. The Commission has taken the view informally that the GDPR does not directly apply to international organisations, but that they must comply with the GDPR's rules affecting data importers when they receive personal data transferred from the EU.[83]

10. Conclusions

Taken as a whole, Article 3—and in particular Article 3(2), and potentially Article 3(3)—clearly casts a wide net indeed, and this has at least four important consequences. First of all, as already alluded to, the broad theoretical reach of Article 3 makes it difficult to predict its actual practical reach. Secondly, it is possible to argue that Article 3—and again, in particular Article 3(2), and potentially Article 3(3)—goes too far, thereby giving the GDPR a scope of application that is difficult to justify on the international stage, as the GDPR may end up applying in situations in relation to which the EU may be argued to lack a legitimate interest to apply its laws and to which it has only a very weak connection. Thirdly, the fact that the GDPR—through Article 3—purports to apply so broadly that it is not possible to ensure its actual enforcement in all situations, means that enforcement will necessarily be selective and thereby may risk being viewed as subjective and, indeed, discretionary. This raises rule of law concerns and could arguably undermine the GDPR's international legitimacy. Fourthly, flowing from the first three observations, it is desirable (not to say necessary) to develop clear guidance as to when a controller or processor not established in the Union will actually be pursued under the GDPR. This may perhaps best be a task for the EDPB.

11. Enforcement

In the context of guidance as to when a controller or processor not established in the Union will actually be pursued under the GDPR, it would seem fruitful to embrace a proportionality approach that goes beyond mere attention given to the criteria set forth in Article 3. For example, it can perhaps be expected that attention will be given to the degree of harm caused (or potentially caused) as well as the type of provision of the GDPR that is alleged to have been violated. This may, for example, be achieved via what may be referred to as a 'layered approach';[84] that is, when determining whether to actually pursue an alleged violation by a controller or processor not established in the Union, the degree

---

[82] See Kuner 2019 regarding the application of the GDPR to international organisations.
[83] See the commentary on Art. 44 in this volume.   [84] Svantesson 2013.

of contact required should be proportionate to the degree of harm caused, as well as the type of provision of the GDPR that is alleged to have been violated. Under such a model for the application of Article 3, a violation of an Article belonging to the more administrative/bureaucratic layer of the GDPR (such as Article 37 requiring a data protection officer) could require a stronger degree of contact with the EU than, for example, a violation of the lawfulness requirements in Article 6 causing significant damage. This would give Article 3 a nuanced application despite its 'all-or-nothing' literal meaning. And this nuanced application is clearly supported by the Commission's call—discussed above— for domestic law that creates cross-border obligations to be applied and interpreted in a manner that is mindful of the restrictions of international law and considerations of international comity, in the light of how the European Union's foundational treaties and case law enshrine the principles of 'mutual regard to the spheres of jurisdiction' of sovereign states and of the need to interpret and apply EU legislation in a manner that is consistent with international law.[85]

Select Bibliography

International agreements

EEA Agreement: Agreement on the European Economic Area, OJ 1994 L 1/3.
Vienna Convention on Consular Relations: Vienna Convention on Consular Relations 1963, 596 UNTS 261.
Vienna Convention on Diplomatic Relations: Vienna Convention on Diplomatic Relations 1961, 500 UNTS 95.
Withdrawal Agreement: Agreement on the withdrawal of the United Kingdom of Great Britain and Northern Ireland from the European Union and the European Atomic Energy Community, as endorsed by leaders at a special meeting of the European Council on 25 November 2018 (25 November 2018).

EU legislation

Brussels I Regulation (recast): Regulation (EU) No. 1215/2012 of the European Parliament and of the Council of 12 December 2012 on jurisdiction and the recognition and enforcement of judgments in civil and commercial matters (recast), OJ 2012 L 351/1.
Decision of the EEA Joint Committee: Decision of the EEA Joint Committee No. 154/2018 of 6 July 2018 amending Annex XI (Electronic communication, audiovisual services and information society) and Protocol 37 (containing the list provided for in Article 101) to the EEA Agreement [2018/1022], OJ 2018 L 183/23.
Rome I Regulation: Regulation (EC) No. 593/2008 of the European Parliament and of the Council of 17 June 2008 on the law applicable to contractual obligations (Rome I), OJ 2008 L 177/6.
Rome II Regulation: Regulation (EC) No. 864/2007 of the European Parliament and of the Council of 11 July 2007 on the law applicable to non-contractual obligations, OJ 2007 L 199/40.

National legislation

Swedish Personal Data Act 1998: Personal Data Act 1998 (Personuppgiftslagen (SFS1998:204)) (repealed).

---

[85] See e.g. Case C-366/10, *Air Transport*, para. 123.

Academic writings

Albrecht 2016: Albrecht, 'Regaining Control and Sovereignty in the Digital Age', in Wright and de Hert (eds.), *Enforcing Privacy: Regulatory, Legal and Technological Approaches* (Springer, 2016), 473.

Azzi, 'The Challenges Faced by the Extraterritorial Scope of the General Data Protection Regulation', 9(2) *Journal of Intellectual Property, Information Technology and E-Commerce Law 'JIPITEC'* (2018), 1.

Blume and Svanberg 2013: Blume and Svanberg, 'The Proposed Data Protection Regulation: The Illusion of Harmonisation, the Private/Public Sector Divide and the Bureaucratic Apparatus', 15 *Cambridge Yearbook of European Legal Studies* (2013), 27.

Brkan, 'Data Protection and Conflict-of-Laws: A Challenging Relationship', 2(3) *European Data Protection Law Review* (2016), 324.

Bygrave, *Data Privacy Law: An International Perspective* (OUP 2014).

Bygrave, 'Determining Applicable Law Pursuant to European Data Protection Legislation', 16(4) *Computer Law & Security Review 'CLSR'* (2000), 218.

Chen, 'How the Best-Laid Plans Go Awry: The (Unsolved) Issues of Applicable Law in the General Data Protection Regulation', 6(4) *International Data Privacy Law 'IDPL'* (2016), 310.

Colonna, 'Article 4 of the EU Data Protection Directive and the irrelevance of the EU–US Safe Harbor Program?', 4(3) *IDPL* (2014), 203.

Czerniawski, 'Do We Need the 'Use of Equipment' as a Factor for the Territorial Applicability of the EU Data Protection Regime?' in Svantesson and Kloza (eds.), *Trans-Atlantic Data Privacy as a Challenge for Democracy* (Intersentia 2017), 221.

D'Aspremont 2009: D'Aspremont, 'Premises of Diplomatic Missions', *Max Planck Encyclopedia of Public International Law* (Article last updated: March 2009) (Online version OUP).

De Hert and Czerniawski, 'Expanding the European Data Protection Scope beyond Territory: Article 3 of the General Data Protection Regulation in its Wider Context', 6(3) *IDPL* (2016), 230.

Gömann, 'The New Territorial Scope of EU Data Protection Law: Deconstructing a Revolutionary Achievement', 54(2) *Common Market Law Review* (2017), 567.

Hijmans, *The European Union as Guardian of Internet Privacy* (Springer 2016).

'Introductory Comment' 1935: 'Introductory Comment to the Harvard Draft Convention on Jurisdiction with Respect to Crime 1935', 29 *Supp American Journal of International Law* (1935), 443.

Jääskinen and Ward 2016: Jääskinen and Ward, 'The External Reach of EU Private Law in the Light of *L'Oréal versus eBay* and *Google and Google Spain*', in Cremona and Micklitz (eds.), *Private Law in the External Relations of the EU* (OUP 2016), 125.

Kindt 2016, 'Why research may no longer be the same: About the territorial scope of the New Data Protection Regulation', 32(5) *CLSR* (2016), 729.

Kohler 2016, 'Conflict of Law Issues in the 2016 Data Protection Regulation of the European Union', 52 *Rivista di diritto internazionale privato e processuale* (2016), 653.

Kuczerawy and Ausloos 2016, 'From Notice-and-Takedown to Notice-and-Delist: Implementing Google Spain', 14(2) *Colorado Technology Law Journal* (2016), 219.

Kühling et al. 2016: Kühling, Martini, Heberlein, Kühl, Nink, Weinzierl and Wenzel, *Die DSGVO und das nationale Recht* (Verlagshaus Monsenstein und Vannderat OHG Münster 2016).

Kuner 2015: Kuner, 'Extraterritoriality and Regulation of International Data Transfers in EU Data Protection Law', 5(4) *IDPL* (2015), 235.

Kuner 2019: Kuner, 'International Organizations and the EU General Data Protection Regulation: Exploring the Interaction between EU Law and International Law', 16 *International Organizations Law Review* (2019), 158.

Kuner, 'Data Protection Law and International Jurisdiction on the Internet (Part 1)', 18(2) *International Journal of Law and Information Technology 'IJLIT'* (2010), 176.

Kuner, 'Data Protection Law and International Jurisdiction on the Internet (Part 2)', 18(3) *IJLIT* (2010), 227.

Kuner, *European Data Protection Law: Corporate Compliance and Regulation* (2nd edn, OUP 2007).

Moerel, 'Back to Basics: When Does EU Data Protection Law Apply?', 1(2) *IDPL* (2011), 92.

Moerel, 'The Long Arm of EU Data Protection Law: Does the Data Protection Directive Apply to Processing of Personal Data of EU Citizens by Websites Worldwide?', 1(1) *IDPL* (2011), 28.

Polčák and Svantesson, *Information Sovereignty: Data Privacy, Sovereign Powers and the Rule of Law* (Edward Elgar 2017).

Revolidis, 'Judicial Jurisdiction over Internet Privacy Violations and the GDPR: A Case of "Privacy Tourism"?', 11(1) *Masaryk University Journal of Law and Technology* (2017), 7.

Svantesson 2013: Svantesson, 'A "Layered Approach" to the Extraterritoriality of Data Privacy Laws', 3(4) *IDPL* (2013), 278.

Svantesson 2014: Svantesson, 'The Extraterritoriality of EU Data Privacy Law: Its Theoretical Justification and Its Practical Effect on U.S. Businesses', 50(1) *Stanford Journal of International Law* (2014), 53.

Svantesson 2017: Svantesson, *Solving the Internet Jurisdiction Puzzle* (OUP 2017).

Svantesson, 'Article 4(1)(a) "Establishment of the Controller" in EU Data Privacy Law—Time to Rein in this Expanding Concept?', 6(3) *IDPL* (2016), 210.

Svantesson, 'Enforcing Privacy across Different Jurisdictions', in Wright and de Hert (eds.), *Enforcing Privacy: Regulatory, Legal and Technological Approaches* (Springer 2016), 195.

Svantesson, 'European Union Claims of Jurisdiction over the Internet: An Analysis of Three Recent Key Developments', 9(2) *JIPITEC* (2018), 113.

Svantesson, 'Extraterritoriality and Targeting in EU Data Privacy Law: The Weak Spot Undermining the Regulation', 5(4) *IDPL* (2015), 226.

Svantesson, *Extraterritoriality in Data Privacy Law* (Ex Tuto Publishing 2013).

Svantesson, 'The CJEU'S *Weltimmo* Data Privacy Ruling: Lost in the Data Privacy Turmoil, Yet So Very Important', 23(2) *Maastricht Journal of European and Comparative Law* (2016), 332.

Taylor, 'The EU's Human Rights Obligations in Relation to Its Data Protection Laws with Extraterritorial Effect', 5(4) *IDPL* (2015), 246.

Taylor, 'Transatlantic Jurisdictional Conflicts in Data Protection Law: How the Fundamental Right to Data Protection Conditions the European Union's Exercise of Extraterritorial Jurisdiction' (2018) (PhD dissertation at Tilburg University).

Van Alsenoy and Koekkoek, 'Internet and Jurisdiction after Google Spain: The Extraterritorial Reach of the "Right to be Delisted"', 5(2) *IDPL* (2015), 105.

Van Alsenoy, 'Reconciling the (Extra)Territorial Reach of the GDPR with Public International Law', in Vermeulen and Lievens (eds.), *Data Protection and Privacy under Pressure: Transatlantic Tensions, EU Surveillance, and Big Data* (Maklu 2017), 77.

Papers of data protection authorities

Article 29 Working Party, 'Opinion 05/2012 on Cloud Computing' (WP 196, 1 July 2012).

Article 29 Working Party, 'Opinion 8/2014 on Recent Developments on the Internet of Things' (WP 223, 16 September 2014).

Article 29 Working Party, 'Guidelines on the Implementation of the Court of Justice of the European Union Judgment on "Google Spain and Inc v. Agencia Española de Protección de Datos (AEPD) and Mario Costeja González" C-131/12' (WP 225, 26 November 2014).

Article 29 Working Party, 'Update of Opinion 8/2010 on Applicable Law in Light of the CJEU Judgement in Google Spain' (WP 179 update, 16 December 2015).

EDPB 2018: European Data Protection Board, 'Guidelines 3/2018 on the Territorial Scope of the GDPR (Article 3)—Version for Public Consultation' (16 November 2018).

WP29 2010: Article 29 Working Party, 'Opinion 8/2010 on Applicable Law' (WP 179, 16 December 2010).

WP29 2017: Article 29 Working Party, 'Statement of the Article 29 Working Party on Data Protection and Privacy Aspects of Cross-Border Access to Electronic Evidence' (29 November 2017).

WP29 General Information Document: Article 29 Working Party, EU General Data Protection Regulation: General Information Document, available at http://ec.europa.eu/newsroom/article29/document.cfm?doc_id=49751&lipi=urn%3Ali%3Apage%3Ad_flagship3_pulse_read%3BaEuuvVHcSFSSShxXB0Rnjg%3D%3D.

Others

Commission Brexit Preparedness Notice: European Commission, 'Notice to Stakeholders: Withdrawal of the United Kingdom from the Union and EU Rules in the Field of Data Protection', 9 January 2018, available at https://ec.europa.eu/info/sites/info/files/file_import/data_protection_en.pdf.

Reding 2014: Reding, 'The EU Data Protection Regulation: Promoting Technological Innovation and Safeguarding Citizens' Rights' (4 March 2014), available at http://europa.eu/rapid/press-release_SPEECH-14-175_en.htm.

Article 4. Definitions

LUCA TOSONI   LEE A. BYGRAVE

For the purposes of this Regulation:

(1) 'personal data' means any information relating to an identified or identifiable natural person ('data subject'); an identifiable natural person is one who can be identified, directly or indirectly, in particular by reference to an identifier such as a name, an identification number, location data, an online identifier or to one or more factors specific to the physical, physiological, genetic, mental, economic, cultural or social identity of that natural person;

(2) 'processing' means any operation or set of operations which is performed on personal data or on sets of personal data, whether or not by automated means, such as collection, recording, organisation, structuring, storage, adaptation or alteration, retrieval, consultation, use, disclosure by transmission, dissemination or otherwise making available, alignment or combination, restriction, erasure or destruction;

(3) 'restriction of processing' means the marking of stored personal data with the aim of limiting their processing in the future;

(4) 'profiling' means any form of automated processing of personal data consisting of the use of personal data to evaluate certain personal aspects relating to a natural person, in particular to analyse or predict aspects concerning that natural person's performance at work, economic situation, health, personal preferences, interests, reliability, behaviour, location or movements;

(5) 'pseudonymisation' means the processing of personal data in such a manner that the personal data can no longer be attributed to a specific data subject without the use of additional information, provided that such additional information is kept separately and is subject to technical and organisational measures to ensure that the personal data are not attributed to an identified or identifiable natural person;

(6) 'filing system' means any structured set of personal data which are accessible according to specific criteria, whether centralised, decentralised or dispersed on a functional or geographical basis;

(7) 'controller' means the natural or legal person, public authority, agency or other body which, alone or jointly with others, determines the purposes and means of the processing of personal data; where the purposes and means of such processing are determined by Union or Member State law, the controller or the specific criteria for its nomination may be provided for by Union or Member State law;

(8) 'processor' means a natural or legal person, public authority, agency or other body which processes personal data on behalf of the controller;

(9) 'recipient' means a natural or legal person, public authority, agency or another body, to which the personal data are disclosed, whether a third party or not. However, public authorities which may receive personal data in the framework of a particular inquiry in accordance with Union or Member State law shall not be regarded as recipients; the processing of those data by those public authorities shall be in compliance with the applicable data protection rules according to the purposes of the processing;

(10) 'third party' means a natural or legal person, public authority, agency or body other than the data subject, controller, processor and persons who, under the direct authority of the controller or processor, are authorised to process personal data;

(11) 'consent' of the data subject means any freely given, specific, informed and unambiguous indication of the data subject's wishes by which he or she, by a statement or by a clear affirmative action, signifies agreement to the processing of personal data relating to him or her;

(12) 'personal data breach' means a breach of security leading to the accidental or unlawful destruction, loss, alteration, unauthorised disclosure of, or access to, personal data transmitted, stored or otherwise processed;

(13) 'genetic data' means personal data relating to the inherited or acquired genetic characteristics of a natural person which give unique information about the physiology or the health of that natural person and which result, in particular, from an analysis of a biological sample from the natural person in question;

(14) 'biometric data' means personal data resulting from specific technical processing relating to the physical, physiological or behavioural characteristics of a natural person, which allow or confirm the unique identification of that natural person, such as facial images or dactyloscopic data;

(15) 'data concerning health' means personal data related to the physical or mental health of a natural person, including the provision of health care services, which reveal information about his or her health status;

(16) 'main establishment' means:

(a) as regards a controller with establishments in more than one Member State, the place of its central administration in the Union, unless the decisions on the purposes and means of the processing of personal data are taken in another establishment of the controller in the Union and the latter establishment has the power to have such decisions implemented, in which case the establishment having taken such decisions is to be considered to be the main establishment;
(b) as regards a processor with establishments in more than one Member State, the place of its central administration in the Union, or, if the processor has no central administration in the Union, the establishment of the processor in the Union where the main processing activities in the context of the activities of an establishment of the processor take place to the extent that the processor is subject to specific obligations under this Regulation;

(17) 'representative' means a natural or legal person established in the Union who, designated by the controller or processor in writing pursuant to Article 27, represents the controller or processor with regard to their respective obligations under this Regulation;

(18) 'enterprise' means a natural or legal person engaged in an economic activity, irrespective of its legal form, including partnerships or associations regularly engaged in an economic activity;

(19) 'group of undertakings' means a controlling undertaking and its controlled undertakings;

(20) 'binding corporate rules' means personal data protection policies which are adhered to by a controller or processor established on the territory of a Member State for transfers or a set of transfers of personal data to a controller or processor in one or more third countries within a group of undertakings, or group of enterprises engaged in a joint economic activity;

(21) 'supervisory authority' means an independent public authority which is established by a Member State pursuant to Article 51;

(22) 'supervisory authority concerned' means a supervisory authority which is concerned by the processing of personal data because:

(a) the controller or processor is established on the territory of the Member State of that supervisory authority;
(b) data subjects residing in the Member State of that supervisory authority are substantially affected or likely to be substantially affected by the processing; or
(c) a complaint has been lodged with that supervisory authority;

(23) 'cross-border processing' means either:

(a) processing of personal data which takes place in the context of the activities of establishments in more than one Member State of a controller or processor in the Union where the controller or processor is established in more than one Member State; or
(b) processing of personal data which takes place in the context of the activities of a single establishment of a controller or processor in the Union but which substantially affects or is likely to substantially affect data subjects in more than one Member State.

(24) 'relevant and reasoned objection' means an objection to a draft decision as to whether there is an infringement of this Regulation, or whether envisaged action in relation to the controller or processor complies with this Regulation, which clearly demonstrates the significance of the risks posed by the draft decision as regards the fundamental rights and freedoms of data subjects and, where applicable, the free flow of personal data within the Union;

(25) 'information society service' means a service as defined in point (b) of Article 1(1) of Directive (EU) 2015/1535 of the European Parliament and of the Council (19);

(26) 'international organisation' means an organisation and its subordinate bodies governed by public international law, or any other body which is set up by, or on the basis of, an agreement between two or more countries.

Article 4(1). Personal data

LEE A. BYGRAVE   LUCA TOSONI

'personal data' means any information relating to an identified or identifiable natural person ('data subject'); an identifiable natural person is one who can be identified, directly or indirectly, in particular by reference to an identifier such as a name, an identification number, location data, an online identifier or to one or more factors specific to the physical, physiological, genetic, mental, economic, cultural or social identity of that natural person;

Relevant Recitals

(26) The principles of data protection should apply to any information concerning an identified or identifiable natural person. Personal data which have undergone pseudonymisation, which could be attributed to a natural person by the use of additional information should be considered to be information on an identifiable natural person. To determine whether a natural person is identifiable, account should be taken of all the means reasonably likely to be used, such as singling out, either by the controller or by another person to identify the natural person directly or indirectly. To ascertain whether means are reasonably likely to be used to identify the natural person, account should be taken of all objective factors, such as the costs of and the amount of time required for identification, taking into consideration the available technology at the time of the processing and technological developments. The principles of data protection should therefore not apply to anonymous information, namely information which does not relate to an identified or identifiable natural person or to personal data rendered anonymous in such a manner that the data subject is not or no longer identifiable. This Regulation does not therefore concern the processing of such anonymous information, including for statistical or research purposes.

(27) This Regulation does not apply to the personal data of deceased persons. Member States may provide for rules regarding the processing of personal data of deceased persons.

(30) Natural persons may be associated with online identifiers provided by their devices, applications, tools and protocols, such as internet protocol addresses, cookie identifiers or other identifiers such as radio frequency identification tags. This may leave traces which, in particular when combined with unique identifiers and other information received by the servers, may be used to create profiles of the natural persons and identify them.

(34) Genetic data should be defined as personal data relating to the inherited or acquired genetic characteristics of a natural person which result from the analysis of a biological sample from the natural person in question, in particular chromosomal, deoxyribonucleic acid (DNA) or ribonucleic acid (RNA) analysis, or from the analysis of another element enabling equivalent information to be obtained.

(35) Personal data concerning health should include all data pertaining to the health status of a data subject which reveal information relating to the past, current or future physical or mental health status of the data subject. This includes information about the natural person collected in the course of the registration for, or the provision of, health care services as referred to in Directive 2011/24/EU of the European Parliament and of the Council to that natural person; a number, symbol or particular assigned to a natural person to uniquely identify the natural

person for health purposes; information derived from the testing or examination of a body part or bodily substance, including from genetic data and biological samples; and any information on, for example, a disease, disability, disease risk, medical history, clinical treatment or the physiological or biomedical state of the data subject independent of its source, for example from a physician or other health professional, a hospital, a medical device or an in vitro diagnostic test.

Closely Related Provisions

Article 4(5) (Definition of 'pseudonymisation') (see too recital 11); Article 4(13) (Definition of 'genetic data') (see too recital 34); Article 4(14) (Definition of 'biometric data') (see also recital 51); Article 4(15) (Definition of 'data concerning health') (see also recital 35); Article 11 (Processing not requiring identification)

Related Provisions in LED [Directive (EU) 2016/680]

Article 3(1) (Definition of 'personal data') (see too recital 21); Article 3(5) (Definition of 'pseudonymisation'); Article 3(12) (Definition of 'genetic data'); Article 3(13) (Definition of 'biometric data'); Article 3(14) (Definition of 'data concerning health')

Related Provisions in EUDPR [Regulation (EU) 2018/1725]

Article 3(1) (Definition of 'personal data') (see too recitals 16 and 18); Article 3(6) (Definition of 'pseudonymisation'); Article 3(17) (Definition of 'genetic data'); Article 3(18) (Definition of 'biometric data'); Article 3(19) (Definition of 'data concerning health')

Relevant Case Law

CJEU

Joined Cases C-465/00, C-138/01 and C-139/01, *Rechnungshof v Österreichischer Rundfunk and Others* and *Christa Neukomm and Joseph Lauermann v Österreichischer Rundfunk*, judgment of 20 May 2003 (ECLI:EU:C:2003:294).

Case C-101/01, *Criminal proceedings against Bodil Lindqvist*, judgment of 6 November 2003 (ECLI:EU:C:2003:596).

Case T-198/03, *Bank Austria Creditanstalt AG v Commission of the European Communities*, CFI, judgment of 30 May 2006 (ECLI:EU:T:2006:136).

Case C-524/06, *Heinz Huber v Bundesrepublik Deutschland*, judgment of 16 December 2008 (Grand Chamber) (ECLI:EU:C:2008:724).

Case C-73/07, *Tietosuojavaltuutettu v Satakunnan Markkinapörssi and Satamedia*, judgment of 16 December 2008 (Grand Chamber) (ECLI:EU:C:2008:727).

Joined Cases C-92/09 and 93/09, *Volker and Markus Schecke GbR* and *Hartmut Eifert v Land Hessen*, judgment of 9 November 2010 (ECLI:EU:C:2010:662).

Case C-291/12, *Michael Schwarz v Stadt Bochum*, judgment of 17 October 2013 (ECLI:EU:C:2013:670).

Joined Cases C-293/12 and C-594/12, *Digital Rights Ireland Ltd v Minister for Communications, Marine and Natural Resources and Others* and *Kärntner Landesregierung and Others*, judgment of 8 April 2014 (Grand Chamber) (ECLI:EU:C:2014:238).

Joined Cases C-141/12 and C-372/12, *YS v Minister voor Immigratie, Integratie en Asiel* and *Minister voor Immigratie, Integratie en Asiel v M and S*, judgment of 17 July 2014 (ECLI:EU:C:2014:2081).
Opinion of Advocate General Sharpston in Joined Cases C-141/12 and C-372/12, *YS v Minister voor Immigratie, Integratie en Asiel* and *Minister voor Immigratie, Integratie en Asiel v M and S*, delivered on 12 December 2013 (ECLI:EU:C:2013:838).
Case C-212/13, *František Ryneš v Úřad pro ochranu osobních údajů*, judgment of 11 December 2014 (ECLI:EU:C:2014:2428).
Case C-201/14, *Smaranda Bara and Others v Casa Naţională de Asigurări de Sănătate and Others*, judgment of 1 October 2015 (ECLI:EU:C:2015:638).
Case C-419/14, *WebMindLicenses kft v Nemzeti Adó- és Vámhivatal Kiemelt Adó- és Vám Főigazgatóság*, judgment of 17 December 2015 (ECLI:EU:C:2015:832).
Opinion of Advocate General Wathelet in Case C-419/14, *WebMindLicenses Kft v Nemzeti Adó- és Vámhivatal Kiemelt Adó- és Vám Főigazgatóság*, delivered on 16 September 2015 (ECLI:EU:C:2015:606).
Case C-582/14, *Patrick Breyer v Bundesrepublik Deutschland*, judgment of 10 October 2016 (ECLI:EU:C:2016:779).
Case T-670/16, *Digital Rights Ireland v European Commission*, GC, order of 22 November 2017 (ECLI:EU:T:2017:838).
Case C-434/16, *Peter Nowak v Data Protection Commissioner*, judgment of 20 December 2017 (ECLI:EU:C:2017:994).
Case C-345/17, *Proceedings brought by Sergejs Buivids*, judgment of 14 February 2019 (ECLI:EU:C:2019:122).
Case C-40/17, *Fashion ID GmbH & Co. KG v Verbraucherzentrale NRW eV.*, judgment of 29 July 2019 (ECLI:EU:C:2019:629).
Opinion of Advocate General Bobek in Case C-40/17, *Fashion ID GmbH & Co. KG v Verbraucherzentrale NRW e.V.*, delivered on 19 December 2018 (ECLI:EU:C:2018:1039).

ECtHR

S and Marper v United Kingdom, Appl. Nos. 30562/04, 30566/04, judgment of 4 December 2008.

United Kingdom

Durant v Financial Services Authority [2003] EWCA Civ 1746.

A. Rationale and Policy Underpinnings

The definition of 'personal data' is of vital importance for determining whether or not the GDPR applies. Indeed, 'personal data' (or equivalents, such as 'personal information') is a threshold concept for the application of data protection law generally: if data being processed are not personal data, their processing is not subject to such law. In data protection discourse, data that are not personal are typically referred to as 'anonymous data',[1] and

---

[1] According to the European Commission, examples of 'anonymous data' or 'non-personal data' are: '[d]ata which are aggregated to the extent that individual events (such as a person's individual trips abroad or travel patterns which could constitute personal data) are no longer identifiable ... Anonymous data are used for instance in statistics or in sales reports (for example to assess the popularity of a product and its features)' and '[h]igh-frequency trading data in the finance sector, or data on precision farming which help to monitor and optimise the use of pesticides, nutrients and water'. See EC Guidance 2019, pp. 6–7.

the process of rendering personal data non-personal is typically termed 'anonymisation'.[2] While non-personal data do not fall within the scope of application of the GDPR, they do fall within the ambit of other EU legal instruments, such as Regulation (EU) 2018/1807 on a framework for the free flow of non-personal data in the European Union, which restricts Member States' ability to introduce or maintain data localisation requirements for non-personal data (Article 4(1)).[3]

The focus of data protection law on personal data reflects its basic aim of safeguarding the privacy and related interests of individual natural/physical persons, particularly within the informational sphere.[4] In Europe, the safeguarding of such interests is regarded as a matter of protecting fundamental human rights and freedoms—manifest in Articles 7–8 of the EU Charter of Fundamental Rights ('CFR'), Article 8 of the European Convention on Human Rights ('ECHR') and CJEU and ECtHR jurisprudence pursuant to these provisions.[5] Thus, European data protection law, including the GDPR, tends to adopt a broad conception of personal data in order to provide a high level of data protection that does justice to the fundamental rights at stake.

It is noteworthy that, during the GDPR legislative process, the Commission originally proposed integrating the guts of the definition of 'personal data' within a definition of 'data subject' (Article 4(1) GDPR Proposal) and defining 'personal data' by reference to the definition of 'data subject' (Article 4(2) GDPR Proposal). This proposed definitional structure found little favour in the Parliament and Council and was accordingly dropped. The Commission also proposed including the identifiability criterion 'by means reasonably likely to be used' (which had been part of recital 26 DPD) in the definition of 'data subject'. Again, this proposal failed to gain traction in the subsequent negotiations and the criterion ended up staying in the preamble to the GDPR (see recital 26 GDPR).

B. Legal Background

1. EU legislation

Article 2(a) DPD defined the term 'personal data' essentially in the same way as the GDPR defines it. Recital 26 DPD elaborated the identifiability criterion inherent in the definition by stating: 'to determine whether a person is identifiable, account should be taken of all the means likely reasonably to be used either by the controller or by any other person to identify the said person'. Again, this is in line with the thrust of recital 26 GDPR.

2. International instruments

Convention 108, both as originally adopted and in its modernised form, defines 'personal data' as 'any information relating to an identified or identifiable individual ('data subject')' (Article 2(a)). The OECD Privacy Guidelines adopt the same definition (paragraph 1(b)), as does the Asia-Pacific Economic Cooperation ('APEC') Privacy Framework (although the latter uses 'about' rather than 'relating to': see paragraph 9).[6]

---

[2] See e.g. WP29 2014. See too rec. 26 and the commentary on Art. 4(5) in this volume.
[3] See Free Flow of Non-Personal Data Regulation.
[4] Further on the range of interests safeguarded by data protection law, see Bygrave 2002, ch. 7.
[5] See further e.g. González Fuster 2014.
[6] OECD Privacy Guidelines 2013; APEC Privacy Framework 2005.

The Explanatory Report to Modernised Convention 108 states that '[a]n individual is not considered "identifiable" if his or her identification would require unreasonable time, effort or resources', and adds that this 'is the case, for example, when identifying a data subject would require excessively complex, long and costly operations'.[7] Further explication of the term 'personal data' in the Explanatory Report indicates that it has essentially the same meaning in Modernised Convention 108 as it does pursuant to the GDPR.[8]

The Explanatory Memorandum to the original OECD Guidelines elaborates on the definition of 'personal data' as follows:

The precise dividing line between personal data in the sense of information relating to identified or identifiable individuals and anonymous data may be difficult to draw and must be left to the regulation of each Member country. In principle, personal data convey information which by direct (e.g. a civil registration number) or indirect linkages (e.g. an address) may be connected to a particular physical person.[9]

3. National developments

European states and, indeed, most other states with data protection laws, have generally operated with definitions of 'personal data' that are basically in line with Article 2(a) DPD, Article 2(a) Convention 108 and para. 1(b) OECD Guidelines. However, European states' interpretation and application of these definitions has not been entirely uniform, nor has it been entirely consistent with EU rules. National (and to some extent international) differences have arisen with respect to, inter alia, the meaning of the terms 'data' and 'information' (a key question being: do they cover, for example, biological material?),[10] the legally relevant agent of identification (in particular, is account to be taken only of the controller's ability to carry out identification?),[11] the type of persons who may be 'data subjects' (in particular, are deceased persons or legal persons—such as corporate entities—data subjects protected by the law concerned?),[12] and the requirement of 'individuation' (i.e. must 'personal data' be capable of being linked to just one person rather than an aggregate of persons, and if not, how large may the aggregate be before the data cease to be 'personal'?).[13]

4. Case law

The CJEU has interpreted the term 'personal data' in numerous cases. This case law is presented directly below. National courts along with the ECtHR have also interpreted the term,[14]

---

[7] Explanatory Report Convention 108 2018, para. 17. See also the Explanatory Report to Convention 108 as originally adopted, which states that an 'identifiable person' is one 'who can be easily identified: it does not cover identification of persons by means of very sophisticated methods'. See Explanatory Report Convention 108 1981, para. 28. For analysis of the latter formulation, see e.g. Bygrave 2002, p. 43.

[8] Explanatory Report Convention 108 2018, paras. 17–20.

[9] OECD Privacy Guidelines 2013, p. 52. The Guidelines were revised in 2013, but without affecting the definition of 'personal data'.

[10] See generally Bygrave 2010 and references cited therein.

[11] See e.g. Bygrave 2014, p. 132 and references cited therein.

[12] See generally Bygrave 2002, ch. 9; Bygrave 2014, pp. 139–140 and references cited therein.

[13] See generally Bygrave 2014, p. 135 and references cited therein.

[14] For a brief overview, see Bygrave 2014, pp. 136–138.

sometimes in ways that have not strictly conformed with its definition under EU data protection law.[15]

C. Analysis

1. Differences to DPD

The definition of 'personal data' in the GDPR is essentially the same as that in the former DPD. Thus, CJEU case law and DPA opinions on the meaning of 'personal data' pursuant to the DPD remain relevant to understanding the term as employed in the GDPR.[16]

The main differences between the two definitions are that the GDPR supplements the DPD's list of potential 'identifiers' with 'location data' and 'online identifier' and adds a 'genetic' dimension to the 'identity' of a person. These additions, however, were implicit in the definition provided by the DPD.

Another difference is the wording of recital 26 GDPR, which provides a lengthier elaboration of the identifiability criterion at the core of the concept of 'personal data' than was provided by recital 26 DPD. The latter stated, in part:

[T]o determine whether a person is identifiable, account should be taken of all the means likely reasonably to be used either by the controller or by any other person to identify the said person.

In contrast, the equivalent passage in recital 26 GDPR states, in part:

[T]o determine whether a natural person is identifiable, account should be taken of all the means reasonably likely to be used, such as singling out, either by the controller or by another person to identify the natural person directly or indirectly.

This is followed by a non-exhaustive list of 'objective factors' that should be taken into account in this regard.

The inclusion of 'singling out' appears to originate—at least partly—from input by the WP29, which pushed to have the criterion, albeit in a lengthier form, inserted in both the definition and preamble. In the view of the WP29, a person is identifiable 'when, within a group of persons, he or she can be distinguished from other members of the group and consequently be treated differently'.[17] The Working Party thus proposed that the wording 'singled out and treated differently' be added to the references to the identification process in both the definition and preamble.[18] Its apparent intention here was to provide an elaboration of identifiability, not to add a new and separate criterion,[19] although the actual

---

[15] A notorious instance being the judgment of the UK Court of Appeal in the *Durant* case, decided in 2003. There the Court restricted the term 'personal data' to information that is 'biographical in a significant sense' or has the data subject as its focus, such that it 'affects his privacy, whether in his personal or family life, business or professional capacity'. See *Durant v Financial Services Authority*, para. 28. Another example in point is the judgment of the ECtHR in the *Marper* case in which samples of human DNA (deoxyribonucleic acid) were held to constitute 'personal data' for the purposes of Convention 108. See ECtHR, *Marper*, para. 68. This differs from the approach taken in the GDPR which distinguishes between biological material and personal data.

[16] This is also the view expressed by Advocate General Bobek in *Fashion ID*: 'as Article 4 of the GDPR largely retains the same key terms as Article 2 of Directive 95/46 (while adding a number of new ones), it would be rather surprising if the interpretation of such key notions, including the notion of controller, processing, or personal data, were to significantly depart (without a very good reason) from the extant case-law'. See Case C-40/17, *Fashion ID* (AG Opinion), para. 87.

[17] WP29 2012B, p. 4. [18] Ibid.

[19] Ibid. ('It is therefore suggested to clarify in Recital 23 and Article 4 that the notion of identifiability also includes singling out in this way').

wording of its proposed legislative text suggested otherwise.[20] The final text of the GDPR operates with a truncated version of this proposal in recital 26 of the preamble and makes clear, through the use of 'such as', that the singling out criterion is part and parcel of the criterion of identifiability. Thus, the end result does not substantially change the way in which the identifiability criterion was understood and applied under the DPD.

Another noteworthy point regarding recital 26 concerns the change from 'means likely reasonably to be used' in the DPD version of the recital to 'means reasonably likely to be used' in the GDPR version. Is this change more than cosmetic? It would seem that the answer is no. The formulation in the DPD is clunky and awkward, at least in the English language, and the change appears to have been instituted in order to bring the text more in line with ordinary grammatical convention.[21]

2. Key constituent elements of the definition

Inspired by the work of the WP29,[22] it is commonplace to analyse the definition of 'personal data' by breaking it down into its four chief constituent elements: (1) 'any information'; (2) 'relating to'; (3) 'identified or identifiable'; (4) 'natural person'.

Regarding the first-listed of these elements, in *Nowak*, the CJEU stated:

[T]he use of the expression 'any information' in the definition of the concept of 'personal data' ... reflects the aim of the EU legislature to assign a wide scope to that concept, which is not restricted to information that is sensitive or private, but potentially encompasses all kinds of information, not only objective but also subjective, in the form of opinions and assessments, provided that it 'relates' to the data subject.[23]

The opinion of Advocate General Sharpston in *YS* is also instructive on this point:

The actual content of that information appears to be of no consequence as long as it relates to an identified or identifiable natural person. It can be understood to relate to any facts regarding that person's private life and possibly, where relevant, his professional life (which might involve a more public aspect of that private life). It may be available in written form or be contained in, for example, a sound or image.[24]

Over the years, the CJEU has found a diverse array of information types to give rise to personal data. These include a person's telephone number or information regarding

---

[20] See ibid., its proposed amended version of Art. 4(2) defining 'data subject' as 'an identified natural person or a natural person who can be identified, directly or indirectly, *or singled out and treated differently*, by means reasonably likely to be used by the controller or by any other natural or legal person': emphasis added. The Parliament included the following text in recital 23 of its proposal: 'or single out the individual directly or indirectly'. See EP Resolution GDPR 2014, rec. 23. In contrast, the Council at one stage considered inserting the following text into the preamble: 'or single out the individual directly or indirectly which means the possibility to isolate some or all records which identify an individual in the dataset'. See Council Report 2015, p. 35 (see also p. 6). This suggestion was inspired by the Working Party's opinion on anonymisation techniques. See WP29 2014.

[21] Indeed, the UK intimated that the phrasing in the DPD was a grammatical error. See Council Report 2012, p. 128. The view that the changes in rec. 26 are only cosmetic in nature would seem to find further support in other language versions of rec. 26. For example, in its Spanish version, rec. 26 DPD referred to the 'medios que puedan ser razonablemente utilizados', while rec. 26 GDPR mentions the 'medios ... que razonablemente pueda utilizar el responsable del tratamiento o cualquier otra persona'. Similarly, the Italian version of rec. 26 DPD used the terms 'mezzi che possono essere ragionevolmente utilizzati', whereas rec. 26 GDPR, in the same language, refers to 'i mezzi ... di cui il titolare del trattamento o un terzo può ragionevolmente avvalersi'.

[22] WP29 2007.   [23] Case C-434/16, *Nowak*, para. 34.

[24] Joined Cases C-141/12 and C-372/12, *YS* (AG Opinion), para. 45.

their working conditions and hobbies;[25] data on personal income and tax;[26] passport details;[27] fingerprints;[28] images of persons recorded on video camera;[29] exam scripts and the comments of examiners on those scripts;[30] and electronic communications traffic data, including, under certain circumstances, IP addresses.[31]

Regarding the second-listed element ('relating to'), again the CJEU has taken a broad view. In *Nowak*, it stated that this element 'is satisfied where the information, by reason of its content, purpose or effect, is linked to a particular person'.[32] This puts another gaping hole in the few borders of the personal data concept, although the reference to 'a particular person' would seem to exclude that data relating to an aggregate of persons (e.g. a household) are personal data, irrespective of the size of the aggregate.

However, in an earlier case dealing with access to data in a dossier about an asylum seeker, the Court held that legal analysis in such a dossier does not constitute personal data.[33] The Court took this line not just in relation to analysis that involves interpreting the law in the abstract (i.e. without any reference to a particular factual situation), but also in relation to 'legal classification of facts relating to an identified or identifiable person (or event involving such persons) and their assessment against the background of the applicable law'.[34] So, whereas the Court had

no doubt that the data relating to the applicant for a residence permit and contained in a minute, such as the applicant's name, date of birth, nationality, gender, ethnicity, religion and language, are information relating to that natural person, who is identified in that minute in particular by his name, and must consequently be considered to be 'personal data',[35]

it held otherwise with respect to the legal analysis in the same minute:

[S]uch a legal analysis is ... at most, in so far as it is not limited to a purely abstract interpretation of the law, ... information about the assessment and application by the competent authority of that law to the applicant's situation, that situation being established inter alia by means of the personal data relating to him which that authority has available to it.[36]

This is a rare instance in which the Court has read the concept of 'personal data' restrictively. However, the current status of the result in *YS* is somewhat uncertain, considering the expansive line the CJEU subsequently took in *Nowak*.

Regarding the third-listed element concerning identifiability, a flexible approach is taken. This is signalled by the wording of both Article 4(1) and recital 26, especially the references to 'singling out', 'directly or indirectly', and 'either by the controller or by another person'.[37] Thus, data may be personal even if the controller cannot make a link to

---

[25] See Case C-101/01, *Lindqvist*, para. 27.

[26] See Joined Cases C-465/00, C-138/01 and C-139/01, *Österreichischer Rundfunk*, para. 64; Case C-73/07, *Satamedia*, para. 35; Case C-201/14, *Smaranda Bara*, para. 29.

[27] See Case C-524/06, *Huber*, paras. 31 and 43.

[28] See Case C-291/12, *Schwarz*, para. 27 (referring also to paras. 68 and 84 of the ECtHR judgment in the *Marper* case).

[29] See Case C-212/13, *Ryneš*, para. 22; Case C-345/17, *Buivids*, para. 32.

[30] See Case C-434/16, *Nowak*, paras. 36 et seq.

[31] Joined Cases C-293/12 and C-594/12, *Digital Rights Ireland*, para. 26; Case C-582/14, *Breyer*, para. 49.

[32] Case C-434/16, *Nowak*, para. 35. Here the Court seems to embrace a position previously taken by the WP29: see WP29 2007, pp. 9–12.

[33] Joined Cases C-141/12 and C-372/12, *YS*, para. 48.

[34] Joined Cases C-141/12 and C-372/12, *YS* (AG Opinion), para. 54.

[35] Joined Cases C-141/12 and C-372/12, *YS*, para. 38   [36] Ibid., paras. 39–40.

[37] For instructive guidance on the operationalisation of these criteria, particularly in the context of online behavioural targeting, see Borgesius 2016.

a particular person without help from other sources: as the CJEU stated in *Breyer*, 'it is not required that all the information enabling the identification of the data subject must be in the hands of one person'.[38] However, as recital 26 states, account is only to be taken of 'means reasonably likely to be used' in the identification process. According to the CJEU, this criterion would not be satisfied 'if the identification of the data subject was prohibited by law or practically impossible on account of the fact that it requires a disproportionate effort in terms of time, cost and man-power, so that the risk of identification appears in reality to be insignificant'.[39]

As for the fourth element ('natural person'), this means that data on corporations, partnerships and other legal/juristic persons are not protected as such by the Regulation. The CJEU has nonetheless held that 'in so far as the official title of the legal person identifies one or more natural persons', the legal person may claim the protection of data linked to it, pursuant to Articles 7 and 8 of the Charter.[40] Given that the GDPR is an elaboration of the overarching safeguards laid down by those Charter provisions,[41] such protection for legal persons may also flow from the GDPR, although this protection pertains not to the legal person as such,[42] but the natural person(s) constituting it and is likely to arise predominantly in cases when the legal person is, in effect, a one-person enterprise or a small family-run enterprise with a transparent 'corporate veil'.[43]

---

[38] Case C-582/14, *Breyer*, para. 43.   [39] Ibid., para. 46.

[40] Joined Cases C-92/09 and 93/09, *Schecke*, para. 53. See also Case C-419/14, *WebMindLicenses*, para. 79; Case T-670/16, *Digital Rights Ireland*, para. 25. The data at issue in *Schecke* concerned an agricultural undertaking in the legal form of a partnership which was a beneficiary of funds deriving from the European Agricultural Guarantee Fund ('EAGF') and the European Agricultural Fund for Rural Development ('EAFRD'). The official title of the partnership in question directly identified the natural persons who were its partners.

[41] However, the extent to which legal persons as such enjoy the protection of Arts. 7 and 8 CFR may change. On this point, Advocate General Wathelet held the following in *WebMindLicenses*: '[a]s regards... the scope *ratione personae* of Articles 7 and 8 of the Charter, it should be noted from the outset that, according to the case-law of both the Court and the European Court of Human Rights, the concept of private life must be interpreted as including the professional or business activities of legal persons. Consequently, Articles 7 and 8 of the Charter and Article 8 of the ECHR concern both natural persons and legal persons'. The Advocate General added that '[i]t is true that, in paragraph 53 of the judgment in *Volker und Markus Schecke and Eifert* (C-92/09 and C-93/09, EU:C:2010:662), the Court held that "legal persons can claim the protection of Articles 7 and 8 of the Charter... only in so far as the official title of the legal person identifies one or more natural persons". However, the case-law in this field has developed considerably, the Court now recognising that legal persons enjoy the protection of Articles 7 and 8 of the Charter. In paragraphs 32 to 37 of the judgment in *Digital Rights Ireland and Others* (C-293/12 and C-594/12, EU:C:2014:238), the Court did not limit the scope of those articles in relation to the first plaintiff, despite the fact that Digital Rights Ireland Ltd was a company under Irish law and was claiming the rights conferred on it by those articles (see paragraphs 17 and 18 of that judgment)'. See Case C-419/14, *WebMindLicenses* (AG Opinion), paras. 111–112 and fn 39. Nonetheless, the GC has refused to move beyond the position taken in *Schecke*: see Case T-670/16, *Digital Rights Ireland*, para. 25.

[42] See, by analogy, the findings of the Court in *Bank Austria Creditanstalt* regarding the protection enjoyed by legal persons under Regulation 45/2001: 'Regulation No 45/2001 seeks to protect individuals with regard to the processing of personal data. The applicant, which is a legal person, does not belong to the circle of persons which the regulation is intended to protect. It cannot therefore invoke an alleged breach of the rules which that regulation prescribes'. See Case T-198/03, *Bank Austria Creditanstalt*, para. 95.

[43] The EPD also provides limited protection for data on legal persons in their capacity as subscribers to the electronic communications services that the Directive covers. This protection arises regardless of the legal persons' size and structure. See Art. 1(2) EPD.

3. Deceased persons

The definition of 'personal data' in Article 4(1) GDPR does not cover data on deceased persons. This is made clear in recital 27, which also provides that Member States may, nevertheless, adopt rules for the protection of deceased person data. While the overwhelming majority of Member States limit the application of their respective data protection regimes to data on living persons, Danish law has long protected data on deceased persons, and continues to do so after the GDPR entered into force. Thus, the Danish Data Protection Act 2018 states that '[t]his Act and the General Data Protection Regulation shall apply to the data of deceased persons for a period of 10 years following the death of the deceased' (Article 2(5)). Italy has also recently introduced limited data protection rights to cater for the interests of deceased persons, allowing—with some qualifications—the estate of a deceased person (the data subject) to exercise the rights in Articles 15–22 GDPR.[44]

At the same time, genetic data relating to deceased persons, along with some types of health data about such persons, may need to be treated as 'personal data' inasmuch as they provide an indication of the genetic or health status of living biological kin.[45]

4. Biological material

For the purposes of the GDPR, 'personal data' does not extend to biological material as such (e.g. blood, saliva, hair or the chemical components of the human body). This follows from recital 35, which distinguishes between bodily samples and the data derived from such samples, and from Article 4(13) and recital 34, both of which refer to data that 'result from the analysis of a biological sample'.[46] The same distinction was made by some supervisory authorities,[47] as well as by WP29 with respect to biometric data.[48]

5. Genetic data, biometric data, health data and pseudonymisation

The concept of 'personal data' is further elaborated in the definitions of 'genetic data' (Article 4(13)), 'biometric data' (Article 4(14)) and 'data concerning health' (Article 4(15)), all of which are formulated as categories of 'personal data'. The definition of 'pseudonymisation' (Article 4(5)) is also relevant, not least because it casts light on the issue of when data are anonymous and hence non-personal.

6. Mixed datasets consisting of both personal and non-personal data

Mixed datasets consisting of both personal and non-personal data are increasingly common because of technological developments such as the Internet of Things, Artificial Intelligence and Big Data Analytics.[49] With respect to these datasets, the Free Flow of

---

[44] See Italian Data Protection Code 2003, Art. 2–terdecies, as amended by Italian Data Protection Legislative Decree 2018.

[45] See too Klabunde 2017, p. 241.

[46] See also the commentaries on Art. 4(13)–(14) in this volume.

[47] For example, the Italian DPA found that the genotypic information contained in a human biological sample qualifies as personal data only if it is extracted from the biological sample and stored in, say, medical records. See Italian Data Protection Authority 2007.

[48] See WP29 2007, p. 9 ('Human tissue samples (like a blood sample) are themselves sources out of which biometric data are extracted, but they are not biometric data themselves'). See also WP29 2012, p. 4.

[49] EC Guidance 2019, p. 8.

Non-Personal Data Regulation provides that: '[I]n the case of a dataset composed of both personal and non-personal data, this Regulation applies to the non-personal data part of the dataset. Where personal and non-personal data in a dataset are inextricably linked, this Regulation shall not prejudice the application of Regulation (EU) 2016/679'.[50]

As aptly noted by the European Commission, this implies that:

1. the Free Flow of Non-Personal Data Regulation applies to the non-personal data part of the dataset;
2. the GDPR's free flow provision applies to the personal data part of the dataset; and
3. if the non-personal data part and the personal data parts are 'inextricably linked', the data protection rights and obligations stemming from the GDPR fully apply to the whole mixed dataset, also when personal data represent only a small part of the dataset.[51]

The term 'inextricably linked' is left undefined in both the GDPR and Free Flow of Non-Personal Data Regulation. However, according to the European Commission, 'it can refer to a situation whereby a dataset contains personal data as well as non-personal data and separating the two would either be impossible or considered by the controller to be economically inefficient or not technically feasible'.[52]

7. The costs of an expansive definition

As made abundantly clear from the preceding text, the term 'personal data' is intentionally defined in a broad and flexible way. As the European Commission stated in relation to the DPD:

The definition of 'personal data' aims at covering all information relating to an identified or identifiable person, either directly or indirectly ... This deliberate approach chosen by the legislator has the benefit of flexibility, allowing it to be applied to various situations and developments affecting fundamental rights, including those not foreseeable when the Directive was adopted.[53]

The Commission went on to note, though, that this flexibility has a cost, in terms of predictability:

[A] consequence of such a broad and flexible approach is that there are numerous cases where it is not always clear, when implementing the Directive, which approach to take, whether individuals enjoy data protection rights and whether data controllers should comply with the obligations imposed by the Directive.[54]

Arguably, though, there is another cost which is that EU data protection law—and other law operating with a similarly broad and flexible conception of 'personal data'—gains an enormous scope of application, perhaps beyond what it can practically cope with in terms of actual compliance and enforcement. This cost looms increasingly large in the era of 'Big Data Analytics' when more and more data that appear to be anonymous are not, and when, concomitantly, more and more data that once would have fallen outside the ambit of data protection law are, in principle, subject to it. Augmenting these technology-induced developments is the tendency of the CJEU to construe 'personal

---

[50] Free Flow of Non-Personal Data Regulation, Art. 2(2). [51] See EC Guidance 2019, p. 9.
[52] Ibid., p. 10. [53] EC Communication 2010, p. 5. [54] Ibid.

data' very liberally—as detailed above. Thus, EU data protection law resembles increasingly a law of everything.[55]

Select Bibliography

International agreements

APEC Privacy Framework 2005: Asia-Pacific Economic Cooperation, 'Privacy Framework' (2005).
OECD Privacy Guidelines 2013: Organisation for Economic Co-operation and Development, 'The OECD Privacy Framework' (2013).

EU legislation

Free Flow of Non-Personal Data Regulation: Regulation (EU) 2018/1807 of the European Parliament and of the Council of 14 November 2018 on a framework for the free flow of non-personal data in the European Union, OJ 2018 L 303/59.
GDPR Proposal: Proposal for a Regulation of the European Parliament and of the Council on the protection of individuals with regard to the processing of personal data and on the free movement of such data (General Data Protection Regulation), COM(2012) 11 final, 25 January 2012.

National legislation

Danish Data Protection Act 2018: Lov nr. 502 av 23. mai 2018 om supplerende bestemmelser til forordning om beskyttelse af fysiske personer i forbindelse med behandling af personoplysninger og om fri udveksling af sådanne oplysninger (databeskyttelsesloven).
Italian Data Protection Code 2003: Decreto legislativo 30 giugno 2003, n. 196: Codice in Materia di Protezione dei Dati Personali.
Italian Data Protection Legislative Decree 2018: Decreto Legislativo 10 agosto 2018 n. 101: Disposizioni per l'adeguamento della normativa nazionale alle disposizioni del regolamento (UE) 2016/679 del Parlamento europeo e del Consiglio, del 27 aprile 2016, relativo alla protezione delle persone fisiche con riguardo al trattamento dei dati personali, nonché alla libera circolazione di tali dati e che abroga la direttiva 95/46/CE (regolamento generale sulla protezione dei dati).

Academic writings

Borgesius 2016: Borgesius, 'Singling Out People without Knowing their Names: Behavioural Targeting, Pseudonymous Data, and the New General Data Protection Regulation', 32(2) *Computer Law & Security Review* (2016), 256.
Bygrave 2002: Bygrave, *Data Protection Law: Approaching its Rationale, Logic and Limits* (Kluwer Law International 2002).
Bygrave 2010: Bygrave, 'The Body as Data? Biobank Regulation via the "Backdoor" of Data Protection Law', 2(1) *Law, Innovation and Technology* (2010), 1.
Bygrave 2014: Bygrave, *Data Privacy Law: An International Perspective* (OUP 2014).
Bygrave 2015: Bygrave, 'Information Concepts in Law: Generic Dreams and Definitional Daylight', 35(1) *Oxford Journal of Legal Studies* (2015), 91.
González Fuster 2014: González Fuster, *The Emergence of Personal Data Protection as a Fundamental Right in the EU* (Springer 2014).
Klabunde 2017: Klabunde, 'Art. 4', in Ehmann and Selmayr (eds.), *Datenschutz-Grundverordnung* (C. H. Beck 2017), 240.

---

[55] See further Purtova 2018.

Purtova 2018: Purtova, 'The Law of Everything: Broad Concept of Personal Data and Future of EU Data Protection Law', 10(1) *Law, Innovation and Technology* (2018), 40.

Papers of data protection authorities

WP29 2007: Article 29 Working Party, 'Opinion 04/2007 on the Concept of Personal Data' (WP 136, 20 June 2007).
WP29 2012A: Article 29 Working Party, 'Opinion 3/2012 on Developments in Biometric Technologies' (WP 193, 27 April 2012).
WP29 2012B: Article 29 Working Party, 'Opinion 08/2012 Providing Further Input on the Data Protection Reform Discussions' (WP 199, 5 October 2012).
WP29 2014: Article 29 Working Party, 'Opinion 05/2014 on Anonymisation Techniques' (WP 216, 10 April 2014).
Italian Data Protection Authority 2007: Garante per la protezione dei dati personali, 'Campione biologico e dato personale genetico' (21 June 2007).

Reports and recommendations

Council Report 2012: Proposal for a regulation of the European Parliament and of the Council on the protection of individuals with regard to the processing of personal data and on the free movement of such data (General Data Protection Regulation), 9897/1/12 REV 1, 24 May 2012.
Council Report 2015: Chapters I and IX, Flexibility for public sector, Preparation for trilogue, 13395/15, 30 October 2015.
EC Communication 2010: Communication from the Commission to the European Parliament, the Council, the Economic and Social Committee and the Committee of the Regions, A comprehensive approach on personal data protection in the European Union, COM(2010) 609 final, 4 November 2010.
EC Guidance 2019: Guidance on the Regulation on a framework for the free flow of non-personal data in the European Union, COM(2019) 250 final, 29 May 2019.
EP Resolution GDPR 2014: European Parliament legislative resolution of 12 March 2014 on the proposal for a regulation of the European Parliament and of the Council on the protection of individuals with regard to the processing of personal data and on the free movement of such data (General Data Protection Regulation), P7_TA(2014)0212, 12 March 2014.
Explanatory Report Convention 108 1981: Council of Europe, 'Explanatory Report to the Convention for the Protection of Individuals with Regard to Automatic Processing of Personal Data' (28 January 1981), available at https://rm.coe.int/16800ca434.
Explanatory Report Convention 108 2018: Council of Europe, 'Explanatory Report to the Protocol Amending the Convention for the Protection of Individuals with Regard to the Automatic Processing of Personal Data' (10 October 2018), available at https://rm.coe.int/cets-223-explanatory-report-to-the-protocol-amending-the-convention-fo/16808ac91a.

Article 4(2). Processing

LUCA TOSONI   LEE A. BYGRAVE

'processing' means any operation or set of operations which is performed on personal data or on sets of personal data, whether or not by automated means, such as collection, recording, organisation, structuring, storage, adaptation or alteration, retrieval, consultation, use, disclosure by transmission, dissemination or otherwise making available, alignment or combination, restriction, erasure or destruction;

Relevant Recital

(15) In order to prevent creating a serious risk of circumvention, the protection of natural persons should be technologically neutral and should not depend on the techniques used. The protection of natural persons should apply to the processing of personal data by automated means, as well as to manual processing, if the personal data are contained or are intended to be contained in a filing system. Files or sets of files, as well as their cover pages, which are not structured according to specific criteria should not fall within the scope of this Regulation.

Closely Related Provisions

Article 2 (Material scope)

Related Provisions in LED [Directive (EU) 2016/680]

Article 3(2) (Definition of 'processing') (see too recital 18)

Related Provisions in EPD [Directive 2002/58/EC]

Article 2 (Definition of 'processing' in DPD)

Related Provisions in EUDPR [Regulation (EU) 2018/1725]

Article 2(1) (Scope); Article 3(3) (Definition of 'processing') (see also recitals 7–8)

Relevant Case Law

CJEU

Case C-101/01, *Criminal proceedings against Bodil Lindqvist*, judgment of 6 November 2003 (ECLI:EU:C:2003:596).
Case C-73/07, *Tietosuojavaltuutettu v Satakunnan Markkinapörssi and Satamedia*, judgment of 16 December 2008 (Grand Chamber) (ECLI:EU:C:2008:727).

Tosoni/Bygrave

Case C-28/08 P, *European Commission v The Bavarian Lager Co. Ltd*, judgment of 29 June 2010 (Grand Chamber) (ECLI:EU:C:2010:378).

Case C-461/10, *Bonnier Audio AB and Others v Perfect Communication Sweden AB*, judgment of 19 April 2012 (ECLI:EU:C:2012:219).

Case C-131/12, *Google Spain v Agencia Española de Protección de Datos (AEPD) and Mario Costeja González*, judgment of 13 May 2014 (Grand Chamber) (ECLI:EU:C:2014:317).

Case C-291/12, *Michael Schwarz v Stadt Bochum*, judgment of 17 October 2013 (ECLI:EU:C:2013:670).

Joined Cases C-293/12 and C-594/12, *Digital Rights Ireland Ltd v Minister for Communications, Marine and Natural Resources and Others* and *Kärntner Landesregierung and Others*, judgment of 8 April 2014 (Grand Chamber) (ECLI:EU:C:2014:238).

Joined Cases C-141/12 and C-372/12, *YS v Minister voor Immigratie, Integratie en Asiel* and *Minister voor Immigratie, Integratie en Asiel v M and S*, judgment of 17 July 2014 (ECLI:EU:C:2014:2081).

Opinion of Advocate General Sharpston in Joined Cases C-141/12 and C-372/12, *YS v Minister voor Immigratie, Integratie en Asiel* and *Minister voor Immigratie, Integratie en Asiel v M and S*, delivered on 12 December 2013 (ECLI:EU:C:2013:838).

Case C-212/13, *František Ryneš v Úřad pro ochranu osobních údajů*, judgment of 11 December 2014 (ECLI:EU:C:2014:2428).

Case C-201/14, *Smaranda Bara and Others v Casa Naţională de Asigurări de Sănătate and Others*, judgment of 1 October 2015 (ECLI:EU:C:2015:638).

Case C-230/14, *Weltimmo s.r.o. v Nemzeti Adatvédelmi és Információszabadság Hatóság*, judgment of 1 October 2015 (ECLI:EU:C:2015:639).

Case C-362/14, *Maximillian Schrems v Data Protection Commissioner*, judgment of 6 October 2015 (Grand Chamber) (ECLI:EU:C:2015:650).

Case C-398/15, *Camera di Commercio, Industria, Artigianato e Agricoltura di Lecce v Salvatore Manni*, judgment of 9 March 2017 (ECLI:EU:C:2017:197).

Case C-73/16, *Peter Puškár v Finančné riaditeľstvo Slovenskej republiky and Kriminálny úrad finančnej správy*, judgment of 27 September 2017 (ECLI:EU:C:2017:725).

Case C-345/17, *Proceedings brought by Sergejs Buivids*, judgment of 14 February 2019 (ECLI:EU:C:2019:122).

Case C-40/17, *Fashion ID GmbH & Co. KG v Verbraucherzentrale NRW e.V.*, judgment of 29 July 2019 (ECLI:EU:C:2019:629).

Opinion of Advocate General Bobek in Case C-40/17, *Fashion ID GmbH & Co. KG v Verbraucherzentrale NRW e.V.*, delivered on 19 December 2018 (ECLI:EU:C:2018:1039).

United Kingdom

UK Court of Appeal, *R v Department of Health; ex parte Source Informatics Ltd* [2000] 1 All ER 786.

A. Rationale and Policy Underpinnings

The GDPR is aimed at regulating all or most stages of the data processing cycle, including registration, storage, retrieval and dissemination of personal data. To this end, Article 4(2) GDPR provides a broad definition of 'processing'. The open wording of the definition ('*any* operations or set of operations': emphasis added) reflects the intention of the legislature to make it technologically neutral in order to prevent risks of circumvention, and to ensure the applicability of the GDPR irrespective of the techniques used to process data (see also recital 15).

B. Legal Background

1. EU legislation

Article 2(b) DPD included a definition of 'processing' that is almost identical to that provided in Article 4(2) GDPR. The only differences between the two definitions are in the non-exhaustive list of examples of 'processing' that they provide. The GDPR adds 'structuring' to the list and replaces the term 'blocking' with the term 'restriction'. This is because the term 'blocking' was considered ambiguous.[1]

2. International instruments

The definition of 'processing' in Article 2(c) Convention 108 is a little narrower than that in Article 4(2) GDPR: it does not cover the mere collection of data, nor data processing carried out by entirely non-automated (manual) means. However, the Modernised Convention 108 aligns its definition of 'processing' with that in Article 4(2) GDPR, albeit with some minor differences (see Article 2(b)).[2]

Neither the OECD Privacy Guidelines (original and revised versions) nor the APEC Privacy Framework contain definitions of 'processing'.[3]

3. National developments

Prior to adoption of the GDPR, national data protection laws normally mirrored the definition of 'processing' provided in the DPD.[4] However, some national laws provided a more elaborate definition of 'processing'. For example, the Hungarian Data Protection Act provided:

[D]ata processing shall mean any operation or the totality of operations performed on the data, irrespective of the procedure applied; in particular, collecting, recording, registering, classifying, storing, modifying, using, querying, transferring, disclosing, synchronising or connecting, blocking, deleting and destructing the data, as well as preventing their further use, taking photos, making audio or visual recordings, as well as registering physical characteristics suitable for personal identification (such as fingerprints or palm prints, DNA samples, iris scans).[5]

4. Case law

The CJEU has interpreted the definition of 'processing' in the DPD in numerous cases. These cases show that the concept of 'processing' covers a very wide range of activities. Given that the definition of 'processing' in the GDPR is essentially the same as that in the former DPD, CJEU jurisprudence on the meaning of 'processing' pursuant to the

---

[1] GDPR Proposal, p. 9. For further details on the definition of 'restriction of processing', see the commentary on Art. 4(3) in this volume.
[2] Art. 2(b) Modernised Convention 108 reads: ' "data processing" means any operation or set of operations performed on personal data, such as the collection, storage, preservation, alteration, retrieval, disclosure, making available, erasure, or destruction of, or the carrying out of logical and/or arithmetical operations on such data'.
[3] OECD Privacy Guidelines 2013. APEC Privacy Framework 2005.
[4] See e.g. Belgian Data Protection Law 1992, Art. 1(2); French Data Protection Act 1978, Art. 2.
[5] See Hungarian Information Act 2011, s. 3(10).

DPD remains relevant to understanding the term as employed in the GDPR.[6] Thus, it is discussed in more detail in the next section.

C. Analysis

As noted above, the GDPR defines 'processing' broadly.[7] The definition must be interpreted in such a way as to avoid threatening the high level of protection conferred by the GDPR (see recitals 9–10). The CJEU has also noted that 'processing' 'may consist in one or a number of operations, each of which relates to one of the different stages that the processing of personal data may involve'.[8] Thus, the definition essentially covers any data processing operation. This would seem to be irrespective of its duration,[9] the amount of data processed and the actual recording of personal data. This was also the view of the WP29, which noted that 'data collection without any recording or storage is nevertheless a processing operation'.[10] In essence, it is difficult to conceive any operation performed on personal data which would fall outside the definition of 'processing'.[11]

The data processing medium and form are *de facto* irrelevant for the purpose of the definition. Indeed, the definition implicitly covers both the 'processing of personal data wholly or partially by automated means', and the 'processing other than by automated means' (see Article 2(1) GDPR). Processing by automated means (often called 'automated processing') refers to all processing done by means of computer technologies, whereas processing other than by automated means primarily refers to any data processing operation executed by humans without the use of computing devices (often termed 'manual processing'). However, not all manual processing entails the application of the GPDR. Manual processing falls within the material scope of application of the GDPR only if two cumulative conditions are met: (i) the personal data must be contained (or intended to be contained) in a 'filing system' (Article 2(1) GDPR); and (ii) the 'filing system' in which the data are contained must be structured according to specific criteria (Article 4(6) GDPR).[12]

---

[6] This was also the view of Advocate General Bobek in *Fashion ID*: 'as Article 4 of the GDPR largely retains the same key terms as Article 2 of Directive 95/46 (while adding a number of new ones), it would be rather surprising if the interpretation of such key notions, including the notion of controller, processing, or personal data, were to significantly depart (without a very good reason) from the extant case-law'. See Case C-40/17, *Fashion ID* (AG Opinion), para. 87.

[7] See Case C-40/17, *Fashion ID* (AG Opinion), para. 99 (noting this in relation to the definition of 'processing' in the DPD). During the legislative process, some Member States argued that this definition was 'too broad in view of the wide variety of data processing operations possibly covered by this'. See e.g. Council Report 2012, p. 45, fn. 58.

[8] Case C-40/17, *Fashion ID*, para 72 (noting this in relation to the definition of 'processing' in the DPD).

[9] For instance, the Italian DPA has found that the recording of images of individuals for 'a few tenths of a second' in the random-access memory of an electronic device constitutes 'processing of personal data': see Italian Data Protection Authority 2017.

[10] WP29 2015, p. 7, fn. 13.

[11] The term 'processing' as used in the DPD was also intended by the Commission to be interpreted very broadly: see DPD Amended Proposal 1992, Explanatory Memorandum, p. 10 (stating that 'the definition [of processing] is ... an *extensive one*, the better to ensure that individuals are protected ... , as it covers everything from the collection to the erasure of data, including organization, use, consultation, disclosure by transmission, dissemination or otherwise making available ... , comparison and suppression': emphasis added). The Amended Proposal's definition of 'processing' was essentially the same as that of Art. 2(b) DPD and Art. 4(2) GDPR.

[12] For further details on the definition of 'filing system', see the commentary on Art. 4(6) in this volume.

Article 4(2) GDPR provides a list of examples of processing operations that are covered by the definition of 'processing': collection, recording, organisation, structuring, storage, adaptation or alteration, retrieval, consultation, use, disclosure by transmission, dissemination or otherwise making available, alignment or combination, restriction, erasure or destruction of personal data. As noted by Advocate General Sharpston in *YS and Others* with regard to equivalent wording in Article 2(b) DPD, the use of the words 'such as' in Article 4(2) indicates that the list is not exhaustive, and also indicates the *type* of operations that constitute 'processing'.[13] These examples of processing operations are complemented by those provided in CJEU jurisprudence concerning the DPD. The CJEU has found that the definition of 'processing' covers, inter alia, the following operations: the loading of personal data on an internet page;[14] the collection of personal data from documents in the public domain, the publication of personal data in printed form, the transfer of personal data on a CD-ROM, the sending of text messages containing personal data, the capture, transmission, manipulation, recording, storage or communication of sound and image data;[15] the communication of personal data in response to a request for access to documents;[16] the communication of the name and address of an internet subscriber or user;[17] the activities of a search engine consisting in exploring the internet automatically, constantly and systematically in search of the information which is published there and the disclosure of such information in the form of lists of search results;[18] the taking and storing of a person's fingerprints;[19] the retention of data for the purpose of possible access to them by the competent national authorities;[20] the video recording of persons;[21] the transfer of personal data from an EU Member State to a third country;[22] the transcription and keeping of personal data in a register and its communication to third parties;[23] the drawing up of a list of individuals;[24] the act of publishing a video recording, which contains personal data, on a video website on which users can send, watch and share videos;[25] and the collection and disclosure by transmission of the personal data of visitors to a website by means of a third-party plug-in.[26]

These interpretations should also apply to the definition of 'processing' in Article 4(2) GDPR as it is essentially the same as that of Article 2(b) DPD.[27] This is the case also for Article 3(2) LED and Article 3(2) EUDPR both of which define 'processing' identically to Article 4(2) GDPR (see also recital 5 EUDPR).

At the same time, it is important to note that some operations have been viewed as not falling within the definition of 'processing'. First, in *YS*, Advocate General Sharpston held that legal analysis—understood as 'a process controlled entirely by individual human intervention through which personal data (in so far as they are relevant

---

[13] Joined Cases C-141/12 and C-372/12, *YS* (AG Opinion), para. 64.
[14] Case C-101/01, *Lindqvist*, para. 25; Case C-131/12, *Google Spain*, para. 26; Case C-230/14, *Weltimmo*, para. 37.
[15] Case C-73/07, *Satamedia*, paras. 35–37.
[16] Case C-28/08 P, *Commission v Bavarian Lager*, para. 69.
[17] Case C-461/10, *Bonnier Audio and Others*, para. 52.
[18] Case C-131/12, *Google Spain*, paras. 26–31.   [19] Case C-291/12, *Schwarz*, paras. 28–29.
[20] Joined Cases C-293/12 and C-594/12, *Digital Rights Ireland*, para. 29.
[21] Case C-212/13, *Ryneš*, para. 25; Case C-345/17, *Buivids*, para. 35. In the latter case, the CJEU made clear that video recording of persons stored on the memory of a digital camera constitutes 'processing' even if the recording is made only once: ibid., para. 36.
[22] Case C-362/14, *Schrems*, para. 45.   [23] Case C-398/15, *Manni*, para. 35.
[24] Case C-73/16, *Puškár*, para. 103.   [25] Case C-345/17, *Buivids*, para. 39.
[26] Case C-40/17, *Fashion ID*, para. 76.   [27] Case C-40/17, *Fashion ID* (AG Opinion), para. 87.

to the legal analysis) are assessed, classified in legal terms and subjected to the application of the law'—did not qualify as a form of 'processing' for the purposes of Article 2(b) DPD.[28]

Secondly, the UK Court of Appeal held (albeit in *obiter dicta*) that the process of anonymising personal data did not qualify as a form of 'processing' for the purposes of the UK Data Protection Act 1998 (repealed), which was intended to transpose the DPD into UK law.[29] The Court justified its line on the grounds of 'justice and common sense alike'.[30] However, the WP29 (including the UK DPA) took the opposite view on this matter.[31]

Select Bibliography

International agreements

APEC Privacy Framework 2005: Asia-Pacific Economic Cooperation, 'Privacy Framework' (2005).
OECD Privacy Guidelines 2013: Organisation for Economic Co-operation and Development, 'The OECD Privacy Framework' (2013).

EU legislation

DPD Amended Proposal 1992: Amended Proposal for a Council Directive on the Protection of Individuals with Regard to the Processing of Personal Data and on the Free Movement of Such Data (COM(92) 422 final—SYN 287, 15 October 1992.
GDPR Proposal: Proposal for a Regulation of the European Parliament and of the Council on the protection of individuals with regard to the processing of personal data and on the free movement of such data (General Data Protection Regulation), COM(2012) 11 final, 25 January 2012.

National legislation

Belgian Data Protection Law 1992: Wet tot bescherming van de persoonlijke levenssfeer ten opzichte van de verwerking van persoonsgegevens, van 8 december 1992; Loi relative à la protection de la vie privée à l'égard des traitements de données à caractère personnel, du 8 decembre 1992) (repealed).
French Data Protection Act 1978: French Act No. 78-17 of 6 January 1978 on Data Processing, Files and Individual Liberties (Loi n° 78-17 du 6 janvier 1978 relative à l'informatique, aux fichiers et aux libertés), as last amended by Law No. 2014-334 of 17 March 2014.
Hungarian Information Act 2011: Hungarian Act CXII of 2011 on the Right of Informational Self-Determination and on Freedom of Information.
UK Data Protection Act 1998: Data Protection Act 1998 (Chapter 29).

Academic writings

Walden 2002: Walden, 'Anonymising Personal Data', 10(2) *International Journal of Law and Information Technology* (2002), 224.

---

[28] Joined Cases C-141/12 and C-372/12, *YS* (AG Opinion), paras. 62–65. The CJEU did not explicitly endorse this view, but decided that the legal analysis nonetheless fell outside the scope of the DPD as it did not qualify as 'personal data'. See further the commentary on Art. 4(1) GDPR in this volume.
[29] UK Court of Appeal, *R v Department of Health*, para. 799. See also UK Data Protection Act 1998.
[30] UK Court of Appeal, *R v Department of Health*, para. 799. For a critical analysis of the decision and the arguments in favour of and against viewing anonymisation as a form of processing, see Walden 2002.
[31] WP29 2014, p. 7.

Papers of data protection authorities

WP29 2014: Article 29 Working Party, 'Opinion 05/2014 on Anonymisation Techniques' (WP 216, 10 April 2014).

WP29 2015: Article 29 Working Party, 'Opinion 1/2015 on Privacy and Data Protection Issues Relating to the Utilisation of Drones' (WP 231, 16 June 2015).

Italian Data Protection Authority 2017: Garante per la protezione dei dati personali, 'Installazione di apparati promozionali del tipo "digital signage" (definiti anche Totem) presso una stazione ferroviaria' (21 December 2017).

Reports and recommendations

Council Report 2012: Proposal for a regulation of the European Parliament and of the Council on the protection of individuals with regard to the processing of personal data and on the free movement of such data (General Data Protection Regulation), 16529/12, 4 December 2012.

Article 4(3). Restriction of processing

LUCA TOSONI

'restriction of processing' means the marking of stored personal data with the aim of limiting their processing in the future;

Relevant Recital

(67) Methods by which to restrict the processing of personal data could include, inter alia, temporarily moving the selected data to another processing system, making the selected personal data unavailable to users, or temporarily removing published data from a website. In automated filing systems, the restriction of processing should in principle be ensured by technical means in such a manner that the personal data are not subject to further processing operations and cannot be changed. The fact that the processing of personal data is restricted should be clearly indicated in the system.

Closely Related Provisions

Article 13(2)(b) (Information to be provided where personal data are collected from the data subject); Article 14(2)(c) (Information to be provided where personal data have not been obtained from the data subject); Article 15(1)(e) (Right of access by the data subject); Article 18 (Right to restriction of processing); Article 19 (Notification obligation regarding restriction of processing); Article 58(2)(g) (Powers of supervisory authorities)

Related Provisions in LED [Directive (EU) 2016/680]

Article 3(3) (Definition of 'restriction of processing') (see also recital 40); Article 13(1)(e) (Information to be made available or given to the data subject) (see too recital 42); Article 14(e) (Right of access by the data subject); Article 16 (Right to rectification or erasure of personal data and restriction of processing) (see too recitals 47–49); Article 47(2)(b) (Powers of supervisory authorities)

Related Provisions in EUDPR [Regulation (EU) 2018/1725]

Article 3(4) (Definition of 'restriction of processing') (see also recital 40); Article 15(2)(b) (Information to be provided where personal data are collected from the data subject); Article 16(2)(b) (Information to be provided where personal data have not been obtained from the data subject); Article 17(1)(e) (Right of access by the data subject); Article 20 (Right to restriction of processing); Article 21 (Notification obligation regarding rectification or erasure of personal data or restriction of processing); Article 58(2)(h) (Powers of the EDPS); Article 79(1)(e) (Information to be made available or given to the data subject); Article 80(e) (Right of access by the data subject); Article 82(3) (Right to rectification or erasure of operational personal data and restriction of processing)

A. Rationale and Policy Underpinnings

A 'restriction of processing' aims to reconcile the interests of the data subject and those of the controller when there is disagreement over whether the personal data of the data subject should be rectified or erased.[1] On the one hand, it allows the controller to retain the data while it assesses the request(s) of the data subject. On the other hand, a restriction ensures that the personal data under dispute are not subject to any further processing (except for storage) during the period in which the controller assesses the data subject's request(s) or until the dispute is otherwise resolved. These objectives are chiefly operationalised in Article 18 GDPR.

B. Legal Background

1. EU legislation

'Restriction of processing' is a term that the GDPR introduces for the first time, but it has its antecedent in the concept of 'blocking' of processing, which was used (but not defined) in Articles 2(b) and 12(b) DPD. Despite the lack of a definition of 'blocking' in the final text of the DPD, the Commission clarified in its initial proposal that '[t]he reference to blocking [in the Directive] relates to data to which access is blocked using more stringent security measures than is normally the case, but stopping short of erasure'.[2] The term 'blocking' remained nonetheless ambiguous, and the EU legislature decided to replace it in the GDPR with the term 'restriction of processing'.[3] The term 'blocking' was also used in Article 15 of Regulation 45/2001,[4] which did not define it but regulated the data subject's right to 'blocking' in a manner that largely coincided with the 'right to restriction of processing' in Article 18 GDPR. This suggests that 'restriction' of processing and 'blocking' of processing have a very similar, though not identical, meaning.

2. International instruments

The term 'restriction of processing' is absent from Convention 108 both in its original and modernised versions. The same applies with respect to the right to 'block' the processing of personal data, although Modernised Convention 108 provides a data subject with a qualified right 'to object, at any time, on grounds relating to his or her situation, to the processing of personal data concerning him or her' (Article 9(1)(d)). The latter right is more closely aligned with Article 21 GDPR than Article 18 GDPR.

Neither the OECD Privacy Guidelines (both original and revised versions) nor the APEC Privacy Framework specifically operate with 'restriction of processing'.

3. National developments

As mentioned above, 'blocking' is the legal antecedent of 'restriction of processing'. While 'blocking' was not defined in the DPD, several national data protection laws

---

[1] See also Voigt and von dem Bussche 2017, p. 164. [2] See DPD Proposal 1990, p. 20.
[3] See GDPR Proposal, p. 9. [4] See Table of Legislation.

defined the term. For example, Part I, section 3(4)(4) of the old German Federal Data Protection Act provided that 'blocking' 'means labelling stored personal data so as to restrict their further processing or use',[5] whereas Article 4(1)(o) of the former Italian Data Protection Code stated that 'blocking' means 'keeping personal data by temporarily suspending any other processing operation'.[6] The latter definition seems to reflect better the original conceptualisation of 'blocking', as it was expressed in the initial DPD proposal.

4. Case law

As 'restriction of processing' is a newly introduced term, the CJEU has not yet had a chance to interpret it.

C. Analysis

A literal reading of Article 4(3) GDPR would suggest, at least prima facie, that 'restriction of processing' consists in the mere singling out or 'earmarking' of certain personal data stored by the controller, namely data the processing of which may be limited in the future. Indeed, the Article employs the term 'marking', which normally refers to the act of putting a sign or a symbol on something in order to distinguish it from something else. It also states that the processing of the 'marked' data may be limited *in the future*.

Yet, recital 67 GDPR makes clear that 'in automated filing systems, the restriction of processing should be ensured by technical means in such a manner that the personal data are not subject to further processing and cannot be changed'. The recital also provides several examples of methods by which the 'restriction of processing' may be achieved, including 'temporarily moving the selected data to another processing system, making the selected personal data unavailable to users, or temporarily removing published data from a website'.

This suggests that the 'restriction of processing' normally entails a prompt (but temporary) limitation of the processing of the selected data, in addition to their singling out or earmarking. This is probably the main difference between the concept of 'blocking' used in the DPD and that of 'restriction of processing' used in the GDPR. In fact, while the former concept arguably refers to the mere temporary stop of any processing operations on certain personal data (with the exception of storage),[7] the latter concept also entails that the data for which the processing is suspended are rendered clearly distinguishable from other data stored by the controller. Recital 67 confirms this when it states that '[t]he fact that the processing of personal data is restricted should be clearly indicated in the system'.

Article 3(3) LED and Article 3(4) EUDPR define 'restriction of processing' identically to Article 4(3) GDPR. Thus, the term should be interpreted homogeneously in all these legal instruments (see recital 5 EUDPR).

---

[5] See German Federal Data Protection Act 1990.
[6] See Italian Data Protection Code 2003, as last amended by Italian Legislative Decree 2015.
[7] See, however, the definition of 'blocking' under the German Federal Data Protection Act 1990.

Select Bibliography

EU legislation

DPD Proposal 1990: Proposal for a Council Directive concerning the protection of individuals in relation to the processing of personal data, COM(90) 314 final—SYN 287, 13 September 1990.
GDPR Proposal: Proposal for a Regulation of the European Parliament and of the Council on the protection of individuals with regard to the processing of personal data and on the free movement of such data (General Data Protection Regulation), COM(2012) 11 final, 25 January 2012.

National legislation

German Federal Data Protection Act 1990: Gesetz zur Fortentwicklung der Datenverarbeitung und des Datenschutzes (Bundesdatenschutzgesetz), BGBl 1990 Teil 1 Nr. 2954 (repealed).
Italian Data Protection Code 2003: Decreto legislativo 30 giugno 2003, n. 196: Codice in Materia di Protezione dei Dati Personali.
Italian Legislative Decree 2015: Decreto Legislativo 14 settembre 2015, n. 151: Disposizioni di razionalizzazione e semplificazione delle procedure e degli adempimenti a carico di cittadini e imprese e altre disposizioni in materia di rapporto di lavoro e pari opportunità, in attuazione della legge 10 dicembre 2014, n. 183.

Academic writings

Voigt and von dem Bussche 2017: Voigt and von dem Bussche, *The EU General Data Protection Regulation (GDPR): A Practical Guide* (Springer 2017).

Article 4(4). Profiling

LEE A. BYGRAVE

'profiling' means any form of automated processing of personal data consisting of the use of personal data to evaluate certain personal aspects relating to a natural person, in particular to analyse or predict aspects concerning that natural person's performance at work, economic situation, health, personal preferences, interests, reliability, behaviour, location or movements;

Relevant Recitals

(24) The processing of personal data of data subjects who are in the Union by a controller or processor not established in the Union should also be subject to this Regulation when it is related to the monitoring of the behaviour of such data subjects in so far as their behaviour takes place within the Union. In order to determine whether a processing activity can be considered to monitor the behaviour of data subjects, it should be ascertained whether natural persons are tracked on the internet including potential subsequent use of personal data processing techniques which consist of profiling a natural person, particularly in order to take decisions concerning her or him or for analysing or predicting her or his personal preferences, behaviours and attitudes.

(30) Natural persons may be associated with online identifiers provided by their devices, applications, tools and protocols, such as internet protocol addresses, cookie identifiers or other identifiers such as radio frequency identification tags. This may leave traces which, in particular when combined with unique identifiers and other information received by the servers, may be used to create profiles of the natural persons and identify them.

(72) Profiling is subject to the rules of this Regulation governing the processing of personal data, such as the legal grounds for processing or data protection principles. The European Data Protection Board established by this Regulation (the 'Board') should be able to issue guidance in that context.

Closely Related Provisions

Article 3(2)(b) (Monitoring of data subjects' behaviour); Article 5 (Principles relating to processing of personal data); Article 6 (Legal grounds for processing of personal data); Article 8 (Conditions applicable to children's consent in relation to information society services) (see also recital 38); Article 13(2)(f) (Information on the existence of automated decision-making, including profiling) (see also recital 60); Article 14(2)(g) (Information on the existence of automated decision-making, including profiling) (see also recital 60); Article 15(1)(h) (Right of access regarding automated decision-making, including profiling) (see also recital 63); Article 21 (Right to object) (see also recital 70); Article 22 (Automated decision-making, including profiling) (see also recital 71); Article 23 (Restrictions) (see also recital 73); Article 35(3)(a) (Data protection impact assessment) (see also recital 91); Article 47(2)(e) (Binding corporate rules); Article 70(1)(f) (EDPB guidelines on automated decisions based on profiling)

Related Provisions in LED [Directive (EU) 2016/680]

Article 3(4) (Definition of 'profiling'); Article 11 (Automated individual decision-making, including profiling) (see too recital 38); Article 12 (Communication and modalities for exercising data subject rights) (see too recital 43); Article 24 (Controller records of data processing activities, including profiling); Article 27 (Data protection impact assessment) (see too recitals 51–52 and 58)

Related Provisions in EPD [Directive 2002/58/EC]

Article 5 (Confidentiality of communications) (see too recitals 24–25)

Related Provisions in EUDPR [Regulation (EU) 2018/1725]

Article 3(5) (Definition of 'profiling') (see also recital 18); Article 5 (Lawfulness of processing); Article 6 (Processing for another compatible purpose); Article 8 (Conditions applicable to children's consent in relation to information society services) (see also recital 27); Article 15(2)(f) (Information on the existence of automated decision-making, including profiling) (see also recital 35); Article 16(2)(f) (Information on the existence of automated decision-making, including profiling) (see also recital 35); Article 17(1)(h) (Right of access regarding automated decision-making, including profiling) (see also recital 37); Article 23(1) (Right to object); Article 24 (Automated individual decision-making, including profiling) (see also recitals 43 and 27); Article 39(3)(a) (Data protection impact assessment) (see too recitals 57–58); Article 77 (Automated individual decision-making, including profiling)

Relevant Case Law

France

Cour de Cassation, Chambre criminelle, audience publique du 24 septembre 1998, No de pourvoi 97-81.748, Publié au bulletin.

Germany

Bundesgerichtshof, Urteil vom 28.1.2014, VI ZR 156/13.

A. Rationale and Policy Underpinnings

The legislative deliberations leading to adoption of the GDPR devoted considerable attention to the topic of profiling, primarily in relation to automated decisional processes and online tracking.[1] Children were singled out as requiring special protection with respect to profiling practices.[2] As a result, profiling is mentioned in a fairly large number of GDPR provisions, thus warranting a specific definition of the term.

---

[1] See further the commentary on Art. 22 in this volume.   [2] Ibid.

B. Legal Background

1. EU legislation

The DPD did not define profiling as such, nor did it specifically address profiling except in one context: the application of profiles in certain types of fully automated decisional processes. These processes were ones that had 'legal or significant effects' on the targeted person and were based on 'automated processing of data intended to evaluate certain personal aspects relating to him, such as his performance at work, creditworthiness, reliability, conduct, etc.' (Article 15(1) DPD).[3] Article 12(a) DPD complemented the restrictions in Article 15 by providing a person with a right to 'knowledge of the logic involved in any automated processing of data concerning him at least in the case of the automated decisions referred to in Article 15(1)'. Numerous other provisions in the DPD indirectly set limits on the process of generating profiles inasmuch as this involved processing of personal data.[4] The same applies with the EPD. Its provisions restricting placement of 'cookies' and other online tracking devices are a case in point (see Article 5(3) EPD).

2. International instruments

Convention 108, both as originally adopted and in its modernised form, does not contain provisions that deal specifically with profiling. The same applies to the OECD Privacy Guidelines and APEC Privacy Framework.[5]

However, in 2010, the Committee of Ministers of the Council of Europe adopted a Recommendation on the protection of individuals with regard to automatic processing of personal data in the context of profiling.[6] The Recommendation defined 'profiling' as 'an automatic data processing technique that consists of applying a "profile" to an individual, particularly in order to take decisions concerning her or him or for analysing or predicting her or his personal preferences, behaviours and attitudes' (section 1(e) of the Appendix to the Recommendation). This definition constituted one of the main sources of inspiration of the definition of 'profiling' in Article 4(4) GDPR.[7]

3. National developments

Prior to adoption of the GDPR, the data protection laws of EU/EEA Member States contained provisions transposing Article 15 DPD, albeit in divergent ways. They otherwise seldom addressed profiling directly, let alone defined the term or variations of it.[8] Swiss law provides a rare instance of a statutory definition of a closely related term—that of 'personality profile' ('Persönlichkeitsprofil'), which is defined in Switzerland's Federal Data Protection Act as a 'combination of data allowing assessment of essential aspects of a natural person's personality'.[9]

---

[3] Further on the operation of Art. 15 DPD, see e.g. Bygrave 2001; Bygrave 2002, ch. 18 (section 18.3.1).
[4] See generally Borgesius 2015; Bygrave 2002, ch. 18 (section 18.4).
[5] OECD Privacy Guidelines 2013. APEC Privacy Framework 2005.
[6] See COM Recommendation 2010. For more details on the Recommendation, see the commentary on Art. 22 in this volume.
[7] See WP29 2013, pp. 2–3.   [8] See generally Borgesius 2015; Bygrave 2002, ch. 18.
[9] Swiss Federal Law on Data Protection, Art. 3(d). See Bygrave 2002, ch. 18 (section 18.3.3).

4. Case law

The CJEU has not yet interpreted the definition of 'profiling' in the GDPR, nor has it construed the meaning of profiling in its jurisprudence pursuant to Article 15 DPD or Articles 7–8 CFR. There is otherwise a small amount of case law at national level construing national provisions that transposed Article 15 DPD or dealt with closely related rules,[10] but none of this case law defines profiling as such.

C. Analysis

In general terms, profiling denotes two processes: (i) inferring a set of characteristics about an individual person or group of persons (i.e. the process of creating a profile); and (ii) treating that person or group (or other persons/groups) in light of these characteristics (i.e. the process of applying a profile).[11] Article 4(4) GDPR builds on this understanding but narrows the scope of profiling for GDPR purposes so that it is limited to *automated* processing of personal data which involves *evaluating* certain personal aspects relating to a natural person.

The automated criterion speaks only to the means of processing;[12] it does not rule out human input[13]—unlike the decisional processes caught by Article 22(1) GDPR.[14] As for the evaluation criterion, this would seem to encompass both the process of profile generation and profile application.[15] Yet, situations in which a controller merely *attempts* to profile a natural person without making an evaluation fall outside the scope of the definition. The particularisation of the criterion ('in particular to analyse or predict') indicates that evaluation need not involve predicting a person's (future) behaviour. Nonetheless, the verb 'to evaluate' ordinarily connotes the act of judging, calculating or assessing. In this respect, the WP29 has opined that a 'simple classification of individuals based on known characteristics such as their age, sex, and height does not necessarily lead to profiling' for the purposes of Article 4(4) GDPR, unless this classification progresses to making predictions or drawing conclusions about an individual.[16]

The definition in Article 4(4) takes up some of the phrasing of Article 15(1) DPD but departs from it by providing more examples of what profiling may embrace. Thus, it is not limited to performance at work, creditworthiness, reliability and conduct, but also embraces health, personal preferences, interests, reliability, behaviour, location or movements. Another difference is that the definition does not include the criterion of 'intention' (unlike Article 15(1) DPD which covered 'processing of data *intended to* evaluate certain personal aspects'). This curtails the possibility whereby profiles that arise only as an ancillary effect of automated processing fall outside the scope of the definition—a possibility that arguably hobbled Article 15(1) DPD.[17]

---

[10] See Cour de Cassation, 97–81.748 and Bundesgerichtshof, Urteil vom 28.1.2014. For details, see the commentary on Art. 22 in this volume.

[11] See e.g. Hildebrandt 2008, p. 19; WP29 2018, p. 7.

[12] Further on the meaning of automated processing, see the commentary on Art. 4(2) in this volume.

[13] See also WP29 2018, p. 7.

[14] Further on these processes, see the commentary on Art. 22 in this volume.

[15] During the legislative process, however, the *evaluation* component of the definition of 'profiling' was understood, at least by some Member States, as pertaining to the purpose for which a profile is created, rather than the means for profiling: see Council Report 2014, p. 7, fn. 2.

[16] WP29 2018, p. 7.   [17] Savin 2015, p. 256.

The definition in Article 4(4) GDPR is replicated in Article 3(4) LED and Article 3(5) EUDPR. Thus, the term 'profiling' should be interpreted uniformly in all these legal instruments (see also recital 5 EUDPR).

Select Bibliography

International agreements

APEC Privacy Framework 2005: Asia-Pacific Economic Cooperation, 'Privacy Framework' (2005).
OECD Privacy Guidelines 2013: Organisation for Economic Co-operation and Development, 'The OECD Privacy Framework' (2013).

National legislation

Swiss Federal Data Protection Act 1992: Bundesgesetz vom 19 Juni 1992 über den Datenschutz/ Loi fédérale du 19 juin 1992 sur la protection des données.

Academic writings

Borgesius 2015: Borgesius, *Improving Privacy Protection in the Area of Behavioural Targeting* (Kluwer Law International 2015).
Bygrave 2001: Bygrave, 'Minding the Machine: Article 15 of the EC Data Protection Directive and Automated Profiling', 17(1) *Computer Law & Security Review* (2001), 17.
Bygrave 2002: Bygrave, *Data Protection Law: Approaching Its Rationale, Logic and Limits* (Kluwer Law International 2002).
Hildebrandt 2008: Hildebrandt, 'Defining Profiling: A New Type of Knowledge?' in Hildebrandt and Gutwirth (eds.), *Profiling the European Citizen* (Springer 2008), 17.
Savin 2015: Savin, 'Profiling in the Present and New EU Data Protection Frameworks', in Nielsen, Schmidt and Dyppel Weber (eds.), *Erhvervsretlige emne: Juridisk Institut CBS* (DJØF 2015), 249.

Papers of data protection authorities

WP29 2013: Article 29 Working Party, 'Advice Paper on Essential Elements of a Definition and a Provision on Profiling within the EU General Data Protection Regulation' (13 May 2013).
WP29 2018: Article 29 Working Party, 'Guidelines on Automated Individual Decision-Making and Profiling for the Purposes of Regulation 2016/679' (WP 251rev.01, as last revised and adopted on 6 February 2018).

Reports and recommendations

COM Recommendation 2010: Committee of the Ministers of the Council of Europe, 'Recommendation on the Protection of Individuals with Regard to Automatic Processing of Personal Data in the Context of Profiling' (Rec(2010)13, 23 November 2010).
Council Report 2014: Profiling, 6079/14, 25 February 2014.

Article 4(5). Pseudonymisation

LUCA TOSONI

'pseudonymisation' means the processing of personal data in such a manner that the personal data can no longer be attributed to a specific data subject without the use of additional information, provided that such additional information is kept separately and is subject to technical and organisational measures to ensure that the personal data are not attributed to an identified or identifiable natural person;

Relevant Recitals

(26) The principles of data protection should apply to any information concerning an identified or identifiable natural person. Personal data which have undergone pseudonymisation, which could be attributed to a natural person by the use of additional information should be considered to be information on an identifiable natural person. To determine whether a natural person is identifiable, account should be taken of all the means reasonably likely to be used, such as singling out, either by the controller or by another person to identify the natural person directly or indirectly. To ascertain whether means are reasonably likely to be used to identify the natural person, account should be taken of all objective factors, such as the costs of and the amount of time required for identification, taking into consideration the available technology at the time of the processing and technological developments. The principles of data protection should therefore not apply to anonymous information, namely information which does not relate to an identified or identifiable natural person or to personal data rendered anonymous in such a manner that the data subject is not or no longer identifiable. This Regulation does not therefore concern the processing of such anonymous information, including for statistical or research purposes.

(28) The application of pseudonymisation to personal data can reduce the risks to the data subjects concerned and help controllers and processors to meet their data-protection obligations. The explicit introduction of 'pseudonymisation' in this Regulation is not intended to preclude any other measures of data protection.

(29) In order to create incentives to apply pseudonymisation when processing personal data, measures of pseudonymisation should, whilst allowing general analysis, be possible within the same controller when that controller has taken technical and organisational measures necessary to ensure, for the processing concerned, that this Regulation is implemented, and that additional information for attributing the personal data to a specific data subject is kept separately. The controller processing the personal data should indicate the authorised persons within the same controller.

(156) The processing of personal data for archiving purposes in the public interest, scientific or historical research purposes or statistical purposes should be subject to appropriate safeguards for the rights and freedoms of the data subject pursuant to this Regulation. Those safeguards should ensure that technical and organisational measures are in place in order to ensure, in particular, the principle of data minimisation. The further processing of personal data for archiving purposes in the public interest, scientific or historical research purposes or statistical purposes is to be carried out when the controller has assessed the feasibility to fulfil those purposes by processing data which do not permit or no longer permit the identification of data subjects,

provided that appropriate safeguards exist (such as, for instance, pseudonymisation of the data). Member States should provide for appropriate safeguards for the processing of personal data for archiving purposes in the public interest, scientific or historical research purposes or statistical purposes. Member States should be authorised to provide, under specific conditions and subject to appropriate safeguards for data subjects, specifications and derogations with regard to the information requirements and rights to rectification, to erasure, to be forgotten, to restriction of processing, to data portability, and to object when processing personal data for archiving purposes in the public interest, scientific or historical research purposes or statistical purposes. The conditions and safeguards in question may entail specific procedures for data subjects to exercise those rights if this is appropriate in the light of the purposes sought by the specific processing along with technical and organisational measures aimed at minimising the processing of personal data in pursuance of the proportionality and necessity principles. The processing of personal data for scientific purposes should also comply with other relevant legislation such as on clinical trials.

Closely Related Provisions

Article 6(4)(e) (Compatibility of processing purposes); Article 9(2)(j) (Processing of special categories of personal data) (see also recital 75); Article 25(1) (Data protection by design and by default) (see also recital 78); Article 32(1)(a) (Security of processing); Article 33(1) (Notification of personal data breach to supervisory authority) (see also recital 85); Article 40(2)(d) (Codes of conduct); Article 89(1) (Safeguards and derogations relating to processing for archiving purposes, scientific or historical research purposes or statistical purposes)

Related Provisions in LED [Directive (EU) 2016/680]

Article 3(5) (Definition of 'pseudonymisation')

Related Provisions in EPD [Directive 2002/58/EC]

Recital 9

Related Provisions in EUDPR [Regulation (EU) 2018/1725]

Article 3(6) (Definition of 'pseudonymisation')

Relevant Case Law

CJEU

Opinion of Advocate General Bobek in Case C-40/17, *Fashion ID*, delivered on 19 December 2018 (ECLI:EU:C:2018:1039).

A. Rationale and Policy Underpinnings

Pseudonymisation is the process of disguising identities by replacing a personal identifier (e.g. name, social security number, date of birth etc.) in a dataset by another attribute (e.g. a randomly assigned code).[1] The inclusion of this term and related definition in the GDPR—a step initiated by the European Parliament[2]—tries to put an end to common misconceptions and longstanding discussions on whether 'pseudonymised data' are personal data subject to EU data protection rules:[3] personal data that have undergone 'pseudonymisation' remain subject to the GDPR rules (see recital 26 GDPR). The introduction of the term in the Regulation is also intended to encourage the use of pseudonymisation techniques as a means to: (i) reduce the risks for data subjects, as pseudonymisation reduces the linkability of a dataset with the original data subject; and (ii) help controllers and processors to meet their obligations under the GDPR, as pseudonymisation can facilitate proving compliance with certain requirements of the Regulation (see recital 28 GDPR).

B. Legal Background

1. EU legislation

The DPD did not mention the term 'pseudonymisation'. However, the EPD refers to 'using anonymous or pseudonymous data where possible' as one of its objectives (recital 9 EPD). Terms such as 'pseudonymisation', 'pseudonymised data' and 'pseudo-identity' have otherwise long been used in Europe in policy discourses concerning data protection.[4]

2. International instruments

The notion of 'pseudonymisation' is not found in Convention 108 as originally adopted or in its modernised version. The same applies with respect to the OECD Privacy Guidelines (both original and revised versions) and APEC Privacy Framework.[5]

3. National developments

As mentioned above, the DPD did not include the concept of 'pseudonymisation'. However, prior to the adoption of the GDPR, the concept was already recognised and defined in the national legislation of several Member States. For example, Part 1, section 3(6a) of the old German Federal Data Protection Act stated that 'pseudonymising' (in German, 'pseudonymisieren') 'means replacing a person's name and other identifying characteristics with a label, in order to preclude identification of the data subject or to render such identification substantially difficult'.[6] The same Act also required that personal data undergo pseudonymisation (or be rendered anonymous) whenever possible (see Part 1, section 3a).[7] The German GDPR Implementation Law operates with a similar requirement (see section 71(1)),[8] which—as elaborated below—may contravene the GDPR.

---

[1] WP29 2007, p. 18. See also WP29 2014, p. 20.
[2] For details on the legislative history of the definition and the context of its inclusion in the GDPR, see the Introduction to this volume.
[3] WP29 2014, pp. 20–25.
[4] See e.g. WP29 1997, p. 8; WP29 2007, p. 18; WP29 2014, pp. 20–25.
[5] See OECD Privacy Guidelines 2013; APEC Privacy Framework 2005.
[6] See German Federal Data Protection Act 1990.   [7] Ibid.
[8] See German GDPR Implementation Law.

An indirect reference to pseudonymisation could also be found in Article 2, Part 1, section 4(1) of the former Austrian Federal Data Protection Act,[9] which defined as 'only indirectly personal' (in German, 'nur indirekt personenbezogen') data that 'relate to the subject in such a manner that the controller, processor or recipient of a transmission cannot establish the identity of the data subject by legal means'. Under the same Act, the processing of data that were 'only indirectly personal' was subject to less stringent requirements: for example, their transfer outside the EU did not need to be authorised by the Austrian DPA (see Article 2, Part 2, section 13(3)(2)).[10]

4. Case law

As 'pseudonymisation' is a newly defined legal concept under EU data protection law, the CJEU has not yet had a chance to interpret it. However, the WP29 has addressed the concept in several of its opinions, which are discussed below.

C. Analysis

In order to meet the conditions of Article 4(6) GDPR and thus be considered pseudonymised, personal data must satisfy two cumulative conditions. First, the data must undergo a process that renders them unlinkable to a specific data subject without the use of additional information. This is normally done by replacing one attribute (e.g. name, social security number, date of birth etc.) in a dataset by another (e.g. a randomly assigned code).[11] After this process, the data subject may still be indirectly identified; accordingly, data that underwent the process in question remain personal data.[12] Secondly, the additional information that is needed to re-identify the original data subject (e.g. an encryption key) must be kept separately from the data it relates to by means of technical or organisational measures. This separation may occur also 'within the same controller', for example, by sharing the information that is needed to re-identify the data subject only with a few selected people within the controller's organisation (see recital 29 GDPR). However, the measures in place must prevent any accidental or unauthorised re-identification.

A classic example of pseudonymisation is the key-coding of data, a process that is frequently used in the context of medical research.[13] Key-coded data are data relating to an individual that have been earmarked by a code.[14] However, there are numerous other pseudonymisation techniques, including encryption with secret key, the use of hash function, the use of keyed-hashed function with stored key, deterministic encryption, and tokenisation.[15]

Pseudonymisation is not a method of anonymisation.[16] Thus, pseudonymised data are not anonymous data. Data are considered anonymous only when the identification

---

[9] See Austrian Federal Data Protection Act 2000. [10] Ibid. [11] WP29 2014, p. 20.
[12] Ibid.
[13] See WP29 2007, pp. 18–21. See further Italian Data Protection Authority 2008. See too EC Guidance 2019, p. 5 (noting that '[f]or instance, a research study on the effects of a new medicine would qualify as pseudonymisation [within the meaning of Art. 4(5) GDPR], if the personal data of study participants would be replaced by unique attributes (e.g. number or code) in the research documentation and their personal data would be kept separately with the assigned unique attributes in a secured document (e.g. in a password protected database)').
[14] WP29 2007, p. 18.   [15] WP29 2014, pp. 20–21.   [16] Ibid., p. 3.

of the data subject is 'no longer possible' (see recital 26 GDPR). While re-identification may almost never be excluded in absolute terms, EU rules set a very high standard for anonymisation, and the WP29 has considered that, in order for data to be considered anonymous, re-identification must be 'reasonably' impossible in the specific context and circumstances of the case.[17]

It is claimed that the GDPR 'treats pseudonymisation, primarily as a data security measure'.[18] This is somewhat misleading: while the Regulation does indeed mention pseudonymisation as a possible means for attaining appropriate security (see Article 32(1)(a)), pseudonymisation techniques are also linked to the more generalised duty of 'data protection by design' (see Article 25(1))[19] and to data minimisation safeguards connected to processing for archival purposes, scientific or historical research purposes or statistical purposes (see Article 89(1)).

On its face, the Regulation does not make pseudonymisation mandatory *by default* (see Article 25(2)). Nevertheless, some national data protection laws impose strict pseudonymisation requirements. For example, as noted above, the German GDPR Implementation Law provides that 'personal data shall be rendered anonymous or pseudonymised as early as possible, as far as possible in accordance with the purpose of processing' (see section 71(1)). Whether this stipulation conforms with the GDPR is questionable as the Regulation does not contain, at least on its face, an equivalent stipulation. As Advocate General Bobek stated, 'national rules implementing a regulation [like the GDPR] may, in principle, only be adopted when *expressly* authorised'.[20] While the rather generally formulated provisions of Articles 25(1) and 32(1) GDPR certainly encourage pseudonymisation, they do not establish an express authorisation for Member States to adopt national rules requiring this measure.

Select Bibliography

International agreements

APEC Privacy Framework 2005: Asia Pacific Economic Cooperation, 'Privacy Framework' (2005).
OECD Privacy Guidelines 2013: Organisation for Economic Co-operation and Development, 'The OECD Privacy Framework' (2013).

National legislation

Austrian Federal Data Protection Act 2000: Bundesgesetz über den Schutz personenbezogener Daten (Datenschutzgesetz 2000 – DSG 2000), BGBl. I Nr 165/1999 zuletzt geändert durch BGBl. I Nr. 132/2015 (repealed).

---

[17] Ibid., pp. 8–10. See further EC Guidance 2019, p. 6 (noting that '[t]he assessment of whether data is [sic] properly anonymised depends on specific and unique circumstances of each individual case' and that 'anonymisation should always be performed using the latest state-of-the-art anonymisation techniques').

[18] Borgesius 2016, p. 267.

[19] Indeed, one of the main reasons that have led to the inclusion of a definition of 'pseudonymisation' in the GDPR would seem to be linked to its use as a 'data protection by design' measure. As the WP29 noted about the absence of such a definition in the GDPR Proposal, 'the concept of pseudonymisation should be introduced more explicitly in the instrument (for example by including a definition on pseudonymised data, consistent with the definition of personal data), as it can help to achieve better data protection, for example, in the context of data protection by design and default'. See WP29 2012, p. 11.

[20] Case C-40/17, *Fashion ID* (AG Opinion), para. 47 (emphasis added). The Advocate General noted this specifically in relation to the GDPR.

German Federal Data Protection Act 1990: Gesetz zur Fortentwicklung der Datenverarbeitung und des Datenschutzes (Bundesdatenschutzgesetz), BGBl 1990 Teil 1 Nr. 2954 (repealed).

German GDPR Implementation Law: Gesetz zur Anpassung des Datenschutzrechts an die Verordnung (EU) 2016/679 und zur Umsetzung der Richtlinie (EU) 2016/680 (Datenschutz-Anpassungs- und Umsetzungsgesetz EU – DsAnpUG-EU), BGBl 2017 Teil 1 Nr. 44.

Academic writings

Borgesius 2016: Borgesius, 'Singling Out People without Knowing their Names: Behavioural Targeting, Pseudonymous Data, and the New General Data Protection Regulation', 32 *Computer Law & Security Review* (2016), 256.

El Emam and Álvarez, 'A Critical Appraisal of the Article 29 Working Party Opinion 05/2014 on Data Anonymization Techniques', 5(1) *International Data Privacy Law* (2015), 73.

Schwartz and Solove, 'The PII Problem: Privacy and a New Concept of Personally Identifiable Information', 86(6) *New York University Law Review* (2011), 1814.

Papers of data protection authorities

WP29 1997: Article 29 Working Party, 'Recommendation 3/97: Anonymity on the Internet' (WP 6, 3 December 1997).

WP29 2007: Article 29 Working Party, 'Opinion 4/2007 on the Concept of Personal Data' (WP 136, 20 June 2007).

WP29 2012: Article 29 Working Party, 'Opinion 01/2012 on the data protection reform proposals' (WP 191, 23 March 2012).

WP29 2014: Article 29 Working Party, 'Opinion 05/2014 on Anonymisation Techniques' (WP 216, 10 April 2014).

Italian Data Protection Authority 2008: Garante per la protezione dei dati personali, 'Guidelines for Data Processing within the Framework of Clinical Drug Trials' (24 July 2008), available (in English) at https://www.garanteprivacy.it/web/guest/home/docweb/-/docweb-display/docweb/1671330.

Reports and recommendations

EC Guidance 2019: European Commission, 'Guidance on the Regulation on a framework for the free flow of non-personal data in the European Union', COM(2019) 250 final (29 May 2019).

Kotschy, 'The New General Data Protection Regulation: Is there Sufficient Pay-Off for Taking the Trouble to Anonymize or Pseudonymize Data?' *Future of Privacy Forum* (2016) available at https://fpf.org/wp-content/uploads/2016/11/Kotschy-paper-on-pseudonymisation.pdf.

Article 4(6). Filing system

LUCA TOSONI

'filing system' means any structured set of personal data which are accessible according to specific criteria, whether centralised, decentralised or dispersed on a functional or geographical basis;

Relevant Recitals

(15) In order to prevent creating a serious risk of circumvention, the protection of natural persons should be technologically neutral and should not depend on the techniques used. The protection of natural persons should apply to the processing of personal data by automated means, as well as to manual processing, if the personal data are contained or are intended to be contained in a filing system. Files or sets of files, as well as their cover pages, which are not structured according to specific criteria should not fall within the scope of this Regulation.

(31) Public authorities to which personal data are disclosed in accordance with a legal obligation for the exercise of their official mission, such as tax and customs authorities, financial investigation units, independent administrative authorities, or financial market authorities responsible for the regulation and supervision of securities markets should not be regarded as recipients if they receive personal data which are necessary to carry out a particular inquiry in the general interest, in accordance with Union or Member State law. The requests for disclosure sent by the public authorities should always be in writing, reasoned and occasional and should not concern the entirety of a filing system or lead to the interconnection of filing systems. The processing of personal data by those public authorities should comply with the applicable data-protection rules according to the purposes of the processing.

(67) Methods by which to restrict the processing of personal data could include, inter alia, temporarily moving the selected data to another processing system, making the selected personal data unavailable to users, or temporarily removing published data from a website. In automated filing systems, the restriction of processing should in principle be ensured by technical means in such a manner that the personal data are not subject to further processing operations and cannot be changed. The fact that the processing of personal data is restricted should be clearly indicated in the system.

Closely Related Provisions

Article 2(1) (Material scope of GDPR)

Related Provisions in LED [Directive (EU) 2016/680]

Article 3(6) (Definition of 'filing system') (see also recitals 18 and 22); Article 2(2) (Scope); Article 28(1) (Prior consultation of the supervisory authority)

Related Provisions in EUDPR [Regulation (EU) 2018/1725]

Article 3(7) (Definition of 'filing system') (see also recitals 7–8); Article 2(5) (Scope); Article 20(4) (Right to restriction of processing); Article 90 (Prior consultation of EDPS when new filing system created for high risk processing of personal data)

Relevant Case Law

CJEU

Case C-73/07, *Tietosuojavaltuutettu v Satakunnan Markkinapörssi Oy and Satamedia Oy*, judgment of 16 December 2008 (Grand Chamber) (ECLI:EU:C:2008:727).
Opinion of Advocate General Kokott in Case C-73/07, *Tietosuojavaltuutettu v Satakunnan Markkinapörssi Oy and Satamedia Oy*, delivered on 8 May 2008 (ECLI:EU:C:2008:266).
Case C-28/08 P, *European Commission v The Bavarian Lager Co. Ltd*, judgment of 29 June 2010 (Grand Chamber) (ECLI:EU:C:2010:378).
Opinion of Advocate General Sharpston in Case C-28/08 P, *European Commission v The Bavarian Lager Co. Ltd*, delivered on 15 October 2009 (ECLI:EU:C:2009:624).
Case C-434/16, *Peter Nowak v Data Protection Commissioner*, judgment of 20 December 2017 (ECLI:EU:C:2017:994).
Opinion of Advocate General Kokott in Case C-434/16, *Peter Nowak v Data Protection Commissioner*, delivered on 20 July 2017 (ECLI:EU:C:2017:582).
Case C-25/17, *Proceedings brought by Tietosuojavaltuutettu (Jehovan todistajat)*, judgment of 10 July 2018 (Grand Chamber) (ECLI:EU:C:2018:551).
Opinion of Advocate General Mengozzi in Case C-25/17, *Proceedings brought by Tietosuojavaltuutettu (Jehovan todistajat)*, delivered on 1 February 2018 (ECLI:EU:C:2018:57).
Case C-40/17, *Fashion ID GmbH & Co. KG v Verbraucherzentrale NRW eV.*, judgment of 29 July 2019 (ECLI:EU:C:2019:629).
Opinion of Advocate General Bobek in Case C-40/17, *Fashion ID GmbH & Co. KG v Verbraucherzentrale NRW e.V.*, delivered on 19 December 2018 (ECLI:EU:C:2018:1039).

Belgium

Belgian Court of Cassation, *D.J-M. v Belfius Banque sa*, judgment of 22 February 2017.
Belgian Court of Appeal of Liège, judgment of 6 February 2006.

Spain

Spanish Supreme Court (*Tribunal Supremo*), judgment No. 383/2011 of 4 February 2011.

United Kingdom

UK Court of Appeal, *Durant v Financial Services Authority* [2003] EWCA Civ 1746.

A. Rationale and Policy Underpinnings

The GDPR retains (at least with respect to manually processed data) the concept of 'filing system', which could be found in Article 2(c) DPD, as well as in many national data protection laws of the 1970s and 1980s.[1] The definition of 'filing system' provided in

---

[1] See e.g. Bygrave 2002, pp. 51–53.

Article 4(6) GDPR—which is crucial to understand the material scope of the Regulation pursuant to Article 2[2]—suggests that the retention of the concept is intended to limit the application of EU data protection rules to data that can be linked to a particular person without great difficulty, as it is in relation to these sorts of data that the risks for data protection interests primarily lie.[3] The retention of the concept is also symptomatic of a concern to prevent data protection rules from overreaching themselves in a practical, regulatory sense.[4]

B. Legal Background

1. EU legislation

The GDPR reproduces *verbatim* the definition of 'filing system' provided in Article 2(c) DPD. This is despite the fact that the concept of 'filing system' as laid down in the latter was often considered 'rather cryptic'[5] and 'completely outdated'.[6] This sameness of definitions, however, entails that the understanding of the concept of 'filing system' developed under the DPD may prove useful to elucidate the definition of the same concept in the GDPR.[7] This is the case also for Article 3(6) LED and Article 3(7) EUDPR both of which define 'filing system' identically to Article 4(6) GDPR (see too recital 5 EUDPR).

2. International instruments

The term 'filing system' is not used in Convention 108. However, the material scope of Convention 108's application is limited to 'automated data files' (Article 3), which the Convention defines as 'any set of data undergoing automatic processing' (Article 2(b)). Modernised Convention 108 extends the material scope of application of the Convention and focuses on 'data processing' regardless of whether the processing is automated or manual. Nonetheless, like the GDPR, the Modernised Convention only covers manual processing of data which form part of a structured filing system. It defines non-automated (manual) processing as 'an operation or set of operations performed upon personal data within a structured set of such data which are accessible or retrievable

---

[2] Art. 2(1) GDPR states that the 'Regulation applies to the processing of personal data wholly or partly by automated means and to the processing other than by automated means of personal data which form part of a filing system or are intended to form part of a filing system'. See further the commentary on Art. 2 GDPR in this volume.

[3] See DPD Amended Proposal, p. 10, explaining that the definition of 'file'—which later become 'filing system' in the DPD and in the GDPR—'allows the scope of the Directive to be confined to sets of data which are structured so as to facilitate access and searches for data on individuals. Personal data which are not organised so that they can be used with reference to the data subjects themselves are thus excluded. In practice data of this kind do not present the same dangers for individuals, and it is more realistic not to subject them to the same obligations'. See further Bygrave 2002, p. 52.

[4] WP29 2007, p. 5. See also Bygrave 2002, p. 52.

[5] Case C-25/17, *Jehovan todistajat* (AG Opinion), para. 55.

[6] This was e.g. the position expressed by the German and Slovenian delegations during the legislative process that led to the adoption of the GDPR: see Council Report 2014, p. 45, fn. 64.

[7] This was also the view of Advocate General Bobek in *Fashion ID*: 'as the GDPR largely retains the same key terms as Article 2 of Directive 95/46 (while adding a number of new ones), it would be rather surprising if the interpretation of such key notions, including the notion of controller, processing, or personal data, were to significantly depart (without a very good reason) from the extant case-law'. See Case C-40/17, *Fashion ID* (AG Opinion), para. 87.

Tosoni

according to specific criteria' (Article 2(c)). Thus, with regard to manual processing, the material scope of application of the Modernised Convention and the GDPR is essentially identical.

Neither the OECD Privacy Guidelines (both original and revised versions) nor the APEC Privacy Framework specifically operate with the concept of 'filing system'.

3. National developments

Historically, some national data protection laws focused mainly on the registration in files, as opposed to the mere collection, of personal data. This was primarily due to a belief, particularly prevalent during the 1970s and 1980s, that systematically structured collections of personal data pose the principal risks for data subjects' privacy-related interests.[8]

Under the DPD, Member States were required to apply the rules laid down in the Directive as much to automated processing as to manual processing of personal data. However, with regard to manual processing, the DPD only required that national data protection laws applied *at least* to the processing of personal data which formed part (or were intended to form part) of a structured 'filing system' (see recital 27 and Article 3(1) DPD). The Directive left Member States free to decide whether to apply its rules to all kinds of manual processing, including the processing of personal data that formed part of unstructured files. This was, for example, the choice made by Italy when it implemented the DPD.[9] Hence, prior to the adoption of the GDPR, the Italian data protection legislation applied to both automated and manual processing regardless of the way in which data were organised.[10] Consequently, it did not include a definition of 'filing system'.[11]

In contrast, other Member States (e.g. Belgium and Finland) decided to limit the ambit of their data protection laws to cover only automated processing and manual processing by means of structured filing systems. The DPD expressly allowed these Member States to establish 'the different [specific] criteria for determining the constituents of a structured set of personal data, and the different criteria governing access to such a set' (recital 27 DPD). Accordingly, some Member States made use of this possibility and included a more detailed definition of 'filing system' in their national laws. For example, section 3(3) of the Finnish Personal Data Law 1999 (repealed) defined a personal data filing system as a 'set of personal data, connected by a common use and processed fully or partially by automatic means or organised using data sheets or lists or any other comparable method permitting the retrieval of data relating to persons easily and without excessive cost'. Finnish law thus required a degree of sophistication of the filing system that was greater than that required by the DPD.[12]

This difference of treatment of manual processing across the EU has disappeared under the GDPR. On the one hand, countries like Italy experience the material scope of application of data protection rules shrink slightly due to the introduction of a definition of 'filing system' and the 'filing system' exemption of Article 2(1) GDPR in their legal systems. On the other hand, countries like Finland are arguably no longer allowed to maintain (or introduce) more specific criteria for determining which filing systems fall under the scope of application of data protection rules. This follows from the objective of

---

[8] See e.g. Bygrave 2002, p. 51. [9] See Italian Data Protection Authority Report 1997, p. 48.
[10] See Italian Data Protection Code 2003 (as last amended by Italian Legislative Decree 2015), Art. 6.
[11] Ibid., Art. 4. [12] Case C-25/17, *Jehovan todistajat* (AG Opinion), para. 58.

the GDPR to prevent fragmentation of data protection rules and to ensure a consistent and high level of protection across the EU (see recitals 9–10 GDPR).

This is also further confirmed by the fact that the EU legislature decided to remove any reference to the possibility of introducing more specific filing system criteria at national level from recital 10 GDPR—a possibility that was expressly included in the homologous recital 27 DPD.

4. Case law

The CJEU has seldom addressed the concept of 'filing system' in its case law.[13] However, several Advocate General opinions provide a fairly thorough analysis of the concept.[14] The CJEU case law on the concept of 'filing system' is discussed in further detail below.[15]

There is also limited national case law on the definition of 'filing system'. This is partly because, under the DPD, not all Member States introduced a definition of 'filing system' in their data protection legislation, as elaborated above. However, some national courts have interpreted (often quite strictly) the definition of 'filing system' as implemented in their national data protection laws.[16] For example, in *Durant v Financial Services Authority*, the UK Court of Appeal found that a manual record of personal data would qualify as a 'filing system' only if it presented the same, or nearly the same, degree of sophistication of accessibility to personal data as a computerised record.[17] Such strict national interpretations of the concept of 'filing system' are unlikely to be upheld under the GDPR, as both the CJEU and several Advocates General have favoured a broad interpretation of the concept under the DPD, and the CJEU is likely to follow the same approach under the GDPR.[18]

C. Analysis

As mentioned above, manual processing falls within the material scope of application of the GDPR only if the personal data to be processed 'form part of a filing system or are intended to form part of a filing system' (Article 2(1) GDPR). This implies that two cumulative conditions must be met. First, the personal data must be contained or intended to be contained in a *file*, which is a set of personal data. Secondly, the file in which the data are contained must be structured according to specific criteria, which make the data easily searchable and accessible.

Article 4(6) GDPR broadly defines the concept of 'filing system', in particular by referring to 'any' structured set of personal data.[19] The definition must therefore be interpreted

---

[13] The most detailed analysis by the CJEU of the notion of 'filing system' occurs in Case C-25/17, *Jehovan todistajat*, paras. 52–62 (concerning the definition of 'filing system' in Art. 2(c) DPD).

[14] See Case C-73/07, *Satamedia* (AG Opinion), para. 34; Case C-28/08 P, *Commission v Bavarian Lager* (AG Opinion), paras. 117–128; Case C-434/16, *Nowak* (AG Opinion), para. 69; Case C-25/17, *Jehovan todistajat* (AG Opinion), paras. 53–59. All these cases concern the definition of 'filing system' in Art. 2(c) DPD.

[15] As mentioned above, the case law on Art. 2(c) DPD remains relevant to interpreting Art. 4(6) GDPR. See Case C-40/17, *Fashion ID* (AG Opinion), para. 87.

[16] See e.g. Belgian Court of Cassation, *D.J-M. v Belfius Banque sa*; Belgian Court of Appeal of Liège, judgment of 6 February 2006; UK Court of Appeal, *Durant v Financial Services Authority*; Spanish Supreme Court (*Tribunal Supremo*), judgment No. 383/2011.

[17] UK Court of Appeal, *Durant v Financial Services Authority*.

[18] See Case C-40/17, *Fashion ID* (AG Opinion), para. 87.

[19] See also Case C-25/17, *Jehovan todistajat*, para. 56.

expansively, also to avoid threatening the high level of protection conferred by the GDPR.[20] Thus, any sets of data grouped together in accordance with specific criteria, which make the data searchable and accessible without great difficulty are likely to be covered by the definition. Indeed, the CJEU has held that the requirement that the data set must be 'structured according to specific criteria' is simply intended to enable personal data to be easily retrieved.[21] In particular, the Court found that the personal data do not need to be 'contained in data sheets or specific lists or in another search method, in order to establish the existence of a filing system'.[22]

In other words, the criteria do not need to be particularly sophisticated:[23] data sets that are organised in accordance with alphabetical, geographical or chronological criteria (or other similar criteria) are likely to be sufficiently structured and accessible to meet the requirements of the definition. In this regard, Advocate General Mengozzi found in *Jehovah's Witnesses* that a 'geographical criterion' is a possible criterion 'lending structure to [a] dataset', and this criterion may simply be based on the geographical allocation given to each agent/individual tasked with the collection of personal data.[24] The CJEU shared the Advocate General's view, and found that 'the concept of a "filing system" ... covers a set of personal data collected in the course of door-to-door preaching, consisting of the names and addresses and other information concerning the persons contacted, if those data are structured according to specific criteria which, in practice, enable them to be easily retrieved for subsequent use'.[25]

The Court stressed that 'the specific criterion and the specific form in which the set of personal data collected by each of the members who engage in preaching is actually structured is irrelevant, so long as that set of data makes it possible for the data relating to a specific person who has been contacted to be easily retrieved'.[26] Similarly, Advocate General Kokott found in *Nowak* that 'a physical set of examination scripts in paper form ordered alphabetically or according to other criteria meets [the] requirements' of the definition of 'filing system'.[27] The WP29 also noted that '[m]ost employment [manual] records are likely to fall within [the] definition' of 'filing system'.[28]

Select Bibliography

EU legislation

DPD Amended Proposal 1992: Amended Proposal for a Council Directive on the Protection of Individuals with Regard to the Processing of Personal Data and on the Free Movement of Such Data (COM(92) 422 final—SYN 287, 15 October 1992).

National legislation

Finnish Personal Data Law 1999: Finnish Law on Personal Data 523/1999 (Henkilötietolaki No. 523/1999) (repealed).

---

[20] See Case C-25/17, *Jehovan todistajat* (AG Opinion), paras. 55–56 (noting this in relation to the DPD).
[21] See Case C-25/17, *Jehovan todistajat*, para. 57.   [22] Ibid., para. 58.
[23] See Case C-25/17, *Jehovan todistajat* (AG Opinion), para. 57.   [24] Ibid.
[25] See Case C-25/17, *Jehovan todistajat*, para. 62.   [26] Ibid., para. 61.
[27] Case C-434/16, *Nowak* (AG Opinion), para. 69.
[28] WP29 2001, p. 13 (noting this in relation to Art. 2(c) DPD).

Italian Data Protection Code 2003: Decreto legislativo 30 giugno 2003, n. 196: Codice in Materia di Protezione dei Dati Personali.

Italian Legislative Decree 2015: Decreto Legislativo 14 settembre 2015, n. 151: Disposizioni di razionalizzazione e semplificazione delle procedure e degli adempimenti a carico di cittadini e imprese e altre disposizioni in materia di rapporto di lavoro e pari opportunità, in attuazione della legge 10 dicembre 2014, n. 183.

Academic writings

Bygrave 2002: Bygrave, *Data Protection Law: Approaching Its Rationale, Logic and Limits* (Kluwer Law International, 2002).

Papers of data protection authorities

WP29 2001: Article 29 Working Party, 'Opinion 8/2001 on the Processing of Personal Data in the Employment Context' (WP 48, 13 September 2001).

WP29 2007: Article 29 Working Party, 'Opinion 4/2007 on the Concept of Personal Data' (WP 136, 20 June 2007).

Italian Data Protection Authority Report 1997: Garante per la protezione dei dati personali, 'Relazione Sull'attività Svolta Dal Garante Per La Protezione Dei Dati Personali (Anno 1997)' (1997).

Reports and recommendations

Council Report 2014: Profiling, 6079/14, 25 February 2014.

Article 4(7). Controller

LEE A. BYGRAVE   LUCA TOSONI

'controller' means the natural or legal person, public authority, agency or other body which, alone or jointly with others, determines the purposes and means of the processing of personal data; where the purposes and means of such processing are determined by Union or Member State law, the controller or the specific criteria for its nomination may be provided for by Union or Member State law;

Closely Related Provisions

Article 5(2) (Principle of accountability); Article 24 (Responsibility of the controller) (see too recital 74); and Article 26 (Joint controllers) (see too recital 79)

Related Provisions in LED [Directive (EU) 2016/680]

Article 3(8) (Definition of 'controller')

Related Provisions in EUDPR [Regulation (EU) 2018/1725]

Article 3(8) (Definition of 'controller')

Relevant Case Law

CJEU

Case C-101/01, *Criminal proceedings against Bodil Lindqvist*, judgment of 6 November 2003 (ECLI:EU:C:2003:596).

Case C-279/12, *Fish Legal, Emily Shirley v Information Commissioner, United Utilities Water plc, Yorkshire Water Services Ltd, Southern Water Services Ltd*, judgment of 19 December 2013 (ECLI:EU:C:2013:853).

Case C-131/12, *Google Spain v Agencia Española de Protección de Datos (AEPD) and Mario Costeja González*, judgment of 13 May 2014 (Grand Chamber) (ECLI:EU:C:2014:317).

Case C-212/13, *František Ryneš v Úřad pro ochranu osobních údajů*, judgment of 11 December 2014 (ECLI:EU:C:2014:2428).

Case C-210/16, *Unabhängiges Landeszentrum für Datenschutz Schleswig-Holstein v Wirtschaftsakademie Schleswig-Holstein GmbH*, judgment of 5 June 2018 (Grand Chamber) (ECLI:EU:C:2018:388).

Case C-25/17, *Proceedings brought by Tietosuojavaltuutettu (Jehovan todistajat)*, judgment of 10 July 2018 (Grand Chamber) (ECLI:EU:C:2018:551).

Case C-40/17, *Fashion ID GmbH & Co. KG v Verbraucherzentrale NRW e.V.*, judgment of 29 July 2019 (ECLI:EU:C:2019:629).

Opinion of Advocate General Bobek in Case C-40/17, *Fashion ID GmbH & Co. KG v Verbraucherzentrale NRW e.V.*, delivered on 19 December 2018 (ECLI:EU:C:2018:1039).

Case C-272/19, *V.Q. v Land Hessen* (pending).

A. Rationale and Policy Underpinnings

Controllers are key actors in the operationalisation of data protection law as they are the primary bearers of the obligations set by such law towards data subjects. Thus, definition of the criteria for attaining the role of controller is essential for understanding the law's application. As detailed below, the tendency under EU data protection law is to apply these criteria in an expansive and flexible way, thus rendering the threshold for attaining controller status quite low. This reflects an underlying concern to ensure that responsibility is taken for implementing data protection measures, thereby ensuring respect for data subjects' fundamental rights. As noted by the WP29, 'the first and foremost role of the concept of controller is to determine who shall be responsible for compliance with data protection rules, and how data subjects can exercise the rights in practice. In other words: to allocate responsibility'.[1]

B. Legal Background

1. EU legislation

Article 2(d) DPD included a definition of 'controller' that was virtually identical to that in Article 4(7) GDPR. Recital 47 DPD elaborated on this definition with regard to providers of telecommunications services, stating:

[W]here a message containing personal data is transmitted by means of a telecommunications or electronic mail service, the sole purpose of which is the transmission of such messages, the controller in respect of the personal data contained in the message will normally be considered to be the person from whom the message originates, rather than the person offering the transmission services; whereas, nevertheless, those offering such services will normally be considered controllers in respect of the processing of the additional personal data necessary for the operation of the service.

2. International instruments

Convention 108 as originally adopted utilises the term 'controller of the file'. This is defined as 'the natural or legal person, public authority, agency or any other body who is competent according to the national law to decide what should be the purpose of the automated data file, which categories of personal data should be stored and which operations should be applied to them' (Article 2(d)). This definition formed the basis for the definition of 'controller' in the DPD,[2] which was later replicated in the GDPR. Under Modernised Convention 108, focus on legal competence and automated data files gives way to focus on decision-making power and processing of personal data. Hence, the Modernised Convention utilises the term 'controller', defining it as 'the natural or legal person, public authority, service, agency or any other body which, alone or jointly with others, has decision-making power with respect to data processing' (Article 2(d)). This definition is in line with the equivalent definitions in the DPD and GDPR, even

---

[1] WP29 2010, p. 4.

[2] DPD Amended Proposal 1992, p. 10 (stating '[t]he definition is borrowed from the definition of the "controller of the file" in the Council of Europe Convention. But as the Directive sets out to regulate the use of data in the light of the object being pursued, it is preferable to speak of the "controller", and to drop any reference to a "file" or to "data"').

though it eschews, on its face, reference to the criterion of 'determination of purposes and means of processing'. This becomes clear from the Explanatory Note to the Modernised Convention which states:

'Controller' refers to the person or body having decision-making power concerning the purposes and means of the processing, whether this power derives from a legal designation or factual circumstances that are to be assessed on a case-by-case basis. In some cases, there may be multiple controllers or co-controllers (jointly responsible for a processing and possibly responsible for different aspects of that processing). When assessing whether the person or body is a controller, special account should be taken of whether that person or body determines the reasons justifying the processing, in other terms its purposes and the means used for it. Further relevant factors for this assessment include whether the person or body has control over the processing methods, the choice of data to be processed and who is allowed to access it. Those who are not directly subject to the controller and carry out the processing on the controller's behalf, and solely according to the controller's instructions, are to be considered processors. The controller remains responsible for the processing also where a processor is processing the data on his or her behalf.[3]

Other important international agreements in the field also employ terms containing the word 'controller' and define these similarly to Article 4(7) GDPR. The OECD Privacy Guidelines use the term 'data controller', defining it as 'a party who, according to domestic law, is competent to decide about the contents and use of personal data regardless of whether or not such data are collected, stored, processed or disseminated by that party or by an agent on its behalf' (paragraph 1(a)). Elaborating on this definition, the Explanatory Memorandum to the Guidelines states:

It attempts to define a subject who, under domestic law, should carry ultimate responsibility for activities concerned with the processing of personal data. As defined, the data controller is a party who is legally competent to decide about the contents and use of data, regardless of whether or not such data are collected, stored, processed or disseminated by that party or by an agent on its behalf. The data controller may be a legal or natural person, public authority, agency or any other body. The definition excludes at least four categories which may be involved in the processing of data, viz.: a) licensing authorities and similar bodies which exist in some Member countries and which authorise the processing of data but are not entitled to decide (in the proper sense of the word) what activities should be carried out and for what purposes; b) data processing service bureaux which carry out data processing on behalf of others; c) telecommunications authorities and similar bodies which act as mere conduits; and d) 'dependent users' who may have access to data but who are not authorised to decide what data should be stored, who should be able to use them, etc. In implementing the Guidelines, countries may develop more complex schemes of levels and types of responsibilities.[4]

The APEC Privacy Framework uses the term 'personal information controller', defining this as:

[A] person or organization who controls the collection, holding, processing or use of personal information. It includes a person or organization who instructs another person or organization to collect, hold, process, use, transfer or disclose personal information on his or her behalf, but excludes a person or organization who performs such functions as instructed by another person or organization (para. 10).[5]

---

[3] Explanatory Report Convention 108 2018, para. 22.   [4] OECD Guidelines 2013, pp. 51–52.
[5] APEC Privacy Framework 2005.

3. National developments

Prior to adoption of the GDPR, EU Member States generally applied the definition of 'controller' given in Article 2(d) DPD, although with occasional discrepancies. For example, the UK Data Protection Act 1998 (repealed) defined 'data controller' as an entity that determines 'the purposes for which and the manner in which any personal data are, or are to be, processed' (section 1(1))—a formulation that eschews express reference to 'means'. To take another example, the current Greek Data Protection Law defines 'controller' as 'any person who determines the scope and manner of the processing of personal data' (Article 2(g))—a formulation that eschews express reference to 'purposes'.[6]

4. Case law

The CJEU has handed down several high-profile judgments that deal, in part, with the definition of 'controller' under the DPD. As that definition is virtually identical to the definition in Article 4(7) GDPR, this case law is relevant for construing the latter.[7]

C. Analysis

1. General approach

The concept of 'controller' must be understood in light of the legislator's aim of placing primary responsibility for protecting personal data on the entity that actually exercises control over the data processing. This entails taking account not simply of legal formalities but factual realities. As the WP29 aptly observed, '[t]he concept of controller is a functional concept, intended to allocate responsibilities where the factual influence is, and thus based on a factual rather than a formal analysis'.[8] Moreover, the CJEU has made clear that the concept is to be construed broadly so as to achieve 'effective and complete protection of data subjects'.[9]

Regard may be had to a wide range of factors when determining controller status. These include express allocations of responsibility/control set out in legislation, contract or other legal instruments, along with implicit allocations of responsibility/control flowing from traditionally recognised roles (e.g. the role of employer vis-à-vis employee).[10] As indicated above, however, it is not the formal legal allocation of responsibility/control that is decisive here, but the factual control.[11] Indeed, an entity may be deemed a controller even if it exceeds its formal legal mandate.[12]

---

[6] The current Greek Data Protection Law is set to be repealed in light of the enactment of the GDPR: see Greek Draft GDPR Law.

[7] This view was also expressed by Advocate General Bobek in *Fashion ID*: 'as Article 4 of the GDPR largely retains the same key terms as Article 2 of Directive 95/46 (while adding a number of new ones), it would be rather surprising if the interpretation of such key notions, including the notion of controller, processing, or personal data, were to significantly depart (without a very good reason) from the extant case-law'. See Case C-40/17, *Fashion ID* (AG Opinion), para. 87.

[8] WP29 2010, p. 9.

[9] Case C-131/12, *Google Spain*, para. 34; Case C-210/16, *Wirtschaftsakademie*, para. 28; Case C-40/17, *Fashion ID*, paras. 65–66.

[10] See further WP29 2010, pp. 10–12.

[11] Case C-25/17, *Jehovan todistajat*, para. 21 (noting that 'in particular, the "effective control" ... must be taken into account'). See also WP29 2010, p. 12.

[12] As illustrated in the SWIFT case: see WP29 2006.

It bears emphasis that, in determining controller status, regard may also be had to the data subject's perspective. According to the WP29, 'the image given to data subjects and reasonable expectations of data subjects on the basis of this visibility' are relevant factors.[13] The CJEU has expressly endorsed the approach of the WP29 here, holding that 'the conception that the data subject has of the controller must be taken into account'.[14] This conception, however, cannot be a decisive factor, and CJEU jurisprudence has not yet openly relied on it when determining controller status. In the view of the WP29, the factor is only relevant 'in case of doubt'.[15]

The type of person or entity that may fulfil the role of controller is cast wide: 'natural or legal person, public authority, agency or other body'.[16] While the typical controller tends to be a corporation, government agency or other organised collective entity, case law shows that an individual natural/physical person acting alone may also be deemed a controller in particular circumstances.[17] However, where an organised collective entity determines the purposes and means of processing, the point of departure is that the entity as such is the controller, rather than any particular individual natural/physical person who is part of that entity. In the words of the WP29, this is due not just to 'the strategic perspective of allocating responsibilities', but also 'in order to provide data subjects with a more stable and reliable reference entity for the exercise of their rights'.[18] Thus, for instance, in the case of a corporation, the controller will usually not be any of the members/employees of the corporation (e.g. Chief Executive Officer, Board Chairperson, Chief Financial Officer, Chief Privacy Officer etc.) who actually decide on the purposes and means of the processing, but the corporation as such. However, an individual member or employee of a collective entity may assume controller status in their own right if they use personal data for their own purposes and these purposes are beyond the boundaries and control regime set by the entity.[19]

Moreover, there may be multiple controllers within one corporate structure—e.g. where responsibility for a distributed database containing personal data is shared between a parent/holding company established in one Member State and its subsidiary company

---

[13] WP29 2010, p. 12.   [14] Case C-25/17, *Jehovan todistajat*, para. 21.

[15] WP29 2010, p. 12.

[16] In Case C-272/19, *Land Hessen* (pending), the CJEU is expected to clarify the meaning of 'public authority' in Art. 4(7) GDPR. In particular, the Court has been asked to clarify whether the committee of a Parliament of a constituent state of a Member State that is responsible for processing the petitions of citizens — namely the Petitions Committee of the *Hessischer Landtag* — should be regarded in that connection as a public authority within the meaning of Art. 4(7). The answer to this question is likely to depend on the specific powers and the legal status that the committee in question enjoys under Hessen law. However, it should be stressed that the term 'public authority' in Art. 4(7) should be given an autonomous EU-wide meaning, and that under EU law the concept of 'public authority' tends to cover: (i) entities which form part of the public administration or the executive of the State; and (ii) legal persons governed by public law or by private law, which are entrusted, under the legal regime which is applicable to them, with the performance of services of public interest, and which are, for this purpose, vested with special powers beyond those which result from the normal rules applicable in relations between persons governed by private law. See e.g. Case C-279/12, *Fish Legal and Shirley*, paras. 42 and 51-52. A non-exhaustive list of entities that should be considered 'public authorities' is also mentioned in rec. 31 GDPR.

[17] See Case C-101/01, *Lindqvist*; Case C-212/13, *Ryneš*.

[18] WP29 2010, p. 15. However, a department within an organisation that enjoys autonomous decision-making powers with regard to the relevant data processing activities might qualify as a controller. For example, the Italian DPA has found that, where a department of a public body (e.g. the department of a Ministry) enjoys autonomous decision-making powers on data processing, it would normally qualify as a separate controller or joint controller with the body to which it belongs: see Italian Data Protection Authority 1997.

[19] WP29 2010, p. 16.

established in another Member State.[20] In other words, as Kuner has memorably stated, 'the rule "one company, one controller" does not apply'.[21]

2. Determination of purposes and means

The crux of controllership for the purposes of the GDPR is the determination of the purposes and means of the processing of personal data. The term 'purposes' connotes the reason and objective for processing—in other words, the 'why' of such processing. The term 'means' is to be construed broadly as connoting the 'how' of such processing, and this encompasses both technical and organisational elements, including the platform for data processing, the accessibility of the data, where the data are stored and for how long.[22]

On its face, Article 4(7) indicates that both the 'why' and 'how' elements are equally important to determine. However, the WP29 has taken the view that the decisive element for attaining controller status is determination of purposes.[23] If a controller delegates the determination of purposes to another entity it ceases to be a controller. The situation is different with respect to determination of means: according to the WP29, some aspects of the means of processing may be delegated to others (namely, processors)[24] without the controller thereby losing controller status.[25] This delegation pertains only to relatively minor technical or organisational measures, such as the type of software to be used, whereas determination of 'essential elements' of the means (i.e. those decisions that may affect the lawfulness of the processing) is reserved for controllers.[26] While some of the distinctions drawn here by the WP29 are not apparent from the wording of Article 4(7), they make sense from a practical perspective.

Regarding the criterion 'determine', this is to be understood as broadly denoting the ability to exercise influence. In the words of the CJEU, to attain controller status, it is sufficient that 'a natural or legal person ... exerts influence over the processing of personal data, for his own purposes, and ... participates, as a result, in the determination of the purposes and means of that processing'.[27] Such influence need not result in the controller performing any of the processing itself; nor, indeed, is it necessary that the controller access the data, at least in situations of joint controllership (as elaborated below).[28] Furthermore, determination of purposes and means need not be done through written instructions.[29]

In the *Jehovah's Witnesses* case, the CJEU considered whether a religious community was a controller with regard to the processing of personal data collected by its members in the course of door-to-door preaching. The community argued that its members who engaged in the preaching determined the specific circumstances for the data collection

---

[20] See further Kuner 2003, p. 64.   [21] Ibid.   [22] WP29 2010, p. 14.

[23] Ibid., p. 13. A stronger focus on the 'why' element of the definition transpires also from the legislative process that led to the adoption of the DPD. Indeed, in its 1992 amended proposal for the DPD, the Commission noted that '[t]he controller is the person ultimately responsible for the choices governing the design and operation of the processing carried out ... , rather than anyone who carries out processing in accordance with the controller's instructions. That is why the definition stipulates that the controller decides the "objective" of the processing': see DPD Amended Proposal 1992, p. 10.

[24] Further on the notion of 'processor', see the commentary on Art. 4(8) GDPR in this volume.

[25] WP29 2010, p. 15.   [26] Ibid., p. 14.

[27] Case C-25/17, *Jehovan todistajat*, para. 68. See also Case C-40/17, *Fashion ID*, para. 68.

[28] Case C-210/16, *Wirtschaftsakademie*, para. 38; Case C-25/17, *Jehovan todistajat*, para. 69; Case C-40/17, *Fashion ID*, para. 69.

[29] Case C-25/17, *Jehovan todistajat*, para. 67.

and that this collection was thereby outside the community's control. The Court, however, held that the community was a controller, together with the preachers, because it organised, coordinated and encouraged the preaching activity, which helped spread the faith of the community.[30] Moreover, the community made some use of the collected data (e.g. keeping records of persons who signalled that they did not want to be visited).[31] Nonetheless, the Court made clear that its finding of controllership did not require establishing that the community had access to those data, or establishing that the community issued written guidelines or instructions for the data processing.[32]

When assessing controller status, the CJEU also places weight on the *effect* that an entity's activity has on the privacy and data protection interests of data subjects. This is well illustrated by the *Google Spain* case, in which the CJEU considered whether Google Inc., as operator of an internet search engine, is a controller in respect of the processing of personal data undertaken by its search engine operations. In reaching an affirmative finding, the Court emphasised, inter alia, that while a search engine operator does not exercise control over what personal data are published on the web pages of third parties, nor is able to index the personal data on all websites, it plays a 'decisive role in the overall dissemination of those data',[33] facilitates the creation of 'a more or less detailed profile of the data subject'[34] and is accordingly 'liable to affect significantly ... the fundamental rights to privacy and to the protection of personal data'.[35] The Court further noted that an opposite finding would be contrary not just to the 'clear wording' of the provision defining the controller concept 'but also to its objective—which is to ensure ... effective and complete protection of data subjects'.[36]

Exercising influence may also involve making basic design choices for information systems. Nonetheless, such choices will not necessarily create controllership for the purposes of Article 4(7) unless they relate to fairly concrete and specific operations involving the processing of personal data. A body that is engaged in designing the fundamental architecture for a large information system that processes personal data is not a controller in respect of that data processing simply because of its design choices. Thus, for instance, the Internet Engineering Task Force ('IETF') and World Wide Web Consortium ('W3C') are not controllers with respect to the processing of personal data on the internet even though they determine the core standards by which data are communicated through that network.[37]

3. Joint controllership

Controllership may be shared. Accordingly, it is not the case that there may be only one controller per data-processing operation:[38] as noted by the CJEU, 'where several operators determine jointly the purposes and means of the processing of personal data, they participate in that processing as [joint] controllers'.[39] Indeed, joint controllership

---

[30] Ibid., para. 70.   [31] Ibid.   [32] Ibid., para. 75.
[33] Case C-131/12, *Google Spain*, para. 36.   [34] Ibid., para. 37.   [35] Ibid., para. 38.
[36] Ibid., para. 34.
[37] Further on the work of the IETF and W3C, see Alvestrand and Wium Lie 2009.
[38] Case C-40/17, *Fashion ID*, para. 67 (noting that 'since, as Article 2(d) of Directive 95/46 expressly provides, the concept of "controller" relates to the entity which "alone or jointly with others" determines the purposes and means of the processing of personal data, that concept does not necessarily refer to a single entity and may concern several actors taking part in that processing'). See further Case C-210/16, *Wirtschaftsakademie*, para. 29; Case C-25/17, *Jehovan todistajat*, para. 65.
[39] Case C-40/17, *Fashion ID*, para. 73.

is increasingly prevalent. This is due to legal factors (in particular, the low threshold for controllership) in combination with technological-organisational developments (in particular, the increasingly interconnected nature of information systems, markets and associated actors). The prevalence of joint controllership is reflected in Article 26 GDPR which deals specifically (although very generally) with the relationship between joint controllers.[40] The DPD did not contain such provisions.

As the WP29 made clear, the criteria for finding joint controllership are essentially the same as for finding sole controllership,[41] but 'the participation of the parties to the joint determination may take different forms and does not have to be equally shared'.[42] Similarly, the CJEU has observed:

[T]he existence of joint responsibility does not necessarily imply equal responsibility of the various operators involved in the processing of personal data. On the contrary, those operators may be involved at different stages of that processing of personal data and to different degrees, so that the level of responsibility of each of them must be assessed with regard to all the relevant circumstances of the particular case.[43]

Hence, a wide range of joint controllership arrangements is possible,[44] as long as they comply with the requirements of Article 26 GDPR.[45] At the same time, care must be taken in delineating between joint controllers, separate controllers operating in cooperative networks, and other entities, such as processors.[46] Making these delineations is often difficult in practice, especially in respect of complex data-processing arrangements involving multiple parties.[47]

In *Wirtschaftsakademie*, the CJEU considered whether the administrator of a Facebook fan page was a joint controller with Facebook in respect of processing the personal data of the visitors to the fan page. The fan page administrator argued that it had no real influence over the processing as Facebook unilaterally sets the terms and conditions of the contract for use of the fan page service. The Court noted that while mere use of Facebook 'does not make a Facebook user a controller jointly responsible for the processing of personal data by that network', the creation of a fan page on Facebook opens up the opportunity for Facebook to place cookies on the computer or other device of persons visiting the fan page, whether or not they have a Facebook account.[48] Further, the administrator

---

[40] See further the commentary on Art. 26 in this volume.   [41] WP29 2010, p. 18.
[42] Ibid., p. 19.
[43] Case C-210/16, *Wirtschaftsakademie*, para. 43; Case C-40/17, *Fashion ID*, para. 70.
[44] See WP29 2010, pp. 19–24 for an overview of typologies for joint control.
[45] Further on these requirements, see the commentary on Art. 26 in this volume.
[46] Regarding processors, see further the commentary on Art. 4(8) in this volume.
[47] See further e.g. Kuner 2007, ch. 2 (section 2.19); Hon et al. 2013; Olsen and Mahler 2007; van Alsenoy 2012; Mahieu et al. 2019. In this regard, a report issued in June 2019 by the Multistakeholder Expert Group to support the application of the GDPR has also stressed the practical difficulties in making a delineation between controllers and processors: '[s]everal members argue that the characterisation of controller and processor is still not clear. They see a "trend" in the market after the European Court of Justice decision on Facebook [i.e. case *Wirtschaftsakademie*, analysed further below] where in some instances former processors now want to become controllers or joint controllers. Differences on roles are less clear for companies and therefore contracts governing the respective responsibilities of business partners in a processing are complex to negotiate. They mention that the contractual assignment of the controller/processor role is sometimes left upon [sic] the will of the strongest company in the market, rather than on who decides on the purposes. In addition, they note that the scope of who falls within the definition of a processor is not always clear; for example some vendors maintaining and supporting software refuse the adaptation of their contracts according to Article 28 GDPR arguing that their tasks do not include processing of personal data'. See GDPR Expert Group 2019, pp. 17–18.
[48] Case C-210/16, *Wirtschaftsakademie*, para. 35.

was able to define parameters for compiling viewing statistics based on visits to the fan page, thus contributing to the processing of the personal data of the visitors to its page.[49] The fact that these statistics were only transmitted to the administrator in anonymised form was irrelevant as joint controllership does not require each of the joint controllers to have access to the personal data concerned.[50] The Court additionally emphasised that as fan pages hosted on Facebook can also be visited by persons who are not Facebook users, the fan page administrator bore even greater responsibility for the processing of the personal data of those persons,[51] and that '[i]n those circumstances, the recognition of joint responsibility ... contributes to ensuring more complete protection of the rights of persons visiting a fan page'.[52]

The Court adopted a similar stance in the *Fashion ID* case,[53] which concerned the legal consequences of a company (Fashion ID) inserting a Facebook plug-in (i.e., a 'Like' button) on its website that caused the browser of a visitor to that website to request content from the provider of that plug-in (i.e., Facebook), and to that end, to transmit to that provider the personal data of the visitor. According to the Court, Fashion ID should be considered a controller jointly with Facebook in respect of the operations involving the collection and transmission (to Facebook), by means of the plug-in, of the personal data of those visiting its website, since it co-determines (together with Facebook) the means and purposes of those operations: its use of the plug-in enabled Facebook to obtain personal data of visitors and allowed Fashion ID to optimize the publicity of its goods by making them more visible on Facebook.[54] By contrast, the Court held that Fashion ID should not be considered a joint controller in respect of the operations carried out by Facebook after the data are transmitted to the latter.[55]

While the CJEU understandably justifies its ready recognition of joint responsibility in terms of ensuring more complete protection of data subjects' rights, its jurisprudence in this regard might, however, paradoxically undermine such protection. In a situation where controller responsibility is shared amongst increasingly large numbers of entities, the risk arises that responsibility becomes diluted if not pulverised. Advocate General Bobek pointed to this risk in his opinion in *Fashion ID*, elegantly stating:

[A] sceptical person from the more eastern parts of the European Union might perhaps suggest, considering his historical experience, that effective protection of something tends to dramatically decrease if everyone is made responsible for it. Making everyone responsible means that no-one will in fact be responsible. Or rather, the one party that should have been held responsible for a certain course of action, the one actually exercising control, is likely to hide behind all those others nominally 'co-responsible', with effective protection likely to be significantly diluted.[56]

To ameliorate this development, he proposed that the liability of a joint controller be limited to 'those operations for which it effectively co-decides on the means and purposes of the processing'.[57] The CJEU essentially agreed with this approach.[58] Hence, a joint controller such as Fashion ID would not be liable for those stages of processing that are outside its sphere of influence.[59]

---

[49] Ibid., paras. 36–37. [50] Ibid., para. 38.
[51] Ibid., para. 41. The Court took a similar stance in *Fashion ID*. See Case C-40/17, *Fashion ID*, para. 83.
[52] Case C-210/16, *Wirtschaftsakademie*, para. 42. [53] Case C-40/17, *Fashion ID*.
[54] Ibid., paras. 64 et seq. [55] Ibid. [56] Case C-40/17, *Fashion ID* (AG Opinion), para. 92.
[57] Ibid., para. 108. [58] Case C-40/17, *Fashion ID*, para. 99. [59] Ibid.

4. Data subject as controller?

A question that regularly arises in practice is whether a data subject can be regarded as a controller of his or her own personal data.[60] This may seem relevant since a data subject often helps to determine the purposes and means of data processing (e.g. if he or she decides to enter personal data on a website, or adds such data to a blockchain, for a particular purpose), which is the key criterion for determination of whether a party is a controller.

However, the GDPR makes a clear distinction between the different actors involved in data processing (i.e. data subject, controller and processor). This is to ensure protection of an individual's personal data (see Article 1(2) and recital 10). Consequently, the CJEU has justified a broad reading of the definition of 'controller' on the basis of the definition's objective which, according to the Court, 'is to ensure ... effective and complete protection of data subjects'.[61] Thus, a contrario, the inclusion of a data subject in that definition would seem contrary to such an objective inasmuch as it would deprive them of their protection by resulting in the imposition of obligations rather than the granting of rights.[62] It would also be nonsensical to require that a data subject comply with the obligations that are imposed on controllers under the GDPR, as such obligations are imposed on controllers specifically to protect others' interests (i.e. those of data subjects), not their own.[63] This is somewhat confirmed in *Wirtschaftsakademie*, where the CJEU held that the administrator of a fan page hosted on Facebook was to be considered a joint controller, not because of the 'mere fact of making use of a social network such as Facebook'—an activity that arguably entails *per se* a partial contribution of the Facebook user to the determination of why and how his/her data are processed by Facebook, e.g. by choosing technical settings—but because the administrator, with its actions, had an influence over the processing of the personal data of *other people* (i.e. the 'visitors of its page').[64] In essence, it would seem logical that a controller must be some party other than the data subject.[65]

5. Definition of controller in the LED and EUDPR

Article 3(8) LED and Article 3(8) EUDPR both define 'controller' in line with Article 4(7) GDPR. However, the definition in the LED is limited to 'competent authorities' (i.e. law enforcement bodies as defined in Article 3(7) LED), while the definition in the

---

[60] For instance, with regard to the use of blockchain technologies (i.e. technologies relying on a digital database updated by a consensus algorithm and stored on multiple nodes in a computer network: a blockchain), Finck notes that 'through blockchains, data subjects can gain control over their own data through the private key, which triggers the question of whether the data subject herself can be considered a controller', and concludes that, at least in some instances, a data subject may be 'able to qualify as a data controller in adding personal data to the blockchain': see Finck 2018, p. 101. See also Edwards et al. 2019.

[61] Case C-131/12, *Google Spain*, para. 34; Case C-210/16, *Wirtschaftsakademie*, para. 28; Case C-40/17, *Fashion ID*, para. 66.

[62] More generally, the fact that the objective of the rules contained in the GDPR is to protect individuals (see Art. 1(2) and rec. 10) should caution against any interpretation of the same rules that would leave individuals deprived of protection of their rights. See also WP29 2007, p. 4 (noting this with regard to the DPD).

[63] As indicated above, the CJEU has made clear that the objective of the definition of 'controller' is to ensure 'effective and complete protection *of data subjects*': emphasis added. See Case C-131/12, *Google Spain*, para. 34; Case C-210/16, *Wirtschaftsakademie*, para. 28; Case C-40/17, *Fashion ID*, para. 66.

[64] Case C-210/16, *Wirtschaftsakademie*, paras. 35–36.

[65] On the basis of ad hoc dialogue with various DPA representatives, it is our impression that this is also the view of many DPAs, although it has not been formalised in an opinion of the WP29 or EDPB.

EUDPR is limited to EU institutions or bodies. The EUDPR makes clear that its application of the term to other entities follows the definitions laid down in Article 4(7) GDPR and Article 3(8) LED (Article 3(9) EUDPR).[66]

Select Bibliography

International agreements

APEC Privacy Framework 2005: Asia-Pacific Economic Cooperation, 'Privacy Framework' (2005).
OECD Guidelines 2013: Organisation for Economic Co-operation and Development, 'The OECD Privacy Framework' (2013).

EU legislation

DPD Amended Proposal 1992: Amended Proposal for a Council Directive on the Protection of Individuals with Regard to the Processing of Personal Data and on the Free Movement of Such Data (COM(92) 422 final—SYN 287, 15 October 1992.

National legislation

Greek Data Protection Law: Law 2472/1997 on the Protection of Individuals with regard to the Processing of Personal Data (as amended).
Greek Draft GDPR Law: Νόμοσ για την Προςταςύα Δεδομϋνων Προςωπικού Φαρακτόρα (20 February 2018), available at http://www.opengov.gr/ministryofjustice/wp-content/uploads/downloads/2018/02/sxedio_nomou_prostasia_pd.pdf.
UK Data Protection Act 1998: Data Protection Act 1998 (Chapter 29).

Academic writings

Alvestrand and Wium Lie 2009: Alvestrand and Wium Lie, 'Development of Core Internet Standards: The Work of IETF and W3C', in Bygrave and Bing (eds.), *Internet Governance: Infrastructure and Institutions* (OUP 2009), 123.
Edwards et al. 2019: Edwards, Finck, Veale and Zingales, 'Data subjects as data controllers: a Fashion(able) concept?', *Internet Policy Review* (2019).
Finck 2018: Finck, *Blockchain Regulation and Governance in Europe* (CUP 2018).
Hon et al. 2013: Hon, Millard and Walden, 'Who Is Responsible for Personal Data in Clouds?', in Millard (ed.), *Cloud Computing Law* (OUP 2013), 193.
Kuner 2003, *European Data Privacy Law and Online Business* (OUP 2003).
Kuner 2007: Kuner, *European Data Protection Law: Corporate Compliance and Regulation* (2nd edn, OUP 2007).
Mahieu et al. 2019: Mahieu, van Hoboken and Asghari, 'Responsibility for Data Protection in a Networked World: On the Question of the Controller, "Effective and Complete Protection" and its Application to Data Access Rights in Europe', 10(1) *Journal of Intellectual Property, Information Technology and E-Commerce Law* (2019), 85.
Olsen and Mahler 2007: Olsen and Mahler, 'Identity Management and Data Protection Law: Risk, Responsibility and Compliance in "Circles of Trust"—Part II', 23(5) *Computer Law & Security Review 'CLSR'* (2007), 415.
Van Alsenoy 2012: Van Alsenoy, 'Allocating Responsibility among Controllers, Processors, and "Everything in Between": The Definition of Actors and Roles in Directive 95/46/EC', 28(1) *CLSR* (2012), 25.

---

[66] See too rec. 5 EUDPR.

Papers of data protection authorities

WP29 2006: Article 29 Working Party, 'Opinion 10/2006 on the Processing of Personal Data by the Society for Worldwide Interbank Financial Telecommunication (SWIFT)' (WP 128, 22 November 2006).

WP29 2007: Article 29 Working Party. 'Opinion 4/2007 on the concept of personal data' (WP 136, 20 June 2007).

WP29 2010: Article 29 Working Party, 'Opinion 01/2010 on the Concepts of "Controller" and "Processor"' (WP 169, 16 February 2010).

WP29 2012: Article 29 Working Party, 'Opinion 05/2012 on Cloud Computing (WP 196, 1 July 2012).

Italian Data Protection Authority 1997: Garante per la protezione dei dati personali, 'Privacy: chi sono i titolari e i responsabili del trattamento dei dati nelle imprese e nelle amministrazioni pubbliche' (11 December 1997).

Reports and recommendations

Explanatory Report Convention 108 2018: Council of Europe, 'Explanatory Report to the Protocol Amending the Convention for the Protection of Individuals with Regard to the Automatic Processing of Personal Data' (10 October 2018), available at https://rm.coe.int/cets-223-explanatory-report-to-the-protocol-amending-the-convention-fo/16808ac91a.

GDPR Expert Group Report 2019: Multistakeholder Expert Group to support the application of Regulation (EU) 2016/679, 'Contribution from the Multistakeholder Expert Group to the stock-taking exercise of June 2019 on one year of GDPR application' (13 June 2019).

Article 4(8). Processor

LEE A. BYGRAVE   LUCA TOSONI

'processor' means a natural or legal person, public authority, agency or other body which processes personal data on behalf of the controller;

Closely Related Provisions

Article 28 (Processor) (see too recital 81); Article 29 (Processing under the authority of the controller or processor)

Related Provisions in LED [Directive (EU) 2016/680]

Article 3(9) (Definition of 'processor'); Articles 22–23 (General obligations of processors)

Related Provisions in EUDPR [Regulation (EU) 2018/1725]

Article 3(12) (Definition of 'processor'); Articles 29–30 (General obligations of processors)

Relevant Case Law

CJEU

Case C-131/12, *Google Spain v Agencia Española de Protección de Datos (AEPD) and Mario Costeja González*, judgment of 13 May 2014 (Grand Chamber) (ECLI:EU:C:2014:317).

Case C-210/16, *Unabhängiges Landeszentrum für Datenschutz Schleswig-Holstein v Wirtschaftsakademie Schleswig-Holstein GmbH*, judgment of 5 June 2018 (Grand Chamber) (ECLI:EU:C:2018:388).

Case C-25/17, *Proceedings brought by Tietosuojavaltuutettu (Jehovan todistajat)*, judgment of 10 July 2018 (Grand Chamber) (ECLI:EU:C:2018:551).

Case C-40/17, *Fashion ID GmbH & Co. KG v Verbraucherzentrale NRW e.V.*, judgment of 29 July 2019 (ECLI:EU:C:2019:629).

Opinion of Advocate General Bobek in Case C-40/17, *Fashion ID GmbH & Co. KG v Verbraucherzentrale NRW e.V.*, delivered on 19 December 2018 (ECLI:EU:C:2018:1039).

A. Rationale and Policy Underpinnings

The 'processor' is one of the principal actors in the operationalisation of data protection law and thus deserves specific definition. Indeed, the role of this actor has increased in importance as the GDPR vests processors with more extensive obligations and liability than was the case under the DPD (see e.g. Articles 30(2), 33(2), 37, 79 and 82 GDPR).[1]

---

[1] See further e.g. van Alsenoy 2016, pp. 284 et seq.

Technological-organisational developments have further increased the significance of the processor role. Growth in the use of outsourcing arrangements, particularly those involving cloud computing, illustrates this well. Providers of cloud services are typically processors for the purposes of data protection law.[2]

B. Legal Background

1. EU legislation

Article 2(e) DPD included a definition of 'processor' that was virtually identical to that in Article 4(8) GDPR. Thus, the WP29 guidance on the concept of 'processor' under the DPD remains relevant to interpreting Article 4(8) GDPR.

2. International instruments

Convention 108 as originally adopted omits specific reference to the term 'processor'. The same applies with the OECD Privacy Guidelines and APEC Privacy Framework.[3] Modernised Convention 108, however, utilises the term and defines it in basically the same way as the DPD and GDPR (see Article 2(f)). The Explanatory Report to the Modernised Convention explains the term as follows:

'Processor' is any natural or legal person (other than an employee of the data controller) who processes data on behalf of the controller and according to the controller's instructions. The instructions given by the controller establish the limit of what the processor is allowed to do with the personal data.[4]

3. National developments

Prior to adoption of the GDPR, EU Member States generally applied the definition of 'processor' given in Article 2(e) DPD, although they did not always directly define the term in their respective national laws. This was the case, for instance, with the Finnish Personal Data Act 1999 (repealed), although it did make clear (in its definition of 'third party') that 'the processor of personal data or someone processing personal data on the behalf of the controller or the processor' was not to be regarded as a 'third party' pursuant to the legislation.[5] The French Data Protection Act 1978 also eschews specific definition of the term, but makes clear (in its definition of 'recipient' ('destinataire')) that the role of 'sub-contractor' ('sous-traitant'), which is apparently intended to equate with that of 'processor', falls outside the definition of 'recipient' for the purposes of the Act.[6]

4. Case law

The CJEU has yet to deal directly with the definition of 'processor'. However, it has handed down several high-profile judgments that deal with the definition of 'controller'

---

[2] See further WP29 2012, p. 8. For general academic analysis of the role of processors in cloud computing contexts, see Hon et al. 2013.
[3] See OECD Privacy Guidelines 2013; APEC Privacy Framework 2005.
[4] Explanatory Report Convention 108 2018, para. 24.
[5] Finnish Personal Data Act 1999, s. 3(6).   [6] French Data Protection Act 1978, Art. 3(2).

under the DPD.[7] As the concepts of 'processor' and 'controller' are inextricably linked and have both remained virtually unchanged in the GDPR compared to the DPD, this case law may prove useful to elucidate the meaning of Article 4(8) GDPR.[8]

C. Analysis

1. Introduction

The role of 'processor' is inextricably linked to that of 'controller' in the sense that the former results from a delegation or 'outsourcing' of tasks determined by the controller. This is clear from the face of Article 4(8) GDPR: a processor is an entity that processes personal data 'on behalf of the controller'. At the same time, a processor is functionally part and parcel of the 'means' of processing referred to in the definition of 'controller' in Article 4(7) GDPR.

2. Legally separate from the controller

Less clear but nonetheless essential is that a processor must be an entity that is legally separate from the controller.[9] Thus, the controller–processor relationship is to be distinguished from an employer–employee relationship: an employee processing personal data in furtherance of obligations towards their employer shall, as such, not be regarded as a processor.[10] At the same time, controllers may also undertake processing operations themselves, in which case there is no separate legal subject (i.e. processor) involved with regard to those specific operations.

3. Nature of the relationship between controller and processor

The processor is sometimes described as an 'agent' of the controller.[11] Caution needs to accompany this characterisation as the controller–processor relationship is not the same as a principal–agent relationship under, say, the rules of commercial law in common law jurisdictions. Under such rules an agent may act on behalf of a principal and bind the latter by creating legal relations with third parties. A processor under the GDPR is not such an agent; nor is the controller a principal.

---

[7] See Case C-131/12, *Google Spain*; Case C-210/16, *Wirtschaftsakademie Schleswig-Holstein*; Case C-25/17, *Jehovan todistajat*; Case C-40/17, *Fashion ID*. See further the commentary on Art. 4(7) in this volume.

[8] In this regard, Advocate General Bobek noted in *Fashion ID*: 'as Article 4 of the GDPR largely retains the same key terms as Article 2 of Directive 95/46 (while adding a number of new ones), it would be rather surprising if the interpretation of such key notions, including the notion of controller, processing, or personal data, were to significantly depart (without a very good reason) from the extant case-law'. See Case C-40/17, *Fashion ID* (AG Opinion), para. 87.

[9] See also WP29 2010, p. 25. Similarly, in its explanatory memorandum to its amended proposal for the DPD, the Commission stated that a controller may have personal data 'processed by members of his staff or by an outside processor, a legally separate person acting on his behalf': DPD Amended Proposal 1992, p. 10.

[10] This was indicated in some national laws implementing the DPD. E.g. Art. 4(1)(h) of the Italian Data Protection Code (as last amended by Italian Legislative Decree 2015) defined as 'persons in charge of the processing' (in Italian, 'incaricati') 'the natural persons [such as employees] who have been authorised by the data controller or processor to carry out processing operations'. See further, by analogy, the Explanatory Report to the Modernised Convention 108, which refers to the 'processor' as a person 'other than an employee of the data controller'.

[11] See e.g. Korff 2010, p. 64.

The controller–processor relationship is basically one of subservience—i.e. the processor must obey the dictates of the controller regarding the purposes and means of the processing.[12] This is apparent from Articles 28 and 29 GDPR, which lay out the specifics of the relationship in considerable detail.[13] Moreover, an entity is *only* a processor in so far as it acts within the remit set by a controller. When a processor undertakes processing of personal data outside the controller's dictates, and in so doing determines the purposes and means of that processing, it ceases to be a processor and assumes the role of controller in respect of that processing. This is made clear in Article 28(10) GDPR, which also indicates that the processor-turned-controller remains liable for infringing Articles 28 and 29 by it having gone beyond the dictates of the original controller. However, care must be taken when assessing whether or not a processor acts beyond the mandate set by a controller as processors may have some discretion when deciding how to process data on controllers' behalf. In the opinion of the WP29, a controller may delegate to a processor the ability to determine particular technical and organisational aspects of the 'means' of processing (e.g. the software to be used) which do not substantially affect the lawfulness of the processing.[14] These aspects are to be contrasted with 'essential elements which are traditionally and inherently reserved to the determination of the controller, such as "which data shall be processed?", "for how long shall they be processed?", "who shall have access to them?", and so on'.[15]

The EDPB also opines that, where a processor in the EU/EEA processes data on behalf of a controller not established in the EU/EEA, the former 'should not be considered to be an establishment [in the EU/EEA] of a data controller ... merely by virtue of its status as processor'.[16] The Board continues by stating that '[t]he existence of a relationship between a controller and a processor does not necessarily trigger the application of the GDPR to both, should one of these two entities not be established in the Union'.[17]

4. Parties that may be processors

Although Article 4(8) refers to a wide range of entities that may be regarded as processors, not any such entity may lawfully be able to fulfil the processor role *in practice*. This is not obvious from Article 4(8), but becomes clear from other provisions in the Regulation. Article 28(1) GDPR stipulates that 'the controller shall use only processors providing sufficient guarantees to implement appropriate technical and organisational measures in such a manner that processing will meet the requirements of this Regulation and ensure the protection of the rights of the data subject'.[18] Thus, taking on the processor role requires considerable expertise, skills and other resources.

---

[12] On the practical challanges linked with this relationship, see GDPR Expert Group Report 2019, pp. 17–18.
[13] For elaboration, see further the commentaries on Arts. 28 and 29 GDPR in this volume.
[14] WP29 2010, pp. 15, 25. See also the commentary on Art. 4(7) GDPR in this volume.
[15] Ibid., p. 14.   [16] EDPB 2018, p. 9.
[17] Ibid. See further the commentary on Art. 3 GDPR in this volume.
[18] See too rec. 81 GDPR which states that 'the controller should use only processors providing sufficient guarantees, in particular in terms of expert knowledge, reliability and resources, to implement technical and organisational measures which will meet the requirements of this Regulation, including for the security of processing'.

5. Other instruments

Article 3(9) LED and Article 3(12) EUDPR both define 'processor' identically to Article 4(8) GDPR, and the term should be interpreted homogeneously in all these legal instruments (see too recital 5 EUDPR).

Select Bibliography

International agreements

APEC Privacy Framework 2005: Asia-Pacific Economic Cooperation, 'Privacy Framework' (2005).
OECD Privacy Guidelines 2013: Organisation for Economic Co-operation and Development, 'The OECD Privacy Framework' (2013).

EU legislation

DPD Amended Proposal 1992: Amended Proposal for a Council Directive on the protection of individuals with regard to the processing of personal data and on the free movement of such data, COM(92) 422 final, 15 October 1992.

National legislation

Finnish Personal Data Law 1999: Finnish Law on Personal Data 523/1999 (Henkilötietolaki No. 523/1999) (repealed).
French Data Protection Act 1978: French Act No. 78-17 of 6 January 1978 on Data Processing, Files and Individual Liberties (Loi n° 78-17 du 6 janvier 1978 relative à l'informatique, aux fichiers et aux libertés), as last amended by Law No. 2014-334 of 17 March 2014.
Italian Data Protection Code 2003: Decreto legislativo 30 giugno 2003, n. 196: Codice in Materia di Protezione dei Dati Personali.
Italian Legislative Decree 2015: Decreto Legislativo 14 settembre 2015, n. 151: Disposizioni di razionalizzazione e semplificazione delle procedure e degli adempimenti a carico di cittadini e imprese e altre disposizioni in materia di rapporto di lavoro e pari opportunità, in attuazione della legge 10 dicembre 2014, n. 183.

Academic writings

Hon et al. 2013: Hon, Millard and Walden, 'Who Is Responsible for Personal Data in Clouds?', in Millard (ed.), *Cloud Computing Law* (OUP 2013), 193.
Olsen and Mahler 2007: Olsen and Mahler, 'Identity Management and Data Protection Law: Risk, Responsibility and Compliance in "Circles of Trust"—Part II', 23(5) *Computer Law & Security Review* (2007), 415.
Van Alsenoy 2012: Van Alsenoy, 'Allocating Responsibility among Controllers, Processors, and "Everything in Between": The Definition of Actors and Roles in Directive 95/46/EC', 28(1) *Computer Law & Security Review* (2012), 25.
Van Alsenoy 2016: Van Alsenoy, 'Liability under EU Data Protection Law: From Directive 95/46 to the General Data Protection Regulation', 7(3) *Journal of Intellectual Property, Information Technology and Electronic Commerce* (2016), 271.

Papers of data protection authorities

EDPB 2018: European Data Protection Board, 'Guidelines 3/2018 on the Territorial Scope of the GDPR (Article 3)—Version for Public Consultation' (16 November 2018).

WP29 2010: Article 29 Working Party, 'Opinion 01/2010 on the Concepts of "Controller" and "Processor"' (WP 169, 16 February 2010).

WP29 2012: Article 29 Working Party, 'Opinion 05/2012 on Cloud Computing' (WP 196, 1 July 2012).

Reports and recommendations

Explanatory Report Convention 108 2018: Council of Europe, 'Explanatory Report to the Protocol Amending the Convention for the Protection of Individuals with regard to the Automatic Processing of Personal Data' (10 October 2018), available at https://rm.coe.int/cets-223-explanatory-report-to-the-protocol-amending-the-convention-fo/16808ac91a.

GDPR Expert Group Report 2019: Multistakeholder Expert Group to support the application of Regulation (EU) 2016/679, 'Contribution from the Multistakeholder Expert Group to the stock-taking exercise of June 2019 on one year of GDPR application' (13 June 2019).

Korff 2010: Korff, 'New Challenges to Data Protection Study—Working Paper No. 2: Data Protection Laws in the EU: The Difficulties in Meeting the Challenges Posed by Global Social and Technical Developments' (2010).

Article 4(9). Recipient

LUCA TOSONI

'recipient' means a natural or legal person, public authority, agency or another body, to which the personal data are disclosed, whether a third party or not. However, public authorities which may receive personal data in the framework of a particular inquiry in accordance with Union or Member State law shall not be regarded as recipients; the processing of those data by those public authorities shall be in compliance with the applicable data protection rules according to the purposes of the processing;

Relevant Recitals

(31) Public authorities to which personal data are disclosed in accordance with a legal obligation for the exercise of their official mission, such as tax and customs authorities, financial investigation units, independent administrative authorities, or financial market authorities responsible for the regulation and supervision of securities markets should not be regarded as recipients if they receive personal data which are necessary to carry out a particular inquiry in the general interest, in accordance with Union or Member State law. The requests for disclosure sent by the public authorities should always be in writing, reasoned and occasional and should not concern the entirety of a filing system or lead to the interconnection of filing systems. The processing of personal data by those public authorities should comply with the applicable data-protection rules according to the purposes of the processing.

(61) The information in relation to the processing of personal data relating to the data subject should be given to him or her at the time of collection from the data subject, or, where the personal data are obtained from another source, within a reasonable period, depending on the circumstances of the case. Where personal data can be legitimately disclosed to another recipient, the data subject should be informed when the personal data are first disclosed to the recipient. Where the controller intends to process the personal data for a purpose other than that for which they were collected, the controller should provide the data subject prior to that further processing with information on that other purpose and other necessary information. Where the origin of the personal data cannot be provided to the data subject because various sources have been used, general information should be provided.

(63) A data subject should have the right of access to personal data which have been collected concerning him or her, and to exercise that right easily and at reasonable intervals, in order to be aware of, and verify, the lawfulness of the processing. This includes the right for data subjects to have access to data concerning their health, for example the data in their medical records containing information such as diagnoses, examination results, assessments by treating physicians and any treatment or interventions provided. Every data subject should therefore have the right to know and obtain communication in particular with regard to the purposes for which the personal data are processed, where possible the period for which the personal data are processed, the recipients of the personal data, the logic involved in any automatic personal data processing and, at least when based on profiling, the consequences of such processing. Where possible, the controller should be able to provide remote access to a secure system which would provide the data subject with direct access to his or her personal data. That right should not adversely affect the rights or freedoms of others, including trade secrets or intellectual property and in particular the copyright protecting

the software. However, the result of those considerations should not be a refusal to provide all information to the data subject. Where the controller processes a large quantity of information concerning the data subject, the controller should be able to request that, before the information is delivered, the data subject specify the information or processing activities to which the request relates.

(101) Flows of personal data to and from countries outside the Union and international organisations are necessary for the expansion of international trade and international cooperation. The increase in such flows has raised new challenges and concerns with regard to the protection of personal data. However, when personal data are transferred from the Union to controllers, processors or other recipients in third countries or to international organisations, the level of protection of natural persons ensured in the Union by this Regulation should not be undermined, including in cases of onward transfers of personal data from the third country or international organisation to controllers, processors in the same or another third country or international organisation. In any event, transfers to third countries and international organisations may only be carried out in full compliance with this Regulation. A transfer could take place only if, subject to the other provisions of this Regulation, the conditions laid down in the provisions of this Regulation relating to the transfer of personal data to third countries or international organisations are complied with by the controller or processor.

(111) Provisions should be made for the possibility for transfers in certain circumstances where the data subject has given his or her explicit consent, where the transfer is occasional and necessary in relation to a contract or a legal claim, regardless of whether in a judicial procedure or whether in an administrative or any out-of-court procedure, including procedures before regulatory bodies. Provision should also be made for the possibility for transfers where important grounds of public interest laid down by Union or Member State law so require or where the transfer is made from a register established by law and intended for consultation by the public or persons having a legitimate interest. In the latter case, such a transfer should not involve the entirety of the personal data or entire categories of the data contained in the register and, when the register is intended for consultation by persons having a legitimate interest, the transfer should be made only at the request of those persons or, if they are to be the recipients, taking into full account the interests and fundamental rights of the data subject.

Closely Related Provisions

Article 13(1)(e) (Information to be provided to data subjects); Article 14(1)(e)–(f) and (3)(c) (Information to be provided to data subjects); Article 15(1)(c) (Right of access by the data subject); Article 19 (Notification regarding rectification or erasure of personal data or restriction of processing); Article 30(1)(d) (Records of processing activities); Article 46(3)(a) (Transfers subject to appropriate safeguards); Article 49(2) (Derogations in the context of transfers of personal data); Article 58(2)(g) and (j) (Powers of supervisory authorities); Article 83(5)(c) (Administrative fines)

Related Provisions in LED [Directive (EU) 2016/680]

Article 3(10) (Definition of 'recipient') (see too recitals 22 and 34)

Related Provisions in EUDPR [Regulation (EU) 2018/1725]

Article 3(13) (Definition of 'recipient')

A. Rationale and Policy Underpinnings

A definition of the term 'recipient' was first included in the DPD and is maintained essentially unmodified in the GDPR. This is primarily to complement the definition of 'third party',[1] and to clarify the categories of persons to whom data may be disclosed and, consequently, must be mentioned in privacy notices, or communicated to the data subjects upon their request (see Articles 10–12 DPD and Articles 13–15 GDPR).[2]

B. Legal Background

1. EU legislation

Article 2(g) DPD included a definition of 'recipient' which was essentially identical to that of Article 4(9) GDPR, apart from the fact that the Directive's definition of 'recipient' did not expressly mention that the processing of data received in the context of a particular inquiry by public authorities must be 'in compliance with the applicable data protection rules according to the purposes of the processing'. However, this specification was implicit in the DPD as well.

2. International instruments

Convention 108 as originally adopted does not use the term 'recipient'. Modernised Convention 108, however, utilises the term and defines it essentially in line with the DPD and GDPR (see Article 2(e)). The Explanatory Report to the Modernised Convention explains the term as follows:

'Recipient' is an individual or an entity who receives personal data or to whom personal data is made available. Depending on the circumstances, the recipient may be a controller or a processor. For example, an enterprise can send certain data of employees to a government department that will process it as a controller for tax purposes. It may send it to a company offering storage services and acting as a processor. The recipient can be a public authority or an entity that has been granted the right to exercise a public function but where the data received by the authority or entity is processed in the framework of a particular inquiry in accordance with the applicable law, that public authority or entity shall not be regarded as a recipient. Requests for disclosure from public authorities should always be in writing, reasoned and occasional and should not concern the entirety of a filing system or lead to the interconnection of filing systems. The processing of personal data by those public authorities should comply with the applicable data protection rules according to the purposes of the processing.[3]

Neither the OECD Privacy Guidelines (both original and revised versions) nor the APEC Privacy Framework specifically operate with the concept of 'recipient'.

---

[1] See Council Report 1992, p. 8 fn. 22. In this document, several Member States expressed concerns that 'the very diversity of [the category of "third parties"] was likely to lead to confusion and that the concept of "third party" needed to be more closely defined; ... therefore proposed a new definition making a clear distinction between "third parties" which had no connection with the processing and the various "recipients" of the processed data'. The definition of 'recipient' was finally included in the text of the DPD to respond to these concerns of Member States: see Council Report 1993, p. 8, fn. 2. On the notion of 'third party', see the commentary on Art. 4(10) GDPR in this volume.

[2] On the information regarding recipients to be provided to data subjects, see WP29 2018.

[3] Explanatory Report Convention 108 2018, para. 23.

3. National developments

Prior to adoption of the GDPR, several national data protection laws implementing the DPD did not include a definition of 'recipient'.[4] In contrast, some other national laws provided a more elaborate (and sometimes more restrictive) definition of 'recipient' than that of the DPD. For example, Article 3(2) of France's Data Protection Act 1978 provided that

[T]he recipient of a processing of personal data is any authorised person to whom the data are disclosed, other than the data subject, the data controller, the sub-contractor and persons who, due to their functions, are in charge of processing the data. However, the authorities who are legally entitled to ask the data controller to send them the personal data, in the context of a particular mission or that of the exercise of a right to receive such data, shall not be regarded as recipients.[5]

Thus, under French law, the data subject, controller, processor and persons who, under the direct authority of the controller or processor, are authorised to process personal data (i.e. non-third parties pursuant to Articles 2(f) DPD and 4(10) GDPR)[6] did not (and still do not)[7] qualify as 'recipients'. This approach is different from that followed by the DPD, GDPR and other national laws,[8] which stipulate(d) that also non-third parties may qualify as 'recipients', as elaborated further below.

C. Analysis

1. Range of actors covered

Article 4(9) GDPR provides a broad definition of 'recipient' that covers essentially any entities or individuals to whom personal data are disclosed or made available. This is despite the many attempts made during the legislative process to limit the definition.[9] Hence, a wide range of actors may potentially be considered as recipients. Indeed, Article 4(9) GDPR specifies that non-third parties are covered by the definition of 'recipient' ('whether a third party or not').[10] This led the WP29 to opine that 'a recipient does not have to be a third party. Therefore, other data controllers, joint controllers and processors to whom data is [sic] transferred or disclosed are covered by the term "recipient"'.[11] Thus, data that are disclosed to, for example, another department of the organisation of the controller are arguably disclosed to a 'recipient',[12] at least when such department enjoys

---

[4] See e.g. Italian Data Protection Code 2003 (as last amended by Italian Legislative Decree 2015), Art. 4; Norwegian Personal Data Act 2000, s. 2.

[5] The Act as in force after the entry into force of the GDPR still includes this definition.

[6] See the commentary on Art. 4(10) GDPR in this volume regarding the concept of 'third party'.

[7] Although maintaining a different definition of 'recipient' under national law seems to run counter to the harmonisation intent of the GDPR: see recitals 9–10 GDPR.

[8] See e.g. Belgian Data Protection Law 1992, Art. 1(7).

[9] E.g. Hungary and Latvia proposed to exclude the controller, processor and data subject from the definition of 'recipient': see Council Report 2012, pp. 73 and 82.

[10] Further on the concept of 'third party', see the commentary on Art. 4(10) GDPR in this volume.

[11] WP29 2018, p. 37.

[12] This was, for instance, the position taken by Belgium under the DPD: see Explanatory Memorandum Belgian Act 1998, p. 16 (stating that 'lorsque des données à caractère personnel sont communiquées à d'autres départements au sein de l'organisation du responsable du traitement, on a également affaire à des destinataires. Il en va de sorte lors de la communication à un autre service au sein du même hôpital de données relatives à des patients'). As mentioned above, the definition of 'recipient' under Belgian law and the DPD was essentially identical to that in Art. 4(9) GDPR.

autonomous decision-making powers with regard to the relevant data processing activities. Indeed, in these circumstances, the department concerned would likely constitute a separate or joint controller.[13]

The broad category of actors that may qualify as a 'recipient' under Article 4(9), coupled with the strict approach normally taken by supervisory authorities on transparency requirements,[14] may present practical difficulties for controllers, as they might find it challenging to collate all the information on recipients that should be provided to data subjects and keep it updated.[15]

2. Exclusion of some public authorities

The definition in Article 4(9) provides for an important exclusion: public authorities that receive personal data in the context of a particular inquiry in accordance with Union or Member State law are not to be regarded as recipients. In some countries, these public authorities are referred to as 'authorised third parties' (in French, 'tiers autorisés').[16] This concept primarily covers judicial, police and tax authorities, but it may extend to other entities or individuals entrusted with functions of a public nature, such as customs officers, social security officers and bailiffs.[17] Similarly, recital 31 GDPR mentions authorities 'such as tax and customs authorities, financial investigation units, independent administrative authorities, or financial market authorities responsible for the regulation and supervision of securities markets'.

A public authority does not qualify as a 'third party' only inasmuch as personal data are disclosed to it 'in accordance with a legal obligation for the exercise of [its] official mission' (recital 31). The use of the word 'inquiry' in Article 4(9) suggests that the authority's request for personal data may have a variety of purposes and does not need to be issued in the context of an enforcement action. Nonetheless, the request must be specific ('a particular inquiry') and have a legal basis ('in accordance with Union or Member State law'). As an example, subject to certain conditions, the French Tax Procedure Code expressly allows the French tax authorities to request disclosure of specified personal information in the context of a tax fraud investigation.[18] Similarly, Article 58(1)(e) GDPR allows national supervisory authorities 'to obtain from the controller or the processor, access to all personal data and to all information necessary for the performance of [their] tasks'. Consequently, the tax authorities and the supervisory authorities that receive personal data pursuant to the above-mentioned legal bases do not qualify as recipients.

Finally, Article 4(9) GDPR reminds public authorities requesting disclosure of personal data that they must comply with the data protection rules that apply to their activities. The rules applicable normally depend on the purposes of the processing. For instance, if the processing occurs for the purposes of the prevention, investigation, detection or prosecution of criminal offences, the rules of the LED (and its national implementing measures) apply (see Article 1(1) LED).

---

[13] For example, the Italian DPA has found that, where a department of a public body (e.g. the department of a Ministry) enjoys autonomous decision-making powers on data processing, it would normally qualify as a separate controller or joint controller of the body to which it belongs. See Italian Data Protection Authority 1997. See also the commentary on Art. 4(7) GDPR in this volume.
[14] WP29 2018, p. 37 (suggesting that privacy notices should normally name every recipient).
[15] See also GDPR Expert Group Report 2019, p. 6.   [16] See e.g. CNIL FAQ.   [17] Ibid.
[18] See French Tax Procedure Code. See further French Guidance on Tax Inspection 2013.

3. LED and EUDPR

Article 3(10) LED and Article 3(13) EUDPR both define 'recipient' identically to Article 4(9) GDPR. Thus, the term should be interpreted homogeneously in all these legal instruments (see too recital 5 EUDPR).

Select Bibliography

National legislation

Belgian Data Protection Law 1992: Wet tot bescherming van de persoonlijke levenssfeer ten opzichte van de verwerking van persoonsgegevens, van 8 december 1992; Loi relative à la protection de la vie privée à l'égard des traitements de données à caractère personnel, du 8 decembre 1992) (repealed).

Explanatory Memorandum Belgian Act 1998: Wetsontwerp tot omzetting van de Richtlijn 95/46/EG van 24 oktober 1995 van het Europees Parlement en de Raad betreffende de beschmerming van natuurlijke personen in verband met de verwerking van persoonsgegevens en betreffende het vrij verkeer van die gegevens – Memorie van toelichting; Project de loi transposant la Directive 95/46/CE du 24 octobre 1995 du Parlement européen et du Conseil relative à la protection des personnes physiques à l'égard du traitement des données à caractère personnel et à la libre circulation de ces données—Expose des motifs (20 May 1998).

French Data Protection Act 1978: French Act No. 78-17 of 6 January 1978 on Data Processing, Files and Individual Liberties (Loi n° 78-17 du 6 janvier 1978 relative à l'informatique, aux fichiers et aux libertés), as last amended by Law No. 2014-334 of 17 March 2014.

French Tax Procedure Code: French Tax Procedure Code (*Livre des procédures fiscales*).

Italian Data Protection Code 2003: Decreto legislativo 30 giugno 2003, n. 196: Codice in Materia di Protezione dei Dati Personali.

Italian Legislative Decree 2015: Decreto Legislativo 14 settembre 2015, n. 151: Disposizioni di razionalizzazione e semplificazione delle procedure e degli adempimenti a carico di cittadini e imprese e altre disposizioni in materia di rapporto di lavoro e pari opportunità, in attuazione della legge 10 dicembre 2014, n. 183.

Norwegian Personal Data Act 2000: Act of 14 April 2000 No. 31 relating to the processing of personal data (Personal Data Act) (lov 14. april 2000 nr. 31 om behandling av personopplysninger) (repealed).

Papers of data protection authorities

WP29 2018: Article 29 Working Party, 'Guidelines on transparency under Regulation 2016/679' (WP260 rev.01, 11 April 2018).

Italian Data Protection Authority 1997: Garante per la protezione dei dati personali, 'Privacy: chi sono i titolari e i responsabili del trattamento dei dati nelle imprese e nelle amministrazioni pubbliche' (11 December 1997).

Reports and recommendations

Council Report 1992: Council document 9388/92, 20 October 1992.
Council Report 1993: Council document 7695/93, 1 July 1993.
Council Report 2012: Proposal for a regulation of the European Parliament and of the Council on the protection of individuals with regard to the processing of personal data and on the free movement of such data (General Data Protection Regulation), 9897/1/12 REV 1, 24 May 2012.
Explanatory Report Convention 108 2018: Council of Europe, 'Explanatory Report to the Protocol Amending the Convention for the Protection of Individuals with Regard to the

Automatic Processing of Personal Data' (10 October 2018), available at https://rm.coe.int/cets-223-explanatory-report-to-the-protocol-amending-the-convention-fo/16808ac91a.

French Guidance on Tax Inspection 2013: French Directorate-General for Public Finances, 'Articulation de la législation sur le droit de communication et de la loi informatique et libertés' (18 October 2013), available at http://bofip.impots.gouv.fr/bofip/8879-PGP.html?identifiant=BOI-CF-COM-10-10-30-30-20131018.

GDPR Expert Group Report 2019: Multistakeholder Expert Group to support the application of Regulation (EU) 2016/679, 'Contribution from the Multistakeholder Expert Group to the stock-taking exercise of June 2019 on one year of GDPR application' (13 June 2019).

Others

CNIL FAQ: Commission nationale de l'informatique et des libertés, 'Besoin d'aide', available at https://www.cnil.fr/fr/cnil-direct/question/649.

Article 4(10). Third party

LUCA TOSONI

'third party' means a natural or legal person, public authority, agency or body other than the data subject, controller, processor and persons who, under the direct authority of the controller or processor, are authorised to process personal data;

Relevant Recitals

(47) The legitimate interests of a controller, including those of a controller to which the personal data may be disclosed, or of a third party, may provide a legal basis for processing, provided that the interests or the fundamental rights and freedoms of the data subject are not overriding, taking into consideration the reasonable expectations of data subjects based on their relationship with the controller. Such legitimate interest could exist for example where there is a relevant and appropriate relationship between the data subject and the controller in situations such as where the data subject is a client or in the service of the controller. At any rate the existence of a legitimate interest would need careful assessment including whether a data subject can reasonably expect at the time and in the context of the collection of the personal data that processing for that purpose may take place. The interests and fundamental rights of the data subject could in particular override the interest of the data controller where personal data are processed in circumstances where data subjects do not reasonably expect further processing. Given that it is for the legislator to provide by law for the legal basis for public authorities to process personal data, that legal basis should not apply to the processing by public authorities in the performance of their tasks. The processing of personal data strictly necessary for the purposes of preventing fraud also constitutes a legitimate interest of the data controller concerned. The processing of personal data for direct marketing purposes may be regarded as carried out for a legitimate interest.

(69) Where personal data might lawfully be processed because processing is necessary for the performance of a task carried out in the public interest or in the exercise of official authority vested in the controller, or on grounds of the legitimate interests of a controller or a third party, a data subject should, nevertheless, be entitled to object to the processing of any personal data relating to his or her particular situation. It should be for the controller to demonstrate that its compelling legitimate interest overrides the interests or the fundamental rights and freedoms of the data subject.

Closely Related Provisions

Article 4(1) (Definition of 'data subject'); Article 4(7) (Definition of 'controller'); Article 4(8) (Definition of 'processor'); Article 4(9) (Definition of 'recipient'); Article 6(1)(f) (Processing based on legitimate interests); Article 13(1)(d) (Information to be provided to data subjects); Article 14(2)(b) (Information to be provided to data subjects); Article 29 (Processing under the authority of the controller or processor)

Related Provisions in LED [Directive (EU) 2016/680]

Article 3(10) (Definition of 'recipient')

Related Provisions in EPD [Directive 2002/58/EC]

Article 2 (Reference to definitions in the DPD); Article 9 (Location data other than traffic data); Article 11 (Automatic call forwarding); Article 12 (see also recital 39)

Related Provisions in EUDPR [Regulation (EU) 2018/1725]

Article 3(14) (Definition of 'third party')

A. Rationale and Policy Underpinnings

The GDPR retains the concept of 'third party' that was found in Article 2(f) DPD. This concept was introduced in the DPD so that entities and individuals which/who have 'no connection with the processing' could be more clearly distinguished from the various 'recipients' of the processed data.[1] This rationale would seem to pertain also in relation to the GDPR.

B. Legal Background

1. EU legislation

Article 2(f) DPD defined 'third party' identically to Article 4(10) GDPR. The same definition may be found in Article 3(14) EUDPR, whereas the term 'third party' is absent in the LED, bar in the definition of 'recipient'.[2]

2. International instruments

The term 'third party' is not found in Convention 108, either as originally adopted or in its modernised form. The same applies with the OECD Privacy Guidelines (both original and revised versions) and the APEC Privacy Framework.

3. National Developments

Prior to adoption of the GDPR, several national data protection laws implementing the DPD did not include a definition of 'third party',[3] whereas some other Member States reproduced, almost *verbatim*, the definition of 'third party' of the DPD in their national laws.[4]

---

[1] See Council Report 1992, p. 8, fn. 22 (noting that 'the very diversity of [the category of "third parties"] was likely to lead to confusion and that the concept of "third party" needed to be more closely defined; ... therefore proposed a new definition making a clear distinction between "third parties" which had no connection with the processing and the various "recipients" of the processed data').

[2] See LED, Art. 3(10).

[3] See e.g. French Data Protection Act 1978, Chapter I; Norwegian Personal Data Act 2000, s. 2.

[4] See e.g. Belgian Data Protection Law 1992, Art. 1(6); Finnish Personal Data Law 1999, s. 3(6).

C. Analysis

The GDPR defines 'third party' in the negative. In essence, anyone who is *not* a (1) data subject,[5] (2) controller,[6] (3) processor[7] or (4) person, who, under the direct authority of the controller or processor, is authorised to process personal data, qualifies as a 'third party'.

The latter category of persons who are not third parties normally comprises the employees, agents and subcontractors of the controller or processor which/who process data for them under their direct authority. Prior to adoption of the GDPR, the status of these persons was formalised under some national data protection laws. For example, Article 4(1)(h) of the former Italian Data Protection Code defined as 'persons in charge of the processing' (in Italian, 'incaricati') 'the natural persons who have been authorised by the data controller or processor to carry out processing operations'.[8] Article 30 of the Code required that the 'persons in charge of the processing' be formally appointed in writing by the controller or processor.[9]

In contrast, individuals working for an organisation different from that of the controller or processor, even if it belongs to the same corporate group, would generally qualify as third parties.[10]

Select Bibliography

EU legislation

DPD Amended Proposal 1992: Amended Proposal for a Council Directive on the Protection of Individuals with Regard to the Processing of Personal Data and on the Free Movement of Such Data, COM(92) 422 final—SYN 287, 15 October 1992.

National legislation

Belgian Data Protection Law 1992: Wet tot bescherming van de persoonlijke levenssfeer ten opzichte van de verwerking van persoonsgegevens, van 8 december 1992; Loi relative à la protection de la vie privée à l'égard des traitements de données à caractère personnel, du 8 decembre 1992) (repealed).

Finnish Personal Data Law 1999: Finnish Law on Personal Data 523/1999 (Henkilötietolaki No. 523/1999) (repealed).

---

[5] See the commentary on Art. 4(1) GDPR in this volume.
[6] See the commentary on Art. 4(7) GDPR in this volume.
[7] See the commentary on Art. 4(8) GDPR in this volume.
[8] See the Italian Data Protection Code 2003, as last amended by Italian Legislative Decree 2015.
[9] Ibid.
[10] See DPD Amended Proposal 1992, p. 11, noting that 'third parties do not include the data subject, the controller, or any person authorised to process the data under the controller's direct authority or on his behalf, as is the case with the processor. Thus, persons working for another organisation, even if it belongs to the same group or holding company, will generally be third parties. On the other hand, branches of a bank processing customers' accounts under the direct authority of their headquarters would not be third parties. The same would apply to the employees of insurance companies; in the case of insurance brokers, on the other hand, the position may vary from case to case'. It bears emphasis that it was the DPD Amended Proposal which first introduced the definition of 'third party'—now included in Art. 4(10) GDPR, and previously included in Art. 2(f) DPD. Thus, its explanation of the term would seem to remain relevant under the GDPR.

French Data Protection Act 1978: Act No. 78-17 of 6 January 1978 on Data Processing, Files and Individual Liberties (Loi n° 78-17 du 6 janvier 1978 relative à l'informatique, aux fichiers et aux libertés), as last amended by Law No. 2014-334 of 17 March 2014.

Italian Data Protection Code 2003: Decreto legislativo 30 giugno 2003, n. 196: Codice in Materia di Protezione dei Dati Personali.

Italian Legislative Decree 2015: Decreto Legislativo 14 settembre 2015, n. 151: Disposizioni di razionalizzazione e semplificazione delle procedure e degli adempimenti a carico di cittadini e imprese e altre disposizioni in materia di rapporto di lavoro e pari opportunità, in attuazione della legge 10 dicembre 2014, n. 183.

Norwegian Personal Data Act 2000: Act of 14 April 2000 No. 31 relating to the processing of personal data (Personal Data Act) (lov 14. april 2000 nr. 31 om behandling av personopplysninger) (repealed).

Reports and recommendations

Council Report 1992: Council document 9388/92, 20 October 1992.

Article 4(11). Consent

LEE A. BYGRAVE   LUCA TOSONI

'consent' of the data subject means any freely given, specific, informed and unambiguous indication of the data subject's wishes by which he or she, by a statement or by a clear affirmative action, signifies agreement to the processing of personal data relating to him or her;

Relevant Recitals

(32) Consent should be given by a clear affirmative act establishing a freely given, specific, informed and unambiguous indication of the data subject's agreement to the processing of personal data relating to him or her, such as by a written statement, including by electronic means, or an oral statement. This could include ticking a box when visiting an internet website, choosing technical settings for information society services or another statement or conduct which clearly indicates in this context the data subject's acceptance of the proposed processing of his or her personal data. Silence, pre-ticked boxes or inactivity should not therefore constitute consent. Consent should cover all processing activities carried out for the same purpose or purposes. When the processing has multiple purposes, consent should be given for all of them. If the data subject's consent is to be given following a request by electronic means, the request must be clear, concise and not unnecessarily disruptive to the use of the service for which it is provided.

(33) It is often not possible to fully identify the purpose of personal data processing for scientific research purposes at the time of data collection. Therefore, data subjects should be allowed to give their consent to certain areas of scientific research when in keeping with recognised ethical standards for scientific research. Data subjects should have the opportunity to give their consent only to certain areas of research or parts of research projects to the extent allowed by the intended purpose.

(42) Where processing is based on the data subject's consent, the controller should be able to demonstrate that the data subject has given consent to the processing operation. In particular in the context of a written declaration on another matter, safeguards should ensure that the data subject is aware of the fact that and the extent to which consent is given. In accordance with Council Directive 93/13/EEC a declaration of consent pre-formulated by the controller should be provided in an intelligible and easily accessible form, using clear and plain language and it should not contain unfair terms. For consent to be informed, the data subject should be aware at least of the identity of the controller and the purposes of the processing for which the personal data are intended. Consent should not be regarded as freely given if the data subject has no genuine or free choice or is unable to refuse or withdraw consent without detriment.

(43) In order to ensure that consent is freely given, consent should not provide a valid legal ground for the processing of personal data in a specific case where there is a clear imbalance between the data subject and the controller, in particular where the controller is a public authority and it is therefore unlikely that consent was freely given in all the circumstances of that specific situation. Consent is presumed not to be freely given if it does not allow separate consent to be given to different personal data processing operations despite it being appropriate in the individual case, or if

the performance of a contract, including the provision of a service, is dependent on the consent despite such consent not being necessary for such performance.

(51) Personal data which are, by their nature, particularly sensitive in relation to fundamental rights and freedoms merit specific protection as the context of their processing could create significant risks to the fundamental rights and freedoms. Those personal data should include personal data revealing racial or ethnic origin, whereby the use of the term 'racial origin' in this Regulation does not imply an acceptance by the Union of theories which attempt to determine the existence of separate human races. The processing of photographs should not systematically be considered to be processing of special categories of personal data as they are covered by the definition of biometric data only when processed through a specific technical means allowing the unique identification or authentication of a natural person. Such personal data should not be processed, unless processing is allowed in specific cases set out in this Regulation, taking into account that Member States law may lay down specific provisions on data protection in order to adapt the application of the rules of this Regulation for compliance with a legal obligation or for the performance of a task carried out in the public interest or in the exercise of official authority vested in the controller. In addition to the specific requirements for such processing, the general principles and other rules of this Regulation should apply, in particular as regards the conditions for lawful processing. Derogations from the general prohibition for processing such special categories of personal data should be explicitly provided, inter alia, where the data subject gives his or her explicit consent or in respect of specific needs in particular where the processing is carried out in the course of legitimate activities by certain associations or foundations the purpose of which is to permit the exercise of fundamental freedoms.

Closely Related Provisions

Article 5 (Principles relating to processing of personal data) (see also recitals 33, 39 and 50); Article 6(1)(a) (Lawfulness of processing on basis of consent) (see too recital 40); Article 7 (Conditions for consent) (see also recital 42); Article 8 (Conditions applicable to child's consent in relation to information society services) (see too recital 38); Article 9(2)(a) (Processing of special categories of personal data on basis of consent) (see too recital 51); Article 13 (Information to be provided where personal data are collected from the data subject) (see too recitals 60–62); Article 14 (Information to be provided where personal data have not been obtained from the data subject); Article 17 (Right to erasure) (see too recital 65); Article 20 (Right to data portability) (see too recital 68); Article 22 (Automated individual decision-making, including profiling) (see too recital 71); Article 49(1)(a) (Transfer of personal data to third country or international organisation on basis of consent) (see too recitals 111–112)

Related Provisions in LED [Directive (EU) 2016/680]

Recitals 35 and 37

Related Provisions in EPD [Directive 2002/58/EC]

Article 2(f) (Definition of 'consent') (see too recital 17)

Related Provisions in EUDPR [Regulation (EU) 2018/1725]

Article 3(15) (Definition of 'consent') (see too recitals 19 and 26); Article 4 (Principles relating to processing of personal data) (see also recitals 20 and 22); Article 5(1)(d) (Lawfulness of processing on basis of consent) (see too recital 26); Article 7 (Conditions for consent) (see also recital 26); Article 8 (Conditions applicable to child's consent in relation to information society services) (see too recital 27); Article 10(2)(a) (Processing of special categories of personal data on basis of consent) (see too recital 29); Article 15 (Information to be provided where personal data are collected from the data subject) (see too recitals 35–36); Article 16 (Information to be provided where personal data have not been obtained from the data subject); Article 19 (Right to erasure) (see also recital 38); Article 22 (Right to data portability) (see too recital 41); Article 24 (Automated individual decision-making, including profiling) (see too recital 43); Article 50(1)(a) (Transfer of personal data to third country or international organisation on basis of consent) (see too recital 68)

Relevant Case Law

CJEU

Joined Cases C-397/01 to C-403/01, *Bernhard Pfeiffer, Wilhelm Roith, Albert Süß, Michael Winter, Klaus Nestvogel, Roswitha Zeller and Matthias Döbele v Deutsches Rotes Kreuz, Kreisverband Waldshut eV*, judgment of 5 October 2004 (Grand Chamber) (ECLI:EU:C:2004:584).

Case C-543/09, *Deutsche Telekom AG v Bundesrepublik Deutschland*, judgment of 5 May 2011 (ECLI:EU:C:2011:279).

Opinion of Advocate General Szpunar in Case C-673/17, *Planet49 GmbH v Bundesverband der Verbraucherzentralen und Verbraucherverbände – Verbraucherzentrale Bundesverband e.V.*, delivered on 21 March 2019 (ECLI:EU:C:2019:246).

Case C-40/17, *Fashion ID GmbH & Co. KG v Verbraucherzentrale NRW e.V.*, judgment of 29 July 2019 (ECLI:EU:C:2019:629).

Case C-61/19, *Orange Romania SA v Autoritatea Națională de Supraveghere a Prelucrării Datelor cu Caracter Personal* (pending).

A. Rationale and Policy Underpinnings

Consent by persons to the processing of data relating to them lies at the heart of the ideals of personal autonomy and privacy, particularly when these are conceived in terms of 'informational self-determination'.[1] Rules requiring data subject consent also make up and manifest a general core principle of data protection law, namely the principle of data subject influence, which holds that individuals should be able to participate in, and have a measure of influence over, the processing of data on them by others.[2]

Data subject consent is singled out for special mention in Article 8(2) CFR as a legitimate basis for processing of personal data. It also figures implicitly in Article 7 CFR, along with Article 8 ECHR, as the absence of consent tends to play a crucial role in establishing interference with the rights laid down in these provisions—interference that requires proper justification if it is not to amount to violation of the rights concerned.[3]

In line with Article 8(2) CFR, the GDPR lays down data subject consent as one of several alternative preconditions for processing of personal data generally

---

[1] See e.g. Bygrave 2002, pp. 150, 154.   [2] See e.g. Bygrave 2014, pp. 158 et seq.
[3] See particularly the criteria for justification laid out in Art. 8(2) ECHR, as elaborated by ECtHR jurisprudence. For an overview, see Bygrave 2014, pp. 86 et seq.

Bygrave/Tosoni

(Article 6(1)(a)),[4] processing of especially sensitive data (Article 9(2)(a)),[5] fully automated decision-making and profiling (Article 22(2)),[6] and transfer of personal data to third countries and international organisations (Article 49(1)(a)).[7] In other words, data subject consent arises as an issue in a multiplicity of data-processing contexts. This warrants its definition in Article 4(11) GDPR.

At the same time, controversy and uncertainty have surrounded the nature of, and requirements for, valid data subject consent, particularly pursuant to the DPD—as elaborated further below.[8] Points of debate in this respect have concerned, inter alia, the amount of information required in order for consent to be 'informed', whether consent may be presumed on the basis of the data subject's failure to object to processing (i.e. 'passive consent'), and what precisely a requirement of 'explicit' consent entails. The drafters of the GDPR were very much aware of these issues and the need to resolve them. The Commission, for instance, declared its intention of 'clarifying and strengthening the rules on consent' as part of the reform process that led to adoption of the GDPR[9]—an intention that was shared by the Parliament and Council. Hence, the definition of consent in Article 4(11) GDPR should also be seen in light of this intention.

B. Legal Background

1. EU legislation

Article 2(h) DPD defined 'the data subject's consent' as 'any freely given specific and informed indication of his wishes by which the data subject signifies his agreement to personal data relating to him being processed'. This is basically in line with the definition given in Article 4(11) GDPR, although there are some differences. One difference concerns the need for consent to be unambiguous, a qualification that was expressly required only in two instances under the DPD: first, when consent was the ground for legitimate processing of personal data (Article 7(a) DPD); and, secondly, when consent was required to permit transfers of data to third countries (Article 26(1) DPD).[10] Another difference is that the DPD's definition of consent lacked the reference to 'by a statement or by a clear affirmative action' that is part of Article 4(11) GDPR.

As for the EPD, its Article 2(f) makes clear that the term 'consent' in the EPD corresponds to the data subject's consent in the DPD.[11] Given that Article 94(2) GDPR

---

[4] See further the commentary on Art. 6 in this volume.
[5] See further the commentary on Art. 9 in this volume.
[6] See further the commentary on Art. 22 in this volume.
[7] See further the commentary on Art. 49 in this volume.
[8] See e.g. Kosta 2013; Bygrave and Schartum 2009.   [9] EC Communication 2010, p. 9.
[10] Advocate General Szpunar noted that the definition in Art. 4(11) GDPR 'is stricter than that of Article 2(h) of Directive 95/46 in that it requires an unambiguous indication of the data subject's wishes and a clear affirmative action signifying agreement to the processing of personal data': see Case C-673/17, *Planet49* (AG Opinion), para. 70.
[11] Rec. 17 EPD further clarifies that the use of the term 'consent' in the EPD is based on the definition provided by the DPD: '[f]or the purposes of this Directive, consent of a user or subscriber, regardless of whether the latter is a natural or a legal person, should have the same meaning as the data subject's consent as defined and further specified in Directive 95/46/EC. Consent may be given by any appropriate method enabling a freely given specific and informed indication of the user's wishes, including by ticking a box when visiting an Internet website'.

states that references to the DPD, subsequent to its repeal, are to be construed as references to the GDPR,[12] the notion of consent in the EPD is to be understood as based on Article 4(11) GDPR. As the WP29 noted, this means that 'the GDPR conditions for obtaining valid consent are applicable in situations falling within the scope of the e-Privacy Directive'.[13]

Consent does not constitute a valid legal basis for processing of personal data under the LED,[14] recital 35 of which makes clear that 'the consent of the data subject, as defined in Regulation (EU) 2016/679, should not provide a legal ground for processing personal data by competent authorities' for the purposes of preventing, investigating, detecting or prosecuting criminal offences. Such exclusion is justified on the following grounds: '[w]here the data subject is required to comply with a legal obligation, the data subject has no genuine and free choice, so that the reaction of the data subject could not be considered to be a freely given indication of his or her wishes'.[15] Furthermore, recital 37 LED states that 'the consent of the data subject should not provide in itself a legal ground for processing ... sensitive personal data by competent authorities'.

Despite the above, Member States remain free to provide under their domestic law that the data subject may agree to the processing of his or her personal data for the above law enforcement purposes, such as for DNA tests in criminal investigations or the monitoring of his or her location with electronic tags for the execution of criminal penalties.[16]

2. International instruments

Convention 108 as originally adopted does not define 'consent'; indeed, the term is absent from its provisions. The Modernised Convention also does not provide a direct definition of 'consent' but stipulates that 'data processing can be carried out on the basis of the free, specific, informed and unambiguous consent of the data subject or of some other legitimate basis laid down by law' (Article 5(2)). Elaboration of the term 'consent' in the Explanatory Report to the Modernised Convention makes clear that the term has essentially the same meaning as it has for the purposes of the GDPR:

The data subject's consent must be freely given, specific, informed and unambiguous. Such consent must represent the free expression of an intentional choice, given either by a statement (which can be written, including by electronic means, or oral) or by a clear affirmative action and which clearly indicates in this specific context the acceptance of the proposed processing of personal data. Mere silence, inactivity or pre-validated forms or boxes should not, therefore, constitute consent. Consent should cover all processing activities carried out for the same purpose or purposes (in the case of multiple purposes, consent should be given for each different purpose). There may be cases with different consent decisions (e.g. where the nature of the data is different even if the purpose is the same—such as health data versus location data: in such cases the data subject may consent to the processing of his or her location data but not to the processing of the health data). The data subject must be informed of the implications of his or her decision (what the fact of consenting entails and the extent to which consent is given). No undue influence or pressure (which can be of an economic or other nature) whether direct or indirect, may be exercised on the data subject and consent should not be regarded as freely given where the data subject has no genuine or free choice or is unable to refuse or withdraw consent without prejudice.[17]

---

[12] See too Case C-673/17, *Planet49* (AG Opinion), para. 50.
[13] WP29 2018, p. 4. See further Case C-673/17, *Planet49* (AG Opinion), paras. 76–81.
[14] Art. 8 LED.   [15] See rec. 35 LED.   [16] Ibid.
[17] Explanatory Report Convention 108 2018, para. 42.

Apart from the reference in Article 5(2) to consent as a basis for processing of personal data generally, the Modernised Convention mentions consent in two other contexts: (i) transfer of personal data to a State or international organisation which is not party to the Convention and which does not provide an 'appropriate level' of data protection—such transfer may occur on the basis of the data subject's 'explicit, specific and free consent, after being informed of risks arising in the absence of appropriate safeguards' (Article 14(4)(a)); and (ii) provision of personal data from a supervisory authority to another—one (alternative) precondition for such provision is 'where the data subject concerned has given explicit, specific, free and informed consent' to it (Article 17(2)).

Neither the OECD Privacy Guidelines (both original and revised versions) nor the APEC Privacy Framework define 'consent', although both make limited use of the concept.[18]

3. National developments

During the lifespan of the DPD, considerable diversity and divergence regarding the conditions for consent reigned at the national level. The European Commission observed in 2010 that these conditions 'are currently interpreted differently in Member States, ranging from a general requirement of written consent to the acceptance of implicit consent'.[19]

4. Case law

The CJEU has yet to tackle directly the definition of 'consent' in the GDPR. However, in its judgment in *Deutsche Telekom*,[20] the Court considered the scope of consent under Article 12(2) EPD,[21] which makes the publication, in printed or electronic directories, of personal data concerning subscribers to electronic communications services (e.g. telephony and electronic mail services) conditional on the consent of those subscribers. Indeed, under the Directive, subscribers are to be free to decide whether their personal data are to be included in a public directory and, if so, which personal data.[22] Part of the dispute in the case concerned whether or not new consent was necessary to enable subscriber data entered into a directory to be passed on to a third-party undertaking (Deutsche Telekom), for the purpose of being included in a new public directory maintained by that undertaking, after the subscriber had consented to being registered in the first directory and having been informed, when giving that initial consent, of the possibility of such data transfer. The Court found that new consent was not necessary in such circumstances.[23]

---

[18] OECD Privacy Guidelines 2013; APEC Privacy Framework.
[19] EC Communication 2010, p. 8.   [20] Case C-543/09, *Deutsche Telekom*.
[21] As mentioned above, the term 'consent' in the EPD corresponds to 'the data subject's consent' in the DPD. See further Case C-543/09, *Deutsche Telekom*, para. 58.
[22] Case C-543/09, *Deutsche Telekom*, paras. 54–55.
[23] Ibid., para. 65: 'where a subscriber has been informed by the undertaking which assigned him a telephone number of the possibility that his personal data may be passed to a third-party undertaking, such as Deutsche Telekom, with a view to being published in a public directory, and where he has consented to the publication of those data in such a directory (in the present case, Deutsche Telekom's directory), renewed consent is not needed from the subscriber for the passing of those same data to another undertaking which intends to publish a printed or electronic public directory, or to make such directories available for consultation through directory enquiry services, if it is guaranteed that the data in question will not be used for purposes other than those for which the data were collected with a view to their first publication. The consent given under Article 12(2) of the Directive on privacy and electronic communications, by a subscriber who has been duly informed, to the

Furthermore, the CJEU has received a request for a preliminary ruling in the *Planet49* case,[24] which concerns whether a company's use of a pre-ticked checkbox for obtaining consent to the installation and use of cookies[25] is compatible with the requirements for valid consent under Articles 5(3) and 2(f) EPD, in conjunction with Article 2(h) DPD and Article 6(1)(a) GDPR, where the consent of the internet user is presumed, unless he or she takes steps to unselect the pre-ticked checkbox. A further question for the Court concerns the type of information that the service provider must give to the user in accordance with Article 5(3) EPD—in particular, whether it must include the duration of the operation of the cookies that are used and the extent to which third parties are given access to the cookies. According to Advocate General Szpunar, the first question should be answered in the negative: there is no valid consent in a situation such as that described above, where the use of cookies is permitted by way of a pre-ticked checkbox which the user must deselect to refuse his consent—this is the case both under the DPD and the GDPR.[26] As for the second question, the Advocate General's view is that the obligation to provide clear and comprehensive information set forth in Article 5(3) EPD implies that the data subject be informed, inter alia, of the duration of the operation of the cookies and on whether third parties are given access to the cookies.[27] The Court has yet to rule on this case, but it is likely to take a similar line.

The CJEU has also been asked—in the *Orange Romania* case— to clarify what are the conditions that must be fulfilled in order for consent to be considered specific, informed and freely given under Article 2(h) DPD.[28] Although the case concerns the definition of 'consent' in the DPD, it will undoubtedly also have an impact on the interpretation of the equivalent definition in the GDPR.

Finally, it is worth noting that the CJEU has ruled on the notion of consent pursuant to legislation concerned with worker safety[29]—an area not unrelated to data protection law. In doing so, the Court has upheld a strict view of what constitutes valid consent by employees to work practices that deviate from EU legislative standards.[30]

---

publication of his personal data in a public directory relates to the purpose of that publication and thus extends to any subsequent processing of those data by third-party undertakings active in the market for publicly available directory enquiry services and directories, provided that such processing pursues that same purpose'.

[24] Case C-673/17, *Planet49*.

[25] As noted by Advocate General Szpunar, '[a] cookie is a way of collecting information generated by a website and saved by an internet user's browser. It is a small piece of data or text file, usually less than one Kbyte in size, that a website asks an internet user's browser to store on the local hard disk of the user's computer or mobile device. A cookie allows the website to "remember" the user's actions or preferences over time. Most web browsers support cookies, but users can set their browsers to decline them. They can also delete them whenever they like. Indeed, many users set their cookie settings in their browsers to automatically delete cookies by default when the browser window is closed. That said, empirical evidence overwhelmingly demonstrates that people rarely change default settings, a phenomenon which has been coined "default inertia"'. See Case C-673/17, *Planet49* (AG Opinion), paras. 36–37.

[26] Ibid., paras. 84–93.   [27] Ibid., paras. 111–21.

[28] Case C-61/19, *Orange Romania* (pending).   [29] Council Directive 93/104/EC.

[30] Joined Cases C-397/01 to C-403/01, *Pfeiffer*, para. 82. Noting that the objective of Directive 93/104/EC is to guarantee workers' health and safety, the CJEU ruled that any derogation from the minimum requirements laid down by the Directive 'must therefore be accompanied by all the safeguards necessary to ensure that, if the worker concerned is encouraged to relinquish a social right which has been directly conferred on him by the directive, he must do so freely and with full knowledge of all the facts. Those requirements are all the more important given that the worker must be regarded as the weaker party to the employment contract and it is therefore necessary to prevent the employer being in a position to disregard the intentions of the other party to the contract or to impose on that party a restriction of his rights without him having expressly given his consent in that regard'.

C. Analysis

1. General interpretation

From the provisions of Article 4(11) GDPR we may discern four key criteria for valid data subject consent: such consent must be (1) freely given, (2) specific, (3) informed and (4) unambiguous. The fact that these criteria are cumulative creates a high threshold for valid consent. Also contributing to this high threshold is the data protection authorities' tendency to interpret each of the criteria strictly. In the words of the WP29, 'inviting people to accept a data processing operation should be subject to rigorous requirements, since it concerns the fundamental rights of data subjects and the controller wishes to engage in a processing operation that would be unlawful without the data subject's consent'.[31] This reasoning is slightly problematic as it is not always the case that a processing operation would be unlawful but for consent—there may sometimes be an alternative lawful basis for the processing[32]—but it does evidence the stringency with which data protection authorities view the preconditions for valid consent.

This stringency made itself felt during the drafting of the GDPR, and is reflected not just in Article 4(11) but in other provisions of the Regulation as well, especially Article 7 and recital 43 both of which take up many of the recommendations made by WP29 in its Opinion 15/2011 on the definition of consent.[33] It bears emphasis, though, that the definition of consent in the GDPR is essentially similar to the DPD's definition of consent.[34] The GDPR has not radically ramped up the requirements for valid consent but rather introduced greater clarity around these requirements.[35] Nonetheless, a common (mis)perception that the consent requirements have become substantially more stringent under the GDPR has reportedly led many organisations to consider switching the legal basis of their processing operations to another legal ground (e.g. performance of a contract, legitimate interest), where possible.[36]

The definition in Article 4(11) must be read in conjunction with other GDPR provisions that expressly lay down conditions regarding the exercise of valid consent, notably Article 7 (for processing generally) and Article 8 (in relation to children). Moreover, there are provisions that implicitly govern the exercise of consent, notably Articles 5(1)(b) and 6(1)(a) (both of which require specification of the purposes of data processing) and Articles 13 and 14 (both of which set out an obligation to provide information to data subjects).[37]

---

[31] WP29 2018, p. 3. See also WP29 2011, p. 8.

[32] Note, though that the EDPB's view is that 'as explained in the Guidelines on consent of the Working Party 29, consent will not be the appropriate legal basis in most cases, and other legal bases than consent must be relied upon': see EDPB 2019, p. 6.

[33] WP29 2011.   [34] See further WP29 2018, p. 4.

[35] This seems to be the position also of Advocate General Szpunar in *Planet49*, as he noted that the GDPR essentially codified the key principles on the giving of consent that applied under the DPD. See Case C-673/17, *Planet49* (AG Opinion), paras., 68, 73, 75 and 97.

[36] See GDPR Expert Group Report 2019, pp. 9–11 (noting in particular that '[m]any organisations indicate that they would now choose where possible to rely on another legal basis [than consent] for their processing ... partially because of the additional requirements for a valid consent').

[37] In this regard, in *Planet49*, Advocate General Szpunar noted that '[t]he obligation to inform is linked to consent in that there must always be information before there can be consent'. See Case C-673/17, *Planet49* (AG Opinion), para. 112.

2. Criterion of freely given

The criterion of 'freely given' consent necessitates that the data subject enjoys a high degree of autonomy when choosing whether or not to give consent. In the words of the WP29, 'if the data subject has no real choice, feels compelled to consent or will endure negative consequences if they do not consent, then consent will not be valid'.[38] The data subject's inability to withdraw consent without incurring detriment to her-/himself does not satisfy the criterion.[39]

It will be difficult to meet the criterion where the data subject is in a position of weakness and dependence vis-à-vis the controller. Recital 43 GDPR refers to this sort of relationship in terms of a 'clear imbalance between the data subject and the controller'. The formulation is somewhat vague as it does not expressly highlight the basic nature of the imbalance, but the context in which it appears makes obvious that the imbalance at issue is one of power. Recital 43 indicates that this imbalance will typically pertain when the controller is a public authority, but not always ('it is ... *unlikely* that consent was freely given in all the circumstances of that specific situation': emphasis added).[40] Hence, there may be exceptional circumstances when a public authority may lawfully process personal data on the basis of consent.[41]

Another relationship usually characterised by a clear power imbalance is that between employer and employee. Thus, in the words of the WP29, 'employees can only give free consent in exceptional circumstances, when it will have no adverse consequences at all whether or not they give consent'.[42]

Yet another example where power imbalance typically pertains is in respect of medical research in the context of clinical trials. The EDPB has stated that consent by participants in clinical trials will not be freely given when 'a participant is not in good health conditions, when participants belong to an economically or socially disadvantaged group or in any situation of institutional or hierarchical dependency'.[43]

Furthermore, the criterion will typically not be satisfied in situations of 'bundled' or 'tied' consent in which consent is tethered to the controller's performance of a contract or to the controller's provision of services, and the processing of the data for which consent is sought is not necessary for the contractual performance or service provision.[44] Article 7(4) GDPR indicates that these sorts of situations demand careful scrutiny, while recital 43 specifies that they create a presumption that consent is not freely given. In *Planet49*, Advocate General Szpunar elaborated on the 'prohibition on bundling' by stating:

---

[38] WP29 2018, pp. 5 and 7: 'consent can only be valid if the data subject is able to exercise a real choice, and there is no risk of deception, intimidation, coercion or significant negative consequences (e.g. substantial extra costs) if he/she does not consent. Consent will not be free in cases where there is any element of compulsion, pressure or inability to exercise free will'.

[39] Ibid., p. 5; rec. 42 GDPR.   [40] See too rec. 35 LED.

[41] For examples, see WP29 2018, pp. 6–7. See too rec. 35 LED.

[42] WP29 2018, p. 7. See too WP29 2017, pp. 6–7; Joined Cases C-397/01 to C-403/01, *Pfeiffer* in which the CJEU observed that 'the worker must be regarded as the weaker party to the employment contract' (para. 82) but nonetheless permitted the employees to agree to derogations from EU legislative standards on working hours by giving their individual express and informed consent.

[43] EDPB 2019, p. 6. However, it would seem logical to understand the EDPB's reference to 'not ... good health conditions' as covering only those conditions capable of affecting the free will of a participant. Otherwise, relying on consent would essentially never be a viable option in a clinical trial context, as clinical trials typically involve people who are not in good health conditions.

[44] See further WP29 2018, pp. 8–10. See also the commentary on Art. 7 in this volume.

For consent to be 'freely given' and 'informed', it must ... be ... separate. The activity a user pursues on the internet (reading a webpage, participating in a lottery, watching a video, etc.) and the giving of consent cannot form part of the same act. In particular, from the perspective of the user, the giving of consent cannot appear to be of an ancillary nature to the participation in [a certain activity or service]. Both actions must, optically in particular, be presented on an equal footing. As a consequence, it appears to me doubtful that a bundle of expressions of intention, which would include the giving of consent, would be in conformity with the notion of consent under Directive 95/46.[45]

However, the Advocate General warned that 'the prohibition on bundling is not absolute in nature', as the terms 'utmost account shall be taken of' in Article 7(4) signify: it must be assessed on a case-by-case basis whether the consent to the processing of personal data is actually necessary for the performance of the relevant contract.[46]

3. Specificity criterion

The requirement that consent be 'specific' concerns the need to link the provision of consent to a particular data processing operation.[47] Part and parcel of this tethering involves the controller clearly defining the parameters of the activity to which the data subject is asked to consent, and then communicating these parameters to the data subject. The latter process helps to make the consent suitably 'informed'. Thus, there is a close relationship between the criterion of specificity and that of being informed.

As intimated above, Articles 5(1)(b) and 6(1)(a) GDPR demand a fairly clear delineation of the purposes of data processing,[48] thus aiding in the fulfilment of the specificity criterion. As noted by the WP29, 'consent must be specific to the purpose',[49] and 'a purpose that is vague or general ... will ... usually not meet the criteria [*sic*] of being "specific"'.[50] At the same time, recital 32 GDPR indicates that one consent may cover multiple processing operations if these are undertaken for the same purpose(s). In respect of consent to scientific research, recital 33 GDPR relaxes the specificity criterion, as it refers to the possibility that consent be given to 'certain areas of scientific research', though the degree of this relaxation will likely vary according to the particular nature of the research. Where, for example, the research involves processing of the special categories of data listed in Article 9 GDPR, 'applying the flexible approach of Recital 33 will be subject to a stricter interpretation and requires a high degree of scrutiny'.[51]

4. Criterion of being informed

The requirement that consent be 'informed' involves ensuring that the data subject is provided with advance knowledge of the parameters of the data processing operation to

---

[45] Case C-673/17, *Planet49* (AG Opinion), para. 66. The Advocate General stated that the same is equally valid under the GDPR: see para. 68.

[46] Ibid., paras. 98–99. The Advocate General suggested that this would be the case with regard to Planet49's activities: 'it is the providing of personal data which constitutes the main obligation of the user in order to participate in the lottery. In such a situation it appears to me that the processing of this personal data *is* necessary for the participation in the lottery': para. 99.

[47] See also DPD Amended Proposal 1992, p. 12 (stating that '[t]he data subject's consent must be "specific", meaning that it must relate to a particular data processing operation concerning the data subject carried out by a particular controller and for particular purposes').

[48] See too rec. 39 GDPR.   [49] WP29 2018, p. 12.   [50] WP29 2013, p. 16.

[51] WP29 2018, p. 28.

which she/he is to consent.[52] The requirement is buttressed by the overarching principle of transparency laid down in Article 5(1)(a) GDPR,[53] together with the general requirements on the provision of information to data subjects as laid down in Articles 7(3) and 12–14 GDPR. Recital 42 GDPR states that '[f]or consent to be informed, the data subject should be aware at least of the identity of the controller and the purposes of the processing for which the personal data are intended'. However, the WP29 elaborated a longer list of what it considered to be the 'minimum content requirements' for consent to be 'informed', adding elements such as the kinds of data processed, the existence of the right to withdraw consent and the identities or categories of the data recipients.[54]

Also relevant is Article 49(1)(a) GDPR which permits personal data to be transferred to a third country or international organisation, in the absence of an adequacy decision or of appropriate safeguards, where the data subject 'has explicitly consented to the proposed transfer, after having been informed of the possible risks of such transfers for the data subject due to the absence of an adequacy decision and appropriate safeguards'.[55]

In *Planet49*, Advocate General Szpunar described the obligation to fully inform the data subject before seeking her/his consent in an online context as follows:

it must be made crystal-clear to a user whether the activity he pursues on the internet is contingent upon the giving of consent. A user must be in a position to assess to what extent he is prepared to give his data in order to pursue his activity on the internet. There must be no room for any ambiguity whatsoever. A user must know whether and, if so, to what extent his giving of consent has a bearing on the pursuit of his activity on the internet.[56]

5. Criterion of non-ambiguity

The criterion of non-ambiguity is elaborated on in recital 32 GDPR, which refers to the need for consent to be provided 'by a clear affirmative act establishing a ... unambiguous indication of the data subject's agreement ... such as by a written statement, including by electronic means, or an oral statement'. The recital goes on to exemplify this requirement by reference to 'ticking a box when visiting an internet website, choosing technical settings for information society services or another statement or conduct which clearly indicates in this context the data subject's acceptance of the proposed processing'. It makes

---

[52] See Case C-40/17, *Fashion ID*, paras. 102–106 (interpreting the consent and transparency requirements under the DPD). See also, by analogy, Joined Cases C-397/01 to C-403/01, *Pfeiffer*, para. 82.

[53] See too rec. 39 GDPR.

[54] See further WP29 2018, p. 13. See also DPD Amended Proposal 1992, p. 11 (stating that for consent to be informed under the DPD '[t]he controller must supply the data subject with the information he needs, such as the name and address of the controller and of his representative if any ... , the purpose of the processing, the data recorded, etc.').

[55] According to the EDPB guidance, 'the general requirement of "informed" consent, requires, in the case of consent as a lawful basis pursuant to Article 6(1)(a) for a data transfer, that the data subject is properly informed in advance of the specific circumstances of the transfer (i.e. the data controller's identity, the purpose of the transfer, the type of data, the existence of the right to withdraw consent, the identity or the categories of recipients)'. Moreover, where personal data are transferred to a third country under Art. 49(1)(a) GDPR, the data subject must also be informed of 'the specific risks resulting from the fact that their data will be transferred to a country that does not provide adequate protection and that no adequate safeguards aimed at providing protection for the data are being implemented'. Notice of risks 'should include for example information that in the third country there might not be a supervisory authority and/or data processing principles and/or data subject rights might not be provided for in the third country'. See EDPB 2018, pp. 7–8.

[56] Case C-673/17, *Planet49* (AG Opinion), para. 67.

clear that passive consent in the form of 'silence, pre-ticked boxes or inactivity' is not acceptable.[57]

It is arguable that the drafters of Article 4(11) and recital 32 did not need to mention that consent must be 'unambiguous', in particular when these provisions also require that consent be expressed 'by a clear affirmative action'. As Kosta writes, '[a] consent given "ambiguously" would amount to an unclear indication of the wishes of the data subject ... and would not qualify as valid consent'.[58] The Commission's proposal for the GDPR used the criterion 'explicit' rather than 'unambiguous' in the definition of consent,[59] justifying this as a measure 'to avoid confusing parallelism with "unambiguous" consent and in order to have one single and consistent definition of consent, ensuring the awareness of the data subject that, and to what, he or she gives consent'.[60] The Parliament favoured this approach in its first reading,[61] but the explicitness criterion ended up being dropped from the final version of the definition of consent in the GDPR, appearing instead as an added qualification for valid consent to the processing of special categories of personal data (Article 9(2)(a) GDPR) and to the transfer of personal data to third countries or international organisations that do not provide adequate protection for the data (Article 49(1)(a) GDPR).[62]

One might question whether the explicitness criterion on its face adds anything of substance to the general requirements for valid consent—one could argue that its role is covered by the phrase 'by a statement or by a clear affirmative action', baked into the definition in Article 4(11). However, as pointed out above, the legislative history indicates that a difference was intended, with the explicitness criterion being considered as stricter than that of 'unambiguous'. This is also the view of the EDPB.[63] The criterion 'unambiguous' essentially means that the data subject's actions must leave no doubt that they have given consent, whereas the criterion 'explicit' means that the process of requesting and providing consent must occur as a formally separate process to the other transaction(s) to which the consent attaches, and that process must involve a specific request by the controller for permission from the data subject to process the data in question, followed by a specific reply in the affirmative.[64]

Both forms of consent probably do not have to be in writing,[65] but Article 7(1) and recital 42 require the controller to be able 'to demonstrate' that the data subject has consented. Hence, there must be at least some sort of documentation of the consent process. In this regard, the WP29 held that:

An obvious way to make sure consent is explicit would be to expressly confirm consent in a written statement. Where appropriate, the controller could make sure the written statement is signed by

---

[57] According to Advocate General Szpunar, passive consent would be equally unacceptable under the DPD: see Case C-673/17, *Planet49* (AG Opinion), paras. 59–66.

[58] Kosta 2013, p. 235. The DPD did not include the criterion of non-ambiguity in its definition of consent, but mentioned the criterion in relation to the use of consent as a ground for the processing of personal data generally (Art. 7(a)) and for the transfer of personal data to third countries (Art. 26(1)).

[59] GDPR Proposal, p. 42.   [60] Ibid., p. 8.   [61] EP Resolution GDPR 2014.

[62] For further details on this aspect of the legislative history, see the Introduction to this volume.

[63] EDPB 2018, p. 6.   [64] See too Bygrave 2014, p. 161.

[65] Ibid. See too DPD Amended Proposal 1992, p. 11 (stating with regard to the definition of 'consent' in the DPD that '[t]he reference to consent being "express" has been removed [from the DPD proposal], lest [*sic*] it be interpreted as requiring written consent (a procedure confined to sensitive data in Article 8 of the amended proposal). It has been replaced by the concept of an "express indication of his wishes", something which may be either oral or in writing').

the data subject, in order to remove all possible doubt and potential lack of evidence in the future. However, such a signed statement is not the only way to obtain explicit consent and, it cannot be said that the GDPR prescribes written and signed statements in all circumstances that require valid explicit consent.[66]

Select Bibliography

International agreements

APEC Privacy Framework 2005: Asia-Pacific Economic Cooperation, 'Privacy Framework' (2005).
OECD Privacy Guidelines 2013: Organisation for Economic Co-operation and Development, 'The OECD Privacy Framework' (2013).

EU legislation

Council Directive 93/104/EC: Council Directive 93/104/EC of 23 November 1993 concerning certain aspects of the organization of working time, OJ 1993 L 307/18.
DPD Amended Proposal 1992: Amended Proposal for a Council Directive on the Protection of Individuals with Regard to the Processing of Personal Data and on the Free Movement of Such Data (COM(92) 422 final—SYN 287).
GDPR Proposal: Proposal for a Regulation of the European Parliament and of the Council on the protection of individuals with regard to the processing of personal data and on the free movement of such data (General Data Protection Regulation), COM(2012) 11 final.

Academic writings

Bygrave 2002: Bygrave, *Data Protection Law: Approaching Its Rationale, Logic and Limits* (Kluwer Law International 2002).
Bygrave 2014: Bygrave, *Data Privacy Law: An International Perspective* (OUP 2014).
Bygrave and Schartum 2009: Bygrave and Schartum, 'Consent, Proportionality and Collective Power', in Gutwirth et al. (eds.), *Reinventing Data Protection?* (Springer 2009), 157.
Kosta 2013; Kosta, *Consent in European Data Protection Law* (Brill/Martinus Nijhoff Publishers 2013).

Papers of data protection authorities

EDPB 2018: European Data Protection Board, 'Guidelines 2/2018 on Derogations of Article 49 under Regulation 2016/679' (25 May 2018).
EDPB 2019: European Data Protection Board, 'Opinion 3/2019 Concerning the Questions and Answers on the Interplay between the Clinical Trials Regulation (CTR) and the General Data Protection regulation (GDPR) (art. 70.1.b))' (23 January 2019).
WP29 2001: Article 29 Working Party, 'Opinion 8/2001 on the Processing of Personal Data in the Employment Context' (WP 48, 13 September 2001)
WP29 2011: Article 29 Working Party, 'Opinion 15/2011 on the Definition of Consent' (WP 187, 13 July 2011).
WP29 2013: Article 29 Working Party, 'Opinion 3/2013 on Purpose Limitation' (WP 203, 2 April 2013).
WP29 2017: Article 29 Working Party, 'Opinion 2/2017 On Data Processing at Work' (WP 249, 8 June 2017).
WP29 2018: Article 29 Working Party, 'Guidelines on Consent under Regulation 2016/679' (WP 259 rev1.0, 10 April 2018).

---

[66] WP29 2018, p. 18.

Reports and recommendations

EC Communication 2010: Communication from the Commission to the European Parliament, the Council, the Economic and Social Committee and the Committee of the Regions, A comprehensive approach on personal data protection in the European Union, COM(2010) 609 final, 4 November 2010.

EP Resolution GDPR 2014: European Parliament legislative resolution of 12 March 2014 on the proposal for a regulation of the European Parliament and of the Council on the protection of individuals with regard to the processing of personal data and on the free movement of such data (General Data Protection Regulation), P7_TA(2014)0212, 12 March 2014.

Explanatory Report Convention 108 2018: Council of Europe, 'Explanatory Report to the Protocol Amending the Convention for the Protection of Individuals with Regard to the Automatic Processing of Personal Data' (10 October 2018), available at https://rm.coe.int/cets-223-explanatory-report-to-the-protocol-amending-the-convention-fo/16808ac91a.

GDPR Expert Group Report 2019: Multistakeholder Expert Group to support the application of Regulation (EU) 2016/679, 'Contribution from the Multistakeholder Expert Group to the stock-taking exercise of June 2019 on one year of GDPR application' (13 June 2019).

Article 4(12). Personal data breach

LUCA TOSONI

'personal data breach' means a breach of security leading to the accidental or unlawful destruction, loss, alteration, unauthorised disclosure of, or access to, personal data transmitted, stored or otherwise processed;

Relevant Recitals

(73) Restrictions concerning specific principles and the rights of information, access to and rectification or erasure of personal data, the right to data portability, the right to object, decisions based on profiling, as well as the communication of a personal data breach to a data subject and certain related obligations of the controllers may be imposed by Union or Member State law, as far as necessary and proportionate in a democratic society to safeguard public security, including the protection of human life especially in response to natural or manmade disasters, the prevention, investigation and prosecution of criminal offences or the execution of criminal penalties, including the safeguarding against and the prevention of threats to public security, or of breaches of ethics for regulated professions, other important objectives of general public interest of the Union or of a Member State, in particular an important economic or financial interest of the Union or of a Member State, the keeping of public registers kept for reasons of general public interest, further processing of archived personal data to provide specific information related to the political behaviour under former totalitarian state regimes or the protection of the data subject or the rights and freedoms of others, including social protection, public health and humanitarian purposes. Those restrictions should be in accordance with the requirements set out in the Charter and in the European Convention for the Protection of Human Rights and Fundamental Freedoms.

(85) A personal data breach may, if not addressed in an appropriate and timely manner, result in physical, material or non-material damage to natural persons such as loss of control over their personal data or limitation of their rights, discrimination, identity theft or fraud, financial loss, unauthorised reversal of pseudonymisation, damage to reputation, loss of confidentiality of personal data protected by professional secrecy or any other significant economic or social disadvantage to the natural person concerned. Therefore, as soon as the controller becomes aware that a personal data breach has occurred, the controller should notify the personal data breach to the supervisory authority without undue delay and, where feasible, not later than 72 hours after having become aware of it, unless the controller is able to demonstrate, in accordance with the accountability principle, that the personal data breach is unlikely to result in a risk to the rights and freedoms of natural persons. Where such notification cannot be achieved within 72 hours, the reasons for the delay should accompany the notification and information may be provided in phases without undue further delay.

(86) The controller should communicate to the data subject a personal data breach, without undue delay, where that personal data breach is likely to result in a high risk to the rights and freedoms of the natural person in order to allow him or her to take the necessary precautions. The communication should describe the nature of the personal data breach as well as recommendations for the natural person concerned to mitigate potential adverse effects. Such communications to data subjects should be made as soon as reasonably feasible and in close cooperation

with the supervisory authority, respecting guidance provided by it or by other relevant authorities such as law-enforcement authorities. For example, the need to mitigate an immediate risk of damage would call for prompt communication with data subjects whereas the need to implement appropriate measures against continuing or similar personal data breaches may justify more time for communication.

(87) It should be ascertained whether all appropriate technological protection and organisational measures have been implemented to establish immediately whether a personal data breach has taken place and to inform promptly the supervisory authority and the data subject. The fact that the notification was made without undue delay should be established taking into account in particular the nature and gravity of the personal data breach and its consequences and adverse effects for the data subject. Such notification may result in an intervention of the supervisory authority in accordance with its tasks and powers laid down in this Regulation.

(88) In setting detailed rules concerning the format and procedures applicable to the notification of personal data breaches, due consideration should be given to the circumstances of that breach, including whether or not personal data had been protected by appropriate technical protection measures, effectively limiting the likelihood of identity fraud or other forms of misuse. Moreover, such rules and procedures should take into account the legitimate interests of law-enforcement authorities where early disclosure could unnecessarily hamper the investigation of the circumstances of a personal data breach.

Closely Related Provisions

Article 33 (Notification of a personal data breach to the supervisory authority); Article 34 (Communication of a personal data breach to the data subject); Article 40(2)(i) (Codes of conduct); Article 58(2)(e) (Powers of supervisory authorities); Article 70(1)(g)–(h) (Tasks of the Board)

Related Provisions in LED [Directive (EU) 2016/680]

Article 3(11) (Definition of 'personal data breach'); Article 30 (Notification of a personal data breach to the supervisory authority) (see too recital 61); Article 31 (Communication of a personal data breach to the data subject) (see also recital 62); Article 51(1)(d)–(e) (Tasks of the Board)

Related Provisions in EPD [Directive 2002/58/EC]

Article 2(i) (Definition of 'personal data breach'); Article 4 (Security of processing) (see too recital 20)

Related Provisions in EUDPR [Regulation (EU) 2018/1725]

Article 3(16) (Definition of 'personal data breach'); Article 34 (Notification of a personal data breach to the EDPS) (see too recital 55); Article 35 (Communication of a personal data breach to the data subject) (see also recital 56); Article 45(1)(d) (Tasks of the data protection officer); Article 58(2)(f) (powers of the EDPS); Article 92 (notification of a personal data breach to the EDPS) (see too recital 55); Article 93 (Communication of a personal data breach to the data subject) (see also recital 56)

A. Rationale and Policy Underpinnings

The GDPR defines 'personal data breach' to clarify which types of security incidents trigger the obligation to notify the competent national supervisory authority and, in certain cases, the data subjects affected (Articles 33–34 GDPR). This obligation builds on the analogous notification requirements provided for in Article 4(3) EPD,[1] which only apply to providers of publicly available electronic communications services (e.g. telephony and internet service providers).

As explained by the European Commission:

[T]he rationale behind such [data breach notification requirements] is that, on the one hand, breach disclosure requirements enable individuals to react and thus prevent possible cases of fraud (or identity theft) and, on the other hand, provide additional incentives to operators to ensure adequate levels of security of their services and networks—or receive complaints from the end-users affected or, at the very least, face adverse consequences of bad publicity in case of a breach.[2]

Thus, the notification of data breaches is seen as a tool for enhancing compliance with data protection rules.[3]

B. Legal Background

1. EU legislation

As mentioned above, the data breach notification requirements established by Article 33 and Article 34 GDPR build on the notification obligations specified in Article 4(3) EPD. Concomitantly, the GDPR's definition of 'personal data breach' is essentially identical to that of Article 2(i) EPD.[4] The only difference between the two definitions lies in the fact that, due to the scope and aim of the EPD,[5] the latter limits its definition of 'personal data breach' to the security incidents that occur 'in connection with the provision of a publicly available electronic communications service in the Community', whereas the definition in the GDPR does not include such a limitation.

Thus, in essence, the definition of 'personal data breach' in the GDPR covers the same kind of security incidents covered by the definition in the EPD but applies regardless of the type of activities in connection to which the incidents occur.

2. International instruments

Convention 108 does not refer to the concept of 'personal data breach'. However, the Modernised Convention 108 introduces an obligation to notify the competent authorities of any 'data breaches which may seriously interfere with the rights and fundamental freedoms of data subjects' (see Article 7(2)). Nevertheless, the Modernised Convention does not define the term 'data breach'.

---

[1] GDPR Proposal, p. 10.   [2] EC Staff Working Document 2007, p. 106.
[3] WP29 2018, p. 5.
[4] See Art. 2(i) EPD (defining 'personal data breach' as 'a breach of security leading to the accidental or unlawful destruction, loss, alteration, unauthorised disclosure of, or access to, personal data transmitted, stored or otherwise processed in connection with the provision of a publicly available electronic communications service in the Community').
[5] Ibid., Art. 1.

Neither the OECD Privacy Guidelines (both original and revised versions) nor the APEC Privacy Framework contain provisions specifically on 'personal data breaches'.

An international definition of 'data breach', which appears to have inspired the drafters of the GDPR, is included in the standard ISO/IEC 27040 of the International Organization for Standardization (ISO), which defines the term as a compromise of security that leads to the accidental or unlawful destruction, loss, alteration, unauthorized disclosure of, or access to protected data transmitted, stored, or otherwise processed.[6]

3. National developments

Prior to the entry into force of the GDPR, only a few Member States imposed data breach notification obligations beyond those specified in Article 4(3) EPD. A very limited number of national laws imposed a general legal obligation on controllers to notify the competent authorities of all serious breaches affecting personal data.[7] However, some DPAs imposed general data breach notification requirements pursuant to 'soft law', such as guidelines and recommendations.[8] Other Member States imposed data breach notification obligations only on specific categories of controllers, in addition to providers of publicly available electronic communications services.[9]

The criteria for defining what equates to a data breach varied between Member States, with several states completely lacking such criteria.[10] Some Member States applied a very broad definition of data breach covering essentially any misuse of personal data,[11] while others considered that only certain specified security incidents qualified as data breaches.[12]

C. Analysis

1. Introduction

Article 4(12) GDPR provides a definition of 'personal data breach' which is broad enough to encompass most, but not all, instances of misuse of or illegal access to data. To be covered by the definition, a breach must have three key attributes: (1) it must concern a violation of 'security measures' (2) leading to the accidental or unlawful destruction, loss, alteration, unauthorised disclosure of, or access to, data (3) which qualify as 'personal data'.

2. Breach of security

The first-listed attribute demands that the breach be the result of a violation of the security measures that the controller or processor has implemented, or should have implemented, pursuant to Article 32 GDPR. This follows from the fact that the definition refers to a 'breach of security', and that Article 32 GDPR and the provisions regarding the obligation to notify a 'personal data breach' are located in the same Section of the Regulation entitled 'Security of personal data'. This is further confirmed by the fact that

---

[6] See ISO 2015, s. 3.7.
[7] See e.g. Dutch Personal Data Protection Act 2015, Art. 34a. See also Dutch Data Protection Authority 2015.
[8] See e.g. Belgian Data Protection Authority 2013; Irish Data Protection Commissioner 2009; ICO 2017.
[9] See e.g. German Federal Data Protection Act 2009, Art. 42a. The data breach notification obligations of Art. 42a only applied to: (i) data concerning bank and credit accounts; (ii) data subject to professional secrecy; (iii) data related to criminal and administrative offences; and (iv) other particularly sensitive data.
[10] ENISA 2011, p. 16.   [11] Ibid.   [12] Ibid.

all the attempts made during the legislative process to modify the definition of 'personal data breach' to cover data breaches that occur without a breach of security were unsuccessful.[13] Thus, a security incident qualifying as a 'personal data breach' would be normally due to a breach of organisational, physical or technical security measures.[14]

3. Types of security incidents covered

Regarding the second-listed attribute, the security incident must lead to the accidental or unlawful destruction, loss, alteration, unauthorised disclosure of, or access to, personal data. In other words, a 'personal data breach' is a *type* of security incident; but not all security incidents are personal data breaches.[15] As a general rule, a personal data breach occurs when one or more of the key elements of information security—i.e. the confidentiality, integrity and availability of the data—is/are compromised.[16] More specifically, 'destruction' of data qualifies as an 'availability breach', and occurs when the data no longer exist in a form that is of any use to the controller.[17] 'Loss' of data also qualifies as an 'availability breach', and refers to situations where the controller has lost control, access or possession of the data, including when this is only temporary.[18] 'Alteration' refers to a situation where the data have been modified, corrupted or are no longer complete, and qualifies as an 'integrity breach'.[19] Finally, unauthorised or accidental 'disclosure of, or access to' data qualifies as a 'confidentiality breach', and refers to situations where the data are communicated or otherwise made available to persons or organisations who/which are not entitled to receive or access them.[20]

4. Personal data

Regarding the third-listed attribute, the breach must concern *personal data*,[21] which have been transmitted, stored or otherwise processed prior to the occurrence of the incident. This means that security incidents that do not affect personal data, fail to qualify as personal data breaches. While these incidents do not need to be reported pursuant to Articles 33–34 GDPR, they may be subject to other notification obligations under different regulatory regimes, such as that of the NIS Directive.[22]

5. Accidental breaches

The definition does not require that the data breach occur wilfully or due to negligence on the part of the controller or processor. Thus, accidental data breaches are also covered by the definition, and should normally be notified, if they reach the threshold required by Articles 33–34 GDPR.[23] However, this does not mean that controllers would necessarily risk being sanctioned for the occurrence of an accidental breach, as the specific criteria to establish liability would vary from country to country. For example, under Spanish

---

[13] See EP Draft Report LIBE 2012, amendment 90. See further the proposals made by Latvia, Hungary and Slovakia in Council Report 2012, pp. 73, 83 and 106.
[14] See Art. 32 GDPR.   [15] See also WP29 2018, p. 7.   [16] Ibid.   [17] Ibid.
[18] Ibid.   [19] Ibid, pp. 7–8.   [20] Ibid.
[21] See further the commentary on Art. 4(1) GDPR in this volume.
[22] See Art. 14(3) NIS Directive.
[23] For a practical example of an accidental disclosure that was considered to fall under the definition of Art. 4(12) GDPR, see Spanish Data Protection Authority 2018. While this decision was adopted before 25 May 2018, it expressly refers to Arts. 33–34 GDPR. See too, for further examples, WP29 2018, pp. 8, 11 and 25.

law, public entities may be subject to administrative sanctions only for wilful misconduct or negligence, and the Spanish DPA has considered this rule when assessing whether to sanction a public entity following a personal data breach affecting its services.[24] The GDPR also assumes that sanctions are imposed only for intentional and negligent infringements of its provisions.[25]

6. Summing up

In light of the above, what the EDPS has noted with respect to the definition of 'personal data breach' in Article 2(i) EPD remains valid under the GDPR:

[T]he definition of 'personal data breach'] is broad enough to encompass most of the relevant situations in which notification of security breaches might be warranted.

First, the definition includes instances when an unauthorised access of personal data by a third party has taken place, such as the hacking of a server containing personal data and retrieving such information.

Second, this definition would also include situations where there has been a loss or disclosure of personal data, while unauthorised access has yet to be demonstrated. This would include such situations as where the personal data may have been lost (e.g. CD-ROMs, USB drives, or other portable devices), or made publicly available by regular users (employee data file made inadvertently and temporarily available to a publicly accessible area through the Internet).[26]

7. Other instruments

Article 3(11) LED and Article 3(16) EUDPR both define 'personal data breach' identically to Article 4(12) GDPR. Therefore, the term should be interpreted homogeneously in all these legal instruments.[27]

Select Bibliography

EU legislation

GDPR Proposal: Proposal for a Regulation of the European Parliament and of the Council on the protection of individuals with regard to the processing of personal data and on the free movement of such data (General Data Protection Regulation), COM(2012) 11 final.
NIS Directive: Directive (EU) 2016/1148 of the European Parliament and of the Council of 6 July 2016 concerning measures for a high common level of security of network and information systems across the Union, OJ 2016 L 194/1.

National legislation

Dutch Personal Data Protection Act 2015: Wet bescherming persoonsgegevens (WBP), versie van 1 januari 2015 (repealed).
German Federal Data Protection Act 2009: Bundesdatenschutzgesetz (BDSG) vom 20. Dezember 1990 (BGBl. I S. 2954), neugefasst durch Bekanntmachung vom 14. Januar 2003 (BGBl. I S. 66), zuletzt geändert durch Gesetz vom 29.07.2009 (BGBl. I, S. 2254), durch Artikel 5 des Gesetzes vom 29.07.2009 (BGBl. I, S. 2355 [2384] und durch Gesetz vom 14.08.2009 (BGBl. I, S. 2814), BGBl 2009 Teil I Nr. 54 (repealed).

---

[24] See Spanish Data Protection Authority 2017.   [25] See Art. 83(2)(b) and (3) GDPR.
[26] EDPS 2009, p. 30.   [27] See also rec. 5 EUDPR.

Academic writings

Esayas, 'Breach Notification Requirements under the European Union Legal Framework: Convergence, Conflicts, and Complexity in Compliance', 31(3) *John Marshall Journal of Information Technology & Privacy Law* (2014), 317.
Schwartz and Janger, 'Notification of Data Security Breaches', 105(5) *Michigan Law Review* (2007), 913.
Wong, *Data Security Breaches and Privacy in Europe* (Springer 2013).

Papers of data protection authorities

EDPS 2009: European Data Protection Supervisor, 'Second Opinion of the European Data Protection Supervisor on the Review of Directive 2002/58/EC Concerning the Processing of Personal Data and the Protection of Privacy in the Electronic Communications Sector (Directive on Privacy and Electronic Communications)' (6 June 2009).
WP29 2014: Article 29 Working Party, 'Opinion 03/2014 on Personal Data Breach Notification' (WP 213, 25 March 2014).
WP29 2018: Article 29 Working Party, 'Guidelines on Personal data Breach Notification under Regulation 2016/679' (WP250rev.01, as last revised and adopted on 6 February 2018).
Belgian Data Protection Authority 2013: Commissie voor de bescherming van de persoonlijke levenssfeer/Commission de la protection de la vie privée, 'Recommendation 1/2013' (21 January 2013).
Dutch Data Protection Authority 2015: Autoriteit Persoonsgegevens, 'The Data Breach Notification Obligation as Laid Down in the Dutch Data Protection Act' (8 December 2015).
ICO 2017: Information Commissioner's Office, 'Notification of Data Security Breaches to the Information Commissioner's Office (ICO)' (6 November 2017).
Irish Data Protection Commissioner 2009: Data Protection Commissioner, 'Breach Notification Guidance' (14 April 2009).
Spanish Data Protection Authority 2017: Agencia Española de Protección de Datos, 'Resolución: R/03494/2017' (AP/00056/2017, 10 August 2017).
Spanish Data Protection Authority 2018: Agencia Española de Protección de Datos, 'Resolución de Archivo de Actuaciones' (E/00255/2018, 5 February 2018).

Reports and recommendations

Council Report 2012: Proposal for a regulation of the European Parliament and of the Council on the protection of individuals with regard to the processing of personal data and on the free movement of such data (General Data Protection Regulation), 9897/1/12 REV 1, 24 May 2012.
EC Staff Working Document 2007: Commission Staff Working Document Impact Assessment of the Proposal for a Directive of the European Parliament of the European Parliament and the Council amending European Parliament and Council Directives 2002/19/EC, 2002/20/EC and 202/21/EC; Proposal for a Directive of the European Parliament of the European Parliament and the Council amending European Parliament and Council Directives 2002/22/EC and 2002/58/EC; Proposal for a Regulation of the European Parliament and the Council establishing the European Electronic Communications Markets Authority, SEC(2007) 1472, 13 November 2007.
ENISA 2011: European Union Agency for Network and Information Security, 'Data Breach Notifications in the EU' (13 January 2011).
EP Draft Report LIBE 2012: Draft report on the proposal for a regulation of the European Parliament and of the Council on the protection of individual with regard to the processing

of personal data and on the free movement of such data (General Data Protection Regulation), 2012/0011 (COD), 17 December 2012.

ISO 2015: International Organization for Standardization, 'Information technology — Security techniques — Storage security', ISO/IEC 27040:2015 (2015).

Others

Agencia Española de Protección de Datos, 'Guía para la gestión y notificación de brechas de seguridad' (19 June 2018), available at https://www.aepd.es/media/guias/guia-brechas-seguridad.pdf.

Article 4(13). Genetic data

LEE A. BYGRAVE   LUCA TOSONI*

'genetic data' means personal data relating to the inherited or acquired genetic characteristics of a natural person which give unique information about the physiology or the health of that natural person and which result, in particular, from an analysis of a biological sample from the natural person in question;

Relevant Recital

(34) Genetic data should be defined as personal data relating to the inherited or acquired genetic characteristics of a natural person which result from the analysis of a biological sample from the natural person in question, in particular chromosomal, deoxyribonucleic acid (DNA) or ribonucleic acid (RNA) analysis, or from the analysis of another element enabling equivalent information to be obtained.

Closely Related Provisions

Article 4(1) (Definition of 'personal data') (see too recital 26); Article 4(15) (Definition of 'data concerning health') (see also recital 35); Article 4(16) (Definition of 'biometric data') (see too recital 51); Article 9(1) (Processing of special categories of personal data) (see also recital 53); Article 22(4) (Automated individual decision-making, including profiling) (see also recital 71); Article 35(3)(b) (Data protection impact assessment) (see too recital 91)

Related Provisions in LED [Directive (EU) 2016/680]

Article 3(12) (Definition of 'genetic data'); Article 3(1) (Definition of 'personal data') (see too recital 21); Article 3(13) (Definition of 'biometric data'); Article 3(14) (Definition of 'data concerning health'); Article 10 (Processing of special categories of personal data) (see too recital 51); Article 11(2) (Automated individual decision-making); Article 29(1) (Security of processing)

Related Provisions in EUDPR [Regulation (EU) 2018/1725]

Article 3(17) (Definition of 'genetic data'); Article 3(1) (Definition of 'personal data') (see too recitals 16 and 18); Article 3(18) (Definition of 'biometric data'); Article 3(19) (Definition of 'data concerning health'); Article 10(1) (Processing of special categories of personal data) (see too recital 29); Article 24(4) (Automated individual decision-making, including profiling); Article 39(3)(b) (Data protection impact assessment); Article 76 (Processing of special categories of operational

---

* Heidi Beate Bentzen also provided useful input to this commentary.

personal data); Article 77(2)–(3) (Automated individual decision-making, including profiling); Article 91(1) (Security of processing of operational personal data)

Relevant Case Law

CJEU

Case C-112/89, *Upjohn Company and Upjohn NV v Farzoo Inc. and J. Kortmann*, judgment of 16 April 1991 (ECLI:EU:C:1991:147).
Case C-101/01, *Criminal proceedings against Bodil Lindqvist*, judgment of 6 November 2003 (ECLI:EU:C:2003:596).

ECtHR

S and Marper v United Kingdom, Appl. Nos. 30562/04, 30566/04, judgment of 4 December 2008.
Aycaguer v France, Appl. No. 8806/12, judgment of 22 June 2017.

A. Rationale and Policy Underpinnings

Recent years have seen huge advances in the ability to derive myriad types of personal information from human biological material. Whole genome sequencing (i.e. the determination of the entire sequence of DNA (deoxyribonucleic acid) of a person's genome (genetic makeup)) has played a key role in this regard. It has enhanced the accuracy, ease and scope of genetic testing, both within and outside the context of medical treatment and research.[1] Especially noteworthy is the dramatic reduction in the financial cost of genome sequencing: in 2008, it cost approximately USD 1 million to sequence a human genome; now it costs less than USD 1,000.[2] This has led in turn to a dramatic reduction in the cost of genetic testing and bolstered the rapid growth of an industry offering 'direct-to-consumer' genetic testing.

These advances have been commonly regarded with a mixture of admiration, wonder and trepidation—as exemplified in the following statement by the WP29, made back in 2000:

[T]he risks of abuse of genetic knowledge race [sic] legitimate concerns about the privacy of individuals ... The decoding of the DNA blueprint paves the way to new discoveries and uses in the field of genetic testing. On the other hand, the information can identify individuals, link them to others, and reveal complex data about the future health and development of those individuals and other people to whom they are genetically related.[3]

Four years later, the WP29 went on to identify what it saw as special features of genetic data that make them 'singular, in particular compared to health data' and warranted subjecting their use to a 'particular legal protection':[4]

– [W]hile genetic information is unique and distinguishes an individual from other individuals, it may also at the same time reveal information about and have implications for that

---

[1] See e.g. Collins 2010.   [2] See US National Human Genome Research Institute 2018.
[3] WP29 2000, p. 2. See too e.g. OECD Privacy Guidelines 2013, p. 85: 'Genetic testing to assess health risks or to determine biological relationships raises issues that affect not only an individual's privacy but also raise the issue of "group privacy", as our genetic makeup is shared by other members of our family and community. At the same time the indelible nature of genetic information and its potential implications for discriminatory treatment make it particularly sensitive'.
[4] WP29 2004, p. 4.

individual's blood relatives (biological family) including those in succeeding and preceding generations. Furthermore, genetic data can characterise a group of persons (e.g. ethnic communities); genetic data can reveal parentage and family links;
- genetic information is often unknown to the bearer him/herself and does not depend on the bearer's individual will since genetic data are non-modifiable;
- genetic data can be easily obtained or be extracted from raw material although this data may at times be of dubious quality;
- taking into account the developments in research, genetic data may reveal more information in the future and be used by an ever increasing number of agencies for various purposes.[5]

Some elements of the above statement by the WP29 are not entirely accurate. The claim that genetic information is unique underplays the fact that the overwhelming majority of human genes are identical; only *circa* 0.1 per cent show variation, although that is typically enough to distinguish one person from another. More importantly, the claim that genetic data are non-modifiable belies the recent advances in genome editing (particularly through use of CRISPR ('Clustered Regularly Interspaced Short Palindromic Repeats')) and the fact that disease and medical treatment for disease can induce changes to DNA characteristics.[6]

Despite its inaccuracies, the WP29's conception of genetic data encapsulated a fairly widespread view in data protection circles at the time. And the inaccuracies did not significantly detract from what has been arguably the predominant worry in those circles about genetic data: that the disclosure of such data to third parties may lead to unfair discrimination and stigma towards the person(s) to whom the data relate, which may in turn detrimentally affect people's willingness to undergo medical treatment that involves genetic testing.[7]

This worry persists—as evidenced by the inclusion in the GDPR of provisions expressly addressing the processing of genetic data. In addition to defining such data, the Regulation places them in its list of 'special' data categories (Article 9(1)) and thereby subjects their processing to all of the other rules pertaining to these data categories.

During the legislative process leading to adoption of the GDPR, differing definitions of 'genetic data' were proffered. The European Commission's GDPR proposal defined 'genetic data' in a considerably more abbreviated way than the definition in the final version of the Regulation ('"genetic data" means all data, of whatever type, concerning the characteristics of an individual which are inherited or acquired during early prenatal development' (Article 4(10) of the Proposal)), while the European Parliament proposed a more detailed definition:

'genetic data' means all personal data, of whatever type, relating to the genetic characteristics of an individual which have been inherited or acquired during early prenatal development as they result from an analysis of a biological sample from the individual in question, in particular by chromosomal, deoxyribonucleic acid (DNA) or ribonucleic acid (RNA) analysis or analysis of any other element enabling equivalent information to be obtained.[8]

In the end, the core of the latter definition was retained and supplemented by the qualification 'which give unique information about the physiology or the health of that natural person',

---

[5] Ibid., pp. 4–5.
[6] As detailed below, this point played a role in the final phrasing of the definition in Art. 4(13) GDPR.
[7] WP29 2004, p. 2 ('the protection of the right to health is conditional upon the assurance that no genetic data may be known to third parties, who might use it to discriminate against and/or stigmatise the data subject').
[8] EP Resolution GDPR 2014, Art. 4(10).

while the clause beginning 'in particular' was moved to recital 34. The reference to characteristics acquired 'during early prenatal development' was eliminated considering that genetic data can change after birth, for instance as a result of cancer treatment or transplantation.[9]

B. Legal Background

1. EU legislation

The DPD did not contain provisions expressly dealing with genetic data. This is also the case with the EPD. However, Article 21(1) CFR prohibits 'any discrimination based ... on genetic features'. The latter term is left undefined in the Charter, but the reference to it in Article 21(1) draws on Article 11 of the Council of Europe's Convention on Human Rights and Biomedicine (elaborated further below).[10]

Both the EUDPR and LED define 'genetic data' identically to the GDPR (see Article 3(17) EUDPR and Article 3(12) LED).[11] This is also the case with Council Regulation 2017/1939 on the establishment of the European Public Prosecutor's Office (see Article 2(19)), whereas Regulation 2016/794 on Europol defines 'genetic data' in essentially the same way but with slightly different syntax (see Article 2(j)).

2. International instruments

Convention 108 in its original form does not contain provisions dealing specifically with genetic data. The Modernised Convention 108, however, includes 'genetic data' in its list of 'special categories of data' (Article 6(1)) but does not define the term. A definition is nonetheless provided in its Explanatory Report:

Genetic data are all data relating to the genetic characteristics of an individual which have been either inherited or acquired during early prenatal development, as they result from an analysis of a biological sample from the individual concerned: chromosomal, DNA or RNA analysis or analysis of any other element enabling equivalent information to be obtained.[12]

The rules on use of genetic data in Modernised Convention 108 build upon the Council of Europe's Convention on Human Rights and Bio-Medicine,[13] Chapter IV of which

---

[9] See Council Report 2015, p. 24 (fn. 54–55).

[10] See Explanations Relating to the Charter of Fundamental Rights 2007 (noting with regard to Art. 21 CFR that '[p]aragraph 1 draws on ... Article 11 of the Convention on Human Rights and Biomedicine as regards genetic heritage').

[11] This entails that the term should be interpreted homogeneously across these legal instruments. See too recital 5 EUDPR.

[12] Explanatory Report Convention 108 2018, para. 57. The reference to genetic characteristics acquired 'during early prenatal development' arguably makes this definition more limited in scope compared to the one included in Art. 4(13) GDPR. In this regard, the Explanatory Report to the Additional Protocol to the Convention on Human Rights and Biomedicine concerning Genetic Testing for Health Purposes is particularly illuminating (para. 29). The latter elaborates on the concept of genetic characteristics 'inherited or acquired during early prenatal development'—a concept that is present in the Additional Protocol to limit its scope of application (Art. 2(1)): '[t]hese genetic characteristics cover those already present in the gametes of the parents and therefore transmitted by the latter, as well as those which appear during the early stage of prenatal development before the differentiation of the germ line. It is sometimes referred to the genetic characteristics inherited or acquired during early prenatal development as "genetic characteristics transmissible to descendants". The genetic modifications acquired during lifetime by only certain somatic cells due for example to external factors in the environment, are therefore not covered'.

[13] Biomedicine Convention.

contains overarching provisions concerned with the human genome. The latter provisions state, inter alia, that '[a]ny form of discrimination against a person on grounds of his or her genetic heritage is prohibited' (Article 11),[14] and that '[t]ests which are predictive of genetic diseases or which serve either to identify the subject as a carrier of a gene responsible for a disease or to detect a genetic predisposition or susceptibility to a disease may be performed only for health purposes or for scientific research linked to health purposes, and subject to appropriate genetic counselling' (Article 12).

In addition, international organisations have adopted a large number of other, predominantly soft law instruments dealing with use of human genetic data. These include recommendations, guidelines and declarations issued by the Council of Europe,[15] the OECD,[16] and the United Nations Educational, Scientific and Cultural Organization ('UNESCO').[17] Some of these instruments contain definitions of genetic data. One example is UNESCO's International Declaration on Human Genetic Data which defines 'human genetic data' as '[i]nformation about heritable characteristics of individuals obtained by analysis of nucleic acids or by other scientific analysis'.[18] Another example is CoE Recommendation R (97) 5 on the Protection of Medical Data which states:

[T]he expression 'genetic data' refers to all data, of whatever type, concerning the hereditary characteristics of an individual or concerning the pattern of inheritance of such characteristics within a related group of individuals. It also refers to all data on the carrying of any genetic information (genes) in an individual or genetic line relating to any aspect of health or disease, whether present as identifiable characteristics or not. The genetic line is the line constituted by genetic similarities resulting from procreation and shared by two or more individuals.[19]

3. National developments

During the life of the DPD, there was considerable variation between EU/EEA Member States' respective data protection regimes for human genetic data. The situation was aptly summed up by the WP29 as follows:

At regulatory level the situation across the EU appears to be uneven. Indeed, while some Member States have explicitly listed genetic data as sensitive data in their Data Protection law with all the safeguards and restrictions associated, in most Member States the issue of the processing of genetic data is not as such regulated by specific legislation. However, some Member States do provide for complementary rules in their laws on patient's rights and legal regulations for the processing of genetic data.[20]

While the processing of human genetic data is now explicitly regulated by the GDPR, thus leading to greater uniformity in national approaches in this area, we cannot expect full cross-national harmony as Article 9(4) of the Regulation leaves Member States with the ability to customise their respective data protection rules for processing genetic data (along with biometric data and data concerning health). Nonetheless, all Member State regimes will have to apply the definition of genetic data laid out in the Regulation.

---

[14] See too Art. 21 CFR (set out above).
[15] See e.g. COM Recommendation 1992A, COM Recommendation 1992B, COM Recommendation 1997 and COM Recommendation 2006.
[16] See OECD 2007 and OECD 2009. [17] See UNESCO 1997 and UNESCO 2003.
[18] UNESCO 2003, Art. 2(i). [19] COM Recommendation 1997, clause 1.
[20] WP29 2004, p. 3. For a comprehensive mapping of the situation as per 2003, see Beyleveld et al. 2004.

4. Case law

The CJEU has not yet ruled on the definition of 'genetic data' in Article 4(13) GDPR or, indeed, on the processing of human genetic data more generally.

The ECtHR handed down a landmark judgment on the use of genetic samples in the case of *S and Marper*.[21] The Court held that the retention by UK policing agencies of the DNA profiles, cellular samples and fingerprints of persons who had been suspected but not convicted of legal offences was a disproportionate interference with those persons' right to respect for private life under Article 8 of the European Convention on Human Rights ('ECHR'). In the course of its judgment, the Court stated that 'all three categories of the personal information retained by the authorities in the present case, namely fingerprints, DNA profiles and cellular samples, constitute personal data within the meaning of the Data Protection Convention as they relate to identified or identifiable individuals'.[22]

The ECtHR has taken a similar line in subsequent jurisprudence on DNA databases. In *Aycaguer v France*, the Court held that the conviction of an already convicted person for refusing to undergo biological testing the result of which would be included in France's national computerised DNA database constituted a disproportionate interference with the person's right under Article 8 ECHR.[23] In this case, the relevant French law did not set a precise limit on the duration of the storage of DNA profiles in the database, did not differentiate the period of storage depending on the nature and gravity of the offences committed by the data subjects, and did not provide any possibility for a data subject who is convicted of crime to request that their profile be deleted.

C. Analysis

The definition of genetic data in Article 4(13) is formulated in relatively generic terms, ostensibly with the aim of 'future-proofing' it in relation to ongoing technological developments. Already now, though, elements of the definition struggle to keep pace with technological change. This is the case with the last part of the definition which assumes that genetic data 'result, in particular, from an analysis of a biological sample from the natural person in question'. It is, for instance, nowadays possible to diagnose genetic disorders on the basis of facial image analysis employing computer vision and deep-learning algorithms.[24] In this respect, though, the continued applicability of the definition in Article 4(13) may be ensured by recital 34, which provides for a broader criterion for deriving genetic data (i.e. 'or from the analysis of another element enabling equivalent information to be obtained'). At the same time, it is questionable whether the latter criterion is also part of the definition in Article 4(13), particularly as the definition uses the words 'in particular', which could be construed as suggesting specification rather than exemplification. However, the equivalent words in other language versions of Article 4(13) suggest that analysis of biological samples is only one of several ways of deriving genetic data, albeit the principal way.[25] Thus, any argument that the broad recital 34 criterion is not implicit in the definition in Article 4(13) faces an uphill battle, also in light of the apparent future-proofing agenda of the legislator combined with the CJEU's teleological approach to construing legislative provisions.

---

[21] ECtHR, *S and Marper v UK*. [22] Ibid., para. 68. [23] ECtHR, *Aycaguer v France*.
[24] See Gurovich et al. 2019.
[25] E.g. the French version uses the term 'notamment' ('most notably'), the German version uses 'insbesondere' ('especially'), while the Swedish version uses 'framför allt' ('above all').

Further, it is worth emphasising that not all information that results from an analysis of a biological sample (e.g. DNA fragments) qualifies as 'genetic data' under the GDPR. Indeed, the definition in Article 4(13) makes clear that it covers only data about the 'genetic characteristics' of a specific individual which 'give unique information about the physiology or the health' of that individual. Thus, as elaborated further below, data about the phenotypic features (i.e. the actual observed properties) of an individual (e.g. eye colour)[26] or that do not clearly distinguish the individual from other individuals in terms of physiological features or health conditions are arguably ordinarily excluded from the definition in Article 4(13), even though they may be derived from the analysis of his/her biological samples.[27]

Genetic data as defined in Article 4(13) are a subcategory of personal data. Accordingly, data must satisfy the criteria baked into the definition in Article 4(1) GDPR, as elaborated in recital 26 GDPR, before they can qualify as genetic under Article 4(13). Back in 2004, the WP29 took the view that genetic data are personal data in most cases, but—using rather ambiguous language—seemed to open up for the possibility that there may be exceptional cases in which they are not.[28] In light of subsequent technological developments,[29] there are solid grounds for claiming that the 'personal data' precondition is now invariably going to be met.

However, any biological material from which genetic data are derived is in itself not personal data and, accordingly, not genetic data. This is fairly clear from the wording of Article 4(13) and recital 34, as these refer to data which 'result from the analysis of a biological sample'. This is made even more clear in recital 35 GDPR, which distinguishes between 'a body part or bodily substance' and 'information derived from the testing or examination of' such part/substance.[30] This distinction was made also by some supervisory authorities, although prior to the adoption of the GDPR.[31] A similar distinction was made by the WP29, in a different but related context: the regulation of biometric data.[32]

The fact that DNA may constitute a biometric reference measure means that the definition of 'genetic data' in Article 4(13) overlaps to some extent with the definition

---

[26] However, as mentioned further below, during the legislative process some Member States noted that the definition 'would also cover data about a person's physical appearance'.

[27] For example, in 2015, the Italian DPA found that data on blood types (ABO, Rh) 'should not be considered as such "genetic data"' within the meaning of the definition of 'genetic data' applicable in Italy at that time, which partly resembled the definition in Art. 4(13) GDPR: '"genetic data" shall mean the result of genetic tests and/or any other information that, regardless of its type, identifies an individual's genotypic characteristics that can be inherited within a related group of individuals'. See Italian Data Protection Authority 2015.

[28] WP29 2004, p. 5: 'a link to a specific person, i.e. the fact that the person concerned is identified or identifiable, is clear in the majority of cases. Nevertheless in some cases it is less clear, e.g. samples of DNA taken in a given place, such as traces at the scene of a crime.'

[29] Increasingly sophisticated methods of analysing data held in current consumer genetic databases, combined with the growth of such databases, makes it increasingly easy to identify persons who have not undergone genetic testing: see further e.g. Erlich et al. 2018; Gymrek et al. 2013. Further, the ability of police authorities to (re)identify individuals on the basis of their families' genetic data has led to successful criminal prosecutions in a number of high-profile cases: see e.g. Murphy 2018.

[30] See also the commentaries on Art. 4(1) and (14) in this volume.

[31] For example, the Italian Data Protection Authority found that the genotypic information contained in a human biological sample qualifies as personal data only if it is extracted from the biological sample and stored in, say, medical records. See Italian Data Protection Authority 2007.

[32] See WP29 2007, p. 9 ('Human tissue samples (like a blood sample) are themselves sources out of which biometric data are extracted, but they are not biometric data themselves'). See also WP29 2012, p. 4.

of biometric data in Article 4(14).[33] Both of these definitions overlap partially with the definition of 'data concerning health' in Article 4(15). However, these overlaps do not appear to be problematic. In this regard, it should be recalled that Member States are given a considerable margin for manoeuvre when drawing up rules for the processing of genetic data, biometric data and data concerning health (see Article 9(4) GDPR).

The wide breadth of the definition in Article 4(13) was also highlighted during the legislative process that led to the adoption of the GDPR. In particular, some Member States expressed their concern that the definition 'would also cover data about a person's physical appearance'.[34] However, the accuracy of this statement ultimately depends on the interpretation of the term *genetic characteristics*. The latter is generally understood as a synonym of 'genetic heritage',[35] which in turn ordinarily refers to the chromosomes and genes of an individual.[36] Thus, it may be argued that the term only covers the genotypic features of an individual, and not his/her phenotypic characteristics (i.e. the actual observed properties of his/her body, like eye color), although it is sometimes possible to identify gene disorders through the identification of phenotypic characteristics.[37] This interpretation is in line with the definition of 'genetic data' with which some Member States operated before the adoption of the GDPR. For example, the Italian DPA operated with a definition of 'genetic data' which only covered 'genotypic characteristics'.[38] In essence, the processing of data that only concerns the phenotypic features of an individual (e.g. the mere taking/storing of a photograph of that individual) would normally not concern the processing of 'genetic data' within the meaning of the GDPR, even though it might accidentally reveal some genetic features of the individual to whom the data relate. This is indirectly supported by recital 51 GDPR, which states that 'the processing of photographs should not systematically be considered to be processing of special categories of personal data'.

Although the definition in Article 4(13) is pitched broadly for the most part, there are two aspects of it that are not. First, the definition is formulated such that it gives the impression that each instance of genetic data revolves around a single human being— the person who provides a biological sample from which the data are derived. As such, the definition regrettably fails to communicate properly the collective dimension of genetic data—i.e. the fact that such data may relate not just to the person from whom the data are derived but also to that person's biological kin. By contrast, the equivalent definition in the above-cited CoE Recommendation on the Protection of Medical Data does far greater justice to this collective dimension.

---

[33] Interestingly, during the Council deliberations on the draft GDPR, one Member State 'did not understand why genetic data were not included in the definition of biometric data', while another took the view that the term 'biometric data' was 'too broadly defined'. See Council Report 2013, p. 67 (fn. 42). See also the commentary on Art. 4(14) in this volume.

[34] See Council Report 2015, p. 24, fn. 55.

[35] See e.g. Additional Protocol to the Convention on Human Rights and Biomedicine, concerning Genetic Testing for Health Purposes, Art. 4 (using both terms in the same provision).

[36] See e.g. Explanatory Report Convention Biomedicine, para. 72.

[37] See Explanatory Report Convention Biomedicine, para. 78.

[38] See Italian Data Protection Authority 2014, s. 1(a).

Secondly, to be covered by the definition, data must give *unique* information about the *physiology* (i.e. the actual functioning of the body or its parts)[39] or *health*[40] of that single human being. This arguably excludes from the definition data on genetic features that do not clearly distinguish that individual from a group in terms of physiological features or health conditions (e.g. XY chromosomes). The reference to the concept of 'physiology' might also present some challenges when trying to assess whether the genetic features studied in the context of certain behavioural genetic studies[41] qualify as 'genetic data' for GDPR purposes, as these features might not necessarily provide information that is strictly about the biological functioning of the human body.

Select Bibliography

International agreements

Biomedicine Convention: Convention for the Protection of Human Rights and Dignity of the Human Being with regard to the Application of Biology and Medicine: Convention on Human Rights and Biomedicine, ETS 164, 4 April 1997.

Additional Protocol to the Convention on Human Rights and Biomedicine, concerning Genetic Testing for Health Purposes: Additional Protocol to the Convention on Human Rights and Biomedicine, concerning Genetic Testing for Health Purposes, ETS 164, 27 November 2008.

OECD Privacy Guidelines 2013: Organisation for Economic Co-operation and Development, 'The OECD Privacy Framework' (2013).

EU legislation

Council Regulation (EU) 2017/1939 of 12 October 2017 implementing enhanced cooperation on the establishment of the European Public Prosecutor's Office ('the EPPO'), OJ 2017 L 283/1.

Directive 65/65: Council Directive 65/65/EEC of 26 January 1965 on the approximation of provisions laid down by Law, Regulation or Administrative Action relating to proprietary medicinal products, OJ 1965 L 22/369.

Explanations Relating to the Charter of Fundamental Rights 2007: Explanations Relating to the Charter of Fundamental Rights, OJ 2007 C 303/17.

GDPR Proposal: Proposal for a Regulation of the European Parliament and of the Council on the protection of individuals with regard to the processing of personal data and on the free movement of such data (General Data Protection Regulation), COM(2012) 11 final, 25 January 2012.

Regulation (EU) 2016/794 of the European Parliament and of the Council of 11 May 2016 on the European Union Agency for Law Enforcement Cooperation (Europol) and replacing and repealing Council Decisions 2009/371/JHA, 2009/934/JHA, 2009/935/JHA, 2009/936/JHA and 2009/968/JHA, OJ 2016 L 135/53.

Academic writings

Beyleveld et al. 2004: Beyleveld, Townend, Rouillé-Mirza and Wright (eds.), *Implementation of the Data Protection Directive in Relation to Medical Research in Europe* (Ashgate 2004).

---

[39] See, by analogy, Case C-112/89, *Upjohn v Farzoo*, para. 21 (interpreting the meaning of 'restoring, correcting or modifying physiological functions' within the definition of 'medicinal product' in Art. 1(2) of Directive 65/65).

[40] The concept of health should normally be interpreted broadly. See Case C-101/01, *Lindqvist*, para. 50 (regarding interpretation of the concept of 'data concerning health').

[41] Behavioural genetics is a field of scientific research which investigates the influence of an organism's genetic features on its behaviour.

Collins 2010: Collins, *The Language of Life: DNA and the Revolution in Personalized Medicine* (HarperCollins 2010).
Erlich et al. 2018: 'Identity Inference of Genomic Data Using Long-Range Familial Searches', 362(6415) *Science*, 690.
Gurovich et al. 2019: Gurovich and others, 'Identifying Facial Phenotypes of Genetic Disorders Using Deep Learning', 25 *Nature Medicine* (2019), 60.
Gymrek et al. 2013: 'Identifying Personal Genomes by Surname Inference', 339(6117) *Science* (2013), 321.

Papers of data protection authorities

WP29 2000: Article 29 Working Party, 'Opinion 6/2000 on the Human Genome and Privacy' (WP 34, 13 July 2000).
WP29 2004: Article 29 Working Party, 'Working Document on Genetic Data' (WP 91, 17 March 2004).
WP29 2007: Article 29 Working Party, 'Opinion 4/2007 on the Concept of Personal Data' (WP 136, 20 June 2007).
WP29 2012: Article 29 Working Party, 'Opinion 3/2012 on Developments in Biometric Technologies' (WP 193, 27 April 2012).
Italian Data Protection Authority 2007: Garante per la protezione dei dati personali, 'Campione biologico e dato personale genetico' (21 June 2007).
Italian Data Protection Authority 2014: Garante per la protezione dei dati personali, 'Autorizzazione n. 8/2014—Autorizzazione generale al trattamento dei dati genetici' (11 December 2014).
Italian Data Protection Authority 2015: Garante per la protezione dei dati personali, 'Parere su uno schema di decreto recante "Disposizioni relative ai requisiti di qualità e sicurezza del sangue e degli emocomponenti"' (25 June 2015).

Reports and recommendations

COM Recommendation 1992A: Committee of Ministers of the Council of Europe, 'Recommendation on the Use of Analysis of Deoxyribonucleic Acid (DNA) within the Framework of the Criminal Justice System' (R (92)1, 10 February 1992).
COM Recommendation 1992B: Committee of Ministers of the Council of Europe, 'Recommendation on Genetic Testing and Screening for Health Care Purposes' (R (92)3, 10 February 1992).
COM Recommendation 1997: Committee of Ministers of the Council of Europe, 'Recommendation on the Protection of Medical Data' (R (97) 5, 13 February 1997).
COM Recommendation 2006: Committee of Ministers of the Council of Europe, 'Recommendation on Research on Biological Materials of Human Origin' (Rec (2006) 4, 15 March 2006).
Council Report 2013: Proposal for a regulation of the European Parliament and of the Council on the protection of individuals with regard to the processing of personal data and on the free movement of such data (General Data Protection Regulation), 17831/13, 16 December 2013.
Council Report 2015: Chapter I and XI, No. 8834/15, 12 May 2015.
EP Resolution GDPR 2014: European Parliament legislative resolution of 12 March 2014 on the proposal for a regulation of the European Parliament and of the Council on the protection of individuals with regard to the processing of personal data and on the free movement of such data (General Data Protection Regulation), P7_TA(2014)0212, 12 March 2014.
Explanatory Report Convention 108 2018: Council of Europe, 'Explanatory Report to the Protocol amending the Convention for the Protection of Individuals with Regard to the Automatic Processing of Personal Data' (10 October 2018), available at https://rm.coe.int/cets-223-explanatory-report-to-the-protocol-amending-the-convention-fo/16808ac91a.

Explanatory Report Convention Biomedicine: Council of Europe, 'Explanatory Report to the Convention for the protection of Human Rights and Dignity of the Human Being with regard to the Application of Biology and Medicine: Convention on Human Rights and Biomedicine' (4 April 1997).

Explanatory Report to the Additional Protocol to the Convention on Human Rights and Biomedicine concerning Genetic Testing for Health Purposes: Council of Europe, 'Explanatory Report to the Additional Protocol to the Convention on Human Rights and Biomedicine concerning Genetic Testing for Health Purposes' (27 December 2008).

OECD 2007: Organisation for Economic Co-operation and Development, 'Recommendation on Quality Assurance in Molecular Genetic Testing', (C(2007)48, May 2007).

OECD 2009: Organisation for Economic Co-operation and Development, 'Recommendation on Human Biobanks and Genetic Research Databases' (October 2009).

UNESCO 1997: United Nations Educational, Scientific and Cultural Organization, 'Universal Declaration on Human Genome and Human Rights' (11 November 1997).

UNESCO 2003: United Nations Educational, Scientific and Cultural Organization, 'International Declaration on Human Genetic Data' (16 October 2003).

Others

Murphy 2018: Murphy, 'How an Unlikely Family History Website Transformed Cold Case Investigations', *New York Times* (25 April 2018).

US National Human Genome Research Institute 2018: US National Human Genome Research Institute, 'DNA Sequencing Costs: Data' (25 April 2018), available at https://www.genome.gov/27541954/dna-sequencing-costs-data/.

Article 4(14). Biometric data

LEE A. BYGRAVE   LUCA TOSONI

'biometric data' means personal data resulting from specific technical processing relating to the physical, physiological or behavioural characteristics of a natural person, which allow or confirm the unique identification of that natural person, such as facial images or dactyloscopic data;

Relevant Recital

(51) Personal data which are, by their nature, particularly sensitive in relation to fundamental rights and freedoms merit specific protection as the context of their processing could create significant risks to the fundamental rights and freedoms. Those personal data should include personal data revealing racial or ethnic origin, whereby the use of the term 'racial origin' in this Regulation does not imply an acceptance by the Union of theories which attempt to determine the existence of separate human races. The processing of photographs should not systematically be considered to be processing of special categories of personal data as they are covered by the definition of biometric data only when processed through a specific technical means allowing the unique identification or authentication of a natural person. Such personal data should not be processed, unless processing is allowed in specific cases set out in this Regulation, taking into account that Member States law may lay down specific provisions on data protection in order to adapt the application of the rules of this Regulation for compliance with a legal obligation or for the performance of a task carried out in the public interest or in the exercise of official authority vested in the controller. In addition to the specific requirements for such processing, the general principles and other rules of this Regulation should apply, in particular as regards the conditions for lawful processing. Derogations from the general prohibition for processing such special categories of personal data should be explicitly provided, inter alia, where the data subject gives his or her explicit consent or in respect of specific needs in particular where the processing is carried out in the course of legitimate activities by certain associations or foundations the purpose of which is to permit the exercise of fundamental freedoms.

Closely Related Provisions

Article 4(1) (Definition of 'personal data') (see too recital 26); Article 4(13) (Definition of 'genetic data') (see too recital 34); Article 4(15) (Definition of 'data concerning health') (see also recital 35); Article 9(1) (Special categories of personal data); Article 22(4) (Automated individual decision-making, including profiling) (see also recital 71); Article 35(3)(b) (Data protection impact assessment) (see too recital 91)

Related Provisions in LED [Directive (EU) 2016/680]

Article 3(13) (Definition of 'biometric data'); Article 3(1) (Definition of 'personal data') (see too recital 21); Article 3(12) (Definition of 'genetic data'); Article 3(14) (Definition of 'data concerning health'); Article 10 (Processing of special categories of personal data) (see too recital 51); and Article 11(2) (Automated individual decision-making); Article 29(1) (Security of processing)

Related Provisions in EUDPR [Regulation (EU) 2018/1725]

Article 3(18) (Definition of 'biometric data'); Article 3(1) (Definition of 'personal data') (see too recitals 16 and 18); Article 3(17) (Definition of 'genetic data'); Article 3(19) (Definition of 'data concerning health'); Article 10(1) (Processing of special categories of personal data) (see too recital 29); Article 24(4) (Automated individual decision-making, including profiling); Article 39(3)(b) (Data protection impact assessment); Article 76 (Processing of special categories of operational personal data); Article 77(2)–(3) (Automated individual decision-making, including profiling); Article 91(1) (Security of processing of operational personal data)

Relevant Case Law

CJEU

Case C-291/12, *Michael Schwarz v Stadt Bochum*, judgment of 17 October 2013 (ECLI:EU:C:2013:670).
Joined Cases C-446/12 to C-449/12, *W. P. Willems and Others v Burgemeester van Nuth and Others*, judgment of 16 April 2015 (ECLI:EU:C:2015:238).

ECtHR

S and Marper v United Kingdom, Appl. Nos. 30562/04 and 30566/04, judgment of 4 December 2008.
M.K. v France, Appl. No. 19522/09, judgment of 18 April 2013.

The Netherlands

Hoge Raad, judgment of 23 March 2010 (ECLI:NL:HR:2010:BK6331).

A. Rationale and Policy Underpinnings

A major technological-organisational development of the last couple of decades is the marked growth in the automated use of biometrics as a basis for establishing or verifying human identity. Biometrics in this context are essentially measurements of human biological or behavioural attributes.[1] Compared to other reference measures, biometrics are special because they are, *in principle*, shared across most if not all of the human population, stable at least for considerable periods of a human's life, and distinctive if not unique for each individual. While the degree to which these characteristics actually are present will differ from biometric to biometric and from individual to individual,[2] they are commonly regarded as allowing a more accurate

---

[1] The notion of 'biometrics' is sometimes used to denote a process rather than attributes: see e.g. Meints and Gasson 2009, p. 138 (defining 'biometrics' as 'the automated recognition of individuals based on their biological and/or behavioural characteristics').
[2] See further e.g. the discussion in Kindt 2013, ch. 2; Liu 2011, ch. 2.

way of distinguishing one person from another than other means of identification or authentication, especially when multiple types of biometrics are used together. This explains in large part the growth in the popularity of their usage for identification or authentication purposes.

Data protection authorities, civil liberties groups and some scholars have followed this growth with a critical eye. A point of departure for their concern is the automation of biometric identification and authentication schemes. In the words of the WP29, these schemes 'change irrevocably the relation between body and identity, because they make the characteristics of the human body "machine-readable" and subject to further use'.[3] With automation comes concern about the potential for the schemes to facilitate systems for social control—a concern aggravated by fear over the schemes' increasing ubiquity and the concomitant growth in 'function creep'.[4] However, concern also revolves around the schemes' potentially poor cost-effectiveness. This relates not simply to the economic but also social costs of the schemes, given that they are rarely error-free and thus can generate incorrect inferences (i.e. in terms of 'false positives' or 'false negatives') about persons.[5]

In light of the above, it is not surprising that the GDPR expressly addresses the processing of biometric data. The Regulation does so primarily in Article 9(1), which includes 'biometric data for the purpose of uniquely identifying a natural person' in its list of 'special' data categories and thus subjects the processing of such data to all of the other rules pertaining to these data categories. It is interesting to note, though, that the European Commission's 2012 proposal for the GDPR did not include biometric data in the Article 9(1) list of 'special' data categories, although the processing of such data was regarded as presenting a 'specific risk' that warranted being subject to a data protection impact assessment (Article 33(2)(d) GDPR Proposal).[6] Further, the definition of 'biometric data' in the GDPR Proposal differed somewhat from its definition in the final version of the GDPR: the former defined 'biometric data' as 'any data relating to the physical, physiological or behavioural characteristics of an individual which allow their unique identification, such as facial images, or dactyloscopic data' (Article 4(11) GDPR Proposal). As elaborated below, the inclusion of biometric data in the Article 9(1) list came at the insistence of the European Parliament. Further, the Parliament and later the Council added the qualification 'personal' to the term 'data' in the definition of biometric data, while the Council subsequently added the remaining textual changes that resulted in the final version of the definition (i.e. the references to 'resulting from specific technical processing' and 'or confirms the ... of that individual').

---

[3] WP29 2012, p. 4.

[4] See e.g. WP29 2003, pp. 2 and 5; WP29 2012B, p. 17; Liu 2011, ch. 3. This is not to say that these actors have only been negative to the use of biometric schemes. Data protection authorities, for example, recognise that these schemes also bring with them significant benefits: see e.g. WP29 2012B, p. 2: 'Biometric data are successfully and efficiently used in scientific research, are a key element of forensic science and a valuable element of access control systems. They can help to raise the security level and make identification and authentication procedures easy, fast and convenient'.

[5] See e.g. WP29 2012, p. 6; Liu 2011, pp. 81–82.

[6] Note too that some jurisdictions, prior to adoption of the GDPR, regarded certain types of biometrics as especially sensitive: see e.g. the Dutch case law discussed below.

B. Legal Background

1. EU legislation

The DPD did not contain provisions expressly dealing with biometric data. This is also the case with the EPD. However, other pieces of EU legislation deal expressly with biometrics, particularly in the context of border control. Examples are Regulation 2252/2004 on standards for security features and biometrics in passports and travel documents issued by Member States, and Regulation 2017/2226 establishing an Entry/Exit System to register entry and exit data and refusal of entry data of third country nationals crossing Member States' external borders. The first-listed of these instruments does not directly define 'biometric data' or related concepts, whereas the second-listed does, defining 'biometric data' as 'fingerprint data and facial image' (Article 3(18)), 'fingerprint data' as 'the data relating to the four fingerprints of the index, middle finger, ring finger and little finger from the right hand where present, and otherwise from the left hand' (Article 3(16), and 'facial image' as 'digital images of the face' (Article 3(17)). This definition of 'biometric data' is obviously narrower than that in Article 4(14) GDPR.

Both the EUDPR and LED define 'biometric data' identically to the GDPR (see Article 3(18) EUDPR and Article 3(13) LED).[7]

2. International instruments

Convention 108 in its original form does not contain provisions dealing specifically with biometrics. However, Modernised Convention 108 includes 'biometric data uniquely identifying a person' in its list of 'special categories of data' (Article 6(1)). While the Modernised Convention does not define 'biometric data', its Explanatory Report states:

Processing of biometric data, that is data resulting from a specific technical processing of data concerning the physical, biological or physiological characteristics of an individual which allows the unique identification or authentication of the individual, is also considered sensitive when it is precisely used to uniquely identify the data subject.[8]

As noted below, the provisions of the Modernised Convention dealing with biometric data were an important point of departure for the trilogue negotiations concerning how such data should be treated under the GDPR.

3. National developments

During the life of the DPD, national data protection authorities dealt with numerous biometrics-based identification or authentication schemes, typically subjecting these to a case-by-case assessment of their necessity and proportionality.[9] Further, case law in some jurisdictions held that certain types of biometrics are especially sensitive.[10]

---

[7] This entails that the term should be interpreted uniformly across these legal instruments. See too rec. 5 EUDPR.

[8] Explanatory Report Convention 108 2018, para. 58.

[9] See e.g. the overviews provided in WP29 2003, p. 7; Liu 2011, pp. 126 et seq.

[10] See e.g. the decision of 23 March 2010 by the Dutch Supreme Court holding that digital images of faces are special data ('bijzondere gegevens'). The decision concerned the status of facial image data on a chip card for the purposes of applying data production orders pursuant to criminal procedure legislation, but the rules reflected essentially the same distinction between ordinary personal data and sensitive data as under Art. 7 DPD. See further Koops 2016, pp. 49–50. The case is also mentioned in WP29 2012A, p. 4, fn. 8.

4. Case law

The CJEU has yet to construe the definition of 'biometric data' in Article 4(14) GDPR. It has, though, handed down judgments dealing with the lawfulness of identification/authentication schemes involving use of fingerprints.

In *Schwarz*, the CJEU assessed whether the inclusion of fingerprint data in EU Member State passports as required by Regulation 2252/2004 violated Articles 7 and 8 CFR. The Court had little difficulty in finding, first, that fingerprints constitute personal data,[11] that their inclusion in passports constitutes a processing of personal data under Article 2(b) DPD,[12] and that this processing threatens the rights to respect for private life and the protection of personal data under the Charter.[13] Applying a multi-pronged proportionality assessment, the Court went on to conclude that the threat in this instance was justified.[14]

In *Willems*,[15] the CJEU considered whether Regulation 2252/2004, in conjunction with Articles 6 and 7 DPD and Articles 7 and 8 CFR, requires Member States to guarantee that the biometric data collected and stored pursuant to that Regulation will not be processed for purposes other than the issue of passports or other travel documents. The Court concluded in the negative.[16]

The use of biometrics has also been examined by the ECtHR. In the case of *S and Marper*,[17] the Court assessed whether aspects of the then existing regulatory regime in England, Wales and Northern Ireland for the retention of the fingerprints, cellular samples and DNA (deoxyribonucleic acid) profiles of particular persons breached the ECHR. It found that the retention of such items with respect to persons who had been suspected but not convicted of legal offences was a disproportionate interference with those persons' right to respect for private life under Article 8 ECHR. The Court has taken a similar line in subsequent jurisprudence.[18]

C. Analysis

1. Relevance of WP29 guidance

The definition of 'biometric data' in Article 4(14) GDPR builds on but does not fully replicate previous definitions of the term by the WP29 or by EU legislation. The WP29 has defined the term as referring to 'biological properties, behavioural aspects, physiological characteristics, living traits or repeatable actions where those features and/or actions are both unique to that individual and measurable, even if the patterns used in practice to technically measure them involve a certain degree of probability'.[19] The latter definition does not fundamentally conflict with that given in the GDPR: Article 4(14) basically prunes the definition by the WP29 and supplements it with general references to the technical process by which biometric data are generated and to the goals of the process, in a way that is not at odds with the conceptualisation of biometric data by the WP29

---

[11] Case C-291/12, *Schwarz*, para. 27. [12] Ibid., para. 29. [13] Ibid., para. 30.
[14] Ibid., para. 64. [15] Joined Cases C-446/12 to C-449/12, *Willems*. [16] Ibid., para. 53.
[17] ECtHR, *S and Marper*.
[18] See ECtHR, *M.K. v France* (concerning retention of fingerprints in a French police database).
[19] WP29 2007, p. 8.

(and, accordingly, the EDPB). Thus, WP29 policy documents on biometrics are relevant for interpreting Article 4(14).

2. The meaning of 'specific technical processing'

Article 4(14) does not so much define the processes of generating or applying biometrics as define a type of data that result from these processes. Its explication of these processes is vague: 'specific technical processing'. Nonetheless, such processes—together with the definition of 'personal data'—set the parameters for the definition of 'biometric data', so it is important to understand what they are.

In general, such processes consist of multiple steps the most important of which involve:

(a) acquiring a reference measure of one or more physical, physiological or behavioural characteristics of a person (often termed 'enrolment')
(b) creating a representation of that measure in a template
(c) linking that template with a code or object which is used to identify the person (the composite of template and code/object being often termed 'master template')
(d) storing the master template in a database
(e) acquiring new measurements (often termed 'live template') of the same biological characteristics
(f) matching the live template with the master template
(g) applying an algorithm to generate a result from the match.[20]

3. Biometric reference measures

Biometric reference measures can be physiographic (e.g. fingerprints, vein patterns), motoric or behavioural (e.g. gait, keystroke patterns), or biochemical (e.g. odour, DNA). The definition in Article 4(14) is phrased broadly so that it embraces a wide range of such measures: 'physical, physiological or behavioural characteristics'.[21] The exemplification it provides of such measures are amongst the most widely employed, although the terminology used for one of the examples ('dactyloscopic data'—more commonly termed fingerprints) will be enigmatic for many readers of the GDPR. A further exemplification of biometric data is provided by recital 51 GDPR, which indicates that photographs may constitute biometric data ('photographs ... are covered by the definition of biometric data when processed through a specific technical means allowing the unique identification or authentication of a natural person'). However, the EDPB took the view that '[t]he video footage of an individual cannot however in itself be considered as biometric data under Article 9, if it has not been specifically technically processed in order to contribute to the identification of an individual'.[22]

Older literature has questioned whether DNA may properly be regarded as a biometric reference measure. A report drawn up for the OECD in 2004 notes several differences between DNA and other biometrics:

---

[20] See further e.g. Wayman et al. 2004, ch. 1; Liu 2011, ch. 2; Kindt 2013, pp. 43 et seq.
[21] The EDPB noted that '[t]o qualify as biometric data as defined in the GDPR, processing of raw data, such as the physical, physiological or behavioural characteristics of a natural person, must imply a measurement of this characteristics'. See EDPB 2019, p. 15.
[22] EDPB 2019, p. 15.

DNA requires an actual physical sample as opposed to an image, photograph or scan; DNA matching is not done in real time and, for the most part, is not automated; DNA matching does not employ templates or feature extraction, but rather represents the comparison of actual samples.[23]

Yet, as the same report goes on to observe, DNA is clearly a physiological characteristic that may be used to determine or confirm human identity, and the policy implications of its use 'share some common attributes with other biometrics'.[24] Further, technological developments over the last decade have brought DNA matching techniques more into line with other biometric matching schemes. There are accordingly good grounds for holding that biometric data as defined in Article 4(14) embrace DNA.

4. Definitional overlap

The fact that DNA may constitute a biometric reference measure means that there is considerable overlap between the definition of 'genetic data' in Article 4(13) and the definition in Article 4(14).[25] There may also be partial overlap between these two definitions and the definition of 'data concerning health' in Article 4(15). These overlaps, however, do not appear to create difficulties in applying the GDPR. In this regard, it bears emphasis that Article 9(4) GDPR accords Member States considerable leeway in how they regulate the processing of genetic data, biometric data and data concerning health.

5. Identification distinguished from authentication/verification

The immediate goal of biometric systems is typically *identification* of a person (i.e. establishing who a person is relative to other persons) or the *authentication* (also termed verification) of a person (i.e. establishing whether a person is who she/he pretends to be). Achieving identification typically involves comparing data on a person with data on multiple other persons (a 1:n comparison), whereas achieving authentication typically involves comparing data on a person with data on one other person (a 1:1 comparison), where a successful match verifies that the former person is the same as the latter person. As elaborated by WP29:

The *identification* of an individual by a biometric system is typically the process of comparing biometric data of an individual (acquired at the time of the identification) to a number of biometric templates stored in a database (i.e. a one-to-many matching process). The *verification* of an individual by a biometric system is typically the process of comparing the biometric data of an individual (acquired at the time of the verification) to a single biometric template stored in a device (i.e. a one-to-one matching process).[26]

The definition in Article 4(14) *appears* to cover both goals ('which allow or confirm the unique identification'). This is also indicated by the wording of recital 51 which links biometric data to processing 'through a specific technical means allowing the unique identification or authentication of a natural person'.

It is important to note, though, that this duality of goals is not replicated in Article 9(1) GDPR, which, in respect of biometric data, is limited to cases when such data

---

[23] OECD 2004, p. 11. [24] Ibid. See too e.g. Liu 2011, p. 11 (taking a similar line).
[25] Interestingly, during the Council deliberations on the draft GDPR, one Member State 'did not understand why genetic data were not included in the definition of biometric data', while another took the view that the term 'biometric data' was 'too broadly defined'. See Council Report 2013, p. 67 fn. 42.
[26] WP29 2012B, pp. 5–6. See also e.g. Liu 2011, pp. 31–32.

are processed 'for the purpose of uniquely identifying a natural person'. In other words, Article 9(1) only pertains to biometric data that are used for the purpose of identification as opposed to authentication/verification. This is presumably because the legislator has deemed biometrics-based identification schemes as presenting a greater threat to data subjects' fundamental rights and freedoms than schemes used for the purpose of verification. Indeed, use of biometric data for identification is often regarded as more problematic from a data protection perspective than their use for verification/authentication, mainly because the latter use does not require storage of personal data in a centralised database and, concomitantly, typically involves processing of data on fewer numbers of persons.[27]

This limitation in the coverage of Article 9 is also evidenced in the trilogue negotiations on the GDPR. Summing up the negotiations held on 24 November 2015, the Council stated:

Concerning Article 9 relating to the processing of special categories of data, the European Parliament insists to include a reference to biometric data in the list of sensitive data in Article 9(1). The modernised Convention 108 of the Council of Europe foresees to restrictively define biometric data that 'uniquely identify a person' to qualify as sensitive data. Such a reference would ensure that biometric data are considered as sensitive only in those situations where they would uniquely identify a person or are used to verify his or her identity. The Presidency invites delegations to indicate their flexibility on a possible inclusion of 'biometric data uniquely identifying a person' in the list of sensitive data, keeping in mind the specific definition of 'biometric data' in Article 4(11).[28]

However, the reference to 'verify his or her identity' in the sentence beginning 'Such a reference ...' does not accurately reflect the intended ambit of Modernised Convention 108. As mentioned above, Article 6(1) of Modernised Convention 108 is intended to cover biometric data only when these are 'precisely used to uniquely identify the data subject'[29]—which seemingly does not include situations where such data are used for authentication/verification purposes.

6. Biometric data as personal data

Biometric data as defined in Article 4(14) are a subcategory of personal data. Accordingly, data must be capable of satisfying the criteria baked into the definition in Article 4(1) GDPR, as elaborated in recital 26 GDPR, before they can qualify as biometric for the purposes of Article 4(14). The extent to which data processed by biometric schemes may be regarded as personal data under EU data protection law has been the subject of a long-running debate.[30] Generally, data protection authorities have taken the view that data processed by biometric schemes are *usually* personal data,[31] but that there may be

---

[27] See also WP29 2003, p. 4: 'In principle, it is not necessary for the purposes of authentication/verification to store the reference data in a database; it is sufficient to store the personal data in a decentralised way. Conversely, identification can only be achieved by storing the reference data in a centralised database, because the system, in order to ascertain the identity of the data subject, must compare his/her templates or raw data (image) with the templates or raw data of all persons whose data are already centrally stored'.
[28] Council Report 2015, p. 3.   [29] Explanatory Report Convention 108 2018, para. 58.
[30] For a detailed survey of the lines of development of this debate, see Kindt 2013, section 3.1.
[31] See WP29 2003, p. 5 ('measures of biometric identification or their digital translation in a template form [are] in most cases ... personal data'); WP 2012B, p. 7 (reiterating this view).

exceptional cases in which they are not.[32] Hence, this 'personal data' precondition is likely to be satisfied, at the very least, in the overwhelming majority of biometric schemes.

At the same time, it bears emphasis that any biological material from which biometric data are derived is in itself not personal data and, concomitantly, not biometric data. This is made clear in recital 35 GDPR, which distinguishes between 'a body part or bodily substance' and 'information derived from the testing or examination of' such part/substance.[33] The distinction also conforms with the line taken by the WP29.[34]

Select Bibliography

EU legislation

GDPR Proposal: Proposal for a Regulation of the European Parliament and of the Council on the protection of individuals with regard to the processing of personal data and on the free movement of such data (General Data Protection Regulation), COM(2012) 11 final, 25 January 2012.

Regulation 2252/2004: Regulation (EC) No. 2252/2004 of the European Parliament and of the Council of 13 December 2004 on standards for security features and biometrics in passports and travel documents issued by Member States, OJ 2004 L 385/1.

Regulation 2017/2226: Regulation (EU) 2017/2226 of the European Parliament and of the Council of 30 November 2017 establishing an Entry/Exit System (EES) to register entry and exit data and refusal of entry data of third-country nationals crossing the external borders of the Member States and determining the conditions for access to the EES for law enforcement purposes, and amending the Convention implementing the Schengen Agreement and Regulations (EC) No. 767/2008 and (EU) No. 1077/2011, OJ 2017 L 327/20.

Academic writings

Kindt 2013: Kindt, *Privacy and Data Protection Issues of Biometric Applications: A Comparative Legal Analysis* (Springer 2013).

Koops 2016, Koops, 'Criminal Investigation and Privacy in Dutch Law', *TILT Law & Technology Working Paper Series* (September 2016), available at https://papers.ssrn.com/abstract=2837483.

Liu 2011: Liu, *Bio-Privacy: Privacy Regulations and the Challenge of Biometrics* (Routledge 2011).

Meints and Gasson 2009: Meints and Gasson, 'High-Tech ID and Emerging Technologies', in Rannenberg, Royer and Deuker (eds.), *The Future of Identity in the Information Society* (Springer 2009), 130.

Wayman et al. 2004: Wayman, Jain, Maltoni and Maio (eds.), *Biometric Systems: Technology, Design and Performance Evaluation* (Springer 2004).

Papers of data protection authorities

EDPB 2019: European Data Protection Board, 'Guidelines 3/2019 on the processing of personal data through video devices (version for public consultation)' (10 July 2019).

---

[32] WP29 2003, p. 5, fn. 11 (referring to 'cases where biometric data, like a template, are stored in a way that no reasonable means can be used by the controller or by any other person to identify the data subject', and stating that those data accordingly 'should not be qualified as personal data'). Cf. Kindt 2013, p. 117 (arguing that biometric data, including biometric templates, will, regardless of their format, 'in principle' be personal data, particularly in light of technological developments).

[33] See also the commentary on Art. 4(1) in this volume.

[34] See WP29 2007, p. 9: 'Human tissue samples (like a blood sample) are themselves sources out of which biometric data are extracted, but they are not biometric data themselves'. See also WP29 2012B, p. 4.

WP29 2003: Article 29 Working Party, 'Working Document on Biometrics' (WP 80, 1 August 2003).
WP29 2007: Article 29 Working Party, 'Opinion 4/2007 on the Concept of Personal Data' (WP 136, 20 June 2007).
WP29 2012A: Article 29 Working Party, 'Opinion 2/2012 on Facial Recognition in Online and Mobile Services' (WP 192, 22 March 2012).
WP29 2012B: Article 29 Working Party, 'Opinion 3/2012 on Developments in Biometric Technologies' (WP 193, 27 April 2012).

Reports and recommendations

Council Report 2013: Proposal for a regulation of the European Parliament and of the Council on the protection of individuals with regard to the processing of personal data and on the free movement of such data (General Data Protection Regulation), 17831/13, 16 December 2013.
Council Report 2015: Written debriefing of trilogue of 24 November, 14461/15, 25 November 2015.
Explanatory Report Convention 108 2018: Council of Europe, 'Explanatory Report to the Protocol Amending the Convention for the Protection of Individuals with Regard to the Automatic Processing of Personal Data' (10 October 2018), available at https://rm.coe.int/cets-223-explanatory-report-to-the-protocol-amending-the-convention-fo/16808ac91a.
OECD 2004: Organisation for Economic Co-operation and Development, 'Biometric-Based Technologies' (DSTI/ICCP/REG(2003)2/FINAL, April 2004).

Article 4(15). Data concerning health

LEE A. BYGRAVE   LUCA TOSONI

'data concerning health' means personal data related to the physical or mental health of a natural person, including the provision of health care services, which reveal information about his or her health status;

Relevant Recital

(35) Personal data concerning health should include all data pertaining to the health status of a data subject which reveal information relating to the past, current or future physical or mental health status of the data subject. This includes information about the natural person collected in the course of the registration for, or the provision of, health care services as referred to in Directive 2011/24/EU of the European Parliament and of the Council to that natural person; a number, symbol or particular assigned to a natural person to uniquely identify the natural person for health purposes; information derived from the testing or examination of a body part or bodily substance, including from genetic data and biological samples; and any information on, for example, a disease, disability, disease risk, medical history, clinical treatment or the physiological or biomedical state of the data subject independent of its source, for example from a physician or other health professional, a hospital, a medical device or an in vitro diagnostic test.

Closely Related Provisions

Article 4(1) (Definition of 'personal data') (see too recital 26); Article 4(13) (Definition of 'genetic data') (see also recital 34); Article 4(16) (Definition of 'biometric data') (see too recital 51); Article 9(1) (Processing of special categories of personal data) (see also recital 53); Article 22(4) (Automated individual decision-making, including profiling) (see also recital 71); Article 35(3)(b) (Data protection impact assessment) (see too recital 91)

Related Provisions in LED [Directive (EU) 2016/680]

Article 3(14) (Definition of 'data concerning health'); Article 3(1) (Definition of 'personal data') (see too recital 21); Article 3(12) (Definition of 'genetic data'); Article 3(13) (Definition of 'biometric data'); Article 10 (Processing of special categories of personal data) (see too recital 51); Article 11(2) (Automated individual decision-making); Article 29(1) (Security of processing)

Related Provisions in EUDPR [Regulation (EU) 2018/1725]

Article 3(19) (Definition of 'data concerning health'); Article 3(1) (Definition of 'personal data') (see too recitals 16 and 18); Article 3(17) (Definition of 'genetic data'); Article 3(18) (Definition of 'biometric data'); Article 10(1) (Processing of special categories of personal data) (see too recital 29); Article 24(4) (Automated individual decision-making, including profiling); Article 39(3)(b) (Data protection impact assessment); Article 76 (Processing of special categories of operational personal data); Article 77(2)–(3) (Automated individual decision-making, including profiling); Article 91(1) (Security of processing of operational personal data)

Relevant Case Law

CJEU

Case C-62/90, *Commission of the European Communities v Federal Republic of Germany*, judgment of 8 April 1992 (ECLI:EU:C:1992:169).
Case C-101/01, *Criminal proceedings against Bodil Lindqvist*, judgment of 6 November 2003 (ECLI:EU:C:2003:596).
Case T-105/03, *Triantafyllia Dionyssopoulou* v *Council of the European Union*, CFI, judgment of 31 May 2005 (ECLI:EU:T:2005:189).
Case T-343/13, *CN v European Parliament*, GC, judgment of 3 December 2015 (ECLI:EU:T:2015:926).

ECtHR

Z v Finland, Appl. No. 22009/93, judgment of 25 February 1997.
MS v Sweden, Appl. No. 20837/92, judgment of 27 August 1997.
I v Finland, Appl. No. 20511/03, judgment of 17 July 2008.

Italian Supreme Court

Judgment No. 18980 of 8 August 2013.
Judgment No. 10280 of 20 May 2015.

UK Court of Appeal

B v The General Medical Council [2018] EWCA Civ 1497.

A. Rationale and Policy Underpinnings

Data concerning the health of natural persons ('health data') have traditionally been regarded as sensitive. This is reflected in long-standing rules to protect the confidentiality of the medical records that doctors keep on their patients—rules that predate the emergence of modern data protection laws. The sensitivity of health data is tied to a commonly held perception that they reveal some of the most intimate and private aspects of ourselves— not least our core vulnerabilities—and to a concomitant fear that if the data are widely disclosed, they may lead to stigma and unfair discrimination. In a more utilitarian perspective, there is also concern that people will not seek health care, communicate candidly with health care providers, or willingly participate in health research projects, for fear of data disclosure.[1]

---

[1] See e.g. ECtHR, *Z v Finland*, para. 95: 'Respecting the confidentiality of health data is ... crucial not only to respect the sense of privacy of a patient but also to preserve his or her confidence in the medical profession and in the health services in general. Without such protection those in need of medical assistance may

As elaborated below, EU data protection laws have consistently included health data in their lists of sensitive data requiring special safeguards. The GDPR continues this tradition.

During the GDPR legislative process, the Commission, Parliament and Council each put forward differing definitions of 'data concerning health'. The European Commission's GDPR Proposal defined the term as 'any information which relates to the physical or mental health of an individual, or to the provision of health services to the individual' (Article 4(13) GDPR Proposal). The European Parliament modified this definition slightly by replacing 'information' with 'personal data',[2] whereas the Council proposed a definition stripped of specific references to personal data and to provision of health care services: 'data related to the physical or mental health of an individual, which reveal information about his or her health status'.[3] The GDPR trilogue discussions ended up adopting a definition that is closer to the Commission and Parliament's proposals than that of the Council.

B. Legal Background

1. EU legislation

The DPD contained provisions that placed relatively stringent limits on the processing of 'data concerning health' (Article 8(1) DPD), but left the term undefined.

Both the EUDPR and LED define 'data concerning health' identically to the GDPR (see Article 3(19) EUDPR and Article 3(14) LED).[4] This is also the case with Council Regulation 2017/1939 on the establishment of the European Public Prosecutor's Office (see Article 2(21)).

Remarkably, Regulation 2016/794 on Europol lays down restrictions on the processing of 'data concerning health' (Article 30(2)) but does not define the term. Nonetheless, its conception of health data is highly likely to conform to that of the GDPR, LED and EUDPR. Moreover, it defines 'genetic data' in essentially the same way as the term is defined in the GDPR, LED and EUDPR and thus makes clear that such data may also reveal information on the health of the data subject (see Article 2(j)).

2. International instruments

Convention 108 as originally adopted includes 'personal data concerning health' in its list of 'special categories of data' (Article 6) but does not define the term. The same applies with regard to Modernised Convention 108. The Explanatory Report to the latter Convention elaborates on the meaning of such data as follows:

Information concerning health includes information concerning the past, present and future, physical or mental health of an individual, and which may refer to a person who is sick or healthy.

---

be deterred, when revealing such information of a personal and intimate nature as may be necessary in order to receive the appropriate treatment, from seeking such assistance thereby endangering their own health but, in the case of transmissible diseases, that of the community'. Further on the empirical basis for such views, see e.g. Mulligan and Braunack-Mayer 2004.

[2] EP Resolution GDPR 2014, Art. 4(12). [3] Council Report 2015, p. 79.

[4] This entails that the term should be interpreted uniformly across these legal instruments. See too recital 5 EUDPR.

Processing images of persons with thick glasses, a broken leg, burnt skin or any other visible characteristics related to a person's health can only be considered as processing sensitive data when the processing is based on the health information that can be extracted from the pictures.[5]

The Council of Europe has adopted a range of other instruments dealing with the processing of health data. Especially significant is the Convention on Human Rights and Biomedicine,[6] which provides for a general right to respect for private life in relation to 'health information' (Article 10(1)) and for a right of data subjects to access their health information, noting at the same time that 'the wishes of individuals not to be so informed shall be observed' (Article 10(2)). However, the Convention and its Explanatory Report do not define 'health information'.

In addition, the Council of Europe has issued numerous recommendations concerning use of health information which provide more detailed specifications of the relatively abstract, high order norms in its treaties.[7] Some of these recommendations define health information or closely related terms. For instance, CoE Recommendation R (97) 5 on the Protection of Medical Data states:

[T]he expression 'medical data' refers to all personal data concerning the health of an individual. It refers also to data which have a clear and close link with health as well as to genetic data.[8]

Another notable source of guidance is provided by the International Organization for Standardization ('ISO'), which has issued guidelines for information security standards and security management practices in respect of 'health informatics'. The guidelines define 'health data' as:

[A]ny information which relates to the physical or mental health of an individual, or to the provision of health service to the individual, and which may include: (a) information about the registration of the individual for the provision of health services; (b) information about payments or eligibility for healthcare with respect to the individual; (c) a number, symbol or particular assigned to an individual to uniquely identify the individual for health purposes; (d) any information about the individual collected in the course of the provision of health services to the individual; (e) information derived from the testing or examination of a body part or bodily substance; and (f) identification of a person (healthcare professional) as provider of healthcare to the individual.[9]

3. National developments

From their inception, national data protection laws in Europe have subjected the processing of health data to special protections. Sweden's Data Act 1973—the world's first data protection law at national level—laid down relatively stringent limits on the processing of such data (section 4), and thereby established a template that other European countries tended to follow.[10] Nonetheless, EU/EEA Member States' respective data protection regimes for the processing of health data varied considerably prior to adoption of the GDPR.[11] This extended also to their respective conceptions of what constitutes such data, particularly as the DPD did not define this data category.[12]

The adoption of the GDPR is intended to iron out this variation, but not to eliminate it entirely. Article 9(4) GDPR permits Member States to customise their respective data

---

[5] Explanatory Report Convention 108 2018, para. 60.　　[6] Biomedicine Convention.
[7] See e.g. COM Recommendation 1981 and COM Recommendation 1997.
[8] COM Recommendation 1997, clause 1.　　[9] ISO 2016.
[10] Swedish Personal Data Act 1973.　　[11] See generally Beyleveld et al. 2004.　　[12] Ibid.

protection rules for processing health data (along with genetic data and biometric data), and this is likely to result in some variation persisting. Member State regimes must nevertheless apply the definition of health data in Article 4(15) GDPR.

4. Case law

In *Lindqvist*, the CJEU adopted a broad interpretation of the term 'data concerning health' as used in Article 8(1) DPD:

In the light of the purpose of the directive, the expression 'data concerning health' used in Article 8(1) thereof must be given a wide interpretation so as to include information concerning all aspects, both physical and mental, of the health of an individual.[13]

The Court went on to hold that 'reference to the fact that an individual has injured her foot and is on half-time on medical grounds constitutes personal data concerning health within the meaning of Article 8(1) of Directive 95/46'.[14] The Court has taken an analogous line in subsequent jurisprudence.[15]

At the same time, the Court has made the relatively trite point in *Dionyssopoulou* that the term 'data concerning health' does not extend to references or expressions that do not give rise to the disclosure of any data regarding a person's health or medical condition.[16]

The Court's teleological approach in *Lindqvist* leveraged off not just the DPD's aim of providing a 'high level' of data protection across the EU (recital 10 DPD), but also previous case law privileging the confidentiality of health data—though this was not made explicit in the judgment. Already in 1992, the Court recognised 'a right to the protection of medical confidentiality' as a 'fundamental right protected by the legal order of the Community'.[17] Moreover, there is a well-established line of ECtHR jurisprudence emphasising the confidentiality of health data as a 'vital principle' in the legal systems of all the Contracting Parties to the European Convention on Human Rights ('ECHR').[18]

National courts have also handed down judgments on the definition of health data under domestic data protection law. Some of the judgments have concerned clear-cut cases of health data,[19] others less clear-cut. Two judgments of the Italian Supreme Court fall within the latter category. In one of the judgments, the Court held that information on a sick leave of an employee constitutes sensitive data even though it does not include information on a specific disease.[20] In the other judgment, the Court found that a bank did not process health data where a payor indicated as the purpose of a bank transfer a reference to an Italian law establishing a compensation scheme for patients damaged by a

---

[13] Case C-101/01, *Lindqvist*, para. 50. [14] Ibid., para. 51.
[15] Case T-343/13, *CN*, para. 50.
[16] See Case T-105/03, *Dionyssopoulou*, which concerned, inter alia, the question whether a reference to 'personal constraints' in a staff report drawn up by the Council on one of its former employees constituted 'data concerning health' of that employee. The Court concluded in the negative, stating at para. 33: 'Il suffit de relever, à cet égard, que l'expression "contraintes personnelles" n'entraîne la divulgation d'aucune donnée relative à la santé ou à la condition médicale de la requérante et ne constitue nullement une donnée à caractère personnel'. The Court reaffirmed this in subsequent case law: see Case T-343/13, *CN*, para. 50.
[17] Case C-62/90, *Commission v Germany*, para. 23.
[18] ECtHR, *Z v Finland*, para. 95; ECtHR, *MS v Sweden*, para. 41; ECtHR, *I v Finland*, para. 38.
[19] E.g. Lord Justice Sales of the UK Court of Appeal had little trouble in holding that information about a person's bladder cancer constituted 'information as to … physical or mental health or condition'. See *B v The General Medical Council*, para. 81, with Lady Justice Arden concurring on this point (para. 96).
[20] Italian Supreme Court, judgment No. 18980 of 8 August 2013.

vaccine or blood transfusion.[21] The Court held this on the basis that the law in question provided that, in certain cases, a compensation could be paid also to the spouse, heirs, parents or siblings of the damaged patient. Thus, a generic reference to the law in question in the bank transfer was not sufficient in itself to learn about the health status of the recipient of the payment. The case has parallels to the above-cited CJEU decision in *Dionyssopoulou*, though the latter was not cited by the Italian Court.

C. Analysis

The definition in Article 4(15) is intentionally cast wide, reflecting the case law of the CJEU and ECtHR set out in the previous section. Recital 35 amplifies this range. In effect, the definition encompasses all elements of the above-cited definition of health data laid down by the ISO,[22] and goes even further.

Guidance from the WP29 is especially instructive in teasing out the various dimensions of the definition.[23] As pointed out by the WP29, health data are more than medical data (in the sense of 'data about the physical or mental health status of a data subject that are generated in a professional, medical context') and more than data on ill-health.[24] Further, the definition covers not just past and present health status but also future status—as recital 35 makes clear. Thus, it extends to 'information where there is scientifically proven or commonly perceived risk of disease in the future'. At the same time, the definition has limits: it does not cover 'data from which no conclusions can be reasonably drawn about the health status of a data subject'. Here, the WP29 gave the example of a step-counting app that is unable to link the data on the number of steps walked with other data on the data subject, and is used outside a specific medical context. But, the WP29 warned, '[r]aw, relatively low privacy impact personal data can quickly change into health data when the dataset can be used to determine the health status of a person'.

As noted in the commentaries on the definitions of 'genetic data' in Article 4(13) and 'biometric data' in Article 4(14) in this volume, there is considerable overlap between both of those data categories and that of health data, but this overlap is not really problematic. In this regard, it should be remembered that Article 9(4) GDPR gives Member States significant leeway when formulating rules for the processing of genetic data, biometric data and data concerning health.

Like genetic data and biometric data, health data are defined as a subcategory of personal data and must therefore satisfy the criteria baked into the definition in Article 4(1) GDPR, as elaborated in recital 26 GDPR, before they can qualify as data concerning health under Article 4(15). If the health data are also genetic or biometric, meeting this precondition will be relatively easy.[25]

---

[21] Italian Supreme Court, judgment No. 10280 of 20 May 2015.

[22] ISO 2016. It is worth noting that the EDPS lobbied for the ISO's definition to form the point of departure for defining health data in the proposal for a directive on patients' rights in cross-border health care, a definition to be possibly replicated in future legal acts. See EDPS 2009, paras. 16–17.

[23] WP29 2015. The following passages are all taken from this document which was published without pagination. More limited guidance is also found in WP29 2007A, p. 7.

[24] In this respect, the EDPS noted that 'health data normally includes medical data (e.g. doctor referrals and prescriptions, medical examination reports, laboratory tests, radiographs etc.), as well as administrative and financial data relating to health (e.g. documents concerning hospital admissions, social security number, medical appointments scheduling, invoices for healthcare service provision, etc.)'. See EDPS 2009, para. 15.

[25] See further the commentaries on Art. 4(13)–(14) in this volume.

However, any biological material from which health data are derived is in itself not personal data and, accordingly, not data concerning health. This is evidenced from the wording of recital 35 GDPR, which distinguishes between 'a body part or bodily substance' and 'information derived from the testing or examination of' such part/substance.[26] The same distinction was made by some supervisory authorities, although prior to the adoption of the GDPR.[27] A similar distinction was made by the WP29 in the context of biometric data.[28]

Select Bibliography

International agreements

Biomedicine Convention: Convention for the Protection of Human Rights and Dignity of the Human Being with regard to the Application of Biology and Medicine: Convention on Human Rights and Biomedicine, ETS 164, 4 April 1997.

EU legislation

Council Regulation (EU) 2017/1939 of 12 October 2017 implementing enhanced cooperation on the establishment of the European Public Prosecutor's Office ('the EPPO'), OJ 2017 L 283/1.

GDPR Proposal: Proposal for a Regulation of the European Parliament and of the Council on the protection of individuals with regard to the processing of personal data and on the free movement of such data (General Data Protection Regulation), COM(2012) 11 final, 25 January 2012.

Regulation (EU) 2016/794 of the European Parliament and of the Council of 11 May 2016 on the European Union Agency for Law Enforcement Cooperation (Europol) and replacing and repealing Council Decisions 2009/371/JHA, 2009/934/JHA, 2009/935/JHA, 2009/936/JHA and 2009/968/JHA, OJ 2016 L 135/53.

National legislation

Swedish Personal Data Act 1973: Personal Data Act 1973 (Datalagen, SFS 298:73) (repealed).

Academic writings

Beyleveld et al. 2004: Beyleveld, Townend, Rouillé-Mirza and Wright (eds.), *Implementation of the Data Protection Directive in Relation to Medical Research in Europe* (Ashgate 2004).

Mulligan and Braunack-Mayer 2004: Mulligan and Braunack-Mayer, 'Why Protect Confidentiality in Health Records? A Review of Research Evidence', 28(1) *Australian Health Review* (2004), 48.

Papers of data protection authorities

EDPS 2009: European Data Protection Supervisor, 'Opinion of the European Data Protection Supervisor on the Proposal for a Directive of the European Parliament and of the Council on the Application of Patients' Rights in Cross-Border Healthcare', OJ 2009 C 128/03.

WP29 2007A: Article 29 Working Party, 'Working Document on the Processing of Personal Data Relating to Health in Electronic Health Records (EHR)' (WP 131, 15 February 2007).

---

[26] See also the commentary on Art. 4(1) in this volume.

[27] For example, the Italian Data Protection Authority found that the genotypic information contained in a human biological sample qualifies as personal data only if it is extracted from the biological sample and stored in, say, medical records. See Italian Data Protection Authority 2007.

[28] See WP29 2007B, p. 9: 'Human tissue samples (like a blood sample) are themselves sources out of which biometric data are extracted, but they are not biometric data themselves'. See also WP29 2012, p. 4.

WP29 2007B: Article 29 Working Party, 'Opinion 4/2007 on the Concept of Personal Data' (WP 136, 20 June 2007).
WP29 2012: Article 29 Working Party, 'Opinion 3/2012 on Developments in Biometric Technologies' (WP 193, 27 April 2012).
WP29 2015: Article 29 Working Party, 'Annex—Health Data in Apps and Devices' (5 February 2015).
Italian Data Protection Authority 2007: Garante per la protezione dei dati personali, 'Campione biologico e dato personale genetico' (21 June 2007).

Reports and recommendations

COM Recommendation 1981: Committee of Ministers of the Council of Europe, 'Recommendation on regulations for automated medical data banks' (Rec(81)1, 23 January 1981).
COM Recommendation 1997: Committee of Ministers of the Council of Europe, 'Recommendation on the Protection of Medical Data', (Rec(1997)5, 13 February 1997).
Council Report 2013: Proposal for a regulation of the European Parliament and of the Council on the protection of individuals with regard to the processing of personal data and on the free movement of such data (General Data Protection Regulation), 17831/13, 16 December 2013.
Council Report 2015: Preparation of a general approach, 9565/15, 15 June 2015.
EP Resolution GDPR 2014: European Parliament legislative resolution of 12 March 2014 on the proposal for a regulation of the European Parliament and of the Council on the protection of individuals with regard to the processing of personal data and on the free movement of such data (General Data Protection Regulation), P7_TA(2014)0212, 12 March 2014.
Explanatory Report Convention 108 2018: Council of Europe, 'Explanatory Report to the Protocol Amending the Convention for the Protection of Individuals with Regard to the Automatic Processing of Personal Data' (10 October 2018), available at https://rm.coe.int/cets-223-explanatory-report-to-the-protocol-amending-the-convention-fo/16808ac91a.
ISO 2016: International Organization for Standardization, 'Health Informatics—Information Security Management in Health Using ISO/IEC 27002', ISO 27799:2016 (2016).

Article 4(16). Main establishment

LUCA TOSONI

'main establishment' means:

(a) as regards a controller with establishments in more than one Member State, the place of its central administration in the Union, unless the decisions on the purposes and means of the processing of personal data are taken in another establishment of the controller in the Union and the latter establishment has the power to have such decisions implemented, in which case the establishment having taken such decisions is to be considered to be the main establishment;
(b) as regards a processor with establishments in more than one Member State, the place of its central administration in the Union, or, if the processor has no central administration in the Union, the establishment of the processor in the Union where the main processing activities in the context of the activities of an establishment of the processor take place to the extent that the processor is subject to specific obligations under this Regulation;

Relevant Recitals

(22) Any processing of personal data in the context of the activities of an establishment of a controller or a processor in the Union should be carried out in accordance with this Regulation, regardless of whether the processing itself takes place within the Union. Establishment implies the effective and real exercise of activity through stable arrangements. The legal form of such arrangements, whether through a branch or a subsidiary with a legal personality, is not the determining factor in that respect.

(36) The main establishment of a controller in the Union should be the place of its central administration in the Union, unless the decisions on the purposes and means of the processing of personal data are taken in another establishment of the controller in the Union, in which case that other establishment should be considered to be the main establishment. The main establishment of a controller in the Union should be determined according to objective criteria and should imply the effective and real exercise of management activities determining the main decisions as to the purposes and means of processing through stable arrangements. That criterion should not depend on whether the processing of personal data is carried out at that location. The presence and use of technical means and technologies for processing personal data or processing activities do not, in themselves, constitute a main establishment and are therefore not determining criteria for a main establishment. The main establishment of the processor should be the place of its central administration in the Union or, if it has no central administration in the Union, the place where the main processing activities take place in the Union. In cases involving both the controller and the processor, the competent lead supervisory authority should remain the supervisory authority of the Member State where the controller has its main establishment, but the supervisory authority of the processor should be considered to be a supervisory authority concerned and that supervisory authority should participate in the cooperation procedure provided for by this Regulation. In any case, the supervisory authorities of the Member State or Member States where the processor has one or more establishments should not be considered to be supervisory authorities concerned where the draft decision concerns only the controller. Where the processing is carried out by a

group of undertakings, the main establishment of the controlling undertaking should be considered to be the main establishment of the group of undertakings, except where the purposes and means of processing are determined by another undertaking.

Closely Related Provisions

Article 4(7) (Definition of 'controller'); Article 4(8) (Definition of 'processor'); Article 4(19) (Definition of 'group of undertakings'); Article 56 (Competence of the lead supervisory authority) (see too recitals 124–128); Article 60 (Cooperation between the lead supervisory authority and the other supervisory authorities concerned) (see too recitals 130–131); Article 65 (Dispute resolution by the Board)

Relevant Case Law

CJEU

Case C-81/87, *The Queen v Treasury and Commissioners of Inland Revenue, ex parte Daily Mail and General Trust plc*, judgment of 27 September 1988 (ECLI:EU:C:1988:456).

Opinion of Advocate General Darmon in Case C-81/87, *The Queen v Treasury and Commissioners of Inland Revenue, ex parte Daily Mail and General Trust plc*, delivered on 7 June 1988 (ECLI:EU:C:1988:286).

Case C-210/06, *Cartesio Oktató és Szolgáltató bt*, judgment of 16 December 2008 (Grand Chamber) (ECLI:EU:C:2008:723).

Case C-131/12, *Google Spain v Agencia Española de Protección de Datos (AEPD) and Mario Costeja González*, judgment of 13 May 2014 (Grand Chamber) (ECLI:EU:C:2014:317).

Case C-230/14, *Weltimmo s.r.o. v Nemzeti Adatvédelmi és Információszabadság Hatóság*, judgment of 1 October 2015 (ECLI:EU:C:2015:639).

Case C-191/15, *Verein für Konsumenteninformation v Amazon EU Sàrl*, judgment of 28 July 2016 (ECLI:EU:C:2016:612).

Case C-210/16, *Unabhängiges Landeszentrum für Datenschutz Schleswig-Holstein v Wirtschaftsakademie Schleswig-Holstein GmbH*, judgment of 5 June 2018 (Grand Chamber) (ECLI:EU:C:2018:388).

Opinion of Advocate General Bot in Case C-210/16, *Unabhängiges Landeszentrum für Datenschutz Schleswig-Holstein v Wirtschaftsakademie Schleswig-Holstein GmbH*, delivered on 24 October 2017 (ECLI:EU:C:2017:796).

Case C-617/15, *Hummel Holding A/S v Nike Inc. and Nike Retail B.V.*, judgment of 18 May 2017 (ECLI:EU:C:2017:390).

Opinion of Advocate General Tanchev in Case C-617/15, *Hummel Holding A/S v Nike Inc. and Nike Retail B.V.*, delivered on 12 January 2017 (ECLI:EU:C:2017:13).

Opinion of Advocate General Szpunar in Case C-673/17, *Planet49 GmbH v Bundesverband der Verbraucherzentralen und Verbraucherverbände—Verbraucherzentrale Bundesverband e.V.*, delivered on 21 March 2019 (ECLI:EU:C:2019:246).

Germany

German Federal Court of Justice (*Bundesgerichtshof*), judgment XII ZB 114/06 of 27 June 2007

United Kingdom

UK Court of Appeal, *Young v Anglo American South Africa Limited* [2014] EWCA Civ 1130

A. Rationale and Policy Underpinnings

The definition of 'main establishment' in Article 4(16) GDPR is primarily intended to determine which national supervisory authority should be the 'lead supervisory authority' in a specific cross-border enforcement case, where the controller or processor has establishments in multiple EU/EEA countries.[1] Article 56 GDPR terms as 'lead supervisory authority' the authority with the chief responsibility for dealing with a given cross-border data processing activity in accordance with the 'one-stop-shop' mechanism.[2] The latter is an enforcement scheme intended to ensure that controllers and processors with multiple EU/EEA establishments, or whose activities substantially affect data subjects in several EU/EEA countries, have one single supervisory authority as their sole interlocutor with respect to cross-border data protection compliance matters. The 'one-stop-shop' mechanism was introduced to help remedy the legal uncertainty and costs linked with the inconsistent enforcement of EU data protection rules across borders. These problems were often cited among the principal shortcomings of the DPD.[3]

The concept of 'main establishment' constitutes the cornerstone on which the 'one-stop-shop' mechanism is built.[4] Indeed, if there is no 'main establishment' (or single establishment where the processing substantially affects or is likely to substantially affect data subjects in more than one Member State) in the EU/EEA, the mechanism does not apply.[5]

In light of the above, the WP29 noted that:

[C]orrect identification of the main establishment is in the interests of controllers and processors because it provides clarity in terms of which supervisory authority they have to deal with in respect of their various compliance duties under the GDPR. These may include, where relevant, designating a data protection officer or consulting for a risky processing activity that the controller cannot mitigate by reasonable means. The relevant provisions of the GDPR are intended to make these compliance tasks manageable.[6]

---

[1] See WP29 2012, p. 16.

[2] Advocate General Bot described the GDPR's one-stop-shop mechanism as a scheme according to which 'a controller that carries out cross-border data processing, such as Facebook, will have only one supervisory authority as interlocutor, namely the lead supervisory authority, which will be the authority for the place where the controller's main establishment is located': see Case C-210/16, *Wirtschaftsakademie* (AG Opinion), para. 103. See also WP29 2017, p. 4 (noting that the 'lead supervisory authority' is 'the authority with the primary responsibility for dealing with a cross-border data processing activity'). See further the commentaries on Arts. 56 and 60 in this volume.

[3] See e.g. EC Staff Working Paper 2012, p. 36.

[4] See also WP29 2012, p. 11 (noting that '[a] clear understanding of the term "main establishment" is crucial, as it is decisive for determining the lead authority ... where processing of personal data takes place in the context of the activities of an establishment of a controller or a processor in the Union, and the controller or processor is established in more than one Member State').

[5] The WP29 opined that 'controllers without any establishment in the EU must deal with local supervisory authorities in every Member State they are active in, through their local representative'. See WP29 2017, p. 10.

[6] Ibid., p. 6.

B. Legal Background

1. EU legislation

The DPD did not use the term 'main establishment' or similar terms. However, the DPD referred to the concept of 'establishment' as a criterion to identify the national law(s) applicable to the processing of personal data (Article 4(1)(a) and recital 19 DPD), and indirectly to determine which supervisory authority or authorities was/were competent under Article 28(1) DPD to apply the relevant national data protection rules to that processing. Nonetheless, the DPD did not lay down any criterion of priority governing the intervention of one supervisory authority as against another in cases where a controller was established on the territory of multiple EU/EEA countries.

The concept of 'place of central administration'—i.e. a key component of the definition of 'main establishment' in Article 4(16) GDPR—was also absent in the DPD. It is, however, found in Article 54 of the Treaty on the Functioning of the European Union ('TFEU') and in several other EU Regulations.[7]

2. International instruments

The concept of 'main establishment' is not found in Convention 108, either in its original or modernised version. The same applies with respect to the OECD Privacy Guidelines (both original and revised versions) and the APEC Privacy Framework.

3. National developments

Some national data protection laws establish specific arrangements to align their national systems with the GDPR's 'one-stop-shop' mechanism, including by laying down rules to identify the competent local supervisory authority based on the location of the controller's or processor's 'main establishment'. For example, section 19 of the German GDPR Implementation Law provides that:

[T]he lead supervisory authority of a *Land* in the one-stop-shop mechanism pursuant to Chapter VII of Regulation (EU) 2016/679 shall be the supervisory authority of the *Land* in which the controller or processor has its main establishment, as referred to in Article 4 no. 16 of Regulation (EU) 2016/679 or its single establishment in the European Union, as referred to in Article 56(1) of Regulation (EU) 2016/679 ... [8]

4. Case law

The CJEU has yet to rule on the definition of 'main establishment' under the GDPR. However, the Court has interpreted the concept of 'establishment' within the meaning of the DPD, as well as that of 'place of central administration' under other EU legal instruments. The latter concept has also been interpreted by national courts. This jurisprudence is referenced in the next section.

---

[7] See e.g. Art. 19(1) Rome I Regulation; Art. 63(1)(b) Regulation 1215/2012; Art. 60(1)(b) Brussels I Regulation (repealed).
[8] German GDPR Implementation Law.

C. Analysis

1. Introduction

The definition of 'main establishment' in Article 4(16) GDPR resembles a house of cards. The Article is subdivided into two parts which delineate the definition slightly differently for controllers and processors. Both of these parts are in turn built around two key concepts which function as connecting factors: (i) establishment; and (ii) place of central administration. As a result, the meaning of these concepts is crucial to identify the 'main establishment' of a controller or processor.

2. The concept of establishment

Before trying to establish where the *main* establishment of a controller or processor is in accordance with the criteria of Article 4(16) GDPR, it is first necessary to assess whether and where the relevant entity has *establishments* in the EU/EEA.[9] Indeed, the incipit of both point (a) and (b) of Article 4(16) makes clear that the definition of 'main establishment' only applies to controllers and processor 'with establishments in more than one Member State'.[10]

The concept of 'establishment' is not defined in the GDPR, but recital 22 states that '[e]stablishment implies the effective and real exercise of activity through stable arrangements. The legal form of such arrangements, whether through a branch or a subsidiary with a legal personality, is not the determining factor in that respect'. This wording essentially reproduces that of recital 19 DPD,[11] which led the CJEU to uphold a flexible understanding of the concept of 'establishment' within the meaning of the DPD.[12] Indeed, according to the Court, the concept 'extends to any real and effective activity— even a minimal one—exercised through stable arrangements'.[13] However, the Court clarified that 'both the degree of stability of the arrangements and the effective exercise of activities [in a Member State] must be interpreted in the light of the specific nature of the economic activities and the provision of services concerned'.[14] In this regard, the Court held that even the presence of a representative in a Member State could, in some circumstances 'suffice to constitute a stable arrangement if that representative acts with a sufficient degree of stability through the presence of the necessary equipment for provision of the specific services concerned in the Member State in question'.[15]

---

[9] Pursuant to s. 8 of Protocol 1 to the EEA Agreement, whenever the acts incorporated in the Annexes to the Agreement (like the GDPR) refer to the territory of the 'Community' (now, 'Union'), such references should be understood as references to the territories of the EEA countries (i.e. the EU Member States plus Iceland, Liechtenstein and Norway).

[10] It should be noted that point (b) of entry 5e of Annex XI to the EEA Agreement specifies that the term 'Member State(s)' in the GDPR shall be understood to include, in addition to its meaning in the Regulation, the three EEA EFTA States (i.e. Iceland, Liechtenstein and Norway).

[11] Rec. 19 DPD stated that 'establishment on the territory of a Member State implies the effective and real exercise of activity through stable arrangements' and that 'the legal form of such an establishment, whether simply [a] branch or a subsidiary with a legal personality, is not the determining factor'. See also Case C-131/12, *Google Spain*, para. 48.

[12] See Case C-230/14, *Weltimmo*, para. 29.

[13] Ibid., para. 31. See further Case C-191/15, *Verein für Konsumenteninformation*, para. 75; Case C-210/16, *Wirtschaftsakademie*, paras. 53–55. For a critical view of the expanding scope of the concept of 'establishment', see Svantesson 2016.

[14] See Case C-230/14, *Weltimmo*, para. 29.   [15] Ibid., para. 30.

Against this background, the CJEU is likely to uphold a flexible understanding of the concept of 'establishment' in Article 4(16) GDPR and to reject a formalistic approach whereby a controller or processor is established in a Member State solely if it is formally registered or incorporated in that Member State.[16]

3. The concept of place of central administration

Under EU law, the concept of place of central administration is intrinsically linked to that of establishment, as the latter may take the form of setting up the former in the territory of a Member State. The place of central administration is generally perceived as the place where the actual running of a company takes place (i.e. where the main decision-making is made).[17] In essence, it normally corresponds to the operational headquarters or real seat of a company (*siège réel*), which does not necessarily coincide with the company's registered office or place of incorporation (*siège statutaire*). This understanding of the term would seem broadly to pertain to Article 4(16) GDPR as well, in particular as recital 36 GDPR states that the concept of 'main establishment ... should imply the effective and real exercise of management activities ... through stable arrangements'.

The term 'place of central administration' is not defined in the GDPR and the Regulation makes no reference to national laws for the purpose of determining its meaning. Thus, the term should be given an autonomous EU-wide meaning.[18] In light of the absence of specific guidance on the meaning of the term in the GDPR's legislative material, this meaning should be determined by recourse to sources going beyond the GDPR.[19] A natural source for guidance in interpreting the term is the case law on freedom of establishment, which under Article 54 TFEU applies to '[c]ompanies or firms formed in accordance with the law of a Member State and having their registered office, *central administration* or principal place of business within the Union' (emphasis added).[20]

While the CJEU has yet to define authoritatively the concept of 'central administration' within the meaning of the Treaties, in *Daily Mail*, Advocate General Darmon referred with approval to Everling's interpretation of the term 'central administration' in Article 58 of the Treaty of Rome (i.e. the legal antecedent of Article 54 TFEU).[21] In particular, the Advocate General opined that:

[E]stablishment may ... take the form of ... the transfer of the central management and control of the company, often regarded as its real head office. That is called 'primary establishment'. It has

---

[16] On the concept of establishment, see further the commentaries on Arts. 3 and 4(23) in this volume.

[17] See Harvey and Schilling 2013, p. 281.

[18] The CJEU has consistently held that the need for uniform application of EU law and the principle of equality require that the terms of a provision of EU law which makes no express reference to the law of the Member States for the purpose of determining its meaning and scope be normally given an autonomous and uniform interpretation throughout the EU, having regard not only to its wording but also to the context of the provision and the objective pursued by the legislation in question: see Case C-617/15, *Hummel Holding*, para. 22 and case law cited therein. An EU-wide meaning of 'place of central administration' is also consistent with the aim of Art. 4(16) GDPR to create a uniform EU-wide criterion for determining which supervisory authority should be the lead supervisory authority in a particular case.

[19] See, by analogy, the way in which Advocate General Tanchev interpreted the term 'establishment' under the Community Trade Mark Regulation (stating that '[i]n the absence of guidance in the legislative material, the term "establishment" under Article 97(1) CTMR necessarily has to be determined by recourse to sources going beyond the CTMR'): see Case C-617/15, *Hummel Holding* (AG Opinion), para. 30.

[20] For an overview of the CJEU case law on freedom of establishment, see EC Guide 2017.

[21] See Everling 1964, p. 75.

been said in that regard that 'central management and control is not a legal concept but an economic one' and that it 'is located where the company organs take the decisions that are essential for the company's operations'.[22]

The CJEU did not directly comment on the above views of the Advocate General, but it would seem to agree with him when noting that:

[T]he transfer of the central management and control of a company to another Member State amounts to the establishment of the company in that Member State because the company is locating its centre of decision-making there, which constitutes genuine and effective economic activity.[23]

Similarly, in *Cartesio*, the Court appears to regard the terms 'central administration' and 'real seat' of a company as equivalent.[24]

The case law on Article 60(1)(b) of the Brussels I Regulation (repealed) is another relevant source of inspiration for interpreting the term 'place of central administration' in Article 4(16) GDPR. Indeed, similarly to the GDPR, the Brussels I Regulation used the term as a connecting factor. For example, also on the basis of the Advocate General opinion cited above, the UK Court of Appeal held that the 'place of central administration' of a company within the meaning of Article 60(1)(b) of the Brussels I Regulation:

[I]s the place where the company concerned, through its relevant organs according to its own constitutional provisions, takes the decisions that are essential for that company's operations. That is ... the same thing as saying it is the place where the company, through its relevant organs, conducts its entrepreneurial management; for that management must involve making decisions that are essential for that company's operations ...[25]

A non-formalistic understanding of the term seems to follow also from the legislative history of Article 4(16) GDPR, as several Member States unsuccessfully tried to modify the definition of 'main establishment' to lay down a formal connecting criterion, which referred to the place of incorporation of the relevant entity.[26]

In view of technological developments, it can be difficult to pinpoint the 'place of central administration' in practice. Indeed, the directors of a company may often take part in the decision-making without being physically present in a given place—e.g. by attending a meeting via videoconference.[27]

---

[22] See Case C-81/87, *Daily Mail* (AG Opinion), para. 4. It is worth noting that the Advocate General uses the term 'central management and control' as equivalent to 'central administration'. This emerges more clearly e.g. in the French and Italian versions of para. 4 of the Opinion which use the term 'administration centrale' and 'amministrazione centrale', respectively.

[23] See Case C-81/87, *Daily Mail*, para. 12. Just like the Advocate General, the Court seems to treat the expressions 'central management and control' and 'central administration' as equivalent.

[24] See Case C-210/06, *Cartesio*, para. 105.

[25] UK Court of Appeal, *Young v Anglo American South Africa Limited*, para. 45. It should be noted that the UK Court held that the meaning of 'central administration' was *acte clair* and so found it unnecessary to refer the case to the CJEU under Art. 267 TFEU. The German Federal Court of Justice (*Bundesgerichtshof*) interpreted the term under the Brussels I Regulation in a similar way in its judgment XII ZB 114/06 of 27 June 2007.

[26] See e.g. Council Report 2014, p. 8, fn. 1.

[27] Interestingly, already in 1988, Advocate General Darmon opined that '[t]he concept of central management is difficult to pin down. Even where it designates the place at which the board of directors meets, it is not sufficient to provide a satisfactory connecting factor. As has been noted, owing to the progress made by means of communication, it is no longer necessary to arrange formal board meetings. The telephone, telex and telecopier enable each director to state his point of view and to take part in the decision-making without

4. Main establishment of a controller

Article 4(16)(a) GDPR provides that, as rule, the 'main establishment' of a controller for GDPR purposes is the 'place of its central administration' in the EU/EEA. The implied assumption in the GDPR is that the place where decisions about the purposes and means of the processing of personal data are taken would normally coincide with the place of central administration in the EU/EEA of the controller.[28] In light of this, the 'main establishment' typically coincides with the controller's European headquarters.[29]

However, there may be cases where an EU/EEA establishment other than the place of central administration makes autonomous decisions concerning the purposes and means of a specific processing activity and has the power to have such decisions implemented.[30] In such case, the establishment having taken the decisions is to be considered the 'main establishment' of the controller. As noted by the WP29, this means that:

> [T]here can be situations where more than one lead authority can be identified, i.e. in cases where a multinational company decides to have separate decision making centres, in different countries, for different processing activities.[31]

Such other establishment may qualify as 'main establishment' under Article 4(16) GDPR only if it is in the EU/EEA. Indeed, the general rule established by Article 4(16)(a) is that the 'main establishment' of a controller is 'the place of its central administration in the Union', the exception to this rule being applicable only where the decisions on the purposes and means of the processing are taken in another establishment *in the Union*. This implies that, at least on the basis of the wording of Article 4(16)(a), there may be cases where the 'main establishment' of a controller coincides with its 'place of central administration' in the EU/EEA, even though the decisions on the purposes and means of a specific processing activity are exclusively taken outside the EU/EEA.[32]

---

being physically present in a given place. The board meetings each director will attend via television will soon form part of a company's everyday life'. See Case C-81/87, *Daily Mail and General Trust* (AG Opinion), para. 7. Similar remarks were also made during the legislative process that led to the adoption of the GDPR: see e.g. Council Report 2014, p. 8, fn. 1.

[28] See also WP29 2017, p. 5 (noting that '[t]he approach implied in the GDPR is that the central administration in the EU is the place where decisions about the purposes and means of the processing of personal data are taken and this place has the power to have such decisions implemented'). See too rec. 36 GDPR.

[29] For example, this seems to be Advocate General Bot's understanding with regard to the data processing activities of Facebook at issue in *Wirtschaftsakademie*: '[under the one-stop-shop mechanism,] a controller that carries out cross-border data processing, such as Facebook, will have only one supervisory authority as interlocutor, namely the lead supervisory authority, which will be the authority for the place where the controller's main establishment is located. Nevertheless, that scheme, and the sophisticated cooperation mechanism which it introduces, are not yet applicable ... Facebook has chosen to set up its main establishment in the European Union in Ireland', as the Facebook group has a European head office in Ireland, which was involved in deciding on the purposes and means of the personal data processing at issue in the case. See Case C-210/16, *Wirtschaftsakademie* (AG Opinion), paras. 51, 95 and 103.

[30] See WP29 2017, p. 5.   [31] Ibid.

[32] The French CNIL seems to take a different approach on this point, as its view appears to be that, in order for a company to have a 'main establishment' in the EU, the company must necessarily make the relevant decisions on the purposes and means of processing in the EU. In its Decision of 21 January 2019 regarding Google, the CNIL found that Google did not have a 'main establishment' in the EU because Google's European headquarters in Ireland did not have a decision-making power with regard to the purposes and means of the relevant processing activities; such decision-making power was rather enjoyed by Google's parent company in the US (i.e. Google LLC). Google has appealed the CNIL's decision and the appeal procedure is still pending. See CNIL 2019. It is worth noting that the CNIL partially justified its decision on the basis that rec. 36 GDPR states: '[t]he main establishment of a controller in the Union should be determined according to objective criteria and should imply the effective and real exercise of management activities *determining the main decisions*

The location of the 'main establishment' of the controller should be carefully determined by the controller itself according to objective criteria, in particular where the central administration criterion does not apply.[33] Pursuant to recital 36 GDPR, the key criterion consists in identifying the location where 'the effective and real exercise of management activities determining the main decisions as to the purposes and means of processing through stable arrangements' takes place.[34] In contrast, the place where the processing of personal data is carried out and the presence and use of certain technical means and technologies for processing personal data are not, in themselves, determining criteria.[35] In practice, according to the WP29, the controller should consider the following non-exhaustive list of queries for determining the location of its 'main establishment' in cases where it is not the location of its central administration in the EU/EEA:

1. Where are decisions about the purposes and means of the processing given final 'sign off'?
2. Where are decisions about business activities that involve data processing made?
3. Where does the power to have decisions implemented effectively lie?
4. Where is the Director (or Directors) with overall management responsibility for the cross-border processing located?
5. Where is the controller or processor registered as a company, if in a single territory?[36]

In this regard, the WP29 has clarified that:

[T]he GDPR does not permit 'forum shopping'. If a company claims to have its main establishment in one Member State, but no effective and real exercise of management activity or decision making over the processing of personal data takes place there, the relevant supervisory authorities (or ultimately EDPB) will decide which supervisory authority is the 'lead', using objective criteria and looking at the evidence. The process of determining where the main establishment is may require active inquiry and co-operation by the supervisory authorities. Conclusions cannot be based solely on statements by the organisation under review. The burden of proof ultimately falls on controllers and processors to demonstrate to the relevant supervisory authorities where the relevant processing decisions are taken and where there is the power to implement such decisions.[37]

In essence, if a controller has a preference for a specific 'lead supervisory authority' (e.g. an authority with an enforcement policy that is perceived as business friendly), it may not simply claim that its 'main establishment' is located in the jurisdiction of that authority

---

as to the purposes and means of processing through stable arrangements' (emphasis added). However, this would not seem conclusive for two main reasons: (i) recitals are descriptive and not prescriptive in nature, and the above passage of rec. 36 does not seem to be accurately reflected in Art. 4(16)(a), at least with respect to the 'central administration' criterion; and (ii) both Art. 4(16)(a) and (b) set out the 'central administration' criterion as the chief rule for identifying the 'main establishment', thus warranting, on their face, a homogeneous interpretation of the notion of 'central administration'—the 'central administration' under point (b) would be barred from deciding on the means and purposes of processing, as it relates to a processor. On the legal nature of recitals, see Case C-673/17, *Planet49* (AG Opinion), para. 71 and case law cited therein. A broader reading of the 'central administration' criterion would also seem to be in line with the GDPR's objective of ensuring a consistent and homogenous application of its rules across the EU/EEA (see rec. 10), an objective that is better ensured when the one-stop-shop mechanism applies, which typically depends on the existence of a 'main establishment' in the Union.

[33] See rec. 36 GDPR. See further WP29 2017, pp. 6–7 (noting that the controller's determination of its 'main establishment' 'can be challenged by the respective supervisory authority concerned afterwards').
[34] See rec. 36. See further WP29 2017, p. 6.   [35] See rec. 36. See too WP29 2017, p. 6.
[36] See WP29 2017, p. 7.   [37] Ibid.

to ensure that the latter be entrusted with the primary responsibility for dealing with the controller's cross-border data processing activities; the controller should instead adapt its operations so that the relevant processing decisions are taken in that jurisdiction.

The GDPR does not specifically clarify how to identify the 'main establishment' in case the relevant data processing activities take place under the responsibility of joint controllers. Nonetheless, the WP29 opined that:

[T]o benefit from the one-stop-shop principle, the joint controllers should designate (among the establishments where decisions are taken) which establishment of the joint controllers will have the power to implement decisions about the processing with respect to all joint controllers. This establishment will then be considered to be the main establishment for the processing carried out in the joint controller situation. The arrangement of the joint controllers is without prejudice to the liability rules provided in the GDPR, in particular in Article 82(4).[38]

While the above suggestion of the WP29 may prove practical, it seems difficult to reconcile with the GDPR's assumption that the 'main establishment' 'be determined according to objective criteria' and not by means of a subjective designation from the part of the (joint) controllers (see recital 36). Moreover, the WP29's guidance does not address the situation in which only one of the joint controllers is established in the EU/EEA, and the others are not. In such a situation, in principle, only the controller established in the EU/EEA may be considered to have a 'main establishment' in the EU/EEA if it meets the criteria of Article 4(16)(a) GDPR, as these apply 'as regards a controller with establishments *in more than one Member State*' (emphasis added). Thus, for the same processing activities, the 'one-stop-shop' mechanism should apply with respect to only one of the joint controllers (i.e. the one with establishments in the EU/EEA), whereas the other controllers should deal with local supervisory authorities in every Member State of relevance, through their local representatives.[39] In such case, it would seem reasonable to expect that the concerned supervisory authorities cooperate to ensure that the GDPR's rules are consistently applied to the processing activities at issue.[40]

5. Main establishment of a processor

In line with the main rule applicable to controllers (illustrated above), Article 4(16)(b) GDPR provides that the 'main establishment' of a processor is 'the place of its central administration in the Union'. However, if the processor has no central administration in the EU/EEA, the establishment where the main processing activities take place is to be considered the 'main establishment' of the processor.[41] The GDPR does not clarify which processing activities should be considered *main* processing activities. The indefinite scope

---

[38] Ibid., pp. 7–8.

[39] As noted above, the WP29 opined that 'controllers without any establishment in the EU must deal with local supervisory authorities in every Member State they are active in, through their local representative'. See ibid., p. 10. However, the EDPB considers that 'the creation of a main or single establishment or its relocation from a third country to the EEA (in a procedure which was initially started without cooperation) mid-procedure will allow the controller to benefit from the one-stop-shop'. See EDPB 2019, p. 8.

[40] See rec. 123 GDPR: 'The supervisory authorities should monitor the application of the provisions pursuant to this Regulation and contribute to its consistent application throughout the Union, in order to protect natural persons in relation to the processing of their personal data and to facilitate the free flow of personal data within the internal market. For that purpose, the supervisory authorities should cooperate with each other and with the Commission, without the need for any agreement between Member States on the provision of mutual assistance or on such cooperation'.

[41] See WP29 2017, p. 9.

of the latter concept makes it quite difficult to apply in practice.[42] However, one could argue—by analogy with what recital 36 states with regard to the 'main establishment' of a controller—that whether an activity qualifies as a 'main processing activity' should be determined according to objective criteria and that these may vary depending on the specific features and nature of the processing activities delegated to the processor.

The second part of Article 4(16)(b) GDPR subjects the application of the main processing activities criterion to two qualifications: (i) the processing activities need to take place 'in the context of the activities of an establishment of the processor'; and (ii) the processor need to be 'subject to specific obligations under [the] Regulation'. The first qualification implies that the processing of personal data does not need to be carried out 'by' the relevant establishment itself, rather that it is sufficient if the processing is carried out 'in the context of the activities' of the establishment.[43] However, if the establishment in the EU/EEA is not involved in any direct way in the processing of data, the data processing activities are normally considered to be carried out 'in the context of the activities' of the EU/EEA establishment only as long as there is an 'inextricable link' between the activities of the EU/EEA establishment and the data processing.[44]

The second qualification seems merely to make clear that the GDPR applies to processors only inasmuch as this is specifically set forth in other provisions of the GDPR, and that the criteria of Article 4(16)(b) are immaterial in this regard.

6. Main establishment of a group of undertakings

Where the processing is carried out by a group of undertakings that has its headquarters in the EU/EEA,[45] the main establishment of the controlling undertaking should be considered to be the main establishment of the group of undertakings, except where the purposes and means of processing are determined by another undertaking (see recital 36 GDPR). In essence, as noted by the WP29:

[T]he establishment of the undertaking with overall control is presumed to be the decision-making centre relating to the processing of personal data, and will therefore be considered to be the main establishment for the group, except where decisions about the purposes and means of processing are taken by another establishment. The parent, or operational headquarters of the group of undertakings in the EU, is likely to be the main establishment, because that would be the place of its central administration.[46]

The above should be considered a general rule of thumb applicable to corporate groups with centralised decision-making headquarters and a branch-type structure. However, the decision system of a corporate group could be more complex, giving independent decision-making powers relating to cross-border processing to different establishments in the EU.[47] In such case, the main establishment for the group should be determined through the above-listed criteria for identifying the main establishment of a controller or processor.[48]

---

[42] This difficulty was also noted during the legislative process where several Member States remarked that 'in view of technological developments, it was very difficult to pinpoint the place of processing and that it was very tricky to establish a main establishment with far-reaching consequences': see Council Report 2014, p. 8, fn. 1.

[43] See Case C-131/12, *Google Spain*, para. 52; Case C-230/14, *Weltimmo*, para. 35. See also rec. 22 GDPR.

[44] See Case C-131/12, *Google Spain*, paras. 55–57. See further WP29 2015, pp. 3–4. On the concept of 'in the context of the activities', see also the commentary on Art. 4(23) in this volume.

[45] Further on the concept of 'group of undertakings', see the commentary on Art. 4(19) in this volume. See also rec. 37 GDPR.

[46] See WP29 2017, p. 7.   [47] Ibid.   [48] Ibid.

7. Change of main establishment

As mentioned above, the identification of the 'main establishment' of a controller/processor is primarily relevant to determine which national supervisory authority should be the 'lead supervisory authority' in a specific cross-border enforcement case. However, this competence should not be considered as definitely fixed. The controller/processor may decide to relocate or disband its main establishment. If this occurs mid-procedure before a final enforcement decision is made, this normally triggers a transfer of the lead competence to another authority (i.e. that of the new main establishment) or the termination of the applicability of the 'one-stop-shop' principle (if the main establishment is moved out of the EEA or disbanded).[49]

8. Conclusions

While the basic contours of the notion of 'main establishment' are fairly clear, applying it in practice is unlikely to be consistently plain sailing. As the WP29 aptly noted, '[t]here will be borderline and complex situations where it is difficult to identify the main establishment or to determine where decisions about data processing are taken'.[50] This difficulty will in turn create complications for the identification of the 'lead supervisory authority' and is thus likely to hinder the smooth operation of the 'one-stop-shop' mechanism.

Select Bibliography

International agreements

EEA Agreement: Agreement on the European Economic Area, OJ 1994 L 1/3.

EU legislation

Brussels I Regulation: Council Regulation (EC) No. 44/2001 of 22 December 2000 on jurisdiction and the recognition and enforcement of judgments in civil and commercial matters, OJ 2001 L 12/1.
Community Trade Mark Regulation: CTMR: Council Regulation (EC) No. 207/2009 of 26 February 2009 on the Community trade mark, 2009 OJ L 78/1.
Regulation 1215/2012: Regulation (EU) No. 1215/2012 of the European Parliament and of the Council of 12 December 2012 on jurisdiction and the recognition and enforcement of judgments in civil and commercial matters, OJ 2012 L 351/1.
Rome I Regulation: Regulation (EC) No. 593/2008 of the European Parliament and of the Council of 17 June 2008 on the law applicable to contractual obligations (Rome I), 2008 OJ L 177/6.

National legislation

German GDPR Implementation Law: Gesetz zur Anpassung des Datenschutzrechts an die Verordnung (EU) 2016/679 und zur Umsetzung der Richtlinie (EU) 2016/680 (Datenschutz-Anpassungs- und -Umsetzungsgesetz EU - DSAnpUG-EU), BGBl 2017 Teil 1 Nr. 44.

Academic writings

Everling 1964: Everling, *The Right of Establishment in the Common Market* (Commerce Clearing House 1964).

---

[49] See EDPB 2019.   [50] Ibid., p. 8.

Harvey and Schilling 2013: Harvey and Schilling, 'Conclusion of Contract', in Dannemann and Vogenauer (eds.), *The Common European Sales Law in Context* (OUP 2013), 248.

Svantesson 2016: Svantesson, 'Article 4(1)(a) 'Establishment of the Controller' in EU Data Privacy Law—Time to Rein in this Expanding Concept?', 6(3) *International Data Privacy Law* (2016), 210.

Papers of data protection authorities

EDPB 2019: European Data Protection Board, 'Opinion 8/2019 on the competence of a supervisory authority in case of a change in circumstances relating to the main or single establishment' (9 July 2019).

WP29 2012: Article 29 Working Party, 'Opinion 01/2012 on the Data Protection Reform Proposals' (WP 191, 23 March 2012).

WP29 2015: Article 29 Working Party, 'Update of Opinion 8/2010 on Applicable Law in Light of the CJEU Judgement in Google Spain' (WP 179 update, 16 December 2015).

WP29 2017: Article 29 Working Party, 'Guidelines for Identifying a Controller or Processor's Lead Supervisory Authority' (WP 244 rev.01, as last revised and adopted on 5 April 2017).

CNIL 2019: Commission nationale de l'informatique et des libertés, 'Délibération de la formation restreinte n° SAN – 2019-001 du 21 janvier 2019 prononçant une sanction pécuniaire à l'encontre de la société GOOGLE LLC' (21 January 2019).

Reports and recommendations

Council Report 2014: One-stop-shop mechanism, 9327/14, 30 April 2014.

EC Guide 2017: Guide to the Case Law of The European Court Of Justice on Articles 49 et seq. TFEU—Freedom Of Establishment, Ref. Ares(2017)1839123, 6 April 2017.

EC Staff Working Paper 2012: Commission Staff Working Paper 'Impact Assessment Accompanying the document Regulation of the European Parliament and of the Council on the protection of individuals with regard to the processing of personal data and on the free movement of such data (General Data Protection Regulation) and Directive of the European Parliament and of the Council on the protection of individuals with regard to the processing of personal data by competent authorities for the purposes of prevention, investigation, detection or prosecution of criminal offences or the execution of criminal penalties, and the free movement of such data', SEC(2012) 72 final, 25 January 2012.

Article 4(17). Representative

LUCA TOSONI

'representative' means a natural or legal person established in the Union who, designated by the controller or processor in writing pursuant to Article 27, represents the controller or processor with regard to their respective obligations under this Regulation;

Relevant Recital

(80) Where a controller or a processor not established in the Union is processing personal data of data subjects who are in the Union whose processing activities are related to the offering of goods or services, irrespective of whether a payment of the data subject is required, to such data subjects in the Union, or to the monitoring of their behaviour as far as their behaviour takes place within the Union, the controller or the processor should designate a representative, unless the processing is occasional, does not include processing, on a large scale, of special categories of personal data or the processing of personal data relating to criminal convictions and offences, and is unlikely to result in a risk to the rights and freedoms of natural persons, taking into account the nature, context, scope and purposes of the processing or if the controller is a public authority or body. The representative should act on behalf of the controller or the processor and may be addressed by any supervisory authority. The representative should be explicitly designated by a written mandate of the controller or of the processor to act on its behalf with regard to its obligations under this Regulation. The designation of such a representative does not affect the responsibility or liability of the controller or of the processor under this Regulation. Such a representative should perform its tasks according to the mandate received from the controller or processor, including cooperating with the competent supervisory authorities with regard to any action taken to ensure compliance with this Regulation. The designated representative should be subject to enforcement proceedings in the event of non-compliance by the controller or processor.

Closely Related Provisions

Article 13(1)(a) (Information to be provided to the data subject); Article 14(1)(a) (Information to be provided to the data subject); Article 27 (Representatives of controllers or processors not established in the Union); Article 30 (Records of processing activities); Article 31 (Cooperation with the supervisory authority); Article 58(1)(a) (Powers of supervisory authorities)

Relevant Case Law

CJEU

Case C-221/89, Case C-221/89, *The Queen v Secretary of State for Transport, ex parte Factortame Ltd and others*, judgment of 25 July 1991 (ECLI:EU:C:1991:320).
Case C-246/89, *Commission of the European Communities v United Kingdom of Great Britain and Northern Ireland*, judgment of 4 October 1991 (ECLI:EU:C:1991:375).
Case C-196/04, *Cadbury Schweppes plc and Cadbury Schweppes Overseas Ltd v Commissioners of Inland Revenue*, judgment of 12 September 2006 (Grand Chamber) (ECLI:EU:C:2006:544).

Case C-201/13, *Johan Deckmyn and Vrijheidsfonds VZW v Helena Vandersteen and Others*, judgment of 3 September 2014 (Grand Chamber) (ECLI:EU:C:2014:2132).
Case C-230/14, *Weltimmo s.r.o. v Nemzeti Adatvédelmi és Információszabadság Hatóság*, judgment of 1 October 2015 (ECLI:EU:C:2015:639).
Case C-191/15, *Verein für Konsumenteninformation v Amazon EU Sàrl*, judgment of 28 July 2016 (ECLI:EU:C:2016:612).
Opinion of Advocate General Saugmandsgaard Øe in Case C-191/15, *Verein für Konsumenteninformation v Amazon EU Sàrl*, delivered on 2 June 2016 (ECLI:EU:C:2016:388).
Case C-210/16, *Unabhängiges Landeszentrum für Datenschutz Schleswig-Holstein v Wirtschaftsakademie Schleswig-Holstein GmbH*, judgment of 5 June 2018 (Grand Chamber) (ECLI:EU:C:2018:388).
Opinion of Advocate General Szpunar in Case C-673/17, *Planet49 GmbH v Bundesverband der Verbraucherzentralen und Verbraucherverbände—Verbraucherzentrale Bundesverband e.V.*, delivered on 21 March 2019 (ECLI:EU:C:2019:246).

A. Rationale and Policy Underpinnings

Article 27 GDPR requires that, as a rule, controllers and processors not established in the EU (or in the EEA) appoint a 'representative' in the EU (or in the EEA),[1] if their activities fall within the territorial scope of application of the GDPR (see Article 3(2) GDPR). The main purpose of this compulsory designation, as expressed in Article 27(4) GDPR, is that of enabling supervisory authorities and data subjects to interact with a person established in the EU/EEA, thus facilitating contacts with non-EU/EEA controllers and processors. Indeed, it can be assumed that individuals and authorities in the EU/EEA would normally prefer to interact with someone nearby who understands their customs and speaks their language.[2]

The designation of a representative in the EU/EEA is also a tool for enhancing compliance with the GDPR and facilitating enforcement, as the Regulation envisages the possibility that the designated representative be subject to enforcement proceedings in the event of non-compliance by the controller or processor. In this regard, the EDPB has noted that:

[T]he concept of the representative was introduced precisely with the aim of ensuring enforcement of the GDPR against controllers or processors that fall under Article 3(2) of the GDPR. To this end, it was the intention to enable enforcers to initiate enforcement action against a representative in the same way as against controllers or processors. This includes the possibility to impose administrative fines and penalties, and to hold representatives liable.[3]

B. Legal Background

1. EU legislation

The definition of the term 'representative' is one of the novelties introduced by the GDPR.[4] The DPD already employed this term, but in a narrower sense (see Article 4(2)

---

[1] Pursuant to s. 8 of Protocol 1 to the EEA Agreement, whenever the acts incorporated in the Annexes to the Agreement (like the GDPR) refer to the territory of the 'Community' (now 'Union'), such references should be understood also as references to the territories of the other EEA countries (i.e. Iceland, Liechtenstein and Norway).

[2] See EDPB 2018, p. 23 (noting that 'communication [with the representative] must take place in the language or languages used by the supervisory authorities and the data subjects concerned').

[3] Ibid.   [4] GDPR Proposal, p. 7.

DPD), as it only conceived the role of representative of a controller, whereas under the GDPR both controllers and processors should appoint a representative in the EU/EEA. Moreover, the DPD required the appointment of a representative in each Member State where a non-EU/EEA controller used 'equipment' to process personal data, whereas the GDPR requires the appointment of a single representative for the whole of the EU/EEA.[5]

The wording of the GDPR's definition of 'representative' is not entirely new. It draws from the terminology used in other EU legal instruments that require that non-EU companies appoint a representative in the EU who should carry out certain tasks on their behalf.[6]

2. International instruments

The concept of 'representative' of the controller or processor is not found in Convention 108, either as originally adopted or in its modernised form. The same applies with the OECD Privacy Guidelines (both original and revised versions) and the APEC Privacy Framework.

3. National developments

In line with the DPD, virtually no national data protection laws in Europe defined the term 'representative' prior to adoption of the GDPR. However, the term was used in some national implementations of Article 4(2) DPD.[7]

4. Case law

The definition of 'representative' is newly introduced and not yet interpreted by the CJEU. However, in *Weltimmo*, the CJEU ruled on a case where a company registered in a Member State appointed a representative in another Member State,[8] a type of appointment that was not formalised in the DPD, nor in the GDPR, but that may be relevant to determine establishment in a certain EU/EEA country under both legal instruments, as elaborated further below.

C. Analysis

1. Introduction

Article 4(17) GDPR defines the 'representative' as a natural or legal person established in the EU (or in the EEA) who represents the non-EU controller or processor with regard to their respective obligations under the GDPR. Thus, the representative may be a legal entity (e.g. a company) or an individual (e.g. an attorney), either internal or external to the organisation of the controller or processor. This is consistent with a longstanding practice that European DPAs have accepted with regard to the appointment of

---

[5] See further the commentary on Art. 27 in this volume.
[6] See e.g. Council Directive 93/42/EEC, Art. 1(2)(j) (which defined 'authorised representative' as 'any natural or legal person established in the Community who, explicitly designated by the manufacturer, acts and may be addressed by authorities and bodies in the Community instead of the manufacturer with regard to the latter's obligations under this Directive'). See further Commission Notice: The Blue Guide, pp. 32–33.
[7] See e.g. French Data Protection Act, Art. 5(2); Norwegian Personal Data Act, s. 4.
[8] See Case C-230/14, *Weltimmo*, paras. 30–33.

representatives pursuant to Article 4(2) DPD. For instance, the WP29 envisaged the possibility that 'the only representative of the controller within the EU [under Article 4(2) DPD] is a law firm'.[9] This has been confirmed by the EDPB under the GDPR:

[T]he function of representative in the Union can be exercised based on a service contract concluded with an individual or an organisation, and can therefore be assumed by a wide range of commercial and non-commercial entities, such as law firms, consultancies, private companies, etc.[10]

However, when the function of representative is assumed by a legal entity, the EDPB recommends that an individual within that entity be appointed as a lead contact and person 'in charge' for each controller or processor represented.[11]

2. Establishment conditions

The person to be appointed as a 'representative' must be established in the EU (or in the EEA). The CJEU tends to accord an autonomous, non-formalistic and EU-wide meaning to the concept of 'establishment', independent from national conceptions.[12] In *Weltimmo*, for instance, the CJEU found that 'the concept of "establishment", within the meaning of Directive 95/46, extends to any real and effective activity—even a minimal one—exercised through stable arrangements'.[13] In light of this, the Court held that the following elements were sufficient for the existence of an 'establishment' in a given jurisdiction within the meaning of the DPD: (i) the pursuance of a real and effective activity in that jurisdiction, such as running a website targeted at customers in that jurisdiction; (ii) the existence of an individual who serves as a point of contact between that company and the data subjects who lodge complaints and represents the company in administrative and judicial proceedings; and (iii) the opening of a bank account and the use of a letter box in that jurisdiction for the management of the company's everyday business affairs.[14]

The Court has given similar interpretations of the concept of establishment in other areas of EU law. In particular, it has found that 'the concept of establishment within the meaning of the Treaty provisions on freedom of establishment involves the actual pursuit of an economic activity through a fixed establishment in that State for an indefinite period',[15] which 'presupposes actual establishment of the company concerned in the host Member State and the pursuit of genuine economic activity there'.[16]

Against this background, the CJEU is likely to uphold a flexible understanding of the concept of 'establishment' in Article 4(17) GDPR and to reject a formalistic approach whereby a representative is 'established in the Union' solely if it is formally registered in

---

[9] WP29 2010, p. 23.   [10] EDPB 2018, p. 20.   [11] Ibid.

[12] This interpretative approach is based on the fact that 'it follows from the requirements of both the uniform application of EU law and the principle of equality that the terms of a provision of EU law which makes no express reference to the law of the Member States for the purpose of determining its meaning and scope must normally be given an autonomous and uniform interpretation throughout the European Union, having regard to the context of the provision and the objective pursued by the legislation in question'. See Case C-191/15, *Verein für Konsumenteninformation* (AG Opinion), para. 78. On the concept of 'establishment' under the GDPR, see generally the commentaries on Arts. 3 and 4(16) in this volume.

[13] See Case C-230/14, *Weltimmo*, para. 31. See also Case C-191/15, *Verein für Konsumenteninformation*, para. 75; Case C-210/16, *Wirtschaftsakademie*, paras. 53–55.

[14] See Case C-230/14, *Weltimmo*, paras. 32–33.

[15] Case C-221/89, *Factortame and Others*, para. 20; Case C-246/89, *Commission v UK*, para. 21.

[16] Case C-196/04, *Cadbury Schweppes and Cadbury Schweppes Overseas*, para. 54.

a Member State. This arguably follows also from the main function of the representative: facilitating contacts in a material, more than a formal, sense.

The obligation to appoint a representative only applies to controllers and processors that are 'not established in the Union'.[17] This implies that, in principle, the mere designation of a representative 'established in the Union' does not trigger the 'establishment' of the non-EU controller or processor in the EU and the consequences that this entails (e.g. the possible applicability of the 'one-stop-shop' mechanism).[18] However, it is arguable that where the controller or processor assigns tasks to the representative that go beyond those specifically envisaged by the GDPR for representatives, the controller or processor may be considered as 'established' in the EU for data protection purposes if those tasks fulfil the criteria for establishment as outlined above.[19] In this regard, it is noteworthy that the CJEU held in *Weltimmo* that the presence of a representative could, in particular circumstances, constitute an establishment for the purposes of Article 4(1)(a) DPD:

[T]he presence of only one representative can, in some circumstances, suffice to constitute a stable arrangement if that representative acts with a sufficient degree of stability through the presence of the necessary equipment for provision of the specific services concerned in the Member State in question.[20]

3. Formalities of appointment

A person qualifies as a 'representative' only if explicitly designated as such by the controller or processor *in writing*. This implies that a *de facto* representative (i.e. a person who acts on behalf of the controller/processor without a formal written mandate) may not be considered a 'representative' for the purposes of the GDPR. It follows, for example, that enforcement proceedings for non-compliance with the Regulation may not be initiated against *de facto* representatives (see recital 80 GDPR).

The GDPR does not specify which form the written designation must take (a contract, letter, email etc.). This should leave some flexibility to controllers and processors, provided that the form of designation they choose allows the representative to act on behalf of the controller or processor with regard to their respective obligations under the GDPR (see recital 80 GDPR).[21] However, supervisory authorities tend to prefer that the tasks delegated to the 'representative' are specified in a written contract.[22] Some commentators suggest that such a written contract should be of a specific type: a contract of mandate (in

---

[17] See Arts. 3(2) and 27(1) GDPR.

[18] In this regard, the WP29 noted that 'the mere presence of a representative in a Member State does not trigger the one-stop-shop system. This means that controllers without any establishment in the EU must deal with local supervisory authorities in every Member State they are active in, through their local representative'. See WP29 2017B, p. 10. See further the commentaries on Arts. 56 and 60 in this volume.

[19] See further the commentary on Art. 27 in this volume.

[20] See Case C-230/14, *Weltimmo*, para. 30.

[21] In practice, there has been at least one case in which a controller established outside the EU has appointed a company of its corporate group as its representative in the EU through a 'simple letter of appointment'. See GDPR Expert Group Report 2019, p. 14.

[22] See EDPB 2018, p. 20 (noting that '[i]n practice, the function of representative in the Union can be exercised based on a service contract concluded with an individual or an organisation'). This is in line with Member States' expectations in other regulatory areas. For example, with regard to the designation of a representative in the EU pursuant to the Council Directive 93/42/EEC, Member States expect that '[m]anufacturers shall delegate tasks explicitly to the authorised representatives, and this *preferably in a written contract*' (emphasis added): see EC Guideline 2012, p. 10.

French, 'mandat'; in Italian and Spanish, 'mandato')[23]—a type of agreement known to many civil law jurisdictions. This is primarily because recital 80 GDPR states that '[t]he representative should be explicitly designated by a written *mandate*' (emphasis added).[24] However, while in some jurisdictions it might be necessary that a representative be designated by means of a contract of mandate for it to be able to act on behalf of the controller or processor, the term 'mandate' in recital 80 should not be understood as referring to this specific type of contract, as terms of a provision of EU law that makes no express reference to the law of the Member States for the purpose of determining its meaning must normally be given an autonomous and uniform interpretation throughout the EU.[25]

4. Requirements to be met by the representative

The designated representative must be able to act on behalf of the controller or processor with regard to their respective obligations under the GDPR. This implies that the representative must be able to assume obligations and to be addressed, in addition to or instead of the controller or processor, regarding all compliance issues related to the processing of personal data. In particular, the representative must be in a position to facilitate the communication between data subjects and the controller or processor, maintain a record of processing activities under the responsibility of the controller or processor and cooperate with the supervisory authorities.[26]

Some Member States have further specified the above requirements, for instance, by imposing that the designated representative be a qualified recipient of formal communications from local authorities, in accordance with their domestic legislation.[27] The compatibility of such an additional requirement with EU law remains dubious, in particular if the domestic law requires that qualified recipients of documents be established in that Member State.

5. Representatives and DPOs

Just like a data protection officer ('DPO'), a single representative can act on behalf of several non-EU/EEA controllers and processors.[28] However, the role of representative is separate and distinct from that of the DPO: the former represents the non-EU controller or processor in the EU/EEA, whereas the latter assists the controller or the processor in complying with the applicable data protection rules. While the GDPR does not expressly prohibit the same person from assuming both the role of representative and that of DPO for the same controller or processor, the simultaneous assumption of the two roles seems incompatible with the degree of autonomy and independence that the GDPR requires

---

[23] See e.g. Bolognini et al. 2016, p. 154; Greco 2017, pp. 269–271.

[24] The French version of rec. 80 reads: '[l]e représentant devrait être expressément désigné par un mandat écrit'; the Italian version of rec. 80 states: '[i]l rappresentante dovrebbe essere esplicitamente designato mediante mandato scritto'; the Spanish version of rec. 80 reads: '[e]l representante debe ser designado expresamente por mandato escrito'.

[25] See Case C-201/13, *Deckmyn and Vrijheidsfonds*, para. 14 and case law cited therein. It should also be stressed that recitals are descriptive and not prescriptive in nature: see Case C-673/17, *Planet49* (AG Opinion), para. 71 and case law cited therein.

[26] See Arts. 27(4) and 30–31 GDPR. See also EDPB 2018, p. 23.

[27] See e.g. German GDPR Implementation Law, s. 44(3), which states that '[i]f the controller or processor has designated a representative pursuant to Art. 27(1) GDPR, this representative shall also be an authorised recipient in civil law proceedings pursuant to subsection 1'.

[28] See EDPB 2018, p. 20.

for DPOs. In particular, Article 38(3) GDPR provides that the DPO 'does not receive any instructions regarding the exercise of [his or her] tasks' (see also recital 97 GDPR). Moreover, Article 38(6) GDPR allows a DPO to 'fulfil other tasks and duties' only inasmuch as 'such tasks and duties do not result in a conflict of interests'. In this regard, the WP29 has noted that:

> [T]he absence of conflict of interests is closely linked to the requirement to act in an independent manner ... This entails in particular that the DPO cannot hold a position within the organisation that leads him or her to determine the purposes and the means of the processing of personal data ... In addition, a conflict of interests may also arise for example if an external DPO is asked to represent the controller or processor before the Courts in cases involving data protection issues.[29]

This suggests that the representative would not normally enjoy the independence required to be appointed as DPO. Indeed, contrary to the DPO, the representative 'should perform its tasks according to the mandate received from the controller or processor' and not of its own volition (recital 80 GDPR). Moreover, as recital 80 states, the representative may be 'subject to enforcement proceedings in the event of non-compliance by the controller or processor', which is likely to affect its impartiality as DPO. This is also the position of the EDPB, which 'does not consider the function of representative in the Union as compatible with the role of an external data protection officer'.[30]

6. Other representatives/actors

The 'representative' defined in Article 4(17) should also be distinguished from other representatives mentioned in the GDPR, such as: the representatives of data subjects (Article 35(9)); the representatives of the supervisory authorities (Article 68(3)–(4)); the representative of the Commission (Article 68(5)); and representatives of third parties (Article 76(2)). In essence, the definition of Article 4(17) only applies to the use of the term 'representative' in Articles 13(1)(a), 14(1)(a), 27, 30–31 and 58(1)(a) GDPR.

Finally, it bears emphasising that although the GDPR assumes a distinction between a representative as defined in Article 4(17) and the controller(s) or processor(s) for which/whom the representative acts, the representative may also be a controller or processor in their own right, if they fulfil the definitional criteria for those actors in Article 4(7) or (8) GDPR.[31]

Select Bibliography

International agreements

EEA Agreement: Agreement on the European Economic Area, OJ 1994 L 1/3.

EU legislation

Council Directive 93/42/EEC: Council Directive 93/42/EEC of 14 June 1993 concerning medical devices, OJ 1993 L 169/1.
GDPR Proposal: Proposal for a Regulation of the European Parliament and of the Council on the protection of individuals with regard to the processing of personal data, COM(2012) 11 final, 25 January 2012.

---

[29] WP 2017A, p. 16. Further on the role of DPOs, see the commentaries on Arts. 37–39 in this volume.
[30] EDPB 2018, p. 20.   [31] See further the commentaries on Art. 4(7)–(8) in this volume.

National legislation

French Data Protection Act 1978: French Act 78-17 of 6 January 1978 on Data Processing, Files and Individual Liberties (Loi 78-17: Loi n° 78-17 du 6 janvier 1978 relative à l'informatique, aux fichiers et aux libertés), as last amended by Law No. 2014-334 of 17 March 2014.

German GDPR Implementation Law: Gesetz zur Anpassung des Datenschutzrechts an die Verordnung (EU) 2016/679 und zur Umsetzung der Richtlinie (EU) 2016/680 (Datenschutz-Anpassungs- und Umsetzungsgesetz EU—DsAnpUG-EU), BGBl 2017 Teil 1 Nr. 44.

Norwegian Personal Data Act 2000: Act of 14 April 2000 No. 31 relating to the processing of personal data (Personal Data Act) (lov 14. april 2000 nr. 31 om behandling av personopplysninger) (repealed).

Academic writings

Bolognini et al. 2016: Bolognini, Pelino and Bistolfi, *Il Regolamento Privacy Europeo: Commentario alla nuova disciplina sulla protezione dei dati personali* (Giuffré 2016).

Greco 2017: Greco, 'I Ruoli: Titolare e Responsabile', in Finocchiaro (ed.), *Il nuovo Regolamento europeo sulla privacy e sulla protezione dei dati personali* (Zanichelli 2017), 251.

Papers of data protection authorities

EDPB 2018: European Data Protection Board, 'Guidelines 3/2018 on the territorial scope of the GDPR (Article 3) -Version for public consultation' (16 November 2018).

WP29 2010: Article 29 Working Party, Opinion 8/2010 on Applicable Law (WP 179, 16 December 2010).

WP29 2017A: Article 29 Working Party, 'Guidelines on the Lead Supervisory Authority' (WP 244 rev.01, as last revised and adopted on 5 April 2017).

WP29 2017B: Article 29 Working Party, 'Guidelines on Data Protection Officers ('DPOs')' (WP 243 rev.01, as last revised and adopted on 5 April 2017).

Reports and recommendations

Commission Notice: Commission Notice: The 'Blue Guide' on the Implementation of EU Products Rules 2016, OJ 2016 C 272/1.

EC Guideline 2012: Guideline for Authorised Representatives, MEDDEV 2.5/10, January 2012.

GDPR Expert Group Report 2019: Multistakeholder Expert Group to support the application of Regulation (EU) 2016/679, 'Contribution from the Multistakeholder Expert Group to the stock-taking exercise of June 2019 on one year of GDPR application' (13 June 2019).

Article 4(18). Enterprise

LEE A. BYGRAVE   LUCA TOSONI

'enterprise' means a natural or legal person engaged in an economic activity, irrespective of its legal form, including partnerships or associations regularly engaged in an economic activity;

Relevant Recitals

(13) In order to ensure a consistent level of protection for natural persons throughout the Union and to prevent divergences hampering the free movement of personal data within the internal market, a Regulation is necessary to provide legal certainty and transparency for economic operators, including micro, small and medium-sized enterprises, and to provide natural persons in all Member States with the same level of legally enforceable rights and obligations and responsibilities for controllers and processors, to ensure consistent monitoring of the processing of personal data, and equivalent sanctions in all Member States as well as effective cooperation between the supervisory authorities of different Member States. The proper functioning of the internal market requires that the free movement of personal data within the Union is not restricted or prohibited for reasons connected with the protection of natural persons with regard to the processing of personal data. To take account of the specific situation of micro, small and medium-sized enterprises, this Regulation includes a derogation for organisations with fewer than 250 employees with regard to record-keeping. In addition, the Union institutions and bodies, and Member States and their supervisory authorities, are encouraged to take account of the specific needs of micro, small and medium-sized enterprises in the application of this Regulation. The notion of micro, small and medium-sized enterprises should draw from Article 2 of the Annex to Commission Recommendation 2003/361/EC.

(98) Associations or other bodies representing categories of controllers or processors should be encouraged to draw up codes of conduct, within the limits of this Regulation, so as to facilitate the effective application of this Regulation, taking account of the specific characteristics of the processing carried out in certain sectors and the specific needs of micro, small and medium enterprises. In particular, such codes of conduct could calibrate the obligations of controllers and processors, taking into account the risk likely to result from the processing for the rights and freedoms of natural persons.

(110) A group of undertakings, or a group of enterprises engaged in a joint economic activity, should be able to make use of approved binding corporate rules for its international transfers from the Union to organisations within the same group of undertakings, or group of enterprises engaged in a joint economic activity, provided that such corporate rules include all essential principles and enforceable rights to ensure appropriate safeguards for transfers or categories of transfers of personal data.

Closely Related Provisions

Article 4(19) (Definition of 'group of undertakings') (see also recital 37); Article 4(20) (Definition of 'binding corporate rules'); Article 30(5) (Records of processing activities) (see too recital 13); Article 40(1) (Codes of conduct) (see too recital 98); Article 42(1) (Certification);

Article 47 (Binding corporate rules) (see too recital 110); Article 83(4)–(6) (General conditions for imposing administrative fines) (see too recital 150); Article 88(2) (Processing in the context of employment)

Relevant Case Law

CJEU

Case C-30/87, *Bodson v Pompes funèbres des régions libérées*, judgment of 4 May 1988 (ECLI:EU:C:1988:225).
Case C-41/90, *Klaus Höfner and Fritz Elser v Macrotron GmbH*, judgment of 23 April 1991 (ECLI:EU:C:1991:161).
Case T-11/89, *Shell International Chemical Company Ltd v Commission of the European Communities*, CFI, judgment of 10 March 1992 (ECLI:EU:T:1992:33).
Case C-364/92, *SAT Fluggesellschaft v Eurocontrol*, judgment of 19 January 1994 (ECLI:EU:C:1994:7).
Case C-343/95, *Diego Calì & Figli Srl v Servizi ecologici porto di Genova SpA (SEPG)*, judgment of 18 March 1997 (ECLI:EU:C:1997:160).
Case C-113/07 P, *SELEX Sistemi Integrati SpA v Commission of the European Communities and Organisation européenne pour la sécurité de la navigation aérienne (Eurocontrol)*, judgment of 26 March 2009 (ECLI:EU:C:2009:191).
Case C-279/12, *Fish Legal, Emily Shirley v Information Commissioner, United Utilities Water plc, Yorkshire Water Services Ltd, Southern Water Services Ltd*, judgment of 19 December 2013 (ECLI:EU:C:2013:853).
Case C-185/14, '*EasyPay' AD and 'Finance Engineering' AD v Ministerski savet na Republika Bulgaria and Natsionalen osiguritelen institut*, judgment of 22 October 2015 (ECLI:EU:C:2015:716).
Case C-90/09 P, *General Química SA and Others v European Commission*, judgment of 20 January 2011 (ECLI:EU:C:2011:21).
Case C-110/13, *HaTeFo GmbH v Finanzamt Haldensleben*, judgment of 27 February 2014 (ECLI:EU:C:2014:114).
Case T-392/13, *Leone La Ferla SpA v Commission and European Chemicals Agency*, GC, judgment of 15 September 2016 (ECLI:EU:T:2016:478).
Case C-516/15 P, *Akzo Nobel NV and Others v European Commission*, judgment of 27 April 2017 (ECLI:EU:C:2017:314).
Case C-617/15, *Hummel Holding A/S v Nike Inc. and Nike Retail B.V.*, judgment of 18 May 2017 (ECLI:EU:C:2017:390).
Case C-74/16, *Congregación de Escuelas Pías Provincia Betania v Ayuntamiento de Getafe*, judgment of 27 June 2017 (Grand Chamber) (ECLI:EU:C:2017:496).
Case T-758/15, *EDF Toruń SA v European Chemicals Agency*, GC, judgment of 18 July 2017 (ECLI:EU:T:2017:519).

A. Rationale and Policy Underpinnings

The term 'enterprise' is principally operationalised by the English language version of the GDPR in two contexts: (i) the simplified requirements for 'micro-, small and medium-sized enterprises' ('SMEs') in their role as controllers or processors; and (ii) the use of binding corporate rules ('BCRs'). Regarding the former context, the GDPR contains several provisions that aim to reduce SMEs' regulatory burden,[1] or to help them meet

---

[1] See e.g. Art. 30(5) which introduces in respect of an enterprise or an organisation employing fewer than 250 persons a qualified derogation from the duty of controllers and processors to keep records of their data processing activities. See too Arts. 40(1) and 42(1) (specifying that account is to be taken of the

their obligations under the Regulation.[2] Regarding the latter context, the BCR scheme established by the GDPR covers data transfers between companies that belong to the same 'group of undertakings' or 'group of enterprises engaged in a joint economic activity' (Article 4(20)).[3]

As elaborated below, the terms 'enterprise' and 'undertaking' are to be regarded as synonyms, and most language versions of the GDPR do not distinguish between them. This means that the term 'enterprise' is operationalised also in those contexts that specifically relate to 'undertakings'. As indicated above, one such context concerns BCRs. Another such context concerns the calculation of administrative fines (Article 83(4)–(6)).[4]

B. Legal Background

1. EU legislation

The term 'enterprise' was mentioned only once in the DPD—in recital 25 of its preamble, which referred to the need for 'the principles of protection' to be 'reflected ... in the obligations imposed on persons, public authorities, enterprises, agencies or other bodies responsible for processing'. The DPD thus used the term to specify a category of controller or processor, but otherwise left it undefined. The same applies with respect to the term 'undertaking': the DPD made passing mention of it just once, also in the preamble, recital 5 of which noted that 'the exchange of personal data between undertakings in different Member States is set to increase'.

The definition in Article 4(18) GDPR is based on the definition of 'enterprise' given in Article 1 of the Annex to Commission Recommendation 2003/361/EC concerning the definition of micro, small and medium-sized enterprises ('SME Recommendation'). The latter definition reads:

An enterprise is considered to be any entity engaged in an economic activity, irrespective of its legal form. This includes, in particular, self-employed persons and family businesses engaged in craft or other activities, and partnerships or associations regularly engaged in an economic activity.

Recital 3 in the preamble to the Recommendation indicates that this definition originates in CJEU jurisprudence concerning the rules on EU competition law:

It should ... be made clear that, in accordance with Articles 48, 81 and 82 of the Treaty, as interpreted by the Court of Justice of the European Communities, an enterprise should be considered to be any entity, regardless of its legal form, engaged in economic activities, including in particular entities engaged in a craft activity and other activities on an individual or family basis, partnerships or associations regularly engaged in economic activities.

---

needs of 'micro, small and medium enterprises' in connection with the drawing up of codes of conduct and certification schemes), and rec. 167 (stipulating that the Commission 'should consider specific measures for micro, small and medium-sized enterprises' in connection with its use of implementing powers under the Regulation).

[2] See rec. 132 ('Awareness-raising activities by supervisory authorities addressed to the public should include specific measures directed at controllers and processors, including micro, small and medium-sized enterprises ... ').
[3] See further the commentaries on Arts. 4(20) and 47 in this volume.
[4] See further the commentary on Art. 83 in this volume.

EU competition law and related case law tend to eschew use of the term 'enterprise', referring instead to 'undertaking'.[5] As shown below, under EU competition law, the latter term is defined essentially as in the definition of 'enterprise' in the SME Recommendation and GDPR.

2. Case law

The definition in Article 4(18) GDPR has yet to be directly interpreted by the CJEU. However, the Court has interpreted aspects of the 'enterprise' concept as employed in the SME Recommendation. It has also defined the concept of 'undertaking' as employed in EU competition law. Both lines of jurisprudence are clearly relevant for understanding the definition in Article 4(18). Recital 13 GDPR states that the notion of SME—and thus by implication, the notion of 'enterprise'—'should draw from' the SME Recommendation, while recital 150 states that 'an undertaking should be understood to be an undertaking in accordance with Articles 101 and 102 TFEU' for the purposes of applying the provisions of Article 83 GDPR on administrative fines. Despite the delimitation of purposes in the latter recital, it is highly likely that other GDPR provisions referring to 'undertakings' and 'enterprises' are to be construed in accordance with CJEU jurisprudence in the field of competition law, particularly as these concepts are rooted in that field, as clearly outlined in recital 3 to the SME Recommendation (mentioned above).[6] This jurisprudence is accordingly elaborated in the section below.

C. Analysis

1. Introduction

Most of the various language versions of the GDPR do not distinguish between the terms 'enterprise' and 'undertaking'. For example, the German version uses the term 'Unternehmen' for both terms, the Swedish version uses the term 'företag', and the French version uses the term 'entreprise'.[7] This reflects the fact that, under EU law, an 'enterprise' is generally considered to be synonymous with an 'undertaking'.[8]

---

[5] See especially Arts. 101–102 TFEU and their antecedents in Arts. 81–82 TEC.

[6] See also the commentary on Art. 4(19) in this volume.

[7] Some of the other language versions use different terms but define the equivalent of 'undertaking' as an 'enterprise'. For example, the Dutch version uses 'onderneming' for 'enterprise' and 'concern' for 'undertaking', and defines 'concern' as 'een onderneming die zeggenschap uitoefent en de ondernemingen waarover die zeggenschap wordt uitgeoefend', while the Italian version defines 'gruppo imprenditoriale' ('group of undertakings') in terms of 'imprese' ('enterprises'), the same term used in the Italian version of Art. 4(18). The Danish version uses the term 'foretagende' for 'enterprise' (defined as 'en fysisk eller juridisk person, som udøver økonomisk aktivitet, uanset dens retlige status, herunder partnerskaber eller sammenslutninger, der regelmæssigt udøver økonomisk aktivitet') and 'koncern' for 'group of undertakings' (defined as 'en virksomhed, der udøver kontrol, og de af denne kontrollerede virksomheder'). There is, though, nothing to indicate that the Danish version treats the notion of 'foretagende' as having a fundamentally different meaning to the notion of 'virksomhed', and the two terms are often used as synonyms in the Danish language. In the latter regard, see e.g. the Danish language version of recital 3 in the preamble to the SME Recommendation ('Det bør præciseres, at begrebet virksomhed i henhold til traktatens artikel 48, 81 og 82 som fortolket af De Europæiske Fællesskabers Domstol omfatter ethvert foretagende, uanset dets retlige form, der udøver en økonomisk aktivitet, herunder især foretagender, der i form af enkeltmandsvirksomheder eller familievirksomheder udøver en håndværksmæssig aktivitet eller andre aktiviteter, samt personselskaber eller foreninger, som regelmæssigt udøver en økonomisk aktivitet').

[8] However, note that in the English-language version of the GDPR, 'enterprise' is used in Art. 4(18) and 'undertaking' is used in Art. 83(4)–(6).

Both terms are to be given an EU-wide meaning independent from national conceptions of them.[9] Basically, both terms denote an economic actor. The classic definition given by the CJEU in the area of competition law is as follows: 'the concept of an undertaking encompasses every entity engaged in an economic activity, regardless of the legal status of the entity and the way in which it is financed'.[10] This formulation constitutes the basis for the definitions of 'enterprise' in the SME Recommendation and GDPR.

2. Economic activity

Thus, 'economic activity' forms the key criterion for determining whether an entity qualifies as an 'enterprise'/'undertaking'. The CJEU has defined such activity fairly broadly as 'any activity consisting in offering goods and services on a given market'.[11] The offering of goods and services does not have to be in pursuit of profit,[12] which means that entities run on a not-for-profit basis—e.g. charities and state-controlled corporations—may qualify as 'undertakings' or 'enterprises', if they regularly offer goods or services in a particular market. However, organisations such as public authorities, private entities entrusted with tasks of public interest and international organisations[13] whose activities are connected with the exercise of powers that are typically those of a public authority or are otherwise not of an economic nature do not qualify as undertakings.[14]

3. Structure and organisation

In respect of the structure and organisation of an enterprise/undertaking, the CJEU lays down fairly liberal requirements. Decisive here is that an entity forms an 'economic unit' which consists 'of a unitary organization of personal, tangible and intangible elements which pursues a specific economic aim on a long-term basis'.[15] While unitary, an enterprise/undertaking may comprise a plurality of natural or legal persons: 'the term "undertaking" must be understood as designating an economic unit even if in law that economic unit consists of several persons, natural or legal'.[16] Thus, it is not the case that there may be, say, only one company per undertaking or enterprise.

4. Temporal criterion

There is, however, a temporal criterion that needs to be met: more specifically, an entity does not qualify as an enterprise/undertaking if its economic activity is fleeting or

---

[9] The CJEU has consistently held that the terms of a provision of EU law which makes no express reference to the law of the Member States for the purpose of determining its meaning and scope must normally be given an autonomous and uniform interpretation throughout the EU, having regard not only to its wording but also to the context of the provision and the objective pursued by the legislation in question. This follows from the need for uniform application of EU law and from the principle of equality. See e.g. Case C-617/15, *Hummel Holding*, para. 22 and case law cited therein.

[10] Case C-41/90, *Höfner and Elser*, para. 21. See too e.g. Case C-516/15 P, *Akzo Nobel and Others*, para. 47; Case C-90/09 P, *General Química*, para. 34.

[11] See e.g. Case C-185/14, *EasyPay and Finance Engineering*, para. 37.

[12] Case C-74/16, *Congregación de Escuelas Pías Provincia Betania*, para. 46.

[13] On the definition of 'international organisation' under the GDPR, see the commentary on Art. 4(26) in this volume.

[14] Case C-364/92, *SAT Fluggesellschaft*, paras. 19–32; Case C-113/07 P, *Selex Sistemi Integrati*, para. 71; Case C-30/87, *Bodson*, para. 18; Case C-343/95, *Calì & Figli*, paras. 16–25. On the notion of 'public authority', see further e.g. Case C-279/12, *Fish Legal and Shirley*, paras. 42 and 51–52.

[15] Case T-11/89, *Shell v Commission*, para. 311.   [16] Case C-90/09 P, *General Química*, para. 35.

ephemeral. This is indicated by the above-cited passage from the *Shell* case, which refers to pursuit of a specific economic aim 'on a long-term basis'.[17] It is also partly reflected in the wording of Article 4(18) GDPR which refers to partnerships or associations being 'regularly engaged in an economic activity'. While the reference to 'regularly' seems to pertain only to a subcategory of enterprises (partnerships and associations), the above-referenced case law makes clear that it must be regarded as pertaining to enterprises/undertakings generally.

5. SMEs

While the SME Recommendation is not binding in itself, the GDPR's express reference to the Recommendation in order to define what is meant by SME is likely to make the applicability of the criteria mentioned in the Recommendation *de facto* mandatory when determining whether an enterprise/undertaking qualifies as an SME for GDPR purposes.[18] In this regard, it is worth noting indications from the CJEU that it will assess the definition of SME in the SME Recommendation stringently.[19] This is particularly so in situations where two or more enterprises are linked with each other through the relations between natural persons in each enterprise, and where the enterprises thus form an economic group in which none of the constituent enterprises is genuinely independent of the other(s).[20] Whether that lack of independence pertains 'depends on the circumstances of the case, and that is not necessarily conditional on the existence of contractual

---

[17] Case T-11/89, *Shell v Commission*, para. 311.

[18] Case T-392/13, *Leone la Ferla SpA*, paras. 79–81. Here the Court ruled on the applicability of the SME Recommendation criteria in light of an express reference to the Recommendation in Regulations 1907/2006 and 340/2008, and concluded for the applicability of such criteria: 'Article 3(36) of Regulation No 1907/2006 defines SMEs as small and medium-sized enterprises "as defined in ... Recommendation [2003/361]". Under Article 2 of Regulation No. 340/2008, a small enterprise is "a small enterprise within the meaning of Recommendation [2003/361]". A similar reference is made in Article 2 of Regulation No. 340/2008 as regards the definition of micro and medium-sized enterprises. Accordingly, the relevant legislation makes express reference to Recommendation 2003/361 in order to define what is meant by, in particular, "small enterprise". In contrast to what the applicant suggests, it cannot be precluded, in principle, that the provisions of a recommendation may be applicable by means of an express reference in a regulation to its provisions, provided that general principles of law and, in particular, the principle of legal certainty, are observed ... In the present case, the applicant has not provided any information to indicate that the reference in Regulations Nos 1907/2006 and 340/2008 is contrary to general principles of law. Furthermore, that reference is designed to ensure, by applying the relevant provisions of Recommendation 2003/361, that the same definition of SMEs is applied in EU policies, which is consistent with the objective of that recommendation'. See also Case T-758/15, *EDF Toruń*, paras. 42–56. It should be noted, however, that in these two cases, the Regulations interpreted by the Court made express reference to the SME Recommendation also in their Articles, whereas the GDPR refers to the Recommendation only in a recital.

[19] See Case C-110/13, *HaTeFo*, paras. 31 and 32: 'The advantages afforded to SMEs are in most cases exceptions to the general rules ... , and therefore the definition of an SME must be interpreted strictly'; 'In that regard, it is apparent from recitals 9 and 12 of the preamble to that recommendation that the definition of linked enterprises aims to gain a better understanding of the economic position of SMEs and to remove from that qualification of SMEs groups of enterprises whose economic power may exceed that of genuine SMEs, with a view to ensuring that only those enterprises which really need the advantages accruing to the category of SMEs from the different rules or measures in their favour actually benefit from them. Those recitals also state that in order to limit to the strict minimum the examination of relations between enterprises which pass through natural persons, the account taken of such relationships must be restricted to cases where those enterprises engage in activities in the relevant market or in adjacent markets'.

[20] Ibid., para. 33: 'In those circumstances, in order to include only enterprises that are genuinely independent SMEs, it is necessary to examine the structure of SMEs which form an economic group, the power of which exceeds the power of an SME, and to ensure that the definition of SMEs is not circumvented by purely formal means'.

relations between those persons or even a finding that they intended to circumvent the definition of an SME'.[21] The CJEU will likely take the same line when assessing whether or not controllers or processors qualify as SMEs under the GDPR.

Select Bibliography

EU legislation

SME Recommendation: Commission Recommendation 2003/361/EC of 6 May 2003 concerning the definition of micro, small and medium-sized enterprises, OJ 2003 L 124/36.

---

[21] Ibid., para. 35. This is not to suggest that as soon as there is a link between two companies they cannot qualify as SMEs. The SME Recommendation sets forth a rather complex mechanism on how to take into account the data of partner and linked companies of an enterprise to assess whether the latter falls within the relevant thresholds that make it an SME under the Recommendation.

Article 4(19). Group of undertakings

LUCA TOSONI

'group of undertakings' means a controlling undertaking and its controlled undertakings;

Relevant Recital

(37) A group of undertakings should cover a controlling undertaking and its controlled undertakings, whereby the controlling undertaking should be the undertaking which can exert a dominant influence over the other undertakings by virtue, for example, of ownership, financial participation or the rules which govern it or the power to have personal data protection rules implemented. An undertaking which controls the processing of personal data in undertakings affiliated to it should be regarded, together with those undertakings, as a group of undertakings.

Closely Related Provisions

Article 4(18) (Definition of 'enterprise'); Article 4(20) (Definition of 'binding corporate rules'); Article 36(3)(a) (Prior consultation); Article 37(2) (Designation of the data protection officer); Article 47 (Binding corporate rules); Article 88 (Processing in the context of employment)

Relevant Case Law

CJEU

Case C-30/87, *Corinne Bodson v SA Pompes funèbres des régions libérées*, judgment of 4 May 1988 (ECLI:EU:C:1988:225).

Case C-41/90, *Klaus Höfner and Fritz Elser v Macrotron GmbH*, judgment of 23 April 1991 (ECLI:EU:C:1991:161).

Case C-364/92, *SAT Fluggesellschaft v Eurocontrol*, judgment of 19 January 1994 (ECLI:EU:C:1994:7).

C-343/95, *Diego Calì & Figli Srl v Servizi ecologici porto di Genova SpA (SEPG)*, judgment of 18 March 1997 (ECLI:EU:C:1997:160).

Case C-113/07 P, *SELEX Sistemi Integrati SpA v Commission of the European Communities and Organisation européenne pour la sécurité de la navigation aérienne (Eurocontrol)*, judgment of 26 March 2009 (ECLI:EU:C:2009:191).

Case C-279/12, *Fish Legal, Emily Shirley v Information Commissioner, United Utilities Water plc, Yorkshire Water Services Ltd, Southern Water Services Ltd*, judgment of 19 December 2013 (ECLI:EU:C:2013:853).

Case C-185/14, *'EasyPay' AD and 'Finance Engineering' AD v Ministerski savet na Republika Bulgaria and Natsionalen osiguritelen institut*, judgment of 22 October 2015 (ECLI:EU:C:2015:716).

Case C-62/99, *Betriebsrat der bofrost* Josef H. Boquoi Deutschland West GmbH & Co. KG v Bofrost* Josef H. Boquoi Deutschland West GmbH & Co. KG.*, judgment of 29 March 2001(ECLI:EU:C:2001:188).

Case C-90/09 P, *General Química SA and Others v European Commission*, judgment of 20 January 2011 (ECLI:EU:C:2011:21).

Case C-516/15 P, *Akzo Nobel NV and Others v European Commission*, judgment of 27 April 2017 (ECLI:EU:C:2017:314).

Case C-617/15, *Hummel Holding A/S v Nike Inc. and Nike Retail B.V.*, judgment of 18 May 2017 (ECLI:EU:C:2017:390).

Case C-74/16, *Congregación de Escuelas Pías Provincia Betania v Ayuntamiento de Getafe*, judgment of 27 June 2017 (Grand Chamber) (ECLI:EU:C:2017:496).

Joined Cases C-61/17, C-62/17 and C-72/17, *Miriam Bichat and Others v APSB - Aviation Passage Service Berlin GmbH & Co. KG*, judgment of 7 August 2018 (ECLI:EU:C:2018:653).

Opinion of Advocate General Sharpston in Joined Cases C-61/17, C-62/17 and C-72/17, *Miriam Bichat and Others v APSB—Aviation Passage Service Berlin GmbH & Co. KG*, delivered on 21 June 2018 (ECLI:EU:C:2018:482).

A. Rationale and Policy Underpinnings

Many of the GDPR's provisions have been drafted with multinational corporate groups in mind (the case, for instance, with the provisions on binding corporate rules and on the appointment of a single data protection officer for a group of companies). Consequently, the Regulation often refers to the concept of 'group of undertakings', thus warranting its definition in Article 4(19).

B. Legal Background

1. EU legislation

While the DPD did not use the term 'group of undertakings', other EU legislation has—most notably, the European Works Council Directive.[1] Article 2(1)(b) of the latter provided the template for the definition of 'group of undertakings' in Article 4(19) GDPR. Indeed, the definition in Article 2(1)(b) is identical to that in the GDPR: 'a controlling undertaking and its controlled undertakings'. The Directive also defines 'controlling undertaking' as 'an undertaking which can exercise a dominant influence over another undertaking (the controlled undertaking) by virtue, for example, of ownership, financial participation or the rules which govern it' (Article 3(1)). The latter definition has been essentially reproduced in recital 37 GDPR.

2. International instruments

The notion of 'group of undertakings' is not found in any other of the principal international instruments on data protection.

3. Case law

The CJEU has yet to interpret the definition of 'group of undertakings' in Article 4(19) GDPR. However, there is long-standing CJEU jurisprudence on the notion of 'undertaking' in the area of EU competition law, and this jurisprudence may help to elucidate the meaning of Article 4(19) GDPR. The preamble to the GDPR indicates that the

---

[1] European Works Council Directive.

term 'undertaking' is normally to be understood in accordance with EU competition law for the purposes of applying the provisions of Article 83 GDPR on administrative fines (recital 150). However, it is highly likely that the same understanding pertains for the purposes of applying other provisions of the GDPR that refer to 'undertakings' (and, indeed, 'enterprises').[2] Hence, the following section sets out and builds on relevant aspects of CJEU jurisprudence on the notion of 'undertaking' in the field of competition law.

C. Analysis

The definition of 'group of undertakings' in Article 4(19) presupposes that each of the entities belonging to the group qualify as an 'undertaking', a term which should be given an autonomous EU-wide meaning independent from national conceptions.[3] In this regard, in the sphere of EU competition law, the CJEU has consistently found that 'the concept of an undertaking covers any entity engaged in an economic activity, irrespective of its legal status and the way in which it is financed'.[4] Therefore, the key test is whether the entity is engaged in an 'economic activity', which is 'any activity consisting in offering goods and services on a given market'.[5] The fact that an entity is engaged in economic activities 'on a not-for-profit basis does not prevent the entity which carries out those operations on the market from being considered an undertaking'.[6] Thus, entities such as public bodies, state-controlled enterprises and charities may all qualify as 'undertakings' under EU competition law, if they carry out economic activities. However, organisations such as public authorities, private entities entrusted with tasks of public interest and international organisations[7] whose activities are connected with the exercise of powers that are typically those of a public authority or are otherwise not of an economic nature do not qualify as undertakings.[8]

On its face, Article 4(19) seems to require that the group have a centralised structure based on hierarchical relations between the participating companies. Indeed, the Article requires the presence of a 'controlling undertaking' which can exert a dominant influence over the other undertakings of the group (see recital 37). Thus, in principle, a group organised on the basis of parity between the various undertakings belonging to the group does not qualify as a 'group of undertakings' within the meaning of Article 4(19) GDPR.[9]

---

[2] See also the commentary on Art. 4(18) in this volume.

[3] The CJEU has consistently held that the terms of a provision of EU law which makes no express reference to the law of the Member States for the purpose of determining its meaning and scope must normally be given an autonomous and uniform interpretation throughout the EU, having regard not only to its wording but also to the context of the provision and the objective pursued by the legislation in question. This follows from the need for uniform application of EU law and from the principle of equality. See e.g. Case C-617/15, *Hummel Holding*, para. 22 and case law cited therein.

[4] See e.g. Case C-41/90, *Höfner and Elser*, para. 21; Case C-90/09 P, *General Química and Others*, para. 34; Case C-516/15 P, *Akzo Nobel and Others*, para. 47. See also the commentary on Art. 4(18) in this volume.

[5] See e.g. Case C-185/14, *EasyPay*, para. 37.

[6] Case C-74/16, *Congregación de Escuelas Pías Provincia Betania*, para. 46.

[7] On the definition of 'international organisation' under the GDPR, see the commentary on Art. 4(26) in this volume.

[8] Case C-364/92, *SAT Fluggesellschaft*, paras. 19–32; Case C-113/07 P, *Selex Sistemi Integrati*, para. 71; Case C-30/87, *Bodson*, para. 18; Case C-343/95, *Calì & Figli*, paras. 16–25. On the notion of 'public authority', see further e.g. Case C-279/12, *Fish Legal and Shirley*, paras. 42 and 51–52.

[9] In Case C-62/99, *Bofrost**, the CJEU ruled on a case involving a group without hierarchical relations between its members under the European Works Council Directive—which, as noted above, included a definition of 'group of undertakings' identical to that of the GDPR—but without concluding on whether such a group was covered by the definition.

However, a group of companies cooperating closely together without hierarchical relations between them might qualify as a 'group of enterprises engaged in a joint economic activity', which is often regulated in the same way as a 'group of undertakings' under the GDPR.[10]

Recital 37 makes clear that a 'controlling undertaking' can exert a dominant influence over the other undertakings of the group by virtue, for example, of ownership, financial participation, the rules which govern it or the power to have personal data protection rules implemented. This broadly mirrors the criteria specified in the definition of 'controlling undertaking' in Article 3(1) of the European Works Council Directive. Thus, the Directive's presumptions regarding the ability to exercise a dominant influence (see Article 3(2) of the Directive) may be useful to understand better the concept of dominant influence in recital 37 GDPR. These presumptions of dominant influence essentially reflect the typical relationship between a parent company and a subsidiary: (i) holding of the majority of the controlled undertaking's subscribed capital; (ii) control of a majority of the votes attached to the controlled undertaking's issued share capital; or (iii) right to appoint more than half of the members of the controlled undertaking's administrative, managerial or supervisory body.[11] Recital 37 provides a further example of a company that should be considered as exerting a dominant influence: '[a]n undertaking which controls the processing of personal data in undertakings affiliated to it should be regarded, together with those undertakings, as a group of undertakings'.

Select Bibliography
EU legislation

European Works Council Directive: Directive 2009/38/EC of the European Parliament and of the Council of 6 May 2009 on the establishment of a European Works Council or a procedure in Community-scale undertakings and Community-scale groups of undertakings for the purposes of informing and consulting employees, OJ 2009 L 122/28.

---

[10] See in particular Arts. 4(20), 47 and 88(2) GDPR. On the notion of 'group of enterprises engaged in a joint economic activity', see the commentary on Art. 4(20) in this volume.

[11] The wording of Art. 3 of the European Works Council Directive has already been employed to interpret by analogy other EU legal instruments: see Joined Cases C-61/17, C-62/17 and C-72/17, *Miriam Bichat* (AG Opinion), para. 45.

Article 4(20). Binding corporate rules

LUCA TOSONI

'binding corporate rules' means personal data protection policies which are adhered to by a controller or processor established on the territory of a Member State for transfers or a set of transfers of personal data to a controller or processor in one or more third countries within a group of undertakings, or group of enterprises engaged in a joint economic activity;

Relevant Recitals

(107) The Commission may recognise that a third country, a territory or a specified sector within a third country, or an international organisation no longer ensures an adequate level of data protection. Consequently the transfer of personal data to that third country or international organisation should be prohibited, unless the requirements in this Regulation relating to transfers subject to appropriate safeguards, including binding corporate rules, and derogations for specific situations are fulfilled. In that case, provision should be made for consultations between the Commission and such third countries or international organisations. The Commission should, in a timely manner, inform the third country or international organisation of the reasons and enter into consultations with it in order to remedy the situation.

(108) In the absence of an adequacy decision, the controller or processor should take measures to compensate for the lack of data protection in a third country by way of appropriate safeguards for the data subject. Such appropriate safeguards may consist of making use of binding corporate rules, standard data protection clauses adopted by the Commission, standard data protection clauses adopted by a supervisory authority or contractual clauses authorised by a supervisory authority. Those safeguards should ensure compliance with data protection requirements and the rights of the data subjects appropriate to processing within the Union, including the availability of enforceable data subject rights and of effective legal remedies, including to obtain effective administrative or judicial redress and to claim compensation, in the Union or in a third country. They should relate in particular to compliance with the general principles relating to personal data processing, the principles of data protection by design and by default. Transfers may also be carried out by public authorities or bodies with public authorities or bodies in third countries or with international organisations with corresponding duties or functions, including on the basis of provisions to be inserted into administrative arrangements, such as a memorandum of understanding, providing for enforceable and effective rights for data subjects. Authorisation by the competent supervisory authority should be obtained when the safeguards are provided for in administrative arrangements that are not legally binding.

(110) A group of undertakings, or a group of enterprises engaged in a joint economic activity, should be able to make use of approved binding corporate rules for its international transfers from the Union to organisations within the same group of undertakings, or group of enterprises engaged in a joint economic activity, provided that such corporate rules include all essential principles and enforceable rights to ensure appropriate safeguards for transfers or categories of transfers of personal data.

Closely Related Provisions

Article 4(7) (Definition of 'controller'); Article 4(8) (Definition of 'processor'); Article 4(18) (Definition of 'enterprise'); Article 4(19) (Definition of 'group of undertakings'); Article 46(2)(b) (Transfers subject to appropriate safeguards); Article 47 (Binding corporate rules); Article 49 (Derogations for specific situations concerned with transfer of personal data to third countries and international organisations); Article 57(1)(s) (Supervisory authorities' tasks); Article 58(3)(j) (Supervisory authorities' powers); Article 64(1)(f) (Opinion of the Board); Article 70(1)(c) and (i) (Tasks of the Board).

Relevant Case Law

CJEU

Case C-30/87, *Corinne Bodson v SA Pompes funèbres des régions libérées*, judgment of 4 May 1988 (ECLI:EU:C:1988:225).

Case C-364/92, *SAT Fluggesellschaft v Eurocontrol*, judgment of 19 January 1994 (ECLI:EU:C:1994:7).

Case C-101/01, *Criminal proceedings against Bodil Lindqvist*, judgment of 6 November 2003 (ECLI:EU:C:2003:596).

Case C-113/07 P, *SELEX Sistemi Integrati SpA v Commission of the European Communities and Organisation européenne pour la sécurité de la navigation aérienne (Eurocontrol)*, judgment of 26 March 2009 (ECLI:EU:C:2009:191).

Case C-279/12, *Fish Legal, Emily Shirley v Information Commissioner, United Utilities Water plc, Yorkshire Water Services Ltd, Southern Water Services Ltd*, judgment of 19 December 2013 (ECLI:EU:C:2013:853).

Case C-230/14, *Weltimmo s.r.o. v Nemzeti Adatvédelmi és Információszabadság Hatóság*, judgment of 1 October 2015 (ECLI:EU:C:2015:639).

Case C-191/15, *Verein für Konsumenteninformation v Amazon EU Sàrl*, judgment of 28 July 2016 (ECLI:EU:C:2016:612).

Case C-74/16, *Congregación de Escuelas Pías Provincia Betania v Ayuntamiento de Getafe*, judgment of 27 June 2017 (Grand Chamber) (ECLI:EU:C:2017:496).

Case C-210/16, *Unabhängiges Landeszentrum für Datenschutz Schleswig-Holstein v Wirtschaftsakademie Schleswig-Holstein GmbH*, judgment of 5 June 2018 (Grand Chamber) (ECLI:EU:C:2018:388).

A. Rationale and Policy Underpinnings

The GDPR restricts the transfer of personal data from the EU and EEA to third countries and international organisations.[1] The basic rule is that such transfers are permitted only when: (i) the European Commission has adopted a decision establishing that a third country or international organisation provides an 'adequate level of protection' for the data (commonly termed as 'adequacy decision') (see Article 45 GDPR); or (ii) the controller or processor has provided 'appropriate safeguards' with respect to the protection of the personal data to be transferred (see Article 46 GDPR).[2] Binding corporate rules

---

[1] On the meaning of 'international organisation', see the commentary on Art. 4(26) in this volume. However, the character of BCRs is such that they are not applicable in cases of transfers of personal data to international organisations.

[2] See WP29 2018C, p. 2. In the absence of a Commission's adequacy decision or of appropriate safeguards, a transfer of personal data to a third country may exceptionally take place where one of the derogations under Art. 49 applies. See further the commentaries on Arts. 45–46 and 49 in this volume.

('BCRs') are one of the tools by means of which such 'appropriate safeguards' may be provided by a 'group of undertakings'[3] or a 'group of enterprises engaged in a joint economic activity'.[4]

BCRs are internal rules developed and followed by a multinational corporation for transfers of personal data between the companies belonging to its corporate group, approved by the competent supervisory authority. Thus, BCRs may be seen as a form of corporate code of conduct. However, their purpose and nature are different from those of more traditional codes of conduct such as those foreseen in Article 40 GDPR. This is reflected in the legislator's choice to refer to them with a term different from 'codes of conduct'.[5]

BCRs were developed under the DPD as a matter of practice by DPAs and by the WP29 on the basis of an extensive interpretation of Articles 25 and 26 DPD, in order to facilitate data transfers within multinational corporate groups operating on a global scale.[6] However, several shortcomings—most notably the inconsistent approach taken by Member States towards BCRs—have often discouraged companies from using them.[7] The EU legislator therefore decided to formalise and restructure the use of BCRs in the GDPR as part of its effort to improve the EU procedures governing the international transfer of data, in particular to ensure a more uniform and coherent EU approach vis-à-vis third countries.[8] As a result, BCRs are mentioned in multiple provisions of the GDPR, thus warranting a specific definition of the term.

B. Legal Background

1. EU legislation

The DPD did not explicitly mention BCRs. However, as of around 2002, some DPAs began approving BCRs as 'adequate safeguards' under Article 26(2) DPD,[9] as the latter provision left Member States with a broad margin of discretion with respect to the assessment of the adequacy of the safeguards put in place by a company to ensure the protection of the personal data to be transferred to a third country.[10] The WP29 expressly endorsed this practice and—starting from 2003—issued a series of guidance documents on BCRs to help streamline the approval process.[11] However, these documents were

---

[3] See the commentary on the definition of 'group of undertakings' in Art. 4(19) in this volume.
[4] Ibid.
[5] The first WP29 document referring to BCRs noted that 'as the purpose of these instruments is different from the codes of conduct foreseen in Article 27 of the Directive, rather than referring to them as "codes of conduct" (which could be misunderstood) it seems more appropriate to find a terminology which fits with the real nature of these instruments, that is, the provision of sufficient safeguards for the protection of personal data transferred outside the Community'. See WP29 2003, p. 8.
[6] See EC Staff Working Paper 2012, p. 16.   [7] Ibid., p. 17.
[8] See EC Communication 2010, p. 16.
[9] See Kuner 2007, p. 221. Art. 26(2) DPD read: '[w]ithout prejudice to paragraph 1, a Member State may authorise a transfer or a set of transfers of personal data to a third country which does not ensure an adequate level of protection within the meaning of Article 25(2), where the controller adduces adequate safeguards with respect to the protection of the privacy and fundamental rights and freedoms of individuals and as regards the exercise of the corresponding rights; such safeguards may in particular result from appropriate contractual clauses'.
[10] See WP29 2003, p. 5.
[11] The WP29 has issued the following guidance documents on BCRs under the DPD: WP29 2015; WP29 2014; WP29 2012A; WP29 2012B; WP29 2008A; WP29 2008B; WP29 2008C; WP29 2007; WP29 2005A;

solely intended to facilitate BCR use and did not force Member States to follow the same approach towards such tools for the transfer of personal data. Thus, as detailed further below, Member States took divergent approaches to BCR usage under the DPD.

BCRs were traditionally limited to controllers.[12] However, in 2012, the WP29 endorsed the expansion of their application to processors as well and started to provide guidance in this regard.[13] This approach was taken over in Articles 4(20) and 47 GDPR, which envisage that BCRs may be adhered to both by controllers and processors.

2. International instruments

There are no international treaties dealing with BCRs. However, in 2014, the WP29 and APEC jointly issued a 'Referential' that maps the respective requirements of the EU BCRs and the APEC's Cross-Border Privacy Rules ('CBPR').[14] The Referential has been used by companies to seek approval of their BCRs, using their CBPR certification as a starting point, thus achieving dual certification and regulatory interoperability in practice.[15]

3. National developments

As mentioned above, prior to adoption of the GDPR, EU Member States took different approaches towards BCRs. A few Member States initially viewed BCRs as creating 'adequate protection' in the third country of import in the sense of Article 25 DPD, and consequently made approval of BCRs optional.[16] Most of the other Member States instead recognised them as 'adequate safeguards' under their national implementation of Article 26(2) DPD, thus requiring approval.[17] Still others considered BCRs as incompatible with their domestic legal systems,[18] primarily because, under these systems, unilateral undertakings in corporate codes of conduct do not create obligations and rights with legal effects.[19]

However, only a few national data protection laws included a definition of BCRs prior to the enactment of the GDPR. A case in point is the Hungarian Information Act of 2011, Article 3(25) of which defined 'binding corporate rules' as:

internal data protection rules adopted by a data controller or a group of data controllers operating in multiple countries, at least in one EEA Member State, and approved by the National Authority for Data Protection and Freedom of Information ... binding upon the data controller or group of data controllers that, in case of a data transfer to third countries, ensures the protection of these data by unilateral commitment of the respective controller or group of controllers.[20]

4. Case law

The CJEU has yet to rule on the definition of 'binding corporate rules' under the GDPR. However, in *Lindqvist*, the CJEU has interpreted the concept of 'transfer of personal

---

WP29 2005B; WP29 2004; WP29 2003. The WP29 has also issued the following guidance documents on BCRs under the GDPR: WP29 2017, WP29 2018A, WP29 2018B, WP29 2018C and WP29 2018D. The latter batch of documents has been endorsed by the EDPB: see EDPB 2018.

[12] See EC Staff Working Paper 2012, p. 17.   [13] See WP29 2012A.   [14] See WP29 2014.
[15] Cooper and Wandall 2017.   [16] Kuner 2007, p. 222.   [17] Ibid.
[18] See Traça and Embry 2011.   [19] See WP29 2003, p. 6.
[20] See Hungarian Information Act 2011.

data to third countries' within the meaning of the DPD, and found that it excluded the loading of personal data onto an internet page of a website which is stored with a hosting provider established in a Member State, thereby making those data accessible to anyone who connects to the internet, including people in a third country.[21] Thus, the judgment suggests that a data transfer should be an active act which involves sending data, and not just making it passively accessible. Yet, this does not mean that granting access to data over the internet would always fail to qualify as a 'transfer'; indeed, the judgment seems to rest on a number of specific factors that may limit the case to its facts.[22]

C. Analysis

The definition of BCRs in Article 4(20) GDPR builds on the conceptualisation of these data transfer instruments that was developed, primarily by the WP29, under the DPD.[23] Thus, Article 4(20) clarifies that BCRs are (internal) 'data protection policies' that may be adopted by multinational companies for transferring personal data. Such policies may be adhered to by companies that qualify as controllers or processors,[24] provided that they 'are established on the territory of a Member State'.[25] This implies that a controller or processor without establishments in the EU/EEA may not rely on BCRs to export data out of the EU/EEA. The concept of 'establishment' is not defined in the GDPR, but recital 22 states that '[e]stablishment implies the effective and real exercise of activity through stable arrangements. The legal form of such arrangements, whether through a branch or a subsidiary with a legal personality, is not the determining factor in that respect'. This wording essentially reproduces that of recital 19 DPD, which led the CJEU to uphold a flexible understanding of the concept of 'establishment' within the meaning of the DPD.[26] Indeed, the Court held that the concept 'extends to any real and effective activity—even a minimal one—exercised through stable arrangements'.[27]

Article 4(20) states that BCRs are tools to be used 'for transfers or a set of transfers of personal data to a controller or processor in one or more third countries'. Thus, BCRs are only applicable to transfers of data outside the EU/EEA. While there is accordingly no need, under the GDPR, for BCRs in the context of intra-EU/EEA transfers, controllers and processors remain free to apply BCRs also in this context.[28]

---

[21] See Case C-101/01, *Lindqvist*, paras. 52–71.

[22] See further the commentary on Art. 44 in this volume.

[23] See e.g. the definition of BCRs provided in EC Staff Working Paper 2012, p. i: 'Codes of practice based on European data protection standards, approved by at least one Data Protection Authority, which multinational organisations draw up and follow voluntarily to ensure adequate safeguards for transfers or categories of transfers of personal data between companies that are part of a same corporate group and that are bound by these corporate rules'.

[24] See the commentaries on the definitions of 'controller' and processor' in Art. 4(7)–(8) in this volume.

[25] It should be noted that point (b) of entry 5e of Annex XI to the EEA Agreement specifies that the term 'Member State(s)' in the GDPR shall be understood to include, in addition to its meaning in the Regulation, the three EEA EFTA States (i.e. Iceland, Liechtenstein and Norway).

[26] See Case C-230/14, *Weltimmo*, para. 29.

[27] See Case C-230/14, *Weltimmo*, para. 31. See further Case C-191/15, *Verein für Konsumenteninformation*, para. 75; Case C-210/16, *Wirtschaftsakademie Schleswig-Holstein*, paras. 53–55. On the concept of establishment, see further the commentaries on Arts. 3, 4(16) and 4(23) in this volume.

[28] During the legislative process, the Commission indicated that 'there was no need for BCRs in the case of intra-EU transfers, but that controllers were free to apply BCRs also in those cases': see Council Report 2014C, p. 16.

The data transfers that may take place on the basis of BCRs are only transfers between companies that belong to the same 'group of undertakings' or 'group of enterprises engaged in a joint economic activity'. A 'group of undertakings' is defined as 'a controlling undertaking and its controlled undertakings' (Article 4(19) GDPR),[29] whereas a 'group of enterprises engaged in a joint economic activity' is not defined in the GDPR.[30] The latter concept was absent from the definition of BCRs which was included in the original Commission proposal for the GDPR,[31] but it was introduced later by the Council.[32] This was to broaden the scope of BCRs and allow their use for transferring data between business partners working very closely together and within joint ventures that do not qualify as groups of undertakings.[33] Thus, the concept may be understood as covering a business partnership (e.g. an alliance among air carriers)[34] or a joint venture. Some degree of stability would seem to be logically inherent in the concept of 'joint economic activity', in the sense that such activity should not be just a one-off business deal.

The reference to groups of 'undertakings' and 'enterprises' in Article 4(20) would seem, on its face, to exclude public authorities and international organisations from making use of BCRs, at least for the purposes of the GDPR.[35] Under the GDPR, the concept of 'undertaking' is normally construed in accordance with EU competition law (see recital 150 GDPR), and is generally considered to be synonymous with that of 'enterprise'.[36] In the sphere of EU competition law, the CJEU has held that an entity does not qualify as an 'undertaking' if its activities are connected with the exercise of powers that are typically those of a public authority or are otherwise not of an economic nature—as will typically be the case for international organisations and public bodies exercising official authority.[37] In contrast, according to settled case law of the CJEU—still in the sphere of EU competition law—an entity engaged in an economic activity, irrespective of its legal status and the way in which it is financed, qualifies as an 'undertaking'; the fact that an entity is engaged in economic activities 'on a not-for-profit basis does not prevent the entity which carries out those operations on the market from being considered an undertaking'.[38] So, to

---

[29] See also rec. 37 GDPR, which states: '[a] group of undertakings should cover a controlling undertaking and its controlled undertakings, whereby the controlling undertaking should be the undertaking which can exert a dominant influence over the other undertakings by virtue, for example, of ownership, financial participation or the rules which govern it or the power to have personal data protection rules implemented. An undertaking which controls the processing of personal data in undertakings affiliated to it should be regarded, together with those undertakings, as a group of undertakings'. See further the commentary on the definition of 'group of undertakings' in Art. 4(19) in this volume.

[30] The GDPR, however, defines the term 'enterprise'. Further on the definition of that term, see the commentary on Art. 4(18) in this volume.

[31] See GDPR Proposal, Art. 3(17).

[32] See Council Report 2014A, p. 16; Council Report 2014B, p. 8.

[33] The need for such broadening of the scope of BCRs was initially expressed by Luxembourg and Finland. See Council Report 2013, pp. 83 and 117.

[34] The example of an alliance among air carriers was given by Finland during the legislative process. See Council Report 2013, p. 117.

[35] Interestingly, during the legislative process, Slovenia 'thought BCRs should also be possible with regard to some public authorities, but [the Commission] stated that it failed to see any cases in the public sector where BCRs could be applied. [Hungary] thought that BCRs were used not only by profit seeking companies but also by international bodies and NGOs'. See Council Report 2014B, p. 17, fn. 66.

[36] See further the commentary on Art. 4(18) in this volume.

[37] See e.g. Case C-30/87, *Bodson*, para. 18; Case C-364/92, *SAT Fluggesellschaft*, paras. 19–32; Case C-113/07 P, *Selex Sistemi Integrati*, para. 71. On the notion of 'public authority', see further e.g. Case C-279/12, *Fish Legal and Shirley*, paras. 42 and 51–52.

[38] Case C-74/16, *Congregación de Escuelas Pías Provincia Betania*, para. 46.

conclude, while international organisations and public bodies exercising public powers will normally be excluded from using BCRs as they will usually not qualify as 'undertakings', other entities (such as, potentially, non-governmental organisations ('NGOs') and state-controlled corporations) that engage in economic activities may use BCRs even where their activities are conducted on a not-for-profit basis.

Select Bibliography

International agreements

EEA Agreement: Agreement on the European Economic Area, OJ 1994 L 1/3.

EU legislation

GDPR Proposal: Proposal for a Regulation of the European Parliament and of the Council on the protection of individuals with regard to the processing of personal data and on the free movement of such data (General Data Protection Regulation), COM(2012) 11 final, 25 January 2012.

National legislation

Hungarian Information Act 2011: Hungarian Act CXII of 2011 on the Right of Informational Self-Determination and on Freedom of Information.

Academic writings

Cooper and Wandall 2017: Cooper and Wandall, 'Scaling Data Protection Globally through Interoperable Accountability', 41(2) *DuD—Datenschutz und Datensicherheit* (2017), 74.

Kuner 2007: Kuner, *European Data Protection Law: Corporate Compliance and Regulation* (2nd edn, OUP 2007).

Moerel, *Binding Corporate Rules: Corporate Self-Regulation of Global Data Transfers* (OUP 2012).

Proust and Bartoli, 'Binding Corporate Rules: A Global Solution for International Data Transfers', 2(1) *International Data Privacy Law 'IDPL'* (2012), 35.

Traça and Embry 2011: Traça and Embry, 'The Portuguese Regulatory Regime for Binding Corporate Rules' 1(3) *IDPL* (2011), 206.

Papers of data protection authorities

EDPB 2018: European Data Protection Board, 'Endorsement 1/2018' (25 May 2018).

WP29 2003: Article 29 Working Party, 'Working Document on Transfers of Personal Data to Third Countries: Applying Article 26(2) of the EU Data Protection Directive to Binding Corporate Rules for International Data Transfers' (WP 74, 3 June 2003).

WP29 2004: Article 29 Working Party, 'Model Checklist, Application for Approval of Binding Corporate Rules' (WP 102, 25 November 2004).

WP29 2005A: Article 29 Working Party, 'Working Document Establishing a Model Checklist Application for Approval of Binding Corporate Rules' (WP 108, 14 April 2005).

WP29 2005B: Article 29 Working Party, 'Working Document Setting Forth a Co-Operation Procedure for Issuing Common Opinions on Adequate Safeguards Resulting From "Binding Corporate Rules"' (WP 107, 14 April 2005).

WP29 2007: Article 29 Working Party, 'Recommendation 1/2007 on the Standard Application for Approval of Binding Corporate Rules for the Transfer of Personal Data' (WP 133, 10 January 2007).

WP29 2008A: Article 29 Working Party, 'Working Document on Frequently Asked Questions (FAQs) related to Binding Corporate Rules' (WP 155 rev. 4, 24 June 2008).

WP29 2008B: Article 29 Working Party, 'Working Document Setting Up a Table with the Elements and Principles to Be Found in Binding Corporate Rules' (WP 153, 24 June 2008).

WP29 2008C: Article 29 Working Party, 'Working Document Setting Up a Framework for the Structure of Binding Corporate Rules' (WP 154, 25 June 2008).

WP29 2012A: Article 29 Working Party, 'Working Document 02/2012 Setting Up a Table with the Elements and Principles to Be Found in Processor Binding Corporate Rules' (WP 195, 6 June 2012).

WP29 2012B: Article 29 Working Party, 'Recommendation 1/2012 on the Standard Application form for Approval of Binding Corporate Rules for the Transfer of Personal Data for Processing Activities' (WP 195a, 17 September 2012).

WP29 2014: Article 29 Working Party, 'Opinion 02/2014 on a Referential for Requirements for Binding Corporate Rules Submitted to National Data Protection Authorities in the EU and Cross Border Privacy Rules Submitted to APEC CBPR Accountability Agents' (WP 212, 27 February 2014).

WP29 2015: Article 29 Working Party, 'Explanatory Document on the Processor Binding Corporate Rules', revised version (WP 204, 22 May 2015).

WP29 2017: Article 29 Working Party, 'Working Document Setting Up a Table with the Elements and Principles to Be Found in Binding Corporate Rules' (WP 256, 29 November 2017).

WP29 2018A: Article 29 Working Party, 'Working Document Setting Forth a Table with the Elements and Principles to Be Found in Processor Binding Corporate Rules' (WP 257 rev.01, as last revised and adopted on 6 February 2018).

WP29 2018B: Article 29 Working Party, 'Working Document Setting Forth a Co-Operation Procedure for the Approval of "Binding Corporate Rules" for Controllers and Processors under the GDPR' (WP 263 rev.01, 11 April 2018).

WP29 2018C: Article 29 Working Party, 'Recommendation on the Standard Application for Approval of Controller Binding Corporate Rules for the Transfer of Personal Data (WP 264, 11 April 2018).

WP29 2018D: Article 29 Working Party, 'Recommendation on the Standard Application form for Approval of Processor Binding Corporate Rules for the Transfer of Personal Data' (WP 265, 11 April 2018).

Reports and recommendations

Council Report 2013: Comments on Chapter V, 6723/4/13 REV 4, 25 March 2013.
Council Report 2014A: Chapter V, 8087/1, 25 March 2014.
Council Report 2014B: Chapter V, 8087/2/14 REV 2, 12 May 2014.
Council Report 2014C: Chapter V, 9865/1/14 REV 1, 22 May 2014.
EC Communication 2010: Communication from the Commission to the European Parliament, the Council, the Economic and Social Committee and the Committee of the Regions: A comprehensive approach on personal data protection in the European Union, COM(2010) 609 final, 4 November 2010.

EC Staff Working Paper 2012: Commission Staff Working Paper 'Impact Assessment Accompanying the document Regulation of the European Parliament and of the Council on the protection of individuals with regard to the processing of personal data and on the free movement of such data (General Data Protection Regulation) and Directive of the European Parliament and of the Council on the protection of individuals with regard to the processing of personal data by competent authorities for the purposes of prevention, investigation, detection or prosecution of criminal offences or the execution of criminal penalties, and the free movement of such data', SEC(2012) 72 final, 25 January 2012.

Article 4(21). Supervisory authority

LEE A. BYGRAVE

'supervisory authority' means an independent public authority which is established by a Member State pursuant to Article 51;

Relevant Recitals

(117) The establishment of supervisory authorities in Member States, empowered to perform their tasks and exercise their powers with complete independence, is an essential component of the protection of natural persons with regard to the processing of their personal data. Member States should be able to establish more than one supervisory authority, to reflect their constitutional, organisational and administrative structure.

(122) Each supervisory authority should be competent on the territory of its own Member State to exercise the powers and to perform the tasks conferred on it in accordance with this Regulation. This should cover in particular the processing in the context of the activities of an establishment of the controller or processor on the territory of its own Member State, the processing of personal data carried out by public authorities or private bodies acting in the public interest, processing affecting data subjects on its territory or processing carried out by a controller or processor not established in the Union when targeting data subjects residing on its territory. This should include handling complaints lodged by a data subject, conducting investigations on the application of this Regulation and promoting public awareness of the risks, rules, safeguards and rights in relation to the processing of personal data.

(123) The supervisory authorities should monitor the application of the provisions pursuant to this Regulation and contribute to its consistent application throughout the Union, in order to protect natural persons in relation to the processing of their personal data and to facilitate the free flow of personal data within the internal market. For that purpose, the supervisory authorities should cooperate with each other and with the Commission, without the need for any agreement between Member States on the provision of mutual assistance or on such cooperation.

Closely Related Provisions

Article 4(22) (Definition of 'supervisory authority concerned'); Article 51 (Supervisory authority); Article 52 (Independence) (see too recitals 118 and 120–121); Article 53 (General conditions for the members of the supervisory authority) (see too recital 121); Article 54 (Rules on the establishment of the supervisory authority); Articles 55–59 (Competence, tasks and powers) (see too recitals 122–124, 129 and 132); Articles 60–62 (Cooperation) (see too recitals 125–128, 130–131 and 133–134); Articles 63–67 (Consistency) (see too recitals 119 and 135–138); Article 68 (European Data Protection Board) (see too recital 139)

Related Provisions in LED [Directive (EU) 2016/680]

Article 3(15) (Definition of 'supervisory authority'); Article 41 (Supervisory authority) (see too recitals 75–77)

Article 4(21)

Related Provisions in EUDPR [Regulation (EU) 2018/1725]

Article 3(22) (Definition of 'national supervisory authority') (see too recitals 72 and 77–78)

Relevant Case Law

CJEU

Case C-188/89, *A. Foster and others v British Gas plc*, judgment of 12 July 1990 (ECLI:EU:C:1990:313).
Case C-518/07, *European Commission v Federal Republic of Germany*, judgment of 9 March 2010 (Grand Chamber) (ECLI:EU:C:2010:125).
Case C-614/10, *European Commission v Republic of Austria*, judgment of 16 October 2012 (Grand Chamber) (ECLI:EU:C:2012:631).
Case C-425/12, *Portgás—Sociedade de Produção e Distribuição de Gás SA v Ministério da Agricultura, do Mar, do Ambiente e do Ordenamento do Território*, judgment of 12 December 2013 (ECLI:EU:C:2013:829).
Case C-279/12, *Fish Legal, Emily Shirley v Information Commissioner, United Utilities Water plc, Yorkshire Water Services Ltd, Southern Water Services Ltd*, judgment of 19 December 2013 (ECLI:EU:C:2013:853).
Case C-288/12, *European Commission v Hungary*, judgment of 8 April 2014 (Grand Chamber) (ECLI:EU:C:2014:237).
Case C-362/14, *Maximillian Schrems v Data Protection Commissioner*, judgment of 6 October 2015 (Grand Chamber) (ECLI:EU:C:2015:650).

ECtHR

Leander v Sweden, Appl. No. 9248/81, judgment of 26 March 1987.

A. Rationale and Policy Underpinnings

A distinguishing feature of European data protection laws is their establishment of special regulatory agencies to oversee, encourage and enforce the implementation of their rules. In the terminology of EU law, these agencies are called 'supervisory authorities'. More generally, they are typically termed 'Data Protection Authorities' ('DPAs'). Such bodies are usually given broad powers to monitor and regulate the processing of personal data by organisations in both the public and private sectors. Their functions extend to handling complaints, providing advice and raising public awareness on data protection matters.

In EU law, the existence of independent DPAs is a *sine qua non* for the operationalisation of data protection. As originally stated in recital 62 DPD, repeated in recital 117 GDPR and confirmed by the CJEU,[1] 'the establishment in Member States of supervisory authorities, exercising their functions with complete independence, is an essential component of the protection of individuals with regard to the processing of personal data'.[2] The definition of 'supervisory authority' in Article 4(21) GDPR reflects this characteristic.

---

[1] See e.g. Case C-518/07, *Commission v Germany*, para. 23; Case C-362/14, *Schrems*, para. 42.
[2] On the notion of independence see further the commentaries on Arts. 52 and 69 in this volume.

B. Legal Background

1. EU legislation

The DPD did not provide a definition of 'supervisory authority'. It did, however, require each Member State to establish 'one or more' such authorities which 'shall act with complete independence in exercising the functions entrusted to them' (Article 28(1); see too recital 62). It also laid down rules regarding supervisory authorities' competence, tasks and roles (see Article 28(2)), but did so in fairly broad-brush fashion.

The DPD's emphasis on the need for independent supervisory authorities was later elevated to a constitutional norm of EU law. Thus, compliance with the right to protection of personal data and associated rules under Article 8(1)–(2) of the EU Charter of Fundamental Rights ('CFR') 'shall be subject to control by an independent authority' (Article 8(3) CFR), while compliance with the equivalent rights and associated rules under Article 16(1)–(2) of the Treaty on the Functioning of the European Union ('TFEU') 'shall be subject to the control of independent authorities' (Article 16(2) TFEU).

Concomitantly, the EDPS is required to act with 'complete independence' similarly to national supervisory authorities (see Article 55(1)–(2) EUDPR and its antecedents in Article 44(1)–(2) of Regulation (EC) 45/2001).[3]

2. International instruments

Convention 108 as originally adopted omitted provisions on DPAs. Such provisions were first introduced by an Additional Protocol to the Convention, adopted in 2001.[4] These provisions basically replicated the thrust of Article 28 DPD. In contrast, Articles 15–21 of Modernised Convention 108 deal extensively with supervisory authorities, along the lines of the GDPR.

The OECD Privacy Guidelines, as originally adopted, did not contain provisions on DPAs. This changed with the revision of the Guidelines in 2013. Thus, the 2013 version of the Guidelines stipulates that Member countries 'should establish and maintain privacy enforcement authorities with the governance, resources and technical expertise necessary to exercise their powers effectively and to make decisions on an objective, impartial and consistent basis' (paragraph 19(c)). The term 'privacy enforcement authority' is defined as 'any public body, as determined by each Member country, that is responsible for enforcing laws protecting privacy, and that has powers to conduct investigations or pursue enforcement proceedings' (paragraph 1(d)). The Supplementary Explanatory Memorandum to the revised Guidelines elaborates on this definition as follows:

The definitions of 'laws protecting privacy' and 'privacy enforcement authorities' allow for flexibility in application. 'Laws protecting privacy' can refer not only to horizontal privacy laws that are common in Member countries, but also to sectoral privacy legislation (e.g. credit reporting or telecommunications laws) or other types of legislation that contain provisions which protect personal data so as to give effect to the Guidelines in practice (e.g. consumer protection laws). Likewise, a 'privacy enforcement authority' refers not only to those public sector entities whose primary mission is the enforcement of national privacy laws, but may for example also extend to regulators with a consumer protection mission, provided they have the powers to conduct investigations or bring proceedings in the context of enforcing 'laws protecting privacy' ... In some countries, the term

---

[3] See Table of Legislation.   [4] Ibid.

'privacy enforcement authority' can also refer to a group of bodies that collectively enforce laws protecting privacy. For example, oversight of public sector data controllers may involve multiple bodies from different branches of government, who may also have the authority to issues guidelines or other data usage requirements. The 'governance, resources, and technical expertise' called for in paragraph 19(c) may not, in such a case, be embodied in a single entity, but rather be found in the enforcement system as a whole.[5]

While the Guidelines do not, on their face, emphasise the need for these authorities to be independent, the Supplementary Explanatory Memorandum makes clear that this need arises as a precondition for the ability of authorities 'to make decisions on an objective, impartial and consistent basis' pursuant to paragraph 19(c).[6]

The UN Guidelines for the Regulation of Computerized Personal Data Files adopted in 1990 also stipulate the need for independent DPAs:

The law of every country shall designate the authority which, in accordance with its domestic legal system, is to be responsible for supervising observance of the principles set forth above. This authority shall offer guarantees of impartiality, independence vis-a-vis persons or agencies responsible for processing and establishing data, and technical competence.[7]

3. National developments

DPAs were initially established in the early 1970s in various European jurisdictions. The German *Land* of Hessen set up the world's first such body in 1970, while Sweden created the first national-level DPA in 1973. Today, almost every country—both within and outside Europe—with a fairly comprehensive statutory regime for data protection has established one or more DPAs.[8]

As noted above, Article 28 DPD required EU/EEA Member States to create independent DPAs but did not otherwise tightly regulate how these bodies were supposed to function or be organised. The result at national level was that, during the life of the DPD, many Member States retained large parts of their pre-DPD frameworks for the operation of their respective DPAs. Not surprisingly, national DPA regimes ended up differing considerably in terms of institutional anchoring, structure, competence and resources.[9] Moreover, these regimes tended to be afflicted by insufficient allocations of funding and staff for them to be able properly to fulfil their remit, and, in some cases, their independence and powers were undermined by institutional arrangements from the pre-DPD era.[10]

4. Case law

CJEU jurisprudence has made a major contribution to defining the criterion of independence for DPAs. In the course of three judgments concerning the DPA regimes of Germany, Austria and Hungary,[11] the CJEU underlined that a supervisory authority must have 'a decision-making power independent of any direct or indirect external influence',[12]

---

[5] OECD Guidelines 2013, pp. 28–29.   [6] Ibid., p. 28.   [7] UNGA 1990, para. 8.
[8] See generally Bygrave 2014, ch. 6, section A.   [9] See generally FRA 2010.   [10] Ibid.
[11] Case C-518/07, *Commission v Germany*; Case C-614/10, *Commission v Austria*; Case C-288/12, *Commission v Hungary*. Further on this jurisprudence, see Hijmans 2016, pp. 354 et seq., along with the commentary on Art. 51 in this volume.
[12] Case C-518/07, *Commission v Germany*, para. 19.

and that 'the mere risk that the scrutinising authorities could exercise a political influence over the decisions of the supervisory authorities is enough to hinder the latter authorities' independent performance of their tasks'.[13] This jurisprudence is reflected in Article 52 GDPR.[14]

The ECtHR has also played a significant role in this regard because it has stressed the need for independent monitoring and supervision of data-processing practices that interfere with the right(s) in Article 8(1) ECHR.[15]

C. Analysis

The definition in Article 4(21) GDPR is brief and provides in itself few concrete indicators of what is meant by 'supervisory authority' under the Regulation. In practice, most of the definitional work is done by Chapter VI of the Regulation, particularly Article 51 (in conjunction with recitals 117 and 122–123) and Article 52 (in conjunction with recitals 118 and 120–121). The purpose of Article 4(21) seems largely to clarify that Article 51 is the first 'point of call' for a reader of the GDPR who is interested in finding out more about supervisory authorities. Nonetheless, the very fact that 'supervisory authority' receives its own place in the list of Article 4 definitions reflects the pronounced importance of DPA regimes in EU law and, concomitantly, the GDPR's central remit of harmonising and strengthening these regimes.[16]

The definition of 'supervisory authority' also reflects the emphasis in EU law on the need for DPA independence. Indeed, the independence criterion is built into the definition so that a body will not even qualify as a supervisory authority unless it meets that criterion, as elaborated in Article 52 GDPR and the CJEU jurisprudence referenced above.

Another important element of the definition is the reference to 'public authority'. This term is not defined in the GDPR nor does the Regulation refer to national laws for the purpose of determining its meaning. Thus, the term should be given an autonomous EU-wide meaning.[17] According to the CJEU, the concept of 'public authority' generally encompasses:

Entities which, organically, are administrative authorities, namely those which form part of the public administration or the executive of the State at whatever level ... This first category includes all legal persons governed by public law which have been set up by the State and which it alone can decide to dissolve;

[and]

entities, be they legal persons governed by public law or by private law, which are entrusted, under the legal regime which is applicable to them, with the performance of services of public interest ... and which are, for this purpose, vested with special powers beyond those which result from the normal rules applicable in relations between persons governed by private law.[18]

---

[13] Ibid., para. 36.   [14] See further the commentary on Art. 52 in this volume.
[15] See e.g. ECtHR, *Leander v Sweden*, para. 65.
[16] For further detail on the ways in which the GDPR fulfils this remit, see Giurgiu and Larsen 2016. Point (b) of entry 5(e) of Annex XI to the EEA Agreement provides that the term 'supervisory authority' in the GDPR shall be understood to include the supervisory authorities of the EFTA States (i.e. Iceland, Liechtenstein and Norway).
[17] See e.g. Case C-279/12, *Fish Legal and Shirley*, para. 42 and case law cited therein.
[18] Ibid., paras. 51–52. See too e.g. Case C-188/89, *Foster*, para. 20; Case C-425/12, *Portgás*, para. 24.

Thus, a purely private body would ordinarily be unable to fulfil the role of supervisory authority for the purposes of the GDPR; a supervisory authority should normally be part of the State apparatus—at the same time as the independence criterion requires it to be accorded a very high degree of functional and institutional autonomy within that apparatus.

While EU law generally permits some flexibility as to the precise legal form taken by a public authority, whatever form is adopted for a supervisory authority under the GDPR will need to be such that the authority can meet the detailed set of requirements laid down in Chapter VI of the Regulation. Further, the reference in Article 4(21) to 'established by a Member State' ordinarily connotes that the supervisory authority is created through a legislative act of the Member State's parliament. Thus, creating a body under the internal rules of an association or organisation that is independent of, and formally separate to, the State is unlikely to be considered 'established by a Member State'.

It is not the case that there can be only one supervisory authority per Member State; the GDPR permits Member States to establish a plurality of authorities if they so wish. This is not made explicit in Article 4(21) but follows from Article 51(3) and recital 117. Moreover, the GDPR envisages the possibility of a Member State creating a sectoral supervisory authority with respect to the processing of personal data by churches and religious associations (Article 91(2)),[19] on the precondition that the authority fulfils the Chapter VI requirements.

Finally, it bears emphasis that a supervisory authority may carry out other functions than simply monitoring and enforcing implementation of data protection law. In other words, they may combine their data protection remit with other roles, such as handling complaints under, say, law on access to government-held information[20]—as long as these functions do not conflict with GDPR requirements. In this regard, it is also noteworthy that the CJEU has stipulated that supervisory authorities are explicitly required to take account of a range of interests that go beyond data protection: 'supervisory authorities must ensure a fair balance between, on the one hand, observance of the fundamental right to private life and, on the other hand, the interests requiring free movement of personal data'.[21]

Select Bibliography

International agreements

OECD Guidelines 2013: Organisation for Economic Co-operation and Development, 'The OECD Privacy Framework' (2013).
UNGA 1990: United Nations General Assembly, 'Guidelines for the Regulation of Computerized Personal Data Files' (14 December 1990).

---

[19] As has been done in Poland, where a Church Data Protection Inspector (*Kościelny Inspektor Ochrony Danych*) has been established to oversee the data-processing activities of the Catholic Church in Poland. See further the commentary on Art. 91 in this volume. However, as this body seems to have been established pursuant to internal rules of the Polish Catholic Church, which is formally independent of the Polish Republic, it is questionable whether it qualifies as an independent public authority 'established by a Member State', and hence supervisory authority, under the GDPR.
[20] The case, for instance, with the UK ICO.
[21] Case C-518/07, *Commission v Germany*, para. 24. See too rec. 123 GDPR.

Academic writings

Bygrave 2014: Bygrave, *Data Privacy Law: An International Perspective* (OUP 2014).
Giurgiu and Larsen 2016: Giurgiu and Larsen, 'Roles and Powers of National Data Protection Authorities', 2(3) *European Data Protection Law Review* (2016), 342.
Hijmans 2016: Hijmans, *The European Union as Guardian of Internet Privacy* (Springer 2016).

Reports and recommendations

FRA 2010: Fundamental Rights Agency of the European Union, *Data Protection in the European Union: The Role of National Data Protection Authorities* (Publications office of the European Union 2010).

Article 4(22). Supervisory authority concerned

LUCA TOSONI

'supervisory authority concerned' means a supervisory authority which is concerned by the processing of personal data because:

(a) the controller or processor is established on the territory of the Member State of that supervisory authority;
(b) data subjects residing in the Member State of that supervisory authority are substantially affected or likely to be substantially affected by the processing; or
(c) a complaint has been lodged with that supervisory authority;

Relevant Recitals

(22) Any processing of personal data in the context of the activities of an establishment of a controller or a processor in the Union should be carried out in accordance with this Regulation, regardless of whether the processing itself takes place within the Union. Establishment implies the effective and real exercise of activity through stable arrangements. The legal form of such arrangements, whether through a branch or a subsidiary with a legal personality, is not the determining factor in that respect.

(36) The main establishment of a controller in the Union should be the place of its central administration in the Union, unless the decisions on the purposes and means of the processing of personal data are taken in another establishment of the controller in the Union, in which case that other establishment should be considered to be the main establishment. The main establishment of a controller in the Union should be determined according to objective criteria and should imply the effective and real exercise of management activities determining the main decisions as to the purposes and means of processing through stable arrangements. That criterion should not depend on whether the processing of personal data is carried out at that location. The presence and use of technical means and technologies for processing personal data or processing activities do not, in themselves, constitute a main establishment and are therefore not determining criteria for a main establishment. The main establishment of the processor should be the place of its central administration in the Union or, if it has no central administration in the Union, the place where the main processing activities take place in the Union. In cases involving both the controller and the processor, the competent lead supervisory authority should remain the supervisory authority of the Member State where the controller has its main establishment, but the supervisory authority of the processor should be considered to be a supervisory authority concerned and that supervisory authority should participate in the cooperation procedure provided for by this Regulation. In any case, the supervisory authorities of the Member State or Member States where the processor has one or more establishments should not be considered to be supervisory authorities concerned where the draft decision concerns only the controller. Where the processing is carried out by a group of undertakings, the main establishment of the controlling undertaking should be considered to be the main establishment of the group of undertakings, except where the purposes and means of processing are determined by another undertaking.

(124) Where the processing of personal data takes place in the context of the activities of an establishment of a controller or a processor in the Union and the controller or processor is established in more than one Member State, or where processing taking place in the context of the activities of

a single establishment of a controller or processor in the Union substantially affects or is likely to substantially affect data subjects in more than one Member State, the supervisory authority for the main establishment of the controller or processor or for the single establishment of the controller or processor should act as lead authority. It should cooperate with the other authorities concerned, because the controller or processor has an establishment on the territory of their Member State, because data subjects residing on their territory are substantially affected, or because a complaint has been lodged with them. Also where a data subject not residing in that Member State has lodged a complaint, the supervisory authority with which such complaint has been lodged should also be a supervisory authority concerned. Within its tasks to issue guidelines on any question covering the application of this Regulation, the Board should be able to issue guidelines in particular on the criteria to be taken into account in order to ascertain whether the processing in question substantially affects data subjects in more than one Member State and on what constitutes a relevant and reasoned objection.

Closely Related Provisions

Article 4(2) (Definition of 'processing'); Article 4(21) (Definition of 'supervisory authority'); Article 4(23) (Definition of 'cross-border processing'); Article 52 (Independence); Article 56 (Competence of the lead supervisory authority); Article 60 (Cooperation between the lead supervisory authority and the other supervisory authorities concerned); Article 63 (Consistency mechanism) (see too recitals 135 and 138); Article 64 (Opinion of the Board); Article 65 (Dispute resolution by the Board); Article 66 (Urgency procedure); Article 74 (Tasks of the Chair); Article 77 (Right to lodge a complaint with a supervisory authority)

Relevant Case Law

CJEU

Case C-230/14, *Weltimmo s.r.o. v Nemzeti Adatvédelmi és Információszabadság Hatóság*, judgment of 1 October 2015 (ECLI:EU:C:2015:639).

Case C-131/12, *Google Spain v Agencia Española de Protección de Datos (AEPD) and Mario Costeja González*, judgment of 13 May 2014 (Grand Chamber) (ECLI:EU:C:2014:317).

Case C-191/15, *Verein für Konsumenteninformation v Amazon EU Sàrl*, judgment of 28 July 2016 (ECLI:EU:C:2016:612).

Case C-617/15, *Hummel Holding A/S v Nike Inc. and Nike Retail B.V.*, judgment of 18 May 2017 (ECLI:EU:C:2017:390).

Case C-210/16, *Unabhängiges Landeszentrum für Datenschutz Schleswig-Holstein v Wirtschaftsakademie Schleswig-Holstein GmbH*, judgment of 5 June 2018 (Grand Chamber) (ECLI:EU:C:2018:388).

A. Rationale and Policy Underpinnings

The one-stop-shop and consistency mechanisms are among the most significant novelties introduced by the GDPR. The former is an enforcement scheme intended to ensure uniform supervision of controllers and processors involved in cross-border processing activities.[1] It is constructed around a 'lead supervisory authority',[2] which steers the

---

[1] See further the commentaries on Arts. 4(23), 56 and 60–62 in this volume.
[2] See Art. 56(1) GDPR.

enforcement process and is empowered to issue the final enforcement decision, but must do so in cooperation with the other 'supervisory authorities concerned'.

The consistency mechanism is intended to ensure that supervisory authorities across the EU/EEA interpret and apply the GDPR in a consistent manner.[3] This includes a dispute resolution system, to be used also where the 'supervisory authorities concerned' take different views in the context of the one-stop-shop mechanism. The chief role within the consistency mechanism is assigned to the EDPB, which is empowered to issue decisions that are binding on supervisory authorities.

The reference to the notion of 'supervisory authority concerned' in the GDPR's provisions dealing with the one-stop-shop and consistency mechanisms,[4] and its definition in Article 4(22), are chiefly intended to identify the supervisory authorities that should participate in such mechanisms. Given that the decisions adopted in the context of these mechanisms may have an impact on data subjects across different EU/EEA countries,[5] the definition of 'supervisory authority concerned' was intentionally drafted quite broadly for ensuring as much 'proximity' as possible between the affected individuals and the relevant decision-making process.[6]

B. Legal Background

1. EU legislation

As mentioned above, the one-stop-shop and consistency mechanisms are among the novelties introduced by the GDPR. Consequently, concepts like 'supervisory authority concerned' that are part and parcel of such mechanisms are not found in the DPD.

2. International instruments

In the data protection context, the one-stop-shop and consistency mechanisms are peculiar to the GDPR. Therefore, notions that pertain to these mechanisms, such as that of 'supervisory authority concerned', are not found in other international instruments on data protection, such as Convention 108, the OECD Privacy Guidelines and the APEC Privacy Framework.

3. Case law

The CJEU has yet to interpret the definition of 'supervisory authority concerned' in Article 4(22) GDPR. However, the Court has provided guidance on the role of supervisory authorities under EU data protection law, as well as on some of the constitutive

---

[3] See the commentaries on Arts. 63–67 in this volume.
[4] See in particular Arts. 60, 64–66 and 74(1)(b) GDPR.
[5] While Art. 4(22) only refers to 'Member State(s)', point (b) of entry 5e of Annex XI to the EEA Agreement provides that the term 'Member State(s)' in the GDPR shall be understood to include, in addition to its meaning in the Regulation, the three EEA EFTA States (i.e. Iceland, Liechtenstein and Norway).
[6] During the legislative process, the Presidency of the Council had suggested to narrow the definition of 'supervisory authority concerned' in the GDPR by incorporating in the definition a reference to a high degree of risk of data subjects being substantially affected in the jurisdiction of the authority concerned. However, this suggestion was rejected by the vast majority of Member States. See Council Report 2015, p. 2. Having a broad definition of 'supervisory authority concerned' implies, for instance, that in the case of personal data processed by social media or other internet platforms, all Member State DPAs are likely to be considered as 'supervisory authorities concerned'. See Council Report 2014, p. 35, fn. 43.

elements of the definition of 'supervisory authority concerned', including on the meaning of 'processing', 'establishment' and 'residence'. This case law is referred to in the following section.

C. Analysis

1. Introduction

The definition of 'supervisory authority concerned' in Article 4(22) GDPR is based on three connecting factors, any of which transforms a 'supervisory authority'[7] into a 'supervisory authority concerned' for the purposes of the GDPR: (1) establishment of the relevant controller or processor in the jurisdiction of that supervisory authority (Article 4(22)(a)); (2) substantial impact (or likelihood thereof) of the relevant processing on data subjects residing in the jurisdiction of that supervisory authority (Article 4(22)(b)); or (3) submission of a complaint with that supervisory authority (Article 4(22)(c)).

The authority in question is 'concerned' both in the sense that it is affected by a certain processing operation, as this presents some connection with its jurisdiction, and in the sense that such connection triggers the authority's involvement in a decision-making process concerning the processing at hand.

2. Establishment of the controller or processor in the EU/EEA country of the supervisory authority

Under Article 4(22)(a), a supervisory authority qualifies as a 'supervisory authority concerned' if the relevant controller or processor is established in its jurisdiction. The concept of 'establishment' is not defined in the GDPR, but recital 22 states that '[e]stablishment implies the effective and real exercise of activity through stable arrangements. The legal form of such arrangements, whether through a branch or a subsidiary with a legal personality, is not the determining factor in that respect'.[8] This wording essentially reproduces that of recital 19 DPD,[9] which led the CJEU to uphold a flexible understanding of the concept of 'establishment' within the meaning of the DPD and reject a formalistic approach whereby a controller or processor is established in an EU/EEA country only if it is formally registered or incorporated in that country.[10] Indeed, according to the Court, the concept 'extends to any real and effective activity—even a minimal one—exercised through stable arrangements'.[11] Thus, an entity does not need to have a branch or subsidiary in a EU/EEA country to be considered as established in that country under EU data protection law.[12]

---

[7] On the notion of 'supervisory authority', see the commentary on Art. 4(21) in this volume.

[8] On the concept of 'establishment', see further the commentaries on Arts. 3, 4(16) and 4(23) in this volume.

[9] Rec. 19 DPD stated that 'establishment on the territory of a Member State implies the effective and real exercise of activity through stable arrangements' and that 'the legal form of such an establishment, whether simply [a] branch or a subsidiary with a legal personality, is not the determining factor'. See also Case C-131/12, *Google Spain*, para. 48.

[10] See Case C-230/14, *Weltimmo*, para. 29.

[11] Ibid., para. 31. See further Case C-191/15, *Verein für Konsumenteninformation*, para. 75; and Case C-210/16, *Wirtschaftsakademie Schleswig-Holstein*, paras. 53–55. For a critical view of the expanding scope of the concept of 'establishment', see Svantesson 2016.

[12] See Case C-191/15, *Verein für Konsumenteninformation*, para. 76. See also EDPB 2018, p. 5.

The reference to the mere establishment of the controller or processor in the jurisdiction of the supervisory authority suggests that it is not necessary that the relevant processing is conducted 'by' or 'in the context of' the activities of such establishment—an authority qualifies as a 'supervisory authority concerned' under Article 4(22)(a) even where the relevant processing takes place abroad or it is 'inextricably linked' only to establishments in other EU/EEA countries, provided that the controller or processor is established in the jurisdiction of the authority at hand.

The establishment criterion arguably brings within the scope of the definition of 'supervisory authority concerned' also the 'lead supervisory authority', which is the authority of the main or single establishment of the controller or processor in the EU/EEA (see Article 56(1) GDPR). This seems to be confirmed by several provisions of the GDPR which state that the 'lead supervisory authority' should cooperate with '*the other* supervisory authorities concerned' (emphasis added), thus suggesting that the lead supervisory authority is one of them.[13] This has important implications: for instance, if the lead authority would not qualify as a 'supervisory authority concerned', it would be unable to adopt urgent interim measures pursuant to Article 66 GDPR, as the latter provision only empowers 'supervisory authorities concerned' to do so.[14]

With regard to the one-stop-shop mechanism, recital 36 GDPR makes clear that:

[i]n cases involving both the controller and the processor, the competent lead supervisory authority should remain the supervisory authority of the Member State where the controller has its main establishment, but the supervisory authority of the processor should be considered to be a supervisory authority concerned and that supervisory authority should participate in the cooperation procedure provided for by [the GDPR].

However, recital 36 continues by stating that 'the supervisory authorities of the Member State or Member States where the processor has one or more establishments should not be considered to be supervisory authorities concerned where the draft decision [prepared by the lead authority in accordance with the one-stop-shop-mechanism] concerns only the controller'.

3. Substantial impact (or likelihood thereof) of the processing on data subjects residing in the EU/EEA country of the supervisory authority

Article 4(22)(b) qualifies as 'supervisory authority concerned' also the authority of the EU/EEA country in which data subjects are substantially affected or likely to be substantially affected by the processing. The GDPR does not elaborate on the criteria that must be applied to assess whether data subjects are 'substantially affected' by a processing operation. However, the use of the term 'affected' suggests that the relevant processing must have some form of meaningful impact on data subjects, whereas the adverb 'substantially' would seem to signify that such impact must be of a considerable magnitude.[15]

Article 4(22)(b) also refers to data subjects being 'likely to' be substantially affected by the processing. On the one hand, this obviously means that individuals need not be

---

[13] See e.g. Art. 60 GDPR.   [14] See further the commentary on Art. 66 in this volume.
[15] WP29 2017, p. 3. On the 'substantial impact' criterion, see further the commentary on Art. 4(23) in this volume.

actually affected: the likelihood of a substantial effect is sufficient to meet the definition of 'supervisory authority concerned'.[16] On the other hand, the existence of a remote possibility in this regard is not sufficient to meet this criterion.[17]

In practice, supervisory authorities will tend to assess whether data subjects are 'substantially affected or likely to be substantially affected' by a processing operation on a case-by-case basis, by reference to a number of factors such as whether the processing:

— causes, or is likely to cause, damage, loss or distress to individuals
— has, or is likely to have, an actual effect in terms of limiting rights or denying an opportunity
— affects, or is likely to affect, individuals' health, well-being, or peace of mind
— affects, or is likely to affect, individuals' financial or economic status or circumstances
— leaves individuals open to discrimination or unfair treatment
— involves analysing the special categories of personal listed in Article 9 GDPR or other intrusive data, particularly the personal data of children
— causes, or is likely to cause individuals to change their behaviour in a significant way
— has unlikely, unanticipated or unwanted consequences for individuals
— creates embarrassment or other negative outcomes, including reputational damage
— involves the processing of a wide range of personal data.[18]

It is worth noting that, under Article 4(22)(b), the data subjects that need to be substantially affected by the processing are those '*residing* in the Member State of that supervisory authority' (emphasis added). This suggests that the data subjects must have stable links with the country in question, which normally exist where data subjects have elected such country as the permanent or habitual centre of their interests. The GDPR does not define the concept of 'residence' and does not contain any express reference to the law of the Member States for the purpose of determining its meaning. Thus, the concept must be given an autonomous EU-wide meaning.[19] In this regard, it bears emphasis that, under EU law, the CJEU tends to consider that the country of residence of an individual is that of their 'habitual residence', a country with which the person has stronger and more stable links than with other countries.[20] Thus, on its face, Article 4(22)(b) seems to require a stronger connection between the individuals affected by the processing and a given country compared to other provisions of the GDPR which also impose a 'substantial effect' test, but do so by referring to data subjects 'in' a Member State, thus suggesting a less stable connection with the State at hand.[21]

---

[16] The WP29 made a similar remark with regard to an analogous likelihood requirement in the definition of 'cross-border processing' in Art. 4(23)(b) GDPR. See WP29 2017, pp. 3–4.

[17] Ibid.   [18] Ibid., p. 4.

[19] The CJEU has consistently held that the terms of a provision of EU law which makes no express reference to the law of the Member States for the purpose of determining its meaning and scope must normally be given an autonomous and uniform interpretation throughout the European Union, having regard not only to its wording but also to the context of the provision and the objective pursued by the legislation in question. This follows from the need for uniform application of EU law and from the principle of equality. See e.g. Case C-617/15, *Hummel Holding*, para. 22 and case law cited therein.

[20] See Wouters 2010, pp. 45–48.

[21] See e.g. Art. 4(23)(b) GDPR, which refers to processing that substantially affects or is likely to substantially affect data subjects 'in' more than one Member State.

4. Submission of a complaint with the supervisory authority

The submission of a complaint in accordance with Article 77 GDPR also transforms the supervisory authority with which such complaint has been lodged into a 'supervisory authority concerned' pursuant to Article 4(22)(c). The latter may also be different from the authority of the country of habitual residence of the data subject, as recital 124 clarifies that 'where a data subject not residing in that Member State has lodged a complaint, the supervisory authority with which such complaint has been lodged should also be a supervisory authority concerned'.

5. Reference to 'supervisory authority concerned' in Article 52(5) GDPR

The GDPR uses the term 'supervisory authority concerned' also in Article 52(5). However, the definition of Article 4(22) does not seem to apply here, as Article 52 elaborates on the independence requirements that each supervisory authority in the EU/EEA must possess, including with respect to its staff. The term 'concerned' in Article 52(5) should thus be understood as 'in question'.

Select Bibliography

International agreements

EEA Agreement: Agreement on the European Economic Area, OJ 1994 L 1/3.

Academic writings

Svantesson 2016: Svantesson, 'Enforcing Privacy across Different Jurisdictions', in Wright and de Hert (eds.), *Enforcing Privacy: Regulatory, Legal and Technological Approaches* (Springer 2016), 195.

Wouters 2010: Wouters, 'Residence of Individuals in EU Law', in Maisto (ed.), *Residence of Individuals under Tax Treaties and EC Law* (IBFD 2010), 41.

Papers of data protection authorities

EDPB 2018: European Data Protection Board, 'Guidelines 3/2018 on the Territorial Scope of the GDPR (Article 3)—Version for Public Consultation' (16 November 2018).

WP29 2017: Article 29 Working Party, 'Guidelines for Identifying a Controller or Processor's Lead Supervisory Authority' (WP 244 rev.01, as last revised and adopted on 5 April 2017).

Reports and recommendations

Council Report 2014: The one-stop-shop mechanism, 14788/1/14, 13 November 2014.
Council Report 2015: The one-stop-shop mechanism, 5627/1/15, 11 February 2015.

Article 4(23). Cross-border processing

LUCA TOSONI

'cross-border processing' means either:

(a) processing of personal data which takes place in the context of the activities of establishments in more than one Member State of a controller or processor in the Union where the controller or processor is established in more than one Member State; or
(b) processing of personal data which takes place in the context of the activities of a single establishment of a controller or processor in the Union but which substantially affects or is likely to substantially affect data subjects in more than one Member State.

Relevant Recitals

(22) Any processing of personal data in the context of the activities of an establishment of a controller or a processor in the Union should be carried out in accordance with this Regulation, regardless of whether the processing itself takes place within the Union. Establishment implies the effective and real exercise of activity through stable arrangements. The legal form of such arrangements, whether through a branch or a subsidiary with a legal personality, is not the determining factor in that respect.

(124) Where the processing of personal data takes place in the context of the activities of an establishment of a controller or a processor in the Union and the controller or processor is established in more than one Member State, or where processing taking place in the context of the activities of a single establishment of a controller or processor in the Union substantially affects or is likely to substantially affect data subjects in more than one Member State, the supervisory authority for the main establishment of the controller or processor or for the single establishment of the controller or processor should act as lead authority. It should cooperate with the other authorities concerned, because the controller or processor has an establishment on the territory of their Member State, because data subjects residing on their territory are substantially affected, or because a complaint has been lodged with them. Also where a data subject not residing in that Member State has lodged a complaint, the supervisory authority with which such complaint has been lodged should also be a supervisory authority concerned. Within its tasks to issue guidelines on any question covering the application of this Regulation, the Board should be able to issue guidelines in particular on the criteria to be taken into account in order to ascertain whether the processing in question substantially affects data subjects in more than one Member State and on what constitutes a relevant and reasoned objection.

Closely Related Provisions

Article 4(2) (Definition of 'processing'); Article 56 (Competence of the lead supervisory authority); Article 62(2) (Joint operations of supervisory authorities); Article 63 (Consistency mechanism) (see too recital 135)

Relevant Case Law

CJEU

Case C-230/14, *Weltimmo s.r.o. v Nemzeti Adatvédelmi és Információszabadság Hatóság*, judgment of 1 October 2015 (ECLI:EU:C:2015:639).

Case C-131/12, *Google Spain v Agencia Española de Protección de Datos (AEPD) and Mario Costeja González*, judgment of 13 May 2014 (Grand Chamber) (ECLI:EU:C:2014:317).

Case C-191/15, *Verein für Konsumenteninformation v Amazon EU Sàrl*, judgment of 28 July 2016 (ECLI:EU:C:2016:612).

Case C-210/16, *Unabhängiges Landeszentrum für Datenschutz Schleswig-Holstein v Wirtschaftsakademie Schleswig-Holstein GmbH*, judgment of 5 June 2018 (Grand Chamber) (ECLI:EU:C:2018:388).

A. Rationale and Policy Underpinnings

The 'one-stop-shop' mechanism is one of the most significant novelties introduced by the GDPR. This is an enforcement scheme intended to ensure uniform supervision of controllers and processors, and consistent application of the GDPR throughout the EU.[1] Within such a mechanism, the chief responsibility is assigned to a 'lead supervisory authority', to be identified in accordance with Article 56(1), which provides that the lead authority is competent for supervising 'cross-border processing' operations. Thus, as noted by WP29, '[i]dentifying a lead supervisory authority is only relevant where a controller or processor is carrying out the cross-border processing of personal data'.[2] This warrants the definition of the term 'cross-border processing' in Article 4(23).

The reference to the notion of 'cross-border processing' in Article 56(1), and its elaboration in Article 4(23), are presumably intended to ensure that the one-stop-shop mechanism only applies to processing operations with a meaningful transnational element.[3] In the initial Commission proposal for the GDPR, the mechanism only covered processing in the context of the activities of an establishment of the same controller or processor established in the territory of multiple Member States.[4] However, the Council later decided to expand its scope to cover also the processing by a controller or processor established in a single Member State which substantially affects (or is likely to substantially affect) data subjects in other Member States.[5] This decision led to the inclusion of a definition of 'cross-border processing' in Article 4(23), which covers both of the above scenarios.[6]

Under the DPD, processing operations with a cross-border impact raised numerous challenges for companies, individuals and supervisory authorities.[7] These were primarily linked with the inconsistent enforcement of data protection rules across the EU.[8] Against this background, the one-stop-shop mechanism is chiefly intended to provide enhanced legal certainty. At the same time, the mechanism's focus on cooperation between the lead authority and the other authorities concerned and its exclusive

---

[1] See further the commentaries on Arts. 56 and 60 in this volume. [2] WP29 2017, p. 3.
[3] See e.g. Council Report 2014A, p. 3 (noting that '[t]he one-stop-shop mechanism should only intervene in important cross-border scenarios').
[4] See Art. 51 GDPR Proposal. [5] See Council Report 2014A, p. 3.
[6] The Council initially used the term 'transnational processing of personal data' but defined this essentially as the current Art. 4(23) GDPR defines 'cross-border processing'. See Council Report 2014B, p. 4.
[7] See Council Report 2014C, p. 5; EC Staff Working Paper 2012, p. 36. [8] Ibid.

applicability to certain cross-border cases are aimed at ensuring enough 'proximity' between the individuals affected by an enforcement decision and the decision-making supervisory authority.[9]

B. Legal Background

1. EU legislation

The DPD did not provide for any enforcement schemes analogous to the one-stop-shop mechanism.[10] Consequently, the Directive did not refer to concepts like 'cross-border processing' that are part and parcel of such a scheme under the GDPR.

2. International instruments

In the data protection context, the one-stop-shop mechanism is peculiar to the GDPR. Therefore, concepts that pertain to this mechanism, such as that of 'cross-border processing', are not found in other international instruments on data protection, such as Convention 108, the OECD Privacy Guidelines and the APEC Privacy Framework.

3. Case law

The CJEU has yet to rule on the definition of 'cross-border processing' in Article 4(23) GDPR. However, the Court has provided guidance—under the DPD—on some of the constitutive elements of this concept, including on the meaning of 'processing', 'establishment' and processing of personal data 'in the context of the activities of an establishment'. This jurisprudence is referred to in the following section.

C. Analysis

1. Introduction

The definition of 'cross-border processing' in Article 4(23) GDPR covers two types of 'processing'[11] operations: (1) processing of personal data that takes place in the context of the activities of establishments in more than one EU/EEA country of a controller or processor established in multiple EU/EEA countries (Article 4(23)(a)); and (2) processing of personal data that takes place in the context of the activities of a single establishment of a controller or processor in the EU/EEA, which substantially affects or is likely to substantially affect data subjects in more than one EU/EEA country (Article 4(23)(b)).[12] Both of these two parts of Article 4(23) are built around the key concept of 'establishment'.

---

[9] Ibid.

[10] On trans-border enforcement of data protection rules under the DPD, see further the commentary on Art. 60 in this volume and Svantesson 2016.

[11] On the concept of 'processing', see further the commentary on Art. 4(2) in this volume.

[12] Pursuant to s. 8 of Protocol 1 to the EEA Agreement, whenever the acts incorporated in the Annexes to the Agreement (like the GDPR) refer to the territory of the 'Community' (now 'Union'), such references should be understood as references to the territories of the EEA countries (i.e. the EU Member States plus Iceland, Liechtenstein and Norway). Moreover, point (b) of entry 5e of Annex X to the EEA Agreement specifies that the term 'Member State(s)' in the GDPR shall be understood to include, in addition to its meaning in the Regulation, the three EEA EFTA States (i.e. Iceland, Liechtenstein and Norway).

However, while under Article 4(23)(a) a given processing operation may qualify as 'cross-border processing' only where the relevant controller or processor has establishments in multiple EU/EEA countries, under Article 4(23)(b) the controller or processor need not be established in multiple EU/EEA countries—a single establishment in the EU/EEA suffices.

Moreover, both parts of Article 4(23) also refer to the concept of processing of personal data that takes place 'in the context of the activities of' an establishment of a controller or processor in the EU/EEA.

As the concepts of 'establishment' and of processing 'in the context of the activities of' an establishment are not new under EU data protection law, and have been interpreted by the CJEU, the following sections of the present commentary begin by addressing these concepts. Thereafter, the notion of processing which 'substantially affects or is likely to substantially affect' data subjects is presented. The commentary then concludes with a few brief remarks on the overall functioning of the criteria that a processing activity must meet to qualify as 'cross-border processing' under either Article 4(23)(a) or (b).

2. The concept of establishment

The concept of 'establishment' is not defined in the GDPR, but recital 22 states that '[e]stablishment implies the effective and real exercise of activity through stable arrangements. The legal form of such arrangements, whether through a branch or a subsidiary with a legal personality, is not the determining factor in that respect'. This wording essentially reproduces that of recital 19 DPD,[13] which led the CJEU to uphold a flexible understanding of the concept of 'establishment' within the meaning of the DPD.[14]

Indeed, according to the Court, the concept 'extends to any real and effective activity—even a minimal one—exercised through stable arrangements'.[15] However, the Court clarified that 'both the degree of stability of the arrangements and the effective exercise of activities [in a Member State] must be interpreted in the light of the specific nature of the economic activities and the provision of services concerned'.[16] As the EDPB has noted, this implies that '[t]he threshold for "stable arrangement" can actually be quite low when the centre of activities of a controller concerns the provision of services online'.[17] In fact, the Court has held that even the presence of a representative in a Member State can, in some circumstances, 'suffice to constitute a stable arrangement if that representative acts with a sufficient degree of stability through the presence of the necessary equipment for provision of the specific services concerned in the Member State in question'.[18] This means that an entity does not need to have a branch or subsidiary in a EU/EEA country to be considered as established in that country under EU data protection law.[19] At the

---

[13] Rec. 19 DPD stated that 'establishment on the territory of a Member State implies the effective and real exercise of activity through stable arrangements' and that 'the legal form of such an establishment, whether simply [a] branch or a subsidiary with a legal personality, is not the determining factor'. See also Case C-131/12, *Google Spain*, para. 48.

[14] See Case C-230/14, *Weltimmo*, para. 29.

[15] Ibid., para. 31. See further Case C-191/15, *Verein für Konsumenteninformation*, para. 75; Case C-210/16, *Wirtschaftsakademie*, paras. 53–55. For criticism of the expanding scope of the concept of 'establishment', see Svantesson 2016.

[16] See Case C-230/14, *Weltimmo*, para. 29.   [17] See EDPB 2018, p. 5.

[18] See Case C-230/14, *Weltimmo*, para. 30.

[19] See Case C-191/15, *Verein für Konsumenteninformation*, para. 76. See also EDPB 2018, p. 5.

same time, the mere fact that the entity's website is accessible from such EU/EEA country does not necessarily entail its establishment in the country in question under EU data protection law.[20]

Against this background, the CJEU is likely to uphold a flexible understanding of the concept of 'establishment' in Article 4(23) GDPR and to reject a formalistic approach whereby a controller or processor is established in an EU/EEA country solely if it is formally registered or incorporated in that country.

3. Processing 'in the context of the activities of' an establishment

Article 4(23) does not require that the processing of personal data be carried out 'by' the relevant establishment itself; it is sufficient that the processing be carried out 'in the context of the activities' of an EU/EEA establishment.[21] In this regard, the CJEU has held that, in order to avoid threatening the high level of protection conferred by EU data protection law,[22] the words 'in the context of the activities of an establishment' cannot be interpreted restrictively.[23] However, the CJEU has also held that, if the relevant EU/EEA establishment is not actually taking any role in the data processing itself, the data processing activities are considered to be carried out 'in the context of the activities' of the EU/EEA establishment only as long as there is an 'inextricable link' between the activities of the EU/EEA establishment and the data processing.[24]

In light of this, the EDPB has made clear that activities of an EU/EEA establishment, which have only remote links to the data processing activities of a non-EU/EEA entity do not meet this criterion: '[s]ome commercial activity led by a non-EU entity within a Member State may indeed be so far removed from the processing of personal data by this entity that the existence of the commercial activity in the EU would not be sufficient' to consider such processing as taking place 'in the context of the activities of' an EU/EEA establishment.[25] Nonetheless, both the Court and the Board have stressed that '[t]he activities of a local establishment in a Member state and the data processing activities of a data controller or processor established outside the EU may be inextricably linked ... even if that local establishment is not actually taking any role in the data processing itself'.[26]

---

[20] Case C-191/15, *Verein für Konsumenteninformation*, para. 76.

[21] This is consistent with the case law on the territorial scope of application of EU data protection rules: see Case C-131/12, *Google Spain*, para. 52; Case C-230/14, *Weltimmo*, para. 35. See further the commentary on Art. 3 GDPR in this volume.

[22] See rec. 9 and 10 GDPR.

[23] See Case C-230/14, *Weltimmo*, para. 25; Case C-131/12, *Google Spain*, para. 53.

[24] In *Google Spain*, the CJEU found that 'the activities of the operator of the search engine [i.e. Google] and those of its establishment situated in the Member State concerned [which was responsible for promoting and selling, in that Member State, advertising space offered by the search engine] are inextricably linked since the activities relating to the advertising space constitute the means of rendering the search engine at issue economically profitable and that engine is, at the same time, the means enabling those activities to be performed'. See Case C-131/12, *Google Spain*, para. 56. See further EDPB 2018, p. 6.

[25] See EDPB 2018, p. 6 (the Board noted this with respect to Art. 3(1) GDPR).

[26] See EDPB 2018, p. 6; Case C-131/12, *Google Spain*, paras. 49–59.

4. Processing which 'substantially affects or is likely to substantially affect' data subjects

The GDPR does not elaborate on the features that a processing operation must present to be considered as 'substantially affecting' data subjects.[27] According to the WP29, '[t]he intention of the wording was to ensure that not all processing activity, with *any* effect and that takes place within the context of a single establishment, falls within the definition of "cross-border processing"'.[28]

The use of the term 'affect' suggests that the relevant processing must have some form of meaningful impact on data subjects, whereas the adverb 'substantially' would seem to signify that such impact must be of a considerable magnitude.[29] Interestingly, the GDPR uses similar—although not identical—wording in other provisions. For example, Articles 22(1) and 35(3)(a) refer to decisions that 'significantly affect' the data subject.[30] In the English language, 'substantially' and 'significantly' may often be used interchangeably, and it should be noted that the difference between 'substantially' and 'significantly' disappears in some language versions of the GDPR.[31] Nonetheless, the term 'substantial' typically denotes something that is fairly large in size, whereas 'significant' generally addresses the importance of something, and such importance can arise regardless of size. The potential difference between these two terms is particularly interesting in light of the WP29's view that the number of individuals affected by a given processing operation is per se not necessarily determinative of whether the operation 'substantially affects' data subjects within the meaning of Article 4(23)(b).[32] However, recital 135 suggests that the number of individuals affected is a material factor here; it refers to the consistency mechanism under Article 63 applying 'in particular ... as regards processing operations which substantially affect a *significant number* of data subjects in several Member States' (emphasis added). Referencing the same recital, the WP29 also acknowledged that '[u]ltimately, the test of "substantial effect" is intended to ensure that supervisory authorities are only required to co-operate formally through the GDPR's consistency mechanism "where a supervisory authority intends to adopt a measure intended to produce legal effects as regards"' such processing operations.[33]

Article 4(23)(b) additionally refers to processing that 'is likely to' substantially affect data subjects. On the one hand, this criterion of likelihood means that 'individuals do not have to be actually affected: the likelihood of a substantial effect is sufficient to bring the processing within the definition of "cross-border processing"'.[34] On the other hand, the likelihood criterion implies that data subjects must be 'more likely than not'

---

[27] During the legislative process, several Member States found that the meaning of 'substantially affecting' should have been further clarified in the Regulation. See Council Report 2015, p. 17, fn. 12.

[28] WP29 2017, p. 3.   [29] Ibid.

[30] On the meaning of 'significantly affect' in Art. 22(1), see WP 2018, pp. 21–22. See further the commentary on Art. 22 in this volume.

[31] E.g. the Romanian and Hungarian versions of the GDPR use the same term in Arts. 4(23)(b), 22(1) and 35(3)(a): 'semnificativ' and 'jelentős', respectively.

[32] WP29 2017, p. 4. However, it would be difficult to argue that 'large-scale processing' within the meaning of Art. 35(3)(b)–(c) does not qualify as processing which 'significantly affects' data subjects, as rec. 91 clarifies that a data protection impact assessment should in particular apply to 'large-scale processing operations which aim to process a considerable amount of personal data at regional, national or supranational level and which could *affect a large number of data subjects* and which are *likely to result in a high risk*, for example, on account of their sensitivity' (emphasis added).

[33] WP29 2017, p. 4.   [34] Ibid., pp. 3–4.

substantially affected by the processing—the existence of a remote possibility in this regard is insufficient.[35]

In practice, supervisory authorities will tend to assess whether a processing operation 'substantially affects or is likely to substantially affect' data subjects on a case-by-case basis, by reference to a broad range of factors, including whether the processing:

– causes, or is likely to cause, damage, loss or distress to individuals
– has, or is likely to have, an actual effect in terms of limiting rights or denying an opportunity
– affects, or is likely to affect, individuals' health, well-being or peace of mind
– affects, or is likely to affect, individuals' financial or economic status or circumstances
– leaves individuals open to discrimination or unfair treatment
– involves analysing the special categories of personal listed in Article 9 GDPR or other intrusive data, particularly the personal data of children
– causes, or is likely to cause individuals to change their behaviour in a significant way
– has unlikely, unanticipated or unwanted consequences for individuals
– creates embarrassment or other negative outcomes, including reputational damage
– involves the processing of a wide range of personal data.[36]

5. Article 4(23)(a): processing taking place within the context of the activities of establishments in multiple EU/EEA countries

As mentioned above, under Article 4(23)(a), a processing operation may be brought within the definition of 'cross-border processing' where it takes place in the context of the activities of establishments in more than one EU/EEA country of a controller or processor. On its face, Article 4(23)(a) seems to require that the processing takes place within the context of the activities of several establishments in multiple EU/EEA countries; concomitantly, processing that takes place within the activities of a single establishment in one EU/EEA country would not qualify as 'cross-border processing' under Article 4(23)(a), even where the relevant controller or processor has establishments in several EU/EEA countries. This would imply that, if the actual processing is carried out by a non-EU/EEA entity, there must be an 'inextricable link' between the activities of several EU/EEA establishments and the data processing—a link with a single EU/EEA establishment would not suffice.

However, there is a misalignment between Article 4(23)(a) and recital 124 GDPR, which elaborates on the identification and the role of the lead supervisory authority within the one-stop-shop mechanism. Article 4(23)(a) refers to processing that 'takes place in the context of the activities of *establishments*' (emphasis added), whereas recital 124 mentions processing that 'takes place in the context of the activities of *an establishment* of a controller or a processor in the Union and the controller or processor is established in more than one Member State' (emphasis added). Thus, if one would interpret Article 4(23)(a) in light of the standard set by recital 124, it would be sufficient that a processing operation be linked to a single establishment in the EU/EEA to qualify as 'cross-border processing', provided that the relevant controller or processor is established in more than one EU/EEA country. In this regard, it should be noted that a similar standard is set by Article 62(2) GDPR, which does not use the term cross-border processing, but provides

---

[35] Ibid., p. 3.   [36] Ibid., p. 4.

that '[w]*here the controller or processor has establishments in several Member States* or where a significant number of data subjects in more than one Member State are likely to be substantially affected by processing operations, a supervisory authority of each of those Member States shall have the right to participate in joint operations' (emphasis added).

Given that the definition of 'cross-border processing' is ultimately relevant to assess whether a certain supervisory authority is competent to act as lead supervisory authority in accordance with the one-stop-shop mechanism, it should be borne in mind that Article 56(2) establishes an exception to the applicability of the one-stop-shop mechanism: 'each supervisory authority shall be competent to handle a complaint lodged with it or a possible infringement of this Regulation, if the subject matter relates only to an establishment in its Member State'.[37] In other words, local cases, although falling within the definition of cross-border processing, should be treated locally. Thus, even if one would follow the second interpretation of Article 4(23)(a) proposed above, the one-stop-shop mechanism would often not be triggered where the relevant processing relates to a single establishment in the EU/EEA.

Finally, it should be stressed that, under Article 4(23)(a), as soon as a processing operation takes place in the context of the activities of establishments in more than one EU/EEA country it qualifies as 'cross-border processing'; the number of individuals affected by the operation, and the impact that this has on them, are irrelevant.

6. Article 4(23)(b): processing substantially affecting data subjects in multiple EU/EEA countries

Under Article 4(23)(b), only processing that substantially affects or is likely to substantially affect data subjects *in more than one Member State* qualifies as 'cross-border processing'. On its face, this seems to imply that the processing must have a *substantial* effect on data subjects in different EU/EEA countries; a processing that substantially affects data subjects in a single EU/EEA country would not qualify as 'cross-border processing' under Article 4(23)(b), even where it affects data subjects also in other EU/EEA countries, although not substantially.[38] However, the latter kind of processing would qualify as 'cross-border processing' under Article 4(23)(a) if it takes places in the context of establishments in more than one EU/EEA of a controller or processor, as elaborated above.

7. Conclusions

While the basic contours of the notion of 'cross-border processing' are fairly clear, there may be borderline and complex situations where it might be difficult to apply in practice, in particular where this involves an assessment of how 'substantially' a certain data processing operation affects data subjects in different countries. This difficulty will in turn create complications for the identification of the 'lead supervisory authority' and is thus likely to hinder the smooth operation of the 'one-stop-shop' mechanism.

---

[37] See further the commentary on Art. 56 in this volume.
[38] Despite this limitation, during the legislative process, several Member States found that the definition of 'cross-border processing' in Art. 4(23)(b) was overly broad, especially as far as online processing was concerned. See Council Report 2015, p. 17, fn. 12.

Select Bibliography

International agreements

EEA Agreement: Agreement on the European Economic Area, OJ 1994 L 1/3.

EU legislation

GDPR Proposal: Proposal for a Regulation of the European Parliament and of the Council on the protection of individuals with regard to the processing of personal data and on the free movement of such data (General Data Protection Regulation), COM(2012) 11 final, 25 January 2012.

Academic writings

Svantesson 2016: Svantesson, 'Enforcing Privacy across Different Jurisdictions', in Wright and de Hert (eds.), *Enforcing Privacy: Regulatory, Legal and Technological Approaches* (Springer 2016), 195.

Papers of data protection authorities

EDPB 2018: European Data Protection Board, 'Guidelines 3/2018 on the Territorial Scope of the GDPR (Article 3)—Version for Public Consultation' (16 November 2018).
WP29 2018: Article 29 Working Party, 'Guidelines on Automated Individual Decision-Making and Profiling for the Purposes of Regulation 2016/679' (WP 251rev.01, as last revised and adopted on 6 February 2018).
WP29 2017: Article 29 Working Party, 'Guidelines for Identifying a Controller or Processor's Lead Supervisory Authority' (WP 244 rev.01, as last revised and adopted on 5 April 2017).

Reports and recommendations

Council Report 2014A: The one-stop-shop mechanism, 14788/14, 31 October 2014.
Council Report 2014B: The one-stop-shop mechanism, 16974/14, 16 December 2014.
Council Report 2014C: The one-stop-shop mechanism, 15656/1/14, 28 November 2014.
Council Report 2015: The one-stop-shop mechanism, 5627/15, 2 February 2015.
EC Staff Working Paper 2012: Commission Staff Working Paper 'Impact Assessment Accompanying the document Regulation of the European Parliament and of the Council on the protection of individuals with regard to the processing of personal data and on the free movement of such data (General Data Protection Regulation) and Directive of the European Parliament and of the Council on the protection of individuals with regard to the processing of personal data by competent authorities for the purposes of prevention, investigation, detection or prosecution of criminal offences or the execution of criminal penalties, and the free movement of such data', SEC(2012) 72 final, 25 January 2012.

Article 4(24). Relevant and reasoned objection

LUCA TOSONI

'relevant and reasoned objection' means an objection to a draft decision as to whether there is an infringement of this Regulation, or whether envisaged action in relation to the controller or processor complies with this Regulation, which clearly demonstrates the significance of the risks posed by the draft decision as regards the fundamental rights and freedoms of data subjects and, where applicable, the free flow of personal data within the Union;

Relevant Recital

(124) Where the processing of personal data takes place in the context of the activities of an establishment of a controller or a processor in the Union and the controller or processor is established in more than one Member State, or where processing taking place in the context of the activities of a single establishment of a controller or processor in the Union substantially affects or is likely to substantially affect data subjects in more than one Member State, the supervisory authority for the main establishment of the controller or processor or for the single establishment of the controller or processor should act as lead authority. It should cooperate with the other authorities concerned, because the controller or processor has an establishment on the territory of their Member State, because data subjects residing on their territory are substantially affected, or because a complaint has been lodged with them. Also where a data subject not residing in that Member State has lodged a complaint, the supervisory authority with which such complaint has been lodged should also be a supervisory authority concerned. Within its tasks to issue guidelines on any question covering the application of this Regulation, the Board should be able to issue guidelines in particular on the criteria to be taken into account in order to ascertain whether the processing in question substantially affects data subjects in more than one Member State and on what constitutes a relevant and reasoned objection.

Closely Related Provisions

Article 60 (Cooperation between the lead supervisory authority and the other supervisory authorities concerned); Article 63 (Consistency mechanism); Article 65 (Dispute resolution by the Board).

A. Rationale and Policy Underpinnings

One of the main novelties introduced by the GDPR consists in establishing an enforcement scheme—known as the 'one-stop-shop' mechanism (see recital 127 GDPR)—according to which a controller or processor that carries out cross-border data processing[1] will normally have a single supervisory authority as interlocutor with respect to data protection compliance matters (Articles 56 and 60 GDPR).[2] This means that such an

---

[1] See the commentary on the definition of 'cross-border processing' in Art. 4(23) in this volume.
[2] On the functioning of the one-stop-shop mechanism, see further the commentaries on Arts. 56 and 60 in this volume.

authority—known as lead supervisory authority—is entrusted with the main responsibility with regard to the adoption of decisions concerning the controller or processor, including the imposition of administrative fines. However, before adopting a decision, the lead authority must allow the other 'supervisory authorities concerned'[3] to express their views on the draft decision (Article 60(3)).

In this context, each of the 'supervisory authorities concerned' may adopt a 'relevant and reasoned objection' to the draft decision. If one does, the lead authority has only two options: (1) follow the objection; or (2) submit the matter to the EDPB (Article 60(4)). While this system tries to accommodate the interests of the various stakeholders involved, it also presents the risk that over-referrals to the EDPB could cause backlogs to decisions being made. This was the primary concern that led the EU legislator to introduce in the GDPR a definition of 'reasoned and relevant objection' that would restrict the subject-matter of the objections that may be successfully mounted against a draft decision to be adopted by the lead authority pursuant to Article 60 GDPR.[4]

B. Legal Background

1. EU legislation

The DPD did not envisage an enforcement mechanism analogous to the one-stop-shop mechanism. Consequently, the Directive did not operate with the concept of 'relevant and reasoned objection'.

The GDPR's 'relevant and reasoned objection' in some ways echoes procedural tools found in other EU legal instruments that have been in force since before the adoption of the GDPR. Several EU legal acts provide for referral mechanisms that allow Member State authorities to resolve their disagreements on the adoption of decisions with a pan-European impact. For example, Directive 2001/83/EC establishes a number of referral procedures, including a procedure that, in case of disagreements between the Member State authorities involved in a mutual recognition or decentralised procedure for the approval of a medicine, allows for the matter to be referred to the European Medicines Agency ('EMA').[5] In this context, 'the reference Member State shall provide the Agency with a detailed statement of the matter(s) on which the Member States concerned have been unable to reach agreement and the reasons for their disagreement'.[6] The matter(s) referred to the EMA must be based on potential serious risks to public health grounds and should be precise.[7]

2. International instruments

The one-stop-shop mechanism is specific to the GDPR. Thus, concepts that pertain to this mechanism, such as that of 'relevant and reasoned objection' are not found in

---

[3] See the commentary on Art. 4(22) in this volume.

[4] The Presidency of the Council of the European Union noted the following on the inclusion in the draft Regulation of a definition of 'serious and reasoned objection' (which was almost identical to the current definition of 'relevant and reasoned objection' in Art. 4(24) GDPR): '[t]he Presidency has inserted a definition of a "serious and reasoned objection" in Article 4(19b) which restricts the subject-matter of the objection'. See Council Report 2015, p. 4.

[5] Directive 2001/83/EC, Art. 29(4).   [6] See EC Notice 2018, p. 5.   [7] Ibid.

other international instruments on data protection, such as Convention 108, the OECD Privacy Guidelines and the APEC Privacy Framework.

3. Case law

The CJEU has yet to rule on the concept of 'relevant and reasoned objection'. However, the EDPB is expected to provide guidance on what constitutes a 'relevant and reasoned objection'.[8]

C. Analysis

All the supervisory authorities concerned may express an objection against a draft decision to be adopted by the lead supervisory authority pursuant to Article 60 GDPR. This objection may lead the supervisory authority to redraft the initially proposed decision (see Article 60(5)). However, the lead supervisory authority may follow an objection only if the latter is 'relevant and reasoned'. If the objection is not relevant or reasoned, the lead authority must dismiss it and submit the matter to the EDPB (Article 60(4)). The lead authority must refer the matter to the Board also where it does not intend to follow an objection, despite finding it relevant and reasoned (Article 60(4)). The EDPB will in turn adopt a binding decision on whether the objection is relevant and reasoned and, if the objection is found to be such, on all the matters which are the subject of it (Article 65(1)(a)).

The definition of 'relevant and reasoned objection' provided in Article 4(24) assists the lead supervisory authority and the EDPB in assessing whether an objection is 'relevant and reasoned', as the definition elaborates on the features that an objection must present to be considered 'relevant and reasoned'. First, the subject-matter of the objection must concern 'whether there is an infringement of [the GDPR], or whether envisaged action in relation to the controller or processor complies with [the GDPR]'. The specific subject-matter of the objection will normally depend on the type of decision to be adopted by the lead authority.[9]

Secondly, the objection must be precise and accompanied by an analysis of 'the significance of the risks posed by the draft decision as regards the fundamental rights and freedoms of data subjects and, where applicable, the free flow of personal data within the Union'. This suggests that the objecting authority must clearly show that the adoption of the draft decision prepared by the lead authority entails non-negligible risks for the data subjects or for the free flow of data. It follows that the supervisory authorities concerned should not raise petty objections. As mentioned above, the intention of the legislator when it stipulated that objections should be 'relevant and reasoned' was primarily to prevent supervisory authorities causing additional costs and delays by raising objections that are not well-founded or based on weak arguments. In this regard, one might question whether the definition does its intended job. In principle, even when a petty objection is raised, the lead authority needs, in effect, to examine it and, if it 'is of the opinion that the objection is not relevant or reasoned', it must refer the matter to the Board (Article 60(4)). However, the 'relevant and reasoned' threshold that objections must meet might partially help to expedite the process, as it allows both the lead authority and the Board to dismiss an objection promptly without dealing with its merits if they find that such

---

[8] See rec. 124 GDPR.   [9] See further the commentary on Art. 60 in this volume.

threshold is not met. In turn, this might discourage supervisory authorities from raising objections that are unlikely to meet this threshold.

Select Bibliography

EU legislation

Directive 2001/83/EC: Directive 2001/83/EC of the European Parliament and of the Council of 6 November 2001 on the Community code relating to medicinal products for human use, OJ 2001 L 311/67.

Reports and recommendations

Council Report 2015: The one-stop-shop mechanism, 5627/15, 2 February 2015.

Others

EC Notice 2018: European Commission, 'Notice to Applicants, Volume 2A, Procedures for Marketing Authorisation' (November 2018), available at https://ec.europa.eu/health/sites/health/files/files/eudralex/vol-2/vol2a_chap3_en.pdf.

Article 4(25). Information society service

LUCA TOSONI

'information society service' means a service as defined in point (b) of Article 1(1) of Directive (EU) 2015/1535 of the European Parliament and of the Council;

Relevant Recitals

(21) This Regulation is without prejudice to the application of Directive 2000/31/EC of the European Parliament and of the Council, in particular of the liability rules of intermediary service providers in Articles 12 to 15 of that Directive. That Directive seeks to contribute to the proper functioning of the internal market by ensuring the free movement of information society services between Member States.

(32) Consent should be given by a clear affirmative act establishing a freely given, specific, informed and unambiguous indication of the data subject's agreement to the processing of personal data relating to him or her, such as by a written statement, including by electronic means, or an oral statement. This could include ticking a box when visiting an internet website, choosing technical settings for information society services or another statement or conduct which clearly indicates in this context the data subject's acceptance of the proposed processing of his or her personal data. Silence, pre-ticked boxes or inactivity should not therefore constitute consent. Consent should cover all processing activities carried out for the same purpose or purposes. When the processing has multiple purposes, consent should be given for all of them. If the data subject's consent is to be given following a request by electronic means, the request must be clear, concise and not unnecessarily disruptive to the use of the service for which it is provided.

Closely Related Provisions

Article 2(4) (Material scope) (see too recital 21); Article 8 (Conditions applicable to child's consent in relation to information society services) (see too recital 38); Article 17(1)(f) (Right to erasure) (see too recital 65); Article 21(5) (Right to object) (see too recitals 69–70)

Related Provisions in EPD [Directive 2002/58/EC]

Article 2 (which refers to the definitions in the DPD); Article 14 (Technical features and standardisation) (see too recitals 25 and 45)

Related Provisions in EUDPR [Regulation (EU) 2018/1725]

Article 3(20) (Definition of 'information society service'); Article 8 (Conditions applicable to a child's consent in relation to information society services) (see too recitals 19 and 27);

Article 19(1)(f) (Right to erasure) (see also recital 38); Article 23(3) (Right to object) (see too recital 42)

Relevant Case Law

CJEU

Case C-275/92, *Her Majesty's Customs and Excise v Gerhart Schindler and Jörg Schindler*, judgment of 24 March 1994 (ECLI:EU:C:1994:119).

Case C-355/00, *Freskot AE v Elliniko Dimosio*, judgment of 22 May 2003 (ECLI:EU:C:2003:298).

Case C-89/04, *Mediakabel BV v Commissariaat voor de Media*, judgment of 2 June 2005 (ECLI:EU:C:2005:348).

Case C-281/06, *Hans-Dieter Jundt, Hedwig Jundt v Finanzamt Offenburg*, judgment of 18 December 2007 (ECLI:EU:C:2007:816).

Joined Cases C-236/08 to C-238/08, *Google France SARL and Google Inc. v Louis Vuitton Malletier SA, Google France SARL v Viaticum SA and Luteciel SARL* and *Google France SARL v Centre national de recherche en relations humaines (CNRRH) SARL and Others*, judgment of 23 March 2010 (Grand Chamber) (ECLI:EU:C:2010:159).

Case C-42/07, *Liga Portuguesa de Futebol Profissional and Bwin International Ltd v Departamento de Jogos da Santa Casa da Misericórdia de Lisboa*, judgment of 8 September 2009 (Grand Chamber) (ECLI:EU:C:2009:519).

Opinion of Advocate General Bot in Case C-42/07, *Liga Portuguesa de Futebol Profissional and Bwin International Ltd v Departamento de Jogos da Santa Casa da Misericórdia de Lisboa*, delivered on 14 October 2008 (ECLI:EU:C:2008:560).

Case C-108/09, *Ker-Optika bt v ÀNTSZ Dél-dunántúli Regionális Intézete*, judgment of 2 December 2010 (ECLI:EU:C:2010:725).

Case C-324/09, *L'Oréal and Others v eBay International AG and Others*, judgment of 12 July 2011 (Grand Chamber) (ECLI:EU:C:2011:474).

Case C-131/12, *Google Spain v Agencia Española de Protección de Datos (AEPD) and Mario Costeja González*, judgment of 13 May 2014 (Grand Chamber) (ECLI:EU:C:2014:317).

Opinion of Advocate General Jääskinen in Case C-131/12, *Google Spain v Agencia Española de Protección de Datos (AEPD) and Mario Costeja González*, delivered on 25 June 2013 (ECLI:EU:C:2013:424).

Case C-291/13, *Sotiris Papasavvas v O Fileleftheros Dimosia Etaireia Ltd and Others*, judgment of 11 September 2014 (ECLI:EU:C:2014:2209).

Case C-484/14, *Tobias Mc Fadden v Sony Music Entertainment Germany GmbH*, judgment of 15 September 2016 (ECLI:EU:C:2016:689).

Case C-339/15, *Criminal proceedings against Luc Vanderborght*, judgment of 4 May 2017 (ECLI:EU:C:2017:335).

Case C-434/15, *Asociación Profesional Elite Taxi v Uber Systems Spain, SL*, judgment of 20 December 2017 (Grand Chamber) (ECLI:EU:C:2017:981).

Opinion of Advocate General Szpunar in Case C-434/15, *Asociación Profesional Elite Taxi v Uber Systems Spain, SL*, delivered on 11 May 2017 (ECLI:EU:C:2017:364).

Case C-255/16, *Criminal proceedings against Bent Falbert and Others*, judgment of 20 December 2017 (ECLI:EU:C:2017:983).

Case C-265/16, *VCAST Limited v RTI SpA*, judgment of 29 November 2017 (ECLI:EU:C:2017:913).

Opinion of Advocate General Szpunar in Case C-265/16, *VCAST Limited v RTI SpA*, delivered on 7 September 2017 (ECLI:EU:C:2017:649).

Case C-320/16, *Criminal proceedings against Uber France*, judgment of 10 April 2018 (Grand Chamber) (ECLI:EU:C:2018:221).

Opinion of Advocate General Szpunar in Case C-390/18, *AIRBNB Ireland*, delivered on 30 April 2019 (ECLI:EU:C:2019:336).

Case C-142/18, *Skype Communications Sàrl v Institut belge des services postaux et des télécommunications (IBPT)*, judgment of 5 June 2019 (ECLI:EU:C:2019:460).

A. Rationale and Policy Underpinnings

Article 4(25) GDPR defines 'information society service' by referring to the definition of 'service' in Article 1(1)(b) of Directive (EU) 2015/1535 laying down a procedure for the provision of information in the field of technical regulations and of rules on Information Society services.[1] The latter reads:

'[S]ervice' means any Information Society service, that is to say, any service normally provided for remuneration, at a distance, by electronic means and at the individual request of a recipient of services.

For the purposes of this definition:

(i) 'at a distance' means that the service is provided without the parties being simultaneously present;
(ii) 'by electronic means' means that the service is sent initially and received at its destination by means of electronic equipment for the processing (including digital compression) and storage of data, and entirely transmitted, conveyed and received by wire, by radio, by optical means or by other electromagnetic means;
(iii) 'at the individual request of a recipient of services' means that the service is provided through the transmission of data on individual request.

This definition was included in the GDPR presumably to ensure that the term 'information society service' is interpreted uniformly across the different EU sectoral instruments that employ the term. Indeed, virtually all EU legal acts that use and define the term refer to the definition in Directive (EU) 2015/1535 (or its antecedent, Directive 98/34/EC),[2] as elaborated further below.

The definition is crucial to clarify the scope of application of the specific safeguards that the GDPR lays down for the processing of personal data of children, particularly regarding: (1) the conditions applicable to a child's consent in relation to information society services;[3] and (2) the right to erasure that may be exercised where a child has given his or her consent to the processing of personal data in relation to the offer of information society services, and later wants to remove such personal data, especially on the internet.[4] In addition, the definition is useful to understand the circumstances under which the data subject may exercise his or her right to object by automated means, as Article 21(5) GDPR specifies that this may occur 'in the context of the use of information society services'.

Article 3(20) EUDPR defines 'information society service' identically to Article 4(25) GDPR, and the definition serves analogous purposes to those under the GDPR.[5] Thus, the provisions referring to 'information society services' in the two Regulations should be interpreted in the same way.[6]

---

[1] Directive (EU) 2015/1535. Annex I of the Directive also includes an indicative list of services not covered by this definition.
[2] Directive 98/34/EC.   [3] See Art. 8 GDPR.   [4] See Art. 17(1)(f) and rec. 65 GDPR.
[5] See Arts. 8, 19(1)(f) and 23(3) EUDPR.   [6] See also rec. 5 EUDPR.

B. Legal Background

1. EU Legislation

The DPD neither defined nor used the term 'information society service'. A definition of the term was first included in Article 1(2) of Directive 98/34/EC by means of an amendment introduced by Directive 98/48/EC.[7] That definition was essentially identical to the one now provided in Article 1(1)(b) of Directive (EU) 2015/1535,[8] referred to by Article 4(25) GDPR and reproduced above. This is because Directive (EU) 2015/1535 was adopted to undertake a codification of Directive 98/34/EC without changes of substance.[9] Thus, the case law concerning the classification of a service as an 'information society service' within the meaning of Directive 98/34/EC may be applied to the provisions of Directive (EU) 2015/1535.[10]

The definition of 'information society service' laid down by Article 1(1)(b) of Directive (EU) 2015/1535 constitutes the standard definition of the term. Many EU legal acts, including most notably the e-Commerce Directive (2000/31/EC),[11] refer to this definition (or its antecedent in Article 1(2) of Directive 98/34/EC).[12]

The definition was intentionally drafted in broad and vague terms for two main reasons: first, 'a detailed and specific definition would be particularly difficult in view of those services' diversity, polymorphous nature and complex architecture'; secondly, a detailed definition 'would be artificial and lacking in clarity' due to the broad diversity of terms used across the EU to refer to the same type of services.[13]

2. International instruments

The term 'information society service' is specific to EU law and accordingly absent from non-EU data protection instruments, such as Convention 108.

3. National developments

In line with the DPD, virtually no national data protection laws in Europe defined or used the term 'information society service' prior to adoption of the GDPR. The term was, however, used in the national implementation of other EU legal instruments employing such term.[14]

---

[7] Directive 98/48/EC, Art. 1(2).
[8] See Case C-390/18, *AIRBNB Ireland* (AG Opinion), para. 4.
[9] See Proposal for Technical Standards Directive, p. 2, stating that '[t]he purpose of this proposal is to undertake a codification of Directive 98/34/EC of the European Parliament and of the Council of 22 June 1998 laying down a procedure for the provision of information in the field of technical standards and regulations and of rules on Information Society services. The new Directive will supersede the various acts incorporated in it; this proposal fully preserves the content of the acts being codified and hence does no more than bring them together with only such formal amendments as are required by the codification exercise itself'.
[10] See Case C-390/18, *AIRBNB Ireland* (AG Opinion), para. 4.
[11] See E-Commerce Directive, Art. 2(a). See further Lodder 2017, pp. 22–25; Edwards 2005, pp. 94–95.
[12] See e.g. Directive 98/84/EC, Art. 2(a); Directive 2002/21/EC, Art. 2(c) and rec. 10; Directive 2014/40/EU, Art. 18(1)(b); Regulation (EU) 2017/746, Art. 6(1).
[13] See Proposal for Directive 83/189/EEC, p. 34. This is the Proposal that resulted in the adoption of Directive 98/48/EC.
[14] See e.g. Italian e-Commerce Law 2003, Art. 2(1)(a); Spanish Information Society Law 2002, Annex, Point (a).

4. Case law

The CJEU has developed a considerable body of case law on the definition of 'information society service' under Directive 98/34/EC and Directive 2000/31/EC. As mentioned above, these Directives define the term identically to the GDPR. Thus, this case law may help to elucidate the meaning of the term also under the GDPR and is referenced in the next section.

C. Analysis

1. Introduction

The definition of 'information society service' encompasses a large number of very different online economic activities.[15] Indeed, Article 4(25) GDPR, read in conjunction with Article 1(1)(b) of Directive (EU) 2015/1535, broadly defines the concept by referring to 'any' service with the following four attributes: (1) the service must be one that is normally provided for remuneration; (2) at a distance; (3) by electronic means; and (4) at the individual request of a recipient of services.

The reference to these four attributes is complemented by a list—laid out in Annex I to Directive (EU) 2015/1535—of examples of services that are not covered by the definition. As expressly indicated in Article 1(1)(b) of Directive (EU) 2015/1535, the list is only 'indicative'. Thus, it should not be considered exhaustive.

2. Services normally provided for remuneration

The first-listed attribute essentially reproduces the definition of 'services' in Article 57 TFEU, which provides that:

[s]ervices shall be considered to be 'services' within the meaning of the Treaties where they are normally provided for remuneration, in so far as they are not governed by the provisions relating to freedom of movement for goods, capital and persons ...[16]

Thus, the term 'service' should be interpreted in light of the CJEU case law on the concept of 'services' under the Treaties.[17] According to the Court's jurisprudence, 'the decisive factor which brings an activity within the ambit of [the definition of "services"] is its economic character, that is to say, the activity must not be provided for nothing. By contrast, ... there is no need in that regard for the person providing the service to be seeking to make a profit'.[18] Thus, a service may be considered to be provided for 'remuneration',

---

[15] See Proposal for e-Commerce Directive, p. 14, stating that '[the] definition encompasses a large number of very different economic activities which may be carried out on line'.

[16] Art. 57 TFEU also specifies that ' "Services" shall in particular include: (a) activities of an industrial character; (b) activities of a commercial character; (c) activities of craftsmen; (d) activities of the professions ...'.

[17] Case C-42/07, *Liga Portuguesa* (AG Opinion), para. 162, noting that 'an "Information Society service", within the meaning of Article 1, point 2, of Directive 98/34, is any service normally provided for remuneration, at a distance, by electronic means and at the individual request of a recipient of services. However, it is clear from the nineteenth recital of the preamble to the directive that it is also necessary to refer to the definition of "services" in Article 50 EC [now Art. 57 TFEU], as interpreted in the Court's case-law'. Similarly, in *Papasavvas*, the CJEU interpreted the definition of 'information society service' in light of the concept of services within the meaning of Art. 57 TFEU. See Case C-291/13, *Papasavvas*, para. 29. For an overview of the case law on the concept of 'services' within the meaning of the Treaties, see EC Guide 2016, pp. 8–15.

[18] See Case C-281/06, *Jundt*, paras. 32–33.

even if it is provided for, say, educational, charitable or recreational purposes.[19] In this regard, the Court has held that 'the essential characteristic of remuneration lies in the fact that it constitutes consideration for the service in question, and is normally agreed upon between the provider and the recipient of the service'.[20]

Moreover, the Court has found that 'the remuneration of a service supplied by a service provider within the course of its economic activity does not require the service to be paid for by those for whom it is performed'.[21] Thus, for example, 'the concept of "information society services" ... covers the provision of online information services for which the service provider is remunerated, not by the recipient, but by income generated by advertisements posted on a website'.[22]

In light of the broad scope of the concept of 'service', the definition in Article 4(25) GDPR appears to encompass both business-to-business and business-to-consumer services.[23]

3. At a distance

Point (i) of Article 1(1)(b) of Directive (EU) 2015/1535 makes clear that ' "at a distance" means that the service is provided without the parties being simultaneously present'. This implies that services provided in the physical presence of the provider and the recipient

---

[19] Ibid., para. 34 (the Court found that '[t]he sum received [by a lawyer for teaching a 16–hour course at a University] constitutes remuneration ... , that is to say, consideration for the service provided by him, even if it is assumed that that activity was carried out on a quasi-honorary basis'). See further Case C-275/92, *H.M. Customs and Excise v Schindler*, paras. 33–34. There the Court held that 'a normal lottery transaction consists of the payment of a sum by a gambler who hopes in return to receive a prize or winnings. The element of chance inherent in that return does not prevent the transaction having an economic nature. It is also the case that, like amateur sport, a lottery may provide entertainment for the players who participate. However, that recreational aspect of the lottery does not take it out of the realm of the provision of services'.

[20] See Case C-355/00, *Freskot*, para. 55 and case law cited therein.

[21] See Case C-484/14, *Mc Fadden*, para. 41. See also rec. 18 of the E-Commerce Directive (stating that 'information society services are not solely restricted to services giving rise to on-line contracting but also, in so far as they represent an economic activity, extend to services which are not remunerated by those who receive them, such as those offering on-line information or commercial communications, or those providing tools allowing for search, access and retrieval of data'). See further Case C-390/18, *AIRBNB Ireland* (AG Opinion), para. 38 (stating that 'the remuneration for a service provided by a service provider in the context of his economic activity is not necessarily paid by the persons who benefit from that service. A fortiori, as regards services consisting in connecting their recipients, who are divided into two categories, it is sufficient that one of those categories pays the remuneration to the provider of an information society service').

[22] See Case C-291/13, *Papasavvas*, para. 30. In this regard, it is interesting to note that Advocate General Jääskinen took the opposite view in *Google Spain*, noting that 'internet search engine service providers like Google who do not provide their service in return for remuneration from the internet users, appear to fall in that capacity outside the scope of application of ecommerce Directive 2000/31'. See Case C-131/12, *Google Spain and Google* (AG Opinion), para. 37. However, in *Google France*, the Court expressly qualified as an 'information society service' a paid referencing service—such as Google's AdWords—that enables any economic operator, by means of the reservation of one or more keywords, to obtain the placing, in the event of a correspondence between one or more of those words and that/those entered as a request in the search engine by an internet user, of an advertising link to its site. See Joined Cases C-236/08 to C-238/08, *Google France and Google*, para. 110.

[23] It should be noted that the explanatory memorandum accompanying the proposal for the e-Commerce Directive states that the definition of 'information society service' includes 'the following:—a business to business or a business to consumer service'. See Proposal for e-Commerce Directive, pp. 14–15. It is worth noting that the CJEU has examined the above explanatory memorandum to confirm whether a certain activity was covered by the definition of 'information society service'. See Case C-108/09, *Ker-Optika*, para. 25.

are normally not considered 'information society services', even if they involve the use of electronic devices.[24]

4. By electronic means

The test as to whether a service is provided 'by electronic means' within the meaning of Article 4(25) GDPR, read in conjunction with Article 1(1)(b) of Directive (EU) 2015/1535, is often more problematic than the tests for the other limbs of the definition elaborated above.[25] Point (ii) of Article 1(1)(b) of Directive 2015/1535 clarifies that

'[B]y electronic means' means that the service is sent initially and received at its destination by means of electronic equipment for the processing (including digital compression) and storage of data, and entirely transmitted, conveyed and received by wire, by radio, by optical means or by other electromagnetic means.

On its face, the key requirement here is that the service be provided *entirely* by the use of electronic equipment.[26] In principle, this excludes from the definition services having material content even though they are provided via electronic devices,[27] offline services[28] and services that are not provided via electronic processing.[29] By contrast, services such as the selling of goods, advertising services and gaming services in so far as they are provided online constitute 'information society services' within the meaning of Article 4(25) GDPR.[30]

With regard to composite services, namely services comprising electronic and non-electronic elements, the WP29 opined on the basis of the CJEU case law that:

[W]here a service has two economically independent components, one being the online component, such as the offer and the acceptance of an offer in the context of the conclusion of a contract

---

[24] This is confirmed by Annex I to Directive (EU) 2015/1535, which lists the following examples of services that are not covered by the definition of 'information society service' because they are not provided 'at a distance': '[s]ervices provided in the physical presence of the provider and the recipient, even if they involve the use of electronic devices: (a) medical examinations or treatment at a doctor's surgery using electronic equipment where the patient is physically present; (b) consultation of an electronic catalogue in a shop with the customer on site; (c) plane ticket reservation at a travel agency in the physical presence of the customer by means of a network of computers; (d) electronic games made available in a video arcade where the customer is physically present'. See further Lodder 2017, pp. 23–25.

[25] See also Case C-390/18, *AIRBNB Ireland* (AG Opinion), para. 37.   [26] Ibid., para. 43.

[27] Annex I to Directive 2015/1535 lists the following examples of services that are not covered by the definition of 'information society service' because they are not provided 'by electronic means': automatic cash or ticket dispensing machines (banknotes, rail tickets); access to road networks, car parks etc., charging for use, even if there are electronic devices at the entrance/exit controlling access and/or ensuring correct payment is made.

[28] Annex I to Directive 2015/1535 lists the following examples of services that are not covered by the definition of 'information society service' because they are not provided 'by electronic means': distribution of CD-ROMs or software on diskettes.

[29] Annex I to Directive 2015/1535 lists the following examples of services that are not covered by the definition of 'information society service' because they are not provided 'by electronic means': voice telephony services; telefax/telex services; services provided via voice telephony or fax; telephone/telefax consultation of a doctor; telephone/telefax consultation of a lawyer; telephone/telefax direct marketing. However, in *Skype Communications*, the CJEU has affirmed that 'the VoIP service provided by SkypeOut is ... covered by the definition of "information society service" within the meaning of Directive 98/34': see Case C-142/18, *Skype Communications*, para. 46. This suggests that voice-over IP services would normally fall within the definition of 'information society service'.

[30] See Case C-108/09, *Ker-Optika*, para. 24; Case C-324/09, *L'Oréal and Others*, paras. 109–110; Case C-339/15, *Vanderborght*, para. 39; Case C-255/16, *Falbert and Others*, para. 29.

or the information relating to products or services, including marketing activities, this component is defined as an information society service, the other component being the physical delivery or distribution of goods is not covered by the notion of an information society service.[31]

Also, as noted by Advocate General Szpunar in *Asociación Profesional Elite Taxi*:

[T]his situation arises, in particular, where an intermediary service provider facilitates commercial relations between a user and an independent service provider (or seller). Platforms for the purchase of flights or hotel bookings are one example of this. In those cases, the supply made by the intermediary represents real added value for both the user and the trader concerned, but remains economically independent since the trader pursues his activity separately.[32]

By contrast, where the two components described above form part of an inseparable whole,[33] a composite service will fall under the definition of 'information society service' only as long as the main component of the service—i.e. the component that gives meaning to the service in economic terms—meets the definition.[34] The CJEU shared this view in *Asociación Profesional Elite Taxi* and in *Uber France* where the Court found that, for instance:

[A]n intermediation service that enables the transfer, by means of a smartphone application, of information concerning the booking of a transport service between the passenger and the non-professional driver who will carry out the transportation using his own vehicle meets, in principle, the criteria for classification as an 'information society service' within the meaning of Article 1(2) of Directive 98/34 and Article 2(a) of Directive 2000/31.[35]

However, the Court noted that the service at issue in these two cases (Uber) was more than just an intermediation service as described above, but had to be regarded as 'forming an integral part of an overall service the main component of which was a transport service and, accordingly, had to be classified, not as an "information society service"'.[36] Conversely, in *AIRBNB Ireland*, Advocate General Szpunar found that a service, like AIRBNB, consisting in connecting, via an online platform, potential guests with hosts offering short-term accommodation qualifies as an 'information society service' as long as the service provider (AIRBNB) does not exercise control over the services having material content, namely the short-term accommodation services, which are linked to its online services.[37]

5. At the individual request of a recipient of services

Point (iii) of Article 1(1)(b) of Directive (EU) 2015/1535 states that '"at the individual request of a recipient of services" means that the service is provided through the transmission of data on individual request'. This means that only services provided

---

[31] WP29 2017, p. 24.
[32] See Case C-434/15, *Asociación Profesional Elite* Taxi (AG Opinion), para. 33.
[33] In *AIRBNB Ireland*, Advocate General Szpunar took the view that '[i]t is the decisive influence exercised by the service provider over the conditions of the supply of the services having material content that is capable of rendering those services inseparable from the service that that provider provides by electronic means': see Case C-390/18, *AIRBNB Ireland* (AG Opinion), para. 67.
[34] Case C-434/15, *Asociación Profesional Elite Taxi* (AG Opinion), para. 35. See further WP29 2017, p. 24, fn. 57.
[35] Case C-434/15, *Asociación Profesional Elite Taxi*, para. 35; see also Case C-320/16, *Uber France*, para. 19.
[36] See Case C-434/15, *Asociación Profesional Elite*, para. 40; Case C-320/16, *Uber France*, para. 22.
[37] See Case C-390/18, *AIRBNB Ireland* (AG Opinion), paras. 18–91.

on individual demand are covered by the definition in Article 4(25) GDPR.[38] In contrast, services provided by transmitting data without individual demand for simultaneous reception by an unlimited number of individual receivers, such as television and radio broadcasting services, are not covered by the definition.[39] For example, in *Mediakabel*, the CJEU excluded from the definition of 'information society service' a pay-per-view service that allows its users to order a film from a catalogue using their remote control or telephone and, after identifying themselves using a personal identification code and paying by automatic debit, watch the film at the times indicated on the television screen or in the programme guide. The Court justified this exclusion on the following grounds:

[A]lthough such a service fulfils the first two criteria for constituting an 'information society service' within the meaning of Article 1(2) of Directive 98/34, that is, it is provided at a distance and transmitted in part by electronic equipment, it does not meet the third criterion of the concept, according to which the service in question must be provided 'at the individual request of a recipient of services'. The list of films offered as part of a service ... is determined by the service provider. That selection of films is offered to all subscribers on the same terms, either through written media or through information transmitted on the television screen, and those films are accessible at the broadcast times determined by the provider. The individual key allowing access to the films is only a means of unencoding images the signals of which are sent simultaneously to all subscribers.

Such a service is thus not commanded individually by an isolated recipient who has free choice of programmes in an interactive setting.[40]

6. Summing up

In light of the above, most (but not all) online services are likely to be covered by the definition of 'information society service'.[41] For instance, the definition would normally cover online professional services (e.g. online legal services, online health services), online information services (e.g. online libraries, online meteorological services, online newspapers), interactive digital entertainment services (e.g. on-demand video services, online videogames), virtual shopping malls and supermarkets, online tourism services, online estate agents, online insurance services, online educational services, search engines and web

---

[38] For example, in *AIRBNB Ireland*, Advocate General Szpunar found that the services offered by AIRBNB are provided at the request of a recipient of the services, and justified this as follows: '... in the judgment in *Google France and Google*, the Court held that a paid referencing service, used in the context of an internet search engine, whereby an economic operator may make an advertising link to its site appear to users of that search engine, satisfies the condition relating to the individual request of that economic operator. As regards AIRBNB Ireland's services, a host must approach the platform managed by that company in order for his accommodation to appear on that platform. Furthermore, it is with the assistance of AIRBNB Ireland's platform that a guest must carry out a search in order to be able to rent accommodation published on that platform': see Case C-390/18, *AIRBNB Ireland* (AG Opinion), para. 39. See further Joined Cases C-236/08 to C-238/08, *Google France and Google*, paras. 23 and 110.

[39] See Annex I to Directive 2015/1535.

[40] Case C-89/04, *Mediakabel*, paras. 38–39. In contrast, services for the cloud recording of free-to-air terrestrial television programmes are covered by the definition of 'information society service'. See also Case C-265/16, *VCAST* (AG Opinion), para. 19 (noting that a service allowing its users to record in the cloud certain programmes broadcasted by certain television channels appear to fulfil the criteria for the definition of information society service). The CJEU seems to agree with the AG's view: see Case C-265/16, *VCAST*, para. 24.

[41] See also ICO 2017. See too rec. 10 Directive 2002/21/EC (stating that the definition of 'information society service' 'spans a wide range of economic activities which take place online').

browsers.[42] By contrast, the definition would exclude, inter alia, non-electronic direct marketing services (e.g. mail order catalogues), automatic bank tellers and traditional telephony services.[43]

Select Bibliography

EU legislation

Directive 98/34/EC: Directive 98/34/EC of the European Parliament and of the Council of 22 June 1998 laying down a procedure for the provision of information in the field of technical standards and regulations, OJ 1998 L 204/37.
Directive 98/48/EC: Directive 98/48/EC of the European Parliament and of the Council of 20 July 1998 amending Directive 98/34/EC laying down a procedure for the provision of information in the field of technical standards and regulations, OJ 1998 L 217/18.
Directive 98/84/EC: Directive 98/84/EC of the European Parliament and of the Council of 20 November 1998 on the legal protection of services based on, or consisting of, conditional access, OJ 1998 L 320/54.
Directive 2002/21/EC: Directive 2002/21/EC of the European Parliament and of the Council of 7 March 2002 on a common regulatory framework for electronic communications networks and services, OJ 2002 L 108/33.
Directive 2014/40/EU: Directive 2014/40/EU of the European Parliament and of the Council of 3 April 2014 on the approximation of the laws, regulations and administrative provisions of the Member States concerning the manufacture, presentation and sale of tobacco and related products and repealing Directive 2001/37/EC, OJ 2014 L 127/1.
Directive (EU) 2015/1535: Directive (EU) 2015/1535 of the European Parliament and of the Council of 9 September 2015 laying down a procedure for the provision of information in the field of technical regulations and of rules on Information Society services, OJ 2015 L 241/1.
E-Commerce Directive: Directive 2000/31/EC of the European Parliament and of the Council of 8 June 2000 on certain legal aspects of information society services, in particular electronic commerce, in the Internal Market, OJ 2000 L 178/1.
Proposal for Directive 83/189/EEC: Proposal for a European Parliament and Council Directive amending for the third time Directive 83/189/EEC laying down a procedure for the provision of information in the field of technical standards and regulations, COM(96) 392 final, 30 August 1996.
Proposal for e-Commerce Directive: Proposal for a European Parliament and Council Directive on certain legal aspects of electronic commerce in the internal market, COM(1998) 586 final, 18 November 1998.
Proposal for Technical Standards Directive: Proposal for a Directive of the European Parliament and of the Council laying down a procedure for the provision of information in the field of technical standards and regulations and of rules on Information Society services, COM(2010)179 final, 23 April 2010.
Regulation (EU) 2017/746: Regulation (EU) 2017/746 of the European Parliament and of the Council of 5 April 2017 on in vitro diagnostic medical devices and repealing Directive 98/79/EC and Commission Decision 2010/227/EU, OJ 2017 L 117/176.

---

[42] These examples are taken from the explanatory memoranda to the proposals for Directive 98/48/EC and Directive 2000/31/EC. See Proposal for Directive 83/189/EEC, pp. 35–36; Proposal for e-Commerce Directive, p. 15. As discussed above, the CJEU has looked at explanatory memoranda to confirm whether a certain activity was covered by the definition of 'information society service': see Case C-108/09, *Ker-Optika*, para. 25.

[43] See Proposal for Directive 83/189/EEC, pp. 35–36; Proposal for e-Commerce Directive, p. 15.

National legislation

Italian e-Commerce Law 2003: Decreto legislativo 9 aprile 2003, n. 70: Attuazione della direttiva 2000/31/CE relativa a taluni aspetti giuridici dei servizi della società dell'informazione, in particolare il commercio elettronico, nel mercato interno.

Spanish Information Society Law 2002: Ley 34/2002, de 11 de julio, de la Sociedad de la Información y de Comercio Electrónico.

Academic writings

Edwards 2005: Edwards, 'Articles 12–15 ECD: ISP Liability: The Problem of Intermediary Service Provider Liability', in Edwards (ed.), *The New Legal Framework for E-Commerce in Europe* (Hart 2005), 93.

Lodder 2017: Lodder, 'Directive 2000/31/EC on Certain Legal Aspects of Information Society Services, in Particular Electronic Commerce, in the Internal Market', in Lodder and Murray (eds.), *EU Regulation of E-Commerce: A Commentary* (Edward Elgar 2017), 15.

Papers of data protection authorities

WP29 2017: Article 29 Working Party, 'Guidelines on Consent under Regulation 2016/679' (WP 259, 28 November 2017).

Reports and recommendations

EC Guide 2016: Guide to the Case Law of the European Court of Justice on Articles 56 et seq. TFEU: 'Freedom to Provide Services', Ref. Ares(2016)2333299, 19 May 2016.

Others

ICO 2017: Information Commissioner's Office, 'What Are the Rules about an ISS and Consent?', available at: https://ico.org.uk/for-organisations/guide-to-data-protection/guide-to-the-general-data-protection-regulation-gdpr/children-and-the-gdpr/what-are-the-rules-about-an-iss-and-consent/.

Article 4(26). International organisation

LEE A. BYGRAVE   LUCA TOSONI

'international organisation' means an organisation and its subordinate bodies governed by public international law, or any other body which is set up by, or on the basis of, an agreement between two or more countries.

Closely Related Provisions

Articles 44–50 (Transfers of personal data to third countries or international organisations) (see too recitals 101–103, 105–107, 112 and 168–169)

Related Provisions in LED [Directive (EU) 2016/680]

Article 3(16) (Definition of 'international organisation'); Articles 35–40 (Transfers of personal data to third countries or international organisations) (see too recitals 64–72)

Related Provisions in EUDPR [Regulation (EU) 2018/1725]

Article 3(21) (Definition of 'international organisation'); Articles 46–51 (Transfers of personal data to third countries or international organisations) (see too recitals 63–71)

Relevant Case Law

CJEU

Case C-364/92, *SAT Fluggesellschaft v Eurocontrol*, judgment of 19 January 1994 (ECLI:EU:C:1994:7).
Case C-386/08, *Firma Brita GmbH v Hauptzollamt Hamburg-Hafen*, judgment of 25 February 2010 (ECLI:EU:C:2010:91).
Case C-113/07 P, *SELEX Sistemi Integrati SpA v Commission of the European Communities and Organisation européenne pour la sécurité de la navigation aérienne (Eurocontrol)*, judgment of 26 March 2009 (ECLI:EU:C:2009:191).
Joined Cases C-103/12 and C-165/12, *European Parliament and European Commission v Council of the European Union*, judgment of 26 November 2014 (Grand Chamber) (ECLI:EU:C:2014:2400).
Opinion of Advocate General Sharpston in Joined Cases C-103/12 and C-165/12, *European Parliament and European Commission v Council of the European Union*, delivered on 15 May 2014 (ECLI:EU:C:2014:334).
Joined Cases C-183/17 P and C-184/17 P, *International Management Group v European Commission*, judgment of 31 January 2019 (ECLI:EU:C:2019:78).

A. Rationale and Policy Underpinnings

The definition of 'international organisation' was not contained in the original Commission proposal for the GDPR,[1] but was introduced later by the Council,[2] presumably due to the term being extensively employed in the provisions dealing with data transfers in Chapter V GDPR. Whereas the equivalent provisions in the DPD governed only transfers of personal data to third countries, the GDPR provisions encompass transfers to international organisations also,[3] as do the equivalent provisions in the LED and EUDPR. The rationale for this extension is rooted in concern to prevent the level of protection offered by the GDPR being undermined (recital 101 GDPR).[4]

B. Legal Background

1. EU legislation

While the DPD did not use the term 'international organisation', other EU legislation has—most notably, Council Decision Europol 2009.[5] That Decision was repealed and replaced by the Europol Regulation 2016/794,[6] the Commission's proposal for which provided the template for the definition of 'international organisation' in Article 4(26) GDPR.[7] Article 2(e) of the Europol Regulation (as finally adopted) defines 'international organisation' identically to the definition in Article 4(26) GDPR, and employs the term in conjunction with its provisions on trans-border data flows to third countries and international organisations.[8] An identical definition of 'international organisation' was also later included in Article 2(23) of Council Regulation (EU) 2017/1939 implementing enhanced cooperation on the establishment of the European Public Prosecutor's Office.[9]

2. International treaties

Convention 108 as originally adopted does not expressly regulate flow of personal data to international organisations. Modernised Convention 108, however, regulates the flow of personal data from States Parties to the Convention to recipients that are 'subject to the jurisdiction of a State or international organisation which is not Party to this Convention'.[10] Moreover, Modernised Convention 108 permits international organisations to accede to the Convention, albeit upon invitation.[11] The term 'international organisation' is not defined in Modernised Convention 108, but its Explanatory Report states that '[i]nternational organisations that can accede to the Convention are solely international organisations which are defined as organisations governed by public

---

[1] See GDPR Proposal.   [2] See Council Report 2014A, p. 8.

[3] See Arts. 44–50. For a discussion of data transfer issues relevant to international organisations see the commentaries on Arts. 44–50 in this volume.

[4] See further the commentary on Art. 44 in this volume.

[5] Council Decision Europol 2009, Art. 23(1)(b), which provided that Europol could maintain relations with 'organisations such as: (i) international organisations and their subordinate bodies governed by public law; (ii) other bodies governed by public law which are set up by, or on the basis of, an agreement between two or more States; and (iii) the International Criminal Police Organisation (Interpol)'.

[6] Europol Regulation.   [7] Europol Proposal 2013, Art. 2(f).

[8] Europol Regulation, Art. 25.   [9] EPPO Regulation.

[10] Modernised Convention 108, Art. 14(2).   [11] Ibid., Art. 27(1).

international law'.[12] This understanding of 'international organisation' presumably applies not just to Article 27(1) but also to Article 14(2) of Modernised Convention 108.

3. Case law

The CJEU has yet to interpret the definition in Article 4(26) GDPR. However, it has developed a body of case law concerning the nature of international organisations. This jurisprudence is referenced in the next section.

C. Analysis

There is no universally accepted definition of 'international organisation'.[13] In public international law, though, the term 'international organisation' is usually defined by reference to four attributes: (i) the organisation has its formal basis in a treaty; (ii) its membership is typically composed of States; (iii) it has its own organs and institutional structure distinct from its Member States; and (iv) it possesses international legal personality.[14] On its face, the definition of an international organisation provided by Article 4(26) GDPR does not include all these attributes,[15] so that it can be viewed as potentially broader than that under public international law.[16] However, the CJEU may consider the public international law definition of 'international organisation' as a source of inspiration for interpreting the GDPR definition, which might result in the definition by the GDPR being brought more in line with that under public international law. In this regard, it is worth noting that the CJEU has affirmed the importance of considering the Vienna Convention on the Law of Treaties as a source of inspiration for interpreting EU law.[17] This is particularly significant given that the Vienna Convention defines 'international organization' as 'an intergovernmental organization'.[18]

Article 4(26) GDPR encompasses two categories of body either of which may qualify as an international organisation for GDPR purposes: (i) organisations (and their subordinate bodies) that are governed by public international law; and (ii) other bodies that are 'set up by, or on the basis of' bilateral or multilateral agreements between States. Neither category is precisely delineated, which gives the impression that the legislator has taken a flexible and accommodating approach to the issue of what may constitute an international organisation. Moreover, if one accepts that the definition is at least partly rooted in Article 23(1)(b) Council Decision Europol 2009 (repealed), this could also further

---

[12] Explanatory Report Convention 108 2018, para. 173. [13] Kuner 2019, p. 168.

[14] Kolb 2012, p. 1. See also UN International Law Commission Report 2011, p. 54 (defining 'international organization' as 'an organization established by a treaty or other instrument governed by international law and possessing its own international legal personality').

[15] The lack of clarity of the definition was noted by several Member States during the legislative process. E.g. the Czech Republic and Latvia 'thought this definition was incomplete and should either be supplemented or deleted': see Council Report 2014B, p. 8, fn. 12.

[16] See also Kuner 2019, pp. 168–169.

[17] See e.g. Case C-386/08, *Brita*, para. 42 (stating that 'the Court has held that, even though the Vienna Convention does not bind either the Community or all its Member States, a series of provisions in that convention reflect the rules of customary international law which, as such, are binding upon the Community institutions and form part of the Community legal order ...').

[18] See Vienna Convention, Art. 2(1)(i). It is noteworthy that Advocate General Sharpston used this definition of 'international organisation' in Joined Cases C-103/12 and C-165/12, *Parliament and Commission v Council* (AG Opinion), para. 68, fn. 29, but without directly referencing the Vienna Convention.

support a flexible interpretation of the phrase 'any other body which is set up by, or on the basis of, an agreement between two or more countries'.[19]

The reference to 'agreement' in the second part of the definition suggests an arrangement that could be less formal than a treaty or convention, while the wording 'set up by, or on the basis of' indicates that an international organisation does not have to be *initially* established through an inter-state agreement if its existence or remit is otherwise tied closely to such an agreement.[20] Thus, the definition seems to embrace more than just intergovernmental organisations in the classic sense (i.e. organisations established by treaty and governed primarily by the States Parties to the treaty) such as the United Nations, its specialised agencies like the International Telecommunications Union,[21] or the World Trade Organisation. Entities which have a treaty-based mandate and enjoy international legal personality, such as the International Committee of the Red Cross ('ICRC'), are covered by the definition under the GDPR as well.[22]

Interestingly, during the legislative process leading to the adoption of the GDPR, some Member States queried whether Interpol would be covered by the definition of 'international organisation' in Article 4(26).[23] However, a systematic interpretation of the GDPR definition indicates that Interpol is indeed covered. First, recital 32 of the Europol Regulation states that 'Europol should ... be able to exchange personal data with authorities of third countries and with international organisations such as the International Criminal Police Organisation—Interpol to the extent necessary for the accomplishment of its tasks'. Secondly, the EPPO Regulation (adopted after the GDPR) includes an identical definition of international organisation,[24] and its recital 108 states: '[f]or the purpose of this Regulation, "international organisations" means international organisations and their subordinate bodies governed by public international law or other bodies which are set up by, or on the basis of, an agreement between two or more countries as well as

---

[19] As pointed out above, Art. 23(1)(b) Council Decision Europol 2009 expressly qualified as 'international organisations' only those under point (i) of its provisions, whereas the organisations under point (ii) seem to cover a much broader group of organisations than those typically considered international organisations under public international law. Point (ii) is broadly mirrored in the second part of the definition in Art. 4(26) GDPR.

[20] The ambiguity of the term 'agreement' was also noted during the legislative process that led to the adoption of the GDPR. For example, the Netherlands queried whether Memoranda of Understanding would also be covered by the definition: see Council Report 2014C, p. 80, fn. 61.

[21] Interestingly, in *International Management Group*, the CJEU held that the fact that a certain organisation was not a specialist UN agency was per se irrelevant to assess whether it qualified as an 'international organisation' under the 2002 and 2012 EU Financial Regulations (i.e. Regulation No. 2342/2002 and Regulation No. 1268/2012), as these Regulations do not require a given entity to be an UN agency in order for it to be classified as an 'international organisation': see Joined Cases C-183/17 P and C-184/17 P, *International Management Group*, para. 96. The notion of 'international organisation' is defined in both Regulations as comprising, inter alia, 'international public-sector organisations set up by intergovernmental agreements, and specialised agencies set up by such organisations' (see Art. 43(2) Regulation No. 2342/2002 and Art. 43(1) Regulation No. 1268/2012).

[22] The ICRC was established as a private association under Swiss law, but draws its mandate from treaty and enjoys a considerable degree of international legal personality. Further on the legal status of the ICRC as an international organisation, see Debuf 2016. The status of the ICRC was specifically discussed in the GDPR legislative deliberations: see Council Report 2015.

[23] See Council Report 2014B, p. 8, fn. 12; Council Report 2014C, p. 80, fn. 61. These doubts appear to be rooted in Art. 23(1)(b) Council Decision Europol 2009 (repealed). As noted above, Art. 23(1)(b) provided that Europol could maintain relations with 'organisations such as: (i) international organisations and their subordinate bodies governed by public law; (ii) other bodies governed by public law which are set up by, or on the basis of, an agreement between two or more States; and (iii) the International Criminal Police Organisation (Interpol)'. The structure of Art. 23(1)(b) suggested that Interpol is different from the organisations mentioned in points (i) and (ii) (which are those also mentioned in the GDPR definition).

[24] See Art. 2(23) EPPO Regulation.

Interpol'. Thirdly, the transfer of data to Interpol is also expressly envisaged in recital 25 LED, which defines 'international organisation' identically to the GDPR.[25]

However, there are a large number of organisations which have an international character in the sense that they operate transnationally, have members from across the globe, or pursue goals that clearly transcend the interests of a single State, but which do not qualify as an international organisation for GDPR purposes.[26] This is typically the case for non-governmental organisations ('NGOs') which are established on private initiative and are governed by the domestic law of the State where they are incorporated or have their headquarters.[27]

Finally, it is worth noting that the CJEU has found that an international organisation does not qualify as an 'undertaking' under EU competition law if its activities—by their nature, their aim and the rules to which they are subject—are connected with the exercise of powers that are typically those of a public authority or are otherwise not of an economic nature.[28] This is particularly relevant in light of the fact that Article 83 GDPR establishes that 'undertakings' may be subject to specific fines if they violate the Regulation,[29] and recital 150 GDPR states that '[w]here administrative fines are imposed on an undertaking, an undertaking should be understood to be an undertaking in accordance with Articles 101 and 102 TFEU for those purposes'.[30] Therefore, in the limited circumstances where the GDPR may directly apply to the data processing activities of international organisations,[31] the latter are likely to escape the fines for 'undertakings' in most cases.

Select Bibliography

International agreements

Vienna Convention on the Law of Treaties 1969, 331 UNTS 1155.

EU legislation

Council Decision Europol 2009: Council Decision 2009/371/JHA of 6 April 2009 establishing the European Police Office (Europol), OJ 2009 L 121/37.

---

[25] See Art. 3(16) LED.

[26] Importantly, in a different context, the CJEU has stressed that whether an entity qualifies as an 'international organisation' should be carefully assessed in light of the applicable legal definition(s) of that term, and that such a qualification may not be excluded on the basis of mere doubts. See Joined Cases C-183/17 P and C-184/17 P, *International Management Group*, paras. 92–97.

[27] Regarding the legal status of NGOs, see Charnovitz 2006, p. 355 and references cited therein.

[28] Case C-364/92, *SAT Fluggesellschaft*, paras. 19–32; Case C-113/07 P, *Selex Sistemi Integrati*, para. 71. The Court noted this with regard to the European Organisation for the Safety of Air Navigation (Eurocontrol), a regionally oriented international organisation established by various European States.

[29] See Art. 83(4)–(6) GDPR.

[30] Arts. 101–102 TFEU lay down competition rules applying to undertakings.

[31] See Kuner 2019, noting that the GDPR does not automatically exclude international organisations, and that determining whether the GDPR applies to international organisations should be based on its material and territorial scope, viewed in light of any privileges and immunities that international organisations may enjoy and the status of international law in the EU legal order. In this regard, it is interesting to note that some international organisations have expressly taken the view that the GDPR does not apply directly to their data processing activities. For example, the European Patent Office ('EPO') stated that '[a]s an international organisation established by its own international treaty signed by 38 member states with its organisational autonomy, the EPO fulfils its mission of providing high quality and efficient services under the European Patent Convention. The European Patent Convention is independent from the regulatory framework of the EU and hence the GDPR is not directly binding to [*sic*] the EPO'. See European Patent Office 2018. On the applicability of the GDPR to international organisations, see further the commentary on Art. 44 in this volume.

EPPO Regulation: Council Regulation (EU) 2017/1939 of 12 October 2017 implementing enhanced cooperation on the establishment of the European Public Prosecutor's Office, OJ 2017 L 283/1.

Europol Proposal 2013: Proposal for a Regulation of the European Parliament and of the Council on the European Union Agency for Law Enforcement Cooperation and Training (Europol) and repealing Decisions 2009/371/JHA and 2005/681/JHA, COM(2013) 173 final, 27 March 2013.

Europol Regulation: Regulation (EU) 2016/794 of the European Parliament and of the Council of 11 May 2016 on the European Union Agency for Law Enforcement Cooperation (Europol) and replacing and repealing Council Decisions 2009/371/JHA, 2009/934/JHA, 2009/935/JHA, 2009/936/JHA and 2009/968/JHA, OJ 2016 L 135/53.

GDPR Proposal: Proposal for a Regulation of the European Parliament and of the Council on the protection of individuals with regard to the processing of personal data and on the free movement of such data (General Data Protection Regulation), COM(2012) 11 final.

Academic writings

Charnovitz 2006: Charnovitz, 'Nongovernmental Organizations and International Law', 100(2) *American Journal of International Law* (2006), 348.

Debuf 2016: Debuf, 'Tools to Do the Job: The ICRC's Legal Status, Privileges and Immunities', 97 *International Review of the Red Cross* (2016), 319.

Kolb 2012: Kolb, 'International Organizations or Institutions, History of', in Wolfrum (ed.), *The Max Planck Encyclopedia of Public International Law* (OUP 2012), 1.

Kuner 2019: Kuner, 'International Organizations and the EU General Data Protection Regulation: Exploring the Interaction between EU Law and International Law', 16 *International Organizations Law Review* (2019), 158.

Reports and recommendations

Council Report 2014A: Chapter V, 8087/14, 25 March 2014.

Council Report 2014B: Chapter V, 8087/1/14, 28 April 2014.

Council Report 2014C: Proposal for a regulation of the European Parliament and of the Council on the protection of individuals with regard to the processing of personal data and on the free movement of such data (General Data Protection Regulation), 11028/14, 30 June 2014.

Council Report 2015: Proposal for a regulation of the European Parliament and of the Council on the protection of individuals with regard to the processing of personal data and on the free movement of such data (General Data Protection Regulation), 7355/15, 25 March 2015.

Explanatory Report Convention 108 2018: Council of Europe, 'Explanatory Report to the Protocol Amending the Convention for the Protection of Individuals with Regard to the Automatic Processing of Personal Data' (10 October 2018), available at https://rm.coe.int/cets-223-explanatory-report-to-the-protocol-amending-the-convention-fo/16808ac91a.

International Law Commission Report 2011: United Nations, 'Report of the International Law Commission on the Work of its Sixty-Sixth Session' (UN Doc. A/66/10, 2011).

Others

European Patent Office 2018: European Patent Office Press Release, 'EU General Data Protection Regulation (GDPR) Comes into Effect' (25 May 2018), available at https://www.epo.org/news-issues/news/2018/20180525.html.

Chapter II Principles (Articles 5–11)

Article 5. Principles relating to processing of personal data

CÉCILE DE TERWANGNE

1. Personal data shall be:
   (a) processed lawfully, fairly and in a transparent manner in relation to the data subject ('lawfulness, fairness and transparency');
   (b) collected for specified, explicit and legitimate purposes and not further processed in a manner that is incompatible with those purposes; further processing for archiving purposes in the public interest, scientific or historical research purposes or statistical purposes shall, in accordance with Article 89(1), not be considered to be incompatible with the initial purposes ('purpose limitation');
   (c) adequate, relevant and limited to what is necessary in relation to the purposes for which they are processed ('data minimisation');
   (d) accurate and, where necessary, kept up to date; every reasonable step must be taken to ensure that personal data that are inaccurate, having regard to the purposes for which they are processed, are erased or rectified without delay ('accuracy');
   (e) kept in a form which permits identification of data subjects for no longer than is necessary for the purposes for which the personal data are processed; personal data may be stored for longer periods insofar as the personal data will be processed solely for archiving purposes in the public interest, scientific or historical research purposes or statistical purposes in accordance with Article 89(1) subject to implementation of the appropriate technical and organisational measures required by this Regulation in order to safeguard the rights and freedoms of the data subject ('storage limitation');
   (f) processed in a manner that ensures appropriate security of the personal data, including protection against unauthorised or unlawful processing and against accidental loss, destruction or damage, using appropriate technical or organisational measures ('integrity and confidentiality').
2. The controller shall be responsible for, and be able to demonstrate compliance with, paragraph 1 ('accountability').

Relevant Recital

(39) Any processing of personal data should be lawful and fair. It should be transparent to natural persons that personal data concerning them are collected, used, consulted or otherwise processed and to what extent the personal data are or will be processed. The principle of transparency requires that any information and communication relating to the processing of those personal data be easily accessible and easy to understand, and that clear and plain language be used. That principle concerns, in particular, information to the data subjects on the identity of the controller and the purposes of the processing and further information to ensure fair and transparent processing in respect of the natural persons concerned and their right to obtain confirmation and communication of personal data concerning them which are being processed. Natural persons should be made aware of risks, rules, safeguards and rights in relation to the processing of personal data and how

to exercise their rights in relation to such processing. In particular, the specific purposes for which personal data are processed should be explicit and legitimate and determined at the time of the collection of the personal data. The personal data should be adequate, relevant and limited to what is necessary for the purposes for which they are processed. This requires, in particular, ensuring that the period for which the personal data are stored is limited to a strict minimum. Personal data should be processed only if the purpose of the processing could not reasonably be fulfilled by other means. In order to ensure that the personal data are not kept longer than necessary, time limits should be established by the controller for erasure or for a periodic review. Every reasonable step should be taken to ensure that personal data which are inaccurate are rectified or deleted. Personal data should be processed in a manner that ensures appropriate security and confidentiality of the personal data, including for preventing unauthorised access to or use of personal data and the equipment used for the processing.

Closely Related Provisions

Article 6(1) (Lawfulness of processing) (see too recitals 40–49); Article 6(4) (Exceptions to the requirement of compatible purposes for further processing and criteria to ascertain whether a purpose of further processing is compatible with the purpose for which the personal data are initially collected) (see too recital 50); Article 12 (Transparent information) (see too recitals 58–59); Articles 13–15 (Information and access to personal data) (see also recitals 60–64); Article 24 (Responsibility of the controller) (see too recitals 74–78) ; Article 32 (Security of processing) (see too recital 83); Article 89(1) (Safeguards and derogations relating to processing for archiving purposes in the public interest, scientific or historical research purposes or statistical purposes) (see too recitals 158–163)

Related Provisions in LED [Directive (EU) 2016/680]

Article 4 (Principles relating to processing of personal data) (see too recitals 26–28); Article 9(1) and (2) (Specific processing conditions) (see too recital 34); Article 13 (Information to be made available or given to the data subject) (see too recitals 39, 40 and 42); Article 19 (Obligations of the controller) (see too recitals 50–51); Article 29 (Security of processing) (see too recital 60)

Related Provisions in EUDPR [Regulation (EU) 2018/1725]

Article 4 (Principles relating to processing of personal data) (see too recitals 20–22); Article 5(1) (Lawfulness of processing) (see also recitals 22–24); Article 6 (Processing for another compatible purpose) (see too recital 25); Article 14 (Transparent information) (see too recitals 34–36); Articles 15–17 (Information and access to personal data) (see also recitals 35–37); Article 26 (Responsibility of the controller) (see too recitals 45–48) ; Article 33 (Security of processing) (see too recitals 53–54); Article 71 (Principles relating to processing of operational personal data); Article 72 (Lawfulness of processing operational personal data); Articles 78–83 (Information and access with respect to operational personal data); Article 91 (Security of processing of operational personal data)

Relevant Case Law

CJEU

Joined Cases C-92/09 and 93/09, *Volker and Markus Schecke GbR* and *Hartmut Eifert v Land Hessen*, judgment of 9 November 2010 (Grand Chamber) (ECLI:EU:C:2010:662).

Case C-342/12, *Worten – Equipamentos para o Lar SA v Autoridade para as Condições de Trabalho (ACT)*, judgment of 30 May 2013 (ECLI:EU:C:2013:355).
Case C-291/12, *Michael Schwarz v Stadt Bochum*, judgment 17 October 2013 (ECLI:EU:C:2013:670).
Joined Cases C-293/12 and C-594/12, *Digital Rights Ireland Ltd v Minister for Communications, Marine and Natural Resources* and *Kärntner Landesregierung and Others*, judgment of 8 April 2014 (Grand Chamber) (ECLI:EU:C:2014:238).
Case C-683/13, *Pharmacontinente – Saude e Higiene SA*, order of 19 June 2014 (ECLI:EU:C:2014:2028).
Case C-201/14, *Smaranda Bara and Others v Casa Națională de Asigurări de Sănătate and Others*, judgment of 1 October 2015 (ECLI:EU:C:2015:638).
Joined Cases C-203/15 and C-698/15, *Tele2 Sverige AB v Post-och telestyrelsen* and *Secretary of State for the Home Department v Tom Watson and Others*, judgment of 21 December 2016 (Grand Chamber) (ECLI:EU:C:2016:970).
Case C-708/18, *TK v Asociația de Proprietari bloc M5A Scara-A* (pending).

ECtHR

Gaskin v United Kingdom, Appl. No. 10454/83, judgment of 7 July 1989.
M.S. v Sweden, Appl. No. 20837/92, judgment of 27 August 1997.
Rotaru v Romania [GC], Appl. No. 28341/95, judgment of 4 May 2000.
Copland v United Kingdom, Appl. No. 62617/00, judgment of 3 April 2007.
S. and Marper v United Kingdom, Appl. No. 30562/04, 30566/04, judgment of 4 December 2008.
Haralambie v Romania, Appl. No. 21737, judgment of 27 October 2009.
K.H. and Others v Slovakia, Appl. No. 32881/04, judgment of 28 April 2009.
Szabo and Vissy v Hungary, Appl. No. 37138/14, judgment of 12 January 2016.

A. Rationale and Policy Underpinnings

Article 5 GDPR lays down all the key principles providing the basis for the protection of personal data: lawfulness, fairness and transparency; purpose limitation; data minimisation; accuracy; storage limitation; integrity and confidentiality; and accountability. Certain principles are further developed in other parts of the Regulation. That is the case for the transparency principle (Article 5(1)(a)) which takes the form of a duty to inform data subjects (Articles 12 and following), as well as for the integrity and confidentiality principle (Article 5(1)(f) which is elaborated in Articles 32 and following), and for the accountability principle (Article 5(2)) which is elaborated in, inter alia, Articles 24 and 25).

Data protection fundamental principles have not been substantially modified compared with the other rules governing this field for several decades. The principles laid down in the 1980 OECD Guidelines[1] and in the Convention 108 of 1981 have demonstrated their capacity to stand the test of time: 'More than 30 years of practical application have proven these principles to be sound'.[2] These principles could indeed be applied in different technical, economic and social contexts. 'So far nobody has been able to claim convincingly that the substantial principles of data protection as contained in Article 6 of the Data Protection Directive 95/46—and in Article 5 of the Convention 108—must be amended'.[3] In consequence, the GDPR does not make fundamental changes to these principles. Nonetheless, certain adjustments and additions have been made in the GDPR, as shown in the following commentary.

---

[1] OECD Guidelines 2013. [2] Kotschy 2016, p. 277. See also de Terwangne 2014.
[3] Kotschy 2016, p. 277.

B. Legal Background

1. EU legislation

Article 6(1) DPD contained virtually the same principles as Article 5 GDPR. It was entitled 'Principles relating to data quality', although it dealt with more than just data quality. It set out principles relating to the lawfulness and fairness of processing; purpose limitation; data minimisation; the accuracy of data; and storage limitation. All these principles were formulated very similarly to the GDPR. Contrary to Article 5 GDPR, Article 6 DPD omitted mention of the principle of integrity and confidentiality, which is arguably logical since this provision was dedicated to data quality—even if certain principles contained therein went beyond the mere matter of data quality. In contrast, Article 5 GDPR is entitled 'Principles relating to processing of personal data' and has a wider scope. Provisions on the integrity and confidentiality of processing were found in Articles 16 and 17 DPD. No accountability principle was stated as such but Article 6(2) DPD clarified all the same that '[i]t shall be for the controller to ensure that paragraph 1 is complied with'.

Article 4 EUDPR contains provisions that are essentially identical to those of Article 5 GDPR, and the former should be interpreted in the same way as the latter (see too recital 5 EUDPR). In contrast, the equivalent principles set out in Article 4 LED, while largely similar to their GDPR and EUDPR counterparts, contain some differences (highlighted in the analysis below), so that care must be taken when applying to them a line of interpretation derived from the GDPR or EUDPR.

2. International instruments

The fundamental principles relating to data protection have been set forth from the very beginning in the international instruments protecting individuals with regard to processing of personal data. Article 5 of Convention 108 inspired Article 6 DPD, which virtually replicated its provisions while adding certain complements, and which in turn has served as a basis for Article 5 GDPR. Article 5 of Convention 108 contains the same principles relating to the lawfulness and fairness of processing; purpose limitation; data minimisation; accuracy of data; and storage limitation. Article 7 entitled 'Data security' requires appropriate security measures to be taken for the protection of personal data 'against accidental or unauthorised destruction or accidental loss as well as against unauthorised access, alteration or dissemination'. There is, however, no specific trace of the accountability principle in the Convention.

The Modernised Convention 108 brings new elements in relation to these last two points. The security requirement is slightly rewritten to state that: 'Each Party shall provide that the controller, and, where applicable the processor, takes appropriate security measures against risks such as accidental or unauthorised access to, destruction, loss, use, modification or disclosure of personal data' (Article 7(1)). It is supplemented by a new data breach notification duty (Article 7(2)). The accountability principle appears in the new Article 10(1) which states that parties shall provide that controllers and processors must take all appropriate measures to comply with the obligations of the Convention as originally adopted and be able to demonstrate their compliance.

3. Case law

The CJEU ruled in the *Bara* case[4] that the requirement of fair processing of personal data mandates that a public administration informs data subjects when it transfers their personal data to another public administration. The Court has also ruled in *Schecke*[5] that a legal obligation to process personal data (*in casu* to publish personal data on every beneficiary of EU agricultural funds) must respect the principle of proportionality (which is part of the requirement for a legitimate purpose). The Court has examined the respect for this principle of proportionality in several cases, one of the most well-known being the *Digital Rights Ireland* case.[6] In that case, the Court found that this principle was not respected. It notably stated that there should be criteria to determine the relevant data as regards the purpose of the processing, as well as to determine the appropriate time-limit for the data retention. The Court went even further in the *Tele2* case,[7] where it stated that legislation prescribing a general and indiscriminate retention of personal data exceeds the limits of what is strictly necessary and cannot be considered as justified. Proportionality considerations also come to the fore in the recent *TK* case[8] where the Court has been asked to assess, inter alia, whether video surveillance is excessive or inappropriate with respect to Article 6(1)(e) DPD where the controller is able to take other measures to protect the legitimate interest in question.

The ECtHR has repeatedly ruled that processing of personal data may in particular circumstances constitute an interference with the data subject's right to respect for private life under Article 8(1) of the European Convention on Human Rights ('ECHR').[9] To be justified, such an interference must, inter alia, be in accordance with the law (Article 8(2) ECHR), which can be correlated with the requirement for lawful processing. This law must be foreseeable as to its effects. In the *Rotaru* case,[10] the Court indicated that, to be foreseeable, domestic law must lay down limits on the powers of the authorities: the law must define the type of information that can be processed, the categories of persons on whom information may be collected, the circumstances in which such measures may be taken, the persons allowed to access these data and the limits of retention of these data.

Concerning the fairness and transparency principle, the ECtHR considers that the collection and storage of personal information relating to telephone, email and internet usage, without the data subject's knowledge, amounts to an interference with his or her right to respect for private life and correspondence within the meaning of Article 8(1) ECHR.[11] The Court has also stated that data subjects have a qualified right of access to their data.[12] In the *M.S.* case, the Court added to this transparency requirement the necessity that operations done with personal data (such as communication of the data to a third party) are within the reasonable expectations of the data subject. The Court noted that the further use of the data at stake pursued a different purpose that was beyond the expectations of the applicant and concluded that this amounted to an interference with the applicant's right to private life.[13]

In the *S. and Marper* case,[14] the Court affirmed that data processing which interferes with rights under Article 8(1) ECHR must be proportionate, that is to say appropriate in

---

[4] Case C-201/14, *Bara*, paras. 34 et seq.
[5] Joined Cases C-92/09 and 93/09, *Schecke*, paras. 86–89.
[6] Joined Cases C-293/12 and C-594/12, *Digital Rights Ireland*.
[7] Joined Cases C-203/15 and C-698/15, *Tele2*, para. 107. [8] Case C-708/18, *TK*.
[9] See generally Bygrave 2014, pp. 86 ff. [10] ECtHR, *Rotaru v Romania*.
[11] ECtHR, *Copland v UK*. [12] See e.g. ECtHR, *Haralambie v Romania*; ECtHR, *Gaskin v UK*.
[13] ECtHR, *M.S. v Sweden*, para. 35. [14] ECtHR, *S. and Marper v UK*.

relation to the legitimate aims pursued and necessary in the sense that there are no other appropriate and less intrusive measures with regard to the interests, rights and freedoms of data subjects or society. Moreover, the processing should not lead to a disproportionate interference with these individual or collective interests in relation to the benefits expected from the controller. In particular, the retention of the data must be proportionate in relation to the purpose of collection and must be limited in time.[15] As stated by the Court in *S. and Marper*: 'The domestic law should ... ensure that such data are relevant and not excessive in relation to the purposes for which they are stored; and preserved in a form which permits identification of the data subjects for no longer than is required for the purpose for which those data are stored'.[16]

C. Analysis

1. Lawfulness, fairness and transparency principle—Article 5(1)(a)

The first basic principle regarding data protection is that personal data be 'processed lawfully, fairly and in a transparent manner in relation to the data subject'.

As in the DPD, the requirement that data processing must be *lawful* essentially means that it respects all applicable legal requirements (for example the obligation of professional secrecy if applicable). Article 6 GDPR has been re-titled 'lawfulness of processing' rather than 'criteria for making data processing legitimate' as in the DPD, and one may find in this provision the core conditions for processing to be lawful. In fact, Article 6(1) GDPR states that processing shall be lawful only if and to the extent that at least one of the conditions it lists applies.[17] In the same way, Article 8 LED sets out the conditions required for processing to be lawful in this field. Following the comment made by the European Union Agency for Fundamental Rights and the Council of Europe,[18] the principle of lawful processing is also to be understood by reference to conditions for lawful limitations of the right to data protection or of the right to respect for private life in light of Article 52(1) of the Charter of Fundamental Rights of the European Union ('CFR') and of Article 8(2) ECHR. Accordingly, to be considered as lawful, processing of personal data should be in accordance with the law, should pursue a legitimate purpose and be necessary and proportionate in a democratic society in order to achieve that purpose.

Fair processing implies that data have not been obtained nor otherwise processed through unfair means, by deception or without the data subject's knowledge.[19] For the sake of clarity, the GDPR authors decided to explicitly include the transparency principle with the requirement that data be processed lawfully and fairly, whereas before the GDPR commentators had read the transparency requirement into the notion of fairness.[20]

The *transparency* principle is explained in recital 39, which starts by specifying that it 'should be transparent to natural persons that personal data concerning them are collected, used, consulted or otherwise processed'. The recital adds that data subjects should know 'to what extent the personal data are or will be processed'. It is not clear what is covered by this phrase, which does not correspond to any specific information requirement. Recital 39

---

[15] See also ECtHR, *Szabo and Vissy v Hungary*. [16] ECtHR, *S. and Marper v UK*, para. 103.
[17] See further the commentary on Art. 6 in this volume. [18] FRA 2014, pp. 64 et seq.
[19] See for a case of unfair processing: ECtHR, *K.H. and Others v Slovakia*.
[20] See e.g. FRA 2014, p. 76 ('Fair processing means transparency of processing, especially vis-à-vis data subjects'); Bygrave 2014, p. 147.

goes on to mention the quality of the information to give to data subjects: it should be easily accessible and easy to understand. To this end, clear and plain language should be used. Moreover, the fairness principle implies that special attention should be paid to the clarity of the language used if addressing information specifically to children. Recital 39 also mentions the content of the information to give in order to be transparent.

Such elements concerning the quality and content of this information duty are the subject of Articles 12–14 dedicated to 'Transparency and modalities'.[21] Certain aspects are more connected to the fairness requirement. This is notably the case where recital 39 indicates that natural persons should be made aware of risks and safeguards in relation to the processing of personal data. One does not find such a requirement in the information obligations in Articles 13 and 14. However, it is difficult to imagine such a requirement to inform about risks concretely implemented. There is—and this could seem logical—no express transparency requirement in the LED since in most cases systematic transparency would hamper the efficiency of crime prevention activity or of the criminal investigation of public authorities. However, fairness of processing is still required and may imply a certain dose of transparency.[22]

2. Purpose limitation principle—Article 5(1)(b)

The purpose limitation principle has long been regarded as a cornerstone of data protection and a prerequisite for most other fundamental requirements. This principle requires data to be collected for specified, explicit and legitimate purposes (the 'purpose specification' dimension)[23] and not further processed in a manner that is incompatible with those purposes (the 'compatible use' dimension).[24] Purposes for processing personal data should be determined from the very beginning, at the time of the collection of the personal data. The processing of personal data for undefined or unlimited purposes is unlawful since it does not enable the scope of the processing to be precisely delimited. The purposes of data processing must also be unambiguous and clearly expressed instead of being kept hidden.[25] Finally, the purposes must be legitimate, which means that they may not entail a disproportionate interference with the rights, freedoms and interests at stake, in the name of the interests of the data controller:[26]

What is considered a legitimate purpose depends on the circumstances as the objective is to ensure that a balancing of all rights, freedoms and interests at stake is made in each instance; the right to the protection of personal data on the one hand, and the protection of other rights on the other hand, as, for example, between the interests of the data subject and the interests of the controller or of society.[27]

In all cases, data processing serving an unlawful purpose (i.e. contrary to the law) cannot be considered to be based on a legitimate purpose.

The second dimension of the purpose limitation principle implies that the controller may perform on these data all the operations that may be considered as compatible with the initial purposes. This notion of 'compatible' processing of data has raised numerous questions in practice. The authors of the GDPR have sought to mark it out better. Thus,

---

[21] See further the commentaries on Arts. 12 to 14 in this volume.
[22] See also Art. 13 LED ('Information to be made available or given to the data subject') and Art. 14 LED ('Right of access by the data subject').
[23] WP29 2013, pp. 11 and 12.   [24] Ibid., pp. 12 and 13.   [25] Ibid., p. 39.
[26] Boulanger et al. 1997.   [27] Explanatory Report Convention 108 2018, p.8.

Article 6(4) offers a series of criteria to determine whether the processing for a purpose other than that for which the personal data have been collected is to be considered as compatible with this initial purpose.[28] Account should be taken of the possible link between both purposes, of the context in which the personal data have been collected in particular regarding the relationship between data subjects and the controller, of the nature of the personal data (ordinary or sensitive), of the possible consequences of the intended further processing for data subjects, and of the existence of appropriate safeguards.[29]

Another new element of the GDPR is the clarification that processing personal data for a purpose other than that for which they have been collected is allowed in certain circumstances even if this new purpose is not compatible with the first one. Indeed, the original Commission Proposal for the GDPR opened up this possibility very widely, which would have reduced the purpose limitation principle to the bare bones. The Council initially wanted to go even further by proposing to authorise further processing for incompatible purposes if done by the same controller and provided that the controller's or a third party's legitimate interests prevailed over the data subject's interests.[30] This proposal, which was heavily criticised,[31] would have rendered the purpose limitation principle well and truly meaningless. The final text has come back to the protective aim of the purpose limitation principle but softens it in the two following cases: if the data subject consents to the new incompatible purpose or if the processing is based on a Union or Member State law.[32] Article 4(2) LED permits the processing of data by public authorities for the purposes of prevention, investigation or prosecution of criminal offences even if those data were initially collected for a different purpose, but on condition that the controller is authorised to process such personal data in accordance with Union or Member State law and that processing is necessary and proportionate to the new purpose in accordance with Union or Member State law.

Finally, certain reuses of data are a priori considered as compatible provided certain conditions are met,[33] as previously permitted under the DPD. These are 'further processing for archiving purposes in the public interest, scientific or historical research purposes or statistical purposes'.[34] These categories of further processing are slightly narrower than before since the previous 'historical purpose' has given place to 'archiving purposes'—and only 'in the public interest'—and to 'historical research purposes'. The 'scientific purpose' is also reduced to 'scientific research purposes'. Some elucidation of these terms is to be found in a recommendation of the Council of Europe which states that processing of data for scientific research purposes aims at providing researchers with information contributing to an understanding of phenomena in varied scientific fields (epidemiology, psychology, economics, sociology, linguistics, political science, criminology, etc.) in view of establishing permanent principles, laws of behaviour or patterns of causality which transcend all the individuals to whom they apply.[35] The category of data processing for statistical purposes has remained unchanged.[36] 'Statistical purpose'

---

[28] This list is based on the one elaborated by the WP29: see WP29 2013, p. 40.
[29] Art. 6(4) GDPR. See also rec. 50 GDPR.
[30] This proposal was aimed at facilitating 'Big Data' operations: see Burton et al. 2016, p. 6.
[31] See notably WP29 Press Release 2015 and WP29 2013, pp. 36 and 37.
[32] See the commentary on Art. 6 in this volume.
[33] These conditions are developed in Art. 89(1) GDPR.   [34] Ibid., Art. 5(1)(b).
[35] Explanatory Report Convention 108 2018, p. 3.
[36] See the detailed regime for processing for statistical purposes in COM Recommendation 1997.

refers to the elaboration of statistical surveys or the production of statistical, aggregated results.[37] Statistics aim at analysing and characterising mass or collective phenomena in a considered population.[38]

The LED has also introduced the notion of archiving purpose in the public interest but has kept the wording of the DPD and Framework Decision 2008/977/JAI as regards 'scientific, statistical or historical' use.[39] Article 4(3) LED states that processing falling within the scope of this text may include such uses for the purposes of prevention, investigation, detection or prosecution of criminal offences, provided appropriate safeguards for the rights and freedoms of data subjects are put in place.

3. Data minimisation principle—Article 5(1)(c)

As was the case under the DPD, processed personal data must be adequate, relevant and limited to what is necessary in relation to the purposes for which they are processed. However, under the GDPR personal data must be 'limited to what is necessary' instead of being 'not excessive' as in the DPD. The LED, though, has kept the wording of the DPD; thus, Article 4(1)(c) LED states that data must be 'not excessive'. This difference of terms should not have a substantial effect on the scope of the data minimisation principle. Recital 39 GDPR specifies that it requires, in particular, that personal data should only be processed if the purposes cannot reasonably be fulfilled by other means. Furthermore, this necessity requirement not only refers to the quantity, but also to the quality of personal data. It is accordingly clear that one may not process an excessively large amount of personal data (asking an employee for her complete medical file to assess her capacity to work, for example). But one may not process a single datum either if this would entail a disproportionate interference in the data subject's rights and interests (for example, collecting information about private drug consumption from a job applicant).[40] The 'limited to what is necessary' criterion also requires 'ensuring that the period for which the personal data are stored is limited to a strict minimum' (see the storage limitation principle below).

4. Accuracy principle—Article 5(1)(d)

The requirement that data be accurate and, where necessary, kept up to date was already present in the DPD and in Convention 108, and has been maintained in the GDPR. All inaccurate data should be rectified or erased. The controller must take every reasonable step to ensure respect of this accuracy principle. The GDPR clarifies that this intervention must be done without delay.

Article 7(2) LED requires that competent authorities take all reasonable steps to ensure that personal data which are inaccurate, incomplete or no longer up to date are not transmitted or made available. These authorities must, as far as practicable, verify the quality of data before communicating them. Article 7(2) LED goes further in specifically providing in the field of police activity that: 'As far as possible, in all transmissions of personal data, necessary information enabling the receiving competent authority to assess the degree of

---

[37] Ibid., Appendix, point 1.   [38] Explanatory Report Convention 108 2018, p. 9.
[39] Council Framework Decision 2008/977/JAI.
[40] See Explanatory Report Convention 108 2018, p. 9, for an explanation of the notion of 'excessive' data.

accuracy, completeness and reliability of personal data, and the extent to which they are up to date shall be added'.

5. Storage limitation principle—Article 5(1)(e)

This provision represents no real change to the prohibition in the DPD against storing personal data in a form which permits identification of data subjects beyond the time necessary to achieve the purposes of processing. However, there is a new element in recital 39, which invites controllers to establish time limits for erasure or for a periodic review. This will ensure that the personal data are not kept longer than necessary.

Article 4(1)(e) LED provides for the same prohibition and Article 5 LED also mandates that appropriate time limits be established for the erasure of the data or for a periodic review of the need for the storage of the data. The text requires procedural measures to be adopted to ensure that those time limits are observed. Article 25 GDPR and Article 20 LED must be taken into account here since they mandate that controllers implement appropriate technical and organisational measures for ensuring notably that, by default, the legitimate period of storage of personal data be respected. Such measures could be expiry dates determined for each set of data.

Moreover, the storage limitation principle permits the storage of personal data for longer periods if it is for archiving purposes in the public interest, scientific or historical research purposes or statistical purposes and is subject to implementation of appropriate technical and organisational measures in order to safeguard the rights and freedoms of the data subject.

6. Integrity and confidentiality principle—Article 5(1)(f)

Under the title of 'integrity and confidentiality' may be found the crucial requirement of security that is now included in the list of fundamental principles of data protection. Personal data must be processed in a manner that ensures their appropriate security, 'including protection against unauthorised or unlawful processing and against accidental loss, destruction or damage, using appropriate technical or organisational measures'. This principle mirrors more or less the terms of Article 17 DPD. A whole section of Chapter IV of the GDPR dedicated to controllers and processors develops this duty of security.[41] This duty includes—and this is new—the requirement to notify personal data breaches to the supervisory authority and in certain cases to the data subjects too.

The LED contains the same articulation of the principle of integrity of data appearing in the list of fundamental protection principles (Article 4(1)(f)) and provisions developing further the security duty in a separate section (Articles 29–31).

7. Accountability principle—Article 5(2)

The list of fundamental principles of data protection ends with the statement that the controller shall be responsible for compliance with all the previous principles. A new element is introduced in comparison to the DPD: the controller must now be able to demonstrate that the processing is in compliance with these legal rules (accountability).[42] This requirement not only to ensure but also to be able to demonstrate compliance to

---

[41] See the commentary on Arts. 32–34 in this volume.   [42] WP29 2010.

GDPR is developed in Article 24 dedicated to the responsibility of the controller.[43] Much important work on accountability has also been done by think-tanks such as the Information Accountability Foundation.[44]

Select Bibliography

International agreements

OECD Guidelines 2013: Organisation for Economic Co-operation and Development, 'The OECD Privacy Framework' (2013).

EU legislation

Council Framework Decision 2008/977/JHA of 27 November 2008 on the protection of personal data processed in the framework of police and judicial cooperation in criminal matters, OJ 2008 L 350/60.

Academic writings

Boulanger et al. 1997: Boulanger, de Terwangne, Léonard, Louveaux, Moreaux and Poullet, 'La Protection des données à caractère personnel en droit communautaire', *Journal des tribunaux— Droit Européen* (1997), 145.

Burton et al. 2016: Burton, De Boel, Kuner, Pateraki, Cadiot and Hoffman, 'The Final European Union General Data Protection Regulation', *Bloomberg Law: Privacy & Data Security* (12 February 2016).

Bygrave 2014: Bygrave, *Data Privacy Law: An International Perspective* (OUP 2014).

De Terwangne 2014: 'The Revision of the Council of Europe Convention 108 for the Protection of Individuals as Regards the Automatic Processing of Personal Data', 28 *International Review of Law, Computers & Technology* (special edition *The Future of Data Protection: Collapse or Revival?*) (2014), 118.

Kotschy 2014: Kotschy, 'The Proposal for a new General Data Protection Regulation—Problems Solved?', 4(4) *International Data Privacy Law* (2014), 274.

Papers of data protection authorities

WP29 2010: Article 29 Working Party, 'Opinion 3/2010 on the Principle of Accountability' (WP 173, 13 July 2010).

WP29 2013: Article 29 Working Party, 'Opinion 03/2013 on Purpose Limitation' (WP 203, 2 April 2013).

WP29 Press Release 2015: Article 29 Working Party, 'Press Release on Chapter II of the Draft Regulation for the March JHA Council' (17 March 2015).

Reports and recommendations

COM Recommendation 1997: Committee of Ministers of the Council of Europe, 'Recommendation Concerning the Protection of Personal Data Collected and Processed for Statistical Purposes' (Rec(1997)18, 30 September 1997).

De Terwangne and Moiny, 'The Lacunae of the Convention for the Protection of Individuals with Regard to Automatic Processing of Personal Data (ETS No. 108) Resulting from Technological

---

[43] See further the commentary on Art. 24 in this volume.
[44] See Information Accountability Foundation website.

Developments' (2010), available at http://www.coe.int/t/dghl/standardsetting/dataprotection/TPD_documents/T-PD-BUR_2010_09_en.pdf.

Explanatory Report Convention 108 2018: Council of Europe, 'Explanatory Report to the Protocol Amending the Convention for the Protection of Individuals with Regard to the Automatic Processing of Personal Data' (10 October 2018), available at https://rm.coe.int/cets-223-explanatory-report-to-the-protocol-amending-the-convention-fo/16808ac91a.

FRA 2014: European Union Agency for Fundamental Rights, European Court of Human Rights, Council of Europe, and European Data Protection Supervisor (eds.), *Handbook on European Data Protection Law* (Publications Office of the European Union 2014).

Others

Information Accountability Foundation Website: Information Accountability Foundation, available at https://informationaccountability.org.

Article 6. Lawfulness of processing

WALTRAUT KOTSCHY

1. Processing shall be lawful only if and to the extent that at least one of the following applies:
    (a) the data subject has given consent to the processing of his or her personal data for one or more specific purposes;
    (b) processing is necessary for the performance of a contract to which the data subject is party or in order to take steps at the request of the data subject prior to entering into a contract;
    (c) processing is necessary for compliance with a legal obligation to which the controller is subject;
    (d) processing is necessary in order to protect the vital interests of the data subject or of another natural person;
    (e) processing is necessary for the performance of a task carried out in the public interest or in the exercise of official authority vested in the controller;
    (f) processing is necessary for the purposes of the legitimate interests pursued by the controller or by a third party, except where such interests are overridden by the interests or fundamental rights and freedoms of the data subject which require protection of personal data, in particular where the data subject is a child.
    Point (f) of the first subparagraph shall not apply to processing carried out by public authorities in the performance of their tasks.
2. Member States may maintain or introduce more specific provisions to adapt the application of the rules of this Regulation with regard to processing for compliance with points (c) and (e) of paragraph 1 by determining more precisely specific requirements for the processing and other measures to ensure lawful and fair processing including for other specific processing situations as provided for in Chapter IX.
3. The basis for the processing referred to in point (c) and (e) of paragraph 1 shall be laid down by:
    (a) Union law; or
    (b) Member State law to which the controller is subject.
    The purpose of the processing shall be determined in that legal basis or, as regards the processing referred to in point (e) of paragraph 1, shall be necessary for the performance of a task carried out in the public interest or in the exercise of official authority vested in the controller. That legal basis may contain specific provisions to adapt the application of rules of this Regulation, inter alia: the general conditions governing the lawfulness of processing by the controller; the types of data which are subject to the processing; the data subjects concerned; the entities to, and the purposes for which, the personal data may be disclosed; the purpose limitation; storage periods; and processing operations and processing procedures, including measures to ensure lawful and fair processing such as those for other specific processing situations as provided for in Chapter IX. The Union or the Member State law shall meet an objective of public interest and be proportionate to the legitimate aim pursued.
4. Where the processing for a purpose other than that for which the personal data have been collected is not based on the data subject's consent or on a Union or Member State law which constitutes a necessary and proportionate measure in a democratic society to safeguard the objectives referred to in Article 23(1), the controller shall, in order to ascertain whether processing for another purpose is compatible with the purpose for which the personal data are initially collected, take into account, inter alia:
    (a) any link between the purposes for which the personal data have been collected and the purposes of the intended further processing;

(b) the context in which the personal data have been collected, in particular regarding the relationship between data subjects and the controller;
(c) the nature of the personal data, in particular whether special categories of personal data are processed, pursuant to Article 9, or whether personal data related to criminal convictions and offences are processed, pursuant to Article 10;
(d) the possible consequences of the intended further processing for data subjects;
(e) the existence of appropriate safeguards, which may include encryption or pseudonymisation.

Relevant Recitals

(40) In order for processing to be lawful, personal data should be processed on the basis of the consent of the data subject concerned or some other legitimate basis, laid down by law, either in this Regulation or in other Union or Member State law as referred to in this Regulation, including the necessity for compliance with the legal obligation to which the controller is subject or the necessity for the performance of a contract to which the data subject is party or in order to take steps at the request of the data subject prior to entering into a contract.

(41) Where this Regulation refers to a legal basis or a legislative measure, this does not necessarily require a legislative act adopted by a parliament, without prejudice to requirements pursuant to the constitutional order of the Member State concerned. However, such a legal basis or legislative measure should be clear and precise and its application should be foreseeable to persons subject to it, in accordance with the case-law of the Court of Justice of the European Union (the 'Court of Justice') and the European Court of Human Rights.

(43) In order to ensure that consent is freely given, consent should not provide a valid legal ground for the processing of personal data in a specific case where there is a clear imbalance between the data subject and the controller, in particular where the controller is a public authority and it is therefore unlikely that consent was freely given in all the circumstances of that specific situation. Consent is presumed not to be freely given if it does not allow separate consent to be given to different personal data processing operations despite it being appropriate in the individual case, or if the performance of a contract, including the provision of a service, is dependent on the consent despite such consent not being necessary for such performance.

(44) Processing should be lawful where it is necessary in the context of a contract or the intention to enter into a contract.

(45) Where processing is carried out in accordance with a legal obligation to which the controller is subject or where processing is necessary for the performance of a task carried out in the public interest or in the exercise of official authority, the processing should have a basis in Union or Member State law. This Regulation does not require a specific law for each individual processing. A law as a basis for several processing operations based on a legal obligation to which the controller is subject or where processing is necessary for the performance of a task carried out in the public interest or in the exercise of an official authority may be sufficient. It should also be for Union or Member State law to determine the purpose of processing. Furthermore, that law could specify the general conditions of this Regulation governing the lawfulness of personal data processing, establish specifications for determining the controller, the type of personal data which are subject to the processing, the data subjects concerned, the entities to which the personal data may be disclosed, the purpose limitations, the storage period and other measures to ensure lawful and fair processing. It should also be for Union or Member State law to determine whether the controller performing a task carried out in the public interest or in the exercise of official authority should be a public authority or another natural or legal person governed by public law, or, where it is in the public interest to do so, including for health purposes such as public health and social protection and the management of health care services, by private law, such as a professional association.

(46) The processing of personal data should also be regarded to be lawful where it is necessary to protect an interest which is essential for the life of the data subject or that of another natural person. Processing of personal data based on the vital interest of another natural person should in principle take place only where the processing cannot be manifestly based on another legal basis. Some types of processing may serve both important grounds of public interest and the vital interests of the data subject as for instance when processing is necessary for humanitarian purposes, including for monitoring epidemics and their spread or in situations of humanitarian emergencies, in particular in situations of natural and man-made disasters.

(47) The legitimate interests of a controller, including those of a controller to which the personal data may be disclosed, or of a third party, may provide a legal basis for processing, provided that the interests or the fundamental rights and freedoms of the data subject are not overriding, taking into consideration the reasonable expectations of data subjects based on their relationship with the controller. Such legitimate interest could exist for example where there is a relevant and appropriate relationship between the data subject and the controller in situations such as where the data subject is a client or in the service of the controller. At any rate the existence of a legitimate interest would need careful assessment including whether a data subject can reasonably expect at the time and in the context of the collection of the personal data that processing for that purpose may take place. The interests and fundamental rights of the data subject could in particular override the interest of the data controller where personal data are processed in circumstances where data subjects do not reasonably expect further processing. Given that it is for the legislator to provide by law for the legal basis for public authorities to process personal data, that legal basis should not apply to the processing by public authorities in the performance of their tasks. The processing of personal data strictly necessary for the purposes of preventing fraud also constitutes a legitimate interest of the data controller concerned. The processing of personal data for direct marketing purposes may be regarded as carried out for a legitimate interest.

(48) Controllers that are part of a group of undertakings or institutions affiliated to a central body may have a legitimate interest in transmitting personal data within the group of undertakings for internal administrative purposes, including the processing of clients' or employees' personal data. The general principles for the transfer of personal data, within a group of undertakings, to an undertaking located in a third country remain unaffected.

(49) The processing of personal data to the extent strictly necessary and proportionate for the purposes of ensuring network and information security, i.e. the ability of a network or an information system to resist, at a given level of confidence, accidental events or unlawful or malicious actions that compromise the availability, authenticity, integrity and confidentiality of stored or transmitted personal data, and the security of the related services offered by, or accessible via, those networks and systems, by public authorities, by computer emergency response teams (CERTs), computer security incident response teams (CSIRTs), by providers of electronic communications networks and services and by providers of security technologies and services, constitutes a legitimate interest of the data controller concerned. This could, for example, include preventing unauthorised access to electronic communications networks and malicious code distribution and stopping 'denial of service' attacks and damage to computer and electronic communication systems.

(50) The processing of personal data for purposes other than those for which the personal data were initially collected should be allowed only where the processing is compatible with the purposes for which the personal data were initially collected. In such a case, no legal basis separate from that which allowed the collection of the personal data is required. If the processing is necessary for the performance of a task carried out in the public interest or in the exercise of official authority vested in the controller, Union or Member State law may determine and specify the tasks and purposes for which the further processing should be regarded as compatible and lawful. Further processing for archiving purposes in the public interest, scientific or historical research purposes or statistical purposes should be considered to be compatible lawful processing

operations. The legal basis provided by Union or Member State law for the processing of personal data may also provide a legal basis for further processing. In order to ascertain whether a purpose of further processing is compatible with the purpose for which the personal data are initially collected, the controller, after having met all the requirements for the lawfulness of the original processing, should take into account, inter alia: any link between those purposes and the purposes of the intended further processing; the context in which the personal data have been collected, in particular the reasonable expectations of data subjects based on their relationship with the controller as to their further use; the nature of the personal data; the consequences of the intended further processing for data subjects; and the existence of appropriate safeguards in both the original and intended further processing operations.

Where the data subject has given consent or the processing is based on Union or Member State law which constitutes a necessary and proportionate measure in a democratic society to safeguard, in particular, important objectives of general public interest, the controller should be allowed to further process the personal data irrespective of the compatibility of the purposes. In any case, the application of the principles set out in this Regulation and in particular the information of the data subject on those other purposes and on his or her rights including the right to object, should be ensured. Indicating possible criminal acts or threats to public security by the controller and transmitting the relevant personal data in individual cases or in several cases relating to the same criminal act or threats to public security to a competent authority should be regarded as being in the legitimate interest pursued by the controller. However, such transmission in the legitimate interest of the controller or further processing of personal data should be prohibited if the processing is not compatible with a legal, professional or other binding obligation of secrecy.

Closely Related Provisions

Article 4(11) (Definition of consent) (see also recital 32); Article 7 (Conditions for consent); Article 8 (Conditions applicable to child's consent); Article 9(2) (Processing of special categories of personal data) (see also recital 51); Article 5 (Principles relating to processing of personal data) (see too recital 39); Article 23 (Restrictions) (see also recital 73); Article 89 (Safeguards relating to processing for archiving, research and statistical purposes) (see too recitals 156–163)

Related Provisions in LED [Directive (EU) 2016/680]

Article 4 (Data processing principles) (see too recital 29); Article 5 (Time-limits for storage and review); Article 8 (Lawfulness of processing) (see too recitals 33–35); Article 9 (Specific processing conditions) (see too recital 36)

Related Provisions in EPD [Directive 2002/58/EC]

Article 5 (Confidentiality of communications); Article 6 (Traffic data); Article 9 (Other location data)

Related Provisions in EUDPR [Regulation (EU) 2018/1725]

Article 3(15) (Definition of consent) (see also recital 26); Article 4 (Principles relating to processing of personal data) (see also recitals 20–21); Article 5 (Lawfulness of processing) (see also recitals 22–23); Article 6 (Processing for another compatible purpose) (see also recital 25); Article 7 (Conditions for consent) (see also recital 26); Article 8 (Conditions applicable to a child's consent in relation to information society services) (see also recital 27); Article 10 (Processing of special categories of personal data) (see also recitals 29–31).

Relevant Case Law

CJEU

Case C-524/06, *Huber v Bundesrepublik Deutschland*, judgment of 16 December 2018 (Grand Chamber) (ECLI:EU:C:2008:724).
Joined Cases C-468/10 and C469/10, *Asociación Nacional de Establecimientos Financieros de Crédito (ASNEF) and Federación de Comercio Electrónico y Marketing Directo (FECEMD) v Administración des Estado*, judgment of 24 November 2011 (ECLI:EU:C:2011:777).
Case C-582/14, *Patrick Breyer v Bundesrepublik Deutschland*, judgment of 10 October 2016 (ECLI:EU:C:2016:779).
C-40/17, *Fashion ID GmbH & Co. KG v Verbraucherzentrale NRW e.V.*, judgment of 29 July 2019 (ECLI:EU:C:2019:629).

ECtHR

Z v Finland, Appl. No. 22009/93, judgment of 25 February 1997.
Von Hannover v Germany, Appl. No. 59320/00, judgment of 24 June 2004.

A. Rationale and Policy Underpinnings

1. Article 6(1)

The principle of 'lawful processing', which is one of several data protection principles under Article 5 GDPR, requires that every processing operation involving personal data has a legal basis. Article 6(1) exhaustively stipulates what may constitute such a legal basis. At the same time, it must be kept in mind that legally sound processing of personal data will necessitate fulfilling also *all other* of the core principles for processing personal data set out by Article 5(1).

The choice of the six grounds corresponds to the general rules for lawful limitations on fundamental rights set out in Article 52(1) Charter of Fundamental Rights of the European Union ('CFR') and Article 8(2) European Convention on Human Rights ('ECHR'). Irrespective of the differences in the respective formulations of the ECHR and the CFR,[1] the effect of the corresponding rules in these two legal instruments is to be considered as equivalent in substance, although protection under the CFR may be more extensive than under the ECHR.[2] According to the CFR, the right to data protection may be limited only if this is explicitly foreseen in an EU or Member State law, and if the content of that law complies with the condition of foreseeing only such limitations which

---

[1] The text of Art. 8(2) ECHR deals only with interferences by public authorities. However, States parties to the Convention are under a positive obligation to provide safeguards against private interference: see e.g. ECtHR, *Von Hannover v Germany*. Thus, processing of personal data by private sector controllers has to be included within the scope of data protection, and adequate measures for effective protection of data subjects must be adopted by the state.
[2] According to Art. 52(3) CFR, 'the meaning and scope' of rights, which are guaranteed under the Charter as well as under the ECHR, 'shall be the same' as those laid down by the ECHR, but EU law may foresee a more extensive protection.

are necessary and apt to achieve the defined purpose of processing, which can be either a public interest or the protection of the rights and freedoms of others. Additionally, the limitation foreseen needs to be proportional and to respect the essence of the fundamental right to data protection.

The function of Article 6(1) GDPR, seen in relation to Article 52(1) CFR, is to specify in more detail what the terms 'objectives of general interest (recognised by the Union)' and 'necessity to protect the rights and freedoms of others' mean in the context of data protection.

2. Article 6(2)

Article 6(2) represents a compromise between the aim of harmonising data protection law throughout the whole Union, which would actually exclude any Member State law in this area, and the fact that more precise rules in the specific areas of application of data protection are advantageous for the legal subjects and cannot be achieved solely by Union law within a reasonable time frame. As harmonisation was felt to be particularly important in the private sector, empowerment of Member States' legislators is limited to rules for the public sector (Article 6(1)(e)) and to special legal obligations for controllers in both sectors (Article 6(1)(c)). For processing on grounds of Article 6(1)(f), which is central to private sector processing, there is no general empowerment for Member States to create data protection rules. Only in those specific areas of processing listed in Chapter IX GDPR may Member State legislation maintain existing rules or adopt new rules. In all cases covered by Article 6(2), Member State law maintaining or introducing more specific data protection rules must fully comply with the rules under the GDPR.

3. Article 6(3)

This provision has two functions: first, to clarify that only legal provisions under EU or Member State law—not foreign law—can provide a legal basis for processing based on Article 6(1)(c) or (e); and secondly, to give guidance as to the appropriate content of such EU or Member State legal provisions. The first-named function is particularly acute in times of globalisation, where controllers acting under different legal systems may be confronted with conflicting legal obligations. Article 6(3) confirms the priority of EU data protection law over obligations derived from foreign legal provisions to which the controller might be subject outside the territorial applicability of the GDPR.

Additionally, Article 6(3) elaborates on those special topics which should be dealt with in provisions of Union or Member State law specifying the conditions for processing based on Article 6(1)(c) or (e). It admonishes legislators to include especially clear statements on the concrete purpose of processing, on the types of data which may be processed for this purpose, on the data subjects concerned, on lawful recipients of data, and, in general, to introduce 'measures to ensure lawful and fair processing'.

4. Article 6(4)

The purpose limitation principle (set out in Article 5(1)(b)) requires that the purpose of processing shall be defined at the time of collection of the data and prescribes, as a point of departure, that all consecutive processing operations shall not exceed the defined purpose. This rule is specified and enhanced by acknowledging that the scope of 'one' defined purpose shall include processing operations that are 'compatible' with the initially named purpose.

The concept of 'compatibility' is not defined in more detail in Article 5(1)(b)—a shortcoming remedied by Article 6(4) which is new in comparison to the DPD. With sharing and repurposing of personal data becoming increasingly prevalent, more guidance on what may be considered as 'compatible further use' was deemed necessary. The WP29 released an opinion on the topic of purpose limitation in 2013 which deals extensively also with the concept of 'compatibility'.[3] The main ideas of this opinion concerning the assessment of 'compatibility' are reflected in Article 6(4).

Moreover, Article 6(4) indirectly deals with the situation that 'incompatible further use' of data might exceptionally be necessary or intended and regulates the conditions for such use. These conditions are logically derived from the fact that incompatible further use is an interference with the principle of purpose limitation and may therefore only take place in compliance with Article 23 GDPR. The latter provision deals with legal restrictions of rights and obligations under, inter alia, Article 5 GDPR, and displaces Article 6(1) in this respect as the relevant provision for determining the bases of lawful processing.

B. Legal Background

1. EU legislation

Article 6(1) is based on and nearly identical to Article 7 DPD. Long experience in applying the latter provisions to the daily practice of information processing has confirmed that the list they contain is comprehensive and serves well, even under rapidly changing technological-organisational developments. Thus, only minor changes were enacted.

2. International instruments

In 1981, the Council of Europe Convention 108 formulated the principles for lawful processing of personal data for the first time in international law. These principles were taken over into Article 6 DPD and, subsequently, into Article 5 GDPR. The Convention did not, however, formulate a list of concrete legal bases for data processing. Developing an exhaustive list of concrete reasons for lawful data processing is one of the special achievements of EU data protection law.

Even the Modernised Convention 108 eschews such a list. In Article 5(2), it adopts the formulation chosen in Article 8(2) CFR, mentioning only 'consent' and 'some legitimate basis laid down by law'.

As concerns 'compatible further use', this qualification of the purpose limitation principle was always inherent in Article 5 of Convention 108, and it has been carried over into Article 5(4) of the Modernised Convention 108. 'Incompatible' further use is subject to Article 11(1) of the Modernised Convention 108, a provision similar to Article 23 GDPR. There is, however, no equivalent to Article 6(4) GDPR in either the original or modernised version of Convention 108.

[3] WP29 2013.

3. Case law

The CJEU has struck down attempts to modify the application of Article 7 DPD by way of national legal provisions, especially concerning limitations on Article 7(f). With reference to its earlier judgment in *ASNEF*,[4] the CJEU remarked:

> The Court has held that Article 7 of Directive 95/46 sets out an exhaustive and restrictive list of cases in which the processing of personal data can be regarded as being lawful and that the Member States cannot add new principles relating to the lawfulness of the processing of personal data or impose additional requirements that have the effect of amending the scope of one of the six principles provided for in that article.[5]

In the *Huber* case,[6] the CJEU interpreted Article 7(e) DPD in the light of the requirement that processing is 'necessary' for the defined purpose(s). Data about the applicant, an Austrian citizen living in Germany, had been entered into a register, which was operated by German authorities on foreigners only, including non-German EU citizens. These data were used by the German authorities to different ends, inter alia, to apply the legislation relating to the right of residence, for statistical purposes, and for the purposes of fighting crime. There was no comparable database for German nationals. The applicant successfully claimed discrimination. One of the questions put to the Court was whether this central register was compatible with the DPD insofar as the legitimacy of processing personal data depends on whether it is 'necessary for the performance of a task carried out in the public interest or in the exercise of official authority'. The Court dealt with the question of 'necessity' of processing in the context of the right of residence and use for statistical purposes. It pointed out that the right of residence of a Union citizen in the territory of a Member State other than his/her own is not unconditional and may be subject to limitations. Therefore, the processing by a centralised register of personal data in order to apply the legislation relating to the right of residence satisfied the requirement of necessity within the meaning of the DPD provided that only the data necessary for that purpose were processed and that the centralised nature of the register enabled the legislation to be more effectively applied. However, the Court took the view that statistics did not necessitate the collection and storage of individualised information as in this case. Accordingly, such processing of personal data did not satisfy the requirement of necessity within the meaning of the DPD.[7]

In *Fashion ID*,[8] the CJEU held that in a situation of joint controllership (i.e. where there are two or more controllers in respect of a particular data-processing operation or set of such operations) and where the processing of personal data is sought justified under the 'legitimate interest' condition pursuant to Article 7(f) DPD, 'it is necessary that *each of those controllers should pursue a legitimate interest*, within the meaning of Article 7(f) of Directive 95/46, through those processing operations in order for those operations to be justified in that regard'.[9]

---

[4] Joined Cases C-468/10 and C469/10, *ASNEF*.   [5] Case C-582/14, *Breyer*, para. 57.
[6] Case C-524/06, *Huber*.
[7] Necessity of the central register for purposes of fighting crime was not examined by the Court in the light of the DPD, as it did not cover matters of public security or the activities of the state in areas of criminal law.
[8] Case C-40/17, *Fashion ID*.   [9] Ibid., para. 96 (emphasis added).

C. Analysis

1. Article 6(1)

1.1 General remarks

Every use of personal data is a potential interference with, or limitation of the right to, data protection. The GDPR, which only deals with the use of data in the form of 'processing by automated means' and 'processing in filing systems',[10] names six grounds in Article 6(1) for making the processing of personal data lawful. In a concrete case, controllers must be able to demonstrate that at least one of these grounds applies to their processing of personal data. The list of legal grounds must be understood as exhaustive and final. As far as Member States' legislators are, at all, allowed to act under Article 6(1),[11] all legislative activities must keep within the strict boundaries it sets.[12] There is no ranking between Article 6(1)(a)–(f) in the sense that one ground has normative priority over the others.[13] However, in the private sector, consent (Article 6(1)(a)) may in practice play a salient role as a potential substitute whenever there is no contractual context, no detailed legal rules about a fitting legal basis or the scope of 'legitimate interests of the controller or of a third party' is particularly difficult to assess. This may also be the reason why it was deemed necessary in the GDPR to define valid consent more extensively than the other legal grounds for processing and—compared to the DPD—to add two articles (Articles 7 and 8) dealing with specific aspects of consenting.

1.2 The bases for lawful processing

1.2.1 Consent of the data subject

According to Article 6(1)(a) GDPR, processing personal data is lawful if the data subject has allowed for processing in a way which satisfies the conditions for valid consent as defined in Article 4(11) and in Articles 7 and 8 GDPR.[14]

Article 6(1)(a) is not substantively different from its antecedent, Article 7(a) DPD.[15] The requirement that consent be 'unambiguous' is now a defining element for valid consent in Article 4(11) and is therefore no longer mentioned in point (a) of the list of reasons for lawful processing.

In addition to the conditions required for valid consent, there are general limits to the use of consent as a legal basis for processing. As allowing for the processing of one's data involves waiving a fundamental right,[16] problems could arise if harmful consequences

---

[10] See further the commentary on Art. 2(1) in this volume on the material scope of application of the GDPR. See also the commentary on Arts. 4(2) and (6) in this volume regarding the definition of 'processing' and 'filing system'.

[11] See Art. 6(2) and (3) GDPR.

[12] Member States were also not permitted to introduce changes or additions to the six grounds for processing personal data under Art. 7 DPD (the direct antecedent to Art. 6 GDPR).

[13] See too WP29 2014, p. 10.

[14] As 'consent' is a declaration of intent, its validity depends, moreover, on the general prerequisites for valid declarations of intent under the law, which means that the person declaring his/her intent must be '*sui iuris*' (i.e. of mature age and with full mental capacity). Art. 8 deals with the validity of 'under age' consent (children's consent) in certain circumstances. For further explication of what constitutes valid consent under the GDPR, see the commentaries on Arts. 4(11), 7 and 8 in this volume.

[15] Art. 7(a) DPD stipulated that processing is lawful if 'the data subject has unambiguously given his consent'.

[16] Contrary to Art. 8(2) ECHR, Art. 8(2) CFR explicitly refers to 'consent' as a possible legal basis for processing personal data. The jurisprudence of the ECtHR pursuant to Art. 8 ECHR shows, however, that

for the protected individual are the result. The WP29 stressed that consent is not an appropriate legal basis for all sorts of processing: 'Where the elements that constitute valid consent are unlikely to be present' and where the data subject cannot decide in the absence of social, financial, psychological or other pressure, the element of 'free' consenting is not secured and consent would therefore not be valid.[17] Similarly, recital 42 states that '[c]onsent should not be regarded as freely given if the data subject ... is unable to refuse or withdraw consent without detriment'.

As a consequence, the use of consent as a legal basis is usually inappropriate in certain areas. This relates especially to the exercise of authoritative power (see further recital 43), which means that the requirements under Article 6(1)(e) for lawful processing by public authorities usually cannot be replaced by asking individuals for consent. Another area is processing in the context of an employment relationship where the lack of legitimate interest on the side of the employer/controller (Article 6(1)(f)) cannot, in all circumstances, be replaced by acquiring consent from employees.[18]

A further general limitation on the use of consent as a legal basis for processing may exist in the context of linking up a pre-formulated consent clause with a contract, so that concluding the contract automatically results in agreement to the consent clause. The 'freeness' of such a decision is questionable.[19]

Moreover, in contractual or quasi-contractual contexts, the WP29 has been sceptical of mixing the legal bases for processing personal data: 'The two lawful bases for the lawful processing of personal data, i.e. consent and contract cannot be merged and blurred'.[20] Concomitantly, where 'a controller seeks to process personal data that are in fact necessary for the performance of a contract, then consent is not the appropriate lawful basis'.[21] The EDPB takes the same line.[22]

1.2.2 Contract and precontractual relationship

Point (b) has been copied in the GDPR from Article 7 DPD without changes. To the extent that processing data about one's contractual partner (the data subject) is necessary for the fulfilment of a contract by the other contractual partner (the controller), the latter has a legal basis for their processing operations on these data. This is laid down explicitly in Article 6(1)(b), but can also be derived more generally from the fact that the controller, as a contractual partner, has a legal obligation to fulfil their contractual obligations according to general legal principles. Legitimacy of processing for fulfilling a contractual obligation could therefore also be understood as a special case of 'legal obligations' and even of 'legitimate interests of the controller', which would shorten the exhaustive list of reasons for lawful processing in the GDPR considerably. However, tradition in European

---

waiving the right to data protection through consent can also be acceptable under the ECHR: see e.g. ECtHR, *Z v Finland*.

[17] WP29 2011, pp. 15 and 13: '[F]ree consent means a voluntary decision, by an individual in possession of all of his faculties, taken in the absence of coercion of any kind, be it social, financial, psychological or other. Any consent given under the threat of non-treatment or lower quality treatment in a medical situation cannot be considered as "free"'. See too WP 2018, pp. 5 and 7.

[18] WP29 2018, p. 7. See also rec. 43 GDPR.

[19] See the last sentence of rec. 43 GDPR; Albrecht and Jotzo 2017, para. 40; WP29 2016, pp. 8–10. See further the commentary on Arts. 4(11) and 7(4) in this volume.

[20] WP29 2018, p. 8. Thus, the act of entering into a contract is not necessarily the same as giving consent under Art. 6(1)(a) GDPR. See EDPB 2019A, p. 6.

[21] WP29 2018, p. 8.   [22] EDPB 2019A, p. 6.

data protection law has been that these cases are kept separate and have their specific meaning, as is explained further in the context of analysing Article 6(1)(c) and (f).

As to the scope of what is necessary for the performance of a contract, this is an objective assessment that must be conducted prior to the commencement of the processing.[23] Assessing what is necessary involves an holistic appraisal of the facts of the situation, including consideration of whether or not there are less intrusive means (than processing the personal data) that can realistically be implemented to perform the contractual service. If such means exist, the necessity criterion cannot be met;[24] if they do exist, the controller 'should be able to demonstrate how the main object of the *specific contract with the data subject* cannot, as a matter of fact, be performed if the specific processing of the *personal data in question* does not occur'.[25]

Assessment of necessity also involves ascertaining the basic purpose of the contract, and this purpose should be identified not just from the controller's perspective but also from the perspective of a 'reasonable data subject' when entering into the contract.[26] As for the phrase 'performance of a contract', this suggests that it comprises all stages necessary for the fulfilment of what was agreed between the contract partners. The purpose of Article 6(1)(b) is to make the legal instrument of 'contract' function also under the aspect of data protection. This requires that Article 6(1)(b) covers all data processing which usually is involved in administering contracts, such as, for instance, processing for billing purposes or processing for defects liability etc.[27] For additional activities, such as enquiries about the creditworthiness of a potential business partner or activities aimed at legal enforcement, Article 6(1)(f) may offer a suitable legal basis.[28]

Contrary to the case where consent is the legal basis for processing, the data subject as a contractual partner cannot freely terminate processing of his/her data based on a contract. Only by terminating the contract will the legal basis for processing (at least partly)[29] be removed. The conditions under which contracting parties are legally able to terminate a contract are defined by civil law.

Article 6(1)(b) additionally mentions precontractual situations as a possible ground for lawful processing. Such a situation could include, for example, the processing of personal data to prepare an offer for a package tour.[30] Processing data to fulfil a request of the data subject in a precontractual relationship could be based also on conclusive consent of the data subject or even on the 'legitimate interest' of the controller. Mentioning it under Article 6(1)(b) as a separate legal basis makes a difference as to the consequences, as in a case of Article 6(1)(b) the data subject cannot terminate lawful processing either by withdrawing consent or by objecting.[31] Considering how vague the concept of 'precontractual relationship' is, it might have been better to leave this case with Article 6(1)(a) or (f) in

---

[23] Ibid., p. 9. [24] Ibid., p. 7. [25] Ibid., p. 8 (emphasis added). [26] Ibid., p. 9.
[27] In this sense, see also Albers 2017, para. 31.
[28] See also WP29 2014, p. 18. See further EDPB 2019A, Part 3, for consideration of the applicability of Art. 6(1)(b) to several types of data-processing purposes and operations ('service improvement', 'fraud prevention', 'online behavioural advertising' and 'personalisation of content') in the context of online services.
[29] However, in many cases some data will have to be retained for purposes of documentation, in particular with respect to the establishment, exercise or defence of legal claims—retention that is permitted under Art. 17(3)(e) GDPR. See EDPB 2019A, p. 11: 'In practice, if controllers see a general need to keep records for legal purposes, they need to identify a legal basis at the outset of processing, and they need to communicate clearly from the start for how long they plan to retain records for these legal purposes after the termination of a contract. If they do so, they do not need to delete the data upon the termination of the contract'.
[30] See Dammann and Simitis 1997, p. 149.   [31] See further Art. 21(1) GDPR.

order to provide the data subject with better legal possibilities for interfering with such processing. To secure the right balance, the scope of lawful processing for precontractual relationships under Article 6(1)(b) must therefore be strictly limited to what is 'necessary' according to general knowledge and practice for complying with the data subject's request. Processing is only justified as far as the reasonable expectations of the data subject would go and as far as it is typically adequate for the kind of request that the data subject expressed.[32]

Lawful processing of sensitive data ('special category' data in the sense of Article 9 GDPR) in the context of a contract or a precontractual relationship is extremely limited.[33] Only in those (few) areas explicitly mentioned in Article 9(2) may a contractual relationship be a legal basis for processing.[34] The most prominent examples are the areas of employment contracts and contracts for medical treatment. It seems justified to assume that typical precontractual situations in these areas would also be covered, such as data processing in the stage of being interviewed for employment or of undergoing preparatory organisational measures for medical treatment. However, data collected in the course of these situations would have to be deleted without delay as soon as the precontractual phase was ended if no further legal basis exists, such as consent or the concluding of the contract.

1.2.3 Processing for compliance with a legal obligation to which the controller is subject

The formulation of Article 6(1)(c) GDPR is identical to the formulation of the corresponding Article 7(c) DPD. Article 6(1)(c) deals with legal obligations under EU or Member State law that necessitate the processing of data of others (e.g. customers, employees, suppliers) in order to be able to fulfil the legal obligation. The purpose of processing needs to be the fulfilling of the obligation. Everyday examples for situations falling under point (c) would be the processing of data about employees by the employer for social insurance purposes or the processing of data of customers by banking institutions for obligations under laws on money laundering.

The wording of Article 6(1)(c) does not clarify the type of legal obligations covered. However, the antecedent to this provision was traditionally understood as relating only to obligations that originate directly from a provision in the law and not from any contractual stipulation between private natural or legal persons.[35] Article 6(1)(c) ought to be understood in the same way.

---

[32] WP29 2014 comes to the same conclusion, giving examples on p. 18. See also EDPB 2019A, p. 11 (opining that the precontractual processing permitted by Art. 6(1)(b) does not cover unsolicited marketing or other processing which is conducted solely on the controller's initiative or a third party's request).

[33] This can result in problems where special categories of data would be needed in the context of a contractual relationship in an area not mentioned specifically in Art. 9 GDPR. In such cases processing could be founded on (explicit) consent; if, however, closing the contract depends on such consent (because the data are needed also by objective standards), Art. 7(4) GDPR might be a hindrance, as consent is not truly free.

[34] Additional cases may be foreseen by Union or Member State law, but only 'for reasons of substantial public interest' and with all special guarantees listed in Art. 9(2)(g).

[35] See e.g. WP29 2014, p. 19: 'For Article 7(c) [DPD] to apply, the obligation must be imposed by law (and not for instance by a contractual arrangement)'. This scope of applicability can also be traced through the provision's history. Art. 7(c) DPD was the final version of a draft provision which initially contained an explicit reference to 'obligations imposed by national or EC law' as opposed to legal obligations founded in a contract or other private law legal instrument. See the Amended Proposal to Directive 95/46, Explanatory statement to Art. 7, as mentioned in Dammann and Simitis 1997, p. 146. See also Frenzel 2017, para. 16.

Article 6(1)(c) would also cover situations where the obligation is not entirely specified in a law but by an additional legal act under public law such as secondary or delegated legislation or even 'by a binding decision of a public authority in a concrete case'.[36] Whether Article 6(1)(c) also covers legal obligations of public authorities is questionable as these are covered under Article 6(1)(e).[37] However, the WP29 favoured an interpretation of Article 7(c) DPD which would lead to applying Article 6(1)(c) to public *and* private controllers,[38] but only if the obligation concerned is derived directly from a legislative provision.[39] Limiting the applicability of Article 6(1)(c) to the private sector or not carries consequences for the data subject's right to object under Article 21(1), as this right exists only in cases of Article 6(1)(e) and (f), not in cases of Article 6(1)(c)—as elaborated further below.

What Article 6(1)(c) clearly does not cover are legal provisions which merely authorise or license legal subjects to do something. Such cases will have to be classified as cases of Article 6(1)(e) if they entitle public authorities to activities which result in processing data, or as cases of Article 6(1)(f) if private parties are licensed to carry out certain data processing activities.

The EDPB has analysed the application of various legal bases for data processing in the context of requests from foreign courts or authorities (in this instance, in the context of the US CLOUD Act), and found that the use of Article 6(1)(c) would require a legal basis in Union or Member State law, which in practice may require an international agreement.[40]

1.2.4 Processing is necessary in order to protect the vital interests of the data subject or of another natural person

In contrast to Article 7(d) DPD, this basis for lawful processing includes not only the vital interests of the data subject but also the equivalent interests of other natural persons. Recital 46 describes a 'vital interest' as one which is 'essential for the life' of an individual. This can include 'when processing is necessary for humanitarian purposes, including for monitoring epidemics and their spread or in situations of humanitarian emergencies, in particular in situations of natural and man-made disasters'. Using information on the data subject in order to be able to assist when his/her basic needs—or the basic needs of others—such as food, housing, medical care etc., are seriously endangered, seems justified, as the right to life[41] takes precedence over the right to data protection. Processing data on grounds of 'vital interests' requires that a situation of concrete and imminent danger exists for the data subject or a third (natural) person.[42]

---

[36] See also WP29 2014, p. 20.

[37] See also Dammann and Simitis 1997, p. 150, who seemed to limit the applicability of Art. 7(c) DPD to private sector controllers.

[38] WP29 2014, p. 19: 'It could also be an obligation to which a public authority is subject, as nothing limits the application of Article 7(c) [DPD] to the private or public sector'. See also Frenzel 2017, para. 18.

[39] WP29 2014, p. 19. However, if it is assumed that Art. 6(1)(c) requires 'an obligation derived directly from a legal provision' in the sense that the legal provision clearly defines the obligation, it could be argued that there is no need for a right to object, as the legal provision already clarifies that there is a legitimate interest in processing certain data which is not overridden by interests of data subjects in protection of their data.

[40] EDPB EDPS Response Cloud Act, p. 4.

[41] See Art. 2 CFR (right to life): '1. Everyone has the right to life. 2. No one shall be condemned to the death penalty, or executed'.

[42] See also Kramer 2017, para. 23.

A specific problem in this context is the role which the data subject should play in the course of taking the decision to process his/her data on grounds of 'vital interests'. Contrary to Article 9 GDPR (dealing with special categories of data), Article 6(1)(d) does not mention that the decision to process may be taken by the controller only if the data subject is incapable of consenting.

The principle of 'fair processing' might require, nevertheless, that the data subject should be consulted if possible. Yet, there may exist legal obligations which override the will of the data subject. In such constellations, the legal basis for processing will rather be found in 'fulfilling legal obligations' than in acting on behalf of vital interests of the data subject. Recital 46 points in this direction, stating that 'vital interests' should be utilised as a legal basis only 'where the processing cannot be manifestly based on another legal basis'—i.e. where Article 6(1)(a), (c), (e) or (f) would seem not to offer a suitable alternative.

The reference to 'vital interests of another natural person' (i.e. a natural person other than the data subject) in Article 6(1)(d) is a change from Article 7 DPD and its significance should be analysed. Survival is a 'legitimate interest' pursued by every individual. If a controller processes data of one individual for the purpose of assisting another individual to survive, this is actually a clear case of processing on the basis of Article 6(1)(f). This latter provision contains a perfect balance of interests. As long as processing data for the vital interests of a third person respects proportionality concerning the interference with the rights of the data subject, all legitimate interests at stake in such a situation are properly taken care of. However, contrary to Article 7(f) DPD, Article 6(1)(f) GDPR is now limited to private sector controllers. This may explain why it was deemed necessary to include a provision on vital interests of third parties in Article 6(1)(d) which can be made use of also by controllers in the public sector.

Understanding processing for the 'vital interests of another natural person' as actually just one case of processing on the basis of 'legitimate interests of others' is also important for the correct interpretation of the vital interest clause in Article 9(2)(c).[43] This clause could be misunderstood as providing the data subject with the power to decide about the life and death of another individual by granting or refusing consent to the processing of his or her data. Irrespective of its formulation, the last part of Article 9(2)(c), prioritising consent, must be read as referring only to the case of 'vital interests *of the data subject*' as the legitimate interest of a third person in survival clearly overrides the data protection interests of the data subject.

The EDPB has analysed the application of various legal bases for data processing in the context of requests from foreign courts or authorities (in this instance, in the context of the US CLOUD Act). It limited the use of Article 6(1)(d) to 'cases of requests to access personal data concerning abducted minors or other obvious situations where the transfer is in the vital interest of data subjects themselves', and found that transfers could not be based on the vital interests of other persons.[44]

---

[43] Art. 9(2)(c) GDPR: 'processing is necessary to protect the vital interests of the data subject or of another natural person where the data subject is physically or legally incapable of giving consent'.
[44] EDPB EDPS Response Cloud Act, p. 4.

1.2.5 Processing for the performance of a task carried out in the public interest or in the exercise of official authority vested in the controller

This provision is the general basis for lawful processing of personal data for public sector purposes. Compared to its antecedent in the DPD,[45] Article 6(1)(e) no longer refers to disclosure of data to other controllers in the public sector. However, this does not result in any substantial changes, as disclosure of data by one public authority to another public authority must be legitimised in the same way as any other type of processing of personal data by an 'authority'.[46] If the transmission of data to a public authority (or another body subject to Article 6(1)(e)) is performed by a controller who is not subject to Article 6(1)(e),[47] this case will now be treated either as processing under Article 6(1)(c) if such transmission is concretely foreseen as legally mandatory, or possibly as processing under Article 6(1)(f) if the controller by transmitting data acts within the limits of their rights or freedoms as a private law subject.[48] Even Article 6(1)(b) might be applicable if the transfer of data to an authority is necessary to fulfil a contract between the transferring controller and the data subject. Under Recital 46, an example of processing based on 'important grounds of public interest' can include 'when processing is necessary for humanitarian purposes, including for monitoring epidemics and their spread or in situations of humanitarian emergencies, in particular in situations of natural and man-made disasters'.

In the English version of Article 6(1)(e) it is ambiguous whether the words 'vested in the controller' relate to 'exercise of official authority' or to 'a task'. The meaning of Article 6(1)(e) is clearer in the German version[49] where commas are set in order to structure the sentence. Transferring this structure into the English version, it would read as follows: 'Processing is necessary for the performance of a task, carried out in the public interest or in the exercise of official authority, vested in the controller'. Thus, the reason for processing under Article 6(1)(e) is the fact that it is necessary for a task, which 'shall be carried out in the public interest or in the exercise of official authority' and has been 'entrusted to the controller'.[50] Vesting such a task in a controller requires a legal provision to this effect.[51] Such understanding excludes cases of assignment of 'tasks' by contract, even if they were 'in the public interest', which will be particularly significant where private entities shall be 'vested with a task' in the sense of Article 6(1)(e). Such understanding also

---

[45] Under Art. 7(e) DPD processing was lawful if it was 'necessary for the performance of a task carried out in the public interest or in the exercise of official authority vested in the controller *or in a third party to whom the data are disclosed*' (emphasis added).

[46] For elaboration of the term 'public authority', see the commentary on Art. 4(7) in this volume. Art. 4(9) GDPR contains a definition of 'recipient' which seems to exclude public authorities when receiving data in form of an inquiry. The reason for this exemption and its consequences are not clear. If it was meant to result in 'free data exchange' between public authorities, it would manifestly infringe the fundamental right to data protection. As 'a particular inquiry' must, however, be 'in accordance with Union or Member State law' according to Art. 4(9), disclosure in the form of an inquiry has in the end to fulfil the same requirements as foreseen in Art. 6(1)(e), because every Member State law must be in accordance with the fundamental right to data protection. On the definition of 'recipient', see further the commentary on Art. 4(9) in this volume.

[47] This is either a private sector controller or could also be a public sector controller when renting office space or contracting a processor etc.

[48] An example of such a situation would be citizens notifying police authorities about suspected crimes.

[49] Art. 6(1) (German version): 'e) die Verarbeitung ist für die Wahrnehmung einer Aufgabe erforderlich, die im öffentlichen Interesse liegt oder in Ausübung öffentlicher Gewalt erfolgt, die dem Verantwortlichen übertragen wurde'.

[50] Authorities acting outside of matters of 'public interest' or 'official authority' (e.g. when renting office space, contracting processors etc.) will, however, act on the basis of Art. 6(1)(b) or (f) GDPR.

[51] See also Albrecht and Jotzo 2017, para. 45; Kramer 2017, para. 24; Frenzel 2017, para. 24.

underlies the provisions of Article 6(2) and (3) which clearly presume that the obligations under Article 6(1)(c) and the tasks under Article 6(1)(e) are conveyed by provisions in the law.

Use of the word 'or' in the description of the nature of the tasks, eligible under Article 6(1)(e), suggests that the remit of this provision is not limited to processing operations of public authorities (in 'exercise of official authority') but extends to processing by private bodies vested with a relevant task. There is some disagreement over whether such private bodies would have to be endowed at the same time with official authority in order to qualify for Article 6(1)(e). For instance, Kramer states that only private entities vested with official authority ('beliehene Unternehmer') are covered by Article 6(1)(e) and that private entities, operating on a commercial basis, although in the public interest, are not covered,[52] whereas Roßnagel does not make such a distinction.[53] Following the text of Article 6(1)(e), which links the two eligibility criteria by 'or' and not by 'and', it seems up to the legislators to decide, when vesting a task of public interest in a private sector controller, whether they want to attribute 'authority' to the controller or not.[54]

Processing may be performed on the basis of Article 6(1)(e) if it is necessary for fulfilling the task which was vested in the controller. Necessity to process personal data must be seen in the context of the area regulated by the respective provision within Article 6(1). Article 6(1)(e) deals with data protection in the context of the performance of intrinsically state or public functions. Building on CJEU jurisprudence in the *Huber* case,[55] processing in this context is necessary if it promotes good governance in the sense that it 'makes the performance more effective' and facilitates activities which are in the public interest and are foreseen by law. The concept of 'necessity' must be interpreted strictly in the light of proportionality.[56] If there are several alternatives to reach a legitimate goal, the least intrusive alternative must be chosen.[57]

Contrary to Article 6(1)(c), the assignment of a task as referred to in Article 6(1)(e) will often not result in precisely determined obligations for the controller but rather in a more general authorisation to act as necessary in order to fulfil the task. Concerning the obligation to interpret and weigh interests, Article 6(1)(e) is therefore not so different from Article 6(1)(f). This may also explain why only these two cases under Article 6(1) are subject to the data subject's right to object pursuant to Article 21 GDPR.[58]

The EDPB has analysed the application of various legal bases for data processing in the context of requests from foreign courts or authorities (in this instance, in the context of the US CLOUD Act). It found that the use of Article 6(1)(e) is not satisfied solely on the basis of a request from a third country authority.[59]

---

[52] Kramer 2017, para. 24. See also Albrecht and Jotzo 2017, para. 73.
[53] Roßnagel 2017, paras. 11 et seq.
[54] This reading of Art. 6(1)(e) evidently also underlies the formulation of Art. 86 GDPR, where the object of 'public access to documents' is defined as 'personal data in official documents held by a public authority or a public body or a private body for the performance of a task carried out in the public interest'. There is no requirement for official authority attributed to the private body in order to qualify under Art. 86.
[55] Case C-524/06, *Huber*.   [56] Ibid., paras. 59–61.
[57] See also rec. 47; Kramer 2017, para. 25; Frenzel 2017, para. 23.
[58] See also WP29 2014, p. 22.   [59] EDPB EDPS Response Cloud Act, p. 4.

1.2.6 Processing on grounds of legitimate interests pursued by the controller or by a third party

In contrast to the antecedent provision in Article 7(f) DPD, 'legitimate interest' in the GDPR refers only to interests of private sector controllers.[60] Other differences to Article 7(f) DPD are the presence of a new and explicit reference to the interest in special protection of children, and the fact that the legitimate interests of third parties are no longer limited to cases of data transmission.

A 'legitimate interest' is an interest which is visibly, although not necessarily explicitly, recognised by law, more precisely by Union or Member State law. Mere commercial interests will not suffice to establish a 'legitimate interest'. Particular relevance must be attributed to the fundamental rights and freedoms recognised in the CFR as they are all potential sources of legitimate interests.[61]

Examples of 'legitimate interests' are given in the recitals to the GDPR. Recital 47 refers to the 'processing of personal data strictly necessary for the purpose of preventing fraud' (an interest based on the right to property) and to 'the processing of personal data for direct marketing purposes' (an interest based on the freedom to conduct a business). Both of the above-mentioned bases are also relevant with respect to recital 48 which names 'the transmission of certain data within groups of companies' as a legitimate interest, and for recital 49 which refers to the processing of data for the purposes of ensuring network and information security.[62]

According to Article 6(1)(f), a controller may process data not only on behalf of their own legitimate interests but also because of legitimate interests of third parties. As a preliminary point, it is important to note that the latter must not qualify as co-controllers in respect of this data processing.[63] If they do qualify as co-controllers, the result in *Fashion ID* indicates that they themselves must each demonstrate their own legitimate interest(s) or the legitimate interest(s) of third parties insofar as they each seek to justify the processing under Art. 6(1)(f).[64] Further, as a controller cannot usurp just anybody's rights or freedoms and process data based on another person's legal position, the applicability of this provision for third party interests can only be very limited. One example is referred to in Article 6(1)(d) where the 'vital interests of another natural person' are mentioned as a legal basis for processing. Another possible and not unimportant scenario is the transmission of data to a third party because of that party's legitimate interests. This situation may occur in particular where a legal provision explicitly entitles or allows a third party to receive data.[65] However, third parties may also have legitimate interests which are not reflected in *specific* legal provisions, and which cannot be exercised unless a certain (type

---

[60] In spite of the fact that the text of Art. 6(1)(f) only refers to 'public authorities' it must be presumed that also private bodies, vested by law with a task in the public interest, are excluded from relying on Art. 6(1)(f) as a legal basis for their processing. The reason given in rec. 47 GDPR for excluding public authorities from relying on Art. 6(1)(f) applies equally to the named private bodies: 'Given that it is for the legislator to provide by law for the legal basis for public authorities to process personal data, that legal basis [i.e. Art. 6(1)(f)] should not apply to the processing by public authorities in the performance of their tasks'. See also above.

[61] See also Frenzel 2017, para. 28.

[62] A list of examples for legitimate interests which are specifically relevant in practice is given in WP29 2014, p. 25.

[63] This follows from the definition of 'third party' in Art. 4(10) GDPR. See further the commentary on that definition in this volume.

[64] Case C-40/17, *Fashion ID*, para. 96 (elaborated above).

[65] This is not a case of processing under Art. 6(1)(c) if the controller who initially collected the data is not legally explicitly obliged to disclose the data to the third party.

of) controller takes care of them by collecting and processing data about other persons.[66] Article 6(1)(f) might provide a legal basis for data processing in such situations. The WP29 discussed, for instance, whether interests of the 'general public' (the third party) in transparency would justify that someone (the controller) publishes information on the income or remuneration of public functionaries (the data subjects).[67] However, the WP29 correctly opined that such delicate situations should preferably be regulated by law and thus handled under Article 6(1)(c) rather than Article 6(1)(f).[68]

All processing for 'legitimate interests' is anyway limited to what is plausibly necessary to pursue this interest. In line with the principle of proportionality processing can only be acknowledged as 'necessary', if there is no better suited and less intrusive alternative available.[69]

Processing on grounds of Article 6(1)(f) is not allowed where the legitimate interests of the controller or of a third party 'are overridden by the interests or fundamental rights and freedoms of the data subject which require protection of personal data, in particular where the data subject is a child'. The reference to 'interests *or* fundamental rights', along with the fact that the interests are not qualified by 'legitimate', means that the position of the data subject is protected extensively.[70] A controller, intending to rely on Article 6(1)(f), must therefore perform a special 'balancing test', in accordance with the principle of proportionality. The WP29 offered a set of criteria for carrying out this test in relation to Article 7(f) DPD;[71] these may be usefully applied in the context of Article 6(1)(f) GDPR. They are, in summary form, as follows: '(a) assessing the controller's legitimate interest, (b) impact on the data subjects, (c) provisional balance and (d) additional safeguards applied by the controller to prevent any undue impact on the data subjects'.[72] It goes without saying that this assessment needs to conform with the principle of proportionality. Moreover, in line with the principle of accountability, this assessment has to be done before starting any processing operations based on Article 6(1)(f), and it needs to be properly documented in order to demonstrate that the controller's obligations have been fulfilled.[73] Processing on grounds of Article 6(1)(f) must, in a proactive way, explore the likely protection interests of the data subjects and construe a design for the processing operations which avoids infringement of such interests.[74] Further, recital 47 stresses the importance of the reasonable expectations of the data subjects based on the time and context of the processing, and indicates that conflict with these expectations could, in certain cases, 'override' a controller's interest in 'further processing'.[75]

---

[66] Credit information systems are, for instance, actually based on the legitimate interests of 'third parties', i.e. the users of such information systems.

[67] WP29 2014, p. 27.

[68] If in such a scenario, the data were initially collected for the purpose of responding to the interests of the third parties, there is no 'further processing' involved, as the interests of the third parties are the explicitly named reason for data collection. If, however, the necessary data were derived from processing for other initial purposes, the rules of Art. 6(4) for 'further processing' would have to be followed.

[69] See also Kramer 2017, para. 34; Plath 2018, para. 23. In the context of installing video-surveillance systems, see also EDPB 2019B, p. 8.

[70] See also WP29 2014, pp. 29–30.   [71] Ibid., pp. 33–42.   [72] Ibid., p. 33.

[73] See also WP29 2012, p. 13 ('Following the accountability principle ... it should be left to the controller to decide whether he has a legitimate interest to justify certain data processing or whether such interests are overridden by the interests or fundamental rights and freedoms of the data subject. This will be subject to supervision, enforcement and judicial review').

[74] See also Art. 25 GDPR.

[75] It should be noted, however, that further processing for an (in)compatible purpose is dealt with under the special provision of Art. 6(4) and cannot be based on Art. 6(1)(f) GDPR.

Building on the above-referenced WP29 opinion, the EDPB has issued guidance on the balancing test in the context of video-surveillance schemes. Emphasising that this test must focus on the case at hand and not abstract situations, the Board takes the view that the 'decisive criterion' for the test is the 'intensity of intervention' that the processing in question poses for 'the rights and freedoms of the individual'.[76] In general terms, this intensity 'can inter alia be defined by the type of information that is gathered (information content), the scope (information density, spatial and geographical extent), the number of data subjects concerned, either as a specific number or as a proportion of the relevant population, the situation in question, the actual interests of the group of data subjects, alternative means, as well as by the nature and scope of the data assessment'.[77]

The EDPB has analysed the application of various legal bases for data processing in the context of requests from foreign courts or authorities (in this instance, in the context of the US CLOUD Act). With regard to Article 6(1)(f), it found that complying with a request from a third country law enforcement authority could potentially be in the legitimate interest of a data controller or third party, but that this interest would be overridden by the interests or fundamental rights and freedoms of the data subject in such situation.[78]

1.3 The relationship between the various grounds of lawful processing

As different consequences are linked to the various grounds of processing under Article 6(1) it is relevant for controllers to consider how their processing operations fit within these grounds. For instance, lawful processing can be stopped at the discretion of the data subject only in case of Article 6(1)(a), by withdrawing consent. Thus, it may be a disadvantage for controllers to rely on consent if they can base their processing on legitimate interests, which cannot be removed at the discretion of the data subject. But if processing is based on Article 6(1)(f), the controller is obliged to perform a special and documented test of weighing 'legitimate interests' in processing against protection interests of the data subject. Undergoing the exercise of weighing legitimate interests against overriding protection interests will be superfluous if processing operations can actually be based on a legal obligation in the sense of Article 6(1)(c). Yet, as elaborated further below, Article 6(3) requires the existence of a special legal basis if processing is based on Article 6(1)(c) or (e).

Moreover, Article 21 grants the data subject a special 'right to object' in case of processing based on Article 6(1)(e) or (f). The applicability of this right, which results in an obligation of controllers to prove that they did not infringe overriding protection interests, is a further reason why distinguishing correctly between the various cases of Article 6(1) is important.

Nonetheless, it is important to keep in mind that, according to Article 52(1) CFR, the conditions for lawful limitations of the right to data protection apply equally to all grounds listed in Article 6(1).[79] Special conditions for lawful processing mentioned in the several points of Article 6(1) can therefore only refer to gradual differences, never to substantial discrepancies. In the absence of consent, all cases of limitations (not only those mentioned specifically in Article 6(3)) must be 'provided for by law', and

---

[76] EDPB 2019B, p. 10.   [77] Ibid.   [78] EDPB EDPS Response Cloud Act, p. 5.
[79] When WP29 2014 explains on p. 9 that, contrary to Art. 6(1)(f), the other cases of Art. 6(1) are 'considered as *a priori* legitimate', that must not be misunderstood. Especially relying on point (e) will very often also require a 'specific test' for assuring that a concrete use of personal data for public interests is proportionate.

proportionality—which is actually 'a balance' between the interest in processing and the interest in protection—must be achieved in all cases of processing, even where consent has been given. All cases of Article 6(1) must be interpreted in a way which avoids gaps or discrepancies when compared to the general provisions of Article 52(1) CFR. In other words, all legal grounds for lawful processing shall only be used in a way which results in respecting the essence of the right to data protection.

2. Article 6(2)

In principle, Member States are not competent to legislate in matters which are subject to an EU Regulation. Exemptions to this rule may, however, be foreseen in Union law. Article 6(2) GDPR contains such exemptions in favour of Member State law concerning legal provisions *specifying and adapting the rules of the GDPR* with regard to processing based on Article 6(1)(c) or (e), or concerning the special processing situations listed in Chapter IX GDPR. This exemption, within its remit, allows for *maintaining* existing Member States' law, as far as is compatible with the GDPR, *as well as introducing new legal provisions* under Member State law in compliance with the GDPR.[80] As a result, Member States can actually keep their sector-specific data protection law as far as the public sector is concerned, as such law would be based on Article 6(1)(e). The only condition is compliance with the GDPR.

Concerning the private sector, it must be stressed that Article 6(1)(f) is not mentioned in Article 6(2).[81] However, as far as Member State law creates obligations for private sector controllers *which necessitate the processing of personal data*, or deal with 'specific processing situations' which are according to provisions in Chapter IX GDPR open for Member States' legislation, it may also 'determine more precisely specific requirements for the processing and other measures to ensure lawful and fair processing' in the private sector. It remains to be seen how these competences of the national legislators comply with the overall purpose of the GDPR to ensure a consistent and high level of protection throughout its entire territorial scope of application. As to the content of Member State laws specifying and adapting the rules of the GDPR in cases of processing under Article 6(1)(c) or (e), paragraph 3 of Article 6 contains more detailed rules.

3. Article 6(3)

Article 6(3) clarifies that processing of personal data can be based on Article 6(1)(c) or (e) *only* if the controller's obligation or the task vested in the controller (which necessitate the processing of personal data) are laid down either in Union law or Member State law to which the controller is subject.[82] It follows that obligations or tasks *based exclusively on foreign law* cannot provide a legal basis for processing.

---

[80] Rec. 8 GDPR mentions that Member State law may even 'incorporate elements of this Regulation into their national law', 'as far as necessary for coherence and for making the national provisions comprehensible to the persons to whom they apply'.

[81] As 'legitimate interests' are, however, derived from the body of law to which the controller (or the third party) is subject, Member State law is relevant also in the context of Art. 6(1)(f) GDPR. Thus, Member State law may contain provisions which create or modify 'legitimate interests', but Member State law may not set up conditions for lawful processing based on 'legitimate interest'. See also Joined Cases C-468/10 and C469/10 *ASNEF* and Case C-582/14, *Breyer*.

[82] Rec. 41 GDPR states that '[w]here this Regulation refers to a legal basis or a legislative measure, this does not necessarily require a legislative act adopted by a parliament' and refers to the constitutional order of the Member State.

The rest of Article 6(3) deals with the nature and content of the provisions in EU or Member State law which are relevant under Article 6(2). The GDPR 'does not require a specific law for each individual processing. A law as a basis for several processing operations ... may be sufficient'.[83] At the same time, there may be one law conveying a task of public interest to a controller and several additional laws dealing with processing operations which are necessary for different purposes under this task.[84]

Apart from the important question of determining the purpose of processing, examples for such added content of legal provisions under paragraph 2 and 3 are given in the third sentence of Article 6(3). A more comprehensive specification is given in recital 45:

> Furthermore, that law could specify the general conditions of this Regulation governing the lawfulness of personal data processing, establish specifications for determining the controller, the type of personal data which are subject to the processing, the data subjects concerned, the entities to which the personal data may be disclosed, the purpose limitations, the storage period and other measures to ensure lawful and fair processing.[85]

Recital 93 mentions, in particular, that laws which delegate tasks to be carried out in the public interest or in the exercise of official authority, might also foresee that an impact assessment has to be done before processing activities may be started.

4. Article 6(4)

Article 6(4) GDPR clarifies the concept of 'compatible further processing' and defines the conditions for lawful further processing in case of incompatibility.

4.1 The concept of 'compatible further processing'

Correctly assessing 'compatibility' of further use of data is highly relevant as only *compatible* further use (processing) does not require an additional legal basis. The legal basis for the initial purpose of processing is extended to compatible further processing.[86] Article 6(4) provides tools for the assessment of compatibility by means of a non-exhaustive list of items which are important to consider in a concrete case.[87] Two main issues emerge from the items listed in Article 6(4)(a)–(e).

First, the relationship between the initial and the 'further' purpose must be examined. 'Compatibility' of further processing does not require that the new additional purpose of processing is just a 'sub-purpose' of the initial purpose of processing.[88] Compatibility of purposes exists also where the new purpose is different but correlates to the initial purpose in the sense that these purposes usually are pursued 'together' in close vicinity in a timely as well as a contextual sense, or that the further purpose is the logical consequence of the initial purpose.[89] Recital 50 introduces 'the reasonable expectations of data subjects based on their relationship with the controller as to their further use' as an additional criterion

---

[83] Rec. 45 GDPR. [84] Such additional laws would be subject to Art. 6(2).
[85] Rec. 45 GDPR.
[86] Rec. 50 GDPR states: 'In such a case, no legal basis separate from that which allowed the collection of the personal data is required'.
[87] This list was modelled according to the deliberations of WP29, put forward in WP29 2013. See also the comments by Frenzel 2017, paras. 48 et seq.
[88] WP29 2013 states on p. 21 that further processing for a different purpose does not necessarily mean that it is incompatible; 'compatibility needs to be assessed on a case-by-case basis'.
[89] See also Kramer 2017, para. 53.

when assessing compatibility.[90] This illustrates that compatibility of purposes depends to a high degree on what is usual and what is to be expected in certain circumstances.[91] Using data collected in the course of selling goods to a customer for mandating a carrier to forward the goods to the customer would constitute a 'compatible further use'. In such cases the transmission of data to certain recipients will be compatible further processing, as such transmission is necessary to complete the initial purpose of processing.[92] The case of a customer receiving marketing information from an enterprise, where he or she had bought goods or services recently is another possible example of 'compatible further use of customer data',[93] as customer relationship management ('CRM') is a usual activity resulting from the customer relationship in which the data have been originally collected.[94] An important and far-reaching example for compatibility is explicitly set out in Article 5(1)(b) GDPR: further processing for purposes of archiving in the public interest, for scientific or historical research purposes or for statistical purposes is considered as compatible with any other initial purpose of processing.

Secondly, it is necessary to consider the extra risks for the data subjects resulting from further processing. The items listed as relevant in Article 6(4)(c)–(e) refer to the necessity of an additional risk assessment concerning the intended further processing and convey the idea that the concept of 'compatibility' contains also an element of risk containment. Further processing must not result in a substantively higher risk than the initial lawful processing if it is to qualify as 'compatible'. This will particularly limit 'compatible' further processing of special category data[95] which are explicitly mentioned in Article 6(4)(c) as a risk factor.[96] Relying on compatibility cannot extend lawful processing of such data beyond the reasons listed in Articles 9 and 10. Risks may be mitigated by special safeguards. Data minimisation might be advantageous. Encryption (of the whole data set) is mentioned in Article 6(4)(e) as one example, pseudonymisation as another. Regarding the special purposes explicitly declared as compatible by Article 5(1)(b),[97] risk containment has to be achieved according to Article 89(1) GDPR. The latter provision requires adequate technical and organisational measures for ensuring appropriate safeguards, pseudonymisation or even anonymisation being a mandatory measure as far as the 'purpose of further processing can be fulfilled in that manner'. Additionally, legal measures could qualify as risk containment. Subjecting recipients of data to requirements

---

[90] In this context, the information given to the data subject at the time of the collection of data can be relevant for determining 'reasonable expectations'.

[91] Compare also the interpretation of 'reasonable expectations of privacy' in US jurisprudence, as elaborated in Feiler et al. 2018, p. 84.

[92] Disclosing a file on the use of public grants to official auditors would be an example for compatible further use founded on the logic of grant procedures. Several highly illustrative examples are given in Annex 4 to WP29 2013.

[93] Whether such procedure is 'compatible further processing' in a given case depends on the fulfilment of additional requirements named in Art. 6(4) GDPR.

[94] Using customer data for keeping up and enhancing an existing customer relationship is essentially different from using customer data for marketing purposes of a third party—this would never qualify as compatible further use. Support for the assessment of CRM as possibly compatible further use of data can be found in the provisions of Art. 13 EPD concerning unsolicited communications.

[95] See Arts. 9 and 10 GDPR.

[96] See too WP29 2013, p. 25: 'In general, the more sensitive the information involved, the narrower the scope for compatible use would be'.

[97] These are archiving purposes in the public interest, scientific or historical research purposes or statistical purposes.

concerning data use limitations and special data security measures are well-established tools to enhance protection and thus lower risks.

If controllers rely on compatibility of further processing, they must be able to demonstrate that a compatibility assessment of all relevant circumstances was done and that, in particular, the key factors explicitly mentioned in Article 6(4) have been appropriately dealt with. This applies to the correlation of purposes as well as to the avoidance of additional risks for the data subjects. Whether the formulation of Article 6(4) might justify an assumption of 'compatibility' also in cases where the new purpose does not specifically 'correlate' to the initial purpose, but where a very high standard of risk containment is implemented (e.g. by secure pseudonymisation), will have to be decided by future jurisprudence. As far as archiving, research and statistics are concerned, compatibility is focused on risk containment as Article 5(1)(b) GDPR presumes a correlation of purposes.

4.2 On the legal conditions for incompatible further processing

The introductory provisions of Article 6(4) regulate quasi 'en passant' how controllers ought to proceed if a case of further processing cannot be considered as compatible with the initial purpose of processing. Where there is no special provision in EU or Member State law allowing for the intended kind of (incompatible) further processing, *the controller must obtain the data subjects' consent* for pursuing this additional purpose.

It is important to note that Article 6(4) does not require a legal basis for further processing under Article 6(1). 'Incompatible further processing' is an interference with the principle of purpose limitation in Article 5(1)(b)); therefore, it is not Article 6(1) that applies in such a case, only Article 23, which deals with lawful restrictions of, inter alia, Article 5.[98] Thus, a 'legitimate interest' pursued by the controller or a third party in the sense of Article 6(1)(f) cannot provide a legal basis for further processing for an incompatible purpose.[99]

According to Article 23, only a special legal provision can be a valid legal basis for interfering with the purpose limitation principle. For the EU or Member State legislators, Article 23 spells out the prerequisites and conditions which such a law ought to fulfil. While Article 6(4) refers alternatively to such legal provisions *or* consent of the data subjects as a valid legal basis for incompatible further processing, Article 23 does not mention consent. The fact that consent is, despite non-applicability of Article 6(1) and despite lack of any reference to consent in Article 23, explicitly named as a legal basis for incompatible further processing in Article 6(4), must be accepted as acknowledgement of the legal possibility for data subjects to waive a fundamental right.

---

[98] The WP29 explained the rationale of such legal assessment in relation to the DPD as follows: 'Processing of personal data in a way incompatible with the purposes specified at collection is against the law and therefore prohibited. The data controller cannot legitimise incompatible processing by simply relying on a new legal ground in Article 7. The purpose limitation principle can only be restricted subject to the conditions set forth in Article 13 of the Directive'. See WP29 2013, p. 3.

[99] The explanation in rec. 47 GDPR that the reasonable expectations of data subjects concerning further processing might result in protection interests which override 'legitimate interests' of the controller (or a third party) is misleading insofar as the introductory sentence of Art. 6(4) excludes 'legitimate interests' as a reason for lawful further processing for an incompatible purpose.

Select Bibliography

Academic writings

Albers 2017: Albers, 'Artikel 6 Rechtmäßigkeit der Verarbeitung', in Brink and Wolff (eds.), *BeckOK Datenschutzrecht* (23rd edn, C. H. BECK 2018) (online version).
Albrecht and Jotzo 2017: Albrecht and Jotzo, *Das neue Datenschutzrecht der EU* (Verlag Nomos 2017).
Dammann and Simitis 1997: Dammann and Simitis, *EG-Datenschutzrichtlinie—Kommentar* (Verlag Nomos 1997).
Feiler et al. 2018: Feiler, Forgó and Weigl, *The EU General Data Protection Regulation (GDPR)* (German Law Publishers 2018).
Frenzel 2017: Frenzel, 'Art. 6 Rechtmäßigkeit der Verarbeitung', in Paal and Pauly (eds.), *Datenschutz-Grundverordnung Bundesdatenschutzgesetz* (2nd edn, Beck Verlag 2017), 86.
Kramer 2017: Kramer, 'Art. 6 Rechtmäßigkeit der Verarbeitung', in Auernhammer, Eßner, Kramer and von Lewinski (eds.), *Heymanns Kommentare DSGVO BDSG* (5th edn, Carl Heymanns Verlag 2017), 105.
Laue, Nink and Kremer, *Das neue Datenschutzrecht in der betrieblichen Praxis* (Nomos Verlag 2017).
Plath 2018: Plath, 'Artikel 6', in Plath (ed.), *DSGVO/BDSG* (3rd edn, Beck-Verlag 2018).
Roßnagel 2017: Roßnagel, 'Das neue Datenschutzrecht – Fort- oder Rückschritt?', in Roßnagel (ed.), *Europäische Datenschutz-Grundverordnung* (Nomos Verlag 2017), 327.

Papers of data protection authorities

EDPB 2019A: European Data Protection Board, 'Guidelines 2/2019 on the processing of personal data under Article 6(1)(b) GDPR in the context of the provision of online services to data subjects' (9 April 2019).
EDPB 2019B: European Data Protection Board, 'Guidelines 3/2019 on processing of personal data through video devices' (10 July 2019).
EDPB EDPS Response Cloud Act: European Data Protection Board and European Data Protection Supervisor, 'EPDB-EDPS Joint Response to the LIBE Committee on the impact of the US Cloud Act on the European legal framework for personal data protection (annex)' (10 July 2019).
WP29 2011: Article 29 Working Party, 'Opinion 15/2011 on the Definition of Consent' (WP 187, 13 July 2011).
WP29 2012: Article 29 Working Party, 'Opinion 08/2012 Providing Further Input on the Data Protection Reform Discussions' (WP 199, 5 October 2012).
WP29 2013: Article 29 Working Party, 'Opinion 03/2013 on Purpose Limitation' (WP 203, 2 April 2013).
WP29 2014: Article 29 Working Party, 'Opinion 06/2014 on the Notion of Legitimate Interests of the Data Controller under Article 7 of Directive 95/46/EC' (WP 217, 9 April 2014).
WP29 2018: Article 29 Working Party, 'Guidelines on Consent under Regulation 2016/679' (WP 259 rev.01, 10 April 2018).

Article 7. Conditions for consent

ELENI KOSTA

1. Where processing is based on consent, the controller shall be able to demonstrate that the data subject has consented to processing of his or her personal data.
2. If the data subject's consent is given in the context of a written declaration which also concerns other matters, the request for consent shall be presented in a manner which is clearly distinguishable from the other matters, in an intelligible and easily accessible form, using clear and plain language. Any part of such a declaration which constitutes an infringement of this Regulation shall not be binding.
3. The data subject shall have the right to withdraw his or her consent at any time. The withdrawal of consent shall not affect the lawfulness of processing based on consent before its withdrawal. Prior to giving consent, the data subject shall be informed thereof. It shall be as easy to withdraw as to give consent.
4. When assessing whether consent is freely given, utmost account shall be taken of whether, *inter alia*, the performance of a contract, including the provision of a service, is conditional on consent to the processing of personal data that is not necessary for the performance of that contract.

Relevant Recitals

(42) Where processing is based on the data subject's consent, the controller should be able to demonstrate that the data subject has given consent to the processing operation. In particular in the context of a written declaration on another matter, safeguards should ensure that the data subject is aware of the fact that and the extent to which consent is given. In accordance with Council Directive 93/13/EEC a declaration of consent pre-formulated by the controller should be provided in an intelligible and easily accessible form, using clear and plain language and it should not contain unfair terms. For consent to be informed, the data subject should be aware at least of the identity of the controller and the purposes of the processing for which the personal data are intended. Consent should not be regarded as freely given if the data subject has no genuine or free choice or is unable to refuse or withdraw consent without detriment.

(43) In order to ensure that consent is freely given, consent should not provide a valid legal ground for the processing of personal data in a specific case where there is a clear imbalance between the data subject and the controller, in particular where the controller is a public authority and it is therefore unlikely that consent was freely given in all the circumstances of that specific situation. Consent is presumed not to be freely given if it does not allow separate consent to be given to different personal data processing operations despite it being appropriate in the individual case, or if the performance of a contract, including the provision of a service, is dependent on the consent despite such consent not being necessary for such performance.

Closely Related Provisions

Article 4(11) (Definition of consent) (see too recitals 32 and 33 on consent for scientific research purposes); Article 6(1)(a) (Lawfulness of processing—consent) (see also recitals 40 and

42–43); Article 8 (Conditions applicable to child's consent in relation to information society services); Article 9(2) (Processing of special categories of personal data—consent) (see too recital 50); Article 13(2)(c) (Information to be provided—withdrawal of consent); Article 14(2)(d) (Information to be provided—withdrawal of consent); Article 17(1)(b) (Right to erasure—withdrawal of consent) (see also recital 65); Article 18(2) (Right to restriction of processing); Article 20(1)(a) (Right to data portability) (see also recital 68); Article 22(2)(c) (Automated decisions and profiling) (see also recital 71); Article 49(1)(a) (Derogations for specific situations) (see also recital 111); Article 83 (General conditions for imposing administrative fines) (see also recitals 155 and 171)

Related Provisions in LED [Directive (EU) 2016/680]

Recitals 35 and 37

Related Provisions in EPD [Directive 2002/58/EC]

Article 2 (Definitions) (see also recital 17); Article 5 (Confidentiality of communications) (see also recital 25); Article 6 (Traffic data) (see also recitals 22, 30–32); Article 9 (Location data other than traffic data) (see also recital 35); Article 12 (Directories of subscribers) (see also recital 39); Article 13 (Unsolicited communications) (see also recitals 40 and 42)

Related Provisions in EUDPR [Regulation (EU) 2018/1725]

Article 3(15) (Definition of consent); Article 7 (Conditions for consent) (see also recitals 19 and 26); Article 8 (Conditions applicable to child's consent in relation to information society services); Article 10(2)(a) (Processing of special categories of personal data—consent) (see too recital 29); Article 15(2)(c) (Information to be provided—withdrawal of consent); Article 16(2)(c) (Information to be provided—withdrawal of consent); Article 19(1)(b) (Right to erasure—withdrawal of consent) (see also recital 38); Article 20(2) (Right to restriction of processing); Article 22(1)(a) (Right to data portability) (see also recital 41); Article 24(2)(c) (Automated decisions and profiling) (see also recital 43); Article 50(1)(a) (Derogations for specific situations) (see also recital 68); Article 66 (Administrative fines) (see also recital 88)

Relevant Case Law

CJEU

Opinion of Advocate General Szpunar in Case C-673/17, *Planet49 GmbH v Bundesverband der Verbraucherzentralen und Verbraucherverbände – Verbraucherzentrale Bundesverband e.V.*, delivered on 21 March 2019 (ECLI:EU:C:2019:246).

Germany

Bundesgerichtshof, *Urteil vom 16. 07. 2008*, VIII ZR 348/06.

A. Rationale and Policy Underpinnings

The conditions for exercising consent under the DPD were construed and applied across EU Member States divergently. The European Commission found that these conditions 'rang[ed] from a general requirement of written consent to the acceptance of implicit consent'.[1] Moreover, the consent requirements under the Directive were criticised for not serving the role they were supposed to for a variety of reasons—e.g. the information provided to the data subject was lengthy or unintelligible; consent to the processing of personal data was given in order for the data subject to get access to services that did not require such processing; or consent was obtained in a context characterised by an imbalance of powers.[2] The GDPR therefore contains a dedicated set of provisions in Article 7 clarifying the conditions for consent, with the aim of ensuring that 'the individual is fully aware that he or she is consenting, and to what data processing, in line with Article 8 of the EU Charter of Fundamental Rights'.[3]

B. Legal Background

1. EU legislation

Article 7 has no exact equivalent in the DPD. The latter did not contain any particular article specifying the operation of consent as a condition for processing in practice. In addition to providing a definition of consent (i.e. 'any freely given specific and informed indication of his wishes by which the data subject signifies his agreement to personal data relating to him being processed' (Article 2(h) DPD)), the DPD referred to consent of the data subject as a legitimate ground for data processing in three instances.

First, Article 7(a) specified the unambiguous consent of the data subject as one of the general criteria for making data processing legitimate. Secondly, the consent of the data subject appeared in relation to especially sensitive data, the processing of which was, in principle, prohibited. The processing of such data was exceptionally allowed when the data subject had given their explicit consent to the processing of the data, except where the laws of a Member State provided that the prohibition of the processing of sensitive data may not be lifted by data subject consent (Article 8(2)(a) DPD). Thirdly, the transfer of personal data to third countries was allowed only when the third country ensured an adequate level of protection (Article 25(2) DPD). A derogation to this rule applied when the unambiguous consent of the data subject was provided (Article 26(1) DPD).

The DPD did not explicitly refer to the withdrawal of consent. However, the possibility to withdraw consent is part and parcel of a data subject's right to informational self-determination, which also entails that the data subject cannot waive their possibility to withdraw their consent in the future.[4]

Similar to the DPD, Regulation 45/2001[5] recognised the unambiguous consent of the data subject as a ground for legitimate data processing (Article 5(d) Regulation 45/2001). Such consent could also be relied upon for the transfer of data from Community institutions or bodies (Article 9(6)(a)), by derogation from the general rules for data transfers (Article 9(1) and (2)). Finally, the 'express' consent of the data subject was recognised as

---

[1] EC Communication 2010, p. 8.   [2] Kosta 2013, pp. 140 ff.
[3] EC Communication 2010, p. 9.   [4] See e.g. Simitis 2003, section 4a, para. 90.
[5] See Table of Legislation.

an exceptional ground for the processing of especially sensitive data, the processing of which was, in principle, prohibited (Article 10 Regulation).

The EUDPR replicates many of the rules of consent in the GDPR and expands the treatment of consent as compared to Regulation 45/2001. The provisions of Article 7 GDPR are mirrored in Article 7 EUDPR, those of recital 42 GDPR are also mirrored in recital 26 EUDPR, while parts of recital 43 GDPR are repeated in recital 19 EUDPR. The EUDPR contains provisions dealing with the definition of consent (Article 3(15)), conditions for consent (Article 7), and children's consent (Article 8). It also allows for the use of explicit consent as a means to process sensitive data (Article 10(2)(a)). Article 50(1)(a) EUDPR allows for the use of explicit consent as a derogation allowing the international transfer of personal data.

In respect of electronic communications, the EPD defines consent as corresponding to the concept of consent in the DPD (Article 2(f) EPD). The EPD reserves a crucial role for consent in relation to the confidentiality of communications (Article 5(3) EPD) and unsolicited communications (Article 13 EPD). Moreover, the EPD allows the processing of traffic and location data on the basis of consent of the user or the subscriber (Articles 6 and 9 EPD). If directories of subscribers are used for any purposes other than the search of contact details of persons, additional consent should be asked of the subscribers.

Delay in reform of the EPD has created some operational difficulties in light of the GDPR's application. As mentioned above, the EPD defines consent by reference to the DPD definition, which is not valid anymore. Article 94 GDPR stipulates that references to the repealed DPD shall be construed as references to the GDPR, while Article 95 GDPR prohibits the imposition of additional obligations in relation to processing governed by the EPD. Thus, although the notion of consent should be understood in light of Article 4(11) GDPR, the specific requirements introduced in Article 7 GDPR do not apply in the electronic communications sector. This situation creates a quandary for the electronic communications industry as to what standard to follow, especially in the context of consent to online marketing and advertising.

2. International instruments

The consent of the data subject as a legitimate basis for personal data processing is explicitly recognised in Article 8(2) of the Charter of Fundamental Rights of the European Union ('CFR'), which stipulates that personal data 'must be processed fairly for specified purposes and on the basis of the consent of the person concerned or some other legitimate basis laid down by law'. This indicates that consent of data subjects is a value that is especially protected at a European constitutional level.

Convention 108 as first adopted did not contain any specific reference to consent. However, the Modernised Convention introduces a provision similar to the GDPR, stipulating that 'data processing can be carried out on the basis of the free, specific, informed and unambiguous consent of the data subject ... ' (Article 5(2)). The data subject's 'explicit, specific and free consent, after being informed of risks arising in the absence of appropriate safeguards' is also mentioned as a ground for legitimising the trans-border transfer of personal data (Article 14(4)(a)). Further, the processing of personal data is allowed when it is necessary for the performance of the duties and exercise of powers of supervisory authorities in the context of cooperation among them or when the data subject has provided their 'explicit, specific, free and informed consent' (Article 17(2)).

3. National developments

Germany's Federal Data Protection Act of 1990 included provisions on the conditions for consent, which have helped shape Article 7 GDPR.[6] Section 4(a) of the Act required that 'if consent is to be given in writing simultaneously with other written declarations, special prominence shall be given to the declaration of consent'. This requirement was interpreted by the German Federal Court of Justice (Bundesgerichtshof) as necessitating that the clause on the consent to the processing of personal data is clearly highlighted, but that the clause does not have to be provided in a separate document requiring, for instance, a special signature from the data subject or the ticking of a box explicitly allowing the processing of his/her personal data.[7] Nonetheless, the Court held that the clause on consent should not be simply part of the general terms and conditions of a contract, without any special highlighting, nor can it be included in the fine print of the contract, as the data subject can easily overlook it.[8]

4. Case law

As Article 7 GDPR is new, there is no case law directly on its provisions. However, the CJEU has ruled in a number of cases concerning the effects of lack of valid consent to the processing of personal data.[9] Further, Case C-673/17, *Planet49* (pending), may provide useful guidance for interpreting Article 7(4) as it concerns the assessment of whether consent may be freely given by means of pre-ticked boxes.

C. Analysis

1. Introduction

Article 7 complements the definition of consent with specific conditions and is only relevant when consent is used as the legitimate ground for data processing, either on a general basis (i.e. pursuant to Article 6(1)(a)) or with respect to particular processing operations, such as those involving processing of especially sensitive data (Article 9(2)(a)) or fully automated decision-making (Article 22(2)(c)).

2. Demonstrating consent

It stipulates first that controllers must be able to demonstrate that consent of the data subjects has been provided (Article 7(1)). As the controllers will be responsible to prove that consent was provided in a valid way for a specific data processing operation, they should use reliable means in order to obtain such consent, taking into account the sensitivity of each specific data processing operation.[10] The Commission Proposal for the GDPR explicitly stated that the controller bore the burden of proving that the consent of the data subject had been provided for specified purposes. Explicit reference to the burden of proof is removed from the final text of the GDPR, yet remains implicit in the

---

[6] German Federal Data Protection Act 1990.
[7] *Urteil vom 16. 07. 2008*. See further Kosta 2013, pp. 195–198.
[8] *Urteil vom 16. 07. 2008*. See also e.g. Hoeren 2010, p. 434; Kosta 2013, p. 152 and references cited therein.
[9] See case law cited in the commentary on Art. 6(1)(a) in this volume.
[10] See also EDPS 2012, p. 21; WP29 2018, p. 9.

wording of Article 7(1) as controllers still have to demonstrate that the data subject has consented to processing of her or his personal data. In practice, controllers need to keep a registry of acquired consents, as they will need to be able to demonstrate that consent has been obtained in situations where the data subject questions her or his provision of consent. In online environments, the consent provided should be logged.

3. Obtaining consent

Article 7(2) requires putting in place measures to ensure that a request for consent, in so far as it forms part of a written declaration concerning another matter, is clearly distinguishable from the other elements of the written declaration, 'in an intelligible and easily accessible form, using clear and plain language'. This requirement builds on pre-existing norms in German law, elaborated above. Therefore, when consent to data processing is provided, for instance, as part of a membership agreement, the section of the agreement where consent is requested, should be highlighted by being placed in a frame or printed in a different font or colour—to name just a few options. The requirement is aimed at stopping the common practice whereby businesses include the text for consenting to processing of personal data in the fine print of agreements. The notion of 'written declaration' covers not just paper-based documents but also digital text in online environments. Thus, when consent is requested by electronic means, it has also to be presented in a separate and easily distinguishable way.[11] Taking into account the difficulties that such a requirement may raise for devices with small screens or similar situations with limited space for information, the relevant information about consent may be presented in a layered way.[12]

Article 7(2) clearly states that any part of the written declaration of the data subject concerning other matters—for instance the Terms and Conditions of a service—which infringes the GDPR shall not be binding. However, Article 7(2) does not specify how the rest of the declaration is to be treated, and the invalidity of the specific part does not, under the GDPR, necessarily extend to the rest of the declaration. Ultimately, the validity of the other parts of the declaration, in so far as they do not fall within the ambit of the GDPR, will depend on the relevant national law. If the declaration is part of a contract, the latter law will be primarily contractual.

Recital 42 GDPR clarifies that where consent to the processing of personal data is given as part of a written declaration on another matter, there should be safeguards in place to ensure that the data subject is aware of the fact that she or he is giving consent and the extent to which consent is provided. In addition, recital 42 refers to declarations of consent that are pre-formulated by the controller, which should be provided 'in an intelligible and easily accessible form, using clear and plain language and … should not contain unfair terms', in accordance with the Unfair Contract Terms Directive ('UCTD'). The reference to the UCTD in the recital is problematic. Whether and under which conditions a contract is formed, which is crucial for the application of the UCTD—in particular as regards free services—is an issue of national law and the answers to these questions differ significantly between civil law and common law countries, as the latter require consideration for the formation of a valid contract. In common law countries, there may often be no valid contract formed for free services unless personal data are regarded as consideration, and any reference to the UCTD would be out of scope.[13]

[11] WP29 2018, p. 14. [12] Ibid. [13] Clifford et al. 2018.

4. Withdrawal of consent

Moving to Article 7(3), this comprises three norms and one qualification. The primary norm is that the data subject has the right to withdraw his consent at any time. A second norm is that the controller must inform the data subject of this right, before providing his/her consent. This requirement is complemented by similar notification duties under Articles 13(2)(c) and 14(2)(d), in so far as the data subject does not 'already ha[ve] the information' (Articles 13(4) and 14(5)(a)). Thirdly, the consent must be as easy to withdraw as to provide. For instance, when consent is provided via electronic means through one mouse-click, its withdrawal shall also be possible by equally expedient means.[14] As for the qualification, Article 7(3) makes clear that withdrawal of consent does not affect the lawfulness of the processing that was based on consent before the withdrawal. If the controller has another legitimate ground for processing personal data, the withdrawal of consent does not lead to the end of the data processing. In such cases, though, the data subject shall be notified about the change in the lawful basis for data processing (Article 13(1)(b) GDPR).

The withdrawal of consent is distinct from data subjects' right to object. The withdrawal of consent refers to consent that has already been given by data subjects for the processing of their personal data, while the right to object is applicable to data processing that is not based on the consent of the data subject, but relies on Article 6(1)(e) or (f) GDPR (see Article 21(1) GDPR) or involves direct marketing (Article 21(2) GDPR). The controller is not required to delete the personal data that were legitimately processed based on the withdrawn consent, unless there is no other legal ground for retaining the data (Article 17(1)(b) GDPR).

5. Freely given

One of the elements for the provision of valid consent is that it should be freely given (see the definition of consent in Article 4(11) GDPR). Various influences can be exercised on data subjects in order to manipulate their decision to agree to the processing of their personal data.[15] However, not every exercise of external pressure leads to the invalidation of consent. The consent of the data subject is still freely given when the data subject is simply convinced to provide it. For example, consent is valid when an individual consents to the processing of their personal data to receive news about their local football club despite being encouraged to do so by a club official, even if later on they wonder whether they are really interested in the progress of the team. However, the exercise of any kind of negative pressure in the form of coercion renders the consent invalid.[16] In this respect, recital 42 indicates that a freely given consent is predicated not only on the data subject's ability to exercise 'genuine or free choice' prior to giving consent but also her or his ability to withdraw consent 'without detriment'.

Article 7(4) specifies one of the factors that shall be taken into account when assessing whether coercion exists in a contractual setting. The reference to 'utmost account' indicates that the factor concerned is central and decisive, at least in the contractual context. At the same time, the reference to 'inter alia' indicates that the factor is but one of

---

[14] WP29 2018, p. 21.
[15] See further Kosta 2013, p. 174. See also the commentary on Art. 4(11) in this volume.
[16] Kosta 2013, p. 176. See too WP29 2018, p. 7 ('Consent will not be free in cases where there is any element of compulsion, pressure or inability to exercise free will').

multiple factors that may be taken into consideration when assessing the voluntariness of consent more generally.

6. Bundling consent

Article 7(4) addresses the common practice of 'bundling' or 'tying' that has required individuals to consent to the processing of their personal data in order to get access to a service or a good as part of a contract. Article 7(4) is implicitly aimed at reducing this practice and at ensuring that 'personal data processing is not disguised or bundled with the provision of a contract of a service for which these personal data are not necessary'.[17]

The GDPR does not fully and utterly forbid such disguising or bundling. As noted by Advocate General Szpunar in his opinion in *Planet49*, the wording of Article 7(4) implies that 'the prohibition on bundling is not absolute in nature'.[18] Recital 43 GDPR indicates that the existence of bundling leads to a 'presumption' that the consent is not freely given. In principle, this presumption may be rebuttable; in practice, though, it is likely to be very difficult to overturn. As pointed out by the WP29, cases in which the presumption is overturned 'will be highly exceptional'.[19] And, in line with Article 7(1) and the overarching principle of accountability (Article 5(2) GDPR), it is the controller that bears the burden of rebuttal.[20] The WP29 has indicated that a controller might be able to overturn the presumption if the controller is able to demonstrate that there is a genuinely equivalent service offered by the same controller, which does not require consenting to the processing of personal data for purposes beyond what is necessary for performance of the contract.[21] In its 2017 guidelines on consent, the WP29 required that both services are 'genuinely equivalent, including no further costs';[22] however, the requirement that the equivalent alternative service offered by the controller should not entail additional costs was deleted from the updated guidelines adopted in 2018.[23]

By contrast, the UK data protection authority (ICO) has suggested that, in some limited circumstances, controllers might be able to overturn the presumption if

there is legitimate reason for the processing that is consistent with the underlying purpose of the service on offer, it is reasonable for it to be bundled with the service, there is a minimal privacy impact, consent is clearly specific, informed and unambiguous, [they] would stop the processing altogether if the individual withdrew their consent and there is no alternative to consent.[24]

However, the ICO admitted that the wording of Article 7(4) and relevant recitals are such that controllers should better rely on the 'legitimate interests' ground as a lawful basis for processing personal data and have a 'clear and transparent privacy notice'.[25]

Recital 43 also states that consent is presumed to be not freely given if it relates to multiple data processing operations and it is not possible to separate out consent on the basis of each of these operations, 'despite it being appropriate in the individual case'. As the WP29 observed, when a 'controller has conflated several purposes for processing and has not attempted to seek separate consent for each purpose, there is a lack of freedom'.[26]

---

[17] WP29 2018, p. 8. The necessity of the data for the performance of the contract should be interpreted narrowly, as discussed in the commentary on Art. 6 in this volume.
[18] Case C-673/17, *Planet49* (AG Opinion), para. 98. See further the commentary on Art. 4(11) in this volume.
[19] WP29 2018, p. 9.   [20] Ibid.   [21] Ibid.   [22] WP29 2017, p. 10.
[23] WP29 2018, p. 9.   [24] ICO 2017, p. 20.   [25] Ibid.   [26] WP29 2018, p. 10.

Moreover, recital 43 states that consent should not constitute a valid ground for data processing when there is, in a 'specific case', a 'clear imbalance between the data subject and the controller, in particular where the controller is a public authority and it is therefore unlikely that consent was freely given in all the circumstances of that specific situation'. As pointed out by the WP29, however, consent may still be valid in certain situations characterised by an imbalance of powers between the parties—for example, when a public school asks students to consent to the use of their photographs in a printed student magazine, or when a local municipality that plans road maintenance work asks citizens to subscribe to an email list to receive updates on the progress of the works and on expected delays.[27] Yet, the ability to use consent in situations characterised by imbalance of powers (typically, the situation pertaining to the relations between state authorities and individual citizens or to employer–employee relationships) will be exceptional.[28]

7. Enforcement

Failure to comply with the obligations relating to Article 7 can result in an administrative fine of up to € 20 million or in the case of an undertaking, up to 4 per cent of the total worldwide annual turnover of the preceding financial year, whichever is higher (Article 83(5)(a) GDPR).

Select Bibliography

EU legislation

UCDT: Council Directive 93/13/EEC of 5 April 1993 on unfair terms in consumer contracts, OJ 1993 L 95/29.

National legislation

German Federal Data Protection Act 1990: Gesetz zur Fortentwicklung der Datenverarbeitung und des Datenschutzes (Bundesdatenschutzgesetz), BGBl 1990 Teil 1 Nr. 2954 (repealed).

Academic writings

Clifford et al. 2018: Clifford, Graef and Valcke, 'Pre-Formulated Declarations of Data Subject Consent: Citizen-Consumer Empowerment and the Alignment of Data, Consumer and Competition Law Protections', 20 *German Law Journal* (forthcoming 2019).
Hoeren 2010: Hoeren, 'Die Einwilligung in Direktmarketing unter datenschutzrechtlichen Aspekten', 9 *Zeitschrift für die Anwaltspraxis* (2010), 434.
Kosta 2013: Kosta, *Consent in European Data Protection Law* (Martinus Nijhoff 2013).
Redeker, 'Teil 12 Internetverträge', in Hoeren and Sieber (eds.), *Handbuch Multimedia-Recht— Rechtsfragen des elektronischen Geschäftsverkehrs (Ergänzungslieferung)* (Verlag C. H. Beck 2010).
Simitis 2003: Simitis (ed.), *Kommentar zum Bundesdatenschutzgesetz* (5th edn, Nomos Verlagsgesellschaft 2003).

Papers of data protection authorities

EDPS 2012: European Data Protection Supervisor, 'Opinion on the Data Protection Reform Package' (7 March 2012).

---

[27] Ibid., p. 6. [28] Ibid. See further the commentary on Art. 6(1)(a) in this volume.

WP29 2017: Article 29 Data Protection Working Party, 'Guidelines on Consent under Regulation 2016/679' (WP259, 28 November 2017).

WP29 2018: Article 29 Data Protection Working Party, 'Guidelines on Consent under Regulation 2016/679' (WP259 rev.01, as last revised and adopted on 10 April 2018).

Article 29 Data Protection Working Party, 'Opinion 15/2011 on the Definition of Consent' (WP187, 13 July 2011).

ICO 2017: UK Information Commissioner's Office, 'Consultation: GDPR Consent Guidance' (March 2017).

Reports and recommendations

EC Communication 2010: Communication from the Commission to the European Parliament, the Council, the Economic and Social Committee and the Committee of the Regions, A Comprehensive Approach on Personal Data Protection in the European Union, COM(2010) 609 final, 4 November 2010.

Article 8. Conditions applicable to child's consent in relation to information society services

ELENI KOSTA

1. Where point (a) of Article 6(1) applies, in relation to the offer of information society services directly to a child, the processing of the personal data of a child shall be lawful where the child is at least 16 years old. Where the child is below the age of 16 years, such processing shall be lawful only if and to the extent that consent is given or authorised by the holder of parental responsibility over the child. Member States may provide by law for a lower age for those purposes provided that such lower age is not below 13 years.
2. The controller shall make reasonable efforts to verify in such cases that consent is given or authorised by the holder of parental responsibility over the child, taking into consideration available technology.
3. Paragraph 1 shall not affect the general contract law of Member States such as the rules on the validity, formation or effect of a contract in relation to a child.

Relevant Recital

(38) Children merit specific protection with regard to their personal data, as they may be less aware of the risks, consequences and safeguards concerned and their rights in relation to the processing of personal data. Such specific protection should, in particular, apply to the use of personal data of children for the purposes of marketing or creating personality or user profiles and the collection of personal data with regard to children when using services offered directly to a child. The consent of the holder of parental responsibility should not be necessary in the context of preventive or counselling services offered directly to a child.

Closely Related Provisions

Article 7 (Conditions for consent); Article 12 (Transparent information, communication and modalities of exercise of the rights of the data subject) (see also recital 58); Article 40(2)(g) (Codes of conduct); Article 22 (Automated individual decision-making) (see also recital 71); Article 35 (Data Protection Impact Assessments)

Related Provisions in LED [Directive (EU) 2016/680]

Article 13, Article 20, recitals 39 and 50–51

Related Provisions in EUDPR [Regulation (EU) 2018/1725]

Article 3(15) (Definition of consent) (see also recital 19); Article 5(1)(d) (Data subject consent); Article 7 (Conditions of consent) (see also recitals 19 and 26); Article 24 (Automated decisions and profiling) (see also recital 43); Article 39 (Data protection impact assessment) (see also recital 46)

Relevant Case Law

ECtHR

K.U. v Finland, Appl. No. 2872/02, judgment of 2 December 2008.

A. Rationale and Policy Underpinnings

From the outset of the discussions about the reform of the EU data protection legal framework, the European Commission identified the need for special protection for children, as 'they may be less aware of risks, consequences, safeguards and rights in relation to the processing of personal data'.[1] This was in line with the EU's express commitment to protecting the rights of the child, as laid down in Article 3(3) Treaty on European Union ('TEU') and Article 24 Charter of Fundamental Rights of the European Union ('CFR'). In the first publicly leaked unofficial drafts of the GDPR, a child was defined as any person under 18 years, but there was no specific article dedicated to consent of children. Article 7, which specified the conditions for consent, included a provision that the consent of a child is only valid when given or authorised by the child's parent or custodian.[2] Article 7 of the draft (which specified the general conditions for consent) simply included a rule that the consent of a child is only valid when given or authorised by the child's parent or custodian.[3] However, the European Commission included in its official proposal for the GDPR a dedicated article, Article 8, on the conditions applicable to the consent of children in relation to information society services.

The preparatory works contain little if any justification for the focus of Article 8 on such services, but it may be seen as a logical progression from the EU's long-standing concern for ensuring a safer internet for children—manifest especially in the Safer Internet programme, which was initiated back in 1999.[4] During the legislative process, the WP29 suggested that the scope of application of Article 8 be broadened in order to cover other areas besides information society services where processing of personal data of children occurs.[5] The suggestion was initially taken up by the European Parliament,[6] but was not adopted in the final text of the Regulation.

B. Legal Background

1. EU legislation

The DPD omitted any reference to minors or children in general or specifically in relation to their capacity to consent. However, during the life of the DPD, the WP29 has published several sets of guidance on the consent of children to the processing of their personal data. Besides a dedicated 2009 opinion on the protection of children's personal

---

[1] EC Communication 2010, p. 6.   [2] GDPR Interservice Draft.   [3] Ibid.
[4] Further on the background for Art. 8 GDPR and the legislative process leading to its adoption, see Macenaite and Kosta 2017, pp. 147–148 and 161–166.
[5] WP29 2012, p. 13.   [6] See Macenaite and Kosta 2017, p. 162.

data,[7] the WP29 made recommendations on the processing of personal data of children in several opinions dealing with specific data-processing operations or challenges, highlighting the need for special attention when processing data of children.[8]

The WP29 considered a child as someone under the age of 18, unless they have acquired legal adulthood before that age.[9] Taking into account the fact that the right to data protection belongs to the child and not to the representative who is appointed to exercise it, the WP29 opined that children, from a certain age, should be consulted on matters relating to them.[10]

Similar to the DPD, the EPD also does not contain any specific reference to children and their capacity to consent, although the need to attribute special protection to children has been discussed in the context of the revision of the EPD. For instance, the European Parliament in its first reading of the European Commission's Proposal for the ePrivacy Regulation proposed amendments that would stress the need to provide additional protection to children.[11]

The provisions of Article 8 GDPR are mirrored in Article 8 EUDPR, which sets 13 as the minimum age for consent. The provisions of recital 38 GDPR are also mirrored in recital 27 EUDPR.

Contrary to the GDPR and EUDPR, the LED does not establish specific safeguards in relation to the processing of data of children. This choice was criticised by, among others, the EDPS, who argued that specific attention should be given to issues relating to the accuracy of children's identification data and their reliability in time.[12]

2. International instruments

The majority of international policy documents set the age of 18 as the 'age of majority'.[13] However, this is not a hard limit for the exercise of rights of children. The central idea in the UN Convention on the Rights of the Child ('UNCRC') is the concept of gradually developing capabilities of a child, and therefore the rights and obligations of caregivers should be 'consistent with the evolving capacities of the child [and provide] appropriate ... guidance in the exercise by the child of the rights' (Article 5). The UNCRC recognises in particular the right of children against any arbitrary or unlawful interference with their privacy, family or correspondence, and not to be subject to unlawful attacks on his or her honour and reputation (Article 16).

Council of Europe Convention 108 as originally adopted did not include any substantive provision dealing specifically with the data protection rights of children, and the Modernised Convention 108 does not introduce any change in this regard except for mentioning in Article 15 (on the duties of supervisory authorities) that 'specific attention shall be given to the data protection rights of children and other vulnerable individuals'. Nonetheless, the Council of Europe has placed privacy and data protection issues high in its Strategy of the Rights of the Child.[14] In July 2018, the Committee of Ministers of the Council of Europe adopted a Recommendation to Member States on Guidelines to respect, protect and fulfil the rights of the child in the digital environment.[15] Part 3.4 of the Guidelines contains provisions dealing specifically with children's privacy and data protection.

---

[7] WP29 2009A. [8] WP29 2008; WP29 2009B: WP29 2010; WP29 2013.
[9] WP 2009A, p. 2. [10] Ibid., p. 5. [11] EPR Proposal. [12] EDPS 2012, para. 321.
[13] Lievens 2010, p. 28. [14] CoE 2016. [15] COM Recommendation 2018.

The issue of consent of children to the processing of their personal data in relation to online services is extensively discussed in the United Nations International Children's Emergency Fund ('UNICEF') discussion paper on 'Privacy, protection of personal information and reputation rights', according to which the explicit consent of children should be obtained for services for which the children can consent themselves. The discussion paper does not recommend a specific age for the provision of valid consent. It rather requires that for children who cannot provide valid consent 'parental consent or offline verification of a child's capacity to consent could be sought. Before seeking parental consent, the potential impacts on children's ability to freely and confidently access online services should also be considered'.[16]

3. National developments

As the DPD omitted specific provisions on the legal capacity of children to consent to the processing of their personal data, the regulatory choices of the Member States on regulating the issue vary significantly. In the UK, for instance, it is broadly accepted that a child above the age of 16 can give valid consent.[17] However, the UK Government and local authorities consider that children can be considered as able to consent from around the age of 12.[18] The age of 16 was also specified in the Dutch Data Protection Act as the age from which onwards children can consent themselves to the processing of their personal data. By contrast, Spain saw minors from the age of 14 as competent to consent to the processing of their personal data. This age was also considered as important in Germany, although this was not officially fixed.[19] Consultation with the parents could still be sought depending on each specific case.[20]

In respect of electronic communications, there have been initiatives at national level which specify issues relating to children's consent. For instance, several UK mobile network operators and location service providers developed a Code of Practice for the use of passive location services in the UK,[21] where they considered the capacity of minors to consent for the provision of child location services. According to the Code of Practice, the parent or guardian must consent to the child signing up to the location service for children under the age of 16, and the additional consent of the child is also required.[22]

4. Case law

The CJEU has not dealt specifically with cases that relate to children's consent in relation to information society services.

The ECtHR has also not yet ruled directly on cases relating to children's consent in relation to information society services, but it has decided cases dealing with the protection of children in relation to the processing of their personal data under Article 8 European Convention of Human Rights ('ECHR'). In *K.U. v Finland*, a child (aged 12 at the time of the alleged infringement) complained that an advertisement on an internet dating site was placed in his name without his knowledge. The ECtHR emphasised 'the potential threat to the applicant's physical and mental welfare brought about by the

---

[16] UNICEF Discussion Paper. [17] Dowty and Korff, 2009, p. 6. [18] Ibid. p. 8.
[19] Ibid., p. 31 [20] Ibid.
[21] UK Code of Practice 2006. The Code was adopted in 2004 and updated in 2006.
[22] Ibid., p. 7.

impugned situation and to his vulnerability in view of his young age' and highlighted that cases where the physical and moral welfare of a child is threatened assume even greater importance.[23]

C. Analysis

1. Introduction

The issue of the legal competence of minors to consent is complicated. As Hodgkin and Nowell have noted, 'setting an age for the acquisition of certain rights or for the loss of certain protections is a complex matter [which] balances the concept of the child as a subject of rights whose evolving capacities must be respected with the concept of the State's obligation to provide special protection'.[24] In the context of data protection, recital 38 GDPR recognises that children deserve special protection due to the fact that 'they may be less aware of the risks, consequences and safeguards concerned and their rights in relation to the processing of personal data'. It highlights this need particularly (but not exclusively) in relation to marketing, the creation of personality or user profiles and the use of services that are offered directly to children. Recital 38 does not make special reference to online services; it rather calls for special protection of children both in online and offline contexts.

Nonetheless, the focus of Article 8 GDPR is quite narrow and specific: it determines the conditions applicable to a child's consent in relation to information society services; it does not regulate issues relating to the consent of children in general. More concretely, Article 8 applies to processing of personal data of a child, when the processing relies on consent as legitimate ground, in accordance with Article 6(1)(a) GDPR. It applies to the offer of information society services directly to a child, and provides, as a general rule, that the child must be at least 16 years old at the time of giving consent for the offer to be lawful. Article 8 thus does not apply to the offer of offline services or to the offer of all online services, but only to information society services. Processing of data on children in the context of other services is governed (where applicable) by the general GDPR provisions and the national laws on the capacity of minors to consent.

Information society services are defined in Article 4(25) GDPR by further reference to the Single Market Transparency Directive (Directive 2015/1535). Article 1(1)(b) of this Directive defines 'service' as:

[A]ny information society service, that is to say, any service normally provided for remuneration, at a distance, by electronic means and at the individual request of a recipient of services. For the purposes of this definition: (i) 'at a distance' means that the service is provided without the parties being simultaneously present; (ii) 'by electronic means' means that the service is sent initially and received at its destination by means of electronic equipment for the processing (including digital compression) and storage of data, and entirely transmitted, conveyed and received by wire, by radio, by optical means or by other electromagnetic means; (iii) 'at the individual request of a recipient of services' means that the service is provided through the transmission of data on individual request.[25]

---

[23] ECtHR, *K.U. v Finland*, paras. 41 and 46.   [24] Hodgkin and Newell 2002, p. 1.

[25] Art. 1(1)b Directive 2015/1535. For analysis of this definition, see the commentary on Art. 4(25) in this volume.

2. Remuneration

The 'remuneration' requirement inherent in the above definition should not be interpreted strictly.[26] For example, an activity that is financed via advertising can also be considered as being provided for remuneration, even if the remuneration does not come directly from the user.[27] This interpretation is also in line with the original idea of the European Commission to protect children on social networks and with the interpretation of Article 8 by the Bavarian Data Protection Authority.[28] Furthermore, the CJEU has ruled that a service can be considered as provided for remuneration even in cases where the provider is a non-profit organisation, when there is an 'element of chance' inherent in the return or when the service is of a recreational or sporting nature.[29]

3. Offering directly to children

Article 8 does not refer to information society services in general, but to information society services that are offered *directly* to children. This requirement should not be read as only covering services that are exclusively offered to children, such as YouTube Kids, as this would limit excessively the scope of Article 8.[30] Information society services falling under this Article should be those that target either only children or both children and adults. Hence, Article 8 does not cover services that clearly exclude users below a certain age from the use of service, unless one could argue that the services are directed *de facto* to children.

4. Age limit and verification

When an information society service is offered directly to a child and the processing of personal data relies on consent, the GDPR differentiates, as a general rule, between children above and below 16 years of age. In the former case, the child can and has to provide valid informed consent to legitimate the processing. In the latter case, when the child is below the age of 16, the processing of their data is lawful only if and to the extent that the child's parent or custodian has given or authorised their consent (Article 8(1)).

In relation to age verification of children in online environments, the WP29 suggested, with respect to the DPD, that this should be based on a 'sliding scale approach', whereby the mechanism that would be used each time for age verification would depend on various factors relating to the specific data processing operation, such as the types of personal data that will be processed, the purposes for which they will be processed, eventual risks arising from the processing etc.[31]

The age limit for the provision of valid consent of children in the context of Article 8 was heavily debated among the European legislative bodies. The European Commission in its 2012 Proposal, proposed the age of 13.[32] Although the national legislation of many Member States favoured 14, 15 or 16 years, the choice of the European Commission can be explained as an attempt to align European rules with the US Children's Online Privacy Protection Act ('COPPA'), which aims at protecting the privacy of minors under 13 years

---

[26] Ibid. See also case references cited therein.
[27] Queck et al. 2010, para. 1-047.
[28] Bavarian DPA 2017.
[29] For an overview see Craig and de Búrca 2008, p. 819. See otherwise the cases listed in the commentary on Art. 4(25) in this volume.
[30] Lievens and Verdoot 2018, p. 272.
[31] WP29 2011, p. 28.
[32] GDPR Proposal.

of age in an online context.[33] The GDPR allows Member States to provide for a lower age provided that such lower age is not below 13 years (Article 8(1)). Unfortunately, the fact that Member States are allowed to lower the threshold of 16 years of age to anything between 13 and 16 does not contribute to the establishment of a harmonised legal framework for children's consent in the EU.[34] Controllers offering their services across multiple Member States should accordingly take into account not only the age limit established in the national law of the Member State where they have their main establishment, but also those established by relevant legislation in the Member States where they offer their information society services.[35]

5. Parental consent

In case parental consent[36] is required in accordance with Article 8, the controller is responsible for verifying that such consent is provided. On its face, Article 8 does not require verification of the age of the child, which would result in a double verification process by controllers: (a) that the child is below the age of 16 (or the diverging national age limit); and (b) if, the child is below the age threshold, that parental consent has been provided. Article 8 explicitly requires verification by the controller only of the latter. Nonetheless, age verification is required in practice when Article 8 applies, as the controller would first need to verify that the data subject is a child below the set minimum age for consent. If a child gives consent although they are under the national age limit for providing consent, the consent is not valid and the processing is unlawful.[37]

The controller has to make 'reasonable efforts' to verify parental consent, taking into account available technology (Article 8(2)). The challenge in such case is to specify what amount to such 'reasonable efforts'. The Belgian DPA has emphasised that this does not require a 'commitment of result' for the controller.[38] The WP29 recommended that a 'proportionate' approach should be adopted, following which the controller should obtain a limited amount of information about the parent or guardian, such as their contact details.[39] What are 'reasonable efforts' will need to be decided on a case-by-case basis, depending on the risks that are inherent in the processing and available technology. For instance, while verification via email may suffice in some low risk cases, in other cases the controller may request more proof.[40] Codes of conduct can be proposed by the associations representing controllers or processors on the way in which parental consent is to be obtained (Article 40(2)(g)). In the US, where COPPA already requires verification of parental consent, several technologies have been proposed to this end.[41]

When the child reaches the age specified in the national legislation, namely between 13 and 16 years, the consent of the child needs to be acquired by the controller. Reliance

---

[33] Council Report GDPR 2014, pp. 87–88.

[34] Indeed, as of 1 November 2018, Germany, Ireland, Hungary, Luxembourg, the Netherlands, Poland, Romania and Slovakia have set 16 years as the minimum age for consent; France the age of 15; Austria, Cyprus, Italy and Lithuania the age of 14; while Belgium, Denmark, Latvia, Malta, Norway, Sweden and the United Kingdom the age of 13.

[35] See also WP29 2018, p. 26.

[36] The term 'parental consent' covers the consent of the holder of parental responsibility, be it a parent, a legal guardian or custodian.

[37] WP29 2018, p. 26. [38] Lievens and Verdoot 2018, p. 274.

[39] WP29 2018, pp. 26–27. [40] Ibid., pp. 26–27.

[41] Examples are the products developed by AssertID and Imperium, respectively. For further information, see Macenaite and Kosta 2017, p. 178.

on parental consent after the child reaches the specified age will render the processing unlawful.[42] Obviously this requirement creates a heavy burden on controllers who need to periodically check the age of their customers and request consent from their customers that reach the specified age.

6. Enforcement

Failure to comply with the obligations relating to Article 8 can result in an administrative fine up to € 10 million or in the case of an undertaking, up to 2 per cent of the total worldwide annual turnover of the preceding financial year, whichever is higher (Article 83(4)(a) GDPR).

Select Bibliography

International agreements

UNCRC: Convention on the Rights of the Child 1989, 1577 UNTS 3.

EU legislation

Directive 2015/1535: Directive (EU) 2015/1535 of the European Parliament and of the Council of 9 September 2015 laying down a procedure for the provision of information in the field of technical regulations and of rules on Information Society services (Text with EEA relevance), OJ 2015 L 241/1.
EPR Proposal: Proposal for a Regulation of the European Parliament and of the Council concerning the respect for private life and the protection of personal data in electronic communications and repealing Directive 2002/58/EC (Regulation on Privacy and Electronic Communications), COM(2017)10 final, 10 January 2017.
GDPR Proposal: Proposal for a Regulation of the European Parliament and of the Council on the protection of individuals with regard to the processing of personal data and on the free movement of such data (General Data Protection Regulation), COM(2012) 11 final, 25 January 2012.

National legislation

COPPA: Children's Online Privacy Protection Act of 1998, 15 U.S.C. 6501–6505.

Academic writings

Craig and de Búrca 2008: Craig and de Búrca, *EU Law: Text, Cases, and Materials* (4th edn, OUP, 2008).
Hodgkin and Newell 2002: Hodgkin and Newell, *Implementation Handbook for the Convention on the Rights of the Child* (UNICEF 2002).
Jasmontaite and de Hert, 'The EU, Children under 13 Years, and Parental Consent: A Human Rights Analysis of a New, Age-Based Bright-Line for the Protection of Children on the Internet', 5(1) *International Data Privacy Law* (2015), 20.
Lievens 2010: Lievens, *Protecting Children in the Digital Era: The Use of Alternative Regulatory Instruments* (Martinus Nijhoff Publishers 2010).
Lievens and Verdoot 2018: Lievens and Verdoot, 'Looking for Needles in a Haystack: Key Issues Affecting Children's Rights in the General Data Protection Regulation', 34(2) *Computer Law & Security Review* (2018), 269.

---

[42] See also WP29 2018, p. 27.

Macenaite and Kosta 2017: Macenaite and Kosta, 'Consent of Minors to their Online Personal Data Processing in the EU: Following in US Footsteps?', 26(2) *Information and Communications Technology Law* (2017), 146.

Queck et al. 2010: Queck, Hou, Jost, Kosta and de Streel, 'The EU Regulatory Framework Applicable to Electronic Communications', in Garzantini and O'Regan (eds.), *Telecommunications, Broadcasting and the Internet* (3rd edn, Sweet & Maxwell, 2010), 1.

Van der Hof and Lievens, 'The Importance of Privacy by Design and Data Protection Impact Assessments in Strengthening Protection of Children's Personal Data Under the GDPR', 23(1) *Communications Law* (2018), 33.

Papers of data protection authorities

EDPS 2012: European Data Protection Supervisor, 'Opinion of the European Data Protection Supervisor on the Data Protection Reform Package' (7 March 2012).

WP29 2008: Article 29 Data Protection Working Party, 'Opinion 1/2008 on Data Protection Issues Related to Search Engines' (WP 148, 04 April 2008).

WP29 2009A: Article 29 Data Protection Working Party, 'Opinion 2/2009 on the Protection of Children's Personal Data (General Guidelines and the Special Case of Schools)' (WP 160, 11 February 2009).

WP29 2009B: Article 29 Data Protection Working Party, 'Opinion 5/2009 on Online Social Networking' (WP 163, 12 June 2009).

WP29 2010: Article 29 Data Protection Working Party, 'Opinion 2/2010 on Online Behavioural Advertising' (WP 171, 22 June 2010).

WP29 2011: Article 29 Data Protection Working Party, 'Opinion 15/2011 on the Definition of Consent' (WP187, 13 July 2011).

WP29 2012: Article 29 Data Protection Working Party, 'Opinion 01/2012 on the Data Protection Reform Proposals' (WP191, 23 March 2012).

WP29 2013: Article 29 Data Protection Working Party, 'Opinion 02/2013 on Apps on Smart Devices' (WP 202, 27 February 2013).

WP29 2018: Article 29 Data Protection Working Party, 'Guidelines on Consent under Regulation 2016/679' (WP259 rev 1, as last revised and adopted on 10 April 2018).

Reports and recommendations

Bavarian Data Protection Authority 2017: Bayrisches Landesamt für Datenschutzaufsicht, 'EU-Datenschutz-Grundverordnung (DS-GVO) – Das BayLDA auf dem Weg zur Umsetzung der Verordnung' (20 January 2017).

CoE 2016: Council of Europe, 'Strategy for the Rights of the Child (2016–2021)' (March 2016).

COM Recommendation 2018: Committee of Ministers of the Council of Europe, 'Recommendation on Guidelines to Respect, Protect and Fulfil the Rights of the Child in the Digital Environment' (CM/Rec(2018)7, 4 July 2018).

Council Report 2014: Proposal for a regulation of the European Parliament and of the Council on the protection of individuals with regard to the processing of personal data and on the free movement of such data (General Data Protection Regulation), 11028/14, 30 June 2014.

Dowty and Korff 2009: Dowty and Korff, 'Protecting the Virtual Child: The Law and Children's Consent to Sharing Personal Data', Report for ARCH (January 2009).

EC Communication 2010: Communication from the Commission to the European Parliament, the Council, the Economic and Social Committee and the Committee of the Regions, A Comprehensive Approach on Personal Data Protection in the European Union, COM(2010) 609 final, 4 November 2010.

GDPR Interservice Draft: Proposal for a Regulation of the European Parliament and of the Council on the protection of individuals with regard to the processing of personal data and on the free movement of such data (General Data Protection Regulation), Version 56, 29 November 2011.

UK Code of Practice 2006: Working Group of location service providers, 'Code of Practice for the Use of Passive Location Services in the UK' (1 October 2006).

UNICEF Discussion Paper: United Nations International Children's Emergency Fund, 'Discussion Paper on Privacy, Protection of Personal Information and Reputation Rights', available at https://www.unicef.org/csr/files/UNICEF_CRB_Digital_World_Series_PRIVACY.pdf.

Article 9. Processing of special categories of personal data

LUDMILA GEORGIEVA*   CHRISTOPHER KUNER

1. Processing of personal data revealing racial or ethnic origin, political opinions, religious or philosophical beliefs, or trade union membership, and the processing of genetic data, biometric data for the purpose of uniquely identifying a natural person, data concerning health or data concerning a natural person's sex life or sexual orientation shall be prohibited.
2. Paragraph 1 shall not apply if one of the following applies:
    (a) the data subject has given explicit consent to the processing of those personal data for one or more specified purposes, except where Union or Member State law provide that the prohibition referred to in paragraph 1 may not be lifted by the data subject;
    (b) processing is necessary for the purposes of carrying out the obligations and exercising specific rights of the controller or of the data subject in the field of employment and social security and social protection law in so far as it is authorised by Union or Member State law or a collective agreement pursuant to Member State law providing for appropriate safeguards for the fundamental rights and the interests of the data subject;
    (c) processing is necessary to protect the vital interests of the data subject or of another natural person where the data subject is physically or legally incapable of giving consent;
    (d) processing is carried out in the course of its legitimate activities with appropriate safeguards by a foundation, association or any other not-for-profit body with a political, philosophical, religious or trade union aim and on condition that the processing relates solely to the members or to former members of the body or to persons who have regular contact with it in connection with its purposes and that the personal data are not disclosed outside that body without the consent of the data subjects;
    (e) processing relates to personal data which are manifestly made public by the data subject;
    (f) processing is necessary for the establishment, exercise or defence of legal claims or whenever courts are acting in their judicial capacity;
    (g) processing is necessary for reasons of substantial public interest, on the basis of Union or Member State law which shall be proportionate to the aim pursued, respect the essence of the right to data protection and provide for suitable and specific measures to safeguard the fundamental rights and the interests of the data subject;
    (h) processing is necessary for the purposes of preventive or occupational medicine, for the assessment of the working capacity of the employee, medical diagnosis, the provision of health or social care or treatment or the management of health or social care systems and services on the basis of Union or Member State law or pursuant to contract with a health professional and subject to the conditions and safeguards referred to in paragraph 3;
    (i) processing is necessary for reasons of public interest in the area of public health, such as protecting against serious cross-border threats to health or ensuring high standards of quality and safety of health care and of medicinal products or medical devices, on the basis of Union or Member State law which provides for suitable and specific measures to safeguard the rights and freedoms of the data subject, in particular professional secrecy;
    (j) processing is necessary for archiving purposes in the public interest, scientific or historical research purposes or statistical purposes in accordance with Article 89(1) based on Union

---

* The views expressed are solely those of the author and do not necessarily reflect those of her current or former employers.

or Member State law which shall be proportionate to the aim pursued, respect the essence of the right to data protection and provide for suitable and specific measures to safeguard the fundamental rights and the interests of the data subject.
3. Personal data referred to in paragraph 1 may be processed for the purposes referred to in point (h) of paragraph 2 when those data are processed by or under the responsibility of a professional subject to the obligation of professional secrecy under Union or Member State law or rules established by national competent bodies or by another person also subject to an obligation of secrecy under Union or Member State law or rules established by national competent bodies.
4. Member States may maintain or introduce further conditions, including limitations, with regard to the processing of genetic data, biometric data or data concerning health.

Relevant Recitals

(10) In order to ensure a consistent and high level of protection of natural persons and to remove the obstacles to flows of personal data within the Union, the level of protection of the rights and freedoms of natural persons with regard to the processing of such data should be equivalent in all Member States. Consistent and homogenous application of the rules for the protection of the fundamental rights and freedoms of natural persons with regard to the processing of personal data should be ensured throughout the Union. Regarding the processing of personal data for compliance with a legal obligation, for the performance of a task carried out in the public interest or in the exercise of official authority vested in the controller, Member States should be allowed to maintain or introduce national provisions to further specify the application of the rules of this Regulation. In conjunction with the general and horizontal law on data protection implementing Directive 95/46/EC, Member States have several sector-specific laws in areas that need more specific provisions. This Regulation also provides a margin of manoeuvre for Member States to specify its rules, including for the processing of special categories of personal data ('sensitive data'). To that extent, this Regulation does not exclude Member State law that sets out the circumstances for specific processing situations, including determining more precisely the conditions under which the processing of personal data is lawful.

(51) Personal data which are, by their nature, particularly sensitive in relation to fundamental rights and freedoms merit specific protection as the context of their processing could create significant risks to the fundamental rights and freedoms. Those personal data should include personal data revealing racial or ethnic origin, whereby the use of the term 'racial origin' in this Regulation does not imply an acceptance by the Union of theories which attempt to determine the existence of separate human races. The processing of photographs should not systematically be considered to be processing of special categories of personal data as they are covered by the definition of biometric data only when processed through a specific technical means allowing the unique identification or authentication of a natural person. Such personal data should not be processed, unless processing is allowed in specific cases set out in this Regulation, taking into account that Member States law may lay down specific provisions on data protection in order to adapt the application of the rules of this Regulation for compliance with a legal obligation or for the performance of a task carried out in the public interest or in the exercise of official authority vested in the controller. In addition to the specific requirements for such processing, the general principles and other rules of this Regulation should apply, in particular as regards the conditions for lawful processing. Derogations from the general prohibition for processing such special categories of personal data should be explicitly provided, inter alia, where the data subject gives his or her explicit consent or in respect of specific needs in particular where the processing is carried out in the course of legitimate activities by certain associations or foundations the purpose of which is to permit the exercise of fundamental freedoms.

(52) Derogating from the prohibition on processing special categories of personal data should also be allowed when provided for in Union or Member State law and subject to suitable safeguards, so as to protect personal data and other fundamental rights, where it is in the public interest to do so, in particular processing personal data in the field of employment law, social protection law including pensions and for health security, monitoring and alert purposes, the prevention or control of communicable diseases and other serious threats to health. Such a derogation may be made for health purposes, including public health and the management of health-care services, especially in order to ensure the quality and cost-effectiveness of the procedures used for settling claims for benefits and services in the health insurance system, or for archiving purposes in the public interest, scientific or historical research purposes or statistical purposes. A derogation should also allow the processing of such personal data where necessary for the establishment, exercise or defence of legal claims, whether in court proceedings or in an administrative or out-of-court procedure.

(53) Special categories of personal data which merit higher protection should be processed for health-related purposes only where necessary to achieve those purposes for the benefit of natural persons and society as a whole, in particular in the context of the management of health or social care services and systems, including processing by the management and central national health authorities of such data for the purpose of quality control, management information and the general national and local supervision of the health or social care system, and ensuring continuity of health or social care and cross-border healthcare or health security, monitoring and alert purposes, or for archiving purposes in the public interest, scientific or historical research purposes or statistical purposes, based on Union or Member State law which has to meet an objective of public interest, as well as for studies conducted in the public interest in the area of public health. Therefore, this Regulation should provide for harmonised conditions for the processing of special categories of personal data concerning health, in respect of specific needs, in particular where the processing of such data is carried out for certain health-related purposes by persons subject to a legal obligation of professional secrecy. Union or Member State law should provide for specific and suitable measures so as to protect the fundamental rights and the personal data of natural persons. Member States should be allowed to maintain or introduce further conditions, including limitations, with regard to the processing of genetic data, biometric data or data concerning health. However, this should not hamper the free flow of personal data within the Union when those conditions apply to cross-border processing of such data.

(54) The processing of special categories of personal data may be necessary for reasons of public interest in the areas of public health without consent of the data subject. Such processing should be subject to suitable and specific measures so as to protect the rights and freedoms of natural persons. In that context, 'public health' should be interpreted as defined in Regulation (EC) No 1338/2008 of the European Parliament and of the Council, namely all elements related to health, namely health status, including morbidity and disability, the determinants having an effect on that health status, health care needs, resources allocated to health care, the provision of, and universal access to, health care as well as health care expenditure and financing, and the causes of mortality. Such processing of data concerning health for reasons of public interest should not result in personal data being processed for other purposes by third parties such as employers or insurance and banking companies.

(55) Moreover, the processing of personal data by official authorities for the purpose of achieving the aims, laid down by constitutional law or by international public law, of officially recognised religious associations, is carried out on grounds of public interest.

(56) Where in the course of electoral activities, the operation of the democratic system in a Member State requires that political parties compile personal data on people's political opinions, the processing of such data may be permitted for reasons of public interest, provided that appropriate safeguards are established.

Closely Related Provisions

Article 4(1) (Definition of personal data); Article 4(2) (Definition of processing); Article 4(11) (Definition of consent); Article 4(13) (Definition of genetic data, see also recital 34); Article 4(14) (Definition of biometric data); Article 4(15) (Definition of data concerning health, see also recital 35); Article 6(4)(c) (Lawfulness of processing, compatibility test) (see too recital 46 on vital interest); Article 13(2)(c) (Information to be provided where personal data are collected from the data subject); Article 17(1)(b), (3)(c) (Right to erasure ('right to be forgotten')); Article 20(1)(a) (Right to data portability); Article 22(4) (Automated individual decision-making, including profiling); Article 27(2)(a) (Representatives of controllers or processors not established in the Union); Article 30(5) (Records of processing activities); Article 35(3)(b) (Data protection impact assessment) (see too recital 91); Article 37(1)(c) (Designation of the data protection officer) (see too recital 97); Article 83(5)(a) (General conditions for imposing administrative fines)

Related Provisions in LED [Directive (EU) 2016/680]

Article 10 (Processing of special categories of personal data) (see too recital 37); Article 11 (Automated individual decision-making) (see too recital 38); Article 19 (Obligations of the controller) (see too recital 50 concerning risk to the rights and freedoms of natural persons); Article 24 (Records of processing activities); Article 27 (Data protection impact assessment) (see too recital 58); Article 29 (Security of processing) (see too recital 60)

Related Provisions in EPD [Directive 2002/58/EC]

Recital 25; Article 2(c) (Definition of location data); Article 5 (Confidentiality of communications) (see too recital 3); Article 9 (Location data other than traffic data) (see too recital 35)

Related Provisions in EUDPR [Regulation (EU) 2018/1725]

Article 3(1) (Definition of personal data); Article 3(3) (Definition of processing); Article 3(15) (Definition of consent); Article 3(17) (Definition of genetic data); Article 3(18) (Definition of biometric data); Article 3(19) (Definition of data concerning health); Article 6 (Processing for another compatible purpose); Article 10 (Processing of special categories of personal data); Article 15(2)(c) (Information to be provided where personal data are collected from the data subject); Article 19(1)(b), (3)(c) (Right to erasure ('right to be forgotten')); Article 22(1)(a) (Right to data portability); Article 24(4) (Automated individual decision-making, including profiling); Article 39(3)(b) (Data protection impact assessment); Article 66(3)(a) (Administrative fines)

Relevant Case Law

CJEU

Case C-101/01, *Criminal proceedings against Bodil Lindqvist*, judgment of 6 November 2003 (ECLI:EU:C:2003:596).

Joined Cases C-465/00, C-138/01 and C-139/01, *Rechnungshof v Österreichischer Rundfunk and Others* and *Christa Neukomm* and *Joseph Lauermann v Österreichischer Rundfunk*, judgment of 20 May 2003 (ECLI:EU:C:2003:294).

Case T-320/02, *Monika Esch-Leonhardt, Tillmann Frommhold and Emmanuel Larue v European Central Bank*, CFI, judgment of 18 February 2004 (ECLI:EU:T:2004:45).

Case F-46/09, *V v European Parliament*, CST, judgment of 5 July 2011 (ECLI:EU:F:2011:101).

Case T-190/10, *Kathleen Egan and Margaret Hackett v European Parliament*, GC, judgment of 28 March 2012 (ECLI:EU:T:2012:165).

Case C-291/12, *Michael Schwarz v Stadt Bochum*, judgment of 17 October 2013 (ECLI:EU:C:2013:670).

Opinion of Advocate General Mengozzi in Case C-291/12, *Michael Schwarz v Stadt Bochum*, delivered on 13 June 2013 (ECLI:EU:C:2013:401).

Opinion 1/15, Opinion of 26 July 2017 (Grand Chamber) (ECLI:EU:C:2017:592).

Opinion of Advocate General Szpunar in Case C-136/17, *G.C., A.F., B.H., E.D. v Commission nationale de l'informatique et des libertés (CNIL)*, delivered on 10 January 2019 (ECLI:EU:C:2019:14).

ECtHR

Z. v Finland, Appl. No. 22009/93, judgment of 25 February 1997.
L.L. v France, Appl. No. 7508/02, judgment of 10 October 2006.
I. v Finland, Appl. No. 20511/03, judgment of 17 July 2008
S. and Marper v UK, Appl. Nos. 30562/04 and 30566/04, judgment of 4 December 2008
L.H. v Latvia, Appl. No. 52019/07, judgment of 29 April 2014.
Vukota-Bojic v Switzerland, Appl. No. 61838/10, judgment of 18 October 2016.

A. Rationale and Policy Underpinnings

Article 9 GDPR is the successor to Article 8 DPD and, like the approach under the latter, contains a prohibition on the processing of certain types of data that the legislator has found to be particularly sensitive together with a list of exceptions under which such data may be processed. These data types are termed 'special categories of personal data', but the designation 'sensitive data' is used for them in this commentary.[1] Article 9 adds new types of data that are considered sensitive that were not listed in the DPD (e.g. biometric and genetic data[2]); several new permitted processing activities (e.g. courts acting in their judicial capacity,[3] employment and social care,[4] and public interest in the area of public health such as serious cross-border threats to health[5]); safeguards in the context of substantial public interest;[6] and several opening clauses (e.g. clauses that allow processing when provided by Union or Member State law[7]).

The history of Europe in the twentieth century shows that the misuse of sensitive data (e.g. data about race or religion) can facilitate human rights abuses on a large scale.[8] Misuse of sensitive data can also have serious consequences for individuals, such as unfair discrimination.[9] As stated in recital 51 GDPR, a high level of protection for sensitive data is regarded as necessary since they 'are, by their nature, particularly sensitive in relation

---

[1] The term 'sensitive data' is also used in rec. 10 GDPR.
[2] See the respective definitions ibid., Arts. 4(14) and 4(13). See also the commentaries on these definitions in this volume.
[3] Ibid., Art. 9(2)(f).   [4] Ibid., Art. 9(2)(h).   [5] Ibid., Art. 9(2)(i).
[6] Ibid., Art. 9(2)(g).   [7] Ibid., Art. 9(2)–(4).   [8] See Seltzer and Anderson 2001.
[9] See Art. 6(2) Modernised Convention 108.

to fundamental rights and freedoms merit specific protection as the context of their processing could create significant risks to the fundamental rights and freedoms'. Some sensitive data (e.g., some types of biometrics data) 'change irrevocably the relation between body and identity, in that they make the characteristics of the human body "machine-readable" and subject to further use ... forever ... '.[10] The processing of sensitive data also has the potential to affect adversely other fundamental rights,[11] and carries a high risk of harm to individuals.[12] At the same time, the processing of sensitive data can also potentially bring great benefits (e.g., the processing of health data in research in order to create new forms of medical treatment). The rapid development of technology thus both poses risks for the processing of sensitive data and creates new opportunities for such processing to benefit both individuals and society in general.

However, providing special protection for certain categories of data has also been controversial. Thus, it has been stated that 'singling out relatively fixed sub-sets of personal data for special protection breaks with the otherwise common assumption in the field that the sensitivity of data is essentially context-dependent'.[13] Extra protections for sensitive data were adopted in the Council of Europe's Convention 108 in 1980, which proved highly influential in Member States enacting similar provisions in their laws and in the adoption of Article 8 DPD.[14] There was also a consensus among Member States for including an equivalent to Article 8 DPD during the legislative process that led to the GDPR's adoption.[15] Hence, the approach and the rules of Article 8 DPD are maintained in Article 9 GDPR, albeit in a modified and updated form.

B. Legal Background

1. EU legislation

As noted above, Article 8 DPD regulated the processing of special categories of data in a similar manner to Article 9 GDPR. Since the DPD was a directive, Article 8 was addressed to the Member States, which had to implement it into their national law. Article 8 listed the same categories of sensitive data listed in Article 9 GDPR except for genetic data, biometric data and data concerning sexual orientation.

Regulation 45/2001[16] also contained a provision on sensitive data in Article 10, which was similar to Article 8 DPD. Article 10 EUDPR contains updated provisions on sensitive data, which track those of the GDPR and are to be construed in the same way (recital 5 EUDPR).

The WP29 issued a number of opinions and papers dealing with the processing of sensitive data. These include a paper on general issues of sensitive data,[17] and papers

---

[10] EDPS 2005, p. 19, cited in the Opinion of Advocate General Megozzi in Case C-291/12, *Schwarz* (AG Opinion), para. 1.

[11] For example, the processing of personal data revealing religious beliefs can affect the freedom of religion under Art. 10 Charter of Fundamental Rights of the European Union ('CFR'), and the processing of personal data revealing trade union membership can affect the freedom of association in trade union matters under Art. 12 CFR.

[12] See WP29 2011, p. 4.

[13] Bygrave 2014, p. 165. See also Simitis and Dammann 1997, p. 160.   [14] Simitis 1999, p. 1.

[15] See DPD Proposal 1992, p. 17 ('there is a broad consensus among the Member States that certain categories of data do by their nature pose a threat to privacy').

[16] See Table of Legislation.   [17] WP29 2011.

on specific topics, such as biometric data[18] and genetic data.[19] The EDPB has also published guidelines on video surveillance which include extensive guidance on the use of biometrics.[20]

2. International instruments

Convention 108 was highly influential in leading to the adoption of provisions on sensitive data in the first Member State laws, as well as in the DPD. Article 6 of the Convention as originally adopted provides as follows:

> Personal data revealing racial origin, political opinions or religious or other beliefs, as well as personal data concerning health or sexual life, may not be processed automatically unless domestic law provides appropriate safeguards. The same shall apply to personal data relating to criminal convictions.[21]

The wording of Article 6 of the Convention can be viewed as more flexible than that of Article 8 DPD,[22] and gives considerable freedom to states to enact data processing rules for sensitive data. The Modernised Convention 108 contains a reformulation of Article 6, which now reads thus:

> 1. The processing of:
>   - genetic data;
>   - personal data relating to offences, criminal proceedings and convictions, and related security measures;
>   - biometric data uniquely identifying a person;
>   - personal data for the information they reveal relating to racial or ethnic origin, political opinions, trade-union membership, religious or other beliefs, health or sexual life,
>   shall only be allowed where appropriate safeguards are enshrined in law, complementing those of this Convention.[23]
> 2. Such safeguards shall guard against the risks that the processing of sensitive data may present for the interests, rights and fundamental freedoms of the data subject, notably a risk of discrimination.

The Explanatory Memorandum to Article 6 notes that appropriate safeguards should be 'adapted to the risks at stake and the interests, rights and freedoms to be protected'.[24] It gives as examples of safeguards, alone or cumulatively, 'the data subject's explicit consent; a law covering the intended purpose and means of the processing or indicating the exceptional cases where processing such data would be permitted; a professional secrecy obligation; measures following a risk analysis; and a particular and qualified organisational or technical security measure (data encryption, for example)'.[25]

The Council of Europe has also issued a number of influential recommendations and reports dealing with the processing of certain types of sensitive data. These include a report on the protection of sensitive data generally,[26] and publications and recommendations dealing with the processing of specific types of sensitive data, such as biometric data,[27] medical data,[28] insurance data[29] and genetic data.[30]

---

[18] WP29 2003; WP29 2004B; WP29 2005; and WP29 2012. [19] WP29 2004A.
[20] EDPB 2019, pp. 15–19. [21] Art. 6 Convention 108. [22] See Simitis 1999, p. 2.
[23] Art. 6 Modernised Convention 108.
[24] See the Explanatory Memorandum to Modernised Convention 108, p. 10. [25] Ibid.
[26] Simitis 1999. [27] Progress Report on Biometric Data 2005; de Hert and Christianen 2013.
[28] COM Recommendation 1997. [29] COM Recommendation 2016.
[30] COM Recommendation 1992; Opinion Insurance Purposes 2014.

3. National developments

There were significant differences in how states implemented Article 6 of Convention 108.[31] These differences continued under Article 8 DPD.[32] Article 9 GDPR contains a number of opening clauses (i.e. Article 9(2)(a)–(b), (2)(g)–(j), (3) and (4)) that allow for national implementation. Article 9(4) grants Member States the power to adopt stricter provisions with regard to the processing of genetic data, biometric data or data concerning health, though such restrictions must not affect the free flow of data within the Union.[33] Provisions of national law enacted under the DPD that do not correspond with the opening clauses of Article 9 will have to be repealed or adapted to the GDPR. In implementing Article 9, Member States must keep in mind Article 16(2) of the Treaty on the Functioning of the European Union ('TFEU') which mandates a high level of protection.[34]

4. Case law

Both the CJEU and the ECtHR have addressed the processing of sensitive data in a number of judgments, which are described below.

In *Lindqvist*, the CJEU adopted a broad interpretation of the expression 'data concerning health' used in Article 8(1) DPD so as to include information concerning all aspects, both physical and mental, of the health of an individual. Therefore, the reference to the fact that an individual had injured a foot and was working half-time on medical grounds constituted personal data concerning health within the meaning of Article 8(1) DPD.[35]

In *Schwarz*, the CJEU considered whether an obligation under EU law to provide two fingerprints for storage in a passport was contrary to Articles 7 and 8 CFR. The Court noted that Regulation 2252/2004[36] did not provide for the storage of fingerprints except within the passport itself, and that this was appropriate and necessary in order to achieve the legitimate purpose of protecting against the fraudulent use of passports.[37]

In *Opinion 1/15*, the Grand Chamber of the CJEU found that a draft agreement between the EU and Canada for the transfer of airline passenger name record data could not be concluded in its current form, since it was adopted on the wrong legal basis and several of its provisions were incompatible with fundamental rights. One of the Court's criticisms was that the transfer of sensitive data to Canada required a 'precise and particularly solid justification, based on grounds other than the protection of public security against terrorism and serious transnational crime',[38] which the Court found did not exist in this case.[39] This demonstrates the Court's concern about the transfer of sensitive data outside the EU, and its conviction that such transfer requires a high level of protection and a strong justification.

In *Esch-Leonhardt*, the CFI considered the inclusion of a letter in the personal file of a staff member of the European Central Bank concerning his use of email to transmit trade union information. The Court found that this did not infringe the prohibition

---

[31] See Simitis 1999.   [32] Korff 2010, pp. 74–75.
[33] Expert Group Minutes 2016, p. 2; rec. 53 GDPR, final sentence.
[34] See Expert Group Minutes 2017, p. 2.
[35] Case C-101/01, *Lindqvist*, paras. 50–51. See also the commentary on Art. 4(15) GDPR in this volume.
[36] Regulation 2252/2004.   [37] Case C-291/12, *Schwarz*.   [38] *Opinion 1/15*, para. 165.
[39] Ibid.

on processing of information revealing trade union membership under Article 10(1) of Regulation 45/2001 as it concerned data which the person himself had manifestly made public within the meaning of the exception under Article 10(2)(d).[40]

In *Egan and Hackett*, the GC considered a request under the Public Access to Documents Regulation[41] for documents containing the names of assistants to former Members of the European Parliament. The European Parliament argued inter alia that such disclosure would reveal the political opinions of the former assistants and would therefore constitute sensitive data, but the Court found that this argument had not been substantiated in any way.[42]

Finally, in *V v EP*, the CST considered the transfer between the medical services of two EU institutions of health information about a job applicant. The applicant had not consented or even been informed of the transfer, nor was it justified. The Court emphasised the particularly sensitive nature of health data and underlined that respect for the confidential nature of health information 'constitutes one of the fundamental rights protected by the legal order of the European Union'.[43]

The growing significance of sensitive data and the continuing development of technology will likely lead to further judgments of the CJEU dealing with complex data processing situations. The ECtHR has also ruled on several occasions on the importance of safeguarding especially sensitive data (e.g. medical data) in the scope of the protection of the right to respect for private and family life under Article 8 ECHR and held that the processing of such data in these cases resulted in a violation of that right.[44]

C. Analysis

1. Defining sensitive data

The list of sensitive data contained in Article 9(1) GDPR is exhaustive, so that additional types of sensitive data may not be added to it. The list includes not just direct indications of sensitive data, but also information that can be used to indicate them indirectly, as evidenced by use of the word 'revealing' in Article 9(1) GDPR.[45] For example, in its report on the Cambridge Analytica scandal, the UK Information Commissioner (ICO) stated that the company processed personal data obtained from Facebook users in order to make predictions about their political affiliations and opinions, and that such data should thus be considered to constitute sensitive data in that context.[46] It is also not necessary to

---

[40] Case T-320/02, *Esch-Leonhardt*. The relevant part of Art.10(2)(d) provided that the prohibition does not apply where 'processing relates to data which are manifestly made public by the data subject'.

[41] Regulation 1049/2001   [42] Case T-190/10, *Egan and Hackett*, para. 101.

[43] Case F-46/09, *V v EP*, para. 123

[44] See e.g. ECtHR, *Z. v Finland* (disclosure during court proceedings and judgment of the applicant's medical records); ECtHR, *L.L. v France* (production and use in court proceedings of medical data without the applicant's consent); *I. v Finland* (failure to control access to medical data and to keep it secure); *S. and Marper v UK* (processing of DNA information); ECtHR, *L.H. v Latvia* (lack of precision of domestic law allowing public authority collection of applicant's medical data); ECtHR, *Vukota-Bojic* (involving secret surveillance of the applicant's medical condition by an insurance company).

[45] See WP29 2011, p. 6, stating with regard to Art. 8 DPD that 'the term "data revealing racial or ethnic origin, political opinions, religious or philosophical beliefs, trade-union membership" is to be understood that not only data which by its nature contains sensitive information is covered by this provision, but also data from which sensitive information with regard to an individual can be concluded'.

[46] ICO 2018, p. 36. Regarding the processing of voter data under EU law, see Bennett 2016.

demonstrate that the processing results in any type of harm or damage for the protections of Article 9 to apply.[47]

At the same time, the broad definition of sensitive data can create questions of interpretation. For example, photographs or paintings may indicate an individual's race (i.e. based on the colour of their skin) or religion (e.g. if they are wearing religious garb), but subjecting all images of individuals in photographs and artistic representations to Article 9 would seem overly broad,[48] and could conflict with other rights. Recital 51 GDPR therefore suggests that photographs are to be considered sensitive data only when they fall under the definition of biometric data.[49] The EDPB has stated that 'video footage showing a data subject wearing glasses or using a wheel chair are not per se considered to be special categories of personal data'.[50] However, if video footage is processed to deduce sensitive data from it, then Article 9 would apply.[51] The EDPB gives the following examples: 'Political opinions could for example be deduced from images showing identifiable data subjects taking part in an event, engaging in a strike, etc. This would fall under Article 9', and 'a hospital installing a video camera in order to monitor a patient's health condition would be considered as processing of special categories of personal data (Article 9)'.[52]

More generally, it has also been argued in the scholarly literature that information about an individual obtained in everyday situations should not be considered sensitive data unless there is an intention to use it based on one of the particular elements of sensitivity contained in the law,[53] but this view has not yet been affirmed by courts or regulators.

2. Categories of sensitive data

Three of the categories of sensitive data listed in Article 9(1) GDPR are defined in Article 4 (i.e. genetic data,[54] biometric data,[55] and data concerning health[56]), and reference should be made to the commentaries on those provisions. There are no definitions provided in the GDPR for the other five categories of sensitive data covered in Article 9, namely personal data revealing racial or ethnic origin, political opinions, religious or philosophical beliefs, trade union membership and data concerning a natural person's sex life or sexual orientation. These categories may be understood as follows:

1. *Racial or ethnic origin*: This category is derived from Article 21(1) CFR, which itself draws on Article 19 TFEU and Article 14 ECHR. It covers information such as minority affiliation and skin colour. From a scientific standpoint, the concept of 'race' can be criticised, since, as the WP29 noted, 'homo sapiens today is not divided into

---

[47] See Case C-465/00, *Rechnungshof*, para. 75, stating 'To establish the existence of such an interference, it does not matter whether the information communicated is of a sensitive character or whether the persons concerned have been inconvenienced in any way ...'

[48] See WP29 2011, p. 8, which refers to the classification of photographs and images of persons as sensitive data under Article 8 DPD as 'especially problematic'.

[49] See further the commentary on Art. 4(14) in this volume.   [50] EDPB 2019, p. 14.
[51] Ibid.   [52] Ibid.
[53] Gola and Schomerus 2010, p. 99, stating that, for example, the Islamic name of an individual which is listed in a company's customer directory should not be considered to be sensitive data unless and until there is the intent to use it for its ethnic or religious character, such as if the company decides to start an advertising campaign directed at individuals of Islamic background.

[54] Art. 4(13) GDPR.   [55] Ibid., Art. 4(14).   [56] Ibid., Art. 4(15).

different races nor sub-types'.[57] For this reason, recital 51 GDPR states that 'the use of the term "racial origin" in this Regulation does not imply an acceptance by the Union of theories which attempt to determine the existence of separate human races'.

2. *Political opinions*: Freedom of expression is protected by Article 11 CFR and Article 10 ECHR. The expression of political opinions can include, for example, affiliation with a political party, participation in demonstrations and political statements or publications.

3. *Religious or philosophical beliefs*: Freedom of religion is protected by Article 10 CFR and Article 9 ECHR, as are non-discrimination based on religion under Article 21(1) CFR and Article 14 ECHR and religious diversity under Article 22 CFR. Religious and philosophical beliefs should be defined to include data such as membership of a religious confession or in an organisation that focuses on a philosophical belief, writings that evidence religious or philosophical beliefs, or behaviour as an expression of religious or philosophical conviction (such as wearing a headscarf or cross or refusing to eat certain foods).

4. *Trade union membership*: Article 28 CFR and Article 11 ECHR protect collective bargaining rights. Data concerning trade union membership could include, for example, information documenting such membership.

5. *A natural person's sex life or sexual orientation*: Protection of a person's sex life is part of the protection of private and family life under Article 7 CFR and Article 8 ECHR, and Article 21(1) CFR protects against discrimination based on sexual orientation. The two categories 'data concerning a natural person's sex life' and 'sexual orientation' are closely connected but not identical. Sexual orientation refers to information concerning whether, for example, an individual is heterosexual, homosexual, bisexual, or of some other orientation. Data concerning a natural person's sex life is to be broadly construed to include not only this, but also information about sexual practices (for example, the consumption of pornography) as well as details on marital status and intimate personal details (for example, concerning change of gender or the use of contraception).

3. Processing of sensitive data

Paragraph 1 of Article 9 prohibits the processing of sensitive data, whilst paragraph 2 lays down exceptions to this prohibition in certain circumstances. As stated above, Article 9 maintains most of the types of processing activities contained in Article 8 DPD, whilst adding refinements to them and a few new ones.

The list of exceptions is exhaustive and all of them are to be interpreted restrictively. The list is similar to that contained in Article 8(2) DPD, with some differences that can be seen in Figure 9.1.

Other provisions of Article 8 DPD dealing with the processing of particular types of sensitive data are dealt with elsewhere in the GDPR. For example, Article 8(5) DPD dealing with offences, criminal convictions and security measures is now covered in Article 10 GDPR. Similarly, processing of national identification numbers, which was covered in Article 8(7) DPD, is dealt with in Article 87 GDPR. Reference should be made to the commentaries on those provisions for further analysis.

[57] WP29 2011, p. 10.

Provision of Article 9(2) GDPR	Difference with Article 8(2) DPD
Article 9(2)(a): explicit consent	GDPR refers to specific purposes of processing and allows derogation by Union law and Member State law.
Article 9(2)(b): legal obligation of the data controller	GDPR also allows processing under social security and social protection law in so far as authorised by Union or Member State law or a collective agreement pursuant to Member State law providing for appropriate safeguards for the fundamental rights and the interests of the data subject.
Article 9(2)(c): vital interests	Identical, except that the GDPR specifies a 'natural' person and 'consent' rather than 'his consent'
Article 9(2)(d): data processing by non-profit bodies	The GDPR refers to 'safeguards' rather than 'guarantees', includes former members of the body and requires that personal data not be 'disclosed outside that body' rather than not be 'disclosed to a third party'.
Article 9(2)(e): personal data manifestly made public by the data subject	The GDPR moves 'necessary for the establishment, exercise or defence of legal claims' to Article 9(2)(f).
Article 9(2)(f): legal claims	New provision in the GDPR, moved from Article 8(2)(e) DPD, plus adds processing by courts acting in their judicial capacity.
Article 9(2)(g): substantial public interest	Article 8(4) DPD allowed Member States to lay down exceptions by law or data protection authority decision for processing based on a substantial public interest; also, the GDPR requires that the public interest 'be proportionate to the aim pursued, respect the essence of the right to data protection and provide for suitable and specific measures to safeguard the fundamental rights and the interests of the data subject'.
Article 9(2)(h)	The GDPR makes many changes in the types of medical and health care situations where sensitive data may be processed compared to Article 8(3) DPD; the GDPR also moves the reference to obligations of secrecy to Article 9(3).
Article 9(2)(i): public health	No corresponding provision in Article 8 DPD.
Article 9(2)(j): archiving in the public interest, scientific or historical research, or statistical purposes	No corresponding provision in Article 8 DPD.

Figure 9.1 Differences between grounds for the processing of sensitive data under the GDPR and the DPD

The processing of sensitive data always requires compliance with other provisions of the GDPR, in addition to those of Article 9.[58] This raises the question of whether Article 9 constitutes a separate legal basis for data processing, or if it only complements Article 6 GDPR and therefore has to be supported by a legal basis in Article 6 as well.[59] The Commission has stated that the processing of sensitive data must always be supported by a legal basis under Article 6 GDPR,[60] in addition to compliance with one of the situations covered in Article 9(2). The EDPB has also stated that 'If a video surveillance system is used in order to process special categories of data, the data controller must identify both an exception for processing special categories of data under Article 9 (i.e. an exemption

---

[58] See rec. 51 GDPR, stating in part with regard to the processing of sensitive data, 'in addition to the specific requirements for such processing, the general principles and other rules of this Regulation should apply, in particular as regards the conditions for lawful processing'.
[59] See Kühling et al. 2016, p. 54. [60] Expert Group Minutes 2016, p. 2.

from the general rule that one should not process special categories of data) and a legal basis under Article 6'.[61]

In a preliminary ruling procedure requested by the French *Conseil d'Etat* concerning implementation of the right to be delisted from search results produced by an internet search engine's operations that was still pending at the time this text was finalised, Advocate General Szpunar proposed that a search engine must, as a matter of course, accede to a request for the de-referencing of sensitive data.[62] When a controller has a legal basis for processing, it may engage a data processor that acts on its behalf, as long as the relevant legal requirements governing data processors (such as under Article 28) are fulfilled.

The following are the exceptions listed in Article 9(2):

1. *Explicit consent of the data subject*:[63] The processing of sensitive data is permitted when the data subject has given 'explicit' consent. This is a higher threshold than in Article 6(1)(a) GDPR, which mentions 'consent' as a legal basis for data processing without requiring that it be explicit. Explicit consent is also required for the derogation under Article 49(1)(a) GDPR for the transfer of personal data outside the EU. Explicit consent means that consent cannot be implied, and requires a high degree of precision and definiteness in the declaration of consent, as well as a precise description of the purposes of processing.[64] In addition, other EU law or Member State law may provide that consent may not provide a legal basis for data processing in particular cases. Controllers must provide data subjects with information about the possibility to withdraw consent at any time when consent is used as the legal basis for processing sensitive data.[65]

2. *Processing necessary to carrying out obligations and exercising specific rights of the controller or of the data subject in the field of employment and social security and social protection law*:[66] This exception covers situations where employers need to process the sensitive data of employees for the purpose of complying with their obligations under employment, social security and social protection law. An example of such a situation can be the need of an employer in Germany to collect data about the employee's religion in order to deduct church tax. Another possible use could be the collection of biometric data for use in access control systems at work. This exception is limited to data processing by employers acting as data controllers.

3. *Protection of the vital interests of the data subject or of another natural person where the data subject is physically or legally incapable of giving consent*:[67] This covers situations where the processing of sensitive data is necessary to protect the vital interests of individuals. It requires an assessment of the data protection interests of individuals, their vulnerability, and their other important interests, and covers both the data subject and other natural persons. Recital 46 GDPR states that this involves processing 'necessary to protect an interest which is essential for the life of the data subject or that of another natural person'. Recital 112 GDPR, which deals with data transfers, defines 'vital interests' as 'including physical integrity or life', indicating that the situation must involve the health and safety of individuals. A situation where this exception could be invoked would be when the processing of sensitive data is needed for medical

---

[61] EDPB 2019, p. 14. [62] Case C-136/17, *G.C., A.F., B.H., E.D* (AG Opinion).
[63] Art. 9(2)(a) GDPR. [64] See further the commentary on Art. 4(11) GDPR in this volume.
[65] Arts. 13(2)(c) and 14(2)(d) GDPR. [66] Ibid., Art. 9(2)(b). [67] Ibid., Art. 9(2)(c).

treatment (either for life-saving treatment, or treatment for a medical condition that is serious but not by itself life-threatening, such as a broken limb), or in humanitarian emergencies. In order for it to apply, the person must be incapable of giving consent either physically (e.g. because they are seriously ill) or legally (e.g. because they are a minor, are under duress or cannot otherwise be expected to understand the consequences of the decision). Like the other exceptions, this is to be narrowly construed. Recital 46 indicates that data processing may serve both the vital interests of data subjects and important grounds of public interest. However, the term 'important grounds of public interest' does not appear in Article 9, and is used in the text of the GDPR only in Article 28(3)(a) (dealing with data processors); it is not clear what (if any) difference there is between these terms.

4. *Processing carried out in the course of its legitimate activities with appropriate safeguards by a foundation, association or any other not-for-profit body with a political, philosophical, religious or trade union aim*:[68] This exception covers non-profit organisations such as political parties,[69] youth groups, non-profit foundations and similar groups that have a 'political, philosophical, religious or trade union aim',[70] and recital 51 GDPR states that they must have the purpose of permitting 'the exercise of fundamental freedoms'. Thus, not every non-governmental organisation ('NGO') or non-profit organisation is covered by this exception. The organisation must be organised on a non-profit basis, though this does not exclude it engaging in fund-raising activities on an occasional basis. The exception only applies to data processing carried out in connection with the purposes of the organisation (e.g. data processing by a religious organisation for the purposes of advertising would not be covered by the exception). Article 9(2)(d) states that the processing must relate solely to members or to former members of the organisation or 'persons who have regular contact with it in connection with its purposes and that the personal data are not disclosed outside that body without the consent of the data subjects'. Thus, the exception only covers internal data processing by the organisation, and not, for example, transfer of the data to third parties. Any disclosure of sensitive data outside the organisation to another controller requires the consent of the data subject.

5. *Data manifestly made public*:[71] Sensitive data may be processed when the data subject has manifestly made them public. In this context, 'making public' should be construed to include publishing the data in the mass media, putting them on online social network platforms or similar actions. However, the data must have been 'manifestly' made public, which requires an affirmative act by the data subject, and that he or she realised that this would be the result. The EDPB has stated that 'data controllers processing those data in the context of video surveillance cannot rely on Article 9(2)(e), which allows processing that relates to personal data that are manifestly made public by the data subject. The mere fact of entering into the range of the camera does not imply that the data subject intends to make public special categories of data relating to him or her'.[72] Data processing will not fall within this exception if the data have been made public illegally.

---

[68] Ibid., Art. 9(2)(d).   [69] With regard to the processing of voter data, see Bennett 2016.
[70] Ibid. See also recital 51 GDPR, stating that the organisations covered must have the purpose of permitting 'the exercise of fundamental freedoms'.
[71] Art. 9(2)(e) GDPR.   [72] EDPB 2019, p. 15.

6. *Legal claims and judicial activities*:[73] This exception is designed to protect the right to an effective remedy and to a fair trial as set out in Article 47 CFR and Article 6 ECHR, and thus applies to court proceedings, whether as plaintiff or defendant, as well as before administrative and private tribunals (such as arbitration tribunals).[74] The concept of legal claims is to be interpreted broadly to include those under both public and private law, for the assertion of which controllers can be viewed as having a legitimate interest under Article 6(1)(f) GDPR. As all the exceptions under Article 9(2) are to be interpreted restrictively, its application here requires, from the perspective of the plaintiff, either a concrete intention to make a claim in the near future or the actual making of a claim, or, from the perspective of the defendant, the existence of an actual claim or judicial or extrajudicial procedure. Thus, it does not apply when sensitive data are processed merely in anticipation of a potential dispute without a formal claim having been asserted or filed, or without any indication that a formal claim is imminent.

7. *Substantial public interest*:[75] The processing of sensitive data based on a 'substantial public interest' requires that it be based on Union or Member State law, and that such law be 'proportionate to the aim pursued, respect the essence of the right to data protection and provide for suitable and specific measures to safeguard the fundamental rights and the interests of the data subject'. These safeguards respond to a criticism by the WP29, which had found that Article 8(4) DPD dealing with substantial public interest was not formulated precisely enough.[76] The GDPR has also split Article 8(4) DPD into several different provisions where a substantial public interest may arise, including a general public interest (Article 9(2)(g)), the provision of health care (Article 9(2)(h)), public interest in the area of public health (Article 9(2)(i)) and archiving purposes in the public interest (Article 9(2)(j)). Finding a substantial public interest requires a balancing between the public interest and the risks for data subjects. To process sensitive data the public interest must be 'substantial', in contrast to the conditions for processing personal data based on a task carried out in the public interest under Article 6(1)(e), where there is no requirement that the public interest be substantial. Recital 46 mentions as examples of data processing serving 'important grounds' of public interest 'when processing is necessary for humanitarian purposes, including for monitoring epidemics and their spread or in situations of humanitarian emergencies, in particular in situations of natural and man-made disasters'. Voter data may be processed based on the public interest when this is required by the operation of the democratic system in a Member State, as long as appropriate safeguards are established.[77] The threshold for satisfying this criterion is thus high.

8. *Health care and health provision*:[78] This provision contains a broad exception for the processing of sensitive data for health care purposes. Data processing for purposes of medical research is not covered by this provision but by Article 9(2)(i) or Article 9(2)(j). This provision covers all types of medical and social care, including diagnosis, treatment and prevention. Moreover, in order for the exception to apply, the requirements of Article 9(3) must be satisfied, which requires that the sensitive data be processed 'by

---

[73] Ibid., Art. 9(2)(f).
[74] See ibid., rec. 52, which refers to 'court proceedings or in an administrative or out-of-court procedure'.
[75] Ibid., Art. 9(2)(g).   [76] WP29 2011, p. 11.   [77] Rec. 56 GDPR. See Bennett 2016.
[78] Art. 9(2)(h) GDPR.

or under the responsibility of a professional subject to the obligation of professional secrecy' such as doctors, dentists, psychologists, hospitals, and insurance companies. This can include data processing carried out with the use of medical devices or apps, as long as they are used under the responsibility of such a professional. Under the opening clause of Article 9(3), professional secrecy is determined 'under Union or Member State law or rules established by national competent bodies or by another person also subject to an obligation of secrecy under Union or Member State law or rules established by national competent bodies'. Since obligations of professional secrecy tend to be governed by Member State law,[79] the conditions under which Article 9(3) applies (and thus the exception itself) will differ depending on national law. The processing must be necessary for medical or social security reasons, so other purposes are not covered. Besides medical care, the exception also covers related purposes, such as assessing whether an employee is medically fit to work. It also covers the processing of sensitive data in the scope of managing health care or social security systems. The provision also covers services performed pursuant to a contract, but a contract is not required. The term 'social care' should be construed broadly to include all types of assistance granted by social security authorities. Under Article 17(3)(c) GDPR, the right to erasure does not apply to data processed under this exception, except in cases where the data subject has withdrawn consent and there is no other legal basis for the processing (Article 17(1)(b)). Where processing of sensitive data is based on consent, the data subject may also exercise the right to data portability (Article 20(1)(a)).

9. *Public interest in the area of public health*:[80] This exception covers the processing of sensitive data for a public interest in the area of public health. According to recital 54, 'public health' is to be understood as set out in Regulation (EC) No. 1338/2008,[81] meaning 'all elements related to health, namely health status, including morbidity and disability, the determinants having an effect on that health status, health care needs, resources allocated to health care, the provision of, and universal access to, health care as well as health care expenditure and financing, and the causes of mortality'.[82] Article 9(2)(i) specifies that it applies in particular in cases of 'protecting against serious cross-border threats to health or ensuring high standards of quality and safety of health care and of medicinal products or medical devices'. The exception only allows processing 'on the basis of Union or Member State law which provides for suitable and specific measures to safeguard the rights and freedoms of the data subject, in particular professional secrecy'.[83] It is forbidden for such data to be processed for other purposes or by third parties.[84] It can be seen that this is a narrow exception that is intended for use by public health authorities, NGOs and other entities working in areas such as disaster relief and humanitarian aid, and similar bodies. Under Article 17(3)(c) GDPR, the right to erasure does not apply to data processed under this exception.

10. *Archiving purposes in the public interest, scientific or historical research purposes or statistical purposes*:[85] Under this exception, the processing of sensitive data may be carried out when it is necessary 'for archiving purposes in the public interest, scientific

---

[79] See also the commentary on Art. 90 GDPR in this volume.   [80] Art. 9(2)(i) GDPR.
[81] Art. 3(c) Public Health Regulation.   [82] Rec. 54 GDPR.   [83] Ibid., Art. 9(2)(i).
[84] Ibid.   [85] Ibid., 9(2)(j).

or historical research purposes or statistical purposes in accordance with Article 89(1) based on Union or Member State law which shall be proportionate to the aim pursued, respect the essence of the right to data protection and provide for suitable and specific measures to safeguard the fundamental rights and the interests of the data subject'. It can be seen that there a number of conditions for this exception to apply. First, the processing must concern archiving purposes in the public interest, scientific or historical research purposes or statistical purposes in accordance with Article 89(1).[86] Such archiving purposes must be in the public interest, meaning that they must further a public purpose.[87] It should be noted that the legislative history indicates that only archiving purposes have to meet the requirement of being 'in the public interest' (i.e., scientific, historical research, and statistical purposes need not be 'in the public interest'). Secondly, the purposes must be based on and in compliance with Union or Member State law, such as Member State laws dealing with archiving or scientific research. Thirdly, the processing activity must be proportionate, respect the essence of the right to data protection, and provide for suitable and specific safeguards. Proportionality in this context will usually require that the data be processed only so far as is strictly necessary.[88] Respecting the essence of the right to data protection goes without saying; the fact that the legislator felt it necessary to mention it explicitly here shows the importance it put on respect for data protection rights in the context of archiving and research.[89] It is not specified what is meant by 'suitable and specific measures to safeguard the fundamental rights and the interests of the data subject'.

4. Appropriate safeguards

A number of provisions of Article 9 require 'safeguards' or 'appropriate safeguards' to protect the fundamental rights and interests of data subject,[90] the processing of sensitive data,[91] and the rights and freedoms of the data subject.[92] The WP29 criticised the failure to define terms such as 'safeguards' more precisely in Article 8 DPD,[93] but no further detail is provided in this regard in Article 9 GDPR. It is also unclear whether there is any difference between 'safeguards' and 'appropriate safeguards', and whether the measures taken to implement them would differ depending on the various rights and interests they are designed to protect (i.e. 'the fundamental rights and interests of data subject', the processing of sensitive data or 'the rights and freedoms of the data subject').

In light of the lack of specificity in the text, and absent more detailed guidance from the EDPB, controllers and processors will have to design safeguards based on principles underlying the GDPR, such as proportionality,[94] data minimisation[95] and data security.[96] This can include a variety of measures based on the purposes of processing and the sensitivity of the data, such as encryption, minimising the amount of sensitive data processed,

---

[86] See the commentary on Art. 89 in this volume.
[87] See rec. 53 GDPR, which gives as an example 'studies conducted in the public interest in the area of public health'.
[88] *Opinion 1/15*, paras. 139–140.
[89] Regarding the essence of the right to data protection, see Brkan 2018.
[90] Art. 9(2)(b), Art. 9(2)(g) and Art. 9(2)(j) GDPR.   [91] Ibid., Art. 9(2)(d).
[92] Ibid., Art. 9(2)(i).   [93] WP29 2011, p. 11.   [94] See rec. 4 GDPR.
[95] See ibid., Art. 5(1)(c).   [96] See ibid., Art. 32.

training personnel who handle personal data and placing personnel under a duty of confidentiality.

Inspiration can also be taken from suggestions for organisational and technical safeguards for the processing of sensitive data made by the WP29, such as:

the introduction of Information Security Management Systems (e.g. ISO/IEC standards) based on the analysis of information resources and underlying threats, measures for cryptographic protection during storage and transfer of sensitive data, requirements for authentication and authorisation, physical and logical access to data, access logging and others. Additional legal safeguards could reinforce information rights of data subjects, accentuate strict relevance of processing or introduce other specific safeguards.[97]

5. Further rules affecting the processing of sensitive data

The processing of sensitive data may have implications for other obligations under the GDPR. Automated individual decision-making, including profiling, may not be carried out based on sensitive data unless they are processed based on consent under Article 9(2)(a) or a substantial public interest based on Article 9(2)(g) and 'suitable measures to safeguard the data subject's rights and freedoms and legitimate interests are in place'.[98] A data protection impact assessment ('DPIA') is required[99] and a data protection officer must be appointed[100] when there is processing of sensitive data 'on a large scale'. The processing of sensitive data must be taken into account by data controllers when deciding if data may be processed for another purpose.[101] The lack of the processing of sensitive data 'on a large-scale' is a factor to indicate that a representative need not be designated by controllers and processors not established in the Union.[102] Finally, the absence of sensitive data being processed may indicate that organisations employing fewer than 250 persons need not keep records of processing operations.[103]

6. Enforcement

The major avenues for enforcement of Article 9 are filing a complaint with a DPA (Article 77) or pursuing a judicial remedy against a controller or processor (Article 79). Infringements of Article 9 are subject to the higher level of administrative fines under Article 83(5)(a), that is, up to € 20 million or, in the case of an undertaking, 4 per cent of its total worldwide turnover of the preceding financial year, whichever is higher.

Select Bibliography

EU legislation

DPD Proposal 1992: Amended Proposal for a Council Directive on the protection of individuals with regard to the processing of personal data and on the free movement of such data, COM(92) 422 final—SYN 287, 15 October 1992.
Public Health Regulation: Regulation (EC) No. 1338/2008 of the European Parliament and of the Council of 16 December 2008 on Community statistics on public health and health and safety at work, OJ 2008 L354/70.

---

[97] WP29 2011, p. 11. [98] Art. 22(4) GDPR. [99] Ibid., Art. 35(3)(b).
[100] Ibid., Art. 37(1)(c). [101] Ibid., Art. 6(4)(c). [102] Ibid., Art. 27(2)(a).
[103] Ibid., Art. 30(5).

Regulation 1049/2001: Regulation (EC) No. 1049/2001 of the European Parliament and of the Council of 30 May 2001 regarding public access to European Parliament, Council and Commission documents, OJ 2001 L 145/43.

Regulation 2252/2004: Council Regulation (EC) No. 2252/2004 of 13 December 2004 on standards for security features and biometrics in passports and travel documents issued by Member States, as amended by Regulation (EC) No. 444/2009 of the European Parliament and of the Council of 6 May 2009, OJ 2009 L 142/1. Corrigendum: OJ 2009 L 188/127.

Academic writings

Bennett 2016: Bennett, 'Voter Databases, Micro-Targeting, and Data Protection Law: Can Political Parties Campaign in Europe as They Do in North America?', 6(4) *International Data Privacy Law* (2016), 261.

Brkan 2018: Brkan, 'The Concept of Essence of Fundamental Rights in the EU Legal Order: Peeling the Onion to Its Core', 14(2) *European Constitutional Law Review* (2018), 332.

Bygrave 2014: Bygrave, *Data Privacy Law: An International Perspective* (OUP 2014).

Gola and Schomerus 2010: Gola and Schomerus, *Bundesdatenschutzgesetz* (10th edn, Verlag C. H. Beck 2010).

Kühling et al. 2016: Kühling, Martini, Heberlein, Kühl, Nink, Weinzierl and Wenzel, *Die DSGVO und das nationale Recht* (Verlagshaus Monsenstein und Vannderat OHG Münster 2016).

Seltzer and Anderson 2001: Seltzer and Anderson, 'The Dark Side of Numbers: The Role of Population Data Systems in Human Rights Abuses', 68(2) *Social Research* (2001), 481.

Simitis and Dammann 1997: Simitis and Dammann, *EG-Datenschutzrichtlinie* (Nomos Verlagsgesellschaft 1997).

Papers of data protection authorities

EDPB 2019: European Data Protection Board, 'Guidelines 3/2019 on the processing of personal data through video devices (version for public consultation)' (10 July 2019).

EDPS 2005: European Data Protection Supervisor, 'Opinion on the Proposal for a Regulation of the European Parliament and of the Council Concerning the Visa Information System (VIS) and the Exchange of Data between Member States on Short-Stay Visas' (23 March 2005).

WP29 2003: Article 29 Working Party, 'Working Document on Biometrics' (WP 80, 1 August 2003).

WP29 2004A: Article 29 Working Party, 'Working Document on Genetic Data' (WP 91, 17 March 2004).

WP29 2004B: Article 29 Working Party, 'Opinion No. 7/2004 on the Inclusion of Biometric Elements in Residence Permits and Visas Taking Account of the Establishment of the European Information System on visas (VIS)' (WP 96, 11 August 2004).

WP29 2005: Article 29 Working Party, 'Opinion 3/2005 on Implementing Council Resolution (EC) No. 2252/2004 of 13 December 2004 on Standards for Security Features and Biometrics in Passports and Travel Documents Issued by Member States' (WP 112, 30 September 2005).

WP29 2011: Article 29 Working Party, 'Advice Paper on Special Categories of Data' (4 April 2011), available at https://ec.europa.eu/justice/article-29/documentation/other-document/files/2011/2011_04_20_letter_artwp_mme_le_bail_directive_9546ec_annex1_en.pdf.

WP29 2012: Article 29 Working Party, 'Opinion 3/2012 on Developments in Biometric Technologies' (WP 193, 27 April 2012).

ICO 2018: Information Commissioner's Office, 'Investigation into the use of Data Analytics in Political Campaigns' (6 November 2018).

Reports and recommendations

COM Recommendation 1992: Committee of Ministers of the Council of Europe, 'Recommendation on Genetic Testing and Screening for Heath Care Purposes' (Rec(1992)3, 10 February 1992).

COM Recommendation 1997: Committee of Ministers of the Council of Europe, 'Recommendation on the Protection of Medical Data', (Rec(1997)5, 13 February 1997).

COM Recommendation 2016: Committee of Ministers of the Council of Europe, 'Recommendation on the Processing of Personal Health-Related Data for Insurance Purposes, including Data Resulting from Genetic Tests' (CM/Rec(2016)8, 26 October 2016).

De Hert and Christianen 2013: De Hert and Christianen, 'Progress Report on the Application of the Principles of Convention 108 to the Collection and Processing of Biometric Data', for the Consultative Committee of the Convention for the Protection of Individuals with regard to Automatic Processing of Personal Data [ETS No. 108] (April 2013).

Korff 2010: Korff for the European Commission, 'Comparative Study on Different Approaches to New Privacy Challenges in Particular in the Light of Technological Developments, Working Paper No. 2: Data Protection Laws in the EU' (20 January 2010).

Opinion Insurance Purposes 2014: Consultative Committee of the Convention for the Protection of Individuals with regard to Automatic Processing of Personal Data (T-PD), 'Opinion on the Draft Recommendation on the Use for Insurance Purposes of Personal Health-Related Information, in Particular Information of a Genetic and Predictive Nature' (27 March 2014).

Progress Report on Biometric Data 2005: Consultative Committee of the Convention for the Protection of Individuals with regard to Automatic Processing of Personal Data (T-PD), 'Progress Report on the Application of the Principles of Convention 108 to the Collection and Processing of Biometric Data' (February 2005).

Simitis 1999: Simitis, 'Revisiting Sensitive Data', Review of the answers to the Questionnaire of the Consultative Committee of the Convention for the Protection of Individuals with regard to Automatic Processing of Personal Data (ETS 108) (Strasbourg, 24–26 November 1999).

Others

Expert Group Minutes 2016: Commission expert group on the Regulation (EU) 2016/679 and Directive (EU) 2016/680, 'Minutes of the Second Meeting' (10 October 2016).

Expert Group Minutes 2017: Commission expert group on the Regulation (EU) 2016/679 and Directive (EU) 2016/680, 'Minutes of the Second Meeting' (6 December 2017).

Article 10. Processing of personal data relating to criminal convictions and offences

LUDMILA GEORGIEVA[*]

Processing of personal data relating to criminal convictions and offences or related security measures based on Article 6(1) shall be carried out only under the control of official authority or when the processing is authorised by Union or Member State law providing for appropriate safeguards for the rights and freedoms of data subjects. Any comprehensive register of criminal convictions shall be kept only under the control of official authority.

Relevant Recital

(19) The protection of natural persons with regard to the processing of personal data by competent authorities for the purposes of the prevention, investigation, detection or prosecution of criminal offences or the execution of criminal penalties, including the safeguarding against and the prevention of threats to public security and the free movement of such data, is the subject of a specific Union legal act. This Regulation should not, therefore, apply to processing activities for those purposes. However, personal data processed by public authorities under this Regulation should, when used for those purposes, be governed by a more specific Union legal act, namely Directive (EU) 2016/680 of the European Parliament and of the Council. Member States may entrust competent authorities within the meaning of Directive (EU) 2016/680 with tasks which are not necessarily carried out for the purposes of the prevention, investigation, detection or prosecution of criminal offences or the execution of criminal penalties, including the safeguarding against and prevention of threats to public security, so that the processing of personal data for those other purposes, in so far as it is within the scope of Union law, falls within the scope of this Regulation.

With regard to the processing of personal data by those competent authorities for purposes falling within scope of this Regulation, Member States should be able to maintain or introduce more specific provisions to adapt the application of the rules of this Regulation. Such provisions may determine more precisely specific requirements for the processing of personal data by those competent authorities for those other purposes, taking into account the constitutional, organisational and administrative structure of the respective Member State. When the processing of personal data by private bodies falls within the scope of this Regulation, this Regulation should provide for the possibility for Member States under specific conditions to restrict by law certain obligations and rights when such a restriction constitutes a necessary and proportionate measure in a democratic society to safeguard specific important interests including public security and the prevention, investigation, detection or prosecution of criminal offences or the execution of criminal penalties, including the safeguarding against and the prevention of threats to public security. This is relevant for instance in the framework of anti-money laundering or the activities of forensic laboratories.

---

[*] The views expressed are solely those of the author and do not necessarily reflect those of her current or former employers.

Closely Related Provisions

Article 5 (Principles relating to processing of personal data); Article 6 (Lawfulness of processing) (see too recital 50); Article 9 (Processing of special categories of personal data); Article 27 (Representatives of controllers or processors not established in the Union) (see too recital 80); Article 30 (Records of processing activities) (see too recital 97); Article 35 (Data protection impact assessment) (see also recitals 75 and 91); Article 37 (Designation of the data protection officer) (see too recital 97)

Related Provisions in LED [Directive (EU) 2016/680]

Article 1 (Subject-matter and objectives); Article 2 (Scope) (see too recital 13); Article 3 (Definitions)

Related Provisions in EPD [Directive 2002/58/EC]

Article 15 (Application of certain provisions of Directive 95/46/EC)

Relevant Case Law

CJEU

Case C-489/10, *Łukasz Marcin Bonda*, judgment of 5 June 2012 (Grand Chamber) (ECLI:EU:C:2012:319).

ECtHR

M.M. v United Kingdom, Appl. No. 24029/07, judgment of 13 November 2012.
Khelili v Switzerland, Appl. No. 16188/07, judgment of 18 October 2011.
Brunet v France, Appl. No. 21010/10, judgment of 18 September 2014.

A. Rationale and Policy Underpinnings

The purpose of Article 10 GDPR is to ensure the responsible handling of personal data relating to criminal convictions and offences or related security measures, since they may have a significant impact on the life of the data subjects concerned. Article 10 does not prohibit the processing of such data but subjects them to a specific regime. Article 10 must be read in conjunction with other GDPR provisions, namely Article 5(1) (concerning the principles for processing personal data), Article 6(1) (which governs the lawfulness of processing), Article 2(2)(d) (which exempts data processing covered by the LED from the scope of the GDPR) and with the LED itself. The LED covers the processing of personal data by competent authorities for the purposes of the prevention, investigation, detection or prosecution of criminal offences, or the execution of criminal penalties, including the safeguarding against and the prevention of threats to public security.[1] Thus, Article 10 applies to processing by private bodies and public bodies which

---

[1] See Art. 1(1) LED.

are not competent authorities in accordance with Article 3(7) LED, or data processing which is not for the purposes listed in Article 2(2)(d) and Article 1(1) LED.

B. Legal Background

1. EU legislation

The wording of Article 10 is close to that of Article 8(5) DPD. The main difference is that the GDPR states that the processing of such data 'shall be carried out only under the control of official authority or when the processing is authorised by Union or Member State law', while Article 8(5) DPD stated that it 'may be carried out only under the control of official authority'. The difference in wording can be attributed to the different nature of the GDPR (i.e. it is an EU regulation rather than a directive like the DPD). Furthermore, Article 8(5) DPD also referred to administrative sanctions and judgments in civil cases. Article 8 DPD was the provision dealing with special categories of data (i.e. 'sensitive data'), although personal data relating to criminal convictions and offences or related security measures were not included in the definition of sensitive data contained in Article 8(1). By contrast, the processing of such data is not specifically mentioned at all in Article 9 GDPR (which covers the processing of special categories of personal data).[2]

2. International instruments

Convention 108 as originally adopted stated that 'personal data relating to criminal convictions' may 'not be processed automatically unless domestic law provides appropriate safeguards' (Article 6). Modernised Convention 108 is more elaborate on this point and includes 'personal data relating to offences, criminal proceedings and convictions, and related security measures' in its specification of 'special categories of data' (Article 6(1)). Such data may only be processed 'where appropriate safeguards are enshrined in law, complementing those of this Convention' (Article 6(1)), and these safeguards 'shall guard against the risks that the processing of sensitive data may present for the interests, rights and fundamental freedoms of the data subject, notably a risk of discrimination' (Article 6(2)).

Unlike the Modernised Convention, the GDPR does not refer to 'criminal proceedings'.

3. National developments

By stating that criminal data may be processed when authorised by Member State law provided there are appropriate safeguards, Article 10 GDPR leaves considerable leeway for national law. Member States often enact legislation to maintain public registers of criminal convictions and related information. For example, in Germany the *Bundeszentralregister* ('BZR') is a public register with information on criminal proceedings before German courts which is maintained by the Federal Ministry of Justice and established by legislation.[3] Recital 19 GDPR recognises that Member States may introduce their own more specific rules for processing such data for other purposes. Differences in Member State law existed already under the DPD: while criminal convictions and offenses were not listed as sensitive data in Article 8 DPD, the WP29 stated that in some cases Member

---

[2] See the commentary on Art. 9 GDPR in this volume. [3] German Federal Registry Act 2017.

States either defined them as an additional category of sensitive data or created a special legal framework including certain conditions for processing such data.[4]

4. Case law

The CJEU has not yet ruled on Article 10. However, the ECtHR has held that a system for the retention and disclosure of criminal record data should afford sufficient safeguards to ensure that data relating to an individual's private life are not disclosed in violation of the right to respect for private life pursuant to Article 8 of the European Convention of Human Rights and Fundamental Freedoms ('ECHR'). In the case of *M.M. v United Kingdom*, the ECtHR held that national arrangements for the indefinite retention and disclosure of criminal data infringed Article 8 ECHR.[5]

C. Analysis

1. Introduction and scope

Although personal data relating to criminal convictions and offences or related security measures are not mentioned in Article 9 GDPR (which concerns the processing of 'special categories of data'), the special sensitivity of such data and their processing is shown by the fact that they are the subject of a separate article. The processing of such data can have severe adverse consequences for data subjects in terms of stigmatisation, the ability to find employment and discrimination in other important areas of life. Article 10 thus lays down strict conditions for the processing of such data. In particular, processing of the data covered by Article 10 must fulfil the requirements of Article 5 GDPR, be based on one of the grounds of Article 6(1) GDPR,[6] and be conducted either under the control of official authority or authorised by Member State or EU law. Other provisions of the GDPR contain further requirements specifying the protections that must be carried out when the data described in Article 10 are processed, including maintaining records of processing activities (see Article 35), carrying out a data protection impact assessment (see Article 35(3)(b) and recital 91) and designating a data protection officer (see Article 37(1)(c) and recital 97).

The scope of Article 10 will largely be determined by Member State law but is also subject to interpretation by the CJEU.[7] For example, the CJEU has held that three criteria must be examined when determining what constitute 'criminal proceedings', namely the legal classification of the offence under national law, the nature of the offence and the nature and degree of severity of the penalty that the person concerned is liable to incur.[8]

The term 'criminal convictions' includes only data relating to actual criminal convictions pronounced by a court or similar public authority. 'Offences' refers to information about criminal offences even if this does not include data about an actual conviction.[9]

---

[4] WP29 2011, p. 8.   [5] ECtHR, *M.M. v UK*.

[6] Note in this regard that rec. 47 GDPR states that 'the processing of personal data strictly necessary for the purposes of preventing fraud also constitutes a legitimate interest of the data controller concerned'.

[7] See rec. 13 LED, stating that 'criminal offence' within the meaning of the LED should be an autonomous concept of Union law as interpreted by the CJEU.

[8] Case C-489/10, *Bonda*, para. 37.

[9] See e.g. ECtHR, *Khelili v Switzerland*, where the Court found that the processing by the police of data that incorrectly designated the complainant as a prostitute violated her right to the respect for private life under Art. 8 ECHR; and ECtHR, *Brunet v France*, where the Court held there was a violation of Art. 8 ECHR when

Data about mere suspicions of criminal activity are not expressly covered by Article 10 or otherwise mentioned in the GDPR, and it is uncertain whether they are within the scope of Article 10. However, the potentially grave consequences for individuals of processing data concerning suspicions of criminal activity[10] suggest that the definition of 'offences' may be expanded by Member States to include suspicions as well. Regarding 'security measures', these refer to measures concerning criminal offences that stop short of a criminal conviction,[11] such as revocation of a driver's license or temporary detention in a psychiatric clinic.

2. Data processing by public authorities

Data processing by public authorities falls within the scope of the LED if they are 'competent authorities'[12] and they process personal data for the purposes of the LED.[13] As stated above, data processing covered by the LED is not covered by the GDPR. Conversely, this suggests that data processing not falling under the LED *is* covered by the GDPR.[14]

With regard to the reference to a 'comprehensive' record of criminal convictions under the control of official authority, the term 'comprehensive' should be liberally interpreted to include registers that are extensive, even if they are not 100 per cent complete. The requirement of control by an official authority requires that a public authority is responsible in practice for the proper functioning of the data processing; a generic right of supervision is not sufficient.[15] An example of such control is the operation of the BZR register by the German Federal Ministry of Justice as referenced above.

3. Data processing by private entities

Private entities and companies such as credit scoring agencies, insurance companies and businesses screening prospective employees may also seek to process data concerning criminal convictions and offences. Since processing by private entities is usually not under the control of official authority, the storing of such data by them is only permissible if EU or Member State law allows it and provides for 'appropriate safeguards for the rights and freedoms of data subjects'.[16] Recital 19 GDPR recognises that more specific national rules may allow processing by private bodies, but only under strict conditions, and that Member State legislation may also restrict 'certain rights and obligations' with regard to such processing.[17] However, the GDPR does not specify which rights and obligations

---

the complainant's data were retained in a criminal database after the criminal proceedings against him were discontinued. See also WP29 2017, p. 7, in which the WP29 suggested that 'offences' under Art. 10 GDPR may include data about traffic safety and violations.

[10] See Dammann and Simitis 1997, p. 170.   [11] Ibid.   [12] Art. 3(7) LED.
[13] Art. 2(2)(d) GDPR and Art. 1(1) LED.   [14] See FRA 2018, p. 282.
[15] See Dammann and Simitis 1997, pp. 170–171.

[16] For example, as of 24 May 2018, credit agencies in Germany were no longer allowed to store data relating to criminal conviction because a specific national regulation permitting the storage had not yet been enacted: see Gola 2017, para. 9.

[17] Rec. 19 states in part: 'When the processing of personal data by private bodies falls within the scope of this Regulation, this Regulation should provide for the possibility for Member States under specific conditions to restrict by law certain obligations and rights when such a restriction constitutes a necessary and proportionate measure in a democratic society to safeguard specific important interests including public security and the prevention, investigation, detection or prosecution of criminal offences or the execution of criminal penalties, including the safeguarding against and the prevention of threats to public security. This is relevant for instance in the framework of anti-money laundering or the activities of forensic laboratories'.

these are. The examples given in recital 19 of 'anti-money laundering or the activities of forensic laboratories' indicate that such national derogations should apply only when there is a strong public interest in the processing of criminal data by private entities. The language of the recital also indicates that such derogations should be interpreted strictly in light of the ECHR and the Charter of Fundamental Rights of the European Union.

4. Enforcement

An infringement of Article 10 can result in a claim for compensation under Article 82 GDPR. In addition, it will automatically involve an infringement of the basic conditions for data processing under Articles 5 and 6 GDPR and can thus also lead to an administrative fine in accordance with Article 83(5)(a) GDPR—i.e. up to € 20 million or up to 4 per cent of an undertaking's total worldwide annual turnover.

Select Bibliography

National legislation

German Federal Registry Act 2017: Bundeszentralregistergesetz in der Fassung der Bekanntmachung vom 21. September 1984 (BGBl. I S. 1229, 1985 I S. 195), das zuletzt durch Artikel 1 des Gesetzes vom 18. Juli 2017 (BGBl. I S. 2732) geändert worden ist.

Academic writings

Dammann and Simitis, *EU-Datenschutzrichtlinie* (Nomos Verlagsgesellschaft 1997).
Gola 2017: Gola, 'Art. 10' in Gola (ed.), *Datenschutz-Grundverordnung VO (EU) 2016/679—Kommentar* (C. H. Beck 2017), 308.

Papers of data protection authorities

WP29 2011: Article 29 Working Party, 'Advice Paper on Special Categories of Data' (4 April 2011).
WP29 2017: Article 29 Working Party, 'Opinion 03/2017 on Processing Personal Data in the Context of Cooperative Intelligent Transport Systems (C-ITS)' (WP 252, 4 October 2017).

Reports and recommendations

FRA 2018: European Union Agency for Fundamental Rights, European Court of Human Rights, Council of Europe, and European Data Protection Supervisor (eds.), *Handbook on European Data Protection Law* (Publications Office of the European Union 2018).

Article 11. Processing which does not require identification

LUDMILA GEORGIEVA[*]

1. If the purposes for which a controller processes personal data do not or do no longer require the identification of a data subject by the controller, the controller shall not be obliged to maintain, acquire or process additional information in order to identify the data subject for the sole purpose of complying with this Regulation.
2. Where, in cases referred to in paragraph 1 of this Article, the controller is able to demonstrate that it is not in a position to identify the data subject, the controller shall inform the data subject accordingly, if possible. In such cases, Articles 15 to 20 shall not apply except where the data subject, for the purpose of exercising his or her rights under those articles, provides additional information enabling his or her identification.

Relevant Recitals

(26) The principles of data protection should apply to any information concerning an identified or identifiable natural person. Personal data which have undergone pseudonymisation, which could be attributed to a natural person by the use of additional information should be considered to be information on an identifiable natural person. To determine whether a natural person is identifiable, account should be taken of all the means reasonably likely to be used, such as singling out, either by the controller or by another person to identify the natural person directly or indirectly. To ascertain whether means are reasonably likely to be used to identify the natural person, account should be taken of all objective factors, such as the costs of and the amount of time required for identification, taking into consideration the available technology at the time of the processing and technological developments. The principles of data protection should therefore not apply to anonymous information, namely information which does not relate to an identified or identifiable natural person or to personal data rendered anonymous in such a manner that the data subject is not or no longer identifiable. This Regulation does not therefore concern the processing of such anonymous information, including for statistical or research purposes.

(57) If the personal data processed by a controller do not permit the controller to identify a natural person, the data controller should not be obliged to acquire additional information in order to identify the data subject for the sole purpose of complying with any provision of this Regulation. However, the controller should not refuse to take additional information provided by the data subject in order to support the exercise of his or her rights. Identification should include the digital identification of a data subject, for example through authentication mechanism such as the same credentials, used by the data subject to log-in to the on-line service offered by the data controller.

Closely Related Provisions

Article 4(1) (Definition of 'personal data'); Article 5 (Principles relating to processing of personal data) (see too recital 39); Article 6 (Lawfulness of processing); Article 12 (Transparent information,

---

[*] The views expressed are solely those of the author and do not necessarily reflect those of her current or former employers.

communication and modalities for the exercise of the rights of the data subject); Articles 15–20 (Data subject rights) (see too recital 64); Article 24 (Responsibility of the controller); Article 25 (Data protection by design and default) (see too recital 78); Article 32 (Security of processing) (see too recital 83)

Related Provisions in EUDPR [Regulation (EU) 2018/1725]

Article 12 (Processing which does not require identification) (see too recital 32); Article 3(1) (Definition of 'personal data') (see too recital 16); Article 4 (Principles relating to processing of personal data) (see also recital 20); Article 5 (Lawfulness of processing); Article 14 (Transparent information, communication and modalities for the exercise of the rights of the data subject); Articles 17–22 (Data subject rights); Article 26 (Responsibility of the controller); Article 27 (Data protection by design and default) (see too recital 48); Article 33 (Security of processing) (see too recital 53)

Relevant Case Law

CJEU

Case C-553/07, *College van burgemeester en wethouders van Rotterdam v M. E. E. Rijkeboer*, judgment of 7 May 2009 (ECLI:EU:C:2009:293).
Case C-131/12, *Google Spain SL and Google Inc. v Agencia Española de Protección de Datos (AEPD) and Mario Costeja González*, judgment of 13 May 2014 (Grand Chamber) (ECLI:EU:C:2014:317).
Case C-582/14, *Patrick Breyer v Bundesrepublik Deutschland*, judgment of 19 October 2016 (ECLI:EU:C:2016:779).

A. Rationale and Policy Underpinnings

Article 11 GDPR pursues a twofold agenda. On the one hand, it emphasises, in accordance with the core data protection principles of purpose limitation, data minimisation and storage limitation,[1] that when the purposes for which a controller processes personal data do not or no longer require the identification of a data subject by the controller, the controller does not have to (re-)identify the data 'for the sole purpose'[2] of complying with the GDPR. In such cases, Articles 15–20 shall not apply. On the other hand, in order to protect data subjects' rights, this norm also contains 'a significant exemption',[3] namely that it does not apply when 'the data subject, for the purpose of exercising his or her rights under those articles, provides additional information enabling his or her identification' (Article 11(2)), which can be viewed as a safeguard to enable data subjects to continue to enforce their rights effectively.

Article 11 provides, generally speaking, that a controller does not need to maintain the data, but also does not contain a requirement to delete them.[4] Article 11 seems mainly designed to target personal data that have undergone pseudonymisation. Thus, recital 57 discusses the scope of Article 11 in situations when 'the personal data processed by a

---

[1] See Art. 5(1)(b)–(c) and (e) GDPR and the commentary on Art. 5 in this volume.
[2] GDPR Proposal, p. 8.   [3] FRA 2018, p. 94.   [4] Nymity 2018, p. 19.

controller do not permit the controller to identify a natural person',[5] which seems to refer to pseudonymous data since anonymous data do not fall within the scope of the GDPR.[6]

Article 11 applies in two main cases, namely where there exists an active communication between controller and data subject (e.g. a request by the data subject under Articles 15–20), and where the GDPR requires a clear identification of, and unambiguous assignment of data to, a data subject (e.g. Articles 15–20). Article 11(2) is also of relevance for Article 12(2), the difference being that Article 11(2) provides for the non-application of data subject rights under Articles 15–20, whilst Article 12(2) provides for a right of refusal for the controller in the context of data subject rights under Articles 15–22.

When considering Article 11 in the context of Cooperative Intelligent Transport Systems ('C-ITS'), the WP29 rejected any interpretation aimed at reducing the responsibility of controllers for compliance with data protection obligations. It advised that Article 11 should be interpreted as 'a way to enforce "genuine" data minimisation, without ... hindering the exercise of data subjects' rights',[7] although this has raised concerns concerning the risks of re-identification, which are discussed below.

B. Legal Background

1. EU legislation

Article 11 has no equivalent in the DPD, EPD or LED. It does, however, have an equivalent in Article 12 EUDPR. The two provisions are to be interpreted homogeneously (recital 5 EUDPR).

2. International instruments

Convention 108 both as originally adopted and in its modernised form does not contain a provision corresponding to Article 11 GDPR. Nonetheless, both versions of the Convention embrace the data protection principles of purpose limitation, data minimisation and storage limitation, although using slightly different formulations from Article 5 GDPR. Other major international instruments, such as the OECD Privacy Guidelines and the APEC Privacy Framework, do not contain equivalent provisions to Article 11 GDPR, nor do they embrace the data protection principles of purpose limitation, data minimisation and storage limitation as set forth in Article 5 GDPR.

3. National developments

The GDPR does not give EU/EEA Member States discretion in the way they are to implement Article 11. Thus, their respective laws must follow the requirements of Article 11 without derogation or other changes.

4. Case law

Given that Article 11 has no equivalent in the DPD, there is no case law on its subject-matter as yet. However, CJEU jurisprudence on the principles of purpose limitation, data minimisation and storage limitation is relevant for elucidating and assessing the framework for Article 11.

---

[5] See also Gola 2017, para. 2.   [6] Rec. 26 GDPR.   [7] WP29 2017, p. 6.

In *Google Spain*, the CJEU noted that 'even initially lawful processing of accurate data may, in the course of time, become incompatible with the directive [DPD] where those data are no longer necessary in the light of the purposes for which they were collected or processed'.[8]

In *Breyer*, the CJEU held that 'it is not required that all the information enabling the identification of the data subject must be in the hands of one person'.[9]

In *Rijkeboer*, the CJEU clarified that, in the context of data subjects' right to access their data, the DPD requires the right of access to be ensured, not only in respect of the present, but also in respect of the past, and that access must be provided on the basis of a fair balance between the interests of the data subject and those of the controller.[10] Thus, the Court considered the situation of data retention from the perspective of protecting the rights of data subjects to access their data and underlined the necessity of a fair balance between the interest of data subjects in protecting their privacy (e.g. by way of the rights to rectification, erasure and blocking of the data in the event that the processing of the data does not comply with the Directive, and the rights to object and to bring legal proceedings) and, on the other hand, the burden which the obligation to store that information represents for the controller.[11] Furthermore, the Court stated that differentiation between different types of data and their storage periods is not acceptable since such distinctions do not constitute a fair balance of interests and obligations.[12] The judgment can also be understood as a practical guidance for putting in place appropriate technical and organisational measures for data subject rights.

C. Analysis

1. The focus of Article 11

Article 11(1) provides that the controller is exempt from the duty to maintain, acquire or process additional information in order to (re)identify the data subject, just for the sake of compliance with the GDPR.[13] Article 11(2) first sentence states that the controller has to inform the data subject about this fact, while the second sentence clarifies when the rights of the data subject prevail over Article 11(1). Article 11 also has implications for other GDPR provisions as well, namely the definition of personal data in Article 4(1) and of pseudonymisation in Article 4(5); the purpose compatibility test pursuant to Article 6(4); and the requirements under Article 24 (responsibility of the controller), Article 25 (data protection by design and default) and Article 32 (security of processing).

The basic remit of Article 11(1) is to provide legal certainty in two cases involving the processing of personal data but when identification of data subjects is not required: first, where the purposes for processing the data have been achieved ('no longer') and, secondly, where data storage is not required in the first place. Article 11(2) in conjunction with recital 57 aims, in line with *Rijkeboer*, to provide a fair balance with data subjects' rights.

---

[8] Case C-131/12, *Google Spain*, para. 93.   [9] Case C-582/14, *Breyer*, para. 43.
[10] Case C-553/07, *Rijkeboer*, paras. 67 and 70.   [11] Ibid., paras. 64 and 70.
[12] Ibid., para. 66 ('In the present case, rules limiting the storage of information on the recipients or categories of recipient of personal data and on the content of the data disclosed to a period of one year and correspondingly limiting access to that information, while basic data is stored for a much longer period, do not constitute a fair balance of the interest and obligation at issue, unless it can be shown that longer storage of that information would constitute an excessive burden on the controller').
[13] Cf. Art. 24 GDPR concerning the responsibility of the controller.

Article 11 concerns only controllers, not processors. It also applies to controllers not established in the EU if their processing is subject to the GDPR under Article 3(2).

While the utility of Article 11 is not at issue, one can raise questions about its classification and legal impact. One the one hand, one could take a systematic approach, qualify the provision as concerned with principle, being in the same chapter as Articles 4–6, and thus as having *de jure* potential impact on each GDPR provision which requires identification, but *de facto* impact (pursuant to Article 11(2)) only on Articles 15–20. Some commentators, however, apply Article 11(1) to the information obligations under Articles 13 and 14, stating that these obligations do not have to be fulfilled when Article 11 applies.[14] In addition, a question mark may be raised about the logic of Article 11(2) given that it appears to be contradictory—it applies when the controller cannot identify the data subject, yet provides that the controller shall inform the data subject if possible.

Article 11 closes a legal gap (or at least attempts to do so) which arises from the definition of personal data. As made clear in *Breyer*, it is not necessary that the controller alone holds all information in order for it to be qualified as personal data.[15] This follows also from recital 26 GDPR, which stipulates that to determine whether a natural person is identifiable, account should be taken of all the means reasonably likely to be used (either by the controller or by another person to identify the natural person directly or indirectly) and therefore of all objective factors (time and costs required for the identification). Still, it was previously unclear what was to happen in cases when the controller cannot undertake identification even though identifiability exists (meaning it can be considered possible according to the objective factors mentioned).

In view of the rights of the data subject and the data protection principles laid down in Article 5(1), especially those of purpose limitation and data minimisation, Article 11 aims to close this gap and underlines that identification (or identifiability) is a matter of objective consideration. Article 11 refers only to 'identification' but not to 'identifiability'. Therefore, Article 11 provides that a controller does not need to retain the data and is not required to destroy them, but has a legitimate interest to process them further. However, at the moment when data are not even identifiable, they have to be deleted or anonymised.

The question arises of why a natural person being identifiable but not identified is a matter of concern from the point of view of data protection. The reason is that storage of data that are identifiable still raises concerns, especially considering the volume of data now being produced and stored in databases, as well as the different possible means of monitoring and analysing the behaviour of data subjects. In the end, even if a data subject is not identified, the datasets can still be used for profiling, including the decision as to whether or not to disclose information or to disclose different information to users responding to certain type of profiles.[16]

2. The privilege of Article 11(1)

As noted above, Article 11(1) stipulates that there is no duty to identify the data subject and the controller is not obliged to take any actions in order to identify the data subject for the purpose of compliance with the GDPR. The principles of data minimisation, integrity and confidentiality enshrined in Articles 5(1)(c) and (e), 24, 25 and 32, require the controller to

---

[14] Gola 2017, para. 8. [15] Case C-582/14, *Breyer*, para. 43.
[16] Klabunde 2017, paras. 8–10.

implement appropriate technical and organisational measures, such as encryption, in order to meet the requirements of the GDPR, to protect the rights of data subjects and to ensure a level of security appropriate to the risk. By applying these measures, the controller gains a privilege under Article 11(1): i.e. no additional information is needed in cases where identification is not or no longer possible, for example due to the use of encryption. However, the WP29 has recalled that pseudonymised data are personal data by definition; concomitantly, in cases of pseudonymisation, the controller is still able to identify the data subject.[17] Nevertheless, an amendment proposed by the Parliament to add the words 'or consists only of pseudonymisation data' was not taken on board for the final compromise.[18] Article 11(1) thus applies when the controller holds personal data but some informational elements are missing and the controller cannot (any longer) identify the data subject.

Article 11(2)[19] was added by the co-legislators (Parliament and Council) to the initial proposal of the Commission. It provides an exemption from Articles 15–20 in the cases mentioned above, if the controller is able to demonstrate its inability to identify the data subject.[20] The demonstration requires a factual justification in order to be upheld by a DPA or a court in the case of *ex post* control.[21] As already stated, the WP29 rejected any interpretation of Article 11 aimed at reducing the responsibility of the controller(s) for compliance with data protection obligations, a position that is presumably shared by the EDPB.

However, if data subjects wish to be identified or to be re-identified by providing additional information in order to exercise their rights under Articles 15–20, the controller may not refuse the receipt of this additional information in order to frustrate the exercise of the data subject's rights. In this respect, the controller cannot request more information than initially needed (e.g. credentials used by the data subject to log-in to the online service offered by the controller). It should be noted, with regard to further processing, that since Article 11 is a separate provision to Article 6, the additional information required under Article 11(2) cannot be interpreted as a legal basis for data processing pursuant to Article 6(1), and that the controller is still required to undertake the purpose compatibility test pursuant to Article 6(4).

As intimated above, the first sentence of Article 11(2) creates confusion since it combines the requirement to demonstrate the non-identification of the data subject and the requirement to inform the data subject, if possible. This raises the question of how a controller can inform a data subject whom it is not able to identify. This confusion is the result of combining the amendments proposed by the Parliament and the Council during the trialogues, where the European Parliament ('EP') amendment continued: '(w)here as a consequence the data controller is unable to comply with a request of the data subject, it shall inform the data subject accordingly'. The only way to resolve this dilemma lies in the caveat 'if possible' at the end of the first sentence. If the controller has reasonable doubts concerning the identity of data subjects exercising their rights under Articles 15–20, the controller may request the provision of additional information necessary to confirm the identity of the data subject, without prejudice to Article 11.[22]

Finally, as noted by WP29, invoking Article 11 without the controller specifying what additional data are necessary to enable identification of the data subjects, would factually prevent the exercise of data subjects' rights (access, rectification, portability etc.).

---

[17] WP29 2017, p .6.   [18] Art. 10(1) EP Position GDPR.   [19] FRA 2018, p. 94.
[20] See the commentary on Art. 15 in this volume for discussion of a possible application of Art. 11(2) in the context of a request for access.
[21] Klabunde 2017, para. 20.   [22] Art. 12(6) GDPR.

In consequence, the controller must clarify which 'additional information' is needed in order to make the provision effective.[23]

3. Enforcement

In the event that a controller invokes Article 11, the data subject has the right to lodge a complaint with a supervisory authority pursuant to Article 77 GDPR (and, consequently, has the right to an effective judicial remedy against a decision of the supervisory authority pursuant to Article 78 GDPR) as well as the right to an effective judicial remedy against the controller pursuant to Article 79 GDPR. An infringement of the obligation under Article 11 is subject to an administrative fine under Article 83(4)(a) GDPR up to a maximum of € 10 million 'or, in the case of an undertaking, up to 2% of the total worldwide annual turnover of the preceding financial year, whichever is higher'.

Select Bibliography

EU legislation

GDPR Proposal: Proposal for a Regulation of the European Parliament and of the Council on the protection of individuals with regard to the processing of personal data and on the free movement of such data (General Data Protection Regulation), COM(2012) 11 final, 25 January 2012.

Academic writings

Gola 2017: Gola, 'Art. 11', in Gola (ed.), *Datenschutz-Grundverordnung VO (EU) 2016/679—Kommentar* (C. H. BECK 2017), 312.
Klabunde 2017: Klabunde, 'Art. 11', in Ehmann and Selmayr (eds.), *Datenschutz-Grundverordnung: DS-GVO* (C. H. BECK 2017), 361.

Papers of data protection authorities

WP29 2017: Article 29 Working Party, 'Opinion 03/2017 on Processing Personal Data in the Context of Cooperative Intelligent Transport Systems (C-ITS)' (WP 252, 4 October 2017).

Reports and recommendations

EP Position GDPR: Position of the European Parliament adopted at first reading on 12 March 2014 with a view to the adoption of Regulation (EU) No. .../2014 of the European Parliament and of the Council on the protection of individuals with regard to the processing of personal data and on the free movement of such data (General Data Protection Regulation), P7_TC1-COD(2012)0011, 12 March 2014.
FRA 2018: European Union Agency for Fundamental Rights (ed.), *Handbook on European Data Protection Law* (Publications Office of the European Union 2018).

Others

Nymity 2018: Nymity, 'GDPR Accountability Handbook 2018' (2018), available at https://info.nymity.com/hubfs/Landing%20Pages/GDPR%20Handbook/Nymity-GDPR-Accountability-Handbook.pdf.

---

[23] WP29 2017, p. 6.

Chapter III Rights of the Data Subject (Articles 12–23)

Section 1 Transparency and modalities

Article 12. Transparent information, communication and modalities for the exercise of the rights of the data subject

RADIM POLČÁK

1. The controller shall take appropriate measures to provide any information referred to in Articles 13 and 14 and any communication under Articles 15 to 22 and 34 relating to processing to the data subject in a concise, transparent, intelligible and easily accessible form, using clear and plain language, in particular for any information addressed specifically to a child. The information shall be provided in writing, or by other means, including, where appropriate, by electronic means. When requested by the data subject, the information may be provided orally, provided that the identity of the data subject is proven by other means.
2. The controller shall facilitate the exercise of data subject rights under Articles 15 to 22. In the cases referred to in Article 11(2), the controller shall not refuse to act on the request of the data subject for exercising his or her rights under Articles 15 to 22, unless the controller demonstrates that it is not in a position to identify the data subject.
3. The controller shall provide information on action taken on a request under Articles 15 to 22 to the data subject without undue delay and in any event within one month of receipt of the request. That period may be extended by two further months where necessary, taking into account the complexity and number of the requests. The controller shall inform the data subject of any such extension within one month of receipt of the request, together with the reasons for the delay. Where the data subject makes the request by electronic form means, the information shall be provided by electronic means where possible, unless otherwise requested by the data subject.
4. If the controller does not take action on the request of the data subject, the controller shall inform the data subject without delay and at the latest within one month of receipt of the request of the reasons for not taking action and on the possibility of lodging a complaint with a supervisory authority and seeking a judicial remedy.
5. Information provided under Articles 13 and 14 and any communication and any actions taken under Articles 15 to 22 and 34 shall be provided free of charge. Where requests from a data subject are manifestly unfounded or excessive, in particular because of their repetitive character, the controller may either:
    (a) charge a reasonable fee taking into account the administrative costs of providing the information or communication or taking the action requested; or
    (b) refuse to act on the request.
    The controller shall bear the burden of demonstrating the manifestly unfounded or excessive character of the request.
6. Without prejudice to Article 11, where the controller has reasonable doubts concerning the identity of the natural person making the request referred to in Articles 15 to 21, the controller may request the provision of additional information necessary to confirm the identity of the data subject.
7. The information to be provided to data subjects pursuant to Articles 13 and 14 may be provided in combination with standardised icons in order to give in an easily visible, intelligible and clearly legible manner a meaningful overview of the intended processing. Where the icons are presented electronically, they shall be machine-readable.

8. The Commission shall be empowered to adopt delegated acts in accordance with Article 92 for the purpose of determining the information to be presented by the icons and the procedures for providing standardised icons.

Relevant Recitals

(11) Effective protection of personal data throughout the Union requires the strengthening and setting out in detail of the rights of data subjects and the obligations of those who process and determine the processing of personal data, as well as equivalent powers for monitoring and ensuring compliance with the rules for the protection of personal data and equivalent sanctions for infringements in the Member States.

(58) The principle of transparency requires that any information addressed to the public or to the data subject be concise, easily accessible and easy to understand, and that clear and plain language and, additionally, where appropriate, visualisation be used. Such information could be provided in electronic form, for example, when addressed to the public, through a website. This is of particular relevance in situations where the proliferation of actors and the technological complexity of practice make it difficult for the data subject to know and understand whether, by whom and for what purpose personal data relating to him or her are being collected, such as in the case of online advertising. Given that children merit specific protection, any information and communication, where processing is addressed to a child, should be in such a clear and plain language that the child can easily understand.

(59) Modalities should be provided for facilitating the exercise of the data subject's rights under this Regulation, including mechanisms to request and, if applicable, obtain, free of charge, in particular, access to and rectification or erasure of personal data and the exercise of the right to object. The controller should also provide means for requests to be made electronically, especially where personal data are processed by electronic means. The controller should be obliged to respond to requests from the data subject without undue delay and at the latest within one month and to give reasons where the controller does not intend to comply with any such requests.

(60) The principles of fair and transparent processing require that the data subject be informed of the existence of the processing operation and its purposes. The controller should provide the data subject with any further information necessary to ensure fair and transparent processing taking into account the specific circumstances and context in which the personal data are processed. Furthermore, the data subject should be informed of the existence of profiling and the consequences of such profiling. Where the personal data are collected from the data subject, the data subject should also be informed whether he or she is obliged to provide the personal data and of the consequences, where he or she does not provide such data. That information may be provided in combination with standardised icons in order to give in an easily visible, intelligible and clearly legible manner, a meaningful overview of the intended processing. Where the icons are presented electronically, they should be machine-readable.

(63) A data subject should have the right of access to personal data which have been collected concerning him or her, and to exercise that right easily and at reasonable intervals, in order to be aware of, and verify, the lawfulness of the processing. This includes the right for data subjects to have access to data concerning their health, for example the data in their medical records containing information such as diagnoses, examination results, assessments by treating physicians and any treatment or interventions provided. Every data subject should therefore have the right to know and obtain communication in particular with regard to the purposes for which the personal data are processed, where possible the period for which the personal data are processed,

the recipients of the personal data, the logic involved in any automatic personal data processing and, at least when based on profiling, the consequences of such processing. Where possible, the controller should be able to provide remote access to a secure system which would provide the data subject with direct access to his or her personal data. That right should not adversely affect the rights or freedoms of others, including trade secrets or intellectual property and in particular the copyright protecting the software. However, the result of those considerations should not be a refusal to provide all information to the data subject. Where the controller processes a large quantity of information concerning the data subject, the controller should be able to request that, before the information is delivered, the data subject specify the information or processing activities to which the request relates.

(166) In order to fulfil the objectives of this Regulation, namely to protect the fundamental rights and freedoms of natural persons and in particular their right to the protection of personal data and to ensure the free movement of personal data within the Union, the power to adopt acts in accordance with Article 290 TFEU should be delegated to the Commission. In particular, delegated acts should be adopted in respect of criteria and requirements for certification mechanisms, information to be presented by standardised icons and procedures for providing such icons. It is of particular importance that the Commission carry out appropriate consultations during its preparatory work, including at expert level. The Commission, when preparing and drawing-up delegated acts, should ensure a simultaneous, timely and appropriate transmission of relevant documents to the European Parliament and to the Council.

Closely Related Provisions

Article 11 (Processing which does not require identification); Article 13 (Information to be provided where personal data are collected from the data subject) (see too recitals 60–62); Article 14 (Information to be provided where personal data have not been obtained from the data subject) (see too recital 61); Article 92 (Exercise of the delegation) (see too recital 166)

Related Provisions in LED [Directive (EU) 2016/680]

Article 11 (Automated individual decision-making) (see too recital 38); Article 12 (Communication and modalities for exercising the rights of the data subject) (see too recitals 39–41); Article 13 (Information to be made available or given to the data subject) (see too recital 39); Article 14 (Right of access by the data subject) (see too recital 43); Article 15 (Limitations to the right of access) (see too recitals 44–46); Article 16 (Right to rectification or erasure of personal data and restriction of processing) (see too recitals 47–48); Article 17 (Exercise of rights by the data subject and verification by the supervisory authority) (see too recital 85); Article 18 (Rights of the data subject in criminal investigations and proceedings) (see too recital 49); Article 31 (Communication of a personal data breach to the data subject) (see too recital 62)

Related Provisions in EPD [Directive 2002/58/EC]

Article 4 (Security) (see too recital 20); Article 5 (Confidentiality of the communications) (see too recitals 24–25); Article 6 (Traffic data) (see too recitals 25–26 and 32); Article 9 (Location data other than traffic data) (see too recitals 32 and 35); Article 12 (Directories of subscribers) (see too recital 38)

Relevant Case Law

CJEU

Case C-553/07, *College van burgemeester en wethouders van Rotterdam v M. E. E. Rijkeboer*, judgment of 7 May 2009 (ECLI:EU:C:2009:293).
Case C-406/10, *SAS Institute Inc. v World Programming Ltd*, judgment of 2 May 2012 (Grand Chamber) (ECLI:EU:C:2012:259).
Case C-486/12, *X*, judgment of 12 December 2013 (ECLI:EU:C:2013:836).
Case C-131/12, *Google Spain v Agencia Española de Protección de Datos (AEPD) and Mario Costeja González*, judgment of 13 May 2014 (Grand Chamber) (ECLI:EU:C:2014:317).
Joined Cases C-141/12 and C-372/12, *YS v Minister voor Immigratie, Integratie en Asiel and Minister voor Immigratie, Integratie en Asiel v M and S*, judgment of 17 July 2014 (ECLI:EU:C:2014:2081).

ECtHR

Klass and Others v Germany, Appl. No. 5029/71, judgment of 6 September 1978.
Sporrong and Lönnroth v Sweden, Appl. No. 7151/75, judgment of 23 September 1982.
Rees v the United Kingdom, Appl. No. 9532/91, judgment of 17 October 1986.
Gaskin v United Kingdom, Appl. No. 10454/83, judgment of 7 July 1989.
Odièvre v France, Appl. No. 42326/98, judgment of 13 February 2003.
Roche v United Kingdom, Appl. No. 32555/96, judgment of 19 October 2005.
Segerstedt-Wiberg and Others v Sweden, Appl. No. 62332/00, judgment of 6 June 2006.
Gabriele Weber and Cesar Richard Saravia v Germany, Appl. No. 54934/00, decision of 29 June 2006.
Dumitru Popescu v Romania No. 2, Appl. No. 71525/01, judgment of 26 April 2007.
Association for European Integration and Human Rights and Ekimdzhiev v Bulgaria, Appl. No. 62540/00, judgment of 30 January 2008.
K. H. and Others v Slovakia, Appl. No. 32881/04, judgment of 28 April 2009.
Haralambie v Romania, Appl. No. 21737/03, judgment of 27 October 2009.
Kennedy v United Kingdom, Appl. No. 26839/05, judgment of 18 May 2010.
Godelli v Italy, Appl. No. 33783/09, judgment of 25 September 2012.
Roman Zakharov v Russia, Appl. No. 47143/06, judgment of 4 December 2015.

A. Rationale and Policy Underpinnings

Article 12 GDPR is aimed at ensuring the efficient exercise of information and access rights, primarily for the benefit of data subjects, and secondarily for the benefit of controllers. It does not define or lay down any substantive rights but provides for technical and procedural provisions regarding the flow of information between controllers and data subjects. The basic rationale of this Article is that substantive rights of data subjects can serve their purpose only if supported by clear, proportionate and effective procedures. In that respect, the Article defines conditions as to how and when data subjects shall be informed, actively or passively, about processing of their personal data.

The nature of information and access rights of data subjects corresponds with the German concept of informational self-determination[1] and with the earlier understanding of privacy advanced by Westin.[2] It is assumed that being able to decide about one's private life requires being informed about quantitative and qualitative aspects of processing

---

[1] See Albers 2005.   [2] See Westin 1970.

of personal data as well as being able to assess the consequences of actual or potential decisions about that processing. Thus, the level of data subjects' actual self-determination directly depends on the form in which information concerning them is presented and communicated.

The subsequent rationale for Article 12 is the need for greater clarity and consistency of rules on information exchange between controllers and data subjects across the Union. Unified rules aim to enhance consumer understanding of and confidence in cross-border transactions while providing for the opportunity for enterprises to develop just one set of compliance procedures for the whole European common market instead of having to invest in different solutions for each jurisdiction.

B. Legal Background

1. EU legislation

The subject-matter of Article 12 GDPR was dealt with partly in Article 12 DPD. However, the overall scope of the latter differed from the former, as its primary purpose was to lay down substantive access rights for data subjects, and it did not specifically mention other rights. Even the form of exercise of access rights was mentioned in Article 12 DPD only briefly. The confirmation obligations under Article 12(a) DPD had to be executed 'without constraint at reasonable intervals and without excessive delay or expense'; rectification, erasure and blocking of unduly processed data under Article 12(b) DPD was supposed to be done 'as appropriate'; and confirmation obligations under Article 12(c) applied unless these 'proved impossible or involved a disproportionate effort'. The form of exercise of information and access rights was also lightly touched upon by the recitals to the DPD. Recital 38 stated that the 'data subject must be in a position to learn of the existence of a processing operation and, where data are collected from him, must be given accurate and full information, bearing in mind the circumstances of the collection'. Recital 41 added that 'any person must be able to exercise the right of access to data'. However, the recitals' main purpose was to lay down the fundamental teleology of information and access rights as such, but not of the ways in which they should be exercised.

The approach to information rights in Article 12 GDPR is essentially analogous to that under EU consumer law. For example, the Consumer Rights Directive (2011/83/EU)[3] demands in Article 6(1) that prior to the conclusion of a distance consumer agreement, information shall be presented to a consumer 'in a clear and comprehensible manner', while other provisions refer to the need for 'clear and prominent' or 'clear and legible' forms of consumer communications. The same Directive also provides for other formal requirements as to the timing of information ('without delay', 'without undue delay') or means of communication ('durable media').

Apart from general EU consumer protection law, specific provisions regarding the exercise of information rights also apply in particular sectors. For example, in relation to the electronic communications sector, Article 11(3) of the Universal Service Directive (2002/22/EC)[4] empowers Member States to implement regulations enabling 'end-users and consumers [to] have access to comprehensive, comparable and user-friendly information'. Another example is the Directive on Distance Marketing of Consumer Financial Services (2002/65/EC)[5]

---

[3] Consumer Rights Directive.   [4] Directive 2002/22/EC.   [5] Directive 2002/65/EC.

which lays down in Article 3 duties to inform 'in good time before the consumer is bound' and to do so in a 'clear and comprehensible manner'.

The exercise of access rights is approached in Article 12 GDPR similarly to the existing EU regulatory framework for public access to environmental data, particularly Directive 2003/4/EC.[6] Although the GDPR covers a much broader range of subjects than Directive 2003/4/EC, both laws share the same general approach to handling of access requests. In both cases, the requested party is obliged to respond (positively or negatively) and there is a specific time frame given. It is also a general rule that access should be granted, unless the request falls under one of relatively restrictively formulated exemptions.

Also noteworthy is that the method of calculation of fees for granting access under Article 12(5) GDPR bears similarity to the general principles of charging laid down in the PSI Directive (Directive 2003/98/EC on the reuse of public sector information)[7] as amended by Directive 2013/37/EU. In comparison with the rather vague requirement in the GDPR that a fee shall be 'reasonable', the PSI Directive uses a slightly more detailed method of calculation that is 'based on marginal costs incurred for ... reproduction, provision and dissemination' of the requested information.

2. International instruments

International cooperation has not progressed far enough for the form of exercise of information or access rights to be explicitly incorporated into multilateral international treaties, with the exception of Modernised Convention 108. However, the ideas underlying Article 12 GDPR have been discussed by the ECtHR, which—as elaborated below—has found that a right to be informed about processing of personal data as well as a right to have access to those data, including necessary forms of their exercise, are inherent in the right to respect for private life stipulated in Article 8 European Convention on Human Rights ('ECHR').

The Modernised Convention 108 contains in Article 8(1)(b) provisions on confirmation and access rights, subject to certain conditions. These provisions use basically the same logic as Article 12 GDPR: confirmation and access rights are to be exercised 'at reasonable intervals and without excessive delay or expense' and data provided upon an access request shall be presented to the requesting party 'in an intelligible form'.

A rather exceptional stipulation regarding the form of exercise of information and access rights is in the bilateral US–EU Umbrella Agreement of 2016 on the protection of personal information relating to the prevention, investigation, detection and prosecution of criminal offences.[8] Articles 16 and 17 lay down neither any specific form nor any time frame in which respective information shall be communicated, but explicitly provide for a duty to decide (positively or negatively with reasons) about access and rectification requests. Both articles also contain a general duty to grant access or rectification unless there is a specific reason for refusal. In addition, Article 16(3) provides for a particular, yet rather vaguely defined, rule for charging, whereby '[e]xcessive expenses shall not be imposed on the individual as a condition to access his or her personal information'.

---

[6] Directive 2003/4/EC. [7] PSI Directive. [8] Umbrella Agreement US.

3. National developments

Under the DPD regime, EU and EEA Member States greatly differed in the ways in which they legislated the form of exercise of information and access rights. Some Member States used formulations closely following Article 12 DPD, while others (such as Austria or Ireland) adopted more detailed and structured rules.[9] Particular rules included time limits for resolving requests of data subjects,[10] principles for charging, and definitions of excessive and abusive requests.

4. Case law

4.1 EU Court of Justice

The CJEU has ruled on access and information rights in several cases.

In *Google Spain*, the CJEU implied that since a search engine operator can be regarded a controller of personal data, it also should have to comply with access and other requests.[11]

In *YS*, the CJEU interpreted the extent and form of exercise of access rights in light of the original purpose of processing and the extent of respective subsequent remedies. The matter here concerned a request for access to data included in particular documents drawn up by government officials in the course of determining applications for residence permits. With respect to the personal data in these documents, the CJEU considered it sufficient that the applicant for a residence permit:

> be in possession of a full summary of all those data in an intelligible form, that is to say a form which allows that applicant to become aware of those data and to check that they are accurate and processed in compliance with that directive [the DPD], so that he may, where relevant, exercise the rights conferred on him by that directive.[12]

In *X*, the CJEU considered principles of charging for access to data, holding that it is in general possible to levy fees for serving access requests under Article 12(a) DPD unless such fees 'exceed the cost of communicating such data'. The main question in these proceedings concerned interpretation of the term 'without excessive delay or expense': did this mean 'without expense' or 'without excessive expense'? The CJEU held it meant the latter. However, the Court also formulated general guidance for the calculation of fees in terms of arriving at 'a fair balance[13] between, on the one hand, the interest of the data subject ... and, on the other, the burden which the obligation to communicate such data represents for the controller'.[14]

The original teleology of processing of personal data proved to be a relevant factor also in *Rijkeboer*. The logic of the dispute was very different here in comparison to other data

---

[9] For Austria, see sections 26–28 Austrian Federal Data Protection Act 2000 (this Act was substantially amended upon the GDPR coming into force); for Ireland, see s. 4(1) Irish Data Protection Act 1988.

[10] E.g. 8 weeks in Austria (see section 26 of the Austrian Federal Data Protection Act 2000 (repealed)), 45 days in Belgium (see section 10 of the Belgian Data Protection Law 1992 (repealed)), or 15 days in Greece (see section 12 of the Greek Data Protection Law 1997).

[11] Case C-131/12, *Google Spain*, paras. 33 and 69.

[12] Joined Cases C-141/12 and C-372/12, *YS*, para. 2 of the operative part.

[13] The term 'fair balance' seems to build on criteria developed by the ECtHR for proportionate balancing of competing rights under the ECHR: see especially ECtHR, *Sporrong and Lönnroth*. See further Christoffersen 2009.

[14] Case C-486/12, *X*, para. 28.

protection cases before the CJEU, as the Court had to interpret the retention duties of the controller (instead of more common duties not to process or to delete personal data). The Court found that Member States have to provide for retention duties of controllers in order to enable data subjects to exercise retrospectively their access rights pursuant to Article 12(a) DPD. In particular, Member States were held to be under a duty 'to ensure a right of access to information on the recipients or categories of recipient of personal data and on the content of the data disclosed not only in respect of the present but also in respect of the past'.[15] The Court went on to stress, as in *X*, the need for a 'fair balance'[16] between the interests at stake:

> It is for Member States to fix a time-limit for storage of that information and to provide for access to that information which constitutes a fair balance between, on the one hand, the interest of the data subject in protecting his privacy, in particular by way of his rights to object and to bring legal proceedings and, on the other, the burden which the obligation to store that information represents for the controller.[17]

The interpretation of Article 12(a) DPD in *Rijkeboer* is implicitly based on Fuller's advocacy of 'congruence between official action and declared rule'.[18] The Court noted that:

> to ensure the practical effect of the provisions referred to in paragraphs 51 and 52 of the present judgment [i.e. Articles 12(b), 12(c), 14, 22, 23 DPD], that right must of necessity relate to the past. If that were not the case, the data subject would not be in a position effectively to exercise his right to have data presumed unlawful or incorrect rectified, erased or blocked or to bring legal proceedings and obtain compensation for the damage suffered.[19]

It was, however, relatively easy for the Court to decide on the particular merits of the case because the time limits of retrospective access rights were here shorter than the duration of the rights of the controller to process the respective data. The CJEU then simply noted that it is disproportionate with regards to the purpose of Article 12(a) DPD if the access rights of data subjects were time-barred, while the rights of the controller to process personal data in question still existed.

4.2 European Court of Human Rights

The ECtHR has implicitly tackled the content of Article 12 GDPR despite the fact that the ECHR lacks explicit definitions of information rights, access rights or their exercise. The ECtHR follows Fuller's above-noted advocacy of congruence between substance and forms of exercise of rights and consistently implies that, first, access and information rights represent integral components of privacy and other fundamental rights (typically fair trial, freedom of expression etc.) and that, secondly, information and access rights can exist only if corresponding forms of their exercise also exist. The Court's jurisprudence on access and information rights builds on its general doctrine of positive obligations that arise with the need for effective and proportionate exercise of Convention rights. This general approach of the ECtHR was explained in *Rees v UK* as follows: 'In determining whether or not a positive obligation exists, regard must be had to the fair balance that has to be struck between the general interest of the community and the interests of the individual, the search for which balance is inherent in the whole of the Convention'.[20]

---

[15] Case C-553/07, *Rijkeboer*, para. 70.   [16] Ibid., paras. 64, 66 and 70.   [17] Ibid., para. 70.
[18] See Fuller 1969, p. 81.   [19] Case C-553/07, *Rijkeboer*, para. 54.
[20] ECtHR, *Rees v UK*, para. 37.

The ECtHR has used the above approach to assess the proportionality of access rights to data stored by public child-care institutions (*Gaskin v UK*, *Odièvre v France*, and *Godelli v Italy*), police records (*Segerstedt-Wiberg*) and communications stored upon security surveillance (*Zakharov v Russia*).[21] In *Roche v UK*, the ECtHR stated that the lack of procedure allowing the applicant to access data concerning his military engagement violated Article 8 ECHR. The Court concluded that 'the respondent State had not fulfilled its positive obligation to provide an effective and accessible procedure enabling the applicant to have access to all relevant and appropriate information which would allow him to assess any risk to which he had been exposed during his participation in the tests'.[22] In *Haralambie*, the ECtHR considered the time frame for serving access requests to data stored by the secret police. A provision of domestic law laying down a delay of six years was considered in the given circumstances disproportionate and in violation of Article 8 ECHR.[23] In *K. H. and Others*, the Court ruled that access rights to health records cannot be limited to individuals (data subjects) or their legal representatives (e.g. parents or court-appointed guardians) but extend also to their contracted representatives or proxies.[24]

The ECtHR has additionally ruled on the right to be informed about processing of personal data. In particular, the Court has assessed the necessity of establishing forms of exercise of this right in cases of security surveillance (*Klass v Germany*, *Weber and Saravia*, *Association for European Integration and Human Rights*, *Popescu* and *Kennedy v UK*).[25] However, the scope of the right to be informed in these cases falls outside the GDPR, according to Article 2(2)(d) GDPR.

C. Analysis

1. Introduction

The purpose of Article 12 is to unify technical and procedural aspects of the exercise of various information and access rights. Paragraphs 1 and 5 set common rules for all rights laid down in Articles 13–22 and 34, while other paragraphs separately define special requirements for exercising information and access rights.

2. Concise and transparent form of information

The first general obligation for the various information and access rights is that all information communicated to data subjects pursuant to Articles 13–22 and 34 should be presented in a 'concise, transparent, intelligible and easily accessible form, using clear and plain language' (Article 12(1)). This formulation is considerably more elaborate than the requirement for 'intelligible form' in Article 12(a) DPD, yet it serves the same basic purpose, i.e. to provide data subjects with information that they can reasonably read and understand. It is somewhat paradoxical that the requirement of 'concise form' is not

---

[21] See ECtHR, *Gaskin v UK*; ECtHR, *Odièvre v France*; ECtHR, *Godelli v Italy*; ECtHR, *Segerstedt-Wiberg*; and ECtHR, *Zakharov v Russia*.
[22] ECtHR, *Roche v UK*, para. 167.   [23] ECtHR, *Haralambie*.
[24] ECtHR, *K. H. and Others*.
[25] ECtHR, *Klass v Germany*; ECtHR, *Weber and Saravia*; ECtHR, *Association for European Integration and Human Rights*; ECtHR, *Popescu*; and ECtHR, *Kennedy v UK*.

entirely obeyed by the text of the GDPR itself—e.g. the need for 'clear and plain language' is replicated in Article 34(2); and the matter of proving identity for access and information requests is tackled simultaneously (and not especially concisely) in both Article 11 and Article 12(2) and (5).

How far the requirement of a 'concise form' reaches is not entirely clear, particularly regarding access rights. Strictly construed, the requirement might entail a time-consuming task for data controllers, especially if they are to transform complexly structured and interlinked datasets originally destined for machine reading into a form concise enough for a data subject. In any case, the explicit inclusion of the requirement of a 'concise form', together with the need for relative transparency (see further below), clearly prohibits operationalising the information rights laid down in Articles 13 and 14 through general or open-ended statements in privacy policies or end-user agreements without clear or specific meanings.

3. Children's data

As already noted, the requirements laid down in Article 12(1) apply commonly for 'any information referred to in Articles 13 and 14 and any communication under Articles 15 to 22 and 34'. It might then seem logically redundant when Article 12(1) speaks particularly about 'any information addressed specifically to a child'.[26] However, the emphasis on communications destined for children has ultimately a punitive function in that it indicates that incompliances with the first sentence of Article 12(1) will be sanctioned more harshly when the affected party is a child. It also indicates that the criteria of 'concise, transparent, intelligible and easily accessible form' as well as 'clear and plain language' have to be interpreted differently by the controller if the anticipated recipient of information is a child. Consequently, the controller has a duty to differentiate between adults and children when choosing forms of expression and of communication of respective information about the processing of personal data. This is also reinforced in the final sentence of recital 58.

4. Logic of processing

Especially in cases of automated processing of personal data, it is unclear from the words of Article 12(1) how far controllers will be required to reveal the logic of that processing, particularly in light of recital 63.[27] It is unlikely that actual algorithms or pieces of computer code will be required to be made transparent to data subjects, as this requirement would probably entail, in the language of recital 63, an 'adverse effect' for 'trade secrets or intellectual property and in particular the copyright protecting the software'. However, recital 63 also points out that the 'result of those considerations should not be a refusal to provide all information to the data subject'. A middle ground could be for data subjects to request controllers in case of processing personal data under Article 22 not to reveal complete algorithms or computer codes, but at least to make them available in compiled form for testing or reverse engineering (in so far as such use does not violate copyright).[28]

---

[26] See also the commentary on Art. 8 in this volume regarding obtaining the consent of a child in relation to information society services.
[27] See also the commentaries on Arts. 13–15 in this volume.
[28] Case C-406/10, *SAS Institute*, para. 61. See also the commentary on Art. 22 in this volume.

5. Form of information

Another common rule for all rights laid down in Articles 13–22 and 34 is to provide information 'in writing, or by other means, including, where appropriate, by electronic means' (Article 12(1)). Although 'other means' might mean practically anything, the simultaneous requirement of 'easy accessibility' and the general rationale of Article 12 limit the choice of means of expressions to those that are reasonably able to communicate the information concerned both concisely and intelligibly. In addition, controllers must bear in mind that there might arise a need for them to prove positively that they have fulfilled their obligations under Article 12. As a result, the only pragmatically available form is here a document (paper or electronic, textual or audio-visual) or a documented procedure (e.g. a document proving that information is given by non-documentary means, e.g. orally).

6. Free of charge

The third common rule for all information and access rights is that they are exercised free of charge (Article 12(5)). An exemption is available for charging for 'manifestly unfounded or excessive' requests made under Articles 15–22. Although no particular meaning has been so far given in secondary EU law to the term 'excessive request', it is possible to base the interpretation upon the established practice of some Member States, i.e. assessing excessiveness by reference to the number of requests in a given time period. The time period and number of requests differed between the Member States, with the most common limitation being one request per year.[29] The EDPB has stated in the context of video surveillance that 'In case of excessive or manifestly unfounded requests from a data subject, the controller may either charge a reasonable fee in accordance with Article 12(5)(a) GDPR, or refuse to act on the request (Article 12 (5) (b) GDPR. The controller needs to be able to demonstrate the excessive or manifestly unfounded character of the request'.[30] It remains questionable whether any special meaning should be given to the term 'manifestly'. If the term were omitted, it would have been enough for the controller to determine whether requests are founded and non-excessive. Instead, it seems controllers will also have to prove, in order to rely on Article 12(5)(a) or (b), that the unfounded or excessive character of requests was apparent at the time they were made. Additionally, it is not entirely certain whether the term 'manifestly' relates only to 'unfounded' or also to 'excessive'. Most likely it relates to both. In any case, if a controller can rely on the second sentence of Article 12(5), there is a choice of two alternatives: either not to comply with the request or to charge 'a reasonable fee taking into account the administrative costs of providing the information or communication or taking the action requested'.

A decision not to comply with the request shall be followed by a corresponding information to the requesting party pursuant to Article 12(3). However, the wording of Article 12(5) does not completely clarify which procedure should follow a decision of the controller according to Article 12(5)(a)—i.e. whether the controller should comply with the request and then charge the 'reasonable fee', or whether it should first inform the requesting party that the request was found 'manifestly unfounded or excessive' before

---

[29] This limit was laid down in the data protection statutes of Austria, Finland, Hungary, Romania, Spain and Sweden. Some EU Member States legislated shorter limitations. For example, Italy operated with one request per 90 days (see section 9 of the Italian Data Protection Code 2003).

[30] EDPB 2019, p. 19.

charging a reasonable fee. It also does not address whether the potential fee should be calculated in advance by the controller.

The issue with charging for manifestly unfounded or excessive requests is problematic not only due to the unclear procedure, but also due to the legislated mechanism for calculation of fees. The actual 'administrative costs of providing the information or communication or taking the action requested' do not represent a basis for the fee, but only have to be taken into account. Moreover, it may be difficult for a data subject to anticipate even the basic extent of actual costs, not only in cases of complex requests, but also regarding requests made to large institutions with costly internal procedures.

Although the GDPR fails to provide particular guidance as to the procedure for charging for manifestly unfound or excessive requests or to the method of calculation of respective fees, it is possible to apply, by analogy, practices that were commonly developed in Member States and in the secondary EU law for charging for public sector information. It should also be noted that fees charged according to Article 12(5)(a) will in most jurisdictions be claimable under standard rules of civil procedure which will often afford protection of a weaker party (i.e. the data subject)—a fortiori where rules on consumer protection apply. Consequently, if a controller chooses to apply Article 12(5)(a), it is advisable first to inform the requesting party about the processing of the request according to the criteria of Article 12(5), second sentence, and about the anticipated fee. Only if the requesting party then confirms that it wants to go forward with the request should the fee be actually charged.

7. Time frame

Article 12(3) provides for the duty to respond to requests made under Articles 15–22 and sets a general time frame of one month from receipt of the request. Within that time, the controller shall either (1) comply with the request, (2) extend the deadline to two further months or (3) refuse to act on the request pursuant to Article 12(5)(b). According to the above-discussed rules for charging, the fourth possible option here is the duty to announce the anticipated fee pursuant to Article 12(5)(a).

8. Unidentified parties

None of the above alternatives applies in a situation when a controller cannot identify the requesting party. According to Article 12(2), unidentified or doubtfully identified requests made under Articles 15–20 should not be complied with.[31] Thus, lack of identification of the requesting party might lead to the situation when a controller has (unlike the above four alternatives) no duty to respond to a request made pursuant to Articles 15–20 within the time frame laid down in Article 12(4). Indeed, complying with an unidentified request made under Articles 15–20 could constitute unlawful processing and/or transfer of personal data by the controller.

Objections made under Article 21 do not fall under the scope of Article 11(2), but they do fall under the scope of Article 12(2) and (6). This means that a controller is entitled to decide whether an unidentified exercise of the right to object will be complied with, additional identification will be required, or no action will be taken at all. This gives rise to a regulatory paradox in that one can well imagine situations when it

---

[31] See also the commentary on Art. 11 in this volume.

will be in the personal interest of data subjects not to object against processing of their personal data pursuant to Article 21, yet, in that case, if an unidentified third party objects to the processing and the objection is complied with by the controller, this will be compliant with Articles 11 and 12 but could harm the personal interests of the data subject concerned.

Even more paradoxical is the handling of unidentified requests made under Article 22. These requests fall neither under Article 11(2) nor Article 12(6), but they still fall under Article 12(2). In result, a controller that receives an unidentified request pursuant to Article 22 has only two options—either to comply with the request or not to do anything at all (i.e. the controller does not even have here the right to request 'additional information necessary to confirm the identity of the data subject').

9. Facilitation of data subject rights

The meaning of Article 12(2), first sentence (i.e. the duty to 'facilitate the exercise of data subject rights under Articles 15 to 22') is rather vague. This duty can be interpreted in conjunction with the broad wording of recitals 59 and 63 to provide for the exercise of information and access right to the maximum possible extent. Concomitantly, Article 12(2), first sentence, requires that controllers, as a general point of departure, act in favour of serving access and information requests and refrain from harming or hindering data subjects' possibilities to exercise their rights under Articles 15–22.

The wording of Article 12(2), first sentence, gives the impression that this duty is not laid down for particular requests (rules for particular requests are specified in other paragraphs of Article 12), but is rather aimed at general and systemic practices of controllers. Similarly to the principles of data protection by design and by default laid down in Article 25, it is arguable that Article 12(2) lays down a general technical and procedural principle of enabling the exercise of information and access rights by design and by default. This is reinforced by the reference in the first sentence of recital 59 to 'modalities' for facilitating the exercise of such rights.

10. Standardised icons and symbols

Article 12(7) lays down a possibility for controllers to fulfil their duty to inform data subjects pursuant to Articles 13 and 14 also through standardised icons. It could be questioned whether the words of Article 12(7) should be interpreted *a contrario* in the sense that standardised icons are the *only* possible addition to the use of 'clear and plain language' (text or speech) for informing data subjects according to Articles 13 and 14. The better view is that Article 12(7) standardises only one of multiple additional options for how a controller can inform data subjects besides textual or spoken form. Thus, a controller can also use pictures or other forms of expression that are not standardised icons under Article 12(7) if these alternative means of expression provide for 'concise, transparent, intelligible and easily accessible' information according to Article 12(1) and/or for a 'meaningful overview' given 'in an easily visible, intelligible and clearly legible manner' (to use the wording of recital 60).

The possibility of using non-standardised graphical or other symbols to inform data subjects can also be indirectly deduced from the wording of Article 12(1), last sentence, which emphasises the need to tackle specifically the problem of properly informing children (see above). If no standardised icons are available or they are not suitable for certain situations, a restrictive interpretation of Article 12(7) would allow controllers only to use language. Especially if data subjects are children, it would quite absurdly mean that controllers could not use other means of expression (e.g. pictures) that typically serve the purpose of 'concise, transparent, intelligible and easily accessible form' much better than text or speech. Thus, there is a good reason to argue for a broad interpretation of Article 12(7) in the sense that a controller is entitled to use not only standardised icons but also any other form of expression of information according to Articles 13 and 14 besides text or speech.

The delegation made in Article 12(8) enables the Commission to legislatively define situations when using standardised icons is mandatory. It also empowers the Commission to lay down standardisation procedures for such icons.

Neither Article 12 nor any other provision in the GDPR defines a 'standardised icon'. Thus, the only possible interpretation of Article 12(7) and (8) is that standardised icons mean (for the purposes of the GDPR) only those that are created through the procedure envisaged in Article 12(8). Consequently, no standardisation of these icons in terms of the GDPR is possible through any other procedure, e.g. by industrial associations, professional guilds etc. It also means that no use of standardised icons pursuant to Article 12(7) is possible unless the Commission enacts relevant standardisation procedures. It should be noted that the Commission has indicated informally that it will be unlikely to enact standardised icons unless there is strong pressure from stakeholders to do so, which thus far has been lacking.

Neither Article 12(7) nor Article 12(8) derogate from the general duty laid down in Article 12(1). Accordingly, even if standardised icons are available or even mandatory for certain situations, their particular use still has to meet the requirement of 'concise, transparent, intelligible and easily accessible form' in which information shall be presented pursuant to Articles 13 and 14.

Select Bibliography

EU legislation

Consumer Rights Directive: Directive 2011/83/EU of the European Parliament and of the Council of 25 October 2011 on consumer rights, amending Council Directive 93/13/EEC and Directive 1999/44/EC of the European Parliament and of the Council and repealing Council Directive 85/577/EEC and Directive 97/7/EC of the European Parliament and of the Council, OJ 2011 L 304/64.

Directive 2002/65/EC: Directive 2002/65/EC of the European Parliament and of the Council of 23 September 2002 concerning the distance marketing of consumer financial services and amending Council Directive 90/619/EEC and Directives 97/7/EC and 98/27/EC, OJ 2002 L 271/16.

Directive 2003/EC: Directive 2003/4/EC of the European Parliament and of the Council of 28 January 2003 on public access to environmental information and repealing Council Directive 90/313/EEC, OJ 2003 L 41/26.

PSI Directive: Directive 2013/37/EU of the European Parliament and of the Council of 26 June 2013 amending Directive 2003/98/EC on the re-use of public sector information, OJ 2013 L 175/1.

Umbrella Agreement US: Agreement between the United States of America and the European Union on the protection of personal information relating to the prevention, investigation, detection, and prosecution of criminal offences, OJ 2016 L 336/3.

Universal Service Directive: Directive 2002/22/EC of the European Parliament and of the Council of 7 March 2002 on universal service and users' rights relating to electronic communications networks and services (Universal Service Directive), OJ 2002 L 108/51.

National legislation

Austrian Federal Data Protection Act 2000: Bundesgesetz über den Schutz personenbezogener Daten (Datenschutzgesetz 2000 – DSG 2000), BGBl. I Nr 165/1999 zuletzt geändert durch BGBl. I Nr. 132/2015 (repealed).

Belgian Data Protection Law 1992: Wet tot bescherming van de persoonlijke levenssfeer ten opzichte van de verwerking van persoonsgegevens, van 8 december 1992; Loi relative à la protection de la vie privée à l'égard des traitements de données à caractère personnel, du 8 decembre 1992) (repealed).

Greek Data Protection Law: Law 2472/1997 on the Protection of Individuals with regard to the Processing of Personal Data (as amended).

Irish Data Protection Act 1988: Data Protection Act (Number 25 of 1988).

Italian Data Protection Code 2003: Decreto legislativo 30 giugno 2003, n. 196: Codice in Materia di Protezione dei Dati Personali.

Academic writings

Albers 2005: Albers, *Informationelle Selbstbestimmung* (Nomos 2005).

Brouwer and Zuiderveen Borgesius, 'Case Report: Access to Personal Data and the Right to Good Governance during Asylum Procedures after the CJEU's YS. and M. and S. judgment', 17 *European Journal of Migration and Law* (2015), 259.

Christoffersen 2009: Christoffersen, *Fair Balance: A Study of Proportionality, Subsidiarity and Primarity in the European Convention on Human Rights* (Martinus Nijhoff Publishers 2009).

Cormack, 'Is the Subject Access Right Now Too Great a Threat to Privacy?', 2(1) *European Data Protection Law Review* (2016), 15

Fuller 1969: Fuller, *The Morality of Law* (Yale University Press 1969).

Galetta and de Hert, 'The Proceduralisation of Data Protection Remedies under EU Data Protection Law: Towards a More Effective and Data Subject-Oriented Remedial System?', 8(1) *Review of European Administrative Law* (2015), 125.

Galetta, Fonio and Ceresa, 'Nothing Is as it Seems: The Exercise of Access Rights in Italy and Belgium: Dispelling Fallacies in the Legal Reasoning from the "Law in Theory" to the "Law in Practice"', 6(1) *International Data Privacy Law* (2016), 16.

Norris, de Hert, L'Hoiry and Galetta (eds.), *The Unaccountable State of Surveillance. Exercising Access Rights in Europe* (Springer 2017).

Raento, 'The Data Subject's Right of Access and to be Informed in Finland: An Experimental Study', 14(3) *International Journal of Law and Information Technology* (2006), 390.

Ticher, *Data Protection vs. Freedom of Information: Access and Personal Data* (IT Governance Publishing 2008).

Westin 1970: Westin, *Privacy and Freedom* (Bodley Head 1970).

Papers of data protection authorities

EDPB 2019: European Data Protection Board, 'Guidelines 3/2019 on the processing of personal data through video devices (version for public consultation)' (10 July 2019).

UK Information Commissioner's Office, 'Subject Access Code of Practice. Dealing with Requests from Individuals for Personal Information' (2014), available at https://ico.org.uk/media/for-organisations/documents/2014223/subject-access-code-of-practice.pdf.

Section 2 Information and access to personal data

Article 13. Information to be provided where personal data are collected from the data subject

GABRIELA ZANFIR-FORTUNA

1. Where personal data relating to a data subject are collected from the data subject, the controller shall, at the time when personal data are obtained, provide the data subject with all of the following information:
   (a) the identity and the contact details of the controller and, where applicable, of the controller's representative;
   (b) the contact details of the data protection officer, where applicable;
   (c) the purposes of the processing for which the personal data are intended as well as the legal basis for the processing;
   (d) where the processing is based on point (f) of Article 6(1), the legitimate interests pursued by the controller or by a third party;
   (e) the recipients or categories of recipients of the personal data, if any;
   (f) where applicable, the fact that the controller intends to transfer personal data to a third country or international organisation and the existence or absence of an adequacy decision by the Commission, or in the case of transfers referred to in Article 46 or 47, or the second subparagraph of Article 49(1), reference to the appropriate or suitable safeguards and the means by which to obtain a copy of them or where they have been made available.
2. In addition to the information referred to in paragraph 1, the controller shall, at the time when personal data are obtained, provide the data subject with the following further information necessary to ensure fair and transparent processing:
   (a) the period for which the personal data will be stored, or if that is not possible, the criteria used to determine that period;
   (b) the existence of the right to request from the controller access to and rectification or erasure of personal data or restriction of processing concerning the data subject or to object to processing as well as the right to data portability;
   (c) where the processing is based on point (a) of Article 6(1) or point (a) of Article 9(2), the existence of the right to withdraw consent at any time, without affecting the lawfulness of processing based on consent before its withdrawal;
   (d) the right to lodge a complaint with a supervisory authority;
   (e) whether the provision of personal data is a statutory or contractual requirement, or a requirement necessary to enter into a contract, as well as whether the data subject is obliged to provide the personal data and of the possible consequences of failure to provide such data;
   (f) the existence of automated decision-making, including profiling, referred to in Article 22(1) and (4) and, at least in those cases, meaningful information about the logic involved, as well as the significance and the envisaged consequences of such processing for the data subject.
3. Where the controller intends to further process the personal data for a purpose other than that for which the personal data were collected, the controller shall provide the data subject prior to that further processing with information on that other purpose and with any relevant further information as referred to in paragraph 2.
4. Paragraphs 1, 2 and 3 shall not apply where and insofar as the data subject already has the information.

Relevant Recitals

(60) The principles of fair and transparent processing require that the data subject be informed of the existence of the processing operation and its purposes. The controller should provide the data subject with any further information necessary to ensure fair and transparent processing taking into account the specific circumstances and context in which the personal data are processed. Furthermore, the data subject should be informed of the existence of profiling and the consequences of such profiling. Where the personal data are collected from the data subject, the data subject should also be informed whether he or she is obliged to provide the personal data and of the consequences, where he or she does not provide such data. That information may be provided in combination with standardised icons in order to give in an easily visible, intelligible and clearly legible manner, a meaningful overview of the intended processing. Where the icons are presented electronically, they should be machine-readable.

(61) The information in relation to the processing of personal data relating to the data subject should be given to him or her at the time of collection from the data subject, or, where the personal data are obtained from another source, within a reasonable period, depending on the circumstances of the case. Where personal data can be legitimately disclosed to another recipient, the data subject should be informed when the personal data are first disclosed to the recipient. Where the controller intends to process the personal data for a purpose other than that for which they were collected, the controller should provide the data subject prior to that further processing with information on that other purpose and other necessary information. Where the origin of the personal data cannot be provided to the data subject because various sources have been used, general information should be provided.

(62) However, it is not necessary to impose the obligation to provide information where the data subject already possesses the information, where the recording or disclosure of the personal data is expressly laid down by law or where the provision of information to the data subject proves to be impossible or would involve a disproportionate effort. The latter could in particular be the case where processing is carried out for archiving purposes in the public interest, scientific or historical research purposes or statistical purposes. In that regard, the number of data subjects, the age of the data and any appropriate safeguards adopted should be taken into consideration.

Closely Related Provisions

Article 5(1) (Principle of fairness, lawfulness and transparency); Article 12 (Transparent information, communication and modalities for the exercise of the rights of the data subject); Article 14 (Information to be provided where personal data have not been obtained from the data subject); Article 15 (Right of access by the data subject); Article 23 (Restrictions); Article 34 (Communication of a personal data breach to the data subject)

Related Provisions in LED [Directive (EU) 2016/680]

Article 13 (Information to be made available or given to the data subject)

Related Provisions in EPD [Directive 2002/58/EC]

Article 4 (Security); Article 5 (Confidentiality of communications); Article 6 (Traffic data); Article 9 (Location data other than traffic data)

Relevant Case Law

CJEU

Case C-473/12, *Institut professionnel des agents immobiliers (IPI) v Geoffrey Englebert and Others*, judgment of 7 November 2013 (ECLI:EU:C:2013:715).

Case C-201/14, *Smaranda Bara and Others v Președintele Casei Naționale de Asigurări de Sănătate, Casa Națională de Asigurări de Sănătate, Agenția Națională de Administrare Fiscală (ANAF)*, judgment of 1 October 2015 (ECLI:EU:C:2015:638).

Opinion 1/15, Opinion of 26 July 2017 (Grand Chamber) (ECLI:EU:C:2017:592).

Case C-40/17, *Fashion ID GmbH & Co. KG v Verbraucherzentrale NRW e.V.*, judgment of 29 July 2019 (ECLI:EU:C:2019:629).

ECtHR

Copland v United Kingdom, Appl. No. 62617/00, judgment of 3 April 2007.
Bărbulescu v Romania, Appl. No. 61496/08, judgment of 5 September 2017.
Lopez Ribalda and Others v Spain, Appl. Nos. 1774/13 and 8567/13, judgment of 9 January 2018.

A. Rationale and Policy Underpinning

Article 13 of the GDPR requires that data subjects are informed by the controller about the details of the processing activity at the time when the controller collects personal data directly from them. There is another provision of the GDPR that details how and when data subjects must be informed when their personal data are obtained from a third party.[1]

One of the principles of processing personal data is transparency, which is closely linked to the principles of lawfulness and fairness, all three of which are covered in one provision.[2] Informing the data subject of the details of the processing activity can be construed as one of the conditions of fair processing, and is certainly a *sine qua non* for transparency. While transparency can be achieved in several ways, its most important building block is the information given to the data subject at the beginning of the processing activity, or before the processing takes place (the 'data protection notice' or the 'privacy notice'), which should then be made easily accessible throughout the processing operation.

Completeness and accuracy of information given to the data subject about the processing activity is also paramount for obtaining valid consent under the GDPR,[3] both when data are obtained directly from the data subject and when they are obtained from another source. It is, however, important to note that the obligation to provide detailed information to the data subject equally applies to all processing activities, irrespective of the legitimate ground for processing upon which they are based. For instance, even when grounding the processing on the necessity to perform a contract, or on the controllers' legitimate interests or those of third parties, the controllers are still under an obligation to provide notice pursuant to the requirements of Article 13.

The rationale for this provision is that protection of personal data would lack effectiveness if the data subject were not aware of the existence of the processing activity, what kind of personal data are used, who is processing the data and for what

---

[1] Art. 14 GDPR.   [2] Ibid., Art. 5(1)(a).

[3] Art. 4(11) requires that consent under the GDPR must be 'informed'. See further the commentary on Art. 4(11) in this volume.

purpose(s) and who else has access to the data. In practice, exercising all the other rights of the data subject is conditional on the knowledge that one's personal data are being processed.[4] Providing individuals with the required elements of information not only puts them in the position of effectively exercising their rights as data subjects, but also contributes to ensuring data quality.[5] As far back as the 1980s, the right to information about the processing operation was called 'chief' among the rights of the data subject.[6] It was later highlighted that the provision encompassing the principles of lawfulness, transparency and fairness 'embraces and generates the other core principles of data protection laws'.[7]

Transparency is all the more important in the emerging age of algorithmic decision-making, AI and machine-learning.[8] This age is described as creating a 'black box society'.[9] Such a society could be defined as a society where decisions taken through the use of algorithms, or AI applications, including applications that involve machine-learning, are pervading all aspects of social life without people knowing how these automated processes function and in what situations they occur.

Understanding that a 'black box' supplied with personal data, even if these data are just part of the input data, exists in the context of a specific activity of an organisation and that the output from the 'black box' may affect a person, is very important. Understanding how a specific 'black box' interacts with one's data and how such processing may affect one's rights and interests, depending on what variables, is equally important.

After the GDPR was adopted, an academic debate ensued over whether a right of the data subject to receive an *ex post* explanation concerning algorithmic and other forms of automated decision-making exists in the GDPR or not.[10] Irrespective of what it is called, such a right is guaranteed in substance by a web of provisions in the GDPR for ensuring transparency regarding specific processing operations.[11]

It is significant to also take into account that providing meaningful transparency about how automated systems work with one's personal data is at the core of the first data protection laws in Europe. The first French data protection law from 1978 already granted persons 'the right to know and to challenge the information and the reasoning used by automated processing whose results concern them'.[12] Thus, from the early days of data protection law, automated processes (or 'the machines') were met with an expectation that they be transparent and comprehensible in the way they work, well before the internet connected them. Meeting these expectations is all the more critical today. Article 13 GDPR, together with the other provisions that ensure transparency under the Regulation, aim to ensure that these expectations are met.

---

[4] Zanfir 2015, pp. 82–83.   [5] EDPS 2014, p. 8.   [6] Gulleford 1986, p. 72.
[7] Bygrave 2002, p. 58.
[8] For understanding of these concepts in a 'data protection' framework, see Norwegian Data Protection Authority 2018, which also specifically addresses the tension between the principle of transparency and the concept of a 'black box' involved in automated decision-making.
[9] See Pasquale 2015.
[10] See Wachter, Mittelstadt and Floridi 2017; Selbst and Powles 2017; Malgieri and Comande 2017; Mendoza and Bygrave 2017. See also the commentary on Art. 20 in this volume.
[11] See e.g. Arts. 5(1)(a), 12, 14 and 15 GDPR.
[12] See French Data Protection Act 1978, Art. 3: 'Toute personne a le droit de connaître et de contester les informations et les raisonnements utilisés dans les traitements automatisés dont les résultats lui sont opposes'.

B. Legal Background

1. EU legislation

1.1 DPD

Article 13 had an equivalent in Article 10 DPD, which regulated 'information in cases of collection of data from the data subject'. The DPD also had a separate provision for information to be given to data subjects when personal data are obtained from a third party.[13] The choice of the EU legislator from the early 1990s to provide separate provisions for the information of data subjects when data are collected directly from them and when data are obtained from a third party was maintained in the GDPR, even though the European Commission in its initial proposal for the GDPR and the European Parliament in its final Report sought to merge the two provisions. Keeping two separate provisions was supported by the European Council during the trialogue.[14]

Article 10 DPD placed the obligation of providing information to the data subject on the controller or the controller's representative, when the controller did not have an establishment in the EU but used equipment on the territory of an EU Member State. Information had to be provided 'except where he [i.e. the data subject] already has it'. Two categories of information always had to be provided: the identity of the controller or its representative and the purposes of the processing.[15] A third category of 'any further information' had to be provided 'in so far as further information is necessary ... to guarantee fair processing in respect of the data subject'.[16] The examples of such further information listed in the DPD were: the recipients and the categories of recipients, whether providing the data is obligatory or voluntary and the consequences of failure to provide it and the existence of the rights of access and rectification.[17]

1.2 EPD

The EPD has several provisions that require information to be provided to the user or subscriber (who can be a data subject in the sense of the GDPR, but also a legal person not protected by the GDPR). The most significant one is Article 5(3), which requires that the subscriber or user of electronic communications networks 'is provided with clear and comprehensive information in accordance with Directive 95/46/EC, inter alia about the purposes of the processing, and is offered the right to refuse such processing by the data controller' as a precondition of using electronic communications networks 'to store information or to gain access to information stored in the terminal equipment' of a user or subscriber. Technically, this provision requires that before a cookie or a similar technology to gather data is placed on a terminal equipment (such as a laptop, a smart mobile phone or any other electronic communications device), the user of that device is informed about it and given the possibility to opt out. The two exceptions to this rule concern (i) technical storage or access for the sole purpose of carrying out the transmission of a communication and (ii) technical storage or access that is 'strictly necessary' to provide an information society service 'explicitly requested by the subscriber or user'.

---

[13] Art. 11 DPD.
[14] For a comparison of the proposed text and the final versions adopted by the Parliament and the Council, see EDPS 2015, pp. 65 et seq.
[15] Art. 10(a) and (b) DPD.
[16] Ibid., Art. 10(c) last indent. This provision also shows the close link between transparency and fairness.
[17] Ibid., Art. 10(c) first indent.

The information to be provided to the user or subscriber must be 'clear and comprehensive' and in accordance with the requirements of the DPD. Therefore, this information must at least contain the identification details of who is placing the cookie or similar technology on a device, as well as the purpose for which they are doing this. In addition, the user or subscriber must be given the possibility to refuse placement of that cookie or similar technology.

Other EPD provisions that impose obligations of informing users and subscribers are:

1. Article 4(2), which requires them being informed of a particular risk of a breach of the security of the network and of any possible remedies to those risks that lay outside the scope of the measures to be taken by the service provider
2. Article 6(4), which requires the service provider to inform subscribers or users of the types of traffic data (metadata) that are being processed and of the duration of this processing
3. Article 9(1), which requires the service provider to inform the users or subscribers, before obtaining their consent, of the type of location data other than traffic data which will be processed, of the purposes and duration of the processing and whether the data will be transmitted to a third party for the purpose of providing a value added service.

1.3 LED

The LED has a similar provision in Article 13, which covers 'information to be made available or given to the data subject', irrespective of the source of the personal data. The provision distinguishes between data that must be provided as a minimum (identity and contact details of the controller and its data protection officer ('DPO'), the purposes of processing, the right to lodge a complaint with a DPA and the existence of the rights to access, rectification, erasure and restriction), and data that must be provided 'in specific cases', that are to be defined by national law. This second layer of information must cover the legal basis for processing, the data retention period or criteria for establishing it, the categories of recipients, and 'further information', especially when data are collected without the knowledge of the data subject.

National law can delay, restrict or omit the provision of this second layer of information to the extent that such a measure constitutes a necessary and proportionate measure in a democratic society with due regard for the fundamental rights and the legitimate interests of the individuals concerned and only for specific purposes exhaustively enumerated in the third paragraph of Article 13. Recital 26 makes it clear, though, that transparency about how personal data are used in the law enforcement area 'does not in itself prevent the law enforcement authorities from carrying out activities such as covert investigations or video surveillance'. Such covert operations can take place if they meet the conditions for lawful restrictions or limitations of fundamental rights, as allowed by the EU Charter of Fundamental Rights ('CFR') and the European Convention on Human Rights ('ECHR'). They must be done for specific legitimate purposes, as long as they are laid down by law and constitute a necessary and proportionate measure in a democratic society.[18] From the way limitations to the right to information are construed, both in recital 26 and Article 13(3) LED, the EU legislator acknowledges that limiting

---

[18] Rec. 26 LED. See also Art. 8(2) ECHR and Arts. 7, 8 and 52(1) CFR.

the right to information of the data subject is an interference with the fundamental right to the protection of personal data.

The first layer of minimum information can be provided on the website of the competent authority, according to recital 42. By leaving out this possibility for the second layer of information, which must be provided only 'in specific cases', the legislator allows the further information to be given in individual notices or in any other way that is not public. Arguably, it could also be provided on the website, together with the minimum information, as long as it is specific enough. Without distinguishing between layers of information, Article 12 LED requires that all information must be provided 'by any appropriate means, including by electronic means'. In any case, all information given to the data subject must be given to the individual 'in a concise, intelligible and easily accessible form, using clear and plain language'.[19]

1.4 Clinical Trials Regulation

EU legislation also provides for specific information to be given to subjects of clinical trials for the purpose of obtaining informed consent for the participation in the trial. According to Article 29 of the Clinical Trials Regulation, all subjects of clinical trials must be given information on the nature, objectives, benefits, implications, risks and inconveniences of the clinical trial, as well as information regarding the subject's rights and guarantees, the conditions under which the clinical trial is to be conducted, the EU trial number and so on.[20] Article 28(1)(d) of the same Regulation requires that a clinical trial may be conducted only when the rights of the subjects to physical and mental integrity, to privacy and to the protection of the data concerning them in accordance with the DPD (replaced by the GDPR on 25 May 2018) are safeguarded.

Therefore, in order to comply with transparency obligations under Article 13 GDPR, the controller must supplement this list of information with details of the processing of personal data associated with the clinical trial. In particular, the subjects must also be informed about the existence of their data protection rights (such as access, erasure), the retention period, the recipients of the clinical trial data etc., as well as details regarding the processing of clinical trial data in the EU database, pursuant to Article 81 of the Clinical Trials Regulation. To avoid lack of clarity, the GDPR information notice can be done using a separate notice rather than the same consent form that results in consenting to the trial itself. One significant difference that must be included in the GDPR information notice is the fact that withdrawing consent for participating in the clinical trial will not affect the activities already carried out and the use of data obtained based on informed consent before its withdrawal.[21] Even though this provision is made 'without prejudice to Directive 95/46/EC', the GDPR establishes in recital 161 that the rules on informed consent in the Clinical Trials Regulation prevail. This is significant because, according to the GDPR, after consent is withdrawn by a data subject, the data subject has the right to also obtain erasure of the data that have been processed, if there is no other legal ground for processing.

---

[19] Art. 12(1) LED.
[20] See the entire list of required information to be included in the consent form in Art. 29(2) Clinical Trials Regulation.
[21] Ibid., Art. 28(3).

2. International instruments

Article 8(a) of Convention 108 grants any person the ability 'to establish the existence of an automated personal data file, its main purposes, as well as the identity and habitual residence of the principal place of business of the controller of the file'. This transparency provision leaves room for interpretation because it does not clearly state that controllers must inform individuals about the existence and other details of an 'automated data file', but that individuals themselves are 'enabled' to 'establish the existence' of such a file. In practice, this could also mean that the individual should not necessarily be informed proactively by the controller, but that he or she could request information from the controller. This would still enable them to 'establish the existence' of a personal data file and other details relating to it. Interestingly, Convention 108 (concluded in 1981) does not include an explicit principle of transparency, even though it does have two transparency provisions, corresponding to the right to information and the right to access one's own data.[22] Article 5(a) of Convention 108 provides for an obligation that personal data 'shall be obtained fairly and lawfully' while none of the other data quality principles refer to transparency. However, it can be argued that the principle of fairness includes transparency.

In fact, transparency of processing was a focus of subsequent Recommendations of the Committee of Ministers of the Council of Europe. For instance, the Recommendation for the protection of privacy on the internet[23] calls on internet service providers to 'inform users of privacy risks before they subscribe or start using services', 'about technical means which they may lawfully use to reduce security risks to data and communications' and to 'highlight a clear statement' on their privacy policy on their 'introductory page', that should include details on the identity of the service providers, the data being collected and how they are processed and stored, for what purposes and for how long.[24] Similarly, the Recommendations on profiling and on privacy in the work environment include detailed transparency requirements, placing a clear obligation on the controller to provide information to data subjects.[25]

Taking into account the vague content of the transparency obligation enshrined in Article 8 of Convention 108 and the focus on transparency in subsequent legal instruments of the Council of Europe, it is not surprising that the text of Modernised Convention 108 places great emphasis on transparency, introducing a new Article 8 dedicated to '[t]ransparency of processing', and requiring that 'the controller inform the data subjects' at least of his or her identity and habitual residence or establishment, the legal basis and the purposes of the intended processing, the categories of personal data processed, the recipients or categories of recipients and the means to exercise the rights of the data subject. This can be supplemented by additional information as necessary 'in order to ensure fair and transparent processing'.

Even though they are not an international treaty, the OECD Privacy Guidelines are noteworthy for including a reference to transparency as part of a general 'Openness principle'.[26] The principle states that 'there should be a general policy of openness about

---

[22] Art. 8(a) and (b) Convention 108.   [23] COM Recommendation 1999.
[24] Ibid., III.2, III.3, III.4 and III.11.
[25] See COM Recommendation 2010, 4.1 ('Information'), and COM Recommendation 2015, 10 ('Transparency of processing').
[26] See para. 12 OECD Guidelines 2013.

developments, practices and policies with respect to personal data' and that 'means should be readily available of establishing the existence and nature of personal data, and the main purpose of their use, as well as the identity and usual residence of the data controller'. This principle was present in the original 1980 Guidelines and remained unchanged during their 2013 revision.

Finally, the EEA Agreement, as amended in July 2018,[27] incorporates the GDPR into its Annexes and provides that the provisions of the GDPR should be read, for the purposes of that Agreement, with a number of adaptations. In this respect, the Agreement provides that, as regards the EFTA States party to the Agreement, the words 'applicable pursuant to the EEA Agreement' shall be inserted in Article 13(1)(f) after the words 'adequacy decision by the Commission'.[28]

3. National developments

The GDPR implementing law in Germany does not provide for any new specifics in regard to the information to be given to data subjects. Exercising the margin left to Member States to restrict data subjects' rights, the German legislator adopted several exceptions to the right to information in the case of further processing. According to section 32 of the law, the obligation to provide notice to the data subject does not apply where the further use of personal data involves 'data stored in analogue form, for which the controller directly contacts the data subject through the further processing',[29] but only if the further purpose of the processing is compatible with the original purpose for which the data were collected, the communication with the data subject does not take place in digital form and the interest of the data subject in receiving the information can be regarded as minimal.

Other exceptions concern public bodies or a public interest: the situation where carrying out tasks of a public body would be impaired,[30] or where public security or the welfare of the Federation or of a land,[31] or a confidential transfer of data to public bodies would be endangered.[32] One last exception concerns the situation where providing information to the data subject would interfere with the establishment, exercise or defence of legal claims.[33] It is important to note that whenever any of these exceptions apply, the controller is under an obligation to protect the legitimate interests of the data subject and to 'set down in writing the reasons for not providing information'.[34]

The Spanish Data Protection Act 2018 includes a pragmatic interpretation of Article 13 GDPR for the processing of personal data obtained directly from the data subject through electronic communications networks or by providing an Information Society service to the data subject, or if the specific processing activity was authorised to be within scope of this provision by the Spanish Data Protection Authority or the law.[35] In these situations, which indeed cover a wide variety of processing activities, controllers are allowed to provide data subjects only with a set of 'basic information' at first, together with an email address or another means of communication where they can 'easily and immediately' access additional information.[36] The basic information consists of the identity of

---

[27] EEA Decision 2018. [28] Ibid., Art. 5e(d).
[29] s. 32(1)(1) German GDPR Implementation Law.
[30] Ibid., s. 32(1)(2); this exception only refers to tasks as enumerated in Art. 23(1)(a)–(e) GDPR.
[31] s. 32(1)(3) German GDPR Implementation Law. [32] Ibid., s. 32(1)(5). [33] Ibid.
[34] Ibid., s. 32(2). [35] Art. 11 Spanish Data Protection Act 2018. [36] Ibid.

the controller and its representative if applicable, the purpose of the processing and the ways in which the data subject can access his or her rights.[37] The Act also provides for specific information to be provided to the data subject if the processing activity involves profiling—specifically, the 'basic information' also includes the fact that the personal data will be used for profiling and the existence of the right to object to the profiling according to Article 22 GDPR. This Spanish implementation of transparency raises questions of conformity with the GDPR. The content of Article 13 is quite clear and precise when requiring a list of pieces of information to be provided to the data subject in all situations where personal data are collected directly from him or her, and thus would seem to exclude the Spanish layered approach.

4. Case law

4.1 CJEU

The CJEU explained in its judgment in *Bara*[38] that 'the requirement to inform the data subjects about the processing of their personal data is all the more important since it affects the exercise by the data subjects of their right of access to, and right to rectify, the data being processed ... and their right to object to the processing of those data'.[39] This case concerned self-employed individuals' personal data collected by the Romanian tax authority ('ANAF') and transferred to the national health insurance authority ('CNAS'). On the basis of the tax data including income, CNAS requested arrear contributions from the self-employed individuals. Several affected individuals challenged the decisions imposing contributions to the national health insurance scheme, arguing that the transfer of personal data from ANAF to CNAS was unlawful since it was not provided for by law but by means of a protocol signed between the two institutions. They submitted that, moreover, the purpose of the transfer, as mentioned in the protocol, was to enable CNAS to determine whether a person qualifies as an insured person and the transferred data were supposed to be limited to name, unique national identification number and home address. The applicants argued that they were not informed about the existence of the transfer of data related to income and that they did not consent to such a transfer.[40] The CJEU was requested to ascertain whether the processing of the data by CNAS required prior information to be given to the data subjects as to the identity of the data controller and the purpose for which the data was transferred.

To provide its answer, the CJEU examined the exceptions to the right to be informed, as laid out by Article 13 DPD. The Court noted that one of the exceptions concerned 'an important economic or financial interest of a Member State ... , including monetary, budgetary and taxation matters'.[41] The Court highlighted, nevertheless, that the DPD 'expressly requires that such restrictions are imposed by legislative measures'.[42] In this case, the definition of transferable information and the detailed arrangements for transferring that information were laid down not in a legislative measure, but in a Protocol agreed between the ANAF and the CNAS, which was not set out in an official publication.[43]

The Court held that, in these circumstances, there was lack of compliance with the conditions permitting a Member State to derogate from the rights and obligations

---

[37] Ibid. [38] Case C-201/14, *Bara*. [39] Ibid., para. 33.
[40] Summary of the facts of the case based on ibid., paras. 14–16. [41] Ibid., para. 39.
[42] Ibid. [43] Ibid., para. 40.

concerning the right of the data subject to be informed.[44] The Court thus found that Articles 10, 11 and 13 DPD (the right of the data subject to be informed and restrictions to this right) preclude 'national measures, such as those at issue in the main proceedings, which allow a public administrative body of a Member State to transfer personal data to another public administrative body and their subsequent processing, without the data subjects having been informed of that transfer and processing'.[45] The Court did not look into whether the transfer also complied with the principles of purpose limitation and fairness of processing; it considered the interinstitutional data sharing unlawful merely based on the lack of transparency.

In *IPI*,[46] the CJEU dealt with the right to information of individuals being investigated by private investigators working for a professional association of real estate agents (IPI). Two individuals acting as real estate agents were asked to cease their activity after IPI concluded an investigation and obtained evidence the two were acting against the rules regulating the profession. The individuals challenged the decision in court claiming it was unlawful due to the fact that the evidence was obtained unlawfully, since they were not informed about the monitoring taking place.[47] The national Court observed that the Belgian data protection law did not provide for an exception to the right of data subjects to be informed in the case provided by Article 13(1)(d) DPD, which covered the prevention, investigation, detection and prosecution of breaches of ethics for regulated professions. It then requested the CJEU to provide a preliminary ruling as to whether Belgium was under an obligation to provide for specific exceptions to the right to be informed, as laid down in Article 13 DPD, or whether that was merely an option that the Member State had.[48]

First, the CJEU found that both Articles 10 and 11 DPD were relevant for the case, since private investigators may collect personal data directly from the data subject or from third parties.[49] The Court considered that Article 13(1) DPD offered Member States the option to provide for one or more of the exceptions that it set out, but they were not compelled to do so.[50] The Court found that 'if a Member State has chosen to implement the exception provided for in Article 13(1)(d), then the professional body concerned and the private detectives acting for it may rely on it and are not subject to the obligation to inform the data subject provided for in Articles 10 and 11 of Directive 95/46'.[51]

In *Opinion 1/15*,[52] the CJEU was called to assess whether the EU-Canada passenger name record ('PNR') agreement as negotiated by the Commission was compatible with the fundamental right to the protection of personal data enshrined in Article 8 ECHR and Article 16 TFEU. One of the aspects of the agreement that the CJEU found problematic was the right of data subjects to be informed about what happens to their personal data once transferred to the Canadian Competent Authorities. The Court observed that the agreement only laid down (in Article 11) a rule regarding transparency requiring the Competent Authority to publish on its website general information relating to the transfer of PNR data and their use.[53] The Court considered that 'the general information provided to air passengers under Article 11 of the envisaged agreement does not afford them the possibility of knowing whether their data have been used by the Canadian Competent Authority for more than those checks'.[54] The Court concluded that 'it is

---

[44] Ibid., para. 41.   [45] Ibid., executive part of the judgment.   [46] Case C-473/12, *IPI*.
[47] Ibid., paras. 14–20.   [48] Ibid., para. 21.   [49] Ibid., para. 24.   [50] Ibid., para. 37.
[51] Ibid., para. 45.   [52] *Opinion 1/15*.   [53] Ibid., para. 222.   [54] Ibid., para. 223.

necessary to notify air passengers individually', in those situations where their PNR data are used by the Canadian authorities beyond the mere transfer and where the data have been disclosed to other government authorities or to individuals.[55] This information must be provided only once it is no longer liable to jeopardise the investigations being carried out by the government authorities.[56] It is notable that the Court considered it a condition for compliance with Articles 7 and 8 CFR that the EU–Canada PNR agreement provide for a right to individual notification of air passengers in the event of use of their PNR data during their stay in Canada and after their departure, and in the event of disclosures of that data to other authorities or to individuals.[57]

Finally, in *Fashion ID*,[58] the CJEU found that a website featuring a Facebook 'Like' button can be a controller jointly with Facebook in respect of the collection and transmission to Facebook of the personal data of visitors to its website, but not in respect of the operations involving data processing carried out by Facebook after those data have been transmitted to the latter. In such a case, the website operator must provide, at the time of their collection, certain information to those visitors such as, for example, its identity and the purposes of the processing.[59]

4.2 Court of Human Rights

The ECtHR also places great importance on transparency when assessing how the obligations under Article 8 ECHR (the right to respect for private life) are complied with by the state parties to the Convention. For example, in *Bărbulescu v Romania*, the Court was asked to decide whether an employer unlawfully dismissed an employee by breaching his right to respect for private life as enshrined in Article 8. The employer had monitored the content of electronic communications of the employee (in particular, his chat messages), after having informed employees that they are not allowed to use the computer equipment from the office for personal reasons. The applicant had messaged his brother and fiancée, resulting in his dismissal. The Grand Chamber of the ECtHR decided that 'domestic authorities should ensure that the introduction by an employer of measures to monitor correspondence and other communications, irrespective of the extent and duration of such measures, is accompanied by adequate and sufficient safeguards against abuse'.[60] One of the relevant safeguards must be the notification of employees 'of the possibility that the employer might take measures to monitor correspondence and other communications', and of 'the implementation of such measures'.[61] The Court acknowledged that, in practice, employees may be notified in various ways depending on the particular factual circumstances of each case. However, the Court considered that for such monitoring to be deemed compatible with the requirements of Article 8 ECHR, 'the notification should normally be clear about the nature of the monitoring and be given in advance'.[62] The absence of such notification in the case at hand contributed to the finding of the Court that there was a breach of Article 8.

In *Copland*, the ECtHR assessed the case of a personal assistant to the College Principal of Carmarthenshire College who complained that during her employment, her telephone, email and internet usage had been monitored at the Deputy Principal's instigation. The Court established that the applicant 'had been given no warning that her

---

[55] Ibid. [56] Ibid., para. 224. [57] Ibid., para. 3(f) of the executive part of the Opinion.
[58] Case C-40/17, *Fashion ID*. [59] Ibid., paras. 102-105.
[60] ECtHR, *Bărbulescu v Romania*, para. 120. [61] Ibid., para. 121(i). [62] Ibid.

calls would be liable to monitoring, therefore she had a reasonable expectation as to the privacy of calls made from her work telephone. The same expectation should apply in relation to the applicant's e-mail and internet usage'.[63] The Court relied on this argument to bring the proceedings under Article 8 of the Convention, finding that the collection and storage of personal information relating to the applicant's use of telecommunication services amounted to an interference with Article 8.[64] The Court decided that this interference was not 'in accordance with the law' and, therefore, violated Article 8.

Yet another example is the case of *Lopez Ribalda and Others*, concerning covert video surveillance of a Spanish supermarket chain's employees after suspicions of theft had arisen. The applicants were dismissed mainly on the basis of the video material, which they alleged had been obtained by breaching their rights related to privacy and data protection. The employer installed both visible and hidden cameras.[65] The ECtHR noted that the video material was processed and examined by several persons working for the applicant's employer before the applicants themselves were informed of the existence of the video recordings.[66] The legislation in force at the time of the events contained specific provisions on providing notice to data subjects 'previously and explicitly, precisely and unambiguously', pursuant to the Spanish law that transposed the DPD into national law.[67] Moreover, the Court also took into account the official guidance adopted by the Spanish Data Protection Authority clarifying that this notification obligation also applied in the specific case of video surveillance, when the controller 'had to place a distinctive sign indicating the areas that were under surveillance, and to make a document available containing the [data protection notice]'.[68] It is undisputed that the controller failed to comply with the notice obligation; however, the domestic Courts considered the lack of notice appropriate to the legitimate aim pursued, necessary and proportionate.[69]

The ECtHR did not agree with this assessment. It highlighted that 'in a situation where the right of every data subject to be informed of the existence, aim and manner of covert video surveillance was clearly regulated and protected by law, the applicants had a reasonable expectation of privacy'.[70] The Court also noted that the covert surveillance was not limited in time, targeted all employees (not only those who were suspected of theft) and was implemented during all working hours.[71] Thus, the Court concluded that the video surveillance measure did not comply with the obligation to previously, explicitly, precisely and unambiguously inform those concerned about the existence and particular characteristics of the personal data collection and found that Article 8 of the Convention was breached.[72]

C. Analysis

1. Introduction

Article 13 GDPR enshrines a positive obligation on the controller to provide a set of information to the data subject, when personal data are obtained directly from him/her, and this provision of information must occur 'at the time' of the data collection. In practice, this means that at every collection point of personal data (e.g. a registration form

---

[63] ECtHR, *Copland*, para. 42. [64] Ibid., para. 44.
[65] ECtHR, *Lopez Ribalda and Others*, para. 58. [66] Ibid., para. 63. [67] Ibid., para. 64.
[68] Ibid. [69] Ibid., paras. 65 and 66. [70] Ibid., para. 67.
[71] ECtHR, *Lopez Ribalda v Spain*, paras. 68. [72] Ibid., paras. 69, 70.

to become member of an association, a registration form to become a user of an online service, an application to university etc.) the data subject must be notified with a set of required details about the processing operation. This information is usually contained in a notice, statement or policy.

2. Notice requirements

Irrespective of what it is called, the notice should be specific to the processing at issue and, to the extent possible, should not cover several completely different processing activities, each one with its own purpose, lawful grounds for processing, rules on international data transfers etc. The components of a notice complying with Article 13 require specificity: while the identity of the controller or the rights of the data subject and how the controller manages them remain the same for all processing activities, the purpose of processing, the lawful ground, recipients of personal data, existence or not of international transfers, retention periods as well as meaningful information about automated decision-making in a specific case will likely be different, and each of them has to be spelled out for each processing operation. For instance, an organisation may have a notice for its website concerning how personal data is collected and processed through the website, and separate notices for direct marketing practices, for organising events, for recruitment and for employee data. The notices can be as granular as is the activity of an organisation involving processing of personal data, but ultimately the controller is responsible to establish their scope in a meaningful way, as part of its accountability.

The EDPB has stated that the principles of Article 13 apply to video surveillance as well,[73] and that 'Video surveillance based on the mere purpose of "safety" or "for your safety" is not sufficiently specific (Article 5 (1) (b)). It is furthermore contrary to the principle that personal data shall be processed lawfully, fairly and in a transparent manner in relation to the data subject (see Article 5 (1) (a))'.[74] The EDPB has further given the following example in this regard: 'A shop owner is monitoring his shop. To comply with Article 13 it is sufficient to place a warning sign at an easy visible point at the entrance of his shop, which contains the first layer information. In addition, he has to provide an information sheet containing the second layer information at the cashier or any other central and easy accessible location in his shop'.[75] The EDPB defines the first layer information as 'the most important information, e.g. the details of the purposes of processing, the identity of controller and the existence of the rights of the data subject, together with information on the greatest impacts of the processing',[76] while the second layer information includes 'further mandatory details'.[77]

While subject to the above obligation and concomitantly liable for non-compliance with it, the controller could, however, rely on processors to provide the necessary notice by stipulating this requirement in the controller–processor agreement pursuant to Article 28 GDPR. Such a clause could be justified in cases where processors have direct contact with data subjects. However, the controller will be ultimately responsible that the content of the notice complies with the requirements of Article 13 and that the data subjects are informed. As a matter of practice, the controller could prepare and validate the text of the notice and then provide it to the processor to be given, displayed or otherwise made

[73] EDPB 2019, p. 21   [74] Ibid., p. 7.   [75] Ibid., p. 23.   [76] Ibid., p. 22.
[77] Ibid.

available to data subjects. The operator of a website featuring a Facebook 'Like' button is a data controller jointly with Facebook regarding the collection and transmission to Facebook of the personal data of visitors to its website, and must provide, at the time of their collection, certain information to those visitors such as, for example, its identity and the purposes of the processing.[78]

3. Transparency

The principle of transparency requires that any information and communication relating to the processing of those personal data be easily accessible and easy to understand, and that clear and plain language be used.[79] The WP29 made it clear that, under Article 13 GDPR, the controller must be proactive in providing the information to the data subject, meaning that 'the data subject must not have to take active steps to seek the information covered ... or find it amongst other information, such as terms and conditions of use of a website or app'.[80] Additionally, the language used for the notice should be short and direct, avoiding complicated legal constructions. It is important that the notice does not contain uncertain statements regarding potential uses of data, such as the data 'may' or 'could' be processed in a certain way.[81]

A best practice for the delivery of information is providing layered notices. As the WP29 explained, layered notices 'can help resolve the tension between completeness and understanding by allowing users to navigate directly to the section of the notice that they wish to read'.[82]

The WP29 clarified that Article 13 applies both to processing of personal data that a data subject consciously provides to a controller (e.g. when completing an online form) and processing of personal data collected by the controller from a data subject through observation (e.g. using automated data capturing devices or data capturing software such as cameras, network equipment, Wi-Fi tracking, RFID or other types of sensors).[83] For these latter cases, the WP29 recommended several specific ways to provide notice, such as icons, QR codes, voice alerts, written details incorporated into paper set-up instructions, written information on the smart device, messages sent by SMS or email, visible boards containing the information, public signage and public information campaigns.[84]

4. Timing

As for timing, the notice must be provided 'at the time when personal data are obtained', meaning simultaneously with the collection of personal data from the data subject and not *post factum*. For example, notice should be given to a subscriber to a newsletter at the time he or she provides the email address for the purpose of subscribing to this service. In the case of 'observed data' collected directly from the data subject through Wi-Fi tracking, notice should be given at the entry in the area covered by this monitoring technology.

5. Information requirements

Article 13 provides for a predetermined set of elements that must be included in the notice, making a distinction between 'information' to be given to the data subject (first

---

[78] Case C-40/17, *Fashion ID*, paras. 102-105.   [79] Rec. 39 GDPR.
[80] WP29 2018B, p. 16.   [81] Ibid., p. 9.   [82] Ibid., p. 17.   [83] Ibid., p. 14.
[84] Ibid., p. 19.

paragraph of Article 13) and 'further information necessary to ensure fair and transparent processing' (second paragraph of Article 13). This distinction does not seem to have any practical consequence, provided that both sets of information are given to the data subject under a positive obligation to act—both use the verb 'shall provide' when instructing the controller. It is to be noted, nevertheless, that the second set of information is explicitly linked to the 'fairness of processing', and this fairness principle will all the more so guide the interpretation of this paragraph.

A number of elements must be included in the notice pursuant to the first paragraph of Article 13. These include the identity and contact details of the controller and, where applicable, of the controller's representative; the contact details of the data protection officer; the purposes of the processing for which the personal data are intended as well as the legal basis for the processing; where the processing is based on point (f) of Article 6(1), the legitimate interests pursued by the controller or by a third party; the recipients or categories of recipients of the personal data, if any; and, where applicable, the fact that the controller intends to transfer personal data to a third country or international organisation and the existence or absence of an adequacy decision by the Commission, or in the case of transfers referred to in Article 46 or 47, or the second subparagraph of Article 49(1), reference to the appropriate or suitable safeguards and the means by which to obtain a copy of them or where they have been made available.

With regard to the obligation to provide information about the controller's representative, the EDPB has stated that such information 'shall for example be included in the privacy notice or upfront information provided to data subjects at the moment of data collection'.[85] Such information should also be easily accessible to the supervisory authorities.[86] If a controller not established in the EU but subject to the GDPR under Article 3(2) does not inform individuals about the identity of its representative, it will be in breach of Article 13.[87]

The elements that must be included in the notice pursuant to the second paragraph of Article 13 'to ensure fair and transparent processing' (in addition to those under paragraph 1) are the following:

1. The period for which the personal data will be stored or, if that is not possible, the criteria used to determine that period: the data retention period for each processing activity should be extracted from the retention schedule adopted by the controller. If a retention schedule is not adopted, the period mentioned should be the one used in practice. If the retention period fluctuates depending on certain factors, those factors must be mentioned instead of an exact number, together with a brief explanation of how the retention period is established for that processing. This information should be phrased in a way that allows the data subject to assess, on the basis of his or her own situation, what the retention period will be for specific data/purposes.[88] In any case, the WP29 made clear that 'it is not sufficient for the data controller to generically state that personal data will be kept as long as necessary for the legitimate purposes of the processing, including, where appropriate, archiving periods'.[89]
2. The existence of the rights of the data subject: the notice must inform individuals that they have the right to request from the controller access to and rectification or erasure

---

[85] EDPB 2018, p. 21.   [86] Ibid.   [87] Ibid.   [88] WP29 2018B, p. 33.
[89] Ibid., p. 34.

of personal data or restriction of processing concerning the data subject or to object to processing as well as the right to data portability. For the latter, it should be kept in mind that it is only applicable where the lawful ground of the processing is consent or necessity to enter or perform a contract. Therefore, if the processing to which the notice refers is grounded in one of the other lawful grounds, the controller should only mention the right to data portability if it was decided to extend this right in practice. The information on the existence of the rights should include a summary of what each right involves and how the individual can take steps to exercise it.[90] In addition, Article 21(4) GDPR requires that the right to object to processing is explicitly brought to the data subject's attention at the latest at the time of first communication with the data subject, and must be presented clearly and separately from any other information.

3. The right to withdraw consent at any time, where processing is based on consent or explicit consent: this information should additionally include a reference to how the individuals can withdraw consent, taking into account that it should be as easy for a data subject to withdraw consent as is to give it.[91]

4. The right to lodge a complaint with a supervisory authority: the WP29 required that this information be accompanied by details concerning where the data subject can lodge a complaint, in particular in the Member State of his or her habitual residence, place of work or of an alleged infringement of the GDPR.[92]

5. Whether providing the personal data is compulsory and if so, which are the consequences of not providing it: this is particularly relevant for online forms, which should clearly identify which fields are required, which are not, and what will be the consequences of not filling in the required fields. Other examples may be in the employment context, where there is a contractual or legal obligation to provide certain information to a current or prospective employer.[93]

6. The existence of automated decision-making, including profiling and, at least in the cases regulated by Article 22(1) and (4) GDPR, meaningful information about the logic involved, as well as the significance and the envisaged consequences of such processing for the data subject. This requires the controller, first, to disclose the existence of automated decision making informed by the personal data processed within the notified processing, regardless of whether it includes profiling or not,[94] as well as the existence of profiling, if that is the case. Merely mentioning that automated decision-making or profiling is taking place will not be enough to meet transparency requirements under the GDPR; additional information must be included in the notice. This is an obligation if the automated decision-making or the profiling is based solely on automated processing, without human involvement, and results in legal effects concerning the data subject or affects the data subject in a significant way. Such effects are present, for instance, where the processing results in potential discrimination, in loss of opportunity (not being selected for a job interview), increased insurance rates, increased mortgage rates, exclusion from a program that would have been beneficial for the data subject and so on.[95] The obligation to provide additional information also

---

[90] Ibid. [91] Ibid. [92] Ibid. [93] Ibid., p. 35.
[94] For what constitutes automated decision-making, see WP29 2018A and the commentary on Art. 22 in this volume.
[95] See further the commentary on Art. 22 in this volume.

applies when such solely automated decision-making is based on special categories of data as defined in Article 9 GDPR. In these two situations, the controller is under an obligation to include in the notice two elements: information about the logic involved in the decision-making and the envisaged consequences of this processing. The 'logic involved in the processing' should be a description of the rationale used to build that specific automated decision-making process, and not the algorithm used, nor lines of code used, nor how machine-learning or algorithmic decision-making work in general. The logic involved in the decision-making process should be framed in such a way that a 'reasonable consumer' or an average person would be able to understand it.

The WP29 suggested that such information could include:

the categories of data that have been or will be used in the profiling or decision-making process, why these categories are considered pertinent, how any profile used in the automated decision-making process is built, including any statistics used in the analysis, why this profile is relevant to the automated decision-making process and how it is used or a decision concerning the data subject.[96]

The second compulsory set of additional information is related to 'the significance and the envisaged consequences' of the processing. After describing the logic involved in the algorithmic decision-making, the controller has to separately inform the data subject about what he or she should expect to happen as a result of the solely automated decision-making. This should include information about what are the potential effects, and it could also include information on how the effects can be challenged and what safeguards the controller has put in place to ensure fairness of the fully automated decision-making process. In the situation where the decision-making, including profiling, is not fully automated or does not result in legal or significant effects for the persons concerned, the controller is not under an obligation to provide information about the logic involved in the processing and its consequences. However, providing this information voluntarily is evidence of accountability and best efforts for ensuring fairness in processing personal data.

6. Processing for different purposes

Article 13(3) GDPR enshrines a provision which deals specifically with the situation of a controller that decides to process the data for a different purpose than the one for which the data were collected. Even if Article 13(3) does not distinguish between a further, completely different purpose and a further compatible purpose, this provision only refers to processing of data for compatible purposes. This is because Article 5(1)(b) GDPR prohibits processing of data for further purposes that are not compatible with the initial one. If the controller intends to start processing the personal data for a new, compatible purpose, the notice to the data subject must be updated to include information about the new purpose. All elements of the notice as required by Article 13(2) must be updated if the processing for the new purpose is not fully covered by the existing information. This update must be done prior to the new processing taking place. The WP29 recommended that a reasonable period should occur between the notification and the processing commencing rather than an immediate start to the processing upon notification, to leave data subjects time to exercise their rights if they consider it necessary.[97] The WP29 also

---

[96] WP29 2018A, p. 31. [97] Ibid., p. 24.

recommended controllers to consider making information available to data subjects in the notice on the compatibility analysis between the original and new purposes carried out under Article 6(4) GDPR.[98]

7. Exemptions

The controller is exempted from providing notice in accordance with Article 13 where and in so far as the data subject already has the information (Article 13(4)). Due to the principle of accountability, the controller will have the burden of proving that the data subject has been provided the information required by Article 13(1)–(3).[99] A claim that the data subject was informed about certain aspects of a processing activity, or the existence itself of a processing activity, must be substantiated with proof such as a time-stamped email sent to the data subject, a time-stamped web page where the notice was published and whose link was made available to the data subject, or any other means that prove the data subject was provided the information. Completeness of information is also important. The WP29 highlighted that even if the data subject has previously been provided with certain categories from the inventory of information set out in Article 13, there is still an obligation on the controller to supplement that information in order to ensure that the data subject now has a complete set of information as required by Article 13.[100]

Select Bibliography

International agreements

EEA Agreement: Agreement on the European Economic Area, OJ 1994 L 1/3.
EEA Decision 2018: Decision of the EEA Joint Committee No. 154/2018 of 6 July 2018 amending Annex XI (Electronic communication, audiovisual services and information society) and Protocol 37 (containing the list provided for in Article 101) to the EEA Agreement [2018/1022], OJ 2018 L 183/23.
OECD Guidelines 2013: Organisation for Economic Co-operation and Development, 'The OECD Privacy Framework' (2013).

EU legislation

Clinical Trials Regulation: Regulation (EU) 563/2014 of the European Parliament and of the Council of 16 April 2014 on clinical trials on medicinal products for human use, OJ 2014 L 158/1.

National legislation

French Data Protection Act 1978: Act No. 78-17 of 6 January 1978 on Data Processing, Files and Individual Liberties (Loi n° 78-17 du 6 janvier 1978 relative à l'informatique, aux fichiers et aux libertés), as last amended by Law No. 2014-334 of 17 March 2014.
German GDPR Implementation Law: Gesetz zur Anpassung des Datenschutzrechts an die Verordnung (EU) 2016/679 und zur Umsetzung der Richtlinie (EU) 2016/680 (Datenschutz-Anpassungs- und Umsetzungsgesetz EU—DsAnpUG-EU), BGBl 2017 Teil 1 Nr. 44.

---

[98] Ibid.   [99] Ibid., p. 27.   [100] Ibid.

Spanish Data Protection Act 2018: Ley Orgánica 3/2018, de 5 de diciembre, de Protección de Datos y de Garantía de los Derechos Digitales.

Academic writings

Bygrave 2002: Bygrave, *Data Protection Law: Approaching Its Rationale, Logic and Limits* (Kluwer Law International 2002).
Gulleford 1986: Gulleford, *Data Protection in Practice* (Butterworths 1986).
Malgieri and Comande 2017: Malgieri and Comande, 'Why a Right to Legibility of Automated Decision-Making Exists in the General Data Protection Regulation', 7 *International Data Privacy Law 'IDPL'* (2017), 243.
Mendoza and Bygrave 2017: Mendoza and Bygrave, 'The Right not to be Subject to Automated Decisions based on Profiling', in Synodinou, Jougleux, Markou and Prastitou (eds.), *EU Internet Law: Regulation and Enforcement* (Springer 2017), 77.
Pasquale 2015: Pasquale, *The Black Box Society: The Secret Algorithms That Control Money and Information* (Harvard University Press 2015).
Selbst and Powles 2017: Selbst and Powles, 'Meaningful information and the right to explanation', 7 *IDPL* (2017), 233.
Wachter, Mittelstadt and Floridi 2017: Wachter, Mittelstadt and Floridi, 'Why a Right to Explanation of Automated Decision-Making Does Not Exist in the General Data Protection Regulation', 7 *IDPL* (2017), 76.
Zanfir 2015: Zanfir, *Protecția datelor personale. Drepturile persoanei vizate* (C. H. Beck 2015).

Papers of data protection authorities

EDPB 2019: European Data Protection Board, 'Guidelines 3/2019 on the processing of personal data through video devices (version for public consultation)' (10 July 2019).
European Data Protection Board, 'Guidelines 3/2018 on the Territorial Scope of the GDPR (Article 3)—Version for Public Consultation' (16 November 2018).
EDPS 2014: European Data Protection Supervisor, 'Guidelines on the Rights of Individuals with Regard to Processing of Personal Data' (25 February 2014).
EDPS 2015: European Data Protection Supervisor, 'Annex to Opinion 3/2015 Comparative Table of GDPR Texts with EDPS Recommendations' (27 July 2015).
WP29 2013: Article 29 Working Party, 'Opinion 3/2013 on Purpose Limitation' (WP203, 2 April 2013).
WP29 2014: Article 29 Working Party, 'Opinion 6/2014 on the Notion of Legitimate Interests of the Data Controller under Article 7 of Directive 95/46/EC' (WP217, 9 April 2014).
WP29 2018A: Article 29 Working Party, 'Guidelines on Individual Automated Decision-Making and Profiling for the Purposes of Regulation 2016/679' (WP251.rev01, as last revised and adopted on 6 February 2018).
WP29 2018B: Article 29 Working Party, 'Guidelines on Transparency under Regulation 2016/269' (WP260rev.01, 11 April 2018).
Norwegian Data Protection Authority 2018: Datatilsynet (Norwegian Data Protection Authority), 'Artificial Intelligence and Privacy' (January 2018).

Reports and recommendations

COM Recommendation 1999: Committee of Ministers of the Council of Europe, 'Recommendation for the Protection of Privacy on the Internet' (R(99)5, 23 February 1999).

COM Recommendation 2010: Committee of Ministers of the Council of Europe, 'Recommendation on the Protection of Individuals with Regard to Automatic Processing of Personal Data in the Context of Profiling' (CM/Rec(2010)13, 23 November 2010).

COM Recommendation 2015: Committee of Ministers of the Council of Europe, 'Recommendation on the Processing of Personal Data in the Context of Employment' (CM/Rec(2015)5, 1 April 2015).

Article 14. Information to be provided where personal data have not been obtained from the data subject

GABRIELA ZANFIR-FORTUNA

1. Where personal data have not been obtained from the data subject, the controller shall provide the data subject with the following information:
   (a) the identity and the contact details of the controller and, where applicable, of the controller's representative;
   (b) the contact details of the data protection officer, where applicable;
   (c) the purposes of the processing for which the personal data are intended as well as the legal basis for the processing;
   (d) the categories of personal data concerned;
   (e) the recipients or categories of recipients of the personal data, if any;
   (f) where applicable, that the controller intends to transfer personal data to a recipient in a third country or international organisation and the existence or absence of an adequacy decision by the Commission, or in the case of transfers referred to in Article 46 or 47, or the second subparagraph of Article 49(1), reference to the appropriate or suitable safeguards and the means to obtain a copy of them or where they have been made available.
2. In addition to the information referred to in paragraph 1, the controller shall provide the data subject with the following information necessary to ensure fair and transparent processing in respect of the data subject:
   (a) the period for which the personal data will be stored, or if that is not possible, the criteria used to determine that period;
   (b) where the processing is based on point (f) of Article 6(1), the legitimate interests pursued by the controller or by a third party;
   (c) the existence of the right to request from the controller access to and rectification or erasure of personal data or restriction of processing concerning the data subject and to object to processing as well as the right to data portability;
   (d) where processing is based on point (a) of Article 6(1) or point (a) of Article 9(2), the existence of the right to withdraw consent at any time, without affecting the lawfulness of processing based on consent before its withdrawal;
   (e) the right to lodge a complaint with a supervisory authority;
   (f) from which source the personal data originate, and if applicable, whether it came from publicly accessible sources;
   (g) the existence of automated decision-making, including profiling, referred to in Article 22(1) and (4) and, at least in those cases, meaningful information about the logic involved, as well as the significance and the envisaged consequences of such processing for the data subject.
3. The controller shall provide the information referred to in paragraphs 1 and 2:
   (a) within a reasonable period after obtaining the personal data, but at the latest within one month, having regard to the specific circumstances in which the personal data are processed;
   (b) if the personal data are to be used for communication with the data subject, at the latest at the time of the first communication to that data subject; or
   (c) if a disclosure to another recipient is envisaged, at the latest when the personal data are first disclosed.

4. Where the controller intends to further process the personal data for a purpose other than that for which the personal data were obtained, the controller shall provide the data subject prior to that further processing with information on that other purpose and with any relevant further information as referred to in paragraph 2.
5. Paragraphs 1 to 4 shall not apply where and insofar as:
   (a) the data subject already has the information;
   (b) the provision of such information proves impossible or would involve a disproportionate effort, in particular for processing for archiving purposes in the public interest, scientific or historical research purposes or statistical purposes, subject to the conditions and safeguards referred to in Article 89(1) or in so far as the obligation referred to in paragraph 1 of this Article is likely to render impossible or seriously impair the achievement of the objectives of that processing. In such cases the controller shall take appropriate measures to protect the data subject's rights and freedoms and legitimate interests, including making the information publicly available;
   (c) obtaining or disclosure is expressly laid down by Union or Member State law to which the controller is subject and which provides appropriate measures to protect the data subject's legitimate interests; or
   (d) where the personal data must remain confidential subject to an obligation of professional secrecy regulated by Union or Member State law, including a statutory obligation of secrecy.

Relevant Recitals

(60) The principles of fair and transparent processing require that the data subject be informed of the existence of the processing operation and its purposes. The controller should provide the data subject with any further information necessary to ensure fair and transparent processing taking into account the specific circumstances and context in which the personal data are processed. Furthermore, the data subject should be informed of the existence of profiling and the consequences of such profiling. Where the personal data are collected from the data subject, the data subject should also be informed whether he or she is obliged to provide the personal data and of the consequences, where he or she does not provide such data. That information may be provided in combination with standardised icons in order to give in an easily visible, intelligible and clearly legible manner, a meaningful overview of the intended processing. Where the icons are presented electronically, they should be machine-readable.

(61) The information in relation to the processing of personal data relating to the data subject should be given to him or her at the time of collection from the data subject, or, where the personal data are obtained from another source, within a reasonable period, depending on the circumstances of the case. Where personal data can be legitimately disclosed to another recipient, the data subject should be informed when the personal data are first disclosed to the recipient. Where the controller intends to process the personal data for a purpose other than that for which they were collected, the controller should provide the data subject prior to that further processing with information on that other purpose and other necessary information. Where the origin of the personal data cannot be provided to the data subject because various sources have been used, general information should be provided.

(62) However, it is not necessary to impose the obligation to provide information where the data subject already possesses the information, where the recording or disclosure of the personal data is expressly laid down by law or where the provision of information to the data subject proves to be impossible or would involve a disproportionate effort. The latter could in particular be the case where processing is carried out for archiving purposes in the public interest, scientific or historical

research purposes or statistical purposes. In that regard, the number of data subjects, the age of the data and any appropriate safeguards adopted should be taken into consideration.

Closely Related Provisions

Article 5(1) (Principle of fairness, lawfulness and transparency); Article 12 (Transparent information, communication and modalities for the exercise of the rights of the data subject); Article 14 (Information to be provided where personal data have not been obtained from the data subject); Article 15 (Right of access by the data subject); Article 23 (Restrictions); Article 34 (Communication of a personal data breach to the data subject)

Related Provisions in LED [Directive (EU) 2016/680]

Article 13 (Information to be made available or given to the data subject)

Related Provisions in EPD [Directive 2002/58/EC]

Article 4 (Security); Article 5 (Confidentiality of communications); Article 6 (Traffic data); Article 9 (Location data other than traffic data)

Relevant Case Law

CJEU

Case C-473/12, *Institut professionnel des agents immobiliers (IPI) v Geoffrey Englebert and Others*, judgment of 7 November 2013 (ECLI:EU:C:2013:715).
Case C-212/13, *František Ryneš v Úřad pro ochranu osobních údajů*, judgment of 11 December 2014 (ECLI:EU:C:2014:2428).
Case C-201/14, *Smaranda Bara and Others v Casa Națională de Asigurări de Sănătate and Others*, judgment of 1 October 2015 (ECLI:EU:C:2015:638).

A. Rationale and Policy Underpinning

Transparency is at the core of Article 14 GDPR as much as it is at the core of Article 13 GDPR.[1] The difference between the two Articles rests in the fact that Article 13 regulates what information must be provided to data subjects by controllers when personal data is collected directly from them (e.g. when they subscribe to a new service), while Article 14 regulates what information must be given to data subjects when they do not provide themselves the personal data, but it is collected from third party sources. Providing details of the processing to the data subject when personal data have not been obtained from him or her is all the more important, since in this situation it is likely that the processing can occur without the knowledge of the person concerned. At the same time, providing

---

[1] See the commentary on Art. 13 in this volume. See there the explanation regarding the importance of transparency for the effectiveness of data protection law in general.

notice in this situation is more difficult to do, since there is no direct contact between the controller and the data subject at the point of collecting data.

Perhaps this paradox explains why the EU legislator ultimately chose to have two separate provisions for informing data subjects, i.e. to show without any doubt that transparency regarding indirect collection of data must be addressed. It also explains why the legislator provided for more exceptions related to reasonableness in the case of indirect collection of data (that is, to acknowledge that it is more difficult to do in practice).

There may also be a historical explanation for having the two situations regulated separately. The first French data protection law, adopted in 1978,[2] partially distinguished between the direct and indirect collection of personal data when providing information to the data subject.[3] Article 3 of the law, in the chapter dedicated to general principles, contained a general transparency principle only with regard to automated processing, and provided that everyone has the right to know and to challenge the information and the 'reasoning' used by automatic processing that resulted in decisions affecting them. Separately, the law required under Article 27 for the controller to provide a set of information to individuals when personal data is directly collected from them, including whether providing the data is obligatory and who are the recipients of the data.

When applying the law, the French data protection authority (CNIL) expanded this obligation of the controller to situations where personal data are obtained from different sources than the data subject, giving as examples obtaining personal data from a telephone book.[4] This may explain why it was considered necessary to have both situations clearly covered by the provisions of the DPD, a distinction that survived the 2012–2016 reform of the DPD and is maintained in the GDPR.

B. Legal Background

1. EU legislation

Article 14 GDPR had an equivalent in Article 11 of the DPD. The latter dealt as well with the obligation of controllers to inform data subjects about the details of the processing activity where the data have not been obtained from the data subject. In this situation, either the controller or its representative had to inform the data subjects about the processing 'at the time of undertaking the recording of personal data or if a disclosure to a third party is envisaged, no later than the time the data are first disclosed'.[5]

The set of information to be provided was very similar to the one in Article 10 DPD (information where the personal data is obtained directly from the data subject). It only differed with regard to disclosing the categories of data concerned, which was not required under Article 10. In the early 1990s, when the DPD was debated and adopted, the legislator likely assumed that when data are collected directly from the data subject, the data subject is aware of the categories of personal data being provided to the controller. Therefore, the need to indicate what data is collected appeared only in the case of indirect collection.

[2] French Data Protection Act 1978.
[3] For a brief history of the provisions regarding the right of information in the first European data protection laws, see Nugter 1990 and Zanfir 2013.
[4] CNIL 1986, pp. 72–76.   [5] Art. 11(1) DPD.

However, the main difference between the two provisions of the DPD was that Article 11 provided for a series of specific exceptions to the right to information. As such, paragraph 2 stated that information did not have to be provided to the data subject in the case of indirect collection in several cases, 'in particular for processing for statistical purposes or for the purposes of historical or scientific research, the provision of such information proves impossible or would involve a disproportionate effort or if recording or disclosure is expressly laid down by law'.[6]

All transparency provisions of the EPD concern direct collection of personal data from the individual. Articles 4(2), 5(3), 6(4) and 9(1) EPD all require service providers to provide certain information about both content and metadata collected from users' or subscribers' devices. In fact, the purpose of the EPD seems to be to act as a shield between the entities that collect personal data from electronic devices and the confidentiality of the communications facilitated by those devices. Controllers who collect personal data indirectly could leverage the fact that all service providers are required by the EPD to inform users about the collection of data from their devices to partner with the service providers or other entities covered by the EPD and who are involved in directly collecting personal data from terminal equipment to make sure that the information given to users or subscribers under the EPD covers, in addition, all the elements required by the GDPR with regard to their own processing. If data subjects would already have all the relevant information, the relevant exception[7] under the GDPR would apply.

The LED does not distinguish between direct and indirect collection of personal data when it provides for the right of data subjects to be informed about the processing. Article 13 LED covers, in general, 'Information to be made available or given to the data subject'. The provision distinguishes between data that must be provided as a minimum and data that must be provided for 'in specific cases', with the latter being defined by national law.

2. International instruments

One of the updates to Council of Europe Convention 108 when it was modernised in 2018 was the introduction of specific transparency requirements. Article 8(1) of the Modernised Convention 108 prescribes a list of information that the controller should give the data subject, which resembles the lists provided by Articles 13 and 14 GDPR,[8] and also refers to 'any necessary additional information in order to ensure fair and transparent processing'. Since there is no specification in Article 8 as to whether the notice must be provided where personal data are collected directly from the data subject or indirectly, from a third party, the controller should provide notice in both situations, according to the principle *ubi lex non distinguit, nec nos distinguere debemus* ('where the law does not distinguish, neither should we distinguish').

The Explanatory Report accompanying the Modernised Convention clarifies that 'certain essential information has to be compulsorily provided in a proactive manner by the

---

[6] Ibid., Art. 11(2).   [7] Art. 14(5)(a) GDPR.

[8] According to Art. 8(1) Modernised Convention 108, the controller must provide information to the data subject about his or her identity and habitual residence or establishment; the legal basis and the purposes of the intended processing; the categories of personal data processed; the recipients or categories of recipients of the personal data, if any; and the means of exercising the rights of the data subject as well as any necessary additional information in order to ensure fair and transparent processing of the personal data.

controller to the data subjects when directly or indirectly (not through the data subject but through a third-party) collecting their data'.[9] To this end, the controller can use 'any available, reasonable and affordable means to inform data subjects collectively (through a website or public notice) or individually'.[10] The Explanatory Report also highlights that the transparency obligation must still be executed, even if it is impossible to provide notice when commencing the processing, since 'it can be done at a later stage, for instance when the controller is put in contact with the data subject for any new reason'.[11]

The Modernised Convention provides for specific exceptions to the obligation of transparency which are similar to the exceptions provided by the GDPR, i.e. where the data subject already has the relevant information[12] and where the personal data are not collected from the data subjects and the processing is expressly prescribed by law (e.g. a national law allowing banks to obtain information from credit bureaus) or providing notice proves to be impossible or involves disproportionate efforts.[13] While the existence of a legal obligation is straightforward, the burden of proof for validly applying the 'impossible or disproportionate efforts' exception rests with the controller, which must make an assessment to this end before deciding it will not proactively give notice to data subjects. Under the regime created by the Modernised Convention, this assessment should take into account the importance of transparency for data protection including. Transparency is needed 'to ensure fair processing and to enable data subjects to understand and thus fully exercise their rights in the context of such data processing'.[14]

As discussed in the commentary on Article 13 GDPR in this volume, the OECD Privacy Principles include a reference to transparency as part of a general 'Openness principle'. This principle is equally applicable to collecting personal data from sources other than the data subject. The OECD Privacy Framework published in 2013 together with the updated Principles questions the importance of transparency towards the data subject, especially with regard to complex data flows (which unequivocally implicate collecting personal data from different sources other than the data subject). In fact, the OECD argues in the Framework that 'as data usage has become more complex, so too have the privacy policies that describe them'[15] and that 'given the implications about how individuals make decisions, questions can be asked about whether this focus on privacy notices and consent can continue to bear the weight they are often assigned in the process of affording protection'.[16] This could explain why the Openness Principle was not updated during the modernisation of the OECD Principles in 2013. It should be noted that this position represents a departure from the importance placed on transparency in the EU and Council of Europe data protection frameworks. In addition, this position seems to link transparency to consent and meaningful choices, whereas the European framework recognises that transparency is relevant regardless of the lawful ground for processing relied on by the controller. Indeed, in order to be valid under the GDPR consent must be 'informed',[17] but transparency towards the data subject is equally required for all processing activities, regardless of the lawful ground relied on.

Finally, the EEA Agreement, as amended in July 2018,[18] incorporates the GDPR into its Annexes and provides that the provisions of the GDPR should be read, for the

---

[9] Explanatory Report Convention 108 2018, p. 12, para. 68. [10] Ibid., para. 70.
[11] Ibid., para. 70.   [12] Art. 8(2) Modernised Convention 108.   [13] Ibid., Art. 8(3).
[14] Explanatory Report Convention 108 2018, p. 12, para. 67.
[15] OECD Guidelines 2013, p. 99.   [16] Ibid., pp. 99–100.
[17] Arts. 4(11) and 7(3) GDPR.   [18] EEA Decision 2018.

purposes of that Agreement, with a number of adaptations. In this respect, the Agreement provides that, as regards the EFTA states party to the Agreement, the words 'applicable pursuant to the EEA Agreement' shall be inserted in Article 14(1)(f) after the words 'adequacy decision by the Commission'.[19]

3. National developments

National law does play a role with regard to exceptions to the obligation to inform data subjects when personal data are not collected directly from them. In particular, the controller does not have to provide information where obtaining or disclosure of personal data is expressly laid down by Union or Member State law which provides appropriate measures to protect the data subject's legitimate interests[20] and where the personal data must remain confidential subject to an obligation of professional secrecy regulated by Union or Member State law.[21] In addition, Article 23 GDPR allows Member States to restrict the scope of all the rights of the data subject in Chapter III, including Article 14.

This may lead to some differences stemming from national implementation. For example, the new German Federal Data Protection Act[22] exempts controllers from informing data subjects when personal data are collected from third party sources where the notification would disclose information which 'by its nature must be kept secret, in particular because of overriding legitimate interests of a third party'.[23] As part of their accountability obligations, controllers that process personal data obtained from third parties which they consider is secret by nature arguably have to keep a record of the decision process not to inform data subjects, why they consider the information to be secret and why third parties have an overriding legitimate interest not to disclose details about the processing.

The German Act provides for additional exceptions to Article 14, both for public and private bodies. These exceptions are only available for processing of personal data collected from other sources than the data subject. Public bodies do not have to provide information if this would endanger the performance of their tasks or if it would threaten public security and public order.[24] On the other hand, private bodies are exempt from providing information if this would interfere with establishing or exercising legal claims, or if the processing includes data from contracts under private law and is intended to prevent harm from criminal offences[25] (for example, this could be the case of processing data from financial or investment contracts for anti-money-laundering purposes). When the public and private controllers make use of these exceptions, they also have the obligation to take appropriate measures to protect the legitimate interests of the data subject. The law mentions that one such measure is providing the information required by Article 14 'for the public' and 'in a precise, transparent, understandable and easily accessible form, in clear and simple language'.[26] Therefore, at least some level of general information must be provided on the website of the controller or on any other public interface it may have.

Some Member States have added additional transparency requirements for specific processing activities. The UK Data Protection Act 2018 provides in section 14(4) that

---

[19] Ibid., Art. 5e(d). [20] Art. 14(5)(c) GDPR. [21] Ibid., Art. 14(5)(d).
[22] German GDPR Implementation Act. [23] Ibid., s. 29(1) (translation by the author).
[24] Ibid., s. 33(1). [25] Ibid. [26] Ibid., s. 33(2) (translation by the author).

where a controller takes a 'qualifying significant decision' in relation to a data subject based solely on automated processing, it must 'as soon as reasonably practicable, notify the data subject in writing that a decision has been taken based solely on automated processing'.[27] The law does not distinguish between the sources of personal data automatically processed to result in a significant decision, which means that this notification must be given both in the situation where the data is collected directly from data subjects and the situation where it is collected from other sources. Following the specific information received with regard to the existence of the decision based solely on automated processing, the data subject will have the right to request the controller, within a month from the receipt of the notification, to reconsider the decision or take a new decision with human involvement.[28]

This increased transparency and control with regard to solely automated decision-making is in fact a consequence of Article 22(3) GDPR, which requires controllers to implement 'suitable measures' to safeguard the data subject's rights and freedoms and legitimate interests when their data is used for solely automated decision-making, and to provide data subjects at least with the right to obtain human intervention and to contest the decision. The specific notification required by the UK Data Protection Act 2018 with regard to an individual decision complements the obligation under both Articles 13 and 14 GDPR for controllers to disclose the existence of solely automatic decision-making, together with the logic involved in the automated decision-making. This specific notification must be given *post factum*, after an individual decision is made, while the information about the existence of solely automated decision-making pursuant to both Articles 13 and 14 must be given at the time of collection (for Article 13) or within a reasonable period after obtaining the data (Article 14).

The draft law implementing the GDPR in Spain provides that for all processing of personal data that has not been obtained from the data subject directly, the controller should inform data subjects, as a first step, about a minimum set of details: identity of the controller, purposes of the processing, the ways in which the rights of the data subject can be exercised and, if this is the case, the existence of solely automated decision-making.[29] The initial notice must also enclose an email address or an indication of other means which would allow access to the rest of information in a simple and immediate way.[30] If the similar provision of the draft law implementing Article 13 raises some questions about conformity with the GDPR, the wording of Article 14 may more easily allow a flexible implementation due to the fact that in this situation information can be provided at a different moment than the moment of collection of data.

4. Case law

Most cases involving the giving of information have involved situations where personal data were collected directly from the data subject, and are thus discussed in the commentary on Article 13 GDPR in this volume. In the cases where the CJEU has dealt with the collection of data and that contributed to establishing the content of the right to information under the DPD, the Court often did not usefully distinguish between

---

[27] s. 14(4)(a) UK Data Protection Act 2018.
[28] Ibid., s. 14(4)(b).   [29] Art. 11(2) and (3) Spanish Draft GDPR Law.   [30] Ibid.

transparency with regard to direct and indirect collection of personal data from the data subjects. In *IPI*,[31] a case concerning the obligation to inform data subjects in the context of investigations carried out by a private detective, the Court established from the outset that this type of activity involves both direct and indirect collection of personal data, and therefore both Articles 10 (direct collection) and 11 (indirect collection) of the DPD were relevant.[32] The Court then continued to refer to both articles when conducting its assessment.[33] Ultimately, in the main part of the judgment, the Court referred solely to the interpretation of Article 13 DPD which provided what types of exceptions Member States could legislate for the exercise of all rights of the data subject, even though the Belgian referring court specifically asked a question concerning the interpretation of both Articles 13 and 11 DPD.[34]

In Case C-201/14 *Bara*[35] the Court took a somewhat similar approach, resulting in an executive part of the judgment that refers in bulk to 'Articles 10, 11 and 13' of the DPD. However, this time the Court did analyse the obligations of the controller under Article 11 separately in the body of the judgment. The case in *Bara* concerned sharing of personal data of self-employed individuals between two authorities of the state, from the Romanian tax authority ('ANAF') to the national health insurance authority ('CNAS'), which resulted in CNAS issuing orders for receiving health insurance payments retroactively from self-employed individuals. This was done without the data subjects being informed either by ANAF (which collected the data directly from them) or by CNAS (which collected the data from ANAF). The Court established that 'the processing by CNAS of the data transferred by the ANAF required that the subjects of the data be informed of the purpose of that processing and the categories of data concerned'[36] and that 'the CNAS did not provide the applicants in the main proceedings with the information listed in Article 11'.[37] The Court further considered that the law relied by the government and the Protocol signed between the two authorities to allow the transfer to take place 'do not establish a basis for applying the derogation under Article 11(2)[38] or that provided for under Article 13 of the directive'.[39] Previously, the CJEU had established that the national law was too vague as the definition of transferable information and the detailed arrangements for transferring that information were laid down in the protocol, which was not subject to an official publication, and was not laid down in the law itself.[40] Therefore, it held, the legislative measures that would justify an exception from informing data subjects about the processing of personal data based on indirect collection must meet a threshold of transparency and sufficient details in order to be lawful.

In *Ryneš* the Court incidentally referred to the obligation to inform data subjects when personal data are not collected directly from them pursuant to Article 11 DPD. The case concerned a home CCTV system installed to capture the public space in front of a private house. The camera recorded an incident which resulted in the windows of the house being broken by a shot from a catapult. The perpetrators were identified with the help of those images.[41] However, the perpetrators challenged the lawfulness of the evidence on several grounds, including that the homeowner did not inform people passing by about the

---

[31] Case C-473/12, *IPI*.   [32] Ibid., para. 24.   [33] See e.g. ibid., paras. 29 and 46.
[34] Ibid., para. 21.   [35] Case C-201/14, *Bara*.   [36] Ibid., para. 43.   [37] Ibid., para. 44.
[38] Which established an exception from the obligation to inform data subjects when the registration or communication of the data are laid down by law.
[39] Case C-201/14, *Bara*, para. 45.   [40] Ibid., para. 40.   [41] Case C-212/13, *Ryneš*, para. 15.

existence of the camera pursuant to the national law transposing the DPD.[42] The national Court stayed proceedings and asked the CJEU whether this particular situation falls under the household exception of the DPD, so the homeowner would not be considered in this case as being a controller and he would not be under an obligation to inform data subjects.[43]

The CJEU found that the household exemption did not apply to the situation at hand, 'to the extent that video surveillance ... covers, even partially, a public space and is accordingly directed outwards from the private setting of the person processing the data in that manner'.[44] However, after replying to the question for a preliminary ruling, the Court stressed that even though the processing in this particular instance was not exempted from data protection law, there are specific provisions of the DPD that makes it possible to process personal data in a lawful manner without obtaining consent and providing notice.[45] In particular with regard to notice, the Court invoked Articles 11(2) and 13(1)(d) DPD. Article 11(2) provided for an exemption from the right to information in the case of indirect collection of personal data when the provision of information proves impossible or would involve a disproportionate effort in certain cases, while the second one allowed Member States to provide for an exception to all rights of data subjects, including the right to information, when this was necessary to safeguard the prevention, investigation, detection and prosecution of criminal offences or of breaches of ethics for regulated professions. Therefore, the Court indicated that the use of the home CCTV system could be lawful without providing notice to data subjects. Since it did not include any reference to Article 10 DPD, the Court also implied that it considers recording of images of people as constituting the indirect collection of personal data. This approach is contrary to the guidance published by the WP29, which included processing of personal data captured by devices such as cameras under Article 13 GDPR.[46]

In an investigation concerning political behavioural advertising during the campaign for Brexit, the British data protection authority (ICO) identified shortcomings related to transparency towards data subjects, and especially with regard to personal data obtained from third parties, including public sources. One of the actions required by the ICO was for parties to review their 'current practices and privacy notices to ensure full and transparent information is provided to individuals'[47] about how their personal data is used. In particular, the ICO asked that parties explain 'how individuals' information gained from sources (such as the electoral register) is supplemented by other information, the source of that information and how it is processed'.[48] The ICO concluded that 'the parties must all make significant efforts to improve the prominence, precision and openness of the information they provide to the public about how their data is used'.[49]

C. Analysis

1. Introduction

Article 14 GDPR enshrines a positive obligation to act on the controller, who must provide to the data subject details about the processing activity where the personal data have not been obtained directly from the data subject. The meaning of the verb used to

---

[42] Ibid., para. 16.   [43] Ibid.   [44] Ibid., para. 33.   [45] Ibid., para. 34.
[46] WP29 Transparency Guidelines, p. 15. The Guidelines were adopted by the WP29 but were endorsed by the EDPB in May 2018.
[47] ICO 2018, p. 50.   [48] Ibid.   [49] Ibid.

describe this obligation—'shall provide'—indicates that the controller has to proactively disclose the required information. The set of information to be disclosed significantly overlaps with the one enshrined in Article 13 GDPR, requiring the controller to identify itself, the purpose of processing, existence of the rights of data subjects etc. Thus, the analysis contained in the commentary to Article 13 in this volume is applicable when applying Article 14 GDPR and should be consulted when dealing with issues under Article 14 as well. In fact, all details required by Article 13 must also be provided pursuant to Article 14, with one exception: since personal data are not collected directly from the data subject, it follows that the notice should not inform whether the provision of personal data is a statutory or contractual requirement, or whether the data subject is obliged to provide the personal data.[50]

In addition to the categories of information that are also required by Article 13 and that have been analysed in the commentary to it in this volume, Article 14 lists two new types of information that should be provided to the data subjects:

1. *The categories of personal data concerned*,[51] which are important to include in the information notice about indirect collection of personal data precisely because the data subject is not providing the personal data herself. To meet the fairness and transparency principle, the description of the categories should be precise enough to allow the data subject to attain an overall understanding about the data processing, especially together with knowing the purposes of the processing,[52] and to cover all personal data items processed, rather than giving an incomplete image. Some examples of categories of personal data are identification data, contact information, location data, political views, religious views, food preferences, biometric data, location data, browsing history data etc. Arguably, some categories of personal data would be too wide in order to include them in a privacy notice that ensures fairness. For example, 'data related to health' is potentially too wide, since it can cover a myriad of information. More specific information, such as 'heart rate', 'blood pressure' and 'age of pregnancy' may be required, depending on the processing and its purposes.
2. *The source from which the personal data originates*, and, if applicable, whether it came from publicly available sources.[53] In order to ensure fairness of processing, it is also important to disclose the source of the personal data. This will allow the data subject to potentially challenge the legality of the initial collection, especially if the personal data in question are publicly available without the data subject being aware of it. The WP29 required in its official guidance that 'the specific source of the data should be provided unless it is not possible to do so'.[54] However, even if it is impossible to specify the source, 'the information provided should include the nature of the sources (i.e. publicly/privately held sources) and types of organization/industry/sector'[55] from which the personal data originated.

The architecture of Article 14 is similar to that of Article 13 to the extent it also provides for two general types of information that should be provided to the data subject, answers the question of when the information should be provided, regulates notice for further processing of personal data and addresses specific exemptions to the right of information.

[50] Art. 13(2)(e) GDPR. [51] Ibid., Art. 14(1)(d). [52] Ibid., Art. 14(1)(c).
[53] Ibid., Art. 14(2)(f). [54] WP29 Transparency Guidelines, p. 40. [55] Ibid.

The first two paragraphs address the list of information that should be provided to data subjects. Even though the list is separated into two paragraphs, just like within Article 13 GDPR, it is clear that both sets of information must equally be provided in the notice, since the wording used does not leave room for optional disclosures. The second paragraph specifies that the information it covers is to be provided in order to ensure fairness and transparency (e.g. the retention period, the legitimate interest pursued if that is the case, the sources of the personal data, the existence of automated decision-making etc.).

2. Timing

A particularly difficult issue is to identify the point in time when the notice covering indirect collection of personal data should be provided to data subjects. Article 14(3)(a) establishes as a general rule that the information should be provided within a reasonable period after obtaining the personal data, but at the latest within one month after having obtained it. The time of delivery should be decided having regard to 'the specific circumstances in which the personal data are processed'. This gives flexibility to the controller to adapt delivery of the notice. For example, it could be relevant what kind of effort the controller needs to identify, how to contact the data subjects or even the number of the data subjects that need to be notified. However, the one-month limit is not extendable, and these circumstances only provide flexibility within this time frame.

There are only two situations that could shorten the one-month time limit. First, if the personal data collected from third parties will be used for communication with the data subject, the privacy notice must be provided at the latest at the time of the first communication to the data subject, according to Article 14(3)(b). If the first communication does not occur within one month from obtaining the data, notice should be given before the one month expires.[56] Secondly, if a disclosure of the personal data to another recipient is envisaged, notice should be provided at the latest when the personal data are first disclosed, according to Article 14(3)(c). Similarly, the one-month limit must be respected if the disclosure is foreseen at a later time.[57] Therefore, when obtaining personal data from data brokers, publicly available sources or any other third party, one of the first concerns should be figuring out how and when to inform the data subjects. The WP29 took the view that the verb 'provide' used in the first paragraph of both Articles 13 and 14 means that the controller must be proactive and seek to inform the data subjects about the processing, as opposed to making the information available somewhere and having the data subjects look for it among other information, such as Terms and Conditions.[58] This may prove particularly difficult in the case of indirect collection of data, especially if there is no direct link that will be established between the controller and the data subjects.

3. Transparency

It is important that at the stage of designing a processing activity which involves the indirect collection of personal data, the controller considers and implements technical or organisational solutions that would ensure transparency and compliance with Article 14.[59] An organisational solution could rely on involving the third party source of the data in

---

[56] Ibid., p. 15.   [57] Ibid., p. 16.   [58] Ibid., p. 18.
[59] This is an obligation under Art. 25(1) GDPR, ensuring data protection by design. See Jasmontaite et al. 2018.

providing an enhanced data protection notice that would cover the processing at issue, especially if the source is collecting the data directly from data subjects. It is relevant here to note that one of the exceptions under Article 14 applies to the situation where the data subject already has the information. Therefore, if the third party source that collected the personal data directly from the data subject had already given full details about the further processing, the controller is likely exempted from providing the information itself. Technical solutions could leverage the work that is being done in the design of privacy notices, scaling delivery of notices depending on timing (at set-up, just in time, context-dependent, periodic, persistent, on demand), the channel of communication (primary, secondary, public), the modality of delivery (visual, auditory, haptic, machine-readable) and the embedded control options (blocking, non-blocking, decoupled).[60]

Article 14, just like Article 13, also provides for rules concerning transparency with regard to further processing. In particular, it provides that where the controller intends to further process the personal data for a purpose other than that for which it was obtained, the controller should provide information identifying the purpose and any other relevant information[61] as referred in the second paragraph of Article 14. The details about the further processing must be made available to the data subjects before the further processing commences.[62] Such further processing can only occur if the new purpose of the processing is compatible with the original one,[63] which explains why 'the purpose' is highlighted in Article 14(4), making it the only element of the notice concerning 'further processing' that must always be provided. It is important to note that even if the GDPR allows processing for compatible purposes relying on the same lawful ground as the original processing, the obligation to inform data subjects about the existence of the further processing still applies.

4. Exemptions

Article 14(5) details the exemptions of the right to information in the case of indirect collection of data:

1. *Where the data subject already has the information*.[64] This means that if the controller that collects the personal data directly from the data subject provides additional details that cover all information that the second controller processing the personal data would need to disclose, the second controller will not have to provide this information. In this case, and in line with the accountability principle, the second controller would have to demonstrate that the information had been already provided in full at the time of collection.
2. *Where providing information proves impossible or would involve a disproportionate effort*, in particular for processing for archiving purposes in the public interest, scientific or historical research purposes or statistical purposes.[65] There are two triggers for this exception: impossibility to deliver information or a disproportionate effort that is required to deliver it. Both of the two conditions must be a result of the indirect collection of personal data in order to be applicable.[66] In the case of 'impossibility', the WP29 clarified that the controller has the burden of proof, so it must demonstrate

---

[60] Schaub et al. 2018.   [61] Art. 14(4) GDPR.   [62] Ibid.   [63] Ibid., Art. 5(1)(b).
[64] Ibid., Art. 14(5)(a).   [65] Ibid., Art. 14(5)(b).   [66] WP29 Transparency Guidelines, p. 30.

the factors that actually prevent it from providing the information in question.[67] In the case of 'disproportionate effort', the WP29 asked that the controller would carry out 'a balancing exercise to assess the effort involved for the data controller to provide the information to the data subject against the impact and effects on the data subject if he or she was not provided with the information'.[68] If either of the two exceptions applies to a processing for archiving purposes in the public interest, scientific or historical research purposes for statistical purposes, according to Article 14(5)(b), they are valid only if the processing is subject to the conditions and safeguards referred to in Article 89(1) GDPR, or in so far as the obligation to provide notice is 'likely to render impossible or seriously impair the achievement of the objectives of that processing'. For example, in the case of a research project that relies on data collected by third parties, if revealing details of the processing such as the identity of the sources would impair the result of the project, it is likely that the obligation to inform data subjects does not apply. According to recital 62, for applying the exception to these particular processing activities, 'the number of data subjects, the age of the data and any appropriate safeguards adopted should be taken into consideration'. The 'impossibility' or 'disproportionate efforts' exceptions can apply to all types of processing, not only to processing for research purposes or statistical purposes. However, the position of the WP29 was that 'this exception should not be routinely relied upon by data controllers who are not processing personal data for the purposes of archiving in the public interest, for scientific or historical research purposes or statistical purposes'.[69] If the controller decides to rely on these exceptions, Article 14(5)(b) requires that it 'shall take appropriate measures to protect the data subject's rights and freedoms and legitimate interests, including making the information publicly available'. The information would be published on the controller's website, without being specifically delivered to the data subjects. Other safeguards could mean undertaking a data protection impact assessment, applying pseudonymisation techniques to the data and minimising the data collected and the storage period.[70] It seems that validly relying on this exception requires a high degree of responsibility and accountability.

3. *Where obtaining or disclosure is expressly laid down by Union or Member State law*, but only if the law in question 'provides appropriate measures to protect the data subject's legitimate interests' and if it specifically addresses the controller.[71] Following the judgment of the CJEU in the *Bara* case, as shown earlier, the law must also meet criteria of publicity.
4. *Where the personal data must remain confidential subject to a professional secrecy obligation regulated by Union or Member State law*.[72] Such a situation may appear for example in the case of lawyers or medical practitioners that cannot disclose information obtained when practicing their job.

The WP29 requires that all exceptions to the right of information in the case of indirect collection should be interpreted and applied narrowly.[73] This consideration is a sign of the importance of transparency in EU data protection law and once again points out that despite the difficulty indirect collection of personal data poses to transparency towards the data subject, controllers are expected to find solutions to provide information about the processing.

---

[67] Ibid., p. 29. [68] Ibid., p. 28. [69] Ibid., p. 30.
[70] Ibid., p. 31. [71] Art. 14(5)(c) GDPR. [72] Ibid., Art. 14(5)(d).
[73] WP29 Transparency Guidelines, p. 28.

Select Bibliography

International agreements

EEA Agreement: Agreement on the European Economic Area, OJ 1994 L 1/3.
EEA Decision 2018: Decision of the EEA Joint Committee No. 154/2018 of 6 July 2018 amending Annex XI (Electronic communication, audiovisual services and information society) and Protocol 37 (containing the list provided for in Article 101) to the EEA Agreement [2018/1022], OJ 2018 L 183/23.
OECD Guidelines 2013: Organisation for Economic Co-operation and Development, 'The OECD Privacy Framework' (2013).

National legislation

French Data Protection Act 1978: Act No. 78-17 of 6 January 1978 on Data Processing, Files and Individual Liberties (Loi n° 78-17 du 6 janvier 1978 relative à l'informatique, aux fichiers et aux libertés), as last amended by Law No. 2014-334 of 17 March 2014.
German GDPR Implementation Law: Gesetz zur Anpassung des Datenschutzrechts an die Verordnung (EU) 2016/679 und zur Umsetzung der Richtlinie (EU) 2016/680 (Datenschutz-Anpassungs- und Umsetzungsgesetz EU—DsAnpUG-EU), BGBl 2017 Teil 1 Nr. 44.
Spanish Draft GDPR Law: Proyecto de Ley Orgánica de Protección de Datos de Carácter Personal (121/000013).
UK Data Protection Act 2018: Data Protection Act 2018 (Chapter 12).

Academic writings

Jasmontaite et al. 2018: Jasmontaite, Kamara, Zanfir-Fortuna and Leucci, 'Data Protection by Design and by Default: Framing Guiding Principles into Legal Obligations in the GDPR', 4(2) *European Data Protection Law Review* (2018), 168.
Nugter 1990: Nugter, *Transborder Flow of Personal Data within the EC* (Springer 1990).
Schaub et al. 2018: Schaub, Balebako, Durity and Cranor, 'A Design Space for Privacy Notices', in Selinger, Polenetsky and Tene (eds.), *The Cambridge Handbook of Consumer Privacy* (CUP 2018), 365.
Zanfir 2013: Zanfir, 'Protecţia Datelor Personale. Drepturile persoanei vizate' (2013) (PhD dissertation at the University of Craiova).

Papers of data protection authorities

WP29 Transparency Guidelines: Article 29 Working Party, 'Guidelines on Transparency under Regulation 2016/269' (WP260rev.01, 11 April 2018).
CNIL 1986: Commission Nationale de l'Informatique et Libertes, '7th Activity Report' (1986).
ICO 2018: Information Commissioner Office, 'Democracy Disrupted? Personal Information and Political Influence' (11 July 2018).

Reports and recommendations

Explanatory Report Convention 108 2018: Council of Europe, 'Explanatory Report to the Protocol Amending the Convention for the Protection of Individuals with Regard to the Automatic Processing of Personal Data' (10 October 2018), available at https://rm.coe.int/cets-223-explanatory-report-to-the-protocol-amending-the-convention-fo/16808ac91a.

Article 15. Right of access by the data subject

GABRIELA ZANFIR-FORTUNA

1. The data subject shall have the right to obtain from the controller confirmation as to whether or not personal data concerning him or her are being processed, and, where that is the case, access to the personal data and the following information:
   (a) the purposes of the processing;
   (b) the categories of personal data concerned;
   (c) the recipients or categories of recipient to whom the personal data have been or will be disclosed, in particular recipients in third countries or international organisations;
   (d) where possible, the envisaged period for which the personal data will be stored, or, if not possible, the criteria used to determine that period;
   (e) the existence of the right to request from the controller rectification or erasure of personal data or restriction of processing of personal data concerning the data subject or to object to such processing;
   (f) the right to lodge a complaint with a supervisory authority;
   (g) where the personal data are not collected from the data subject, any available information as to their source;
   (h) the existence of automated decision-making, including profiling, referred to in Article 22(1) and (4) and, at least in those cases, meaningful information about the logic involved, as well as the significance and the envisaged consequences of such processing for the data subject.
2. Where personal data are transferred to a third country or to an international organisation, the data subject shall have the right to be informed of the appropriate safeguards pursuant to Article 46 relating to the transfer.
3. The controller shall provide a copy of the personal data undergoing processing. For any further copies requested by the data subject, the controller may charge a reasonable fee based on administrative costs. Where the data subject makes the request by electronic means, and unless otherwise requested by the data subject, the information shall be provided in a commonly used electronic form.
4. The right to obtain a copy referred to in paragraph 3 shall not adversely affect the rights and freedoms of others.

Relevant Recitals

(58) The principle of transparency requires that any information addressed to the public or to the data subject be concise, easily accessible and easy to understand, and that clear and plain language and, additionally, where appropriate, visualisation be used. Such information could be provided in electronic form, for example, when addressed to the public, through a website. This is of particular relevance in situations where the proliferation of actors and the technological complexity of practice make it difficult for the data subject to know and understand whether, by whom and for what purpose personal data relating to him or her are being collected, such as in the case of online advertising. Given that children merit specific protection, any information and communication, where processing is addressed to a child, should be in such a clear and plain language that the child can easily understand.

(59) Modalities should be provided for facilitating the exercise of the data subject's rights under this Regulation, including mechanisms to request and, if applicable, obtain, free of charge, in particular, access to and rectification or erasure of personal data and the exercise of the right to object. The controller should also provide means for requests to be made electronically, especially where personal data are processed by electronic means. The controller should be obliged to respond to requests from the data subject without undue delay and at the latest within one month and to give reasons where the controller does not intend to comply with any such requests.

(63) A data subject should have the right of access to personal data which have been collected concerning him or her, and to exercise that right easily and at reasonable intervals, in order to be aware of, and verify, the lawfulness of the processing. This includes the right for data subjects to have access to data concerning their health, for example the data in their medical records containing information such as diagnoses, examination results, assessments by treating physicians and any treatment or interventions provided. Every data subject should therefore have the right to know and obtain communication in particular with regard to the purposes for which the personal data are processed, where possible the period for which the personal data are processed, the recipients of the personal data, the logic involved in any automatic personal data processing and, at least when based on profiling, the consequences of such processing. Where possible, the controller should be able to provide remote access to a secure system which would provide the data subject with direct access to his or her personal data. That right should not adversely affect the rights or freedoms of others, including trade secrets or intellectual property and in particular the copyright protecting the software. However, the result of those considerations should not be a refusal to provide all information to the data subject. Where the controller processes a large quantity of information concerning the data subject, the controller should be able to request that, before the information is delivered, the data subject specify the information or processing activities to which the request relates.

(64) The controller should use all reasonable measures to verify the identity of a data subject who requests access, in particular in the context of online services and online identifiers. A controller should not retain personal data for the sole purpose of being able to react to potential requests.

Closely Related Provisions

Article 5(1) (Principles of fairness, lawfulness and transparency) (see too recital 39); Article 11 (Processing which does not require identification) (see too recital 57); Article 12 (Transparent information, communication and modalities for the exercise of the rights of the data subject) (see too recitals 58–59); Article 13 (Information to be provided where personal data are collected from the data subject) (see too recital 60); Article 14 (Information to be provided where personal data have not been obtained from the data subject); Article 23 (Restrictions) (see too recital 73)

Related Provisions in LED [Directive (EU) 2016/680]

Article 12 (Communication and modalities for exercising the rights of the data subject) (see too recital 40); Article 14 (Right of access by the data subject) (see too recital 43): Article 15 (Limitations to the right of access) (see too recital 44)

Related Provisions in EPD [Directive 2002/58/EC]

Article 5 (Confidentiality of communications) (see too recitals 3 and 21–23); Article 6 (Traffic data) (see too recital 35); Article 9 (Location data other than traffic data) (see too recital 14)

Related Provisions in EUDPR [Regulation (EU) 2018/1725]

Article 17 (Right to access by the data subject) (see too recital 34)

Relevant Case Law

CJEU

Case C-553/07, *College van burgemeester en wethouders van Rotterdam v M.E.E. Rijkeboer*, judgment of 7 May 2009 (ECLI:EU:C:2009:293).
Case C-28/08 P, *European Commission v The Bavarian Lager Co. Ltd*, judgment of 29 June 2010 (Grand Chamber) (ECLI:EU:C:2010:378).
Joined Cases C-141/12 and C-372/12, *YS v Minister voor Immigratie, Integratie en Asiel* and *Minister voor Immigratie, Integratie en Asiel v M and S*, judgment of 17 July 2014 (ECLI:EU:C:2014:2081).
Case C-486/12, *X*, judgment of 12 December 2013 (ECLI:EU:C:2013:836).
Case T-115/13, *Gert-Jan Dennekamp v European Parliament*, GC, judgment of 15 July 2015 (ECLI:EU:T:2015:497).
Case C-434/16, *Peter Nowak v Data Protection Commissioner*, judgment of 20 December 2017 (ECLI:EU:C:2017:994).
Case C-272/19, *V.Q. v Land Hessen* (pending).

ECtHR

Leander v Sweden, Appl. No. 9248/81, judgment of 26 March 1987.
Gaskin v United Kingdom, Appl. No. 10454/83, judgment of 7 July 1989.
Odièvre v France, Appl. No. 42326/98, judgment of 13 February 2003.
Segerstedt-Wiberg and Others v Sweden, Appl. No. 62332/00, judgment of 6 June 2006.
K.H. and Others v Slovakia, Appl. No. 32881/04, judgment of 23 April 2009.
Haralambie v Romania, Appl. No. 21737/03, judgment of 27 October 2009.
Jarnea v Romania, Appl. No. 41838/05, judgment of 19 July 2011.
Godelli v Italy, Appl. No. 33783/09, judgment of 25 September 2012.
Joanna Szulc v Poland, Appl. No. 43932/08, judgment of 13 November 2012.
Antoneta Tudor v Romania, Appl. No. 23445/04, judgment of September 24 2013.

United Kingdom

England and Wales Court of Appeal, *Ittihadieh v Cheyne Gardens joined with Deer v University of Oxford* [2017] EWCA Civ 121, 3 March 2017.

A. Rationale and Policy Underpinning

The exercise of the right of access by the data subject to his or her own personal data gives rise to the most common topic for complaints filed with supervisory authorities. For example, the UK Information Commissioner (ICO) reported that 42 per cent of the complaints received in 2017 and 39 per cent of the complaints received in 2018 were about the right of access.[1] Similarly, the Irish Data Protection Commissioner ('DPC') noted that the most complaints it received in 2018 prior to the GDPR entering into force were about the right of access—571 of 1,249 complaints (45 per cent).[2]

---

[1] ICO 2018B, p. 30.   [2] DPC 2018, p. 15.

The right of access has two main functions, namely enhancing transparency and facilitating control. It enhances transparency because it provides a second, deeper and more detailed layer of information that the data subject can obtain beyond what the controller discloses in the data protection notices pursuant to Article 13 or 14 GDPR. It allows the data subject to obtain copies of the personal data being processed and to obtain updated information compared to what was included in the notice, at any time after the point of collection and in principle free of charge. 'Clarity about what is going to happen, is happening or has happened with personal data is crucial for the person concerned', as Kranenborg has argued.[3]

The right of access also facilitates control by the data subject over the personal data being processed. By obtaining confirmation that their personal data is processed and a copy of those data, the person concerned can exercise all other rights, as applicable. For example, access allows the data subject to identify incorrect or incomplete information, making it possible to ask for rectification pursuant to Article 16 GDPR. It also allows the data subject to obtain a copy of the personal data they may want erased by the controller, ensuring that erasure does not mean the data subject will forever lose the information.

It is important to distinguish between the right to access one's own personal data and the right to request access to public information. The two rights have different policy underpinnings, one guaranteeing transparency towards the person whose personal information is being collected and used by a controller (*inter partes* transparency), while the other ensures transparency towards the public with regard to information that has public value or relevance (*erga omnes* transparency). Sometimes, information which is valuable for the public and is thus subject to public access requests, such as access to public documents,[4] may be personal data. In those situations, the two legal regimes governing the same data are in conflict and a balancing exercise between the public interest and the rights of the data subject must be made on a case-by-case basis.[5]

To understand the importance of the right of access personal data, it is also worth mentioning that a historically relevant aspect of it is the right to access one's own file held by the secret police in the former totalitarian regimes in Europe. The ECtHR has developed a line of jurisprudence[6] to ensure that the victims of these regimes enjoy the right of accessing their own file usually held by specialised state archive services. The right of access is undoubtedly one of the main instruments that individuals have against any system or product meant to surreptitiously collect personal information about them, regardless of whether its source is a public power or a private entity.

Finally, it is notable that the right of access is a component of the fundamental right to personal data protection as enshrined in Article 8 CFR. It is specifically provided by Article 8(2) CFR as one of the prerogatives that any person has with regard to processing of their personal data. Considering its fundamental role to ensure transparency

---

[3] Kranenborg 2014, p. 254.

[4] See Art. 42 Charter of Fundamental Rights of the European Union ('CFR'), the right of access to public documents and Regulation 1049/2001. This Regulation only concerns public documents of the EU institutions and bodies. At Member State level there are national legal regimes that apply to access to public documents or access to public information, a field which is not harmonized at EU level and which depends on the constitutional traditions of each Member State.

[5] See Case C-28/08 P, *Bavarian Lager*; Case T-115/13, *Dennekamp*. See also Docksey 2016 and Kranenborg 2008.

[6] See e.g. ECtHR, *Haralambie*; ECtHR, *Szulc v Poland*; ECtHR, *Jarnea v Romania*; ECtHR, *Tudor v Romania*.

and facilitate control, its specific inclusion in the Charter, and its historical significance, it could be argued that the right to access one's own personal data is part of the essence[7] of the right to the protection of personal data, and any measure tempering with the existence of the right of access in general may in fact touch the essence of the fundamental right to the protection of personal data. In this respect Article 23 GDPR allows for restrictions of the right of access so long as such a restriction respects the essence of the right, illustrating the difference between a restriction of the scope of the right and a measure that endangers the existence itself of the right.

B. Legal Background

1. EU legislation

The DPD provided for a right of access under Article 12(a), which required Member States to guarantee that data subjects 'have the right to obtain from the controller' three types of information: (i) confirmation that personal data are being processed and details about the processing, including what are its purposes, the categories of data concerned and the recipients and categories of recipients of data; (ii) communication in an intelligible form of the personal data undergoing processing; and (iii) knowledge of the logic involved in any automated processing concerning the data subject, 'at least' where it lead to a decision which produced legal effects or significantly affected the data subject.

No other details were prescribed by the DPD with regard to the modalities of exercising this right, the form under which personal data should be communicated, any authentication requirements for the requester of the personal data or time frames to reply to requests. It is no surprise that a comparative analysis of ten national laws[8] that transposed the DPD found that 'substantial differences at national level exist as to how access rights can be exercised'.[9] For example, in some countries data subjects could only submit their requests in writing,[10] while other countries allowed for more informal ways of exercising the right of access.[11] There were also differences with regard to time limits for replying to requests, ranging from 15 days in Italy to 56 days in Austria.[12] Despite these disparities, the Commission's first report on the implementation of the DPD in 2003 did not find any problems with its disparate implementation.[13] This conclusion fundamentally changed over the following years. In 2010, the Commission's Communication on the overhaul of the data protection legislation in the EU contained a specific call to strengthen the individual rights of data subjects, including transparency rights, given that 'the way in which these rights can be exercised is not harmonised, and therefore exercising them is actually easier in some Member States than in others'.[14]

In the law enforcement area Article 14 of the LED requires Member States to provide a similar right of access to that in Article 15 GDPR, save that it does not include a right to know the logic involved in automated processing that results in a decision

---

[7] Art. 52(1) CFR only allows limitations of the exercise of fundamental rights to the extent such limitations respect the 'essence' of the right in question. For background on this concept, see Brkan 2018.

[8] These countries were Austria, Belgium, Germany, Hungary, Italy, Luxembourg, Norway, Slovakia, Spain and the United Kingdom.

[9] Galetta et al. 2014, p. 4.

[10] This is the case in Belgium, Hungary, Slovakia and the United Kingdom.

[11] This is the case in Italy and Austria.   [12] See Table 1 in Galetta et al. 2014, p. 5.

[13] EC Report 2003.   [14] EC Communication 2010, pp. 6 and 7.

adversely affecting the data subject. However, decisions solely based on automated processing which produce an adverse legal effect concerning the data subject are specifically prohibited by Article 11(1) LED, unless such decisions are authorised either by EU law or by the law of the Member State. Nevertheless, the fact that there are no conditions for lawfulness related to disclosing the logic involved in such decisions seems to be misaligned with the principles of transparency and fairness, all the more so in an area where the effects of automated decision-making on persons subject to criminal procedures may be particularly serious.

In fact, Article 15(1) LED allows Member States to restrict 'wholly or partly' the data subject's right of access for several reasons, including to avoid prejudicing the prevention, detection, investigation or prosecution of criminal offences or the execution of criminal penalties and to protect the rights and freedoms of others. A 'partial or complete restriction' of the right of access pursuant to a legislative measure would be lawful only 'to the extent that, and for as long as' it constitutes a 'necessary and proportionate measure in a democratic society with due regard for the fundamental rights and legitimate interests of the natural person concerned', according to Article 15(1) LED.

Given the importance of the right of access for the fundamental right to the protection of personal data as provided for by the Charter, it is unlikely that a complete and perpetual elimination of the right of access through a legislative measure of general application would be found compatible with Article 8(2) Charter, which specifically provides for a right of access to one's own data as part of the fundamental right to the protection of personal data. When implementing restrictions, Member States should take into account that such restrictions are lawful only 'to the extent that' and 'for as long as' providing transparency puts in jeopardy official or legal inquiries, the rights of other persons or any of the reasons enumerated in Article 15(1). In practice, this means that the possibility to request access, including confirmation that personal data are being processed, should be available once the reason that triggers any of the conditions for exceptions in Article 15(1) ceases to exist. Any other solution would raise considerable issues of conformity with Article 8(2) CFR, read together with Article 52(1) CFR.

Regulation 45/2001,[15] applicable to EU institutions and bodies, contained a provision dedicated to the right of access, namely Article 13. The EU institutions and bodies had to provide to the data subject all information required by Article 12 DPD, and in addition 'knowledge of the logic involved in any automated decision process concerning him or her'. Replying to access requests had to be done 'within three months from the receipt of the request and free of charge'. The EDPS interpreted this right in Guidelines addressed to EU institutions as meaning that 'access shall be granted to the fullest extent' and that 'it must not be restricted more broadly than necessary'.[16] Nonetheless, when establishing the scope of the right of access, the EDPS acknowledged that 'the fact that a person's name is mentioned in a document does not necessarily mean that all information in that document should be considered as data *relating to* that person',[17] since this depends on a further analysis. In 2018 Regulation 45/2001 was updated and replaced by the EUDPR, which provides for a right of access under Article 17 that is very similar to the right enshrined in the GDPR and must be read together with it.

---

[15] See Table of Legislation.   [16] EDPS 2014, pp. 11 and 12.   [17] Ibid., p. 12.

2. International instruments

Article 8(b) of Convention 108 provides for the right to obtain 'at reasonable intervals and without excessive delay or expense' both confirmation that personal data were being processed and communication of that data in an 'intelligible form'. Article 9(b) of the Modernised Convention 108 of 2018 maintains and enhances the right of access to include details about the processing. The details that need to be communicated to the data subject specifically refer to the origin of the personal data, the retention period and any other information that the controller is required to provide in the notice to be given to the data subject by virtue of obligations for ensuring 'transparency of processing' under Article 8 thereof.

In contrast to the GDPR, the Convention does not specify from whom the data subject should obtain confirmation that personal data are being processed or from whom the personal data are to be communicated. The Explanatory Report to the Modernised Convention clarifies that 'in most cases, this will be the controller, or the processor on his or her behalf'.[18] This is a departure from the legal regime of the GDPR, which provides unequivocally that the controller is the entity responsible to reply to access requests. The Modernised Convention is prima facie more protective towards data subjects, given that in a complex processing environment it could be easier for data subjects to ask for access to their personal data from the entity closest to them, which may often be the processor. However, as the Explanatory Report highlights, the processor may only reply on behalf of the controller. Under the GDPR it is also conceivable that the controller and the processor could reach an agreement that the processor replies to requests from data subjects in the exercise of their rights, including access, following instructions from the controller.[19]

The OECD Privacy Framework 2013 enshrines an Individual Participation Principle, which remained virtually unchanged during the 2013 revision. It recommends that individuals 'should have' the right to obtain confirmation 'from a data controller, or otherwise' whether the controller holds personal data relating to them and, if this is the case, to have communicated to them the concerned data. The Principle requires that such communication be done within a reasonable time; at a charge, if any, that is not excessive; in a reasonable manner (including taking geographical distance[20] and intervals between the times when requests for access must be met[21] into account); and in a form that is readily intelligible to the persons concerned.

3. National developments

The right of access to personal data was present in the first national legislation regulating data protection in European states. In Germany, Article 4(1) of the first Federal Data Protection Act of 1977 enshrined an incipient right of access, providing that the data subject shall have the right to 'information about one's own personal data that are stored'.[22] The Act enshrined a bundled transparency right, with elements from the present day right to information and right of access. It is notable that this transparency right did not presuppose access to a copy of the personal data.

---

[18] Explanatory Report Convention 108 2018, p. 13.   [19] See Art. 28(3)(e) GDPR.
[20] OECD Guidelines 2013, p. 58.   [21] Ibid.
[22] Original: 'Jeder hat nach Maßgabe dieses Gesetzes ein Recht auf... (1) Auskunft über die zu seiner Person gespeicherten Daten'.

The French Data Protection Act of 1978, on the other hand, already distinguished between a right to know that personal data are being automatically processed, provided by Article 3, and a right of access to personal data, provided by Article 34. The former specifically recognised the right of data subjects 'to know' and 'to challenge ... the logic used by automated processing whose results are opposed to them'. The latter guaranteed the right 'to ask' the organisations that were registered in the public register of data controllers whether they were processing the individual's personal data and, in that case, it also guaranteed the right to obtain 'communication' of the personal data. Article 35 further provided for modalities to implement this right, such as providing the personal data 'in clear language'.

Similarly, section 21 of the UK Data Protection Act 1984 also provided for a right of access to personal data which had two manifestations: first, informing the individual 'whether the data held ... include personal data of which that individual is the data subject' and, secondly, supplying the individual 'with a copy of the information constituting any such personal data held by him'. The right of access was, thus, one of the fundamental components of the first data protection laws in Europe.

The Member States implemented the right of access in very different ways under the DPD.[23] Following the adoption of Article 15 of the GDPR, there is no room for Member States to further implement the right of access. However, variations are allowed with regard to the restrictions that may apply to the right of access, including those situations which would allow controllers to refuse access altogether. These derogations are allowed by Article 23 GDPR dealing with general restrictions to the rights of the data subject; by Article 89 on processing for scientific or historical research, archiving in the public interest or statistical purposes; and by Article 85 concerning processing of personal data and freedom of expression and information.

As a result, the German GDPR Implementation Law provides for significant carve-outs to the right of access, in particular, section 34, which compiles all exceptions previously mentioned throughout the law with regard to specific processing operations, such as scientific research, archiving purposes and overriding legitimate interests of a third party, and adds national security and other objectives of general public interest.

The UK Data Protection Act 2018 provides for even wider carve-outs than the German implementation law, to such an extent that questions may rise about the compatibility of such measures with Article 8(2) CFR. Schedule 2 of the Act details limitations of data subject rights, including the right of access, for purposes relating to taxation, criminal law and legal proceedings, immigration control, public protection, audit, the health service and children's services and many other detailed exceptions.

4. Case law

4.1 Introduction

There is extensive case law on the right of access to one's own personal information, developed both under the DPD and earlier under Article 8 of the European Convention on Human Rights ('ECHR').

---

[23] See Galetta et al. 2016.

4.2 CJEU

The CJEU has issued several judgments under the preliminary ruling procedure that interpret the right of access to one's own personal data as enshrined in the DPD.

The first case, *Rijkeboer*,[24] concerned data retention and a request for access to all instances of disclosure of the data subject's personal data to third parties in the two years preceding the request. The controller provided the information only for one year preceding the request, since older information on data sharing was automatically erased in accordance with a specific legal obligation to only retain details of any communication of data to third parties for one year following that communication. This requirement was part of the transposition of the DPD in the Netherlands. In its judgment the Court established a clear link between the 'meaning' of the right to personal data protection and the right to access—that is, that the data subject has the right to be 'certain that his personal data are processed in a correct and lawful manner, that is to say, in particular, that the basic data regarding him are accurate and that they are disclosed to authorised recipients'.[25] An important distinction that the court took into account was that the personal data related to the data subject, which the court called 'basic data', were stored longer than information related to the communication of that data to third parties.[26] Under these circumstances, the Court found that the:

> rules limiting the storage of information on the recipients or categories of recipients of personal data and on the content of the data disclosed to a period of one year and correspondingly limiting access to that information, while basic data is stored for a much longer period, do not constitute a fair balance of the interest and obligation at issue, unless it can be shown that longer storage of that information would constitute an excessive burden on the controller.[27]

The conclusion of the Court was that the DPD granted a right of access to information 'not only in respect of the present, but also in respect of the past', leaving it to the Member States to establish a fair balance between the competing interests.[28]

Two subsequent cases were concerned with the scope of the data protection rules, related to what information is considered personal data. In *YS*,[29] third-country nationals that unsuccessfully applied for asylum or resident permits to the Netherlands had their requests for access to the minutes of the Dutch Ministry of Immigration concerning their cases partially rejected. They were only given access to a summary of the data contained in the minutes, the origin of those data and the bodies to which the data had been disclosed.[30] The CJEU considered whether the legal analysis on the basis of which the Ministry reached its decision was personal data and also whether the right of access can be complied with only by sharing a summary of the personal data undergoing processing, or whether a copy of the data is in fact required.

The Court relied on a utilitarian argument to answer these two questions. For the first one, it linked the ability of accessing and correcting information with the classification of that information as 'personal data', concluding that the information identifying the applicants and related to the facts of their case contained in the minute is personal

---

[24] Case C-553/07, *Rijkeboer*, para. 23.　　[25] Ibid., para. 49.　　[26] Ibid., para. 42.
[27] Ibid., para. 66.　　[28] Ibid., para. 70.　　[29] Joined Cases C-141/12 and C-372/12, *YS*.
[30] Ibid., para. 20.

data, whereas the legal analysis on the basis of this information was not. The Court argued that:

> extending the right of access of the applicant for a residence permit to that legal analysis would not in fact serve the directive's purpose of guaranteeing the protection of the applicant's right to privacy with regard to the processing of data relating to him, but would serve the purpose of guaranteeing him a right of access to administrative documents, which is not however covered by Directive 95/46.[31]

Following the same type of reasoning to answer the second question, the Court found that there is no right under Article 12(a) DPD and Article 8(2) CFR to a copy of the document containing the personal data, since sometimes a summary of the personal data is sufficient, 'in so far as the objective pursued by that right of access may be fully satisfied by another form of communication' and 'in order to avoid giving the data subject access to information other than the personal data relating to him'.[32]

In *Nowak*,[33] three years later, the CJEU took the opportunity to revisit its rather isolated utilitarian approach in *YS*. the Court found that both the written answers submitted by a candidate to an exam and any comments made by an examiner on those scripts were personal data, in the context of a request to access a copy of those exam scripts and comments under the DPD. Otherwise, the Court held, 'if such information ... were not to be classified as "personal data", that would have the effect of entirely excluding that information from the obligation to comply ... with the rights of access, rectification and objection of the data subject'.[34] However, the Court partly upheld its reasoning in *YS*, stating that candidates have the right to access their exam scripts 'in so far' as those scripts are liable to be checked for accuracy,[35] after explaining that accuracy could also refer to situations such as mixing up exam scripts[36] and in any case does not mean correcting a posteriori answers that are incorrect.[37]

In *X*[38] the Court was asked to interpret what an 'excessive' fee for complying with a request for access means. The Court decided that 'in order to ensure that fees levied when the right to access personal data is exercised are not excessive ... , the level of those fees must not exceed the cost of communicating such data'.[39] The Court left it to the national courts to carry out the necessary verifications on a case-by-case basis.

In the case *V.Q. v Land Hessen*,[40] which was pending when this text was finalised, the CJEU is asked to opine on whether Article 15 GDPR is applicable to the committee of a parliament of a constituent state of a Member State that is responsible for processing the petitions of citizens.

4.3 European Court of Human Rights

The ECtHR has a rich case law regarding the right of access to one's own personal data that goes back to *Leander v Sweden* in 1987. This case concerned a request of access made by a Swedish citizen to see his own file held by the National Police Boards' Security Department (a 'secret police'), on the basis of which his job application for a Naval Museum was rejected. The Court found that there was an interference with the right to respect private life guaranteed by Article 8 ECHR when 'both the storing and the release' of information relating to the applicant's private life, 'coupled with a refusal to allow [the applicant] an opportunity to refute it'[41] take place, though it found that the interference

---

[31] Ibid., para. 46.   [32] Ibid., paras. 58–59.   [33] Case C-434/16, *Nowak*.
[34] Ibid., para. 49   [35] Ibid., para. 56.   [36] Ibid., para. 54.   [37] Ibid., para. 52.
[38] Case C-486/12, *X*.   [39] Ibid., para. 31.
[40] Case C-272/19, *V.Q. v. Land Hessen* (pending).   [41] ECtHR *Leander v Sweden*, para. 48.

was justified under Article 8(2). This was the first case recognising that there is a specific component related to the processing of personal data under the right protected by Article 8 of the Convention.

In 1989, the *Gaskin* case centred around the request of an applicant to access his personal file held by the social services of the Liverpool City Council documenting his case as a child in social care, and who alleged that he was mistreated during his childhood. His request was rejected on the ground that the file contained confidential information provided by different case workers, medical staff and other persons. The ECtHR found a violation of Article 8 ECHR, because inter alia of 'the interest of the individual to have access to his private and family life'.[42]

A specific positive obligation of the state to provide access to one's own file was recognised under Article 8 of the Convention in *K.H. and Others*.[43] This case concerned eight Roma women who asked for access to their medical files, after suspecting they had been secretly sterilised during their stay in hospital. The women complained that they could not take photocopies of the medical records. The ECtHR, taking into account that the exercise of the right to private life 'must be practical and effective', decided that the positive obligations of the state under Article 8 'should extend, in particular in cases like the present one where personal data are concerned, to the making available to the data subject of copies of his or her data files'.[44] Importantly, before reaching the conclusion that there had been a breach of Article 8 in this case, the Court also established that it 'does not consider that data subjects should be obliged to specifically justify a request to be provided with a copy of their personal data files. It is rather for the authorities to show that there are compelling reasons for refusing this facility'.[45]

In *Segerstedt-Wiberg* five Swedish citizens, who all had either political or mass-media background, complained that the Secret Police did not give them full access to their own files. Some of them had obtained partial access. The Court found there was a violation of Article 8 only with respect to the storage of information by the Secret Police regarding four of the applicants, given that they were not linked to 'any actual relevant national security interests'[46] and primarily referred to events that happened decades earlier. However, there was no violation of Article 8 with respect to not granting full access to those files. The Court noted that 'a refusal of full access to a national secret police register is necessary where the State may legitimately fear that the provision of such information may jeopardise the efficacy of a secret surveillance system designed to protect national security and to combat terrorism'.[47]

4.4 National courts

At national level, the England and Wales Court of Appeal had to decide in joined cases of *Ittihadieh* and *Deer*[48] whether a controller could refuse to carry out searches to reply to a request for access on the grounds of proportionality, of the improper purpose of the request (e.g. the request is manifestly made for the purpose of legal proceedings) or of

---

[42] ECtHR, *Gaskin*. Cf. ECtHR, *Odièvre v France* and ECtHR, *Godelli v Italy*.
[43] ECtHR, *K.H. and Others*.   [44] Ibid., para. 47.   [45] Ibid., para. 48.
[46] ECtHR, *Segerstedt-Wiberg*, para. 90.
[47] Ibid., para. 102. Cf. ECtHR, *Haralambie v Romania* and ECtHR, *Jarnea v Romania*, which relate to secret police files from former totalitarian regimes, most of which are now archived by public bodies which do not have any intelligence or law enforcement-related competences.
[48] England and Wales Court of Appeal, *Ittihadieh and Deer*.

specific exceptions. The judge decided that the right of access 'is not subject to any express purpose or motive test. Nor is a data subject required to state any purpose when making a SAR ('subject access request').[49] Additionally, a controller cannot refuse to disclose information on the grounds that it will not tell the individual anything he did not already know.[50] With regard to the proportionality of the search following a request for access, the judge noted that even though neither the DPD nor the law transposing it in the UK contain any express obligation on the data controller to search for personal data in response to such a request, 'such an obligation must necessarily be implied'.[51] Nevertheless, the judge also pointed out that he considers this implied obligation as being limited to a 'reasonable and proportionate search', which means that 'it is not an obligation to leave no stone unturned'.[52]

C. Analysis

The right of access has three components, or layers, in the benefit it grants to data subjects: receiving confirmation of the processing; receiving information (details) about the processing; and receiving access to the personal data themselves, including a copy of the personal data. This section will look at who can exercise the right of access, against whom, and what are the components of the right of access.

It should be noted that the original version of the GDPR published in May 2016 had mistakes in some language versions of Article 15; these have since been corrected.[53]

1. Who can exercise access

The right of access pertains to the 'data subject' and can only be exercised by the data subject. In particular, Article 12(6) GDPR allows controllers that have 'reasonable doubts' about the identity of the 'natural person making the request' to ask for additional information if they consider that it is 'necessary to confirm the identity of the data subject'. Recital 64 further asks the controller to use 'all *reasonable* measures to verify the identity of a data subject who requests access', with special attention to be paid to 'online services and online identifiers'.

Making personal data available to someone else than the data subject pursuant to an access request may amount to a data breach, which is defined also as 'unauthorised disclosure of, or access to, personal data transmitted'.[54] It may also breach confidentiality and the right to respect for private life of the data subject. It is therefore important for controllers to ascertain that the requester is the data subject. However, asking for additional information in order to comply with an access request is only lawful if that information is necessary to identify the data subject (therefore, kept as long as necessary to identify the data subject) and if it meets a reasonableness test. For example, asking for a copy of the passport of a person who requests access to all personal data made available to third parties by a mobile application installed on their phone will likely be unnecessary. Under its accountability obligations, a controller should identify the minimal information needed

---

[49] Ibid., para. 85.   [50] Ibid., para. 90.   [51] Ibid., para. 95.   [52] Ibid., para. 103.
[53] For example, in the German language version of the GDPR, Art. 15(4) contained an incorrect cross-reference to para. 1(b) rather than para. (3).
[54] Art. 4(12) GDPR. See the commentary on Art. 4(12) and the commentary on Art. 33 in this volume.

for authentication of the requester as a data subject in relation to the nature of the processing and include it in the internal procedure on handling access requests.

The GDPR does not regulate representation with regard to access requests, which means that any legal representation is regulated under Member State law (for example, via power of attorney). A third party could, nonetheless, support the data subject in filing a request with the controller.

As for processing the personal data of children, the GDPR is silent with regard to who should submit an access request. The rule that the right of access pertains to the data subject fully applies. Therefore, it should be acceptable that children themselves make valid access requests. This is all the more so when children consent themselves for the processing of their personal data. In fact, recital 58 of the GDPR implies that not only 'information' about processing addressed to a child, but also 'communication' about that processing could be done, and if so, it must be done 'in a clear and plain language that the child can easily understand'. This can be seen as a reference to communication under the right of access. The question remains to what extent and up to what age of the data subjects the holders of parental responsibility can make requests on their behalf. The answer will also depend on the national legal systems of the Member State concerned and how legal responsibility in private law is regulated. For example, the ICO advises that in the UK controllers should 'only allow parents to exercise these rights on behalf of a child if the child authorises them to do so, when the child does not have sufficient understanding to exercise these rights him or herself, or when it is evident that this is in the best interests of the child'.[55]

2. Against whom can the right be exercised

While the right of access pertains to the data subject, the corresponding obligations pertain to the controller of the processing. This means that the controller is legally responsible for compliance with the right of access. In order to comply with its obligations, the controller can contractually agree with processors that the latter provide support for handling access requests, pursuant to Article 28(3)(e). In particular, the mandatory contract between a controller and a processor can include an arrangement for the processor to 'assist the controller by appropriate technical and organisational means' to comply with its obligation to respond to requests for access. In practice this could mean that, for example, the processor is tasked with searching its systems for personal data subject to an access request and making the relevant personal data available to the controller. The processor could also conceivably be tasked with setting up an interface of its systems which would allow the controller to search directly the personal data at issue. Regardless of any contractual arrangement, the controller should always be able to assess any access request on the merits and should also decide with regard to the scope of valid access requests. Any contractual arrangements between the controller and the processor to comply with the right of access will depend on the nature of the processing and on the types of services the processor is providing to the controller.

The controller has an implied positive obligation to act, which corresponds to the right of the data subject 'to obtain confirmation', 'access to the personal data', and details about the processing, since Article 15(1) specifies that such confirmation, access and details are

---

[55] ICO 2018A, p. 41.

to be obtained 'from the controller'. In addition, the controller has a clear positive obligation to act resulting from Article 15(3), which prescribes that 'the controller *shall provide a copy* of the personal data undergoing processing'.

Contrary to the right of information in Articles 13 and 14 GDPR, which presupposes that the controller proactively informs data subjects from the outset about the existence and details of the processing, the right of access presupposes that the data subject must actively exercise the right (submitting a request or otherwise asking for access).

3. Components of the right of access

3.1 *Confirmation of processing*

The first layer of the right of access is obtaining confirmation that personal data are being processed. This means that the controller should include in its reply to a valid request for access a simple confirmation or denial that personal data of the requester are being processed.

3.2 *Details about the processing*

The second layer of the right of access is receiving details about the processing, as prescribed by Article 15(1) GDPR. The list of details to be provided to the data subject overlaps with the type of information that must be included in the data protection notices under Articles 13 and 14 GDPR. These articles envisage information such as, for example, the purpose of the processing; the categories of personal data concerned; the recipients or categories of recipient to whom the personal data have been or will be disclosed; any available information on the source of personal data where they are not collected directly from the data subject; and the right to lodge a complaint with a supervisory authority.[56] In addition, Article 15(2) provides that where the personal data have been transferred to a third country or international organisation that has not been found to offer adequate protection, controllers have to disclose the safeguards on the basis of which the transfer took place from the list provided in Article 46 GDPR[57] (such as binding corporate rules, standard contractual clauses, etc.).

Importantly, as opposed to the information included in notices, the details given to the data subject pursuant to an access request must inevitably be more precise and granular, specifically tailored to the exact pieces of personal data of the person making the request and their processing. Notices, by their nature, are general in the sense that usually they cover processing of personal data of multiple data subjects. They are a priori, meaning that they provide information about what will happen to the personal data being collected directly or obtained from third parties, as opposed to what has happened already to the personal data. On the contrary, an answer to a request for access will need to specifically address the information about the personal data items related to the person making the request, for example individualising the specific recipients or categories of recipients that received that person's data or disclosing the exact retention period or retention policy applied to the specific data of the requester.

When communicating details of the processing to the data subject, one type of information required by Article 15(1)(h) is of particular importance in the current digital environment, namely 'the existence of automated decision-making, including profiling

---

[56] See Art. 15(1)(a)–(h) GDPR.   [57] See the commentary on Art. 46 GDPR in this volume.

referred to in Article 22(1) and (4)' and 'at least in those cases, meaningful information about the logic involved, as well as the significance and the envisaged consequences of such processing for the data subject'. As noted above, the roots of the right to know the logic involved in automated decision-making are old and go back to the first French data protection law in 1978, Article 3 of which provided for a right 'to know' and 'to challenge ... the logic used by automated processing whose results are opposed to them'. In fact, the right of access under the DPD, which was adopted in 1995, also comprised communication of 'knowledge of the logic involved in any automatic processing ... at least in the case of automated decisions' that significantly affect the data subject. This point was important enough to be individualised and mentioned at the third paragraph of Article 12(a), instead of being enumerated under the first paragraph of Article 12(a) together with the other details of the processing that need to be revealed to the data subject making a request. Therefore, the right to know about the logic involved in certain automated decision-making is not a regulatory response to recent developments in the use of algorithms and AI. Legislators in Europe have been mindful of automated processing and the impact of automated decision-making since the beginnings of data protection law.

As for what should be communicated to the data subject in this regard pursuant to Article 15(1)(h) GDPR, first and foremost, the controller should confirm whether the person making the request is subjected to automated decision-making as referred in Article 22(1) and (4) GDPR, meaning automated decision-making based *solely* on automated processing and which produces legal effects concerning the data subject or similarly significantly affecting the data subject, including such decisions based on processing sensitive data.[58] Pursuant to its accountability obligations, the controller should immediately verify at the time when receiving an access request whether it engages in this type of processing. Certain obligations result when this kind of processing is engaged in. For example, a systematic evaluation and extensive evaluation of personal aspects relating to natural persons which is based on automated processing, and on which decisions are based that produce legal effects concerning the person or similarly significantly affect the person, require a Data Protection Impact Assessment ('DPIA').[59] Secondly, if this type of processing exists, the controller must communicate meaningful information about the logic involved.[60] However, the EDPB has explained that the GDPR does not require 'necessarily a complex explanation of the algorithms used or disclosure of the full algorithm'.[61] The EDPB has further advised that the controller should provide the data subject with general information, for example on factors taken into account for the decision-making process, and on their respective 'weight' on an aggregate level.[62] In any case, the information should be sufficiently comprehensive to understand the reasons for the decisions.[63] Moreover, recital 58 of the GDPR mentions that the communication of information to data subjects must be concise, easily accessible and easy to understand, using clear and plain language and, where appropriate, relying on visualisation. Thirdly, the controller should explain the significance and envisaged consequences of this type of processing. For example, if the envisaged consequence is exclusion of the data subject from a benefit or from competing for a job, these consequences should be spelled out.

---

[58] See the commentary on Art. 22 in this volume for an explanation of what this type of automated decision-making entails.
[59] See Art.35 (3)(a) GDPR.
[60] This is described as a 'right to legibility of automated decision-making' in Malgieri and Comande 2017.
[61] WP29 2018, p. 25.   [62] Ibid., p. 27.   [63] Ibid., p. 25.

3.3 Providing access to the data

The third layer of the right of access is providing access to the personal data being processed. While Article 15(1) generally refers to the data subject having the right 'to obtain ... access to personal data', Article 15(3) is more prescriptive and specifically enshrines an obligation of the controller to 'provide a copy of the personal data undergoing processing'. This is one significant difference compared to the former provision for the right of access under the DPD, which did not specifically refer to providing 'a copy' of the data, but referred to 'communication' of the data being processed. By requiring controllers to provide copies, the right of access has been strengthened, since it does not allow anymore a limitation of the scope of this right to only cover a summary of the personal data being processed. According to recital 63, where possible, the controller should be able to provide 'remote access to a secure system which would provide the data subject with direct access to his or her personal data'. It is interesting, in view of the distinction noted above between the rights to subject access and access to public documents, that Article 15(3) does not require the provision of a copy of the document containing the personal data, being limited to the personal data undergoing processing. However, it may well be appropriate, for example where all the information in the document relates to the data subject, simply to provide a copy of that document.

The legislator seems to have differentiated between the access offered on the basis of Article 15(1) and the access offered on the basis of Article 15(3), since a specific exemption to the right of access applies only to the latter. As such, Article 15(4) provides that 'the right to obtain a copy' shall not 'adversely affect the rights and freedoms of others'. For example, as recital 63 provides, direct access to the personal data should not breach trade secrets or intellectual property rights, including 'copyright protecting the software'. The EDBP has also found that, with regard to access requests for video footage, data controllers should implement technical measures (such as the masking or scrambling of images) to avoid other data subjects being identified.[64]

The relationship between Article 15(1) access and Article 15(3) access seems to be one of inclusion, in the sense that offering access to personal data as provided under the first paragraph includes obtaining a copy of the data as provided under the third paragraph. However, Article 15(1) access could additionally cover summaries of personal data being processed, direct access without the possibility of making copies or other types of communication of personal data that do not presuppose making copies available. One important question is whether controllers are under an obligation to always provide a copy of the personal data when they receive a general access request. This is debatable, given the differentiation made by the legislator. In order to make sure a copy is provided, the person making the access request should specifically ask for a copy of personal data. Otherwise, it may be left to the controller to decide under what form access will be granted (albeit under the form of a copy).

How specific, then, should the data subject be when making an access request? If the data subject submits a general request simply asking for access to his or her own personal data under Article 15 GDPR, the controller has to provide all three layers of information—confirmation, details about the processing and communication of the personal data, with regard to all personal data being processed. If the controller processes

---

[64] EDPB 2019, p. 19.

personal data of the requester, it may ask for confirmation from the data subject in a follow-up whether he or she is seeking both information about the processing and communication of the personal data. Pursuant to recital 63, where the controller processes a large quantity of information concerning the data subject, the controller can request that, before the information is delivered, the data subject specify the information or processing activities to which the request relates. However, if the data subject requests access to all his or her personal data being processed and to all the meta-information about the processing (e.g. the purpose, the recipients, the logic involved in automated decision-making etc.), the controller will have to comply with the request.

3.4 Modalities of access

The modalities for the exercise of the right of access are governed by Article 12 GDPR,[65] which establishes a duty for the controller 'to facilitate' the exercise of data subjects' rights, including the right of access. This means that the controller has to provide an accessible way for the data subject to submit requests and to set up internal processes that would facilitate the exercise of the right of access. There are no limitations on the means a data subject can use to ask for access. According to the ICO, a valid request may even be submitted through social media and does not have to include a reference to the right of access or Article 15 GDPR, 'as long as it is clear that the individual is asking for their own personal data'.[66] As for the reply to access requests, according to Article 12(1) GDPR they may be done 'in writing or by other means', including orally. However, only where data subjects specifically request an oral reply may the controller do this, provided that the identity of the data subject is proven by other means. Pursuant to Article 12(3), if the data subject made the request by electronic form means (e.g. through electronic mail), the controller has to provide the information by electronic means where possible, unless otherwise requested by the data subject.

Research has shown that controllers exceed reasonable time limits when replying to access requests, if they reply at all: after five months, from the start to the end of the experiment, only 74 per cent of the investigated online services had responded, whether with a satisfying answer or not, while 26 per cent of them remained completely silent.[67] According to Article 12(1) GDPR, the controller has to provide information on the action taken pursuant to an access request 'without undue delay and in any event within one month of receipt of the request'. The wording 'information on action taken' seems to imply that the controller does not necessarily have to resolve the request within the imposed deadline, but that it must substantially take action towards doing so in order to inform the data subject about the steps taken. For example, in the case of a complex request, the controller may need to inform the data subject that his or her personal data are being searched in specific systems or jurisdictions, an operation which requires more time. Even if it is accepted that the time limit only applies to communication of intermediate steps towards solving the request, any excessive and unjustified delay of the final answer is likely to amount to non-compliance with Article 15, in the light of Article 8(2) CFR. The one-month period may be extended by two further months, if necessary, but the controller has to inform the data subject of this delay within the first month that has passed from the receipt of the request, together with the reasons for the delay.

[65] See the commentary on Art. 12 GDPR in this volume.   [66] ICO Website 2018.
[67] Ausloos and Dewitte 2018.

Brkan 2018: Brkan, 'The Concept of Essence of Fundamental Rights in the EU Legal Order: Peeling the Onion to Its Core', 14(2) *European Constitutional Law Review* (2018), 332.

Docksey 2016: Docksey, 'Four Fundamental Rights: Finding the Balance', 6(3) *IDPL* (2016), 195.

Galetta et al. 2014: Galetta, de Hert, L'Hoiry and Norris, 'Mapping the Legal and Administrative Frameworks of Access Rights in Europe: A Cross-European Comparative Analysis', Work Package 5 for the IRISS Project (2014), available at http://irissproject.eu/wp-content/uploads/2014/06/IRISS-WP5-Summary-Meta-Analyses-for-Press-Release.pdf.

Galetta et al. 2016: Galetta, Fonio and Ceresa, 'Nothing Is as it Seems. The Exercise of Access Rights in Italy and Belgium: Dispelling Fallacies in the Legal Reasoning from the "Law in Theory" to the "Law in Practice"', 6(1) *IDPL* (2016), 16.

Kranenborg 2008: Kranenborg, 'Access to Documents and Data Protection in the European Union: On the Public Nature of Personal Data', 45(4) *Common Market Law Review* (2008), 1079.

Kranenborg 2014: Kranenborg, 'Article 8', in Peers, Hervey, Kenner and Ward (eds.), *The EU Charter of Fundamental Rights: A Commentary* (Hart Publishing 2014), 222.

Malgieri and Comande 2017: Malgieri and Comande, 'Why a Right to Legibility of Automated Decision-Making Exists in the General Data Protection Regulation', 7(4) *IDPL* (2017), 243.

Papers of data protection authorities

EDPB 2019: European Data Protection Board, 'Guidelines 3/2019 on the processing of personal data through video devices (version for public consultation)' (10 July 2019).

EDPS 2014: European Data Protection Supervisor, 'Guidelines on the Rights of Individuals with Regard to Processing of Personal Data' (25 February 2014).

WP29 2018: Article 29 Working Party, 'Guidelines on Automated Individual Decision-Making and Profiling for the Purposes of Regulation 2016/679' (WP 251 rev.01, as last revised and adopted 6 February 2018).

DPC 2018: Data Protection Commissioner, 'Final Report 1 January–24 May 2018' (2018).

ICO 2018A: Information Commissioner's Office, 'Children and the GDPR' (22 March 2018).

ICO 2018B: Information Commissioner's Office, 'Annual Report and Financial Statements 2017–18' (19 July 2018).

Reports and recommendations

EC Communication 2010: Communication from the Commission to the European Parliament, the Council, the Economic and Social Committee and the Committee of the Regions: A comprehensive approach on personal data protection in the European Union, COM(2010) 609 final, 4 November 2010.

EC Report 2003: Report from the Commission: First report on the implementation of the Data Protection Directive (95/46/EC), COM(2003) 265 final, 15 May 2003.

Explanatory Report Convention 108 2018: Council of Europe, 'Explanatory Report to the Protocol Amending the Convention for the Protection of Individuals with Regard to the Automatic Processing of Personal Data' (10 October 2018), available at https://rm.coe.int/cets-223-explanatory-report-to-the-protocol-amending-the-convention-fo/16808ac91a.

Others

ICO Website 2018: Information Commissioner's Office, 'Right of Access', available at https://ico.org.uk/for-organisations/guide-to-data-protection/guide-to-the-general-data-protection-regulation-gdpr/individual-rights/right-of-access/.

Section 3 Rectification and erasure

Article 16. Right to rectification

CÉCILE DE TERWANGNE

The data subject shall have the right to obtain from the controller without undue delay the rectification of inaccurate personal data concerning him or her. Taking into account the purposes of the processing, the data subject shall have the right to have incomplete personal data completed, including by means of providing a supplementary statement.

Relevant Recitals

(39) Any processing of personal data should be lawful and fair. It should be transparent to natural persons that personal data concerning them are collected, used, consulted or otherwise processed and to what extent the personal data are or will be processed. The principle of transparency requires that any information and communication relating to the processing of those personal data be easily accessible and easy to understand, and that clear and plain language be used. That principle concerns, in particular, information to the data subjects on the identity of the controller and the purposes of the processing and further information to ensure fair and transparent processing in respect of the natural persons concerned and their right to obtain confirmation and communication of personal data concerning them which are being processed. Natural persons should be made aware of risks, rules, safeguards and rights in relation to the processing of personal data and how to exercise their rights in relation to such processing. In particular, the specific purposes for which personal data are processed should be explicit and legitimate and determined at the time of the collection of the personal data. The personal data should be adequate, relevant and limited to what is necessary for the purposes for which they are processed. This requires, in particular, ensuring that the period for which the personal data are stored is limited to a strict minimum. Personal data should be processed only if the purpose of the processing could not reasonably be fulfilled by other means. In order to ensure that the personal data are not kept longer than necessary, time limits should be established by the controller for erasure or for a periodic review. Every reasonable step should be taken to ensure that personal data which are inaccurate are rectified or deleted. Personal data should be processed in a manner that ensures appropriate security and confidentiality of the personal data, including for preventing unauthorised access to or use of personal data and the equipment used for the processing.

(65) A data subject should have the right to have personal data concerning him or her rectified and a 'right to be forgotten' where the retention of such data infringes this Regulation or Union or Member State law to which the controller is subject. In particular, a data subject should have the right to have his or her personal data erased and no longer processed where the personal data are no longer necessary in relation to the purposes for which they are collected or otherwise processed, where a data subject has withdrawn his or her consent or objects to the processing of personal data concerning him or her, or where the processing of his or her personal data does not otherwise comply with this Regulation. That right is relevant in particular where the data subject has given his or her consent as a child and is not fully aware of the risks involved by the processing, and later wants to remove such personal data, especially on the internet. The data subject should be able to exercise that right notwithstanding the fact that he or she is no longer a child. However, the further retention of the personal data should

be lawful where it is necessary, for exercising the right of freedom of expression and information, for compliance with a legal obligation, for the performance of a task carried out in the public interest or in the exercise of official authority vested in the controller, on the grounds of public interest in the area of public health, for archiving purposes in the public interest, scientific or historical research purposes or statistical purposes, or for the establishment, exercise or defence of legal claims.

Closely Related Provisions

Article 5(d) (Principles relating to processing of personal data—accuracy) (see too recital 39); Article 12 (Transparent information, communication and modalities for the exercise of the rights of the data subject) (see too recital 59); Article 19 (Notification obligation regarding rectification or erasure of personal data or restriction of processing); Article 23 (Restrictions) (see too recital 73); Article 89 (Safeguards and derogations relating to processing for archiving purposes in the public interest, scientific or historical research purposes or statistical purposes) (see too recital 156)

Related Provisions in LED [Directive (EU) 2016/680]

Article 4(1)(d) (Principles relating to processing of personal data) (see too recital 30); Article 13(1)(e) (Information to be made available or given to the data subject) (see too recital 40); Article 16(1) and (4)–(6) (Right to rectification or erasure of personal data and restriction of processing) (see too recital 47); Article 17 (Exercise of rights by the data subject and verification by the supervisory authority) (see too recitals 48–49)

Related Provisions in EUDPR [Regulation (EU) 2018/1725]

Article 18 (right to rectification) (see too recital 34)

Relevant Case Law

CJEU

Case C-553/07, *College van burgemeester en wethouders van Rotterdam v M. E. E. Rijkeboer*, judgment of 7 May 2009 (ECLI:EU:C:2009:293).
Case C-362/14, *Maximilian Schrems v Data Protection Commissioner*, judgment of 6 October 2015 (Grand Chamber) (ECLI:EU:C:2015:650)
Case C-434/16, *Peter Nowak v Data Protection Commissioner*, judgment of 20 December 2017 (ECLI:EU:C:2017:994).

ECtHR

Leander v Sweden, Appl. No. 9248/81, judgment of 26 March 1987.
Rotaru v Romania, Appl. No. 28341/95, judgment of 4 May 2000.
Cemalettin Canli v Turkey, Appl. No. 22427/04, judgment of 18 November 2008.
Dalea v France, Appl. No. 964/07, judgment of 2 February 2010.
Ciubotaru v Moldova, Appl. No. 27138/04, judgment of 27 July 2010.

de Terwangne

A. Rationale and Policy Underpinnings

Article 16 GDPR is the expression of the data subjects' power of control of (the quality of) their data. The right to rectification is intrinsically linked to the right of access; once data subjects have accessed their personal information and discovered that it is inaccurate or incomplete with regard to the purpose of the processing, they have the correlated right to have the data rectified or completed.[1] This right to rectification echoes, in terms of data subjects' rights, the principle of accuracy under Article 5(1)(d) GDPR, that requires the controller to take every reasonable step 'to ensure that personal data that are inaccurate, having regard to the purposes for which they are processed, are erased or rectified without delay'. This right has a very interesting second component, in Article 19, namely the obligation to forward justified rectifications or complements to previous recipients of the data.[2] The importance of this right to have the rectifications forwarded is shown by the fact that it allows the data subject to stop or at least limit the spreading of erroneous or false information.

B. Legal Background

1. EU legislation

Article 12(b) DPD listed three distinct rights that are laid down in three different articles in the GDPR (Articles 16–18). The right to rectification is one of these rights. Article 12(b) DPD provides that 'Member States shall guarantee every data subject the right to obtain from the controller as appropriate the rectification, erasure or blocking of data the processing of which does not comply with the provisions of this Directive, in particular because of the incomplete or inaccurate nature of the data'.

Article 12(c) DPD added a duty to inform recipients downstream about the rectifications or other actions done with the data. It states that every data subject has the right to obtain from the controller 'notification to third parties to whom the data have been disclosed of any rectification, erasure or blocking carried out in compliance with (b), unless this proves impossible or involves a disproportionate effort'. This duty to inform is maintained in the GDPR, but in a separate article (Article 19) dedicated to the notification obligation linked to the exercise of the three rights: rectification, erasure and blocking.

Article 14 of Regulation 45/2001,[3] applicable to the EU institutions and bodies, laid down the right to rectification. The data subject had the right to obtain from the controller the 'rectification without delay of inaccurate or incomplete personal data'. In 2018 Regulation 45/2001 was updated and replaced by the EUDPR, Article 18 of which provides for the right to rectification. Article 18 is formulated in identical terms to the right to rectification under Article 16 GDPR.

Article 16(1) LED also provides for a right to rectification in parallel to and in the same terms as the GDPR. Recital 47 LED explains that the rectification of inaccurate data should in particular be carried out where these data relate to facts, and that 'the right to rectification should not affect, for example, the content of a witness testimony'. In effect,

---

[1] See Case C-553/07, *Rijkeboer*, para. 51.   [2] See the commentary on Art. 19 in this volume.
[3] See Table of Legislation.

opinions cannot be considered as accurate or not, whereas the facts on which they are based can be regarded as true, false or incomplete, and can be rectified where appropriate.

Where inaccurate personal data have been rectified, the LED requires the controller to communicate the rectification to the competent authority from which the inaccurate personal data originate[4] and to the recipients of this data.[5]

2. International instruments

The right to have one's data rectified was one of the first rights granted to data subjects in the international instruments related to data protection. Article 8(c) of Convention 108 provides that any person should be enabled to obtain, as the case may be, rectification of personal data relating to him or her if these data have been processed contrary to the basic data protection principles. The Explanatory Report of the Convention specifies that this means rectification of 'erroneous or inappropriate information'.[6]

Article 9(e) of the modernised text of the Convention maintains a similar formulation to the original, although it contains some new elements. Obtaining the rectification of data, if justified, is now expressed as a right instead of as a safeguard (although the Explanatory Report of the original text specified that in domestic legislation implementing the provisions of the Convention, the content of Article 8 should clearly correspond to subjective rights). The modernised text also contains concrete details on the exercise of this right: rectification must be provided on request, free of charge and without excessive delay. In line with the original Explanatory Report (paragraph 54), the Explanatory Report of the Modernised Convention (paragraph 81) provides that 'justified rectifications should, where possible, be brought to the attention of the recipients of the original information, unless this proves to be impossible or involves disproportionate efforts'.[7]

3. National developments

As early as 1978, the French Data Protection Act,[8] in addition to the right of access under Article 34, provided in Article 36 that the person who has the right of access to their own personal data 'can request that the data are rectified, completed, clarified, updated or erased', if they are incomplete, expired or if their collection, use, retention or dissemination are forbidden.

4. Case law

The ECtHR has ruled in several cases that the storage of private information and its release, coupled with a refusal to allow the data subject an opportunity to refute it, amounts to an interference with the right to respect for private life.[9] In the *Ciubotaru* case, the Court held that there is a positive obligation for a State Party to the ECHR to allow natural persons to provide objective evidence in view of having personal data relating to them (*in casu* their official ethnicity) changed.[10] 'For the Court, the State's failure consists in the inability for the applicant to have examined his claim to belong to a certain

---

[4] Art. 16(5) LED.   [5] Ibid., Art. 16(6). See the commentary on Art. 19 in this volume.
[6] Explanatory Report Convention 108 1981.   [7] Explanatory Report Convention 108 2018.
[8] French Data Protection Act 1978.
[9] ECtHR, *Leander v Sweden*, para. 48; ECtHR, *Rotaru v* Romania, para. 46.
[10] ECtHR, *Ciubotaru v Moldova*, paras. 58–59.

ethnic group in the light of the objectively verifiable evidence adduced in support of that claim'.[11] The Court has indicated in the *Cemalettin Canli* case[12] that not only the keeping of false, inaccurate information but also the communication of incomplete information (such as the omission of a mention of the applicant's acquittal) amount to interferences with the right to respect for private life.

The CJEU has consistently emphasised the significance of the right to rectification. In *Schrems*, the CJEU considered the validity of the Safe Harbor decision authorising transfers of personal data to the United States. Interestingly, it made an explicit link between data protection rights, including the right to rectification, and the fundamental right to effective legal protection enshrined in Article 47 of the Charter. According to the Court, the essence of the fundamental right to effective judicial protection is not respected if an individual does not have the possibility to 'pursue legal remedies in order to have access to personal data relating to him, or to obtain the rectification or erasure of such data'.[13]

In *Nowak*, the CJEU considered a request for access under the DPD to the written answers submitted by a candidate to an exam and any comments made by an examiner on those scripts, with a view inter alia to possible rectification of this material. The Court found that such information was 'personal data', and that finding otherwise, in reasoning comparable to that in *Schrems*, 'would have the effect of entirely excluding that information from the obligation to comply ... with the rights of access, rectification and objection of the data subject'.[14] The Court found that candidates had the right to access their exam scripts 'in so far' as those scripts are liable to be checked for accuracy,[15] after explaining that accuracy could refer to situations such as mixing up exam scripts[16] but does not mean correcting a posteriori answers that are incorrect.[17]

C. Analysis

The right to rectification is a key element of the fundamental right to data protection, one of the elements specifically enshrined in Article 8(2) of the Charter. Its significance has been emphasised in the case law of the CJEU and that of the ECtHR relating to the fundamental right of privacy, as noted above.

Article 16 GDPR affirms and specifies the right to rectify inaccurate personal data, requiring the controller to implement a request for rectification 'without undue delay'.

In addition to the rectification of false or inaccurate data, Article 16 also gives data subjects the right to have incomplete personal data completed. This notion of incompleteness must be assessed with regard to the purposes of the processing. Certain data could be considered as complete in one context of processing, while the same data could be seen as incomplete in another. The right to rectification may then become a right to add missing elements instead of to correct existing data. In this respect, Article 16 specifies that completing the data can be done by providing a supplementary statement (such as the mention of the data subject's acquittal and of the discontinuation of the criminal proceedings, as in the *Cemalettin Canli* case).[18]

It should be noted that Article 12(2) requires controllers to facilitate the exercise of the data subject's rights. Recital 59 explains that modalities should be provided to this

---

[11] Ibid., para. 59.   [12] ECtHR, *Cemalettin Canli*, paras. 41–42.
[13] Case C-362/14, *Schrems*, para. 95   [14] Case C-434/16, *Nowak*, para. 49
[15] Ibid., para. 56.   [16] Ibid., para. 54.   [17] Ibid., para. 52.   [18] Ibid.

effect. The modalities should include mechanisms to request and, if applicable, obtain, free of charge, rectification of personal data. The controller should also provide means for requests to be made electronically. Finally, recital 59 states that the controller should be obliged to respond to requests from the data subject without undue delay and at the latest within one month and to give reasons where the controller does not intend to comply with any such requests. It should be noted however that these requirements are set forth in a recital, not in the text itself.

The obligation for the controller to notify the rectifications carried out to all the recipients of the data concerned (see the discussion of Article 19) should also be born in mind. As stated above, this obligation to forward justified rectifications or complements to previous recipients of the data is valuable, as it avoids multiple separate requests for rectification from the data subject while allowing to stop or at least limit the spreading of erroneous or false information.

Select Bibliography

National legislation

French Data Protection Act 1978: Act No. 78-17 of 6 January 1978 on Data Processing, Files and Individual Liberties (Loi n° 78-17 du 6 janvier 1978 relative à l'informatique, aux fichiers et aux libertés), as last amended by Law No. 2014-334 of 17 March 2014.

Reports and recommendations

Explanatory Report Convention 108 1981: Council of Europe, 'Explanatory Report to the Convention for the Protection of Individuals with regard to Automatic Processing of Personal Data' (28 January 1981), available at https://rm.coe.int/16800ca434.

Explanatory Report Convention 108 2018: Council of Europe, 'Explanatory Report to the Protocol Amending the Convention for the Protection of Individuals with Regard to the Automatic Processing of Personal Data' (10 October 2018), available at https://rm.coe.int/cets-223-explanatory-report-to-the-protocol-amending-the-convention-fo/16808ac91a.

Article 17. Right to erasure ('right to be forgotten')

HERKE KRANENBORG*

1. The data subject shall have the right to obtain from the controller the erasure of personal data concerning him or her without undue delay and the controller shall have the obligation to erase personal data without undue delay where one of the following grounds applies:
   (a) the personal data are no longer necessary in relation to the purpose for which they were collected or otherwise processed;
   (b) the data subject withdraws consent on which the processing is based according to point (a) of Article 6(1), or point (a) of Article 9(2), and where there is no other legal ground for the processing;
   (c) the data subject objects to the processing pursuant to Article 21(1) and there are no overriding legitimate grounds for the processing, or the data subject objects to the processing pursuant to Article 21(2);
   (d) the personal data have been unlawfully processed;
   (e) the personal data have to be erased for compliance with a legal obligation in Union or Member State law to which the controller is subject;
   (f) the personal data have been collected in relation to the offer of information society services referred to in Article 8(1).
2. Where the controller has made the personal data public and is obliged pursuant to paragraph 1 to erase the personal data, the controller, taking account of the available technology and the cost of implementation, shall take reasonable steps, including technical measures, to inform controllers which are processing the personal data that the data subject has requested the erasure by such controllers of any links to, or copy or replication of, those personal data.
3. Paragraphs 1 and 2 shall not apply to the extent that processing is necessary:
   (a) for exercising the right of freedom of expression and information;
   (b) for compliance with a legal obligation which requires processing by Union or Member State law to which the controller is subject or for the performance of a task carried out in the public interest or in the exercise of official authority vested in the controller;
   (c) for reasons of public interest in the area of public health in accordance with points (h) and (i) of Article 9(2) as well as Article 9(3);
   (d) for archiving purposes in the public interest, scientific or historical research purposes or statistical purposes in accordance with Article 89(1) in so far as the right referred to in paragraph 1 is likely to render impossible or seriously impair the achievement of the objectives of that processing; or
   (e) for the establishment, exercise or defence of legal claims.

Relevant Recitals

(65) A data subject should have the right to have personal data concerning him or her rectified and a 'right to be forgotten' where the retention of such data infringes this Regulation or Union or

---

* The views expressed are solely those of the author and do not necessarily reflect those of the European Commission.

Member State law to which the controller is subject. In particular, a data subject should have the right to have his or her personal data erased and no longer processed where the personal data are no longer necessary in relation to the purposes for which they are collected or otherwise processed, where a data subject has withdrawn his or her consent or objects to the processing of personal data concerning him or her, or where the processing of his or her personal data does not otherwise comply with this Regulation. That right is relevant in particular where the data subject has given his or her consent as a child and is not fully aware of the risks involved by the processing, and later wants to remove such personal data, especially on the internet. The data subject should be able to exercise that right notwithstanding the fact that he or she is no longer a child. However, the further retention of the personal data should be lawful where it is necessary, for exercising the right of freedom of expression and information, for compliance with a legal obligation, for the performance of a task carried out in the public interest or in the exercise of official authority vested in the controller, on the grounds of public interest in the area of public health, for archiving purposes in the public interest, scientific or historical research purposes or statistical purposes, or for the establishment, exercise or defence of legal claims.

(66) To strengthen the right to be forgotten in the online environment, the right to erasure should also be extended in such a way that a controller who has made the personal data public should be obliged to inform the controllers which are processing such personal data to erase any links to, or copies or replications of those personal data. In doing so, that controller should take reasonable steps, taking into account available technology and the means available to the controller, including technical measures, to inform the controllers which are processing the personal data of the data subject's request.

Closely Related Provisions

Article 5 (Principles relating to processing of personal data); Article 19 (Notification obligation regarding rectification or erasure of personal data or restriction of processing); Article 21 (Right to object) (see also recitals 69–70)

Related Provisions in LED [Directive (EU) 2016/680]

Article 16 (Right to rectification or erasure of personal data and restriction of processing) (see also recitals 47–49)

Related Provisions in EPD [Directive 2002/58/EC]

Article 6(1) (Traffic data)

Relevant Case Law

CJEU

Case C-131/12, *Google Spain SL v Agencia Española de Protección de Datos (AEPD) and Mario Costeja González*, judgment of 13 May 2014 (Grand Chamber)(ECLI:EU:C:2014:317).

Opinion of Advocate General Jääskinen in Case C-131/12, *Google Spain SL v Agencia Española de Protección de Datos (AEPD) and Mario Costeja González*, delivered on 25 June 2013 (ECLI:EU:C:2013:424).

Case C-398/15, *Camera di Commercio, Industria, Artigianato e Agricoltura di Lecce v Salvatore Manni*, judgment of 9 March 2017 (ECLI:EU:C:2017:197).

Kranenborg

Case C-136/17, *G.C., A.F., B.H., E.D. v Commission nationale de l'informatique et des libertés (CNIL)* (pending).
Opinion of Advocate General Szpunar in Case C-136/17, *G.C., A.F., B.H., E.D. v Commission nationale de l'informatique et des libertés (CNIL)*, delivered on 10 January 2019 (ECLI:EU:C:2019:14).
C-507/17, *Google Inc. v Commission nationale de l'informatique et des libertés (CNIL)* (pending).
Opinion of Advocate General Szpunar in Case C-507/17, *Google Inc. v Commission nationale de l'informatique et des libertés (CNIL)*, delivered on 10 January 2019 (ECLI:EU:C:2019:15).

ECtHR

Węgrzynowski and Smolczewski v Poland, Appl. No. 33846/07, judgment of 16 July 2013.
Delfi AS v Estonia, Appl. No. 64569/09, judgment of 16 June 2015.
M.L. and W.W. v Germany, Appl. Nos. 60798/10 and 65599/10, judgment of 28 June 2018.

A. Rationale and Policy Underpinnings

The right to be forgotten in Article 17 has been perceived as one of the novelties of the GDPR and as an illustration of the modernisation of the European data protection rules. A closer look shows, however, that the right to be forgotten is in fact more of a detailed elaboration of the already existing right of erasure. This is also illustrated by the actual title of Article 17 'the right to erasure' which is followed by a reference to the right to be forgotten between brackets.

That being said, compared to the previous rules, the right to erasure or to be forgotten is given more prominence in the GDPR. This recognises its increased importance in today's society, in which personal data is generated, made public and shared on a massive scale, as an instrument for the data subject to retain a certain control over personal data.

If personal data are being processed in breach of the provisions of the GDPR, the data subject can require the controller to erase the data. The controller must take reasonable steps to inform other controllers with whom the data were shared. As follows from Article 17, the right, as well as the obligation on the controller, is not absolute. There are several reasons which justify a limitation of the right of erasure, such as the reconciliation with the freedom of expression or the establishment, exercise or defence of legal claims.

B. Legal Background

1. EU legislation

The right to erasure was also contained in the DPD in the provision on the right of access, Article 12.[1] The provision granted data subjects the right to obtain from the controller, as appropriate, the rectification, erasure and blocking of data the processing of which did not comply with the provisions of the DPD (see Article 12(b) thereof). Data subjects also had the right to obtain from the controller notification to third parties to whom the data were disclosed of any rectification erasure or blocking carried out in compliance with Article 12(b), unless it proved impossible or involved disproportionate effort (see Article 12(c) of the DPD). Thus Article 12 of the DPD already contained the basic components of what is referred to in Article 17 GDPR as the right to be forgotten.

---

[1] See on the roots of the right to be forgotten Bartolini and Siry 2016.

2. International instruments

The right to erasure can be found in Article 8(c) of the current version of Convention 108, which refers to the right 'to obtain, as the case may be, rectification or erasure of such data if these have been processed contrary to the provisions of domestic law giving effect to the basic principles set out in Articles 5 and 6 of this Convention'. In the modernised version of the Convention, this has been revised in Article 9(e) to refer to the right 'to obtain, on request, free of charge and without excessive delay, rectification or erasure, as the case may be, of such data if these are being, or have been, processed contrary to the provisions of this Convention'. Neither version of the Convention contains an additional reference to the right to be forgotten as in Article 17 GDPR.

3. National developments

The right to erasure does not apply if, amongst other things, the processing is necessary for exercising the right to freedom of expression and information. The scope of this exception depends on Member State law. This follows from Article 85 GDPR which requires Member States by law to reconcile the right to the protection of personal data pursuant to the GDPR with the right to freedom of expression and information, including processing for journalistic purposes and the purpose of academic, artistic and literary expression.

4. Case law

The leading ruling of the CJEU on the right to be forgotten is the *Google Spain* case in which a Spanish citizen asked Google Spain to remove a link to two publications in a Spanish newspaper from the list of results when searching on his name. The publications, upon order of a Spanish Ministry, announced a real-estate auction connected with proceedings for the recovery of social security debts, mentioning the name of the person. This judgment was based on the provisions of the DPD and will be further discussed below.[2] The right to erasure was also considered by the CJEU in the *Manni* case, which concluded that this right did not require a Member State to remove certain personal data from a public companies register, or at least to end the general public nature of such information after a certain period of time. In the accompanying press release, the CJEU presented the decision as considering that 'there is no right to be forgotten in respect of personal data in the companies register'.[3] Nevertheless, the CJEU did not exclude the possibility that in specific situations, overriding and legitimate reasons relating to the specific case of the person concerned could justify, exceptionally, that access to personal data concerning him should be limited.[4]

The closest the ECtHR has come to discussing a 'right to be forgotten' was in *Węgrzynowski and Smolczewski v Poland*. The question was whether a press article concerning the applicant had to be removed from the archives of a newspaper's website, after it was established in Court that the publication of the article as such had infringed the rights of the applicant. The ECtHR had to reconcile the freedom of expression, in

---

[2] At the time this commentary was finalised, several questions were put to the CJEU by the French *Conseil d'État* asking for a clarification of the right to be forgotten with regard to the responsibility of search engines in case of processing of special categories of data (reference registered under Case C-136/17), and with regard to the territorial scope of the right. See Case C-136/17, *G.C., A.F., B.H., E.D.*; and Case C-507/17, *Google Inc.* See further the Opinion of Advocate General Szpunar in both cases.

[3] EC Press Release Manni, p 1.   [4] Case C-398/15, *Manni*, para. 60.

particular freedom of the press, with the right to privacy of the applicant. Building on its well-established case law on conflicts between Article 8 and 10 European Convention on Human Rights ('ECHR'), the ECtHR considered that an adequate remedy to protect the rights of the applicant would be to add a comment to the article on the website informing the public of the outcome of the court proceedings. Deleting the whole article from the archive could amount to rewriting history and would be contrary to the legitimate interest of the public in access to the public internet archives of the press which is protected under Article 10 ECHR.[5]

C. Analysis

1. Introduction

The right to be forgotten has triggered a significant debate. This is illustrated by the great number of academic, journalistic and (other) internet publications. A big driver behind the production of all these publications was the CJEU ruling in *Google Spain*. The case constituted a perfect example of the challenges surrounding the right to erasure in modern society. It revealed the tension between freedom of expression and the personal rights of individuals and the particular impact of the internet on the dissemination of information, and it raised questions about the role and responsibilities of a search engine like Google.

Strictly speaking, however, the *Google Spain* ruling did not deal with the right to be forgotten. It concerned the possibility of finding a public document by searching the internet for the individual's name. In the *Google Spain* case, the outcome was that the document should no longer show up in the list of results produced by the search engine when searching on the applicant's name. However, the document itself—an article published in a Spanish newspaper—remained publicly accessible. Still, the impossibility of finding the document by searching against the data subject's name clearly reduces the 'public impact' of the publication on the data subject. The information about the person is not really 'forgotten', but removed from the 'active memory' of the internet.

Whether the right to be forgotten could also relate to the removal of the information from the internet as such, is not addressed in the *Google Spain* case. The CJEU did not deal with this question as it made a clear distinction between the responsibilities of Google as the search engine on the one hand, and the responsibilities of the publisher of a website on the other hand. Since the questions put before it only related to Google, the CJEU did not go into the responsibility of the publisher of the website. The Court only stated that the search engine might be obliged to remove the results from the list, even when the publication of the information to which a result refers in itself was lawful.[6]

The ruling of the ECtHR in the *Węgrzynowski and Smolczewski v Poland* steps into this lacuna.[7] It follows from that ruling that when the freedom of the press is at stake, it is not easy to invoke the right to be forgotten. The ECtHR concluded that even if it was found that a publication about a person was incorrect or unlawful, the publication should still remain available, in light of the fact that a correct balance with the interests of the person

---

[5] See ECtHR, *Węgrzynowski and Smolczewski v Poland*, paras. 65 and 66.
[6] Case C-131/12, *Google Spain*, para. 88. See on the liability of a news website for comments on its articles posted by third persons, ECtHR, *Delfi AS v Estonia*, para. 140 and further.
[7] On the right to be forgotten and the ECHR, see Wechsler 2015.

concerned was found by adding a comment to the article on the website informing the public of the outcome of the court proceedings. The ECtHR thus took into account the risk that deleting the article from the public domain could amount to rewriting history.[8]

2. Freedom of expression

The main challenge regarding the right to be forgotten is thus its relationship with freedom of expression. In *Węgrzynowski and Smolczewski v Poland*, the ECtHR applied its well-established case law on the conflict between Article 8 and 10 ECHR. In the *Google Spain* case the CJEU did not expend many words on the freedom of expression as such.[9] When it put all interests at stake in the balance, the CJEU referred to the economic interest of Google, the legitimate interests of internet users potentially interested in having access to the information, and the interests of the data subject.[10] The interest of the newspaper itself in the wider accessibility of its website was not taken into account.[11] The role of Google as an instrument of freedom of expression in that respect was also not directly acknowledged by the CJEU.[12] That being said, when giving guidance as to what elements should be taken into account when striking the balance, the CJEU referred to elements which seem to be directly taken from the case law of the ECtHR on Article 8 and 10 ECHR. The point of departure, according to the CJEU, is that the rights of the data subject 'as a rule' override the other interests. However, in some circumstances the right of the general public might prevail. According to the CJEU, this depends on the nature of the information in question, its sensitivity for the data subject's private life and on the interest of the public in having that information, an interest which may vary, in particular, according to the role played by the data subject in public life.[13]

The CJEU's ruling in *Google Spain* has been criticised for placing the burden on the search engine provider as data controller, a position that Advocate General ('AG') Jääskinen had warned against in his opinion. He stated that internet search-engine service providers should not be saddled with such an obligation. According to the AG this would lead to an interference with the freedom of expression of the publisher of the web page, who would not enjoy adequate legal protection in such a situation, and would amount to the censorship of published content by a private party.[14] This position has been echoed in academic literature.[15]

---

[8] See in relation to online press archives ECtHR, *M.L. and W.W. v Germany*.
[9] See for criticism on this point Frantziou 2014, Kuner 2015, Kulk and Zuiderveen Borgesius 2015. On tension between the right to be forgotten and freedom of expression in general, see Fazlioglu 2013.
[10] Case C-131/12, *Google Spain*, para. 81.
[11] Advocate General Szpunar in his opinion in Case C-136/17, *G.C., A.F., B.H., E.D* (still pending) advised the CJEU to require the inclusion of the freedom of expression of the website holder as guaranteed by Art. 11 of the Charter of Fundamental rights of the European Union ('CFR') in the balancing exercise to be made by Google when assessing a request for delisting, see Case C-136/17, *G.C., A.F., B.H., E.D* (AG Opinion), para. 89.
[12] The Court does point at the 'important role' played by search engines, but only to underline that its activities constitute a more significant interference with the data subject's fundamental right to privacy than the publication on the website, see Case C-131/12, *Google Spain*, paras. 80 and 87. See for criticism on this point Hijmans 2014.
[13] Case C-131/12, *Google Spain*, paras. 81 and 97. See on this also Kranenborg 2015, pp. 77–79.
[14] Case C-131/12, *Google Spain* (AG Opinion), para. 134. See Allen 2015 for an elaborate comparison of the opinion of the AG and the CJEU ruling.
[15] See e.g. Spiecker 2015, p. 1053.

3. Implementation and territorial scope of the right

In order to help Google and other search engines to organise compliance with the CJEU ruling, the WP29 issued guidelines on the implementation of the ruling.[16] When it turned out that Google was delisting persons from search results only when the search was performed from Google websites with EU domains, the WP29 sent a letter to Google, warning that the decision of delisting must guarantee the effective and complete protection of data protection rights and that EU law cannot be circumvented.[17] At the time of writing, the question of whether the right to be forgotten should be implemented by Google with worldwide effect was under consideration by the CJEU.[18] Advocate General Szpunar in his opinion in this case advised the CJEU not to give the right global scope, but to require that it be limited to searches executed within the EU, thus preventing persons located within EU territory from seeing the delisted results when using the Google search engine.[19]

As indicated, Articles 17(3)(a) and 85 GDPR leave it to the Member States to reconcile the right to protection of personal data with the right to freedom of expression and information.[20]

4. Grounds for exercising the right

The right to erasure or to be forgotten is not only relevant in relation to freedom of expression. It can be invoked against any controller who processes personal data, if one of the grounds listed in Article 17(1) GDPR applies. The different grounds partly overlap. Three of them assume the lack of a basis for processing, such as if the personal data are no longer necessary for the purpose for which they were collected or otherwise processed (subparagraph (a)), consent is withdrawn (subparagraph (b)) or the personal data are unlawfully processed (subparagraph (d)). Article 17(1)(d) can be seen as a general clause, which is confirmed by recital 65 in which it is stated that the right to erasure can be invoked by a data subject, where the processing of his or her personal data does not otherwise comply with this Regulation.

The three other grounds do not as such assume unlawful data processing. Article 17(1)(c) is based on an invocation of the right to object in Article 21 when processing is based on Article 6(1)(e) or (f) GDPR.[21] Under Article 21(1), the burden of proof following an objection has been reversed: the data controller, rather than the data subject, has to demonstrate compelling legitimate grounds for processing the data. If the controller fails to do so, the data have to be erased. In case of direct marketing, the controller has to erase the data upon a simple objection of the data subject. In the situation of personal data processing of a child in relation to the offer of information society services based on the child's consent,[22] the data have to be erased upon simple request. It follows from recital

---

[16] See WP29 2014. It is to be noted that the WP29 in an opinion of 2008 on search engines had taken the view that a search engine provider was generally not to be held primarily responsible under European data protection law, see WP29 2008, p. 23.
[17] See WP29 Letter Google Spain. See also Kranenborg 2015, pp. 76–77.
[18] The French *Conseil d'État* put a question to the CJEU asking for a clarification on the territorial scope of the right to be forgotten, see Case C-507/17, *Google Inc*. See also Van Calster 2018.
[19] Case C-507/17, *Google Inc.* (AG Opinion), paras. 63 and 74–75.
[20] See the commentary on Art. 85 in this volume.
[21] See the commentary on Art. 21 in this volume.
[22] See also the commentary on Art. 8 in this volume.

65 that the data subject should be able to exercise that right notwithstanding the fact that he or she no longer is a child. It is emphasised that the right to erasure is relevant in particular where the data subject has given his or her consent as a child and is not fully aware of the risks involved by the processing, and later wants to remove such personal data, especially on the internet. Finally, Article 17(1)(e) requires erasure if this is mandated under Union or Member State law.

In cases where video recordings are stored, data subjects may request them to be erased under Article 17 GDPR.[23] If the video footage has been made public (e.g., by broadcasting or streaming online), the controller must take reasonable steps to inform other controllers of the request pursuant to Article 17 (2) GDPR.[24] These steps should include technical measures that take into account available technology and the cost of implementation.[25] In addition, to the extent possible, the controller should notify anyone to whom the personal data previously have been disclosed in accordance with Article 19 GDPR.[26] The personal data can be considered erased if the picture is blurred with no retroactive ability to recover the personal data the picture previously contained.[27]

5. Exemptions

The right to erasure does not apply in the situations indicated in the third paragraph of Article 17. These situations apply regardless of the ground in the first paragraph on which the right to erasure is based. The processing necessary for exercising the right of freedom of expression and information (subparagraph (a)) was discussed above. Other situations are the necessity for compliance with a legal obligation or for the performance of a task carried out in the public interest or in the exercise of official authority vested in the controller (subparagraph (b)). These situations refer to the grounds for processing contained in Article 6(1)(c) and (e) GDPR. The right to erasure does not apply either in cases in which the processing is necessary for certain grounds provided for in Article 9, the provision on the processing of special categories of personal data (subparagraph (c)).[28] The same holds true for processing necessary for archiving purposes in the public interest, scientific or historical research purposes or statistical purposes in accordance with Article 89(1) GDPR (subparagraph (d)).[29] It is added that this exception can be invoked in so far as the right to erasure is likely to render impossible or seriously impair the achievement of the objectives of that processing. The last situation in which the right does not apply is in case of processing necessary for the establishment, exercise or defence of legal claims (subparagraph (e)).

An example of a legal obligation in Article 17(3)(b) is provided in the *Manni* ruling. In this case, the question was whether the right to erasure could be invoked with regard to certain personal data (data relating to the identity and the respective functions of persons in relation to a specific company) contained in a public companies register. The CJEU first assessed whether the continued inclusion of the personal data in the public register was justified and necessary for the objective pursued (to protect the interests of third parties in relation to joint stock companies and limited liability companies).[30] After reaching

---

[23] EDPB 2019, p. 20.   [24] Ibid.   [25] Ibid.   [26] Ibid.   [27] Ibid.
[28] See the commentary on Art. 9 in this volume.
[29] See the commentary on Art. 89 in this volume.
[30] Case C-398/15, *Manni*, para. 52. A similar question appeared in *Google Spain*, where the newspaper was under a legal obligation to publish the information about the real-estate auction.

a positive conclusion on this, the CJEU considered that the Member States could not guarantee that the natural persons whose personal data is contained in the public register have the right to obtain, as a matter of principle, after a certain period of time, erasure of the personal data concerning them.[31] According to the CJEU this did not result in a disproportionate interference with the rights of the individuals as laid down in Articles 7 and 8 CFR. However, the CJEU did not exclude the possibility that in specific situations, overriding and legitimate reasons relating to the specific case of the person concerned could justify, exceptionally, that access to personal data concerning him should be limited.[32] In such circumstances the right to erasure does not result in the actual deletion of the personal data, but rather takes the data from the public domain.

6. Notification

Once the right to erasure or to be forgotten is successfully invoked, and none of the situations in the third paragraph apply, the controller, if it has made the personal data public, is obliged to inform the controllers who are processing such personal data to erase any links to, or copies or replications of, those personal data (see Article 17(2)). In doing so, the controller has to take reasonable steps, taking into account available technology and the means available to it, including technical measures, to inform the controllers which are processing the personal data of the data subject's request. This obligation on the controller has been slightly weakened compared to the initial proposal of the Commission. In the proposed Article 17, the controller had to take *all* reasonable steps and was 'considered responsible' for the publication of the personal data if it 'authorised' a third party to do so.[33]

Select Bibliography

EU legislation

GDPR Proposal: Proposal for a Regulation of the European Parliament and of the Council on the protection of individuals with regard to the processing of personal data and on the free movement of such data (General Data Protection Regulation), COM(2012) 11 final, 25 January 2012.

Academic writings

Ausloos, 'The Right to Erasure: Safeguard for Informational Self-Determination in a Digital Society?' (2018) (PhD dissertation at the University of Leuven).
Allen 2015: Allen, 'Remembering and Forgetting: Protecting Privacy Rights in the Digital Age', 1(3) *European Data Protection Law Review 'EDPL'* (2015), 164.
Bartolini and Siry 2016: Bartolini and Siry, 'The Right to Be Forgotten in the Light of the Consent of the Data Subject', 32(2) *Computer Law & Security Review* (2016), 218.
Fazlioglu, 'Forget Me Not: The Clash of the Right to Be Forgotten and Freedom of Expression on the Internet', 3 *International Data Privacy Law* (2013), 149.
Frantziou 2014: Frantziou, 'Further Developments in the Right to be Forgotten: The European Court of Justice's Judgment in Case C-131/12, Google Spain, SL, Google Inc v Agencia Española de Protección de Datos', 14(4) *Human Rights Law Review* (2014), 761.

---

[31] Case C-398/15, *Manni*, para. 56. [32] Ibid., paras. 57–61.
[33] See Art. 17(2) GDPR Proposal.

Hijmans 2014: Hijmans, 'Right to Have Links Removed: Evidence of Effective Data Protection', 21(3) *Maastricht Journal of European and Comparative Law* (2014), 555.

Kuczerawy and Ausloos 2016, 'From Notice-and-Takedown to Notice-and-Delist: Implementing Google Spain', 14(2) *Colorado Technology Law Journal* (2016), 219.

Kranenborg 2015: Kranenborg, 'Google and the Right to be Forgotten', 1(1) *EDPL* (2015), 70.

Kulk and Zuiderveen Borgesius 2015: Kulk and Zuiderveen Borgesius, '"Freedom of Expression" and "Right to Be Forgotten" Cases in the Netherlands after Google Spain', 1(2) *EDPL* (2015), 113.

Kuner 2015: Kuner, 'The Court of Justice of the EU Judgment on Data Protection and Internet Search Engines: Current Issues and Future Challenges', in Hess and Mariottini (eds.), *Protecting Privacy in Private International and Procedural Law and by Data Protection* (Ashgate/Nomos 2015), 19.

Mayer-Schönberger, *Delete: The Virtue of Forgetting in the Digital Age* (Princeton University Press 2011).

Spiecker 2015: Spiecker, 'A New Framework for Information Markets: Google Spain', 52(4) *Common Market Law Review* (2015), 1033.

Van Calster 2018: Van Calster, 'Not Just One, but Many 'Rights to Be Forgotten', 7(2) *Internet Policy Review* (2018), 1.

Wechsler 2015: Wechsler, 'The Right to Remember: The European Convention on Human Rights and the Right to be Forgotten', 49(1) *Columbia Journal of Law and Social Problems* (2015), 135.

Papers of data protection authorities

EDPB 2019: European Data Protection Board, 'Guidelines 3/2019 on the processing of personal data through video devices (version for public consultation)' (10 July 2019).

WP29 2008: Article 29 Working Party, 'Opinion 1/2008 on Data Protection Issues Related to Search Engines' (WP148, 4 April 2008).

WP29 2014: Article 29 Working Party, 'Guidelines on the Implementation of the Court of Justice of the European Union Judgment on "Google Spain and Inc. v Agencia Española de Protección de Datos (AEPD) and Mario Costeja González C-131/12"' (WP 225, 26 November 2014).

WP29 Letter Google Spain: Article 29 Working Party, 'Letter of 6 January 2015 to Google on the Right to Be Delisted' (6 January 2015).

Others

EC Press Release Manni: European Commission, 'The Court Considers that There Is No Right to Be Forgotten in Respect of Personal Data in the Companies Register' (9 March 2017), available at https://curia.europa.eu/jcms/upload/docs/application/pdf/2017-03/cp170027en.pdf.

Article 18. Right to restriction of processing

GLORIA GONZÁLEZ FUSTER

1. The data subject shall have the right to obtain from the controller restriction of processing where one of the following applies:
   (a) the accuracy of the personal data is contested by the data subject, for a period enabling the controller to verify the accuracy of the personal data;
   (b) the processing is unlawful and the data subject opposes the erasure of the personal data and requests the restriction of their use instead;
   (c) the controller no longer needs the personal data for the purposes of the processing, but they are required by the data subject for the establishment, exercise or defence of legal claims;
   (d) the data subject has objected to processing pursuant to Article 21(1) pending the verification whether the legitimate grounds of the controller override those of the data subject.
2. Where processing has been restricted under paragraph 1, such personal data shall, with the exception of storage, only be processed with the data subject's consent or for the establishment, exercise or defence of legal claims or for the protection of the rights of another natural or legal person or for reasons of important public interest of the Union or of a Member State.
3. A data subject who has obtained restriction of processing pursuant to paragraph 1 shall be informed by the controller before the restriction of processing is lifted.

Relevant Recitals

(67) Methods by which to restrict the processing of personal data could include, inter alia, temporarily moving the selected data to another processing system, making the selected personal data unavailable to users, or temporarily removing published data from a website. In automated filing systems, the restriction of processing should in principle be ensured by technical means in such a manner that the personal data are not subject to further processing operations and cannot be changed. The fact that the processing of personal data is restricted should be clearly indicated in the system.

(156) The processing of personal data for archiving purposes in the public interest, scientific or historical research purposes or statistical purposes should be subject to appropriate safeguards for the rights and freedoms of the data subject pursuant to this Regulation. Those safeguards should ensure that technical and organisational measures are in place in order to ensure, in particular, the principle of data minimisation. The further processing of personal data for archiving purposes in the public interest, scientific or historical research purposes or statistical purposes is to be carried out when the controller has assessed the feasibility to fulfil those purposes by processing data which do not permit or no longer permit the identification of data subjects, provided that appropriate safeguards exist (such as, for instance, pseudonymisation of the data). Member States should provide for appropriate safeguards for the processing of personal data for archiving purposes in the public interest, scientific or historical research purposes or statistical purposes. Member States should be authorised to provide, under specific conditions and subject to appropriate safeguards for data subjects, specifications and derogations with regard to the information requirements and rights to rectification, to erasure, to be forgotten, to restriction of processing, to data portability, and to

object when processing personal data for archiving purposes in the public interest, scientific or historical research purposes or statistical purposes. The conditions and safeguards in question may entail specific procedures for data subjects to exercise those rights if this is appropriate in the light of the purposes sought by the specific processing along with technical and organisational measures aimed at minimising the processing of personal data in pursuance of the proportionality and necessity principles. The processing of personal data for scientific purposes should also comply with other relevant legislation such as on clinical trials.

Closely Related Provisions

Article 4(3) (Definition of 'restriction of processing'); Article 5(1)(d) (Principle of accuracy); Article 16 (Right to rectification); Article 5(1)(a) (Principle of lawfulness); Article 17(1)(d) (Right to erasure based on unlawful processing); Article 5(1)(c) (Principle of data minimisation); Article 17(3)(e) (Limitations to the right to erasure); Article 19 (Notification obligation); Article 21 (Right to object); Article 89 (Derogations relating to processing for archiving purposes in the public interest, scientific or historical research purposes or statistical purposes); Article 58(1)(g) (Powers of supervisory authorities)

Related Provisions in LED [Directive (EU) 2016/680]

Recital 47; Article 3(3) (Definition of 'restriction of processing'); Article 16 (Right to rectification or erasure of personal data and restriction of processing)

Relevant Case Law

CJEU

Case C-553/07, *College van burgemeester en wethouders van Rotterdam v M. E. E. Rijkeboer*, judgment of 7 May 2009 (ECLI:EU:C:2009:293).
Opinion of Advocate General Ruiz-Jarabo Colomer in Case C-553/07, *College van burgemeester en wethouders van Rotterdam v M.E.E. Rijkeboer*, delivered on 22 December 2008 (ECLI:EU:C:2008:773).
Case C-131/12, *Google Spain SL and Google Inc. v Agencia Española de Protección de Datos (AEPD) and Mario Costeja González*, judgment of 13 May 2014 (Grand Chamber) (ECLI:EU:C:2014:317).

A. Rationale and Policy Underpinnings

The right to restriction of processing is a novelty of the GDPR, which has introduced it as a multifaceted notion. To a certain extent, this right might be regarded as a fundamentally adjunct right, closely connected to the exercise of other, more established data subject rights (in particular, the right to rectification, and the right to object): in this sense, it allows the temporarily curtailment of the processing of personal data pending the granting of such rights, and thus prevents processing that would otherwise be lawfully processed.

From another perspective, the right to restriction can also function as an alternative right in the hands of data subjects, who might choose to exercise it instead of the right to erasure when other solutions fit their interests better. From this point of view, the most relevant effect of having recourse to the right to restriction of processing is that it might prevent the deletion of personal data that could otherwise have been lawfully deleted.

The right to restriction can indeed be used by data subjects basically in three types of situations: when they have exercised the right to rectification and the right to object, to ensure that the processing of the personal data at stake is limited while the applicability of such rights is being confirmed; when the data processing is unlawful, but the data subject nevertheless prefers to prevent the erasure of the data; and when the data are no longer of use for the data controller (which means they could be deleted), but the data subject needs them for the establishment, exercise or defence of legal claims. When the right to restriction of processing is granted, the 'restricted data' will not be erased, but their further processing, beyond storage as such, will be conditioned to the applicability of a particularly limited of possible grounds for processing.

In the GDPR, restriction of processing has been substantially configured as a prerogative of data subjects, who are entitled to be granted such a restriction under specified circumstances. In the LED, by contrast, restriction of processing is an obligation imposed on data controllers in some cases: data controllers must avoid the erasure of data, opting instead to merely restrict the use of such data, when that is to be regarded as necessary to either preserve data the accuracy of which is contested but cannot be ascertained, or to maintain the data for the purposes of evidence.[1] The coexistence of these divergent approaches can be seen as another manifestation of the dualities accompanying the rationale(s) behind the right to restriction of processing.

B. Legal Background

1. EU legislation

Although legal antecedents regarding different rights and obligations connected to the right to restriction of processing can be found in prior EU legislation, there is no direct antecedent to this provision as such. The DPD did refer to the possibility for data subjects to request the 'blocking of data', the processing of which did not comply with its provisions,[2] but the nature and implications of such 'blocking' were not specified. The Commission deliberately replaced in its proposal for the GDPR references to 'blocking' of data with 'restriction of processing', arguing that the term 'blocking' was ambiguous.[3] However, the right to restriction of processing in the GDPR is not completely identical with blocking as set out in such provisions.

2. International instruments

The original Convention 108 did not include any reference to the possibility for data subjects to obtain a blocking of data or restriction of processing. The Modernised Convention 108 also lacks any mention of such a right.

---

[1] Art. 16 LED.
[2] Art. 12(b) DPD; see also Art. 28(3) DPD on the possibility for supervisory authorities to order the 'blocking of data'.
[3] GDPR Proposal, section 3.4.3.3.

3. National developments

Member States may enact legislation implementing Article 18 with regard to processing for archiving purposes in the public interest, scientific or historical research purposes or statistical purposes.[4] Article 89 GDPR foresees, in its second and third paragraphs, that where personal data are processed for scientific or historical research purposes or statistical purposes, or for archiving purposes in the public interest, Union or Member State law may provide for derogations from the right to restriction of processing in so far as such rights are likely to render impossible or seriously impair the achievement of the mentioned purposes, and such derogations are necessary for the fulfilment of those purposes. However, Article 89(1) also requires that such processing shall be subject to appropriate safeguards for the rights and freedoms of the data subject, ensuring that technical and organisational measures are in place in particular in order to guarantee respect for the principle of data minimisation.

4. Case law

The *Rijkeboer* case decided by the CJEU concerned the interpretation of the provisions of the right of access in the DPD and the tension between, on the one hand, the interest of data subjects in accessing data (in particular in view of bringing legal proceedings to protect their rights), and, on the other hand, the burden of obligations imposed on data controllers to store data which are not to be used by them for other purposes.[5] In that judgment, the Court noted that it is for Member States to achieve a fair balance between the interests of data subjects and that burden imposed on controllers with regard to the storage of information.[6]

The judgment of the CJEU in *Google Spain*, although commonly envisioned as concerned with the right to erasure or the 'right to be forgotten', is also related to the right to restriction of processing as established in the GPDR. In that ruling, the Court observed that a data subject may, in light of his or her fundamental rights under Articles 7 and 8 of the Charter of Fundamental Rights of the European Union ('CFR'), request that some data no longer be made available to the general public on account of their inclusion in a list of search results.[7] Making some data unavailable to users and temporarily removing published data from a website, both of which reflect the measures upheld by the CJEU in *Google Spain*, are mentioned in recital 67 GDPR as methods by which the processing of data may be restricted.

C. Analysis

The right to restriction of processing is regulated in Section 3 of the GDPR, which is entitled 'Rectification and erasure'. While this section is indeed partially concerned with the exercise of these rights, it has a broader reach. The GDPR configures restriction of processing not only as a right of data subjects, but also as a measure that supervisory authorities have the power to order in accordance with Article 58(1)(g).[8]

---

[4] See the commentary on Art. 89 in this volume. [5] Case C-553/07, *Rijkeboer*.
[6] Ibid., para. 64.   [7] Case C-131/12, *Google Spain*, para. 99.
[8] See the commentary on Art. 58 in this volume.

In the original GDPR proposal of the Commission, the processing of data was advanced as an obligation imposed on data controllers when confronted with certain requests for data erasure,[9] and the Commission suggested empowering itself to adopt delegated acts determining the criteria and conditions for such restrictions.[10] As a result of the legislative process, the right to restriction of processing emerged as a right deserving a distinct provision, which can be broadly welcomed for addressing some of the persistent uncertainties surrounding the 'blocking' of data mentioned in the DPD.[11]

The right to restriction of processing has received relatively little attention in policy debates and academic literature. Article 18, nonetheless, can be perceived as an example of how EU data protection law often foresees difficult exercises in order to determine the possibility or the obligation to process personal data. In this sense, it has emerged from the very core of what Advocate General Ruiz-Jarabo Colomer once described as the internal conflict inside the right to personal data protection, split between two personalities like Dr Jekyll and Mr Hyde,[12] in this case between 'the obligation to provide for time-limits for the deletion of files containing personal data and the obligation to guarantee the right of access of the individuals to whom such data relate'.[13]

However, the terminological choice of the term 'restriction' as the key term for this new right might be questioned, as it is more generally traditionally used to refer to permissible limitations on data subject rights, and not to limitations curtailing data processing, and can thus lead to confusion. Indeed, the Commission appears to be confused by the term, as its Guidelines on the right to restriction of processing reference recital 73 as relevant, even though this recital is concerned with restrictions to data protection principles and data subject rights rather than the right to restriction of processing.[14]

1. Circumstances allowing restriction of processing

In line with the GDPR, the right to restriction of processing can be invoked by data subjects against data controllers in any one of four different instances.

First, restriction of processing can be obtained following the data subject contesting the accuracy of data held by the data controller (Article 18(1)(a)). Restriction shall be granted for the period necessary for the controller to verify the accuracy (or inaccuracy) of the contested data. This period should on paper be very limited, as according to the principle of accuracy (Article 5(1)(d)), inaccurate data must be rectified by data controllers 'without delay'. Similarly, when data subjects exercise their right to rectification (Article 16), the GDPR foresees that the data controller must rectify the inaccurate data 'without undue delay'.

Secondly, restriction shall apply when the processing is unlawful, but the data subject opposes the erasure of the data, and requests instead restriction of the data processing. This situation would seem a priori to be related to cases where the right of erasure could have been exercised by the data subject under Article 17(1)(d), allowing them to obtain the erasure of personal data unlawfully processed, but they prefer to refrain from requesting such an irreversible measure. Strictly speaking, however, in such a scenario the data subject would not *oppose* the erasure of the data, but rather simply avoid requesting

---

[9] See GDPR Proposal, Art. 17(4).   [10] Ibid., Art. 17(9).
[11] See Zanfir 2015 concerning the coexistence of the notions of erasure and blocking in German law.
[12] Case C-553/07, *Rijkeboer* (AG Opinion), para. 25.   [13] Ibid.   [14] EC Guidelines.

it. Restriction would in any case be applicable also when the erasure is decided or demanded by any another actor.

Thirdly, restriction shall be granted when the controller no longer needs the data for the purposes of the processing, but they are nevertheless required by the data subject for the establishment, exercise or defence of legal claims. In this case, the controller could be regarded as being obliged in principle to erase the data, in accordance with the principle of data minimisation (Article 5(1)(c)), but this general obligation would be counterbalanced by the existence of the interest of the data subject in using the data to establish, exercise or defend legal claims.

Fourthly, and finally, restriction can be obtained when the data subject has exercised the right to object enshrined in Article 21(1), pending verification (presumably, in principle, by the data controller) of whether the legitimate grounds of the controller override those of the data subject. This situation concerns cases where a data subject objects, on grounds relating to their particular situation, to the processing of personal data about them based either on the performance of a task carried out in the public interest or in the exercise of official authority vested in the controller (Article 6(1)(e)), or on the legitimate interests pursued by the controller or by a third party (Article 6(1)(f)), unless these legitimate interests are overridden by the interests or fundamental rights and freedoms of the data subject.

The fact that Article 18(1) refers to the need to verify the *legitimate grounds* of the controller, whereas Article 6(1)(f) mentions the *legitimate interests* of the controller, can be interpreted as meaning that the right to restriction of processing might also apply when the data subject objected to processing which was grounded on Article 6(1)(e), and not exclusively when the controller is occupied carrying out the specific balancing exercise between its legitimate interests and the interests and fundamental rights and freedoms of the data subject under Article 6(1)(f).

2. Modalities and implications of restriction

The notion of 'restriction of processing' is defined in Article 4(3) GDPR as 'the marking of stored personal data with the aim of limiting their processing in the future'.[15] Article 18 GDPR, however, does not refer to marking, focusing instead on describing the consequences of obtaining the right to restriction as the limitation of the possible grounds for further processing of such data.

Under Article 18(2) GDPR, the granting of the right to restriction of processing limits any further processing of the 'restricted data' beyond their storage. The data shall only be processed for purposes other than storage if based on the data subject's consent; on the establishment, exercise or defence of legal claims; on the protection of the rights of another natural or legal person; or if for reasons of important public interest of the Union or of a Member State. This list of lawful grounds constitutes a limitation of the general grounds of processing listed in Article 6(1).

The way in which the use of data must in practice be 'restricted' when Article 18 GDPR applies is elaborated in more detail in recital 67. The recital does not refer explicitly to marking, indicating for instance that moving the selected data to a different processing system can be regarded as a method by which to restrict the processing of data,

---

[15] See the commentary on Art. 4(3) in this volume.

although it points out that '[t]he fact that the processing of personal data is restricted should be clearly indicated in the system'.

The right to restriction of processing grants the data subject the right to be informed by the controller before restriction is lifted, as established by Article 18(3) GDPR. It is important to emphasise that the information about the lifting needs to be provided *before* the lifting as such, allowing data subjects to consider requesting other measures, or exercise other rights, before the de-selection or the deletion of the data.

When the right is exercised under Article 18(1)(a), the lifting of restriction should take place as soon as the data controller has finished verifying the accuracy (or inaccuracy) of the data affected by the contestation. When it is granted under Article 18(1)(c), then this should take place as soon as the data are no longer required by the data subject for the establishment, exercise or defence of legal claims. When the right is exercised following Article 18(1)(d), then the restriction should be lifted as soon as the verification of whether the legitimate grounds of the controller override those of the data subject has taken place. The timing of the lifting of a restriction granted under Article 18(1)(b), whereby the data subject has opposed the erasure of unlawfully processed data but requested restriction of processing instead (for unspecified reasons), is unclear.

Granting restriction of processing imposes on the controller notification obligations towards each recipient to whom the personal data have been disclosed, as specified in Article 19 GDPR.

Select Bibliography

EU legislation

GDPR Proposal: Proposal for a Regulation of the European Parliament and of the Council on the protection of individuals with regard to the processing of personal data and on the free movement of such data (General Data Protection Regulation), COM(2012) 11 final, 25 January 2012.

Academic writings

Zanfir 2015: Zanfir, 'Tracing the Right to Be Forgotten in the Short History of Data Protection Law: The "New Clothes" of an Old Right', in Gutwirth, Leenes and de Hert (eds.), *Reforming European Data Protection Law* (Springer 2015).

Others

EC Guidelines: European Commission, 'When Should I Exercise my Right to Restriction of Processing of my Personal Data?', available at https://ec.europa.eu/info/law/law-topic/data-protection/reform/rights-citizens/my-rights/when-should-i-exercise-my-right-restriction-processing-my-personal-data_en.

Article 19. Notification obligation regarding rectification or erasure of personal data or restriction of processing

GLORIA GONZÁLEZ FUSTER

The controller shall communicate any rectification or erasure of personal data or restriction of processing carried out in accordance with Article 16, Article 17(1) and Article 18 to each recipient to whom the personal data have been disclosed, unless this proves impossible or involves disproportionate effort. The controller shall inform the data subject about those recipients if the data subject requests it.

Closely Related Provisions

Article 4(9) (Definition of 'recipient'); Article 12 (Transparent information, communication and modalities for the exercise of the rights of the data subject); Article 16 (Right to rectification); Article 17(1) (Right to erasure ('right to be forgotten')); Article 18 (Right to restriction of processing); Article 58(2)(g) (Powers of supervisory authorities); Article 89(3) (Safeguards and derogations relating to processing for archiving purposes in the public interest, scientific or historical research purposes or statistical purposes)

Related Provisions in LED [Directive (EU) 2016/680]

Article 16(6) in LED (Right to rectification or erasure of personal data and restriction of processing)

Relevant Case Law

CJEU

Case C-553/07, *College van burgemeester en wethouders van Rotterdam v M.E.E. Rijkeboer*, judgment of 7 May 2009 (ECLI:EU:C:2009:293).
Case C-582/14, *Patrick Breyer v Bundesrepublik Deutschland*, judgment of 19 October 2016 (ECLI:EU:C:2016:779).
Case C-398/15, *Camera di Commercio, Industria, Artigianato e Agricoltura di Lecce v Salvatore Manni*, judgment of 9 March 2017 (ECLI:EU:C:2017:197).

A. Rationale and Policy Underpinnings

The notification obligations under Article 19 of the GDPR constitute a duty for controllers to inform recipients to whom they had disclosed data about the fact they have carried out a rectification, erasure or restriction of processing affecting such data. The obligations concern thus the communication of an action taken by the controller following the exercise of a limited subset of data subject rights (rectification, erasure and restriction of processing). This duty aims to ease the burden falling on data subjects wishing to have some data rectified or erased, or some processing restricted, by obliging controllers to attempt to reach out to previously contacted recipients who are possibly still holding the data.

Article 19 of the GDPR does not specify what is expected from the recipients receiving such notifications from the controller. The LED, in contrast, explicitly foresees that upon being notified 'the recipients shall rectify or erase the personal data or restrict processing of the personal data under their responsibility'.[1] Under the GDPR, recipients might consider the notification as an invitation to consider whether they should also proceed to an equivalent rectification, erasure or restriction of processing, even though the notification is not necessarily linked to any request in that sense emanating from the data subject, and even though the necessity to comply with the rectification, erasure or restriction of processing, applicable to the controller, might not be applicable to them. This uncertainty, and its consequences, do not appear to have received much attention in policy discussions.

The obligations imposed on controllers to notify recipients are accompanied by a subjective right granted to data subjects to be informed about the recipients involved. This right to be informed about the recipients goes beyond the information potentially received by data subjects under general information obligations, or through the exercise of the right to access, which could be limited to obtaining information on *categories* of recipients. It constitutes, therefore, a clear strengthening of data subject rights.

B. Legal Background

1. EU legislation

With regard to the right of access, the DPD foresaw in Article 12 the right of data subjects to obtain from the controller 'the notification to third parties to whom the data have been disclosed of any rectification, erasure or blocking carried out ... , unless this proves impossible or involves a disproportionate effort'.[2] The original Commission proposal for the GDPR built on such a clause and contained a provision entitled 'Rights in relation to recipients', mandating notification regardless of any individual request, and broadening the scope of parties to be notified to 'recipients',[3] which might or might not be a third party.

2. International instruments

Council of Europe Convention 108 and the Modernised Convention do not contain a provision similar to Article 19. However, the Council of Europe's 'Recommendation No. R(87)15 on the use of personal data in the police sector' states that if data which are no longer accurate or up to date have been communicated, the communicating body should inform as far as possible all the recipients of the data of their non-conformity.[4]

3. National developments

Member State law can restrict the scope of obligations and rights derived from Article 19 of the GDPR by the general rules for restrictions of rights under Article 23, or under Article 89(3) concerning derogations relating to processing for archiving purposes in the public interest (see below).

---

[1] Art. 16(6) LED.   [2] Art. 12(c) DPD.   [3] Art. 13 GDPR Proposal.
[4] COM Recommendation 1987, principle 5(5)ii.

4. Case law

In the *Rijkeboer* judgment, the CJEU stressed that the access by data subjects to information on the recipients to whom personal data about them has been disclosed is necessary for them to 'be in a position effectively to exercise' their data protection rights, such as the 'right to have data presumed unlawful or incorrect rectified, erased or blocked'.[5] Limits with regard to the right to access to information on the recipients of personal data are possible, but must nevertheless allow data subjects to effectively exercise their rights under EU data protection law.[6]

The judgment in *Rijkeboer* concerned specifically national obligations imposed on data controllers to store information on recipients, and the possible limits of such storage. In this regard, the Court concluded that it is for Member States to find a fair balance between, on the one hand, the interest of the data subject in exercising their rights, and, on the other, the burden which the obligation to store that information on recipients represents for the controller.[7] It also found that 'a number of parameters may accordingly be taken into account by the Member States', such as applicable provisions of national law on time limits for bringing related actions, the more or less sensitive nature of the personal data at stake, the length of time for which those data are to be stored, and the number of recipients.[8]

In its ruling in *Breyer*, the CJEU discussed the notion of 'disproportionate effort' in relation to the means which may likely reasonably be used by a controller in order to identify the data subject, with the assistance of other persons. The CJEU noted in that context that such disproportionate effort could be conceived 'in terms of time, cost and man-power'.[9]

Finally, in *Manni*, regarding the determination of which data stored in a register shall be made subject to disclosure or disclosure limitations, the CJEU emphasised that generic determinations were not possible in the case at stake. It was for Member States to determine, the Court pointed out, whether in some instances data subjects may apply to a responsible authority to determine this 'on the basis of a case-by-case assessment',[10] and if justified, to limit access to some data to certain third parties. In doing so, the Court warned against the suitability of automatically generalising assessments on (limitations to) access to data. This can be interpreted as being in tension with the suitability of automatically assuming that a rectification, erasure or restriction of processing relevant for a controller will be applicable to the recipients.

C. Analysis

The notification obligations under Article 19 of the GDPR apply to data controllers carrying out any rectification or erasure of personal data, or restriction of processing, under the respective provisions of the GDPR (that is, Articles 16, 17(1) and 18). The obligations concern the notification to each recipient to whom the personal data has been disclosed. Article 19 does not detail what exactly needs to be notified to recipients, but

---

[5] Case C-553/07, *Rijkeboer*, paras. 53–54. [6] Ibid., paras. 57. [7] Ibid., paras. 64.
[8] Ibid., paras. 63. [9] Case C-582/14, *Breyer*, para. 46.
[10] Case C-398/15, *Manni*, para. 61.

presumably it shall be that the rectification, erasure or restriction of processing in question have been carried out.

Article 19 of the GDPR is not to be conflated with Article 17(2), which imposes on controllers, when they have made personal data public and have to erase some personal data, the obligation to notify other controllers 'that the data subject has requested the erasure by such controllers of any links to, or copy or replication of, those personal data'. For the purposes of Article 17(2), it is necessary that the data subject has requested the erasure by the other controllers of links to, or copies of, the data at stake. Article 19, on the contrary, imposes an overall obligation to notify recipients, even when the data subject did not request any action by them. In addition, the notification obligations described in Article 17(2) are accompanied by a list of specific, ad hoc derogations,[11] which is not the case for Article 19.

1. Scope of the notification obligations

Communication to recipients shall not be required when 'this proves impossible or involves disproportionate effort' for the controller. It is relevant to note, for this assessment, that the controllers' records of processing activities under their responsibility do not necessarily need to contain information on all recipients, as they are only obliged to generally record 'categories of recipients'.[12] In relation to other notification obligations imposed on controllers, the GDPR suggests 'taking account of available technology and the cost of implementation' in order to 'take reasonable steps' to inform them.[13]

'Public authorities which may receive personal data in the framework of a particular inquiry in accordance with Union or Member State law' are not to be given notifications under Article 19, as they are formally not regarded as 'recipients' under the GDPR.[14] Situations in which a controller has to erase data following a notification received from another data controller under Article 17(2) are also outside the scope of Article 19, as the provision limits its scope to erasure of data in accordance with Article 17(1) of the GDPR.

Article 19 is silent on the possible need for controllers to inform recipients which have been notified about a restriction of processing of the eventual lifting of such restriction, about which however they must inform data subjects.[15] In such cases, data subjects are then left with the burden to, if suitable, notify by themselves the (by then mis-)informed recipients.

Both EU and Member State law may provide for derogations from Article 19, subject to certain conditions and safeguards, 'where personal data are processed for archiving purposes in the public interest' and 'in so far as such rights are likely to render impossible or seriously impair the achievement of the specific purposes, and such derogations are necessary for the fulfilment of those purposes'.[16] In principle, the requirement of processing data 'for archiving purposes in the public interest' would appear to apply to the controller potentially obliged to notify recipients under Article 19, for whom derogations could be introduced. It is nevertheless not self-evident to think of instances where a controller processing data for archiving purposes in the public interest would have to comply with a request to rectify or erase data, or restrict processing, but notifying this to recipients (who are possibly processing the data for other purposes) would obstruct the archiving purposes of the controller.

---

[11] Art.17(3) GDPR.   [12] Ibid., Art. 30(1)(d).   [13] Ibid., Art. 17(2).
[14] Ibid., Art. 4(9).   [15] Ibid., Art. 18(3).
[16] Ibid., Art. 89(3). Art. 89(2) does not refer to possible equivalent derogations where personal data are processed for scientific or historical research purposes or statistical purposes.

2. Right of the data subject to be informed about the recipients

The controller must also inform data subjects, if they request it, 'about those recipients'. It is not clear whether 'those recipients' refers to all recipients to whom the personal data at stake have been disclosed, or only those who are actually notified (excluding, therefore, those for which notification proved impossible, or involved a disproportionate effort). In line with the objectives of the GDPR, the latter reading should in principle be excluded, as the data subject has a special interest in knowing precisely which recipients might hold the data but have not been notified, in order to reach out to them by other means, if appropriate. Exercise of the right to obtain information under Article 19 about the recipients of personal data in the context of the exercise of the rights to rectification, erasure and restriction of processing is interdependent with the provision of transparent information about the rights of data subjects under Article 12 GDPR.

Article 19 does not specify whether the communication of recipients to data subjects shall take place before or after the recipients have been notified, which could be problematic in some instances. As explained above, the fact that a controller has been obliged to rectify, erase or restrict the processing of some date does not necessarily imply that each and every recipient of such data must do the same. In this sense, for instance, it is possible that an obligation to erase some data, which needs to be respected by a controller, may not apply to all the recipients to whom the data were disclosed. In these cases, the notification might however mislead the recipients into believing that they should automatically also carry out the same action as the controller. In relation to the erasure of personal data, this might have irreparable consequences.

The GDPR endorses (through the right to rectification) the principle according to which the erasure of data is not systematically the most protective or beneficial option for the data subject. In some circumstances, the data subject may wish a controller to erase some data, while preferring that all or some recipients should simply restrict their processing rather than erasing the data. It would then be preferable that data subjects can contact recipients before these receive any notifications from the controller.

The GDPR additionally foresees, in the realm of supervisory authority's corrective powers, the possibility for them to order the notification of any rectification or erasure of personal data, or restriction of processing, to recipients to whom the personal data have been disclosed, 'pursuant to ... Article 19'.[17] It is not specified what occurs in such a case with regard to the right of the data subject to request information about recipients, i.e. whether it applies or not.

Select Bibliography

EU legislation

GDPR Proposal: Proposal for a Regulation of the European Parliament and of the Council on the protection of individuals with regard to the processing of personal data and on the free movement of such data (General Data Protection Regulation), COM(2012) 11 final, 25 January 2012.

Reports and recommendations

COM Recommendation 1987: Committee of Ministers of the Council of Europe, 'Recommendation Regulating the Use of Personal Data in the Police Sector' (Rec(1987)15, 17 September 1987).

---

[17] Ibid., Art. 58(2)(g).

Article 20. Right to data portability

ORLA LYNSKEY

1. The data subject shall have the right to receive the personal data concerning him or her, which he or she has provided to a controller, in a structured, commonly used and machine-readable format and have the right to transmit those data to another controller without hindrance from the controller to which the personal data have been provided, where:
   (a) the processing is based on consent pursuant to point (a) of Article 6(1) or point (a) of Article 9(2) or on a contract pursuant to point (b) of Article 6(1); and
   (b) the processing is carried out by automated means.
2. In exercising his or her right to data portability pursuant to paragraph 1, the data subject shall have the right to have the personal data transmitted directly from one controller to another, where technically feasible.
3. The exercise of the right referred to in paragraph 1 of this Article shall be without prejudice to Article 17. That right shall not apply to processing necessary for the performance of a task carried out in the public interest or in the exercise of official authority vested in the controller.
4. The right referred to in paragraph 1 shall not adversely affect the rights and freedoms of others.

Relevant Recitals

(68) To further strengthen the control over his or her own data, where the processing of personal data is carried out by automated means, the data subject should also be allowed to receive personal data concerning him or her which he or she has provided to a controller in a structured, commonly used, machine-readable and interoperable format, and to transmit it to another controller. Data controllers should be encouraged to develop interoperable formats that enable data portability. That right should apply where the data subject provided the personal data on the basis of his or her consent or the processing is necessary for the performance of a contract. It should not apply where processing is based on a legal ground other than consent or contract. By its very nature, that right should not be exercised against controllers processing personal data in the exercise of their public duties. It should therefore not apply where the processing of the personal data is necessary for compliance with a legal obligation to which the controller is subject or for the performance of a task carried out in the public interest or in the exercise of an official authority vested in the controller. The data subject's right to transmit or receive personal data concerning him or her should not create an obligation for the controllers to adopt or maintain processing systems which are technically compatible. Where, in a certain set of personal data, more than one data subject is concerned, the right to receive the personal data should be without prejudice to the rights and freedoms of other data subjects in accordance with this Regulation. Furthermore, that right should not prejudice the right of the data subject to obtain the erasure of personal data and the limitations of that right as set out in this Regulation and should, in particular, not imply the erasure of personal data concerning the data subject which have been provided by him or her for the performance of a contract to the extent that and for as long as the personal data are necessary for the performance of that contract. Where technically feasible, the data subject should have the right to have the personal data transmitted directly from one controller to another.

(73) Restrictions concerning specific principles and the rights of information, access to and rectification or erasure of personal data, the right to data portability, the right to object, decisions

based on profiling, as well as the communication of a personal data breach to a data subject and certain related obligations of the controllers may be imposed by Union or Member State law, as far as necessary and proportionate in a democratic society to safeguard public security, including the protection of human life especially in response to natural or manmade disasters, the prevention, investigation and prosecution of criminal offences or the execution of criminal penalties, including the safeguarding against and the prevention of threats to public security, or of breaches of ethics for regulated professions, other important objectives of general public interest of the Union or of a Member State, in particular an important economic or financial interest of the Union or of a Member State, the keeping of public registers kept for reasons of general public interest, further processing of archived personal data to provide specific information related to the political behaviour under former totalitarian state regimes or the protection of the data subject or the rights and freedoms of others, including social protection, public health and humanitarian purposes. Those restrictions should be in accordance with the requirements set out in the Charter and in the European Convention for the Protection of Human Rights and Fundamental Freedoms.

(156) The processing of personal data for archiving purposes in the public interest, scientific or historical research purposes or statistical purposes should be subject to appropriate safeguards for the rights and freedoms of the data subject pursuant to this Regulation. Those safeguards should ensure that technical and organizational measures are in place in order to ensure, in particular, the principle of data minimisation. The further processing of personal data for archiving purposes in the public interest, scientific or historical research purposes or statistical purposes is to be carried out when the controller has assessed the feasibility to fulfil those purposes by processing data which do not permit or no longer permit the identification of data subjects, provided that appropriate safeguards exist (such as, for instance, pseudonymisation of the data). Member States should provide for appropriate safeguards for the processing of personal data for archiving purposes in the public interest, scientific or historical research purposes or statistical purposes. Member States should be authorised to provide, under specific conditions and subject to appropriate safeguards for data subjects, specifications and derogations with regard to the information requirements and rights to rectification, to erasure, to be forgotten, to restriction of processing, to data portability, and to object when processing personal data for archiving purposes in the public interest, scientific or historical research purposes or statistical purposes. The conditions and safeguards in question may entail specific procedures for data subjects to exercise those rights if this is appropriate in the light of the purposes sought by the specific processing along with technical and organisational measures aimed at minimising the processing of personal data in pursuance of the proportionality and necessity principles. The processing of personal data for scientific purposes should also comply with other relevant legislation such as on clinical trials.

Closely Related Provisions

Recital 68; Article 6 (Lawfulness of processing); Article 9 (Processing of special categories of personal data); Article 13 (Information to be provided when the personal data are collected from the data subject) (see too recitals 61–62); Article 14 (Information to be provided when the personal data have not been obtained from the data subject); Article 23 (Restrictions) (see further recital 73)

Related Provisions in LED [Directive (EU) 2016/680]

Article 12 (Communication and modalities for exercising the rights of the data subject) (see also recitals 40 and 46); Article 13 (Information to be made available or given to the data subject) (see further recital 42); Article 14 (Right of access by the data subject) and Article 15 (Limitations to the right of access) (see also recitals 43–45); Article 16 (Right to rectification or erasure of personal data and restriction of processing) (see also recital 47); Article 17 (Exercise of rights by the data subject and verification by the supervisory authority) (see also recital 48); Article 18 (Rights of the data subject in criminal investigations and proceedings) (see too recital 49)

Relevant Case Law

CJEU

Case T-201/04, *Microsoft Corp. v Commission of the European Communities*, CFI, judgment of 17 September 2007 (ECLI:T:2007:289).

A. Rationale and Policy Underpinnings

A number of distinct yet interconnected rationales are said to underpin the right to data portability. These range from the rights-based rationale to enhance informational self-determination and empower data subjects to the more economic rationale of reducing switching costs for consumers and promoting competition by potentially lowering barriers to entry to digital markets and encouraging the development of new products and services. Data portability may also enhance the free flow of personal data in keeping with the market integration objectives of EU data protection regulation. For instance, in its 2015 Digital Single Market Strategy for Europe, the Commission suggested that a lack of interoperability and portability between digital services acts as a barrier to the cross-border flow of data and to the development of new services.[1]

During the legislative process, the UK expressed a reservation in the Council that data portability should not be within the scope of data protection law but rather consumer or competition law and recommended that the provision should therefore be deleted. Other Member States (in particular, Denmark, Germany, France, Ireland, the Netherlands, Poland and Sweden) raised similar concerns regarding the nature and scope of the right to data portability.[2] This objective of promoting competition has been noted in several policy documents. For instance, the WP29 acknowledged that data portability is 'expected to foster opportunities for innovation',[3] while in its 'Questions and Answers' on data protection reform, the Commission notes that providing individuals with more control over their personal data through data portability will benefit business as '[s]tart-ups and smaller companies will be able to access data markets dominated by digital giants and attract more consumers with privacy-friendly solutions'.[4] Commentators on data portability, such as Graef, have suggested that lock-in in online social networks, such as Facebook, may be preventing users from switching despite fierce opposition to privacy policy changes by users.[5] Data portability may reduce the risk of lock-in by lowering the costs of switching services for data subjects.

---

[1] EC Communication 2015, pp. 14–15. [2] Council Report 2014, p. 3.
[3] WP29 2017, p. 5.   [4] EC Factsheet 2015.   [5] Graef 2015, p. 506.

Yet, the role of competition as an objective for data portability, as well as the relationship between the human rights orientated and economic rationales for data portability, remains contested. This is evidenced by the guidelines of the WP29 on data portability. In the initial draft of these guidelines, the WP29 stated that: 'the primary aim of data portability is to facilitate switching, from one service provider to another, thus enhancing competition between services' and that it enables 'the creation of new services in the context of the digital single market strategy'.[6] The final draft of the guidelines deletes this sentence and highlights that data portability 'aims to empower data subjects regarding their own personal data, as it facilitates their ability to move, copy or transmit personal data easily from one IT environment to another'.[7] To emphasise this point it states that whilst 'the right to data portability may enhance competition between services (by facilitating service switching), the GDPR is regulating personal data and not competition'.[8] Thus, it will likely be for the EDPB, in the first instance, and later perhaps the CJEU to clarify which of the underpinning rationales for data portability should prevail in case of conflict.

B. Legal Background

1. EU legislation

There is no legal antecedent for data portability in the EU, and it has thus been classified as a 'brand new right'.[9] The right has been linked within the data protection regime to the data subject's right of access to personal data. The European Parliament rapporteur suggested, on first reading, that the right to data portability should be merged with the right of access in Article 15 GDPR. Data portability would then strengthen the right of access. Ultimately however the Council resisted the merger of the two rights. Nevertheless, parts of the doctrine view data portability as an extension of the right of access,[10] and contend that portability should be 'modulated in practice' to mirror the right of access in some ways (for instance, to allow the data subject to select what should be transferred and the data controller to distinguish between categories of personal data).[11] However, the right to data portability is narrower in scope than the right of access (for example, it only applies to personal data 'provided by' the data subject), while others suggest that the right to data portability—at least as described in the WP29 guidelines—is 'something much more radical' than the existing right of access.[12]

Data portability may have been inspired by the concept of number portability, introduced by the EU's Universal Service Directive, which entitles consumers to switch from one mobile phone provider to another while retaining their mobile phone number.[13] The GDPR impact assessment notes that portability is 'a key factor for effective competition, as evidenced in other market sectors, e.g. number portability in the telecom sector'[14] while the EDPS notes that data portability would allow 'users to transfer between online services in a similar way that users of telephone services may change providers but keep their telephone numbers'.[15]

---

[6] WP29 2017, p. 4.   [7] Ibid.   [8] Ibid.
[9] Scudiero 2017, p. 119. See also CIPL 2017, p. 1.   [10] Vanberg and Ünver 2017, p. 2.
[11] Rec. 63 facilitates this in the context of the access right. See also CIPL 2017, p. 3.
[12] Cormack 2017.   [13] Art. 30 Universal Services Directive.
[14] EC Impact Assessment, p. 30.   [15] EDPS 2014, p. 15.

2. International instruments

The right to data portability has, thus far, also been absent from international treaties although a right to access personal data is set out in several treaties. For instance, Council of Europe Convention No. 108 provides for a right of access in Article 8(b) which provides that 'any person shall be enabled to obtain at reasonable intervals and without excessive delay or expense confirmation of whether personal data relating to him are stored in the automated data file as well as communication to him of such data in an intelligible form'. The text of the Modernised Convention 108 does not explicitly mention data portability. However, the Explanatory Report to the Modernised Convention states with regard to Article 10(3) that 'There should also be easy-to-use tools to enable data subjects to take their data to another provider of their choice or keep the data themselves (data portability tools)'.[16]

A sector-specific right to data portability exists in the United States for medical data. Patients can access and obtain a copy of their data pursuant to the 1996 Health Insurance Portability and Accountability Act ('HIPAA'). The rights of patients to, amongst other things, access, correct and obtain a copy of their medical records from public and private healthcare providers was initially enacted to improve the efficiency and effectiveness of the health-care system.[17] However, the right of individuals to 'get it, check it, use it' is now regarded as a consumer empowerment tool, and enforced by the US Office for Civil Rights.

Voluntary sector-specific initiatives also exist in the United States. The US Government introduced a series of 'My Data' schemes in 2010 with the aim of enabling consumers to access their own personal data in certain sectors. For example, the 'Green Button' scheme enabled consumers to access their electricity utility data, while the 'Get Transcript' scheme allowed them to access the tax data held by the Internal Revenue Service about them. The White House Office of Science and Technology Policy launched a consultation in 2016 to ascertain whether a broader right to data portability—more akin to that set out in the GDPR—would be desirable. This consultation concluded that although a more general data portability scheme might be incentivised, it should not be mandated.[18]

The Philippines is the only non-EU state, to date, to enact a general right to data portability as part of its domestic data protection legislation. In 2012, it signed into law a data protection act and implementing legislation. The 2012 Act sets out a right that is broader than the GDPR right as it does not require that the personal data should be 'provided by the data subject'.[19] However, this broad right is qualified by the accompanying implementing rules which state that the exercise of the right shall 'primarily take into account the right of data subject to have control over his or her personal data being processed based on consent or contract, for commercial purpose, or through automated means'.[20] These qualifications were likely introduced in order to align the right to its GDPR equivalent. While the right was part of a 2012 Act, the final version of the 'Implementing Rules and Regulations' that accompany the 2012 Act were adopted only in August 2016.[21] There is therefore no decisional practice to draw upon yet.

---

[16] Explanatory Report Convention 108 2018, p. 25.   [17] See HIPAA 1996, preamble.
[18] MacGillivray 2017.   [19] Philippine Data Privacy Act 2012, s. 18.   [20] Ibid., s. 36.
[21] Hunton and Williams 2016.

3. National developments

In the UK, the government eschewed legislation to mandate data portability and instead took a power pursuant to the Enterprise and Regulatory Reform Act 2013.[22] Data portability is therefore operating on a voluntary basis, but the Secretary of State can introduce regulations to make it compulsory should the government be unsatisfied with the progress made on a voluntary basis. The 'midata' initiative introduced in 2011 was part of a wider consumer empowerment strategy and sought to give individuals access to electronic data regarding their transactions in a machine-readable and portable format. Such transaction data would exclude personal data regarding transactions made using an unregistered guest account, or other complaints or communications data held by companies.[23] The midata scheme was also only focused on three sectors: namely, the financial sector, energy supply and the mobile phone sector. Thus, like the US 'My Data' schemes, the UK initiative is more limited in scope and application than the GDPR right.

4. Case law

Given that there is no predecessor to the right to data portability in the DPD, there is no case law concerning the right to data portability. The jurisprudence on the right to access[24] may however be of relevance in light of the relationship between the two rights.

It is also worth noting that data portability may be a remedy mandated under EU competition law (Article 102 Treaty on the Functioning of the European Union 'TFEU') in cases where the failure to provide access to the data might be deemed 'abusive' (as it would have an exclusionary effect on equally efficient competitors) if undertaken by a company with a position of market dominance.[25]

C. Analysis

1. Introduction

The right to data portability is the latest addition to the rights of the data subject and is intended to empower data subjects. Concerns have however been expressed regarding its broad scope of application, particularly when compared to the data portability remedy available pursuant to competition law.[26] The right is however qualified in important ways. Four criteria might be said to define the limits of the GDPR right to data portability: (i) 'personal data'; (ii) 'provided by' the data subject; (iii) processed pursuant to consent or contract; and (iv) processed by automated means.

2. The limits of the right to data portability

Unlike, for instance, competition law portability remedies, the right to data portability only applies to 'personal data'.[27] According to the WP29, the right covers pseudonymous

---

[22] UK Enterprise and Regulatory Reform Act 2013. [23] BIS 2012, p. 5.
[24] See the commentary on Art. 15 in this volume.
[25] Consider for example that Microsoft was ordered to provide interoperability information for its software to providers of alternative software products to enable them to interact with servers equipped with Microsoft software in EC Microsoft Decision, para. 782. This finding was upheld by the General Court in Case T-201/04, *Microsoft Corp.*
[26] Lynskey 2017. [27] See the commentary on Art. 4(1) in this volume.

data provided that they can be clearly linked to the data subject. Indeed, it follows from Article 11(2) GDPR that the right to data portability shall not apply if the controller is able to demonstrate that it is not in a position to identify the data subject unless the data subject then provides more information that enables the data controller to identify him/her. The controller therefore appears to have no autonomous obligation to acquire additional information for the identification of the data subject.[28]

The personal data must also be 'provided by' the data subject. The WP29 suggests that a distinction should be made between observed data and data actively and knowingly provided by the data subject, which would be included within the scope of the right, and, inferred and derived data, which would be excluded from the scope of the right.[29] According to this suggestion, data collected by a device such as a 'quantified self' application that tracks an individual's movements (exercise, sleep etc.) would be within the scope of the right while any insights gleaned on the basis of that information (for example, about the individual's health status or working patterns) would be excluded from the scope of the right. Such a distinction would ostensibly respect the intellectual property of data controllers (for instance, their application of data analytics to the data 'provided by' the data subject) although some practitioners suggest that the actual data provided to individuals may be where intellectual property lies. This is because it may provide an insight into the data gathering process and the types of data collected by the data controller.[30]

Intellectual property aside, others—such as the European Commission and the Centre for Information Policy and Leadership ('CIPL')—have suggested a narrower definition of 'provided by'. The European Commission's position is that the WP29 guidelines 'might go beyond what was agreed by the co-legislators in the legislative process'.[31] CIPL distinguishes between the wording of Articles 13 and 20 GDPR: Article 13 refers to information to be provided where personal data are 'collected from' the data subject, which, it is implied, is broader than data 'provided by' the data subject. CIPL therefore suggests that pursuant to Article 20 'there must be a voluntary, affirmative element of 'providing' data to the controller, as opposed to collecting data from an individual who may be passive'.[32] They distinguish between varieties of 'observed data' suggesting that data relating to a wearable device where the individuals 'willingly and knowingly provide tracking data and sensed data because it is part of the desired service to the individual and conveys a desired benefit to the individual' should fall within the scope. However, other observed data should not, including network traffic data, as such data 'falls under the category of technical analysis as it is data generated by systems and not provided by the individual in return for a specific benefit or as part of the service he or she intended to receive'.[33] This vision seems to conflict with that of the WP29 which suggested that the personal data provided to individuals exercising their right to data portability should include 'as many metadata with the data as possible at the best possible level of granularity' as this 'preserves the precise meaning of exchanged information'.[34]

Whatever the interpretation of 'provided by' adopted, however, it is noteworthy that important personal data, such as the online 'reputation' that an individual develops as a seller or host in digital marketplaces based on customer reviews, are likely to be excluded from the scope of the right to data portability.

---

[28] CIPL 2017, p. 7.   [29] WP29 2017, p. 8.   [30] Boardman and Mole 2017.
[31] Meyer 2017.   [32] CIPL 2017, p. 8.   [33] Ibid.   [34] WP29 2017, p. 14.

The right also only applies where the individual has either consented to the personal data processing or where the information is processed pursuant to a contract.[35] In instances where personal data processing is reliant on another legal basis (e.g. public interest), the WP29 suggests that it would be good practice nevertheless to develop data portability processes by 'following the principles governed by the right to data portability'.[36] It gives the example of government services ensuring that past personal income tax filings could be downloaded. Any such processes would however be developed on a voluntary basis. Indeed, Article 17(3) GDPR provides that the GDPR right 'shall not apply to processing necessary for the performance of a task carried out in the public interest or in the exercise of official authority vested in the controller'.

The right applies to processing carried out by automated means. It was noted, with concern, in Council that 'processing carried out by an automated processing system' (the wording of an earlier draft) could cover almost anything; however attempts to limit the right to providers of 'information society services' or internet services were rejected.[37] It has been suggested that to be automated 'the means used by the data controller will have to exclude any human intervention during the whole processing'.[38] However, given that the rights of the data subject are generally interpreted expansively, such a restriction seems unlikely.

It is useful to recall that when the right to data portability does not apply to particular personal data (for instance, a user profile) other rights, such as the right of access, the right to object or the right to delete, may remain applicable provided the data concerned are personal data.

3. The responsibilities of the data controller

According to Article 20(1) GDPR the data should be provided to the data subject in a 'structured, commonly used and machine-readable format' and the data subject should have the right to transmit those data to another data controller without hindrance. Moreover, Article 20(2) stipulates that, where technically feasible, the data should be transferred directly from one data controller to another.

The GDPR is silent as to the format of the data transmitted save to stipulate that they should be 'machine-readable'. Recital 68 does however specify that the data should be available in an 'interoperable format', which data controllers 'should be encouraged to develop', and that data portability 'should not create an obligation for the controllers to adopt or maintain processing systems which are technically compatible'. The WP29 defines interoperability as the 'capability to communicate, execute programs, or transfer data among various functional units in a manner that requires the user to have little or no knowledge of the unique characteristics of those units'.[39] It also notes that '"structured, commonly used and machine readable" are specifications for the means, whereas interoperability is the desired outcome'.[40] Yet, whether interoperability is desirable is contestable. For instance, it is legitimate to query whose privacy and data use policy will prevail in such circumstances. It is for this reason that some privacy scholars fear a 'privacy race to the bottom' if data portability is mandated.[41] Moreover, sceptics suggest that without standards leading to interoperability, the right to data portability may 'remain more a declaration of principle than a real and effective tool for individual self-determination in

[35] Art. 20(3) and rec. 68. [36] WP29 2017, p. 7. [37] Council Report 2014, p. 4.
[38] Scudiero 2017, p. 6. [39] WP29 2017, p. 14. [40] Ibid., p. 13.
[41] Grimmelmann 2009, p. 1194.

the digital environment'.[42] The Commission has published a Communication on 'ICT Standardization Priorities for the Digital Single Market', which may be used as a basis on which to develop standards for the purposes of data portability.

The responsibilities of the data controller are therefore difficult to grasp. As 'technically feasible' is not defined by the GDPR, some data controllers may claim that direct controller-to-controller data transfers are not possible. Scudiero suggests that a new export–import model will be needed, and that controllers will need to 'plan specific investments in order to adapt their IT systems to this new legal perspective'.[43] For its part, the WP29 recommends that data controllers offer several options to the data subject. They suggest, for instance, that data subjects should be offered an opportunity to directly download the data as well as to transmit it directly to another data controller, and that this could be implemented by making an Application Programme Interface ('API') available.[44] Cormack expresses doubt regarding the viability of this solution, noting that many organisations will hold their data on internal databases that are securely firewalled from internet access as opposed to APIs. He also warns that as the majority of data subjects are unlikely to ever use their own account on this API, it 'will create a large number of idle accounts, likely to have simple or default passwords' while good security practice has been to remove such accounts.[45]

A further query for data controllers concerns the data of third party data subjects. The WP29 guidelines suggest that the recipient data controller is responsible for ensuring that portable data provided are relevant and not excessive with regard to the new data processing. This obligation is however contestable. As CIPL notes, it is not clear that there is an obligation to receive this data on the recipient controller: 'it may be impractical or disproportionate to require the receiving controller to assess the data it receives; unrealistic to require the receiving controller to provide individuals with a full notice about data use before the request for transmission'.[46]

Article 20(4) GDPR explicitly states that the right to data portability should not adversely affect the rights and freedoms of others. Scudiero notes that this seems to imply that the right enjoys a lower rank compared to the rights and freedoms of others.[47] However, the WP29 stated that, for example, 'a potential business risk cannot, in and of itself serve as a basis for a refusal to answer a portability request'.[48]

4. The challenges of data portability

Data security will be a major challenge for data controllers. The opportunities for data breach are numerous: an individual may attempt to exercise the right fraudulently (which would also constitute a data security breach); the data may be interfered with during transmission between controllers; or, the data may be accessed once on the data subject's personal devices. For instance, where controllers have had no significant prior contact with the data subject, or where they hold only indirect identifiers for him or her, authentication of identity may be difficult. Articles 11(2) and 12(6) GDPR might be of use in such circumstances as they respectively allow the data subject to provide more information to the data controller to enable his or her identification and enable controllers with reasonable doubts regarding the identity of a data subject to request further information to confirm identity.

These data security risks should be taken into consideration by the data controller when conducting its data protection impact assessment. For its part, the WP29 simply recognised

---

[42] Scudiero 2017, p. 1.   [43] Ibid., p. 3.   [44] WP29 2017, p. 5.   [45] Cormack 2017.
[46] CIPL 2017, p. 5.   [47] Scudiero 2017, p. 9.   [48] WP29 2017, p. 10.

that data portability 'may also raise some security issues' while highlighting that the data controller will remain responsible for 'taking all the security measures needed to ensure that personal data is securely transmitted'.[49] Commentators have offered various solutions to alleviate these concerns: for instance, Scudiero suggests that Article 20 'should have been drafted so as to provide a clear reference to a minimum standard of security measures',[50] while CIPL recommends that solutions be found 'allowing individuals to suspend or freeze the portability mechanisms with respect to their accounts if there is suspicion that the account has been compromised, and a delay feature to enable robust verification of identity'.[51]

Select Bibliography

EU legislation

EC Microsoft Decision 2007: Commission Decision 2007/53/EC of 24 March 2004 (Case COMP/C-3/37.792 *Microsoft*), OJ 2007 L 32/23.
Universal Services Directive: Directive 2002/22/EC of the European Parliament and of the Council of 7 March 2002 on universal service and users' rights relating to electronic communications networks and services (Universal Service Directive), OJ 2002 L 108/51.

National legislation

HIPAA 1996: Health Insurance Portability and Accountability Act, Public Law 104-191 (104th Congress).
Philippine Data Privacy Act 2012: Act Protecting Individual Personal Information in Information and Communications Systems in the Government and the Private Sector, Creating for this Purpose a National Privacy Commission, and for Other Purposes, Republic Act No. 10173 ('the Data Privacy Act of 2012').
UK Enterprise and Regulatory Reform Act 2013: Enterprise and Regulatory Reform Act 2013 (Chapter 24).

Academic writings

Graef 2015: Graef, 'Mandating Portability and Interoperability in Online Social Networks', 39(6) *Telecommunications Policy* (2015), 502.
Grimmelmann 2009: Grimmelmann, 'Saving Facebook', 94(4) *Iowa Law Review* (2009), 1137.
Lynskey 2017: Lynskey, 'Aligning Data Protection Rights with Competition Law Remedies? The GDPR Right to Data Portability', 42(6) *European Law Review* (2017), 793.
Scudiero 2017: Scudiero, 'Bringing Your Data Everywhere: A Legal Reading of the Right to Data Portability', 3(1) *European Data Protection Law Review* (2017), 119.
Swire and Lagos, 'Why the Right to data Portability Likely Reduces Consumer Welfare: Antitrust and Privacy Critique', 72(2) *Maryland Law Review* (2013), 335.
Vanberg and Ünver 2017: Vanberg and Ünver, 'The Right to Data Portability in the GDPR and EU Competition Law: Odd Couple or Dynamic Duo?', 8(1) *European Journal of Law and Technology* (2017), 1.
Van der Auwermeulen, 'How to Attribute the Right to Data Portability in Europe: A Comparative Analysis of Legislations', 33(1) *Computer Law and Security Review* (2017), 57.

Papers of data protection authorities

EDPS 2014: EDPS, 'Preliminary Opinion Privacy and Competitiveness in the Age of Big Data: The Interplay between Data Protection, Competition Law and Consumer Protection in the Digital Economy' (March 2014).

---

[49] Ibid., p.15.   [50] Scudiero 2017, p. 7.   [51] CIPL 2017, p. 11.

WP29 2017: Article 29 Working Party, 'Guidelines on the Right to Data Portability' (WP 242 rev.01, as last revised and adopted on 5 April 2017).

Reports and recommendations

BIS 2012: BIS, 'Midata: Government Response to 2012 Consultation', available at https://assets.publishing.service.gov.uk/government/uploads/system/uploads/attachment_data/file/34700/12-1283-midata-government-response-to-2012-consultation.pdf.

Boardman and Mole 2017: Boardman and Mole, 'Data Portability Guidance' (9 January 2017), available at https://www.twobirds.com/en/news/articles/2016/global/data-portability-guidance.

CIPL 2017: Centre for Information Policy Leadership, 'Comments on the Article 29 Data Protection Working Party's "Guidelines on the Right to Data Portability" Adopted on 13 December 2016' (2017).

Cormack 2017: Cormack, 'Portability Right: A Data Protection Challenge' (27 January 2017), available at https://community.jisc.ac.uk/blogs/regulatory-developments/article/portability-right-data-protection-challenge.

Council Report 2014: Proposal for a regulation of the European Parliament and of the Council on the protection of individuals with regard to the processing of personal data and on the free movement of such data (General Data Protection Regulation)—Data Portability (Revision of Article 18), 10614/14, 6 June 2014.

EC Communication 2015: Communication from the Commission to the European Parliament, the Council, the European Economic and Social Committee and the Committee of the Regions, 'A Digital Single Market Strategy for Europe' COM(2015) 192 final, 6 May 2015.

EC Impact Assessment: Commission Staff Working Paper 'Impact Assessment Accompanying the document Regulation of the European Parliament and of the Council on the protection of individuals with regard to the processing of personal data and on the free movement of such data (General Data Protection Regulation) and Directive of the European Parliament and of the Council on the protection of individuals with regard to the processing of personal data by competent authorities for the purposes of prevention, investigation, detection or prosecution of criminal offences or the execution of criminal penalties, and the free movement of such data', SEC(2012) 72 final, 25 January 2012.

Explanatory Report Convention 108 2018: Council of Europe, 'Explanatory Report to the Protocol Amending the Convention for the Protection of Individuals with Regard to the Automatic Processing of Personal Data' (10 October 2018), available at https://rm.coe.int/cets-223-explanatory-report-to-the-protocol-amending-the-convention-fo/16808ac91a.

Others

EC Factsheet 2015: European Commission, 'Fact Sheet: Questions and Answers—Data Protection Reform' (2015), available at http://europa.eu/rapid/press-release_MEMO-15-6385_en.htm.

Hunton and Williams 2016: Hunton and Williams, Privacy & Information Security Law Blog, 'Final Rules for the Data Privacy Act Published in the Philippines' (13 September 2016), available at https://www.huntonprivacyblog.com/2016/09/13/final-rules-data-privacy-act-published-philippines/.

MacGillivray 2017: MacGillivray, 'Summary of Comments Received Regarding Data Portability' (10 January 2017), available at https://obamawhitehouse.archives.gov/blog/2017/01/10/summary-comments-received-regarding-data-portability.

Meyer 2017: Meyer, 'European Commission Experts Uneasy over WP29 Data Portability Interpretation' (25 April 2017), available at https://iapp.org/news/a/european-commission-experts-uneasy-over-wp29-data-portability-interpretation-1/.

Section 4 Right to object and automated individual decision-making

Article 21. Right to object

GABRIELA ZANFIR-FORTUNA

1. The data subject shall have the right to object, on grounds relating to his or her particular situation, at any time to processing of personal data concerning him or her which is based on point (e) or (f) of Article 6(1), including profiling based on those provisions. The controller shall no longer process the personal data unless the controller demonstrates compelling legitimate grounds for the processing which override the interests, rights and freedoms of the data subject or for the establishment, exercise or defence of legal claims.
2. Where personal data are processed for direct marketing purposes, the data subject shall have the right to object at any time to processing of personal data concerning him or her for such marketing, which includes profiling to the extent that it is related to such direct marketing.
3. Where the data subject objects to processing for direct marketing purposes, the personal data shall no longer be processed for such purposes.
4. At the latest at the time of the first communication with the data subject, the right referred to in paragraphs 1 and 2 shall be explicitly brought to the attention of the data subject and shall be presented clearly and separately from any other information.
5. In the context of the use of information society services, and notwithstanding Directive 2002/58/EC, the data subject may exercise his or her right to object by automated means using technical specifications.
6. Where personal data are processed for scientific or historical research purposes or statistical purposes pursuant to Article 89(1), the data subject, on grounds relating to his or her particular situation, shall have the right to object to processing of personal data concerning him or her, unless the processing is necessary for the performance of a task carried out for reasons of public interest.

Relevant Recitals

(69) Where personal data might lawfully be processed because processing is necessary for the performance of a task carried out in the public interest or in the exercise of official authority vested in the controller, or on grounds of the legitimate interests of a controller or a third party, a data subject should, nevertheless, be entitled to object to the processing of any personal data relating to his or her particular situation. It should be for the controller to demonstrate that its compelling legitimate interest overrides the interests or the fundamental rights and freedoms of the data subject.

(70) Where personal data are processed for the purposes of direct marketing, the data subject should have the right to object to such processing, including profiling to the extent that it is related to such direct marketing, whether with regard to initial or further processing, at any time and free of charge. That right should be explicitly brought to the attention of the data subject and presented clearly and separately from any other information.

Closely Related Provisions

Article 12 (Transparent information, communication and modalities for the exercise of the rights of the data subject) (see too recital 59); Article 17 (Right to erasure) (see too recital 65);

Article 18 (Right to restriction of processing) (see to recital 67); Article 23 (Restrictions) (see too recital 73)

Related Provisions in LED [Directive (EU) 2016/680]

Article 16 (Right to rectification or erasure of personal data and restriction of processing) (see too recital 47)

Related Provisions in EPD [Directive 2002/58/EC]

Article 13 (Unsolicited communications) (see too recital 40)

Relevant Case Law

CJEU

Case C-131/12, *Google Spain v Agencia Española de Protección de Datos (AEPD) and Mario Costeja González*, judgment of 13 May 2014 (Grand Chamber) (ECLI:EU:C:2014:317).
Case C-398/15, *Camera di Commercio, Industria, Artigianato e Agricoltura di Lecce v Salvatore Manni*, judgment of 9 March 2017 (ECLI:EU:C:2017:197).
Case C-434/16, *Peter Nowak v Data Protection Commissioner*, judgment of 20 December 2017 (ECLI:EU:C:2017:994).
Opinion of Advocate General Kokott in Case C-434/16, *Peter Nowak v Data Protection Commissioner*, delivered on 20 July 2017 (ECLI:EU:C:2017:582).

ECtHR

Österreichischer Rundfunk v Austria, Appl. No. 35841/02, judgment of 7 December 2005.
Verlagsgruppe News GmbH v Austria (no. 2), Appl. No. 10/520/02, judgment of 14 December 2006.
Mosley v United Kingdom, Appl. No. 48009/08, judgment of 10 May 2011.
Węgrzynowski and Smolczewski v Poland, Appl. No. 33846/07, judgment of 16 July 2013.
Von Hannover v Germany (No. 3), Appl. No. 8772/10, judgment of 19 September 2013.

A. Rationale and Policy Underpinning

The right to object is another manifestation of the 'control centric' nature of the EU data protection legal framework. It has two forms: the general right to object, under Article 21(1) GDPR, and the right to object to direct marketing, under Article 21(2) GDPR.

On one hand, the general right to object allows data subjects to oppose processing of personal data that is lawful, based on their particular situation. Its rationale is that the circumstances of an individual may justify ending a processing operation at the request of the data subject, even if the controller engages in lawful processing. However, its scope is limited to those processing activities that are grounded in the necessity for the performance of a task carried out in the public interest or in the exercise of official authority,[1] and in the necessity for the legitimate interests pursued by the controller or by a third party.[2] Thus, it is the equivalent of the right to withdraw consent at any time when processing is based on consent, but in the context of processing of personal data based on a task in the public interest, official authority or on legitimate interests. If the processing of personal data is conducted on any other lawful basis under Article 6, the right to object is not applicable.

---

[1] Art. 6(1)(e) GDPR.   [2] Ibid., Art. 6(1)(f).

On the other hand, the right to object to direct marketing grants the data subjects an unconditional right to ask for their personal data not to be processed anymore for direct marketing purposes, including for profiling to the extent that it is related to direct marketing. The right is 'unconditional' in the sense that in order for an objection to be effective, the data subject does not need to invoke his or her particular situation and the controller does not have the possibility to show that it has compelling legitimate grounds to continue the processing.

The right to object has its origin in the French data protection law of 1978[3] and was not generally recognised throughout Europe before the adoption of the DPD in 1995.[4] Article 26 of the 1978 French law provided that everyone had the right to object, for legitimate reasons, to personal data concerning him or her being subject to processing. Therefore, from the very beginning, the right to object was linked to the particular situation of the data subject rather than to the lawfulness of the processing.

B. Legal Background

1. EU legislation

The right to object was provided in Article 14 DPD, which enshrined the two forms of this right that continued to be provided in the GDPR—the general right to object and the right to object to processing of personal data for direct marketing.[5] At first sight, the DPD provided for a wider general right to object, since it mentioned that Member States have to grant a right to object 'at least' for processing based on legitimate interests and for processing based on a task in the public interest or in the exercise of public authority. However, upon closer examination, the DPD in fact allowed Member States to widely derogate from the right to object altogether, providing in Article 14(1)(a) that this right shall be granted at least in those two cases, 'save where otherwise provided by national legislation'.

In principle, Article 14(a) DPD allowed the data subjects to object 'at any time' and 'on compelling legitimate grounds' to the processing of personal data. Therefore, it was implied that the data subjects had the burden of proof to show that their particular situation involved compelling legitimate grounds for the objection to be justified. According to the same provision, the consequence of a successful right to object was the fact that the processing 'may no longer involve those data'.[6] In practice, however, the text of Article 14(a) was not clear enough on the consequences of a justified objection, leaving room for different national implementations.

The right to object to direct marketing was provided by Article 14(b) DPD and provided for two possibilities: the data subject could either directly request the controller to stop processing his or her personal data for direct marketing, or the data subject could be informed by the controller before the personal data were made available to third parties for direct marketing and be provided the possibility to object to the disclosure or uses of such data. These two alternatives were described as 'surprisingly' having a notably

---

[3] French Data Protection Act 1978.   [4] See Church and Millard 2006, p. 82.

[5] As shown by Kosta, this right amounted to an 'opt-out' under the DPD, highlighting that 'any reference to the so-called "opt-out" consent, as is commonly the case in the UK, is incorrect, and that "opt-out" refers to an opportunity to object'. See Kosta 2015, p. 17.

[6] See also Dammann and Simitis 1997, p. 214.

different content.[7] However, Member States transposed both options equally in their national laws.[8] Just like its successor in the GDPR, the right to object to processing of personal data for direct marketing under the DPD did not need to be justified in any way, a mere objection being sufficient for it to be effective.

The right to object to direct marketing was further clarified by the EPD when regulating unsolicited communications. Article 13(2) of the EPD allows entities to use the contact details of their existing customers obtained in the context of the sale of a product or service, to send direct marketing messages without obtaining specific consent for this purpose. However, it specifically requires that such communications can only be done if the customers are given 'clearly and distinctly' the right to object to such use of their contact details. The EPD also imposes that the opportunity to object must be given 'free of charge and in an easy manner' and 'on the occasion of each message in case the customer has not initially refused such use'. The provisions of the EPD are considered *lex specialis* in relation to the GDPR, and therefore should have priority in a case of conflict.

Importantly, the LED does not provide for a right to object to the processing of personal data. It would indeed conflict with the nature of processing personal data by public entities in the law enforcement sector for purposes related to their core activity, were the data subject given the opportunity to object grounded on his or her particular situation and not on the lawfulness of the processing. However, the data subject does have the right to obtain erasure from controllers 'without undue delay' where processing infringes the principles relating to processing of personal data as enshrined in Article 4 LED, the rules relating to lawful grounds for processing as detailed in Article 8 LED and the conditions to process special categories of personal data as provided by Article 10 thereof. Personal data whose processing fall under the LED must also be erased if this is required by a legal obligation to which the controller is subject. Additionally, if the data subject opposes the processing and considers that any of his or her rights provided by the LED are infringed, he or she has the possibility to lodge a complaint with the competent supervisory authority (Article 52) and also has the right to an effective judicial remedy against a controller or processor (Article 54).

The EUDPR, which governs the processing of personal data by EU institutions and bodies, provides for a general right to object at Article 23. Data subjects have the right to object only to processing that is necessary for the performance of a task carried out in the public interest or in the exercise of official authority vested in the Union institution or body.[9] In addition, when processing is based on consent, the data subject has the right to withdraw consent at any time, in accordance with Article 7(3). The EUDPR does not provide for a right to object to the processing of personal data for direct marketing purposes, which is surprising given that EU institutions also engage in promotional activities. The only provision that deals with direct marketing is Article 38, which requires Union institutions and bodies to prevent personal data contained in directories of users they maintain from being used for direct marketing purposes, regardless of whether such directories are accessible to the public or not. According to the EDPS, the right to object cannot be restricted under Article 25(1) of the Regulation: 'In practice, ... the data subject always

---

[7] Korff 2005, 100.   [8] Church and Millard 2006, p. 82.
[9] Note that the EUDPR does not provide for the possibility to process personal data on the basis of legitimate interests, since controllers whose activity falls under it are all public authorities.

has the right to complain. However, the controller has to examine the objection and may demonstrate that there are compelling legitimate grounds not to accept it'.[10]

2. International instruments

Providing for a right to object is one of the improvements the Modernised Convention 108 brought as compared to the original version. Article 9(1)(d) of the Modernised Convention provides that every individual has a right to object 'at any time, on grounds relating to his or her situation to the processing of personal data concerning him or her, unless the controller demonstrates legitimate grounds for the processing which override his or her interests or rights and fundamental freedoms', a right that is not contained in the original version of Convention 108. Thus, the burden of proof to show 'legitimate grounds' in this case rests on the controller.

As compared to the GDPR, it seems that the threshold to overturn an objection is lower. While the GDPR refers to 'compelling legitimate grounds' of the controller,[11] the Convention seems to allow an objection to be dismissed based on any legitimate ground that overrides the interests and rights of the data subject. This may be problematic in jurisdictions that recognise processing on the basis of legitimate interests as one of the lawful grounds for processing (the Modernised Convention 108 provides for processing based on a 'legitimate basis laid down by law',[12] leaving it to the signatory parties to define what this means). Not imposing 'compelling' legitimate grounds as the counterbalance to objection could technically mean that any processing lawfully based on legitimate interests is immune from the right to object, given that one of the main conditions (at least under the GDPR) for this lawful ground to be applicable is that the legitimate interests of the controller or the third party override those of the data subject.[13] It will thus be interesting to see how these provisions will interplay in practice in the signatory countries that will ratify the Convention. On another hand, it is important to note that the Convention does not limit the right to object to specific lawful grounds for processing, as the GDPR does in Article 21.

The Explanatory Report accompanying the Modernised Convention 108 specifies that, for example, the establishment, exercise or defence of legal claims or reasons of public safety could be considered as overriding legitimate grounds justifying the continuation of the processing when an individual objects to it.[14] In any case, such justifications would have to be demonstrated on a case by case basis.[15] The Explanatory Report also clarifies that 'objection to data processing for marketing purposes should lead to unconditional erasing or removing of the personal data covered by the objection'.[16]

The OECD Privacy Framework[17] does not provide for a right to object. However, it does provide under the 'individual participation principle' for a right of individuals to 'challenge data relating to them', and if the challenge is successful, the right to have the data 'erased, rectified or amended'.[18] According to the explanations accompanying the OECD Framework, the right to challenge 'is broad in scope and includes first instance challenges to data controllers as well as subsequent challenges in courts, administrative bodies, professional organs or other institutions according to domestic rules of

---

[10] EDPS 2018, p. 7. [11] Art. 21(1) GDPR.
[12] See Art. 5(2) Modernised Convention 108. [13] Art. 6(1)(f) GDPR.
[14] Explanatory Report Convention 108 2018, para. 78. [15] Ibid. [16] Ibid., para. 79.
[17] OECD Guidelines 2013. [18] Ibid., Art. 13(d).

procedure'.[19] One could argue that the scope of this principle is perhaps too broad, given that it guarantees neither a judicial remedy nor a right to oppose processing based on compelling grounds resulting from a particular situation of the individual.

3. National developments

While Article 21 does not explicitly refer to Member State law, national laws do contain some interesting divergences, as is shown by a few examples.

According to the German implementation of the GDPR, the right to object as provided by Article 21(1) of the GDPR is not applicable with regard to a public body if there is an urgent public interest in the processing which outweighs the interests of the data subject or if processing is required by law.[20] The law does not define what an 'urgent public interest' means. Thus, the only limitation of this right is provided with regard to processing based on Article 6(1)(e) GDPR, while the right to object to processing based on Article 6(1)(f) is not affected by restrictions under the German act.

The Irish Data Protection Act 2018 enshrines a specific carve out of the right to object for processing carried out in the course of electoral activities in Ireland by a political party or a candidate for election to, or a holder of, elective political office in that state, as well as by the Irish Referendum Commission in the performance of its functions.[21]

The UK Data Protection Act[22] provides a detailed list of exemptions to all rights of the data subject in Schedules 2 and 3, including the right to object, but only with regard to the general right to object and not with regard to the right to object to processing for direct marketing. The list of exemptions is very wide. For example, the general right to object does not apply to processing for the purposes of the assessment and collection of taxes;[23] processing of personal data for the maintenance of effective immigration control;[24] personal data consisting of information that the controller is obliged to make available to the public, to the extent that the application of the right to object would prevent the controller from complying with its legal obligations;[25] disclosures of personal data necessary for the purpose or in connection with legal proceedings;[26] as well as some processing of health, social work, education and child abuse data.[27]

In addition, exercise of the right to object may be restricted by Member State law pursuant to Article 23 GDPR.

4. Case law

In *Nowak*, the CJEU placed the right to object among the building blocks of the data protection legal framework, highlighting that this framework is a mixture of accountability of controllers and rights of individuals to control their personal data. The case involved a preliminary ruling procedure originating in Ireland and concerning the question of whether exam scripts are personal data, and, if that is the case, whether the data subject has the right to access that personal data. Specifically, the Court held that the principles of protection provided by the DPD:

are reflected, on the one hand, in the obligations imposed on those responsible for processing data, obligations which concern in particular data quality, technical security, notification to the

---

[19] Ibid., p. 59.   [20] German GDPR Implementation Law, s. 36.
[21] Irish Data Protection Act 2018, Art. 59.   [22] UK Data Protection Act 2018.
[23] Ibid., Sched. 2, Art. 2(1)(c).   [24] Ibid., Sched. 2, Art. 4(1)(a).
[25] Ibid., Sched. 2, Art. 5(1).   [26] Ibid., Sched. 2, Art. 5(3)(a).   [27] Ibid., Sched. 3.

supervisory authority, and the circumstances under which processing can be carried out, and, on the other hand, in the rights conferred on individuals, the data on whom are the subject of processing, to be informed that processing is taking place, to consult the data, to request correction and even to object to processing in certain circumstances.[28]

Moreover, the Court upheld the view of Advocate General Kokott that an examination candidate has 'a legitimate interest, based on the protection of his private life, in being able to object to the processing of the answers submitted by him at that examination and of the examiner's comments with respect to those answers outside the examination procedure and, in particular, to their being sent to third parties, or published, without his permission'.[29] The Court relied on this argument to highlight that considering exam scripts and examiner's comments to be personal data would allow the individual to exercise some of the rights of a data subject, even if correction of the exam scripts or the comments would not be possible.

In *Manni*, a case where the right to object was analysed by the CJEU in parallel with the right of erasure, the Court was asked whether the obligation of Member States to keep public Companies Registers, and data retention requirements to keep personal data in a form which permits identification of data subjects for no longer than is necessary for the purposes for which the data were collected, must be interpreted as allowing individuals to 'request the authority responsible for maintaining the Companies Register to limit, after a certain period has elapsed from the dissolution of the company concerned and on the basis of a case-by-case assessment, access to personal data concerning them and entered in that register'.[30] The case was initiated by an Italian citizen who had requested his regional Chamber of Commerce to erase his personal data from the Public Registry of Companies, after he found out that he was losing clients who performed background checks on him through a private company that specialised in finding information in the Public Register. This happened because the applicant had been an administrator of a company that was declared bankrupt more than ten years before the facts in the main proceedings.

Analysing the applicability of the right to erasure through the lens of the data retention principle and in the context of Directive 68/151/EEC,[31] the Court found it impossible to identify a single time limit from the dissolution of a company at the end of which the inclusion of personal data in the register and their disclosure would no longer be necessary.[32] The Court thus concluded that data subjects in this case are not guaranteed a right of erasure by the DPD after a certain period of time has passed from the dissolution of the company.[33] The Court further analysed the applicability of Article 14 DPD in this case and established that, in principle, the need to protect the interests of third parties in relation to joint-stock companies and limited liability companies and to ensure legal certainty, fair trading and thus the proper functioning of the internal market take precedence over the right of the data subject to object.[34]

Nonetheless, highlighting the exceptional character of the right to object to lawful processing and related to specific circumstances of a person, the Court also noted that:

it cannot be excluded however, that there may be specific situations in which the overriding and legitimate reasons relating to the specific case of the person concerned justify exceptionally that access to personal data entered in the register is limited, upon expiry of a sufficiently long period

---

[28] Case C-434/16, *Nowak*, para. 48.   [29] Case C-434/16, *Nowak* (AG Opinion), para. 50.
[30] Case C-398/15, *Manni*, para. 30.   [31] Directive 68/151/EEC.
[32] Case C-398/15, *Manni*, para. 55.   [33] Ibid., para. 56.   [34] Ibid., para. 60.

after the dissolution of the company in question, to third parties who can demonstrate a specific interest in their consultation.[35]

While acknowledging that theoretically such a limited right to object exists for particular reasons, the Court pointed out that in the specific case of the complainant it is not applicable, since:

> the mere fact that, allegedly, the properties of a tourist complex built ... do not sell because of the fact that potential purchasers of those properties have access to that data in the company register, cannot be regarded as constituting such a reason, in particular in view of the legitimate interest of those purchasers in having that information.[36]

The *Google Spain*[37] case of the CJEU is usually recalled in the literature as being the landmark judgment on the right of erasure.[38] However, the judgment is as much about the right to object as about the erasure right.[39] In fact, all the key findings of the Court, and especially the finding that a data subject has the right to have internet search results on the basis of his name removed, are made by the Court interpreting and equally applying both Article 12(b) DPD (the right to erasure) and Article 14(a) DPD (the general right to object).[40] However, the judgment does not always refer to the two rights in tandem, the Court differentiating them at one point by highlighting that while the right of erasure entails an assessment of whether the processing of personal data complies with lawfulness requirements, this is not the case for the general right to object, which may be relied on 'in addition' to an erasure request which is made based on the unlawfulness of the processing.[41] The Court further dwells on the general right to object and explains that 'the balancing to be carried out under subparagraph (a) of the first paragraph of Article 14 thus enables account to be taken in a more specific manner of all the circumstances surrounding the data subject's particular situation. Where there is a justified objection, the processing instigated by the controller may no longer involve those data'.[42]

In *Google Spain*, the Court also focuses separately on the right to object in analysing how requests to remove personal data may have different results when applying Article 14(a) DPD when the context of the processing differs, and in this particular case when personal data are processed by a newspaper and when they are processed by an internet search engine bringing a newspaper article out of obscurity. The Court specifically states that:

> the outcome of the weighing of the interests at issue to be carried out under Article 7(f) and subparagraph (a) of the first paragraph of Article 14 of the directive *may differ* according to whether the processing carried out by the operator of a search engine or that carried out by the publisher of the web page is at issue, given that, first, the legitimate interests justifying the processing may be different and, second, the consequences of the processing for the data subject, and in particular for his private life, are not necessarily the same.[43]

On the basis of this argument, the Court finds that both Article 12(b) and Article 14(a) DPD mean that, when all of their conditions are satisfied:

> the operator of a search engine is obliged to remove from the list of results displayed following a search made on the basis of a person's name links to web pages, published by third parties and

---

[35] Ibid. [36] Ibid., para. 63. [37] Case C-131/12, *Google Spain*.
[38] See the commentary on Art. 17 GDPR in this volume.
[39] For a detailed analysis of this judgment see Zanfir 2015.
[40] Case C-131/12, *Google Spain*, paras. 3 and 4 of the executive part. [41] Ibid., para. 75.
[42] Ibid., para. 76. [43] Ibid., para. 86 (emphasis added).

containing information relating to that person, also in a case where that name or information is not erased beforehand or simultaneously from those web pages, and even, as the case may be, when its publication in itself on those pages is lawful.[44]

The right to respect for private life as enshrined in Article 8 of the European Convention on Human Rights and Fundamental Freedoms ('ECHR') protects under its wide umbrella certain aspects of the right to personal data protection.[45] The right to object to processing is not yet clearly one of those aspects, which may also partially be explained by the fact that Convention 108 did not enshrine a right to object until its modernisation in 2018. Nonetheless, there are certain similarities between the right to object and requests to have news articles removed from websites,[46] or injunctions to stop the publication of images in printed publications or over the internet,[47] which often find their way to the Court in Strasbourg. In such cases the Court always engages in a balancing exercise between freedom of expression under Article 10 ECHR and the right to respect for private life, including one's own image, under Article 8 ECHR. On the other hand, one could say that such cases are perhaps more similar to the right of erasure under Article 17 GDPR, since it specifically makes a reference to freedom of expression under its limitations.

C. Analysis

1. Introduction

The right to object as provided by the GDPR has evolved compared to the DPD. Hustinx has characterised it as 'stronger', since 'it does not require the data subject to show a compelling legitimate ground to object and instead requires the controller to justify the compelling need for the processing'.[48]

Two perspectives shine a useful light on the right to object under the GDPR. The first arises when the right to object is compared with the withdrawal of consent per Article 7(3) GDPR. Just as withdrawal of consent provides the data subject the opportunity to halt a processing operation which was lawfully initiated on the basis of his or her consent, the right to object provides an opportunity to halt a processing operation which was initiated by the controller without the consent of the data subject, but on the basis of either the controller's legitimate interests or those of third parties, or on the basis of performing a task in the public interest or in the exercise of official authority. The main difference between the two types of opposition to processing is that unlike the general right to object, the withdrawal of consent is unconditional. While the general right to object is also strong, the controller nonetheless has the possibility to demonstrate it has compelling grounds to continue the processing.

The second perspective can be seen when comparing the right to object with the right of erasure as provided by Article 17 GDPR. Both rights, when exercised successfully, in principle lead to erasure of the personal data in question.[49] However, there are some fundamental differences in the way they operate. As explained by recitals 65 and 69 GDPR, the right of erasure applies where the retention of the personal data infringes the GDPR

---

[44] Ibid., para. 88.
[45] See further e.g. Bygrave 2014, pp. 86 et seq.
[46] See e.g. ECtHR, *Węgrzynowski*.
[47] See e.g. ECtHR, *Mosley*; ECtHR, *Von Hannover*; ECtHR, *Österreichischer Rundfunk;* and ECtHR, *Verlagsgruppe*.
[48] Hustinx 2017, p. 153.
[49] However, Art. 21(3) GDPR raises some questions in this regard, which are explored below.

or Union or Member State law to which the controller is subject, while, on the contrary, the right to object applies when personal data is processed lawfully, but the data subject wants the processing to stop on the basis of his or her particular situation. Another significant difference is that the right of erasure applies irrespective of the lawful ground relied upon by the controller to process the personal data as long as the conditions for erasure are met, while the general right to object only applies when processing is done on the basis of letters (e) and (f) of Article 6(1). It should also be noted that the right to object for direct marketing purposes, following the second paragraph of Article 21, is in fact applicable irrespective of the lawful ground relied on for such processing.

In fact, there is a connection between withdrawal of consent, the right to object and the right of erasure. Pursuant to Article 17(1)(b) and Article 17(1)(c), the data subject has the right to obtain erasure from the controller where he or she withdraws consent and where he or she successfully objects to the processing of personal data under both Article 21(1) and Article 21(2) GDPR.

Exercise of the right to object may be restricted by Union or Member State law pursuant to Article 23 GDPR, as is the case with other rights of the data subject, within the limits set by that article.[50] Of relevance for the right to object is that most of the restrictions that could be implemented under Article 23 are based on public interest objectives, meaning that such restrictions mainly apply to objection to processing based on Article 6(1)(e) and may affect less those based on Article 6(1)(f).

2. Compelling legitimate grounds

The general right to object is provided by Article 21(1) GDPR, which confers the data subject a right to object to processing, 'on grounds relating to his or her particular situation', and at the same time imposes on the controller a correlated duty to 'no longer process the personal data unless the controller demonstrates compelling legitimate grounds for the processing'. In order for the compelling legitimate grounds to be valid, they need to either 'override the interests, rights and freedoms of the data subject', or to be necessary 'for the establishment, exercise or defence of legal claims'. However, it will not suffice that the rights of the data subjects are overridden by legitimate grounds of the controller, since the latter also have to be 'compelling', meaning 'overwhelming' or that they override the rights of the individual in a strong, significant way.[51] Otherwise, if it were accepted that it is sufficient for the controller to have overriding legitimate interests in order to dismiss an objection, it would mean that any processing of personal data lawfully based on Article 6(1)(f) cannot be subject to a successful objection. This is because all processing allowed under Article 6(1)(f) presupposes that the legitimate interests of the controller or a third party outweigh the rights of the data subject.

If a controller decides to reject an objection on the basis of Article 21(1), the controller has the burden of proof that the conditions are met. Therefore, it is not for the data subject to prove that his or her particular circumstances justify the objection, but it is for the controller to prove that it has compelling legitimate grounds to continue the processing. As such, the reasoning for any rejection to a request in the exercise of the right to object should be included by the controller in the correspondence with the data subject.

---

[50] See the commentary on Art. 23 in this volume.   [51] In this sense see also WP29 2018, p. 19.

3. Effect of the right of objection

Irrespective of whether an objection is successful or not, immediately after a request to exercise the right to object is received from the data subject, the controller has to restrict the processing, pursuant to Article 18(1)(d) GDPR, 'pending the verification whether the legitimate grounds of the controller override those of the data subject'. Restricting the processing means that, with the exception of storage, the personal data can only be processed with the consent of the data subject or for the establishment, exercise or defence of legal claims, for the protection of the rights of other persons or for reasons of important public interest of the Union or of a Member State.[52]

If after verifying the request the controller finds that the objection has merit, then it must 'no longer process' that personal data, according to Article 21(1). Given that 'storing' personal data is part of the definition of 'processing' under Article 4(2) GDPR, this means that the controller cannot even merely retain the data. As mentioned above, Article 17(1)(c) GDPR in fact provides that the controller has the obligation to erase personal data 'without undue delay' where the data subject successfully objects to the processing pursuant to Article 21(1). The two provisions interpreted together mean that the data subject does not have to submit an additional request for erasure of the data after he or she successfully objected to the processing pursuant to Article 21(1) GDPR. The controller, being under an obligation to no longer process the personal data, should immediately erase that personal data that is subject to the objection.

4. Objections for direct marketing purposes

A data subject has the right to object 'at any time' to processing for direct marketing purposes under Article 21(2), including profiling to the extent that it relates to direct marketing. There are no conditions attached to effectively exercising this right, neither with regard to a specific lawful ground of the processing, nor with regard to the existence of particular circumstances of the data subject or of rights that override compelling legitimate interests of the controller. Therefore, 'there is no need for any balancing of interests'.[53] It is enough that the data subject objects for the objection to be successful.

Article 21(3) provides that where such an objection to direct marketing occurs, 'the personal data shall no longer be processed *for such purposes*' (emphasis added). This means that, unlike a successful objection under Article 21(1), the controller can keep processing the personal data, but only for purposes other than direct marketing. However, if the data subject makes a specific request under Article 17(1)(b) for erasure of the personal data pursuant to an objection made under Article 21(2), then the controller would have to erase the personal data. It is conceivable, though, that the controller could argue the personal data should only be erased from a dedicated list or database kept for direct marketing and continue to process the personal data for other purposes under Article 21(3). In addition, some DPAs (such as the UK Information Commissioner or ICO) suggest that some personal data of the individuals who object to direct marketing should be kept in order to ensure that 'their preference not to receive direct marketing is respected in the future'.[54]

[52] Art. 18(2) GDPR. [53] WP29 2018, p. 19. [54] ICO Website.

5. Scientific or historical research purposes or statistical purposes

According to Article 21(6) GDPR, there are specific rules with regard to the right to object to processing of personal data for scientific or historical research purposes or statistical purposes that satisfy the conditions of Article 89(1) GDPR.[55] In these cases, the right to object is not applicable if it concerns processing based on Article 6(1)(e), and in particular processing on the basis of necessity 'for the performance of a task carried out for reasons of public interest'. However, the right to object is still applicable against processing for research or archiving purposes based on Article 6(1)(f) and on the second branch of Article 6(1)(e) (processing of personal data in the exercise of official authority vested in the controller).[56] In these cases, the data subject would have to invoke his or her particular situation when he or she objects, which means that the right to object in this case is not unconditional. However, the text of Article 21(6) does not make reference to the existence of compelling legitimate grounds of the controller for the right to object to be rejected, which means that the threshold for rejecting an objection might be lower and even the burden of proof might be reversed when the purpose of the processing is related to research or archiving in the public interest. These aspects need further guidance from supervisory authorities and courts.

6. Transparency

Article 21(4) GDPR provides for a special transparency rule, requiring the right to object be 'explicitly brought to the attention of the data subject' and 'presented clearly and separately from any other information'. This often means in practice that the data subject should be provided with an 'opt-out' possibility at the first communication from the controller. This is especially applicable for processing for direct marketing purposes. As for other types of processing, whenever the processing relies on Article 6(1)(e) and(f), at least the data protection notice must contain a specific reference to the existence of the right to object, and the reference must be made in a distinct paragraph or pictogram.[57] The distinct information with regard to the right to object must be provided 'at the latest at the time of the first communication with the data subject', according to Article 21(4) GDPR. As for any other information that needs to be disclosed to the data subject, Articles 13 and 14 GDPR apply regarding the content and the timing.

7. Modalities for exercising the right

Article 21(5) GDPR specifies that when processing of personal data is conducted through the use of information society services,[58] the data subject may exercise his or her right to object 'by automated means using technical specifications'. For example, clicking on an 'opt-out' link in a direct marketing email would meet this criterion, as would providing a dedicated Wi-Fi network for mobile phone users that want not to be tracked when passing through a monitored area.

---

[55] See the commentary on Art. 89 in this volume.
[56] See also ICO Website.
[57] See e.g. the Guidance that the CNIL issued on audience measuring in public spaces (for instance by collecting unique mobile phone identifiers on a certain area), and in particular the requirement that when such processing is allowed based on necessity for legitimate interests, the controller would have to prominently offer the right to opt out as one of the safeguards that ensures the processing is lawful. See CNIL 2018.
[58] On the meaning of such services, see the commentary on Art. 4(25) GDPR in this volume.

Otherwise, the modalities to exercise the right to object are provided under Article 12 GDPR,[59] including the time limit of the controller to inform data subjects about the action taken following requests (one month, which may be extended by two further months); the fact that the controller needs to inform the data subject of the reasons for rejecting a request; and that the right to object must be free of charge. Just as with the other rights of the data subject, if an objection is manifestly unfounded or excessive, the controller may either charge a reasonable fee taking into account the administrative costs of dealing with the request, or may refuse to act on the request.[60] However, in such cases, the controller must prove that the request was manifestly unfounded or excessive.

Select Bibliography

International agreements

OECD Guidelines 2013: Organisation for Economic Co-operation and Development, 'The OECD Privacy Framework' (2013).

EU legislation

Directive 68/151/EEC: First Council Directive 68/151/EEC of 9 March 1968 on co-ordination of safeguards which, for the protection of the interests of members and others, are required by Member States of companies within the meaning of the second paragraph of Article 58 of the Treaty, with a view to making such safeguards equivalent throughout the Community, OJ 1968 L 65/8.

National legislation

French Data Protection Act 1978: Act No. 78-17 of 6 January 1978 on Data Processing, Files and Individual Liberties (Loi n° 78-17 du 6 janvier 1978 relative à l'informatique, aux fichiers et aux libertés), as last amended by Law No. 2014-334 of 17 March 2014.
German GDPR Implementation Law: Gesetz zur Anpassung des Datenschutzrechts an die Verordnung (EU) 2016/679 und zur Umsetzung der Richtlinie (EU) 2016/680 (Datenschutz-Anpassungs- und Umsetzungsgesetz EU—DsAnpUG-EU), BGBl 2017 Teil 1 Nr. 44.
Irish Data Protection Act 2018: Data Protection Act 2018 (Number 7 of 2018).
UK Data Protection Act 2018: Data Protection Act 2018 (Chapter 12).

Academic writings

Bygrave 2014: Bygrave, *Data Privacy Law: An International Perspective* (OUP 2014).
Church and Millard 2006: Church and Millard, 'Article 14 of Directive 95/46/EC', in Bullesbach, Poullet and Prins (eds.), *Concise European IT Law* (Kluwer Law International (2006), 82.
Dammann and Simitis 1997: Dammann and Simitis, *EG-Datenschutzrichtlinie* (Nomos Verlagsgesellschaft 1997).
Hustinx 2017: Hustinx, 'EU Data Protection Law: The Review of Directive 95/46/EC and the General Data Protection Regulation', in Cremona (ed.), *New Technologies and EU Law* (OUP 2017), 123.
Korff 2005: Korff, *Data Protection Laws in the European Union* (Federation of European Direct Marketing and Direct Marketing Association 2005).

---

[59] See the commentary on Art. 12 in this volume.   [60] Art. 12(5) GDPR.

Kosta 2015: Kosta, 'Construing the Meaning of "Opt-Out"—An Analysis of the European, U.K. and German Data Protection Legislation', 1(1) *European Data Protection Law Review* (2015), 16.

Zanfir 2015: Zanfir, 'How CJEU's "Privacy Spring" Construed the Human Rights Shield in the Digital Age', in Kuzelewska, Kloza, Krasnicka and Strzyczkowski (eds.), *European Judicial Systems as a Challenge for Democracy* (Intersentia 2015), 111.

Papers of data protection authorities

EDPS 2018: European Data Protection Supervisor, 'Guidance on Article 25 of the New Regulation and Internal Rules' (20 December 2018).

WP29 2018: Article 29 Working Party, 'Guidelines on Automated Individual Decision-Making and Profiling for the Purposes of Regulation 2016/679' (WP 251 rev.01, as last revised and adopted 6 February 2018).

CNIL 2018: Commission nationale de l'informatique et des libertés, 'Dispositifs de mesure d'audience et de fréquentation dans des espaces accessibles au public: la CNIL rappelle les règles' (17 October 2018).

Reports and recommendations

Explanatory Report Convention 108 2018: Council of Europe, 'Explanatory Report to the Protocol Amending the Convention for the Protection of Individuals with Regard to the Automatic Processing of Personal Data' (10 October 2018), available at https://rm.coe.int/cets-223-explanatory-report-to-the-protocol-amending-the-convention-fo/16808ac91a.

Others

ICO Website: Information Commissioner's Office, 'Right to Object', available at https://ico.org.uk/for-organisations/guide-to-data-protection/guide-to-the-general-data-protection-regulation-gdpr/individual-rights/right-to-object/.

Article 22. Automated individual decision-making, including profiling

LEE A. BYGRAVE

1. The data subject shall have the right not to be subject to a decision based solely on automated processing, including profiling, which produces legal effects concerning him or her or similarly significantly affects him or her.
2. Paragraph 1 shall not apply if the decision:
   (a) is necessary for entering into, or performance of, a contract between the data subject and a data controller;
   (b) is authorised by Union or Member State law to which the controller is subject and which also lays down suitable measures to safeguard the data subject's rights and freedoms and legitimate interests; or
   (c) is based on the data subject's explicit consent.
3. In the cases referred to in points (a) and (c) of paragraph 2, the data controller shall implement suitable measures to safeguard the data subject's rights and freedoms and legitimate interests, at least the right to obtain human intervention on the part of the controller, to express his or her point of view and to contest the decision.
4. Decisions referred to in paragraph 2 shall not be based on special categories of personal data referred to in Article 9(1), unless point (a) or (g) of Article 9(2) apply and suitable measures to safeguard the data subject's rights and freedoms and legitimate interests are in place.

Relevant Recitals

(4) The processing of personal data should be designed to serve mankind. The right to the protection of personal data is not an absolute right; it must be considered in relation to its function in society and be balanced against other fundamental rights, in accordance with the principle of proportionality. This Regulation respects all fundamental rights and observes the freedoms and principles recognised in the Charter as enshrined in the Treaties, in particular the respect for private and family life, home and communications, the protection of personal data, freedom of thought, conscience and religion, freedom of expression and information, freedom to conduct a business, the right to an effective remedy and to a fair trial, and cultural, religious and linguistic diversity.

(24) The processing of personal data of data subjects who are in the Union by a controller or processor not established in the Union should also be subject to this Regulation when it is related to the monitoring of the behaviour of such data subjects in so far as their behaviour takes place within the Union. In order to determine whether a processing activity can be considered to monitor the behaviour of data subjects, it should be ascertained whether natural persons are tracked on the internet including potential subsequent use of personal data processing techniques which consist of profiling a natural person, particularly in order to take decisions concerning her or him or for analysing or predicting her or his personal preferences, behaviours and attitudes.

(38) Children merit specific protection with regard to their personal data, as they may be less aware of the risks, consequences and safeguards concerned and their rights in relation to the processing of personal data. Such specific protection should, in particular, apply to the use of personal data of children for the purposes of marketing or creating personality or user profiles and the collection of personal data with regard to children when using services offered directly to a child. The consent of the holder

The discussions on various proposals for its provisions prior to the final adoption of the Regulation focused more on profiling per se than was the case with Article 15 DPD. Indeed, the European Commission's initial proposal for rules on the subject matter of Article 22 GDPR was titled 'Measures based on profiling' (Article 20 GDPR Proposal). Although the final wording of Article 22 GDPR does not fully replicate any one of the proposals from the Commission, Parliament or the Council, all of these proposals targeted profiling. The most radical proposal came from the Parliament's Committee on Civil Liberties, Justice and Home Affairs ('LIBE'), which wanted to afford individuals a right to object to profiling in general, not just particular types of decisions that might arise from profiling.[6] All three institutions took the view that some decisions based on profiling should be subject to relatively stringent regulation, namely the decisions based on sensitive data as specified in Article 9(1) GDPR. The pronounced focus on profiling is reflected in the title of Article 22 along with the use, in its provisions, of the term 'profiling' instead of the longer phrase 'automated processing of data intended to evaluate certain personal aspects relating to him', used in Article 15(1) DPD (elaborated further below). The term 'profiling' also receives its own definition in Article 4(4) GDPR.

The protection of children deserves special mention. Whereas the status of children as data subjects received little if any specific attention in the drafting of the DPD, it was extensively discussed in the drafting of the GDPR, also with respect to profiling. Thus, recital 38 GDPR states that 'specific protection' of personal data on children 'should, in particular, apply to the use of ... [such data] for the purposes of ... creating personality or user profiles', while recital 71 states that a measure involving the making of an automated decision based on profiling 'should not concern a child'.[7]

B. Legal Background

1. EU legislation

Article 22 GDPR is based closely on Article 15 DPD which provided individual natural persons with a qualified right 'not to be subject to a decision which produces legal effects concerning him or significantly affects him and which is based solely on automated processing of data intended to evaluate certain personal aspects relating to him, such as his performance at work, creditworthiness, reliability, conduct, etc.'.[8] This right was complemented by a right to knowledge of the logic involved in such decisions (Article 12(a) DPD).

---

[6] EP GDPR Draft Report 2013, p. 93 (outlining proposed Art. 20(1)). However, two other committees in the Parliament, namely the Committee on Internal Market and Consumer Protection ('IMCO') and the Committee on Industry, Research and Energy ('ITRE'), were more friendly to profiling than the LIBE Committee (which had the lead role in negotiating the GDPR). See further EP GDPR Draft Report 2013, pp. 308, 309, 471 and 472.

[7] See also the commentary on Art. 8 in this volume.

[8] The initial draft forerunner to Art. 15(1) DPD gave a person the right 'not to be subject to an administrative or private decision involving an assessment of his conduct which has as its sole basis the automatic processing of personal data defining his profile or personality' (Art. 14(1) DPD Proposal 1990). These provisions were changed in 1992 such that a person was granted a right 'not to be subjected to an administrative or private decision adversely affecting him which is based solely on automatic processing defining a personality profile' (Art. 16(1) DPD Amended Proposal 1992).

Both rights were rarely applied during their lifespan under the DPD. Article 15 DPD scarcely figured in court litigation or in enforcement actions by national DPAs.[9] It also played a marginal role in assessments of the adequacy of third countries' data protection regimes with a view to regulating the flow of personal data to those countries.[10] In this context, the WP29 opined that Article 15 did not establish a 'basic' principle but an 'additional principle to be applied to specific types of processing'.[11]

2. International instruments

The ideals of Article 22 are poorly reflected in Convention 108 as first adopted. The same applies with respect to the OECD Privacy Guidelines and APEC Privacy Framework: neither of these instruments contains a right that bears similarity to Article 22.

However, Article 9(1) of Modernised Convention 108 stipulates:

Every individual shall have a right: (a) not to be subject to a decision significantly affecting him or her based solely on an automated processing of data without having his or her views taken into consideration; ... (c) to obtain, on request, knowledge of the reasoning underlying data processing where the results of such processing are applied to him or her; (d) to object at any time, on grounds relating to his or her situation, to the processing of personal data concerning him or her unless the controller demonstrates legitimate grounds for the processing which override his or her interests or rights and fundamental freedoms.

Article 9(2) derogates from the right in Article 9(1)(a) 'if the decision is authorised by a law to which the controller is subject and which also lays down suitable measures to safeguard the data subject's rights, freedoms and legitimate interests'.

These provisions build not just on Article 22 GDPR and Article 15 DPD but also earlier norms issued by the Council of Europe, in particular its 2010 'Recommendation on the Protection of Individuals with Regard to Automatic Processing of Personal Data in the Context of Profiling',[12] and 2017 Guidelines on the Protection of Individuals with Regard to the Processing of Personal Data in the World of Big Data.[13]

---

[9] A notable exception being an action by the French CNIL, in which the CNIL found that an automated system for determining admission to French universities violated the French rules transposing Art. 15 DPD: see CNIL 2017.

[10] WP29 1998, pp. 6–7.   [11] Ibid.

[12] See COM Recommendation 2010, principle 5.5 ('Where a person is subject to a decision having legal effects concerning her or him, or significantly affecting her or him, taken on the sole basis of profiling, she or he should be able to object to the decision unless: *a.* this is provided for by law, which lays down measures to safeguard data subjects' legitimate interests, particularly by allowing them to put forward their point of view; *b.* the decision was taken in the course of the performance of a contract to which the data subject is party or for the implementation of pre-contractual measures taken at the request of the data subject and that measures for safeguarding the legitimate interests of the data subject are in place') and principle 5.1 ('The data subject who is being, or has been, profiled should be entitled to obtain from the controller, at her or his request, within a reasonable time and in an understandable form, information concerning: *a.* her or his personal data; *b.* the logic underpinning the processing of her or his personal data and that was used to attribute a profile to her or him, at least in the case of an automated decision; *c.* the purposes for which the profiling was carried out and the categories of persons to whom or bodies to which the personal data may be communicated').

[13] See T-PD Guidelines 2017, principle 7.1 ('The use of Big Data should preserve the autonomy of human intervention in the decision-making process'), principle 7.3 ('Where decisions based on Big Data might affect individual rights significantly or produce legal effects, a human decision-maker should, upon request of the data subject, provide her or him with the reasoning underlying the processing, including the consequences for the data subject of this reasoning'), and principle 7.4 ('On the basis of reasonable arguments, the human decision-maker should be allowed the freedom not to rely on the result of the recommendations provided using Big Data').

3. National developments

The legislative roots of Article 22 GDPR and Article 15 DPD reach back to France's Data Protection Act 1978. In its original form, Article 2 of the Act prohibited judicial, administrative or personal decisions involving assessment of human behaviour in so far as these were based solely on automatic data processing which defined the profile or personality of the individual concerned.[14]

National transposition of Article 15 DPD diverged considerably. Some EU/EEA Member States implemented Article 15(1) as a right to be exercised at the discretion of each person (thereby permitting the targeted decision-making to occur in the absence of the right being exercised, provided that the data-processing operation involved in the decision-making met the other requirements of the law).[15] This form of transposition conformed closely to the actual wording of Article 15(1). However, transposition by some other Member States involved laying down a qualified prohibition on the targeted decision-making.[16] Yet other states adopted a hybrid approach, creating a prohibition for some types of decision and a right to object to other types.[17]

4. Case law

The CJEU has yet to rule directly on Article 22 and never ruled on Article 15 DPD. In *Opinion 1/15*, it addressed a somewhat similar provision in the draft EU-Canada passenger name record agreement, but only very briefly (as elaborated in footnote 38 below).

In 2014, the German Federal Court of Justice ('Bundesgerichtshof') handed down a judgment in a case that touched briefly on the scope of the German rules transposing Article 15 DPD. The case concerned the use of automated credit-scoring systems. The Court held that the contested decision-making system fell outside the scope of the national rules transposing Article 15 DPD because decisions to provide credit were ultimately made by a person and therefore not fully automated.[18]

---

[14] Art. 2 of the Act stated: 'Aucune décision de justice impliquant une appréciation sur en comportement humain ne peut avoir pour fondement un traitement automatisé d'informations donnant une définition du profil ou de la personnalité de l'intéressé. Aucune décision administrative ou privée impliquant une appréciation sur en comportement humain ne peut avoir seul fondement un traitement automatisé d'informations donnant une définition du profil ou de la personnalité de l'intéressé'. Art. 3 of the Act stated: 'Toute personne a le droit de connaître et de contester les informations et les raisonnements utilisés dans les traitements automatisés dont les résultats lui sont opposes'. In amendments to the Act in 2004, the provisions of Art. 2 were moved to Art. 10 while the provisions of Art. 3 were moved to Art. 39(1). Both sets of provisions were also reformulated to align better with the DPD.

[15] See e.g. s. 29 Swedish Personal Data Act 1998 (repealed).

[16] See e.g. Art. 12bis Belgian Data Protection Law 1992 (repealed).

[17] See e.g. Art. 14 Italian Data Protection Code 2003, prior to the Code's amendment in August 2018. This prohibited judicial or administrative decisions involving assessment of a person's conduct that were based solely on the automated processing of personal data aimed at defining the person's profile or personality, whereas similar decisions made by private sector actors were simply subject to a qualified right to object by the data subject.

[18] See Bundesgerichtshof, *Urteil vom 28.1.2014*, para. 34. In the words of the Court: 'Von einer automatisierten Einzelentscheidung kann im Falle des Scorings nur dann ausgegangen werden, wenn die für die Entscheidung verantwortliche Stelle eine rechtliche Folgen für den Betroffenen nach sich ziehende oder ihn erheblich beeinträchtigende Entscheidung ausschließlich aufgrund eines Score-Ergebnisses ohne weitere inhaltliche Prüfung trifft, nicht aber, wenn die mittels automatisierter Datenverarbeitung gewonnenen Erkenntnisse lediglich Grundlage für eine von einem Menschen noch zu treffende abschließende Entscheidung sind'. Also noteworthy is an earlier judgment of the French Supreme Court (Cour de cassation) concerning, inter alia, judges' utilisation, in the course of criminal court proceedings, of statistical analysis of the activities of masseur-physiotherapists by means of computer systems; see *Cour de Cassation 1998*. The Court held that the statistics usage was not affected by the French rules restricting automated judicial decision-making as the

C. Analysis

1. Scope of application

Although Article 22 bears close similarity to its antecedent in Article 15 DPD, its scope of application is broader. Decisions caught by Article 15 DPD had to involve a form of profiling (in as much as they had to be based on 'processing intended to evaluate certain personal aspects' of the targeted person). This is not the case with Article 22(1) GDPR which states that the decision concerned must be based on 'automated processing, including profiling'. The use of the comma to separate 'automated processing' and 'including profiling' indicates—at least on a conventional reading—that profiling is one of two alternative baseline criteria of application, the other being 'automated processing'.[19] The latter can but need not involve profiling. Data protection authorities ('DPAs') have generally embraced this line of interpretation.[20] In practice, however, many if not most types of automated decision-making caught by Article 22 will likely involve profiling.[21]

Further, whereas Article 15 DPD did not specifically address use of especially sensitive data as listed in Article 8(1) DPD (now listed more expansively in Article 9(1) GDPR), Article 22(4) GDPR does. The latter lays down a qualified prohibition on automated decisions based on these data types.

2. The nature of the right in Article 22(1)

The basic nature of the rule laid down by Article 22(1) is subject to considerable disagreement: does the rule lay down a right to be exercised by a data subject or is it really laying down a qualified prohibition on a particular type of decisional process, independently of a data subject's objections? This issue presents a real conundrum with good arguments able to be mounted both ways. As noted in section B above, Article 15(1) DPD, although worded as a right, was operationalised by some Member States as a prohibition. In the view of the WP29, Article 22(1) GDPR is also a form of qualified prohibition despite being formulated as a right[22]—a view that the EDPB thus far has not altered. The WP29 justified its view on logical grounds, claiming that the consent derogation in Article 22(2)(c) 'would not make much sense' if Article 22(1) were interpreted as a right to object: 'a data subject cannot object and consent to the same processing'.[23] The WP29 also pointed out that treating Article 22(1) as a qualified prohibition preserves the operational functionality of the safeguard of 'human

---

statistics had not been generated and used in such a way as to define the profile or personality of the person concerned. This case formally did not turn on French transposition of Art. 15 DPD but on application of Art. 2 of the French Data Protection Act 1978. As noted above, Art. 2 was an antecedent to Art. 15 DPD and prohibited, inter alia, judicial decisions involving assessment of human behaviour when these were based solely on automatic data processing which defined the profile or personality of the targeted person. The provisions of Art. 2 were later reformulated and moved to Art. 10 of the French legislation to align better with Art. 15 DPD.

[19] Not all language versions of the GDPR use a comma here. Punctuation in the German version uses the em-dash ('— einschließlich Profiling —'), but the effect is the same as using a comma and there is no other indication in the German version that automated processing must involve profiling.

[20] WP29 2018, p. 8. Cf. Mendoza and Bygrave 2017, pp. 90– 91 (mounting a tenuous argument that this line of interpretation runs counter to the provisions' rationale and background, and that the use of 'including' must accordingly be read as equivalent to 'involving'). See too Brkan 2019, p. 97 (seemingly agreeing with Mendoza and Bygrave).

[21] See also Brkan 2019, p. 97.

[22] WP29 2018, p. 19. See also e.g. Mendoza and Bygrave 2017, p. 87; Brkan 2019, pp. 98–99.

[23] WP29 2018, p. 35.

involvement' laid down in Article 22(3) and of the derogations of consent and contract laid down in Article 22(2).[24] Other commentators have additionally argued that treating Article 22(1) as a qualified prohibition strengthens its bite and thus does greater justice to the Regulation's overarching aim of strengthening protection of the fundamental rights to privacy and data protection.[25] Furthermore, this line of interpretation brings the GDPR into alignment with the approach of the LED (Article 11(1) of which, as elaborated below, explicitly places a qualified prohibition on the sort of decision making covered by Article 22 GDPR), thus helping to make the EU's broader framework for data protection more coherent.[26]

These are strong arguments, but they run counter to the actual wording of Article 22(1). Arguably, the text of Article 22(1) would have been formulated more like Article 22(4) GDPR or Article 11(1) LED if it was to be treated as laying down a prohibition. The lawmakers would seem to be aware that such differences in formulation ordinarily bring about different effects. Moreover, the drafting history of the GDPR does not evidence firm intention by the lawmakers that Article 22(1) is meant to function as a prohibition.[27] It might also be argued that the placement of Article 22 in Chapter III of the GDPR—i.e. the chapter termed 'rights of the data subject'—indicates that Article 22(1) is to be treated as a right. However, this placement is hardly decisive as, first, some of the other provisions in the same chapter are not formulated directly as data subject rights but as duties cast upon controllers (see particularly Articles 13 and 14), and, secondly, elements of Article 22 (other than Article 22(1)) are indeed phrased as data subject rights.[28]

A more decisive factor undermining the prohibition line is the fact that other provisions of the GDPR (in particular, Article 13(2)(f)) seem to assume the existence of the decisional processes caught by Article 22(1).[29] Further, treating Article 22(1) as a right to be exercised at the data subject's discretion implicitly recognises that the decisional processes targeted by the right are already used extensively in both private and government sectors where digitalisation is advanced, and sometimes with socially justifiable benefits.[30]

Finally, the prohibition-contra-right issue must also be approached in light of the managerial requirements the GDPR brings to bear on fully automated decisional systems that involve systematic and extensive evaluation of data subjects. Such systems must undergo an *ex ante* 'data protection impact assessment' ('DPIA').[31] This goes some way towards fulfilling the control function that a qualified prohibition would institute. More specifically, controllers must undertake a DPIA when planning 'a systematic and extensive evaluation of personal aspects relating to natural persons which is based on automated processing, including profiling, and on which decisions are based that produce legal effects concerning the natural person or similarly significantly affect the natural person' (Article 35(3)(a)). As already indicated, this DPIA must take place 'prior' to using the automated decisional system referenced here (Article 35(1)). Moreover, when the DPIA 'indicates that the processing would result

---

[24] Ibid. See also Mendoza and Bygrave 2017, p. 87.
[25] Mendoza and Bygrave 2017, p. 87.   [26] Brkan 2019, p. 99.
[27] See further Tosoni 2019.   [28] See also WP29 2018, p. 34.
[29] See also Tosoni 2019. Art. 13(2)(f) requires a controller to provide the data subject, 'at the time when personal data are obtained', with information about 'the existence of automated decision-making, including profiling, referred to in Art. 22(1) and (4) and, at least in those cases, meaningful information about the logic involved, as well as the significance and the envisaged consequences of such processing for the data subject'. The WP29 seems to have overlooked the significance of this provision when casting Art. 22(1) as a qualified prohibition.
[30] Bygrave 2019, p. 251.   [31] See further the commentary on Art. 35 in this volume.

in a high risk in the absence of measures taken by the controller to mitigate the risk', the controller must consult the relevant DPA (Article 36(1)), which may then apply its powers under Article 58. These powers include banning (temporarily or permanently) the decisional system (Article 58(2)(f)). Thus, it is not the case that operationalising Article 22(1) as a qualified prohibition is the sole means by which to give its provisions bite *ex ante*.

3. Conditions for applying the right in Article 22(1)

Application of the right afforded by Article 22(1) rests on three cumulative conditions: (i) a decision is made that is (ii) based solely on automated processing or profiling and (iii) has either legal effects or similarly significant effects. These conditions are for the most part identical to those that inhered in Article 15(1) DPD; hence, their explication may build on previous explication of the latter.

Regarding the first-listed condition, the term 'decision' obviously covers official acts of authorities that provide a determination or ruling on a matter with legal effects on those persons covered or targeted by the determination/ruling. This is a conception of decision found elsewhere in EU law.[32] However, Article 22 GDPR covers a larger range of situations than those involving exercise of government agency authority, and, in light of its rationale, there are good grounds for holding that its notion of 'decision' should be viewed in a fairly generic sense. Thus, a decision probably means that a particular attitude or stance is taken towards a person and this attitude/stance has a degree of binding effect in the sense that it must—or, at the very least, is likely to—be acted upon.[33] This attitude/stance might, for instance, manifest itself as a specific choice amongst a set of variables. It follows from the rationale for the provisions that the decisional process may consist entirely of steps taken by computer software.[34] While there is no prima facie requirement that the decision takes a particular form, it must be formalised to the extent that it can be distinguished from other stages that prepare, support, complement or head off decision-making.[35] At the same time, the mere fact that a decision is not labelled as such but, say, as a 'plan' or 'design' would not of itself take the decision outside the scope of Article 22 if it has a basis and effect that Article 22(1) otherwise requires.[36] Concomitantly, if a decision has that basis and effect, it may be caught by Article 22 even if it is an interim action in a broader process potentially involving multiple decisions (e.g. in some sort of appeal system).

The second-listed condition (that the decision is based solely on automated data processing) means that a person fails to exercise any real influence on the outcome of the decision-making process. Even if formally ascribed to a person, a decision is to be regarded as based solely on automated processing if a person does not actively assess the result of the processing prior to its formalisation as a decision. According to the WP29, genuine human involvement presumes 'meaningful' rather than just 'token' human oversight by 'someone who has the authority and competence to change the decision' and

---

[32] See e.g. Art. 5(39) Regulation 952/2013. This defines 'decision' as 'any act by the customs authorities pertaining to the customs legislation giving a ruling on a particular case, and having legal effects on the person or persons concerned'.

[33] See also Mendoza and Bygrave 2017, p. 87; Bygrave 2001, pp. 18–19 (regarding Art. 15(1) DPD).

[34] See also Mendoza and Bygrave 2017, p. 87; Bygrave 2001, pp. 18–19 (regarding Art. 15(1) DPD).

[35] See Veale and Edwards 2018, p. 401 (querying whether online advertisements per se may qualify as decisions, but implicitly going on to accept that they may so qualify).

[36] See also Bygrave 2001, p. 19 (regarding Art. 15(1) DPD).

who 'consider[s] all the relevant data'.[37] Thus, an automated process falls clear of Article 22 when it remains a decisional *support* tool for a human being, and the latter considers the merits of the results of that process prior to reaching her or his decision, rather than being blindly or automatically steered by the process.[38] This would be the case even when the predominant part of the preliminary decisional process is automated.[39]

Another issue in relation to the second-listed condition concerns the data basis for processing. The term 'automated processing' suggests prima facie that the data upon which the decision is based are in digital form.[40] In principle, the term might even suggest that the initial collection and registration of such data must be automated (e.g. through use of sensor devices that operate independently of human action).[41] The latter requirement, however, would mean that many automated decisional processes that have potentially deleterious effects on targeted persons fall outside the scope of Article 22, thus undermining the purpose of the provisions. It is therefore sensible to delimit the automation requirement to the use of data as a secondary source, thereby permitting manual or semi-automated processes for the initial data capture.

A further point regarding data basis is that the decision need not be based on personal data relating to the person targeted by the decision; instead, it could encompass personal data relating to other persons or even non-personal data.[42] Nonetheless, while the data involved probably need not relate, at least initially, to the person targeted by the decision, Article 22(1) presumes that the decision will ultimately involve processing of data on that person as the right it lays down is operationalised by reference to the 'data subject'. And where a decision is based on 'profiling' as opposed to 'automated processing', it must involve automated processing of *personal* data. This follows from the definition of 'profiling' in Article 4(4) GDPR, which refers to 'any form of automated processing of personal data'. The definition goes on to elaborate 'profiling' as 'consisting of using those data to evaluate certain personal aspects relating to a natural person, in particular

---

[37] WP29 2018, p. 19. In CNIL 2017, the system for determining admission to French universities was found to be fully automated for the purposes of the French rules transposing Art. 15 DPD. Admission was determined entirely by use of computer algorithms. One algorithm automatically ranked university applicants; another algorithm automatically directed an offer of university admission solely on the basis of that ranking. Human staff at a university had no possibility of influencing the final decision regarding offer of admission.

[38] See also DPD Amended Proposal 1992, p. 26 ('what is prohibited is the strict application by the user [data controller] of the results produced by the system. Data processing may provide an aid to decision-making, but it cannot be the end of the matter; human judgment must have its place. It would be contrary to this principle, for example, for an employer to reject an application from a job-seeker on the sole basis of his results in a computerised psychological evaluation, or to use such assessment software to produce lists giving marks and classing job applicants in order of preference on the sole basis of a test of personality'). The CJEU indirectly supports this view in its Opinion 1/15 concerning the EU-Canada passenger name records (PNR) agreement. The Court stated that Article 15 of the agreement (stipulating that 'Canada shall not take any decisions significantly adversely affecting a passenger solely on the basis of automated processing of PNR data') means that 'any positive result obtained following the automated processing of [PNR] data must ... be subject to an individual re-examination by non-automated means before an individual measure adversely affecting the air passengers concerned is adopted', and, '[c]onsequently, such a measure may not ... be based solely and decisively on the result of automated processing of PNR data': para. 173.

[39] The European Parliament's Committee on Civil Liberties, Justice and Home Affairs ('LIBE') proposed provisions to capture profiling when it is based 'solely *or predominantly*' on automated processing' (proposed Art. 20(5)); see EP GDPR Draft Report, p. 94.

[40] See also Schartum 2018, p. 394.

[41] Ibid., p. 395 ('individual decisions are not *really* totally automated unless automatic procedures cover everything from sensing all legally relevant aspects of the real world, to valid decision').

[42] See also WP29 2018, p. 8 (noting that automated decisions 'can be based on any type of data').

to analyse or predict aspects concerning that natural person's performance at work, economic situation, health, personal preferences, interests, reliability, behaviour, location or movements'. From this definition, it is clear that profiling must involve evaluation of personal aspects of a natural person, but need not involve prediction as to their future behaviour.[43]

The third-listed condition (that the decision has legal effects or similarly significant effects) means that the decision changes, shapes or otherwise determines (partly or fully) a person's legal rights or duties, or it brings consequences that have a seriously adverse impact on a person's welfare. In the latter respect, it bears highlighting that the formulation of Article 22(1) differs slightly from its predecessor: whereas Article 15(1) DPD did not draw a link between significant effects and 'legal effects', Article 22(1) does do so by using 'similarly' before 'significantly affects'. This linkage signals an intention that such effects must have a degree of significance that is roughly equivalent to that of legal effects (although they do not need to be legal in nature).[44] It may also signal that such effects must have, at the very least, a non-trivial impact on the *status* of a person relative to other persons (as legal effects usually do).[45] Noting the difficulty of being precise about the significant effects threshold, the WP29 opined that the threshold may be met when the decision has the potential to 'significantly affect the circumstances, behaviour or choices of the individuals concerned', 'have prolonged or permanent impact on the data subject' or 'at its most extreme, lead to the exclusion or discrimination of individuals'.[46] Recital 71 GDPR mentions the refusal of 'online credit applications' and 'e-recruiting practices' as two examples of automated decisions with significant effects. It also suggests other measures that the decision-maker should avoid in order to have a fair and transparent processing, such as decisions with discriminatory effects on the basis of racial and ethnic origins, political opinions, religion and other beliefs, health status and sexual orientation. Further, recital 38 GDPR intimates that a decision will meet the significant effects threshold if it targets a child.

In respect of meeting the significant effects threshold for Article 15(1) DPD, it was claimed that the effects probably need not be pecuniary.[47] It was also claimed that a significant effect might arguably lie 'merely in the insult to a data subject's integrity and dignity which is occasioned by the simple fact of being judged by a machine, at least in certain circumstances (e.g., when there is no reasonable justification for [such decision-making])'.[48] The validity of these claims is more tenuous with respect to Article 22(1) in light of the linkage factor pointed to above. The linkage factor suggests that significant effects cannot be purely emotional. It also buttresses doubts that targeted online advertising will ordinarily meet the significant effects threshold.[49] Such advertising might nonetheless meet the threshold if it involves blatantly

---

[43] See further the commentary on Art. 4(4) in this volume.   [44] See also WP29 2018, p. 21.
[45] See also Mendoza and Bygrave 2017, p. 89.
[46] WP29 2018, pp. 21–22. The WP29 also listed decisions affecting a person's financial circumstances, access to health services, employment opportunities or access to education as examples of decisions that may pass the threshold.
[47] Church and Millard 2010, p. 84.   [48] Bygrave 2001, p. 19.
[49] WP29 2018, p. 22 (opining that advertisements based on simple demographic profiles will typically fall short of the threshold). In relation to Art. 15 DPD, see e.g. Simitis and Damman 1997, p. 220. The Commission appeared to take the view that simply sending a commercial brochure to a list of persons selected by a computer did not significantly affect the persons for the purposes of Art. 15(1) DPD; see DPD Proposal 1992, pp. 26–27. This view, though, related to a draft provision expressly requiring an *adverse* effect—a requirement that was omitted from the wording of the final version of Art. 15(1).

unfair discrimination with non-trivial economic consequences (e.g. the data subject must pay a substantially higher price for services than other persons, effectively preventing her/him from accessing these services)[50]—a fortiori if this occurs repeatedly. The WP29 listed a range of factors that need to be considered when determining whether targeted advertising meets the threshold. These include the intrusiveness of the profiling process involved, the expectations and desires of the data subject, the pitch of the advertisement and the exploitation of data subject vulnerabilities.[51]

The wording of Article 22(1) suggests that the significant effects threshold is to be assessed primarily by reference to the data subject *qua* individual.[52] This does not shut out the possibility of considering the threshold also by reference to attitudes and actions towards a particular collective entity to which the data subject belongs or is otherwise linked. If these attitudes/actions give rise to decisions that have a sufficiently significant effect not just on the collective entity but also on the data subject, they may fall within Article 22(1), even if they are originally triggered by the behaviour of persons other than the data subject—the case, for example, where the latter's creditworthiness is determined not by her or his own specific financial credentials but those of other persons in her or his geophysical neighbourhood.[53] However, a decision targeting a group to which the data subject belongs is unlikely to meet the requisite threshold if, due to the particular privileges or other circumstances of the data subject, it does not have a significant effect on the latter even if it has a detrimental effect on other group members.[54]

Evaluation and application of the significant effects threshold will obviously vary to some degree according to the attributes and sensibilities of the particular data subject concerned. While the threshold must be applied using objective (inter-subjective) standards (i.e. standards that are regarded as reasonable or well-founded by a fairly large number of people—and ultimately the judiciary in the event of litigation), some regard must be permitted of a data subject's own perceptions of what is significant, particularly given the rationale for Article 22.[55] As indicated above, some regard must also be permitted of the attributes of any particular group to which the data subject belongs and which is relevant for the decisional process concerned. Thus, if the data subject belongs to a vulnerable group, this vulnerability will likely lower the threshold. This is most clearly evidenced with respect to children, who are singled out in recitals 71 and 38 GDPR as warranting special protection. These recitals do not create on their own a legally binding prohibition on automated decisions or profiling directed at children, but will, at the very least, likely

---

[50] See also WP29 2018, p. 22; Mendoza and Bygrave 2017, p. 89; Bygrave 2001, p. 20.

[51] Ibid. See also Veale and Edwards 2018, pp. 401–402 (querying whether the WP29 guidance here 'is drawing more from consumer protection principles than the underlying [legislative] text' and, at the same time, remarking that it is 'odd' that the guidance does not refer to 'the theory that targeted adverts are significant because . . . they reduce the universe of those deemed not suitable, not rich or not persuadable enough by certain offers and this create [*sic*] social sorting').

[52] See also Brkan 2019, p. 100. [53] See also WP29 2018, p. 22.

[54] See further Veale and Edwards 2018, p. 402 (leaving this issue open, but noting 'an irreconcilable tension between [data protection] as a creature of the individual rights paradigm, and the inevitable conclusion that algorithmic decision-making leads to group harms'). See further Brkan 2019, p. 101 (arguing in favour of Art. 22 GDPR and Art. 11 LED extending – in terms of both *lex lata* and *lex ferenda* – to 'collective' automated decisions, although leaving somewhat unclear whether such decisions would necessarily be based on anonymized (non-personal) data or would otherwise not have significant effects on the group members as individuals).

[55] See also Bygrave 2001, p. 19. See further Brkan 2019, p. 103 (noting that Art. 22 GDPR and Art. 11 LED 'require that the decision significantly affects a particular data subject ("him or her") and not an average one').

lead to these processes being subjected to more stringent national controls, particularly in terms of what decisions may qualify as having a 'significant' effect.[56]

4. Qualifications in Article 22(2)

Article 22(2) introduces a first layer of qualifications to Article 22(1). It essentially states that the 'right' provided by Article 22(1) does not exist in three alternative sets of circumstances: contract, statutory authority and consent. The EDPB is specifically tasked with publishing 'guidelines, recommendations and best practices' on how these qualifications are to be interpreted and implemented (Article 70(1)(f) GDPR). Such documentation has been issued in the form of guidelines first developed by the WP29 and subsequently endorsed by the EDPB.[57]

The qualifications laid down by Article 22(2) are themselves subject to sets of qualifications in Article 22(3) and (4)—elaborated further below.

4.1 Contracts

The contractual derogation under Article 22(2)(a) follows a similar derogation that was laid down in Article 15(2)(a) DPD, but does so in a considerably tightened form. Unlike for Article 15(2)(a) DPD, application of Article 22(2)(a) is *always* subjected to the imposition of 'suitable measures to protect the data subject's rights and freedoms and legitimate interests' (including, as a minimum, the right of the data subject 'to obtain human intervention on the part of the controller, to express his or her point of view and to contest the decision' (Article 22(3))).[58] Article 22(2)(a) also introduces an explicit necessity criterion not found in Article 15(2)(a) DPD—i.e. the decision must be '*necessary* for entering into, or performance of, a contract'. This criterion is not elaborated in the preamble or preparatory works, and it will ultimately be left to courts to clarify, but it signals at least that the decision must have been *required* for the purpose of entering into or fulfilling the contract with the data subject. Yet, it is unlikely that the necessity criterion connotes indispensability: it is hard to think of an example where an automated decision *has* to occur without human involvement.[59] The criterion has presumably been inserted to make it difficult for the controller to escape Article 22(1) simply by pointing to a standardised contract with the data subject.[60]

In one respect, Article 22(2)(a) widens the derogation previously laid down in Article 15(2)(a) DPD. Whereas the latter required that the contract be requested by the data subject, this is no longer the case. In other words, the derogation now applies also to contracts that the controller requests. Overall, however, data subjects are afforded a higher level of protection in contractual situations than they were afforded under the DPD, due largely to the provisions of Article 22(3) (elaborated below).

---

[56] See also WP29 2018, pp. 28–29; Mendoza and Bygrave 2017, p. 85; Veale and Edwards 2018, p. 403.
[57] WP29 2018, pp. 23 et seq.
[58] In contrast, Art. 15(2)(a) DPD allowed a fully automated decision based on profiling where the decision was taken in the course of entering into or executing a contract, *and either* the data subject's request for the entering into or execution of the contract was fulfilled, *or* provision was made for 'suitable measures' to safeguard the person's 'legitimate interests'. The derogation was duly criticised for wrongly assuming that fulfilment of a person's request to enter into or execute a contract will never be problematic for that person. See Bygrave 2001, p. 21.
[59] Mendoza and Bygrave 2017, p. 92; Brkan 2019, p. 104.
[60] Mendoza and Bygrave 2017, p. 92.

4.2 Statutory authority

The allowance in Article 22(2)(b) for automated decisions pursuant to EU or Member State law replicates Article 15(2)(b) DPD. National legislation will likely play a major part in determining the level of protection under Article 22. This follows not just from Article 22(2)(b) but also Article 22(4) (explicated further below). Member States are given fairly broad discretionary powers in this regard, particularly as the 'suitable measures' required to safeguard data subjects are specified in relatively general terms. It will not be surprising if significant differences between the various national legislative regimes emerge.[61]

On their face, the 'suitable measures' required of these regimes do not need to include the safeguards specified in Article 22(3). In many if not all contexts, however, these safeguards (or elements of them) are likely to figure as measures for the purposes of Article 22(2)(b). The key safeguard in this respect will be the right to obtain human intervention.[62] Significantly, this safeguard is expressly required for national legislation authorising automated decision-making in the areas covered by, respectively, the LED and the EUDPR—in addition to being included in Article 22(3) GDPR.

4.3 Consent

The exception for consent is new relative to the derogations under Article 15 DPD.[63] The consent must be 'explicit'—i.e. the same standard as laid down for the processing of especially sensitive personal data pursuant to Article 9(2)(a) GDPR. The consent derogation must otherwise be applied in light of the definition of consent in Article 4(11) GDPR and the provisions of Article 7(4) and recital 43 GDPR concerning what is a *freely given* consent particularly in the context of entering into or performing a contract.[64]

The issue of when consent is freely given arises especially with conditional offers that create 'take-it-or-leave-it' situations. Article 7(4) states that one should examine whether the data processing is actually 'necessary' for the realisation of the contract or service provided. In the context of Article 22(2)(c), one should ask whether a conditional automated decision is actually necessary for the offered services. This assessment is similar to the above-noted assessment of 'necessity' under Art. 22(2)(a). However, in the context of Article 22(2)(c), the interest the data subject has in the automated decision will likely figure in the assessment. When an automated decision is in the data subject's interest (e.g. the situation with applications for credit or insurance), it is easier to argue that consent is freely given than when the decision is not.[65]

---

[61] For example, it is unlikely that a large number of Member States will follow the recent move by the Italian legislature to permit—with some qualifications—the estate of a deceased person (the data subject) to exercise the 'right' in Article 22(1) (see Art. 2 Italian Data Protection Code 2003, as amended by Italian Data Protection Code 2018). The GDPR applies only to processing of data on living persons, but permits Member States to enact rules on the processing of data on deceased persons as well (rec. 27 GDPR). Few Member States have done so.

[62] WP29 2018, p. 27. See too WP29 2017, p. 13 (reiterating human intervention as a 'key element', also in the context of the LED).

[63] Prior to 25 May 2018, Ireland, however, operated with such an exception during the lifetime of the DPD (see s. 6B(2)(b) Irish Data Protection Act 2003), but was the only country in Europe to do so.

[64] See further the commentaries on Arts. 4(11) and 7 in this volume.

[65] Mendoza and Bygrave 2017, p. 95.

Article 22(2)(c) omits specifying whether consent can be withdrawn for future automated decision-making. It follows from Article 7(3), however, that consent generally may be withdrawn at any time, and this presumably applies also in the context of Article 22.

5. Qualifications in Article 22(3)

Article 22(3) introduces a set of qualifications on two of the derogations under Article 22(2): those for contract and consent. The qualifications build on similar wording to Article 15(2)(a) DPD but are considerably more expansive than the latter.[66] The overall result is that, unlike the situation under the DPD, a data subject will *always* have the right to demand human review of a fully automated decision, except where the decision is pursuant to statute. Hence, there will ultimately be very little difference between the level of protection offered by exercise of the 'right' in Article 22(1) and that offered by exercise of the rights in Article 22(3), particularly in the situation where the former 'right' is exercised *ex post* (i.e. after a decision is adopted).[67] As indicated above, even where the decision is pursuant to statute, a right of human intervention is likely to exist as part of the requisite 'suitable measures to safeguard the data subject's rights and freedoms and legitimate interests' (Article 22(2)(b)).

The list of rights mentioned in Article 22(3) is not exhaustive. Which other rights it encompasses is contested. In particular, scholars have clashed over whether Article 22(3) requires data subjects to be provided with a right of *ex post* explanation of automated decisions affecting them.[68] This debate extends to how several other provisions in the Regulation (Articles 13(2)(f), 14(2)(g) and 15(1)(h)) are to be interpreted. Recital 71 GDPR explicitly references such a right in its elaboration of Article 22(3), but this does not of itself make the right a legally enforceable part of the Regulation.

Nonetheless, solid grounds exist for viewing the right as inherent in the penumbra of the right to contest a decision referenced in Article 22(3),[69] in the overarching requirement that personal data be processed 'fairly and in a transparent manner' (Article 5(1)(a) GDPR),[70] and in those provisions of the Regulation that provide a right to 'meaningful information about the logic involved, as well as the significance and envisaged consequences' of automated decision-making (Articles 13(2)(f), 14(2)(g) and 15(1)(h)).[71] It is also arguable that the right to *ex post* explanation of automated decisions follows from the general requirements for controller accountability in Articles 5(2) and 24 GDPR.

---

[66] Art. 15(2)(a) DPD elaborated 'suitable measures' only by reference to arrangements allowing a data subject 'to put his point of view'.

[67] This situation assumes, of course, that Art. 22(1) does not operate as a qualified prohibition.

[68] See WP29 2017 (which fails to take a clear and unambiguous stand on this issue).

[69] Mendoza and Bygrave 2017, pp. 93–94 ('if such a right is to be meaningful, it must set in train certain obligations for the decision maker, including (at the very least) an obligation to hear and consider the merits of the appeal. If the appeal process is to be truly fair, it must additionally carry a qualified obligation to provide the appellant with reasons for the decision'). See also WP 2017, p. 27 (which seems implicitly to take this view by stating that data subjects 'will only be able to challenge a decision or express their view if they fully understand how it has been made and on what basis').

[70] Mendoza and Bygrave 2017, p. 94.

[71] Selbst and Powles 2017; Brkan 2019, pp. 113 et seq. Cf. Wachter et al. 2017 (arguing that Arts. 13(2)(f), 14(2)(g) and 15(1)(h) concern supply of information *prior* to an automated decision being made, and only require

6. Prohibition on decisions based on sensitive data

The final paragraph of Article 22 lays down a qualified prohibition on decisions 'referred to in paragraph 2' when they are based on the categories of sensitive data listed in Article 9(1) GDPR. Paragraph 2 refers to the automated decisions in the first paragraph. The reason the prohibition refers to paragraph 2 and not paragraph 1 is presumably in order to stress that the prohibition takes precedence over the exceptions.

There are two derogations to this prohibition: (i) where the data subject explicitly consents to the decision for one or more specific purposes under Article 9(2)(a) GDPR; or (ii) when the decision is necessary for reasons of substantial public interest and has a basis in EU or Member State law under Article 9(2)(g) GDPR. Explicit consent in this context must be interpreted in the same manner as for Article 22(2)(c). For both derogations, 'suitable measures' to safeguard data subject rights, freedoms and interests must be in place, similar to the requirements in Article 22(2). Article 22(4) does not spell out what these measures involve, but they are presumably to be interpreted in the same manner as the measures specified in Article 22(3).[72]

7. Binding corporate rules

As one of the prerequisites for DPA approval of binding corporate rules ('BCRs'), Article 47(2)(e) stipulates that the rules provide for 'the right not to be subject to decisions based solely on automated processing, including profiling, in accordance with Article 22'.[73]

8. Article 11 LED

The provisions of Article 22 are replicated in Article 11 LED, albeit with multiple differences, the bulk of which are quite minor. The first difference, which is relatively major, is that Article 11(1) LED is clearly expressed as a qualified prohibition on fully automated decisions and profiling.[74] Secondly, this prohibition targets only decisions or profiling that have an 'adverse' legal effect on the data subject (or otherwise 'significantly affect' him or her). Thirdly, the qualifications to this prohibition pertain only to situations in which Union or Member State law 'provides appropriate safeguards' for the rights and freedoms of the data subject' and 'at least the right to obtain human intervention on the part of the controller'. Fourthly, Article 11(2) LED prohibits basing fully automated decisions as referred to in Article 11(1) on the 'special categories' of relatively sensitive

---

fairly generalised explication of system functionality, not *ex post* explanation of a particular decision); and WP29 2017 (adopting a similar line).

[72] Additionally, Art. 9(2)(g) GDPR requires the legislation concerned to be 'proportionate to the aim pursued, respect the essence of the right to data protection and provide for suitable and specific measures to safeguard the fundamental rights and the interests of the data subject'.

[73] Further on BCRs, see the commentaries on Arts. 4(20) and 47 in this volume.

[74] Art. 11(1) replicates, with some differences, Art. 7 of the predecessor to the LED—i.e. Council Framework Decision 2008/977/JHA. Art. 7 was expressed as a permission rather than prohibition (i.e. automated decisions involving profiling with adverse legal effects or other significant effects for the data subject were 'permitted only if authorised by a law which also lays down measures to safeguard the data subject's legitimate interests'), but the effect was the same as for Art. 11(1) LED. Like Art. 15(1) DPD but in contrast to Art. 11(1) LED and Art. 22(1) GDPR, Art. 7 of the Framework Decision only covered decisions involving profiling (i.e. evaluation of the data subject's 'personal aspects'). The Framework Decision did not contain equivalents to the second and third paragraphs of Art. 11 LED.

personal data listed in Article 10 LED (these categories are largely commensurate with the data categories listed in Article 9 GDPR) 'unless suitable measures to safeguard the data subject's rights and freedoms and legitimate interests are in place'. Fifthly, Article 11(3) LED prohibits '[p]rofiling that results in discrimination against natural persons on the basis of special categories of personal data referred to in Article 10 ... in accordance with Union law'.

A further difference between the GDPR and the LED regime—at least on the face of the latter—arises with respect to DPIA requirements. As noted in respect of the GDPR, automated decision-making that is caught by Article 22 and involves systematic and extensive evaluation of data subjects is explicitly subject to *ex ante* DPIA pursuant to Article 35(3)(a) GDPR. The provisions on DPIA in Article 27 LED do not expressly extend to the decision-making caught by Article 11 LED. However, such decision-making will be subject to *ex ante* DPIA inasmuch as it presents a 'high risk' to persons' rights and freedoms.[75]

Additional LED provisions address other aspects of profiling (which is defined in Article 3(4) in the same way as under the GDPR). For example, Article 24(1)(e) mandates Member States to provide that controllers maintain a record of profiling practices, where applicable.

Traces of Article 22 GDPR are further found in Article 6(5) of the Directive on Processing of Passenger Name Record Data (Directive (EU) 2016/681).[76] Article 6(5) provides:

> Member States shall ensure that any positive match [leading to the identification of persons who may be involved in terrorism or serious crime and who thus need to be subject to further examination by the competent authorities] resulting from the automated processing of PNR data ... is individually reviewed by non-automated means to verify whether the competent authority ... needs to take action under national law.

9. Articles 24 and 77 EUDPR

Article 22 GDPR is identically replicated in Article 24 EUDPR. The decisions covered by the latter are also subject to DPIA requirements similar to those pertaining under the GDPR—see especially Articles 39(3)(a) and 40(2) EUDPR—with the EDPS ultimately able to ban such decisions (Article 58(2)(g) EUDPR).

However, Chapter IX EUDPR lays down a subset of special rules for processing of 'operational' personal data in the course of activities that are within the ambit of Chapters 4 or 5 of Title V of Part Three Treaty on the Functioning of the European Union ('TFEU'). These are activities concerning judicial cooperation in criminal matters and police cooperation. Accordingly, fully automated decisions, including decisions based on profiling, which fall within the scope of Chapter IX EUDPR are essentially subject to the same controls as Article 11 LED (elaborated above) lays down (see Article 77 EUDPR).

---

[75] The criterion of 'high risk' is the touchstone triggering a DPIA under both Art. 27(1) LED (see also rec. 52 LED) and Art. 35(1) GDPR. Rec. 51 LED mentions profiling as one instance of data processing with the potential to become a 'high risk' operation. Accordingly, WP29 'recommends' (but does not require) Member States to require controllers to carry out DPIAs in connection with automated decision-making. See WP29 2017, p. 14.
[76] PNR Directive.

Select Bibliography

EU legislation

Council Framework Decision 2008/977/JHA: Council Framework Decision 2008/977/JHA of 27 November 2008 on the protection of personal data processed in the framework of police and judicial cooperation in criminal matters, OJ 2008 L 350/60.

DPD Proposal 1990: Proposal for a Council Directive concerning the protection of individuals in relation to the processing of personal data, COM(90) 314 final, 13 September 1990.

DPD Amended Proposal 1992: Amended Proposal for a Council Directive on the protection of individuals with regard to the processing of personal data and on the free movement of such data, COM(92) 422 final, 15 October 1992.

GDPR Proposal: Proposal for a Regulation of the European Parliament and ofthe Council on the protection of individuals with regard to the processing ofpersonaldata and on the free movement of such data (General DataProtection Regulation), COM(2012) 11 final,25 January 2012.

PNR Directive: Directive (EU) 2016/681 of the European Parliament and of the Council of 27 April 2016 on the use of passenger name record (PNR) data for the prevention, detection, investigation and prosecution of terrorist offences and serious crime, OJ 2016 L 119/132.

Regulation 952/2013: Regulation (EU) No. 952/2013 of the European Parliament and of the Council of 9 October 2013 laying down the Union Customs Code, OJ 2013 L 269/1.

National legislation

Belgian Data Protection Law 1992: Wet tot bescherming van de persoonlijke levenssfeer ten opzichte van de verwerking van persoonsgegevens, van 8 december 1992; Loi relative à la protection de la vie privée à l'égard des traitements de données à caractère personnel, du 8 decembre 1992) (repealed).

French Data Protection Act 1978: Act No. 78-17 of 6 January 1978 on Data Processing, Files and Individual Liberties (Loi n° 78-17 du 6 janvier 1978 relative à l'informatique, aux fichiers et aux libertés), as last amended by Law No. 2014-334 of 17 March 2014.

Irish Data Protection Act 2003: Data Protection Act 2003 (Number 6 of 2003).

Italian Data Protection Code 2003: Decreto legislativo 30 giugno 2003, n. 196: Codice in Materia di Protezione dei Dati Personali.

Italian Data Protection Code 2018: Decreto Legislativo 10 agosto 2018 n. 101: Disposizioni per l'adeguamento della normativa nazionale alle disposizioni del regolamento (UE) 2016/679 del Parlamento europeo e del Consiglio, del 27 aprile 2016, relativo alla protezione delle persone fisiche con riguardo al trattamento dei dati personali, nonche' alla libera circolazione di tali dati e che abroga la direttiva 95/46/CE (regolamento generale sulla protezione dei dati).

Swedish Personal Data Act 1998: Personal Data Act 1998 (Personuppgiftslagen (SFS1998:204)) (repealed).

Academic writings

Brkan 2019: Brkan, 'Do Algorithms Rule the World? Algorithmic Decision Making and Data Protection in the Framework of the GDPR and Beyond', 27(2) *International Journal of Law and Information Technology* (2019), 91.

Bygrave 2001: Bygrave, 'Minding the Machine: Article 15 of the EC Data Protection Directive and Automated Profiling', 17(1) *Computer Law & Security Review 'CLSR'* (2001), 17.

Bygrave 2019: Bygrave, 'Minding the Machine v2.0: The EU General Data Protection Regulation and Automated Decision Making', in Yeung and Lodge (eds.), *Algorithmic Regulation* (OUP 2019), 246.

Church and Millard 2010: Church and Millard, 'Commentary on Article 15 of the Data Protection Directive', in Büllesbach, Gijrath, Poullet and Prins (eds.) *Concise European IT Law* (2nd edn, Kluwer Law International 2010), 83.

Edwards and Veale, 'Slave to the Algorithm: Why a "Right to an Explanation" Is Probably Not the Remedy You Are Looking For', 16(1) *Duke Law & Technology Review* (2017), 18.

Mendoza and Bygrave 2017: Mendoza and Bygrave, 'The Right Not to Be Subject to Automated Decisions Based on Profiling', in Synodinou, Jougleux, Markou and Prastitou (eds.), *EU Internet Law: Regulation and Enforcement* (Springer 2017), 77.

Schartum 2018: Schartum, 'From Facts to Decision Data: About the Factual Basis of Automated Individual Decisions', 65 *Scandinavian Studies in Law* (2018), 379.

Selbst and Powles 2017: Selbst and Powles, 'Meaningful Information and the Right to Explanation', 7(4) *International Data Privacy Law 'IDPL'* (2017), 233.

Simitis and Damman 1997: Simitis and Dammann, *EU-Datenschutzrichtlinie* (Nomos Verlag 1997).

Tosoni 2019: Tosoni, 'The Right to Object to Automated Individual Decisions: Resolving the Ambiguity of Article 22(1) of the General Data Protection Regulation', 9 *IDPL* (2019) (forthcoming).

Veale and Edwards 2018: Veale and Edwards, 'Clarity, Surprises, and Further Questions in the Article 29 Working Party Draft Guidance on Automated Decision-Making and Profiling', 34(2) *CLSR* (2018), 398.

Wachter et al. 2017: Wachter, Mittelstadt and Floridi, 'Why a Right to Explanation of Automated Decision-Making Does Not Exist in the General Data Protection Regulation', 7(2) *IDPL* (2017), 76.

Papers of data protection authorities

WP29 1998: Article 29 Working Party, 'Transfers of Personal Data to Third Countries: Applying Articles 25 and 26 of the EU Data Protection Directive' (WP 12, 24 July 1998).

WP29 2017: Article 29 Working Party, 'Opinion on Some Key Issues of the Law Enforcement Directive (EU 2016/680)' (WP 258, 29 November 2017).

WP29 2018: Article 29 Working Party, 'Guidelines on Automated Individual Decision-Making and Profiling for the Purposes of Regulation 2016/679' (WP 251rev.01, as last revised and adopted on 6 February 2018).

CNIL 2017: Commission nationale de l'informatique et des libertés, 'Décision n° MED-2017-053 du 30 août 2017' (30 August 2017).

Reports and recommendations

COM Recommendation 2010: Committee of the Ministers of the Council of Europe, 'Recommendation on the Protection of Individuals with Regard to Automatic Processing of Personal Data in the Context of Profiling' (Rec(2010)13, 23 November 2010).

EP GDPR Draft Report: Draft Report on the proposal for a regulation of the European Parliament and of the Council on the protection of individual with regard to the processing of personal data and on the free movement of such data (General Data Protection Regulation), 2012/0011(COD), 16 January 2013.

T-PD Guidelines 2017: Consultative Committee of the Convention for the Protection of Individuals with regard to Automatic Processing of Personal Data, 'Guidelines on the Protection of Individuals with Regard to the Processing of Personal Data in the World of Big Data' (T-PD(2017)01, 23 January 2017).

Section 5 Restrictions

Article 23. Restrictions

DOMINIQUE MOORE*

1. Union or Member State law to which the data controller or processor is subject may restrict by way of a legislative measure the scope of the obligations and rights provided for in Articles 12 to 22 and Article 34, as well as Article 5 in so far as its provisions correspond to the rights and obligations provided for in Articles 12 to 22, when such a restriction respects the essence of the fundamental rights and freedoms and is a necessary and proportionate measure in a democratic society to safeguard:
   (a) national security;
   (b) defence;
   (c) public security;
   (d) the prevention, investigation, detection or prosecution of criminal offences or the execution of criminal penalties, including the safeguarding against and the prevention of threats to public security;
   (e) other important objectives of general public interest of the Union or of a Member State, in particular an important economic or financial interest of the Union or of a Member State, including monetary, budgetary and taxation a matters, public health and social security;
   (f) the protection of judicial independence and judicial proceedings;
   (g) the prevention, investigation, detection and prosecution of breaches of ethics for regulated professions;
   (h) a monitoring, inspection or regulatory function connected, even occasionally, to the exercise of official authority in the cases referred to in points (a) to (e) and (g);
   (i) the protection of the data subject or the rights and freedoms of others;
   (j) the enforcement of civil law claims.
2. In particular, any legislative measure referred to in paragraph 1 shall contain specific provisions at least, where relevant, as to:
   (a) the purposes of the processing or categories of processing;
   (b) the categories of personal data;
   (c) the scope of the restrictions introduced;
   (d) the safeguards to prevent abuse or unlawful access or transfer;
   (e) the specification of the controller or categories of controllers;
   (f) the storage periods and the applicable safeguards taking into account the nature, scope and purposes of the processing or categories of processing;
   (g) the risks to the rights and freedoms of data subjects; and
   (h) the right of data subjects to be informed about the restriction, unless that may be prejudicial to the purpose of the restriction.

Relevant Recital

(73) Restrictions concerning specific principles and the rights of information, access to and rectification or erasure of personal data, the right to data portability, the right to object, decisions

---

* The views expressed are solely those of the author and do not necessarily reflect those of the European Parliament.

based on profiling, as well as the communication of a personal data breach to a data subject and certain related obligations of the controllers may be imposed by Union or Member State law, as far as necessary and proportionate in a democratic society to safeguard public security, including the protection of human life especially in response to natural or manmade disasters, the prevention, investigation and prosecution of criminal offences or the execution of criminal penalties, including the safeguarding against and the prevention of threats to public security, or of breaches of ethics for regulated professions, other important objectives of general public interest of the Union or of a Member State, in particular an important economic or financial interest of the Union or of a Member State, the keeping of public registers kept for reasons of general public interest, further processing of archived personal data to provide specific information related to the political behaviour under former totalitarian state regimes or the protection of the data subject or the rights and freedoms of others, including social protection, public health and humanitarian purposes. Those restrictions should be in accordance with the requirements set out in the Charter and in the European Convention for the Protection of Human Rights and Fundamental Freedoms.

Closely Related Provisions

Article 5 (Principles relating to processing of personal data) (see too recitals 41, 45 and 50); Article 12 (Transparent information, communication and modalities for the exercise of the rights of the data subject); Article 13 (Information to be provided where personal data are collected from the data subject); Article 14 (Information to be provided where personal data have not been obtained from the data subject); Article 15 (Right of access by the data subject); Article 16 (Right to rectification); Article 17 (Right to erasure, 'right to be forgotten'); Article 18 (Right to restriction of processing); Article 20 (Right to data portability); Article 21 (Right to object); Article 22 (Automated individual decision-making, including profiling); Article 34 (Communication of a personal data breach to the data subject)

Related Provisions in LED [Directive (EU) 2016/680]

Article 13(3) (Information to be made available or given to the data subject) (see too recital 44); Article 15 (Limitations to the right of access) (see too recital 46); Article 16(4) (Right to rectification or erasure of personal data and restriction of processing)

Related Provisions in EPD [Directive 2002/58/EC]

Article 15 (Application of certain provisions of Directive 95/46/EC) (see too recital 11)

Relevant Case Law

CJEU

Joined Cases C-465/00, C-138/01 and C-139/01, *Rechnungshof v Österreichischer Rundfunk and Others and Christa Neukomm and Joseph Lauermann v Österreichischer Rundfunk*, judgment of 20 May 2003 (ECLI:EU:C:2003:294).
Case C-275/06, *Productores de Música de España (Promusicae) v Telefónica de España SAU*, judgment of 29 January 2008 (Grand Chamber) (ECLI:EU:C:2008:54).
Joined Cases C-92/09 and 93/09, *Volker and Markus Schecke GbR and Hartmut Eifert v Land Hessen*, judgment of 9 November 2010 (Grand Chamber) (ECLI:EU:C:2010:662).

Joined Cases C-293/12 and C-594/12, *Digital Rights Ireland Ltd v Minister for Communications, Marine and Natural Resources and Others* and *Kärntner Landesregierung, Michael Seitlinger, Christof Tschohl and Others*, judgment of 8 April 2014 (Grand Chamber) (ECLI:EU:C:2014:238).

Case C-201/14, *Smaranda Bara and Others v Președintele Casei Naționale de Asigurări de Sănătate, Casa Națională de Asigurări de Sănătate, Agenția Națională de Administrare Fiscală (ANAF)*, judgment of 1 October 2015 (ECLI:EU:C:2015:638).

Case C-362/14, *Maximillian Schrems v Data Protection Commissioner*, judgment of 6 October 2015 (Grand Chamber) (ECLI:EU:C:2015:650).

Joined Cases C-203/15 and C-698/15, *Tele2 Sverige AB v Post-och telestyrelsen* and *Secretary of State for Home Department v Tom Watson and Others*, judgment of 21 December 2016 (Grand Chamber) (ECLI:EU:C:2016:970).

Opinion 1/15, judgment of 26 July 2017 (Grand Chamber) (ECLI:EU:C:2017:592).

Case C-207/16, *Ministerio Fiscal*, judgment of 2 October 2018 (Grand Chamber) (ECLI:EU:C:2018:788).

ECtHR

Zakharov v Russia, Appl. No. 47143/06, judgment of 4 December 2015.
Szabo and Vissy v Hungary, Appl. No. 37138/14, judgment of 12 January 2016.

A. Rationale and Policy Underpinnings

Article 23 GDPR reflects the nature of the fundamental right to the protection of natural persons with regard to the processing of personal data. As the CJEU has underlined,[1] the right to the protection of personal data is not an absolute right, but must be considered in relation to its function in society. Article 8(2) of the Charter of Fundamental Rights of the European Union ('CFR') thus authorises the processing of personal data if certain conditions are satisfied. It provides that personal data 'must be processed fairly for specified purposes and on the basis of the consent of the person concerned or some other legitimate basis laid down by law'. Moreover, Article 52(1) of the Charter accepts that limitations may be imposed on the exercise of rights such as those set forth in Articles 7 and 8 of the Charter, as long as the limitations are provided by law, respect the essence of those rights and freedoms and, subject to the principle of proportionality, are necessary and genuinely meet objectives of general interest recognised by the European Union or the need to protect the rights and freedoms of others. Also, in line with Article 52(3) of the Charter, the limitations which may lawfully be imposed on the right to the protection of personal data correspond to those tolerated in relation to Article 8 of the Convention for the Protection of Human Rights and Fundamental Freedoms ('ECHR').[2]

Article 23, together with recital 73, thus recognises that certain rights foreseen in the GDPR may be restricted, but only subject to explicit conditions which are set out in this provision which are themselves inspired by the provisions of the Charter, and in particular its Article 52, read in the light of the case law of the Court of Justice and Article 8 of the Convention and the corresponding case law of the ECtHR.

[1] Joined Cases C-92/09 and C-93/09, *Schecke*, para. 48. [2] Ibid., para. 52.

B. Legal Background

1. EU legislation

Article 23 is the equivalent of Article 13 DPD, which was part of Section VI entitled 'Exemptions and restrictions'. Article 13 DPD already provided that Member States may adopt 'legislative measures' to restrict the scope of the obligations and rights provided for in Article 6(1) (on principles relating to data quality), Articles 10 and 11(1) (on information to be given to the data subject), Article 12 (on the data subject's right of access to data) and Article 21 (on publicising of processing operations) in the DPD, on comparable, though not identical, grounds set out in Article 13(1) (a)–(g) DPD.

Article 15 EPD—read in the light of recital 11 EPD which explains that it does not seek to 'alter the existing balance' between the individual's right to privacy and the possibility for Member States to take 'necessary' measures for the protection of certain interests—is also relevant, as it foresees the possibility for Member States to adopt legislative measures to restrict the scope of certain rights and obligations specifically provided for in the EPD (including rights relating to confidentiality of communications, to erasure of traffic data and to processing of location data), on certain grounds, with reference also to Article 13 DPD. To this end, Article 15 EPD expressly recognises that Member States may, inter alia, adopt legislative measures providing for the retention of data for a limited period justified on these same grounds, which has subsequently given rise to significant litigation before the courts, at both the national and European level, on the legality of national legislation adopted on this basis.[3]

2. International instruments

Article 23 GDPR now reflects the general concept first set out in Article 9 of Convention 108 as first adopted, under the heading 'Exceptions and restrictions'. Article 9 provides that derogation from the provisions of Articles 5 (on quality of data), 6 (on special categories of data) and 8 (on additional safeguards for the data subject) of the Convention shall be allowed when such derogation is provided for by the law of the party and constitutes a necessary measure in a democratic society in certain specified interests themselves drawn from Article 8 ECHR. Article 8(2) ECHR provides that interference with the exercise of the right to respect for private and family life can only be made by public authorities in accordance with law, and as necessary in a democratic society for certain listed interests.[4] As will be seen, Article 8 has often been cited in the judgments of the CJEU in this field.

The general scheme of Article 9 of Convention 108 was the model for Article 13 DPD under the very similar heading 'Exemptions and restrictions', albeit with some significant changes to the wording of its contents. The same scheme was also followed in Article 15 EPD which reincorporated some of the original wording initially included in Article 9 of Convention 108, but which was not found in Article 13 DPD, such as the phrase 'constitutes a necessary ... measure within a democratic society'.[5]

---

[3] See in particular Joined Cases C-203/15 and C-698/15, *Tele2*.

[4] The interests listed in Art. 8(2) ECHR include 'national security, public safety or the economic well-being of the country, for the prevention of disorder or crime, for the protection of health or morals, or for the protection of the rights and freedoms of others'. See regarding interpretation of these interests by the ECtHR, Lynskey 2015, p. 115.

[5] With regard to the importance of this particular phrase, see Joined Cases C-203/15 and C-698/15, *Tele2*, para. 107.

The modernised version of Convention 108, which has not yet entered into force, provides in Article 11 more detailed provisions concerning exceptions than in the current Article 9 of the Convention. The new Article 11 provides in paragraph 1 that the only exceptions allowed to the general provisions of the Convention are to Article 5 paragraph 4 (concerning certain rules on the legitimacy and quality of data processing), Article 7 paragraph 2 (dealing with notification of data breaches to supervisory authorities), Article 8 paragraph 1 (the obligation of data controllers to inform individuals of their habitual residence or establishment), and Article 9 (rights of data subjects), when such an exception is provided for by law, respects the essence of the fundamental rights and freedoms and constitutes a necessary and proportionate measure in a democratic society for certain defined purposes. Article 11(2) also allows for restrictions on the exercise of the provisions specified in Article 8 (transparency of processing) and Article 9 (rights of data subjects) with respect to 'data processing for archiving purposes in the public interest, scientific or historical research purposes or statistical purposes when there is no recognisable risk of infringement of the rights and fundamental freedoms of data subjects'. Finally, Article 11(3) allows for certain exceptions by law with regard to data processing for national security and defence purposes.

3. National developments

Although a significant body of national legislation, in diverse fields, has been adopted within the scope of Article 13 DPD and Article 15 EPD, not to mention Article 9 of Convention 108, as reflected in the case law of both the CJEU and the ECtHR, such national legislation merely provides concrete examples of how certain rights set out at European and international level may actually be 'restricted' in specific cases by national legislation. In those circumstances, such national legislation does not though aim to provide a model for creating a general scheme for defining the broad range of rights which may be subject to restrictions and for setting the general conditions which determine whether such restrictions will be lawful, as is the aim of Article 23 GDPR, Article 13 DPD, Article 15 EPD, Article 9 Convention 108 and Article 11 Modernised Convention 108.

4. Case law

An important body of case law now exists on the interpretation given by the CJEU to Articles 7, 8 and 52(1) CFR, specifically in relation to EU legislation adopted in the field of data protection. In this regard, the CJEU has repeatedly made reference to the case law of the ECtHR which has itself also developed in tandem in this field, referring back in turn to the case law of the CJEU. This case law of both the CJEU and the ECtHR will be of direct relevance to the proper interpretation to be given to Article 23 GDPR.

As regards the CJEU, the application of Article 13 DPD has consistently been analysed with reference also to the case law of the ECtHR. The judgment of 20 May 2003 in *Österreichischer Rundfunk*[6] provides an early example where Article 13(e) and (f) DPD were to be applied to Austrian legislation on the publication of salaries and pensions paid by public bodies, as a derogation from the principles in Article 6(1) DPD, to protect 'an

---

[6] Joined Cases C-465/00, C-138/01 and C-139/01, *Österreichischer Rundfunk*, paras. 64–90.

important economic or financial interest of a Member State' or 'a monitoring, inspection or regulatory function'. In this context, the CJEU examined the existence of an interference with private life and the justification of that interference by reference to Article 8 ECHR and the relevant case law of the ECtHR, although it left the final assessment of that matter for the national courts to ascertain.

A subsequent example is to be found in the judgment of 29 January 2008 in the *Promusicae* case,[7] which concerned the interpretation of both Article 13 of the DPD and also Article 15 of the EPD, in the context of the refusal of an internet access service provider to disclose, to a third party, personal data relating to use of the internet. Here, the CJEU explained that this case raised the question of the need to reconcile the requirements of the protection of different fundamental rights, namely the right to respect for private life, in accordance with Articles 7 and 8 CFR and Article 8 ECHR, on the one hand, and the rights to protection of property, including intellectual property, and to an effective remedy, in accordance with Articles 17 and 47 CFR, respectively, on the other. In this context, the CJEU ruled that Member States must, when transposing the directives in question, take care to rely on an interpretation which allows a 'fair balance' to be struck between the various fundamental rights protected by the EU legal order and, specifically as regards Article 15(1) EPD, the CJEU insisted that any restrictions on those rights must be adopted by Member States in compliance with the general principles of EU law, such as the principle of proportionality.

The requirement in Article 13 DPD for any restriction to be imposed by a 'legislative measure' was considered in the judgment of 1 October 2015 in the *Bara* case, where Romanian legislation was found lacking in this regard as concerns the restriction of the right to provide information to data subjects, in the context of the transfer of personal tax data by one public administrative body to another.[8]

More recent case law has further clarified the interpretation of Articles 7, 8 and 52(1) CFR, with the findings being made by the CJEU that certain measures had exceeded the limits imposed by compliance with the principle of proportionality in the light of those provisions of the Charter. Of particular importance in this regard is the judgment of 8 April 2014 in *Digital Rights Ireland*[9] in which Directive 2006/24/EC on data retention was declared invalid and also the subsequent judgment of 6 October 2015 in *Schrems*[10] in which a Commission adequacy decision, adopted under Article 25 DPD, on the transfer of data to the USA was also declared invalid. In addition, in July 2017 the CJEU in *Opinion 1/15*[11] declared that a proposed international agreement between the EU and Canada could not be concluded since some of its provisions were inconsistent with EU fundamental rights. These cases dramatically demonstrate the legal consequences of a failure to properly justify, in accordance with the requirements of Article 52 of the Charter, serious interferences with the fundamental rights guaranteed by Articles 7 and 8 of the Charter.

Finally, the CJEU judgment of 21 December 2016 in the *Tele2* case is of particular relevance to this field. In that case, the CJEU not only referred to both the previous *Digital Rights Ireland* and *Schrems* cases, together with the most recent ECtHR judgments[12] (*Zakharov v Russia* and *Szabó and Vissy v Hungary*), but also examined in detail

---

[7] Case C-275/06, *Promusicae*.   [8] Case C-201/12, *Bara*, see paras. 39–41.
[9] Joined Cases C-293/12 and C-594/12, *Digital Rights Ireland*.   [10] Case C-362/14, *Schrems*.
[11] *Opinion 1/15*.   [12] Joined Cases C-203/15 and C-698/15, *Tele2*, paras. 119–120.

the interpretation of Article 15 EPD, in the light of Articles 7, 8 and 52 CFR, before finding that these provisions of EU law preclude national legislation which, for the purpose of fighting crime, provides for the general and indiscriminate retention of all traffic and location data of all subscribers and registered users relating to all means of electronic communication. This ruling of the CJEU may thus well become the 'touchstone' for the interpretation of Article 23 GDPR in the future.

The previous rulings in the *Tele2* and *Digital Rights Ireland* cases must also be read in the light of the more recent judgment of the Grand Chamber of the CJEU of 2 October 2018 in the *Ministerio Fiscal* case which also concerned the interpretation of Article 15 EPD, read in the light of Articles 7 and 8 CFR.[13] Here, the Spanish police sought judicial authorisation to access personal data retained by providers of electronic communications services, based on national law governing the access of public authorities to such data. That national legislation permitted the police, in the event that judicial authorisation is granted, to require providers of electronic communications services to make personal data available to it and, in so doing, to 'process' those data within the meaning of the DPD and EPD. The CJEU confirmed that this national legislation therefore governs the activities of providers of electronic communications services and, as a result, falls within the scope of the EPD. As a result, the fact that the request for access was made in connection with a criminal investigation does not make the EPD inapplicable by virtue of Article 1(3) EPD.

The CJEU also recalled in the *Ministerio Fiscal* ruling that that it had previously ruled in the *Tele2* case that the objective pursued by national legislation governing access to personal data must be proportionate to the seriousness of the interference with the fundamental rights in question that that access entails.[14] In accordance with the principle of proportionality, serious interference can be justified, in areas of prevention, investigation, detection and prosecution of criminal offences, only by the objective of fighting crime which must also be defined as 'serious'.[15] By contrast, when the interference that such access entails is not serious, that access is capable of being justified by the objective of preventing, investigating, detecting and prosecuting 'criminal offences' generally.[16] In this case, the sole purpose of the police request for judicial authorisation to access personal data was to identify the owners of SIM cards activated over a period of 12 days with the IMEI code[17] of a stolen mobile telephone. The data requested did not concern the communications carried out with the stolen mobile telephone or its location. Those data would not therefore allow precise conclusions to be drawn concerning the private lives of the persons whose data is concerned. In those circumstances, the Court found, access to only the data referred to in the police request at issue cannot be defined as a 'serious' interference with the fundamental rights of the persons whose data is concerned.[18] The interference that access to such data entails is therefore capable of being justified by the objective, to which the first sentence of Article 15(1) EPD refers, of preventing,

---

[13] Case C-207/16, *Ministerio Fiscal*.   [14] See ibid., para. 55.   [15] Ibid., para. 56.
[16] Ibid., para. 57.
[17] IMEI is the abbreviation of the expression *'International Mobile Equipment Identity'*. The IMEI is a unique identification code, consisting of around 15 digits, which is generally found inside the battery compartment of the mobile telephone and also on the box and the invoice issued when the device is purchased.
[18] Case C-207/16, *Ministerio Fiscal*, para. 61.

investigating, detecting and prosecuting 'criminal offences' generally, without it being necessary that those offences be defined as 'serious'.

As regards the ECtHR, the well-developed case law on the application of Article 8 ECHR has often been cited in the judgments of the CJEU in this field, as explained above. The degree to which the case law of the ECtHR and the CJEU has become intertwined is perhaps best demonstrated by the judgment of the ECtHR of 4 December 2015 in the *Zakharov v Russia* case[19] and by the judgment of 12 January 2016 in the *Szabó and Vissy v Hungary* case,[20] relating to the compatibility of certain surveillance measures in Russia and Hungary, respectively, both of which make reference to the *Digital Rights Ireland* judgment of the CJEU.[21] As noted above, the subsequent *Tele2* judgment of the CJEU later referred in turn to each of these rulings of the ECtHR.[22] The reasoning of the CJEU and ECtHR in this field is thus closely aligned.

C. Analysis

1. Introduction

Given that the fundamental right to the protection of personal data is not absolute but may, under certain limited conditions, take into account other legitimate interests in a democratic society, Article 23 seeks to create a mechanism for striking an appropriate balance in this regard. This reflects the concept initially recognised in Article 9 of Convention 108 which was itself inspired by the case law of the ECtHR notably in respect of the application of Article 8 ECHR. It also builds on Article 13 DPD and Article 15 EPD, together with the relevant case law of the CJEU which now takes account of Articles 7, 8 and 52 CFR in this context, having due regard still to the case law of the ECtHR.

Given this rich background, the core components of the new text of Article 23 will be readily understood with reference to these antecedents, such as for example the need for a 'legislative measure', the need to 'respect the essence of the fundamental rights and freedoms' and the requirement for a 'necessary and proportionate measure in a democratic society'.

2. Changes in the GDPR

However, whilst Article 23 clearly builds on existing concepts, it nevertheless also brings certain changes with respect to the previous legislative rules contained in Article 13 DPD. As regards the scope of these provisions, Article 23 GDPR may, at first sight, appear to have a broader scope, as it refers to a wider list of provisions which may now be subject to restrictions: i.e. restrictions are possible for the obligations and rights provided for in Article 12–22 GDPR and Article 34 GDPR, as well as Article 5 GDPR in certain respects, whereas Article 13 DPD referred only to Articles 6(1), 10, 11(1), 12 and 21 DPD. However, this longer list of provisions affected by Article 23 merely reflects the fact that new obligations and rights have been recognised by the GDPR in Chapter III under the

---

[19] ECtHR, *Zakharov v Russia*.   [20] ECtHR, *Szabó and Vissy v Hungary*.
[21] ECtHR, *Zakharov v Russia*, para. 147; ECtHR, *Szabó and Vissy v Hungary*, paras. 23 and 73.
[22] See Joined Cases C-203/15 and C-698/15, *Tele2*, paras. 119–120.

heading 'Rights of the data subject', which were not previously included in the DPD, such as the 'right to rectification' and the 'right to erasure (right to be forgotten)' which are now separate to the 'right of access', as well as the 'right to restriction of processing' and the 'right to data portability'. In this sense, Article 23 takes the logical approach of applying to all of the various obligations and rights which fall under the heading of 'Rights of the data subject' in Chapter III of the GDPR, which is also the heading under which Article 23 is now found.

Following this approach of focusing on the rights of the data subject, Article 23 now applies in a significantly more limited way to the 'principles relating to data quality' when compared with Article 13 DPD. Whilst Article 13 DPD previously permitted the restriction of the obligations and rights provided for in 'Article 6(1)', thus potentially making all of the principles relating to data quality contained in points (a)–(e) of Article 6(1) DPD open to restrictions, Article 23 GDPR now only applies to Article 5 in so far as its provisions correspond to the rights and obligations provided for in Articles 12–22.[23] A link must therefore now be shown to the data subject 'rights' provided for in Articles 12–22 (under Chapter III), before any restriction of the 'principles' set out in Article 5, under Chapter II, GDPR can be envisaged.

It remains to be seen how this apparently subtle shift of focus towards data subjects' rights, when comparing Article 13 DPD and Article 23 GDPR, will affect the more limited scope for legislative measures to be adopted, in future, in order to impose restrictions on aspects of 'principles' set out in Article 5, under Chapter II, GDPR (at least in cases where there is no obvious link to specific data subject 'rights' provided for in Articles 12–22 under Chapter III). For example, this question could arise in relation to a proposed restriction of the 'purpose limitation' principle under Article 5(b) or a restriction of the 'storage limitation' principle under Article 5(e), where a legislative measure seeks to change the specified purpose for which data was initially collected (e.g. a commercial purpose of a private entity) to an entirely different purpose (e.g. a law enforcement purpose pursued by a public authority, unconnected with the commercial purpose initially pursued by a private commercial entity).[24]

Furthermore, it may also be of interest to compare Article 23 GDPR with Article 15 EPD, even if this latter provision has a somewhat different scope than Article 23 GDPR, given that it refers expressly to the possibility to restrict the scope of the rights and obligations 'provided for in Article 5, Article 6, Article 8(1), (2), (3), and (4) and Article 9 of this [EPD] Directive'. In particular, Article 5 EPD provides for the confidentiality of communications to be ensured, in order to respect Article 7 of the Charter and Article 8 ECHR on the right to privacy, and as a result Article 15 EPD, by authorising restrictions

---

[23] The initial GDPR proposal included an express reference to 'points (a) to (e) of Art. 5', which would have made it possible to adopt restrictions to all of these principles, but the Parliament proposed instead to simply delete the whole of this text. The Council took an intermediate approach proposing instead to include the following text in this provision: 'as well as Art. 5 in so far as its provisions correspond to the rights and obligations provided for in Arts. 12 to 20'. The final text agreed in trilogues was then based on the Council's proposal which referred to the possibility of adopting restrictions to the principles set out in Art. 5, but only in this limited sense. The EU legislator has thus deliberately adopted an approach which is now somewhat narrower than the initial proposal of the Commission, which was first based on the previous text of Art. 13 DPD.

[24] See in this regard WP 29 2013, which explains that such a change of purpose for further use by law enforcement authorities would be incompatible with the initial (commercial) purpose for which the data were collected by a commercial entity and, as a result, the only possibility to nevertheless lawfully process data for these further (law enforcement) purposes must be based on Art. 13 DPD (or Art. 15 EPD as the case may be), as illustrated by the various examples 17–22 at the end of this opinion.

to the confidentiality of communications, foresees the limitation of the right to privacy under Article 7 CFR, in addition to other limitations of the right to the protection of personal data under Article 8 of the Charter. In this respect, the scope of Article 15 EPD is significantly broader than that of Article 23 GDPR.

The judgment of the CJEU in the *Tele2* case should be considered in this context, given that it examines the scope of the EPD, and in particular Article 15 EPD, with particular emphasis on the protection of confidentiality, guaranteed in Article 5 EPD.[25] Given this focus on the confidentiality of communications guaranteed in Article 5 EPD (on the basis of Article 7 of the Charter and Article 8 ECHR), which has no obvious counterpart in the GDPR (which is based exclusively on Article 16 Treaty on the Functioning of the European Union ('TFEU') and, correspondingly, on Article 8 CFR), it remains to be seen whether the CJEU would still reach the same conclusions in respect of restrictions adopted purely on the basis of Article 23 GDPR, outside of the field of electronic communications,[26] or whether the conclusions to be drawn from Article 23 GDPR may perhaps need to be nuanced in this respect, depending on the circumstances of each particular case.

3. Application to Union law

It is worth noting that Article 23 now concerns not only the ability of 'Member State law' to impose restrictions by way of a 'legislative measure', which was already the case under Article 13 DPD, but, by virtue of the fact that this provision is included in a Regulation, 'Union law' is also now expressly covered too. In other words, Article 23 GDPR regulates how the EU legislature may adopt, by a 'legislative measure' any 'restriction' of the rights and obligations in question, in accordance with Articles 8 and 52 of the Charter. This could be of particular relevance to Union legislation adopted in other fields—outside of the scope of the legislative competence in Article 16(2) in Part One of the TFEU—such as in one of the fields of legislative competence in Part Three of the TFEU (for example, in the fields of border checks, asylum and immigration or police and judicial cooperation) which may nevertheless have an important impact on the processing of personal data of individuals covered by the GDPR. In effect, EU legislation adopted in other fields will have to take account of this requirement included in Article 23 GDPR, to the extent that the envisaged EU legislation may create a 'restriction' of the rights and obligations now covered here.

Such a 'legislative measure'—be it adopted as Union or Member State law—will also now have to respect the new provisions of Article 23(2) which imposes an obligation for such legislative measures to contain, where relevant, specific provisions on the matters listed in points (a)–(h) of this Article. Failure by a Member State to respect these requirements set out in a regulation may clearly entail the invalidity of national law, according to well established principles of the primacy of EU law. However, it remains unclear whether the same will also apply to any failure by the EU legislator to respect these new formal requirements when adopting other EU 'legislative measures', such as another regulation

---

[25] C-203/15 and C-698/15, *Tele2*, paras. 77 and 84–89.
[26] Such as, for example, an obligation imposed on other commercial entities, in fields other than the provision of electronic communications services (such as cross-border transport), to retain data, initially collected for commercial purposes, for a longer period for the purposes of law enforcement (or to transfer that data to public authorities for law enforcement purposes).

adopted in another field of EU competence, given that these measures would normally be regarded as having an equivalent rank in the EU legal order.[27]

4. Essence of fundamental rights and freedoms

Finally, under Article 23(1) GDPR, any restriction must respect 'the essence of the fundamental rights and freedoms'. The CJEU has opined several times on the essence of the fundamental rights to privacy and data protection,[28] finding that (1) mass data retention did not affect the essence of the right to privacy under Article 7 CFR, since it did not lead to knowledge of the content of electronic communications;[29] (2) mass data retention did not affect the essence of the right to data protection under Article 8 CFR, since certain principles of data protection and data security had to be respected by providers of electronic communications services or of public communications networks;[30] (3) legislation permitting public authorities to have access to electronic communications on a generalised basis compromised the essence of Article 7;[31] (4) legislation not providing legal remedies for an individual to have access to their personal data or to obtain the rectification or erasure of it violated the essence of the fundamental right to effective judicial protection enshrined in Article 47 CFR;[32] and (5) the transfer of PNR data to Canada did not violate the essence of Articles 7 and 8 CFR, based on the nature of the information at issue being limited to certain aspects of private life, in particular to air travel between Canada and the EU (with regard to Article 7), the fact that the Draft Agreement limited the purposes for which PNR data may be processed, and that it contained rules protecting the security, confidentiality and integrity of the data (with regard to Article 8).[33]

It is difficult to find a common thread between these holdings that would identify the essence of the rights to private life and data protection, and further elucidation of it by the Court will be required.[34]

Select Bibliography

EU legislation

GDPR Proposal: Proposal for a Regulation of the European Parliament and of the Council on the protection of individuals with regard to the processing of personal data and on the free movement of such data (General Data Protection Regulation), COM(2012) 11 final, 25 January 2012.

Academic writings

Brkan 2018: Brkan, 'The Concept of Essence of Fundamental Rights in the EU Legal Order: Peeling the Onion to Its Core', 14(2) *European Constitutional Law Review* (2018), 332.
Docksey, 'Case note, *Ministerio Fiscal*: holding the line on ePrivacy', 26(4) *Maastricht Journal of European and Comparative Law* (2019), 1.

---

[27] Unless the GDPR, adopted under Art. 16 TFEU, is now recognised as having special status, above other EU legislative acts, in view of its unique role in applying Arts. 8 and 52 CFR.
[28] See Kuner 2018, pp. 875–876.
[29] Joined Cases C-293/12 and C-594/12, *Digital Rights Ireland*, para. 39.   [30] Ibid., para. 40.
[31] Case C-362/14, *Schrems*, para. 94.   [32] Ibid., para. 95.   [33] *Opinion 1/15*, para. 150.
[34] See regarding the essence of the rights to private life and data protection, Brkan 2018.

Granger and Irion, 'The Court of Justice and the Data Retention Directive in Digital Rights Ireland: Telling Off the EU Legislator and Teaching a Lesson in Privacy and Data Protection', 39(6) *European Law Review* (2014), 850.

Kuner 2018: Kuner, 'International Agreements, Data Protection, and EU Fundamental Rights on the International Stage: *Opinion 1/15*', 55(3) *Common Market Law Review 'CMLRev.'* (2018), 857.

Kuner, 'Data Protection and Rights Protection on the Internet: The Promusicae Judgment of the European Court of Justice', 30(5) *European Intellectual Property Review* (2008), 202.

Lynskey 2015: Lynskey, *The Foundations of EU Data Protection Law* (OUP 2015).

Lynskey, 'The Data Retention Directive Is Incompatible with the Rights to Privacy and Data Protection and Is Invalid in its Entirety: Digital Rights Ireland', 51(6) *CMLRev.* (2014), 1789.

Papers of data protection authorities

European Data Protection Supervisor, 'Background Paper: Developing a "Toolkit" for Assessing the Necessity of Measures that Interfere with Fundamental Rights' (16 June 2016).

WP29 2013: Article 29 Working Party, 'Opinion 03/2013 on Purpose Limitation' (WP 203, 2 April 2013).

Article 29 Working Party, 'Opinion 1/2014 on the Application of Necessity and Proportionality Concepts and Data Protection within the Law Enforcement Sector' (WP 211, 27 February 2014).

Article 29 Working Party, 'Opinion 4/2014 on Surveillance of Electronic Communications for Intelligence and National Security Purposes' (WP 215, 10 April 2014).

Article 29 Working Party, 'Working Document on Surveillance of Electronic Communications for Intelligence and National Security Purposes' (WP 228, 5 December 2014).

Reports and recommendations

Council Position GDPR: Proposal for a Regulation of the European Parliament and of the Council on the protection of individuals with regard to the processing of personal data and on the free movement of such data (General Data Protection Regulation), Preparation of a general approach, 9565/15, 11 June 2015.

EP Position GDPR: Position of the European Parliament adopted at first reading on 12 March 2014 with a view to the adoption of Regulation (EU) No .../2014 of the European Parliament and of the Council on the protection of individuals with regard to the processing of personal data and on the free movement of such data (General Data Protection Regulation), P7_TA(2014)0212, 12 March 2014.

Chapter IV Controller and Processor (Articles 24–43)

Section 1 General obligations

Article 24. Responsibility of the controller

CHRISTOPHER DOCKSEY

1. Taking into account the nature, scope, context and purposes of processing as well as the risks of varying likelihood and severity for the rights and freedoms of natural persons, the controller shall implement appropriate technical and organisational measures to ensure and to be able to demonstrate that processing is performed in accordance with this Regulation. Those measures shall be reviewed and updated where necessary.
2. Where proportionate in relation to processing activities, the measures referred to in paragraph 1 shall include the implementation of appropriate data protection policies by the controller.
3. Adherence to approved codes of conduct as referred to in Article 40 or approved certification mechanisms as referred to in Article 42 may be used as an element by which to demonstrate compliance with the obligations of the controller.

Relevant Recitals

(74) The responsibility and liability of the controller for any processing of personal data carried out by the controller or on the controller's behalf should be established. In particular, the controller should be obliged to implement appropriate and effective measures and be able to demonstrate the compliance of processing activities with this Regulation, including the effectiveness of the measures. Those measures should take into account the nature, scope, context and purposes of the processing and the risk to the rights and freedoms of natural persons.

(75) The risk to the rights and freedoms of natural persons, of varying likelihood and severity, may result from personal data processing which could lead to physical, material or non-material damage, in particular: where the processing may give rise to discrimination, identity theft or fraud, financial loss, damage to the reputation, loss of confidentiality of personal data protected by professional secrecy, unauthorised reversal of pseudonymisation, or any other significant economic or social disadvantage; where data subjects might be deprived of their rights and freedoms or prevented from exercising control over their personal data; where personal data are processed which reveal racial or ethnic origin, political opinions, religion or philosophical beliefs, trade union membership, and the processing of genetic data, data concerning health or data concerning sex life or criminal convictions and offences or related security measures; where personal aspects are evaluated, in particular analysing or predicting aspects concerning performance at work, economic situation, health, personal preferences or interests, reliability or behaviour, location or movements, in order to create or use personal profiles; where personal data of vulnerable natural persons, in particular of children, are processed; or where processing involves a large amount of personal data and affects a large number of data subjects.

(76) The likelihood and severity of the risk to the rights and freedoms of the data subject should be determined by reference to the nature, scope, context and purposes of the processing. Risk should be evaluated on the basis of an objective assessment, by which it is established whether data processing operations involve a risk or a high risk.

(77) Guidance on the implementation of appropriate measures and on the demonstration of compliance by the controller or the processor, especially as regards the identification of the risk related to the processing, their assessment in terms of origin, nature, likelihood and severity, and the identification of best practices to mitigate the risk, could be provided in particular by means of approved codes of conduct, approved certifications, guidelines provided by the Board or indications provided by a data protection officer. The Board may also issue guidelines on processing operations that are considered to be unlikely to result in a high risk to the rights and freedoms of natural persons and indicate what measures may be sufficient in such cases to address such risk.

Closely Related Provisions

Article 5 (Principles relating to processing of personal data) (see too recital 39); Article 25 (Data protection by design and by default) (see too recital 78); Article 30 (Records of processing activities) (see too recital 82); Article 32 (Security of processing) (see too recital 83); Article 35 (Data protection impact assessment) (see too recitals 84 and 89–93); Articles 37–39 (Data protection officer) (see too recital 97); Articles 40–41 (Codes of conduct) (see too recitals 98–99); Articles 42–43 (Certification) (see too recital 100); Article 47 (Binding corporate rules) (see also recitals 108 and 110); Article 83 (General conditions for imposing administrative fines) (see too recitals 148 and 150–151)

Related Provisions in LED [Directive (EU) 2016/680]

Article 19 (Obligations of the controller) (see too recitals 50–52); Article 20 (Data Protection by Design and by Default) (see too recital 53); Article 24 (Records of processing activities) (see too recital 56); Article 25 (Logging) (see too recital 57); Article 27 (Data Protection Impact Assessment) (see too recital 58); Article 29 (security of processing) (see too recital 60); Articles 32–34 (Data Protection Officer) (see too recital 63)

Related Provisions in EPD [Directive 2002/58/EC, as amended]

Article 4(1) and (1a) (Security of processing and implementation of a security policy) (see too recital 20)

Related Provisions in EUDPR [Regulation (EU) 2018/1725]

Article 4(2) ('accountability') (see too recital 45); Article 26 (Responsibility of the controller) (see too recital 48).

Relevant Case Law

CJEU

Case C-553/07, *College van burgemeester en wethouders van Rotterdam v M. E. E. Rijkeboer*, judgment of 7 May 2009 (ECLI:EU:C:2009:293).
Case C-362/14, *Maximillian Schrems v Data Protection Commissioner*, judgment of 6 October 2015 (Grand Chamber) (ECLI:EU:C:2015:650).

Case C-210/16, *Unabhängiges Landeszentrum für Datenschutz Schleswig-Holstein v Wirtschaftsakademie Schleswig-Holstein GmbH*, judgment of 5 June 2018 (Grand Chamber) (ECLI:EU:C:2018:388).

Case C-25/17, *Proceedings brought by Tietosuojavaltuutettu (Jehovan todistajat)*, judgment of 10 July 2018 (Grand Chamber) (ECLI:EU:C:2018:551).

Case C-40/17, *Fashion ID GmbH & Co.KG v Verbraucherzentrale NRW eV*, judgment of 29 July 2019 (Grand Chamber) (ECLI:EU:C:2019:629).

A. Rationale and Policy Underpinnings

Article 24 GDPR is entitled 'Responsibility of the controller', but can be viewed as imposing accountability obligations, alongside Article 5(2) GDPR. The principle of accountability is one of the central pillars of the GDPR and one of its most significant innovations. It places responsibility firmly on the controller to take proactive action to ensure compliance and to be ready to demonstrate that compliance.

The term 'accountability' is not new for data protection law. In its original sense of responsibility for specific tasks and duties it was present in the original OECD Guidelines and was implicit in the data quality requirements of Convention 108 and in Article 6(2) of the DPD, now Article 5(2) GDPR, specifically labelled 'accountability'.

However, the new meaning of the accountability principle could already be seen in the security requirements in Article 17 of the DPD and in the extra-statutory procedure for binding corporate rules ('BCRs') (see discussion below). Accountability in this sense requires that controllers put in place internal policies and mechanisms to ensure compliance and provide evidence to demonstrate compliance to external stakeholders, including supervisory authorities.

The problem that the new accountability principle seeks to resolve was summarised by the WP29 in 2009 as follows:

[C]ompliance with existing legal obligations often is not properly embedded in the internal practices of organizations. Frequently, privacy is not embedded in information processing technologies and systems. Furthermore, management, including top level managers, generally are not sufficiently aware of and therefore actively responsible for the data processing practices in their own organizations ... Unless data protection becomes part of the shared values and practices of an organization, and unless responsibilities for it are expressly assigned, effective compliance will be at risk and data protection mishaps will continue ... The principles and obligations of [data protection law] should permeate the cultural fabric of organizations, at all levels, rather than being thought of as a series of legal requirements to be ticked off by the legal department.[1]

To address this situation, the WP29 proposed that the Commission consider accountability-based mechanisms, with particular emphasis on the possibility to include a principle of 'accountability' in the legislative reform. This principle would strengthen the role of the data controller and increase its responsibility.[2] The following year, the WP29 developed its analysis in detail in its Opinion on Accountability. It warned that the then legal framework had not been fully successful in ensuring that data protection requirements translate into effective mechanisms that deliver real protection, and proposed a draft accountability clause for new legislation:

---

[1] WP29 2009, p. 19. [2] WP29 2010, p. 3.

Article X—Implementation of data protection principles

1. The controller shall implement appropriate and effective measures to ensure that the principles and obligations set out in the Directive are complied with.
2. The controller shall demonstrate compliance with paragraph 1 to the supervisory authority on its request.[3]

B. Legal Background

1. EU legislation

The precursor to the principle of accountability is the principle of responsibility, which can be found in Article 6(2) DPD: 'It shall be for the controller to ensure that paragraph 1 is complied with'. In addition, Article 17(1) DPD required data controllers to implement measures of both a technical and organisational nature to ensure security of processing.

Article 4 EPD imposes an obligation to take appropriate technical and organisational measures to ensure a level of security appropriate to the risk presented.

2. International instruments

The 1980 OECD Privacy Guidelines included an Accountability Principle similar to the principle of responsibility in Article 6(2) DPD. Article 14 of the Guidelines states: 'A data controller should be accountable for complying with measures which give effect to the principles stated above'.[4] The updated OECD Privacy Guidelines from 2013 maintain the original Accountability Principle but add the new meaning of accountability, in the sense of proactive and demonstrable compliance, in a new Part Three on Implementing Accountability.[5] This sets out the key elements of what it means to be an accountable organisation, including basic elements such as those set forth in Article 24 GDPR and common elements of the principle (discussed below).

The OECD approach forms the basis of the Asia–Pacific Economic Cooperation ('APEC') Privacy Framework of 2005, which includes a similarly worded accountability principle as the final principle in a list of nine Information Privacy Principles. An accountability mechanism, certified by an APEC-recognised independent third party known as an Accountability Agent, also features in the APEC Cross Border Privacy Rules ('CBPR'). The CBPR System consists of four elements: (1) self-assessment of data privacy policies and practices against the requirements of the APEC Privacy Framework; (2) compliance review; (3) recognition/acceptance; and (4) dispute resolution and enforcement.[6] In 2014, the WP29 together with the APEC group issued jointly a 'Referential' that maps the differences and similarities between BCRs in the EU and the CPPR system among the APEC countries.[7]

---

[3] Ibid., p. 10.
[4] See also Art. 16 OECD Guidelines 1980, with regard to trans-border flows of personal data: 'A data controller remains accountable for personal data under its control without regard to the location of the data'.
[5] OECD Guidelines 2013.
[6] The APEC group is an intergovernmental forum comprised of the 21 Pacific Rim member economies, focused primarily upon trade and economic issues. See APEC Privacy Framework.
[7] WP29 2014A.

required to demonstrate compliance to supervisory authorities will depend on the processing in question. In its Opinion on the principle of accountability, the WP29 gave two examples:

[I]n simple and basic cases, such as for the processing of personal data related to human resources for the establishment of a corporate directory, the 'obligation to demonstrate' ... could be fulfilled easily (through for instance the information notices that were used; the description of basic security measures etc.). On the contrary, in other more complex cases, such as for instance the use of innovative biometric devices, fulfilling the 'obligation to demonstrate' could need further requirements. The controller may have for instance to demonstrate that it undertook a privacy impact assessment, that the staff involved in the processing are trained and informed regularly, etc.[28]

The WP29 also recalled that:

Transparency is an integral element of many accountability measures. Transparency vis-à-vis the data subjects and the public in general contributes to the accountability of data controllers. For example, a greater level of accountability is achieved by publishing privacy policies on the Internet, by providing transparency in regard to internal complaints procedures, and through the publication in annual reports.[29]

4. The common elements of accountability in practice

In 2009, the Global Accountability Dialogue, also known as the *Galway Project*, brought together experts from a wide range of sectors—industry, civil society, academia, government, data protection commissioners and privacy regulators. They identified, for the first time, five 'common elements' of accountability.[30] Later that year, an accountability principle was included in the 'Madrid Resolution' and the WP29 made initial comments on accountability in its 'Future of Privacy' Opinion.[31] This opinion was followed by a detailed list of elements in the WP29 Opinion on the principle of accountability.[32] In 2015 the Privacy Bridges Report presented to the 37th Annual International Privacy Conference in Amsterdam considered elements that could be implemented in both the EU and the United States.[33] The explanatory report on Modernised Convention 108 also explains the elements of the principle of accountability.[34] Finally the Explanatory Memorandum to the GDPR sets out elements of accountability in addition to the core, statutory elements of accountability in the GDPR itself.

The common elements in these various documents may be summarised as follows:

1. Appointment of data protection professionals to assure internal implementation: the GDPR requires DPOs to have expert knowledge,[35] to report to top management,[36] and for there to be provision for their professional development and necessary resources.[37]

---

[28] WP29 2010, p. 13.   [29] Ibid., p. 14.
[30] The five elements were: (1) organisational commitment to accountability and adoption of internal policies consistent with external criteria; (2) mechanisms to put privacy policies into effect, including tools, training and education; (3) systems for internal ongoing oversight and assurance reviews and external verification; (4) transparency and mechanisms for individual participation; and (5) means for remediation and external enforcement. See CIPL 2009.
[31] WP29 2009, p. 19.   [32] WP29 2010, pp. 11–12.
[33] International Privacy Conference 2015, Bridge 8.
[34] Explanatory Report Convention 108 2018, p. 25.   [35] Rec. 97 GDPR.
[36] Ibid., Art. 38(3).   [37] Ibid., Art. 38(2).

2. Organisational commitment to accountability and the approval and oversight of internal policies by top management.[38]
3. Mapping of processing activities, assessment of purpose specification,[39] and assessment of the risks to individuals 'by virtue of their nature, their scope or their purpose'.[40] The WP29 has also referred to 'economic and reputational risks'.[41] The risk assessment may lead to conducting a data protection impact assessment ('DPIA').[42]
4. Adoption of internal policies and processes to implement relevant data protection requirements for the particular processing operations carried out by the controller, which are binding on all corporate units and staff members in the organisation.[43]
5. Assignment of responsibility for data protection to designated persons at different levels in the organisation with responsibility for compliance.
6. Mechanisms to put internal policies and processes into effect and make them effective in practice. These may include tools, staff training and awareness, and instructions about the collection and processing of data. In particular there should be internal policies to implement the principles of data protection by design and data protection by default.[44]
7. Systems for internal and ongoing oversight, review and updating[45] and for external verification—internal compliance reports, external audits, third party certification and/or seals to monitor and assess whether the internal measures are effective.[46]
8. Transparency of these adopted measures for data subjects, regulators and the general public.[47]
9. Means for remediation and external enforcement, including response mechanisms that provide means for individuals to complain about privacy violations,[48] means for data breach notification,[49] and means for organisations to address any discovered deficiencies, and redress for violations of the privacy requirements.

5. Scalability—Nature of Processing and Level and Likelihood of Risk

Controllers must tailor the measures to the concrete specifics of their organisations and the data processing operations in question. The technical and organisational measures required under the principle of accountability must be 'appropriate' in view of the two factors specified in Article 24, namely the nature of the processing and the likelihood and severity of risk. The GDPR introduces the criterion of likelihood of risk in addition to that of the level or severity of risk in Article 17 DPD. Recital 74 explains that the 'likelihood and severity of the risk to the rights and freedoms of the data subject should be determined by reference to the nature, scope, context and purposes of the processing'.

The WP29 has stressed that:

[T]he rights of individuals ... must be just as strong even if the processing in question is relatively 'low risk'. Rather, the scalability of legal obligations based on risk addresses compliance mechanisms. This means that a data controller whose processing is relatively low risk may not have to do as much to comply with its legal obligations as a data controller whose processing is high-risk.[50]

---

[38] EDPS Website 2016, p. 2.   [39] WP29 2013.   [40] Rec. 74 GDPR.
[41] See WP29 2010, p. 3.   [42] WP29 2017B, pp. 8–12.
[43] Canadian Privacy Commissioners 2012, p. 10.   [44] Rec. 78 GDPR.
[45] Ibid., Art. 24(1).   [46] Ibid., rec. 100.   [47] Raab 2017, p. 344.
[48] Art. 38(4) GDPR.   [49] Ibid., recs. 85 and 86.   [50] WP29 2014B, p. 2.

Normally the size of the organisation concerned does not per se determine the level of compliance required. Only one provision of the GDPR, Article 30, provides that organisations employing fewer than 250 persons do not have to respect the obligation to keep records of processing activities. This is subject to two caveats. First, the obligation applies if the processing they carry out is likely to result in a risk to the rights and freedoms of data subjects, the processing is not occasional or the processing includes sensitive data. Secondly, controllers remain subject to the general obligation in Article 24 to be able to demonstrate compliance, which would normally require the keeping of some written records.

Recital 75 GDPR explains that risks 'may result from personal data processing which could lead to physical, material or non-material damage'. It contains an extensive but not exhaustive list of examples of processing which may give rise to such risks and thus should be borne in mind. Examples given by the EU legislator include processing which may give rise to discrimination, identity theft or fraud, the processing of sensitive data and the processing of a large amount of personal data which affects a large number of data subjects. The WP29 has pointed out that some measures are 'staples' that will have to be implemented in most data processing operations. These would include drafting internal policies and procedures implementing those policies, e.g. procedures to handle access requests and complaints.[51] Where the organisation is larger and more complex, and/or where there is a higher level of risk, the GDPR requires controllers to do more, and sets out a number of specific accountability-based mechanisms to this effect.

6. Accountability-based mechanisms

The GDPR accompanies the principle of accountability with a suite of tools for controllers, described by the WP29 as 'accountability based mechanisms ... as a way of encouraging data controllers to implement practical tools for effective data protection'.[52] Article 22(2) GDPR Proposal listed five measures 'in particular': documentation, security, data protection impact assessments, prior authorisation or consultation, and the DPO. These examples are not retained in the text finally adopted. Instead Article 24(3) of the GDPR specifies two different mechanisms, codes of conduct and certification, which may be used as an element by which to demonstrate compliance with the obligations of the controller. In addition, the GDPR underlines the importance for accountability of a number of other mechanisms: the principles of data protection by design and default under Article 25,[53] the keeping of records under Article 30, DPIAs under Article 35,[54] the Data Protection Officer ('DPO') under Articles 37–39,[55] and BCRs under Article 47.[56]

Many of these accountability-based mechanisms are good practice for controllers, which the GDPR has rendered legally binding in some cases. The Commission,[57] the

---

[51] WP29 2010, p. 13.   [52] Ibid., p. 3.

[53] See rec. 78 GDPR and the commentary on Art. 25 in this volume.

[54] The WP29 regards DPIAs as 'important tools for accountability' as they can help controllers both to comply with the GDPR and to demonstrate compliance with it, see WP29 2017B.

[55] The WP29 regards the DPO as a 'cornerstone of accountability' in the sense that the DPO can facilitate compliance through the implementation of other accountability tools such as DPIAs and audits and can act as an intermediary between internal and external stakeholders, see WP29 2017A, p. 4. See also EDPS 2012, p. 3, where the EDPS stressed the role of DPOs in accountability.

[56] The WP29 has identified binding corporate rules as 'a way to implement data protection principles on the basis of the accountability principle', see WP29 2010, p. 15.

[57] EC Communication 2010, pp. 6–7.

WP29 and national DPAs have strongly underlined the complementary nature of these tools, which all promote accountability and good governance.

In its 2010 Opinion, the WP29 distinguished between the minimum requirements of a future accountability obligation, a 'first tier' binding on all controllers, and a 'second tier' of accountability architecture, whereby controllers may achieve a higher level of compliance through voluntary use of tools such as DPIAs and DPOs. In the meantime, although minimum standards are now enshrined in the GDPR, the WP29 in its various Opinions and Guidelines has consistently urged controllers as a matter of good practice to use accountability mechanisms to the full and not to limit their use to the minimum required by statute (see discussion below), the aim being to aim for a high standard of effective compliance.

7. Accountability and the law

The CJEU has developed a broad approach to the scope of the data protection rules, developing the notion of joint controllership (now specified in Article 26 GDPR) in order to 'ensure, through a broad definition of the concept of "controller", effective and complete protection of the persons concerned'.[58] The President of the Court, Koen Lenaerts, has characterised this case law as confirming the Court's attachment to 'high levels of accountability' of individuals that process personal data, in light of the 'central theme' of accountability in the GDPR.[59] The Court has made it clear that it will hold to account those who process personal data for the processing for which they are responsible.[60]

In this respect, two questions arise. First, does the principle of accountability itself impose new obligations on data controllers and processors? Secondly, if a controller respects the principle of accountability and implements all the necessary measures, does this provide a 'safe harbour' in the event of an unexpected violation, such as a data breach?

Turning to the first question, the responsibility of the controller under Article 5(2) to ensure compliance with the principles relating to processing of personal data in Article 5(1) already existed under Article 6(2) DPD. However, the proactive obligation to adopt appropriate measures and the obligation to be able to demonstrate compliance are new obligations which, quite apart from any failure to respect applicable accountability-related obligations, would in themselves render controllers liable for non-compliance. In this respect, the wording of Article 24 is significant. The references to 'risks of varying likelihood and severity for the rights and freedoms of natural persons' are echoed both in the accountability-based mechanisms[61] and in the provisions on administrative fines in Article 83. This requires due regard to be paid in the first instance to the nature, gravity and duration of the infringement and to any other applicable aggravating or mitigating factors. Article 24(3) itself refers to two mitigating factors that may be taken into account, the use of codes of practice and certification.

This link between accountability and sanctions was specifically made by the WP29 in 2010:

---

[58] Case C-210/16, *Wirtschaftsakademie*, para. 28; Case C-25/17, *Jehovan todistajat*, para. 66; Case C-40/17, *Fashion ID*, para. 66.
[59] Lenaerts speech 2018   [60] Case C-40/17, *Fashion ID*, para.74.
[61] Regarding privacy by design, see Art. 25(1) GDPR. Regarding security, see Art. 32. Regarding DPIAs, see recs. 84 and 90.

The proposed system can only work if data protection authorities are endowed with meaningful powers of sanction. In particular, when and if data controllers fail to fulfil the accountability principle, there is a need for meaningful sanctions. For example, it should be punishable if a data controller does not honour the representations it made in binding internal policies. Obviously, this is in addition to the actual infringement of substantive data protection principles.[62]

As can be seen, the WP29 also noted the difference between formal accountability and genuine accountability, where the controller has taken action to implement its representations. This underlines the need for management at all levels to commit to implementing the privacy policies adopted by the organisation. The recent FTC settlement mentioned above requiring Facebook to implement accountability mechanisms at Board level and at individual level is an interesting example of this need to engage controllers at all levels, imposing it as a requirement.

In consequence, turning to the second question, the response is that a genuinely accountable controller will have put in place robust programmes that are more likely to be in compliance and less likely to be in breach of the law. Indeed, as noted in the commentary on Article 83 in this volume, fines can play an important role in encouraging accountability.[63] They not only have a 'deterrent' effect, by changing the balance of the expected benefits and expected costs of non-compliance, but also a 'supportive' effect, reinforcing controllers' commitment to compliance.

In this respect, Article 83(4)(a) specifies that an administrative fine may be imposed up to € 10 million, or in the case of an undertaking, up to 2 per cent of the total worldwide annual turnover of the preceding financial year, whichever is higher, for infringement inter alia of the obligations of controllers and/or processors under Articles 25–39. This includes failure to implement the accountability mechanisms of data protection by design and by default, records, impact assessments, data protection officer, and preparation for data breaches.

Thus, the presence of such programmes, documented as necessary, would certainly be an element taken into account should a problem arise. Article 83(2)(b)–(d) lays down the general conditions for imposing administrative fines, and requires due regard to be taken of the circumstances when deciding on whether to impose a fine and on the amount of the administrative fine, and, in particular for present purposes: 'the intentional or negligent character of the infringement; any action taken by the controller or processor to mitigate the damage suffered by data subjects; and the degree of responsibility of the controller or processor taking into account technical and organisational measures implemented by them pursuant to Articles 25 and 32' (that is, notably, respect for the requirements of data protection by design and by default and of security of processing).

Finally, with regard to individual cases brought by data subjects, the accountability obligation on controllers to be able to demonstrate compliance may well affect the burden of proof. Whilst the legal burden of proof is still borne by the data subject, it is argued that 'the evidential burden of proof should de facto shift to the controller as soon as the data subject has offered prima facie evidence of an unlawful processing activity'.[64] This strong relation between accountability and key obligations and sanctions in the GDPR is a powerful incentive for encouraging proactive compliance. A fully accountable controller

---

[62] WP29 2010, p. 17.
[63] See Wils 2006, pp. 185-190, on the use of fines in competition law. See also FTC 2019.
[64] Van Alsenoy 2016, p. 9.

is unlikely to be in a situation of non-compliance and thus less likely to be sanctioned in the event of unexpected events.

8. Conclusion: accountability at the heart of the GDPR

The concept of accountability lies at the root of the new approach to compliance demanded by the GDPR. It is crucial for controllers to take active responsibility for ensuring compliance and develop an accountability culture at all levels of their organisation. For some controllers the link to sanctions for non-compliance will provide the necessary motivation. For others, respect for privacy and data protection will become part of their ethical framework,[65] and ethical standards will drive the use of the accountability-based mechanisms discussed above, in particular DPIAs and data protection by design and data protection by default.

Finally, accountability is an international concept, based on powerful examples of law and best practice in jurisdictions across the globe. It will be key to facilitating compliance by controllers using the new technologies of big data, cloud computing and artificial intelligence,[66] and to building bridges between legal systems in the EU and abroad.

Select Bibliography

International agreements

APEC Privacy Framework: Asia Pacific Economic Cooperation, 'Privacy Framework' (2005).
OECD Guidelines 1980: Organisation for Economic Co-operation and Development, 'Guidelines on the Protection of Privacy and Transborder Flows of Personal Data' (1980).
OECD Guidelines 2013: Organisation for Economic Co-operation and Development, 'The OECD Privacy Framework' (2013).

EU legislation

GDPR Proposal: Proposal for a Regulation of the European Parliament and of the Council on the protection of individuals with regard to the processing of personal data and on the free movement of such data (General Data Protection Regulation), COM(2012) 11 final, 25 January 2012.

National legislation

Australian Privacy Act 1988: Privacy Act 1988 (No. 199, 1988).
PIPEDA 2018: Personal Information Protection and Electronic Documents Act, S.C. 2000, c. 5, last amended on November 1, 2018.

Academic writings

De Hert et al. 2014: De Hert, Papakonstantinou and Kamara, 'The New Cloud Computing ISO/IEC 27018 Standard through the Lens of the EU Legislation on Data Protection', 1(2) *Brussels Privacy Hub Working Paper* (November 2014).
Koppel 2005: Koppell, 'Pathologies of Accountability: ICANN and the Challenge of Multiple Accountabilities Disorder', 65(1) *Public Administration Review* (2005), 94.

---

[65] EDPS 2015. See also Abrams 2015.
[66] The Information Accountability Foundation has updated the five essential elements of the Galway Project to respond to the challenges of big data and most recently artificial intelligence, see AI Essential Elements in IAF 2017, p. 11. See also Raab 2017 and materials referred to therein.

Raab 2017: Raab, 'Information Privacy: Ethics and Accountability', in Brand, Heesen, Kröber, Müller and Potthast (eds.), *Ethik in den Kulturen—Kulturen in der Ethik: Eine Festschrift für Regina Ammicht Quinn* (Narr Francke Attempto 2017), 335.

Van Alsenoy 2016: Van Alsenoy, 'Liability under EU Data Protection Law: From Directive 95/46 to the General Data Protection Regulation', 7(3) *Journal of Intellectual Property, Information Technology and Electronic Commerce Law* (2016), 270.

Wils 2006: Wils, 'Optimal Antitrust Fines: Theory and Practice', 29(2) *World Competition* (2006), 183.

Papers of data protection authorities

ICDPPC 2009: International Conference of Data Protection and Privacy Commissioners, 'Joint Proposal for a Draft of International Standards on the Protection of Privacy with Regard to the Processing of Personal Data' (5 November 2009).

EDPS 2012: European Data Protection Supervisor, 'Policy on Consultations in the Field of Supervision and Enforcement' (23 November 2012).

EDPS 2015: European Data Protection Supervisor, 'Opinion 4/2015 Towards a New Digital Ethics: Data, Dignity and Technology' (11 September 2015).

WP29 2009: Article 29 Working Party, 'The Future of Privacy: Joint Contribution to the Consultation of the European Commission on the Legal Framework for the Fundamental Right to Protection of Personal Data' (WP 168, 1 December 2009).

WP29 2010: Article 29 Working Party, 'Opinion 3/2010 on the Principle of Accountability' (WP 173, 13 July 2010).

WP29 2013: Article 29 Working Party, 'Opinion 3/2013 on Purpose Limitation' (WP 203, 2 April 2013).

WP29 2014A: Article 29 Working Party, 'Opinion 02/2014 on a Referential for Requirements for Binding Corporate Rules Submitted to National Data Protection Authorities in the EU and Cross Border Privacy Rules Submitted to APEC CBPR Accountability Agents' (WP 212, 27 February 2014).

WP29 2014B: Article 29 Working Party, 'Statement on the Role of a Risk-Based Approach in Data Protection Legal Frameworks' (WP 218, 30 May 2014).

WP29 2017A: Article 29 Working Party, 'Guidelines on Data Protection Officers ('DPOs')' (WP 243 rev.01, as last revised and adopted on 5 April 2017).

WP29 2017B: Article 29 Working Party, 'Guidelines on Data Protection Impact Assessment (DPIA) and Determining whether Processing Is "Likely to Result in a High Risk" for the Purposes of Regulation 2016/679' (WP 248 rev.01, as last revised and adopted on 4 October 2017).

Canadian Privacy Commissioners 2012: Office of the Information and Privacy Commissioner of Alberta, Office of the Privacy Commissioner of Canada, Office of the Information and Privacy Commissioner for British Colombia, 'Getting Accountability Right with a Privacy Management Program' (April 2012).

CNIL 2014: Commission nationale de l'informatique et des libertés, 'Privacy Seals on Privacy Governance Procedures' (11 December 2014).

Columbian Data Protection Authority 2017: Superintendencia de Industria y Comercio, 'Guía para la Implementación del Principio de Responsabilidad Demostrada' (19 January 2017).

FTC Settlement Order: Federal Trade Commission, 'Plaintiff's Consent Motion for entry of stipulated order for civil penalty, monetary judgment, and injunctive relief, and memorandum in support (Case No. 19-cv-2184)' (July 24, 2019).

Hong Kong Privacy Commissioner 2014: Hong Kong Privacy Commissioner for Personal Data, 'Privacy Managaement Programme: A Best Practice Guide (February 2014), available at https://www.pcpd.org.hk/pmp/files/PMP_guide_e.pdf.

Reports and recommendations

Abrams 2015: Abrams et al., 'Unified Ethical Frame for Big Data Analysis' (March 2015), available at http://informationaccountability.org/wp-content/uploads/IAF-Unified-Ethical-Frame.pdf.

CIPL 2009: Centre for Information Policy Leadership, 'Data Protection Accountability: The Essential Elements, a Document for Discussion' (October 2009).

EC Communication 2010: Communication from the Commission to the European Parliament, the Council, the Economic and Social Committee and the Committee of the Regions, 'A Comprehensive Approach on Personal Data Protection in the European Union', COM(2010) 609 final, 4 November 2010.

Explanatory Report Convention 108 2018: Council of Europe, 'Explanatory Report to the Protocol Amending the Convention for the Protection of Individuals with Regard to the Automatic Processing of Personal Data' (10 October 2018), available at https://rm.coe.int/cets-223-explanatory-report-to-the-protocol-amending-the-convention-fo/16808ac91a.

IAF 2017: Information Accountability Foundation, 'Artificial Intelligence, Ethics and Enhanced Data Stewardship' (20 September 2017).

International Privacy Conference 2015: 37th International Privacy Conference, 'Privacy Bridges: EU and US Privacy Experts in Search of Transatlantic Privacy Solutions' (21 October 2015), available at https://privacybridges.mit.edu/sites/default/files/documents/PrivacyBridges-FINAL.pdf.

ISO/IEC 29190:2015: ISO, 'ISO/IEC 29190:2015 Information Technology—Security Techniques—Privacy Capabilities Assessment Model' (2015), available at https://www.iso.org/obp/ui/#iso:std:iso-iec:29190:ed-1:v1:en.

Others

Australian Information Commissioner Website: Office of the Australian Information Commissioner, 'Privacy Management Framework: Enabling Compliance and Encouraging Good Practice', available at https://www.oaic.gov.au/resources/agencies-and-organisations/guides/privacy-management-framework.pdf.

EDPS Website 2016: European Data Protection Supervisor, 'EDPS Launches Accountability Initiative' (7 June 2016), available at https://edps.europa.eu/sites/edp/files/publication/16-06-07_accountability_factsheet_en.pdf.

FTC Press Release: Federal Trade Commission, 'FTC Imposes $5 Billion Penalty and Sweeping New Privacy Restrictions on Facebook' (24 July 2019), available https://www.ftc.gov/news-events/press-releases/2019/07/ftc-imposes-5-billion-penalty-sweeping-new-privacy-restrictions.

Lenaerts speech 2018: Lenaerts, 'The EU General Data Protection Regulation Five Months On', speech by CJEU President Koen Lenaerts at the 40th International Conference of Data Protection and Privacy Commissioners (25 October 2018), available at https://www.youtube.com/watch?v=fZaKPaGbXNg.

Article 25. Data protection by design and by default

LEE A. BYGRAVE

1. Taking into account the state of the art, the cost of implementation and the nature, scope, context and purposes of processing as well as the risks of varying likelihood and severity for rights and freedoms of natural persons posed by the processing, the controller shall, both at the time of the determination of the means for processing and at the time of the processing itself, implement appropriate technical and organisational measures, such as pseudonymisation, which are designed to implement data-protection principles, such as data minimisation, in an effective manner and to integrate the necessary safeguards into the processing in order to meet the requirements of this Regulation and protect the rights of data subjects.
2. The controller shall implement appropriate technical and organisational measures for ensuring that, by default, only personal data which are necessary for each specific purpose of the processing are processed. That obligation applies to the amount of personal data collected, the extent of their processing, the period of their storage and their accessibility. In particular, such measures shall ensure that by default personal data are not made accessible without the individual's intervention to an indefinite number of natural persons.
3. An approved certification mechanism pursuant to Article 42 may be used as an element to demonstrate compliance with the requirements set out in paragraphs 1 and 2 of this Article.

Relevant Recital

(78) The protection of the rights and freedoms of natural persons with regard to the processing of personal data require that appropriate technical and organisational measures be taken to ensure that the requirements of this Regulation are met. In order to be able to demonstrate compliance with this Regulation, the controller should adopt internal policies and implement measures which meet in particular the principles of data protection by design and data protection by default. Such measures could consist, inter alia, of minimising the processing of personal data, pseudonymising personal data as soon as possible, transparency with regard to the functions and processing of personal data, enabling the data subject to monitor the data processing, enabling the controller to create and improve security features. When developing, designing, selecting and using applications, services and products that are based on the processing of personal data or process personal data to fulfil their task, producers of the products, services and applications should be encouraged to take into account the right to data protection when developing and designing such products, services and applications and, with due regard to the state of the art, to make sure that controllers and processors are able to fulfil their data protection obligations. The principles of data protection by design and by default should also be taken into consideration in the context of public tenders.

Closely Related Provisions

Article 4(5) (Definition of 'pseudonymisation') (see too recital 28); Article 5(2) (Accountability) (see too recital 11); Article 6(4)(e) (Compatibility); Article 22 (Automated individual decision-making, including profiling) (see too recital 71); Article 24 (Responsibility of controllers);

Article 28 (Processors) (see too recital 81); Article 32 (Security of processing) (see too recital 83); Article 34(3)(a) (Communication of personal data breach to data subject) (see too recitals 87–88); Article 35 (Data protection impact assessment) (see too recital 84); Article 40 (Codes of conduct); Article 83(2)(d) and 83(4) (Fines); Article 89(1) (Safeguards relating to processing of personal data for archiving purposes in the public interest, scientific or historical research purposes or statistical purposes)

Related Provisions in LED [Directive (EU) 2016/680]

Article 4(4) (Controller responsibility) (see too recital 50); Article 19 (Obligations of controller); Article 20 (Data protection by design and by default) (see too recital 53); Article 22 (Processor) (see too recital 55); Article 24(1)(i) (Records of technological and organisational security measures); Article 25 (Logging) (see too recital 57); Article 27 (Data protection impact assessment) (see too recital 58); Article 29 (Security of processing) (see too recital 60); Article 31(3)(a) (Communication of personal data breach to data subject)

Related Provisions in EPD [Directive 2002/58/EC]

Article 14 (Technical features and standardisation) (see too recital 33)

Related Provisions in EUDPR [Regulation (EU) 2018/1725]

Article 3(6) (Definition of 'pseudonymisation') (see too recital 17); Article 4(2) (Accountability) (see too recital 45); Article 6(e) (Compatibility); Article 13 (Safeguards for processing of personal data for archiving purposes, scientific or historical research, or statistical purposes) (see too recital 33); Article 24 (Automated individual decision-making, including profiling) (see too recital 43); Article 26 (Responsibility of controllers); Article 27 (Data protection by design and by default) (see too recital 48); Article 29 (Processors) (see too recital 51); Article 33 (Security of processing) (see too recital 53); Article 35(3)(a) (Communication of personal data breach to data subject) (see too recitals 55–56); Article 36 (Confidentiality of electronic communications); Article 37 (Protection of information with respect to users' terminal equipment); Article 39 (Data protection impact assessment) (see too recital 58); Article 40 (Prior consultation); Article 66(1)(c) and 66(2) (fines)

Relevant Case Law

CJEU

Case C-400/10 PPU, *J. McB v L. E.*, judgment of 5 October 2010 (ECLI:EU:C:2010:582).
Joined Cases C-293/12 and C-594/12, *Digital Rights Ireland Ltd v Minister for Communications, Marine and Natural Resources and Others* and *Kärntner Landesregierung and Others*, judgment of 8 April 2014 (Grand Chamber) (ECLI:EU:C:2014:238).
Case C-131/12, *Google Spain v Agencia Española de Protección de Datos (AEPD) and Mario Costeja González*, judgment of 13 May 2014 (Grand Chamber) (ECLI:EU:C:2014:317).

ECtHR

I v Finland, Appl. No. 20511/03, judgment of 17 July 2008.

A. Rationale and Policy Underpinnings

Article 25 GDPR is aimed at ensuring that the design and development of systems for processing personal data take due account of core data protection principles such that the latter are effectively integrated into the resulting systems. This entails ensuring that the safeguarding of privacy-related interests receives serious consideration throughout the lifecycle of information systems development—and not just towards the end of the lifecycle. The basic rationale for this endeavour is a belief that building data protection principles into information systems architecture will substantially improve the principles' traction. Part and parcel of this rationale is recognition of the powerful regulatory potential of information systems architecture, particularly its ability to shape human conduct in ways that are often more effective than the imposition of law laid down by statute or contract.

At the same time, Article 25 exemplifies and elaborates the increased emphasis in the GDPR on making controllers accountable and responsible for their data processing operations. Article 25 is thus closely linked to the provisions of Articles 5(2) and 24.

Article 25 springs out of a policy discourse that commonly goes under the nomenclature 'Privacy by Design' ('PbD'). Closely linked to this discourse is an older policy discourse centred on the creation of 'Privacy-Enhancing Technologies' ('PETs')—i.e. technological mechanisms that promote respect for privacy-related interests.[1] During the last decade, PbD ideals have become a staple part of data protection authorities' regulatory approach. In 2010, the 32nd International Conference of Data Protection and Privacy Commissioners ('ICDPPC') unanimously passed a resolution recognising 'Privacy by Design as an essential component of fundamental privacy protection' and encouraging 'the adoption of Privacy by Design's Foundational Principles ... as guidance to establishing privacy as an organisation's default mode of operation'. The WP29 followed up this resolution in, *inter alia*, policy pronouncements concerning internet technology.[2]

B. Legal Background

1. EU legislation

Article 25 has no exact equivalent in the DPD. The latter contained, however, provisions with a similar thrust as Article 25, albeit with a pronounced security focus. Recital 46 DPD mentioned the need to take 'appropriate technical and organizational measures' for protection of data subjects' rights and freedoms 'both at the time of the design of the processing system and at the time of the processing itself, particularly in order to maintain security and thereby to prevent any unauthorized processing'. The recital went on to stipulate that 'these measures must ensure an appropriate level of security, taking into account the state of the art and the costs of their implementation in relation to the risks inherent in the processing and the nature of the data to be protected'. Article 17 DPD was in a similar vein, although the protective measures it listed concerned information security rather than data protection more generally.

---

[1] Further on the evolution and parameters of these policy discourses, see e.g. Cavoukian 2009, Schaar 2010, Rubinstein 2012, Klitou 2014, ENISA 2014, Schartum 2016, Bygrave 2017A, Hartzog 2018.

[2] See e.g. WP29 2014.

In respect of electronic communications, Article 4(1) EPD replicates the security focus of the DPD by requiring a 'provider of a publicly available electronic communications service' to 'take appropriate technical and organisational measures to safeguard security of its services'. However, recital 30 EPD reaches beyond a security remit by encouraging design measures that give effect to the minimisation principle: 'Systems for the provision of electronic communications networks and services should be designed to limit the amount of personal data necessary to a strict minimum'. Article 14(3) EPD also reaches beyond a security remit by requiring the adoption of measures 'to ensure that terminal equipment is constructed in a way that is compatible with the right of users to protect and control the use of their personal data'. This provision parallels Article 3(3)(e) of the Radio Equipment Directive (2014/53/EU)[3] which empowers the Commission to issue delegated legislation requiring that certain classes of radio equipment 'incorporate safeguards to ensure that the personal data and privacy of the user and of the subscriber are protected'.

2. International instruments

The ideals of Article 25 are poorly reflected in Convention 108 as first adopted. However, the Modernised Convention 108 introduced a set of provisions that embrace requirements for 'data protection by design' but using different formulations than found in Article 25. Article 10(2) of the Modernised Convention stipulates that a state party shall require 'controllers and, where applicable processors' to 'examine the likely impact of intended data processing on the rights and fundamental freedoms of data subjects prior to the commencement of such processing, and shall design the data processing in such a manner as to prevent or minimise the risk of interference with those rights and fundamental freedoms'. Article 10(3) requires a state party to provide 'that controllers, and, where applicable, processors, implement technical and organisational measures which take into account the implications of the right to the protection of personal data at all stages of the data processing'. Article 10(4) permits a state party, 'having regard to the risks arising for the interests, rights and fundamental freedoms of the data subjects', to modify its law giving effect to the requirements of the preceding provisions 'according to the nature and volume of the data, the nature, scope and purpose of the processing and, where appropriate, the size of the controller or processor'.

Revisions to the OECD Privacy Guidelines in 2013 also introduced some support for the ideals of Article 25 GDPR. In their revised form, the Guidelines stipulate that OECD Member countries should, when implementing the Guidelines, 'consider ... the promotion of technical measures which help to protect privacy' (para. 19(g)). The Supplementary Explanatory Memorandum to the revised Guidelines states:

Technical measures also play an increasingly important role in complementing laws protecting privacy. Paragraph 19(g) encourages measures to foster the development and deployment of privacy-respecting and privacy-enhancing technologies (PETs). For example, Member countries may choose to support the development of technical standards which advance privacy principles. International standardisation initiatives may also advance technical interoperability among PETs, which may in turn help promote wider adoption of these technologies. Accreditation and seal programmes may further foster the adoption of technologies beneficial to privacy. Other measures

---

[3] Radio Equipment Directive.

include the promotion of research and development, exchange of best practices, and the issuance of regulatory guidance.[4]

3. National developments

Prior to adoption of the GDPR, Germany's Federal Data Protection Act of 1990[5] came closest, at the national level, to embracing the thrust of Article 25. Under the nomenclature 'Datenvermeidung und Datensparsamkeit' (data avoidance and data economy), section 3a of the Act required information systems to be designed with the aim of processing as little personal data as possible. Elaborating on this requirement, section 3a stipulated that personal data shall be pseudonymised or anonymised in so far as is reasonable in relation to the desired level of protection. A similar stipulation is contained in section 71(1) German GDPR Implementation Law.[6] The provisions of section 71 otherwise reproduce the requirements of Article 25 GDPR, albeit with slight differences in syntax.

4. Case law

The CJEU has yet to rule directly on the subject-matter of Article 25. It has, though, strongly implied that the 'essence' of Article 8 Charter of Fundamental Rights of the EU ('CFR') requires adoption of 'technical and organisational measures' to ensure that personal data are given 'effective protection' against 'risk of abuse and against any unlawful access and use'.[7] This requirement is in line with the thrust of Article 25, particularly the provisions of Article 25(2) on data protection by default. The requirement suggests that data protection by design and by default is part of the EU's constitutional fabric. This may have repercussions for how stringently the provisions of Article 25 (and, indeed, the equivalent provisions in the LED) are to be construed and applied.

Additionally, the CJEU has indirectly fostered the aims of Article 25 in some of its decisions dealing with internet mechanisms. A prime example is its judgment in the *Google Spain* case.[8] While the Court did not require any substantial modification of the design of Google's search engine, it did require Google (and other search engine operators) to reconfigure systemic aspects of search engine operations so that they are more privacy friendly.

The ECtHR has also embraced the ideals manifest in Article 25. Already in 2008, the Court issued a judgment holding that Finland violated Article 8 European Convention on Human Rights ('ECHR') due to its failure to secure, through technological-organisational measures, the confidentiality of patient data at a public hospital.[9] While Finnish law provides legal remedies for breaches of data confidentiality, this was judged insufficient in order for Finland to meet its positive obligations under Article 8: 'What is required in this connection is practical and effective protection to exclude any possibility of unauthorised access occurring in the first place. Such protection was not given here'.[10] Although the Court made no reference to 'data protection by design and by default' or closely linked notions, such as PbD, the basic thrust of its judgment necessitates adoption of a mindset

---

[4] OECD 2013, p. 32.   [5] German Federal Data Protection Act 1990.
[6] German GDPR Implementation Law.
[7] Joined Cases C-293/12 and C-594/12, *Digital Rights Ireland*, paras. 40 and 66; see also para. 67.
[8] Case C-131/12, *Google Spain*.   [9] ECtHR, *I v Finland*.   [10] Ibid., para. 47.

and methods in line with these notions. Further, the above-cited paragraph of the Court's judgment implies a requirement for data accessibility limits that, as a point of departure, guarantee confidentiality of data. This is akin to the requirement of data protection by default in Article 25(2) GDPR. On the basis of this judgment, a solid argument can be made that data protection by design and by default is, in effect, an integral element of a state's positive obligations to secure respect for private life pursuant to Article 8 ECHR, at least with respect to personal health data.

It is not unlikely that the CJEU would rule similarly with respect to the obligations flowing from Articles 7 and 8 CFR and Article 16 Treaty on the Functioning of the European Union ('TFEU') (independently of GDPR Article 25). This is particularly in light of the so-called homogeneity clause in Article 52(3) CFR together with CJEU recognition that Article 7 CFR 'must ... be given the same meaning and the same scope as Article 8(1) of the ECHR, as interpreted by the case-law of the European Court of Human Rights'.[11]

C. Analysis

1. Basic thrust

The overall thrust of Article 25 is to impose a qualified duty on controllers to put in place technical and organisational measures that are designed to implement effectively the data protection principles of the GDPR and to integrate necessary safeguards into the processing of personal data so that the processing will meet its requirements and otherwise ensure protection of data subjects' rights. The duty is a key element of the principle of accountability mentioned in Article 5(2) and developed in Article 24. The initial wording of the duty is similar to the initial wording of the duty under Article 32 to ensure adequate security of processing. Yet, unlike the latter, the duty under Article 25 expressly applies not just at the time of processing but also beforehand when the controller determines the means for processing—i.e. the stage of designing an information system. Moreover, it extends (in Article 25(2)) to ensuring—apparently without qualification—*default* application of particular data protection principles—most notably minimisation and proportionality—and *default* limits on data accessibility.

2. Qualifications

The duty imposed by Article 25(1) is qualified by an extensive list of contextual factors. These will be determined largely (but not exclusively) by the data protection impact assessment that controllers are required to conduct pursuant to Article 35.[12] There is accordingly a link between impact assessments and Article 25 requirements. However, the requirement to undertake an impact assessment arises only where processing 'is likely to result in a high risk' to persons' rights and freedoms (Article 35(1)), whereas the duty imposed by Article 25 does not. Nonetheless, the contextual factors listed at the start of Article 25(1) evidence a more general risk-based approach to assessing what measures are required.

---

[11] Case C-400/10 PPU, *J. McB*, para. 53. For further elaboration, see Bygrave 2017B.
[12] See further the commentary on Art. 35 in this volume.

3. Types of measures

In keeping with common conceptions of PbD,[13] the measures referred to in Article 25 are not just technical but also organisational. In other words, they embrace not simply the design and operation of software or hardware; they extend to business strategies and other organisational practices as well, such as rules determining which and under what circumstances employees in an organisation are authorised to access or otherwise process particular categories of personal data. The reference to 'pseudonymisation' as an example of a suitable measure is supplemented by other examples listed in recital 78. At the same time, Article 25(1) stipulates that the measures concerned must be 'designed to implement data protection principles'. The latter denote primarily the principles listed in Article 5.[14] This is confirmed by the reference to 'data minimisation' as an example (listed in Article 5(1)(c)). Whether Article 25(1) embraces other data protection principles than those listed in Article 5 is a moot point and arguably of academic interest only, as the pith of such principles is adequately covered by Article 5, at least at an operational level.

Further guidance on the parameters of Article 25 measures is expected to come from codes of conduct prepared by industry bodies (Article 40(2)(h)), from certification schemes (Article 25(3) in combination with Article 42) and from advice provided by data protection authorities. In respect of the latter, the WP29 issued brief guidance on Article 20 LED, which lays down similar requirements as Article 25 GDPR (see further below). The guidelines focus on design of data storage systems and procedures.[15] They place special emphasis on the need to ensure that data are automatically deleted or anonymised once the maximum period for their storage is exceeded, and on the need for automated periodic reminders of the need to review the necessity of storing data. The Norwegian DPA (Datatilsynet) has also issued guidelines on data protection by design and by default in respect of software development.[16] Both sets of guidelines are pertinent for application of Article 25 GDPR.

4. Differentiating between 'by design' and 'by default' requirements

There are significant differences between the 'by design' requirements of Article 25(1) and the 'by default' requirements of Article 25(2). First, the former cover a potentially wider range of data protection measures than the latter, which focus on ensuring data minimisation and confidentiality. Secondly, the former appears to be largely process-oriented, while the latter are concerned with results that guarantee data minimisation and confidentiality, at least as a point of departure. The CJEU and ECtHR jurisprudence mentioned above buttresses the relatively absolutist orientation of Article 25(2) requirements, as does the omission from Article 25(2) of the various contextual qualifications that introduce the requirements of Article 25(1). However, it is arguable that these qualifications are to be read into the adjective 'appropriate' used to describe Article 25(2) measures. If they are, the latter are less absolutist than first appears.

As indicated above, Article 25(1) measures are to be taken at both the design stage and processing stage. The same necessarily applies for Article 25(2) measures even if Article 25(2) does not spell this out.

---

[13] See e.g. Cavoukian 2009.
[14] For elaboration of these principles, see the commentary on Art. 5 in this volume.
[15] WP29 2017, pp. 5–6.   [16] Norwegian Data Protection Authority 2017.

5. Actors

On their face, both 'by design' and 'by default' measures are to be taken by controllers only. Controllers are basically defined as entities that determine or co-determine the purposes and means of processing personal data (Article 4(7)).[17] Whether and to what extent basic design decisions in information systems development will be taken by persons or organisations acting in a controller capacity are open questions. Article 25(1) formulates the design stage in terms of when the controller assumes controller status ('the time of the determination of the means for processing'). This might not equate with the time when a particular data-processing device is actually designed and manufactured, thus undermining the goal of ensuring that privacy interests are fully integrated into information systems architecture. However, recital 78 brings PbD ideals to bear on actors other than controllers—namely, 'producers' of products, services and applications that involve processing of personal data. These actors are subject to less stringent requirements ('should be encouraged') than those imposed on controllers.

At the same time, Article 25 prevents, on its face, controllers from using technologies that collect more personal data than are strictly necessary for technological functionality or that 'leak' personal data to outsiders. This might shape the market and technology foundations for information systems development in a privacy-friendly direction. PbD ideals are also brought to bear on processors inasmuch as controllers are only permitted to use processors 'providing sufficient guarantees to implement appropriate technical and organisational measures' (Article 28(1)); see too recital 81). Thus, the Regulation evinces an expectation that the duty imposed by Article 25 on controllers will be passed both to processors and to technology developers.

6. Role of Article 25 with respect to other provisions of GDPR

The duty imposed by Article 25 plays a role in the application of numerous other GDPR provisions. For instance, in assessing whether processing of personal data for another purpose is compatible with the initial purpose for which the data are collected, account shall be taken of, *inter alia*, 'the existence of appropriate safeguards, which may include encryption or pseudonymisation' (Article 6(4)(e)). Further, the requirement imposed by Article 34 on a controller to communicate a personal data breach to the data subject may be relaxed if the controller 'has implemented appropriate technical and organisational protection measures' (Article 34(3)(a); see too recitals 87 and 88). Additionally, Article 83(2)(d) stipulates that in determining the imposition of fines for breach of the Regulation, 'due regard' shall be taken of, inter alia, 'the degree of responsibility of the controller or processor taking into account technical and organisational measures implemented by them' pursuant to Article 25. Moreover, recital 78 states that the 'principles of data protection by design and by default' are to play a role in public procurement tenders: the principles 'should ... be taken into consideration' in this context. The latter phrasing falls short of making data protection by design and by default a prerequisite for such tenders, but is otherwise ambiguous as to how much weight the principles should be given.

Elements of the duty imposed by Article 25 also come into play in other contexts, even though no specific mention is made of Article 25. An example concerns safeguards

---

[17] See further the commentary on Art. 4(7) in this volume.

with respect to processing of personal data for archiving purposes in the public interest, scientific or historical research purposes or statistical purposes. The GPDR stipulates that these safeguards require implementation of 'technical and organisational measures ... in particular in order to ensure respect for the principle of data minimisation ... and may include pseudonymisation' (Article 89(1)).

7. Sanctions

Breach of the requirements of Article 25 may result in the imposition of administrative fines of up to € 10 million or, in the case of an undertaking, up to 2 per cent of its annual turnover of the preceding financial year, whichever is higher (Article 83(4) GDPR). It has been claimed that handing down heavy fines for violation of Article 25 will be difficult due to the vague and relatively abstract formulation of its requirements.[18] This difficulty afflicts the 'by design' requirements of Article 25(1) to a greater degree than the more concrete and seemingly stringent 'by default' requirements of Article 25(2). Nonetheless, recent fines meted out by the Romanian DPA for breach of Article 25(1) show that controllers cannot realistically expect to escape any sanction for their failure to comply with these provisions.[19]

8. Other EU legislation

The provisions of Article 25 are replicated in Article 27 EUDPR, and the latter should be interpreted in the same way as the former (see too recital 5 EUDPR). The provisions of Article 25 GDPR are further replicated in Article 20 LED, albeit with two minor differences. One difference is that Article 20 omits reference to certification mechanisms. The other difference occurs in the elaboration of Article 20 in recital 53 where it is stated that the implementation of the measures referred to in Article 20 'should not depend solely on economic considerations'. As noted above, the WP29 provided guidance on Article 20 LED with respect to the design of systems and procedures for storing personal data.[20]

Furthermore, the Cybersecurity Act flags the promotion of 'privacy-by-design'—along with 'security-by-design'—as part of the remit of the EU Agency for Cybersecurity ('ENISA').[21] We can accordingly expect policy developments under the aegis of the Cybersecurity Act to attempt to complement the aims of Article 25 GDPR.

---

[18] Bygrave 2017A, p. 771; Bygrave 2017B, p. 117; Bygrave 2019, p. 255. Tamò-Larrieux goes so far as to characterise Art. 25 in itself as a 'hollow norm' because it 'relies on all the legal principles elaborated in other articles of the GDPR' and 'does not provide much guidance on how these legal principles must be achieved in a particular scenario'. See Tamò-Larrieux 2018, p. 209.

[19] On 27 June 2019, the Romanian DPA fined an Italian bank (UNICREDIT BANK S.A.) the equivalent of € 130,000 for failure to implement appropriate technical and organisational measures pursuant to Art. 25(1). See Romanian Data Protection Authority Press Release 2019. Note also that the settlement reached on 24 July 2019 between the US Federal Trade Commission ('FTC') and Facebook Inc., in which Facebook had to pay a penalty of $ 5 billion, included various PbD-related requirements. While the settlement does not apply or reference the GDPR, it shows that the ideals of Art. 25 GDPR may receive support in third countries. See FTC Settlement Order and FTC Press Release. See also the commentary on Art. 83 in this volume.

[20] WP29 2017, pp. 5–6.

[21] See rec. 41 Cybersecurity Act ('ENISA should play a central role in accelerating end-user awareness of the security of devices and the secure use of services, and should promote security-by-design and privacy-by-design at Union level').

Select Bibliography

International agreements

OECD Guidelines 2013: Organisation for Economic Co-operation and Development, 'The OECD Privacy Framework' (2013).

EU legislation

Cybersecurity Act: Regulation (EU) 2019/881 of the European Parliament and of the Council of 17 April 2019 on ENISA (the European Union Agency for Cybersecurity) and on information and communications technology cybersecurity certification and repealing Regulation (EU) No 526/2013 (Cybersecurity Act), OJ 2019 L 151/15.

Radio Equipment Directive: Directive 2014/53/EU of the European Parliament and of the Council of 16 April 2014 on the harmonisation of the laws of the Member States relating to the making available on the market of radio equipment and repealing Directive 1999/5/EC, OJ 2014 L 153/62.

National legislation

German Federal Data Protection Act 1990: Gesetz zur Fortentwicklung der Datenverarbeitung und des Datenschutzes (Bundesdatenschutzgesetz), BGBl 1990 Teil 1 Nr. 2954 (repealed).

German GDPR Implementation Law: Gesetz zur Anpassung des Datenschutzrechts an die Verordnung (EU) 2016/679 und zur Umsetzung der Richtlinie (EU) 2016/680 (Datenschutz-Anpassungs- und Umsetzungsgesetz EU—DsAnpUG-EU), BGBl 2017 Teil 1 Nr. 44.

Academic writings

Bygrave 2017A: Bygrave, 'Hardwiring Privacy', in Brownsword, Scotford and Yeung (eds.), *The Oxford Handbook of Law, Regulation, and Technology* (OUP 2017), 754.

Bygrave 2017B: Bygrave, 'Data Protection by Design and by Default: Deciphering the EU's Legislative Requirements', 4(2) *Oslo Law Review* (2017), 105.

Bygrave 2019: Bygrave, 'Minding the Machine v2.0: The EU General Data Protection Regulation and Automated Decision Making', in Yeung and Lodge (eds.), *Algorithmic Regulation* (OUP 2019), 246.

Cavoukian 2009: Cavoukian, 'Privacy by Design: The 7 Foundational Principles' (August 2009; revised January 2011), available at https://www.ipc.on.ca/wp-content/uploads/Resources/7foundationalprinciples.pdf.

Hartzog 2018: Hartzog, *Privacy's Blueprint: The Battle to Control the Design of New Technologies* (Harvard University Press 2018).

Klitou 2014: Klitou, 'A Solution But Not a Panacea for Defending Privacy: The Challenges, Criticism and Limitations of Privacy by Design', in Preneel and Ikonomou (eds.), *Privacy Technologies and Policy: First Annual Privacy Forum, APF 2012* (Springer Verlag 2014), 86.

Rubinstein 2012: Rubinstein, 'Regulating Privacy by Design', 26 *Berkeley Technology Law Journal* (2012), 1409.

Schaar 2010: Schaar, 'Privacy by Design', 3(2) *Identity in the Information Society* (2010), 267.

Schartum 2016: Schartum, 'Making Privacy by Design Operative', 24(2) *International Journal of Law & Information Technology* (2016), 151.

Tamò-Larrieux 2018: Tamò-Larrieux, *Designing for Privacy and its Legal Framework: Data Protection by Design and Default for the Internet of Things* (Springer Verlag 2018).

Papers of data protection authorities

WP29 2014: Article 29 Working Party, 'Opinion 8/2014 on Recent Developments on the Internet of Things' (WP 223, 16 September 2014).

WP29 2017: Article 29 Working Party, 'Opinion on Some Key Issues of the Law Enforcement Directive (EU 2016/680)' (WP 258, 29 November 2017).

FTC Settlement Order: Federal Trade Commission, 'Plaintiff's Consent Motion for entry of stipulated order for civil penalty, monetary judgment, and injunctive relief, and memorandum in support (Case No. 19-cv-2184)' (24 July 2019).

Norwegian Data Protection Authority 2017: Datatilsynet, 'Software Development with Data Protection by Design and by Default' (November 2017), available https://www.datatilsynet.no/en/regulations-and-tools/guidelines/data-protection-by-design-and-by-default.

Reports and recommendations

ENISA 2014: European Union Agency for Network and Information Security, *Privacy and Data Protection by Design—From Policy to Engineering* (ENISA 2014).

Others

FTC Press Release: Federal Trade Commission, 'FTC Imposes $5 Billion Penalty and Sweeping New Privacy Restrictions on Facebook' (24 July 2019), available https://www.ftc.gov/news-events/press-releases/2019/07/ftc-imposes-5-billion-penalty-sweeping-new-privacy-restrictions.

Romanian Data Protection Authority Press Release 2019: Autoritatea Națională de Supraveghere a Prelucrării Datelor cu Caracter Personal, 'First fine for the application of GDPR' (27 June 2019), available at https://www.dataprotection.ro/index.jsp?page=Comunicat_Amenda_Unicredit&lang=en.

Article 26. Joint controllers

CHRISTOPHER MILLARD   DIMITRA KAMARINOU

1. Where two or more controllers jointly determine the purposes and means of processing, they shall be joint controllers. They shall in a transparent manner determine their respective responsibilities for compliance with the obligations under this Regulation, in particular as regards the exercising of the rights of the data subject and their respective duties to provide the information referred to in Articles 13 and 14, by means of an arrangement between them unless, and in so far as, the respective responsibilities of the controllers are determined by Union or Member State law to which the controllers are subject. The arrangement may designate a contact point for data subjects.
2. The arrangement referred to in paragraph 1 shall duly reflect the respective roles and relationships of the joint controllers *vis-à-vis* the data subjects. The essence of the arrangement shall be made available to the data subject.
3. Irrespective of the terms of the arrangement referred to in paragraph 1, the data subject may exercise his or her rights under this Regulation in respect of and against each of the controllers.

Relevant Recital

(79) The protection of the rights and freedoms of data subjects as well as the responsibility and liability of controllers and processors, also in relation to the monitoring by and measures of supervisory authorities, requires a clear allocation of the responsibilities under this Regulation, including where a controller determines the purposes and means of the processing jointly with other controllers or where a processing operation is carried out on behalf of a controller.

Closely Related Provisions

Article 4(7) (Definitions) (see too recital 79); Article 5 (Principles relating to the processing of personal data) (see too recital 39); Article 24 (Responsibility of the controller) (see too recital 74); Article 28 (Processors) (see too recital 81); Article 82 (Right to compensation and liability) (see too recital 146)

Related Provisions in LED [Directive (EU) 2016/680]

Article 3 (Definitions); Article 19 (Obligations of the controller) (see too recital 50); Article 21 (Joint controller) (see too recital 54 and 63).

Related Provisions in EPD [Directive 2002/58/EC]

Recital (10) and (32); Article 4 (Security) (see too recital 20); Article 5 (Confidentiality of the communications) (see too recitals 3–4)

Relevant Case Law

CJEU

Case C-131/12, *Google Spain v Agencia Española de Protección de Datos (AEPD) and Mario Costeja González*, judgment of 13 May 2014 (Grand Chamber) (ECLI:EU:C:2014:317).

Case C-210/16, *Unabhängiges Landeszentrum für Datenschutz Schleswig-Holstein v Wirtschaftsakademie Schleswig-Holstein GmbH*, judgment of 5 June 2018 (Grand Chamber) (ECLI:EU:C:2018:388).

Case C-25/17, *Proceedings brought by Tietosuojavaltuutettu (Jehovan todistajat)*, judgment of 10 July 2018 (Grand Chamber) (ECLI:EU:C:2018:551).

Case C-40/17, *Fashion ID GmbH & Co. KG v Verbraucherzentrale NRW e.V.*, judgment of 29 July 2019 (ECLI:EU:C:2019:629).

A. Rationale and Policy Underpinnings

Article 26 GDPR aims to provide clarity as to how responsibility is to be allocated in cases in which more than one data controller determines the purposes and means of processing of personal data.

Article 26 is also aimed at ensuring that joint controllers comply with their obligations to process data in a way that is transparent to data subjects. The rationale for this is that controllers' roles, relationships and respective responsibilities may not be obvious unless the essential information is provided by the controllers directly to the data subjects. Nevertheless, explicit arrangements to allocate responsibilities between joint controllers will not prevent individual data subjects from exercising their rights in respect of and against each of the controllers. This provision is supported by Article 82(4) GDPR on compensation and liability which states that where more than one controller is involved in the same processing operation and is liable for the damage caused by that processing, each controller shall be liable to compensate a data subject for the entire damage caused. The rationale for this provision is that the Regulation should ensure complete and effective protection of data subjects and it should not impose on them the burden of ascertaining each controller's part in the shared responsibility to comply with data subjects' rights. It is up to joint controllers to make arrangements amongst themselves as to how to allocate their joint responsibility and how to compensate each other in a situation where one of them has paid full compensation to a data subject for the damage suffered. This form of joint and several liability did not exist explicitly in the wording of the DPD, and the WP29 had argued that it should be considered only if an alternative, clear allocation of responsibility between joint controllers was not established either by themselves or by relevant circumstances.[1]

B. Legal Background

1. EU legislation

Article 26 did not have an exact equivalent in the DPD in the form of an article dedicated to 'joint controllers'. Article 2(d) of the DPD on 'definitions', however, recognised the

---

[1] WP29 2010, p. 29.

possibility that multiple natural or legal actors may jointly determine the purposes and means of processing.

2. International instruments

The concept of two or more persons acting as joint controllers was not mentioned in the original text of Convention 108. However, the Modernised Convention 108 refers to the concept of 'joint controllers' in Article 2 on 'definitions'. According to Article 2(d), '"controller" means the natural or legal person, public authority, service, agency or any other body which, alone or jointly with others, has decision-making power with respect to data processing'.

3. National developments

At the national level, section 1(1) of the 1998 UK Data Protection Act[2] went a step further and included in the definition of data controller not only joint controllers but also controllers in common, thus recognising two different ways in which controllers may share responsibility for processing. A controller in common was a person who 'in common with other persons determines the purposes for which and the manner in which any personal data are, or are to be, processed'. This provision covered cases where two or more persons share personal data but process them independently of each other, such as where two or more parties collaborate on a research project. Data controllers in common were also required to have contractual agreements in place to ensure that all their obligations under data protection law were met.[3] The concept of 'controller in common' does not appear in the 2018 Data Protection Act[4] which, like the DPD and GDPR, refers only to the exercise of control by a controller 'alone or jointly with others'.

Other Member States, for example Poland, did not recognise the concept of joint controllers in their law, but the concept was sometimes recognised in practice by the national DPA.[5] In France, the CNIL published a set of guidelines on cloud computing in 2012[6] discussing the roles of 'controller', 'processor' and 'joint controller' in the cloud and indicating that providers of public SaaS ('Software as a Service') and PaaS ('Platform as a Service') cloud services will often be joint controllers with the cloud customer.[7]

4. Case law

In the context of the ruling in *Google Spain*,[8] the CJEU held that the definition of 'controller' under the DPD should be interpreted broadly in a way that reflects the wording and objective of the specific provision in the DPD and ensures effective and complete protection of data subjects. The Court found that it was undisputed that search engines play a decisive role in the dissemination of the data published on third party websites as they facilitate the users' access to such information and present it in such a way that users see a list of results with a structured overview of the information about the data subject which allows them to create a profile of that data subject. This activity by the search engine operators, which may significantly affect data subjects' fundamental rights to privacy and data protection, was interpreted by the Court to mean that search engine operators

---

[2] UK Data Protection Act 1998 (repealed). [3] IGA 2016, p. 2.
[4] UK Data Protection Act 2018. [5] Kuner 2007, p. 70, FN30. [6] CNIL 2012.
[7] Maxwell 2012. [8] Case C- 131/12, *Google Spain*, para. 34.

'determine the purposes and means' of this activity and therefore they assume the role of controller.[9] The Court went on to add that the publishers of the relevant websites may also determine the purposes and means of the specific processing but that does not relieve search engine operators from their responsibilities as controllers; rather, it means that the operators and the publishers are 'joint controllers'.[10]

In *Wirtschaftsakademie*, the CJEU found that the operator of a social network and an administrator of a fan page hosted on that network are jointly responsible for the processing of the personal data of visitors to that page.[11] This was the case even if the administrator of the fan page does not have access to personal data, as the DPD did not require each of the operators to have access to the personal data concerned.[12] The Court held that the concept of 'controller' within the meaning of Article 2(d) of the DPD should encompass the administrator of a fan page hosted on a social network, when such administrator contributes to the processing of personal data of visitors to its page.[13] The contribution lies in that, in creating a fan page, an administrator defines the parameters of that page, 'depending inter alia on the target audience and the objectives of managing and promoting its activities' and this 'has an influence on the processing of personal data for the purpose of producing statistics based on visits to the fan page'.[14] The administrator may also 'define the criteria in accordance with which the statistics are to be drawn up and even designate the categories of persons whose personal data is to be made use of'.[15] Therefore, the administrator must be recognised as a joint controller together with the operator of the social network under Article 2(d) DPD.[16] Moreover, the Court stated that recognising the administrator of the fan page and the operator of the social network as jointly responsible enhances the protection of the visitors' rights,[17] but does not necessarily imply that the administrator and the operator share an equal responsibility, as they 'may be involved at different stages of that processing of personal data and to different degrees'.[18]

These principles for determining joint controllership for the purposes of Article 2(d) DPD were applied by the CJEU in *Jehova's Witnesses*, where the Court found that the Jehovah's Witness Community and its individual members who engage in door-to-door preaching, are joint controllers for the processing of personal data carried out by the members in the context of that preaching, because the activity is 'organised, coordinated and encouraged by' the Community.[19] Again, in establishing this status, the Court held that it was not necessary for the Community to have access to the data, nor to establish that the data processing occurred pursuant to written guidelines or instructions from the Community to its members.[20]

Following its reasoning in *Wirtschaftsakademie* and *Jehova's Witnesses*, the CJEU held in *Fashion ID* that a website operator which embeds in its website a social plug-in, such as the Facebook 'Like' button, in a way that triggers the collection of website visitors' personal data and their transmission to Facebook, is a controller[21] as it 'exerts a decisive influence over the collection and transmission of the personal data of visitors to that website to the provider of that plugin, Facebook Ireland, which would not have occurred without that plugin'.[22] As a result, the Court concluded that for those processing operations (i.e.

[9] Ibid., para. 33. [10] Ibid., para. 40. [11] Case C-210/16, *Wirtschaftsakademie*, para. 42.
[12] Ibid., para. 38. [13] Ibid., para. 36. [14] Ibid., para. 36. [15] Ibid., para. 36.
[16] Ibid., para. 39. [17] Ibid., para. 42. [18] Ibid., para. 43.
[19] Case C-25/17, *Jehovan todistajat*, para. 75. [20] Ibid., para. 75.
[21] Case C-40/17, *Fashion ID*, para. 85. [22] Ibid., para. 78.

the collection and transmission of such personal data to Facebook), Fashion ID was a joint controller together with Facebook Ireland as they both determined the means (i.e. the use of the social plug-in) by which the personal data of the visitors to the Fashion ID website were collected and disclosed by transmission to Facebook.[23] As Fashion ID embedded the 'Like' button in its website to make its products more visible on the Facebook network when a website visitor clicked on that button and, thus, benefit from the commercial advantage of such advertising, the Court found that Fashion ID seemed to 'have consented, at least implicitly' to the collection and disclosure by transmission of the website visitors' personal data to Facebook.[24] Moreover, as that processing activity was carried out in the economic interests of both Fashion ID and Facebook Ireland, the Court ruled that they also jointly determined the purposes of the relevant processing.[25] The fact that Fashion ID did not have access to the personal data collected did not prevent the Court from classifying it as a controller.[26] However, as Fashion ID could not determine the purposes and means of any subsequent processing operation by Facebook, the Court held that Fashion ID could not be held responsible for such subsequent processing.[27] The Court once again reiterated that joint responsibility does not necessarily mean equal responsibility as different actors may be responsible for different stages of the processing and to different degrees.[28] For instance, the Court clarified that it is the website operator's obligation to ask for the website visitors' consent at the time of the collection of their personal data triggered by the social plug-in, and also to provide the information required under data protection legislation, as this ensures the 'efficient and timely protection of data subjects' rights'.[29]

C. Analysis

1. Introduction

The overall aim of Article 26 is to recognise the possibility that more than one controller may jointly determine the means and purposes of processing in such a way that each assumes the role of 'joint controller'. The term 'joint' in this context has been interpreted to mean 'together with' or 'not alone' and the joint activity may take different forms.[30] It does not necessarily mean that the joint controllers participate equally in determining the means and purposes of the processing.[31] For instance, in the context of social networking sites ('SNS'), the WP29 argued that SNS providers will be controllers under the DPD because they provide the means for the processing and all the basic services for the users to manage their data, and they also determine the purposes of use when they process users' data for advertising or marketing purposes. Providers of applications that use data in a way separate to the SNS providers may also be controllers. And, finally, users of SNS may themselves also assume the role of controllers when their processing of third party personal data ceases to be 'in the course of a purely personal or household activity' either because they use the SNS for commercial purposes or to promote political or charitable causes, or because they are indiscriminate in accepting contact requests.[32]

---

[23] Ibid., para. 79.   [24] Ibid., para. 80.   [25] Ibid., para. 80-81.   [26] Ibid., para. 82.
[27] Ibid., para. 76.   [28] Ibid., para. 70.   [29] Ibid., paras. 102-104.
[30] WP29 2010, p. 18.   [31] Ibid., p. 19.
[32] WP29 2009, pp. 5–6; WP29 2010, p. 17 and pp. 21–22.

The WP29 provided a number of use cases to illustrate the possibility of joint controllership. One example concerns online publishers and advertising networks that collect users' personal data and exchange information for behavioural advertising purposes.[33] Yet, collaboration between controllers will not always mean that they have joint control because they may process data for their own purposes, independently of each other.[34]

2. Arrangements between joint controllers

Article 26 also imposes on joint controllers the obligation to have an arrangement with a clear and transparent allocation of roles and relationships between them in order to resolve the potential uncertainty that may have existed in similar situations under the DPD. The arrangement should reflect the controllers' respective responsibilities for compliance in relation to the exercise of data subjects' rights and their duties to provide data subjects with essential information about the processing under Articles 13 and 14 GDPR. The aim here is to ensure that even in complex processing situations the level of data protection is not reduced,[35] and that all the obligations deriving from the GDPR continue to be fulfilled by (at least) one of the controllers. Irrespective of the stated arrangement, however, if that arrangement does not reflect the reality of the processing, the factual circumstances may prevail over it.[36] This argument is supported by Article 28(10) which recognises that, in practice, a processor may fail to comply with the controller's instructions or may go beyond the contractual obligation to process data only under the controller's instructions and may determine the means and purposes of processing.[37] If that happens, the processor may assume the role of controller or joint controller in regards to that processing. In the view of the WP29, this may occur in cloud computing relationships where the cloud customer, for example a small and medium-sized enterprise ('SME'), may not have effective control over the way in which the cloud services are delivered by the cloud provider.[38]

The obligation to have an arrangement in place does not apply when the respective responsibilities are determined by Union or Member State law to which the controllers are subject.

Even though there is no explicit obligation for the arrangement to be recorded in writing, the requirement to make 'the essence of the arrangement ... available to the data subject' implies that there will be at least a written summary of the arrangement. Also, the data controllers' obligations to maintain records of processing activities (Article 30) will provide a further driver for the arrangement to be recorded in writing.[39] The 'essence' of the arrangement should be made available to the data subject, and it has been argued that the reference to 'essence' means that controllers should at least provide data subjects with information on the specific purposes of processing and other information required in Articles 13 and 14.[40] The arrangement may also designate a point of contact but this will not constrain data subjects in exercising their rights against each of the controllers irrespective of the arrangement.

---

[33] WP29 2010, p. 23.   [34] Van Alsenoy 2012, p. 34.   [35] WP29 2010, p. 22.
[36] This approach would be consistent with the WP29 Opinion on the concept of 'controller' and 'processor' which states that 'the factual circumstances should be considered also in this case with a view to assessing whether the arrangements reflect the reality of the underlying data processing'. See ibid., p. 24.
[37] See the commentary on Art. 28 in this volume.   [38] WP29 2012, p. 23.
[39] Jay 2017, para. 9-019.   [40] Ibid., para. 9-020.

Select Bibliography

National legislation

UK Data Protection Act 1998: Data Protection Act 1998 (Chapter 29) (repealed).
UK Data Protection Act 2018: Data Protection Act 2018 (Chapter 12).

Academic writings

Blume, 'Controller and Processor: Is there a Risk of Confusion?' 3(2) *International Data Privacy Law* (2013), 140.
Hon, Millard and Walden, 'Who Is Responsible for Personal Data in Clouds?' in Millard (ed.), *Cloud Computing Law* (OUP 2014), 193.
Jay 2017: Jay, 'Accountability' in Jay (ed.), *Guide to The General Data Protection Regulation* (Sweet & Maxwell 2017), 169.
Kuner 2007: Kuner, *European Data Protection Law: Corporate Compliance and Regulation* (2nd edn, OUP 2007).
Van Alsenoy 2012: Van Alsenoy, 'Allocating Responsibility among Controllers, Processors, and "Everything in Between": The Definition of Actors and Roles in Directive 95/46/EC', 28(1) *Computer Law & Security Review 'CLSR'* (2012), 25.
Van Eecke and Truyens, 'Privacy and Social Networks' 25(5) *CLSR* (2010), 535.

Papers of data protection authorities

CNIL 2012: Commission nationale de l'informatique et des libertés, 'Recommendations for Companies Planning to use Cloud Computing Services' (2012).
Information Commissioner's Office, 'Data Controllers and Data Processors: What the Difference Is and what the Governance Implications Are' (6 May 2014).
WP29 2009: Article 29 Working Party, 'Opinion 5/2009 on Online Social Networking' (WP 163, 12 June 2009).
WP29 2010: Article 29 Working Party, 'Opinion 1/2010 on the Concepts of "Controller" and "Processor"' (WP 169, 16 February 2010).
WP29 2012: Article 29 Working Party, 'Opinion 05/2012 on Cloud Computing' (WP 196, 1 July 2012).

Reports and recommendations

IGA 2016: Information Governance Alliance, 'Integrated Digital Care Records: Data Controller Issues' (18 May 2016).
Maxwell 2012: Maxwell, 'CNIL Cloud Guidelines Address Controller vs. Processor Issues', *Hogan Lovell's Chronicle of Data Protection* (25 June 2012), available at https://www.hldataprotection.com/2012/06/articles/international-eu-privacy/cnil-cloud-guidelines-address-controller-vs-processor-issues/.

Article 27. Representatives of controllers or processors not established in the Union

CHRISTOPHER MILLARD   DIMITRA KAMARINOU

1. Where Article 3(2) applies, the controller or the processor shall designate in writing a representative in the Union.
2. The obligation laid down in paragraph 1 of this Article shall not apply to:
   (a) processing which is occasional, does not include, on a large scale, processing of special categories of data as referred to in Article 9(1) or processing of personal data relating to criminal convictions and offences referred to in Article 10, and is unlikely to result in a risk to the rights and freedoms of natural persons, taking into account the nature, context, scope and purposes of the processing; or
   (b) a public authority or body.
3. The representative shall be established in one of the Member States where the data subjects, whose personal data are processed in relation to the offering of goods or services to them, or whose behaviour is monitored, are.
4. The representative shall be mandated by the controller or processor to be addressed in addition to or instead of the controller or the processor by, in particular, supervisory authorities and data subjects, on all issues related to processing, for the purposes of ensuring compliance with this Regulation.
5. The designation of a representative by the controller or processor shall be without prejudice to legal actions which could be initiated against the controller or the processor themselves.

Relevant Recital

(80) Where a controller or a processor not established in the Union is processing personal data of data subjects who are in the Union whose processing activities are related to the offering of goods or services, irrespective of whether a payment of the data subject is required, to such data subjects in the Union, or to the monitoring of their behaviour as far as their behaviour takes place within the Union, the controller or the processor should designate a representative, unless the processing is occasional, does not include processing, on a large scale, of special categories of personal data or the processing of personal data relating to criminal convictions and offences, and is unlikely to result in a risk to the rights and freedoms of natural persons, taking into account the nature, context, scope and purposes of the processing or if the controller is a public authority or body. The representative should act on behalf of the controller or the processor and may be addressed by any supervisory authority. The representative should be explicitly designated by a written mandate of the controller or of the processor to act on its behalf with regard to its obligations under this Regulation. The designation of such a representative does not affect the responsibility or liability of the controller or of the processor under this Regulation. Such a representative should perform its tasks according to the mandate received from the controller or processor, including cooperating with the competent supervisory authorities with regard to any action taken to ensure compliance with this Regulation. The designated representative should be subject to enforcement proceedings in the event of non-compliance by the controller or processor.

Closely Related Provisions

Article 3 (Territorial scope) (see also recitals 23–24); Article 4(17) (Definitions); Article 9 (Processing of special categories of personal data) (see also recitals 10, 51–54); Article 10 (Processing of personal data relating to criminal convictions and offences) (see also recital 97); Article 13 (Information to be provided where personal data are collected from the data subject) and Article 14 (Information to be provided where personal data have not been obtained from the data subject) (see also recitals 60–62); Article 30 (Records of processing activities) (see also recital 82); Article 31 (Cooperation with the supervisory authority); Article 35 (Data protection impact assessment) (see also recitals 89–93); Article 36 (Prior consultation) (see also recital 94); Article 79 (Right to an effective judicial remedy against a controller or processor) (see also recital 145)

Related Provisions in EPD [Directive 2002/58/EC]

Recital 10

Relevant Case Law

CJEU

Case C-131/12, *Google Spain SL and Google Inc. v Agencia Española de Protección de Datos (AEPD) and Mario Costeja González*, judgment of 13 May 2014 (Grand Chamber) (ECLI:EU:C:2014:317).

Case C-230/14, *Weltimmo s. r. o. v Nemzeti Adatvédelmi és Információszabadság Hatóság*, judgment of 1 October 2015 (ECLI:EU:C:2015:639).

Case C-191/15, *Verein für Konsumenteninformation v Amazon EU Sàrl*, judgment of 28 July 2016 (ECLI:EU:C:2016:612).

Case C-210/16, *Unabhängiges Landeszentrum für Datenschutz Schleswig-Holstein v Wirtschaftsakademie Schleswig-Holstein GmbH*, judgment of 5 June 2018 (Grand Chamber) (ECLI:EU:C:2018:388).

A. Rationale and Policy Underpinnings

Article 27 GDPR aims to enhance the practical-procedural traction of the GDPR on controllers and processors who are not established in an European Economic Area ('EEA') Member State but who are nonetheless subject to the Regulation pursuant to Article 3(2). A key objective is to ensure that the level of protection of data subjects is not reduced where such controllers or processors fail to comply with the Regulation. Article 27 provides data subjects and supervisory authorities with an additional (or alternative) point of contact (i.e. the representative) for all issues regarding the processing of personal data while, at the same time, maintaining their right to initiate legal actions directly against the controllers or processors. In addition, if Article 27 is interpreted in light of recital 80, enforcement against controllers or processors could be facilitated, as the Regulation allows for the representative to be subject to enforcement proceedings in the event of non-compliance by the controller or processor. A secondary objective of Article 27 is to clarify some of a controller's or processor's obligations when designating a representative in a Member State, and to relieve the controller or processor from the administrative burdens that accompany those obligations in cases where the processing of personal data is likely to present a low risk to the rights and freedoms of data subjects.

B. Legal Background

1. EU legislation

The obligation for controllers not established in the Union to designate a representative in the Union existed pursuant to Article 4(2) DPD but in a significantly different and more limited form than mandated by Article 27 GDPR. Under the DPD, controllers established outside the Union (or EEA) who, in order to process personal data, made use of equipment located in a Member State, were required to designate a representative in that Member State to be the point of contact for data subjects to request information or submit complaints. The representative could be a subsidiary or an agent of the controller. Article 4(2) DPD further stipulated that designation of a representative was 'without prejudice to legal actions which could be initiated against the controller himself'. As elaborated below, considerable variation existed between Member States' laws regarding the extent to which data subjects were permitted to initiate legal proceedings against the representative without prejudice to direct legal actions against the controller.[1]

The EPD does not have a territoriality provision. However, the 2017 proposal for a Regulation to replace this Directive contains such a provision in Article 3, which requires the provider of an electronic communications service who is not established in the Union to designate in writing a representative in the Union (Article 3(2)), and this representative 'shall be established in one of the Member States where the end-users of such electronic communications services are located' (Article 3(3)).[2] Article 3(4) sets out briefly the powers of the representative, while Article 3(5) stipulates that the designation of the representative is 'without prejudice to legal actions, which could be initiated against a natural or legal person who processes electronic communications data in connection with the provision of electronic communications services from outside the Union to end-users in the Union'. The fate of the 2017 proposal is, at the time of writing, unclear.

Article 2(13) of Directive 2014/53/EU on the harmonisation of the laws of the Member States relating to the making available on the market of radio equipment and repealing Directive 1999/5/EC defines an 'authorised representative' as 'any natural or legal person established within the Union who has received a written mandate from a manufacturer to act on his behalf in relation to specified tasks'. In relation to those tasks, Article 11(2) of the Directive provides that the mandate shall allow the authorised representative to perform at least three tasks:

a) keep the EU declaration of conformity and the technical documentation at the disposal of national market surveillance authorities for 10 years after the radio equipment has been placed on the market;
(b) further to a reasoned request from a competent national authority, provide that authority with all the information and documentation necessary to demonstrate the conformity of radio equipment;
(c) cooperate with the competent national authorities, at their request, on any action taken to eliminate the risks posed by radio equipment covered by the authorised representative's mandate.[3]

---

[1] WP29 2010, p. 23.   [2] EPR Proposal.   [3] Art. 11(2) Directive 2014/53/EU.

The requirement to appoint an authorised representative in the EU exists in other EU legislation, such as that concerning medical devices. Article 11 of Regulation 2017/745 on medical devices and of Regulation 2017/746 on in vitro diagnostic medical devices prescribes that '[w]here the manufacturer of a device is not established in a Member State, the device may only be placed on the Union market if the manufacturer designates a sole authorised representative',[4] while Article 11(5) of both Regulations goes on to impose on the authorised representative legal liability for defective devices, 'on the same basis as, and jointly and severally with, the manufacturer' without prejudice to those obligations that the manufacturer cannot delegate to others.[5] These provisions build on earlier legislation predating the GDPR, such as Article 10(3) of Directive 98/79/EC (repealed) on in vitro diagnostic medical devices.

2. International instruments

Convention 108, either in its original or modernised form, does not impose an obligation on signatory states to require controllers or processors established outside these states to appoint a representative along the lines mandated by Article 27 GDPR.

3. National developments

National laws differed significantly in their respective transpositions of the requirements of Article 4(2) DPD. In particular, there was little uniformity regarding whether or not a representative could be held liable for the actions of a controller and sanctioned, either on a civil or criminal law basis.[6] As noted by the WP29:

> In some Member States, the representative substitutes for the controller, also with regard to enforcement and sanctions, while in others it has a simple mandate. Some national laws explicitly foresee fines applicable to the representatives, while in other Member States this possibility is not envisaged.[7]

Accordingly, the WP29 urged greater pan-European harmonisation on these matters, 'with the objective of giving more effectiveness to the role of the representative'.[8]

The status of the UK's departure from the EU ('Brexit') was unclear at the time this commentary was finalised, and is subject to political factors that were unresolved. However, guidance from the UK Information Commissioner ('ICO') indicates that a UK-based controller falling under Article 27 will be required to appoint a representative in the Union (or EEA).[9]

4. Case law

Designating a representative in a Member State is an obligation only for controllers or processors not established in the Union (or EEA). As a result, the meaning of 'establishment' in the Regulation is vitally important for whether a controller or processor is under an obligation to designate a representative or not. The CJEU has dealt with the concept of 'establishment' in the cases of *Google Spain*, *Weltimmo*, *Verein für Konsumenteninformation*

---

[4] Regulation 2017/745; Regulation 2017/746.
[5] See Arts. 11(4) and (5) Regulation 2017/745 and Arts. 11(4) and (5) Regulation 2017/746.
[6] WP29 2010, p. 23. [7] Ibid. [8] Ibid. [9] ICO 2018, pp. 14-16.

and *Wirtschaftsakademie*, and, in doing so has developed a broad and flexible interpretation of the term.

In *Google Spain*, the Court concluded that processing of personal data is carried out in the context of the activities of an establishment of the controller on the territory of a Member State when the controller sets up a branch or a subsidiary which is intended to carry out activities that make the service offered by the controller economically profitable,[10] and when the service provided by the controller is the means enabling the activities of the subsidiary to be performed,[11] thereby rendering the activities of the two actors 'inextricably linked'.[12] Therefore, it could be argued that when the controller designates a representative in a Member State, the representative should not go beyond carrying out the specific tasks assigned to representatives under the Regulation to include processing personal data for other activities for the controller, as this processing may be interpreted as the controller being 'established' in that Member State.

In *Weltimmo*, the CJEU confirmed that the concept of 'establishment' under the DPD covers any 'real and effective activity', and that this activity could be a 'minimal one' as long as it is 'exercised through stable arrangements'.[13] This was reaffirmed in *Wirtschaftsakademie*.[14]

The Court, in *Weltimmo*, held that even 'the presence of only one representative can, in some circumstances, suffice to constitute a stable arrangement if that representative acts with a sufficient degree of stability through the presence of the necessary equipment for provision of the specific services concerned in the Member State in question'.[15] By contrast, in *Verein für Konsumenteninformation*, the Court held that the mere accessibility of an undertaking's website in a Member State is not enough to amount to 'establishment' in that Member State.[16] The Court also held that, taking into account all the relevant circumstances, it is for the national court to decide whether the processing of personal data concerned is carried out 'in the context of the activities' of an establishment within the meaning of Article 4(1) DPD.[17] If that is the case, then 'the processing of personal data carried out by an undertaking engaged in electronic commerce is governed by the law of the Member State to which that undertaking directs its activities'.[18]

C. Analysis

1. Introduction

The broad thrust of Article 27 GDPR can be summarised as follows: when a controller or processor not established in the Union (or EEA) offers goods or services to, or monitors the behaviour of, data subjects in the Union, the controller or processor is under a qualified obligation to designate, in writing, a representative in one of the Member States where such data subjects 'are'. This obligation is both more extensive and more limited than the obligation that previously existed pursuant to Article 4(2) DPD. On the one hand, the latter applied only to controllers, whereas Article 27 GDPR extends to

---

[10] Case C-131/12, *Google Spain*, para. 55.   [11] Ibid., para. 56.   [12] Ibid., para. 56.
[13] Case C-230/14, *Weltimmo*, para. 31.   [14] Case C-210/16, *Wirtschaftsakademie*, para. 54.
[15] Case C-230/14, *Weltimmo*, para. 30.
[16] Case C-191/15, *Verein für Konsumenteninformation*, paras. 75–76 (referencing extensively the *Weltimmo* case).
[17] Ibid., paras. 78–79.   [18] Ibid., para. 81.

processors as well. Further, the rather narrow and clumsy equipment location criterion utilised by the DPD has been replaced by broader criteria relating to processing in the context of offering goods or services to, or monitoring the behaviour of, data subjects in the EU. On the other hand, only one representative needs to be appointed under Article 27 GDPR for the whole of the EU (or EEA),[19] whereas the DPD required the appointment of a representative in each Member State where equipment was used by a non-EU controller to process personal data. This is a key practical change. Moreover, the DPD's obligation to appoint a representative applied, in theory at least, in cases where there was no substantive connection to any data subject in the EU, for example where a US controller stored personal data relating to its US employees or customers on a server in an EU member state. This type of scenario has long been an incidental feature of the data management arrangements of multinational corporations, and has become increasingly common with the widespread adoption of distributed public cloud computing services.

2. No one-stop-shop

Even if a non-EU controller need only appoint one representative in the EU, the mere presence of such a representative does not trigger the 'one-stop-shop' mechanism for the purposes of Article 56, as the presence of the representative does not constitute an 'establishment' under Article 3(1).[20] This means that the supervisory authority of the Member State of the representative is not considered as the lead supervisory authority, and the representative acting on behalf of the non-EU controller 'must deal with local supervisory authorities in every Member State [the controller] is active in'.[21]

3. Obligations towards DPAs

Under Article 31 GPDR, the controller, processor and their representatives shall co-operate generally with supervisory authorities. Under Article 30, they should also keep records of processing activities (which include, inter alia, information on the identity and contact details of the representatives themselves) and make them available to supervisory authorities on request.[22] However, there is no obligation under the GDPR for controllers/processors to publish and communicate to supervisory authorities the contact details of the representatives—as is the case for their Data Protection Officers ('DPOs').[23] Nevertheless, controllers and processors are obliged to provide such details to data subjects,[24] and supervisory authorities have the investigatory power to order a controller's or processor's representative to provide any information the supervisory authority requires for the performance of its tasks.[25] As a supervisory authority would find it very difficult to order a representative to provide information if it did not have its contact details, it may be that supervisory authorities require controllers and processors to provide such information *ex ante*, even without a specific requirement to do so in the GDPR. The

---

[19] If a significant number of data subjects are located in one Member State, the EDPB has proposed that the representative be established in that Member State, while remaining easily accessible to other data subjects in Member States where the non-EU controller or processor offers goods or services or monitors the behaviour of such data subjects: EDPB 2018, p. 22.
[20] Ibid., p. 20.   [21] WP29 2017A, p. 10.   [22] Art. 30(1)(a) and Art. 30(2)(a) GDPR.
[23] Art. 37(7) GDPR.   [24] Art. 13(1)(a) and Art. 14(1)(a) GDPR.
[25] Art. 58(1)(a) GDPR.

EDPB has proposed that controllers should make the representative's details easily accessible to supervisory authorities.[26]

4. Exemptions

The obligation under Article 27(1) is qualified by Article 27(2), which makes clear that the obligation does not apply to public sector controllers or processors, and otherwise lays down three conditions for exempting a private sector controller or processor from the obligation: (i) the relevant processing is occasional; (ii) it does not include, on a large scale, special categories of personal data or data relating to criminal offences; and (iii) it is unlikely to result in a risk for the rights and freedoms of data subjects. These three conditions seem to apply cumulatively. The term 'occasional' could be interpreted to mean 'non-systematic', so controllers or processors could still process personal data on an ad hoc and infrequent basis but not in a systematic, regular way. In addition, the term 'on a large scale' is not defined in Article 27, but recital 91 GDPR (concerning the data protection impact assessment requirements under Article 35) provides some guidance as to what kind of processing would constitute processing 'on a large scale'—this may include processing a considerable amount of personal data at regional, national or supranational level or processing which could affect a large number of data subjects, or both. In addition, in the context of its guidelines on DPOs, the WP29 recommended that, when deciding whether the processing is carried out on a large scale, the following factors should be considered: 'the number of data subjects concerned—either as a specific number or as a proportion of the relevant population, the volume of data and/or the range of different data items being processed, the duration or permanence, of the data processing activity and the geographical extent of the processing activity'.[27] As a result, according to the WP29, a search engine processing personal data for behavioural advertising purposes would constitute large-scale processing but an individual lawyer processing personal data relating to criminal convictions would not.[28]

It also follows logically that prior to any personal data processing, controllers or processors should carry out a risk assessment to identify whether such processing poses a 'high' or 'low' risk for the rights and freedoms of data subjects. Then, based on that risk assessment, they should decide whether they are required to designate a representative in the Union or not. Controllers or processors who are public bodies or authorities are also exempt from the obligation to designate a representative. This could include, for example, a tax authority which monitors data subjects' tax behaviour in the Union to calculate their worldwide tax.

5. Designation of a representative

The representative should be explicitly designated by a written mandate from the controller or processor to act on their behalf with regard to their obligations under the Regulation and the representative should cooperate with the supervisory authorities with regards to any action taken to comply with the Regulation (recital 80 GDPR) It is not clear under the Regulation whether the requirement of a 'written mandate' implies that the representative's designation and tasks should be governed by a written contract or another form of written authorisation (e.g. a letter or an email), but it should confer on

---

[26] EDPB 2018, p. 21. [27] WP29 2017B, p 8. [28] Ibid.

the representative the legal authority to represent the controller or processor in relation to their respective obligations under the GDPR.[29] The representative can be a natural or legal person established in the Union (Article 4(17) GDPR). Where an organisation assumes the role of the representative, the EDPB recommends that the service contract between the controller (or processor) and the representative indicates the individual in that organisation who is the point of contact for the specific controller or processor.[30]

6. Obligations of the representative

The representative has limited direct obligations under the Regulation, such as maintaining records of the processing activities under its responsibility (Article 30), making available such records to the supervisory authority as requested (Article 30(4)), and, as mentioned previously, the representative must cooperate with the supervisory authority as requested in the performance of its tasks according to Article 31 on 'cooperation' and Article 58 on the powers of supervisory authorities. In contrast to Articles 10 and 11 DPD under which the controller's representative was one of the persons responsible (the other being the controller itself) for providing information to data subjects about the processing of their personal data both when the data were collected from the data subject (Article 10 DPD) and when the data had not been obtained directly from the data subject (Article 11 DPD), this obligation is not included in the equivalent Articles 13 and 14 of the Regulation. However, under Article 27(4), the representative may be addressed by data subjects on all issues relating to the processing of their personal data, for the purposes of ensuring compliance with the Regulation. This provision implies that the representative will have to respond to data subjects' requests addressed to the representative in relation to Articles 15–21, and, thus, may need to provide some of the information relating to the processing of their personal data. According to the EDPB, however, the representative is not itself responsible for responding to such data subjects' requests but must facilitate the communication between data subjects and the controllers or processors represented.[31]

7. DPO and representative

The role of the representative is separate and different from the role of the DPO, who has a number of formal tasks listed in Articles 38 and 39 of the Regulation.[32] Indeed, the EDPB has suggested that the two roles are not only different but incompatible, as the representative acts under a direct mandate from the controller whereas the DPO is required to maintain a degree of autonomy and independence from the controller in carrying out its tasks and duties.[33] Furthermore, the EDPB argues that due to a potential conflict of interests during enforcement proceedings, the role of representative is also incompatible with that of a processor acting for the same controller.[34]

---

[29] See the commentary on Art. 4(17) in this volume concerning the formal requirements for the appointment of a representative.

[30] EDPB 2018, p. 20. The EDPB also notes that a particular representative may act on behalf of several controllers and processors.

[31] Ibid., p. 23. The EDPB further argues that the representative's team must be able to communicate with the data subjects and supervisory authorities of a Member State in the language used by such data subjects and supervisory authorities.

[32] See further the commentary on Art. 4(17) in this volume concerning the likely incompatibility of the two roles.

[33] EDPB 2018, pp. 20–21. [34] Ibid., p 21.

8. Enforcement

If the controller or the processor fails to designate a representative or infringes any of the provisions in Article 27 GDPR they may face administrative fines of up to € 10 million or 2 per cent of the total worldwide annual turnover of the preceding financial year, whichever is higher, according to Article 83(4)(a) GDPR. These fines would be calculated on a case-by-case basis depending on the nature, gravity and duration of the infringement.

Article 27 does not impose any direct liability on representatives. However, there is some inconsistency between its provisions and recital 80 GDPR, which states: 'The designated representative should be subject to enforcement proceedings in the event of non-compliance by the controller or processor'. Even though recitals are not legally binding, if Article 27 is interpreted, in the light of recital 80, to mean that a supervisory authority may initiate enforcement proceedings against a representative, this might indirectly enhance data subjects' protection in cases where the controller or processor does not comply with the Regulation. In fact, some Member States' laws adapting the Regulation have addressed this issue of the representative's liability by going one step further than the obligations imposed by the Regulation itself.[35] For instance, Article 30(1) of the Spanish GDPR Implementation Law provides that the Spanish supervisory authorities may impose on representatives (who are jointly and severally responsible with controllers and/or processors) all the 'measures' established in the GDPR.[36] Whether such 'measures' include administrative fines would be a matter of interpretation but, under Article 30(2) of the Law, representatives would be jointly and severally liable to provide compensation to data subjects for any damage caused by an infringement of the Regulation.[37]

In the EU Commission's original Proposal for the GDPR, Article 78 stated that any penalties imposed by Member States on controllers for infringing the provisions of the Regulation should also apply to their representatives ('without prejudice to any penalties which could be initiated against the controller').[38] This provision did not survive in the final text of the Regulation where there are no direct administrative fines or explicit penalties imposed on representatives. Notwithstanding the fact that the statement regarding penalties in an article in the original proposal was replaced by a reference in a recital to 'enforcement proceedings' in the final text, the EDPB has interpreted the final provisions to mean that a representative may be found liable for an infringement by a controller or processor in the same way as the controller or processor could be liable directly. If the EDPB's interpretation is correct, supervisory authorities may impose administrative fines and penalties on representatives themselves and not merely on the controllers or processors that they represent.[39] According to the EDPB, this result is not merely an interpretation of Article 27(5) and recital 80, but the 'intention' of the GDPR.[40] However, the EDPB does not elaborate on how this intention is evidenced in the Regulation. If the EDBP's proposed position is confirmed in the final version of the Guidelines, this is likely to deter prospective representatives or, at least, lead to intense contractual negotiations between controllers, processors and their respective representatives regarding limitations of liability and indemnities to protect representatives' interests.

---

[35] See the commentary on Art. 82 in this volume.
[36] Art. 30(1) Spanish Data Protection Act 2018.
[37] Ibid., Art. 30(2).
[38] GDPR Proposal.
[39] EDPB 2018, p 22.
[40] Ibid.

Select Bibliography

EU legislation

Directive 2014/53/EU: Directive 2014/53/EU of the European Parliament and of the Council of 16 April 2014 on the harmonisation of the laws of the Member States relating to the making available on the market of radio equipment and repealing Directive 1999/5/EC, OJ 2014 L 153/62.

EPR Proposal: Proposal for a Regulation of the European Parliament and of the Council concerning the respect for private life and the protection of personal data in electronic communications and repealing Directive 2002/58/EC (Regulation on Privacy and Electronic Communications), COM(2017)10 final, 10 January 2017.

GDPR Proposal: Proposal for a Regulation of the European Parliament and of the Council on the protection of individuals with regard to the processing of personal data and on the free movement of such data (General Data Protection Regulation), COM(2012) 11 final, 25 January 2012.

Regulation 2017/745: Regulation (EU) 2017/745 of the European Parliament and of the Council of 5 April 2017 on medical devices, amending Directive 2001/83/EC, Regulation (EC) No. 178/2002 and Regulation (EC) No. 1223/2009 and repealing Council Directives 90/385/EEC and 93/42/EEC (OJ L 117/1, 5 May 2017) and Regulation (EU) 2017/746 of the European Parliament and of the Council of 5 April 2017 on in vitro diagnostic medical devices and repealing Directive 98/79/EC and Commission Decision 2010/227/EU, OJ 2017 L 117/176.

Regulation 2017/746: Regulation EU 2017/746 of the European Parliament and of the Council of 5 April 2017 on in vitro diagnostic medical devices and repealing Directive 98/79/EC and Commission Decision 2010/227/EU, OJ 2017 L117/176.

National legislation

Spanish Data Protection Act 2018: Ley Orgánica 3/2018, de 5 de diciembre, de Protección de Datos y de Garantía de los Derechos Digitales.

Papers of data protection authorities

EDPB 2018: European Data Protection Board, 'Guidelines 3/2018 on the Territorial Scope of the GDPR (Article 3)—Version for Public Consultation' (16 November 2018).

ICO 2018: UK Information Commissioner, (ICO) 'ICO guidance for UK businesses and organisations which operate within the European Economic Area (EEA)', available at https://ico.org.uk/media/for-organisations/data-protection-and-brexit/data-protection-if-there-s-no-brexit-deal/-1-0.pdf

WP29 2010: Article 29 Working Party, 'Opinion 8/2010 on Applicable Law' (WP 179, 16 December 2010).

WP29 2017A: Article 29 Working Party, 'Guidelines for Identifying a Controller's or Processor's Lead Supervisory Authority' (WP244, 5 April 2017).

WP29 2017B: Article 29 Working Party, 'Guidelines on Data Protection Officers ("DPOs")' (WP243 rev.01, as last revised and adopted 5 April 2017).

Others

Determann, 'Representatives under Art. 27 of the GDPR: All your Questions Answered' (12 June 2018), available at https://iapp.org/news/a/representatives-under-art-27-of-the-gdpr-all-your-questions-answered/.

Article 28. Processor

CHRISTOPHER MILLARD   DIMITRA KAMARINOU

1. Where processing is to be carried out on behalf of a controller, the controller shall use only processors providing sufficient guarantees to implement appropriate technical and organisational measures in such a manner that processing will meet the requirements of this Regulation and ensure the protection of the rights of the data subject.
2. The processor shall not engage another processor without prior specific or general written authorisation of the controller. In the case of general written authorisation, the processor shall inform the controller of any intended changes concerning the addition or replacement of other processors, thereby giving the controller the opportunity to object to such changes.
3. Processing by a processor shall be governed by a contract or other legal act under Union or Member State law, that is binding on the processor with regard to the controller and that sets out the subject-matter and duration of the processing, the nature and purpose of the processing, the type of personal data and categories of data subjects and the obligations and rights of the controller. That contract or other legal act shall stipulate, in particular, that the processor:
    (a) processes the personal data only on documented instructions from the controller, including with regard to transfers of personal data to a third country or an international organisation, unless required to do so by Union or Member State law to which the processor is subject; in such a case, the processor shall inform the controller of that legal requirement before processing, unless that law prohibits such information on important grounds of public interest;
    (b) ensures that persons authorised to process the personal data have committed themselves to confidentiality or are under an appropriate statutory obligation of confidentiality;
    (c) takes all measures required pursuant to Article 32;
    (d) respects the conditions referred to in paragraphs 2 and 4 for engaging another processor;
    (e) taking into account the nature of the processing, assists the controller by appropriate technical and organisational measures, insofar as this is possible, for the fulfilment of the controller's obligation to respond to requests for exercising the data subject's rights laid down in Chapter III;
    (f) assists the controller in ensuring compliance with the obligations pursuant to Articles 32 to 36 taking into account the nature of processing and the information available to the processor;
    (g) at the choice of the controller, deletes or returns all the personal data to the controller after the end of the provision of services relating to processing, and deletes existing copies unless Union or Member State law requires storage of the personal data;
    (h) makes available to the controller all information necessary to demonstrate compliance with the obligations laid down in this Article and allow for and contribute to audits, including inspections, conducted by the controller or another auditor mandated by the controller.
    With regard to point (h) of the first subparagraph, the processor shall immediately inform the controller if, in its opinion, an instruction infringes this Regulation or other Union or Member State data protection provisions.

4. Where a processor engages another processor for carrying out specific processing activities on behalf of the controller, the same data protection obligations as set out in the contract or other legal act between the controller and the processor as referred to in paragraph 3 shall be imposed on that other processor by way of a contract or other legal act under Union or Member State law, in particular providing sufficient guarantees to implement appropriate technical and organisational measures in such a manner that the processing will meet the requirements of this Regulation. Where that other processor fails to fulfil its data protection obligations, the initial processor shall remain fully liable to the controller for the performance of that other processor's obligations.

5. Adherence of a processor to an approved code of conduct as referred to in Article 40 or an approved certification mechanism as referred to in Article 42 may be used as an element by which to demonstrate sufficient guarantees as referred to in paragraphs 1 and 4 of this Article.

6. Without prejudice to an individual contract between the controller and the processor, the contract or the other legal act referred to in paragraphs 3 and 4 of this Article may be based, in whole or in part, on standard contractual clauses referred to in paragraphs 7 and 8 of this Article, including when they are part of a certification granted to the controller or processor pursuant to Articles 42 and 43.

7. The Commission may lay down standard contractual clauses for the matters referred to in paragraph 3 and 4 of this Article and in accordance with the examination procedure referred to in Article 93(2).

8. A supervisory authority may adopt standard contractual clauses for the matters referred to in paragraph 3 and 4 of this Article and in accordance with the consistency mechanism referred to in Article 63.

9. The contract or the other legal act referred to in paragraphs 3 and 4 shall be in writing, including in electronic form.

10. Without prejudice to Articles 82, 83 and 84, if a processor infringes this Regulation by determining the purposes and means of processing, the processor shall be considered to be a controller in respect of that processing.

Relevant Recital

(81) To ensure compliance with the requirements of this Regulation in respect of the processing to be carried out by the processor on behalf of the controller, when entrusting a processor with processing activities, the controller should use only processors providing sufficient guarantees, in particular in terms of expert knowledge, reliability and resources, to implement technical and organisational measures which will meet the requirements of this Regulation, including for the security of processing. The adherence of the processor to an approved code of conduct or an approved certification mechanism may be used as an element to demonstrate compliance with the obligations of the controller. The carrying-out of processing by a processor should be governed by a contract or other legal act under Union or Member State law, binding the processor to the controller, setting out the subject- matter and duration of the processing, the nature and purposes of the processing, the type of personal data and categories of data subjects, taking into account the specific tasks and responsibilities of the processor in the context of the processing to be carried out and the risk to the rights and freedoms of the data subject. The controller and processor may choose to use an individual contract or standard contractual clauses which are adopted either directly by the Commission or by a supervisory authority in accordance with the consistency mechanism and then adopted by the Commission. After the completion of the processing on behalf of the controller, the processor should, at the choice of the controller, return or delete the personal data, unless there is a requirement to store the personal data under Union or Member State law to which the processor is subject.

Closely Related Provisions

Article 4(8) (Definitions); Article 29 (Processing under the authority of the controller or processor); Article 30 (Records of processing activities) (see also recitals 13 and 82); Article 79 (Right to an effective judicial remedy against a controller or processor) (see also recital 145); Article 82 (Right to compensation and liability) (see also recitals 146–147)

Related Provisions in LED [Directive (EU) 2016/680]

Article 3 (Definitions); Article 22 (Processor) (see also recitals 11 and 55); Article 24 (Records of processing activities) (see also recital 56); Article 26 (Cooperation with the supervisory authority) (see also recital 59); Article 28 (Prior consultation of the supervisory authority); Article 29 (Security of processing) (see also recital 60); Article 30 (Notification of personal data breach to the supervisory authority); Article 54 (Right to an effective judicial remedy against a controller or processor)

Related Provisions in EPD [Directive 2002/58/EC]

Article 4 (Security) (see also recital 20); Article 6(5) (Traffic data) (see also recital 32); Article 9 (Location data other than traffic data) (see also recital 32)

Relevant Case Law

CJEU

Case C-73/07, *Tietosuojavaltuutettu v Satakunnan Markkinapörssi Oy and Satamedia Oy*, judgment of 16 December 2008 (Grand Chamber) (ECLI:EU:C:2008:727).
Opinion of Advocate General Kokott in Case C-73/07, *Tietosuojavaltuutettu v Satakunnan Markkinapörssi Oy and Satamedia Oy*, delivered on 8 May 2008 (ECLI:EU:C:2008:266).
Case C-119/12, *Josef Probst v mr.nexnet GmbH*, judgment of 22 November 2012 (ECLI:EU:C:2012:748).
Joined Cases C-293/12 and C-594/12, *Digital Rights Ireland Ltd v Minister for Communications, Marine and Natural Resources* and *Kärntner Landesregierung and Others*, judgment of 8 April 2014 (Grand Chamber) (ECLI:EU:C:2014:238).
Opinion of Advocate General Cruz Villalón in Joined Cases C-293/12 and C-594/12, *Digital Rights Ireland Ltd v Minister for Communications, Marine and Natural Resources* and *Kärntner Landesregierung and Others*, delivered on 12 December 2013 (ECLI:EU:C:2013:845).
Case C-210/16, *Unabhängiges Landeszentrum für Datenschutz Schleswig-Holstein v Wirtschaftsakademie Schleswig-Holstein GmbH*, judgment of 5 June 2018 (Grand Chamber) (ECLI:EU:C:2018:388).

ECtHR

M.M. v United Kingdom, Appl. No. 24029/07, judgment of 13 November 2012.

A. Rationale and Policy Underpinnings

The introduction of a separate article on 'processors'[1] in Article 28 GDPR, was necessary to reflect the increased responsibilities and liabilities that the Regulation imposes on

---

[1] For the definition of 'processor', see the commentary on Art. 4(8) in this volume.

processors. Under the DPD, controllers and processors were required to have a contract documenting the controller's instructions to processors but the Directive did not go into detail regarding the content of such an agreement, in contrast with Article 28 which lists a number of different obligations to be included in the contract.

In addition, under the DPD only the controller was responsible to compensate data subjects for the damage suffered by an unlawful processing (see Article 23(1)), whereas under the Regulation, processors are also liable (see Article 82(2)) up to a certain extent. This is a significant change introduced by the Regulation, as data subjects can choose to claim compensation against processors directly. Under the Regulation, processors are liable for the damage caused by the processing only when they have not complied with their direct obligations or where they have acted outside the instructions of the controller. In the latter case, they may be liable as separate controllers or joint controllers. If multiple controllers or processors are involved in the processing, each of them is liable for the entirety of the damage against the data subjects (Article 82(4)) and can only claim back from the other controllers or processors the part of the compensation corresponding to their part of responsibility for the damage caused (Article 82(5)).

Article 28 also aims at ensuring that processors have increased responsibilities as regards international transfers of personal data. Processors not only have to abide by the rules on transfers and the documented instructions by the controllers but, additionally, when they have to carry out a transfer independent of those instructions because the Union or Member State law to which they are subject requires them to, they should inform controllers in advance, unless that law prohibits such information on important grounds of public interest. A function of having processors inform controllers in advance of such a potential conflict is perhaps to encourage controllers to be more transparent about the recipients of their data and the potential disclosure of their data to law enforcement authorities.

B. Legal Background

1. EU legislation

Under the DPD, a processor's obligations and relationship with a controller was established in Article 17(2)–(4) on 'security of processing'.[2] Under Article 17 DPD, processors had two main obligations: (i) to follow the controller's instructions about the processing of data; and (ii) to guarantee the security of data by taking appropriate technical and organisational measures. The obligation to implement appropriate security measures was dependent on the provisions of Member State law, in contrast with the Regulation, which imposes the same security obligations on controllers and processors alike. The DPD mandated that, for evidentiary purposes, the parts of the contract of the controller and processor that referred to data protection and the relevant security measures had to be in writing but implied that that was not necessary for the whole agreement (Article 17(4)). In order to assist compliance with the obligations under Article 17, in 2005, the

---

[2] Art. 28 GDPR (previously Art. 26 GDPR Proposal) 'clarifies the position and obligation of processors, partly based on Article 17(2) of Directive 95/46/EC, and adding new elements, including that a processor who processes data beyond the controller's instructions is to be considered as a joint controller': GDPR Proposal, p. 10.

European Committee for Standardization ('CEN') adopted a model data processing contract reflecting the requirements of Article 17.[3]

2. International instruments

The concept of 'processor' was not mentioned in the original text of Convention 108.[4] However, in the Modernised Convention 108, Article 2(f) contains a definition of 'processor' with similar wording to the one in Article 4(8) GDPR. In addition, the Modernised Convention obliges each signatory Party to provide that controllers and, where applicable, processors take appropriate measures against data security risks (Article 7(1)) and take appropriate measures to ensure compliance with the provisions of the Convention and be able to demonstrate such compliance to the competent supervisory authority (Article 10(1)). Under Article 10(2), it seems that the modernised Convention mirrors the concepts of 'data protection impact assessments' and 'data protection by design' found in the GDPR when imposing on signatory Parties the obligation to provide that controllers and, where applicable, processors shall pre-assess the likely impact of their intended processing on the rights and freedoms of data subjects and design their processing in a way that prevents or minimises the risk of interference with those rights and freedoms. Controllers and processors shall also implement appropriate technical and organisational measures which take into account the implications of the right to the protection of personal data at all stages of processing (Article 10(3)). When the Parties impose such obligations upon controllers and processors, they shall take into account the nature and volume of data, the nature, scope and context of processing and, where appropriate, the size of the controller or processor (Article 10(4)).

3. National developments

Member State laws transposing the DPD addressed processors' obligations and liabilities quite differently. For instance, the Belgian Data Protection Act of 1992, as amended, implied limited obligations directly on processors and mandated that the agreement between the controller and the processor included not only the standard processor obligations but also an allocation of liability between the two actors.[5] In addition, in 2009, the German Federal Data Protection Act was amended to cover in more detail the required elements of the written agreement between a controller and a processor. The agreement had to include, among other things, the subject and duration of the processing and the processor's obligation to return any data storage media to the controller and erase the data following the end of processing[6]—obligations which are now explicitly mentioned in Article 28 GDPR.

Even though controllers and processors may choose to provide additional data protection safeguards in their data processing agreements, it is unclear whether Article 28 allows for Member States to introduce in their national laws further obligations on processors or additional requirements in connection with the controller-processor relationship. Considering that one of the drivers behind adopting a regulation was to resolve

---

[3] European Committee for Standardization 2005.
[4] The concept of 'processor' was first introduced in the Commission's proposal for the Data Protection Directive and subsequently operationalised in the final text of the Directive. See WP29 2010A, p. 24.
[5] Art. 16(1)(3) and Art. 16(4) Belgian Data Protection Law 1992 (repealed).
[6] ss. 11(2)(1) and 11(2)(10) German Federal Data Protection Act 2009 (repealed).

the fragmentation in the implementation of data protection across the Union (recital 9 GDPR), the level of data protection should be equivalent in all Member States to ensure both a consistent and high level of data protection and to remove the obstacles to flow of data in the Union (recital 10 GDPR). Where the Regulation allows for Member States to introduce national provisions to further specify the rules of the Regulation, this is clearly stated in the Recitals or the Articles of the Regulation (e.g. recitals 10, 19 and 20 GDPR, Article 8(1) GDPR, etc.). Article 28 GDPR and its relevant recital 81 do not address this issue, so it could be argued that Member States should not introduce additional obligations on the controller-processor relationship in their national laws unless such obligations deal with an issue for which the Regulation clearly allows Member States to add further requirements, such as processing of personal data by competent authorities (recital 19 second paragraph).

4. Case law

In the *Probst* case, the CJEU interpreted Article 6(5) EPD which provides, inter alia, that processing of electronic communications traffic data must be restricted to persons 'acting under the authority' of providers of publicly available electronic communications services. An issue in the case was what this restriction means for the relationship between an internet service provider ('ISP') and the assignee of claims for payment for the ISP's provision of its services. The Court concluded that 'under the authority' means 'act(ing) exclusively on the instructions and under the control of that provider',[7] and added that the contract between the provider and the assignee must contain provisions to ensure that the assignee guarantees the lawful processing of data and that the provider can check that the assignee is complying with those provisions.[8] This interpretation of the relationship between the provider and the assignee seems to reflect the relationship between a controller and a processor, whereby the processor should only act under the instructions of the controller and must commit contractually to make available all the necessary information to enable the controller to check that the processor complies with all of its data protection obligations.

With regards to the technical and organisational measures taken to ensure security of processing, the CJEU in *Digital Rights Ireland* argued that Article 7 of the (now invalid) Data Retention Directive, if read together with the second subparagraph of Article 17(1) DPD and Article 4(1) EPD, did not ensure a sufficiently high level of protection and security as these articles permitted providers (and controllers/processors) to take into account economic considerations and the cost of the implementation of any security measures.[9] This is still the case under the GDPR as controllers and processors are allowed to take these considerations into account before deciding which security measures to implement (Article 32(1)). However, the potential administrative fines in the Regulation are very high for a security breach, and it may be very difficult for a controller or processor to prove that they were not liable for such a breach. Accordingly, controllers and processors may well think twice before trying to depend on a defence based on economic considerations.

---

[7] Case C-119/12, *Probst*, para. 30.   [8] Ibid.
[9] Joined Cases C-293/12 and C-594/12, *Digital Rights Ireland*, para. 67.

In *M.M. v United Kingdom*—a case assessing compliance with Article 8 European Convention on Human Rights ('ECHR'), the ECtHR held that the lawfulness of the measures taken for the retention and deletion of criminal record data and 'in particular the adequacy of the safeguards in place'[10] must be assessed against the specific background of the case. In addition, the Court said that 'the greater the scope of the recording system, and thus the greater the amount and sensitivity of data held and available for disclosure, the more important the content of the safeguards to be applied at the various crucial stages in the subsequent processing of the data'.[11] This makes it clear that any technical or organisational measures taken to ensure lawful processing must be context specific.

C. Analysis

1. Introduction

Article 28 GDPR sets out the relationship between the controller and the processor and some of the direct obligations imposed on processors under the Regulation. Most importantly, when a controller uses a processor to carry out processing of personal data on its behalf, the controller must only use a processor who can provide sufficient guarantees to implement appropriate technical and organisational measures in such a manner that the processing will meet the requirements of the Regulation and ensure the protection of the rights of the data subject. Therefore, the controller must use a processor who is reliable and can demonstrate the required technical knowledge, expertise and resources to provide adequate guarantees.

As the processor must only act under the instructions of the controller, it should obtain from the controller prior specific or general authorisation to use sub-processors or to make changes to arrangements with existing sub-processors, in order to give the controller the possibility to object. In the context of the DPD, the WP29 had recommended that processors obtain the general (or specific) written consent of the controller when transferring data to sub-processors outside the European Economic Area ('EEA').[12] All the rules that apply to processors should also apply to sub-processors by virtue of a contract or other binding legal act between a processor and any sub-processors, ensuring in particular that sub-processors provide appropriate technical and organisational measures so that the processing complies with the Regulation. If any sub-processor fails to fulfil its obligations under the Regulation, the initial processor remains liable to the controller to fulfil such obligations, in the same way as the controller remains liable towards the data subject for all such obligations. However, this does not preclude the initial processor from claiming compensation from the sub-processor based on the existing contract between them. According to Article 82(3), a processor may be exempt from liability if it proves that it is not in any way responsible for the event giving rise to the damage.[13]

2. Contract between controller and processor

To ensure a transparent allocation of responsibilities and liabilities both internally (between controllers and processors) and externally towards data subjects and regulators,

---

[10] ECtHR, *M.M. v UK*, para. 201.   [11] Ibid., para. 200.
[12] WP29 2010B, p. 10 and WP29 2012A, p. 10.
[13] See the commentary on Art. 82 in this volume.

processing by a processor must be covered by a contract or other binding legal act between the controller and processor which documents the instructions of the controller as well as the subject-matter and duration of the processing, the nature and purpose of the processing, the type of personal data and categories of data subjects, and the obligations and rights of the controller. Regarding the subject-matter, this should refer clearly to the nature, scope and context of the processing. The duration of the processing may be specified by a start and end date and the purpose should comply with the purpose limitation principle laid down in Article 5(1)(b). Such a contract may take the form of a Service Level Agreement or a Framework Service Agreement or a Data Transfer Agreement.[14]

3. Standard contractual clauses

Without prejudice to any individual contract between them, the controller and processor can also manage the requirements of Article 28(3) and (4) via standard contractual clauses that the European Commission has issued or a supervisory authority has adopted under Article 28(8). Where a supervisory authority adopts a draft decision on standard contractual clauses, it must follow the consistency mechanism referred to in Article 63 and communicate to the European Data Protection Board the draft document, so that the Board can issue its opinion on the matter according to Article 64(3), so as to ensure a harmonized implementation of the GDPR.

As of July 2019, neither the European Commission nor any supervisory authority has adopted any such standard contractual clauses. However, the Board has issued an opinion on a draft set of standard clauses submitted by the Danish supervisory authority[15] and concluded that, if all the recommended changes suggested by the Board are implemented, the Danish supervisory authority will be able to use this draft agreement as standard contractual clauses without any required adoption by the European Commission.[16] Even though the Board's overarching view is that 'clauses which merely restate the provisions of Article 28(3) and (4) are inadequate to constitute standard contractual clauses',[17] in a number of instances, the Board suggests that the Danish supervisory authority uses the same wording as in the GDPR.[18]

Additional recommendations include, among others, the need for the standard contractual clauses to provide details on technical and organisational measures, on how a processor may assist a controller,[19] and on options regarding the erasure and return of data to a controller.[20] The Board welcomes the inclusion of clauses that provide additional safeguards, such as the possibility that a sub-processor accepts that it may be liable to the controller if an initial processor becomes bankrupt,[21] but warns against using clauses that contradict the relevant provisions of the GDPR, particularly on issues of liability, governing law and jurisdiction.[22]

According to Article 28(6) GDPR, standard contractual clauses may also form part of a certification granted to the controller or the processor under Article 42. The contract

---

[14] See too Terstegge 2010, pp. 88–89 (regarding data processor contracts under Art. 17(3) DPD).
[15] EDPB Opinion 14/2019.   [16] Ibid., para. 52.   [17] Ibid., para. 7.
[18] Ibid., paras. 19, 26, 28, 30 and 40. In contrast, where para. 38 discusses the controller's obligation to provide information to data subjects on personal data processing, the Board recommends that the Danish supervisory authority changes the phrase 'notification obligation' to 'right to be informed'. However, this is not in line with the wording of the GDPR, as Arts. 13 and 14 GDPR do not provide a right to data subjects but rather impose an obligation on controllers.
[19] Ibid., para. 38.   [20] Ibid., para. 42.   [21] Ibid., para. 30.   [22] Ibid., para. 47.

between a controller and processor must be in writing and it must include the specific provisions listed in Article 28(3).

The contract must obligate the processor to act only under the detailed instructions of the controller, including with regard to international transfers, except where the processing is required under Union or Member State law (Article 28(3)(a)). The processor should inform the controller of any such requirement prior to the processing unless prohibited to do so by the relevant law. Under the GDPR, a processor is now directly liable for complying with the rules of international transfers (Article 44; see too recital 101). This means that if there is no Commission decision regarding the adequacy of a third country, the controller and processor should have in place standard contractual clauses (or binding corporate rules for intra-group transfers) to comply with the rules on international transfers.

The contract must also stipulate that persons authorised to process personal data should be subject to confidentiality obligations (Article 28(3)(b); as was also the case under Article 16 DPD), and the processor should concomitantly have confidentiality agreements in place with its employees and contractors. In addition, when the contract ends the processor should delete or return all personal data to the controller and delete all existing copies unless required to retain them by Union or Member State law (Article 28(3)(g)). The processor must also comply with all the security obligations under Article 32 GDPR (Article 28(3)(c)).[23] Relevant security measures could include pseudonymisation (Article 32); encryption (recital 83); ability to ensure the confidentiality, integrity and availability of data (Article 32(1)(b)); ability to restore access to data in a timely manner after a security incident (Article 32(1)(c)); and putting in place a process for regular testing of the security measures to ensure their effectiveness (Article 32(1)(d)).

Processors must additionally take appropriate technical and organisational measures, if possible, to assist the controller to comply with its obligation to exercise the data subjects' rights (Article 28(3)(e)). In regards to providing assistance to the controller, the processor also has the obligation to assist the controller in complying with Articles 32-36 (on security, notification of a personal data breach to a supervisory authority, notification of a personal data breach to data subject, carrying out a data protection impact assessment and consultation with the supervisory authority) depending on the nature of the processing and on whether the processor has the necessary information to assist the controller (Article 28(3)(f)).

Finally, the contract must include the processor's obligation to make available to the controller all information necessary to demonstrate compliance with the obligations laid down in Article 28(3)(h) and to permit and contribute to audits, including inspections, conducted by the controller or another auditor mandated by the controller (Article 28(3)(h)). The processor should have processes in place to identify whether any of the instructions given by the controller infringe the Regulation or Union or Member State law and, if that happens, it should immediately inform the controller (Article 28(3)(h)). According to recital 83, the processor should also carry out a risk assessment to identify the risks inherent to the specific processing and put in place measures to mitigate such risks such as incorporating 'privacy by design' (depending on the state of the art and the cost of the implementation). Adhering to approved codes of conduct (Article 40 GDPR)

---

[23] For processors in the electronic communications sectors, see also the commentary on Art. 95 in this volume.

or approved certification mechanisms (Article 42 GDPR) may demonstrate compliance with obligations under Article 28(1)–(4) and obligations under Article 32.

As processors must demonstrate their own compliance first in order to assist controllers in demonstrating theirs, it may be that the contract between them will also need to include additional provisions determining responsibilities and liabilities. Indeed, recital 109 encourages controllers and processors to provide additional data protection safeguards in their contractual agreements. For example, processors must make available to controllers all information necessary to demonstrate compliance with Article 28 (Article 28(3)(h)) and they also have an obligation to maintain records of their processing activities under Article 30(2). Maintaining records of processing could facilitate processors' obligation to demonstrate compliance for themselves and for controllers and contribute to required audits. There is an exemption from the records-keeping obligation for processors with fewer than 250 employees but the scope is very limited as it is only available to processors who carry out processing that is only occasional, low risk and does not involve special categories of personal data or criminal convictions and offences (Article 30(5)). Moreover, regardless of whether or not the exemption is available in theory, controllers may in practice still insist that processors accept a contractual obligation to keep appropriate records and make them available to the controller.

4. Relationship between non-EU controllers and EU processors

In the context of its guidance on the territorial scope of Article 3 GDPR, the EDPB deals with a more complicated situation, where a non-EU controller who is not subject to the GDPR under Article 3 engages an EU processor.[24] If this processor is processing in the context of an establishment in the Union, the processor will be subject to the GDPR.

As the non-EU controller is not subject to the GDPR, it is not subject to any of the obligations addressed to controllers under the Regulation. As a result, one would think that this non-EU controller is not required to have a GDPR-mandated contract with its processor nor give its processor GDPR-mandated instructions. Also, the EDPB confirms that this non-EU controller does not become subject to the GDPR simply because it uses an EU processor.[25]

From the perspective of the EU processor, however, the situation is more complex. Clearly the EU processor must fulfil all the GDPR obligations addressed directly to processors, such as the obligation to implement appropriate technical and organisational security measures (Article 32) and the obligation to keep records of processing activities (Article 30). However, the EDPB goes on to suggest that such an EU processor is also required to comply with Article 28(2)–(5).[26] This would mean that the EU processor must have a contract with its non-EU controller which stipulates, among all the other conditions of Article 28, the non-EU controller's instructions to the processor on how to process personal data, including in relation to international transfers of data, and that the EU processor must notify the non-EU controller without undue delay after becoming aware of a personal data breach according to Article 33 GDPR.

In the first place, the required contract under Article 28 must be binding on the processor 'with regard to the controller', which implies that the obligation to put this contract in place rests primarily with the controller. Even though, in practice, major

[24] EDPB 2018, p. 10. [25] Ibid. [26] Ibid., p. 11.

processors (such as global cloud service providers) have drafted such contracts themselves, in the form of Data Processing Agreements that reflect (or sometimes even replicate) the wording of Article 28[27] and essentially pre-determine the controllers' instructions, it could be argued that this is an obligation that rests primarily with the controller, which must provide the relevant instructions. In addition, the contract must set out, among other things, the rights and obligations of the controller under the GDPR, which, in this scenario, do not exist. As the non-EU controller is not subject to GDPR obligations, the EDPB proposal implies that it is the EU processor who must draft the contract and impose it on the non-EU controller who, in order to be able to use that specific processor, must comply with GDPR-related obligations, even if not subject to them. From a policy perspective, it is perhaps not surprising that the EDPB would want the non-EU controller to be subject to the GDPR, but it is contradictory to the letter of the GDPR as well as the Board's view that the non-EU controller does not become subject to the GDPR simply because it uses an EU processor.

Secondly, in case of a personal data breach, it is the controller who has an obligation to notify the competent supervisory authority within 72 hours, while the processor *only* has an obligation to notify the controller (Article 33(1) and (2)). Consequently, in a case where the EU processor notifies the non-EU controller who is not subject to the GDPR, that non-EU controller has no obligation to notify the competent supervisory authority as the non-EU controller has no GDPR obligations. In that case, it is not clear whether or how a personal data breach should be notified to the supervisory authority or, indeed, be communicated to the data subjects if it is likely to result in a high risk for the rights and freedoms of natural persons (as, under Article 34, the obligation to communicate a data breach to data subjects is also the controller's obligation). The EDPB does not provide a suggestion on how to resolve this legal gap, which may result in personal data breaches going unreported. In some cases, the relevant obligations may be imposed contractually, for example, where an EU processor and a non-EU controller implement the Standard Contractual clauses as a basis for international transfers of personal data.

5. Change in status from processor to controller

If a processor infringes the controller's instructions and itself determines the means and purposes of processing, then the processor will become a controller (or joint controller) in its own right. In the context of cloud computing, the WP29 argued that cloud service providers are processors unless they go beyond a controller's instructions to process personal data for their own purposes and, thus, assume the role of the controller.[28] However, it has also been stated that both the notion of the controller 'giving instructions' and the blanket interpretation that all cloud providers are at least processors are problematic in the cloud context.[29] Unlike a traditional outsourcing arrangement, where a cloud client as a controller is itself undertaking a processing activity using resources provided passively by a cloud provider, there may be no 'instructions' to be given.[30] Also, where infrastructure cloud providers merely provide IT resources, do not persistently store data, do not even know the nature of the data they store and have no practical ability to access such data in an intelligible form, it has been argued that they should not even be considered

---

[27] Kamarinou, Millard and Oldani 2018, p. 4.   [28] WP29 2012B, p. 4.
[29] Hon, Millard and Walden 2013, pp. 198 and 208.
[30] Ibid., pp. 198–201 for a discussion on what the term 'instructions' may refer to in cloud computing.

'processors', unless they access personal data for their own purposes.[31] This view, however, is not supported by DPAs, which consider that the cloud provider is at least a 'data processor'.[32]

6. Enforcement

Infringements of the obligations deriving from Article 28 can lead to the imposition on the controller or processor of administrative fines of up to € 10 million or, in the case of an undertaking, 2 per cent of the worldwide total annual turnover of the preceding financial year, whichever is higher (Article 83(4) GDPR). Moreover, infringements of the obligations deriving from Articles 44–49 on transfers of personal data outside the EEA or non-compliance with an order by a supervisory authority could incur higher administrative fines of up to € 20 million or 4 per cent of the worldwide annual turnover (Article 83(5)(c) GDPR).

Select Bibliography

EU legislation

GDPR Proposal: Proposal for a Regulation of the European Parliament and of the Council on the protection of individuals with regard to the processing of personal data and on the free movement of such data (General Data Protection Regulation), COM(2012) 11 final, 25 January 2012.

National legislation

Belgian Data Protection Law 1992: Wet tot bescherming van de persoonlijke levenssfeer ten opzichte van de verwerking van persoonsgegevens, van 8 december 1992; Loi relative à la protection de la vie privée à l'égard des traitements de données à caractère personnel, du 8 decembre 1992) (repealed).

German Federal Data Protection Act 2009: Bundesdatenschutzgesetz (BDSG) vom 20. Dezember 1990 (BGBl. I S. 2954), neugefasst durch Bekanntmachung vom 14. Januar 2003 (BGBl. I S. 66), zuletzt geändert durch Gesetz vom 29.07.2009 (BGBl. I, S. 2254), durch Artikel 5 des Gesetzes vom 29.07.2009 (BGBl. I, S. 2355 [2384] und durch Gesetz vom 14.08.2009 (BGBl. I, S. 2814), BGBl 2009 Teil I Nr. 54 (repealed).

Academic writings

Hon, Millard and Walden 2013: Hon, Millard and Walden, 'Who Is Responsible for Personal Data in Clouds?' in Millard (ed.), *Cloud Computing Law* (OUP 2013), 193.

Kamarinou, Millard and Oldani 2018: Kamarinou, Millard and Oldani, 'Compliance as a Service', 287 *Queen Mary School of Law Legal Studies Research Paper* (2018).

Terstegge 2010: Terstegge, 'Article 17' in Büllesbach, Poullet and Prins (eds.), *Concise European IT Law* (2nd edn, Kluwer Law International 2010), 86.

Papers of data protection authorities

EDPB 2018: European Data Protection Board, 'Guidelines 3/2018 on the Territorial Scope of the GDPR (Article 3)—Version for Public Consultation' (16 November 2018).

EDPB 2019: European Data Protection Board, 'Opinion 14/2019 on the draft Standard Contractual Clauses submitted by the DK SA (Article 28(8) GDPR)' (9 July 2019).

---

[31] Ibid., pp. 208–215.   [32] WP29 2012B; ICO 2012, p. 7.

WP29 2010A: Article 29 Data Protection Working Party, 'Opinion 1/2010 on the Concepts of "Controller" and "Processor"' (WP 169, 16 February 2010).

WP29 2010B: Article 29 Data Protection Working Party, 'FAQs in Order to Address Some Issues Raised by the Entry into Force of the EU Commission Decision 2010/87/EU of 5 February 2010 on Standard Contractual Clauses for the Transfer of Personal Data to Processors Established in Third Countries under Directive 95/46/EC' (WP176, 12 July 2010).

WP29 2012A: Article 29 Data Protection Working Party, 'Working Document 02/2012 Setting Up a Table with the Elements and Principles to Be Found in Processor Binding Corporate Rules' (WP195, 6 June 2012).

WP29 2012B: Article 29 Data Protection Working Party, 'Opinion 05/2012 on Cloud Computing' (WP 196, 1 July 2012).

ICO 2012: Information Commissioner's Office, 'Guidance on the Use of Cloud Computing' (2 October 2012).

Information Commissioner's Office, 'Data Controllers and Data Processors: What the Difference Is and What the Governance Implications Are' (6 May 2014).

Reports and recommendations

European Committee for Standardization 2005: European Committee for Standardization, 'Standard Form Contract to Assist Compliance with Obligations Imposed by Article 17 of the Data Protection Directive 95/46/EC (and Implementation Guide)' (CWA 15292, May 2005), available at https://ico.org.uk/media/for-organisations/documents/2014483/cwa15292-00-2005-may.pdf.

Article 29. Processing under the authority of the controller or processor

CHRISTOPHER MILLARD DIMITRA KAMARINOU

The processor and any person acting under the authority of the controller or of the processor, who has access to personal data, shall not process those data except on instructions from the controller, unless required to do so by Union or Member State law.

Relevant Recital

(81) To ensure compliance with the requirements of this Regulation in respect of the processing to be carried out by the processor on behalf of the controller, when entrusting a processor with processing activities, the controller should use only processors providing sufficient guarantees, in particular in terms of expert knowledge, reliability and resources, to implement technical and organisational measures which will meet the requirements of this Regulation, including for the security of processing. The adherence of the processor to an approved code of conduct or an approved certification mechanism may be used as an element to demonstrate compliance with the obligations of the controller. The carrying-out of processing by a processor should be governed by a contract or other legal act under Union or Member State law, binding the processor to the controller, setting out the subject-matter and duration of the processing, the nature and purposes of the processing, the type of personal data and categories of data subjects, taking into account the specific tasks and responsibilities of the processor in the context of the processing to be carried out and the risk to the rights and freedoms of the data subject. The controller and processor may choose to use an individual contract or standard contractual clauses which are adopted either directly by the Commission or by a supervisory authority in accordance with the consistency mechanism and then adopted by the Commission. After the completion of the processing on behalf of the controller, the processor should, at the choice of the controller, return or delete the personal data, unless there is a requirement to store the personal data under Union or Member State law to which the processor is subject.

Closely Related Provisions

Article 28 (Processor) (see also recital 81 in its entirety)

Related Provisions in LED [Directive (EU) 2016/680]

Article 23 (Processing under the authority of the controller or processor) (see also recital 55)

Related Provisions in EPD [Directive 2002/58/EC]

Article 6(5) (Traffic data) (see also recital 32); Article 9(3) (Location data other than traffic data)

Relevant Case Law

CJEU

Case C-119/12, *Josef Probst v mr. nexnet GmbH*, judgment of 22 November 2012 (ECLI:EU:C:2012:748).

A. Rationale and Policy Underpinnings

The basic purpose of Article 29 GDPR is, first, to reinforce a processor's obligation to act solely in conformity with a controller's instructions. Secondly, it is to clarify that this obligation—including a duty of confidentiality—extends to persons acting under the authority of the processor or controller who are able to access personal data managed by the processor or controller.

B. Legal Background

1. EU legislation

The antecedent to Article 29 is to be found in Article 16 DPD, which, under the heading 'confidentiality of processing', stipulated: 'Any person acting under the authority of the controller or of the processor, including the processor himself, who has access to personal data must not process them except on instructions from the controller, unless he is required to do so by law'. Article 16 recognised that the people actually carrying out the processing of personal data are likely to be employees or contractors of the controller or processor and required the controller to issue proper instructions to these people on how to process the data.[1] Anyone processing personal data under the authority of the controller or the processor was accordingly required to keep the data confidential and secure unless data disclosure was explicitly authorised by the controller or required under law. In this context, it was argued that the authority of the controller may be established in various contractual agreements between the controller, the processor and its employees or contractors, or it may be derived from the circumstances.[2]

Article 6(5) EPD on 'traffic data' and Article 9(3) EPD on 'location data other than traffic data' restrict the processing of such data to persons 'acting under the authority of the provider of the public communications network or publicly available communications service'. As elaborated below, the CJEU has interpreted the phrase 'under the authority' to mean acting 'exclusively under the instructions and the control of that provider'.[3]

2. International instruments

In the context of 'mutual assistance' between data protection authorities, Convention 108 as first adopted provides for 'safeguards concerning assistance rendered by designated authorities' to include obligations on persons belonging to or acting on behalf of these authorities to be bound by secrecy and confidentiality in regards to the information processed (Article 15(2)). This requirement is replicated, with somewhat different wording, in Article 15(8) of the Modernised Convention 108. Although the requirement deals with confidentiality obligations imposed on employees or other agents of *regulators*, it

---

[1] See further Terstegge 2010, p. 85. [2] Ibid. [3] Case C-119/12, *Josef Probst*, para. 30.

nevertheless set a precedent for the approach taken in Article 29 GDPR (and Article 16 DPD).

3. National developments

Member States have long had provisions that transpose Article 16 DPD into their national law and are thus in line with the thrust of Article 29 GDPR.[4]

4. Case law

In the *Josef Probst* case, the CJEU interpreted Article 6(5) EPD which provides, inter alia, that processing of electronic communications traffic data must be restricted to persons 'acting under the authority' of providers of publicly available electronic communications services. An issue in the case was what this restriction means for the relationship between an internet service provider ('ISP') and the assignee of claims for payment for the ISP's provision of its services. The Court concluded that 'under the authority' means 'act(ing) exclusively on the instructions and under the control of that provider'.[5] The Court added that the contract between the provider and the assignee must contain provisions to ensure that the assignee guarantees the lawful processing of data and that the provider can check that the assignee is complying with those provisions.[6] This interpretation of the relationship between the provider and the assignee seems to reflect the relationship between a controller and a processor, whereby the processor should only act under the instructions of the controller and must commit contractually to make available all the necessary information to enable the controller to check that the processor complies with its data protection obligations.

C. Analysis

Article 29 GDPR obliges the processor and any person acting under the authority of the controller or the processor, who has access to personal data, to refrain from processing that data except on instructions from the controller, unless EU or Member State law requires otherwise. As indicated earlier, the provision reflects its antecedent in Article 16 DPD.

However, the provisions of Article 28(3)(b)[7] already go a long way to fulfilling the objective of Article 29. Article 28(3)(b) states that the processor shall ensure 'that persons authorised to process the personal data have committed themselves to confidentiality or are under an appropriate statutory obligation of confidentiality'.[8] Arguably, this makes Article 29 somewhat redundant. Indeed, several Member States (Spain, France, Slovenia and the UK) stated during the legislative process that it was difficult to discern the added value of Article 29 (at the time Article 27) as compared to Article 28(3)(b) (then Article 26(2)(b)). They suggested that a controller will always be liable for data protection violations carried out by its employees so there was no added value in having a separate article on this matter. They further suggested that the confidentiality provision could be covered

---

[4] See e.g. Art. 10 Greek Data Protection Law, Art. 35 French Data Protection Act 1978, and Art. 13 Icelandic Data Protection Act.
[5] Case C-119/12, *Josef Probst*, para. 30.   [6] Ibid.
[7] See the commentary on Art. 28 in this volume.   [8] Council Report 2014, p. 133 fn. 243.

by then Article 30 concerning security of processing. In the Council's Preparation for a general approach document in June 2015, the Council suggested deleting then Article 27. However, in November 2015, the Council, European Parliament and Commission agreed to reinstate then Article 27 with the same wording as in the Commission's original proposal from 2012.[9] It is assumed that the provision survived the trilogue deliberations in order to make clear that confidentiality and security obligations extend to the employees, contractors and agents processing personal data on behalf of the controller or processor. It could also be assumed that Article 29 exists to reiterate that, despite the processor's increased responsibilities under the GDPR, it is ultimately the controller's instructions which should be followed at every stage of the processing.

As the processor or any person acting under the authority of the controller or processor may process personal data without, or indeed contrary to, the controller's instructions when required to do so by Union or Member State law, it may be that Article 29 was included in the Regulation to clarify that such an exemption extends to *any* person processing personal data and not only to a controller or processor. Therefore, this could mean that if Union or Member State law to which a person is subject requires them to disclose personal data to a law enforcement authority, they would be permitted to do so, even if that disclosure was contrary to the controller's instructions.

Select Bibliography

National legislation

French Data Protection Act 1978: Act No. 78-17 of 6 January 1978 on Data Processing, Files and Individual Liberties (Loi n° 78-17 du 6 janvier 1978 relative à l'informatique, aux fichiers et aux libertés), as last amended by Law No. 2014-334 of 17 March 2014.
Greek Data Protection Law: Law 2472/1997 on the Protection of Individuals with regard to the Processing of Personal Data (as amended).
Icelandic Data Protection Act: The Data Protection Act on the Protection of Privacy as regards the Processing of Personal Data, No. 77/2000 (repealed).

Academic writings

Terstegge 2010: Terstegge, 'Article 16', in Büllesbach, Poullet and Prins (eds.), *Concise European IT Law* (2nd edn, Kluwer Law International 2010).

Reports and recommendations

Council Report 2014: Proposal for a regulation of the European Parliament and of the Council on the protection of individuals with regard to the processing of personal data and on the free movement of such data (General Data Protection Regulation), 11028/14, 30 June 2014.
Council Report 2015: Proposal for a Regulation of the European Parliament and of the Council on the protection of individuals with regard to the processing of personal data and on the free movement of such data (General Data Protection Regulation)—Chapter IV—Presidency debriefing on the outcome of the trilogue on 11/12 November and preparation for trilogue, 13885/15, 13 November 2015.

---

[9] Council Report 2015, p. 70.

Article 30. Records of processing activities

WALTRAUT KOTSCHY

1. Each controller and, where applicable, the controller's representative, shall maintain a record of processing activities under its responsibility. That record shall contain all of the following information:
   (a) the name and contact details of the controller and, where applicable, the joint controller, the controller's representative and the data protection officer;
   (b) the purposes of the processing;
   (c) a description of the categories of data subjects and of the categories of personal data;
   (d) the categories of recipients to whom the personal data have been or will be disclosed including recipients in third countries or international organisations;
   (e) where applicable, transfers of personal data to a third country or an international organisation, including the identification of that third country or international organisation and, in the case of transfers referred to in the second subparagraph of Article 49(1), the documentation of suitable safeguards;
   (f) where possible, the envisaged time limits for erasure of the different categories of data;
   (g) where possible, a general description of the technical and organisational security measures referred to in Article 32(1).
2. Each processor and, where applicable, the processor's representative shall maintain a record of all categories of processing activities carried out on behalf of a controller, containing:
   (a) the name and contact details of the processor or processors and of each controller on behalf of which the processor is acting, and, where applicable, of the controller's or the processor's representative, and the data protection officer;
   (b) the categories of processing carried out on behalf of each controller;
   (c) where applicable, transfers of personal data to a third country or an international organisation, including the identification of that third country or international organisation and, in the case of transfers referred to in the second subparagraph of Article 49(1), the documentation of suitable safeguards;
   (d) where possible, a general description of the technical and organisational security measures referred to in Article 32(1).
3. The records referred to in paragraphs 1 and 2 shall be in writing, including in electronic form.
4. The controller or the processor and, where applicable, the controller's or the processor's representative, shall make the record available to the supervisory authority on request.
5. The obligations referred to in paragraphs 1 and 2 shall not apply to an enterprise or an organisation employing fewer than 250 persons unless the processing it carries out is likely to result in a risk to the rights and freedoms of data subjects, the processing is not occasional, or the processing includes special categories of data as referred to in Article 9(1) or personal data relating to criminal convictions and offences referred to in Article 10.

Relevant Recitals

(82) In order to demonstrate compliance with this Regulation, the controller or processor should maintain records of processing activities under its responsibility. Each controller and processor

should be obliged to cooperate with the supervisory authority and make those records, on request, available to it, so that it might serve for monitoring those processing operations.

(89) Directive 95/46/EC provided for a general obligation to notify the processing of personal data to the supervisory authorities. While that obligation produces administrative and financial burdens, it did not in all cases contribute to improving the protection of personal data. Such indiscriminate general notification obligations should therefore be abolished, and replaced by effective procedures and mechanisms which focus instead on those types of processing operations which are likely to result in a high risk to the rights and freedoms of natural persons by virtue of their nature, scope, context and purposes. Such types of processing operations may be those which in, particular, involve using new technologies, or are of a new kind and where no data protection impact assessment has been carried out before by the controller, or where they become necessary in the light of the time that has elapsed since the initial processing.

Closely Related Provisions

Article 13 (Information to be provided where personal data are collected from the data subject); Article 14 (Information to be provided where personal data have not been obtained from the data subject); Article 15 (Right of access by the data subject); Article 24 (Responsibility of the controller); Article 32 (Security of processing); Article 35 (Data protection impact assessment); Article 37 (Designation of a data protection officer); Article 49 (Derogations for specific situations concerning transborder data flows); Article 83 (General conditions for imposing administrative fines)

Related Provisions in LED [Directive (EU) 2016/680]

Article 19 (Obligations of the controller); Article 24 (Records of processing activities); Article 25 (Logging); Article 29 (Security of processing); Article 32 (Designation of the data protection officer)

Related Provisions in EUDPR [Regulation (EU) 2018/1725]

Article 31 (Records of processing activities) (see also recital 52); Article 15 (Information to be provided where personal data are collected from the data subject); Article 16 (Information to be provided where personal data have not been obtained from the data subject); Article 17 (Right of access by the data subject); Article 26 (Responsibility of the controller); Article 33 (Security of processing); Article 39 (Data protection impact assessment); Article 43 (Designation of a data protection officer); Article 50 (Derogations for specific situations concerning transborder data flows); Article 66 (Administrative fines)

A. Rationale and Policy Underpinnings

Article 30 GDPR stipulates a duty for controllers as well as for processors to maintain records on their processing operations. Generally exempted from this duty are controllers and processors in small or medium-sized enterprises (SMEs) having up to 250 employees,[1] provided that their processing is only occasional and not specifically

---

[1] According to a Commission recommendation, a staff headcount of up to 250 staff along with an annual turnover not exceeding € 50 million and/or an annual balance sheet total not exceeding € 43 million, characterises an enterprise as belonging to the category of 'micro, small and medium-sized enterprises (SMEs)': see Annex to EC Recommendation 2003, Art. 2.

risky. The records must be kept available for checking by the supervisory authority. Infringements of the duty to keep correct and comprehensive records is punishable under Article 83(4)(a) GDPR.

The duty of controllers (and processors) to keep records on processing operations is one of the means to reinforce accountability.[2] Controllers (and also processors) must be able to demonstrate compliance with their obligations under the GDPR.[3] Knowing which data are processed about what kind of data subjects and for what purpose is a prerequisite for being able to be held accountable. Even when the exemption from the duty to document under Article 30(5) applies, the controller must nevertheless be able to give account to the data protection authority about the categories of data and data subjects and the purpose of its processing operations.

However, unlike the regime created by the DPD, there is no longer an obligation to notify the data protection authority in advance about the processing operations to be performed. Under the GDPR, records concerning a controller's/processor's processing operations must be made available to the supervisory authority only upon request. Transparency of processing by notification that the DPA keeps in a public register is no longer provided for in the GDPR. Taking leave of such public registration was evidently deemed justified as automated processing of personal data is no longer the exception but the rule. On the other hand, it cannot be denied that publicity of processing operations is in itself a potentially potent safeguard against infringements of the rights of data subjects—a safeguard that now has been lost.

The formal duty of processors to document their processing operations is new compared to the DPD. It goes hand in hand with the fact that the role of processors in assisting the controller to comply with its obligations under the accountability principle is better defined and more prominent in the GDPR than before.[4] This may justify this new special duty of processors to keep records on processing operations performed on behalf of controllers.

B. Legal Background

1. EU legislation

Article 19 DPD contained a whole section on 'notification' which included maintaining a publicly accessible register of notifications by the supervisory authorities. Controllers were obliged to provide the data protection authority with a documentation of the processing operations performed by or on behalf of them. The minimum content of the documentation under Article 19 DPD is equivalent to what is now prescribed as standard in Article 30(1).

Exemptions from the duty to notify could be foreseen in the national implementation of the DPD for low risk categories of processing operations and/or, generally, if the controller appointed a data protection officer with the task of keeping records on data processing operations available for inspection by the data protection authority and for informing the public.[5]

---

[2] This concept is specifically referenced in Art. 5(2) GDPR. For further elaboration of the accountability concept, see the commentary on Art. 24 GDPR in this volume.
[3] See Art. 24 GDPR for controllers and Art. 32 GDPR for processors.
[4] See e.g. Art. 28(3)(e) and (f) GDPR.   [5] Art. 21(1) DPD.

For processing operations with high risks, a 'prior checking' procedure was foreseen, which meant that before starting a high-risk processing operation the data protection authority had to be consulted. The definition of high-risk processing operations was left to national implementation, which resulted in considerable divergences.

The notifications had to be entered into the register of processing operations kept by the data protection authority, if the notified processing operations were found to be compliant. This register had to be publicly available in order to provide everybody with the opportunity to gain information on the kind of processing operations performed by a controller.

2. International instruments

The original version of Convention 108 does not discuss documentation of processing operations. There is, however, apart from the right to access dealt with in Article 8(b), an 'additional safeguard' foreseen in Article 8(a), which results in a duty for the national legislator to provide 'any person' with the opportunity 'to establish the existence of an automated personal data file, its main purposes, as well as the identity and habitual residence or principal place of business of the controller of the file'. This duty seems to be best fulfilled by having a public register where controllers have their processing operations recorded.[6] In the modernised version of the Convention, this duty is no longer foreseen.

3. National developments

The provisions in the DPD on notification were fairly general, leaving the regulation of the details of the notification system to the Member States. Some Member States developed comprehensive systems, even with detailed description of those categories of processing operations which were exempt from the obligation to notify the supervisory authority.[7]

Under the GDPR, further enhancement of Article 30 by Member State legislation is no longer foreseen, and further specification of details will now be the task of the supervisory authorities.

C. Analysis

The notification system under the DPD has been replaced by a duty for controllers and processors to have records (in writing)[8] on their processing operations available for inspection by the supervisory authority. If a controller or processor is not established in the

---

[6] The Explanatory Report to Convention 108 gives, however, more leeway to the national legislator. Concerning 'knowledge about the existence of an automated data file', the Memorandum explains that the variety of rules of domestic law giving effect to this principle must be taken into account. 'There are States where the name of the controller of the file is listed in a public index. In other States which have no such publicity rule, the law will provide that the name of the controller of the file must be communicated to a person at his request'. Evidently, the states having ratified Convention 108 may choose how to establish the necessary amount of transparency of processing vis-à-vis the public. See Explanatory Report to Convention 108 1981, para. 51.

[7] E.g. such a system was provided in Austria for categories of processing operations resulting from legal duties of the controller. See Austrian Regulation on Standards and Templates 2004.

[8] Under Art. 30(3) GDPR, 'in writing' includes electronic form.

Union,[9] but is subject to the GDPR under Article 3(2), its representative in the Union must have these records available.

1. Information to be recorded by controllers and their representatives

A controller's records, and that of its representatives, must contain the kind of general information which is the basis for assessing lawful processing,[10] namely:

1. The *controller* or controllers (in case of joint controllership) must be identified in the records by name and contact details; this is true also for the controller's *representative*, where applicable, and also for existing *data protection officer(s)* (Article 30(1)(a)).
2. The essential features of the processing activity must be described, that is its *purpose*, the *categories of data subjects* and the *categories of data processed*; where possible, also the 'envisaged *time limits for erasure* of the different categories of data'; and 'a general description of the *technical and organisational security measures* referred to in Article 32(1)' (Article 30(1)(b), (c), (f) and (g)).

Naming the legal basis (in the sense of Article 6) which the controller claims to have for its processing activities is not mandatory. Such an obligation was also not mentioned in Article 19 DPD, but experience in the meantime suggests that clarity on this topic is essential. The omission of a mandatory reference to the legal basis of processing in Article 30(1) also runs counter to the principle of accountability. Article 24 GDPR states that every controller must 'be able to demonstrate that processing is performed in accordance with this Regulation', which means that the controller must have a firm and reasoned notion about the legal basis of processing before it starts any operation, and this notion should be verifiable by means of its records.[11] Thus, in order for the keeping of records to be meaningful, it will be necessary for the controller to be able to demonstrate on which legal basis it relies in its processing.

In case of disclosure, 'the categories of recipients' must be named (Article 30(1)(d). 'Disclosure' is not defined in the GDPR.[12] The term is used here to denote the transmission of data to 'a recipient'. A 'recipient' is any 'natural or legal person, public authority, agency or another body to which personal data are disclosed'.[13] 'Disclosure' must therefore be understood in a very broad sense: recipients are not only other controllers, but also processors or even employees of the controller or of a processor.

Consequently, the records will have to contain information not only concerning transmissions of data to other controllers, but also to processors. As individuals *inside the organisation* of the controller (or even of the processor) are actually also 'recipients', the question arises to what extent such data flows within the organisation of the

---

[9] This also applies to Iceland, Liechtenstein and Norway, which are the Member States of the European Economic Area ('EEA') and which must have the same data protection law as the EU Member States do.

[10] The items which have to be dealt with in the records are the same as are mentioned in Art. 19 DPD. However, under the Directive, this was the minimum standard which could be extended by Member State legislation.

[11] A statement on the legal basis is also required in the context of the information which has to be given to data subjects according to Arts. 13 or 14 GDPR.

[12] The word 'disclosure' is used repeatedly in the definitions contained in Art. 4 GDPR, e.g. as an example for 'processing data', but is not defined itself.

[13] See further the commentary on Art. 4(9) GDPR in this volume.

controller—or of a processor—must be reflected in the documentation. The purpose of maintaining documentation suggests that a very general outline of these internal data flows should be sufficient as far as such data flows are fully covered by the initial purpose named at the time of collecting the data. However, when internal data flows amount to further processing in the sense of Article 5(1)(b) GDPR, mentioning such cases seems mandatory, as the question arises as to how far further processing is legally admissible in a concrete case.

Article 30(1)(d) GDPR requires the keeping of records 'on the *categories* of recipients' of data. This evidently does not oblige the controller to name the recipients in an identified form; it is sufficient to denominate the recipients as 'customers', 'suppliers', 'processors', 'employees' etc. However, comparison of Article 30 with Articles 13–15 GDPR suggests that some additional documentation might be required on identified 'recipients', as the said articles require naming '*recipients or* categories of recipients', although without defining criteria for the one or the other procedure. In some cases, 'recipients' will be named because there is only 'one of a category', as e.g. in groups of companies in case of data transfer to the holding (parent) company. In other cases, in the absence of explicit regulation, it seems justified to resort to the principles of the Regulation. Giving information according to Articles 13 and 14 and answering an access request according to Article 15 are both governed by the principle of fairness and transparency; therefore, where naming a 'category of recipients' would not create the necessary transparency, 'the recipient' will have to be named. This means, in the context of Article 30, that additional documentation about legally delicate cases of data disclosure should be kept by the controller, even if they are not part of the (formal) documentation according to Article 30.

Article 30(1)(d) further requires that disclosures have to be documented which 'have been or will be' carried out. Considering that only *categories* of recipients have to be named, disclosures will also only have to be dealt with on the level of categories. Therefore, the reference to what 'has been and or will be' disclosed does not refer to concrete cases of disclosure but to what was planned to happen in the past and is planned to happen in the future.

Whether disclosure really took place in concrete cases cannot be shown by means of the documentation required under Article 30. Exploring whether a specific disclosure actually happened needs a different kind of documentation. It would need logging protocols and would require organisational measures to extract the necessary information from these protocols. However, even if documentation according to Article 30 refers only to categories of disclosure, it will be necessary to check from time to time, by analysing concrete cases of disclosure, whether the actual data flows coincide with the controller's intentions.

A further item to be documented under Article 30(1) GDPR is transfer of data to 'a third country or an international organisation'. In such cases, the third country, or international organisation respectively, must be named in the records (Article 30(1)(e), but evidently not the identity of the recipient, as the text does not add anything to point d for cases of international data transfer.

If the nature of the purpose of data transfer does not allow for limiting the recipient countries, it will be necessary to mention 'all countries' as possible recipients, in which cases lawful data transfers will be limited to Article 49(1)(a)–(g) (since data transfers under these legal grounds are not limited to particular countries), unless data transfers could be based on existing binding corporate rules[14] which may also cover all countries of the world.

There is no obligation to name the means by which the controller intends to ensure an adequate level of protection on the part of the foreign recipient of the data. Additional information is needed only if a data transfer shall, exceptionally, be based on Article 49(1), second subparagraph, which pertains to occasional ('non-repetitive') transfers of data about a limited number of data subjects and for compelling legitimate interests.[15] In such cases, where the usual instruments for verifying or establishing adequate protection on the part of the foreign recipient are not required due to the exceptional character of the transfer, documentation is needed on how the controller avoids the special risks for the data subjects which are likely to arise in the course of transferring data to a recipient established outside the EU data protection regime.

Finally, the technical and organisational security measures foreseen by the controller for its processing operations should be described in general terms, 'where possible'.[16] Concerning the nature of the security measures which should exist at the controller or processor, reference is made to Article 32(1).

2. Information to be recorded by processors

Under Article 30(2) GDPR, processors must maintain records, which are, however, less detailed than those of controllers. This obligation did not exist under the DPD. The obligation refers to 'all categories of processing activities' which a processor carries out on behalf of a controller.

Foreign processors not established in the EU or in the EEA (see above) but rendering services to controllers in the EU/EEA, do not have an obligation to keep records pursuant to Article 30, unless they take part in processing operations which fall under Article 3(2) GDPR. In such cases, the foreign processor should name a representative in the Union, who acts as a contact point concerning the processor's duties under the GDPR. The documentation required by Article 30 on relevant processing operations must be available from the representative.

The mandatory content of the records to be kept by processors or their representatives pertains to the following information:

1. The name and contact details of the documenting processor and, where applicable, its representative; further, where applicable, the data protection officer of the processor.
2. The name and contact details of each controller on whose behalf the processor is acting and, where applicable, the controller's representative. In this regard, it is not entirely clear from the formulation of Article 30(2)(a) whether the data protection officer of the controller has to be included in the documentation.

---

[14] In accordance with Art. 47 GDPR.
[15] According to that provision, this legal basis to transfer data extends only to a transfer which is 'not repetitive, concerns only a limited number of data subjects, is necessary for the purposes of compelling legitimate interests pursued by the controller which are not overridden by the interests or rights and freedoms of the data subject, and the controller has assessed all the circumstances surrounding the data transfer and has on the basis of that assessment provided suitable safeguards with regard to the protection of personal data'.
[16] No criteria are cited for what would be accepted as 'impossible'. In WP29 2018A, p. 29, the WP29 stated as follows in a comparable case of exemption because of 'impossibility': 'Thus if a data controller seeks to rely on this exemption it must demonstrate the factors that actually *prevent it* from providing the information in question ...'

3. The name and contact details of other 'processors'.[17] Which kind of processors should be included is not explained: they could be involved either by having delegated processing tasks to the documenting processor or by being sub-processors of the documenting processor. In both cases there would have to exist a contract between the documenting processor and the other processor or processors, in which case their identity must be known and recorded anyway by the documenting processor, which is also the case with regard to the names of the representative (Article 27) and data protection officer (Article 37) both of which are also required under Article 30(2)(a).
4. The 'categories of processing' carried out 'on behalf of each controller'. Note that there is no reference to 'categories of processing' carried out on behalf of another processor having delegated some of the processing tasks to the documenting processor. The content and the degree of detail of a description of 'the categories of processing' by the processor are not discussed in Article 30(2). Distinctions of services offered by processors are often made along the lines of 'technical services' (such as web-hosting or cloud computing), 'application services' (such as financial accounting or personnel administration), 'security services' (such as anti-virus services) and other types of services. As long as the data protection authorities have not introduced other schemes for describing 'the categories of processing' performed by a processor, proceeding in the manner suggested above should be sufficient.
5. Transfers of data to third countries or international organisations. These will be either transfers which have been ordered by the controller and are facilitated by the processor on behalf of the controller, or transfers which the documenting processor initiates itself by employing sub-processors in third countries.[18] In this respect, the documentation should refer to the same topics and details as foreseen for controllers.
6. A general description of the technical and organisational security measures which are put in place by the processor. These can be determined based on Article 32(1) (dealing with the security of processing).

3. Derogations for SMEs

The duty to maintain records is, in principle, limited to controllers and processors that employ at least 250 persons. Article 30(5) provides, however, that there are situations where also smaller-sized controllers and processors must keep records of processing activities as mentioned in Article 30(1) and (2). These situations are where the processing carried out 'is likely to result in a risk to the rights and freedoms of data subjects, the processing is not occasional, or the processing includes special categories of data as referred to in Article 9(1) or personal data relating to criminal convictions and offences referred to in Article 10'. These three categories of processing are alternatives, so the occurrence of any one of them triggers the obligation to maintain records of processing.[19] Nonetheless, the threefold categorisation of processing employed in Article 30(5) is somewhat artificial and confusing as the processing of special categories of data or personal data relating to criminal convictions and offences under Articles 9 or 10 GDPR always results in a risk.

---

[17] Art. 30(2)(a) reads as follows: 'the name and contact details of the processor or processors and of each controller on behalf of which the processor is acting'.
[18] Lawful use of sub-processors must adhere to the specific requirements of Art. 28(4) GDPR.
[19] See also WP29 2018B, p. 2.

Further criteria for assessing 'a risk' will have to be taken from the supervisory authorities' deliberations on data protection impact assessment according to Article 35 GDPR. In a paper of the WP29 that was endorsed by the EDPB,[20] the regular processing of employee data by a small organisation was stated as an example of processing that cannot be regarded as 'occasional' under Article 30(5) GDPR.[21]

The WP29 has encouraged DPAs to support small enterprises 'by providing tools to facilitate the set up and management of records of processing activities'.[22] As an example, the WP29 mentioned a DPA making available on its website 'a simplified model that can be used by SMEs to keep records of processing activities not covered by the derogation in Article 30(5)'.[23]

Select Bibliography

EU legislation

EC Recommendation 2003: Commission Recommendation of 6 May 2003 concerning the definition of micro, small and medium-sized enterprises, OJ 2003 L 124/36.

National legislation

Austrian Regulation on Standards and Templates 2004: Standard- und Muster-Verordnung 2004, BGBl II Nr. 312/2004.

Papers of data protection authorities

EDPB 2018: European Data Protection Board, 'Endorsement 1/2018' (25 May 2018).
WP29 2018A: Article 29 Working Party, 'Guidelines on Transparency under Regulation 2016/269' (WP260rev.01, 11 April 2018).
WP29 2018B: Article 29 Working Party, 'Position Paper on the Derogations from the Obligation to Maintain Records of Processing Activities Pursuant to Article 30(5) GDPR' (19 April 2018).

Reports and recommendations

Explanatory Report to Convention 108 1981: Council of Europe, 'Explanatory Report to the Convention for the Protection of Individuals with Regard to Automatic Processing of Personal Data' (28 January 1981).

---

[20] EDPB 2018.   [21] WP29 2018B, p. 2.   [22] Ibid.   [23] Ibid.

Article 31. Cooperation with the supervisory authority

WALTRAUT KOTSCHY

The controller and the processor and, where applicable, their representatives, shall cooperate, on request, with the supervisory authority in the performance of its tasks.

Relevant Recital

(82) In order to demonstrate compliance with this Regulation, the controller or processor should maintain records of processing activities under its responsibility. Each controller and processor should be obliged to cooperate with the supervisory authority and make those records, on request, available to it, so that it might serve for monitoring those processing operations.

Closely Related Provisions

Article 57 (Tasks of the supervisory authorities) (see too recital 122); Article 58 (Powers of the supervisory authorities) (see also recital 129); Article 83 (General conditions for imposing fines) (see also recitals 148 and 150)

Related Provisions in LED [Directive (EU) 2016/680]

Article 26 (Cooperation with the supervisory authority) (see too recital 56); Article 46 (Tasks of the supervisory authorities) (see too recital 76); Article 47 (Powers of the supervisory authorities) (see too recital 82)

Related Provisions in EUDPR [Regulation (EU) 2018/1725]

Article 32 (obligation to cooperate) (see too recital 42); Article 59 (powers of the EDPS) (see too recital 62)

Relevant Case Law

CJEU

Case C-374/87, *Orkem v Commission of the European Communities*, judgment of 18 October 1989 (ECLI:EU:C:1989:387).

Case T-34/93, *Société Générale v Commission of the European Communities*, judgment of 8 March 1995 (ECLI:EU:T:1995:46).

Case T-112/98, *Mannesmannröhren-Werke AG v Commission of the European Communities*, CFI, judgment of 20 February 2001 (ECLI:EU:T:2001:61).

Joined Cases C-204/00 P, C-205/00 P, C-211/00 P, C-213/00 P, C-217/00 P and C-219/00 P, *Aalborg Portland A/S, Irish Cement Ltd, Ciments français SA, Italcementi - Fabbriche Riunite Cemento SpA, Buzzi Unicem SpA and Cementir - Cementerie del Tirreno SpA v Commission of the European Communities*, judgment of 7 January 2004 (ECLI:EU:C:2004:6).

Case C-301/04 P, *Commission of the European Communities v SGL Carbon AG*, judgment of 29 June 2006 (ECLI:EU:C:2006:432).

ECtHR

Engel and Others v Netherlands, Appl. Nos. 5100/71; 5101/71; 5102/71; 5354/72; 5370/72, judgment of 23 November 1976.

A. Rationale and Policy Underpinnings

The relationship between the supervisory authority on the one side and controller and processor on the other side is complex, as the authority has a wide range of competences ranging from guidance and advice, approving, monitoring and investigating, and finally to enforcing compliance with the GDPR.[1] Article 31 obliges controllers and processors to cooperate with all requests[2] from the authority, regardless of whether the context of such a request is advisory, investigative or enforcement.

Assessing compliance in matters of data protection is very often not a clear and easy task; especially where intricate processing activities are performed, involving the latest technological developments with societal effects which are not yet fully foreseen. A duty for controllers and processors to cooperate with the supervisory authority in order to facilitate assessment is therefore particularly necessary.

As to the legal consequences of this duty, Article 31 does not give any details. Some guidance may, however, be taken from the relevant provisions of the former Regulation 45/2001,[3] now replaced by the EUDPR, and from the case law of the CJEU dealing with the legal duty to cooperate with requests of a supervisory authority for information in the context of investigations of infringements of competition law.

B. Legal Background

1. EU legislation

An obligation for controllers/processors to cooperate with the supervisory authority was not explicitly mentioned in the DPD. However, Article 30 of Regulation 45/2001 on the obligation to cooperate provided:

At his or her request, controllers shall assist the European Data Protection Supervisor in the performance of his or her duties, in particular by providing the information referred to in Article 47(2)(a) and by granting access as provided in Article 47(2)(b).[4]

In addition, Article 47(2)(a) of that Regulation empowered the EDPS 'to obtain from a controller or Community institution or body access to all personal data and to all

---

[1] This accumulation of functions, especially those of an investigator and of a 'judge', is not entirely unproblematic when assessed in the light of Art. 6 European Convention on Human Rights ('ECHR') and its principles for a fair trial. However, as Art. 78 GDPR requires an effective judicial remedy against a decision of a supervisory authority, it may be argued that the system of supervision and remedies against fines in the GDPR is adequate when regarded in its entirety, provided that the court is entitled also to review the assessment of the facts underlying the decision of a supervisory authority.
[2] Disputes about the reasonableness of requests would have to be finally resolved according to Art. 78, which affords the right to an effective judicial remedy against a legally binding decision of a supervisory authority.
[3] See Table of Legislation.   [4] See Art. 32 EUDPR.

information necessary for his or her enquiries',[5] and Article 47(2)(b) empowered the EDPS 'to obtain access to any premises in which a controller ... carries on its activities'.[6]

2. International instruments

Convention 108 leaves all questions of enforcing the guarantees under this Convention to the legislation of the contracting parties.[7] The Modernised Convention 108 does not contain an obligation similar to that of Article 31 GDPR.

3. National developments

Under the DPD the adoption of the procedural rules necessary for exercising the tasks of supervisory authorities and for the role of the controllers or processors in these procedures was left to Member State legislation. The introduction by the GDPR of an explicit obligation on the side of controllers and processors to cooperate with the supervisory authority may therefore alter the legal situation in some of the Member States.

4. Case law

There is no case law on this point at present. However, the case law in the context of competition law lays down a comprehensive duty to cooperate, subject to the right not to incriminate oneself, as discussed below.

C. Analysis

1. Introduction

Article 31 establishes a legal obligation for controllers and processors, including their representatives, to cooperate with the supervisory authority when exercising its tasks. Such cooperation must be provided on request of the authority.

'Cooperation' is not defined in the GDPR, as concerns the means of fulfilling this obligation: it will have to be fulfilled as requested by the supervisory authority, which may include providing information, granting access to processing facilities and to documentation, and explaining processing operations. While recital 82 mentions 'cooperation' in the context of making the records of processing activities available, which are to be kept according to Article 30, neither the texts of the recital nor of Article 31 signify that 'cooperation' is limited to showing these records.

Violations of the obligation to cooperate are punishable under Article 83(4)(a) GDPR. Moreover, the degree of cooperation shown by the controller or processor vis-à-vis the supervisory authority in the context of mitigating the effects of an infringement is specifically mentioned in Article 83(2)(f) as a point to which the authority must have due regard when considering whether to impose an administrative fine and the amount of such a fine.

---

[5] See ibid., Art. 59(1)(d).   [6] See ibid., Art. 59(1)(e).
[7] Supervisory authorities were only introduced to the system of protection under Convention 108 in 2001, when an Additional Protocol to the Convention was adopted. There are no provisions on obligations of controllers/processors in relation to these authorities. For the Additional Protocol, see Table of Legislation.

2. Right against self-incrimination

A legal issue arises from the fact that, according to the right to a fair trial, enshrined in Article 6 ECHR, there is a right against self-incrimination.[8] Having to give information to the supervisory authority upon its request may have the effect of self-incrimination, as the result of answering such a request may be the imposition of a sanction pursuant to Article 83 GDPR.[9]

This legal issue is not fundamentally different from that which arises under EU competition law, where a duty to cooperate with a supervisory authority (here, the Commission) which may result in heavy fines has been in place for many years.[10] It is therefore interesting to consider the relevant jurisprudence of the CJEU in this regard.

In the context of competition law, the Court assumes that there is in principle a comprehensive duty to cooperate, based at present on Regulation 1/2003.[11] The right not to incriminate oneself is acknowledged by the CJEU's jurisprudence in so far as nobody may be forced to accuse himself or herself; however, documents, even with incriminating content, must be delivered,[12] and inquiries for mere facts must be answered.[13] In the leading case of *Orkem*,[14] the Court concluded, at paragraphs 34 and 35, that:

> [W]hile the Commission is entitled ... to compel an undertaking to provide all necessary information concerning such facts as may be known to it and to disclose to it, if necessary, such documents relating thereto as are in its possession, even if the latter may be used to establish against it or another undertaking, the existence of anti-competitive conduct, it may not, by means of a decision calling for information, undermine the rights of defence of the undertaking concerned.
>
> Thus, the Commission may not compel an undertaking to provide it with answers which might involve an admission on its part of the existence of an infringement which it is incumbent on the Commission to prove.[15]

This would result in the duty to answer, e.g. when and where a meeting of certain competitors had taken place, but not what was the purpose of the meeting.

Whether the Court will apply the same reasoning to the duty of cooperation under the GDPR remains to be seen, but seems likely.

Select Bibliography

EU legislation

Regulation 1/2003: Council Regulation (EC) No. 1/2003 of 16 December 2002 on the implementation of the rules on competition laid down in Articles 81 and 82 of the Treaty (Text with EEA relevance), OJ 2003 L 1/1.

---

[8] The case law of the CJEU has acknowledged that Art. 47 of the Charter of Fundamental Rights of the European Union ('CFR') also affords a right to fair trial, which includes a right not to have to incriminate oneself (*nemo tenetur se ipsum accusare*), e.g. in Case C-374/87, *Orkem*, paras. 32–35; Joined Cases C-204/00 P, C-205/00 P, C-211/00 P, C-213/00 P, C-217/00 P and C-219/00 P, *Aalborg and Others*, para. 65; and Case C-301/04 P, *SGL Carbon*, para. 42ff.

[9] Although fines under Art. 83 are administrative fines, Art. 6 ECHR seems relevant for Art. 31 GDPR as the ECtHR's 'Engel-criteria' (see ECtHR, *Engel*, paras. 82–83) apply, especially the criterion of 'severity of the penalty that the person concerned risks incurring'.

[10] See especially Regulation (EC) 1/2003.   [11] Ibid.

[12] Case C-301/04, *SGL Carbon*, paras. 44 and 48; Joined Cases C-204/00 P, C-205/00 P, C-211/00 P, C-213/00 P, C-217/00 P and C-219/00 P, *Aalborg and Others*, para. 61; Case C-374/1987, *Orkem*, para. 34.

[13] Case T-112/98, *Mannesmannröhren-Werke*, paras. 70 and 78, Case T-34/93, *Société Générale*, para. 75

[14] Case C-374/87, *Orkem*.   [15] Ibid., paras. 34–35.

Academic writings

Willis, 'The Privilege against Self-Incrimination in Competition Investigations—Speaker's Notes' (2006), available at https://www.law.ox.ac.uk/sites/files/oxlaw/cclp_l_01-06.pdf.

Reports and recommendations

ECtHR Guide 2018: European Court of Human Rights, 'Guide on Article 6 of the European Convention on Human Rights (Civil Limb)' (30 April 2018).

Section 2 Security of personal data

Article 32. Security of processing

CÉDRIC BURTON*

1. Taking into account the state of the art, the costs of implementation and the nature, scope, context and purposes of processing as well as the risk of varying likelihood and severity for the rights and freedoms of natural persons, the controller and the processor shall implement appropriate technical and organisational measures to ensure a level of security appropriate to the risk, including inter alia as appropriate:
   (a) the pseudonymisation and encryption of personal data;
   (b) the ability to ensure the ongoing confidentiality, integrity, availability and resilience of processing systems and services;
   (c) the ability to restore the availability and access to personal data in a timely manner in the event of a physical or technical incident;
   (d) a process for regularly testing, assessing and evaluating the effectiveness of technical and organisational measures for ensuring the security of the processing.
2. In assessing the appropriate level of security account shall be taken in particular of the risks that are presented by processing, in particular from accidental or unlawful destruction, loss, alteration, unauthorised disclosure of, or access to personal data transmitted, stored or otherwise processed.
3. Adherence to an approved code of conduct as referred to in Article 40 or an approved certification mechanism as referred to in Article 42 may be used as an element by which to demonstrate compliance with the requirements set out in paragraph 1 of this Article.
4. The controller and processor shall take steps to ensure that any natural person acting under the authority of the controller or the processor who has access to personal data does not process them except on instructions from the controller, unless he or she is required to do so by Union or Member State law.

Relevant Recital

(83) In order to maintain security and to prevent processing in infringement of this Regulation, the controller or processor should evaluate the risks inherent in the processing and implement measures to mitigate those risks, such as encryption. Those measures should ensure an appropriate level of security, including confidentiality, taking into account the state of the art and the costs of implementation in relation to the risks and the nature of the personal data to be protected. In assessing data security risk, consideration should be given to the risks that are presented by personal data processing, such as accidental or unlawful destruction, loss, alteration, unauthorised disclosure of, or access to, personal data transmitted, stored or otherwise processed which may in particular lead to physical, material or non-material damage.

Closely Related Provisions

Recitals 75–79; recital 88; Article 4(12) (Definition of a personal data breach); Article 28(1) (Choice of processor providing sufficient guarantees) (see too recital 81); Article 28(3)(c) (Processor must be contractually bound to implement security measures); Article 33 (Personal data breach notification

* The author is grateful for the research assistance of Rossana Fol and Bastiaan Suurmond.

requirement to the supervisory authority) (see too recitals 85 and 87); Article 34 (Communication of a personal data breach to the data subject) (see too recital 86)

Related Provisions in LED [Directive (EU) 2016/680]

Recital 57; recital 96; Article 3(11) (Definition of a personal data breach); Article 4(1)(f) (Principle of secure processing); Article 24(1)(i) (Records) (see too recital 56); Article 29 (Security of processing) (see too recitals 28 and 60); Article 30 (Notification of a breach to the supervisory authority) (see too recital 61); Article 31 (Communication of a breach to the data subject) (see too recital 62); Article 51(1)(d)(e) (Tasks of the Board)

Related Provisions in EPD [Directive 2002/58/EC]

Article 2(i) (Definition of a personal data breach); Article 4(1) (Security measures) (see too recital 20); Article 4(1a) (Details regarding security measures) (see too recital 21); Article 4(2) (Information to subscribers about a particular risk of a network security breach) (see too recital 20); Article 4(3) (Personal data breach notification to the competent national authority)

Relevant Case Law

CJEU

Case C-342/12, *Worten — Equipamentos para o Lar SA v Autoridade para as Condições de Trabalho (ACT)*, judgment of 30 May 2013 (ECLI:EU:C:2013:355).
Joined Cases C-293/12 and C-594/12, *Digital Rights Ireland Ltd v Minister for Communications, Marine and Natural Resources and Others* and *Kärntner Landesregierung and Others*, judgment of 8 April 2014 (Grand Chamber) (ECLI:EU:C:2014:238).

ECtHR

Z v Finland, Appl. No. 22009/93, judgment of 25 February 1997.
I v Finland, Appl. No. 20511/03, judgment of 17 July 2008.

A. Rationale and Policy Underpinnings

Data security has become increasingly important in today's data-driven society, just as data breaches have become increasingly common.[1] Indeed, it could be said that the issue is not *if* a data controller or data processor will suffer a data breach, but *when*. Data breaches can result in the accidental loss of entire databases or the disclosure of personal data to unauthorised parties, and thus pose substantial data protection risks. To prevent such breaches, the GDPR imposes a general security obligation on both data controllers and data processors. Recital 83 summarises the essence of this general obligation as follows: 'the controller or processor should evaluate the risks inherent in the processing and implement measures to mitigate those risks'.

Data security also underlies many of the obligations to which data controllers and data processors are subject under the GDPR. For example, compliance with the 'integrity and confidentiality' principle enshrined in Article 5(1)(f) or the accountability principle

---

[1] See ENISA Report, p. 1, stating that 'Cyber attacks are increasing in complexity and severity, with reported incidents growing at 41% p.a'.

directed at controllers under Article 5(2) cannot be ensured unless adequate security is provided for the data being processed. This is also demonstrated by Recital 83, which explains that security measures need to be implemented 'in order to maintain security and to prevent processing in infringement of this Regulation'. The Commission's impact assessment accompanying the proposal for the GDPR and the LED also notes that 'the reform leaves space to actors to implement appropriate measures to achieve the purpose of the instruments, e.g. by strengthening accountability and responsibility of data controllers and processors for assessing and mitigating data protection risks'.[2]

There is an obvious connection between Article 32, Article 33 (notification of a personal data breach to the supervisory authority) and Article 34 (communication of a personal data breach to the data subject) GDPR. As a practical matter, whether or not Article 32 has been complied with often becomes clear in the context of a potential data breach.[3] The definition of 'personal data breach' is contained in Article 4(12).[4]

B. Legal Background

1. EU legislation

Article 17 DPD was the equivalent to Article 32 GDPR. Article 17 DPD specified that 'the controller must implement appropriate technical and organizational measures to protect personal data against accidental or unlawful destruction or accidental loss, alteration, unauthorized disclosure or access, in particular where the processing involves the transmission of data over a network, and against all other unlawful forms of processing'. Recital 46 DPD also articulated the need to maintain an appropriate level of security by controllers in order to prevent any unauthorised processing and lists the criteria to be taken into account when identifying the most appropriate security measures. The major difference between the security provisions of the DPD and those of the GDPR is that, unlike the DPD, the GDPR also brings processors directly under the scope of data security obligations. In other words, Article 17 DPD applied directly to data controllers, and applied to data processors only indirectly by providing in Article 17(3) that the use of data processors had to be governed by a contract between the controller and the processor and requiring the security obligations of Article 17(1) to apply to the processor as well.[5] By contrast, Article 32(1) GDPR applies explicitly to both controllers and processors.

With respect to electronic communications, Article 4(1) EPD imposes security requirements similar to the DPD, but it is limited to providers of publicly available electronic communications services. Recital 20 EPD also reflects the obligation of service providers to safeguard the security of their services. The Commission's Proposal for an e-Privacy Regulation issued in January 2017[6] does not contain a security provision, but refers to the level of security required in Article 32 GDPR in order to avoid a potential overlap between the two instruments,[7] since the e-Privacy Regulation will act as a *lex specialis* to the

---

[2] EC Staff Working Paper 2012, p. 39.

[3] See WP29 2018, p. 10, stating that 'the failure to notify a breach could reveal either an absence of existing security measures or an inadequacy of the existing security measures'. On 25 May 2018 the EDPB adopted Endorsement 1/2018, in which it endorsed the WP29 paper on data breaches (inter alia), see EDPB 2018.

[4] See the commentary on Art. 4(12) in this volume.

[5] However, some national laws implementing the DPD already imposed security obligations directly on processors even before the GDPR. See e.g. Art. 16(4) Belgian Data Protection Law 1992.

[6] Art. 8(2)(b) EPR Proposal.   [7] Wolters 2017, p. 170.

GDPR. The Directive establishing the European Electronic Communications Code also mandates that providers take 'appropriate and proportionate technical and organisational measures' to manage the risks posed to the security of networks and service.[8]

In the context of law enforcement cooperation, Article 32 finds an equivalent in Article 29 LED. However, the LED specifically refers to the risks related to the processing of special categories of data and identifies a number of specific measures to be implemented in case of automated processing (e.g. equipment access control, data media control, storage control, user control etc.).

Other EU legislation may also contain data security requirements; examples include the Payment Services Directive 2015/2366/EU (the recast PSD2 Directive)[9] and the Network and Information Systems Directive 2016//1148 (the NIS Directive).[10] On 26 June 2019 the EU Cybersecurity Act[11] entered into force. The Cybersecurity Act strengthens the role of ENISA (the European Union Agency for Cybersecurity), and establishes an EU-wide cybersecurity certification framework for digital products, services, and processes.

The EDPB has also described security measures that data controllers should consider when they create video surveillance policies and procedures.[12]

2. International instruments

Article 7 of the Council of Europe's Convention 108 contains a security obligation.[13] It provides that 'appropriate security measures shall be taken for the protection of personal data stored in automated data files against accidental or unauthorised destruction or accidental loss as well as against unauthorised access, alteration or dissemination'. However, this provision uses more flexible wording and does not contain the same level of specificity as Article 32. The Modernised Convention 108 contains a similar provision in Article 7(1), stating that 'Each Party shall provide that the controller, and, where applicable the processor, takes appropriate security measures against risks such as accidental or unauthorised access to, destruction, loss, use, modification or disclosure of personal data'.[14]

3. National developments

Article 17 DPD already required EU Member States to impose security obligations on controllers. Post-GDPR, Member States may also implement detailed data security provisions. An example is provided by Article 64 of the German Federal Data Protection Act 2017 that was amended to implement certain requirements of the GDPR, and which contains a detailed list of requirements to ensure the security of data processing.[15] The security requirements of the German Act have also become influential in practice and are often agreed by parties as the standard for measures required by Article 28 GDPR and the EU-approved standard contractual clauses for data transfers. Differing national legislation enacted in response to the GDPR may lead to divergences in the degree of harmonisation with regard to data security requirements.[16]

---

[8] EECC Directive, Art. 40(1).   [9] PSD2 Directive.
[10] NIS Directive. See in particular Arts. 14 and 16.
[11] Cybersecurity Act.   [12] EDPB 2019, pp. 27-28.   [13] Art. 7 Convention 108.
[14] Art. 7(1) Modernised Convention 108.
[15] German Federal Data Protection Act 2017.   [16] See Wolters 2017, p. 165.

4. Case law

In 2014, the CJEU seemed to equate data security with the 'essence' of the right to data protection in *Digital Rights Ireland*.[17] In that case, the Court stated:

> Nor is that retention of data such as to adversely affect the essence of the fundamental right to the protection of personal data enshrined in Article 8 of the Charter, because Article 7 of Directive 2006/24 provides, in relation to data protection and data security, that, without prejudice to the provisions adopted pursuant to Directives 95/46 and 2002/58, certain principles of data protection and data security must be respected by providers of publicly available electronic communications services or of public communications networks. According to those principles, Member States are to ensure that appropriate technical and organisational measures are adopted against accidental or unlawful destruction, accidental loss or alteration of the data.[18]

In 2013, the CJEU ruled on Article 17 DPD (the equivalent of Article 32 GDPR) in *Worten*.[19] In this case, Worten (a private company in Portugal) adopted a system of restricted access to working hour records of staff to which the national authority responsible for monitoring working conditions did not have access. The Court recalled that the obligation for an employer, as a controller of personal data, to provide the national authority responsible for monitoring working conditions immediate access to the record of working time does not imply that the personal data contained in the record must necessarily be made accessible to persons not authorised for that purpose, so the requirement of security of processing in Article 17 DPD was not jeopardised.

The ECtHR has also ruled on the adequacy of data security obligations. In *Z v Finland*, the Court held that domestic law must afford appropriate safeguards to prevent any such communication or disclosure of personal health data as may be inconsistent with the guarantees in Article 8 of the European Convention of Human Rights ('ECHR').[20] And then in 2008, the ECtHR ruled directly on security obligations related to data processing in *I v Finland*.[21] In this case, the ECtHR ruled that Finland violated Article 8 ECHR on the right to respect for private and family life. The judgment held that Finland failed to secure patient's medical data against unauthorised access at a public hospital due to the lack of adequate technical and organisational measures.

C. Analysis

1. Scope of the security obligation

Article 32 imposes data security obligations on both data controllers and data processors. Beyond the direct obligations that Article 32 places on data controllers, the GDPR makes changes in particular with regard to the controller's engagement of data processors. While the DPD only required the controller to impose a contractual security obligation on the processor, Article 32 GDPR directly imposes this obligation on the processor itself. Thus, processors also have a statutory obligation to ensure an appropriate level of security of the processing under the GDPR. In addition, Article 28(4) requires data controllers to conclude a written contract with the data processor that, among other things, requires the processor to take all measures required by Article 32, as well as to assist the controller in ensuring compliance with its own obligations under Article 32.

---

[17] Joined Cases C-293/12 and C-594/12, *Digital Rights Ireland*.
[18] Ibid., para. 40. See regarding this point Lynskey 2015, p. 271.   [19] Case C-342/12, *Worten*.
[20] ECtHR, *Z v Finland*, paras. 95–96.   [21] ECtHR, *I v Finland*.

From the data controller's perspective, and already under the DPD, security considerations must be taken into account in the selection of the processor. In this context, Article 17(2) DPD provided that controllers must choose a processor 'providing sufficient guarantees in respect of the technical security measures and organizational measures governing the processing to be carried out'. Under the GDPR, this provision was introduced in modified form in Article 28(1) in much more general terms, which are no longer limited to security, but extend to all GDPR requirements.

Article 28(4) requires the processor to bind sub-processors by a contract containing the 'same data protection obligations' as imposed on the processor by the controller, which includes measures related to data security. Article 32(4) also has implications for the use of sub-processors and for employees. Externally, under Article 32(4) data controllers and data processors must 'take steps to ensure that any natural person acting under the authority of the controller or the processor who has access to personal data' (which can include sub-processors) does not process them except on instructions from the controller, unless this is required by EU law or Member State law. This requires the conclusion of written contracts with sub-processors. Internally, both controllers and processors must require their employees—or anyone acting under their authority—to only process personal data under the instructions of the controller (Article 32(4)). In practice, such instructions should reflect the controller's obligations under Article 32, which means that the security safeguards required by Article 32 must also be made binding internally within each data controller's or processor's structure.

2. Compliance with the security obligation

Article 32 GDPR imposes a data security duty on controllers and processors by requiring them to implement technical and organisational measures appropriate to the risks of the data processing. As a first step, controllers and processors must identify and assess the particular risks presented by the data processing, paying attention in particular to risks of accidental or unlawful destruction, loss, alteration, unauthorised disclosure of, or access to personal data. As a second step, they must identify and implement security measures as a mitigating response.

The word 'appropriate' appears not less than three times in Article 32(1): 'the controller and the processor shall implement *appropriate* technical and organisational measures to ensure a level of security *appropriate* to the risk, including inter alia as *appropriate*' (emphasis added). This indicates that controllers and processors must identify the situation-specific risks, assess their potential impact having regard to the particular circumstances of the processing and implement measures to mitigate (at least) those risks which are the most likely to materialise and those whose impact would be the most severe.

The references to 'appropriateness' can be seen as a way of expressing the importance of the principle of proportionality, which is a general principle of EU law, in determining how to ensure data security. A proportionality analysis generally inquires whether the means used to achieve an aim corresponds to the importance of the aim and whether it is necessary for its achievement.[22] Thus, the use of security measures should be evaluated based on whether they are reasonably likely to achieve their objectives, and on weighing competing interests, i.e. assessing the consequences that a measure has on an interest worthy of legal

---

[22] Tridimas 2009, p. 139.

protection (in this case, the security of data processing), and determining whether those consequences are justified in view of the importance of the objective pursued.[23]

The GDPR does provide some specific guidance on assessing security risks and identifying what security measures may be 'appropriate'. In particular, Article 32(1) provides a (non-exhaustive) list of criteria to be taken into account, namely: the state of the art; the costs of implementation; the nature, scope, context and purposes of the processing; and the risk of varying likelihood and severity for the rights and freedoms of individuals. Article 32(2) further specifies the major risks to be alerted of in the following terms: 'In assessing the appropriate level of security account shall be taken in particular of the risks that are presented by processing, in particular from accidental or unlawful destruction, loss, alteration, unauthorised disclosure of, or access to personal data transmitted, stored or otherwise processed'. Thus, this second paragraph impliedly elaborates on the last two criteria of paragraph 1, as it gives examples of the most likely and/or severe risks to be mitigated. These examples show some similarities to the criteria to be used in determining whether to carry out a data protection impact assessment ('DPIA') pursuant to Article 35 GDPR, and the WP29 has emphasised the importance of data security in the context of DPIAs.[24]

The GDPR does not require the use of any particular technology or technical standard with regard to data security.[25] However, Article 32(1) lists four types of security measures that controllers and processors should implement 'as appropriate', including the following: the pseudonymisation and encryption of personal data (Article 32(1)(a)); the ability to ensure the ongoing confidentiality, integrity, availability and resilience of processing systems (Article 32(1)(b)); the ability to restore the availability and access to personal data in a timely manner in case of an incident (Article 32(1)(c), for example by setting up a disaster recovery plan); and a process for regularly testing, assessing and evaluating the effectiveness of security measures (Article 32(1)(d)). While these measures are not mandatory, Article 32 expresses a clear preference for them, making it likely that regulators will expect data controllers and processors to use them whenever possible.

3. Accountability, liability and fines

While both controllers and processors must abide by the data security requirements, the responsibility of controllers is more pronounced. Controllers are subject to the accountability principle enshrined in Article 5(2), which includes the obligation to demonstrate that they ensure appropriate security. The GDPR does not explicitly impose this accountability obligation on processors, although they are subject to a number of legal requirements, particular under Article 28.

Article 32(3) provides that data controllers and processors may demonstrate compliance with data security requirements by adhering to an approved code of conduct or an approved certification mechanism regarding the security of processing. The conditions for and the consequences of this are to be determined under Article 40 (for codes of conduct) and Article 42 (for certification mechanisms).

Compensation and liability for violations of Article 32 can be imposed under Article 82 GDPR. Regarding administrative fines, the amount of such fines is supposed to give due regard to 'the degree of responsibility of the controller or processor taking into account

[23] Ibid.   [24] WP29 2017.
[25] See rec. 15 GDPR, explaining that 'the protection of natural persons should be technologically neutral and should not depend on the techniques used'.

technical and organisational measures implemented by them pursuant to Articles 25 and 32'.[26] However, Article 32 only imposes an obligation of means,[27] not an obligation to provide a result. This means that if a data breach occurs despite the implementation of appropriate security measures, there may still not be an infringement of the GDPR.

Fines for violations of Article 32 can range up to € 10 million or 2 per cent of the total worldwide annual turnover of the preceding financial year, whichever is higher (Article 83(4)(a)). In its guidance on data breach notification under the GDPR,[28] the WP29 explained that a sanction for absence of appropriate security measures can be distinct from a sanction for failure to notify a data breach to the supervisory authority or affected individuals in accordance with Articles 33 and 34.[29] It has been stated that the imposition of criminal sanctions for violation of Article 32 could violate the principle of legality because its requirements are formulated in vague and general terms;[30] this was the reason that the Italian legislature decided not to provide for criminal sanctions for violation of security requirements under the GDPR.[31]

DPAs have issued large fines for breaches of data security. For example, on 8 July 2019 the UK Information Commissioner (ICO) announced that she planned to fine British Airways £183.39 million (approximately € 204 million and approximately 1.5% of the company's annual worldwide turnover) for breaches of the GDPR regarding data security.[32] And on 9 July 2019, the ICO also announced that she intended to fine Marriott International more than £99 million (approximately € 110 million) under the GDPR for a data breach.[33]

4. Security measures in the context of other obligations imposed by the GDPR

References to the obligation to ensure appropriate security measures are made throughout the GDPR. For instance, data processing for the purpose of ensuring network and information security, such as to prevent data breaches, constitutes a legitimate interest of the controller and does not require reliance on any other legal ground for processing (recital 49). Another example is that, whenever possible, controllers and processors must include a general description of the technical and organisational security measures in their records of processing activities (Articles 30(1)(g) and 30(2)(d)). Security measures are also important in the context of Binding Corporate Rules ('BCRs'), when an organisation wishes to obtain regulatory approval of them (Article 47(2)(d)).

Select Bibliography

EU legislation

Cybersecurity Act: Regulation (EU) 2019/881 of the European Parliament and of the Council of 17 April 2019 on ENISA (the European Union Agency for Cybersecurity) and on information and communications technology cybersecurity certification and repealing Regulation (EU) No 526/2013 (Cybersecurity Act), OJ 2019 L 151/15.

EECC Directive: Directive (EU) 2018/1972 of the European Parliament and of the Council of 11 December 2018 establishing the European Electronic Communications Code (Recast), OJ 2018 L 321/36.

---

[26] Art. 83(2)(d) GDPR. [27] Wolters 2017, p. 172. [28] WP29 2018, p. 10.
[29] Ibid., p. 8. [30] Tosoni 2018, p. 1200. [31] Ibid. [32] ICO British Airways fine.
[33] ICO Marriott fine.

EPR Proposal: Proposal for a Regulation of the European Parliament and of the Council concerning the respect for private life and the protection of personal data in electronic communications and repealing Directive 2002/58/EC (Regulation on Privacy and Electronic Communications), COM(2017)10 final, 10 January 2017.

NIS Directive: Directive (EU) 2016/1148 of the European Parliament and of the Council of 6 July 2016 concerning measures for a high common level of security of network and information systems across the Union, OJ 2016 L 194/1.

PSD2 Directive: Directive 2015/2366/EU of the European Parliament and of the Council of 25 November 2015 on payment services in the internal market, amending Directives 2002/65/EC, 2009/110/EC and 2013/36/EU and Regulation (EU) No. 1093/2010, and repealing Directive 2007/64/EC, OJ 2015 L 337/35.

National legislation

Belgian Data Protection Law 1992: Wet tot bescherming van de persoonlijke levenssfeer ten opzichte van de verwerking van persoonsgegevens, van 8 december 1992; Loi relative à la protection de la vie privée à l'égard des traitements de données à caractère personnel, du 8 decembre 1992) (repealed).

German Federal Data Protection Act 2017: Bundesdatenschutzgesetz vom 30. Juni 2017, BGBl. 2017 Teil I Nr. 2097.

Academic writings

Lynskey 2015: Lynskey, *The Foundations of EU Data Protection Law* (OUP 2015).

Tosoni 2018: Tosoni, 'Rethinking Privacy in the Council of Europe's Convention on Cybercrime', 34(6) *Computer Law & Security Review* (2018), 1197.

Tridimas 2009: Tridimas, *The General Principles of EU Law* (2nd edn, OUP 2009).

Wolters 2017: Wolters, 'The Security of Personal Data under the GDPR: A Harmonized Duty or a Shared Responsibility?', 7 *International Data Privacy Law* (2017), 165.

Papers of data protection authorities

EDPB 2018: European Data Protection Board, 'Endorsement 1/2018' (25 May 2018).

EDPB 2019: European Data Protection Board, 'Guidelines 3/2019 on the processing of personal data through video devices (version for public consultation)' (10 July 2019).

WP29 2017: Article 29 Working Party, 'Guidelines on Data Protection Impact Assessment (DPIA) and Determining Whether Processing is "Likely to Result in a High Risk" for the Purposes of Regulation 2016/679' (WP 248 rev.01, as last revised and adopted on 4 October 2017).

WP29 2018: Article 29 Working Party, 'Guidelines on Personal data Breach Notification under Regulation 2016/679' (WP 250 rev.01, as last revised and adopted on 6 February 2018).

ICO British Airways fine: UK Information Commissioner's Office, 'Intention to fine British Airways £183.39m under GDPR for data breach' (8 July 2019), available at https://ico.org.uk/about-the-ico/news-and-events/news-and-blogs/2019/07/ico-announces-intention-to-fine-british-airways/.

ICO Marriott fine: UK Information Commissioner's Office, 'Intention to fine Marriott International, Inc more than £99 million under GDPR for data breach' (9 July 2019), available at https://ico.org.uk/about-the-ico/news-and-events/news-and-blogs/2019/07/intention-to-fine-marriott-international-inc-more-than-99-million-under-gdpr-for-data-breach/.

Reports and recommendations

EC Staff Working Paper 2012: Commission Staff Working Paper 'Impact Assessment Accompanying the document Regulation of the European Parliament and of the Council on the protection of individuals with regard to the processing of personal data and on the free movement of such data (General Data Protection Regulation) and Directive of the European Parliament and of the Council on the protection of individuals with regard to the processing of personal data by competent authorities for the purposes of prevention, investigation, detection or prosecution of criminal offences or the execution of criminal penalties, and the free movement of such data', SEC(2012) 72 final, 25 January 2012.

ENISA Report: European Union Agency for Network and Information Security, 'ENISA's Role in the European Digital Single Market (DSM)' (2018), available at https://www.enisa.europa.eu/publications/enisa-position-papers-and-opinions/enisa2019s-role-in-the-european-digital-single-market-dsm.

Article 33. Notification of a personal data breach to the supervisory authority

CÉDRIC BURTON*

1. In the case of a personal data breach, the controller shall without undue delay and, where feasible, not later than 72 hours after having become aware of it, notify the personal data breach to the supervisory authority competent in accordance with Article 55, unless the personal data breach is unlikely to result in a risk to the rights and freedoms of natural persons. Where the notification to the supervisory authority is not made within 72 hours, it shall be accompanied by reasons for the delay.
2. The processor shall notify the controller without undue delay after becoming aware of a personal data breach.
3. The notification referred to in paragraph 1 shall at least:
   (a) describe the nature of the personal data breach including where possible, the categories and approximate number of data subjects concerned and the categories and approximate number of personal data records concerned;
   (b) communicate the name and contact details of the data protection officer or other contact point where more information can be obtained;
   (c) describe the likely consequences of the personal data breach;
   (d) describe the measures taken or proposed to be taken by the controller to address the personal data breach, including, where appropriate, measures to mitigate its possible adverse effects.
4. Where, and in so far as, it is not possible to provide the information at the same time, the information may be provided in phases without undue further delay.
5. The controller shall document any personal data breaches, comprising the facts relating to the personal data breach, its effects and the remedial action taken. That documentation shall enable the supervisory authority to verify compliance with this Article.

Relevant Recitals

(85) A personal data breach may, if not addressed in an appropriate and timely manner, result in physical, material or non-material damage to natural persons such as loss of control over their personal data or limitation of their rights, discrimination, identity theft or fraud, financial loss, unauthorised reversal of pseudonymisation, damage to reputation, loss of confidentiality of personal data protected by professional secrecy or any other significant economic or social disadvantage to the natural person concerned. Therefore, as soon as the controller becomes aware that a personal data breach has occurred, the controller should notify the personal data breach to the supervisory authority without undue delay and, where feasible, not later than 72 hours after having become aware of it, unless the controller is able to demonstrate, in accordance with the accountability principle, that the personal data breach is unlikely to result in a risk to the rights and freedoms of natural persons. Where such notification cannot be achieved within 72 hours, the reasons for the delay should accompany the notification and information may be provided in phases without undue further delay.

* The author is grateful for the research assistance of Rossana Fol and Bastiaan Suurmond.

Member State law applies by virtue of public international law. The WP29 has stated that data controllers not established in the EU but subject to the GDPR under Article 3(2) or (3) are bound by the notification obligation of Article 33 when it experiences a breach.[33] In such cases, notification should be made to the DPA in the Member State where the representative of the controller is established.[34] The same applies to a data processor established outside the EU but subject to the GDPR under Article 3.[35]

When a processor is established in the EU but carries out processing for a data controller outside the EU who is not subject to the GDPR, the processor must notify the controller without undue delay after it becomes aware of a data breach.[36]

3. Data breaches subject to notification

The GDPR defines a personal data breach as any 'breach of security leading to the accidental or unlawful destruction, loss, alteration, unauthorised disclosure of, or access to, personal data transmitted, stored or otherwise processed'.[37] The broad scope of 'personal data' under the GDPR[38] also reinforces the wide coverage of data breaches. At the same time, there is a distinction between data breaches, which involve breaches of personal data, and security incidents (i.e. incidents where there is a breach of security principles), which may not.[39] The WP29 has classified data breaches in three categories as either (1) confidentiality breaches (where there is an unauthorised or accidental disclosure of, or access to, personal data); (2) integrity breaches (where there is an unauthorised or accidental alteration of personal data); or (3) availability breaches (where there is an accidental or unauthorised loss of access to, or destruction of, personal data).[40] However, a particular breach may also be a combination of any of these three categories.[41] The unavailability of personal data due to planned system maintenance is not considered to be a data breach.[42]

As a practical matter, when there is a doubt as to whether a data breach should be notified to a DPA, data controllers often err on the side of doing so, in order to protect themselves in case it is later found that a breach occurred. This has led to a flood of notifications, with some DPAs requesting informally that not all breaches be notified.[43] However, as a matter of law, a number of elements determine whether there is a duty to notify, which will now be examined in turn, and the conditions for which differ between data controllers and data processors.

4. Obligations of data controllers

For data controllers, Article 33(1) requires the notification to the DPA of a personal data breach, without undue delay and, where feasible, not later than 72 hours after having become aware of it, unless the breach is unlikely to result in a risk to the rights and freedoms of natural persons. The WP29 has provided a flow chart as to how notification to the DPA is to be made, together with a table giving concrete examples.[44]

The GDPR does not define precisely what is meant by 'without undue delay'. The only explanation is provided by recital 87, which states that 'the fact that the notification was

---

[33] WP29 2018, p. 18. [34] Ibid. [35] Ibid. [36] EDPB 2018B, p. 11.
[37] Art. 4(12) GDPR. See the commentary on Art. 4(12) in this volume.
[38] See Art. 4(1) GDPR. [39] See WP29 2018, p. 7. [40] Ibid. [41] Ibid., p. 8.
[42] Ibid. [43] See e.g. Website ICO, stating that 'you do not need to report every breach to the ICO'.
[44] WP29 2018, pp. 30–33.

made without undue delay should be established taking into account in particular the nature and gravity of the personal data breach and its consequences and adverse effects for the data subject'. Thus, 'undue delay' will have to be defined on a case-by-case basis.

The criteria of notifying 'where feasible, not later than 72 hours after having become aware of it' raises the question of what is meant by 'feasible', and when the controller becomes aware of the breach. The guidance of the WP29 as endorsed by the EDPB indicates that the DPAs are prepared to grant a certain amount of flexibility regarding the 72 hour notification requirement.[45] Thus, the WP29 has indicated that the DPAs are willing to allow notification in phases, as long as a convincing explanation is provided for the delay.[46] Indeed, Article 33(1) requires that 'where the notification to the supervisory authority is not made within 72 hours, it shall be accompanied by reasons for the delay'. The WP29 has given examples of what may be considered to be acceptable reasons for delay, such as when 'a controller experiences multiple, similar confidentiality breaches over a short period of time, affecting large numbers of data subjects in the same way'.[47] In the case of multiple breaches, it may also be possible to 'bundle' them into a single notification, assuming there is sufficient similarity between them.[48]

As to when the data controller becomes aware of the breach, this is when it 'has a reasonable degree of certainty that a security incident has occurred that has led to personal data being compromised'.[49] As the WP29 has stated, this will necessarily depend on the facts of each particular case.[50] The controller may undertake a short period of investigation after being informed of a potential breach in order to establish whether a breach has in fact occurred, during which time the controller is not to be considered as being aware of the breach.[51] In addition, if a data processor becomes aware of a breach of data it is processing for a data controller, the controller is deemed to be aware of the breach when it has been notified about it by the processor.[52]

Notification to a DPA is not required when 'the personal data breach is unlikely to result in a risk to the rights and freedoms of natural persons'. There is no precise definition in the GDPR as to when there is a risk to the rights and freedoms of natural persons in the context of a data breach. In practice, data controllers tend to notify data breaches in most cases under the GDPR, rather than take the risk of not notifying and then being found later to be in violation.

Recital 75 gives a number of examples of risks to rights and freedoms. In particular, it suggests that such risks should be broadly interpreted to include cases that could lead to physical, material or nonmaterial damage, including 'discrimination, identity theft or fraud, financial loss, damage to the reputation, loss of confidentiality of personal data protected by professional secrecy, unauthorised reversal of pseudonymisation, or any other significant economic or social disadvantage'; situations 'where data subjects might be deprived of their rights and freedoms or prevented from exercising control over their personal data'; where sensitive data are processed; the use of data analytics, particularly with regard to 'performance at work, economic situation, health, personal preferences or interests, reliability or behaviour, location or movements, or in order to create or use

---

[45] Ibid., p. 15, stating 'This means that the GDPR recognises that controllers will not always have all of the necessary information concerning a breach within 72 hours of becoming aware of it, as full and comprehensive details of the incident may not always be available during this initial period'.
[46] Ibid.   [47] Ibid., p. 16.   [48] Ibid.   [49] Ibid., pp. 10–11.   [50] Ibid., p. 11.
[51] Ibid.   [52] Ibid., p. 13.

personal profiles'; the processing of personal data of vulnerable natural persons, particularly children; or where processing 'involves a large amount of personal data and affects a large number of data subjects'. The WP29 has also given examples of situations where the rights and freedoms of natural persons are not at issue, such as where the personal data are already publicly available and their disclosure does not present a likely risk to the individuals concerned,[53] and when data have been properly encrypted so that they have been made unintelligible to unauthorised parties and a copy or a backup exists.[54]

There is a presumption of a high risk to rights and freedoms when 'the breach may lead to physical, material or non-material damage for the individuals whose data have been breached', which is the case with regard to situations involving discrimination, identity theft or fraud, financial loss, damage to reputation, the processing of sensitive data, or criminal convictions and offences or related security measures.[55]

The WP29 has identified the following factors that can be used to assess risk: the type of breach; the nature, sensitivity and volume of personal data; ease of identification of individuals; the severity of consequences for individuals; special characteristics of the individual; special characteristics of the data controller; and the number of affected individuals.[56]

With regard to joint controllers, it is recommended that in the agreements they are required to conclude under Article 26 to determine their respective compliance responsibilities under the GDPR they enter into contractual arrangements between themselves concerning compliance with breach notification obligations as well.[57]

Associations of data controllers and data processors are empowered to prepare codes of conduct to specify the application of the GDPR with regard to the notification of personal data breaches to DPAs and the communication of such personal data breaches to data subjects.[58]

5. Obligations of data processors

The tasks of data processors differ from those of data controllers with regard to data breaches. In particular, data processors are supposed to notify breaches of which they become aware to the data controller that has engaged them, rather than to the DPA.[59] Notification by data processors is also not subject to the various conditions that apply to data controllers under Article 33(1) (i.e. notifying without delay, where feasible within 72 hours of becoming aware of the breach etc.). The reason for the different rules for data processors regarding notification is that it is the data controller that engaged them that should determine whether a breach triggers the requirement to notify the DPA.

The processor must assist the controller in ensuring compliance with its obligation to notify a breach to the supervisory authority.[60] A key factor is the point at which the processor informs the controller about the breach, since it is from this point that the controller is deemed to be 'aware' of it.[61]

The GDPR provides that processors must notify the controller 'without undue delay after becoming aware of a personal data breach', and the WP29 recommends prompt notification by the processor to the controller, with further information about the breach being provided in phases as information becomes available.[62] The rationale behind this is

[53] Ibid., p. 18. [54] Ibid., p. 19. [55] Ibid. [56] Ibid., pp. 24–26.
[57] Ibid., p. 13. [58] Art. 40(2)(i) GDPR. [59] Ibid., Art. 33(2).
[60] Ibid., Art. 28(3)(f). [61] WP29 2018, p. 13. [62] Ibid., pp. 13–14.

to allow the controller to contain the breach by implementing mitigating measures and, if appropriate, to inform the supervisory authority and affected individuals as soon as possible. A data processing agreement between a controller and a processor may also contractually oblige the processor to report a breach within a certain time limit and specify the type of information to be provided to the controller.[63]

6. What to notify

Article 33(3) describes the information to be notified to the DPA, which must include the nature of the personal data breach, including the categories and approximate number of data subjects concerned and the categories and approximate number of personal data records concerned; the name and contact details of the data protection officer or other contact point where more information can be obtained; the likely consequences of the personal data breach; and the measures taken or proposed to be taken by the controller to address the personal data breach, including, where appropriate, measures to mitigate its possible adverse effects.

The above information is the minimum to notify, and the controller may, and often should, provide further details. Details about how to notify and the form in which notification should be made is typically provided in online forms[64] or information notes[65] published by the DPAs.

The lack of precise information being available should not be used as an excuse to delay timely notification.[66] In cases where some of the necessary information is lacking, approximations may be made,[67] and notification made be made in phases, as long as the information is provided without undue further delay and reasons are given for the delay.[68] In the case of multiple breaches, it may also be possible to 'bundle' them into a single notification, assuming there is sufficient similarity between them.[69]

7. Whom to notify

Under Article 33(1), the DPA to be notified is the one that is competent under Article 55 GDPR, meaning the DPA of the Member State of the data controller's establishment in the context of which the data processing activities take place.

However, data breaches will often take place in the context of cross-border data processing.[70] In cases when a data controller has at least one establishment in the EU and undertakes cross-border processing, then the competence for such processing is invested in the lead supervisory authority.[71] The WP29 has stated that this means that notification for breaches that take place in the context of cross-border processing should be made to the lead supervisory authority.[72] However, it has also said that 'if the controller has any doubt as to the identity of the lead supervisory authority then it should, at a minimum, notify the local supervisory authority where the breach has taken place'.[73] Since

---

[63] Ibid., p. 14.
[64] See e.g. Austrian Data Protection Authority 2018; Website Belgian Privacy Commission Notification Form; Website CNIL Notification Form.
[65] See e.g. Website Belgian Privacy Commission Guidance; Website CNIL Guidance; Website Luxembourg Data Protection Commission Guidance; ICO 2013.
[66] WP29 2018, p. 14. [67] Ibid. [68] Ibid., pp. 15–16. [69] Ibid., p. 16.
[70] See Art. 4(23) GDPR regarding the definition of cross-border processing.
[71] See ibid., Art. 56(1). [72] WP29 2018, p. 17. [73] Ibid.

identification of the lead supervisory authority is not always straightforward, this means that, depending on the facts of the breach, it may sometimes be necessary to notify other DPAs as well.

8. Accountability and documentation of breaches

Article 33(5) requires controllers to document all personal data breaches, including the facts relating to the breach, its effects and the remedial action taken. This obligation is an illustration of the accountability principle enshrined in Article 5(2) GDPR. The obligation to maintain documentation related to breaches should be distinguished from the obligation to keep records of processing under Article 30 GDPR.

Controllers are advised to go beyond this minimum and keep additional documentation, since they will need much more detailed information in order to respond to breaches, respond to queries from DPAs and individuals, and implement their information security programs. The keeping of documentation is also important to protect against legal liability. For example, recital 85 GDPR emphasises that, if controllers do not report a data breach, they will need to 'be able to demonstrate, in accordance with the accountability principle, that the personal data breach is unlikely to result in a risk to the rights and freedoms of natural persons'. Thus, the failure to properly document a breach can lead to a DPA taking action under Article 58 or levying an administrative fine under Article 83.[74]

The WP29 recommends that controllers establish an internal register of data breaches, whether or not they are required to notify them.[75] Article 33 does not impose obligations on data processors to keep documentation of data breaches, though it is in the data processor's interest to do so, particularly in order to allow it to fulfil its obligations to assist the controller with regard to data security and data breach matters.[76]

Data controllers are expected to have internal processes in place to detect and address breaches.[77] While these measures can differ, the following are some practical steps that the WP29 has stated that it expects to be taken in all cases:

1. Information concerning all security-related events should be directed towards a responsible person or persons with the task of addressing incidents, establishing the existence of a breach and assessing risk.
2. Risk to individuals as a result of a breach should then be assessed (likelihood of no risk, risk or high risk), with relevant sections of the organisation being informed.
3. Notification to the supervisory authority, and potentially communication of the breach to the affected individuals should be made, if required.
4. At the same time, the controller should act to contain and recover the breach.
5. Documentation of the breach should take place as it develops.[78]

The specific details of documenting breaches are left up to the data controller.[79] The WP29 has suggested that data controllers and data processors may find the recommendations of the European Union Agency for Network and Information Security ('ENISA') concerning the assessment of the severity of data breaches[80] helpful in designing a breach management response plan.

[74] Ibid., p. 27.   [75] Ibid., p. 26.   [76] See Art. 28(3)(f) GDPR.
[77] WP29 2018, p. 13.   [78] Ibid. p. 12.
[79] Ibid. pp. 26–27 for further recommendations of the WP29 in this regard.   [80] ENISA 2013.

The data protection officer ('DPO') of the controller or processor has an important role to play in data breaches. In particular, DPOs appointed under the GDPR have a number of mandatory tasks under Article 37 that are relevant to data breaches, such as providing data protection advice, cooperating with the DPAs, and acting as a contact point for the supervisory authority and for data subjects.[81] The data controller is also required under Article 33(3)(b) to provide the name and contact details of its DPO or other contact point when it notifies the data breach to the DPA.

9. Conflict with third country legal requirements

In some cases of cross-border breaches, such as when it is suspected that a breach was caused by criminal activity, law enforcement requirements of third countries may restrict disclosure of the breach and its details. This can create legal conflicts for data controllers, who may be expected by third country law enforcement authorities not to disclose the breach while they are conducting an investigation, while at the same time controllers are under an obligation to notify it to a DPA.

Recital 88 GDPR grants some flexibility in this regard, as it states that notification of a breach should take into account 'the legitimate interests of law-enforcement authorities where early disclosure could unnecessarily hamper the investigation of the circumstances of a personal data breach'. The WP29 states that 'this may mean that in certain circumstances, where justified, and on the advice of law-enforcement authorities, the controller may delay communicating the breach to the affected individuals until such time as it would not prejudice such investigations'.[82] However, the reference in recital 88 to 'notification' seems to mean that the possibility of delaying disclosure could apply to notification of the breach to DPAs as well as communication to individuals. Since DPAs are likely to view the possibility of delaying notification restrictively,[83] data controllers are advised to be cautious in delaying notification, and to attempt to negotiate with third country law enforcement authorities to minimise any delay in notifying a breach to the greatest extent possible.

10. Penalties

Recital 87 deals with the consequences of breach notification and states that it can result in an intervention of the supervisory authority. Penalties for violation of Article 33 can include administrative fines and corrective measures under Article 58(2) (such as warnings, reprimands, orders etc.). Fines for non-compliance with the obligations resulting from Article 33 can reach up to € 10 million or up to 2 per cent of total worldwide annual turnover of the preceding year, whichever is higher.[84] Because the failure to notify a breach in violation of Article 33 may reveal other security-related violations (such as the absence of adequate security measures under Article 32 or the failure to communicate the breach to data subjects), administrative sanctions may be imposed at a level which is effective, proportionate and dissuasive within the limit of the gravest infringement.[85] In such a case, the DPA will also have the possibility 'to issue sanctions for failure to

---

[81] WP29 2018, p. 28.   [82] Ibid., p. 21.
[83] Ibid., p. 20, stating 'controllers should recall that notification to the supervisory authority is mandatory unless there is unlikely to be a risk to the rights and freedoms of individuals as a result of a breach'.
[84] Art. 83(4)(a) GDPR.   [85] WP29 2018, p. 10.

notify or communicate the breach (Articles 33 and 34) on the one hand, and absence of (adequate) security measures (Article 32) on the other hand, as they are two separate infringements'.[86]

DPAs have begun issuing large fines for breaches of data security, which includes violations related to a failure to notify breaches.[87] For instance, in November 2018 the Dutch DPA fined Uber € 600,000 for notifying a data breach a year late.[88]

Select Bibliography

EU legislation

Citizens Rights Directive: Directive 2009/1136/EC of the European Parliament and of the Council of 25 November 2009 amending Directive 2002/22/EC on universal service and users' rights relating to electronic communications networks and services, Directive 2002/58/EC concerning the processing of personal data and the protection of privacy in the electronic communications sector and Regulation (EC) No. 2006/2004 on cooperation between national authorities responsible for the enforcement of consumer protection laws, OJ 2009 L 337/11.

Commission Regulation 611/2013: Commission Regulation 611/2013 of 24 June 2013 on the measures applicable to the notification of personal data breaches under Directive 2002/58/EC of the European Parliament and of the Council on privacy and electronic communications, OJ 2013 L 173/2.

Cybersecurity Act: Regulation (EU) 2019/881 of the European Parliament and of the Council of 17 April 2019 on ENISA (the European Union Agency for Cybersecurity) and on information and communications technology cybersecurity certification and repealing Regulation (EU) No 526/2013 (Cybersecurity Act), OJ 2019 L 151/15.

EECC Directive: Directive (EU) 2018/1972 of the European Parliament and of the Council of 11 December 2018 establishing the European Electronic Communications Code (Recast), OJ 2018 L 321/36.

eIDAS Regulation: Regulation (EU) 910/2014 on electronic identification and trust services for electronic transactions in the internal market, OJ 2014 L 257/73.

EPR Proposal: Proposal for a Regulation of the European Parliament and of the Council concerning the respect for private life and the protection of personal data in electronic communications and repealing Directive 2002/58/EC (Regulation on Privacy and Electronic Communications), COM(2017)10 final, 10 January 2017.

NIS Directive: Directive 2016/1148 of the European Parliament and of the Council of 6 July 2016 concerning measures for a high common level of security of network and information systems across the Union, OJ 2016 L 194/1

PSD2 Directive: Directive 2015/2366/EU of the European Parliament and of the Council of 25 November 2015 on payment services in the internal market, amending Directives 2002/65/EC, 2009/110/EC and 2013/36/EU and Regulation (EU) No. 1093/2010, and repealing Directive 2007/64/EC, OJ 2015 L 337/35.

National legislation

Austrian Federal Data Protection Act: Bundesgesetz zum Schutz natürlicher Personen bei der Verarbeitung personenbezogener Daten (Datenschutzgesetz—DSG), BGBl. I Nr. 165/1999 zuletzt geändert durch BGBl. I Nr. 24/2018.

[86] Ibid.　[87] See the commentary on Art. 32 in this volume.
[88] Website Dutch DPA Uber fine.

Dutch GDPR Implementation Law: Uitvoeringswet Algemene verordening gegevensbescherming, versie van 25 mei 2018.

German Federal Data Protection Act 2017: Bundesdatenschutzgesetz vom 30. Juni 2017, BGBl. 2017 Teil I Nr. 2097.

Spanish Data Protection Law 2007: Real Decreto 1720/2007, de 21 de diciembre, por el que se aprueba el Reglamento de desarrollo de la Ley Orgánica 15/1999, de 13 de diciembre, de protección de datos de carácter personal.

Papers of data protection authorities

EDPB 2018A: European Data Protection Board, 'Endorsement 1/2018' (25 May 2018).

EDPB 2018B: European Data Protection Board, 'Guidelines 3/2018 on the Territorial Scope of the GDPR (Article 3)—Version for Public Consultation' (16 November 2018).

WP29 2014: Article 29 Working Party, 'Opinion 03/2014 on Personal Data Breach Notification' (WP 213, 25 March 2014).

WP29 2018: Article 29 Working Party, 'Guidelines on Personal data Breach Notification under Regulation 2016/679' (WP 250rev.01, as last revised and adopted on 6 February 2018).

Article 29 Working Party, 'Guidelines for Identifying a Controller or Processor's Lead Supervisory Authority' (WP 244, 5 April 2017)

Article 29 Working Party, 'Guidelines on Personal Data Breach Notification under Regulation 2016/679' (WP 250, 3 October 2017)

Article 29 Working Party, 'Guidelines on the Application and Setting of Administrative Fines for the Purposes of the Regulation 2016/679' (WP 253, 3 October 2017).

Austrian Data Protection Authority 2018: Datenschutzbehörde, 'Meldung von Verletzungen des Schutzes personenbezogener Daten gemäß Art. 33 DSGVO' (2018).

Dutch Data Protection Authority 2017: Autoriteit Persoonsgegevens, 'Meldeplicht datalekken: facts & figures, Overzicht feiten en cijfers 2017' (2018).

ICO 2013: Information Commissioner's Office 'ICO', 'Notification of PECR Security Breaches' (19 March 2013).

Reports and recommendations

EC GDPR Impact Assessment: Commission Staff Working Paper 'Impact Assessment Accompanying the document Regulation of the European Parliament and of the Council on the protection of individuals with regard to the processing of personal data and on the free movement of such data (General Data Protection Regulation) and Directive of the European Parliament and of the Council on the protection of individuals with regard to the processing of personal data by competent authorities for the purposes of prevention, investigation, detection or prosecution of criminal offences or the execution of criminal penalties, and the free movement of such data', SEC(2012) 72 final, 25 January 2012.

ENISA 2013: European Union Agency for Network and Information Security, 'Recommendations for a Methodology of the Assessment of Severity of Personal Data Breaches' (2013), available at https://www.enisa.europa.eu/publications/dbn-severity.

Others

Website Belgian Privacy Commission Guidance: Autorité de protection des donnés, 'Notification des fuites de données à l'Autorité', available at https://www.autoriteprotectiondonnees.be/notification-des-fuites-de-données-à-la-commission-vie-privée.

Website Belgian Privacy Commission Notification Form: Autorité de protection des donnés, 'La notification de fuites de données', available at https://www.autoriteprotectiondonnees.be/la-notification-de-fuites-de-données.

Website CNIL Guidance: Commission Nationale de l'Informatique et des Libertés, 'Notifier une violation de données personnelles', available at https://www.cnil.fr/fr/notifier-une-violation-de-donnees-personnelles.

Website CNIL Notification Form: Commission Nationale de l'Informatique et des Libertés 'CNIL', 'Notification d'une violation de données personnelles', available at https://notifications.cnil.fr/notifications/index.

Website Dutch DPA Breach Notification: Autoriteit Persoongegevens, 'Data breach notification obligation', https://autoriteitpersoonsgegevens.nl/en/news/data-breach-notification-obligation.

Website Dutch DPA Uber fine: Autoriteit Persoongegevens, 'Dutch DPA: Fine for Data Breach Uber', 27 November 2018, https://www.autoriteitpersoonsgegevens.nl/en/news/dutch-dpa-fine-data-breach-uber.

Website ICO: Information Commissioner's Office, 'Report a Breach', available at https://ico.org.uk/for-organisations/report-a-breach/.

Website Irish Data Protection Commission Code of Practice: Irish Data Protection Commission, 'Personal Data Security Breach Code of Practice', available at https://www.dataprotection.ie/docs/Data-Security-Breach-Code-of-Practice/y/1082.htm.

Website Irish Data Protection Commission Notification Form: Irish Data Protection Commission, 'National Breach Notification Form', available at https://www.dataprotection.ie/docs/Data-Breach-Handling/901.htm.

Website Luxembourg Data Protection Commission Guidance: Commission nationale pour la protection des données, 'Violations de données (Règlement général sur la protection des données)', available at https://cnpd.public.lu/fr/professionnels/obligations/violation-de-donnees/violation-donnees-rgpd.html.

Article 34. Communication of a personal data breach to the data subject

CÉDRIC BURTON[*]

1. When the personal data breach is likely to result in a high risk to the rights and freedoms of natural persons, the controller shall communicate the personal data breach to the data subject without undue delay.
2. The communication to the data subject referred to in paragraph 1 of this Article shall describe in clear and plain language the nature of the personal data breach and contain at least the information and measures referred to in points (b), (c) and (d) of Article 33(3).
3. The communication to the data subject referred to in paragraph 1 shall not be required if any of the following conditions are met:
   (a) the controller has implemented appropriate technical and organisational protection measures, and those measures were applied to the personal data affected by the personal data breach, in particular those that render the personal data unintelligible to any person who is not authorised to access it, such as encryption;
   (b) the controller has taken subsequent measures which ensure that the high risk to the rights and freedoms of data subjects referred to in paragraph 1 is no longer likely to materialise;
   (c) it would involve disproportionate effort. In such a case, there shall instead be a public communication or similar measure whereby the data subjects are informed in an equally effective manner.
4. If the controller has not already communicated the personal data breach to the data subject, the supervisory authority, having considered the likelihood of the personal data breach resulting in a high risk, may require it to do so or may decide that any of the conditions referred to in paragraph 3 are met.

Relevant Recitals

(86) The controller should communicate to the data subject a personal data breach, without undue delay, where that personal data breach is likely to result in a high risk to the rights and freedoms of the natural person in order to allow him or her to take the necessary precautions. The communication should describe the nature of the personal data breach as well as recommendations for the natural person concerned to mitigate potential adverse effects. Such communications to data subjects should be made as soon as reasonably feasible and in close cooperation with the supervisory authority, respecting guidance provided by it or by other relevant authorities such as law-enforcement authorities. For example, the need to mitigate an immediate risk of damage would call for prompt communication with data subjects whereas the need to implement appropriate measures against continuing or similar personal data breaches may justify more time for communication.

(87) It should be ascertained whether all appropriate technological protection and organisational measures have been implemented to establish immediately whether a personal data breach has taken place and to inform promptly the supervisory authority and the data subject. The fact that the notification was made without undue delay should be established taking into account in particular the nature and gravity of the personal data breach and its consequences and adverse effects

---

[*] The author is grateful for the research assistance of Rossana Fol and Bastiaan Suurmond.

for the data subject. Such notification may result in an intervention of the supervisory authority in accordance with its tasks and powers laid down in this Regulation.

(88) In setting detailed rules concerning the format and procedures applicable to the notification of personal data breaches, due consideration should be given to the circumstances of that breach, including whether or not personal data had been protected by appropriate technical protection measures, effectively limiting the likelihood of identity fraud or other forms of misuse. Moreover, such rules and procedures should take into account the legitimate interests of law-enforcement authorities where early disclosure could unnecessarily hamper the investigation of the circumstances of a personal data breach.

Closely Related Provisions

Article 4(12) (Definition of a personal data breach); Article 23(1) (Restriction of communication obligation by EU Member States) (see too recital 73); Article 28(3)(f) (Processor); Article 32 (Security of processing); Article 33 (Notification of a breach to the supervisory authority) (see too recital 85); Article 70(1)(g)(h) (Tasks of the Board); Article 83(4)(a) (Fines for infringement of Article 34)

Related Provisions in LED [Directive (EU) 2016/680]

Article 3(11) (Definition of a personal data breach); Article 13(3) (Grounds on which communication can be restricted); Article 30 (Notification of a breach to the supervisory authority) (see too recital 61); Article 31 (Communication of a breach to the data subject) (see too recital 62); Article 51(1)(d)(e) (Tasks of the Board)

Related Provisions in EPD [Directive 2002/58/EC]

Article 2(i) (Definition of a personal data breach); Article 4(3) (Notification of a breach to the national authority and notification of a breach to the subscriber or individual); Article 4(2) (Information to subscribers about a particular risk of a network security breach) (see too recital 20); recital 21

A. Rationale and Policy Underpinnings

Article 34 GDPR is intended to prevent the negative consequences that may result from a personal data breach by specifically providing affected individuals with the opportunity to take appropriate mitigating measures. The sooner that an individual becomes aware of a breach, the sooner they may undertake the necessary precautions in order to prevent or minimise the damage resulting from it. Breach communication may also enable individuals to seek financial compensation for the damage suffered, and provide an incentive for data controllers to improve data security by motivating them to avoid the damage to reputation that notification can bring. In a paper that has been endorsed by the EDPB,[1] the WP29 has explained the benefits of communicating breaches to individuals as follows:

Communicating a breach to individuals allows the controller to provide information on the risks presented as a result of the breach and the steps those individuals can take to protect themselves

[1] EDPB 2018.

from its potential consequences. The focus of any breach response plan should be on protecting individuals and their personal data. Consequently, breach notification should be seen as a tool enhancing compliance in relation to the protection of personal data.[2]

Article 34 is closely related to the obligations to provide appropriate security measures pursuant to Article 32 and to notify data breaches to the competent supervisory authority (DPA) under Article 33. However, the obligation to communicate a breach to data subjects exists independently of the duty to notify it to the DPA, so that notification of the DPA may not serve as a justification for failure to communicate the breach to the data subject.[3]

B. Legal Background

1. EU legislation

The DPD had no equivalent to Article 33 GDPR. While Article 17 DPD required controllers to prevent breaches ('to protect personal data against accidental or unlawful destruction or accidental loss, alteration, unauthorized disclosure or access, and ... against all other unlawful forms of processing'), and Article 10 and Article 11 DPD required them to provide information about data processing to individuals, the DPD did not contain a specific requirement to communicate data breaches.

An obligation to notify data breaches exists in the EPD for providers of electronic communications services; this includes both notification to the 'competent national authority', and, when a personal data breach 'is likely to adversely affect the personal data or privacy of a subscriber or individual', notification to 'the subscriber or individual of the breach without undue delay' as well.[4] The EPD empowers the Commission to specify further notification requirements, which it did by issuing a detailed Regulation 611/2013.[5] The Commission's 2017 proposal for an e-Privacy Regulation[6] to replace the EPD did not contain a data breach notification requirement.

Other sector-specific notification requirements may also apply. Under the eIDAS Regulation, trust service providers must notify individuals in case of a breach of security or loss of integrity 'likely to adversely affect a natural or legal person to whom the trusted service has been provided' without undue delay'.[7] In addition, the notified supervisory body shall inform the public or require the trust service provider to do so where it determines that disclosure of the breach of security or loss of integrity is in the public interest.[8] Under the NIS Directive the competent authority or the Computer Security Incident Response Team ('CSIRT') may inform the public about such incidents[9] or require digital service providers to do so.[10] For payment services providers, the recast PSD2 Directive also contains a breach notification obligation, though this only foresees notification to competent authorities.[11] The Directive establishing the European Electronic Communications Code ('EECC') also contains a breach notification requirement to the competent authority on 'providers of public electronic communications networks or of

---

[2] WP29 2018A, p. 7.   [3] Ibid., p. 16.
[4] Art. 4 EPD. See also Art. 3 Citizens Rights Directive.   [5] Commission Regulation 611/2013.
[6] Art. 4 EPR Proposal.   [7] Art. 19(2) eIDAS Regulation.   [8] Ibid.
[9] Arts. 14(6) and 16(7) NIS Directive.   [10] Ibid., Art. 16(7).   [11] Art. 96 PSD2 Directive.

publicly available electronic communications services'.[12] Under the EECC, providers are also supposed to notify their users when there is 'a particular and significant threat of a security incident in public electronic communications networks or publicly available electronic communications services'.[13]

Article 31 LED replicates the provisions of Article 34 and also allows EU Member States to restrict the communication obligation by way of a legislative act. Communication may thus be delayed, restricted, or omitted to the extent that such a measure constitutes a necessary and proportionate measure in a democratic society, and duly regards the fundamental rights and the legitimate interests of the individuals. Article 13(3) LED lists public interest grounds based on which such restrictions may be introduced.

The existence of multiple breach notification regimes raises the question of how they interact. Generally speaking, each instrument of EU law dealing with breach notification has its own tests for when the notification requirement applies, who should be notified, the information to be provided and other relevant details. This means that the requirements for when each notification regime applies have to be determined individually.[14] However, there may be overlaps between these requirements in certain cases. For example, the NIS Directive[15] clarifies that its breach notification obligation does not apply to undertakings that are already subject to the security and notification requirements under Article 19 of the eIDAS Regulation or Articles 13(a) and 13(b) of the Electronic Privacy Directive.

On 26 June 2019 the EU Cybersecurity Act[16] entered into force. The Cybersecurity Act strengthens the role of ENISA (the European Union Agency for Cybersecurity), and establishes an EU-wide cybersecurity certification framework for digital products, services, and processes.

2. International instruments

Council of Europe Convention 108 does not include a provision dealing with personal data breach notification. However, the modernised version of the Convention contains a new provision stating that 'Each Party shall provide that the controller notifies, without delay, *at least* the competent supervisory authority within the meaning of Article 15 of this Convention, of those data breaches which may seriously interfere with the rights and fundamental freedoms of data subjects'[17] (emphasis added), implying that individuals should be informed of breaches in certain circumstances.

3. National developments

At the national level, some EU Member States had personal data breach notification requirements in place before the enactment of the GDPR, a few of which covered notification to affected individuals.[18]

4. Case law

To date, neither the CJEU nor the ECtHR has ruled directly on the subject-matter of Article 34.

---

[12] Art. 40(2) EECC Directive.   [13] Ibid. Art. 40(3).
[14] The guidance in WP29 2018A implies this; see p. 28.   [15] Art. 1(3) NIS Directive.
[16] Cybersecurity Act.   [17] Art. 7(2) Modernised Convention 108.
[18] E.g. s. 42a German Federal Data Protection Act 2017.

C. Analysis

1. Member State law and practice

In contrast to Article 33, the obligations and rights provided for in Article 34 may be limited by EU or Member State law under the conditions of Article 23 GDPR, which means it is likely that there will be divergences between the Member States regarding communication of data breaches to data subjects. In addition, the role of the DPAs in having to deal with data breaches presupposes that they have procedures in place to deal with them. Recital 86 also states that communications to data subjects should be made 'in close cooperation with the supervisory authority'.

A number of Member States have developed their own guidance and requirements for notifying data breaches. For example, Belgium,[19] France,[20] Austria[21] and Ireland[22] provide online forms to notify breaches. Some have also provided information notes on data breaches (for example, Belgium,[23] France,[24] Luxemburg[25] and the United Kingdom).[26] Ireland also has a code of practice dealing with personal data security breaches.[27] Some national laws post-GDPR also deal with the notification of data breaches (such as in Austria).[28]

Under Article 70(1)(h) GDPR, the EDPB is tasked with issuing 'guidelines, recommendations and best practices in accordance with point (e) of this paragraph as to the circumstances in which a personal data breach is likely to result in a high risk to the rights and freedoms of the natural persons referred to in Article 34(1)'. The Working Paper of the WP29 that was endorsed by the EDPB[29] is a first step in providing such guidance, and also contains a flow chart as to how notification to the DPA is to be made, together with a table giving examples.[30]

2. Territorial scope of the communication requirement

Under Article 3(2), the GDPR may apply to controllers and processor not established in the EU in certain circumstances, and under Article 3(3) it may also apply to the processing of personal data by a controller not established in the Union but in a place where Member State law applies by virtue of public international law. The WP29 has stated that data controllers not established in the EU but subject to the GDPR under Article 3(2) or Article 3(3) are bound by the communication requirement of Article 34 when they experience a breach.[31] In such cases, the competent DPA will be the one of the Member State where the controller's representative is established.[32]

---

[19] Website Belgian Privacy Commission Notification Form.
[20] Website CNIL Notification Form   [21] Austrian Data Protection Authority 2018.
[22] Website Irish Data Protection Commission Notification Form.
[23] Website Belgian Privacy Commission Guidance.   [24] Website CNIL Guidance.
[25] Website Luxembourg Data Protection Commission Guidance.   [26] See ICO 2013.
[27] Website Irish Data Protection Commission Code of Practice.
[28] Section 55 Austrian Federal Data Protection Act.
[29] WP29 2018A. See also WP29 2014, which mainly deals with data breach notification under the DPD but also contains some discussion of the (at that time) proposed GDPR.
[30] WP29 2018A, pp. 30–33.
[31] Ibid., p. 18.   [32] Ibid.

3. Data breaches covered

The GDPR defines a personal data breach broadly as any 'breach of security leading to the accidental or unlawful destruction, loss, alteration, unauthorised disclosure of, or access to, personal data transmitted, stored or otherwise processed'.[33] The broad scope of 'personal data' under the GDPR[34] also reinforces the wide coverage of data breaches. At the same time, there is a distinction to be made between data breaches, which involve breaches of personal data, and security incidents (i.e. incidents where there is a breach of security principles), which may not.[35] As a practical matter, when there is a doubt as to whether a data breach is covered by the obligations of the GDPR, data controllers often err on the side of doing so, in order to protect themselves in case it is later found that a breach occurred.

4. Application of the communication obligation

Article 34 requires controllers to communicate a personal data breach to the data subject without undue delay, when the breach is likely to result in a high risk to the rights and freedoms of natural persons. The obligation of communication to data subjects under Article 34 applies only to data controllers, not to data processors.

The threshold for communication of a data breach to data subjects is higher than that of notification of a breach to a DPA, in order to protect data subjects from 'unnecessary notification fatigue'.[36] There is no precise definition in the GDPR of what constitutes a 'high risk to the rights and freedoms of natural persons' within the context of Article 34, or how it is to be differentiated from mere risk (which is the threshold required under Article 33).[37]

The WP29 has identified the following factors that can be used to assess risk: the type of breach; the nature, sensitivity and volume of personal data; ease of identification of individuals; the severity of consequences for individuals; special characteristics of the individual; special characteristics of the data controller; and the number of affected individuals.[38] It has also stated that there is a presumption of high risk to rights and freedoms when 'the breach may lead to physical, material or non-material damage for the individuals whose data have been breached', which is the case with regard to situations involving discrimination, identity theft or fraud, financial loss, damage to reputation, the processing of sensitive data, or criminal convictions and offences or related security measures.[39] Annex B of the WP29 guidance contains a non-exhaustive list of examples when a breach may result in a high risk to individuals.[40]

Article 34(3) specifies three situations in which communication to data subjects is not required. Data controllers will have to be able to demonstrate to DPAs that any of these conditions applies.[41]

First, communication is not necessary when technical and organisational measures have been implemented and applied to the personal data affected by the breach, such

---

[33] Art. 4(12) GDPR. See the commentary on Art. 4(12) in this volume.
[34] See Art. 4(1) GDPR.   [35] See WP29 2018A, p. 7.   [36] Ibid., p. 20.
[37] The concept of high risk to the rights and freedoms of natural persons is also used in Art. 35 regarding data protection impact assessments ('DPIAs'), but the WP29 has argued that the concept of risk has a different focus in the context of DPIAs than it does with regard to notification of data breaches. Ibid., p. 23.
[38] Ibid., pp. 24–26.   [39] Ibid., p. 23.   [40] Ibid., pp. 31–33.   [41] Ibid., p. 22.

as encryption (but not pseudonymisation),[42] or other measures aimed at rendering the data unintelligible to any unauthorised person who may access it.[43] The encryption technology used must be state-of-the-art.[44]

Secondly, notification is not required where the controller has taken subsequent measures which ensure that the high risk to individuals' rights 'is no longer likely to materialize'.[45] For example, this could be the case where the controller has immediately taken action against the individual who has accessed the data before they were able to do anything with it.[46] While the GDPR simply refers to 'subsequent' measures, the WP29 requires that such measures be taken 'immediately' following the breach.[47]

Thirdly, controllers do not need to notify affected individuals where this would involve 'disproportionate effort'.[48] In such cases, the controller should instead make a public communication in a way that informs individuals in an equally effective manner. In the context of Article 34, the WP29 has given as an example of 'disproportionate effort' a situation when 'the warehouse of a statistical office has flooded and the documents containing personal data were stored only in paper form',[49] and has analysed the concept further in its Guidelines on transparency.[50] In addition to the public communication, the WP29 recommends that 'technical arrangements' be made to provide information about the breach on demand, particularly to assist individuals whom the controller cannot otherwise contact.[51]

With regard to joint controllers, it is recommended that in the agreements they are required to conclude under Article 26 to determine their respective compliance responsibilities under the GDPR they enter into contractual arrangements between themselves concerning compliance with breach notification obligations as well.

Associations of data controllers and data processors are empowered to prepare codes of conduct to specify the application of the GDPR with regard to the notification of personal data breaches to DPAs and the communication of such personal data breaches to data subjects.[52]

5. Timing of the communication

A personal data breach is to be communicated to the data subject by the data controller 'without undue delay'.[53] This term is not defined in the GDPR, but the WP29 has explained that it means 'as soon as possible'.[54] Recital 86 GDPR provides that communication should be made 'as soon as reasonably feasible', and further explains that the need to undertake mitigating measures against an immediate risk of damage calls for prompt communication, while the need to implement appropriate measures against continuing or similar breaches may justify communication at a later stage. The WP29 has also emphasised that timely communication is important 'to help individuals to take steps to protect themselves from any negative consequences of the breach'.[55] In case it is not possible to communicate a breach (for example, because the controller does not have sufficient contact details of the individuals affected), then the individual should be contacted as soon as it is reasonably feasible to do so.[56]

---

[42] Ibid., p. 25.　[43] Art. 34(3)(a) GDPR.　[44] WP29 2018A, p. 22.
[45] Art. 34(3)(b) GDPR.　[46] WP29 2018A, p. 22.　[47] Ibid.
[48] Art. 34(3)(c) GDPR.　[49] WP29 2018A, p. 22.　[50] WP29 2018B, pp. 30–34.
[51] WP29 2018A, p. 22.　[52] Art. 40(2)(i) GDPR.　[53] Ibid., Art. 34(1).
[54] WP29 2018A, p. 20.　[55] Ibid.　[56] Ibid., p. 22.

6. Content of the communication

The content of a communication under Article 34 is similar, but not identical, to the notification to be made to the competent supervisory authority as per Article 33. Under Article 34(2), the communication 'shall describe in clear and plain language the nature of the personal data breach and contain at least the information and measures referred to in points (b), (c) and (d) of Article 33(3)'. This means that the following mandatory elements must be included: (i) a description of the nature of the breach; (ii) the name and contact details of the data protection officer or other contact point; (iii) the likely consequences of the breach; and (iv) the measures taken or proposed to be taken by the controller to address the breach. The phrase 'at least' means that additional information can and should be communicated depending on the details of the breach.

However, Article 33 calls for a more detailed and technical description of the nature of the breach, including the categories and approximate number of individuals and records concerned,[57] while Article 34 focuses on the intelligibility of the communication to individuals. The requirements of Article 12(1) GDPR concerning transparency of information and communication apply to communications under Article 34. Thus, the WP29 recommends that the communication be in the language used during the normal course of business, or, if the controller has not previously interacted with the individuals concerned, the local national language.[58] In addition, controllers should provide recommendations for the concerned individuals as to how to mitigate potential adverse effects of the breach.[59] Such mitigating measures could include, for example, advice to individuals on resetting passwords in case their access credentials have been compromised.[60] The supervisory authority may advise controllers on the appropriate message to be sent to individuals and the most appropriate way to contact them.[61]

7. Method of communicating

Communication of a data breach must be sent separately from other information, using dedicated messages, and cannot be coupled with other communication, in particular regular messages to which the individual would likely not pay special attention (e.g. a newsletter).[62] The WP29 has given as examples of clear and transparent communication methods 'direct messaging (e.g. email, SMS, direct message), prominent website banners or notification, postal communications and prominent advertisements in print media'.[63] However, a press release or corporate blog by itself would not be sufficient.[64] The WP29 has recommended using multiple communication channels at the same time to maximise the chances of informing the individual.[65] Information provided under Article 34 must be provided free of charge.[66] Again, controllers may turn to the supervisory authority for advice regarding the most appropriate method to contact individuals.[67]

8. Role of data processors

Data processors are not directly involved in communicating with data subjects, but they do have an important role to play. First of all, as is made clear in Article 33(2), they must notify the data controller of a breach 'without undue delay' when they become aware of one, which allows the controller to take action and communicate with data subjects.[68]

---

[57] See Art. 33(3)(a) GDPR. [58] WP29 2018A, p. 21.
[59] Rec. 86 GDPR. [60] WP29 2018A, p. 20. [61] Ibid., p. 21. [62] Ibid.
[63] Ibid. [64] Ibid. [65] Ibid.
[66] Art. 12(5) GDPR. [67] WP29 2018, p. 18. [68] Ibid., p. 13.

Secondly, data processors must assist controllers in ensuring compliance with their communication obligations under Article 34, taking into account the nature of the processing and the information available to them.[69] This should be reflected in contractual arrangements between the controller and processor.

9. Conflict with third country legal requirements

In some cases of cross-border breaches, such as when it is suspected that a breach was caused by criminal activity, law enforcement requirements of third countries may restrict disclosure of the breach and its details. This can create legal conflicts for data controllers, who may be expected by third country law enforcement authorities not to disclose the breach while they are conducting an investigation, while at the same time controllers are under an obligation to notify it to a DPA.

Recital 86 GDPR states that 'the need to mitigate an immediate risk of damage would call for prompt communication with data subjects whereas the need to implement appropriate measures against continuing or similar personal data breaches may justify more time for communication'. In addition, recital 88 calls for considering 'the legitimate interests of law-enforcement authorities where early disclosure could unnecessarily hamper the investigation of the circumstances of a personal data breach'.

The WP29 states that 'this may mean that in certain circumstances, where justified, and on the advice of law-enforcement authorities, the controller may delay communicating the breach to the affected individuals until such time as it would not prejudice such investigations. However, data subjects would still need to be promptly informed after this time'.[70] Since DPAs are likely to view the possibility of delaying communication restrictively, data controllers are advised to be cautious in doing so, and to attempt to negotiate with third country law enforcement authorities to minimise any delay in communicating with data subjects, when this is required under the GDPR.

10. Enforcement

Penalties for violation of Article 34 can include administrative fines and corrective measures under Article 58(2) (such as warnings, reprimands, orders etc.). Fines for non-compliance with the obligations resulting from Article 34 can reach up to € 10 million or up to 2 per cent of total worldwide annual turnover of the preceding year, whichever is higher.[71] Because the failure to communicate with data subjects in violation of Article 34 may reveal other security-related violations, administrative sanctions may be imposed at a level which is effective, proportionate and dissuasive within the limit of the gravest infringement.[72] In such a case, the DPA will also have the possibility 'to issue sanctions for failure to notify or communicate the breach (Articles 33 and 34) on the one hand, and absence of (adequate) security measures (Article 32) on the other hand, as they are two separate infringements'.[73] Article 34(4) empowers the supervisory authority to require the controller to communicate with affected individuals, or to confirm that there is no need for a notification if it considers that the conditions of one of the three exemption scenarios are met or that the processing is unlikely to result in a high risk to individuals.[74]

---

[69] Art. 28(3)(f) GDPR.　　[70] WP29 2018A, p. 21.　　[71] Art. 83(4)(a) GDPR.
[72] WP29 2018A, p. 10.　　[73] Ibid.
[74] The DPAs are also empowered to do this under Art. 58(2)(e) GDPR.

Select Bibliography

EU legislation

Citizens Rights Directive: Directive 2009/1136/EC of the European Parliament and of the Council of 25 November 2009 amending Directive 2002/22/EC on universal service and users' rights relating to electronic communications networks and services, Directive 2002/58/EC concerning the processing of personal data and the protection of privacy in the electronic communications sector and Regulation (EC) No. 2006/2004 on cooperation between national authorities responsible for the enforcement of consumer protection laws, OJ 2009 L 337/11.

Commission Regulation 611/2013: Commission Regulation 611/2013 of 24 June 2013 on the measures applicable to the notification of personal data breaches under Directive 2002/58/EC of the European Parliament and of the Council on privacy and electronic communications, OJ 2013 L 173/2.

Cybersecurity Act: Regulation (EU) 2019/881 of the European Parliament and of the Council of 17 April 2019 on ENISA (the European Union Agency for Cybersecurity) and on information and communications technology cybersecurity certification and repealing Regulation (EU) No 526/2013 (Cybersecurity Act), OJ 2019 L 151/15.

EECC Directive: Directive (EU) 2018/1972 of the European Parliament and of the Council of 11 December 2018 establishing the European Electronic Communications Code (Recast), OJ 2018 L 321/36.

eIDAS Regulation: Regulation (EU) 910/2014 on electronic identification and trust services for electronic transactions in the internal market, OJ 2014 L 257/73.

EPR Proposal: Proposal for a Regulation of the European Parliament and of the Council concerning the respect for private life and the protection of personal data in electronic communications and repealing Directive 2002/58/EC (Regulation on Privacy and Electronic Communications), COM(2017)10 final, 10 January 2017.

NIS Directive: Directive 2016/1148 of the European Parliament and of the Council of 6 July 2016 concerning measures for a high common level of security of network and information systems across the Union, OJ 2016 L 194/1

PSD2 Directive: Directive 2015/2366/EU of the European Parliament and of the Council of 25 November 2015 on payment services in the internal market, amending Directives 2002/65/EC, 2009/110/EC and 2013/36/EU and Regulation (EU) No. 1093/2010, and repealing Directive 2007/64/EC, OJ 2015 L 337/35.

National legislation

Austrian Federal Data Protection Act: Bundesgesetz zum Schutz natürlicher Personen bei der Verarbeitung personenbezogener Daten (Datenschutzgesetz—DSG), BGBl. I Nr. 165/1999 zuletzt geändert durch BGBl. I Nr. 24/2018.

German Federal Data Protection Act 2017: Bundesdatenschutzgesetz vom 30. Juni 2017, BGBl. 2017 Teil I Nr. 2097.

Papers of data protection authorities

EDPB 2018: European Data Protection Board, 'Endorsement 1/2018' (25 May 2018).

WP29 2014: Article 29 Working Party, 'Opinion 03/2014 on Personal Data Breach Notification' (WP 213, 25 March 2014).

WP29 2018A: Article 29 Working Party, 'Guidelines on Personal data Breach Notification under Regulation 2016/679' (WP 250rev.01, as last revised and adopted on 6 February 2018).

WP29 2018B: Article 29 Working Party, 'Guidelines on Transparency under Regulation 2016/679' (WP 260rev.01, as last revised and adopted on 11 April 2018).

Austrian Data Protection Authority 2018: Datenschutzbehörde, 'Meldung von Verletzungen des Schutzes personenbezogener Daten gemäß Art. 33 DSGVO' (2018).

ICO 2013: Information Commissioner's Office 'ICO', 'Notification of PECR Security Breaches' (19 March 2013).

Others

Website Belgian Privacy Commission Guidance: Autorité de protection des donnés, 'Notification des fuites de données à l'Autorité', available at https://www.autoriteprotectiondonnees.be/notification-des-fuites-de-données-à-la-commission-vie-privée.

Website Belgian Privacy Commission Notification Form: Autorité de protection des donnés, 'La notification de fuites de données', available at https://www.autoriteprotectiondonnees.be/la-notification-de-fuites-de-données.

Website CNIL Guidance: Commission Nationale de l'Informatique et des Libertés, 'Notifier une violation de données personnelles', available at https://www.cnil.fr/fr/notifier-une-violation-de-donnees-personnelles.

Website CNIL Notification Form: Commission Nationale de l'Informatique et des Libertés 'CNIL', 'Notification d'une violation de données personnelles', available at https://notifications.cnil.fr/notifications/index.

Website Irish Data Protection Commission Code of Practice: Irish Data Protection Commission, 'Personal Data Security Breach Code of Practice', available at https://www.dataprotection.ie/docs/Data-Security-Breach-Code-of-Practice/y/1082.htm.

Website Irish Data Protection Commission Notification Form: Irish Data Protection Commission, 'National Breach Notification Form', available at https://www.dataprotection.ie/docs/Data-Breach-Handling/901.htm.

Website Luxembourg Data Protection Commission Guidance: Commission nationale pour la protection des données, 'Violations de données (Règlement général sur la protection des données)', available at https://cnpd.public.lu/fr/professionnels/obligations/violation-de-donnees/violation-donnees-rgpd.html.

Section 3 Data protection impact assessment and prior consultation

Article 35. Data protection impact assessment

ELENI KOSTA

1. Where a type of processing in particular using new technologies, and taking into account the nature, scope, context and purposes of the processing, is likely to result in a high risk to the rights and freedoms of natural persons, the controller shall, prior to the processing, carry out an assessment of the impact of the envisaged processing operations on the protection of personal data. A single assessment may address a set of similar processing operations that present similar high risks.
2. The controller shall seek the advice of the data protection officer, where designated, when carrying out a data protection impact assessment.
3. A data protection impact assessment referred to in paragraph 1 shall in particular be required in the case of:
   (a) a systematic and extensive evaluation of personal aspects relating to natural persons which is based on automated processing, including profiling, and on which decisions are based that produce legal effects concerning the natural person or similarly significantly affect the natural person;
   (b) processing on a large scale of special categories of data referred to in Article 9(1), or of personal data relating to criminal convictions and offences referred to in Article 10; or
   (c) a systematic monitoring of a publicly accessible area on a large scale.
4. The supervisory authority shall establish and make public a list of the kind of processing operations which are subject to the requirement for a data protection impact assessment pursuant to paragraph 1. The supervisory authority shall communicate those lists to the Board referred to in Article 68.
5. The supervisory authority may also establish and make public a list of the kind of processing operations for which no data protection impact assessment is required. The supervisory authority shall communicate those lists to the Board.
6. Prior to the adoption of the lists referred to in paragraphs 4 and 5, the competent supervisory authority shall apply the consistency mechanism referred to in Article 63 where such lists involve processing activities which are related to the offering of goods or services to data subjects or to the monitoring of their behaviour in several Member States, or may substantially affect the free movement of personal data within the Union.
7. The assessment shall contain at least:
   (a) a systematic description of the envisaged processing operations and the purposes of the processing, including, where applicable, the legitimate interest pursued by the controller;
   (b) an assessment of the necessity and proportionality of the processing operations in relation to the purposes;
   (c) an assessment of the risks to the rights and freedoms of data subjects referred to in paragraph 1; and
   (d) the measures envisaged to address the risks, including safeguards, security measures and mechanisms to ensure the protection of personal data and to demonstrate compliance with this Regulation taking into account the rights and legitimate interests of data subjects and other persons concerned.
8. Compliance with approved codes of conduct referred to in Article 40 by the relevant controllers or processors shall be taken into due account in assessing the impact of the processing

operations performed by such controllers or processors, in particular for the purposes of a data protection impact assessment.

9. Where appropriate, the controller shall seek the views of data subjects or their representatives on the intended processing, without prejudice to the protection of commercial or public interests or the security of processing operations.

10. Where processing pursuant to point (c) or (e) of Article 6(1) has a legal basis in Union law or in the law of the Member State to which the controller is subject, that law regulates the specific processing operation or set of operations in question, and a data protection impact assessment has already been carried out as part of a general impact assessment in the context of the adoption of that legal basis, paragraphs 1 to 7 shall not apply unless Member States deem it to be necessary to carry out such an assessment prior to processing activities.

11. Where necessary, the controller shall carry out a review to assess if processing is performed in accordance with the data protection impact assessment at least when there is a change of the risk represented by processing operations.

Relevant Recitals

(75) The risk to the rights and freedoms of natural persons, of varying likelihood and severity, may result from personal data processing which could lead to physical, material or non-material damage, in particular: where the processing may give rise to discrimination, identity theft or fraud, financial loss, damage to the reputation, loss of confidentiality of personal data protected by professional secrecy, unauthorised reversal of pseudonymisation, or any other significant economic or social disadvantage; where data subjects might be deprived of their rights and freedoms or prevented from exercising control over their personal data; where personal data are processed which reveal racial or ethnic origin, political opinions, religion or philosophical beliefs, trade union membership, and the processing of genetic data, data concerning health or data concerning sex life or criminal convictions and offences or related security measures; where personal aspects are evaluated, in particular analysing or predicting aspects concerning performance at work, economic situation, health, personal preferences or interests, reliability or behaviour, location or movements, in order to create or use personal profiles; where personal data of vulnerable natural persons, in particular of children, are processed; or where processing involves a large amount of personal data and affects a large number of data subjects.

(84) In order to enhance compliance with this Regulation where processing operations are likely to result in a high risk to the rights and freedoms of natural persons, the controller should be responsible for the carrying-out of a data protection impact assessment to evaluate, in particular, the origin, nature, particularity and severity of that risk. The outcome of the assessment should be taken into account when determining the appropriate measures to be taken in order to demonstrate that the processing of personal data complies with this Regulation. Where a data-protection impact assessment indicates that processing operations involve a high risk which the controller cannot mitigate by appropriate measures in terms of available technology and costs of implementation, a consultation of the supervisory authority should take place prior to the processing.

(89) Directive 95/46/EC provided for a general obligation to notify the processing of personal data to the supervisory authorities. While that obligation produces administrative and financial burdens, it did not in all cases contribute to improving the protection of personal data. Such indiscriminate general notification obligations should therefore be abolished, and replaced by effective procedures and mechanisms which focus instead on those types of processing operations which are likely to result in a high risk to the rights and freedoms of natural persons by virtue of their nature, scope, context and purposes. Such types of processing operations may be those which in, particular, involve using new technologies, or are of a new kind and where no data protection impact

assessment has been carried out before by the controller, or where they become necessary in the light of the time that has elapsed since the initial processing.

(90) In such cases, a data protection impact assessment should be carried out by the controller prior to the processing in order to assess the particular likelihood and severity of the high risk, taking into account the nature, scope, context and purposes of the processing and the sources of the risk. That impact assessment should include, in particular, the measures, safeguards and mechanisms envisaged for mitigating that risk, ensuring the protection of personal data and demonstrating compliance with this Regulation.

(91) This should in particular apply to large-scale processing operations which aim to process a considerable amount of personal data at regional, national or supranational level and which could affect a large number of data subjects and which are likely to result in a high risk, for example, on account of their sensitivity, where in accordance with the achieved state of technological knowledge a new technology is used on a large scale as well as to other processing operations which result in a high risk to the rights and freedoms of data subjects, in particular where those operations render it more difficult for data subjects to exercise their rights. A data protection impact assessment should also be made where personal data are processed for taking decisions regarding specific natural persons following any systematic and extensive evaluation of personal aspects relating to natural persons based on profiling those data or following the processing of special categories of personal data, biometric data, or data on criminal convictions and offences or related security measures. A data protection impact assessment is equally required for monitoring publicly accessible areas on a large scale, especially when using optic-electronic devices or for any other operations where the competent supervisory authority considers that the processing is likely to result in a high risk to the rights and freedoms of data subjects, in particular because they prevent data subjects from exercising a right or using a service or a contract, or because they are carried out systematically on a large scale. The processing of personal data should not be considered to be on a large scale if the processing concerns personal data from patients or clients by an individual physician, other health care professional or lawyer. In such cases, a data protection impact assessment should not be mandatory.

(92) There are circumstances under which it may be reasonable and economical for the subject of a data protection impact assessment to be broader than a single project, for example where public authorities or bodies intend to establish a common application or processing platform or where several controllers plan to introduce a common application or processing environment across an industry sector or segment or for a widely used horizontal activity.

(93) In the context of the adoption of the Member State law on which the performance of the tasks of the public authority or public body is based and which regulates the specific processing operation or set of operations in question, Member States may deem it necessary to carry out such assessment prior to the processing activities.

Closely Related Provisions

Article 24 (Responsibility of controller); Article 25 (Data protection by design and by default); Article 32 (Security of processing); Article 36 (Prior consultation) (see too recitals 94–95); Article 39 (Tasks of data protection officer); Article 40 (Codes of conduct); Article 63 (Consistency mechanism); Article 64 (Opinions of EDPB)

Related Provisions in LED [Directive (EU) 2016/680]

Article 19 (Obligations of controller) (see too recitals 51–53); Article 20 (Data protection by design and by default) (see too recital 53); Article 27 (Data protection impact assessment) (see too recital 58); Article 28 (Prior consultation of supervisory authority)

Related Provisions in EPD [Directive 2002/58/EC]

Article 4 (Security of processing) (see too recital 20)

Related Provisions in EUDPR [Regulation (EU) 2018/1725]

Article 26 (Responsibility of the controller) (see also recital 45); Article 27 (Data protection by design and by default) (see too recital 48); Article 39 (Data protection impact assessment) (see too recitals 57, 46–47); Article 40 (Prior consultation of European Data Protection Supervisor) (see too recital 58)

Relevant Case Law

CJEU

Joined Cases C-92/09 and 93/09, *Volker and Markus Schecke GbR* and *Hartmut Eifert v Land Hessen*, judgment of 9 November 2010 (Grand Chamber) (ECLI:EU:C:2010:662).

Joined Cases C-293/12 and C-594/12, *Digital Rights Ireland Ltd v Minister for Communications, Marine and Natural Resources and Others and Kärntner Landesregierung and Others*, judgment of 8 April 2014 (Grand Chamber) (ECLI:EU:C:2014:238).

Case C-362/14, *Maximillian Schrems v Data Protection Commissioner*, judgment of 6 October 2015 (Grand Chamber) (ECLI:EU:C:2015:650).

Case C-582/14, *Patrick Breyer v Bundesrepublik Deutschland*, judgment of 19 October 2016 (ECLI:EU:C:2016:779).

ECtHR

S and Marper v United Kingdom, Appl. Nos. 30562/04, 30566/04, judgment of 4 December 2008.

A. Rationale and Policy Underpinnings

Article 35 GDPR introduces an obligation to carry out a data protection impact assessment ('DPIA') when a data processing operation, or a set of similar operations, especially those making use of new technologies, is likely to result in high risk to the rights and freedoms of individuals. This obligation reflects the main objective of the GDPR, which is to ensure a high level of protection of the fundamental rights and freedoms of natural persons in general and in particular their right to the protection of personal data (see Article 1(2) GDPR, along with recitals 9 and 10 GDPR).

Impact assessments have been used in many regulatory areas to assess the (impact of) risks raised by a specific technology or in a specific context. For instance, technology assessments were developed in the 1960s to study the consequences of technological inventions. Environmental impact assessments are also a common practice.[1] Privacy Impact Assessments ('PIAs')—and later DPIAs—were first carried out in the 1990s in Canada, New Zealand and Australia,[2] initially by public sector bodies and later by industry, as an instrument to safeguard privacy-related interests and to demonstrate accountability.[3]

DPIAs are introduced as an accountability measure, as their outcomes shall 'be taken into account when determining the appropriate measures to be taken in order to demonstrate that the data processing operation is compliant with the [GDPR]' (recital 84 GDPR).[4]

---

[1] See for Environmental Impact Assessments, Directive 2015/52/EU. [2] Kloza et al. 2017, p. 1.
[3] Wright and de Hert 2012, p. 3; Clarke 2009. [4] See also WP29 2017C, p. 4.

At the same time, DPIAs are also *ex ante* regulatory mechanisms that function as 'early warning systems' aimed at identifying potential negative consequences of processing operations at an early stage and at mitigating the impact of the potential risks.[5] The requirements pertaining to data protection by design (see Article 25 GDPR) have a similar function, as these are aimed at ensuring that early account is taken of data protection requirements in information systems development.[6]

The introduction of DPIA requirements in the GDPR must also be understood in light of problems with the notification and prior checking procedures pursuant to the DPD. These procedures (elaborated in the next section) were complicated and entailed a heavy workload for DPAs. Moreover, their efficacy in producing actual data protection gains was questionable.[7] Indeed, the WP29 concluded that the notification system was 'not a useful or appropriate tool to provide information and transparency'.[8] To remedy these problems, the EU legislature chose to introduce requirements for DPIAs, described as 'effective procedures and mechanisms which focus instead on those types of processing operations which are likely to result in a high risk to the rights and freedoms of natural persons by virtue of their nature, scope, context and purposes' (recital 89 GDPR).

B. Legal Background

1. EU legislation

The DPD did not contain specific provisions on DPIAs. In certain circumstances, however, it required controllers to notify the competent data protection authority before they carried out a specific data processing operation (Article 18 DPD). It additionally established a procedure of prior checking according to which Member States were required to determine the processing operations likely to present specific risks to the rights and freedoms of data subjects and to check that these processing operations were examined prior to the start thereof (Article 20(1) DPD). This procedure may be seen as the predecessor to DPIAs, as it was aimed at ensuring that processing operations likely to present a high risk complied with the data protection legislation. Such prior checking, though, was able to be carried out only on an exceptional basis (recital 54 DPD), as the '*ex post facto* verification by the competent authorities' was considered 'a sufficient measure' (recital 52 DPD).[9]

The DPD entrusted DPAs with the primary role in prior checking: they had to carry out prior checks when a controller or a data protection official notified them of data processing operations that were likely to present specific risks to the rights and freedoms of the data subjects (Article 20(2) DPD). The elements to be taken into account in order to decide whether data processing operations were likely to pose specific risks concerned 'their nature, their scope or their purposes, such as that of excluding individuals from a right, benefit or a contract, or by virtue of the specific use of new technologies' (recital 53 DPD).

Like the DPD, the EPD does not contain any provisions about DPIAs. Rather it establishes an obligation for service providers to take appropriate technical and organisational

---

[5] Kloza et al. 2017, p. 1.   [6] See further the commentary on Art. 25 in this volume.
[7] See the commentary on Art. 30 in this volume.   [8] WP29 2011, p. 8.
[9] Confirmed in Joined Cases C-92/09 and 93/09, *Schecke* and *Eifert*, paras. 104–105.

measures to safeguard the security of their services (Article 4 EPD). In order to determine the most appropriate measures, service providers need to assess the risks of a breach of security (recital 20 EPD).

2. International instruments

Council of Europe Convention 108 as first adopted did not contain any specific reference to impact assessments. However, the Modernised Convention 108, Article 10(2) requires that:

controllers and, where applicable, processors, examine the likely impact of intended data processing on the rights and fundamental freedoms of data subjects prior to the commencement of such processing, and shall design the data processing in such a manner as to prevent or minimise the risk of interference with those rights and fundamental freedoms.

The Explanatory Report to the Modernised Convention states that the examination required by Article 10(2) 'can be done without excessive formalities'.[10] This might suggest that the examination need not amount to a full DPIA as envisaged by Article 35 GDPR. Nonetheless, such an examination could, in certain situations, end up being similar in scale and formality to procedures under the GDPR. At the same time, the extension of impact assessment obligations to processors in addition to controllers goes further than the GDPR. Moreover, the Modernised Convention 108—contrary to the GDPR—does not tie these obligations to the existence of a likely 'high' risk of interference with data subjects' rights and freedoms.

3. National developments

When transposing the DPD, EU and European Economic Area ('EEA') Member States included in their national legislation provisions relating to the DPD's above-described requirements of notification and prior checking. Some Member States operated with relatively extensive prior checking requirements. Norway, for instance, required prior authorisation (licensing) by the Norwegian Data Inspectorate for the processing of sensitive data (with some exceptions),[11] and for data processing operations by telecommunication service providers, insurance companies and financial bodies.[12] Moreover, the Data Inspectorate was given the power to require licensing for data processing operations when they 'obviously infringe weighty data protection interests'.[13]

Some national DPAs were active in producing guidance on privacy/data protection impact assessments prior to the GDPR's adoption. For instance, the UK ICO first published in 2007 a handbook on PIAs which was formalised seven years later as a code of conduct on 'Conducting privacy impact assessments',[14] while the French DPA (CNIL), published in 2015 three manuals on PIAs, focusing on methodology, tools and good practices respectively.[15] Guidelines on PIAs and DPIAs in specific areas were also published by other DPAs, such as the Slovenian Privacy Impact Assessment in e-Government Projects (2010),[16] and the Irish Guidance on Privacy Impact Assessment in Health and Social Care (2017).[17]

---

[10] Explanatory Report Convention 108 2018, para. 88.
[11] s. 33 Norwegian Personal Data Act 2000.   [12] Ibid., chapter 7.
[13] Ibid., s. 33. See further on the old Norwegian licensing scheme, e.g. Bygrave 2002, 18.4.7.
[14] ICO 2014.   [15] CNIL 2015.   [16] Slovenian Data Protection Authority 2010.
[17] HIQA 2017.

4. Case law

Although the DPD did not include dedicated provisions on DPIAs, the CJEU has subjected data processing operations to special protection when they present a high risk to data subjects' rights. In doing so, the Court has repeatedly examined 'the risk of abuse' of personal data in the context of laying down guarantees for effectively safeguarding the right to protection of personal data.[18] This approach builds on and parallels the jurisprudence of the ECtHR pursuant to Article 8 European Convention on Human Rights ('ECHR').[19]

C. Analysis

1. Scope of application

Article 35(1) requires controllers to carry out a DPIA when a data processing operation, or a set of similar operations, 'is likely to result in a high risk to the rights and freedoms of natural persons', particularly if it makes use of new technologies. Despite the reference here to 'natural persons' as opposed to 'data subjects', the overall thrust of Article 35 focuses on the impact on the protection of the individuals whose personal data are being processed (see especially Article 35(7)(c)). At the same time, the general reference to 'rights and freedoms of natural persons' means that the factors giving rise to the need to conduct a DPIA may concern not just data protection and privacy rights but also other fundamental rights and freedoms, such as freedom of expression or freedom of movement.[20]

As recital 84 GDPR makes clear, the DPIA should, inter alia, evaluate the origin, nature, particularity and severity of the risk. If it is not clear whether a data processing operation is likely to result in such high risk, it is advisable that the controller perform a DPIA nonetheless.[21] Moreover, although DPIAs are not mandatory for all data processing operations, in practice, controllers must always carry out a preliminary assessment in order to identify whether the processing is likely to result in a high risk and thus require a DPIA.

A DPIA may cover a single category of data processing operation or a set of similar operations. Recital 92 provides examples of DPIAs covering a set of similar operations—i.e. 'where public authorities or bodies intend to establish a common application or processing platform or where several controllers plan to introduce a common application or processing environment across an industry sector or segment or for a widely used horizontal activity'. Such a situation might arise, for instance, where a group of municipal authorities set up similar CCTV systems.[22]

When controllers or processors assess the impact of data processing operations, they shall take due account of approved codes of conduct (as referred to in Article 40 GDPR) with which they comply (Article 35(8) GDPR).

2. Roles

The Commission and the Parliament initially proposed that both controllers and processors carry out DPIAs. However, the GDPR as finally adopted requires that only controllers carry them out after receiving the advice of the data protection officer ('DPO'),

---

[18] See e.g. Joined Cases C-293/12 and C-594/12, *Digital Rights Ireland*, paras. 54–55; Case C-362/14, *Schrems*, para. 91; Case C-582/14, *Breyer*, para. 74.
[19] See e.g. ECtHR, *S and Marper*, para. 99 ff.   [20] See also WP29 2017C, p. 6.
[21] Ibid., p. 8.   [22] Ibid., p. 7.

where designated (Article 35(2)).[23] The assignment of DPIA responsibility to controllers only is in line with the general increase in controller accountability under the GDPR (see especially Articles 5(2) and 24 GDPR). However, if a processor performs all or part of the processing, it will be contractually obliged to assist the controller(s) in carrying out the DPIA 'taking into account the nature of the processing and the information available to the processor' (Article 28(3)(f) GDPR).

Article 35(2) GDPR grants DPOs an advisory role in relation to the performance of a DPIA. DPOs are also entrusted with monitoring the performance of the DPIA (Article 39(1)(c) GDPR). The WP29 initially envisaged additional tasks for DPOs, proposing that they 'could suggest that the controller carries out a DPIA on a specific processing operation, and should help the stakeholders on the methodology, help to evaluate the quality of the risk assessment and whether the residual risk is acceptable, and to develop knowledge specific to the data controller context'.[24] In its revised DPIA guidelines, the WP29 deleted these tasks from the DPO's remit, indicating that they could instead be carried out by a controller's Chief Information Security Officer ('CISO').[25] The latter is one of many possible 'in-house' actors that, depending on the structure of the controller's organisation, may collaborate in the carrying out of DPIAs—in addition to DPOs.[26] Independent (external) experts may be also consulted.[27]

Article 35(9) GDPR requires the controller to seek the views of the data subjects (or of their representatives) on the intended processing, 'without prejudice to the protection of commercial or public interests or the security of processing operations', when this is deemed 'appropriate'. The latter qualification implicitly recognises that involving data subjects in DPIA processes could engender excessively high administrative and financial burdens for controllers. However, the GDPR provides no further guidance regarding the assessment of the appropriateness qualification, thus leaving this to the controllers' discretion, at least initially. The WP29 advised that various means (e.g. surveys, questionnaires) should be deployed in order to seek the views of data subjects, and that controllers must provide documented explanation both in cases where they adopt decisions that differ from the views of the data subjects and where they choose not to seek those views at all.[28]

Although not explicitly required in Article 35, the developers of particular technology products or implementing applications (as opposed to the controllers deploying the products/applications) may also undertake DPIAs. The WP29 suggested that this would be useful where the product/application is likely to be used by multiple controllers for various processing operations. However, as the WP29 made clear, 'the data controller deploying the product remains obliged to carry out its own DPIA with regard to the specific implementation, but this can be informed by a DPIA prepared by the product provider, if appropriate'.[29] Thus, a utility company deploying smart meters would have to conduct a DPIA in so far as it is a controller and the processing of personal data by the smart meters is likely to result in a high risk to the data subjects' rights and freedoms, and this DPIA could be informed by a DPIA conducted by the smart meter manufacturer. The WP29 further indicated that '[e]ach product provider or processor should share useful information without neither [sic] compromising secrets nor [sic] leading to security risks by disclosing vulnerabilities'.[30] In strict legal terms, though, the product

---

[23] Further on the role of the DPO, see WP29 2017B. See also the commentary on Art. 39 in this volume.
[24] WP29 2017A, p. 15. See also Gellert 2017, p. 215 (claiming that the WP29 guidance on this point contradicted the advisory role that the GDPR entrusts to DPOs).
[25] WP29 2017C, p. 15. [26] Ibid., p. 14. [27] Ibid.
[28] Ibid., p. 13. [29] WP29 2017A, p. 6. [30] Ibid., p. 8.

provider's DPIA and sharing of information occur at the provider's discretion, unless the provider is a controller or is a processor subject to contractual obligations pursuant to Article 28(3)(f) GDPR.

3. Specific cases of high risk

Following the general reference to processing likely to result in high risk for data subjects' rights and freedoms (Article 35(1) GDPR), paragraph 3 of Article 35 lists three specific cases when a DPIA would be required. The list is non-exhaustive (as indicated by the formulation 'in particular' in the first line of Article 35(3)). The listed cases are:

1. The systematic and extensive evaluation of personal aspects relating to natural persons which is based on automated processing, including profiling, and on which decisions are based that produce legal effects concerning the natural person or similarly significantly affect the natural person.[31] This includes cases where the processing operations may lead to exclusion or discrimination against individuals.[32]
2. Processing on a large scale of special categories of data[33] or of personal data relating to criminal convictions and offences.[34] Examples of processing operations falling under this category are hospitals keeping medical records of patients, or private investigators keeping data about offenders.[35]
3. Systematic monitoring of a publicly accessible area on a large scale, 'especially when using optic-electronic devices' or 'in particular' when data processing operations 'prevent data subjects from exercising a right or using a service or a contract' (recital 91 GDPR). However, data processing operations on patients or clients by individual physicians, health professionals or lawyers shall not be considered to be on a large scale (recital 91 GDPR). In such cases, a DPIA is not mandatory (recital 91 GDPR), but, of course, the controller can decide to carry out one on their own volition.

During the legislative process, the Parliament proposed a dedicated Article 32a on risk analysis, which included a list of nine cases that would be likely to present specific risks, such as the processing of personal data relating to more than 5,000 data subjects during any consecutive 12-month period or where a personal data breach would likely adversely affect the protection of the personal data, the privacy, the rights or the legitimate interests of the data subject.[36]

While this proposal was not adopted, elements of it may be found in the WP29 DPIA guidelines, which lay out a set of nine criteria that should be considered in defining whether a data processing operation is 'likely to result in a high risk'. These criteria take into account the specific cases referred in Article 35(3), as well as the relevant recitals of the GDPR, but are not legally binding. The criteria comprise:

1. Evaluation or scoring, including profiling and predicting, especially from 'aspects concerning the data subject's performance at work, economic situation, health, personal preferences or interests, reliability or behaviour, location or movements' (recitals 71 and 91), such as credit screening by financial institutions or marketing profiling by companies analysing the use of a website.

---

[31] See the commentary on Art. 22 in this volume.
[32] WP29 2017C, p. 9.
[33] See the commentary on Art. 9(1) in this volume.
[34] See the commentary on Art. 10 in this volume.
[35] WP29 2017C, p. 9.
[36] EP Resolution GDPR 2014.

2. Automated decision-making with legal or similar significant effect (Article 35(3)(a)).
3. Systematic monitoring, including the collection of data through 'a systematic monitoring of a publicly accessible area' (Article 35(3)(c)). The EDBP has stated that 'given the typical purposes of video surveillance (protection of people and property, detection, prevention and control of offences, collection of evidence and biometric identification of suspects), it is reasonable to assume that many cases of video surveillance will require a DPIA'.[37]
4. Sensitive data or data relating to criminal convictions and offences, or data of highly personal nature. This criterion goes beyond Article 35(3)(b) and relates to processing that can have an impact on daily life of individuals or the exercise of fundamental rights.
5. Data processed on a large scale, which can be determined on the basis of the following factors: (a) the number of data subjects concerned, either as a specific number or as a proportion of the relevant population; (b) the volume of data and/or the range of different data items being processed; (c) the duration, or permanence, of the data processing activity; (d) the geographical extent of the processing activity.[38]
6. Matching or combining datasets in a way that would exceed the expectations of the data subject.[39]
7. Data concerning vulnerable data subjects (recital 75), such as employees, children, mentally ill, asylum seekers, elderly, patients etc. This criterion pertains in general cases when there is an increased imbalance of powers between the data subjects and the controllers.
8. Innovative use or applying new technologies or organisational solutions, such as the combined use of fingerprints or face recognition to control access to dedicated areas. New technologies are defined in relation to the achieved state of technological knowledge (recital 91). New technologies can involve novel ways of collecting and using data with unknown personal and social consequences that would justify the need to carry out a DPIA, such as for instance certain 'Internet of Things' applications.
9. The processing in itself 'prevents data subjects from exercising a right or using a service or a contract' (Article 22 and recital 91), such as bank credit screening of customers in order to decide on granting a loan.

This list of criteria is non-exhaustive, but the more criteria that a processing operation or set of similar operations meets, the more likely it is that the processing presents a high risk to the rights and freedoms of data subjects. The WP29 suggested that, as a general rule, when a data processing operation meets two criteria, a DPIA would be required.[40] However, as the aforementioned criteria refer to processing that in most cases could potentially result in high risk, the controller should carry out a DPIA even when only one of these criteria is met. Conversely, a controller may decide not to carry out a DPIA even when a processing operation falls under these criteria. In such a case, the controller should document the reasons for not carrying out a DPIA, and in doing so refer specifically to the views of the DPO.[41]

---

[37] EDPB 2019, p. 29.   [38] Further on these factors, see WP29 2017B.
[39] For further explanation, see WP29 2013, p. 24.
[40] WP29 2017C, p. 11.   [41] Ibid., p. 12.

4. Timing, review, reassessment and transparency of DPIAs

Article 35(1) clearly indicates that the DPIA must take place before the processing begins. Nevertheless, DPIAs should be seen as a continuous process rather than as a one-time exercise. Concomitantly, DPIAs should undergo regular review and re-assessment.[42] The WP29 initially suggested a reassessment of DPIAs every three years,[43] but in the revised version of its guidelines, it did not refer to any concrete time periods.[44] It is thus left initially up to controllers to decide how often they should update their DPIAs, but this decision needs to be justified.

The GDPR requires that, where necessary, the controller shall carry out a review to assess if processing is performed in accordance with the DPIA at least when there is a change of the risk represented by processing operations (Article 35(11)). This could relate, for example, to a change in the source of risk for the actual processing operation or to a change in the context for that operation (such as its repurposing).[45] The GDPR does not specify who is responsible to judge whether there is a need to carry out a reassessment of the DPIA. It seems logical to assign primary responsibility to the controller, but a DPA may also initiate such a decision, given its wide-ranging competence under Article 57 GDPR.

Although the GDPR does not, on its face, require publication of DPIAs, controllers should consider publishing them either in full or, at the very least, in summary form. This is in line with the overarching principles of transparency and accountability.[46]

5. Exemptions

As a rule, a DPIA is not required in cases where the processing is not likely to result in a high risk to the rights and freedoms of natural persons. This follows from the wording of Article 35(1) GDPR. A DPIA is also not required when the nature, scope, context and purposes of the processing are very similar to the processing for which a DPIA has already been carried out,[47] following a justified opinion of the controller. Moreover, a DPIA is not required when a national DPA has checked the data processing operation prior to the application of the GDPR (recital 171 GDPR) in accordance with Article 20 DPD.[48]

Article 35(10) GDPR lays down additional exemptions from the obligation to perform a DPIA in specific cases, but only when the legitimate ground for data processing is compliance with a legal obligation (Article 6(1)(c) GDPR) or performance of a task carried out in the public interest or in the exercise of official authority vested in the controller (Article 6(1)(e) GDPR), in accordance with European or national legislation. Such exemption applies when: (a) the relevant law regulates the specific processing in question; and (b) a DPIA has already been carried out 'as part of a general impact assessment in the context of the adoption of [the] legal basis' of the aforementioned two cases. However, Member States may override this exemption where they deem necessary (see also recital 93 GDPR).

Finally, a DPIA is not required when the national DPA has decided so and has included the specific type of data processing operation in the optional list foreseen in Article 35(5) GDPR.

[42] Ibid., p. 14.   [43] WP29 2017A, p. 12.   [44] WP29 2017C, p. 12.
[45] Ibid.   [46] Ibid., p. 18.   [47] Ibid., p. 12.   [48] Ibid., p. 13.

6. Prior consultation with DPAs

In cases when the controller carries out a DPIA which concludes that the data processing operations at stake involve a high risk that cannot be mitigated by appropriate measures taking into account available technology and the costs of implementation ('residual risk'), the controller must consult with the DPA before carrying out the processing of personal data (recital 84 and Article 36 GDPR).[49]

7. List requirements for DPAs

Article 35(4) GDPR requires DPAs to establish and make public a list of the kind of processing operations which are subject to the requirement for a DPIA. In addition to such an inclusion list, Article 35(5) GDPR offers DPAs the possibility to prepare an exclusion list—i.e. a list of the kind of processing operations for which no DPIA is required. Both lists must be communicated to the EDPB, which should issue further guidance on DPIAs.[50] Prior to the adoption of the aforementioned lists, each DPA shall collaborate with other DPAs under the consistency mechanism established pursuant to Article 63 GDPR, 'where such lists involve processing activities that relate to the offering of goods or services to data subjects or to the monitoring of their behaviour in several Member States, or may substantially affect the free movement of personal data within the European Union' (Article 35(6)).

The DPAs of all EU Member States have submitted draft inclusion lists, drawn up pursuant to Article 35(4), to the EDPB, which has in turn issued opinions on each list with a view to establishing common criteria for such lists across the EEA.[51] The lists cover a range of topics, including the processing of biometric and genetic data, location data, health and non-health data carried out with the aid of an implant, and employee monitoring. The EDPB has not accommodated all DPA proposals as to activities that would result in a high risk. For instance, it did not acknowledge the proposal of the German and Portuguese authorities to cover interfaces for personal electronic devices that are unprotected from unauthorised readout, nor did it accede to the proposal of the Bulgarian authority to cover activities relating to cross-border information systems. Lists under Article 35(4) have also been submitted by DPAs of Iceland, Liechtenstein, and Norway.[52]

The EDPB has highlighted that all supervisory authorities shall include an explicit statement that the lists are non-exhaustive and that they build on and complement the WP29 DPIA guidelines. It is noteworthy that the EDPB requested the deletion of explicit figures in definitions of 'large-scale' processing—included, for instance, in the Czech, Estonian and Greek lists—and required instead reference to the definitions adopted in the WP29 guidelines on DPIA and DPO's respectively. Further, in relation to employee monitoring, the EDPB criticised supervisory authorities for failing to make explicit the reference to the two criteria that the WP29 identified in its DPIA guidelines: systematic monitoring and data concerning vulnerable data subjects. The EDPB requested that the lists be updated to make explicit reference to these two criteria.

In addition, the EDPB has thus far issued opinions on draft lists submitted by DPAs of three Member States (Czech Republic, France, and Spain) on draft lists they submitted

---

[49] See the commentary on Art. 36 in this volume.
[50] WP29 2017C, p. 5.   [51] The opinions are available online. See EDPB Website.   [52] Ibid.

pursuant to Article 35(5) GDPR regarding processing operations exempt from the requirement of a DPIA.[53]

8. Content of a DPIA

A DPIA shall at least contain the following elements:

1. a description of the envisaged processing operations and the purposes of the processing, including, where applicable, the legitimate interest pursued by the controller;
2. an assessment of the necessity and proportionality of the processing operations;
3. an assessment of the risks to the rights and freedoms of data subjects, in terms of likelihood and severity (recital 90 GDPR);
4. the measures envisaged to address the risks and to demonstrate compliance with the GDPR (Article 35(7)).

The Parliament in its first reading proposed a more extensive list of elements to be included in a DPIA, such as a general indication of the time limits for erasure of the different categories of data, and also an explanation of the data protection by design and default practices to be implemented.[54] This proposal was not adopted.

9. Sanctions

Failure to comply with the obligations relating to DPIAs can result in an administrative fine of up to € 10 million or, in the case of an undertaking, up to 2 per cent of the total worldwide annual turnover of the preceding financial year, whichever is higher (Article 83(4)(a) GDPR).

10. DPIA obligations under the LED

The regulation of DPIAs in the LED is a simplified counterpart of Article 35 GDPR. The LED mandates the carrying out of DPIAs by controllers when a type of processing—in particular, using new technologies, and taking into account the nature, scope, context and purposes of the processing—is likely to result in a high risk to the rights and freedoms of natural persons (Article 27(1) LED). Recital 58 clarifies that DPIAs should cover relevant systems and processes of processing operations, but not individual cases. Article 27(2) LED contains the minimum requirements that should be contained in the DPIA, which are a general description of the envisaged processing operations; an assessment of the risks to the rights and freedoms of data subjects; the measures envisaged to address those risks; and safeguards, security measures and mechanisms to ensure the protection of personal data and to demonstrate compliance with the LED, taking into account the rights and legitimate interests of the data subjects and other persons concerned.

The results of the DPIAs should be taken into account when the controllers decide on the appropriate technical and organisational measures for the protection of the security of the data (recital 53). The data protection officer shall provide advice on the carrying out of DPIAs and monitor their performance (Article 34(c) LED).

[53] Ibid. [54] EP Resolution GDPR 2014, Art. 33(3).

Select Bibliography

EU legislation

Directive 2015/52/EU: Directive 2014/52/EU of the European Parliament and of the Council of 16 April 2014 amending Directive 2011/92/EU on the assessment of the effects of certain public and private projects on the environment, OJ 2014 L 124/1.

National legislation

Norwegian Personal Data Act 2000: Act of 14 April 2000 No. 31 relating to the processing of personal data (Personal Data Act) (lov 14. april 2000 nr. 31 om behandling av personopplysninger) (repealed).

Academic writings

Beslay and Lacoste, 'Double-Take: Getting to the RFID PIA Framework', in Wright and de Hert (eds.), *Privacy Impact Assessment* (Springer 2012), 347.
Bygrave 2002: Bygrave, *Data Protection Law: Approaching its Rationale, Logic and Limits* (Kluwer Law International 2002).
Clarke 2009: Clarke 'Privacy Impact Assessment: Its Origins and Development', 25(2) *Computer Law and Security Review* (2009), 123.
De Hert 2012: De Hert, 'A Human Rights Perspective on Privacy and Data Protection Impact Assessments', in Wright and de Hert (eds.), *Privacy Impact Assessment* (Springer 2012), 33.
Gellert 2017: Gellert, 'The Article 29 Working Party's Provisional Guidelines on Data Protection Impact Assessment', 3(2) *European Data Protection Law Review* (2017), 212.
Kloza et al. 2017: Kloza, van Dijk, Gellert, Böröcz, Tanas, Mantovani and Quinn, 'Data Protection Impact Assessments in the European Union: Complementing the New Legal Framework towards a More Robust Protection of Individuals', 1 *d.pia.lab Policy Brief* (2017).
Wright and de Hert 2012: Wright and de Hert, 'Introduction to Privacy Impact Assessment', in Wright and de Hert (eds.), *Privacy Impact Assessment* (Springer 2012), 3.
Wright et al. 2014: Wright, Wadhwa, Lagazio, Raab and Charikane, 'Integrating Privacy Impact Assessment into Risk Management'. 4 *International Data Privacy Law* (2014), 155.
Wright et al. 2015: Wright, Friedewald and Gellert, 'Developing and Testing a Surveillance Impact Assessment Methodology', 5 *International Data Privacy Law* (2015), 40.

Papers of data protection authorities

EDPB 2019: European Data Protection Board, 'Guidelines 3/2019 on the processing of personal data through video devices (version for public consultation)' (10 July 2019).
WP29 2011: Article 29 Data Protection Working Party, 'Advice Paper on Notification' (20 April 2011).
WP29 2013: Article 29 Working Party, 'Opinion 03/2013 on Purpose Limitation' (WP 203, 02 April 2013).
WP29 2017A: Article 29 Working Party, 'Guidelines on Data Protection Impact Assessment (DPIA) and Determining whether Processing Is "Likely to Result in a High Risk" for the Purposes of Regulation 2016/679' (WP 248, 4 April 2017).
WP29 2017B: Article 29 Working Party, 'Guidelines on Data Protection Officers ('DPOs')' (WP 243 rev. 1, as last revised and adopted on 5 April 2017).
WP29 2017C: Article 29 Working Party, 'Guidelines on Data Protection Impact Assessment (DPIA) and Determining whether Processing Is "Likely to Result in a High Risk" for the Purposes of Regulation 2016/679' (WP 248 rev.01, as last revised and adopted on 4 October 2017).
CNIL 2015: Commission nationale de l'informatique et des libertés, 'Privacy Impact Assessments Manual' (2015).

ICO 2014: Information Commissioner's Office 'Conducting Privacy Impact Assessments—Code of Conduct' (2014).

Information Commissioner's Office, 'Privacy Impact Assessment Handbook' (June 2009).

Slovenian Data Protection Authority 2010: Informacijski pooblaščenec, 'Privacy Impact Assessment in e-Government Projects' (2010).

Reports and recommendations

EP Resolution GDPR 2014: Legislative resolution of 12 March 2014 on the proposal for a regulation of the European Parliament and of the Council on the protection of individuals with regard to the processing of personal data and on the free movement of such data (General Data Protection Regulation), 2012/0011(COD), 12 March 2014.

Explanatory Report Convention 108 2018: Council of Europe, 'Explanatory Report to the Protocol amending the Convention for the Protection of Individuals with regard to the Automatic Processing of Personal Data' (10 October 2018), available at https://rm.coe.int/cets-223-explanatory-report-to-the-protocol-amending-the-convention-fo/16808ac91a.

HIQA 2017: Irish Health Information and Quality Authority, 'Guidance on Privacy Impact Assessment (PIA) in Health and Social Care' (version 2, 2017).

Others

EDPB Website: European Data Protection Board, 'Opinions', available at https://edpb.europa.eu/our-work-tools/consistency-findings/opinions_en.

Article 36. Prior consultation

CECILIA ALVAREZ RIGAUDIAS   ALESSANDRO SPINA[*]

1. The controller shall consult the supervisory authority prior to processing where a data protection impact assessment under Article 35 indicates that the processing would result in a high risk in the absence of measures taken by the controller to mitigate the risk.
2. Where the supervisory authority is of the opinion that the intended processing referred to in paragraph 1 would infringe this Regulation, in particular where the controller has insufficiently identified or mitigated the risk, the supervisory authority shall, within period of up to eight weeks of receipt of the request for consultation, provide written advice to the controller and, where applicable to the processor, and may use any of its powers referred to in Article 58. That period may be extended by six weeks, taking into account the complexity of the intended processing. The supervisory authority shall inform the controller and, where applicable, the processor, of any such extension within one month of receipt of the request for consultation together with the reasons for the delay. Those periods may be suspended until the supervisory authority has obtained information it has requested for the purposes of the consultation.
3. When consulting the supervisory authority pursuant to paragraph 1, the controller shall provide the supervisory authority with:
   (a) where applicable, the respective responsibilities of the controller, joint controllers and processors involved in the processing, in particular for processing within a group of undertakings;
   (b) the purposes and means of the intended processing;
   (c) the measures and safeguards provided to protect the rights and freedoms of data subjects pursuant to this Regulation;
   (d) where applicable, the contact details of the data protection officer;
   (e) the data protection impact assessment provided for in Article 35; and
   (f) any other information requested by the supervisory authority.
4. Member States shall consult the supervisory authority during the preparation of a proposal for a legislative measure to be adopted by a national parliament, or of a regulatory measure based on such a legislative measure, which relates to processing.
5. Notwithstanding paragraph 1, Member State law may require controllers to consult with, and obtain prior authorisation from, the supervisory authority in relation to processing by a controller for the performance of a task carried out by the controller in the public interest, including processing in relation to social protection and public health.

Relevant Recitals

(84) In order to enhance compliance with this Regulation where processing operations are likely to result in a high risk to the rights and freedoms of natural persons, the controller should be responsible for the carrying-out of a data protection impact assessment to evaluate, in particular, the origin, nature, particularity and severity of that risk. The outcome of the assessment should be taken into account when determining the appropriate measures to be taken in order to demonstrate

---

[*] The views expressed are solely those of the author and do not necessarily reflect those of the European Commission.

that the processing of personal data complies with this Regulation. Where a data-protection impact assessment indicates that processing operations involve a high risk which the controller cannot mitigate by appropriate measures in terms of available technology and costs of implementation, a consultation of the supervisory authority should take place prior to the processing.

(89) Directive 95/46/EC provided for a general obligation to notify the processing of personal data to the supervisory authorities. While that obligation produces administrative and financial burdens, it did not in all cases contribute to improving the protection of personal data. Such indiscriminate general notification obligations should therefore be abolished, and replaced by effective procedures and mechanisms which focus instead on those types of processing operations which are likely to result in a high risk to the rights and freedoms of natural persons by virtue of their nature, scope, context and purposes. Such types of processing operations may be those which in, particular, involve using new technologies, or are of a new kind and where no data protection impact assessment has been carried out before by the controller, or where they become necessary in the light of the time that has elapsed since the initial processing.

(94) Where a data protection impact assessment indicates that the processing would, in the absence of safeguards, security measures and mechanisms to mitigate the risk, result in a high risk to the rights and freedoms of natural persons and the controller is of the opinion that the risk cannot be mitigated by reasonable means in terms of available technologies and costs of implementation, the supervisory authority should be consulted prior to the start of processing activities. Such high risk is likely to result from certain types of processing and the extent and frequency of processing, which may result also in a realisation of damage or interference with the rights and freedoms of the natural person. The supervisory authority should respond to the request for consultation within a specified period. However, the absence of a reaction of the supervisory authority within that period should be without prejudice to any intervention of the supervisory authority in accordance with its tasks and powers laid down in this Regulation, including the power to prohibit processing operations. As part of that consultation process, the outcome of a data protection impact assessment carried out with regard to the processing at issue may be submitted to the supervisory authority, in particular the measures envisaged to mitigate the risk to the rights and freedoms of natural persons.

(95) The processor should assist the controller, where necessary and upon request, in ensuring compliance with the obligations deriving from the carrying out of data protection impact assessments and from prior consultation of the supervisory authority.

(96) A consultation of the supervisory authority should also take place in the course of the preparation of a legislative or regulatory measure which provides for the processing of personal data, in order to ensure compliance of the intended processing with this Regulation and in particular to mitigate the risk involved for the data subject.

Closely Related Provisions

Article 24 (Responsibility of the controller) (see too recital 74); Article 30 (Records of processing activities) (see too recital 82); Article 35 (Data Protection Impact Assessment) (see too recital 84); Article 39 (Tasks of the data protection officer) (see too recitals 77 and 97); Article 58 (Powers of the supervisory authorities) (see too recital 129)

Related Provisions in LED [Directive (EU) 2016/680]

Article 19 (Obligations of the controller) (see too recitals 51–53); Article 27 (Data protection impact assessment) (see too recital 58); Article 28 (Prior consultation of the supervisory authority)

Alvarez Rigaudias/Spina

Related Provisions in EUDPR [Regulation (EU) 2018/1725]

Article 42(1) (Legislative consultation), Article 57(1)(g) (Advisory task); Article 58(3)(c) (Advisory power) (see too recitals 58–60)

A. Rationale and Policy Underpinnings

The prior consultation procedure foreseen by Article 36 GDPR is part of the compliance obligations that the controller has to meet under the accountability principle enshrined in Article 24. It creates a procedural step by which controllers are required to consult supervisory authorities on processing operations that present residual high risks, which cannot be mitigated with measures taken pursuant to a data protection impact assessment.

The obligation of prior consultation with the supervisory authority can be seen as the summit of a pyramid of obligations concerning the activities by a controller for managing the risks arising from the processing operations under its responsibility. The base of the pyramid is formed by the obligation under Article 30 to maintain records of all processing activities.[1] Higher up the pyramid, under Article 35 the controller must conduct data protection impact assessments ('DPIAs') of those recorded processing activities that present high risks for the rights and freedoms of natural persons.[2] At the summit of the pyramid is the present obligation to consult the supervisory authority in those cases in which, notwithstanding the DPIA and in the absence of measures adopted by the controller to mitigate risks, the processing results in residual high risks for the rights and freedoms of natural persons.

Thus, prior consultation under Article 36 should not be seen in isolation, but as the final and exceptional step in the risk management methodology adopted by the controller. Such prior consultation is strictly interlinked with the other compliance activities of the controller and in particular with the obligation to conduct data protection impact assessments.

B. Legal Background

1. EU legislation

Article 20(1) DPD contained a provision on prior checking. However, as the rationale of prior consultation under Article 36 is linked to the new data protection impact assessment, the procedure for prior checking under the DPD would have a limited relevance for the interpretation of the scope and nature of prior consultation under the GDPR.

Article 20(2) of the DPD entrusted an important role to supervisory authorities. It required a DPA to carry out prior checks when a data controller or a data protection official notified the DPA of data processing operations likely to present specific risks to the rights and freedoms of the data subjects.

The GDPR has replaced notification of prior checking with the appointment of the data protection officer ('DPO') and data protection impact assessments, which are described in recital 89 as 'effective procedures and mechanisms which focus instead on those

---

[1] See the commentary on Art. 30 in this volume.
[2] See the commentary on Art. 35 in this volume.

types of processing operations which are likely to result in a high risk to the rights and freedoms of natural persons by virtue of their nature, scope, context and purposes'.

2. International instruments

Council of Europe Convention 108 as first adopted did not contain any specific reference to impact assessments and to prior consultations on impact assessments. However, the Modernised Convention requires that:

> [C]ontrollers and, where applicable, processors, examine the likely impact of intended data processing on the rights and fundamental freedoms of data subjects prior to the commencement of such processing, and shall design the data processing in such a manner as to prevent or minimise the risk of interference with those rights and fundamental freedoms.[3]

There is however no specific reference to the obligation for controllers to consult supervisory authorities in case of residual high-risk processing operations.

3. National developments

When adopting legislation in order to implement the GDPR, the Member States should include provisions relating to prior consultation, in particular, as regard the procedural aspects of the prior consultation under Article 36(4) and the prior consultation and prior authorisation under Article 36(5).

C. Analysis

1. Introduction

Article 36 requires data controllers to launch a prior consultation procedure in cases where the high risk identified during a DPIA cannot be mitigated by appropriate measures. This prior consultation should be distinguished from other informal consultations concerning any other matter taking place between the DPO of a controller or processor and the supervisory authorities, for example, under Article 39(1)(e). Prior consultation under Article 36 is a formal procedure triggered by the combination of two elements: (a) the controller has completed a DPIA, and (b) the controller is not in a position to take measures to mitigate the risk of the processing to an acceptable level.

2. Time of consultation

Under normal circumstances, the controller should begin the consultation prior to the start of the processing operation, more exactly in the period between the completion of the DPIA and the start of the data processing activities. However, in very exceptional cases, the need to submit a prior consultation to the supervisory authority may materialise even *ex post*, i.e. when processing operations have already started. This will be the case when, as a result of organisational or technical changes, the risk assessment of the original DPIA carried out by the controller must be revised and the updated DPIA results in residual high risk which cannot be mitigated.

---

[3] Art. 10(2) Modernised Convention 108.

Although not explicitly described in the legislation, this possibility stems from the dynamic nature of the DPIA and the obligation of the controller to review the DPIA laid down in Article 35(11). As clarified by the DPIA Guidelines adopted by the WP29 and endorsed by the EDPB:

Updating the DPIA throughout the lifecycle process will ensure that data protection and privacy are considered and will encourage the creation of solutions which promote compliance ... The DPIA is an on-going process, especially if a processing operation is dynamic and subject to ongoing change.[4]

3. Absence of measures by the controller

The second element of the provision of Article 36(1) refers to the 'absence of measures taken by controller to mitigate the risk'. In this respect, it seems more likely that these processing operations would be linked to a public interest (e.g. anti-money laundering, anti-corruption, scientific research) or to a technology that is inherently unable to comply with all of the GDPR principles (e.g. blockchain[5]). Taking into account the context (high risk that a data controller has been unable to mitigate sufficiently), it seems that the consultation should assess whether the intended processing activity is deemed necessary and proportionate in a democratic society (see Article 11(1) Modernised Convention 108 and Article 23(1) GDPR). The principle of proportionality, traditionally applied in EU law to assess the limitation to a fundamental right, is aligned with the above and could provide guidance in this respect. According to this principle, the processing activity would need to be suitable (i.e. at least suitable to attain its aim, that should be legitimate), necessary (i.e. the least restrictive among equally effective means) and proportional *stricto sensu* (i.e. a proper balance should exist between the risk to an individual on the one hand and the interest of the controller and society on the other).

4. Focus of prior consultation

In this respect, the prior consultation should focus on assessing not only the data protection risks but also the benefits that should have been identified in the controller's DPIA as well as the actual impact of the intended processing operation on the GDPR ultimate goals. Indeed, the scope of the consultation seems to be focused on the complete assessment of the processing operation not only in terms of the identified risks but also on the trade-off between these risks and the broader social benefits and interests of the processing operation. The rationale of the consultation procedure would be undermined if the scope of the consultation was only the question of whether risks were correctly identified in the DPIA.

In support of this interpretation, recitals 84 and 94 GDPR explain the need to carry out a consultation with the supervisory authority when high risk cannot be mitigated 'by appropriate measures in terms of available technology and costs of implementation' or 'by reasonable means in terms of available technologies and costs of implementation'. This implies that the request for prior consultation must include a reasoned discussion of the technological and social context in which the processing operation should take place and its proportionality in order to justify it. Hence, the scope of the prior consultation

---

[4] WP29 2017, p. 14.   [5] Regarding the GDPR and blockchain, see Finck 2018.

should not only be about whether the identification of the risk is correct or the adopted mitigation measures are reasonably possible and appropriate (even if not sufficient), but about whether, even in the presence of a high risk for the rights and freedoms of natural persons, the processing operation is still proportionate taking into account the interests at stake. This could be the case where there is a public or private interest underlying the processing operation that is proportionate and must be protected, and the controller is under an objective impossibility to adopt mitigation measures.

In practice, this seems to support the view that the legal framework on data protection created by the GDPR has moved towards traditional areas of 'risk regulation'.[6] Hence, supervisory authorities will need to consider both the risk and the benefits of the intended processing operation. In a similar fashion, other public authorities carry out a pre-market or preventive assessment of the relative risks and benefits of a commercial product (for example, a pharmaceutical product) or a project having an environmental impact where the risks are balanced against the intended benefits. In this way, the prior consultation review would be a powerful instrument in the hands of data protection authorities acting as regulatory bodies. However, as later discussed, if the resulting advice were to be understood as a legally binding decision, it could contradict Article 23 GDPR, which requires the existence of a specific law to protect specific interests, in order to permit the restriction of certain GDPR provisions (in particular, transparency duties or data protection rights).

The existing WP29 Guidelines on DPIAs offer only a very brief clarification. They describe examples of 'unacceptable high residual risks' rather than cases in which the controller is not in a position to adopt mitigation measures. Focusing on the two negative variables of risk (the size of the harm and the frequency of its occurrence), the Guidelines refer to cases where the data subjects would 'encounter significant, or even irreversible, consequences which they may not overcome (e.g. an illegitimate access to data leading to a threat to the lives of data subjects, a layoff, a financial jeopardy)' or where it is 'obvious' that the risks will occur.[7]

Ultimately it will be for the supervisory authorities to elaborate what could be those instances in which, in the absence of measures that the controller may reasonably adopt to mitigate the risk to an acceptable level, processing operations would still be considered acceptable. In any event, the supervisory authority may still propose or recommend the adoption of alternative measures not envisaged by the data controller and/or not foreseen in the GDPR but appropriate to meet the GDPR's ultimate goals (e.g. to make public in a website specific information on the processing activities rather than to try to send a notice to each individual).[8]

5. Procedural aspects

The procedural aspects of the prior consultation are laid down in Article 36(2). The normal deadline for a DPA to provide the written advice on a prior consultation is eight

---

[6] Gellert 2015, p. 3; Maceinate 2017, p. 506.   [7] WP29 2017, p. 19

[8] For instance, under the Spanish pre-GDPR law, controllers were able to apply for a DPA authorisation to be exempted from the right to provide information when the data were obtained from a source different from the data subjects. This authorisation was conditional on the fact that the controller was required to provide evidence that the compliance with the duty to inform was disproportionate in terms of cost or effectiveness and to adopt, where possible, alternative measures (sometimes proposed by the controllers and approved by the DPO and in other occasions proposed by the DPA). See Spanish Data Protection Act 1999.

weeks, but it is possible to extend this deadline by six weeks. These deadlines are also subject to 'stop the clock' suspensions when the supervisory authority requests additional information for the purposes of the consultation. Recital 94 states that the absence of a reaction by the supervisory authority within the period laid down should be 'without prejudice to any intervention of the supervisory authority within its tasks and powers'. Therefore, from the wording of Article 36, one may reasonably assume that the deadline provisions create a legitimate expectation that the supervisory authority concerned will deliver a written advice on time.

However, prior consultation is arguably not a prior authorisation. Therefore, it is entirely conceivable that the controller would not infringe the GDPR by starting the processing operation in the absence of written advice received within the aforementioned deadlines. Moreover, it is doubtful whether the advice provided by the supervisory authority under the prior consultation procedure may be considered as a 'legally binding decision' and thus subject to the judicial remedies of Article 78. After the expiry of the deadline, any other intervention of the supervisory authority, in particular that of a 'legally binding' nature, would still be possible, though it would need to meet the standards of proportionality and necessity laid down in Member States law concerning the exercise of public power.

Article 36(3) provides the list of necessary documents and information to be submitted as part of the prior consultation procedure. In accordance with Article 39(1)(e), the DPO of the controller is required to act as the contact point in prior consultation procedures.

6. Role of DPAs

Article 36(4) requires Member States to consult the supervisory authority on the submission of a proposal for primary or secondary legislation under national law. In this case, the scope and nature of the consultation procedure is completely different from that under Article 36(1). In particular, Article 36(4) binds Member States, not controllers; it concerns draft primary or secondary legislation; it could concern any type of processing operations and not only those resulting in high risk in the absence of mitigation measures; and it is not subject to the same deadline as Article 36(1).

It is unclear whether the outcome of the procedure referred to in Article 36(4) would be advice similar to that to controllers under Article 58(3)(a). On the one hand this could be seen as the preferred outcome of a systematic interpretative approach based on the mitigation of risks for data subjects (recital 96). On the other hand, the prior consultation procedure under Article 36(4) seems to be closer to that contemplated under Article 58(3)(b), under which national parliaments and Member State governments, amongst others, may request supervisory authorities to issue opinions on any matter related to data protection.

In this respect, Article 28(2) of Regulation 45/2001[9] contained an obligation, similar to that under Article 36(4) GDPR, for the Commission to consult the EDPS on draft legislative measures. In addition, similarly to Article 58(3)(b) GDPR, Articles 41(2) second indent and 46(d) of Regulation 45/2001 (taken together for present purposes) provided that the EDPS should advise the Community institutions and bodies and data subjects, either on its own initiative or in response to a consultation, on all matters concerning

[9] See Table of Legislation.

the processing of personal data. The EDPS has consistently stressed since 2005 the importance of this consultative role on proposed legislative measures as a means of ensuring consistency.[10]

This approach in Regulation 45/2001 has been carried over into the EUDPR, which aligns the provisions of the former Regulation 45/2001 with the GDPR whilst preserving its specific characteristics.[11] Recital 60 EUDPR explains that these provisions requiring the EDPS to be consulted are '(i)n order to ensure consistency of data protection rules throughout the Union'.

Finally, under Article 36(5), Member States can request controllers to submit to supervisory authorities for prior consultation and prior authorisation processing operations for the performance of a task carried out in the public interest. It is important to note that in these particular cases the outcome of the prior consultation is clearly not merely an advice but rather an authorisation to perform the intended processing operation.

Select Bibliography

National legislation

Spanish Data Protection Act 1999: Ley Orgánica 15/1999, de protección de datos de carácter personal (repealed).

Academic writings

Finck 2018: Finck, 'Blockchains and Data Protection in the European Union', 4 *European Data Protection Law Review* (2018), 17.
Gellert 2015: Gellert, 'Data Protection: A Risk Regulation? Between the Risk Management of Everything and The Precautionary Alternative', 5(1) *International Data Privacy Law* (2015), 3.
Maceinate 2017: Macenaite, 'The Riskification of European Data Protection Law through a Two-Fold Shift', 8(3) *European Journal of Risk Regulation* (2017), 506.
Wright and de Hert, 'Introduction to Privacy Impact Assessment', in de Hert and Wright (eds.), *Privacy Impact Assessment* (Springer 2012), 3.

Papers of data protection authorities

EDPS 2014: European Data Protection Supervisor, 'The EDPS as an Advisor to EU Institutions on Policy and Legislation: Building on Ten Years of Experience' (4 June 2014).
WP29 2017: Article 29 Working Party, 'Guidelines on Data Protection Impact Assessment (DPIA) and Determining whether Processing Is "Likely to Result in a High Risk" for the Purposes of Regulation 2016/679' (WP 248, 4 April 2017).

Others

EDPS Website: European Data Protection Supervisor, 'Our Role as an Advisor', available at https://edps.europa.eu/data-protection/our-role-advisor_en.

---

[10] EDPS 2014, p. 4. See further EDPS Website.
[11] See Arts. 42(1), 57(1)(g) and 58(3)(c) EUDPR.

Section 4 Data protection officer

Article 37. Designation of the data protection officer

CECILIA ALVAREZ RIGAUDIAS   ALESSANDRO SPINA*

1. The controller and the processor shall designate a data protection officer in any case where
   (a) the processing is carried out by a public authority or body, except for courts acting in their judicial capacity;
   (b) the core activities of the controller or the processor consist of processing operations which, by virtue of their nature, their scope and/or their purposes, require regular and systematic monitoring of data subjects on a large scale; or
   (c) the core activities of the controller or the processor consist of processing on a large scale of special categories of data pursuant to Article 9 or personal data relating to criminal convictions and offences referred to in Article 10.[1]
2. A group of undertakings may appoint a single data protection officer provided that a data protection officer is easily accessible from each establishment.
3. Where the controller or the processor is a public authority or body, a single data protection officer may be designated for several such authorities or bodies, taking account of their organisational structure and size.
4. In cases other than those referred to in paragraph 1, the controller or processor or associations and other bodies representing categories of controllers or processors may or, where required by Union or Member State law shall, designate a data protection officer. The data protection officer may act for such associations and other bodies representing controllers or processors.
5. The data protection officer shall be designated on the basis of professional qualities and, in particular, expert knowledge of data protection law and practices and the ability to fulfil the tasks referred to in Article 39.
6. The data protection officer may be a staff member of the controller or processor, or fulfil the tasks on the basis of a service contract.
7. The controller or the processor shall publish the contact details of the data protection officer and communicate them to the supervisory authority.

Relevant Recital

(97) Where the processing is carried out by a public authority, except for courts or independent judicial authorities when acting in their judicial capacity, where, in the private sector, processing is carried out by a controller whose core activities consist of processing operations that require regular and systematic monitoring of the data subjects on a large scale, or where the core activities of the controller or the processor consist of processing on a large scale of special categories of personal data and data relating to criminal convictions and offences, a person with expert knowledge of data protection law and practices should assist the controller or processor to monitor internal compliance with this Regulation. In the private sector, the core activities of a controller

---

* The views expressed are solely those of the author and do not necessarily reflect those of the European Commission.

[1] Corrigenda to the English text of Art. 37(1)(c) were published on 23 May 2018. The text printed reflects the updated version of the Corrigendum GDPR 2018. For the Corrigendum GDPR 2018, see Table of Legislation.

relate to its primary activities and do not relate to the processing of personal data as ancillary activities. The necessary level of expert knowledge should be determined in particular according to the data processing operations carried out and the protection required for the personal data processed by the controller or the processor. Such data protection officers, whether or not they are an employee of the controller, should be in a position to perform their duties and tasks in an independent manner.

Closely Related Provisions

Article 30 (Records of processing activities) (see too recital 82); Article 33 (Notification of a personal data breach to the supervisory authority) (see too recital 85); Article 35 (Data protection impact assessment) (see too recitals 90–91); Article 36 (Prior consultation) (see too recital 94); Article 38 (Position of the data protection officer) (see too recital 97); Article 39 (Tasks of the data protection officer) (see too recitals 77 and 97)

Related Provisions in LED [Directive (EU) 2016/680]

Article 32 (Designation of the data protection officer) (see too recital 63)

Related Provisions in EUDPR [Regulation (EU) 2018/1725]

Article 43 (Designation of the data protection officer); Article 44 (Position of the data protection officer); Article 45 (Tasks of the data protection officer) (see too recital 62)

Relevant Case Law

CJEU

Case C-518/07, *European Commission v Federal Republic of Germany*, judgment of 9 March 2010 (Grand Chamber) (ECLI:EU:C:2010:125).
Case T-483/13, *Athanassios Oikonomopoulos v European Commission*, GC, judgment of 20 July 2016 (ECLI:EU:T:2016:421).

Italy

Balducci Romano v Azienda per l'Assistenza Sanitaria n. 3 Alto Friuli Collinare Medio Friuli, Tribunale Amministrativo Regionale- Friuli Venezia Giulia Reg. Ric. 00135/2018.

A. Rationale and Policy Underpinnings

Article 37 GDPR confirms the importance of the role assigned by the GDPR to the data protection officer ('DPO'). It sets out the conditions in which appointment of a DPO is mandatory for data controllers and data processors and the qualifications that DPOs must have in order to be appointed and to exercise their function within the relevant organisations. The choices made reflect a compromise solution between the rigid and prescriptive nature of the professional status of a DPO, mandatory appointment in certain circumstances, and the relative flexibility, almost generic nature, of the professional experience required. It can therefore be expected that the implementation of this provision will bring about not only the development of a new and increasingly important professional role but also a high level of variation and adaptation of this role across various organisations, industries and institutional contexts, depending not only on the size of the private or public body, but on the concrete elements of the data processing operations. The WP29 has adopted Guidelines for Data Protection Officers[2] which provide detailed clarifications on the appointment and designation of DPOs.

B. Legal Background

1. EU legislation

Article 37 is partly inspired by the limited provision in the DPD for a 'data protection official'. Under Article 18(2) DPD, the designation of a data protection official was not mandatory. The appointment of a data protection official was merely a condition for the data controller to be exempted from the duty to notify its processing activities to the supervisory authority (if so provided by the national legislation implementing the DPD). In such a case, Article 18 DPD laid down the role and tasks of the data protection official, discussed in the commentary to Article 39 in this volume. Article 18 DPD also mentioned the need to ensure their independence, and recital 49 DPD added that the 'data protection official' could or could not be an employee of the controller.

In fact, the GDPR provisions relating to the DPO are principally inspired by Regulation 45/2001,[3] which provided for the mandatory appointment of a DPO in each EU institution, body and agency. As stated by the EDPS, 'the Data Protection Officer (DPO) is fundamental in ensuring the respect of data protection principles within institutions/bodies'.[4]

Regulation 45/2001 has been replaced by the EUDPR, which retains the characteristics of Regulation 45/2001 whilst aligning itself more closely with the GDPR. Article 43 EUDPR builds on Article 37(1)(a) GDPR and Article 24 of Regulation 45/2001 to provide a mandatory DPO for EU institutions and bodies and determine the conditions for the appointment of the DPO. These EU-level provisions closely resemble the provisions of Article 37 GDPR but with the following specific differences from the GDPR:

1. Article 24(4) of Regulation 45/2001 laid down a minimum term for the DPO of between two and five years, with a maximum total term of ten years. Article 44(8) EUDPR extends this minimum term to three (to five) years and simply provides for reappointment without any maximum term.
2. Article 44(9) EUDPR, like the former Article 24(5) of Regulation 45/2001, requires DPOs to be registered with the competent supervisory authority, the EDPS, after their designation.
3. Article 24(1) of Regulation 45/2001 provided the possibility for the EU institutions or bodies to appoint more than one DPO ('Each Community institution shall appoint at least one person as Data Protection Officer'). However, this possibility of appointing multiple DPOs never materially occurred and has not been maintained in Article 44(1) EUDPR. In contrast, there is some experience in the EU bodies of appointing an Assistant DPO, who assists the DPO and represents them in case

---

[2] WP29 2017.   [3] See Table of Legislation.   [4] EDPS 2005, p. 3.

of absence, as witness the implementing rules adopted by various EU institutions, agencies and bodies. In addition, the larger EU institutions have appointed a Data Protection Coordinator or Contact Person for their component parts, such as the Directorates-General of the European Commission.[5]

Another important consequence of the mandatory designation of DPOs under Regulation 45/2001 was the self-establishment of an informal network of the DPOs of the EU institutions, agencies and bodies, which meets on a regular basis in order to exchange best practices and professional experiences.[6] Laudati has provided an insightful account of the establishment of the DPO role in one EU body.[7]

In conclusion, the provisions on the DPO in the GDPR are very similar to those under Regulation 45/2001 and the EUDPR, save for the additional provisions affecting EU bodies discussed. In consequence, the EDPS opinions and guidelines issued to date are particularly valuable for construing homogeneously the comparable GDPR provisions.[8]

2. International instruments

The DPO is not mentioned in Convention 108 nor in its modernised version of 2018. The OECD Privacy Guidelines 2013[9] do not themselves refer to privacy officers, but the Supplementary explanatory memorandum to the Guidelines mentions the 'important role' of privacy officers in 'designing and implementing a privacy management programme'.[10]

3. National development

As noted above, the DPD enabled Member States to provide an exemption from the duty to notify data processing to the DPAs when the controller appointed a data protection official. According to the comparative analysis of the role of DPOs in many EU Member States undertaken by the Confederation of European Data Protection Organisations ('CEDPO') in 2012, the option to appoint data protection officials was implemented in France, Germany, Sweden, Netherlands and Luxembourg, but there was no uniformity regarding the appointment and designation of DPOs.[11]

4. Case law

The CJEU has yet to rule directly on data protection officers or officials. However, the General Court has underlined the gravity of failure to notify the DPO under Article 25(1) of Regulation 45/2001 before personal data were processed, discussed in the commentary to Article 39 in this volume.[12] In addition, the discussion of the case law on the 'independence' of supervisory authorities in the commentaries on Articles 38, 52 and 69 may also be relevant in assessing the professional status of a DPO within organisations and the possibility for their dismissal.

---

[5] See Art. 14 EC Decision 2008; Art. 10 Council Decision 2004; EP Decision 2015; and EP Guide.
[6] EDPS 2004, p. 25; EDPS 2005, p. 4. [7] Laudati 2014.
[8] See Case C-518/07, *Commission v Germany*, para. 28: 'In view of the fact that Article 44 of Regulation No 45/2001 and Article 28 of Directive 95/46 are based on the same general concept, those two provisions should be interpreted homogeneously ... '
[9] OECD Privacy Guidelines 2013. [10] Ibid., p. 24. [11] CEDPO 2012.
[12] Case T-483/13, *Oikonomopoulos*, para. 100.

During the first months of application of the GDPR, a first instance Italian administrative tribunal handed down a ruling on the professional qualification of DPOs under the GDPR.[13] The tribunal annulled the tender notice of a public authority concerning the provision of professional assistance for the function of DPO. The tender notice had included, as mandatory professional requirements for tenderers, both the possession of a university degree in the relevant fields (IT, law or similar academic degrees) and the possession of a certification ISO/IEC/27001 Auditor/Lead Auditor for IT management and security. In its decision, the administrative tribunal noted that the ISO/IEC 27001 certification cannot be considered a degree qualifying per se the holder for the functions of DPO. Regardless of the possession of such professional certification, the essential requirement for the role of DPO is the specific expertise and legal knowledge necessary to exercise the safeguard function with regard to the fundamental right to the protection of personal data; it is not the establishment of efficient procedures for the management and security of IT systems.

C. Analysis

1. Mandatory designation

The appointment of a DPO is mandatory in three specific cases under Article 37(1) GDPR.

1.1 For public authorities and bodies, except for courts exercising judicial authority

The focus here is the public nature of the processing operations performed by the relevant organisation or body in accordance with public law, as the objective sought by this provision seems to guarantee the control of personal data in situations where there is little or no choice for the data subjects. The exclusion of judicial authorities from the mandatory designation of a DPO derives from the general principle of independence of the judiciary from the enforcement provisions of the GDPR, in particular the absence of competence from the supervisory authorities (Article 55(3) and recital 20 GDPR).

This exceptional derogation, however, would not apply in case of processing operations of personal data carried out by court administrations in the exercise of a public authority which are not directly linked to their judicial mandate. Such processing would either be considered an expression of exercise of public authority or as falling under another specific case.

Moreover, as clarified by the WP29, the reference to public authorities would also imply the application of the mandatory designation in the case of 'natural or legal persons governed by public or private law, which exercise a public task' in sectors such as public transport services, water and energy supply, public housing, public broadcasting or disciplinary bodies for regulated professions.[14] As the other grounds established by Article 37(1)(b) and (c) for the application of the mandatory DPO would in any event apply to many large private companies operating in the public sector, it seems that the clarification by the WP29 would make this broad interpretation a residual instance which only applies in very exceptional cases.

---

[13] Italian Court, *Balducci Romano*.   [14] WP29 2017, p. 6.

1.2 For entities whose 'core activities' require 'regular and systematic monitoring of personal data on a large scale'

The concept of 'core activity' is associated with the idea that processing personal data 'forms an inextricable part of the controller's or processor's activity', as clarified by the guidance of the WP29.[15] In this respect, CEDPO proposed that 'core activities must be construed in accordance with the description of the corporate purpose of the organization and the P&L revenues'.[16]

Similarly, the concept of 'large scale' processing of personal data is not defined in the GDPR although recital 91 offers some clarification with regard to the application of the provision concerning the need to perform a data protection impact assessment in the case of processing on a large scale of special categories of data under Article 35(3)(b) GDPR. The WP29 DPO Guidelines mention four criteria for assessing the large scale nature of the processing: (a) the number of data subjects concerned; (b) the volume of data and/or the range of specific items being processed; (c) the duration, or permanence, of the data processing activity; and (d) the geographical extent of data processing activity.[17]

Finally, the meaning of regular and systematic[18] 'monitoring of the behaviour' has also raised issues. The WP29 noted that 'the notion of monitoring is not restricted to the online environment and online tracking should only be considered as one example of monitoring the behaviour of data subjects'. It provided a number of examples, including operating a telecommunications network; providing telecommunications services; email re-targeting; data-driven marketing activities; profiling and scoring for purposes of risk assessment (e.g. for purposes of credit scoring, establishment of insurance premiums, fraud prevention, detection of money-laundering); location tracking, for example, by mobile apps; loyalty programmes; behavioural advertising; monitoring of wellness, fitness and health data via wearable devices; closed-circuit television; and connected devices (e.g. smart meters, smart cars, home automation).[19]

1.3 For entities whose core activity is the processing, again on a large scale, of special category of data under Article 9 GDPR or data relating to criminal convictions and offences under Article 10 GDPR

It is important to recall that entities processing personal data as data processors also fall under the mandatory scope if the processing is regular and systematic or relates to special categories of data or to data relating to criminal convictions and offences and is carried out on a large scale. The situation of a data controller and a data processor with regard to the mandatory designation of DPOs may not coincide; for example there may be situations in which the data controller is a small business and uses the services (as data processor) of a company operating large scale data centres. In this case, the data processor only and not the data controller may be under the obligation to appoint a DPO.

Additionally, in accordance with Article 37(4), Union or Member State law could adopt specific legislative measures to increase the number of situations in which the

---

[15] Ibid., p. 7.   [16] CEDPO 2017, p. 3.   [17] WP29 2017, pp. 7–8.
[18] According to the WP29 (i) regular would mean ongoing or occurring at particular intervals for a particular period or recurring or repeated at fixed times; and (ii) systematic would refer to any of the following meanings: occurring according to a system, prearranged, organised or methodical, taking place as part of a general plan for data collection, or carried out as part of a strategy, see ibid., p. 9.
[19] Ibid.

appointment of a DPO by a public or private organisation is mandatory. An example of this can be seen in the Italian legislation which has introduced provisions for the modification of the Italian legal framework ('Italian Data Protection Code') on data protection and privacy following the application of the GDPR.[20]

In any event, the WP29 notes that, once appointed, the 'DPO, whether mandatory or voluntary, is designated for all the processing operations carried out by the controller or the processor'.[21]

2. DPOs of group of undertakings and several public authorities

Article 37(2) and (3) GDPR provide for the possibility that a single DPO may be appointed for a 'group of undertakings' and for several public authorities respectively. This provision aims at bringing some rationalisation and efficiency in ensuring compliance by certain data controllers and data processors, especially those which are separate legal persons from a formal legal point of view but which from a practical point of view would appear as one single data controller or processor. This possibility would also depend upon the condition that single DPOs are in a position to exercise their function effectively by being involved in the definition of the essential characteristics of the processing activities concerned.

Article 37(2) GDPR also requires that a group DPO should be 'easily accessible from each establishment'. In addition to the questions that this provision raises in terms of the group DPO's location (see below), the issue of communication skills was also considered by the WP29, which recommended that in order to ensure accessibility 'communication must take place in the language or languages used by the supervisory authorities and the data subjects concerned'.[22] However, as pointed out by CEDPO:

[T]he GDPR cannot expect that any Group DPO speaks all the 24 EU languages of each EU establishment of its group. We therefore suggest adding that it is not required that the DPO himself/herself speaks the languages of all countries where the controller/processor is established but that, in practice, this need can be met through translations of documents/media, resort to local contacts assisting the DPO. The GDPR is another piece of how the EU internal market is built and should not impose any restriction to the freedom of movement of the DPO professionals and services within the EU. The language(s) requirement should not be a barrier to the construction of the EU.[23]

3. Voluntary DPO

As the designation of the DPO constitutes both a key aspect of the governance of personal data established by the GDPR and a tangible implementation of the principle of accountability by a data controller or data processor,[24] organisations may also decide to appoint a DPO even when they are not legally obliged to do so.

The WP29 Guidelines on DPOs welcome and promote this possibility, but also make clear that when an organisation appoints a DPO on a voluntary basis, the requirements of the DPO laid down in Article 37–39 GDPR should apply to their designation, position

---

[20] Italian Data Protection Code 2018. [21] WP29 2017, p. 6. [22] Ibid, p. 10.
[23] CEDPO 2017, p. 5.
[24] The WP29 has characterised the DPO as a 'cornerstone of accountability', see WP29 2017, p. 4. See also EDPS 2012, p. 3, where the EDPS stressed the role of DPOs in accountability.

and task as if the designation had been mandatory, in order to prevent nominal and superficial DPO appointments aimed to convey to the public or to supervisory authorities a façade of compliance. The same document clarified that organisations which may employ staff or outside consultants with tasks relating to protection of personal data but that do not fulfil the requirements described in Articles 37–39 GDPR, should refrain from using the title of DPO for these other roles either inside the organisation or in relation to communications to the public or to supervisory authorities.[25]

Article 37(4) GDPR also refers to the possibility that associations or bodies representing categories of data controllers and data processors may appoint a DPO who may act for such associations and other bodies 'representing controllers or processors'. In this context, such a DPO could provide important assistance by advising on data protection issues frequently encountered by the categories of data controllers and data processors represented and by serving as a focal point in the communication between the represented data controllers and data processors and the competent supervisory authorities.

4. Professional and personal qualities, relevant expertise and DPO by contract

Article 37(5) GDPR requires that the DPO must have expert knowledge of data protection law and practices but it does not specify the minimum requirements for this level of expertise. Recital 97 states that the necessary level of expertise should be measured by taking into account the processing operations carried out by the organisation concerned rather than *in abstracto* on the basis of formal requirements.

It would be excessive to read into this provision the existence of additional professional qualities which could be presumptively assumed to be mandatory such as the necessity for the DPO to be a qualified lawyer or have a law degree. To the contrary, the legislation refers to relevant expertise 'in data protection law and practices', which could be also demonstrated by continuous professional exposure to data protection matters. In fact, the WP29 guidance stresses that 'knowledge of the business sector and the organization of the controller' (to be also read as 'of the data processor') also helps to contribute to the establishment of the required professional qualities and in case of public authorities the DPO should have 'a sound knowledge of administrative rules and procedures of the administration'.[26] However, it must also be noted that, in order to avoid conflicts of interest, the WP29 considers that certain positions would not be appropriate to be combined with the role of DPO, namely chief executive, chief operating officer, chief financial officer, chief medical officer, head of the marketing department, head of Human Resources or head of the IT department.

The Spanish Data Protection Authority (Agencia Española de Protección de Datos) has published an official certification scheme for DPOs (Esquema AEPD-DPD), to be managed by Entidade Nacional de Acreditação ('ENAC'), the Spanish official certification body, which will accredit any certification body which is interested in using this scheme to certify DPOs in Spain.[27] This certification scheme will coexist with other certification schemes for privacy professionals (not limited to DPOs) launched some years ago and with new schemes that will probably be created. In any event, this seems to be the first example of the involvement of an EU data protection authority in the current trend

[25] WP29 2017, pp. 5–6.   [26] Ibid, p. 11   [27] Spanish Data Protection Authority 2018.

towards accreditation and certification schemes with regard to the role of DPOs that was already anticipated by the doctrine.[28]

It is more difficult to spell out the personal as opposed to the professional qualities required of a DPO and how it would be possible to determine qualities such as integrity or ethics referred to in the WP29 Guidelines, in the absence of voluntary professional and specific deontology regimes for DPOs. However, in 2010 the Network of Data Protection Officers ('NDPO') of the EU institutions and bodies already considered that a DPO should possess the following personal qualities:

(a) It is recommended that the DPO should have the following experience/maturity: at least 3 years of relevant experience to serve as DPO in a body where data protection is not related to the core business (and thus personal data processing activities are mainly administrative); and at least 7 years of relevant experience to serve as DPO in an EU institution or in those EU bodies where data protection is related to the core business or which have an important volume of processing operations on personal data.
(b) Personal skills: integrity, initiative, organization, perseverance, discretion, ability to assert himself/herself in difficult circumstances, interest in data protection and motivation to be a DPO.
(c) Interpersonal skills: communication, negotiation, conflict resolution, ability to build working relationships.[29]

In any event, it would be natural that, with the gradual establishment and maturity of the DPO profession, specific deontology and ethical codes will be generated. Some national associations of DPOs have already published such codes (e.g. Asociación Profesional Española de Privacidad ('APEP') in Spain, Association Française des Correspondants à la protection des Données à caractère Personnel ('AFCDP') in France or Association of Data Protection Officers ('ADPO') in Ireland)[30] or are preparing codes of conduct.

It may also be noted with regard to these characteristics of level of expertise and personal and professional qualities that the GDPR offers a certain degree of flexibility and creativity for organisations to develop practical ways to reach the necessary level of compliance with the accountability principle, which would not be compatible with ceremonial and formalistic approaches. In this context the provision that enables controllers and processors to use external DPOs is relevant. An external DPO serving on the basis of a 'service contract' under Article 37(6) should be subject to the same provisions concerning the tasks and position of the DPO laid down in Articles 38 and 39, and the controllers or processors concerned should be able to demonstrate that they are effectively responsible for the processing operations supervised by the external DPO. Indeed, the size and activities of each organisation as well as its private or public status should determine whether an internal or external DPO is appropriate at the time. As stated by CEPDO:

There are instances in which it could make sense to share the same external DPO, such as small organisations and organisations dealing with similar data processing activities. External DPOs may include legal entities even though the client organization may expect certain stability, to the extent compatible with local laws, regarding the actual individual(s) ultimately assuming the outsourced DPO tasks. The choice between an internal or external DPO shall not be influenced by the employment protection of internal DPOs.[31]

---

[28] Lachaud 2014, p. 189. [29] NDPO 2010, p. 4.
[30] APEP 2011; AFCDP 2017, Art. 14; ADPO Code. [31] CEPDO 2017, p. 3.

5. Location and visibility of the DPO

As a general rule, DPOs should be located in proximity to the processing activities of the organisations concerned in order to enable the effective exercise of their functions. However, the specific physical location of a group DPO or the DPO of a single organisation with several establishments seems to be irrelevant nowadays so long as the organisation may ensure their accessibility, an appropriate business involvement and a good local network (e.g. local privacy links).

According to CEDPO,[32] 'the GDPR is another piece of how the EU internal market is built and should not impose any restriction to the freedom of movement of the DPO professionals and services within the EU'. The existence of a group DPO entails that 'the DPO's accessibility is not necessarily dependent only on his/her own skills but rather on the combination of his/her skills and those of his/her local "network"', e.g. local privacy liaisons to ensure appropriate local legal and language knowledge when required.[33] In consequence, a supervisory authority is not entitled to impose on any organisation the appointment of a DPO of the nationality or residence of its own country, in particular, when a group DPO has been appointed (irrespective of whether the one-stop-shop applies or not).

In any event, as clarified by the WP29 guidance,[34] the DPO should generally be located in the EU, in order to engage more rapidly with the competent supervisory authorities. It is only in exceptional cases, in which the core activities of the organisation with regard to the processing of personal data are not located in the EU, that DPOs may be able to carry out their activities outside the EU.

Article 37(7) GDPR establishes that the data controller or data processor shall publish the contact details of the DPO and communicate them to the supervisory authority. This provision should be read in conjunction with other provisions of the GDPR which increase the visibility of the DPO vis-à-vis supervisory authorities and data subjects; for example, Articles 13(1)(b) and 14(1)(b) require the data controller to inform the data subject not only of the identity of the data controller but also of the 'contact details of the data protection officer'; similarly Article 33(3)(b) requires the name and contact details of the DPO to be communicated to the supervisory authority by the data controller together with other information concerning a personal data breach.

However, the WP29 clearly states that 'Article 37(7) does not require that the published contact details should include the name of the DPO'.[35] As CEDPO pointed out:

[O]rganisations should be able to provide generic contact details such as dpo@company.com. The organisation must be able to decide the level of information to be provided in order to ensure smooth communication with external stakeholders (including but not limited to data subjects) and respect for the DPO's privacy.[36]

6. Notification to the lead supervisory authority under the one-stop-shop

A group that is entitled to benefit from the one-stop-shop mechanism for cross-border processing activities, under the lead of a specific supervisory authority of its 'main

---

[32] Ibid., p. 3. [33] Ibid., pp. 2 and 5. [34] WP29 2017, p. 11.
[35] Ibid., p. 13. [36] CEDPO 2017, p. 6.

establishment' in the EU (as defined in the GDPR), is required under Article 37(7) to communicate the contact details of its DPO *only* to this lead supervisory authority ('LSA'). This is clear from Article 56(6), which designates the LSA as the 'sole interlocutor' in these circumstances. However, it appears that some supervisory authorities are 'recommending' that such an organisation notifies the DPO details to the DPA in each jurisdiction in the EU, which would not be aligned to the GDPR's requirements and goals.

The situation is different where such an organisation does not have a clear LSA because it does not have a clear 'main establishment' in the EU. In such situations, the organisation will need to make a notification in each EU country where it has an establishment ('main' or not).

In any event, any such multiple cross-border notification should be subject to two caveats. First, the contents and format of such notifications are not yet harmonised across the EU. Secondly, such a multiple notification should not preclude any future decisions of the organisation affecting its ability to benefit from the one-stop-shop in the future.

7. Final remarks

The increased visibility of the DPO is a further element showing the mutual fiduciary relationship that DPOs will have with the data controller and the data processor with regard to the way in which the latter organise the processing operations of personal data. DPOs may be compared with similar figures of 'regulatory intermediaries' in other sectoral legislation such as, for example, the 'qualified person for pharmacovigilance' in the case of pharmaceutical regulation or the independent financial accountant in the case of financial rules.

Under the GDPR the DPO plays a key and strategic role in ensuring that organisations comply with data protection rules by embedding cultural and regulatory practices and mechanisms into the fabric of the organisation.

Select Bibliography

International agreements

OECD Privacy Guidelines 2013: Organisation for Economic Co-operation and Development, 'The OECD Privacy Framework' (2013).

EU legislation

Council Decision 2004: Council Decision of 13 September 2004 adopting implementing rules concerning Regulation (EC) No. 45/2001 of the European Parliament and of the Council on the protection of individuals with regard to the processing of personal data by the Community institutions and bodies and on the free movement of such data (2004/644/EC), OJ 2004 L 296/16.

EC Decision 2008: Commission Decision of 3 June 2008 adopting implementing rules concerning the Data Protection Officer pursuant to Article 24(8) of Regulation (EC) No. 45/2001 on the protection of individuals with regard to the processing of personal data by the Community institutions and bodies and on the free movement of such data, OJ 2008 L 193/7.

EP Decision 2015: Décision relative à la fonction de Coordinateur pour la protection des données et du réseau DPD/CPD, 12 March 2015 (unpublished).

National legislation

Italian Data Protection Code 2018: Decreto Legislativo 10 agosto 2018 n. 101: Disposizioni per l'adeguamento della normativa nazionale alle disposizioni del regolamento (UE) 2016/679 del Parlamento europeo e del Consiglio, del 27 aprile 2016, relativo alla protezione delle persone fisiche con riguardo al trattamento dei dati personali, nonche' alla libera circolazione di tali dati e che abroga la direttiva 95/46/CE (regolamento generale sulla protezione dei dati).

Academic writings

Lachaud 2014: Lachaud, 'Should the DPO Be Certified?', 4(3) *International Data Privacy Law* (2014), 189.

Laudati 2014: Laudati, 'Ten Years of Supervision of the EU Institutions and Bodies: The Perspective of a DPO', in Hijmans and Kranenborg (eds.), *Data Protection Anno 2014: How to Restore Trust?: Contributions in Honour of Peter Hustinx (2004–2014)* (Intersentia 2014), 261.

Papers of data protection authorities

EDPS 2004: European Data Protection Supervisor, 'Annual Report 2004' (18 March 2005).

EDPS 2005: European Data Protection Supervisor, 'Position Paper on the Role of Data Protection Officers in Ensuring Effective Compliance with Regulation (EC) 45/2001' (28 November 2005).

EDPS 2012: European Data Protection Supervisor, 'Monitoring Compliance of EU Institutions and Bodies with Article 24 of Regulation (EC) 45/2001—Report on the Status of Data Protection Officers' (17 December 2012).

WP29 2017: Article 29 Working Party, 'Guidelines on Data Protection Officers ("DPOs")' (WP 243 rev.01, as last revised and adopted on 5 April 2017).

Spanish Data Protection Authority 2018: Agencia Española de Protección de Datos, 'Esquema De Certificación De Delegados De Protección De Datos (Esquema AEPD-DPD)' (13 June 2018).

Reports and recommendations

ADPO Code: Association of Data Protection Officers, 'Code of Professional Conduct', available at https://www.dpo.ie/about/code.

AFCDP 2017: Association Française des Correspondants à la protection des Données à caractère Personnel, 'Règlement intérieur de l'AFCDP' (19 January 2017).

APEP 2011: Asociación Profesional Española de Privacidad, 'Código de Ética Profesional' (5 July 2011).

CEDPO 2012: Confederation of European Data Protection Organisations, 'Comparative Analysis of Data Protection Officials Role and Status in the EU and More' (2012), available at http://www.cedpo.eu/wp-content/uploads/2015/01/CEDPO_Studies_Comparative-Analysis_DPO_20120206.pdf.

NDPO 2010: Network of Data Protection Officers of the EU institutions and bodies, 'Professional Standards for Data Protection Officers of the EU Institutions and Bodies Working under Regulation (EC) 45/20011' (14 October 2010).

Others

CEDPO 2017: Confederation of European Data Protection Organisations, 'CEDPO Follow-Up Letter on the WP29 DPO Guidelines Published in WP242', available at http://www.cedpo.eu/wp-content/uploads/2015/01/CEDPO-Follow-Up_Letter_on_WP_29_DPO-Guidelines_20170215.pdf.

EP Guide: European Parliament, 'Data Protection, A Guide for Users', available at http://www.europarl.europa.eu/pdf/data_protection/guide_en.pdf.

Article 38. Position of the data protection officer

CECILIA ALVAREZ RIGAUDIAS   ALESSANDRO SPINA*

1. The controller and the processor shall ensure that the data protection officer is involved, properly and in a timely manner, in all issues which relate to the protection of personal data.
2. The controller and processor shall support the data protection officer in performing the tasks referred to in Article 39 by providing resources necessary to carry out those tasks and access to personal data and processing operations, and to maintain his or her expert knowledge.
3. The controller and processor shall ensure that the data protection officer does not receive any instructions regarding the exercise of those tasks. He or she shall not be dismissed or penalised by the controller or the processor for performing his tasks. The data protection officer shall directly report to the highest management level of the controller or the processor.
4. Data subjects may contact the data protection officer with regard to all issues related to processing of their personal data and to the exercise of their rights under this Regulation.
5. The data protection officer shall be bound by secrecy or confidentiality concerning the performance of his or her tasks, in accordance with Union or Member State law.
6. The data protection officer may fulfil other tasks and duties. The controller or processor shall ensure that any such tasks and duties do not result in a conflict of interests.

Relevant Recital

(97) Where the processing is carried out by a public authority, except for courts or independent judicial authorities when acting in their judicial capacity, where, in the private sector, processing is carried out by a controller whose core activities consist of processing operations that require regular and systematic monitoring of the data subjects on a large scale, or where the core activities of the controller or the processor consist of processing on a large scale of special categories of personal data and data relating to criminal convictions and offences, a person with expert knowledge of data protection law and practices should assist the controller or processor to monitor internal compliance with this Regulation. In the private sector, the core activities of a controller relate to its primary activities and do not relate to the processing of personal data as ancillary activities. The necessary level of expert knowledge should be determined in particular according to the data processing operations carried out and the protection required for the personal data processed by the controller or the processor. Such data protection officers, whether or not they are an employee of the controller, should be in a position to perform their duties and tasks in an independent manner.

Closely Related Provisions

Article 13(1)(b) (Information to be provided where personal data are collected from the data subject) (see too recitals 60–61); Article 14(1)(b) (Information to be provided where personal data have not been obtained from the data subject) (see too recital 61); Article 30 (Records of processing activities) (see too recital 82); Article 33 (Notification of a personal data breach to the

---

* The views expressed are solely those of the author and do not necessarily reflect those of the European Commission.

supervisory authority) (see too recital 85); Article 35 (Data protection impact assessment) (see too recitals 90–91); Article 36 (Prior consultation) (see too recital 94); Article 37 (Designation of the Data Protection Officer) (see too recital 97); Article 39 (Tasks of the data protection officer) (see too recitals 77 and 97); Article 47 (Binding corporate rules) (see too recital 108); Article 52(1) (Independence of supervisory authorities) (see too recitals 117–118 and 120–121); Article 57 (Tasks of supervisory authorities) (see too recital 122); Article 69 (Independence of the EDPB) (see too recital 139)

Related Provisions in LED [Directive (EU) 2016/680]

Article 33 (Position of the data protection officer) (see too recital 63)

Related Provisions in EUDPR [Regulation (EU) 1725/2018]

Article 43 (Designation of the data protection officer), Article 44 (Position of the data protection officer) and Article 45 (Tasks of the data protection officer) (see too recital 62).

Relevant Case Law

CJEU

Case C-518/07, *European Commission v Federal Republic of Germany*, judgment of 9 March 2010 (Grand Chamber) (ECLI:EU:C:2010:125).

Case C-614/10, *European Commission v Republic of Austria*, judgment of 16 October 2012 (Grand Chamber) (ECLI:EU:C:2012:631).

Case C-288/12, *European Commission v Hungary*, judgment of 8 April 2014 (Grand Chamber) (ECLI:EU:C:2014:237).

Case C-362/14, *Maximillian Schrems v Data Protection Commissioner*, 6 October 2015 (Grand Chamber) (ECLI:EU:C:2015:650).

A. Rationale and Policy Underpinnings

The GDPR considers the data protection officer ('DPO') as a cornerstone of the accountability principle.[1] This function plays an essential role in the effective application by controllers and processors of the provisions concerning the processing of personal data. The DPO has been presented as a 'chef d'orchestre'[2] to highlight the DPO's *sui generis* role of leadership based on authority and expertise rather than on formal powers over the governance of personal data within organisations.

Article 38 GDPR (DPO position), to be read jointly with Article 39 (DPO tasks), establishes a statutory regime aimed at ensuring that the DPO (or the DPO team, where appropriate) has the appropriate qualifications, resources and support to carry out this strategic role.

---

[1] Recio 2017, pp. 114–115.
[2] This image has been used by the CNIL in public communications related to the appointment of a DPO under the GDPR. See CNIL 2018.

The GDPR makes clear that the formal appointment and the conditions under which the DPO should operate, including the guarantee of independence and the resources necessary for carrying out the tasks laid down in Article 39, is an obligation of the data controller or data processor. The infringement of this obligation is subject to administrative fines laid down in Article 83(4)(a) GDPR.

B. Legal Background

1. EU legislation

As pointed out in the commentary to Article 37 in this volume, the DPO regime under the GDPR is partly inspired by the DPD regarding the 'data protection official' and principally inspired by Regulation 45/2001[3] regarding the 'data protection officer' required for every European Union institution, body or agency. As a result, the GDPR provisions on the DPO are very similar to the DPO provisions under Regulation 45/2001, now replaced by the EUDPR, as explained in the commentary to Article 37 in this volume.

2. International instruments

The DPO is not mentioned in either the original or the modernised versions of Convention 108, nor does it figure in the OECD Privacy Guidelines 2013,[4] although the Supplementary explanatory memorandum to the Guidelines mentions the 'important role' of Privacy Officers in 'designing and implementing a privacy management programme'.

3. National developments

As pointed out in the commentary to Article 37 in this volume, the DPD enabled Member States to provide that data controllers could appoint a DPO and then be exempt from the duty to notify data processing to the DPAs.[5] This option was implemented in a certain number of EEA countries but, according to the comparative analysis regarding the DPO role in many EU member states undertaken by the Confederation of European Data Protection Organisations ('CEDPO'),[6] there is no uniformity regarding their mandatory role, tasks, liability, qualifications, relationships vis-à-vis the supervisory authority, independence and legal protection.

4. Case law

The CJEU has yet to rule directly on data protection officials or officers. However, there are several rulings regarding the 'independence' of DPAs' that could be relevant in order to assess whether any of the elements that comprise the independence of a DPA could be applied to a DPO, as set out in Figure 38.1.[7]

Many of these elements could be appropriate to assess the independence of a DPO, with one main exception: DPOs cannot be fully independent of any influence

---

[3] See Table of Legislation.   [4] OECD Privacy Guidelines 2013.   [5] Art. 18(2) DPD.
[6] CEDPO 2012.
[7] See also the commentary on Art. 52 in this volume on the independence of supervisory authorities and the commentary on Art. 69 in this volume on the independence of the EDPB.

CJEU Ruling	Elements of DPA independence
Case C-518/07 *Commission v Germany*	Complete freedom, no instructions, no pressure Independent of any influence exercised by the supervised entities
Case C614/10 *Commission v Austria*	Operational autonomy Adequate budget DPA staff shall not be under the authority of government (one of its supervised bodies)
Case C288/12 *Commission v Hungary*	Objective reasons required to terminate the mandate prematurely
Case C-362/14 *Schrems*	Independence aim: ensuring effectiveness and reliability of the monitoring of compliance

Figure 38.1 CJEU rulings on the independence of DPAs

exercised by the data controller or the data processor which appoints them. Indeed, a DPO does not have enforcement powers over the data controller or data processor and is appointed and paid by them. This is an extremely pertinent difference which also determines that the DPO's effectiveness should also be assessed in a realistic manner and jointly with the effective support obtained from the organisation which appoints them.

C. Analysis

1. Independence

Both Article 38(3) and recital 97 focus on the DPO's 'independent' manner of acting. As we have seen above, DPO independence cannot be equated in essence to the requirement of independence of a DPA due to the lack of enforcement powers of the DPO and the fact that DPOs are integrated in the organisations that have appointed them as a trusted counsellor.

According to the WP29, the meaning of a DPO acting 'in an independent manner' is that:

[I]n fulfilling their tasks under Article 39, DPOs must not be instructed how to deal with a matter, for example, what result should be achieved, how to investigate a complaint or whether to consult the supervisory authority. Furthermore, they must not be instructed to take a certain view of an issue related to data protection law, for example, a particular interpretation of the law. The autonomy of DPOs does not, however, mean that they have decision-making powers extending beyond their tasks pursuant to Article 39.[8]

It would appear that the DPO does not exercise a form of power independently from the organisation in which the DPO is embedded but rather a form of expert-based autonomy, adequately supported by relevant norms of professional conduct.

When examining the 2010 professional standards for DPOs of the EU institutions and bodies prepared by the Network of DPOs of EU institutions[9] as well as the 2012 EDPS report on the status of DPOs,[10] we may conclude that the following elements are relevant

[8] WP29 2017, p. 15.   [9] NDPO 2010.   [10] EDPS 2012.

to guarantee DPOs' autonomy and independence (of which only two are expressly included in Article 38 of the GDPR):

1. Nature and stability of the job:
   – as a general rule, not a part-time job, in order to avoid conflicts of interest;
   – as a general rule, a permanent contract, in order not to be concerned lest their actions negatively influence the renewal of their contract;
   – no penalties imposed as a result of carrying out their duties as a DPO (Article 38(3) GDPR).
2. Appropriate age and work experience:
   – not too young and inexperienced, in order to have work experience as well as skills to standing up to the organisation.
3. Status and power:
   – report to, and performance review by, top management (Article 38(3) GDPR);
   – management-level position;
   – resources, including their own staff (HR autonomy) and budget (financial autonomy);
   – signing power (regarding data protection matters).

It must also be noted that Article 38(5) GDPR mentions certain confidentiality requirements which raise a number of questions, in particular regarding the DPO's duties regarding their appointing organisation. The WP29 only provided limited guidance regarding confidentiality vis-à-vis the DPA: '[h]owever, the obligation of secrecy/confidentiality does not prohibit the DPO from contacting and seeking advice from the supervisory authority'.[11]

Even though the DPO under the GDPR is not the same as the DPO under German data protection law, it is worth knowing that, according to a 2010 resolution of German DPAs responsible for the private sector on the minimum requirements for the (qualifications and) independence of company DPOs, confidentiality was considered a necessary measure to protect such independence:

In order to ensure the DPO's independence, certain of company internal organizational measures are necessary: ... DPOs are bound to confidentiality about the identity of the data subjects, as well as the circumstances under which they obtained information about a data subject, unless otherwise specifically authorized by the data subject in question.[12]

However, none of these statements actually answer the question of how the confidentiality requirement should work regarding the relationship between the DPO and their appointing organisation. This must depend in part on the kind of privacy issues that the organisation faces and how they are addressed. In addition, the question arises how, if the DPO's work is protected by legal privilege (in particular, for external DPOs who are lawyers), the confidentiality duty can operate vis-à-vis the client.

Additional guidance can also be found in the second sentence of Article 44(7) EUDPR (formerly point 3 of the Annex to Regulation 45/2001):

No one shall suffer prejudice on account of a matter brought to the attention of the competent data protection officer alleging that a breach of the provisions of this Regulation has taken place.

[11] WP29 2017, p. 18.   [12] Hladjk 2010.

Under this provision the confidentiality to which the DPO is subject is mainly interpreted as a way to protect sources of potential complaints against institutions with regard to processing of personal data (whistleblowing).

2. Conflicts of interests

Under Article 38(6), the GDPR allows part-time DPOs to be appointed, provided that their non-DPO duties do not result in a conflict of interest. However, it would appear that, according to the EU DPO Network, a part-time DPO faces per se 'a permanent conflict between allocating time and efforts to his/her DPO tasks versus other tasks'.[13] Therefore, DPOs should ideally be able to dedicate their time fully to their DPO duties, especially for large entities and for smaller ones in the initial phase of establishing a data protection culture.[14]

In any event, the EDPS considered that a conflict of interest is present when 'the other duties which a DPO is asked to perform may have directly adverse interests to that of protection of personal data within his/her institution'.[15] In particular, the EDPS seems to identify a clear conflict of interest for DPOs who also act as data controller in their primary activity, such as the Head of Administration/HR or IT.[16] This is also the view of the Bavarian Data Protection Authority, which imposed a fine in 2016 on a Bavarian company which appointed the IT manager as DPO. The Bavarian authority considered that no independent control was possible due to the DPO's significant operational responsibility for data processing activities.[17]

The WP29 enlarged this list of potential conflicts, as follows:

[A]s a rule of thumb, conflicting positions may include senior management positions (such as chief executive, chief operating, chief financial, chief medical officer, head of marketing department, head of Human Resources or head of IT departments) but also other roles lower down in the organisational structure if such positions or roles lead to the determination of purposes and means of processing.[18]

Assuming that an organisation appoints a part-time DPO, the EDPS has recommended a separate evaluation of the tasks of DPOs and their other concurrent tasks. In addition, the EDPS has warned against the weight placed on non-DPO activities both in terms of time (i.e. DPOs should not be prevented from exercising their tasks to lack of time as a result of non-DPO activities) as well as with respect to career development and performance review, since this 'creates pressure on the DPO to concentrate his/her efforts on the non-DPO tasks'.[19]

Some of the above considerations would mainly apply to internal DPOs. However, external DPOs may face other conflicts of interest when they are, at the same time, the legal advisor of the organisation that appointed them or the DPO of other clients of the same sector or engaged in the same transaction (since the DPO has a strategic role regarding the use of the personal data). The WP29 also refers to the fact that 'a conflict of interests may also arise for example if an external DPO is asked to represent the controller or processor before the Courts in cases involving data protection issues'. This limitation, in principle, could also apply by analogy to internal DPOs in those rare cases where they are qualified to represent the controller before a court of law. However, a complete

---

[13] NDPO 2010, p. 6. [14] Ibid. [15] Ibid, p. 15. [16] EDPS 2012, p. 14.
[17] Bavarian DPO 2016. [18] WP29 2017, p. 16. [19] EDPS 2005, p. 4.

prohibition for DPOs to participate in court proceedings as an expert or witness of the controller or processor would be not only disproportionate but also not beneficial for the operation of the judicial function. Any limitation should be interpreted narrowly because the DPO is responsible for cooperating with the supervisory authority[20] and for acting as the contact point with the supervisory authority.[21] Indeed, the DPO should not be restricted, based on the possibility of conflict of interests, from participating in any administrative procedures or other interactions with the competent supervisory authorities (in particular, inspections or enforcement procedures).

Finally, the WP29 consistently stressed, as noted above, that both Article 38(3) and recital 97 focus on the 'independent' manner of acting of the DPO and that the DPO should 'not receive any instructions regarding the exercise of [his or her] tasks'.[22] In this respect, the EDPB has considered whether the role of external DPO may be combined with the function of a representative in the Union designated under Article 27 GDPR. Such a representative is subject to a mandate by the controller or processor[23] and will act on its behalf[24] and therefore under its direct instruction. In view of the requirement for a DPO to enjoy a 'sufficient degree of autonomy and independence', the EDPB has concluded that the role of external DPO 'does not appear to be compatible with the function of representative in the Union'.[25]

3. Obligations of the appointing organisations

In order for DPOs to carry out their tasks (further described in the commentary to Article 39 in this volume) in an independent manner, and in view of their strategic role, it is crucial that the organisation provides them with the appropriate resources. This requires a broad construction of Article 38. In this regard, the EDPS[26] and the WP29[27] have provided valuable comments on what the DPO needs from the appointing organisation, which may be classified into the following categories:

1. Support by top management:
   - by senior management providing active support for the DPO's function;
   - by designating the DPO through an official communication addressed to all staff to ensure that the DPO's existence and function are known throughout the organisation;
   - by ensuring that the DPO is involved in good time in all relevant business planning and design processes (Article 38(1) GDPR).

2. Resources:
   - by providing DPOs with access to infrastructure (facilities, equipment and technology) as well as financial resources and staff[28] that are necessary to carry out their tasks, including adequate support, input and information if needed from other

---

[20] Art. 39(1)(d) GDPR.   [21] Ibid., Art. 39(1)(e).
[22] See WP29 2017, pp. 15 and 24.   [23] Art. 27(4) GDPR.   [24] Ibid., rec. 80.
[25] EDPB 2018, p. 20. See also the commentary on Art. 27 in this volume.
[26] EDPS 2015.   [27] WP29 2017.
[28] Ibid., p. 14: 'Given the size and structure of the organisation, it may be necessary to set up a DPO team (a DPO and his/her staff). In such cases, the internal structure of the team and the tasks and responsibilities of each of its members should be clearly drawn up. Similarly, when the function of the DPO is exercised by an external service provider, a team of individuals working for that entity may effectively carry out the tasks of a DPO as a team, under the responsibility of a designated lead contact for the client'.

services (HR, legal, IT, security) within the organisation and access to training facilities (Article 38(2) GDPR);
– by giving the DPO full access to data and processing operations and ensuring that all staff members cooperate with the DPO.

3. Continuous training:
– by maintaining their expert knowledge through continuous training[29] (Article 38(2) GDPR).
4. Time:
– by ensuring that DPOs have adequate time necessary to both complete their tasks and to maintain their qualifications. The WP29 recommends that organisations should determine the percentage of time required for the DPO function regarding part-time DPOs, the appropriate level of priority for DPO duties, and the drawing up of a work plan.[30]

4. Liability

The GDPR does not mention the DPO's liability. However, this issue has raised concerns in the community of privacy professionals, notably, in view of the high level of sanctions that can be imposed under the GDPR.

Articles 5(2) and 24(1) of the GDPR make it clear that it is the controller, not the DPO, who is required to ensure and to be able to demonstrate that processing is performed in accordance with the GDPR. This is of course without prejudice to the professional liability of the DPO as an employee or contractor of the controller or processor, as in the case of any other employee or contractor. This might explain why the WP29 included reassuring statements in their 2017 Guidelines:

> Monitoring of compliance does not mean that it is the DPO who is personally responsible where there is an instance of non-compliance ... Data protection compliance is a corporate responsibility of the data controller, not of the DPO.[31]

As noted above, failure to comply with Article 38 concerning the position of the DPO may be subject, for the controller or processor concerned, to administrative fines established by Article 83(4)(a) GDPR.

Select Bibliography

International agreements

OECD Privacy Guidelines 2013: Organisation for Economic Co-operation and Development, 'The OECD Privacy Framework' (2013).

---

[29] Ibid., p. 14: 'they should be encouraged to participate in training courses on data protection and other forms of professional development, such as participation in privacy fora, workshops, etc'. On 25 November 2010, the German DPAs responsible for the private sector (also known as the 'Düsseldorfer Kreis') issued a resolution on the minimum requirements for the (qualifications and) independence of company DPOs, where it considered that in order to maintain the appropriate qualifications, the company has to enable the DPO to participate in professional educational seminars and events, and cover costs associated with such training. See Düsseldorfer Kreis 2010, p. 2.
[30] WP29 2017, p. 14.   [31] Ibid, p. 17.

Academic writings

Recio 2007, 'Data Protection Officer: The Key Figure to Ensure Data Protection and Accountability', 3(1) *European Data Protection Law Review* (2017), 114.

Papers of data protection authorities

EDPB 2018: European Data Protection Board, 'Guidelines 3/2018 on the Territorial Scope of the GDPR—Version for Public Consultation' (16 November 2018).
EDPS 2005: European Data Protection Supervisor, 'Position Paper on the Role of Data Protection Officers in Ensuring Effective Compliance with Regulation (EC) 45/2001' (28 November 2005).
EDPS 2012: European Data Protection Supervisor, 'Monitoring Compliance of EU Institutions and Bodies with Article 24 of Regulation (EC) 45/2001—Report on the Status of Data Protection Officers' (17 December 2012).
WP29 2017: Article 29 Working Party, 'Guidelines on Data Protection Officers ("DPOs")' (WP 243 rev.01, as last revised and adopted on 5 April 2017).
CNIL 2018: CNIL, 'Désigner un pilote', 29 March 2018, available at https://www.cnil.fr/fr/designer-un-pilote.
Düsseldorfer Kreis 2010: Düsseldorfer Kreis, 'Mindestanforderungen an Fachkunde und Unabhängigkeit des Beauftragten für den Datenschutz nach § 4f Abs. 2 und 3 Bundesdatenschutzgesetz (BDSG)' (24/25 November 2010), available at https://www.bfdi.bund.de/SharedDocs/Publikationen/Entschliessungssammlung/DuesseldorferKreis/24112010-MindestanforderungenAnFachkunde.html?nn=5217016.

Reports and recommendations

CEDPO 2012: Confederation of European Data Protection Organisations, 'Comparative Analysis of Data Protection Officials Role and Status in the EU and More' (2012), available at http://www.cedpo.eu/wp-content/uploads/2015/01/CEDPO_Studies_Comparative-Analysis_DPO_20120206.pdf.
NDPO 2010: Network of Data Protection Officers of the EU institutions and bodies, 'Professional Standards for Data Protection Officers of the EU Institutions and Bodies Working under Regulation (EC) 45/20011' (14 October 2010).

Others

Bayerisches Landesamt für Datenschutzaufsicht, 'Datenschutzbeauftragter darf keinen Interessenkonflikten unterliegen' (20 October 2016), available at https://www.lda.bayern.de/media/pm2016_08.pdf.
Hladjk 2010: Hladjk, 'German DPAs Set Minimum Qualification and Independence Requirements for Company Data Protection Officer' (17 December 2010), available at http://www.lexology.com/library/detail.aspx?g=29b11019-fde6-48fe-a54e-4d6bdf4619b2.

Article 39. Tasks of the data protection officer

CECILIA ALVAREZ RIGAUDIAS   ALESSANDRO SPINA*

1. The data protection officer shall have at least the following tasks:
   (a) to inform and advise the controller or the processor and the employees who carry out processing of their obligations pursuant to this Regulation and to other Union or Member State data protection provisions;
   (b) to monitor compliance with this Regulation, with other Union or Member State data protection provisions and with the policies of the controller or processor in relation to the protection of personal data, including the assignment of responsibilities, awareness-raising and training of staff involved in processing operations, and the related audits;
   (c) to provide advice where requested as regards the data protection impact assessment and monitor its performance pursuant to Article 35;
   (d) to cooperate with the supervisory authority;
   (e) to act as the contact point for the supervisory authority on issues relating to processing, including the prior consultation referred to in Article 36, and to consult, where appropriate, with regard to any other matter.
2. The data protection officer shall in the performance of his or her tasks have due regard to the risk associated with processing operations, taking into account the nature, scope, context and purposes of processing.

Relevant Recitals

(77) Guidance on the implementation of appropriate measures and on the demonstration of compliance by the controller or the processor, especially as regards the identification of the risk related to the processing, their assessment in terms of origin, nature, likelihood and severity, and the identification of best practices to mitigate the risk, could be provided in particular by means of approved codes of conduct, approved certifications, guidelines provided by the Board or indications provided by a data protection officer. The Board may also issue guidelines on processing operations that are considered to be unlikely to result in a high risk to the rights and freedoms of natural persons and indicate what measures may be sufficient in such cases to address such risk.

(97) Where the processing is carried out by a public authority, except for courts or independent judicial authorities when acting in their judicial capacity, where, in the private sector, processing is carried out by a controller whose core activities consist of processing operations that require regular and systematic monitoring of the data subjects on a large scale, or where the core activities of the controller or the processor consist of processing on a large scale of special categories of personal data and data relating to criminal convictions and offences, a person with expert knowledge of data protection law and practices should assist the controller or processor to monitor internal compliance with this Regulation. In the private sector, the core activities of a controller relate to its primary activities and do not relate to the processing of personal data as ancillary activities. The necessary level of expert knowledge should be determined in particular according

---

* The views expressed are solely those of the author and do not necessarily reflect those of the European Commission.

to the data processing operations carried out and the protection required for the personal data processed by the controller or the processor. Such data protection officers, whether or not they are an employee of the controller, should be in a position to perform their duties and tasks in an independent manner.

Closely Related Provisions

Article 30 (Records of processing activities) (see too recital 82); Article 33 (Notification of a personal data breach to the supervisory authority) (see too recital 85); Article 35 (Data protection impact assessment) (see too recitals 90–91); Article 36 (Prior consultation) (see too recital 94); Article 37 (Designation of the data protection officer) (see too recital 97); Article 38 (Position of the data protection officer) (see too recital 97); Article 47 (Binding corporate rules) (see too recital 108); Article 57 (Tasks of supervisory authorities) (see too recital 122).

Related Provisions in LED [Directive (EU) 2016/680]

Article 34 (Tasks of the data protection officer) (see too recital 63).

Related Provisions in EUDPR [Regulation (EU) 1725/2018]

Article 43 (Designation of the data protection officer), Article 44 (Position of the data protection officer); Article 45 (Tasks of the data protection officer) (see too recital 62).

Relevant Case Law

CJEU

Case C-518/07, *European Commission v Federal Republic of Germany*, judgment of 9 March 2010 (Grand Chamber) (ECLI:EU:C:2010:125).
Case T-483/13, *Athanassios Oikonomopoulos v European Commission*, GC, judgment of 20 July 2016 (ECLI: EU:T:2016:421).

A. Rationale and Policy Underpinnings

Article 39 GDPR, jointly with Article 38, is aimed at providing a statutory regime for the data protection officer ('DPO'), which was previously lacking under the DPD.

The DPO under the GDPR is not simply the same as the previous positions of German Datenschutzbeauftragter, French Correspondant Informatique et Libertés ('CIL') or Spanish Security Manager; the DPO is the person who must assist the organisation to navigate data protection and to change their data protection culture.[1] The task of a DPO is not only to facilitate data protection compliance but also to play a strategic role, taking into account in particular that appropriate handling of personal data may (or not) provide the business a competitive advantage. As shown by the survey carried out by

---

[1] The WP29 has characterised the DPO as a 'cornerstone of accountability', see WP29 2017, p. 4. See also EDPS 2012, p. 3, where the EDPS stressed the role of DPOs in accountability.

the authors of 'Privacy on the Ground' in the US and some EU jurisdictions including France, Germany and Spain:

[R]espondents uniformly rejected an understanding of privacy as a compliance function. '[T]he law in privacy,' one respondent summarized, 'will only get you so far'. Despite all that 'privacy' requires, said another, 'there's no law that says "you have to do this."' In sum, explained a third, broader principles have to be developed that can guide privacy decisions consistently in a variety of contexts—privacy must be 'strategic, part of the technical strategy and the business strategy'.[2]

B. Legal Background

1. EU legislation

Article 39 is partly inspired by the limited provision in the DPD for a 'data protection official'. Under Article 18 of the DPD, the role of the data protection official was simply to ensure 'that the rights and freedoms of the data subjects are unlikely to be adversely affected by the processing operations' by performing the following tasks: (i) to ensure 'in an independent manner the internal application' of the national data protection legislation; and (ii) to keep an internal register of processing operations carried out by the controller.

In addition, under Article 20 and recital 54 DPD, the data protection official could also be involved in the prior checking of processing operations likely to present specific risks to the rights and freedoms of data subjects 'in cooperation with the authority'.

The DPO regime under the GDPR is principally inspired by the provisions of Regulation 45/2001[3] requiring a 'data protection officer' for every EU institution, body or agency. As a result, the GDPR provisions on the DPO are very similar to the DPO provisions under Regulation 45/2001, now replaced by the EUDPR, save as discussed in the commentary on Article 37 in this volume. As early as 2005 the EDPS stated that 'the Data Protection Officer is fundamental in ensuring the respect of data protection principles within institutions/bodies'.[4] In consequence, the EDPS opinions and guidelines issued to date are particularly valuable for construing homogeneously the comparable GDPR provisions.[5]

2. International instruments

The data protection officer is mentioned neither in Convention 108 nor in the Modernised Convention of 2018. The revised OECD Privacy Guidelines[6] do not themselves refer to privacy officers, but the Supplementary explanatory memorandum to the Guidelines

---

[2] Bamberger and Mulligan 2011, p. 269. The study examines how the people charged with protecting privacy in US and EU corporations actually do their work, and what kinds of regulation effectively shape their behaviour.

[3] See Table of Legislation. [4] EDPS 2005, p. 3.

[5] See Case C-518/07, *Commission v Germany*, para. 28: 'In view of the fact that Article 44 of Regulation No 45/2001 and Article 28 of Directive 95/46 are based on the same general concept, those two provisions should be interpreted homogeneously ... '

[6] OECD Privacy Guidelines 2013.

mentions the 'important role' of Privacy Officers in 'designing and implementing a privacy management programme'.[7]

3. National developments

The DPD enabled Member States to provide that appointment of a DPO could exempt data controllers from notifying data processing to the DPAs.[8] This option was implemented in a certain number of European Economic Area ('EEA') countries. However, according to the comparative analysis regarding the role of the DPO in many EU member states undertaken by the Confederation of European Data Protection Organisations ('CEDPO')[9], there is no uniformity regarding their mandatory role, tasks, liability, qualifications, relationships vis-à-vis the supervisory authority, independence and legal protection.

4. Case law

The CJEU has yet to rule directly on data protection officials or officers. However, the General Court has underlined the gravity of failure to notify the DPO under Article 25(1) of Regulation 45/2001 before personal data were processed. In *Oikonomopoulos*, the Court found that the failure to notify the DPO was sufficiently serious to found a claim for damages. It highlighted that, without adequate and timely information about data processing operations, the DPO was not in a position to notify the EDPS and therefore 'cannot effectively fulfil the essential task of supervision assigned to him by the European legislature'.[10]

C. Analysis

Article 39 contains a list of the tasks to be carried out by or with the assistance of the DPO. These tasks refer to activities vis-à-vis the data controller or processor that appointed the DPO as well as vis-à-vis the supervisory authorities and data subjects.

1. Tasks vis-à-vis the appointing organisations

The tasks vis-à-vis the appointing organisations may be summarised as set out in Figure 39.1.

One relevant connotation of the set of tasks of the DPO in terms of monitoring compliance by the controller or processor concerned is the reference to conducting audits. Indeed, Article 39(1)(b) GDPR expressly refers to the monitoring of 'the assignment of responsibilities, awareness-raising and training of staff involved in processing operations, and the related audits'. The question arises whether this reference is intended to mirror the use of audits by data protection authorities ('DPAs') under Article 58(1)(b) GDPR, which explicitly gives them the power of carrying out investigations in the form of 'data

---

[7] Ibid., p. 24. [8] Art. 18(2) DPD. [9] CEDPO 2012.
[10] Case T-483/13, *Oikonomopoulos*, para. 100.

GDPR cf.	Task	Comment
Art. 39(1)(a)	To inform and raise awareness	According to the EDPS, 'raising awareness can take the form of staff information notes, training sessions, setting up of a web site, privacy statements'.[11]
Art. 39(1)(b)	To (internally) monitor compliance	According to the WP29, as part of these duties to monitor compliance, DPOs may, in particular: □ collect information to identify processing activities, □ analyse and check the compliance of processing activities, and □ inform, advise and issue recommendations to the controller or the processor. Monitoring of compliance does not mean that it is the DPO who is personally responsible where there is an instance of non-compliance. DPOs must receive sufficient support in the organisation, to investigate matters directly relating to their tasks.
Art. 39(1)(c)	To provide advice	The DPO shall provide the organisation with advice on data protection laws and in particular advice on data protection impact assessments ('DPIA'),[12] risk (i.e., how to prioritise efforts on issues that present higher data protection risks)[13], the inventory[14] and, in general, how to comply with the accountability principle.

Figure 39.1 Tasks of DPAs vis-à-vis the appointing organisations

protection audits'.[15] It is perhaps important to recall that audits are generally considered to be based on a structured and formalised methodology to inspect specific processes or corporate practices by an external independent body. However, the WP29 has provided a more flexible approach regarding the DPO tasks in this respect by reference to Article 32:

This selective and pragmatic approach should help DPOs advise the controller what methodology to use when carrying out a DPIA, which areas should be subject to an internal or external data

---

[11] EDPS 2005, p. 5.

[12] Art. 35(2) GDPR specifically requires that the controller 'shall seek the advice' of the DPO when carrying out a DPIA. This should be construed as advice regarding whether a DPIA is necessary, and the methodology to be used to both assess the risks and to determine the appropriate risk minimisation measures in line with the GDPR. See WP29 2017, p. 18.

[13] Art. 39(2) GDPR requires that the DPO 'have due regard to the risk associated with processing operations, taking into account the nature, scope, context and purposes of processing'.

[14] Under Art. 30(1) and (2) GDPR, it is the controller or the processor, not the DPO, who is required to 'maintain a record of processing operations under its responsibility' or 'maintain a record of all categories of processing activities carried out on behalf of a controller'. However, as stated by the WP29, 'nothing prevents the controller or the processor from assigning the DPO with the task of maintaining the record of processing operations under the responsibility of the controller. Such a record should be considered as one of the tools enabling the DPO to perform its tasks of monitoring compliance, informing and advising the controller or the processor.' WP29 2017, p. 19.

[15] There seems to be an interpretative problem with the idea that the DPO is responsible for monitoring compliance under Art. 39(1)(b) and the 'related audits' at the end of that clause, the meaning of which is unclear. In particular in public organisations, the performance of audits is restricted to specialised bodies/officials that conduct audits in accordance with specific methodologies and norms of conduct.

protection audit, which internal training activities to provide to staff or management responsible for data processing activities, and which processing operations to devote more of his or her time and resources to.[16]

2. Tasks vis-à-vis the data subjects

Under Article 39(4), it is expected that the DPO could be contacted by data subjects, who could be part of the organisation (e.g. employees) or not (e.g. customers, vendors etc.).

This task is clearly linked to Article 37(7) regarding the publication of details enabling data subjects to contact DPOs and the obligations of controllers to provide information about the contact details of the DPO as part of the information about processing operations in the specific privacy statements under Article 13(1)(b) and 14(1)(b) GDPR. This seems to be aimed at facilitating the possibility that the DPO assists data subjects in exercising their rights. Further, the DPO is also well placed to play a primary role in investigating and handling queries or complaints before these are referred to the supervisory authority (if not resolved to the satisfaction of both the data subject and the organisation).

Indeed, the EDPS experience seems to favour this approach:

The handling of complaints and queries by the DPO at a local level is to be encouraged at least as concerns a first phase of investigation and resolution ... DPOs should try to investigate and resolve complaints at a local level before referring to the EDPS. The DPO should also be invited to consult the EDPS whenever he/she has doubts on the procedure or content of complaints. This does not however prevent the data subject from addressing him/herself directly to the EDPS ... [17]

3. Tasks vis-à-vis the supervisory authorities

It is intended that the DPO should facilitate cooperation between the DPA and the organisation, in particular, in the frame of investigations, complaint handling or prior consultation. The DPO not only has inside knowledge of the institution and speaks the same 'privacy language' as the DPA, but is also likely to know who is the best person to contact within the organisation. Conversely, the contact point function foreseen by Article 39(1)(e) of the DPO would imply an obligation for organisations to involve the DPO in any communication or interaction with DPAs.

It seems clear that, in order for DPOs to carry out their tasks according to Article 38, in particular in view of their strategic role and autonomy and independence, it is crucial that organisations provide them with the appropriate resources. This and the liability of the DPO are further discussed in the commentary to Article 38 in this volume.

Select Bibliography

International agreements

OECD Privacy Guidelines 2013: Organisation for Economic Co-operation and Development, 'The OECD Privacy Framework' (2013).

---

[16] WP29 2017, p. 18 (emphasis added).   [17] EDPS 2005, p. 6 (emphasis added).

Academic writings

Bamberger and Mulligan 2011: Bamberger and Mulligan, 'Privacy on the Books and on the Ground', 63(2) *Stanford Law Review* (2011), 247.

Papers of data protection authorities

EDPS 2005: European Data Protection Supervisor, 'Position Paper on the Role of Data Protection Officers in Ensuring Effective Compliance with Regulation (EC) 45/2001' (28 November 2005).
EDPS 2012: European Data Protection Supervisor, 'Monitoring Compliance of EU Institutions and Bodies with Article 24 of Regulation (EC) 45/2001—Report on the Status of Data Protection Officers' (17 December 2012).
WP29 2017: Article 29 Working Party, 'Guidelines on Data Protection Officers ("DPOs")' (WP 243 rev.01, as last revised and adopted on 5 April 2017).

Reports and recommendations

CEDPO 2012: Confederation of European Data Protection Organisations, 'Comparative Analysis of Data Protection Officials Role and Status in the EU and More' (2012), available at http://www.cedpo.eu/wp-content/uploads/2015/01/CEDPO_Studies_Comparative-Analysis_DPO_20120206.pdf.
NDPO 2010: Network of Data Protection Officers of the EU institutions and bodies, 'Professional Standards for Data Protection Officers of the EU Institutions and Bodies Working under Regulation (EC) 45/20011' (14 October 2010).

Section 5 Codes of conduct and certification

Article 40. Codes of Conduct

IRENE KAMARA

1. The Member States, the supervisory authorities, the Board and the Commission shall encourage the drawing up of codes of conduct intended to contribute to the proper application of this Regulation, taking account of the specific features of the various processing sectors and the specific needs of micro, small and medium-sized enterprises.
2. Associations and other bodies representing categories of controllers or processors may prepare codes of conduct, or amend or extend such codes, for the purpose of specifying the application of this Regulation, such as with regard to:
   (a) fair and transparent processing;
   (b) the legitimate interests pursued by controllers in specific contexts;
   (c) the collection of personal data;
   (d) the pseudonymisation of personal data;
   (e) the information provided to the public and to data subjects;
   (f) the exercise of the rights of data subjects;
   (g) the information provided to, and the protection of, children, and the manner in which the consent of the holders of parental responsibility over children is to be obtained;
   (h) the measures and procedures referred to in Articles 24 and 25 and the measures to ensure security of processing referred to in Article 32;
   (i) the notification of personal data breaches to supervisory authorities and the communication of such personal data breaches to data subjects;
   (j) the transfer of personal data to third countries or international organisations; or
   (k) out-of-court proceedings and other dispute resolution procedures for resolving disputes between controllers and data subjects with regard to processing, without prejudice to the rights of data subjects pursuant to Articles 77 and 79.
3. In addition to adherence by controllers or processors subject to this Regulation, codes of conduct approved pursuant to paragraph 5 of this Article and having general validity pursuant to paragraph 9 of this Article may also be adhered to by controllers or processors that are not subject to this Regulation pursuant to Article 3 in order to provide appropriate safeguards within the framework of personal data transfers to third countries or international organisations under the terms referred to in point (e) of Article 46(2). Such controllers or processors shall make binding and enforceable commitments, via contractual or other legally binding instruments, to apply those appropriate safeguards including with regard to the rights of data subjects.
4. A code of conduct referred to in paragraph 2 of this Article shall contain mechanisms which enable the body referred to in Article 41(1) to carry out the mandatory monitoring of compliance with its provisions by the controllers or processors which undertake to apply it, without prejudice to the tasks and powers of supervisory authorities competent pursuant to Article 55 or 56.
5. Associations and other bodies referred to in paragraph 2 of this Article which intend to prepare a code of conduct or to amend or extend an existing code shall submit the draft code, amendment or extension to the supervisory authority which is competent pursuant to Article 55. The supervisory authority shall provide an opinion on whether the draft code, amendment or extension complies with this Regulation and shall approve that draft code, amendment or extension if it finds that it provides sufficient appropriate safeguards.

6. Where the draft code, or amendment or extension is approved in accordance with paragraph 5, and where the code of conduct concerned does not relate to processing activities in several Member States, the supervisory authority shall register and publish the code.
7. Where a draft code of conduct relates to processing activities in several Member States, the supervisory authority which is competent pursuant to Article 55 shall, before approving the draft code, amendment or extension, submit it in the procedure referred to in Article 63 to the Board which shall provide an opinion on whether the draft code, amendment or extension complies with this Regulation or, in the situation referred to in paragraph 3 of this Article, provides appropriate safeguards.
8. Where the opinion referred to in paragraph 7 confirms that the draft code, amendment or extension complies with this Regulation, or, in the situation referred to in paragraph 3, provides appropriate safeguards, the Board shall submit its opinion to the Commission.
9. The Commission may, by way of implementing acts, decide that the approved code of conduct, amendment or extension submitted to it pursuant to paragraph 8 of this Article have general validity within the Union. Those implementing acts shall be adopted in accordance with the examination procedure set out in Article 93(2).

Relevant Recitals

(77) Guidance on the implementation of appropriate measures and on the demonstration of compliance by the controller or the processor, especially as regards the identification of the risk related to the processing, their assessment in terms of origin, nature, likelihood and severity, and the identification of best practices to mitigate the risk, could be provided in particular by means of approved codes of conduct, approved certifications, guidelines provided by the Board or indications provided by a data protection officer. The Board may also issue guidelines on processing operations that are considered to be unlikely to result in a high risk to the rights and freedoms of natural persons and indicate what measures may be sufficient in such cases to address such risk.

(81) To ensure compliance with the requirements of this Regulation in respect of the processing to be carried out by the processor on behalf of the controller, when entrusting a processor with processing activities, the controller should use only processors providing sufficient guarantees, in particular in terms of expert knowledge, reliability and resources, to implement technical and organisational measures which will meet the requirements of this Regulation, including for the security of processing. The adherence of the processor to an approved code of conduct or an approved certification mechanism may be used as an element to demonstrate compliance with the obligations of the controller. The carrying-out of processing by a processor should be governed by a contract or other legal act under Union or Member State law, binding the processor to the controller, setting out the subject- matter and duration of the processing, the nature and purposes of the processing, the type of personal data and categories of data subjects, taking into account the specific tasks and responsibilities of the processor in the context of the processing to be carried out and the risk to the rights and freedoms of the data subject. The controller and processor may choose to use an individual contract or standard contractual clauses which are adopted either directly by the Commission or by a supervisory authority in accordance with the consistency mechanism and then adopted by the Commission. After the completion of the processing on behalf of the controller, the processor should, at the choice of the controller, return or delete the personal data, unless there is a requirement to store the personal data under Union or Member State law to which the processor is subject.

(98) Associations or other bodies representing categories of controllers or processors should be encouraged to draw up codes of conduct, within the limits of this Regulation, so as to facilitate the effective application of this Regulation, taking account of the specific characteristics of the processing carried out in certain sectors and the specific needs of micro, small and medium enterprises. In particular, such codes of conduct could calibrate the obligations of controllers and processors,

taking into account the risk likely to result from the processing for the rights and freedoms of natural persons.

(99) When drawing up a code of conduct, or when amending or extending such a code, associations and other bodies representing categories of controllers or processors should consult relevant stakeholders, including data subjects where feasible, and have regard to submissions received and views expressed in response to such consultations.

(168) The examination procedure should be used for the adoption of implementing acts on standard contractual clauses between controllers and processors and between processors; codes of conduct; technical standards and mechanisms for certification; the adequate level of protection afforded by a third country, a territory or a specified sector within that third country, or an international organisation; standard protection clauses; formats and procedures for the exchange of information by electronic means between controllers, processors and supervisory authorities for binding corporate rules; mutual assistance; and arrangements for the exchange of information by electronic means between supervisory authorities, and between supervisory authorities and the Board.

Closely Related Provisions

Article 24 (Responsibility of the controller) (see too recitals 74–77 and 83); Article 35 (Data protection impact assessment) (see too recital 84); Article 41 (Monitoring of approved codes of conduct); Article 46 (Transfers subject to appropriate safeguards) (see too recitals 108–109); Article 57 (Tasks); Article 58 (Powers); Article 64 (Opinion of the Board); Article 70 (Tasks of the Board); Article 83 (General conditions for imposing administrative fines) (see too recitals 150–151); Article 93 (Committee procedure)

A. Rationale and Policy Underpinnings

Codes of conduct, alongside with data protection impact assessments and data protection certification mechanisms, are introduced in the GDPR as tools for facilitating effective application of the Regulation.

The Commission explained in its 2010 Communication that codes of conduct, as prescribed in the DPD, were largely a tool that had rarely been used and were considered unsatisfactory by private stakeholders.[1] Nevertheless, in the same Communication the Commission expressed its encouragement for self-regulatory initiatives, updating the provision covering codes of conduct and including it in the GDPR.

The rationale for codes of conduct is dual, namely to serve both controllers/processors and supervisory authorities. First, they assist controllers' and processors' compliance with their legal obligations and demonstration thereof by considering different sectors' characteristics of processing. In this manner, codes of conduct may calibrate the obligations of controllers and processors to the level of risk relevant to different sectors. In addition, as highlighted in the UK by ICO, they can collectively address the specific needs of small and medium-sized enterprises ('SMEs').[2]

Secondly, supervisory authorities are assisted in their task of supervising the application of the GDPR. Codes of conduct entail independent private bodies being responsible for monitoring the compliance of the controller or processor with them, an activity that produces documentation of the measures taken by the controller or processor to comply

---

[1] EC Communication 2010. [2] ICO 2018, p. 201.

with their legal obligations. The *voluntary* adherence to codes of conduct may have an impact on the fines imposed on a controller or processor, either as an aggravating or mitigating factor.[3]

Overall, codes of conduct are linked to the principle of accountability of Article 5(2) GDPR. The shift in the GDPR from a set of principles and obligations in the previous regime under the DPD, to an accountability-based data protection legal framework, is demonstrated by the reinforced role assigned to codes of conduct.

B. Legal Background

1. EU Legislation

Article 27 DPD provided trade associations and other bodies representing categories of controllers with the possibility to draw up codes of conduct. The aim was to facilitate the proper implementation of the national provisions of the Member States and the specific features of different sectors. The draft codes of conduct would be submitted to the opinion of the competent supervisory authorities or the WP29 in the case of draft Community codes. The supervisory authorities would, in turn, approve the codes if they were in accordance with the national provisions transposing the DPD. As Hirsch has noted, a Community code represented compliance with the data protection laws of all EU Member States.[4] Recital 26 DPD also provided that codes of conduct could be an instrument for providing guidance for anonymisation of personal data.

In 1998, the WP29 published an assessment guidance setting out a procedure for the acceptance and consideration of codes of conduct. The WP29 would first assess whether the code was in accordance with the DPD, and, where necessary, under the national laws adopted pursuant to it. Secondly, the WP29 would examine the quality, consistency and added value of the codes. The added value was assessed by looking at whether the draft code was focused on the specific data protection issues of the sector or organisation, and whether the code offered sufficient solutions to the problems.[5]

There are only a few examples of approved codes of conduct under the DPD. In 2003, the WP29 formally approved the Federation of European Direct and Interactive Marketing ('FEDMA') Community Code of Conduct on direct marketing.[6] Other draft community codes submitted to the WP29 for approval, such as the World Anti-Doping Agency ('WADA') International Anti-doping standard, the C-SIG Code of Conduct on Cloud Computing, and the Code of Conduct for Cloud Infrastructure Service Providers were not approved, as not meeting the minimum legal requirements of the DPD or not adding sufficient value to it.[7]

At Member State level, DPAs encouraged the drafting of codes and provided guidance on the content and matters to be potentially addressed in codes of conduct. In this regard, the example of the Irish DPA stands out. The Irish DPA provided very detailed guidance on the elements of a code, namely: types of personal data, the purposes of processing, means of collection and processing, disclosure and retention periods.[8] Codes of conduct have been drawn up in various fields, such as on the secondary use of medical data in

---

[3] Art. 83(2)(j) GDPR; EDPB 2018; WP29 2018B.   [4] Hirsch 2013, p. 1056.
[5] WP29 1998.   [6] WP29 2003.   [7] WP29 2009, WP29 2015, WP29 2018A.
[8] Irish Data Protection Commissioner 2001.

scientific research, without receiving DPA approval.[9] Despite the encouragement and guidance, the numbers of approved codes of conduct in Member States are negligible.

Codes of conduct have been recognised in Union law in other fields. The Unfair Commercial Practices Directive 2005/29/EC (hereinafter 'UCPD') provides an example. The UCPD defines codes of conduct as 'an agreement or set of rules not imposed by law, regulation or administrative provision of a Member State which defines the behaviour of traders who undertake to be bound by the code in relation to one or more particular commercial practices or business sectors'.[10] The UCPD obliges traders to comply with codes of conduct to which they have committed themselves in commercial communications.[11] Article 10 UCPD explicitly allows for the control of unfair commercial practices by owners of codes of conduct in the field, to which traders have committed.

2. International instruments

The OECD Privacy Guidelines (which date from 1980 but were revised in 2013) require OECD member countries to encourage and support self-regulation such as codes of conduct.[12] Furthermore, the Explanatory Memorandum to the original 1980 Guidelines clarifies that the principle of accountability refers to accountability supported by legal sanctions and established by codes of conduct.[13]

The Explanatory Report to the current version of Convention 108 provides that the measures taken by State Parties to the Convention to incorporate data protection into their respective systems may be reinforced by voluntary measures such as codes of good practice or codes of professional conduct.[14] The modernised version of Convention 108 does not refer to codes of conduct.

3. National developments

Common law countries broadly use codes of conduct due to the heightened role self-regulation plays in their legal traditions. Other countries with legal systems that combine both common law and civil law traditions may also use codes of conduct in data protection, whether mandated by law or not.

For example, the Canadian Personal Information Protection and Electronic Documents Act ('PIPEDA') of 2000 introduced in its Annex the Model Code for the Protection of Personal Information, a standard developed by the Canadian Standards Association in 1996.[15] The mandatory Annex listed the principles of the Model Code, which were inspired by the 1980 OECD Guidelines. In the national legislation of the Member States, the laws transposing the DPD included relevant provisions on codes of conduct, with some differences in terminology such as deontological codes or sectoral agreements.[16]

4. Case Law

Despite the existence of Article 27 DPD, there is no relevant case law on codes of conduct. This is perhaps unsurprising given the low interest that Article 27 attracted and the

---

[9] See Bahr and Schlünder 2015. [10] Art. 2(f) UCPD. [11] Ibid., Art. 6(2)(b).
[12] Art. 19(d) OECD Guidelines 2013.
[13] See Original explanatory memorandum to the OECD Privacy Guidelines, ibid, p. 59.
[14] Explanatory Report Convention 108, p. 8.
[15] PIPEDA 2018, sched. 1; CSA Model Code 1996. [16] Korff 2002, pp. 196–199.

nature of codes of conduct as self-regulatory instruments, which usually include out-of-court dispute resolution mechanisms.

C. Analysis

1. Status and target group

Article 40 introduces the purpose, content and checks and balances of codes of conduct. As mentioned earlier, the main aim of such codes is to contribute to the proper application of the Regulation. This is possible through sector-specific and/or SME-specific codes, which include issues to be addressed by controllers or processors and solutions or recommended best practices on how to respond to those issues. An example would be a code of conduct for cloud computing, which explains the classification of controllers, joint controllers and processors in respect of cloud computing actors (e.g. when a cloud service provider is a processor or a joint controller), highlights key issues about how personal data are collected or how data subjects can exercise their rights and provides answers to those issues that are commonly encountered in the application of the Regulation to the sector.

A novelty of codes of conduct under the GDPR is the expansion of their target group. While Article 27 DPD was addressed only to controllers, Articles 40 and 41 GDPR also foresee processors as possible adopters of codes of conduct. This shift is justified by the growing role and responsibility of processors in the GDPR, as provided in Article 28, and the growing economic importance and role of processors.

Article 40(3) provides that the Commission may also approve as having general validity codes of conduct adhered to by controllers and processors not subject to the GDPR; this could presumably include, for example, a trade association in a third country whose members are not subject to the GDPR but who want to make it easier for EU business partners to transfer personal data to them. Article 40(3) states that by having such a code approved under Article 40(5) and having it declared as having general validity under Article 40(9), such third country organisations would be providing 'appropriate safeguards within the framework of personal data transfers to third countries or international organisations under the terms referred to in point (e) of Article 46(2)'. However, Article 46(1) refers to appropriate safeguards that are provided by the controller or processor transferring personal data from the EU, not by the parties receiving the data, which seems to present a contradiction with Article 40(3). Even though this provision is explicitly designed to apply to controllers and processors not subject to the GDPR, once the relevant organisations adopt such a code they would be subject to the 'binding and enforceable commitments' (Article 40(3)) under the GDPR that they have to assume in order for the code to be approved.

Codes of conduct are drafted by associations and other bodies representing categories of controllers or processors. The element of representation is important, although the GDPR does not set any quantitative criteria concerning the number of members of such associations or qualitative criteria regarding associations' activities. The question of binding effect also arises. In this respect, the GDPR does not expressly oblige controllers or processors to adhere to codes of conduct; Article 40(4) simply refers to 'controllers or processor which undertake to apply' such codes, which seems to suggest that adherence could be voluntary. Nonetheless, mandatory adherence might pertain in some circumstances, for instance as a membership requirement of an association, such as the case of codes of conduct in fields or professions where they are mandatory for all registered members (as, for example, a code of conduct of a Bar Association).

2. Subject-matter and governance

Regarding the content of the code of conduct, there are two distinctive layers, namely the subject-matter and the governance of the code. In terms of subject-matter, Article 40(2) provides a non-exhaustive list ('such as with regard to') of general topics. The list is extensive, and it covers the majority, but not the full spectrum of principles and legal obligations under the GDPR. Recommended topics include fair and transparent processing (Article 5(1)); the legitimate interests pursued by the controller in specific contexts (Article 6(1)(f)); the collection of personal data, information provided to the public and the data subjects (Articles 13 and 14); the exercise of data subjects rights (Articles 15–18 and 20–22); the measures and procedures for complying with the obligations of the controller (Article 24); data protection by design and by default (Article 25); security measures, including pseudonymisation (Article 32); data breach notification (Articles 33 and 34); transnational data transfers (Article 46); and alternative dispute resolution mechanisms.[17]

Codes of conduct are governed by accredited monitoring bodies, as explained in Article 41. The GDPR does not leave the implementation and monitoring of conformity to the complete discretion of the monitoring bodies. The codes need to have monitoring mechanisms embedded that are known to and approved by supervisory authorities.

After a code has been drafted by an association or an existing code is amended or extended, the association shall submit the code for approval to the competent supervisory authority. When the code concerns processing activities in the territory of one Member State, the competent supervisory authority is the authority of that Member State. When, however, more jurisdictions are involved, the supervisory authority to which the code is submitted should follow the procedure of Article 63 (consistency mechanism): the EDPB provides an Opinion on whether the draft code complies with the GDPR in case of codes in line with Article 40(1) or, in case of codes pursuant to Article 40(3), provides the appropriate safeguards.

As opposed to the DPD involving only the supervisory authorities, the GDPR also gives a role to the European Commission. Where the Opinion of the EDPB is positive and the code is approved, the Board informs the Commission about the Opinion. The Commission may decide to give the approved code of conduct general validity within the Union by adopting an implementing act. The power of the Commission to adopt an implementing act was mentioned in the relevant article on codes of conduct (Article 38) already in the original 2012 Proposal for the GDPR[18] and survived the debates during the legislative process. Codes of conduct of general validity may also be used to provide safeguards for data transfers.[19]

3. Checks and Balances

Korff has reported that under the national laws and the DPD regime, codes of conduct would get approved after a rigorous assessment and often a 'tortuous' process.[20] This

---

[17] The WP29 has acknowledged that the list could be broader than the above issues, including topics such as data portability. See WP29 2018C.
[18] GDPR Proposal.   [19] Art. 40(3) GDPR.   [20] Korff 2002, p. 198.

might have been caused by the lack of other checks and balances beyond the approval of the supervisory authority and a relatively unclear landscape concerning the content and governance of the codes.

The GDPR includes a reformed system of checks and balances to address these concerns, which apply both before and after the code is operational. The opinion and approval of the supervisory authority constitutes a check as to whether the code complies with the GDPR and can offer the solutions it promises. The approval of the supervisory authority is an administrative act. Recital 99 stipulates an obligation for the drafters of the codes to consult relevant stakeholders, including data subjects.

After the code is operational, monitoring of controllers or processors that have adhered to a code of conduct is mandatory for the accredited monitoring bodies.[21] The system of checks and balances for codes of conduct also foresees a public register maintained by the EDPB.[22] Other transparency and publicity measures include the registration and publication of the codes of conduct by the competent supervisory authority and the guarantees for publicity offered by the Commission for codes of conduct with general validity.[23]

Select Bibliography

International agreements

OECD Guidelines 2013: Organisation for Economic Co-operation and Development, 'The OECD Privacy Framework' (2013).

EU legislation

GDPR Proposal: Proposal for a Regulation of the European Parliament and of the Council on the protection of individuals with regard to the processing of personal data and on the free movement of such data (General Data Protection Regulation), COM(2012) 11 final, 25 January 2012.
UCPD: Directive 2005/29/EC of the European Parliament and of the Council of 11 May 2005 concerning unfair business-to-consumer commercial practices in the internal market and amending Council Directive 84/450/EEC, Directives 97/7/EC, 98/27/EC and 2002/65/EC of the European Parliament and of the Council and Regulation (EC) No. 2006/2004 of the European Parliament and of the Council ('Unfair Commercial Practices Directive'), OJ 2005 L 149/22.

National legislation

PIPEDA 2018: Personal Information Protection and Electronic Documents Act, S.C. 2000, c. 5, last amended on November 1, 2018.

Academic writings

Bahr and Schlünder 2015: Bahr and Schlünder, 'Code of Practice on Secondary Use of Medical Data in European Scientific Research Projects', 5(4) *International Data Privacy Law* (2015), 279.
Bennett and Mulligan, 'The Governance of Privacy through Codes of Conduct: International Lessons for US Privacy Policy' (13 July 2014), available at https://papers.ssrn.com/sol3/papers.cfm?abstract_id=2230369.
Bennett and Raab, *The Governance of Privacy: Policy Instruments in Global Perspective* (Routledge 2017).

---

[21] Art. 40(4) GDPR.   [22] Ibid., Art. 40(11).   [23] Ibid., Art. 40(6) and (10).

Christiansen and Dobbels 'Non-Legislative Rule Making after the Lisbon Treaty: Implementing the New System of Comitology and Delegated Acts', 19(1) *European Law Journal* (2013), 42.

Hirsch 2013: Hirsch, 'In Search of the Holy Grail: Achieving Global Privacy Rules through Sector-Based Codes of Conduct', 74(6) *Ohio State Law Journal* (2013), 1029.

Papers of data protection authorities

EDPB 2018: European Data Protection Board, 'Guidelines 1/2018 on Certification and Identifying Certification Criteria in Accordance with Articles 42 and 43 of the Regulation 2016/679' (25 May 2018).

WP29 1998: Article 29 Working Party, 'Future Work on Codes of Conduct: Working Document on the Procedure for the Consideration by the Working Party of Community Codes of Conduct' (WP 13, 10 September 1998).

WP29 2003: Article 29 Working Party, 'Opinion 3/2003 on the European Code of Conduct of FEDMA for the Use Of Personal Data in Direct Marketing' (WP 77, 13 June 2003).

WP29 2009: Article 29 Working Party, 'Second Opinion 4/2009 on the World Anti-Doping Agency (WADA) International Standard for the Protection of Privacy and Personal Information, on Related Provisions of the WADA Code and on Other Privacy Issues in the Context of the Fight against Doping in Sport by WADA and (National) Anti-Doping Organisations' (WP 162, 6 April 2009).

WP29 2015: Article 29 Working Party, 'Opinion 2/2015 on C-SIG Code of Conduct on Cloud Computing' (WP 232, 22 September 2015).

WP29 2018A: Article 29 Working Party, 'Guidelines on the Application and Setting of Administrative Fines for the Purposes of the Regulation 2016/679,' (WP 253, 13 February 2018).

WP29 2018B: Article 29 Working Party, 'Letter to Alban Schmutz' (23 February 2018).

WP29 2018C: Article 29 Working Party, 'Fablab GDPR/from Concepts to Operational Toolbox, DIY—Results of the Discussion' (26 July 2016).

Article 29 Working Party, 'Opinion 4/2010 on the European Code of Conduct of FEDMA for the Use of Personal Data in Direct Marketing' (WP174, 13 July 2010).

ICO 2018: Information Commissioner's Office, 'Guide to the General Data Protection Regulation (GDPR)' (2018).

Irish Data Protection Commissioner 2001: Data Protection Commissioner, 'Thirteenth Annual Report of the Data Protection Commissioner' (2001).

Reports and recommendations

CSA Model Code 1996: Canadian Standards Association, Model Code for the Protection of Personal Information, approved by Standards Council of Canada, CAN/CSA-830-96, March 1996.

Dumortier and Goemans, 'Data Privacy and Standardization. Discussion Paper Prepared for the CEN/ISSS Open Seminar on Data Protection' (2000).

EC Communication 2010: European Commission, 'Communication from the Commission to the European Parliament, the Council, the Economic and Social Committee and the Committee of the Regions, "A Comprehensive Approach on Personal Data Protection in the European Union"', COM (2010) 609 final, 4 November 2010.

Explanatory Report Convention 108 1981: Council of Europe, 'Explanatory Report to the Convention for the Protection of Individuals with Regard to Automatic Processing of Personal Data' (28 January 1981), available at https://rm.coe.int/16800ca434.

Korff 2002: Korff for the European Commission, 'EC Study on Implementation of Data Protection Directive 95/46/EC' (2002).

Article 41. Monitoring of approved codes of conduct

IRENE KAMARA

1. Without prejudice to the tasks and powers of the competent supervisory authority under Articles 57 and 58, the monitoring of compliance with a code of conduct pursuant to Article 40 may be carried out by a body which has an appropriate level of expertise in relation to the subject-matter of the code and is accredited for that purpose by the competent supervisory authority.
2. A body as referred to in paragraph 1 may be accredited to monitor compliance with a code of conduct where that body has:
   (a) demonstrated its independence and expertise in relation to the subject-matter of the code to the satisfaction of the competent supervisory authority;
   (b) established procedures which allow it to assess the eligibility of controllers and processors concerned to apply the code, to monitor their compliance with its provisions and to periodically review its operation;
   (c) established procedures and structures to handle complaints about infringements of the code or the manner in which the code has been, or is being, implemented by a controller or processor, and to make those procedures and structures transparent to data subjects and the public; and
   (d) demonstrated to the satisfaction of the competent supervisory authority that its tasks and duties do not result in a conflict of interests.
3. The competent supervisory authority shall submit the draft requirements for accreditation of a body as referred to in paragraph 1 of this Article to the Board pursuant to the consistency mechanism referred to in Article 63.[1]
4. Without prejudice to the tasks and powers of the competent supervisory authority and the provisions of Chapter VIII, a body as referred to in paragraph 1 of this Article shall, subject to appropriate safeguards, take appropriate action in cases of infringement of the code by a controller or processor, including suspension or exclusion of the controller or processor concerned from the code. It shall inform the competent supervisory authority of such actions and the reasons for taking them.
5. The competent supervisory authority shall revoke the accreditation of a body as referred to in paragraph 1 if the requirements for accreditation are not, or are no longer, met or where actions taken by the body infringe this Regulation.[2]
6. This Article shall not apply to processing carried out by public authorities and bodies.

Relevant Recitals

(77) Guidance on the implementation of appropriate measures and on the demonstration of compliance by the controller or the processor, especially as regards the identification of the risk related to the processing, their assessment in terms of origin, nature, likelihood and severity,

---

[1] Corrigenda to the English text of Art. 41(3) were published on 23 May 2018. The text printed reflects the updated version of the Corrigendum GDPR 2018. For the Corrigendum GDPR 2018, see Table of Legislation.
[2] Corrigenda to the English text of Art. 41(5) were published on 23 May 2018. The text printed reflects the updated version of the Corrigendum GDPR 2018.

and the identification of best practices to mitigate the risk, could be provided in particular by means of approved codes of conduct, approved certifications, guidelines provided by the Board or indications provided by a data protection officer. The Board may also issue guidelines on processing operations that are considered to be unlikely to result in a high risk to the rights and freedoms of natural persons and indicate what measures may be sufficient in such cases to address such risk.

(81) To ensure compliance with the requirements of this Regulation in respect of the processing to be carried out by the processor on behalf of the controller, when entrusting a processor with processing activities, the controller should use only processors providing sufficient guarantees, in particular in terms of expert knowledge, reliability and resources, to implement technical and organisational measures which will meet the requirements of this Regulation, including for the security of processing. The adherence of the processor to an approved code of conduct or an approved certification mechanism may be used as an element to demonstrate compliance with the obligations of the controller. The carrying-out of processing by a processor should be governed by a contract or other legal act under Union or Member State law, binding the processor to the controller, setting out the subject- matter and duration of the processing, the nature and purposes of the processing, the type of personal data and categories of data subjects, taking into account the specific tasks and responsibilities of the processor in the context of the processing to be carried out and the risk to the rights and freedoms of the data subject. The controller and processor may choose to use an individual contract or standard contractual clauses which are adopted either directly by the Commission or by a supervisory authority in accordance with the consistency mechanism and then adopted by the Commission. After the completion of the processing on behalf of the controller, the processor should, at the choice of the controller, return or delete the personal data, unless there is a requirement to store the personal data under Union or Member State law to which the processor is subject.

(98) Associations or other bodies representing categories of controllers or processors should be encouraged to draw up codes of conduct, within the limits of this Regulation, so as to facilitate the effective application of this Regulation, taking account of the specific characteristics of the processing carried out in certain sectors and the specific needs of micro, small and medium enterprises. In particular, such codes of conduct could calibrate the obligations of controllers and processors, taking into account the risk likely to result from the processing for the rights and freedoms of natural persons.

(168) The examination procedure should be used for the adoption of implementing acts on standard contractual clauses between controllers and processors and between processors; codes of conduct; technical standards and mechanisms for certification; the adequate level of protection afforded by a third country, a territory or a specified sector within that third country, or an international organisation; standard protection clauses; formats and procedures for the exchange of information by electronic means between controllers, processors and supervisory authorities for binding corporate rules; mutual assistance; and arrangements for the exchange of information by electronic means between supervisory authorities, and between supervisory authorities and the Board.

Closely Related Provisions

Article 24 (Responsibility of the controller) (see too recitals 74–77, 83); Article 35 (Data protection impact assessment) (see too recital 84); Article 40 (Codes of conduct); Article 46 (Transfers subject to appropriate safeguards) (see too recitals 108–109); Article 57 (Tasks); Article 58 (Powers); Article 64 (Opinion of the Board); Article 70 (Tasks of the Board); Article 83 (General conditions for imposing administrative fines) (see too recitals 150–151); Article 93 (Committee procedure)

A. Rationale and Policy Underpinnings

Codes of conduct have sometimes been viewed as a regulatory failure due to their lack of accountability, poor transparency and weak oversight and enforcement.[3] To address such issues, the DPD introduced the requirement for a mandatory opinion and approval from supervisory authorities on draft codes of conduct.[4] The 2012 Commission proposal[5] and the Parliament First Reading[6] maintained the requirement for an opinion and approval, without adding safeguards to the provisions on codes of conduct. Article 41 thus has a relatively short history, since it was first inserted in the 2015 General Approach of the Council.[7] Article 38a (Article 41 in the final version) of the Council General Approach aimed at adding the layer of safeguards missing from the DPD, the Commission Proposal and the Parliament First Reading. By dedicating a separate article to the issue of monitoring of codes of conduct, the GDPR demonstrates that the post-approval period, when the codes become operational, is equally important to the drafting and approval stage.

Corrigenda to the English text of Article 41 were published on 23 May 2018. This resulted in 'the draft criteria' in Article 41(3) being replaced with 'the draft requirements', and 'the conditions' in Article 41(5) being replaced with 'the requirements'.

B. Legal Background

1. EU legislation

Article 27 DPD provided general requirements on the purpose and approval of codes. However, the DPD detailed neither the process and requirements of complying with a code, nor the characteristics of bodies responsible for monitoring the compliance of controllers to the approved code. Such matters were left to be dealt with either in national laws or in guidance from the supervisory authorities.

2. International instruments

International data protection legal instruments and guidelines referring to codes of conduct, such as the Council of Europe Convention 108 and the OECD Privacy Guidelines,[8] avoid any mention of the monitoring of compliance with codes of conduct; nor do they specify how such codes are to operate and be enforced.

3. National developments

Member States' laws transposing the DPD sometimes addressed the approval process for codes of conduct along with other similar aspects concerning, for example, the validity of such codes,[9] but did not include provisions similar to Article 41 GDPR.

4. Case law

Since the DPD did not include any requirements on the monitoring of codes of conduct, there is as yet no relevant case law.

---

[3] Rubinstein 2011, p. 356.   [4] Art. 27 DPD.   [5] GDPR Proposal.
[6] EP Position GDPR.   [7] Council Report 2015.   [8] OECD Guidelines 2013.
[9] See e.g. Art. 25 Dutch Personal Data Protection Act 2015. See also Korff 2002, pp. 196–199.

C. Analysis

Article 41 firstly specifies the qualifications of the bodies monitoring the enforcement of approved codes and, secondly, places emphasis on the obligation of monitoring bodies to impose sanctions in the case of code infringements. As with Article 40, Article 41 applies only in respect of data processing undertaken by private sector bodies (Article 41(6)).

1. Monitoring bodies

The first question that arises is what qualifies as a monitoring body. In contrast to Article 40, which clarifies that only associations and bodies representing controllers or processors may submit a code of conduct for approval to the supervisory authorities, Article 41 leaves the identity of the monitoring body intentionally vague. Instead of naming an association or other type of body, Article 41 provides characteristics and qualities that should be met by any candidate monitoring body. It thereby follows that any organisation meeting the requirements of Article 41 can be accredited to monitor compliance with approved codes of conduct. While the evident candidate for a monitoring body would be the association that drafted the code, another reasonable option could be conformity assessment bodies—that is bodies offering conformity assessment services such as sampling, testing, inspections and audits.[10] Conformity assessment bodies are organisations dedicated to assess professionally the conformity of a given product, system or service with a technical standard or another type of normative document, which in this case could be a code of conduct as specified in Article 40.

2. Characteristics and qualities of monitoring bodies

The requirements of Article 41(2) relate to the expertise, integrity and readiness of an organisation to become an accredited monitoring body. The candidate organisation needs to demonstrate its expertise in relation to the subject-matter of the code, which could concern one or more of the topics listed in Article 40(2)—for example, data security, data protection by design and by default, or transnational data transfers. Where the codes relate to a specific sector or to the needs of small or medium-sized enterprises ('SMEs'), the organisation needs to show its expertise and prior experience in dealing with such specificities as well. In addition, the organisation must demonstrate its independence and the absence of conflict of interests.[11] This may be challenging to demonstrate a priori to the competent supervisory authority before the organisation starts working on the monitoring of actual cases. The demonstration of these elements can only be done by the organisation showing that it has implemented preventive organisational measures to avoid interference with its independence and mechanisms to identify and raise alert about conflicts of interests. The supervisory authorities should also audit the monitoring bodies regarding these two elements, after accreditation. The GDPR provides that the candidate monitoring bodies should demonstrate the independence, expertise and absence of conflict of interest to the satisfaction of the supervisory authorities. To ensure due process in the treatment of candidate bodies across the Union, supervisory authorities should establish a common approach in this regard.

---

[10] ISO/IEC 17000.   [11] Art. 41(2)(a) and (d) GDPR.

Further, the candidate monitoring bodies should have established procedures for assessing the eligibility of controllers and processors to apply the code, monitor their compliance with the code's provisions and periodically review its operation.[12] Article 41 indirectly indicates the steps for compliance with a code of conduct. The controller or processor that voluntarily decides to apply the code should be prepared to be periodically monitored on whether it complies with the code. The initial assessment and the monitoring of compliance procedures would need to be developed by the monitoring body, but the code could already indicate appropriate ways to assess compliance and address other governance and organisational issues. This would facilitate the harmonised application of the codes when there is a plurality of monitoring bodies for the same code in a Member State, or in the case of codes of general validity across the Union. The harmonised application thus depends not only on the content of the code (common requirements), but also on the manner the compliance thereof is assessed so that the assessment results would be replicable, should another body perform the assessment.

Article 41(2)(c) makes clear that the monitoring body must have in place complaint mechanisms covering infringements by controllers or processors claiming to comply with the code, and that these mechanisms are to be transparent to the data subjects and the public. This requirement helps facilitate the data subjects' need to know what sort of behaviour constitutes a code infringement, to be put in the position to file a complaint against the infringing party, to be notified of the result of the complaint, and to be made aware of other relevant post-complaint procedure.

3. Accreditation

Based on the elements prescribed in Article 41(1) and (2), the supervisory authorities need to develop accreditation requirements. Such requirements should be submitted to the EDPB for an opinion via the consistency mechanism. Once an organisation fulfils the requirements of Article 41 as specified in the accreditation requirements provided by the competent supervisory authority, the latter accredits the organisation to monitor the compliance of controllers and processors with the approved code.

In comparison to the accreditation of certification bodies as provided in Article 43, the accreditation of bodies monitoring codes of conduct is more straightforward: accreditation is provided only by supervisory authorities, without the involvement of National Accreditation Bodies. There is also no reference made to any technical conformity assessment standards, such as the ISO/IEC 17065 standard, unlike in Article 43(2) GDPR. The reason for this difference lies with the identity of the monitoring body: Regulation 765/2008 provides that National Accreditation Bodies ('NAB') accredit conformity assessment bodies (i.e. certification bodies).[13] Thus, if codes of conduct were to be accredited by NABs, only conformity assessment bodies could be accredited as monitoring bodies. Accreditation may be revoked by the supervisory authority when the conditions for accreditation are not or no longer met. The GDPR does not specify how the supervisory authority will be informed, so this could be in any manner, for example during a regular or sporadic audit by the supervisory authority of the accredited body or by a complaint of any interested party. Another ground for revocation of the accreditation of the monitoring body is that the latter infringes the GDPR, meaning any provision of

---

[12] Ibid., Art. 41(2)(c).   [13] Accreditation Regulation 2008.

the Regulation, not only those referring to codes of conduct. As opposed to the five-year duration of the accreditation of certification bodies in Article 43, the GDPR does not provide an expiry date for the accreditation of bodies monitoring codes of conduct.

4. The obligation to sanction infringing controllers and processors

The monitoring body has not only the power but also the obligation to monitor the compliance of the code by a controller or a processor and take action in case of infringement.[14] The accredited monitoring body acts as a trusted third party towards the supervisory authority, providing assurance that controllers and processors adhering to a code actually comply with its provisions. Article 41(4) provides that the sanctions could include suspension or exclusion of the controller or processor from the code. The sanctions and conditions for imposing them should be clearly determined in each code. Beyond suspension for a limited period (for example until the infringer performs a corrective action and reinstates a good practice) or exclusion, other sanctions could also be imposed, such as a monetary penalty. However, it should be kept in mind that both monitoring body and infringing party are private parties, so that these penalties cannot be seen as administrative fines.[15] The monitoring body also bears the obligation to inform the relevant supervisory authority of sanctions and the reasons for taking them. When the infringing actions relate to matters other than procedural elements (i.e., incomplete documentation), such as to processing activities, the reporting obligation of the monitoring body may result in an alert being given to the supervisory authority that the controller's or processor's activities not only infringe the code, but also the GDPR on which the code is based.

Select Bibliography

International agreements

OECD Guidelines 2013: Organisation for Economic Co-operation and Development, 'The OECD Privacy Framework' (2013).

EU legislation

Accreditation Regulation 2008: Regulation (EC) No. 765/2008 of the European Parliament and of the Council of 9 July 2008 setting out the requirements for accreditation and market surveillance relating to the marketing of products and repealing Regulation (EEC) No. 339/93, OJ 2008 L 218/30.

GDPR Proposal: Proposal for a Regulation of the European Parliament and of the Council on the protection of individuals with regard to the processing of personal data and on the free movement of such data (General Data Protection Regulation), COM(2012) 11 final, 25 January 2012.

---

[14] Art. 43(4) GDPR.
[15] An obligation to intervene from the side of the monitoring body presupposes that the perpetrator has a legal duty to follow the code of conduct. However, the GDPR's point of departure seems to be that adherence is voluntary, although there will be circumstances when it could be mandatory. See further the commentary on Art. 40 in this volume. . See also the commentary on Art. 83 in this volume.

National legislation

Dutch Personal Data Protection Act 2015: Wet bescherming persoonsgegevens (WBP), versie van 1 januari 2015 (repealed).

Academic writings

Rubinstein 2011: Rubinstein, 'Privacy and Regulatory Innovation: Moving Beyond Voluntary Codes' 6 *I/S: A Journal of Law and Policy for the Information Society* (2011), 356.

Papers of data protection authorities

Article 29 Working Party, 'Guidelines on the Application and Setting of Administrative Fines for the Purposes of the Regulation 2016/679' (WP 253, 3 October 2017).

Reports and recommendations

Council Report 2015: Preparation of a general approach, 965/15, 11 June 2015.

EP Position GDPR: Position of the European Parliament adopted at first reading on 12 March 2014 with a view to the adoption of Regulation (EU) No. .../2014 of the European Parliament and of the Council on the protection of individuals with regard to the processing of personal data and on the free movement of such data (General Data Protection Regulation), P7_TC1-COD(2012)0011, 12 March 2014.

Korff 2002: Korff for the European Commission, 'EC Study on Implementation of Data Protection Directive 95/46/EC' (2002).

Others

ISO/IEC 17000: ISO/IEC 17000:2004 Conformity assessment—Vocabulary and general principles.

Article 42. Certification

RONALD LEENES

1. The Member States, the supervisory authorities, the Board and the Commission shall encourage, in particular at Union level, the establishment of data protection certification mechanisms and of data protection seals and marks, for the purpose of demonstrating compliance with this Regulation of processing operations by controllers and processors. The specific needs of micro, small and medium-sized enterprises shall be taken into account.
2. In addition to adherence by controllers or processors subject to this Regulation, data protection certification mechanisms, seals or marks approved pursuant to paragraph 5 of this Article may be established for the purpose of demonstrating the existence of appropriate safeguards provided by controllers or processors that are not subject to this Regulation pursuant to Article 3 within the framework of personal data transfers to third countries or international organisations under the terms referred to in point (f) of Article 46(2). Such controllers or processors shall make binding and enforceable commitments, via contractual or other legally binding instruments, to apply those appropriate safeguards, including with regard to the rights of data subjects.
3. The certification shall be voluntary and available via a process that is transparent.
4. A certification pursuant to this Article does not reduce the responsibility of the controller or the processor for compliance with this Regulation and is without prejudice to the tasks and powers of the supervisory authorities which are competent pursuant to Article 55 or 56.
5. A certification pursuant to this Article shall be issued by the certification bodies referred to in Article 43 or by the competent supervisory authority, on the basis of criteria approved by that competent supervisory authority pursuant to Article 58(3) or by the Board pursuant to Article 63. Where the criteria are approved by the Board, this may result in a common certification, the European Data Protection Seal.
6. The controller or processor which submits its processing to the certification mechanism shall provide the certification body referred to in Article 43, or where applicable, the competent supervisory authority, with all information and access to its processing activities which are necessary to conduct the certification procedure.
7. Certification shall be issued to a controller or processor for a maximum period of three years and may be renewed, under the same conditions, provided that the relevant criteria continue to be met. Certification shall be withdrawn, as applicable, by the certification bodies referred to in Article 43 or by the competent supervisory authority where the criteria for the certification are not or are no longer met.[1]
8. The Board shall collate all certification mechanisms and data protection seals and marks in a register and shall make them publicly available by any appropriate means.

Relevant Recital

(100) In order to enhance transparency and compliance with this Regulation, the establishment of certification mechanisms and data protection seals and marks should be encouraged, allowing data subjects to quickly assess the level of data protection of relevant products and services.

---

[1] Corrigenda to the English text of Art. 42(7) were published on 23 May 2018. The text printed reflects the updated version of the Corrigendum GDPR 2018. For the Corrigendum GDPR 2018, see Table of Legislation.

Closely Related Provisions

Article 5(2) (Principle of accountability); Article 24(3) (Responsibility of the controller); Article 25(3) (Data protection by design and by default); Article 28(5) (Responsibilities of the processor) (see too recital 81); Article 32(3) (Security of processing); Article 43 (Certification bodies); Article 46(2)(f) (Transfers subject to appropriate safeguards); Article 55 (Competence of the supervisory authorities); Article 56 (Tasks of the supervisory authorities); Articles 57(1)(n)–(q) (Tasks of the supervisory authorities) (see too recital 77); Article 58(h) (Powers of the supervisory authorities); Article 63 (Consistency mechanism); Article 64(1)(c) (Opinion of the Board); Article 70(1)(n)–(q) (Tasks of the Board); Article 93(4)(b) (General conditions for imposing administrative fines)

A. Rationale and Policy Underpinnings

The GDPR has introduced the risk-based approach and accountability as new cornerstones of the data protection framework. Certification, data protection impact assessments and codes of conduct are among the primary means in the GDPR's accountability framework. Certification is an accountability-based mechanism that assists controllers and processors to achieve and demonstrate compliance of their processing operations with the obligations imposed by the GDPR.

The rationale for incorporating certification can be found in its dual function. On the one hand it allows controllers to achieve and demonstrate compliance to the regulatory authorities. On the other hand it provides transparency to the market. Certifications, data protection seals and marks allow 'data subjects to quickly assess the level of data protection of relevant products and services'.[2]

Certifications, seals and marks are well established instruments to enhance transparency and trust, facilitate consumer choice and promote legal compliance.[3] Certification is a generic mechanism that generally involves third party assessment against objective pre-existing requirements. It is a flexible mechanism which has led to many different ways in which conformity assessment takes place, as well as to a multitude of seals and marks available in various sectors and to different forms of oversight. Oversight, usually by accreditation bodies, is an important element of certification that aims to guarantee that the entities that provide the certification (certification bodies) do their job properly. The flexibility and variety are part of the popularity of certification[4] as an instrument to increase compliance and conformity, but are also cited as reasons[5] why certification often does not deliver the envisaged safeguards to consumers. Certifications disconnected from adequate oversight may actually deceive consumers.[6] Hence, certification is sometimes a contested and controversial mechanism.

Nevertheless, self-regulatory instruments, such as certification and codes of conduct, are seen by some as important in promoting a real data protection culture within organisations and requiring less prescriptive rules and reducing administrative burdens without

---

[2] Rec. 100 GDPR.   [3] Kamara and de Hert 2018; Lachaud 2018.
[4] E.g. according to ISO 2018, in 2017 there were 1,058,504 ISO 9001 certificates granted.
[5] Lachaud 2018.
[6] The US online privacy seal provider TRUSTe, for instance, has faced complaints regarding its failure to conduct promised annual re-certifications on a large scale. Ultimately, these complaints have been settled with the FTC. See FTC 2015.

reducing compliance.[7] Also, the WP29 subscribes to the idea that certification can have a changing impact on the data protection landscape by promoting transparency and consumer choice. It envisions data protection as a market differentiator in which certification can have a signalling function to consumers. As the WP29 has stated,

> data controllers may decide to use the option of trustworthy services delivering certificates. As certain seals become known for their rigorous testing, controllers are likely to favour them insofar as they would give more compliance 'comfort' in addition to offering a competitive advantage.[8]

A corrigendum to the English text of Article 42 was published on 23 May 2018. This resulted in 'the relevant requirements' in Article 42(7) being replaced with 'the relevant criteria'.

B. Legal Background

1. EU Legislation

There is no legal antecedent for certification in the DPD, though certification bears some resemblance to codes of conduct under Article 27 of the DPD. Codes of conduct are self-regulatory instruments that allow parties to define rules to cope with sectoral specificities both under the Directive and the national provisions implementing the Directive. Certification is also based on rules elaborating provisions in the GDPR and is voluntary.

Although certification was not regulated in the DPD, there are examples of certification in the data protection field.[9] Notable is the EuroPriSe seal, which originated from an EU-funded project. Its criteria are based on the DPD, the EPD and other EU legislation.[10] Seals such as these had no legal effect, which may be one of the reasons why their uptake has been very limited.[11]

The history of certification as a data protection instrument goes back to at least 2008 when the WP29 issued its opinion on the Future of Privacy as a joint response (with the Working Party on police and justice) to the Commission's consultation on the legal framework for the fundamental right to protection of personal data. In the opinion, the Working Party states that 'the technological data protection principles and the ensuing concrete criteria should be used as a basis for awarding labels of quality (seals) in a framework of a data protection audit'.[12] In this context, the WP29 had in mind schemes such as the abovementioned EuroPriSe seal. This attention to certification as a mechanism to further data protection was reaffirmed in the 2010 WP29 opinion on the accountability principle,[13] where certification programmes and seals were discussed as accountability-based tools that could contribute to prove that a data controller has fulfilled the applicable requirements, allow data controllers to differentiate themselves in the market and, in the case of 'seals known for their rigorous testing', provide them with a competitive advantage in the market.

Around the same time, certification appeared on the agenda of the Commission in its policy objectives in the Digital Agenda for Europe, where the Commission called for the creation of online trustmarks for retail websites to enhance user trust regarding security of payments and privacy.[14] Also within the context of cybersecurity generally,

---

[7] Council Statement GDPR, p. 4.   [8] WP29 2010, p. 17.
[9] Rodrigues et al. 2014; Lachaud 2018.   [10] See EuroPriSe 2017.
[11] E.g. EuroPriSe awarded 11 seals in 2017, of which nine were re-certifications. EuroPriSe seals are valid for two years. See EuroPriSe Website.
[12] WP29 2009, p. 15.
[13] WP29 2010, p. 17.   [14] EC Communication 2010.

where technical standards play a prominent role, certification has gained the attention of EU policy makers. The 2013 Cybersecurity Strategy, for instance, promoted voluntary certification in cloud computing which should be based on 'industry-led standards for companies' performance on cybersecurity'.[15] More recently, the 2019 Cybersecurity Act (Regulation (EU) 2019/881) provides for the establishment of an elaborate 'European cybersecurity certification framework'.[16] This will be, in practice, complementary but 'without prejudice' to the GDPR's certification scheme.[17]

The GDPR Proposal incorporated certification mechanisms in Article 39.[18] The proposed provision set out the aims of data protection certification: transparency, allowing data subjects to assess quickly the level of data protection provided by controllers and processors, and contributing to the proper application of the GDPR. The provision stipulated further that Member States and the Commission should encourage these mechanisms, especially at European level. Article 39 GDPR Proposal was silent on the certification criteria, requirements, technical standards, procedure and parties involved, with this left to be specified by the Commission through the adoption of delegated acts. The Parliament in its first reading[19] aimed to strip away the discretion of the Commission to elaborate the practical details of certification at a later stage and instead provided a much more thoroughly developed framework. Article 39 of the Parliament first reading came to include detailed provisions on the role of supervisory authorities, the procedure and the legal significance of certification based on the GDPR.

The Council's general approach[20] took a middle ground between the Commission and Parliament. It assigned a role for Member States, the Commission and the EDPB to encourage the establishment of data protection certification mechanisms, especially at Union level. It further suggested strengthening the role of certification by adding that the purpose of certification would be to demonstrate compliance with the GDPR of processing operations carried out by controllers and processors. The Council also added that the needs of small and medium sized enterprises needed to be taken into account in this context, without further elaboration of what this means. The Council identified the certification bodies and the data protection authorities (supervisory authorities) as the main actors for the GDPR certification. Both could act as entities granting certification. Furthermore, the Council specified the procedure and constraints of certification, such as validity periods for the certification; withdrawal of certifications; and a public register with all data protection certification mechanisms, seals and marks maintained by the EDPB for transparency purposes. The Council's proposal is close to what has become Articles 42 and 43 in the GDPR.[21]

2. National developments

A few national data protection laws included provisions on certifications or seals prior to the GDPR. An example is the French Data Protection Act of 1978, which after an amendment in 2009, authorised the French Data Protection Authority to deliver privacy seals for products or procedures intended to protect individuals.[22] Also, the federal state (*Bundesland*) of Schleswig-Holstein in Germany had regulations in place for instance for

---

[15] EC Communication 2013, p. 13.   [16] Cybersecurity Act, Title III.   [17] Ibid., rec. 74.
[18] GDPR Proposal.   [19] EP Resolution 2014.   [20] Council Report 2015.
[21] Kamara and de Hert 2018.
[22] French Data Protection Act 1978. See further Carvais-Palut 2018.

the certification of IT products by the regional DPA (the Unabhängige Landeszentrum für Datenschutz 'ULD').[23]

3. Case law

Given that there is no predecessor to certification in the DPD, there is no case law concerning certification.

C. Analysis

The data protection certification mechanism introduced in the GDPR is complex and involves multiple layers and actors. At the time of its introduction it left many details to be sorted out by the Commission (through delegated (Article 43(8) GDPR) and implementing (Article 43(9) GDPR) acts), supervisory authorities, the EDPB and certification bodies. In the following analysis, the certification system introduced in Article 42 is dissected into six blocks: aims, concepts, scope, actors and roles, criteria and process. Because GDPR certification consists of two elements—certification (Article 42) and certification bodies (Article 43)—the analysis herein of Article 42 should be read in conjunction with the commentary on Article 43 in this volume.

1. Aims

The purpose of certification, according to Article 42(1), is to allow controllers or processors to demonstrate compliance with the GDPR. This is done by having their processing operation or chain of operations assessed by an independent certification body against a set of data protection certification criteria. If the assessment is positive, the certification body grants certification that demonstrates compliance. Certification contributes to transparency and accountability in line with the accountability principle in Article 5(2) GDPR and allows data subjects to assess quickly the level of data protection of products and services.[24]

Demonstration of compliance does not equal compliance. Controllers or processors are still accountable for complying with the GDPR, independently of whether they are certified or not. Under Article 42(4), being certified does not reduce the responsibility of controllers and processors to comply with their legal obligations, nor does it interfere with the tasks and powers of the DPAs. Thus, Article 42 certification does not offer a presumption of conformity with the Regulation,[25] unlike in some other domains.[26]

GDPR certification introduces a dual compliance obligation. Not only is the certified controller or processor obliged to comply with the GDPR, but due to the certification, it also has contractual obligations towards the certification body to adhere to the certification criteria. Non-compliance with these may trigger corrective measures or withdrawal of certification.

The availability of an Article 42 certification has an effect on potential administrative fines by the supervisory authorities because adherence to an approved certification

---

[23] Schleswig-Holstein Regulation 2013.   [24] Rec. 100 GDPR
[25] Kamara et al. 2019.
[26] Most notably this is the case of certification based on the 'New Approach' Directives. The New Approach policy has been adopted in Europe by Council Resolution 85/C136/01.

mechanism is one of the factors to be taken into account in the establishment of such fines.[27]

2. Concepts

The certification mechanism introduced in the GDPR is based on existing certification schemes[28] as well as the International Organization for Standardization ('ISO') conformity assessment framework and Union legislation.[29] However, many terms in Articles 42 and 43 are not defined, or not consistently used compared to their use in other domains. In particular, 'data protection certification mechanisms', 'seals' and 'marks' are not defined in the GDPR or Union legislation. Furthermore, the terms are sometimes used collectively, as in 'data protection mechanisms, seals and marks' (Article 42(1) GDPR).

A common starting point for assessing what certification is, can be found in the standard ISO/IEC 17000:2004 developed by ISO, which defines certification as a 'third party attestation ... related to products, processes, and services'.[30] Article 42 implies third party attestation in the process outlined in the provision and narrows down the object of certification to 'processing operations' by controllers and processors (Article 42(1) GDPR). Data protection certification is a certification process that, if successful, results in awarding a certification or data protection certification, which is attested by a certificate. Data protection marks and seals are visual representations of data protection certifications. Marks (such as trust marks) and seals (e.g. the EuroPriSe privacy seal) already exist in the privacy and security domain, but there is no established definition of them, and the GDPR does nothing to change this. Generally, marks are used to represent that some object meets certain qualities or requirements (e.g. CE marking). A data protection mark could thus be interpreted as a mark that signals that a controller or a processor has been awarded a certification.

Whereas marks are familiar in EU regulation, 'seals' or data protection seals as introduced in the GDPR certification framework are not. Seals are neither defined in the ISO/IEC conformity assessment framework, nor in the Accreditation Regulation 765/2008. Seals are traditionally used as a sign of authenticity that is inseparably attached to some object (e.g. wax seals). This is also how we encounter electronic seals, for instance in the context of electronic identification and trust services: 'data in electronic form, which is attached to or logically associated with other data in electronic form to ensure the latter's origin and integrity'.[31]

Data protection marks and data protection seals could both refer to some visual indicator that a controller or processor has been awarded certification for its processing operation(s). Is there a difference between the two types of symbols? The EDPB in its guidelines on certification treats them as having the same legal meaning, namely a logo or a symbol 'whose presence (in addition to a certificate) indicates that the object of certification has been independently assessed and conforms to specified requirements, stated in normative documents such as regulations, standards, or technical specifications'.[32]

---

[27] Art. 83(2)(j) GDPR.
[28] Especially the German scheme EuroPriSe seems to have been influential. See Rodrigues et al. 2014.
[29] See Accreditation Regulation 765/2008 and Standardisation Regulation 1025/2012.
[30] ISO/IEC 17000:2004, section 5.5.
[31] Art. 3(25) Regulation 910/2014.   [32] EDPB 2019, p. 8.

A data protection certification mechanism is the set of all the rules, processes and requirements that regulate what is certified; how and under which conditions the evaluation takes place; and when the certification is granted, revoked or renewed. A specific instance of a data protection certification mechanism is commonly called a 'certification scheme'.

3. Scope

The scope of data protection certification entails the object that can be certified as well as the subject-matter that can be certified. As to the object, recital 100 GDPR mentions products and services, while Article 42(1) and (6) GDPR define the objects as processing operation(s). This may create confusion but given the binding legal nature of the provision compared to the explanatory value of recitals and the fact that processing operations are always embedded into something (products, such as a household robot; or services, such as an online shop), the scope is clearer than it may first seem.

It is the data processing operation that can be certified because this is where the personal data are handled. Certification of persons (such as data protection officers[33] (Article 37 GDPR)) or management systems are out of the scope of Articles 42 and 43. The GDPR is also clear about who can apply for certification: Article 42(7) states that 'certification shall be issued to a controller or processor'. This means that other entities involved in the creation of processing operations, such as software or hardware developers, are outside the scope of Article 42 certification.

Regarding the subject-matter, the GDPR provides a number of pointers. First, Article 42(1) mentions 'demonstrating compliance with this regulation'. This suggests that the conformity assessment should take into account all relevant provisions of the GDPR. This excludes, for instance, provisions aimed at supervisory authorities (e.g. Articles 51–59), but leaves unanswered which provisions should be taken into account in what Kamara et al. have termed 'comprehensive GDPR certification'.[34] In view of the breadth of GDPR certification, the EDPB has pointed out that the lawfulness of processing (Article 6), the principles of data processing (Article 5), data subjects' rights (Articles 12–23), data breach notification (Article 33), the obligations of data protection by design and by default (Article 25), data protection impact assessments (Article 35(7)(d)) and technical and organisational security measures of the applicant organisation (Article 32) should all be taken into account, where applicable.[35]

Elsewhere in the GDPR, certification is mentioned as a means to demonstrate compliance with respect to specific types of obligations. For controllers, this concerns Article 24(3) GDPR to demonstrate compliance with the obligations of the controller; Article 25(3) GDPR to demonstrate compliance with the requirements of data protection by design and by default; Article 32(3) to demonstrate compliance with the requirements of security of processing as provided in Article 32(1) GDPR. For processors, Article 28(5) GDPR mentions certification as a mechanism to demonstrate sufficient guarantees to implement appropriate technical and organisational measures under Article 28(1) and (4) GDPR, and Article 32(3) GDPR mentions it to demonstrate compliance with the

---

[33] EDPB 2019 p. 16. See Lachaud 2014 for an analysis of the opportunity, feasibility and limits of certifying DPO competences.
[34] Kamara et al. 2019, p. 37.   [35] EDPB 2019, p. 15.

requirements of security of processing pursuant to Article 32(1) GDPR. These provisions suggest that 'single-issue schemes', focusing on specific aspects of GDPR compliance, are also foreseen in the GDPR. The list provided above should not be seen as exhaustive; there is room for other topics as well.[36]

However, it is not always clear which set of provisions should be taken into account in an actual certification scheme. For example, certification of the GDPR's security requirements under Article 32 may be relatively limited in scope, but certification based on the obligations of the processor under Article 28 certainly does not only involve Article 28, but also a broad range of controller obligations such as data protection by design and by default, as well as data security. Article 42(2) GDPR also makes clear that certification can additionally play a role in demonstrating that appropriate safeguards are available in the context of data transfer to third countries or international organisations. Specific certification mechanisms, seals or marks may be developed for this purpose.[37]

Certification bodies may opt to develop 'comprehensive' or 'single-issue' certification schemes.[38] They may also develop schemes for specific types of processing operations, such as cloud computing, or certain jurisdictions incorporating criteria based on specific Member State law, and/or offering the certification scheme in a specific language, thus targeting a specific group of controllers/processors.

4. Actors and roles

Any certification mechanism is a multi-layered construct. At the bottom, we have the applicant, a controller or processor who wants their processing operation certified. ISO/IEC 170000:2004 and other regulations, including Articles 42 and 43 GDPR consider certification to be a 'third party' attestation. This means that an entity independent of the applicant has to assess conformity with the criteria embedded in the certification scheme. Article 42(6) GDPR opens the way to two types of assessors, namely certification bodies accredited in line with Article 43 GDPR, or certification by the competent supervisory authorities.[39] Certification bodies are private or public entities[40] that conduct (or outsource to external auditors) conformity assessments in view of criteria based on some normative standard (minimally the GDPR in the case of Article 42 GDPR certification). Independent of whether a supervisory authority chooses to offer data protection certification, they are tasked with approving certification criteria provided to them for approval by certification bodies (Article 42(5)).

It is unusual for supervisory authorities to be assigned a role that can potentially conflict with their roles regarding investigation and enforcement. Hence, the EDPB has argued that supervisory authorities should be transparent in the exercise of their functions and make sure there is a clear separation of powers relating to investigations and enforcement to prevent conflicts of interests from occurring.[41]

Although the exact legal effects of a certification are not entirely clear (see above), aside from the compliance obligations resting on controllers and processors, those that have been awarded certification are also contractually obliged to meet the requirements of the

---

[36] See Kamara et al. 2019, pp. 82 et seq.   [37] Kamara et al. 2019, pp. 174-226.
[38] Kamara et al. 2019.   [39] See Art. 55 GDPR on the competence of supervisory authorities.
[40] While certification bodies are usually private entities that offer certification as a commercial service, Art. 42(5) clears a path for supervisory authorities (i.e. public entities) to offer data protection certification.
[41] EDPB 2019, p. 10.

Leenes

certification scheme. This will have to be assessed at least when the applicant requests renewal of the certification (which has a validity of three years maximum under Article 42(7)). The supervisory authorities are tasked with periodic reviews of certifications issued in accordance with Article 42 (Article 57(1)(o)), and certification bodies must withdraw certifications when they discover that the certification requirements or conditions are no longer met (Article 42(7)).[42] Withdrawal of certification does not directly imply a violation of the GDPR obligations, because a certification scheme may contain conditions that go beyond what the GDPR requires.

5. Criteria

Certification under Article 42 GDPR aims to demonstrate compliance with the GDPR. However, the assessment of compliance is not done on the basis of the provisions of the GDPR, but rather on the basis of criteria that follow from transforming its high-level and abstract provisions into auditable criteria. Such criteria should be sufficiently clear and precise so that the need for subjective interpretation by the assessors/auditors is limited. In principle, two independent assessors should arrive at the same conclusion regarding the assessment of a particular applicant in light of the material regarding the target of evaluation (a specific processing operation) available to them (comparability). However, in this respect certification of the safety of chairs, for instance, is much more straightforward than assessing whether appropriate technical and organisational measures have been taken in a data-processing operation. In the former case, the requirements can be specified in terms such as the weight a chair has to withstand, stability properties etc. In the latter, there are many factors to take into account partially depending on the context of the processing operation.

The GDPR does not specify how assessment criteria should be developed or by whom. However, it does specify that once developed, the criteria to be used in a particular certification scheme need to be approved by the competent supervisory authority or by the EDPB (Article 42(5)). In cases where the certifying entity aims to establish a Union-wide (common) certification scheme (the so-called 'European Data Protection Seal'), the approval should come from the EDPB (Article 42(5)).[43] The supervisory authorities at the time of introduction of the GDPR had not yet received any clear guidance on how to assess the appropriateness of certification schemes under the GDPR. In its 2019 guidelines on certification, the EDPB indicated that the approval of the criteria should aim at properly reflecting the requirements and principles of the GDPR, and contribute to the consistent application of the GDPR.[44] The certification criteria for the European Data Protection Seal in specific must be ready to use in all Member States and reflect national legal requirements, where relevant.[45] The EDPB also provided guidance to the supervisory authorities for review and assessment of the certification criteria in line with Article 42(5).[46]

Certification under the GDPR is not restricted to the GDPR alone as a normative source for criteria. Especially, but not confined to, the security aspects of processing, international (ISO/IEC) standards exist that may be incorporated into certification

---

[42] See also with regard to the DPAs, Art. 58(2)(h) GDPR.
[43] See too EDPB 2019, pp. 12 et seq.   [44] Ibid., p. 12.
[45] Ibid., p. 14.   [46] Ibid., Annex 2.

mechanisms. A data protection certification mechanism will not only have to reflect material criteria derived from the GDPR, but also procedural ones that relate to the certification procedure and that specify, for instance, how the assessment process is implemented, who makes the certification decision, what documentation is provided and will be produced, timeline, conflict resolution procedures etc.

6. Process

Article 42 certification is a voluntary process. Controllers and processors may opt to have their processing operation(s) certified if they see a value of such certification in the market and/or in relation to the supervisory authorities. The GDPR requires the certification process to be transparent (Article 42(3)). This means that the assessment criteria should be transparent to both the applicants and the data subjects. They should be able to assess the scope and rigour of the certification process in order to establish what entering the process entails (controller/processor) and what the value of the certification is (controller/processor/data subjects). In practice, transparency should in any case mean making public the scope of certification, the certification criteria, assessment methodology, conflict resolution and sanctions.

The application process for certification is not described in the GDPR. However, based on the commonly followed practice outlined in ISO/IEC 17065, such processes consist in review of the application by the certification body and evaluation by expert auditors/assessors leading to an evaluation report. Next, a decision on the basis of this report is taken by a different person than the assessor and, if positive, certification is granted. Part of the process is an elaborate document review and possibly site visits. The whole assessment process must be amply documented, as the EDPB has explained.[47] In particular, demonstration of compliance requires documentation, including reports describing how certification criteria are met, proof and reasoning of the decision of the entity granting the certification, and the conclusions from facts or premises collected throughout the certification process.[48]

Select Bibliography

EU legislation

Accreditation Regulation 765/2008: Regulation (EC) No. 765/2008 of the European Parliament and of the Council of 9 July 2008 setting out the requirements for accreditation and market surveillance relating to the marketing of products and repealing Regulation (EEC) No. 339/93, OJ 2008 L 218/30.

Council Resolution 85/C136/01: Council Resolution of 7 May 1985 on a new approach to technical harmonization and standards, OJ 1985 C 136/1.

Cybersecurity Act: Regulation (EU) 2019/881 of the European Parliament and of the Council of 17 April 2019 on ENISA (the European Union Agency for Cybersecurity) and on information and communications technology cybersecurity certification and repealing Regulation (EU) No 526/2013 (Cybersecurity Act), OJ 2019 L 151/15.

---

[47] EDPB 2019, pp. 19 et seq.   [48] EDPB 2019, p. 5.

GDPR Proposal: Proposal for a Regulation of the European Parliament and of the Council on the protection of individuals with regard to the processing of personal data and on the free movement of such data (General Data Protection Regulation), COM(2012) 11 final, 25 January 2012.

Regulation 910/2014: Regulation (EU) No. 910/2014 of the European Parliament and of the Council of 23 July 2014 on electronic identification and trust services for electronic transactions in the internal market and repealing Directive 1999/93/EC, 2014 OJ L 257/73.

Standardisation Regulation 1025/2012: Regulation (EU) No. 1025/2012 of the European Parliament and of the Council of 25 October 2012 on European standardisation, amending Council Directives 89/686/EEC and 93/15/EEC and Directives 94/9/EC, 94/25/EC, 95/16/EC, 97/23/EC, 98/34/EC, 2004/22/EC, 2007/23/EC, 2009/23/EC and 2009/105/EC of the European Parliament and of the Council and repealing Council Decision 87/95/EEC and Decision No. 1673/2006/EC of the European Parliament and of the Council, OJ 2012 L 316/12.

National legislation

French Data Protection Act 1978: Act No. 78-17 of 6 January 1978 on Data Processing, Files and Individual Liberties (Loi n° 78-17 du 6 janvier 1978 relative à l'informatique, aux fichiers et aux libertés), as last amended by Law No. 2014-334 of 17 March 2014.

Schleswig-Holstein Regulation 2013: Landesverordnung über ein Datenschutzgütesiegel, (Datenschutzgütesiegelverordnung – DSGSVO) vom 30. November 2013, GVOBl. 2013 S. 536.

Academic writings

Carvais-Palut 2018: Carvais-Palut, 'The French Privacy Seal Scheme: A Successful Test' in Rodrigues and Papakonstantinou (eds.), *Privacy and Data Protection Seals* (Springer 2018), 49.

Kamara and de Hert 2018: Kamara and de Hert, 'Data Protection Certification in the EU: Possibilities, Actors and Building Blocks in a Reformed Landscape' in Rodrigues and Papakonstantinou (eds.), *Privacy and Data Protection Seals* (Springer 2018), 7.

Lachaud 2014: Lachaud, 'Should the DPO Be Certified', 6(4) *International Data Privacy Law* (2014), 189.

Lachaud 2018: Lachaud, 'The General Data Protection Regulation and the Rise of Certification as a Regulatory Instrument', 34(2) *Computer Law & Security Review* (2018), 244.

Rodrigues et al. 2014: Rodrigues, Barnard-Wills, de Hert and Papakonstantinou, 'The Future of Privacy Certification in Europe: An Exploration of Options under Article 42 of the GDPR', 30(3) *International Review of Law, Computers & Technology* (2014), 248.

Rodrigues, Barnard-Wills, Wright, de Hert and Papakonstantinou, *EU Privacy Seals Project: Inventory and Analysis of Privacy Certification Schemes. Final Report* (Publications Office of the European Union 2013)

Papers of data protection authorities

EDPB 2019: European Data Protection Board, 'Guidelines 1/2018 on Certification and Identifying Certification Criteria in Accordance with Articles 42 and 43 the Regulation 2016/679' (4 June 2019).

WP29 2009: Article 29 Working Party and Working Party on Police and Justice, 'The Future of Privacy—Joint Contribution to the Consultation of the European Commission on the Legal Framework for the Fundamental Right to Protection of Personal Data' (WP168, 1 December 2009).

WP29 2010: Article 29 Working Party, 'Opinion 3/2010 on the Principle of Accountability' (WP173, 13 July 2010).

Reports and recommendations

Centre for Information Policy Leadership, 'Certifications, Seals and Marks under the GDPR and Their Roles as Accountability Tools and Cross-Border Data Transfer Mechanisms' (12 April 2017).
Council Report 2015: Preparation of a general approach, 965/15, 11 June 2015.
Council Statement GDPR: Position of the Council at first reading with a view to adoption of a Regulation of the European Parliament and of the Council on the protection of natural persons with regard to the processing of personal data and on the free movement of such data, and repealing Directive 95/45/EC (General Data Protection Regulation), Statement of the Council's reasons, 5419/1/16, 8 April 2016.
EC Communication 2010: Communication from the Commission to the European Parliament, the Council, the European Economic and Social Committee and the Committee of the Regions, 'A Digital Agenda for Europe', COM(2010) 245 final/2, 26 August 2010.
EC Communication 2013: Joint Communication to the European Parliament, the Council, the European Economic and Social Committee and the Committee of the Regions, 'Cybersecurity Strategy of the European Union: An Open, Safe and Secure Cyberspace', JOIN(2013) 1 final, 7 February 2013.
EP Resolution 2014: European Parliament legislative resolution of 12 March 2014 on the proposal for a regulation of the European Parliament and of the Council on the protection of individuals with regard to the processing of personal data and on the free movement of such data (General Data Protection Regulation), 2012/0011(COD), 12 March 2014.
European Commission, 'Comparative Study on Different Approaches to New Privacy Challenges, in Particular in the Light of Technological Developments, Final Report' (January 2010).
European Union Agency for Network and Information Security, 'Recommendations on European Data Protection Certification' (November 2018).
Kamara et al. 2019: Kamara, Leenes, Lachaud, Stuurman, van Lieshout, and Bodea, 'Data Protection Certification Mechanisms. Study on Articles 42 and 43 of the Regulation (EU) 2016/679', Study commissioned by the European Commission (2019).

Others

EuroPriSe 2017: EuroPriSe, 'European Privacy Seal—EuroPriSe Criteria for Certification of IT Products and IT-Based Services' (January 2017), available at https://www.european-privacy-seal.eu/AppFile/GetFile/6a29f2ca-f918-4fdf-a1a8-7ec186b2e78a.
EuroPriSe Website: EuroPriSe, 'Register of Awarded Seals', available at https://www.european-privacy-seal.eu/EPS-en/awarded-seals.
FTC 2015: Federal Trade Commission, 'FTC approves Final Order in TRUSTe Privacy Case' (18 March 2015), available at https://www.ftc.gov/news-events/press-releases/2015/03/ftc-approves-final-order-truste-privacy-case.
ISO 2018: International Organization for Standardization, 'The ISO Survey of Management System Standard Certifications—2017—Explanatory Note' (August 2018), available at https://isotc.iso.org/livelink/livelink/fetch/-8853493/8853511/8853520/18808772/00._Overall_results_and_explanatory_note_on_2017_Survey_results.pdf?nodeid=19208898&vernum=-2.
ISO/IEC 17000:2004: International Organization for Standardization, 'ISO/IEC 17000:2004' (2004), available at https://www.iso.org/obp/ui/#iso:std:iso-iec:17000:ed-1:v1:en.

Article 43. Certification bodies

RONALD LEENES

1. Without prejudice to the tasks and powers of the competent supervisory authority under Articles 57 and 58, certification bodies which have an appropriate level of expertise in relation to data protection shall, after informing the supervisory authority in order to allow it to exercise its powers pursuant to point (h) of Article 58(2) where necessary, issue and renew certification. Member States shall ensure that those certification bodies are accredited by one or both of the following:
   (a) the supervisory authority which is competent pursuant to Article 55 or 56;
   (b) the national accreditation body named in accordance with Regulation (EC) No 765/2008 of the European Parliament and of the Council in accordance with EN-ISO/IEC 17065/2012 and with the additional requirements established by the supervisory authority which is competent pursuant to Article 55 or 56.
2. Certification bodies referred to in paragraph 1 shall be accredited in accordance with that paragraph only where they have:
   (a) demonstrated their independence and expertise in relation to the subject-matter of the certification to the satisfaction of the competent supervisory authority;
   (b) undertaken to respect the criteria referred to in Article 42(5) and approved by the supervisory authority which is competent pursuant to Article 55 or 56 or by the Board pursuant to Article 63;
   (c) established procedures for the issuing, periodic review and withdrawal of data protection certification, seals and marks;
   (d) established procedures and structures to handle complaints about infringements of the certification or the manner in which the certification has been, or is being, implemented by the controller or processor, and to make those procedures and structures transparent to data subjects and the public; and
   (e) demonstrated, to the satisfaction of the competent supervisory authority, that their tasks and duties do not result in a conflict of interests.
3. The accreditation of certification bodies as referred to in paragraphs 1 and 2 of this Article shall take place on the basis of requirements approved by the supervisory authority which is competent pursuant to Article 55 or 56 or by the Board pursuant to Article 63. In the case of accreditation pursuant to point (b) of paragraph 1 of this Article, those requirements shall complement those envisaged in Regulation (EC) No 765/2008 and the technical rules that describe the methods and procedures of the certification bodies.[1]
4. The certification bodies referred to in paragraph 1 shall be responsible for the proper assessment leading to the certification or the withdrawal of such certification without prejudice to the responsibility of the controller or processor for compliance with this Regulation. The accreditation shall be issued for a maximum period of five years and may be renewed on the same conditions provided that the certification body meets the requirements set out in this Article.
5. The certification bodies referred to in paragraph 1 shall provide the competent supervisory authorities with the reasons for granting or withdrawing the requested certification.

---

[1] Corrigenda to the English text of Art. 43(3) were published on 23 May 2018. The text printed reflects the updated version of the Corrigendum GDPR 2018. For the Corrigendum GDPR 2018, see Table of Legislation.

6. The requirements referred to in paragraph 3 of this Article and the criteria referred to in Article 42(5) shall be made public by the supervisory authority in an easily accessible form. The supervisory authorities shall also transmit those requirements and criteria to the Board.[2]
7. Without prejudice to Chapter VIII, the competent supervisory authority or the national accreditation body shall revoke an accreditation of a certification body pursuant to paragraph 1 of this Article where the conditions for the accreditation are not, or are no longer, met or where actions taken by a certification body infringe this Regulation.
8. The Commission shall be empowered to adopt delegated acts in accordance with Article 92 for the purpose of specifying the requirements to be taken into account for the data protection certification mechanisms referred to in Article 42(1).
9. The Commission may adopt implementing acts laying down technical standards for certification mechanisms and data protection seals and marks, and mechanisms to promote and recognise those certification mechanisms, seals and marks. Those implementing acts shall be adopted in accordance with the examination procedure referred to in Article 93(2).

Relevant Recital

(100) In order to enhance transparency and compliance with this Regulation, the establishment of certification mechanisms and data protection seals and marks should be encouraged, allowing data subjects to quickly assess the level of data protection of relevant products and services.

Closely Related Provisions

Recital 77; Article 5(2) (Principle of accountability); Article 42 (Certification); Article 55 (Competence of the supervisory authorities); Article 56 (Competence of the lead supervisory authority); Articles 57(1)(p)–(q) (Tasks of the supervisory authorities); Article 58(3)(e) (Powers of the supervisory authorities); Article 63 (Consistency mechanism); Article 64(1)(c) (Opinions of the board); Article 70(1)(o)–(q) (Tasks of the board) (see too recital 77); Article 92 (Exercise of delegated acts by Commission) (see too recitals 166 and 168)

A. Rationale and Policy Underpinnings

Article 42 GDPR has introduced 'certification mechanisms, data protection seals and marks' as an accountability-based mechanism to assist controllers and processors to achieve and demonstrate compliance of their processing operations with the obligations imposed by the GDPR. Certification is a mechanism that generally involves third party assessment against objective pre-existing requirements. The positive result of the assessment leads to granting a certification, seal and/or mark. Certification usually includes oversight over the entity granting the certification ('certifying the certifiers'). The process of certifying the certifiers is commonly called accreditation. This multiple-layer model aims to foster consumer trust in the mechanism of certification, which in essence is a form of self-regulation because the criteria against which the applicant of certification is assessed are defined by the certification body, albeit

---

[2] Corrigenda to the English text of Art. 43(6) were published on 23 May 2018. The text printed reflects the updated version of the Corrigendum GDPR 2018.

based on a normative source. Certifications disconnected from adequate oversight may deceive consumers.[3]

The Commission, Parliament and Council as well as the supervisory authorities consider certification to have a potential major impact on the data protection landscape by promoting transparency and consumer choice. As the WP29 has formulated it:

Data controllers may decide to use the option of trustworthy services delivering certificates. As certain seals become known for their rigorous testing, data controllers are likely to favour them insofar as they would give more compliance 'comfort' in addition to offering a competitive advantage.[4]

Supervising certification bodies and their actions, including correcting irregularities when necessary, is thus an important factor in achieving the potential of this new mechanism in the data protection legal framework.

Corrigenda to the English text of Article 43 were published on 23 May 2018. This resulted in 'criteria' in the first sentence of Article 43(3) being replaced with 'requirements', and in the third sentence of Article 43(6) being deleted ('The Board shall collate all certification mechanisms and data protection seals in a register and shall make them publicly available by any appropriate means').

B. Legal Background

1. EU Legislation

There is no legal antecedent for certification in the DPD, but certification plays a role in other domains governed by EU legislation and there is legislation regarding accreditation of certification bodies. Regulation (EC) 765/2008 (the Accreditation Regulation)[5] regulates the accreditation of certification and conformity assessment bodies, such as inspection bodies and laboratories, and requires Member States to establish a National Accreditation Body ('NAB').

2. International instruments

Although technically neither EU legislation nor an international treaty, standards of the International Organization for Standardization ('ISO') play an important role for certification bodies. ISO/IEC standards not only concern substance, but also the processes of certification and accreditation. In particular the ISO/IEC 17065:2012 is relevant in this respect.[6] This standard describes issues that need to be considered by certification bodies, which in turn are assessed by accreditation bodies.

3. National developments

Some national data protection laws included provisions on certifications or seals prior to the GDPR. In some of these countries, certification was provided by the data protection authorities without any accreditation of the organisations offering certification, such as in France where the French CNIL delivered privacy seals for products or procedures intended to protect individuals.[7] In other cases, such as in the Bundesland of

---

[3] E.g. the US online privacy seal provider TRUSTe has faced complaints regarding its failure to conduct promised annual re-certifications on a large scale. Ultimately, these complaints were settled with the US Federal Trade Commission (FTC). See FTC 2015.
[4] WP29 2010, p. 17.   [5] Regulation 765/2008.   [6] ISO/IEC 17065:2012.
[7] Carvais-Palut 2018.

Schleswig-Holstein in Germany, the Data Protection Authority ('ULD') 'accredited' auditors who assessed the IT products of applicants for certification.[8]

4. Case law

Given that there is no predecessor to certification in the DPD, there is no case law concerning certification or accreditation in this context.

C. Analysis

Articles 42 and 43 GDPR introduce a new mechanism in the data protection legal framework. Whereas Article 42 deals with the certification itself, Article 43 addresses the second layer of certification—the certification of certifiers—i.e. accreditation. Article 43 furthermore contains two paragraphs regarding the power of the Commission in specifying and clarifying the certification mechanism in Article 43(8)–(9) GDPR.

The following topics are addressed in this analysis: the different accreditation models introduced in Article 43; the roles and tasks of the entities involved; the accreditation requirements; the legal effects; and the role of the Commission through delegated and implementing acts. The commentary on Article 43 should be read in conjunction with that on Article 42.

1. Accreditation models

As mentioned above, certification is a multilayered construct. At the basis is the *applicant*, a controller or processor who wants their processing operation certified. The certification is done by a *certification body*. In the case of Article 42 GDPR certification, this certification body is the competent supervisory authority (or the EDPB) or an entity that is accredited pursuant to Article 43 GDPR. In this framework, accreditation is mandatory for certain types of entities. Non-accredited certification bodies are not allowed to certify controllers or processors pursuant to Articles 42 and 43 GDPR.

Article 43 GDPR regulates how certification bodies shall be accredited. It does not, however, define the terms adopted in this provision. A definition of accreditation can be found in Article 2(10) of Regulation 765/2008, which defines it as 'an attestation by a national accreditation body that a conformity assessment body meets the requirements set by harmonised standards and, where applicable, any additional requirements including those set out in relevant sectoral schemes, to carry out a specific conformity assessment activity'. Accreditation in the context of GDPR certification mechanisms can be understood as 'an attestation by a national accreditation body and/or by a supervisory authority, that a certification body is qualified to carry out certification pursuant to Articles 42 and 43 GDPR, taking into account ISO/IEC 17065/2012 and the additional requirements established by the supervisory authority and or by the Board'.[9]

Article 43(1) GDPR provides that Member States shall ensure that certification bodies are accredited. The GDPR allows for three alternative models: accreditation by the competent supervisory authority, by the NAB in the country where the certification body is

---

[8] Schleswig-Holstein Regulation 2013.   [9] WP29 2018, p. 8; EDPB 2019B, p. 8 no. 28.

established, or by a combination of these two. Each Member State has to decide which of the three models will be followed in its jurisdiction.

The *first option* in Article 43(1)(a) GDPR adopts the supervisory authorities as the accreditation bodies.[10] This model involves two actors: the certification body requesting accreditation and the (accrediting) supervisory authority. Which supervisory authority is competent to assess a particular accreditation request is determined by Article 55 GDPR, according to which the supervisory authority in the territory where the requesting certification body has its main or single establishment is competent. In the case of a certification body intending to offer GDPR certification services in more than one Member State, Article 56 GDPR determines which supervisory authority is competent.

The *second option* described in Article 43(1)(b) GDPR is accreditation of the certification body by the NAB of the Member State in which the certification body has its establishment.[11] Every Member State has in principle a NAB pursuant to Regulation 765/2008, but not all NABs provide all accreditation services. In such a case a NAB of another country may be involved to accredit an applicant certification body.[12] Having NABs provide the accreditation of certification bodies is the standard practice in certification and hence this is an established model. Article 43 GDPR goes beyond this, taking both the established model and the competent supervisory authority on board. The DPA does not directly participate in the accreditation process,[13] but is tasked to provide the NAB with 'additional requirements' that the NABs have to take into account in accrediting certification bodies.[14]

The *third option* is a combination of both previously mentioned options. Although the GDPR is silent on how this should work, it seems reasonable to presume that the supervisory authority and NAB each conduct part of the accreditation in their field of competence and expertise. Given their roles and experience, it would be reasonable for the NAB to focus on the procedural, organisational and integrity requirements, as prescribed in the Accreditation Regulation and the ISO/IEC 17065:2012 standard. The DPA would focus on the data protection competence and expertise of the applicant certification body. Given the silence of the GDPR on how such a joint accreditation process would work,[15] the authorities will have to establish procedures for collaboration, and guidance to applicants on issues such as where to apply, who provides the accreditation certificate and who monitors and renews the accreditation.

The choice of the legislator to provide three (potential) roles for the supervisory authorities (approval of criteria, certification body, accreditation body) has raised concerns.[16] Not only do the various roles potentially put strains on the resources of the DPAs,[17] but there is also concern that they lack experience with the procedural requirements of conformity assessments, such as checks and controls on the independence and transparency of the applicant for certification.[18] Furthermore, there are also potential conflicts of

---

[10] Austria, for instance, has adopted this option. See s. 21(3) Austrian Federal Data Protection Act.

[11] Art. 7 Regulation 765/2008. Ireland, for instance, has adopted this model, designating the Irish National Accreditation Board as the accreditation body for the purposes of Art. 43(1) GDPR. See s. 35 Irish Data Protection Act 2018.

[12] See more on this in Kamara et al. 2019, ch. 5.

[13] Art. 43(1)(b) GDPR. This model is adopted by the Netherlands. See Dutch Data Protection Certificate.

[14] WP29 2018, p. 6. The Board has suggested concrete additional requirements in EDPB 2019B Annex 1.

[15] The Board is also silent on this point in its guidelines. See EDPB 2019.

[16] See e.g. ENISA 2017; Kamara et al. 2018; Rodrigues et al. 2016; EDPB 2019, p. 9, no. 33.

[17] See also Rodrigues et al. 2016.   [18] Kamara and de Hert 2018.

interest if the supervisory authority acts as an accreditation body and at the same time is involved in the certification process. An example is where the DPA should carry out periodic review of certifications in line with Article 57(1)(o) GDPR or order the certification body to withdraw or refuse to issue certification in line with Article 58(2)(h) GDPR.[19]

2. Roles and tasks

The entities involved in GDPR accreditation depend on the option chosen by the individual Member States. Their roles can, however, be described more generally. The competent supervisory authority first has to draft and publish the requirements for accreditation (Article 57(1)(p) GDPR). The GDPR is silent as to whom these requirements are addressed. Given the need for transparency in the certification process, it seems plausible, though, that these are targeted at the applicant certification bodies. However, the supervisory authorities are also competent to create 'additional requirements' to be taken into account by NABs in cases where the NABs are competent to perform accreditation services pursuant to Article 43(2)(b) GDPR. These requirements likely pertain to data protection requirements, because the NABs are already bound by ISO/IEC 17065/2012 for the non-data protection accreditation requirements.[20] The second role for supervisory authorities is to conduct the accreditation process of the applicant certification body in cases where a Member State has empowered the supervisory authority to conduct accreditation.[21] In the case of the European Data Protection Seal, applicant certification bodies are accredited on the basis of accreditation requirements approved by the EDPB.[22]

The NABs established in accordance with Regulation 765/2008 can be assigned by Member States to conduct accreditation pursuant to Article 43(1)(b) GDPR, either alone or jointly with the supervisory authority. The roles of the NAB are outlined in Regulation (EC) 765/2008. Their primary task is to evaluate, when requested by a conformity assessment body, whether that conformity assessment body is competent to carry out a specific conformity assessment activity.[23] Furthermore, the NAB must monitor the conformance of the accredited bodies.[24] If a certification body is no longer competent to carry out a specific conformity assessment activity or has committed a serious breach of its obligations, the NAB shall take all appropriate measures within a reasonable time frame to restrict, suspend or withdraw the accreditation certificate.[25] Article 43(7) GDPR specifies that both the NAB and supervisory authority shall revoke accreditations of certification bodies that do not, or no longer meet the accreditation requirements or where actions taken by a certification body infringe the GDPR.

According to Article 43(4) GDPR accreditation is valid for a period up to five years and may be renewed by the entity or entities that provided the initial accreditation on the same conditions provided that the certification body meets the various requirements set out in Article 43 GDPR.

---

[19] ENISA 2017.
[20] The Board argues that these requirements should be 'focused on facilitating the assessment, amongst others, of the independence and level of data protection expertise of certification bodies': see EDPB 2019B, p. 10. Annex 1 to EDPB 2019 contains suggested 'additional' accreditation requirements with respect to ISO/IEC 17065/2012 and in accordance with Art. 43(1) and (3) GDPR. See also the results of a survey targeted at supervisory authorities and NABs on the meaning of the 'accreditation requirements' of Art. 43(1)(b) in Kamara et al. 2019, p. 122 et seq.
[21] Art. 57(1)(q) and 58(3)(e) GDPR.   [22] Ibid., Art. 70(1)(p).
[23] Art. 5(1) Regulation 765/2008.   [24] Ibid., Art. 5(3).   [25] Ibid., Art. 5(4).

The GDPR is silent on an important aspect of GDPR accreditation: acceptance of accreditation granted in another Member State. The Accreditation Regulation establishes a system of peer evaluation for the NABs which helps establish mutual trust and confidence among the NABs on the quality of the assessments. Once a certification body is accredited in one Member State, this accreditation is also valid in other Member States, and the national authorities accept (recognise) the accreditation granted in another Member State. In the case that supervisory authorities act as Accreditation Bodies (Model 1), there is no explicit obligation of supervisory authorities to recognise accreditation certificates issued in other Member States. We can thus distinguish the following cases: in case of accreditation certificates issued by a NAB in one Member State, the supervisory authority of another Member State is not obliged to recognise the accreditation certificate.[26] However, in the case of accreditation certificates issued by other DPAs, the view that there is a general obligation of recognition, deriving from Article 63 GDPR (Consistency mechanism) and Article 64(1)(c) GDPR (Opinion of the EDPB) could be supported. In either case, such issues demand clarification and preferably a common approach that does not allow for forum-shopping and ensures consistency in the implementation of the GDPR.[27]

3. Accreditation requirements

Certification bodies need to meet both substantial requirements pertaining to, for instance, knowledge about data protection regulation, as well as legal, organisational, procedural and competence-related requirements. Article 43(2) GDPR specifies a list of general requirements that provide minimum guarantees to non-data protection accreditation requirements. These requirements are inspired by ISO/IEC 17065:2012, are primarily aimed at accreditation by supervisory authorities[28] and concern: (1) the independence of the certification body and the expertise in relation to the subject-matter; (2) adherence to the certification criteria the certification body has put forward to, and have been approved by the competent supervisory authority in view of Article 42(5) GDPR; (3) establishing procedures for issuing, periodic review, and withdrawal of data protection certification, seals and marks; (4) putting in place transparent and public mechanisms for handling complaints about infringement of certification by the controller or processor; and (5) demonstrating that no conflicts of interest arise in view of the entities to be certified.

Independence, impartiality and expertise are particularly important aspects of certification mechanisms because the public needs to be able to trust that an attestation provided is valid. A certification body needs to be independent of the applicant body, and the certification body needs to be independent of the accreditation body, and it is difficult to determine what is sufficient in terms of the independence, impartiality and expertise. Article 43(2) GDPR provides that all three qualities need to be demonstrated to the

---

[26] The EDPB argues that the GDPR is *lex specialis* to Regulation 765/2008. See EDPB 2019B, p. 9. The Board in its Guidelines 1/2018 states that certification bodies that intend to offer schemes only in selected Member States will have to be accredited in these Member States as accreditation requirements may differ. Accreditation for the scope of an EU Seal will only require accreditation in the Member State of the headquarters of the certifying body intending to operate the scheme. See EDPB 2019A p. 12 no. 45.

[27] Kamara et al. 2019, pp. 115-117.

[28] The Board adds that 'in the interest of contributing to a harmonised approach to accreditation, the accreditation criteria used by supervisory authorities should be guided by ISO/IEC 17065'. See EDPB 2019B, p. 10 no. 39.

satisfaction of the supervisory authority, but no information is provided as to what would be the standard required to satisfy the DPA. This is an area where guidance from, and collaboration between the DPAs are critical for a harmonised practice throughout the EU Member States. Expertise of the certification body with respect to the subject-matter is crucial for the success of the data protection certification mechanisms: the certification body is the body that examines whether a controller or processor processed personal data in line with the approved criteria of certification. Certification bodies need to have proven track records of experience and expertise in the field of data protection in general, but also in the specific field or sector of application where the controller or processor is active. That means that, if a certification body wishes to provide services to controllers and processors active in the health-care sector, the certification body needs to be accredited that it has sufficient expertise in the processing of personal data in that sector.[29]

NABs are bound to apply the more elaborate set of accreditation requirements specified in ISO/IEC 17065:2012 as well as the 'additional' accreditation requirements in accordance with Articles 43(1) and 43(3) GDPR. The EDPB has provided guidance and suggested requirements that supervisory auhorities can use in this respect.[30] ISO/IEC 17065:2012 includes legal and contractual matters, such as: the legal status of the cetification body; liability of the certification body regarding certification activities; arrangements for inspection, monitoring before, during and after certification; and availability of measures to record and deal with complaints, disputes and various types of transgressions. Furthermore, ISO/IEC 17065:2012 contains requirements regarding conflict of interests and impartiality, confidentiality, non-discrimination and liability, and transparency. These requirements resemble those in Article 43(2) GDPR but are more elaborate. For instance, transparency is specified in terms of transparency of criteria, assessment methods and the status of awarded and withdrawn certifications. The standard requires that information on the requirements, process and results of certification is publicly available.

Accreditation bodies themselves, and NABs in particular, also need to meet organisational and operational requirements. These are specified in Regulation 765/2008 and relate, inter alia, to independence and integrity of the organisation and its personnel, competence of the personnel, quality of assessment, and efficiency of procedures.

The proposed accreditation requirements of the Board include process requirements regarding, for instance, the evaluation process documentation and accessability of certification results, and it opens the way for supervisory authorities to define management system requirements.[31]

4. Legal effects

The granting of an accreditation certification has legal effects and decisions on accreditation are contestable. In case of accreditation by a supervisory authority, the decision is an administrative act with binding legal effect. In principle, these decisions can be challenged before the competent national administrative courts. Next to national law, the GDPR provides the right to any natural or, in this case, legal person to an effective judicial remedy against a legally binding decision made by an authority concerning them.[32]

---

[29] Ibid. See also EDPB 2019A, p. 9. [30] EPDP 2019B, Annex 1.
[31] EDPB 2019B, Annex 1. [32] Art. 78 GDPR.

In the case of accreditation by a NAB, the remedies depend on the legal status of the NAB, which may be either a public or private body. In the latter case, the NAB needs to be granted formal recognition by the Member State in which it conducts the accreditation activity as a public authority operating as a not-for-profit organisation.[33] According to Article 5(5) Regulation 765/2008, Member States shall establish procedures for the resolution of appeals, including, where appropriate, legal remedies against accreditation decisions or the absence thereof.

In case of joint accreditation by supervisory authority and NAB, the options to appeal are less clear. If the accreditation is granted by one of them, the above applies. An alternative joint accreditation model splits the process in two parts: the NAB grants an accreditation certificate, which is followed by, and is only valid on the condition of, the supervisory authority granting a specific accreditation certification on the basis of its accreditation requirements. In such a case, the applicant certification body could proceed against the decision of the authority which is harmful to its interests.[34]

5. Implementing and delegated acts

The original Commission draft of the GDPR gave significant power to the Commission to further shape data protection certification mechanisms, seals and marks.[35] The adopted GDPR assigns a more limited role to the Commission. Article 43(8) and (9) GDPR grants the Commission the power to adopt delegated and implementing acts respectively. Implementing acts aim to ensure uniform conditions for the application of the GDPR.[36] Delegated acts aim to help with the fulfilment of the objectives of the GDPR.[37]

Article 43(8) GDPR empowers the Commission to adopt delegated acts for the purpose of specifying requirements to be taken into account for the data protection certification mechanisms of Article 42(1) GDPR. The GDPR does not define the terms 'requirements' and 'criteria', but from the context of the use of the terms in the GDPR in relation to certification, and the Corrigendum to the GDPR, it can be deduced that the term 'criteria' corresponds to certification, while the term 'requirements' relates to the procedural accreditation requirements. However, Article 43(8) requirements seem to have a broader scope and not be limited to accreditation only, taking into account recital 166 GDPR[38] and the general role of the Commission in the establishment of the data protection certification mechanisms.[39] This interpretation[40] implies that the Commission has the power to adopt delegated acts pursuant to Article 43(8) GDPR with requirements regarding the data protection certification mechanisms.

Article 43(9) GDPR empowers the Commission to adopt implementing acts which lay down technical standards for certification mechanisms, data protection seals and marks. Technical standards may relate to issues such as conformity assessment safeguards, the scope of certification mechanisms or other relevant topics. It is not clear from the text whether such standards are intended to be related also to the content of the GDPR and the certification criteria. Both approaches, namely technical standards for conformity assessment and standards for GDPR-based certification criteria, are plausible.

---

[33] Art. 4(5) and (7) Regulation 765/2008. [34] Kamara et al. 2019.
[35] See Arts. 38(4), 39(2) and 39(3) GDPR Proposal. [36] Rec. 167 GDPR.
[37] Ibid., rec. 166. [38] Rec. 166 GDPR. [39] Art. 42(1) GDPR.
[40] Kamara et al. 2019, p. 28 et seq.

Article 43(9) GDPR also empowers the Commission to adopt implementing acts on mechanisms to promote and recognise certification mechanisms, seals and marks. These mechanisms might relate, for example, to procedures and conditions for recognition of issued certifications across Member States, or to the size, visual representation and other characteristics of seals and marks.[41]

Select Bibliography

EU legislation

GDPR Proposal: Proposal for a Regulation of the European Parliament and of the Council on the protection of individuals with regard to the processing of personal data and on the free movement of such data (General Data Protection Regulation), COM(2012) 11 final, 25 January 2012.
Regulation 765/2008: Regulation (EC) No. 765/2008 of the European Parliament and of the Council of 9 July 2008 setting out the requirements for accreditation and market surveillance relating to the marketing of products and repealing Regulation (EEC) No. 339/93, OJ 2008 L 218/30.
Regulation (EU) No. 182/2011 of the European Parliament and of the Council of 16 February 2011 laying down the rules and general principles concerning mechanisms for control by Member States of the Commission's exercise of implementing powers. OJ 2011 L 55/13.
Regulation (EU) No. 1025/2012 of the European Parliament and of the Council of 25 October 2012 on European standardisation, amending Council Directives 89/686/EEC and 93/15/EEC and Directives 94/9/EC, 94/25/EC, 95/16/EC, 97/23/EC, 98/34/EC, 2004/22/EC, 2007/23/EC, 2009/23/EC and 2009/105/EC of the European Parliament and of the Council and repealing Council Decision 87/95/EEC and Decision No. 1673/2006/EC of the European Parliament and of the Council, OJ 2012 L 316/12.

National legislation

Austrian Federal Data Protection Act: Bundesgesetz zum Schutz natürlicher Personen bei der Verarbeitung personenbezogener Daten (Datenschutzgesetz – DSG), BGBl. I Nr. 165/1999 zuletzt geändert durch BGBl. I Nr. 24/2018.
Irish Data Protection Act 2018: Data Protection Act 2018 (Number 7 of 2018).
Schleswig-Holstein Regulation 2013: Landesverordnung über ein Datenschutzgütesiegel (Datenschutzgütesiegelverordnung – DSGSVO) vom 30. November 2013, GVOBl. 2013 S. 536.

Academic writings

Carvais-Palut 2018: Carvais-Palut, 'The French Privacy Seal Scheme: A Successful Test' in Rodrigues and Papakonstantinou (eds.), *Privacy and Data Protection Seals* (Springer 2018), 49.
Kamara and de Hert 2018: Kamara and de Hert, 'Data Protection Certification in the EU: Possibilities, Actors and Building Blocks in a Reformed Landscape' in Rodrigues and Papakonstantinou (eds.), *Privacy and Data Protection Seals* (Springer 2018), 7.
Rodrigues et al. 2016: Rodrigues, Barnard-Wills, de Hert and Papakonstantinou, 'The Future of Privacy Certification in Europe: An Exploration of Options under Article 42 of the GDPR', 30(3) *International Review of Law, Computers & Technology* (2016), 248.

---

[41] Kamara et al. 2019.

Papers of data protection authorities

EDPB 2019A: European Data Protection Board, 'Guidelines 1/2018 on Certification and Identifying Certification Criteria in Accordance with Articles 42 and 43 of the Regulation 2016/679' (4 June 2019).

EDPB 2019B: European Data Protection Board, 'Guidelines 4/2018 on the Accreditation of Certification Bodies under Article 43 of the General Data Protection Regulation (2016/679)' (4 June 2019).

WP29 2010: Article 29 Working Party, 'Opinion 3/2010 on the Principle of Accountability' (WP173, 13 July 2010).

WP29 2018: Article 29 Working Party, 'Draft Guidelines on the Accreditation of Certification Bodies under Regulation (EU) 2016/679' (WP 261, 6 February 2018).

Reports and recommendations

ENISA 2017: European Union Agency for Network and Information Security, 'Recommendations on European Data Protection Certification' (27 November 2017).

Kamara et al. 2019: Kamara, Leenes, Lachaud, Stuurman, van Lieshout and Bodea, 'Data Protection Certification Mechanisms. Study on Articles 42 and 43 of the Regulation (EU) 2016/679', Commissioned by the European Commission (2019).

Others

Dutch Data Protection Certificate: Autoriteit Persoonsgegevens, 'AVG-certificaat', available at https://www.autoriteitpersoonsgegevens.nl/nl/zelf-doen/avg-certificaat.

FTC 2015: Federal Trade Commission, 'FTC Approves Final Order in TRUSTe Privacy Case' (18 March 2015), available at https://www.ftc.gov/news-events/press-releases/2015/03/ftc-approves-final-order-truste-privacy-case.

ISO/IEC 17065:2012: International Organisation for Standardization, 'ISO/IEC 17065:2012: Conformity Assessment—Requirements for Bodies Certifying Products, Processes and Services' (2012), available at https://www.iso.org/standard/46568.html.

Chapter V Transfers of Personal Data to Third Countries or International Organisations (Articles 44–50)

Article 44. General principle for transfers

CHRISTOPHER KUNER

Any transfer of personal data which are undergoing processing or are intended for processing after transfer to a third country or to an international organisation shall take place only if, subject to the other provisions of this Regulation, the conditions laid down in this Chapter are complied with by the controller and processor, including for onward transfers of personal data from the third country or an international organisation to another third country or to another international organisation. All provisions in this Chapter shall be applied in order to ensure that the level of protection of natural persons guaranteed by this Regulation is not undermined.

Relevant Recitals

(6) Rapid technological developments and globalisation have brought new challenges for the protection of personal data. The scale of the collection and sharing of personal data has increased significantly. Technology allows both private companies and public authorities to make use of personal data on an unprecedented scale in order to pursue their activities. Natural persons increasingly make personal information available publicly and globally. Technology has transformed both the economy and social life, and should further facilitate the free flow of personal data within the Union and the transfer to third countries and international organisations, while ensuring a high level of the protection of personal data.

(101) Flows of personal data to and from countries outside the Union and international organisations are necessary for the expansion of international trade and international cooperation. The increase in such flows has raised new challenges and concerns with regard to the protection of personal data. However, when personal data are transferred from the Union to controllers, processors or other recipients in third countries or to international organisations, the level of protection of natural persons ensured in the Union by this Regulation should not be undermined, including in cases of onward transfers of personal data from the third country or international organisation to controllers, processors in the same or another third country or international organisation. In any event, transfers to third countries and international organisations may only be carried out in full compliance with this Regulation. A transfer could take place only if, subject to the other provisions of this Regulation, the conditions laid down in the provisions of this Regulation relating to the transfer of personal data to third countries or international organisations are complied with by the controller or processor.

(102) This Regulation is without prejudice to international agreements concluded between the Union and third countries regulating the transfer of personal data including appropriate safeguards for the data subjects. Member States may conclude international agreements which involve the transfer of personal data to third countries or international organisations, as far as such agreements do not affect this Regulation or any other provisions of Union law and include an appropriate level of protection for the fundamental rights of the data subjects.

Closely Related Provisions

Recital 6; recital 48; recital 102; Article 45 (Adequacy decision) (see too recitals 103–107); Article 46 (Transfers subject to appropriate safeguards) (see too recitals 108–109); Articles 4(20) and 47 (BCRs) (see too recital 110); Article 48 (Transfers not authorised by EU law) (see too recital 115); Article 49 (Derogations) (see too recitals 111–114); Article 50 (see too recital 116); Article 83(5)(c) (Fines for non-compliance with data transfer restrictions); Article 96 (Relationship with previously concluded agreements of the EU Member States)

Related Provisions in LED [Directive (EU) 2016/680]

Recital 4; recital 25; recital 36; Article 35 (General principles for data transfers) (see too recitals 64–65)

Relevant Case Law

CJEU

Case 22/70, *Commission of the European Communities v Council of the European Communities (AETR/ERTA)*, judgment of 31 March 1971 (ECLI:EU:C:1971:32).

Case C-101/01, *Criminal proceedings against Bodil Lindqvist*, judgment of 6 November 2003 (ECLI:EU:C:2003:596).

Joined Cases C-317/04 and C-318/04, *European Parliament v Council of the European Union and Commission of the European Communities*, judgment of 30 May 2006 (Grand Chamber) (ECLI:EU:C:2006:346).

Joined Cases C-402 and 415/05 P, *Yassin Abdullah Kadi and Al Barakaat International Foundation v Council of the European Union and Commission of the European Communities*, judgment of 3 September 2008 (Grand Chamber) (ECLI:EU:C:2008:461).

Case C-366/10, *Air Transport Association of America, American Airlines Inc., Continental Airlines Inc., United Airlines Inc. v Secretary of State for Energy and Climate Change*, judgment of 21 December 2011 (Grand Chamber) (ECLI:EU:C:2011:864).

Case C-617/10, *Åkerberg Fransson*, judgment of 26 February 2013 (ECLI:EU:C:2013:105).

Case C-362/14, *Maximillian Schrems v Data Protection Commissioner*, judgment of 6 October 2015 (Grand Chamber) (ECLI:EU:C:2015:650).

Opinion 1/15, Opinion of 26 July 2017 (Grand Chamber) (ECLI:EU:C:2017:592).

Case C-505/19, *Bundesrepublik Deutschland* (pending).

ECtHR

Zakharov v Russia, Appl. No. 47143/06, judgment of 4 December 2015.

Germany

Verwaltungsgericht Wiesbaden, case no. Az 6 K 565/17.Wl, referred to the CJEU on 27 June 2019.

A. Rationale and Policy Underpinnings

Article 44 GDPR introduces Chapter V of the GDPR dealing with international data transfers. Chapter V contains a number of important changes from the corresponding articles of the DPD (Chapter IV, Articles 25–27), but does not represent a radical departure from the approach taken there.

The EU legislator has in effect split former Article 25 DPD into two parts, with Article 44 GDPR dealing with the general principles for data transfers, and Article 45 GDPR describing the conditions for adequacy. The rationale of Article 44 is set out in recital 101. On the one hand, this recital stresses the importance of the free flow of data internationally, a point that is also set out in recital 6. On the other hand, it makes clear that the level of protection provided for in the GDPR should not be 'undermined'; indeed, recital 10 clarifies that it is a consistent high level of protection that makes the free flow of personal data possible. The prohibition against the level of protection in the GDPR being undermined can be interpreted to mean that flows of personal data outside the EU should not be allowed to circumvent the protections contained in EU data protection regulation, in particular the GDPR.

Under Article 44, all other relevant provisions of the GDPR must be complied with before personal data may be transferred outside the EU (this is the so-called 'two-step' approach to data transfers). In particular, the GDPR contains a number of provisions relevant to international data transfers in addition to those found in Chapter V, such as the obligation to inform data subjects that data are to be transferred internationally (Article 13(1)(e)–(f), Article 14(1)(e)–(f), Article 15(1)(c) and Article 15(2)); duties of data processors (Article 28(3)(a)); and the obligation to keep records concerning data processing (Article 30(1)(d)–(e) and Article 30(2)(c)). The principle of accountability must also be complied with (Article 5(2) and Article 24). Thus, the rules of Chapter V build on those of the rest of the GDPR, but do not supplant them. In addition, the provisions of Chapter V must be read in light of Charter, since, as the CJEU has found, the applicability of EU law entails the applicability of the Charter.[1]

The prevention of circumvention of the law is the most frequently cited policy underlying regulation of international data transfers under data protection law.[2] There is considerable diversity in data protection and privacy laws around the world, and some countries do not have any such law at all, which is what raises the risk of circumvention of EU law when data are transferred to and processed in third countries. Most data protection legislation is based on the same international instruments, so that the fundamental, high-level principles of the law are similar across regions and legal systems. However, the differences in the cultural, historical and legal approaches to data protection mean that once one descends from the highest level of abstraction, there are significant differences in detail. Moreover, some major countries (such as China and the United States) do not have data protection laws based on the EU model.

There has never been a clear explanation of what constitutes 'circumvention' of the law in the context of trans-border data flows, and whether the term should be understood in a subjective sense, such as when a party transfers data with the primary purpose of evading application of the law, or in an objective one, such as that the primary purpose is to transfer the data without regard to the motivation behind it. Under the CJEU's *Schrems* judgment,[3] it seems that an objective definition should be used. In *Schrems* the Court found that, based on the Charter of Fundamental Rights of the European Union ('CFR'), the term 'an adequate level of protection' as used in the DPD must be understood as 'requiring the third country in fact to ensure, by reason of its domestic law or its international commitments, a level of protection of fundamental rights and freedoms

---

[1] See Case C-617/10, *Åkerberg Fransson*, para. 21. See also Rauchegger 2015.
[2] See Kuner 2013, pp. 107–113. [3] Case C-362/14, *Schrems*.

that is essentially equivalent to that guaranteed within the European Union by virtue of Directive 95/46 read in the light of the Charter'.[4] The Court went on to note that without this requirement, 'the high level of protection guaranteed by Directive 95/46 read in the light of the Charter could easily be circumvented by transfers of personal data from the European Union to third countries for the purpose of being processed in those countries'.[5] This seems to support an objective definition of circumvention based on an evasion of EU legal standards.

There is overlap between Article 3 GDPR, which can result in the GDPR applying to data controllers and data processors not established in the EU, and Chapter V, which regulates the transfer of personal data outside EU boundaries. Indeed, by requiring protections under EU law for personal data that are transferred outside the EU, the GDPR's rules on trans-border data flows can be viewed as a form of applicable law provision.[6] The interaction between Article 3 and Chapter V can result in situations where the GDPR both applies to a non-EU data controller or processor, and a data transfer mechanism must be used in order to transfer data to such parties. It is a pity that proposals made in the GDPR legislative process to merge applicable law rules with those on trans-border data flows and produce a single provision dealing with the protection of personal data processed or transferred outside the EU were not adopted. The relationship between Article 3 and Chapter V has also been the subject of discussions in the EDPB. However, as things now stand, Article 3 and Chapter V must be applied separately, and compliance with one does not remove the obligation to comply with the other when it is applicable.

B. Legal Background

1. EU legislation

The antecedent of Article 44 was Article 25 DPD, the history of which reaches back into the 1970s. The European Commission began conducting studies on the regulation of trans-border data flows as early as 1973,[7] spurred by cases in which the free flow of data between the Member States of the European Communities was threatened by the varying levels of data protection applicable in them. For example, an Austrian government ordinance from 1980 required the prior authorisation of the Austrian Data Protection Commission before personal data of legal persons could be transferred to France, Germany or Sweden, since the data protection laws of those countries did not cover such data.[8] In the 1970s the Swedish Data Protection Board refused to authorise the transfer of personal data to the United Kingdom in several cases.[9] And in 1989, the French subsidiary of the Italian automobile company Fiat was only allowed by the French data protection authority to transfer employee data to Italy once a data transfer agreement between the two companies had been signed, owing to a lack of data protection legislation in Italy.[10]

These situations led to the enactment of Article 25 DPD. Under the DPD, the transfer of personal data within the EU Member States and the three European Economic Area

---

[4] Ibid., para. 73.   [5] Ibid. See also *Opinion 1/15*, para. 93.
[6] See Kuner 2013, pp. 125–129.   [7] See Mengel 1984, p. 52.
[8] Austrian Regulation on Equivalence 1980. See also Mengel 1984, p. 14.
[9] See Bing 1980, p. 73.   [10] See CNIL 1989, p. 32.

('EEA') Member Countries (Iceland, Liechtenstein and Norway)[11] could not be restricted based on the level of data protection.[12] Article 25 DPD contained a similar restriction on transferring personal data outside the EU as Article 44 GDPR. Article 25(1) DPD provided that 'The Member States shall provide that the transfer to a third country of personal data which are undergoing processing or are intended for processing after transfer may take place only if, without prejudice to compliance with the national provisions adopted pursuant to the other provisions of this Directive, the third country in question ensures an adequate level of protection'.

The following are some of the major differences between Article 25 DPD and Article 44 GDPR:

1. Article 25 specifically required an adequate level of protection in the third country to which personal data are transferred. Article 44 does not mention the requirement that an adequate level of protection be required in all instances when data are transferred; rather, adequacy is mentioned in Article 45 in relation to decisions by the Commission regarding the adequacy of protection.
2. Article 44 does not contain specifics regarding Commission adequacy decisions (these have been moved to Article 45 GDPR).
3. Article 44 also mentions transfers to international organisations, whereas Article 25 referred solely to transfers to third countries.
4. Article 44 emphasises more explicitly than Article 25 DPD did that any legal basis for data transfers is 'subject to' the other legal rules for data processing set forth in the GDPR.

The EU Free Flow of Non-Personal Data Regulation[13] does not deal with the topics covered in Article 44, since it applies only to non-personal data (Article 2(1)) and to the free movement of data within the Union (Article 4), and does not affect the GDPR.[14]

2. International instruments

There are several international treaties that deal with international transfers of personal data in the context of data protection. International agreements between the EU and Australia,[15] Canada[16] and the US[17] have resulted in transfers to the latter of airline passenger name record (PNR) data being declared as offering adequate protection (sometimes but not always[18] in conjunction with a Commission adequacy decision), and an international agreement has also been reached with the US regarding the transfer of financial

---

[11] See EEA Decision 1999. [12] Art. 1(2) DPD.
[13] Free Flow of Non-Personal Data Regulation. [14] See ibid., rec. 8.
[15] PNR Agreement Australia 2012. A similar agreement was entered into between Australia and the EU in 2008 but never entered into force. See PNR Agreement Australia 2008; Council Decision Australia 2008.
[16] PNR Agreement Canada 2006. See also Commission Decision Canada 2006; Council Decision Canada 2006. In addition, in July 2017 the CJEU found that a treaty between the EU and Canada concerning the transfer of airline passenger record data could not be concluded because certain provisions of it were not in compliance with the CFR, see *Opinion 1/15*.
[17] PNR Agreement US 2012. See also Council Decision US 2007, and PNR Agreement US 2007; Council Decision US 2006, and PNR Agreement US 2006 (both annulled, see Joined Cases C-317/04 and C-318/04, *Parliament v Council and Commission*); Council Decision US 2004; Commission Decision US 2004.
[18] E.g. transfers of PNR data to Australia are covered by Art. 5 PNR Agreement Australia, without any separate adequacy decision having been issued.

messaging data.[19] The EU and the US have also agreed on an 'Umbrella Agreement' to provide safeguards for the protection of personal data exchanged between EU and US law enforcement authorities;[20] however, the Umbrella Agreement does not by itself provide a legal basis for data transfers from the EU.[21] In January 2017 the European Commission announced that it will seek to use international agreements to set the parameters for international data flows.[22] Member States have also become parties to some international agreements that result in data transfers (e.g. the Hague Convention on the Taking of Evidence Abroad in Civil or Commercial Matters).[23]

The major multilateral agreements of relevance to international data transfers are the European Convention on Human Rights ('ECHR') and the Council of Europe Convention 108.[24] The ECHR does not specifically regulate international data transfers, but its interpretation by the ECtHR carries implications for the international transfer of personal data. For instance, the judgment of the ECtHR in *Zakharov v Russia*,[25] in which the Court strongly criticised the interception of electronic communications by the Russian government, could be seen as complementing *Schrems* in similarly setting a high standard for the test of essential equivalence, even though the case did not specifically deal with international data transfers.

The Council of Europe Convention 108 is supplemented by an Additional Protocol[26] that was enacted in 2001 and contains restrictions on the transfer of personal data to third countries and international organisations. The Modernised Convention 108 also contains such rules.[27] The European Commission has stated that it will 'will actively promote the swift adoption of the modernised text with a view to the EU becoming a Party'.[28]

There are other important international instruments dealing with international data transfers, such as the OECD Privacy Guidelines and APEC Privacy Framework,[29] but they are not legally binding.

3. National developments

Article 96 GDPR provides that 'international agreements involving the transfer of personal data to third countries or international organisations which were concluded by Member States prior to 24 May 2016, and which comply with Union law as applicable prior to that date, shall remain in force until amended, replaced or revoked'.[30] Under recital 102, 'Member States may conclude international agreements which involve the transfer of personal data to third countries or international organisations, as far as such agreements do not affect this Regulation or any other provisions of Union law and include an appropriate level of protection for the fundamental rights of the data subjects'. However, the Member States may not undertake obligations with third countries that affect common rules laid down by the EU,[31] and Member States may act with regard

---

[19] TFTP US 2010. See also Council Decision TFTP US 2010.   [20] Umbrella Agreement US.
[21] Ibid., Art. 1(3).   [22] EC Communication 2017, p. 9.
[23] Hague Evidence Convention. See regarding this Convention, Cooper and Kuner 2017, pp. 131–137; Borchers 2003.
[24] In May 2018 a modernised version of the Convention was approved by the Committee of Ministers.
[25] ECtHR, *Zakharov v Russia*. See de Hert and Bocos 2015.   [26] See Table of Legislation.
[27] See Art. 12 Modernised Convention 108.   [28] EC Communication 2017, p. 12.
[29] See OECD Guidelines 2013; APEC Privacy Framework 2005.
[30] See the commentary on Art. 96 in this volume.
[31] See Case 22/70, *AETR/ERTA*. See also Eeckhout 2011, pp. 71–76.

to areas of shared competence only to the extent that the EU has not done so.[32] Since the GDPR has comprehensively regulated data protection and the rules covering international data transfers in the Union, in practice, Member States have only a limited margin to enter into international agreements governing international data transfers, if at all.[33]

4. Case law

The first case in which the CJEU dealt with restrictions on international data transfers was *Bodil Lindqvist*.[34] In that case, the defendant was a parishioner in a Swedish church who had published information about fellow members of the church community in the church's internet home page, and then had criminal charges brought against her by the public prosecutor for failure to respect the data protection rules. The CJEU found that placing material on a server located in the EU which was accessible worldwide via the internet did not constitute an international data transfer under the restrictions of Article 25 DPD, based on the following factors:

1. The information was not being sent automatically from the server to other internet users, but the users would themselves have to carry out the actions necessary to access the information.[35]
2. There was thus no direct transfer of personal data between the person loading the information on the server and the person accessing the data from the server, i.e. the data was transmitted via the infrastructure of the hosting provider where the information was stored on the server.[36]
3. Given the state of the internet when the DPD was enacted, one could not assume that the data transfer restrictions contained in Article 25 were intended to apply in such a situation.[37]
4. The restrictions on trans-border data flows contained in Article 25 constitute a 'regime of special application', which the Court contrasted with the 'general regime' under Chapter II DPD that set forth the conditions for the lawful processing of personal data.[38] The Court stated that it did not want the 'special regime' to become a 'regime of general application'.[39]

The two other CJEU judgments dealing with the issues relevant to Article 44 are *Schrems* and *Opinion 1/15*, which are analysed at length in the commentary on Article 45 in this volume.

C. Analysis

1. Introduction

Article 44 maintains the general focus of Article 25 DPD, while introducing several changes. It does not specifically mention the need for an 'adequate level of data protection' provided for by a third country before data transfers may take place (as in

---

[32] Art. 2(2) Treaty on the Functioning of the European Union ('TFEU'). See Rosas and Armati 2012, p. 246.
[33] See Hijmans 2016, pp. 468–470.   [34] Case C-101/01, *Lindqvist*.   [35] Ibid., paras. 60–61.
[36] Ibid., paras. 61–62.   [37] Ibid., para. 68.   [38] Ibid., paras. 63 and 69.   [39] Ibid., para. 69.

Article 25(1) DPD), instead making transfers dependent on the satisfaction of three conditions: (1) the transfer is subject to 'the other provisions of this Regulation'; (2) 'the conditions laid down in this Chapter are complied with by the controller and processor', including those relating to onward transfers; and (3) 'all provisions in this Chapter' are applied in order to ensure that the level of protection contained in the GDPR is not undermined. The provisions of Article 25 DPD regarding adequacy decisions have been moved into Article 45 GDPR. Chapter V contains a closed list of methods for international transfers of personal data, i.e. no other ones are possible. The two-step approach requires that both the provisions of Chapter V concerning international data transfers as well as all other provisions of the GDPR be complied with. Both the EDPB[40] and the European Commission[41] interpret compliance with Chapter V as requiring both a legal basis for the transfer under Article 6 GDPR and a legal mechanism for it under Chapter V, in addition to a legal basis for the processing prior to the transfer, i.e., in effect requiring three steps rather than two.

The provisions of Chapter V (including Article 44) do not always state whether they are addressed to data controllers, data processors or both. Generally speaking, it should be assumed that the data transfer mechanisms included in Chapter V can be used by controllers or processors,[42] unless this would conflict with their text or spirit, or would lead to a gap in protection or a lowering of the level of protection.

On 29 March 2017, the UK invoked Article 50 of the Treaty on European Union ('TEU') and indicated its intention to leave the EU, at which point it will become a third country by operation of law ('Brexit') and all Union primary and secondary law will cease to apply to the UK.[43] The EDPB[44] and the UK Information Commissioner[45] have published guidance for dealing with international data transfers post-Brexit.

2. Definition of international data transfer

The GDPR does not define what constitutes an international data transfer (just as the DPD did not). This concept is of central importance, since it determines when Article 44 (and the other provisions of Chapter V) applies. Article 4(23) defines the term 'cross-border processing', which at first glance might seem relevant here, but actually deals with situations where a controller or processor has establishments in more than one Member State or where processing substantially affects or is likely to substantially affect data subjects in more than one Member State, in order to help determine the lead supervisory authority under Article 56.

The *Lindqvist* judgment suggests that a data transfer should be an active act which involves sending data, and not just making it passively accessible. However, this does not mean that granting access may not also constitute a 'transfer'; indeed, the judgment seems to rest on a number of specific factors (the necessity for an internet user to personally take

---

[40] See, e.g., EDPB EDPS Response Cloud Act, p. 3, stating that 'any order under the CLOUD Act for transfer of personal data from the EU could only be lawful if there is a legal basis under Article 6 and Article 49 of the GDPR ...'

[41] See EC Microsoft Brief, p. 9-10.

[42] See rec. 101 GDPR, which specifically mentions compliance with data transfer rules by both data controllers and data processors.

[43] Commission Brexit Preparedness Notice, p. 1.   [44] EDPB Brexit information note.

[45] ICO 2018. See also the commentary on Art. 47 in this volume regarding the legal status of binding corporate rules (BCRs) post-Brexit.

action to consult the website, the fact that the information was all in Swedish and was not intended to be read and used outside that country, and the early state of development of internet technologies at the time) that may limit the case to its facts.

The judgment in *Schrems* goes beyond *Lindqvist* by relating the requirement of an adequate level of data protection under the DPD to the level of data protection required by the Charter,[46] which was elevated to the status of primary law several years after *Lindqvist*.[47] The *Schrems* judgment demonstrates that the CJEU views the concept of an international data transfer in terms of requiring a high level of protection based on EU standards with regard to personal data that are sent or made accessible across national borders, rather than based on a set definition. The Grand Chamber of the Court then affirmed the *Schrems* rationale in *Opinion 1/15*.[48] Thus, if the CJEU were faced today with a case involving facts similar to those in *Lindqvist*, it would likely be reluctant to find that the GDPR does not apply to placing personal data on an internet site.

3. Onward transfer

The GDPR also does not define 'onward transfer', although the term is used not only in Article 44 but also in other provisions (such as recital 101, Article 45(2)(a) and Article 47(2)(d)). There is also no definition of the term in relevant documents relating to international data transfers such as the standard contractual clauses issued by the Commission. Based on common usage of the term, an onward transfer refers to a further transfer of personal data after they have been transferred to a data importer outside the EU or EEA, as can be seen, for example, in the way it is used by the WP29.[49] Onward transfers are common in practice, since data are often re-exported to third parties by a data importer. This situation can arise, for example, when a company (the data exporter) outsources the operation of a database to a service provider (the data importer), which then subcontracts some of the maintenance to another company; this would result in an onward transfer of the data from the service provider to the third party maintenance company.

An onward transfer should be defined broadly to require the same high level of protection as that for data transfers. In *Opinion 1/15*, the CJEU held that onward transfers also require a level of protection essentially equivalent to that under EU law, in order to prevent its protections from being circumvented.[50] The reasons for requiring a high level of protection for onward transfers under the GDPR can be explained in light of concerns that arose under the EU–US Safe Harbour system invalidated by the CJEU in *Schrems*, in which data transferred first to the US could then be sent easily on to other third countries. The importance of restrictions on onward transfers for the adequacy of protection was emphasised by the WP29.[51]

4. International organisations

Article 44 raises questions about the interaction between the GDPR and public international law with regard to data transfers to international organisations.[52] International organisations generally enjoy privileges and immunities under public international law

---

[46] See Case C-362/14, *Schrems*, para. 73. See also González Fuster 2016. [47] See Art. 6(1) TEU.
[48] *Opinion 1/15*, para. 214. See Kuner 2018.
[49] See e.g. WP29 2008, p. 7, referring to onward transfers as transfers to entities 'outside the group'.
[50] *Opinion 1/15*, para. 214. [51] See WP29 2017, p. 7.
[52] See the commentary on Art. 4(26) in this volume regarding the definition of international organisation.

and may expect that once they receive data from the EU its further transfer would be subject to international law or their own internal rules, not EU law. Article 44 addresses its obligations to controllers and processors, but also seems to suggest that parties (including international organisations) conducting onward transfers of personal data received from the EU may only do so under the conditions set forth in Chapter V. In addition, international organisations may be subject to pressure from third parties (such as contract partners and funding agencies, including EU entities) to certify that they comply with the GDPR when personal data are transferred to them, even though this may not be legally required.

Since public international law (in particular treaty law) has primacy over secondary law (such as the GDPR) in the EU legal system,[53] if an international organisation enjoys privileges and immunities under international law, then its data transfers should not be subject to the GDPR. However, a different view could be taken if protection of data transfers is considered to be a matter of EU primary law (such as with regard to the fundamental right to data protection in EU law), in which case it would prevail over rules of international law.[54] The Commission has taken the view informally that the GDPR does not directly apply to international organisations, but that they must comply with the GDPR's data transfer rules when they receive personal data from the EU (in theory, this means that these rules may apply as well to transfers to international organizations located in the EU or EEA).

There is no easy way for international organisations to cope with the data transfer requirements of the GDPR.[55] No single data transfer mechanism can provide a solution to all data transfer issues faced by all international organisations; rather, they will have to use solutions to cover the specific situation they find themselves in. These could include, for example, administrative arrangements under Article 46(3)(b), or derogations for data transfers made for important reasons of the public interest (Article 49(1)(d)) or when the transfer is necessary to protect the vital interests of the data subject or of other persons (Article 49(1)(f)); these are all discussed in the commentaries on the above articles in this volume. However, these mechanisms may not provide a ready answer to all the data transfer issues that international organisations are faced with.

In June 2019, a German administrative court made a reference for a preliminary ruling to the CJEU in a case involving the adequacy of data transfers to the International Criminal Police Organization ('INTERPOL') under the LED, among other issues.[56] Although it concerns the LED rather than the GDPR, this case could give the CJEU an opportunity to clarify how EU data protection law applies to international organisations.

5. Conflicts between data transfer mechanisms

The GDPR does not deal with conflicts between data transfer mechanisms. Chapter V GDPR establishes a three-tiered structure for legal bases for data transfers, with adequacy decisions at the top, appropriate safeguards in the middle, and derogations at the bottom.

---

[53] See e.g. Case C-366/10, *Air Transport Association of America*, para. 50. See also Rosas and Armati 2012, p. 59.
[54] See Joined Cases C-402 and 415/05P, *Kadi*, para. 285. See also Rosas and Armati 2012, p. 59.
[55] See Kuner 2019.
[56] Case C-505/19, *Bundesrepublik Deutschland*; Verwaltungsgericht Wiesbaden. See also Presseerklärung Verwaltungsgericht Wiesbaden.

This means that if an adequacy decision has been issued then that should be relied on; if not, then appropriate safeguards should be used; and only if neither of these legal bases is available should the derogations be relied on.

Any conflicts between these three types of mechanisms should be resolved with this hierarchy in mind, and with an aim to maximise the level of data protection for the transfer. For example, if one party to a transfer is located in a third country that has been declared to provide adequate protection, and the other party wants to base the transfer on the consent of the data subject, then the adequacy decision rather than consent should be used, since this results in a higher level of protection, whereas consent is a derogation that is not designed to lead to any protection at all. This does not mean that the parties cannot agree to provide extra protections in addition to those that are needed to provide a legal basis; for example, in the case above the parties could also agree on contractual clauses to provide extra protection for the transfer.

Further problems arise when different parties use the same level of data transfer mechanism. For example, there may be a difference in the rules for onward transfers between the use of standard contractual clauses and binding corporate rules ('BCRs'), which can create questions about which one applies if parties using those mechanisms transfer personal data between them. Such conflicts will have to be resolved keeping in mind which solution results in the higher level of data protection. In a legal sense either solution at the same level of the hierarchy (e.g. either standard contractual clauses or binding corporate rules) would be acceptable, since they both provide the same level of protection under the GDPR.

6. Data transfers and data security

The GDPR addresses data security and information security in Chapter V in only two provisions, namely in Article 45(2)(a) (stating that the Commission must take 'security measures' into account when conducting an adequacy assessment) and in Article 47(2)(d) (stating that binding corporate rules must specify 'measures to ensure data security'). No other article of the GDPR specifically addresses data security or information security in the context of international data transfers, which is odd given the importance of this topic. However, transferring personal data is a form of data processing,[57] and any data processing must be carried out in a manner that ensures appropriate security of the personal data, including protection against unauthorised or unlawful processing and against accidental loss, destruction or damage, using appropriate technical or organisational measures.[58] Data controllers and data processors are under general data security requirements,[59] and some other provisions of the GDPR that may be particularly relevant in the context of international data transfers also contain data security requirements.[60] Thus, there is no doubt that data security and information security is a crucial component of complying with the GDPR when transferring personal data, no matter which data transfer mechanism is used.

---

[57] See Art. 4(2) GDPR, which includes in the definition of processing such actions as 'disclosure by transmission, dissemination or otherwise making available', and thus clearly indicates that conducting international data transfers is a form of processing.
[58] Ibid., Art. 5(1)(f).   [59] Ibid., Art. 32.
[60] See e.g. ibid., Art. 35 dealing with data protection impact assessments (DPIAs), which requires that data security measures and mechanisms be taken into account when performing a DPIA.

7. LED

Article 44 GDPR has a counterpart in Article 35 LED, which provides for the possibility of data transfers to third countries and international organisations. Chapter V LED is structured similarly to Chapter V GDPR, and includes articles dealing with general provisions for data transfers (Article 35 LED, corresponding to Article 44 GDPR); adequacy decisions (Article 36 LED, corresponding to Article 45 GDPR); appropriate safeguards (Article 37 LED, corresponding to Article 46 GDPR); derogations (Article 38 LED, corresponding to Article 49 GDPR); and international cooperation (Article 40 LED, corresponding to Article 50 GDPR). These provisions are modelled on the corresponding ones of the GDPR, but with some important differences that cannot be described in detail here. As a Directive rather than a Regulation like the GDPR, the LED requires implementation in the Member States and compliance with requirements of national law. The LED is generally more liberal about allowing data transfers and contains bases for them that do not appear in the GDPR. For example, Article 39 LED allows both EU and Member State law to permit data transfers from competent authorities to recipients in third countries for reasons such as that the competent authority believes that otherwise the transfer cannot be carried out 'in good time'.[61]

8. Enforcement

Infringements of Articles 44–49 are subject to the higher level of administrative fines under Article 83(5)(c), i.e. up to € 20 million or 4 per cent of the total worldwide turnover of the preceding financial year, whichever is higher.

Select Bibliography

International agreements

APEC Privacy Framework: Asia Pacific Economic Cooperation, 'Privacy Framework' (2005).
EEA Agreement: Agreement on the European Economic Area, OJ 1994 L 1/3.
Hague Evidence Convention: Hague Convention on the Taking of Evidence Abroad in Civil or Commercial Matters, 18 March 1970, 847 UNTS 231.
OECD Guidelines 2013: Organisation for Economic Co-Operation and Development, 'The OECD Privacy Framework' (2013).

EU legislation

Commission Decision Canada 2006: Commission Decision of 6 September 2005 on the adequate protection of personal data contained in the Passenger Name Record of air passengers transferred to the Canada Border Services Agency, OJ 2006 L 91/49 (expired).
Commission Decision US 2004: Commission Decision of 14 May 2004 on the adequate protection of personal data contained in the Passenger Name Record of air passengers transferred to the United States' Bureau of Customs and Border Protection, OJ 2004 L 235/11.
Council Decision Australia 2008: Council Decision of 30 June 2008 on the signing, on behalf of the European Union, of an Agreement between the European Union and Australia on the processing and transfer of European Union-sourced passenger name record (PNR) data by air carriers to the Australian Customs Service, OJ 2008 L 213/47.

---

[61] Art. 39(1)(c) LED.

Council Decision Canada 2006: Council Decision of 18 July 2005 on the conclusion of an Agreement between the European Community and the Government of Canada on the processing of API/PNR data, OJ 2006 L82/14.

Council Decision TFTP US 2010: Council Decision of 13 July 2010 on the conclusion of the Agreement between the European Union and the United States of America on the processing and transfer of Financial Messaging Data from the European Union to the United States for the purposes of the Terrorist Finance Tracking Program, OJ 2010 L 195/3.

Council Decision US 2004: Council Decision of 17 May 2004 on the conclusion of an Agreement between the European Community and the United States of America on the processing and transfer of PNR data by Air Carriers to the United States Department of Homeland Security, Bureau of Customs and Border Protection, OJ 2004 L 183/83.

Council Decision US 2006: Council Decision 2 of 16 October 2006 on the signing, on behalf of the European Union, of an Agreement between the European Union and the United States of America on the processing and transfer of passenger name record (PNR) data by air carriers to the United States Department of Homeland Security, OJ 2006 L 298/27.

Council Decision US 2007: Council Decision 2007/551/CFSP/JHA of 23 July 2007 on the signing, on behalf of the European Union, of an Agreement between the European Union and the United States of America on the processing and transfer of Passenger Name Record (PNR) data by air carriers to the United States Department of Homeland Security (DHS) (2007 PNR Agreement), OJ 2007 L 204/16.

EEA Decision 1999: Decision of the EEA Joint Committee No. 83/1999 of 25 June 1999 amending Protocol 37 and Annex XI (Telecommunication services) to the EEA Agreement, OJ 2000 L 296/41.

Free Flow of Non-Personal Data Regulation: Regulation (EU) 2018/1807 of the European Parliament and of the Council of 14 November 2018 on a framework for the free flow of non-personal data in the European Union, OJ 2018 L 303/59.

PNR Agreement Australia 2008: Agreement between the European Union and Australia on the processing and transfer of European Union-sourced passenger name record (PNR) data by air carriers to the Australian customs service, OJ 2008 L 213/49 (never entered into force).

PNR Agreement Australia 2012: Agreement between the European Union and Australia on the processing and transfer of Passenger Name Record (PNR) data by air carriers to the Australian Customs and Border Protection Service, OJ 2012 L 186/4.

PNR Agreement Canada 2006: Agreement between the European Community and the Government of Canada on the processing of Advance Passenger Information and Passenger Name Record data, OJ 2006 L 82/15 (expired).

PNR Agreement US 2006: Agreement between the European Community and the United States of America on the processing and transfer of PNR data by air carriers to the United States Department of Homeland Security, OJ 2006 L 298/29.

PNR Agreement US 2007: Agreement between the European Union and the United States of America on the processing and transfer of Passenger Name Record (PNR) data by air carriers to the United States Department of Homeland Security (DHS) (2007 PNR Agreement), OJ 2007 L 204/18.

PNR Agreement US 2012: Agreement between the United States of America and the European Union on the use and transfer of passenger name records to the United States Department of Homeland Security, OJ 2012 L 215/5.

TFTP US 2010: Agreement between the European Union and the United States of America on the processing and transfer of Financial Messaging Data from the European Union to the United States for purposes of the Terrorist Finance Tracking Program, OJ 2010 L 8/11.

Umbrella Agreement US: Agreement between the United States of America and the European Union on the protection of personal information relating to the prevention, investigation, detection, and prosecution of criminal offences, OJ 2016 L 336/3.

National legislation

Austrian Regulation on Equivalence 1980: Verordnung des Bundeskanzlers vom 18. Dezember 1980 über die Gleichwertigkeit ausländischer Datenschutzbestimmungen, BGBl II Nr. 612/3403.

Academic writings

Bing 1980: Bing, 'Transnational Data Flows and the Scandinavian Data Protection Legislation', 24 *Scandinavian Studies in Law* (1980), 65.
Blume, 'Transborder Data Flow: Is There a Solution in Sight?', 8(1) *International Journal of Law and Information Technology* (2000), 65.
Borchers 2003: Borchers, 'The Incredible Shrinking Hague Evidence Convention', 38(1) *Texas International Law Journal* (2003), 73.
Brühann, 'Die Veröffentlichung personenbezogener Daten im Internet als Datenschutzproblem', 28 *Datenschutz und Datensicherheit* (2004), 201.
Bygrave, *Data Privacy Law: An International Perspective* (OUP 2014).
Cooper and Kuner 2017: Cooper and Kuner, 'Data Protection Law and International Dispute Resolution', 382 *Recueil des cours de l'Académie de droit international de La Haye* (2017), 9.
Eeckhout 2011: Eeckhout, *EU External Relations Law* (OUP 2011) (Kindle edition).
Freese, *International Data Flow* (Studentlitteratur 1979).
González Fuster 2016: González Fuster, 'Un-Mapping Personal Data Transfers', 2(2) *European Data Protection Law Review* (2016), 160.
Hijmans 2016: Hijmans, *The European Union as Guardian of Internet Privacy* (Springer 2016).
Hondius, 'A Decade of International Data Protection', 30(2) *Netherlands International Law Review* (1983), 103.
Kirby, 'Transborder Data Flows and the "Basic Rules of Data Privacy"', 16(2) *Stanford Journal of International Law* (1980), 27.
Kuner 2013: Kuner, *Transborder Data Flow Regulation and Data Privacy Law* (OUP 2013).
Kuner 2018: Kuner, 'International Agreements, Data Protection, and EU Fundamental Rights on the International Stage: *Opinion 1/15*', 55(3) *Common Market Law Review* (2018), 857.
Kuner 2019: Kuner, 'International Organizations and the EU General Data Protection Regulation: Exploring the Interaction between EU Law and International Law', 16 *International Organizations Law Review* (2019), 158.
Kuner, 'An International Legal Framework for Data Protection: Issues and Prospects', 25(4) *Computer Law and Security Review* (2009), 307.
Kuner, *European Data Protection Law: Corporate Compliance and Regulation* (2nd edn, OUP 2007).
Kuner, 'Reality and Illusion in EU Data Transfer Regulation Post *Schrems*', 18(4) *German Law Journal* (2017), 881.
Mengel 1984: Mengel, *Internationale Organisationen und transnationaler Datenschutz* (Wissenschaftlicher Autoren-Verlag 1984).
Ploman, *International Law Governing Communications and Information* (Frances Pinter Ltd 1982).
Rauchegger 2015: Rauchegger, 'The Interplay Between the Charter and National Constitutions after *Åkerberg Fransson* and *Melloni*', in de Vries, Bernitz and Weatherill (eds.), *The EU Charter of Fundamental Rights as a Binding Instrument* (Hart Publishing 2015), 93.
Rosas and Armati 2012: Rosas and Armati, *EU Constitutional Law: An Introduction* (Hart Publishing 2012) (Kindle edition).
Schwartz, 'European Data Protection Law and Restrictions on International Data Flows', 80(3) *Iowa Law Review* (1995), 471.
Shaffer, 'Reconciling Trade and Regulatory Goals: Prospects and Limits of New Approaches to Transatlantic Governance through Mutual Recognition and Safe Harbour Agreements', 9(1) *Columbia Journal of European Law* (2002), 29.

Simitis and Dammann, *EU-Datenschutzrichtlinie* (Nomos-Verlag 1997).
Svantesson, 'Privacy, the Internet and Transborder Data Flows: An Australian Perspective', 4(1) *Masaryk University Journal of Law and Technology* (2010), 1.
Swire and Litan, *None of Your Business: World Data Flows, Electronic Commerce, and the European Privacy Directive* (Brookings Institution Press 1998).
Wochner, *Der Persönlichkeitsschutz im grenzüberschreitenden Datenverkehr* (Schulthess Polygraphischer Verlag 1981).

Papers of data protection authorities

EDPB EDPS Response Cloud Act: European Data Protection Board and European Data Protection Supervisor, 'EPDB-EDPS Joint Response to the LIBE Committee on the impact of the US Cloud Act on the European legal framework for personal data protection (annex)' (10 July 2019), available at https://edpb.europa.eu/our-work-tools/our-documents/letters/epdb-edps-joint-response-libe-committee-impact-us-cloud-act_en.
WP29 2008: Article 29 Working Party, 'Working Document Setting up a Framework for the Structure of Binding Corporate Rules' (WP 154, 24 June 2008).
WP29 2017: Article 29 Working Party, 'Adequacy Referential (updated)' (WP 254, 28 November 2017).
Article 29 Working Party, 'Working Document: Transfers of Personal Data to Third Countries: Applying Articles 25 and 26 of the EU Data Protection Directive' (WP 12, 24 July 1998).
Article 29 Working Party, 'Working Document on Determining the International Application of EU Data Protection Law to Personal Data Processing on the Internet by Non-EU Based Websites' (WP 56, 30 May 2002).
Article 29 Working Party, 'Opinion 2/2002 on the Use of Unique Identifiers in Telecommunication Terminal Equipment: The Example of IPv6' (WP 58, 30 May 2002).
Article 29 Working Party, 'Opinion 10/2006 on the Processing of Personal Data by the Society for Worldwide Interbank Financial Telecommunication (SWIFT)' (WP 128, 22 November 2006).
Article 29 Working Party, 'Opinion 5/2009 on Online Social Networking' (WP 163, 12 June 2009).
Article 29 Working Party, 'Opinion 3/2010 on the Principle of Accountability' (WP 173, 13 July 2010).
Article 29 Working Party, 'Opinion 8/2010 on Applicable Law' (WP 179, 16 December 2010).
Article 29 Working Party, 'Opinion 05/2012 on Cloud Computing' (WP 196, 1 July 2012).
Article 29 Working Party, 'The Future of Privacy' (WP 168, 1 December 2009).
Article 29 Working Party, 'Working Document 1/2009 on Pre-Trial Discovery for Cross Border Civil Litigation' (WP 158, 11 February 2009).
Agencia Española de Protección de Datos, 'Report on International Data Transfers: Ex officio Sectorial Inspection of Spain-Colombia at Call Centres' (July 2007).
CNIL 1989: Commission nationale de l'informatique et des libertés, '10ᵉ rapport d'activité' (1989).
ICO 2018: UK Information Commissioner, 'International Data Transfers', available at https://ico.org.uk/for-organisations/data-protection-and-brexit/data-protection-if-there-s-no-brexit-deal/the-gdpr/international-data-transfers/.

Reports and recommendations

EC Communication 2017: Communication from the Commission to the European Parliament and the Council, 'Exchanging and Protection Personal Data in a Globalised World', COM(2017) 7 final, 10 January 2017.
Kropf, *Guide to U.S. Government Practice on Global Sharing of Personal Information* (American Bar Association 2012).

Others

Commission Brexit Preparedness Notice: European Commission, 'Notice to Stakeholders: Withdrawal of the United Kingdom from the Union and EU Rules in the Field of Data Protection' (9 January 2018), available at https://ec.europa.eu/info/sites/info/files/file_import/data_protection_en.pdf.

De Hert and Bocos 2015: De Hert and Bocos, 'Case of Roman Zakharov v. Russia: The Strasbourg Follow Up to the Luxembourg Court's Schrems Judgment' (23 December 2015), available at https://strasbourgobservers.com/2015/12/23/case-of-roman-zakharov-v-russia-the-strasbourg-follow-up-to-the-luxembourg-courts-schrems-judgment/.

EC Microsoft Brief: Amicus Brief of the European Commission on behalf of the European Union as *Amicus Curiae* in support of neither party in: United States v. Microsoft Corporation 584 U.S. (2018).

Presseerklärung Verwaltungsgericht Wiesbaden: Verwaltungsgericht Wiesbaden, 'Verwaltungsgericht Wiesbaden legt EuGH Fragen zu Interpol vor' (3 July 2019), available at https://verwaltungsgerichtsbarkeit.hessen.de/pressemitteilungen/verwaltungsgericht-wiesbaden-legt-eugh-fragen-zu-interpol-vor.

Article 45. Transfers on the basis of an adequacy decision

CHRISTOPHER KUNER

1. A transfer of personal data to a third country or an international organisation may take place where the Commission has decided that the third country, a territory or one or more specified sectors within that third country, or the international organisation in question ensures an adequate level of protection. Such a transfer shall not require any specific authorisation.
2. When assessing the adequacy of the level of protection, the Commission shall, in particular, take account of the following elements:
    (a) the rule of law, respect for human rights and fundamental freedoms, relevant legislation, both general and sectoral, including concerning public security, defence, national security and criminal law and the access of public authorities to personal data, as well as the implementation of such legislation, data protection rules, professional rules and security measures, including rules for the onward transfer of personal data to another third country or international organisation which are complied with in that country or international organisation, case-law, as well as effective and enforceable data subject rights and effective administrative and judicial redress for the data subjects whose personal data are being transferred;
    (b) the existence and effective functioning of one or more independent supervisory authorities in the third country or to which an international organisation is subject, with responsibility for ensuring and enforcing compliance with the data protection rules, including adequate enforcement powers, for assisting and advising the data subjects in exercising their rights and for cooperation with the supervisory authorities of the Member States; and
    (c) the international commitments the third country or international organisation concerned has entered into, or other obligations arising from legally binding conventions or instruments as well as from its participation in multilateral or regional systems, in particular in relation to the protection of personal data.
3. The Commission, after assessing the adequacy of the level of protection, may decide, by means of implementing act, that a third country, a territory or one or more specified sectors within a third country, or an international organisation ensures an adequate level of protection within the meaning of paragraph 2 of this Article. The implementing act shall provide for a mechanism for a periodic review, at least every four years, which shall take into account all relevant developments in the third country or international organisation. The implementing act shall specify its territorial and sectoral application and, where applicable, identify the supervisory authority or authorities referred to in point (b) of paragraph 2 of this Article. The implementing act shall be adopted in accordance with the examination procedure referred to in Article 93(2).
4. The Commission shall, on an ongoing basis, monitor developments in third countries and international organisations that could affect the functioning of decisions adopted pursuant to paragraph 3 of this Article and decisions adopted on the basis of Article 25(6) of Directive 95/46/EC.
5. The Commission shall, where available information reveals, in particular following the review referred to in paragraph 3 of this Article, that a third country, a territory or one or more specified sectors within a third country, or an international organisation no longer ensures an adequate level of protection within the meaning of paragraph 2 of this Article, to the extent necessary, repeal, amend or suspend the decision referred to in paragraph 3 of this Article by means of implementing acts without retro-active effect. Those implementing acts shall be

adopted in accordance with the examination procedure referred to in Article 93(2). On duly justified imperative grounds of urgency, the Commission shall adopt immediately applicable implementing acts in accordance with the procedure referred to in Article 93(3).

6. The Commission shall enter into consultations with the third country or international organisation with a view to remedying the situation giving rise to the decision made pursuant to paragraph 5.
7. A decision pursuant to paragraph 5 of this Article is without prejudice to transfers of personal data to the third country, a territory or one or more specified sectors within that third country, or the international organisation in question pursuant to Articles 46 to 49.
8. The Commission shall publish in the Official Journal of the European Union and on its website a list of the third countries, territories and specified sectors within a third country and international organisations for which it has decided that an adequate level of protection is or is no longer ensured.
9. Decisions adopted by the Commission on the basis of Article 25(6) of Directive 95/46/EC shall remain in force until amended, replaced or repealed by a Commission Decision adopted in accordance with paragraph 3 or 5 of this Article.

Relevant Recitals

(102) This Regulation is without prejudice to international agreements concluded between the Union and third countries regulating the transfer of personal data including appropriate safeguards for the data subjects. Member States may conclude international agreements which involve the transfer of personal data to third countries or international organisations, as far as such agreements do not affect this Regulation or any other provisions of Union law and include an appropriate level of protection for the fundamental rights of the data subjects.

(103) The Commission may decide with effect for the entire Union that a third country, a territory or specified sector within a third country, or an international organisation, offers an adequate level of data protection, thus providing legal certainty and uniformity throughout the Union as regards the third country or international organisation which is considered to provide such level of protection. In such cases, transfers of personal data to that third country or international organisation may take place without the need to obtain any further authorisation. The Commission may also decide, having given notice and a full statement setting out the reasons to the third country or international organisation, to revoke such a decision.

(104) In line with the fundamental values on which the Union is founded, in particular the protection of human rights, the Commission should, in its assessment of the third country, or of a territory or specified sector within a third country, take into account how a particular third country respects the rule of law, access to justice as well as international human rights norms and standards and its general and sectoral law, including legislation concerning public security, defence and national security as well as public order and criminal law. The adoption of an adequacy decision with regard to a territory or a specified sector in a third country should take into account clear and objective criteria, such as specific processing activities and the scope of applicable legal standards and legislation in force in the third country. The third country should offer guarantees ensuring an adequate level of protection essentially equivalent to that ensured within the Union, in particular where personal data are processed in one or several specific sectors. In particular, the third country should ensure effective independent data protection supervision and should provide for cooperation mechanisms with the Member States' data protection authorities, and the data subjects should be provided with effective and enforceable rights and effective administrative and judicial redress.

(105) Apart from the international commitments the third country or international organisation has entered into, the Commission should take account of obligations arising from the third

country's or international organisation's participation in multilateral or regional systems in particular in relation to the protection of personal data, as well as the implementation of such obligations. In particular, the third country's accession to the Council of Europe Convention of 28 January 1981 for the Protection of Individuals with regard to the Automatic Processing of Personal Data and its Additional Protocol should be taken into account. The Commission should consult the Board when assessing the level of protection in third countries or international organisations.

(106) The Commission should monitor the functioning of decisions on the level of protection in a third country, a territory or specified sector within a third country, or an international organisation, and monitor the functioning of decisions adopted on the basis of Article 25(6) or Article 26(4) of Directive 95/46/EC. In its adequacy decisions, the Commission should provide for a periodic review mechanism of their functioning. That periodic review should be conducted in consultation with the third country or international organisation in question and take into account all relevant developments in the third country or international organisation. For the purposes of monitoring and of carrying out the periodic reviews, the Commission should take into consideration the views and findings of the European Parliament and of the Council as well as of other relevant bodies and sources. The Commission should evaluate, within a reasonable time, the functioning of the latter decisions and report any relevant findings to the Committee within the meaning of Regulation (EU) No 182/2011 of the European Parliament and of the Council as established under this Regulation, to the European Parliament and to the Council.

(107) The Commission may recognise that a third country, a territory or a specified sector within a third country, or an international organisation no longer ensures an adequate level of data protection. Consequently the transfer of personal data to that third country or international organisation should be prohibited, unless the requirements in this Regulation relating to transfers subject to appropriate safeguards, including binding corporate rules, and derogations for specific situations are fulfilled. In that case, provision should be made for consultations between the Commission and such third countries or international organisations. The Commission should, in a timely manner, inform the third country or international organisation of the reasons and enter into consultations with it in order to remedy the situation.

Closely Related Provisions

Recital 6; recital 102; Articles 13(1)(f) and 14(1)(f) (Information to a data subject); Article 15(1)(c) (Right to access information about data recipients in third countries); Article 23(2)(d) (Member States can restrict individuals' rights but must provide for safeguards to prevent abuse or unlawful transfer) (see too recital 153); Article 28(3)(a) (Provisions of a data processing agreement stipulating controller's instructions regarding data transfers); Article 30(1)(e) and (2)(c) (Internal records about data transfers); Article 40(2)(j) (Data transfer codes of conduct); Article 44 (General principles for transfers); Article 70(1)(s) (Assessment by the Board of the level of protection in a third country); Article 83(5)(c) (Fines for non-compliance with data transfer restrictions); Article 96 (Relationship with previously concluded agreements of the EU Member States)

Related Provisions in LED [Directive (EU) 2016/680]

Recital 36; Article 35 (General principles for data transfers); Article 36 (Transfers on the basis of an adequacy decision) (see too recitals 66–70); Article 51(1)(g) (Assessment by the Board of the level of protection in a third country)

Relevant Case Law

CJEU

Case C-101/01, *Criminal proceedings against Bodil Lindqvist*, judgment of 6 November 2003 (ECLI:EU:C:2003:596).

Joined Cases C-317/04 and C-318/04, *European Parliament v Council of the European Union and Commission of the European Communities*, judgment of 30 May 2006 (Grand Chamber) (ECLI:EU:C:2006:346).

Joined Cases C-293/12 and C-594/12, *Digital Rights Ireland Ltd v Minister for Communications, Marine and Natural Resources and Others and Kärntner Landesregierung and Others*, judgment of 8 April 2014 (Grand Chamber) (ECLI:EU:C:2014:238).

Case C-362/14, *Maximillian Schrems v Data Protection Commissioner*, judgment of 6 October 2015 (Grand Chamber) (ECLI:EU:C:2015:650).

Opinion of Advocate General Bot in Case 362/14, *Maximilian Schrems v Data Protection Commissioner*, delivered on 23 September 2015 (ECLI:EU:C:2015:650).

Joined Cases C-203/15 and C-698/15, *Tele2 Sverige AB v Post-och telestyrelsen* and *Secretary of State for Home Department v Tom Watson and Others*, judgment of 21 December 2016 (Grand Chamber) (ECLI:EU:C:2016:970).

Opinion 1/15, Opinion of 26 July 2017 (Grand Chamber) (ECLI:EU:C:2017:592).

Opinion of Advocate General Mengozzi in *Opinion 1/15*, delivered on 8 September 2016 (ECLI:EU:C:2016:656).

Case T-670/16, *Digital Rights Ireland Ltd v European Commission*, GC, order of 22 November 2017 (ECLI:EU:T:2017:838).

Case C-311/18, *Data Protection Commissioner v Facebook Ireland Limited, Maximillian Schrems* (pending).

Ireland

Schrems v Data Protection Commissioner [2014] IEHC 310, [2014] 2 ILRM 441.

Schrems v Data Protection Commissioner (No. 2) [2014] IEHC 351, [2014] 2 ILRM 506.

Data Protection Commissioner and Facebook Ireland Limited and Maximilian Schrems, Irish High Court, 2016 No. 4809 P, 3 October 2017.

A. Rationale and Policy Underpinnings

Article 45 GDPR sets forth the procedure and standards for determining when third countries (including territories or one or more specified sectors within such countries) and international organisations can be found to provide an adequate level of data protection.

Chapter V of the GDPR creates a three-tiered structure for legal bases for international data transfers, with adequacy decisions at the top, appropriate safeguards in the middle and derogations at the bottom. An adequacy decision requires that the legal system of a third country or international organisation be 'essentially equivalent' to that of EU data protection law, which represents the highest standard of protection. When there is no adequacy, adequate safeguards may be used, which can be seen as the middle level of protection.[1] Finally, derogations may be used in certain cases when there is no essential equivalence and appropriate safeguards cannot be used, making them the lowest standard.[2]

---

[1] See the commentary on Art. 46 in this volume.
[2] See the commentary on Art. 49 in this volume regarding derogations.

Adequacy requires both that the content of data protection rules in third countries or international organisations meet the standards of EU law, and that such rules be effective in practice.[3] It is not required that the rules be identical to those of the EU; rather, they must be 'essentially equivalent' to EU rules. As the WP29 has stated,[4] this means that they must comply with a 'core' of principles relating both to the content of data protection rules and their enforcement, based on the GDPR, the Charter of Fundamental Rights of the European Union ('CFR') and other relevant international instruments, such as Council of Europe Convention 108. This also requires that attention be paid to the legal framework for the access of public authorities to personal data.[5]

B. Legal Background

1. EU legislation

Article 25 DPD contained rules concerning the adequacy of protection in third countries. The following are the main differences between Article 25 DPD and Article 45 GDPR:

1. Article 25 required an adequate level of protection in a third country to which personal data are transferred, while Article 45 sets out an adequate level of protection in a third country or international organisation as one option under which personal data may be transferred.
2. Article 45(2) contained a more detailed and exhaustive list of conditions for adequacy than what was contained in Article 25.
3. Article 45 does not allow the Commission to find that a third country does *not* provide an adequate level of data protection, a possibility that was provided in Article 25(4) DPD. However, the removal of this possibility is only relevant with regard to third countries for which no adequacy decision is in force, since the Commission may repeal, amend or suspend adequacy decisions that are in force under Article 45(5) GDPR.
4. Article 45 provides only for EU adequacy decisions, whereas Article 25 also mentioned decisions of the Member States.
5. Article 45 also mentions adequacy decisions covering transfers to international organisations, specific sectors or territories of a third country, whereas Article 25 referred solely to transfers to third countries.
6. Article 45 requires a periodic review of adequacy decisions at least every four years.

There are thirteen Commission adequacy decisions currently in force.[6] Two former adequacy decisions are no longer in force after the data transfers mechanisms upon which they were based were invalidated (i.e. the 2004 decision on the transfer of passenger name record data to the United States' Bureau of Customs and Border Protection[7]

---

[3] WP29 2017, p. 3.   [4] Ibid.   [5] Ibid., p. 4. See also WP29 2016.

[6] The decisions cover Andorra (Commission Decision Andorra 2010); Argentina (Commission Decision Argentina 2003); the Canadian Personal Information Protection and Electronic Documents Act ('PIPEDA') (Commission Decision PIPEDA 2002); Switzerland (Commission Decision Switzerland 2000); the Faroe Islands (Commission Decision Faroe Islands 2010); Guernsey (Commission Decision Guernsey 2003); Israel (Commission Decision Israel 2011); the Isle of Man (Commission Decision Isle of Man 2004); the Japanese Act on the Protection of Personal Information (Commission Decision Japan 2019); Jersey (Commission Decision Jersey 2008); New Zealand (Commission Decision New Zealand 2013); the EU–U.S. Privacy Shield (Commission Decision Privacy Shield 2016); and Uruguay (Commission Decision Uruguay 2012).

[7] Commission Decision US 2004.

which was invalidated by the Court of Justice of the EU,[8] and the 2000 decision on the EU–US Safe Harbour arrangement[9] which CJEU invalidated in its *Schrems*[10] judgment in 2015). In addition, the adequacy decision issued in 2005 covering the transfer of Passenger Name Record data of air passengers to the Canada Border Services Agency expired in 2009.[11]

In December 2016 the Commission issued a decision that amended eleven existing adequacy decisions to take into account the requirements of the *Schrems* judgment.[12] The decision amends the previous adequacy decisions covering Andorra, Argentina, the Canadian Personal Information Protection and Electronic Documents Act, the Faeroese Act on the processing of personal data, Guernsey, the Isle of Man, Israel, Jersey, New Zealand, Switzerland and Uruguay. It makes changes to each decision that require Member State data protection authorities to inform the Commission when they take decisions to suspend or ban data flows; require the Commission to monitor developments in the respective third country that could affect the functioning of the decision; order the Commission and the Member States to keep each other informed about cases where the action of bodies in the third country responsible for ensuring compliance fail to do so; obligate the Member States and the Commission to inform each other of indications that interferences by public authorities responsible for national security, law enforcement or other public interests go beyond what is strictly necessary or that there is no effective legal protection against such interferences; and require the Commission to inform the competent authorities of the third country and to propose draft measures to repeal or suspend the decision or limit its scope when evidence shows that an adequate level of protection is no longer ensured.

In January 2017 the Commission announced that it will 'actively engage with key trading partners in East and South-East Asia, starting from Japan and Korea in 2017, and, depending on progress towards the modernisation of its data protection laws, with India, but also with countries in Latin America, in particular Mercosur, and the European neighbourhood which have expressed an interest in obtaining an "adequacy finding"'.[13] In 2018, the Commission stated the following concerning its strategy for adequacy decisions:

Under its framework on adequacy findings, the Commission considers that the following criteria should be taken into account when assessing with which third countries a dialogue on adequacy should be pursued:

(i) the extent of the EU's (actual or potential) commercial relations with a given third country, including the existence of a free trade agreement or ongoing negotiations;
(ii) the extent of personal data flows from the EU, reflecting geographical and/or cultural ties;
(iii) the pioneering role the third country plays in the field of privacy and data protection that could serve as a model for other countries in its region; and
(iv) the overall political relationship with the third country in question, in particular with respect to the promotion of common values and shared objectives at international level.[14]

---

[8] Joined Cases C-317/04 and C-318/04, *Parliament v Council and Commission*. Regarding this judgment, see Docksey 2014, pp. 100–106.
[9] Safe Harbour 2000.   [10] Case C-362/14, *Schrems*.
[11] Art. 7 Commission Decision Canada 2006.   [12] Commission Decision 2016/2295.
[13] EC Communication 2017A, p. 9.   [14] Ibid., p. 8.

On 23 January 2019 the Commission adopted an adequacy decision covering the Japanese Act on the Protection of Personal Information,[15] which is the first adequacy decision covering a non-Western legal system. The Japanese government has also issued a reciprocal adequacy decision covering the EU.[16]

In 2012 the WP29 found that the Principality of Monaco guaranteed an adequate level of protection under Article 25(6) DPD.[17] However, a Commission adequacy decision was never issued, and thus data transfers to Monaco are subject to the same restrictions as those to any other third country.

2. International instruments

In *Opinion 1/15* the Court found that the transfer of personal data may be legalised by an international agreement.[18] Such agreements must meet the *Schrems* standard of 'essential equivalence' with EU law,[19] and must also fulfil the requirements of EU primary law, in particular the Charter. The GDPR does not further specify the conditions under which international agreements may provide a legal basis to transfer personal data, beyond stating in recital 102 that the GDPR is 'without prejudice to international agreements concluded between the Union and third countries regulating the transfer of personal data including appropriate safeguards for the data subjects'. Requiring 'appropriate safeguards for data subjects' is a weaker standard than that contained in Article 44 GDPR, which provides that any data transfers must comply with both the conditions laid down in Chapter V and with the other provisions of the GDPR, and it can be questioned whether this standard complies with the standard for adequacy set out by the CJEU.

In addition, Article 96 provides that 'international agreements involving the transfer of personal data to third countries or international organisations which were concluded by Member States prior to 24 May 2016, and which comply with Union law as applicable prior to that date, shall remain in force until amended, replaced or revoked'. However, it is questionable whether this is compatible with the dynamic approach to fundamental rights protection that the CJEU adopted in *Schrems* (discussed below).

Whether an adequacy decision or an international agreement is used as a legal basis for data transfers depends on a variety of factors, both legal and political. An adequacy decision is based on a more thorough investigation of data protection standards in third countries than is usually possible when negotiating an international agreement. Changes to the law have also made it easier to adopt adequacy decisions for data sharing; for example, the Commission may now also issue such decisions under the LED.[20] The Commission has determined that data transfers in the context of international trade are to be legalised by adequacy decisions rather than by international agreements, based on a desire to avoid political controversy.[21]

However, the legal relationship between international agreements and adequacy decisions remains confused, as illustrated by the so-called Umbrella Agreement between the EU and the US dealing with the protection of personal information relating to the prevention, investigation, detection and prosecution of criminal offences.[22] While stating

---

[15] Commission Decision Japan 2019. In December 2018 the EDPB published its opinion on the Commission decision; see EDPB 2018.
[16] See EU-Japan Joint Statement 2019.   [17] WP29 2012, p. 19.
[18] *Opinion 1/15*, para. 214. See Kuner 2018.   [19] *Opinion 1/15*, paras. 93, 134 and 214.
[20] Art. 36 LED.
[21] See Hanke 2017, stating that 'diplomats and Commission insiders' say the preference for adequacy decisions points to the Commission's desire to 'keep trade deals uncontroversial'.
[22] Umbrella Agreement US.

on the one hand that it does not provide a legal basis for data transfers,[23] the Umbrella Agreement also proclaims that data processing under it shall be deemed to comply with laws restricting the international transfer of data,[24] which makes it sound like an adequacy decision. Several other treaties provide a legal basis for transfers of personal data to third countries; these are discussed in the commentary to Article 44 in this volume.

Adequacy decisions also have implications for the EEA and EFTA states. The EEA is comprised of the EU Member States plus Iceland, Liechtenstein and Norway, which three countries together plus Switzerland comprise the EFTA. The EEA Agreement, as amended in July 2018,[25] incorporates the GDPR into its Annexes and provides that the provisions of the GDPR should be read, for the purposes of that Agreement, with a number of adaptations affecting the three EEA/EFTA States[26] and the EFTA Surveillance Authority. In this respect, the amended Agreement provides that, as regards the EEA/EFTA States, the following shall be inserted after Article 45(1) GDPR:

1a. Pending a decision by the EEA Joint Committee to incorporate into the EEA Agreement an implementing act adopted pursuant to paragraphs 3 or 5 of this Article an EFTA State may decide to apply the measures contained therein.

Each EFTA State shall decide and inform the Commission and the EFTA Surveillance Authority, before the entry into force of any implementing act adopted pursuant to paragraphs 3 or 5 of this Article, whether it, pending a decision by the EEA Joint Committee to incorporate the implementing act into the EEA Agreement, will apply the measures contained therein at the same time as the EU Member States or not. In the absence of a decision to the contrary, each EFTA State shall apply the measures contained in an implementing act adopted pursuant to paragraphs 3 or 5 of this Article at the same time as the EU Member States.

Notwithstanding Article 102 of the Agreement, if an agreement on the incorporation into the EEA Agreement of an implementing act adopted pursuant to paragraphs 3 or 5 of this Article cannot be reached in the EEA Joint Committee within twelve months of the entry into force of that implementing act, any EFTA State may discontinue the application of such measures and shall inform the Commission and the EFTA Surveillance Authority thereof without delay.

The other Contracting Parties to the EEA Agreement shall, by way of derogation from Article 1(3), restrict or prohibit the free flow of personal data to an EFTA State which does not apply the measures contained in an implementing act adopted pursuant to paragraph 5 of this Article in the same way as these measures prevent the transfer of personal data to a third country or an international organisation.[27]

In addition, the amended EEA Agreement states the following:

Whenever the EU enters into consultations with third countries or international organisations with the aim of adopting an adequacy decision pursuant to Article 45, the EFTA States shall be kept duly informed. In cases where the third country or the international organisation undertakes specific obligations regarding the processing of personal data from the member states, the EU will take into account the situation of EFTA States and discuss with third countries or international organisation possible mechanisms for subsequent possible application by the EFTA States.[28]

---

[23] Ibid., Art. 1(3). See also EDPS 2016, p. 7, finding that the Umbrella Agreement is not itself an adequacy decision.
[24] Art. 5(3) Umbrella Agreement US.   [25] EEA Decision 2018.
[26] Switzerland, the fourth EFTA State is not a signatory to the EEA.
[27] Art. 5e(m) EEA Decision 2018.   [28] Ibid.

3. National developments

Article 45 does not foresee implementation by the Member States. Legislation of some Member States provides for DPAs to suspend their proceedings and refer questions about adequacy decisions of the Commission for a court decision,[29] as provided for in CJEU's *Schrems* judgment.[30]

4. Case law

The two most significant CJEU judgments to date dealing with adequate protection for international data transfers are *Schrems* and *Opinion 1/15*. These two cases are discussed at length because of their importance. The CJEU also dealt with the DPD's provisions on international data transfers in *Lindqvist*,[31] which is discussed in the commentary on Article 44 in this volume.

4.1 Schrems

The complainant Maximilian Schrems brought several complaints against Facebook before the Irish Data Protection Commissioner ('DPC'), based on, among other things, Facebook's membership in the EU–US Safe Harbour.[32] In 2013, Schrems sought judicial review in the Irish High Court against the DPC's decision not to proceed against Facebook. On 18 June 2014, Mr Justice Hogan of the High Court referred two questions about the case to the CJEU.[33] In its judgment, the CJEU broadly agreed with the conclusions of Advocate General Bot,[34] finding that the DPAs were not prevented by Article 25(6) from examining claims related to the adequacy of protection under a Commission decision, and that the decision underlying the Safe Harbour was invalid.

The CJEU found that all provisions of the DPD must be interpreted in light of a high level of fundamental rights protection under the Charter. In considering the powers of the DPAs, it stressed the importance of their independence, and mentioned that their powers do not extend to data processing carried out in a third country. It further held that the transfer of personal data to a third country is itself an act of data processing, and thus falls within Member State law and the supervisory powers of the DPA. The Court went on to find that a Commission decision cannot preclude an individual from filing a claim with a DPA concerning the adequacy of protection, nor can such a decision eliminate or reduce their powers.

Thus, when an individual makes a claim to a DPA contesting the compatibility of a data transfer based on an adequacy decision with the protection of privacy and fundamental rights, the DPA must examine the claim 'with all due diligence'.[35] When the DPA rejects such a claim as unfounded, the individual must have access to judicial remedies allowing him to contest this decision before national courts, and such courts 'must stay proceedings and make a reference to the Court for a preliminary ruling on validity where they consider that one or more grounds for invalidity put forward by the parties or, as the case may be, raised by them of their own motion are well founded'.[36] Conversely, when the DPA finds such claim to be well-founded, it must 'be able to engage in legal

---

[29] See e.g. German GDPR Implementation Law, s. 21. [30] Case C-362/14, *Schrems*, para. 65.
[31] Case C-101/01, *Bodil Lindqvist*. [32] The following analysis is adapted from Kuner 2017.
[33] See the Irish High court in *Schrems* [2014]; and *Schrems* (No. 2) [2014].
[34] Case C-362/14, *Schrems* (Opinion AG). [35] Case C-362/14, *Schrems*, para. 63.
[36] Ibid., para. 64.

proceedings', and the national legislature must 'provide for legal remedies enabling the national supervisory authority concerned to put forward the objections which it considers well founded before the national courts in order for them, if they share its doubts as to the validity of the Commission decision, to make a reference for a preliminary ruling for the purpose of examination of the decision's validity'.[37]

The CJEU went on to find that the term 'an adequate level of protection' as used in the DPD must be understood as 'requiring the third country in fact to ensure, by reason of its domestic law or its international commitments, a level of protection of fundamental rights and freedoms that is essentially equivalent to that guaranteed within the European Union by virtue of Directive 95/46 read in the light of the Charter', while not requiring that the level be identical to that under EU law.[38] Without this requirement, 'the high level of protection guaranteed by Directive 95/46 read in the light of the Charter could easily be circumvented by transfers of personal data from the European Union to third countries for the purpose of being processed in those countries'.[39] While the means to which a third country has recourse for ensuring a high level of protection may differ from those employed within the EU, they must prove to be effective in practice.

Assessing the level of protection in a third country requires the Commission to 'take account of all the circumstances surrounding a transfer of personal data to a third country',[40] to check periodically whether the adequacy assessment is still justified and to take account of circumstances that have arisen after adoption of the decision. This means that 'the Commission's discretion as to the adequacy of the level of protection ensured by a third country is reduced, with the result that review of the requirements stemming from Article 25 of Directive 95/46, read in the light of the Charter, should be strict'.[41]

The CJEU then dealt with the validity of the Safe Harbour adequacy decision. While it found that 'a system of self-certification is not in itself contrary to the requirement laid down in Article 25(6) of Directive 95/46 that the third country concerned must ensure an adequate level of protection "by reason of its domestic law or ... international commitments"', the reliability of such a system is based on 'the establishment of effective detection and supervision mechanisms enabling any infringements of the rules ensuring the protection of fundamental rights, in particular the right to respect for private life and the right to protection of personal data, to be identified and punished in practice'.[42] It noted that public authorities in the US were not required to comply with the Safe Harbour principles, and that the Safe Harbour decision of the Commission did not contain sufficient findings explaining how the US ensures an adequate level of protection.

The CJEU stated that under the Safe Harbour decision, the applicability of the principles could be limited to meet, for example, national security, public interest or law enforcement requirements, and that the decision stated that '[c]learly, where US law imposes a conflicting obligation, US organisations whether in the Safe Harbor or not must comply with the law'.[43] It found that these provisions in effect gave US law primacy over EU fundamental rights in situations where they conflict, and that to establish an interference with fundamental rights, 'it does not matter whether the information in question relating to private life is sensitive or whether the persons concerned have suffered any adverse consequences on account of that interference'.[44] Moreover, the Safe Harbour decision did not contain any finding concerning limitations on the powers of

---

[37] Ibid., para. 65.   [38] Ibid., para. 73.   [39] Ibid.   [40] Ibid., para. 75.
[41] Ibid., para. 78.   [42] Ibid., para. 81.   [43] Ibid., para. 85.   [44] Ibid., para. 87.

public authorities (such as law enforcement authorities) in the US to interfere with fundamental rights.

The CJEU stated that:

> legislation is not limited to what is strictly necessary where it authorises, on a generalised basis, storage of all the personal data of all the persons whose data has been transferred from the European Union to the United States without any differentiation, limitation or exception being made in the light of the objective pursued and without an objective criterion being laid down by which to determine the limits of the access of the public authorities to the data, and of its subsequent use, for purposes which are specific, strictly restricted and capable of justifying the interference which both access to that data and its use entail.[45]

It found that 'legislation permitting the public authorities to have access on a generalised basis to the content of electronic communications must be regarded as compromising the essence of the fundamental right to respect for private life, as guaranteed by Article 7 of the Charter',[46] and that 'legislation not providing for any possibility for an individual to pursue legal remedies in order to have access to personal data relating to him, or to obtain the rectification or erasure of such data, does not respect the essence of the fundamental right to effective judicial protection, as enshrined in Article 47 of the Charter'.[47]

In the judgment, the CJEU gave the following points of orientation to interpret the concept of essential equivalence:

1. There must be a high level of fundamental rights protection, which must be evaluated strictly.
2. The third country in question must have a means for ensuring a high level of protection that is effective in practice, in light of all the circumstances surrounding a transfer of personal data to a third country. This must include periodic checks as to whether the adequacy assessment is still justified and take into account all circumstances that have arisen after adoption of the decision.
3. Adequate protection must take into account the country's domestic law or international commitments.
4. Any system of self-certification must be reliable based on effective detection and supervision mechanisms enabling infringements of the rules, in particular the right to respect for private life and the protection of personal data, to be identified and punished in practice.
5. An adequacy decision must include a detailed explanation of how a country ensures an adequate level of protection.
6. There must not be limitations based on national security, public interest or law enforcement requirements that give third country law primacy over EU law.
7. Limitations must be placed on the power of public authorities (such as law enforcement authorities) to interfere with fundamental rights. In particular, any such access must be strictly necessary and proportionate to the protection of values such as national security, there must be clear and precise rules regarding the scope of application of a measure, and for effective protection against the risk of abuse of data, and derogations and limitations in relation to data protection should apply only when strictly necessary.

---

[45] Ibid., para. 93.   [46] Ibid., para. 94.   [47] Ibid., para. 95.

8. Third country legislation must not authorise, on a generalised basis, storage of all the personal data transferred without any differentiation, limitation or exception being made in light of the objective pursued and without an objective criterion being laid down to determine the limits to the data, and its subsequent use, for purposes which are specific, strictly restricted and capable of justifying the interference entailed by access to that data and its use.

The significance of *Schrems* goes beyond its data protection implications. As President of the CJEU Koen Lenaerts has stated, the *Schrems* judgment is 'a landmark case' in EU procedural law 'because it has made clear that the preliminary reference for controlling the validity of an act of the Union is not only without limit in time ... but also may be reviewed in terms of the legal framework existing at the date of the Court's judgment'.[48] Thus, the Charter, under which the CJEU evaluated the Safe Harbour Framework in *Schrems*, had not been elevated to the level of EU primary law at the time the Safe Harbour was enacted in 2000, but the Court still used it as the standard of reference. More specifically, the Court's dynamic approach to fundamental rights protection in *Schrems* can also be seen in its choice of 'essential equivalence' with EU law as the measure of 'adequate protection', even though when the DPD was adopted, the EU legislator specifically preferred the term 'adequate protection' over 'equivalent protection'.[49] This indicates that in cases involving the validity of adequacy decisions (and possibly other data transfer mechanisms as well), the CJEU will make a 'dynamic assessment' and evaluate whether they meet the legal standards in force at the time that it makes its judgment and not just those that applied when the case was brought.

4.2 Opinion 1/15

An agreement for the processing and transfer of passenger name records ('PNR') data between the EU and Canada was initialled by the EU Council of Ministers and Canada on 6 May 2013[50] (referred to here as the Draft Agreement) and signed on 25 June 2014,[51] following which the Council sought approval of it by the European Parliament.[52] On 25 November 2014, the Parliament adopted a resolution seeking an opinion from the CJEU pursuant to Article 218(11) on two questions,[53] which application was lodged with the Court on 10 April 2015.[54] The two questions were as follows:

Is the envisaged agreement compatible with the provisions of the Treaties (Article 16 TFEU) and the Charter of Fundamental Rights of the European Union (Articles 7, 8 and Article 52(1)) as regards the right of individuals to protection of personal data?

Do Articles 82(1)(d) and 87(2)(a) TFEU constitute the appropriate legal basis for the act of the Council concluding the envisaged agreement or must that act be based on Article 16 TFEU?

In his Opinion issued on 8 September 2016,[55] Advocate General Mengozzi responded negatively to both questions, as he found several provisions of the Draft Agreement incompatible with the Charter. He also found that the correct legal basis of the Agreement was provided by Articles 16(2) (the right to data protection) and 87(2)(a) Treaty on the Function of the European Union ('TFEU') (police cooperation among the Member

---

[48] Lenaerts speech 2018, between 27'07" and 30'35". [49] Simitis and Dammann 1997, p. 273.
[50] Proposal PNR Canada 2013. [51] Press Release PNR Canada 2014.
[52] The following analysis is adapted from Kuner 2018. [53] EP Resolution 2014.
[54] EP Request Opinion 1/15. [55] *Opinion 1/15* (Opinion AG).

States in criminal matters) and not by Article 82(1)(d) TFEU (judicial cooperation in criminal matters in the Union).

In its Opinion of July 2017,[56] the Court first noted that an international agreement must be entirely compatible with the treaties and constitutional principles of the EU.[57] The CJEU found that the Draft Agreement had the dual objectives of protecting public security and data protection, both of which are inextricably linked.[58] Thus, the Court agreed with the above conclusions of the Advocate General concerning the legal basis.

The Court found that PNR data may reveal considerable detail about an individual, such as their travel habits, relationships and financial situation, which may also include sensitive information. It stressed that the data were to be systematically analysed by automated means before arrival in Canada, and that they could be stored for up to five years. Thus, the Court observed that the transfer of PNR data to Canada and the rules foreseen in the Draft Agreement would entail an interference with the fundamental rights to respect for private life under Article 7[59] and to the protection of personal data under Article 8 of the Charter.[60]

Since Article 7 and Article 8 are not absolute rights,[61] the Court then examined whether such interferences could be justified. It found that the processing of PNR data under the Draft Agreement pursued a different objective from that for which it was collected by air carriers, and thus required a different legal basis, such as separate consent by passengers or some other legal basis laid down by law.[62] The Court next found that an international agreement may meet the requirements of being a 'law' as defined in Articles 8(2) and 52(1) of the Charter.[63] It went on to note that in this case such interferences are justified by the need to fight terrorism and serious transnational crime in order to ensure public security, and that the transfer of PNR data to Canada and its subsequent processing may be appropriate to meet that objective.[64]

The CJEU then analysed the protections provided in the Draft Agreement, and had the following criticisms:

1. The Draft Agreement was not sufficiently precise in specifying the PNR data to be transferred.
2. It did not provide sufficient protections for the transfer of sensitive data. In addition, it stated that 'a transfer of sensitive data ... requires a particularly solid justification, based on grounds other than the protection of public security against terrorism and serious transnational crime'.[65]
3. With regard to automated analyses of PNR data, because of the margin of error, any positive result had to be subject to 'individual re-examination by non-automated means' before any measure adversely affecting a passenger was taken.[66]
4. Language permitting Canada to process PNR data on a case-by-case basis to 'ensure the oversight or accountability of the public administration' and to 'comply with the subpoena or warrant issues, or an order made, by a court' lacked sufficient clarity and precision.[67]

---

[56] Opinion 1/15.   [57] Ibid., para. 67.   [58] Ibid., para. 94.   [59] Ibid., para. 125.
[60] Ibid., para. 126.   [61] Ibid., para. 136.   [62] Ibid., para. 143.
[63] Ibid., paras. 145–147.   [64] Ibid., paras. 151 and 153.   [65] Ibid., para. 165.
[66] Ibid., para. 173.   [67] Ibid., para. 181.

The Court also noted that the coverage of all air passengers flying between the EU and Canada was not unacceptably broad, particularly since Article 13 of Convention on Civil Aviation (the Chicago Convention)[68] require signatories (which include Canada and all EU Member States, but not the EU itself) to comply with admission and departure formalities of passengers from their territory, which can include security checks laid down by Canadian law.[69]

The Court then discussed at length the compatibility of the Draft Agreement with EU law requirements for data retention. With regard to the retention and use of PNR data before the arrival of passengers, during their stay in Canada, and on their departure, the Court found that some elements of the retention of data under the Draft Agreement were acceptable, such as the use of data for security checks and border control checks;[70] verifying the reliability and topicality of models for the automated processing of data;[71] or cases when data are collected by the Canadian authorities during the individuals' stay in Canada indicating that use of it may be necessary to combat terrorism and serious transnational crime.[72] However, the Court stated that the use of PNR data should be subject to prior review by a court or an administrative body, and that otherwise it may be found to go beyond what is strictly necessary.[73]

With regard to the retention and use of PNR data after passengers' departure from Canada, the Court found that this was not strictly necessary,[74] but that it could be stored in Canada in cases where certain passengers may present a risk of terrorism or serious transnational crime. It stated that the five-year retention period in the Draft Agreement does not exceed the limits of what is strictly necessary,[75] but that use of such data should be subject to prior review by a court or 'independent administrative body'.[76]

Concerning the disclosure of PNR data to government authorities, the Court reiterated the standard it set forth in *Schrems* that data transfers to third countries require a level of protection that is 'essentially equivalent' to that under EU law,[77] and held that this also applies to PNR transfers to Canada. The Court went on to say that this required either an international agreement between the EU and a third country, or an adequacy decision of the Commission.[78] It held that individuals must have a right to have their data rectified,[79] and that they must be notified individually when their data are used by a judicial authority or independent administrative body[80] unless this would jeopardise an investigation.[81] Finally, the Court held that the Draft Agreement did not sufficiently guarantee that oversight of compliance with its rules would be carried out by an independent authority within the meaning of Article 8(3) of the Charter.[82] Thus, the Court found that the Draft Agreement could not be concluded in its current form.

C. Analysis

1. Procedure for adequacy decisions

Article 45 deals with the issuance of formal decisions concerning adequacy by the Commission. Such decisions are implementing acts issued based on the examination

---

[68] Aviation Convention 1944.   [69] *Opinion 1/15*, paras. 188–189.   [70] Ibid., para. 197.
[71] Ibid., para. 198.   [72] Ibid., para. 199.   [73] Ibid., paras. 201–203.
[74] Ibid., paras. 206 and 211.   [75] Ibid., para. 209.   [76] Ibid., para. 208.
[77] Ibid., paras. 134 and 214.   [78] Ibid., para. 214.   [79] Ibid., para. 220.
[80] Ibid., para. 223.   [81] Ibid., para. 224.   [82] Ibid., para. 231.

procedure set out in Article 5 of the so-called Comitology Regulation.[83] The adoption of implementing acts is covered in detail in the commentary on Article 93 GDPR in this volume.

The issuance and negotiation of an adequacy decision typically begins with a third country approaching the Commission and requesting that discussions be opened. Negotiations between the Commission and a third country concerning adequacy generally take several years, and can become entangled in political factors[84] that can lead to tensions.[85] In the course of the procedure, the Commission has typically made its own investigations about the adequacy of protection in third countries, including through reports by academic experts.[86] Documents concerning the Commission's deliberations, including such academic studies, have typically not been made public, and there is a lack of transparency concerning the entire procedure.

Decisions by the Commission concerning adequacy, or decisions finding that an adequate level of protection is or is no longer ensured, must be published in the Official Journal of the EU.[87] Before reaching a decision on adequacy, the Commission must consult the EDPB. The EDPB is to be provided by the Commission with all relevant documentation, including correspondence, findings and the Commission's report on the level of protection in the third country or international organisation.[88] The EDPB will then issue its own opinion on the Commission's findings.[89] The fact that the GDPR does not mention a power by the EDPB to approve the Commission's decision[90] indicates that its opinion is not binding.[91] In enacting adequacy decisions, the Commission is assisted by a committee of Member State representatives[92] (the successor to the 'Article 31 Committee' under the DPD) that must approve decisions in line with the examination procedure provided for by Article 5 of the Comitology Regulation.

An adequacy decision must contain at least the following:

1. It must state specifically that the third country or international organisation ensures adequate protection by virtue of its domestic law or international commitments (this follows from para. 97 of the *Schrems* judgment).
2. It must give the territorial and sectoral application of the decision (GDPR Article 45(3)).
3. It must provide for a mechanism for periodic review of the decision (Article 45(3)).
4. It must identify the supervisory authority or authorities with responsibility for ensuring and enforcing compliance with the data protection rules (Article 45(2)(b) and (3)).

---

[83] Regulation 182/2011. See Art. 93(2) GDPR.

[84] E.g. in July 2010 the government of Ireland delayed an EU adequacy decision for Israel based on alleged Israeli government involvement in the forging of Irish passports (see Ihle 2010). Israel later received an adequacy decision from the European Commission.

[85] See e.g. Stoddart, Chan and Joly 2016 (concerning tensions with Quebec concerning adequacy).

[86] See e.g. Commission Staff Working Document 2006, p. 3, referring to such an academic study.

[87] Art. 45(8) GDPR.   [88] WP29 2017, p. 4.   [89] Ibid.

[90] See Art. 70(1)(s), stating that the EDPB is to 'provide the Commission with an opinion' concerning adequacy, and rec. 105, stating that the Commission 'should consult' the EDPB.

[91] Thus, the Commission approved an adequacy decision covering the Japanese Act on the Protection of Personal Information in 2019 despite the fact that the opinion of the EDPB on the decision (EDPB 2018) contained some criticisms of it.

[92] Art. 93(2) GDPR.

In addition, the adequacy decision must not limit the power of the DPAs to investigate complaints about whether the level of protection set forth in a Commission adequacy decision is compatible with fundamental rights.[93] Transfers under adequacy decisions do not require any further authorisation by DPAs or other authorities.[94]

2. Scope of adequacy decisions

Adequacy decisions can be issued for any country that is not an EU Member State or party to the EEA. This means that no adequacy decision is needed with regard to data transfers to the three EEA countries. Commission adequacy decisions apply in the EEA countries once they are adopted into the list of EEA Joint Committee Decisions,[95] which has been done with existing decisions (minus that of Japan, which had not been incorporated at the time this text was finalised).[96] Thus, they also apply for data transfers from Iceland, Liechtenstein and Norway as well. The GDPR was marked as EEA relevant and has been incorporated into the EEA Agreement.[97]

Article 45 allows Commission decisions to be issued concerning not only third countries, but also 'a territory or one or more specified sectors within that third country' or, unlike the DPD, an international organisation. The reference to territories includes, for example, Overseas Countries and Territories ('OCTs') that have special links with either Denmark, France, the Netherlands or the UK,[98] and to which EU law does not apply under the TFEU.[99] All such territories can thus be the subject of an adequacy decision. However, EU law applies in Guadeloupe, French Guiana, Martinique, Réunion, Saint-Barthélemy, Saint-Martin, the Azores, Madeira and the Canary Islands,[100] so personal data can be transferred to them without an adequacy decision.

There have been three adequacy decisions issued under the DPD that cover a specific legal framework in a third country, namely those covering the Canadian Personal Information Protection and Electronic Documents Act;[101] the Japanese Act on the Protection of Personal Information;[102] and the EU–US Privacy Shield.[103] The Commission has mentioned 'financial services or IT sectors' as potential subjects of sectoral adequacy decisions,[104] and has indicated that sectoral decisions 'will need to be considered in light of elements such as, for instance, the nature and state of development of the privacy regime (stand-alone law, multiple or sectorial laws etc.), the constitutional structure of the third country or whether certain sectors of the economy are particularly exposed to data flows from the EU'.[105]

The concept of international organisation is defined under Article 4(26),[106] and data transfers to international organisations are also covered in Article 45. Thus far there have been no adequacy decisions covering an international organisation. Many international organisations enjoy privileges and immunities under international law, and a waiver of

---

[93] See Case C-362/14, *Schrems*, para. 102. [94] Art. 45(1) GDPR. [95] See EFTA 2017.
[96] See EEA Agreement, Annex XI, pp. 13–16. [97] EEA Decision 2018.
[98] Under Annex II TFEU, OCTs include Greenland, New Caledonia and Dependencies, French Polynesia, French Southern and Antarctic Territories, Wallis and Futuna Islands, Mayotte, Saint Pierre and Miquelon, Aruba, Netherlands Antilles (Bonaire, Curaçao, Saba, Sint Eustatius and Sint Maarten), Anguilla, Cayman Islands, Falkland Islands, South Georgia and the South Sandwich Islands, Montserrat, Pitcairn, Saint Helena and Dependencies, British Antarctic Territory, British Indian Ocean Territory and Turks.
[99] Art. 355 TFEU. See also the commentary on Art. 3 in this volume. [100] Art. 355(1) TFEU.
[101] See Commission Decision PIPEDA 2002. [102] See Commission Decision Japan 2019.
[103] See Commission Decision Privacy Shield 2016. [104] EC Communication 2017A, p. 8.
[105] Ibid. [106] See the commentary on Art. 4(26) in this volume.

them must generally be express.[107] It is an open question whether an international organisation requesting and agreeing to be subject to an adequacy decision could be interpreted as a waiver of privileges and immunities.

On 29 March 2017, the UK invoked Article 50 of the Treaty on European Union ('TEU') and indicated its intention to leave the EU, at which point it will become a third country by operation of law ('Brexit') and all Union primary and secondary law will cease to apply to the UK.[108] On 14 November 2018, the parties agreed on a Withdrawal Agreement that sets forth the terms of the UK's withdrawal. The Withdrawal Agreement includes a 21-month implementation period during which the GDPR would continue to apply to all personal data which has been collected and processed in the UK until 31 December 2020.[109] However, during this period, the UK will have exited the EU and will no longer be an EU Member State, so that the rules on the transfer of personal data to third countries will apply, subject to the Withdrawal Agreement.[110] The Withdrawal Agreement will only come into effect if it is approved by the UK House of Commons and then by the Parliament. A political declaration agreed between the EU and the UK government states with regard to an EU adequacy decision for the UK that 'the European Commission will start the assessments with respect to the United Kingdom as soon as possible after the United Kingdom's withdrawal, endeavouring to adopt decisions by the end of 2020, if the applicable conditions are met'.[111] However, since Brexit is subject to political factors that were unresolved at the time this text was finalised, the legal status of data transfers from the EU to the UK post-Brexit remains uncertain. The EDPB[112] and the UK Information Commissioner[113] have published guidance for dealing with international data transfers post-Brexit.

3. Criteria for adequacy

The approach to assessing adequacy has traditionally been based on determining whether law and practice in third countries results in the implementation of certain core EU data protection practices and principles.[114] These principles were set out by the WP29 in 1998 as including the purpose limitation principle; the data quality and proportionality principle; the transparency principle; the security principle; the rights of access, rectification and opposition; and restrictions on onward transfers.[115] In addition, the Working Party found that adequacy required the realisation of the basic objectives of a data protection system, namely delivering a good level of compliance with the rules; providing support and help to individual data subjects; and providing appropriate redress to the injured party when the rules are not complied with.[116] Article 25(2) DPD built on these criteria and required assessing the adequacy of protection 'in the light of all the circumstances surrounding a data transfer operation or set of data transfer operations', with particular consideration being given to 'the nature of the data, the purpose and duration of the proposed processing operation or operations, the country of origin and country of final

---

[107] Regarding the waiver of privileges and immunities by international organisations, see Wickremasinghe 2012, pp. 12–13. See also Kuner 2019.
[108] Commission Brexit Preparedness Notice, p. 1.   [109] Art. 71 Withdrawal Agreement.
[110] Commission Brexit Preparedness Notice, p. 1.   [111] EU–UK Political Declaration, p. 4.
[112] EDPB Brexit information note.
[113] ICO 2018. See also the commentary on Art. 47 in this volume regarding the legal status of binding corporate rules (BCRs) post-Brexit.
[114] See WP29 1998; WP29 1997.   [115] WP29 1998, p. 6.   [116] Ibid., p. 7.

destination, the rules of law, both general and sectoral, in force in the third country in question and the professional rules and security measures which are complied with in that country'.

The criteria for adequacy in the GDPR have been significantly influenced by the CJEU's judgment in *Schrems*, as discussed above. Article 45(2) contains a list of criteria that the Commission shall use when assessing the adequacy of protection which are much more detailed and extensive than those contained in Article 25(2) DPD and are partially derived from the *Schrems* judgment.

Article 45(2)(c) states that a decision concerning adequacy should take into account 'the international commitments the third country or international organisation concerned has entered into, or other obligations arising from legally binding conventions or instruments as well as from its participation in multilateral or regional systems, in particular in relation to the protection of personal data'. This does not allow adequacy to be based solely on application of such an international convention or instrument, but indicates that it should be taken into account when assessing adequacy (this is of particular relevance with regard to a third country's membership in the Council of Europe Convention 108[117]). The list of criteria to be taken into account when determining adequacy is not exhaustive, as shown by the fact that Article 45(2) states that the elements shall 'in particular' be taken into account.

In 2017 the WP29 published a paper setting out its interpretation of the adequacy criteria contained in the GDPR; the paper has since been endorsed by the EDPB.[118] In it, the Working Party found that a number of content and procedural or enforcement principles and mechanisms should exist in the data protection system of a third country or international organisation in order for it to be considered adequate.[119] The following are the content principles that the WP29 enumerated:

1. Basic data protection concepts or principles (e.g. personal data, data controller, sensitive data, etc.).
2. Grounds for lawful and fair processing for legitimate purposes.
3. The purpose limitation principle.
4. The data quality and proportionality principle.
5. The data retention principle.
6. The security and confidentiality principle.
7. The transparency principle.
8. The right of access, rectification, erasure and objection.
9. Restrictions on onward transfers.

In addition, the WP29 required that additional content principles be applied when specific types of data processing are involved, in particular the processing of sensitive data, direct marketing and automated decision-making and profiling.[120] The WP29 indicated that the non-existence of the rights to data portability or the restriction of processing in the third country's or international organisation's system should not be an obstacle for it to be recognised as essentially equivalent,[121] although it did not explain why it singled out those two rights. The WP29 neither supported nor excluded the possibility of an adequacy decision being issued if one of these content principles

---

[117] Rec. 105 GDPR.   [118] EDPB Endorsement.   [119] WP29 2017, pp. 5–7.
[120] Ibid., p. 7.   [121] Ibid., p. 6.

is excluded from the scope of an adequacy decision, e.g. whether an adequacy decision could be issued with regard to a third country whose data protection system did not provide special protections for sensitive data if the scope of the decision excluded the transfer of sensitive data.

The WP29 also enumerated the following procedural and enforcement mechanisms that the data protection system of a third country or international organisation must contain:[122]

1. A competent independent supervisory authority.
2. The data protection system must ensure a good level of compliance.
3. Accountability (i.e. obliging data controllers and/or those processing personal data on their behalf to comply with it and to be able to demonstrate such compliance in particular to the competent supervisory authority).
4. Providing support and help to data subjects in the exercise of their rights and appropriate redress mechanisms.

Finally, the WP29 also required, in line with Article 45(2)(a) GDPR, that third countries provide essential guarantees for law enforcement and national security access to limit interference with fundamental rights.[123] This means, in particular:

1. Data processing should be based on clear, precise and accessible rules.
2. Necessity and proportionality must be demonstrated with regards to the legitimate objectives pursued.
3. The processing must be subject to independent oversight.
4. Effective remedies must be available to individuals.

4. Repeal, amendment or suspension of adequacy decisions

Article 45 contains detailed provisions dealing with situations where a third country, a territory or one or more specified sectors within a third country, or an international organisation no longer ensures an adequate level of protection. Such situations can arise when 'information reveals' that adequate protection no longer applies, which is to be broadly interpreted (e.g. when such information becomes known through reports in the news media). When this occurs, the Commission must repeal, amend or suspend its adequacy decision by means of an implementing act under the examination procedure referred to in Article 93(2),[124] except for 'duly justified imperative grounds of urgency', in which case the Commission must 'adopt immediately applicable implementing acts in accordance with the procedure referred to in Article 93(3)'.[125] Article 45(5) says that the Commission 'shall' take such actions, so it has a duty to do so in such situations. Repeal, amendment or suspension of an adequacy decision shall not have retroactive effect,[126] which is a departure from normal EU law, since generally when an EU act is annulled, it disappears from the EU legal order from the date on which it entered into force (*ex tunc*).[127]

When the Commission repeals, amends or suspends an adequacy decision, it must enter into consultations with the third country or international organisation in order to remedy the situation. Such a decision is without prejudice to transfers of personal data

---

[122] Ibid., p. 8.   [123] Ibid., p. 9.   [124] Art. 45(5) GDPR.   [125] Ibid.   [126] Ibid.
[127] Lenaerts, Maselis and Gutman 2014, locations 18058–18065.

carried out under Articles 46–49. This means that even if an adequacy decision is repealed by the Commission, data transfers to the affected third country or international organisation made pursuant to appropriate safeguards under Article 46, binding corporate rules under Article 47, or derogations under Article 49 are not affected.

5. Periodic review

The CJEU in *Schrems* found that the Commission must check 'periodically whether the finding relating to the adequacy of the level of protection ensured by the third country in question is still factually and legally justified'.[128] The GDPR requires that the implementing act determining adequacy provides for a periodic review at least every four years,[129] though the review period may be shorter than this depending on the particular circumstances at hand.[130] For example, the adequacy decision covering the EU–US Privacy Shield foresees a joint annual review.[131] In cases where incidents or changes in the legal framework of the third country or international organisations require it, a review may need to be conducted ahead of schedule.[132]

With regard to the procedure for conducting a periodic review, the GDPR states only that it should be 'conducted in consultation with the third country or international organisation in question and take into account all relevant developments in the third country or international organisation'; that the Commission should 'take into consideration the views and findings of the European Parliament and of the Council as well as of other relevant bodies and sources'; and that the Commission should report 'any relevant findings' to the Committee established under Article 93.[133] In light of the CJEU's findings in *Schrems* that the Commission's discretion in determining the adequacy of protection is 'reduced', and that its review of the adequacy requirements should be 'strict',[134] it seems that a periodic review must be rigorous and comprehensive. The EDPB has stated that it expects to be kept informed of the review process and to participate in it.[135]

Adequacy decisions of the Commission issued pre-GDPR also contained review clauses, though these were formulated more vaguely than under the GDPR.[136] The requirements of the GDPR concerning periodic review also apply to these previous adequacy decisions, so that the Commission will have to review them as well. Thus far, information concerning periodic review has been published by the Commission only with regard to the Privacy Shield.[137]

Before the GDPR, there was little transparency concerning monitoring and review of adequacy decisions. However, this will have to change in light of the Court's judgment in *Schrems* and the requirements of Article 45, which have raised the stakes with regard to periodic review considerably.

---

[128] Case C-362/14, *Schrems*, para. 76.   [129] Art. 45(3) GDPR.
[130] Ibid., stating that the periodic review shall happen 'at least' every four years. See WP29 2017, p. 4.
[131] Commission Decision Privacy Shield 2016, section 6.   [132] Ibid.
[133] See rec. 106 and the commentary on Art. 93 in this volume.
[134] Case C-362/14, *Schrems*, para. 78.   [135] WP29 2017, p. 4.
[136] See e.g. Commission Decision Argentina 2003 (Art. 4), Commission Decision Guernsey 2003 (Art. 5) and Commission Decision Israel 2011 (Art. 5), all stating merely that 'The Commission shall monitor the functioning of this Decision'.
[137] See e.g. Privacy Shield Press Release December 2018.

6. Status of past adequacy decisions

Article 45(9) GDPR specifies that adequacy decisions previously issued under the DPD shall remain in force until amended, replaced or repealed by a Commission Decision as specified in this Article. Thus, existing adequacy decisions remain in effect under the GDPR. However, as explained above, they must be reviewed periodically as set out in Article 45(3). Since adequacy decisions issued pre-GDPR may not all meet the requirements of Article 45,[138] the Commission may have to amend them in the future.

7. Enforcement

A Commission adequacy finding is a 'decision' under Article 288 TFEU, the legality of which may be reviewed by the CJEU, and it is binding on all organs of Member States, including DPAs. Under the CJEU's *Schrems* judgment, an individual must be able to make a claim to a DPA contesting the compatibility of a data transfer based on an adequacy decision with the protection of privacy and fundamental rights, and the DPA must examine the claim with all due diligence.[139] If the DPA rejects the claim, the individual must have access to judicial remedies allowing her to contest this decision before national courts, and the courts must stay proceedings and make a reference to the Court for a preliminary ruling.[140] If the DPA finds such claim to be well-founded, it must be able to engage in legal proceedings based on national legislation to enable the courts to make a reference for a preliminary ruling concerning the decision's validity.[141]

These requirements are reflected in provisions of the GDPR such as Articles 77 and 78, which give individuals the right to lodge a complaint against a DPA and to exercise an effective judicial remedy against one. In addition, under Article 58(2)(j) a DPA may order the suspension of data flows to a third country and international organisation, and Article 58(5) gives DPAs the power to bring infringements of the GDPR to the attention of judicial authorities and to engage in legal proceedings in order to enforce it. The important role of DPAs is also shown by the fact that while the CJEU in both *Digital Rights Ireland*[142] and *Tele2*[143] indicated that locating databases in third countries might raise fundamental rights issues, in *Opinion 1/15* Advocate General Mengozzi found that the retention of data outside the EU is not in itself problematic unless it 'does not fully ensure a review of the requirements of protection and security by an independent authority' (i.e. an EU-based DPA).[144]

The General Court has held inadmissible a claim brought by a not for profit company on behalf of itself and its members, supporters and the general public to seek annulment of the EU–US Privacy Shield pursuant to Article 263 TFEU.[145]

On 12 April 2018 the Irish High Court[146] referred to the CJEU[147] a series of questions that could put in question the continued validity of the EU-US Privacy Shield;[148] the case was still pending when this text was finalised.

---

[138] E.g. with regard to periodic review, as explained above.
[139] Case C-362/14, *Schrems*, para. 63. [140] Ibid., para. 64. [141] Ibid., para. 65.
[142] See Joined Cases C-293/12 and C-594/12, *Digital Rights Ireland*, para. 68.
[143] See Joined Cases C-203/15 and C-698/15, *Tele2*, para. 122.
[144] *Opinion 1/15* (Opinion AG), para. 277. [145] Case T-670/16, *Digital Rights Ireland*.
[146] Irish High Court, *Data Protection Commissioner and Facebook Ireland Limited and Maximilian Schrems*.
[147] Case C-311/18, *Facebook Ireland Limited*.
[148] Ibid., containing one of the following questions referred to the CJEU: 'For the purposes of Article 25(6) of the Directive, does Decision (EU) 2016/1250⁴ ("the Privacy Shield Decision") constitute a finding of general application binding on data protection authorities and the courts of the member states to the effect that the

Infringements of Articles 44–49 are subject to the higher level of administrative fines under Article 83(5)(c) GDPR, i.e. up to € 20 million or 4 per cent of the total worldwide turnover of the preceding financial year, whichever is higher.

8. Adequacy decisions under the LED

The LED also allows adequacy decisions to be issued by the Commission in the area of law enforcement, which is outside the scope of the GDPR.[149] Under Article 36 LED, the Commission may issue adequacy decisions applying to a third country, a territory or one or more specified sectors within such third country, or an international organisation. The procedures and conditions for the issuance of adequacy decisions are based on those in Article 45 GDPR, with several differences. Of particular significance is the requirement that the third country or international organisation be subject to an 'independent supervisory authority' (Article 36(2)(b) LED), which may be difficult for foreign law enforcement authorities to meet since independent data protection authorities are a specific feature of EU data protection law that is not replicated in all other legal systems.

Select Bibliography

International agreements

Aviation Convention 1944: Convention on Civil Aviation 1944, 15 U.N.T.S. 295.
EEA Agreement: Agreement on the European Economic Area, OJ 1994 L 1/3.
EEA Decision 2018: Decision of the EEA Joint Committee No 154/2018 of 6 July 2018 amending Annex XI (Electronic communication, audiovisual services and information society) and Protocol 37 (containing the list provided for in Article 101) to the EEA Agreement [2018/1022], OJ 2018 L 183/23.

EU legislation

Commission Decision 2016/2295: Commission Implementing Decision (EU) 2016/2295 of 16 December 2016 amending Decisions 2000/518/EC, 2002/2/EC, 2003/490/EC, 2003/821/EC, 2004/411/EC, 2008/393/EC, 2010/146/EU, 2010/625/EU, 2011/61/EU and Implementing Decisions 2012/484/EU, 2013/65/EU on the adequate protection of personal data by certain countries, pursuant to Article 25(6) of Directive 95/46/EC of the European Parliament and of the Council (notified under document C(2016) 8353), OJ 2016 L 344/83.
Commission Decision Andorra 2010: Commission Decision of 19 October 2010 pursuant to Directive 95/46/EC of the European Parliament and of the Council on the adequate protection of personal data in Andorra, OJ 2010 L 277/27.
Commission Decision Argentina 2003: Commission Decision 2003/1731 of 30 June 2003 pursuant to Directive (EC) 95/46 of the European Parliament and of the Council on the adequate protection of personal data in Argentina, OJ 2003 L 168/19.
Commission Decision Canada 2006: Commission Decision of 6 September 2005 on the adequate protection of personal data contained in the Passenger Name Record of air passengers transferred to the Canada Border Services Agency, 2006 OJ L 91/49.

US ensures an adequate level of protection within the meaning of Article 25(2) of the Directive by reason of its domestic law or of the international commitments it has entered into?'.

[149] See Art. 2(2)(d) GDPR.

Commission Decision Faroe Islands 2010: Commission Decision of 5 March 2010 pursuant to Directive 95/46/EC of the European Parliament and of the Council on the adequate protection provided by the Faeroese Act on the processing of personal data, OJ 2010 L 58/17.

Commission Decision Guernsey 2003: Commission Decision 2003/821 of 21 November 2003 on the adequate protection of personal data in Guernsey, OJ 2003 L 308/27.

Commission Decision Isle of Man 2004: Commission Decision 2004/411 of 28 April 2004 on the adequate protection of personal data in the Isle of Man, OJ 2004 L 151/1.

Commission Decision Israel 2011: Commission Decision 2011/61/EU of 31 January 2011 pursuant to Directive 95/46/EC of the European Parliament and of the Council on the adequate protection of personal data by the State of Israel with regard to automated processing of personal data, OJ 2011 L 27/39.

Commission Decision Japan 2019: Commission Implementing Decision (EU) 2019/419 of 23 January 2019 pursuant to Regulation (EU) 2016/679 of the European Parliament and of the Council on the adequate protection of personal data by Japan under the Act on the Protection of Personal Information, OJ 2019 L 76/1.

Commission Decision Jersey 2008: Commission Decision of 8 May 2008 pursuant to Directive 95/46/EC of the European Parliament and of the Council on the adequate protection of personal data in Jersey, OJ 2008 L 138/21.

Commission Decision New Zealand 2013: Commission Implementing Decision of 19 December 2012 pursuant to Directive 95/46/EC of the European Parliament and of the Council on the adequate protection of personal data by New Zealand, OJ 2013 L 28/12.

Commission Decision PIPEDA 2002: Commission Decision (EC) 2002/2 of 20 December 2001 pursuant to Directive (EC) 95/46 of the European Parliament and of the Council on the adequate protection of personal data provided by the Canadian Personal Information Protection and Electronic Documents Act, OJ 2002 L 2/13.

Commission Decision Privacy Shield 2016: Commission Implementing Decision (EU) 2016/1250 of 12 July 2016 pursuant to Directive 95/46/EC of the European Parliament and of the Council on the adequacy of the protection provided by the EU-U.S. Privacy Shield, OJ 2016 L 207/1.

Commission Decision Switzerland 2000: Commission Decision of 26 July 2000 pursuant to Directive 95/46/EC of the European Parliament and of the Council on the adequate protection of personal data provided in Switzerland, OJ 2000 L215/1.

Commission Decision Uruguay 2012: Commission Implementing Decision of 21 August 2012 pursuant to Directive 95/46/EC of the European Parliament and of the Council on the adequate protection of personal data by the Eastern Republic of Uruguay with regard to automated processing of personal data, OJ 2012 L 227/11.

Commission Decision US 2004: Commission Decision of 14 May 2004 on the adequate protection of personal data contained in the Passenger Name Record of air passengers transferred to the United States' Bureau of Customs and Border Protection, OJ 2004 L 235/11.

Decision of the EEA Joint Committee: Decision of the EEA Joint Committee, No 154/2018 of 6 July 2018 amending Annex XI (Electronic communication, audiovisual services and information society) and Protocol 37 (containing the list provided for in Article 101) to the EEA Agreement [2018/1022], OJ 2018 L183/23.

EP Request Opinion 1/15: Request for an opinion submitted by the European Parliament pursuant to Article 218(11) TFEU (Opinion 1/15), OJ 2015 C 138/24.

Proposal PNR Canada 2013: Proposal for a Council Decision on Conclusion of the Agreement between Canada and the European Union on the Transfer and Processing of Passenger Name Record Data, COM/2013/0528 final.

Regulation 182/2011: Regulation (EU) No. 182/2011 of the European Parliament and of the Council of 16 February 2011 laying down the rules and general principles concerning mechanisms for control by Member States of the Commission's exercise of implementing powers, OJ 2011 L 55/13.

Safe Harbour 2000: European Commission Decision 2000/520 of 26 July 2000 pursuant to Directive 95/46 of the European Parliament and of the Council on the adequacy of the protection provided by the safe harbor privacy principles and related frequently asked questions issued by the US Department of Commerce, OJ 2000 L 215/7 (annulled).

Umbrella Agreement US: Agreement on the Protection of Personal Information Relating to the Prevention, Investigation, Detection and Prosecution of Criminal Offenses, OJ 2017 L 336/3.

National legislation

German GDPR Implementation Law: Gesetz zur Anpassung des Datenschutzrechts an die Verordnung (EU) 2016/679 und zur Umsetzung der Richtlinie (EU) 2016/680 (Datenschutz-Anpassungs- und Umsetzungsgesetz EU – DsAnpUG-EU), BGBl 2017 Teil 1 Nr. 44.

Academic writings

Bing, 'Transnational Data Flows and the Scandinavian Data Protection Legislation', 24 *Scandinavian Studies in Law* (1980), 65.

Bygrave, *Data Privacy Law: An International Perspective* (OUP 2014).

Docksey 2014: Docksey, 'The European Court of Justice and the Decade of Surveillance', in Hijmans and Kranenborg (eds.), *Data Protection Anno 2014: How to Restore Trust?* (Intersentia 2014), 97.

González Fuster 2016: González Fuster, 'Un-Mapping Personal Data Transfers', 2(2) *European Data Protection Law Review* (2016), 160.

Hondius, 'A Decade of International Data Protection', 30(2) *Netherlands International Law Review* (1983), 103.

Kirby, 'Transborder Data Flows and the "Basic Rules of Data Privacy"', 16(2) *Stanford Journal of International Law* (1980), 27.

Kuner 2017: Kuner, 'Reality and Illusion in EU Data Transfer Regulation Post *Schrems*', 18(4) *German Law Journal* (2017), 881.

Kuner 2018: Kuner, 'International Agreements, Data Protection, and EU Fundamental Rights on the International Stage: Opinion 1/15', 55(3) *Common Market Law Review* (2018), 857.

Kuner 2019: Kuner, 'International Organizations and the EU General Data Protection Regulation: Exploring the Interaction between EU Law and International Law', 16 *International Organizations Law Review* (2019),158.

Kuner, *European Data Protection Law: Corporate Compliance and Regulation* (2nd edn., OUP 2007).

Kuner, *Transborder Data Flow Regulation and Data Privacy Law* (OUP 2013).

Lenaerts, Maselis and Gutman 2014: Lenaerts, Maselis and Gutman, *EU Procedural Law* (OUP 2014) (Kindle edition).

Schwartz, 'European Data Protection Law and Restrictions on International Data Flows', 80(3) *Iowa Law Review* (1995), 471.

Shaffer, 'Reconciling Trade and Regulatory Goals: Prospects and Limits of New Approaches to Transatlantic Governance through Mutual Recognition and Safe Harbour Agreements', 9(1) *Columbia Journal of European Law* (2002), 29.

Simitis and Dammann 1997: Simitis and Dammann, *EU-Datenschutzrichtlinie* (Nomos-Verlag 1997).

Stoddart, Chan and Joly 2016: Stoddart, Chan and Joly, 'The European Union's Adequacy Approach to Privacy and International Data Sharing in Health Research', 44(1) *The Journal of Law, Medicine & Ethics* (2016), 143.

Swire and Litan, *None of Your Business: World Data Flows, Electronic Commerce, and the European Privacy Directive* (Brookings Institution Press 1998).

Wickremasinghe 2012: Wickremasinghe, 'International Organizations or Institutions, Immunities before National Courts', in Wolfrum (ed.), *The Max Planck Encyclopedia of Public International Law Vol. VI* (OUP 2012), 10.

Wochner, *Der Persönlichkeitsschutz im grenzüberschreitenden Datenverkehr* (Schulthess Polygraphischer Verlag 1981).

Papers of data protection authorities

EDPB Brexit information note: EDPB, 'Information Note on Data Transfers under the GDPR in the Event of a No-Deal Brexit' (12 February 2019).

EDPB Endorsement: European Data Protection Board, 'Endorsement 1/2018' (25 May 2018).

EDPB 2018: European Data Protection Board, 'Opinion 28/2018 Regarding the European Commission Draft Implementing Decision on the Adequate Protection of Personal Data in Japan' (5 December 2018).

EDPS 2016: European Data Protection Supervisor, 'Opinion 1/2016: Preliminary Opinion on the Agreement between the United States of America and the European Union on the Protection of Personal Information Relating to the Prevention, Investigation, Detection and Prosecution of Criminal Offences' (12 February 2016).

WP29 1997: Article 29 Working Party, 'First Orientations on Transfers of Personal Data to Third Countries—Possible Ways Forward in Assessing Adequacy' (WP 4, 26 June 1997).

WP29 1998: Article 29 Working Party, 'Working Document: Transfers of Personal Data to Third Countries: Applying Articles 25 and 26 of the EU Data Protection Directive' (WP 12, 24 July 1998).

WP29 2012: Article 29 Working Party, 'Opinion on the level of protection of personal data in the Principality of Monaco' (WP 198, 19 July 2012).

WP29 2016: Article 29 Working Party, 'Working Document 01/2016 on the Justification of Interferences with the Fundamental Rights to Privacy and Data Protection through Surveillance Measures when Transferring Personal Data (European Essential Guarantees)' (WP 237, 13 April 2016).

WP29 2017: Article 29 Working Party, 'Adequacy Referential (updated)' (WP 254, 28 November 2017).

ICO 2018: UK Information Commissioner, 'International Data Transfers', available at https://ico.org.uk/for-organisations/data-protection-and-brexit/data-protection-if-there-s-no-brexit-deal/the-gdpr/international-data-transfers/.

Reports and recommendations

Commission Staff Working Document 2006: Commission Staff Working Document: The application of Commission Decision 2002/2/EC of 20 December 2001 pursuant to Directive 95/46/EC of the European Parliament and of the Council on the adequate protection of personal data provided by the Canadian Personal Information Protection and Electronic Documentation Act', SEC(2006) 1520, 20 November 2006.

EC Communication 2017A: Communication from the Commission to the European Parliament and the Council, 'Exchanging and Protection Personal Data in a Globalised World', COM(2017) 7 final, 10 January 2017.

EP Resolution 2014: European Parliament resolution of 25 November 2014 on seeking an opinion from the Court of Justice on the compatibility with the Treaties of the Agreement between Canada and the European Union on the transfer and processing of Passenger Name Record data, 2014/2966(RSP), 25 November 2014.

Others

Commission Brexit Preparedness Notice: European Commission, 'Notice to Stakeholders: Withdrawal of the United Kingdom from the Union and EU Rules in the Field of Data

Protection', 9 January 2018, available at https://ec.europa.eu/info/sites/info/files/file_import/data_protection_en.pdf.

EFTA 2017: European Free Trade Association, 'Overview of Adopted EEA Joint Committee Decisions and EU Acts Contained Therein' (11 September 2017), available at https://www.efta.int/sites/default/files/documents/legal-texts/eea/other-legal-documents/List-Adopted-Joint-Committee-Decisions/2017%20List%20of%20Adopted%20Joint%20Committee%20Decisions.pdf .

EU–Japan Joint Statement 2019: Personal Information Protection Commission, 'Joint Statement by Haruhi Kumazawa, Commissioner of the Personal Information Protection Commission of Japan and Věra Jourová, Commissioner for Justice, Consumers and Gender Equality of the European Commission' (23 January 2019), available at https://www.ppc.go.jp/files/pdf/310123_pressstatement_en.pdf.

EU–UK Political Declaration: Council of the European Union, 'Outline of the Political Declaration Setting out the Framework for the Future Relationship between the European Union and the United Kingdom', 22 November 2018, available at https://www.consilium.europa.eu/media/37059/20181121-cover-political-declaration.pdf.

Hanke 2017: Hanke, 'EU Trade, the Martin Selmayr Way', *POLITICO* (7 November 2017), available at https://www.politico.eu/article/eu-trade-the-martin-selmayr-way/.

Ihle 2010: Ihle, 'Ireland Blocks EU Data Sharing with Israel', *JTA* (8 July 2010), available at http://www.jta.org/2010/07/08/news-opinion/world/ireland-blocks-eu-data-sharing-with-israel.

Lenaerts speech 2018: Lenaerts, 'The EU General Data Protection Regulation Five Months On', speech by CJEU President Koen Lenaerts at the 40th International Conference of Data Protection and Privacy Commissioners (25 October 2018), available at https://www.youtube.com/watch?v=fZaKPaGbXNg.

Press Release PNR Canada 2014: Council of the European Union, 'Press Release: Signature of the EU–Canada Agreement on Passenger Name Records (PNR)' (25 June 2014).

Privacy Shield Press Release December 2018: European Commission, 'Press Release: EU–U.S. Privacy Shield: Second Review Shows Improvements but a Permanent Ombudsperson Should Be Nominated by 28 February 2019' (19 December 2018).

Article 46. Transfers subject to appropriate safeguards

CHRISTOPHER KUNER

1. In the absence of a decision pursuant to Article 45(3), a controller or processor may transfer personal data to a third country or an international organisation only if the controller or processor has provided appropriate safeguards, and on condition that enforceable data subject rights and effective legal remedies for data subjects are available.
2. The appropriate safeguards referred to in paragraph 1 may be provided for, without requiring any specific authorisation from a supervisory authority, by:
   (a) a legally binding and enforceable instrument between public authorities or bodies;
   (b) binding corporate rules in accordance with Article 47;
   (c) standard data protection clauses adopted by the Commission in accordance with the examination procedure referred to in Article 93(2);
   (d) standard data protection clauses adopted by a supervisory authority and approved by the Commission pursuant to the examination procedure referred to in Article 93(2);
   (e) an approved code of conduct pursuant to Article 40 together with binding and enforceable commitments of the controller or processor in the third country to apply the appropriate safeguards, including as regards data subjects' rights; or
   (f) an approved certification mechanism pursuant to Article 42 together with binding and enforceable commitments of the controller or processor in the third country to apply the appropriate safeguards, including as regards data subjects' rights.
3. Subject to the authorisation from the competent supervisory authority, the appropriate safeguards referred to in paragraph 1 may also be provided for, in particular, by:
   (a) contractual clauses between the controller or processor and the controller, processor or the recipient of the personal data in the third country or international organisation; or
   (b) provisions to be inserted into administrative arrangements between public authorities or bodies which include enforceable and effective data subject rights.
4. The supervisory authority shall apply the consistency mechanism referred to in Article 63 in the cases referred to in paragraph 3 of this Article.
5. Authorisations by a Member State or supervisory authority on the basis of Article 26(2) of Directive 95/46/EC shall remain valid until amended, replaced or repealed, if necessary, by that supervisory authority. Decisions adopted by the Commission on the basis of Article 26(4) of Directive 95/46/EC shall remain in force until amended, replaced or repealed, if necessary, by a Commission Decision adopted in accordance with paragraph 2 of this Article.

Relevant Recitals

(108) In the absence of an adequacy decision, the controller or processor should take measures to compensate for the lack of data protection in a third country by way of appropriate safeguards for the data subject. Such appropriate safeguards may consist of making use of binding corporate rules, standard data protection clauses adopted by the Commission, standard data protection clauses adopted by a supervisory authority or contractual clauses authorised by a supervisory authority. Those safeguards should ensure compliance with data protection requirements and the rights of the data subjects appropriate to processing within the Union, including the availability of enforceable data subject rights and of effective legal remedies, including to obtain effective administrative or judicial redress and to claim compensation, in the Union or in a third country. They should relate

in particular to compliance with the general principles relating to personal data processing, the principles of data protection by design and by default. Transfers may also be carried out by public authorities or bodies with public authorities or bodies in third countries or with international organisations with corresponding duties or functions, including on the basis of provisions to be inserted into administrative arrangements, such as a memorandum of understanding, providing for enforceable and effective rights for data subjects. Authorisation by the competent supervisory authority should be obtained when the safeguards are provided for in administrative arrangements that are not legally binding.

(109) The possibility for the controller or processor to use standard data-protection clauses adopted by the Commission or by a supervisory authority should prevent controllers or processors neither from including the standard data-protection clauses in a wider contract, such as a contract between the processor and another processor, nor from adding other clauses or additional safeguards provided that they do not contradict, directly or indirectly, the standard contractual clauses adopted by the Commission or by a supervisory authority or prejudice the fundamental rights or freedoms of the data subjects. Controllers and processors should be encouraged to provide additional safeguards via contractual commitments that supplement standard protection clauses.

(114) In any case, where the Commission has taken no decision on the adequate level of data protection in a third country, the controller or processor should make use of solutions that provide data subjects with enforceable and effective rights as regards the processing of their data in the Union once those data have been transferred so that that they will continue to benefit from fundamental rights and safeguards.

Closely Related Provisions

Recital 6; Article 15(2) (Right to access information about appropriate safeguards pursuant to Article 46); Article 44 (General principles for transfers); Article 58(3)(g)–(h) (Powers of supervisory authorities to adopt standard contractual clauses and authorise contractual clauses); Article 64(1)(d)(e) (Opinion of the Board regarding determination of standard data protection clauses and authorisation of contractual clauses)

Related Provisions in LED [Directive (EU) 2016/680]

Recital 36; Article 37 (transfers subject to appropriate safeguards) (see too recital 71)

Relevant Case Law

CJEU

Case C-617/10, *Åkerberg Fransson*, judgment of 26 February 2013 (ECLI:EU:C:2013:105).
Case C-362/14, *Maximillian Schrems v Data Protection Commissioner*, judgment of 6 October 2015 (Grand Chamber) (ECLI:EU:C:2015:650).
Case C-311/18, *Data Protection Commissioner v Facebook Ireland Limited, Maximillian Schrems* (pending).

Ireland

Data Protection Commissioner and Facebook Ireland Limited and Maximilian Schrems, Irish High Court, 2016 No. 4809 P, 3 October 2017.
Judgment of Mr Justice Clark, Irish Supreme Court, 2018 No. 2018/68, 31 July 2018.

A. Rationale and Policy Underpinnings

Article 46 GDPR provides that when an adequacy decision has not been issued under Article 45(3), a controller or processor may transfer personal data to a third country or an international organisation only if it has provided appropriate safeguards,[1] and on the condition that enforceable data subject rights and effective legal remedies for data subjects are available. Such appropriate safeguards are based not on a detailed evaluation of the legal system of the country or international organisation to which the data are to be transferred, as is the case when an adequacy decision has been issued under Article 45, but on a set of protections that apply to the particular data transfer or set of transfers. The rules of Article 46 build and expand on those of Article 26 DPD. The multi-tiered structure of Chapter V means that if an adequacy decision[2] has been issued then that should be relied on; if not, then appropriate safeguards may be used.

B. Legal Background

1. EU legislation

Article 26(2) DPD allowed data transfers to be carried out absent adequate protection in the third country or international organisation to which personal data are transferred 'where the controller adduces adequate safeguards with respect to the protection of the privacy and fundamental rights and freedoms of individuals and as regards the exercise of the corresponding rights; such safeguards may in particular result from appropriate contractual clauses'. Under the DPD, two main types of 'adequate safeguards' were recognised, namely contractual clauses and binding corporate rules ('BCRs', though they were not mentioned explicitly in the DPD). The GDPR maintains and expands the concept of adequate safeguards, which it renames 'appropriate safeguards'.

Contractual clauses are concluded between the data exporter in the EU and the data importer outside the EU to whom the data are sent and contain obligations on each to provide certain protections to the personal data. They can either be 'standard contractual clauses', the text of which is standardised and adopted by a formal decision of the European Commission or by a DPA with approval of the Commission, or 'ad hoc' clauses that are drafted in each specific case and must be approved by the DPAs before use. BCRs are internal, legally binding data protection rules that are adopted by a company or companies; since they are dealt with in detail in Article 47 in this volume, they will not be discussed further here.[3]

Contractual clauses were the type of adequate safeguards that were most used under the DPD.[4] The history of the standard contractual clauses began in 1992, when the Council of Europe, European Commission and International Chamber of Commerce ('ICC') jointly approved a set of model clauses for international data

---

[1] This is the language used in Art. 46(1) GDPR; of course, data transfers may also be made using the derogations, as discussed in the commentary on Art. 49 in this volume.
[2] See the commentary on Art. 45 in this volume.
[3] See the commentary on Art. 47 in this volume.
[4] See, regarding the use of contractual clauses under the DPD, Kuner 2007, pp. 191–210; Kuner 2013, pp. 43–44.

transfers.[5] While this contract was never formally approved by the Commission, it served as inspiration for later work to draft model clauses. In 2001, the Commission approved a set of standard contractual clauses for controller to controller transfers,[6] and a set of standard contractual clauses for controller to processor transfers later the same year.[7] The Commission then entered into consultations with a coalition of various business groups led by the ICC[8] and approved an alternative set of controller to controller clauses in 2004,[9] and an alternative set of controller to processor clauses in 2010.[10] The 2004 controller to controller clauses apply in addition to those adopted in 2001 (i.e. either set can be used for controller to controller transfers), while the 2010 controller to processor clauses replace those adopted earlier (i.e. the 2001 controller to processor clauses were repealed by the 2010 set).[11]

In 2016 the Commission adopted a decision amending the 2001 controller to controller clauses and the 2010 controller to processor clauses to take into account the *Schrems*[12] judgment of the CJEU.[13] The 2016 decision replaces Article 4 of each of the two sets of clauses with the following text:

Whenever the competent authorities in Member States exercise their powers ... leading to the suspension or definitive ban of data flows to third countries in order to protect individuals with regard to the processing of their personal data, the Member State concerned shall, without delay, inform the Commission, which will forward the information to the other Member States.

However, this decision of 2016 does not make reference to the third standard clauses decision that is still in force (Commission Decision 2004/915). Perhaps this was found unnecessary since Decision 2004/915 merely amends Decision 2001/497,[14] but a reference could have been made to the 2004 decision, if only to note that it amended the earlier 2001 decision, particularly since the 2004 decision includes a new set of model clauses in the Annex.

Article 46 also adds four new forms of appropriate safeguards to those contained in the DPD, namely a legally binding and enforceable instrument between public authorities or bodies; an approved code of conduct together with binding and enforceable commitments of the controller or processor; an approved certification mechanism together with binding and enforceable commitments; and provisions to be inserted into administrative arrangements between public authorities or bodies.

2. International instruments

The EEA is comprised of the EU Member States plus Iceland, Liechtenstein and Norway, which three countries together plus Switzerland comprise the EFTA. The EEA Agreement, as amended in July 2018,[15] incorporates the GDPR into its Annexes and provides that

---

[5] Data Flow Model Contract 1992.   [6] EC Standard Contractual Clauses 2001.
[7] EC Standard Contractual Clauses Processors 2001.
[8] The author led negotiations on behalf of the ICC and the business groups.
[9] EC Standard Contractual Clauses 2004. See Kuner 2005, p. 2; Kuner and Hladjk 2005.
[10] EC Standard Contractual Clauses Processors 2010. See Kuner 2010, p. 1.
[11] See EC Standard Contractual Clauses Processors 2010, rec. 25, stating that 'Decision 2002/16/EC should be repealed'.
[12] Case C-362/14, *Schrems*. See the commentary on Art. 45 in this volume for a detailed explanation of the judgment.
[13] EC Standard Contractual Clauses Processors 2016.
[14] EC Standard Contractual Clauses 2004, p. 1.   [15] EEA Decision 2018.

the provisions of the GDPR should be read, for the purposes of that Agreement, with a number of adaptations affecting the three EEA/EFTA States[16] and the EFTA Surveillance Authority. In this respect, the amended EEA Agreement provides that, as regards the EFTA States, the following text shall be inserted in Article 46(2)(d) GDPR: 'The supervisory authorities of the EFTA States shall have the same right as EU supervisory authorities to submit standard data protection clauses to the Commission for approval pursuant to the examination procedure referred to in Article 93(2)'.[17] In addition, the amended Agreement states that as regards the EFTA States, the following paragraph shall be inserted after Article 46(2) GDPR:[18]

2a. Pending a decision by the EEA Joint Committee to incorporate into the EEA Agreement an implementing act, the appropriate safeguards referred to in paragraph 1 may be provided for by standard data protection clauses referred to in points (c) and (d) of Article 46(2) where an EFTA State applies the measures contained therein.

Each EFTA State shall decide and inform the Commission and the EFTA Surveillance Authority, before the entry into force of implementing acts adopted pursuant to points (c) and (d) of Article 46(2), whether it, pending a decision by the EEA Joint Committee to incorporate the implementing act into the EEA Agreement, will apply the measures contained therein at the same time as the EU Member States or not. In the absence of a decision to the contrary, each EFTA State shall apply the measures contained in an implementing act adopted pursuant to points (c) and (d) of Article 46(2) at the same time as the EU Member States.

Notwithstanding Article 102 of the Agreement, if an agreement on the incorporation into the EEA Agreement of an implementing act adopted pursuant to points (c) and (d) of Article 46(2) cannot be reached in the EEA Joint Committee within twelve months of the entry into force of that implementing act, any EFTA State may discontinue the application of such measures and shall inform the Commission and the EFTA Surveillance Authority thereof without delay.

3. National developments

Under the DPD, approval of adequate safeguards by the competent data protection authority was required in a number of Member States, particularly for ad hoc contractual clauses and BCRs.[19] This is no longer the case under the GDPR with regard to use of standard contractual clauses approved either by the Commission alone (Article 46(2)(c)) or adopted by a DPA and then approved by the Commission (Article 46(2)(d)). Approval of custom-drafted (ad hoc) contractual clauses by the competent DPA is still required under the GDPR (Article 46(3)), with its determination subject to the consistency mechanism referred to in Article 63 (Article 46(4) GDPR). The competent DPA is determined under Article 55. Adoption by the Commission of standard contractual clauses, and approval by the Commission of standard clauses adopted by DPAs, are both carried out under the examination procedure referred to in Article 93(2) (Article 46(2)(c)–(d) GDPR). Adoption by a DPA of its own standard contractual clauses or of ad hoc contractual clauses requires an opinion of the EDPB (Article 64(1)(d)–(e)).

---

[16] Switzerland, the fourth EFTA State, is not a signatory to the EEA.
[17] Art. 5e(m) EEA Decision 2018.   [18] Ibid.
[19] See Kuner 2007, Appendix 12, regarding national filing requirements for the standard contractual clauses under the DPD.

4. Case law

There are no judgments of the CJEU or the ECtHR dealing with the subject-matter of Article 46. However, on 12 April 2018 the Irish High Court[20] referred to the CJEU[21] a series of questions that could put in doubt the use of both the existing standard contractual clauses[22] and the use of standard contractual clauses to transfer personal data in general.[23] The Irish Supreme Court then subsequently granted Facebook leave to appeal the referral to the CJEU,[24] but the challenge was ultimately unsuccessful. The case was still pending when this text was finalised.

C. Analysis

1. Introduction

The use of appropriate safeguards allows the transfer of personal data when no adequacy decision has been issued by the Commission regarding a country or international organisation (including a territory or one or more specified sectors within that third country as specified in the decision). The GDPR does not contain a concise definition of 'appropriate safeguards', but describes them as follows in recital 108:

Those safeguards should ensure compliance with data protection requirements and the rights of the data subjects appropriate to processing within the Union, including the availability of enforceable data subject rights and of effective legal remedies, including to obtain effective administrative or judicial redress and to claim compensation, in the Union or in a third country. They should relate in particular to compliance with the general principles relating to personal data processing, the principles of data protection by design and by default.

Appropriate safeguards are more limited in scope than an adequacy decision, which is issued based on the totality of conditions in the third country or international organisation, including such factors as the rule of law, respect for human rights and other factors that relate to the legal system as a whole. By contrast, appropriate safeguards are tailored to particular transfers or types of transfers. Thus, appropriate safeguards cannot provide protection against certain data protection risks that must be taken into account when an adequacy decision is issued (e.g. access to the data by public authorities in the country to which the data are transferred, as provided for in Article 45(2) GDPR). The provisions of Article 46 must be read in light of Charter, since, as the CJEU has found, the applicability of EU law entails the applicability of the Charter.[25]

The list of appropriate safeguards provided for in Article 46 is not exclusive (this follows from the words 'may be provided for'). As recital 109 makes clear, this means that

---

[20] Irish High Court, *Data Protection Commissioner and Facebook Ireland Limited and Maximilian Schrems*.
[21] Case C-311/18, *Facebook Ireland Limited*.
[22] Ibid., which raises as one of the questions whether the EC Standard Contractual Clauses Processors 2010 violate Arts. 7, 8 or 47 of the Charter of Fundamental Rights of the European Union ('CFR').
[23] Case C-311/18, *Facebook Ireland Limited*, which raises as one of the questions 'Does the fact that the standard contractual clauses apply as between the data exporter and the data importer and do not bind the national authorities of a third country who may require the data importer to make available to its security services for further processing the personal data transferred pursuant to the clauses provided for in the SCC Decision preclude the clauses from adducing adequate safeguards as envisaged by Article 26(2) of the Directive?'
[24] Irish Supreme Court, *Judgment of Mr Justice Clark*.
[25] See Case C-617/10, *Åkerberg Fransson*, para. 21. See also Rauchegger 2015.

nothing in the GDPR prevents the parties to a data transfer from providing extra protection beyond what the GDPR requires, so that its provisions regarding data transfers should be seen as providing a floor of protection rather than a ceiling. Recital 114 also invites parties involved in data transfers to make use of innovative solutions to protect them beyond those listed in the GDPR.[26]

Additional safeguards should provide 'enforceable data subject rights and effective legal remedies for data subjects'.[27] Recital 108 also states that any appropriate safeguards 'should relate in particular to compliance with the general principles relating to personal data processing, the principles of data protection by design and by default', which may refer to the principles of Article 5 GDPR.

As explained above, under a decision of the EEA Joint Committee, 'pending a decision by the EEA Joint Committee to incorporate into the EEA Agreement an implementing act, the appropriate safeguards referred to in paragraph 1 may be provided for by standard data protection clauses referred to in points (c) and (d) of Article 46(2) where an EFTA State applies the measures contained therein'.[28] This means that EEA controllers or EEA processors may use standard data protection clauses, unless an EEA or EFTA State decides not to apply the measure at the same time as the EU Member States.[29]

The Commission has taken the view informally that the GDPR does not directly apply to international organisations,[30] but that they must comply with the GDPR's rules affecting data importers when they receive personal data transferred from the EU.[31]

On 29 March 2017, the UK invoked Article 50 of the Treaty on European Union ('TEU') and indicated its intention to leave the EU, at which point it will become a third country by operation of law ('Brexit') and all Union primary and secondary law will cease to apply to the UK.[32] The EDPB[33] and the UK Information Commissioner[34] have published guidance for dealing with international data transfers post-Brexit, including the use of appropriate safeguards.

2. Harmonisation

Under the principle of the primacy of EU law over national law,[35] data transfers under national systems that do not comply with the requirements of Article 46 are not allowed under the GDPR. Thus, for example, the prior system in the UK whereby parties transferring personal data under the DPD were able to determine on their own whether the contractual clauses they put in place provided sufficient safeguards, with the UK ICO refusing to review them or issue authorisation of such transfers absent 'exceptional circumstances',[36] is no longer viable under the GDPR, given the requirement in Article 46(3)(a) that ad hoc contractual clauses be authorised by the competent DPA.

---

[26] See also rec. 113, stating 'Controllers and processors should be encouraged to provide additional safeguards via contractual commitments that supplement standard protection clauses'.
[27] Art. 46(1) GDPR.   [28] EEA Agreement, Annex XI, Art. 5e(m), p. 13.
[29] Art. 5e(h) EEA Decision 2018.
[30] See the commentary on Art. 4(26) in this volume regarding the definition of international organisation.
[31] See the commentary on Art. 44 in this volume. See also Kuner 2019.
[32] Commission Brexit Preparedness Notice, p. 1.   [33] EDPB Brexit information note.
[34] ICO 2018. See also the commentary on Art. 47 in this volume regarding the legal status of binding corporate rules (BCRs) post-Brexit.
[35] See Rosas and Armati 2012, p. 15.   [36] See ICO 2017.

The regime for appropriate safeguards under Article 46 is designed to remedy the fragmented legal situation that existed under Article 26 DPD, pursuant to which, for example, some DPAs required authorisation of the use of the Commission-approved standard contractual clauses and some did not. Article 46(2) GDPR provides that the following forms of appropriate safeguards do not require further authorisation by a DPA: 'a legally binding and enforceable instrument between public authorities or bodies'; binding corporate rules; standard contractual clauses adopted by the Commission; standard clauses adopted by a DPA and approved by the Commission; approved codes of conduct; and approved certification mechanisms. Under Article 46(2), standard contractual clauses are adopted by the Commission and standard clauses adopted by a DPA are approved by the Commission pursuant to the examination procedure under Article 93(2), which refers to Article 5 of the so-called Comitology Regulation.[37]

However, under Article 46(3), other appropriate safeguards do require DPA authorisation. This includes ad hoc contractual clauses, and provisions to be inserted into administrative arrangements between public authorities, authorisation for both of which must be obtained based on the consistency mechanism under Article 63 GDPR.

Some Member States have imposed formal requirements on the use of appropriate safeguards such as contractual clauses; for example, some of them have required that the signatures of data exporters and data importers to standard contractual clauses be notarised. The primacy of EU law is to be broadly construed,[38] which means that any requirement of Member State law or practice that would in effect result in the DPA needing to approve use of the standard clauses should no longer be permissible under the GDPR.

3. Other requirements

The transfer of personal data based on appropriate safeguards is subject to compliance with all other requirements for data processing besides those concerning international data transfers (this follows from Article 44). This includes in particular, but not exclusively, provisions of the GDPR specifically relevant to international data transfers under Article 46, for example the obligation to inform data subjects that data are to be transferred internationally (Articles 13(1)(e)–(f), 14(1)(e)–(f), 15(1)(c) and 15(2)); duties of data processors (Article 28(3)(a)); and the obligation to keep records concerning data processing (Article 30(1)(d)–(e) and (2)(c)). Also, contractual clauses to transfer personal data under Article 46 should not be confused with contractual clauses mentioned in the GDPR to be used for other purposes (e.g. Article 28(3) GDPR, which requires that processing by a data processor be carried out based on a written contract[39]).

4. Prior authorisations under the DPD

Under Article 46(5) GDPR, authorisations issued by a Member State or supervisory authority on the basis of Article 26(2) DPD (such as regarding ad hoc contractual clauses or BCRs) remain in effect, as do decisions adopted by the Commission on the basis of Article 26(4) DPD (such as concerning standard contractual clauses). Thus, data transfers may continue to be carried out under such instruments. The competent DPA may amend, replace or repeal authorisations granted on the basis of Article 26(2) DPD, but

---

[37] Regulation 182/2011. [38] See Lenaerts and Corthaut 2006, p. 289.
[39] See EDPB 2019C, p. 10.

does not have to, just as the Commission may (but need not) amend, replace or repeal decisions it adopted under Article 26(4) DPD. Any amendment, replacement or repeal of Commission decisions must be carried out in accordance with the examination procedure referred to in Article 93(2) (as provided in Article 46(2)). Unlike the case with adequacy decisions, there is no requirement for periodic review of the standard contractual clauses, but it can be expected that the Commission will in time adopt new sets of them to replace those approved under the DPD, and possibly also clauses dealing with further data processing situations (such as with regard to processor-to-processor transfers). In June 2019 Commissioner Věra Jourová of DG Justice announced publicly that the Commission was 'already working to modernise standard contractual clauses'.[40]

5. Practical use of contractual clauses

The GDPR does not contain requirements as to how contractual clauses, whether standard or otherwise, should be signed, beyond stating that parties may include contractual clauses 'in a wider contract, such as a contract between the processor and another processor' (recital 109). This gives the parties considerable latitude in determining how to implement them in practice, e.g. by signing them separately, incorporating them into an existing contract or otherwise.

Parties may attempt to organise their signature of contractual clauses (whether the standard ones or otherwise) based on their corporate structure. For example, if Company A and Company B are both data exporters in the EU, and Company B is a subsidiary of Company A, then the question may arise as to whether Company A may sign the clauses as a data exporter also on behalf of Company B. Furthermore, the question may also arise as to whether Company B may grant a power of attorney ('POA') to Company A to sign on its behalf. Similar questions may arise with regard to signature of the clauses by data importers.

Signature of the clauses is based on a party's status either as a data exporter or a data importer, and not on its particular status under company or corporate law. Thus, the fact that Company B may be a subsidiary of Company A is not relevant with regard to signature of the clauses: if Company A and Company B are both data controllers, then they should both sign the clauses, and Company A may not sign on Company B's behalf merely because it stands higher in the corporate hierarchy. In such a situation it could be possible for Company B to grant a power of attorney to Company A and thus have it sign on Company B's behalf. However, the granting of powers of attorney is often fraught with difficulties under company law, particularly when the party to which a power of attorney is given is located outside the EU.

It can be difficult to decide which set of clauses to use (controller to controller or controller to processor), since it is not always clear whether the data importer is a controller or a processor. Parties signing the clauses will have to use their best judgment in deciding which types of clauses to use, based on the characterisation of the parties as data controllers or data processors under the GDPR.[41]

While the WP29 has issued a draft opinion on a proposed set of ad hoc contractual clauses for data transfers from EU data processors to non-EU sub-processors,[42] this has

---

[40] Jourová speech 2019.
[41] See the definition of these terms the commentary on Art. 4(20) in this volume.
[42] See WP29 2014.

not yet been officially approved by the Commission. However, recital 109 GDPR states that 'The possibility for the controller or processor to use standard data-protection clauses adopted by the Commission or by a supervisory authority should prevent controllers or processors neither from including the standard data-protection clauses in a wider contract, such as a contract between the processor and another processor ... ' Thus, parties may consider using one of the sets of standard contractual clauses in a processor-to-processor scenario as well.

The Commission-approved standard contractual clauses may not be amended in any way (i.e. they must be adopted verbatim),[43] aside from filling out the annexes. In practice, any amendment of the standard clauses means that they will be considered to be ad hoc clauses that require the authorisation of the competent DPA. However, the GDPR makes it clear that there is no prohibition against 'adding other clauses or additional safeguards provided that they do not contradict, directly or indirectly, the standard contractual clauses adopted by the Commission or by a supervisory authority or prejudice the fundamental rights or freedoms of the data subjects' (recital 109). Additional clauses are to be recommended in cases involving data transfers where there is a particularly high risk of the transfer or sensitivity of the data. In addition, parties often add further detail in documents annexed to the clauses in order to provide additional protections, such as through detailed data security requirements.[44]

6. New forms of appropriate safeguards

Article 46 also adds four new forms of appropriate safeguards for the transfer of personal data beyond those contained in the DPD, namely the following: 'a legally binding and enforceable instrument between public authorities or bodies' (Article 46(2)(a)); 'an approved code of conduct pursuant to Article 40 together with binding and enforceable commitments of the controller or processor in the third country to apply the appropriate safeguards, including as regards data subjects' rights' (Article 46(2)(e)); 'an approved certification mechanism pursuant to Article 42 together with binding and enforceable commitments of the controller or processor in the third country to apply the appropriate safeguards, including as regards data subjects' rights' (Article 46(2)(f)); and 'provisions to be inserted into administrative arrangements between public authorities or bodies which include enforceable and effective data subject rights' (Article 46(3)(b)). Each of these will now be considered in turn.

6.1 Legally binding and enforceable instruments

The reference to 'a legally binding and enforceable instrument between public authorities or bodies' (Article 46(2)(a)) allows data transfers based on enforceable legal instruments (such as contractual clauses) between public authorities or bodies in the EU and those in third countries. This could include, for example, an international agreement (i.e. a treaty) to share data between an EU-based public authority and one in a third country. Under Article 46(2), no DPA authorisation is required for the use of such an instrument.

---

[43] See e.g. EC Standard Contractual Clauses 2004, rec. 3, stating that 'data exporters should not, however, be allowed to amend these sets or totally or partially merge them in any manner'.

[44] See the commentary on Art. 32 in this volume.

6.2 Codes of conduct

The reference to 'an approved code of conduct' refers to a code drawn up by 'associations or other bodies' pursuant to Article 40.[45] The GDPR does not contain a definition of 'code of conduct'. That article contains a detailed list of provisions that a code of conduct must contain and how it must be adopted and implemented. Under Article 40(5), such a code must be approved by the competent DPA as determined by Article 55, which is confirmed by Article 46(2)(e) (referring to 'an approved code of conduct'); however, no further authorisation is required (Article 46(2)). Use of a code of conduct to transfer data requires 'binding and enforceable commitments of the controller or processor in the third country to apply the appropriate safeguards, including as regards data subjects' rights' (Article 46(2)(e)), indicating that it must be legally binding between the parties that have adopted it (for example, on a contractual level). The Commission may issue implementing acts finding that approved codes of conduct have general validity within the EU (Article 40(9)), though the GDPR does not explain what 'general validity' means in a legal sense (e.g. whether adherence to an approved code of conduct would lead to a presumption of compliance with the GDPR's provisions on international data transfers).

The Commission may also approve as having general validity codes of conduct adhered to by data controllers and data processors not subject to the GDPR (Article 40(3)); this could presumably include, for example, a trade association in a third country whose members are not subject to the GDPR but who want to make it easier for EU business partners to transfer personal data to them. Article 40(3) states that by having such a code approved under Article 40(5) and having it declared as having general validity under Article 40(9), such third country organisations would be providing 'appropriate safeguards within the framework of personal data transfers to third countries or international organisations under the terms referred to in point (e) of Article 46(2)'. However, Article 46(1) refers to appropriate safeguards that are provided by the data controller or data processor transferring personal data from the EU, not by the parties receiving the data, which seems to present a contradiction with Article 40(3). Even though this provision is explicitly designed to apply to data controllers and data processors not subject to the GDPR, once the relevant organizations adopt such a code they would be subject to the 'binding and enforceable commitments' (Article 40(3)) under the GDPR that they have to assume in order for the code to be approved. The EDPB has stated that it will prepare guidelines on codes of conduct as a tool for transfers of data as per Article 40(3).[46]

6.3 Approved certification mechanisms

The reference to 'an approved certification mechanism' means a certification mechanism adopted pursuant to Article 42.[47] The GDPR does not contain a definition of 'certification mechanism', though it does mention them in the same breath as 'data protection seals and marks' (Article 42(1)). An example of a certification mechanism would thus presumably be a trustmark placed on a website, which would have to be backed up by some sort of code of conduct or code of practice; the GDPR does not address the interaction of certification mechanisms with codes of conduct, though presumably if they were to

---

[45] See also Art. 40(2)(j) GDPR, listing one of the potential purposes for a code of conduct as 'the transfer of personal data to third countries or international organisations'. See also the commentary on Art. 40 in this volume.
[46] EDPB 2019B, p. 6.   [47] See the commentary on Art. 42 in this volume.

be used together then both would have to be approved under the relevant provisions of the GDPR. Certification mechanisms are voluntary, but under Article 42(5) they may be approved either by a DPA or a national certification body as set out in Article 43. A certification mechanism must contain 'binding and enforceable commitments of the controller or processor in the third country to apply the appropriate safeguards, including as regards data subjects' rights' (Article 46(2)(f)), and must thus be legally binding. Under Article 46(2), no additional DPA authorisation is required for the use of a certification mechanism as providing adequate safeguards once it has been approved as provided in Article 46(2)(f). According to Article 42(5), a 'common certification, the European Data Protection Seal' may 'result' from criteria approved by the EDPB, but it is unclear whether this would have any legal effect with regard to international data transfers.

As is the case with codes of conduct (see above), data protection certification mechanisms may be established for data controllers and data processors not subject to the GDPR (Article 42(2)); this could presumably include, for example, a trade association in a third country whose members are not subject to the GDPR but who want to make it easier for EU business partners to transfer personal data to them. Such certification mechanisms may 'be established for the purpose of demonstrating the existence of appropriate safeguards ... under the terms referred to in point (f) of Article 46(2)' (Article 42(2)). Such a certification mechanism has to be approved either by a certification authority under Article 43 or a DPA (Article 42(5)). Article 46(1) refers to appropriate safeguards that are provided by the data controller or data processor transferring personal data from the EU, not by the parties receiving the data, which seems to present a contradiction with Article 42(2). Even though this provision is explicitly designed to apply to data controllers and data processors not subject to the GDPR, once the relevant organisations adopt such a certification mechanism they would be subject to the 'binding and enforceable commitments' (Article 42(2)) under the GDPR that they have to assume in order for it to be approved.

6.4 Provisions inserted into administrative arrangements

Article 46(3)(b) allows data transfers based on 'provisions to be inserted into administrative arrangements between public authorities or bodies which include enforceable and effective data subject rights'. As recital 108 makes clear, these arrangements are presumed not to be legally binding,[48] which is how they are distinguished from the 'legally binding and enforceable instrument between public authorities or bodies' referred to in Article 46(2)(a). Data transfers based on such administrative arrangements require authorisation from the competent DPA in accordance with the examination procedure referred to in Article 93(2) (as provided in Article 46(3)). It is unclear how 'enforceable and effective' rights for data subjects can be provided when the arrangements under which such rights are to be secured are themselves not legally binding. Satisfying the high standard the CJEU has set for data subject rights should also involve something more elaborate than a simple memorandum of understanding between public authorities or bodies, which is the only example of such administrative arrangements given in the GDPR.[49]

---

[48] See rec. 108, stating that 'authorisation by the competent supervisory authority should be obtained when the safeguards are provided for in administrative arrangements that are not legally binding'.

[49] Ibid., referring to a 'memorandum of understanding' as an example of such a provision to be inserted administrative arrangements.

The EDPB has issued an opinion approving a set of draft administrative arrangements[50] under Article 46(3)(b), for use in the transfer of personal data between EEA financial supervisory authorities and non-EEA financial supervisory authorities.[51] Administrative arrangements may also prove to be an option for use in data transfers to international organisations.

7. LED

The LED also allows data transfers to be carried out based on appropriate safeguards in the area of law enforcement, which is outside the scope of the GDPR.[52] Article 37(1) LED mentions two types of appropriate safeguards, namely 'appropriate safeguards with regard to the protection of personal data are provided for in a legally binding instrument; or (b) the controller has assessed all the circumstances surrounding the transfer of personal data and concludes that appropriate safeguards exist with regard to the protection of personal data'. Data transfers carried out under (b) require that the DPA be informed and that certain documentation about the transfer must be kept and made available to the DPA upon request; these seem to provide less protection than the specific safeguards mentioned in Article 46(3)(b) GDPR, which refers to 'enforceable and effective data subject rights'.

8. Enforcement

Under the CJEU's *Schrems* judgment, an individual must be able to make a claim to a DPA contesting the compatibility of data transfers based on an adequacy decision with the protection of privacy and fundamental rights, and the DPA must examine the claim with all due diligence. If the DPA rejects the claim, the individual must have access to judicial remedies allowing him to contest this decision before national courts, and the courts must stay proceedings and make a reference to the Court for a preliminary ruling. If the DPA finds such claim to be well-founded, it must be able to engage in legal proceedings based on national legislation to enable the courts to make a reference for a preliminary ruling concerning the decision's validity. Given the high value that the CJEU has set on the fundamental right to data protection, these requirements should apply to appropriate safeguards under the GDPR as well.

These requirements are reflected in provisions of the GDPR such as Articles 77 and 78, which give individuals the right to lodge a complaint against a DPA and to exercise an effective judicial remedy against one. In addition, under Article 58(2)(j) a DPA may order the suspension of data flows to a third country and international organisation, and Article 58(5) gives DPAs the power to bring infringements of the GDPR to the attention of judicial authorities and to engage in legal proceedings in order to enforce it.

Infringements of Article 46 are subject to the higher level of administrative fines under Article 83(5)(c), i.e. up to € 20 million or 4 per cent of the total worldwide turnover of the preceding financial year, whichever is higher.

---

[50] Draft Administrative Arrangements 2019. [51] EDPB 2019A.
[52] See Art. 2(2)(d) GDPR.

Select Bibliography

International agreements

EEA Agreement: Agreement on the European Economic Area, OJ 1994 L 1/3.
EEA Decision 2018: Decision of the EEA Joint Committee No. 154/2018 of 6 July 2018 amending Annex XI (Electronic communication, audiovisual services and information society) and Protocol 37 (containing the list provided for in Article 101) to the EEA Agreement [2018/1022], OJ 2018 L 183/23.

EU legislation

Council Decision 2018: Council Decision (EU) 2018/893 of 18 June 2018 on the position to be adopted, on behalf of the European Union, within the EEA Joint Committee concerning the amendment of Annex XI (Electronic communication, audiovisual services and information society) and Protocol 37 containing the list provided for in Article 101 to the EEA Agreement (General Data Protection Regulation), OJ 2018 L 159/31.
Decision of the EEA Joint Committee: Decision of the EEA Joint Committee, No. 154/2018 of 6 July 2018 amending Annex XI (Electronic communication, audiovisual services and information society) and Protocol 37 (containing the list provided for in Article 101) to the EEA Agreement [2018/1022], OJ 2018 L 183/23.
EC Standard Contractual Clauses 2001: Commission Decision (EC) 2001/497 of 15 June 2001 on standard contractual clauses for the transfer of personal data to third countries, under Directive (EC) 95/46, OJ 2001 L181/19.
EC Standard Contractual Clauses Processors 2001: Commission Decision (EC) 2001/16 of 27 December 2001 on standard contractual clauses for the transfer of personal data to processors established in third countries, under Directive (EC) 95/46, OJ 2002 L 6/52.
EC Standard Contractual Clauses Processors 2004: Commission Decision (EC) 2004/915 of 27 December 2004 amending Decision (EC) 2001/497 as regards the introduction of an alternative set of standard contractual clauses for the transfer of personal data to third countries, OJ 2004 L 385/74.
EC Standard Contractual Clauses Processors 2010: Commission Decision (EC) 2010/87/EU of 5 February 2010 on standard contractual clauses for the transfer of personal data to processors established in third countries under Directive (EC) 95/46/EC of the European Parliament and of the Council, OJ 2010 L 39/5.
EC Standard Contractual Clauses Processors 2016: Commission Implementing Decision (EU) 2016/2297 of 16 December 2016 amending Decisions 2001/497/EC and 2010/87/EU on standard contractual clauses for the transfer of personal data to third countries and to processors established in such countries, under Directive 95/46/EC of the European Parliament and of the Council, 2016 OJ L 344/100.
Regulation 182/2011: Regulation (EU) No. 182/2011 of the European Parliament and of the Council of 16 February 2011 laying down the rules and general principles concerning mechanisms for control by Member States of the Commission's exercise of implementing powers, OJ 2011 L 55/13.

Academic writings

Blume, 'Transborder Data Flow: Is there a Solution in Sight?', 8(1) *International Journal of Law and Information Technology* (2000), 65.
Kuner 2005: Kuner, 'The E.U. Alternative Standard Contractual Clauses for International Data Transfers', *BNA World Data Protection Reporter* (February 2005), 17.
Kuner 2007: Kuner, *European Data Protection Law: Corporate Compliance and Regulation* (2nd edn, OUP 2007).

Kuner 2010: Kuner, 'The New EU Standard Contractual Clauses for International Data Transfers to Data Processors', *BNA Privacy & Security Law Reporter* (19 April 2010), 1.

Kuner 2013: Kuner, *Transborder Data Flows and Data Protection Law* (OUP 2013).

Kuner 2019: Kuner, 'International Organizations and the EU General Data Protection Regulation: Exploring the Interaction between EU Law and International Law', 16 *International Organizations Law Review* (2019), 158.

Kuner, 'Reality and Illusion in EU Data Transfer Regulation Post-*Schrems*', 18(4) *German Law Journal* (2017), 881.

Kuner and Hladjk 2005: Kuner and Hladjk, 'Die alternativen Standardvertragsklauseln der EU für internationale Datenübermittlungen', 21(5) *Recht der Datenverarbeitung* (2005), 193.

Lenaerts and Corthaut 2006: Lenaerts and Corthaut, 'Of Birds and Hedges: The Role of Primacy in Invoking Norms of EU Law', 31(3) *European Law Review* (2006), 287.

Rauchegger 2015: Rauchegger, 'The Interplay between the Charter and National Constitutions after *Åkerberg Fransson* and *Melloni*', in de Vries, Bernitz and Weatherill (eds.), *The EU Charter of Fundamental Rights as a Binding Instrument* (Hart Publishing 2015), 93.

Rosas and Armati 2012: Rosas and Armati, *EU Constitutional Law: An Introduction* (Hart Publishing 2012) (Kindle edition).

Simitis and Dammann, *EU-Datenschutzrichtlinie* (Nomos Verlag 1997).

Papers of data protection authorities

EDPB 2019A: European Data Protection Board, 'Opinion 4/2019 on the draft Administrative Arrangement for the transfer of personal data between European Economic Area ("EEA") Financial Supervisory Authorities and non-EEA Financial Supervisory Authorities' (12 February 2019).

EDPB 2019B: European Data Protection Board, 'Guidelines 1/2019 on Codes of Conduct and Monitoring Bodies under Regulation 2016/679' (4 June 2019).

EDPB 2019C: European Data Protection Board, 'Opinion 14/2019 on the draft Standard Contractual Clauses submitted by the DK SA (Article 28(8) GDPR)' (9 July 2019).

EDPB Brexit information note: European Data Protection Board, 'Information Note on Data Transfers under the GDPR in the Event of a No-Deal Brexit' (12 February 2019).

WP29 2014: Article 29 Working Party, 'Working Document 01/2014 on Draft Ad Hoc Contractual Clauses "EU Data Processor to Non-EU Sub-Processor"' (WP 214, 21 March 2014).

Article 29 Working Party, 'Working Document: Transfers of Personal Data to Third Countries: Applying Articles 25 and 26 of the EU Data Protection Directive' (WP 12, 24 July 1998).

ICO 2017: UK Information Commissioner's Office, 'Sending Personal Data outside the European Economic Area (Principle 8)' (2017).

ICO 2018: UK Information Commissioner, 'International Data Transfers', available at https://ico.org.uk/for-organisations/data-protection-and-brexit/data-protection-if-there-s-no-brexit-deal/the-gdpr/international-data-transfers/.

Others

Commission Brexit Preparedness Notice: European Commission, 'Notice to Stakeholders: Withdrawal of the United Kingdom from the Union and EU Rules in the Field of Data Protection', 9 January 2018, available at https://ec.europa.eu/info/sites/info/files/file_import/data_protection_en.pdf.

Data Flow Model Contract 1992: Council of Europe/European Commission/ICC, 'Model Contract to Ensure Equivalent Protection in the Context of Transborder Data Flows with Explanatory Memorandum' (2 November 1992), available at https://rm.coe.int/16806845b2.

Draft Administrative Arrangements 2019: European Data Protection Board, 'Draft administrative arrangement for the transfer of personal data between each of the European Economic Area ("EEA") Authorities set out in Appendix A and each of the non-EEA Authorities set out in Appendix B' (7 January 2019), available at https://edpb.europa.eu/sites/edpb/files/files/file1/edpb-2019-02-12-draft-aa-esma-annex_en_0.pdf.

Jourová speech 2019: Jourová, 'Commissioner Jourová's intervention at the event "The General Data Protection Regulation one year on: Taking stock in the EU and beyond"' (13 June 2019), available at http://europa.eu/rapid/press-release_SPEECH-19-2999_en.htm.

Article 47. Binding corporate rules

CHRISTOPHER KUNER

1. The competent supervisory authority shall approve binding corporate rules in accordance with the consistency mechanism set out in Article 63, provided that they:
   (a) are legally binding and apply to and are enforced by every member concerned of the group of undertakings, or group of enterprises engaged in a joint economic activity, including their employees;
   (b) expressly confer enforceable rights on data subjects with regard to the processing of their personal data; and
   (c) fulfil the requirements laid down in paragraph 2.
2. The binding corporate rules referred to in paragraph 1 shall specify at least:
   (a) the structure and contact details of the group of undertakings, or group of enterprises engaged in a joint economic activity and of each of its members;
   (b) the data transfers or set of transfers, including the categories of personal data, the type of processing and its purposes, the type of data subjects affected and the identification of the third country or countries in question;
   (c) their legally binding nature, both internally and externally;
   (d) the application of the general data protection principles, in particular purpose limitation, data minimisation, limited storage periods, data quality, data protection by design and by default, legal basis for processing, processing of special categories of personal data, measures to ensure data security, and the requirements in respect of onward transfers to bodies not bound by the binding corporate rules;
   (e) the rights of data subjects in regard to processing and the means to exercise those rights, including the right not to be subject to decisions based solely on automated processing, including profiling in accordance with Article 22, the right to lodge a complaint with the competent supervisory authority and before the competent courts of the Member States in accordance with Article 79, and to obtain redress and, where appropriate, compensation for a breach of the binding corporate rules;
   (f) the acceptance by the controller or processor established on the territory of a Member State of liability for any breaches of the binding corporate rules by any member concerned not established in the Union; the controller or the processor shall be exempt from that liability, in whole or in part, only if it proves that that member is not responsible for the event giving rise to the damage;
   (g) how the information on the binding corporate rules, in particular on the provisions referred to in points (d), (e) and (f) of this paragraph is provided to the data subjects in addition to Articles 13 and 14;
   (h) the tasks of any data protection officer designated in accordance with Article 37 or any other person or entity in charge of the monitoring compliance with the binding corporate rules within the group of undertakings, or group of enterprises engaged in a joint economic activity, as well as monitoring training and complaint-handling;
   (i) the complaint procedures;
   (j) the mechanisms within the group of undertakings, or group of enterprises engaged in a joint economic activity for ensuring the verification of compliance with the binding corporate rules. Such mechanisms shall include data protection audits and methods for ensuring corrective actions to protect the rights of the data subject. Results of such verification should be communicated to the person or entity referred to in point (h) and to the board of the controlling undertaking of a group of undertakings, or of the group of enterprises engaged in a joint economic activity, and should be available upon request to the competent supervisory authority;

(k) the mechanisms for reporting and recording changes to the rules and reporting those changes to the supervisory authority;
(l) the cooperation mechanism with the supervisory authority to ensure compliance by any member of the group of undertakings, or group of enterprises engaged in a joint economic activity, in particular by making available to the supervisory authority the results of verifications of the measures referred to in point (j);
(m) the mechanisms for reporting to the competent supervisory authority any legal requirements to which a member of the group of undertakings, or group of enterprises engaged in a joint economic activity is subject in a third country which are likely to have a substantial adverse effect on the guarantees provided by the binding corporate rules; and
(n) the appropriate data protection training to personnel having permanent or regular access to personal data.
3. The Commission may specify the format and procedures for the exchange of information between controllers, processors and supervisory authorities for binding corporate rules within the meaning of this Article. Those implementing acts shall be adopted in accordance with the examination procedure set out in Article 93(2).

Relevant Recital

(110) A group of undertakings, or a group of enterprises engaged in a joint economic activity, should be able to make use of approved binding corporate rules for its international transfers from the Union to organisations within the same group of undertakings, or group of enterprises engaged in a joint economic activity, provided that such corporate rules include all essential principles and enforceable rights to ensure appropriate safeguards for transfers or categories of transfers of personal data.

Closely Related Provisions

Recital 6; Articles 13(1)(f) and 14(1)(f) (Information to a data subject); Article 15(1)(c) (Right to access information about data recipients in third countries); Article 23(2)(d) (Member States can restrict individuals' rights but must provide for safeguards to prevent abuse or unlawful transfer) (see too recital 153); Article 28(3)(a) (Provisions of a data processing agreement stipulating controller's instructions regarding data transfers); Articles 30(1)(e) and 30(2)(c) (Internal records about data transfers); Article 40(2)(j) (Data transfer codes of conduct); Article 58(3)(j) (Power of supervisory authorities to approve BCRs); Article 64(1)(f) (Opinion of the Board regarding the approval of BCRs); Article 70(1)(c) (Advice by the Board to the Commission regarding the format and procedures for the exchange of information for BCRs); Article 83(5)(c) (Fines for non-compliance with data transfer restrictions).

Relevant Case Law

CJEU

Case C-362/14, *Maximillian Schrems v Data Protection Commissioner*, judgment of 6 October 2015 (Grand Chamber) (ECLI:EU:C:2015:650).

A. Rationale and Policy Underpinnings

Article 47 GDPR sets out the conditions for using binding corporate rules ('BCRs') as a legal basis for transferring personal data. Article 4(20) GDPR defines BCRs as 'personal data protection policies which are adhered to by a controller or processor established on the territory of a Member State for transfers or a set of transfers of personal data to a controller or processor in one or more third countries within a group of undertakings, or group of enterprises engaged in a joint economic activity'.[1] BCRs can be approved for data controllers or data processors; in some cases, DPAs have been willing to approve BCRs that mix these two roles.

Chapter V of the GDPR sets up a three-tiered structure for legal bases for data transfers, with adequacy decisions at the top, appropriate safeguards in the middle and derogations at the bottom. This means that if an adequacy decision has been issued then that should be relied on as the legal basis for the data transfer;[2] if not, then appropriate safeguards (including BCRs[3]) should be used if possible.

B. Legal Background

1. EU legislation

The DPD did not explicitly mention BCRs. However, beginning in approximately 2002, some DPAs began approving BCRs as adequate safeguards under Article 26(2) DPD.

The following were some of the earliest approvals of BCRs:

1. In July 2002, two sets of BCRs (covering, respectively, employee data and customer/supplier data) of DaimlerChrysler were approved by the conference of German data protection authorities (Düsseldorfer Kreis).
2. In November 2002, a set of BCRs proposed by the German Insurance Association (Gesamtverband der Deutschen Versicherungswirtschaft) was also approved by the Düsseldorfer Kreis.
3. The BCRs of General Electric ('GE') covering employee data were approved in July 2003.
4. On 4 May 2004, the Austrian DPA approved the BCRs of an unnamed Austrian bank (known to be Bank Austria Creditanstalt).[4]
5. Deutsche Telekom's BCRs (covering both employee and customer data) were approved in November 2003.

The first meeting of the WP29 ever with outside stakeholders took place in The Hague in November 2004 and focused on BCRs.

The Member State DPAs differed substantially in their approach to BCRs. Some viewed them as, in effect, creating 'adequate protection' in the country of import in the sense of Article 25 DPD. Since Article 25 did not require formal approval of a DPA for a transfer to take place, these DPAs made approval of BCRs optional. Other DPAs viewed BCRs as analogous to contractual clauses under Article 26(2) DPD, thus requiring approval.

The WP29 issued a number of papers over the years on the subject of BCRs.[5] These papers have formed the basis of the substantive requirements for BCRs, and for the approval process for them. Eventually the WP29 developed a mutual recognition procedure among the DPAs to speed up approvals and harmonise procedures.[6] Most but not all of

---

[1] See the commentary on Art. 4(20) in this volume concerning the definition of BCRs.
[2] See the commentary on Art. 45 in this volume regarding the standard of 'essential equivalency' to EU law for adequacy decisions, which was first set by the CJEU in Case C-362/14, *Schrems*.
[3] See Art. 46(2)(b), listing BCRs as a type of appropriate safeguard.
[4] Austrian Data Protection Authority 2004.
[5] See the following papers issued by the WP29: WP29 2015; WP29 2014; WP29 2012A; WP29 2012B; WP29 2008A; WP29 2008B; WP29 2008C; WP29 2007; WP29 2005A; WP29 2005B; WP29 2004; WP29 2003.
[6] See BCR EC Website.

the DPAs were members of the so-called 'mutual recognition' group that applied these procedures.[7] The system of mutual recognition is no longer needed under the GDPR, though the DPAs continue to coordinate informally concerning the approval of BCRs. The EDPB has also endorsed five of the papers issued by the WP29 on BCRs (see below).

2. International instruments

There are no international treaties dealing with BCRs. In 2014 the WP29 together with the Asia-Pacific Economic Cooperation ('APEC')[8] group issued jointly a 'Referential' that maps the differences and similarities between BCRs and the Cross-Border Privacy Rules ('CBPR') system among the APEC countries.[9]

3. National developments

Article 47 does not provide for Member State implementation; indeed, one of the main purposes of including the article in the GDPR was to create a more harmonised standard for what BCRs should contain and a more streamlined procedure for their approval. However, national implementation of BCRs requirements can still be important in practice.

C. Analysis

1. Substantive requirements and scope

The substantive requirements for BCRs in Article 47 are largely taken from the Article 29 documents on the topic, but are far less detailed. Pursuant to Article 47(3), the Commission is empowered to adopt implementing acts specifying the format and procedures for the exchange of information between controllers, processors and DPAs under the procedure set out in Article 93(2). In addition, the EDPB has endorsed five papers of the WP29 relating to BCRs,[10] and they will remain influential. Since Article 47 does not differentiate between application of the requirements to BCRs for data controllers and BCRs for data processors, it will be up to the EDPB to indicate more detailed criteria for each type of BCRs. BCRs already in force remain valid after entry into force of the GDPR (see Article 46(5)).

BCRs must fulfil the following requirements (Article 47(1) GDPR):

1. They must be 'legally binding and apply to and are enforced by every member concerned of the group of undertakings, or group of enterprises engaged in a joint economic activity, including their employees' (47(1)(a)).
2. They must 'expressly confer enforceable rights on data subjects with regard to the processing of their personal data' (47(1)(b).
3. They must 'fulfil the requirements laid down in paragraph 2' (47(1)(c).

---

[7] See ibid., indicating that the following 21 Member States were members of the group: Austria, Belgium, Bulgaria, Cyprus, the Czech Republic, Estonia, France, Germany, Iceland, Ireland, Italy, Latvia, Liechtenstein, Luxembourg, Malta, the Netherlands, Norway, Slovakia, Slovenia, Spain and the United Kingdom.
[8] The APEC group is an intergovernmental forum comprised of the 21 Pacific Rim member economies, focused primarily upon trade and economic issues. The APEC group issued the APEC Privacy Framework in 2005. See APEC Privacy Framework.
[9] WP29 2014.
[10] EDPB 2018. The papers it endorsed are WP 2017, WP 2018A, WP 2018B, WP 2018C and WP 2018D.

Article 47(2) then sets forth the provisions that BCRs must contain. The GDPR adds new requirements to those contained in papers of the WP29 under the DPD. Figure 47.1 indicates the differences between the substantive requirements for BCRs set out by the WP29 under the DPD and those included in Article 47 GDPR.

Topic	Requirements under the DPD	Requirements under the GDPR	Comments
Remedies	Data subjects were entitled to take action against the corporate group, as well as to choose to file a complaint (i) either in the jurisdiction of the member that is at the origin of the transfer, or (ii) in the jurisdiction of the European headquarters or the European member with delegated data protection responsibilities. *WP29 2003, p. 19*	The BCRs must specify that data subjects have the right to bring proceedings against the controller/processor before the courts of the Member State either where the controller or processor is established or where the data subject has his or her habitual residence (unless the controller/processor is a public authority). *Article 47(2)(e) in conjunction with Article 79(2) GDPR*	Individuals are offered the possibility to seek a remedy in their own country. Before the GDPR, this option was only available for BCRs for processors, and only where the other possibilities (i.e., in the court of the EU processor/ data exporter/EU processor's headquarters/EU member with delegated data protection responsibilities/ EU controller) were not applicable. *WP29 2015, p. 9*
Data Protection Principles	The BCRs had to specify the application of general data protection principles (e.g., purpose limitation, data quality, security, requirements in respect of onward transfers to bodies not bound by the BCRs).	The BCRs must specify the application of general data protection principles, including purpose limitation, data minimisation, limited storage periods, data quality, data protection by design and by default, legal basis for processing, processing of special categories of personal data, measures to ensure data security, and the requirements in respect of onward transfers to bodies not bound by the binding corporate rules'. *Article 47(2)(d) GDPR*	New data protection principles are added to the list. In addition to data minimization, limited storage periods, and data protection by design and by default, the GDPR also requires the BCRs to specify the legal basis of the processing and the processing of special categories of personal data. In the WP29 documents, this was only suggested in the (non-mandatory) framework for the structure of BCRs (WP29 2008C). Hence, this is not new, but the GDPR makes it mandatory to include the legal basis of the processing and the processing of special categories of personal data in the text of the BCRs.

Figure 47.1 Differences in BCR requirements between the DPD and the GDPR

Topic	Requirements under the DPD	Requirements under the GDPR	Comments
Individual rights	The BCRs had to specify the rights of data subjects. WP29 2003 and WP29 2005A	The BCRs must specify the rights of data subjects in regard to processing and the means to exercise those rights, including the right not to be subject to decisions based solely on automated processing, including profiling in accordance with Article 22, the right to lodge a complaint with the competent supervisory authority and before the competent courts of the Member States in accordance with Article 79, and to obtain redress and, where appropriate, compensation for a breach of the binding corporate rules. *Article 47(2)(e) GDPR*	New rights for individuals are added to the list.
Notice	The BCRs had to specify how the information on BCRs is provided to data subjects. WP29 2003	The BCRs must specify how the information on BCRs is provided to data subjects, in particular: information on the application of general data protection principles (e.g., including data minimization, limited storage periods, data protection by design and by default, and others) *(Article 47(2)(g) GDPR referring to Article 47(2)(d) GDPR)*; information on the rights of data subjects, including the right not to be subject to decisions based solely on automated processing, including profiling in accordance with Article 22 GDPR, and others *(Article 47(2)(g) GDPR referring to Article 47(2)(e) GDPR)*; and information on the acceptance, by the controller or processor established in the EU, of liability for any breaches of the BCRs by a non-EU member *(Article 47(2)(g) GDPR referring to Article 47(2)(f) GDPR)*.	This change affects the content of the notice to be provided, rather than the content of the BCRs. The specified information is to be provided in addition to the general notice requirements in Article 13 and 14 GDPR.

Figure 47.1 Continued

Topic	Requirements under the DPD	Requirements under the GDPR	Comments
Conflicting legislation	The BCRs had to specify that where a member of the corporate group had reasons to believe that the legislation applicable to it could prevent it from fulfilling its obligations under the BCRs and had a substantial adverse effect on the guarantees provided by them, it would promptly inform the EU headquarters (or the EU member with delegated data protection responsibilities), unless otherwise prohibited by a law enforcement authority. WP29 2012A, p. 11 In this case, the EU headquarters (or the EU member with delegated data protection responsibilities) had to take a responsible decision on what action to take and had to consult the DPA in case of doubt. WP29 2008C, p. 8	The BCRs must specify the mechanisms for reporting to the DPA any legal requirement to which a member of the group of undertakings (or group of enterprises engaged in a joint economic activity) is subject in a third country which are likely to have a substantial adverse effect on the guarantees provided by the BCRs. Article 47(2)(m) GDPR	The GDPR suggests that all situations of potential conflict between national legislation and BCRs will need to be reported to the DPA, whereas before, the EU headquarters were free to assess whether such notification is necessary, and were only required to report to the DPA in case of doubt. On the other hand, the threshold for such requirements is lowered under the GDPR, which only refers to the second criterion (i.e. 'substantial adverse effect on the guarantees provided by the BCRs'), without referring to the member being prevented from fulfilling its obligations under the BCRs.
Duty to respect the BCRs	The BCRs had to be binding on, and applied by, those having data protection responsibilities within the organization. WP29 2003, p. 14	The BCRs must specify that they are enforced by every member of the group (in addition to being binding on, and applied by, every member of the group). Article 47(1)(a) GDPR	The BCRs need to include a duty for all members to enforce, not only to comply with, the rules they contain.
Structure and contact details	The application for approval of BCRs had to specify the structure and contact details of the corporate group. WP29 2005A, p. 4	The BCRs (not only the application for approval of BCRs) must specify the structure and contact details of the group of undertakings (or group of enterprises engaged in a joint economic activity) and of each of its members. Article 47(2)(a) GDPR	It is not clear whether the phrase 'and of each of its members' refers to (i) both a group of undertakings and a group of enterprises engaged in a joint economic activity, or (ii) only to a group of enterprises engaged in a joint economic activity (see punctuation in Article 47(2)(a)).

Figure 47.1 Continued

Topic	Requirements under the DPD	Requirements under the GDPR	Comments
Ensuring compliance	The BCRs had to provide a brief description of the internal structure, role and responsibilities of the network or privacy officers or similar function created to ensure compliance with the BCRs. WP29 2012A, p. 7	The BCRs must specify the tasks of the data protection officer designated in accordance with Article 37 (or any other person or entity in charge of monitoring compliance with the BCRs). Article 47(2)(h) GDPR	The GDPR puts more emphasis on the role of the data protection officer.
Other	The Commission had no executive powers in the context of BCRs.	The GDPR provides that the Commission may specify the format and procedures for the exchange of information between controllers, processors and DPAs by adopting implementing acts in accordance with the examination procedure set out in Article 93(2) GDPR.	The GDPR grants more power to the Commission.

Figure 47.1 Continued

The EDPB has endorsed a paper of the WP29 setting up a table with the elements and principles to be found in BCRs,[11] and a separate one setting up such a table for processor BCRs.[12] The WP29 has also issued standard application forms for BCRs[13] and BCRs for processors,[14] both of which have been endorsed by the EDPB.

BCRs may be adopted by data controllers or data processors established in the EU.[15] Data transfers under BCRs may be 'to a controller or processor in one or more third countries within a group of undertakings, or group of enterprises engaged in a joint economic activity'.[16] An enterprise is defined as 'a natural or legal person engaged in an economic activity, irrespective of its legal form, including partnerships or associations regularly engaged in an economic activity' (Article 4(18)),[17] while a group of undertakings means 'a controlling undertaking and its controlled undertakings' (Article 4(19)).[18] The GDPR does not explain what a 'group of enterprises engaged in a joint economic activity' is, but an example of this could be a joint venture or an alliance, as long as it is stable.[19]

Since BCRs extend to data processing within the corporate group, transfers of personal data to entities of the group that have enacted BCRs are covered by them. The GDPR does not address data transfers between different groups, each of which has enacted BCRs separately. Presumably such transfers will have to comply with the conditions for onward transfers set out in each of the sets of BCRs. In theory these should be the same or similar, since the GDPR sets out harmonised rules for the content of BCRs, but in practice there can be differences between different BCRs based on factors such as the type of data covered and the purposes for which they will be processed.[20]

[11] WP29 2017.   [12] WP29 2018A.   [13] WP29 2018C.   [14] WP29 2018D.
[15] See Art. 4(20) GDPR.   [16] Ibid.
[17] This definition was taken from Commission Recommendation 2003, Annex, Art. 1.
[18] This definition was taken from Art. 2(b) Council Directive 94/45/EC.
[19] In the negotiations of the GDPR, the EU institutions agreed that a joint economic activity should be stable and mentioned an airline alliance as an example.
[20] See the commentary on Art. 44 in this volume regarding conflicts between data transfer mechanisms.

2. Approval process

The DPD did not contain an approval procedure for BCRs, but this is now set out in the GDPR. Under Article 47(1) GDPR, approval must be obtained from the applicant's competent DPA (the 'lead DPA') in accordance with the consistency mechanism set forth in Article 63. This means that the applicant company should first apply to its lead supervisory authority as determined under Articles 55 and 56. If the lead DPA intends to approve them, then the EDPB has to give its opinion.[21] If approval from the EBPD is obtained, no further authorisation is required.[22] Approval of BCRs used to be a multi-year process, but can now often be obtained much more quickly than this, making BCRs a realistic option for many companies, not just for the largest multinationals.

The Figure 47.2 explains the differences between the approval under the requirements set by the WP29 when the DPD was in force and those contained in the GDPR.

Topic	Requirements set by the WP29	Requirements under the GDPR	Comments
Applicant	BCRs could be adopted by a corporate group. WP29 2003	BCRs can be adopted by a group of undertakings or by a group of enterprises engaged in a joint economic activity. Article 47(1)(a) GDPR	The GDPR grants a broader scope to the entities that can apply for approval of BCRs.
Competent DPA	Selection of the lead authority was done on the basis of relevant criteria such as: location of the group's European headquarters; location of the company within the group with delegated data protection responsibilities; location of the company which is best placed (in terms of management function, administrative burden etc.) to deal with the application and to enforce the BCRs; the place where most decisions in terms of the purposes and the means of the processing are taken; and Member States within the EU from which most transfers outside the EEA will take place. WP29 2005B, p. 2	If the conditions of Article 56(1) GDPR are met, the competent DPA will be the lead DPA, i.e. the DPA of the group's main establishment in the EU. Article 56(1) GDPR	Main establishment under the GDPR: For a controller, the main establishment will be the place of its central administration, unless the decisions on the purposes and means of the processing are taken in another establishment which has the power to implement them. For a processor, the main establishment will also be the place of its central administration, or, if it has no central administration in the EU, where the main processing activities take place. Article 4(16) GDPR
National transfer authorizations	After the EU cooperation procedure was closed, the corporate group had to obtain national transfer authorizations, where required by national law.	Under the GDPR, no national transfer authorization is necessary, once the BCRs have been approved.	The GDPR abolishes the necessity for national authorizations.

Figure 47.2 Differences in approval requirements between the DPD and the GDPR

---

[21] See Art. 64(1)(f) GDPR.   [22] Ibid., Art. 46(2)(b).

The GDPR does not address the mutual recognition procedure that has been used previously to approve BCRs across multiple countries, and which has now been replaced by the approval scheme of Article 47. The EDPB has endorsed a paper issued by the WP29 setting forth a co-operation procedure for the approval of BCRs.[23]

3. Brexit and BCRs

On 29 March 2017, the UK invoked Article 50 of the Treaty on European Union ('TEU') and indicated its intention to leave the EU, at which point it will become a third country by operation of law ('Brexit') and all Union primary and secondary law will cease to apply to the UK.[24] On 14 November 2018, the parties agreed on a Withdrawal Agreement that sets forth the terms of the UK's withdrawal. The Withdrawal Agreement includes a 21-month implementation period during which the GDPR would continue to apply to all personal data which has been collected and processed in the UK until 31 December 2020.[25] During this period, the UK will have exited the EU and will no longer be an EU Member State, so that the rules on the transfer of personal data to third countries will apply, subject to the Withdrawal Agreement.[26] However, the Withdrawal Agreement will only come into effect if it is approved by the UK House of Commons and then by the Parliament. Since Brexit is subject to political factors that were unresolved at the time this text was finalised, the legal status of data transfers from the EU to the UK post-Brexit remains uncertain.[27]

Brexit has implications for BCRs. According to the EDPB, if the UK exits the EU without the Withdrawal Agreement coming into effect, then the UK Information Commissioner (ICO) will no longer have a role in dealing with BCRs.[28] This means that the ICO will not be able to serve as lead supervisory authority for companies applying for BCRs.[29] In such cases, 'the Supervisory Authority that may be approached to act as the new BCR Lead Supervisory Authority will consider in cooperation with other concerned Supervisory Authorities whether it is the appropriate BCR Lead on a case by case basis'.[30]

4. Remedies

Companies whose BCRs are rejected by a DPA can sue it in the courts of the DPA's Member State (Article 78 GDPR). A natural or legal person can also bring an action for annulment under Article 263 of the Treaty on the Functioning of the European Union ('TFEU') against a decision of the EDPB in cases where the Board reaches a binding decision under Article 65 GDPR, including one concerning BCRs. An action for annulment must be brought within two months of the publication of the binding decision, or its notification to the claimant or, in the absence thereof, the day on which it came to the knowledge of the latter.[31]

Article 77 provides individuals with the right to make a complaint to a DPA with regard to alleged violations of his or her rights, which includes cases involving BCRs. Under Article 79 GDPR, an individual also has a right to a judicial remedy and may bring a case in the Member State where he or she has their habitual residence, as well as the courts of the Member State where the data controller or data processor has an establishment.

---

[23] WP29 2018B.   [24] Commission Brexit Preparedness Notice, p. 1.
[25] Art. 71 Withdrawal Agreement.   [26] Commission Brexit Preparedness Notice, p. 1.
[27] ICO 2018.   [28] EDPB 2019.   [29] Ibid.   [30] Ibid.   [31] Art. 263 TFEU.

Article 47(2)(f) requires the controller or processor established on the territory of a Member State to assume liability for any breaches of the BCRs by any member concerned not established in the EU, with the controller or the processor being exempt from that liability only if it proves that that member is not responsible for the event giving rise to the damage. Infringements of Article 47 are subject to the higher level of administrative fines under Article 83(5)(c), i.e. up to € 20 million or 4 per cent of the total worldwide turnover of the preceding financial year, whichever is higher.

Select Bibliography

International agreements

APEC Privacy Framework: Asia Pacific Economic Cooperation, 'Privacy Framework' (2005).

EU legislation

Council Directive 94/45/EC: Council Directive 94/45/EC of 22 September 1994 on the establishment of a European Works Council or a procedure in Community-scale undertakings and Community-scale groups of undertakings for the purposes of informing and consulting employees, OJ 1994 L 254/64.

Academic writings

Kuner, *European Data Protection Law: Corporate Compliance and Regulation* (2nd edn, OUP 2007).
Kuner, 'The European Commission's Proposed Data Protection Regulation: A Copernican Revolution in European Data Protection Law', *Bloomberg BNA Privacy and Security Law Report* (6 February 2012), 6.
Kuner, *Transborder Data Flow Regulation and Data Privacy Law* (OUP 2013).
Moerel, *Binding Corporate Rules: Corporate Self-Regulation of Global Data Transfers* (OUP 2012).

Papers of data protection authorities

EDPB 2018: European Data Protection Board, Endorsement 1/2018 (25 May 2018).
EDPB 2019: European Data Protection Board, 'Information Note on BCRs for Companies which Have ICO as BCR Lead Supervisory Authority' (12 February 2019).
WP29 2003: Article 29 Working Party, 'Working Document on Transfers of Personal Data to Third Countries: Applying Article 26(2) of the EU Data Protection Directive to Binding Corporate Rules for International Data Transfers' (WP 74, 3 June 2003).
WP29 2004: Article 29 Working Party, 'Model Checklist, Application for Approval of Binding Corporate Rules' (WP 102, 25 November 2004).
WP29 2005A: Article 29 Working Party, 'Working Document Establishing a Model Checklist Application for Approval of Binding Corporate Rules' (WP 108, 14 April 2005).
WP29 2005B: Article 29 Working Party, 'Working Document Setting Forth a Co-Operation Procedure for Issuing Common Opinions on Adequate Safeguards Resulting From "Binding Corporate Rules"' (WP 107, 14 April 2005).
WP29 2007: Article 29 Working Party, 'Recommendation 1/2007 on the Standard Application for Approval of Binding Corporate Rules for the Transfer of Personal Data' (WP 133, 10 January 2007).
WP29 2008A: Article 29 Working Party, 'Working Document on Frequently Asked Questions (FAQs) Related to Binding Corporate Rules' (WP 155 rev. 4, 24 June 2008).
WP29 2008B: Article 29 Working Party, 'Working Document Setting Up a Table with the Elements and Principles to be Found in Binding Corporate Rules' (WP 153, 24 June 2008).

WP29 2008C: Article 29 Working Party, 'Working Document Setting Up a Framework for the Structure of Binding Corporate Rules' (WP 154, 25 June 2008).

WP29 2012A: Article 29 Working Party, 'Working Document 02/2012 Setting Up a Table with the Elements and Principles to Be Found in Processor Binding Corporate Rules' (WP 195, 6 June 2012).

WP29 2012B: Article 29 Working Party, 'Recommendation 1/2012 on the Standard Application form for Approval of Binding Corporate Rules for the Transfer of Personal Data for Processing Activities' (WP 195a, 17 September 2012).

WP29 2014: Article 29 Working Party, 'Opinion 02/2014 on a Referential for Requirements for Binding Corporate Rules Submitted to National Data Protection Authorities in the EU and Cross Border Privacy Rules Submitted to APEC CBPR Accountability Agents' (WP 212, 27 February 2014).

WP29 2015: Article 29 Working Party, 'Explanatory Document on the Processor Binding Corporate Rules', revised version (WP 204, 22 May 2015).

WP29 2017: Article 29 Working Party, 'Working Document Setting Up a Table with the Elements and Principles to Be Found in Binding Corporate Rules' (WP 256, 29 November 2017).

WP29 2018A: Article 29 Working Party, 'Working Document Setting Forth a Table with the Elements and Principles to Be Found in Processor Binding Corporate Rules' (WP 257 rev.01, 28 November 2017, as last revised and adopted on 6 February 2018).

WP29 2018B: Article 29 Working Party, 'Working Document Setting Forth a Co-Operation Procedure for the Approval of "Binding Corporate Rules" for Controllers and Processors under the GDPR' (WP 263 rev.01, 11 April 2018).

WP29 2018C: Article 29 Working Party, 'Recommendation on the Standard Application for Approval of Controller Binding Corporate Rules for the Transfer of Personal Data' (WP 264, 11 April 2018).

WP29 2018D: Article 29 Working Party, 'Recommendation on the Standard Application Form for Approval of Processor Binding Corporate Rules for the Transfer of Personal Data' (WP 265, 11 April 2018).

Article 29 Working Party, 'Opinion 1/2010 on the Concepts of 'Controller' and 'Processor'' (WP 169, 16 February 2010).

Article 29 Working Party, 'Opinion 3/2010 on the Principle of Accountability' (WP 173, 13 July 2010).

Article 29 Working Party, 'Working Document: Transfers of Personal Data to Third Countries: Applying Articles 25 and 26 of the EU Data Protection Directive' (WP 12, 24 July 1998).

Austrian Data Protection Authority 2004: Datenschutzkommission, 'Bescheid internationaler Datenverkehr', K178.173/0007-DSK/2004, 4 May 2004.

Reports and recommendations

Commission Brexit Preparedness Notice: European Commission, 'Notice to Stakeholders: Withdrawal of the United Kingdom from the Union and EU Rules in the Field of Data Protection', 9 January 2018, available at https://ec.europa.eu/info/sites/info/files/file_import/data_protection_en.pdf.

Commission Recommendation 2003: Commission Recommendation of 6 May 2003 concerning the definition of micro, small and medium-sized enterprises, OJ 2003 L 124/36.

Others

BCR EC Website: European Commission Website, 'Binding Corporate Rules', available at https://ec.europa.eu/info/law/law-topic/data-protection/data-transfers-outside-eu/binding-corporate-rules_en.

Article 48. Transfers or disclosures not authorised by Union law

CHRISTOPHER KUNER

Any judgment of a court or tribunal and any decision of an administrative authority of a third country requiring a controller or processor to transfer or disclose personal data may only be recognised or enforceable in any manner if based on an international agreement, such as a mutual legal assistance treaty, in force between the requesting third country and the Union or a Member State, without prejudice to other grounds for transfer pursuant to this Chapter.

Relevant Recitals

(102) This Regulation is without prejudice to international agreements concluded between the Union and third countries regulating the transfer of personal data including appropriate safeguards for the data subjects. Member States may conclude international agreements which involve the transfer of personal data to third countries or international organisations, as far as such agreements do not affect this Regulation or any other provisions of Union law and include an appropriate level of protection for the fundamental rights of the data subjects.

(115) Some third countries adopt laws, regulations and other legal acts which purport to directly regulate the processing activities of natural and legal persons under the jurisdiction of the Member States. This may include judgments of courts or tribunals or decisions of administrative authorities in third countries requiring a controller or processor to transfer or disclose personal data, and which are not based on an international agreement, such as a mutual legal assistance treaty, in force between the requesting third country and the Union or a Member State. The extraterritorial application of those laws, regulations and other legal acts may be in breach of international law and may impede the attainment of the protection of natural persons ensured in the Union by this Regulation. Transfers should only be allowed where the conditions of this Regulation for a transfer to third countries are met. This may be the case, inter alia, where disclosure is necessary for an important ground of public interest recognised in Union or Member State law to which the controller is subject.

Closely Related Provisions

Article 83(5)(c) (Fines for non-compliance with data transfer restrictions)

Relevant Case Law

CJEU

Case C-327/91, *French Republic v Commission*, judgment of 9 August 1994 (ECLI:EU:C:1994:305).
Joined Cases C-402 and 415/05 P, *Yassin Abdullah Kadi and Al Barakaat International Foundation v Council of the European Union and Commission of the European Communities*, judgment of 3 September 2008 (Grand Chamber) (ECLI:EU:C:2008:461).
Case C-617/10, *Åkerberg Fransson*, judgment of 26 February 2013 (ECLI:EU:C:2013:105).

Case C-362/14, *Maximillian Schrems v Data Protection Commissioner*, judgment of 6 October 2015 (Grand Chamber) (ECLI:EU:C:2015:650).
Opinion 1/15, Opinion of 26 July 2017 (Grand Chamber) (ECLI:EU:C:2017:592).

United States

Société Nationale Industrielle Aérospatiale v United States, 482 US 522 (1987).
Volkswagen v Valdez, 909 SW2d 900 (Tex. 1995).
United States v Microsoft Corporation, 584 US ___ (2018) (per curiam).
In the matter of a warrant to search a certain e-mail account controlled and maintained by Microsoft Corporation, 829 F3d 197 (2nd Cir. 2016), *cert. granted*, 16 October 2017, *dismissed per curiam*, 584 US ___ (2018).

A. Rationale and Policy Underpinnings

The history of EU data protection law is marked by conflicts with the law and policy of third countries. Such cases often involve requirements of third country law that compel the transfer of personal data from the EU or access to it, without there being a valid legal basis for the transfer or access under EU law. It is this situation that Article 48 GDPR addresses.

One example involves US requirements concerning discovery, which is the process that allows parties in US civil litigation to obtain facts and information from their opponents. US courts have interpreted such requirements to apply to discovery taking place abroad[1] notwithstanding US accession to the Hague Convention on the Taking of Evidence Abroad in Civil or Commercial Matters (the 'Hague Evidence Convention'),[2] which establishes methods of international cooperation for the taking of evidence abroad in civil and commercial matters. For their part, the EU and its Member States regard the procedures under the Convention as mandatory, thus setting up a conflict with the US view. This situation led the WP29 in February 2009 to publish an opinion on pre-trial discovery for cross-border civil litigation.[3]

Another such conflict concerns so called 'whistle-blower hotlines'. Many US corporations interpret the provisions of the US Sarbanes-Oxley Act[4] ('SOX') to require their audit committees to establish hotlines for the confidential, anonymous submission of employee complaints (commonly called whistle-blowing) regarding questionable auditing or accounting matters in their operations outside the US. On the other hand, such anonymous whistle-blower hotlines have been found to violate EU data protection law. For example, on 26 May 2005, the French CNIL refused to authorise the implementation of employee hotlines by French subsidiaries of two US companies.[5] In February 2006, the WP29 issued guidance on how internal whistle-blowing schemes can be implemented in compliance with the EU data protection law.[6]

In addition, there has been an increase in recent years in governmental authorities accessing personal data for law enforcement, anti-terrorism or national security purposes.[7]

---

[1] US Supreme Court, *Société Nationale Industrielle Aérospatiale*, pp. 533–547.
[2] Hague Evidence Convention. See regarding the Hague Evidence Convention, Cooper and Kuner 2017, pp. 131–137; Borchers 2003.
[3] WP29 2009.   [4] Sarbanes-Oxley Act 2002, s. 301(4)(A), (B).
[5] CNIL 2005A, CNIL 2005B (concerning Exide).   [6] WP29 2006.
[7] See Cate, Dempsey and Rubenstein 2012; Cate and Dempsey 2017.

The best-known such case involves the so-called 'Snowden revelations', which concerned widespread electronic surveillance by US intelligence agencies and gained global notoriety in 2013.[8] A related phenomenon concerns the issuance of orders by governmental or law enforcement authorities in third countries to transfer data stored in the EU. Particularly significant in this regard is the US Clarifying Lawful Overseas Use of Data (CLOUD) Act[9], which allows US authorities to require the production of data stored abroad by a service provider subject to US jurisdiction.[10]

A provision similar to Article 48 first surfaced in the GDPR Interservice Draft dated 29 November 2011, where it was contained in Article 42(1). In addition, this article contained a provision (Article 42(2)) that prohibited data controllers or processors from complying with such a foreign order unless they first obtained DPA authorisation.[11] The Explanatory Memorandum to the Interservice Draft explained the purpose of Article 42 as follows:

Article 42 clarifies that in accordance with international public law and existing EU legislation, in particular Council Regulation (EC) No 227/96, a controller operating in the EU is prohibited to disclose personal [sic] to a third country if so requested by a third country's judicial or administrative authority, unless this is expressly authorized by an international agreement or provided for by a mutual legal assistance treaties or approved by a supervisory authority.[12]

However, this article was not contained in the Commission's original proposal for the GDPR when it was published in January 2012. A text resembling Article 48 first appeared as Article 43a in the text proposed by the Parliament.[13] The Parliament's amendment would have required data controllers to notify DPAs about requests to disclose personal data to courts or regulatory authorities in countries outside of the EU, and to obtain formal approval from DPAs before turning over European data for law enforcement purposes. It also proposed a recital 82 stating that 'any legislation which provides for extra-territorial access to personal data processed in the Union without authorization under Union or Member State law should be considered as an indication of a lack of adequacy', but that was not adopted.

The final version of Article 48 represents a compromise between the Parliament and the Council and purports to shift responsibility from data controllers and DPAs to Member States, the Union and third countries, which are to resolve such conflicts through the conclusion of international agreements. Moreover, language was added at the end of Article 48 indicating that its operation is without prejudice to other grounds for data transfers pursuant to Chapter V GDPR. However, Article 48 does not by itself resolve conflicts between EU and foreign legal requirements, and still leaves parties potentially subject to them. Article 48 must be read in light of the Charter, since, as the CJEU has found, the applicability of EU law entails that of the Charter as well.[14]

As will be explained later, Article 48 is essentially a form of blocking statute that has been adapted to the data protection context. Basedow defines blocking statutes as 'political instruments' that 'are meant to increase political leverage on the government of the foreign state whose acts and policy are disapproved. The individuals and corporate entities involved are only tools to achieve that purpose',[15] which is also the case with

---

[8] See Greenwald 2014; Milanovic 2015.　[9] CLOUD Act 2018.
[10] See EDPB EDPS Response Cloud Act, p. 1.　[11] GDPR Interservice Draft.
[12] Ibid., p. 12.　[13] EP GDPR Report 2013.
[14] See Case C-617/10, *Åkerberg Fransson*, para. 21. See also Rauchegger 2015.
[15] Basedow 2017, pp. 213-214.

regard to Article 48. In other areas besides data protection, blocking statutes have been sparingly used, and their use has often been terminated after the legal conflict that gave rise to them was resolved, typically through the conclusion of an international agreement.[16] The question is whether such an approach can be realized in the case of Article 48. While initiatives are underway for the EU to negotiate such agreements, only time will tell if they are successful. In addition, government requests to access data stored in other countries are a global phenomenon not limited to the US, and the challenges posed by Article 48 will likely be even greater when they involve requests from third countries that do not share Western concepts of human rights and the rule of law.

B. Legal Background

1. EU legislation

The forerunners of Article 48 are the so-called blocking statutes that restrict compliance with the extraterritorial scope of third country law. Though it did not deal with data protection, a blocking statute was enacted at EU level in 1996, in response to a dispute between the EU and the US regarding the so-called Helms-Burton Act, which was US legislation that enforced that country's embargo against Cuba with extraterritorial effect. In response, the EU enacted Council Regulation 2271/96,[17] which declared the Act to be unenforceable within the EU. In 2018 the EU also adopted legislation to mitigate the effect of US sanctions against companies doing business in Iran.[18] EU blocking legislation contains no mention of data protection or the regulation of international data transfers.

Also relevant to Article 48 are the efforts that the EU is taking to enact a legal framework for cross-border access to electronic evidence (the so-called 'e-evidence' package).[19] At the internal EU level, this comprises a proposal for a regulation[20] on European production and preservation orders for electronic evidence in criminal matters, and a proposal for a directive[21] laying down authorizing rules on the appointment of legal representatives for the purpose of gathering evidence in criminal proceedings; and at the international level, a recommendation for a Council decision[22] authorizing the opening of negotiations in view of an agreement between the European Union and the United States of America on cross-border access to electronic evidence for judicial cooperation in criminal matters, and a proposal for a Second Additional Protocol[23] to the Council of Europe 'Budapest' Convention on Cybercrime.[24] If it is concluded, an EU-US agreement on cross-border access to electronic evidence for judicial cooperation in criminal matters could help resolve some of the conflicts of laws issues that were the motivation for including Article 48 in the GDPR, at least with regard to the US.[25]

[16] Ibid., p. 214.
[17] Council Regulation 2271/96. The annex to the Regulation was amended in June 2018.
[18] Commission Implementing Regulation August 2018.
[19] See EC E-Evidence page. Ironically, it seems that the e-evidence proposal may itself create conflicts with foreign law by requiring the production of electronic evidence held outside the EU, which may be forbidden by foreign blocking statutes. See Christakis 2019, pp. 16-17.
[20] E-Evidence Regulation Proposal.   [21] E-Evidence Directive Proposal.
[22] EU-US E-Evidence Recommendation. See also EDPS 2019.
[23] Council of Europe Cybercrime Additional Protocol Proposal.
[24] Convention on Cybercrime.   [25] See Christakis 2019, p. 17.

2. International instruments

A number of international instruments are relevant to Article 48. This includes mutual legal assistance treaties ('MLATs'), which are specifically referred to therein. Another is the Hague Evidence Convention,[26] which allows for different methods for the taking of evidence abroad in civil and commercial matters, such as by one judicial authority of a State Party requesting an authority of another State Party to obtain evidence to be used in judicial proceedings in the requesting state, or by having this done by diplomatic or consular agents. Some other relevant international agreements include the Council of Europe Cybercrime Convention[27] and the EU-US Umbrella Agreement.[28]

3. National developments

Some Member States have enacted blocking statutes that specifically target the extraterritorial scope of third country discovery requirements. An example is the French law of 16 July 1980 on the taking of evidence in view of judicial or administrative proceedings abroad,[29] which amended the law of 26 July 1968.[30]

4. Case law

The CJEU has held that constitutional principles set out in the EU treaties are to be given priority over other rules in case of conflict.[31] The fundamental right to data protection is such a constitutional principle, and in its *Schrems* judgment, the CJEU invalidated the Commission decision upon which the EU-US Safe Harbour arrangement was based, since it gave third country law precedence over EU data protection law.[32] In addition, in *Opinion 1/15* the Court found that a draft international agreement of the EU could not be concluded in its current form since several of its provisions were incompatible with fundamental rights.[33]

In a significant US case, in December 2013 the US Federal Bureau of Investigation sought the production by Microsoft of content and non-content related data of a specific customer under a warrant. Microsoft provided account information kept on its US servers, but withheld content data located on its Irish data servers, citing the potential that such unilateral legal demands could conflict with other countries' data protection laws. In July 2016, the US Second Circuit Court of Appeals ruled in favour of Microsoft, holding that search warrants served on US internet companies and cloud service providers cannot obtain customer data stored overseas.[34] In October 2017 the US Supreme Court granted the US government's petition for a writ of certiorari, but subsequently dismissed the case as moot[35] in light of the passage of the US CLOUD Act.[36]

Other US cases have also dealt with the conflict between US legal requirements and EU data protection law. For example, in the case of *Volkswagen v Valdez*,[37] the Texas Supreme Court vacated the order of a lower court that had ordered Volkswagen to transfer to it a

---

[26] Hague Evidence Convention.   [27] Convention on Cybercrime. See also Tosoni 2018.
[28] Umbrella Agreement US.   [29] French Access to Evidence for Foreigners Act 1980.
[30] French Access to Evidence for Foreigners Act 1968.
[31] See Joined Cases C-402 and 415/05P, *Kadi*, para. 285.
[32] See Case C-362/14, *Schrems*, paras. 84–87.   [33] *Opinion 1/15*. See also Kuner 2018.
[34] Second Circuit Court of Appeals, *Microsoft Corporation*.
[35] US Supreme Court, *United States v Microsoft Corporation*.   [36] CLOUD Act 2018.
[37] Texas Supreme Court, *Volkswagen v Valdez*.

company phone book containing the names and details of Volkswagen staff in potential violation of German data protection requirements.

C. Analysis

1. Introduction

Article 48 GDPR is designed to restrict the effect of extraterritorial assertions of jurisdiction by third country courts, tribunals and administrative authorities. It provides that their judgments and decisions requiring a data controller or a data processor to transfer or disclose personal data to them are not to be recognised or enforced in the EU unless they are based on an international agreement (i.e. a treaty) in force between the requesting third country and the EU or a Member State (with an important exception, as discussed below). It is also designed to prevent the circumvention of EU data protection law by the application of third country legal requirements.[38] While many of the cases that underlie the motivation for Article 48 relate to US law, it is applicable to judgments and decisions from any third country.

2. Nature and purpose of Article 48

Article 48 does not actually deal with 'transfers or disclosures not authorised by Union law' in general, as one might assume from its title, but with the narrower topic of the recognition and enforcement of judgments and decisions of third country courts, tribunals, and administrative authorities. In fact, the best way to understand Article 48 is as a blocking statute adapted to a data protection context. It is not an absolute blocking statute, since, as described below, it does allow for data transfers to be made under other legal grounds of Chapter V.[39] However, it is the first time a form of blocking statute has appeared in EU data protection law, which can account for much of the confusion surrounding it. As explained above, the original Interservice draft of the GDPR contained both a provision prohibiting the recognition or enforcement of third country judgments and decisions, and one that prohibited controllers from complying with such orders without DPA approval.[40] The final version of Article 48 GDPR retained the first provision, but not the second. However, the EDPB still views Article 48 as imposing a duty on data controllers and data processors not to comply with orders of foreign courts, tribunals, and administrative authorities unless there is a legal basis for doing so,[41] and that when an international agreement covering the transfer exists, they should demand that the foreign authority make use of it.[42] Article 48 does not mention this duty of controllers and processors, but only speaks of such foreign orders not being recognisable or enforceable, so that the EDPB's interpretation goes considerably beyond the text of Article 48.

---

[38] See regarding prevention of circumvention of EU data protection law, Kuner 2013, pp. 107–113.

[39] See Christakis 2019, pp. 7 and 14.

[40] A true blocking statute, such as the original 1996 version of Council Regulation 2271/96, Art. 4, contains both types of clauses (see Arts. 4 and 5 of that instrument).

[41] See, e.g., EDPB EDPS Response Cloud Act, p. 3; EDPB 2018, p. 5.

[42] See EDPB 2018, p. 5, stating 'In situations where there is an international agreement, such as a mutual legal assistance treaty (MLAT), EU companies should generally refuse direct requests and refer the requesting third country authority to existing MLAT or agreement'.

In fact, judgments and decisions of foreign authorities are often not used in the way that Article 48 seems to assume, i.e., they are often not presented to a court or other governmental authority in the EU by the third country for formal recognition and enforcement, but instead are routinely presented directly to the data controller or processor. Stating that they may not be recognised or enforced may thus have little effect in practice. Another oddity of Article 48 is the reference in it to mutual legal assistance treaties, which result in data transfers between law enforcement authorities, a topic that is outside the scope of the GDPR.[43] One can also ask whether Article 48 adds any extra protection for data transfers, since it could be argued that transferring data based on foreign judgments and decisions without a legal basis for processing and transfer would already violate other provisions of the GDPR (e.g., Articles 6 and 44). In this sense, Article 48 seems to be largely superfluous.

3. Legal bases for processing and transfer

The EDPB has found that compliance with foreign judgments and decisions under Article 48 is only permissible if there is a legal basis under Article 6 and Article 49[44] (this is the so-called 'two-step' test for data transfers).[45] The EDPB has analysed the application of various legal bases for data processing in the context of requests from foreign courts or authorities (in this instance, in the context of the US CLOUD Act), i.e. processing is necessary for compliance with a legal obligation (Article 6(1)(c));[46] processing is necessary in order to protect the vital interests of the data subject or another natural person (Article 6(1)(d));[47] processing is necessary of the performance of a task carried out in the public interest or in the exercise of official authority vested in the controller (Article 6(1)(e));[48] and processing is necessary for the purposes of the legitimate interests pursued by the controller or by a third party, except where such interests are overridden by the interests or fundamental rights and freedoms of the data subject (Article 6(1)(f)).[49] As can be seen from the EDPB's analysis of the individual legal bases, it has questioned whether they could be sufficient for processing in the context of complying with foreign judgments and decisions.[50]

The EDPB has also found that justifying a data transfer on the basis of the derogations of Article 49 would be 'very difficult'.[51] In doing so, it discussed the various derogations of that article that could in theory be applicable in such a situation (again in the context of the US Cloud Act), and found them all wanting in some way, at least in most cases (i.e., transfers

---

[43] Art. 2(2)(d) GDPR. Regarding the use of MLATs in practice, see Kent 2014.
[44] EDPB EDPS Response Cloud Act, p. 3.
[45] See the commentary on Art. 44 in this volume regarding the two-step test.
[46] See EDPB EDPS Response Cloud Act, p. 4, finding that this would require a legal basis in Union or Member State law, which in practice may require an international agreement.
[47] Ibid., limiting this legal basis to 'cases of requests to access personal data concerning abducted minors or other obvious situations where the transfer is in the vital interest of data subjects themselves', and that transfers could not be based on the vital interests of other persons.
[48] Ibid., p. 4, finding that this legal basis is not satisfied solely on the basis of a request from a third country authority.
[49] Ibid., p. 5, finding that complying with a request from a third country law enforcement authority could potentially be in the legitimate interest of a data controller or third party, but that this interest would be overridden by the interests or fundamental rights and freedoms of the data subject in such situation.
[50] See the commentary on Art. 6 in this volume for further discussion of these legal bases.
[51] EDPB EDPS Response Cloud Act, p. 8. See also the commentary on Article 49 in this volume.

necessary for important reasons of public interest (Article 49(1)(d));[52] transfers necessary for the establishment, exercise or defence of legal claims (Article 49(1)(e));[53] transfers necessary to protect the vital interests of the data subject or of other persons where the data subject is physically or legally incapable of giving consent (Article 49(1)(f));[54] and transfers necessary for the purpose of compelling legitimate interests pursued by the controller which are not overridden by the interests or rights and freedoms of the data subject (Article 49(1) last paragraph)).[55]

4. Conditions for application

For Article 48 to apply, there must be a 'judgment of a court or tribunal' or a 'decision of an administrative authority of a third country' that requires a 'controller or processor' to 'transfer or disclose' personal data.

4.1 'Judgment of a court or tribunal' or 'decision of an administrative authority of a third country'

The terms 'judgment of a court or tribunal and any decision of an administrative authority' should be interpreted broadly to include any such judgment or decision of a third-country court, tribunal or other public authority. However, they do not cover requests for data from private parties; thus, for example, the provision does not apply to orders or awards of private arbitral institutions. In order to be covered by Article 48, a judgment or decision must be directed to a data controller or a data processor, and must have been issued by a court, tribunal, or administrative authority of a third country (i.e., it does not apply to such orders from EU or EEA countries).

4.2 'Requiring a controller or processor'

For Article 48 to apply, the controller or processor must also be 'required' to transfer or disclose the data, which means being required upon pain of legal penalty. However, this should be broadly construed to also include situations where data controllers and processors agree to cooperate with the authorities when such an order to compel data transfer or disclosure would otherwise be issued, if their intention in doing so is to evade the requirements of Article 48.

The terms 'controller' and 'processor' are to be construed as defined in Articles 4(7) and 4(8) GDPR respectively. Article 48 applies only to those controllers and processors who are subject to the GDPR. It can also apply to requests directed to data controllers and processors not established in the EU, in so far as they come within the material and territorial scope of the GDPR under Articles 2 and 3.

When personal data have already been transferred to a third country with a valid legal basis under EU law, Article 48 should not apply, since the language of the Article makes it clear that it applies when personal data are sought to be transferred from the EU,

---

[52] EDPB EDPS Response Cloud Act, p. 6, finding that for this derogation to apply, it is not sufficient for a data transfer to be requested 'for an investigation which serves a public interest of a third county which, in an abstract sense, also exists in EU or Member State law'.

[53] Ibid., p. 7, stating that 'a close link is necessary between a data transfer and a specific procedure and the derogation cannot be used to justify the transfer of personal data on the grounds of the mere possibility that legal proceedings or formal proceedings may be brought in the future'.

[54] Ibid., p. 7, finding that the vital interests of the data subject can be validly used as a legal basis to answer foreign law enforcement requests only in 'certain exceptional, specific and necessary circumstances ... '.

[55] Ibid., finding that this provision 'cannot provide a valid lawful ground to transfer personal data' based on a foreign law enforcement request.

meaning before a data transfer has occurred. Many of the mechanisms for transferring personal data from the EU (such as adequacy decisions,[56] standard contractual clauses,[57] and binding corporate rules)[58] already contain rules for dealing with foreign government requests for data, and they should apply when personal data have already been validly transferred, not Article 48. Thus, for example, data transferred under the EU-US Privacy Shield[59] and the EU-US Umbrella Agreement[60] are not subject to Article 48.[61]

4.3 'Transfer or disclose'

As discussed at length in the commentary on Article 44 in this volume, there is no definition of the term 'data transfer' in EU data protection law, and the term 'disclose' is also not defined in the GDPR. However, in the context of Article 48, these terms should be broadly construed to include transferring, sending, making available, or disclosing the data in any way to the third country authorities.

5. Consequences of application

If the above conditions are met, then such judgment or decision may only be 'recognised or enforceable' in any manner if based on an 'international agreement', without prejudice to other grounds for transfer pursuant to Chapter V. According to the EDPB, the application of Article 48 should result in data controllers and processors refusing to transfer personal data and referring the foreign authorities to the relevant international agreement instead.[62]

5.1 'Recognised or enforceable' in any manner

Article 48 states its consequences in terms of conditions for the recognition and enforcement of a foreign judgment or decision of an administrative authority; thus, on its face it would seem to apply only when such recognition or enforcement is sought. However, the EDPB seems to interpret it more broadly as a prohibition against data controllers and data processors disclosing or transferring personal data in response to foreign governmental requests.[63]

The recognition and enforcement of foreign judgments is an area of private international law dealing with extending the legal effects of a foreign judgment or decision to the domestic territory of the State of recognition, so that the claimant can then execute it by making use of domestic enforcement mechanisms.[64] The term 'recognised and enforceable' in Article 48 is used in this formal legal sense, so that a data controller or data processor cannot be said to 'recognise or enforce' a foreign judgment or decision by transferring personal data to a foreign party that has requested them. The EDPB's more expansive interpretation of the Article seems to be based on its title ('Transfers or Disclosures not authorised by Union Law'),[65] but it seems questionable whether this interpretation can be supported in light of the clear wording of the text of Article 48.[66] While Recital 115 does state that 'Transfers should only be allowed where the conditions of this Regulation for a transfer to third countries are met', this could also be seen as a

---

[56] See e.g. Art. 3 Commission Decision Argentina 2003, as amended by Commission Decision 2016/2295.
[57] See e.g. Art. 5 (b) EC Standard Contractual Clauses Processors 2010.
[58] See e.g. WP29 2015, p. 12.　　[59] Commission Decision Privacy Shield 2016.
[60] Umbrella Agreement US.　　[61] EDPB EDPS Response Cloud Act, p. 3.
[62] EDPB 2018, p. 5.　　[63] EDPB EDPS Response Cloud Act, pp. 3-8.
[64] See Wurmnest 2012, p. 1424.　　[65] EDPB EDPS Response Cloud Act, p. 3.
[66] See Beck 2012, pp. 189-190, noting that in interpreting a provision of EU law, the CJEU 'attaches very great importance to the words used', and that 'the words used, where reasonably clear, thus raise a strong presumptiom in favour of a literal interpretation'.

restatement of Article 44. The discrepancy between the title of Article 48 and its text can only lead to confusion.

The formal recognition or enforcement of a decision or request of a court or authority of a third country is provided for in a number of international agreement to which the EU and/or the Member States are parties.[67] This is the case, for example, with regard to a formal request (known as Letters Rogatory) sent by a judicial authority of one contracting State of the Hague Evidence Convention[68] to a judicial authority in a Member State that is also party to the Convention, which then has to execute it under the methods and procedures of its own domestic law.[69]

The widespread government electronic surveillance that was brought to light by the Snowden revelations will not fall under Article 48, since it typically involves third country authorities accessing EU data without first requesting data controllers or processors to transfer the data and without seeking to have an order recognised or enforced in the EU. In this regard, the EU legislator's intention 'to enshrine by law a protection against unauthorised access to personal data'[70] has not been effectively realised.

5.2 'Based on an international agreement'

The judgment or decision must be 'based' on an international agreement in order to be recognisable or enforceable. This presumably means that it must be foreseen in the international agreement in question or issued pursuant to it. An example would be a judgment or decision of a national court issued pursuant to the Hague Evidence Convention, which provides for the taking of evidence based on letters of request issued by national courts and directed to competent authorities of other State parties.[71]

Questions may arise as to whether particular international agreements are covered by Article 48. With regard to an agreement between the requesting third country and the Union, this would require that it fall within the scope of Union law,[72] and that it be an international agreement within the meaning of Title V of the Treaty on the Functioning of the European Union ('TFEU'). The CJEU has taken a broad view of what constitutes an international agreement, finding that it indicates an undertaking entered into by entities subject to international law and that has binding force, regardless of its formal designation.[73] The agreement must be legally binding under international law, so that adherence to non-binding international standards would not be sufficient. Examples of agreements concluded by the EU that would be covered include those governing the transfer of airline passenger name record ('PNR') data.[74] International agreements in force between a third country and a Member State, such as the Hague Evidence Convention (to which some but not all EU Member States are parties), and MLATs, are expressly covered by Article 48.

The question also arises of whether Article 48 applies to international agreements in areas that may be within the scope of Union law but outside the scope of the GDPR (e.g. those dealing with criminal law or procedure,[75] such as the Council of Europe

---

[67] See regarding recognition and enforcement of foreign judgments in the EU, Van Calster 2013.
[68] Hague Evidence Convention.   [69] Hanloser 2011, pp. 32-33.
[70] EDPB EDPS Response Cloud Act, p. 3.
[71] Hague Evidence Convention, Art, 1. See Hartley 2015, p. 529.
[72] See Art. 2(2)(a) GDPR. This could mean, for example, that an international agreement covering defence or military matters would not be covered, since these areas generally do not fall within EU law.
[73] See Case C-327/91, *French Republic v Commission*, para. 27. See also Koutrakos 2015, 6339–6353.
[74] See, e.g., PNR Agreement Australia 2012 and PNR Agreement US 2012.
[75] See Art. 2(2)(d) GDPR, which exempts from its scope the processing of personal data 'by competent authorities for the purposes of the prevention, investigation, detection or prosecution of criminal offences or

Convention on Cybercrime.[76] In Article 48, the EU legislator intended to require that data transfers pursuant to third country orders be conducted under international agreements. In light of this, it would be wrong to take too restrictive a view of what constitutes an 'international agreement' under Article 48. Thus, Article 48 should apply also with regard to international agreements of the EU that may not fall within the scope of the GDPR, as long as they are within the scope of Union law and contain 'an appropriate level of protection for the fundamental rights of data subjects' as required in recital 102. Article 48 does not contain any data protection standards that international agreements must meet (besides the vague standard of 'appropriate safeguards for data subjects' in recital 102 GDPR). Data protection is not mentioned in most international agreements, though in recent years more attention has been paid to data protection standards in areas such as mutual legal assistance.[77] In this regard, the CJEU has in *Opinion 1/15* provided the standard for judging the compatibility of international agreements with fundamental rights.[78]

6. Relationship to other grounds for transfer

Article 48 concludes with the phrase 'without prejudice to other grounds for transfer pursuant to this Chapter'. Thus, even if the transfer or disclosure of personal data would not be allowed because of a clash with third country law, it may still take place as long as there is a legal basis for the transfer under another provision of Chapter V. This interpretation is supported by the amicus brief of the Commission before the US Supreme Court in the *Microsoft* case, where the Commission acknowledged that data transfers falling under Article 48 may still take place when another ground for data transfer is present.[79] The reference to data transfers being permissible when there are other grounds for transfer seems to remove much of its power to restrain third country extraterritorial jurisdictional assertions.

In practice, the only legal bases for transfer that will be relevant in the context of Article 48 are the derogations under Article 49 GDPR (aside from the possibility of an international agreement being concluded); their applicability is discussed above. The derogations of Article 49 are all to be interpreted restrictively.[80]

7. Enforcement

Infringements of Article 48 are subject to the higher level of administrative fines under Article 83(5)(c) GDPR, i.e. up to € 20 million or 4 per cent of the total worldwide turnover of the preceding financial year, whichever is higher. The EDPB interprets Article 48 as placing an obligation on controllers and processors to provide a legal basis for

---

the execution of criminal penalties, including the safeguarding against and the prevention of threats to public security'. However, there is Union law dealing with data protection in the law enforcement context (such as the LED).

[76] Convention on Cybercrime.

[77] See e.g. Umbrella Agreement US, which entered into force on 1 February 2017. The European Commission has stated that the Umbrella Agreement 'puts in place a comprehensive high-level data protection framework for EU–US law enforcement cooperation'. See EC Fact Sheet 2016. Note that Art. 1(3) of the Umbrella Agreement US states 'This Agreement in and of itself shall not be the legal basis for any transfers of personal information. A legal basis for such transfers shall always be required'.

[78] *Opinion 1/15*. See also Kuner 2018.   [79] EC Microsoft Brief, pp. 14–15.

[80] EDPB EDPS Response Cloud Act, p. 6.

processing and for transfer for data transfers to foreign authorities.[81] In practice this means that infringements of it will involve such transfers being carried out without legal bases for processing under Article 6 and for transfer under Article 49 being present.

Any court judgment or decision of a third country administrative authority may not be recognised or enforced unless it complies with the conditions of Article 48. Judgments and decisions of third countries do not fall under the rules for recognition and enforcement provided in Regulation 1215/2012 (the recast Brussels I Regulation),[82] and are thus subject to the national rules on recognition and enforcement in each Member State.[83] Since the primacy of EU law is to be broadly construed,[84] any judgment or decision falling under Article 48 should also not be enforceable under Member State law.

8. Application to the UK

The UK has taken the position that Article 48 does not apply to it,[85] since under Protocol 21 to the TFEU the UK is not bound by measures dealing with justice and home affairs unless it decides to participate in them. However, the UK declared its intention to leave the EU under Article 50 TEU,[86] at which point it will cease to be a Member State.[87] The UK Data Protection Act enacted in 2018 to implement the GDPR contains no mention of Article 48.[88]

Select Bibliography

International agreements

Cybercrime Convention: Convention on Cybercrime, CETS No. 185 (2001).
Hague Evidence Convention: Hague Convention on the Taking of Evidence Abroad in Civil or Commercial Matters, 18 March 1970, 847 UNTS 231.
OECD Guidelines 2013: Organisation for Economic Co-operation and Development, 'The OECD Privacy Framework' (2013).

EU legislation

Brussels I Regulation (recast): Regulation (EU) No. 1215/2012 of the European Parliament and of the Council of 12 December 2012 on jurisdiction and the recognition and enforcement of judgments in civil and commercial matters (recast), OJ 2012 L 351/1.
Commission Decision 2016/2295: Commission Implementing Decision (EU) 2016/2295 of 16 December 2016 amending Decisions 2000/518/EC, 2002/2/EC, 2003/490/EC, 2003/821/EC, 2004/411/EC, 2008/393/EC, 2010/146/EU, 2010/625/EU, 2011/61/EU and Implementing Decisions 2012/484/EU, 2013/65/EU on the adequate protection of personal data by certain countries, pursuant to Article 25(6) of Directive 95/46/EC of the European Parliament and of the Council (notified under document C(2016) 8353), OJ 2016 L 344/83.
Commission Decision Argentina 2003: Commission Decision 2003/1731 of 30 June 2003 pursuant to Directive (EC) 95/46 of the European Parliament and of the Council on the adequate protection of personal data in Argentina, OJ 2003 L 168/19.

---

[81] See EDPB EDPS Response Cloud Act, p. 3. [82] Brussels I Regulation (recast).
[83] Requejo Isidro 2014, p. 10. [84] See Lenaerts and Corthaut 2006, p. 289.
[85] Council Report 2012, Annex 2, Statement by the UK, p. 4. [86] UK Notification Art. 50.
[87] The final results of Brexit, and their legal implications, were unresolved at the time this text was finalised.
[88] UK Data Protection Act 2018.

Commission Decision Privacy Shield 2016: Commission Implementing Decision (EU) 2016/1250 of 12 July 2016 pursuant to Directive 95/46/EC of the European Parliament and of the Council on the adequacy of the protection provided by the EU–US Privacy Shield, OJ 2016 L 207/1.

Commission Implementing Regulation August 2018: Commission Implementing Regulation (EU) 2018/1101 of 3 August 2018 laying down the criteria for the application of the second paragraph of Article 5 of Council Regulation (EC) No. 2271/96 protecting against the effects of the extra-territorial application of legislation adopted by a third country, and actions based thereon or resulting therefrom, 2018 OJ LI 199/7.

Council Decision MLA US 2009: Council Decision 2009/820/CFSP of 23 October 2009 on the conclusion on behalf of the European Union of the Agreement on extradition between the European Union and the United States of America and the Agreement on mutual legal assistance between the European Union and the United States of America, OJ 2009 L 291/40.

Council of Europe Cybercrime Additional Protocol Proposal: European Commission, 'Recommendation for a Council Decision authorising the participation in negotiations on a second Additional Protocol to the Council of Europe Convention on Cybercrime (CETS No. 185)', COM(2019) 71 final, 5 May 2019.

Council Regulation 2271/96: Council Regulation (EC) No. 2271/96 of 22 November 1996 protecting against the effects of the extra-territorial application of legislation adopted by a third country, and actions based thereon or resulting therefrom, OJ 1996 L 309/1, *amended by* Commission Delegated Regulation (EU) 2018/1100 of 6 June 2018 amending the Annex to Council Regulation (EC) No. 2271/96 protecting against the effects of extra-territorial application of legislation adopted by a third country, and actions based thereon or resulting therefrom, OJ LI 199/1.

EC Standard Contractual Clauses Processor 2010: Commission Decision 2010/87 of 5 February 2010 on Standard Contractual Clauses for the Transfer of Personal Data to Processors Established in Third Countries Under Directive 95/46/EC of the European Parliament and of the Council, OJ 2010 L 39/5.

E-Evidence Directive Proposal: European Commission, 'Proposal for a Directive of the European Parliament and of the Council laying down harmonised rules on the appointment of legal representatives for the purpose of gathering evidence in criminal proceedings', COM(2018) 226 final, 17 April 2018.

E-Evidence Regulation Proposal: European Commission, 'Proposal for a Regulation of the European Parliament and of the Council on European Production and Preservation Orders for electronic evidence in criminal matters', COM(2018) 225 final, 17 April 2018.

EU-US E-Evidence Recommendation: European Commission, 'Recommendation for a Council Decision authorising the opening of negotiations in view of an agreement between the European Union and the United States of America on cross-border access to electronic evidence for judicial cooperation in criminal matters', COM(2019) 70 final, 5 May 2019.

MLA EU US 2003: Agreement on mutual legal assistance between the European Union and the United States of America, OJ 2003 L 181/34.

PNR Agreement Australia 2012: Agreement between the European Union and Australia on the processing and transfer of Passenger Name Record (PNR) data by air carriers to the Australian Customs and Border Protection Service, OJ 2012 L 186/4.

PNR Agreement US 2012: Agreement between the United States of America and the European Union on the use and transfer of passenger name records to the United States Department of Homeland Security, OJ 2012 L 215/5.

Umbrella Agreement US: Agreement between the United States of America and the European Union on the Protection of Personal Information relating to the Prevention, Investigation, Detection and Prosecution of Criminal Offenses, OJ 2017 L 336/3.

National legislation

CLOUD Act 2018: Clarifying Lawful Overseas Use of Data Act (CLOUD Act), HR 1625, Division V, 115th Congress, 23 March 2018.
French Access to Evidence for Foreigners Act 1968: Loi n° 68-678 du 26 juillet 1968 relative à la communication de documents et renseignements d'ordre économique, commercial, industriel, financier ou technique à des personnes physiques ou morales étrangères.
French Access to Evidence for Foreigners Act 1980: Loi n° 80-538 du 16 juillet 1980 relative à la communication de documents ou renseignements d'ordre économique, commercial ou technique à des personnes physiques ou morales étrangères.
Sarbanes-Oxley Act 2002: Sarbanes-Oxley Act of 2002, Pub. L. No. 107-204.
UK Data Protection Act 2018: Data Protection Act 2018 (Chapter 12).

Academic writings

Basedow 2017: Basedow, 'Blocking Statutes', in Basedow, Rühl, Ferrari and Asensio (eds.), *Encyclopedia of Private International Law* (Edward Elgar 2017), 209.
Beck 2012: Beck, *The Legal Reasoning of the Court of Justice of the EU* (Hart 2012) (Kindle edition).
Borchers 2003: Borchers, 'The Incredible Shrinking Hague Evidence Convention', 38(1) *Texas International Law Journal* (2003), 73.
Cate and Dempsey 2017: Cate and Dempsey, *Bulk Collection: Systematic Government Access to Private-Sector Data* (OUP 2017).
Cate, Dempsey and Rubenstein 2012: Cate, Dempsey and Rubenstein, 'Systematic Government Access to Private-Sector Data', 2(4) *International Data Privacy Law* (2012), 195.
Christakis 2019: Christakis, 'Transfer of EU Personal Data to U.S. Law Enforcement Authorities After the CLOUD Act: Is There a Conflict with the GDPR?' (14 June 2019), available at https://papers.ssrn.com/sol3/papers.cfm?abstract_id=3397047.
Cooper and Kuner 2017: Cooper and Kuner, 'Data Protection Law and International Dispute Resolution', 382 *Recueil des cours/Collected Courses of the Hague Academy of International Law* (2017), 9.
Greenwald 2014: Greenwald, *No Place to Hide: Edward Snowden, the NSA, and the US Surveillance State* (MacMillan 2014).
Hanloser 2011: Hanloser, 'Hague Convention on the Taking of Evidence Abroad', in Noorda and Hanloser (eds.), *E-Discovery and Data Privacy* (Wolters Kluwer 2011), 29.
Hartley 2015: Hartley, *International Commercial Litigation* (2nd edn, CUP 2015).
Kent 2014: Kent, 'Sharing Investigation Specific Data with Law Enforcement: an International Approach', *Stanford Public Law Working Paper* (2014), available at https://papers.ssrn.com/sol3/papers.cfm?abstract_id=2472413.
Koutrakos 2015: Koutrakos, *EU External Relations Law* (Hart Publishing 2015) (Kindle edition).
Kuner 2013: Kuner, *Transborder Data Flow Regulation and Data Privacy Law* (OUP 2013).
Kuner 2018: Kuner, 'International Agreements, Data Protection, and EU Fundamental Rights on the International Stage: *Opinion 1/15*', 55(3) *Common Market Law Review* (2018), 857.
Lenaerts and Corthaut 2006: Lenaerts and Corthaut, 'Of Birds and Hedges: The Role of Primacy in Invoking Norms of EU Law', 31(3) *European Law Review* (2006), 287.
Milanovic 2015: Milanovic, 'Human Rights Treaties and Foreign Surveillance: Privacy in the Digital Age', 56(1) *Harvard International Law Journal* (2015), 81.
Rauchegger 2015: Rauchegger, 'The Interplay between the Charter and National Constitutions after *Åkerberg Fransson* and *Melloni*', in de Vries, Bernitz and Weatherill (eds.), *The EU Charter of Fundamental Rights as a Binding Instrument* (Hart Publishing 2015), 93.
Requejo Isidro 2014: Requejo Isidro, 'Recognition and Enforcement in the new Brussels I Regulation (Regulation 1215/2012, Brussels I recast): The Abolition of Exequatur' (11 July 2014), available at http://www.ejtn.eu/PageFiles/6333/Requejo_Doc.pdf.

Tosoni 2018: Tosoni, 'Rethinking Privacy in the Council of Europe's Convention on Cybercrime', 34(6) *Computer Law & Security Review* (2018), 1197.
Van Calster 2013: Van Calster, *European Private International Law* (Hart Publishing 2013) (Kindle edition).
Wurmnest 2012: Wurmnest, 'Recognition and Enforcement of Foreign Judgments', in Basedow, Hopt, Zimmerman and Stier (eds.), *The Max Planck Encyclopedia of European Private Law* (OUP 2012), 1424.

Papers of data protection authorities

EDPB 2018: European Data Protection Board, 'Guidelines 2/2018 on Derogations of Article 49 under Regulation 2016/679' (25 May 2018).
EDPB EDPS Response Cloud Act: European Data Protection Board and European Data Protection Supervisor, 'EPDB-EDPS Joint Response to the LIBE Committee on the impact of the US Cloud Act on the European legal framework for personal data protection (annex)' (10 July 2019).
EDPS 2019: European Data Protection Supervisor, 'Opinion 2/2019: EDPS Opinion on the negotiating mandate of an EU-US agreement on cross-border access to electronic evidence' (2 April 2019).
WP29 2006: Article 29 Working Party, 'Opinion 1/2006 on the Application of EU Data Protection Rules to Internal Whistleblowing Schemes in the Fields of Accounting, Internal Accounting Controls, Auditing Matters, Fight against Bribery, Banking and Financial Crime' (WP 117, 1 February 2006).
WP29 2009: Article 29 Working Party, 'Working Document 1/2009 on Pre-Trial Discovery for Cross Border Civil Litigation' (WP 158, 11 February 2009).
WP29 2015: Article 29 Working Party, 'Explanatory Document on the Processor Binding Corporate Rules' (WP 204 rev.01, 22 May 2015).
WP29 2017: Article 29 Working Party, 'Adequacy Referential (updated)' (WP 254, 28 November 2017).
CNIL 2005A: CNIL, 'Délibération n° 2005-110 du 26 mai 2005 relative à une demande d'autorisation de McDonald's France pour la mise en œuvre d'un dispositif d'intégrité professionnelle' (26 May 2005).
CNIL 2005B: CNIL, 'Délibération n° 2005-111 du 26 mai 2005 relative à une demande d'autorisation de la Compagnie européenne d'accumulateurs pour la mise en œuvre d'un dispositif de ligne éthique' (26 May 2005).

Reports and recommendations

Council Report 2012: Adoption of the Council's position at first reading and of the statement of the Council's reasons, 7920/16, 14 April 2016.
EP GDPR Report 2013: Report on the proposal for a regulation of the European Parliament and of the Council on the protection of individual with regard to the processing of personal data and on the free movement of such data (General Data Protection Regulation), 2012/0011(COD), 22 November 2013.
GDPR Interservice Draft: Proposal for a Regulation of the European Parliament and of the Council on the protection of individuals with regard to the processing of personal data and on the free movement of such data (General Data Protection Regulation), Version 56, 29 November 2011.

Others

EC E-Evidence page: European Commission, 'E-evidence—cross-border access to electronic evidence', available at https://ec.europa.eu/info/policies/justice-and-fundamental-rights/criminal-justice/e-evidence-cross-border-access-electronic-evidence_en.

EC Fact Sheet 2016: European Commission, 'Fact Sheet: Questions and Answers on the EU–U.S. Data Protection 'Umbrella Agreement' (1 December 2016), available at http://europa.eu/rapid/press-release_MEMO-16-4183_en.htm.

EC Microsoft Brief: Amicus Brief of the European Commission on behalf of the European Union as *Amicus Curiae* in support of neither party in: United States v. Microsoft Corporation 584 U.S. (2018).

UK Notification Article 50: Letter of 29 March 2017 from the Prime Minister of the United Kingdom to the President of the European Council (United Kingdom Notification under Article 50 TEU) (29 March 2017), available at http://data.consilium.europa.eu/doc/document/XT-20001-2017-INIT/en/pdf.

Article 49. Derogations for specific situations

CHRISTOPHER KUNER

1. In the absence of an adequacy decision pursuant to Article 45(3), or of appropriate safeguards pursuant to Article 46, including binding corporate rules, a transfer or a set of transfers of personal data to a third country or an international organisation shall take place only on one of the following conditions:
    (a) the data subject has explicitly consented to the proposed transfer, after having been informed of the possible risks of such transfers for the data subject due to the absence of an adequacy decision and appropriate safeguards;
    (b) the transfer is necessary for the performance of a contract between the data subject and the controller or the implementation of pre-contractual measures taken at the data subject's request;
    (c) the transfer is necessary for the conclusion or performance of a contract concluded in the interest of the data subject between the controller and another natural or legal person;
    (d) the transfer is necessary for important reasons of public interest;
    (e) the transfer is necessary for the establishment, exercise or defence of legal claims;
    (f) the transfer is necessary in order to protect the vital interests of the data subject or of other persons, where the data subject is physically or legally incapable of giving consent;
    (g) the transfer is made from a register which according to Union or Member State law is intended to provide information to the public and which is open to consultation either by the public in general or by any person who can demonstrate a legitimate interest, but only to the extent that the conditions laid down by Union or Member State law for consultation are fulfilled in the particular case.

    Where a transfer could not be based on a provision in Article 45 or 46, including the provisions on binding corporate rules, and none of the derogations for a specific situation referred to in the first subparagraph of this paragraph is applicable, a transfer to a third country or an international organisation may take place only if the transfer is not repetitive, concerns only a limited number of data subjects, is necessary for the purposes of compelling legitimate interests pursued by the controller which are not overridden by the interests or rights and freedoms of the data subject, and the controller has assessed all the circumstances surrounding the data transfer and has on the basis of that assessment provided suitable safeguards with regard to the protection of personal data. The controller shall inform the supervisory authority of the transfer. The controller shall, in addition to providing the information referred to in Articles 13 and 14, inform the data subject of the transfer and on the compelling legitimate interests pursued.

2. A transfer pursuant to point (g) of the first subparagraph of paragraph 1 shall not involve the entirety of the personal data or entire categories of the personal data contained in the register. Where the register is intended for consultation by persons having a legitimate interest, the transfer shall be made only at the request of those persons or if they are to be the recipients.

3. Points (a), (b) and (c) of the first subparagraph of paragraph 1 and the second subparagraph thereof shall not apply to activities carried out by public authorities in the exercise of their public powers.

4. The public interest referred to in point (d) of the first subparagraph of paragraph 1 shall be recognised in Union law or in the law of the Member State to which the controller is subject.

5. In the absence of an adequacy decision, Union or Member State law may, for important reasons of public interest, expressly set limits to the transfer of specific categories of personal data to a third country or an international organisation. Member States shall notify such provisions to the Commission.
6. The controller or processor shall document the assessment as well as the suitable safeguards referred to in the second subparagraph of paragraph 1 of this Article in the records referred to in Article 30.

Relevant Recitals

(111) Provisions should be made for the possibility for transfers in certain circumstances where the data subject has given his or her explicit consent, where the transfer is occasional and necessary in relation to a contract or a legal claim, regardless of whether in a judicial procedure or whether in an administrative or any out-of-court procedure, including procedures before regulatory bodies. Provision should also be made for the possibility for transfers where important grounds of public interest laid down by Union or Member State law so require or where the transfer is made from a register established by law and intended for consultation by the public or persons having a legitimate interest. In the latter case, such a transfer should not involve the entirety of the personal data or entire categories of the data contained in the register and, when the register is intended for consultation by persons having a legitimate interest, the transfer should be made only at the request of those persons or, if they are to be the recipients, taking into full account the interests and fundamental rights of the data subject.

(112) Those derogations should in particular apply to data transfers required and necessary for important reasons of public interest, for example in cases of international data exchange between competition authorities, tax or customs administrations, between financial supervisory authorities, between services competent for social security matters, or for public health, for example in the case of contact tracing for contagious diseases or in order to reduce and/or eliminate doping in sport. A transfer of personal data should also be regarded as lawful where it is necessary to protect an interest which is essential for the data subject's or another person's vital interests, including physical integrity or life, if the data subject is incapable of giving consent. In the absence of an adequacy decision, Union or Member State law may, for important reasons of public interest, expressly set limits to the transfer of specific categories of data to a third country or an international organisation. Member States should notify such provisions to the Commission. Any transfer to an international humanitarian organisation of personal data of a data subject who is physically or legally incapable of giving consent, with a view to accomplishing a task incumbent under the Geneva Conventions or to complying with international humanitarian law applicable in armed conflicts, could be considered to be necessary for an important reason of public interest or because it is in the vital interest of the data subject.

(113) Transfers which can be qualified as not repetitive and that only concern a limited number of data subjects, could also be possible for the purposes of the compelling legitimate interests pursued by the controller, when those interests are not overridden by the interests or rights and freedoms of the data subject and when the controller has assessed all the circumstances surrounding the data transfer. The controller should give particular consideration to the nature of the personal data, the purpose and duration of the proposed processing operation or operations, as well as the situation in the country of origin, the third country and the country of final destination, and should provide suitable safeguards to protect fundamental rights and freedoms of natural persons with regard to the processing of their personal data. Such transfers should be possible only in residual cases where none of the other grounds for transfer are applicable. For scientific or historical research purposes or statistical purposes, the legitimate expectations of society for an increase of knowledge should be taken into consideration. The controller should inform the supervisory authority and the data subject about the transfer.

(114) In any case, where the Commission has taken no decision on the adequate level of data protection in a third country, the controller or processor should make use of solutions that provide data subjects with enforceable and effective rights as regards the processing of their data in the Union once those data have been transferred so that that they will continue to benefit from fundamental rights and safeguards.

Closely Related Provisions

Recital 6; recital 48; Articles 13(1)(f) and 14(1)(f) (Information to a data subject); Article 15(1)(c) (Right to access information about data recipients in third countries); Article 23(2)(d) (Member States can restrict individuals' rights but must provide for safeguards to prevent abuse or unlawful transfer) (see too recital 153); Article 28(3)(a) (Provisions of a data processing agreement stipulating controller's instructions regarding data transfers); Article 30(1)(e) and (2)(c) (Internal records about data transfers); Article 40(2)(j) (Data transfer codes of conduct); Article 70(1)(j) (Guidelines of the Board specifying criteria for data transfers on the basis of derogations); Article 83(5)(c) (Fines for non-compliance with data transfer restrictions)

Related Provisions in LED [Directive (EU) 2016/680]

Recital 36; Article 38 (Derogations for specific situations); Article 39 (Transfers of personal data to recipients established in third countries) (see too recital 72)

Relevant Case Law

CJEU

Joined Cases C-92/09 and 93/09, *Volker and Markus Schecke GbR and Hartmut Eifert v Land Hessen*, judgment of 9 November 2010 (Grand Chamber) (ECLI:EU:C:2010:662).
Case C-617/10, *Åkerberg Fransson*, judgment of 26 February 2013 (ECLI:EU:C:2013:105).
Joined Cases C-293/12 and C-594/12, *Digital Rights Ireland Ltd v Minister for Communications, Marine and Natural Resources and Others* and *Kärntner Landesregierung and Others*, judgment of 8 April 2014 (Grand Chamber) (ECLI:EU:C:2014:238).
Case C-362/14, *Maximillian Schrems v Data Protection Commissioner*, judgment of 6 October 2015 (Grand Chamber) (ECLI:EU:C:2015:650).

A. Rationale and Policy Underpinnings

The rationale of having derogations from restrictions on international data transfers was set out by the WP29 soon after the DPD entered into force. As the WP29 stated, the derogations are meant to cover situations in which there is no adequate protection in the country to which the data are to be transferred, but 'the risks to the data subject are relatively small' or 'other interests (public interests or those of the data subject himself) override the data subject's right to privacy'.[1] Thus, the derogations in effect function as a 'safety valve' to allow transfers when there is an overriding societal interest that they take place, whether because the risks to the transfers are small, or because such risks are overridden by other important rights and interests. As the CJEU has held, data protection is

[1] WP29 1998, p. 24.

not an absolute right,[2] which implies that there must be situations when respect for other important rights and freedoms requires that international data transfers be allowed.[3] However, this rationale also requires that the derogations be narrowly construed,[4] and cannot generally provide a long-term framework for repeated or structural data transfers.[5] The GDPR maintains the derogations of the DPD, makes explicit some restrictions on their use that had heretofore been implicit, and also adds to their number. The LED also contains derogations for specific data transfer situations.[6]

B. Legal Background

1. EU legislation

The DPD contained a list of derogations in Article 26(1) that provide the basis for Article 49 GDPR.[7] It required Member States to provide that transfers to a third country that did not ensure an adequate level of protection could take place on the following conditions:

1. Consent: 'the data subject has given his consent unambiguously to the proposed transfer' (Article 26(1)(a)).
2. Performance of a contract: 'the transfer is necessary for the performance of a contract between the data subject and the controller or the implementation of precontractual measures taken in response to the data subject's request' (Article 26(1)(b)).
3. Conclusion or performance of a contract in the interest of a data subject: 'the transfer is necessary for the conclusion or performance of a contract concluded in the interest of the data subject between the controller and a third party' (Article 26(1)(c)).
4. Important public interest grounds or defence of legal claims: 'the transfer is necessary or legally required on important public interest grounds, or for the establishment, exercise or defence of legal claims' (Article 26(1)(d)).
5. Vital interest of the data subject: 'the transfer is necessary in order to protect the vital interests of the data subject' (Article 26(1)(e)).
6. Transfers from a register to provide information to the public: 'the transfer is made from a register which according to laws or regulations is intended to provide information to the public and which is open to consultation either by the public in general or by any person who can demonstrate legitimate interest, to the extent that the conditions laid down in law for consultation are fulfilled in the particular case' (Article 26(1)(f)).

Under Article 26(1), the derogations were available unless 'otherwise provided by domestic law governing particular cases'.

---

[2] Joined Cases C-92/09 and C-93/09, *Schecke*, para. 48.
[3] See Art. 19 UDHR, stating 'Everyone has the right to freedom of opinion and expression; this right includes freedom to hold opinions without interference and to seek, receive and impart information and ideas through any media and *regardless of frontiers*' (emphasis added); Art. 19 (2) ICCPR, stating 'Everyone shall have the right to freedom of expression; this right shall include freedom to seek, receive and impart information and ideas of all kinds, *regardless of frontiers*, either orally, in writing or in print, in the form of art, or through any media of his choice' (emphasis added).
[4] See WP29 1998, p. 24.   [5] WP29 2005, p. 11 (regarding consent).   [6] Art. 38 LED.
[7] Regarding the derogations under the DPD, see Kuner 2007, pp. 210–218.

2. International instruments

The Council of Europe Convention 108 does not provide specific derogations from the restrictions on trans-border data flows provided for in Article 12. However, the Additional Protocol to Convention 108[8] contains the following derogations to the obligation of States Parties to allow data transfers to states and organisations that are not party to the Convention only if they provide an adequate level of protection:

By way of derogation from paragraph 1 of Article 2 of this Protocol, each Party may allow for the transfer of personal data:

a. if domestic law provides for it because of :
   - specific interests of the data subject, or
   - legitimate prevailing interests, especially important public interests, or
b. if safeguards, which can in particular result from contractual clauses, are provided by the controller responsible for the transfer and are found adequate by the competent authorities according to domestic law.[9]

The Explanatory Report to the Additional Protocol states as follows with regard to these provisions:

The parties have discretion to determine derogations from the principle of an adequate level of protection. The relevant domestic law provisions must nevertheless respect the principle inherent in European law that clauses making exceptions are interpreted restrictively, so that the exception does not become the rule. Domestic law exceptions can therefore be made for a legitimate prevailing interest. That interest may be to protect an important public interest, such as is specified in the context of Article 8 paragraph 2 of the European Convention on Human Rights and Article 9 paragraph 2 of Convention ETS No. 108; the exercise or defence of a legal claim; or the extraction of data from a public register. Exceptions may also be made for the specific interest of the data subject as for the fulfilment of a contract with the data subject or in his interest, or for protecting his vital interest or when he has given his consent. In this case, before consenting, the data subject would have to be informed in an appropriate way about the intended transfer.[10]

The Modernised Council of Europe Convention 108 provides for the following derogations with regard to international data transfers:

Notwithstanding the provisions of the previous paragraphs, each Party may provide that the transfer of personal data may take place if:

a. the data subject has given explicit, specific and free consent, after being informed of risks arising in the absence of appropriate safeguards; or
b. the specific interests of the data subject require it in the particular case; or
c. prevailing legitimate interests, in particular important public interests, are provided for by law and such transfer constitutes a necessary and proportionate measure in a democratic society; or
d. it constitutes a necessary and proportionate measure in a democratic society for freedom of expression.[11]

---

[8] See Table of Legislation.　　[9] Additional Protocol Convention 108, Art. 2(2).
[10] Explanatory Report Additional Protocol Convention 108 2001, para. 31.
[11] Art. 14(4) Modernised Convention 108.

3. National developments

Article 49 allows for Member State law (along with Union law) to determine the scope of derogations in the following two cases:[12] under Article 49(1)(g), when Member State law specifies the conditions for public registers providing information to the public, and under Article 49(4), in specifying important reasons of public interest. In addition, under Article 49(5) Member State law may, for important reasons of public interest, expressly set limits to the transfer of specific categories of personal data to a third country or an international organisation (discussed further below).

4. Case law

There are no judgments of the CJEU specifically dealing with derogations.

C. Analysis

1. Introduction

As provided in Article 49(1) GDPR, the derogations under Article 49 are designed to be used in situations when no adequacy decision has been issued with regard to the third country of data transfer, and appropriate safeguards cannot be used. That is, Chapter V of the GDPR sets up a three-tiered structure for legal bases for data transfers, with adequacy decisions at the top, appropriate safeguards in the middle, and derogations at the bottom. This means that if an adequacy decision has been issued then it should be relied on; if not, then appropriate safeguards should be used; and only if neither of these legal bases is available should the derogations be relied on.[13] The derogations in Article 49 represent an exclusive list (i.e. there are no other ones).

The language of some of the derogations refers specifically to international transfers by data controllers,[14] while others also mention data processors.[15] Whether a particular derogation applies only to data transfers made by data controllers or also to those made by data processors will have to be determined based on the language and purpose of the respective derogation.

It is important to note that the derogations are to be interpreted restrictively and used sparingly. This is made clear by several provisions of Article 49 that place restrictions on their use.[16] In addition, under EU law derogations from fundamental rights must be interpreted restrictively.[17]

Use of the derogations of Article 49 by their nature provides no extra protection for data transfers. However, any relevant provisions of the GDPR continue to apply when personal data are transferred based on a derogation.[18] In addition, such provisions must

---

[12] See below for more information about each of these derogations.
[13] The EDPB has affirmed this 'layered' approach. See EDPB 2018, pp. 3–4.
[14] See e.g. Art. 49(1)(b)–(c) GDPR; ibid., second subparagraph of Art. 49(1); and ibid., Art. 49(4).
[15] See e.g. ibid., Art. 49(6), referring to data controllers and data processors with regard to the second subparagraph of Art. 49(1).
[16] E.g. in Arts. 49(2)–(4) GDPR. See also EDPB 2018, p. 4.
[17] See e.g. Case C-362/14, *Schrems*, para. 92; Joined Cases C-293/12 and C-594/12, *Digital Rights Ireland*, para. 52.
[18] See Art. 44 GDPR, providing that data transfers made under Chapter V can only be made 'subject to the other provisions of this Regulation'. See also the commentary on Art. 44 in this volume.

be read in light of the Charter, since, as the CJEU has found, the applicability of EU law entails the applicability of the Charter.[19]

The structure of Article 49 is confusing. Paragraphs (2)–(4) and (6) contain qualifications or specifications of the various derogations and would better have been included in those respective paragraphs rather than having been set out separately, and the second subparagraph of paragraph (1) is set out separately and is not given a number. Also, Article 49(5) dealing with limitations on data transfers under Union or Member State law seems out of place in Article 49 (see below).

On 29 March 2017, the UK invoked Article 50 of the Treaty on European Union ('TEU') and indicated its intention to leave the EU, at which point it will become a third country by operation of law ('Brexit') and all Union primary and secondary law will cease to apply to the UK.[20] The EDPB[21] and the UK Information Commissioner[22] have published guidance for dealing with international data transfers post-Brexit, including the use of derogations.

2. Consent

Article 49(1)(a) allows a transfer or set of transfers to take place when 'the data subject has explicitly consented to the proposed transfer, after having been informed of the possible risks of such transfers for the data subject due to the absence of an adequacy decision and appropriate safeguards'.

Article 49(1)(a) requires explicit consent for international data transfers, which is a higher level of consent than that under Article 26(1) DPD that required unambiguous consent. Thus, consent for data transfers must be at the same level as that for the processing of sensitive data under Article 9(2)(a) GDPR, and is more stringent than the definition of consent contained in Article 4(11) GDPR (which defines consent as 'any freely given, specific, informed and unambiguous indication of the data subject's wishes by which he or she, by a statement or by a clear affirmative action, signifies agreement to the processing of personal data relating to him or her'). This means that giving consent to transfer personal data cannot be implied, and must be evidenced by some positive, affirmative action (such as checking an unchecked box on a web form, providing an electronic signature, or using a two-step verification procedure).[23]

Consent must also be specific for a particular data transfer or set of transfers. This means that 'blanket' consent for undetermined data transfers in the future is not valid, and it may be impossible to obtain valid consent if the occurrence and specific circumstances of the transfer are not known.[24] In addition, consent may only be obtained after the data subject has been informed about the risks of the transfer that exist owing to the absence of an adequacy decision and appropriate safeguards. Consent can also always be withdrawn at any time.[25]

With regard to consent that has already been given before the GDPR enters into force, recital 171 indicates that it can be used as long as it complies with the requirements of the GDPR. This seems to indicate that consent for data transfers obtained under the

---

[19] See Case C-617/10, *Åkerberg Fransson*, para. 21. See also Rauchegger 2015.
[20] Commission Brexit Preparedness Notice, p. 1.   [21] EDPB Brexit information note.
[22] ICO 2018.
[23] See WP29 2017, pp. 18–19. See also the commentary on Art. 9 in this volume.
[24] EDPB 2018, p. 7.   [25] Ibid., p. 8.

DPD will have to be 'upgraded' to comply with the GDPR, i.e. that if may need to be confirmed under the GDPR's more stringent requirements. Under Article 49(3) GDPR, public authorities may not rely on consent to conduct international data transfers when they are acting in the exercise of their public powers.

3. Necessary for the performance of a contract between the data subject and the controller or for the implementation of precontractual measures taken at the data subject's request

Article 49(1)(b) allows a transfer or set of transfers to take place when 'the transfer is necessary for the performance of a contract between the data subject and the controller, or for the implementation of pre-contractual measures taken at the data subject's request'.

A strict definition of when a data transfer is 'necessary' is applied to this derogation, which limits the situations in which it may be used. The WP29 made this clear with regard to Article 26(1)(b) DPD:

This 'necessity test' here requires a close and substantial connection between the data subject and the purposes of the contract. Thus, certain international groups would like to be able to avail themselves of this exception in order to transfer data of their employees from a subsidiary to the parent company, for example in order to centralise the group's payment and human resources management functions. They believe that such transfers could be deemed necessary for performance of the employment contract concluded between the employee and the data controller. The Working Party holds this interpretation as excessive since it is highly questionable whether the concept of an employment contract can be interpreted so broadly, as there is no direct and objective link between performance of an employment contract and such a transfer of data.[26]

Based on recital 111, this derogation may only be used if the transfer is 'occasional'. The EDPB has explained that this excludes data transfers 'regularly occurring within a stable relationship', and that it cannot apply to many transfers within a business relationship.[27] Examples of situations when the derogation could apply would be when a hotel chain transfers data about a guest's reservation to the hotel the guest will be staying at in a third country, or when payment information is transferred to a third country in order to effectuate a bank transfer that an individual has initiated. Also, occasional transfers are covered by this derogation.[28] The reference to precontractual measures should be broadly construed to mean measures that the data subject has initiated before a contractual relationship has been created (for example, a preliminary booking for a trip made by a travel agent for a customer).[29]

Article 49(1)(b) GDPR is identical to Article 26(1)(b) DPD, except that it uses the formulation 'taken at the data subject's request' rather than 'in response to the data subject's request'. The formulation used in the GDPR is more explicit in making it clear that the implementation of precontractual measures must be initiated by request of the data subject.

Under Article 49(3) GDPR, public authorities may not rely on the performance of a contract as a legal basis to conduct international data transfers when they are acting in the exercise of their public powers.

---

[26] WP29 2005, p. 13. See also EDPB 2018, pp. 8–9.　　[27] EDPB 2018, p. 9.
[28] Rec. 111 GDPR.　　[29] See Dammann and Simitis 1997, p. 149.

4. Necessary for the conclusion or performance of a contract concluded in the interest of the data subject between the controller and another natural or legal person

Article 49(1)(c) allows a transfer or set of transfers to take place when 'the transfer is necessary for the conclusion or performance of a contract concluded in the interest of the data subject between the controller and another natural or legal person'. The difference between this provision and Article 49(1)(b) is that under Article 49(1)(c), the data subject is not a party to the contract in question, but it was concluded in their interest. The same conditions that the transfer be necessary and occasional that apply with regard to Article 49(1)(b) also apply to this provision. Also, occasional transfers are covered by this derogation.[30] This derogation could apply, for example, when the data subject is the beneficiary of an international bank transfer, or when a travel agent forwards the details of a flight booking to an airline.[31]

Article 49(1)(c) GDPR is identical to Article 26(1)(c) DPD, except that it uses the formulation 'between the controller and another natural or legal person' rather than 'between the controller and a third party'. There is no substantive difference in this new formulation. Under Article 49(3) GDPR, public authorities may not rely on this derogation to conduct international data transfers when they are acting in the exercise of their public powers.

5. Necessary for important reasons of public interest

Article 49(1)(d) allows a transfer or set of transfers to take place when 'the transfer is necessary for important reasons of public interest'. This requires satisfaction of the necessity test discussed above.

It is not sufficient to come under this derogation that a particular policy be recognised as falling within the public interest both in the EU and in a third country. For example, the prevention of crime is in the public interest both in the EU and third countries, but crime prevention in an abstract sense would not be sufficient to qualify under this derogation. Rather, as the EDPB has stated, '[T]he derogation only applies when it can also be deduced from EU law or the law of the member state to which the controller is subject that such data transfers are allowed for important public interest purposes including in the spirit of reciprocity for international cooperation'.[32]

Transferring personal data based on important reasons of public interest requires that such public interest be laid down in EU law or Member State law to which the data controller is subject, as required in Article 49(4).[33] This also covers international commitments to which Member States are subject and which have thus become part of Member State law. In order to fall within the derogation, the public interest grounds must be 'important',[34] so that not every public interest will qualify. A public interest that does not have a basis in EU or Member State law, or that is only laid down in the law of a third

---

[30] Ibid.   [31] See EC Communication 2015, p. 10.   [32] EDPB 2018, p. 10.
[33] See also Art. 6(3) GDPR.
[34] See ibid., Art. 9(2)(g), which refers to 'substantial public interest' as grounds for the processing of sensitive data.

country, does not provide a legal basis for data transfers based on important reasons of public interest.[35] The existence of an international agreement that is designed to foster cooperation with regard to the particular issue is an indicator of an important reason of public interest.[36]

This derogation could cover, for example, 'cases of international data exchange between competition authorities, tax or customs administrations, between financial supervisory authorities, between services competent for social security matters, or for public health, for example in the case of contact tracing for contagious diseases or in order to reduce and/ or eliminate doping in sport'.[37] The GDPR also refers to humanitarian action as serving important grounds of public interest. Thus, under recital 46 this includes data processing necessary for humanitarian purposes such as monitoring epidemics, or humanitarian action in natural and man-made disasters. Recital 112 also states that transfers to international humanitarian organisations of the personal data of an individual who is physically or legally incapable of giving consent may be found necessary for an important reason of public interest or because it is in the vital interest of the data subject when this is necessary to accomplish a task under the Geneva Conventions or to comply with international humanitarian law in armed conflicts, which would apply to the work of the International Committee of the Red Cross ('ICRC').[38]

Questions have arisen about whether the transfer of personal data to foreign law enforcement authorities could be covered by the public interest derogation, particularly in cases involving the US CLOUD Act.[39] Generally speaking, foreign law enforcement requirements cannot by themselves provide a legal basis for the transfer of personal data.[40] The EDPB has also indicated that derogations under Article 49 cannot generally provide a legal basis for complying with orders from non-EU public authorities,[41] and has stated that for the application of the public interest exception, 'it is not sufficient that the data transfer is requested (for example by a third country authority) for an investigation which serves a public interest of a third country which, in an abstract sense, also exists in EU or Member State law'.[42] The Commission has suggested that the derogation may be satisfied when the foreign request is based on important reasons of public interest that are recognised in EU law or the law of the Member State to which the data controller is subject, such as 'particularly serious areas of crime' that are listed in Article 83(1) of the Treaty on the Functioning of the European Union ('TFEU'), namely 'terrorism, trafficking in human beings and sexual exploitation of women and children, illicit drug trafficking, illicit arms trafficking, money laundering, corruption, counterfeiting of means of payment, computer crime and organised crime'.[43] However, there seems to be no reason to limit important reasons of public interest to the types of crime

---

[35] This is also made clear ibid., Art. 48.
[36] EDPB 2018, p. 10.   [37] Rec. 112 GDPR.
[38] See also the commentary on Art. 4(26) in this volume regarding the definition of international organisation.
[39] CLOUD Act 2018. See the commentary on Art. 48 in this volume. See also Christakis 2019.
[40] Thus, the WP29 rejected the argument that the transfer of airline passenger name record (PNR) data should be allowed based on US legal requirements, stating 'firstly, the need for the transfer is not proven and secondly it does not seem acceptable that a unilateral decision taken by a third country for reasons of its own public interest should lead to the routine and wholesale transfer of data protected under the directive'. WP29 2002, p. 6.
[41] EDPB 2018, p. 5.   [42] EDPB EDPS Response Cloud Act, p. 6.
[43] EC Microsoft Brief, p. 15.

in Article 83(1), or even to crime-fighting in general; indeed, the TFEU[44] and other EU treaties[45] identify a number of other important values of the EU besides law enforcement. This suggests that the derogation may be available to a limited extent in cases that involve a strong public interest that can be clearly identified under EU or Member State law, but that it cannot justify transfers under third country legislation such as the CLOUD ACT on a large scale or on a regular basis. Other derogations relevant to data transfers under the CLOUD Act are discussed herein under the relevant heading.

6. Necessary for the establishment, exercise or defence of legal claims

Article 49(1)(e) allows a transfer to take place when it 'is necessary for the establishment, exercise or defence of legal claims'.

According to recital 111 GDPR, the derogation can apply to a 'contract or a legal claim, regardless of whether in a judicial procedure or whether in an administrative or any out-of-court procedure, including procedures before regulatory bodies'. Thus, it may also apply to arbitration proceedings or to proceedings before an administrative or regulatory agency, as long as these are based on a formal process defined in law. It can also apply to formal pre-trial discovery procedures in civil litigation.[46] The derogation covers not only defence of claims, but actions by a data exporter to institute legal claims in a third country.[47] As an example, the WP29 has been willing to allow data transfers based on a defence of legal claims when 'the parent company of a multinational group, established in a third country, might be sued by an employee of the group currently posted to one of its European subsidiaries'.[48]

The necessity test means that the derogation does not apply to the large-scale transfer of personal data based on the mere possibility that litigation might occur sometime in the future.[49] However, occasional transfers are also covered by this derogation.[50] The EDPB has recommended a layered approach to situations involving legal claims, with data exporters first determining if export of the data in anonymised form would suffice, then considering the transfer of pseudonymised data, and only relying on this derogation if these solutions would be insufficient and if the transfer is both necessary and relevant.[51] The EDPB has also stated that 'a close link is necessary between a data transfer and a specific procedure and the derogation cannot be used to justify the transfer of personal data on the grounds of the mere possibility that legal proceedings or formal proceedings may be brought in the future'.[52] The restrictive nature of this derogation means that it is unlikely to provide a legal basis for the transfer of personal data to respond to data requests from foreign law enforcement authorities except in a small number of cases.[53]

---

[44] See, e.g., Art. 214 TFEU concerning humanitarian aid, and Arts. 12 and 169 TFEU concerning consumer protection.

[45] See, e.g., Art. 2 TEU identifying the core values on which the Union is based as 'respect for human dignity, freedom, democracy, equality, the rule of law and respect for human rights, including the rights of persons belonging to minorities'.

[46] EDPB 2018, p. 11.   [47] Ibid.   [48] WP29 2005, p. 15.
[49] Ibid. See also EDPB 2018, pp. 11–12.   [50] Rec. 111 GDPR.   [51] EDPB 2018, p. 12.
[52] EDPB EDPS Response Cloud Act, p. 7.   [53] See the commentary on Art. 48 in this volume.

7. Necessary in order to protect the vital interests of the data subject or of other persons, where the data subject is physically or legally incapable of giving consent

Article 49(1)(f) allows a transfer when it 'is necessary in order to protect the vital interests of the data subject or of other persons, where the data subject is physically or legally incapable of giving consent'.

Article 49(1)(f) sets a high standard,[54] and requires that the data transfer is necessary to protect an individual's life, health or physical integrity. It requires that the data subject be physically or legally incapable of giving consent, which means that the conditions for valid consent under the other provisions of the GDPR must not be able to be satisfied.[55] This could be applicable, for example, in cases involving the transfer of a patient's medical data which are necessary for treatment.[56] However, it would not apply in other cases when medical treatment is not necessary or when the life or health of the individual is not at stake, such as when data are to be transferred for purposes of medical research. A key criterion is that the individual must be incapable of giving consent, either legally or factually; if the individual can give consent, then the derogation cannot be used.[57]

Recital 112 also states that transfers to international humanitarian organisations of the personal data of an individual who is physically or legally incapable of giving consent may be found necessary for an important reason of public interest or because it is in the vital interest of the data subject when this is necessary to accomplish a task under the Geneva Conventions or to comply with international humanitarian law in armed conflicts, which would apply to the work of the ICRC. Individuals who are victims of natural disasters or similar unexpected catastrophic events are considered not to be able to provide consent for transfer of their data.[58] The EDBP has recognised with regard to data transfers compelled under the US CLOUD Act that 'in certain exceptional, specific and necessary circumstances, the vital interests of the data subject could be validly used as a legal basis to answer US CLOUD Act requests'.[59]

8. Transfers made from a public register

Article 49(1)(g) allows a transfer that is:

> made from a register which according to Union or Member State law is intended to provide information to the public and which is open to consultation either by the public in general or by any person who can demonstrate a legitimate interest, but only to the extent that the conditions laid down by Union or Member State law for consultation are fulfilled in the particular case.

This derogation concerns the transfer of data from public registers which exist in various forms throughout the EU and the Member States. The EDPB has given as examples of such registries 'registers of companies, registers of associations, registers of criminal convictions, (land) title registers or public vehicle registers'.[60] The form of the registry is not determinative; rather, what is important is that it is open to consultation to the public or to a person who can demonstrate a legitimate interest to consult it.

---

[54] See Dammann and Simitis 1997, pp. 150–151. See also the commentary on Art. 9 in this volume concerning the processing of sensitive data based on the vital interests of the data subject.
[55] See the commentaries on Arts. 7 and 8 in this volume.   [56] WP29 2005, p. 15.
[57] See EDPB 2018, p. 13.   [58] Ibid.   [59] EDPB EDPS Response Cloud Act, p. 7.
[60] Ibid., p. 14.

At the same time, the transfer of such data is made subject to strict conditions. This means that, as stated in Article 49(2), the transfer cannot involve the entirety of the register or entire categories of the data contained in it, and that, if the register is accessible only to persons having a legitimate interest in it, then 'the transfer should be made only at the request of such persons or if they are to be the recipients'.[61] The WP29 has in the past published two opinions relevant to the derogation that may provide insight into how the data protection authorities are likely to interpret it.[62]

9. Compelling legitimate interests of the controller

The second subparagraph of paragraph 1 sets forth a derogation based on the compelling legitimate interests of the data controller that did not exist in the DPD. The text of the derogation indicates that it can be used only when none of the other data transfer mechanisms set out in Chapter V are applicable ('Where a transfer could not be based on a provision in Article 45 or 46, including the provisions on binding corporate rules, and none of the derogations for a specific situation referred to in the first subparagraph of this paragraph is applicable ... '). This derogation was a controversial addition to the GDPR, having been supported by the Commission and the Council and added to the text late in the negotiation process. The EDPB regards it as a 'last resort',[63] meaning that in order to use this derogation, the data exporter must be able to demonstrate that it was not possible to use appropriate safeguards under Article 46 or to use one of the derogations in Article 49(1)(1).[64]

In order for this derogation to apply, the second subparagraph of Article 49(1) requires that all the following conditions be fulfilled: (1) the data transfer must not be repetitive; (2) the transfer must concern only a limited number of data subjects; (3) it must be necessary for the purposes of compelling legitimate interests pursued by the controller which are not overridden by the interests or rights and freedoms of the data subject; (4) it must be based on an assessment by the data controller of all the circumstances surrounding the data transfer on the basis of which it provides suitable safeguards with regard to the protection of personal data; (5) the data controller must inform the data protection authority of the transfer (but need not obtain the DPA's authorisation); and (6) the data controller must, in addition to providing the information referred to in Articles 13 and 14 GDPR, inform the data subject about the transfer and on the compelling legitimate interests pursued. In addition to these conditions, Article 49(6) requires that the data controller or data processor document the assessment as well as the suitable safeguards in the records of data processing activities referred to in Article 30.[65] The data exporter may also have to apply additional protections as safeguards if these are called for, such as pseudonymising or encrypting the data.[66]

The derogation was introduced to provide additional flexibility for data transfers, but the conditions for using it are so restrictive that it seems to be available only in a very limited set of situations. The legitimate interest leading to the need to data transfer must

---

[61] Rec. 111 GDPR adds 'taking into full account the interests and fundamental rights of the data subject'.
[62] WP29 2016; WP29 2013.   [63] EDPB 2018, p. 14.   [64] Ibid.
[65] With regard to the risk assessment, rec. 113 GDPR states that the data controller should assess all the circumstances surrounding the data transfer, and should 'give particular consideration to the nature of the personal data, the purpose and duration of the proposed processing operation or operations, as well as the situation in the country of origin, the third country and the country of final destination'.
[66] EDPB 2018, p. 16.

be 'compelling', suggesting that it may not be applied in routine situations, and that it was designed to be used in exceptional cases only. As the EDPB notes, this is a higher standard than that of data processing based on the legitimate interests of the data controller under Article 6(1)(f) GDPR.[67] In general, the derogation seems designed mainly for use when important societal issues are at stake (such as for data transfers carried out in the context of academic or scientific research).[68] It does not seem suitable for most commercial situations, though the EDPB has suggested that it could be of use for small or medium-sized enterprises that may not be able to implement appropriate safeguards.[69] The text of Article 49(3) indicates that the derogation does not apply to activities carried out by public authorities in the exercise of their public powers.

The Commission has suggested that the derogation may be relevant in cases involving requests from non-EU law enforcement authorities for the transfer of data, particularly those under the US CLOUD Act,[70] but the EDPB has said that this derogation cannot provide a lawful ground to transfer personal data on the basis of requests under the Act.[71] However, even if it is found to be possible in theory, the use of this derogation seems so restricted that it is hard to imagine that it would be practicable to justify transfers based on foreign law enforcement requests under it except in a very small number of cases.

Many other questions about the derogation remain unanswered (e.g. how 'suitable safeguards' are to be adduced), so that the conditions for its use will have to be determined based on how it is interpreted by data protection authorities and the courts. Whenever it is used, data exporters are advised to keep detailed records of all aspects of the data transfer, including the compelling legitimate interests pursued, the competing interests of the individual, the nature of the data transferred and the purpose of the transfer.[72]

10. Limitation of transfers based on important reasons of public interest

Article 49(5) allows Union or Member State law, for important reasons of public interest, to expressly set limits on the transfer of specific categories of personal data to third countries or international organisations, as long as the transfer is not covered by an adequacy decision.

This provision is to be distinguished from the derogation allowing data transfers for important reasons of public interest under Article 49(1)(d), i.e. it is an empowerment of Union and Member State law to set limits on data transfers rather than a derogation from them. It seems out of place in Article 49, since it has nothing to do with the derogations from data transfer restrictions that are the subject of this article, and would have fit better somewhere else (such as in Article 44 dealing with general principles for transfers).

The provision allows such limits to be placed on transfers of 'specific categories of personal data', indicating that it is intended to cover specific, limited cases only, and cannot be used as a *carte blanche* to impose wide-ranging limitations on the transfer of personal data. Limits may be imposed only when 'important reasons of public interest'

---

[67] EDPB 2018, p. 15.
[68] See rec. 113 GDPR, which refers to its use in 'scientific or historical research purposes or statistical purposes', in which case 'the legitimate expectations of society for an increase of knowledge should be taken into consideration'.
[69] EDPB 2018, p. 14.
[70] EC Microsoft Brief, p. 15. See the commentary on Art. 48 in this volume.
[71] EDPB EDPS Response Cloud Act, p. 7. [72] EDPB 2018, p. 17.

are involved. The term 'important reasons of public interest' (which is the same one used in the derogation of Article 49(1)(d)) is not defined, but the legislative history suggests that it could cover situations where national databases of strategic importance, such as passport databases or electronic patient dossiers, were to be transferred to third countries.[73] Any limits on data transfers must be 'expressly' stated in Member State or Union law, i.e. they may not be implied. Limits on data transfers cannot be set with regard to those covered by an adequacy decision.[74] Although the provision states that such limits may be imposed by 'Union or Member State law', it seems intended to apply mainly to the Member States, since it states that 'Member States shall notify such provisions to the Commission'. When this text was finalized, five Member States (Cyprus, Denmark, Estonia, France, and Germany) had made such notifications to the Commission under Article 49(5).[75]

11. Enforcement

Infringements of Article 49 are subject to the higher level of administrative fines under Article 83(5)(c), i.e. up to € 20 million or 4 per cent of the total worldwide turnover of the preceding financial year, whichever is higher.

Select Bibliography

International agreements

ICCPR: International Covenant on Civil and Political Rights 1966, 999 UNTS 171.
UDHR: Universal Declaration of Human Rights 1948, GA res. 217A (III), UN Doc. A/810.

National legislation

CLOUD Act 2018: Clarifying Lawful Overseas Use of Data Act (CLOUD Act), HR 1625, Division V, 115th Congress, 23 March 2018.

Academic writings

Christakis 2019: Christakis, 'Transfer of EU Personal Data to U.S. Law Enforcement Authorities After the CLOUD Act: Is There a Conflict with the GDPR' (14 June 2019), available at https://papers.ssrn.com/sol3/papers.cfm?abstract_id=3397047.
Dammann and Simitis 1997: Dammann and Simitis, *EG-Datenschutzrichtlinie* (Nomos Verlagsgesellschaft 1997).
Kuner 2007: Kuner, *European Data Protection Law: Corporate Compliance and Regulation* (2nd edn, OUP 2007).
Rauchegger 2015: Rauchegger, 'The Interplay between the Charter and National Constitutions after *Åkerberg Fransson* and *Melloni*', in de Vries, Bernitz and Weatherill (eds.), *The EU Charter of Fundamental Rights as a Binding Instrument* (Hart Publishing 2015), 93.

Papers of data protection authorities

EDPB 2018: European Data Protection Board, 'Guidelines 2/2018 on Derogations of Article 49 under Regulation 2016/679' (25 May 2018).

---

[73] See Council Non Paper 2014.
[74] See the commentary on Art. 45 in this volume regarding Commission adequacy decisions.
[75] Member State notifications to the Commission under the GDPR.

EDPB Brexit information note: EDPB, 'Information Note on Data Transfers under the GDPR in the Event of a No-Deal Brexit' (12 February 2019).

EDPB EDPS Response Cloud Act: European Data Protection Board and European Data Protection Supervisor, 'EPDB-EDPS Joint Response to the LIBE Committee on the impact of the US Cloud Act on the European legal framework for personal data protection (annex)' (10 July 2019).

WP29 1998: Article 29 Working Party, 'Working Document: Transfers of Personal Data to Third Countries: Applying Articles 25 and 26 of the EU Data Protection Directive' (WP 12, 24 July 1998).

WP29 2002: Article 29 Working Party, 'Opinion 6/2002 on Transmission of Passenger Manifest Information and Other Data from Airlines to the United States' (WP 66, 24 October 2002).

WP29 2005: Article 29 Working Party, 'Working Document on a Common Interpretation of Article 26(1) of Directive 95/46/EC of October 24 1995' (WP 114, 25 November 2005).

WP29 2013: Article 29 Working Party, 'Opinion 06/2013 on Open Data and Public Sector Information ('PSI') Reuse' (WP 207, 5 June 2013).

WP29 2016: Article 29 Working Party, 'Opinion 02/2016 on the Publication of Personal Data for Transparency Purposes in the Public Sector' (WP 239, 8 June 2016).

WP29 2017: Article 29 Working Party, 'Guidelines on Consent under Regulation 2016/679' (WP 259, 28 November 2017).

ICO 2018: UK Information Commissioner, 'International Data Transfers', available at https://ico.org.uk/for-organisations/data-protection-and-brexit/data-protection-if-there-s-no-brexit-deal/the-gdpr/international-data-transfers/.

Reports and recommendations

Commission Brexit Preparedness Notice: European Commission, 'Notice to Stakeholders: Withdrawal of the United Kingdom from the Union and EU Rules in the Field of Data Protection', 9 January 2018, available at https://ec.europa.eu/info/sites/info/files/file_import/data_protection_en.pdf.

Council Non Paper 2014: Non paper on Article 44, paragraph 5 of the Regulation, 9703/14, 12 May 2014.

EC Communication 2015: Communication from the Commission to the European Parliament and the Council on the Transfer of Personal Data from the EU to the United States of America under Directive 95/46/EC following the Judgment by the Court of Justice in Case C-362/14 (Schrems), COM(2015) 566 final, 6 November 2015.

Explanatory Report Convention 108 2018: Council of Europe, 'Explanatory Report to the Protocol amending the Convention for the Protection of Individuals with Regard to the Automatic Processing of Personal Data' (10 October 2018), available at https://rm.coe.int/cets-223-explanatory-report-to-the-protocol-amending-the-convention-fo/16808ac91a.

Others

EC Microsoft Brief: Amicus Brief of the European Commission on behalf of the European Union as *Amicus Curiae* in support of neither party in: United States v. Microsoft Corporation 584 U.S. (2018).

Member State notifications to the Commission under the GDPR: European Commission, 'EU Member States notifications to the European Commission under the GDPR', available at https://ec.europa.eu/info/law/law-topic/data-protection/data-protection-eu/eu-countries-gdpr-specific-notifications_en.

Article 50. International cooperation for the protection of personal data

CHRISTOPHER KUNER

In relation to third countries and international organisations, the Commission and supervisory authorities shall take appropriate steps to:

(a) develop international cooperation mechanisms to facilitate the effective enforcement of legislation for the protection of personal data;
(b) provide international mutual assistance in the enforcement of legislation for the protection of personal data, including through notification, complaint referral, investigative assistance and information exchange, subject to appropriate safeguards for the protection of personal data and other fundamental rights and freedoms;
(c) engage relevant stakeholders in discussion and activities aimed at furthering international cooperation in the enforcement of legislation for the protection of personal data;
(d) promote the exchange and documentation of personal data protection legislation and practice, including on jurisdictional conflicts with third countries.

Relevant Recitals

(102) This Regulation is without prejudice to international agreements concluded between the Union and third countries regulating the transfer of personal data including appropriate safeguards for the data subjects. Member States may conclude international agreements which involve the transfer of personal data to third countries or international organisations, as far as such agreements do not affect this Regulation or any other provisions of Union law and include an appropriate level of protection for the fundamental rights of the data subjects.

(116) When personal data moves across borders outside the Union it may put at increased risk the ability of natural persons to exercise data protection rights in particular to protect themselves from the unlawful use or disclosure of that information. At the same time, supervisory authorities may find that they are unable to pursue complaints or conduct investigations relating to the activities outside their borders. Their efforts to work together in the cross-border context may also be hampered by insufficient preventative or remedial powers, inconsistent legal regimes, and practical obstacles like resource constraints. Therefore, there is a need to promote closer cooperation among data protection supervisory authorities to help them exchange information and carry out investigations with their international counterparts. For the purposes of developing international cooperation mechanisms to facilitate and provide international mutual assistance for the enforcement of legislation for the protection of personal data, the Commission and the supervisory authorities should exchange information and cooperate in activities related to the exercise of their powers with competent authorities in third countries, based on reciprocity and in accordance with this Regulation.

Closely Related Provisions

Recital 6; Article 15(1)(c) (Right to access information about data recipients in third countries); Articles 70(1)(v) and (w) (Board's tasks to facilitate exchanges with supervisory authorities in third countries and exchanges of knowledge on data protection legislation with supervisory authorities worldwide); Article 96 (Relationship with previously concluded agreements of the EU Member States)

Related Provisions in LED [Directive (EU) 2016/680]

Recital 25; Article 40 (International cooperation for the protection of personal data) (see too recitals 73–74); Articles 51(1)(i)–(j) (Board's tasks to facilitate exchanges with supervisory authorities in third countries and exchanges of knowledge on data protection law with supervisory authorities worldwide)

A. Rationale and Policy Underpinnings

Since the DPD entered into force in 1998, data processing has become globalised through the growth of the internet and other electronic communications networks; the reduction of capital controls and the liberalisation of international trade by the foundation of the World Trade Organization ('WTO'); the increasing economic and political power of developing countries outside of Europe and North America; and the increased movement of persons across national borders.

These forces pose challenges for EU data protection law. First of all, they challenge the ability of the law to protect the processing of personal data across national borders. The internet allows parties in third countries to interact with EU individuals and process their data, which creates the risk that data processing may not be subject to the protections of EU law. These risks were recognised by the Commission when it made its original proposal[1] for the GDPR. The rules of Article 3(2) (extending the territorial scope of the GDPR to data controllers and processors not established in the EU) and Chapter V (dealing with transfers of personal data) are designed to help extend the reach of EU data protection law to the processing of personal data in third countries and international organisations in order to deal with these risks. However, these provisions cannot by themselves guarantee the seamless protection of personal data on a global level. Article 50 foresees the possibility of cooperation between EU data protection authorities and authorities in third countries and international organisations, in order to ensure a higher level of protection.[2]

In addition, these factors challenge the EU to develop means for cooperation with third countries and international organisations with regard to data protection. Data protection law has grown exponentially around the world in recent years. This includes international and regional standards, such as the Council of Europe Convention 108, the OECD Privacy Guidelines,[3] the Asia-Pacific Economic Cooperation ('APEC') Privacy Framework,[4] the Economic Community of West African States ('ECOWAS') Supplementary Act on Data Protection,[5] and others.[6] In addition, data protection law has been enacted in all regions of the world at the national and local level. EU data protection law has also had considerable influence around the world.[7] The growth of data protection law and the influence of EU law make it necessary for the EU to interact with other data

---

[1] EC Communication 2012, p. 10.   [2] See EC Communication 2017, p. 5.
[3] OECD Guidelines 2013.   [4] APEC Privacy Framework.
[5] ECOWAS Supplementary Act.   [6] See Bygrave 2014.   [7] See Kuner 2019B.

protection systems, both politically and legally. This can include measures such as discussions between regulators and public authorities, bilateral agreements, participation by the EU in international organisations, and others.

B. Legal Background

1. EU legislation

The DPD did not contain a provision that corresponds to Article 50 GDPR.

2. International instruments

There have not yet been any international agreements enacted pursuant to Article 50. The OECD has established the Global Privacy Enforcement Network ('GPEN'), which is a network of data protection regulators worldwide that includes those of many EU Member States that cooperate across borders in enforcing data protection and privacy laws. The GPEN was established to implement the 2007 OECD Recommendation on Cross-Border Co-operation in the Enforcement of Laws Protecting Privacy.[8]

A number of data protection authorities (including those of many Member States) who are members of the International Conference of Data Protection and Privacy Commissioners ('ICDPPC') also participate in the 'Global Cross Border Enforcement Cooperation Arrangement'[9] that is designed to foster cross-border privacy enforcement.

3. National developments

Article 50 contains no opening clauses that allow implementation by the Member States. There are several examples of agreements between data protection authorities in EU Member States and those in third countries that are designed to enhance cooperation between them in regulatory and enforcement matters.[10]

C. Analysis

1. Addressees

Article 50 is addressed to both the Commission and the national data protection authorities. The article is designed both to further international cooperation between the EU institutions and the DPAs with third countries and international organisations, and between the Commission and the DPAs themselves[11] (the GDPR also assumes that third countries should develop cooperation mechanisms with EU data protection authorities[12]).

---

[8] OECD Recommendation 2007.   [9] See ICDPCC 2014.
[10] E.g. the Privacy Commissioner of Canada has concluded a number of Memoranda of Understanding regarding enforcement with various Member State data protection authorities, including those of Germany, Ireland, the Netherlands, Romania and the UK (see Website Privacy Commissioner Canada). See also OECD Report 2006, p. 24.
[11] See rec. 116 GDPR, stating 'the Commission and the supervisory authorities should exchange information and cooperate in activities related to the exercise of their powers with competent authorities in third countries, based on reciprocity and in accordance with this Regulation'.
[12] See ibid., rec. 104.

Article 50 in effect supplements other provisions of the GDPR that require the data protection authorities to cooperate,[13] and extends them globally.[14]

The GDPR assigns the EDPB certain tasks relating to international cooperation (e.g. to 'promote common training programmes and facilitate personnel exchanges between the supervisory authorities and, where appropriate, with the supervisory authorities of third countries or with international organisations', Article 70(1)(v), and to 'promote the exchange of knowledge and documentation on data protection legislation and practice with data protection supervisory authorities worldwide', Article 70(1)(w)). However, Article 50 contains a fuller list of such tasks, and, given that most individual data protection authorities will not have the resources to engage in extensive international outreach, Article 50 envisions that in practice the Commission has the broadest powers to engage in tasks relating to international outreach and cooperation. In fact, the Commission has already announced that the EU 'will continue to engage actively in dialogue with its international partners, at both bilateral and multilateral level, to foster convergence by developing high and interoperable personal data protection standards globally'.[15]

2. Forms of international cooperation

The substance of Article 50 is oriented around the 2007 OECD recommendation referred to earlier.[16] Basically, it can be divided into two areas, namely tasks that are designed to enhance cross-border enforcement of data protection violations, and exhortations to the Commission and data protection authorities to cooperate with other actors on the international data protection stage.

In the first category are Articles 50(a) and 50(b), and in the second category are Articles 50(c) and 50(d). With regard to cross-border enforcement, Article 50(a) foresees the development of international cooperation mechanisms to facilitate the effective enforcement of data protection legislation. Such mechanisms are being developed at the international level, and a number of Member State data protection authorities are involved in them. Article 50(b) is in effect a specification of the preceding provision, as it provides in detail that mechanisms should be developed for mutual assistance in the enforcement of legislation, including 'notification, complaint referral, investigative assistance and information exchange'. As discussed above, some Member States already have concluded such agreements with data protection authorities in third countries.

With regard to the second category, the Member States, the WP29, and the Commission have been involved for years in the work of international organisations, and organisations in other regions, that deal with data protection issues; for example, in 2014 the WP29 together with the APEC group issued jointly a 'Referential' that maps the differences and similarities between binding corporate rules ('BCRs') and the Cross-Border Privacy Rules ('CBPR') system among the APEC countries.[17] When engaging in international cooperation, the Commission and the data protection authorities are supposed to 'engage relevant stakeholders', meaning that they should give a hearing to parties with a stake in such discussions, such as non-governmental organisations ('NGOs'), consumer organisations, academia and the business community. In addition, in their international

---

[13] E.g. ibid., Art. 57(1)(g).
[14] See also the commentary on Art. 61 in this volume regarding international cooperation.
[15] EC Communication 2017, p. 11.   [16] OECD Recommendation 2007.
[17] WP29 2014.

outreach activities they are supposed to focus in particular on 'jurisdictional conflicts with third countries', a topic that is dealt with in the commentary to Article 48 GDPR in this volume. As an example, there is a need for guidance about how to interpret the GDPR in light of the privileges and immunities granted to international organisations by the Member States.[18]

On 29 March 2017, the UK invoked Article 50 TEU and indicated its intention to leave the EU, at which point it will become a third country by operation of law ('Brexit') and all Union primary and secondary law will cease to apply to the UK.[19] This means that international cooperation between the EU and the UK in data protection will be necessary (for example, with regard to cooperation between the EDPB and the UK Information Commissioner or ICO post-Brexit). Article 50 may thus also be important in the context of Brexit.

Select Bibliography

International agreements

APEC Privacy Framework: Asia Pacific Economic Cooperation, 'Privacy Framework' (2005).
ECOWAS Supplementary Act: Economic Community of West African States 'ECOWAS', 'Supplementary Act A/SA.1/01/10 on Personal Data Protection within ECOWAS' (16 February 2010).
OECD Guidelines 2013: Organisation for Economic Co-Operation and Development, 'The OECD Privacy Framework' (2013).

Academic writings

Bygrave 2014: Bygrave, *Data Privacy Law: An International Perspective* (OUP 2014).
Kuner 2019A: Kuner, 'International Organizations and the EU General Data Protection Regulation: Exploring the Interaction between EU Law and International Law', 16 *International Organizations Law Review* (2019), 158.
Kuner 2019B: Kuner, 'The Internet and the Global Reach of EU Law', in Cremona and Scott (eds.), *EU Law Beyond EU Borders: The Extraterritorial Reach of EU Law* (OUP 2019), 112.
Kuner, *Transborder Data Flow Regulation and Data Privacy Law* (OUP 2013).

Papers of data protection authorities

ICDPCC 2014: International Conference of Data Protection and Privacy Commissioners, 'Global Cross Border Enforcement Cooperation Arrangement' (14 October 2014).
WP29 2014: Article 29 Working Party, 'Opinion 02/2014 on a Referential for Requirements for Binding Corporate Rules Submitted to National Data Protection Authorities in the EU and Cross Border Privacy Rules Submitted to APEC CBPR Accountability Agents' (WP 212, 27 February 2014).

Reports and recommendations

EC Communication 2012: Communication from the Commission to the European Parliament, the Council, the European Economic and Social Committee and the Committee of the Regions, 'Safeguarding Privacy in a Connected World—A European Data Protection Framework for the 21st Century', COM(2012) 9 final, 25 January 2012.

---

[18] See Kuner 2019A.   [19] Commission Brexit Preparedness Notice, p. 1.

EC Communication 2017: Communication from the Commission to the European Parliament and the Council, 'Exchanging and Protection Personal Data in a Globalised World', COM(2017) 7 final, 10 January 2017.

OECD Recommendation 2007: OECD, 'Recommendation on Cross-Border Co-Operation in the Enforcement of Laws Protecting Privacy' (2007).

OECD Report 2006: OECD, 'Report on the Cross-Border Enforcement of Privacy Law' (2006).

Others

Commission Brexit Preparedness Notice: European Commission, 'Notice to Stakeholders: Withdrawal of the United Kingdom from the Union and EU Rules in the Field of Data Protection', 9 January 2018, available at https://ec.europa.eu/info/sites/info/files/file_import/data_protection_en.pdf.

Website Privacy Commissioner Canada: Office of the Privacy Commissioner of Canada, 'International Memorandums of Understanding', available at https://www.priv.gc.ca/en/about-the-opc/what-we-do/international-collaboration/international-memorandums-of-understanding/.

Chapter VI Independent Supervisory Authorities (Articles 51–59)

Section 1 Independent status

Article 51. Supervisory authority

HIELKE HIJMANS[*]

1. Each Member State shall provide for one or more independent public authorities to be responsible for monitoring the application of this Regulation, in order to protect the fundamental rights and freedoms of natural persons in relation to processing and to facilitate the free flow of personal data within the Union ('supervisory authority').
2. Each supervisory authority shall contribute to the consistent application of this Regulation throughout the Union. For that purpose, the supervisory authorities shall cooperate with each other and the Commission in accordance with Chapter VII.
3. Where more than one supervisory authority is established in a Member State, that Member State shall designate the supervisory authority which is to represent those authorities in the Board and shall set out the mechanism to ensure compliance by the other authorities with the rules relating to the consistency mechanism referred to in Article 63.
4. Each Member State shall notify to the Commission the provisions of its law which it adopts pursuant to this Chapter, by 25 May 2018 and, without delay, any subsequent amendment affecting them.

Relevant Recitals

(117) The establishment of supervisory authorities in Member States, empowered to perform their tasks and exercise their powers with complete independence, is an essential component of the protection of natural persons with regard to the processing of their personal data. Member States should be able to establish more than one supervisory authority, to reflect their constitutional, organisational and administrative structure.

(119) Where a Member State establishes several supervisory authorities, it should establish by law mechanisms for ensuring the effective participation of those supervisory authorities in the consistency mechanism. That Member State should in particular designate the supervisory authority which functions as a single contact point for the effective participation of those authorities in the mechanism, to ensure swift and smooth cooperation with other supervisory authorities, the Board and the Commission.

(122) Each supervisory authority should be competent on the territory of its own Member State to exercise the powers and to perform the tasks conferred on it in accordance with this Regulation. This should cover in particular the processing in the context of the activities of an establishment of the controller or processor on the territory of its own Member State, the processing of personal data carried out by public authorities or private bodies acting in the public interest, processing affecting data subjects on its territory or processing carried out by a controller or processor not established in the Union when targeting data subjects residing on its territory. This should include

---

[*] The views expressed are solely those of the author and do not necessarily reflect those of the Belgian Data Protection Authority.

handling complaints lodged by a data subject, conducting investigations on the application of this Regulation and promoting public awareness of the risks, rules, safeguards and rights in relation to the processing of personal data.

(123) The supervisory authorities should monitor the application of the provisions pursuant to this Regulation and contribute to its consistent application throughout the Union, in order to protect natural persons in relation to the processing of their personal data and to facilitate the free flow of personal data within the internal market. For that purpose, the supervisory authorities should cooperate with each other and with the Commission, without the need for any agreement between Member States on the provision of mutual assistance or on such cooperation.

Closely Related Provisions

Article 4 (21) (Definition of supervisory authority); Article 52 (Independence) (see too recitals 118 and 120–121); Article 53 (General conditions for the members of the supervisory authority) (see too recital 121); Article 54 (Rules on the establishment of the supervisory authority); Articles 55–59 (Competence, tasks and powers) (see too recitals 122–124, 129 and 132); Articles 60–62 (Cooperation) (see too recitals 125–128, 130–131 and 133–134); Articles 63–67 (Consistency) (see too recitals 135–138); Article 68 (European Data Protection Board) (see too recital 139)

Related Provisions in LED [Directive (EU) 2016/680]

Article 41 (Supervisory authority) (see too recitals 75–77)

Relevant Case Law

CJEU

Case C-518/07, *European Commission v Federal Republic of Germany*, judgment of 9 March 2010 (Grand Chamber) (ECLI:EU:C:2010:125).

Case C-614/10, *European Commission v Republic of Austria*, judgment of 16 October 2012 (Grand Chamber) (ECLI:EU:C:2012:631).

Case C-288/12, *European Commission v Hungary*, judgment of 8 April 2014 (Grand Chamber) (ECLI:EU:C:2014:237).

Case C-362/14, *Maximillian Schrems v Data Protection Commissioner*, judgment of 6 October 2015 (Grand Chamber) (ECLI:EU:C:2015:650).

Case C-582/14, *Patrick Breyer v Bundesrepublik Deutschland*, judgment of 26 October 2016 (ECLI:EU:C:2016:779).

Case C-210/16, *Unabhängiges Landeszentrum für Datenschutz Schleswig-Holstein v Wirtschaftsakademie Schleswig-Holstein GmbH*, judgment of 5 June 2018 (Grand Chamber) (ECLI:EU:C:2018:388).

A. Rationale and Policy Underpinnings

Article 51 GDPR introduces one of the main elements of the EU mechanism of data protection, namely control by an independent supervisory authority. This control is guaranteed under EU law at Treaty level by a supervisory authority (Article 8(3) Charter of Fundamental Rights of the European Union ('CFR') or by supervisory authorities

(Article 16 (2), second sentence, Treaty on the Functioning of the European Union ('TFEU')). As confirmed by recital 117 GDPR, the establishment of these authorities, performing their tasks and powers in an independent manner, is an essential component of the individual's right to data protection. This recital underpins the consistent case law of the CJEU which qualifies control by an independent authority as an essential component of the fundamental right to data protection.[1]

Article 51(1) GDPR lays down that the control by a DPA has a double purpose, both protecting fundamental rights and facilitating the free flow of personal data within the EU. This wording is in line with the case law of the CJEU[2] and with the double purpose of the GDPR itself. It also allows Member States to establish more than one DPA. This enables federal states such as, in particular, Germany and Spain, to maintain existing responsibilities for (the control of) data protection law at a decentralised level.

Article 51(2) is a new provision that illustrates the growing cross-EU responsibilities of DPAs. In the internet environment many processing operations have a cross-border nature. This changed reality is reflected in Article 51(2), which applies the general notion of sincere cooperation under Article 4(3) Treaty on European Union ('TEU') to DPAs.

Article 51(3) ensures the link between decentralisation at national level and a clear allocation of responsibilities at EU level. This provision is again relevant for Germany and for Spain, where supervisory authorities are established at national as well as at regional level. The obligation to designate one single supervisory authority to represent all the authorities in each Member State in the EDPB, together with the obligation to appoint that joint representative in accordance with national law, is also set forth in Article 68(4) GDPR.

Article 51 and the related GDPR provisions implement one of the main objectives of the GDPR, namely providing a stronger institutional arrangement for the effective enforcement of the data protection rules.[3] The GDPR strengthens this institutional framework at EU level, but at the same time respects the EU as a federal system based on executive federalism,[4] where implementation and enforcement takes place at the national level. It remains the responsibility of Member States to provide for the supervisory authorities.

B. Legal Background

1. EU legislation

Article 51 and the subsequent GDPR articles on supervisory authorities modify and replace Article 28 DPD. However, in contrast to the wide discretion conferred by the DPD on Member States, the GDPR lays down detailed provisions on the establishment, tasks and powers of DPAs. Nonetheless, the essential elements of the establishment and functioning of independent supervisory authorities were already present in Article 28 DPD.

Under Article 28(1) DPD each Member State had to provide that 'one or more public authorities are responsible for monitoring the application within its territory of the provisions adopted by the Member States pursuant to this Directive. These authorities shall

---

[1] E.g. Case C-518/07, *Commission v Germany*, para. 23.   [2] Ibid., para. 30.
[3] EC Communication 2010, p. 4.   [4] Lenaerts and van Nuffel 2011, para. 17-002.

act with complete independence in exercising the functions entrusted to them'. Article 28 DPD also provided that the supervisory authorities had to have the necessary means to perform their duties, including powers of investigation and intervention, deal with complaints from individuals and powers to engage in legal proceedings.[5]

Article 28 DPD, together with its accompanying recital 62 was the inspiration for the CJEU case law emphasising the complete nature of independence of supervisory authorities. It was also the source for the provisions of EU primary law safeguarding independence, namely Article 16(2) TFEU and Article 8(2) CFR. Chapter VI GDPR was founded upon these provisions.

The consistency obligation under Article 51(2) GDPR does not have an equivalent in the DPD. However, Article 28 DPD required DPAs to 'cooperate with one another to the extent necessary for the performance of their duties, in particular by exchanging all useful information'.

2. International instruments

Convention 108 of the Council of Europe, the first legally binding international instrument on data protection, initially did not include provisions on independent authorities. These provisions were included in an Additional Protocol, adopted in 2001.[6] Article 1 of this Protocol, which should be regarded by the parties to the Convention as an additional article to Convention 108, is similar to Article 28 DPD. Modernised Convention 108 contains an entire chapter (Chapter IV, Articles 15–21) dealing with supervisory authorities.

The concept of the independent DPA is not included in the OECD Privacy Guidelines,[7] which are, strictly speaking, not an international treaty but a non-binding instrument with wide global influence. These guidelines refer to privacy enforcement authorities which are public bodies responsible for enforcing laws protecting privacy. However, there is no reference to the independence of these bodies, which is due to the fact that not all member countries of the OECD are familiar with the EU concept of independence. The United States, for instance, has a different system.[8]

3. National developments

The whole concept of DPAs is founded in national law. Several European countries established independent DPAs in the 1970s. For example, the French CNIL started work in 1978 under the French data protection law.[9]

Other often cited examples are the early laws in Sweden and in some German Länder which provided for the establishment of independent DPAs before their existence was addressed at EU or international level.[10]

Currently, all Member States have national provisions on the establishment and functioning of DPAs, in their laws implementing the DPD. The big differences between these laws, and the resulting deficiencies of DPAs in a number of Member States,[11] were important factors for strengthening and harmonising these roles in Chapter VI GDPR.

[5] See rec. 63 DPD.   [6] See Table of Legislation.   [7] OECD Guidelines 2013.
[8] Hijmans 2016A, 7.5.   [9] French Data Protection Act 1978.
[10] See González Fuster 2014, ch. 3.   [11] As illustrated in FRA 2010.

4. Case law

The CJEU played an important role in the definition of the role of independent DPAs. Judgments in three infringement proceedings under Article 258 TFEU against Germany, Austria and Hungary for inadequate implementation of the DPD developed the position of supervisory authorities.[12]

The CJEU regards these authorities as the guardians of data protection.[13] It has asserted the supervision by DPAs as an essential component of the individual's right to data protection[14] and has set high standards for the independence of these authorities.

This independence precludes any external influence, requiring not only functional but also institutional independence. The level of independence is high in comparison to most national and EU bodies in other areas of law, such as competition authorities or consumer authorities. It is moreover similar to the independence of the judiciary. To be able to act independently, these authorities must also have effective powers and resources. Finally, without prejudice to their independence, these authorities remain accountable in a democratic society.[15] In the words of the CJEU, 'the absence of any parliamentary influence over those authorities is inconceivable'.[16]

The *Schrems* judgment confirmed and refined this status of DPAs, e.g. by considering that they should examine claims by individuals 'with all due diligence'.[17]

C. Analysis

1. Article 51 illustrates a trend: Making DPAs stronger and more European

Article 51 GDPR is not only the first article of Chapter VI on independent supervisory authorities, but also marks the start of the second, more procedural part of the GDPR, in which these authorities have a key role. Chapter VII deals with the cooperation of these authorities with each other and—under the heading of consistency—within the EDPB. Chapter VIII, entitled 'Remedies, liabilities and penalties', not only ensures the embedding of DPAs within the system of legal remedies, but also provides for sanctioning powers, ensuring that these authorities are a comprehensive part of administrative law.

In this wider perspective, Article 51 GDPR reflects an important underpinning of the reform of EU data protection law: the role of the supervisory authorities needs to be significantly strengthened, to ensure that data protection is not only delivered in the books, but also on the ground.[18]

Strengthening their role has two features in the GDPR: DPAs themselves should be better equipped, and DPAs should work in a more European fashion. Article 51 confirms the importance of strong DPAs, mainly in its first paragraph, emphasises their Europeanisation in its second paragraph and deals with one specific consequence of this Europeanisation in its third paragraph.

---

[12] See Case C-518/07, *Commission v Germany*; Case C-614/10, *Commission v Austria*; Case C-288/12, *Commission v Hungary*.
[13] Case C-518/07, *Commission v Germany*, para. 23.
[14] This was confirmed in Case C-362/14, *Schrems*, para. 42.   [15] Hijmans 2016A, 7.9 and 7.10.
[16] Case C-518/07, *Commission v Germany*, para. 43.   [17] Case C-362/14, *Schrems*, para. 63.
[18] This metaphor is derived from the work of Bamberger and Mulligan 2015.

2. Article 51(1): Confirming the dual objectives of DPAs

Article 51(1) GDPR requires Member States to provide for one or more DPAs. Normally, they will have one national DPA responsible for monitoring the application of the Regulation. The GDPR uses the terms 'monitoring the application', which should be understood as being equal to control of compliance, the terminology included in Article 16(2) TFEU and Article 8(3) CFR.

As explained before, the control (or monitoring) by a DPA is an essential component of the right to data protection under the Court's case law, as confirmed by recital 117 GDPR. Within the scope of EU law, individuals are entitled to control by a DPA. The DPA derives its position and its responsibilities from primary EU law, which includes the Charter. It is logical in this context that Article 51(1) GDPR should reiterate that the task of DPAs is to protect the fundamental rights and freedoms of natural persons, even though the DPD did not make any such reference[19] and it is not strictly necessary from a legal perspective.

However, it is less logical that the provision also mentions the responsibility to facilitate the free flow of personal data within the Union. On the one hand, this reference does not take account of the shift in emphasis of EU data protection after the entry into force of the Lisbon Treaty. The centre of gravity of data protection is no longer the free flow of data but rather the protection of fundamental rights.[20] This shift towards fundamental rights protection is not confined to the domain of data protection but is a broader development. In the Court's case law, fundamental rights have become more important and the Charter has become the yardstick for a strict scrutiny of acts of the EU and the Member States within the scope of EU law.[21]

On the other hand, this reference to the free flow of personal data is a link to the dual overall objectives of the GDPR laid down in Article 1(1) thereof. It also affirms the case law of the CJEU which requires DPAs to establish 'a fair balance between the protection of the right to private life and the free movement of personal data'.[22] This quotation is taken from the ruling in *Commission v Germany* of March 2010, in an era where the shift in emphasis had not started.

Arguably, Article 51(1) is in line with the views of Lynskey who argues that there indeed is a shift in emphasis.[23] However, as a result of this shift, the free flow or internal market perspective is no longer predominant, but the two objectives (free movement and the internal market versus fundamental rights) are now of equal importance. According to her view, data protection is not predominantly a fundamental rights issue.

In any event, the reference to facilitating the free flow of personal data in Article 51(1) clarifies that economic considerations should play a role in the performance of the tasks of the DPAs. This is also in line with more recent case law of the Court.[24]

3. Article 51(2): National DPAs contributing to EU-wide protection

Supervisory authorities are under an obligation to contribute to the consistent application of the GDPR throughout the entire EU. This obligation is in addition to the primary

---

[19] Jay 2017, para. 19-005. [20] Hijmans 2016A, 2.10. [21] Ibid., paras. 5.6 and 5.7.
[22] Case C-518/07, *Commission v Germany*, para. 30. [23] Lynskey 2015, ch. 3.
[24] Case C-582/14, *Breyer*, para. 58.

task of each DPA of monitoring the application of the GDPR within the territory of its own Member State (see recitals 122–123 GDPR).

The addition of this specific legal requirement is a novelty within EU data protection law.[25] Article 51(2) GDPR is an illustration of a wider trend towards the Europeanisation of DPAs. This started with purely national authorities in the seventh decade of the last century; step by step they are becoming more European.[26] This trend can be seen in the precise descriptions of the duties and powers of DPAs under the GDPR (Articles 57–58). It can also be seen in the key role of the EDPB, within which DPAs cooperate and which also deals with the enforcement of EU data protection law. It may be argued that DPAs are no longer only part of the national administration, but also have become part of the EU administration.[27] This is confirmed by their membership of the EDPB, an EU body according to Article 68(1) GDPR.

Under Article 51(2), the contribution to EU wide protection is an essential feature of the DPA role. This means that considerable resources should be reserved for this task and that, in case of conflicting priorities, national responsibilities do not necessarily prevail.[28]

Cooperation with other DPAs and with the Commission is treated by Article 51(2) as an instrument which gives effect to the DPAs' obligation to contribute to consistent protection. Cooperation is also included as a DPA task in Article 57(1)(g). This gives rise to two comments.

First, although other instruments are not mentioned, cooperation is arguably not the only instrument giving effect to this task. DPAs should in the performance of their duties always have in mind the need for consistent application of the law. Only then do they play their role in achieving some of the wider objectives of the GDPR, harmonising the protection of fundamental rights in the EU[29] and contributing to the accomplishment of an area of freedom, security and justice and of an economic union.[30]

Secondly, cooperation should be seen as a *lex specialis* of the principle of sincere cooperation of Article 4(3) TEU, which requires the Union and the Member States, in full mutual respect, to assist each other in carrying out tasks which flow from the Treaties. Article 51(2) complements and specifies this provision under primary law.

Moreover, cooperation as an instrument relating to the consistent application of the EU is closely linked to the task of the Commission as Guardian of the Treaties, as defined in TEU Article 17, ensuring the (consistent) application of EU law. It is understandable in this context that the GDPR should specifically provide that DPAs should cooperate with the Commission. The right of the Commission to participate in the activities and meetings of the EDPB[31] has the same background.

However, the cooperation between DPAs and the Commission also has limits in view of the independence of DPAs and the fact that this independence precludes any external influence, as specified in the case law of the CJEU. This was why the possibility of interference by the Commission in the consistency mechanism, as included in the Commission proposal for the GDPR was heavily criticised.[32] Arguably, the Commission's

---

[25] Although, arguably, the responsibility also existed implicitly in the DPD: see rec. 65 and Arts. 29 and Art. 30(1)(a) DPD.
[26] Hijmans 2016B. See also Hijmans 2016A, ch. 7.8.   [27] Hijmans 2016A, ch. 8.
[28] See more in detail, Hijmans 2016B.   [29] Rec. 3 GDPR.   [30] Ibid., rec. 2.
[31] Ibid., Art. 68(5).   [32] E.g. EDPS 2012, 248–255.

participation in the activities and meetings of the EDPB is not always necessarily in line with the DPAs' independence.[33]

Cooperation by DPAs serves to ensure the consistent application of the law in the EU and should be performed on the basis of equality of the DPAs concerned and on trust and transparency.[34] However, it should also be recognised that DPAs also operate in a national legal environment and that differences of legal systems exist. Moreover, in several instances the GDPR allows for national specifications. The need to respect national differences is a further aspect that should be taken into account.[35]

Article 51(2) confirms the hybrid position of DPAs between the EU and national levels. DPAs are not the only such hybrid bodies within the EU, since many EU agencies and national agencies are similarly positioned.[36] However, the status of DPAs is specific, in view of their complete independence, which excludes any direct or indirect influence by national governments or the Commission.

4. Article 51(3): The case of (federal) states with more than one DPA

Article 51(3) GDPR sets out the consequences for the EU data protection system of the situation of Member States which provide for more than one DPA. This is mainly the case in federal states where responsibilities for data protection are exercised at the level of provinces or states, often in addition to national authorities. However, Article 51(3) may also be applied in situations where different DPAs have powers vis-à-vis different categories of controllers. An example of the latter is the possibility of supervision by a specific DPA for churches and religious organisations under Article 91(2) GDPR. Belgian law provides a further example, albeit strictly speaking outside of the scope of Article 53, by establishing a different authority for supervising the LED.[37]

Article 51(3) is particularly relevant for Germany as a federation of 16 states which are not just provinces but federal states with their own sovereign rights and legislative responsibilities. This federal system of government also affects the supervision of data protection. At present, the division of competences means that the Federal DPA mainly supervises the public sector at federal level, as well as the telecommunications sector, whereas the DPAs in the 16 states supervise the remainder of the public and the private sector.[38] Spain is also a country with certain federalist features, where the central government has granted different levels of autonomy to communities and there are regional DPAs for Catalonia and the Basque Country.

The existence of more than one DPA in a Member State already required national coordination under the DPD, to ensure, for instance, that the authorities spoke with one voice and were able to use their one vote within the WP29. In Germany, this coordination took place in a structured conference of the national and regional DPAs.[39]

This coordination has entered a new phase under the GDPR, because, as stipulated by Article 51(3), it must not only ensure representation in the EDPB but also ensure that all DPAs in a Member State comply with the consistency mechanism. This means, for instance, that they should communicate draft decisions to the Board under Article 63(1),

---

[33] Hijmans 2016A, 8.11. See also the commentary on Art. 69 in this volume.
[34] Barnard-Wills et al. 2017, ch. 3.   [35] Ibid., 3.3.
[36] See on this Everson, Monda and Vos 2014.
[37] This is laid down in the Belgian GDPR Implementation Law.   [38] Zell 2014.
[39] Website Düsseldorfer Kreis. This conference must ensure a coordinated approach.

that they have the power to submit requests to the Board under Article 63(2) and that opinions and decisions of the Board in the consistency mechanism should be complied with by DPAs which do not participate in the deliberations of the Board. Again, this has significant implications for the German situation, where DPAs in the states have in recent years taken strong positions vis-à-vis processing operations by big internet companies.[40]

Member State law must set out this mechanism. The GDPR, however, is silent on the application of the cooperation mechanism of Chapter VII, Section 1, in the case of multiple DPAs in one Member State and, related to this, the designation of the lead supervisory authority under Article 56(1). The GDPR does not expressly state that a Member State must lay down a mechanism for identifying the lead authority within a Member State and it is not clear whether the dispute resolution mechanism by the Board could also be invoked in case of conflicting views on the competent DPA within a Member State.

However, it may be assumed that the Member States concerned must provide for legal certainty within their national laws, in view of the requirement of effective application of the GDPR. The German federal data protection act aims to provide this legal certainty in a chapter on the cooperation between the German DPAs and on the representation of the DPAs in the Board.[41]

Select Bibliography

International agreements

OECD Guidelines 2013: Organisation for Economic Co-operation and Development, 'The OECD Privacy Framework' (2013).

National legislation

Belgian GDPR Implementation Law: Wet betreffende de bescherming van natuurlijke personen met betrekking tot de verwerking van persoonsgegevens, van 30 juli 2018; Loi relative à la protection des personnes physiques à l'égard des traitements de données à caractère personnel, du 30 juillet 2018.

French Data Protection Act 1978: Act No. 78-17 of 6 January 1978 on Data Processing, Files and Individual Liberties (Loi n° 78-17 du 6 janvier 1978 relative à l'informatique, aux fichiers et aux libertés), as last amended by Law No. 2014-334 of 17 March 2014.

German Federal Data Protection Act 2017: Bundesdatenschutzgesetz vom 30. Juni 2017, BGBl. 2017 Teil I Nr. 2097.

Academic writings

Bamberger and Mulligan 2015: Bamberger and Mulligan, *Privacy on the Ground: Driving Corporate Behaviour in the United States and Europe* (MIT Press 2015).

Everson, Monda and Vos 2014: Everson, Monda and Vos, *EU Agencies in between Institutions and Member States* (Kluwer Law International 2014).

González Fuster 2014: González Fuster, *The Emergence of Personal Data Protection as a Fundamental Right of the EU* (Springer 2014).

---

[40] Zell mentions e.g. interventions by the Scheswig-Holstein DPA against Facebook and by the Hamburg DPA against Google; see Zell 2014, pp. 480–486. See also Case C-210/16, *Wirtschaftsakademie Schleswig-Holstein*.

[41] German Federal Data Protection Act 2017, Chapter 5.

Hijmans 2016A: Hijmans, *The European Union as Guardian of Internet Privacy* (Springer 2016).

Hijmans 2016B: Hijmans, 'The DPAs and their Cooperation: How Far Are We in Making Enforcement of Data Protection Law More European?', 3(2) *European Data Protection Law Review* (2016), 362.

Jay 2017: Jay, *Guide to the General Data Protection Regulation* (Sweet & Maxwell 2017).

Lenaerts and van Nuffel 2011: Lenaerts and van Nuffel, *European Union Law* (3rd edn, Sweet & Maxwell 2011).

Lynskey 2015: Lynskey, *The Foundations of EU Data Protection Law* (Oxford Studies in European Law 2015).

Zell 2014: Zell, 'Data Protection in the Federal Republic of Germany and the European Union: An Unequal Playing Field', 15(3) *German Law Journal* (2014), 461.

Papers of data protection authorities

EDPS 2012: European Data Protection Supervisor, 'Opinion on the Data Protection Reform Package' (7 March 2012).

Reports and recommendations

Barnard-Wills et al. 2017: Barnard-Wills, Papakonstantinou, Pauner Chulvi and Díaz Lafuente, 'Recommendations for Improving Practical Cooperation between European Data Protection Authorities', Deliverable D4.1 for the PHAEDRA II project (14 January 2017), available at http://www.phaedra-project.eu/wp-content/uploads/PHAEDRA2_D41_final_20170114.pdf.

EC Communication 2010: Communication from the Commission to the European Parliament, the Council, the European Economic and Social Committee and the Committee of the Regions, 'A Comprehensive Approach on Personal Data Protection in the European Union' COM (2010) 609 final, 4 November 2010.

FRA 2010: Fundamental Rights Agency of the European Union, 'Data Protection in the European Union: The Role of National Data Protection Authorities' (2010).

Others

Website Düsseldorfer Kreis: Bundesbeauftragte für den Datenschutz und die Informationsfreiheit, 'Entschließungen der Konferenz der Datenschutzbeauftragten des Bundes und der Länder (Düsseldorfer Kreis)', available at https://www.bfdi.bund.de/DE/Infothek/Entschliessungen/DSBundLaender/Functions/DSK_table.html.

Article 52. Independence

THOMAS ZERDICK*

1. Each supervisory authority shall act with complete independence in performing its tasks and exercising its powers in accordance with this Regulation.
2. The member or members of each supervisory authority shall, in the performance of their tasks and exercise of their powers in accordance with this Regulation, remain free from external influence, whether direct or indirect, and shall neither seek nor take instructions from anybody.
3. Member or members of each supervisory authority shall refrain from any action incompatible with their duties and shall not, during their term of office, engage in any incompatible occupation, whether gainful or not.
4. Each Member State shall ensure that each supervisory authority is provided with the human, technical and financial resources, premises and infrastructure necessary for the effective performance of its tasks and exercise of its powers, including those to be carried out in the context of mutual assistance, cooperation and participation in the Board.
5. Each Member State shall ensure that each supervisory authority chooses and has its own staff which shall be subject to the exclusive direction of the member or members of the supervisory authority concerned.
6. Each Member State shall ensure that each supervisory authority is subject to financial control which does not affect its independence and that it has separate, public annual budgets, which may be part of the overall state or national budget.

Relevant Recitals

(117) The establishment of supervisory authorities in Member States, empowered to perform their tasks and exercise their powers with complete independence, is an essential component of the protection of natural persons with regard to the processing of their personal data. Member States should be able to establish more than one supervisory authority, to reflect their constitutional, organisational and administrative structure.

(118) The independence of supervisory authorities should not mean that the supervisory authorities cannot be subject to control or monitoring mechanisms regarding their financial expenditure or to judicial review.

(120) Each supervisory authority should be provided with the financial and human resources, premises and infrastructure necessary for the effective performance of their tasks, including those related to mutual assistance and cooperation with other supervisory authorities throughout the Union. Each supervisory authority should have a separate, public annual budget, which may be part of the overall state or national budget.

(121) The general conditions for the member or members of the supervisory authority should be laid down by law in each Member State and should in particular provide that those members are to be appointed, by means of a transparent procedure, either by the parliament, government or the head of State of the Member State on the basis of a proposal from the government,

---

* The views expressed are solely those of the author and do not necessarily reflect those of the EDPS.

a member of the government, the parliament or a chamber of the parliament, or by an independent body entrusted under Member State law. In order to ensure the independence of the supervisory authority, the member or members should act with integrity, refrain from any action that is incompatible with their duties and should not, during their term of office, engage in any incompatible occupation, whether gainful or not. The supervisory authority should have its own staff, chosen by the supervisory authority or an independent body established by Member State law, which should be subject to the exclusive direction of the member or members of the supervisory authority.

Closely Related Provisions

Article 4(21) (Definitions: 'supervisory authority'); Article 45 (Transfers on the basis of an adequacy decision) (see also recital 104); Article 69 (EDPB Independence) (see also recital 139); Article 85 (Freedom of expression) (see also recital 153)

Related Provisions in LED [Directive (EU) 2016/680]

Article 42 (Independence of the Board) (see also recitals 75, 78–79)

Related Provisions in EUDPR [Regulation (EU) 2018/1725]

Article 55 (Independence of EDPS) (see too recitals 2, 72 and 87)

Relevant Case Law

CJEU

Case C-518/07, *European Commission v Federal Republic of Germany*, judgment of 9 March 2010 (Grand Chamber) (ECLI:EU:C:2010:125).

Case C-614/10, *European Commission v Republic of Austria*, judgment of 16 October 2012 (Grand Chamber) (ECLI:EU:C:2012:631).

Case C-288/12, *European Commission v Hungary*, judgment of 8 April 2014 (Grand Chamber) (ECLI:EU:C:2014:237).

Joined Cases C-293/12 and C-594/12, *Digital Rights Ireland Ltd v Minister for Communications, Marine and Natural Resources and Others and Kärntner Landesregierung and Others*, judgment of 8 April 2014 (Grand Chamber) (ECLI:EU:C:2014:238).

Case C-362/14, *Maximillian Schrems v Data Protection Commissioner*, judgment of 6 October 2015 (Grand Chamber) (ECLI:EU:C:2015:650).

Joined Cases C-203/15 and C-698/15, *Tele2 Sverige AB v Post-och telestyrelsen* and *Secretary of State for Home Department v Tom Watson and Others*, judgment of 21 December 2016 (Grand Chamber) (ECLI:EU:C:2016:970).

Opinion 1/15, Opinion of 26 July 2017 (Grand Chamber) (ECLI:EU:C:2017:592).

Germany

Bundesverfassungsgerichtshof, *Urteil vom 15.12.1983*, VZG 83 1 BVerfGE 65 ('Volkzählungsurteil').

A. Rationale and Policy Underpinnings

The guarantee of the independence of national supervisory authorities is intended to ensure the effectiveness and reliability of the monitoring of compliance with the provisions concerning protection of individuals with regard to the processing of personal data. The guarantee of 'complete independence' was established not to grant a special status to those authorities themselves as well as their agents, but in order to strengthen the protection of individuals and bodies affected by their decisions.[1] The establishment of supervisory authorities in Member States, empowered to perform their tasks and exercise their powers with complete independence, is an essential component of the protection of natural persons with regard to the processing of their personal data:[2] supervisory authorities cannot effectively safeguard individual rights and freedoms unless they exercise their functions in complete independence. Any failure to ensure their independence and powers has a wide-ranging negative impact on the enforcement of the data protection legislation.[3]

At the level of EU primary law, Article 8(3) of the Charter of Fundamental Rights of the European Union ('Charter' or 'CFR') as well as Article 16(2) of the Treaty on the Functioning of the European Union ('TFEU') and Article 39 of the Treaty on European Union ('TEU') therefore require independent authorities to check that the rules for the processing of personal data are complied with. In consequence, whilst Article 51 GDPR sets out the obligation for Member States to provide for independent data protection supervisory authorities, Article 52 clarifies the conditions in detail for such independence of supervisory authorities. In particular this requires Member States to provide supervisory authorities with sufficient resources. The wording of Article 52 builds on Article 28(1) DPD and takes inspiration from Article 44 of Regulation 45/2001,[4] which has now been replaced by Article 55 EUDPR. It also codifies case law by the CJEU, in particular *Commission v Germany*.[5]

The different implementations of Article 28(1) DPD in national data protection laws had led data protection authorities to be subject to widely diverging rules in the Member States, particularly with regard to their status, resources and powers. The lack of independence of several supervisory authorities was recognised by both the Commission[6] and the European Union Agency for Fundamental Rights[7] as a major problem at a structural level. In addition, understaffing and lack of financial resources of supervisory authorities also posed problems in several Member States, restricting supervisory authorities in the proper exercise of their tasks.[8] These concerns had also been raised by business organisations, citizens and public authorities during the 2009 public consultation.[9]

In consequence, a clarification of the concept of 'complete independence' had become necessary. The Commission indicated early on that it would examine how to 'strengthen, clarify and harmonise the status and the powers of the national Data Protection Authorities in the new legal framework, including the full implementation of the concept of "complete independence"'.[10] This call was echoed by the European Parliament[11]

---

[1] Case C-518/07, *Commission v Germany*, para. 25; Case C-362/14, *Schrems*, para. 41.
[2] Rec. 117 GDPR, and stated previously already in rec. 62 DPD.   [3] EC Communication 2007.
[4] See Table of Legislation.   [5] Case C-518/07, *Commission v Germany*.
[6] See the EC Staff Working Paper, 2.12.1.   [7] FRA 2010, 5.1.1.
[8] '[O]ne European DPA even had to shut down its operations for several months at the end of 2010 because it had completely run out of funds', Kuner, Cate, Millard and Svantesson 2012, p. 1.
[9] EC Consultation Website.
[10] EC Communication 2010, p.18. See also EC Communication 2012, p. 8. See also Reding 2012.
[11] EP Resolution 2011.

and the Council.[12] Given this general consensus, the 2012 Commission's proposals[13] as regards the independence of the supervisory authorities remained largely unchanged in the ensuing legislative process.[14]

The GDPR emphasises the requirement of independence in numerous parts: in Article 4(12) in the definition of a 'supervisory authority', in Article 45(2)(b) as regards transfers to third countries and also in the title of Chapter VI ('Independent supervisory authorities'), in the title of Section 1 of that Chapter ('Independent status') and in the title of Article 52 itself ('Independence'). The requirement of independence is also a feature of the European Data Protection Board ('EDPB') under Article 69 GDPR, which is also titled 'Independence'.[15]

B. Legal Background

1. EU legislation

Since 1995, the second subparagraph of Article 28(1) DPD required data protection supervisory authorities to act with 'complete independence' in exercising the functions entrusted to them. However, the exact nature of this 'independence' was not further elaborated upon in the DPD.

Adopted on the basis of the former Article 286 of the EC Treaty, which was replaced by Article 16 TFEU, Regulation 45/2001 established the EDPS. Article 44 of Regulation 45/2001 required the EDPS to 'act in complete independence in the performance of his or her duties' and sets out in greater detail further requirements, such as the obligations 'to neither seek nor take instructions from anybody' or to 'refrain from any action incompatible with his or her duties' (Article 44(2) and (3) of Regulation 45/2001). Article 55 EUDPR is very similar to Article 44 of Regulation 45/2001, but includes some extra detail. Thus, Article 55(1) EUDPR states that the EDPS shall act 'with complete independence in performing his or her tasks and exercising his or her powers in accordance with this Regulation'; and Article 55(2) provides that he or she 'shall, in the performance of his or her tasks and exercise of his or her powers in accordance with this Regulation, remain free from external influence, whether direct or indirect, and shall neither seek nor take instructions from anybody'.

2. International instruments

As a legally binding international treaty on the protection of personal data, Convention 108 of 1981 does not explicitly require the States Parties to establish independent supervisory authorities.

In order to remedy that situation, and in view of the subsequently adopted DPD, which contained such a requirement, Article 1(3) of the 2001 Additional Protocol,[16] regarding supervisory authorities and trans-border data flows, requires the establishment of supervisory authorities and their acting in 'complete independence'.

---

[12] Council Conclusions 2011, para. 16.
[13] See Art. 47 GDPR Proposal. See also Art. 40 LED Proposal.
[14] Albrecht and Jotzo 2017, p. 108.   [15] See the commentary on Art. 69 in this volume.
[16] See Table of Legislation.

Modernised Convention 108 intends to achieve synchronisation with the EU reform and has therefore introduced a set of provisions as regards the independence of supervisory authorities in a new Article 15(5). It specifically requires that supervisory authorities 'shall act with complete independence and impartiality in performing their duties and exercising their powers and in doing so shall neither seek nor accept instructions'. In addition, Article 15(6) requires that '[e]ach Party shall ensure that the supervisory authorities are provided with the resources necessary for the effective performance of their functions and exercise of their powers'. The Amending Protocol modernising the Convention was adopted on 18 May 2018, just before the entry into application of the GDPR, and will enter into force after the accession of five Member States of the Council of Europe. Once that is achieved, Modernised Convention 108 will further cement the clear consensus amongst European States on 'completely independent' data protection supervisory authorities.

3. National developments

The need for independent supervision in personal data protection matters led some Member States such as France, Germany or Sweden early on since the 1970s to establish supervisory authorities.[17] By way of example, in 1981, the German Federal Constitutional Court (*Bundesverfassungsgericht*) argued in its landmark judgment concerning data protection that 'due to the lack of transparency of the storage and use of data for the public in the context of automated data processing as well as in the interest of anticipatory legal protection in the form of timely precautions, the involvement of independent data protection commissioners is of significant importance for effective protection of the right to informational self-determination'.[18]

Following the adoption of the DPD, at national level all EU (and European Economic Area 'EEA') Member States implemented their obligations stemming from Article 28(1) DPD to set up one or more national data protection supervisory authorities, as evidenced in the Commission's reports on the implementation of the DPD.[19] However, the Commission brought infringement proceedings before the CJEU against Germany, Austria and Hungary for incorrect implementation of the requirement of 'complete independence' of supervisory authorities in these Member States.

4. Case law

The case law of the CJEU has had a significant influence on the wording of Article 52, given that the Court had interpreted Article 28(1) DPD relating to the independence of supervisory authorities in three rulings during the data protection reform legislative process.

In its landmark judgment of 2010, the Court ruled that Germany had incorrectly implemented Article 28(1) DPD by subjecting the data protection supervisory authorities for the private sector at state (*Land*) level to governmental supervision and state scrutiny which in principle allowed the government of the respective *Land* or an administrative body subject to that government to influence, directly or indirectly, the decisions of the

---

[17] For an overview on the history of supervisory authorities in the EU, see Hijmans 2016, p. 330.
[18] Bundesverfassungsgerichtshof, *Urteil vom 15.12.1983*.
[19] EC Report 2003; EC Communication 2007; EC Communication 2010; EC Communication 2012.

supervisory authorities or, as the case may be, to cancel and replace those decisions.[20] In that ruling the Court clarified furthermore that the words 'with complete independence' must be given an autonomous and broad interpretation, and that the existence of public data protection supervisory authorities outside the classic hierarchical administration and independent of the government was in line with the principle of democracy.[21] In addition, the CJEU found that Article 44 of Regulation 45/2001 and Article 28 DPD should be interpreted homogeneously, given they are based on the same general concept of independence.[22] This interpretation allowed the Commission to largely model its proposal for the GDPR provisions on independence on the corresponding articles of Regulation 45/2001.

Likewise, in a similar case in 2012, the Court ruled that Austria had failed to comply with the requirement of ensuring 'complete independence' of its national data protection supervisory authority due to the following aspects of organisational influence by the Austrian government: a regulatory framework under which the 'managing member' of the Austrian data protection supervisory authority was a federal official of the Federal Chancellery (the executive office of the Federal Chancellor, the Austrian head of government) and subject to direct supervision by the Federal Chancellery; the integration of the office of the Austrian data protection supervisory authority with the departments of the Federal Chancellery; and the unconditional right of the Federal Chancellor to information covering all aspects of the work of the Austrian data protection supervisory authority.[23]

In 2014, the Court found against Hungary for not ensuring 'complete independence' by prematurely bringing to an end the term served by the Hungarian Commissioner for the protection of personal data, due to a statutory restructuring of the supervisory authority.[24]

In three later judgments, the Court reiterated the importance of data protection control within the Union by an 'independent authority',[25] i.e. by independent data protection supervisory authorities. The Court has also applied its interpretation of 'complete independence' for supervisory authorities as regards oversight by a non-EU authority.[26]

C. Analysis

The overall objective of Article 52 is to set out in greater detail—when compared to Article 28(1) DPD—the requirements and conditions for ensuring the 'complete independence' of a data protection supervisory authority in all its possible forms, i.e. institutional, organisational, budgetary, financial, functional and personal independence and independence in decision-making. To achieve that objective, Article 52 contains obligations for the member(s) of the supervisory authority as well as for Member States when setting up the legal and organisational structures required by the GDPR (and by Article 8(3) CFR) for such a supervisory authority.

[20] Case C-518/07, *Commission v Germany*. [21] Ibid, paras. 17–28 and 46.
[22] Ibid., para. 28. [23] Case C-614/10, *Commission v Austria*.
[24] Case C-288/12, *Commission v Hungary*.
[25] Joined Cases C-293/12 and C-594/12, *Digital Rights Ireland*, para. 68; Case C-362/14, *Schrems*, para. 41; Joined Cases C-203/15 and C-698/15, *Tele2*, para. 123.
[26] *Opinion 1/15*, para. 230.

1. Complete independence

First, paragraph 1 lays down the obligation that data protection supervisory authorities need to act with 'complete independence'. This wording follows that of Article 28(1) DPD and Article 55 EUDPR, and is now reflected in primary law of the European Union, in particular in Article 8(3) of the Charter and Article 16(2) TFEU. The prior case law of the CJEU as regards the interpretation of Article 28(1) DPD and Article 44 of Regulation 45/2001 remains fully applicable to the interpretation of Article 52.

Given that Article 51 authorises Member States to set up not only one but several supervisory authorities, Article 52(1) clarifies that 'each' of these supervisory authorities must act with complete independence.

In its broad interpretation of the requirement of 'complete independence', the Court ruled that independence was not limited to the direct relationship between the supervisory authorities and the organisations or bodies subject to that supervision but that it also necessitates a decision-making power independent of *any* (direct or indirect) external influence on the supervisory authority.[27] In other words: a so-called 'functional independence' or 'organisational independence' which sets up a supervisory authority in such a way that it would be independent only from the organisation or body it directly supervises (as was the case in the German *Land* supervisory authority supervising the private companies within its jurisdiction) does not suffice.[28]

Moreover, while Member States are free (within the parameters of the GDPR) to adopt or amend the institutional model that they consider to be the most appropriate for their supervisory authorities,[29] in order to comply with the requirement of 'complete independence', the supervisory authority must be placed outside the classic hierarchical administration.[30] Equally, a change of the national institutional model cannot compromise the independence of the supervisory authority.[31]

'Complete independence' however does not mean that supervisory authorities cannot be appointed by a national parliament or the government: Article 53(1) on the general conditions for the members of the supervisory authority itself allows for that possibility. Equally, all actions (and/or inactions) by a supervisory authority are subject to judicial review of a court or tribunal, in accordance with Article 78 (and as required by Article 47 of the Charter). The independence by supervisory authorities also extends to their relationship with the European Commission:[32] thus, even if the Commission has adopted an adequacy decision pursuant to Article 45, the national supervisory authorities, when hearing a claim lodged by a person concerning the protection of his rights and freedoms in regard to the processing of personal data relating to him, must be able to examine, with complete independence, whether the transfer of personal data outside the Union complies with the requirements laid down by the GDPR.[33]

Supervisory authorities must act independently in any action they are taking. In consequence, the references made to 'tasks' and 'powers' refer not only to the tasks spelt out

---

[27] Case C-518/07, *Commission v Germany*, para. 19.
[28] Case C-614/10, *Commission v Austria*, para. 42.
[29] Case C-288/12, *Commission v Hungary*, para. 60.
[30] Case C-518/07, *Commission v Germany*, para. 42.
[31] Case C-288/12, *Commission v Hungary*, para. 61.
[32] Art. 17(3) TEU equally requires the European Commission to be 'completely independent' in carrying out its responsibilities.
[33] Case C-362/14, *Schrems*, para. 57.

in Article 57 and the powers as defined in Article 58 but also to generally to any other duties laid down in the GDPR, such as the obligation to produce an annual activity report in Article 59.

2. Further elements of complete independence

Article 52 GDPR details four further elements to guarantee the 'complete independence' of supervisory authorities: the freedom from any external influence (paragraph 2); a prohibition from incompatible actions (paragraph 3); and the need for sufficient resources, including their own staff (paragraphs 4–5). Lastly, a clarification on the limits on financial control over supervisory authorities and the budgetary status is provided for in paragraph 6.[34]

2.1 Freedom from external influence

Paragraph 2 specifies two obligations: first, that supervisory authorities must remain free from external influence, whether direct or indirect, and secondly, an obligation that supervisory authorities may neither seek nor take instructions from anybody. The wording of the first obligation codifies the findings of the Court in the case *Commission v Germany*[35] whereas the second obligation directly reflects similar wording in Article 44(1) of Regulation 45/2001, now in Article 55(2) EUDPR.

In this context, according to the case law of the Court, 'free from external influence' means that supervisory authorities must be able to act objectively and impartially and therefore carry out their activities free from any influence which may have an effect on their decisions.[36] In consequence, in practice any 'direct influence' in the form of instructions to a supervisory authority is prohibited, not only as regards service or performance-related aspects, but also as regards issues of legality.[37]

As regards 'indirect influences', which are equally prohibited by Article 52 GDPR, supervisory authorities must remain above all suspicion of partiality.[38] Therefore, the mere risk that state scrutinising authorities could exercise political influence over the decisions of the supervisory authorities is enough to hinder the latter in the independent performance of their tasks. The Court argues that there could be the danger of 'prior compliance' on the part of those authorities in the light of the scrutinising authority's decision-making practice. Such indirect influence on the supervisory authority, or its members and staff may equally result from possible effect on career prospects or disciplinary actions.

The CJEU has found that such indirect influence was present in a service-related link between the 'managing member' of the Austrian data protection supervisory authority, who was an official of the Federal Chancellery, which allowed the activities of the managing member to be supervised by her hierarchical superior within the Federal

---

[34] Apart from those, there are a number of other elements which contribute to safeguarding the independence of the supervisory authority. The Explanatory Report to the Additional Protocol to Convention 108 mentions 'the composition of the authority, the method for appointing its members, the duration of exercise and conditions of cessation of their functions'; see Explanatory Report Additional Protocol Convention 108 2001. All of these elements mentioned are addressed by Art. 54 GDPR and need to be provided by Member States within the legislative framework for setting up supervisory authorities.

[35] Case C-518/07, *Commission v Germany*, paras. 19, 25, 30 and 50.

[36] Ibid., paras. 19, 25, 30 and 50.

[37] Ibid., where this was the case as the national data protection supervisory authorities for entities outside the public sector in all the German *Länder* were subject to such oversight.

[38] Ibid., para. 36. See also Case C-614/10, *Commission v Austria*, para. 52.

Chancellery. Equally, the Court found that if a Member State were allowed to compel a supervisory authority to vacate office before serving its full term, then the threat of a premature termination to which a supervisory authority would be exposed throughout its term of office could lead it to enter into a form of prior compliance with the political authority, which is incompatible with the requirement of independence.[39] Therefore, a mere change in institutional model cannot therefore objectively justify compelling the person or persons entrusted with the duties of supervisor to vacate office before expiry of their full term, without providing for transitional measures to ensure that they allowed to serve his term of office in full.[40]

2.2 Prohibition against incompatible actions

Paragraph 3 contains the additional requirement that the member or members of the supervisory authority should act with integrity, refrain from any action that is incompatible with their duties and should not, during their term of office, engage in any incompatible occupation, whether gainful or not. While Article 52(3) GDPR does not specify examples of such occupations directly in the text, Article 54(1)(f) GDPR requires Member States to regulate this aspect by way of national legislation. This provision therefore allows for the practice that in a number of jurisdictions inside and outside the EU, the national data protection supervisory authority is at the same time the public authority in charge of freedom of information legislation.[41]

2.3 Sufficient resources

It is evident that in order to exercise their tasks independently, supervisory authorities need to be equipped with sufficient resources. As a consequence, Article 52(4) GDPR obliges Member States (and not the EU) to ensure that their supervisory authority is provided with the human, technical and financial resources, premises and infrastructure necessary for the effective performance of its tasks and exercise of its powers.[42] This wording of the requirements incorporates some of the elements already contained in the 1993 UN Principles relating to the Status of National Institutions for the Promotion and Protection of Human Rights[43] and is designed to eliminate the understaffing and lack of financial resources of supervisory authorities which posed problems in several Member States, restricting supervisory authorities in the proper exercise of their tasks.[44]

As regards human resources, the supervisory authority should be able to rely on lawyers, as well as on information and communication technologies' specialists to take prompt and effective action. In addition, the adequacy of resources should be kept under review.[45]

---

[39] Case C-288/12, *Commission v Hungary*, para. 60.   [40] Ibid., para. 61.

[41] See e.g. in Germany the Federal Commissioner for Data Protection and Freedom of Information (Bundesbeauftragter für den Datenschutz und die Informationsfreiheit—'BfDI'), the ICO in the UK, and the Mexican National Institute for Transparency, Access to Information and Personal Data Protection (Instituto Nacional de Transparencia, Acceso a la Información y Protección de Datos Personales—'INAI').

[42] Art. 52(4) GDPR. See also rec. 120 GDPR.

[43] 'The national institution shall have an infrastructure which is suited to the smooth conduct of its activities, in particular adequate funding. The purpose of this funding should be to enable it to have its own staff and premises, in order to be independent of the Government and not be subject to financial control which might affect its independence'. UNGA Resolution 1993, Annex, 'Composition and guarantees of independence and pluralism', point 2.

[44] Kuner, Cate, Millard and Svantesson 2012, p. 1.

[45] As mentioned in the Explanatory Report Convention 108 2018, para 118.

However, the attribution of the necessary equipment and staff to supervisory authorities must not prevent them from acting 'with complete independence' in exercising the functions entrusted to them within the meaning of paragraph 1.[46] Therefore, paragraph 5 specifies that, in addition, each supervisory authority must be able to choose and be able to employ its own staff, who then must be subject to the exclusive direction of the member or members of the supervisory authority.[47] By way of example, this excludes making available staff to the supervisory authority whilst that staff remains linked in an organisational way to or remains subject to any form of supervision by the body which made the staff available.

2.4 Financial control and budgetary status

The independence of supervisory authorities should not mean that supervisory authorities cannot be subject to control or monitoring mechanisms regarding their financial expenditure, as clarified by paragraph 6. However, such a financial control may under no circumstances affect the supervisory authority's independence and may therefore not result in direct supervision, instructions to the supervisory authority or the government temporarily taking over the management of the supervisory authority for reasons of achieving 'budgetary compliance'.

It should be noted that paragraph 6 now requires that each supervisory authority has to have a separate (and public) annual budget (which however may be part of the overall state or national budget). Member States can no longer therefore provide that, from the point of view of budgetary law, the supervisory authorities are to come under a specified ministerial department, contrary to the situation under the DPD.[48]

Select Bibliography

International agreements

UNGA Resolution 1993: Resolution 48/134 'National Institutions for the Promotion and Protection of Human Rights', A/RES/48/134, 20 December 1993.

EU legislation

GDPR Proposal: Proposal for a Regulation of the European Parliament and of the Council on the protection of individuals with regard to the processing of personal data and on the free movement of such data (General Data Protection Regulation), COM(2012) 11 final, 25 January 2012.
LED Proposal: Proposal for a Directive of the European Parliament and of the Council on the protection of individuals with regard to the processing of personal data by competent authorities for the purposes of prevention, investigation, detection or prosecution of criminal offences or the execution of criminal penalties, and the free movement of such data, COM(2012) 10 final, 25 January 2012.

Academic writings

Albrecht and Jotzo 2017: Albrecht and Jotzo, *Das neue Datenschutzrecht der EU* (Nomos Verlag 2017).
Hijmans 2016: Hijmans, *The European Union as Guardian of Internet Privacy* (Springer 2016).

---

[46] Case C-614/10, *Commission v Austria*, para. 58.   [47] Art. 52(5) GDPR. See also rec. 121.
[48] Compare Case C-614/10, *Commission v Austria*, para. 58.

Kuner, Cate, Millard and Svantesson 2012: Kuner, Cate, Millard and Svantesson, 'The Intricacies of Independence', 2(1) *International Data Privacy Law 'IDPL'* (2012), 1.

Reding 2012: Reding, 'The European Data Protection Framework for the Twenty-First Century', 2(3) *IDPL* (2012), 199.

Reports and recommendations

Council Conclusions 2011: Council conclusions on the Communication from the Commission to the European Parliament and the Council—A comprehensive approach on personal data protection in the European Union, 5980/4/11 REV 4, 15 February 2011.

EC Communication 2007: Communication from the Commission to the European Parliament and the Council on the follow-up of the Work Programme for better implementation of the Data Protection Directive, COM(2007) 87 final, 7 March 2007.

EC Communication 2010: Communication from the Commission to the European Parliament, the Council, the Economic and Social Committee and the Committee of the Regions, 'A Comprehensive Approach on Personal Data Protection in the European Union', COM(2010) 609 final, 4 November 2010.

EC Communication 2012: Communication from the Commission to the European Parliament, the Council, the European Economic and Social Committee and the Committee of the Regions, 'Safeguarding Privacy in a Connected World—A European Data Protection Framework for the 21st Century', COM(2012) 9/3, 25 January 2012.

EC Report 2003: Report from the Commission 'First Report on the Implementation of the Data Protection Directive (95/46/EC)', COM(2003) 265 final, 15 May 2003.

EC Staff Working Paper 2012: Commission Staff Working Paper 'Impact Assessment Accompanying the document Regulation of the European Parliament and of the Council on the protection of individuals with regard to the processing of personal data and on the free movement of such data (General Data Protection Regulation) and Directive of the European Parliament and of the Council on the protection of individuals with regard to the processing of personal data by competent authorities for the purposes of prevention, investigation, detection or prosecution of criminal offences or the execution of criminal penalties, and the free movement of such data', SEC(2012) 72 final, 25 January 2012.

EP Resolution 2011: Resolution on a comprehensive approach on personal data protection in the European Union, 2011/2025(INI), P7_TA(2011)032, 6 July 2011.

Explanatory Report Additional Protocol Convention 108 2001: Council of Europe, 'Explanatory Report to the Additional Protocol to the Convention for the Protection of Individuals with Regard to Automatic Processing of Personal Data, Regarding Supervisory Authorities and Transborder Data Flows' (8 November 2001).

Explanatory Report Convention 108 2018: Council of Europe, 'Explanatory Report to the Protocol Amending the Convention for the Protection of Individuals with Regard to the Automatic Processing of Personal Data' (10 October 2018), available at https://rm.coe.int/cets-223-explanatory-report-to-the-protocol-amending-the-convention-fo/16808ac91a.

FRA 2010: Fundamental Rights Agency of the European Union, 'Data Protection in the European Union: The Role of National Data Protection Authorities' (2010).

Others

EC Consultation Website: European Commission, 'Public Consultations', available at https://ec.europa.eu/home-affairs/what-is-new/public-consultation/2009/consulting_0003_en#top-page.

Article 53. General conditions for the members of the supervisory authority

HIELKE HIJMANS[*]

1. Member States shall provide for each member of their supervisory authorities to be appointed by means of a transparent procedure by:
   - their parliament;
   - their government;
   - their head of State; or
   - an independent body entrusted with the appointment under Member State law.
2. Each member shall have the qualifications, experience and skills, in particular in the area of the protection of personal data, required to perform its duties and exercise its powers.
3. The duties of a member shall end in the event of the expiry of the term of office, resignation or compulsory retirement, in accordance with the law of the Member State concerned.
4. A member shall be dismissed only in cases of serious misconduct or if the member no longer fulfils the conditions required for the performance of the duties.

Relevant Recital

(121) The general conditions for the member or members of the supervisory authority should be laid down by law in each Member State and should in particular provide that those members are to be appointed, by means of a transparent procedure, either by the parliament, government or the head of State of the Member State on the basis of a proposal from the government, a member of the government, the parliament or a chamber of the parliament, or by an independent body entrusted under Member State law. In order to ensure the independence of the supervisory authority, the member or members should act with integrity, refrain from any action that is incompatible with their duties and should not, during their term of office, engage in any incompatible occupation, whether gainful or not. The supervisory authority should have its own staff, chosen by the supervisory authority or an independent body established by Member State law, which should be subject to the exclusive direction of the member or members of the supervisory authority.

Closely Related Provisions

Article 4(21) (Definition of a supervisory authority); Article 51 (Establishment of supervisory authorities) (see too recital 117); Article 52 (Independence of supervisory authorities) (see too recitals 118–120); Article 54 (Rules on the establishment of supervisory authorities); Article 68 (European Data Protection Board) (see too recital 139).

Related Provisions in LED [Directive (EU) 2016/680]

Article 3(15) (Definition of a supervisory authority); Article 43 (General conditions for the members of the supervisory authority) (see too recital 79); Article 41 (Establishment of supervisory

---

[*] The views expressed are solely those of the author and do not necessarily reflect those of the Belgian Data Protection Authority.

authorities) (see too recitals 75–77); Article 42 (Independence of supervisory authorities) (see too recital 78); Article 44 (Rules on the establishment of supervisory authorities)

Related Provisions in EPD [Directive 2002/58/EC]

Article 15a (Implementation and enforcement)

Related Provisions in EUDPR [Regulation (EU) 2018/1725]

Article 53 (Appointment of the EDPS) (see also recitals 72 and 87)

Relevant Case Law

CJEU

Case C-518/07, *European Commission v Federal Republic of Germany*, judgment of 9 March 2010 (Grand Chamber) (ECLI:EU:C:2010:125).

Case C-614/10, *European Commission v Republic of Austria*, judgment of 16 October 2012 (Grand Chamber) (ECLI:EU:C:2012:631).

Case C-288/12, *European Commission v Hungary*, judgment of 8 April 2014 (Grand Chamber) (ECLI:EU:C:2014:237).

Opinion of Advocate General Wathelet in Case C-288/12, *European Commission v Hungary*, delivered on 10 December 2013 (ECLI:EU:C:2013:816).

Case C-362/14, *Maximillian Schrems v Data Protection Commissioner*, judgment of 6 October 2015 (Grand Chamber) (ECLI:EU:C:2015:650).

Case C-424/15, *Xabier Ormaetxea Garai and Bernardo Lorenzo Almendros v Administración del Estado*, judgment of 19 October 2016 (ECLI:EU:C:2016:780).

A. Rationale and Policy Underpinnings

Article 53 GDPR is a further provision to safeguard the independent status of supervisory authorities, by specifying the conditions for the members of a data protection authority.

It aims at reconciling, on the one hand, the institutional autonomy of the Member States as regards the establishment, the organisation and the structuring of supervisory authorities[1] with, on the other hand, the basic requirements ensuring independence of DPAs, in particular their members. It must be read in close connection with Article 54 GDPR, which requires the Member States to specify (most of) the provisions of Article 53 in their national laws.

Whilst Member States have full discretion on organising the appointment of the members of DPAs, Article 53(1) aims at ensuring an impartial and transparent procedure

---

[1] See Case C-424/15, *Garai*, para. 30. This case concerned the regulatory authorities in the telecommunications sector.

for this appointment, which is one of the most critical factors for influencing DPA independence.[2]

Further conditions for the independence of members are included in the other provisions of Article 53. These conditions include qualifications, experience and skills, in order to prevent purely political appointments, as well as protection against dismissal for reasons relating to the exercise of the functions as member of an authority. The conditions included in the article may be compared to those relating to members of the judiciary.

In the broader context, Article 53 GDPR may be regarded as one of the provisions implementing the requirements for DPA independence stemming from the case law of the CJEU. It should also guarantee respect for the rule of law, a core value of the European Union and its Member States enshrined in Article 2 of the Treaty on European Union ('TEU').

B. Legal Background

1. EU legislation

The text of Article 53 GDPR is based on Article 42 of Regulation 45/2001.[3] The latter article lays down the requirements for the appointment of the EDPS, including the procedure for appointment, personal qualifications, ending of the term and dismissal. That regulation has now been replaced with the EUDPR, Article 53 of which contains similar provisions.

The transparency of the EDPS appointment procedure was further developed in Article 3 of Decision 1247/2002.[4] The objectives of Article 3 are reflected in Article 53(1) GDPR, although without copying the specific assurances for transparency, for reasons relating to procedural autonomy of the Member States.

2. International instruments

The ideals of Article 53 GDPR are in line with the Additional Protocol to Convention 108 of the Council of Europe, adopted in 2001.[5] Article 1(3) of this Protocol requires complete DPA independence, but does not contain the specific elements in Article 53. Modernised Convention 108 provides in Article 15 that the supervisory authorities are to act with complete independence and impartiality, but also does not contain all the details of Article 53 GDPR.

3. National developments

Article 53, in particular its first paragraph, is rooted in the national legislation of the Member States. A variety of procedures for the appointment of supervisory authorities exist. According to the European Union Agency for Fundamental Rights ('FRA'), in some Member States the parliaments appoint, in others the governments. The FRA also mentions that France, Spain, Portugal and Belgium 'provide for a combined procedure to nominate the officers of the national Data Protection Authority, involving the executive, the legislature and the judiciary or other organized societal groups'.[6]

---

[2] Hijmans 2016, 7.10.3.   [3] See Table of Legislation.   [4] Decision 1247/2002.
[5] See Table of Legislation.   [6] FRA 2010, p. 19.

This variety in the national legislation of the Member States explains why Article 53(1) leaves so many options for appointing DPA members.

4. Case law

Article 53 GDPR must be understood against the background of the CJEU case law on DPA independence.[7] *Commission v Hungary* dealt more specifically with issues relating to the end of the term of office and the dismissal of a member of a DPA as included in Article 53(3) and (4) GDPR.[8] Furthermore, *Garai* concerned the dismissal of board members of a telecom regulator before the expiry of their terms of office.

C. Analysis

1. Article 53 as a further safeguard for independent, effective and accountable DPAs

Article 53 is a further provision that limits the institutional autonomy of the Member States, which may be exercised only in accordance with the objectives and obligations laid down in the GDPR. The objectives are clear. Under the GDPR, DPAs should operate as independent, effective and accountable expert bodies.[9] Vibert explains that amongst the main advantages of expert bodies is that they are independent fact-gatherers and sources of expert knowledge and judgment.[10] Independence and expertise enables these bodies to become authoritative and to play their role as leaders in the area of data protection, capable of influencing behaviour.[11]

Hodges emphasises that in his view the essence of the role of DPAs is influencing behaviour through relationships of trust, rather than enforcement *strictu sensu*, which may lead to large fines.[12] It is evident that a high level of independence and expertise is a prerequisite for creating these relationships of trust. Ottow describes this as regulatory expertise with bodies operating with professional judgment.[13]

Selecting the right people is an essential precondition for DPAs to operate as independent, effective and accountable leaders in the area of data protection, performing the wide range of tasks of Article 57 GDPR. This is the key objective of Article 53(1) and (2).

A second precondition for the proper functioning of DPAs is the assurance that the people working for DPAs do not suffer on account of performing their duties, which may in certain situations not concur with the preferences of their governments. This is the key objective of Article 53(3) and (4), which apply to members of DPAs. The staff of DPAs are protected—in a similar but more indirect manner—by Article 52(5) GDPR on the independence of DPAs, which provides that staff are subject to the exclusive direction of DPA members.[14]

---

[7] Case C-518/07, *Commission v Germany*; Case C-614/10, *Commission v Austria*; Case C-288/12, *Commission v Hungary*.
[8] See also the commentary on Art. 52 in this volume.   [9] As explained in Hijmans 2016, ch. 7.
[10] Vibert 2007, pp. 42–43.   [11] Hodges 2018. See also Hijmans 2018.   [12] Hodges 2018.
[13] Ottow 2015, p. 11.   [14] See rec. 121 GDPR and the commentary on Art. 52 in this volume.

2. Article 53(1) on the appointment of DPA Members

The appointment of DPA members is one of the most critical factors from the perspective of DPA independence.[15] If the appointment procedure is not surrounded by sufficient checks and balances, the appointing authority could appoint persons for reasons of political loyalty and not necessarily on the grounds of proven expertise or independent attitude.

Article 53(1) provides various options for the Member States for the appointment of DPA Members. This provision has some notable features. First, it contains one single procedural safeguard: the procedure must be transparent. Secondly, it mentions the branches of government with one exception: the judiciary. Thirdly, it does not foresee the option of a joint appointment by the different branches.

First, as to the requirement that the procedure must be transparent, the GDPR does not specify the meaning of transparency in this specific context. Transparency is a general principle of EU law.[16] Article 10(3) of the Treaty on the Functioning of the European Union ('TFEU') provides that '(e)very citizen shall have the right to participate in the democratic life of the Union. Decisions shall be taken as openly and as closely as possible to the citizen'. This is developed in Article 15 TFEU and the corresponding Article 42 of the Charter of Fundamental Rights of the European Union ('CFR'), both addressed to EU institutions and bodies. Article 15(1) TFEU provides that '(i)n order to promote good governance and ensure the participation of civil society, the Union institutions, bodies, offices and agencies shall conduct their work as openly as possible'. Article 15(3) TFEU develops this to include a right to access to documents and an obligation for institutions and bodies to 'ensure that its proceedings are transparent'.

The Member States—although not addressees of Article 15 TFEU and the Charter—should also act transparently as far as the appointment of DPA members is concerned, in order to serve the right to participation of the citizens in a democratic society. Although Article 53(1) leaves the Member States a wide margin of manoeuvre in organising the appointment, they must ensure that the procedure is transparent. They could do this, for example, by an open call for candidature and by selecting from a public short list.[17]

Secondly, the Commission proposal only provided for two options for an appointing authority: appointment by the national government or by the parliament. The final text of Article 53(1) adds the possibility of appointment by the head of state. For instance, in The Netherlands the members of the authority are appointed by the King. In France, the President of the authority is appointed by the President of the Republic.[18] The final text also adds the option of appointment by an independent body. It is not specified how this body should be composed. Remarkably, neither Article 53 nor recital 121 refer to a judicial body. Although it is not excluded that members of the judiciary participate in the independent body, the option of entrusting the appointment to a judicial body was not even considered during the legislative procedure.[19]

Thirdly, the text of Article 53(1) does not provide for a joint appointment by government and by parliament, whereas the Council had opened up this possibility explicitly.

---

[15] See Hijmans 2016, 7.10.3. See also Scholten 2014, p. 174.
[16] Lenaerts and van Nuffel 2011, paras. 20.08 and 20.10.
[17] This procedure was applied for the selection of the EDPS and the Assistant Supervisor in 2014.
[18] French GDPR Implementation Law, Art. 9.   [19] Hijmans 2016, 7.10.3.

By deleting 'and/or' as proposed by the Council, it may be assumed that the EU legislator deliberately excluded the option of a joint appointment.

Finally, according to Article 54(1)(c) the rules and procedures for appointment should be laid down in national law.

3. Article 53(2) on the qualifications, experiences and skills of DPA members

The members of supervisory authorities should have the qualifications, experiences and skills, in particular in the area of data protection, to carry out their tasks. This provision aims at ensuring that the members are experts in the field. However, the provision is fairly open. It does not formulate this expertise as a requirement for appointment. Article 53(2) uses the formulation 'in particular', which does not exclude that other relevant qualifications, experiences and skills may be sufficient, nor that these qualifications, experiences and skills may be acquired during the mandate.

This wording is slightly different from Article 42(2) of Regulation 45/2001 which provided that the European Data Protection Supervisor and the Assistant Supervisor are 'acknowledged' as having the required experience and skills, 'for example' because they belong or have belonged to a supervisory authority. It can be seen, however, that it reflects the same ratio: experience in the field (or in a DPA) is an asset but is not required. In contrast, the vacancy notices for appointment of the European Data Protection Supervisor and the Assistant Supervisor in 2014 were more stringent. Very good knowledge of and proven experience in data protection issues were prerequisites for appointment.[20] Currently, Article 53(2) EUDPR (replacing Regulation 45/2001) provides that candidates shall be acknowledged as having expert knowledge in data protection as a requirement for the appointment of the European Data Protection Supervisor.[21]

Article 53(2) GDPR confirms that the supervisory authority should be a non-majoritarian expert body and not a political body. Hence, the members should possess professional qualifications, experiences and skills, and not solely have a political background. However, professional experience should not necessarily include data protection.

Moreover, although the GDPR stipulates that DPA members should be experts, it does not lay down any requirement about their independence. In contrast, EU law requires that members of the Court of Justice and the General Court are chosen 'from persons whose independence is beyond doubt', under Articles 253 and 254 TFEU respectively. Article 42(2) of Regulation 45/2001—now replaced by Article 53(2) EUDPR—imposed the same requirement on the choice of the European Data Protection Supervisor and the Assistant Supervisor.

Nonetheless, Article 53(2) does restrict national autonomy concerning the choice of suitable candidates for supervisory authorities. In this respect it is remarkable that provisions similar to Article 53(2) do not exist in other areas of EU law. For instance, the NIS Directive contains a provision on national authorities for network security, however without any reference to the qualifications of the members of these authorities.[22] Equally, the Antitrust Regulation 1/2003[23] delegates important tasks to national competition authorities, without however prescribing who should be their members.

---

[20] EDPS Vacancy 2014.
[21] As explained below, the function of Assistant Supervisor will disappear.
[22] Art. 8 NIS Directive.   [23] Council Regulation 1/2003.

4. Article 53(3) on the ending of the duties of DPA members

Article 53(3) concerns the coming to an end of the duties of DPA members. Normally their duties will end 'in the event of the expiry of the term of office'. The term of office is dealt with in Article 54(1), as an obligation for the Member States to include a provision in their national laws. Although it is not fully clear from Article 54(1) whether a fixed term is required by the GDPR, the assumption is that the DPA members' appointment is for a specified term of office. However, an appointment for life or until a legal age of retirement is reached, is not excluded. Such an appointment would be fully in line with the objective of independence.

The duties of DPA members may only end—apart from the expiry of the term of office—in case of voluntary resignation or compulsory retirement. It should be underlined that resignation should be voluntary, so not pressured by government or parliament.

5. Article 53(4) on the dismissal of DPA Members

Article 53(4) protects the DPA against dismissal and contains an important safeguard for protecting the independence of DPAs. The threshold for dismissal is high. Dismissal is only allowed in two situations: serious misconduct, or no longer fulfilling the conditions required for the performance of the duties.

This is comparable to the protection enjoyed by the members of the European Commission in Article 247 TFEU. In the same way Article 6 of the Protocol to the TEU on the Statute of the Court of Justice provides that a judge of the Court may be deprived of office if 'he no longer fulfils the requisite conditions or meets the obligations arising from his office'.

There is, however, an important difference in this protection of members of the European Commission or the Court of Justice. EU law does not provide for any procedural guarantee against dismissal of members of DPAs. It does not lay down what authority is entitled to establish that the criteria for dismissal are fulfilled. This is, for instance, not necessarily a judicial authority. The matter is left to national law.

Nonetheless, the performance of DPAs per se cannot be a ground for dismissal. One may assume that even members of a supervisory authority who do not perform their duties at all cannot be dismissed, unless they have lost their skills to act as a DPA. Possibly, not performing at all could be qualified as serious misconduct, yet this is not evident.

As noted above, the threshold for dismissal is high. According to recital 121, the members of supervisory authorities are under specific obligations during their term of office. They 'should act with integrity, refrain from any action that is incompatible with their duties and should not, during their term of office, engage in any incompatible occupation, whether gainful or not'. National law should specify, under Article 54(1)(f), the incompatible occupations and benefits. However, it should be noted that these obligations of DPA members are not laid down in a substantive provision of the GDPR, but only in a recital, with the result that these obligations are not enforceable. Moreover, it is far from clear whether non-respect of these obligations would amount to 'serious misconduct' in the sense of Article 53(4).

Even institutional reform may not by itself be a ground for dismissal, as may be seen in *Commission v Hungary*. This ruling showed that, whilst Member States are free to determine the duration of the term of office of a DPA member,[24] they are not allowed to limit

---

[24] The discretion of the Member States is to a certain extent limited in Art. 54(1)(d) GDPR which provides for a minimum term of office of four years.

the term of office of DPAs during their term, even if this limitation is connected to an institutional reform. Member States cannot change the rules during the game.[25]

The CJEU explained the reasons for its strict construction of the prohibition to end the term of office prematurely. The risk of such premature termination could lead the DPA member 'to enter into a form of prior compliance with the political authority'.[26] Moreover, in such a situation, a DPA member would risk not to be 'able, in all circumstances, to operate above all suspicion of partiality'.[27] Referring to the work of Brkan,[28] this may be a situation where the essence of DPA independence is at stake.

Commission v Hungary may be the result of the specific context, where a new Hungarian government initiated an institutional reform which may have been inspired by the intention to bypass the prohibition in the DPD and to end the term of a specific head of a DPA.[29]

However, in *Garai* the CJEU confirmed in more general terms that the dismissal of a regulator resulting from an institutional reform does not satisfy the requirements of EU law unless there are rules guaranteeing that such dismissals do not jeopardise the regulator's independence and impartiality. This case concerned the dismissal of members of the Spanish national regulatory authority for electronic communications networks and services. This authority was merged with other authorities and a single body for the supervision of markets and competition was created. The CJEU did not object to this institutional reform, but to the fact that this reform *de facto* meant the dismissal of certain members of the old authority in the absence of rules on dismissal guaranteeing their independence and impartiality.

This is the background to Article 100 EUDPR which, for instance, provides that 'the current terms of office of the European Data Protection Supervisor and the Assistant Supervisor shall not be affected by this Regulation'.[30]

In practical terms, whilst the function of Assistant Supervisor disappears under the new regime for data protection at the EU institutions and bodies, the current Assistant Supervisor will remain in office until his term ends on 5 December 2019.

Select Bibliography

EU legislation

Council Regulation 1/2003: Council Regulation (EC) No. 1/2003 of 16 December 2002 on the implementation of the rules on competition laid down in Articles 81 and 82 of the Treaty, OJ 2003 L 1/1.
Decision 1247/2002: Decision No. 1247/2002/EC of the European Parliament and of the Council and of the Commission of 1 July 2002 on the regulations and general conditions governing the performance of the European Data Protection Supervisor's duties, OJ 2002 L 183/1.
NIS Directive: Directive (EU) 2016/1148 of the European Parliament and of the Council of 6 July 2016 concerning measures for a high common level of security of network and information systems across the Union, OJ 2016 L 194/1.

---

[25] Case C-288/12, *Commission v Hungary*, para. 38. [26] Ibid., para. 54.
[27] Ibid., para. 55. [28] Brkan 2018.
[29] These specific circumstances are explained by Advocate General Wathelet, see Case C-288/12, *Commission v Hungary* (AG Opinion), para. 81.
[30] Art. 100(1) EUDPR.

National legislation

French GDPR Implementation Law: Ordonnance n° 2018-1125 du 12 décembre 2018 prise en application de l'article 32 de la loi n° 2018-493 du 20 juin 2018 relative à la protection des données personnelles et portant modification de la loi n° 78-17 du 6 janvier 1978 relative à l'informatique, aux fichiers et aux libertés et diverses dispositions concernant la protection des données à caractère personnel.

Academic writings

Brkan 2018: Brkan, 'The Concept of Essence of Fundamental Rights in the EU Legal Order: Peeling the Onion to its Core', 14(2) *European Constitutional Law Review* (2018), 332.
Hijmans 2016: Hijmans, *The European Union as Guardian of Internet Privacy* (Springer 2016).
Hijmans 2018: Hijmans, 'How to Enforce the GDPR in a Strategic, Consistent and Ethical Manner? A Reaction to Christopher Hodges', 4(1) *European Data Protection Law Review 'EDPL'* (2018), 80.
Hodges 2018: Hodges, 'Delivering Data Protection: Trust and Ethical Culture', 4(1) *EDPL* (2018), 65.
Hodges, *Law and Corporate Behaviour: Integrating Theories of Regulation, Enforcement, Culture and Ethics* (Hart Publishing 2015).
Lenaerts and van Nuffel 2011: Lenaerts and van Nuffel, *European Union Law* (3rd edn, Sweet & Maxwell 2011).
Ottow 2015: Ottow, *Market & Competition Authorities, Good Agency Principles* (OUP 2015).
Scholten 2014: Scholten, 'The Political Accountability of EU Agencies: Learning from the US Experience' (2014) (PhD dissertation at Maastricht University).
Vibert 2007: Vibert, *The Rise of the Unelected, Democracy and the New Separation of Powers* (CUP 2007).
Wright and de Hert (eds.), *Enforcing Privacy, Regulatory, Legal and Technological Approaches* (Springer 2016).

Papers of data protection authorities

EDPS Vacancy 2014: European Data Protection Supervisor—Vacancy for the European Data Protection Supervisor, COM/2014/10354, OJ 2014 C 163A/6.

Reports and recommendations

Centre for Information Policy Leadership, 'Regulating for Results, Strategies and Priorities for Leadership and Engagement' (10 October 2017).
FRA 2010: Fundamental Rights Agency of the European Union, 'Data Protection in the European Union: The Role of National Data Protection Authorities' (2010).

Article 54. Rules on the establishment of the supervisory authority

HIELKE HIJMANS[*]

1. Each Member State shall provide by law for all of the following:
   (a) the establishment of each supervisory authority;
   (b) the qualifications and eligibility conditions required to be appointed as member of each supervisory authority;
   (c) the rules and procedures for the appointment of the member or members of each supervisory authority;
   (d) the duration of the term of the member or members of each supervisory authority of no less than four years, except for the first appointment after 24 May 2016, part of which may take place for a shorter period where that is necessary to protect the independence of the supervisory authority by means of a staggered appointment procedure;
   (e) whether and, if so, for how many terms the member or members of each supervisory authority is eligible for reappointment;
   (f) the conditions governing the obligations of the member or members and staff of each supervisory authority, prohibitions on actions, occupations and benefits incompatible therewith during and after the term of office and rules governing the cessation of employment.
2. The member or members and the staff of each supervisory authority shall, in accordance with Union or Member State law, be subject to a duty of professional secrecy both during and after their term of office, with regard to any confidential information which has come to their knowledge in the course of the performance of their tasks or exercise of their powers. During their term of office, that duty of professional secrecy shall in particular apply to reporting by natural persons of infringements of this Regulation.

Relevant Recitals

(117) The establishment of supervisory authorities in Member States, empowered to perform their tasks and exercise their powers with complete independence, is an essential component of the protection of natural persons with regard to the processing of their personal data. Member States should be able to establish more than one supervisory authority, to reflect their constitutional, organisational and administrative structure.

(121) The general conditions for the member or members of the supervisory authority should be laid down by law in each Member State and should in particular provide that those members are to be appointed, by means of a transparent procedure, either by the parliament, government or the head of State of the Member State on the basis of a proposal from the government, a member of the government, the parliament or a chamber of the parliament, or by an independent body entrusted under Member State law. In order to ensure the independence of the supervisory authority, the member or members should act with integrity, refrain from any action that is incompatible with their duties and should not, during their term of office, engage in

---

[*] The views expressed are solely those of the author and do not necessarily reflect those of the Belgian Data Protection Authority.

any incompatible occupation, whether gainful or not. The supervisory authority should have its own staff, chosen by the supervisory authority or an independent body established by Member State law, which should be subject to the exclusive direction of the member or members of the supervisory authority.

Closely Related Provisions

Article 4(21) (Definition of a supervisory authority); Article 38 (Position of the data protection officer); Article 51 (Establishment of supervisory authorities); Article 52 (Independence of supervisory authorities) (see too recitals 118–120); Article 53 (General conditions for the members of supervisory authorities); Article 76 (EDPB Confidentiality)

Related Provisions in LED [Directive (EU) 2016/680]

Article 3(15) (Definition of a supervisory authority); Article 44 (Rules on the establishment of supervisory authorities) (see too recital 79); Article 41 (Establishment of supervisory authorities) (see too recitals 75–77); Article 42 (Independence of supervisory authorities) (see too recital 78); Article 43 (General conditions for the members of the supervisory authority)

Related Provisions in EPD [Directive 2002/58/EC]

Article 15a (Implementation and enforcement)

Related Provisions in EUDPR [Regulation (EU) 2018/1725]

Article 53 (Appointment of the EDPS); Article 54 (Regulations and general conditions governing the performance of the European Data Protection Supervisor's duties, staff and financial resources); Article 55 (Independence); Article 56 (Professional secrecy)

Relevant Case Law

CJEU

Case C-518/07, *European Commission v Federal Republic of Germany*, judgment of 9 March 2010 (Grand Chamber) (ECLI:EU:C:2010:125).

Case C-614/10, *European Commission v Republic of Austria*, judgment of 16 October 2012 (Grand Chamber) (ECLI:EU:C:2012:631).

Case T-380/08, *Kingdom of the Netherlands v European Commission*, GC, judgment of 13 September 2013 (ECLI:EU:T:2013:480).

Case C-288/12, *European Commission v Hungary*, judgment of 8 April 2014 (Grand Chamber) (ECLI:EU:C:2014:237).

Case C-140/13, *Annett Altmann and Others v Bundesanstalt für Finanzdienstleistungsaufsicht*, judgment of 12 November 2014 (ECLI:EU:C:2014:2362).

Case C-362/14, *Maximillian Schrems v Data Protection Commissioner*, judgment of 6 October 2015 (Grand Chamber) (ECLI:EU:C:2015:650).

Case C-424/15, *Xabier Ormaetxea Garai and Bernardo Lorenzo Almendros v Administración del Estado*, judgment of 19 October 2016 (ECLI:EU:C:2016:780).

A. Rationale and Policy Underpinnings

Article 54(1) GDPR is a further elaboration of the notion of data protection authority independence,[1] which stems from the case law of the CJEU and is laid down in Treaty provisions. It mainly specifies the obligations of the Member States when they establish the supervisory authorities and, more in detail, how the appointment of DPA members should be organised.

Article 54(1) should not only ensure that DPAs effectively operate in an independent manner, but also serves as a good example of the reconciliation of the two objectives of the GDPR.[2] The GDPR is intended to ensure a level playing field in the EU and, at the same time, to respect the general features of the EU as a mechanism of executive federalism,[3] with enforcement by national authorities and respect for national institutional autonomy. As to the latter, Member States are autonomous as regards the organisation and the structuring of their national authorities, but that autonomy may be exercised only in accordance with the objectives and obligations laid down in EU law.[4] Article 54(2) is of a different nature. It contains a directly applicable norm that deals with the professional secrecy of the DPA and its members. This does not necessarily aim at safeguarding the independence of the DPAs, but it does aim to contribute to the DPAs operating in an effective and professional manner.

B. Legal Background

1. EU legislation

Article 54 was inspired by Regulation 45/2001,[5] in particular Articles 42 and 43 thereof, on the appointment and regulations and general conditions governing the performance of the EDPS duties, staff and financial resources. In particular, Article 44 thereof dealt with situations that may be incompatible with the nature of the DPAs, in particular the requirement that they act with complete independence (these situations are referred to here as 'incompatibilities'). A good example may be found in Article 44(4): 'The European Data Protection Supervisor shall, after his or her term of office, behave with integrity and discretion as regards the acceptance of appointments and benefits'. The EUDPR, which replaces Regulation 45/2001, contains an even more detailed set of provisions dealing with how the EDPS should be set up and act.[6]

Articles 11, 11a, 16 and 17 of the EU Staff Regulations[7] have similar objectives and content to Article 54 GDPR in relation to incompatibilities and professional secrecy.

2. International instruments

The ideals of Article 54 are, like the ideals of Article 53, in line with the Additional Protocol to Convention 108 of the Council of Europe, adopted in 2001.[8] Article 1(3) of this Protocol requires complete DPA independence, but does not deal specifically with the topics included in Article 53 GDPR. Modernised Convention 108 also requires complete independence of supervisory authorities and also contains provisions to ensure

---

[1] See the commentary on Art. 52 in this volume.
[2] See the commentary on Art. 1 in this volume.   [3] Lenaerts and van Nuffel 2011, para. 17-002.
[4] See e.g. Case C-424/15, *Garai*, para. 30.   [5] See Table of Legislation.
[6] EUDPR, Arts. 53–56.   [7] EU Staff Regulations.   [8] See Table of Legislation.

that this independent role can be exercised.[9] The Explanatory Report to the Modernised Convention also discusses issues relating to the duration of the exercise of the functions of DPA members and the conditions under which they may cease their functions, which are also a component of Article 54(1) GDPR.[10]

Article 15(8) of the Modernised Convention also contains requirements on the confidentiality obligations of DPA members and their staff, the subject of Article 54(2) GDPR. However, it does not say anything about the appointment of DPA members, a key subject of Article 54(1) GDPR.

3. National developments

At the national level, under the DPD a wide variety of national provisions on the appointment, terms of office and further conditions for DPA members were enacted.[11] These provisions will need to be renewed and strengthened in the various national laws implementing the GDPR in respect of supervisory authorities. These national laws inspired the drafting of Article 54 GDPR, and this provision is addressed—to a large extent—to national legislators, who should update their national laws accordingly.

4. Case law

Article 54 must be understood against the background of the CJEU case law on DPA independence.[12] Other relevant case law relates to confidentiality obligations, which are the subject of GDPR Article 54(2).[13]

C. Analysis

1. The contribution of Article 54 for DPA independence

Article 54 is part of a section of the GDPR dealing with the independent status of DPAs, consisting of four articles (Chapter VI Section 1 GDPR, Articles 51–54). While they are closely connected, their organisation is not entirely logical.

To give a few examples: first, Article 51 provides that a Member State shall establish a DPA. Article 54(1)(a) basically repeats this obligation, without adding anything. It would be difficult to imagine that a Member State would establish a DPA—with all duties and powers provided by the GDPR—outside a legislative framework. Secondly, Article 53 is entitled 'general conditions for the members of the supervisory authority' and the article refers to national law and procedures. The provisions of Article 54(1)(b)–(f) GDPR could have been included in the previous article on the conditions for members of the DPAs.[14] Thirdly, three provisions—Articles 52(4), 54(1)(f) and 54(2)—address the staff of DPAs, but they are not consolidated into the same article.

[9] Modernised Convention 108, Art. 15.   [10] Explanatory Report Convention 108 2018.
[11] FRA 2010, p. 19.
[12] Case C-518/07, *Commission v Germany*; Case C-614/10, *Commission v Austria*; Case C-288/12, *Commission v Hungary*; Case C-362/14, *Schrems*. See also the commentaries on Arts. 52 and 69 in this volume.
[13] Case C-140/13, *Altmann*; Case T-380/08, *Netherlands v Commission*.
[14] See the commentary on Art. 53 in this volume.

In consequence, the way Chapter VI, Section 1 GDPR is organised requires Article 54 to be read in direct connection with Articles 51–53. It cannot be read in an autonomous manner.

2. Obligations for the national legislator

Article 54(1), though part of an EU regulation, is a provision with features of a directive. It requires the Member States to implement in their national laws a number of the elements for the establishment of a DPA and the appointment of its members.

Article 54(1) requires Member States to specify the elements of Article 54(1) in their national law. Some of these elements follow directly from the preceding provisions of the GDPR, including those concerning the establishment of a DPA under Article 54(1)(a), the qualifications and eligibility conditions of DPA members under Article 54(1)(b), and the rules and procedures for the appointment of the members under Article 54(1)(c). The provisions of Article 54 do not further specify the obligations of Member States already laid down in the preceding articles.

Other provisions contain new substantive elements. These relate to the duration of the term, a possible reappointment under Article 54(1)(d)–(e) and the incompatibilities with the function of DPA member under Article 54(1)(f).

Article 54(2) is more of a hybrid provision, because it contains a directly applicable provision on professional secrecy, with however a reference to both Union and Member State law.

3. Term of office and reappointment

The starting point of the GDPR is that DPA members are appointed for a fixed period. Although DPA independence is to a certain extent comparable to the independence of members of the judiciary, it is not provided that DPAs are appointed for life.[15]

However, Article 54(1)(d) GDPR does provide a minimum period for appointment of four years, leaving it up to the Member States to choose a longer period. This does not preclude Member States from providing in national law for an appointment of undetermined duration.

The terms of office of DPA members are renewable, again as specified in national law, which not only should determine whether the terms of members are renewable, but also, if so, on how many occasions. A comparison can be made with the terms of office of the Chair of the EDPB according to Article 73(2) GDPR providing that the term of office of the Chair shall be five years and renewable once.[16]

The possibility for renewal of the term of office is a sensitive issue, since it may encourage a form of 'prior compliance' on the part of the DPA member seeking renewal[17] which might detract from the independence of the DPA itself.

4. Incompatibilities as components of integrity

Recital 121 explains the concept of integrity as follows: '(i)n order to ensure the independence of the supervisory authority, the member or members should act with integrity,

---

[15] Ibid.   [16] See the commentary on Art. 73 in this volume.

[17] See to that effect, Case C-518/07, *Commission v Germany*, para. 36; Case C-614/10, *Commission v Austria*, para. 51. See more in general on the vulnerability of appointment procedures, Scholten 2014.

refrain from any action that is incompatible with their duties and should not, during their term of office, engage in any incompatible occupation, whether gainful or not'.

This concept of integrity is set forth in Article 54(1)(f), which lays down that national law should provide for prohibitions on actions, occupations and benefits incompatible with DPA tasks, as a part of integrity. These prohibitions should also cover incompatibilities after the term of office and, moreover, they should apply not only to DPA members, but also to DPA staff.

This is based on the principle that the 'authorities should remain above any suspicion of partiality'.[18] The CJEU has emphasised that any direct or indirect influence should be avoided.[19] Similarly, (potential) conflicts of interests should be prevented, even though the term 'conflict of interest' is not used in this context, contrary to Article 38(6) GDPR on data protection officers.

The following examples show the diverging ways incompatibility is regarded in national law. Belgian law provides that members of the board of the Data Protection Authority, which is composed of five members, cannot be members of the European Parliament or a national or regional parliament, nor members of a national or regional government or as a policy adviser of a minister, nor exercise a public mandate.[20] In contrast, French law provides that the CNIL, which is composed of 18 members, can include members of parliament and of other public bodies.[21] French law does not consider the main (political) affiliation of DPA members as compromising their independence. Dutch law is of a different nature and mainly provides that members of the Dutch DPA should refrain from incompatible external activities and be transparent about any external activity they perform.[22]

Member States law should also deal with incompatibilities after the term of office of a DPA member or a member of the staff. This has to do with so-called 'revolving door' situations where members or staff leave the DPA to work for the private sector (and, equally, for the public sector). This 'revolving door' has attracted some attention in recent years, e.g. at EU level where the European Ombudsman has made a number of suggestions in the context of enquiries.[23] These suggestions include the development of Codes of ethics and integrity. These suggestions could also be relevant in relation to DPAs.

For a better understanding of the objectives and content of these incompatibility and integrity obligations included in Article 54(1)(f) GDPR, it can be helpful to consult provisions of the EU Staff Regulations. These rules apply directly to the staff of the EDPS and the EDPB, but may also play a role in the interpretation of national provisions implementing Article 54(1)(f) GDPR. Article 11 of the Staff Regulations provides:

An official shall carry out his duties and conduct himself solely with the interests of the Union in mind. He shall neither seek nor take instructions from any government, authority, organisation or person outside his institution. He shall carry out the duties assigned to him objectively, impartially and in keeping with his duty of loyalty to the Union.[24]

Article 11a (1) specifies this as follows: 'An official shall not, in the performance of his duties ... deal with a matter in which, directly or indirectly, he has any personal interest

---

[18] Hijmans 2016, 7.9.1.   [19] Case C-518/07, *Commission v Germany*, para. 19.
[20] Art. 38 Belgian DPA Law 2017. The same obligation applies to members of the knowledge centre and of the litigation chamber, separate unities within the Belgian DPA.
[21] French Data Protection Act 1978.   [22] This is laid down in Dutch DPA Law 2006.
[23] European Ombudsman Website 2017.   [24] Art. 11 EU Staff Regulations.

such as to impair his independence, and, in particular, family and financial interests'. Finally, Article 16 sets a rule for behaviour after the term of duty: 'An official shall, after leaving the service, continue to be bound by the duty to behave with integrity and discretion as regards the acceptance of certain appointments or benefits'.

5. Professional secrecy for members and staff

Professional secrecy obligations exist in EU law and Member States law for several professions which handle confidential information on a regular basis. Examples are doctors, lawyers and public officials in a variety of domains.

For officials and holders of public office at EU level as well as for EU officials, Article 339 Treaty on the Functioning of the European Union ('TFEU') provides that they 'shall be required, even after their duties have ceased, not to disclose information of the kind covered by the obligation of professional secrecy, in particular information about undertakings, their business relations or their cost components'. This is, for officials and other servants, further developed in Article 17 of the EU Staff Regulations as a general rule that: '(a)n official shall refrain from any unauthorised disclosure of information received in the line of duty, unless that information has already been made public or is accessible to the public'. One may assume that Article 339 TFEU binds members of DPAs acting in their capacity of members of the EDPB. The staff of the EDPS and the EDPB are bound by both Article 339 TFEU, Article 17 of the Staff Regulations and Article 56 EUDPR.

In general, one of the main reasons for applying professional secrecy obligations for DPA members and staff relates to enforcement procedures. In EU competition law, the CJEU held that there exists 'a general presumption that disclosure of [certain][25] documents ... in the context of a proceeding under Article 81 EC undermines, in principle, both the protection of the purpose of investigation activities and the protection of the commercial interests of the undertakings involved in such a proceeding'.[26] In another case, on professional secrecy in relation to financial supervision, the Court ruled that the obligation to maintain professional secrecy prevailed over the interest of an individual who requested access to certain information.[27]

A similar presumption of secrecy exists in the context of DPA investigations, although commercial interests by themselves will in this domain in many cases not justify secrecy.

A further reason relates to the protection of individuals' rights. There is a clear link with Article 38(5) GDPR, according to which the data protection officer is bound by obligations of secrecy and confidentiality, which is particularly important in relation to individuals exercising their rights. The second sentence of Article 54(2) GDPR mentions the reporting by individuals of infringements as a particular interest to be protected by the duty of professional secrecy.

Finally, obligations of secrecy should be performed in a proportionate manner, so as not to unduly restrict the transparency of DPA performance, one of the main elements of public accountability of DPAs.[28] Curtin explains this—in a slightly different context—as follows: 'If executive officials are given largely unchecked power to conceal from the public and from parliament(s) whatever information they consider sensitive, part of the essential machinery of democracy is disconnected'.[29]

---

[25] Addition inserted by author.
[26] Case T-380/08, *Netherlands v Commission*, para. 68.
[27] Case C-140/13, *Altmann*.
[28] Hijmans 2016, 7.14.1.
[29] Curtin 2014, p. 684.

For this reason, where relevant, the obligations of professional secrecy should be balanced with public access to document rules, at national level and, in accordance with Article 15 TFEU and Regulation 1049/2001,[30] at EU level.

Select Bibliography

EU legislation

EU Staff Regulations: Regulation No. 31 (EEC), 11 (EAEC) of 14 June 1962 laying down the Staff Regulations of Officials and the Conditions of Employment of Other Servants of the European Economic Community and the European Atomic Energy Community as amended, OJ 1962 L 45/1385.
Regulation 1049/2001: Regulation (EC) No. 1049/2001 of the European Parliament and of the Council of 30 May 2001 regarding public access to European Parliament, Council and Commission documents, OJ 2001 L 145/43.

National legislation

Belgian DPA Law 2017: Loi portant création de l'Autorité de protection des données, du 3 decembre 2017; Wet tot oprichting van de Gegevensbeschermingsautoriteit, van 3 december 2017.
Dutch DPA Law 2006: Kaderwet zelfstandige bestuursorganen van 2 november 2006.
French Data Protection Act 1978: Act No. 78-17 of 6 January 1978 on Data Processing, Files and Individual Liberties (Loi n° 78-17 du 6 janvier 1978 relative à l'informatique, aux fichiers et aux libertés), as last amended by Law No. 2014-334 of 17 March 2014.

Academic writings

Curtin 2014: Curtin, 'Overseeing Secrets in the EU: A Democratic Perspective', 52(3) *Journal of Common Market Studies* (2014), 684.
Hijmans 2016: Hijmans, *The European Union as Guardian of Internet Privacy* (Springer 2016).
Hijmans, 'The European Data Protection Supervisor: The Institutions of the EC Controlled by an Independent Authority', 43(5) *Common Market Law Review* (2006), 1313.
Hijmans, 'The DPAs and their Cooperation: How Far Are We in Making Enforcement of Data Protection Law More European?', 3(2) *European Data Protection Law Review* (2016), 362.
Lenaerts and van Nuffel 2011: Lenaerts and van Nuffel, *European Union Law* (3rd edn, Sweet & Maxwell 2011).
Scholten 2014: Scholten, 'The Political Accountability of EU Agencies: Learning from the US Experience' (2014) (PhD dissertation at Maastricht University).

Reports and recommendations

Centre for Information Policy Leadership, 'Regulating for Results, Strategies and Priorities for Leadership and Engagement' (10 October 2017).
Explanatory Report Convention 108 2018: Council of Europe, 'Explanatory Report to the Protocol Amending the Convention for the Protection of Individuals with Regard to the Automatic Processing of Personal Data' (10 October 2018), available at https://rm.coe.int/cets-223-explanatory-report-to-the-protocol-amending-the-convention-fo/16808ac91a.

---

[30] Regulation 1049/2001.

FRA 2010: Fundamental Rights Agency of the European Union, 'Data Protection in the European Union: The Role of National Data Protection Authorities' (2010).

Others

European Ombudsman Website 2017: European Ombudsman, 'The Commission's Management of 'Revolving Doors' Situations Concerning EU Staff' (27 March 2017), available at https://www.ombudsman.europa.eu/en/correspondence/en/77544.

Section 2 Competence, tasks and powers

Article 55. Competence

HIELKE HIJMANS*

1. Each supervisory authority shall be competent for the performance of the tasks assigned to and the exercise of the powers conferred on it in accordance with this Regulation on the territory of its own Member State.
2. Where processing is carried out by public authorities or private bodies acting on the basis of point (c) or (e) of Article 6(1), the supervisory authority of the Member State concerned shall be competent. In such cases Article 56 does not apply.
3. Supervisory authorities shall not be competent to supervise processing operations of courts acting in their judicial capacity.

Relevant Recitals

(20) While this Regulation applies, inter alia, to the activities of courts and other judicial authorities, Union or Member State law could specify the processing operations and processing procedures in relation to the processing of personal data by courts and other judicial authorities. The competence of the supervisory authorities should not cover the processing of personal data when courts are acting in their judicial capacity, in order to safeguard the independence of the judiciary in the performance of its judicial tasks, including decision-making. It should be possible to entrust supervision of such data processing operations to specific bodies within the judicial system of the Member State, which should, in particular ensure compliance with the rules of this Regulation, enhance awareness among members of the judiciary of their obligations under this Regulation and handle complaints in relation to such data processing operations.

(122) Each supervisory authority should be competent on the territory of its own Member State to exercise the powers and to perform the tasks conferred on it in accordance with this Regulation. This should cover in particular the processing in the context of the activities of an establishment of the controller or processor on the territory of its own Member State, the processing of personal data carried out by public authorities or private bodies acting in the public interest, processing affecting data subjects on its territory or processing carried out by a controller or processor not established in the Union when targeting data subjects residing on its territory. This should include handling complaints lodged by a data subject, conducting investigations on the application of this Regulation and promoting public awareness of the risks, rules, safeguards and rights in relation to the processing of personal data.

(128) The rules on the lead supervisory authority and the one-stop-shop mechanism should not apply where the processing is carried out by public authorities or private bodies in the public interest. In such cases the only supervisory authority competent to exercise the powers conferred to it in accordance with this Regulation should be the supervisory authority of the Member State where the public authority or private body is established.

---

* The views expressed are solely those of the author and do not necessarily reflect those of the Belgian Data Protection Authority.

Closely Related Provisions

Article 3(1) (Territorial scope) (see too recital 22); Article 4(21) (Definition of supervisory authority); Articles 51–54 (Independent Status) (see too recitals 117–121); Article 56 (Competence of the lead authority) (see too recitals 124–131), Article 57 (Tasks) (see too recitals 122–123 and 132–133) Article 58 (Powers) (see too recital 129); Article 59 (Activity reports)

Related Provisions in LED [Directive (EU) 2016/680]

Article 45 (Competence) (see also recital 80)

Relevant Case Law

CJEU

Case C-54/96, *Dorsch Consult Ingenieurgesellschaft mbH v Bundesbaugesellschaft Berlin mbH*, judgment of 17 September 1997 (ECLI:EU:C:1997:413).
Case C-614/10, *European Commission v Republic of Austria*, judgment of 16 October 2012 (Grand Chamber) (ECLI:EU:C:2012:631).
Case C-131/12, *Google Spain v Agencia Española de Protección de Datos (AEPD) and Mario Costeja González*, judgment of 13 May 2014 (Grand Chamber) (ECLI:EU:C:2014:317).
Joined Cases C-293/12 and C-594/12, *Digital Rights Ireland Ltd v Minister for Communications, Marine and Natural Resources and Others and Kärntner Landesregierung and Others*, judgment of 8 April 2014 (Grand Chamber) (ECLI:EU:C:2014:238).
Case C-230/14, *Weltimmo s.r.o. v Nemzeti Adatvédelmi és Információszabadság Hatóság*, judgment of 1 October 2015 (ECLI:EU:C:2015:639).
Opinion of Advocate General Cruz Villalón in C-230/14, *Weltimmo s.r.o. v Nemzeti Adatvédelmi és Információszabadság Hatóság*, delivered on 25 June 2015 (ECLI:EU:C:2015:426).
Case C-362/14, *Maximillian Schrems v Data Protection Commissioner*, judgment of 6 October 2015 (Grand Chamber) (ECLI:EU:C:2015:650).
Case C-191/15, *Verein für Konsumenteninformation v Amazon EU Sàrl*, judgment of 28 July 2016 (ECLI:EU:C:2016:612).
Case C-210/16, *Unabhängiges Landeszentrum für Datenschutz Schleswig-Holstein v Wirtschaftsakademie Schleswig-Holstein GmbH*, judgment of 5 June 2018 (Grand Chamber) (ECLI:EU:C:2018:388).

A. Rationale and Policy Underpinnings

Article 55 lays down the territorial competence of the independent supervisory authorities and is the direct consequence of one of the main features of the GDPR. The GDPR as a law of the Union is directly applicable in the Member States. However, the enforcement of the law is a matter of national authorities. Lenaerts and van Nuffel call this executive federalism.[1]

The main rule, as laid down in Article 55(1) GDPR is simple: the DPA is competent on the territory of its own Member State. This rule should be read in connection with Article 3(1) on territorial scope. The competence of a DPA applies to the processing of personal data in the context of an activity of an establishment of the controller in that Member State. Hence, the criterion for processing is not the physical place where the

---

[1] Lenaerts and van Nuffel 2011, para. 17-002.

processing takes place, but the establishment of the controller. As explained in recital 22 GDPR, '[e]stablishment implies the effective and real exercise of activity through stable arrangements'.[2] Article 55(1) GDPR confirms the territorial sovereignty of the Member States which includes that the administrative authorities of a state are competent to act on national territory.[3] It also confirms the role of authorities as enforcement authorities, having competence on national territory, equal to other public bodies and judicial authorities.

Article 55(2) confirms the territorial sovereignty of the Member States in more specific terms for the processing by public bodies and by private bodies acting in the public interest. This concerns processing necessary for compliance with a legal obligation and necessary for the performance of a task carried out in the public interest or in the exercise of official authority (with reference to Article 6(1)(c) and (e) GDPR). Within this context, there are no exceptions to the territorial competence and there cannot be a lead supervisory authority (as introduced in Article 56 GDPR). The one-stop-shop mechanism with a lead DPA leading the enforcement by all concerned DPAs is not applicable either. Article 55(2) links the territorial competence to the Member State concerned. This must be understood as the Member State imposing the legal obligation or the Member State of which the public interest is served. The fact that the legal obligation or the public interest may be grounded in EU law or international law does not affect this competence.

Article 55(3) GDPR excludes supervisory authorities from supervising the processing activities of courts acting in their judicial capacity. This provision seeks a solution for the position of courts as a result of the separation of powers in a democratic state. Courts are subject to data protection law, but not to data protection authorities. The provision is based on the view that judges should not be supervised by an administrative authority nor by persons that do not belong to the judicial branch of government. Thus, recital 20 specifies that it is up to the Member States to set up specific bodies within the judicial system, with similar roles as supervisory authorities for data protection.

The exception in Article 55(3) is limited to the judicial activity of the court, which means that for instance the processing of staff data by courts falls within the competence of supervisory authorities.

B. Legal Background

1. EU legislation

Article 55(1) GDPR is a further article modifying and replacing Article 28 DPD on the supervisory authority. The provision is more specific than its predecessor, since it refers to the tasks and powers of the supervisory authorities. The DPA's competence extends to all tasks and powers. Article 55(2) does not have an antecedent in EU legislation, which is logical since it is included solely in connection to the lead supervisory authority (in Article 56). The lead supervisory authority is a novelty in EU law introduced by the GDPR.

Nor is there any equivalent to Article 55(3) in the DPD. However, the limited competence of data protection authorities vis-à-vis the judiciary is not new in EU legislation.

---

[2] EDPB 2018, Chapter 1.   [3] See Case 230/14, *Weltimmo* (AG Opinion).

A similar provision was included in Regulation 45/2001[4] on data protection within the EU institutions.[5] The Regulation is now replaced by the EUDPR which equally provides for an exception to the monitoring competence of the European Data Protection Supervisor with regard to the processing of personal data by the Court of Justice acting in its judicial capacity.[6] This provision aims to avoid having judicial authorities supervised by authorities of an administrative nature. The same policy rationale—judges should not be supervised by non-judges—was reflected in the provisions in the Eurojust Decision on the Joint Supervisory Body for Eurojust.[7] Members of this body were normally judges and the three permanent members of this body who play a key role in its functioning always had to be judges.

2. International instruments

Convention 108 of the Council of Europe, the first binding international instrument on data protection, initially did not include provisions on independent supervisory authorities. These provisions were included in an Additional Protocol, adopted in 2001.[8] Article 1 of this Protocol is quite similar to Article 28 DPD and contains elements of Article 55(1) GDPR.

The modernised text of Convention 108 contains a more extensive provision on supervisory authorities. Article 15(10) of the text provides that the 'supervisory authorities shall not be competent with respect to processing carried out by bodies when acting in their judicial capacity'. This provision is the equivalent of Article 55(3) GDPR.

3. National developments

Before 25 May 2018, national law of all Member States contained provisions assigning tasks to DPAs implementing Article 28 DPD.[9] There was no reason, in those laws, to specifically lay down that these authorities were competent on national territory. This competence of DPAs follows from the fact that they are national administrative authorities.

Article 55(3) GDPR, the exemption of courts acting in their judicial capacity from DPA competence, is inspired by Regulation 45/2001 on data protection within the EU institutions, not by national law.

4. Case law

The territorial competence of supervisory authorities was addressed by the CJEU in the *Weltimmo* judgment.[10] Although this judgment mainly dealt with applicable law in cross-border situations,[11] it also explains some basics about the competence of national supervisory authorities to perform tasks and to exercise powers.[12] The *Weltimmo* judgment dealt with the situation of a company having its seat in one Member State (Slovakia) and directing its activities online mainly or entirely to another Member State (Hungary) in the language of the latter Member State.

---

[4] See Table of Legislation.   [5] Art. 46(c) Regulation 45/2000.   [6] Art. 57(1) EUDPR.
[7] Art. 23 Council Decision Eurojust, repealed with effect from 12 December 2019.
[8] See Table of Legislation.
[9] An overview (neither fully complete nor up to date) can be found in FRA 2010, section 4.
[10] Case C-230/14, *Weltimmo*.
[11] Interpreting Art. 4(1)(b) DPD. See on this also Case C-191/15, *Verein für Konsumenteninformation*.
[12] Case C-230/14, *Weltimmo*, paras. 42–60.

As a first step in its analysis, the CJEU underlined the flexibility of the definition of the concept of 'establishment'. This flexibility means an interpretation 'in the light of the specific nature of the economic activities and the provision of services concerned. This is particularly true for undertakings offering services exclusively over the Internet'. The DPA competence is linked to the existence of an establishment of a company in its Member State, yet for an establishment to exist a (formalistic) registration in that Member State is not required.[13] However, the mere accessibility of a website in a Member State is not sufficient, as was confirmed in *Verein für Konsumenteninformation*.[14] The CJEU has confirmed the territorial nature of the DPAs powers in the DPD, however with a reference to Article 28(6) DPD specifying the need for DPAs to cooperate with one another as a necessary provision to ensure the free flow of personal data.[15]

In *Weltimmo*, the CJEU underlined that the law should make it possible for individuals to enforce their right to protection.[16] The CJEU ruled that the Hungarian authority pursuant to Article 28 DPD may hear claims by persons who consider themselves victims of unlawful processing of their personal data.[17] The CJEU explained that, under the circumstances of the case, DPD Article 28(6) entitles the Hungarian DPA to examine a claim irrespective of the applicable law, even if the applicable law would be that of another Member State (i.e. Slovakia).[18] The powers of the Hungarian DPA extend to the exercise of investigative powers vis-à-vis the company established in Slovakia which was directing its activities to residents in Hungary. It cannot, however, impose penalties on the company not established in Hungary. Instead, the Hungarian DPA should ask the DPA of the Member State whose law is applicable (Slovakia) to act.

C. Analysis

1. Territorial competence in a digital world

Article 55(1) GDPR states the obvious: DPAs are competent on national territory.[19] Within this territory, they perform the tasks assigned to them and exercise the powers conferred to them by the GDPR. Article 55(1) is a rule of jurisdiction. It is a confirmation of a key jurisdictional rule under public international law that within its territory a state has the power to enforce the law. This power normally is an exclusive power.[20] However, in a digital environment territoriality is not straightforward, particularly because the place of processing of data is not necessarily relevant for the effect this processing has on individuals. The vulnerability of individuals for processing outside their national territory has made the legislator define a wide territorial scope of the GDPR— for instance in Article 3 GDPR—which scholars have characterised as a territorial overreach.[21] It has also prompted the legislator to link the territorial competence of the DPAs to the establishment of a company.

As a rule, territorial competence of a DPA is vested when processing takes place in the context of the activities an establishment of a company on the territory of its Member

---

[13] Ibid., para. 29. [14] Case C-191/15, *Verein für Konsumenteninformation*, para. 76.
[15] Case C-230/14, *Weltimmo*, paras. 52–53. [16] Ibid., para. 53. [17] Ibid., para. 45.
[18] Ibid., para. 54.
[19] See also Case C-230/14, *Weltimmo*, para. 57, where the CJEU stated that a DPA 'cannot impose penalties outside the territory of its own Member State'.
[20] See Hijmans 2016, 9.9. [21] Kuner 2019; Gömann 2017.

State.[22] It is thus not necessary to prove that the establishment has effectively processed the data. The concept is flexible and appropriate to ensure effective and complete protection of the individual, as demonstrated in the CJEU ruling in *Google Spain*[23] where advertising activities of a local subsidiary of a globally operating search engine was sufficient to vest jurisdiction.

Its flexibility was even increased in the *Weltimmo* judgment as explained above. Under the DPD and also the GDPR,[24] 'establishment' implies the effective and real exercise of activity through stable arrangements. The CJEU even seemed to accept the fact that a website was written in the Hungarian language as a decisive element for the effective and real exercise of activity in Hungary. The presence of a representative was qualified as a stable arrangement.[25] Admittedly, *Weltimmo* was decided in a specific context, but the emphasis on flexibility is evident.[26]

This flexibility can be justified, on the one hand, by the variety and volatility in complex data processing operations[27] and, on the other hand, by the need for the law to keep up and deliver effective protection, even when personal data are processed in the context of an establishment of a controller outside of the Member State where the individuals concerned have their habitual residence.[28] It must be ensured that the protection does not remain symbolic or, as Svantesson explains, 'bark jurisdiction' of DPAs is not enough. 'Bite jurisdiction' is required.[29]

The GDPR has solved this problem for intra-EU situations, by determining that a DPA is competent within its own territory and at the same time by providing a cooperation and consistency mechanism between DPAs, in Articles 56 and 60–67 GDPR. This mechanism is particularly relevant because a DPA is not competent to exercise its investigative and corrective powers under Article 58 GDPR outside the national territory.

The complex balance between a globalised digital world and the territorial limitation of DPA competence prompted the CJEU to require in *Digital Rights Ireland*[30] that certain personal data that should be retained for law enforcement purposes should remain within the European Union. Although this requirement should not be applied outside the specific context of the case, it illustrates the dilemma at stake.

2. Competence or obligation?

This territorial competence does not only imply a competence to act, but may, under EU law, also contain an obligation to act. The *Schrems* judgment of the CJEU confirmed that such an obligation may exist, by considering that the DPAs should examine claims by individuals 'with all due diligence'.[31]

Arguably, under the regime of the DPD, the DPAs had full discretion to setting their priorities. However, this full discretion is to a certain extent limited as far as

---

[22] The concept of 'context of the activities' is used in Art. 4(1)(a) GDPR and in a number of provisions and recitals of the GDPR, e.g. in relation to DPA competence in rec. 124 GDPR.
[23] Case C-131/12, *Google Spain*, paras. 53–54.
[24] See rec. 22 GDPR.
[25] Case C-230/14, *Weltimmo*, paras. 30–33.
[26] This was heavily criticised by Gömann 2018.
[27] For instance, since controllers and processors are organised in different ways, see CIPL 2016, p. 4.
[28] Criterion of habitual residence is included in Arts. 77 and 79 GDPR, on remedies.
[29] Svantesson 2016, p. 201.
[30] Joined Cases C-293/12 and C-594/12, *Digital Rights Ireland*, para. 68.
[31] Case C-362/14, *Schrems*, para. 63.

complaints—the DPD uses the term claims—are lodged with them. Article 28 (4) DPD provided that DPAs shall hear claims, and this obligation was specified in the *Schrems* judgment.

Article 57(1) GDPR brings about a change, since it provides that each DPA 'shall' perform in its territory the tasks assigned to it. This is not evident in view of the number of tasks and the availability of resources.

3. No rules for applicable law

Article 55 is a rule on competence. However, the GDPR does not contain rules on applicable law when data are processed within the EU. The existence of a regulation, directly applicable on EU territory, seems to justify the absence of such rules on applicable law. Since there is one law on the whole territory of the EU, there would be no longer need for rules on the conflict of laws, as formerly included in Article 4(1)(a) DPD. This is the starting point. However, this starting point does not reflect the legal reality. The EU legislator does not take account of the fact that the GDPR mandates the national legislator to adopt legislation specifying the EU rules on data protection at many instances.[32] Hence, differences in substantive law remain and jurisdictional issues will occur.[33]

The use of opening clauses and possible derogations for the national legislator may pose problems in cross border situations, where a DPA has competence because an organisation has its main establishment on its national territory, but where nevertheless the laws of another Member State have relevance, because data relating to individuals in that Member State are being processed.[34] Examples are national rules on special categories of data (Article 9 GDPR) or human resources data of staff located in that other Member State. It is not evident which national law is applicable in these situations. On the one hand, one can argue with regard to Article 1(3) GDPR, that also in these situations the law of the country of main establishment should apply. On the other hand, one could argue the opposite: this kind of national provisions is meant to protect everyone on the territory of the country where the law was issued. Additionally, specific rules on applicable law within the EU are absent in the GDPR and, on the other hand, DPAs do not always have competence to enforce data protection law in order to protect individuals where personal data are processed by a controller established in another Member State.

Under the GDPR, individuals are entitled to the effective protection of their fundamental right to data protection, which not only includes control by a DPA[35]—although not necessarily the DPA of the country of the individual usually resides—but also the national laws designed to give them additional protection. In short, a DPA may be obliged to apply the national law of another Member State, in order to ensure the effective protection of a national of the latter Member State. In *Weltimmo*, the CJEU confirmed that such a duty already existed under the DPD.[36]

---

[32] This is also explained by Gömann 2017, pp. 574–575.
[33] See more in general on this: Svantesson 2016.
[34] See also the commentary on Art. 3 in this volume.
[35] Independent supervision is an essential component of data protection, see e.g. rec. 117 GDPR.
[36] Case C-230/14, *Weltimmo*, para. 54.

4. Article 55(2): Exclusive competence only in relation to public tasks

As a rule, the DPAs are competent on their national territory, but this competence is no longer exclusive in situations of cross border processing. Yet, as a result of Article 55(2) GDPR, when the processing takes place in the context of public tasks, the DPA remains exclusively competent. Article 56 GDPR on the lead supervisory authority does not apply, nor does Article 60 which is inextricably linked to Article 56. However, the co-operation mechanisms of Articles 61 (mutual assistance) and 62 (joint DPA operations) GDPR can be applied where data are processed in relation to public tasks.

Article 55(2) GDPR applies to data processing by public authorities. When public authorities give effect to a legal obligation imposed on them, exercise official authority or otherwise carry out a task in the public interest, they are supervised by their national DPA. This makes sense, because the exercise of these public tasks will often be the result of national law or the national public interest. Moreover, it is hard to imagine how a DPA of one Member State would exercise its powers over a public body in another Member State, without infringing national institutional sovereignty.

However, the exception of Article 55(2) GDPR relates to tasks, not to public bodies as such. The exception does not apply where public bodies are active in the commercial domain or otherwise process data independently of their public tasks. This means in any event that publicly owned undertakings ('public undertakings'), as meant in Article 106(1) Treaty on the Functioning of the European Union ('TFEU'),[37] which operate on the market may have a lead authority.

Article 55(2) GDPR also applies to private bodies that process personal data in order to comply with a legal obligation or to perform a task in the public interest. This may have the effect that private bodies may have to deal with different DPAs, sometimes in connection to the same or related processing activities. For example, when airlines collect Passenger Name Records ('PNR') data for commercial purposes, they are subject to the control by the DPA of the country of their main establishment. When they transfer these data to a public authority under Article 8 of Directive 2016/681,[38] they are subject to the control of the DPA of the Member State on the territory of which a specific flight will land or from the territory of which the flight will depart.[39]

5. Article 55(3): DPA competence and the judiciary

The application of data protection law and supervision to the judiciary is a complex issue. On the one hand, the fundamental right to data protection fully applies when personal data are processed by judicial authorities, even when the personal data are included in judicial files in pending procedures. This rule is explained in recital 20 GDPR and is also the consequence of data protection as a fundamental right under Article 16(1) TFEU and Article 8 Charter of Fundamental Rights of the European Union ('CFR') which can be invoked under all circumstances, no matter who processes personal data.

Often specific rules apply to judicial files, in the context of national procedural law. Recital 20 mentions that national law and Union law could specify the GDPR provisions. There is no equivalent to recital 20 in the substantive GDPR provisions, but one may

---

[37] See Lenaerts and van Nuffel 2011, para. 11-017.   [38] PNR Directive.
[39] Another example on telecommunications data can be found in the commentary on Art. 56(1) in this volume.

assume that the Member States may use their power under Article 6(2) GDPR to adopt these specifications. One may also assume that—especially in the context of criminal proceedings—restrictions to the rights of the data subject can be adopted, in accordance with Article 23 GDPR. An important issue, outside the scope of data protection law, will be the admissibility of evidence obtained in breach of data protection law. This is mostly left to Member States' law.

On the other hand, and this is the subject of Article 55(3) GDPR, judicial authorities acting in their judicial capacity should not be subject to the control of DPAs, since these are authorities with an administrative status. This is recognised as a matter of principle under EU law. Exempting judicial authorities acting in judicial capacity from DPA control may be a matter of principle, but this does not mean that other choices could not be made. DPAs may be administrative bodies, but they are independent from the executive branch of government and it is not contested that they are competent to supervise the processing of personal data by parliaments. If one accepts that DPAs are bodies outside of the traditional *trias politica*,[40] there is *prima vista* no legal principle stating that these bodies may supervise the executive and the legislative branch, but not the judiciary branch. An argument in support of this view can be found in the CJEU's case law itself, since the requirements of independence of DPAs are similar to or—in respect of the organisational structure—even higher[41] than those of independent tribunals.[42]

Article 55(3) GDPR applies to courts. It is remarkable that the similar provision in the LED enables the Member States to 'provide for their supervisory authority not to be competent to supervise processing operations of other independent judicial authorities when acting in their judicial capacity'.[43] This mandate refers mainly, however not exclusively, to the public prosecutor's office.[44] The absence of such a mandate in the GDPR means that, where the public prosecutor's office performs tasks outside of the domain of criminal law, it is subject to control by DPAs.

Furthermore, recital 80 LED confirms that courts (and other independent judicial authorities) should always be subject to independent supervision in accordance with Article 8(3) CFR. This confirmation is not included in the GDPR. However, since independent supervision is an essential component of data protection,[45] it is obvious that this legal obligation also applies within the scope of application of the GDPR. Where recital 20 GDPR states that it should be possible to entrust supervision to specific bodies within the judicial system of the Member State, this must be read as an obligation for Member States to ensure this.

Finally, the exemption to DPA competence only applies to courts acting in their judicial capacity. It is clear that the processing of administrative data of courts is subject to full DPA control.[46] However, the boundary of the exception is not clear. Does it, for instance, apply to the publication of names in judgments on the website of a court? This is one of many questions that one could ask.

---

[40] DPAs could even be qualified as a new branch of government, see Hijmans 2016, ch. 7.
[41] This conclusion can be reached when comparing Case C-54/96, *Dorsch* (on independence of tribunals) with Case C-614/10, *Commission v Austria* (on DPA independence).
[42] This is heavily criticised by Balthasar 2013. See also Hijmans 2016, 7.10.1.
[43] Art. 45(2) LED. See also ibid., rec. 80.   [44] See ibid., rec. 80.   [45] E.g. rec. 117 GDPR.
[46] A range of examples can be found in the prior checks register of the EDPS, see EDPS Website.

Select Bibliography

EU legislation

Council Decision Eurojust: Council Decision 2002/187/JHA of 28 February 2002 setting up Eurojust with a view to reinforcing the fight against serious crime as amended by Council Decision 2003/659/JHA and by Council Decision 2009/426/JHA of 16 December 2008 on the strengthening of Eurojust, OJ 2002 L 63/1.

Eurojust Regulation 2018: Regulation (EU) 2018/1727 of the European Parliament and of the Council of 14 November 2018 on the European Union Agency for Criminal Justice Cooperation (Eurojust), and replacing and repealing Council Decision 2002/187/JHA, OJ 2018 L 295/138.

PNR Directive: Directive (EU) 2016/681 of the European Parliament and of the Council of 27 April 2016 on the use of passenger name record (PNR) data for the prevention, detection, investigation and prosecution of terrorist offences and serious crime, OJ 2016 L 119/132.

Academic writings

Balthasar 2013: Balthasar, '"Complete Independence" of National Data Protection Supervisory Authorities', 9(3) *Utrecht Law Review* (2013), 26.

Gömann 2017: Gömann, 'The New Territorial Scope of EU Data Protection Law: Deconstructing a Revolutionary Achievement', 54(2) *Common Market Law Review* (2017), 567.

González Fuster, *The Emergence of Personal Data Protection as a Fundamental Right of the EU* (Springer 2014).

Hijmans 2016: Hijmans, *The European Union as Guardian of Internet Privacy* (Springer 2016).

Hijmans, 'The DPAs and their Cooperation: How Far Are We in Making Enforcement of Data Protection Law More European?', 3(2) *European Data Protection Law Review* (2016), 362.

Jay, *Guide to the General Data Protection Regulation* (Sweet & Maxwell 2017).

Kuner 2019: Kuner, 'The Internet and the Global Reach of EU Law', in Cremona and Scott (eds.), *EU Law Beyond EU Borders: The Extraterritorial Reach of EU Law* (OUP 2019) 112.

Lenaerts and van Nuffel 2011: Lenaerts and van Nuffel, *European Union Law* (3rd edn, Sweet & Maxwell 2011).

Lynskey, *The Foundations of EU Data Protection Law* (Oxford Studies in European Law 2015).

Svantesson 2016: Svantesson, 'Enforcing Privacy across Jurisdictions', in Wright and de Hert (eds.), *Enforcing Privacy, Regulatory, Legal and Technological Approaches* (Springer 2016), 195.

Papers of data protection authorities

EDPB 2018: European Data Protection Board, 'Guidelines 3/2018 on the Territorial Scope of the GDPR (Article 3)—Version for Public Consultation' (16 November 2018).

European Data Protection Supervisor, 'Opinion on the Data Protection Reform Package' (7 March 2012).

Article 29 Working Party, 'Guidelines on the Lead Supervisory Authority' (WP 244 rev.01, as last revised and adopted on 5 April 2017).

Reports and recommendations

Barnard-Wills, Papakonstantinou, Pauner Chulvi and Díaz Lafuente, 'Recommendations for Improving Practical Cooperation between European Data Protection Authorities', Deliverable D4.1 for the PHAEDRA II project (14 January 2017), available at http://www.phaedra-project.eu/wp-content/uploads/PHAEDRA2_D41_final_20170114.pdf.

CIPL 2016: Centre for Information Policy Leadership, 'The One-Stop-Shop and the Lead DPA as Co-Operation Mechanisms in the GDPR' (30 November 2016).

Communication from the Commission to the European Parliament, the Council, the European Economic and Social Committee and the Committee of the Regions, 'A Comprehensive Approach on Personal Data Protection in the European Union' COM(2010) 609 final, 4 November 2010.

FRA 2010: Fundamental Rights Agency of the European Union, 'Data Protection in the European Union: The Role of National Data Protection Authorities' (2010).

Others

EDPS Website: Website of the European Data Protection Supervisor, 'Prior Checks Register', available at https://edps.europa.eu/data-protection/our-role-supervisor/register_en.

Article 56. Competence of the lead supervisory authority

HIELKE HIJMANS[*]

1. Without prejudice to Article 55, the supervisory authority of the main establishment or of the single establishment of the controller or processor shall be competent to act as lead supervisory authority for the cross-border processing carried out by that controller or processor in accordance with the procedure provided in Article 60.
2. By derogation from paragraph 1, each supervisory authority shall be competent to handle a complaint lodged with it or a possible infringement of this Regulation, if the subject matter relates only to an establishment in its Member State or substantially affects data subjects only in its Member State.
3. In the cases referred to in paragraph 2 of this Article, the supervisory authority shall inform the lead supervisory authority without delay on that matter. Within a period of three weeks after being informed the lead supervisory authority shall decide whether or not it will handle the case in accordance with the procedure provided in Article 60, taking into account whether or not there is an establishment of the controller or processor in the Member State of which the supervisory authority informed it.
4. Where the lead supervisory authority decides to handle the case, the procedure provided in Article 60 shall apply. The supervisory authority which informed the lead supervisory authority may submit to the lead supervisory authority a draft for a decision. The lead supervisory authority shall take utmost account of that draft when preparing the draft decision referred to in Article 60(3).
5. Where the lead supervisory authority decides not to handle the case, the supervisory authority which informed the lead supervisory authority shall handle it according to Articles 61 and 62.
6. The lead supervisory authority shall be the sole interlocutor of the controller or processor for the cross-border processing carried out by that controller or processor.

Relevant Recitals

(124) Where the processing of personal data takes place in the context of the activities of an establishment of a controller or a processor in the Union and the controller or processor is established in more than one Member State, or where processing taking place in the context of the activities of a single establishment of a controller or processor in the Union substantially affects or is likely to substantially affect data subjects in more than one Member State, the supervisory authority for the main establishment of the controller or processor or for the single establishment of the controller or processor should act as lead authority. It should cooperate with the other authorities concerned, because the controller or processor has an establishment on the territory of their Member State, because data subjects residing on their territory are substantially affected, or because a complaint has been lodged with them. Also, where a data subject not residing in that Member State has lodged a complaint, the supervisory authority with which such complaint has been lodged should also be a supervisory

---

[*] The views expressed are solely those of the author and do not necessarily reflect those of the Belgian Data Protection Authority.

authority concerned. Within its tasks to issue guidelines on any question covering the application of this Regulation, the Board should be able to issue guidelines in particular on the criteria to be taken into account in order to ascertain whether the processing in question substantially affects data subjects in more than one Member State and on what constitutes a relevant and reasoned objection.

(125) The lead authority should be competent to adopt binding decisions regarding measures applying the powers conferred on it in accordance with this Regulation. In its capacity as lead authority, the supervisory authority should closely involve and coordinate the supervisory authorities concerned in the decision-making process. Where the decision is to reject the complaint by the data subject in whole or in part, that decision should be adopted by the supervisory authority with which the complaint has been lodged.

(126) The decision should be agreed jointly by the lead supervisory authority and the supervisory authorities concerned and should be directed towards the main or single establishment of the controller or processor and be binding on the controller and processor. The controller or processor should take the necessary measures to ensure compliance with this Regulation and the implementation of the decision notified by the lead supervisory authority to the main establishment of the controller or processor as regards the processing activities in the Union.

(127) Each supervisory authority not acting as the lead supervisory authority should be competent to handle local cases where the controller or processor is established in more than one Member State, but the subject matter of the specific processing concerns only processing carried out in a single Member State and involves only data subjects in that single Member State, for example, where the subject matter concerns the processing of employees' personal data in the specific employment context of a Member State. In such cases, the supervisory authority should inform the lead supervisory authority without delay about the matter. After being informed, the lead supervisory authority should decide, whether it will handle the case pursuant to the provision on cooperation between the lead supervisory authority and other supervisory authorities concerned ('one-stop-shop mechanism'), or whether the supervisory authority which informed it should handle the case at local level. When deciding whether it will handle the case, the lead supervisory authority should take into account whether there is an establishment of the controller or processor in the Member State of the supervisory authority which informed it in order to ensure effective enforcement of a decision vis-à-vis the controller or processor. Where the lead supervisory authority decides to handle the case, the supervisory authority which informed it should have the possibility to submit a draft for a decision, of which the lead supervisory authority should take utmost account when preparing its draft decision in that one-stop-shop mechanism.

(128) The rules on the lead supervisory authority and the one-stop-shop mechanism should not apply where the processing is carried out by public authorities or private bodies in the public interest. In such cases the only supervisory authority competent to exercise the powers conferred to it in accordance with this Regulation should be the supervisory authority of the Member State where the public authority or private body is established.

Closely Related Provisions

Article 4(16) (Definition of 'main establishment'); Article 4(22) (Definition of 'supervisory authority concerned'); Article 4(23) (Definition of 'cross-border processing'); Article 57 (Tasks of supervisory authorities) (see too recitals 122–123 and 132–133); Article 58 (Powers of supervisory authorities) (see too recital 129); Article 59 (Activity reports); Articles 60–67 (Cooperation and Consistency) (see also recitals 126 and 130–138)

Relevant Case Law

CJEU

Case C-131/12, *Google Spain v Agencia Española de Protección de Datos (AEPD) and Mario Costeja González*, judgment of 13 May 2014 (Grand Chamber) (ECLI:EU:C:2014:317).

A. Rationale and Policy Underpinnings

Article 56 GDPR lays down the foundation of possibly the most significant novelty of the GDPR, the mechanism of enforcement for the cross-border processing within the EU/EEA.[1] This mechanism is constructed around a lead supervisory authority cooperating with other concerned authorities in a 'one-stop-shop mechanism' in an endeavour to reach consensus. The mechanism must lead to one single enforcement decision with wide applicability, without centralising enforcement by a supervisory authority at EU/EEA level. This mechanism must reconcile the need for a level playing field within the EU/EEA—which requires consistent enforcement within the jurisdiction—with the concepts of proximity of decision-making close to the citizen[2] and of executive federalism.[3]

This objective, aimed at satisfying the need for both the consistency of enforcement and for justified demands for national treatment, is not just a feature of the one-stop-shop mechanism itself, but is also reflected in the derogation in Article 56(2) GDPR. This derogation is designed to ensure the competence of local supervisory authorities to handle complaints of individuals with a local nature and to deal with subject-matter relating only to establishments of organisations within the national borders.

The one-stop-shop mechanism with a lead authority is established by Article 56 and elaborated in Article 60. It ensures that controllers and processors with multiple establishments in the EU/EEA or whose activities substantially affect data subjects in multiple Member States have one single supervisory authority as their sole interlocutor. This is the lead DPA, which also takes the final decision in respect of the processing by the controller or processor concerned. However, this single interlocutor does not have exclusive competence in the course of the process; it has the lead role in a cooperative process.

A further rationale for Article 56 is the need for effectiveness. Procedural rules are inserted in Article 56(3)–(5), to avoid legal uncertainty about the application of the derogation to the one-stop-shop mechanism.

B. Legal Background

1. EU legislation

Article 56 GDPR is a novelty within EU data protection law. However, the need for reconciling consistent enforcement within the EU with the competences of national authorities is also apparent in other areas of EU law, although the models for cross-border enforcement are different.

---

[1] The GDPR applies across the EEA, which comprises the EU Member States and the three EEA EFTA States (Iceland, Liechtenstein and Norway). See the discussion of the EEA Agreement below.
[2] Council Report 2013.
[3] On executive federalism, see further Lenaerts and van Nuffel 2011, section 17-002.

The enforcement of EU competition law and in particular the regime of Regulation 1/2003[4] is the most obvious example. This regulation facilitates the cooperation of the enforcement bodies at EU level and at national level. Unlike the area of data protection, a centralised EU enforcement body exists (the European Commission itself), but the system is also characterised by decentralised enforcement. National competition authorities are competent to supervise infringements of EU competition law. These national competition authorities cooperate with each other and with the European Commission in a European Network of Competition Authorities.[5]

A different model may be found in the sector of electronic communications, a sector with links to data protection.[6] National regulatory authorities ('NRAs') are responsible for enforcing the EU regulatory framework for electronic communications. However, they are obliged to cooperate with each other (and with the Commission) in the Body of European Regulators for Electronic Communications ('BEREC'). NRAs and the Commission have to take the utmost account of any opinion, recommendation, guidelines, advice or regulatory best practice adopted by BEREC.[7]

Further models of (enforcement) cooperation between authorities (agencies) of Member States in an EU framework exist in a variety of sectors, such as the supervision of financial markets.[8]

2. International instruments

The subject-matter of Article 56 GDPR is not specifically addressed in any international treaty. Article 1(5) of the Additional Protocol to Convention 108 of the Council of Europe, adopted in 2001,[9] imposes a limited obligation on supervisory authorities to 'co-operate with one another to the extent necessary for the performance of their duties, in particular by exchanging all useful information'. This is taken over by Article 17 of Modernised Convention 108, which also contains new provisions which may be relevant. Article 17(1)(b) imposes the obligation of 'coordinating ... investigations or interventions, or conducting joint actions', and Article 17(3) provides that, in order to organise their cooperation and to perform their duties, supervisory authorities should 'form a network'.

The European Economic Area ('EEA') Agreement, as amended in July 2018,[10] incorporates the GDPR into its Annexes and provides that the provisions of the GDPR should be read, for the purposes of that Agreement, with a number of adaptations. In this respect, the Agreement as amended provides that 'the terms "Member State(s)" and "supervisory authorities" shall be understood to include, in addition to their meaning in the Regulation, the three EEA EFTA States[11] and their supervisory authorities, respectively'.[12]

---

[4] Council Regulation 1/2003.   [5] Lenaerts and van Nuffel 2011, section 11-013.
[6] Notably because of the EPD, which allows Member States to assign enforcement tasks to national regulators for electronic communications.
[7] Art. 3(3) BEREC Regulation.   [8] Ottow 2014.   [9] See Table of Legislation.
[10] EEA Decision 2018.
[11] Switzerland, the fourth EFTA State, is not a signatory to the EEA Agreement.
[12] Art. 5b EEA Decision 2018.

3. National developments

The German GDPR Implementation Law contains arrangements to align the federal system of Germany—is many cases a DPA of a *Land* (State) is competent and not the Federal German DPA—with the GDPR.[13] The Implementation Law contains a provision on the lead supervisory authority of a *Land* in the one-stop-shop mechanism pursuant to the GDPR, as well as a mechanism in cases where complaints are lodged in Germany with a DPA which is not the lead authority. It also contains a procedure in case there is no agreement on determining the lead authority. Finally, it defines how the German DPAs establish a common position, also vis-à-vis the lead DPA in another EU Member State.

C. Analysis

1. The concept of the lead supervisory authority: a primus inter pares?

As a rule, DPAs are competent on their national territory, but this competence is no longer exclusive in situations of cross-border processing. Article 56(1) contains an exception to the normal rule, which is founded on notions of territorial competence under public international law. As a result of the one-stop-shop mechanism, the DPA of the country of main or single establishment leads, in situations of cross-border processing, enforcement by all DPAs concerned.[14] The WP29 has underlined that the task consists of coordinating investigations.[15]

The legislative history illustrates the concept of lead supervisory authority well. The 2012 Commission Proposal contained a different concept: in cases of cross-border processing, only one DPA would be competent. This competence was an exclusive competence, not a competence to lead/coordinate an enforcement action. This exclusive competence was strongly criticised, precisely because it did not lead to a system of structural DPA cooperation.[16]

The Commission proposal was simple: one DPA is competent. The proposal followed the logic of the internal market and was based on the principle of mutual recognition whereby a Member State should, normally, recognise decisions taken in other Member States. This principle also applies in other areas of EU law, particularly in the area of freedom, security and justice.[17] The proposal provided one safeguard enabling other DPAs to get involved: before taking a decision, the competent DPA was to notify the EDPB, which could trigger the consistency mechanism on request by another DPA or the Commission.[18] This safeguard could be characterised as a sort of emergency brake, aimed at ensuring a consistent enforcement of EU data protection law.

This mechanism was not considered robust enough to prevent a single DPA from acting without considering the views of the DPAs in countries where individuals are affected. As noted by the Presidency of the Council: the 'lead authority cannot adopt a "go-it-alone" attitude but needs to cooperate'.[19] This position was based on the view that any

---

[13] German GDPR Implementation Law, ss. 18–19.
[14] This has been termed a 'collaborative competence': see Giurgiu and Larsen 2016, p. 348.
[15] WP29 2017, p. 4.   [16] EDPS 2012, p. 39. See also Hijmans 2016, pp. 403-405.
[17] E.g. Arts. 81(1) and 82(1) Treaty on the Functioning of the European Union ('TFEU').
[18] Art. 58 and rec. 97 and 98 GDPR Proposal.   [19] Council Report 2014, p. 4.

DPA should be able to protect effectively individuals within its country; this role cannot be performed by or delegated to a DPA in another Member State.

As a result, Articles 56(1) and 60 ensure that the DPA of the Member State where the controller or processor has its main or single establishment in the EU/EEA cannot act alone. This DPA must take account of relevant and reasoned objections by concerned DPAs.[20] If the DPAs do not agree on the outcome, the dispute resolution mechanism of Article 65 is triggered.

The concept of 'leading' should be understood mainly as a procedural role. The lead DPA is responsible for the procedure and it drafts the enforcement decisions. However, at the end of the day, its position on substance is no stronger than that of any other DPA. Cooperation should take place 'in an endeavour to reach consensus'.[21]

The term *primus inter pares* may nevertheless be used. The lead DPA drafts the decision, takes the decision and defends the decision before the judiciary, where relevant. Moreover, it acts as the 'sole interlocutor' of the controller or processor.[22] This gives the lead DPA at least a stronger information position than that of the other DPAs. In short, all DPAs are equal but the lead DPA is more equal than the others.[23]

2. The scope of application of Article 56(1)

The competence of a lead DPA is limited to situations of cross-border processing, as defined in Article 4(23) GDPR.[24] Cross-border processing includes two types of situations. The processing of personal data must take place in the context of activities of establishments of the controller or processor in more than one Member State. This requires that the controller (or processor) has establishments in more than one Member State. Alternatively, when the processing only relates to an establishment in one Member State, it is required that the processing substantially affects or is likely to substantially affect data subjects in multiple Member States.

The competence of a lead DPA has two clear limitations. First, the exception to the exclusive competence of a DPA on its national territory does not apply when the processing of personal data takes place in the context of public tasks. Within this context, the DPA remains exclusively competent on its own territory, as a result of Article 55(2) GDPR.[25] The latter could lead to complexity. Imagine the provider of telecommunications services which stores the same communications data for commercial purposes—such as billing—and for the purpose of access by law enforcement authorities. This provider deals with a lead DPA (because of the commercial purpose) and with one or more local DPAs (because of the law enforcement purpose). This complexity also arises in relation to passenger name records ('PNR' data), which are collected for commercial purposes and subsequently used for law enforcement.[26]

Secondly, there must be an establishment within the EU/EEA. As confirmed by the WP29 and the EDPB, organisations without any establishment in the EU/EEA—whose

---

[20] Art. 60(4) GDPR.   [21] Ibid., Art. 60(1).   [22] Ibid., Art. 56(6).
[23] To adapt the famous quote in George Orwell's *Animal Farm*.
[24] See the commentary on Art. 4(23) in this volume.
[25] Art. 55(2) stipulates: 'Where processing is carried out by public authorities or private bodies acting on the basis of point (c) or (e) of Article 6(1), the supervisory authority of the Member State concerned shall be competent. In such cases Article 56 does not apply'.
[26] As explained in the commentary on Art. 55 in this volume.

activities fall within the scope of the GDPR on the basis of Article 3(2)—must deal with local DPAs in every Member State.[27]

However, it is not clear if an organisation with an establishment in the EU/EEA can have a lead authority also for processing activities which are conducted in the context of an establishment in a third country.[28] An argument in favour of the position that in many situations there can be a lead DPA can be drawn from the CJEU's ruling in *Google Spain*[29] where the CJEU broadly interpreted the notion 'in the context of the activities of an establishment'.[30] Following this ruling, in many cases processing activities can be attributed to an establishment in the EU/EEA. The EDPB elaborates this, e.g. with the example of a local establishment in the EU/EEA that raises revenues for a company having its main seat outside the EU/EEA.[31]

Article 56(1) is drafted with the example of businesses in mind.[32] The guidance of the WP29 also seems to mainly address multinational companies.[33] However, one may assume that the GDPR does not exclude that the mechanism also applies to not-for-profit organisations which have establishments in more than one Member State.

In the event that the UK leaves the EU ('Brexit'), the UK Information Commissioner ('ICO') will no longer be the supervisory authority of an EU or EEA/EFTA Member State under Article 4(22) GDPR. As a result, if a UK controller or processor, whose main or single establishment is in the UK, carries out cross-border processing within the EU/EEA, the ICO will no longer be the lead supervisory authority under Article 56 GDPR, although of course it will remain the supervisory authority within the UK under UK law.[34] In this case, the one-stop-shop principle will cease to apply and each concerned EU/EEA authority will regain full jurisdiction, unless an establishment in the EU/EEA becomes the main or single establishment of the controller/processor, and the relevant processing continues to qualify as 'cross-border' under Article 4(23) GDPR. If this occurs, the DPA of the country where the main or single establishment is located will become the lead supervisory authority under Article 56(1), and the one-stop-shop will apply to the establishment(s) of the controller or processor within the EU/EEA.[35]

3. The identification of the lead supervisory authority

Article 56(1) provides that in certain situations, there *shall* be a competent lead DPA. This lead DPA shall be the authority for the single or main establishment of the controller or processor.

It is clear from the text of the GDPR that the competence of the lead DPA follows directly from the law and is not based on a constitutive decision of any administrative body. The only procedural rule in the GDPR relates to a situation 'where there are conflicting views on which of the supervisory authorities concerned is competent for the main establishment'.[36]

---

[27] WP29 2017, p. 10; EDPB 2018, p. 12; EDPB 2019A. See also Jay 2017, section 21-018. Note too that the establishment of a representative in the EU/EEA as stipulated in Art. 27 GDPR does not trigger the one-stop-shop mechanism: see further WP29 2017, p. 10.
[28] This point is addressed in CIPL 2016A, p. 6. The Centre asks for guidance.
[29] Case C-131/12, *Google Spain*, para. 60.
[30] See e.g. Gömann 2017, section 2.1.1. See also Brkan 2016, p. 327.   [31] EDPB 2018, p. 7.
[32] Council Report 2013, pp. 4–5.   [33] WP29 2017, p. 5.
[34] See the ICO guidance in ICO 2018, pp. 17–22.
[35] See further the commentary on Art. 4(16) in this volume.   [36] Art. 65(1)(b) GDPR.

The GDPR, however, provides scant detail about the identification of the lead DPA. This is an omission of the legislator since, in view of the wide range of organisational models of companies, it is often not evident what DPA will be the lead DPA. This already starts with the definition of main establishment in Article 4(16), with its key notion of the establishment where decisions on the 'purposes and means of processing' are taken. Given the wide variety of organisational models of companies, it is often not evident what entity within a company has the say over personal data processing. There are many situations where the central administration does not have the final say. There are also situations where companies provide a certain service in one establishment and another service in an establishment in another Member State. Does such a company only deal with one DPA? To give an even more complicated practical example, how may the lead DPA be identified in the situation of groups of companies operating in multiple Member States, where the organisation comprises both controller(s) and processor(s)?[37]

The WP29 guidance takes as a starting point that, in situations which are not clear cut, the controller or processor itself should designate its main establishment. However, the organisation does not have a final say on this, since the GDPR does not permit forum shopping,[38] which would mean in this context choosing the DPA with the most agreeable enforcement policy as perceived by the organisation.[39] This does not mean that an organisation is precluded from having a preference for a specific lead DPA, for instance because of language, size and resources, as well as regulatory approaches. In this case, the organisation may adapt its operations in line with the GDPR. An example is an organisation ensuring the effective control of the processing activities in a specific Member State, for reasons relating to its preference for a specific lead DPA.[40]

In July 2019 the EDPB published further guidance in Opinion 8/2019 to clarify the competence of a supervisory authority in the event of a change relating to the main or single establishment.[41] The Board took the view that an authority's competence is only definitely fixed at the final moment of a one-stop-shop procedure, when a decision is made putting an end to the procedure. Until then, competences may change, according to the following considerations.

First, if the main or single establishment of an organisation relocates to the territory of another EU/EEA Member State during a one-stop-shop procedure, the existing lead supervisory authority will lose that competence at the moment the relocation becomes effective and the new lead supervisory authority will take over. Second, if a main or single establishment is relocated from a third country to the EU/EEA, the one-stop-shop mechanism will enter into application and the DPA of the Member State in which the main establishment has been located will become the lead supervisory authority responsible for all pending proceedings. Third, where the main or single establishment disappears (either because the main establishment has been moved outside the EU/EEA or because it has been disbanded), the controller will cease to benefit from the one-stop-shop mechanism and the existing lead supervisory authority will lose its competence as lead authority. Since the processing can no longer be considered as 'cross-border', all the authorities concerned should thereafter exercise their individual jurisdiction.

This guidance is useful, since the GDPR does not address the changes of circumstances at all. However, there are doubts whether the chosen solution is the most effective one.

---

[37] Example from CIPL 2016A, p. 4.   [38] WP29 2017, p. 8.
[39] Hijmans 2016, pp. 390–393.   [40] Jay 2017, section 21-017.   [41] EDPB 2019C.

Cooperation in the one-stop-shop mechanism takes time, also because of national procedural law in the country of the lead supervisory authority. The result of this guidance may be that—because of the change of the lead supervisory authority during an enforcement procedure—the procedure has to start all over again.

Finally, the Board cautioned against the risk of forum shopping, where controllers or processors artificially change their main establishment for the purpose of changing the competent authority, so that a relocation of the main establishment must be 'a real one, made with a lasting purpose'.[42]

It is safe to say that the GDPR does not provide legal certainty. This is recognised by the Centre for Information Policy Leadership ('CIPL') which has suggested a procedure for organisations to register with the lead DPA.[43] Such a procedure is, however, not foreseen in the GDPR.[44]

Finally it should be noted that the EDPB has created workflows in the Internal Market Information System ('IMI') to enable DPAs to identify their respective roles as lead and concerned supervisory authorities. The Board has noted that the 'main purpose of this procedure is to define the roles at an early stage and to avoid objections on the question of competences at a later stage of the procedure'. Between May 2018 and February 2019 the Board reported that 642 procedures have been initiated to identify the lead supervisory authority and the concerned supervisory authorities in cross-border cases, and that over that period no dispute arose on the selection of the lead supervisory authority.[45]

4. Article 56(2): Subject-matter of a local nature

Whilst Article 56(1) is an exception to the territorial competence of a DPA, Article 56(2) creates an exception to the exception which restores the competence of the local DPA in certain limited cases of cross-border processing. Local cases, although falling within the definition of cross-border processing, should be treated locally. Recital 127 mentions as an example of a local case 'where the subject matter concerns the processing of employees' personal data in the specific employment context of a Member State'.

This exception to the exception was included in the GDPR after discussions in the Council and relates to the concept of proximity, an important aspect of the protection of individual rights.[46] These discussions referred to proximity to the data subject as requiring a role of the local supervisory authority. They also mentioned that a local supervisory authority should treat 'local cases'.[47]

However, the result laid down in Article 56(2) is ambiguous. The applicability of this exception does not interfere with the mechanism where the relevant controller or processor deals with a lead DPA as its sole interlocutor. Moreover, although this paragraph states that the local DPA is competent to deal with subject-matters of a local nature, the following paragraph empowers the lead DPA to decide whether this competence can be used in a specific case.[48] It is also remarkable that a possible disagreement on competence between the local DPA and the lead DPA is not an issue which can lead to dispute

---

[42] Ibid., para 26 [43] CIPL 2016B, p. 4.
[44] During the legislative process there had been attempts to establish a one-stop-shop register kept by the EDPB, but this was not retained. See e.g. Art. 51c in Council Doc. 16090/14 of 25 November 2014.
[45] EDPB 2019B, p. 3. [46] Council Press Release 2013, p. 7. [47] Council Report 2014.
[48] Art. 56(3).

resolution by the EDPB under Article 65(1) GDPR. Of course, the local DPA can always ask for an opinion of the EDPB under Article 64(2) GDPR.

The ambiguity of the applicability of the exception to the exception continues in Article 56(4). Even in cases where the lead authority decides to handle the case, the local DPA remains in a strong position. It may submit a draft decision and the lead DPA must take the utmost account of this draft. Also, it should be underlined that, whereas the cooperation mechanism in enforcement cases—under Articles 56(1) and 60 GDPR—is governed by a presumption of equality of DPAs and an endeavour to reach consensus, the handling of local cases is based on a different approach. Arguably, the lead DPA is in charge of the procedure and the local DPA is in charge of the substance.

It can be questioned whether this approach by the EU legislator is practical, especially since it will often not be evident in practice which cases fall within the scope of Article 56(2). It may be for this reason that the guidance of the WP29 departs from the text of the GDPR. The Working Party underlines cooperation, with due respect for each other's views, and describes the case of two DPAs agreeing on who is the most appropriate to take the lead in dealing with the matter, also based on input of the controller or processor concerned.[49]

Finally, the scope of the exception under Article 56(2) gives rise to the following considerations.

First, Article 56(2) applies to situations where the subject-matter relates only to 'an establishment' in one Member State. This wording is different to the definition of cross-border processing, which refers to 'the context of the activities' of an establishment, and which has been given a broad meaning in the case law.[50] Article 56(2) does not clarify whether its formulation is intended to have a different, possibly narrower, meaning. Recital 127—already mentioned—gives the example of the processing of employees' personal data in the specific employment context of a Member State; the WP29 simply repeats this in its 2017 Guidelines.[51] There is as yet no indication whether the meaning of 'subject matter' in Article 56(2) differs from the normal meaning of 'context of the activities' with regard to cross-border processing.

Secondly, Article 56(2) is applicable when the subject-matter substantially affects data subjects only in one Member State. In this respect, the WP29's Guidelines can contribute to the assessment of whether data subjects in other Member States are substantially affected. The Guidelines explain that the processing must have some form of impact on the data subjects, to be examined on a case-by-case basis. In addition, they provide some examples of this impact, which—to a certain extent—are comparable to the examples of risk for the data subject mentioned in recital 75 GDPR. The WP29 also mentions recital 135, which—in the consistency mechanism—substantially requires 'a significant number of data subjects in several Member States' to be affected.[52]

Thirdly, the 'substantially criterion in Article 56(2) is slightly different from the definition of cross-border processing, which also includes 'likely to substantially affect'. It can be argued that the narrower formulation of Article 56(2) means that this provision should not be applied in cases where there is doubt whether data subjects in other Member States

---

[49] WP29 2017, p. 9.
[50] See further commentary on Art. 4(23) GDPR in this volume. The related provision in the DPD was broadly interpreted in Case C-131/12, *Google Spain*, paras. 50–58. See also e.g. Gömann 2017, section 2.1.1.
[51] WP29 2017, p. 5.   [52] Ibid., p. 3.

are substantially affected. In short, when it is uncertain whether there is a risk to a significant number of data subjects in another Member State, the local exception in Article 56(2) should not be applied.

5. Article 56(3)–(5): Procedural matters

Article 56 paragraphs (3)–(5) lay down the procedure to be respected when Article 56(2) applies. The procedure is included in the law to ensure that the exception of Article 56(2) does not disrupt the effective handling of enforcement cases. The starting point is that the local DPA takes the initiative and the lead DPA decides whether it takes the case. This is the division of tasks laid down in Article 56(3). However, it remains to be seen if this division will be applied in practice.

One can very well imagine the situation that a lead DPA considers that a case it investigates is mainly of a local nature. In that situation, it can ask the local DPA to take the case. This would be in compliance with the GDPR, although the procedural rules in Article 56 paragraphs (3)–(4) would not be applicable. This situation would be governed by Article 56(5).

Article 56 paragraphs (3)–(4) govern the procedure starting with the initiative of the local DPA. Article 56(3) lays down a deadline for deciding on the request of the local DPA—three weeks—and includes a consideration that should be taken into account by the lead DPA. If the controller or the processor has an establishment in the country of the local DPA, it makes more sense that the local DPA takes the case, for reasons of effective enforcement.[53] The GDPR, however, does not specify that the presence of this establishment requires the case to be taken by the local DPA and that the absence of such establishment means that the lead DPA is competent.

GDPR Article 56(4) is a remarkable provision. Even in situations where the lead DPA takes the case, the local DPA is empowered (though not required) to prepare a draft decision, in which case the lead DPA must take the utmost account of that draft.

All in all, one can argue that the legislator has a clear preference for local cases to be handled by the local DPA. However, this clear preference has not led to a clear legislative text.

6. Article 56(6): The concept of a single interlocutor

The lead DPA is the sole interlocutor. The term interlocutor is commonly understood as 'a person who takes part in a dialogue or conversation'.[54] This is also the meaning that can be deduced from other language versions of the GDPR.[55]

This provision is part of the wider consequence of Articles 56 and 60 GDPR where normally the lead DPA is the master of the procedure. The lead DPA takes the initiative, interacts with the controller and processor (and possibly other concerned parties), and takes the decision.

The added value of Article 56(6) may not be the notion of 'interlocutor' per se but rather the emphasis that this is the *sole* interlocutor, which suggests exclusiveness. It may very well be that this is precisely what the legislator had in mind: to preclude a controller (or processor) which operates in multiple Member States from discussing issues with multiple DPAs, in order to seek the best outcome. On the basis of Article 56(6), other

---

[53] See too rec. 127 GDPR.   [54] English Oxford Living Dictionaries.
[55] E.g. 'gesprekspartner' in Dutch, or 'Ansprechpartner' in German. The French version uses 'interlocuteur'.

(concerned) DPAs must refer the controller to the lead DPA. Exclusive contacts with a controller or processor are a means to streamline the procedure.

This does not mean that the lead DPA must always operate as the sole contact point of the local DPA. In view of the strong position of the local DPA on substance, as described, it would be illogical to preclude the local DPA from interacting with the controller or processor. How could the local DPA prepare a draft decision, as required by Article 56(4), if it were not in a position to verify the facts directly with the controller or processor?

Furthermore, it is not clear whether Article 56(6) also has implications for the consistency mechanism and whether it means that the EDPB should refer a controller or processor, which is directly impacted by a case before the consistency mechanism, to the lead DPA, instead of the EDPB itself being an interlocutor for the controller or processor. Would such an approach not be contrary to the right to good administration by EU bodies enshrined in Article 41 of the Charter? Article 41(2) provides the right of every person to be heard, before any individual measure which would affect him or her adversely is taken, and to have access to his or her file. It also includes an obligation of the EU administration to give reasons for its decisions. The EDPB as an EU body under Article 68(1) GDPR is part of the EU administration.

These are just two examples of a multitude of situations that may exist under the GDPR and where guidance by the EDPB might be required.

Finally, the fact that a local DPA handles a case in accordance with Article 56(2) does not mean that the lead DPA is no longer the sole interlocutor, even for this case. This may be an awkward result, since Article 56(5) requires the local DPA to handle the practical conduct of the case with regard to other authorities under Articles 61 and 62, but this is what the text of Article 56 implies. A common sense approach will be required where the lead DPA recognises the practical consequences of its decision under Article 56(5) not to handle the case. Indeed, DPAs will have to apply common sense and goodwill generally for this part of the GDPR to work effectively.

Select Bibliography

International agreements

EEA Agreement: Agreement on the European Economic Area, OJ 1994 L 1/3.
EEA Decision 2018: Decision of the EEA Joint Committee No 154/2018 of 6 July 2018 amending Annex XI (Electronic communication, audiovisual services and information society) and Protocol 37 (containing the list provided for in Article 101) to the EEA Agreement [2018/1022], OJ 2018 L 183/23.

EU legislation

BEREC Regulation: Regulation (EC) No 1211/2009 of the European Parliament and of the Council of 25 November 2009 establishing the Body of European Regulators for Electronic Communications (BEREC) and the Office, OJ 2009 L 337/1.
Council Regulation 1/2003: Council Regulation (EC) No 1/2003 of 16 December 2002 on the implementation of the rules on competition laid down in Articles 81 and 82 of the Treaty, OJ 2003 L1/1.
GDPR Proposal: Proposal for a Regulation of the European Parliament and of the Council on the protection of individuals with regard to the processing of personal data and on the free movement of such data (General Data Protection Regulation), COM(2012) 11 final, 25 January 2012.

National legislation

German GDPR Implementation Law: Gesetz zur Anpassung des Datenschutzrechts an die Verordnung (EU) 2016/679 und zur Umsetzung der Richtlinie (EU) 2016/680 (Datenschutz-Anpassungs- und Umsetzungsgesetz EU – DsAnpUG-EU), BGBl 2017 Teil 1 Nr. 44.

Academic writings

Brkan 2016: Brkan, 'Data Protection and Conflict-of-laws: A Challenging Relationship', 3(2) *European Data Protection Law Review 'EDPL'* (2016), 324.

Giurgiu and Larsen 2016: Giurgiu and Larsen, 'Roles and Powers of National Data Protection Authorities', 2(3) *EDPL* (2016), 342.

Gömann 2017: Gömann, 'The New Territorial Scope of EU Data Protection Law: Deconstructing a Revolutionary Achievement', 54(2) *Common Market Law Review* (2017), 567.

Hijmans 2016: Hijmans, *The European Union as Guardian of Internet Privacy* (Springer 2016).

Hijmans, 'The DPAs and their Cooperation: How Far Are We in Making Enforcement of Data Protection Law More European?', 2(3) *EDPL* (2016), 362.

Jay 2017: Jay, *Guide to the General Data Protection Regulation: A Companion to Data Protection Law and Practice* (Sweet & Maxwell 2017).

Lenaerts and van Nuffel 2011: Lenaerts and van Nuffel, *European Union Law* (3rd edn, Sweet & Maxwell 2011).

Ottow 2014: Ottow, 'The New European Supervisory Architecture of the Financial Markets', in Everson, Monda and Vos (eds.), *European Agencies in between Institutions and Member States* (Kluwer Law International 2014), 123.

Papers of data protection authorities

EDPB 2018: European Data Protection Board, 'Guidelines 3/2018 on the Territorial Scope of the GDPR (Article 3)—Version for Public Consultation' (16 November 2018).

EDPB 2019A: European Data Protection Board, 'Information Note on Data Transfers under the GDPR in the Event of a No-Deal Brexit' (12 February 2019).

EDPB 2019B: European Data Protection Board, 'First overview on the implementation of the GDPR and the roles and means of the national supervisory authorities' (26 February 2019).

EDPB 2019C: European Data Protection Board, 'Opinion 8/2019 on the competence of a supervisory authority in case of a change in circumstances relating to the main or single establishment' (9 July 2019).

EDPS 2012: EDPS, 'Opinion on the Data Protection Reform Package' (March 2012).

WP29 2017: Article 29 Working Party, 'Guidelines on the Lead Supervisory Authority' (WP 244 rev.01, as last revised and adopted on 5 April 2017).

ICO 2018: Information Commissioner's Office, 'Data protection if there's no Brexit deal' (December 2018), available at https://ico.org.uk/media/for-organisations/data-protection-and-brexit/data-protection-if-there-s-no-brexit-deal-1-0.pdf.

Reports and recommendations

CIPL 2016A: Centre for Information Policy Leadership (CIPL), 'The One-Stop-Shop and the Lead DPA as Co-Operation Mechanisms in the GDPR' (2016).

CIPL 2016B: Centre for Information Policy Leadership (CIPL), 'Comments on the Article 29 Data Protection Working Party's "Guidelines for Identifying a Controller or Processor's Lead Supervisory Authority" Adopted on 13 December 2016' (13 December 2016).

Council Press Release 2013: Council of the European Union, 'Press Release: 3260th Council Meeting, Justice and Home Affairs, 7 and 8 October 2013', PRESSE 393 PR CO 46, 7 and 8 October 2013.

Council Report 2013: Effective judicial protection of data subject's fundamental rights in the context of the envisaged 'one-stop shop' mechanism, 18031/13, 19 December 2013 (Document partially accessible to public, full text available at lobbyplag.eu).
Council Report 2014: Orientation debate on one-stop-shop mechanism, 10139/14, 26 May 2014.

Others

English Oxford Living Dictionaries: English Oxford Living Dictionaries, 'Definition of Interlocutor in English', available at https://en.oxforddictionaries.com/definition/interlocutor.

Article 57. Tasks

HIELKE HIJMANS*

1. Without prejudice to other tasks set out under this Regulation, each supervisory authority shall on its territory:
   (a) monitor and enforce the application of this Regulation;
   (b) promote public awareness and understanding of the risks, rules, safeguards and rights in relation to processing. Activities addressed specifically to children shall receive specific attention;
   (c) advise, in accordance with Member State law, the national parliament, the government, and other institutions and bodies on legislative and administrative measures relating to the protection of natural persons' rights and freedoms with regard to processing;
   (d) promote the awareness of controllers and processors of their obligations under this Regulation;
   (e) upon request, provide information to any data subject concerning the exercise of their rights under this Regulation and, if appropriate, cooperate with the supervisory authorities in other Member States to that end;
   (f) handle complaints lodged by a data subject, or by a body, organisation or association in accordance with Article 80, and investigate, to the extent appropriate, the subject matter of the complaint and inform the complainant of the progress and the outcome of the investigation within a reasonable period, in particular if further investigation or coordination with another supervisory authority is necessary;
   (g) cooperate with, including sharing information and provide mutual assistance to, other supervisory authorities with a view to ensuring the consistency of application and enforcement of this Regulation;
   (h) conduct investigations on the application of this Regulation, including on the basis of information received from another supervisory authority or other public authority;
   (i) monitor relevant developments, insofar as they have an impact on the protection of personal data, in particular the development of information and communication technologies and commercial practices;
   (j) adopt standard contractual clauses referred to in Article 28(8) and in point (d) of Article 46(2);
   (k) establish and maintain a list in relation to the requirement for data protection impact assessment pursuant to Article 35(4);
   (l) give advice on the processing operations referred to in Article 36(2);
   (m) encourage the drawing up of codes of conduct pursuant to Article 40(1) and provide an opinion and approve such codes of conduct which provide sufficient safeguards, pursuant to Article 40(5);
   (n) encourage the establishment of data protection certification mechanisms and of data protection seals and marks pursuant to Article 42(1), and approve the criteria of certification pursuant to Article 42(5);
   (o) where applicable, carry out a periodic review of certifications issued in accordance with Article 42(7);

---

* The views expressed are solely those of the author and do not necessarily reflect those of the Belgian Data Protection Authority.

(p) draft and publish the requirements for accreditation of a body for monitoring codes of conduct pursuant to Article 41 and of a certification body pursuant to Article 43;[1]
(q) conduct the accreditation of a body for monitoring codes of conduct pursuant to Article 41 and of a certification body pursuant to Article 43;
(r) authorise contractual clauses and provisions referred to in Article 46(3);
(s) approve binding corporate rules pursuant to Article 47;
(t) contribute to the activities of the Board;
(u) keep internal records of infringements of this Regulation and of measures taken in accordance with Article 58(2); and
(v) fulfil any other tasks related to the protection of personal data.
2. Each supervisory authority shall facilitate the submission of complaints referred to in point (f) of paragraph 1 by measures such as a complaint submission form which can also be completed electronically, without excluding other means of communication.
3. The performance of the tasks of each supervisory authority shall be free of charge for the data subject and, where applicable, for the data protection officer.
4. Where requests are manifestly unfounded or excessive, in particular because of their repetitive character, the supervisory authority may charge a reasonable fee based on administrative costs, or refuse to act on the request. The supervisory authority shall bear the burden of demonstrating the manifestly unfounded or excessive character of the request.

Relevant Recitals

(122) Each supervisory authority should be competent on the territory of its own Member State to exercise the powers and to perform the tasks conferred on it in accordance with this Regulation. This should cover in particular the processing in the context of the activities of an establishment of the controller or processor on the territory of its own Member State, the processing of personal data carried out by public authorities or private bodies acting in the public interest, processing affecting data subjects on its territory or processing carried out by a controller or processor not established in the Union when targeting data subjects residing on its territory. This should include handling complaints lodged by a data subject, conducting investigations on the application of this Regulation and promoting public awareness of the risks, rules, safeguards and rights in relation to the processing of personal data.

(123) The supervisory authorities should monitor the application of the provisions pursuant to this Regulation and contribute to its consistent application throughout the Union, in order to protect natural persons in relation to the processing of their personal data and to facilitate the free flow of personal data within the internal market. For that purpose, the supervisory authorities should cooperate with each other and with the Commission, without the need for any agreement between Member States on the provision of mutual assistance or on such cooperation.

(129) In order to ensure consistent monitoring and enforcement of this Regulation throughout the Union, the supervisory authorities should have in each Member State the same tasks and effective powers, including powers of investigation, corrective powers and sanctions, and authorisation and advisory powers, in particular in cases of complaints from natural persons, and without prejudice to the powers of prosecutorial authorities under Member State law, to bring infringements of this Regulation to the attention of the judicial authorities and engage in legal proceedings. Such powers should also include the power to impose a temporary or definitive limitation,

---

[1] Corrigenda to the English text of Art. 57(1)(p) were published on 23 May 2018. The text printed reflects the updated version of the Corrigendum GDPR 2018. For the Corrigendum GDPR 2018, see Table of Legislation.

including a ban, on processing. Member States may specify other tasks related to the protection of personal data under this Regulation. The powers of supervisory authorities should be exercised in accordance with appropriate procedural safeguards set out in Union and Member State law, impartially, fairly and within a reasonable time. In particular each measure should be appropriate, necessary and proportionate in view of ensuring compliance with this Regulation, taking into account the circumstances of each individual case, respect the right of every person to be heard before any individual measure which would affect him or her adversely is taken and avoid superfluous costs and excessive inconveniences for the persons concerned. Investigatory powers as regards access to premises should be exercised in accordance with specific requirements in Member State procedural law, such as the requirement to obtain a prior judicial authorisation. Each legally binding measure of the supervisory authority should be in writing, be clear and unambiguous, indicate the supervisory authority which has issued the measure, the date of issue of the measure, bear the signature of the head, or a member of the supervisory authority authorised by him or her, give the reasons for the measure, and refer to the right of an effective remedy. This should not preclude additional requirements pursuant to Member State procedural law. The adoption of a legally binding decision implies that it may give rise to judicial review in the Member State of the supervisory authority that adopted the decision.

(132) Awareness-raising activities by supervisory authorities addressed to the public should include specific measures directed at controllers and processors, including micro, small and medium-sized enterprises, as well as natural persons in particular in the educational context.

(133) The supervisory authorities should assist each other in performing their tasks and provide mutual assistance, so as to ensure the consistent application and enforcement of this Regulation in the internal market. A supervisory authority requesting mutual assistance may adopt a provisional measure if it receives no response to a request for mutual assistance within one month of the receipt of that request by the other supervisory authority.

Closely Related Provisions

Article 4(21) (Definition of a supervisory authority); Article 28(8) (Adoption of processors' standard contractual clauses); Article 36(2) (Prior consultation) (see too recitals 84 and 94); Articles 40(1), (5) and 41(3) (Codes of conduct) (see too recital 98); Article 42(1), (5), (7) and 43(1) (Certification) (see too recital 100); Article 46(2)(d), (3) and (4) (Standard data protection clauses for data transfers) (see too recitals 108–109); Article 47 (Approval of binding corporate rules); Article 50 (International cooperation for the protection of personal data) (see too recitals 104 and 116); Article 58 (Powers) (see too recitals 129, 148 and 150); Article 59 (Activity reports); Article 60 (Cooperation between supervisory authorities); Article 61 (Mutual assistance between supervisory authorities); Article 62 (Joint operations of supervisory authorities); Article 70 (Tasks of the Board, including promotion of cooperation between supervisory authorities; contribution to activities of the Board); Article 77 (Complaint handling and investigations) (see too recital 141); Article 83 (Administrative fines) (see too recital 148)

Related Provisions in LED [Directive (EU) 2016/680]

Article 3(15) (Definition of a supervisory authority); Article 17 (Exercise of rights by the data subject and verification by the supervisory authority) (see too recital 43); Article 28 (Prior consultation of the supervisory authority) (see too recital 59); Article 40 (International cooperation for the protection of personal data) (see too recital 74); Article 41 (Establishment of supervisory authorities) (see too recitals 75–76); Article 42(1) (Exercise of powers with complete independence) (see too recital 79); Article 45 (Competence); Article 46 (Tasks) (see too recital 82); Article 47 (Powers) (see too recital 82); Article 50 (Mutual assistance) (see too recital 83); Article 51 (Tasks of the Board, including promotion of cooperation between supervisory authorities) (see too recital 84); Article 52 (Complaint handling) (see too recitals 81 and 85)

Related Provisions in EPD [Directive 2002/58/EC]

Article 15 (Application of certain provisions of Directive 95/46/EC); Article 15a (Implementation and enforcement)

Related Provisions in EUDPR [Regulation (EU) 2018/1725]

Article 42 (Legislative consultation) (see too recital 60); Article 51 (International cooperation) (see too recital 71); Article 57 (Tasks of the European Data Protection Board) (see too recitals 60 and 73)

Relevant Case Law

CJEU

Case C-518/07, *European Commission v Federal Republic of Germany*, judgment of 9 March 2010 (Grand Chamber) (ECLI:EU:C:2010:125).

Case C-614/10, *European Commission v Republic of Austria*, judgment of 16 October 2012 (Grand Chamber) (ECLI:EU:C:2012:631).

Case C-288/12, *European Commission v Hungary*, judgment of 8 April 2014 (Grand Chamber) (ECLI:EU:C:2014:237).

Case C-230/14, *Weltimmo s.r.o. v Nemzeti Adatvédelmi és Információszabadság Hatóság*, judgment of 1 October 2015 (ECLI:EU:C:2015:639).

Case C-362/14, *Maximillian Schrems v Data Protection Commissioner*, judgment of 6 October 2015 (Grand Chamber) (ECLI:EU:C:2015:650).

Case C-192/15, *T. D. Rease, P. Wullems v College bescherming persoonsgegevens*, order of 9 December 2015 (ECLI:EU:C:2015:861).

ECtHR

Roman Zakharov v Russia, Appl. No. 47143/06, judgment of 4 December 2015.

A. Rationale and Policy Underpinnings

Article 57 empowers the DPAs and harmonises their tasks. 'A stronger institutional arrangement for better enforcement of data protection rules' with strong DPAs and harmonised rules on DPAs was a key objective[2] behind the reform of the data protection framework that resulted in the GDPR. This has to do with a fundamental criticism of the EU data protection framework existing before 25 May 2018: its presumed lack of effectiveness.[3] It also has to do with the Europeanisation of data protection and the internal market rationale. The GDPR cannot create a level playing field if there is too much divergence in enforcement. Divergence in enforcement might not only adversely affect

---

[2] EC Communication 2010, 2.5.   [3] See Hijmans 2016A, para. 7.11.

the functioning of the internal market but may also incentivise forum shopping by controllers and processors which could result in a lower level of protection of data subjects within the EU. Providing the same tasks and powers to DPAs is a means to prevent these effects from happening. Other means are the cooperation and consistency mechanisms in Articles 60–66 GDPR.

Both rationales—empowering and Europeanising DPAs—also explain why the DPAs *shall* exercise the tasks assigned to them. They must exercise all these tasks and do not have the discretion to only take up some of the tasks inserted in Article 57 GDPR. This does not mean that they should refrain from prioritising certain tasks, as will be explained in the analysis below.

Another rationale relates to the wide range of tasks, reflecting the various roles of DPAs. Control by these authorities—as mandated by Article 16(2) of the Treaty on the Functioning of the European Union ('TFEU') and Article 8(3) of the Charter of Fundamental Rights of the European Union ('CFR')—is a wide concept which extends beyond enforcement of the various GDPR provisions *strictu sensu*. This is a continuation of the role the DPAs already have. The purpose of DPAs can be summarised as contributing to a high level of privacy in society.

The range of tasks was already wide under the DPD, and will be even wider in the GDPR, for instance because the GDPR specifies public awareness raising as a separate task.

B. Legal Background

1. EU legislation

Article 57 is the successor of Article 28(3) and (4) DPD, although with a different nature since Article 28 DPD only identifies a few more general tasks, leaving a wide discretion to Member States law. Article 57 GDPR draws inspiration from Article 46 of Regulation 45/2001 (data protection at EU institutions and bodies),[4] now Article 57 EUDPR. The latter provision contains a longer list, including many of the same tasks of the EDPS as national DPAs,[5] in order, according to recital 73 EUDPR, to ensure consistent monitoring and enforcement of the data protection rules throughout the EU.

2. International instruments

The ideals of Article 57 are a reflection and elaboration of the Additional Protocol to the Convention for the Protection of Individuals with regard to Automatic Processing of Personal Data regarding supervisory authorities and trans-border data flows, of the Council of Europe (Convention 108).[6] The modernised version of Convention 108 contains a lengthy list of tasks that supervisory authorities should perform.[7]

3. National developments

Until the entry into application of the GDPR, national law of all Member States contained provisions assigning tasks to DPAs implementing Article 28 DPD.[8]

---

[4] See Table of Legislation.   [5] See e.g. Hijmans 2006.
[6] See Table of Legislation.   [7] See Art. 15 Modernised Convention 108.
[8] An overview (neither fully complete nor up to date) can be found in FRA 2010, section 4.

4. Case law

A general characterisation of the tasks of the DPAs was given by the CJEU in its three infringement rulings on DPA independence.[9] In essence, DPAs should establish 'a fair balance between the protection of the right to private life and the free movement of personal data'.[10] The CJEU considered, in addition, in *Schrems* that the DPAs should examine claims by individuals 'with all due diligence'.[11] The ECtHR has not discussed the tasks of DPAs in its jurisprudence.

C. Analysis

1. Article 57 as a pivotal provision

Article 57 GDPR is a pivotal provision in Chapter VI. It links the provisions on institutional matters and on competence of the supervisory authorities with the exercise of powers by these authorities. The tasks included in Article 57 GDPR give meaning to the establishment of these authorities, whereas the powers are needed to make the assignment of tasks meaningful. As recital 63 DPD explains, powers constitute the necessary means for DPAs to perform their tasks.[12]

The attribution of powers to the DPAs received much more attention during the legislative process than the attribution of tasks, which is remarkable because the attribution of tasks is neither obvious nor always a continuation of the past. An example is recital 129 GDPR, stating that DPAs in the EU should have the same tasks and powers. However, this is a long recital that further only explains the powers of DPAs. The EDPS commented on the powers of the DPAs as proposed by the legislator, but not on the tasks.[13] Also, in its summary of the negotiations, the Council did not devote many words to the DPAs' tasks and simply referred to enhancing the independence of supervisory authorities while harmonising their tasks (and powers).[14]

2. Characterising the 22 tasks of Article 57 GDPR

Article 57 GDPR distinguishes between 22 tasks. The twenty-second task, included in Article 57(1)(v), is open-ended and requires DPAs to fulfil any other tasks related to data protection. Although Article 57 gives the impression of being exhaustive, it is not. Various other GDPR provisions provide for tasks of the DPAs which are not included in Article 57. For example, Article 58 provides for a number of DPA tasks requiring them to authorise certain activities. Article 58 also provides for tasks in relation to certification, whereas the general task of DPAs to cooperate in Article 57(1)(g) is elaborated in a number of specific tasks in Chapter VII GDPR. Moreover, Article 59 provides for DPAs to draw up activity reports. In short, despite the fact that Article 57 provides for an extensive number of tasks for the DPAs, it is not all they have to do. In addition, national law may also provide for tasks for DPAs.

---

[9] Case C-518/07, *Commission v Germany*; Case C-614/10, *Commission v Austria*; Case C-288/12, *Commission v Hungary*.
[10] Case C-518/07, *Commission v Germany*, para. 30.   [11] Case C-362/14, *Schrems*, para. 63.
[12] This statement is not included in the GDPR recitals.   [13] EDPS 2012, pp. 238–240.
[14] Council Position 2016.

The roles and tasks of DPAs have been characterised by various scholars. Particularly influential has been the work of Bennett and Raab, who distinguish between the roles of ombudsmen, auditors, consultants, educators, policy advisors, negotiators and enforcers.[15] Another description highlights a range of roles 'varying from policy oriented tasks (like advising on new legislation) to quasi-judicial functions where decisions must be taken vis-à-vis individuals'.[16] In essence, DPAs advise on data protection issues, whereas—at the same time—they enforce data protection laws. The GDPR adds the role of communicators raising awareness of the public on privacy issues. Recitals 122 and 123 GDPR provide some further clarity on the variety of tasks. They mention: complaints handling, conducting investigations, promoting public awareness, as well as monitoring the GDPR application and cooperation. These tasks are all put on equal footing.

A paper by the Centre for Information Policy Leadership ('CIPL') distinguishes four DPA roles.[17] They are leader, authoriser, police officer and complaint-handler. This distinction is useful, for two reasons. First, it recognises the main dichotomy in DPA tasks: the policy or leader role, on the hand and the enforcement role, on the other hand. Secondly, it broadens the tasks of DPAs beyond compliance. Whereas the role of DPAs in Article 16(2) TFEU and Article 8(2) CFR is dedicated to 'control', which could be interpreted as emphasising the enforcement role, Article 57 GDPR takes a wider approach. Since neither the handling of complaints, nor prior authorisation, necessarily falls into one of these categories, they are qualified as separate roles by CIPL and are discussed separately below.

3. The duty of supervisory authorities to perform their tasks

Under Article 57, the DPAs 'shall' perform all their tasks. This is mandatory. The GDPR does not permit the DPAs to disregard one of the 22 tasks as such. However, Article 57 does not address the question of *how* these tasks shall be performed. The independence of DPAs makes it possible for them to prioritise their tasks, despite the fact that this is not mentioned in Article 57 (nor in any other GDPR article). Prioritisation, normally, is within the full discretion of DPAs, with one exception: as a result of the CJEU ruling in *Schrems*, complaints of data subjects should be handled with 'due diligence'.[18]

The need for prioritising is linked to the resources of a DPA. Whereas Article 52(5) GDPR stipulates that Member States must provide a DPA with the necessary human, technical and financial resources, there are concerns that these resources are not sufficient.[19] Probably even more important, resources will never be sufficient to perform all the tasks of DPAs in an intensive manner in view of the developing digital society. Prioritising is mainly needed because DPAs as independent bodies are required to act in an effective[20] and accountable manner, also vis-à-vis democratic bodies. As the CJEU has underlined, the principle of democracy forms part of EU law and the absence of any parliamentary influence over DPAs is inconceivable.[21] DPAs should not act in a non-controllable and arbitrary manner.[22]

The need for effectiveness and accountability justifies the conclusion that strategic approaches are not just optional for DPAs but required by the GDPR. The emphasis in

---

[15] Bennett and Raab 2003, pp. 109–114.   [16] Hijmans 2016A, 7.4.5.   [17] CIPL 2017.
[18] Case C-362/14, *Schrems*, para. 63.   [19] Some evidence can be found in ICDPPC 2017.
[20] E.g. as a result of the general principle of effectiveness in EU law.
[21] Case C-518/07, *Commission v Germany*, paras. 41–43.   [22] Hijmans 2016A, 7.15.

Article 51(2) GDPR on the responsibility for contributing to a consistent application also argues in favour of a common strategic approach by EU DPAs, which could be done within the framework of the EDPB.[23] The need for effectiveness and accountability is also one of the reasons why there are concerns that DPAs will be swamped by complaints of data subjects, which would make it impossible for them to perform their other tasks in an appropriate manner.[24] Experiences in Spain where the DPA had to investigate all complaints provide evidence for this concern.[25] A similar concern is valid in connection with notifications of personal data breaches under Article 33 GDPR. Both tasks are demand-driven, limiting the discretion of DPAs to act strategically.

Finally, prioritising also involves strategic choices of a DPA. A key strategic choice of a DPA is whether to focus on an enforcement approach, using corrective powers and sanctions (in other words, using the 'stick'), or to focus on an approach based on consultation and engagement with organisations they supervise (in other words, using the 'carrot').[26] A third way would be to combine both approaches in a strategic manner. This is sometimes characterised as speaking softly while carrying a big stick.[27]

4. Enforcement related tasks

Only a few tasks within Article 57 are strictly related to enforcement of the various GDPR provisions. Article 57(1)(a) sets out the task of monitoring and enforcing the application of the GDPR, whereas in accordance with Article 57(1)(h) the DPA conducts investigations. Possibly, also the task of keeping internal records of infringements can qualify as an enforcement-related task.

However, this does not mean that the GDPR ignores the importance of enforcement. On the contrary, as already stated, strengthening the enforcement of EU data protection law is one of the main policy objectives behind the GDPR. As part of an enforcement regime, Article 58 provides for a wide set of investigative and corrective powers and Article 83 includes a mechanism for imposing administrative fines.

In short, enforcement is an essential component of the notion of control included in Article 16(2) TFEU and Article 8(3) CFR and therefore a core task of DPAs. As a first step, the DPA must monitor the application of the GDPR, which necessarily includes the existence of breaches. As discussed below, complaints can be a welcome source of information for the DPAs in performing this task. As a second step, investigations can also play an important role in this regard. DPAs should perform these tasks in accordance with the principle of effectiveness, in an accountable manner. However, enforcement is not the only DPA task.

5. Policy or leadership-oriented tasks

The DPAs have a wide range of tasks which cannot be qualified as directly relating to enforcement, and are of a more policy-oriented nature, the core of which is giving advice and guidance. The term leadership is also mentioned in this context.[28] Others describe DPAs as authoritative champions in the domain of data protection.[29] It is sometimes

---

[23] Under Art. 70(1)(e) GDPR the EDPB may issue guidelines, recommendations and best practices to encourage consistent application of the GDPR.
[24] E.g. CIPL 2017.   [25] Lombarte 2016, p. 126.   [26] Further: CIPL 2017.
[27] As reported by Greenleaf 2016, p. 239.
[28] E.g. in CIPL 2017.   [29] Bennett and Raab 2003.

argued that amongst this range of roles, that of leader should prevail. DPAs have a wide responsibility under the GDPR; most important of all is to achieve the best outcomes in terms of data protection. Enforcing breaches of the law is not sufficient to achieve this goal.[30]

The policy or leadership-oriented tasks include the following: promote public awareness of risks (Article 57(1)(b)); advise parliament, government etc. (Article 57(1)(c)); promote the awareness of controllers and processors of their obligations (Article 57(1)(d)); provide information on request to data subjects (Article 57(1)(e)); monitor relevant developments, in particular technologies and commercial practices (Article 57(1)(i)); give advice on processing operations requiring a data protection impact assessment ('DPIA') (Article 57(1)(l)); and encourage and facilitate codes of practice and certification mechanisms (including seals and marks) (Article 57(1)(m)–(n)).

The variety of these tasks is wide and includes engagement with various stakeholders, in particular law and policy makers (including democratically elected bodies, as well as the European Commission), controllers and processors, data subjects and the public at large. They include advising on draft legislation or policy documents, but also quasi-legislative activities. An example of the latter is the task of a DPA to establish and make public a list of the kind of processing operations which are subject to the requirement for a data protection impact assessment (Article 35(4) GDPR).

They also include engaging with accountable controllers and processors, which Article 57(1)(d) describes as promoting the awareness of controllers and processors of their obligations. This engagement is also known as responsive regulation which, by some, is considered the most effective way of getting to compliance.[31] In this view, the emphasis is on engagement and mutual understanding rather than on sanctions (in other words, the carrot and not the stick).

Furthermore, DPAs should be available to data subjects to help them in exercising their rights. They also have the proactive task of raising public awareness. This is a task of the DPAs which was not included in the DPD but fits very well within the concept of DPAs as authoritative champions, by encouraging individuals to contribute to a higher level of data protection (and, hence, more effective compliance). Public campaigns for better privacy by DPAs can be qualified as the performance of a task under the GDPR.

6. Complaint handling (including Article 57(2)–(4))

The task of handling and investigating complaints is enshrined in Article 57(1)(f) GDPR. Article 57(2)–(4) includes safeguards and requirements, mainly related to this task.

Complaints under the GDPR are primarily a remedy for the data subject, as will be explained below. However, complaints also serve as a source of intelligence for DPAs, enabling them to focus their activities in an effective manner. In this sense, the mechanism is comparable to the complaints of individuals to the European Commission reporting an alleged breach of EU law.[32] These latter complaints do not provide individuals with a remedy; they contribute to the monitoring by the Commission of breaches of EU law.

The complaint-handling role of the DPAs was at stake in *Schrems*, where the CJEU decided that a DPA has a certain obligation to handle claims.[33] The ruling in *Weltimmo* also

---

[30] This argument is based on general theories on 'responsive regulation', as explained in Hodges 2015.
[31] This is a key message ibid. See also CIPL 2017.
[32] See EC Website Complaints.   [33] Case C-362/14, *Schrems*, para. 63.

found its origins in complaints and resulted in a decision on the territorial competence of DPAs to handle complaints in a cross-border situation.

A more fundamental issue was at stake in *Rease and Wullems*, a case which was brought before the CJEU, but was removed from the register before the Court could rule on it.[34] This case concerned a situation where a DPA decided not to deal with a case for policy reasons, but also based on the reasoning that a data subject had an alternative remedy.[35] The argument was that, instead of complaining to a DPA, the complainant could directly invoke his or her right before a court, and hence the refusal to handle a complaint did not deprive the DPA of his fundamental right to an effective remedy guaranteed by Article 47 CFR. While this argument was not decided by the CJEU since the case was withdrawn, it remains relevant to the GDPR. It is not evident to what extent a DPA is obliged to investigate a complaint or, alternatively, is entitled to refer the data subject to its right to an effective judicial remedy against a controller or processor (Article 79 GDPR).

In any event, the GDPR aims at creating a wide possibility for data subjects to make complaints. Article 57(2)–(4) GDPR requires DPAs to facilitate the submission of complaints, e.g. by electronic complaint forms, and not to charge fees, except for manifestly unfounded or excessive requests, in which case a DPA may refuse to act on a request. Article 77 ensures that a data subject can issue a complaint before the DPA of his or her Member State of residence, whilst not excluding complaints before other DPAs.

It is safe to say, in view of the above, that DPAs are normally obliged to consider complaints when they are submitted to them. The notion of 'due diligence' from the *Schrems* ruling is illustrative. On the one hand, data subjects must have the assurance that their complaints are assessed in a serious manner. On the other hand, complaints must not result in DPAs being swamped because they need to dedicate a large part of their resources to complaint handling.

7. Authorisations

Authorisations by DPAs are the exceptions to the main rule in the GDPR that compliance is primarily based on the principle of accountability of controllers. The latter should ensure and demonstrate that processing is performed in accordance with the law, having discretion in choosing the best means for compliance. This is laid down in Articles 5(2) and 24 GDPR.

However, in several circumstances, prior authorisation by DPAs is required. This task is formulated (mainly in Article 58 GDPR) with regard to the DPAs' powers, i.e.: to authorise high-risk processing on public interest grounds if required by national law (Article 58(3)(c)); to authorise contractual clauses for international transfers (Article 58(3)(h)); to authorise administrative arrangements for international transfers (Article 58(3)(i)); and to authorise Binding Corporate Rules ('BCRs') (Article 58(3)(j)). Moreover, DPAs have a variety of tasks in relation to codes and conduct and certification mechanisms which include some form of authorisation.[36]

---

[34] Case C-192/15, *Rease and Wullems*. This case was based on the DPD.
[35] Explained in Hijmans 2016A, 7.4.3.
[36] Arts. 57(1)(q), 58(3)(d)–(f) GDPR. See also the various roles of the DPAs in Arts. 40–43 GDPR.

8. Cooperation

Cooperation with other supervisory authorities is identified as an explicit task of DPAs task in Article 57(1)(e) and (g). Cooperation includes the sharing of information and providing mutual assistance and should envisage ensuring the consistency of application and enforcement of the GDPR. Article 57(1)(g) elaborates the general DPA role of contributing to the consistent application of the GDPR throughout the EU (Article 51(2)). In turn, Article 57(1)(g) is elaborated in several provisions of Chapter VII on cooperation and consistency, including the tasks of the DPAs as member of the EDPB.

The cooperation tasks of DPAs give a further explanation of the need for a common strategic approach by EU DPAs. The obligation of DPAs to provide assistance to another DPA might interfere with national priorities and investigations,[37] but common strategic approaches may mitigate this undesired effect.

Select Bibliography

Academic writings

Bennett and Raab 2003: Bennett and Raab, *The Governance of Privacy* (Ashgate Publishing 2003).
Giurgiu and Larsen, 'Roles and Powers of National Data Protection Authorities', 2(3) *European Data Protection Law Review 'EDPL'* (2016), 342.
González Fuster, *The Emergence of Personal Data Protection as a Fundamental Right of the EU* (Springer 2014).
Greenleaf 2016: Greenleaf, 'Responsive Regulation of Data Privacy: Theory', in Wright and de Hert (eds.), *Enforcing Privacy, Regulatory, Legal and Technological Approaches* (Springer 2016), 233.
Hijmans 2006: Hijmans, 'The European Data Protection Supervisor: The Institutions of the EC Controlled by an Independent Authority', 43(5) *Common Market Law Review* (2006), 1313.
Hijmans 2016A: Hijmans, *The European Union as Guardian of Internet Privacy* (Springer 2016).
Hijmans 2016B: Hijmans, 'The DPAs and their Cooperation: How Far Are We in Making Enforcement of Data Protection Law More European?', 3(2) *EDPL* (2016), 362.
Hodges 2015: Hodges, *Law and Corporate Behaviour, Integrating Theories of Regulation, Enforcement, Compliance and Ethics* (Hart Publishing 2015).
Lombarte 2016: Lombarte, 'The Spanish Experience of Enforcing Privacy Norms: Two Decades of Evolution from Sticks to Carrots', in Wright and de Hert (eds.), *Enforcing Privacy, Regulatory, Legal and Technological Approaches* (Springer 2016), 123.
Lynskey, *The Foundations of EU Data Protection Law* (Oxford Studies in European Law 2015).
Ottow, *Market & Competition Authorities, Good Agency Principles* (OUP 2015).

Papers of data protection authorities

ICDPPC 2017: International Conference of Data Protection and Privacy Commissioners, 'Counting on Commissioners: High Level Results of the ICDPPC Census 2017' (6 September 2017).
EDPS 2012: European Data Protection Supervisor, 'Opinion on the Data Protection Reform Package' (7 March 2012).
Article 29 Working Party, 'Guidelines for Identifying a Controller or Processor's Lead Supervisory Authority' (WP 244 rev.01, as last revised and adopted on 5 April 2017).
Article 29 Working Party, 'Guidelines on the Application and Setting of Administrative Fines for the Purpose of the Regulation 2016/679' (WP 253, 3 October 2017).

---

[37] Hijmans 2016B.

Reports and recommendations

CIPL 2017: Centre for Information Policy Leadership, 'Regulating for Results, Strategies and Priorities for Leadership and Engagement' (10 October 2017).

Council Position 2016: Position of the Council at first reading with a view to the adoption of a Regulation of The European Parliament and of the Council on the protection of natural persons with regard to the processing of personal data and on the free movement of such data, and repealing Directive 95/46/EC (General Data Protection Regulation)—Statement of the Council's Reasons, 5419/1/16 REV 1 ADD 1, 8 April 2016.

EC Communication 2010: Communication from the Commission to the European Parliament, the Council, the European Economic and Social Committee and the Committee of the Regions, 'A Comprehensive Approach on Personal Data Protection in the European Union', COM (2010) 609 final, 4 November 2010.

FRA 2010: Fundamental Rights Agency of the European Union, 'Data Protection in the European Union: The Role of National Data Protection Authorities' (2010).

Others

EC Website Complaints: European Commission Website, 'Submit a Complaint', available at https://ec.europa.eu/info/about-european-commission/contact/problems-and-complaints/how-make-complaint-eu-level/submit-complaint_en.

Article 58. Powers

LUDMILA GEORGIEVA[*]   MATTHIAS SCHMIDL[**]

1. Each supervisory authority shall have all of the following investigative powers:
   (a) to order the controller and the processor, and, where applicable, the controller's or the processor's representative to provide any information it requires for the performance of its tasks;
   (b) to carry out investigations in the form of data protection audits;
   (c) to carry out a review on certifications issued pursuant to Article 42(7);
   (d) to notify the controller or the processor of an alleged infringement of this Regulation;
   (e) to obtain, from the controller and the processor, access to all personal data and to all information necessary for the performance of its tasks;
   (f) to obtain access to any premises of the controller and the processor, including to any data processing equipment and means, in accordance with Union or Member State procedural law.
2. Each supervisory authority shall have all of the following corrective powers:
   (a) to issue warnings to a controller or processor that intended processing operations are likely to infringe provisions of this Regulation;
   (b) to issue reprimands to a controller or a processor where processing operations have infringed provisions of this Regulation;
   (c) to order the controller or the processor to comply with the data subject's requests to exercise his or her rights pursuant to this Regulation;
   (d) to order the controller or processor to bring processing operations into compliance with the provisions of this Regulation, where appropriate, in a specified manner and within a specified period;
   (e) to order the controller to communicate a personal data breach to the data subject;
   (f) to impose a temporary or definitive limitation including a ban on processing;
   (g) to order the rectification or erasure of personal data or restriction of processing pursuant to Articles 16, 17 and 18 and the notification of such actions to recipients to whom the personal data have been disclosed pursuant to Article 17(2) and Article 19;
   (h) to withdraw a certification or to order the certification body to withdraw a certification issued pursuant to Articles 42 and 43, or to order the certification body not to issue certification if the requirements for the certification are not or are no longer met;
   (i) to impose an administrative fine pursuant to Article 83, in addition to, or instead of measures referred to in this paragraph, depending on the circumstances of each individual case;
   (j) to order the suspension of data flows to a recipient in a third country or to an international organisation.
3. Each supervisory authority shall have all of the following authorisation and advisory powers:
   (a) to advise the controller in accordance with the prior consultation procedure referred to in Article 36;

---

[*] The views expressed are solely those of the author and do not necessarily reflect those of her current or former employers.

[**] The views expressed are solely those of the author and do not necessarily reflect those of the Austrian Data Protection Authority.

(b) to issue, on its own initiative or on request, opinions to the national parliament, the Member State government or, in accordance with Member State law, to other institutions and bodies as well as to the public on any issue related to the protection of personal data;
(c) to authorise processing referred to in Article 36(5), if the law of the Member State requires such prior authorisation;
(d) to issue an opinion and approve draft codes of conduct pursuant to Article 40(5);
(e) to accredit certification bodies pursuant to Article 43;
(f) to issue certifications and approve criteria of certification in accordance with Article 42(5);
(g) to adopt standard data protection clauses referred to in Article 28(8) and in point (d) of Article 46(2);
(h) to authorise contractual clauses referred to in point (a) of Article 46(3);
(i) to authorise administrative arrangements referred to in point (b) of Article 46(3);
(j) to approve binding corporate rules pursuant to Article 47.
4. The exercise of the powers conferred on the supervisory authority pursuant to this Article shall be subject to appropriate safeguards, including effective judicial remedy and due process, set out in Union and Member State law in accordance with the Charter.
5. Each Member State shall provide by law that its supervisory authority shall have the power to bring infringements of this Regulation to the attention of the judicial authorities and where appropriate, to commence or engage otherwise in legal proceedings, in order to enforce the provisions of this Regulation.
6. Each Member State may provide by law that its supervisory authority shall have additional powers to those referred to in paragraphs 1, 2 and 3. The exercise of those powers shall not impair the effective operation of Chapter VII.

Relevant Recitals

(129) In order to ensure consistent monitoring and enforcement of this Regulation throughout the Union, the supervisory authorities should have in each Member State the same tasks and effective powers, including powers of investigation, corrective powers and sanctions, and authorisation and advisory powers, in particular in cases of complaints from natural persons, and without prejudice to the powers of prosecutorial authorities under Member State law, to bring infringements of this Regulation to the attention of the judicial authorities and engage in legal proceedings. Such powers should also include the power to impose a temporary or definitive limitation, including a ban, on processing. Member States may specify other tasks related to the protection of personal data under this Regulation. The powers of supervisory authorities should be exercised in accordance with appropriate procedural safeguards set out in Union and Member State law, impartially, fairly and within a reasonable time. In particular each measure should be appropriate, necessary and proportionate in view of ensuring compliance with this Regulation, taking into account the circumstances of each individual case, respect the right of every person to be heard before any individual measure which would affect him or her adversely is taken and avoid superfluous costs and excessive inconveniences for the persons concerned. Investigatory powers as regards access to premises should be exercised in accordance with specific requirements in Member State procedural law, such as the requirement to obtain a prior judicial authorisation. Each legally binding measure of the supervisory authority should be in writing, be clear and unambiguous, indicate the supervisory authority which has issued the measure, the date of issue of the measure, bear the signature of the head, or a member of the supervisory authority authorised by him or her, give the reasons for the measure, and refer to the right of an effective remedy. This should not preclude additional requirements pursuant to Member State procedural law. The adoption of a legally binding

decision implies that it may give rise to judicial review in the Member State of the supervisory authority that adopted the decision.

(148) In order to strengthen the enforcement of the rules of this Regulation, penalties including administrative fines should be imposed for any infringement of this Regulation, in addition to, or instead of appropriate measures imposed by the supervisory authority pursuant to this Regulation. In a case of a minor infringement or if the fine likely to be imposed would constitute a disproportionate burden to a natural person, a reprimand may be issued instead of a fine. Due regard should however be given to the nature, gravity and duration of the infringement, the intentional character of the infringement, actions taken to mitigate the damage suffered, degree of responsibility or any relevant previous infringements, the manner in which the infringement became known to the supervisory authority, compliance with measures ordered against the controller or processor, adherence to a code of conduct and any other aggravating or mitigating factor. The imposition of penalties including administrative fines should be subject to appropriate procedural safeguards in accordance with the general principles of Union law and the Charter, including effective judicial protection and due process.

(150) In order to strengthen and harmonise administrative penalties for infringements of this Regulation, each supervisory authority should have the power to impose administrative fines. This Regulation should indicate infringements and the upper limit and criteria for setting the related administrative fines, which should be determined by the competent supervisory authority in each individual case, taking into account all relevant circumstances of the specific situation, with due regard in particular to the nature, gravity and duration of the infringement and of its consequences and the measures taken to ensure compliance with the obligations under this Regulation and to prevent or mitigate the consequences of the infringement. Where administrative fines are imposed on an undertaking, an undertaking should be understood to be an undertaking in accordance with Articles 101 and 102 TFEU for those purposes. Where administrative fines are imposed on persons that are not an undertaking, the supervisory authority should take account of the general level of income in the Member State as well as the economic situation of the person in considering the appropriate amount of the fine. The consistency mechanism may also be used to promote a consistent application of administrative fines. It should be for the Member States to determine whether and to which extent public authorities should be subject to administrative fines. Imposing an administrative fine or giving a warning does not affect the application of other powers of the supervisory authorities or of other penalties under this Regulation.

Closely Related Provisions

Article 4(21) (Definition of a supervisory authority); Article 36 (Advisory and other powers concerning prior consultation, national legislative measures and mandatory prior consultation or authorisation) (see too recital 94); Article 50 (Supervisory authorities to take steps to provide international mutual assistance in enforcement, including through investigative assistance) (see too recital 116); Article 52 (Exercise of powers with complete independence) (see too recital 117); Article 55 (Competence with regard to the exercise of powers, competence over public bodies) (see too recitals 122, 128 and 131); Article 57 (Tasks of supervisory authorities) (see too recitals 122, 123, 132 and 133); Articles 60(2) and 61 (Mutual assistance) (see too recital 133); Article 62 (Joint operations of supervisory authorities, including joint investigations and conferring of powers) (see too recitals 130 and 134); Article 90 (Possibility for Member States to adopt specific rules to set out supervisory authorities' powers) (see too recital 164)

Related Provisions in LED [Directive (EU) 2016/680]

Article 3(15) (Definition of a supervisory authority); Article 28 (Possibility to make use of advisory and any other powers when requested for prior consultation); Article 41 (Establishment of supervisory authorities) (see too recitals 75–76); Article 43 (General conditions for supervisory authorities) (see too recital 79); Article 45 (Competence of supervisory authorities); Article 46 (Tasks of supervisory authorities) and Article 47 (Powers of supervisory authorities) (see too recitals 82–83); Article 51 (Tasks of the Board, including cooperation between supervisory authorities) (see too recital 84); Article 53 (Effective judicial remedy) (see too recital 86)

Related Provisions in EPD [Directive 2002/58/EC]

Article 4(3) (Competent national authorities may require the provider to notify the individual of the personal data breach); Article 4(4) (Inventory of personal data breaches enabling competent national authorities to verify providers' compliance with breach notification requirement); Article 15(1b) (Competent national authorities may ask providers for information on how they respond to data access requests); Article 15a (Implementation and enforcement)

Related Provisions in EUDPR [Regulation (EU) 2018/1725]

Article 42 (Legislative consultation) (see too recital 60); Article 51 (International cooperation) (see too recital 71); Article 57 (Tasks of the European Data Protection Board) (see too recitals 60 and 73)

Relevant Case Law

CJEU

Case C-617/10, *Åklagaren v Hans Åkerberg Fransson*, judgment of 26 February 2013 (Grand Chamber) (ECLI:EU:C:2013:105).

Case C-230/14 and C-227/88, *Weltimmo s.r.o. v Nemzeti Adatvédelmi és Információszabadság Hatóság*, 1 October 2015 (ECLI:EU:C:2015:639).

Case C-362/14, *Maximillian Schrems v Data Protection Commissioner*, judgment of 6 October 2015 (Grand Chamber) (ECLI:EU:C:2015:650).

ECtHR

Centrum För Rättvisa v Sweden, Appl. No. 35252/08, judgment of 19 June 2018.

A. Rationale and Policy Underpinnings

Article 58 GDPR follows the logic of the new legal framework proposed in 2012 for the protection of personal data in the EU, which the Commission stated should include 'strong enforcement that will allow the digital economy to develop across the internal market, put individuals in control of their own data and reinforce legal and practical certainty for economic operators and public authorities'.[1] The GDPR thus strengthens the system of the supervisory authorities and their independence and powers within

[1] GDPR Proposal, p. 2.

a dedicated Chapter VI, and creates a mechanism for cooperation and consistency in Chapter VII.

The fragmentation in national implementation led to the need for a regulation to replace the DPD, and the fragmentation in enforcement and application by supervisory authorities led to the need to define a binding set of far-reaching tasks[2] in Article 57 and respective powers in Article 58 necessary for the performance of the tasks in order to meet the objectives laid down in Article 1. In this regard, Member States had on the one hand to adapt their national legislation since contradictory national provisions should not be in place, and on the other hand to provide corresponding provisions in their procedural law[3] subject to appropriate safeguards.[4]

The data protection authorities must adapt their structure and organisation in accordance with the new requirements of the GDPR. Article 58 does not distinguish between measures against public and private controllers and processors, so that powers of the DPAs extend also to public bodies (while Member States are allowed to enact rules about the extent to which administrative fines and penalties may be levied against public bodies, this is without prejudice to the powers of the DPAs under Article 58(2)).[5]

Article 58 provides for 26 'effective powers'[6] of the supervisory authorities, in part building on Article 28(3) DPD and Article 47 Regulation 45/2001,[7] and adding some new elements, including the power to impose fines and to sanction administrative offences. The latter is a new element in order to increase the effectiveness of enforcement and to prevent forum shopping, since under the DPD some DPAs had this power and some not. Article 58 foresees new investigative, corrective, authorisation and advisory powers for the supervisory authorities in paragraphs 1–3, subject to appropriate safeguards (e.g. measures to ensure appropriateness, necessity and proportionality), in accordance with paragraph 4. Furthermore, Article 58 also contains an opening clause for Member States to stipulate additional powers in para 6 in so far as these do not affect the cooperation and consistency mechanism.

B. Legal Background

1. EU legislation

Article 28(3) DPD already provided that each DPA shall in particular be endowed with investigative powers,[8] effective powers of intervention[9] and the power to engage in legal proceedings where national provisions transposing the DPD have been violated or the power to bring these violations to the attention of the judicial authorities.

---

[2] Ibid., p. 77, referring in Art. 52 of the draft proposal to 'duties'.
[3] See C-230/14, *Weltimmo*, para. 50, stating 'The powers granted to the supervisory authorities must be exercised in accordance with the procedural law of the Member State to which they belong'.
[4] See rec. 129 GDPR. [5] See ibid., Art. 83(7). [6] Ibid., rec. 129.
[7] See Table of Legislation.
[8] Such as powers of access to data forming the subject matter of processing operations and powers to collect all the information necessary for the performance of its supervisory duties.
[9] Such as e.g. that of delivering opinions before processing operations are carried out, in accordance with Art. 20 GDPR, and ensuring appropriate publication of such opinions, of ordering the blocking, erasure or destruction of data, of imposing a temporary or definitive ban on processing, of warning or admonishing the controller, or that of referring the matter to national parliaments or other political institutions.

However, due to the nature of a directive, Member States had a discretion when transposing this provision into their national laws, hence the powers of the DPAs differed substantially between the Member States. As a result, DPAs in some Member States had the power to impose fines and others did not. This and other differences made cross-border cooperation difficult in many cases, since DPAs could not assume that other DPAs had similar powers.

2. International instruments

The Additional Protocol to Council of Europe Convention 108 is so far the only international treaty which deals exclusively with independent DPAs and their powers.[10] Article 1(2)(a) and (b) of the Additional Protocol provides that each DPA shall have, in particular, powers of investigation and intervention, as well as the power to engage in legal proceedings or bring to the attention of the competent judicial authorities violations of provisions of domestic law giving effect to the principles mentioned in Article 1(1) of the Additional Protocol. Each supervisory authority shall also hear claims lodged by any person concerning the protection of his/her rights and fundamental freedoms with regard to the processing of personal data within its competence.[11] A similar provision can be found in Article 15(2) of Modernised Convention 108.

The EEA Agreement, as amended in July 2018,[12] incorporates the GDPR into its Annexes and provides that the provisions of the GDPR should be read, for the purposes of that Agreement, with a number of adaptations. With regard to Article 58(4) GDPR, the Agreement provides that, as regards the EFTA States, the words 'in accordance with the Charter' shall not apply.[13]

3. National developments

Article 58 is directly applicable. Hence, DPAs can rely on it directly when exercising their powers. However, Article 58 also leaves room for national legislation, both with regard to questions of procedural law[14] and those of additional tasks.[15] While paragraphs 1–3 of Article 58 contain the powers that each DPA must have in any case and, unlike Art 28(3) DPD, do not just provide for minimum powers, the questions of how to exercise them and which additional tasks can be assigned to the DPAs are left to Member State law. The powers of the DPAs are subject to appropriate safeguards (paragraph 4), and additional powers conferred by the Member States may not have a negative impact on the effective operation of Chapter VII (paragraph 6).

Article 58(1)(f), for example, provides that the right of a DPA to obtain access to any premises of the controller and the processor must be carried out 'in accordance with Union or Member State procedural law'. According to Article 58(3)(b) each DPA shall have the power to issue, on its own initiative or on request opinions to certain public institutions or 'in accordance with Member State law, to other institutions and bodies as well as to the public' on any issue related to the protection of personal data. A further reference to Member State law can be found in Article 58(3)(c) which requires a DPA to

---

[10] See Table of Legislation. [11] Art. 1(2)(b) Additional Protocol Convention 108.
[12] EEA Decision 2018. [13] Ibid., Art. 5e(i). [14] See e.g. Art. 58(1)(f) GDPR.
[15] See ibid., Art. 58(6).

authorise processing referred to in Article 36(5), 'if the law of the Member State requires such prior authorisation'.

The following examples of Member State law illustrate how they have used this room for manoeuvre. Section 22 of the Austrian Federal Data Protection Act[16] provides for procedural safeguards when exercising the powers (including onsite inspections) conferred upon the Austrian DPA. Sections 24 and 25 of the said Act contain procedural provisions when dealing with complaints of data subjects. The German Federal Data Protection Act[17] provides procedural measures and safeguards in section 16 when the Federal DPA is exercising its powers. The French Data Protection Act[18] contains procedural provisions on how to exercise on-site inspections and on how to exercise corrective powers in Articles 44 et seq.

4. Case law

The rulings by the CJEU concern Article 28 DPD, but are also of relevance for the understanding of Article 58. However, since Article 58 is a further developed version of Article 28 DPD, not all the case law on Article 28 DPD can be applied mutatis mutandis.

The CJEU decided in *Schrems* that a decision taken by the Commission in accordance with Article 25(6) DPD (now Article 45(3) GDPR) does not prevent a DPA from examining the claims of persons concerning the protection of their rights and freedoms with regard to the processing of personal data relating to them which have been transferred from a Member State to a third country when such a person contends that the law and practices in force in the third country do not ensure an adequate level of protection.[19]

In *Weltimmo*, the CJEU ruled that, when the DPA of a Member State to which complaints have been submitted in accordance with Article 28(4) DPD decides that the law applicable is that of another Member State, paragraphs 1, 3 and 6 of Article 28 DPD must be interpreted as meaning that such supervisory authority will be able to exercise the effective powers of intervention conferred on it in accordance with Article 28(3) DPD only in accordance with the procedural law and within the territory of its own Member State.[20] However, the GDPR has introduced a new model of cooperation between DPAs in Articles 56 and 60, so this judgment cannot be relied on completely under the GDPR.

It is important to remember that Article 58(4) takes into account the CJEU's holding in *Åkerberg Fransson* that 'the fundamental rights guaranteed in the legal order of the European Union are applicable in all situations governed by European Union law, but not outside such situations'.[21] Thus supervisory authorities have to respect the rights enshrined in the Charter of Fundamental Rights of the European Union ('CFR') when exercising their powers. In the same judgment the Court also clarified that a criminal penalty can be imposed alongside an administrative penalty without violating the principle *ne bis in idem*.[22]

The ECtHR has alluded to data protection authorities as a significant element to be taken into account when assessing safeguards in the context of Article 8 ECHR.[23]

---

[16] Austrian Federal Data Protection Act.   [17] German GDPR Implementation Law.
[18] French Data Protection Act 1978.   [19] Case C-362/14, *Schrems*, paras. 38 et seq.
[20] Case C-230/14, *Weltimmo*, paras. 50–51.   [21] Case C-617/10, *Åkerberg Fransson*, para. 19.
[22] Ibid, para. 37.   [23] ECtHR, *Centrum För Rättvisa*, paras. 111 and 153–161.

C. Analysis

1. General remarks

Article 58 must be read in conjunction with Article 57 which stipulates the tasks of a DPA. The powers according to Article 58 are those needed to give effect to the tasks enshrined in Article 57. Without a task under Article 57 there is no action for the supervisory authorities to take.

Furthermore, Article 58 is relevant for understanding Articles 60–62, which deal with cross-border cooperation between DPAs. It was the clear intention of the legislator to provide all DPAs with identical minimum tasks and powers which should facilitate co-operation and ensure a largely harmonised application of the GDPR.

As already stated above, Article 58(6) is an opening clause for Member States to assign additional tasks to DPAs not covered by paragraphs 1–3 of Article 58.

2. Overview of the powers and the possibility for additional powers

Paragraph 1 of Article 58 contains *investigative powers*, which are powers that are needed to establish the facts of a case. This includes the power to order a controller and a processor (or their representative according to Article 27) to provide any information that is needed for the performance of tasks, to carry out investigations in the form of data protection audits, to carry out a review on certifications issued pursuant to Article 42(7), to notify the controller or the processor of an alleged infringement of the GDPR, and to obtain access to all personal data and to all information necessary and to obtain access to any premises of the controller and the processor, including to any data processing equipment and means in accordance with Union and Member State procedural law.[24]

Each DPA is only competent to exercise these (and other) powers on the territory of its own Member State. If, in cross-border cases, investigations must be carried out in another Member State, the competent DPA may request mutual assistance (Article 61) or joint operations (Article 62) from the local DPA.[25]

Paragraph 2 of Article 58 provides for *corrective powers* a DPA may exercise in order to ensure compliance with the GDPR. This includes, inter alia, the power to issue warnings that intended processing operations are likely to infringe provisions of the GDPR. The wording of Article 58(2)(a) clearly shows that a warning is a power to be exercised *ex ante* (when a violation of the GDPR has not yet occurred but is likely to happen if the controller puts the intended processing operation into effect).[26]

A DPA may also issue reprimands where processing operations have infringed provisions of the GDPR. Further corrective powers according to Article 58(2) include orders to a controller and a processor (e.g. to bring processing operations into compliance with the GDPR, to comply with a data subject's request, to suspend data flows to recipients in third countries etc.); imposing a temporary or a definitive limitation including a ban on processing; to withdraw certifications or to give orders to certification bodies; and to impose an administrative fine in addition to, or instead of, other corrective measures.[27]

---

[24] In particular, the power to obtain access to premises can differ from Member State to Member State under the relevant provisions of national procedural law.
[25] See in that regard the CJEU in C-230/14, *Weltimmo*, and rec. 122 GDPR.
[26] A warning can be used to conclude a consultation pursuant to Art. 36 GDPR.
[27] As discussed above, the CJEU has ruled that imposing a criminal penalty in addition to an administrative measure does not violate the principle of *ne bis in idem*; see Case C-617/10, *Åkerberg Fransson*, para. 37.

However, as indicated by Recital 148, a reprimand can be used in a case of a minor infringement or if the fine (pursuant to Article 83) likely to be imposed would constitute a disproportionate burden to a natural person. This raises the question whether a reprimand is of a punitive nature and hence cannot be issued in addition to an administrative fine without violating the principle of *ne bis in idem*.

Paragraph 3 lists the *authorisation and advisory powers* of a DPA. This includes giving *advice* to the controller in accordance with the prior consultation procedure pursuant to Article 36, and to issue opinions[28] to the national parliament, governments or other institutions and bodies as well as to the public on any issue related to data protection. Other powers pursuant to paragraph 3 relate to the approval of codes of conducts and binding corporate rules, the adoption of standard contractual clauses and questions concerning certifications and certification bodies.

Paragraph 4 obliges a DPA to exercise powers in accordance with procedural safeguards as set out in Union and Member State law in accordance with the CFR. Since questions of procedural law in principle fall within the competence of the Member States,[29] the effective exercise of powers can differ between DPAs. This can make cross-border cooperation difficult, e.g. when carrying out joint operations according to Article 62 GDPR.

Paragraph 5 obliges Member States to provide by law that DPAs have the power to bring infringements of the GDPR to the attention of the judicial authorities[30] and to commence or engage otherwise in legal proceedings in order to enforce the provisions of the GDPR. Again, depending on the relevant provisions of national law there are differences in the effective exercise of that power between DPAs.

Paragraph 6 of Article 58 allows Member States to provide DPAs with additional powers to those referred to in paragraphs 1–3. For example, in several Member States (e.g. Germany and Hungary) DPAs are also responsible for enforcing the right of freedom of information, and in Austria the DPA is responsible for providing natural and legal persons with their electronic identity. However, under paragraph 6 the exercise of such additional powers shall not impair the effective operation of Chapter VII, i.e. the effective cooperation in cross-border cases and the consistency mechanism.

All powers exercised by a DPA that lead to a binding decision, which affects the legal situation of the person(s) to whom it applies, are subject to judicial review according to Article 78. These include the corrective powers imposing a positive obligation listed in Article 58(2) and negative powers such as a decision to reject a complaint as unfounded.[31]

Select Bibliography

International agreements

EEA Agreement: Agreement on the European Economic Area, OJ 1994 L 1/3.
EEA Decision 2018: Decision of the EEA Joint Committee No. 154/2018 of 6 July 2018 amending Annex XI (Electronic communication, audiovisual services and information society)

---

[28] See Art. 57(1)(c) GDPR.
[29] The GDPR itself contains procedural provisions only in a few provisions, e.g. ibid., Arts. 60, 83(2)–(3), 77(2) and 78(2).
[30] This might be the case if a DPA is of the opinion that a controller or processor has violated provisions of criminal law; see in this regard Art. 84 GDPR.
[31] Case C-362/14, *Schrems*, para. 64.

and Protocol 37 (containing the list provided for in Article 101) to the EEA Agreement [2018/1022], OJ 2018 L 183/23.

EU legislation

GDPR Proposal: Proposal for a Regulation of the European Parliament and the Council on the protection of individuals with regard to the processing of personal data and on the free movement of such data (General Data Protection Regulation), COM(2012) 11, 25 January 2012.

National legislation

Austrian Federal Data Protection Act: Bundesgesetz zum Schutz natürlicher Personen bei der Verarbeitung personenbezogener Daten (Datenschutzgesetz – DSG), BGBl. I Nr. 165/1999 zuletzt geändert durch BGBl. I Nr. 24/2018.

French Data Protection Act 1978: Act No. 78-17 of 6 January 1978 on Data Processing, Files and Individual Liberties (Loi n° 78-17 du 6 janvier 1978 relative à l'informatique, aux fichiers et aux libertés), as last amended by Law No. 2014-334 of 17 March 2014.

German GDPR Implementation Law: Gesetz zur Anpassung des Datenschutzrechts an die Verordnung (EU) 2016/679 und zur Umsetzung der Richtlinie (EU) 2016/680 (Datenschutz-Anpassungs- und Umsetzungsgesetz EU – DsAnpUG-EU), BGBl 2017 Teil 1 Nr. 44.

Article 59. Activity reports

HIELKE HIJMANS[*]

Each supervisory authority shall draw up an annual report on its activities, which may include a list of types of infringement notified and types of measures taken in accordance with Article 58(2). Those reports shall be transmitted to the national parliament, the government and other authorities as designated by Member State law. They shall be made available to the public, to the Commission and to the Board.

Closely Related Provisions

Article 57 (DPA tasks) (see too recital 129); Article 57(1)(u) (Obligation for supervisory authorities to keep internal records of infringements of the GDPR and of measures taken under Article 58(2)); Article 58 (DPA powers) (see too recital 129); Article 71 (European Data Protection Board annual report); Article 97 (European Commission reports on the evaluation and review of the GDPR)

Related Provisions in LED [Directive (EU) 2016/680]

Article 49 (Activity reports of supervisory authorities); Article 62 (European Commission reports on the evaluation and review of the LED)

Related Provisions in EPD [Directive 2002/58/EC]

Article 18 (Review)

Related Provisions in EUDPR [Regulation 2018/1725]

Article 60 (EDPS annual activities report) (see too recital 75)

Relevant Case Law

CJEU

Case C-518/07, *European Commission v Federal Republic of Germany*, judgment of 9 March 2010 (Grand Chamber) (ECLI:EU:C:2010:125).

---

[*] The views expressed are solely those of the author and do not necessarily reflect those of the Belgian Data Protection Authority.

A. Rationale and Policy Underpinnings

Activity reports as described in Article 59 GDPR are one of the tools for accountability of the independent DPAs. They also encourage the DPAs to act in accordance with the principle of democracy, particularly in view of the obligation to report to the national parliament.

Moreover, activity reports enhance the transparency of these public bodies. In accordance with Article 15 Treaty on the Functioning of the European Union ('TFEU'), EU bodies shall conduct their work as openly as possible, in order to promote good governance and ensure the participation of civil society. Although—strictly speaking—DPAs are not EU bodies, these principles of EU law are relevant for DPAs, as they represent legal principles common to the Member States, and because DPAs perform their tasks under EU law, particularly the GDPR.

Both these rationales explain why activity reports are addressed to the national parliament and national government (and to the Commission and the EDPB), as well to the public. In a wider sense, the drawing up of these reports expresses the notion of good administration, which is a fundamental right under EU law in the Charter of Fundamental Rights of the European Union ('CFR').[1]

B. Legal Background

1. EU legislation

This provision is the successor of Article 28(5) DPD, which provided that each DPA shall draw up a public report on its activities at regular intervals. A provision similar to Article 59 GDPR can also be found in Article 46 of Regulation 45/2001[2] that covered data protection at EU institutions and bodies and is now replaced by the EUDPR.[3] These provisions contain the obligation of the EDPS to draw up an annual activity report.

2. International instruments

Modernised Convention 108 requires each supervisory authority to prepare and publish a periodical report outlining its activities.[4]

The EEA Agreement, as amended in July 2018,[5] incorporates the GDPR into its Annexes and provides that the provisions of the GDPR should be read, for the purposes of that Agreement, with a number of adaptations. With regard to Article 59, the Agreement provides that the words 'to the EFTA Surveillance Authority' shall be inserted after the words 'to the Commission'.[6]

3. National developments

At the national level, the laws of the Member States included provisions about the activity reports of DPAs, implementing Article 28(5) DPD.

---

[1] Art. 41 CFR.   [2] See Table of Legislation.   [3] Art. 60 EUDPR covers activity reports.
[4] Art. 15(7) Modernised Convention 108.   [5] EEA Decision 2018.   [6] Ibid., Art. 5e(j).

4. Case law

The CJEU has emphasised that the principle of democracy forms part of EU law and the absence of any parliamentary influence over DPAs is inconceivable. The legislator may thus require DPAs to report their activities to the parliament.[7]

C. Analysis

1. Article 59 as a separate provision

From the perspective of good legislative technique, there is no reason to include the obligation to draw up an annual activity report in a separate article. Article 57 GDPR provides the DPAs with 22 tasks. There is no specific reason why the obligation to draw up an annual report was not included in the same Article 57 as a further task. In proposing this obligation as a separate provision in the GDPR, the Commission probably followed the example of Regulation 45/2001 (now the EUDPR).[8] However, the inclusion of the activity report in a separate provision can also be interpreted as reflecting the importance of reporting on activities by DPAs as part of their accountability.

The legislative process resulted in a specification under which the DPAs may specifically report on types of infringement notified and types of measures taken in accordance with Article 58(2).[9] This addition in Article 59 was the result of the trilogue negotiations, although neither the European Parliament nor the Council had previously proposed it.[10] It reflects the practice of the ICO in the UK to publish the outcome of complaints in the annual report.[11]

Finally, during the legislative process, the draft report of the rapporteur of the European Parliament proposed to make the obligation to draw up an activity report more flexible, by providing that this should happen at least every two years.[12] This proposal for flexibility did not receive sufficient support to lead to a change in the final text.

2. Activity reports and DPA accountability

The accountability of data controllers is one of the pillars of the GDPR. In addition, and partly for different reasons, DPAs are accountable for the way they implement their tasks and powers under the GDPR.[13] This accountability has two main components. First, DPAs are accountable for their acts before a court, under the rule of law. Secondly, DPAs are independent, yet they are public bodies and as such accountable to democratically elected bodies and also to the wider public. The activity reports are instruments enhancing this democratic or public accountability. They can be used to assess general DPA performance, by giving account of how public money is spent and how their activities contribute to fundamental rights and freedoms in relation to data processing and to the free flow of personal data.[14]

Article 59 GDPR provides that the activity report may include a list of types of infringements notified and types of measures taken in accordance with Article 58(2). This

---

[7] Case C-518/07, *Commission v Germany*, paras. 41–45.   [8] Art. 54 GDPR Proposal.
[9] Under Art. 57(1)(u) GDPR, they are also required to keep internal records thereof.
[10] Council Preparation 2015.   [11] Jay 2017, 19-027.
[12] EP Draft Report GDPR, amendment 276.   [13] See also Hijmans 2016, 7.13 and 7.14.
[14] DPA responsibilities are defined in Art. 51(1) GDPR.

is a helpful specification, in view of DPA accountability. However, it should not be interpreted to mean that activity reports should not specify how the DPAs have performed their other tasks under Article 57 or used their powers under Article 58. Equally, and in view of the relevant public interest, it makes sense for DPAs to specify in their activity reports how they gave effect to their powers to impose administrative fines under Article 83 GDPR. Annual activity reports are also instruments for DPAs to give account of their commitment to the principles of transparency and good governance in EU law, such as are laid down in Article 15 TFEU and Article 41 CFR.

Finally, annual activity reports—as well as the annual report of the EDPB under Article 71 GDPR[15]—may be expected to provide useful input to the Commission reports on the evaluation and review of the GDPR, as required by Article 97 GDPR. This further enhances the accountability of the EU data protection regime.

Select Bibliography

International agreements

EEA Agreement: Agreement on the European Economic Area, OJ 1994 L 1/3.
EEA Decision 2018: Decision of the EEA Joint Committee No. 154/2018 of 6 July 2018 amending Annex XI (Electronic communication, audiovisual services and information society) and Protocol 37 (containing the list provided for in Article 101) to the EEA Agreement [2018/1022], OJ 2018 L 183/23.

EU legislation

GDPR Proposal: Proposal for a Regulation of the European Parliament and of the Council on the protection of individuals with regard to the processing of personal data and on the free movement of such data (General Data Protection Regulation), COM(2012) 11 final, 25 January 2012.

Academic writings

Hijmans 2016: Hijmans, *The European Union as Guardian of Internet Privacy* (Springer 2016).
Jay 2017: Jay, *Guide to the General Data Protection Regulation* (Sweet & Maxwell 2017).

Reports and recommendations

Council Preparation 2015: Preparation for trilogue, 13394/15, 30 October 2015.
EP Draft GDPR Report: Draft Report on the proposal for a regulation of the European Parliament and of the Council on the protection of individual with regard to the processing of personal data and on the free movement of such data (General Data Protection Regulation), 2012/0011(COD), 17 December 2012.

---

[15] See the commentary on Art. 71 in this volume.

Chapter VII Cooperation and Consistency (Articles 60–76)

Section 1 Cooperation

Article 60. Cooperation between the lead supervisory authority and the other supervisory authorities concerned

LUCA TOSONI

1. The lead supervisory authority shall cooperate with the other supervisory authorities concerned in accordance with this Article in an endeavour to reach consensus. The lead supervisory authority and the supervisory authorities concerned shall exchange all relevant information with each other.
2. The lead supervisory authority may request at any time other supervisory authorities concerned to provide mutual assistance pursuant to Article 61 and may conduct joint operations pursuant to Article 62, in particular for carrying out investigations or for monitoring the implementation of a measure concerning a controller or processor established in another Member State.
3. The lead supervisory authority shall, without delay, communicate the relevant information on the matter to the other supervisory authorities concerned. It shall without delay submit a draft decision to the other supervisory authorities concerned for their opinion and take due account of their views.
4. Where any of the other supervisory authorities concerned within a period of four weeks after having been consulted in accordance with paragraph 3 of this Article, expresses a relevant and reasoned objection to the draft decision, the lead supervisory authority shall, if it does not follow the relevant and reasoned objection or is of the opinion that the objection is not relevant or reasoned, submit the matter to the consistency mechanism referred to in Article 63.
5. Where the lead supervisory authority intends to follow the relevant and reasoned objection made, it shall submit to the other supervisory authorities concerned a revised draft decision for their opinion. That revised draft decision shall be subject to the procedure referred to in paragraph 4 within a period of two weeks.
6. Where none of the other supervisory authorities concerned has objected to the draft decision submitted by the lead supervisory authority within the period referred to in paragraphs 4 and 5, the lead supervisory authority and the supervisory authorities concerned shall be deemed to be in agreement with that draft decision and shall be bound by it.
7. The lead supervisory authority shall adopt and notify the decision to the main establishment or single establishment of the controller or processor, as the case may be and inform the other supervisory authorities concerned and the Board of the decision in question, including a summary of the relevant facts and grounds. The supervisory authority with which a complaint has been lodged shall inform the complainant on the decision.
8. By derogation from paragraph 7, where a complaint is dismissed or rejected, the supervisory authority with which the complaint was lodged shall adopt the decision and notify it to the complainant and shall inform the controller thereof.
9. Where the lead supervisory authority and the supervisory authorities concerned agree to dismiss or reject parts of a complaint and to act on other parts of that complaint, a separate decision shall be adopted for each of those parts of the matter. The lead supervisory authority shall adopt the decision for the part concerning actions in relation to the controller, shall notify it to the main establishment or single establishment of the controller or processor on the territory of its Member State and shall inform the complainant thereof, while the supervisory authority of the complainant shall

adopt the decision for the part concerning dismissal or rejection of that complaint, and shall notify it to that complainant and shall inform the controller or processor thereof.

10. After being notified of the decision of the lead supervisory authority pursuant to paragraphs 7 and 9, the controller or processor shall take the necessary measures to ensure compliance with the decision as regards processing activities in the context of all its establishments in the Union. The controller or processor shall notify the measures taken for complying with the decision to the lead supervisory authority, which shall inform the other supervisory authorities concerned.

11. Where, in exceptional circumstances, a supervisory authority concerned has reasons to consider that there is an urgent need to act in order to protect the interests of data subjects, the urgency procedure referred to in Article 66 shall apply.

12. The lead supervisory authority and the other supervisory authorities concerned shall supply the information required under this Article to each other by electronic means, using a standardised format.

Relevant Recitals

(130) Where the supervisory authority with which the complaint has been lodged is not the lead supervisory authority, the lead supervisory authority should closely cooperate with the supervisory authority with which the complaint has been lodged in accordance with the provisions on cooperation and consistency laid down in this Regulation. In such cases, the lead supervisory authority should, when taking measures intended to produce legal effects, including the imposition of administrative fines, take utmost account of the view of the supervisory authority with which the complaint has been lodged and which should remain competent to carry out any investigation on the territory of its own Member State in liaison with the competent supervisory authority.

(131) Where another supervisory authority should act as a lead supervisory authority for the processing activities of the controller or processor but the concrete subject matter of a complaint or the possible infringement concerns only processing activities of the controller or processor in the Member State where the complaint has been lodged or the possible infringement detected and the matter does not substantially affect or is not likely to substantially affect data subjects in other Member States, the supervisory authority receiving a complaint or detecting or being informed otherwise of situations that entail possible infringements of this Regulation should seek an amicable settlement with the controller and, if this proves unsuccessful, exercise its full range of powers. This should include: specific processing carried out in the territory of the Member State of the supervisory authority or with regard to data subjects on the territory of that Member State; processing that is carried out in the context of an offer of goods or services specifically aimed at data subjects in the territory of the Member State of the supervisory authority; or processing that has to be assessed taking into account relevant legal obligations under Member State law.

Closely Related Provisions

Article 4(16) (Definition of 'main establishment') (see too recital 36); Article 4(22) (Definition of 'supervisory authority concerned') (see also recital 36); Article 4(23) (Definition of 'cross-border processing'); Article 4(24) (Definition of 'relevant and reasoned objection') (see too recital 124); Article 50 (International cooperation for the protection of personal data) (see too recitals 102 and 116); Article 55 (Competence of the supervisory authorities) (see too recitals 122 and 128); Article 56 (Competence of the lead supervisory authority) (see also recitals 124–128); Article 57(1)(g) (Supervisory authorities' task to cooperate with other supervisory authorities) (see too recitals 123 and 133); Article 58 (Powers of supervisory authorities) (see too recitals 122 and 129); Article 61 (Mutual assistance) (see too recitals 123 and 133); Article 62 (Joint operations of supervisory authorities) (see too recital 134); Article 63 (Consistency mechanism) (see too recitals 13, 136 and 138); Article 64 (Opinion of the Board) (see also recitals 135–136); Article 65 (Dispute resolution by the Board) (see too recitals 136 and 143); and Article 66 (Urgency procedure) (see too recitals 137–138)

Related Provisions in LED [Directive (EU) 2016/680]

Article 40 (International cooperation for the protection of personal data) (see too recitals 25, 67, 71 and 73–74); Article 46(1)(h)–(i) (Tasks of supervisory authorities) (see to recitals 74, 81 and 83–85); and Article 50 (Mutual assistance) (see too recitals 77, 83 and 90)

Related Provisions in EPD [Directive 2002/58/EC]

Article 15a(4) (Cross-border enforcement cooperation)

Related Provisions in EUDPR [Regulation (EU) 2018/1725]

Article 51 (International cooperation for the protection of personal data) (see too recital 71); Article 61 (Cooperation between the European Data Protection Supervisor and national supervisory authorities) (see also recitals 71 and 78)

Relevant Case Law

CJEU

Case C-230/14, *Weltimmo s.r.o. v Nemzeti Adatvédelmi és Információszabadság Hatóság*, judgment of 1 October 2015 (ECLI:EU:C:2015:639).
Case T-242/12, *Société nationale des chemins de fer français (SNCF) v European Commission*, GC, judgment of 17 December 2015 (ECLI:EU:T:2015:1003).
Case C-566/14 P, *Jean-Charles Marchiani v European Parliament*, judgment of 14 June 2016 (Grand Chamber) (ECLI:EU:C:2016:437).
Case C-210/16, *Unabhängiges Landeszentrum für Datenschutz Schleswig-Holstein v Wirtschaftsakademie Schleswig-Holstein GmbH*, judgment of 5 June 2018 (Grand Chamber) (ECLI:EU:C:2018:388).
Opinion of Advocate General Bot in Case C-210/16, *Unabhängiges Landeszentrum für Datenschutz Schleswig-Holstein v Wirtschaftsakademie Schleswig-Holstein GmbH*, delivered on 24 October 2017 (ECLI:EU:C:2017:796).

Belgium

Court of Appeal of Brussels, judgment of 8 May 2019 (18N – 2018/AR/410).

Tosoni

A. Rationale and Policy Underpinnings

Article 60 GDPR lays down the procedure which operationalises one of the most significant novelties introduced by the Regulation: the 'one-stop-shop' mechanism. This is an enforcement scheme intended to ensure uniform supervision of controllers and processors that conduct cross-border processing of personal data.[1] The mechanism is construed around the idea that, as a rule, a company operating in several Member States should have only one supervisory authority as its sole interlocutor with regard to data protection compliance matters. This is to increase the consistent application of the GDPR throughout the European Union, provide legal certainty and reduce administrative burdens. These were among the key objectives of the data protection reform that led to the adoption of the GDPR,[2] as the legal uncertainty and the red tape linked with the inconsistent enforcement of the DPD across borders were often cited among the main shortcomings of the Directive.[3] Against this background, the one-stop-shop mechanism purports to be an advantage for businesses.[4]

The original GDPR Proposal envisaged that only the supervisory authority of the main establishment in the EU of a controller or processor should be competent for the supervision of the processing activities of the controller or processor in all Member States.[5] However, during the legislative process, such concept of exclusive competence triggered several reservations. This was mainly because it was felt that the concept was not compatible with the effective legal protection of the fundamental rights of data subjects, as it would not ensure enough 'proximity' between the individuals affected by an enforcement decision and the decision-making supervisory authority.[6] In light of this, the EU legislator endeavoured to strike a balance in Article 60 between uniform supervision and proximity by providing that, as a rule, cross-border enforcement decisions should be agreed upon jointly by all the supervisory authorities concerned, but should be formally adopted by a single supervisory authority. In other words, Article 60 aims to ensure that the authority empowered to issue the final decision does not adopt a 'go-it-alone' attitude, but cooperates with the supervisory authorities of the other Member States concerned and takes due account of their views.

B. Legal Background

1. EU legislation

Article 60 and its operationalisation of the one-stop-shop principle established by Article 56 are a novelty under EU data protection law. However, one-stop-shop enforcement mechanisms as such are not new to EU law. Indeed, the GDPR borrowed the

---

[1] See the commentary on Art. 4(23) in this volume for the definition of 'cross-border processing'.
[2] See EC Communication 2010, pp. 17–18. See also EC Staff Working Paper 2012, pp. 67–68.
[3] See EC Staff Working Paper 2012, p. 36.
[4] After one year of GDPR application, 'those organisations that have a main establishment in the EU and therefore benefit from the one-stop-shop report that this new system contributes to deal more efficiently with pan-EU issues. However they indicate that it is too early to say how well this new system is working'. See GDPR Expert Group Report 2019, p. 14. During the first year of application of the Regulation, there have been 205 one-stop-shop procedures. See EDPB 2019B.
[5] See Art. 51(2) GDPR Proposal.
[6] See Council Report 2013A. See also Council Legal Service 2013.

one-stop-shop concept from pre-existing EU legal instruments dealing with other regulatory areas, in particular competition law,[7] but it operationalised the concept in a way that is essentially unique to EU data protection law.

Under the DPD, a company operating in more than one Member State normally had to deal with several supervisory authorities, but without any guarantee that these would align their actions when enforcing data protection rules. In fact, the Directive did not establish any detailed obligation for supervisory authorities to cooperate and coordinate their enforcement activities.[8] Article 28(6) DPD simply provided that '[t]he supervisory authorities shall cooperate with one another to the extent necessary for the performance of their duties, in particular by exchanging all useful information'. However, the practical implementation of Article 28(6) was generally seen as problematic.[9] Moreover, under the DPD, when the processing of a company established only in one Member State affected data subjects in other Member States, in principle, only the supervisory authority of the country where the company was established was empowered to decide on the processing (see Articles 4(1) and 28(4) DPD).[10] This situation resulted in the inconsistent enforcement of the rules of the Directive across the EU, and consequently in legal uncertainty for companies and fragmented protection for data subjects in respect to processing activities with a cross-border impact.[11]

2. International instruments

The specific subject-matter of Article 60 is not dealt with in any international instrument on data protection, as no international treaty has yet embraced the one-stop-shop principle. However, Convention 108 establishes mechanisms for mutual assistance between supervisory authorities (see Articles 13–17). Moreover, the Additional Protocol to Convention 108 regarding Supervisory Authorities and Transborder Data Flows[12] requires that supervisory authorities cooperate with one another to the extent necessary for the performance of their duties, in particular by exchanging all useful information (see Article 1(5)). These obligations are taken over and further expanded in Articles 16–21 of the modernised version of the Convention.

The establishment of cooperation mechanisms was also envisaged in the Recommendation on Cross-border Co-operation in the Enforcement of Laws Protecting Privacy, adopted in 2007 by the OECD.[13] The Recommendation called on OECD Member countries to improve cross-border cooperation between privacy enforcement authorities to address the challenges of protecting the personal data of individuals wherever

---

[7] See e.g. rec. 8 Merger Regulation: 'The provisions to be adopted in this Regulation should apply to significant structural changes, the impact of which on the market goes beyond the national borders of any one Member State. Such concentrations should, as a general rule, be reviewed exclusively at Community level, in application of a "one-stop shop" system and in compliance with the principle of subsidiarity ... ' See also the enforcement regime of Council Regulation 1/2003. Other examples of one-stop-shop systems under EU law may be found in Art. 13 Regulation 913/2010; Art. 47(1) Regulation 952/2013; and Art. 12 Regulation 2016/796. See also the commentary on Art. 56 in this volume.

[8] The Council summarised the situation under the DPD in similar terms during the legislative process that led to the adoption of the GDPR. See e.g. Council Report 2014F, p. 2.

[9] See WP29 2011.

[10] However, it should be noted that the CJEU upheld a flexible understanding of the concept of 'establishment' under the DPD, and rejected a formalistic approach whereby companies are established solely in the place where they are registered. See Case C-230/14, *Weltimmo*, paras. 28–31.

[11] See Council Report 2014F, p. 2.   [12] See Table of Legislation.

[13] OECD Recommendation 2007.

the data or individuals may be located. In response to this call, a group of OECD countries decided to set up the Global Privacy Enforcement Network ('GPEN'), an informal network of privacy authorities from more than 50 countries.[14]

Some European countries have also formalised their cooperation with non-European privacy enforcement authorities in bilateral agreements. For example, the Dutch Data Protection Authority has signed a memorandum of understanding with the US Federal Trade Commission ('FTC') to enhance information sharing and enforcement cooperation on privacy-related matters.[15]

3. National developments

Several national data protection laws establish specific arrangements to align their national systems with the one-stop-shop mechanism introduced by the GDPR. For example, the German Federal Data Protection Act provides for a procedure to identify which of the *Länder* supervisory authorities should be considered the 'lead supervisory authority' pursuant to Article 56(1) GDPR. It also allocates specific responsibilities on each of the *Länder* authorities involved in a one-stop-shop procedure.[16] Similarly, Spanish Law 3/2018 lays down procedural rules that the Spanish supervisory authority ('AEPD') and the supervisory authorities of the Spanish autonomous communities must follow where Article 60 GDPR applies.[17]

4. Case law

The CJEU has yet to rule on the subject-matter of Article 60.[18] However, the Court has ruled on the supervisory authorities' powers and duty to cooperate under the DPD in the following two cases with a cross-border impact: the *Weltimmo* case and the *Wirtschaftsakademie* case.

The *Weltimmo* case concerned the data processing activities of a company registered in Slovakia, but whose services were exclusively targeted at customers in Hungary. Against this background, the CJEU had to clarify which powers the Hungarian data protection authority was entitled to exercise under the DPD. While the Court adopted a broad interpretation of the territorial scope of application of the national rules implementing the DPD[19]—which in that case favoured the applicability of Hungarian law—the Court also pointed out that:

[I]t follows from the requirements derived from the territorial sovereignty of the Member State concerned, the principle of legality and the concept of the rule of law that the exercise of the power to impose penalties cannot take place, as a matter of principle, outside the legal limits within which an administrative authority is authorised to act subject to the law of its own Member State.

Thus, when a supervisory authority receives a complaint, in accordance with Article 28(4) of Directive 95/46, that authority may exercise its investigative powers irrespective of the applicable law and before even knowing which national law is applicable to the processing in question. However, if it reaches the conclusion that the law of another Member State is applicable, it cannot

---

[14] See GPEN Website. [15] See Memorandum FTC and Dutch Data Protection Authority 2015.
[16] See ss. 18 and 19 German GDPR Implementation Law.
[17] See in particular Arts. 61, 64, 66, 68 and 75 of the Spanish GDPR Implementation Law.
[18] However, the CJEU is expected to interpret Art. 60 GDPR pursuant to a reference for a preliminary ruling submitted by the Court of Appeal of Brussels. See Court of Appeal of Brussels 2019.
[19] See Case C-230/14, *Weltimmo*, paras. 19–41.

impose penalties outside the territory of its own Member State. In such a situation, it must, in fulfilment of the duty of cooperation laid down in Article 28(6) of that directive, request the supervisory authority of that other Member State to establish an infringement of that law and to impose penalties if that law permits, based, where necessary, on the information which the authority of the first Member State has transmitted to the authority of that other Member State.[20]

In light of the above, the Court concluded that the Hungarian data protection authority was entitled to exercise the powers to impose penalties only inasmuch as Hungarian law was applicable to the relevant data processing activities.[21]

The *Wirtschaftsakademie* case dealt with the activities of a German company offering educational services by means of a fan page hosted on Facebook, a social network with its European headquarters in Ireland, but with establishments in many other Member States, including Germany. In the case, the Court had to answer the following question regarding the monitoring of the data processing activities of a corporate group, like Facebook, with establishments in several Member States: is the supervisory authority of a Member State entitled to exercise the powers conferred on it by the DPD:

with respect to an establishment situated in the territory of that Member State even if, as a result of the division of tasks within the group, first, that establishment is responsible solely for the sale of advertising space and other marketing activities in the territory of that Member State and, second, exclusive responsibility for collecting and processing personal data belongs, for the entire territory of the European Union, to an establishment situated in another Member State[?][22]

The Court answered this question in the affirmative.[23]

However, in connection to the above, the Court also stated:

[W]hile under the second subparagraph of Article 28(6) of Directive 95/46 the supervisory authorities are to cooperate with one another to the extent necessary for the performance of their duties, in particular by exchanging all useful information, that directive does not lay down any criterion of priority governing the intervention of one supervisory authority as against another, nor does it lay down an obligation for a supervisory authority of one Member State to comply with a position which may have been expressed by the supervisory authority of another Member State.

A supervisory authority which is competent under its national law is not therefore obliged to adopt the conclusion reached by another supervisory authority in an analogous situation.[24]

The above cases illustrate some of the main issues that supervisory authorities, as well as companies and individuals, had to face when they dealt with cross-border cases in accordance with the DPD. They also show the key differences between the enforcement model for cross-border cases embraced by the Directive, based on multiple (often uncoordinated) enforcement decisions, and the model adopted by the GDPR, constructed around the one-stop-shop principle.[25]

---

[20] See ibid., paras. 56–57. [21] Ibid., para. 59.
[22] Case C-210/16, *Wirtschaftsakademie*, para. 45. [23] Ibid., paras. 45–64.
[24] Ibid., paras. 69–70.
[25] In this regard, it is interesting to note that, in the *Wirtschaftsakademie* case, Advocate General Bot invited the Court to decide the case exclusively on the basis of the enforcement model of the DPD, and without pre-empting 'the scheme established by the general regulation on data protection which will apply from 25 May 2018 onwards. As part of that scheme a one-stop-shop mechanism is instituted. This means that a controller that carries out cross-border data processing, such as Facebook, will have only one supervisory authority as interlocutor, namely the lead supervisory authority, which will be the authority for the place where the controller's main establishment is located. Nevertheless, that scheme, and the sophisticated cooperation mechanism which it introduces, are not yet applicable'. See Case C-210/16, *Wirtschaftsakademie* (AG Opinion), para. 103.

C. Analysis

1. Subject-matter and scope of application of Article 60

Contrary to what the reference to 'cooperation' in the title of Article 60 might suggest, the Article does not deal—at least not directly—with the typical mechanisms for cooperation between supervisory authorities that are often included in data protection instruments, such as mechanisms for mutual assistance and joint enforcement operations.[26] These are laid down in other Articles of the GDPR. More specifically, Articles 61 and 62 establish mechanisms for cooperation between supervisory authorities in the EU/ European Economic Area ('EEA'), while Article 50 requires the establishment of mechanisms for cooperation with authorities outside the EU/EEA.

Instead, Article 60 provides for a specific type of cooperation between supervisory authorities in the EU/EEA,[27] namely the co-decision making process to be followed when the one-stop-shop mechanism applies.[28] As discussed above, the one-stop-shop mechanism is an enforcement scheme according to which a controller or processor that carries out cross-border processing of personal data will normally have one sole supervisory authority as interlocutor, in respect of such cross-border processing: the supervisory authority of its main or single establishment in the EU/EEA, referred to in the Regulation as 'lead supervisory authority' (see Article 56(1) and the commentary thereon in this volume). This means that such lead supervisory authority is entrusted with the main responsibility with regard to the adoption of decisions concerning the controller or processor, including the imposition of administrative fines. However, in order to ensure proximity of the decision-making process to the data subjects affected by it, the GDPR envisages that the lead supervisory authority should 'closely involve and coordinate the supervisory authorities concerned in the decision-making process' (see recital 125). To this end, Article 60 lays down a complex procedure in which all 'supervisory authorities concerned' may express their views and object to draft decisions prepared by the lead supervisory authority.

Article 60 only applies where a controller or processor's lead supervisory authority may be identified in accordance with Article 56(1).[29] In turn, this implies that the controller or processor conducts 'cross-border processing'[30] of personal data, is established in the EU/EEA, and that, if the controller or processor has establishments in several

---

[26] The specific subject-matter of Art. 60 emerged perhaps more clearly in previous draft versions of that Article. Indeed, at some point during the legislative process, the Article was entitled 'Co-operation and *co-decision* between lead supervisory authority and concerned supervisory authority' (emphasis added). See Art. 54aa Council Report 2014H, p. 7.

[27] While the text of the GDPR only refers to the supervisory authorities of the EU Member States, point (b) of entry 5e of Annex XI to the EEA Agreement (version dated 6.12.2018, p. 12) specifies that 'the terms "Member State(s)" and "supervisory authorities" [in the GDPR] shall be understood to include, in addition to their meaning in the Regulation, the EFTA States and their supervisory authorities, respectively'. Note: in the EEA Agreement and related legal texts the term 'EFTA States' refers to the three EEA EFTA States and is understood to exclude Switzerland.

[28] For further details regarding the applicability of the one-stop-shop mechanism see the commentaries on Arts. 4(16) and 56 in this volume.

[29] This of course presupposes that Art. 56 applies, which depends, among other things, on the public or private nature of the entity conducting the relevant processing. If the latter is carried out by public authorities or private bodies in the public interest, Art. 56 does not apply (see Art. 55(2) and rec. 128 GDPR). See also WP29 2017.

[30] See the commentary on the definition of 'cross-border processing' in Art. 4(23) GDPR in this volume.

EU/EEA countries, one of its establishments qualifies as 'main establishment' under Article 4(16).[31] In this regard, the WP29 has noted that:

> The GDPR's cooperation and consistency mechanism only applies to controllers with an establishment, or establishments, within the European Union. If the company does not have an establishment in the EU, the mere presence of a representative in a Member State does not trigger the one-stop-shop system. This means that controllers without any establishment in the EU must deal with local supervisory authorities in every Member State they are active in, through their local representative.[32]

In the event that the UK leaves the EU ('Brexit'), the UK Information Commissioner ('ICO') will no longer be the supervisory authority of an EU or EEA/EFTA Member State under Article 4(22) GDPR. As a result, if a UK controller or processor, whose main or single establishment is in the UK, carries out cross-border processing within the EU/EEA, the ICO will no longer be the lead supervisory authority under Article 56 GDPR, although of course it will remain the supervisory authority within the UK under UK law.[33] In this case, the one-stop-shop principle will cease to apply and each concerned EU/EEA authority will regain full jurisdiction, unless an establishment in the EU/EEA becomes the main or single establishment of the controller/processor, and the relevant processing continues to qualify as 'cross-border' under Article 4(23) GDPR. If this occurs, the DPA of the country where the main or single establishment is located will become the lead supervisory authority under Article 56(1), and the one-stop-shop will apply to the establishment(s) of the controller or processor within the EU/EEA.[34]

The text of Article 60 is not entirely clear with respect to its scope of application. On its face, the Article 60 procedure would seem to be intended only for adopting enforcement decisions *stricto sensu*.[35] However, the legislative history of Article 60 and a broader reading of its text would seem to suggest that supervisory authorities must follow the Article 60 procedure not only to impose administrative sanctions and other corrective measures, but also to adopt other legally binding decisions with a cross-border impact. For example, during the legislative process, the Presidency of the Council aptly noted:

> [t]he principle is that in cross-border cases the lead DPA, which acts as supervisory authority, proposes the single supervisory decision. When deciding on BCR, standard contractual clauses, but also on a ban of processing or other corrective measures, the lead DPA will be the best placed to deliver more effective and comprehensive protection. The proximity, of which the importance was emphasised repeatedly at the Council, is ensured by the involvement of the local supervisory authorities in the decision-making process by the lead DPA.[36]

Consequently, the Presidency explained how, under the Article 60 procedure, 'the lead supervisory authority must, where appropriate, draw up a draft *decision on the (corrective, authorisation or advisory) measure* to be taken and submit it to all authorities concerned for their opinion and take due account of their views' (emphasis added).[37]

---

[31] See the commentary on Art. 4(16) in this volume on the definition of 'main establishment'.
[32] See WP29 2017, p. 10.   [33] See the ICO guidance in ICO 2018, pp. 17-22.
[34] See further the commentary on Art. 4(16) in this volume.
[35] This is partially due to the fact that the bulk of the provisions now included in Art. 60 GDPR were first introduced in the draft text of the GDPR under the title 'Cooperation between the main establishment authority and other supervisory authorities regarding the *exercise of corrective powers*' (emphasis added). See Art. 54a Council Report 2013B, pp. 25–26. However, as elaborated further below, the reference to corrective measures was removed in later drafts. See Council Report 2014E, p. 4.
[36] Council Report 2014F, p. 4.   [37] See Council Report 2014E, p. 4.

Such wider scope of application of Article 60 seems to follow also from the rationale of the one-stop-shop mechanism, which is to ensure that a controller or processor that carries out cross-border data processing have only one supervisory authority as interlocutor with regard to data protection compliance matters in general (see Article 56(6)). This appears to be further confirmed in recital 130 GDPR, which states that 'the lead supervisory authority should, when taking *measures intended to produce legal effects, including the imposition of administrative fines*, take utmost account of the view of the supervisory authority with which the complaint has been lodged' (emphasis supplied). This suggests that the lead supervisory authority must follow the Article 60 procedure to adopt a variety of legally binding decisions, and that such decisions are not limited to corrective measures such as administrative fines.[38] Nonetheless, in practice, the Article 60 process is likely to be more frequently followed to impose corrective measures.[39]

2. Article 60(1)–(9) and (12): the decision-making process for adopting decisions in accordance with the one-stop-shop mechanism

2.1 The initial stage of the one-stop-shop mechanism

As noted above, Article 60 establishes the enforcement procedure that supervisory authorities must follow where a lead supervisory authority may be identified in accordance with Article 56(1). This procedure is geared towards the adoption of binding decisions with an EU wide impact (see recitals 126 and 129).

The identification of the lead authority—and of the other authorities concerned—typically occurs on the basis of the information that is made available in the EDPB's Internal Market Information ('IMI') case registry, discussed below. The EDPB has made clear that it 'created workflows in the IMI system to enable the SAs to identify their respective roles. The main purpose of this procedure is to define the roles at an early stage and to avoid objections on the question of competences at a later stage of the procedure'.[40]

The Article 60 procedure involves the lead supervisory authority and any other supervisory authority that is concerned by the relevant cross-border processing because: (i) the controller or processor is established in the jurisdiction of that other supervisory authority; (ii) data subjects residing in the jurisdiction of that other supervisory authority are substantially affected or likely to be substantially affected by the processing; or (iii) a

---

[38] A further indication in this sense may be read into Art. 4(24) GDPR, which defines 'relevant and reasoned objection' as 'an objection to a draft decision as to whether there is an infringement of this Regulation, or whether *envisaged action in relation to the controller or processor complies with this Regulation*, which clearly demonstrates the significance of the risks posed by the draft decision as regards the fundamental rights and freedoms of data subjects and, where applicable, the free flow of personal data within the Union' (emphasis added). Arguably, the reference to the 'envisaged action' concerns measures different from the corrective measures that may be imposed to sanction 'an infringement of this Regulation'.

[39] According to a report issued by the EDPB in February 2019, the 'first final One-Stop-Shop decisions relate to the exercise of the rights of individuals (such as the right to erasure), the appropriate legal basis for data processing and data breach notifications'. See EDPB 2019A, p. 4. A more recent example of the one-stop-shop mechanism is the Swedish DPA investigation into possible infringements of the GDPR by Spotify, a company with establishments in several Member States, including Sweden. See Swedish Data Protection Authority 2019, p. 4.

[40] EDPB 2019A, p. 3. In July 2019 the EDPB published further guidance to clarify the competence of a supervisory authority in the event of a change in circumstances relating to the main or single establishment over the course of a one-stop-shop procedure. See EDPB 2019C and the commentary on Art. 56 in this volume.

complaint has been lodged with that other supervisory authority.[41] Thus, where an investigation concerns, for instance, personal data processed by social media or other internet platforms, all Member State supervisory authorities are likely to be concerned.[42]

Arguably, the procedure may be triggered both by the lead supervisory authority and by any supervisory authority concerned, in particular by the authority with which a complaint has been lodged. Indeed, if an authority which received a complaint were not to refer the matter to the lead supervisory authority, the latter would be unable to fulfil its duty to prepare a draft decision pursuant to Article 60(3). Moreover, the legislative history of Article 60 suggests that the EU legislator envisaged that both the lead authority and the authorities concerned could trigger the cooperation mechanism.[43]

Article 60 assigns the main role in the procedure to the lead supervisory authority. In fact, it is the lead supervisory authority that must prepare a draft decision and that normally will ultimately adopt it.[44] However, Article 60(1) makes clear that the lead supervisory authority must cooperate with the other supervisory authorities concerned 'in an endeavour to reach consensus'. This means that the final decision should normally 'be agreed jointly by the lead supervisory authority and the supervisory authorities concerned' (recital 126). To this end, Article 60(1)–(3) tries to ensure that the cooperation between supervisory authorities works both ways: the lead supervisory authority may request the other supervisory authorities concerned to provide relevant information and mutual assistance pursuant to Article 61, and to participate in joint operations (e.g. joint investigations) pursuant to Article 62; at the same time, the lead supervisory authority must communicate the relevant information on the matter to the other supervisory authorities concerned. Such cooperation is essential in the context of cross-border enforcement as each national supervisory authority remains competent to carry out investigations on the territory of its Member State (see Articles 55(1), 60(2) and recital 130). Where a supervisory authority does not comply with a request for assistance or cooperation, the matter may be submitted to the EDPB (see Article 64(2)).

The exchange of information between supervisory authorities should occur 'by electronic means, using a standardised format' (Article 60(12)). Since May 2018 the Board and DPAs have been using the IMI case registry, in which cases with a cross-border component are normally logged in.[45] In due course the European Commission is empowered to draw up a standardised format (see Article 61(9)).[46] The existence of a standardised format may partially alleviate the administrative burdens and costs linked with the exchange of documents (e.g. translations), which may nonetheless remain substantial.[47]

---

[41] See the definition of 'supervisory authority concerned' in Art. 4(22) and the commentary on Art. 4(22) in this volume.

[42] This was pointed out by some Member States (e.g. Ireland) during the legislative process. See Council Report 2014D, p. 20, fn. 34.

[43] During the legislative process, the Presidency of the Council noted that '[t]he compromise text could be further clarified by providing that the cooperation can be triggered both by the lead DPA and any concerned DPA and in particular by the one to which a complaint has been lodged'. While this was not made explicit in the final text of the GDPR, this statement provides an indication of how the legislator envisaged the practical functioning of the one-stop-shop mechanism. See Council Report 2014A, p. 6.

[44] The preparation of a draft decision normally follows an investigation led by the lead supervisory authority in accordance with its national procedural rules. See EDPB 2019A, p. 4.

[45] For details of the IMI system see the commentary on Art. 67 in this volume.

[46] For further details on the procedure to be followed by the Commission to establish the standardised format see the commentary on Art. 93 in this volume.

[47] During the legislative process, several Member States noted that one of the potential weaknesses of the system to be introduced by Art. 60 was that it would imply heavy administrative burdens. For example,

The obligation to cooperate 'in an endeavour to reach consensus' necessarily implies that all the authorities involved in the procedure are able to express their views on the matter under scrutiny by the lead supervisory authority. This is made clear in Article 60(3), which requires that the lead authority 'without delay submit a draft decision to the other supervisory authorities concerned for their opinion and take due account of their views'. This should ensure that all the interests at stake are taken into account.

After being notified of the draft decision, the supervisory authorities concerned have four weeks to scrutinise it and express objections to it. If at least one of the authorities does object, the lead authority has only two options: (i) follow the objection(s); or (ii) submit the matter to the Board with a view to obtaining a binding decision on the matter (Article 60(4)). In practice, any single supervisory authority concerned enjoys the power to suspend the adoption of a draft decision and trigger the intervention of the Board—even if not just the lead supervisory authority, but all other supervisory authorities concerned, disagree.

However, the Regulation does circumscribe the objections that the supervisory authorities concerned may successfully raise in this initial stage of the procedure, as the lead authority may follow an objection only if it is 'relevant and reasoned'.[48] Indeed, if the lead authority is of the opinion that the objection is not relevant or reasoned, it *shall* dismiss the objection and submit the matter to the EDPB (Article 60(4)). This is primarily intended to try to prevent the supervisory authorities concerned causing additional costs and delays by raising objections that are not well-founded or based on weak arguments.

2.2 Following a relevant and reasoned objection

If the lead authority intends to follow a relevant and reasoned objection, it must submit a revised draft decision to the other supervisory authorities concerned for their opinion (Article 60(5)). This time the authorities have only two weeks to scrutinise the revised draft and raise further objections (Article 60(5)). The Regulation is unclear about what should be done in case further objections are raised against the revised draft decision. However, given that Article 60(5) provides that 'the revised draft decision shall be subject to the procedure referred to in paragraph 4' of Article 60, it would seem logical that, if the lead authority intends to follow one of such further objections, it must submit once again a new revised draft decision to the other supervisory authorities for their opinion. Otherwise, it must submit the matter to the Board.

2.3 Referral to the Board

If the lead authority decides to dismiss an objection and refer the matter to the Board, the consistency mechanism set out in Articles 63 and 65 must be followed. This means that the Board must adopt a decision on whether the objection is relevant and reasoned and, if so, on all the matters which are the subject of the relevant and reasoned objection (Article 65(1)(a) and recital 136). The Board's decision is binding for all the supervisory

---

Hungary stated that '[t]his provision and the system as a whole seem to lead to the permanent involvement of DPAs in the decision-making process and to a massive exchange of information and documents among DPAs as well. This implies a heavy burden (time, translations, staff, etc. ...) and costs that might be difficult to bear by some, if not many, DPAs. It could be a weakness of the proposal'. See Council Report 2014C, p. 30.

[48] See the commentary on Art. 4(24) in this volume on the definition 'relevant and reasoned objection'.

authorities concerned, including the lead supervisory authority, and should normally be adopted within one month (or two, if the matter is particularly complex) from the referral of the matter to the Board (Article 65(2)). As a rule, the Board must adopt its decision by a two-thirds majority of its members (Article 65(2) and recital 136). However, if the Board is unable to adopt a decision within the periods mentioned above, the opinion may be adopted by a simple majority of the members of the Board (Article 65(3)). This implies that, although an objection of a single supervisory authority is sufficient to trigger the consistency mechanism, once the matter reaches the Board it might be relatively easy to dismiss objections that are not shared by several authorities and thus to oblige the dissenting authority to comply with the majority position.[49] This might discourage authorities from raising formal objections that are unlikely to be supported by at least a few other authorities concerned.[50]

As elaborated further below, once the Board adopts its decision, the lead supervisory authority or, as the case may be, the supervisory authority with which the complaint has been lodged, must 'adopt its final decision on the basis of the decision' of the Board (Article 65(6)). This means that the actual content of the final measure adopted towards the controller or processor will substantially depend on the decision of the Board. This is despite the fact that the GDPR does not expressly envisage the participation of the final addressee of the enforcement decision in the procedure before the Board. This might be problematic if viewed in light of the right to be heard enshrined in Article 41(2) of the Charter of Fundamental Rights of the European Union ('CFR').[51] However, the EDPB has adopted Rules of Procedure,[52] Article 11(1) of which provides that '[b]efore taking decisions, the Board shall make sure that all persons that might be adversely affected have been heard'. Interpreted in the light of the Charter, Article 11(1) would require the Board to give a controller or processor the opportunity to make known its views on the matter referred to the Board before the latter adopts its decision, even though this is not expressly envisaged by the GDPR. This finding is supported by the CJEU's view that 'the principle of respect for the rights of the defence is, in all proceedings initiated against a person which are liable to culminate in a measure adversely affecting that person, a general principle of EU law which is applicable even in the absence of any specific rules in that regard'.[53]

Whether and how the Board will provide this opportunity in practice remains to be seen. This is likely to depend on whether the Board considers that receiving from the lead authority 'the written observations of the persons that might be adversely affected by the Board's decision'—as required by Article 11(2) of the Rules of Procedure—is sufficient to ensure that the addressee of the final decision is properly heard in the specific circumstances of a given referral. Arguably, Article 11(2) only provides for a minimum safeguard, but in specific cases additional safeguards may be warranted under Article 11(1),

---

[49] Of course, the dissenting supervisory authority may challenge the binding decision of the Board before the CJEU within two months of being notified of it, in accordance with Art. 263 Treaty on the Functioning of the European Union ('TFEU'). See rec. 143 GDPR.

[50] During the legislative process it was even proposed to establish that a matter could be referred to the Board only if a minimum number of supervisory authorities objected to a draft decision of the lead authority, but this rule was left out in the final text of the GDPR. See Council Report 2015, p. 2.

[51] Art. 41(2) CFR states that '[e]very person has the right to be heard, before any individual measure which would affect him or her adversely is taken'. See further the commentary on Art. 65 in this volume.

[52] EDPB Rules of Procedure. See the commentary on Art. 72 in this volume.

[53] See Case C-566/14 P, *Marchiani*, para. 51. See further Case T-242/12, *SNCF*, para. 347 and case law cited.

read in light of the Charter.[54] For example, while the right to be heard does not always require an oral hearing,[55] the latter may be necessary in a particular case. A right to an oral hearing is often granted under the procedural rules applicable in other regulatory areas.[56]

2.4 Final adoption of a decision

If the authorities involved in the procedure do not raise any objection to a draft decision—either in its first or revised version—within the time limits specified above, 'the lead supervisory authority and the supervisory authorities concerned shall be deemed to be in agreement with that draft decision and shall be bound by it' (Article 60(6)). As mentioned above, the authorities are similarly bound by the outcome of the Board's review of the draft decision in accordance with the consistency mechanism.

Thereafter, the lead supervisory authority must formally adopt the decision, except where the authorities have jointly agreed, or the Board has found, that a complaint should be dismissed or rejected (see Articles 60(7)–(8) and 65(6) and recital 125).[57] In such case, the supervisory authority which received the complaint must formally adopt the decision (Article 60(8)). Where the same complaint was received by several authorities, in principle, each of these authorities must adopt a decision formalising the dismissal or rejection of the complaint. However, if the supervisory authorities involved in the cooperation procedure jointly agree to dismiss or reject only parts of a complaint and to act on other parts, or if the Board decides so after a referral, the lead authority must adopt a decision on the part(s) of the complaint for which the authorities have decided to act, while the supervisory authority (or authorities) of the complainant(s) must adopt another decision for the part(s) concerning dismissal or rejection of the complaint (see Articles 60(9) and 65(6) and recital 125).[58]

This system was designed to ensure proximity of the decision-making to the data subjects affected, and in particular to allow them to have 'adverse' decisions reviewed by a national court in their Member State (see recital 143).[59] In this respect, Article 78(3)

---

[54] See, by analogy, rec. 129 GDPR, which states that 'each measure [adopted by a supervisory authority] should … *taking into account the specific circumstances of each individual case*, respect the right of every person to be heard before an individual measure which would affect him or her adversely is taken' (emphasis added).

[55] Craig 2014, p. 1081.

[56] See e.g. Art. 12 Commission Regulation 773/2004 (providing that '[t]he Commission shall give the parties to whom it has addressed a statement of objections the opportunity to develop their arguments at an oral hearing, if they so request in their written submissions').

[57] In this regard, it should be noted that '[e]ach legally binding measure of the supervisory authority should be in writing, be clear and unambiguous, indicate the supervisory authority which has issued the measure, the date of issue of the measure, bear the signature of the head, or a member of the supervisory authority authorised by him or her, give the reasons for the measure, and refer to the right of an effective remedy'. See rec. 129 GDPR.

[58] It should be noted that Art. 60(9) only states that '[t]he lead supervisory authority shall adopt the decision for the part concerning actions *in relation to the controller*' (emphasis added). Thus, a literal reading of the provision would suggest that the lead authority should not adopt the decision for the part concerning the processor. However, a contextual interpretation of Art. 60(9) suggests that the decision of the lead authority could also deal with the position of the processor. In fact, first, Art. 60(9) provides that the processor should be notified of the decision. Therefore, it may be assumed that the decision could concern the processor directly. Secondly, rec. 125 states that '[w]here the decision is to reject the complaint by the data subject in whole or in part, that decision should be adopted by the supervisory authority with which the complaint has been lodged'. This is reflected in the second part of Art. 60(9), which provides that 'the supervisory authority of the complainant shall adopt the decision for the part concerning dismissal or rejection of that complaint'. This suggests that, for the part of the complaint for which the authorities have decided to act, it is the lead authority which should adopt the decision, including where the decision only concerns the processor.

[59] This objective clearly emerges also from the legislative history of Art. 60. In fact, the Presidency of the Council justified its proposal to require that, where a complaint is rejected, dismissed or granted only in part,

GDPR provides that appeals against decisions of a supervisory authority must be brought 'before the courts of the Member State where the supervisory authority is established'. If it were for the lead authority to adopt a decision dismissing or rejecting a complaint lodged with another supervisory authority, the data subjects affected would normally be unable to challenge such a decision before the courts of the country where the complaint was initially brought.

However, the way in which the system is structured is not unproblematic. For instance, if a complainant wishes to appeal a decision of the lead authority upholding their complaint (e.g. to challenge the suitability of the corrective measures imposed on the controller), in order to comply with Article 78(3), they would arguably need to bring the proceedings before the courts of the Member State of the lead supervisory authority, even where the complaint was initially brought in a different Member State.[60]

Moreover, while the decision adopted by the lead authority in accordance with the one-stop-shop mechanism would normally not take account of relevant Member State legislation,[61] one could envisage some limited cases in which such decision would need to deal with certain national law aspects (e.g. to assess whether the processing was carried out to comply with a national legal obligation to which the controller was subject), most likely with input from the supervisory authority of the relevant Member State. In such case, it might be difficult for a court of the jurisdiction of the lead authority to conduct a proper review of any foreign law aspects of the decision, and for the lead authority to defend them in court.

Furthermore, as discussed above, where a complaint is rejected, dismissed or granted only in part, the enforcement process would often end with the adoption of several decisions by different authorities. This multiplies the avenues for judicial review and might create risks for legal certainty, as it may result in contradictory court judgments on the same underlying matter.

3. Article 60(7) and (9)–(10): notification and enforcement of a decision adopted in accordance with the one-stop-shop mechanism

Once the lead authority has adopted a decision in accordance with the one-stop-shop mechanism, it must notify the decision to the main establishment or single establishment

each supervisory authority that have received such complaint must adopt the single decision concerning that complaint as follows: '[t]he Presidency proposal that in all such cases all concerned DPAs adopt an identical decision is an essential element of the one-stop-shop mechanism, because it guarantees that all affected data subjects will have the possibility to challenge the DPA decision before their local court'. See Council Report 2014G, p. 10.

[60] In theory, one could also take a less formalistic approach and argue that the decision adopted by the lead authority is also a decision of the authority concerned with which the complaint was initially lodged. This is because, pursuant to Art. 60(6), the latter authority is 'deemed to be in agreement' with the final decision adopted by the lead authority. This interpretation would allow the complainant to appeal a decision of the lead authority upholding a complaint in his/her jurisdiction in accordance with Art. 78(3) GDPR. Nonetheless, this interpretation seems to run counter to the rationale of having a decision formally adopted by the authority of the complainant in case of dismissal or rejection of the complaint, an obligation which was introduced in the GDPR precisely to ensure that the affected data subjects have the possibility to challenge the decision before their local courts. See also rec. 143 GDPR.

[61] During the legislative process, the Presidency of the Council expressed its understanding that: 'the single decision to be agreed upon in the context of the one-stop-shop mechanism cannot take account of relevant Member State legislation, such as, for example, (constitutional) rules on the freedom of expression'. See Council Report 2014G, p. 5.

Tosoni

of the controller or processor. At the same time, it must inform the other supervisory authorities concerned and the Board of the decision in question, and provide them with a summary of the relevant facts and grounds. Subsequently, each of the supervisory authorities with which a complaint has been lodged must inform the complainant(s) of the decision (Article 60(7)).

After being notified of the decision, the controller or processor must take all the measures necessary to comply with it, and inform the lead supervisory authority of the measures taken (Article 60(10)). However, where the addressee of the decision has several establishments in the EU, in principle, the decision is formally binding only for the 'main establishment' of the controller or processor. It is then for such establishment to ensure—e.g. through the internal rules of its corporate group—that the decision is implemented in the subsidiaries in other Member States. The EU legislator envisaged the enforcement of one-stop-shop decisions in this way,[62] in order to alleviate the concerns that several Member States (e.g. Denmark and Slovakia) had voiced regarding the possible incompatibility with their national constitutions of a mechanism that would allow a decision adopted by the lead supervisory authority to be directly binding for the concerned establishments in other Member States.[63]

It was specifically to allay these concerns that the legislator (i) provided in Article 60(7) that the lead authority must direct its final decision, on its own territory, to the main establishment of the controller or processor; and (ii) made clear in Article 60(10) that it is the controller or processor that must 'take the necessary measures to ensure compliance with the decision as regards processing activities in the context of all its establishments in the Union'.[64] However, the text of Article 60 is not entirely clear on this point. In fact, given that pursuant to Article 60(10) the controller or processor must ensure compliance with the decision throughout the EU, one might also argue that the controller is *de facto* bound by the decision in each of the Member States where it operates. Otherwise, there may be situations where a supervisory authority concerned is bound by a decision adopted by the lead authority (see Article 60(6)), but the relevant establishment in its territory is not. In such case, the only remedy available where the latter establishment does not voluntary comply with the decision seems to be that of imposing a corrective measure on the main establishment for non-compliance with its obligations under Article 60(10). This is because the rationale and envisaged functioning of the one-stop-shop mechanism seem to exclude that the supervisory authority concerned could adopt a separate decision against the establishment in its territory, unless there is an urgent need to act to protect the interests of data subjects pursuant to Article 60(11) (as elaborated below). In

---

[62] During the legislative process the Commission stated that 'a decision by the "lead authority" should be directed towards the "main establishment" and should only be binding for this establishment. It would then be for the "main establishment"—e.g. through internal business/cooperation rules—to implement the decision in subsidiaries in other Member States'. See Council Report 2014B, p. 7.

[63] E.g. during the legislative process, Denmark noted that 'the Danish Constitution does not allow for Denmark to submit powers or competences that belong to Danish authorities to authorities in other countries. Denmark can therefore not accept that authorities in other Member States take decisions that are directly binding for citizens or businesses in Denmark as if the decisions were taken by Danish authorities. This gives raise to serious constitutional concerns in Denmark ... As Denmark will have a constitutional problem if the lead authority in another Member States takes decisions that are directly binding for citizens and businesses in Denmark, it is crucial for us that this will not be the case if the one-stop-shop mechanism is agreed upon'. See Council Report 2014B, pp. 12–13. Similar concerns have been raised by Slovakia. See p. 19.

[64] See further Council Report 2014E, p. 6.

any event, it will ultimately be for the competent national and EU judicature to decide whether a decision adopted by the lead authority in accordance with the one-stop-shop mechanism is directly binding for all the establishments of a controller or processor in the EU.

As mentioned above, where a complaint is rejected or dismissed, each supervisory authority that has received such complaint must adopt a separate decision, which formalises the rejection or dismissal of the complaint (or parts of it). In such case, each of the supervisory authorities in question must notify its decision to the complainant(s). In addition, it must inform 'the controller' of the decision (Article 60(8)). Article 60(8) does not expressly provide that the processor must be informed of the decision. However, there seem to be no objectively justified reasons for treating controllers and processors differently in this regard. Thus, where the rejected or dismissed complaint concerns a processor, it would seem logical to inform the processor of the rejection or dismissal.[65]

If the complaint is upheld only in part, the lead supervisory authority must notify the decision it adopted to the main or single establishment of the controller or processor on the territory of its Member State and must inform the complainant(s) thereof. The decision(s) for the part concerning dismissal or rejection of the complaint must be notified to the complainant(s) by each of supervisory authorities with which the complaint was lodged. The latter must also inform the controller or processor of the partial dismissal or rejection of the complaint (Article 60(9)).

4. Article 60(11): urgency procedure

The adoption of a single enforcement decision with an EU wide applicability constitutes the general rule where the one-stop-shop mechanism applies. Nonetheless, if there is an urgent need to act to protect the rights of data subjects, any supervisory authority concerned may adopt an interim measure in accordance with the procedure laid down in Article 66 GDPR[66] (see recital 137). Such measure has a maximum validity of three months and applies only in the territory of the Member State of the supervisory authority that adopted it. The need to adopt an interim measure might present itself, for example, in case of failure to act of the lead supervisory authority.

5. Cooperation between supervisory authorities in the LED, EPD and EUDPR

The one-stop-shop principle is not embraced by any other EU data protection instrument. However, the LED, the EPD and the EUDPR all provide for different forms of cooperation between supervisory authorities.

1. LED: The cooperation regime of the LED mirrors that of the GDPR,[67] but is more limited (see Article 50 LED). This is mainly for reasons of national sovereignty, which are stronger in the law enforcement realm.[68] Article 40 LED also provides, similarly to Article 50 GDPR, that Member States must ensure international cooperation on data protection enforcement. Member States tend to understand this as an obligation

---

[65] Note in this regard that Art. 60(9) provides that both the controller and processor must be informed of a partial dismissal or rejection.
[66] See the commentary on Art. 66 in this volume.   [67] See in particular Art. 61 GDPR.
[68] See EDPS 2012, p. 67.

of endeavour and most of them have assigned to their supervisory authorities the task to cooperate globally with their counterparts.[69]

2. EPD: The EPD includes very limited provisions on cross-border cooperation. Article 15a(4) EPD simply empowers the relevant regulatory authorities to 'adopt measures to ensure effective cross-border cooperation in the enforcement of the national laws adopted pursuant to this Directive and to create harmonised conditions for the provision of services involving cross-border data flows'. Such measures must be notified to the European Commission before being adopted.

3. EUDPR: The EUDPR also establishes limited cooperation requirements. Article 51 provides, similarly to Article 50 GDPR and Article 40 LED, that the European Data Protection Supervisor, in cooperation with the Commission and the European Data Protection Board, must take appropriate steps to ensure international cooperation for the protection of personal data. In addition, Article 61 EUDPR provides that the European Data Protection Supervisor must cooperate with Member State supervisory authorities and with the Joint Supervisory Authority of Customs to the extent necessary for the performance of their respective duties, in particular by providing each other with relevant information.[70]

Select Bibliography

International agreements

EEA Agreement: Agreement on the European Economic Area, OJ 1994 L 1/3.

EU legislation

Commission Regulation 773/2004: Commission Regulation (EC) No. 773/2004 of 7 April 2004 relating to the conduct of proceedings by the Commission pursuant to Articles 81 and 82 of the EC Treaty, OJ 2004 L 123/18.

Council Regulation 1/2003: Council Regulation (EC) No. 1/2003 of 16 December 2002 on the implementation of the rules on competition laid down in Articles 81 and 82 of the Treaty (Text with EEA relevance), OJ 2003 L 1/1.

GDPR Proposal: Proposal for a Regulation of the European Parliament and of the Council on the protection of individuals with regard to the processing of personal data and on the free movement of such data (General Data Protection Regulation), COM(2012) 11 final, 25 January 2012.

Merger Regulation: Council Regulation (EC) No. 139/2004 of 20 January 2004 on the control of concentrations between undertakings (the EC Merger Regulation) (Text with EEA relevance), OJ 2004 L 24/1.

Regulation 913/2010: Regulation (EU) No. 913/2010 of the European Parliament and of the Council of 22 September 2010 concerning a European rail network for competitive freight, OJ 2010 L 276/22.

Regulation 952/2013: Regulation (EU) No. 952/2013 of the European Parliament and of the Council of 9 October 2013 laying down the Union Customs Code, OJ 2013 L 269/1.

Regulation 2016/796: Regulation (EU) 2016/796 of the European Parliament and of the Council of 11 May 2016 on the European Union Agency for Railways and repealing Regulation (EC) No. 881/2004, OJ 2016 L 138/1.

---

[69] See GDPR Expert Group Minutes 2017, p. 1.
[70] With regard to future cooperation and coordination tasks see the commentary on Art. 70 in this volume.

National legislation

German GDPR Implementation Law: Gesetz zur Anpassung des Datenschutzrechts an die Verordnung (EU) 2016/679 und zur Umsetzung der Richtlinie (EU) 2016/680 (Datenschutz-Anpassungs- und Umsetzungsgesetz EU – DsAnpUG-EU), BGBl 2017 Teil 1 Nr. 44.

Spanish GDPR Implementation Law: Ley Orgánica 3/2018, de 5 de diciembre, de Protección de Datos Personales y garantía de los derechos digitales.

Academic writings

Bernard-Willis, Pauner Chulvi and de Hert, 'Data Protection Authority Perspectives on the Impact of Data Protection Reform on Cooperation in the EU', 32(4) *Computer Law & Security Review* (2016), 587.

Craig 2014: Craig, 'Art 41—Right to Good Administration', in Peers, Hervey, Kenner and Ward (eds.), *The EU Charter of Fundamental Rights: A Commentary* (Hart Publishing 2014), 1069.

Hijmans, 'The DPAs and their Cooperation: How Far Are We in Making Enforcement of Data Protection Law More European?', 2(3) *European Data Protection Law Review* (2016), 362.

Kloza and Moscibroda, 'Making the Case for Enhanced Enforcement Cooperation between Data Protection Authorities: Insights from Competition Law', 4(2) *International Data Privacy Law* (2014), 120.

Svantesson, 'Enforcing Privacy across Different Jurisdictions', in Wright and de Hert (eds.), *Enforcing Privacy: Regulatory, Legal and Technological Approaches* (Springer 2016), 195.

Papers of data protection authorities

EDPB 2019A: European Data Protection Board, 'First overview on the implementation of the GDPR and the roles and means of the national supervisory authorities' (26 February 2019).

EDPB 2019B: European Data Protection Board, '1 year GDPR – taking stock' (22 May 2019).

EDPB 2019C: European Data Protection Board, 'Opinion 8/2019 on the competence of a supervisory authority in case of a change in circumstances relating to the main or single establishment' (9 July 2019).

EDPB Rules of Procedure: European Data Protection Board, 'Rules of Procedure' (25 May 2018).

EDPS 2012: European Data Protection Supervisor, 'Opinion of the European Data Protection Supervisor on the Data Protection Reform Package' (7 March 2012).

WP29 2011: Article 29 Working Party, 'Advice Paper on the Practical Implementation of the Article 28(6) of the Directive 95/46/EC' (20 April 2011).

WP29 2017: Article 29 Working Party, 'Guidelines on the Lead Supervisory Authority' (WP 244 rev.01, as last revised and adopted on 5 April 2017).

ICO 2018: Information Commissioner's Office, 'Data protection if there's no Brexit deal' (December 2018), available at https://ico.org.uk/media/for-organisations/data-protection-and-brexit/data-protection-if-there-s-no-brexit-deal-1-0.pdf.

Memorandum FTC and Dutch Data Protection Authority 2015: Federal Trade Commission and Dutch Data Protection Authority, 'Memorandum of Understanding Between the United States Federal Trade Commission and the Dutch Data Protection Authority on Mutual Assistance in the Enforcement of Laws Protecting Personal Information in the Private Sector' (6 March 2015).

Swedish Data Protection Authority 2019: Datainspektionen, 'Letter to Spotify' (11 June 2019), available at https://www.datainspektionen.se/globalassets/dokument/ovrigt/skrivelse-till-spotify.pdf.

Reports and recommendations

Council Legal Service 2013: Effective judicial protection of data subject's fundamental rights in the context of the envisaged 'one-stop shop' mechanism, 18031/13, 19 December 2013.

Council Report 2013A: The one-stop shop mechanism, 13643/13, 18 September 2013.

Council Report 2013B: The one-stop-shop mechanism: partial general approach on essential concepts, 16626/1, 22 November 2013.
Council Report 2014A: One-stop-shop mechanism, 5882/14, 31 January 2014.
Council Report 2014B: One-stop-shop mechanism, Doc. 7464/14, 11 March 2014.
Council Report 2014C: One-stop-shop mechanism, 7464/2/14, 3 April 2014.
Council Report 2014D: One-stop-shop mechanism, 9327/14, 30 April 2014.
Council Report 2014E: Orientation debate on one-stop-shop mechanism, 10139/14, 26 May 2014.
Council Report 2014F: The one-stop-shop mechanism, 14788/14, 31 October 2014.
Council Report 2014G: The one-stop-shop mechanism, 14788/1/14, 13 November 2014.
Council Report 2014H: The one-stop-shop mechanism, 16974/14, 16 December 2014.
Council Report 2015: The one-stop-shop mechanism, 6286/15, 19 February 2015.
EC Communication 2010: Communication from the European Commission to the European Parliament, the Council, the Economic and Social Committee and the Committee of the Regions: 'A Comprehensive Approach on Personal Data Protection in the European Union', COM(2010) 609 final, 4 November 2010.
EC Staff Working Paper 2012: Commission Staff Working Paper 'Impact Assessment Accompanying the document Regulation of the European Parliament and of the Council on the protection of individuals with regard to the processing of personal data and on the free movement of such data (General Data Protection Regulation) and Directive of the European Parliament and of the Council on the protection of individuals with regard to the processing of personal data by competent authorities for the purposes of prevention, investigation, detection or prosecution of criminal offences or the execution of criminal penalties, and the free movement of such data', SEC(2012) 72 final, 25 January 2012.
OECD Recommendation 2007: Organisation for Economic Co-operation and Development, 'Recommendation on Cross-Border Co-Operation in the Enforcement of Laws Protecting Privacy' (2007).

Others

GDPR Expert Group Minutes 2017: Commission expert group on the Regulation (EU) 2016/679 and Directive (EU) 2016/680, 'Minutes of the Twelfth Meeting' (2 October 2017).
GDPR Expert Group Report 2019: Multistakeholder Expert Group to support the application of Regulation (EU) 2016/679, 'Contribution from the Multistakeholder Expert Group to the stock-taking exercise of June 2019 on one year of GDPR application' (13 June 2019).
GPEN Website: Global Privacy Enforcement Network, 'Website', available at https://www.privacyenforcement.net/.

Article 61. Mutual assistance

PETER BLUME

1. Supervisory authorities shall provide each other with relevant information and mutual assistance in order to implement and apply this Regulation in a consistent manner, and shall put in place measures for effective cooperation with one another. Mutual assistance shall cover, in particular, information requests and supervisory measures, such as requests to carry out prior authorisations and consultations, inspections and investigations.
2. Each supervisory authority shall take all appropriate measures required to reply to a request of another supervisory authority without undue delay and no later than one month after receiving the request. Such measures may include, in particular, the transmission of relevant information on the conduct of an investigation.
3. Requests for assistance shall contain all the necessary information, including the purpose of and reasons for the request. Information exchanged shall be used only for the purpose for which it was requested.
4. The requested supervisory authority shall not refuse to comply with the request unless:
   (a) it is not competent for the subject-matter of the request or for the measures it is requested to execute; or
   (b) compliance with the request would infringe this Regulation or Union or Member State law to which the supervisory authority receiving the request is subject.
5. The requested supervisory authority shall inform the requesting supervisory authority of the results or, as the case may be, of the progress of the measures taken in order to respond to the request. The requested supervisory authority shall provide reasons for any refusal to comply with a request pursuant to paragraph 4.
6. Requested supervisory authorities shall, as a rule, supply the information requested by other supervisory authorities by electronic means, using a standardised format.
7. Requested supervisory authorities shall not charge a fee for any action taken by them pursuant to a request for mutual assistance. Supervisory authorities may agree on rules to indemnify each other for specific expenditure arising from the provision of mutual assistance in exceptional circumstances.
8. Where a supervisory authority does not provide the information referred to in paragraph 5 of this Article within one month of receiving the request of another supervisory authority, the requesting supervisory authority may adopt a provisional measure on the territory of its Member State in accordance with Article 55(1). In that case, the urgent need to act under Article 66(1) shall be presumed to be met and require an urgent binding decision from the Board pursuant to Article 66(2).
9. The Commission may, by means of implementing acts, specify the format and procedures for mutual assistance referred to in this Article and the arrangements for the exchange of information by electronic means between supervisory authorities, and between supervisory authorities and the Board, in particular the standardised format referred to in paragraph 6 of this Article. Those implementing acts shall be adopted in accordance with the examination procedure referred to in Article 93(2).

Relevant Recitals

(123) The supervisory authorities should monitor the application of the provisions pursuant to this Regulation and contribute to its consistent application throughout the Union, in order

to protect natural persons in relation to the processing of their personal data and to facilitate the free flow of personal data within the internal market. For that purpose, the supervisory authorities should cooperate with each other and with the Commission, without the need for any agreement between Member States on the provision of mutual assistance or on such cooperation.

(133) The supervisory authorities should assist each other in performing their tasks and provide mutual assistance, so as to ensure the consistent application and enforcement of this Regulation in the internal market. A supervisory authority requesting mutual assistance may adopt a provisional measure if it receives no response to a request for mutual assistance within one month of the receipt of that request by the other supervisory authority.

(138) The application of such mechanism should be a condition for the lawfulness of a measure intended to produce legal effects by a supervisory authority in those cases where its application is mandatory. In other cases of cross-border relevance, the cooperation mechanism between the lead supervisory authority and supervisory authorities concerned should be applied and mutual assistance and joint operations might be carried out between the supervisory authorities concerned on a bilateral or multilateral basis without triggering the consistency mechanism.

Closely Related Provisions

Article 50 (International cooperation) (see too recital 116); Article 51(2) (Obligation of supervisory authorities to cooperate to ensure consistency) (see too recital 124); Article 56 (Competence of lead supervisory authority) (see too recitals 124–128); Article 57(1)(g) (Tasks of supervisory authorities); Article 60 (Cooperation between lead supervisory authority and supervisory authorities concerned) (see too recitals 130–31); Article 62 (Joint operations of DPAs) (see too recital 134); Article 64(2) (Opinion of the Board in case of non-compliance with Articles 61 or 62) (see too recital 136)

Related Provisions in LED [Directive (EU) 2016/680]

Article 40 (International cooperation) (see too recitals 67 and 74); Article 46(1)(h) and (i) (Tasks of supervisory authorities) (see too recitals 81 and 83-85); Article 47(1) (Investigative powers) (see too recital 82); and Article 50 (Mutual assistance) (see too recitals 77, 83 and 90)

Related Provisions in EPD [Directive 2002/58/EC]

Article 15a(4) (Cross-border enforcement cooperation)

Related Provisions in EUDPR [Regulation (EU) 2018/1725]

Article 51 (International cooperation) (see too recital 71); Article 61 (Cooperation between the European Data Protection Supervisor and national supervisory authorities) (see too recitals 71 and 78)

Relevant Case Law

CJEU

Case C-503/03, *Commission of the European Communities v Kingdom of Spain*, judgment of 31 January 2006 (Grand Chamber) (ECLI:EU:C:2006:74).

Case C-230/14, *Weltimmo s.r.o. v Nemzeti Adatvédelmi és Információszabadság Hatóság*, judgment of 1 October 2015 (ECLI:EU:C:2015:639).

Case C-362/14, *Maximilian Schrems v Data Protection Commissioner*, judgment of 6 October 2015 (Grand Chamber) (ECLI:EU:C:2015:650).

Case C-210/16, *Unabhängiges Landeszentrum für Datenschutz Schleswig-Holstein v Wirtschaftsakademie Schleswig-Holstein GmbH*, judgment of 5 June 2018 (Grand Chamber) (ECLI:EU:C:2018:388).

A. Rationale and Policy Underpinnings

Article 61 GDPR concerns cooperation between supervisory authorities by way of information exchange and mutual assistance. Its general purpose is to contribute to the correct and consistent implementation and application of the GDPR, in particular, but not exclusively, as part of the 'one-stop-shop' mechanism laid down by Article 60 GDPR. This mechanism is intended to ensure uniform supervision of controllers and processors that conduct cross-border processing of personal data and to ensure the consistent application of the GDPR throughout the EU. Under this mechanism, a company operating in two or more Member States normally has one supervisory authority—termed as 'lead supervisory authority' by the GDPR as its sole interlocutor with regard to data protection compliance matters.[1]

Article 60(2) provides that the 'lead supervisory authority may request at any time other supervisory authorities concerned to provide mutual assistance pursuant to Article 61 ..., in particular for ... monitoring the implementation of a measure concerning a controller or processor established in another Member State'. As noted below, Article 61 may also apply beyond the one-stop-shop mechanism, and is not restricted to cases triggered under Article 60(2).

Article 61 thus applies in cases where one DPA is responsible but requires information from another DPA or where the case can only be concluded after measures carried out in another Member State. It is presumed that the competent DPA cannot make a fully informed decision on its own, as information from or measures taken (such as prior authorisations or investigations) in another Member State are necessary in order to achieve the full picture of the case.

B. Legal Background

1. EU legislation

As Chapter VII GDPR is novel, most of its constituent Articles, including Article 61, have limited antecedents under the DPD. The DPD contained only one single binding provision dealing with cooperation between European DPAs, Article 28(6), which

---

[1] See the commentary on Art. 56 in this volume.

provided: 'The supervisory authorities shall cooperate with one another to the extent necessary for the performance of their duties, in particular by exchanging all useful information'. Recital 64 DPD explained that 'the authorities in the different Member States will need to assist one another in performing their duties so as to ensure that the rules of protection are properly respected throughout the European Union'.

Under this previous EU framework, supervisory authorities have cooperated by exchanging information and providing assistance on an informal basis in specific cases. However, the practical implementation of Article 28(6) was generally seen as problematic.[2]

Research has shown that 'cooperation among DPAs has been taking place for a long time. This cooperation has been characterized for being irregular, heterogeneous and often based on questions of geographical proximity and trust'.[3] DPAs have reported that 'exchanges of information have been taking place in the context of activities of a very different nature and DPAs have informed about the wide plethora of types of information that they share, including plans and intentions, case law, decisions, experiences and best practices, informal thinking, opinions, and requests for opinions'.[4]

In practice, the main multilateral forum for EU DPAs to exchange information was the former WP29, now the EDPB, where DPAs and their staff met regularly in the plenary and the working subgroups, in particular the Cooperation and Enforcement subgroups.[5] In this context a number of DPAs would sometimes establish a task force to cooperate on a specific case.[6]

Other European fora for the exchange of experience and information are the European Conference of Data Protection Authorities ('Spring Conference'), the Council of Europe Consultative Committee on the protection of personal data, regional fora such as the Nordic DPAs, the Central Eastern European Data Protection Authorities ('CEEDPA') and the Conference of Balkan Data Protection Authorities.[7]

As the GDPR aims to provide a higher degree of harmonisation, DPAs will have to increase the intensity of their cooperation, and Article 61 lays down a specific, mandatory framework for this. In this respect, the LED, the EPD and the EUDPR all provide for forms of cooperation between supervisory authorities.

Article 50 LED addresses mutual assistance between supervisory authorities in the law enforcement area. Many of these authorities will also be the supervisory authorities under the GDPR. The LED's mutual assistance provisions, unlike those in the GDPR, have to be implemented by Member States. However, in substance, these two components of the data protection reform package are aligned on mutual assistance.

Article 15a(4) EDP provides for cross-border cooperation by empowering the relevant data protection or telecoms regulators to 'adopt measures to ensure effective cross-border cooperation in the enforcement of the national laws adopted pursuant to this Directive and to create harmonised conditions for the provision of services involving cross-border data flows'.

---

[2] See WP29 2011. [3] Papakonstantinou et al. 2016, p. 65.
[4] Barnard-Wills and Wright 2015, p. 16.
[5] Now established under Art. 25 EDPB Rules of Procedure. Current work of the subgroups can be seen on each meeting agenda of the EDPB.
[6] E.g. the drafting of the WP29 2013. Another example is the taskforce on the UBER data breach case established by the WP29 in 2017. This taskforce, led by the Dutch DPA, is composed of representatives from the French, Italian, Spanish, Belgian and German DPAs as well as ICO, and coordinates the national investigations on the Uber case.
[7] See Papakonstantinou et al. 2016, pp. 65–66.

Finally, the EUDPR also establishes specific cooperation requirements. Article 61 EUDPR requires the EDPS to cooperate with national supervisory authorities[8] 'to the extent necessary for the performance of their respective duties, in particular by providing each other with relevant information, asking each other to exercise their powers and responding to each other's requests'. Article 51 EUDPR requires the EDPS, in cooperation with the Commission and the EDPB, to take appropriate steps to ensure international cooperation for the protection of personal data. In addition, recital 78 recalls that a specific cooperation model has been established concerning Europol. In this context the EDPS, as the supervisory authority of Europol, and national supervisory authorities cooperate within the frame of an advisory cooperation board.[9]

2. International instruments

Article 13(3)(b) of Convention 108 lays down an obligation of mutual assistance. Designated authorities are required to 'take, in conformity with … domestic law and for the sole purpose of protection of privacy, all appropriate measures for furnishing factual information relating to specific automatic processing carried out in its territory, with the exception however of the personal data being processed'. Article 1(5) of the Additional Protocol[10] adds the obligation on supervisory authorities, 'without prejudice' to Article 13 of Convention 108, to 'co-operate with one another to the extent necessary for the performance of their duties, in particular by exchanging all useful information'.

Once it enters into force, Modernised Convention 108 will strengthen these provisions. In the new Chapter V on cooperation and mutual assistance, Article 17(1)(a) makes explicit the duty to provide mutual assistance and adds in subparagraph (b) the obligation of 'coordinating … investigations or interventions, or conducting joint actions'. Article 17(2) provides that the 'information referred to in paragraph 1 shall not include personal data undergoing processing unless such data are essential for co-operation, or where the data subject concerned has given explicit, specific, free and informed consent to its provision'. Finally, Article 17(3) provides that, in order to organise their cooperation and to perform their duties, supervisory authorities should 'form a network'.

In the international context,[11] the two most important fora where EU DPAs are able to exchange information and experiences with third party DPAs are the International Conference of Data Protection and Privacy Commissioners ('ICDPPC')[12] and the Global Privacy Enforcement Network ('GPEN').[13] Two documents adopted under the framework of the ICDPPC may be noted. First, the International Standards on the Protection of Personal Data and Privacy, which provided that supervisory authorities should '(s)hare

---

[8] The EDPS must also cooperate with the joint supervisory authority for coordinated supervision in the ex-third pillar customs area, the CIS SCG. See also Art. 62 EUDPR for coordinated supervision between the EDPS and national supervisory authorities.

[9] See Regulation 2016/794.   [10] See Table of Legislation.

[11] See Papakonstantinou et al. 2016, pp. 66–67.

[12] The purposes of the ICDPPC are, inter alia, to promote and enhance internationally personal data protection, to draft and adopt joint resolutions and to encourage and facilitate cooperation and the exchange of information.

[13] The GPEN was inspired by OECD Recommendation 2007, which called on OECD member economies to 'foster the establishment of an informal network … to discuss the practical aspects of privacy law enforcement co-operation, share best practices … work to develop shared enforcement priorities, and support joint enforcement initiatives and awareness raising campaigns'. See OECD Recommendation 2007 and GPEN Website.

reports, investigation techniques, communication and regulatory strategies and any other useful information for exercising their functions more effectively, in particular following a request for cooperation by another supervisory authority in conducting an investigation or intervention'.[14] Secondly, the Global Cross Border Enforcement Cooperation Arrangement, which included the identification of 'possible issues or incidents for coordinated action and the active seeking of opportunities to coordinate cross-border actions where feasible and beneficial amongst the elements for the coordination of cross border enforcement activities'.[15]

3. Case law

The CJEU has yet to rule on the subject-matter of Article 61. However, the Court has ruled in a number of cases on the supervisory authorities' powers and duty to cooperate under the DPD, which already establish that cooperation is an active, not a passive obligation.

In *Commission v Spain*, the Court considered the automatic implementation of an alert under the Schengen Agreement, without further investigation or information. The Court found that the principle of 'genuine cooperation' underpinning the Schengen acquis required the provision of supplementary information to enable the case to be correctly assessed.[16]

In *Weltimmo* the CJEU considered the compatibility with EU law of the imposition of a fine on Weltimmo by the Hungarian supervisory authority. Weltimmo was a company registered in Slovakia but whose services and data processing activities were exclusively targeted at customers in Hungary. The CJEU found that the Hungarian data protection legislation could be applied to Weltimmo because it exercised through stable arrangements a real and effective activity in that Member State. The CJEU also considered the situation where the law of a DPA investigating a case is not applicable. On the one hand it affirmed the investigative jurisdiction of such a DPA, on the other it preserved the enforcement jurisdiction of the DPA of the Member State of the applicable law.[17] In such a case, the Court underlined the necessity for cooperation under Article 28(6) DPD, and ruled that the investigating DPA must, in fulfilment of that duty of cooperation, request the supervisory authority of the Member State of the applicable law 'to establish an infringement of that law and to impose penalties if that law permits, based, where necessary, on the information which the [requesting] authority has transmitted to the [requested] authority'.[18] The Court emphasised that enforcement cooperation is an obligation for the requested supervisory authority, which 'may, in the context of that cooperation, find it necessary to carry out other investigations, on the instructions of the [requesting] supervisory authority'.[19]

Shortly afterwards, the CJEU referred in *Schrems* to the 'wide range of powers' of supervisory authorities on a non-exhaustive basis in Article 28(3) DPD, including, 'in particular, investigative powers, such as the power to collect all the information necessary

[14] ICDPPC 2009, Art. 2(a).
[15] ICDPPC 2014, section (i). See the commentary on Art. 50 in this volume for more detail on international cooperation.
[16] Case C-503/03, *Commission v Spain*, para. 56.
[17] See Svantesson 2015 for the distinction between investigative and enforcement jurisdiction.
[18] Case C-230/14, *Weltimmo*, para. 57.
[19] Ibid., para. 58.

for the performance of their supervisory duties', and stressed that DPAs should exercise those powers with regard to a complaint 'with all due diligence'.[20]

Finally, in *Wirtschaftsakademie*, a German company was offering educational services by means of a fan page hosted on Facebook. The Court affirmed its approach in *Weltimmo* and ruled that supervisory authorities were required under Article 28(6) DPD to co-operate with one another to the extent necessary for the performance of their duties, in particular by exchanging all useful information. However, the Court also found that there was no obligation under Article 28(6) for a supervisory authority of one Member State 'to comply with a position which may have been expressed by the supervisory authority of another Member State' nor to 'adopt the conclusion reached by another supervisory authority in an analogous situation'.[21]

C. Analysis

1. Introduction

One of the main objectives of the GDPR is the effective and consistent application and enforcement of the GDPR throughout the EU, in order to protect natural persons in relation to the processing of their personal data and to facilitate the free flow of personal data within the internal market. To this end, the GDPR lays down specific rules to ensure that mutual assistance and cooperation are implemented in practice, based on specific procedural steps. In essence, cooperation is made mandatory following a request for assistance, subject to very limited grounds for refusal.

Article 61 falls within the completely new procedures for cross-border cases in Chapter VII, in particular the cooperation mechanism between supervisory authorities in Section 1 (the so-called 'one-stop-shop') as well as other forms of cooperation. Article 61 establishes a binding mechanism for mutual assistance between EU supervisory authorities, such as information requests and requests to carry out prior authorisations and consultations, inspections and investigations.

It should be considered alongside three other provisions of the GDPR which require DPAs to cooperate so as to ensure consistency of application and enforcement under the GDPR. Article 57(1)(g) requires national DPAs to cooperate with other supervisory authorities, including sharing information and providing mutual assistance; Article 60 lays down the one-stop-shop cooperation mechanism (see the commentary on Article 60 in this volume); and Article 62 requires supervisory authorities to conduct, where appropriate, joint operations including joint investigations and joint enforcement measures. Article 50(1)(b) GDPR should also be borne in mind, requiring the Commission and supervisory authorities to take appropriate steps to 'provide international mutual assistance in the enforcement of legislation for the protection of personal data, including through notification, complaint referral, investigative assistance and information exchange'.

Under Article 60(2) the lead supervisory authority may request the other supervisory authorities concerned to provide relevant information and mutual assistance pursuant to Article 61. Article 60(3) requires the lead supervisory authority to communicate the relevant information on the matter without delay to the other supervisory authorities

---

[20] Case C-362/14, *Schrems*, paras. 43 and 63.
[21] Case C-210/16, *Wirtschaftsakademie*, paras. 69–70.

concerned. Such cooperation is essential in the context of cross-border enforcement as each national supervisory authority remains competent to carry out investigations on the territory of its Member State.[22]

2. Cooperation

The main goal of cooperation is that the GDPR is applied effectively and in the same way in all Member States. According to recital 123, cooperation is the duty of each individual DPA, as also underlined in recital 133. Article 61 lays down both specific and general instructions. The mechanism is mandatory.

Paragraph 1 generally requires supervisory authorities to provide each other with relevant information and mutual assistance, and to put in place measures for effective cooperation with one another. The exchange of information is the core of this procedural cooperation between authorities. Paragraph 1 then details what mutual assistance should normally cover ('requests to carry out prior authorisations and consultations, inspections and investigations').

Paragraphs 2 and 8 specify the deadlines to be respected. Under paragraph 2, when a DPA makes a request for help, the requested DPA must answer without undue delay and at the latest within a month after receiving the request.

Paragraph 3 requires the request to contain relevant information, including the purpose of and reasons for the request. The case in question must accordingly be described. The purpose sets the limits of the request, as paragraph 3 expressly limits the use of information exchanged to the purpose for which it was requested.

Under paragraph 4, the requested supervisory authority can reject the request only if it is not the competent authority or when the request contradicts provisions of the GDPR, EU law or the national law to which the requested DPA is subject. The requested DPA must substantiate the reasons for rejection, under the second sentence of paragraph 5.

Under the first sentence of paragraph 5, the requested supervisory authority must inform the requesting supervisory authority of the results or the progress of the measures it has taken in order to respond to the request.

Paragraph 6 requires requested supervisory authorities to, as a rule, supply the information requested by other supervisory authorities by electronic means, using a standardised format. This requirement can also be seen in Articles 60(12) and 64(4). Paragraph 9 of Article 61 and Article 67 empower the Commission to delegated legislation to specify the arrangements for the exchange of information by electronic means, including the standardised format to be used.[23]

Paragraph 7 precludes requested supervisory authorities from charging a fee for any action taken by them pursuant to a request for mutual assistance but notes that supervisory authorities may agree on rules to indemnify each other for specific expenditure arising from the provision of mutual assistance in exceptional circumstances.

---

[22] See Art. 55(1) and rec. 130 GDPR.

[23] See the commentary on Art. 93 in this volume on the procedure to be followed by the Commission to specify the arrangements for the exchange of information by electronic means. See also the commentary on Art. 67 in this volume, which discusses the IMI system used by DPAs and the Board since the GDPR entered into application.

3. Provisional measures and enforcement

DPAs are obliged to respond to requests for mutual assistance. When a competent DPA does not meet this obligation within a month, and measures have not been instigated according to paragraph 5, then paragraph 8 authorises the requesting supervisory authority to take provisional measures within its own Member State, pursuant to the normal rule of competence under Article 55(1).

Moreover, whilst the provisions on cooperation in Section 1 are separate to those on consistency in Section 2, both fall under Chapter VII, and the consistency mechanism in Section 2 is designed to serve as an enforcement mechanism for cases of failure to cooperate under Section 1.

Thus, Article 61(8) further provides that if a request for assistance is not answered within a month, the urgency procedure under Article 66(1) is triggered, including an urgent binding decision by the EDPB prescribed under Article 66(2).

In addition, when a requested DPA does not comply with its obligations under Article 61, Article 64(2) provides that the requesting DPA can request that the matter be considered by the EDPB with a view to obtaining an opinion. Failure to respect the opinion can then lead to a binding decision by the Board under Article 64(8) and Article 65(1)(c).

Finally, if a DPA continuously resorts to Article 61 without good reason, this can probably also be considered by the EDPB.

4. Relevant information

The term 'relevant information' in Article 61(1), which also figures in Article 60(1), allows a certain flexibility, so as to encompass all conceivable elements of the information. The advantage of using such a general term instead of a limitative exhaustive list is that it leaves open what information may be considered as 'relevant'.

Research shows that the practice of DPAs has been to determine relevancy through contextual criteria, ranging from 'all pieces of information that are useful in assessing the issue at hand', to the information needed to 'take the appropriate procedural and material measures in order to solve a case', and 'the information which we consider as necessary for adoption of a decision'. Relevancy is determined by informing a DPA, 'with the possibility of negotiation and discussion if the receiving DPA felt there was some information missing'.[24]

5. Exchange of information and languages

The GDPR requires relevant information to be provided but does not directly address the question of languages and translations, which inevitably arise in a cross-border and multicultural jurisdiction like the EU. This question is not regulated as in principle all official EU languages are equal but is underpinned by practical reasons. As mentioned in connection with Article 60, it may be assumed that information provided between authorities, including accounts on the results of measures, will normally be in English. However, if two DPAs agree to and prefer the use of another language, this remains

---

[24] See Barnard-Wills et al. 2016, pp. 591–592.

possible. For example, German would be used in a situation involving only German and Austrian DPAs.

Nonetheless, some translation will always be necessary for authorities not working in English and this raises the issue of the costs. The common practice found in parallel systems of cooperation is that translation is provided by the Member State that introduces a request for information, and the GDPR has followed this approach. As noted above, Article 61(7) provides that requested supervisory authorities may not charge a fee for their actions taken in responding to a request for mutual assistance. However, the impact of this provision will be much greater on smaller DPAs with less resources, who will probably need to resort to the second sentence of Article 61(7), which provides that DPAs may agree on rules to indemnify each other for specific expenditure arising from the provision of mutual assistance in exceptional circumstances.

6. Confidential information and personal data

The sharing of information is a key element of the mandatory procedure laid down by Article 61 and generally for the new cooperation mechanisms laid down in Section 1 of Chapter VII. However, Article 61(4)(b) GDPR does not address the issue of the exchange of confidential information and simply carves out national rules on confidentiality, providing that a request for assistance may be refused if 'compliance with the request would infringe ... Member State law to which the supervisory authority receiving the request is subject'.[25]

Nonetheless, national laws often protect information held by supervisory authorities as confidential, restricted or secret.[26] In particular, the obligation of professional secrecy may limit a DPA's powers to share such information with DPAs in other Member States, and information containing personal data may be regarded as confidential and unable to be shared.

One solution may be practical, to share information for cross-border investigations which is neither confidential to the authority concerned nor the personal data involved in the case. For example, this could include 'information on the nature of the incident, circumstances, and the opportunities for cross-border working, including identifying the jurisdiction in which a data controller is located'.[27]

Another solution may arise from developments in the Council of Europe and the ICDPPC. As noted above, Article 13(3)(b) of Convention 108 subjects the obligation of mutual assistance to an exception for personal data being processed. However, Article 17(2) of Modernised Convention 108 provides that personal data may be included if they 'are essential for co-operation, or where the data subject concerned has given explicit, specific, free and informed consent to its provision'. In addition, the ICDPPC Global Cross Border Enforcement Cooperation Arrangement included criteria on confidentiality[28] and a provision that personal data may be shared 'where it is strictly necessary'.[29]

---

[25] See the commentary on Art. 90 in this volume regarding data processing by data controllers and processors subject to a duty of confidentiality.

[26] For national laws on confidential information, see Papakonstantinou et al. 2016, pp. 70–78.

[27] Barnard-Wills et al. 2016, p. 587.

[28] ICDPPC 2014, section 6 on the confidentiality principle.   [29] Ibid., section (1)(i).

7. Informal cooperation

Finally, Article 61 does not preclude cooperation by DPAs in a more informal way on the basis of Article 57(1)(g). The one-stop-shop mechanism has the potential to constitute the standard cooperation tool among DPAs, but this should not be to the detriment of other already operating examples of cooperation. It has been argued that, 'while informal cooperation is mostly undocumented, it is nevertheless crucial for DPA cooperation' and that the formal cooperation mechanism under the GDPR 'risks abolishing the cooperation paths already in existence ... which is something that could ultimately harm DPA effectiveness'.[30]

Moreover, Article 61 may serve as an important regulatory tool to ensure the consistent application of the GDPR where it is enforced, for example, against non-EU controllers or processors. In such case, the one-stop-shop mechanism would not apply, but it would be most effective to have a close cooperation and exchange of information between the supervisory authorities affected by the processing activities of such controllers or processors.

The wording of Article 57(1)(g), read in conjunction with Article 61, would support this broader approach. It is also supported by recital 138, which explains that, in cases where cooperation is not mandatory under the GDPR, 'mutual assistance and joint operations might be carried out between the supervisory authorities concerned on a bilateral or multilateral basis without triggering the consistency mechanism'.

In the event that the UK leaves the EU, the Information Commissioner's Office ('ICO') will no longer be the supervisory authority of an EU or EEA/EFTA Member State under Article 4(22) GDPR. As a result, if a UK controller or processor carries out cross-border processing within the EU/EEA, the ICO will no longer be the lead or other supervisory authority under Article 56 GDPR, although of course it will remain the supervisory authority within the UK under UK law, and neither Article 61 nor Article 57(1)(g) will apply. However the ICO has announced that it will continue to cooperate with EU/EEA supervisory authorities, outside the one-stop-shop and the consistency mechanism, regarding any breaches of GDPR that affect individuals in the UK and other EU and EEA states.[31] In this respect it may expect to benefit from the provisions for international cooperation under Article 50 GDPR.[32]

The EDPB has confirmed that mutual assistance can be used not only on a formal basis, for cross-border cases subject to the one-stop-shop procedure, but also on an informal basis, for national cases with a 'cross-border component'. To this end it has designed the IMI system to input informal mutual assistance cases (in a 'voluntary mutual assistance' field), without any legal deadline as well as formal mutual assistance cases, where the requested supervisory authority has a legal deadline of 1 month to reply to the request.[33]

When this text was finalised, mutual assistance seems to have been working satisfactorily. The EDPB reported that, between 25 May 2018 to 31 January 2019, there were 444 mutual assistance requests, both formal and informal, by DPAs from 18 different EEA countries, 353 of which were answered within 23 days.[34]

---

[30] Barnard-Wills et al. 2017, p. 38. [31] See the ICO guidance in ICO 2018, p. 22.
[32] See the commentary on Art. 50 in this volume.   [33] EDPB 2019, p. 5.   [34] Ibid.

Select Bibliography

EU legislation

Regulation 2016/794: Regulation (EU) 2016/794 of the European Parliament and of the Council of 11 May 2016 on the European Union Agency for Law Enforcement Cooperation (Europol) and replacing and repealing Council Decisions 2009/371/JHA, 2009/934/JHA, 2009/935/JHA, 2009/936/JHA and 2009/968/JHA, OJ 2016 L 135/53.

Academic writings

Barnard-Wills et al. 2016: Barnard-Wills, Pauner Chulvi and de Hert, 'Data Protection Authority Perspectives on the Impact of Data Protection Reform on Cooperation in the EU', 32(4) *Computer Law & Security Review* (2016), 587.

Papers of data protection authorities

ICDPPC 2009: International Conference of Data Protection and Privacy Commissioners, 'Joint Proposal for a Draft of International Standards on the Protection of Privacy with Regard to the Processing of Personal Data' (5 November 2009).
ICDPPC 2014: International Conference of Data Protection and Privacy Commissioners, 'Global Cross Border Enforcement Cooperation Arrangement' (14 October 2014).
EDPB 2019: EDPB, 'First overview on the implementation of the GDPR and the roles and means of the national supervisory authorities' (26 February 2019).
EDPB Rules of Procedure: European Data Protection Board, 'Rules of Procedure' (25 May 2018).
WP29 2011: Article 29 Working Party, 'Advice Paper on the Practical Implementation of the Article 28(6) of the Directive 95/46/EC' (20 April 2011).
WP29 2013: Article 29 Working Party, 'Opinion 04/2013 on the Data Protection Impact Assessment Template for Smart Grid and Smart Metering Systems ("DPIA Template") Prepared by Expert Group 2 of the Commission's Smart Grid Task Force' (WP 205, 22 April 2013).
ICO 2018: Information Commissioner's Office, 'Data protection if there's no Brexit deal' (December 2018), available at https://ico.org.uk/media/for-organisations/data-protection-and-brexit/data-protection-if-there-s-no-brexit-deal-1-0.pdf.

Reports and recommendations

Barnard-Wills and Wright 2015: Barnard-Wills and Wright, 'Authorities' Views on the Impact of the Data Protection Framework Reform on their Co-Operation in the EU', Deliverable D1 for the PHAEDRA II project (20 July 2015), available at http://www.phaedra-project.eu/wp-content/uploads/PHAEDRA2_D1_20150720.pdf.
Barnard-Wills et al. 2017: Barnard-Wills, Papakonstantinou, Pauner Chulvi and Díaz Lafuente, 'Recommendations for Improving Practical Cooperation between European Data Protection Authorities', Deliverable D4.1 for the PHAEDRA II project (14 January 2017), available at http://www.phaedra-project.eu/wp-content/uploads/PHAEDRA2_D41_final_20170114.pdf.
OECD Recommendation 2007: Organisation for Economic Co-operation and Development, 'Recommendation on Cross-border Co-operation in the Enforcement of Laws Protecting Privacy' (2007).
Papakonstantinou et al. 2016: Papakonstantinou, Pauner Chulvi, Cuella and Barnard-Wills, 'European and National Legal Challenges when Applying the New General Data Protection Regulation Provisions on Co-Operation', Deliverable D3.1 for the PHAEDRA II

project (15 September 2016), available at http://www.phaedra-project.eu/wp-content/uploads/PHAEDRA2_D31_final_15092016.pdf.

Svantesson 2015: Svantesson, 'Will Data Privacy Change the Law?' (31 May 2015), available at https://blog.oup.com/2015/05/investigative-jurisdiction-law/.

Others

GPEN Website: Global Privacy Enforcement Network, 'Website', available at https://www.privacyenforcement.net/.

Article 62. Joint operations of supervisory authorities

PETER BLUME

1. The supervisory authorities shall, where appropriate, conduct joint operations including joint investigations and joint enforcement measures in which members or staff of the supervisory authorities of other Member States are involved.
2. Where the controller or processor has establishments in several Member States or where a significant number of data subjects in more than one Member State are likely to be substantially affected by processing operations, a supervisory authority of each of those Member States shall have the right to participate in joint operations. The supervisory authority which is competent pursuant to Article 56(1) or (4) shall invite the supervisory authority of each of those Member States to take part in the joint operations and shall respond without delay to the request of a supervisory authority to participate.
3. A supervisory authority may, in accordance with Member State law, and with the seconding supervisory authority's authorisation, confer powers, including investigative powers on the seconding supervisory authority's members or staff involved in joint operations or, in so far as the law of the Member State of the host supervisory authority permits, allow the seconding supervisory authority's members or staff to exercise their investigative powers in accordance with the law of the Member State of the seconding supervisory authority. Such investigative powers may be exercised only under the guidance and in the presence of members or staff of the host supervisory authority. The seconding supervisory authority's members or staff shall be subject to the Member State law of the host supervisory authority.
4. Where, in accordance with paragraph 1, staff of a seconding supervisory authority operate in another Member State, the Member State of the host supervisory authority shall assume responsibility for their actions, including liability, for any damage caused by them during their operations, in accordance with the law of the Member State in whose territory they are operating.
5. The Member State in whose territory the damage was caused shall make good such damage under the conditions applicable to damage caused by its own staff. The Member State of the seconding supervisory authority whose staff has caused damage to any person in the territory of another Member State shall reimburse that other Member State in full any sums it has paid to the persons entitled on their behalf.
6. Without prejudice to the exercise of its rights *vis-à-vis* third parties and with the exception of paragraph 5, each Member State shall refrain, in the case provided for in paragraph 1, from requesting reimbursement from another Member State in relation to damage referred to in paragraph 4.
7. Where a joint operation is intended and a supervisory authority does not, within one month, comply with the obligation laid down in the second sentence of paragraph 2 of this Article, the other supervisory authorities may adopt a provisional measure on the territory of its Member State in accordance with Article 55. In that case, the urgent need to act under Article 66(1) shall be presumed to be met and require an opinion or an urgent binding decision from the Board pursuant to Article 66(2).

Relevant Recitals

(116) When personal data moves across borders outside the Union it may put at increased risk the ability of natural persons to exercise data protection rights in particular to protect themselves

from the unlawful use of disclosure of that information. At the same time, supervisory authorities may find that they are unable to pursue complaints or conduct investigations relating to the activities outside their borders. Their efforts to work together in the cross-border context may also be hampered by insufficient preventative or remedial powers, inconsistent legal regimes, and practical obstacles like resource constraints. Therefore, there is a need to promote closer cooperation among data protection supervisory authorities to help them exchange information and carry out investigations with their international counterparts.

(134) Each supervisory authority should, where appropriate, participate in joint operations with other supervisory authorities. The requested supervisory authority should be obliged to respond to the request within a specified time period.

(138) The application of such mechanism should be a condition for the lawfulness of a measure intended to produce legal effects by a supervisory authority in those cases where its application is mandatory. In other cases of cross-border relevance, the cooperation mechanism between the lead supervisory authority and supervisory authorities concerned should be applied and mutual assistance and joint operations might be carried out between the supervisory authorities concerned on a bilateral or multilateral basis without triggering the consistency mechanism.

Closely Related Provisions

Article 50 (International cooperation for the protection of personal data); Article 56 (Competence of lead supervisory authority) (see too recitals 124–128); Article 57(1)(g) (Tasks of supervisory authorities); Article 60 (Cooperation between lead supervisory authority and supervisory authorities concerned) (see too recitals 130–31); Article 61 (Mutual assistance) (see too recitals 123 and 133)

Related Provisions in LED [Directive (EU) 2016/680]

Article 40 (International cooperation) (see too recitals 67 and 74); Article 46(1)(h)–(i) (Tasks of supervisory authorities) (see too recitals 81 and 83–85); Article 47(1) (Investigative powers) (see too recital 82); Article 50 (Mutual assistance) (see too recitals 77, 83 and 90)

Related Provisions in EPD [Directive 2002/58/EC]

Article 15a(4) (Cross-border enforcement cooperation)

Related Provisions in EUDPR [Regulation (EU) 2018/1725]

Article 51 (International cooperation) (see too recital 71); Article 61 (Cooperation between the European Data Protection Supervisor and national supervisory authorities) (see also recital 71)

A. Rationale and Policy Underpinnings

Article 62 GDPR concerns situations where it is expedient that supervisory authorities work together in order to investigate and clarify a certain kind of data processing in order to enable the competent DPA(s) to make a decision in accordance with the GDPR.

Blume

Like Article 61, Article 62 is intended to ensure the correct and consistent application of the GDPR, in particular, but not exclusively, as part of the 'one-stop-shop' mechanism laid down by Article 60 GDPR.[1] This mechanism is intended to ensure uniform supervision of controllers and processors that conduct cross-border processing of personal data and to ensure the consistent application of the GDPR throughout the EU. Under this mechanism, a company operating in two or more Member States normally has one supervisory authority—termed as 'lead supervisory authority' by the GDPR—as its sole interlocutor with regard to data protection compliance matters.[2]

Article 60(2) provides that the 'lead supervisory authority ... may conduct joint operations pursuant to Article 62, in particular for carrying out investigations or for monitoring the implementation of a measure concerning a controller or processor established in another Member State'. As noted below, Article 62 may also apply beyond the one-stop-shop mechanism, and is not restricted to cases triggered under Article 60(2).

Article 62 thus applies in cases where one DPA is responsible but where the case is more effectively investigated by another DPA. It is presupposed that the competent DPA cannot fully investigate the case on its own and requires input by another DPA into the investigation in order to achieve the full picture of the case.

B. Legal Background

1. EU legislation

As Chapter VII GDPR is novel, most articles including Article 62 have limited antecedents under the DPD. The DPD contained only one single binding provision dealing with co-operation between European DPAs, Article 28(6), which provided: 'The supervisory authorities shall cooperate with one another to the extent necessary for the performance of their duties, in particular by exchanging all useful information'. Recital 64 DPD explained that 'the authorities in the different Member States will need to assist one another in performing their duties so as to ensure that the rules of protection are properly respected throughout the European Union'.

Under this previous EU framework, supervisory authorities have cooperated by exchanging information and providing assistance on an informal basis in specific cases. However, the practical implementation of Article 28(6) was generally seen as problematic.[3]

Research has shown that 'cooperation among DPAs has been taking place for a long time. This cooperation has been characterized for being irregular, heterogeneous and often based on questions of geographical proximity and trust'.[4]

In practice, the main multilateral forum for EU DPAs to exchange information was the former WP29, now the EDPB, where DPAs and their staff met regularly in the plenary and the working subgroups, in particular the Cooperation and Enforcement subgroups.[5]

DPAs have sometimes established a working group in this context to cooperate on a specific case. For example, following a Facebook statement regarding the amendment of its privacy policy, a working group was set up in March 2015 in the framework of the

---

[1] See the commentary on Art. 60 in this volume.
[2] See the commentary on Art. 56 in this volume.
[3] See WP29 2011.
[4] Papakonstantinou et al. 2016, p. 65.
[5] Established under Art. 25 EDPB Rules of Procedure. Current work of the subgroups can be seen on each meeting agenda of the EDPB.

WP29 composed by five DPAs that decided to investigate the matter (France, Belgium, The Netherlands, Spain and Hamburg).

In addition, the WP29 itself has also set up task forces to investigate certain matters. For example, in February 2012 the WP29 asked the CNIL, the French DPA, to take the lead ad hoc in the examination on behalf of the WP29 of Google's single privacy policy, which was nonetheless adopted on 1 March 2012. This initiative was followed up in 2013 by the constitution of a WP29 task force of 6 DPAs, led by the CNIL, and the launching of national level investigations by DPAs from France, Germany, Italy, the Netherlands, Spain and the UK. These investigations concluded with a number of separate and binding decisions of national DPAs in 2013 and 2014.[6]

In October 2017, the WP29 set up another task force, chaired by ICO in the UK, to take action on the sharing of data by WhatsApp with the Facebook group of companies.[7]

Other European fora for the exchange of experience and information are the European Conference of Data Protection Authorities ('Spring Conference'), the Council of Europe Consultative Committee on the protection of personal data, and regional fora such as the Nordic DPAs. The national DPAs in the Nordic area (Denmark, Sweden, Finland, Norway and Iceland) organise joint Nordic Inspections on an annual basis.[8]

2. International instruments

At present, the cooperation obligations in Convention 108 are limited to an obligation of mutual assistance. Article 13(3)(b) requires designated authorities to 'take, in conformity with … domestic law and for the sole purpose of protection of privacy, all appropriate measures for furnishing factual information relating to specific automatic processing carried out in its territory'. However, Article 17(1)(b) of Modernised Convention 108, once it enters into force, will include in the new Chapter V on Co-operation and mutual assistance the obligation of 'conducting joint actions'.

In the international context,[9] the two most important fora where EU DPAs are able to exchange information and experiences with third party DPAs are the International Conference of Data Protection and Privacy Commissioners ('ICDPPC')[10] and the Global Privacy Enforcement Network ('GPEN').[11] Two documents adopted under the framework of the ICDPPC may be noted: first, the International Standards on the Protection of Personal Data and Privacy, which provided that supervisory authorities should '[c]onduct co-ordinated investigations or interventions, at both national and international level, in

---

[6] Kloza and Moscibroda 2014, pp. 125–127.

[7] See WP29 Letter 2017. See also CNIL Press Release 2017.

[8] See Papakonstantinou et al. 2016, p. 66.

[9] Ibid., pp. 66–67. See also the commentaries on Arts. 50 and 61 in this volume regarding international cooperation.

[10] The purposes of the ICDPPC are, inter alia, to promote and enhance internationally personal data protection, to draft and adopt joint resolutions and to encourage and facilitate cooperation and the exchange of information.

[11] The GPEN was inspired by OECD Recommendation 2007, which called on OECD member economies to 'foster the establishment of an informal network … to discuss the practical aspects of privacy law enforcement co-operation, share best practices … , work to develop shared enforcement priorities, and support joint enforcement initiatives and awareness raising campaigns'. See OECD Recommendation 2007 and GPEN Website.

matters where the interests of two or more authorities are shared';[12] secondly, the Global Cross Border Enforcement Cooperation Arrangement, which included 'Participating in Coordinated Actions' amongst the elements for the coordination of cross border enforcement activities.

C. Analysis

1. Introduction

One of the main objectives of the GDPR is the effective and consistent application and enforcement of the GDPR throughout the EU, in order to protect natural persons in relation to the processing of their personal data and to facilitate the free flow of personal data within the internal market. As a result, the GDPR lays down specific rules to ensure that practical cooperation on cross-border investigations take place.

Article 62 falls within the completely new procedures for cross-border cases in Chapter VII, in particular the cooperation mechanism between supervisory authorities in Section 1, the so-called 'one-stop-shop'. Article 62 establishes a mechanism for joint enforcement operations between EU supervisory authorities, including joint investigations and audits, to reinforce the one-stop-shop cooperation mechanism laid down in Article 60.

It should be considered alongside three other provisions which are aimed at ensuring consistency of application and enforcement under the GDPR: Article 57(1)(g), which requires national DPAs to cooperate with other supervisory authorities, including sharing information and providing mutual assistance;[13] Article 60, which lays down the one-stop-shop cooperation mechanism, and Article 61, which establishes a binding mechanism for mutual assistance between EU supervisory authorities.[14]

In the event that the UK leaves the EU ('Brexit'), the UK Information Commissioner ('ICO') will no longer be the supervisory authority of an EU or EEA/EFTA Member State under Article 4(22) GDPR. As a result, if a UK controller or processor carries out cross-border processing within the EU/EEA, the ICO will no longer be the lead or other supervisory authority under Article 56 GDPR, although of course it will remain the supervisory authority within the UK under UK law, and neither Article 62 nor Article 57(1)(g) will apply. However the ICO has announced that it will continue to cooperate with EU/EEA supervisory authorities, outside the one-stop-shop and the consistency mechanism, regarding any breaches of GDPR that affect individuals in the UK and other EU and EEA states.[15]

In this respect, Article 50(1)(b) GDPR should also be borne in mind, requiring the Commission and supervisory authorities to take appropriate steps to 'provide international mutual assistance in the enforcement of legislation for the protection of personal data, including through notification, complaint referral, investigative assistance and information exchange'.[16]

---

[12] ICDPPC 2009, Art. 2(b). [13] See the commentary on Art. 57 in this volume.
[14] See the commentary on Art. 61 in this volume.
[15] See the ICO guidance in ICO 2018, p. 22.
[16] See the commentary on Art. 50 in this volume.

Under Article 60(2) the lead supervisory authority may conduct joint operations pursuant to Article 61.[17] Article 60(3) requires the lead supervisory authority to communicate the relevant information on the matter without delay to the other supervisory authorities concerned. Such cooperation is essential in the context of cross-border enforcement as each national supervisory authority remains competent to carry out investigations on the territory of its Member State.[18] Article 62 lays down a number of specific instructions. The mechanism is mandatory.

2. Scope and participants

Paragraph 1 provides that supervisory authorities shall, where appropriate, conduct joint operations including joint investigations and joint enforcement measures. It specifies that such operations will involve members or staff of the supervisory authorities of multiple Member States.

Paragraph 2 states that joint operations may take place in cases that involve controllers or processors that are established in several Member States or when processing is likely to substantially affect data subjects in more than one Member State.[19] This corresponds with the definition of cross-border processing in Article 4(23).[20] According to recital 134, any DPA can where appropriate participate in joint operations, as discussed below, but Article 62(2) regulates who has the right to participate in joint operations where the one-stop-shop mechanism applies, namely the supervisory authorities of any Member State concerned.

Paragraph 2 further requires the lead supervisory authority in the case to request the other supervisory authorities concerned to participate in joint operations. Recital 134 notes that the requested supervisory authority should be obliged to respond to the request within a specified time period. The lead supervisory authority must also respond without delay to the request of a supervisory authority to participate.

It is evident that this process will be more demanding the greater the number of DPAs involved, which supports the view that only the DPAs who have the right to be involved are actually invited. However, it would be prudent for the host DPA to be 'generous' with invitations to participate in joint operations, so as to avoid the risk of excluding a potential partner.[21]

3. The actual operation

Paragraph 3 provides that the host DPA may, subject to specific limitations, confer powers, including investigative powers, on the members or staff seconded by the other supervisory authority involved in joint operations, or allow that other DPA's members or staff to exercise their investigative powers.

These elements of joint operations are a delicate matter as they take place within one particular Member State, and paragraph 3 thus provides that it is dependent on the host's

---

[17] The 'lead supervisory authority' is the authority with the primary responsibility for dealing with a cross-border data processing activity. See further the commentaries on Arts. 56 and 60 in this volume.
[18] See Art. 55(1) and rec. 130 GDPR.
[19] On the concept of 'establishment' under the GDPR, see rec. 22 GDPR and EDPB 2018, pp. 5–6. On the notion of processing that 'substantially affects' data subjects in multiple Member States, see WP29 2017, pp. 3–4.
[20] See further the commentary on Art. 4(23) in this volume.
[21] Papakonstantinou et al. 2016, p. 96.

national law whether foreign DPAs may conduct activities on its territory. This may not always be an option.

Similarly, the host DPA may confer powers to the seconding DPAs if this is authorised under its national law. The host authority may even when legally possible authorise the seconding DPA to conduct operations according to their own national law. This will probably not often be the case. In any event, the host DPA must always be present and the seconding DPA's members and staff are subject to the law of the host country.

Research has suggested a number of best practices for joint operations, based on the experience of DPAs. These included developing good communications between DPAs in advance and laying down procedures for regular communication during a joint exercise, using the different legal and technical resources available to different authorities in a complementary manner; ensuring senior management support for teams involved in joint exercises; and limiting requests for assistance to cases of necessity, to reduce the burden on resources of other DPAs.[22]

As indicated, joint operations are challenging with respect to national sovereignty and also for controllers and processors who may be confronted with foreign DPAs. Although the international nature of data processing makes cross-border operations necessary, it remains to be seen whether such investigations and inspections will often take place. The EDPB has reported that, between 25 May 2018 to 31 January 2019, no joint operations had been initiated.[23]

4. Damages and reimbursement

Paragraphs 4–6 address the question of damages caused by officials seconded to the host DPA by the other DPAs involved. Under paragraph 4, when the staff of other DPAs are involved, the host DPA must assume responsibility for their actions, including liability for damages caused by them, under its own national law. Paragraph 5 requires the host DPA to make good any such expenses as if they were caused by its own staff. However, the other DPAs involved must reimburse such payments in full. Finally, paragraph 6 provides that Member States themselves shall refrain from requesting reimbursement from other Member States for such damages.

5. Provisional measures and enforcement

As detailed above, where the one-stop-shop mechanism applies, the lead authority must invite the supervisory authorities of the other Member States concerned to participate in the relevant joint operations, and when it refrains and does not meet this obligation within a month then paragraph 7 authorises the other supervisory authorities to adopt provisional measures on their own territory, pursuant to the normal rule of competence under Article 55(1).

Moreover, whilst the provisions on cooperation in Section 1 are separate to those on consistency in Section 2, both fall under Chapter VII, and the consistency mechanism in Section 2 is designed to serve as an enforcement mechanism for cases of failure to co-operate under Section 1.

Thus, Article 61(8) further provides that such default at the same time triggers the urgency procedure under Article 66(1), including an urgent binding decision by the EDPB

[22] Ibid., pp. 94–96.   [23] EDPB 2019, p. 5.

prescribed under Article 66(2). Accordingly, a DPA is prevented from blocking the operation or making it less efficient.

In addition, when a requested DPA does not comply with its obligations under Article 62, Article 64(2) provides that any DPA can request that the matter be considered by the EDPB with a view to obtaining an opinion. Failure to respect the opinion can then lead to a binding decision by the Board under Articles 64(8) and 65(1)(c).

6. Informal cooperation

Finally, Article 62(1) does not in any way preclude joint operations or investigations by DPAs in a more informal way on the basis of Article 57(1)(g). The one-stop-shop mechanism has indeed the potential to constitute the standard cooperation tool among DPAs, but this should not be to the detriment of other already operating examples of cooperation. It has been argued that, 'while informal cooperation is mostly undocumented, it is nevertheless crucial for DPA cooperation', and that the formal cooperation mechanism under the GDPR 'risks abolishing the cooperation paths already in existence ... which is something that could ultimately harm DPA effectiveness'.[24]

In this respect, Article 62(1) provides that DPAs should conduct joint operations 'where appropriate', which is not limited to cases where the one-stop-shop mechanism applies. A joint operation may be considered to be 'appropriate' to investigate, for example, the data processing operations of a controller with no establishments in the EU, but whose processing operations affect data subjects in multiple Member States.

The wording of Article 57(1)(g), read in conjunction with Article 62, would support this broader approach. It is also supported by recital 138, which explains that in cases where cooperation is not mandatory under the GDPR, 'the cooperation mechanism between the lead supervisory authority and supervisory authorities concerned should be applied and mutual assistance and joint operations might be carried out between the supervisory authorities concerned on a bilateral or multilateral basis without triggering the consistency mechanism'.

Select Bibliography

Academic writings

Kloza and Moscibroda 2014: Kloza and Moscibroda, 'Making the Case for Enhanced Enforcement Cooperation between Data Protection Authorities: Insights from Competition Law', 4(2) *International Data Privacy Law* (2014), 120.

Papers of data protection authorities

ICDPPC 2009: International Conference of Data Protection and Privacy Commissioners, 'Joint Proposal for a Draft of International Standards on the Protection of Privacy with Regard to the processing of Personal Data' (5 November 2009).
ICDPCC 2014: International Conference of Data Protection and Privacy Commissioners, 'Global Cross Border Enforcement Cooperation Arrangement' (14 October 2014).
EDPB 2018: European Data Protection Board, 'Guidelines 3/2018 on the Territorial Scope of the GDPR (Article 3)—Version for Public Consultation' (16 November 2018).

---

[24] Barnard-Wills et al. 2017, p. 38.

EDPB Rules of Procedure: European Data Protection Board, 'Rules of Procedure' (25 May 2018).
EDPB 2019: EDPB, 'First overview on the implementation of the GDPR and the roles and means of the national supervisory authorities' (26 February 2019).
WP29 2011: Article 29 Working Party, 'Advice Paper on the Practical Implementation of the Article 28(6) of the Directive 95/46/EC' (20 April 2011).
WP29 2017: Article 29 Working Party, 'Guidelines for Identifying a Controller or Processor's Lead Supervisory Authority' (WP 244 rev.01, as last revised and adopted on 5 April 2017).
ICO 2018: Information Commissioner's Office, 'Data protection if there's no Brexit deal' (December 2018), available at https://ico.org.uk/media/for-organisations/data-protection-and-brexit/data-protection-if-there-s-no-brexit-deal-1-0.pdf.

Reports and recommendations

Barnard-Wills et al. 2017: Barnard-Wills, Papakonstantinou, Pauner Chulvi and Díaz Lafuente, 'Recommendations for Improving Practical Cooperation between European Data Protection Authorities', Deliverable D4.1 for the PHAEDRA II project (14 January 2017), available at http://www.phaedra-project.eu/wp-content/uploads/PHAEDRA2_D41_final_20170114.pdf.
OECD Recommendation 2007: Organisation for Economic Co-operation and Development, 'Recommendation on Cross-Border Co-Operation in the Enforcement of Laws Protecting Privacy' (2007).
Papakonstantinou et al. 2016: Papakonstantinou, Pauner Chulvi, Cuella and Barnard-Wills, 'European and National Legal Challenges when Applying the New General Data Protection Regulation Provisions on Co-Operation', Deliverable D3.1 for the PHAEDRA II project (15 September 2016), available at http://www.phaedra-project.eu/wp-content/uploads/PHAEDRA2_D31_final_15092016.pdf.

Others

CNIL Press Release 2017: Commission nationale de l'informatique et des libertés, 'Data Transfers from WHATSAPP to FACEBOOK: CNIL Publicly Serves Formal Notice for Lack of Legal Basis' (18 December 2017).
GPEN Website: Global Privacy Enforcement Network, 'Website', available at https://www.privacyenforcement.net/.
WP29 Letter 2017: Article 29 Working Party, 'Letter to Jan Koom Regarding WhatsApp' (24 October 2017).

Section 2 Consistency

Article 63. Consistency mechanism

PATRICK VAN EECKE   ANRIJS ŠIMKUS

In order to contribute to the consistent application of this Regulation throughout the Union, the supervisory authorities shall cooperate with each other and, where relevant, with the Commission, through the consistency mechanism as set out in this Section.

Relevant Recitals

(135) In order to ensure the consistent application of this Regulation throughout the Union, a consistency mechanism for cooperation between the supervisory authorities should be established. That mechanism should in particular apply where a supervisory authority intends to adopt a measure intended to produce legal effects as regards processing operations which substantially affect a significant number of data subjects in several Member States. It should also apply where any supervisory authority concerned or the Commission requests that such matter should be handled in the consistency mechanism. That mechanism should be without prejudice to any measures that the Commission may take in the exercise of its powers under the Treaties.

(138) The application of such mechanism should be a condition for the lawfulness of a measure intended to produce legal effects by a supervisory authority in those cases where its application is mandatory. In other cases of cross-border relevance, the cooperation mechanism between the lead supervisory authority and supervisory authorities concerned should be applied and mutual assistance and joint operations might be carried out between the supervisory authorities concerned on a bilateral or multilateral basis without triggering the consistency mechanism.

Closely Related Provisions

Article 28(8) (Adopting standard contractual clauses in accordance with the consistency mechanism) (see too recital 81); Article 35(6) (Adopting rules on data protection impact assessments in accordance with the consistency mechanism); Article 40(7) (Adopting or modifying draft codes of conduct in accordance with the consistency mechanism); Article 41(3) (Adopting draft criteria for bodies monitoring codes of conduct in accordance with the consistency mechanism); Article 42(5) (Issuing certification in accordance with the consistency mechanism); Article 43(3) (Establishing criteria for certification body accreditation in accordance with the consistency mechanism); Article 46 (Using the consistency mechanism in relation to transfers subject to appropriate safeguards); Article 47 (Approving binding corporate rules in accordance with the consistency mechanism); Article 60(4) (Submitting objections of a lead supervisory authority's draft decision to the consistency mechanism) (see too recitals 124 and 130); Article 64 (Opinion of the Board) (see too recital 136); Article 65 (Dispute Resolution by the Board) (see too recital 136); Article 66 (Urgency Procedure) (see too recital 137); Article 67 (Exchange of Information) (see too recital 168)

Related Provisions in LED [Directive (EU) 2016/680]

Article 41(2) (obligation of supervisory authorities to contribute to the consistent application of the Directive); Article 51 (tasks of the Board to encourage consistent application of the Directive)

Related Provisions in EPD [Directive 2002/58/EC]

Article 4(5) (Obligation to ensure consistency in implementation of measures relating to the security of processing); Article 15a(4) (Obligation of national regulatory authorities to consult the Commission regarding measures of a cross-border nature)

Relevant Case Law

CJEU

Case C-518/07, *European Commission v Federal Republic of Germany*, judgment of 9 March 2010 (Grand Chamber) (ECLI:EU:C:2010:125).
Case C-210/16, *Unabhängiges Landeszentrum für Datenschutz Schleswig-Holstein v Wirtschaftsakademie Schleswig-Holstein GmbH*, judgment of 5 June 2018 (Grand Chamber) (ECLI:EU:C:2018:388).
Case C-25/17, *Proceedings brought by Tietosuojavaltuutettu (Jehovan todistajat)*, judgment of 10 July 2018 (Grand Chamber) (ECLI:EU:C:2018:551).

A. Rationale and Policy Underpinnings

One of the main goals of the GDPR was to solve the problem of having a fragmented system of EU data protection rules, which the DPD had not been able to prevent from happening. One of the preconditions to achieve this goal was to have in place a mechanism which would ensure that every data protection supervisory authority in the EU interprets and applies the provisions and principles of the GDPR in the same way. This would then increase the effectiveness and transparency of the EU data protection system, as well as decrease the administrative and financial burden for both data subjects and companies.

In consequence, a consistency mechanism was introduced in the GDPR. Generally speaking, this mechanism serves two purposes. First, it seeks to ensure that all DPAs interpret and apply the GDPR in a consistent, harmonious and uniform manner. Secondly, it assists in solving disputes which arise either between the DPAs over the course of the one-stop-shop mechanism ('one-stop-shop'), or when a DPA disregards or fails to seek the opinion of the EDPB in those cases where it is required by the consistency mechanism. The important role of ensuring the effectiveness of the consistency mechanism has been assigned to the EDPB.

The consistency mechanism consists of different procedures designed for different scenarios, where issues concerning the consistent interpretation and application of the GDPR would arise. Thus, Article 64 concerns cases where a supervisory authority considers adopting a decision which might substantially affect a significant number of data subjects in several Member States. Article 65 lays down a procedure for resolving disputes, which have arisen either in the course of the one-stop-shop, or when a DPA disregards the procedure laid down in Article 64. Article 66 provides for an urgency procedure, when due to exceptional circumstances a DPA needs to derogate from the one-stop-shop or the consistency mechanisms. Finally, Article 67 provides that the Commission may adopt an implementing act establishing arrangements for information exchange to facilitate cooperation between supervisory authorities and the Board.

These specific procedures will be analysed separately in the commentaries to Articles 64–67 in this volume. The present analysis will focus on the rationale of having a consistency mechanism in the first place, and the potential risks and downsides of this mechanism.

B. Legal Background

1. EU legislation

Article 30(2) DPD provided that the WP29 should 'inform the Commission accordingly' if it found that 'divergences likely to affect the equivalence of protection for persons with regard to the processing of personal data in the Community are arising between the laws or practices of Member States'. However, this provision alone could not be regarded as a proper consistency mechanism.

Instead, the GDPR found the inspiration for its present consistency mechanism in another area of EU law, namely, electronic communications law and, in particular, the provisions concerning the role and tasks of the Body of European Regulators for Electronic Communications ('BEREC').[1] The Regulation establishing BEREC provides for several cases where BEREC, like the EDPB, must be consulted before a national competent authority may adopt a measure, which could substantially affect the functioning of the EU telecom sector.[2]

Another comparable form of consistency mechanism can be found in EU competition law. Regulation 1/2003[3] lays down specific rules on the cooperation between the Commission and Member States' competition authorities through the European Competition Network ('ECN').[4] This particular consistency mechanism also deals with such matters as the obligation to consult on certain decisions before their adoption and the identification of a single national authority to deal with a particular cross-border case. However, the major difference to the GDPR model lies in the role of the Commission. While under the GDPR, the EDPB is an independent and separate entity, whose decisions cannot be influenced by the Commission, in competition matters the ECN does not have separate legal personality and only serves as a forum for better cooperation, and the Commission has a much more authoritative role including binding decision powers. The existence of this model may help to explain the much greater (and much criticised) role envisaged by the Commission in its original proposal for the GDPR.[5]

---

[1] See Hijmans 2016, p. 411. [2] Art. 3 BEREC Regulation.
[3] Council Regulation 1/2003. [4] Galetta et al. 2016, p. 63.
[5] See EDPS 2012, pp. 39–42; and WP29 2012, p. 7. See also the commentary on Art. 69 in this volume.

2. International instruments

The EEA Agreement, as amended in July 2018,[6] incorporates the GDPR into its Annexes and provides that the provisions of the GDPR should be read, for the purposes of that Agreement, with a number of adaptations. In this respect the Agreement provides that, where it is relevant to the exercise of its functions under Article 109 of this Agreement, the EFTA Surveillance Authority shall have the right to request advice or opinions from, and to communicate matters to, the Board pursuant to Article 63 and to that effect provides that the words 'and, where relevant, the EFTA Surveillance Authority' shall be added after the words 'the Commission' in Article 63.[7]

3. National developments

Article 63 does not give any room to Member States for national implementation. However, the practices of the national DPAs will play a role in how it functions.

4. Case law

Article 63 is a novel and unique provision that is not based on previous case law of the CJEU or the ECtHR. However, this does not mean that the case law is not relevant for interpretation of this provision which, in particular, must be compatible with the CJEU case law on DPA independence.[8]

C. Analysis

1. The consistency mechanism's role and scope in creating a uniform EU data protection regime

While the DPD successfully established strong objectives and principles with regard to protection of personal data in the EU, it fell short of achieving the ultimate goal—a transparent and uniform EU system of data protection rules, applied in a consistent manner by all DPAs. This shortcoming was highlighted not only throughout the entire legislative process of the GDPR,[9] but also in several other strategically important documents, such as the Commission's Action Plan implementing the Stockholm Programme,[10] the Digital Agenda for Europe[11] and the EU's growth strategy Europe 2020.[12] The Commission neatly summarised this issue as follows:

> Despite the current Directive's objective to ensure an equivalent level of data protection within the EU, there is still considerable divergence in the rules across Member States ... The result is a fragmented legal environment which has created legal uncertainty and uneven protection for individuals. This has caused unnecessary costs and administrative burdens for businesses and is a disincentive for enterprises operating in the Single Market that may want to expand their operations across borders.[13]

---

[6] EEA Decision 2018.   [7] Ibid., Art. 5e(l).
[8] E.g. Case C-518/07, *Commission v Germany*. See the commentary on Art. 52 in this volume.
[9] GDPR Proposal, p. 2. See also: EC Communication 2010D; EC Communication 2012, p. 2; EESC Opinion 2011.
[10] EC Communication 2010B.   [11] EC Communication 2010C.
[12] EC Communication 2010A.   [13] EC Communication 2012, p. 7.

To solve the issue of a fragmented EU data protection system, the GDPR has introduced two wholly new mechanisms, the one-stop-shop and the consistency mechanism, which together form part and parcel of the broader agenda to unify the EU data protection system. Although contributing to the same goal, both mechanisms do not necessarily achieve identical results.

The one-stop-shop mechanism creates clear rules for DPAs on how to handle cross-border cases in order to improve cooperation and avoid uncertainty for affected data subjects and undertakings. This mechanism does not, however, prevent possible situations where a particular DPA might decide to use its influence or resources to abuse the one-stop-shop, for example, by declaring itself in a given case as the lead supervisory authority and disregarding the objections raised by other DPAs.[14] Nor does the one-stop-shop solve issues with the uniform application of the GDPR when a DPA is acting outside the context of a cross-border case.

Due to these considerations a consistency mechanism was required to address these issues. However, the consistency mechanism appears to be more of a complementary forum for cooperation, which is only to be used in situations where the one-stop-shop cannot effectively ensure that the GDPR will be applied in a uniform manner. Treating the consistency mechanism largely as an exception to the one-stop-shop is logical, as it is consistent with the paramount goal of a speedy and effective EU data protection system. The one-stop-shop mechanism was specifically designed to allow cooperation between DPAs and the handling of cross-border cases to be done in a quicker, simpler and more effective way. However, the consistency mechanism conflicts with the one-stop-shop precisely on this point, as the consistency mechanism prolongs the cooperation process and leaves the parties involved uncertain as to whether the initial approach taken by a DPA in their case will or will not be confirmed later by the EDPB. This view has been taken by other commentators[15] and seems to be supported by the GDPR drafters as well: recital 138 states that in cases where the consistency mechanism is not expressly mandated by the GDPR, the one-stop-shop mechanism 'should be applied and mutual assistance and joint operations might be carried out between the supervisory authorities concerned on a bilateral or multilateral basis without triggering the consistency mechanism'.

Finally, in the event that the UK leaves the EU ('Brexit'), the UK Information Commissioner ('ICO') will no longer be the supervisory authority of an EU or EEA/EFTA Member State under Article 4(22) GDPR and the consistency mechanism will no longer apply to it However the ICO has announced that it will continue to cooperate with EU/EEA supervisory authorities, outside the consistency mechanism regarding any breaches of GDPR that affect individuals in the UK and other EU and EEA states.[16]

2. Triggering the consistency mechanism, and the EDPB's role and powers as the promoter and guardian of consistency

There are three distinct scenarios when a consistency mechanism is triggered. These scenarios are set forth in Articles 64–65, with additional guidance provided in recitals 135–136. First, the consistency mechanism is triggered when a supervisory authority plans to adopt a measure intended to produce legal effects as regards processing operations

---

[14] For a similar view, see: Balboni et al. 2014, p. 396.   [15] Ibid., pp. 394 and 397–398.
[16] See the ICO guidance in ICO 2018, p. 22.

which substantially affect a significant number of data subjects in several Member States.[17] Secondly, the mechanism also applies where any concerned DPA or the Commission[18] requests that any other matter which produces similar effects as in the first scenario should be handled under the consistency mechanism.[19] In both of these scenarios, the EDPB is required to issue an opinion, providing guidance to the concerned DPA on the manner in which to deal with the case at hand, so that consistency is maintained. According to Article 64(7), the DPA concerned must then take the utmost account of this opinion.

The third scenario occurs when the Board either has to resolve a conflict which has arisen in the context of the one-stop-shop, or when the supervisory authority concerned does not request the EDPB to issue an opinion under the first two scenarios, or when that DPA did not follow the Board's opinion.[20] In this scenario the EDPB can issue a decision on how to resolve the aforementioned situations. This decision is legally binding on the supervisory authorities concerned.

Under the consistency mechanism, neither the EDPB's opinions delivered in accordance with Article 64, nor its binding decisions under Article 65 can replace or overturn any measure adopted by a DPA. Furthermore, the GDPR does not regulate situations when a DPA disregards the guidance provided by the EDPB entirely. While this prima facie might lead to think that the EDPB's role is merely advisory, as the DPAs apparently would not face any repercussions by not adhering to the consistency mechanism, such reasoning cannot hold true for two main reasons. First, should a DPA adopt a measure, which does not adhere to the EDPB's opinion, a data subject or undertaking affected by this measure would be able to challenge its lawfulness before a national court and ask for its annulment based on non-compliance of the consistency mechanism. This argument is supported by recital 138, which reads that 'the application of such mechanism should be a condition for the lawfulness of a measure intended to produce legal effects by a supervisory authority in those cases where its application is mandatory'.[21] Secondly, a failure to abide by the provisions of the GDPR, in general, would be grounds for the Commission to start infringement proceedings against the respective DPA's Member State in accordance with Article 258 Treaty on the Functioning of the European Union ('TFEU').

As a result, regardless of how the consistency mechanism is triggered, the EDPB plays a crucial and decisive role in all three scenarios, as it is placed in a highly authoritative position, allowing it to steer any case in the direction it sees as necessary for ensuring consistency. Thus, by providing it with real and effective powers of oversight, the consistency mechanism allows the Board to meaningfully carry out its tasks as the promoter and guardian of consistency.

3. Risks and downsides of the consistency mechanism

3.1 Possible conflict with DPA independence

As described above, the existing consistency mechanism affords the EDPB strong powers to compel any DPA to conform with the required approach determined by the former. However, although this enables the consistency mechanism to achieve the desired result, it risks undermining the independent status of supervisory authorities[22] required by

---

[17] See Art. 64(1) GDPR.
[18] And where relevant the EFTA Surveillance Authority, pursuant to Art. 5e(l) EEA Decision 2018.
[19] See Art. 64(2) GDPR.   [20] See ibid., Art. 65(1).   [21] Ibid., rec. 138.
[22] See the discussion of the case law of the CJEU in the commentary on Art. 69 in this volume.

Article 52 GDPR.[23] This is because any case brought within the scope of the consistency mechanism is no longer independently decided by the DPA, but by the EDPB, as the former is obliged to 'voluntarily' accept the latter's approach.

There are, of course, several counter-arguments to support the position that the EDPB does not interfere with the independent status of supervisory authorities. Several of these arguments relate to the structure and powers of the Board. First, the EDPB itself is composed of DPA representatives, thus ultimately giving them control over the Board. Secondly, the EDPB is not a higher judicial body which can overturn DPA decisions: a DPA can always stand its ground against the EDPB and force the dispute to be resolved before national courts and ultimately before the CJEU. Thirdly, independence in this context is not a right but rather a privilege of the DPAs. This means that independence is granted to a DPA not for itself alone but so that it can effectively fulfil its tasks and ensure respect for data subjects' rights. Thus, so long as the EDPB and the consistency mechanism assist supervisory authorities in achieving such objectives, this should not be considered as hindering DPA independence. These arguments are discussed in more detail in the commentary in this volume on the EDPB's independence under Article 69 GDPR.

3.2 The mechanism does not cover exclusively internal DPA decisions

In addition to the issue of maintaining a balance between the efficiency of the consistency mechanism and DPA independence, it is also worth recalling that the mechanism itself has been limited to certain exceptional situations, as described previously. The limited scope of the consistency mechanism was one of the main ways to avoid overly affecting DPA independence.[24]

The common denominator for all the situations which trigger the consistency mechanism is that a DPA measure must produce legal effects in, or otherwise concern, more than one Member State. This means that the consistency mechanism does not apply where a particular measure creates legal effects only within a single Member State.

Such limitations are natural, given that the GDPR in general leaves several areas of competence to Member States' discretion. Many of these can be found in Chapter IX GDPR,[25] which includes specific rules on processing personal data within the context of freedom of expression, public access to official documents, national identification numbers, employment and various research purposes. This nevertheless means that rules adopted in these areas will not be harmonised (though they must not detract from the EU level of protection under the GDPR), and anyone operating in these areas in several Member States will not necessarily be able to use a single global formula to ensure compliance with such rules.[26]

3.3. The risk of lowering GDPR standards to accommodate consistency

The DPD created a system with differing data protection standards around the EU. While some DPAs adopted a stringent interpretation of data protection rules, others took a more flexible approach. As the GDPR is applied by these authorities, the inevitable differences of opinion on the best approach to follow will arise. Having been

---

[23] Hijmans 2016, p. 386.   [24] See WP29 2012, p. 20.
[25] Arts. 85–91 Chapter IX GDPR.   [26] Tene and Wolf 2013, p. 9.

charged with resolving such issues, the EDPB will have to find a fair balance between fundamental rights and the single market, whereby the GDPR is applied in a way which not only guarantees the effective protection of data subjects' rights but also does not inhibit market players and deter economic growth. Furthermore, the EDPB will have to take into account the actual capabilities and resources of national supervisory authorities, as not all of them may be able to uphold very high standards. Thus, in order to avoid interpreting the GDPR to impose standards which are difficult for some DPAs to apply, there is a possibility that the EDPB might opt for a 'golden mean' to accommodate a consistent application which would oblige other DPAs to lower previously adopted higher standards. This risk that national standards could be lowered was raised in some Member States (such as Germany[27]) when the GDPR was first proposed. As Giurgiu and Larsen argue:

> The aim of the Regulation to create the same level of data protection all over the EU through the direct applicability of the GDPR with the strong position of the EDPB might also raise issues of a possible race 'towards' the bottom. This could especially be the case for countries with a strong data protection culture forced to succumb to perhaps more moderate opinions of the EDPB that would ensure consistency at the cost of having a lower level or protection. This might be the price that will have to be paid for harmonisation through a regulation instead of having a directive which allows more flexibility in its transposition by Member States.[28]

However, any such interpretation by the Board would need, none the less, to ensure the 'effective and complete protection' of the data subjects concerned.[29]

4. Conclusions

The new consistency mechanism appears to be well suited to ensure that the GDPR is applied in a uniform manner throughout the whole EU. In those cases where this mechanism is triggered, any DPA facing scrutiny from the EDPB will have to either align its decision to match the latter's preferences or risk the consequences. These may include the DPA decision being annulled before a national court or even infringement proceedings brought by the Commission against the Member State concerned for non-compliance with the GDPR.

Although the consistency mechanism has been carefully designed, it still has certain flaws which could potentially prevent it from achieving complete uniformity in all Member States. How these flaws will be addressed by supervisory authorities and the Board remains to be seen.

Select Bibliography

International agreements

EEA Agreement: Agreement on the European Economic Area, OJ 1994 L 1/3.
EEA Decision 2018: Decision of the EEA Joint Committee No. 154/2018 of 6 July 2018 amending Annex XI (Electronic communication, audiovisual services and information society) and Protocol 37 (containing the list provided for in Article 101) to the EEA Agreement [2018/1022], OJ 2018 L 183/23.

---

[27] See Masing 2012.   [28] Giurgiu and Larsen 2016, p. 351.
[29] Case C-25/17, *Jehovan todistajat*, para. 66. See also Case C-210/16, *Wirtschaftsakademie*, para. 42.

EU legislation

BEREC Regulation: Regulation (EC) No. 1211/2009 of the European Parliament and of the Council of 25 November 2009 establishing the Body of European Regulators for Electronic Communications (BEREC) and the Office, OJ 2009 L 337/1.

Council Regulation 1/2003: Council Regulation (EC) No. 1/2003 of 16 December 2002 on the implementation of the rules on competition laid down in Articles 81 and 82 of the Treaty, OJ 2003 L 1/1.

GDPR Proposal: Proposal for a Regulation of the European Parliament and of the Council on the protection of individuals with regard to the processing of personal data and on the free movement of such data (General Data Protection Regulation), COM(2012) 11 final, 25 January 2012.

Academic writings

Balboni et al. 2014: Balboni, Pelino and Scudiero, 'Rethinking the One-Stop-Shop Mechanism: Legal Certainty and Legitimate Expectation' 30 *Computer Law & Security Review* (2014), 392.

Giurgiu and Larsen 2016: Giurgiu and Larsen, 'Roles and Powers of National Data Protection Authorities' 2(3) *European Data Protection Law Review* (2016), 342.

Hijmans 2016: Hijmans, *The European Union as Guardian of Internet Privacy* (Springer 2016).

Masing 2012: Masing, 'Herausforderungen des Datenschutzes', 32 *Neue Juristische Wochenschrift* (2012), 2305.

Tene and Wolf 2013: Tene and Wolf, 'Overextended: Jurisdiction and Applicable Law under the EU General Data Protection Regulation' *Future of Privacy Forum White Paper* (January 2013).

Papers of data protection authorities

EDPS 2012: European Data Protection Supervisor, 'Opinion on the Data Protection Reform Package' (March 2012).

WP29 2012: Article 29 Working Party, 'Opinion 01/2012 on the Data Protection Reform Proposals' (WP 191, 23 March 2012).

ICO 2018: Information Commissioner's Office, 'Data protection if there's no Brexit deal' (December 2018), available at https://ico.org.uk/media/for-organisations/data-protection-and-brexit/data-protection-if-there-s-no-brexit-deal-1-0.pdf.

Reports and recommendations

EC Communication 2010A: EUROPE 2020: A strategy for smart, sustainable and inclusive growth, COM(2010)2020 final, 3 March 2010.

EC Communication 2010B: Communication from the Commission to the European Parliament, the Council, the European Economic and Social Committee and the Committee of the Regions of 20 April 2010—Delivering an area of freedom, security and justice for Europe's citizens—Action Plan Implementing the Stockholm Programme, COM(2010) 171 final, 20 April 2010.

EC Communication 2010C: Communication from the Commission to the European Parliament, the Council, the European Economic and Social Committee and the Committee of the Regions: A Digital Agenda for Europe, COM(2010)245 final, 19 May 2010.

EC Communication 2010D: Communication from the Commission to the European Parliament, the Council, the Economic and Social Committee and the Committee of the Regions: A comprehensive approach on personal data protection in the European Union, COM(2010)609 final, 4 November 2010.

EC Communication 2012: Communication from the Commission to the European Parliament, the Council, the European Economic and Social Committee and the Committee of the Regions: Safeguarding Privacy in a Connected World A European Data Protection Framework for the 21st Century, COM/2012/09 final, 25 January 2012.

EESC Opinion 2011: Opinion of the European Economic and Social Committee on the Communication from the Commission to the European Parliament, the Council, the European Economic and Social Committee and the Committee of the Regions—Tackling the challenges in commodity markets and on raw materials, OJ 2011 C 318/76, 29 October 2011.

Galetta et al. 2016: Galetta, Kloza and de Hert, 'Cooperation among Data Privacy Supervisory Authorities by Analogy: Lessons from Parallel European Mechanisms', Deliverable D2.1 for the PHAEDRA II project (16 April 2016), available at http://www.phaedra-project.eu/wp-content/uploads/PHAEDRA2_D21_final_20160416.pdf.

Article 64. Opinion of the Board

PATRICK VAN EECKE   ANRIJS ŠIMKUS

1. The Board shall issue an opinion where a competent supervisory authority intends to adopt any of the measures below. To that end, the competent supervisory authority shall communicate the draft decision to the Board, when it:
   (a) aims to adopt a list of the processing operations subject to the requirement for a data protection impact assessment pursuant to Article 35(4);
   (b) concerns a matter pursuant to Article 40(7) whether a draft code of conduct or an amendment or extension to a code of conduct complies with this Regulation;
   (c) aims to approve the requirements for accreditation of a body pursuant to Article 41(3), of a certification body pursuant to Article 43(3) or the criteria for certification referred to in Article 42(5);[1]
   (d) aims to determine standard data protection clauses referred to in point (d) of Article 46(2) and in Article 28(8);
   (e) aims to authorise contractual clauses referred to in point (a) of Article 46(3); or
   (f) aims to approve binding corporate rules within the meaning of Article 47.
2. Any supervisory authority, the Chair of the Board or the Commission may request that any matter of general application or producing effects in more than one Member State be examined by the Board with a view to obtaining an opinion, in particular where a competent supervisory authority does not comply with the obligations for mutual assistance in accordance with Article 61 or for joint operations in accordance with Article 62.
3. In the cases referred to in paragraphs 1 and 2, the Board shall issue an opinion on the matter submitted to it provided that it has not already issued an opinion on the same matter. That opinion shall be adopted within eight weeks by simple majority of the members of the Board. That period may be extended by a further six weeks, taking into account the complexity of the subject matter. Regarding the draft decision referred to in paragraph 1 circulated to the members of the Board in accordance with paragraph 5, a member which has not objected within a reasonable period indicated by the Chair, shall be deemed to be in agreement with the draft decision.
4. Supervisory authorities and the Commission shall, without undue delay, communicate by electronic means to the Board, using a standardised format any relevant information, including as the case may be a summary of the facts, the draft decision, the grounds which make the enactment of such measure necessary, and the views of other supervisory authorities concerned.
5. The Chair of the Board shall, without undue, delay inform by electronic means:
   (a) the members of the Board and the Commission of any relevant information which has been communicated to it using a standardised format. The secretariat of the Board shall, where necessary, provide translations of relevant information; and
   (b) the supervisory authority referred to, as the case may be, in paragraphs 1 and 2, and the Commission of the opinion and make it public.
6. The competent supervisory authority referred to in paragraph 1 shall not adopt its draft decision referred to in paragraph 1 within the period referred to in paragraph 3.[2]

---

[1] Corrigenda to the English text of Art. 64(1)(c) were published on 23 May 2018. The text printed reflects the updated version of the Corrigendum GDPR 2018. For the Corrigendum GDPR 2018, see Table of Legislation.

[2] Corrigenda to the English text of Art. 64(6) were published on 23 May 2018. The text printed reflects the updated version of the Corrigendum GDPR 2018.

7. The competent supervisory authority referred to in paragraph 1 shall take utmost account of the opinion of the Board and shall, within two weeks after receiving the opinion, communicate to the Chair of the Board by electronic means whether it will maintain or amend its draft decision and, if any, the amended draft decision, using a standardised format.[3]
8. Where the competent supervisory authority referred to in paragraph 1 informs the Chair of the Board within the period referred to in paragraph 7 of this Article that it does not intend to follow the opinion of the Board, in whole or in part, providing the relevant grounds, Article 65(1) shall apply.[4]

Relevant Recitals

(135) In order to ensure the consistent application of this Regulation throughout the Union, a consistency mechanism for cooperation between the supervisory authorities should be established. That mechanism should in particular apply where a supervisory authority intends to adopt a measure intended to produce legal effects as regards processing operations which substantially affect a significant number of data subjects in several Member States. It should also apply where any supervisory authority concerned or the Commission requests that such matter should be handled in the consistency mechanism. That mechanism should be without prejudice to any measures that the Commission may take in the exercise of its powers under the Treaties.

(136) In applying the consistency mechanism, the Board should, within a determined period of time, issue an opinion, if a majority of its members so decides or if so requested by any supervisory authority concerned or the Commission. The Board should also be empowered to adopt legally binding decisions where there are disputes between supervisory authorities. For that purpose, it should issue, in principle by a two-thirds majority of its members, legally binding decisions in clearly specified cases where there are conflicting views among supervisory authorities, in particular in the cooperation mechanism between the lead supervisory authority and supervisory authorities concerned on the merits of the case, in particular whether there is an infringement of this Regulation.

(138) The application of such mechanism should be a condition for the lawfulness of a measure intended to produce legal effects by a supervisory authority in those cases where its application is mandatory. In other cases of cross- border relevance, the cooperation mechanism between the lead supervisory authority and supervisory authorities concerned should be applied and mutual assistance and joint operations might be carried out between the supervisory authorities concerned on a bilateral or multilateral basis without triggering the consistency mechanism.

Closely Related Provisions

Article 61 (Mutual assistance) (see too recitals 123 and 133); Article 62 (Joint operations of supervisory authorities) (see too recital 134); Article 63 (Aim of consistency mechanism); Article 65 (Procedure for the consistency mechanism where Article 64 is not complied with); Article 67 (Information exchange arrangements for the standardised format under Article 64(4)); Article 70(1) (Tasks of the Board) (see too recitals 136 and 139)

---

[3] Corrigenda to the English text of Art. 64(7) were published on 23 May 2018. The text printed reflects the updated version of the Corrigendum GDPR 2018.

[4] Corrigenda to the English text of Art. 64(8) were published on 23 May 2018. The text printed reflects the updated version of the Corrigendum GDPR 2018.

Van Eecke/Šimkus

Relevant Case Law

CJEU

Case C-518/07, *European Commission v Federal Republic of Germany*, judgment of 9 March 2010 (Grand Chamber) (ECLI:EU:C:2010:125).

A. Rationale and Policy Underpinnings

Article 64 GDPR establishes a precise procedure for carrying out the consistency mechanism in situations when a supervisory authority intends to adopt a measure 'intended to produce legal effects as regards processing operations which substantially affect a significant number of data subjects in several Member States'.[5] Article 64(1) lays down a list of concrete measures, which have to be subjected to the consistency mechanism before they can be adopted by a DPA, while Article 64(2) allows any other unspecified matter of general application or producing effects in more than one Member State, provided that the applicable criteria are met. In both scenarios the EDPB shall deliver an opinion on the matter at hand. Finally, paragraphs 3–8 of Article 64 contain both procedural rules on how an EDPB opinion is issued and substantive rules on the intended consequences of the opinion and, more generally, on the consistency mechanism as a whole.

B. Legal Background

1. EU legislation

The DPD did not oblige the DPAs to consult any central authority before adopting a particular measure. The WP29, unlike its successor, did not have any review powers. As a result, any form of review of DPA measures in the pre-GDPR era could only have been done post factum by national courts or, in due course, the CJEU.

The consistency mechanism, and in particular, the procedure laid down in Article 64 GDPR was primarily inspired by the EU telecommunications sector and its main supervisory authority, the Body of European Regulators for Electronic Communications ('BEREC').[6] All Member State national regulatory authorities ('NRAs') must consult the BEREC before adopting a measure which could substantially affect the functioning of the EU telecoms sector. These measures are laid down in Article 3 of the BEREC Regulation and mostly concern situations where a NRA exercises its powers under one of the EU laws forming the telecoms sector.[7] In those situations the BEREC must also issue an opinion, and the NRA, to whom this opinion is addressed, must take the utmost account of it.[8]

2. International instruments

The EEA Agreement, as amended in July 2018,[9] incorporates the GDPR into its Annexes and provides that the provisions of the GDPR should be read, for the purposes of that Agreement, with a number of adaptations. In this respect the Agreement provides that,

---

[5] Rec. 135 GDPR [6] See Hijmans 2016, pp. 408–412. [7] Art. 3(1) BEREC Regulation.
[8] Ibid., Art. 3(3). [9] EEA Decision 2018.

where it is relevant to the exercise of its functions under Article 109 of this Agreement, the EFTA Surveillance Authority shall have the right to request advice or opinions from, and to communicate matters to, the Board pursuant to Article 64(2) and to that effect provides that the words 'and, where relevant, the EFTA Surveillance Authority' shall be added after the words 'the Commission' in Article 64(2).[10]

3. National developments

Article 64 does not give any room to Member States for national implementation. However, the practices of the national DPAs will play a role in how it functions, for example, with regard to the adoption of a draft decision by the competent supervisory authority (Article 64(6) and its obligation to take the utmost account of the Board's opinion (Article 64(7).

4. Case law

Article 64 is a novel and unique provision that is not based on previous case law of the CJEU or the ECtHR. However, this does not mean that the case law is not relevant for interpretation of this provision which, in particular, must be compatible with the CJEU case law on DPA independence.[11]

C. Analysis

1. Two consistency mechanism triggering scenarios

Article 64 deals with two distinct scenarios where the procedure for the consistency mechanism will be triggered. The first scenario relates to an exhaustive list of measures explicitly provided for in the GDPR, whereas the second scenario acts as a catch-all for cases which are not defined in any of the Articles in the GDPR but which could produce effects equal to those occurring in the first scenario.

In the first scenario the consistency mechanism is triggered if a DPA plans to adopt one of six concrete measures provided for in the first paragraph of Article 64. These measures are: adopting a list of the processing operations subject to the requirement for a data protection impact assessment;[12] ruling on a draft code of conduct's compliance with the GDPR;[13] approving requirements for accreditation bodies, certification bodies or the criteria for certification;[14] determining standard data protection clauses;[15] authorising contractual clauses;[16] approving binding corporate rules.[17] In these situations, a DPA must communicate its draft decision to the EDPB, and the latter must issue an opinion on it.

The second scenario is set forth in the second paragraph of Article 64. This complements the exhaustive list laid down in the first paragraph, as it allows any other matter which is not listed in paragraph 1 but which nevertheless is of general application or producing effects in more than one Member State, to be subjected to the consistency

---

[10] Ibid., Art. 5e(l).
[11] E.g. Case C-518/07, *Commission v Germany*. See the commentaries on Arts. 52 and 69 in this volume.
[12] Art. 64(1)(a); see also Art. 35(4) GDPR.   [13] Ibid., Art. 64(1)(b); see also Art. 40(7).
[14] Ibid., Art. 64(1)(c); see also Arts. 41(3), 42(5), 43(3).
[15] Ibid., Art. 64(1)(d); see also Arts. 28(8) and 46(2)(d).
[16] Ibid., Art. 64(1)(e); see also Art. 46(3)(a).   [17] Ibid., Art. 64(1)(f); see also Art. 47.

mechanism. Such matters can be brought before the Board by any DPA, the Chair (in effect, the Board itself), the Commission and, where relevant, the EFTA Surveillance Authority.[18] Paragraph 2 provides further guidance by stating that this scenario should apply in particular where a DPA does not comply with the obligations for mutual assistance in accordance with Article 61 or for joint operations in accordance with Article 62. The EDPB Rules of Procedure add that the request for an opinion pursuant to Article 64(2) must be reasoned and the EDPB may without undue delay and within a deadline set by the Chair decide not to issue an opinion if the applicable criteria are not met.[19]

The Board reported in February 2019[20] that 34 opinions had been adopted or were being prepared under these scenarios, concerning national lists of processing subject to a DPIA, binding corporate rules, a draft standard contract between Controllers and Processors (first scenario), together with an administrative arrangement for the transfer of personal data between financial supervisory authorities and the interplay between the GDPR and the EPD, in particular as regards the competence of the national data protection supervisory authorities (second scenario).

Finally, in the event that the UK leaves the EU ('Brexit'), the UK Information Commissioner ('ICO') will no longer be the supervisory authority of an EU or EEA/EFTA Member State under Article 4(22) GDPR and thus will no longer be subject to the consistency mechanism.

2. Procedure for issuing an opinion

When the consistency mechanism is triggered under one of the above two scenarios, the Board will have to issue an opinion in the matter at hand. The draft opinion is prepared and drafted by the EDPB secretariat, and then presented for approval to the Board. If necessary, the Chair can invite a rapporteur and expert subgroups to assist with the preparation of the draft opinion.[21] Paragraph 3 of Article 64 lays down three elements which this procedure must entail.

First, paragraph 3 limits this procedure to those cases where the Board has not already issued an opinion on the same matter. The EDPB Rules of Procedure further clarify that the EDPB may decide not to issue an opinion pursuant to Article 64(1) or (2), if the criteria have not been met or another opinion on the same matter may have already been issued.[22] This decision must be taken without undue delay and within a deadline set by the Chair.[23]

Secondly, the opinion of the EDPB must be adopted by a simple majority of its members. The final sentence of paragraph 3 provides that this majority can be obtained tacitly. The Chair is to indicate a reasonable amount of time for members to comment on a draft DPA decision up for consideration, and a member that does not respond within the time limit is presumed to be in agreement with the draft DPA decision. The EDPB Rules of Procedure add that the time limit must be clearly defined by the Chair when the case is initiated.[24]

---

[18] Art. 5e(l) EEA Decision 2018. With regard to the role of the Commission and the independence of the EDPB, see the commentary on Art. 69 in this volume. Under Art. 64(2) GDPR the role of the Commission is limited to requesting that a matter be examined by the Board.
[19] Art. 10(3) EDPB Rules of Procedure.   [20] EDPB 2019, p.6   [21] Ibid., Art. 10(5).
[22] Ibid., Art. 10(4).   [23] Ibid.   [24] Ibid., Art. 10(1).

Thirdly, the opinion must be adopted within no more than 14 weeks—that is, within an initial time limit of eight weeks which can be extended for an additional six weeks, given the complexity of the case. Again, the EDPB Rules of Procedure contain two important clarifications concerning this time-limit rule. First, the initial eight-week time-limit will start to run only when the Chair, as well as the authority concerned responsible for triggering the consistency mechanism (a DPA or the Commission), have decided that the case file is complete, i.e. that all relevant documents have been submitted to the Chair.[25] Secondly, the eight-week time-limit can be extended by the further amount of six weeks either by the EDPB Chair's own initiative, or at the request of one-third of the members of the Board.[26]

3. Cooperation and information sharing

Article 64 paragraphs 4 and 5 lay down specific information sharing rules and obligations. Thus, Article 64(4) provides that any concerned DPA and the Commission shall communicate by electronic means to the EDPB any relevant information, which is needed in order for the EDPB to adopt an opinion in a given case. The paragraph mentions in a non-exhaustive manner that such information can include a summary of the facts, the draft decision of the relevant DPA, the grounds which make the enactment of the DPA's measure necessary and the views of other DPAs concerned. According to the EDPB Rules of Procedure, all documents have to be sent to the Board's secretariat via the designated IT system.[27] Furthermore, the secretariat of the EDPB should pre-check if all the documents are complete, and it may request the concerned DPA to provide within a specific timeframe additional information, which is needed for the file to be complete.[28] It should be noted in this respect that DPAs are expected to transmit to the Board fully formed draft decisions, and not merely questions, since the consistency mechanism has been envisaged as a resolution and not as a consulting mechanism.[29]

Article 64(4) further requires that the aforementioned information should be sent to the EDPB in a standardised format. In this regard, Article 67 GDPR grants the Commission the power to adopt an implementing act, with which any such standardised format could be created. When this text was finalised the Board and DPAs were using the Internal Market Information ('IMI') electronic system for information exchange, discussed in the commentary to Article 67 in this volume, and the Commission had not yet exercised its powers under Article 67. For the time being it can be presumed that all information exchange arrangements between the involved parties will be coordinated based on the IMI system and the discretionary powers and instructions of the EDPB.

Article 64(5) establishes additional rules on cooperation and information sharing by requiring the Chair of the EDPB, first, to communicate any relevant information received pursuant to Article 64(4) to the members of the EDPB and to the Commission[30]; secondly, to communicate the adopted opinion to the respective DPA and the Commission; and thirdly, to make the adopted opinion available to the public. Article 64(5) also provides that, where necessary, translations of relevant information will be provided by the secretariat of the EDPB.[31]

---

[25] Ibid., Arts. 10(1)–(2) and (4). [26] Ibid., Arts. 10(2) and (4). [27] Ibid., Art. 10(1).
[28] Ibid. [29] Papakonstantinou et al. 2016, p. 15.
[30] See also Art. 10(1) EDPB Rules of Procedure. [31] Ibid.

4. Effects and consequences of the Article 64 procedure

Article 64(6)–(8) establish certain legal effects, which come about, when the consistency mechanism is triggered in accordance with this Article. First, Article 64(6) suspends the adoption of the intended draft DPA decision, due to which the consistency mechanism was triggered, until an opinion by the EDPB in the matter has been given. Secondly, Article 64(7) requires that the concerned DPA must take the utmost consideration of the EDPB opinion.

Thirdly, Article 64(7) also requires the concerned DPA to inform the EDPB within two weeks from receiving the latter's opinion whether it intends to amend or maintain its draft decision. While the GDPR itself places no obligation for DPAs to motivate their decision not to adhere to the EDPB's opinion, the latter nevertheless expects this to happen. In its first batch of opinions concerning DPAs' data protection impact assessment lists, the Board noted in the final remarks section that in such situations the concerned DPA 'shall provide the relevant grounds for which it does not intend to follow this opinion, in whole or in part'.[32]

In this respect it should be noted that Article 41 of the Charter of Fundamental Rights of the European Union (Charter) enshrines the fundamental right to good administration, including the obligation of the administration under Article 41(2)(c) to give reasons for its decisions. Whilst DPAs are not EU bodies, they have a unique position under EU primary law, having been enshrined in Article 16(2) Treaty on the Functioning of the European Union ('TFEU') and Article 8(3) of the Charter, and it has been argued that they are 'hybrid' bodies with an EU function as well as a national constitutional role, and thus may be regarded as subject to the rights and obligations under the Charter, including Article 41 addressed to the EU administration.[33]

Fourthly, and finally, in the case that the concerned DPA does not follow the EDPB's opinion, then Article 64(8) provides that any further resolution of this dispute must be resolved in accordance with the Article 65 procedure, where the EDPB can then adopt a binding decision in the matter.

The set-up described above places the EDPB in a highly authoritative and powerful position to ensure one of its main objectives—a uniform and consistent application of the GDPR by the DPAs. Thus, even if the opinions issued by it under the Article 64 procedure are not legally binding, a DPA not willing to adhere to such an opinion will have to provide relevant and sufficient reasons for its disobedience, and in any event, prepare for the dispute settlement procedure under Article 65, and possibly even litigation before national courts and the CJEU. Due to these considerations, some even argue that the EDPB's opinion is likely to result in the creation of legal rules of a general nature, applicable *erga omnes*, within their territorial scope.[34]

5. A risk of overextending the consistency mechanism

Overall, Article 64 lays down a very clear and straightforward procedure on how the consistency mechanism should function. Thus, the few issues and uncertainty surrounding Article 64 comes not from the procedure and effects of Article 64, but from its scope and, more concretely, the scope of Article 64(2).

---

[32] See, among the other similar opinions, EDPB 2018.   [33] Hijmans 2016, pp. 327–328.
[34] Barnard-Wills et al. 2017, p. 37.

As already described, Article 64(2) allows any DPA, regardless of competence, the Commission[35] and the Chair of the Board to request that any matter of general application or producing effects in more than one Member State be examined by the Board with a view to obtaining an opinion. At first, this paragraph appears to allow all of these actors to bring an endless amount of potential cases to be examined within the consistency mechanism. While such an interpretation would theoretically assist the EDPB to reach its goal of a uniform application of the GDPR by all DPAs, it could also prove counter-productive, as the numerous requests for opinions would overburden the EDPB and render it dysfunctional and inefficient.

In light of the above, a better approach in this respect would be to interpret Article 64(2) in the light of the practical goal of the consistency mechanism, i.e. to solve disputes between DPAs which arise from the application of the GDPR. It could be argued that alongside the two criteria mentioned in Article 64(2)—a matter of general applicability and a cross-border element—a third criterion could be that the matter at hand also has to stem from an existing dispute between two or more DPAs. The stress on Articles 61 and 62 in Article 64(2) support this argument, as a DPA's unwillingness to respond to a request for mutual assistance or to participate in joint operations naturally creates a conflict with the DPA making such a request.[36] This also fits well with the idea that Article 64(2) should be used as the first avenue for solving all potential disputes arising from the one-stop-shop which are not related to those issues expressly regulated under Article 65(1). Indeed, since there are no similar open-ended provisions in Article 65, Article 64(2) is the only way such a dispute can be examined under the consistency mechanism.

This approach, which would exclude in principle all other matters not originating from a dispute would not prevent the EDPB from having its say on them. Of course, the Board may always decide that in a specific urgent case it would be appropriate to use the mechanism under Article 64(2). In other cases, the Board may use its powers under Article 70(1)(e) to issue guidelines, recommendations and best practices on any question covering the application of the GDPR in order to encourage its consistent application.

With this approach the consistency mechanism would be concentrated on the more urgent cases which require a clearly defined procedure for obtaining a fast and enforceable solution. In other cases which are not time-sensitive, the EDPB has the option to handle such cases without triggering the consistency mechanism and avoid the strict deadlines mandated by that mechanism. This should be to the benefit of all, as the EDPB would not be overrun by a landslide of requests for an opinion, and DPAs would encounter less situations where their independence and sovereignty could arguably be undermined due to the intrusive nature of the consistency mechanism.

At this moment the consistency mechanism has not yet been properly tested, so it is premature to make definite conclusions on whether the interpretation of Article 64(2) suggested above would be adopted by the EDPB in its practice. In any event, however, the Board will have to find a good balance between submitting enough cases to the consistency mechanism to ensure greater uniformity whilst at the same time limiting the number of such cases in order to avoid overextending the mechanism and thereby rendering it ineffective.

---

[35] And, where relevant, the EFTA Surveillance Authority, per Art. 5e(l) EEA Decision 2018.
[36] See Papakonstantinou et al. 2016, p.14.

Select Bibliography

International agreements

EEA Agreement: Agreement on the European Economic Area, OJ 1994 L 1/3.
EEA Decision 2018: Decision of the EEA Joint Committee No. 154/2018 of 6 July 2018 amending Annex XI (Electronic communication, audiovisual services and information society) and Protocol 37 (containing the list provided for in Article 101) to the EEA Agreement [2018/1022], OJ 2018 L 183/23.

EU legislation

BEREC Regulation: Regulation (EC) No. 1211/2009 of the European Parliament and of the Council of 25 November 2009 establishing the Body of European Regulators for Electronic Communications (BEREC) and the Office, OJ 2009 L 337/1.

Academic writings

Hijmans 2016: Hijmans, *The European Union as Guardian of Internet Privacy* (Springer 2016).

Papers of data protection authorities

EDPB 2018: European Data Protection Board, 'Opinion 2/2018 on the Draft List of the Competent Supervisory Authority of Belgium Regarding the Processing Operations Subject to the Requirement of a Data Protection Impact Assessment (Article 35.4 GDPR)' (25 September 2018).
EDPB 2019: European Data Protection Board, 'First overview on the implementation of the GDPR and the roles and means of the national supervisory authorities' (26 February 2019).
EDPB Rules of Procedure: European Data Protection Board, 'Rules of Procedure' (25 May 2018).

Reports and recommendations

Barnard-Wills et al. 2017: Barnard-Wills, Papakonstantinou, Pauner Chulvi and Díaz Lafuente, 'Recommendations for Improving Practical Cooperation between European Data Protection Authorities', Deliverable D4.1 for the PHAEDRA II project (14 January 2017), available at http://www.phaedra-project.eu/wp-content/uploads/PHAEDRA2_D41_final_20170114.pdf.
Papakonstantinou et al. 2016: Papakonstantinou, Pauner Chulvi, Cuella and Barnard-Wills, 'European and National Legal Challenges when Applying the New General Data Protection Regulation Provisions on Co-Operation', Deliverable D3.1 for the PHAEDRA II project (15 September 2016), available at http://www.phaedra-project.eu/wp-content/uploads/PHAEDRA2_D31_final_15092016.pdf.

Article 65. Dispute resolution by the Board

HIELKE HIJMANS[*]

1. In order to ensure the correct and consistent application of this Regulation in individual cases, the Board shall adopt a binding decision in the following cases:
    (a) where, in a case referred to in Article 60(4), a supervisory authority concerned has raised a relevant and reasoned objection to a draft decision of the lead supervisory authority and the lead supervisory authority has not followed the objection or has rejected such an objection as being not relevant or reasoned. The binding decision shall concern all the matters which are the subject of the relevant and reasoned objection, in particular whether there is an infringement of this Regulation;[1]
    (b) where there are conflicting views on which of the supervisory authorities concerned is competent for the main establishment;
    (c) where a competent supervisory authority does not request the opinion of the Board in the cases referred to in Article 64(1), or does not follow the opinion of the Board issued under Article 64. In that case, any supervisory authority concerned or the Commission may communicate the matter to the Board.
2. The decision referred to in paragraph 1 shall be adopted within one month from the referral of the subject-matter by a two-thirds majority of the members of the Board. That period may be extended by a further month on account of the complexity of the subject-matter. The decision referred to in paragraph 1 shall be reasoned and addressed to the lead supervisory authority and all the supervisory authorities concerned and binding on them.
3. Where the Board has been unable to adopt a decision within the periods referred to in paragraph 2, it shall adopt its decision within two weeks following the expiration of the second month referred to in paragraph 2 by a simple majority of the members of the Board. Where the members of the Board are split, the decision shall by adopted by the vote of its Chair.
4. The supervisory authorities concerned shall not adopt a decision on the subject matter submitted to the Board under paragraph 1 during the periods referred to in paragraphs 2 and 3.
5. The Chair of the Board shall notify, without undue delay, the decision referred to in paragraph 1 to the supervisory authorities concerned. It shall inform the Commission thereof. The decision shall be published on the website of the Board without delay after the supervisory authority has notified the final decision referred to in paragraph 6.
6. The lead supervisory authority or, as the case may be, the supervisory authority with which the complaint has been lodged shall adopt its final decision on the basis of the decision referred to in paragraph 1 of this Article, without undue delay and at the latest by one month after the Board has notified its decision. The lead supervisory authority or, as the case may be, the supervisory authority with which the complaint has been lodged, shall inform the Board of the date when its final decision is notified respectively to the controller or the processor and to the data subject. The final decision of the supervisory authorities concerned shall be adopted under the terms of Article 60(7), (8) and (9). The final decision shall refer

---

[*] The views expressed are solely those of the author and do not necessarily reflect those of the Belgian Data Protection Authority.

[1] Corrigenda to the English text of Art. 65(1)(a) were published on 23 May 2018. The text printed reflects the updated version of the Corrigendum GDPR 2018. For the Corrigendum GDPR 2018, see Table of Legislation.

to the decision referred to in paragraph 1 of this Article and shall specify that the decision referred to in that paragraph will be published on the website of the Board in accordance with paragraph 5 of this Article. The final decision shall attach the decision referred to in paragraph 1 of this Article.

Relevant Recitals

(136) In applying the consistency mechanism, the Board should, within a determined period of time, issue an opinion, if a majority of its members so decides or if so requested by any supervisory authority concerned or the Commission. The Board should also be empowered to adopt legally binding decisions where there are disputes between supervisory authorities. For that purpose, it should issue, in principle by a two-thirds majority of its members, legally binding decisions in clearly specified cases where there are conflicting views among supervisory authorities, in particular in the cooperation mechanism between the lead supervisory authority and supervisory authorities concerned on the merits of the case, in particular whether there is an infringement of this Regulation.

(143) Any natural or legal person has the right to bring an action for annulment of decisions of the Board before the Court of Justice under the conditions provided for in Article 263 TFEU. As addressees of such decisions, the supervisory authorities concerned which wish to challenge them have to bring action within two months of being notified of them, in accordance with Article 263 TFEU. Where decisions of the Board are of direct and individual concern to a controller, processor or complainant, the latter may bring an action for annulment against those decisions within two months of their publication on the website of the Board, in accordance with Article 263 TFEU. Without prejudice to this right under Article 263 TFEU, each natural or legal person should have an effective judicial remedy before the competent national court against a decision of a supervisory authority which produces legal effects concerning that person. Such a decision concerns in particular the exercise of investigative, corrective and authorisation powers by the supervisory authority or the dismissal or rejection of complaints. However, the right to an effective judicial remedy does not encompass measures taken by supervisory authorities which are not legally binding, such as opinions issued by or advice provided by the supervisory authority. Proceedings against a supervisory authority should be brought before the courts of the Member State where the supervisory authority is established and should be conducted in accordance with that Member State's procedural law. Those courts should exercise full jurisdiction, which should include jurisdiction to examine all questions of fact and law relevant to the dispute before them.

Where a complaint has been rejected or dismissed by a supervisory authority, the complainant may bring proceedings before the courts in the same Member State. In the context of judicial remedies relating to the application of this Regulation, national courts which consider a decision on the question necessary to enable them to give judgment, may, or in the case provided for in Article 267 TFEU, must, request the Court of Justice to give a preliminary ruling on the interpretation of Union law, including this Regulation. Furthermore, where a decision of a supervisory authority implementing a decision of the Board is challenged before a national court and the validity of the decision of the Board is at issue, that national court does not have the power to declare the Board's decision invalid but must refer the question of validity to the Court of Justice in accordance with Article 267 TFEU as interpreted by the Court of Justice, where it considers the decision invalid. However, a national court may not refer a question on the validity of the decision of the Board at the request of a natural or legal person which had the opportunity to bring an action for annulment of that decision, in particular if it was directly and individually concerned by that decision, but had not done so within the period laid down in Article 263 TFEU.

Closely Related Provisions

Article 4(16) (Definition of the main establishment) (see too recital 36); Article 4(24) (Definition of a relevant and reasoned objection) (see too recital 124); Article 60(4) (Objection by a concerned supervisory authority to a draft decision of the lead supervisory authority); Articles 60(7)–(9) (Procedure to adopt a final decision by a supervisory authority); Article 63 (Consistency mechanism) (see too recitals 123, 135 and 150 *in fine*); Article 64 (Cases when opinions of the Board are mandatory); Article 66 (Derogations from the consistency mechanism in case of urgency) (see too recitals 137–138); Article 74(1)(b) (Notification of binding decisions by the Chair of the Board); Article 74(1)(c) (Chair of the Board to ensure the timely performance of the Board's tasks); Article 75(6)(g) (Secretariat to prepare, draft and publish decisions on the settlement of disputes between supervisory authorities) (see too recital 140); Article 76(1) (Confidentiality of Board's discussions when necessary)

Relevant Case Law

CJEU

Case C-322/88, *Salvatore Grimaldi v Fonds des maladies professionnelles*, judgment of 13 December 1989 (ECLI:EU:C:1989:646).

Case C-188/92, *TWD Textilwerke Deggendorf GmbH v Bundesrepublik Deutschland*, judgment of 9 March 1994 (ECLI:EU:C:1994:90).

Case C-241/01, *National Farmers' Union v Secrétariat général du gouvernement*, judgment of 22 October 2002 (ECLI:EU:C:2002:604).

Case C-518/07, *European Commission v Federal Republic of Germany*, judgment of 9 March 2010 (Grand Chamber) (ECLI:EU:C:2010:125).

Case C-362/14, *Maximillian Schrems v Data Protection Commissioner*, judgment of 6 October 2015, (Grand Chamber) (ECLI:EU:C:2015:650).

Case C-191/15, *Verein für Konsumenteninformation v Amazon EU Sàrl*, judgment of 28 July 2016 (ECLI:EU:C:2016:612).

Case C-210/16, *Unabhängiges Landeszentrum für Datenschutz Schleswig-Holstein v Wirtschaftsakademie Schleswig-Holstein GmbH*, judgment of 5 June 2018 (Grand Chamber) (ECLI:EU:C:2018:388).

Opinion of Advocate General Bot in Case C-210/16, *Unabhängiges Landeszentrum für Datenschutz Schleswig-Holstein v Wirtschaftsakademie Schleswig-Holstein GmbH*, delivered on 24 October 2017 (ECLI:EU:C:2017:796).

A. Rationale and Policy Underpinnings

Article 65 GDPR provides for decision-making by the EDPB in three types of situations. It provides for a last resort, in case the normal processes, including the consistency rules of Article 64 GDPR resulting in an opinion of the EDPB, do not deliver an outcome, or—as seems to be the case in Article 65(1)(c)—an unsatisfactory outcome.

Article 65(1)(a) may be considered the hard core of the consistency mechanism. It provides for dispute resolution, in case data protection authorities cooperate in the one-stop-shop mechanism on a possible violation of the GDPR, but do not manage to reach consensus. In this situation, the EDPB is empowered to adopt a binding decision. This provision is included for reasons of effectiveness, in order to ensure that the one-stop-shop mechanism with its emphasis on consensus will always lead to a single decision, also in the (rare) cases that consensus cannot be reached. However, it is also driven by the rationale of efficiency.

Article 65(1)(a) should only be applied in exceptional cases, neither overburdening the EDPB nor adding a further stage to the procedure. Its application is triggered solely on the basis of a relevant and reasoned objection of a DPA.

Article 65(1)(b) deals with the identification of the lead DPA. The GDPR starts from the presumption that the identification of the lead DPA is a natural process that does not require any constitutive decision.[2] However, although a decision on the designation of a lead DPA is not required under the GDPR—or maybe precisely because of the absence of such a decision—there may be a conflict of competence between DPAs. Such a conflict must be resolved, for reasons of legal certainty.

Article 65(1)(c) is directly linked to Article 64 and is of a slightly different nature. It does not address a situation where there is no outcome, but seems to be meant to reinforce the procedure of Article 64 in cases where this procedure is not respected or where there is a risk that the outcome of the procedure could be unsatisfactory from the perspective of consistent data protection in the EU, because the competent DPA does not follow the opinion of the EDPB. The rationale is ensuring consistent and harmonised data protection in the EU. This rationale also explains why the Commission (and, where relevant, the EFTA Surveillance Authority[3]) is also empowered to initiate the procedure. Article 65(1)(c) is not meant to resolve disputes between individual DPAs, but between the Board and the lead DPA or another competent DPA. In the situations identified in Article 65(1)(c), the EDPB is empowered to overrule a decision of a national DPA. In this specific context, the legislator demonstrates a preference for a centralised decision over proximity of decision-making close to the citizen.[4]

Paragraphs (2)–(5) of Article 65 contain procedural provisions. They balance the need for wide support within the Board for a decision, with the objective of ensuring a smooth and efficient process. This explains why, in principle, a two-thirds majority is required, but if this majority cannot be obtained within the defined time frame, a simple majority will suffice. These provisions should also contribute to legal certainty. They specify the nature of the nature of the decision by the EDPB, which is addressed to the lead DPA and other concerned DPAs. This means that the decision of the Board is not addressed to controllers, processors or data subjects. Nonetheless, the decision may be of direct and individual concern to them, as recognised in recital 145. This is why Article 65(5), last sentence, provides that the EDPB decision must be published, but only after the lead DPA (or another DPA concerned) has taken a final decision based on Article 65(6). This final decision is addressed to controllers, processors and/or data subjects.

Article 65(6) specifies the interaction between the decision of the EDPB and the final decision of the lead DPA (or another DPA concerned). This is needed for reasons of a smooth and efficient process and to contribute to legal certainty. It must, moreover, ensure that an effective remedy under the rule of law is always available, either before the CJEU (which includes the General Court) or before the national judiciary.

---

[2] Guidance by the WP29 is provided, see WP29 2017A. [3] Art. 5e(l) EEA Decision 2018.
[4] Council Report 2013.

Under Article 47 of the Charter of Fundamental Rights of the European Union ('CFR'), everyone whose rights and freedoms guaranteed by the law of the Union have been violated has the right to an effective remedy before a tribunal. This is explained in recital 143, which also contains an attempt to avoid multiplication of legal procedures.

Finally, it may be noted that in the event that the UK leaves the EU ('Brexit'), the UK Information Commissioner ('ICO') will no longer be the supervisory authority of an EU or EEA/EFTA Member State under Article 4(22) GDPR and thus will no longer be subject to the consistency mechanism.

B. Legal Background

1. EU legislation

Article 65 GDPR is a novel provision which is not based on antecedents in EU law.

2. International instruments

The European Economic Area ('EEA') Agreement, as amended in July 2018,[5] incorporates the GDPR into its Annexes and provides that the provisions of the GDPR should be read, for the purposes of that Agreement, with a number of adaptations. In this respect the Agreement provides that, where it is relevant to the exercise of its functions under Article 109 of this Agreement, the EFTA Surveillance Authority ('ESA') shall have the right to request advice or opinions from, and to communicate matters to, the Board pursuant to Article 65(1)(c) and to that effect provides that the words 'and, where relevant, the EFTA Surveillance Authority' shall be added after the words 'the Commission' in Article 65(1)(c).[6]

3. National developments

At the national level, a comparison could be made with decision-making processes in federal states, which requires consistency between decisions of the authorities of the states. This would be particularly relevant in Germany where the DPAs of the states are competent vis-à-vis the private sector in their respective jurisdictions. The federal German data protection law ('Bundesdatenschutzgesetz') provides for a cooperation mechanism between the DPAs of the states but does not provide for a binding dispute resolution mechanism comparable to GDPR Article 65.[7]

4. Case law

Article 65 is a novel and unique provision that is not based on previous case law of the CJEU or the ECtHR. However, this does not mean that the case law is not relevant for the interpretation of this provision which, in particular, must be compatible with the CJEU case law on DPA independence.[8]

---

[5] EEA Decision 2018.   [6] Ibid., Art. 5e(l).
[7] See German GDPR Implementation Law, s. 18.
[8] E.g. Case C-518/07, *Commission v Germany*. See the commentary on Art. 52 in this volume.

C. Analysis

1. The overall thrust of Article 65

Article 65 is a component of the consistency mechanism which aims at contributing to the consistent application of the GDPR throughout the Union.[9] Article 65 establishes a mechanism enabling the EDPB to resolve disputes on the application of the GDPR. Recital 136 explains that its scope relates to disputes between DPAs. It is evident that a mechanism to resolve disputes between DPAs may contribute to consistency, especially for the cases covered by Article 65(1)(a). These are the cases when the enforcement co-operation of the DPAs in the one-stop-shop mechanism of Article 60 does not lead to consensus between the DPAs concerned and, hence, a single decision cannot be taken. However, it is less evident how substantial this contribution will be.

Arguably consistency not only requires that in specific cases one single decision is taken, but also that this single decision is consistent with decisions taken in other cases.[10] Article 70(1)(a) goes even further, by providing that the task of the EDPB in the consistency mechanism is to monitor and ensure the correct application of the GDPR. A correct application of the law is not the same as consistent application. It adds a further requirement. The application of the law should also be in accordance with EU law. It is arguable that Article 65 does not provide the EDPB with the instruments to perform this task, since it seems to be mainly designed to solve disputes between DPAs. Admittedly, Article 65(1)(c) does have a slightly wider nature, as discussed below.

The dispute resolution mechanism was designed with a view to limiting its application to exceptional situations. Various documents on the negotiations in the Council mention concern lest the Board be overburdened.[11] This explains why qualitative thresholds are included in the GDPR. The application of Article 65(1)(a) can only be triggered after a reasoned and relevant objection[12] which is subsequently rejected by the lead DPA. In the negotiations in the Council, the mechanism now laid down in Article 65 was proposed as a system of binding corrective measures.[13] The mechanism can be qualified as an *ultimum remedium* where the cooperation does not lead to a (satisfactory) result.

This has been confirmed by practice between 25 May 2018 and 18 February 2019, when, according to a survey by the EDPB, no dispute resolutions were initiated. The EDPB commented that '[t]his means that up to now, the SAs were able to reach consensus in all current cases, which is a good sign in terms of cooperation'.[14]

Another issue is the limitation in scope of Article 65 to disputes between DPAs. Although this limitation seems to be intended by the legislators and is referred to in recital 136, it is not explicitly laid down in Article 65, so it is not excluded that Article 65 could be applied in other types of situations. For instance, Article 65(1)(b) refers to situations where there are conflicting views on which DPA is competent for the main establishment (in other words: which is the lead DPA for a specific organisation). These conflicting views may occur in a dispute between DPAs, but also in a dispute between a DPA and an organisation. Moreover, the power of the Commission (and, where relevant, the ESA[15]) to refer cases to the EDPB, in accordance with Article 65(1)(c), seems to imply that the dispute must not necessarily be a dispute between DPAs.

---

[9] As stipulated in Art. 63 GDPR.　　[10] This is explained in Hijmans 2016B, 5.
[11] Council Report 2015A; Council Report 2015B.　　[12] As defined in Art. 4(24) GDPR.
[13] Council Report 2013.　　[14] EDPB 2019, p. 6.　　[15] Art. 5e(l) EEA Decision 2018.

2. Article 65(1)(a): Disputes in the context of the one-stop-shop mechanism

Article 65(1)(a) represents the situation where the cooperation mechanism does not lead to consensus. DPAs are under an obligation to attempt to reach consensus in cases of enforcement of the GDPR, not under an obligation of result. This dispute resolution mechanism must be applied exceptionally and also be limited to circumstances where dispute resolution is really needed. It is not meant to replace the cooperation mechanisms. This explains the high threshold and a scope of application restricted to matters of dispute.

The qualitative threshold for triggering the application of this provision is a relevant or reasoned objection of a concerned DPA, as defined in Article 4(24) GDPR. The objection must be relevant. It must concern either a difference in views between DPAs on the existence of a breach of the Regulation or on the legality of an enforcement action. It must be reasoned, meaning that it must clearly demonstrate the risks for the data subject, on the one hand, or for the free flow of data, on the other hand, or for both risks. During the legislative process it was emphasised that the objection must be serious.[16]

The binding EDPB decision in the dispute resolution mechanism will only apply to the subject-matter of the objection. For example, the lead DPA may observe in an enforcement action that a controller has breached several provisions of the GDPR. A concerned DPA may object only to the alleged breach of one article. In this circumstance, the EDPB will only decide on the matter of dispute, being the breach of this particular article, not on the breach of the other provisions. Another obvious limitation might involve the situation where the dispute involves the existence of a breach. In that case, the EDPB might decide on the breach itself, but not necessarily on the corrective measures or sanctions to be imposed on the controller or processor if this is not part of the dispute between the DPAs.

Recital 136 adds that the conflicting views should, in particular, concern the merits of the case. This should not exclude disputes which concern corrective measures or sanctions. On the contrary, as stipulated in the last phrase of Article 65(1)(a), the intervention by the EDPB concerns all the matters which are the subject of the objection, in particular in case of an infringement. The specific reference to an infringement justifies the presumption that the nature, scope and level of corrective measures or sanctions can also be the object of an EDPB intervention. In view of the wide discretion of the DPAs in this field and the potential size of administrative sanctions, disputes on corrective measures or sanctions may well arise. A role of the EDPB in these disputes would be fully in line with the objective of a consistent approach on sanctions.[17]

Finally, the interpretation that the dispute resolution mechanism may only be relevant to some elements of an enforcement case—and not necessarily concern the entire case—is consistent with the coexistence of a decision by the EDPB and a final decision of the lead DPA (or of the DPA where a complaint was launched).

3. Article 65 (1)(b): Disputes on DPA competence

The competence of supervisory authorities is dealt with in essence in Articles 55 and 56 GDPR. However, whilst the GDPR provides for the principles of DPA competence, it

---

[16] 'Serious' is the term used in Council Report 2015A, p. 2.
[17] As underlined in WP29 2017B, p. 1.

does not include a procedure for identifying the competent (lead) supervisory authority in complex realities. This explains why the WP29 addressed this issue in one of its first guidance papers.[18] It also explains why a provision needed to be included in the GDPR to deal with conflicting views on competence.

A dispute on DPA competence was one of the factors leading to the preliminary questions in *Wirtschaftsakademie*.[19] Although this case concerned the interpretation of the DPD and, as stipulated explicitly by Advocate General Bot, does not pre-empt the GDPR,[20] it illustrates that disputes on DPA competence may actually arise. These disputes may arise, for instance, within a group of undertakings or in situations of joint controllership under Article 26, when there is no evident single controller. *Wirtschaftsakademie* concerned Facebook, with its main EU establishment in Ireland, but with legal entities in various EU Member States responsible for advertising and marketing services. Apart from the specificities of this particular case, in these types of situations the dispute may concern the question whether there is one controller (with a main establishment and other establishments)[21] or multiple controllers. One DPA might want to invoke the cooperation mechanism of Article 56, whereas another DPA might prefer to exercise its control directly on the basis of Article 55(1).

The question also arises whether the GDPR requires that there must be conflicting views between DPAs or whether controllers, processors or data subjects may also initiate the procedure before the EDPB, in case a decision on DPA competence is of direct or indirect concern to them,[22] for example where a company identifies a certain DPA as its lead and the DPA decides that another one should be the lead.[23] The text of the GDPR does not exclude the application of Article 65 in this situation, although it was probably not intended by the legislator, as may be seen in recital 136, second sentence, which only refers to disputes between DPAs. As will be seen, Article 65(1)(c) is also not limited to disputes between DPAs.

4. Article 65(1)(c): Disputes resulting from the 'normal' consistency mechanism

Article 65(1)(c) concerns two different situations which are both related to the 'normal' consistency mechanism, the procedure ending with an opinion of the EDPB. First, the dispute resolution procedure can be triggered in cases where a DPA does not respect its obligation under Article 64(1)(a) to submit certain draft measures to the EDPB for an opinion. A DPA that does not follow the obligatory procedure can be sanctioned, meaning that the competence to adopt the measure will pass to the EDPB. This sanction does not follow automatically. A concerned DPA or the Commission (or, where relevant, the ESA)[24] must initiate it.

Secondly, and perhaps the most remarkable component of Article 65, is the possibility for the EDPB to adopt a binding decision if a competent DPA does not follow the opinion of the EDPB under Article 64. Notably, the competent DPA is not obliged to follow the EDPB opinion, but instead it is supposed to take the utmost account

---

[18] WP29 2017A.   [19] Case C-210/16, *Wirtschaftsakademie*.
[20] Case C-210/16, *Wirtschaftsakademie* (AG Opinion), para. 103.
[21] In the meaning of Case C-191/15, *Verein für Konsumenteninformation*, paras. 74–75.
[22] Wording from Art. 263 Treaty on the Functioning of the European Union ('TFEU').
[23] WP29 2017A.   [24] Art. 5e(l) EEA Decision 2018.

of it.[25] This requirement is similar to the CJEU's case law on recommendations of the Commission. These are explicitly non-binding, but this does not mean that they are without any legal effect. As the CJEU has stated, 'the national courts are bound to take recommendations into consideration in order to decide disputes brought before them'.[26] This limited legal effect is apparently insufficient for purposes of consistency, so that a binding decision can be requested under Article 65.

The dispute resolution under Article 65(1)(c) can be triggered by any DPA concerned and by the Commission (and, where relevant, the ESA),[27] reading its second sentence as referring to both situations included in the first sentence. This wording has two remarkable elements. First, it is not clear if the limitation to the supervisory authorities concerned has any meaning. Which, for instance, are the DPAs concerned in the hypothesis of the list of processing operations subject to a data protection impact assessment ('DPIA')? Secondly, it establishes a role for the Commission and the ESA. This role is not unique within the framework of the GDPR, but is not logical in view of recital 136, second sentence, referring to the mechanism as resolution for disputes between DPAs. Moreover, it is not necessarily in line with the complete independence of DPAs.

The GDPR provides a role for the Commission in Article 64(2), where it can request that in various situations matters may be examined by the EDPB. Article 68(5) also gives the Commission the right to participate in activities and meetings of the EDPB.[28] As said, the Commission may trigger the application of the dispute resolution mechanism in certain cases under Article 65(1)(c). Arguably, these powers are a remnant of the much more extensive role of the Commission in the consistency mechanism that it had originally proposed.[29] This role of the Commission was heavily criticised for its incompatibility with DPA independence[30] and significantly limited in the legislative procedure. However, it was not completely removed, despite the strong arguments for non-involvement of the Commission in the activities of the EDPB where the Board acts as a DPA in the enforcement of individual cases.[31] The involvement of the Commission or the ESA could possibly jeopardise DPA independence, explained by the CJEU as the absence of any external influence,[32] or the independence of the Board itself.[33]

5. The internal workings of the EDPB

Paragraphs (2)–(5) of Article 65 mainly describe the internal procedures of the EDPB, including its relation to the supervisory authorities concerned. Decisions must be taken within clearly specified deadlines, in principle by a two-thirds majority of its members and if this qualified majority is not reached, even after an extension of the deadline, by a simple majority. The provisions are drafted to ensure that procedural requirements do not stand in the way of a decision.

Moreover, Article 65(2) specifies that the—reasoned[34]—decision is addressed to the lead DPAs and all DPAs concerned and binding upon them. Article 65(4) prohibits these

[25] Art. 64 (7) GDPR. [26] E.g. Case C-322/88, *Grimaldi*, para. 18.
[27] Art. 5e(l) EEA Decision 2018.
[28] For the purposes of the Agreement the EFTA Surveillance Authority also has this right, Art. 5e(k) EEA Decision 2018.
[29] Arts. 59 and 60 GDPR Proposal. [30] E.g. EDPS 2012, pp. 248–255.
[31] Hijmans 2016A, 8.10.4 and 8.11.3. [32] Case C-518/07, *Commission v Germany*, para. 19.
[33] See the commentary on Art. 69 in this volume.
[34] This specification is strictly speaking not necessary, since each decision of an administration under EU law should be reasoned, see Art. 41(2) CFR.

DPAs from taking a unilateral decision during the process before the EDPB and can be seen as a specification of the general obligation of sincere cooperation of Article 4(3) Treaty on European Union ('TEU').

Article 65(5) deals with the notification by the Board of its decision to the DPAs concerned and the Commission and the communication of the decision to the public at large on its website. The GDPR does not contain any provision about the transparency of the procedure or the participation in the procedure of the parties concerned. In theory, the procedure before the EDPB could happen without the parties concerned being aware of it. Only afterwards is there a requirement that the decision be published on the EDPB website and attached to the final decision of the DPA, as well as the requirement that the annual report should include a review of the decision, under Article 71(2). The only GDPR provision on involvement of interested parties in the activities of the EDPB (Article 70(4)) does not address the dispute resolution mechanism, and indeed is specifically 'without prejudice' to the confidentiality of the discussions of the Board under Article 76. However, Article 41 of the Charter on the right to good administration includes a 'right of every person to be heard, before any individual measure which would affect him or her adversely is taken'. It also includes a right 'to have access to his or her file'. More generally, the parties could benefit from their right to access to documents, as laid down in Article 15 TFEU and Article 42 of the Charter.

Article 11(1) of the EDPB Rules of Procedure provides that 'before taking decisions, the Board shall make sure that all persons that might be adversely affected have been heard'. Article 11(2) of those Rules does not provide for a direct right to be heard by the Board itself but rather that, in cases under Article 65(1)(a), the lead supervisory authority provide the secretariat with 'the written observations of the persons that might be adversely affected by the Board's decision'. The same requirement is not imposed in cases under Article 65(1)(b)–(c).

The question arises whether Article 11 EDPB Rules of Procedure is in line with the right to be heard enshrined in Article 41 CFR. There are three main reasons for doubt. First, the absence of a procedure to be heard as such in the Rules of Procedure is critical, since Article 11(2) only mentions written observations and does not specify any procedure. It does not, for instance, mention the possibility of a hearing. Secondly, Article 41 CFR presupposes that EU bodies themselves ensure good administration and do not mandate this task to a national authority. Article 41 lays down that '(e)very person has the right to have his or her affairs handled impartially, fairly and within a reasonable time by the institutions and bodies of the Union'. 'By' does not include 'on behalf of'. Moreover, Article 41 CFR is only binding upon EU institutions and bodies, not upon national authorities.[35] Thirdly, no procedure is foreseen relating to a right to be heard in connection with the decisions based on Article 65(1)(b)–(c).

6. The relation between the EDPB decision and the final DPA decision

The difference between the EDPB decision and the final decision is not obvious. EU law does not make a difference between decisions and final decisions. Moreover, the EDPB

---

[35] Normally, provisions of the Charter are binding upon the Member States under the conditions of Art. 51 CFR. This is not the case for Art. 41 CFR.

decision is binding and is final, within the limits of its scope. As explained before, the EDPB decision does not necessarily address all elements of an enforcement case. For instance, the imposition of sanctions and corrective measures may remain outside of the scope of the involvement of the EDPB.[36]

As noted above, Article 65(2) specifies that the EDPB decision is addressed to the lead supervisory authority and to all concerned DPAs and is binding upon them. On this basis, the lead supervisory authority (or another DPA concerned) shall adopt a final decision. Hence, the EDPB decision is not addressed to the controllers, processors and data subjects who are the parties concerned in an enforcement case, and it is not even required to notify the parties.[37] However, recital 143 recognises that the EDPB decision may be of direct and individual concern to a controller, processor or complainant.

The parties concerned may thus be confronted with two decisions. Since these two decisions will be inextricably linked, Article 65(6) ensures that the parties concerned will be informed of both decisions at the same time. This is guaranteed through the publication of the EDPB decision on the EDPB website 'without delay' upon the notification of the final DPA decision, by including a reference to the EDPB decision in the final DPA decision and by attaching the EDPB decision to the latter. This inextricable link is also the rationale behind the delayed transparency of the EDPB decision. The parties concerned should be informed simultaneously of the two decisions. Before the final decision is taken, the EDPB decision should remain secret. Time will tell whether this mechanism, and the mechanism for ensuring the right to be heard discussed in Section C.5 above, is in accordance with transparency principles of EU law enshrined in Article 41 CFR.

7. Parallel judicial review mechanisms

The existence of two decisions is reflected in the judicial review mechanism explained in recital 143. The recital explains the existence of two parallel review mechanisms. First, in accordance with Article 263 TFEU, any legal or natural person can bring an action for annulment before the CJEU against a decision which is of direct and individual concern to him or her. As recital 143 explains, this remedy is available for the DPAs concerned and for controllers, processors and complainants. There does not seem to be any reason why other interested parties (such as data subjects affected that did not issue a complaint or even not-for-profit bodies, organisations or associations under Article 80 GDPR) would not be in the same position.

Secondly, any natural or legal person should have an effective judicial remedy before a national court against a decision by a supervisory authority, in the present case a remedy against the final decision. Recital 143 mentions that this remedy concerns in particular the exercise of DPA powers or the dismissal or rejections of complaints. The national court of the jurisdiction where the DPA which takes the decision is established is competent. In the case where a decision of the Board requires final decisions by multiple DPAs (e.g. because complaints have been lodged in more than one Member State), there can also be parallel national procedures. This is the subject of Article 81, dealing with suspension of parallel proceedings concerning the same subject-matter.

---

[36] Although, as explained, this is not a necessary consequence of Art. 65(1)(a) GDPR.
[37] Notification to the parties is the task of the lead supervisory authority, under Art. 65(6).

Thirdly, in accordance with Article 267 TFEU, the national court is entitled—and, in the case of the court of last resort, is obliged—to ask the CJEU for a preliminary ruling in a case where an issue arises that requires interpretation of the GDPR. In any event, the national court is not in a position to declare an EDPB decision invalid. Invalidity requires a reference to the CJEU. These are general requirements under EU law[38] which are explained in recital 143 GDPR.

Fourthly, recital 143 expresses a preference for challenging an EDPB decision before the CJEU, rather than before a national court as part of a procedure against the final decision of the national DPA. The recital states that a question of validity may not be referred at the request of a natural or a legal person who had the possibility to bring an action against the EDPB decision but had not done so. This statement would seem to be based on case law of the CJEU in the area of state aid in particular,[39] which in essence precludes challenging a decision of an EU body in a case before a national court after the deadline for an appeal at the CJEU has expired.

This seems to be a questionable statement, for a number of reasons. First, there is considerable debate as to the scope of the above case law. Secondly, there is a fundamental difference between the situation covered by this case law and the situation contemplated by recital 143. The EDPB decision is not addressed to the parties and only covers specific elements of a final decision of a national DPA. Thirdly, the statement is not in line with Article 65, which underlines the inextricable link between the decision and specifies that only the final decision is addressed to the parties concerned. It is submitted that the parties cannot be asked to challenge a decision which is not addressed to them instead of challenging a decision which is addressed to them. Finally, a recital cannot limit a right of a national court under primary EU law.[40]

Select Bibliography

International agreements

EEA Agreement: Agreement on the European Economic Area, OJ 1994 L 1/3.
EEA Decision 2018: Decision of the EEA Joint Committee No. 154/2018 of 6 July 2018 amending Annex XI (Electronic communication, audiovisual services and information society) and Protocol 37 (containing the list provided for in Article 101) to the EEA Agreement [2018/1022], OJ 2018 L 183/23.

EU legislation

GDPR Proposal: Proposal for a Regulation of the European Parliament and of the Council on the protection of individuals with regard to the processing of personal data and on the free movement of such data (General Data Protection Regulation), COM(2012) 11 final, 25 January 2012.

National legislation

German GDPR Implementation Law: Gesetz zur Anpassung des Datenschutzrechts an die Verordnung (EU) 2016/679 und zur Umsetzung der Richtlinie (EU) 2016/680 (Datenschutz-Anpassungs- und Umsetzungsgesetz EU – DsAnpUG-EU), BGBl 2017 Teil 1 Nr. 44.

---

[38] See Case C-362/14, *Schrems*, para. 64.
[39] See Case C-188/92, *TWD Textilwerke Deggendorf*, paras. 17–18; and Case C-241/01, *National Farmers' Union*, para. 35.
[40] See also the commentary on Art. 78 in this volume.

Hijmans

Academic writings

Giurgiu and Larsen, 'Roles and Powers of National Data Protection Authorities', 2(3) *European Data Protection Law Review 'EDPL'* (2016), 342.
Hijmans 2016A: Hijmans, *The European Union as Guardian of Internet Privacy* (Springer 2016).
Hijmans 2016B: Hijmans, 'The DPAs and their Cooperation: How Far Are We in Making Enforcement of Data Protection Law More European?' 2(3) *EDPL* (2016), 362.
Jay, *Guide to the General Data Protection Regulation: A Companion to Data Protection Law and Practice* (Sweet & Maxwell 2017).
Lenaerts and van Nuffel, *European Union Law* (3rd edn, Sweet & Maxwell 2011).

Papers of data protection authorities

EDPB 2019: European Data Protection Board, 'First overview on the implementation of the GDPR and the roles and means of the national supervisory authorities' (26 February 2019).
EDPB Rules of Procedure: European Data Protection Board, 'Rules of Procedure' Version 2 (Adopted on 25 May 2018, as last modified and adopted on 23 November 2018).
EDPS 2012: EDPS, 'Opinion on the Data Protection Reform Package' (March 2012).
WP29 2017A: Article 29 Working Party, 'Guidelines on The Lead Supervisory Authority' (WP 244 rev.01, as last revised and adopted on 5 April 2017).
WP29 2017B: Article 29 Working Party, 'Guidelines on the Application and Setting of Administrative Fines for the Purpose of the Regulation 2016/679' (WP 253, 3 October 2017).

Reports and recommendations

Council Report 2013: Effective judicial protection of data subjects' fundamental rights in the context of the envisaged 'one-stopshop' mechanism, 18031/13, 19 December 2013.
Council Report 2015A: Contributions of the German and French delegations: General Data Protection Regulation – The one-stop-shop mechanism, 5315/15, 15 January 2015.
Council Report 2015B: Discussion note on possible thresholds for submitting cases to the EDPB, 5331/15, 21 January 2015.

Article 66. Urgency procedure

LUDMILA GEORGIEVA[*]

1. In exceptional circumstances, where a supervisory authority concerned considers that there is an urgent need to act in order to protect the rights and freedoms of data subjects, it may, by way of derogation from the consistency mechanism referred to in Articles 63, 64 and 65 or the procedure referred to in Article 60, immediately adopt provisional measures intended to produce legal effects on its own territory with a specified period of validity which shall not exceed three months. The supervisory authority shall, without delay, communicate those measures and the reasons for adopting them to the other supervisory authorities concerned, to the Board and to the Commission.
2. Where a supervisory authority has taken a measure pursuant to paragraph 1 and considers that final measures need urgently be adopted, it may request an urgent opinion or an urgent binding decision from the Board, giving reasons for requesting such opinion or decision.
3. Any supervisory authority may request an urgent opinion or an urgent binding decision, as the case may be, from the Board where a competent supervisory authority has not taken an appropriate measure in a situation where there is an urgent need to act, in order to protect the rights and freedoms of data subjects, giving reasons for requesting such opinion or decision, including for the urgent need to act.
4. By derogation from Article 64(3) and Article 65(2), an urgent opinion or an urgent binding decision referred to in paragraphs 2 and 3 of this Article shall be adopted within two weeks by simple majority of the members of the Board.

Relevant Recitals

(137) There may be an urgent need to act in order to protect the rights and freedoms of data subjects, in particular when the danger exists that the enforcement of a right of a data subject could be considerably impeded. A supervisory authority should therefore be able to adopt duly justified provisional measures on its territory with a specified period of validity which should not exceed three months.

(138) The application of such mechanism should be a condition for the lawfulness of a measure intended to produce legal effects by a supervisory authority in those cases where its application is mandatory. In other cases of cross-border relevance, the cooperation mechanism between the lead supervisory authority and supervisory authorities concerned should be applied and mutual assistance and joint operations might be carried out between the supervisory authorities concerned on a bilateral or multilateral basis without triggering the consistency mechanism

Closely Related Provisions

Article 4(21)–(22) (Definitions, supervisory authority and supervisory authority concerned); Article 60 (Cooperation between the lead supervisory authority and the other supervisory

---

[*] The views expressed are solely those of the author and do not necessarily reflect those of her current or former employers.

authorities concerned); Article 61 (Mutual assistance) (see too recital 133); Article 62 (Joint operations of supervisory authorities) (see too recital 134); Article 63 (Consistency mechanism) (see too recital 135); Article 64 (Opinion of the Board), Article 65 (Dispute resolution by the Board) (see too recital 136); Article 70 (Tasks of the Board) (see too recital 136)

A. Rationale and Policy Underpinnings

One of the main objectives of the GDPR is a strong and more coherent data protection framework in the Union, backed by strong enforcement (recital 7) and effective protection of the fundamental rights of the data subjects. For this reason, the GDPR places the system of the supervisory authorities and their independence, establishment, powers and tasks on a new foundation with its own Chapter VI, and creates a new system for cooperation and consistency in Chapter VII. Thus, Chapter VII sets out completely new procedures for cross-border cases: a cooperation mechanism between the supervisory authorities, the so-called 'one-stop-shop' (Section 1) and a consistency mechanism (Section 2) as well as the establishment of the EDPB as a formal body able to adopt binding decisions (Section 3). This is because cooperation and consistency are needed to ensure consistent application and enforcement of the GDPR throughout the EU, in order to protect natural persons in relation to the processing of their personal data and to facilitate the free flow of personal data within the internal market.[1] However, these procedures between the EU Member States are also complex and time consuming.[2]

The GDPR foresees a derogation in 'exceptional circumstances' from this principle of cooperation and consistency in cross-border cases—the urgency procedure in Article 66. By doing so, it underlines the even greater importance of an effective protection of fundamental rights compared to the coherent enforcement of the data protection framework.[3]

Nevertheless, the provision is designed as an exception. If the requirements of Article 66 are fulfilled, a supervisory authority concerned can immediately adopt provisional measures which are limited in time (max. three months) and space (to its own territory). Thereafter it must communicate and explain its measures without delay to the other supervisory authorities concerned, to the EDPB and to the European Commission ('Commission'). If the measures are considered to be final and urgent, it can request an urgent opinion or an urgent binding decision from the EDPB to be adopted within two weeks by simple majority. The same applies for any supervisory authority, if a competent supervisory authority has not taken appropriate measure in need of urgent action.

B. Legal Background

1. EU legislation

As Chapters VI and VII are new, most articles of these two chapters including Article 66 have no equivalent in the DPD. The DPD contains only one single article on supervisory

---

[1] Art. 51 and rec. 123, 133 and 135 GDPR.
[2] Under Art. 64(3) GDPR the EDPB must adopt its opinion within eight weeks, which may be extended by six weeks; under Art. 65(2) GDPR the EDPB must adopt its decision within one month, which may be extended by one month.
[3] Klabunde 2017, para. 2.

authorities and their powers, including one sentence on mutual assistance, all together in Article 28 and recitals 62–64. Article 18 of the EPR Proposal[4] (replacing and repealing the EDP) stipulates that the independent supervisory authority or authorities responsible for monitoring the application of the GDPR shall also be responsible for monitoring the application of the new ePrivacy Regulation and that Chapter VI and VII of the GDPR shall apply *mutatis mutandis*.

2. International instruments

Modernised Convention 108 of 2018 includes provisions on cooperation and mutual assistance but no urgency procedure or comparable provision is foreseen.

3. National developments

Since the GDPR is a regulation no national implementation is needed. Article 66 sets out the urgency procedure and its paragraphs 1–3 foresee information obligations and powers to request measures, and define the categories of measures and their maximum duration. Although these provisions are directly applicable, Article 66 does not regulate the process of decision-making within the supervisory authorities concerned regarding the type, duration and content of the measures. In consequence the national law of the authority taking action is relevant and these procedures are at the disposal of Members States' law.

C. Analysis

Article 66 is short and relatively uncomplicated. It states who is entitled to do what and when (under which circumstances), and who has to inform whom, in case of an urgent need to protect the rights and freedoms of data subjects. The provision creates an exception to the principle of cooperation and consistency in order to ensure effective protection. However, Article 66 is not meant to prevent the EDPB from acting urgently and adopting an opinion or a binding decision.

The urgency procedure also does not affect an ongoing procedure pursuant to Articles 60, 64 or 65,[5] or have any impact on the questions of competence, tasks and powers or judicial protection laid down in Articles 55, 57, 58 or 78. The only purpose of this provision is to allow the supervisory authority to act unilaterally despite the joint mechanisms in the case of urgent need.

1. Who may act

The authority addressed under Article 66(1)–(2) is the 'supervisory authority concerned' within the meaning of Article 4(22). In contrast, under Article 66(3) *any* 'supervisory authority' within the meaning of Article 4(21) may request an urgent opinion or binding decision from the EDPB in cases where the competent supervisory authority within the meaning of Article 55 has not acted appropriately in case of urgent need, thus requiring a decision to be made.

[4] EPR Proposal. [5] Klabunde 2017, para. 6.

2. What to do, and against whom

Article 66 entitles its addressee, the supervisory authority concerned, to adopt urgent measures outside the cooperation and consistency system of Article 60 and Articles 63–65, including provisional, final or replacement measures. Depending on the type of the measures, different requirements are to be fulfilled. Thus, the provisional measures adopted under paragraph 1 are limited in time to a maximum of three months and in space to the territory of the supervisory authority concerned. If measures pursuant to paragraph 1 have been undertaken and final measures need to be urgently adopted, then paragraph 2 requires an urgent opinion or urgent binding decision by the EDPB. Replacement measures in the form of an urgent opinion or urgent binding decision by the EDPB can be requested by any data protection authority in case the competent supervisory authority has not undertaken an appropriate measure in a situation where there is an urgent need (to act in order to protect the rights and freedoms of data subjects).

However, the urgent measure can only be addressed when its addressee has either an establishment or a representative in the territory of the DPA concerned. This means that the provision does not apply if the DPA is 'concerned' by the processing of personal data under Article 4(22)(b) or (c) (i.e. when data subjects are substantially affected or a complaint has been lodged with that DPA) but there is no one on its territory against whom the measures can be addressed. At the same time, Article 66 creates a duplication of powers because the lead DPA pursuant to Article 56 remains the lead DPA even if a concerned authority has adopted urgent measures.

3. When to act

Article 66 creates strict conditions for cross-border cases when a DPA wishes to act on its own without consulting the other DPAs concerned. Three conditions must be fulfilled in this regard, namely (1) exceptional circumstances, (2) an urgent need to act and (3) the need for protection of the rights and freedoms of data subjects. The latter is fulfilled if a concrete and immediate damage or disadvantage is to be expected. Only if these three elements are present may 'duly justified' (recital 137) territorially and time limited provisional measures be adopted immediately. This assessment is a matter of discretion by the authority taking action, and requires it to weigh all facts and interests (i.e. of the data subject, controller/processor and other supervisory authorities concerned). However, the urgency procedure can be applied *only* to protect rights and freedoms of data subjects, not of the controller or processor.

Recital 137 describes as an 'urgent need to act' the situation 'in particular when the danger exists that the enforcement of a right of a data subject could be considerably impeded'. The urgent measures should provide immediate and direct protection. The GDPR itself foresees two cases where the urgent need to act is presumed to be met, namely those when a supervisory authority does not react or take the necessary measures within one month in the context of mutual assistance (Article 61(8)) or joint operations (Article 62(7)). Both cases require an urgent opinion or a binding decision from the EDPB because of the inaction of a supervisory authority.

4. Whom to inform and how to request an opinion

Article 66(1) second sentence stipulates an information obligation *ex-post*: the provisional measures adopted and the reasons for adopting them have to be communicated without delay to the other DPAs concerned, to the EDPB, and to the Commission.

Article 66(2) has two aspects. First it gives the opportunity[6] to a supervisory authority which has taken a measure pursuant to paragraph 1, and considers that final measures need urgently be adopted, to request an urgent opinion or urgent binding decision from the EDPB. Given the exceptional character of Article 66 and the limited discretion for unilateral action, it may be assumed that in such cases the authority will normally want the provisional measures already adopted to be considered final. Secondly, the EDPB must be consulted in cases of Articles 61(8) and 62(7), where the urgent need to act under Article 66(1) is presumed to be met (see above).

5. Procedure for adoption of a decision by the EDPB

Article 66(4) requires the EDPB to adopt an urgent opinion or an urgent binding decision as provided in Article 66(2)–(3). In such cases it derogates from the procedures foreseen in Articles 64(3) and 65(2). Article 66(4) specifies only the deadline (two weeks) and the voting majority (simple majority) required for the adoption of an urgent opinion or binding decision of the EDPB. This allows a certain amount of procedural flexibility, so that, for example, a request for such an opinion or binding decision can be made in electronic form.

Select Bibliography

EU legislation

EPR Proposal: Proposal for a Regulation of the European Parliament and of the Council concerning the respect for private life and the protection of personal data in electronic communications and repealing Directive 2002/58/EC (Regulation on Privacy and Electronic Communications), COM(2017)10 final, 10 January 2017.

Academic writings

Klabunde 2017: Klabunde, 'Art. 66', in Ehmann and Selmayr (eds.), *Datenschutz-Grundverordnung: DS-GVO* (C. H. BECK 2017), 1013.

---

[6] Expressed in the English version with 'may', in German with 'kann'.

Article 67. Exchange of information

PATRICK VAN EECKE   ANRIJS ŠIMKUS

The Commission may adopt implementing acts of general scope in order to specify the arrangements for the exchange of information by electronic means between supervisory authorities, and between supervisory authorities and the Board, in particular the standardised format referred to in Article 64.

Those implementing acts shall be adopted in accordance with the examination procedure referred to in Article 93(2).

Relevant Recital

(168) The examination procedure should be used for the adoption of implementing acts on standard contractual clauses between controllers and processors and between processors; codes of conduct; technical standards and mechanisms for certification; the adequate level of protection afforded by a third country, a territory or a specified sector within that third country, or an international organisation; standard protection clauses; formats and procedures for the exchange of information by electronic means between controllers, processors and supervisory authorities for binding corporate rules; mutual assistance; and arrangements for the exchange of information by electronic means between supervisory authorities, and between supervisory authorities and the Board.

Closely Related Provisions

Article 51(2) (Obligation for supervisory authorities to cooperate with each other) (see too recital 123); Article 60(12) (Obligation for supervisory authorities to use a standardised format for communicating information to each other); Article 61(9) (Commission power to adopt implementing acts concerning the exchange of information by electronic means); Article 64(4) (Obligation to use a standardised format for communicating information to the Board); Article 93(2) (Committee procedure for adopting implementing acts) (see too recital 167)

Related Provisions in LED [Directive (EU) 2016/680]

Article 50(8) (Commission's powers to specify information exchange) (see too recitals 90–91)

A. Rationale and Policy Underpinnings

Compared to the DPD, the GDPR has put much greater emphasis on the cooperation between the Member State supervisory authorities themselves and between DPAs and the EDPB. A major reason to do so was the ever-increasing amount of cross-border cases and the need to have in place a concrete, coherent and effective system to handle such cases. The one-stop-shop[1] and consistency mechanisms[2] are the most important novelties in this regard, but the GDPR also provides for mandatory cooperation between national DPAs. Up to now, DPAs have used email communication, phone calls and the existing networks discussed below. However, the new context of the GDPR requires a free flow of information between supervisory authorities and between them and the EDPB.

In addition, along with these mechanisms, the GDPR has introduced new and stringent obligations for DPAs, including, in particular, strict time limits for carrying out the aforementioned mechanisms. Consequently, an effective system of cooperation is not only an important element in raising the overall standards of EU data protection, but also a *sine que non* for meeting several time-sensitive requirements laid down by the GDPR. As a result, Article 64(4) specifically requires supervisory authorities and the Commission to, 'without undue delay, communicate by electronic means to the Board, using a standardised format', the information required for EDPB to issue an opinion under the consistency mechanism.[3]

In this light, Article 67 may be seen as a means to implement these obligations and to help improve cooperation by minimising administrative burdens which supervisory authorities and the EDPB will inevitably face in the one-stop-shop and the consistency mechanisms. A solid and well-designed information exchange system, as contemplated by Article 67, would allow DPAs and the EDPB to save valuable time and resources, which could then be better used for completing other tasks, such as responding to data subjects' requests.

Article 67 mandates the Commission to establish specific arrangements for the exchange of information, by adopting an implementing act following the committee procedure laid down in Article 93(2). However, the Commission is not obliged to adopt such an implementing act, nor is there any concrete guidance provided by the GDPR on what criteria the information exchange arrangements should meet. Given the different approaches in information exchange developed and used by the DPAs under the DPD (Communication and Information Resource Centre for Administrations, Businesses and Citizens – 'CIRCABC') and now under the GDPR (Internal Market Information system – 'IMI'), together with the technical and political complexities of implementing a truly effective information exchange system, it is appropriate that the Commission has been given discretion on both whether and how to use the powers granted to it under Article 67 GDPR.

B. Legal Background

1. EU legislation

Article 28(6) DPD stated that 'supervisory authorities shall cooperate with one another to the extent necessary for the performance of their duties, in particular by exchanging all useful information'. Thus, while the DPD laid down a general rule that exchanging information between DPAs formed an essential part of the requirement of cooperation,

---

[1] See the commentary on Art. 60 in this volume.
[2] See the commentaries on Arts. 63–66 in this volume.
[3] See also the obligation under Art. 60(12) to use a standardised format.

it did not provide any further guidance on how exactly exchange of information should take place.

2. International instruments

Several international documents have called for countries to cooperate with each other in the field of data protection, in particular, by exchanging all relevant information, but have not provided any further guidance in what form or manner such exchange should take place. This has been the case with the OECD Recommendation on Cross-border Co-operation in the Enforcement of Laws Protecting Privacy,[4] as well as with many memoranda of understanding, which are bilateral agreements signed between countries' data protection authorities.[5]

In the case of the Council of Europe, Convention 108 is similarly limited,[6] but Modernised Convention 108 will add an obligation on supervisory authorities to provide mutual assistance by 'exchanging relevant and useful information and co-operating with each other'[7] and, to this end, to 'form a network'.[8]

There are some initiatives at the global level, which are aimed specifically at improving information exchange between data protection authorities around the world. Thus, the Global Privacy Enforcement Network ('GPEN') was founded in 2010 and currently has 46 Members, including EU DPAs. This network aims to facilitate cross-border cooperation in the enforcement of privacy laws with the help of the GPEN Alert—a secure internet-based platform that allows GPEN members to alert other members about investigations and find out whether other members are investigating the same company or practice.[9]

Another international forum which focuses inter alia on developing effective information exchange methods is the International Complaints Handling Workshop. Although originally born from the 1999 Spring Conference of European Data Protection Authorities with the principal aim of seeking ways on how to best comply with Article 28(6) DPD, in time this workshop has drawn in not only EU DPAs but also DPAs from other EU accession and European countries.[10]

3. National developments

Since there are no EU or international rules requiring specific information exchange arrangements to be in place, there are thus no concrete or common set of national laws implemented in the Member States. Although Member States should avoid adopting national rules which might impede cooperation under the GDPR, they are otherwise free to decide whether these matters should be regulated by law. However, certain provisions of a general nature might affect information sharing indirectly. For example, a Member State might have in place stricter privacy or confidentiality rules or laws on state secrets, which in certain cases might restrict sharing certain information with other Member States.

---

[4] OECD Recommendation 2007.
[5] For more information and concrete examples of memoranda of understanding, see: Barnard-Wills and Wright 2014, p. 133.
[6] Convention 108, Art. 13(3).   [7] Modernised Convention 108, Art. 17(1)(a).
[8] Ibid, Art. 17(3).   [9] For more information on GPEN, see ibid., p. 117; Blair 2015.
[10] International Complaints Handling Workshop 2004.

C. Analysis

1. Introduction

While Article 67 GDPR is essentially an enabling provision and does not form part of substantive EU data protection law, it could nevertheless play an important role in ensuring that the GDPR is effectively enforced. This commentary looks first at what information exchange arrangements existed under the DPD regime. Then it examines the scope of Article 67 and the potential challenges for the Commission in adopting the implementing act in accordance with this Article. Finally, it looks at the current situation and how DPAs and the EDPB are implementing the exchange of information between each other.

2. Information exchange arrangements between DPAs under the DPD

Since the DPD did not have such stringent rules and concrete requirements on cooperation, DPAs adopted different ways and methods for cooperating with other DPAs, including how to exchange information. Most of the information exchange occurred either through informal ad hoc arrangements, such as an email conversation between several DPAs to discuss a cross-border case, or by using one of the many information sharing platforms offered by EU or international bodies.

In a survey conducted shortly before the GDPR came into effect, DPAs were asked to share their perspectives on a number of issues related to the EU data protection reform on cooperation, including matters concerning the exchange of information.[11] This survey revealed that cooperation and, more specifically, information exchange was done primarily on an informal basis; that DPAs shared the information which they deemed necessary and relevant for a particular case; that the information was shared mainly via focused email messages, or bilateral meetings; and that there were no pre-agreed, binding standards for either the format or the contents of the information.

Along with the international fora mentioned above, such as the GPEN and the International Complaints Handling Workshop, DPAs also had at their disposal certain fora and information exchange systems exclusive to the EU. The European Conference of Data Protection Commissioners, known as the 'Spring Conference', has often featured cooperation between DPAs in its discussions. Some DPAs were also members of the Working Party on Information Exchange and Data Protection ('DAPIX')[12], a working group of the Council of Ministers aimed at improving the exchange of information between law enforcement authorities. The principal information exchange system used by European DPAs and the Commission, acting as the secretariat of the WP29, was the CIRCABC.[13] This is a tool for the sharing of information and resources and for the distribution and management of documents across multiple languages in collaborative online working spaces.

The fora and tools discussed above worked to improve the experience of exchanging certain information, but there were no legally binding obligations for DPAs to use any particular sharing method or application.

---

[11] Barnard-Wills et al. 2016.   [12] DAPIX Website.   [13] CIRCABC Website.

3. The scope of Article 67—arrangements not only for the one-stop-shop and consistency mechanisms

Article 67 GDPR is situated in Chapter VII of the GDPR, which deals with cooperation and consistency. However, the wording of this provision suggests that the drafters of the GDPR did not exclude the possibility that arrangements for information exchange adopted pursuant to Article 67 could relate to the work of the DPAs and the EDPB in a broader sense, covering more aspects than those needed for the two mechanisms. Thus, such arrangements could also relate to the sharing of general knowledge and case law among those involved, which is not related to any particular individual case.

Although the GDPR places an obligation to cooperate and exchange information only in order to deal with cross-border cases, this does not mean that any other forms of cooperation should be neglected. As Raab writes: 'Collaboration outside of enforcement provides opportunities for DPAs to increase their regulatory capacity and effectiveness in relation to globalised threats to privacy'.[14] It would be to everyone's advantage if effective and practical information exchange arrangements could be put in place to permit DPAs and the EDPB to exchange information regarding upcoming meetings and conferences, whether formal or informal, about case law and best practices in handling different cases and data subject complaints. Sharing knowledge in these fields can also contribute to the consistent application of the GDPR in the broadest sense.

The power to adopt an implementing act for introducing information exchange arrangements under Article 67 has been granted to the Commission for good reason. The Commission has extensive experience and knowledge in how to handle large amounts of information being exchanged between several Member State authorities, as seen inter alia in the CIRCABC and IMI systems discussed herein, and has a vast amount of technical, financial and human resources to facilitate any such arrangements. Most importantly, it is the Union institution empowered and accustomed to propose changes to Union law.

Among its many advantages, the Commission's translation services certainly rank as crucial for establishing an effective and beneficial information exchange system, as they are one of the largest in the world and are well-equipped to handle translation requests in the 24 official EU languages.[15]

Many DPAs have pointed out that language diversity among EU Member States is one of the main factors, which could impede putting into place any systematic arrangements.[16] The PHAEDRA project recommended that translation should be kept to an absolute minimum for routine cooperation between authorities,[17] and found that in practice English is, and is likely to remain, the default lingua franca of internationally active staff at DPAs.[18] In this respect, the EDPB has decided that the 'working language of the Board shall be English'[19] and that '[d]ocuments drafted by the supervisory authorities for the procedures foreseen under Articles 64–66 and 70 GDPR shall be submitted in English.[20]

In contrast, the PHAEDRA project recommended that translation of collectively generated material (guidance notes, education material, press releases) should be maximised to make the best use of the intellectual and policy effort required to generate the content.[21]

---

[14] Raab 2010. [15] EC Website Translation.
[16] Barnard-Wills et al. 2016, pp. 590 and 597. [17] Ibid., p. 27. [18] Ibid., p. 28.
[19] Art. 23(1) EDPB Rules of Procedure. [20] Ibid., Art. 23(2).
[21] Barnard-Wills et al. 2017, p.27.

In this respect, the Board has decided that '[d]ocuments adopted pursuant to Article 64–66 GDPR and Article 70 GDPR shall be translated into all official languages of the EU'.[22] However, its annual report will be available in English, with only its executive summary available in all official languages of the EU.[23] Similarly, the EDPB website will be in English, whilst its static parts and press releases are available in all official languages of the EU.[24]

It should also be noted that in many situations DPAs would need to translate certain documents back into the local language for presentation before national authorities and data subjects. This is particularly the case where a lead DPA adopts a final decision in a cross-border case, which might then be challenged by data subjects in a Member State with a language different from the one in which the decision was issued.

Whatever the final outlook of such arrangements might be, all key stakeholders will need to make hard choices in finding the best balance between costs and efficiency when it comes to translation.

4. Challenges in creating a one-size-fits-all information exchange system

The cautious wording of Article 67 indicates the drafters' limited expectations about coming up with meaningful information exchange arrangements, which would be a real benefit rather than another tedious administrative formality. The previously mentioned issue of having multiple languages alone presents considerable difficulties in achieving this task. Unfortunately, there are many other considerations to take into account in this regard.

Another indicator of the difficulty of adopting an implementing act under Article 67 is the number of the different information exchange mechanisms already in place. One might wonder, if after all this time nobody has been able to come up with a one-size-fits-all system, then why would it suddenly be a different story with Article 67? Moreover, some of the previously mentioned information exchange platforms have been criticised by the DPAs themselves. For instance, some DPAs have expressed doubts about the design and control of CIRCABC,[25] and others are reluctant to use the GPEN system for case-sensitive information sharing because of the US influence there.[26]

Before the entry into application of the GDPR, some DPAs did not even regard a universal and binding information exchange system as necessary. They believed that the lack of such a system would not be a severe barrier or challenge to effective cooperation, and for this reason it would have little positive impact.[27] Instead, these DPAs were keen on keeping flexible working conditions and the ability to determine their own strategies in both dealing with specific cross-border cases, and achieving effective cooperation in general. These are indeed very legitimate considerations, but it remains to be seen whether the same approach will continue in the face of the much greater cooperation required under the GDPR and the information exchange arrangements which have now been put in place. The Commission will have to take all these factors into careful consideration when considering whether to adopt an implementing act under Article 67.

---

[22] Art. 23(4) EDPB Rules of Procedure.   [23] Ibid., Art. 35.   [24] Ibid., Art. 38.
[25] Barnard-Wills et al. 2016, p. 593.   [26] Ibid., p. 595.   [27] Ibid., p. 592.

5. Current information exchange arrangements in place

In view of the entry into application of the GDPR, the EDPB and DPAs have resorted to an existing Commission information sharing system, and adapted it to serve the GDPR.

The IMI is an IT-based information network developed and managed by the Commission's DG GROW, which links up national, regional and local authorities across borders. The network was first created in 2008, but the IMI Regulation adopted in 2012 made clear the network's scope and rules of operation for exchanges of information for the purpose of administrative cooperation.[28] Currently more than 7,000 EU Member State authorities, which manage more than ten different areas of EU law, are registered on this network. IMI's main goal is to assist these authorities in their daily tasks when communicating and exchanging information with other EU Member State authorities. IMI has the following main features: a multilingual search function that helps competent authorities identify their counterparts in another country; pre-translated questions and answers for all cases where they are likely to need information from abroad; a tracking mechanism allowing users to follow the progress of their information; requests and that enabling IMI coordinators at national or regional level to intervene if there are problems.[29]

IMI has now been specially tailored for DPAs and the Board. At the EDPS' request, as part of its preparations for the Board, the Commission introduced amendments to the IMI Regulation via the Single Digital Gateway Regulation to 'clarify the coordinated supervision mechanism foreseen for IMI and ... enable the new European Data Protection Board ... to benefit from the technical possibilities offered by IMI for information exchange under the GDPR'.[30] Previously Article 5(g) of the IMI Regulation had a narrower scope limited to 'competent authorities, IMI coordinators and the Commission', but this was extended for GDPR purposes to 'Union bodies, offices and agencies'.[31] Thus, whilst national supervisory authorities already fell within the scope of the IMI Regulation, the modification enabled access to IMI for the EDPB Secretariat and the EDPS itself, as a member of the Board, for GDPR purposes.

In consequence, IMI has been used by DPAs and the Board since 25 May 2018[32] to assist them in fulfilling their cooperation and consistency tasks under the GDPR. The EDPB requires that all documents have to be sent to the Board's secretariat via the designated IT system.[33] DPAs are able to use IMI to identify the lead DPA and concerned DPAs for a cross-border case, cooperate for the resolution of cross-border cases, request and provide assistance to other DPAs, arrange joint operations involving multiple DPAs, and consult the EDPB to obtain an opinion or a binding decision.[34]

Shortly after the IMI started operating for GDPR purposes, the EDPB announced that more than 100 cross-border cases had already been registered in the network.[35] In May 2019 the Board reported that a total of 446 cross-border cases had been registered, of which 205 had led to One-Stop-Shop procedures and 19 to final outcomes.[36] Overall, the Board reported that the 'feedback of the national regulators in this system is really positive'.[37]

---

[28] IMI Regulation.   [29] EC Website IMI 2017.   [30] EDPS Annual Report 2017, p. 39.
[31] Art. 38 Single Digital Gateway Regulation.
[32] In the period from 25 May until the Single Digital Gateway Regulation, the GDPR bodies used IMI for GDPR purposes under the Implementing Decision 2018/743.
[33] Art. 10(1) EDPB Rules of Procedure.   [34] EC Website IMI 2018; EDPB Website 2018A.
[35] EDPB Website 2018B.   [36] EDPB 2019A.   [37] EDPB 2019B, p. 2.

6. Conclusion

At the time of writing, the Commission has not adopted any implementing act pursuant to Article 67. In light of the above, a certain amount of time should certainly be allowed to pass in order to determine the efficiency and potential of the one-stop-shop and consistency mechanisms, how cooperation in general is carried out by DPAs and the EDPB, and the extent to which the IMI responds to these needs. Once such feedback is obtained the Commission will be able to consider whether Article 67 needs to come into play. In the meantime, it can be presumed that all information exchange arrangements between the involved parties will be coordinated based on the discretionary powers and instructions of the EDPB.

Select Bibliography

EU legislation

IMI Regulation: Regulation (EU) No. 1024/2012 of the European Parliament and of the Council of 25 October 2012 on administrative cooperation through the Internal Market Information System and repealing Commission Decision 2008/49/EC ('the IMI Regulation'), OJ 2012 L 316/1.
Implementing Decision 2018/743: Commission Implementing Decision (EU) 2018/743 of 16 May 2018 on a pilot project to implement the administrative cooperation provisions set out in Regulation (EU) 2016/679 of the European Parliament and of the Council by means of the Internal Market Information System, OJ 2018 L 123/115.
Single Digital Gateway Regulation: Regulation (EU) 2018/1724 of the European Parliament and the Council of 2 October 2018 establishing a single digital gateway to provide access to information, to procedures and to assistance and problem-solving services and amending Regulation (EU) No. 1024/2012, OJ 2018 L 295/1.

Academic writings

Barnard-Wills et al. 2016: Barnard-Willis, Pauner Chulvi and de Hert, 'Data Protection Authority Perspectives on the Impact of Data Protection Reform on Cooperation in the EU', 32 *Computer Law & Security Review* (2016), 587.
Raab 2010: Raab, 'Information Privacy: Networks of Regulation at the Subglobal Level', 1(3) *Global Policy* (2010), 291.

Papers of data protection authorities

EDPB 2019A: European Data Protection Board, '1 year GDPR – taking stock' (22 May 2019).
EDPB 2019B: European Data Protection Board, 'First overview on the implementation of the GDPR and the roles and means of the national supervisory authorities' (26 February 2019).
EDPB Rules of Procedure: European Data Protection Board, 'Rules of Procedure' (25 May 2018).
EDPS Annual Report 2017: European Data Protection Supervisor, 'Annual Report 2017' (19 March 2018).

Reports and recommendations

Barnard-Wills and Wright 2014: Barnard-Wills and Wright, 'Co-Ordination and Co-Operation between Data Protection Authorities', Workstream 1 report for the PHAEDRA I project (1 April 2014), available at http://www.phaedra-project.eu/wp-content/uploads/PHAEDRA-D1-30-Dec-2014.pdf.

Barnard-Wills et al. 2017: Barnard-Wills, Papakonstantinou, Pauner Chulvi and Díaz Lafuente, 'Recommendations for Improving Practical Cooperation between European Data Protection Authorities', Deliverable D4.1 for the PHAEDRA II project (14 January 2017), available at http://www.phaedra-project.eu/wp-content/uploads/PHAEDRA2_D41_final_20170114.pdf.

Blair 2015: Blair, 'Big Year for Global Privacy Enforcement Network: GPEN Releases 2014 Annual Report' (1 April 2015), available at https://www.privacyenforcement.net/node/513.

OECD Recommendation 2007: Organisation for Economic Co-operation and Development, 'OECD Recommendation on Cross-Border Co-Operation in the Enforcement of Laws Protecting Privacy' (2007).

Others

CIRCABC Website: Communication and Information Resource Centre for Administrations, Businesses and Citizens (CIRCABC), 'About', available at https://joinup.ec.europa.eu/collection/communication-and-information-resource-centre-administrations-businesses-and-citizens/about.

DAPIX Website: Council of the European Union, 'Working Party on Information Exchange and Data Protection (DAPIX)', available at https://www.consilium.europa.eu/en/council-eu/preparatory-bodies/working-party-information-exchange-data-protection/.

EC Website IMI 2017: European Commission, 'Internal Market Information System' (2017), available at http://ec.europa.eu/internal_market/scoreboard/performance_by_governance_tool/internal_market_information_system/index_en.htm.

EC Website IMI 2018: European Commission, 'IMI Helps Enforce GDPR' (2 August 2018), available at http://ec.europa.eu/internal_market/imi-net/news/2018/07/index_en.htm.

EC Website Translation: European Commission, 'Translation', available at http://ec.europa.eu/languages/policy/linguistic-diversity/official-languages-eu_en.htm.

EDPB Website 2018A: European Data Protection Board, 'State of Play—IMI for GDPR Purposes', (27 June 2018), available at https://edpb.europa.eu/news/news/2018/state-play-imi-gdpr-purposes_en.

EDPB Website 2018B: European Data Protection Board, 'Second Plenary Meeting: ICANN, PSD2, Privacy Shield', (5 July 2018), available at https://edpb.europa.eu/news/news/2018/european-data-protection-board-second-plenary-meeting-icann-psd2-privacy-shield_en.

International Complaints Handling Workshop 2004: Spring Conference of the European Data Protection Authorities, 'The International Complaints Handling Workshop: Evolution & Consolidation' (2004), available at https://giodo.gov.pl/data/filemanager_pl/667.pdf.

Section 3 European Data Protection Board

Article 68. European Data Protection Board

CHRISTOPHER DOCKSEY

1. The European Data Protection Board (the 'Board') is hereby established as a body of the Union and shall have legal personality.
2. The Board shall be represented by its Chair.
3. The Board shall be composed of the head of one supervisory authority of each Member State and of the European Data Protection Supervisor, or their respective representatives.
4. Where in a Member State more than one supervisory authority is responsible for monitoring the application of the provisions pursuant to this Regulation, a joint representative shall be appointed in accordance with that Member State's law.
5. The Commission shall have the right to participate in the activities and meetings of the Board without voting right. The Commission shall designate a representative. The Chair of the Board shall communicate to the Commission the activities of the Board.
6. In the cases referred to in Article 65, the European Data Protection Supervisor shall have voting rights only on decisions which concern principles and rules applicable to the Union institutions, bodies, offices and agencies which correspond in substance to those of this Regulation.

Relevant Recital

(139) In order to promote the consistent application of this Regulation, the Board should be set up as an independent body of the Union. To fulfil its objectives, the Board should have legal personality. The Board should be represented by its Chair. It should replace the Working Party on the Protection of Individuals with Regard to the Processing of Personal Data established by Directive 95/46/EC. It should consist of the head of a supervisory authority of each Member State and the European Data Protection Supervisor or their respective representatives. The Commission should participate in the Board's activities without voting rights and the European Data Protection Supervisor should have specific voting rights. The Board should contribute to the consistent application of this Regulation throughout the Union, including by advising the Commission, in particular on the level of protection in third countries or international organisations, and promoting cooperation of the supervisory authorities throughout the Union. The Board should act independently when performing its tasks.

Closely Related Provisions

Article 57 (Tasks of supervisory authorities), Article 58 (Powers of supervisory authorities) (see too recital 129); Article 69 (Independence of the EDPB); Article 70 (Tasks of the EDPB); Article 71 (Reports); Article 72 (Procedure within the EDPB); Article 73 (Chair of the EDPB); Article 74 (Tasks of the Chair); Article 75 (Secretariat of the EDPB) (see too recitals 118 and 140); Article 76 (Confidentiality within the EDPB).

Related Provisions in LED [Directive (EU) 2016/680]

Article 51 (Tasks of the EDPB) (see too recital 84)

Related Provisions in EUDPR [Regulation 2018/1725]

Article 55 (Independence) (see too recitals 2 and 72); Article 57(1)(k) (Participation in the activities of the European Data Protection Board) (see too recital 60)

Relevant Case Law

CJEU

Case C-9/56, *Meroni & Co., Industrie Metallurgiche, SpA v High Authority of the European Coal and Steel Community*, judgment of 13 June 1958 (ECLI:EU:C:1958:7).
Case C-317/04, *European Parliament v Council of the European Union ('PNR')*, order of 17 March 2005 (Grand Chamber) (ECLI:EU:C:2005:189).
Case C-518/07, *European Commission v Federal Republic of Germany*, judgment of 9 March 2010 (Grand Chamber) (ECLI:EU:C:2010:125).
Case C-614/10, *European Commission v Republic of Austria*, judgment of 16 October 2012 (Grand Chamber) (ECLI:EU:C:2012:63).
Case C-270/12, *United Kingdom of Great Britain and Northern Ireland v European Parliament and Council of the European Union ('ESMA')*, judgment of 22 January 2014 (Grand Chamber) (ECLI:EU:C:2014:18).

A. Rationale and Policy Underpinnings

The rationale behind the establishment of the EDPB was to create an independent EU body which could promote a more effective and consistent application of the data protection rules across the Union, as part of the structured cooperation laid down in Chapter VII, as well as having its own advisory tasks, quite distinct from the consistency mechanism.

In 2010 the Commission set out its approach to modernising the EU data protection legal framework in its Communication on 'A Comprehensive Approach on Personal Data Protection in the European Union'.[1] It stressed the role of supervisory authorities and the WP29 but noted the 'continuing divergent application and interpretation of EU rules by Data Protection Authorities'. The Commission therefore called for a 'strengthening of the Working Party's role in coordinating DPAs' positions, ensuring a more uniform application at national level and thus an equivalent level of data protection'. Specifically, it undertook to examine, amongst others:

[H]ow to ensure a more consistent application of EU data protection rules across the internal market. This may include strengthening the role of national data protection supervisors, better coordinating their work via the Article 29 Working Party (which should become a more transparent body), and/or creating a mechanism for ensuring consistency in the internal market under the authority of the European Commission.[2]

Some ideas were retained in the GDPR, notably the aim of greater transparency of the Board and the aim of creating a consistency mechanism. Others were not, notably the aim of placing the consistency mechanism under the authority of the Commission.

As for the supervisory authorities themselves, the WP29 welcomed the 'brand new governance model' under the GDPR and forecast the role of the Board as one of 'three

---

[1] EC Communication 2010.   [2] Ibid., pp. 17–18.

pillars' of this new 'distributed governance' model: 'national data protection authorities, enhanced co-operation between authorities and EDPB level for consistency'.[3]

B. Legal Background

1. EU legislation

Article 29 DPD established the WP29. Recital 65 DPD explained that 'having regard to its specific nature, [the WP29] must advise the Commission and, in particular, contribute to the uniform application of the national rules adopted pursuant to this Directive'. Although the WP29 did not have legal personality under the DPD, it was supposed to act independently.

Article 29(2) of the DPD included a representative of the Commission as a member of the WP29. However, the Commission had no right to vote, which was restricted under Article 29(3) to the representatives of the supervisory authorities.

Article 29(4) DPD concerning the chair of the WP29 made no provision for the salary of the Chair. Over the history of the WP29 its chairs served part-time at the same time as serving and being remunerated as the head of their national supervisory authorities.

2. International instruments

The two Council of Europe Conventions on data protection in force when this text was finalised are limited to mutual assistance[4] and coooperation.[5] However Article 17(3) of Modernised Convention 108 provides that, in order to organise their cooperation and to perform their duties, supervisory authorities should 'form a network'. Article 143 of the Explanatory Report explains that such a network would be a 'means to contribute to the rationalisation of the co-operation process and thus to the efficiency of the protection of personal data'. It also stresses that 'the Convention refers to "a network" in singular form'.

The EEA Agreement, as amended in July 2018,[6] incorporates the GDPR into its Annexes and provides that the provisions of the GDPR should be read, for the purposes of that Agreement, with a number of adaptations concerning the participation of the supervisory authorities of Norway, Iceland and Liechtenstein, the three EFTA States participating in the EEA,[7] and the EFTA Surveillance Authority in the composition and workings of the EDPB. In this respect, the amended Agreement provides:[8]

(a) The supervisory authorities of the EFTA States shall participate in the activities of the European Data Protection Board, hereinafter referred to as "the Board". To that effect, they shall, but for the right to vote and to stand for election as chair or deputy chairs of the Board, have the same rights and obligations as supervisory authorities of the EU Member States in the Board, unless otherwise provided in this Agreement. The positions of the supervisory authorities of the EFTA States shall be recorded separately by the Board. The rules of procedures of the Board shall give full effect to the participation of the supervisory authorities of the EFTA States and the EFTA Surveillance Authority with the exception of voting rights and to stand for election as chair or deputy chairs of the Board.

[3] WP29 2016, p. 2. [4] Art. 13(3)(b) Convention 108.
[5] Art. 1(5) Additional Protocol Convention 108, see Table of Legislation.
[6] EEA Decision 2018.
[7] Switzerland, the fourth EFTA State is not a signatory to the EEA Agreement.
[8] Art. 5e EEA Decision 2018.

(b) Notwithstanding the provisions of Protocol 1 to this Agreement, and unless otherwise provided for in this Agreement, the terms 'Member State(s)' and 'supervisory authorities' shall be understood to include, in addition to their meaning in the Regulation, the EFTA States and their supervisory authorities, respectively.

...

(k) The EFTA Surveillance Authority shall have the right to participate in the meetings of the Board without voting right. The EFTA Surveillance Authority shall designate a representative.
(l) Where it is relevant to the exercise of its functions under Article 109 of this Agreement, the EFTA Surveillance Authority shall have the right to request advice or opinions from, and to communicate matters to, the Board pursuant to Articles 63, 64(2), 65(1)(c) and 70(1)(e). In Articles 63, 64(2), 65(1)(c), and 70(1)(e), the words 'and, where relevant, the EFTA Surveillance Authority' shall be added after the words 'the Commission'.
(m) The Chair of the Board, or the secretariat, shall communicate to the EFTA Surveillance Authority the activities of the Board, where relevant pursuant to Articles 64(5)(a) and (b), 65(5), and 75(6)(b). In Articles 64(5)(a) and (b), 65(5), and 75(6)(b), the words 'and, where relevant, the EFTA Surveillance Authority' shall be added after the words 'the Commission'.
(n) In Article 71(1), the words ', to the Standing Committee of the EFTA States, to the EFTA Surveillance Authority' shall be inserted after the words 'to the Council'.
(o) In Article 73(1), the following sentence shall be added: 'The EFTA States' members of the Board shall not be eligible to be elected as chair or deputy chairs'.

3. Case law

The case law of the CJEU is discussed below concerning the question whether the conferral of powers on the Board is consistent with the *Meroni* doctrine[9] and the question of the independence of supervisory authorities in the context of the Board.[10]

C. Analysis

1. Presentation

The provisions governing the EDPB are set forth in Section 3 of Chapter VII of the GDPR. This places the Board squarely within the provisions governing cooperation between supervisory authorities and the consistency mechanism. These provisions confer a wide range of tasks on the Board, including interpretation, authorisation and adjudication.

Article 68 addresses the nature, status and composition of the Board and its Chair. Recital 139, common to the articles in Section 3 GDPR, introduces the other main elements enshrined in Section 3, including independence, governance and transparency.

Article 3 of the EDPB Rules of Procedure sets out seven Guiding Principles underpinning the work of the Board, namely the principles of independence and impartiality; good governance; integrity and good administrative behaviour; collegiality and inclusiveness; cooperation, transparency; efficiency and modernisation; and proactivity.

---

[9] See Case C-9/56, *Meroni*; Order in Case C-317/04, *'PNR'*; Case C-518/07, *Commission v Germany*; and Case C-270/12, *'ESMA'*.
[10] See Case C-518/07, *Commission v Germany* and Case C-614/10, *Commission v Austria*. See also the commentary on Art. 69 in this volume.

2. Replacing the Article 29 Working Party

Recital 139 explains that the Board 'should replace the Working Party on the Protection of Individuals with Regard to the Processing of Personal Data established by Directive 95/46/EC'. As will be seen, whilst the membership of the two bodies is the same, the nature of the WP29 and the Board are completely different. On the one hand, the Board will continue the advisory work of the WP29, in particular the provision of advice by way of Guidelines on the interpretation of the GDPR, adopted after the consultation of stakeholders. On the other hand, the Board is an independent EU body with significant new powers in the context of the consistency mechanism. Robert comments that both of these functions will contribute to laying down a 'European jurisprudence' on data protection.[11] Lynskey argues that the new role of the Board, at the heart of the consistency mechanism, will lead to the 'Europeanisation' of data protection law in the sense of the 'institutionalisation at European level of a system of governance with the authority to enact European-wide binding rules and to formalise interactions between domestic authorities'.[12] This central governance role of the Board, in comparison to that of the WP29, will require effective management by the Chair, clear input by the Secretariat and a great deal of good will and cooperation by its members.[13]

The question arises whether the conferral of powers on the Board is consistent with the *Meroni* doctrine. This doctrine only permits the delegation of powers by the Commission to EU bodies or agencies provided they are clearly defined and they do not empower the delegated agency to exercise a 'wide margin of discretion'.[14] In terms of this case law, the Board is an autonomous, *sui generis* EU body with its own legal personality and prerogatives, and is expected to enjoy a 'high degree of professional expertise'.[15] Moreover the Board exercises its powers within the 'strictly circumscribed circumstances'[16] of the enforcement of the data protection legal framework,[17] which forms part of the fundamental rights architecture of the EU.[18] More important, the Board is not a body or agency exercising executive powers delegated from the Commission; its powers are directly conferred by the EU legislator and they are only appropriate for an independent authority. Indeed, in view of the extensive case law of the CJEU on Article 18(3) of the Charter, the powers of the Board, affecting as they do those of national supervisory authorities and the EDPS, could not be conferred on the Commission. The establishment of the Board is therefore unlikely to infringe the *Meroni* doctrine.[19]

3. EU body with legal personality

Article 68(1) provides that '[t]he European Data Protection Board (the 'Board') is hereby established as a body of the Union and shall have legal personality'. Article 69 adds that it shall 'act independently when performing its tasks or exercising its powers'. Recital 139 explains that '[i]n order to promote the consistent application of this Regulation, the

---

[11] Robert 2017, p. 82.
[12] Lynskey 2017, p. 254. See also Hijmans 2016B, pp. 4–5; and Risse, Caporoso and Cowles 2001, p. 3.
[13] Robert 2017, p. 58.   [14] Case C-9/56, *Meroni*, para. 152. See Busuioc 2013, p. 19.
[15] Case C-270/12, *'ESMA'*, para. 85.   [16] Ibid., paras. 64 and 98.
[17] Order in Case C-317/04, *'PNR'*, paras. 16–18 (intervention of the EDPS).
[18] Case C-518/07, *Commission v Germany*, paras. 22–24.
[19] See the discussion and literature cited in Hijmans 2016A, pp. 359–360.

Board should be set up as an independent body of the Union. To fulfil its objectives, the Board should have legal personality'.

The Commission proposal did not give legal personality to the Board as an independent EU body. The Board may be contrasted with the Body of European Regulators for Electronic Communications ('BEREC'), the collective body of telecoms regulators, which neither is a Community agency nor has legal personality.[20] In this respect, the Commission had originally proposed the establishment of a European Electronic Communications Market Authority, but this was resisted by Member States and their national regulators, who preferred the looser model embodied in the BEREC.[21]

The legal personality of the Board was added by the Council during the negotiations[22] and supported by the WP29.[23] Legal personality strengthens the nature of the Board as a government body in its own right, deriving its legitimacy directly from legislation rather than by delegation from the Commission.[24] In practical terms it means that the Board may take action before the courts.[25]

The question arises as to the legal nature of the Board. On the one hand it is not an EU institution in the sense of Article 13 Treaty on the European Union ('TEU') nor is it treated as an institution for budgetary[26] or staffing[27] purposes, as in the case of the Committee of the Regions, the Economic and Social Committee, the European Ombudsman and the EDPS. The GDPR provides that the Board must depend on the EDPS to provide its facilities and its staff and the EDPS also hosts and defends the Board's budget.[28] However the Board will have to be accountable for its decisions, in particular to the European Parliament; indeed, the CJEU has stressed that the absence of parliamentary control over supervisory authorities is 'inconceivable',[29] and the fact that Board does not have its own independent budget does not affect its independence.[30]

Moreover, unlike national supervisory authorities, the Board is an EU body, subject to the obligations of such bodies under EU law and to the oversight of the various supervisory bodies of the EU system. This means that its decisions may be appealed to the General Court under Article 263 Treaty on the Functioning of the European Union ('TFEU'); its budgetary and administrative activity is supervised by the Court of Auditors under Article 287 TFEU; it is accountable to the European Parliament, in particular to the Committee on Budgetary Control ('CONT') and the Committee on Civil Liberties, Justice and Home Affairs ('LIBE'); it is subject to the oversight of the European Ombudsman with regard to the right to good administration enshrined in Article 41 of the Charter of Fundamental Rights of the European Union ('CFR'); under Article 76(2) GDPR it will have to respect the rules on public access to documents enshrined in Article 42 CFR and Article 15 TFEU and developed in Regulation 1049/2001;[31] and its respect for the EU-level data protection rules is supervised by the EDPS. All these features

---

[20] Rec. 6 Regulation 1211/2009.   [21] Thatcher 2011, pp. 802–803.
[22] Art. 64(1a) of the Council text in the trilogue.   [23] WP Propositions 2015, p. 1.
[24] Vibert 2007, pp. 114–128.
[25] See Art. 36 EDPB Rules of Procedure, empowering the Chair to appoint the agents representing the Board before the Court of Justice.
[26] Art. 2(b) Regulation 966/2012.   [27] Art. 1b EU Staff Regulations.
[28] Section VI.1.iv EDPB EDPS MoU.   [29] Case C-518/07, *Commission v Germany*, para. 43.
[30] Case C-614/10, *Commission v Austria*, para. 58.
[31] Regulation 1049/2001.

contribute to the political and legal accountability, also characterised as the 'social responsiveness',[32] of the Board as an independent EU body.

Unlike the WP29, the Board has, in addition to its legal personality, decision-making powers which are legally binding on independent supervisory authorities. The question arises whether the fact that such decisions interfere with the independence of these authorities requires the Board itself to be an independent supervisory authority within the meaning of Article 8(3) CFR. The nature, characteristics and powers of the Board and its constituent parts are further defined in Articles 69–75 of the GDPR.[33]

4. Chair

Article 68(2) provides that the Board shall be represented by its Chair. The Commission proposal did not provide for this, it was added by the European Parliament during negotiations. The function of 'representation' is both public and formal.

Like the Chair of the WP29, the Chair of the Board will represent the Board and its supervisory authorities in public. She will appear as Chair at conferences inside the EU and abroad, she will meet the press after meetings of the Board, and she will represent the Board at discussions of the European Parliament and when presenting the Annual Report to the Parliament.

Unlike the Chair of the WP29, the Chair of the Board will also have a formal role, representing the Board legally. The Chair will sign the decisions of the Board, represent the Board before the European Courts, and nominate its Agents before those Courts.

The appointment and tasks of the Chair (and deputy chairs) are laid down in Articles 73 and 74.[34]

The EEA Agreement provides that EEA EFTA supervisory authorities may not serve as the Chair or as a deputy Chair of the Board.[35]

5. National supervisory authorities

As proposed by the Commission, Article 68(3) provides that the Board shall be composed of the head of one supervisory authority in each Member State and the EDPS, or their respective representatives.[36] Article 29(2) DPD was similarly worded to Article 68(3) but there are a number of specific differences. The DPD only provided for a 'representative' of the national DPA or DPAs, whereas the Board is composed of the *head* of the supervisory authority. This consolidates the practice that heads of the supervisory authorities attend the plenary meetings of the WP29. It also emphasises that the Board is intended to be a high-level body, composed of the heads of European supervisory authorities, with the aim of ensuring effective interaction and coherence between the EU and national levels. This significantly increases the 'self-binding' effect on national authorities of discussions and decisions by their heads at the Board. According to the principle of reliance and legitimate expectations, a 'body will be bound itself by guidance it gives'.[37]

In addition, Article 68(3) provides for *one* supervisory authority. Where a Member State has established more than one supervisory authority, for example in Germany and

---

[32] Zemánek 2012, p. 1765.   [33] See the commentaries on Arts. 69 to 75 in this volume.
[34] See the commentaries on Arts. 73 and 74 in this volume.   [35] Art. 5e(o) EEA Decision.
[36] See also Art. 4(1) EDPB Rules of Procedure.   [37] Meijers Committee 2018, p. 3.

Spain, Article 68(4) provides that those authorities should be represented by a joint representative, similarly to Article 51(3) GDPR. However, unlike the DPD, the Commission proposal and Article 51(3), Article 68(4) specifies that the joint representative should be appointed in accordance with the national law of that Member State. This was added by the European Parliament during negotiations. Pursuant to the EEA Agreement, Article 4(3) of the EDPB Rules of Procedure provides that the same rule applies to EFTA EEA supervisory authorities.

Article 68(4) also deals with the case of the absence of the head of a supervisory authority acting as the representative, or joint representative, of the EU or EEA EFTA authority or authorities concerned. In this case a representative should be designated by the respective supervisory authority, who is entitled to attend and participate with voting rights. It adds that, in the case of a joint representative, that person may be accompanied by the head of another supervisory authority of their state or its representative, who could also act as a representative in the case of absence, again in accordance with that Member State's law. This both weakens and tries to compensate for the emphasis on the attendance of the head of the designated authority, faced with the inevitable problem of absence caused by illness and by the competing agendas of the head of the authority acting both in Brussels and at home.

Finally, Article 8(5) provides that the members and participants of the Board may be assisted by their staff members. No doubt in view of considerations of available space at the meetings, it advises that the 'number of staff members per delegation attending the meetings should be limited to the minimum necessary taking into account the importance and variety of issues to be addressed'. In any event, Article 16 of the EDPB Rules of Procedure provides that only one representative of each Member State will be reimbursed for travel expenses for attending plenary meetings and expert subgroups. Representatives from EFTA EEA States do not enjoy this entitlement.

The GDPR does not lay down provisions on the eligibility and qualifications required, or the mandate and the end of mandate of the members of the Board, unlike Article 53 GDPR with regard to the members of supervisory authorities. The only qualification required is to be the head of a supervisory authority, or their representative, and thus questions of eligibility and mandate will follow the governance of the authority concerned, as provided under Article 53.

6. European Data Protection Supervisor (EDPS)

The EDPS had not been established at the time of the adoption of the DPD in 1995. In consequence there was only a general enabling clause in Article 29(2) DPD for one or more future European-level supervisory authorities. This provided that where there was more than one supervisory authority established for the Community institutions and bodies in the future, those authorities should be represented by a joint representative. In the event there was only ever one such body, the EDPS. Although other supervisory bodies were established (the Joint Supervisory Bodies ('JSB') for Europol and Eurojust), they were not Community bodies and thus fell outside the scope of the DPD and hence of the WP29. The EDPS was therefore designated as a member of the Board in Article 68(3), and there is no provision for any joint representative.

In May 2017 the EDPS took over supervision of Europol under the new Europol Regulation.[38] The EDPS will be responsible for supervision of the new European Public Prosecutor's Office ('EPPO')[39] and will take over supervision of Eurojust from 12 December 2019.[40] These developments confirm the policy of providing membership of the Board for only one supervisory body at EU level, the EDPS.

Article 68(6) limits the voting rights of the EDPS in the Board in the dispute resolution procedure under Article 65 to cases which concern principles and rules applicable to EU bodies which correspond in substance to those of the GDPR. That is, to cases where the principles and rules applicable to EU institutions and bodies under the EUDPR are similarly applicable under the GDPR.

This formula was a compromise. On the one hand the Council contained a number of Member States that wished to completely exclude the voting rights of the EDPS within the Board, on the basis that the EDPS should not be involved in cases which do not concern them. On the other hand, the Commission wished to treat the EDPS in the same way as any other supervisory authority. In view of the undeniable status of the EDPS as an independent supervisory authority in the sense of Article 8(3) CFR,[41] it was agreed in the trilogue to limit the restriction on voting rights in the dispute resolution procedure to the scope of the EDPS's jurisdiction, using the formula in Article 68(6). The compromise is designed to reconcile the principle that the EDPS should not be involved in cases which do not concern him and the countervailing principle that the EDPS is a supervisory authority in the sense of Article 8(3) CFR and should be treated as such in order to ensure the effective protection of individuals.

Having reconciled these principles in theory, there is little difference in practice to the participation of the EDPS in the Board. The legal framework in which the EDPS operates, the EUDPR, and the EDPS' mission as a public sector supervisory authority, have been very closely aligned with those of the GDPR.

7. EEA EFTA supervisory authorities

As noted above, the amended EEA Agreement provides that the provisions of the GDPR should be read, for the purposes of that Agreement, with a number of adaptations concerning the composition and workings of the EDPB. In this context, EEA EFTA supervisory authorities are now members of the Board,[42] with the same rights and obligations as EU supervisory authorities save that they have no right to vote nor to stand for election as chair or deputy chairs of the Board.

The EDPB Rules of Procedure are required to give full effect to the participation of the supervisory authorities of the EFTA States and the EFTA Surveillance Authority with the exception of voting rights and to stand for election as chair or deputy chairs of the Board.[43] Article 4(1) of the modified Rules of Procedure implements this obligation, and adds that they 'have the right to express their positions on all items discussed and/or voted'.

8. European Commission

Unlike its former status in the WP29, the Commission is not a member of the Board nor under Article 68(5) does it enjoy voting rights in the Board. However, Article 68(5)

---

[38] Art. 43 Europol Regulation. [39] Art. 85 Regulation 2017/1939.
[40] Art. 101(2) EUDPR. [41] Zemánek 2012. [42] See Art. 4(1) EDPB Rules of Procedure.
[43] Art. 5e EEA Decision.

provides that the Commission has the right to 'participate in the activities and meetings of the Board' and that 'the Chair of the Board shall communicate to the Commission the activities of the Board'.

As noted above, the amended EEA Agreement provides that the provisions of the GDPR should be read, for the purposes of that Agreement, with a number of adaptations. In this respect, the EFTA Surveillance Authority ('ESA') has, like the Commission, the right to participate in the meetings of the Board without voting right and to designate a representative to this effect.[44] Similarly, the ESA has the right, where relevant, to request advice or opinions from, and to communicate matters to, the Board pursuant to Articles 63, 64(2), 65(1)(c) and 70(1)(e) GDPR,[45] and to receive information on the activities of the Board from the Chair of the Board, or the secretariat, pursuant to Articles 64(5)(a)–(b), 65(5) and 75(6)(b).[46]

The participation and information of the Commission in the Management Board of an EU Agency is standard,[47] but its right to participate in meetings of the Board and to be informed of its activities is remarkable. The significance for the independence of the Board of these rights to information and to participate in its activities is discussed in the commentary on Article 69 in this volume.

9. Observers, external experts, guests or other external parties

Articles 8 and 9 of the Board's Rules of Procedure provide for the presence of observers, external experts, guests or other external parties at plenary meetings and meetings of subgroups. These provisions develop and specify the practice under Article 9 of the former WP29's Rules of Procedure,[48] whereby the Chair could invite observers or experts, pursuant to a decision of the Working Party, to participate in the meetings.

Article 8(1) of the EDPB Rules of Procedure provides that independent data protection authorities from outside the EU may be granted the status of permanent or temporary observers, and sets out the criteria for deciding to grant this status: namely, that it must be in the interest of the Board, it must be upon request and it must concern a public authority which supervises the implementation of data protection legislation and which demonstrates a substantial interest in the implementation of EU data protection legislation. Article 8(2) lays down the general rule that such observers may only participate in meetings of the Board or expert subgroups to the extent that they relate to work on drawing up guidelines. However, the Board or the Chair may decide otherwise.

Article 8 is plainly intended to permit the Board to invite supervisory authorities from outside the EU to participate as observers on a regular basis in meetings drawing up guidelines, and permits the Board or its Chair to decide that such authorities may attend plenary meetings as observers. In the past, unlike the Board, the WP29 was formally a Commission committee, even if it was supposed to act independently, and thus was subject to the Commission's view on the extent to which it could lawfully invite third parties to its meetings without detracting from its nature as an EU body made up of supervisory bodies with the task of interpreting and enforcing the EU *acquis* on data protection. In this context, the WP29 had invited third country supervisory authorities as observers in

---

[44] Ibid., Art. 5e(k). [45] Ibid., Art. 5e(l). [46] Ibid., Art. 5e(m).
[47] See Joint Statement EP, Council and EC 2012. [48] WP29 Rules of Procedure.

three specific cases, all where there was a legally binding nexus to the relevant EU rules, either generally or specifically:

- The supervisory authorities of Norway, Iceland and Liechtenstein[49] were permanent observers at WP29 meetings in their capacity as representing EEA Member States, which had accepted the DPD. As noted above, the amended EEA Agreement now provides that these authorities are members of the Board, albeit with limited rights, as specified in Article 4 of the EDPB Rules of Procedure.
- By specific agreement between Switzerland and the EU related to Swiss membership of Schengen and Eurodac, Switzerland was invited to attend WP29 meetings for the discussion of agenda items related to Schengen or Eurodac.[50] This approach has been consolidated in the opening passage of Article 8 of the EDPB Rules of Procedure, which states that it is 'without prejudice to any relevant international agreement between the Union and a non-EU country, providing for a specific status for the data protection authority of this non-EU country within the Board'.
- The WP29 had also invited as observers the supervisory authorities of candidate countries before accession but after the ratification of the accession agreements, or even after the adoption by the Council of an Accession Partnership.[51]

It remains to be seen how the Board will exercise its new power. There is an obvious interest in inviting the supervisory authority of a third state to join discussions of proposed guidelines on a matter where it has significant expertise. For example, the Privacy Commissioner of Canada could make a huge contribution to updated guidelines on accountability. A counter-argument is that such specific input could also be achieved by inviting representatives of such an authority as experts under Article 9 of the EDPB Rules of Procedure. The situation of the UK Information Commissioner ('ICO') in the event that the UK leaves the EU ('Brexit')[52] also raises interesting questions about the scope of Article 8. The ICO will no longer be the supervisory authority of an EU or EEA/EFTA Member State under Article 4(22) GDPR and thus will no longer be eligible to be a member of the Board.

This authority would satisfy the criterion of independence and supervise a legal regime which after departure from the EU would be fully equivalent to the EU framework, even though it is no longer subject to the jurisdiction of the CJEU. Would such an authority be eligible to be invited as an observer? The criteria to be taken into account will undoubtedly include the benefit of the regular involvement of such an authority in the deliberations of the Board and the question whether there is a sufficiently binding nexus (in the sense of close rather than 'essential' equivalence) to EU law.

It should be noted that Article 8(3) provides that observers, unlike members of the Board, will not receive any reimbursement for their travel costs.

---

[49] The WP29 Annual Report 2013, the most recent Annual Report available, included the DPAs of Iceland, Liechtenstein and Norway as observers in 2012.

[50] Agreement EU Switzerland 2008; Joint Declaration EU Switzerland 2008.

[51] E.g. Council Decision 2008. It was significant that there was a data protection regime in that candidate country and a plan to address data protection. The WP29 Annual Report 2013 included the DPAs of Croatia and the former Yugoslav Republic of Macedonia as observers in 2012.

[52] The question of Brexit and the GDPR is discussed in the introduction to this volume.

Docksey

Finally, Article 9 of the EDPB Rules of Procedure provides that external experts, guests or other external parties may be invited to take part in Board meetings. They can be invited to plenary meetings by invitation of the Chair and to expert subgroup meetings by invitation of the coordinator of the expert subgroup concerned. Unlike observer status, such invitations are limited to specific items on the agenda.

Select Bibliography

International agreements

Agreement EU Switzerland 2008: Agreement between the European Union, the European Community and the Swiss Confederation of 27 February 2008 on the Swiss Confederation's association with the implementation, application and development of the Schengen acquis, OJ 2008 L 53/77.

EEA Agreement: Agreement on the European Economic Area, OJ 1994 L 1/3.

EEA Decision 2018: Decision of the EEA Joint Committee No. 154/2018 of 6 July 2018 amending Annex XI (Electronic communication, audiovisual services and information society) and Protocol 37 (containing the list provided for in Article 101) to the EEA Agreement [2018/1022], OJ 2018 L 183/23.

EU legislation

Council Decision 2008: Council Decision of 12 February 2008 on the principles, priorities and conditions contained in the Accession Partnership with Croatia and repealing Decision 2006/145/EC, OJ 2008 L 42/51.

Council Regulation 2017/1939: Council Regulation (EU) 2017/1939 of 31 October 2017 implementing enhanced cooperation on the establishment of the European Public Prosecutor's Office ('the EPPO'), OJ 2017 L 283/1.

EU Staff Regulations: Regulation No. 31 (EEC), 11 (EAEC) of 14 June 1962 laying down the Staff Regulations of Officials and the Conditions of Employment of Other Servants of the European Economic Community and the European Atomic Energy Community as amended, OJ 1962 L 45/1385.

Europol Regulation: Regulation (EU) 2016/794 of the European Parliament and of the Council of 11 May 2016 on the European Union Agency for Law Enforcement Cooperation (Europol) and replacing and repealing Council Decisions 2009/371/JHA, 2009/934/JHA, 2009/935/JHA, 2009/936/JHA and 2009/968/JHA, OJ 2016 L 135/53.

Joint Declaration EU Switzerland 2008: Joint Declaration of the Contracting Parties of 27 February 2008 on Directive 95/46/EC of the European Parliament and the Council on data protection, annexed to the Agreement between the European Community and the Swiss Confederation concerning the criteria and mechanisms for establishing the State responsible for examining a request for asylum lodged in a Member State or in Switzerland, OJ 2008 L 53/15.

Regulation 1049/2001: Regulation (EC) No. 1049/2001 of the European Parliament and of the Council of 30 May 2001 regarding public access to European Parliament, Council and Commission documents, OJ 2001 L 145/43.

Regulation 1211/2009: Regulation (EC) No. 1211/2009 of the European Parliament and of the Council of 25 November 2009 establishing the Body of European Regulators for Electronic Communications (BEREC) and the Office, OJ 2009 L 337/1.

Regulation 966/2012: Regulation (EU, EURATOM) No. 966/2012 of the European Parliament and of the Council of 25 October 2012 on the financial rules applicable to the general budget of the Union and repealing Council Regulation (EC, Euratom) No. 1605/2002 as amended by

Regulation (EU, Euratom) No. 547/2014 of the European Parliament and of the Council of 15 May 2014 and Regulation (EU, Euratom) 2015/1929 of the European Parliament and of the Council of 28 October 2015, OJ 2012 L 298/1.

Academic writings

Busuioc 2013: Busuioc, 'Rule-Making by the European Financial Supervisory Authorities: Walking a Tight Rope', 19(1) *European Law Journal* (2013), 111.
Hijmans 2016A: Hijmans, *The European Union as Guardian of Internet Privacy* (Springer 2016).
Hijmans 2016B: Hijmans, 'The DPAs and their Cooperation: How Far Are We in Making Enforcement of Data Protection Law More European?', 3(2) *European Data Protection Law Review* (2016), 362.
Lynskey 2017: Lynskey, 'The Europeanisation of Data Protection Law', 19 *Cambridge Yearbook of European Legal Studies* (2017), 252.
Risse, Caporoso and Cowles 2001: Risse, Caporoso and Cowles, 'Europeanisation and Domestic Change. Introduction', in Cowles, Caporaso and Risse (eds.), *Transforming Europe: Europeanisation and Domestic Change* (Cornell University Press 2001), 1.
Robert 2017: Robert, 'Les Autorités de contrôle dans le nouveau règlement général sur la protection des données: statut, coopération et gouvernance européenne', in Docquir (ed.), *Vers un droit européen de la protection des données?* (Larcier 2017), 21.
Thatcher 2011: Thatcher, 'The Creation of European Regulatory Agencies and its Limits: A Comparative Analysis of European Delegation', 18(6) *Journal of European Public Policy* (2011), 790.
Vibert 2007: Vibert, *The Rise of the Unelected, Democracy and the New Separation of Powers* (Cambridge University Press 2007).
Zemánek 2012: Zemánek, 'Comment on Case C-518/07, Commission v Germany', 49(5) *Common Market Law Review* (2012), 1755.

Papers of data protection authorities

EDPB Rules of Procedure: European Data Protection Board 'Rules of Procedure' Version 2 (Adopted on 25 May 2018, as last modified and adopted on 23 November 2018).
EDPB EDPS MoU: European Data Protection Board and European Data Protection Supervisor, 'Memorandum of Understanding' (25 May 2018), available at https://edpb.europa.eu/sites/edpb/files/files/file1/memorandum_of_understanding_signed_en.pdf.
European Data Protection Supervisor, 'Opinion of 5 March 2014 on the Package of Legislative Measures Reforming Eurojust and Setting Up the European Public Prosecutor's Office ("EPPO")' (2014).
WP29 2016: Article 29 Working Party, 'Statement on the 2016 Action Plan for the Implementation of the General Data Protection Regulation (GDPR)' (WP 236, 2 February 2016).
WP29 Annual Report 2013: Report of the Article 29 Working Party on Data Protection, covering the year 2013, European Commission (2016).
WP29 Rules of Procedure: Article 29 Working Party, 'Rules of Procedure' (15 February 2010).

Reports and recommendations

EC Communication 2010: Communication from the Commission to the European Parliament, the Council, the European Economic and Social Committee and the Committee of the Regions, 'A Comprehensive Approach on Personal Data Protection in the European Union', COM (2010) 609 final, 4 November 2010.

Joint Statement EP, Council and EC 2012: Joint Statement of the European Parliament, the Council of the EU and the European Commission on Decentralised Agencies (19 July 2012), available at https://europa.eu/european-union/sites/europaeu/files/docs/body/joint_statement_and_common_approach_2012_en.pdf.

Meijers Committee 2018: Meijers Committee, '1806 Note on the Use of Soft Law Instruments under EU law, in Particular in the Area of Freedom, Security and Justice, and its Impact on Fundamental Rights, Democracy and the Rule of Law' (2018), available at https://www.commissie-meijers.nl/sites/all/files/cm1806_note_on_soft_law_instruments.pdf.

Article 69. Independence

CHRISTOPHER DOCKSEY

1. The Board shall act independently when performing its tasks or exercising its powers pursuant to Articles 70 and 71.
2. Without prejudice to requests by the Commission referred to in Article 70(1) and (2), the Board shall, in the performance of its tasks or the exercise of its powers, neither seek nor take instructions from anybody.[1]

Relevant Recital

(139) In order to promote the consistent application of this Regulation, the Board should be set up as an independent body of the Union. To fulfil its objectives, the Board should have legal personality. The Board should be represented by its Chair. It should replace the Working Party on the Protection of Individuals with Regard to the Processing of Personal Data established by Directive 95/46/EC. It should consist of the head of a supervisory authority of each Member State and the European Data Protection Supervisor or their respective representatives. The Commission should participate in the Board's activities without voting rights and the European Data Protection Supervisor should have specific voting rights. The Board should contribute to the consistent application of this Regulation throughout the Union, including by advising the Commission, in particular on the level of protection in third countries or international organisations, and promoting cooperation of the supervisory authorities throughout the Union. The Board should act independently when performing its tasks.

Closely Related Provisions

Article 51(1) (Supervisory authority) and Article 52 (Independence of supervisory authorities) (see too recitals 117–118 and 120–121); Article 64(2) (Commission right to request the Board concerning an opinion) (see too recitals 135–136); Article 68(5) (Participation of the Commission in the activities and meetings of the Board)

Related Provisions in EUDPR [Regulation (EU) 2018/1725]

Article 55 (Independence of EDPS) (see too recitals 2, 72 and 87)

Relevant Case Law

CJEU

Case C-322/88, *Salvatore Grimaldi v Fonds des maladies professionnelles*, judgment of 13 December 1989 (ECLI:EU:C:1989:646).

---

[1] Corrigenda to the English text of Art. 37(1)(c) were published on 23 May 2018. The text printed reflects the updated version of the Corrigendum GDPR 2018. For the Corrigendum GDPR 2018, see Table of Legislation.

Case C-207/01, *Altair Chimica SpA v ENEL Distribuzione SpA*, judgment of 11 September 2003 (ECLI:EU:C:2003:451)
Case C-518/07, *European Commission v Federal Republic of Germany*, judgment of 9 March 2010 (Grand Chamber) (ECLI:EU:C:2010:125).
Joined Cases C-317/08, C-318/08, C-319/08 and C-320/08 *Rosalba Alassini v Telecom Italia SpA, Filomena Califano v Wind SpA, Lucia Anna Giorgia Iacono v Telecom Italia SpA* and *Multiservice Srl v Telecom Italia SpA*, judgment of 18 March 2010 (ECLI:EU:C:2010:146).
Case C-614/10, *European Commission v Republic of Austria*, judgment of 16 October 2012 (Grand Chamber) (ECLI:EU:C:2012:63).
Case C-288/12, *European Commission v Hungary*, judgment of 8 April 2014 (Grand Chamber) (ECLI:EU:C:2014:237).
Case C-230/14, *Weltimmo s.r.o. v Nemzeti Adatvédelmi és Információszabadság Hatóság*, judgment of 1 October 2015 (ECLI:EU:C:2015:639).
Case C-362/14, *Maximillian Schrems v Data Protection Commissioner*, judgment of 6 October 2015 (Grand Chamber) (ECLI:EU:C:2015:650).
Case C-424/15, *Xabier Ormaetxea Garai and Bernardo Lorenzo Almendros v Administración del Estado*, judgment of 19 October 2016 (ECLI:EU:C:2016:780).
Opinion of Advocate General Bot in C-424/15, *Xabier Ormaetxea Garai and Bernardo Lorenzo Almendros v Administración del Estado*, delivered on 30 June 2016 (ECLI:EU:C:2016:503).
Opinion 1/15, Opinion of 26 July 2017 (Grand Chamber) (ECLI:EU:C:2017:592).
Case C-73/16, *Peter Puškár v Finančné riaditeľstvo Slovenskej republiky and Kriminálny úrad finančnej správy*, judgment of 27 September 2017 (ECLI:EU:C:2017:725).

A. Rationale and Policy Underpinnings

Article 69 GDPR provides that the Board shall act independently when performing its tasks or exercising its powers and that it shall, in the performance of its tasks or the exercise of its powers, neither seek nor take instructions from anybody. These requirements are similar to those required of supervisory authorities, although the Board does not have all the features of such authorities.

The right to independent supervision is enshrined in Article 8(3) of the Charter of Fundamental Rights of the European Union ('Charter' or 'CFR'), Article 16(2) of the Treaty on the Functioning of the European Union ('TFEU') and Article 39 of the Treaty on European Union ('TEU'). It has been characterised in the case law of the CJEU as an 'essential component' of the fundamental right to protection of personal data.

Article 52(1) GDPR implements the requirement of 'complete independence' with regard to national supervisory authorities. Article 52(2) adds:

The member or members of each supervisory authority shall, in the performance of their tasks and exercise of their powers in accordance with this Regulation, remain free from external influence, whether direct or indirect, and shall neither seek nor take instructions from anybody.

The same formulation is applied with regard to the EDPS under Article 55(2) of the EUDPR. Both these texts, in the GDPR and the EUDPR, were based on Article 44(2) of Regulation 45/2001.[2]

[2] See Table of Legislation.

B. Legal Background

1. EU legislation

Article 8(3) of the Charter provides that 'Compliance with these rules shall be subject to control by an independent authority'. Similar wording is enshrined in Article 16(2) TFEU and in Article 39 TEU.

Article 28 of the DPD provided that national supervisory authorities 'shall act with complete independence in exercising the functions entrusted to them'. Recital 62 explained that 'the establishment in Member States of supervisory authorities, exercising their functions with complete independence, is an essential component of the protection of individuals with regard to the processing of personal data'. Recital 65 added that the WP29 had to be 'completely independent in the performance of its functions'.

Article 16(1) of Regulation (EC) No. 168/2007 establishing the Agency for Fundamental Rights[3] provides that '(t)he Agency shall fulfil its tasks in complete independence'.

Article 52(1) of the EUDPR provides that the 'European Data Protection Supervisor is hereby established'.[4] Article 55(1) provides that the EDPS 'shall act in complete independence in performing his or her tasks and exercising his or her powers in accordance with this Regulation'.[5]

The Eurojust Decision[6] established an independent data protection authority made up of representatives of national supervisory authorities, the Joint Supervisory Body ('JSB'), responsible for the supervision of Eurojust. Article 23 thereof provided that an 'independent JSB shall be established to monitor collectively the Eurojust activities in order to ensure that the processing of personal data is carried out in accordance with this Decision'.

In contrast, the new Europol Regulation confers the task of independent supervision on the EDPS and establishes a Cooperation Board made up of and responsible for co-operation between the EDPS and national supervisory authorities.[7] Article 45(2) of that Regulation provides that '(t)he Cooperation Board shall act independently when performing its tasks pursuant to paragraph 3 and shall neither seek nor take instructions from any body'. Recital 52 of the Europol Regulation notes that the Cooperation Board is 'an advisory body'.

In the EU telecoms sector, a type of consistency mechanism exists under Regulation 1211/2009[8] whereby national regulatory authorities must consult the Body of European Regulators for Electronic Communications ('BEREC') before adopting a measure which could substantially affect the functioning of that sector. Article 1(3) of that Regulation provides that the BEREC 'shall carry out its tasks independently, impartially and transparently'.

---

[3] FRA Council Regulation.

[4] Formerly Art. 41(1) of Regulation 45/2001, which provided that an 'independent supervisory authority is hereby established referred to as the European Data Protection Supervisor'.

[5] Formerly ibid., Art. 44(1), which provided that the EDPS 'shall act in complete independence in the performance of his or her duties'.

[6] See Council Decision Eurojust. This Decision has been repealed and replaced by the Eurojust Regulation with effect from 12 December 2019.

[7] Art. 45 Europol Regulation. There is no Cooperation Board in the subsequent Eurojust Regulation, see Art. 42 on cooperation between the EDPS and national supervisory authorities.

[8] Regulation 1211/2009.

2. International instruments

The European Economic Area ('EEA') Agreement, as amended in July 2018,[9] incorporates the GDPR into its Annexes and provides that the provisions of the GDPR should be read, for the purposes of that Agreement, with a number of adaptations. With regard to the composition and workings of the EDPB, the amended Agreement provides that the EFTA Surveillance Authority ('ESA') shall have the right to participate in the meetings of the Board without voting right and shall designate a representative.[10] The Agreement further provides that, where relevant to the exercise of its functions under the Agreement, the ESA has the right to request advice or opinions from, and to communicate matters to, the Board pursuant to Articles 63, 64(2), 65(1)(c) and 70(1)(e). To that effect the Agreement provides that the words 'and, where relevant, the EFTA Surveillance Authority' shall be added after the words 'the Commission' in those Articles.[11] Finally, the Agreement provides that the ESA has the right to receive information on the activities of the Board from the Chair of the Board, or the secretariat, where relevant pursuant to Articles 64(5)(a)–(b), 65(5) and 75(6)(b).[12]

3. Case law

The case law on the independence of supervisory authorities was summarised by the CJEU as follows:

The Court has held that the second subparagraph of Article 28(1) of Directive 95/46 must be interpreted as meaning that the supervisory authorities responsible for supervising the processing of personal data must enjoy an independence allowing them to perform their duties free from external influence. That independence precludes inter alia any directions or any other external influence in whatever form, whether direct or indirect, which may have an effect on their decisions and which could call into question the performance by those authorities of their task of striking a fair balance between the protection of the right to private life and the free movement of personal data.[13]

According to the Court there are two sources for this high standard of independence of data protection supervisory authorities:

[T]he second subparagraph of Article 28(1) of Directive 95/46 requires Member States to set up one or more supervisory authorities with complete independence in the exercise of the duties entrusted to them. In addition, the requirement that compliance with the EU rules on the protection of individuals with regard to the processing of personal data is subject to control by an independent authority derives from the primary law of the European Union and, in particular, from Article 8(3) of the Charter of Fundamental Rights of the European Union and Article 16(2) TFEU.[14]

This may be distinguished from the standard of independence required of other national regulators, who are required to be independent and impartial but not to the same extent as data protection authorities.

In Case C-424/15, *Garai and Almendros*, the referring court asked whether the standard of independence applied to data protection authorities should be applied to a national telecom regulatory authority ('NRA'). Whilst Advocate General Bot took the view that the same standard should be applied to both, he noted the argument by Member States and the Commission that 'the fundamental differences between the tasks assigned to the

---

[9] EEA Decision 2018. [10] Ibid., Art. 5e(k). [11] Ibid., Art. 5e(l)
[12] Ibid., Art. 5e(m) [13] Case C-288/12, *Commission v Hungary*, para. 51.
[14] Ibid., para. 47.

authorities responsible for supervising the protection of personal data and those tasks assigned to NRAs justify a different definition being given to the notion of independence in the present case from that adopted by the Court'.[15] The CJEU followed the Member States and the Commission and ruled that 'as long as the objectives and obligations laid down by the Framework Directive are fully complied with, Member States enjoy institutional autonomy as regards the organisation and the structuring of their NRAs'.[16]

C. Analysis

Recital 139 explains that 'in order to promote the consistent application of this Regulation, the Board should be set up as an independent body of the Union'. Article 69 requires the Board is required to 'act independently' and 'neither seek nor take instructions from anybody' when performing its tasks or exercising its powers. This echoes Article 29(1) DPD which stated that the WP29 should 'act independently'. The Board itself in Article 3 of its Rules of Procedure has emphasised in the first of its Guiding Principles that it 'shall act independently when performing its tasks or exercising its powers'.

The discussion of independence also raises the question whether the Board may be regarded as an independent supervisory authority in the sense of Article 8(3) of the Charter. As will be seen, the GDPR confers many but not all of the elements of a supervisory authority upon the Board. Three issues arise for consideration. First, the level of independence enjoyed by the Board in comparison to its constituent members. Secondly, whether it is permissible under Article 8(3) CFR for the exercise of the Board's tasks to interfere with the powers of supervisory authorities at national level and hence with their complete independence (for example, the exercise of certain tasks such as adopting decisions, which are legally binding on supervisory authorities, and authoritative opinions, of which supervisory authorities must take the utmost account). Finally, the effect of the role of the Commission on the independence of the Board will be considered.

1. The level of independence enjoyed by the Board

1.1 The standard of independence of data protection authorities

Ottow distinguishes between the standard of independence applied to data protection authorities and other regulators:

> Overlooking the European landscape of ... regulated areas, three levels of protection can be distinguished. First, there is the area of data protection, where the European legislator and court have recognised the importance of independence and have secured a high level of protection of independence. A middle category is the energy and communications area, with legal requirements, which qualify as a medium level of protection of independence. Finally, there are sectors, such as the media sector, where so far the level of protection is low.[17]

Thus, both national telecoms regulators and their EU counterpart, the BEREC, fall within the 'middle' category, as confirmed by the CJEU in *Garai and Almendros*.

This difference between data protection and other regulators may be explained by the unique status of data protection authorities under primary law, noted above. The Court

---

[15] Case C-424/15, *Garai and Almendros* (AG Opinion), para. 41.
[16] Case C-424/15, *Garai and Almendros*, judgment, para. 49.   [17] Ottow 2013, p. 139.

has consistently held that supervision by independent data protection authorities is regarded as an essential component[18] of the right to data protection under Article 8 of the Charter and Article 16 TFEU.[19] The question arises whether the Board may be equated to a data protection authority enjoying a high level of independence, or to the middle category defined by Ottow, where only a 'medium level' of independence is required.

1.2 The nature and structure of the Board and its advisory role

The nature and structure of the Board may be compared with other means of collective supervision. First, as well as working together in the Board, representatives of national supervisory authorities and the EDPS cooperate in the various 'coordinated supervision' bodies.[20] These 'coordinated supervision' bodies are clearly collective, cooperative bodies rather than independent supervisory bodies.

Secondly, in 2017 the new Europol Regulation came into application. Article 42 of that Regulation established the EDPS as the supervisory authority of Europol, in place of the former Europol JSB. Article 45 of the Europol Regulation also established a new Cooperation Board bringing together the EDPS and national supervisory authorities. The Cooperation Board is required under the second paragraph of Article 45 of that Regulation to 'act independently when performing its tasks [and to] neither seek nor take instructions from any body'. However, recital 52 of the Europol Regulation makes it clear that the Cooperation Board is an 'advisory body' rather than a supervisory body, intended to 'facilitate the cooperation between the EDPS and the national supervisory authorities, but without prejudice to the independence of the EDPS and his or her responsibility for data protection supervision of Europol'. The tasks and powers of the Cooperation Board set forth in paragraphs 3 and 4 of Article 45 of the Europol Regulation are essentially concerned with discussion, interpretation and advice and do not include any of the decision-making powers of a supervisory authority.

In this respect, the advisory tasks of the Board may be equated with those of its predecessor, the WP29, and with those of the Europol Cooperation Board. These are clearly 'middle level' independent bodies.

1.3 The legal nature and regulatory tasks of the Board

Unlike the Europol Cooperation Board, the Board is an EU body with legal personality, and it has a distinct role and specific decision-making powers in dispute resolution cases under the consistency mechanism.

On the one hand, the Board does not have the same range of direct enforcement powers and duties as national supervisory authorities under Articles 57 and 58 GDPR, which enable them to play their role as the 'guardians'[21] at national level of the rights to privacy and data protection. Nor does it have the power to take the final decision under the dispute resolution procedure, which is reserved to the lead authority concerned. On the other hand, the Board has a wide range of tasks, discussed below under Article 70, which range from purely advisory, to authoritative advice on how supervisory authorities

---

[18] See the discussion of the case law below. See also rec. 117 GDPR and rec. 72 EUDPR.
[19] This uniquely high standard has, however, been criticised as excessive in comparison to the standard of independence required of the courts, see Balthazar 2013, p. 31.
[20] For a brief description of the coordinated supervision bodies, see Hijmans 2016A, pp. 401–402.
[21] Case C-518/07, *Commission v Germany*, paras. 23 and 36.

should exercise their tasks (guidelines, recommendations and best practises) and finally to a definitive adjudicative role in ensuring consistency of enforcement.

Under Article 64 the Board has the power to issue opinions on a number of matters falling within the competence of supervisory authorities before such authorities may adopt draft measures on those matters. Whilst such an opinion is not legally binding on the supervisory authority concerned, Article 64(7) requires it to take the 'utmost account' of such opinion. This authoritative advice is essentially soft law. Furthermore, where the supervisory authority informs the Board under Article 64(8) that it does not intend to follow the opinion of the Board, Article 65 empowers the Board to adopt a decision which is legally binding on that authority.

These strong powers over independent supervisory authorities militate against an interpretation that the Board enjoys a lower level of independence than they do. As a result, Hijmans has described the Board as more than an advisory body and as 'something equating to a European DPA'. He argues that, to the extent that the Board has binding powers to ensure compliance with data protection rules, it qualifies as a supervisory authority within the meaning of Article 16(2) TFEU and Article 8(3) of the Charter. Under these circumstances, he concludes, 'the EDPB must fulfil the requirements of independence as laid down in the case law of the Court of Justice'.[22]

1.4 'Complete' independence

At first glance the GDPR imposes less strict conditions on the Board than on national supervisory authorities. In comparison with the requirement on the Board to 'act independently', Article 52 GDPR requires supervisory authorities to 'act with complete independence', the same wording as Article 28(1) DPD.[23]

In the first case on independence, *Commission v Germany*, the CJEU emphasised this stronger requirement under the DPD to act with 'complete independence'. The Court interpreted Article 28(1) DPD to lay down a strict approach to independence which precluded any external influence, direct or indirect, on decision-making by a supervisory authority or on carrying out their duties.[24] Moreover the Court has subsequently stressed that independence is an 'essential component' of the right to data protection under primary law, namely Article 8(3) of the Charter.[25]

However, there are a number of factors that suggest that the presence or absence of the word 'complete' is simply an important factor to be taken into consideration when considering the nature and function of the body concerned. First, neither Article 8(3) of the Charter nor Article 16(2) TFEU apply the word 'complete' to the requirement of 'control by an independent authority', but this has had no effect on the independence required of data protection authorities as an essential component of the right. Secondly, the JSB of Eurojust was established as an 'independent' supervisory authority without any reference to 'complete' independence. However, the JSB was nonetheless a supervisory authority within the meaning of Article 8(3) of the Charter, and the absence of the word 'complete' in its mandate had no effect on its obligation to be completely independent. As a result,

---

[22] Hijmans 2016A, p. 433.
[23] See also rec. 65 DPD. For a full discussion of the notion of 'complete independence' see the commentary on Art. 52 of this volume.
[24] Case C-518/07, *Commission v Germany*, para. 19. In Case C-614/10, *Commission v Austria*, para. 40, the CJEU added that the expression 'complete independence' must be given an autonomous interpretation.
[25] See *Opinion 1/15*, para. 229 and the case law cited therein.

the absence of the adjective 'complete' applied to independence in Article 69 has no conclusive effect on the level of independence required of the Board. To the contrary, the Board may be regarded as falling under the highest standard of independence reserved for data protection supervisory authorities under Article 8(3) of the Charter.

2. Whether interference by the Board with the powers of its constituent supervisory authorities undermines the right to effective supervision

As noted above, Article 64 GDPR empowers the Board to issue authoritative opinions on draft measures proposed by supervisory authorities and Article 65 empowers the Board to adopt a binding decision on a supervisory authority which does not intend to follow an opinion under Article 64. These powers are clearly intended to circumscribe the powers of the independent supervisory authorities concerned and it has been argued that, when the EDPB uses its binding powers, 'national DPAs are no longer sovereign to ensure the control of the EU rules on data protection'.[26] However there are both substantive and procedural reasons why this power of the Board does not detract from the effectiveness of supervision which underlies the requirement of independence, imposed on both the Board and on supervisory authorities.

First, national supervisory bodies and the EDPS are represented in the Board itself, directly or indirectly, and constitute its membership. It has been stressed that 'the EU legislator ensured that the national DPAs are fully in charge of this new body'.[27] Like the concept of shared sovereignty underpinning the European project, the Board may be regarded as embodying the shared independence of its constituent bodies. Similarly it is possible to talk of competences that are not divided, but shared.[28] It has been argued that 'the data protection governance system ... is an integral part of the "emerging fundamental rights architecture"[29] of the EU' and that 'when decision-making formerly conducted by supervisory authorities is conducted by the EDPB it too will be acting as part of this fundamental rights architecture'.[30] In the broader context of EU administrative law, the consistency mechanism bringing together the Board and the supervisory authorities may be regarded as an integrated administration or a composite decision-making procedure, where EU and national authorities have distinct functions and a clear allocation of responsibilities, but are interdependent.[31]

Secondly, Article 65(6) GDPR reserves the final decision-making power for the supervisory authority concerned. The Board has the power to take a decision binding the lead supervisory authority and the other supervisory authorities concerned, and this undoubtedly has both legal and moral effect on those authorities, and hence has both direct and indirect influence on them. However, the 'final decision' is made by the lead supervisory authority.

The GDPR does not address the situation where the lead supervisory authority refuses to follow the decision of the Board, which might suggest that the authority's discretion to take the decision it thinks fit is unaffected. However, the authority is bound by a number of both general and specific obligations under EU law to cooperate with its fellow authorities in the Board. The duty of sincere cooperation under Article 4(3) Treaty on European

---

[26] Hijmans 2016B, p. 10. [27] Ibid. [28] Bignami 2005, p. 821.
[29] Szydło 2013, p 1826. [30] Lynskey 2017, p. 283.
[31] Hofmann, Schneider and Ziller 2014, p. 29; see also Hofmann and Tidghi 2014, p. 148.

Union ('TEU') applies,[32] and in addition the authority is specifically bound to contribute to the consistent application of the GDPR under Article 51(2) GDPR and to cooperate with other supervisory authorities with a view to ensuring the consistency of application and enforcement of the GDPR under Article 57(g) GDPR. Moreover, as in *Schrems*, its decision may be challenged in court and ultimately reviewed on reference to the Court of Justice under Article 267 TFEU,[33] where it would have to defend its minority view. Finally, in the event of a manifest failure to apply the GDPR correctly by the authority concerned, it would be the Commission's duty to open an infringement action against the Member State concerned, under Article 258 TFEU.

Thirdly, because the Board can circumscribe the powers of independent supervisory authorities, whether by adopting by legally binding decisions or opinions—the latter being soft law which DPAs must take into account[34]—the independence of the Board should not be lower than that of the independent authorities affected by its rulings.

Finally, and most important, the independence of supervisory authorities is not a *right* enjoyed by the authority itself but rather a *privilege* to guarantee its ability to ensure the effective protection of individuals' personal data. In *Commission v Germany* the CJEU stressed that 'the guarantee of the independence of national supervisory authorities ... was established not to grant a special status to those authorities themselves ... but in order to strengthen the protection of individuals and bodies affected by their decisions'.[35] The Court felt that the key issue was the 'effectiveness and reliability of the supervision of compliance ... and must be interpreted in the light of that aim'.[36] This approach is explained in recital 117 of the GDPR:

The establishment of supervisory authorities in Member States, empowered to perform their tasks and exercise their powers with complete independence, is an essential component of the protection of natural persons with regard to the processing of their personal data.[37]

Independence is thus the means to ensure the effective protection of the individual, it is not a right of the supervisory authority itself.

At paragraph 24 of *Commission v Germany* the Court also approved the imposition on supervisory authorities of the requirement to cooperate under Article 28(6) DPD 'and even, if necessary, to exercise their powers at the request of an authority of another Member State'. The obligation to cooperate was not seen as inconsistent with the requirement of independence, since both contribute to the protection of individuals.[38] The GDPR now lays down stronger obligations to cooperate, which further emphasise the need for effective supervision and consistency over purely formal autonomy.

The *Puškár* ruling concerning effective judicial protection under Article 47 of the Charter is also relevant for the right to effective supervision. The CJEU held that national legislation which subjects the exercise of a judicial remedy to the prior exhaustion of administrative remedies does not detract from effective judicial protection 'provided that

---

[32] Described as 'the most important and most dynamic single Article in the E.C. Treaty', in Temple Lang 2000, pp. 373–426, quoted by Klamert 2014, p. 2.
[33] Case C-362/14, *Schrems*, paras. 63–65.
[34] Case C-322/88, *Grimaldi*, paras. 7, 16 and 18; Case C-207/01, *Altair Chimica*, para. 41; Joined Cases C-317/08, C-318/08, C-319/08 and C-320/08, *Alassini and Others*, para. 40.
[35] Case C-518/07, *Commission v Germany*, para. 25.
[36] Affirmed in Case C-362/14, *Schrems*, para. 41.   [37] Rec. 117 GDPR.
[38] There is a similar emphasis on cooperation in Case C-230/14, *Weltimmo*, paras. 57–58.

the practical arrangements for the exercise of such remedies do not disproportionately affect the right to an effective remedy before a court'.[39]

Therefore, the issue for independence is not whether the powers of the Board have any effect on the powers of its constituent supervisory authorities but rather whether they contribute to or detract from the 'effectiveness and reliability' of supervision. In this respect, it has been strongly argued that the role of the Board within the consistency mechanism is a guarantee of *greater* effectiveness of supervision and enforcement than the previous situation under the DPD. Indeed, the previous regulatory framework, made up of different interpretations and levels of enforcement between the various supervisory authorities and a correspondingly unequal level of data protection throughout the EU, has even been criticised as incompatible with the protection required by the Charter.[40]

In this respect, Lynskey argues that the centralisation under the Board imposed by the GDPR is compatible with EU law, as 'independence must be interpreted in a teleological way that enhances the effectiveness of individual rights protection'.[41]

In light of the above, it may be concluded that, in so far as the interaction between supervisory authorities and the Board contributes to effective protection rather than diminishes it, then the individual's right to independent supervision by supervisory authorities is unaffected.

3. The Commission's role in the Board and the consistency mechanism and its possible effect on the independence of the Board

Under Article 68 GDPR the Commission has the right to attend meetings of the Board and to receive information. In addition, Article 64(2) provides that the Commission, as well as any supervisory authority and the Chair of the Board, may request the Board to examine certain horizontal matters with a view to producing an opinion. Finally, Article 69(2) provides that the right of the Commission to receive and request advice from the Board, even subject to a time limit, is without prejudice to the independent performance of the Board's tasks or exercise of its powers.

As noted above, the EEA Agreement, as amended, provides a number of rights to the EFTA Surveillance Authority (ESA). Like the Commission, the ESA has the right to participate in the meetings of the Board without voting right and to designate a representative, together with the rights, where relevant, to request advice or opinions from, and to communicate matters to, the Board pursuant to Articles 63, 64(2), 65(1)(c) and 70(1)(e) GDPR and to receive information on the activities of the Board from the Chair or the secretariat, pursuant to Articles 64(5)(a)–(b), 65(5) and 75(6)(b) GDPR.[42] The following analysis may therefore be applied, *mutatis mutandis*, to this role of the ESA.

The Commission's role in the Board should first be compared with the situation of the Austrian supervisory authority, the Austrian DPA, considered by the CJEU in infringement proceedings against Austria.[43] The Court held that the Austrian DPA did not meet the requirement of independence for three reasons: first, because its managing member was an official of the federal government; secondly, because the office of the

---

[39] Case C-73/16, *Puškár*, para. 76. See also Case C-320/08 *Alassini and Others*, paras. 53–57.
[40] Zemánek 2012, p. 1766. [41] Lynskey 2017, p. 277. [42] Art. 5e(k)–(m) EEA Decision.
[43] Case C-614/10, *Commission v Austria*, para. 66.

Austrian DPA was integrated with the departments of the Federal Chancellery; and, finally, because the Federal Chancellor had an unconditional right to information covering all aspects of the work of the Austrian DPA.

The first two grounds do not apply to the Commission and the Board. The Secretariat of the Board is made up of staff of the EDPS, an independent institution, who work exclusively under the instructions of the Chair, and the Board is hosted by the EDPS rather than by the Commission. However, there is an issue with regard to the third ground. First Article 68(5) stipulates that 'the Commission shall have the right to participate in the activities and meetings of the Board without voting right'. Although this is a lesser status than that enjoyed by the Commission under Article 29(2) DPD, under which the Commission was a member of the WP29,[44] the Commission still has the right to attend the Board's meetings.

Article 68(5) further provides that 'The Chair of the Board shall communicate to the Commission the activities of the Board'. The Commission had originally proposed that the Commission should be informed 'without delay' on 'all' activities of the Board. This proposal for an intrusive and unconditional obligation was directly comparable to the unconditional right of the Austrian Chancellor to be informed of the activities of the Austrian DPA discussed above. These extra elements of 'without delay' and 'all' activities were opposed by the Council, supported by the EDPS, and were not retained.

The question therefore arises whether the Commission's role in the Board, namely its rights to participate in the activities and the meetings of the Board and to be informed on its activities, detracts from the independence of the Board.

On the one hand, the Commission is the guardian of the treaties, tasked with the oversight of Member States and their supervisory authorities and the power to bring infringement proceedings before the Court under Article 258 TFEU. In this respect, the Commission is the natural ally of the Board in promoting consistency, and indeed has specific powers under the GDPR to trigger an opinion under Article 64(2) and to request advice and impose a deadline under Article 69(2). It is clear that the presence of the Commission at the discussions of the Board and its right to receive information on its activities could strengthen this role. Moreover, the presence of the Commission as guardian of the treaties could support and add 'clout'[45] to the work of the Board in promoting consistency. These elements may well contribute to the 'effectiveness and reliability of the monitoring of compliance' and hence the 'protection of individuals and bodies affected by the decisions of (supervisory) authorities', the foundations of the high standard of independence developed by the CJEU.[46]

On the other hand, the Commission is also the executive of the EU administration. The CJEU has referred to a number of situations where the executive 'may have an interest in not complying with the provisions with regard to the protection of personal data'.[47] In 2012 the EDPS noted that national supervisory authorities may have to assess the conduct of public or private actors in which the Commission has a specific interest, for instance in competition law issues, or cases of financial support from EU funds.[48] In the same year the WP29 expressed its 'strong reservations with regard to the role foreseen for the Commission in individual cases which have been dealt with under the consistency

---

[44] Although only supervisory authorities had the right to vote under Art. 29(3) DPD.
[45] Kuner et al. 2012, p. 1.   [46] Case C-362/14, *Schrems*, para. 41.
[47] Case C-518/07, *Commission v Germany*, para. 35.   [48] EDPS 2012, p. 41.

mechanism', as it encroaches upon the independent position of supervisory authorities.[49] Indeed, it is possible that the Commission itself might be one of the controllers concerned in a consistency case, with the EDPS acting either as lead authority or a concerned authority. In this role it is difficult to see how the Commission may legitimately participate in, or indeed have any influence over, a matter being considered by the Board in which the Commission has its own economic or political interest as the EU executive.

Hustinx has warned that 'Articles 7 and 8, as well as other relevant provisions of the Charter have to be kept in mind when the details of the Regulation are discussed and adopted, and eventually applied in practice'.[50] His approach was subsequently confirmed by the CJEU, which has held that 'national supervisory authorities must be able to examine, with complete independence, any claim concerning the protection of a person's rights and freedoms in regard to the processing of personal data relating to him', including whether a provision of Union law was incompatible with a superior norm of Union law.[51]

Hijmans suggests that there could be a procedural solution, that the 'EDPB acting as a DPA should have the possibility to deliberate in enforcement cases without the Commission being present'.[52] At the very least, the Commission should be prepared to recuse itself from discussions and information in cases where it has a potential conflict of interest as the executive arm of the Union.

Finally, it may be recalled that the Commission is also a part of the EU legislator, with the prerogative of proposing legislation to Parliament and the Council and its own delegated and implementing powers, including those under the GDPR.[53] As noted above, it has the right to request advice from the Board in this role, which Article 69(2) expressly states to be without prejudice to the independent activities of the Board.

4. Conclusions

In light of the above, the Board may be regarded as an independent supervisory authority within the meaning of Article 8(3) of the Charter when it exercises its power to adopt binding decisions and soft law. Although the Board may interfere with the discretion of supervisory authorities when exercising these powers, the effect of the 'composite' decision-making under the consistency mechanism is to strengthen the protection of the individual and hence does not detract from the independence of its component parts. In view of the high standard of independence required under Article 8(3) of the Charter, care must be taken with regard to participation of the Commission in Board discussions of certain cases, particularly those where the Commission has a specific interest as the executive of the European Union.

Select Bibliography

International agreements

EEA Agreement: Agreement on the European Economic Area, OJ 1994 L 1/3.
EEA Decision 2018: Decision of the EEA Joint Committee No. 154/2018 of 6 July 2018 amending Annex XI (Electronic communication, audiovisual services and information society) and Protocol 37 (containing the list provided for in Article 101) to the EEA Agreement [2018/1022], OJ 2018 L 183/23.

---

[49] WP29 2012, p. 7.   [50] Hustinx 2017, p. 167.
[51] Case C-362/14, *Schrems*, paras. 99–104.   [52] Hijmans 2016A, p. 436.
[53] See the commentaries on Arts. 92 and 93 in this volume.

EU legislation

Council Decision Eurojust: Council Decision 2002/187/JHA of 28 February 2002 setting up Eurojust with a view to reinforcing the fight against serious crime as amended by Council Decision 2003/659/JHA and by Council Decision 2009/426/JHA of 16 December 2008 on the strengthening of Eurojust, OJ 2002 L 63/1.

Eurojust Regulation: Regulation (EU) 2018/1727 of the European Parliament and of the Council of 14 November 2018 on the European Union Agency for Criminal Justice Cooperation (Eurojust), and replacing and repealing Council Decision 2002/187/JHA, OJ 2018 L 295/138.

Europol Regulation: Regulation (EU) 2016/794 of the European Parliament and of the Council of 11 May 2016 on the European Union Agency for Law Enforcement Cooperation (Europol) and replacing and repealing Council Decisions 2009/371/JHA, 2009/934/JHA, 2009/935/JHA, 2009/936/JHA and 2009/968/JHA, OJ 2016 L 135/53.

FRA Council Regulation: Council Regulation (EC) No. 168/2007 of 15 February 2007 establishing a European Union Agency for Fundamental Rights, OJ 2007 L 53/1.

Regulation 1211/2009: Regulation (EC) No. 1211/2009 of the European Parliament and of the Council of 25 November 2009 establishing the Body of European Regulators for Electronic Communications (BEREC) and the Office, OJ 2009 L 337/1.

Academic writings

Balthazar 2013: Balthasar, '"Complete Independence" of National Data Protection Supervisory Authorities—Second Try', 9(3) *Utrecht Law Review* (2013), 26.

Bignami 2005: Bignami, 'Transgovernmental Networks vs. Democracy: The Case of the European Information Privacy Network', 26(3) *Michigan Journal of International Law* (2005), 807.

Hijmans 2016A: Hijmans, *The European Union as Guardian of Internet Privacy* (Springer 2016).

Hijmans 2016B: Hijmans, 'The DPAs and their cooperation: How Far Are We in Making Enforcement of Data Protection Law More European?', 3(2) *European Data Protection Law Review* (2016), 362.

Hofmann and Tidghi 2014: Hofmann and Tidghi, 'Rights and Remedies in Implementation of EU Policies by Multi-Jurisdictional Networks', 20(1) *European Public Law* (2014), 147.

Hustinx 2017: Hustinx, 'EU Data Protection Law: The Review of Directive 95/46/EC and the General Data Protection Regulation', in Cremona (ed.), *New Technologies and EU Law* (OUP 2017), 123.

Klamert 2014: Klamert, *The Principle of Loyalty in EU Law* (Oxford University Press 2014)

Kuner et al. 2012: Kuner, Cate, Millar and Svantesson, 'The Intricacies of Independence', 2(1) *International Data Privacy Law* (2012), 1.

Lynskey 2017: Lynskey, 'The Europeanisation of Data Protection Law', 19 *Cambridge Yearbook of European Legal Studies* (2017), 252.

Ottow 2013: Ottow, 'The Different Levels of Protection of National Supervisors' Independence in the European Landscape', in Comtois and de Graaf (eds.), *On Judicial and Quasi-Judicial Independence* (Eleven International Publishing 2013), 139.

Szydło 2013: Szydło, 'Principles Underlying Independence of National Data Protection Authorities: Commission v. Austria', 50(6) *Common Market Law Review 'CMLRev'* (2013), 1809.

Temple Lang 2000: Temple Lang, 'General Report: The Duties of Cooperation of National Authorities and Courts and the Community Institutions under Article 10 EC Treaty', 1, *XIX F.I.D.E. Congress* (2000), 373.

Zemánek 2012: Zemánek, 'Comment on Case C-518/07, Commission v Germany', 49(5) *CMLRev* (2012), 1755.

Papers of data protection authorities

European Data Protection Board, 'Rules of Procedure' (version 2, as last modified and adopted on 23 November 2018).

EDPS 2012: European Data Protection Supervisor, 'Opinion of the European Data Protection Supervisor on the Data Protection Reform Package' (7 March 2012).

WP29 2012: Article 29 Working Party, 'Opinion 01/2012 on the Data Protection Reform Proposals' (WP 191, 23 March 2012).

Reports and recommendations

Council Report EUDPR: Proposal for a Regulation of the European Parliament and of the Council on the protection of individuals with regard to the processing of personal data by the Union institutions, bodies, offices and agencies and on the free movement of such data, and repealing Regulation (EC) No. 45/2001 and Decision No. 1247/2002/EC, Confirmation of the final compromise text with a view to agreement, 9296/18, 1 June 2018.

Hofmann, Schneider and Ziller 2014: Hofmann, Schneider and Ziller (ed.), *ReNEUAL Model Rules on EU Administrative Procedure* (2014), available at http://www.reneual.eu/images/Home/ReNEUAL-Model_Rules-Compilation_BooksI_VI_2014-09-03.pdf.

Article 70. Tasks of the Board

CHRISTOPHER DOCKSEY

1. The Board shall ensure the consistent application of this Regulation. To that end, the Board shall, on its own initiative or, where relevant, at the request of the Commission, in particular:
   (a) monitor and ensure the correct application of this Regulation in the cases provided for in Articles 64 and 65 without prejudice to the tasks of national supervisory authorities;
   (b) advise the Commission on any issue related to the protection of personal data in the Union, including on any proposed amendment of this Regulation;
   (c) advise the Commission on the format and procedures for the exchange of information between controllers, processors and supervisory authorities for binding corporate rules;
   (d) issue guidelines, recommendations, and best practices on procedures for erasing links, copies or replications of personal data from publicly available communication services as referred to in Article 17 (2);
   (e) examine, on its own initiative, on request of one of its members or on request of the Commission, any question covering the application of this Regulation and issue guidelines, recommendations and best practices in order to encourage consistent application of this Regulation;
   (f) issue guidelines, recommendations and best practices in accordance with point (e) of this paragraph for further specifying the criteria and conditions for decisions based on profiling pursuant to Article 22(2);
   (g) issue guidelines, recommendations and best practices in accordance with point (e) of this paragraph for establishing the personal data breaches and determining the undue delay referred to in Article 33(1) and (2) and for the particular circumstances in which a controller or a processor is required to notify the personal data breach;
   (h) issue guidelines, recommendations and best practices in accordance with point (e) of this paragraph as to the circumstances in which a personal data breach is likely to result in a high risk to the rights and freedoms of the natural persons referred to in Article 34(1).
   (i) issue guidelines, recommendations and best practices in accordance with point (e) of this paragraph for the purpose of further specifying the criteria and requirements for personal data transfers based on binding corporate rules adhered to by controllers and binding corporate rules adhered to by processors and on further necessary requirements to ensure the protection of personal data of the data subjects concerned referred to in Article 47;
   (j) issue guidelines, recommendations and best practices in accordance with point (e) of this paragraph for the purpose of further specifying the criteria and requirements for the personal data transfers on the basis of Article 49(1);
   (k) draw up guidelines for supervisory authorities concerning the application of measures referred to in Article 58(1), (2) and (3) and the fixing of administrative fines pursuant to Articles 83;
   (l) review the practical application of the guidelines, recommendations and best practices;[1]
   (m) issue guidelines, recommendations and best practices in accordance with point (e) of this paragraph for establishing common procedures for reporting by natural persons of infringements of this Regulation pursuant to Article 54(2);

---

[1] Corrigenda to the English text of Art. 70(1)(l) were published on 23 May 2018. The text printed reflects the updated version of the Corrigendum GDPR 2018. For the Corrigendum GDPR 2018, see Table of Legislation.

(n) encourage the drawing up of codes of conduct and the establishment of data protection certification mechanisms and data protection seals and marks pursuant to Articles 40 and 42;

(o) approve the criteria of certification pursuant to Article 42(5) and maintain a public register of certification mechanisms and data protection seals and marks pursuant to Article 42(8) and of the certified controllers or processors established in third countries pursuant to Article 42(7);[2]

(p) approve the requirements referred to in Article 43(3) with a view to the accreditation of certification bodies referred to in Article 43;[3]

(q) provide the Commission with an opinion on the certification requirements referred to in Article 43(8);

(r) provide the Commission with an opinion on the icons referred to in Article 12(7);

(s) provide the Commission with an opinion for the assessment of the adequacy of the level of protection in a third country or international organisation, including for the assessment whether a third country, a territory or one or more specified sectors within that third country, or an international organisation no longer ensures an adequate level of protection. To that end, the Commission shall provide the Board with all necessary documentation, including correspondence with the government of the third country, with regard to that third country, territory or specified sector, or with the international organisation.

(t) issue opinions on draft decisions of supervisory authorities pursuant to the consistency mechanism referred to in Article 64(1), on matters submitted pursuant to Article 64(2) and to issue binding decisions pursuant to Article 65, including in cases referred to in Article 66;

(u) promote the cooperation and the effective bilateral and multilateral exchange of information and best practices between the supervisory authorities;

(v) promote common training programmes and facilitate personnel exchanges between the supervisory authorities and, where appropriate, with the supervisory authorities of third countries or with international organisations;

(w) promote the exchange of knowledge and documentation on data protection legislation and practice with data protection supervisory authorities worldwide.

(x) issue opinions on codes of conduct drawn up at Union level pursuant to Article 40(9); and

(y) maintain a publicly accessible electronic register of decisions taken by supervisory authorities and courts on issues handled in the consistency mechanism.

2. Where the Commission requests advice from the Board, it may indicate a time limit, taking into account the urgency of the matter.

3. The Board shall forward its opinions, guidelines, recommendations, and best practices to the Commission and to the committee referred to in Article 93 and make them public.

4. The Board shall, where appropriate, consult interested parties and give them the opportunity to comment within a reasonable period. The Board shall, without prejudice to Article 76, make the results of the consultation procedure publicly available.

Relevant Recitals

(124) Where the processing of personal data takes place in the context of the activities of an establishment of a controller or a processor in the Union and the controller or processor is established

---

[2] Corrigenda to the English text of Art. 70(1)(o) were published on 23 May 2018. The text printed reflects the updated version of the Corrigendum GDPR 2018.

[3] Corrigenda to the English text of Art. 70(1)(p) were published on 23 May 2018. The text printed reflects the updated version of the Corrigendum GDPR 2018.

in more than one Member State, or where processing taking place in the context of the activities of a single establishment of a controller or processor in the Union substantially affects or is likely to substantially affect data subjects in more than one Member State, the supervisory authority for the main establishment of the controller or processor or for the single establishment of the controller or processor should act as lead authority. It should cooperate with the other authorities concerned, because the controller or processor has an establishment on the territory of their Member State, because data subjects residing on their territory are substantially affected, or because a complaint has been lodged with them. Also where a data subject not residing in that Member State has lodged a complaint, the supervisory authority with which such complaint has been lodged should also be a supervisory authority concerned. Within its tasks to issue guidelines on any question covering the application of this Regulation, the Board should be able to issue guidelines in particular on the criteria to be taken into account in order to ascertain whether the processing in question substantially affects data subjects in more than one Member State and on what constitutes a relevant and reasoned objection.

(136) In applying the consistency mechanism, the Board should, within a determined period of time, issue an opinion, if a majority of its members so decides or if so requested by any supervisory authority concerned or the Commission. The Board should also be empowered to adopt legally binding decisions where there are disputes between supervisory authorities. For that purpose, it should issue, in principle by a two-thirds majority of its members, legally binding decisions in clearly specified cases where there are conflicting views among supervisory authorities, in particular in the cooperation mechanism between the lead supervisory authority and supervisory authorities concerned on the merits of the case, in particular whether there is an infringement of this Regulation.

(139) In order to promote the consistent application of this Regulation, the Board should be set up as an independent body of the Union. To fulfil its objectives, the Board should have legal personality. The Board should be represented by its Chair. It should replace the Working Party on the Protection of Individuals with Regard to the Processing of Personal Data established by Directive 95/46/EC. It should consist of the head of a supervisory authority of each Member State and the European Data Protection Supervisor or their respective representatives. The Commission should participate in the Board's activities without voting rights and the European Data Protection Supervisor should have specific voting rights. The Board should contribute to the consistent application of this Regulation throughout the Union, including by advising the Commission, in particular on the level of protection in third countries or international organisations, and promoting cooperation of the supervisory authorities throughout the Union. The Board should act independently when performing its tasks.

(172) The European Data Protection Supervisor was consulted in accordance with Article 28(2) of Regulation (EC) No 45/2001 and delivered an opinion on 7 March 2012.

Closely Related Provisions

Article 12 (Transparent information, communication and modalities for the exercise of the rights of the data subject) (see too recital 60); Article 42 (Certification) (see too recital 100); Article 43 (Certification bodies); Article 57 (Tasks of supervisory authorities) (see too recitals 123, 129 and 133); Article 58 (Powers of supervisory authorities) (see too recital 129); Article 63 (Consistency mechanism) (see too recital 135); Article 64 (Opinion of the Board) (see too recital 136); Article 65 (Dispute resolution by the Board); Article 66 (Urgency procedure); Article 68 (European Data Protection Board) (see too recital 139); Article 69 (Independence) (see too recital 139)

Related Provisions in LED [Directive (EU) 2016/680]

Recital 106 (Consultation of EDPS); Article 46 (Tasks of supervisory authorities); Article 47 (Powers of supervisory authorities) (see too recitals 82–83); Article 51 (Tasks of the Board) (see too recitals 68 and 84)

Related Provisions in EPD [Directive 2002/58/EC]

Article 4 (Security of processing) (see too recital 20); Article 15(3) (Application of WP29) (see too recital 48); Article 15(a) (Consultation of WP29 on national measures on cross-border cooperation)

Related Provisions in EUDPR [Regulation (EU) 2018/1725]

Recital 172 (Consultation of EDPS); Article 39(6) (Examination by EDPB of lists of processing operations requiring or not requiring a DPIA); Article 42 (Legislative consultation) (see too recital 60); Article 51 (International cooperation) (see too recital 71); Article 54(2) (Provision of secretariat of the Board) (see too recital 61); Article 57 (Tasks of the European Data Protection Board, in particular paragraphs 1(g) (Advice on legislative measures) and 1(k) (Participation in the activities of the Board) (see too recitals 60 and 73); Article 62 (Coordinated supervision by the European Data Protection Supervisor and national supervisory authorities) (see too recital 78)

Relevant Case Law

CJEU

Case C-131/12, *Google Spain SL and Google Inc. v Agencia Española de Protección de Datos (AEPD) and Mario Costeja González*, judgment of 13 May 2014 (Grand Chamber) (ECLI:EU:C:2014:317).

A. Rationale and Policy Underpinnings

Article 70 GDPR is a core provision of Section 3, which sets forth the main tasks of the Board and links those tasks to its various powers and duties under Chapter VII. It demonstrates that the principal role of the Board is to ensure consistency of the interpretation and application of the GDPR by the various EU/EEA supervisory authorities. Article 70 is the main, but not the only source of tasks, which can also be found in other Articles of the GDPR and in the other EU instruments on data protection.

The broad range of tasks of the Board, combined with the powers set forth in the various provisions of Chapter VII, stand in sharp contrast to the role of its predecessor. Under Article 30 DPD the WP29 was confined to a more limited role, to 'advise the Commission and, in particular, contribute to the uniform application' of national implementation of the DPD, per recital 65 DPD.

B. Legal Background

1. EU legislation

Article 30 of the DPD set out the tasks of the WP29 as follows:

1. The Working Party shall:
   (a) examine any question covering the application of the national measures adopted under this Directive in order to contribute to the uniform application of such measures;
   (b) give the Commission an opinion on the level of protection in the Community and in third countries;
   (c) advise the Commission on any proposed amendment of this Directive, on any additional or specific measures to safeguard the rights and freedoms of natural persons with regard to the processing of personal data and on any other proposed Community measures affecting such rights and freedoms;
   (d) give an opinion on codes of conduct drawn up at Community level.
2. If the Working Party finds that divergences likely to affect the equivalence of protection for persons with regard to the processing of personal data in the Community are arising between the laws or practices of Member States, it shall inform the Commission accordingly.
3. The Working Party may, on its own initiative, make recommendations on all matters relating to the protection of persons with regard to the processing of personal data in the Community.
4. The Working Party's opinions and recommendations shall be forwarded to the Commission and to the committee referred to in Article 31.
5. The Commission shall inform the Working Party of the action it has taken in response to its opinions and recommendations. It shall do so in a report which shall also be forwarded to the European Parliament and the Council. The report shall be made public.

Recital 65 of the DPD explained:

Whereas, at Community level, a Working Party on the Protection of Individuals with regard to the Processing of Personal Data must be set up and be completely independent in the performance of its functions; whereas, having regard to its specific nature, it must advise the Commission and, in particular, contribute to the uniform application of the national rules adopted pursuant to this Directive.

2. International instruments

Article 17(3) of Modernised Convention 108 provides that, in order to organise their cooperation and to perform their duties, supervisory authorities should 'form a network'. Article 143 of the Explanatory Report explains that such a network would be a 'means to contribute to the rationalisation of the co-operation process and thus to the efficiency of the protection of personal data'. It also stresses that 'the Convention refers to "a network" in singular form'.

The European Economic Area ('EEA') Agreement, as amended in July 2018,[4] incorporates the GDPR into its Annexes and provides that the provisions of the GDPR should be read, for the purposes of that Agreement, with a number of adaptations. These concern the participation in the composition and workings of the EDPB of the supervisory authorities of Norway, Iceland and Liechtenstein, the three EFTA States participating in the

---

[4] EEA Decision 2018.

EEA[5] and of the EFTA Surveillance Authority. In this respect, the amended Agreement provides that, where it is relevant to the exercise of its functions under Article 109 of the Agreement, the EFTA Surveillance Authority shall have the right to request advice or opinions from, and to communicate matters to, the Board pursuant to Articles 63, 64(2), 65(1)(c) and 70(1)(e), and that in Articles 63, 64(2), 65(1)(c) and 70(1)(e), 'the words "and, where relevant, the EFTA Surveillance Authority" shall be added after the words 'the Commission'.[6]

C. Analysis

1. Introduction

Article 70(1) GDPR confers an extensive and detailed list of tasks on the Board, which are both unique to the Board and complementary to the tasks of the supervisory authorities under Article 57 GDPR.[7] The task placed at the head of the list demonstrates that the primary role of the Board is to 'ensure the consistent application' of the GDPR, acting within the consistency mechanism laid down in Articles 64 and 65. Recital 139 confirms that the Board was set up '(i)n order to promote the consistent application' of the GDPR and that its primary role is to 'contribute to the consistent application of this Regulation throughout the Union'. Included within this mandate the recital gives two specific examples, of 'advising the Commission, in particular on the level of protection in third countries or international organisations', and of 'promoting cooperation of the supervisory authorities throughout the Union'. The same approach may be found in recital 84 of the LED, save without the specific reference to advice on international transfers.

The 'consistency' tasks of the Board under Article 70(1) include the giving of advice, often in specific circumstances, the power for the first time to adopt decisions binding upon supervisory authorities, and the promotion of practical cooperation between supervisory authorities.

2. Advice

This task carries forward the advisory role of the predecessor WP29, although with greater weight and influence, providing specific advice to the Commission as well as advice to stakeholders and individuals on the interpretation of the legislation in the form of opinions, guidelines and best practices. The Board is required to forward its opinions, guidelines, recommendations and best practices to the Commission and, where relevant, to the EFTA Surveillance Authority[8] and to the rule-making committee referred to in Article 93 (that is, to representatives of the Member States) and to make them public.[9]

2.1 Advice to the Commission

Under Article 70(1)(b) the Board has the general task of advising the Commission on 'any issue related to the protection of personal data in the Union'; that is, on any issue falling within the scope of EU data protection law. This may be regarded as essentially

---

[5] Switzerland, the fourth EFTA State is not a signatory to the EEA Agreement.
[6] Art. 5e(l) EEA Decision 2018.
[7] Which may be summarised as supervisory tasks, advice and information, see Robert 2017, p. 17.
[8] Added Art. 5e(l) EEA Decision. [9] Art. 70(3) GDPR.

the same task as the various advisory mandates of the WP29 under Article 30 paragraphs 1(c) and 2–4 of the DPD.

There was in the past a certain overlap between the advisory tasks of the WP29 and the EDPS. Sometimes the two bodies would collaborate in drafting a sole advice by the WP29, the EDPS often acting as a rapporteur or the principal rapporteur in such cases. Less frequently, they would both provide complementary advice on the same matter, for example on the Commission proposal on the legislative reform package,[10] on drones and on ePrivacy.[11] This practice has now been consolidated and regulated in the EUDPR, which imposes obligations on the Commission, the EDPS and the Board itself to this effect.

Article 57(1)(g) EUDPR reiterates the general advisory task of the EDPS. This is specified in Article 42(1) EUDPR, which requires the Commission to consult the EDPS on draft legislation where there is an 'impact' on the protection of individuals' rights and freedoms with regard to the processing of personal data. This obligation applies either once a legislative proposal has been adopted, or when delegated or implementing measures are being prepared. The convention has developed to cite the consultation of and opinion of the EDPS in one of the final recitals to the legislative act concerned.[12]

Recital 60 EUDPR adds a significant obligation of 'endeavour', to consult the EDPS prior to adoption of a proposal, 'when preparing proposals or recommendations', usually at the same time as the internal inter-service consultation procedure. Such upstream consultation can be highly effective in practice, as it enables the Commission services to take account of informal and uncontroversial advice before the Commission finalises its position.[13]

Article 41(4) EUDPR provides that the obligation to consult the EDPS does not apply where the GDPR specifically requires the Board to be consulted. In this respect, Article 70(1) GDPR requires the Board to provide opinions to the Commission on a number of specific issues where tasks are imposed on the Commission and the Board is required to inform the Commission's decision-making. These are the certification requirements under Article 43(8),[14] the icons referred to in Article 12(7)[15] and specific issues relating to international data transfers, namely advice on the format and procedures for the exchange of information between controllers, processors and supervisory authorities for binding corporate rules[16] and opinions on the assessment of the adequacy of the level of protection in a third country or international organisation.[17] In such cases the consultation of and opinion of the Board will have to be cited in one of the final recitals to the legislative act concerned, in the same way as the advice of the EDPS noted above.

Article 41(2) EUDPR lays down a threshold where the EDPB may be consulted in addition to the EDPS, and how the two EU bodies should interact. Where a proposed act under Article 41(1) EUDPR is of 'particular importance' for the protection of rights and freedoms of natural persons with regard to the processing of personal data, the Commission may also consult the Board. In such cases, the EDPS and the EDPB should coordinate their work 'with a view to issuing a joint opinion'. This obligation can also be

---

[10] EDPS 2012 and WP29 2012.   [11] See EDPS 2017, para. 55.   [12] See rec. 172 GDPR.
[13] See EDPS 2017, para. 51 and fn. 50, and EDPS Rules of Procedure, Art. 27.
[14] Art. 70(1)(q) GDPR.   [15] Ibid., Art. 70(1)(r).   [16] Ibid., Art. 70(1)(c).
[17] Ibid., Art. 70(1)(s).

seen as a specification of the EDPS's task of participation in the activities of the European Data Protection Board under Article 57(1)(k) EUDPR.

Finally, paragraph 3 of Article 41 EUDPR provides that the advice requested under paragraphs 1 and 2 must be provided in writing within eight weeks of receipt of the request. The Commission may shorten this period in urgent cases or cases where a shorter period is appropriate, such as, according to recital 60 EUDPR, when the Commission is preparing delegated and implementing acts.

These tasks of advising the Commission, both on specific issues and in cases of 'particular importance', constitute one of the most important roles of the Board, second only to its role in ensuring consistency. The importance of the Board's advisory role for the Commission can also be seen in Articles 70(2) and 69(2). Article 70(2) empowers the Commission to fix a time limit in urgent cases within which the Board must provide its advice. Article 69(1) requires the Board to act independently and to 'neither seek nor take instructions from anybody'. However, Article 69(2) states that this requirement is without prejudice to requests by the Commission for advice under Article 70(1)(b) and to time limits fixed by the Commission for receiving such advice under Article 70(2).

2.2 Advice to stakeholders, including guidelines, recommendations and best practice

Article 70(1)(e) lays down a general requirement on the Board to examine—either on its own initiative, on request of one of its members or on request of the Commission and, where relevant, the EFTA Surveillance Authority[18]—any question covering the application of the GDPR.

In addition, Article 70(1)(e) lays down the general task of the Board to issue 'guidelines, recommendations and best practice' at EU level. This general clause is complemented by clauses requiring the Board to provide specific guidance on the right to be forgotten,[19] profiling,[20] data breaches and high risk,[21] binding corporate rules,[22] personal data transfers[23] and complaints procedures.[24] Under this provision, Article 39(6) EUDPR requires the EDPS to request the Board to examine proposed lists of the kind of processing operations which are subject to the requirement for a data protection impact assessment, or for which no data protection impact assessment is required, where they refer to processing operations by a controller acting jointly with one or more controllers other than Union institutions and bodies.

Whilst the Board has the task of providing guidance on these topics, the Board is not required to provide specific advice to individuals or to handle complaints, unlike supervisory authorities which have these tasks under Article 57(e) and (f), respectively.

Article 70(1)(l) requires the Board to review the practical application of the guidelines, recommendations and best practices. The 2018 Corrigendum to the GDPR removed two references in Article 70(1)(l)—namely, to the general guidance clause of Article 70(1)(e) and to the specific guidance clause on profiling under (f)—and thus clarified that *all* the guidance by the Board, including that under (d), (f)–(j) and (m), is subject to the review

---

[18] Added Art. 5e(l) EEA Decision.　[19] Art. 70(1)(d) GDPR.　[20] Ibid., Art. 70(1)(f).
[21] Ibid., Art. 70(1)(g)–(h).　[22] Ibid., Art. 70(1)(i).　[23] Ibid., Art. 70(1)(j).
[24] Ibid., Art. 70(1)–(m).

obligation under (l). The misleading reference to only one specific guidance clause, that in (f), had been a drafting error during the negotiations. In addition, (d) does not refer to the general guidance clause under (e). The removal by the Corrigendum of the two references to (e) and (f) from (l) thus precludes any interpretation that might have limited the scope of Article 70(1)(l).

With regard to the preparation of such guidance, Article 70(4) requires the Board—'where appropriate'—to consult interested parties and give them the opportunity to comment within a reasonable period. Without prejudice to the confidentiality requirement under Article 76, the Board must make the results of the consultation procedure publicly available.

The work of the WP29 from 2016 onwards gives an indication of what data protection authorities regard as 'appropriate', namely the adoption of guidelines on the application of the GDPR. In order to prepare for the GDPR the WP29 adopted a new methodology for adopting a series of guidelines:[25] the adoption and publication of draft guidelines, the fixing of a period of six weeks to submit comments, and the finalisation and publication of the final guidelines after taking into consideration the comments received. In addition, the WP29 prepared its work on a number of guidelines beforehand by organising a Fablab workshop in 2016[26] and 2017.[27] These procedures have given stakeholders the chance to comment upon and to have some influence on these often highly technical documents.

The Board has not formally consolidated either of these procedures in the EDPB Rules of Procedure. Instead, Article 30 simply provides that the 'Board shall, where appropriate, organize consultations of interested parties in accordance with Article 70 (4) GDPR. The means and consultation period shall be decided on a case-by-case basis'.[28]

In the meantime, the Board has formally endorsed the preparatory work by its predecessor. On 25 May 2018 it adopted Endorsement 1/2018 in which it endorsed the sixteen existing WP29 guidelines and other documents on various aspects of the GDPR.[29] These were '(w)ithout prejudice to any future revision, as appropriate', noting that the Board may in due course update these guidelines in the light of experience.

2.3 Advice to supervisory authorities

Under Article 70(1)(k) the Board has the task of supporting supervisory authorities by drawing up guidelines on the exercise of their powers under Article 58 and on the fixing of administrative fines. The WP29 already had some experience of providing such authoritative advice for its member authorities in the guidelines on implementing the CJEU ruling on the 'right to be forgotten' in *Google Spain*.[30] These guidelines set out in detail how the members of the WP29 intended to implement the ruling and listed the

---

[25] See list in EDPB 2018. Guidelines adopted by the Board itself after 25 May 2018 can be found on the EDPB Website.

[26] See WP29 GDPR Fablab 2016, discussing DPO, portability, DPIA and certification.

[27] See WP29 GDPR Fablab 2017, discussing consent, data breach notifications and profiling.

[28] EDPB Rules of Procedure.

[29] These sixteen papers are WP29 2017A, WP29 2017B, WP29 2017C, WP29 2017D, WP29 2017E, WP29 2018A, WP29 2018B, WP29 2018C, WP29 2018D, WP29 2018E, WP29 2018F, WP29 2018G, WP29 2018H, WP29 2018I, WP29 2018J, WP29 2018K.

[30] Case C-131/12, *Google Spain*. See WP29 2014. See also a description of coordinated enforcement action in respect of Google's privacy policy, in Kloza and Moscibroda 2014, pp. 125–127.

common criteria which supervisory authorities would apply to handle complaints against refusals of de-listing by search engines.[31]

2.4 Advice and opinions on codes of conduct and certification

Article 70(1)(n) requires the Board to encourage the drawing-up of codes of conduct and the establishment of data protection certification mechanisms and data protection seals and marks pursuant to Articles 40(1) and 42(1).

With regard to encouraging the drawing-up of codes of conduct, the Board has the task of providing an opinion to the supervisory authority concerned[32] and to the Commission[33] on whether a draft cross-frontier code of conduct complies with the GDPR.[34] In addition, the Board must collate all approved codes of conduct, amendments and extensions in a register and make them publicly available by way of appropriate means.[35]

As well as encouraging the establishment of data protection certification mechanisms, the Board may approve criteria of certification pursuant to Article 42(5)[36] including approving[37] and advising the Commission[38] on the requirements for the accreditation of certification bodies. In addition, the Board must collate all certification mechanisms and data protection seals and marks pursuant to Article 42(8) and maintain a public register of those certification mechanisms and data protection seals and marks and of the certified controllers or processors established in third countries pursuant to Article 42(7).[39]

3. Consistency mechanism: opinions and binding decisions

Under Article 70(1)(t) the Board shall issue opinions on draft decisions of supervisory authorities on the six matters laid down in Article 64(1) and on matters of general application submitted pursuant to Article 64(2), and to issue binding decisions pursuant to the dispute resolution procedure laid down in Article 65 and the urgency procedure laid down in Article 66. In effect the Board has the power under the consistency mechanism laid down in Articles 63–66 to conciliate between EU/EEA supervisory authorities and to determine disputes between them, so as to ensure the consistent application of the GDPR.

In the event of disputes, the Board has the power to adopt binding decisions under the dispute resolution procedure laid down in Article 65. This procedure applies in three cases: where there is a disagreement on a draft decision between the lead authority and a supervisory authority concerned, where there is disagreement on which is the lead authority and where a supervisory authority has failed to follow the procedure under Article 64.[40] An urgent decision may also be adopted by the Board in cases of urgency under Article 66.

The Board reported in February 2019 that 34 opinions had been adopted or were being prepared under this procedure, concerning national lists of processing subject to a DPIA, a draft administrative arrangement for the transfer of personal data between financial supervisory authorities, binding corporate rules, a draft standard contract between Controllers and Processors, and the interplay between the GDPR and the ePrivacy Directive, in particular as regards the competence of the national data protection

---

[31] WP29 2014, p. 5.   [32] Art. 40(7) GDPR.   [33] Ibid., Art. 40(8).
[34] Ibid., Arts. 40(9) and 70(1)(x).   [35] Ibid., Art. 40(11).   [36] Ibid., Art. 70(1)(o).
[37] Ibid., Art.70(1)(p).   [38] Ibid., Art. 70(1)(q).   [39] Ibid., Art. 70(1)(o).
[40] See also ibid., Art. 64(8).

supervisory authorities. The Board further reported that no dispute resolution procedures had been initiated by that time.[41]

The GDPR lays down the rules on voting for these procedures but does not provide any further detailed rules on the procedure within the Board for adopting such decisions nor whether the Board may limit itself to commenting upon the draft decision or whether the Board may substitute its own appreciation for that proposed in the draft decision[42]—for example, on the assessment and amount of an administrative fine.

Title III of the Rules of Procedure of the Board lay down detailed rules for each of these procedures. Under Article 10(2) of those Rules, normally an opinion should be adopted within eight weeks from the first working day after the Chair and the competent supervisory authority have decided that the file is complete, and under Article 11(4) normally a decision should be adopted within one month from the first working day after the Chair and the competent supervisory authority have decided that the file is complete. Article 11(1) lays down two specific safeguards for taking binding decisions. The Board must respect the right to good administration as set out by Article 41 CFR, and the Board must make sure that all persons that might be adversely affected have been heard before taking decisions.

As legally binding decisions[43] these decisions may be challenged before the General Court by those directly and individually concerned, such as the controller, processor or person affected by the decision as well as any supervisory authority that wishes to contest the decision.[44] Finally, Article 70(1)(y) GDPR requires the Board to maintain a publicly accessible electronic register of decisions taken by supervisory authorities and courts on issues handled in the consistency mechanism.

4. Promoting cooperation between supervisory authorities

The Board is tasked with the promotion of a number of cooperation initiatives between EU/EEA supervisory authorities and with cooperation initiatives at international level. Article 3 of the Rules of Procedure stresses the need for effective cooperation between supervisory authorities in its fourth Guiding Principle, the Principle of Cooperation:

In accordance with the principle of cooperation, the Board shall promote cooperation between supervisory authorities and endeavour to operate where possible by consensus, and subject to the GDPR and the Police and Criminal Justice Data Protection Directive.[45]

The cooperation tasks of the Board include the bilateral and multilateral exchange of information and best practices among supervisory authorities,[46] common training programmes and staff exchanges between supervisory authorities and, where appropriate, third country supervisory authorities and international organisations,[47] and exchanges of knowledge and documentation with supervisory authorities worldwide.[48]

By conferring these tasks on the Board, the EU legislator has firmly established the role of the Board both as a coordinator within the EU and an important actor at international level.

---

[41] EDPB 2019, p.6   [42] Robert 2017, p. 75.
[43] These decisions are *sui generis* by nature, termed 'Beschluss' in German, and hence do not necessarily have specific addressees, unlike a traditional decision or 'Entscheidung'. See Lenaerts and van Nuffel 2011, para. 22-096.
[44] Robert 2017, p. 76.   [45] EDPB Rules of Procedure.   [46] Art. 70(1)(u) GDPR.
[47] Ibid., Art. 70(1)(v).   [48] Ibid., Art. 70(1)(w).

5. The tasks of the Board under the LED

Article 51 LED lays down a similar list of tasks to Article 70(1) GDPR. However, it does not have the same emphasis on ensuring consistency. Although recital 84 LED sets forth the same priority for contributing to the consistent application of the Directive as recital 139 GDPR, the LED omits a number of the tasks conferred on the Board under the GDPR. Tasks under the GDPR which do not feature in Article 51 LED are monitoring under Article 70(1)(a), the adoption of guidelines for supervisory authorities on consistency measures and fines under sub-paragraph (k) and of consistency opinions under sub-paragraph (t). In addition, the LED omits the tasks relating to BCRs under Article 70(1)(c), links under sub-paragraph (d), data transfers under sub-paragraph (j), complaints under sub-paragraph (m), codes under sub-paragraphs (n)–(q), certification under sub-paragraph (r) and icons under sub-paragraph (t).

6. Future coordination tasks

The GDPR does not impose any obligation on the Board to coordinate cooperation between the EDPS and national supervisory authorities with regard to coordinated supervision and supervision in the law enforcement area. However, the present situation has been criticised for its 'fragmentation and increasing complexity', particularly in the area of freedom, security and justice.[49] In consequence, the EUDPR has laid the groundwork for developing the role of the Board in the future, as the first stage of what is effectively a two-stage procedure.

Recital 78 EUDPR refers to the model of coordinated supervision developed and shared between the EDPS and national supervisory authorities, principally in the area of large-scale IT systems.[50] The Research Network on EU Administrative Law suggested in 2014 that the role of coordination of these systems should be given to the future EDPB.[51] This suggestion was not followed. Instead, Article 62 EUDPR, paragraphs 1 and 2, requires the EDPS and national supervisory authorities, each acting within the scope of their respective competences, to (continue to) cooperate actively within the framework of their responsibilities to ensure effective supervision of such systems.

In addition, recital 78 EUDPR refers to a new model of cooperation between the EDPS, as the responsible DPA, and national supervisory authorities concerning the supervision of Europol, where they cooperate in a Cooperation Board with an advisory function.[52] Cooperation is also required between the EDPS, as the responsible DPA, and national supervisory authorities concerning supervision of EPPO[53] and Eurojust.[54] In this respect, it is significant that Article 62 EUDPR has not been limited to coordination of large-scale IT systems. It also requires the EDPS and national supervisory authorities to cooperate actively to ensure effective supervision of 'Union bodies, offices and agencies', a much broader scope, which capable of embracing Europol, Eurojust and EPPO, as well as traditional coordinated supervision. To this end Article 62(3)

---

[49] EDPS 2017 paras. 13 and 14. See also Eurojust Regulation recital 29.
[50] Consisting of CIS Regulation, Art. 37; Eurodac Regulation, Art. 32; SIS II Regulation, Art. 46; SIS II Decision, Art. 62; IMI Regulation, Art. 21; VIS Regulation, Art. 43. For information on coordinated supervision, see the EDPS Supervision Coordination website.
[51] ReNEUAL Model Rules, Art. VI-39, pp. 262–263
[52] Europol Regulation, Art. 45 and rec. 52   [53] EPPO Regulation, Art. 87
[54] Eurojust Regulation, Art. 42.

requires the EDPS and national supervisory authorities to meet at least twice a year within the framework of the EDPB and provides that the Board may develop further working methods as necessary.

Article 98 EUDPR contemplates the second stage of this reform, requiring the Commission to review these various measures, in particular their consistency with the LED and the EUDPR and any divergencies that may hamper the exchange of personal data or create legal fragmentation, and on the basis of that review to submit appropriate legislative proposals.

To conclude, recital 78 EUDPR explains what the legislator has in mind for the second stage of the reform and the future role of the Board in this area:

In order to improve the effective supervision and enforcement of substantive data protection rules, a single, coherent model of coordinated supervision should be introduced in the Union. The Commission should therefore make legislative proposals where appropriate with a view to amending Union legal acts providing for a model of coordinated supervision, in order to align them with the coordinated supervision model of this Regulation. The European Data Protection Board should serve as a single forum for ensuring effective coordinated supervision in all areas.

Select Bibliography

International agreements

EEA Agreement: Agreement on the European Economic Area, OJ 1994 L 1/3.
EEA Decision 2018: Decision of the EEA Joint Committee No. 154/2018 of 6 July 2018 amending Annex XI (Electronic communication, audiovisual services and information society) and Protocol 37 (containing the list provided for in Article 101) to the EEA Agreement [2018/1022], OJ 2018 L 183/23.

EU legislation

CIS Regulation: Council Regulation (EC) No. 515/97 of 13 March 1997 on mutual assistance between the administrative authorities of the Member States and cooperation between the latter and the Commission to ensure the correct application of the law on customs and agricultural matters, OJ L 82, 22.3.1997, p. 1, as amended by Regulation (EC) No. 766/2008 of 9 July 2008, OJ L 218, 13.8.2008, p. 48. See also Council Decision 2009/917/JHA of 30 November 2009 on the use of information technology for customs purposes, OJ L323,10.11.2009, p. 20
EPPO Regulation: Council Regulation (EU) 2017/1939 of 12 October 2017 implementing enhanced cooperation on the establishment of the European Public Prosecutor's Office, OJ L 283, 31.10.2017, p.1
Eurodac Regulation: Regulation (EU) No. 603/2013 of the European Parliament and of the Council of 26 June 2013 on the establishment of 'Eurodac' for the comparison of fingerprints for the effective application of Regulation (EU) No. 604/2013 establishing the criteria and mechanisms for determining the Member State responsible for examining an application for international protection lodged in one of the Member States by a third-country national or a stateless person and on requests for the comparison with Eurodac data by Member States' law enforcement authorities and Europol for law enforcement purposes, and amending Regulation (EU) No. 1077/2011 establishing a European Agency for the operational management of large-scale IT systems in the area of freedom, security and justice (recast), OJ L 180, 29.6.2013, p. 1.

Eurojust Regulation: Regulation (EU) 2018/1727 of the European Parliament and of the Council of 14 November 2018 on the European Union Agency for Criminal Justice Cooperation (Eurojust), and replacing and repealing Council Decision 2002/187/JHA, OJ L 295, 21.11.2018, p. 138.

Europol Regulation: Regulation (EU) 2016/794 of the European Parliament and of the Council of 11 May 2016 on the European Union Agency for Law Enforcement Cooperation (Europol) and replacing and repealing Council Decisions 2009/371/JHA, 2009/934/JHA, 2009/935/JHA, 2009/936/JHA and 2009/968/JHA, OJ L 135, 24.5.2016, p. 53.

IMI Regulation: Regulation (EU) No. 1024/2012 of the European Parliament and of the Council of 25 October 2012 on administrative cooperation through the Internal Market Information System and repealing Commission Decision 2008/49/EC, OJ L 316, 14.11.2012, p. 1.

SIS II Decision: Council Decision 2007/533/JHA of 12 June 2007 on the establishment, operation and use of the second generation Schengen Information System (SIS II), OJ L 205, 7.8.2007, p. 63.

SIS II Regulation: Regulation (EC) No. 1987/2006 of the European Parliament and of the Council of 20 December 2006 on the establishment, operation and use of the second generation Schengen Information System (SIS II), OJ L 381, 28.12.2006, p. 4.

VIS Regulation: Regulation (EC) No. 767/2008 of the European Parliament and of the Council of 9 July 2008 concerning the Visa Information System (VIS) and the exchange of data between Member States on short-stay visas (VIS Regulation), OJ L 218, 13.8.2008, p. 60.

Academic writings

Kloza and Moscibroda 2014: Kloza and Moscibroda, 'Making the Case for Enhanced Enforcement Cooperation between Data Protection Authorities: Insights from Competition Law', 4(2) *International Data Privacy Law* (2014), 120.

Lenaerts and van Nuffel 2011: Lenaerts and van Nuffel, *European Union Law* (3rd edn, Sweet and Maxwell 2011).

Robert 2017: Robert 2017: Robert, 'Les Autorités de contrôle dans le nouveau règlement général sur la protection des données: statut, coopération et gouvernance européenne', in Docquir (ed.), *Vers un droit européen de la protection des données?* (Larcier 2017), 21.

Papers of data protection authorities

EDPB 2018: European Data Protection Board, 'Endorsement 1/2018' (25 May 2018).

EDPB 2019: European Data Protection Board, 'First overview on the implementation of the GDPR and the roles and means of the national supervisory authorities' (26 February 2019).

EDPB Rules of Procedure: European Data Protection Board, 'Rules of Procedure' Version 2 (Adopted on 25 May 2018, as last modified and adopted on 23 November 2018).

EDPS 2012: European Data Protection Supervisor, Opinion on the data protection reform package, 7 March 2012.

EDPS 2017: European Data Protection Supervisor, 'Upgrading Data Protection Rules for EU Institutions and Bodies', EDPS Opinion 5/2017 on the proposal for a Regulation on the protection of individuals with regard to the processing of personal data by the Union institutions, bodies, offices and agencies and on the free movement of such data, and repealing Regulation (EC) No. 45/2001 and Decision No. 1247/2002/EC, 15 March 2017.

EDPS Rules of Procedure: Decision of the European Data Protection Supervisor of 17 December 2012 on the adoption of Rules of Procedure, OJ L 274, 15.10.2013, p. 41.

WP29 2012: Article 29 Working Party, Opinion 1/2012 on the data protection reform proposals, WP 191, 23 March 2012.

WP29 2014: Article 29 Working Party, 'Guidelines on the Implementation of the Court of Justice of the European Union Ruling on "Google Spain and inc v. Agencia Española de Protección de Datos (AEPD) and Mario Costeja González"' (WP 225, 26 November 2014).

WP29 2017A: Article 29 Working Party, 'Guidelines on Data Protection Impact Assessment (DPIA) and Determining Whether Processing Is "Likely to Result in a High Risk" for the Purposes of Regulation 2016/679' (WP 248 rev.01, as last revised and adopted on 4 October 2017).

WP29 2017B: Article 29 Working Party, 'Guidelines on the Application and Setting of Administrative Fines for the Purposes of the Regulation 2016/679' (WP 253, 3 October 2017).

WP29 2017C: Article 29 Working Party, 'Guidelines on the Right to Data Portability' (WP 242 rev.01, as last revised and adopted on 5 April 2017).

WP29 2017D: Article 29 Working Party, 'Guidelines on Data Protection Officers ("DPOs")' (WP 243 rev.01, as last revised and adopted on 5 April 2017).

WP29 2017E: Article 29 Working Party, 'Guidelines for Identifying a Controller or Processor's Lead Supervisory Authority' (WP 244 rev.01, as last revised and adopted on 5 April 2017).

WP29 2018A: Article 29 Working Party, 'Guidelines on Personal data Breach Notification under Regulation 2016/679' (WP 250 rev.01, as last revised and adopted on 6 February 2018).

WP29 2018B: Article 29 Working Party, 'Guidelines on Automated Individual Decision-Making and Profiling for the Purposes of Regulation 2016/679' (WP 251 rev.01, as last revised and adopted on 6 February 2018).

WP29 2018C: Article 29 Working Party, 'Adequacy Referential' (WP 254 rev.01, as last revised and adopted on 6 February 2018).

WP29 2018D: Article 29 Working Party, 'Working Document Setting Up a Table with the Elements and Principles to Be Found in Binding Corporate Rules' (WP 256 rev.01, as last revised and adopted on 6 February 2018).

WP29 2018E: Article 29 Working Party, 'Working Document Setting Up a Table with the Elements and Principles to Be Found in Processor Binding Corporate Rules' (WP 257 rev.01, as last revised and adopted on 6 February 2018).

WP29 2018F: Article 29 Working Party, 'Guidelines on Consent under Regulation 2016/679' (WP 259 rev.01, as last revised and adopted on 10 April 2018).

WP29 2018G: Article 29 Working Party, 'Guidelines on Transparency under Regulation 2016/679' (WP 260 rev.01, as last revised and adopted on 11 April 2018).

WP29 2018H: Article 29 Working Party, 'Working Document Setting Forth a Co-Operation Procedure for the Approval of "Binding Corporate Rules" for Controllers and Processors under the GDPR' (WP 263 rev.01, as last revised and adopted on 11 April 2018).

WP29 2018I: Article 29 Working Party, 'Recommendation on the Standard Application for Approval of Controller Binding Corporate Rules for the Transfer of Personal Data' (WP 264, 11 April 2018).

WP29 2018J: Article 29 Working Party, 'Recommendation on the Standard Application form for Approval of Processor Binding Corporate Rules for the Transfer of Personal Data' (WP 265, 11 April 2018).

WP29 2018K: Article 29 Working Party, 'Working Party 29 Position Paper on the Derogations from the Obligation to Maintain Records of Processing Activities Pursuant to Article 30(5) GDPR' (19 April 2018).

Others

EDPB Website: Website of the European Data Protection Board, 'GDPR: Guidelines, Recommendations, Best Practices', available at https://edpb.europa.eu/our-work-tools/general-guidance/gdpr-guidelines-recommendations-best-practices_en.

EDPS coordination supervision website: https://edps.europa.eu/data-protection/supervision-coordination_en.

EDPS supervision of Europol website: https://edps.europa.eu/data-protection/our-role-supervisor/supervision-europol_en

ReNEUAL Model Rules: ReNEUAL Model Rules on EU Administrative Procedure, Research Network on EU Administrative Law, Version for online publication, 2014

WP29 GDPR Fablab 2016: Article 29 Working Party, 'Fablab "GDPR/from Concepts to Operational Toolbox, DIY"—Results of the Discussion' (26 July 2016), available at https://ec.europa.eu/justice/article-29/documentation/other-document/files/2016/20160930_fablab_results_of_discussions_en.pdf.

WP29 GDPR Fablab 2017: Article 29 Working Party, '2017 GDPR Fablab—Results of the Discussions' (6 April 2017), available at https://ec.europa.eu/newsroom/document.cfm?doc_id=44645.

Article 71. Reports

CHRISTOPHER DOCKSEY

1. The Board shall draw up an annual report regarding the protection of natural persons with regard to processing in the Union and, where relevant, in third countries and international organisations. The report shall be made public and be transmitted to the European Parliament, to the Council and to the Commission.
2. The annual report shall include a review of the practical application of the guidelines, recommendations and best practices referred to in point (l) of Article 70(1) as well as of the binding decisions referred to in Article 65.

Closely Related Provisions

Recital 100; recital 139; Article 42 (Certification); Article 59 (Activity reports of supervisory authorities); Article 68 (European Data Protection Board); Article 70 (Tasks of the Board); Article 97 (European Commission reports on the evaluation and review of the GDPR)

Related Provisions in LED [Directive (EU) 2016/680]

Article 49 (Activity reports of supervisory authorities); Article 62 (European Commission reports on the evaluation and review of the LED)

Related Provisions in EPD [Directive 2002/58/EC]

Article 18 (Review)

Related Provisions in EUDPR [Regulation 2018/1725]

Article 60 (EDPS annual activities report) (see too recital 75)

Relevant Case Law

CJEU

Case C-518/07, *European Commission v Federal Republic of Germany*, judgment of 9 March 2010 (Grand Chamber) (ECLI:EU:C:2010:125).

A. Rationale and Policy Underpinnings

Under Article 30(6) DPD the WP29 issued an annual report in which it highlighted data protection developments across the EU and within each EU and European Economic Area ('EEA') country. No review was required of the work of the WP29 itself.

In 2010 the Commission set out its approach to modernising the EU data protection legal framework in its Communication on 'A comprehensive approach on personal data protection in the European Union'.[1] The Commission stressed that the WP29 should become a more transparent body.[2]

Whilst the Board must act independently, it must also be fully accountable, in compliance with the principles of transparency and good governance in EU law enshrined in Article 15 of the Treaty on the Functioning of the European Union ('TFEU') and Article 41 of the Charter of Fundamental Rights. The new requirement on the Board under Article 71(2) to include in its annual report a review of the practical application of the guidelines, recommendations and best practices and the binding decisions adopted, supports the enhanced transparency intended by the legislator.

B. Legal Background

1. EU legislation

Article 30(6) DPD provided:

The Working Party shall draw up an annual report on the situation regarding the protection of natural persons with regard to the processing of personal data in the Community and in third countries, which it shall transmit to the Commission, the European Parliament and the Council. The report shall be made public.

Article 15(2) of the WP29 Rules of Procedure added: 'The report referred to in the first paragraph above shall be adopted by the Working Party, transmitted by the Chairman to the Institutions mentioned in the said paragraph and made public by the Secretariat'.[3]

The report included two main elements. First, a section on the issues addressed by the WP29 over the year, consisted of both a report on its own activities and on the main developments in data protection at EU and international level. Secondly, a section on the main developments in Member States reported on developments in legislation and case law and on the activities of national supervisory authorities. In this respect, at national level Article 28(5) DPD required supervisory authorities to draw up a report on their activities 'at regular intervals'.[4]

Article 33 DPD also required the Commission to report at regular intervals on the implementation of the DPD to the Council and the European Parliament.

A comparable requirement on the Commission to the obligation under Article 71(2) was imposed under Article 18 EPD, to report after three years on the 'application of this Directive and its impact on economic operators and consumers'.

2. International instruments

The Additional Protocol to Convention 108[5] did not include a requirement for supervisory authorities to publish a regular report. This lacuna is filled by Art. 15(7) of Modernised Convention 108, which requires each supervisory authority to prepare and publish a periodical report outlining its activities.

---

[1] EC Communication 2010.   [2] Ibid., pp. 17–18.
[3] WP29 Rules of Procedure. The Annual Reports of the WP29 from 1998 to 2012 may be consulted on their archived website, hosted by the Commission. See WP29 Website.
[4] The most recent report available is WP29 Annual Report 2013.
[5] Additional Protocol Convention 108.

The EEA Agreement, as amended in July 2018,[6] incorporates the GDPR into its Annexes and provides that the provisions of the GDPR should be read, for the purposes of that Agreement, with a number of adaptations. With regard to the composition and workings of the EDPB, the amended Agreement provides that the Board should also report under Article 71(1) GDPR to the Standing Committee of the EFTA States and to the EFTA Surveillance Authority.[7]

3. Case law

The CJEU has pointed out that, in accordance with the principle of democracy enshrined in the Treaties, the absence of parliamentary influence over supervisory authorities is 'inconceivable', and that the legislator may impose an obligation on them to report their activities to the parliament.[8]

C. Analysis

Under Article 71(1) the EDPB must draw up an annual report regarding the protection of natural persons with regard to processing in the Union and, where relevant, in third countries and international organisations. The report has to be made public and transmitted to the European Parliament, to the Council, to the Standing Committee of the EFTA States, to the EFTA Surveillance Authority[9] and to the Commission. Article 35 of the EDPB Rules of Procedure provides that the annual report should be in English and that its executive summary should be available in all the official languages of the EU.

The obligation under Article 71(1) GDPR is effectively the same as the reporting obligation on the WP29 under Article 30(6) DPD, save for the additional reference to international organisations. This was added by the Council to reflect the extension to international organisations of the transfer provisions in Chapter V GDPR.

The obligation to publish an annual review and report is a core element of the transparency and accountability of the Board, both to the public and to the three key EU institutions involved in the legislative and budgetary processes, namely the Parliament, the Council and the Commission. Under Article 97 the Commission is itself required to submit a report on the evaluation and review of the GDPR to the European Parliament and to the Council by 25 May 2020 and every four years thereafter, and to take into account the positions and findings of 'other relevant bodies or sources', which should of course include the information furnished by the Board in its Annual Reports. In the same way, the Board will take account of national developments described in the annual activity reports by national supervisory authorities under Article 59.[10]

In this respect, Article 71(2) is quite significant. This new obligation requires the Board in effect to carry out an annual review of the practical application of the guidelines, recommendations and best practices referred to in Article 70(1)(l) and the binding decisions referred to in Article 65, and to include that review in the annual report. It may have been inspired by the obligation on the Commission under Article 18 EPD to report on the application of the EPD and its 'impact on economic operators and consumers'.

---

[6] EEA Decision 2018. [7] Ibid., Art. 5e(n).
[8] Case C-518/07, *Commission v Germany*, paras. 43-45. [9] Art. 5e(n) EEA Decision.
[10] See the commentary on Art. 59 in this volume.

The Commission proposed the review clause relating to the Board's guidance activities, and the Council added the requirement to review the application of the binding decisions adopted under the dispute resolution procedure.

This requirement to review the practical application of its key activities underpins the transparency and accountability of the Board and strengthens its role in ensuring the consistency of interpretation and application of the GDPR. It also underlines the central role of the Board within the consistency mechanism.

Article 38 of the EDPB Rules of Procedure provides that all the final documents adopted by the Board should be made public on the Board's website. The reporting obligation should serve, together with the website, as a significant source of information on the Board's activities, its advice to the legislator and guidance to stakeholders, and its opinions and decisions under the consistency mechanism.

As noted above the Board also has the specific tasks of maintaining and publicising registers of certification mechanisms and seals,[11] of accredited certification bodies and certified controllers or processors established in third countries,[12] and of decisions taken by supervisory authorities and courts on issues handled in the consistency mechanism.[13] Again, these provisions are intended to enhance transparency.[14]

Based on the experience of the EDPS, the Board as an EU body will present its report to the relevant committee of the Parliament, in this case the Committee on Civil Liberties, Justice and Home Affairs ('LIBE'), thus enabling the necessary political scrutiny. At the same time, it may organise a press conference in order to present its work to the public. In view of the scope and importance of the Board's work compared to that of the WP29, not least the work which must be reviewed under Article 71(2), political and press interest in the annual report is likely to be high.

Similarly, the Board will have to justify its annual budgetary request, based in part on the annual report for the previous year, before the Council and the Parliament. Under the Memorandum of Understanding between the EDPB and the EDPS, the EDPS has the task of defending the budget,[15] in close consultation with the Board.[16] The budgetary request is considered in public by the Parliament, and hence guarantees the transparency of the Board's planning on the disposition of its resources.

Select Bibliography

International agreements

Additional Protocol Convention 108: Additional Protocol to the Convention for the Protection of Individuals with regard to Automatic Processing of Personal Data, regarding supervisory authorities and transborder data flows [ETS 181])

EEA Agreement: Agreement on the European Economic Area, OJ 1994 L 1/3.

EEA Decision 2018: Decision of the EEA Joint Committee No. 154/2018 of 6 July 2018 amending Annex XI (Electronic communication, audiovisual services and information society) and Protocol 37 (containing the list provided for in Article 101) to the EEA Agreement [2018/1022], OJ 2018 L 183/23.

---

[11] Art. 42(8) GDPR. [12] Ibid., Art. 70(1)(o). [13] Ibid., Art. 70(1)(y).
[14] Ibid., rec. 100. [15] EDPS EDPB MoU, section VI.1(iv).
[16] Ibid., section VI.6, see also section VI.7.

Docksey

Papers of data protection authorities

EDPB EDPS MoU: European Data Protection Board and European Data Protection Supervisor, 'Memorandum of Understanding' (25 May 2018), available at https://edpb.europa.eu/sites/edpb/files/files/file1/memorandum_of_understanding_signed_en.pdf.

EDPB Rules of Procedure: European Data Protection Board, 'Rules of Procedure' Version 2 (Adopted on 25 May 2018, as last modified and adopted on 23 November 2018).

WP29 Annual Report 2013: Report of the Article 29 Working Party on Data Protection, covering the year 2013. European Commission (2016).

WP29 Rules of Procedure: Article 29 Working Party, 'Rules of Procedure' (5 October 2017).

Reports and recommendations

EC Communication 2010: Communication from the Commission to the European Parliament, the Council, the European Economic and Social Committee and the Committee of the Regions, 'A Comprehensive Approach on Personal Data Protection in the European Union', COM (2010) 609 final, 4 November 2010.

Others

WP29 Website: Article 29 Working Party, 'Annual Report', available at http://ec.europa.eu/justice/article-29/documentation/annual-report/index_en.htm.

Article 72. Procedure

CHRISTOPHER DOCKSEY

1. The Board shall take decisions by a simple majority of its members, unless otherwise provided for in this Regulation.
2. The Board shall adopt its own rules of procedure by a two-thirds majority of its members and organise its own operational arrangements.

Closely Related Provisions

Article 64 (Opinion of the Board) (see too recital 136); Article 65 (Dispute resolution by the Board) (see too recital 136); Article 66 (Urgency procedure) (see too recital 137); Article 68 (European Data Protection Board) (see too recital 139); Article 69 (Independence) (see too recital 139); Article 70 (Tasks of the Board) (see too recital 139); Article 71 (Reports); Article 73 (Chair) (see too recital 139); Article 74 (Tasks of the chair); Article 75 (Secretariat) (see too recital 140); Article 76 (Confidentiality)

A. Rationale and Policy Underpinnings

It is standard practice for the measures establishing EU bodies to provide for the adoption of internal Rules of Procedure laying down their governance, procedures and organisation.[1] Such internal rules are binding EU law. They cannot override the provisions of the instrument on the basis of which they are adopted, but they specify and complement those provisions, laying down the detailed framework which governs the internal workings of the organisation.

Article 3 of the EDPB Rules of Procedure lays down the Principle of collegiality and inclusiveness, which provides:

In accordance with the principle of collegiality and inclusiveness, and pursuant to the provisions of the GDPR and the Police and Criminal Justice Data Protection Directive, the Board shall be organised and shall act collectively as a collegiate body.

B. Legal Background

1. EU legislation

Article 29 DPD laid down a single voting rule of adopting decisions by a simple majority of the representatives of the supervisory authorities, in paragraph 3, and provided that the WP29 should adopt its own rules of procedure, in paragraph 6. The final version of the WP29 Rules of Procedure was adopted on 15 February 2010. Article 16(1) of those

---

[1] See e.g. EDPS Rules of Procedure.

Rules provided that 'The Working Party may establish one or more subgroups to prepare its position on certain matters and shall decide on their mandate'.[2]

2. International instruments

The EEA Agreement, as amended in July 2018,[3] provides that the provisions of the GDPR should be read, for the purposes of that Agreement, with a number of adaptations. With regard to the composition and workings of the EDPB, the amended Agreement provides that the supervisory authorities of the EFTA States shall participate in the activities of the Board, with the same rights and obligations as supervisory authorities of the EU Member States in the Board, save for the right to vote and to stand for election as chair or deputy chairs of the Board.[4]

C. Analysis

Article 72 GDPR lays down the voting arrangements of the Board and requires the Board to adopt its own Rules of Procedure and to organise its operational arrangements.

1. Voting

Under Article 72(1) GDPR the EDPB normally takes decisions by a simple majority of its members, unless otherwise provided for in the GDPR. Similarly, all decisions of the WP29 were adopted by simple majority, and the Commission followed this approach in its original proposal. However, the GDPR requires majority voting (two-third majority of members) in two cases.

First, a two-thirds majority is required for the adoption of Rules of Procedure themselves under the second paragraph of Article 72. Article 37(2) of the Rules of Procedure extends this entrenched majority vote to amendments. This entrenched requirement to adopt or amend the Rules of Procedure reflects the enhanced nature and tasks of the Board compared to that of the WP29.

Secondly, a two-thirds majority is required for the adoption of binding decisions under the dispute resolution procedure under Article 65(2) GDPR. This is subject to the possibility in case of deadlock of voting by simple majority and ultimately to the tie-break vote of the Chair, under Article 65(3), an important element of the decision-making process. The Chair's tie-breaking vote may be contrasted with the voting procedure of the WP29, where, in the event of a tie, a proposed decision was treated as not carried.[5]

As noted above, the representatives of the three EEA EFTA supervisory authorities do not have the right to vote. However, they do have the right to express their positions on all items discussed and/or voted.[6] The Board is required to record the positions of the EEA EFTA supervisory authorities separately.[7]

Article 72 does not lay down any time limits for voting, but specific time limits are laid down in Articles 64(3) (Opinions), 65(2) and (3) (Decisions) and 66(4) (Urgency procedure) and further specified, respectively, in Articles 10, 11 and 13 of the Rules of

---

[2] WP29 Rules of Procedure.   [3] EEA Decision 2018.   [4] Ibid., Art. 5e(a) and (k).
[5] Art. 12(2) WP29 Rules of Procedure.   [6] EDPB Rules of Procedure, rec. 7.
[7] Art. 5e(a) EEA Decision, and Art. 21(2) EDPB Rules of Procedure.

Procedure.[8] In this respect, under Article 74, the Chair has the specific task 'to ensure the timely performance of the tasks of the Board, in particular in relation to the consistency mechanism referred to in Article 63'.

The decisions of the Board may be challenged before the European courts under Article 263 Treaty on the Functioning of the European Union ('TFEU'), like those of any EU body.

2. Rules of Procedure

The Rules of Procedure of the Board were adopted on 25 May 2018 and modified on 23 November 2018 to implement the adaptations under the amended EEA Agreement[9] and to allocate the tasks between the Chair and deputy chairs under the access to documents procedure.[10] They specify and complement the provisions of the GDPR, providing the necessary detail to govern its procedures and internal workings. The Board's duty to organise its own operational arrangements underlines the need for the Memorandum of Understanding of 25 May 2018 agreed with the EDPS on financial, administrative and staffing matters under Article 75(4) GDPR.

The GDPR already contains a number of provisions governing the Board and its activities, namely on the Chair, deputy chairs and membership in Articles 68, 73 and 74; on independence in Articles 68–69; on the convening of meetings in Article 74; on transparency and confidentiality in Articles 70–71 and 76; on consultations by the Commission and consultation of interested parties under Article 70; and on the establishment and functioning of the Secretariat under Article 75.

Some of these Articles specifically refer to the EDPB Rules of Procedure. Article 74(2) GDPR provides that the Board should lay down the allocation of tasks between the Chair and the deputy chairs in its Rules of Procedure.[11] Article 76 GDPR provides that the Rules of Procedure should lay down that the discussions of the Board shall be confidential 'where the Board deems it necessary'.[12]

The original Commission proposal, supported by Parliament, listed a number of specific matters which should be addressed by the Rules of Procedure:

In particular it shall provide for the continuation of exercising duties when a member's term of office expires or a member resigns, for the establishment of subgroups for specific issues or sectors and for its procedures in relation to the consistency mechanism referred to in Article 57.[13]

Although these elements were removed from the final text of the GDPR, they now figure expressly or implicitly in the EDPB Rules of Procedure, as adopted and modified.

The Rules are divided into seven Titles:

1. *Title I. The Board.* This includes its identity, missions and guiding principles.
2. *Title II. Composition.* This deals with membership, the mandate and duties of the Chair and deputy chairs, and the presence of observers, experts, guests and other external

---

[8] See the commentaries on Arts. 64–66 in this volume.
[9] Rec. 7 and Arts. 4, 16, 17, 21 and 23 EDPB Rules of Procedure.
[10] Ibid., Art. 32(2). See the commentary on Art. 74 in this volume.
[11] See Art. 7(2) EDPB Rules of Procedure on the allocation of tasks among the Chair and deputy chairs, and Art. 32(2) for the allocation of tasks between the Chair and deputy chairs under the access to documents procedure.
[12] See ibid., Art. 33 on confidentiality of discussions.   [13] Art. 68(2) GDPR Proposal.

parties. It does not expressly provide for the situation envisaged by the Commission proposal where a member ceases to hold office, which is left by Article 53 GDPR to the national law of the Member State concerned. However, Article 4(3) Rules of Procedure provides that in the absence of the head of a supervisory authority, that authority may designate a representative to attend and participate with voting rights, thus guaranteeing the continued participation of the authority.

3. *Title III. Adoption of Documents and Procedure.* Articles 10–13 of the Rules of Procedure lay down the procedures to adopt advisory opinions and binding decisions under the consistency mechanism.

4. *Title IV. Secretariat and Organisation.* This provides that the head of secretariat is responsible for the due and timely performance of the tasks of the secretariat[14] and that the Chair in liaison with the EDPS should provide regular financial reports to the plenary.[15] It also provides for the reimbursement of travel costs for meetings of one representative of each Member State[16] and for the provision of an information and communication system to support the exchange of documents.[17]

5. *Title V. Working Methods.* This is the largest Title of the Rules. It provides for the convocation and direction of plenary meetings by the Chair and the possibility of remote participation by videoconferencing,[18] the preparation of the agenda and the submission of documents and minutes. It provides for voting procedures, including a written voting procedure,[19] and stipulates that, in principle voting should not be secret.[20] The working language of the Board is English, accompanied by provisions on interpretation and translation.[21] Most importantly, Articles 25–28 of the Rules of Procedure make detailed provision for the role of subgroups, their coordinators and rapporteurs, based on the procedures developed under the DPD. These expert subgroups were crucial to the work of the WP29 and will inevitably remain an essential part of the work of the Board. Finally Articles 29 and 30 provide for a two-year work programme and for consultation of interested parties.

6. *Title VI. General Provisions.* These provide for the restricted access to meetings laid down in Title II,[22] the right to public access to documents under Regulation 1049/2001,[23] confidentiality of discussions,[24] appointment of a DPO reporting to the Chair,[25] publication of the annual report[26] and representation of the Board before the CJEU.[27]

7. *Title VII. Final Provisions.* As noted above, these provide for amendment of the Rules. In particular, Article 37(2) provides that the Rules of Procedure shall be reviewed within two years after their adoption by the Board—that is, by 25 May 2020. They also provide for publication of all final documents adopted by the Board on its website[28] and for the entry into force of the Rules of Procedure on the date of their adoption, namely 25 May 2018.[29]

There is a fuller discussion of certain provisions of the Rules of Procedure under the commentaries in this volume dealing with specific articles of the GDPR relating to the Board.[30]

---

[14] Art. 14(3) EDPB Rules of Procedure.　[15] Ibid., Art. 15(2).　[16] Ibid., Art. 16.
[17] Ibid., Art. 17.　[18] Ibid., Art. 18.　[19] Ibid., Art. 24.　[20] Ibid., Art. 22(4).
[21] Ibid., Art. 23.　[22] Ibid., Art. 31.　[23] Ibid., Art. 33.　[24] Ibid.
[25] Ibid., Art. 34.　[26] Ibid., Art. 35.　[27] Ibid., Art. 36.　[28] Ibid., Art. 38.
[29] Ibid., Art. 39.
[30] See the commentaries on Arts. 68–87 on the Board, Arts. 60 and 65 on the right to be heard, and on Art. 67 on the exchange of information in this volume.

Select Bibliography

International agreements

EEA Agreement: Agreement on the European Economic Area, OJ 1994 L 1/3.
EEA Decision 2018: Decision of the EEA Joint Committee No. 154/2018 of 6 July 2018 amending Annex XI (Electronic communication, audiovisual services and information society) and Protocol 37 (containing the list provided for in Article 101) to the EEA Agreement [2018/1022], OJ 2018 L 183/23.

EU legislation

GDPR Proposal: Proposal for a Regulation of the European Parliament and of the Council on the protection of individuals with regard to the processing of personal data and on the free movement of such data (General Data Protection Regulation), COM(2012) 11 final, 25 January 2012.

Papers of data protection authorities

EDPB Rules of Procedure: European Data Protection Board, 'Rules of Procedure' Version 2 (Adopted on 25 May 2018, as last modified and adopted on 23 November 2018).
EDPB EDPS MoU: European Data Protection Board and European Data Protection Supervisor, 'Memorandum of Understanding' (25 May 2018), available at https://edpb.europa.eu/sites/edpb/files/files/file1/memorandum_of_understanding_signed_en.pdf.
EDPS Rules of Procedure: European Data Protection Supervisor, 'Rules of Procedure' (17 December 2012).
WP29 Rules of Procedure: Article 29 Working Party, 'Rules of Procedure' (15 February 2010).

Article 73. Chair

CHRISTOPHER DOCKSEY

1. The Board shall elect a chair and two deputy chairs from amongst its members by simple majority.
2. The term of office of the Chair and of the deputy chairs shall be five years and be renewable once.

Closely Related Provisions

Article 64 (Opinion of the Board); Article 68 (European Data Protection Board) (see too recital 139); Article 72 (Procedure); Article 74 (Tasks of the Chair)

Related Provisions in EUDPR
[Regulation 2018/1725]

Article 54(1) (EDPS remuneration, allowances, retirement pension and any other benefit in lieu of remuneration)

A. Rationale and Policy Underpinnings

In view of the central role of the Chair, it is important to determine the election of the Chair and the deputy chairs and to determine their terms of office.

B. Legal Background

1. EU legislation

Article 29(4) DPD provided that 'The Working Party shall elect its chairman. The chairman's term of office shall be two years. His appointment shall be renewable'. Article 3(1) of the WP29 Rules of Procedure provided in addition for the election of two Vice-Chairs.[1] Article 31(3) provided that the term of office of the Chairman and Vice-Chairs shall be renewable only once.

2. International instruments

The EEA Agreement, as amended in July 2018,[2] incorporates the GDPR into its Annexes and provides that the provisions of the GDPR should be read, for the purposes of that Agreement, with a number of adaptations. With regard to the composition and workings of the EDPB, the amended Agreement provides that the supervisory authorities of

---

[1] WP29 Rules of Procedure. [2] EEA Decision 2018.

Norway, Iceland and Liechtenstein, the three EFTA States participating in the EEA,[3] are members of the Board but do not have the right to vote or to stand for election as Chair or deputy chairs of the Board.[4] To that end, the Agreement adds to Article 73(1) the sentence: 'The EFTA States' members of the Board shall not be eligible to be elected as chair or deputy chairs'.[5]

C. Analysis

Like its predecessor, the WP29, the EDPB elects a Chair and two deputy chairs from amongst its members, save for the supervisory authorities of the EEA EFTA States, by simple majority. Differences between the Chair and the deputies in the WP29 have been removed by the GDPR and both the Chair and the deputy chairs serve for five years, renewable once.[6]

Article 5 of the EDPB Rules of Procedure lays down the election procedure for these three posts, adding that the election is by secret ballot.[7] Article 6 provides for the end of term and dismissal of the Chair and the deputy chairs. If their term ends abruptly and they cannot give two months' notice to the Secretariat, they do not continue in office and new elections are organised as soon as possible.[8] They are subject to dismissal by a simple majority vote following a reasoned proposal by at least one third of the members of the Board.[9]

There were two main controversies concerning Article 73 GDPR. First, the role of the EDPS. The Commission had proposed that the Supervisor should ex officio be one of the two deputy chairs, unless he or she was elected Chair. The Council was opposed to this, and the clause was removed. Of course, as a member of the Board the Supervisor may be elected as Chair or as a deputy chair, but the Supervisor has no special status per se within the Board compared to any other member representing a national authority.

Secondly, the status of the Chair was discussed. The Commission proposal made no provision for the status or remuneration of the Chair of the Board. However, the WP29 argued, supported by the European Parliament,[10] that, in view of the broad responsibility of the EDPB and its independence, the post of Chair should be 'a full-time position to be performed at EU level',[11] In fact, on the basis of the experience of Chairs of the WP29, it was believed that the task of Chair of the Board would be too demanding to be performed part-time, in addition to the role of head of a national authority. However, there was a strong counter-argument, that the Chair should remain a full representative of his or her authority, to ensure the close link between the Board and national authorities required to ensure effective consistency in practice. The Commission and the Council were opposed

---

[3] Switzerland, the fourth EFTA State is not a signatory to the EEA Agreement.
[4] Art. 5e(a), (k) and (o) EEA Decision 2018.   [5] Ibid, Art. 5e(o).
[6] During its first plenary meeting on 25 May 2018 the Board elected Andrea Jelinek, Head of the Austrian Data Protection Authority, as Chair; and Ventsislav Kirilov Karadjov, Chairman of the Bulgarian Commission for Personal Data Protection, and Willem Debeuckelaere, Head of the Belgian Commission for the Protection of Privacy, as deputy chairs. On 15 May 2019 Judge Debeuckelaere was replaced as deputy chair by Aleid Wolfsen, Chairman of the Dutch Data Protection Authority.
[7] Art. 5(1) EDPB Rules of Procedure.   [8] Ibid., Art. 6(1).   [9] Ibid., Art. 6(2).
[10] Art. 69.2a EP Report GDPR.
[11] WP29 2015, p. 2. The Chair could have been a full-time post comparable in salary and status to the EDPS, who is on a par with a judge of the CJEU as regards remuneration, allowances, retirement pension and any other benefit in lieu of remuneration. See Art. 54(1) EUDPR.

to a full-time Chair, and the European Parliament's proposal was dropped. As a result, the Chair of the Board has to carry out both roles, that of Chair of the Board and that of head of her national supervisory authority.

Select Bibliography

International agreements

EEA Agreement: Agreement on the European Economic Area, OJ 1994 L 1/3.
EEA Decision 2018: Decision of the EEA Joint Committee No 154/2018 of 6 July 2018 amending Annex XI (Electronic communication, audiovisual services and information society) and Protocol 37 (containing the list provided for in Article 101) to the EEA Agreement [2018/1022], OJ 2018 L 183/23.

Papers of data protection authorities

EDPB Rules of Procedure: European Data Protection Board, 'Rules of Procedure' Version 2 (Adopted on 25 May 2018, as last modified and adopted on 23 November 2018).
WP29 2015: Article 29 Working Party 'Propositions Regarding the European Data Protection Board Internal Structure' (25 September 2015), available at https://ec.europa.eu/justice/article-29/documentation/other-document/files/2015/20150925_edpb_internal_structure.pdf.
WP29 Rules of Procedure: Article 29 Working Party, 'Rules of Procedure' (15 February 2010).

Reports and recommendations

EP Report GDPR: Report on the proposal for a regulation of the European Parliament and of the Council on the protection of individuals with regard to the processing of personal data and on the free movement of such data (General Data Protection Regulation), A7-0402/2013, 21 November 2013.

Article 74. Tasks of the Chair

CHRISTOPHER DOCKSEY

1. The Chair shall have the following tasks:
   a. to convene the meetings of the Board and prepare its agenda;
   b. to notify decisions adopted by the Board pursuant to Article 65 to the lead supervisory authority and the supervisory authorities concerned;
   c. to ensure the timely performance of the tasks of the Board, in particular in relation to the consistency mechanism referred to in Article 63.
2. The Board shall lay down the allocation of tasks between the Chair and the deputy chairs in its rules of procedure.

Closely Related Provisions

Article 63 (Consistency mechanism) (see too recital 135); Article 64 (Opinion of the Board) (see too recital 136); Article 65 (Dispute resolution by the Board) (see too recital 136); Article 68 (European Data Protection Board) (see too recital 139); Article 72 (Procedure); Article 73 (Chair) (see too recital 136); Article 75 (Secretariat) (see too recital 140).

A. Rationale and Policy Underpinnings

The tasks of the Chair demonstrate both the role of the Chair and the potential effectiveness of the EDPB in carrying out its activities under the leadership of the Chair. Under the new consistency mechanism, the Board has a more powerful and influential role than its predecessor, the WP29, and the tasks of the Chair have increased in turn.

B. Legal Background

1. EU legislation

The tasks of the Chair of the WP29 were briefly set forth in Article 29(7) of the DPD, which provided that:

The Working Party shall consider items placed on its agenda by its chairman, either on his own initiative or at the request of a representative of the supervisory authorities or at the Commission's request.

2. International instruments

There is as yet no international equivalent to the tasks of the Chair of the EDPB, which is a unique institution in the data protection field, an EU body with its own legal personality. However, it is worth mentioning developments of networks of data protection authorities at European and international level.

At European level Article 17(3) of Modernised Convention 108 provides that, in order to organise their cooperation and to perform their duties, supervisory authorities should 'form a network'. The role of this network, and the tasks of its Chair, will undoubtedly be influenced by the precedent of the Board.

At international level, the International Conference of Data Protection & Privacy Commissioners ('ICDPPC') has been developing the role of its Executive Committee according to a series of Strategic Plans in 2013, 2015 and 2019. In this respect, the Chair has the key task of steering the work of the Executive Committee.[1]

C. Analysis

In essence the task of the Chair is to organise the work of the Board. The role of the Chair of the WP29 was limited to setting the agenda and organising the meetings of the WP29. In contrast there is a much greater catalogue of tasks conferred on the Chair of the Board.

First there are the tasks listed in Article 74(1), namely to convene the meetings of the Board and prepare its agenda; to notify decisions adopted by the Board pursuant to Article 65 to the lead supervisory authority and the supervisory authorities concerned; and to ensure the timely performance of the tasks of the Board, in particular in relation to the consistency mechanism referred to in Article 63. These tasks are supplemented by the tasks described in Article 68(2), of representing the Board, and Article 75(2), of being responsible for directing the work of the Secretariat.

With regard to the consistency mechanism, the Chair has a specific role in administering the procedures under Articles 64 and 65. Some tasks of the Chair are purely administrative or procedural, such as sending (under Articles 64(5) and 65(5)) or receiving communications (under paragraph 7 of Article 64) or information (under paragraph 8 of Article 64)—all without undue delay, by electronic means, using a standardised format.

Other consistency mechanism tasks are more substantive. Under Article 64(3) the Chair may determine a reasonable period in which members may object to draft decisions. Under Article 64(2), in addition to any supervisory authority or the Commission, the Chair has the right to request an opinion of the Board on any matter of general application or producing effects in more than one Member State. The subject-matter is thus not limited to the matters listed in Article 64(1) and could concern, for example, the determination of a data breach or the validity of consent in a specific technological context.[2]

A task which is procedural, substantive and potentially sensitive is the obligation to communicate to the Commission the activities of the Board under Article 68(5).[3]

Perhaps most important is the tie-breaking power of the Chair under Article 65(3), that is, the power to adopt a decision where the members of the Board are split. This may be contrasted with the voting procedure of the WP29, where, in the event of a tie, a proposed decision was treated as not carried.[4]

Article 74(2) addresses the question of the functions of the two deputy chairs. The appointment of two deputy chairs was uncontroversial from the outset. The Commission had proposed that the Chair should be helped by two deputy chairpersons, elected from the members of the EDPB. The other institutions and the WP29 agreed. In addition the WP29 felt they should be entrusted with specific tasks and, together with the Chair,

---

[1] See ICDPPC 2018.   [2] Robert 2017, p. 21.
[3] See the commentary on Art. 69 in this volume.   [4] Art. 12(2) WP29 Rules of Procedure.

should constitute the Executive Committee of the EDPB.[5] The fact that the Chair is a post held by the head of a supervisory authority and hence necessarily part-time inevitably heightens the role of the two deputy chairs, who, it was thought, would need to share the work of leading the Board.

Article 74(2) does not itself address the tasks that should be performed by the deputy chairs but rather leaves this to the Board, requiring the Board to lay down the allocation of tasks between the Chair and the deputy chairs in its Rules of Procedure.[6]

In consequence, Article 7(2) of the EDPB Rules of Procedure provides that after each election the Chair shall consult with the deputy chairs and submit a proposal to the Board for the allocation of tasks among them, including the acting on behalf of each other in cases of non-availability or incapacity. The Chair may also delegate to the deputies the power to sign documents. In addition, Article 7(1) provides that the Chair may designate not only a deputy chair but also any member of a supervisory authority or of the secretariat to represent the Board externally in her place. These various options should make it more practicable for the Chair to combine both her EU and national roles, although they will incur greater reliance on coordination by the secretariat, especially its head.

When this text was finalised, the Board had decided on the allocation of tasks between the Chair and deputy chairs with regard to one specific issue, the access to documents procedure under Regulation 1049/2001.[7] This procedure distinguishes between two phases: the initial application, pursuant to Article 7 of that Regulation and, in the event of the rejection of the access request in whole or in part, the confirmatory application, pursuant to Article 8 of that Regulation. Article 32(2) of the EDPB Rules of Procedure lays down that one of the deputy chairs shall be responsible for handling any initial application for access to documents held by the Board, whilst the Chair should be responsible for handling any confirmatory application. It may be assumed that the Chair and the deputy chairs are otherwise building up a body of experience to inform a more general allocation of tasks in the future.

Finally, the Union legislator has left the internal management of the secretariat, under the instructions of the Chair pursuant to Article 75(2), to be governed by the Rules of Procedure, as well as the Memorandum of Understanding between the Board and the EDPS.[8]

Select Bibliography

EU legislation

Regulation 1049/2001: Regulation (EC) No. 1049/2001 of the European Parliament and of the Council of 30 May 2001 regarding public access to European Parliament, Council and Commission documents, OJ 2001 L 145/43.

Academic writings

Robert 2017: Robert, 'Les Autorités de contrôle dans le nouveau règlement général sur la protection des données: statut, coopération et gouvernance européenne', in Docquir (ed.), *Vers un droit européen de la protection des données*? (Larcier 2017), 21.

---

[5] WP29 2015, p. 2. [6] EDPB Rules of Procedure.
[7] Regulation 1049/2001. See the commentary on Art. 76 in this volume.
[8] EDPB EDPS MoU.

Papers by data protection authorities

EDPB Rules of Procedure: European Data Protection Board, 'Rules of Procedure' Version 2 (Adopted on 25 May 2018, as last modified and adopted on 23 November 2018).
EDPB EDPS MoU: European Data Protection Board and European Data Protection Supervisor, 'Memorandum of Understanding' (25 May 2018), available at https://edpb.europa.eu/sites/edpb/files/files/file1/memorandum_of_understanding_signed_en.pdf.
WP29 2015: Article 29 Working Party 'Propositions Regarding the European Data Protection Board Internal Structure', (25 September 2015), available at https://ec.europa.eu/justice/article-29/documentation/other-document/files/2015/20150925_edpb_internal_structure.pdf.
WP29 Rules of Procedure: Article 29 Working Party, 'Rules of Procedure' (15 February 2010).

Others

ICDPPC 2018: Elizabeth Denham, 'Chair News: End of Year Message' (22 December 2018), available at https://icdppc.org/chair-news-end-of-year-message/.

Article 75. Secretariat

CHRISTOPHER DOCKSEY

1. The Board shall have a secretariat, which shall be provided by the European Data Protection Supervisor.
2. The secretariat shall perform its tasks exclusively under the instructions of the Chair of the Board.
3. The staff of the European Data Protection Supervisor involved in carrying out the tasks conferred on the Board by this Regulation shall be subject to separate reporting lines from the staff involved in carrying out tasks conferred on the European Data Protection Supervisor.
4. Where appropriate, the Board and the European Data Protection Supervisor shall establish and publish a Memorandum of Understanding implementing this Article, determining the terms of their cooperation, and applicable to the staff of the European Data Protection Supervisor involved in carrying out the tasks conferred on the Board by this Regulation.
5. The secretariat shall provide analytical, administrative and logistical support to the Board.
6. The secretariat shall be responsible in particular for:
    (a) the day-to-day business of the Board;
    (b) communication between the members of the Board, its Chair and the Commission;
    (c) communication with other institutions and the public;
    (d) the use of electronic means for the internal and external communication;
    (e) the translation of relevant information;
    (f) the preparation and follow-up of the meetings of the Board;
    (g) the preparation, drafting and publication of opinions, decisions on the settlement of disputes between supervisory authorities and other texts adopted by the Board.

Relevant Recitals

(118) The independence of supervisory authorities should not mean that the supervisory authorities cannot be subject to control or monitoring mechanisms regarding their financial expenditure or to judicial review.

(140) The Board should be assisted by a secretariat provided by the European Data Protection Supervisor. The staff of the European Data Protection Supervisor involved in carrying out the tasks conferred on the Board by this Regulation should perform its tasks exclusively under the instructions of, and report to, the Chair of the Board.

Closely Related Provisions

Article 52 (Independence of supervisory authorities); Article 68 (European Data Protection Board) (see too recital 139); Article 69 (Independence of the EDPB); Article 70 (Tasks of the EDPB); Article 71 (Reports); Article 72 (Procedure within the EDPB); Article 73 (Chair of the EDPB); Article 74 (Tasks of the Chair)

Related Provisions in EUDPR [Regulation 2018/1725]

Article 54(4) (EDPS secretariat); Article 57(1)(l) (Provision of the secretariat for the EDPB) (see too recital 61)

Relevant Case Law

CJEU

Case C-614/10, *European Commission v Republic of Austria*, judgment of 16 October 2012 (Grand Chamber) (ECLI:EU:C:2012:63).

A. Rationale and Policy Underpinnings

In view of the central role of the EDPB in the new consistency mechanism, its own distinct advisory and decision-making tasks,[1] and the consequent need for it to act independently,[2] the EU legislator was concerned to ensure the independence and efficiency of this new EU body. In view of its small size, it was felt that it would greatly benefit from being attached for purely administrative purposes to a suitable larger body. In consequence the Commission proposal aimed to:

[U]pgrade the Article 29 Working Party to an independent European Data Protection Board ... and to enhance synergies and effectiveness by foreseeing that the secretariat of the European Data Protection Board will be provided by the European Data Protection Supervisor.[3]

To this effect, Article 75(4) GDPR provides that, where appropriate, the Board and the EDPS shall establish and publish a Memorandum of Understanding ('MoU') determining the terms of their cooperation and applicable to the staff of the EDPS. On 25 May 2018 the MoU between the Board and the EDPS was signed and took effect. Section I.7 of the MoU notes:

Given the positive spirit of cooperation among the community of supervisory authorities in the EU, the EDPB and the EDPS have agreed that a Memorandum of Understanding (hereinafter 'MoU') serve as a valuable guide and additional point of reference as to the common commitment of the EDPB and the EDPS concerned towards sound administrative management and synergies and the effectiveness of the EDPB.[4]

In this respect the Board has also adopted a sixth Guiding Principle, the Principle of efficiency and modernisation, in Article 3 of its Rules of Procedure. This states that:

In accordance with the principle of efficiency and modernisation, the Board shall operate efficiently and as flexible as possible so to achieve internally the highest level of synergies among its members. The efficiency and modernisation principle shall be realised by using new technologies to help bring efficiencies to current working methods such as the minimisation of formalities and providing efficient administrative support.[5]

---

[1] See the commentary on Art. 70 in this volume.
[2] See the commentary on Art. 69 in this volume.   [3] See EC Communication 2010, p. 9.
[4] EDPB EDPS MoU.   [5] EDPB Rules of Procedure.

B. Legal Background

1. EU legislation

Article 29(5) DPD stated that the WP29's secretariat should be provided by the Commission, and Article 29(6) provided that the WP29 should adopt its own rules of procedure. Article 16(1) of the WP29 Rules of Procedure of 15 February 2010 stated that: 'The Working Party may establish one or more subgroups to prepare its position on certain matters and shall decide on their mandate'.[6]

2. International instruments

The EEA Agreement, as amended in July 2018,[7] incorporates the GDPR into its Annexes and provides that the provisions of the GDPR should be read, for the purposes of that Agreement, with a number of adaptations. With regard to the composition and workings of the EDPB, the amended Agreement provides that the Chair of the Board, or the secretariat, shall communicate to the EFTA Surveillance Authority ('ESA') the activities of the Board, where relevant pursuant to Articles 64(5)(a)–(b), 65(5) and 75(6)(b) and that, in Articles 64(5)(a)–(b), 65(5) and 75(6)(b), the words 'and, where relevant, the EFTA Surveillance Authority' shall be added after the words 'the Commission'.[8]

3. Case law

In *Commission v Austria*, the CJEU considered the composition of the staff of the Austrian supervisory authority, the budget of that authority and their implications for its independence. The Court first considered the fact that the managing member of the authority, in effect the Commissioner, was an official subject to the supervision of her hierarchical superior in the administration. It found that this position was inconsistent with the required level of independence because it could lead to a form of 'prior compliance' with the administration and raise a suspicion of partiality.[9] The same considerations applied to the staff of the authority, who were also officials subject to the supervision of the executive.[10] Secondly, the Court considered the fact that the authority fell within the administrative organisation of the executive and did not enjoy a separate budget line. However this did not per se detract from independence so long as the attribution of equipment and staff did not prevent them from acting with 'complete independence'.[11] Finally the Court criticised the fact that the head of the executive had the unconditional right to be informed at all times of all aspects of the work of the authority. The Court found that this unconditional right precluded the authority from being capable of operating above all suspicion of partiality.[12]

C. Analysis

1. Provision of the secretariat by the EDPS

Article 75(1) GDPR provides that the EDPS shall provide the secretariat of the Board. In contrast, under the DPD the Commission was responsible for providing the secretariat

---

[6] WP29 Rules of Procedure.   [7] EEA Decision 2018.   [8] Ibid., Art. 5e(m).
[9] Case C-614/10, *Commission v Austria*, paras. 51–52.   [10] Ibid, para. 59.
[11] Ibid, para. 58.   [12] Ibid, paras. 62–64.

of the WP29. That secretariat was made up of Commission officials in the Unit responsible for data protection, who reported to their superiors in the Commission rather than to the WP29 itself. In the early years the Commission secretariat officials played a significant role in drafting papers for the WP29, but this role declined, and by the time that the Commission proposed the data protection reform package in 2012 the role of the WP29 secretariat had become purely logistical, organising meetings and the WP29 website and sending out communications. Substantive work was carried out by members of the WP29 and their officials in subgroups, recognised in Article 16(1) of the WP29 Rules of Procedure.

The formulation of Article 75 GDPR shows that the secretariat of the Board is intended to have a much broader role. The choice of the EDPS rather than the Commission to provide its secretariat was grounded on a number of compelling considerations: it is itself an independent supervisory authority; it has the necessary data protection expertise; and it is an independent EU institution for the purposes of financial administration and budget[13] and human resources.[14]

This choice must also be seen in the light of the ruling in *Commission v Austria*, which made it plain that the EDPB could not be attached to and be dependent upon the Commission and its services for its operation. It was also out of the question for the officials of the Board to be Commission officials. It therefore made sense to attach the Board for such administrative purposes to another, larger independent authority which was completely in control over its own human and budgetary resources.[15]

However, the provision of the secretariat by the EDPS was only one of a number of possible options. Another possibility could have been to merge the Board and the EDPS and transform the EDPS into a single European data protection authority. The Commission may have discussed this option internally, but it was never submitted for discussion to the legislator.

Another possibility, favoured by the WP29, could have been to establish the Board as a completely separate body with its own staff and budget. The WP29 opined that the 'desirable option would be to have a completely independent secretariat', and stressed the 'need to ensure independence of the members of the secretariat' and to reflect on the 'legal and institutional consequences of entrusting the secretariat of the EDPB to one of its members'.[16] The Council made an alternative proposal, intended to distance the Supervisor personally from the Board's secretariat. It proposed that the secretariat of the Board should be provided by the secretariat of the EDPS rather than directly by the EDPS.[17] However the Council was unable to convince the Commission and the Parliament to accept this rather abstruse approach. Either approach would have deprived the EDPB of the potential synergies and economies of scale resulting from the provision of its human and material resources by the EDPS.

The approach in Article 75 GDPR is also the most compatible with standard practice for setting up a new EU body. This can be seen in the norms for setting up a new EU agency set forth in the 'Common Approach on decentralised agencies'. In particular, in view of the small size of the Board as an EU body, it may be noted that the Common

---

[13] Art. 2(b) Regulation 966/2012.   [14] Art. 1b EU Staff Regulations.
[15] For the implications of the third element of the ruling, concerning the right to information, see the commentary on Art. 69 in this volume.
[16] WP29 2012, p. 22.   [17] Art. 71(1) Council Report 2015.

Approach states that 'merging agencies should be considered in cases where their respective tasks are overlapping, where synergies can be contemplated or when agencies would be more efficient if inserted in a bigger structure'.[18] The configuration decided by the EU legislator in Articles 68 and 75 follows this objective of 'enhancing synergies and effectiveness'.

To that effect, the EDPS developed in consultation with the WP29 a system of shared administrative resources between the EDPS and the Board to benefit from synergies and avoid duplication of functions. The aim was to allocate most of the Board's human resources budget to staff carrying out analytical, administrative and logistical tasks exclusively under the instructions of the Chair.

2. The budget of the Board

The consequence of the EDPS providing the secretariat of the Board is that the EDPS as an institution will be responsible for administering the budget of the Secretariat and for implementing and respecting the EU Financial Regulation and Staff Regulations.

The EDPS is one of the limited number of EU institutions and bodies[19] which enjoy formal budgetary and administrative autonomy. Nonetheless they are under the external control, first, of the Commission in establishing their draft budgets[20] and then under the control of the EU budgetary authority responsible for adopting the budget (Council and Parliament).[21] Recital 118 GDPR notes in this respect that the 'independence of supervisory authorities should not mean that the supervisory authorities cannot be subject to control or monitoring mechanisms regarding their financial expenditure'. With regard to the administration of the Board's budget by the EDPS, the CJEU has taken the view, noted above, that the lack of a separate budget does not affect per se the independence of a supervisory authority.[22]

3. The preparation of the Secretariat

Unlike national authorities preparing for the GDPR, the secretariat of the Board had to be set up from scratch by the EDPS and delivered ready to service the Board upon its entry into function in May 2018.

With regard to budget preparations, in 2013 the EDPS included a new Title III 'EDPB' in the EDPS budgetary request for 2014,[23] to which resources have been progressively allocated since 2015.[24] It also included planning for the Board in the EDPS submission for the Multiannual Financial Framework ('MFF') for the current period 2014–2020.[25]

In the same year, with regard to administration, the EDPS began work on adapting existing Service Level Agreements with the larger institutions or negotiating new ones to ensure that the Board could benefit from essential services such as translation and interpretation. In 2015 two task forces to prepare the Board were set up, one within the EDPS and one within the WP29,[26] and in 2016 the EDPS produced four factsheets designed to inform members of the WP29 about the EDPS preparations for the Board.[27]

---

[18] Joint Statement EP, Council and EC 2012.   [19] Art. 2(b) Regulation 966/2012.
[20] Art. 314(1) Treaty on the Function of European Union ('TFEU'), introduced by the Lisbon Treaty.
[21] Ibid., Art. 314(2) et seq.   [22] Case C-614/10, *Commission v Austria*, para. 58.
[23] EDPS Annual Report 2013, pp. 87–88.   [24] EDPS Annual Report 2017, p. 57.
[25] Ibid., p. 86.   [26] EDPS Annual Report 2015, p. 44.
[27] EDPS Annual Report 2016, p. 49.

With regard to staff, it was necessary to ensure the necessary expertise in future recruitments for the Board. In 2014 the EDPS organised a specialist data protection competition[28] which resulted in a reserve list of 21 candidates to cover the recruitment needs of the EDPS and the Board in the short and medium term.[29] The resulting pool of data protection experts included specialists from both the public and private sectors who would be available for recruitment for both the EDPS and the Board secretariat. In 2015 the EDPS recruited the first two qualified staff members to assist with the provision of the secretariat to the Board.[30] In 2017 a liaison coordinator was appointed to coordinate all the preparations for the Secretariat,[31] and a separate sector for EDPB matters was created.[32] On 25 May 2018 the sector became the Secretariat of the Board, led by a head of secretariat who is responsible for the 'due and timely performance of the tasks of the secretariat'.[33] A further specialist data protection competition was launched in 2018 which resulted in a reserve list of 33 candidates, to permit the further recruitment of expert staff from mid-2019 onwards.[34]

4. The staff of the secretariat

The staff of the EDPB are provided by the EDPS, which as noted above is regarded as an institution for the purposes of the EU Staff Regulations.

Article 75 GDPR does not speak of staff members belonging to one entity or the other but rather of EDPS staff members 'involved in carrying out the tasks conferred on the Board' and EDPS staff members 'involved in carrying out tasks conferred on the European Data Protection Supervisor'.

In this respect there are three categories of staff employed by the EDPS: staff working on EDPS core activities under the direction of the EDPS, defined as 'EDPS staff';[35] staff working on budget, human resources and administration under the direction of the EDPS, who are also 'EDPS staff' but carry out these support tasks for both the EDPS and the Board,[36] in the latter case in consultation with the Board;[37] and staff carrying out analytical, administrative and logistical tasks to support the Board and under its direction, defined as 'Secretariat staff'.[38]

The GDPR lays down two requirements for the Secretariat staff assigned to the Board. Under Article 75(2) the Board secretariat must 'perform its tasks exclusively under the instructions of the Chair', and under Article 75(3) 'the staff of the EDPS involved in carrying out the tasks conferred on the Board … shall be subject to separate reporting lines'. In this respect recital 140 clarifies that the staff concerned should report to the Chair and the MoU specifies that they carry out their tasks 'exclusively under the instructions of the Chair of the EDPB and subject to separate reporting lines as provided in Article 75 of the GDPR'.[39] These requirements are intended to preserve the independence and autonomy of the Board in carrying out its tasks.

[28] EDPS Annual Report 2014, pp. 54–55.   [29] EDPS Annual Report 2015, p. 42.
[30] Ibid., p. 44.   [31] EDPS Annual Report 2016, p. 20.
[32] EDPS Annual Report 2017, pp. 59–60.   [33] Art. 14(2) EDPB Rules of Procedure.
[34] EPSO/AD/360/18.   [35] EDPB EDPS MoU, section II.5.
[36] Ibid., section VI (EDPS responsibilities to provide the Secretariat).
[37] Ibid., section V.4. See also EDPS Annual Report 2017, p. 60.
[38] EDPB EDPS MoU, section II.4.   [39] Ibid.

Article 75 left the details of how its requirements should be implemented to the Rules of Procedure of the Board under Article 72(2) and to the MoU under Article 75(4) between the Board and the EDPS 'determining the terms of their cooperation'.

Section VI of the MoU lists the EDPS responsibilities to provide the Secretariat under paragraph 1 thereof relating to (i) staff, including recruitment, (ii) offices, (iii) IT infrastructure, (iv) budget and financial support and (v) security. Section VI provides for close cooperation between the two bodies in this respect and requires the EDPS under paragraph 4 to take the 'utmost account of any opinion of the Board and endeavour to reach consensus'. If consensus cannot be achieved, the EDPS will give reasons for not following the view of the Board.[40] The MoU is also designed to ensure that information handled by the EDPS staff working for the Board secretariat is not accessible to the EDPS itself save in so far as it is information the EDPS should normally receive as a member of the Board.[41]

Both the EDPS and the Board potentially suffer from the problem posed by staff recruitment and career patterns for the independence of small supervisory authorities, who often have to recruit from the general public service and lose staff to the same. This is both a practical problem and a potential interference with their independence. Lynskey has observed that:

[A]lthough the personnel of supervisory authorities must not be employed by other public bodies, it is unclear whether this prevents supervisory authorities from hiring employees from amongst members of a national civil service.[42]

This problem was considered by the CJEU in *Commission v Austria*, where the Court held that the fact that the Austrian supervisory authority was composed of officials of the Federal Chancellery, which is itself subject to supervision by that authority, carried a 'risk of influence' over the decisions of the supervisory authority.[43] As a result, Article 52(5) GDPR lays down the necessary safeguards to ensure that national supervisory authorities may control their own staffing:

Each Member State shall ensure that each supervisory authority chooses and has its own staff which shall be subject to the exclusive direction of the member or members of the supervisory authority concerned.[44]

Similarly, the Secretariat of the Board is provided by the EDPS rather than the Commission, so that there is no risk of the executive influencing the decisions of the Board by way of its staff.

As noted above, the EDPS has taken up the practice of organising specialist data protection competitions, to enable the direct recruitment of expert staff by the EDPS and the Board.

5. Analytical, administrative and logistical support under Article 75(5)–(6)

The secretariat of the Board has a broader range of tasks than the simple administrative and logistical tasks provided by the Commission secretariat to the WP29. Article 75(5)

---

[40] Ibid. [41] Ibid., sections V.8 and III.5 (principle of confidentiality for restricted information).
[42] Lynskey 2016, p. 261. See also Szydło 2013, p. 1819.
[43] Case C-614/10, *Commission v Austria*, para. 61. See also paras. 50–55 on the risk of influence due to the fact that the managing member of the supervisory authority was a federal government official.
[44] Robert 2017, p. 21.

states generally that the secretariat shall provide 'analytical, administrative and logistical support'. This requires the secretariat to carry out two different types of activity for the Board: analytical tasks on the one hand, and logistical and administrative tasks on the other.

Article 75(6) provides more detail on both types of task. It lists standard administrative and logistical tasks, such as (a) the day-to-day business of the Board; (b) communication between the members of the Board, its Chair and the Commission, and, where relevant, the EFTA Surveillance Authority;[45] (d) the use of electronic means for the internal and external communication; and (e) the translation of relevant information. In addition it includes substantive analytical tasks such as (c) communication with other institutions and the public; (f) the preparation and follow-up of the meetings of the Board; and (g) the preparation, drafting and publication of opinions, decisions on the settlement of disputes between supervisory authorities and other texts adopted by the Board.

Section IV.2 of the MoU sets forth a number of further support tasks regarded as included under Article 75(6) GDPR: (i) organisation of meetings, (ii) IT communications, (iii) handling access to document requests, (iv) record management, (v) security of information, (vi) information and communication tasks, (vii) relations with other institutions, including representation of the Board before the Courts, and (viii) DPO activities.

This substantive work will require specific legal or technological expertise in the secretariat, complementing the expertise of the staff of the supervisory authorities themselves. The interaction between these two groups of staff will be crucial in enabling the Board to function effectively.

Select Bibliography

International agreements

EEA Agreement: Agreement on the European Economic Area, OJ 1994 L 1/3.
EEA Decision 2018: Decision of the EEA Joint Committee No. 154/2018 of 6 July 2018 amending Annex XI (Electronic communication, audiovisual services and information society) and Protocol 37 (containing the list provided for in Article 101) to the EEA Agreement [2018/1022], OJ 2018 L 183/23.

EU legislation

EU Staff Regulations: Regulation No. 31 (EEC), 11 (EAEC) of 14 June 1962 laying down the Staff Regulations of Officials and the Conditions of Employment of Other Servants of the European Economic Community and the European Atomic Energy Community as amended, OJ 1962 L 45/1385.
Regulation 966/2012: Regulation (EU, EURATOM) No. 966/2012 of the European Parliament and of the Council of 25 October 2012 on the financial rules applicable to the general budget of the Union and repealing Council Regulation (EC, Euratom) No. 1605/2002 as amended by Regulation (EU, Euratom) No. 547/2014 of the European Parliament and of the Council of 15 May 2014 and Regulation (EU, Euratom) 2015/1929 of the European Parliament and of the Council of 28 October 2015, OJ 2012 L 298/1.

---

[45] Added by the EEA Decision, Art. 5e(m).

Academic writings

Lynskey 2017: Lynskey, 'The Europeanisation of Data Protection Law', 19 *Cambridge Yearbook of European Legal Studies* (2017), 252.
Robert 2017: Robert, 'Les Autorités de contrôle dans le nouveau règlement général sur la protection des données: statut, coopération et gouvernance européenne', in Docquir (ed.), *Vers un droit européen de la protection des données?* (Larcier 2017), 21.
Szydło 2013: Szydło, 'Principles Underlying Independence of National Data Protection Authorities: Commission v. Austria', 50(6) *Common Market Law Review* (2013), 1809.

Papers of data protection authorities

EDPB EDPS MoU: European Data Protection Board and European Data Protection Supervisor, 'Memorandum of Understanding' (25 May 2018).
EDPB Rules of Procedure: European Data Protection Board, 'Rules of Procedure' Version 2 (Adopted on 25 May 2018, as last modified and adopted on 23 November 2018).
EDPS Annual Report 2013: European Data Protection Supervisor, 'Annual Report 2013' (1 April 2014).
EDPS Annual Report 2014: European Data Protection Supervisor, 'Annual Report 2014' (2 July 2015).
EDPS Annual Report 2015: European Data Protection Supervisor, 'Annual Report 2015' (24 May 2016).
EDPS Annual Report 2016: European Data Protection Supervisor, 'Annual Report 2016' (4 May 2017).
EDPS Annual Report 2017: European Data Protection Supervisor, 'Annual Report 2017' (19 March 2018).
WP29 2012: Article 29 Working Party, 'Opinion 01/2012 on the Data Protection Reform Proposals' (WP 191, 23 March 2012).
WP29 Rules of Procedure: Article 29 Working Party, 'Rules of Procedure' (15 February 2010).

Reports and recommendations

Council Report 2015: Preparation of a general approach, 965/15, 11 June 2015.
EC Communication 2010: Communication from the Commission to the European Parliament, the Council, the European Economic and Social Committee and the Committee of the Regions, 'A Comprehensive Approach on Personal Data Protection in the European Union' COM (2010) 609 final, 4 November 2010.

Others

EPSO/AD/360/18: European Personnel Selection Office, 'Selection Procedure for Administrators in the field of Data Protection', available at https://epso.europa.eu/epsocrs-ref-numbers/epso-ad-360-18_en.
Joint Statement EP, Council and EC 2012: Joint Statement of the European Parliament, the Council of the EU and the European Commission on Decentralised Agencies (19 July 2012), available at https://europa.eu/european-union/sites/europaeu/files/docs/body/joint_statement_and_common_approach_2012_en.pdf.

Article 76. Confidentiality

CHRISTOPHER DOCKSEY

1. The discussions of the Board shall be confidential where the Board deems it necessary, as provided for in its rules of procedure.
2. Access to documents submitted to members of the Board, experts and representatives of third parties shall be governed by Regulation (EC) No. 1049/2001 of the European Parliament and of the Council.

Closely Related Provisions

Recital 164; Article 54(2) (Rules on the establishment of the supervisory authority); Article 76 (Secretariat of the EDPB)

Related Provisions in LED [Directive (EU) 2016/680]

Article 44(2) (Rules on the establishment of the supervisory authority)

Related Provisions in EUDPR [Regulation 2018/1725]

Article 52(4) (Application of Regulation 1049/2001 to documents held by the EDPS) (see also recital 76); Article 56 (Professional secrecy of the EDPS and EDPS staff); Article 54(5) (Obligations of EDPS staff) (see also recital 83)

Relevant Case Law

CJEU

Case C-28/08 P, *European Commission v The Bavarian Lager Co. Ltd*, judgment of 29 June 2010 (Grand Chamber) (ECLI:EU:C:2010:378).

Case C-362/14, *Maximillian Schrems v Data Protection Commissioner*, judgment of 6 October 2015 (Grand Chamber) (ECLI:EU:C:2015:650).

Case T-540/15, *Emilio De Capitani v European Parliament*, GC, judgment of 22 March 2018 (ECLI:EU:T:2018:167).

A. Rationale and Policy Underpinnings

The deliberations of the WP29 were regarded as confidential under Article 11(1) of its Rules of Procedure, which provided that the minutes and any draft documents of the Working Party should be restricted documents, unless the Working Party decided otherwise.[1] However, in view of the settled case law of the Court and of the status of public access to documents as a fundamental right under Article 42 of the Charter of

---

[1] WP29 Rules of Procedure.

Fundamental Rights of the European Union ('Charter') and Article 15(3) of the Treaty on the Functioning of the European Union ('TFEU'), it was necessary to provide for a more modern approach in the EDPB, where transparency rather than confidentiality should be the norm save where confidentiality is specifically required.

B. Legal Background

1. EU legislation

Article 11 WP29 Rules of Procedure provided that:

In line with Article 339 of the Treaty on the Functioning of the European Union, the members of the Working Party experts and observers shall exercise discretion with regard to the Working Party's discussions. The minutes and any draft documents of the Working Party shall be restricted documents, unless the Working Party decides otherwise. Opinions, recommendations and any other document adopted by the Working Party shall be published on the website, unless the Working Party decides otherwise.

Article 42 of the Charter provides that:

Any citizen of the Union, and any natural or legal person residing or having its registered office in a Member State, has a right of access to documents of the institutions, bodies, offices and agencies of the Union, whatever their medium.

Article 15(3) TFEU adds a reference to and a legal basis for principles and conditions:

Any citizen of the Union, and any natural or legal person residing or having its registered office in a Member State, shall have a right of access to documents of the Union's institutions, bodies, offices and agencies, whatever their medium, subject to the principles and the conditions to be defined in accordance with this paragraph.

General principles and limits on grounds of public or private interest governing this right of access to documents shall be determined by the European Parliament and the Council, by means of regulations, acting in accordance with the ordinary legislative procedure.

Each institution, body, office or agency shall ensure that its proceedings are transparent and shall elaborate in its own Rules of Procedure specific provisions regarding access to its documents, in accordance with the regulations referred to [above].

The general principles and limits on grounds of public or private interest governing the right of access to documents are laid down in Regulation 1049/2001.[2] Article 2(3) of that Regulation provides that it applies 'to all documents held by an institution, that is to say, documents drawn up or received by it and in its possession'.

Article 52(4) EUDPR applies Regulation 1049/2001 to documents held by the EDPS and requires the EDPS to adopt detailed rules for applying Regulation 1049/2001 to those documents.[3]

Article 339 TFEU provides that:

The members of the institutions of the Union, the members of committees, and the officials and other servants of the Union shall be required, even after their duties have ceased, not to disclose information of the kind covered by the obligation of professional secrecy, in particular information about undertakings, their business relations or their cost components.

---

[2] Regulation 1049/2001. [3] See also rec. 76 EUDPR.

Article 56 EUDPR[4] (Professional secrecy) provides that:

The European Data Protection Supervisor and his or her staff shall, both during and after their term of office, be subject to a duty of professional secrecy with regard to any confidential information which has come to their knowledge in the course of the performance of their official duties.

2. Case law

The abundant case law of the CJEU and the General Court has stressed the need for transparency of documents held by the EU institutions and the 'close relationship that, in principle, exists between legislative procedures and the principles of openness and transparency'.[5] However, it has recognised that there is not the same need for transparency with regard to administrative documents.[6]

C. Analysis

The Board has stressed the need for transparency in its fifth Guiding Principle, the Principle of transparency, laid down in Article 3 of its Rules of Procedure:[7]

In accordance with the principle of transparency, the Board shall operate as openly as possible so as to be more effective and more accountable to the individual. The Board shall explain its activities in a clear language which is accessible to all.

In contrast, the fifth principle underpinning the Memorandum of Understanding between the Board and the EDPS refers instead to the principle of 'confidentiality for restricted information'.[8] The fifth principle is the only principle to differ between the principles in the Rules of Procedure and the MoU. The fifth principle in the MoU is relevant in particular to the working relationship between the Board and the EDPS laid down in Section V of the MoU dealing with Cooperation and Confidentiality and to the restricted approach to the confidentiality of discussions of the Board and to documents held by the Board.

1. Confidentiality of discussions of the Board

Article 76(1) GDPR provides that '(t)he discussions of the Board shall be confidential where the Board deems it necessary, as provided for in its rules of procedure'. This is less sweeping than the proposal by the Commission, supported by the Council, which simply stated that the 'discussions of the Board shall be confidential'.[9] The Commission and the Council clearly intended that as a general rule the discussions of the Board should not be public. However, the European Parliament successfully advanced an approach much closer to the final wording, according to which Board discussions 'may' be confidential 'where necessary, unless otherwise provided in its rules of procedure'.[10] As a result, Article 76(1) confirms that discussions of the Board shall be confidential following a specific appreciation of the Board, as embodied in the Rules of Procedure.

---

[4] Which has taken over the same formulation as Art. 45 of Regulation 45/2001, see Table of Legislation.
[5] Case T-540/15, *De Capitani*, para. 77. See the case law referred to in paras. 57–58 and 77–80.
[6] Compare the critical assessment of the case law in EP Study 2016.
[7] EDPB Rules of Procedure.   [8] EDPB EDPS MoU.   [9] Art. 72(1) GDPR Proposal.
[10] Art. 72(1) EP Report 2013.

In this respect Article 33(1) of the EDPB Rules of Procedure dealing with the Confidentiality of discussions provides:

In accordance with Art 76 (1) GDPR, discussions of the Board and of expert subgroups shall be confidential when:

a. they concern a specific individual;
b. they concern the consistency mechanism;
c. the Board decides that the discussions on a specific topic shall remain confidential for instance when the discussions concern international relations and/or where the absence of confidentiality would seriously undermine the institution's decision-making process, unless there is an overriding public interest in disclosure.

The confidentiality of discussions concerning a specific individual appears to be aimed at protecting the privacy and personal data of the individuals concerned. Whether their names may be disclosed following a request for public access to any documents recording such discussions will depend on the reconciliation of the rights to protection of personal data and of public access to documents following the interpretation of Article 4(1)(b) of Regulation 1049/2001 in the *Bavarian Lager* ruling.[11]

The confidentiality of discussions concerning the consistency mechanism is aimed at protecting information produced and positions advanced during discussions from being disclosed in situations where they could undermine the final position of the Board and the positions of the member authorities concerned when discussing an authoritative opinion or a decision legally binding the authorities concerned. In this respect the case law of the CJEU has recognised that there is not the same need for transparency in administrative matters as there is in legislative matters.[12]

The Board has reserved the right to decide on a case-by-case basis whether the discussions on a specific topic outside these two cases should remain confidential. The examples given, where the discussions concern international relations and/or where the absence of confidentiality would seriously undermine the institution's decision-making process, are inspired by elements of the exceptions to the right to public access to documents under Article 4 paragraphs 1(a) and 2 of Regulation 1049/2001.

Finally, it should be noted that observers, external experts, guests or other external parties who may attend meetings of the Board under Articles 8 and 9 of the Rules of Procedure are bound under those Articles by the same confidentiality requirements as the members of the Board as provided for in Article 54(2) and Article 33 of the EDPB Rules of Procedure.

2. Public access to documents

Article 76(2) GDPR provides that access to documents *submitted to* members of the Board, experts and representatives of third parties shall be governed by Regulation 1049/2001. The scope of the right of public access is significantly narrower under this rubric than under Regulation 1049/2001 itself, which applies pursuant to Article 2(3) thereof to 'all documents *held* by an institution, that is to say, documents *drawn up* or *received by* it and in its possession'. As a result, documents drawn up by the Board itself are not intended to be covered. This limitation of the application of Regulation 1049/2001 to documents *submitted* was common to all three institutions in the trilogue and shows a very clear legislative

---

[11] See EDPS 2011 and Docksey 2016, pp. 202–205.
[12] See Case T-540/15, *De Capitani*, paras. 77–80 and the critical assessment in EP Study 2016.

intention. It is an extra limitation of the right to public access to documents, in addition to the exceptions discussed above, and simply removes documents drawn up by the Board itself, its members, experts and representatives of third parties from the scope of the rules, so that there is no need to discuss whether the exceptions apply to such documents.

Subject to this narrower scope, Regulation 1049/2001 applies to 'any citizen of the Union, and any natural or legal person residing or having its registered office in a Member State', and to all documents, whatever their medium. It lays down a two-stage procedure for requesting access, an initial application, pursuant to Article 7 thereof and, in the event of the rejection of the request in whole or in part, a confirmatory application, pursuant to Article 8 thereof, triggering an administrative review of the initial decision. In this respect, Article 32(2) of the EDPB Rules of Procedure lays down that one of the deputy chairs shall be responsible for handling any initial application for access to documents, whilst the Chair should be responsible for handling any confirmatory application.

Article 4 of Regulation 1049/2001 sets forth certain limitations to the right of public access to documents based on grounds of public or private interest. Recital 11 to that Regulation explains in particular that '(t)he institutions should be entitled to protect their internal consultations and deliberations where necessary to safeguard their ability to carry out their tasks'. However, since these exceptions derogate from the principle of the widest possible public access to documents, the Court of Justice has stressed that such exceptions must be interpreted and applied strictly.[13]

The most relevant exceptions related to the work of the Board under Article 33(1)(c) of the EDPB Rules of Procedure, in addition to the protection of the public interest as regards international relations, will include the protection of inspections, investigations and audits under Article 4(2) and the 'space to think' under Article 4(3) of Regulation 1049/2001.

Finally, it may be recalled that Article 42 of the Charter and Article 15(3) TFEU express the right to public access to documents in broad terms, subject only to secondary legislation laying down general principles and limits on grounds of public or private interest—that is, the exceptions laid down in Article 4 of Regulation 1049/2001. However, as noted above, Article 76(2) GDPR excludes all documents held by the Board but not submitted to its members from the scope of the right to public access to documents enshrined in Article 42 of the Charter and Article 15(3) TFEU. Hustinx has warned that 'relevant provisions of the Charter have to be kept in mind when the details of the Regulation are discussed and adopted, and eventually applied in practice'.[14] The question arises therefore whether Article 76(2) GDPR may exclude a whole class of documents from the scope of a fundamental right laid down in primary law.[15]

3. Duty of professional secrecy

There is no reference to the duty of confidentiality on members of the Board and members of staff of the Secretariat. However, members of the Board who are representatives of national authorities will be bound by Article 54(2) GDPR, which provides that:

The members or members and the staff of each supervisory authority shall, in accordance with Union or State law, be subject to a duty of professional secrecy both during and after their term of office, with regard to any confidential information which has come to their knowledge in the

---

[13] Case T-540/15, *De Capitani*, para. 61.   [14] Hustinx 2017, p. 167.
[15] See by analogy the reasoning of the CJEU in Case C-362/14, *Schrems*, paras. 53–7 and 99–104.

course of the performance of their tasks or exercise of their powers. During their term of office, that duty of professional secrecy shall in particular apply to reporting by natural persons of infringements of this Regulation.

Recital 164 adds that:

As regards the powers of the supervisory authorities to obtain from the controller or processor access to personal data and access to their premises, Member States may adopt by law, within the limits of this Regulation, specific rules in order to safeguard the professional or other equivalent secrecy obligations, in so far as necessary to reconcile the right to the protection of personal data with an obligation of professional secrecy. This is without prejudice to existing Member State obligations to adopt rules on professional secrecy where required by Union law.

Similarly, there is no comparable reference to the duty of confidentiality of the staff of the Secretariat of the Board, but such staff, as officials of the EDPS, are subject to the provisions of confidentiality binding them under Article 56 EUDPR.

Select Bibliography

EU legislation

GDPR Proposal: Proposal for a Regulation of the European Parliament and of the Council on the protection of individuals with regard to the processing of personal data and on the free movement of such data (General Data Protection Regulation), COM(2012) 11 final, 25 January 2012.
Regulation 1049/2001: Regulation (EC) No. 1049/2001 of the European Parliament and of the Council of 30 May 2001 regarding public access to European Parliament, Council and Commission documents, OJ 2001 L 145/43.

Academic writings

Docksey 2016: Docksey, 'Four Fundamental Rights: Finding the Balance', 6(3) *International Data Privacy Law* (2016), 195.
Hustinx 2017: Hustinx, 'EU Data Protection Law: The Review of Directive 95/46/EC and the Proposed General Data Protection Regulation', in Cremona (ed), *New Technologies and EU Law* (OUP 2017), 123.

Papers of data protection authorities

EDPB Rules of Procedure: European Data Protection Board, 'Rules of Procedure' Version 2 (Adopted on 25 May 2018, last modified on 23 November 2018).
EDPB EDPS MoU: European Data Protection Board and European Data Protection Supervisor, 'Memorandum of Understanding' (25 May 2018).
EDPS 2011: European Data Protection Supervisor, 'Public Access to Documents Containing Personal Data after the Bavarian Lager Ruling' (24 March 2011).
WP29 Rules of Procedure: Article 29 Working Party, 'Rules of Procedure' (15 February 2010).

Reports and recommendations

EP Report 2013: Report on the proposal for a regulation of the European Parliament and of the Council on the protection of individuals with regard to the processing of personal data and on the free movement of such data (General Data Protection Regulation), A7-0402/2013, 21 November 2013.
EP Study 2016: Curtin and Leino-Sandberg, 'Openness, Transparency and the Right of Access to Documents in the EU' (2016) PE 556.973.

Chapter VIII Remedies, Liability and Penalties (Articles 77–84)

Article 77. Right to lodge a complaint with a supervisory authority

WALTRAUT KOTSCHY

1. Without prejudice to any other administrative or judicial remedy, every data subject shall have the right to lodge a complaint with a supervisory authority, in particular in the Member State of his or her habitual residence, place of work or place of the alleged infringement if the data subject considers that the processing of personal data relating to him or her infringes this Regulation.
2. The supervisory authority with which the complaint has been lodged shall inform the complainant on the progress and the outcome of the complaint including the possibility of a judicial remedy pursuant to Article 78.

Relevant Recitals

(141) Every data subject should have the right to lodge a complaint with a single supervisory authority, in particular in the Member State of his or her habitual residence, and the right to an effective judicial remedy in accordance with Article 47 of the Charter if the data subject considers that his or her rights under this Regulation are infringed or where the supervisory authority does not act on a complaint, partially or wholly rejects or dismisses a complaint or does not act where such action is necessary to protect the rights of the data subject. The investigation following a complaint should be carried out, subject to judicial review, to the extent that is appropriate in the specific case. The supervisory authority should inform the data subject of the progress and the outcome of the complaint within a reasonable period. If the case requires further investigation or coordination with another supervisory authority, intermediate information should be given to the data subject. In order to facilitate the submission of complaints, each supervisory authority should take measures such as providing a complaint submission form which can also be completed electronically, without excluding other means of communication.

(146) The controller or processor should compensate any damage which a person may suffer as a result of processing that infringes this Regulation. The controller or processor should be exempt from liability if it proves that it is not in any way responsible for the damage. The concept of damage should be broadly interpreted in the light of the case-law of the Court of Justice in a manner which fully reflects the objectives of this Regulation. This is without prejudice to any claims for damage deriving from the violation of other rules in Union or Member State law. Processing that infringes this Regulation also includes processing that infringes delegated and implementing acts adopted in accordance with this Regulation and Member State law specifying rules of this Regulation. Data subjects should receive full and effective compensation for the damage they have suffered. Where controllers or processors are involved in the same processing, each controller or processor should be held liable for the entire damage. However, where they are joined to the same judicial proceedings, in accordance with Member State law, compensation may be apportioned according to the responsibility of each controller or processor for the damage caused by the processing, provided that full and effective compensation of the data subject who suffered the damage is ensured. Any controller

or processor which has paid full compensation may subsequently institute recourse proceedings against other controllers or processors involved in the same processing.

Closely Related Provisions

Article 52 (Independence of supervisory authorities) (see too recital 121); Article 57 (Tasks of supervisory authorities) (see too recital 122); Article 78 (Right to an effective judicial remedy against a supervisory authority) (see too recital 141); Article 79 (Right to an effective judicial remedy against a controller or processor) (see too recital 145); Article 80 (Representation of data subjects) (see too recital 142)

Related Provisions in LED [Directive (EU) 2016/680]

Article 52 (Right to lodge a complaint with a supervisory authority) (see too recital 85)

Related Provisions in EPD [Directive 2002/58/EC]

Article 15 (Application of certain provisions of Directive 95/46/EC); Article 15a (Implementation and enforcement)

Related Provisions in EUDPR [Regulation (EU) 2018/1725]

Article 57 (Tasks of the EDPS); Article 58 (Powers of the EDPS) (see too recital 62); Article 63 (Right to lodge a complaint with the EDPS) (see too recital 79)

Relevant Case Law

CJEU

Case C-288/12, *European Commission v Hungary*, judgment of 8 April 2014 (Grand Chamber) (ECLI:EU:C:2014:237).

Joined Cases C-293/12 and C-594/12, *Digital Rights Ireland Ltd v Minister for Communications, Marine and Natural Resources and Others and Kärntner Landesregierung and Others*, judgment of 8 April 2014 (Grand Chamber) (ECLI:EU:C:2014:238).

Case C-230/14, *Weltimmo s.r.o. v Nemzeti Adatvédelmi és Információszabadság Hatóság*, judgment of 1 October 2015 (ECLI:EU:C:2015:639).

Case C-362/14, *Maximillian Schrems v Data Protection Commissioner*, judgment of October 2015 (Grand Chamber) (ECLI:EU:C:2015:650).

Case C-337/15 P, *European Ombudsman v Claire Staelen*, judgment of 4 April 2017 (Grand Chamber) (ECLI:EU:C:2017:256).

A. Rationale and policy underpinning

Article 8 of the Charter of Fundamental Rights of the European Union ('CFR' or 'Charter') guarantees individuals the right to protection of their personal data. Article 77 GDPR deals with enforcing this right on the initiative of the data subject: everybody[1] has a right to 'lodge a complaint with a supervisory authority'.

---

[1] Art. 77 GDPR mentions only 'data subjects' as entitled to lodge a complaint. However, this must not be understood literally, as in many cases only the final decision will show whether the complainant is indeed a

The legal provisions governing the procedures to be followed before administrative or judicial authorities in the Member States are not harmonised by Union law. The procedural autonomy[2] of the Member States is, however, not absolute—it may be exercised only within the limits set by the Charter, especially Article 47, which enshrines the right to an effective remedy and to a fair trial, and by specific provisions under EU law which may exist in the different legal fields.

Chapter VIII of the GDPR contains specific provisions on procedures before administrative and judicial authorities in matters of data protection (within the material scope of the GDPR). These provisions set forth several objectives which must be achieved by national law. Again, the means for doing so are left to the Member States in acknowledgement of their procedural autonomy. The objectives enumerated in Article 77–79 must be fulfilled in national law irrespective of any other remedies which may exist under national law.

Article 77 GDPR addresses the first objective, for national law to provide 'a right to lodge a complaint with a supervisory authority ... if the data subject considers that the processing of personal data relating to him or her infringes this Regulation'. No other remedy under national law can substitute for the right to appeal to a supervisory authority.

However, the fact that Member State law must enable data subjects to address the supervisory authority in cases of alleged infringements of their right to data protection does not result in an obligation for the national legislator to foresee an exclusive competence for the supervisory authority to hear complaints on infringements of the right to data protection. This right to appeal to a supervisory authority is, first of all, limited by the remit of tasks and powers of the supervisory authorities according to the GDPR, especially Articles 57 and 58 thereof: in particular, supervisory authorities are not competent to decide in matters of alleged infringements of data protection by the judiciary[3] and have no obligatory power to decide on matters of the right to compensation.[4]

Moreover, Article 79(1) refers to a complaint handling system where data subjects must have the right to approach a court to obtain an 'effective judicial remedy' for their complaint 'without prejudice to any available administrative or non-judicial remedy, including the right to lodge a complaint with a supervisory authority'. The meaning of this reference to the subject matter of Article 77 in Article 79(1) will be discussed in more detail in the commentary on Article 79 in this volume.

B. Legal Background

1. EU legislation

The legal remedies against infringements of the right to data protection which had to exist in the Member States under the DPD were intrinsically the same as those now in the GDPR: national law had to and still must foresee for everybody the possibility, inter alia, to bring a complaint before a national supervisory authority.[5] The GDPR differs from the DPD in the scope of the tasks and powers to be given to data protection authorities.

'data subject'. Thus, more precisely: everybody who claims to be a data subject is entitled to lodge a complaint with the supervisory authority.

[2] Dashwood et al. 2011, p. 288   [3] As is explicitly stated in Art. 55(3) GDPR.
[4] See ibid., Art. 58(2).   [5] Art. 28(4) and rec. 63 DPD, now Art. 77 GDPR.

Article 28(3) DPD only required a minimum standard and left a wide margin of manoeuvre for the Member States to implement their system of legal remedies. Most significantly, there was no duty for them to vest the national supervisory authorities with the power of delivering legally binding decisions; as a minimum standard, it was sufficient if the supervisory authority was entitled by national law to appeal to a court in order to achieve legally binding decisions.[6] In contrast, the EDPS has always been empowered to take legally binding decisions, which could be challenged before the CJEU.[7]

In consequence, the procedural legal position of supervisory authorities varied considerably among the different Member States: models for supervisory authorities varying from an Ombudsman to tribunal-like institutions could be found in the national law of the Member States. This has been changed by the GDPR, in which Articles 57 and 58 lay down a long and mandatory list of tasks and powers of supervisory authorities, inspired by those of the EDPS under Regulation 45/2001.[8]

2. International instruments

A right to a remedy for violations of the right to data protection was foreseen in Article 10 of Convention 108.[9] Article 12 of Modernised Convention 108 contains the obligation for the contracting parties 'to establish appropriate judicial and non-judicial sanctions[10] and remedies for violations of the provisions of this Convention'. Concerning the necessary judicial remedies, the rules of the European Convention on Human Rights ('ECHR') on the right to a fair trial apply. Concerning non-judicial remedies before supervisory authorities, the provisions of the Additional Protocol[11] to the Convention, adopted in 2001, are now incorporated and enhanced in Article 15 of Modernised Convention 108. These authorities 'shall have powers to issue decisions' and 'to impose fines'.[12]

In 2016, the EU and the US concluded another international agreement with special provisions on remedies against infringements of the right to protection of personal data in the course of trans-border data flows to the US: the Privacy Shield.[13] Supervisory authorities in the EU Member States are empowered to assist complainants vis-à-vis controllers, processors and other institutions in the US under this agreement.[14]

3. National developments

As concerns the establishment of supervisory authorities and the right to approach them with complaints about infringements of the right to data protection, such provisions were already required under the DPD in every Member State.

---

[6] Art. 28(3), last indent, DPD
[7] Arts. 47 (powers) and 32(3) (actions against EDPS decisions) of Regulation 45/2001. Compare now, respectively, Arts. 58, 63(2) and 64 EUDPR. For Regulation 45/2001, see Table of Legislation.
[8] Ibid. See EDPS 2010 for a description of EDPS policy and practice on the use of its enforcement powers.
[9] At present Convention 108 has been ratified by 50 states, three of them (Mauritius, Senegal and Uruguay) not being members of the Council of Europe.
[10] Insofar as disputes about infringements of the right to data protection are disputes 'of a civil nature' under Art. 6 ECHR, the (final) remedy under national law would have to be a judicial one.
[11] The Additional Protocol had been ratified by 39 states when this text was finalised, including Mauritius, Senegal and Uruguay. For the Additional Protocol Convention 108, see Table of Legislation.
[12] Art. 15(2)(c) Modernised Convention 108.
[13] See Commission Decision Privacy Shield 2016.
[14] See the commentary on Art. 45 in this volume.

4. Case law

In *Digital Rights Ireland*, the CJEU has stressed the importance of ensuring control of compliance by independent supervisory authorities.[15] *Commission v Hungary* considered the requirements of 'independence'.[16] In *Weltimmo* the Court considered when a company registered in one Member State but carried out its data processing activities in another Member State could fall under the jurisdiction of a data protection authority in that second Member State.[17] In *Schrems*, the CJEU ruled that such authorities must examine claims with all due diligence,[18] the requirements of which were considered in *Staelen*.[19]

C. Analysis

1. Introduction

Article 8(3) CFR enshrines the role of the 'independent authority'[20] that is given the task of controlling compliance with the rules set out in paragraphs 1 and 2 of the said article, and the CJEU has stressed the importance of ensuring this control, 'explicitly required by Article 8(3) of the Charter, by an independent authority of compliance'.[21] Chapter VI of the GDPR contains detailed regulation of how the independent 'supervisory authority' defined in Article 51(1) shall be established and organised and how the task of controlling compliance shall be achieved within the framework of the GDPR.[22]

2. The task of hearing complaints

One of the tasks of a supervisory authority, listed in Article 57(1)(f) GDPR, is to 'handle complaints lodged by a data subject'. Correspondingly, Article 77(1) GDPR establishes the right for every individual[23] to lodge a complaint with a supervisory authority because of alleged infringements of their right to data protection.[24]

The competence of a supervisory authority to perform the task of hearing complaints, is derived directly from EU law. However, the determination of the procedural framework for receiving and handling complaints falls within the procedural autonomy of Member States, to the extent that no special provisions are foreseen under EU law. The Member States are obliged to provide—within the limits of EU law—procedural law appropriate for the supervisory authorities to fulfil their tasks and for the individuals to exercise their rights. In the present context, what is 'appropriate' is to a large extent defined by the rules on 'fair trial' according to Article 47 CFR[25] and Article 6 ECHR.[26]

---

[15] Joined Cases C-293/12 and C-594/12, *Digital Rights Ireland*, para. 68.
[16] Case C-288/12, *Commission v Hungary*. [17] Case C-230/14, *Weltimmo*, paras. 44–45.
[18] Case C-362/14, *Schrems*, para. 63. [19] Case C-337/15 P, *Staelen*, para. 11.
[20] See 'independent authorities' in Art. 16 Treaty on the Functioning of the European Union ('TFEU').
[21] Joined Cases C-293/12 and C-594/12, *Digital Rights Ireland*, para. 68
[22] See the commentary on Art. 51 in this volume.
[23] If it turns out in the end that the complainant is not a data subject, the complaint will be dismissed, unless the complaint falls under the EPD and the supervisory authority is competent – see the commentary on Art. 95 in this volume.
[24] See the commentary on Art. 77 in this volume.
[25] Art. 47 CFR guarantees, inter alia, 'a right to a fair trial in case of violations of rights and freedoms guaranteed by the law of the Union'.
[26] Seen from the perspective of the complainant, it would be the rules concerning the so called 'civil limb' of Art. 6 ECHR which have to be fulfilled. For details see ECtHR Guide 2018.

In this respect, Article 77 must not be assessed as a single provision, but must be seen in the context of the whole of Chapter VIII, especially Articles 78–79. As the notion of a 'fair trial' demands that 'everybody is entitled to a fair and public hearing within a reasonable time by an independent and impartial tribunal previously established by law',[27] the sole possibility to approach a supervisory authority would not suffice per se to respect Article 47 CFR. On the one hand, a DPA must be fully independent, as required under Article 8(3) of the Charter.[28] On the other hand, supervisory authorities are not 'tribunals' but administrative bodies.[29] The 'hearing before a tribunal' is therefore achieved by the combination of Articles 77–78 GDPR. In effect, Article 79 obliges the Member States to respect Article 47 CFR when implementing procedures according to Articles 77 and 78.[30]

3. Territorial competence of supervisory authorities to handle complaints

The territorial competence of supervisory authorities is, as a starting point, tied to the territory of their own Member States.[31] Thus complaints against public sector controllers can be brought only before the supervisory authority of the same Member State.[32]

However, where complaints relate to the private sector, the duty of cooperation and the consistency mechanism result in a substantial enlargement of the territorial sphere of lawful action of each authority. Whenever a case includes cross-border elements, the competence to organise the handling of the case is transferred to the lead supervisory authority, cooperating with all 'authorities concerned'.[33] An authority which receives a complaint is always a 'concerned authority'[34] which therefore can rely on the cooperation and help of all other authorities concerned, including especially the lead authority, if a complaint surpasses the sole involvement of that authority. It would therefore be possible for a supervisory authority to deal with complaints referring to events which happened outside its original territorial competence.[35]

Whilst it is, in principle, up to national law to define the territorial limits of hearing complaints, Article 77(1) sets a minimum standard; 'in particular', complaints are to be handled if they are brought in by individuals having their habitual residence or their place of work in the territory of the Member State, or if they allege an infringement on the territory of the Member State for which the supervisory authority is established. This is strikingly similar to the test enunciated by the CJEU in *Weltimmo* when interpreting the less detailed wording of Article 28(4) DPD. In that case, a company was registered in Slovakia but targeted its services and its data processing activities exclusively at customers in Hungary. The Court concluded that the Hungarian data protection authority could hear claims against a Slovakian company lodged by data subjects in Hungary, such as the

---

[27] Art. 47(2) CFR.
[28] See the commentaries on Arts. 52 and 60 in this volume and Case C-288/12, *Commission v Hungary*, para. 48 and the case law cited therein.
[29] See the commentary on Art. 78 in this volume.
[30] See the commentary on Art. 79 in this volume.   [31] Art. 55(1) GDPR.
[32] Art. 55(2) GDPR.   [33] Art. 60 GDPR. See the commentary on Art. 60 in this volume.
[34] See Art. 60 and also rec. 124: 'Also where a data subject not residing in that Member State has lodged a complaint, the supervisory authority with which such complaint has been lodged should also be a supervisory authority concerned'.
[35] See Svantesson 2015.

advertisers of properties on the company's website, who considered themselves victims of unlawful processing of their personal data in the Member State (Hungary) in which they held those properties. [36]

4. Obligations to provide information to the complainant

According to Article 77(2) the complainant must be informed by the supervisory authority with which the complaint has been lodged 'about the progress and the outcome of the complaint' and about 'the possibility of a judicial remedy pursuant to Article 78'. More details on the judicial remedies which must be available are contained in Article 78, paragraphs 2 and 3.[37]

Recital 141 mentions that the data protection authorities themselves could at their level also contribute reasonable rules for complaint procedures, e.g. by developing a form (which can also be submitted electronically) that helps the data subject to formulate the complaint and to attach the necessary information.

5. Procedural rules for supervisory authorities

In the event of receiving a complaint, the supervisory authority is expected to perform all steps necessary to establish compliance with the GDPR in making use of its powers according to Article 58 GDPR. Under the DPD the CJEU held in *Schrems* that, when considering a claim by an individual concerning the transfer of personal data outside the EU, 'it is incumbent upon the national supervisory authority to examine the claim with all due diligence', subject to review by a national court and a possible reference to the CJEU.[38] With respect to the principle of diligence, the Court recalled in *Staelen* that, 'where an administration is called upon to conduct an inquiry, it is for that administration to conduct it with the greatest possible diligence in order to dispel the doubts which exist and to clarify the situation'.[39]

The obligation under the GDPR includes investigation of the facts, assessment of the merits of the case and a decision about compliance or non-compliance, plus, eventually, enforcement activities and/or sanctioning if non-compliance is encountered. This will also include starting a coordination procedure according to Articles 56 and 60, if the case contains elements of cross-border processing.[40] The national procedural rules for supervisory authorities must be appropriate to achieving all these tasks in a way which guarantees an effective remedy to data subjects.[41]

Select Bibliography

EU legislation

Commission Decision Privacy Shield 2016: Commission Implementing Decision (EU) 2016/1250 of 12 July 2016 pursuant to Directive 95/46/EC of the European Parliament and of the Council on the adequacy of the protection provided by the EU–US Privacy Shield, OJ 2016 L 207/1.

---

[36] Case C-230/14, *Weltimmo*, paras. 44–45.
[37] See the commentary on Art. 78 in this volume.
[38] Case C-362/14, *Schrems*, paras. 63–64.
[39] Case 337/15P, *Staelen*, para. 114
[40] 'Cross-border processing' is defined in Art. 4(23) GDPR. It is essentially a processing activity which creates effects in more than just one Member States. This is why several supervisory authorities shall jointly perform their tasks in relation to such processing activities. See also the commentary on Art. 4(23) in this volume.
[41] Dashwood et al. 2011, pp. 294 et seq.

Academic writings

Dashwood et al. 2011: Dashwood, Dougan, Rodger, Spaventa and Wyatt, *Wyatt and Dashwood's European Union Law* (6th edn, Hart Publishing 2011).

Hijmans, *The European Union as Guardian of Internet Privacy* (Springer 2016).

Papers of data protection authorities

EDPS 2010: European Data Protection Supervisor, 'Monitoring and Ensuring Compliance with Regulation (EC) 45/2001—Policy Paper' (13 December 2010).

Reports and recommendations

ECtHR Guide 2018: European Court of Human Rights, 'Guide on Article 6 of the European Convention on Human Rights (Civil Limb)' (30 April 2018).

Svantesson 2015: Svantesson, 'Will Data Privacy Change the Law?', *OUPblog* (31 May 2015), available at https://blog.oup.com/2015/05/investigative-jurisdiction-law/.

Article 78. Right to an effective judicial remedy against a supervisory authority

WALTRAUT KOTSCHY

1. Without prejudice to any other administrative or non-judicial remedy, each natural or legal person shall have the right to an effective judicial remedy against a legally binding decision of a supervisory authority concerning them.
2. Without prejudice to any other administrative or non-judicial remedy, each data subject shall have the right to an effective judicial remedy where the supervisory authority which is competent pursuant to Articles 55 and 56 does not handle a complaint or does not inform the data subject within three months on the progress or outcome of the complaint lodged pursuant to Article 77.
3. Proceedings against a supervisory authority shall be brought before the courts of the Member State where the supervisory authority is established.
4. Where proceedings are brought against a decision of a supervisory authority which was preceded by an opinion or a decision of the Board in the consistency mechanism, the supervisory authority shall forward that opinion or decision to the court.

Relevant Recitals

(141) Every data subject should have the right to lodge a complaint with a single supervisory authority, in particular in the Member State of his or her habitual residence, and the right to an effective judicial remedy in accordance with Article 47 of the Charter if the data subject considers that his or her rights under this Regulation are infringed or where the supervisory authority does not act on a complaint, partially or wholly rejects or dismisses a complaint or does not act where such action is necessary to protect the rights of the data subject. The investigation following a complaint should be carried out, subject to judicial review, to the extent that is appropriate in the specific case. The supervisory authority should inform the data subject of the progress and the outcome of the complaint within a reasonable period. If the case requires further investigation or coordination with another supervisory authority, intermediate information should be given to the data subject. In order to facilitate the submission of complaints, each supervisory authority should take measures such as providing a complaint submission form which can also be completed electronically, without excluding other means of communication.

(143) Any natural or legal person has the right to bring an action for annulment of decisions of the Board before the Court of Justice under the conditions provided for in Article 263 TFEU. As addressees of such decisions, the supervisory authorities concerned which wish to challenge them have to bring action within two months of being notified of them, in accordance with Article 263 TFEU. Where decisions of the Board are of direct and individual concern to a controller, processor or complainant, the latter may bring an action for annulment against those decisions within two months of their publication on the website of the Board, in accordance with Article 263 TFEU. Without prejudice to this right under Article 263 TFEU, each natural or legal person should have an effective judicial remedy before the competent national court against a decision of a supervisory authority which produces legal effects concerning that person. Such a decision concerns in particular the exercise of investigative, corrective and

authorisation powers by the supervisory authority or the dismissal or rejection of complaints. However, the right to an effective judicial remedy does not encompass measures taken by supervisory authorities which are not legally binding, such as opinions issued by or advice provided by the supervisory authority. Proceedings against a supervisory authority should be brought before the courts of the Member State where the supervisory authority is established and should be conducted in accordance with that Member State's procedural law. Those courts should exercise full jurisdiction, which should include jurisdiction to examine all questions of fact and law relevant to the dispute before them.

Where a complaint has been rejected or dismissed by a supervisory authority, the complainant may bring proceedings before the courts in the same Member State. In the context of judicial remedies relating to the application of this Regulation, national courts which consider a decision on the question necessary to enable them to give judgment, may, or in the case provided for in Article 267 TFEU, must, request the Court of Justice to give a preliminary ruling on the interpretation of Union law, including this Regulation. Furthermore, where a decision of a supervisory authority implementing a decision of the Board is challenged before a national court and the validity of the decision of the Board is at issue, that national court does not have the power to declare the Board's decision invalid but must refer the question of validity to the Court of Justice in accordance with Article 267 TFEU as interpreted by the Court of Justice, where it considers the decision invalid. However, a national court may not refer a question on the validity of the decision of the Board at the request of a natural or legal person which had the opportunity to bring an action for annulment of that decision, in particular if it was directly and individually concerned by that decision, but had not done so within the period laid down in Article 263 TFEU.

(147) Where specific rules on jurisdiction are contained in this Regulation, in particular as regards proceedings seeking a judicial remedy including compensation, against a controller or processor, general jurisdiction rules such as those of Regulation (EU) No. 1215/2012 of the European Parliament and of the Council should not prejudice the application of such specific rules.

Closely Related Provisions

Article 58 (Powers of supervisory authorities) (see too recital 129); Article 77 (Right to lodge a complaint with a supervisory authority) (see too recital 141); Article 79 (Right to an effective judicial remedy against a controller or processor) (see too recital 145); Article 80 (Representation of data subjects) (see too recital 142); Article 81 (Suspension of proceedings) (see too recital 144); Article 82 (Right to compensation and liability) (see too recital 146); Recital 147 (jurisdiction); Article 83 (General conditions for imposing administrative fines) (see too recitals 150 and 152)

Related Provisions in LED [Directive (EU) 2016/680]

Article 53 (Right to an effective judicial remedy against a supervisory authority) (see too recital 86)

Related Provisions in EPD [Directive 2002/58/EC]

Article 15 (Application of certain provisions of Directive 95/46/EC); Article 15a (Implementation and enforcement)

Related Provisions in EUDPR [Regulation (EU) 2018/1725]

Article 63(2) (Information on the possibility of a judicial remedy); Article 64 (Right to an effective judicial remedy) (see too recital 79)

Relevant Case Law

CJEU

Case C-188/92, *TWD Textilwerke Deggendorf GmbH v Bundesrepublik Deutschland*, judgment of 9 March 1994 (ECLI:EU:C:1994:90).

Case C-241/01, *National Farmers' Union v Secrétariat général du gouvernement*, judgment of 22 October 2002 (ECLI:EU:C:2002:604).

Joined Cases C-346/03 and C-529/03, *Giuseppe Atzeni and Others* and *Marco Scalas and Renato Lilliu v Regione autonoma della Sardegna*, judgment of 23 February 2006 (ECLI:EU:C:2006:130).

Opinion of Advocate General Ruiz-Jarabo Colomer in Joined Cases C-346/03 and C-529/03, *Giuseppe Atzeni and Others* and *Marco Scalas and Renato Lilliu v Regione autonoma della Sardegna*, delivered on 28 April 2005 (ECLI:EU:C:2005:256).

Case C-362/14, *Maximillian Schrems v Data Protection Commissioner*, judgment of October 2015 (Grand Chamber) (ECLI:EU:C:2015:650).

Case T-458/17, *Harry Shindler and Others v Council of the European Union*, GC, judgment 26 November 2018 (ECLI:EU:T:2018:838).

A. Rationale and Policy Underpinnings

The supervisory authorities under the GDPR are entrusted, inter alia, with the task of hearing complaints against infringements of the rights of individuals under the GDPR and also with imposing fines up to a considerable maximum amount on controllers or processors.[1] They have to be established by Member State law as independent authorities[2] with a fixed term of office and legal guarantees against premature removal from office[3] and full jurisdiction in the matters entrusted to their powers of investigation and decision.[4]

Nevertheless, supervisory authorities are not 'tribunals', as is best illustrated by the fact that it was deemed necessary to foresee a right to an effective judicial remedy against them in Article 78;[5] the wide range of functions of supervisory authorities and the rather limited (minimum) term of office for the members of the authority are untypical of 'tribunals'.[6] As data protection supervisory authorities do not satisfy the requirements for being 'tribunals', their decisions must undergo full review by a court. Article 78 sets forth the consequences of the principle of fair trial for the organisational context created by the GDPR.

---

[1] This is why procedures before a supervisory authority have to fulfil all the conditions for a fair trial under the so-called 'civil limb' as well as under the 'criminal limb' of the right to a fair trial according to Art. 6 European Convention on Human Rights ('ECHR').

[2] Art. 52 GDPR. [3] Arts. 53 and 54 GDPR. [4] See Arts. 57 and 58 GDPR.

[5] The nature of supervisory authorities as administrative bodies can also be deduced from Art. 55(3) which states that these bodies 'shall not be competent to supervise processing operations of courts acting in their judicial capacity', the evident reason being separation of powers; and from the heading of Art. 83 which explicitly denominates the fines imposed by the supervisory authorities according to Art. 83 as 'administrative fines'.

[6] For details concerning the legal concept of a 'tribunal' see ECtHR Guide 2018, part III A.

The legal provisions governing the procedures to be followed before administrative or judicial authorities in the Member States are not harmonised by Union law. Chapter VIII of the GDPR contains specific provisions on procedures before administrative and judicial authorities in matters of data protection (within the material scope of the GDPR). These provisions set forth several objectives which must be achieved by national law, whereas the precise means for doing so are left to the Member States in acknowledgement of their procedural autonomy.[7] The objectives enumerated in Articles 77–79 must be fulfilled effectively[8] in national law irrespective of any other remedies which may exist under national law.

Judicial remedies can be construed in different ways. Article 78(1) requires there to be the opportunity under national law *to appeal to a court against* legally binding *decisions of a supervisory authority*. In addition, Article 78(2) requires a judicial remedy to be available against the *inactivity (failing to act)* of a supervisory authority which has been seized of a complaint. Indeed, the CJEU has emphasised that it is incumbent on supervisory authorities to examine such complaints 'with all due diligence'.[9]

An effective judicial remedy requires full jurisdiction on the part of the court: 'Only an institution that has full jurisdiction merits the designation "tribunal" within the meaning of Article 6 § 1', which means that a 'tribunal ... must have jurisdiction to examine all questions of fact and law relevant to the dispute before it'.[10]

B. Legal Background

1. EU legislation

Article 28 DPD not only provided for the tasks and powers of supervisory authorities but also for some procedural aspects of their activities. For instance, the last sentence of Article 28(3) provided that 'decisions by the supervisory authority which give rise to complaints may be appealed against through the courts'. This provision is comparable to Article 78 GDPR, which requires Member States to ensure in their legal systems that decisions of supervisory authorities can be appealed against before a national court. At EU level, the decisions of the EDPS have always been susceptible to challenge before the CJEU.[11]

2. International instruments

Article 1(4) of the Additional Protocol to Convention 108[12] contains a provision to the same effect as Article 78—that is, the possibility to appeal to a court against decisions of a supervisory authority which give rise to complaints. Article 15 of Modernised Convention 108 deals with appeal to the courts: 'Decisions of the supervisory authorities may be subject to appeal through the courts'. This has to be read as compulsory in so far as Article 6 ECHR applies.

---

[7] Dashwood et al. 2011, p. 288.   [8] Ibid., pp. 294 et seq.
[9] Case C-362/14, *Schrems*, para. 63.   [10] See ECtHR Guide 2018, part III A. 3.
[11] Arts. 47(powers) and 32(3) (actions against EDPS decisions) of Regulation 45/2001, now, respectively, Arts. 58, 63(2) and 64 EUDPR. For Regulation 45/2001, see Table of Legislation.
[12] See Table of Legislation.

3. National developments

As has been pointed out above under EU legislation, provisions already existed under national law implementing the DPD which provided for a judicial remedy against decisions of supervisory authorities. Such provisions existed in every Member State.

4. Case law

In *Shindler*, the General Court affirmed the settled case law of the CJEU that an action for annulment must be available in the case of all measures adopted by the institutions, whatever their nature or form, which are intended to have legal effects that are binding on, and capable of affecting the interests of, the applicant by bringing about a distinct change in his legal position.[13] In *Deggendorf*, the CJEU considered the case where a complainant in a national case could have brought an action for annulment against a decision by the Commission but failed to do so and allowed the mandatory time limit to expire. It ruled that such a person is precluded from subsequently calling into question the lawfulness of the original decision before the national courts in an action against measures taken at national level in implementation of that decision.[14] The applicability of the rule in *Deggendorf* to proceedings against a supervisory authority which has implemented a binding decision by the EDPB is discussed below.

In *Schrems*, the CJEU considered the situation where a supervisory authority rejected a complaint against the allegedly unlawful transfer of personal data to a third country. It concluded that, on the basis of Article 28(3) DPD read in the light of Article 47 of the Charter of Fundamental Rights of the European Union ('CFR'), the claimant 'must ... have access to judicial remedies enabling him to challenge such a decision adversely affecting him before the national courts'.[15] However the Court recalled that where a national court considered that the validity of a decision by an EU institution was in question, it should suspend its proceedings and refer the question to the CJEU for a preliminary ruling on validity.[16]

C. Analysis

The GDPR has vested supervisory authorities with extensive powers including the issue of legally binding decisions. As such authorities are considered to be administrative authorities,[17] their decisions must be open to judicial review in order to comply with Article 47 CFR, granting a general right to an effective judicial remedy.

Recital 143 GDPR explains that 'each natural or legal person should have an effective judicial remedy before the competent national court against a decision of a supervisory authority which produces legal effects concerning that person. Such a decision concerns in particular the exercise of investigative, corrective and authorisation powers by the supervisory authority or the dismissal or rejection of complaints'. The settled case law

---

[13] Case T-458/17, *Shindler*, para. 30.
[14] Case C-188/92, *TWD Textilwerke Deggendorf*, paras. 17–18; and C-241/01, *National Farmers' Union*, para. 35.
[15] Case C-362/14, *Schrems*, para. 64.
[16] Ibid. See the commentary on Art. 79 in this volume for the extensive case law on the right to an effective judicial remedy enshrined in Art. 47 CFR.
[17] See Hijmans 2016, p. 351, qualifying DPAs as 'a new branch of government'.

of the CJEU on acts which are susceptible of review under Article 263 Treaty on the Functioning of the European Union ('TFEU') has provided guidance on what constitutes a decision which produces legal effects. It is a measure, whatever its nature or form, which is 'intended to have legal effects that are binding on, and capable of affecting the interests of, the applicant by bringing about a distinct change in his legal position'.[18]

Recital 129 GDPR lays down a series of requirements that should be observed by supervisory authorities when adopting legally binding measures, for example that it should be in writing and be clear and unambiguous, and notes that 'adoption of a legally binding decision implies that it may give rise to judicial review in the Member State of the supervisory authority that adopted the decision'. This right of review is limited to such legally binding decisions by a supervisory authority, it does not extend to any other measures by such an authority.[19]

Judicial review of a decision of a supervisory authority must cover all aspects of the decision, including 'the exercise of investigative, corrective and authorisation powers by the supervisory authority or the dismissal or rejection of complaints'. Moreover, the competent 'courts should exercise full jurisdiction, which should include jurisdiction to examine all questions of fact and law relevant to the dispute before them'.[20]

The GDPR also requires there to be a judicial remedy against inaction of the supervisory authority. If the supervisory authority does not handle a complaint, partially or wholly rejects or dismisses a complaint or does not act where such action is necessary to protect the rights of the data subject[21] there must be the possibility to appeal to a court. A judicial remedy because of inactivity of the supervisory authority may also be sought if the authority does not inform the complainant about the progress or outcome of the procedure within three months after bringing in the claim.[22]

Any other means available under national law for review of the activities of a supervisory authority in pursuance of a complaint, cannot substitute for the right to a proper judicial remedy according to Article 78.

Article 78(3) provides that '[p]roceedings against a supervisory authority shall be brought before the courts of the Member State where the supervisory authority is established'[23] and will be conducted in accordance with that Member State's procedural law. The competent court has to be defined by the law of the Member State where the supervisory authority is established. In the case of cross-border procedures the territorially competent court is to be determined according to Article 60 paragraphs 7–10. Article 81 foresees the possibility of a suspension or consolidation of court proceedings where appeals against decisions of supervisory authorities could—exceptionally—lead to court procedures in several Member States concerning the same subject-matter.[24]

In the case of a cross-border complaint procedure, if a decision could only be reached by involving the EDPB in the course of applying the consistency mechanism, the supervisory authority, which implements the opinion or decision of the Board, shall forward the opinion or decision of the Board to the court where the remedy is sought.[25] Recital

---

[18] Case T-458/17, *Shindler*, para. 30.
[19] Rec. 143 clarifies that 'the right to an effective judicial remedy does not encompass measures taken by supervisory authorities which are not legally binding, such as opinions issued by or advice provided by the supervisory authority'.
[20] Rec. 143 GDPR. [21] Rec. 141 GDPR. [22] Art. 78(2) GDPR.
[23] Art. 78(3) GDPR. [24] See the commentary on Art. 81 in this volume.
[25] Art. 78(4) GDPR.

143 recalls that the national court does not, however, have the power to declare the Board's decision invalid but must refer the question of validity to the Court of Justice under the preliminary ruling procedure laid down in Article 267 TFEU.[26]

If a direct judicial remedy against a decision of the Board is sought under Article 263 TFEU, it must follow the specific rules of that Article as the Board is established under Article 68(1) GDPR as a body of the Union with legal personality.

In this respect, recital 143 asserts that if the complainant had had the opportunity to bring an action for annulment of a decision of the Board, in particular if it was directly and individually concerned by that decision, but had not done so within the period laid down in Article 263 TFEU,[27] then national courts are precluded from referring the question of the validity of the decision of the Board for a preliminary ruling under Article 267 TFEU. Since a recital cannot itself limit the right of a national court to refer a question to the CJEU for a preliminary ruling under primary EU law, the justification for this assertion must be sought elsewhere.

In this respect, the *Deggendorf* case law of the CJEU precludes the questioning of the validity of a measure adopted by an EU institution in certain circumstances after the mandatory deadline for directly challenging that measure at EU level has expired.[28] *Deggendorf* was a state aid case, where the Court was concerned to prevent the use of national courts in cases where the real nature of the claim is one which should have been protected by recourse to a direct action under Article 263 TFEU.[29] The CJEU has ruled that the rule in *Deggendorf* is not limited to state aid measures and applies to other kinds of Union acts,[30] but there has been considerable debate as to its appropriate scope.[31] In particular Advocate General Ruiz-Jarabo Colomer has argued that the 'rule in *Deggendorf* is highly questionable and at some point the Court of Justice must resolve to formulate it more precisely or overrule it, since it is open to significant objections'.[32]

For present purposes it may be noted that the rule in *Deggendorf* only applies where there is 'absolutely no doubt' that the complainant in a national case could have brought an action for annulment against the original EU level decision itself and failed to do so.[33] However, a binding decision of the Board under Article 65 GDPR is not addressed to a natural or legal person at national level but rather to the lead supervisory authority and the other supervisory authorities concerned; the final decision binding on the parties is then taken by the supervisory authority concerned. In this respect, it may be noted that the decision of the Board is not of direct concern to the parties concerned by the final decision by the supervisory authority because it does not directly affect their legal situation.[34] Finally Article 65(5) provides that the decision of the Board is only required to be

---

[26] See Case C-362/14, *Schrems*, paras. 61–64 and the case law cited therein.

[27] See Art. 263(6) TFEU: 'The proceedings provided for in this Article shall be instituted within two months of the publication of the measure, or of its notification to the plaintiff, or, in the absence thereof, of the day on which it came to the knowledge of the latter, as the case may be'.

[28] Case C-188/92, *TWD Textilwerke Deggendorf*, paras. 17–18; and C-241/01, *National Farmers' Union*, para. 35.

[29] Dashwood et al. 2011, p. 874.

[30] See Lenaerts et al. 2014, p. 466 and case law referred to in fn. 55 and 56; Dashwood et al. 2011, p. 225, fn. 105.

[31] Compare Lenaerts et al. 2014, pp. 465–466, fn. 5 and Dashwood et al. 2011, p. 225, fn. 106.

[32] See Joined Cases C-346/03 and C-529/03, *Atzeni* (Opinion AG), paras. 85–88, in particular the arguments set forth in para. 88.

[33] See Lenaerts et al. 2014, pp. 465–466.   [34] Case T-458/17, *Shindler*, para. 33.

published after the national supervisory authority concerned has notified its final decision to the parties at national level.

In such circumstances it is doubtful that the rule in *Deggendorf* would be applicable to restrain national proceedings pursuant to Article 78, notwithstanding the final sentence of recital 143 GDPR.[35]

Select Bibliography

Academic writings

Dashwood et al. 2011: Dashwood, Dougan, Rodger, Spaventa and Wyatt, *Wyatt and Dashwood's European Union Law* (6th edn, Hart Publishing 2011).
Hijmans 2016: Hijmans, *The European Union as Guardian of Internet Privacy* (Springer 2016).
Lenaerts et al. 2014: Lenaerts, Maselis and Gutman, *EU Procedural Law* (OUP 2014).

Papers of data protection authorities

WP29 2018: Article 29 Working Party, 'Guidelines on Automated Individual Decision-Making and Profiling for the Purposes of Regulation 2016/679' (WP 251rev.01, as last revised and adopted on 6 February 2018).

Reports and recommendations

ECtHR Guide 2018: European Court of Human Rights, 'Guide on Article 6 of the European Convention on Human Rights (Civil Limb)' (30 April 2018).

---

[35] See also the commentary on Art. 65 in this volume.

Article 79. Right to an effective judicial remedy against a controller or processor

WALTRAUT KOTSCHY

1. Without prejudice to any available administrative or non-judicial remedy, including the right to lodge a complaint with a supervisory authority pursuant to Article 77, each data subject shall have the right to an effective judicial remedy where he or she considers that his or her rights under this Regulation have been infringed as a result of the processing of his or her personal data in non-compliance with this Regulation.
2. Proceedings against a controller or a processor shall be brought before the courts of the Member State where the controller or processor has an establishment. Alternatively, such proceedings may be brought before the courts of the Member State where the data subject has his or her habitual residence, unless the controller or processor is a public authority of a Member State acting in the exercise of its public powers.

Relevant Recitals

(145) For proceedings against a controller or processor, the plaintiff should have the choice to bring the action before the courts of the Member States where the controller or processor has an establishment or where the data subject resides, unless the controller is a public authority of a Member State acting in the exercise of its public powers.

(147) Where specific rules on jurisdiction are contained in this Regulation, in particular as regards proceedings seeking a judicial remedy including compensation, against a controller or processor, general jurisdiction rules such as those of Regulation (EU) No. 1215/2012 of the European Parliament and of the Council should not prejudice the application of such specific rules.

Closely Related Provisions

Article 77 (Right to lodge a complaint with a supervisory authority) (see too recital 141); Article 78 (Right to an effective judicial remedy against a supervisory authority); Article 80 (Representation of data subjects) (see too recital 142); Article 81 (Suspension of proceedings) (see too recital 144); Article 82 (Right to compensation and liability) (see too recital 146); Article 83(8) (Safeguards for imposing administrative fines) (see too recital 148)

Related Provisions in LED [Directive (EU) 2016/680]

Article 54 (Right to an effective judicial remedy against a controller or processor) (see too recital 85)

Related Provisions in EPD [Directive 2002/58/EC]

Article 15 (Application of certain provisions of Directive 95/46/EC); Article 15a (Implementation and enforcement)

Related Provisions in EUDPR [Regulation 2018/1725]

Article 63(2) (Information on the possibility of a judicial remedy); Article 64 (Right to an effective judicial remedy) (see too recital 79)

Relevant Case Law

CJEU

Case C-33/76, *Rewe-Zentralfinanz eG and Rewe-Zentral AG v Landwirtschaftskammer für das Saarland*, judgment of 16 December 1976 (ECLI:EU:C:1976:188).
Case C-199/82, *Amministrazione delle Finanze dello Stato v SpA San Giorgio*, judgment of 9 November 1983 (ECLI:EU:C:1983:318).
Case C-312/93, *Peterbroeck, Van Campenhout & Cie SCS v Belgian State*, judgment of 14 December 1995 (ECLI:EU:C:1995:437).
Case C-50/00 P, *Unión de Pequeños Agricultores v Council of the European Union*, judgment of 25 July 2002 (ECLI:EU:C:2002:462).
Case C-201/02, *The Queen, on the application of Delena Wells v Secretary of State for Transport, Local Government and the Regions*, judgment of 7 January 2004 (ECLI:EU:C:2004:12).
Case T-461/08, *Evropaïki Dynamiki - Proigmena Systimata Tilepikoinonion Pliroforikis kai Tilematikis AE v European Investment Bank*, GC, judgment of 20 September 2011 (ECLI:EU:T:2011:494).
Case C-362/14, *Maximillian Schrems v Data Protection Commissioner*, judgment of October 2015 (Grand Chamber) (ECLI:EU:C:2015:650).
Case C-429/15, *Evelyn Danqua v Minister for Justice and Equality and Others*, judgment of 20 October 2016 (ECLI:EU:C:2016:789).
Case C-327/15, *TDC A/S v Teleklagenævnet and Erhvervs- og Vækstministeriet*, judgment of 21 December 2016 (ECLI:EU:C:2016:974).
Case C-73/16, *Peter Puškár v Finančné riaditeľstvo Slovenskej republiky and Kriminálny úrad finančnej správy*, judgment of 27 September 2017 (ECLI:EU:C:2017:725).
Case C-687/18, *SY v Associated Newspapers Ltd* (pending).

ECtHR

Vučković and Others v Serbia [GC], Appl. Nos. 17153/11, 17157/11, 17160/11, 17163/11, 17168/11, 17173/11, 17178/11, 17181/11, 17182/11, 17186/11, 17343/11, 17344/11, 17362/11, 17364/11, 17367/11, 17370/11, 17372/11, 17377/11, 17380/11, 17382/11, 17386/11, 17421/11, 17424/11, 17428/11, 17431/11, 17435/11, 17438/11, 17439/11, 17440/11 and 17443/11, judgment of 25 March 2014.

A. Rationale and Policy Underpinnings

Article 47 of the Charter of Fundamental Rights of the European Union ('CFR') guarantees *a right to an effective remedy before a tribunal* to everyone who deems his rights under Union law to have been violated.

The settled case law of the CJEU and of the ECtHR has clarified what constitutes the 'effectiveness' of a judicial remedy. An individual must 'have a clear, practical opportunity to challenge an act that is an interference with his rights' and this opportunity must not be impaired by either prohibitive costs, unjustified timely constraints or special procedural bars preventing or seriously hindering the possibility to apply to a court.[1] An additional condition for 'effectiveness' is that the remedy must be capable of providing redress in respect of the applicant's complaints and that it offers reasonable prospects of success within a reasonable timeframe.[2] For remedies under EU law, the Member States have additionally to respect equivalence in the sense that the conditions relating to claims arising from EU law are not less favourable than those relating to similar actions of a domestic nature.[3]

The Member States are autonomous in laying down the procedures to be followed before national administrative or judicial authorities. This procedural autonomy,[4] however, is not absolute; it may be exercised only within the limits set by the Charter and by specific provisions under EU law which may exist in the different legal fields. What is decisive is the result of the exercise by a Member State of its legal margin of manoeuvre, to ensure the availability of an effective judicial remedy for every individual claiming an infringement of one or more of their rights under EU law.

When Article 79(1) GDPR proclaims that each data subject shall have a right to an effective judicial remedy, it actually only repeats Article 47 of the Charter. Its special role within Chapter VIII GDPR is to stress that an effective legal remedy is not automatically present where *any* remedies are available under national law. For example, the opportunity to lodge a complaint with a supervisory authority according to Article 77 GDPR is explicitly mentioned as not constituting an effective judicial remedy, as supervisory authorities are considered not to be courts but administrative bodies (albeit vested with special independence).[5]

Even the obligation under Article 78 GDPR to provide an effective judicial remedy in national law against legally binding decisions of a supervisory authority does not guarantee in itself the general and complete existence of an 'effective judicial remedy' against violations of the GDPR, as there are legal claims derived from the GDPR which do not fall under the remit of a supervisory authority. This is true, for instance, for the special right provided by Article 82 GDPR to receive compensation from the controller or processor for damage suffered, cannot be brought (successfully) before a supervisory authority as the power to order compensation for damages is not mentioned among the corrective powers of such authorities listed in Article 58(2) GDPR,[6] this power being traditionally reserved for the judiciary. Additionally, alleged infringements of the GDPR by data processing operations performed by courts in the course of their judicial functions are not subject to investigation and decisions by supervisory authorities according to Article 55(3) GDPR.

---

[1] ECtHR Guide 2018, para. 44; Dashwood et al. 2011, pp. 294 et seq.

[2] ECtHR, *Vučković*, paras. 71 and 74.

[3] Case C-50/00 PP, *Union de Pequeños Agricultores*, paras. 39–41; Case T-461/08, *Evropaiki Dynamiki*, para. 46.

[4] Wyatt and Dashwood 2011, p. 288

[5] See the commentaries on Arts. 4(21) and 58 in this volume. The nature of supervisory authorities as administrative bodies can be deduced from Art. 55(3) which states that these bodies 'shall not be competent to supervise processing operations of courts', the evident reason being separation of powers; and from the heading of Art. 83 which explicitly denominates the fines imposed by the supervisory authorities according to Art. 83 as 'administrative fines'.

[6] Considering the relatively high level of precision with which Art. 58(2) GDPR is formulated (where, for instance, the power of imposing administrative fines according to Art. 83 GDPR is specifically mentioned), the fact that Art. 82 is not mentioned must be interpreted as not conferring upon supervisory authorities the competence to decide about compensation.

All in all, there are a number of situations where the possibility to lodge a complaint under Article 77 with a supervisory authority in data protection matters - and thus subsequently reach a court under Article 78 - does not exist under the GDPR, so that in such cases the right to an effective judicial remedy must be established outside Article 78. Thus, the purpose of Article 79(1) is primarily to guarantee that access to a court must exist *in every case*, regardless of all other possibly existing legal remedies in a Member State.

A specific problem of 'effectiveness' of judicial remedies was raised before the CJEU in *Puškár*,[7] which considered whether the right to seek an effective judicial remedy is compatible with a national requirement to previously exhaust a procedure before an administrative authority. The CJEU found that a condition of prior recourse to an administrative procedure could be imposed, so long as it did not disproportionately affect the right to an effective remedy before a court (see the discussion below). This ruling confirms that national legislators enjoy a far-reaching autonomy in designing the organisational and procedural components of their system of legal remedies, and is relevant not only for national law but also for EU law. The judicial remedy under Article 78 GDPR, which must be available against every decision (and lack of decision) of a supervisory authority, is an 'effective judicial remedy' so long as its detailed design under national law does not disproportionately affect the right to an effective remedy before a court. Thus it is the effect of the design which conditions compatability with Article 47 of the Charter.[8]

B. Legal Background

1. EU legislation

Under the DPD the Member States enjoyed a wide discretion to determine the organisational and procedural role of supervisory authorities. This was especially true concerning the power to issue legally binding decisions. The text of Article 28(3) DPD suggests that the mere possibility for supervisory authorities to appeal to a court in order to invoke legally binding decisions might have been sufficient and thus a feasible model for Member States' law implementing the Directive. Where national law had chosen an ombudsman-like legal role for the supervisory authority, it was only logical that data subjects should have the opportunity to choose between approaching the supervisory authority or approaching a competent court. On the one hand, bringing the claim before the supervisory authority usually had the advantage of a less formal, quicker and possibly less costly procedure. On the other hand, going directly to court would usually have produced a legally enforceable result.

However, for those Member States or those categories of cases, where the supervisory authorities were themselves vested with the power to make legally binding decisions, having to establish a system of choice between different remedial procedures seemed less desirable, as such a system is prone to produce conflicting decisions which would require an additional legal procedure to resolve such conflicts. A prominent commentary on the DPD denied that the Directive laid down a general obligation for the Member States to

---

[7] Case C-73/16, *Puškár*.

[8] This issue will be considered again in the pending Case C-687/18, *Associated Newspapers*, discussed below.

provide for a genuine choice of remedies:[9] Member States were free either to provide a choice of legal remedies or provide a consecutive competence for deciding on complaints.

2. International instruments

Regulation 1215/2012, known as the recast Brussels I Regulation on jurisdiction and the recognition and enforcement of judgments in civil and commercial matters, generally determines which national court will be responsible for particular proceedings.[10] Recital 147 GDPR clarifies, however, that the specific rules on jurisdiction in Article 79 GDPR are, in effect, *lex specialis* and should accordingly have precedence in GDPR-related disputes over the general rules in the recast Brussels I Regulation.

3. National developments

The European Union Agency for Fundamental Rights has carried out an EU-wide comparative analysis of the remedies available as a means of ensuring individuals' rights in the area of data protection, in which national legislation on judicial remedies is briefly discussed.[11]

4. Case law

In *Schrems*, the CJEU recalled that, on the basis of Article 28(3) DPD read in the light of Article 47 of the Charter, the claimant 'must ... have access to judicial remedies enabling him to challenge such a decision adversely affecting him before the national courts'.[12] The Court found that the complete absence of 'any possibility for an individual to pursue legal remedies ... does not respect the essence of the fundamental right to effective judicial protection, as enshrined in Article 47 of the Charter'.[13]

As mentioned above, the CJEU was asked in *Puškár* for a preliminary ruling on the interpretation of Article 22 DPD, which is in substance equivalent to Article 79 GDPR.[14] The referring court asked whether Article 47 of the Charter must be interpreted as precluding national legislation which subjects the exercise of a judicial remedy to the prior exhaustion of the administrative remedies available before the national administrative authorities.

In response to the argument that the mandatory introduction of an administrative complaint procedure before bringing a court action may contribute to the efficiency of the judicial procedure and therefore pursues legitimate general interest objectives, the CJEU found that 'it is not evident that any disadvantages caused by the obligation to exhaust available administrative remedies are clearly disproportionate to those objectives'.[15] The Court went on to conclude that Article 47 CFR does not preclude mandatory prior exhaustion of available administrative remedies, 'provided that the practical arrangements

---

[9] Dammann and Simitis 1997, para. 7: 'The Directive does not determine the procedural arrangements. It does not, for instance, preclude making the availability of a judicial remedy in certain cases dependent on having first gone through an administrative procedure, as e.g. the procedure according to Article 28(4). What is decisive is whether the (judicial) remedy is effective'. (Translation by the author).

[10] Brussels I Regulation (recast). [11] FRA 2014, pp. 21–22.

[12] Case C-362/14, *Schrems*, para. 64. [13] Ibid., para. 95.

[14] Art. 22 DPD ('Remedies'): 'Without prejudice to any administrative remedy for which provision may be made, inter alia before the supervisory authority referred to in Article 28, prior to referral to the judicial authority, Member States shall provide for the right of every person to a judicial remedy for any breach of the rights guaranteed him by the national law applicable to the processing in question'.

[15] Case C-73/16, *Puškár*, para. 69.

for the exercise of such remedies do not disproportionately affect the right to an effective remedy before a court referred to in that article'.[16] The Court also stressed that '[i]t is important, in particular, that the prior exhaustion of the available administrative remedies does not lead to a substantial delay in bringing a legal action, that it involves the suspension of the limitation period of the rights concerned and that it does not involve excessive costs'.[17]

The right to an effective judicial remedy will be considered in the pending case of *Associated Newspapers*, a reference from the Court of Appeal in London requesting the interpretation of 9, 22 and 23 DPD (now Articles 79, 82 and 85 GDPR) and Articles 7, 8 and 47 of the Charter.[18] This case concerns national legislation which automatically imposes a stay on proceedings brought by a data subject which concern the processing of unpublished material for journalistic purposes. The national court cannot review the substance of whether the stay should be imposed, and it remains in place unless the Information Commissioner's Office ('ICO'), the UK data protection authority, makes a determination that the necessary criteria (journalistic purposes and unpublished material) have not been met. The legislation is intended to be a strong disincentive to data protection law being used to inhibit the freedom of the press. However it does not permit any judicial review of matters such as the degree of sensitivity of the personal data, the lawfulness of the proposed publication, and thus the balance between freedom of expression and the rights of privacy and protection of personal data.

C. Analysis

1. Effective judicial remedy

Article 79(1) GDPR requires Member States to create procedural rules which make an effective judicial remedy available to everyone who claims that their rights under the Regulation have been infringed. Such a remedy must be available 'without prejudice to any available administrative or non-judicial remedy, including the right to lodge a complaint with a supervisory authority pursuant to Article 77'. The type of remedies involved are left to Member State law.[19]

Article 79(1) must be seen against the background of the extensive autonomy of the Member States in the areas of procedural and organisational law. Article 79 clarifies that, whatever the specificities of national organisational and procedural law, national legislation must provide 'an effective judicial remedy' against infringements of the GDPR for all procedural situations, and must not make the exercise of this right 'practically impossible or excessively complicated'.[20]

As a result of the CJEU's decision in *Puškár*, where the Court confirmed the far-reaching autonomy of Member States concerning procedural law, and found that prior recourse to another procedure before being allowed to address a court does not in itself infringe the right to an effective judicial remedy, Article 79(1) can be interpreted as having the following functions:

---

[16] Ibid., para. 76. [17] Ibid. See also the case law cited in support in para. 70 of the judgment.
[18] Case C-687/18, *SY v Associated Newspapers Ltd*. [19] Kohler 2016, p. 667.
[20] See Case C-33/76, *Rewe-Zentralfinanz*, para. 5; Case 199/82, *San Giorgio*, para. 12; Case C-312/93, *Peterbroeck*, para. 12; Case C-201/02, *Wells*, para. 67; Case C-429/15, *Danqua*, para. 29; and Case C-327/15, *TDC*.

1. Article 79(1) reminds the Member States that procedures, installed under national law in fulfillment of Articles 77 and 78, must, as the outcome of their design under national law, result in an 'effective judicial remedy' in the sense of Article 47 of the Charta.
2. Where a specific complaint cannot be lodged with a supervisory authority according to the GDPR, the Member States have, additionally, to install an 'effective judicial remedy' outside the procedures implementing Articles 77 and 78.
3. Article 79(1) does, however, *not* require, as is occasionally claimed,[21] that direct access to a court must be foreseen *additionally* to an existing remedy according to Articles 77 and 78.

Since the CJEU clarified that prior recourse to an administrative instance before being able to seize a court is not as such contrary to the effectiveness of a judicial remedy, it may be assumed that implementation of Articles 77 and 78 will result in an 'effective judicial remedy' - and thus satisfy Article 79(1) – only if the special conditions for efficiency spelled out by the CJEU are fulfilled under national law.

Where Member States, nevertheless, choose to set up remedial judicial proceedings additional to the ones implementing Articles 77 and 78, care must be taken that such parallel procedures do not in themselves violate the principle of efficiency if they result in contradicting legally binding decisions without a smoothly functioning system of resolving such conflicts.[22]

Whatever the system chosen by national law, it must result in the possibility to obtain in any case an effective remedy before a court without substantial hindrance, delay or excessive costs.

Since claims under the GDPR are without prejudice to those deriving from other legal bases,[23] claims for compensation under Article 79 may be combined with other types of claims, such as those for violation of personality rights under Article 7(2) of the recast Brussels I Regulation.[24]

2. Territorial aspects of seeking a judicial remedy

Article 79(2) deals with the territorial aspect of seeking a judicial remedy. In the event of an alleged infringement of the GDPR by a controller or processor, the courts of the Member State where the controller or processor is established are competent to deal with the case. Alternatively, data subjects may choose to bring the case before a court in their country of habitual residence, if the controller or processor belongs to the private sector. This ability for data subjects to apply to a court in the country where they reside, regardless of where the controller or processor is established, should make it easier for data subjects to assert their rights. The jurisdictional grounds of Article 79(2) cannot be derogated from by contract.[25]

The rules in Article 79(2) on jurisdiction of courts are different from those contained in Article 78(3) GDPR, where the country of establishment *of the supervisory authority* is the decisive factor. Evidently, a difference is made in the GDPR between 'proceedings

---

[21] See further Nemitz 2018, para. 8.
[22] Conflicts would also arise in cross-border cases if a national supervisory authority were not the only competent authority to deal with a complaint at first instance.
[23] See rec. 146 GDPR.   [24] Kohler 2016, pp. 672–673.   [25] Hess 2018, pp. 170–171.

against a (decision of a) supervisory authority' (Article 78) and 'proceedings against a controller or processor' (Article 79), although proceedings against (the decision of) a supervisory authority may often be, at the same time, 'proceedings against a controller or processor'. This is due to the margin of manoeuvre allowed to Member States on procedural matters. Whenever a court can be approached directly, without first having to lodge a complaint with a supervisory authority, Article 79 is relevant for the territorial aspect of the competence of courts.

It may be expected that, as a consequence of divergent legal procedural systems in the Member States, there will be cases of judicial procedures *concerning the same subject-matter* before courts in different Member States. Such situations should be resolved according to Article 81 GDPR on 'suspension of proceedings' before courts in the Member States.

3. Relationship to the recast Brussels I Regulation

The jurisdictional grounds under Article 79(2) deviate considerably from those of the recast Brussels I Regulation on jurisdiction and the recognition and enforcement of judgments in civil and commercial matters.[26] As noted above, recital 147 GDPR underlines that the specific GDPR rules on jurisdiction concerning infringements of the right to data protection should have precedence over general jurisdiction rules, in particular those of the recast Brussels I Regulation. However, it has been argued that the rules of the recast Brussels I Regulation should continue to apply to the extent that they are compatible with the GDPR.[27] This interpretation would allow the plaintiff to choose additional fora if provided under the recast Brussels I Regulation.[28]

Select Bibliography

EU legislation

Brussels I Regulation (recast): Regulation (EU) No. 1215/2012 of the European Parliament and of the Council of 12 December 2012 on jurisdiction and the recognition and enforcement of judgments in civil and commercial matters (recast), OJ 2012 L 351/1.

Academic writings

Brkan 2015: Brkan, 'Data Protection and European Private International Law: Observing a Bull in a China Shop', 5 *International Data Privacy Law* (2015), 257.
Damann and Simitis 1997: Dammann and Simitis, *EG-Datenschutzrichtlinie – Kommentar* (Verlag Nomos 1997).
Dashwood et al 2011: Dashwood, Dougan, Rodger, Spaventa and Wyatt, *Wyatt and Dashwood's European Union Law* (6th edn, Hart Publishing 2011).
Hess 2018: Hess, *The Private–Public Divide in International Dispute Resolution* (Brill/Nijhoff 2018).
Kohler 2016: Kohler, 'Conflict of Law Issues in the 2016 Data Protection Regulation of the European Union', 52 *Rivista di diritto internazionale privato e processuale* (2016), 653.
Nemitz 2018: Nemitz, 'Artikel 79', in Ehmann and Selmayr (eds.), *Datenschutz-Grundverordnung - DS-GVO* (2nd ed., Beck 2018).

---

[26] See Hess 2018, p. 170. Further on the relationship between EU rules on jurisdiction and data protection law, see also Brkan 2015.
[27] Kohler 2016, p. 669.
[28] Ibid., pp. 669–670, giving as examples the *forum contractus* and *forum delicti* under, respectively, Art. 7(1) and (2) of the Brussels I Regulation.

Reports and recommendations

ECtHR Guide 2018: European Court of Human Rights, 'Guide on Article 6 of the European Convention on Human Rights (Civil Limb)' (30 April 2018), available at https://www.echr.coe.int/Documents/Guide_Art_6_ENG.pdf.

FRA 2013: European Union Agency for Fundamental Rights, *Access to Data Protection Remedies in EU Member States* (Publication Office of the European Union 2013).

Article 80. Representation of data subjects

GLORIA GONZÁLEZ FUSTER

1. The data subject shall have the right to mandate a not-for-profit body, organisation or association which has been properly constituted in accordance with the law of a Member State, has statutory objectives which are in the public interest, and is active in the field of the protection of data subjects' rights and freedoms with regard to the protection of their personal data to lodge the complaint on his or her behalf, to exercise the rights referred to in Articles 77, 78 and 79 on his or her behalf, and to exercise the right to receive compensation referred to in Article 82 on his or her behalf where provided for by Member State law.
2. Member States may provide that any body, organisation or association referred to in paragraph 1 of this Article, independently of a data subject's mandate, has the right to lodge, in that Member State, a complaint with the supervisory authority which is competent pursuant to Article 77 and to exercise the rights referred to in Articles 78 and 79 if it considers that the rights of a data subject under this Regulation have been infringed as a result of the processing.

Relevant Recital

(142) Where a data subject considers that his or her rights under this Regulation are infringed, he or she should have the right to mandate a not-for-profit body, organisation or association which is constituted in accordance with the law of a Member State, has statutory objectives which are in the public interest and is active in the field of the protection of personal data to lodge a complaint on his or her behalf with a supervisory authority, exercise the right to a judicial remedy on behalf of data subjects or, if provided for in Member State law, exercise the right to receive compensation on behalf of data subjects. A Member State may provide for such a body, organisation or association to have the right to lodge a complaint in that Member State, independently of a data subject's mandate, and the right to an effective judicial remedy where it has reasons to consider that the rights of a data subject have been infringed as a result of the processing of personal data which infringes this Regulation. That body, organisation or association may not be allowed to claim compensation on a data subject's behalf independently of the data subject's mandate.

Closely Related Provisions

Article 57(1)(f) (Tasks of supervisory authorities); Article 77 (Right to lodge a complaint with a supervisory authority); Article 78 (Right to an effective judicial remedy against a supervisory authority); Article 79 (Right to an effective judicial remedy against a controller or processor); Article 82 (Right to compensation and liability)

Related Provisions in LED [Directive (EU) 2016/680]

Article 55 (Representation of data subjects), Article 52 (Right to lodge a complaint with a supervisory authority), 53 (Right to an effective judicial remedy against a supervisory authority), Article 54 (Right to an effective judicial remedy against a controller or processor); recital (87)

González Fuster

Relevant Case Law

CJEU

Joined Cases C-293/12 and C-594/12, *Digital Rights Ireland Ltd v Minister for Communications, Marine and Natural Resources and Others and Kärntner Landesregierung and Others*, judgment of 8 April 2014 (Grand Chamber) (ECLI:EU:C:2014:238).

Case C-498/16, *Maximilian Schrems v Facebook Ireland Limited*, judgment of 25 January 2018 (ECLI:EU:C:2018:37).

Opinion of Advocate General Bobek in Case C-498/16, *Maximilian Schrems v Facebook Ireland Limited*, delivered on 14 November 2017 (ECLI:EU:C:2017:863).

Case C-40/17, *Fashion ID GmbH & Co. KG v Verbraucherzentrale NRW e.V.*, judgment of 29 July 2019 (ECLI:EU:C:2019:629).

Opinion of Advocate General Bobek in Case C-40/17, *Fashion ID GmbH & Co. KG v Verbraucherzentrale NRW e.V.*, delivered on 19 December 2018 (ECLI:EU:C:2018:1039).

Austria

Verfassungsgerichtshof, 27.06.2014, G47/2012 ua (ECLI:AT:VFGH:2014:G47.2012).

France

Tribunal de Grand Instance de Paris, ¼ social, jugement du 7 août 2018, *UFC-Que choisir / Société Twitter Inc. et Société Twitter International Company*, N° RG 14/07300.

Tribunal de Grand Instance de Paris, ¼ social, jugement du 12 février 2019, *UFC - Que choisir / Société Google Inc.*, N° RG: 14/07224.

Tribunal de Grand Instance de Paris, ¼ social, jugement du 9 avril 2019, *UFC - Que choisir / Société Facebook Ireland Limited*, N° RG: 14/07298.

Ireland

Digital Rights Ireland Ltd v Minister for Communication and Others [2010] IEHC 221, judgment by McKechnie J delivered on 5 May 2010.

A. Rationale and Policy Underpinnings

The right to representation aims to strengthen and facilitate the defence of the interests of data subjects, by allowing individuals to mandate an association to act in their name lodging a complaint with a supervisory authority or bringing proceedings before the courts, whether against supervisory authorities or against controllers and processors. In addition, Member States can also allow associations to lodge complaints with a supervisory authority, and to bring proceedings before the courts, without the mandate of any particular data subject. Finally, it is also possible for Member States to allow data subjects to mandate an association to exercise their right to compensation.

The general background of Article 80 of the GDPR, establishing such right, can be traced back to Article 47(1) of the Charter of Fundamental Rights of the European Union, which provides that everyone has the right to an effective remedy for violations of EU law.[1] From a policy perspective, Article 80 is deeply entrenched in the work of the EU's Agency for Fundamental Rights. A report published in 2013 by the FRA on access

---

[1] Sorace 2018, p. 8.

to data protection remedies notably highlighted as one of the major factors hampering the effectiveness of remedy mechanisms in place across Member States the persistent lack of knowledge about the protection of personal data among data subjects, but also across the judiciary. To mitigate this problem, and to ease the pressure on supervisory authorities in assisting victims of breaches of data protection law, the report put forward a series of recommendations on the role of 'specialised NGOs'.[2] It notably called for sufficient funding for these associations, but also for a relaxation of rules on legal standing, and for the possibility for them to lodge complaints while acting in the public interest, therefore opening the door 'to a much wider collective action'.[3]

These policy considerations intersected partially with EU policy discussions on collective redress. In 2013, the European Commission published a Recommendation on this subject in which the protection of personal data was highlighted as one of the areas where the private enforcement of rights 'in the form of collective redress' would be of value.[4]

In practice, Article 80 of the GDPR gives EU-wide validity only to some possible dimensions of the right to representation, leaving a number of controversial questions in the hands of Member States, such as the ability of non-governmental organisations ('NGOs') to act without an individual's mandate, and the role of NGOs in collective claims for compensation.

B. Legal Background

1. EU legislation

There was no equivalent provision to Article 80 of the GDPR in the DPD. Article 28(4) DPD, nevertheless, established that supervisory authorities had to hear 'claims lodged by any person, or by an association representing that person, concerning the protection of his rights and freedoms in regard to the processing of personal data'.

2. International instruments

There is no equivalent provision in Convention 108 or Modernised Convention 108, which leaves to each party the freedom to establish appropriate remedies for violations of its provisions.

3. National developments

The DPD left to Member States the determination of how associations could represent data subjects. In relation to collective redress, there has traditionally been a marked—and until now persistent—disparity of approaches among the Member States.[5]

4. Case law

NGOs, as well as different groups of concerned individuals, have already played an important role in challenging EU legislation on data protection grounds. The judgment of the CJEU in *Digital Rights Ireland*,[6] in which the Data Retention Directive[7] was declared invalid, is a prime example of this.

---

[2] In the words of Morten Kjaerum; see the Foreword in FRA 2013, p. 3.   [3] Ibid., p. 53.
[4] EC Recommendation 2013, rec. 7.   [5] See EP Study 2012.
[6] Joined Cases C-293/12 and C-594/12, *Digital Rights Ireland*.
[7] Data Retention Directive 2006/24/EC.

The *Digital Rights Ireland* case brought together two requests for preliminary rulings. The first one, emanating from the Irish High Court, referred to proceedings initiated by Digital Rights Ireland Ltd, which contested the legality of national legislative and administrative measures concerning the retention of data relating to electronic communications. Digital Rights Ireland Ltd is a limited liability company which pursues the promotion and protection of civil and human rights, particularly those arising in the context of modern communication technologies. The *locus standi* of this company to initiate proceedings was discussed at length by the High Court, which eventually granted Digital Rights Ireland both *locus standi* in its personal capacity, on the grounds that it owned a mobile phone which could have been affected by infringement to its rights, but also recognised its *locus standi* to litigate generally as what might could be termed an '*actio popularis*', on the basis that the impugned legislation could have a possible effect on virtually all persons.[8] The High Court judgment notably argued that where issues of EU law arise in litigation, the courts may be required to take a more liberal approach to the issue of standing so individual rights are not unduly hampered or frustrated.[9]

The other request for preliminary ruling submitted to the CJEU came from the Austrian *Verfassungsgerichtshof* (Constitutional Court), and concerned, inter alia, a constitutional action brought before that court by Mr Tschohl together with 11,128 other applicants, on the compatibility between the Federal Constitutional Law (*Bundesverfassungsgesetz*) and the law transposing the Data Retention Directive into Austrian national law. Described by the Constitutional Court as a 'collective individual application', it found that such a massive application did not trigger any particular concern. Thus, the Constitutional Court directly accepted the admissibility of these joint individual applications.[10]

The CJEU ruling in *Schrems v Facebook*[11] concerned the interpretation of Regulation No. 44/2001 on jurisdiction and the recognition and enforcement of judgments in civil and commercial matters, in relation to proceedings between Mr Maximilian Schrems, domiciled in Austria, and Facebook Ireland Limited, registered in Ireland. Mr Schrems had brought an action before the *Landesgericht für Zivilrechtssachen Wien* (Regional Civil Court, Vienna) seeking certain declarations, an injunction, disclosure and the production of accounts, as well as compensation for damages in respect of the variation of contract terms, harm suffered and unjustified enrichment. In relation to damages, a payment in the amount of € 4,000 was requested related to private Facebook accounts of both Mr Schrems and seven other persons who had assigned to him their claims relating to their accounts. While the case did not directly concern the interpretation of an EU data protection law instrument, it is of interest on at least two grounds.

First, in this case the Court was confronted with the question of whether the activities of Mr Schrems in the area of data protection, which include publishing books, lecturing, operating websites, fundraising, founding a non-profit organisation seeking to uphold the fundamental right to data protection,[12] and the fact of being assigned the claims of numerous consumers for the purpose of their enforcement, entailed the loss of his private Facebook account user's status as a 'consumer' within the meaning of the mentioned Regulation on judgments in civil and commercial matters.

---

[8] *Digital Rights Ireland Ltd*, IEHC 221.   [9] Ibid., para. 46.
[10] Verfassungsgerichtshof, *G47/2012 ua*, in particular paras. 5.1. and 1.6. In its judgment, the Austrian Constitutional Court refers to 11,129 'other applicants'.
[11] Case C-498/16, *Schrems v Facebook*.   [12] Ibid., paras. 12–13.

The Court noted that in this context the concept of 'consumer' had to be strictly construed,[13] but nevertheless indicated that neither the expertise which a person may acquire in the field covered by some services, nor their assurances given for the purposes of representing the rights and interests of the users of those services, could deprive them of the status of a 'consumer' within the meaning of said Regulation.[14] Excluding such activities, the Court added, would prevent an effective defence of consumer rights, among which it explicitly mentioned 'those rights which relate to the protection of their personal data', recalling that Article 169(1) Treaty on the Functioning of the European Union ('TFEU') identifies as an EU objective the promotion of the right of consumers to organise themselves in order to safeguard their interests.

Secondly, the CJEU also examined in this ruling the provision of Regulation No. 44/2001 according to which a consumer may bring proceedings against the other party to a contract in the courts for the place where the consumer is domiciled. Concretely, the Court was asked whether it was possible, on the basis of this provision, for a consumer to assert in the courts of the place where they are domiciled not only their own claims, but also claims assigned to them by other consumers, possibly domiciled in the same Member State, in other Member States or in third countries.[15] Observing that such a rule was a derogation from the general principles of jurisdiction under the Regulation No. 44/2001, and had therefore to be interpreted strictly,[16] the Court concluded that consumers could only bring proceedings where they are domiciled but only if a contract has been concluded between them and the trader or professional concerned.[17]

In *Fashion ID*,[18] the CJEU considered whether the DPD precluded national legislation from granting standing to consumer protection associations to bring actions against alleged infringers of data protection laws. The CJEU, following the same approach as Advocate General Bobek, found that the DPD did not prohibit such legislation, notably arguing that recognising such as a possibility does not affect DPAs' freedom of action or their liberty to decide.[19] The Court also dismissed the argument that Article 80 GDPR showed that such a possibility did not previously exist in EU law. To the contrary, the CJEU felt that Article 80 confirmed that the Court's interpretation of the DPD reflected the wishes of the EU legislator,[20] in addition to being fully in line with the Directive's objectives.[21]

In a number of Member States, litigation predating the GDPR brought by consumer organisations has recently resulted in data protection related condemnations.[22] Since the GDPR became fully applicable, several NGOs have begun using Article 80 as a basis for representing data subjects in claims filed in courts and before data protection authorities. Two of the most well-known NGOs are None of your Business ('nyob')[23] (based in Austria) and La Quadrature du Net[24] (based in France), but more such organisations will undoubtedly be created.[25]

---

[13] Ibid., para. 29.   [14] Ibid., para. 39.   [15] Ibid., para. 42.   [16] Ibid., para. 43.
[17] Ibid., paras. 44-46.   [18] Case C-40/17, *Fashion ID*.   [19] Ibid., para. 60.
[20] Ibid., para. 62.   [21] Ibid., paras. 51-59.
[22] In France, for instance, litigation by UFC-Que Choisir resulted in judgments by the *Tribunal de grande instance de Paris* against Twitter (August 2018), Google (February 2019) and Facebook (April 2019).
[23] See None of Your Business cases.   [24] See La Quadrature du Net cases.
[25] See, for instance, the recently launched Civil Liberties Union for Europe (Liberties), headquartered in Berlin and aiming at *'promoting the civil liberties of everyone in the EU'*. See Civil Liberties Union Website.

González Fuster

C. Analysis

In the original proposal of the Commission, the representation of data subjects was mentioned both in an Article on the right to lodge complaints with supervisory authorities,[26] and in a provision on 'Common rules for court proceedings' where it was stated that some associations shall have the right to exercise, on behalf of one or more data subjects, the right to a judicial remedy against a supervisory authority and against a controller or processor.[27] The Commission's proposal provided the possibility for associations to lodge complaints independently of any data subjects' endorsement, exceptionally, in case of a personal data breach.[28] In any case, it repeatedly and explicitly endorsed the entitlement for associations legally established in a Member State to generally lodge complaints with supervisory authorities 'in any Member State'.[29] During its first reading of the legislative procedure, the European Parliament proposed that associations should have the right to lodge complaints with a supervisory authority in any Member State if they considered that any breach of the Regulation had occurred,[30] and thus not only in case of a personal data breach.

In its final version, Article 80 GDPR contains most of these elements, but not all, and some merely as a possible national choice. Its title refers to 'representation' of data subjects, in the singular, but might be best described as establishing a number of rights or modalities of a single right, and foreseeing the possibility, at national level, of others.

The first part of the first paragraph of Article 80 of the GDPR generally establishes a right for data subjects to mandate an entity to exercise their rights under Articles 77–79, which gives rise to a number of questions.

1. Who can be mandated

Data subjects can mandate bodies, organisations or associations that comply with four cumulative requirements. These requirements can be seen as aimed to prevent the rise of professional litigators who are primarily interested in their personal profit.[31] These requirements are the following:

1. Being *not-for-profit*: This requires that the organisation is not constituted for commercial gain and that its purposes as set out in its articles of association or incorporation indicate that it is organised to benefit the public. In the English text of Article 80(1), the term 'not-for-profit' occurs directly before 'body', but reference to other language texts indicates that 'not-for-profit' applies generally to all the entities covered by the provision (i.e. to organisations and associations as well).[32]
2. Being *properly constituted* in accordance with a national law: This may refer to being properly constituted as a legal body, association or organisation in general terms, or under requirements that are foreseen by law for the constitution of bodies, associations or organisations capable of being mandated for the specific purposes of Article 80 of the GDPR. They key point is that the entity must be legally constituted in accordance with the law of a Member State.

---

[26] Art. 73 GDPR Proposal.   [27] Ibid., Art. 76, in conjunction with Arts. 74 and 75.
[28] Ibid., Art. 73(3).   [29] Ibid., Art. 73(2).
[30] EP Resolution GDPR 2014, amendment 182.   [31] See Sorace 2018, p. 14.
[32] See e.g. the French version of Art. 80(1), which refers to 'un organisme, une organisation ou une association à but non lucratif'.

3. Having *statutory objectives in the public interest*: This is a logical precondition for allowing Member States to foresee the possibility for these entities to act without an individual mandate.
4. Being *active in the field of data protection*: A mention of data protection in the statutory objectives of the organisation is not explicitly required, and such objectives might thus be wider, or possibly indirectly connected; the key issue here is that the entity is de facto active in relation to data protection. More specifically, they should be involved in protecting 'data subjects' rights and freedoms'—a particular formulation, since, the notion of data subjects' 'freedoms' is yet unexplored (typically, EU data protection law refers to their 'interests').

2. Content of the mandate

The data subject shall have the right to mandate any of these entities 'to lodge the [*sic*] complaint on his or her behalf' and 'to exercise the rights referred to in Articles 77, 78 and 79 on his or her behalf'. The wording of this part of the provision is unfortunate, not only because it refers to lodging 'the complaint', instead of just alluding to lodging *a complaint*, but also because immediately afterwards it mentions the right to mandate the exercise of the right referred to in Article 77 of the GDPR, which is, precisely, the 'right to lodge a complaint with a supervisory authority',[33] and is thus an unnecessary repetition. In any case, the data subject has also the right to mandate the exercise of both the right to an effective judicial remedy against a supervisory authority (Article 78), and the right to an effective judicial remedy against a controller or processor (Article 79). These are clearly configured as dimensions of a right to representation of data subjects, as the mentioned entities shall exercise the rights of the data subject 'on his or her behalf'.

3. Who can mandate

These modalities of the right of representation are directly applicable, so in principle all data subjects can exercise them, although in practice this will be dependent on the existence of entities capable of being mandated in the Member States where the data subject wishes to exercise the right of representation. Connected to this question, the GDPR does not require data subjects to mandate entities established in any specific Member State—they just need to be established in accordance with the law of *a* Member State. Since once mandated they will exercise the rights to lodge a complaint or bring proceedings before the courts on behalf of the data subject, the entities will be restricted in the choice of forum by the jurisdictional provisions relevant to the rights they have been mandated to exercise by the data subject.[34]

4. The right to representation for compensation

The final part of the first paragraph of Article 80 of the GDPR provides that data subjects shall be able to mandate the mentioned entities 'to exercise the right to receive compensation referred to in Article 82 on his or her behalf where provided for by Member State law'.[35] This thus permits Member States to allow data subjects to mandate certain

---

[33] This is the title of Art. 77 GDPR.   [34] See the commentaries on Arts. 77–79 in this volume.

[35] The clause 'where provided for by Member State law' could conceivably be read as potentially applying to the whole paragraph. However, rec. 142 makes clear that it is supposed to qualify only the exercise the right to

entities to exercise their right to receive compensation, potentially under certain conditions, as provided by their law. It is unclear, from the wording of the provision, *which* Member State law shall provide for such a right: potentially, it could be the law of the Member State of the data subjects given the right to mandate such exercise, or the law of the Member State of the entities able to accept such a mandate, or even the law of any Member State where a data subject could exercise the right to receive compensation. It may also be unclear whether a lawsuit brought by an entity for the compensation of individuals when the sums obtained are not to be paid to the individual victims can be regarded as civil in nature or as an atypical administrative fine.[36] What is certain is that there is no general right for all data subjects to mandate the exercise of their right to receive compensation, which will be dependent on the existence of national law applicable to the situation at stake.

5. The right of associations to bring complaints and proceedings on their own initiative

The second paragraph of Article 80 GDPR gives Member States the possibility to grant any of the mentioned entities the right to, 'independently of a data subject's mandate', lodge complaints with supervisory authorities and exercise the rights referred to in Articles 78 and 79, 'if it considers that the rights of a data subject under this Regulation have been infringed as a result of the processing'. Again, this is not a generally applicable right, but an option that Member States are free to embrace.

The option does not, strictly speaking, concern the same type of representation as the rights previously discussed. Here, the entities do not act on behalf of a data subject, or with their mandate. This does not mean, however, that these entities should act on the basis of an abstract interest in data protection issues, or any other theoretical public interest concern: rather, they shall be able to act only if they consider that the GDPR rights of (at least) one data subject have been breached due to some data processing. They can thus be perceived as representing such potentially unidentified but presumably affected data subject, even if without the data subject's mandate.

Member States are free to allow for such non-mandated actions to be valid in relation to their own supervisory authorities and their courts.[37] Article 80 further indicates that associations shall have the right to lodge complaints with the supervisory authority 'which is competent pursuant to Article 77', a wording that appears to result from wishing to prevent the right of associations to lodge complaints with *any* supervisory authority. The consequences of the adopted wording are however not completely clear, as Article 77 grants to data subjects the right to lodge a complaint 'in particular in the Member State of his or her habitual residence, place of work or place of the alleged infringement', and there might not always be an identified data subject, which might make it difficult to predict the possible fora.

---

receive compensation on behalf of data subjects ('or, if provided for in Member State law, exercise the right to receive compensation on behalf of data subjects').

[36] See Hess 2018, pp. 174–175.

[37] This possibility for entities to act without mandate can be foreseen by Member States for the right to lodge complaints with the supervisory authority 'in that Member State'. There is no equivalent reference with regard to Arts. 78–79 GDPR, but the exercise of the rights they establish is in any case dependent on national law.

6. Concluding remarks

The right to representation is consistent with the objectives of the GDPR, and in particular with the strengthening of data subject rights. The fact that some of its modalities are not equally available to all data subjects, however, could be perceived as being in tension with the fundamental rights nature of EU data protection, the need to provide effective remedies for breaches of EU law, and EU's commitment to the promotion of the right of consumers to organise themselves in order to safeguard their interests.

The relationship between EU data protection and consumer law is multifaceted.[38] Data protection issues can be integrated into consumer law litigation, and data protection law can find a source of inspiration in consumer law, though it is far from having embraced all the potential of such possible influence. In this sense, it is striking that the GDPR configures the right to representation of data subjects with a national accent, and in a fragmented fashion, whereas in the area of consumer protection the EU has an established tradition of supporting consumers who face cross-border challenges. For example, the EU co-funds the European Consumer Centres Network ('ECC-Net'), which is committed to boosting consumer confidence across the EU by specifically assisting consumers who buy goods and services in another EU Member State. Data subjects confronted with cross-border data issues would certainly benefit from a 'strong and more coherent' framework for the exercise of their right to representation in cross-border scenarios, which would be fully coherent with 'the importance of creating the trust that will allow the digital economy to develop across the internal market'.[39]

Policy hesitations regarding collective redress in EU consumer law have also affected the construction of Article 80. As the EU legislator appears to advance towards supporting such collective redress,[40] which includes integrating also data protection concerns,[41] what remains to be explored is whether any upcoming rules in that regard could compensate for the limitations of Article 80 of the GDPR. Beyond learning from consumer law, EU data protection law has undoubtedly also to assimilate the full range of constitutional issues connected to the imperative of guaranteeing effective remedies in case of breach of its fundamental requirements.

Select Bibliography

EU legislation

Council Regulation 44/2001: Council Regulation (EC) No. 44/2001 of 22 December 2000 on jurisdiction and the recognition and enforcement of judgments in civil and commercial matters, OJ 2001 L 12/1.

Directive 2006/24/EC: Directive 2006/24/EC of the European Parliament and of the Council of 15 March 2006 on the retention of data generated or processed in connection with the provision of publicly available electronic communications services or of public communications networks and amending Directive 2002/58/EC, OJ 2006 L 105/54 (no longer in force).

EC Proposal 2018: Proposal for a Directive of the European Parliament and of the Council on representative actions for the protection of the collective interests of consumers, and repealing Directive 2009/22/EC, COM(2018) 184 final, 11 April 2018.

---

[38] See on this subject Helberger et al. 2017. See also on the role of information in EU data protection and consumer law, González Fuster 2014.
[39] Rec. 7 GDPR.   [40] See EC Proposal 2018.   [41] Ibid., rec. (6).

GDPR Proposal: Proposal for a Regulation of the European Parliament and of the Council on the protection of individuals with regard to the processing of personal data and on the free movement of such data (General Data Protection Regulation), COM(2012) 11 final, 25 January 2012.

Academic writings

González Fuster 2014: González Fuster, 'How Uninformed Is the Average Data Subject? A Quest for Benchmarks in EU Personal Data Protection', 19 *Revista d'Internet, Dret i Política (IDP)* (2014), 92.

Helberger et al. 2017: Helberger, Zuiderveen Borgesius and Reyna, 'The Perfect Match? A Closer Look at the Relationship Between EU Consumer Law and Data Protection Law', 54(5) *Common Market Law Review* (2017), 1427.

Hess 2018: Hess, *The Private–Public Divide in International Dispute Resolution* (Brill/Nijhoff 2018).

Sorace 2018: Sorace, 'Collective Redress in the General Data Protection Regulation: An Opportunity to Improve Access to Justice in the European Union?', 7/2018 *Working Papers Jean Monnet Chair* (2018), available at http://diposit.ub.edu/dspace/handle/2445/123425.

Reports and recommendations

EC Recommendation 2013: Commission Recommendation of 11 June 2013 on common principles for injunctive and compensatory collective redress mechanisms in the Member States concerning violations of rights granted under Union Law, OJ 2013 L 201/60.

EP Resolution GDPR 2014: European Parliament legislative resolution of 12 March 2014 on the proposal for a regulation of the European Parliament and of the Council on the protection of individuals with regard to the processing of personal data and on the free movement of such data (General Data Protection Regulation), 2012/0011(COD), 12 March 2014.

EP Study 2012: European Parliament, 'Standing Up for Your Right(s) in Europe. A Comparative Study on Legal Standing (Locus Standi) before the EU and Member States' Courts' (15 August 2012).

FRA 2013: European Union Agency for Fundamental Rights, *Access to Data Protection Remedies in EU Member States* (Publication Office of the European Union 2013).

Others

Civil Liberties Union Website: Civil Liberties Union For Europe, 'Prevent the Online Ad Industry from Misusing Your Data – Join the #StopSpyingOnUs Campaign', available at https://www.liberties.eu.

None of Your Business cases: Cases filed by None of Your Business ('noyb'), an Austrian non-profit organisation ('Verein') established in 2017 by Max Schrems and others, information available at https://noyb.eu. All cases are pending at the time of writing.

1. Complaint on 'forced consent' against Google LLC (Android), filed with the CNIL based on Article 80 and Article 77(1) GDPR, available at https://noyb.eu/wp-content/uploads/2018/05/complaint-android.pdf.
2. Complaint on 'forced consent' against Instagram (Facebook Ireland Ltd), filed with the Belgian DPA ('CPP') based on Article 80 and Article 77(1) GDPR, available at https://noyb.eu/wp-content/uploads/2018/05/complaint-instagram.pdf.
3. Complaint on 'forced consent' against WhatsApp Ireland Ltd, filed with the Hamburg DPA ('HmbBfDI') based on Article 80 and Article 77(1) GDPR, available at https://noyb.eu/wp-content/uploads/2018/05/complaint-whatsapp.pdf.
4. Complaint on 'forced consent' against Facebook, before the Austrian DPA based on Article 80 and Article 77(1) GDPR, available at https://noyb.eu/wp-content/uploads/2018/05/complaint-facebook.pdf.

5. Right to Access case before the Austrian Federal Administrative Court. Noyb represents a customer of an Austrian bank, who wanted access to his bank account details but was denied access. The Austrian DPA has decided in favour of the customer, but the bank appealed to the Federal Administrative Court ('BVwG'). Noyb made submissions on behalf of the customer under Article 80 GDPR.

La Quadrature du Net cases: Cases filed by La Quadrature du Net, a French organisation active since 2008 but formally established as an association in 2013, information available at https://www.laquadrature.net/. All cases are pending at the time of writing.

1. Complaint filed with the Commission nationale de l'informatique et des libertés ('CNIL'), against Google LLC based on Article 80 and Article 77(1) GDPR, following an online upon call for individuals using the services at stake and residing in France to mandate them (mandates were received from 9,973 data subjects), available at https://gafam.laquadrature.net/wp-content/uploads/sites/9/2018/05/google.pdf.
2. Complaint filed with the CNIL, against Apple, based on Article 80 and Article 77(1) GDPR, following an online upon call for individuals using the services at stake and residing in France to mandate them (mandates were received from 6,880 data subjects), available at https://gafam.laquadrature.net/wp-content/uploads/sites/9/2018/05/apple.pdf.
3. Complaint filed with the CNIL, against Facebook based on Article 80 and Article 77(1) GDPR, following an online upon call for individuals using the services at stake and residing in France to mandate them (mandates were received from 10,569 data subjects), available at https://gafam.laquadrature.net/wp-content/uploads/sites/9/2018/05/facebook.pdf.
4. Complaint filed with the CNIL, against Amazon based on Article 80 and Article 77(1) GDPR, following an online upon call for individuals using the services at stake and residing in France to mandate them (mandates were received from 10,065 data subjects), available at https://gafam.laquadrature.net/wp-content/uploads/sites/9/2018/05/amazon.pdf.
5. Complaint filed with the CNIL, against LinkedIn based on Article 80 and Article 77(1) GDPR, following an online upon call for individuals using the services at stake and residing in France to mandate them (mandates were received from 8,540 data subjects), available at https://gafam.laquadrature.net/wp-content/uploads/sites/9/2018/05/linkedin.pdf.

Article 81. Suspension of proceedings

WALTRAUT KOTSCHY

1. Where a competent court of a Member State has information on proceedings, concerning the same subject matter as regards processing by the same controller or processor, that are pending in a court in another Member State, it shall contact that court in the other Member State to confirm the existence of such proceedings.
2. Where proceedings concerning the same subject matter as regards processing of the same controller or processor are pending in a court in another Member State, any competent court other than the court first seized may suspend its proceedings.
3. Where those proceedings are pending at first instance, any court other than the court first seized may also, on the application of one of the parties, decline jurisdiction if the court first seized has jurisdiction over the actions in question and its law permits the consolidation thereof.

Relevant Recital

(144) Where a court seized of proceedings against a decision by a supervisory authority has reason to believe that proceedings concerning the same processing, such as the same subject matter as regards processing by the same controller or processor, or the same cause of action, are brought before a competent court in another Member State, it should contact that court in order to confirm the existence of such related proceedings. If related proceedings are pending before a court in another Member State, any court other than the court first seized may stay its proceedings or may, on request of one of the parties, decline jurisdiction in favour of the court first seized if that court has jurisdiction over the proceedings in question and its law permits the consolidation of such related proceedings. Proceedings are deemed to be related where they are so closely connected that it is expedient to hear and determine them together in order to avoid the risk of irreconcilable judgments resulting from separate proceedings.

Closely Related Provisions

Article 78 (Right to an effective judicial remedy against a supervisory authority) (see too recital 141);
Article 79 (Right to an effective judicial remedy against a controller or processor) (see too recital 145)

Relevant Case Law

Case 144/86, *Gubisch Maschinenfabrik KG v Giulio Palumbo*, judgment of 8 December 1987 (ECLI:EU:C:1987:528).
Case C-406/92, *The owners of the cargo lately laden on board the ship 'Tatry' v the owners of the ship 'Maciej Rataj'*, judgment of 6 December 1994 (ECLI:EU:C:1994:400).

A. Rationale and Policy Underpinnings

One of the main purposes of the new EU data protection legal framework was to achieve greater harmonisation and consistency of application of data protection law throughout the Member States. Even if this goal is partly impeded by the many opening clauses in the GDPR, there has been a great step forward at the level of the supervisory authorities, where the GDPR has created a detailed framework of cooperation obligations in order to achieve consistency of decisions throughout the Union. At the level of judicial authorities of the Member States such consistency would be equally desirable, but this is more difficult to achieve, considering the abundant diversity of legal rules and traditions governing judicial proceedings in the Member States.

Within the limits determined by the Charter of Fundamental Rights of the European Union ('CFR') and special procedural rules which may exist under Union law, the Member States are autonomous in laying down the procedural rules for their national judicial authorities. Achieving consistency of jurisprudence in data protection matters within the framework of national courts is a responsibility left to the Member States under the principle of procedural autonomy.[1] In this context Article 81 may be understood as having the limited aim of 'cross-border consistency' in the sense of consistent application of the GDPR in cases dealt with in the courts of different Member States.[2]

Article 81 foresees two possibilities to promote consistency: suspension of proceedings, or consolidation[3] of proceedings. In the case of suspension the decision is postponed until after the court first seized has decided; in the case of consolidation two closely related proceedings are combined into one proceeding. The purpose of both instruments is to avoid contradicting or inconsistent decisions.

It is important to note that Article 81 is relevant only for the private sector: complaint proceedings against controllers and processors in the public sector are handled only by the national courts of the Member State where the controller or processor is established.[4]

B. Legal Background

1. EU legislation

The DPD contained no provisions on cases where the subject-matter of similar cases is pending in courts of different Member States. The language of some of Article 81 recalls provisions of the Brussels I Regulation recast dealing with *lis pendens*; for example, Article 81(2) GDPR echoes Article 29(1) of the Brussels Regulation,[5] though suspension under the Brussels Regulation is mandatory whereas under the GDPR it is optional.

2. International instruments

There are no international instruments dealing with suspension of judicial proceedings in the context of data protection.

---

[1] Dashwood et al. 2011, p. 288.

[2] The final means for achieving consistency of judicial decisions is a request of national courts or tribunals to the CJEU for interpretation of EU law in form of a preliminary ruling.

[3] In this respect the title of Art. 81 is actually incomplete. The Council carved out the subject-matter of Art. 81 from the broader Art. 76 GDPR Proposal, but only proposed 'suspension of proceedings' for the title of the new provision.

[4] See Arts. 55(2) and 79(2) GDPR.

[5] Art. 29(1) Brussels I Regulation recast reads as follows: 'Without prejudice to Article 31(2), where proceedings involving the same cause of action and between the same parties are brought in the courts of different Member States, any court other than the court first seised shall of its own motion stay its proceedings until such time as the jurisdiction of the court first seised is established'. See Hartley 2015, pp. 261–267.

3. National developments

Article 81 GDPR does not foresee implementation by the Member States. However, within the limits determined by special procedural rules under Union law and the Charter, the Member States are autonomous in laying down the procedural rules for their national judicial authorities. National procedural law is also important in the context of Article 81 since consolidation is only possible when this is allowed by national law.

4. Case law

There is no case law dealing with suspension of judicial proceedings in multiple Member States in the context of data protection.

C. Analysis

Article 81 GDPR is designed to prevent contradictory decisions of courts of different Member States about cases which concern intrinsically the same (data protection) legal issues. The means provided by Article 81 for achieving this goal are 'suspension' (paragraph 2) and 'consolidation' (paragraph 3) of proceedings.

In case of suspension, the suspending court remains competent to decide and will eventually decide after the court first seized has given its decision. The purpose of suspension is to enable the suspending court to have regard to the arguments and opinions laid down in the first decision, so that the second decision may be consistent with the first decision. However, due to the independence of the judiciary, there is no legal obligation to follow the reasoning of the court first seized.

The purpose of consolidation is the combining of two closely related proceedings into one proceeding, with the result that there is only one competent court and only one decision. Consolidation of the case with the court first seized is achieved by all other courts involved declining jurisdiction. Prerequisites are that consolidation was demanded by one of the parties to the proceedings, that the proceedings are still pending at first instance, that the court first seized has acknowledged jurisdiction and consolidation is permitted according to the national law governing this court and that the other courts seized are entitled by law to abstain from deciding the case.

1. The same subject-matter

There are two types of cases where questions regarding the similarity of the subject-matter may arise. The first type are proceedings which could be called 'similar cases' or 'related cases',[6] as they have been brought before different courts by different claimants alleging the same kind of infringement of the GDPR by the same processing performed by the same controller and/or processor. It may occur that different cases brought in different Member States concern the same underlying situation, but that there are some differences between them. This raises the question of what can be considered 'the same subject-matter' under Article 81. The other kind of cases covered by Article 81 are identical cases or more precisely, 'the same case', which means that the same claimant approached different courts with exactly the same issues.

---

[6] See rec. 144 GDPR, which speaks of 'related proceedings'.

The question may arise whether Article 81 should be limited to certain types of parallel claims. There is a contradiction between Article 81 and recital 144 in this regard: Article 81 speaks about 'proceedings concerning the same subject matter', but does not specify their nature or type, whereas recital 144 refers to 'proceedings against a decision by a supervisory authority', i.e. it seems to contemplate coverage only of appeals against DPA decisions. It is submitted that Article 81 must have a broader scope than proceedings against DPA decisions, and should encompass both proceedings under administrative law and civil law. Limiting its scope to DPA decisions would severely curtail the coverage of the provision, and contradict its aim of increasing consistency among judicial decisions in Member States.

In a case involving *lis pendens* in the civil context, the CJEU took a liberal view of what constitutes 'the same cause of action' under Article 29(2) of the Brussels I Regulation recast.[7] It is submitted that the same broad view should be taken under Article 81 GDPR as well, and that the criterion of 'the same subject matter' should be satisfied if decisions in different proceedings could contradict one another. This interpretation also fits the criteria of recital 144, which states that 'Proceedings are deemed to be related where they are so closely connected that it is expedient to hear and determine them together in order to avoid the risk of irreconcilable judgments resulting from separate proceedings'.

Article 81 also requires that proceedings concern 'the same controller or processor'. Different cases may involve different constellations of parties even when the same subject-matter is involved, which can raise questions in this regard. In an admiralty case, the CJEU ruled in 1994 that the rule of *lis pendens* applied only with regard to parties in the first action that were the same as those in the second action.[8] For example, if A and B sue C and D in Member State X, while A and E subsequently sue D and F in Member State Y, then the court in Member State Y could suspend the proceedings or decline jurisdiction with regard to A's claim against D, but should otherwise let the case continue.

Whether this approach should be followed in interpreting Article 81 is an open question. On the one hand Article 81 seems to be a form of *lis pendens* and Article 81(2) explicitly refers to the 'same controller or processor'. On the other hand, the focus of Article 81 on cross-border consistency and the fact that nonetheless *a* 'same controller or processor' is present in both proceedings militates in favour of interpreting Article 81 to suspend the second proceeding in its entirety.

2. Cases eligible for suspension or consolidation

The cases eligible for suspension or consolidation are defined in Article 81 as 'concerning the same subject matter as regards processing by the same controller or processor'. This definition actually covers two different types of cases:

1. 'Similar cases' or 'related cases',[9] brought before different courts *by different claimants* alleging the same kind of infringement of the GDPR, constituted by the same processing, and performed by the same controller and/or processor.
2. 'Identical cases' or more precisely 'the same case', where *the same claimant* has approached different courts with the same legal problem involving the same controller and/or processor.

---

[7] E.g. Case 144/86, *Gubisch*. See Hartley 2015, p. 264.
[8] Case C-406/92, *Tatry*. See Hartley 2015, p. 264.
[9] Rec. 144 GDPR uses this denomination.

In the private sector there exist various reasons why, according to the provisions of the GDPR on complaint procedures and territorial competence, several courts, especially in different Member States, may have been approached in the same case *and are actually competent to decide*. Some of the more common reasons include the following:

1. The GDPR allows data subjects to bring complaints before supervisory authorities *in several* Member States. Although multiple procedures before supervisory authorities should normally be addressed by the duty of those authorities to cooperate,[10] it could nevertheless happen that decisions are taken by different supervisory authorities who have no knowledge of proceedings in another Member State; this could lead to parallel appeals to courts and in consequence to court proceedings about the same case in different Member States.
2. Under Article 79(1), national law can enable the complainant to approach a supervisory authority as well as *directly* a court. Due to a possible obligation to cooperate with a lead authority it could happen that the judicial proceeding against the decision of the competent data protection authority is situated in a Member State other than the court which was competent to receive a direct complaint.
3. When seeking a judicial remedy against a controller or processor, Article 79(2) foresees that proceedings can be brought *either* before the courts of the Member State where the controller or processor has an establishment, *or* before the courts of the Member State where the data subject habitually resides. This might also lead to procedures about the same case in the courts of different Member States.

Article 81 provides the means to achieve a consistent jurisprudence in such cases.

3. Knowledge of the existence of proceedings in another Member State

Implementing Article 81 presupposes that a court has knowledge of proceedings in another court. Knowledge of the existence of proceedings about 'the same case' before a court in another Member State will most likely be based on information provided by the *defendant*. This party will know whether it is defending the same infringement before multiple courts and will normally[11] have a special interest in not being involved in avoidable court proceedings. However, there is no legal obligation to inform the courts. This sort of situation will most likely lead to the application of Article 81(3), where a party (especially the defendant) can request the consolidation of proceedings with the effect that only the court first seized by the claimant is further competent to decide the consolidated case.

Where 'similar cases' are dealt with in the courts of different Member States, there is no guarantee that they will all be informed. It may be that supervisory authorities have information on appeals to multiple courts against their decisions and, being naturally interested in consistent jurisprudence, impart such information to the courts involved. The EDBP could also play an important role as a provider of useful information,

---

[10] Ibid., Art. 60.
[11] However, it is also possible that the defendant might prefer to have a second decision by the court in another Member State and bring the less favourable decision, via appeal to a higher court, before the CJEU for a preliminary ruling. There is no obligation on the side of a party to the proceeding to inform the court about related proceedings.

possibly based on the Internal Market Information System ('IMI') database which has been adapted to assist the cooperation of national supervisory authorities.[12] It may also be in the interest of one of the parties to the proceedings to inform the courts involved. There is, however, no legal obligation for anyone to inform a court about the fact that proceedings in a similar case are pending before a court of another Member state.

However, once such information is received by a court involved in proceedings about infringements of the GDPR, that court is required to act accordingly. 'It shall contact the court in the other Member State to confirm the existence of such proceedings'.[13]

4. Suspension of proceedings

The rules for dealing with cases, which have been assessed as being 'the same' or, at least, 'similar' in the sense of Article 81, afford some discretion to the courts on how to proceed. Article 81(2) GDPR states that 'Any competent court other than the court first seized *may* suspend its proceedings'. There is, however, no prohibition against the second court deciding the case without delay. Whether the parties to the proceedings can oppose a suspension of proceedings depends on national procedural law: it might enable an appeal against a decision of suspension.

In case of suspension of proceedings, the suspending court will nevertheless have to decide the case in due course, in principle only after a decision has been taken in the court first seized.[14] The suspending court is not bound by the opinion of the first court. However, it is presumed that the suspending court would take full account of the reasoning developed by the first court in substantiating its decision and, hopefully, come to the same conclusions. If not, it is possible and indeed desirable for the second court to refer the case to the CJEU under the second paragraph of Article 267 Treaty on the Functioning of the European Union ('TFEU'). Otherwise if the second court were to hand down a decision inconsistent with the first court, the losing party can only appeal to a higher court (if provided under national law) to demonstrate that there are irreconcilable judgments and bring forward the arguments used in the more favourable ruling.

In the end, only a preliminary ruling of the CJEU can provide the interpretation necessary to decide the similar cases. In any event, should the question be appealed to a national court of last instance, the third paragraph of Article 267 TFEU requires that court to refer the matter to the CJEU for a preliminary ruling.

5. Consolidation of proceedings

Consolidation of cases is legally possible only if all the requirements under Article 81(3) are fulfilled:

1. One of the parties to the proceedings has made an application for consolidation.
2. The cases are still pending at first instance.
3. The court first seized has acknowledged jurisdiction over the action in question.
4. The national law governing the court first seized permits consolidation.
5. The other courts seized are entitled by law to abstain from deciding the case.

---

[12] See the EDPB Website, for a state of play of IMI for GDPR purposes, and the commentary on Art. 67 in this volume.
[13] Art. 81(1) GDPR, last sentence.
[14] In exceptional cases the court might decide in due course, despite the suspension, not to wait any longer for a decision of the other court—such questions will depend on national procedural law.

Consolidation is finally achieved by all the courts involved declining jurisdiction, with the exception of the court first seized. The wording of Article 81(3) does not imply a legal obligation to decline jurisdiction as soon as the requirements are fulfilled. Questions have been raised as to whether consolidation under this Article will be effective in practice, in light of the fact that 'the domestic rules of civil procedure of the EU Member States do not provide for any rules on the cross-border consolidation of proceedings (a practice which has no tradition in Continental Europe)'.[15]

Select Bibliography

EU legislation

Brussels I Regulation (recast): Regulation (EU) No. 1215/2012 of the European Parliament and of the Council of 12 December 2012 on jurisdiction and the recognition and enforcement of judgments in civil and commercial matters (recast), OJ 2012 L 351/1.

GDPR Proposal: Proposal for a Regulation of the European Parliament and of the Council on the protection of individuals with regard to the processing of personal data and on the free movement of such data (General Data Protection Regulation), COM(2012) 11 final, 25 January 2012.

Academic writings

Dashwood et al. 2011: Dashwood, Dougan, Rodger, Spaventa and Wyatt, *Wyatt and Dashwood's European Union Law* (6th edn, Hart Publishing 2011).

Hartley 2015: Hartley, *International Commercial Litigation* (2nd edn, OUP 2015) (Kindle edition).

Hess 2018: Hess, *The Private–Public Divide in International Dispute Resolution* (Brill/Nijhoff 2018).

Others

EDPB Website: European Data Protection Board, 'State of Play—IMI for GDPR Purposes' (27 June 2018), available at https://edpb.europa.eu/news/news/2018/state-play-imi-gdpr-purposes_en.

---

[15] Hess 2018, p. 171.

Article 82. Right to compensation and liability

GABRIELA ZANFIR-FORTUNA

1. Any person who has suffered material or non-material damage as a result of an infringement of this Regulation shall have the right to receive compensation from the controller or processor for the damage suffered.
2. Any controller involved in processing shall be liable for the damage caused by processing which infringes this Regulation. A processor shall be liable for the damage caused by processing only where it has not complied with obligations of this Regulation specifically directed to processors or where it has acted outside or contrary to lawful instructions of the controller.
3. A controller or processor shall be exempt from liability under paragraph 2 if it proves that it is not in any way responsible for the event giving rise to the damage.
4. Where more than one controller or processor, or both a controller and a processor, are involved in the same processing and where they are, under paragraphs 2 and 3, responsible for any damage caused by processing, each controller or processor shall be held liable for the entire damage in order to ensure effective compensation of the data subject.
5. Where a controller or processor has, in accordance with paragraph 4, paid full compensation for the damage suffered, that controller or processor shall be entitled to claim back from the other controllers or processors involved in the same processing that part of the compensation corresponding to their part of responsibility for the damage, in accordance with the conditions set out in paragraph 2.
6. Court proceedings for exercising the right to receive compensation shall be brought before the courts competent under the law of the Member State referred to in Article 79(2).

Relevant Recitals

(145) For proceedings against a controller or processor, the plaintiff should have the choice to bring the action before the courts of the Member States where the controller or processor has an establishment or where the data subject resides, unless the controller is a public authority of a Member State acting in the exercise of its public powers.

(146) The controller or processor should compensate any damage which a person may suffer as a result of processing that infringes this Regulation. The controller or processor should be exempt from liability if it proves that it is not in any way responsible for the damage. The concept of damage should be broadly interpreted in the light of the case-law of the Court of Justice in a manner which fully reflects the objectives of this Regulation. This is without prejudice to any claims for damage deriving from the violation of other rules in Union or Member State law. Processing that infringes this Regulation also includes processing that infringes delegated and implementing acts adopted in accordance with this Regulation and Member State law specifying rules of this Regulation. Data subjects should receive full and effective compensation for the damage they have suffered. Where controllers or processors are involved in the same processing, each controller or processor should be held liable for the entire damage. However, where they are joined to the same judicial proceedings, in accordance with Member State law, compensation may be apportioned according to the responsibility of each controller or processor for the damage caused by the processing, provided that full and effective compensation of the data subject who suffered the damage is ensured. Any controller or processor which has paid full compensation may subsequently institute recourse proceedings against other controllers or processors involved in the same processing.

(147) Where specific rules on jurisdiction are contained in this Regulation, in particular as regards proceedings seeking a judicial remedy including compensation, against a controller or processor, general jurisdiction rules such as those of Regulation (EU) No. 1215/2012 of the European Parliament and of the Council should not prejudice the application of such specific rules.

Closely Related Provisions

Article 77 (Right to lodge a complaint with a supervisory authority) (see too recital 141); Article 78 (Right to an effective judicial remedy against a supervisory authority) (see too recital 141); Article 79 (Right to an effective judicial remedy against a controller or processor) (see too recitals 141 and 145), Article 80 (Representation of data subjects) (see too recital 142); Article 81 (Suspension of proceedings) (see too recital 144)

Related Provisions in LED [Directive (EU) 2016/680]

Article 52 (Right to lodge a complaint with a supervisory authority) (see too recital 85); Article 53 (Right to an effective judicial remedy against a supervisory authority) (see too recital 86); Article 54 (Right to an effective judicial remedy against a controller or processor) (see too recital 85); Article 55 (Representation of data subjects) (see too recital 87); Article 56 (Right to compensation) (see too recital 88)

Related Provisions in EPD [Directive 2002/58/EC]

Article 15 (Application of certain provisions of Directive 95/46/EC) (see too recital 47)

Related Provisions in EUDPR [Regulation 2018/1725]

Article 65 (Right to compensation) (see too recital 80)

Relevant Case Law

CJEU

Case C-403/98, *Azienda Agricola Monte Arcosu Srl v Regione Autonoma della Sardegna, Organismo Comprensoriale n° 24 della Sardegna and Ente Regionale per l'Assistenza Tecnica in Agricoltura (ERSAT)*, judgment of 11 January 2001 (ECLI:EU:C:2001:6).
Case C-278/02, *Herbert Handlbauer GmbH*, judgment of 24 June 2004 (ECLI:EU:C:2004:388).
Case T-259/03, *Kalliopi Nikolaou v Commission of the European Communities*, CFI, judgment of 12 September 2007 (ECLI:EU:T:2007:254).
Case T-452/05, *Belgian Sewing Thread (BST) NV v European Commission*, GC, judgment of 28 April 2010 (ECLI:EU:T:2010:167).
Case F-46/09, *V. v European Parliament*, Civil Service Tribunal, judgment of 5 July 2011 (ECLI:EU:F:2011:101).
Case C-362/14, *Maximillian Schrems v Data Protection Commissioner*, judgment of 6 October 2015 (Grand Chamber) (ECLI:EU:C:2015:650).
Case T-343/13, *CN v European Parliament*, GC, judgment of 3 December 2015 (ECLI:EU:T:2015:926).

Case C-413/15, *Elaine Farrell v Alan Whitty and Others*, judgment of 10 October 2017 (Grand Chamber) (ECLI:EU:C:2017:745).
Opinion of Advocate General Sharpston in Case C-413/15, *Elaine Farrell v Alan Whitty and Others*, delivered on 22 June 2017 (ECLI:EU:C:2017:492).
Case C-378/17, *The Minister for Justice and Equality and The Commissioner of the Garda Síochána v Workplace Relations Commission*, judgment of 4 December 2018 (Grand Chamber) (ECLI:EU:C:2018:979).
Case C-687/18, *SY v Associated Newspapers Ltd* (pending).

ECtHR

I v Finland, Appl. No. 20511/03, judgment of 17 July 2008.
Biriuk v Lithuania, Appl. No. 23373/03, judgment of 25 November 2008.
Armoniene v Lithuania, Appl. No. 36919/02, judgment of 25 November 2008.
Pruteanu v Romania, Appl. No. 30181/05, judgment of 3 February 2015.

France

Cour de Cassation, Chambre Civile 1, 94-14.798, 5 November 1996.

Ireland

Collins v FBD Insurance plc, [2013] IEHC 137, 14 March 2013.

Romania

Court of First Instance (Judecătoria Sectorului 1), Bucharest, Sector 1, Case No. 19326/299/2008, Judgment of 16 March 2009.
Court of Appeal, Cluj, Decision No. 88/A of 25 September 2012.

United Kingdom

Court of Appeal, Case [2015] EWCA Civ 311 *Google Inc. v Vidal-Hall, Hann and Bradshaw*, Judgment of 27 March 2015.

A. Rationale and Policy Underpinning

The rationale of the right to compensation and liability under the GDPR, as provided in Article 82, stems from the universally acknowledged principle of law *ubi jus, ibi remedium* (where there is a right, there is a remedy).[1] Or, as AG Sharpston has pointed out, 'because rights under EU law must be effective, no right can exist without a corresponding remedy'.[2] In order to understand, generally, what is a right and what is a remedy, one can rely on Van Gerven's succinct definition of both: 'the concept of right refers ... to a legal position which a person recognized as such by the law—thus a legal "subject" (hence the name "subjective" right)—may have, and which in its normal state can be enforced by that person against (some or all) others before a court of law by means of one or more remedies',[3] whereas remedies are 'classes of action, intended to make good infringements

---

[1] For an analysis of this principle under US constitutional law, see Thomas 2004.
[2] Case C-413/15, *Farell* (AG Opinion), para. 32.
[3] Van Gerven 2000, p. 502.

of the rights concerned, in accordance with procedures governing the exercise of such classes of action and intended to make the remedy concerned operational'.[4]

Unlike many—if not most—areas of EU law which often require creativity from the CJEU to ensure that the rights provided by legal acts of the EU are effectively protected within national jurisdictions by national courts (and especially when these rights are granted by directives and the applicant seeks enforcement against a private party),[5] data protection is a rather privileged field in that the Regulation that governs it specifically enshrines not only a general right to an effective judicial remedy,[6] but also a specific right to receive compensation for the damage suffered as a result of a breach of the Regulation's provisions.[7] This is particularly relevant with regard to the application of these rules at national level, and especially in disputes between private parties, that the source of the remedial action is a regulation, given that, unlike directives, [8] regulations are directly applicable[9] at national level and their provisions usually have direct effect (including between private parties), as long as they are sufficiently clear, precise and relevant to the situation of an individual litigant.[10]

In fact, the CJEU has established as a rule that 'by virtue of the very nature of regulations and of their function in the system of sources of Community law, the provisions of those regulations generally have immediate effect in the national legal systems without it being necessary for the national authorities to adopt measures of application'.[11] Hence, provisions of regulations do not have direct effect only in exceptional cases. In particular, this may happen where Member States enjoy discretion in respect of the implementation of those provisions,[12] and the CJEU indeed found in *Azienda*[13] that a provision of a regulation did not have direct effect since it specifically provided that Member States are to define a concept directly related to the personal scope of application of that regulation.[14] In contrast, in *Handlbauer*,[15] the CJEU found that a provision of a regulation had direct effect since it 'leaves the Member States no discretion nor does it require them to adopt implementation measures'.[16]

Article 82 GDPR does not leave any discretion to Member States to implement it, and it is clear and precise in establishing a right of any person who suffered material or non-material damage as a result of unlawful processing of personal data to receive compensation. Therefore, more than likely, Article 82 GDPR enjoys direct effect regardless of its implementation in national legislations,[17] and creates an EU-wide individual cause

---

[4] Ibid.   [5] See ibid. and Micklitz 2011.   [6] Art. 79 GDPR.

[7] The question whether the right to receive compensation after the damage has been suffered is sufficient to constitute an effective judicial remedy is at issue in the pending Case C-687/18, *Associated Newspapers*. See the commentaries on Arts. 79 and 85 in this volume.

[8] On the difference between regulations and directives see Craig and de Burca 2015, pp. 184 and 225.

[9] Art. 288 Treaty on the Functioning of the European Union ('TFEU').

[10] Craig and de Burca 2015, p. 198 and the case law cited therein.

[11] Case C-403/98, *Azienda*, para. 26.   [12] Ibid., para. 28.

[13] Ibid., in which the provisions of a regulation were not sufficiently precise and therefore could not be directly relied upon in national courts.

[14] This finding concerns the last paragraph of Art. 2(5) Council Regulation 797/85 and the last paragraph of Art. 5(5) Council Regulation 2328/91, which were identical and specifically stated that 'On the basis of the criteria referred to in the foregoing paragraph, the Member States shall define what is meant by this same expression in the case of persons other than natural persons'. The finding that they do not have direct effect was made in Case C-403/98, *Azienda*.

[15] Case C-278/02, *Handlbauer*.   [16] Ibid., para. 27.

[17] For a contrary opinion, see O'Dell 2017.

of action for any person that feels wronged with regard to processing of personal data falling under the GDPR, to initiate remedial actions in civil courts. The person can seek compensation from controllers and processors alike, under specific conditions which will be analysed below.

Ultimately, the detailed provisions in the GDPR concerning the remedies available to individuals to ensure that their data protection rights are effectively protected merely mirrors Article 47 of the Charter of Fundamental Rights of the European Union ('CFR' or 'Charter'), i.e. the right to an effective judicial remedy. This fundamental right has central importance in EU data protection law, since the CJEU has found that 'legislation not providing for any possibility for an individual to pursue legal remedies in order to have access to personal data relating to him, or to obtain the rectification or erasure of such data, does not respect the essence of the fundamental right to effective judicial protection as enshrined in Article 47 of the Charter'.[18] The Court added that 'the very existence of effective judicial review designed to ensure compliance with provisions of EU law is inherent in the existence of the rule of law'.[19] Whenever Article 82 GDPR is invoked before a court, as such or as implemented in national law, it will have to be applied in accordance with Article 47.

Finally, it should be highlighted that the possibility to bring a legal action against breaches of the GDPR and to seek compensation for any damages suffered, material or non-material, is also a manifestation of the principle of 'individual control' in EU data protection law. An individual challenging the processing of their personal data and causing judicial scrutiny of a breach of data protection law provides a means of individual control, beyond the rights of the data subject or the possibility to withdraw consent at any time. In contrast, one can observe the lack of individual causes of action in other systems, such as the US legal framework for protecting privacy, and in particular informational privacy. There, even the California Consumer Privacy Act, which is generally considered stringent and is set to enter into force on 1 January 2020, only provides for a limited individual cause of action in the case of data breaches.[20]

B. Legal Background

1. EU legislation

The DPD enshrined a similar right to compensation under Article 23, which under its first paragraph required Member States to provide that 'any person who has suffered damage as a result of an unlawful processing operation or of any act incompatible with the national provisions adopted pursuant to [the DPD] is entitled to receive compensation from the controller for the damage suffered'. Under the second paragraph, Article 23 DPD also established that the controller may be exempted from liability wholly or partially 'if he proves that he is not responsible for the event giving rise to the damage'. There are two main criticisms that can be made of the text of the DPD, the first being that it did not specifically include a reference to non-material damage,[21]

---

[18] Case C-362/14, *Schrems*, para. 95.   [19] Ibid.

[20] CCPA 2018. For a comparison of the judicial remedies available under the GDPR and the CCPA, see FPF and Dataguidance 2018, p. 39.

[21] Even though seemingly this was not the purpose of Art. 23 DPD, the lack of clarity allowed some Member States to exclude non-material damages from compensation following a remedial action for the breach

and the second that it did not contain any provisions regarding the liability exposure of processors.[22]

According to a report issued by the EU Fundamental Rights Agency on data protection remedies in the EU under the DPD, several Member States reported that compensation for non-material damages can also be granted by courts, with some Member States having set limits of the amount of compensation that can be awarded.[23] For example, the report noted that 'Austria sets an upper limit of € 20,000 for non-pecuniary damages, but the range of cases in other Member States suggests that awards of compensation are often much lower, ranging from € 300 to € 800 in Finland, up to €600 in Sweden, and from € 1,200 to € 12,000 in Poland'.[24] In fact, the survey conducted by FRA among individuals that sought redress in 16 EU Member States showed that they most commonly tended to describe damage caused them by breach of data protection law 'in psychological or social terms'[25] rather than in material form. For example, 'they focused on their emotions' and 'on the opinion of other people or the impact on their relations with other people', mentioning 'varying degrees of emotional distress, offence, insecurity (including feelings of being persecuted or under surveillance), helplessness or damage to their professional or personal reputation, loss of trust and other forms of moral damage'.[26]

The LED includes a right to compensation in Article 56, which requires Member States to provide 'for any person who has suffered material or non-material damage as a result of an unlawful processing operation or of any act infringing national provisions adopted pursuant to [the LED] to have the right to receive compensation for the damage suffered from the controller or any other authority competent under Member State law'. Notably, compared to Article 13 DPD, this provision specifically refers to making good non-material damage as well as material damage. Also, in contrast to the DPD, Article 56 LED does not include a clause that puts the burden of proof on controllers to show they did not give rise to the event causing the damage in order to be exonerated of liability. One important aspect with regard to liability of controllers under the LED is that controllers are always public authorities or bodies exercising public authority,[27] which means that the provisions of the LED that are sufficiently clear and precise are capable of direct effect in all situations that may give rise to a claim for damage under Article 56,[28] and also that the positive and negative obligations of the state stemming from Article 8 of the European Convention on Human Rights ('ECHR') on the respect of private life and the confidentiality of correspondence are directly visible in any relationship between controllers and the persons concerned.

One last observation with regard to Article 56 LED is that it does not provide for any specific rules on the liability of processors. However, the title of Article 54 LED is the 'right to an effective judicial remedy against a controller or processor', and the provision itself ensures this right for the data subject 'where he or she considers that his or her rights laid down in provisions adopted pursuant to [the LED] have been infringed as a result of the processing of his or her personal data in non-compliance with those provisions'. Just

---

of data protection law. See e.g. *Collins v FBD Insurance plc*, where the Irish court found that a requirement for actual damage precluded claims for non-pecuniary loss such as distress, pain and suffering, and the commentary in O'Dell 2017, p. 28.

[22] For a detailed analysis of liability exposure of processors under Art. 23 DPD, see van Alsenoy 2016, p. 277.

[23] FRA 2013, p. 21.   [24] Ibid.   [25] Ibid., p. 28.   [26] Ibid.   [27] Art. 3(8) LED.

[28] Under the doctrine of the vertical direct effect of directives, see Craig and de Burca 2015, pp. 200–206.

like the GDPR, the LED also provides for some specific obligations for processors, therefore it is conceivable that data subjects can bring an action against a breach of the LED committed by a processor in order to sanction non-compliance or to obtain an order or an injunction. However, if the data subject also seeks compensation for any damage that may have been caused by the action or omission of a processor, it seems that he or she can only receive compensation from the controller that has contracted with the processor. It is then between the controller and processor, under national rules on contractual liability or even non-contractual liability, depending on the facts, to re-equilibrate the losses taking into account the distribution of fault or negligence between the two.

The EPD contains a clause with a cross-reference to the DPD concerning judicial redress, namely Article 15(2), which establishes that the provisions of the DPD on judicial remedies, liability and sanctions apply with regard to national provisions adopted to transpose the EPD and 'with regard to the individual rights derived from this Directive'. As Article 94 GDPR that repeals the DPD specifies under the second paragraph that 'references to the repealed Directive shall be construed as references to this Regulation', this probably means that the entire GDPR chapter on remedies, liability and penalties (Chapter VIII), including Article 82, is *de jure* applicable to the national laws transposing the EPD and to the individual rights derived from the EPD. The situation of an entire modernised chapter on remedies transplanted from a regulation to an outdated directive that has been transposed in a disparate way by Member States in their national laws, including with regard to enforcement of sanctions,[29] creates legal uncertainty and is yet another reason for the reform of the ePrivacy framework to be pushed across the finish line as soon as possible.[30]

The EUDPR governing data processing by the EU institutions and bodies provides for a right to compensation under Article 65, ensuring that any person who has suffered material or non-material damage as a result of an infringement of that regulation has the right to receive compensation from the Union institution or body for the damage suffered, subject to the conditions provided for in the treaties. It is thus relevant to recall that Article 340(2) TFEU specifically provides that in the case of non-contractual liability, the Union shall 'make good any damage caused by its institutions or by its servants in the performance of their duties'. However, losses are recoverable only if they are certain and specific, proven and quantifiable.[31] Additionally, it is settled case law that a number of conditions must be satisfied to engage the non-contractual liability of the Union on behalf of its institutions, namely that the institution's conduct must be unlawful, actual damage must have been suffered and there must be a causal link between the conduct and the damage pleaded.[32] In general, the CJEU grants damages for losses actually sustained, and will only exceptionally award compensation for non-material damage.[33] One of the

---

[29] One aspect where the disparate transposition of the EPD is evident concerns the appointing of the competent authority to enforce sanctions. According to the Commission, Member States have often allocated competences to enforce the provisions of the EPD to multiple authorities within their country rather than to one: data protection authorities, telecom national regulatory authorities and other types of bodies (consumer protection bodies). Overall, in the majority of Member States, DPAs are the bodies most appointed as enforcers of the EPD, but they are the sole competent authority in charge of EPD rules only in Italy, Luxembourg, Spain and Romania and the main authority in Portugal, Lithuania and Czech Republic. See EC Staff Working Document 2017, p. 19.

[30] See EPR Proposal. The proposal had not yet been adopted when this text was finalised.

[31] Craig and de Burca 2015, p. 599 and the case law cited therein.

[32] Case C-452/05, *Belgian Sewing Thread*, para. 163.

[33] Craig and de Burca 2015, p. 600.

cases where the CJEU granted compensation for non-material damage (*V. v EP*) concerns the application of the predecessor to the EUDPR, the former data protection Regulation 45/2001,[34] and will be discussed below.

2. International instruments

Modernised Convention 108 does not provide for an individual cause of action to sanction non-compliance with its provisions, nor for obtaining compensation as a result of those breaches. However, Article 12 creates an obligation for the signatory countries 'to establish appropriate judicial and non-judicial sanctions and remedies for violations of the provisions of this Convention'. The Explanatory Report to the Modernised Convention confirms that in the absence of 'sanctions and remedies' an effective level of data protection will not in fact be guaranteed.[35] The Convention allows a wide margin of appreciation to the signatory states on how to implement the remedial aspect of guaranteeing the rights it enshrines. As such, each party may determine the nature—be it 'civil, administrative, criminal'[36]—of the judicial or non-judicial sanctions. However, the Explanatory Report clarifies with regard to remedies that 'data subjects must have the possibility to judicially challenge a decision or practice'.[37] Additionally, the Convention does have a stronger mandate for its signatories to provide for a 'remedy' when any of the rights enshrined in it are breached. Article 9(f) specifically requires that every individual has a right 'to have a remedy under Article 12 where his or her rights under this Convention have been violated'. This provision seems to specifically address the rights enumerated in Article 9, such as information, access, erasure and objection; read together with the Explanatory Report it implies that remedies for breaching these rights should be of a judicial nature.[38]

As for the possibility to ask for compensation for any damages caused by a breach of the Convention, the recommendation made in the Explanatory Report is quite weak, since parties are only encouraged to potentially consider such a remedy: 'Financial compensation for material and non-material damages, where applicable, caused by the processing and collection actions could also be considered'.[39] While the effects of this provision will entirely depend on the national legal systems of the parties to the Convention, some general observations can be made with regard to those parties that are also members of the Council of Europe and, thus, parties to the ECHR and fall under the jurisdiction of the ECtHR. These countries can be held responsible, pursuant to Article 41 ECHR, to provide just satisfaction including compensation for material and non-material damages for any breaches of the ECHR, including breaches of Article 8—the right to respect for private and family life and the confidentiality of correspondence, whose adjudication oftentimes involves considerations stemming from Convention 108 made by the ECtHR. In fact, a quantitative study has found that awards under Article 41 ECHR 'made in respect of non-pecuniary damage in cases concerning the protected legal interest

---

[34] See Table of Legislation.   [35] Explanatory Report Convention 108 2018, para. 99.
[36] Ibid., para. 100.   [37] Ibid.
[38] Explanatory Report Convention 108 2018 differentiates, ibid., para. 100 between 'sanctions', which according to the first sentence of the paragraph can be judicial or non-judicial, and 'remedies', for which the third sentence of the paragraph specifically states that 'data subjects must have the possibility to judicially challenge a decision or practice, the definition of the modalities to do so being left with the Parties'.
[39] Ibid.

of "private and family life" are considerably high, ranging second after "life, physical and mental integrity".[40]

The OECD Guidelines,[41] on the other hand, do not enshrine any provision or recommendation that would entitle an individual to seek a remedy, be it judicial or non-judicial, against a practice that breaches the Guidelines, a fact which ultimately makes them lack effectiveness. The original explanatory memorandum to the 1980 OECD guidelines mentions 'the right to challenge data' that individuals have, as meaning that they also have the right to challenge data in 'courts, administrative bodies, professional organs or other institutions according to domestic rules of procedures'.[42] However, such challenges only relate to accuracy of the personal data being processed since, according to Principle 13(d), a successful challenge can only lead to data being 'erased, rectified, completed or amended'. Principle 19 of the updated 2013 Guidelines provides that OECD Members, when implementing the Guidelines, should, among other things, adopt laws protecting privacy and provide for adequate sanctions and remedies in case of failures to comply with laws protecting privacy.

The weak provisions from Convention 108 regarding judicial remedies and compensation, and the virtual non-existence of such provisions in the OECD Guidelines, heighten the extraordinary character of the prerogatives that individuals have under EU data protection law to seek an effective judicial redress, including the right to receive compensation for any material or non-material damages caused to them as provided by Article 82 GDPR.

3. National developments

Non-contractual liability is a legal institution deeply entrenched in national legal systems, most of the time provided for in general terms by civil codes or other statutes,[43] unless developed through common law as specific torts.[44] In practice, this means that national courts may apply different criteria to quantify damage or to find that non-contractual liability is engaged in a particular case. However, in the field of data protection law, this should happen only to the extent the national provisions or mechanisms are not contrary to Articles 79 and 82 of the GDPR and Article 47 of the Charter.

The type of remedial action provided by Article 82 GDPR is closely connected to the general non-contractual liability regimes of the EU Member States. Therefore, any effects of Article 82 in actual litigation will be highly dependent on these regimes and the practice developed by national courts applying them. Some examples on how compensation for breaches of data protection law has developed at national level will be provided below. It is important to point out, though, that Article 82 GDPR is directly applicable to all national legal systems of the EU Member States, since it is provided by an EU regulation,

---

[40] Altwicker-Hamori et al. 2015, p. 35.   [41] OECD Guidelines 2013.   [42] Ibid., p. 59.

[43] See e.g. Art. 1240 French Civil Code (former Art. 1382); Art. 1382 Belgian Civil Code; Art. 823 German Civil Code; Art. 1357 (the general clause for compensation for damages caused by non-contractual liability) and Art. 253(4) (compensation for damages caused to personality rights) Romanian Civil Code; Art. 1902 Spanish Civil Code.

[44] According to von Bar and Drobnig, it is possible to distinguish among at least three groups of jurisdictions in Europe on the construction of the law of liability for breach of duty: English and Irish Common Law with its system of individual torts; Continental Europe, which has its starting point in one (sometimes subdivided) basic tort law provision; and Scandinavia, which relies on a similar basic tort law provision called the 'culpa-rule'. Von Bar and Drobnig 2004, pp. 26 and 27.

and likely has direct effect. Together with the principle of the supremacy of EU law, this means that any application of liability rules by national courts must comply and align with the conditions set out in Article 82, even when they contradict or supplement the law and practice of non-contractual liability in the national legal systems concerned.

Beyond the specifics of national regimes for non-contractual liability, there are also national flavours to implementation of Article 82. For example, the UK Data Protection Act[45] clarifies under Article 182(1) that 'non-material damage includes distress' pursuant to Article 82 GDPR. In addition, Article 182(3) of the Act establishes that a court may make an order providing for the compensation to be paid not only directly to the data subject, but also to the representative body that brought a case on behalf of the data subject or to 'such other person as the court thinks fit'. This provision primarily concerns the scenario laid out by Article 80 GDPR on representation of data subjects.[46]

The Spanish law implementing the GDPR[47] contains some specific provisions with regard to the application of Article 82 GDPR to controllers or processors not established in the Union. Article 30(2) of the law provides that when liability is engaged pursuant to the conditions of Article 82 GDPR, 'controllers, processors and legal representatives shall be jointly and severally liable for the damages and losses caused'. Thus, the Spanish law establishes the liability of legal representatives for breaches of the GDPR, seemingly going beyond the requirements of Article 27 GDPR, which under paragraph 4 merely requires legal representatives to be 'addressed' in addition to or instead of controllers or processors by data subjects, making them more like an official point of contact (like an 'inbox' for requests, legal actions, complaints) than actually responsible entities for failure of controllers or processors to comply with their obligations under the GDPR. This provision also builds on Article 82 GDPR, which only provides for liability of controllers and processors.

The German implementation of the GDPR[48] also addresses the role of the legal representative in judicial proceedings. First, it provides under section 44(1) that the proceedings against a controller or processor for a violation of data protection law, including actions under Article 82 GDPR, may be brought by a data subject 'before the court in the place where the controller or processor has an establishment' or 'before the court in the place where the data subject has his or her habitual residence'. Section 44(3) further establishes that where controllers and processors have designated a legal representative, the latter 'shall also be an authorized recipient in civil law proceedings' and that 'Section 184 of the Code of Civil Procedure shall remain unaffected'. This particular section of the German Code of Civil Procedure provides that a court may order a party to a civil litigation 'to name, within a reasonable period of time, an authorized recipient who is a resident of Germany or who has business premises in Germany, unless the party has appointed an attorney of record'. The provision also refers to the timeline for serving court documents. Therefore, section 44(3) of the law implementing the GDPR in Germany read together with section 184 of the German Code of Civil Procedure seem to indicate that indeed the legal representative has more of a procedural role than actually being held responsible together with the controller and/or processor for their failure to comply with the GDPR.

---

[45] UK Data Protection Act 2018.
[46] See commentary on Art. 80 in this volume.
[47] Spanish Data Protection Act 2018.
[48] German GDPR Implementation Law.

4. Case law

4.1 CJEU

The CJEU has not been called upon to interpret Article 23 DPD, the predecessor of Article 82 GDPR, in a preliminary ruling procedure. However, it has had the opportunity to analyse and apply rules concerning compensation for breaching data protection obligations in the context of adjudicating upon former Regulation 45/2001 on the processing of personal data by EU institutions and bodies, together with rules on compensation stemming from the non-contractual liability of the Union.[49]

In *Nikolaou v Commission*,[50] the Court of First Instance found that the unauthorised disclosure to the media of certain information about an investigation of the European Anti-Fraud Office ('OLAF') concerning the applicant constituted unlawful processing in violation of Article 5 of Regulation 45/2001.[51] In particular, a leak of personal data constituted a serious and manifest breach of the law.[52] Moreover, the further publication of a press release about an ongoing investigation containing personal data of the applicant was also done in breach of Article 5 of the Regulation.[53] In consequence, OLAF seriously and manifestly exceeded the limits of its discretion in the application of Article 5 of Regulation 45/2001, which was sufficient to engage the liability of the Union.[54] In view of all these findings, the Court of First Instance established that both the leaks and the publication of the press release were attributable to illegal acts committed by OLAF which were the source of some but not all of the negative information published about the applicant in the media.[55] Hence, the Court decided to award € 3,000 as compensation for non-material damage.

The case of *V. v EP*[56] concerned a complaint regarding misuse of health data by the Parliament and the Commission, in particular stemming from an inter-institutional data transfer of the complainants' health file, during a selection procedure, which led to a job offer being retracted. The applicant complained that the medical officer of the Parliament, instead of proceeding to a consultation, issued his opinion about her general health condition on the basis of documents received from the Commission, which were collected exclusively with a view to recruiting the applicant into the services of that institution[57] two years prior to the events in the main proceedings, and were not to be shared across EU institutions whenever the person would apply for a new job, without her consent. The Court found that in this case the Parliament breached the right to privacy of the applicant and several provisions of Regulation 45/2001. The Court took into account that 'medical data are particularly sensitive data', that 'those data were collected nearly two years beforehand, for a well-defined purpose, by an institution with which the applicant did not, as a consequence of the procedure for ascertaining medical fitness for recruitment, have an employment relationship' and that the Parliament 'could have fulfilled its task under conditions involving less interference with the applicant's fundamental rights'. In consequence, the applicant received both material and non-material compensation following this breach, including € 5,000 for material damage'.[58] As for the non-material

---

[49] Art. 340(2) TFEU and the case law developed by the CJEU in its application.
[50] Case T-259/03, *Nikolaou v Commission*.
[51] Ibid., para. 206–209. For a summary, see Laudati 2016, p. 32.
[52] Case T-259/03, *Nikolaou v Commission*, para. 213.   [53] Ibid., paras. 230–231.
[54] Ibid., para. 232.   [55] Ibid., para. 333.   [56] Case F-46/09, *V. v EP*.   [57] Ibid.
[58] Ibid., para. 166.

damage, the Court took into account that 'the annulment of the administration's unlawful act cannot constitute full reparation for the non-material damage if that act contains an assessment of the abilities and conduct of the person concerned which is capable of offending the person'.[59] It further held that 'the Parliament's assessment concerning the applicant's attitude, made in the decision at issue and in the reply to the complaint, can, to a certain extent, be regarded as offensive to her' since the European Parliament alleged that she intentionally withheld information, 'calling into question the applicant's good faith'.[60] Thus, 'the Parliament's assessments, set out in a decision already characterized as unlawful ... , directly caused non-material damage to the applicant',[61] and the Court awarded € 20,000 as compensation for non-material damage.

In another case brought against the Parliament, which concerned the publication on the internet of a summary of a petition which disclosed the name of the applicant and information about his and his son's health condition,[62] the Court did not find a breach of Regulation 45/2001 and, as a consequence, did not award any damages. After he discovered that the personal data from the petition were published on the internet, the applicant had requested the Parliament to delete the data and after insisting managed to obtain deletion.[63] The applicant had requested compensation for both material damages—the cost of fees he paid to legal counsel to request erasure of the information prior to the legal proceedings, and non-material damages. First, the Court found that the publication of the personal data included in the summary of the petition was lawful, since the applicant had been informed about the possibility of such publication when submitting the online form and had not expressly requested that his petition be treated confidentially, which the Court considered as being an informed, express consent.[64] The Court did not grant any compensation for material damage to the applicant, since it found that the cost of seeking legal advice could not be imputed to the Parliament.[65] With regard to non-material damage, the Court held that 'it is for the party seeking to establish the European Union's liability to adduce proof as to the existence or extent of the damage alleged and to establish a sufficiently direct causal link between that damage and the conduct complained of on the part of the institution concerned'.[66] The Court finally found that 'the applicant has not demonstrated the existence of such damage', since he 'merely claimed that the Parliament's dismissive and dilatory attitude hurt him deeply and caused him considerable stress, without providing any evidence in support of his claim'.[67]

4.2 ECtHR

In *I. v Finland*,[68] the ECtHR made some important findings on the effectiveness of awarding damages for non-contractual liability for breaches of Article 8 ECHR involving the unlawful processing of personal data. The case was initiated by a former nurse in an ophthalmologic polyclinic whose detailed health condition (she was infected with HIV) was discovered by her colleagues unlawfully accessing her patient data, which led her to change employers. The Court noted that the applicant had lost her civil action in national courts because she was unable to prove a causal connection between the deficiencies of the process for accessing medical records in the hospital and the dissemination of information about her medical condition. The Court considered that the applicant should not

---

[59] Ibid., para. 169 and the case law cited therein. [60] Ibid., para. 170. [61] Ibid.
[62] Case T-343/13, *CN v EP*. [63] Ibid., paras. 7–13. [64] Ibid., paras. 76 and 80.
[65] Ibid., para. 124. [66] Ibid., para. 119. [67] Ibid., para. 121.
[68] ECtHR, *I v Finland*.

have been put under such a strict burden of proof,[69] and found it decisive that the case management system used by the hospital was in breach of the legal requirements of the national data protection law in Finland, 'a fact that was not given due weight by the domestic courts'.[70] Ultimately, the Court held that the mere fact that domestic legislation 'provided the applicant with an opportunity to claim compensation for damages caused by an alleged unlawful disclosure of personal data was not sufficient to protect her private life. What is required in this connection is practical and effective protection to exclude any possibility of unauthorised access occurring in the first place',[71] which was not the case here. The Court thus found a breach of Article 8 ECHR and also decided to award € 8,000 in non-material damage under Article 41 ECHR 'as a result of the State's failure to adequately secure her patient record against the risk of unauthorized access'.[72]

In two cases concerning Lithuanian citizens, the ECtHR had the opportunity to decide whether a ceiling for damages awarded by national courts as a result of breaches of Article 8 ECHR complied with the Convention. Both applicants complained that the state had breached their right to respect for private life 'as a result of the derisory sum of non-pecuniary damages awarded' to them, even though the domestic courts had found that a serious violation of their privacy occurred, given that the national law established an unsatisfactory maximum ceiling for compensation of damages caused by mass media for unintentional breach of privacy (set at LTL 10,000—or approximately € 3,500, for regular breaches and LTL 50,000 for breaches degrading the dignity of the person).[73] Both cases concerned the publication by a daily newspaper of an article claiming that the threat of AIDS was imminent in a remote village of Lithuania, since it was confirmed by medical staff that the applicants were HIV positive. One of the applicants was described as 'notoriously promiscuous' and was said to have had two illegitimate children with the first applicant, who was married to another woman.[74] The publication of the article caused public humiliation and the applicants' exclusion from the social life of the village.[75] The Court found that while the government enjoys a certain margin of appreciation in deciding what respect for private life requires in particular circumstances, any financial limits with regard to compensation for non-pecuniary damage 'must not be such as to deprive the individual of his or her privacy and thereby empty the right of its effective content'.[76] The Court further found that 'severe legislative limitations on judicial discretion in redressing the damage suffered by the victim and sufficiently deterring the recurrence of such abuses failed to provide the applicant with the protection that could have legitimately been expected under Article 8 of the Convention'.[77] Therefore, according to the ECtHR, a legislative framework that impairs just satisfaction for damages resulting from the breach of the right to respect for private life is in itself a breach of that right.

Insufficient legal means to seek judicial redress for breach of Article 8 was also at the core of the ECtHR's findings in *Pruteanu*.[78] This case concerned the interception of conversations between a lawyer, the applicant in this case, and one of his clients as part of an investigation for fraud. The client was a business partner of two other persons who were

---

[69] Ibid., para. 44. [70] Ibid. [71] Ibid., para. 47. [72] Ibid., para. 55.
[73] ECtHR, *Biriuk v Lithuania*, para. 22; and ECtHR, *Armoniene v Lithuania*, para. 22.
[74] ECtHR, *Biriuk v Lithuania*, para. 6. [75] Ibid., para. 41.
[76] ECtHR, *Armoniene v Lithuania*, para. 46.
[77] ECtHR, *Biriuk v Lithuania*, para. 46; and ECtHR, *Armoniene v Lithuania*, para. 47.
[78] ECtHR, *Pruteanu*.

indicted by prosecutors but was not herself among those officially accused. However, the interceptions of her conversations with her lawyer were included as evidence in the file. Considering that the only way the applicant could have challenged the lawfulness of the interceptions was during a criminal trial against himself or against his client, the Court concluded that the accessibility of a remedy for the applicant was uncertain.[79] As regards a possible action for damages (which was pointed out by the Romanian government as an alternative means of redress), the Court stated that the government did not provide any example of case law which would prove the effectiveness of this particular remedy. In addition, a complaint in civil court regarding the non-contractual civil liability of the state could not be seen as an 'effective control' for the purposes of Article 8 ECHR.[80] The Court concluded there was a violation of Article 8 since the interference was disproportionate and the applicant had not had access to an effective judicial remedy in order to limit the interference to what is necessary in a democratic society.[81]

4.3 National courts

A brief review of judicial practice in some EU Member States prior to the entry into force of the GDPR shows that non-contractual liability for breaches of data protection law and personality resulting from the unlawful processing of personal data bears the strong imprint of national liability regimes. At the same time, they also show how national courts are sometimes willing to consider matters of EU law or European human rights law when deciding on the effects of non-contractual liability in the context of data protection.

The UK case *Google v Vidal-Hall*[82] recognised for the first time a tort of misuse of private information[83] and acknowledged that individuals can also seek compensation for non-material damage for a breach of data protection law. The essence of the complaint was that Google collected private information about the claimants' internet usage via the Apple Safari browser, without the claimants' knowledge and consent, by using cookies. This private information was aggregated and used to create targeted ads which revealed private information that might have been viewed by third parties. The claimants alleged that their personal dignity, autonomy and integrity were violated and claimed damages for anxiety and distress.[84] One of the questions at issue was the meaning of 'damage' in Article 13 of the UK Data Protection Act (prior to the GDPR implementation), which expressly allowed compensation for non-material damages caused by breaches of data protection law only in the cases where there is also a pecuniary loss, or where processing of data occurs for journalistic, artistic and literary purposes. The Court first established that the situation of the claimants did not fall in any of the two conditions necessary for them to be awarded compensation for non-pecuniary damage. Acknowledging that the UK Data Protection Act was transposing the DPD, the Court further analysed whether 'damage in Article 23 of the Directive includes non-pecuniary loss' and decided that:

Since what the Directive purports to protect is privacy rather than economic rights, it would be strange if the Directive could not compensate those individuals whose data privacy had been invaded by a data controller so as to cause them emotional distress (but not pecuniary damage). It is the distressing invasion of privacy which must be taken to be the primary form of damage

[79] Ibid., para. 54. [80] Ibid., para. 55. [81] Ibid., para. 56.
[82] Court of Appeal of England and Wales, *Google Inc. v Vidal-Hall*. [83] Ibid., para. 51.
[84] For a summary of the judgment see EDPS 2015, pp. 58–61.

(commonly referred to in the European context as 'moral damage') and the data subject should have an effective remedy in respect of that damage.[85]

Grounding its decision on Articles 7, 8 and 47 of the Charter, the Court of Appeal decided to disapply Article 13(2) of the national law, which meant that compensation would be recoverable under Article 13(1) 'for any damage suffered as a result of a contravention by a data controller of any of the requirements of the Data Protection Act'.[86]

In contrast, in civil law systems non-contractual liability of the controller caused by unlawful processing of personal data can be engaged on the basis of the general clauses that are usually enshrined in the Civil Code. For example, in a case before the Romanian courts,[87] the applicant sought compensation for non-material damage caused by unlawful processing of personal data, grounding his claim in (former) Articles 998 and 999 of the Civil Code (which provide that everyone who, through his or her fault or negligence, causes damage to another must compensate that person for the damage caused). The municipality of *Sectorul 1* Bucharest published online personal data related to health of the applicant, and in particular about his infection with the HIV virus, after he had applied for a subsidised public transportation subscription. The Municipality published online the unredacted decision concerning the applicant, including the reason for which he was granted the subsidy. In order to reach its decision, the Court assessed whether an unlawful act had occurred, whether the respondent was responsible for that act, whether the act caused damage to the applicant and, finally, whether there was a causal link between the act and the damage. It found that all four conditions were met in this case and awarded € 10,000 in moral damages. Thus, it seems that the mere finding of unlawful processing of personal data is sufficient to establish the existence of an unlawful act and the causal link, while the existence of damage seems to be dependent on the nature of the personal data subject to the unlawful processing and the nature of the subjective rights breached by that unlawful processing.

C. Analysis

1. Introduction

National courts are the ones that have to deal with whether damages should be awarded for breaches of data protection law in the first instance, and actions before them are usually based on the general clauses in national civil law for engaging non-contractual liability. In an exhaustive study published in 2004, von Bar and Drobnig noted that 'the existing national laws of tort in the European Union differ substantially in their taxonomy and structure'.[88] With the successive waves of enlargement, the landscape of European tort law has become even more diverse.[89] To add to the complexity, in addition to the general liability clauses usually found in civil codes (or principles of general tort law in common law systems), and due to the fact that 'the main focus of the protection of human dignity from a private law point of view runs all through non-contractual liability',[90] many European states have also adopted special legislation dedicated to the

---

[85] Court of Appeal of England and Wales, *Google Inc. v Vidal-Hall*, para. 77.
[86] Ibid, para. 105.
[87] Romanian Court of First Instance, judgment of 16 March 2009. The decision was upheld in appeal by the Tribunal of Bucharest on 10 October 2010.
[88] Von Bar and Drobnig 2004, p. 26.   [89] See e.g. Oliphant 2012.
[90] Von Bar and Drobnig 2004, p. 32.

protection of incorporeal patrimonial and non-patrimonial rights, such as personality rights.[91] The task of finding common ground to interpret and apply Article 82 GDPR across the EU is not easy, but also not impossible.

2. Article 82 directly applicable

First of all, as discussed above, Article 82 GDPR is directly applicable in the national systems of the Member States, since it is provided in an EU Regulation and more than likely meets the conditions for direct effect. This means that even if Article 82 is not implemented in national legislation, or if it is implemented in a way that is not compatible with the GDPR (e.g. by allowing compensation only for material damage), both national courts and other public authorities,[92] as the case may be, can disapply the national law and apply Article 82 directly. Article 82 also reverses the situations in some Member State prior to the GDPR, in which the burden of proof rested with the claimant, and national law did not allow for the recovery of immaterial damages. This was the case, for example, under German law.[93]

3. Clear and cumulative rules

Secondly, Article 82 GDPR establishes clear, cumulative rules with regard to identifying and engaging the non-contractual liability of the controller or processor. This requires the following elements:

1. the existence of an infringement of any provision of the GDPR, including processing that infringes delegated and implementing acts adopted in accordance with the GDPR and Member State law[94]
2. the existence of a material or non-material damage caused to the person claiming compensation (who does not necessarily need to fit the definition of a 'data subject', since Article 82(1) confers the right to compensation to 'any person who has suffered' damage) and
3. a causal link between the infringement and the damage.

What will likely vary in national application of these rules is the threshold relied on by civil courts to identify damage as a consequence of a breach of data protection law, and especially non-material damage, as well as the scrutiny with which the causal link between the unlawful processing of personal data and the damage will be assessed. For example, courts in some civil law systems may find a breach of data protection rights is sufficient to

---

[91] Ibid., where the author gives as example the Portugese Civil Code which has 'especially numerous' rules about the protection of particular rights of personality (Arts. 70–81). To this example, one can add the Romanian Civil Code that entered into force in 2011, which dedicates one Chapter to 'the respect owed to the human being and his or her inherent rights' (Arts. 58–81), and another one specifically to judicial remedies for protecting 'non-patrimonial rights' (Arts. 252–257). For a detailed analysis of how the general non-contractual civil liability clause, the special non-contractual liability clause for breach of non-patrimonial rights and the special non-contractual liability clause stemming from data protection law interact in the Romanian legal system, see Zanfir 2015, pp. 233–306.

[92] See e.g. Case C-378/17, *Minister for Justice and Equality*, where the Court established that EU law, in particular the principle of primacy, must be interpreted as precluding national legislation under which a national body established by law in order to ensure enforcement of EU law lacks jurisdiction to disapply a rule of national law that is contrary to EU law.

[93] See Hess 2017, p. 256.   [94] Rec. 146 GDPR.

receive compensation, meaning that proving the existence of some quantifiable damage is not required.[95]

4. Existence of fault

Thirdly, Article 82 GDPR does not require the existence of fault when establishing the liability of controllers or processors. This needs to be emphasised, since another instance of disparate practice across the Union concerns the issue of 'fault' or 'strict' liability, meaning that depending on the practice related to non-contractual liability in a given legal system, civil courts may be tempted to seek to establish 'fault' or 'responsibility' of the controller or processor in order to engage their liability. The rule imposed by Article 82(2) is that 'any controller involved' in the unlawful processing is liable for the damage caused. This means that once it is shown that the processing at issue breaches any provision of the GDPR, the controller (or the joint controllers, as the case may be) is responsible for that unlawful processing and, to the extent that damage was caused by it, the controller will have to provide compensation for that damage. This conclusion is also supported by the accountability principle, which provides that the controller is responsible for demonstrating compliance with the principles relating to the processing of personal data under the GDPR,[96] meaning that any unlawful processing is imputable to the controller, regardless of intention, fault or negligence. Article 82(2) also clarifies that processors are only liable for damages in two situations: when they breach obligations specifically imposed on them under the GDPR, and where the processor has acted outside or contrary to the instructions of the controller.

5. Exemption from liability

Article 82(3) provides controllers and processors with a possible defence, namely that they may be exempt from liability if they prove that they are not 'in any way responsible for the event giving rise to the damage'. Following the logic of Article 82(1) GDPR, the event giving rise to the damage could only be an 'infringement of the Regulation'. Therefore, controllers may be exempt from liability if they prove that, in fact, they are not controllers of the unlawful processing causing the damage, or if they prove that the damage was caused by a processor acting outside of or contrary to the mandate received from the controller. Similarly, processors may be exempt from liability if they prove that the event giving rise to the damage is in fact a consequence of an action they conducted on behalf of the controller within their mandate.

6. Joint and several liability

To the extent they are responsible for the unlawful processing causing the damage, controllers and processors are jointly and severally liable for it. Article 82(4) establishes that

---

[95] See e.g. French Cour de Cassation, 94-14.798, where the court found that the mere finding there was an invasion of privacy as provided by Art. 9 French Civil Code gives a right to compensation; and the Romanian court in Curtea de Apel Cluj, Decizia nr. 88/A, where the court found that 'there are situations where the existence of damage is not required as one of the conditions to receive compensation. The violations of the right to respect for private life as they are detailed in Article 73(a) to (i) of the New Civil Code may justify compensation by themselves, without having the need to prove damage exists, being self-sufficient in order to obtain compensation as provided by the New Civil Code'.
[96] See Art. 5(2) GDPR.

where more than one controller or processor, or both a controller and a processor, 'are involved in the same processing' and they are responsible for any damage caused by that processing, 'each controller or processor shall be held liable for the entire damage in order to ensure effective compensation of the data subject'. This provision can be seen as a consequence of the fundamental right to effective judicial protection provided by Article 47 of the Charter, applied together with the right to personal data protection provided by Article 8 of the Charter. Indeed, 'full and effective compensation of the data subject'[97] must be the goal of any compensatory measure. However, the GDPR allows compensation to be 'apportioned according to the responsibility of each controller or processor for the damage caused by the processing'.[98] In accordance with Article 82(5), if one of the entities held jointly and severally responsible for compensation of damages pays the entire compensation for the damage incurred, that entity has the right to claim back from the other controllers and processors involved in the unlawful processing 'that part of the compensation corresponding to their part of responsibility for the damage'.

7. Jurisdiction

Finally, it should be noted that pursuant to Article 82(6), court proceedings for exercising the right to receive compensation can be brought either before the courts of the Member State where the controller or processor has an establishment, or before the courts of the Member State where the data subject has his or her habitual residence. The person claiming compensation does not have a choice of jurisdictions when the controller is a public authority of a Member State acting in the exercise of its public powers: in such situations, the Member State where that authority is established has jurisdiction. As *lex specialis*, these provisions of the GDPR will have priority over other general jurisdictional rules, in particular regarding proceedings seeking a judicial remedy including compensation.[99] However, it has also been argued that the rules of the recast Brussels I Regulation should continue to apply to the extent that they are compatible with the GDPR.[100]

Select Bibliography

International agreements

OECD Guidelines 2013: Organisation for Economic Co-operation and Development, 'The OECD Privacy Framework' (2013).

EU legislation

Brussels I Regulation (recast): Regulation (EU) No. 1215/2012 of the European Parliament and of the Council of 12 December 2012 on jurisdiction and the recognition and enforcement of judgments in civil and commercial matters (recast), OJ 2012 L 351/1.
Council Regulation 797/85: Council Regulation (EEC) No. 797/85 of 12 March 1985 on improving the efficiency of agricultural structures, OJ 1985 L 93/1.
Council Regulation 2328/91: Council Regulation (EEC) No. 2328/91 of 15 July 1991 on improving the efficiency of agricultural structures, OJ 1991 L 218/1.
EPR Proposal: Proposal for a Regulation of the European Parliament and of the Council concerning the respect for private life and the protection of personal data in electronic communications

---

[97] Rec. 146 GDPR. [98] Ibid. [99] See rec. 147 GDPR.
[100] See the commentary on Art. 79 in this volume.

and repealing Directive 2002/58/EC (Regulation on Privacy and Electronic Communications), COM(2017)10 final, 10 January 2017.

National legislation

Belgian Civil Code: Burgerlijk Wetboek van 21 maart 1804; Code civil du 21 mars 1804.
CCPA 2018: California Consumer Privacy Act of 2018, AB375, Title 1.81.5.
French Civil Code: Code civil, version consolidée au 1 octobre 2018.
German Civil Code: Bürgerliches Gesetzbuch, in der Fassung der Bekanntmachung vom 02.01.2002, BGBl. 2003 Teil I Nr. 42.
German GDPR Implementation Law: Gesetz zur Anpassung des Datenschutzrechts an die Verordnung (EU) 2016/679 und zur Umsetzung der Richtlinie (EU) 2016/680 (Datenschutz-Anpassungs- und Umsetzungsgesetz EU – DsAnpUG-EU), BGBl 2017 Teil 1 Nr. 44.
Portugese Civil Code: Código Civil, DL n.º 47344/66, de 25 de Novembro.
Romanian Civil Code: Noul Cod Civil actualizat 2018 – Legea 287/2009.
Spanish Civil Code: Real Decreto de 24 de julio de 1889 por el que se publica el Código Civil.
Spanish Data Protection Act 2018: Ley Orgánica 3/2018, de 5 de diciembre, de Protección de Datos y de Garantía de los Derechos Digitales.
UK Data Protection Act 2018: Data Protection Act 2018 (Chapter 12).

Academic writings

Altwicker-Hamori et al. 2015: Altwicker-Hamori, Altwicker and Peters, 'Measuring Violations of Human Rights: An Empirical Analysis of Awards in Respect of Non-Pecuniary Damage under the European Convention on Human Rights', 76 *Heidelberg Journal of International Law* (2016), 1.
Craig and de Burca 2015: Craig and de Burca, *EU Law: Text, Cases and Materials* (6th edn, OUP 2015).
Hess 2017: Hess, 'Die EU-Datenschutzverordnung und das europäische Prozessrecht', in Schütze (ed.), *Fairness Justice Equity: Festschrift für Reinhold Geimer zum 80. Geburtstag* (C. H. Beck 2017), 255.
Micklitz 2011: Micklitz, 'The ECJ between the Individual Citizen and the Member States—A Plea for a Judge-Made European Law on Remedies', 15 *EUI Working Paper LAW* (2011), available at http://cadmus.eui.eu/handle/1814/19494.
O'Dell 2017: O'Dell, 'Compensation for Breach of the General Data Protection Regulation', 40(1) *Dublin University Law Journal* (2017), 97.
Oliphant 2012: Oliphant, 'Cultures of Tort Law in Europe', 3(2) *Journal of European Tort Law* (2012), 147.
Thomas 2004: Thomas, 'Ubi Jus, Ibi Remedium: The Fundamental Right to a Remedy under Due Process', 41(4) *San Diego Law Review* (2004), 1633.
Van Alsenoy 2016: Van Alsenoy, 'Liability under EU Data Protection Law: From Directive 95/46 to the General Data Protection Regulation', 7(3) *Journal of Intellectual Property, Information Technology and Electronic Commerce Law* (2016), 271.
Van Gerven 2000: Van Gerven, 'Of Rights, Remedies and Procedures', 37(3) *Common Market Law Review* (2000), 501.
Von Bar and Drobnig 2004: Von Bar and Drobnig, *The Interaction of Contract Law and Tort and Property Law in Europe. A Comparative Study* (Sellier European Law Publishers 2004).
Zanfir 2015: Zanfir, *Protecția datelor personale. Drepturile persoanei vizate* (C. H. Beck 2015).

Papers of data protection authorities

EDPS 2015: European Data Protection Supervisor, 'Case Law Overview. 1 December 2014–31 December 2015' (15 March 2016).

Reports and recommendations

EC Staff Working Document 2017: Commission Staff Working Document 'Ex-post REFIT Evaluation of the ePrivacy Directive 2002/58/EC', SWD(2017) 5 final, 10 January 2017.

Explanatory Report Convention 108 2018: Council of Europe, 'Explanatory Report to the Protocol Amending the Convention for the Protection of Individuals with Regard to the Automatic Processing of Personal Data' (10 October 2018), available at https://rm.coe.int/cets-223-explanatory-report-to-the-protocol-amending-the-convention-fo/16808ac91a.

FPF and Dataguidance 2018: The Future of Privacy Forum and Dataguidance, 'Comparing Privacy Laws: GDPR v CCPA' (November 2019), available at https://fpf.org/wp-content/uploads/2018/11/GDPR_CCPA_Comparison-Guide.pdf.

FRA 2013: European Union Agency for Fundamental Rights, *Access to data protection remedies in EU Member States* (Publication Office of the European Union 2013).

Laudati 2016: Larraine Laudati, 'Summaries of EU Court Decisions Relating to Data Protection 2000–2015' (28 January 2016).

Article 83. General conditions for imposing administrative fines

WALTRAUT KOTSCHY

1. Each supervisory authority shall ensure that the imposition of administrative fines pursuant to this Article in respect of infringements of this Regulation referred to in paragraphs 4, 5 and 6 shall in each individual case be effective, proportionate and dissuasive.
2. Administrative fines shall, depending on the circumstances of each individual case, be imposed in addition to, or instead of, measures referred to in points (a) to (h) and (j) of Article 58(2). When deciding whether to impose an administrative fine and deciding on the amount of the administrative fine in each individual case due regard shall be given to the following:
   (a) the nature, gravity and duration of the infringement taking into account the nature scope or purpose of the processing concerned as well as the number of data subjects affected and the level of damage suffered by them;
   (b) the intentional or negligent character of the infringement;
   (c) any action taken by the controller or processor to mitigate the damage suffered by data subjects;
   (d) the degree of responsibility of the controller or processor taking into account technical and organisational measures implemented by them pursuant to Articles 25 and 32;
   (e) any relevant previous infringements by the controller or processor;
   (f) the degree of cooperation with the supervisory authority, in order to remedy the infringement and mitigate the possible adverse effects of the infringement;
   (g) the categories of personal data affected by the infringement;
   (h) the manner in which the infringement became known to the supervisory authority, in particular whether, and if so to what extent, the controller or processor notified the infringement;
   (i) where measures referred to in Article 58(2) have previously been ordered against the controller or processor concerned with regard to the same subject-matter, compliance with those measures;
   (j) adherence to approved codes of conduct pursuant to Article 40 or approved certification mechanisms pursuant to Article 42; and
   (k) any other aggravating or mitigating factor applicable to the circumstances of the case, such as financial benefits gained, or losses avoided, directly or indirectly, from the infringement.
3. If a controller or processor intentionally or negligently, for the same or linked processing operations, infringes several provisions of this Regulation, the total amount of the administrative fine shall not exceed the amount specified for the gravest infringement.
4. Infringements of the following provisions shall, in accordance with paragraph 2, be subject to administrative fines up to 10 000 000 EUR, or in the case of an undertaking, up to 2 % of the total worldwide annual turnover of the preceding financial year, whichever is higher:
   (a) the obligations of the controller and the processor pursuant to Articles 8, 11, 25 to 39 and 42 and 43;
   (b) the obligations of the certification body pursuant to Articles 42 and 43;
   (c) the obligations of the monitoring body pursuant to Article 41(4).
5. Infringements of the following provisions shall, in accordance with paragraph 2, be subject to administrative fines up to 20 000 000 EUR, or in the case of an undertaking, up to 4 % of the total worldwide annual turnover of the preceding financial year, whichever is higher:
   (a) the basic principles for processing, including conditions for consent, pursuant to Articles 5, 6, 7 and 9;

(b) the data subjects' rights pursuant to Articles 12 to 22;
(c) the transfers of personal data to a recipient in a third country or an international organisation pursuant to Articles 44 to 49;
(d) any obligations pursuant to Member State law adopted under Chapter IX;
(e) non-compliance with an order or a temporary or definitive limitation on processing or the suspension of data f lows by the supervisory authority pursuant to Article 58(2) or failure to provide access in violation of Article 58(1).

6. Non-compliance with an order by the supervisory authority as referred to in Article 58(2) shall, in accordance with paragraph 2 of this Article, be subject to administrative fines up to 20 000 000 EUR, or in the case of an undertaking, up to 4 % of the total worldwide annual turnover of the preceding financial year, whichever is higher.
7. Without prejudice to the corrective powers of supervisory authorities pursuant to Article 58(2), each Member State may lay down the rules on whether and to what extent administrative fines may be imposed on public authorities and bodies established in that Member State.
8. The exercise by the supervisory authority of its powers under this Article shall be subject to appropriate procedural safeguards in accordance with Union and Member State law, including effective judicial remedy and due process.
9. Where the legal system of the Member State does not provide for administrative fines, this Article may be applied in such a manner that the fine is initiated by the competent supervisory authority and imposed by competent national courts, while ensuring that those legal remedies are effective and have an equivalent effect to the administrative fines imposed by supervisory authorities. In any event, the fines imposed shall be effective, proportionate and dissuasive. Those Member States shall notify to the Commission the provisions of their laws which they adopt pursuant to this paragraph by 25 May 2018 and, without delay, any subsequent amendment law or amendment affecting them.

Relevant Recitals

(13) In order to ensure a consistent level of protection for natural persons throughout the Union and to prevent divergences hampering the free movement of personal data within the internal market, a Regulation is necessary to provide legal certainty and transparency for economic operators, including micro, small and medium-sized enterprises, and to provide natural persons in all Member States with the same level of legally enforceable rights and obligations and responsibilities for controllers and processors, to ensure consistent monitoring of the processing of personal data, and equivalent sanctions in all Member States as well as effective cooperation between the supervisory authorities of different Member States. The proper functioning of the internal market requires that the free movement of personal data within the Union is not restricted or prohibited for reasons connected with the protection of natural persons with regard to the processing of personal data. To take account of the specific situation of micro, small and medium-sized enterprises, this Regulation includes a derogation for organisations with fewer than 250 employees with regard to record-keeping. In addition, the Union institutions and bodies, and Member States and their supervisory authorities, are encouraged to take account of the specific needs of micro, small and medium-sized enterprises in the application of this Regulation. The notion of micro, small and medium-sized enterprises should draw from Article 2 of the Annex to Commission Recommendation 2003/361/EC.

(148) In order to strengthen the enforcement of the rules of this Regulation, penalties including administrative fines should be imposed for any infringement of this Regulation, in addition to, or instead of appropriate measures imposed by the supervisory authority pursuant to this Regulation. In a case of a minor infringement or if the fine likely to be imposed would constitute a disproportionate burden to a natural person, a reprimand may be issued instead of a fine. Due regard should

however be given to the nature, gravity and duration of the infringement, the intentional character of the infringement, actions taken to mitigate the damage suffered, degree of responsibility or any relevant previous infringements, the manner in which the infringement became known to the supervisory authority, compliance with measures ordered against the controller or processor, adherence to a code of conduct and any other aggravating or mitigating factor. The imposition of penalties including administrative fines should be subject to appropriate procedural safeguards in accordance with the general principles of Union law and the Charter, including effective judicial protection and due process.

(149) Member States should be able to lay down the rules on criminal penalties for infringements of this Regulation, including for infringements of national rules adopted pursuant to and within the limits of this Regulation. Those criminal penalties may also allow for the deprivation of the profits obtained through infringements of this Regulation. However, the imposition of criminal penalties for infringements of such national rules and of administrative penalties should not lead to a breach of the principle of ne bis in idem, as interpreted by the Court of Justice.

(150) In order to strengthen and harmonise administrative penalties for infringements of this Regulation, each supervisory authority should have the power to impose administrative fines. This Regulation should indicate infringements and the upper limit and criteria for setting the related administrative fines, which should be determined by the competent supervisory authority in each individual case, taking into account all relevant circumstances of the specific situation, with due regard in particular to the nature, gravity and duration of the infringement and of its consequences and the measures taken to ensure compliance with the obligations under this Regulation and to prevent or mitigate the consequences of the infringement. Where administrative fines are imposed on an undertaking, an undertaking should be understood to be an undertaking in accordance with Articles 101 and 102 TFEU for those purposes. Where administrative fines are imposed on persons that are not an undertaking, the supervisory authority should take account of the general level of income in the Member State as well as the economic situation of the person in considering the appropriate amount of the fine. The consistency mechanism may also be used to promote a consistent application of administrative fines. It should be for the Member States to determine whether and to which extent public authorities should be subject to administrative fines. Imposing an administrative fine or giving a warning does not affect the application of other powers of the supervisory authorities or of other penalties under this Regulation.

(151) The legal systems of Denmark and Estonia do not allow for administrative fines as set out in this Regulation. The rules on administrative fines may be applied in such a manner that in Denmark the fine is imposed by competent national courts as a criminal penalty and in Estonia the fine is imposed by the supervisory authority in the framework of a misdemeanour procedure, provided that such an application of the rules in those Member States has an equivalent effect to administrative fines imposed by supervisory authorities. Therefore the competent national courts should take into account the recommendation by the supervisory authority initiating the fine. In any event, the fines imposed should be effective, proportionate and dissuasive.

(152) Where this Regulation does not harmonise administrative penalties or where necessary in other cases, for example in cases of serious infringements of this Regulation, Member States should implement a system which provides for effective, proportionate and dissuasive penalties. The nature of such penalties, criminal or administrative, should be determined by Member State law.

Closely Related Provisions

Article 58 (Powers of supervisory authorities) (see too recital 129); Article 78 (Right to an effective judicial remedy against a supervisory authority) (see too recital 141); Article 79 (Right to an effective judicial remedy against a controller or processor) (see too recital 145); Article 82 (Right to compensation and liability); Article 84 (Penalties) (see too recitals 149 and 152)

Related Provisions in LED [Directive (EU) 2016/680]

Article 53 (Right to an effective judicial remedy against a supervisory authority) (see too recital 86); Article 57 (Penalties) (see too recital 89)

Related Provisions in EPD [Directive 2002/58/EC]

Article 15a (Implementation and enforcement)

Related Provisions in EUDPR [Regulation (EU) 2018/1725]

Article 66 (Administrative fines) (see too recital 81).

Relevant Case Law

CJEU

Case C-41/90, *Klaus Höfner and Fritz Elser v Macrotron GmbH*, judgment of 23 April 1991 (ECLI:EU:C:1991:161).
Case C-217/05, *Confederación Española de Empresarios de Estaciones de Servicio v Compañía Española de Petróleos SA*, judgment of 14 December 2006 (ECLI:EU:C:2006:784).
Case C-328/05 P, *SGL Carbon AG v Commission of the European Communities*, judgment of 10 May 2007 (ECLI:EU:C:2007:277).
Case C-109/10 P, *Solvay SA v Commission*, judgment of 25 October 2011 (ECLI:EU:C:2011:686).
Case C-386/10 P, *Chalkor AE Epexergasias Metallon v European Commission*, judgment of 8 December 2011 (ECLI:EU:C:2011:815).
Case F-46/09, *V v European Parliament*, judgment of 5 July 2011, Civil Service Tribunal (ECLI:EU:F:2011:101).
Case C-67/13 P, *Groupement des cartes bancaires (CB) v European Commission*, judgment of 11 September 2014 (ECLI:EU:C:2014:2204).
Case C-583/13 P, *Deutsche Bahn AG and Others v European Commission*, judgment of 18 June 2015 (ECLI:EU:C:2015:404).
Case C-73/16, *Peter Puškár v Finančné riaditeľstvo Slovenskej republiky and Kriminálny úrad finančnej správy*, judgment of 27 September 2017 (ECLI:EU:C:2017:725).
Case T-612/17, *Google v Commission* (pending).

ECtHR

Engel and Others v The Netherlands, Appl. Nos. 5100/71, 5101/71, 5102/71, 5354/72 and 5370/72, judgment of 8 June 1976.
Adolf v Austria, Appl. No. 8269/78, judgment of 26 March 1982.
Öztürk v Germany, Appl. No. 8544/79, judgment of 21 February 1984.
Campbell and Fell v United Kingdom, Appl. Nos. 7819/77 and 7878/77, judgment of 28 June 1984.
Lutz v Germany, Appl. No. 9912/82, judgment of 25 August 1987.
Demicoli v Malta, Appl. No. 13057/87, judgment of 27 August 1991.
A. Menarini Diagnostics S.R.L v Italy, Appl. No. 43509/08, judgment of 27 September 2011.
Nicoleta Gheorghe v Romania, Appl. No. 23470/05, judgment of 3 April 2012.

Austria

Verfassungsgerichtshof, 27.06.2014, G47/2012 ua (ECLI:AT:VFGH:2014:G47.2012).

A. Rationale and Policy Underpinnings

Before the entry into force of the GDPR, the penalties foreseen in the national law of the Member States for infringements of EU data protection law did not in many cases reach the level of being 'dissuasive'. The GDPR not only extends its remit to foreign controllers and processors acting in EU markets,[1] but also opens up the possibility to impose effective, dissuasive fines.

Fines can play an important role in discouraging violations and encouraging accountability.[2] They can have a 'deterrent' effect, by creating a credible threat of being investigated and fined, which changes the perceived balance of the expected benefits and expected costs of non-compliance sufficiently to encourage controllers to choose in favour of compliance. At the same time they can have a 'moral and supportive' effect, in that they send a message to the spontaneously law-abiding and their internal advisors and data protection officers, reinforcing their commitment to accountability and compliance.

The fines laid down in Article 83 are explicitly designated as 'administrative fines', the reason being that they are to be imposed by supervisory authorities,[3] which are considered by the GDPR as administrative authorities.[4] Although supervisory authorities must be established as independent bodies,[5] they are not considered by the GDPR to belong to the judiciary.[6] This follows, for instance, from Article 55(3), which does not consider supervisory authorities as 'competent to supervise processing operations of courts acting in their judicial capacity', and from Article 79, which groups complaints to a supervisory authority together with 'administrative or non-judicial remedies'.

The qualification of supervisory authorities as *administrative* authorities poses questions as to the compatibility of the administrative fines foreseen in Article 83 with the requirements of a 'fair trial'.[7] Under Article 6 ECHR, fines under Article 83 would fall within the category of 'criminal charges'[8] under the so-called 'Engel criteria',[9] in particular

---

[1] See commentary on Art. 3 GDPR in this volume for an explanation of the territorial scope of the GDPR.

[2] See Wils 2006, pp. 185-190, on the use of fines in competition law.

[3] See Art. 83(9) GDPR regarding exemptions from the duty to foresee in national law the power to impose fines.

[4] The nature of supervisory authorities as administrative bodies can also be deduced from Art. 55(3) which states that these bodies 'shall not be competent to supervise processing operations of courts acting in their judicial capacity', the evident reason being separation of powers; and from the heading of Art. 83 which explicitly denominates the fines imposed by the supervisory authorities according to Art. 83 as 'administrative fines'.

[5] See ibid., Art. 52 ('Independence').

[6] See also commentary on the definition of 'supervisory authority' in Art. 4(21) GDPR in this volume.

[7] The right to a 'fair trial' is a fundamental right under Art. 47 of the Charter of Fundamental Rights of the European Union ('CFR') and under Art. 6 of the European Convention of Human Rights and Fundamental Freedoms ('ECHR'). According to Art. 52(3) CFR, 'the meaning and scope' of corresponding rights under the Charter and under the ECHR 'shall be the same as those laid down by the said Convention'. This specifically also incorporates the jurisprudence of the ECtHR to corresponding rights under the Charter. The ECtHR's jurisprudence on Art. 6 ECHR is comprehensively commented on by the ECtHR itself in the document ECtHR Guide 2018.

[8] ECtHR Guide, para. 4: 'The concept of a "criminal charge" has an "autonomous" meaning, independent of the categorisations employed by the national legal systems of the member States'. See also ECtHR, *Adolf v Austria*, para. 30; and ECtHR, *Menarini Diagnostic* (dealing with fines under competition law).

[9] The assessment of the applicability of the criminal aspect of Art. 6 ECHR is based on the criteria outlined in *Engel*, namely classification in domestic law, nature of the offence, and severity of the penalty: see ECtHR, *Engel*, paras. 82–83. See further ECtHR Guide 2018, para. 8: 'For Article 6 to be held to be applicable, it suffices that the offence in question should by its nature be regarded as "criminal" from the point of view of the Convention, or that the offence rendered the person liable to a sanction which, by its nature and degree of severity, belongs in general to the "criminal" sphere'. See also ECtHR, *Lutz v Germany*, para. 55; ECtHR,

the third criterion thereof concerning the severity of the (highest) punishment foreseen.[10] Whilst not 'criminal' within the meaning of EU law, they are 'criminal within the wider, autonomous meaning of Article 6 ECHR.[11] The procedure leading to the imposition of a fine under Article 83 must therefore respect the special conditions developed by the jurisprudence of the ECtHR for lawfully deciding on 'criminal charges'. In particular, Article 6 ECHR enshrines the 'right to be heard in court'[12] with regard to criminal charges, a right which is also inherent in Article 47 CFR.[13] This legal obligation may, under certain conditions, also be fulfilled by providing for the possibility to appeal from an administrative body to a 'court'.[14]

This is the system foreseen in the GDPR: whilst the 'right to a court' does not exclude administrative authorities—here, the supervisory authorities—from deciding in cases of 'criminal charges', Article 78 GDPR lays down 'the right to an effective judicial remedy against a supervisory authority' concerning all legally binding decisions of such authorities.[15] This obliges the Member States to provide a procedural system which entitles controllers and processors to appeal to a court against fines under Article 83. Such a court must be competent to review the decision of the data protection supervisory authority concerning the assessment of the legal questions involved as well as the facts on which the decision was based.[16]

B. Legal Background

1. EU legislation

The DPD contained only one short provision on sanctions, in Article 24, which recognised the prerogative of the Member States to regulate this topic:

The Member States shall adopt suitable measures to ensure the full implementation of the provisions of this Directive and shall in particular lay down the sanctions to be imposed in case of infringement of the provisions adopted pursuant to this Directive.

Öztürk v Germany, para. 54. The fact that an offence is not punishable by imprisonment is not in itself decisive, since the relative lack of seriousness of the penalty at stake cannot divest an offence of its inherently criminal character: see ECtHR, *Öztürk v Germany*, para. 53; ECtHR, *Nicoleta Gheorghe*, para. 26.

[10] ECtHR Guide 2018, para. 7: 'The third criterion is determined by reference to the maximum potential penalty for which the relevant law provides'. See also ECtHR, *Campbell and Fell*, para. 72; ECtHR, *Demicoli v Malta*, para. 34. The Engel criteria are not to be applied cumulatively but alternatively: even if an offence is *not* designated as 'criminal' under national law, it has to be considered as being 'criminal' in the sense of Art. 6 ECHR if one of the other two Engel criteria applies, see e.g. ECtHR, *Lutz v Germany*, para. 55.

[11] See the discussion of Art. 6 ECHR in the context of competition law fines in Wils 2010, pp. 16-18.

[12] Art. 6(1) ECHR: 'In the determination of ... any criminal charge against him, everyone is entitled to a ... hearing ... by [a] tribunal ... ' Concerning the concept of a 'tribunal' see ECtHR Guide 2018, p. 19.

[13] Art. 47 CFR requires that the case must be heard before 'an independent and impartial tribunal previously established by law'.

[14] This specific question has been dealt with extensively by the CJEU: see Case C-73/16, *Puškár*. See the commentary on Art. 79 GDPR in this volume.

[15] The importance of an effective judicial remedy in this context has been stressed in a change of jurisprudence of the Austrian Constitutional Court. As a consequence of the introduction of a new system of administrative courts with full guarantees of judicial independence and full power of reviewing administrative decisions in Austria in 2012, the Austrian Constitutional Court held it permissible for an administrative authority to be entrusted by law with imposing particularly high fines: see Verfassungsgerichtshof, *G47/2012 ua*.

[16] The importance of both elements for effective judicial control is stressed e.g. in Case C-386/10 P, *Chalkor*, para. 62, and Case C-67/13 P, *CB*, para. 44.

Article 28 DPD, which dealt with the powers of the supervisory authorities, did not mention any competence for imposing fines; paragraph 3, third indent, only conveyed a 'power to engage in legal proceedings where the national provisions adopted pursuant to this Directive have been violated or to bring these violations to the attention of the judicial authorities'. Some Member States nevertheless endowed their supervisory authorities with a competence to impose 'fines'—that is, pecuniary sanctions—evidently interpreting Article 28(3) as listing only the mandatory minimum of tasks and powers.

2. International instruments

Article 10 of Council of Europe Convention 108 provides that Contracting Parties must establish 'appropriate sanctions and remedies for violations of provision of domestic law giving effect to the basic principles for data protection set out in this chapter'. Article 12 of Modernised Convention 108 obliges the Contracting Parties to foresee 'appropriate judicial and non-judicial sanctions and remedies for violations of the provision of this Convention'. However, neither of them prescribes any further details for such provisions under national law.

3. National developments

In several Member States, such as Germany, France, the UK and Spain, the imposition of considerable fines by supervisory authorities has a long tradition. In Germany, for instance, so-called 'Bußgelder' could be imposed for infringements of data protection law up to a maximum of € 300,000 under the Federal Data Protection Act.[17] The French data protection authority (CNIL) imposed a sanction of € 150,000 in 2017 which was said to be the highest fine it ever imposed.[18] In the UK, the ICO has also imposed substantial fines in the same order.[19] Spain reported in 2013 fining a global company € 900,000.[20] Thus, Article 83 GDPR is in line with these developments under national data protection law, though the potential fines under the GDPR are significantly higher than any national DPA ever imposed under the DPD. In consequence, with regard to the maximum amount for fines under the GDPR, it is not Member States' data protection law but rather EU competition law which will set the example.[21]

Outside the EU, the US Federal Trade Commission ('FTC') has recently imposed a $5 Billion penalty on Facebook, for violation of a 2012 FTC order by deceiving users about their ability to control the privacy of their personal information. In addition to the fine the FTC imposed 'sweeping' accountability requirements including an independent Board-level privacy committee and independent compliance officers at individual level responsible for Facebook's privacy program. [22]

---

[17] German Federal Data Protection Act 1990.   [18] See the CNIL Website 2017.

[19] In July 2019, the ICO issued a notice of its intention to fine British Airways £183.39 million, and was awaiting representations by British Airways and the results of consultation of other concerned supervisory authorities. See the ICO Website 2019.

[20] See the EDRi Website 2014.

[21] See currently the pending proceedings in Case T-612/17, *Google v Commission*, appealing Commission Decision 2017 to impose a fine of € 2.42 billion on Google. The Commission has been developing its approach to fines, see EC Guidelines 2006 and EC Communication 2014. See generally Wils 2006, and Wils 2010, pp. 10-12.

[22] See FTC Settlement Order and FTC Press Release. See also the commentary on Art. 24 in this volume.

4. Case law

As Article 83 GDPR has no precedent in EU data protection law there is no relevant case law yet on its provisions. However, there is ample case law on fundamental principles such as *ne bis in idem*[23] and the right to a fair trial, as well as on procedural questions of imposing fines to a very high maximum amount. The ECtHR's extensive case law on the right to a fair trial is best described in the Court's own guide.[24] The CJEU has dealt with similar procedural questions in the context of competition law, such as in *SGL Carbon AG*,[25] *Deutsche Bahn AG*,[26] *Chalkor*,[27] and *CB*.[28]

C. Analysis

1. Administrative fines as an enforcement power available to supervisory authorities

The WP29 has pointed out that consistent enforcement is central to the harmonised data protection regime under the GDPR:

Administrative fines are a central element in the new enforcement regime introduced by the Regulation, being a powerful part of the enforcement toolbox of the supervisory authorities together with the other measures provided by article 58.[29]

According to Article 58 GDPR, supervisory authorities have a wide array of corrective powers at their disposal, such as the power to issue warnings or reprimands, to give orders to the controller or processor, and to impose a limitation or ban on processing. The imposition of a fine is only one of the several means available to supervisory authorities to enforce compliance with the GDPR.[30]

Recital 150 shows that the authors of the GDPR decided that fines can be imposed not only on individual persons or legal persons, but also on undertakings that meet the conditions set in EU law to be considered an undertaking. The recital states, inter alia: 'Where administrative fines are imposed on an undertaking, an undertaking should be understood to be an undertaking in accordance with Articles 101 and 102 Treaty on the Functioning of the European Union ("TFEU") for those purposes'. Articles 101 and 102 TFEU do not themselves contain any definition of the concept of 'undertaking'. Consequently, the reference in recital 150 should be understood as a reference to the whole body of jurisprudence concerning the definition of an 'undertaking' under the TFEU.[31]

In this respect, the case law of the EU courts in the area of competition law has defined an undertaking as an economic unit, which may comprise several natural or legal persons

---

[23] See the commentary on Art. 84 GDPR in this volume with regard to the principle of *ne bis in idem* under the GDPR.
[24] See ECtHR Guide 2018.   [25] Case C-328/05 P, *SGL Carbon*.
[26] Case C-583/13 P, *Deutsche Bahn AG*.   [27] Case C-386/10 P, *Chalkor*.
[28] Case C-67/13 P, *CB*.   [29] WP29 2017, p. 4.
[30] Rec. 150 GDPR: 'Imposing an administrative fine or giving a warning does not affect the application of other powers of the supervisory authorities or of other penalties under this Regulation'.
[31] See WP29 2017, p. 6, fn. 4: 'The CJEU case law definition is: "the concept of an undertaking encompasses every entity engaged in an economic activity regardless of the legal status of the entity and the way in which it is financed"'; see Case C-41/90, *Höfner and Elsner*, para. 21. An undertaking 'must be understood as designating an economic unit even if in law that economic unit consists of several persons, natural or legal': see Case C-217/05, *Confederación Española*, para. 40.

or 'which may be formed by the parent company and all involved subsidiaries',[32] together referred to as a 'single economic entity'.[33] Moreover, under this case law, each person forming part of a single economic entity may be held liable for an infringement of EU competition law committed by that economic entity.[34]

Whether fines may also be imposed on controllers or processors *in the public sector* shall, according to Article 83(7), be determined by Member State law. Adequate regulation will depend on a number of conditions which are not uniform in the Member States, due to their 'procedural autonomy'[35] in questions of procedural law and of sanctions and their different ways of funding public institutions. At the EU level, the EDPS may impose fines on the EU institutions and bodies, but only up to a maximum of up to € 50,000 per infringement and up to a total of € 500,000 per year.[36] However, even if fines are not applied to the public sector of a Member State, there are usually disciplinary or other measures to follow up infringements of data protection law by public sector controllers or processors.[37]

In addition to the measures listed in Article 58(2), Article 84 requires Member States to foresee additional penalties other than administrative fines, e.g. under criminal law. According to recital 149 GDPR, 'the imposition of criminal penalties for infringements of such national rules and of administrative penalties should not lead to a breach of the principle of *ne bis in idem*, as interpreted by the Court of Justice'.[38] The principle of *ne bis in idem* is a fundamental right enshrined in Article 50 CFR, which corresponds to Article 4 of Protocol No. VII to the ECHR.[39] It means that the same infringement should not be punished both by criminal penalties and by administrative fines of a criminal nature. However, according to CJEU jurisprudence, the principle of *ne bis in idem* may be restricted under the strict conditions laid down under Article 52 CFR.[40]

The procedures for supervisory authorities to exercise their power of imposing fines are to be determined by the Member States. Article 83(8) reminds the national (and also the EU) legislators that Article 47 CFR must be respected, which requires a 'fair trial' before imposing fines, 'including effective judicial remedy and due process'.[41]

2. Fines must be effective, proportionate and dissuasive

As the main guideline for imposing adequate fines, Article 83(1) invokes the principles developed in the CJEU's interpretation of the right to a fair trial under Article 47 CFR.

---

[32] WP29 2017, p. 6.   [33] Odudu and Bailey 2014, see case law cited at fnn. 1 and 5–6.
[34] Subject to a determination of its participation in the infringement: see Odudu and Bailey 2014, pp. 1742–1755.
[35] Dashwood et al. 2011, p. 288.   [36] Art. 66(2)–(3) EUDPR.
[37] For example, Case F-46/09, *V v Parliament* concerned an action in damages.
[38] Rec. 149 GDPR.
[39] See the commentary on Art. 84 in this volume with regard to the principle of *ne bis in idem* under the GDPR.
[40] See the discussion of the recent case law of the CJEU and the ECtHR in Lo Schiavo 2018.
[41] 'Due process', often also referred to as 'the rights of defence', comprises a number of rights which have been formulated initially in ECtHR jurisprudence on Art. 6 ECHR and are explained in ECtHR Guide 2018. On this basis, the CJEU developed its own jurisprudence on due process, especially in the area of competition law, see for example Case C-109/10 P, *Solvay*, paras. 52-53. Several aspects of due process have been regulated by EU Directives over the last years, such as Directive 2010/64/EU, Directive 2012/13/EU, Directive 2013/48/EU and Directive 2016/343/EU.

Thus, the fine imposed in a concrete case must be 'effective, proportionate and dissuasive' in order to be justified.[42]

Article 83(2), paras. (a)–(k) enumerate a number of criteria which help to determine the appropriate amount of the fine to be imposed in a concrete case. The main criteria are the nature, gravity and duration of the infringement; its intentional or negligent character; the degree of effort on the side of the controller or processor to avoid damage and to cooperate with the supervisory authority; and the previous history of the controller or processor concerning infringements of data protection law.[43]

Recital 150 points out that the consistency mechanism may be used to promote a consistent application of administrative fines. In this respect, in cases of dispute between the supervisory authorities concerned, the EDPB will be able to consider 'how the principles of effectiveness, proportionality and deterrence are observed'.[44]

Recital 148 considers the case of 'minor' infringements, and advises, inter alia, that a reprimand should be issued rather than a fine in such cases. This should be seen as a consequence of the principle of proportionality and of the fact that fines are only one of the several means at the disposal of supervisory authorities to produce compliance with the GDPR in the most suitable manner.[45]

Recital 148 follows the same approach of replacing a fine with a reprimand where a fine would constitute a disproportionate burden on a natural person. Recital 150 adds that:

Where administrative fines are imposed on persons that are not an undertaking, the supervisory authority should take account of the general level of income in the Member State as well as the economic situation of the person in considering the appropriate amount of the fine.[46]

If several infringements have occurred within the same or linked processing operations 'the total amount of the administrative fine shall not exceed the amount specified for the gravest infringement'.[47] For example, if there is an infringement of Articles 8 and 12, the graver assessment under Article 83(5) will be triggered by Article 12.[48] Thus, Article 83 does not support the principle of accumulation of penalties but rather adheres to the principle of absorption,[49] under which a DPA has to decide which infringement is the most serious one and calculate the fine for it, and then determine the fine based on the number of infringements.

3. Punishable infringements under paragraphs 4–6 of Article 83

In paragraphs 4 and 5 of Article 83, the punishable infringements are determined solely by referring to certain articles of the GDPR, without any specific description of the punishable facts and circumstances. The following remarks can therefore only be an approximation of

---

[42] Art. 83(1) GDPR.
[43] See rec. 148. These assessment criteria are discussed in detail in WP29 2017, pp. 9-16.
[44] WP29 2017, p. 7.
[45] Within the limits of such understanding, national law provisions might refer to details of Art. 83(2) GDPR. They should, however, not interfere with the independent interpretation of Art. 83(2) by the national supervisory authority/authorities.
[46] Ibid., rec. 150.   [47] Ibid., Art. 83(3).   [48] See WP29 2017, p. 10.
[49] Whether this provision really results in absorption depends on the interpretation of the term 'same or linked processing operations'.

the whole array of offences punishable under the Articles enumerated in Article 83 paragraphs 4 and 5.

Under Article 83(4), the following infringements of specific articles of the GDPR are—approximately—punishable with a maximum fine of € 10 million (or in the case of an undertaking, up to 2 per cent of the total worldwide annual turnover of the preceding financial year, whichever is higher):

1. *Article 8*: Processing of data of children based on consent which is not valid according to the conditions set out in Article 8.
2. *Article 11*: Unjustified denial of complying with the rights of data subjects on grounds of not being able to identify the data subject.
3. *Articles 25–39*: Neglect of the general obligations of controllers and/or processors which are prerequisites for achieving lawful processing; these obligations are, inter alia:
    (a) to implement appropriate technical and organisational measures to ensure compliance with the GDPR
    (b) in certain cases: to designate a data protection officer
    (c) to stipulate the obligations of processors acting on behalf of the controller in a clear and comprehensive way
    (d) to keep records on all processing operations
    (e) to perform impact assessment and, accordingly, prior consultation
    (f) to implement data protection by design and by default
    (g) to provide security of processing
    (h) to notify the data protection authority and, under certain circumstances, also the data subjects in case of data breach and
    (i) to cooperate with the supervisory authorities.
4. *Articles 42 and 43:* In this context, Article 83(4) refers to infringements of 'the obligations of the controller or processor' and to infringements of 'the certification body'. Infringements of Articles 42 or 43 *by the certification bodies* are evidently centred on attaining accreditation under falsified conditions, on unjustified certifications and lack of due supervision of certified data processing operations. Infringements of these Articles *by a controller or processor* could, for instance, occur in the context of Article 42(6) if a controller or processor were to provide falsified or incomplete information in the course of a certification procedure, or if a controller or processor purports in public to perform a processing operation in accordance with a (non-existing) certification. Deviation from a certified procedure is not as such punishable under Article 83, unless the deviant procedure is at the same time unlawful.[50]
5. *Article 41(4):* Infringement of the duties of monitoring bodies to supervise and take appropriate action if a controller or processor is not compliant with an applicable[51] code of conduct.

Under Article 83 paragraphs 5 and 6, the following infringements of specific articles of the GDPR are punishable with a higher maximum fine of € 20 million (or in the case of

---

[50] See the commentaries on Arts. 42 and 43 in this volume.

[51] An obligation to intervene from the side of the monitoring body presupposes that the perpetrator has a legal duty to follow the code of conduct. This will be the case only where a controller or processor formally undertook to apply the code according to Art. 40(4) GDPR. See also the commentaries on Arts. 40–41 in this volume.

an undertaking, up to 4 per cent of the total worldwide annual turnover of the preceding financial year, whichever is higher):

1. *Articles 5–7 and 9*: processing personal data contrary to 'the basic principles' for lawful processing contained in these articles of the GDPR
2. *Articles 12–22*: not correctly answering as a controller[52] to rights evoked by individuals under these Articles
3. *Articles 44—49*: transfer of personal data to third countries[53] in violation of the conditions spelt out in Articles 44–49
4. *Chapter IX*: violations of Member State law which regulates in more detail the topics mentioned in Chapter IX of the GDPR[54]
5. *Article 58*: non-compliance with an order by a supervisory authority or with a temporary or definitive limitation on processing or the suspension of data flows according to Article 58(2)[55] or with an order of a supervisory authority to provide access according to Article 58(1).

In effect, lesser breaches which would otherwise potentially fall under Article 83(4) may end up being addressed with higher sanctions under Article 83 paragraphs (5) or (6) where the controller has failed to comply with an order previously made concerning such a lesser breach.

Select Bibliography

EU legislation

Commission Decision 2017: Summary of Commission decision of 27 June 2017 relating to a proceeding under Article 102 of the Treaty on the Functioning of the European Union and Article 54 of the EEA Agreement (Case AT.39740 — Google Search (Shopping)), OJ 2018 C 9/14.
Directive 2010/64/EU: Directive 2010/64/EU of the European Parliament and of the Council of 20 October 2010 on the right to interpretation and translation in criminal proceedings, OJ 2010 L 289/1.
Directive 2012/13/EU: Directive 2012/13/EU of the European Parliament and of the Council of 22 May 2012 on the right to information in criminal proceedings, OJ 2012 L 142/1.
Directive 2013/48/EU: Directive 2013/48/EU of the European Parliament and of the Council of 22 October 2013 on the right of access to a lawyer in criminal proceedings and in European arrest warrant proceedings, and on the right to have a third party informed upon deprivation of liberty and to communicate with third persons and with consular authorities while deprived of liberty, OJ 2013 L 294/1.

---

[52] Processors might be fined in this context where they do not comply with their duty under Art. 28 (3) to support the controller in fulfilling its duties under Arts. 15-22

[53] These are countries outside the European Economic Area ('EEA'). The EEA consists of the Member States of the EU plus Iceland, Liechtenstein and Norway.

[54] These topics are: freedom of expression and information; public access to official documents; national identification numbers; employment; archiving in the public interest and scientific research and statistics; professional obligations of secrecy; and data protection rules for churches and religious associations that existed at the time of entry into force of the GDPR.

[55] Non-compliance with an order of the supervisory authority based on Art. 58(2) is sanctioned similarly by Art. 83 (5)e and by Art.83(6).

Directive 2016/343/EU: Directive (EU) 2016/343 of the European Parliament and of the Council of 9 March 2016 on the strengthening of certain aspects of the presumption of innocence and of the right to be present at the trial in criminal proceedings, OJ 2016 L 65/1.

National legislation

German Federal Data Protection Act 1990: Gesetz zur Fortentwicklung der Datenverarbeitung und des Datenschutzes (Bundesdatenschutzgesetz), BGBl 1990 Teil 1 Nr. 2954 (repealed).

Academic writings

Dashwood et al. 2011: Dashwood, Dougan, Rodger, Spaventa and Wyatt, *Wyatt and Dashwood's European Union Law* (6th edn, Hart Publishing 2011).
Lo Schiavo 2018: Lo Schiavo, 'The Principle of *ne bis in idem* and the Application of Criminal Sanctions: Of Scope and Restrictions: ECJ 20 March 2018, Case C-524/15, Luca Menci ECJ 20 March 2018, Case C-537/16, Garlsson Real Estate SA and Others v Commissione Nazionale per le Società e la Borsa (Consob) ECJ 20 March 2018, Joined Cases C-596/16 and C-597/16, Enzo Di Puma v Consob and Consob v Antonio Zecca', 14(3) *European Constitutional Law Review* (2018), 644.
Odudu and Bailey 2014: Odudu and Bailey, 'The Single Economic Entity Doctrine in EU Competition Law', 51(6) *Common Market Law Review* (2014), 1721.
Wils 2006: Wils, 'Optimal Antitrust Fines: Theory and Practice', 29(2) *World Competition* (2006), 183.
Wils 2010: Wils, 'The Increased Level of EU Antitrust Fines, Judicial Review and the ECHR', 33(1) *World Competition* (2010), 5.

Papers of data protection authorities

WP29 2017: Article 29 Working Party, 'Guidelines on the Application and Setting of Administrative Fines for the Purpose of the Regulation 2016/679' (WP 253, 3 October 2017).
FTC Settlement Order: Federal Trade Commission, 'Plaintiff's Consent Motion for entry of stipulated order for civil penalty, monetary judgment, and injunctive relief, and memorandum in support (Case No. 19-cv-2184)' (July 24, 2019).

Reports and recommendations

EC Guidelines 2006: Guidelines on the method of setting fines imposed pursuant to Article 23(2)(a) of Regulation No 1/2003, OJ 2006 C 210/2, 1 September 2006.
EC Communication 2014: Communication from the Commission to the European Parliament and the Council, 'Ten Years of Antitrust Enforcement under Regulation 1/2003: Achievements and Future Perspectives', COM/2014/0453 final, 9 July 2014.
ECtHR Guide 2018: European Court of Human Rights, 'Guide on Article 6 of the European Convention on Human Rights (civil limb)' (30 April 2018).

Others

CNIL Website 2017: Commission nationale de l'informatique et des libertés, 'FACEBOOK Sanctioned for Several Breaches of the French Data Protection Act' (16 May 2017), available at https://www.cnil.fr/en/facebook-sanctioned-several-breaches-french-data-protection-act.
EDRi Website 2014: European Digital Rights, 'Google Was Fined by French and Spanish Data Protection Authorities' (15 January 2014), available at https://edri.org/google-fined-french-spanish-data-protection-authorities/.

FTC Press Release: Federal Trade Commission, 'FTC Imposes $5 Billion Penalty and Sweeping New Privacy Restrictions on Facebook' (24 July 2019), available https://www.ftc.gov/news-events/press-releases/2019/07/ftc-imposes-5-billion-penalty-sweeping-new-privacy-restrictions.

ICO Website 2019: Information Commissioner's Office, 'Intention to fine British Airways £183.39m under GDPR for data breach' (8 July 2019), available at https://ico.org.uk/about-the-ico/news-and-events/news-and-blogs/2019/07/ico-announces-intention-to-fine-british-airways/.

Article 84. Penalties

ORLA LYNSKEY

(1) Member States shall lay down the rules on other penalties applicable to infringements of this Regulation in particular for infringements which are not subject to administrative fines pursuant to Article 83, and shall take all measures necessary to ensure that they are implemented. Such penalties shall be effective, proportionate and dissuasive.
(2) Each Member State shall notify to the Commission the provisions of its law which it adopts pursuant to paragraph 1, by 25 May 2018 and, without delay, any subsequent amendment affecting them.

Relevant Recitals

(149) Member States should be able to lay down the rules on criminal penalties for infringements of this Regulation, including for infringements of national rules adopted pursuant to and within the limits of this Regulation. Those criminal penalties may also allow for the deprivation of the profits obtained through infringements of this Regulation. However, the imposition of criminal penalties for infringements of such national rules and of administrative penalties should not lead to a breach of the principle of ne bis in idem, as interpreted by the Court of Justice.

(150) In order to strengthen and harmonise administrative penalties for infringements of this Regulation, each supervisory authority should have the power to impose administrative fines. This Regulation should indicate infringements and the upper limit and criteria for setting the related administrative fines, which should be determined by the competent supervisory authority in each individual case, taking into account all relevant circumstances of the specific situation, with due regard in particular to the nature, gravity and duration of the infringement and of its consequences and the measures taken to ensure compliance with the obligations under this Regulation and to prevent or mitigate the consequences of the infringement. Where administrative fines are imposed on an undertaking, an undertaking should be understood to be an undertaking in accordance with Articles 101 and 102 TFEU for those purposes. Where administrative fines are imposed on persons that are not an undertaking, the supervisory authority should take account of the general level of income in the Member State as well as the economic situation of the person in considering the appropriate amount of the fine. The consistency mechanism may also be used to promote a consistent application of administrative fines. It should be for the Member States to determine whether and to which extent public authorities should be subject to administrative fines. Imposing an administrative fine or giving a warning does not affect the application of other powers of the supervisory authorities or of other penalties under this Regulation.

(151) The legal systems of Denmark and Estonia do not allow for administrative fines as set out in this Regulation. The rules on administrative fines may be applied in such a manner that in Denmark the fine is imposed by competent national courts as a criminal penalty and in Estonia the fine is imposed by the supervisory authority in the framework of a misdemeanour procedure, provided that such an application of the rules in those Member States has an equivalent effect to administrative fines imposed by supervisory authorities. Therefore the competent national courts should take into account the recommendation by the supervisory authority initiating the fine. In any event, the fines imposed should be effective, proportionate and dissuasive.

(152) Where this Regulation does not harmonise administrative penalties or where necessary in other cases, for example in cases of serious infringements of this Regulation, Member

States should implement a system which provides for effective, proportionate and dissuasive penalties. The nature of such penalties, criminal or administrative, should be determined by Member State law.

Closely Related Provisions

Article 58 (Powers of supervisory authorities) (see recital 129); Article 79 (Right to an effective judicial remedy against a controller or processor) (see too recital 145); Article 82 (Right to compensation and liability) (see too recital 146); Article 83 (General conditions for imposing administrative fines) (see recitals 148 and 150)

Related Provisions in LED [Directive (EU) 2016/680]

Article 57 (Penalties) (see too recital 89)

Related Provisions in EPD [Directive 2002/58/EC]

Recital 47

Relevant Case Law

CJEU

Case C-33/76, *Rewe-Zentralfinanz eG and Rewe-Zentral AG v Landwirtschaftskammer für das Saarland*, judgment of 16 December 1976 (ECLI:EU:C:1976:188).
Case C-68/88, *Commission of the European Communities v Hellenic Republic ('Greek Maize')*, judgment of 21 September 1989 (ECLI:EU:C:1989:339).
Case C-78/98, *Shirley Preston and Others v Wolverhampton Healthcare NHS Trust and Others and Dorothy Fletcher and Others v Midland Bank plc*, judgment of 16 May 2000 (ECLI:EU:C:2000:247).
Case C-176/03, *Commission of the European Communities v Council of the European Union ('Environmental Sanctions')*, judgment of 13 September 2005 (Grand Chamber) (ECLI:EU:C:2005:542).
Case C-617/10, *Åklagaren v Hans Åkerberg Fransson*, judgment of 26 February 2013 (Grand Chamber) (ECLI:EU:C:2013:105).
Joined Cases C-596/16 and C-597/16, *Enzo Di Puma v Commissione Nazionale per le Società e la Borsa (Consob)* and *Commissione Nazionale per le Società e la Borsa (Consob) v Antonio Zecca*, judgment of 20 March 2018 (Grand Chamber) (ECLI:EU:C:2018:192).
Case C-537/16, *Garlsson Real Estate SA and Others v Commissione Nazionale per le Società e la Borsa (Consob)*, judgment of 20 March 2018 (Grand Chamber) (ECLI:EU:C:2018:193).

ECtHR

Engel and Others v The Netherlands, Appl. No. 5100/71, judgment of 8 June 1976.
A. Menarini Diagnostics S.r.l. v Italy, Appl. No. 43509/08, judgment of 27 September 2011.

A. Rationale and Policy Underpinnings

Article 24 DPD left Member States with the discretion to adopt 'suitable measures' to ensure the full implementation of its provisions and to adopt sanctions in case of their infringement. Member States were thus given the choice to opt for criminal or administrative sanctions, or a combination of the two. The EU Fundamental Rights Agency concluded in a 2013 report on access to data protection remedies in EU Member States that 'in almost all member states criminal sanctions can be imposed, in the form of a fine or imprisonment'.[1] This, however, is ostensibly where the similarities in practice ended as there was differentiation across Member States in terms of both the data protection infringements that were criminalised and the ultimate outcome of such criminalisation.

De Hert and Boulet provide a helpful overview of the type of data protection crimes enacted across EU Member States. One common violation, criminalised in the majority of EU Member States, was the failure to notify personal data processing activities to the relevant regulatory authority. Other violations treated as criminal conduct in more than a handful of Member States include: the violation of the duty of confidentiality; the illegitimate processing of sensitive personal data; and, the failure to fulfil security obligations. The UK and Ireland both made it a criminal offence to force a data subject to exercise their subject access rights (for instance, to circumvent existing criminal disclosure rules).[2] Belgium is cited by these authors as an example of a jurisdiction that opted for extensive criminalisation, as the relevant data protection legislation enumerates a long list of provisions the violation of which results in the imposition of a criminal fine.[3]

In addition to this substantive differentiation across Member States in terms of the conduct criminalised, the outcome of criminal proceedings also differed between them. Such outcomes, for instance, included the issuing of court warnings; the prohibition of specified individuals from managing future data processing operations; and, compulsory community service for relevant individuals.[4] Moreover, of those states that imposed custodial sentences for data protection violations, these sentences ranged in length from, for the most part, between six months and five years.[5]

Nevertheless, despite the widespread availability of criminal sanctions on paper, the FRA concluded that such sanctions were only rarely used in the 16 EU Member States covered in its report.[6] This reluctance might be attributed to the loss of influence this may entail for data protection authorities. This is because the vast majority of DPAs do not have the competence to impose criminal sanctions (with the notable exceptions of the Estonian and Macedonian DPAs, who could impose misdemeanour fines) and thus reliance on criminal sanctions would require them to transfer the case to the relevant prosecuting authorities to be brought before the Courts.[7]

The DPD thus led to widespread differentiation in terms of enforcement practice across EU Member States, which may at first glance seem odd given the Directive's aim to harmonise.[8] The failure of the Directive to specify the criminal penalties applicable for its infringement can however be explained by the EU's lack of explicit competence to enact criminal law measures.[9] Indeed, it was this understanding—that the (then) European Community lacked a general competence to enact criminal law measures applicable to

---

[1] FRA 2013, p. 7. [2] De Hert and Boulet 2016, p. 362. [3] Ibid.
[4] FRA 2013, p. 22. [5] Ibid. [6] Ibid., p. 35.
[7] De Hert and Boulet 2016, pp. 364–365. [8] See Art. 1(1) DPD.
[9] Dawes and Lynskey 2008.

the former First Pillar—that prompted the EU institutions to resort to a 'double text' practice. It followed from this practice that 'the main thrust of a Community policy [was] included in a Regulation or a Directive while the criminal law aspects of such a policy [were] hived off and included in a Framework Decision'.[10] However, following a series of judgments of the CJEU, it became apparent that the European Community could enact criminal law provisions when 'the application of effective, proportionate and dissuasive criminal penalties by the competent national authorities is an essential measure for combatting serious [environmental] offences'.[11]

This matter was put beyond doubt by Article 83(2) Treaty on the Functioning of the European Union ('TFEU') which provides that if the approximation of criminal rules proves 'essential to ensure the effective implementation of a Union policy' in an area which has been harmonised, 'directives may establish minimum rules with regard to the definition of criminal offences and sanctions in the area'. Article 83(2) TFEU does however continue to assume a 'double text' practice: it states that '[s]uch directives should be adopted by the same legislative procedure as that used to adopt the harmonisation measure in question'.

In its 2010 Communication on data protection reform, the European Commission suggested that it would avail of this possibility to enact criminal law measures in the data protection context. In particular, it stated that it would 'assess the need for strengthening the existing provisions on sanctions, for example by explicitly including criminal sanctions in case of serious data protection violations, in order to make them more effective'.[12] Yet, in its 2012 GDPR Proposal, Article 78 of the Proposal[13]—like Article 84 GDPR— left Member States the discretion to lay down penalties (beyond the listed 'administrative sanctions', then in Article 79). Therefore, Article 83 GDPR sets out detailed prescription of the administrative fines applicable for infringement of the GDPR, and thus greatly curtails the discretion of Member States in this regard. Yet, once again, Article 84 GDPR leaves the decision as to whether to impose alternative penalties (such as criminal sanctions) entirely at the discretion of Member States, subject only to the proviso that the penalties shall be 'effective, proportionate and dissuasive'.

De Hert and Boulet are damning of this failure to harmonise noting, correctly, that 'a future of sustained differences between Member States goes against the aim of a regulation to establish a uniform data protection framework'.[14] They also suggest that this failure to harmonise will be detrimental to legal certainty and may encourage forum shopping.

B. Legal Background

1. EU legislation

Article 24 DPD (entitled 'Sanctions') provides that:

The Member States shall adopt suitable measures to ensure the full implementation of the provisions of this Directive and shall in particular lay down the sanctions to be imposed in case of infringement of the provisions adopted pursuant to this Directive.

---

[10] Ibid., p. 132. [11] Case C-176/03, *'Environmental Sanctions'*, paras. 47–48.
[12] EC Communication 2010, p. 9   [13] Art. 78 GDPR Proposal.
[14] De Hert and Boulet 2016, p. 372. See also de Hert 2014.

All Member States had implemented this provision, though in very different ways.[15] The harmonisation of sanctions was one of the purposes of the GDPR.

2. International instruments

Modernised Convention 108 provides in Article 12 that 'each Party undertakes to establish appropriate judicial and non-judicial sanctions and remedies for violations of the provisions of this Convention'.

C. Analysis

1. Introduction

Article 84 in conjunction with recital 150 obliges the Member States to lay down rules on both administrative fines and 'other penalties' that they enact for infringements of Article 83.[16] Recital 151 makes an exception to these requirements for Denmark and Estonia, with Denmark being allowed to implement the rules on administrative fines as criminal penalties, and Estonia being allowed to implement them in the framework of a misdemeanour procedure. Under recital 149, Member States are also allowed to lay down rules for criminal penalties for infringements of the GDPR, as long as they do not violate the principle of *ne bis in idem* as set forth by the CJEU.

Several elements of Article 84 warrant further analysis. In particular, what the 'effective, persuasive and proportionate' criteria entail; what data protection violations could, or should, be subject to additional penalties; and how compliance with *ne bis in idem* will be assured in this context.

2. Effectiveness and proportionality

The stipulation that penalties should be 'effective, persuasive and proportionate' was set out by the CJEU in the '*Greek Maize*' case.[17] In that judgment, the Hellenic Republic was found to have breached its EU law obligations through its failure to act, in particular by 'omitting to initiate all the criminal or disciplinary proceedings provided for by national law against the perpetrators of the fraud'.[18] The Court specified that Member States were under a general obligation to ensure that infringements of EU law 'are penalised under conditions, both procedural and substantive, which are analogous to those applicable to infringements of national law of a similar nature and importance and which, in any event, make the penalty effective, persuasive and proportionate'.[19]

The principle of effectiveness and of proportionality are well-established as general principles of EU law and as limitations on national procedural autonomy.[20] For instance, the principle of effectiveness dictates that national procedural rules and rules on sanctions may not render impossible or excessively difficult the exercise of rights conferred by Union law.[21] However, limitations such as reasonable limitation periods to initiate proceedings are permissible.[22] In assessing the compatibility of national penalties introduced pursuant to Article 84 GDPR with these general principles, it will however be necessary

---

[15] See Korff 2010, pp. 104–108. [16] See Tosoni 2018, p. 1202.
[17] Case C-68/88, '*Greek Maize*'. [18] Ibid., para. 22. [19] Ibid., para. 24.
[20] Lenaerts, Maselis and Gutman 2015, ch. 4. [21] Case C-33/76, *Rewe*.
[22] Case C-78/98, *Preston and Others*.

to identify 'comparator' infringements (of a similar nature and importance) against which the effectiveness and equivalence of these penalties can be benchmarked.

3. Types of violations subject to further penalties

A second query is what data protection violations should be subject to further penalties. The English language version of Article 84 GDPR ('shall lay down the rules') suggests that this is an imperative. Given that criminalisation is currently a widespread practice across EU Member States, this should not be contentious. However, there is reasonable divergence on the question of whether conduct that is subject to an Article 83 administrative sanction should be excluded from Article 84 penalties. Jay remarks that this is simply 'not clear whether these penalties can apply to the same breaches which are the subject of administrative fines under Art 83'.[23] De Hert and Boulet are more decisive in arguing that it would be incorrect to assume that because particular conduct is subject to an administrative sanction under Article 83 GDPR, it should not be subject to further penalties under Article 84 GDPR. They argue, to the contrary, that 'overlaps between crimes and between criminal wrongs and administrative wrongs are deliberately chosen and, as such, are not always illegitimate, since they allow an approach where the criminal is only used where the administrative fails'.[24] The text of Article 84 GDPR seems to support this conclusion. While the Council had inserted the specification that the penalties enacted should be '*in particular* for infringements which are not subject to administrative fines pursuant to Article 83 GDPR' (emphasis added), the words 'in particular' would suggest that penalties for infringements which are also subject to administrative fines can be introduced. This would be subject to the proviso that such additional penalties respect the principle of *ne bis in idem*.

4. Ne bis in idem

The principle of *ne bis in idem* is set out in Article 50 of the Charter of Fundamental Rights of the European Union ('CFR'). This right entitled 'Right not to be tried or punished twice in criminal proceedings for the same criminal offence' provides that 'No one shall be liable to be tried or punished again in criminal proceedings for an offence for which he or she has already been finally acquitted or convicted within the Union in accordance with the law'. The administrative fines pursuant to Article 83 GDPR are likely to be classified as 'criminal' as they meet the *Engel* criteria which, when determining whether a law is criminal in nature, take into account three alternative criteria: whether the domestic law treat the contested penalties as criminal law; whether the offence is of general concern and application; and, whether the penalty operates as a punishment and/ or a deterrent (or is merely designed, for instance, to compensate for harm suffered).[25] Given that the ECtHR has held that competition law fines constitute, as a result of their severity, criminal sanctions, a similar finding is inevitable for data protection sanctions.[26] In *Åkerberg Fransson* the CJEU held that, following the imposition of a final administrative penalty of a criminal nature, Article 50 CFR precludes criminal proceedings in relation to the same acts brought against the same person.[27]

---

[23] Jay 2017, p. 331.   [24] De Hert and Boulet 2016, p. 383.
[25] ECtHR, *Engel and Others v The Netherlands*, para. 82.
[26] ECtHR, *A. Menarini Diagnostics S.r.l. v Italy*, para. 42.
[27] Case C-617/10, *Åkerberg Fransson*, para. 34.

The Court had the opportunity to consider this principle more recently in the context of insider dealing. The EU Directive in question allowed Member States to enact administrative sanctions, without prejudice to any existing criminal law sanctions, and required them to ensure that penalties were effective, persuasive and proportionate. The Directive did not specify however what effect a final criminal judgment would have on proceedings for an administrative fine. The Court held that the bringing of proceedings for an administrative fine of a criminal nature, based on the same facts, constitutes a limitation of Article 50 CFR[28] that may however be justified on the basis of Article 51(1) CFR.[29] In *Di Puma*, the criminal proceedings had resulted in an acquittal of the individual on the grounds that the facts had not been established. The Court held that the criminal proceedings had *res judicata* effect[30] and 'clearly exceeds what is necessary' in order to achieve the objective of protecting the integrity of financial markets'.[31]

In *Garlsson Real Estate SA*, the individual concerned had already been convicted of the insider trading offence when administrative proceedings were launched. The Court recalled that when assessing the existence of the same offence the relevant criterion is the 'identity of the material facts, understood as the existence of a set of concrete circumstances which are inextricably linked together and which resulted in the final acquittal or conviction of the person concerned'.[32] The Court once again held that the duplication in proceedings constituted a limitation of Article 50 CFR[33] and sought to assess its justification. Interestingly, the Court held that the duplication respected the essence of Article 50 since duplication is allowed 'only under certain conditions which are exhaustively defined, thereby ensuring that [Article 50] is not called into question as such'.[34] More interesting still is the Court's proportionality analysis. It specified that the national rules should exist to ensure coordination so as 'to reduce to what is strictly necessary the additional disadvantage associated with such a duplication for the persons concerned'[35] and to 'ensure that the severity of the sum of all penalties imposed does not exceed the seriousness of the offence identified'.[36] It concluded however that Italian legislation in question had these safeguards in place solely for the duplication of pecuniary penalties and not to the duplication of an administrative fine of a criminal nature and a term of imprisonment.[37] It was thus incompatible with Article 50 CFR.

This jurisprudence provides an interesting insight into how the principle of *ne bis in idem* may apply to Articles 83–84 GDPR. As Eurojust has noted, it is possible that *ne bis in idem* will arise not just at national level but 'Member States might be confronted with the transnational application of *ne bis in idem* for punitive sanctions imposed in other Member States'.[38] It is also noteworthy that the GDPR itself does not stipulate criteria to be taken into account when choosing between administrative and criminal enforcement.[39] Such a rule of 'coordination' will therefore need to be introduced by Member States.

The WP29 guidance on this is limited. It states that Member States will need to ensure compliance through all corrective measures available to them and that supervisory authorities 'will also be required to choose the most appropriate channel for pursuing regulatory action' (including via penal sanctions where available at national level).[40] De

---

[28] Joined Cases C-596/16 and C-597/16, *Di Puma*, para. 40.   [29] Ibid, para. 41.
[30] Ibid., para. 45.   [31] Ibid., para. 44.
[32] Case C-537/16, *Garlsson Real Estate SA*, para. 37.   [33] Ibid., para. 41.
[34] Ibid., para. 45.   [35] Ibid., para. 55.   [36] Ibid., para. 56.   [37] Ibid., para. 60.
[38] Eurojust 2017, p. 25.   [39] De Hert and Boulet 2016, p. 386.   [40] WP29 2017, p. 17.

Hert and Boulet suggest that the coordination rule in Austria under the Data Protection Directive had 'a certain charm'. It provided that administrative law sanctions would apply in so far as the contested action does not fulfil the requisite legal elements of a criminal offence.[41]

Select Bibliography

EU legislation

GDPR Proposal: Proposal for a Regulation of the European Parliament and of the Council on the protection of individuals with regard to the processing of personal data and on the free movement of such data (General Data Protection Regulation), COM(2012) 11 final, 25 January 2012.

Academic writings

Dawes and Lynskey 2008: Dawes and Lynskey, 'The Ever-Longer Arm of EC Law: The Extension of Community Competence into the Field of Criminal Law', 45(1) *Common Market Law Review* (2008), 131.
De Hert 2014: De Hert, 'The EU Data Protection Reform and the (Forgotten) Use of Criminal Sanctions', 4 *International Data Privacy Law* (2014), 262.
De Hert and Boulet 2016: De Hert and Boulet, 'The Co-Existence of Administrative and Criminal Law Approaches to Data Protection Wrongs' in Wright and de Hert (eds.), *Enforcing Privacy: Regulatory, Legal and Technological Approaches* (Springer 2016), 357.
Jay 2017: Jay, *Guide to the General Data Protection Regulation* (Sweet & Maxwell 2017).
Lenaerts, Maselis and Gutman 2015: Lenaerts, Maselis and Gutman, *EU Procedural Law* (OUP 2015).
Tosoni 2018: Tosoni, 'Rethinking Privacy in the Council of Europe's Convention on Cybercrime', 34(6) *Computer Law & Security Review* (2018), 1197.

Papers of data protection authorities

WP29 2017: Article 29 Working Party, 'Guidelines on the Application and Setting of Administrative Fines for the Purposes of the Regulation 2016/679' (WP 253, 3 October 2017).

Reports and recommendations

EC Communication 2010: Communication from the Commission to the European Parliament, the Council, the Economic and Social Committee and the Committee of Regions, 'A Comprehensive Approach to on Personal Data Protection in the European Union', COM(2010) 609 final, 4 November 2010.
Eurojust 2017: Eurojust, 'The Principle of Ne Bis in Idem in Criminal Matters in the Case Law of the Court of Justice of the European Union' (September 2017).
FRA 2013: European Union Agency for Fundamental Rights, *Access to Data Protection Remedies in EU Member States* (Publication Office of the European Union 2013).
Korff 2010: Korff for the European Commission, 'Comparative Study on Different Approaches to New Privacy Challenges in Particular in the Light of Technological Developments, Working Paper No. 2: Data Protection Laws in the EU' (20 January 2010).

---

[41] De Hert and Boulet, p. 363.

Chapter IX Provisions Relating to Specific Processing Situations (Articles 85–91)

Article 85. Processing and freedom of expression and information

HERKE KRANENBORG*

1. Member States shall by law reconcile the right to the protection of personal data pursuant to this Regulation with the right to freedom of expression and information, including processing for journalistic purposes and the purposes of academic, artistic or literary expression.
2. For processing carried out for journalistic purposes or the purpose of academic artistic or literary expression, Member States shall provide for exemptions or derogations from Chapter II (principles), Chapter III (rights of the data subject), Chapter IV (controller and processor), Chapter V (transfer of personal data to third countries or international organisations), Chapter VI (independent supervisory authorities), Chapter VII (cooperation and consistency) and Chapter IX (specific data processing situations) if they are necessary to reconcile the right to the protection of personal data with the freedom of expression and information.
3. Each Member State shall notify to the Commission the provisions of its law which it has adopted pursuant to paragraph 2 and, without delay, any subsequent amendment law or amendment affecting them.

Relevant Recitals

(4) The processing of personal data should be designed to serve mankind. The right to the protection of personal data is not an absolute right; it must be considered in relation to its function in society and be balanced against other fundamental rights, in accordance with the principle of proportionality. This Regulation respects all fundamental rights and observes the freedoms and principles recognised in the Charter as enshrined in the Treaties, in particular the respect for private and family life, home and communications, the protection of personal data, freedom of thought, conscience and religion, freedom of expression and information, freedom to conduct a business, the right to an effective remedy and to a fair trial, and cultural, religious and linguistic diversity.

(153) Member States law should reconcile the rules governing freedom of expression and information, including journalistic, academic, artistic and or literary expression with the right to the protection of personal data pursuant to this Regulation. The processing of personal data solely for journalistic purposes, or for the purposes of academic, artistic or literary expression should be subject to derogations or exemptions from certain provisions of this Regulation if necessary to reconcile the right to the protection of personal data with the right to freedom of expression and information, as enshrined in Article 11 of the Charter. This should apply in particular to the processing of personal data in the audio-visual field and in news archives and press libraries. Therefore, Member States should adopt legislative measures which lay down the exemptions and derogations necessary for the purpose of balancing those fundamental rights. Member States should adopt such

---

* The views expressed are solely those of the author and do not necessarily reflect those of the European Commission.

exemptions and derogations on general principles, the rights of the data subject, the controller and the processor, the transfer of personal data to third countries or international organisations, the independent supervisory authorities, cooperation and consistency, and specific data-processing situations. Where such exemptions or derogations differ from one Member State to another, the law of the Member State to which the controller is subject should apply. In order to take account of the importance of the right to freedom of expression in every democratic society, it is necessary to interpret notions relating to that freedom, such as journalism, broadly.

Closely Related Provisions

Article 17(3)(a) (Right to erasure ('right to be forgotten') (see too recitals 65 and 66); Article 86 (Processing and public access to official documents) (see too recital 154)

Related Provisions in EUDPR [Regulation (EU) 2018/1725]

Article 19(3)(a) (Right to erasure ('right to be forgotten') (see too recital 38)

Relevant Case Law

CJEU

Case C-101/01, *Criminal proceedings against Bodil Lindqvist*, judgment of 6 November 2003 (ECLI:EU:C:2003:596).
Case C-73/07, *Tietosuojavaltuutettu v Satakunnan Markkinapörssi Oy and Satamedia Oy*, judgment of 16 December 2008 (ECLI:EU:C:2008:727).
Opinion of Advocate General Kokott in Case C-73/07, *Tietosuojavaltuutettu v Satakunnan Markkinapörssi Oy and Satamedia Oy*, delivered on 8 May 2008 (ECLI:EU:C:2008:266).
Case C-131/12, *Google Spain v Agencia Española de Protección de Datos (AEPD) and Mario Costeja González*, judgment of 13 May 2014 (Grand Chamber) (ECLI:EU:C:2014:317).
Case C-345/17, *Sergejs Buivids v Datu valsts inspekcija*, judgment of 14 February 2019 (ECLI:EU:C:2019:122).
Opinion of Advocate-General Szpunar in Case C-136/17, *G. C., A. F., B. H., E. D. v Commission nationale de l'informatique et des libertés (CNIL)*, delivered on 10 January 2019 (ECLI:EU:C:2019:14).
Case C-687/18, *SY v Associated Newspapers Ltd* (pending).

ECtHR

Von Hannover v Germany, Appl. No. 59320/00, judgment of 24 September 2004.
K.U. v Finland, Appl. No. 2872/02, judgment of 2 December 2008.
Von Hannover v Germany (No.2), Appl. Nos. 40660/08 and 60641/08, judgment of 7 February 2012.
Delfi AS v Estonia, Appl. No. 64569/09, judgment of 16 June 2015.
Satakunnan Markkinapörssi Oy and Satamedia Oy v Finland, Appl. No. 931/13, judgment of 21 July 2015.
Couderc and Hackette Filipacchi Associés v France, Appl. No. 40454/07, judgment of 10 November 2015.
Magyar Helsinki Bizottság v Hungary, Appl. No. 18030/11, judgment of 8 November 2016.
Satakunnan Markkinapörssi Oy and Satamedia Oy v Finland, Appl. No. 931/13, judgment of 27 June 2017.

United Kingdom

Stunt v Associated Newspapers Ltd [2018] EWCA Civ 1780.

A. Rationale and Policy Underpinnings

Rules on privacy and data protection do not necessarily fit easily with the freedom of expression, which, according to Article 11 of the Charter of Fundamental Rights of the European Union ('CFR') and Article 10 European Convention on Human Rights ('ECHR'), includes the freedom to receive and impart information. Already in the early 1980s the drafters of Council of Europe Convention 108 were conscious of the tension between both fundamental rights. Article 9(2)(b) of Convention 108 allows for derogation from certain provisions if this constitutes a necessary measure in a democratic society in the interest of protecting the rights and freedoms of others.

As a consequence of the development of the information society, the tension between the two rights has become increasingly apparent. This is also recognised in Modernised Convention 108. A recital has been added recalling that 'the right to protection of personal data is to be considered in respect of its role in society and has to be reconciled with other rights and freedoms, including the freedom of expression'. In the revised provision on restrictions, Article 11(1)(b), freedom of expression is explicitly mentioned as a ground for restrictions.

In the DPD the European Union gave a more explicit recognition of the need for exemptions or derogations when data are processed in the context of the freedom of expression. In a dedicated provision, Article 9, Member States were allowed to provide for exemptions or derogations for the processing of personal data carried out solely for journalistic purposes or the purpose of artistic or literary expression, however only if they were necessary to reconcile the right to privacy with the rules governing freedom of expression.

The reconciliation of the rights to privacy and data protection with the right to freedom of expression and to receive and impart information is a matter which the Union legislator has basically preferred to leave to Member States, as in Article 85 of the GDPR. Member States are obliged to notify the European Commission of their laws on the matter which allows the Commission to keep a certain control. However, this control will be performed against the general parameters set out by Article 85 GDPR.

B. Legal Background

1. EU legislation

Article 85 GDPR is the successor of Article 9 DPD. The latter provision already required Member States to provide for exemptions or derogations from the provisions in several chapters of the DPD (Chapters II, IV and VI). The exemptions or derogations could be made for the processing of personal data carried out solely for journalistic purposes or the purpose of artistic or literary expression only if they were necessary to reconcile the right to privacy with the rules governing freedom of expression. If the two provisions are compared, what stands out is that the word 'solely', although still used in recital 153, can no longer be found in Article 85 itself. Another change is that 'academic' has been added to artistic and literary expression, and that 'the right to privacy' is replaced by 'the right to the protection of personal data'.

2. International instruments

Article 9(2)(b) of Convention 108 allows for derogation from certain provisions of the Convention if it constitutes a necessary measure in a democratic society in the interest of protecting the rights and freedoms of others. In the Explanatory Report to Convention 108 freedom of the press is given as an example.[1] In Modernised Convention 108, in the revised provision on restrictions (the new Article 11(1)(b)), freedom of expression is explicitly mentioned as a ground for restrictions.

3. National developments

Article 9 DPD already required Member States to provide for exemptions and derogations where necessary to reconcile the right to privacy with the rules governing freedom of expression. In consequence many Member States had national laws in place when the GDPR entered into application. A report from 2010 shows that the laws in the Member States are 'clearly widely divergent, and range from stipulating the overall primacy of freedom of expression, for the benefit of everyone, through wide exemptions for the press (but not for non-professionals), to a system which is tantamount to imposing prior restraint on the publication of certain information by the press'.[2]

4. Case law

The CJEU seems reluctant to take a firm position on how to reconcile the rights to privacy and data protection with the right to freedom of expression. In *Lindqvist*,[3] *Satamedia*[4] and *Buivids*[5] the Court clearly kept it as a matter to be resolved at national level. In *Google Spain*,[6] the CJEU did express itself on the balance of the different interests at stake when a person requested the search engine to take certain links from the list of results when searching on his name, with a default position in favour of data protection, albeit outside the remit of Article 9 DPD. However, when balancing the interests at stake, the CJEU did not explicitly refer to freedom of expression, an omission for which the decision was criticised.

When it is up to the Member States to reconcile both rights, this should still be done in conformity with the ECHR. Throughout the years, the ECtHR has built up an impressive body of case law in which the right to privacy in Article 8 ECHR is reconciled with the right to freedom of expression in Article 10 ECHR. The Court has developed a standard set of criteria. One of the decisive elements for the outcome of the balance is whether the personal information published contributed to a debate of public interest. However, the ECtHR leaves a wide margin of appreciation for the parties to the ECHR. If the balancing exercise was undertaken by the national authorities in conformity with the criteria laid down in its case law, the Court required strong reasons to substitute its view for that of the domestic courts.[7]

---

[1] Explanatory Report Convention 108 1981, p. 11.
[2] Korff 2010. See also Erdos 2015A.
[3] Case C-101/01, *Lindqvist*.
[4] Case C-73/07, *Satamedia*.
[5] Case C-345/17, *Buivids*.
[6] Case C-131/12, *Google Spain*.
[7] See ECtHR, *Von Hannover v Germany (No. 2)*, para. 107.

C. Analysis

1. Introduction

Article 9 DPD was criticised for being 'opaque' and manifestly or far 'too restricted'.[8] This criticism basically concerned two elements in Article 9. First, the provision referred only to three types of activities, namely processing for journalistic, artistic and literary purposes. As a result, this excluded the possibility to reconcile the data protection rules with the right to freedom of expression when personal data was processed for other (also 'non-professional') purposes which fell none the less within the scope of freedom of expression. Secondly, the provision only applied when the processing was carried out 'solely' for those three purposes, which seemed to exclude from the scope of the provision all activities which were not exclusively performed for such purposes.[9]

2. CJEU

In the *Lindqvist* ruling of 2003, the CJEU considered whether, despite the existence of Article 9, the provisions of the DPD as such brought about a restriction which conflicted with the general principle of freedom of expression.[10] This case concerned the publication on a Swedish internet site, of certain personal information by Mrs Lindqvist about fellow parishioners in her church. The Court concluded that the provisions of the DPD did not as such bring about such a restriction. It considered that it was for the national authorities and courts responsible for applying the implementing national law to ensure a fair balance between the rights and interests in question, including fundamental rights.[11]

In *Satamedia* the CJEU had the occasion to clarify Article 9 of the DPD. The case concerned two companies which, through a newspaper and through a paid SMS service, provided details of the financial situation of 1.2 million natural persons in Finland, information which they obtained from publicly available governmental sources. The CJEU was asked whether these activities could be seen as processing activities carried out 'solely for journalistic purposes'. The CJEU emphasised that the object of Article 9 was to reconcile two fundamental rights and that the obligation to do so lay with the Member States.[12] With a view to the importance of the right to freedom of expression in every democratic society, the CJEU considered that the notions relating to that freedom, such as journalism, had to be interpreted broadly.[13] On the other hand, the derogations and limitations to the right to data protection applied only in so far as strictly necessary. The CJEU went on to find that the derogations and limitations provided for in Article 9 did not only apply to media undertakings but also to every person engaged in journalism. Moreover, the fact that a publication was done for profit-making purposes did not preclude such a publication from being considered as an activity undertaken 'solely for journalistic purposes'.[14] Furthermore, the medium used to transmit the data was not

---

[8] See Korff 2010, p. 12; Erdos 2015B, p. 151.
[9] For a very elaborate and thorough analysis of this provision, and on the broader issue of reconciling EU data protection rules with the freedom of expression, see Erdos 2015B.
[10] Case C-101/01, *Lindqvist*, para. 72.
[11] Ibid., para. 90. See on Art. 9 DPD also Kranenborg 2014, pp. 231–232 and pp. 262–263.
[12] Case C-73/07, *Satamedia*, para. 54.
[13] Ibid., para. 56. This is in stark contrast with opinion of the Advocate-General in this case who advised a restrictive approach, see Case C-73/07, *Satamedia* (AG Opinion), para. 60.
[14] Case C-73/07, *Satamedia*, para. 59.

determinative for whether the activity undertaken was done 'solely for journalistic purposes'. The CJEU concluded that the activities of the two companies could be classified as 'journalistic activities' if their 'sole object [was] the disclosure to the public of information, opinion or ideas'.[15]

With the *Satamedia* ruling the CJEU considerably lowered the impact of the two elements in Article 9 of the DPD that had been regarded as 'too restrictive'.

As to, first, the notion of journalistic activities, it was interpreted very broadly and not restricted to professional entities. This broad interpretation brought more activities within the scope of the provision. In particular, the placing of material on the internet could easily be considered to have the object of disclosing information, opinion or ideas to the public. This was confirmed by the CJEU in *Buivids*.[16] The question in that case was whether putting a film on YouTube by someone who openly filmed a police officer when being interrogated, constituted a journalistic activity. The CJEU considered that not all information published on the internet, involving personal data, comes under the concept of 'journalistic activities'.[17] Still, the CJEU took the view that the activity in the case at issue might have been done solely for journalistic purposes, provided its sole objective was the disclosure to the public of information, opinions or ideas, which was for the referring court to determine.[18] In this respect, the CJEU pointed to the fact that, according to Mr Buivids, the video in question was published on an internet site to draw to the attention of society alleged police malpractice which, as Mr Buivids had claimed, occurred while he was making his statement.[19]

In the *Satamedia* ruling the second element, the notion of 'solely', was also interpreted broadly. According to the Court it did not imply exclusivity: one could perfectly well (also) earn money by disclosing information to the public without falling outside of the scope of the derogations and limitations under Article 9 DPD.

The lenient approach of the CJEU may have accommodated to a certain extent the criticism from the perspective of freedom of expression, but it triggered criticism from the perspective of the opposing interest: the protection of personal data. The ruling has been criticised for not respecting the parameters set by the EU legislator within which the two fundamental rights should be reconciled. In particular, it has been argued that because of the broad possibilities for derogations and limitations, freedom of expression could actually 'trump' the right to data protection.[20]

This issue is raised in *Associated Newspapers*.[21] This pending case concerns national legislation imposing a stay on proceedings by a data subject relating to unpublished material held for the purposes of journalism. The stay is automatic where two conditions concerning the personal data at issue are met: they must be processed for journalistic purposes, and with a view to publication. The court does not review the substance of whether the stay should be imposed, and it remains in place until the ICO, the UK data protection authority, makes a determination on whether the two factual conditions have been met. The legislation is intended to be a strong disincentive to data protection law being used to inhibit the freedom of the press and stifle stories pre-publication, but the Court of Appeal in London was divided on its interpretation.[22] The majority felt that it

---

[15] Ibid., para. 62.   [16] Case C-345/17, *Buivids*.   [17] Ibid., para. 58.
[18] Ibid., para. 69.   [19] Ibid., para. 60.
[20] See Lynskey 2015, p. 145. See for a critical view on the ruling also Oliver 2009, pp. 1459–1463.
[21] Case C-687/18, *Associated Newspapers*   [22] See *Stunt v Associated Newspapers Ltd.*

was necessary to reconcile the rights to privacy and freedom of expression and that it fell within the broad margin of discretion given to member states in balancing those rights under the ECHR. However, the minority felt that the legislation was incompatible with the right to an effective judicial remedy because it did not permit the review by the court in each case of the balance between freedom of expression and the rights of privacy and protection of personal data.[23]

Returning to the *Google Spain* ruling, which concerned a request to have certain search results on a name removed, the CJEU concluded that Article 9 DPD was only relevant for the holder of the website on which the information was published (*in casu* the Spanish newspaper). Processing carried out by Google, the operator of a search engine, according to the CJEU, appeared not to be carried out 'solely for journalistic purposes'.[24] Placing the activities of Google outside the remit of Article 9 DPD allowed the CJEU to apply the data protection rules in full to the situation without having to consider any possible derogations and limitations put in place to reconcile the data protection rules with the freedom of expression. When balancing the different interests at stake (on the basis of the ground for processing contained in Article 7(f) of the DPD, now Article 6(1)(f) GDPR), which arguably included the interests of the user of the search engine in finding information and the interest of the website holder to have his website found, the CJEU did not refer to freedom of expression and information in so many words. Instead, the CJEU referred to the interest of the general public in finding information upon a search relating the data subject's name and disregarded the interest of the website holder.[25] The CJEU subsequently formulated the default rule that in the situation at hand, the rights of the data subject override not only the economic interest of the search engine operator but also the interest of its users.[26] None the less, using some elements of the case law of the ECtHR, the CJEU described situations in which the default rule would be set aside.[27]

In *Buivids*, as regards the balance to be made between the right to privacy and the right to freedom of expression, the CJEU pointed to a number of relevant criteria laid down by the ECtHR which had to be taken into account. These include the contribution to a debate of public interest, the degree of notoriety of the person affected, the subject of the news report, the prior conduct of the person concerned, the content, form and consequences of the publication, and the manner and circumstances in which the information was obtained and its veracity.[28] Similarly, according to the CJEU, the possibility for the controller to adopt measures to mitigate the extent of the interference with the right to privacy had to be taken into account.

The above case law illustrates the difficulties which surround the reconciliation of the two fundamental rights. In *Satamedia* and *Buivids* the CJEU gave a wide interpretation of Article 9 of the DPD, leaving more situations to reconciliation at the national level. On the other hand, in *Google Spain*, the Court apparently felt compelled to give more substantive guidance and moved the issue outside the scope of Article 9 of the DPD, turning the conflict of the two fundamental rights into a balancing of the different interests at stake under the 'unrestricted' data protection rules.

---

[23] See the commentary on Art. 79 in this volume.   [24] Case C-131/12, *Google Spain*, para. 85.
[25] Ibid., para. 97. In the opinion of the Advocate-General in Case C-136/17, *G.C.* (still pending), the Advocate-General has invited the CJEU to take the right to freedom of expression into account in its analysis of the lawfulness of Google's search engine activities. See Case C-136/17, *G.C.* (AG Opinion), paras. 89–92.
[26] Case C-131/12, *Google Spain*, paras. 81 and 97.   [27] See Docksey 2016, p. 206.
[28] Case C-345/17, *Buivids*, para. 66.

As already mentioned, Article 85 GDPR contains two main changes which relate precisely to the two elements of criticism regarding Article 9 DPD: academic activities were added and the word 'solely' disappeared from the provision. This provision and in particular its recitals are less explicit in codifying the approach under Article 9 of the DPD than the proposal of the European Commission had envisaged. In the proposed recital several phrases were taken from the CJEU's ruling in *Satamedia*, including clarification of the notion of 'journalistic' activities.[29] However, in the legislative process most of these phrases were deleted. What remained was the statement that in order to take account of the importance of the right to freedom of expression in a democratic society, notions relating to that freedom, such as journalism, must necessarily be interpreted broadly. No new language was introduced which would indicate any deviation from the previous approach. The word 'solely' was taken from the provision, although, as stated, recital 153 still uses the word 'solely'. It may therefore be assumed that Article 85 GDPR will not bring about any major changes to the approach developed under the old rules.

3. ECtHR

Although some elements of guidance on how actually to reconcile both fundamental rights can be found in the *Google Spain* case, albeit outside the remit of Article 9 of the DPD, it is clear from *Buivids* that for more substantive guidance one has to look at the case law of the ECtHR. As said, the Court developed a standard set of criteria to be taken into account when a situation in which both rights collide has to be assessed. These criteria are:

1. the contribution to a debate of public interest
2. the degree of notoriety of the person affected
3. the subject of the news report
4. the prior conduct of the person concerned
5. the method of obtaining the information and its veracity/circumstances in which, in case of pictures, the photographs were taken
6. the content, form and consequences of the publication.[30]

Most famous in this respect are the cases concerning the Princess of Monaco, Caroline von Hannover. In the first case concerning this applicant the ECtHR developed a notion which became a cornerstone in subsequent case law on this matter. Private pictures of the Princess in a gossip magazine—the sole purpose of which, according to the ECtHR, was to satisfy the curiosity of a particular readership regarding the details of the applicant's private life—did not contribute to any debate of general interest to society despite the applicant being known to the public.[31] According to the ECtHR a distinction needed to be made between reporting details of the private life of an individual and reporting facts—even controversial ones—capable of contributing to a debate in a democratic society; e.g. relating to politicians in the exercise of their official functions. While in the latter case the press exercises its vital role of public 'watchdog' it does not do so in the former.[32] The

---

[29] See rec. 121 and Art. 80 GDPR Proposal.
[30] ECtHR, *Couderc and Hackette Filipacchi Associés*, para. 93. This case gives a very elaborate overview of the different criteria.
[31] ECtHR, *Von Hannover v Germany*, para. 65.
[32] Ibid., para. 63. See also ECtHR, *Couderc and Hackette Filipacchi Associés*, para. 118.

ECtHR considered that anyone, even if they are known to the general public, must be able to enjoy a 'legitimate expectation' of protection of and respect for their private life.[33] A member of a royal family obviously has a peculiar public position since the person concerned did not willingly and knowingly subject herself to public scrutiny. This is the difference, for instance, with politicians. The ECtHR took the view that certain private actions by public figures cannot be regarded as private, given their potential impact in view of the role played by those persons on the political or social scene and the public's resultant interest in being informed of them.[34]

The ECtHR was also confronted with the follow-up to the *Satamedia* ruling of the CJEU.[35] After the CJEU ruling, despite the broad interpretation given by the CJEU to the notion of 'journalistic activities', the Finnish court concluded that the activities of Satakunnan and Satamedia could not be qualified as such. In order to assess whether the activities were journalistic, the national court did not just check whether the activities had as sole object the disclosure to the public of information, opinion or ideas, but used the criterion of whether the publication of the information contributed to a public debate. Since it did not, the national court concluded that the activities were not journalistic. It could be argued that the Finnish court took a more restrictive approach than the CJEU in the *Satamedia* ruling. However, the ECtHR stayed away from expressing itself on this in *Satakunnan and Satamedia*. It recalled the judgment of the CJEU but noted that the national court came to its conclusion with an acceptable reasoning attaching importance to both rights.[36]

The ruling in *Satakunnan and Satamedia* shows that the ECtHR still leaves a wide margin of appreciation for the parties to the ECHR.[37] If the balancing exercise is undertaken by the national authorities in conformity with the criteria laid down in the ECtHR's case law, the Court requires strong reasons to substitute its view for that of the domestic Courts.[38]

4. Exceptions

In so far as necessary to reconcile the right to the protection of personal data with the freedom of expression and information, Member States shall provide for exemptions and restrictions from the rules of the GDPR, but not from all. No exemptions are possible with regard to the provisions contained in Chapter I (which includes the definitions) and in Chapter VIII (on remedies, liability and penalties).

5. Notification to the Commission

According to Article 85(3) GDPR, Member States shall notify to the European Commission the provisions of their laws adopted on the basis of Article 85(2). Member States also have to notify, without delay, any subsequent amendment law or amendment affecting them. The Commission publishes these notifications online, together with the

---

[33] ECtHR, *Von Hannover v Germany*, para. 69.
[34] ECtHR, *Couderc and Hackette Filipacchi Associés*, paras. 120–121.
[35] ECtHR *Satakunnan and Satamedia*.
[36] Ibid., paras. 69–72. The conclusion was confirmed by the Grand Chamber of the ECtHR.
[37] See also ECtHR, *Delfi AS v Estonia*, para. 139.
[38] See ECtHR, *Von Hannover v Germany (No. 2)*, para. 107.

other notifications required under the GDPR.[39] The question is what the Commission will do after receiving the different notifications. As said, a study from 2010 shows that there are wide divergences between the Member States.[40] Even more than under the previous *Directive*, the Commission will feel compelled to search for a certain coherence in this area in order not to undermine the harmonising effects of the present *Regulation*. The existence of national law also raises questions about the national law applicable in cross-border situations, which can be 'particularly sensitive'.[41] The issue was recognised by the legislator, which stated in recital 153 that where such exemptions or derogations differ from one Member State to another, the law of the Member State to which the controller is subject should apply.

Select Bibliography

EU legislation

GDPR Proposal: Proposal for a Regulation of the European Parliament and of the Council on the protection of individuals with regard to the processing of personal data and on the free movement of such data (General Data Protection Regulation), COM(2012) 11 final, 25 January 2012.

Academic writings

Docksey 2016: Docksey, 'Four Fundamental Rights: Finding the Balance', 6(3) *International Data Privacy Law* (2016), 195
Erdos 2015A: Erdos, 'Data Protection Confronts Freedom of Expression on the "New Media" Internet: The Stance of European Regulatory Authorities', 40 *European Law Review* (2015), 531.
Erdos 2015B: Erdos, 'From the Scylla of Restrictions to the Charybdis of Licence? Exploring the Scope of the "Special Purposes" Freedom of Expression Shield in European Data Protection', 52(1) *Common Market Law Review 'CMLRev.'* (2015), 119.
Jozwiak, 'Balancing the Right to Data Protection and Freedom of Expression and Information by the Court of Justice of the European Union', 23(3) *Maastricht Journal of European and Comparative Law* (2016), 404.
Kranenborg 2014: Kranenborg, 'Article 8', in Peers, Hervey, Kenner and Ward (eds.), *The EU Charter of Fundamental Rights: A Commentary* (Hart Publishing 2014), 223.
Lynskey 2015: Lynskey, *The Foundations of EU Data Protection Law* (OUP 2015).
Oliver 2009: Oliver, 'The Protection of Privacy in the Economic Sphere before the European Court of Justice', 46(5) *CMLRev.* (2009), 1443.

Papers of data protection authorities

Article 29 Working Party, 'Opinion 1/2008 on Data Protection Issues Related to Search Engines' (WP148, 4 April 2008).
Article 29 Working Party, 'Recommendation 1/97 on Data Protection Law and the Media' (WP1, 25 February 1997).

---

[39] Such as notifications required under Arts. 51(4) (data protection authorities) and 84(2) (penalties) and notifications in the case of national legislation, such as Art. 88(3). See Member State notifications to the Commission under the GDPR. See also the commentary on Art. 88 in this volume.
[40] Korff 2010.   [41] Ibid., pp. 12–13.

Reports and recommendations

Explanatory Report Convention 108 1981: Council of Europe, 'Explanatory Report to the Convention for the Protection of Individuals with Regard to Automatic Processing of Personal Data' (28 January 1981), available at https://rm.coe.int/16800ca434.

Korff 2010: Korff for the European Commission, 'Comparative Study on Different Approaches to New Privacy Challenges in Particular in the Light of Technological Developments, Working Paper No. 2: Data Protection Laws in the EU' (20 January 2010).

Member State notifications to the Commission under the GDPR: European Commission, 'EU Member States notifications to the European Commission under the GDPR', available at https://ec.europa.eu/info/law/law-topic/data-protection/data-protection-eu/eu-countries-gdpr-specific-notifications_en.

Article 86. Processing and public access to official documents

HERKE KRANENBORG[*]

Personal data in official documents held by a public authority or a public body or a private body for the performance of a task carried out in the public interest may be disclosed by the authority or body in accordance with Union or Member State law to which the public authority or body is subject in order to reconcile public access to official documents with the right to the protection of personal data pursuant to this Regulation.

Relevant Recital

(154) This Regulation allows the principle of public access to official documents to be taken into account when applying this Regulation. Public access to official documents may be considered to be in the public interest. Personal data in documents held by a public authority or a public body should be able to be publicly disclosed by that authority or body if the disclosure is provided for by Union or Member State law to which the public authority or public body is subject. Such laws should reconcile public access to official documents and the reuse of public sector information with the right to the protection of personal data and may therefore provide for the necessary reconciliation with the right to the protection of personal data pursuant to this Regulation. The reference to public authorities and bodies should in that context include all authorities or other bodies covered by Member State law on public access to documents. Directive 2003/98/EC of the European Parliament and of the Council leaves intact and in no way affects the level of protection of natural persons with regard to the processing of personal data under the provisions of Union and Member State law, and in particular does not alter the obligations and rights set out in this Regulation. In particular, that Directive should not apply to documents to which access is excluded or restricted by virtue of the access regimes on the grounds of protection of personal data, and parts of documents accessible by virtue of those regimes which contain personal data the re-use of which has been provided for by law as being incompatible with the law concerning the protection of natural persons with regard to the processing of personal data.

Closely Related Provisions

Article 85 (Processing and freedom of expression and information) (see also recital 153)

Related Provisions in LED [Directive (EU) 2016/680]

Recital 16

Related Provisions in EUDPR [Regulation (EU) 2018/1725]

Article 9(3) (Transmissions of personal data to recipients established in the EU); Article 52(4) (Application of Regulation 1049/2001 to EDPS) (see too recital 76)

---

[*] The views expressed are solely those of the author and do not necessarily reflect those of the European Commission.

Relevant Case Law

CJEU

Case T-194/04, *The Bavarian Lager Co. Ltd v Commission of the European Communities*, CFI, judgment of 8 November 2007 (ECLI:EU:T:2007:334).
Case C-28/08 P, *European Commission v The Bavarian Lager Co. Ltd*, judgment of 29 June 2010 (Grand Chamber) (ECLI:EU:C:2010:378).
Joined Cases C-92/09 and 93/09, *Volker and Markus Schecke GbR* and *Hartmut Eifert v Land Hessen*, judgment of 9 November 2010 (Grand Chamber) (ECLI:EU:C:2010:662).
Case T-82/09, *Gert-Jan Dennekamp v European Parliament*, GC, judgment of 23 November 2011 (ECLI:EU:T:2011:688).
Case T-190/10, *Kathleen Egan and Margaret Hackett v European Parliament*, GC, judgment of 28 March 2012 (ECLI:EU:T:2012:165).
Case T-115/13, *Gert-Jan Dennekamp v European Parliament*, GC, judgment of 15 July 2015 (ECLI:EU:T:2015:497).
Case C-615/13 P, *ClientEarth and Pesticide Action Network Europe (PAN Europe) v European Food Safety Authority*, judgment of 16 July 2015 (ECLI:EU:C:2015:489).

ECtHR

The Sunday Times v United Kingdom, Appl. No. 6538/74, judgment of 26 April 1979.
Leander v Sweden, Appl. No. 9248/81, judgment of 26 March 1987.
Gaskin v United Kingdom, Appl. No. 10454/83, judgment of 7 July 1989.
Guerra v Italy, Appl. No. 14967/89, judgment of 19 February 1998.
Sdružení Jihočeské Matky v Czech Republic, Appl. No. 19101/03 (decision on admissibility), judgment of 10 July 2006.
Társaság a Szabadságjogokért v Hungary, Appl. No. 37374/05, judgment of 14 April 2009.
Magyar Helsinki Bizottság v Hungary, Appl. No. 18030/11, judgment of 8 November 2016.

A. Rationale and Policy Underpinnings

Article 15 of the Treaty on the Functioning of the European Union ('TFEU') contains rules on transparency and the right of public access to documents. However, these rules apply only to the EU legislative process and the Union institutions, bodies, offices and agencies. Additionally, Article 42 of the Charter of Fundamental Rights of the European Union ('CFR'), which recognises a right of access to documents, together with the EU provisions on access to documents in Regulation 1049/2001, are restricted to the EU level. The EU has no general competence to set rules on public access to official documents at the national level. Only in specific areas may the EU address the issue of public access to the information concerned. The main example in this respect is public access to environmental information.[1]

As a consequence, in the DPD and again in the GDPR, the EU legislator maintains a distance from the national rules on public access to documents. In fact, Article 86 GDPR only acknowledges the importance of public access to official documents. No further guidance is given on how public access to official documents should be reconciled with the data protection rules.

---
[1] See Directive 2003/4/EC. These rules stem from the Aarhus Convention.

B. Legal Background

1. EU legislation

The DPD only contained recital 72 in which reference was made to the principle of public access to official documents. It was stated that the DPD allowed this principle to be taken into account when implementing the principles set out in the DPD.

At the EU level, Article 9(3) EUDPR requires the EU institutions and bodies, when transferring personal data to recipients established in the Union, to reconcile the right to protection of personal data with the right of access to documents in accordance with EU law.

2. International instruments

Within the Council of Europe, the issue of public access to document and data protection is referred to, not in Convention 108, but in instruments on public access to documents. After several recommendations of the Committee of Ministers ('COM'),[2] in 2009 the Council of Europe agreed on a Convention on Access to Official Documents.[3] When this text was finalised it had not yet entered into force, as it required ten ratifications and only nine members of the Council of Europe had done so. Article 3(1)(f) of the Convention allows parties to limit the right of access to official documents by law, if necessary, in a democratic society and proportionate to the aim of protecting, inter alia, 'privacy and other legitimate private interest'.

In Modernised Convention 108, a new preamble is introduced stating that the Convention 'permits account to be taken, in the implementation of the rules laid down therein, of the principle of the right of access to official documents'.

3. National developments

Around half of the EU Member States recognise public access to documents as a fundamental right enshrined in their constitution. Almost all Member States have a law on public access to documents, although the level of transparency reached through these laws may vary.[4] With regard to the reconciliation of these rules with rules on privacy and data protection, the national legislation of the EU Member States shows a wide variety of approaches. It should be noted that already under the DPD almost all Member States chose to address the possible conflict in the legislation on public access to documents and not in the national data protection law which transposed the DPD.[5] The conflict rules in the national laws on public access range from a plain privacy exception to an explicit and detailed reconciliation with the data protection rules.[6] In a significant number of Member States the legislature formulates a category or categories of data which fall outside the privacy or data protection exception to the right of public access to documents. Most often these data relate to a person acting in an official capacity.[7]

---

[2] See COM Recommendation 1991 and COM Recommendation 2002.
[3] Convention on Access to Official Documents.
[4] See for an elaborate study from 2005: Kranenborg and Voermans 2005.
[5] See Kranenborg 2008, pp. 1102–1105.
[6] Ibid., p. 1103.   [7] Ibid., p. 1104.

4. Case law

In the case law of the CJEU the clash between transparency on the one hand and privacy and data protection on the other has occurred several times. A distinction can be made between situations in which the CJEU had to assess the validity of a Union law prescribing the publication of certain personal data (rules on 'active' disclosure), and situations in which a request for public access was made to a document held by an Union institution which contained personal data (so-called 'passive' disclosure, i.e. disclosure upon request).

Rules on 'active' disclosure were considered in the *Schecke* case. In *Schecke* the CJEU was asked about the validity of a Union law which required the publication of personal data of farmers who received money from Union funds. The CJEU accepted that the aim of increasing the transparency of Union funds pursued an objective of general interest recognised by the EU; however, since the Union legislator had not considered whether the same objective could be achieved with less intrusive means concerning privacy and data protection, the CJEU declared the Union law invalid on this point.[8] The necessity of the measure to achieve the intended objective had not been established.

'Passive' disclosure has been the subject of several cases before the General Court and the Court of Justice. The leading case is *Bavarian Lager*, which will be discussed below, in which the CJEU overturned a decision of the General Court.[9] The case concerned a request for public access to the minutes of a meeting which contained the names of the participants. The CJEU had to assess the matter on the basis of the rules on access to documents and on data protection which apply to the EU institutions: Regulation 1049/2001[10] on public access to European Parliament, Council and Commission documents and Regulation 45/2001.[11] The decision of 29 June 2010 put an end to a long debate about the interpretation of the relevant Article 4(1)(b) of Regulation 1049/2001, which also involved the European Ombudsman and the EDPS.

Two strands of case law of the ECtHR are relevant here. The first is case law in which the Court gradually acknowledged a right of public access to documents under Article 10 of the European Convention on Human Rights ('ECHR'). The second strand is the well-established case law on the conflict between Article 8 and Article 10. Once a right of public access is recognised under Article 10, a conflict with privacy and data protection is closely linked to the situations subject of the 'standard' case law on the collision of Article 8 and Article 10 ECHR. In the case *Magyar Helsinki Bizottság*,[12] which will be discussed below, both strands of case law came together.

C. Analysis

1. Introduction

When examining Article 86 GDPR one can wonder what normative value it actually has. This question becomes particularly apparent when Article 86 is compared with Article 85 GDPR which deals with the right to freedom of expression and information. In both

---

[8] Joined Cases C-92/09 and C-93/09, *Schecke*, paras. 71 and 81.
[9] Case C-28/08 P, *Bavarian Lager*.   [10] See Regulation 1049/2001.
[11] See Table of Legislation.   [12] ECtHR, *Magyar Helsinki Bizottság*.

provisions the EU legislator refrained from regulating the matter on substance, but the approach taken is completely different. Article 85 creates room for manoeuvre for the Member States, albeit within certain limits and subject to certain conditions. It requires Member States to adopt laws which provide for exemptions and derogations from almost all provisions in the GDPR necessary to reconcile the right to protection of personal data with the freedom of expression and information. These laws have to be notified to the European Commission.

Article 86 does not provide Member States such a circumscribed leeway. It only states that personal data in official documents may be disclosed in accordance with Union or Member State law to which the authority or body is subject in order to reconcile public access with the right to data protection pursuant to the GDPR. No exemptions and derogations from the data protection rules are allowed. In fact, it seems that the Union or Member State law referred to in Article 86 on which disclosure can be based is no different from a Union or Member State law referred to in Article 6 GDPR.[13] Article 86 seems to be intended to confirm that public access to official documents is a legitimate objective pursued by a legal obligation, or a necessary processing activity for the performance of a task in the public interest. Support for this 'declaratory' nature of the provision can be found in recital 154, in which it is stated that public access to official documents may be considered to be in the public interest.[14] It follows from Article 86 that the solution for reconciling the two principles, if any, must be laid down in the national law on access to documents. However, no further guidance is given on how to actually reconcile public access to official documents with the data protection rules.

2. ECtHR

As with freedom of expression,[15] guidance must first of all be found in the case law of the ECtHR. However, in this respect a preliminary issue for some time was whether the right of public access to official documents was as such protected under the ECHR.[16] The case law shows a gradual process of acceptance of a right of public access to official documents under Article 10 ECHR with the ruling in *Magyar Helsinki Bizottság* of November 2016 as the final step so far.

Article 10 ECHR provides that the right to freedom of expression shall include the freedom to hold opinions and to receive and impart information and ideas without interference by a public authority. The provision does not specify that it entails a freedom to seek information. In its earlier case law, the ECtHR interpreted this provision as preventing the government from interfering in the exchange of information between individuals (unless justified on the basis of Article 10(2) ECHR).[17] In 'vertical' relationships, i.e. information exchange between an individual and public authorities, the ECtHR first discussed a right of access under other provisions of the ECHR, since the

---

[13] See for an assessment of the grounds for disclosing personal data for transparency purposes, on the basis of the DPD, WP29 2001.

[14] Art. 86 GDPR seems to have more the character of a recital. In the initial proposal of the European Commission no provision on the matter was included, but only a recital stating that the Regulation allowed the principle of public access to official documents to be taken into account when applying the provisions set out in the Regulation, see rec. 18 GDPR Proposal.

[15] See the commentary on Art. 85 in this volume.   [16] See e.g. Curtin and Meijers 1995.

[17] See e.g. ECtHR, *The Sunday Times*, para. 65.

individual concerned had a particular personal interest in the disclosure (such as the right of access to information about oneself under the right to privacy in Article 8 ECHR).[18]

However, the ECtHR had to express itself directly on the matter when it was confronted with requests for access to information refused by national authorities which were made in the public interest, or at least in the interest of a group of individuals. In *Guerra v Italy* the ECtHR ruled that the freedom to receive information under Article 10 ECHR could not be construed as imposing on a state, in such circumstances, positive obligations to collect and disseminate information of its own motion.[19] This raised the question whether the state, when it had already collected information, could be under an obligation to disseminate such information upon request. In *Sdružení Jihočeské Matky* the ECtHR considered 'that it is difficult to derive from Article 10 a general right to have access to administrative documents'.[20] However, since the Czech legislation itself provided for such a right, the ECtHR assessed whether the refusal was justified under the conditions of Article 10(2) ECHR and concluded it was. In *Társaság a Szabadságjogokért* the ECtHR once again did not expressly recognise a right of public access to official documents under Article 10 ECHR, but considered it a form of indirect censorship if a request for access was refused that had been made by a 'watchdog' (the Civil Liberties Union) gathering information about a subject of public interest.[21] The ECtHR stated that the function of public 'watchdog' was not limited to the press, but could also be performed by an association involved in human rights litigation with various objectives, including the protection of freedom of information.[22]

In *Magyar Helsinki Bizottság*, the ECtHR finally took a more principled position. It considered that the time had come to clarify the classic principles on access to information under Article 10 ECHR.[23] It 'relaxed' the conditions set in *Társaság a Szabadságjogokért*: the right of access is not necessarily restricted to public watchdogs but can be invoked by any individual in circumstances where the information is instrumental for the individual's exercise of their right to freedom of expression, in particular the freedom to receive and impart information and where its denial constitutes an interference with that right.[24] The ECtHR then set out the criteria to be taken into account for assessing to what extent a denial of access to information constitutes an interference with the applicant's rights.

After the recognition of a more general right of public access to official documents under Article 10 ECHR, more specific guidance was provided by the ECtHR on the relationship of this right with the right to privacy in Article 8 ECHR. In the *Magyar Helsinki Bizottság* case, access to the information was refused since it concerned personal data not subject to disclosure.[25] Under Hungarian law disclosure of such information was only possible if expressly provided for by law or if the information was related to the performance of municipal or governmental (state) functions or was related to other persons performing public duties. Hungary took the view that the public defenders about whom information was requested on their appointments in the case did not qualify as other persons performing public duties.[26] In its assessment

---

[18] See ECtHR, *Leander v Sweden*, para. 74 and also ECtHR, *Gaskin v UK*, para. 52.
[19] ECtHR, *Guerra v Italy*, para. 53.   [20] ECtHR, *Sdružení Jihočeské Matky*.
[21] ECtHR, *Társaság a Szabadságjogokért*, para. 26.   [22] Ibid., para. 27.
[23] ECtHR, *Magyar Helsinki Bizottság*, para. 156.   [24] Ibid.
[25] Ibid., para. 188.   [26] Ibid.

the ECtHR acknowledged that the request for access concerned personal data but added that it did not involve information outside the public domain. It concluded that the privacy rights of the public defenders would not have been negatively affected had the request for access been granted.[27]

In this respect, the ECtHR pointed at the fact that the information related predominantly to the conduct of professional activities in the context of public proceedings. In that sense, according to the ECtHR, these professional activities could not be considered to be a private matter. The ECtHR also considered that the disclosure would not have exposed the public defenders to a degree surpassing that which they could possibly have foreseen when registering as public defenders: there was no reason to assume that the information could not be known to the public through other means.[28]

In *Magyar Helsinki Bizottság*, the ECtHR used the distinction between professional and private matters of an individual to assess whether the restriction of the right to public access for privacy reasons was justified.

3. CJEU

The conflict between rules on access to documents and rules on data protection applicable to EU institutions was subject of a long debate involving many actors. With its *Bavarian Lager* ruling, the CJEU put an end to it. But in subsequent case law further clarification had to be provided. The discussion focussed on the meaning of the 'conflict rule' in the EU provisions on access to documents, i.e. Article 4(1)(b) of Regulation 1049/2001, which determined that 'institutions shall refuse access to a document where disclosure would undermine the protection of ... privacy and the integrity of the individual, in particular in accordance with Community legislation regarding the protection of personal data'. In short, two opposing interpretations were advocated. The first interpretation (advocated by the Commission) was the so-called 'renvoi' interpretation implying that the provision should be seen as a direct referral to applicable regulation on data protection (Regulation 45/2001). The other interpretation, the 'threshold' interpretation (defended by the applicant and the EDPS, and supported by the European Ombudsman), argued that it should be assessed whether the privacy of the individual was undermined by disclosing the information without moving directly to the data protection rules.[29] Although the General Court followed the 'threshold' approach, the CJEU overturned its ruling on appeal and decided in favour of the 'renvoi' interpretation.[30]

As a consequence, requests for access to documents containing personal data were governed by the rules of Regulation 45/2001 in as far as access to the personal data was concerned. It follows from Article 8(b) of this Regulation that personal data can only be transferred if the person requesting the transfer shows that it is necessary and that there is no reason to assume that the data subject's legitimate interest might be prejudiced. Since in *Bavarian Lager*, the applicant had not given any reasons for accessing the data—under the access to documents

---

[27] Ibid., para. 198.   [28] Ibid., paras. 194–195.
[29] See for the EDPS position before and after the *Bavarian Lager* ruling of the CJEU: EDPS 2005 and EDPS 2011. See on the distinction between privacy and data protection: Kranenborg 2008, Hustinx 2017, Kranenborg 2014, Kokott and Sobotta 2014, Lynskey 2015, Docksey 2016 and Hijmans 2016.
[30] See Case T-194/04, *Bavarian Lager*; and Case C-28/08 P, *Bavarian Lager*.

rules an applicant is not required to do so—the CJEU concluded that the Commission had not been able to make the assessment of Article 8(b) of Regulation 45/2001.[31]

In subsequent case law, the General Court further clarified the circumstances in which the necessity of having *public* access to personal data could be proven. In *Dennekamp*[32] the General Court annulled a refusal of the European Parliament to grant access to a document containing information about the participation of Members of the European Parliament ('MEPs') in an additional pension scheme. The Court did not accept the reasoning of the applicant, a Dutch journalist, that publication of the data was necessary for informing the public and enabling it to take part in a debate on the legitimacy of the scheme. It did, however, accept the necessity of access for the aim of bringing to light potential conflicts of interest.[33] According to the Court, disclosure would not prejudice the legitimate interests of the MEPs as the personal data belongs 'in the public sphere of MEPs'.[34]

The existence of the necessity of disclosure of personal data in the public interest was also recognised by the CJEU in its judgment in *ClientEarth*,[35] which concerned a request for access to an EU guidance document on the interpretation of a provision relating to the acceptance of substances when placing plant protection products on the market. A draft version of the document contained remarks of appointed experts. The CJEU concluded that the disclosure of the information was necessary to ensure transparency of the process of adoption of a measure likely to have an impact on the activities of economic operators, in particular, in order to appreciate how the form of participation by each expert in that process might, through that expert's own scientific opinion, have influenced the context of that measure.[36] The CJEU concluded that the claim that the legitimate interests of the expert would be prejudiced was not supported by any evidence.[37]

4. Effects of Article 86

It follows from all of the above that Member States are left to reconcile their rules on public access to official documents without much concrete guidance. The interest of reconciliation as such is acknowledged in Article 86 GDPR, but the provision does not allow for exemptions and derogations from the rules contained in the GDPR nor does it set any further conditions. A law which regulates public access to official documents containing personal data has to fulfil the conditions of Article 6 GDPR. Existing conflict rules in the Member States, the case law of the ECtHR as well as the case law of the CJEU show that there are two criteria to assess whether disclosure of data is justified: the distinction between private and professional matters and the 'public nature' of the data. However, these serve only as general indications, leaving the actual assessment to a case by case analysis. It remains to be seen, in particular after the ECtHR ruling in *Magyar Helsinki Bizottság*, in how far public access to official documents can be reconciled with the data protection rules under Article 85 GDPR on the freedom of expression and information.

5. Relation to Directive 2003/98/EC

A final point concerns the reference in recital 154 to Directive 2003/98/EC on the reuse of public sector information.[38] The recital states that Directive 2003/98/EC leaves intact

---

[31] Case C-28/08 P, *Bavarian Lager*, para. 78. [32] Case T-115/13, *Dennekamp*.
[33] Ibid., paras. 87 and 113. [34] Ibid., para. 121. [35] Case C-615/13 P, *ClientEarth*.
[36] Ibid., paras. 55–56. [37] Ibid., paras. 68–70.
[38] Directive 2003/98/EC. See Jaatinen 2016.

and in no way affects the level of protection of natural persons with regard to the processing of personal data under the provisions of Union and Member State law, and in particular does not alter the obligations and rights set out in the GDPR. This is unusual, since such a statement should normally be contained in Directive 2003/98/EC itself, just as Article 1(4) of that Directive explicitly refers to the DPD. The recital then continues with a specification: in particular that Directive should not apply to documents to which access is excluded or restricted by virtue of the access regimes on the grounds of protection of personal data, and parts of documents accessible by virtue of those regimes which contain personal data the reuse of which has been provided for by law as being incompatible with the law concerning the protection of natural persons with regard to the processing of personal data. This suggests that the legislator wanted to ensure that, once data protection is relied upon to refuse public access to a document, this should not be 'circumvented' by application of the rules on reuse of public sector data.

Select Bibliography

International agreements

Aarhus Convention: Convention on Access to Information, Public Participation in Decision-Making and Access to Justice in Environmental Matters, 25 June 1998.
Convention on Access to Official Documents: Council of Europe Convention on Access to Official Documents, CETS No. 205.

EU legislation

Directive 2003/4/EC: Directive 2003/4/EC of the European Parliament and of the Council of 28 January 2003 on public access to environmental information, OJ 2003 L41/26.
Directive 2003/98/EC: Directive 2003/98/EC on the re-use of public sector information, OJ 2003 L 345/90.
GDPR Proposal: Proposal for a Regulation of the European Parliament and of the Council on the protection of individuals with regard to the processing of personal data and on the free movement of such data (General Data Protection Regulation), COM(2012) 11 final, 25 January 2012.
Regulation 1049/2001: Regulation (EC) No. 1049/2001 of the European Parliament and of the Council of 30 May 2001 regarding public access to European Parliament, Council and Commission document, OJ 2001 L 145/43.

Academic writings

Curtin and Meijers 1995: Curtin and Meijers, 'The Principle of Open Government in Schengen and the European Union: Democratic Retrogression?', 32(2) *Common Market Law Review* 'CMLRev.* (1995), 391.
Docksey 2016: Docksey, 'Four Fundamental Rights: Finding the Balance', 6(3) *International Data Privacy Law* (2016), 195.
Driessen, *Transparency in EU Institutional Law: A Practitioner's Handbook* (Kluwer Law International 2012).
Hijmans 2016: Hijmans, *The European Union as Guardian of Internet Privacy* (Springer 2016).
Hustinx 2017: Hustinx, 'EU Data Protection Law: The Review of Directive 95/46/EC and the General Data Protection Regulation', in Cremona (ed.), *New Technologies and EU Law* (OUP 2017), 123.
Jaatinen 2016: Jaatinen, 'The Relationship between Open Data Initiatives, Privacy, and Government Transparency: A Love Triangle?', 6 *International Data Privacy Law* (2016), 28.

Kokott and Sobotta 2014: Kokott and Sobotta, 'The Distinction between Privacy and Data Protection in the Jurisprudence of the CJEU and the ECtHR', in Kranenborg and Hijmans (eds.), *Data Protection Anno 2014: How to Restore Trust?* (Intersentia 2014).

Kranenborg 2008: Kranenborg, 'Access to Documents and Data Protection in the European Union: On the Public Nature of Personal Data', 45(4) *CMLRev.* (2008), 1079.

Kranenborg 2014: Kranenborg, 'Article 8', in Peers, Hervey, Kenner and Ward (eds.), *The EU Charter of Fundamental Rights: A Commentary* (Hart Publishing 2014), 223.

Kranenborg and Voermans 2005: Kranenborg and Voermans, *Access to Information in the European Union: A Comparative Analysis of EC and Member State Legislation* (Europa Law Publishing 2005).

Lynskey 2015: Lynskey, *The Foundations of EU Data Protection Law* (OUP 2015).

Papers of data protection authorities

EDPS 2005: European Data Protection Supervisor, 'Public Access to Documents and Data Protection' (July 2005).

EDPS 2011: European Data Protection Supervisor, 'Public Access to Documents Containing Personal Data after the Bavarian Lager Ruling' (March 2011).

WP29 2001: Article 29 Working Party, 'Opinion 5/2001 on the European Ombudsman Special Report to the European Parliament Following the Draft Recommendation to the European Commission in Complaint 713/98/IJH' (WP 44, 17 May 2001).

Reports and recommendations

COM Recommendation 1991: Committee of Ministers of the Council of Europe, 'Recommendation on the Access to Information Held by Public Authorities', R(91)10, 9 September 1991.

COM Recommendation 2002: Committee of Ministers of the Council of Europe, 'Recommendation No. R(2002)2 on Access to Official Documents', R(2002)2, 21 February 2002.

Article 87. Processing of the national identification number

PATRICK VAN EECKE   ANRIJS ŠIMKUS

Member States may further determine the specific conditions for the processing of a national identification number or any other identifier of general application. In that case the national identification number or any other identifier of general application shall be used only under appropriate safeguards for the rights and freedoms of the data subject pursuant to this Regulation.

Closely Related Provisions

Article 83 (Fines for breaches of any obligations pursuant to Member State law adopted under Article 87) (see too recital 148)

Relevant Case Law

ECtHR

Jäggi v Switzerland, Appl. No. 58757/00, judgment of 13 July 2006.
Odièvre v France [GC], Appl. No. 42326/98, judgment of 13 February 2003.

A. Rationale and Policy Underpinnings

The DPD did not provide for any specific rules on the use of national identification numbers or other identifiers of general nature ('national ID numbers') but left it to the Member States to determine the conditions under which a national identification number or any other identifier of general application may be processed. Member States were therefore left with a very broad margin of appreciation in this field. As a result, they adopted different approaches in regulating not only the use of national ID numbers, but the concept of such identifiers in general. Given the sensitive and complex nature of this topic, the EU legislator decided not to attempt harmonisation through the GDPR.

Thus, the idea behind Article 87 GDPR was to allow Member States to maintain their right to set their own conditions for processing national ID numbers, which was initially provided for by Article 8(7) DPD. Although the core concept contained in both Articles is the same, Article 87 GDPR has introduced certain changes.

First, according to the first sentence of Article 87 GDPR, there is no longer an obligation for Member States to have in place specific rules on the processing of national ID numbers. This means that a Member State may choose to apply only data protection rules of general application to existing or newly created national ID numbers. Previously, under the DPD, Member States had to provide rules governing the conditions under which national ID numbers or other identifiers of general application could be processed.[1]

---

[1] DPD, Art. 8(7).

Secondly, if Member States do however decide to lay down specific rules on national ID numbers (or maintain the ones they had already established in accordance with the DPD), then the second sentence of Article 87 GDPR requires that the use of these identifiers pursuant to such rules be accompanied with appropriate safeguards to protect individuals' rights and interests. What this also means, in essence, is that whatever rules Member States decide to adopt pursuant to Article 87, such rules must also conform with the minimum standards imposed by the GDPR as a whole, and no derogations in this respect are permitted.

Thirdly, although national ID numbers were not explicitly classified as a special category of data anywhere in the DPD, it could have been assumed that the EU legislator saw such identifiers as a special category of sensitive personal data, for the obvious reason that the relevant provision was placed under Article 8 DPD titled 'The processing of special categories of data'. If this was the case, then any use of national ID numbers had to also respect the additional rules applicable to sensitive data. The GDPR has cleared up this confusion, since there are no references in Article 87 or anywhere else in the GDPR linking national ID numbers to sensitive data. Given that national ID numbers have been developed differently across the EU, especially in terms of which categories of personal data are associated with each identifier, and what personal information the ID number itself reveals, then not all such identifiers will necessarily constitute sensitive data. Therefore, since the GDPR leaves it up to the Member States to develop, implement and decide on the use of any national ID numbers, it is only logical that the determination of whether these identifiers constitute sensitive data should also be left to their discretion.

B. Legal Background

1. EU legislation

The legal antecedent of Article 87 GDPR was Article 8(7) DPD, which provided that 'Member States shall determine the conditions under which a national identification number or any other identifier of general application may be processed'. As described above, while the core concept in both Articles is essentially the same, the DPD's version was different in several aspects.

2. International instruments

There are no international instruments dealing explicitly with the topic of national ID numbers. However, the Council of Europe Convention 108 and the Modernised Convention 108 are of relevance, since a national identification number would clearly constitute personal data under them.[2]

3. National developments

As noted above, since the DPD left it up to the Member States to decide how they set their rules regarding the processing of national ID numbers, national legislation in this field was not harmonised at EU level. As a result, the regulatory approach differs greatly among Member States.[3]

---

[2] See e.g. Explanatory Report Convention 108 2018, p. 4.
[3] See IDABC 2007, p. 3, stating that the Member States 'apply vastly different standards' for the lawful use of national identifiers.

For example, countries such as Belgium[4] and Sweden[5] deploy the system of a national identification number of general application as referred to in Article 8(7) DPD. This number is composed of the date of birth, a number referencing the citizen's gender and a control number. The identifier is of general application and is used in all fields of the public sector.

Other countries such as Austria[6] and Portugal[7] have not opted for an identification number of general application but use one that is limited to use within one particular sector only (e.g. an identification number issued for tax purposes, for instance, could identify every subject for tax-related matters within the issuing state).

Using and accessing the national identification number is also regulated differently among Member States. For example, in Belgium the use of the National Register number and the access to the data from the National Register is not free and must be authorised by either a statutory or regulatory provision or the Sector Committee of the National Register.[8]

4. Case law

There is as yet no case law applicable specifically to national ID numbers under the GDPR. Case law establishing rules on principles of processing of personal data would apply in the field of national ID numbers in a general fashion. Some cases of the ECtHR relevant to identity are mentioned below.

C. Analysis

1. Introduction

The idea to have some form of identification is as old as civilisation. Evidence of the use of unique identifiers assigned to each person can even be found in the New Testament, which contains the following passage: 'And he causeth all, both small and great, rich and poor, free and bond, to receive a mark in their right hand, or in their foreheads ... And that no man might buy or sell, save he that had the mark, or the name of the beast, or the number of his name'.[9] Restrictions on the processing of national identity numbers in data protection law derive from the historical experience in Europe of how they can be used to facilitate serious human rights abuses.[10]

2. Types of identifiers

A national ID number forms part of the much broader concept of identity. The latter concept has quickly grown from a rather philosophical notion of a person seeking the meaning of his or her life and place in society, to a more rationalised idea, where identity is treated as a form of intellectual property, capable of being monetised by state governments and corporate entities.[11] Fearing that the general right to privacy

---

[4] See IDABC Belgium 2009.   [5] See IDABC Sweden 2009.   [6] See IDABC Austria 2009.
[7] See IDABC Portugal 2009.   [8] See IDABC Belgium 2009, p. 15.
[9] Book of Revelations, Chapter 13, verses 16–17 (King James version). See also Angell 2008, p. 34.
[10] For example, the registration systems and related national identity card introduced in the Netherlands in the 1930s 'played an important role in the apprehension of Dutch Jews and Gypsies prior to their eventual deportation to the death camps'. Seltzer and Anderson 2001, p. 486.
[11] Angell 2008, pp. 24–34.

might not be sufficiently tailored to provide adequately protection, some authors urge that identity be acknowledged as a separate human right, in order to afford additional safeguards.[12] They have also argued that the ECtHR has implicitly recognised such a right.[13] Without going into further details, this brief introduction demonstrates the need for careful consideration of all elements enshrined in the notion of identity, including national ID numbers.

A national ID number serves, in essence, as a type of pseudonym. However, unlike the commonly associated use of pseudonyms for hiding one's true identity (e.g. when participating in a political debate on the internet), national ID numbers, as understood in Article 87 GDPR, are used as a unique and trustworthy method of identifying a particular person by state authorities, so that public services might be provided while also respecting that person's confidentiality.

Article 87 GDPR mentions two kinds of identifiers—national identification numbers and any other identifiers of general application. This denotes the existing situation among Member States, where several types of identifiers exist and are used for different purposes. In practical terms, national ID numbers can be categorised in two main groups—general purpose identifiers used by all state authorities for any public administration purpose, and identifiers used only for a specific sector or purpose (e.g. separate ID numbers only for social security or tax purposes). Moreover, Member States can not only choose how many national ID numbers they wish to have and for which purposes, but they can also regulate the categories of personal data collected under each identifier, and even what information will the ID number itself show. For example, several Member States issue ID numbers which are partly composed of such elements as an individual's date and place of birth, gender or nationality.

3. Risks and uses

Nowadays national ID numbers issued to individuals by state authorities can serve multiple purposes and facilitate a more efficient and expedited processing of personal data for public administration purposes. In this respect, the concept of a single data collection is one of the most important goals which such identifiers aim to achieve. This concept entails that all public authorities of a state should be treated as a single body. Therefore, if an individual has provided certain data to one state authority, then that person should not be obliged to provide the same data again to a different authority. Instead, whenever data is submitted to a state authority, it can be associated with a national ID number, which is known to and can be accessed by all other state authorities.

There are, however, risks associated with the use of national ID numbers. In the case of the previously mentioned single data collection concept, a national ID number assigned to an individual will need to be shared among all state authorities. For this reason, it is crucial that any national ID number system is accompanied by appropriate and sufficient safeguards to protect individuals' data. However, the question of what level of protection must be applied to national ID numbers will need to be answered by the Member States themselves, as this will largely depend on how much personal data they store alongside each identifier, with whom this identifier is shared

---

[12] Gutwirth 2009, pp. 124–126.
[13] Ibid., citing ECtHR, *Jäggi v Switzerland* and ECtHR, *Odièvre v France*.

and whether a particular ID number, due to its characteristics and functions, would amount to sensitive data.

The need for enhanced protection of national ID numbers is, in fact, ever increasing, as such identifiers are becoming more widespread and are shared not only between public authorities of a single state, but also in some situations between different states, and even disclosed to certain private institutions (e.g. to banks and insurance companies for anti-money laundering purposes). As an example, these concerns clearly relate to the application of the eIDAS Regulation,[14] which sets out a set of standards for electronic identification in the EU Single Market. In particular, Article 6(1) of this Regulation states that in certain circumstances a Member State is obliged to recognise, for the purpose of cross-border authentication for a given online service, the electronic identification means provided by a public sector body of another Member State. In practice, this means, for example, that a Belgian citizen would be able to use his Belgian national ID card (which is a recognised means of authentication in Belgium and contains a national ID number) to access the Spanish social security services provided online.

Another field where national ID numbers might come into play, is the prevention and combating of money laundering. For example, Article 28 of the Belgian Anti-Money Laundering Law[15] provides that the companies subject to it can request a professional organisation designated by the King to verify the identity of a natural person that did not physically appear during the identification process by using the national ID number or by accessing the National Register.

4. Member State protections

Due to the above-mentioned considerations, Member States will need to pay particular attention to whether the use of their national ID numbers is in compliance with the GDPR and whether individuals' personal data is sufficiently protected.[16] Furthermore, some Member States may need to re-evaluate or even modify their national ID number schemes in light of the stricter data protection standards of the GDPR. In particular, with the principle of data minimisation now enhanced in the GDPR,[17] Member States will need to put forward very strong arguments as to why a national ID number itself should contain an individual's personal data and why it is necessary to reveal such data every time the ID number is requested by private institutions and foreign states.

Select Bibliography

EU legislation

eIDAS Regulation: Regulation (EU) 910/2014 of the European Parliament and of the Council of 23 July 2014 on electronic identification and trust services for electronic transactions in the internal market and repealing Directive 1999/93/EC, OJ 2014 L 257/73.

---

[14] eIDAS Regulation.   [15] Belgian AML Law.
[16] For additional information concerning the issues presented in this article, and other related topics, see Vandezande 2011, with further references.
[17] See Art. 5(1)(c) GDPR.

National legislation

Belgian AML Law: Loi relative à la prévention du blanchiment de capitaux et du financement du terrorisme et à la limitation de l'utilisation des espèces, Moniteur Belge 6 October 2017, p. 90839.

Academic writings

Angell 2008: Angell, 'As I See It: Enclosing Identity', 1(1) *Identity Journal Limited* (2008), 23.
Gutwirth 2009: Gutwirth, 'Beyond Identity?', 1(1) *Identity Journal Limited* (2008), 123.
Seltzer and Anderson 2001: Seltzer and Anderson, 'The Dark Side of Numbers: The Role of Population Data Systems in Human Rights Abuses', 68(2) *Social Research* (2001), 481.
Vandezande 2011: Vandezande, 'Identification Numbers as Pseudonyms in the EU Public Sector', 2(2) *European Journal of Law and Technology* (2011), 1.

Reports and recommendations

EIDAS 2015 Study: European Commission, 'EIDAS Study to Support the Implementation of a Pan-European Framework on Electronic Identification and Trust Services for Electronic Transactions in the Internal Market', Annex D3: 'Monitoring eID and eTS—Country Profiles' (2015), available at https://publications.europa.eu/en/publication-detail/-/publication/c9192a82-0494-11e7-8a35-01aa75ed71a1/language-en.
Explanatory Report Convention 108 2018: Council of Europe, 'Explanatory Report to the Protocol Amending the Convention for the Protection of Individuals with Regard to the Automatic Processing of Personal Data' (10 October 2018), available at https://rm.coe.int/cets-223-explanatory-report-to-the-protocol-amending-the-convention-fo/16808ac91a.
IDABC 2007: European eGovernment Services ('IDABC'), 'eID Interoperability for PEGS: Analysis and Assessment of Similarities and Differences—Impact on eID Interoperability' (November 2007), available at http://ec.europa.eu/idabc/servlets/Doc0939.pdf?id=29618.
IDABC Austria 2009: European eGovernment Services, 'eID Interoperability for PEGS: Update of Country Profiles Study—Austrian Country Profile' (July 2009), available at http://ec.europa.eu/idabc/servlets/Doca375.pdf?id=32296.
IDABC Belgium 2009: European eGovernment Services, 'eID Interoperability for PEGS: Update of Country Profiles Study—Belgian Country Profile' (July 2009), available at http://ec.europa.eu/idabc/servlets/Doc3e95.pdf?id=32297.
IDABC Portugal 2009: European eGovernment Services, 'eID Interoperability for PEGS: Update of Country Profiles Study—Portuguese Country Profile' (July 2009), available at http://ec.europa.eu/idabc/servlets/Doc9e74.pdf?id=32289.
IDABC Sweden 2009: European eGovernment Services: 'eID Interoperability for PEGS: Update of Country Profiles Study—Sweden Country Profile' (July 2009), available at http://ec.europa.eu/idabc/servlets/Doc09e0.pdf?id=32291.

Article 88. Processing in the context of employment

PATRICK VAN EECKE   ANRIJS ŠIMKUS

1. Member States may, by law or by collective agreements, provide for more specific rules to ensure the protection of the rights and freedoms in respect of the processing of employees' personal data in the employment context, in particular for the purposes of the recruitment, the performance of the contract of employment, including discharge of obligations laid down by law or by collective agreements, management, planning and organisation of work, equality and diversity in the workplace, health and safety at work, protection of employer's or customer's property and for the purposes of the exercise and enjoyment, on an individual or collective basis, of rights and benefits related to employment, and for the purpose of the termination of the employment relationship.
2. Those rules shall include suitable and specific measures to safeguard the data subject's human dignity, legitimate interests and fundamental rights, with particular regard to the transparency of processing, the transfer of personal data within a group of undertakings, or a group of enterprises engaged in a joint economic activity and monitoring systems at the work place.
3. Each Member State shall notify to the Commission those provisions of its law which it adopts pursuant to paragraph 1, by 25 May 2018 and, without delay, any subsequent amendment affecting them.

Relevant Recital

(155) Member State law or collective agreements, including 'works agreements', may provide for specific rules on the processing of employees' personal data in the employment context, in particular for the conditions under which personal data in the employment context may be processed on the basis of the consent of the employee, the purposes of the recruitment, the performance of the contract of employment, including discharge of obligations laid down by law or by collective agreements, management, planning and organisation of work, equality and diversity in the workplace, health and safety at work, and for the purposes of the exercise and enjoyment, on an individual or collective basis, of rights and benefits related to employment, and for the purpose of the termination of the employment relationship.

Closely Related Provisions

Article 4 (Definition of consent) (see too recital 42); Article 7 (Conditions for consent) (see too recital 43); Article 9 (Processing of special categories of personal data in the context of employment) (see too recital 52); Article 83 (Fines for breaches of any obligations pursuant to Member State law adopted under Article 88) (see too recital 148)

Relevant Case Law

CJEU

Joined Cases C-465/00, C-138/01 and C-139/01, *Rechnungshof v Österreichischer Rundfunk and Others and Christa Neukomm and Joseph Lauermann v Österreichischer Rundfunk*, judgment of 20 May 2003 (ECLI:EU:C:2003:294).

Van Eecke/Šimkus

Case F-46/09, *V European Parliament*, CST, judgment of 5 July 2011 (ECLI:EU:F:2011:101).
Case C-342-12, *Worten — Equipamentos para o Lar SA v Autoridade para as Condições de Trabalho (ACT)*, judgment of 30 May 2013 (ECLI:EU:C:2013:355).

ECtHR

Copland v United Kingdom, Appl. No. 62617/00, judgment of 3 April 2007.
Bărbulescu v Romania, Appl. No. 61496/08, judgment of 5 September 2017.
Antović and Mirković v Montenegro, Appl. No. 70838/13, judgment of 28 November 2017.
López Ribalda and Others v Spain, Appl. Nos. 1874/13 and 8567/13, judgment of 9 January 2018.
Libert v France, Appl. No. 588/13, judgment of 22 February 2018.

Austria

Verfassungsgerichtshof, 28.11.2003, KR1/00 (ECLI:AT:VFGH:2003:KR1.2000)

A. Rationale and Policy Underpinnings

Under the predecessor to the GDPR—the DPD—the rules relating to data protection and privacy in the context of employment were implemented in varying ways across the different EU Member States. Thus, Article 88 was inserted in the GDPR to guarantee continuity of these rules, as well as the national interpretations of these rules given by the competent authorities.

Article 88 gives Member States the freedom to adopt, by laws or by collective agreement, specific rules for processing personal data in the employment context. However, for many Member States this Article will more likely serve as a legal basis simply to maintain the rules already put in place under the DPD, rather than adopting a new set of national rules.

B. Legal Background

1. EU legislation

The antecedent of Article 88 was Article 8(2)(b) DPD. Like the Directive, the GDPR leaves room for Member States to create laws governing the relationship between the GDPR and national employment law and lays down a number of principles with particular relevance to the employment relationship, such as consent and transparency. However, the DPD specifically referred to employment relations only in the context of the processing of sensitive data. The GDPR maintains this provision in Article 9(2), but also contains Article 88.

Before the adoption of the GDPR there was never any specific legal framework in the EU governing data processing in the context of employment.[1] While there had been proposals to adopt a directive specifying the application of the data protection principles in the employment context, these attempts have never materialised.[2]

---

[1] Compare FRA Handbook 2014, p. 170 and FRA Handbook 2018, p. 331.
[2] For an analysis of such a draft submitted for consultation by the EU Commission in 2004, see de Hert and Lammerant 2013, p. 22.

2. International instruments

There are a number of international instruments dealing, either directly or indirectly, with data processing in the context of employment.

Article 8 of the European Convention on Human Rights ('ECHR') guarantees to everyone the right to private life. While this article does not explicitly mention any employment aspects, the ECtHR has interpreted Article 8 to cover also the right to data protection of employees (see below). In particular, the Court has laid down several criteria, which apply to the monitoring of employee personal correspondence and to secret video surveillance in the workplace.

The first international treaty dealing specifically with data protection was Council of Europe Convention 108. While this convention established several principles and safeguards applicable to automated data processing, no provision explicitly addressed employee rights. Modernised Convention 108 also does not explicitly mention the processing of employee data.

There are other international instruments, which directly address data processing in the context of employment, however, they are not legally binding. One such instrument is the CoE Employment Recommendation.[3] Adopted in 1989, this recommendation was aimed at providing guidance for the Contracting States in implementing national legislation in the employment sector in a manner consistent with applicable privacy and data protection laws. Following a study on the proposed revision,[4] in 2015 the Employment Recommendation was replaced with a new version, which, in addition to the principles already proclaimed by the former recommendation, also takes into account the ever-increasing use of information and communication technologies, and the globalisation of employment and services.[5]

Finally, another authoritative, yet non-binding source worth mentioning is the International Labour Organisation's Code of Conduct on the protection of workers' personal data, adopted in 1997.[6] This code may serve as inspiration for stakeholders when drafting national legislation, collective agreements or working rules and policies.

3. National developments

Since the DPD gave Member States a wide margin of appreciation as to the implementation of data protection principles and rules in the context of employment (as is now done by the GDPR), there have been different national approaches in this field, and these differences appear in various forms. For example, the relevant provisions for each Member State might be provided for either in their labour codes, or in the general data protection laws, or both. Additionally, some Member States might choose to enact stricter rules than the ones now provided for in the GDPR, while others will stick to the minimum thresholds.

Germany was the first Member State to enact national legislation pursuant to Article 88 GDPR. Section 26 of the Federal Data Protection Act[7] lays down several rules on data processing in the field of employment, so that any such processing taking place in Germany complies with the GDPR. Many of the rules contained in the German Federal Data Protection Act 2017 specify the application of the general legal obligations imposed

---

[3] CoE Recommendation 1989. [4] Butarelli 2011. [5] CoE Recommendation 2015.
[6] ILO 1997. [7] German Federal Data Protection Act 2017.

by the GDPR to accommodate them for the employment field, e.g. by laying down conditions on video surveillance, how to document employee data processing, and compensating employees for data breaches.

4. Case law

4.1 CJEU

The CJEU has delivered numerous judgments on the interpretation of relevant data protection rules, which are also applicable when processing data in the context of employment. However, the CJEU has not provided any legal guidance aimed particularly at the employment field. Even when the factual circumstances of certain cases dealt by the CJEU related to employment, the legal issues dealt by the Court in those cases concerned the application of EU data protection laws in general.

For example, in the *Rundfunk* case the CJEU was requested to rule on the interpretation of a provision in the Austrian legal system, which required to make publicly available information about the salaries of certain persons employed in the public sector.[8] Austria claimed that the publication of the names of the persons concerned, as well as information on their salaries, was necessary in the public interest, in order to ensure transparency of public governance and proper management of public funds. The Court replied, in essence, that any national measures which interfere with the private life of individuals must comply with Article 8 ECHR. In particular, such measures must be in accordance with law, must pursue a legitimate aim and must be proportional to the aims pursued. The interpretation of the provision in question in compliance with this test was a matter for the Austrian courts to decide.[9]

The *Worten* case concerned a Portuguese law, which required an employer to make the record of employee working times available to the national authority responsible for monitoring working conditions, so as to allow its immediate consultation.[10] The aim of this law was to ensure that the national authority could effectively monitor whether an employer complies with the national rules of employee working times. Worten, a small company established in Portugal, was fined for a breach of this provision, as it had implemented a mechanism which restricted access to its employee working times records. It contested this decision and the case ultimately came before the CJEU.

The Court was first asked to clarify whether employee working times constituted personal data, to which it replied in the affirmative. It noted that the data contained in a record of working time, which concerned each worker's daily work periods and rest periods, constituted personal data, because they represented 'information relating to an identified or identifiable natural person'. Secondly, the CJEU established that national rules, such as the one in question, were not precluded per se under the DPD. However, such rules, as well as the applicable fines had to be necessary for the performance by the national authority of its monitoring task, by contributing to the more effective application of the legislation relating to working conditions. Whether that was the case in the present circumstances was for the national courts to decide.

---

[8] Joined Cases C-465/00, C-138/01 and C-139/01, *Österreichischer Rundfunk*.
[9] See the ruling of the Austrian Constitutional Court (Verfassungsgerichtshof, KR1/00), where the Court found that publication of the names as well as the salaries of the persons concerned was neither necessary nor proportionate.
[10] Case C-342-12, *Worten*.

Finally, the ruling by a lower EU court in the *V v EP* case is worthy of note.[11] In this case the Civil Service Tribunal found that the defendant institution had obtained the medical data of a candidate for recruitment in violation of both Regulation 45/2001[12] and Article 8 ECHR. In particular, the Tribunal found that there was no express consent for transferring the sensitive data concerned and that the transfer was not necessary as the purpose could have been achieved in a less intrusive manner. As a result of the seriousness of the infringement, the Tribunal ordered the Parliament to pay € 25,000 in damages, the only data protection ruling where an EU institution has been condemned in damages.

4.2 European Court of Human Rights

The ECtHR has delivered numerous rulings which have covered a wide range of issues on data protection and privacy in the workplace. Two aspects, which have been dealt by the Strasbourg Court, are of particular relevance—monitoring and accessing personal files of employees, and secret surveillance in the workplace.

As to the first aspect, one of the landmark cases in this respect is *Bărbulescu v Romania*,[13] where the Grand Chamber of the Court found a violation of the right to private life under Article 8 ECHR due to secret monitoring by an undertaking of its employee's private emails. The Court held that the Romanian authorities had failed to reach a fair balance between the interests of the undertaking and those of the employee. In particular, it ruled that the national courts had failed to determine whether the applicant had received prior notice from his employer of the possibility that his communications might be monitored; nor had they had regard either to the fact that he had not been informed of the nature or the extent of the monitoring, or the degree of intrusion into his private life and correspondence. In addition, the national courts had failed to determine, first, the specific reasons justifying the introduction of the monitoring measures; secondly, whether the employer could have used measures entailing less intrusion into the applicant's private life and correspondence; and thirdly, whether the communications might have been accessed without his knowledge.[14]

However, in the case of *Libert v France*[15] the Court came to a different conclusion, finding that the opening of an employee's personal files placed on the work computer by the employer did not amount to a violation of Article 8 ECHR. It is worth pointing out that in this case the employer had discovered that the applicant was storing pornographic files and forged certificates drawn up for third persons. Accordingly, in circumstances such as these, the Court ruled that the employer had a legitimate interest in making sure that the work computers are not used contrary to any internal policies or national law.

As regards the second aspect of video surveillance, the ECtHR found a violation of Article 8 ECHR in the case *Antović and Mirković v Montenegro*,[16] which concerned the monitoring of employees in their workplace. In this case the Court held that the national courts had erred in finding that the applicants—professors of one of Montenegro's universities—did not have the right to privacy, as they were being monitored in a public area. Here the Court recalled its well-established case law that professional activities may also fall within the ambit of private life.[17] Thus, the national courts had to examine

---

[11] Case F-46/09, *V v EP*. [12] See Table of Legislation. [13] ECtHR, *Bărbulescu v Romania*.
[14] See the summary of this case in ECtHR Factsheet 2018. [15] ECtHR, *Libert v France*.
[16] ECtHR, *Antović and Mirković v Montenegro*.
[17] As one of the well-known cases in this respect, see ECtHR, *Copland v UK*.

the interference of the applicants' right to privacy, which they had failed to do in the present case.

The ECtHR has also underlined the need for transparency when carrying out video surveillance. In *López Ribalda v Spain*[18] a supermarket suspected that staff were stealing from it and installed covert video surveillance which proved this to be the case. The staff concerned were dismissed on disciplinary grounds. On appeal to the national courts the recordings were accepted as proof of theft, and the interference with the applicants' rights was accepted as necessary and proportionate in order to protect the rights of the employer. The ECtHR noted that the employer had failed to provide general information to its staff about the video surveillance, contrary to Spanish data protection law, and that the video surveillance had been extensive both in scope and in duration. It found that the national courts had failed to strike a fair balance between the employer's right to property and the employees' right to privacy, and that there had thus been a violation of Article 8 ECHR.

C. Analysis

Article 88 GDPR enshrines all the data processing rules and principles laid down by the GDPR and obliges Member States to integrate these rules and principles in the field of employment. The following section will outline only some of the main issues relating to data processing in the context of employment, i.e. those issues, which have attracted the biggest debates among scholars and may cause uncertainty in terms of legal interpretation.

1. Requirements for Member States when adopting specific rules in the context of employment

1.1 Requirement to maintain the minimum standards set by GDPR

The EU has given Member States a certain margin of appreciation when regulating data processing in the context of employment, as Paragraph 1 of Article 88 GDPR provides that 'Member States may, by law or by collective agreements, provide for more specific rules ... in the employment context ... ' The first paragraph also gives a non-exhaustive list of the particular aspects, which Member States may choose to regulate. This list has been termed in a very broad fashion, covering everything from employee recruitment up to the termination of the employment relationship.

However, the discretion afforded to Member States to adopt such rules should not be interpreted as allowing derogations from the minimum standards imposed by the GDPR.[19] To the contrary, paragraph 1 of Article 88 stipulates that the specific rules must 'ensure the protection of the rights and freedoms in respect of the processing of employees' personal data', and paragraph 2 thereof states that '[t]hose rules shall include suitable and specific measures to safeguard the data subject's human dignity, legitimate interests and fundamental rights'. In other words, the aim of Article 88 is to allow Member States to implement such rules on data processing in the employment context as would best suit the needs of their own particular legal system, while at the same time keeping in line with the rules set by the GDPR.

---

[18] ECtHR, *López Ribalda and Others v Spain*. [19] De Hert and Lammerant 2013, p. 67.

In practice, however, for many Member States this Article serves as legal grounds to maintain national laws which already exist and were adopted whilst the DPD was in force. For example, Germany was the first Member State to introduce specific rules pursuant to Article 88 GDPR. Section 26 German Federal Data Protection Act 2017 contains provisions on data processing for employment purposes. This section lays down, inter alia, elaborate rules on obtaining consent for processing employee data, and conditions for processing sensitive employee data. However, section 26 was built upon rules already in place under Germany's previous data protection law, and no significant amendments were introduced in the German Federal Data Protection Act 2017.

1.2 Requirement to notify the adopted specific rules to the European Commission

Undertakings operating their business on a multi-jurisdiction level will need to pay the utmost attention to the specific rules adopted by Member States under Article 88. There might be circumstances where the national rules are stricter than the baseline set by the GDPR, or alternatively where such rules require undertakings to exercise their rights or obligations in a particular manner.

For this reason, Paragraph 3 of Article 88 requires Member States to notify the European Commission of any specific rules adopted pursuant to this Article, and also of any subsequent amendments affecting these rules. The Commission publishes these notifications online, together with the other notifications required under the GDPR.[20] In this way, a register of all existing rules adopted under Article 88 by Member States could be created. In practice, this would mean that undertakings operating within the EU would have a single and easy-to-access source of domestic legislation, which they will need to respect when processing personal data of their employees.

2. Choosing the appropriate legal grounds for processing employee data

Just as the DPD previously, the GDPR provides for several legal grounds to process personal data.[21] While in principle any of the grounds can be also used for the purposes of processing personal data in the context of employment, there are however several aspects which must be taken into account in this field. This section of the Article will cover some of those aspects, which are likely to arise and/or cause legal uncertainty when using a particular legal ground for data processing.

One of the most debated issues in this regard stems from the question whether consent may be used as a legal ground for processing personal data of employees by the employer. Article 4(11) of the GDPR defines consent as one being 'freely given, specific, informed and unambiguous'.[22] While the latter three conditions are rather straightforward and do not cause problems for the employer, the story is different for the first condition.

The WP29 has argued in its opinions that a consent obtained by the employer from an employee cannot usually be considered as obtained freely and, thus, such consent also

---

[20] Such as the notifications required under Arts. 51(4) (data protection authorities), 84(2) (penalties) and 85(3) (freedom of expression). See Member State notifications to the Commission under the GDPR.
[21] Art. 6 GDPR.
[22] See the commentaries on Art. 4(11) (definition of consent) and on Art. 7 (conditions for consent) in this volume.

cannot be deemed as lawful.[23] Such reasoning arises from the presumption that the employer and the employee are not in an equal position of power, as the latter is dependent upon the former. Namely, in most cases the employee, when asked for consent for a specific data processing activity, will feel coerced in providing the consent in order to avoid any potential negative consequences, such as a loss of a prospective pay raise or promotion, or even dismissal. For these reasons, it is generally the preferred position in practice that employers should avoid consent as a legal ground for processing employee data and instead rely on the other grounds available whenever possible.[24]

Moreover, unlike the DPD, the notion that consent is not freely given where an imbalance of power exists has been mentioned explicitly in the GDPR. Recital 43 states that '[i]n order to ensure that consent is freely given, consent should not provide a valid legal ground for the processing of personal data in a specific case where there is a clear imbalance between the data subject and the controller'.

Since consent as a legal ground for processing employee data has thus been made undesirable, and most other grounds (such as performance of a contract and fulfilment of an obligation arising from law) usually can cover only the bare essentials of an employer's processing activities, legitimate interest has become the primary legal ground in the field of employment. Processing activities for the purpose of improving work efficiency and for protecting the employer's material and intellectual assets fall easily under the notion of a legitimate interest. However, this ground requires that a balancing exercise be conducted to weight the employer's interests against those of the employees, as Article 6(f) states that this ground may not be used if the employer's interests are 'overridden by the interests or fundamental rights and freedoms of the data subject'.[25]

In particular, the WP29 has explained that when relying on a legitimate interest ground, that interest must be legitimate; the technology or method utilised for processing employee data must be necessary and proportionate; and the processing must be carried out in the least intrusive manner possible.[26] In essence, this means that an employer cannot rely on this legal ground to process employee data simply because it would be in his economic interest; he or she must also duly consider the other side of the coin.[27]

It might not always be easy to find the correct balance between competing interests in the employment field. This is becoming especially difficult given the advances in different technologies, which now afford the employer an even greater degree of personal data processing and thus intrusion into employees' private life, by way of surveillance both on and off the premises and the monitoring of electronic communications. Thus, employers will need to pay careful attention as to the measures they may take to optimise their profits and workplace efficiency at the expense of their employees' rights. In this regard the WP29 has done extensive research on the impact and lawfulness of different surveillance methods and communications monitoring in the workplace, and also provided several guidelines on how the employer can comply with the conditions of data processing based on legitimate interests.[28]

[23] WP29 2001; WP29 2017. [24] Kuner 2007, pp. 260–261.
[25] See the commentary on Art. 6 in this volume. [26] WP29 2017.
[27] As in ECtHR, *López Ribalda v Spain*, para. 38, citing WP29 2001 with regard to monitoring of employees.
[28] See, in general: WP29 2001; WP29 2002; WP 29 2017.

3. Maintaining transparency in employee data processing

Transparency is one of the key elements which any personal data processing activity must have in order to comply with the proportionality test. A requirement of transparency acts as a mitigating measure to ensure that a proper balance is struck between competing interests. However, as technological advances continue to overwhelm the workplace, transparency is becoming a particularly sensitive topic in the field of employment.

Modern technologies enable employees to be tracked over time, across workplaces and their homes, through many different devices such as smartphones, desktops, tablets, vehicles and wearables. If there are no limits to the processing, and if it is not transparent, there is a high risk that the legitimate interest of employers in the improvement of efficiency and the protection of company assets turns into unjustifiable and intrusive monitoring.[29]

In order to avoid infringing employees' rights, the employer should always give the employees a general notice of what monitoring measures are in place, determine to what extent personal data will be collected via these measures and make clear the consequences of misconduct discovered using these measures.[30]

In particular, employers are now also required to conduct a data protection impact assessment under Article 35 GDPR. This explicitly refers to situations where the use of new technologies 'is likely to result in a high risk to the rights and freedoms of natural persons'. It is highly probable that supervisory authorities will find that employers wishing to implement surveillance measures in the workplace will need to conduct an impact assessment in accordance with Article 35.

4. Conclusion

Article 88 was inserted in the GDPR in order to allow Member States to accommodate its requirements with the needs and peculiarities of their own legal systems. While this gives Member States a certain margin of appreciation in how exactly to achieve this aim, Article 88 also mandates that the specific rules adopted pursuant to this Article cannot derogate from the minimum threshold of data protection standards imposed by the GDPR.

Differing rules on data processing in the field of employment among EU Member States will create a challenge, especially for those employers who operate their business on a global scale, as they will need to be aware of their obligations under the relevant legal norms of all the Member States where their employees are posted. Fortunately, keeping track of all national rules adopted pursuant to Article 88 will be facilitated by the EU, as the GDPR requires Member States to notify such rules to the European Commission.

Processing personal data in the field of employment poses several challenges, as the GDPR rules need to be interpreted in the light of this specific context. The most highly debated issues in this regard concern the seeking of appropriate legal grounds for processing employee data, as well as ensuring that employers who use new and privacy-intrusive surveillance technologies, respect the principle of transparency and generally strike a fair balance between their interests and those of the employees.

Quite obviously, this brief analysis could not cover all aspects concerning this topic. For example, employers also need to be aware of issues which arise from transferring

---

[29] WP29 2017.   [30] See the recent case law of the ECtHR discussed above.

employee data between entities located in different countries,[31] or from implementing the principles of data protection by design and by default in all the technologies which employees will use in their work.[32] Furthermore, it is not unlikely that new and unforeseen legal complexities will arise as supervisory authorities start applying and interpreting the GDPR.

For these reasons, employers, whenever they are processing employee data, should always pay careful regard to all applicable data protection rules, both at the EU, international and national level, and should keep track of any amendments of such rules and any relevant interpretations thereof by the courts.

Select Bibliography

International agreements

ILO 1997: International Labour Organization, *Protection of Workers' Personal Data: An ILO Code of Practice* (International Labour Office 1997).

National legislation

German Federal Data Protection Act 2017: Bundesdatenschutzgesetz vom 30. Juni 2017, BGBl. 2017 Teil I Nr. 2097.

Academic writings

Kuner 2007: Kuner, *European Data Protection Law* (OUP 2007).

Papers of data protection authorities

WP29 2001: Article 29 Working Party, 'Opinion 8/2001 on the Processing of Personal Data in the Employment Context' (WP 48, 13 September 2001).
WP29 2002: Article 29 Working Party, 'Working Document on the Surveillance of Electronic Communications in the Workplace' (WP 55, 29 May 2002).
WP29 2017: Article 29 Working Party, 'Opinion 02/2017 on Data Processing at Work' (WP 249, 8 June 2017).

Reports and recommendations

Butarelli 2011: Butarelli for the Council of Europe, 'Study on Recommendation No. R (89) 2 on the Protection of Personal Data Used for Employment Purposes and to Suggest Proposals for the Revision of the Above-Mentioned Recommendation' (June 2011).
CoE Recommendation 1989: Council of Europe, 'Recommendation of the Committee of Ministers to Member States on the Protection of Personal Data Used for Employment Purposes', R(89) 2, 18 January 1989.
CoE Recommendation 2015: Council of Europe, 'Recommendation of the Committee of Ministers to Member States on the Processing of Personal Data in the Context of Employment', CM/Rec(2015)5, 1 April 2015.
De Hert and Lammerant 2013: De Hert and Lammerant for the European Parliament, 'Protection of Personal Data in Work-Related Relations' (April 2013).
FRA Handbook 2014: Council of Europe, EU Agency for Fundamental Rights, *Handbook on European Data Protection Law* (Publications Office of the European Union 2014).

---

[31] Arts. 44–50 GDPR.   [32] Ibid., Art. 25.

FRA Handbook 2018: Council of Europe, EU Agency for Fundamental Rights, European Data Protection Supervisor, *Handbook on European Data Protection Law* (Publication Office of the European Union 2018).

Member State notifications to the Commission under the GDPR: European Commission, 'EU Member States notifications to the European Commission under the GDPR', available at https://ec.europa.eu/info/law/law-topic/data-protection/data-protection-eu/eu-countries-gdpr-specific-notifications_en.

Others

ECtHR Factsheet 2018: European Court of Human Rights, 'Factsheet: Surveillance at Workplace' (February 2018), available at: https://www.echr.coe.int/Documents/FS_Workplace_surveillance_ENG.pdf.

Article 89. Safeguards and derogations relating to processing for archiving purposes in the public interest, scientific or historical research purposes or statistical purposes

CHRISTIAN WIESE SVANBERG*

1. Processing for archiving purposes in the public interest, scientific or historical research purposes or statistical purposes, shall be subject to appropriate safeguards, in accordance with this Regulation, for the rights and freedoms of the data subject. Those safeguards shall ensure that technical and organisational measures are in place in particular in order to ensure respect for the principle of data minimisation. Those measures may include pseudonymisation provided that those purposes can be fulfilled in that manner. Where those purposes can be fulfilled by further processing which does not permit or no longer permits the identification of data subjects, those purposes shall be fulfilled in that manner.
2. Where personal data are processed for scientific or historical research purposes or statistical purposes, Union or Member State law may provide for derogations from the rights referred to in Articles 15, 16, 18 and 21 subject to the conditions and safeguards referred to in paragraph 1 of this Article in so far as such rights are likely to render impossible or seriously impair the achievement of the specific purposes, and such derogations are necessary for the fulfilment of those purposes.
3. Where personal data are processed for archiving purposes in the public interest, Union or Member State law may provide for derogations from the rights referred to in Articles 15, 16, 18, 19, 20 and 21 subject to the conditions and safeguards referred to in paragraph 1 of this Article in so far as such rights are likely to render impossible or seriously impair the achievement of the specific purposes, and such derogations are necessary for the fulfilment of those purposes.
4. Where processing referred to in paragraphs 2 and 3 serves at the same time another purpose, the derogations shall apply only to processing for the purposes referred to in those paragraphs.

Relevant Recitals

(156) The processing of personal data for archiving purposes in the public interest, scientific or historical research purposes or statistical purposes should be subject to appropriate safeguards for the rights and freedoms of the data subject pursuant to this Regulation. Those safeguards should ensure that technical and organisational measures are in place in order to ensure, in particular, the principle of data minimisation. The further processing of personal data for archiving purposes in the public interest, scientific or historical research purposes or statistical purposes is to be carried out when the controller has assessed the feasibility to fulfil those purposes by processing data which do not permit or no longer permit the identification of data subjects, provided that appropriate safeguards exist (such as, for instance, pseudonymisation of the data). Member States should provide for appropriate safeguards for the processing of personal data for archiving purposes in the public interest, scientific or historical research purposes or statistical purposes. Member States should be authorised to provide, under specific conditions and subject to appropriate safeguards for data subjects, specifications and derogations with regard to the information requirements and rights to rectification, to erasure, to be forgotten, to restriction of processing, to data portability, and to

---

* The views expressed are solely those of the author and do not necessarily reflect those of the Danish Police.

object when processing personal data for archiving purposes in the public interest, scientific or historical research purposes or statistical purposes. The conditions and safeguards in question may entail specific procedures for data subjects to exercise those rights if this is appropriate in the light of the purposes sought by the specific processing along with technical and organisational measures aimed at minimising the processing of personal data in pursuance of the proportionality and necessity principles. The processing of personal data for scientific purposes should also comply with other relevant legislation such as on clinical trials.

(157) By coupling information from registries, researchers can obtain new knowledge of great value with regard to widespread medical conditions such as cardiovascular disease, cancer and depression. On the basis of registries, research results can be enhanced, as they draw on a larger population. Within social science, research on the basis of registries enables researchers to obtain essential knowledge about the long-term correlation of a number of social conditions such as unemployment and education with other life conditions. Research results obtained through registries provide solid, high-quality knowledge which can provide the basis for the formulation and implementation of knowledge-based policy, improve the quality of life for a number of people and improve the efficiency of social services. In order to facilitate scientific research, personal data can be processed for scientific research purposes, subject to appropriate conditions and safeguards set out in Union or Member State law.

(158) Where personal data are processed for archiving purposes, this Regulation should also apply to that processing, bearing in mind that this Regulation should not apply to deceased persons. Public authorities or public or private bodies that hold records of public interest should be services which, pursuant to Union or Member State law, have a legal obligation to acquire, preserve, appraise, arrange, describe, communicate, promote, disseminate and provide access to records of enduring value for general public interest. Member States should also be authorised to provide for the further processing of personal data for archiving purposes, for example with a view to providing specific information related to the political behaviour under former totalitarian state regimes, genocide, crimes against humanity, in particular the Holocaust, or war crimes.

(159) Where personal data are processed for scientific research purposes, this Regulation should also apply to that processing. For the purposes of this Regulation, the processing of personal data for scientific research purposes should be interpreted in a broad manner including for example technological development and demonstration, fundamental research, applied research and privately funded research. In addition, it should take into account the Union's objective under Article 179(1) TFEU of achieving a European Research Area. Scientific research purposes should also include studies conducted in the public interest in the area of public health. To meet the specificities of processing personal data for scientific research purposes, specific conditions should apply in particular as regards the publication or otherwise disclosure of personal data in the context of scientific research purposes. If the result of scientific research in particular in the health context gives reason for further measures in the interest of the data subject, the general rules of this Regulation should apply in view of those measures.

(160) Where personal data are processed for historical research purposes, this Regulation should also apply to that processing. This should also include historical research and research for genealogical purposes, bearing in mind that this Regulation should not apply to deceased persons.

(161) For the purpose of consenting to the participation in scientific research activities in clinical trials, the relevant provisions of Regulation (EU) No. 536/2014 of the European Parliament and of the Council should apply.

(162) Where personal data are processed for statistical purposes, this Regulation should apply to that processing. Union or Member State law should, within the limits of this Regulation, determine statistical content, control of access, specifications for the processing of personal data for statistical purposes and appropriate measures to safeguard the rights and freedoms of the data subject and for ensuring statistical confidentiality. Statistical purposes mean any operation of collection

and the processing of personal data necessary for statistical surveys or for the production of statistical results. Those statistical results may further be used for different purposes, including a scientific research purpose. The statistical purpose implies that the result of processing for statistical purposes is not personal data, but aggregate data, and that this result or the personal data are not used in support of measures or decisions regarding any particular natural person.

(163) The confidential information which the Union and national statistical authorities collect for the production of official European and official national statistics should be protected. European statistics should be developed, produced and disseminated in accordance with the statistical principles as set out in Article 338(2) TFEU, while national statistics should also comply with Member State law. Regulation (EC) No. 223/2009 of the European Parliament and of the Council provides further specifications on statistical confidentiality for European statistics.

Closely Related Provisions

Article 4 (Definitions) (see too recital 26); Article 5 (Principles relating to processing of personal data); Article 6 (Lawfulness of processing) (see too recital 50); Article 9 (Processing of special categories of personal data) (see too recitals 52–53)

Related Provisions in LED [Directive (EU) 2016/680]

Article 4 (Principles relating to processing of personal data) (see too recital 26); Article 9 (Specific processing conditions)

Relevant Case Law

CJEU

Case C-524/06, *Heinz Huber v Bundesrepublik Deutschland*, judgment of 16 December 2008 (grand Chamber) (ECLI:EU:C:2008:724).
Case C-131/12, *Google Spain SL and Google Inc. v Agencia Española de Protección de Datos (AEPD) and Mario Costeja González*, judgment of 13 May 2014 (Grand Chamber) (ECLI:EU:C:2014:317).
Opinion of Advocate General Jääskinen in C-131/12, *Google Spain SL and Google Inc. v Agencia Española de Protección de Datos (AEPD) and Mario Costeja González*, delivered on 25 June 2013 (ECLI:EU:C:2013:424).

ECtHR

Times Newspapers Ltd v United Kingdom (nos. 1 and 2), Appl. Nos. 3002/03 and 23676/03, judgment of 10 March 2009.

A. Rationale and Policy Underpinnings

As is the case with the other provisions of Chapter IX, Article 89 GDPR enumerates specific processing situations in regard to which the EU legislator has deemed it necessary to allow the processing of personal data, subject to appropriate safeguards. The fundamental reason for providing what is in practice a broad margin for Member States to accommodate archiving purposes in the public interest, or processing carried out for scientific, historical research or statistical purposes, is the recognition of the important role they each play in society,[1] and the fact that they cannot be accomplished without the processing of personal data. In practice, this means that the fundamental question from a data protection standpoint is often not whether processing may take place, but rather which safeguards should be imposed and adhered to when it does.

B. Legal Background

1. EU legislation

The DPD recognised the fundamental interests enumerated in Article 89 with regards to data processing for historical, statistical or scientific purposes.[2] While the DPD did not contain a provision directly equivalent to Article 89, Member States could under Article 8(4) of the DPD, subject to the provision of suitable safeguards, lay down exemptions from the prohibition on the processing of special categories of personal data for reasons of substantial public interest.[3] In practice this allowed for national legislation with a scope similar to that now mandated under Article 89.

Recital 29 of the DPD stated that the further processing of personal data for historical, statistical or scientific purposes was not generally to be considered incompatible with the purposes for which the data had previously been collected, provided that Member States furnished suitable safeguards. It also contained the only mention in the DPD of safeguards that could be imposed on processing of personal data for historical, statistical or scientific purposes, which were supposed to 'rule out the use of the data in support of measures or decisions regarding any particular individual'.[4] The DPD also recognised in other provisions derogations that could be used for research purposes.[5]

Finally, the WP29 recognised processing for historical, scientific, statistical or research purposes as interests that could be invoked to provide a legal basis for data processing under Article 7(f) of the DPD.[6]

2. International instruments

Article 9(3) of Convention 108 provides that 'Restrictions on the exercise of the rights specified in Article 8, paragraphs b, c and d, may be provided by law with respect to automated personal data files used for statistics or for scientific research purposes when there is obviously no risk of an infringement of the privacy of the data subjects'. The Modernised Convention 108 provides in Article 5(4)(b) that 'further processing for archiving purposes in the public interest, scientific or historical research purposes or statistical purposes is, subject to appropriate safeguards, compatible with those purposes'. In addition, the Modernised Convention allows restrictions on the exercise of the provisions concerning the transparency of processing (Article 8(3)) and on rights of the data subject (Article 9(2)). Finally, Article 11 of the Modernised Convention states that 'Restrictions

---

[1] E.g. research is a key objective of the EU as set out in Art. 179 Treaty on the Functioning of the European Union ('TFEU').
[2] See rec. 29 and 40, and Art. 6(1)(b) and (e) DPD.   [3] See further Pormeister 2017.
[4] DPD recital 29.
[5] E.g. in Art. 6(1)(e) GDPR (allowing the Member States to provide for longer storage of personal data) and Art. 11(2) GDPR (allowing derogations from the obligation to provide information to the data subject). See also Pormeister 2017, p. 142.
[6] WP29 2014B, p. 28.

on the exercise of the provisions specified in Articles 8 and 9 may be provided for by law with respect to data processing for archiving purposes in the public interest, scientific or historical research purposes or statistical purposes when there is no recognisable risk of infringement of the rights and fundamental freedoms of data subjects'.

3. National developments

National laws governing data processing for archiving or research purposes are present in many Member States, many of which deal with medical research.[7] A notable example from the realm of scientific research is the research authorisation regime in Denmark, where the national DPA—in addition to an authorisation provided to the individual researcher by the National Committee on Health Research Ethics—authorises and sets conditions for, inter alia, the publication of personal data collected in the course of research projects.[8] It has been stated that considerable variation exists between the Member States with regard to data protection requirements for medical research under the DPD,[9] and that this lack of harmonisation will likely continue under the GDPR.[10]

4. Case law

The *Huber*[11] judgment of the CJEU concerned an Austrian national resident in Germany who requested the deletion of personal data relating to him in the German Central Register of Foreign Nationals ('AZR'), which was used for statistical purposes and by security and police services and judicial authorities for the prosecution and investigation of criminal activities. The Court held that only the processing of anonymous information was required in order for the statistical objectives of the database to be attained, so that it could not be said that the processing of personal data in this case was 'necessary'.[12]

In his Opinion in *Google Spain*,[13] Advocate General Jääskinen cited with approval the decision of the European Court of Human Rights ('ECtHR') in *Times Newspapers Ltd v United Kingdom (nos. 1 and 2)*, where the ECtHR had stated that newspaper archives 'constitute an important source for education and historical research, particularly as they are readily accessible to the public and are generally free'.[14] However, the Court disagreed with the Advocate General's conclusion that there was no so-called 'right to be forgotten' with regard to links to search results derived from online newspaper archives,[15] and found that such a right did exist in this case.[16]

C. Analysis

1. Introduction

The interaction between data protection law, archiving in the public interest and research has been complex and controversial.[17] The strengthening in the GDPR of rules

---

[7] See e.g. Beyeveld et al. 2004; Timmers et al. 2018.
[8] See section 10 Danish Data Protection Act 2000.   [9] Timmers et al. 2018, p. 7.
[10] Ibid., p. 19.   [11] Case C-524/06, *Huber*.   [12] Ibid., para. 65.
[13] Case C-131/12, *Google Spain* (Opinion AG).
[14] ECtHR, *Times Newspapers Ltd v UK*, para. 27. See Case C-131/12, *Google Spain* (Opinion AG), para. 123.
[15] *Google Spain* (Opinion AG), para. 137.   [16] See Case C-131/12, *Google Spain*, para. 99.
[17] For a discussion of the issues in the context of research, see Forgó 2015; Pormeister 2017; Rumbold 2017; and Timmers et al. 2018.

in areas such as consent could be seen as potentially harmful to archiving and research, while the creation in Article 89 of a more detailed framework for reconciling the needs of data protection and research than was the case under the DPD could be viewed as helpful. It should be noted that many of the specific issues concerning the tension between archiving and research on the one hand and data protection on the other hand are also mirrored in other provisions of the GDPR.[18]

During the negotiations of the GDPR, the issue of whether to require the explicit consent of the data subject for processing of personal data for scientific research purposes was debated extensively. The WP29 took the position that the further processing of health data for historical, statistical and scientific research purposes should only be permitted after having obtained the explicit consent of the data subjects or if certain narrow exceptions apply,[19] but this position has not been reflected in the GDPR.

Article 89 is addressed both to parties that conduct archiving and research (with regard to their practices in these areas), and to the EU and Member State legislators (with regard to the enactment of derogations). Article 89 encompasses the processing of both personal data under Article 6 and special categories of personal data under Article 9. Article 89 does not by itself provide a legal basis for data processing. Under the GDPR, potential legal bases for archiving and research covered by Article 89 could include, among others, the legitimate interests of the data controller as set forth in Article 6(1)(f).[20] Article 5(1)(b) also provides that further processing for archiving purposes in the public interest, scientific or historical research purposes or statistical purposes will not be considered to be incompatible with the initial purpose, provided that Article 89(1) is complied with.

With regard to special categories of personal data, Article 9(2)(j) allows for the processing hereof:

when processing is necessary for archiving purposes in the public interest, scientific or historical research purposes or statistical purposes in accordance with Article 89(1) based on Union or Member State law which shall be proportionate to the aim pursued, respect the essence of the right to data protection and provide for suitable and specific measures to safeguard the fundamental rights and the interests of the data subject.[21]

The sensitive nature of personal data covered by Article 9 is reflected by the requirement in Article 9(2)(j) whereby the Union or Member State law allowing for the processing of such data, in addition to meeting the general criteria stated in Article 89(1), 'shall be proportionate to the aim pursued, respect the essence of the right to data protection and provide for suitable and specific measures to safeguard the fundamental rights and the interests of the data subject'. Throughout Article 89, the 'public interest' must be based on Union or Member State law;[22] i.e. the public interest of a third country does not suffice.

---

[18] See in particular Art. 5 (principles relating to the processing of personal data); Art. 9 (processing of special categories of personal data); Art. 14 (information to be provided where personal data have not been obtained from the data subject); Art. 17 (right to erasure); and Art. 21 (right to object) GDPR.
[19] WP29 2015.
[20] Ibid, p. 28, finding that the legitimate interests of the controller 'will often' be a 'well-considered use' of Art. 7(f) DPD (which corresponds to Art. 6(1)(f) GDPR) with regard to data processing for historical or other kinds of scientific research.
[21] See the commentary on Art. 9 in this volume.
[22] See Art. 6(3) and the commentary on Art. 6 in this volume.

Articles 89(2)–(3) provide for derogations from the exercise of certain rights, in order to provide 'specific conditions' for their exercise.[23] However, even when the derogations apply, the protections of Article 89(1) are still applicable. In addition, other relevant legislation will continue to apply even when the derogations are used.[24]

Certain conditions apply to the derogations contained in Article 89(2)–(3). First of all, the conditions of Article 89(1) still apply notwithstanding any derogations. Thus, appropriate safeguards must be in place to protect the rights and freedoms of data subjects even when derogations apply. Secondly, use of the rights from which derogations are given must be 'likely to render impossible or seriously impair the achievement of the specific purposes, and such derogations are necessary for the fulfilment of those purposes'.[25] Thus, Member States should tailor the scope of the derogations narrowly so that they will apply only when exercise of the rights in question would make the relevant data processing impossible or seriously impair it. Finally, the derogations only apply to the purposes mentioned in the respective paragraphs.[26] This means, for example, that when a company conducts scientific research then such data processing may fall under a derogation, but its subsequent use of the research results for commercial purposes would not; in practice, it may not always be easy to differentiate between the original research purposes of data processing and any subsequent purposes. It should be noted that the phrase 'in the public interest' in Article 89 modifies only 'processing for archiving purposes'; thus, data processing for scientific or historical research purposes or statistical purposes is covered by the Article even if they are not 'in the public interest'.

2. Safeguards and purposes of processing

Article 89 GDPR regulates three distinct and separate purposes: archiving in the public interest, scientific or historical research purposes and statistical purposes. The provision mandates that appropriate safeguards for the rights and freedoms of the data subject must be observed when processing personal data for all of the listed purposes (paragraph (1)). Further, it provides in paragraphs (2) and (3) for derogations from the rights referred to in the enumerated provisions. Paragraph (4) makes clear that the derogations provided for in paragraphs (2) and (3) only apply to the purposes described in those paragraphs and not to any other purpose.

Common to all three purposes is that the formal definition of the individual purpose is largely left to the discretion of the Member States. Similarly, the extent to which the pursuit of one of these purposes can be a task delegated wholly or partly to private entities is left to Member States to set out. This means that in practice, the detailed requirements for the types of data processing described in Article 89 are likely to be determined largely under Member State law.

Under Article 89(1) GDPR, safeguards must be used whenever personal data are processed for archiving purposes in the public interest, scientific or historical research purposes or statistical purposes. In particular, the provision requires the use of technical and organisational measures to achieve data minimisation, which is defined in Article 5(1)(c)

---

[23] Rec. 156 GDPR.
[24] Ibid. See also rec. 161, stating that 'For the purpose of consenting to the participation in scientific research activities in clinical trials, the relevant provisions of Regulation (EU) No. 536/2014 of the European Parliament and of the Council should apply'.
[25] This formulation is used in both Art. 89(2) and (3) GDPR.   [26] See ibid., Art. 89(4).

GDPR as personal data being processed in a way that is 'adequate, relevant and limited to what is necessary in relation to the purposes for which they are processed'. Recital 156 mentions anonymisation in this regard, and the reference in Article 89(1) to 'further processing which does not permit or no longer permits the identification of data subjects' could be interpreted as including anonymisation. In addition, Article 89(1) specifically mentions pseudonymisation. Thus, anonymisation and pseudonymisation are favoured as safeguards under Article 89, though the list of safeguards mentioned in the article is non-exhaustive. The generality and limited scope of the safeguards in Article 89(1) have been criticised,[27] and it remains to be seen how much protection they will provide in practice.

The phrase at the end of Article 89(1), that 'those purposes *shall* be fulfilled in that manner' (emphasis added), may seem to require anonymisation or pseudonymisation, though this will to a large degree depend on which purposes are being pursued. In some areas, such as in medical research, they are widely used. But in others, a requirement to anonymise or pseudonymise personal data that have been deemed worthy of preservation (e.g. that are processed for archiving purposes) may make little sense, as removing the nexus between people and events would negate the purpose of the processing. The fact that anonymisation and pseudonymisation should only be used when this would not defeat the purpose of the processing is emphasised by the statement in Article 89(1) 'Where those purposes can be fulfilled by further processing …'

3. Archiving in the public interest

Article 89(3) GDPR permits derogations for 'archiving in the public interest'. Services covered by this definition include ones 'which, pursuant to Union or Member State law, have a legal obligation to acquire, preserve, appraise, arrange, describe, communicate, promote, disseminate and provide access to records of enduring value for general public interest'.[28] Thus, not every archive will fall under the scope of Article 89, but only those that have a legal obligation to maintain records as described above. This means that archives such as personal or family archives or company records will generally not be covered by Article 89, unless they somehow fulfil the criteria of being kept in the 'public interest'. The requirement that archiving must take place 'in the public interest' should be regarded as satisfied as long as any individual archiving activity is set out—even broadly—in Member State law. Thus, the GDPR does not limit the extent to which Member States can delimit what materials are of sufficient historical interest to warrant subjecting them to achieving rules.

Under Article 89(3) GDPR, where personal data are processed for archiving purposes in the public interest, Union or Member State law may provide for derogations from the rights referred to in Articles 15 (right of access by the data subject), 16 (right to rectification), 18 (right to restriction of processing), 19 (notification obligation regarding rectification or erasure of personal data or restriction of processing), 20 (right to data portability) and 21 (right to object) GDPR. However, such derogations are still subject to the conditions and safeguards referred to in Article 89(1).

The GPDR provides in the recitals that it should not apply to deceased persons,[29] even though many of the archives to which Article 89 applies will necessarily contain

---

[27] See Pormeister 2017, p. 139.   [28] Rec. 158 GDPR.   [29] See ibid., rec. 27, 158 and 160.

the personal data of such persons. However, Member States are authorised to provide for rules regarding the processing of personal data of the deceased,[30] and they are also authorised to provide for the further processing of personal data in archives that include 'specific information related to the political behaviour under former totalitarian state regimes, genocide, crimes against humanity, in particular the Holocaust, or war crimes',[31] which would seem to consist mainly of persons who are deceased. Thus, the processing of the personal data of the deceased is a matter left to national law and to European human rights law. With regard to archiving under the GDPR, the best view seems to be that, while archives containing only the personal data of deceased persons are not subject to the GDPR, archives are not removed from the rules of Article 89 (and the GDPR in general) solely because they contain some data of deceased persons. Moreover, Member State law may also be relevant in such cases.

The GDPR does not require that archiving be carried out in a particular manner. Thus, it may be centralised with one or more state-owned or private bodies, may make use of private sector entities and may encompass flexible arrangements whereby relevant materials are archived locally with the entity which originally produced them, as long as such a practice is governed by relevant legislation and subject to appropriate safeguards as required in Article 89.

4. Scientific or historical research purposes

Recital 159 states that 'the processing of personal data for scientific research purposes should be interpreted in a broad manner including for example technological development and demonstration, fundamental research, applied research and privately funded research'.

Further, the Regulation provides a broad enumeration of the types of scientific research that can be carried out under Article 89, including as examples medical research into cardiovascular disease, cancer and depression, and registry-based research whereby information from registries is coupled to enable researchers to obtain essential knowledge about the long-term correlation of a number of social conditions such as unemployment and education with other life conditions.[32] The term also includes studies conducted in the public interest in the area of public health.[33]

The exact meaning of historical research is not set out. The term does, however, include both historical research and research for genealogical purposes.[34] As discussed above with regard to archiving in the public interest, the GDPR does not apply to deceased persons in the context of scientific or historical research purposes as well.[35] However, scientific and historical research is not removed from the rules of Article 89 (and the GDPR in general) just because it results in the processing of some data of deceased persons. Member State law may also be relevant in such cases.

It is clear that the legislator has intended to ensure a broad mandate for Member States to allow scientific research purposes to be pursued at least to the extent possible under the DPD. Many types of scientific research are covered, including those in the 'hard sciences', social sciences etc. Parties involved in scientific research, particularly in the health context, should be prepared to implement further protections if they are in the interest of

[30] See ibid., rec. 27. [31] Ibid., rec. 158. [32] Ibid., rec. 157. [33] Ibid., rec. 159.
[34] Ibid., rec. 160. [35] Ibid.

the data subject, and to apply the general rules of the GDPR with regard to such further protections.[36] Regarding the question on how the result of scientific research may be disseminated to the public via publication, and thus ensure the public value of the research is realised, Member States are required to ensure specific conditions apply 'in particular as regards the publication or otherwise disclosure of personal data in the context of scientific research purposes'.[37]

Under Article 89(2), where personal data are processed for scientific or historical research purposes, Union or Member State law may provide for derogations from the rights referred to in Articles 15 (right of access by the data subject), 16 (right to rectification), 18 (right to restriction of processing) and 21 (right to object) GDPR. However, such derogations are still subject to the conditions and safeguards referred to in Article 89(1).

The GDPR as a whole, and Article 89 in particular, do not distinguish between scientific research pursuing public interests and that pursuing private or purely commercial research.[38] As long as the requirements of the GDPR and applicable Member State law are met, purely private or commercial interests can be pursued through the processing of personal data for scientific research purposes. Any other relevant legislation (such as legislation on clinical trials in the case of medical or scientific research) will also continue to apply.[39] Furthermore, if the result of scientific research gives reason for further measures in order to protect the interests of data subjects, then the general rules of the GDPR will apply to such further measures.[40]

Although consent is not dealt with in Article 89, it should be noted that the use of consent as a processing basis for the purpose of scientific research should be allowed even though it often is not possible to fully identify the purpose of personal data processing at the time when consent is given.[41]

5. Statistical purposes

Recital 162 defines 'statistical purposes' as 'any operation of collection and the processing of personal data necessary for statistical surveys or for the production of statistical results'. The non-personal nature of aggregate or statistical data means that it is not to be used 'in support of measures or decisions regarding any particular natural person'.[42] Union or Member State law must also enact a number of protections for data used for statistical purposes, within the limit of the GDPR. In particular, they should 'determine statistical content, control of access, specifications for the processing of personal data for statistical purposes and appropriate measures to safeguard the rights and freedoms of the data subject and for ensuring statistical confidentiality'.[43] There are also special rules covering information which the EU institutions and national statistical authorities collect for the production of official European and national statistics;[44] in particular, Article 338(2) TFEU applies to the development, production and dissemination of European statistics,[45] and national statistics must comply with Member State law. Regulation EC No. 223/2009 also applies with regard to statistical confidentiality for European statistics.[46]

Under Article 89(2), where personal data are processed for statistical purposes, Union or Member State law may provide for derogations from the rights referred to in Articles

---

[36] Ibid., rec. 159.   [37] Ibid.
[38] See also the example of 'privately funded research' listed ibid., rec. 159.   [39] Ibid., rec. 156.
[40] Ibid., rec. 159.   [41] See ibid., Art. 6(1)(a) and rec. 33.   [42] Ibid.   [43] Ibid.
[44] See ibid., rec.163.   [45] Ibid.   [46] Ibid. See further Regulation 223/2009.

15 (right of access by the data subject), 16 (right to rectification), 18 (right to restriction of processing) and 21 (right to object) GDPR. However, such derogations are still subject to the conditions and safeguards referred to in Article 89(1).

The material scope of the GDPR extends only to personal data,[47] and recital 162 states that the processing of personal data for statistical purposes results in aggregate data (i.e. non-personal data).[48] A literal reading of this recital would suggest that the aggregated datasets produced for statistical purposes are always non-personal data. This literal reading is, however, likely to be precluded by the broad definition of 'personal data' in GDPR Article 4(1)[49] and by the high level of protection conferred by the GDPR (see recitals 9–10). Such an interpretation would also be at odds with the high threshold for anonymisation that the GDPR sets, and with the WP29's finding (under the DPD) that aggregate statistical data may remain personal data if aggregation and anonymisation are not done effectively.[50]

A better reading of recital 162 is that it is only intended to make clear that data processed for statistical purposes remain personal data (subject to the GDPR) until they are anonymised through aggregation (i.e. until the 'result' of the statistical processing operation is achieved). This is in line with the WP29's view on the scope of application of the DPD, as the WP29 considered the process of data anonymisation as an instance of 'further processing' that requires a legal basis.[51]

6. Enforcement

Infringements of Article 89 are subject to the higher level of administrative fines under Article 83(5)(c), i.e. up to € 20 million or 4 per cent of the total worldwide turnover of the preceding financial year, whichever is higher.

Select Bibliography

EU legislation

Regulation 223/2009: Regulation (EC) No. 223/2009 of the European Parliament and of the Council of 11 March 2009 on European statistics and repealing Regulation (EC, Euratom) No. 1101/2008 of the European Parliament and of the Council on the transmission of data subject to statistical confidentiality to the Statistical Office of the European Communities, Council Regulation (EC) No. 322/97 on Community Statistics, and Council Decision 89/382/EEC, Euratom establishing a Committee on the Statistical Programmes of the European Communities, OJ 2009 L 87/164.

Regulation (EU) No. 536/2014 of the European Parliament and of the Council of 16 April 2014 on clinical trials on medicinal products for human use, and repealing Directive 2001/20/EC, OJ 2014 L 158/1.

National legislation

Danish Data Protection Act 2000: Act No. 429 of 31 May 2000 on the Processing of Personal Data.

---

[47] See ibid., Art. 2(1). [48] Ibid., rec. 162.
[49] See the commentary on Art. 4(1) in this volume. [50] See WP29 2013, pp. 12–18.
[51] See WP29 2014A, p. 7.

Academic writings

Beyeveld et al. 2004: Beyeveld, Townend, Rouillé-Mirza and Wright (eds.), *The Data Protection Directive and Medical Research across Europe* (Routledge 2004).

Forgó 2015: Nikolaus Forgó, 'My Health Data—Your Research: Some Preliminary Thoughts on Different Values in the General Data Protection Regulation', 5(1) *International Data Privacy Law 'IDPL'* (2015), 54.

Jaatinen 2016: Jaatinen, 'The Relationship between Open Data Initiatives, Privacy, and Government Transparency: A Love Triangle?', 6 *IDPL* (2016), 28.

Pormeister 2017: Pormeister, 'Genetic Data and the Research Exemption: Is the GDPR Going too Far?', 7(2) *IDPL* (2017), 137.

Rumbold 2017: Rumbold, 'The Effect of the General Data Protection Regulation on Medical Research', 19(2) *Journal of Medical Internet Research* (2017), 1.

Timmers et al. 2018: Timmers, van Veen, Maas and Kompanje, 'Will the EU Data Protection Regulation 2016/679 Inhibit Critical Care Research?', 26 *Medical Law Review* (2018) (forthcoming).

Papers of data protection authorities

WP29 2013: Article 29 Working Party, 'Opinion 06/2013 on Open Data and Public Sector Information ("PSI") Reuse' (WP 207, 5 June 2013).

WP29 2014A: Article 29 Working Party, 'Opinion 05/2014 on Anonymisation Techniques' (WP 216, 10 April 2014).

WP29 2014B: Article 29 Working Party, 'Opinion 06/2014 on the Notion of Legitimate Interests of the Data Controller under Article 7 of Directive 95/46/EC' (WP 217, 9 April 2014).

WP29 2015: Article 29 Working Party, 'Letter from the Art 29 WP to the European Commission, DG CONNECT on mHealth' (with annex) (5 February 2015).

Article 29 Working Party, 'Opinion 4/2007 on the Concept of Personal Data' (WP 136, 20 June 2007).

Article 29 Working Party, 'Opinion 06/2014 on the Notion of Legitimate Interests of the Data Controller under Article 7 of Directive 95/46/EC' (WP 217, 9 April 2014).

Reports and recommendations

Korff for the European Commission, 'Comparative Study on Different Approaches to New Privacy Challenges in Particular in the Light of Technological Developments, Working Paper No. 2: Data Protection Laws in the EU' (20 January 2010).

Article 90. Obligations of secrecy

CHRISTIAN WIESE SVANBERG[*]

1. Member States may adopt specific rules to set out the powers of the supervisory authorities laid down in points (e) and (f) of Article 58(1) in relation to controllers or processors that are subject, under Union or Member State law or rules established by national competent bodies, to an obligation of professional secrecy or other equivalent obligations of secrecy where this is necessary and proportionate to reconcile the right of the protection of personal data with the obligation of secrecy. Those rules shall apply only with regard to personal data which the controller or processor has received as a result of or has obtained in an activity covered by that obligation of secrecy.
2. Each Member State shall notify to the Commission the rules adopted pursuant to paragraph 1, by 25 May 2018 and, without delay, any subsequent amendment affecting them.

Relevant Recital

(164) As regards the powers of the supervisory authorities to obtain from the controller or processor access to personal data and access to their premises, Member States may adopt by law, within the limits of this Regulation, specific rules in order to safeguard the professional or other equivalent secrecy obligations, in so far as necessary to reconcile the right to the protection of personal data with an obligation of professional secrecy. This is without prejudice to existing Member State obligations to adopt rules on professional secrecy where required by Union law.

Closely Related Provisions

Article 9(3) (Processing of special categories of personal data); Article 25 (Data protection by design and by default) (see too recital 75); Article 33 (Notification of a personal data breach to the supervisory authority) (see too recital 85); Article 54(2) (Rules on the establishment of the supervisory authority); Article 58(1) (Investigatory powers) (see too recital 129)

Relevant Case Law

CJEU

Case C-275/06, *Productores de Música de España (Promusicae) v Telefónica de España SAU*, judgment of 29 January 2008 (Grand Chamber) (ECLI:EU:C:2008:54).
Case C-73/07, *Tietosuojavaltuutettu v Satakunnan Markkinapörssi Oy and Satamedia Oy*, judgment of 16 December 2008 (Grand Chamber) (ECLI:EU:C:2008:727).
Case C-518/07, *European Commission v Federal Republic of Germany*, judgment of 9 March 2010 (Grand Chamber) (ECLI:EU:C:2010:125).
Case C-614/10, *European Commission v Republic of Austria*, judgment of 16 October 2012 (Grand Chamber) (ECLI:EU:C:2012:63).
Case C-288/12, *European Commission v Hungary*, judgment of 8 April 2014 (Grand Chamber) (ECLI:EU:C:2014:237).

---

[*] The views expressed are solely those of the author and do not necessarily reflect those of the Danish Police.

Joined Cases C-293/12 and C-594/12, *Digital Rights Ireland Ltd v Minister for Communications, Marine and Natural Resources and Others and Kärntner Landesregierung and Others*, judgment of 8 April 2014 (Grand Chamber) (ECLI:EU:C:2014:238).

Joined Cases C-203/15 and C-698/15, *Tele2 Sverige AB v Post- och telestyrelsen and Secretary of State for the Home Department v Tom Watson and Others*, judgment of 21 December 2016 (Grand Chamber) (ECLI:EU:C:2016:970).

A. Rationale and Policy Underpinnings

When supervisory authorities exert their competence to gain access to personal data being processed by controllers and processors or to access relevant premises, access may in certain instances also entail the disclosure of information subject to professional secrecy. Article 90 GDPR grants Member States a mandate to strike a balance between the—often strict and sometime absolute—rules of non-disclosure applicable in regard to certain professions and the right of the protection of personal data.

The rationale of the provision is the need to ensure that the enforcement of the GDPR does not undermine the legitimate interests of individuals—or, if so provided, legal persons—that the individual Member State or Union law has deemed should be protected by an obligation of professional secrecy. The provision is thus another substantive example of cases where data protection—in this case its enforcement by the competent authorities—must take a countervailing interest into account.[1] Further, Member States, their authorities and courts—and thereby also the data protection authorities—have an obligation to make sure that they do not rely on an interpretation of data protection law which would be in conflict with other fundamental rights or with the other general principles of Community law, such as the principle of proportionality.[2]

The DPD does not contain a similar provision limiting the competence of the supervisory authority.[3] Article 28(7) DPD imposed a duty of professional secrecy on members and staff of the supervisory authority, which is now laid down under Article 54(2) GDPR.[4]

B. Legal Background

1. EU legislation

The DPD provided in recital 33 that there should be a derogation from the prohibition against processing 'data which are capable by their nature of infringing fundamental freedoms or privacy' in cases when processing is carried out by 'persons subject to a legal obligation of professional secrecy' (among other things). Also, Article 8 DPD that prohibited the processing of sensitive data did not apply under Article 8(3) when such data were processed 'by a health professional subject under national law or rules established by national competent bodies to the obligation of professional secrecy or by another person also subject to an equivalent obligation of secrecy'. These rules covered not only doctors but also other medical personnel subject to duties of confidentiality, such as pharmacists,

---

[1] Another example of countervailing interests includes the right to freedom of expression and information, including processing for journalistic purposes and the purposes of academic, artistic or literary expression; see the commentary on Art. 85 GDPR in this volume. See also C-73/07, *Satamedia*, para. 53–55.

[2] See C-275/06, *Promusicae*, para. 68.   [3] See Art. 28(3) DPD.

[4] See the commentary on Art. 54 in this volume.

Wiese Svanberg

midwives, therapists and administrative and technical personnel covered by duties of confidentiality.[5]

The EUDPR also contains provisions dealing with data processing of controllers and processors that is subject to professional secrecy.[6]

2. International instruments

Neither the Council of Europe Convention 108 nor the Modernised Convention 108 mention the topic of professional secrecy of data controllers or data processors.

3. National developments

National laws regulating professional secrecy are widespread and apply (depending on the traditions and customs of the particular Member State) to e.g. members of the legal profession, accountants, Members of Parliaments, health care professionals, representatives of religious communities and similar.

4. Case law

In both *Digital Rights Ireland*[7] and *Tele2*[8] the CJEU placed emphasis on the fact that the relevant rules on the retention of telecommunications data did not exempt persons whose communications are subject, according to rules of national law, to the obligation of professional secrecy.

C. Analysis

1. Introduction

Article 90 GDPR contains what can for illustrative purposes be termed procedural and substantive elements. Procedurally, Member State law must provide that an existing professional obligation of secrecy or other equivalent obligations of secrecy falls within the ambit of Article 90 in order for the relevant rules to be covered by Article 90. Further, under Article 90(2), rules adopted pursuant to paragraph 1 had to be notified to the Commission by 25 May 2018 and, without delay, any subsequent amendment affecting them must also be notified.

2. Substantive elements

Substantively, Article 90 grants Member States the right to set out the powers of the supervisory authorities laid down in points (e) and (f) of Article 58(1) in order to reflect rules on professional secrecy provided under Union or Member State law. The full extent of the competence provided gives rise to some uncertainty in regard to how extensively Member States can curtail the powers in question. In light of the fact that Article 90(1) only allows Member States to set out the powers of the supervisory authorities it may be argued on the one hand that a full curtailment of the relevant powers provided in Article 58 cannot take place (see below in light of the duty of the professional secrecy incumbent

---

[5] See Dammann and Simitis 1997, p. 168. [6] See Arts. 10(2)(i), 10(3) and 16(5)(d) EUDPR.
[7] Joined Cases C-293/12 and C-594/12, *Digital Rights Ireland*, para. 58.
[8] Joined Cases C-203/15 and C-698/15, *Tele2*, para. 105.

upon members and the staff of each supervisory authority under Article 54 para. 2). On the other hand, it could be argued that any setting out of residual powers—however limited it may be—would still fall within the wording of the provision. In any event, the obligation under Article 90 to establish the proper balance between the rights to data protection, in particular the right to independent supervision, and professional secrecy must be interpreted in light of the case law of the CJEU characterising independent supervision under Articles 8(3) Charter of Fundamental Rights of the European Union ('CFR') and 16(2) Treaty on the Functioning of the European Union ('TFEU') as an essential component of the right to data protection.[9]

3. Competences of supervisory authorities

Further, Article 90 only provides Member States a mandate to derogate from the Regulation in regard to the processing of personal data a data controller or data processor has received as a result of or has obtained in an activity covered by the obligation of secrecy or other equivalent obligations of secrecy. This means, inter alia, that specific rules adopted by Member States under Article 90 cannot exclude other information from the enforcement competences of the supervisory authority provided under points (e) and (f) of Article 58(1). Given that professional obligations of secrecy often protect more than just personal data—and in some instances may prevent the party subject to the obligation to even confirm that e.g. an attorney/client relationship with a legal person exists—it is notable that Article 58(1) point (e) gives the supervisory authority the right to obtain access to all personal data and to all information necessary. Such information could, depending on the circumstances, include non-personal data documenting an otherwise confidential relationship between legal entities or the content of advice provided under privilege.

Under Article 90 the supervisory authority's competences can be set out in regard to both data controllers and data processors. This must be construed as allowing e.g. a medical doctor—acting as a data controller in a matter covered by national or Union rules on doctor/patient confidentiality recognised under Member State law with reference to Article 90—to invoke relevant Member State rules with regard to requests for information by a supervisory authority made under points (e) and (f) of Article 58(1). In the same way, a lawyer acting for a client has an obligation of professional secrecy under national law covering client information processed as a data controller. Indeed, there is an obligation on such controllers under Article 25, interpreted in the light of recital 75, to take measures to ensure that personal data protected by professional secrecy retains that protection.

Article 90 also applies to data processors. For example, to the extent an attorney-at-law is acting as a data processor on behalf of a client (assuming again that the formal requirements of Article 90 are met) they can, where provided, resist the handing over of personal data to the supervisory authority, assuming such a provision is set out in Union or Member State law.[10] However, it must be assumed that Member State or Union law cannot preclude the supervisory authority from seeking the same information from the data controller. Whether such a request will comply with other fundamental rights—notably the right to a fair trial of Article 6 European Convention of Human Rights

---

[9] See Case C-518/07, *Commission v Germany*, para. 23; Case C-614/10, *Commission v Austria*, para. 37; and Case C-288/12, *Commission v Hungary*, para. 48.

[10] But see WP29 2010, p. 28, stating that a barrister is likely to be a data controller rather than a data processor.

('ECHR') and the privilege against self-incrimination[11]—will be subject to a separate determination. In this respect Article 58(4) provides that the exercise of the powers conferred on the supervisory authority pursuant to Article 58 shall be subject to appropriate safeguards, including effective judicial remedy and due process, set out in Union and Member State law in accordance with the Charter.

4. National competent bodies

The reference in Article 90 to rules on professional secrecy or other equivalent obligations of secrecy established by national competent bodies allow Member States to entrust competent bodies such as professional organisations, boards and committees with setting out—on the basis of national law—the specific rules on secrecy applicable to a profession, sector or similar.

5. Exemptions

Finally, Article 90 requires that Union and Member State law only allow exemptions from Article 58(1) points (e) and (f) where this is necessary and proportionate to reconcile the right of the protection of personal data with the obligation of secrecy. Given the substantive interest generally reflected by the creation of rules on professional secrecy, the material reach of this requirement may be limited in practice.

However, any exemption from Article 58(1) points (e) and (f) must also take into account the fact that the duty of professional secrecy is also incumbent upon members and the staff of each supervisory authority.[12] Thus, it can be argued that an exemption generally can only be adopted in those instances where a duty of professional secrecy has an absolute or near-absolute reach, so that that, for example, it cannot be revoked without the consent of the protected party.

Further, if the interests protected by a duty of professional secrecy can remain unaffected while still allowing some DPA competence to obtain information, this must arguably be reflected in Member State law. For instance, a DPA may have the competence to obtain information about the way a controller has handled medical data, which is subject to an obligation of secrecy placed on health care professionals, but may not be able to obtain the medical data itself. Such considerations would especially be relevant in ensuring that the DPA can obtain relevant data on the circumstances surrounding a personal data breach.[13]

Select Bibliography

Academic writings

Dammann and Simitis 1997: Dammann and Simitis, *EG-Datenschutzrichtlinie* (Nomos Verlagsgesellschaft 1997).

Papers of data protection authorities

WP29 2010: Article 29 Working Party, 'Opinion 1/2010 on the Concepts of "Controller" and "Processor"' (WP 169, 16 February 2010).

---

[11] See also the commentary on Art. 31 in this volume regarding the privilege against self-incrimination.
[12] See the commentary on Art. 54 in this volume.
[13] See the commentary on Arts. 4(12), 33 and 34 in this volume.

Article 91. Existing data protection rules of churches and religious associations

LUCA TOSONI

1. Where in a Member State, churches and religious associations or communities apply, at the time of entry into force of this Regulation, comprehensive rules relating to the protection of natural persons with regard to processing, such rules may continue to apply, provided that they are brought into line with this Regulation.
2. Churches and religious associations which apply comprehensive rules in accordance with paragraph 1 of this Article shall be subject to the supervision of an independent supervisory authority, which may be specific, provided that it fulfils the conditions laid down in Chapter VI of this Regulation.

Relevant Recitals

(4) The processing of personal data should be designed to serve mankind. The right to the protection of personal data is not an absolute right; it must be considered in relation to its function in society and be balanced against other fundamental rights, in accordance with the principle of proportionality. This Regulation respects all fundamental rights and observes the freedoms and principles recognised in the Charter as enshrined in the Treaties, in particular the respect for private and family life, home and communications, the protection of personal data, freedom of thought, conscience and religion, freedom of expression and information, freedom to conduct a business, the right to an effective remedy and to a fair trial, and cultural, religious and linguistic diversity.

(165) This Regulation respects and does not prejudice the status under existing constitutional law of churches and religious associations or communities in the Member States, as recognised in Article 17 TFEU.

Closely Related Provisions

Article 4(21) (Definition of 'supervisory authority'); Article 9(2)(d) (Processing of special categories of personal data by religious organisations); Articles 51–59 (Independent supervisory authorities); Article 99 (Entry into force and application)

Relevant Case Law

CJEU

Case C-223/98, *Adidas AG*, judgment of 14 October 1999 (ECLI:EU:C:1999:500).
Opinion of Advocate General Cosmas in Case C-223/98, *Adidas AG*, delivered on 10 June 1998 (ECLI:EU:C:1999:300).
Case C-101/01, *Criminal proceedings against Bodil Lindqvist*, judgment of 6 November 2003 (ECLI:EU:C:2003:596).
Opinion of Advocate General Tizzano in Case C-101/01, *Criminal proceedings against Bodil Lindqvist*, delivered on 19 September 2002 (ECLI:EU:C:2002:513).

Case C-212/13, *František Ryneš v Úřad pro ochranu osobních údajů*, judgment of 11 December 2014 (ECLI:EU:C:2014:2428).

Case C-362/14, *Maximillian Schrems v Data Protection Commissioner*, judgment of 6 October 2015 (Grand Chamber) (ECLI:EU:C:2015:650).

Case C-25/17, *Proceedings brought by Tietosuojavaltuutettu (Jehovan todistajat)*, judgment of 10 July 2018 (Grand Chamber) (ECLI:EU:C:2018:551).

Opinion of Advocate General Mengozzi in Case C-25/17, *Proceedings brought by Tietosuojavaltuutettu (Jehovan todistajat)*, delivered on 1 February 2018 (ECLI:EU:C:2018:57).

Case C-426/16, *Liga van Moskeeën en Islamitische Organisaties Provincie Antwerpen, VZW and Others v Vlaams Gewest*, judgment of 29 May 2018 (Grand Chamber) (ECLI:EU:C:2018:335).

Case C-193/17, *Cresco Investigation GmbH v Markus Achatzi*, judgment of 22 January 2019 (Grand Chamber) (ECLI:EU:C:2019:43).

Opinion of Advocate General Bobek in Case C-193/17, *Cresco Investigation GmbH v Markus Achatzi*, delivered on 25 July 2018 (ECLI:EU:C:2018:614).

ECtHR

Węgrzynowski and Smolczewski v Poland, Appl. No. 33846/07, judgment of 16 July 2013.

Italy

Court of Padua, judgment of 26 May 2000 (case No. 3531/99).

A. Rationale and Policy Underpinnings

Article 91 GDPR complements the rules on the processing of special categories of personal data by religious organisations set out in Article 9(2)(d) GDPR. It does so by introducing a minor innovation compared to the DPD.[1] The innovation consists in providing for a limited derogation from the requirements of the Regulation for those churches and religious associations that applied comprehensive data protection rules prior to the entry into force of the Regulation. The derogation implies that, in the Member States where they exist, special rules for churches and religious associations may continue to apply, provided that they are amended to ensure consistency with the GDPR. Although this derogation was absent from the DPD, some Member States granted similar derogations under their national data protection laws, in particular those where religious groups enjoy a special status under constitutional law, such as Italy and Poland.[2]

In light of this, the primary aim of Article 91 is to maintain the status quo to the extent necessary to ensure that, in accordance with Article 17 Treaty on the Functioning of the European Union ('TFEU'),[3] the entry into force of the GDPR does not prejudice the constitutional status of churches and religious associations in the Member States (see recital 165).[4] More generally, Article 91 tries to balance the fundamental freedom of

---

[1] See Buttarelli 2016, p. 2.

[2] See Arts. 7–8 of the Italian Constitution and Art. 25 of the Polish Constitution. See on the status of religious groups in the EU and in the Member States: Zucca and Ungureanu 2012; Doe 2011; McCrea 2010; Madeley and Leuştean 2010.

[3] Art. 17(1) TFEU reads: '[t]he Union respects and does not prejudice the status under national law of churches and religious associations or communities in the Member States'.

[4] This objective was also made clear in the GDPR Proposal, which stated that its Art. 85 (which became Art. 91 in the final text of the GDPR) 'allows in the light of Article 17 of the Treaty on the Functioning of the European Union for the continuous application of existing comprehensive data protection rules of churches if brought in line with this Regulation'. See GDPR Proposal, p. 16.

religion and the related need to respect the autonomy of religious communities, on the one hand, against the no less fundamental right to the protection of personal data, on the other (see recital 4). This balance is achieved by: (i) giving the Article 91 derogation a narrow scope of application; (ii) bringing the pre-existing data protection rules of religious organisations into line with the GDPR; and (iii) subjecting religious organisations to the supervision of an independent authority with regard to compliance with data protection requirements. Indeed, as noted by Advocate General Mengozzi in the *Jehovah's Witnesses* case, 'the EU legislature ... saw no contradiction between, on the one hand, recognising the status of religious communities as determined by the Member States and, on the other hand, confirming that data processing by those same communities is to be subject to specific rules'.[5]

B. Legal Background

1. EU legislation

Under the DPD, the processing of personal data by religious organisations was neither excluded from the scope of application of the Directive (see Article 3(2) DPD)[6] nor subject to derogations similar to that of Article 91 GDPR. However, part of the roots of Article 91 GDPR can be traced back to the original DPD proposal.[7] The latter excluded from the scope of application of the proposed Directive all files held by 'non-profit-making bodies, notably of ... religious ... nature, as part of their legitimate aims, on condition that they relate only to those members and corresponding members who have consented to being included therein and that they are not communicated to third parties' (Article 3(2)(b)). Such an exclusion was not retained in the text of the DPD as finally adopted in 1995. This was primarily due to a fear that, if too many organisations were exempted from compliance with the obligations of the DPD, the rights of individuals would not be sufficiently guaranteed.[8] Instead, the EU legislator decided to partially simplify the rules governing the processing of personal data by religious organisations.[9] This resulted in the adoption of Article 8(2)(d) DPD. The latter provision lifted the general ban on the processing of sensitive data (including data revealing religious beliefs), imposed as a rule by Article 8(1) DPD, where it was a non-profit body with a religious aim which processed such data and the processing was conducted in the course of the body's legitimate activities; was subject to appropriate guarantees; related solely to the members of the body or to persons who had regular contact with it in connection with its purposes; and was merely internal to the body (i.e. the data could not be disclosed outside that body without the consent of the data subject).[10] The above exemption survives, essentially unmodified, in Article 9(2)(d) GDPR.[11]

In addition, the DPD allowed Member States to provide for an exemption from the obligation to notify the local supervisory authority before beginning an automatic

---

[5] The Advocate General made this observation mainly on the basis of his reading of recital 165 GDPR. See Case C-25/17, *Jehovan todistajat* (AG Opinion), para. 34.

[6] This is also made clear in the CJEU's case law on Art. 3(2) DPD. See Case C-25/17, *Jehovan todistajat*, paras. 34–51; Case C-101/01, *Lindqvist*, paras. 29–51.

[7] DPD Proposal 1990.   [8] DPD Proposal 1992, p. 13.   [9] Ibid.

[10] It should be emphasised that data coming under this exemption were not removed from protection under the DPD, but rather only from the special protection under Art. 8 DPD.

[11] See the commentary on Art. 9 in this volume.

processing operation, or for a simplification of the notification, in the case of processing operations referred to in Article 8(2)(d) (see Article 18(4)). This exemption disappeared under the GDPR, as the latter abolished the general obligation to notify supervisory authorities.

2. International instruments

Convention 108, both in its original and modernised form, does not contain any provision specifically regulating the processing of personal data by religious organisations.

3. National developments

Legal antecedents of Article 91 may be found primarily at domestic level. In fact, the Article in some ways mirrors provisions that could be found in some of the national data protection laws in force before the GDPR became applicable. This does not clearly emerge from the legislative history of Article 91, but a closer look at these national provisions suggests that they were probably a source of inspiration for the EU legislature. The old Italian and Polish data protection laws are a case in point.

The Italian Data Protection Code of 2003[12] transposed Article 8(2)(d) DPD into Italian law and materially reflected its rules.[13] However, the Code also provided that religious groups (in Italian, *confessioni religiose*) that, prior to the enactment of the Code, had adopted specific data protection safeguards were allowed to continue to process data in accordance with such safeguards, provided that the safeguards complied with certain principles to be specified by the Italian DPA (see Articles 181(6) and 26(3)(a)). In Italy, the only religious group which could practically benefit from this specific derogation was the Catholic Church, as it was the sole religious organisation to adopt its own data protection rules prior to the entry into force of the Data Protection Code. In fact, in 1999, the Italian Episcopal Conference had adopted a General Decree that laid down the rules to be followed by parishes and other catholic bodies when processing data of Christian faithful and people who have contacts with the Catholic Church for religious reasons.[14] Both the Italian DPA[15] and courts[16] have confirmed (at least implicitly) the adequacy of the data protection safeguards of the General Decree on several occasions. It should be noted, however, that the Italian Constitution recognises the Catholic Church as an 'independent and sovereign' legal order.[17] Thus, Italian authorities would normally scrutinise the data processing activities of the Catholic Church only to verify whether such activities are exclusively relevant for the legal order of the Church in view of their religious nature, and to ensure that other fundamental rights recognised by the State (e.g. the right to privacy) are not substantially affected by the activities in question.[18] For example, Italian authorities have consistently taken the view that the keeping of baptismal records is only relevant for the legal order of the Church, and that the rights of those individuals who

---

[12] See Italian Data Protection Code 2003.
[13] The DPD was initially transposed into the Italian Data Protection Law 1996. The latter was later repealed and substituted by the Italian Data Protection Code 2003. For further details on the protection of religious data under the Code see Resta 2005.
[14] See Italian Episcopal Decree 1999. See further Redaelli 1999.
[15] See, inter alia, Italian Data Protection Authority 2004, 2006A, 2006B and 2009.
[16] See judgment of the Court of Padua 2000.   [17] See Art. 7 Italian Constitution.
[18] See, in particular, judgment of the Court of Padua 2000.

intend to leave the Church are sufficiently safeguarded by adding a note in the margin of the relevant baptismal record, as opposed to removing their names from the record.[19]

The Polish Act on the Protection of Personal Data of 1997[20] implemented and essentially mirrored the rules of Article 8(2)(d) DPD (see Article 27(2)(4)). It also exempted churches and other religious groups from the obligation to register their data filing systems with the Polish DPA with regard to the data that they processed for their institutional purposes (see Article 43(1)(3)).[21] In addition, the Act considerably limited the enforcement powers of the Polish DPA with regard to the data processing activities of religious organisations (see Article 43(2)). This reflected the special status that churches and religious organisations enjoy under Polish constitutional law,[22] as clarified in a Guidance jointly issued by the Polish DPA and the Polish Episcopal Conference.[23] The Guidance also clarified that, under Polish law, the Catholic Church may adopt its own internal rules and that the data processing activities of the Church are also governed by the Code of Canon Law of 1983 (*Codex Iuris Canonici*).[24]

4. Case law

As mentioned above, Article 91 GDPR tries to reconcile freedom of religion with the protection of personal data. The CJEU has addressed the relationship between these two rights in two cases: the *Lindqvist* case and the *Jehovah's Witnesses* case.[25]

The *Lindqvist* case[26] concerned the activities of a catechist in a parish in Sweden, which consisted in setting up an internet page providing information to parishioners preparing for their confirmation. One of the questions that the Court had to answer in the case was whether such activities fell outside the scope of application of the DPD in light of the exceptions of Article 3(2) of the DPD (now largely reproduced in Article 2(2) GDPR). Article 3(2) DPD read:

This Directive shall not apply to the processing of personal data:

– in the course of an activity which falls outside the scope of Community law, such as those provided for by Titles V and VI of the Treaty on European Union and in any case to processing operations concerning public security, defence, State security (including the economic well-being of the State when the processing operation relates to State security matters) and the activities of the State in areas of criminal law,
– by a natural person in the course of a purely personal or household activity.

The Court found that the activities of the catechist were not covered by those exceptions, as the exceptions only related to specific activities of the state falling outside the scope of EU law and to activities carried out in the course of private or family life of

---

[19] See, inter alia, Italian Data Protection Authority 1999 and 2009. See also judgment of the Court of Padua 2000.
[20] See Polish Data Protection Act 1997. [21] Ibid. [22] See Art. 25 Polish Constitution.
[23] See Polish Data Protection Authority and Polish Episcopal Conference 2009. A similar Guidance was jointly issued by the Polish DPA and the Council of Bishops of the Polish Autocephalous Orthodox Church. See Polish Data Protection Authority and Council of Bishops of the Polish Autocephalous Orthodox Church 2011.
[24] Polish Data Protection Authority and Polish Episcopal Conference 2009, pp. 10–11. See also the Polish Data Protection Authority FAQ 2013.
[25] See also the commentary on Art. 2 in this volume regarding the *Lindqvist* and *Jehovan todistajat* cases.
[26] Case C-101/01, *Lindqvist*.

individuals.[27] Thus, according to the Court, religious activities such as those carried out by the catechist in Sweden remained subject to the requirements of the DPD.

The *Jehovah's Witnesses* case[28] concerned the activities of the Jehovah's Witnesses community consisting in manually collecting and processing personal data in the context of door-to-door preaching. These activities were also scrutinised by the Court in light of the exceptions of Article 3(2) DPD. Reading the latter provision together with Article 10 of the Charter of Fundamental Rights of the European Union ('CFR') ('freedom of thought, conscience and religion') and Article 17 TFEU, the Court reaffirmed that the exceptions must be strictly interpreted.[29] On this basis, it held that the collection of personal data by members of a religious community in the course of door-to-door preaching does not fall within the exemptions of Article 3(2) DPD.[30] Thus, according to the Court, religious communities (and their members) must comply with the EU data protection rules when carrying out such activities. In this context, the CJEU noted that '[t]he obligation for every person to comply with the rules of EU law on the protection of personal data cannot be regarded as an interference in the organisational autonomy of those communities [as recognised in Article 17 TFEU]'.[31]

C. Analysis

1. Introduction

Article 91 provides for a limited derogation from the requirements of the GDPR. The applicability of the derogation is subject to stringent conditions. Thus, the derogation applies only if: (i) the entities that intend to benefit from it qualify as 'churches and religious associations or communities'; (ii) such religious organisations applied special and comprehensive data protection rules prior to the entry into force of the GDPR; and (iii) the pre-existing data protection rules are amended to ensure consistency with the GDPR.

Where the derogation applies, it arguably has limited consequences, the main one being that a religious organisation may apply special data protection rules in certain limited circumstances while remaining subject to the supervision of a DPA.

2. Conditions for applying the derogation

2.1 *The concepts of churches and religious associations or communities*

As mentioned above, the derogation of Article 91 applies only to 'churches and religious associations or communities'. As a result, the meaning of these concepts is vitally important to assess whether a given entity falls under the scope of application of Article 91.

The GDPR does not define the above concepts. However, EU law tends to adopt a broad understanding of the concept of 'religion'.[32] For example, Article 10(1)(b) of Directive 2011/95/EU states that:

[T]he concept of religion shall in particular include the holding of theistic, non-theistic and atheistic beliefs, the participation in, or abstention from, formal worship in private or in public, either alone or in community with others, other religious acts or expressions of view, or forms of personal

---

[27] Ibid., paras. 37–48.   [28] Case C-25/17, *Jehovan todistajat*.   [29] Ibid., para. 37.
[30] Ibid., para. 51.   [31] Ibid., para. 74.
[32] See Case C-426/16, *Liga van Moskeeën*, para. 44 and the case law cited.

or communal conduct based on or mandated by any religious belief and as a consequence of religious organisation.[33]

Therefore, in principle, the concepts of 'churches and religious associations or communities' should also be interpreted broadly. For instance, in the *Jehovah's Witnesses* case, the CJEU seems to (implicitly) recognise that the Jehovah's Witnesses community should be considered a religious association or community for the purposes of Article 17 TFEU and the DPD,[34] and the Advocate General's Opinion in the same case suggests that this may be true also under Article 91 GDPR.[35]

While Article 91 only refers to 'churches and religious associations or communities', one could argue that the derogation it grants implicitly applies also to 'philosophical and non-confessional organisations'. This is because the derogation of Article 91 is primarily intended to ensure compliance with Article 17 TFEU (see recital 165), and the latter Article provides that, in addition to respecting the status of religious organisations in the Member States, '[t]he Union equally respects the status under national law of philosophical and non-confessional organisations'.[36]

In this regard, Advocate General Bobek observed in the *Cresco Investigation* case that this formulation of Article 17 TFEU implies that 'any "exemption" hypothetically granted to churches and religious associations or communities would immediately become applicable to any philosophical organisations (largely undefined and left to the law of the Member States)'.[37] Nevertheless, in practice, philosophical organisations are unlikely to be able to benefit from the derogation of Article 91, as most of these organisations, if not all of them, did not apply special data protection rules before the entry into force of the GDPR.[38]

2.2 Pre-existing comprehensive data protection rules

The derogation of Article 91 only applies where in a Member State a religious organisation applied 'comprehensive rules relating to the protection of natural persons with regard to processing' before 24 May 2016.[39] Neither the text of the GDPR nor its legislative history clarifies which features the rules must present to be considered comprehensive. However, the comprehensiveness threshold that the rules should meet is arguably high. This is indicated in the *Adidas* case where Advocate General Cosmas opined that even the rules of the DPD were not 'comprehensive'.[40] Thus, only rules that regulate the data processing activities of religious organisations in extensive detail are likely to be considered 'comprehensive rules' under Article 91.

Moreover, Article 91 refers to rules that religious organisations 'apply'. This suggests that they may be able to benefit from the Article 91 derogation not only when they

---

[33] See Directive 2011/95/EU.
[34] The Court refers to the Jehovah's Witnesses community as a 'religious community' throughout the entire decision. See Case C-25/17, *Jehovan todistajat*.
[35] Ibid. (AG Opinion), para. 34 and fn. 30.   [36] See Art. 17(2) TFEU.
[37] See Case C-193/17, *Cresco Investigation* (AG Opinion), para. 28.
[38] See, however, the comments made further below on the possible incompatibility with the principle of equality of the rule establishing that only organisations that applied special data protection rules in the past may benefit from the derogation of Art. 91 GDPR.
[39] 24 May 2016 is the date of the entry into force of the GDPR (see Art. 99).
[40] In the *Adidas* case, Advocate General Cosmas noted that, even after the adoption of the DPD, '[t]he Community institutions have not introduced comprehensive rules governing the protection of personal data'. See Case C-223/98, *Adidas* (AG Opinion), para. 37.

adopted (and applied) their own internal data protection rules (like the Catholic Church did in Italy), but also when they were subject to a special data protection regime under the legislation of a Member State.[41]

There are likely only a handful of Member States where comprehensive rules for religious organisations existed prior to the entry into force of the GDPR. For example, the UK Information Commissioner ('ICO') noted that it was 'not aware of any such rules currently being applied in the UK and therefore provisions relating to the continuation of such rules are not relevant in UK legislation'.[42] On the contrary, as discussed above, Italy and Poland are countries where the Article 91 derogation may be relevant.

The requirement that only religious organisations that applied special data protection rules in the past may benefit from the derogation of Article 91 could be problematic if viewed in light of the principle of equality.[43] Indeed, it is hard to see any objectively justified reason for not allowing a religious organisation to adopt and apply its own internal data protection rules (for the first time) after the entry into force of the GDPR. This is particularly so if these rules are in line with the GDPR and if the constitutional arrangements in place in the relevant Member State would permit this.

2.3 Revision of the pre-existing rules

Article 91(1) provides that the pre-existing rules may continue to apply only if they are 'brought into line' with the GDPR. This wording is rather cryptic, but it suggests that the pre-existing rules must be amended to ensure that they materially reflect and conform to the requirements of the GDPR, albeit with minor, largely cosmetic, differences. In other words, divergences should be allowed only if duly justified. This is confirmed by the fact that the GDPR also mandates that the rules on the processing of personal data by the EU institutions, bodies, offices and agencies be adapted to the principles and rules laid down in the GDPR (see Articles 2(3) and 98 and recital 17). It was in response to this requirement that the EUDPR, which closely mirrors the requirements of the GDPR, was enacted.

The rules as amended must be 'precise and clear' in order to meet the foreseeability criterion set both by the CJEU and by the ECtHR.[44] This is because 'citizens must be able to predict the effect of a law, especially where the law may interfere with their fundamental rights'.[45] Article 91(1) does not specify by when the pre-existing rules must be amended. Yet, as the special rules for churches may not apply until they are amended to be consistent with the GDPR, the pre-existing rules should have been amended by 25 May 2018 to ensure their seamless continuation.

In light of the above requirement of Article 91(1), the Italian and Polish Episcopal Conferences have adopted new rules that broadly reflect the requirements of the GDPR.[46] However, these rules also present some differences compared to the GDPR. For instance, the General Decree adopted by the Italian Episcopal Conference provides that a data subject

---

[41] Note, in this regard, the difference between Art. 91 GDPR and Art. 181(6) Italian Data Protection Code, which referred to safeguards 'adopted' by the religious group.

[42] See ICO 2017, p. 19. The UK Government made a similar statement on Art. 91 during the legislative process that led to the adoption of the GDPR: '[t]his Article does not have any specific effect on the UK. We have no objection to its inclusion if it deals with particular situations in other Member States'. See Council Document 2014, p. 140.

[43] See Art. 20 CFR. [44] Buttarelli 2016, p. 4. [45] Ibid.

[46] See Italian Episcopal Decree 2018; Polish Episcopal Decree 2018. For example, both the Italian and the Polish General Decrees establish record-keeping, DPO and data breach notification requirements.

may not request the deletion from the Church records of data on the sacraments that he/she received, but only an annotation in the margins of the records (see Article 8(8)).[47] Whether these differences are compatible with the Article 91 requirement that the Church's rules be brought into line with the GDPR is unclear. However, in a different context, an annotation in the margins of a document was considered a viable compromise to reconcile the conflicts between the right to privacy and other fundamental rights, such as freedom of expression.[48] In any event, it should be noted that the WP29's understanding during the legislative process was that Article 91:

> obliges churches and religious organisations that currently have separate legal regimes, to bring it [sic] in line with the Regulation. It shall in any case not grant churches and religious organisations the possibility to adopt a separate legal regime that is incompatible with the Regulation in those Member States where constitutional arrangements do not permit this.[49]

3. Consequences of the derogation

3.1 Continuation of pre-existing rules

Where it applies, Article 91 does not exclude religious organisations from the scope of application of the Regulation: churches and religious associations are by default within the scope of EU data protection rules, unless one of the limited exceptions of Article 2(2) GDPR applies (e.g. pure personal or household activity).[50]

However, Article 91 arguably allows the pre-existing data protection rules of religious organisations to operate as a *lex specialis* where such organisations process data for strictly religious purposes. Indeed, while Article 91 does not clarify the relationship between the GDPR and the special rules for religious organisations, it does state that the latter rules 'may continue to apply'. Thus, it seems to give precedence to the special rules of religious organisations in case of overlap with the requirements of the GDPR. Nonetheless, this should apply only where a religious organisation processes data for its purely institutional purposes. This is because 'derogations and limitations in relation to the protection of personal data must apply only in so far as is strictly necessary'.[51] Therefore, the derogation of Article 91 should not go beyond what is necessary to ensure its objective, namely guaranteeing that the entry into force of the GDPR does not prejudice the organisational autonomy of religious associations in the Member States. Achieving such an objective arguably requires only minimal adaptation of the rules of the GDPR, as the CJEU found that, in principle, 'the obligation for every person to comply with the rules of EU law on the protection of personal data cannot be regarded as an interference in the organisational autonomy of those communities'.[52] Consequently, where a religious organisation processes data for purposes that are not strictly religious, the GDPR applies in its entirety.

3.2 Supervision of an independent supervisory authority

Religious organisations that continue to apply their special rules pursuant to Article 91(1) must be subject to the supervision of an independent authority. The latter may be the authority generally responsible for monitoring the application of the GDPR or an authority

---

[47] Similar rules are also established by the Polish Episcopal Decree 2018 (see Arts. 13 and 14(4)).
[48] See ECtHR, *Węgrzynowski*.   [49] See WP29 2012, p. 25.   [50] Buttarelli 2016, pp. 1–3.
[51] See Case C-212/13, *Ryneš*, para. 28. See also Case C-362/14, *Schrems*, para. 92.
[52] See Case C-25/17, *Jehovan todistajat*, para. 74.

specifically responsible for supervising the processing of personal data by one or several religious organisations. However, such an authority must fulfil all the conditions specified in Chapter VI GDPR; in particular, it must be independent according to the criteria established by Article 52 GDPR.[53]

In light of the above requirement, the General Decree of the Polish Episcopal Conference establishes a specific supervisory authority (Church Data Protection Inspector or *Kościelny Inspektor Ochrony Danych*) in charge of supervising the data processing activities of the Catholic Church in Poland (see Articles 35–40).[54]

Select Bibliography

EU legislation

Directive 2011/95/EU: Directive 2011/95/EU of the European Parliament and of the Council of 13 December 2011 on standards for the qualification of third-country nationals or stateless persons as beneficiaries of international protection, for a uniform status for refugees or for persons eligible for subsidiary protection, and for the content of the protection granted, OJ 2011 L 337/9.

DPD Proposal 1990: Proposal for a Council Directive concerning the protection of individuals in relation to the processing of personal data, COM(90) 314 final, 13 September 1990.

DPD Proposal 1992: Amended Proposal for a Council Directive on the protection of individuals with regard to the processing of personal data and on the free movement of such data, COM(92) 422 final, 15 October 1992.

GDPR Proposal: Proposal for a Regulation of the European Parliament and of the Council on the protection of individuals with regard to the processing of personal data and on the free movement of such data (General Data Protection Regulation), COM(2012) 11 final, 25 January 2012.

National legislation

Italian Constitution: Senato della Repubblica, 'Constitution of the Italian Republic', available (in English) at https://www.senato.it/documenti/repository/istituzione/costituzione_inglese.pdf.

Italian Data Protection Code 2003: Decreto legislativo 30 giugno 2003, n. 196: Codice in Materia di Protezione dei Dati Personali.

Italian Data Protection Law 1996: Legge n. 675 del 31 dicembre 1996 - Tutela delle persone e di altri soggetti rispetto al trattamento dei dati personali.

Italian Episcopal Decree 1999: Decreto Generale: Disposizioni per la Tutela del Diritto alla Buona Fama e alla Riservatezza del 30 ottobre 1999.

Italian Episcopal Decree 2018: Decreto Generale: Disposizioni per la Tutela del Diritto alla Buona Fama e alla Riservatezza del 25 maggio 2018.

Polish Constitution: The Constitution of the Republic of Poland, available (in English) at https://www.senat.gov.pl/en/about-the-senate/konstytucja/.

Polish Data Protection Act 1997: USTAWA z dnia 29 sierpnia 1997 r.o ochronie danych osobowych.

Polish Episcopal Decree 2018: Dekret ogólny w sprawie ochrony osób fizycznych w związku z przetwarzaniem danych osobowych w Kościele katolickim wydany przez Konferencję Episkopatu Polski, w dniu 13 marca 2018 r., podczas 378.

---

[53] See Buttarelli 2016, p. 4. See further the commentary on Art. 52 in this volume.

[54] See Polish Episcopal Decree 2018. See further the commentary on Art. 4(21) in this volume regarding the fact that it is questionable whether such Polish authority qualifies as an independent public authority 'established by a Member State', and hence as a supervisory authority, under the GDPR.

Academic writings

Doe 2011: Doe, *Law and Religion in Europe: A Comparative Introduction* (OUP 2011).
McCrea 2010: McCrea, *Religion and the Public Order of the European Union* (OUP 2010).
Madeley and Leuştean 2010: Madeley and Leuştean (eds.), *Religion, Politics and Law in the European Union* (Routledge 2010).
Redaelli 1999: Redaelli, 'Il Decreto generale della CEI sulla Privacy', 4 *Ex lege* (1999), 66.
Zucca and Ungureanu 2012: Zucca and Ungureanu (eds.), *Law, State and Religion in the New Europe: Debates and Dilemmas* (CUP 2012).

Papers of data protection authorities

WP29 2012: Article 29 Working Party, 'Opinion 01/2012 on the Data Protection Reform Proposals' (WP 191, 23 March 2012).
ICO 2017: Information Commissioner's Office, 'The Information Commissioner's Office (ICO) Response to DCMS General Data Protection Regulation (GDPR) Derogations Call for Views' (10 May 2017).
Italian Data Protection Authority 1999: Garante per la Protezione dei Dati Personali, Dati sensibili (convinzioni religiose): richiesta di cancellazione dal registro dei battezzati – 13 settembre 1999 [1090502] (1999).
Italian Data Protection Authority 2004: Garante per la Protezione dei Dati Personali, Diritti dell'interessato – Diritto all'aggiornamento dei dati nel registro dei battezzati – 30 giugno 2004 [1039664] (2004).
Italian Data Protection Authority 2006A: Garante per la Protezione dei Dati Personali, Provvedimento del 20 settembre 2006 [1353369] (2006).
Italian Data Protection Authority 2006B: Garante per la protezione dei Dati Personali, Provvedimento del 28 settembre 2006 [1357386] (2006).
Italian Data Protection Authority 2009: Garante per la protezione dei Dati Personali, Provvedimento dell'8 luglio 2009 [1638541] (2009).
Polish Data Protection Authority and Council of Bishops of the Polish Autocephalous Orthodox Church 2011: Polish Data Protection Authority and the Council of Bishops of the Polish Autocephalous Orthodox Church. 'Ochrona Danych Osobowych W Działalności Polskiego Autokefalicznego Kościoła Prawosławnego' (22 March 2011).
Polish Data Protection Authority and Polish Episcopal Conference 2009: Polish Data Protection Authority and the Polish Episcopal Conference, 'Ochrona Danych Osobowych W Działalności Kościoła Katolickiego W Polsce' (23 September 2009).

Reports and recommendations

Council Document 2014: Comments on Chapters IX–XI, 5406/2/14 REV 2, 10 February 2014.
Resta 2005: Resta, 'La protezione dei dati personali di interesse religioso dopo l'entrata in vigore del Codice del 2003', (16 September 2005), available at https://www.olir.it/areetematiche/80/documents/Resta_Privacy.pdf.

Others

Buttarelli 2016: Buttarelli, 'Personal Data Protection in Churches and Religious Organisation', Speech to a Conference in Warsaw (25 February 2016), available at https://edps.europa.eu/sites/edp/files/publication/16-02-25_personal_data_protection_church_warsaw_en.pdf.
Polish Data Protection Authority FAQ 2013: Polish Data Protection Authority, 'FAQ Document on Data Protection and Churches' (28 November 2013), available at https://www.giodo.gov.pl/392.

Chapter X Delegated Acts and Implementing Acts (Articles 92–93)

Article 92. Exercise of the delegation

LUCA TOSONI

1. The power to adopt delegated acts is conferred on the Commission subject to the conditions laid down in this Article.
2. The delegation of power referred to in Article 12(8) and Article 43(8) shall be conferred on the Commission for an indeterminate period of time from 24 May 2016.
3. The delegation of power referred to in Article 12(8) and Article 43(8) may be revoked at any time by the European Parliament or by the Council. A decision of revocation shall put an end to the delegation of power specified in that decision. It shall take effect the day following that of its publication in the Official Journal of the European Union or at a later date specified therein. It shall not affect the validity of any delegated acts already in force.
4. As soon as it adopts a delegated act, the Commission shall notify it simultaneously to the European Parliament and to the Council.
5. A delegated act adopted pursuant to Article 12(8) and Article 43(8) shall enter into force only if no objection has been expressed by either the European Parliament or the Council within a period of three months of notification of that act to the European Parliament and the Council or if, before the expiry of that period, the European Parliament and the Council have both informed the Commission that they will not object. That period shall be extended by three months at the initiative of the European Parliament or of the Council.

Relevant Recital

(166) In order to fulfil the objectives of this Regulation, namely to protect the fundamental rights and freedoms of natural persons and in particular their right to the protection of personal data and to ensure the free movement of personal data within the Union, the power to adopt acts in accordance with Article 290 TFEU should be delegated to the Commission. In particular, delegated acts should be adopted in respect of criteria and requirements for certification mechanisms, information to be presented by standardised icons and procedures for providing such icons. It is of particular importance that the Commission carry out appropriate consultations during its preparatory work, including at expert level. The Commission, when preparing and drawing-up delegated acts, should ensure a simultaneous, timely and appropriate transmission of relevant documents to the European Parliament and to the Council.

Closely Related Provisions

Article 12(7)–(8) (Standardised icons) (see too recitals 60 and 166); Article 42(1) (Certification); Article 43(8) (Certification bodies) (see too recitals 100 and 166); Article 70(1)(q)–(r) (Tasks of the Board); Article 93 (Committee procedure)

Related Provisions in EUDPR [Regulation (EU) 2018/1725]

Article 14(8) (Standardised icons) (see too recital 35); Article 42 (Legislative consultation) (see too recital 60)

Relevant Case Law

CJEU

Case C-355/10, *European Parliament v Council of the European Union*, judgment of 5 September 2012 (Grand Chamber) (ECLI:EU:C:2012:516).

Case C-427/12, *European Commission v European Parliament and Council of the European Union*, judgment of 18 March 2014 (Grand Chamber) (ECLI:EU:C:2014:170).

Case C-88/14, *European Commission v European Parliament and Council of the European Union*, judgment of 16 July 2015 (Grand Chamber) (ECLI:EU:C:2015:499).

Case C-286/14, *European Parliament v European Commission*, judgment of 17 March 2016 (ECLI:EU:C:2016:183).

A. Rationale and Policy Underpinnings

The GDPR grants the Commission the power to supplement the rules of the Regulation through the adoption of 'delegated acts'.[1] This power may only be used to: (i) determine the information to be presented by the standardised icons mentioned in Article 12(7)[2] and the procedures for providing such icons (Article 12(8)); and (ii) specify the requirements for the certification mechanisms to be used to demonstrate compliance with the GDPR (Article 43(8)).[3] This delegation of 'quasi-legislative' powers to the Commission was done primarily in the interest of efficiency.[4] In fact, the result of the delegation is that decisions can be taken more quickly and without taking up much time of the already overburden legislative bodies of the European Union (i.e. the European Parliament and the Council). In turn, this allows the regulator to respond more swiftly to technological and societal changes. However, since the Commission is empowered to add new elements to the regulatory framework established by a legislative act (i.e. the GDPR), the Commission remains accountable to the EU legislature and its powers must be subject to strict limits, so as to ensure democratic legitimacy (see Article 290 TFEU). The aim of Article 92 is to specify such limits.

---

[1] Delegated acts are non-legislative acts of general application that may be adopted by the Commission to supplement or amend certain non-essential elements of a legislative act in accordance with Art. 290 Treaty on the Functioning of the European Union ('TFEU'). See Craig and de Búrca 2015, pp. 114–116.

[2] Art. 12(7) GDPR reads: '[t]he information to be provided to data subjects pursuant to Articles 13 and 14 may be provided in combination with standardised icons in order to give in an easily visible, intelligible and clearly legible manner a meaningful overview of the intended processing. Where the icons are presented electronically they shall be machine-readable'. The Parliament proposed in its first reading position the inclusion of similar icons in the GDPR, accompanied by essential information, but these were finally left out. See Annex 1, EP Position GDPR.

[3] During the legislative process, the WP29 found it appropriate to spell out the criteria and requirements for certification mechanisms in a delegated act. This was to ensure legal certainty and '[s]ince it would be hard to spell out all criteria and requirements in full in the text of the Regulation'. See WP29 2012B, p. 36.

[4] This is typical of any conferral of delegated powers. As noted by the Commission, 'the legislator delegates its powers to the Commission [in accordance with Art. 290 TFEU] in the interests of efficiency'. See EC Communication 2009, p. 3.

B. Legal Background

1. EU legislation

Under the DPD, the Commission was not empowered to adopt delegated acts. This is essentially because delegated acts are a creation of the Treaty of Lisbon, which entered into force in 2009, after the adoption of the DPD.[5] However, the DPD gave the Commission some limited implementing powers with regard to the international transfer of data (see Articles 25(4)–(6), 26(3)–(4) and 31).[6] These are taken over in Articles 45(3)–(5), 46(2) and 93 GDPR.

2. Case law

There is extensive case law of the CJEU on the delegation of powers to the European Commission under EU law,[7] but no case law on the delegations under the GDPR.

C. Analysis

1. Delegated acts under the GDPR

The GDPR confers on the Commission the power to adopt a number of delegated acts (see Articles 12(8) and 43(8)). These are quasi-legislative acts that may be adopted by the Commission to 'supplement or amend' certain elements of the GDPR that are considered 'non-essential'.[8] In this regard, the delegated acts to be adopted pursuant to Articles 12(8) and 43(8) GDPR are more likely to 'supplement' than 'amend' the GDPR, as these provisions do not envisage any changes to the text of the Regulation or the addition of an Annex to it.[9]

The number of empowerments for delegated acts was far greater in the GDPR Proposal compared to the text of the GDPR that was finally adopted in 2016.[10] The Commission had proposed these empowerments to ensure a more consistent application of the GDPR

---

[5] On the creation of delegated acts by the Treaty of Lisbon, see Craig and de Búrca 2015, pp. 114–116.

[6] See further on the difference between delegated powers and implementing powers, before and after the Treaty of Lisbon: ibid., pp. 114–123. See also the commentary on Art. 93 in this volume.

[7] See, inter alia, Case C-355/10, *Parliament v Council*; Case C-427/12, *Commission v Parliament and Council*; Case C-88/14, *Commission v Parliament and Council*; Case C-286/14, *Parliament v Commission*. For an analysis of some of this case law, see Chamon 2015 and van der Mei 2016.

[8] This follows directly from Art. 290 TFEU, which allows the legislature to delegate to the Commission the power to adopt non-legislative acts of general application to supplement or amend certain non-essential elements of a legislative act (in this case the GDPR).

[9] On this point, the Commission noted that 'it believes that by using the verb "amend" the authors of [Art. 290 TFEU] wanted to cover hypothetical cases in which the Commission is empowered formally to amend a basic instrument. Such a formal amendment might relate to the text of one or more articles in the enacting terms or to the text of an annex that legally forms part of the legislative instrument ... [Instead, if] the future measure specifically adds new non-essential rules which change the framework of the legislative act, leaving a margin of discretion to the Commission ... the measure could be deemed to "supplement" the basic instrument'. See EC Communication 2009, p. 4. See also EC Guidelines 2011, paras. 34 and 40. See further Case C-286/14, *Parliament v Commission*, paras. 28–64, where the Court found that the Commission may not, in the context of the exercise of a power to 'supplement' a legislative act, change the actual text of that act: it must adopt a separate act.

[10] See in particular Arts. 6(5), 8(3), 9(3), 12(5), 14(7), 15(3), 17(9), 20(6), 22(4), 23(3), 26(5), 28(5), 30(3), 31(5), 32(5), 33(6), 34(8), 35(11), 37(2), 39(2), 43(3), 44(7), 79(6), 81(3), 82(3) and 83(3) GDPR Proposal.

across the EU, but also 'to avoid the Regulation being over prescriptive, to ensure technological neutrality and openness to future technological developments'.[11] Nonetheless, this solution was met with strong opposition during the legislative process, mainly due to the large extent to which further regulation was left to delegated powers.[12] As a result, the EU legislator decided to grant only limited delegated powers to the Commission in the final text of the GDPR. In particular, the GDPR provides that the Commission may adopt delegated acts only for two purposes: (i) determining the information to be presented by the standardised icons mentioned in Article 12(7) and the procedures for providing such icons (Article 12(8)); and (ii) specifying the requirements for the certification mechanisms to be used to demonstrate compliance with the GDPR (Article 43(8)). It should be noted, however, that granting the Commission the power to adopt delegated acts does not mean that the Commission is obliged to adopt them. Indeed, the acts should be adopted only when there is a clear need to do so.[13]

Article 92 and recital 166 GDPR contain the standard provisions for the exercise of the delegations in line with Article 290 TFEU.[14] These provisions subject the Commission's delegated powers to strict material and procedural limits. First, recital 166 specifies that the Commission should make use of its delegated powers only to 'fulfil the objectives of [the GDPR], namely to protect the fundamental rights and freedoms of natural persons and in particular their right to the protection of personal data and to ensure the free movement of personal data within the Union'. In turn, Articles 12(8) and 43(8) circumscribe the context in which such objectives may be pursued by means of delegated acts. Therefore, the Commission may not use its quasi-legislative powers beyond the boundaries of Articles 12(8) and 43(8) or to attain other objectives. In particular, the Commission may not change the 'essential elements' of the GDPR or supplement it by new 'essential elements'.[15] Elements of an act are generally considered 'essential' where they entail 'political choices falling within the responsibilities of the European Union legislature'.[16] According to the CJEU, a measure entails 'political choices' where, inter alia, it is liable to interfere with fundamental rights (e.g. the right to privacy) to a considerable extent.[17]

Secondly, Article 92 and recital 166 establish the procedural conditions that the Commission must respect when exercising its delegated powers under the GDPR. The conditions include consulting experts in the preparation of the delegated acts and submitting the latter acts to the scrutiny of the European Parliament and the Council.

Thirdly, Article 92 makes clear that the Parliament and the Council may express objections to the delegated acts adopted by the Commission, and revoke the delegations at any time. These are radical powers and are likely to be used parsimoniously.[18] In fact, the power to revoke a delegation has never been used.[19] Should it be used to revoke the delegations granted in Articles 12(8) and 43(8) GDPR, the revocation will not affect the

---

[11] See Council Report 2012, p. 3.
[12] Strong reservations were expressed in the Parliament, in the Council, by the EDPS and by the WP29. See, inter alia, EP GDPR Draft Report, p. 214; Council Questionnaire 2012; EDPS 2012, pp. 12–13; WP29 2012A, p. 7; and WP29 2012B, pp. 8–12.
[13] WP29 2012B, p. 9.
[14] See GDPR Proposal, p. 16. See also the Appendix to the Annex to the Interinstitutional Agreement 2016.
[15] See Case C-355/10, *Parliament v Council*, paras. 64–68. See further Chamon 2014.
[16] See Case C-355/10, *Parliament v Council*, para. 65. See further Bradley 2016, pp. 60–62; Ritleng 2016, pp. 133–155.
[17] See Case C-355/10, *Parliament v Council*, para. 77.   [18] See Mendes 2016, p. 236.
[19] Best 2016, p. 62.

validity of any of the delegated acts that the Commission may have already adopted and which are in force at that point (Article 92(3)).

2. Procedure for adopting delegated acts

The procedure for adopting a delegated act is not regulated in detail in any biding EU legal act. Article 290 TFEU establishes the general procedural principles. These are operationalised and complemented, for the purposes of the GDPR, by the provisions of Article 92 and recital 166. Moreover, the EU institutions have adopted in 2016 a (non-binding) Interinstitutional Agreement on Better Law-Making[20] which sets out the procedural steps and the practical arrangements for adopting delegated acts.[21] Thus, the Commission enjoys a certain degree of procedural autonomy in this matter, but it committed to follow the procedural steps laid down in the Interinstitutional Agreement.

2.1 Preparation and adoption of delegated acts

The Commission may decide to exercise its delegated powers under the GDPR at any time. This is made clear in Article 92(2) GDPR, which provides that '[t]he delegation of power referred to in Article 12(8) and Article 43(8) shall be conferred on the Commission for an indeterminate period of time from 24 May 2016'.

Should it decide to exercise its delegated powers, the Commission will involve national experts in the preparation of the delegated acts.[22] Indeed, the Commission systematically consults experts from the national authorities of the Member States in the drawing-up of draft delegated acts.[23] This practice is echoed in recital 166 GDPR, which states that '[i]t is of particular importance that the Commission carry out appropriate consultations during its preparatory work, including at expert level'.

Each of the Member States designates one or more experts to be consulted.[24] The experts should be consulted in a timely manner on each draft prepared by the Commission services and should be given enough time to prepare and provide comments.[25] The drafts are also transmitted to the European Parliament and Council (see recital 166)[26] and are normally published in the Register of Delegated Acts.[27]

In practice, the consultations take place either via existing expert groups (e.g. the Commission expert group on the GDPR and LED)[28] or via ad hoc meetings with experts from the Member States.[29] In this context, the experts have a consultative rather than an institutional role.[30] However, draft delegated acts are normally refined in light of the experts' observations. This is done to ensure that 'from a political and institutional point of view everything possible is done to avoid any objections being made by Parliament or the Council'.[31]

The EDPB must also be involved in the consultations. This is because the GDPR specifically assigns to the EDPB the task of providing the Commission with a (non-binding)

---

[20] See Interinstitutional Agreement 2016.   [21] Ibid., in the Annex.
[22] In the preparation of a delegated act, the Commission may occasionally decide to seek advice also from experts from civil society, industry, and academia, such as the experts who sit in the Commission Multistakeholder expert group to support the application of the GDPR. See GDPR Expert Group 2018.
[23] See Interinstitutional Agreement 2016, in the Annex, point 4. See also EC Communication 2009, p. 6.
[24] See Annex to the Interinstitutional Agreement 2016, point 4.   [25] Ibid.
[26] Ibid., point 10.   [27] For the Register of Delegated Acts, see EU Website Register.
[28] This is the expert group which was set up to assist the Commission in relation to the implementation of existing EU data protection legislation, programmes and policies, see EC Website Register.
[29] Annex to the Interinstitutional Agreement 2016, point 4.   [30] EC Communication 2009, p.7.
[31] Ibid., p. 6.

opinion on: (i) the icons referred to in Article 12(7) (Article 70(1)(r)); and (ii) the certification requirements referred to in Article 43(8) (Article 70(1)(q)).[32] The mandatory nature of the EDPB consultation in these cases is reaffirmed by the EUDPR, recital 60 of which states that 'Regulation (EU) 2016/679 provides for mandatory consultation of the European Data Protection Board [on] delegated acts on standardised icons and requirements for certification mechanisms'.

In contrast, the Commission does not need to consult the EDPS before adopting a delegated act pursuant to the GDPR. Indeed, Article 42(4) EUDPR exempts the Commission from its obligation to consult the EDPS under Article 42(1)[33] where it is required, pursuant to the GDPR, to consult the EDPB (see also recital 60 EUDPR).

At the end of the consultations with the experts, the College of Commissioners formally adopts the delegated act in accordance with its internal decision-making procedures.[34] The adopted delegated act is then published in the Register of Delegated Acts.

2.2 Scrutiny of delegated acts

As soon as it adopts a delegated act, the Commission must notify it simultaneously to the European Parliament and to the Council (Article 92(4)). This allows the latter institutions to scrutinise the act adopted by the Commission to decide whether they want to express objections. They have three months to do so but may request an extension of additional three months (Article 92(5)). The period for expressing objections starts when all official language versions of the delegated act have been received by the European Parliament and the Council.[35]

In practice, both the European Parliament and the Council enjoy a veto power over delegated acts. In fact, the power to propose objections does not formally entail the possibility of introducing modifications in the delegated act adopted by the Commission,[36] and the Parliament and the Council may only reject the act *in toto*. If one of them does, the act may not enter into force. This threat may 'act as a lever to secure amendment' by the Commission.[37]

2.3 Publication in the Official Journal and entry into force

A delegated act adopted by the European Commission may (and should) be published in the Official Journal of the European Union ('OJ') only after the expiry of the period for objections, unless the European Parliament and the Council have both informed the Commission that they will not object (Article 92(5))—in such case the delegated act may be published in the OJ before the expiry of the above period.[38] After the publication in the OJ, the delegated act enters into force at the date specified in the act itself or, in the absence thereof, on the twentieth day following that of its publication.[39]

The lifecycle of a delegated act under the GDPR is summarised in Figure 92.1.

---

[32] This task was assigned to the EDPB also in response to an express demand of the WP29 during the legislative process. See WP29 2012A, p. 8; WP29 2012B, p. 8. The task is consistent with the role that the WP29 *de facto* had in the context of past procedures for the adoption of delegated acts with an impact on data protection: see e.g. WP29 2015.

[33] Art. 42(1) EUDPR reads: 'The Commission shall … when preparing delegated acts or implementing acts, consult the European Data Protection Supervisor where there is an impact on the protection of individuals' rights and freedoms with regard to the processing of personal data'.

[34] See Craig and de Búrca 2015, p. 34.
[35] See Annex to the Interinstitutional Agreement 2016, point 15.
[36] See Mendes 2016, p. 236; Craig and de Búrca 2015, p. 141.
[37] See Craig and de Búrca 2015, p. 141.
[38] See Annex to the Interinstitutional Agreement 2016, point 24.
[39] See Art. 297(2) TFEU.

Procedural Step	Timeframe	Comments
Drafting of delegated act	The drafting may start at any time as of 24 May 2016 (delegation for an indeterminate period of time).	▫ The initial drafting of a planned delegated act is done by the competent Commission services. These are typically within the jurisdiction of Directorate-General for Justice and Consumers ('DG JUST').
Consultations with experts	Experts should be consulted in a timely manner.	▫ The Commission consults experts designated by each Member State. The experts normally come from the national authorities of the Member States. ▫ The experts are provided with the draft delegated act and any other relevant documentation. The draft is also normally published in the Register of Delegated Acts. ▫ The EDPB must also be consulted and issue an opinion (see Art. 70(1)(q) and (r) GDPR). ▫ The consultations may occur via existing expert groups (e.g., the Commission expert group on the GDPR and LED) or via ad hoc meetings with experts from the Member States. ▫ Experts from the European Parliament and the Council may also attend the meetings with the Member States' experts. ▫ Occasionally, the preparation of the delegated act may include consultations with other stakeholders (including a public consultation). ▫ The draft is normally refined in light of experts' observations.
Adoption and notification to the European Parliament and the Council	Adoption: after the consultations (delegation for an indeterminate period of time). Notification: as soon as the delegated act is adopted (except in the periods from 22 December to 6 January and from 15 July to 20 August).	▫ The delegated act is formally adopted by the College of Commissioners. ▫ After its adoption, the act must be simultaneously notified to the European Parliament and the Council. ▫ The adopted delegated act is published in the Register of Delegated Acts.
Scrutiny by the European Parliament and the Council	Within three (or six) months from the official notification.	▫ The European Parliament and the Council may express objections to the delegated act adopted by the Commission (i.e., each of them have a veto power). If they do, the act may not enter into force. ▫ The period of three months for expressing objections starts when all official language versions of the delegated act have been received by the European Parliament and the Council. ▫ Before the expiry of the scrutiny period, the European Parliament and the Council may decide to inform the Commission that they will not object. ▫ The standard three-month scrutiny period may be extended by three months at the initiative of the European Parliament or of the Council.

Figure 92.1 Lifecycle of a delegated act under the GDPR

Procedural Step	Timeframe	Comments
Publication in the OJ	After the expiry of the period for objection (or earlier if the European Parliament and the Council have both informed the Commission that they will not object).	☐ If it has successfully passed the scrutiny of the European Parliament and the Council, the delegated act is published in the Official Journal of the European Union.
Entry into force	After the publication in the OJ.	☐ The date of entry into force is normally specified in the delegated act itself.

Figure 92.1 Continued

3. The Commission's use of its power to adopt delegated acts under the GDPR

As discussed above, the European Commission should make a careful use of the empowerments for delegated acts under the GDPR. This was recognised by the Commission itself, which stated that it 'will only make use of these empowerments when there is a clearly demonstrated added-value and based on feedback from stakeholders' consultation'.[40] In particular, the Commission stated that it 'will look into the issue of certification based on a study contracted with external experts and input and advice on this issue from the multi-stakeholder group on the Regulation established at the end of 2017'.[41] In light of this, the Commission should assess the need to make use of its power to adopt delegated acts in the course of 2018–2019.[42] At the time of writing, the Commission had not yet exercised its delegated powers under the GDPR.

Select Bibliography

EU legislation

GDPR Proposal: Proposal for a Regulation of the European Parliament and of the Council on the protection of individuals with regard to the processing of personal data and on the free movement of such data (General Data Protection Regulation), COM(2012) 11 final, 25 January 2012.
Interinstitutional Agreement 2016: Interinstitutional Agreement between the European Parliament, the Council of the European Union and the European Commission of 13 April 2016 on Better Law-Making, OJ 2016 L 123/1.

Academic writings

Best 2016: Best, *Understanding EU Decision-Making* (Springer 2016).
Bradley 2016: Bradley, 'Delegation of Powers in the European Union: Political Problems, Legal Solutions?', in Bergström and Ritleng (eds.), *Rulemaking by the European Commission: The New System for Delegation of Powers* (OUP 2016), 55.

---

[40] EC Communication 2018, p. 14.
[41] Ibid. The study referred to by the Commission is a study on certification mechanisms led by the Tilburg Institute for Law, Technology, and Society ('TILT'), see TILT study. The multi-stakeholder group mentioned by the Commission is the GDPR expert group. The expert group discussed the TILT study in a meeting of 20 March 2018. See GDPR Expert Group 2018.
[42] EC Communication 2018, p. 17.

Brandsma and Blom-Hansen, *Controlling the EU Executive? The Politics of Delegation in the European Union* (OUP 2017).

Chamon 2014: Chamon, 'How the Concept of Essential Elements of a Legislative Act Continues to Elude the Court: Parliament v. Council', 50(3) *Common Market Law Review 'CMLRev.'* (2014), 849.

Chamon 2015: Chamon, 'The Dividing Line between Delegated and Implementing Acts, Part Two: The Court of Justice Settles the Issue in Commission v. Parliament and Council (Visa Reciprocity)', 52(6) *CMLRev.* (2015), 1617.

Craig and de Búrca 2015: Craig and de Búrca, *EU Law: Text, Cases, and Materials* (6th ed., OUP 2015).

Mendes 2016: Mendes, 'The Making of Delegated and Implementing Acts: Legitimacy beyond Institutional Balance', in Bergström and Ritleng (eds.), *Rulemaking by the European Commission: The New System for Delegation of Powers* (OUP 2016), 233.

Ritleng 2016: Ritleng, 'The Reserved Domain of the Legislature: The Notion of "Essential Elements of an Area"', in Bergström and Ritleng (eds.), *Rulemaking by the European Commission: The New System for Delegation of Powers* (OUP 2016), 136.

Van der Mei 2016: Van der Mei, 'Delegation of Rulemaking Powers to the European Commission Post-Lisbon', 12(3) *European Constitutional Law Review* (2016), 538.

Papers of data protection authorities

EDPS 2012: European Data Protection Supervisor, 'Opinion of the European Data Protection Supervisor on the Data Protection Reform Package' (7 March 2012).

WP29 2012A: Article 29 Working Party, 'Opinion 01/2012 on the Data Protection Reform Proposals' (WP 191, 23 March 2012).

WP29 2012B: Article 29 Working Party, 'Opinion 08/2012 Providing Further Input on the Data Protection Reform Discussions' (WP 199, 5 October 2012).

WP29 2015: Article 29 Working Party, 'Letter to DG FISMA on Possible Delegated Acts for the Implementation of EU Legislation on Both Markets in Financial Instruments (MIFID II) and on Market Abuse Regulation (MAR)' (7 July 2015).

Reports and recommendations

Council Questionnaire 2012: Replies to questionnaire on delegated/implementing acts, 14609/1/12 REV 1, 11 October 2012.

Council Report 2012: Data protection package—Report on progress achieved under the Cyprus Presidency, 16525/12, 26 November 2012.

EC Communication 2009: Communication from the Commission to the European Parliament and the Council, 'Implementation of Article 290 of the Treaty on the Functioning of the European Union', COM(2009) 673 final, 9 December 2009.

EC Communication 2018: Communication from the Commission to the European Parliament and the Council, 'Stronger Protection, New Opportunities—Commission Guidance on the Direct Application of the General Data Protection Regulation as of 25 May 2018', COM(2018) 43 final, 24 January 2018.

EC Guidelines 2011: European Commission, 'Implementation of the Treaty of Lisbon Delegated Acts—Guidelines for the Services of the Commission' (24 June 2011).

EP GDPR Draft Report: Draft Report on the proposal for a regulation of the European Parliament and of the Council on the protection of individual with regard to the processing of personal data and on the free movement of such data (General Data Protection Regulation), 2012/0011(COD), 16 January 2013.

EP Position GDPR: Position of the European Parliament adopted at first reading on 12 March 2014 with a view to the adoption of Regulation (EU) No. …/2014 of the European Parliament and of the Council on the protection of individuals with regard to the processing of personal data and on the free movement of such data (General Data Protection Regulation), P7_TC1-COD(2012)0011, 12 March 2014.

Others

EC Website Register: European Commission, 'Register of Commission Expert Groups', available at http://ec.europa.eu/transparency/regexpert/index.cfm?do=groupDetail.groupDetail&groupID=3461.
EU Website Register: European Union, 'Interinstitutional Register of Delegated Acts', available at https://webgate.ec.europa.eu/regdel/#/home.
GDPR Expert Group 2018: Multistakeholder expert group to support the application of Regulation (EU) 2016/679 (E03537), 'Minutes of the 2nd Meeting of the Multistakeholder Expert Group to Support the Application of the Regulation (EU) 2016/679' (20 March 2018), available at http://ec.europa.eu/transparency/regexpert/index.cfm?do=groupDetail.groupMeetingDoc&docid=17326.
TILT Study: Tilburg Institute for Law, Technology, and Society, 'Research Projects Tilburg Institute for Law, Technology, and Society (TILT)', available at https://www.tilburguniversity.edu/research/institutes-and-research-groups/tilt/research/current-major-research-projects/.

Article 93. Committee procedure

LUCA TOSONI

1. The Commission shall be assisted by a committee. That committee shall be a committee within the meaning of Regulation (EU) No. 182/2011.
2. Where reference is made to this paragraph, Article 5 of Regulation (EU) No. 182/2011 shall apply.
3. Where reference is made to this paragraph, Article 8 of Regulation (EU) No. 182/2011, in conjunction with Article 5 thereof, shall apply.

Relevant Recitals

(167) In order to ensure uniform conditions for the implementation of this Regulation, implementing powers should be conferred on the Commission when provided for by this Regulation. Those powers should be exercised in accordance with Regulation (EU) No. 182/2011. In that context, the Commission should consider specific measures for micro, small and medium-sized enterprises.

(168) The examination procedure should be used for the adoption of implementing acts on standard contractual clauses between controllers and processors and between processors; codes of conduct; technical standards and mechanisms for certification; the adequate level of protection afforded by a third country, a territory or a specified sector within that third country, or an international organisation; standard protection clauses; formats and procedures for the exchange of information by electronic means between controllers, processors and supervisory authorities for binding corporate rules; mutual assistance; and arrangements for the exchange of information by electronic means between supervisory authorities, and between supervisory authorities and the Board.

(169) The Commission should adopt immediately applicable implementing acts where available evidence reveals that a third country, a territory or a specified sector within that third country, or an international organisation does not ensure an adequate level of protection, and imperative grounds of urgency so require.

Closely Related Provisions

Article 28(7) (Standard contractual clauses); Article 40(9) (Codes of conduct); Article 43(9) (Certification mechanisms); Article 45(3) and (5) (Adequacy decisions); Article 46(2)(c)–(d) (Standard data protection clauses); Article 47(3) (Binding corporate rules); Article 61(9) (Format and procedures for mutual assistance); Article 67 (Exchange of information); Article 70(1) and (3) (Tasks of the Board); and Article 92 (Exercise of the delegation)

Related Provisions in LED [Directive (EU) 2016/680]

Article 36(3)–(5) (Adequacy decisions); Article 50(8) (Format and procedures for mutual assistance); Article 51(1) and (3) (Tasks of the Board); Article 58 (Committee procedure) (see too recitals 90–92)

Related Provisions in EPD [Directive 2002/58/EC]

Article 14a (Committee procedure)

Related Provisions in EUDPR [Regulation (EU) 2018/1725]

Article 29(7) (Standard contractual clauses between controllers and processors and between processors); Article 40(4) (Processing operations requiring prior consultation of the EDPS); Article 42 (Legislative consultation) (see too recital 60); Article 48(2)(b)–(c) (Transfers subject to appropriate safeguards); Article 96 (Committee procedure) (see too recital 84)

Relevant Case Law

CJEU

Case C-427/12, *European Commission v European Parliament and Council of the European Union*, judgment of 18 March 2014 (Grand Chamber) (ECLI:EU:C:2014:170).

Case C-65/13, *European Parliament v European Commission*, judgment of 15 October 2014 (ECLI:EU:C:2014:2289).

Case C-88/14, *European Commission v European Parliament and Council of the European Union*, judgment of 16 July 2015 (Grand Chamber) (ECLI:EU:C:2015:499).

Case C-362/14, *Maximillian Schrems v Data Protection Commissioner*, judgment of 6 October 2015 (Grand Chamber) (ECLI:EU:C:2015:650).

Case C-183/16 P, *Tilly-Sabco SAS v European Commission*, judgment of 20 September 2017 (ECLI:EU:C:2017:704).

Case T-738/16, *La Quadrature du Net and Others v Commission* (pending).

Case C-311/18, *Data Protection Commissioner v Facebook Ireland Limited, Maximillian Schrems* (pending).

A. Rationale and Policy Underpinnings

Under European Union law, the power to adopt the measures necessary to implement EU legislation normally lies with the Member States.[1] However, where uniform conditions for the implementation of legally binding EU acts (e.g. a Directive or a Regulation) are needed, those acts are to confer implementing powers on the European Commission in accordance with Article 291 of the Treaty on the Functioning of the European Union ('TFEU'). This is what the GDPR does, as several of its provisions grant the Commission the power to adopt 'implementing acts'. These are acts that the Commission may adopt to give effect to rules that are already laid down in the GDPR while ensuring uniform conditions of application across the EU.[2] Nonetheless, the Commission's exercise of its implementing powers must be subject to control mechanisms.[3] The aim of Article 93 GDPR is to specify which control mechanisms apply by referring to the procedural requirements of the Comitology Regulation.[4]

---

[1] See Art. 291(1) TFEU.
[2] Implementing acts should be distinguished from delegated acts, which are dealt with in the commentary on Art. 92 in this volume. On the distinction between implementing acts and delegated acts, see EC Guidelines 2011, points 14–44; Craig and de Búrca 2015, pp. 114–20 and pp. 137–145.
[3] These control mechanisms have been established in accordance with Art. 291(3) TFEU.
[4] See Comitology Regulation.

B. Legal Background

1. EU legislation

The legal antecedent of Article 93 GDPR is Article 31 DPD. Article 31 established the control mechanisms that applied to the Commission's use of its implementing powers under the DPD in relation to the international transfer of personal data (see Articles 25(4)–(6) and 26(3)–(4) DPD). These powers largely coincided with those that are now conferred on the Commission by Articles 45(3)–(5) and 46(2) GDPR and were subject to control mechanisms analogous to those established by Article 93 GDPR. Provisions similar to Article 93 GDPR may also be found in other EU legal acts, including data protection instruments such as the EPD (see Article 14a), the LED (see Article 58) and the EUDPR (see Article 96).

2. Case law

The Commission's use of its implementing powers under EU law has been scrutinised by the CJEU on various occasions,[5] including in the data protection context. In particular, the Court has reviewed or currently is in the process of reviewing in several cases two Commission Decisions on the adequacy of the protection provided by specific arrangements for the transfer of personal data to the United States (commonly known as 'Safe Harbour' and 'Privacy Shield'), as well as Commission Decisions on standard contractual clauses for the transfer of personal data to third countries.[6] None of these cases directly concern the procedural requirements that the Commission had to comply with when adopting the challenged Decisions. Thus, their relevance for interpreting Article 31 DPD and Article 93 GDPR is limited. However, for the purposes of the present commentary, it is worth noting that, in the *Schrems* case, the CJEU invalidated Commission Decision 2000/520 (i.e. the Safe Harbour Decision) also because, according to the Court, when the Commission adopted the Decision it exceeded its implementing powers under the DPD.[7]

It should also be noted that the CJEU found that some of the procedural requirements laid down in the Comitology Regulation are 'essential procedural requirements' (e.g. the time limits for submitting a draft implementing act to the competent Comitology Committee—specified further below),[8] and held that an act adopted in violation of an 'essential procedural requirement' must be annulled by the EU judicature, if necessary, of its own motion.[9] Therefore, if an implementing act adopted pursuant to the GDPR is challenged before the CJEU, the Court may spontaneously decide to examine whether the act was adopted in violation of an 'essential procedural requirement' of the Comitology Regulation and, if so, invalidate the act.

---

[5] See, inter alia, Case C-427/12, *Commission v Parliament and Council*; Case C-65/13, *Parliament v Commission*; Case C-88/14, *Commission v Parliament and Council*; Case C-183/16 P, *Tilly-Sabco*.

[6] See Case C-362/14, *Schrems*; Case T-738/16, *La Quadrature du Net*; Case C-311/18, *Facebook Ireland and Schrems*. The Decisions scrutinised by the CJEU are Safe Harbour Decision 2000; Commission Decision Privacy Shield 2016; and Commission Decision Standard Contractual Clauses 2010, as amended by Commission Decision Standard Contractual Clauses 2016.

[7] See Case C-362/14, *Schrems*, paras. 67–106.

[8] See Case C-183/16 P, *Tilly-Sabco*, para. 114 and case law cited.

[9] Ibid., para. 115–116 and case law cited.

C. Analysis

1. Implementing powers under the GDPR

As discussed above, the GDPR contains a number of provisions which confer on the Commission implementing powers in accordance with Article 291 TFEU. In particular, the GDPR allows the Commission to adopt implementing acts to:

1. lay down standard contractual clauses to be included in the data processing contracts between controllers and processors and between processors and sub-processors (Article 28(7));
2. decide that a code of conduct has general validity within the EU (Article 40(9));
3. lay down technical standards for certification mechanisms and data protection seals and marks, and mechanisms to promote and recognise those certification mechanisms, seals and marks (Article 43(9));
4. determine whether a third country, a territory or one or more specified sectors within a third country, or an international organisation ensures (or no longer ensures) an adequate level of data protection (Article 45(3) and (5));
5. adopt or approve standard data protection clauses for the international transfer of data (Article 46(2)(c)–(d));
6. specify the format and procedures for the exchange of information between controllers, processors and supervisory authorities for binding corporate rules (Article 47(3));
7. specify the format and procedures for mutual assistance between supervisory authorities and the arrangements for the exchange of information by electronic means between supervisory authorities, and between supervisory authorities and the EDPB (Articles 61(9) and 67).[10]

The above provisions essentially call on the Commission to execute certain provisions of the GDPR or provide further technical detail in relation to the content of the provisions, to ensure that they are implemented under uniform conditions in all Member States.

The original GDPR proposal contained a much larger number of instances in which the Commission was empowered to adopt implementing acts compared to the text of the Regulation that was finally adopted in 2016.[11] Nonetheless, most of these proposed empowerments met with strong opposition during the legislative process, as it was felt that, in most cases, there was no need to adopt implementing acts to ensure further harmonisation, and that it would be sufficient to have guidance by the

---

[10] Similarly, the LED provides for the adoption of implementing acts on the adequate level of protection afforded by a third country, a territory or a specified sector within a third country, or an international organisation and on the format and procedures for mutual assistance and the arrangements for the exchange of information by electronic means between supervisory authorities, and between supervisory authorities and the Board (see Arts. 36(3)–(5) and 50(8) LED). Instead, the EUDPR provides that the Commission should follow the examination procedure for the adoption of standard contractual clauses between controllers and processors and between processors, for the adoption of a list of processing operations requiring prior consultation of the EDPS by controllers processing personal data for the performance of a task carried out in the public interest, and for the adoption of standard contractual clauses providing appropriate safeguards for international transfers (see Arts. 29(7), 40(4) and 48(2)(b)–(c) EUDPR).

[11] See in particular Arts. 87(4), 12(6), 14(8), 15(4), 18(3), 23(4), 28(6), 30(4), 31(6), 32(6), 33(7), 34(9), 38(4), 39(3), 41(3)–(5), 42(2)(b), 43(4), 55(10), 62(1)–(2) and 87 GDPR Proposal.

national supervisory authorities and the Board.[12] As a result, the EU legislator decided to grant more limited implementing powers to the Commission in the final text of the GDPR. It should be noted, however, that granting the Commission the power to adopt implementing acts does not necessarily mean that it is obliged to adopt them; in general, these acts should be adopted only when there is a need to do so.[13] In principle, the implementing acts to be adopted by the Commission are all legally binding and should take the form of Commission regulations, directives or decisions, in conformity with Article 288 TFEU.[14]

2. The procedure for adopting implementing acts

Should the Commission decide to use its implementing powers under the GDPR, it must follow the 'examination procedure' referred to in Article 5 of the Comitology Regulation (Article 93(2) GDPR). This procedure is primarily intended to allow the Member States to review draft implementing acts before they are adopted by the Commission.

Under the examination procedure, a committee composed of representatives of all the Member States and chaired by a representative of the Commission (often referred to as a 'Comitology Committee') must assist the Commission in the exercise of its implementing powers by giving opinions on the draft implementing acts prepared by the Commission.[15] To this end, Article 93(1) GDPR provides for the establishment of a specific Comitology Committee that must assist the Commission in the exercise of its implementing powers under the GDPR. The Committee in question (commonly called the 'Article 93 Committee') was set up in 2018 and held its first meeting on 21 September 2018.[16] This Committee has also been given the task of assisting the Commission in the exercise of its implementing powers under the LED[17] and the EUDPR.[18] Its workings are regulated by specific internal rules of procedure.[19]

The examination procedure envisages two stages. The first stage is mandatory and is intended to allow the competent Comitology Committee to deliver an opinion on a draft implementing act. The second stage is optional and is meant to allow the Commission to try to bypass a negative opinion of the competent Comitology Committee by submitting the same draft implementing act to the scrutiny of another Comitology Committee, known as the Appeal Committee.

---

[12] See, inter alia, EP GDPR Draft Report, p. 214; Council Questionnaire 2012; EDPS 2012, pp. 12–13 and pp. 40–42; WP29 2012A, p. 7; WP29 2012B, pp. 8–9; and WP29 2013.

[13] WP29 2012B, p. 9.

[14] EC Guidelines 2012, p. 3 (noting that '[o]nly legally binding acts may be adopted by means of implementing acts. These acts take the form of regulations, directives or decisions, in conformity with Art. 288 TFEU. By contrast, acts that are not legally binding but only offer guidance are adopted by the Commission under its own autonomous right under the TFEU').

[15] See Art. 3(2) Comitology Regulation. See further EC Guidelines 2012, p. 9. The representatives of Iceland, Lichtenstein and Norway are normally invited to attend the meetings of the Committee, but do not participate in the voting.

[16] See GDPR Committee 2018. This Committee should be distinguished from the Commission expert group on the GDPR and the LED (E03461), and from the Multistakeholder expert group to support the application of the GDPR (E03537).

[17] See Art. 58(1) LED.   [18] See Art. 96(1) EUDPR.

[19] See GDPR Committee Rules of Procedure.

2.1 Preparation of a draft implementing act and review by the Article 93 Committee

The first stage begins with the preparation of a draft implementing act by the competent Commission services. With regard to implementing acts to be adopted pursuant to the GDPR, the competent services are typically within the Commission's Directorate-General for Justice and Consumers ('DG JUST').

Subsequently, the Commission must submit the draft implementing act to the Article 93 Committee together with the draft agenda of the meeting in which the draft implementing act will be discussed.[20] The Commission must submit the draft implementing act to the Committee no less than 14 calendar days before the meeting.[21] However, the time limit for submission may be shortened in exceptional cases.[22]

At the same time as the draft implementing act is sent to the Article 93 Committee members, the Commission must make it available to the European Parliament and the Council.[23] To this end, the draft implementing act is published in the Comitology Register.[24] The Parliament and the Council are normally not involved in the preparation of implementing acts and do not participate in the meetings of the Article 93 Committee.[25] They can neither block the adoption of a draft implementing act nor 'call back' the implementing powers.[26] However, at any stage of the procedure, the Parliament or the Council may indicate to the Commission that, in its view, a draft implementing act exceeds the implementing powers provided for in the GDPR.[27] In such case, the Commission must review the draft and inform the other institutions whether it intends to maintain, amend or withdraw it.[28]

The Commission should normally send the draft implementing act also to the EDPS and/or to the EDPB. Indeed, as a rule, when preparing implementing acts with an impact on data protection, the Commission must consult the EDPS (see Article 42(1) EUDPR). The Commission is, however, exempted from this obligation where it is required, pursuant to GDPR, to consult the Board (see Article 42(4) GDPR). For example, the GDPR provides for mandatory consultation of the Board on adequacy decisions (see Article 70(1)(s) GDPR and recital 60 EUDPR).[29] Where the consultation of the Board is not mandatory but the implementing act to be adopted is of particular importance for the protection of rights and freedoms of natural persons with regard to the processing of

---

[20] The basic rule is to have a meeting. However, in duly justified cases, the Commission may request the Committee's opinion by means of a written procedure. See Art. 3(5) Comitology Regulation.

[21] See Art. 3(3) Comitology Regulation.

[22] Except in cases of extreme urgency for the protection of individuals with respect to the processing of personal data, the time limit must not be shorter than five calendar days. See Art. 3(2) GDPR Committee Rules of Procedure.

[23] See Art. 10(5) Comitology Regulation.

[24] See EC Guidelines 2012, p. 11. The Comitology Register is online, see EC Website Comitology Register.

[25] See EC Guidelines 2012, p. 22.   [26] Ibid.   [27] See Art. 11 Comitology Regulation.

[28] Ibid.

[29] For further details on the role of the EDPB within the process for adequacy findings under the GDPR, see WP29 2018, pp. 4–5. In principle, the Board must be consulted also on: (i) the format and procedures for the exchange of information between controllers, processors and supervisory authorities for binding corporate rules (Art. 70(1)(c) GDPR); and (ii) codes of conduct with a general validity within the EU (Art. 70(1)(x) GDPR).

personal data, the Commission may, in addition to consulting the EDPS, seek advice from the Board (see Article 42(2) and recital 60 EUDPR). Indeed, the GDPR assigns to the EDPB the task of advising the Commission on any issue related to the protection of personal data (see Article 70(1)(b) GDPR). If the Commission consults both the EDPS and the Board, these should coordinate their work with a view to issuing a joint opinion (see Article 42(2) EUDPR). The EDPS, and where applicable, the Board should provide their written advice within eight weeks, or the different deadline set by the Commission (see Article 70(2) GDPR and Article 42(3) and recital 60 EUDPR). The EDPB must forward all of its opinions on draft implementing acts to the Article 93 Committee (see Article 70(3) GDPR and Article 51(3) LED).[30]

Once the Article 93 Committee has received the draft implementing act, it examines the draft act in view of expressing an opinion. Until the Committee delivers an opinion, any Committee member may suggest amendments and the Commission may present amended versions of the draft implementing act.[31] It is in this context that the draft act is normally refined in light of the EDPB's and/or the EDPS's opinion.

The Article 93 Committee must deliver its opinion within the time limit laid down by its chair (i.e. the Commission representative who chairs the Committee).[32] As a rule, the opinion must be adopted by qualified majority.[33] The latter is reached where, within the Committee, 55 per cent of the Member States representing 65 per cent of the EU population vote in the same way (in favour or against the draft act).[34] However, the adoption of an opinion supported by a qualified majority of the Committee members may be halted by a blocking minority of at least four members representing more than 35 per cent of the EU population.[35] The Committee may also adopt an opinion in favour of the draft delegated act ('positive opinion') by consensus, without proceeding to a formal vote, unless one of the members of the Committee objects.[36] The voting results are normally published in the Comitology Register.

Where there is a qualified majority in favour of the draft implementing act ('positive opinion'), the Commission must adopt the act.[37] In contrast, where there is a qualified majority against the draft implementing act ('negative opinion'), the Commission

---

[30] In the preparation of an implementing act, the Commission may also decide to seek advice from experts from civil society, industry and academia, such as the experts who sit in the Commission Multistakeholder expert group to support the application of the GDPR.

[31] See Art. 3(4) Comitology Regulation.

[32] See ibid., Art. 3(3). See also Art. 4(1) GDPR Committee Rules of Procedure.

[33] See Art. 5(1) Comitology Regulation. See also Art. 4(2) GDPR Committee Rules of Procedure.

[34] See Art. 16 Treaty on European Union ('TEU') and Art. 238 TFEU. In cases where not all the Member States participate in the vote, Art. 238(3)(a) TFEU defines a qualified majority as at least 55% of the participating Member States, comprising at least 65% of the population of these States.

[35] In cases where not all the Member States participate in the vote, a blocking minority must include at least a minimum number of Member States representing more than 35% of the population of the participating Member States, plus one Member State.

[36] See Art. 4(3) GDPR Committee Rules of Procedure.

[37] See Art. 5(2) Comitology Regulation. In very exceptional cases, the Commission may take into consideration new circumstances that have arisen after the vote and decide not to adopt the draft implementing act, after having duly informed the Committee and the legislator. See EC Guidelines 2012, pp. 14–15.

cannot adopt the act.[38] In such case, the Commission has three options: (i) drop the draft implementing act altogether; (ii) submit an amended version of the draft implementing act to the Article 93 Committee within two months of the delivery of the 'negative opinion'; or (iii) refer the same draft to the Appeal Committee within one month of the delivery of the 'negative opinion'.[39]

If there is no qualified majority for or against the draft implementing act ('no opinion'), in principle, the Commission may decide to: (i) adopt the draft implementing act; (ii) drop the draft implementing act; or (iii) submit an amended version of the draft implementing act to the Article 93 Committee.[40] However, if a simple majority of the Committee members oppose the draft implementing act, a 'no opinion' is considered equivalent to a 'negative opinion' and the Commission cannot adopt the act, but has the same alternative options as for a 'negative opinion'.[41] The decision of the Commission in case of 'no opinion' will normally depend on the political sensitivity of the matter.

2.2 The Appeal Committee

As discussed above, if the Article 93 Committee delivers a 'negative opinion' on a draft implementing act, the Commission may try to overcome the effects of such an opinion by submitting the same draft to the Appeal Committee.

The Appeal Committee is made up of Member State representatives, is chaired by the Commission, and follows the same voting rules as the Article 93 Committee.[42] However, contrary to the Article 93 Committee, the Appeal Committee is not a permanent body and its members should normally have a higher professional rank (e.g. Ministers) than those who sit in the Article 93 Committee.[43] Its workings are governed by specific internal rules of procedure.[44]

There is no obligation to refer a draft implementing act to the Appeal Committee. Hence, the Commission will normally try to settle the matter within the Article 93 Committee and go before the Appeal Committee only where 'all possibilities of discussion within the [Article 93 Committee] have been exhausted and no amended draft can be envisaged'.[45] Indeed, the Appeal Committee merely works as 'a procedural tool, giving Member States the opportunity to have a second discussion at a higher level of representation'.[46]

The referral to the Appeal Committee initiates a new stage of the examination procedure, which is subject to specific time limits: the Appeal Committee must meet no sooner than 14 days, except in duly justified cases, no later than six weeks after the date of the referral,[47] and must deliver its opinion within two months of the date of the referral.[48] If the Appeal Committee delivers a 'positive opinion' or fails

---

[38] See Art. 5(3) Comitology Regulation.
[39] Ibid.   [40] See ibid., Art. 5(4).   [41] Ibid.
[42] See ibid., Arts. 3(7) and 6. It should be noted that the Appeal Committee stage of the examination procedure is currently under review, including the voting rules of the Appeal Committee. See Comitology Regulation Proposal.
[43] EC Guidelines 2012, p. 9.   [44] See Rules of Procedure for the Appeal Committee.
[45] EC Guidelines 2012, p. 17.
[46] Ibid., p. 9.   [47] See Comitology Regulation Art. 3(7).   [48] Ibid.

to adopt an opinion, the act must and may be adopted, respectively.[49] In contrast, if the Appeal Committee delivers a 'negative opinion', the Commission cannot adopt the act.[50]

Once the draft has successfully passed the scrutiny of Member States, either within the Article 93 Committee or the Appeal Committee, the College of Commissioners (i.e. the political body comprising the European Commissioners) formally adopts the implementing act in accordance with its internal decision-making procedures.[51] The act is then published in the Official Journal of the European Union ('OJ') and enters into force on the date specified in it or, in the absence thereof, on the twentieth day following that of its publication.[52]

2.3 Urgency procedure

If a third country, a territory or a specified sector within that third country, or an international organisation no longer ensures an adequate level of protection, the Commission should repeal, amend or suspend the relevant adequacy decision (see recital 169 and Article 45(5) GDPR). Where imperative grounds of urgency so require, this should be done by adopting an implementing act without its prior submission to the Article 93 Committee. In such case, the Commission must follow the urgency procedure set out in Article 8 of the Comitology Regulation.[53]

Implementing acts adopted through the urgency procedure are immediately applicable. However, their applicability is only provisional, as they can remain in force for no longer than six months.[54]

The urgency procedure is not a separate procedure but rather a 'variant' of the examination procedure.[55] Indeed, the consultation of the Article 93 Committee is not eliminated, but it is simply held after the adoption of the implementing act: no later than 14 days after adoption, the Commission must submit the act to the Article 93 Committee to obtain its opinion in accordance with the procedure described above.[56] If at the end of this process the Committee delivers a 'negative opinion', the Commission must immediately repeal the implementing act adopted in accordance with the urgency procedure.[57] In contrast, if the Committee delivers a 'positive opinion' or fails to deliver an opinion, the act remains in force for a maximum of six months.[58] Of course, the Commission may decide to launch another examination procedure to adopt a definitive act that should replace the provisional act.

---

[49] Ibid., Art. 6(3).   [50] Ibid.
[51] See Craig and de Búrca 2015, p. 34.   [52] See Art. 297(2) TFEU.
[53] See rec. 169 and Arts. 45(5) and 93(3) GDPR.   [54] See Art. 8(2) Comitology Regulation.
[55] See EC Guidelines 2012, p. 8.   [56] See Art. 8(3) Comitology Regulation.
[57] See ibid., Art. 8(4).   [58] See EC Guidelines 2012, pp. 21–22.

2.4 Normal life cycle of implementing acts

The normal life cycle of an implementing act under the GDPR is summarised in Figure 93.1.

Procedural Step	Timeframe	Comments
Article 93 Committee Stage		
Drafting of the implementing act (e.g., adequacy decision; standard contractual clauses; etc.)	The drafting may start at any time.	□ The competent Commission services will typically be located within the Directorate-General for Justice and Consumers ('DG JUST').
Submission to the Article 93 Committee and publication of the draft implementing act	Submission: normally no less than 14 calendar days before the meeting of the Article 93 Committee in which the draft will be discussed. Publication in the Comitology Register: normally, at the same time as the submission to the Committee members.	□ The chair of the Article 93 Committee sends the invitation, the draft agenda, and the draft implementing act to the Committee members. □ The representatives of Iceland, Lichtenstein, and Norway are also invited to attend the meeting, but do not participate in the voting. □ The chair may decide to invite other experts to the meeting, unless a simple majority of the members oppose their participation in the meeting. □ Draft implementing acts are also sent to the European Parliament and the Council and are normally published in the Comitology Register. □ If there are urgent needs to repeal, amend or suspend an adequacy decision, the Commission may adopt the necessary act without its prior submission to the Article 93 Committee. In such case, the consultation of the Committee is postponed until no later than 14 days after the adoption.
Delivery of an opinion by the EDPB and/or EDPS	Within eight weeks or the different deadline set by the Commission.	□ The opinion of the EDPB and/or EDPS is not legally binding.
Delivery of an opinion by the Article 93 Committee (Committee Code: C49000)	Within the deadline set by the chair of the Article 93 Committee for the adoption of the Committee's opinion.	□ The Article 93 Committee must adopt its opinion by qualified majority or consensus.
Adoption of the act by the College of Commissioners	After the Article 93 Committee's positive opinion or no opinion.	□ If there is a qualified majority in favour of the draft implementing act ('positive opinion'), the Commission must adopt it. □ If there is a qualified majority against the draft implementing act ('negative opinion'), the Commission cannot adopt it but may refer the same draft to the Appeal Committee. □ If there is no qualified majority for or against the draft implementing act ('no opinion'), in principle, the Commission may adopt the act.

Figure 93.1 Life cycle of an implementing act under the GDPR

Procedural Step	Timeframe	Comments
Appeal Committee Stage		
Referral to the Appeal Committee	Within one month of the delivery of a negative opinion by the Article 93 Committee.	▫ The Commission is not obliged to refer a draft implementing act to the Appeal Committee.
Delivery of an opinion by the Appeal Committee	Within two months of the date of the referral.	▫ The Appeal Committee must adopt its opinion by qualified majority or consensus.
Adoption of the act by the College of Commissioners	After the Appeal Committee's positive opinion or no opinion.	▫ If the Appeal Committee delivers a positive opinion, the Commission must adopt the act. ▫ If the Appeal Committee delivers a negative opinion, the Commission cannot adopt the act. ▫ If the Appeal Committee delivers no opinion, in principle, the Commission may adopt the act.
Publication in the OJ	After the adoption of the act by the College of Commissioners.	▫ Implementing acts are published in the non-legislative acts section of the OJ.
Entry into force	After the publication in the OJ.	▫ The adopted act enters into force on the date specified in it or, in the absence thereof, on the twentieth day following that of its publication in the OJ.

Figure 93.1 Continued

3. The Commission's use of its implementing powers under the GDPR

The Commission should make careful use of the empowerments for implementing acts under the GDPR. This was recognised by the Commission itself, which stated that, in principle, it 'will only make use of these empowerments when there is a clearly demonstrated added-value and based on feedback from stakeholders' consultation'.[59]

The Commission's assessment on whether to adopt an implementing act should be particularly careful in the field of certification. This is because the GDPR empowers the Commission both to: (i) adopt delegated acts to specify the requirements to be considered for data protection certification mechanisms (Article 43(8));[60] and (ii) adopt implementing acts laying down technical standards for certification mechanisms and mechanisms to promote and recognise those certification mechanisms (Article 43(9)). Making a clear distinction between these two tasks is not self-evident. However, given that the GDPR requires the adoption of two different legal instruments (i.e. delegated act vs. implementing act), the Commission must carefully consider whether an act on certification that it intends to adopt falls under Article 43(8) or (9). Indeed, failing to adopt the appropriate act (or adopting an act that covers more than it is supposed to under the chosen legal basis) may result in the act being annulled by the CJEU.

---

[59] EC Communication 2018, p. 14.

[60] For further details on the adoption of delegated acts under the GDPR, see the commentary on Art. 92 in this volume.

The Commission is expected to assess the need to make use of its power to adopt implementing acts.[61] An example of an implementing act adopted by the Commission pursuant to the GDPR is the adequacy decision on Japan.[62]

Select Bibliography

EU legislation

Comitology Regulation: Regulation (EU) No. 182/2011 of the European Parliament and of the Council of 16 February 2011 laying down the rules and general principles concerning mechanisms for control by Member States of the Commission's exercise of implementing powers, OJ 2001 L 55/13.

Comitology Regulation Proposal: Proposal for a Regulation of the European Parliament and of the Council amending Regulation (EU) No. 182/2011 laying down the rules and general principles concerning mechanisms for control by Member States of the Commission's exercise of implementing powers, COM(2017) 85 final, 14 February 2017.

Commission Decision Japan 2019: Commission Implementing Decision (EU) 2019/419 of 23 January 2019 pursuant to Regulation (EU) 2016/679 of the European Parliament and of the Council on the adequate protection of personal data by Japan under the Act on the Protection of Personal Information, OJ 2019 L 76/1.

Commission Decision Standard Contractual Clauses 2010: Commission Decision of 5 February 2010 on standard contractual clauses for the transfer of personal data to processors established in third countries under Directive 95/46/EC of the European Parliament and of the Council, OJ 2010 L 39/5.

Commission Decision Standard Contractual Clauses 2016: Commission Implementing Decision (EU) 2016/2297 of 16 December 2016 amending Decisions 2001/497/EC and 2010/87/EU on standard contractual clauses for the transfer of personal data to third countries and to processors established in such countries, under Directive 95/46/EC of the European Parliament and of the Council, OJ 2016 L 344/100.

Commission Decision Privacy Shield 2016: Commission Implementing Decision (EU) 2016/1250 of 12 July 2016 pursuant to Directive 95/46/EC of the European Parliament and of the Council on the adequacy of the protection provided by the EU-U.S. Privacy Shield, OJ 2016 L 207/1.

GDPR Proposal: Proposal for a Regulation of the European Parliament and of the Council on the protection of individuals with regard to the processing of personal data and on the free movement of such data (General Data Protection Regulation), COM(2012) 11 final, 25 January 2012.

Rules of Procedure for the Appeal Committee: Rules of Procedure for the Appeal Committee, OJ 2011 C 183/13.

Safe Harbour Decision 2000: European Commission Decision 2000/520 of 26 July 2000 pursuant to Directive 95/46 of the European Parliament and of the Council on the adequacy of the protection provided by the safe harbor privacy principles and related frequently asked questions issued by the US Department of Commerce, OJ 2000 L 215/7 (annulled).

Academic writings

Bergström and Ritleng, *Rulemaking by the European Commission: The New System for Delegation of Powers* (OUP 2016).

Best, *Understanding EU Decision-Making* (Springer 2016).

Craig and de Búrca 2015: Craig and de Búrca, *EU Law: Text, Cases, and Materials* (6th edn, OUP 2015).

---

[61] EC Communication 2018, p. 17. [62] See Commission Decision Japan 2019.

Papers of data protection authorities

EDPS 2012: European Data Protection Supervisor, 'Opinion of the European Data Protection Supervisor on the Data Protection Reform Package' (7 March 2012).
WP29 2012A: Article 29 Working Party, 'Opinion 01/2012 on the Data Protection Reform Proposals' (WP 191, 23 March 2012).
WP29 2012B: Article 29 Working Party, 'Opinion 08/2012 Providing Further Input on the Data Protection Reform Discussions' (WP 199, 5 October 2012).
WP29 2013: Article 29 Working Party, 'Working Document 01/2013 Input on the Proposed Implementing Acts' (WP 200, 22 January 2013).
WP29 2018: Article 29 Working Party, 'Adequacy Referential' (WP 254 rev.01, as last revised and adopted on 6 February 2018).

Reports and recommendations

Council Questionnaire 2012: Replies to questionnaire on delegated/implementing acts, 14609/1/12 REV 1, 11 October 2012.
EC Communication 2018: Communication from the Commission to the European Parliament and the Council, 'Stronger Protection, New Opportunities—Commission Guidance on the Direct Application of the General Data Protection Regulation as of 25 May 2018', COM(2018) 43 final, 24 January 2018.
EC Guidelines 2011: European Commission, 'Implementation of the Treaty of Lisbon Delegated Acts—Guidelines for the Services of the Commission' (24 June 2011).
EC Guidelines 2012: European Commission, 'Implementation of the Treaty of Lisbon Implementing Acts—Guidelines for the Services of the Commission' (25 October 2012).
EP GDPR Draft Report: Draft Report on the proposal for a regulation of the European Parliament and of the Council on the protection of individual with regard to the processing of personal data and on the free movement of such data (General Data Protection Regulation), 2012/0011(COD), 16 January 2013.
GDPR Committee 2018: Committee on the protection of individuals with regard to the processing of personal data and on the free movement of such data, 'Minutes of the 1st Meeting' (21 September 2018).
GDPR Committee Rules of Procedure: Committee on the protection of individuals with regard to the processing of personal data and on the free movement of such data, 'Rules of Procedure' (21 September 2018).

Others

EC Website Comitology Register: European Commission, 'Comitology Register', available at http://ec.europa.eu/transparency/regcomitology/index.cfm.

Chapter XI Final Provisions (Articles 94–99)

Article 94. Repeal of Directive 95/46/EC

DOMINIQUE MOORE*

1. Directive 95/46/EC is repealed with effect from 25 May 2018.
2. References to the repealed Directive shall be construed as references to this Regulation. References to the Working Party on the Protection of Individuals with regard to the Processing of Personal Data established by Article 29 of Directive 95/46/EC shall be construed as references to the European Data Protection Board established by this Regulation.

Relevant Recital

(171) Directive 95/46/EC should be repealed by this Regulation. Processing already under way on the date of application of this Regulation should be brought into conformity with this Regulation within the period of two years after which this Regulation enters into force. Where processing is based on consent pursuant to Directive 95/46/EC, it is not necessary for the data subject to give his or her consent again if the manner in which the consent has been given is in line with the conditions of this Regulation, so as to allow the controller to continue such processing after the date of application of this Regulation. Commission decisions adopted and authorisations by supervisory authorities based on Directive 95/46/EC remain in force until amended, replaced or repealed.

Closely Related Provisions

Article 68 (European Data protection Board) (see too recital 139): Article 98 (Review of other Union legal acts on data protection) (see too recital 173); Article 99 (Entry into force and application)

Related Provisions in LED [Directive (EU) 2016/680]

Article 59 (Repeal of Framework Decision 2008/977/JHA) (see too recital 98)

Related Provisions in EPD [Directive 2002/58/EC]

Article 15 (Application of certain provisions of Directive 95/46/EC) (see too recitals 10–11)

A. Rationale and Policy Underpinnings

The repeal of the DPD is the logical consequence of the entry into force and application of the GDPR. The date set for the repeal of that Directive coincides with the date set, in

---

* The views expressed are solely those of the author and do not necessarily reflect those of the European Parliament.

Article 99(2), for the application of the GDPR. Thus, the DPD was repealed at the same time that the GDPR became applicable, namely midnight on 25 May 2018.[1] Article 94 and the related recital 171 also clarify a number of important points concerning repeal of the DPD.

B. Analysis

To ensure the proper continuation of other existing EU acts which already refer to the DPD, but which themselves remain applicable despite its repeal on that date, any references to the repealed Directive are to be construed as references to the GDPR, following a standard formula in EU legislation. The replacement of the WP29 by the EDPB in the context of other such EU acts is also a logical consequence of this. The replacement of references to the DPD with the GDPR applies to any type of EU legislation. An example of the relevance of this provision can be found in Article 15 EPD on the 'Application of certain provisions of Directive 95/46/EC' which is to be construed as referring instead to the GDPR. The reference in Article 15(3) EPD to the WP29 will then also refer to the EDPB. However, this should also be considered together with Article 98 GDPR which foresees the review of other Union legal acts on data protection and, in particular, recital 173 which states that the EPD should be reviewed and amended accordingly.[2]

The replacement of references to the DPD in other EU legislation with references to the GDPR may sometimes give rise to problems of interpretation, since there is not necessarily a one-to-one correspondence between provisions of the DPD and those of the GDPR. In such cases, all that can be done is to attempt to identify the provision of the GDPR that most closely corresponds to that of the DPD, though in some cases it may be that no such provision exists (for example, because the relevant provision of the DPD concerns a topic that is not dealt with in the GDPR).

Recital 171 deals with some important issues that go beyond repeal of the DPD. Under that recital, data processing already underway on the GDPR's date of application (i.e. as of 25 May 2018) must be brought into conformity with it. Given the broad definition of data processing under Article 4(2) GDPR, this means that virtually any data processing that began before the date of application and has not completely ceased by that date is subject to the GDPR; for example, data that were stored electronically prior to the date of application and continue to be stored after that date will be subject to it. The recital also makes clear that consent given under the DPD will only remain valid if it 'is in line with the conditions' of the GDPR, meaning in effect that consent would have to be valid under the rules of the GDPR. Commission decisions (such as adequacy decisions) and authorisations by DPAs made under the DPD remain in force unless otherwise amended, repealed or replaced.

---

[1] Note that the entry into force and application of the GDPR are dealt with in Art. 99 GDPR.
[2] The Commission has in fact proposed the revision of the EPD, with all references to the DPD being replaced by references to the GDPR. See EPR Proposal.

Select Bibliography

EU legislation

EPR Proposal: Proposal for a Regulation of the European Parliament and of the Council concerning the respect for private life and the protection of personal data in electronic communications and repealing Directive 2002/58/EC (Regulation on Privacy and Electronic Communications), COM(2017)10 final, 10 January 2017.

Article 95. Relationship with Directive 2002/58/EC

PIEDADE COSTA DE OLIVEIRA[*]

This Regulation shall not impose additional obligations on natural or legal persons in relation to processing in connection with the provision of publicly available electronic communications services in public communication networks in the Union in relation to matters for which they are subject to specific obligations with the same objective set out in Directive 2002/58/EC.

Relevant Recital

(173) This Regulation should apply to all matters concerning the protection of fundamental rights and freedoms *vis-à-vis* the processing of personal data which are not subject to specific obligations with the same objective set out in Directive 2002/58/EC of the European Parliament and of the Council, including the obligations on the controller and the rights of natural persons. In order to clarify the relationship between this Regulation and Directive 2002/58/EC, that Directive should be amended accordingly. Once this Regulation is adopted, Directive 2002/58/EC should be reviewed in particular in order to ensure consistency with this Regulation.

Closely Related Provisions

Article 94 (Repeal of Directive 95/46/EC)

Related Provisions in EPD [Directive 2002/58/EC]

Article 1(2) (Relationship with Directive 95/46/EC) (see also recitals 10 and 12)

Relevant Case Law

CJEU

Case C-450/06, *Varec SA v Belgian State*, judgment of 14 February 2008 (ECLI:EU:C:2008:91).
Joined Cases C-293/12 and C-594/12, *Digital Rights Ireland Ltd v Minister for Communications, Marine and Natural Resources* and *Kärntner Landesregierung, Seitlinger and Others*, judgment of 8 April 2014 (Grand Chamber) (ECLI:EU:C:2014:238).
Case C-419/14, *WebMindLicenses kft v Nemzeti Adó- és Vámhivatal Kiemelt Adó- és Vám Főigazgatóság*, judgment of 17 December 2015 (ECLI:EU:C:2015:832).
Joined Cases C-203/15 and C-698/15, *Tele2 Sverige AB v Post-och telestyrelsen* and *Secretary of State for the Home Department v Tom Watson and Others*, judgment of 21 December 2016 (Grand Chamber) (ECLI:EU: C:2016:970).

---

[*] The views expressed are solely those of the author and do not necessarily reflect those of the European Commission.

ECtHR

Niemietz v Germany, Appl. No. 13710/88, judgment of 16 December 1992.
Société Colas Est and Others v France, Appl. No. 37971/97, judgment of 16 April 2002.
Peck v United Kingdom, Appl. No. 44647/98, judgment of 28 January 2003.
Vinci Construction and GTM Génie Civil et Services v France, Appl. Nos. 63629/10 and 60567/10, judgment of 2 April 2015.
Bărbulescu v Romania [GC], Appl. No. 61496/08, judgment of 5 September 2017.

A. Rationale and Policy Underpinnings

Article 95 establishes the relationship between the GDPR and the EPD by laying down the principle that the GDPR should not impose additional obligations with the same objective on controllers that are subject to the specific obligations laid down in the EPD. This means that regarding matters specifically governed by the EPD, including rights conferred on natural persons,[1] the EPD should apply instead of the general rules. However, in all other cases the GDPR should apply.

The basic rationale for this endeavour is to offer more legal certainty as to the provisions on the processing of personal data that are applicable in the context of the use of publicly available electronic communications services in public communication networks in the EU. This was considered necessary by the Commission[2] and was confirmed by the EU legislator. Given the novelties introduced by the GDPR, including the range of new obligations for data controllers (and joint controllers and processors), without Article 95 it could be argued that providers of electronic communications services might need to comply also with certain obligations laid down by the GDPR, notably, because it is *lex posterior* (i.e. it was enacted later in time).

For a correct understanding of the relationship between the GDPR and EPD, it is useful to recall that both acts have as their main purpose to implement to different degrees Articles 7–8 of the Charter of Fundamental Rights of the European Union ('CFR' or 'Charter'). Indeed, the GDPR constitutes a detailed elaboration of Article 8 whereas the EPD implements Articles 7–8. It should be noted that the EPD is so far the only instrument in EU secondary law that comprehensively implements the principle of confidentiality of communications in Article 7 of the Charter, by laying down rules on the processing of traffic, communication and location data and the protection of terminal equipment. Vis-à-vis the GDPR it particularises data protection rules for the specific economic sector to which it applies. The EPD also ensures the confidentiality of communications of legal persons and protects their legitimate interests in this regard.

The need to protect confidentiality of communications has long been recognised. It is part of Article 8 of the European Convention on Human Rights ('ECHR') as interpreted by the ECtHR[3] and is in line with the constitutional traditions of EU Member States. Indeed, the majority of EU Member States recognise confidentiality of communications as a distinct constitutional right.[4] At EU level, Directive 97/66/EC,[5] adopted in 1997, was the first specific Directive for the processing of personal data in the telecommunications sector, the predecessor of Directive 2002/58/EC. The obligation to protect the

[1] See rec. 173 GDPR. [2] Art. 89 GDPR Proposal.
[3] See most recently ECtHR, *Bărbulescu v Romania*, paras. 72–73.
[4] See the examples listed in EDPS Preliminary Opinion 5/2016, fn. 11. [5] Directive 97/66/EC.

confidentiality of traditional correspondence has been integrated into EU law with the adoption of Directive 97/67/EC on postal services[6] (see Article 2(19)).

B. Legal Background

1. EU legislation

Article 95 GDPR has no equivalent in the DPD. The relationship between the two Directives is laid down in Article 1(2) EPD, according to which the 'provisions of this Directive particularise and complement Directive 95/46/EC for the purposes mentioned in paragraph 1'.[7]

Recital 10 EPD further states that 'in the electronic communications sector, Directive 95/46/EC applies in particular to all matters concerning the protection of fundamental rights and freedoms, which are not specifically covered by the provisions of this directive, including the obligations on the controller and the rights of individuals'.

2. National developments

A list of national transposition measures communicated by the Member States concerning the EPD is available online.[8] Certain provisions of these national laws will be unaffected by the entry into application of the GDPR because of Article 95.

3. Case law

The CJEU ruled on several occasions on the interpretation of the EPD together with the DPD. In situations which concerned the processing of personal data and privacy in the electronic communications sector, the Court focused on the relevant provisions of the EPD. Such was the case in its landmark judgments in *Digital Rights Ireland*[9] and *Tele2*,[10] both concerning the compatibility of data retention measures (EU and national, respectively) with the Charter.

In *Digital Rights Ireland*, the Court declared Directive 2006/24/EC invalid, leaving national data protection measures under the aegis of the derogation in Article 15 EPD.

In *Tele2*, the Court first determined whether the national measures in question constituted implementation of EU law in the sense of Article 51(1) of the Charter. To that effect, the Court looked, in the first place, at the scope of the EPD as defined by Article 1(3) thereof, which excludes 'activities of the state' in specified fields, including the activities of the state in areas of criminal law and in the areas of public security, defence and state security, including the economic well-being of the state when the activities relate to state security matters. The Court noted, however, that Article 3 EPD states that this Directive is to apply to the processing of personal data in connection with the provision of 'electronic communications services'. It further considered that, having regard to the general structure of the EPD, Article 15(1) necessarily presupposes that the national

---

[6] Directive 97/67/EC.
[7] An equivalent provision already existed in Art. 2(1) Directive 97/66/EC, the predecessor of the current EPD.
[8] See EUR-Lex EPD transposition measures.
[9] Joined Cases C-293/12 and C-594/12, *Digital Rights Ireland*.
[10] Joined Cases C-203/15 and C-698/15, *Tele2*.

measures referred to therein, fall within the scope of that Directive. The Court therefore concluded that the Directive must be regarded as regulating the activities of the providers of such services, including the granting of access to the retained data to authorities.

Secondly, the Court interpreted Article 15(1) EPD in the light of Articles 7–8, 11 and 52(1) of the Charter. It observed that, as stated in recital 2 thereof, the EPD seeks to ensure, in particular, full respect for the rights set out in Articles 7–8 of the Charter and that the EU legislature sought 'to ensure that a high level of protection of personal data and privacy will continue to be guaranteed for all electronic communications services regardless of the technology used'.[11] The Court further observed that the principle of confidentiality of communications established by the EPD implies, inter alia, that, as a general rule, any person other than the users is prohibited from storing, without the consent of the users concerned, the traffic data related to electronic communications. The only exceptions relate to persons lawfully authorised in accordance with Article 15(1) of that Directive and to the technical storage necessary for conveyance of a communication.[12]

After examining the compatibility of the national measures at issue in light of Articles 7–8 and 11 of the Charter, the Court concluded that national legislation such as that at issue exceeded the limits of what was strictly necessary. Hence, it could not be considered to be justified, within a democratic society, as required by Article 15(1) EPD, read in the light of Articles 7–8, 11 and 52(1) of the Charter.[13]

C. Analysis

1. From lex generalis to lex specialis

Before analysing Article 95 GDPR, it is appropriate to explain briefly the rationale for including both natural and legal persons as beneficiaries of the rights conferred by the EPD. The main purpose of this Directive is to ensure confidentiality of communications and, to that effect, its provisions particularise and complement the general rules on the protection of personal data. The reason for including legal persons in its scope is connected with the scope of Article 7 of the Charter. This provision contains rights corresponding to those guaranteed by Article 8(1) ECHR. In accordance with Article 52(3) CFR, Article 7 thereof is thus to be given the same meaning and the same scope as Article 8(1) ECHR, as interpreted by the ECtHR.[14] Concerning the scope of Article 7 as concerns legal persons, the case law of the CJEU[15] and of the ECtHR confirms that professional activities of legal persons may not be excluded from the protection of the right guaranteed by both Article 7 of the Charter and Article 8 ECHR.[16]

As the EPD specifically governs the processing of personal data by providers of electronic communications services falling within its scope, it must be regarded as a *lex specialis*,[17] as is explicit in Article 1(2) thereof.

---

[11] Ibid., para. 82.   [12] Ibid., para. 85.   [13] Ibid., para. 107.
[14] Case C-419/14, *WebMind Licenses*, para. 70 and case law cited therein.
[15] C-450/06, *Varec SA*, para. 48.
[16] See, inter alia, ECtHR, *Niemietz v Germany*, para. 29; ECtHR, *Société Colas Est and Others v France*, para. 41; ECtHR, *Peck v UK*, para. 57, ECtHR, *Vinci Construction v France*, para. 63.
[17] This is also explicit in rec. 173 GDPR: it states that the GDPR applies to all matters concerning the processing of personal data which are not subject to specific obligations with the same objective set out in the EPD, including the obligations on the controller and the rights of natural persons.

Article 95 GDPR was part of the Commission's proposal of 2012.[18] The then Article 89 of the proposal contained two paragraphs: paragraph 1, which corresponds to Article 95, and a second paragraph intended to amend the EPD by deleting its Article 1(2). The amendment to the EPD was not retained by the co-legislators.[19] The result is that the relationship between the EPD and the GDPR is therefore established in both acts. Indeed, given that any references to Directive 95/46/EC must be construed as references to the GDPR (see Article 94(2) GDPR), arguably Article 95 was not necessary. In the author's view, it is nevertheless a useful clarification as to the obligations that are applicable to communications service providers, notably during the period pending the adoption of the proposed ePrivacy Regulation.[20]

Regarding the matters for which controllers are subject to 'specific obligations with the same objective', as referred to in Article 95, an example is Article 4 EPD on security of processing. Article 4(1) requires communications service providers to take appropriate technical and organisational measures to safeguard the security of their services, and thus departs from the objective of protecting personal data. However, Article 4(1a), introduced by Directive 2009/136/EC, obliges communications service providers to put in place a number of mandatory measures aimed specifically at ensuring the protection of personal data (access limited to authorised personnel for legally authorised purposes; protection against accidental or unlawful destruction, accidental loss or alteration; implementation of a security policy with respect to processing). Furthermore, Article 4(3) imposes on the same providers the obligation to notify the competent authority (and in certain circumstances, the person concerned) of a personal data breach, falling within the same objective as the GDPR.

This means that these obligations will coexist in parallel under the two different pieces of legislation, according to their respective scope of application. Pursuant to Article 95, the GDPR shall not impose additional obligations on natural or legal persons in relation to matters for which they are subject to specific obligations with the same objective set out in the EPD. However, as a *lex specialis* to the GDPR, the EPD should not lead to a lower level of data protection than that provided by the GDPR.[21] Article 95 is thus the logical consequence of a specific regime that is not modified by the GDPR and which regulates the core aspects of the processing of personal data (grounds for processing, purposes, retention periods, security measures, personal data breach notifications) in connection with the provision and use of electronic communications in publicly available communications services and networks.[22]

---

[18] GDPR Proposal.
[19] Rec. 173 GDPR still makes reference to the amendment of that Directive (as proposed in rec. 135).
[20] See EPR Proposal.
[21] Art. 32 GDPR on security of processing builds on Art. 17 DPD, and Arts. 33–34 on data breach notification build on Art. 4(3) EPD. Also, the definition of personal data breach under Art. 4(12) GDPR is based on Art. 2(i) EPD. In view of the new GDPR provisions, the security obligations in Art. 4 EPD were not carried over into the proposal for the ePrivacy Regulation, see EPR Proposal, point 1.2.
[22] It is interesting to note that Art. 95 GDPR was adopted almost without modifications as compared to Art. 89 of the EPR Proposal, with the sole difference that the Commission proposed to amend the EPD by deleting Art. 1(2). Rec. 173 GDPR still makes reference to the amendment of that Directive (as proposed in rec. 135).

2. The EPR proposal

Recital 173 states that once the GDPR is adopted, the EPD should be reviewed, in particular to ensure consistency with this Regulation. In reply to this call by the co-legislators, the Commission adopted the proposal for the EPR on 10 January 2017.[23] The text of Article 1(3) of that proposal is similar to current Article 1(2) EPD and provides that the provisions of the EPR particularise and complement the GDPR by laying down specific rules for the purposes that it covers. This means that all matters concerning the processing of personal data not specifically addressed by the proposal are covered by the GDPR. As the EPR had not yet been adopted at the time this volume was finalised, there is currently overlap between the GDPR and the EPD, as contemplated by Article 95.

The Commission's choice of the instrument (a Regulation) for electronic communications privacy follows the same rationale as for the GDPR: to ensure legal certainty for users and businesses alike by avoiding divergent interpretation and implementation in the Member States. It is also justified for reasons of consistency with the GDPR.

The proposal contains a set of targeted measures aimed at ensuring effective protection of the fundamental right to privacy and communications. To that effect, it lays down the principle of confidentiality of communications and identifies exhaustively the permitted processing of communications data. It enlarges the personal scope of the current EPD to extend to Over-the-Top communications services ('OTTs').[24] This takes into account the reality that users increasingly replace traditional voice telephony, text messages ('SMS') and electronic mail conveyance services in favour of functionally equivalent online services such as Voice over IP, messaging services and web-based email services.

The proposal also extends the principle of confidentiality of communications to the transmission of machine-to-machine communications and reinforces the protection of privacy of terminal equipment.[25] The alignment with the GDPR resulted in incorporating its definitions, territorial scope and the supervision and consistency mechanism into the EPR. It also resulted in the omission in the proposal of some provisions, such as the security and data breach notification obligations of Article 4 EPD, to ensure that those provisions already in the GDPR will apply. Finally, as some of the rules in the EPD apply also to legal persons, certain provisions of the GDPR will be applicable to this category of end-users, notably those on consent and on legal remedies and compensation, as provided for under Articles 77–79 and 82 GDPR.

On 26 October 2017 the plenary of the European Parliament confirmed the decision to enter into interinstitutional negotiations based on the report of the Civil Liberties, Justice and Home Affairs ('LIBE').[26] This report, which contains 56 amendments, goes

---

[23] EPR Proposal. See also EP Report EPR and Council Report EPR 2017.

[24] The EPD is part of the regulatory framework for electronic communications. This framework was revised in 2016 following which the Commission adopted the EECC Proposal (the EECC Directive, which is based on the EEEC Proposal, entered into force on 20 December 2018). The EPR Proposal partially relies on definitions provided in the EECC Proposal, including that of 'electronic communications services', 'interpersonal communications service', 'number based communications services' and number-independent communications services'.

[25] The Explanatory Memorandum accompanying the EPR Proposal states that 'the consent rule to protect the confidentiality of terminal equipment failed to reach its objectives as end-users face requests to accept tracking cookies without understanding their meaning and, in some cases, are even exposed to cookies being set without their consent. The consent rule is over-inclusive, as it also covers non-privacy intrusive practices, and under-inclusive, as it does not clearly cover some tracking techniques (e.g. device fingerprinting) which may not entail access/storage in the device. Finally, its implementation can be costly for businesses'.

[26] EP Report EPR.

in the direction of reinforcing the protection of confidentiality of communications and of terminal equipment of end-users, as illustrated, in particular by the amendments on Articles 5–6, 8 and 10.

When this text was finalised, the Council had had several meetings on the proposal at Working Party level under the Maltese, Estonian, Bulgarian, Austrian and Romanian Presidencies. As can be seen from the relevant texts,[27] the work focused on certain key provisions of the draft Regulation, such as Article 6 (permitted processing), 8 (protection of end-users' terminal equipment) and 18 (supervision). The first two documents show an increased alignment with Article 6 of the GDPR, by the addition of more permitted grounds for processing, such as statistical or scientific research purposes, and the addition of further compatible processing of electronic communications metadata, taking inspiration from Article 6(4) of the GDPR. When this text was finalised, it was not clear whether the Council would agree on a general approach that could be a basis for entering into interinstitutional negotiations with the Parliament and the Commission.

Select Bibliography

EU legislation

Directive 97/66/EC: Directive 97/66/EC of the European Parliament and of the Council of 15 December 1997 concerning the processing of personal data and the protection of privacy in the telecommunications sector, OJ 1998 L 24/1.

Directive 97/67/EC: Directive 97/66/EC of the European Parliament and of the Council of 15 December 1997 on common rules for the development of the internal market for Community postal services and the improvement of quality of service, OJ 1997 L 15/14.

EECC Directive: Directive (EU) 2018/1972 of the European Parliament and of the Council of 11 December 2018 establishing the European Electronic Communications Code (Recast), OJ 2018 L 321/36.

EECC Proposal: Proposal for a Directive of the European Parliament and of the Council establishing the European Electronic Communications Code (Recast), COM(2016) 590 final/2, 12 October 2016.

EPR Proposal: Proposal for a Regulation of the European Parliament and of the Council concerning the respect for private life and the protection of personal data in electronic communications and repealing Directive 2002/58/EC (Regulation on Privacy and Electronic Communications), COM(2017)10 final, 10 January 2017

GDPR Proposal: Proposal for a Regulation of the European Parliament and of the Council on the protection of individuals with regard to the processing of personal data and on the free movement of such data (General Data Protection Regulation), COM(2012) 11 final, 25 January 2012.

Papers of data protection authorities

EDPS Preliminary Opinion 5/2016: EDPS, 'Opinion 5/2016: Preliminary Opinion on the Review of the EPD (2002/58/3C)' (22 July 2016).

Article 29 Working Party, 'Opinion 3/2016 on the Evaluation and Review of the ePrivacy Directive (2002/58/EC)' (WP 240, 19 July 2016).

---

[27] Council Report EPR 2018A and Council Report EPR 2018B.

Reports and recommendations

Council Report EECC: Proposal for a Directive of the European Parliament and of the Council establishing the European Electronic Communications Code (Recast), Outcome of proceedings, 10692/18, 29 June 2018.

Council Report EPR 2017: Proposal for a Regulation of the European Parliament and of the Council concerning the respect for private life and the protection of personal data in electronic communications and repealing Directive 2002/58/EC (Regulation on Privacy and Electronic Communications), Examination of the Presidency text, 15333/17, 5 December 2017.

Council Report EPR 2018A: Proposal for a Regulation of the European Parliament and of the Council concerning the respect for private life and the protection of personal data in electronic communications and repealing Directive 2002/58/EC (Regulation on Privacy and Electronic Communications), Examination of the Presidency text, 10975/1, 10 July 2018.

Council Report EPR 2018B: Proposal for a Regulation of the European Parliament and of the Council concerning the respect for private life and the protection of personal data in electronic communications and repealing Directive 2002/58/EC (Regulation on Privacy and Electronic Communications), Examination of the Presidency text, 12336/18, 20 September 2018.

EP Report EPR: Report on the proposal for a Regulation of the European Parliament and of the Council concerning the respect for private life and the protection of personal data in electronic communications and repealing Directive 2002/58/EC (Regulation on Privacy and Electronic Communications), PE606.011v02-00, A8-0324/2017, 20 October 2017.

Others

EUR-Lex EPD transposition measures: EUR-Lex, 'National transposition measures communicated by the Member States concerning: Directive 2002/58/EC of the European Parliament and of the Council of 12 July 2002 concerning the processing of personal data and the protection of privacy in the electronic communications sector (Directive on privacy and electronic communications)', available at https://eur-lex.europa.eu/legal-content/EN/NIM/?uri=CELEX:32002L0058&qid=1508243542130.

Article 96. Relationship with previously concluded Agreements

DOMINIQUE MOORE[*]

International agreements involving the transfer of personal data to third countries or international organisations which were concluded by Member States prior to 24 May 2016, and which comply with Union law as applicable prior to that date, shall remain in force until amended, replaced or revoked.

Closely Related Provisions

Article 44 (General principle for transfers); Article 45 (Transfers on the basis of an adequacy decision)

Related Provisions in LED [Directive (EU) 2016/680]

Article 61 (Relationship with previously concluded international agreements in the field of judicial cooperation in criminal matters and police cooperation) (see too recital 95)

Relevant Case Law

CJEU

Case C-205/06, *Commission of the European Communities v Republic of Austria*, judgment of 3 March 2009 (Grand Chamber) (ECLI:EU:C:2009:118).
Case C-249/06, *Commission of the European Communities v Kingdom of Sweden*, judgment of 3 March 2009 (Grand Chamber) (ECLI:EU:C:2009:119).
Case C-118/07, *Commission of the European Communities v Republic of Finland*, judgment of 19 November 2009 (ECLI:EU:C:2009:715).
Joined Cases C-203/15 and C-698/15, *Tele2 Sverige AB v Post-och telestyrelsen* and *Secretary of State for the Home Department v Tom Watson and Others*, judgment of 21 December 2016 (Grand Chamber) (ECLI:EU: C:2016:970).
Opinion 2/15, Opinion of 16 May 2017 (Full Court) (ECLI:EU:C:2017:376).
Opinion 1/15, Opinion of 26 July 2017 (Grand Chamber) (ECLI:EU:C:2017:592).

A. Rationale and Policy Underpinnings

There are a number of international agreements concluded by Member States with third countries on cooperation or exchange of information between national authorities in areas such as law enforcement, tax and competition. However, the scope and number of these agreements is uncertain.

[*] The views expressed are solely those of the author and do not necessarily reflect those of the European Parliament.

Perhaps as a result, the initial proposal presented by the Commission for the GDPR did not contain any provision relating to this matter. However, the proposal presented in parallel by the Commission for the LED did contain a comparable, though not identical, provision, and corresponding recital, relating to international agreements concluded by Member States in the field of criminal justice cooperation.[1]

During the course of trilogues held concurrently on both the GDPR[2] and the LED,[3] a compromise text was agreed on this issue for both of these (separate) legislative procedures.[4] The provisions contained in Article 96 GDPR are thus now identical, save for necessary changes to the heading and date referred to therein, to those in Article 61 LED.[5] Although no recital was included in the GDPR in this respect (apparently as an oversight),[6] it is still relevant to refer now to recital 95 LED on this matter, even though it merely alludes to the need 'to ensure a comprehensive and consistent protection of personal data in the Union' in this context.

Nevertheless, the EU legislator clearly intended to adopt a common approach, in both the GDPR and LED on this matter. The need to address this issue in the LED is perhaps more obvious, given the fact that EU competence in the field of police and judicial cooperation was far more restricted until the entry into force of the Lisbon Treaty, thereby leading to a situation where Member States were free to conclude international agreements with third countries or international organisations in this field, on account of the EU either having no competence here or having only exercised that competence to a very limited degree.

The situation was somewhat different with regards to the ability of Member States to conclude international agreements with third countries or international organisations

---

[1] LED Proposal.

[2] Given that the Commission had not proposed any provision on this matter (GDPR Proposal), the Parliament did not take any position on this issue either in its first reading adopted in plenary on 12 March 2014 (EP Position GDPR). The Council's general approach agreed on 15 June 2015 subsequently proposed an entirely new provision (then Art. 89a) worded as follows: 'International agreements involving the transfer of personal data to third countries or international organisations which were concluded by Member States prior to the entry into force of this Regulation, and which are in compliance with Directive 95/46/EC, shall remain in force until amended, replaced or revoked'. See Council Report 2015A.

[3] The LED Proposal initially foresaw an obligation for Member States to amend international agreements in this field within five years, in the following terms: 'International agreements concluded by Member States prior to the entry force of this Directive shall be amended, where necessary, within five years after the entry into force of this Directive'. The Parliament's first reading adopted on 12 March 2014 did not foresee any changes to this provision (EP Position LED). However, the Council's general approach subsequently agreed on 9 October 2015 reworded the Commission's proposal as follows: 'International agreements *involving the transfer of personal data to third countries or international organisations which were* concluded by Member States prior to the entry *into* force of this Directive *and which are in compliance with Union law applicable prior to the entry into force of this Directive shall remain in force until amended, replaced or revoked*'. (Emphasis added.) See Council Report 2015B.

[4] In effect, the final text agreed in both legislative procedures derives from the Council Report 2015B.

[5] The final text of Art. 61 LED now reads as follows, under the title 'Relationship with previously concluded international agreements in the field of judicial cooperation in criminal matters and police cooperation': 'International agreements involving the transfer of personal data to third countries or international organisations which were concluded by Member States prior to 6 May 2016 and which comply with Union law as applicable prior to that date shall remain in force until amended, replaced or revoked'.

[6] Rec. 102 GDPR provides that 'This Regulation is without prejudice to international agreements concluded between the Union and third countries regulating the transfer of personal data including appropriate safeguards for the data subjects. Member States may conclude international agreements which involve the transfer of personal data to third countries or international organisations, as far as such agreements do not affect this Regulation or any other provisions of Union law and include an appropriate level of protection for the fundamental rights of the data subjects'. However, this is different than the subject matter of Art. 96.

in the fields covered by the DPD, which are clearly more extensively covered by the exercise of EU legislative competence over a much longer time, with the result that the competence of Member States was correspondingly reduced in this respect.[7] Article 25 DPD on transfers of personal data to third countries also confers on the Commission the power to find that a third country ensures an adequate level of protection, as well as the power to enter into negotiations with a third country with a view to remedying a situation where the Commission finds to the contrary. Notwithstanding these powers of the Commission, it still remained conceivable that the Member States might also act in this field—at least to the extent that the Commission had not itself taken any action under its own powers— given the structure of this Directive which imposed the primary obligation on Member States to provide in national law that transfers to a third country must ensure an adequate level of protection.[8]

It is unclear though to what extent this abstract possibility was in actual fact used by Member States in the field covered by the DPD (particularly given the absence of any proposal from the Commission or corresponding recital as regards the provision in the GDPR in this regard). However, to the extent that any such international agreements had indeed been concluded by Member States prior to 24 May 2016, and assuming that they complied with Union law applicable at that time, the provisions of Article 96 GDPR will now preserve their effects, until amended, replaced or revoked.

This situation does, to some degree, reflect the provisions of Article 351 Treaty on the Functioning of the European Union ('TFEU') albeit in the very different context of international agreements concluded with third countries prior to accession to the Union. As the CJEU has explained,[9] the purpose of that provision is to make it clear, in accordance with the principles of international law, that application of the Treaty is not to affect the duty of the Member State concerned to respect the rights of third countries under a prior agreement and to perform its obligations.

B. Legal Background

This is a comparatively novel provision, at least in the field of data protection legislation, and its inclusion in the GDPR derives largely from the corresponding provision in Article 61 LED, which was itself prompted by the relatively unique legal situation arising from the previously limited EU competences in the field of police and judicial cooperation, before the entry into force of the Lisbon Treaty. In these particular circumstances, this matter is without legal background to mention here.

C. Analysis

It should be underlined that Article 96 GDPR is subject to a number of limitations. First, this provision can only apply to international agreements that the Member States may have actually concluded prior to 24 May 2016, 'involving the transfer of personal data to third countries or international organisations'. This issue now therefore concerns only a

---

[7] See Arts. 2(2) and 216(1) TFEU.   [8] See rec. 102 GDPR.
[9] Case C-205/06, *Commission v Austria*, para. 33. See also Case C-249/06 *Commission v Sweden*, para. 34 and Case C-118/07, *Commission v Finland*, para. 27.

'closed list' of international agreements already concluded by Member States before the adoption of the GDPR by the EU legislator. Any international agreements concluded by Member States after this date will not be covered. Also, this provision cannot apply either to any international agreements concluded by the Union under EU law. There is no provision of the GDPR dealing with international agreements of the EU, but it is clear that such agreements must comply with both the TFEU and the Charter.[10]

Secondly, the international agreements in question must 'comply with Union law as applicable prior to that date', i.e. 24 May 2016. Accordingly, the issue here is not to assess whether the international agreements in question still comply with the GDPR, after its entry into force, but rather it must be assessed whether these international agreements did in fact previously comply with Union law in force from the time when they were initially concluded[11] and throughout the intervening period up to and including 24 May 2016.

Clearly, 'Union law' applicable prior to 24 May 2016 includes both primary and secondary EU law in this context. It must therefore be ascertained not only that an international agreement complied with the DPD then in force but, perhaps more importantly, that the international agreement also complied with applicable provisions of the Treaties, including the Charter. As a result, Article 96 GDPR cannot, in any event, apply to international agreements that are shown to be incompatible with relevant provisions of primary law, such as Article 16 TFEU and Articles 7–8 and 47 of the Charter of Fundamental Rights of the European Union ('CFR').[12]

Where it is shown that the international agreement was indeed in compliance with 'Union law' in this broad sense up to 24 May 2016, then Article 96 GDPR now ensures that it still remains in force afterwards, even if the entry into force and application of the new provisions of the GDPR would have otherwise called into question the issue of compliance of that international agreement with EU law. Such agreements are thus to be 'preserved' notwithstanding any potential incompatibility with other provisions of the GDPR.

Thirdly, it should be noted that Article 96 GDPR foresees that the international agreements in question 'remain in force until amended, replaced or revoked'. Where an agreement is replaced or revoked it will obviously have no further application under international law in any event (and any replacement will not be covered by Article 96 GDPR, given that it will have been concluded after the date of 24 May 2016). However, where an international agreement is simply 'amended' then it would appear that Article 96 GDPR will also cease to apply, with the effect that the international agreement which continues to apply in its amended form will then no longer be protected by Article 96 GDPR in the event that it is found to be incompatible with other provisions of the GDPR.

---

[10] See *Opinion 1/15*, paras. 119–141 (and the case law cited therein, as regards compatibility of an international agreement concluded by the EU with a third country with regard to Art. 16 TFEU and Arts. 7–8 CFR) and para. 227 (as regards compatibility of an international agreement with Art. 47 CFR). See also Kuner 2018.

[11] Of course, the international agreement must have been concluded by a Member State in compliance with EU law from the outset, when it was first signed and ratified by that Member State and the third country (for example, the Member State must not have exercised a competence in breach of Art. 2 TFEU in an area where the EU has also exercised its competence at that same time). This thus also requires an examination of the situation under EU law at an earlier time (well before 24 May 2016) when the international agreement was first concluded by the Member State.

[12] See *Opinion 1/15*, paras. 119–141 and 227. Regarding the status of international agreements of Member States in EU law in general, see Rosas 2010.

Finally, the duty of sincere cooperation under Article 4(3) Treaty on European Union ('TEU') should also be considered in this context, where an international agreement protected by Article 96 GDPR may derogate from one or more provisions of the GDPR or the LED implementing the fundamental right to data protection. Provisions which derogate from fundamental rights must, in accordance with settled case law, be interpreted strictly.[13] Arguably, there may still be a positive obligation on Member States, arising under Article 4(3) TEU, to take any opportunities which exist under an existing agreement to 'amend, replace or revoke' the international agreement concerned, so as to remove any potential incompatibility with the fundamental right, for example under a provision in the agreement which provides for review and possible amendment after a certain period of time. By analogy with the case law on Article 351 TFEU,[14] the underlying purpose of Article 96 GDPR would be to permit Member States to respect the rights which third states derive, in accordance with international law, from existing international agreements.

However, this same purpose can be also achieved where it is possible for a Member State to amend, replace or revoke an agreement whilst respecting the wishes of a third state, for example where the third state expresses the wish for an existing agreement to come to an end upon the entry into force of a new agreement.[15] In this light, it may be argued that Article 96 GDPR should be interpreted to mean that incompatible provisions of such agreements may continue to remain in force only for so long as there is no means available for the Member State to rectify this situation with due respect for the rights which third states derive under international law, such as under a review procedure included in the provisions of the agreement itself.

Select Bibliography

EU legislation

GDPR Proposal: Proposal for a Regulation of the European Parliament and of the Council on the protection of individuals with regard to the processing of personal data and on the free movement of such data (General Data Protection Regulation), COM (2012) 11 final, 25 January 2012.

LED Proposal: Proposal for a Directive of The European Parliament and of the Council on the protection of individuals with regard to the processing of personal data by competent authorities for the purposes of prevention, investigation, detection or prosecution of criminal offences or the execution of criminal penalties, and the free movement of such data, COM(2012) 10 final, 25 January 2012.

Academic writings

Kuner 2018: Kuner, 'International Agreements, Data Protection, and EU Fundamental Rights on the International Stage: *Opinion 1/15*', 55(3) *Common Market Law Review* (2018), 857.

---

[13] See, by analogy, the judgment in Joined Cases C-203/15 and C-698/15, *Tele2*, para. 89.

[14] See Case C-205/06, *Commission v Austria*; Case C-249/06, *Commission v Sweden* and Case C-118/07, *Commission v Finland*.

[15] See, by analogy, *Opinion 2/15*, para. 254, where the Court noted, in respect of Art. 351 TFEU and the related case law, that the rights of a third state (the Republic of Singapore) could be duly respected as that third state had expressed the wish that certain bilateral agreements with a number of Member States would come to an end upon the entry into force of an envisaged agreement with the EU.

Rosas 2010: Rosas, 'The Status in EU Law of International Agreements Concluded by EU Member States', 34 *Fordham International Law Journal* (2010), 1304.

Reports and recommendations

Council Report 2015A: Preparation of a general approach, 965/15, 11 June 2015.
Council Report 2015B: General approach, 12555/15, 2 October 2015.
EP Position GDPR: Position of the European Parliament adopted at first reading on 12 March 2014 with a view to the adoption of Regulation (EU) No. .../2014 of the European Parliament and of the Council on the protection of individuals with regard to the processing of personal data and on the free movement of such data (General Data Protection Regulation), P7_TC1-COD(2012)0011, 12 March 2014.
EP Position LED: Position of the European Parliament adopted at first reading on 12 March 2014 with a view to the adoption of Directive 2014/.../EU of the European Parliament and of the Council on the protection of individuals with regard to the processing of personal data by competent authorities for the purposes of prevention, investigation, detection or prosecution of criminal offences or the execution of criminal penalties, and the free movement of such data, P7_TC1-COD(2012)0010, 12 March 2014.

Article 97. Commission reports

THOMAS ZERDICK*

1. By 25 May 2020 and every four years thereafter, the Commission shall submit a report on the evaluation and review of this Regulation to the European Parliament and to the Council. The reports shall be made public.
2. In the context of the evaluations and reviews referred to in paragraph 1, the Commission shall examine, in particular, the application and functioning of:
   (a) Chapter V on the transfer of personal data to third countries or international organisations with particular regard to decisions adopted pursuant to Article 45(3) of this Regulation and decisions adopted on the basis of Article 25(6) of Directive 95/46/EC;
   (b) Chapter VII on cooperation and consistency.
3. For the purpose of paragraph 1, the Commission may request information from Member States and supervisory authorities.
4. In carrying out the evaluations and reviews referred to in paragraphs 1 and 2, the Commission shall take into account the positions and findings of the European Parliament, of the Council, and of other relevant bodies or sources.
5. The Commission shall, if necessary, submit appropriate proposals to amend this Regulation, in particular taking into account of developments in information technology and in the light of the state of progress in the information society.

Closely Related Provisions

Chapter V (Transfers of personal data to third countries or international organisations); Chapter VII (Cooperation and consistency)

Related Provisions in LED [Directive (EU) 2016/680]

Article 62 (Commission reports) (see too recital 94)

Related Provisions in EPD [Directive 2002/58/EC]

Article 18 (Review)

Relevant Case Law

Case C-362/14, *Maximillian Schrems v Data Protection Commissioner*, judgment of 6 October 2015 (Grand Chamber) (ECLI:EU:C:2015:650).

* The views expressed are solely those of the author and do not necessarily reflect those of the EDPS.

A. Rationale and Policy Underpinnings

Article 97 lays down an obligation for the Commission to evaluate and review the GDPR and then make this review and evaluation public in a report. As such it is an obligation to conduct an *ex post* evaluation of the GDPR as part of the Union institution's policy towards better regulation, i.e. better law-making.[1] The first report will need to be published by 25 May 2020, i.e. two years after the entry into application of the GDPR (Article 99 paragraph 2). The subsequent reports then have to follow every four years afterwards.

Paragraph 1 establishes a reviewing and reporting obligation for the Commission. Paragraph 2 sets out specific provisions to report on in particular. Paragraph 3 lays down an information right for the Commission to request information from Member States and supervisory authorities. Paragraph 4 provides the basis on which the review and report should be conducted. Paragraph 5 spells out the Commission's obligation to submit proposals for amending the GDPR, if necessary.

B. Legal Background

Article 33 DPD contained a similar obligation to report on the implementation of that Directive.[2]

C. Analysis

The Commission is obliged to produce the first report by 25 May 2020 (paragraph 1). After that, the time frame for reporting is every four years. The mandatory recipients of the reports are both the European Parliament and the Council. The Commission's obligation extends to conduct both an evaluation and a review of the GDPR. This evaluation means that the Commission should look at the application and functioning of the GDPR, in light of the two objectives of the protection of natural persons with regard to the processing of personal data as well as the free movement of personal data (see Article 1 paragraph 1).[3] In its ensuing review the Commission will have to assess if amendments to the GDPR need to be proposed (see paragraph 5). In addition, the Commission is obliged to make this report and all following reports public. As a mandatory publication required by this article, this will have to be done by the EU's Publication Service via a publication in the Official Journal ('OJ') of the EU.[4] Normally the Commission will also publish its reports on its website.

Similarly to Article 33(2) DPD, paragraph 2 sets out specific provisions of the GDPR where the legislator stresses a particular need of the European Parliament and the Member States in the Council to be informed. However, it is clear from the wording in paragraph 2 'in particular' that not only the provisions referred to on this paragraph but also any other provisions of the GDPR should be made subject to the evaluations and review of paragraph 1. Paragraph 2 mentions specifically Chapter V (transfers of personal data to third countries or international organisations) and Chapter VII (cooperation and

---

[1] See e.g. Interinstitutional Agreement 2016.
[2] The Commission produced the following reports on the DPD: EC Report 2003; EC Communication 2007; EC Communication 2010; EC Communication 2012.
[3] See the commentary on Art. 1 in this volume.   [4] Decision 2009/496/EC, Euratom.

consistency). In particular, the Commission is tasked to report on the application and functioning of its adequacy decisions adopted as implementing acts pursuant to Article 45(3) of the GDPR as well as on existing adequacy decisions adopted on the basis of Article 25(6) of Directive 95/46. By way of an such adequacy decision, the Commission has the power to determine whether a third country or an international organisation ensures an adequate level of protection, in particular by reason of its domestic law or of the international commitments it has entered into.[5] Although the GDPR repeals the DPD with effect from 25 May 2018 in accordance with Article 94(1)), Article 45(9) provides that adequacy decisions adopted by the Commission on the basis of Article 25(6) DPD remain in force until amended, replaced or repealed by the Commission.

As a direct reaction to the CJEU judgment in *Schrems*,[6] the legislators of the GDPR agreed, first, that every single adequacy decision will need to provide for an explicit mechanism for a periodic review, at least every four years, in accordance with Article 45(3) second sentence. In addition, they also decided that the application and functioning of adequacy decisions in general should be subject to a regular reporting obligation laid down in Article 97(2).[7]

In order to comply with its obligation under Article 97, the Commission is authorised to request information from Member States and supervisory authorities (paragraph 3). This corresponds to an information obligation by Member States and supervisory authorities. The Commission has no such right to information from the EDPB. However, Article 70 (1b) imposes on the Board the task of advising the Commission on any issue related to the protection of personal data in the Union including on any proposed amendment of the GDPR, in addition to its duty to provide the Commission with an opinion for the assessment of the adequacy of the level of protection in a third country or international organisation.[8] In addition, Article 71(2) GDPR requires the Board to provide annual reports to the Commission, together with the European Parliament and the Council, on the practical application of its guidelines, recommendations and best practices under Article 70(1)(l) and its binding decisions adopted under Article 65.[9]

Paragraph 4 requires the Commission to take into account the positions and findings of the European Parliament, of the Council, and of other relevant bodies or sources (e.g. the Board or civil society associations) during the evaluations and reviews. This obligation writes into law the already existing general Commission policy on listening more to the people affected by its policy and law-making as part of the Commission's better regulation agenda.[10] Where the Commission, after having carried out the evaluations and reviews, comes to the conclusion that further improvements of the GDPR are necessary, it is authorised in accordance with paragraph 5 to propose amendments to the GDPR, having considered developments in information technology and progress in the information society. This is a reflection of the general power of the Commission to propose new EU legislation in line with Article 17(2) of the Treaty on European Union ('TEU').

---

[5] See the commentary on Art. 45 in this volume.   [6] Case C-362/14, *Schrems*.
[7] Albrecht 2016, p. 95.   [8] See the commentary on Art. 70 in this volume.
[9] See the commentary on Art. 71 in this volume.
[10] For more information see EC Website law-making.

Select Bibliography

EU legislation

Decision 2009/496/EC, Euratom: Decision 2009/496/EC, Euratom of the European Parliament, the Council, the Commission, the Court of Justice, the Court of Auditors, the European Economic and Social Committee and the Committee of the Regions of 26 June 2009 on the organisation and operation of the Publications Office of the European Union, OJ 2009 L 168/41.

Interinstitutional Agreement 2016: Interinstitutional Agreement between the European Parliament, the Council of the European Union and the European Commission on Better Law-Making, OJ 2016 L 123/1.

Academic writings

Albrecht 2016: Albrecht, 'Das neue EU-Datenschutzrecht – von der Richtlinie zur Verordnung', 32(2) *Computer und Recht* (2016), 88.

Reports and recommendations

EC Communication 2007: Communication from the Commission to the European Parliament and the Council on the follow-up of the Work Programme for better implementation of the Data Protection Directive, COM(2007) 87 final, 7 March 2007.

EC Communication 2010: Communication from the Commission to the European Parliament, the Council, the Economic and Social Committee and the Committee of the Regions, 'A Comprehensive Approach on Personal Data Protection in the European Union', COM(2010) 609 final, 4 November 2010.

EC Communication 2012: Communication from the Commission to the European Parliament, the Council, the European Economic and Social Committee and the Committee of the Regions, 'Safeguarding Privacy in a Connected World—A European Data Protection Framework for the 21st Century', COM(2012) 9/3, 25 January 2012.

EC Report 2003: Report from the Commission 'First Report on the Implementation of the Data Protection Directive (95/46/EC)', COM(2003) 265 final, 15 May 2003.

Others

EC Website law-making: European Commission, 'Contribute to Law-Making', available at https://ec.europa.eu/info/law/contribute-law-making_en.

Article 98. Review of other Union legal acts on data protection

LUCA TOSONI

The Commission shall, if appropriate, submit legislative proposals with a view to amending other Union legal acts on the protection of personal data, in order to ensure uniform and consistent protection of natural persons with regard to processing. This shall in particular concern the rules relating to the protection of natural persons with regard to processing by Union institutions, bodies, offices and agencies and on the free movement of such data.

Relevant Recitals

(17) Regulation (EC) No. 45/2001 of the European Parliament and of the Council applies to the processing of personal data by the Union institutions, bodies, offices and agencies. Regulation (EC) No. 45/2001 and other Union legal acts applicable to such processing of personal data should be adapted to the principles and rules established in this Regulation and applied in the light of this Regulation. In order to provide a strong and coherent data protection framework in the Union, the necessary adaptations of Regulation (EC) No. 45/2001 should follow after the adoption of this Regulation, in order to allow application at the same time as this Regulation.

(173) This Regulation should apply to all matters concerning the protection of fundamental rights and freedoms *vis-à-vis* the processing of personal data which are not subject to specific obligations with the same objective set out in Directive 2002/58/EC of the European Parliament and of the Council, including the obligations on the controller and the rights of natural persons. In order to clarify the relationship between this Regulation and Directive 2002/58/EC, that Directive should be amended accordingly. Once this Regulation is adopted, Directive 2002/58/EC should be reviewed in particular in order to ensure consistency with this Regulation.

Closely Related Provisions

Article 2(3) (Material scope); Article 97(5) (Review of the GDPR)

Related Provisions in LED [Directive (EU) 2016/680]

Article 62(6) (Review of other legal acts); recital 19

Related Provisions in EPD [Directive 2002/58/EC]

Article 18 (Review)

Related Provisions in EUDPR [Regulation (EU) 2018/1725]

Article 2(3) (Scope); Article 42 (Legislative consultation); Article 97 (Review clause); Article 98 (Review of Union legal acts) (see too recital 13)

Relevant Case Law

CJEU

Case C-241/01, *National Farmers' Union v Secrétariat général du gouvernement*, judgment of 22 October 2002 (ECLI:EU:C:2002:604).

Opinion of Advocate General Misho in Case C-241/01, *National Farmers' Union v Secrétariat général du gouvernement*, delivered on 2 July 2002 (ECLI:EU:C:2002:415).

Case C-504/04, *Agrarproduktion Staebelow GmbH v Landrat des Landkreises Bad Doberan*, judgment of 12 January 2006 (ECLI:EU:C:2006:30).

Case C-134/15, *Lidl GmbH & Co. KG v Freistaat Sachsen*, judgment of 30 June 2016 (ECLI:EU:C:2016:498).

Opinion of Advocate General Bobek in Case C-134/15, *Lidl GmbH & Co. KG v Freistaat Sachsen*, delivered on 16 March 2016 (EU:C:2016:169).

Case C-528/16, *Confédération paysanne and Others v Premier ministre and Ministre de l'agriculture, de l'agroalimentaire et de la forêt*, judgment of 25 July 2018 (Grand Chamber) (ECLI:EU:C:2018:583).

Opinion of Advocate General Bobek in Case C-528/16, *Confédération paysanne and Others v Premier ministre and Ministre de l'agriculture, de l'agroalimentaire et de la forêt*, delivered on 18 January 2018 (ECLI:EU:C:2018:20).

A. Rationale and Policy Underpinnings

Article 98 GDPR includes a review clause[1] that requires the Commission to examine the existing EU legal acts on the protection of personal data in view of their possible amendment. The primary aim of the Article is to ensure that all of the EU rules on data protection be brought into line with the GDPR, so as to guarantee a uniform and consistent protection of data subjects in the European Union ('EU') (see recitals 17 and 173 GDPR).[2] Thus, the Article triggers a process that should complete and complement the general data protection framework established by the GDPR.[3] Article 98 requires in particular that the EU rules governing the processing of personal data by the Union institutions, bodies, offices and agencies be updated to ensure consistency with the GDPR.[4] Indeed, as noted by the EDPS, 'it would be inacceptable if the European Commission and the other EU institutions were not bound by rules equivalent to those which [are] applicable at Member State level'.[5] This is because Article 8 of the Charter of Fundamental

---

[1] Kiendl Krišto and Poutouroudi 2018, pp. 258–259. See further on review clauses in EU legislation Weber, Edwards and Huber 2017.

[2] This was also the justification given in the European Parliament's LIBE Committee Draft Report on the GDPR proposal, which is where the provisions now included in Art. 98 GDPR first originated (albeit with a slightly different formulation). The Draft Report's justification for the amendment No. 75, which proposed the introduction in the GDPR proposal of an Art. 89a (i.e. the antecedent of Art. 98 GDPR) stated: '[t]his amendment seeks to ensure consistency between the Regulation and the laws regulating EU institutions, bodies and agencies, such as Regulation No. 45, but equally of all the EU agencies that currently have their own data protection regulations, leading to a patchwork of rules that makes it very hard for the data subject to exercise its rights'. See EP GDPR Draft Report, pp. 207–208.

[3] EDPS 2017, p. 6.

[4] See also Art. 2(3) GDPR. At the time of the adoption of the GDPR, the processing of personal data by the Union institutions, bodies, offices and agencies was primarily governed by Regulation 45/2001. For Regulation 45/2001, see Table of Legislation. Art. 2(3) GDPR reads: '[R]egulation (EC) No. 45/2001 and other Union legal acts applicable to such processing of personal data shall be adapted to the principles and rules of this Regulation in accordance with Article 98'. An analogous requirement is also mentioned in rec. 19 LED.

[5] EDPS 2017, p. 6.

Tosoni

Rights of the EU ('CFR') and Article 16 of the Treaty on the Functioning of the EU ('TFEU') imply that the fundamental right to the protection of personal data should be ensured in a consistent and homogeneous manner throughout the EU.

B. Legal Background

1. EU legislation

The DPD was meant as a general framework for data protection, which could be complemented by specific sectoral data protection regimes.[6] Moreover, as the DPD was adopted as a first pillar instrument,[7] the Directive's scope of application covered neither the processing by EU institutions and bodies nor processing operations that fell outside the former first pillar (e.g. processing for law enforcement purposes).[8] As a result, after the adoption of the DPD, the EU legislature established a patchwork of EU data protection regimes and introduced specific data protection rules in several pieces of sectoral legislation.[9] A few notable examples of this regulatory approach are Regulation 45/2001, the EPD, Council Framework Decision 2008/977/JHA,[10] the Third Anti-Money Laundering Directive,[11] the SIS II Regulation,[12] the Eurodac Regulation,[13] the Europol Regulation[14] and the PNR Directive.[15] Although the EDPS had recommended in the past to partially depart from this approach and specifically demanded that the data protection rules for EU institutions and bodies be incorporated in the GDPR,[16] the EU legislature finally decided to maintain separate data protection regimes in place, including a specific legal instrument applicable to the EU institutions and bodies. Thus, the legislature committed in Articles 2(3) and 98 GDPR to review the existing EU legal acts on the protection of personal data to ensure their consistency with the GDPR.[17]

Article 98 had no exact equivalent in the DPD. Nonetheless, the DPD did include a limited review clause in Article 33(2). The latter Article required the Commission to examine the application of the DPD to the data processing of sound and image data and to submit the appropriate proposals which would prove to be necessary, taking account of developments in information technology and in the light of the state of progress in the information society.

2. Case law

The CJEU has not yet interpreted Article 98 GDPR. However, the Article may be seen as an operationalisation of the legislature's duty to update legislation in light of technological

---

[6] WP29 2009, p. 6.

[7] See the preamble to the DPD, which refers to Art. 100a of the Treaty establishing the European Community (which is now Art. 114 TFEU) as the legal basis of the Directive.

[8] WP29 2009, p. 6. See generally on the old three pillar structure of the EU Craig and de Búrca 2015, pp. 965–967.

[9] WP29 2009, pp. 6–7.

[10] See Council Framework Decision 2008/977/JHA. The latter Decision was reviewed in parallel with the GDPR to ensure consistency with the Regulation, and was ultimately substituted and repealed by the LED.

[11] See Third Anti-Money Laundering Directive. The Directive was later repealed by the Fourth Anti-Money Laundering Directive, which also includes specific data protection rules (see, in particular, Arts. 40–44).

[12] See SIS II Regulation.   [13] See Eurodac Regulation.   [14] See Europol Regulation.

[15] See PNR Directive.   [16] See EDPS 2011, pp 11–12. See also EDPS 2012, p. 5.

[17] This solution partially reflects the 'second best' regulatory option suggested by the EDPS. See EDPS 2012, pp. 6–7.

and social developments, a duty that according to some Advocate General Opinions exists under EU law.[18] In particular, in *Confédération paysanne and Others*, Advocate General Bobek opined that 'the [EU] legislature is obliged to keep its regulation reasonably up to date' and that 'there is a constitutional duty for legislation to be relevant, in the sense of being technically and socially responsive, and, provided that it is necessary in view of later evolution, to be updated'.[19] The CJEU has not yet expressly recognised this duty, but some of its judgments seem to echo it.[20]

C. Analysis

1. The requirements of Article 98

Article 98 implicitly envisages that, as a first step, the Commission should review the existing EU legal acts on the protection of personal data to assess whether they are consistent with the principles and requirements of the GDPR. At the time of the adoption of the GDPR and the LED, the other EU legal acts dealing specifically with the protection of personal data were: (i) Regulation 45/2001 and (ii) the EPD.[21] A narrow reading of Article 98 would suggest that these are the only acts to be reviewed by the Commission.[22] This is because Article 98 refers exclusively to 'Union legal acts *on the protection of personal data*' (emphasis added).

However, under a broader reading, the Commission should also review all EU sectoral legislation which includes specific data protection rules, such as the Fourth Anti-Money Laundering Directive and the Europol Regulation. Indeed, the objective of ensuring a uniform and consistent protection throughout the EU may only be achieved if all of the data protection rules existing under EU law are aligned with the GDPR. This reading is supported by the wording of Article 2(3) GDPR, which states that, in addition to updating Regulation 45/2001, the Commission should update, 'in accordance with Article 98', 'other Union legal acts' applicable to the processing of personal data by the Union institutions, bodies, offices and agencies.[23]

Following the above-mentioned preliminary assessment, the Commission must 'submit legislative proposals' with a view to amending the acts it reviewed, but only if it finds it 'appropriate'. Article 98 does not set any concrete timetables.[24] Therefore, Article 98 leaves the Commission a certain margin of discretion in deciding whether and when to table a proposal. Nonetheless, if one accepts that the EU legislature 'is obliged to keep its regulation reasonably up to date',[25] such a margin of discretion is

---

[18] See Case C-241/01, *National Farmers' Union* (AG Opinion), para. 51; Case C-134/15, *Lidl* (AG Opinion), para. 90; Case C-528/16, *Confédération paysanne* (AG Opinion), para. 139.

[19] Case C-528/16, *Confédération paysanne* (AG Opinion), para. 139.

[20] For instance, the CJEU has found that 'when new elements change the perception of a risk or show that that risk can be contained by less restrictive measures than the existing measures, it is for the institutions and in particular the Commission, which has the power of legislative initiative, to bring about an amendment to the rules in the light of the new information'. See Case C-504/04, *Agrarproduktion Staebelow*, para. 40.

[21] A list of the EU legal acts on data protection may be found in Annex 1 to EC GDPR Impact Assessment.

[22] The review of the EPD is also envisaged in its Art. 18.

[23] The 'other Union acts' mentioned in Art. 2(3) are arguably those EU acts that include special data protection rules for specific Union bodies, such as Europol (see Arts. 28–46 of the Europol Regulation). The review of the Europol Regulation is also envisaged by the EUDPR (see Arts. 2(3) and 98).

[24] The initial idea was, however, to update the rules for EU institutions and bodies by 25 May 2018 (see rec. 17 GDPR), but this did not occur.

[25] See Case C-528/16, *Confédération paysanne* (AG Opinion), para. 139.

not without limits. Indeed, Advocate General Bobek opined that '[f]ailing to meet such a duty could result, in *extreme* cases of technical or social lack of responsiveness, in a potential declaration of invalidity of the specific legislative provisions because of inactivity, namely, because of the failure to amend'.[26] However, the Advocate General underlined 'the very exceptional nature of such a step, which could only be contemplated in cases of clear and paramount dissonance between changed reality and effectively obsolete legislation'.[27]

The proposals for amendments to be submitted by the Commission after the initial review of the relevant legal acts should be 'legislative proposals'. This implies that the Commission should submit proposals for a Regulation, a Directive or a Decision, as under EU law these are the only legal acts that can be legislative (i.e. acts adopted by a legislative procedure).[28] Following the adoption of a legislative proposal on data protection, the Commission must consult the EDPS (see Article 42(1) and recital 60 EUDPR). The EDPS must then provide the Commission with its advice in writing within a period of up to eight weeks of receipt of the request for consultation, unless the Commission considers it necessary to shorten the deadline (see Article 42(3) EUDPR).

As discussed above, the update of the existing EU legal acts on data protection should be aimed at ensuring their consistency with the GDPR. This means that the legislature should seek the maximum alignment possible with the provisions of the GDPR. Nonetheless, as noted by the EDPS:

[A]lignment with the GDPR can be neither full, nor automatic. The GDPR includes numerous clauses allowing Member States to maintain or introduce specific legislation in certain areas, including for public authorities. In those cases where the GDPR provides specific rules for public authorities or leaves room for implementation of its provisions by Member States, the [legislation to be adopted in accordance with Article 98] can be considered to play a role comparable to a national law 'implementing' the GDPR.[29]

2. The application of Article 98: the ePrivacy Regulation and the EUDPR

In light of the requirements of Articles 2(3) and 98 GDPR, the EPD is currently under review[30] and Regulation 45/2001 was repealed by the EUDPR, which applies to the processing of personal data by EU institutions and bodies. The EUDPR closely mirrors the principles and rules of the GDPR. In fact, among other things, it establishes: conditions applicable to a child's consent in relation to information society services; a right to data portability; rules on automated individual decision-making, including profiling; rules on data protection by design and by default; record-keeping requirements; data breach notification requirements; data protection impact assessment ('DPIA') requirements; and data protection officer ('DPO') requirements.

The existence of a close relationship between the GDPR and the EUDPR is further stressed in recital 5 of the latter, which states that '[w]henever the provisions of this Regulation follow the same principles as the provisions of Regulation (EU) 2016/679, those two sets of provisions should, under the case law of the Court of Justice of the European Union (the "Court of Justice"), be interpreted homogeneously, in particular

---

[26] Ibid., para. 140. [27] Ibid.
[28] See Art. 289 TFEU. See further Craig and de Búrca 2015, pp. 113–114.
[29] EDPS 2017, p. 7. [30] See EPR Proposal. See further Buttarelli 2017.

because the scheme of this Regulation should be understood as equivalent to the scheme of Regulation (EU) 2016/679'.

3. Provisions related to Article 98

As mentioned above, the process of updating the EU data protection rules across sectors in light of the changes introduced by the GDPR does not stop with the adoption of the LED and the review of the EPD and Regulation 45/2001. This is made clear in several review clauses analogous to Article 98 GDPR. In particular, Article 62(6) LED requires that, by 6 May 2019, the Commission review other EU legal acts which regulate the processing by police and criminal justice authorities to assess the need to align them with the LED. Similarly, Article 98 EUDPR provides that:

1. By 30 April 2022, the Commission shall review legal acts adopted on the basis of the Treaties which regulate the processing of operational personal data by Union bodies, offices or agencies when carrying out activities which fall within the scope of Chapter 4 or Chapter 5 of Title V of Part Three TFEU, in order to:
   (a) assess their consistency with Directive (EU) 2016/680 and Chapter IX of this Regulation;
   (b) identify any divergences that may hamper the exchange of operational personal data between Union bodies, offices or agencies when carrying out activities in those fields and competent authorities; and
   (c) identify any divergences that may create legal fragmentation of the data protection legislation in the Union.
2. On the basis of the review, in order to ensure uniform and consistent protection of natural persons with regard to processing, the Commission may submit appropriate legislative proposals, in particular with a view to applying Chapter IX of this Regulation to Europol and the European Public Prosecutor's Office and including adaptations of Chapter IX of this Regulation, if necessary.[31]

The GDPR itself will need to be reviewed in light of future technological and social developments. This is specifically envisaged by Article 97(5) GDPR.

Select Bibliography

EU legislation

Council Framework Decision 2008/977/JHA: Council Framework Decision 2008/977/JHA of 27 November 2008 on the protection of personal data processed in the framework of police and judicial cooperation in criminal matters, OJ 2008 L 350/60.
EPR Proposal: Proposal for a Regulation of the European Parliament and of the Council concerning the respect for private life and the protection of personal data in electronic communications and repealing Directive 2002/58/EC (Regulation on Privacy and Electronic Communications), COM(2017)10 final, 10 January 2017.
Eurodac Regulation: Regulation (EU) No. 603/2013 of the European Parliament and of the Council of 26 June 2013 on the establishment of 'Eurodac' for the comparison of fingerprints for the effective application of Regulation (EU) No. 604/2013 establishing the criteria and mechanisms for determining the Member State responsible for examining an application for

---

[31] See also rec. 13 EUDPR. Operational personal data are 'all personal data processed by Union bodies, offices or agencies when carrying out activities which fall within the scope of Chapter 4 or Chapter 5 of Title V of Part Three TFEU to meet the objectives and tasks laid down in the legal acts establishing those bodies, offices or agencies' (see Art. 3(2) EUDPR).

international protection lodged in one of the Member States by a third-country national or a stateless person and on requests for the comparison with Eurodac data by Member States' law enforcement authorities and Europol for law enforcement purposes, and amending Regulation (EU) No. 1077/2011 establishing a European Agency for the operational management of large-scale IT systems in the area of freedom, security and justice (recast), OJ 2013 L 180/1.

Europol Regulation: Regulation (EU) 2016/794 of the European Parliament and of the Council of 11 May 2016 on the European Union Agency for Law Enforcement Cooperation (Europol) and replacing and repealing Council Decisions 2009/371/JHA, 2009/934/JHA, 2009/935/JHA, 2009/936/JHA and 2009/968/JHA, OJ 2016 L 135/53.

Fourth Anti-Money Laundering Directive: Directive (EU) 2015/849 of the European Parliament and of the Council of 20 May 2015 on the prevention of the use of the financial system for the purposes of money laundering or terrorist financing, amending Regulation (EU) No. 648/2012 of the European Parliament and of the Council, and repealing Directive 2005/60/EC of the European Parliament and of the Council and Commission Directive 2006/70/EC, OJ 2015 L 141/73.

PNR Directive: Directive (EU) 2016/681 of the European Parliament and of the Council of 27 April 2016 on the use of passenger name record (PNR) data for the prevention, detection, investigation and prosecution of terrorist offences and serious crime, OJ 2016 L 119/132.

SIS II Regulation: Regulation (EC) No. 1987/2006 of the European Parliament and of the Council of 20 December 2006 on the establishment, operation and use of the second generation Schengen Information System (SIS II), OJ 2006 L 381/4.

Third Anti-Money Laundering Directive: Directive 2005/60/EC of the European Parliament and of the Council of 26 October 2005 on the prevention of the use of the financial system for the purpose of money laundering and terrorist financing, OJ 2005 L 309/15.

Academic writings

Buttarelli 2017: Buttarelli, 'The Commission Proposal for a Regulation on ePrivacy: Why Do We Need a Regulation Dedicated to ePrivacy in the European Union?', 3(2) *European Data Protection Law Review* (2017), 155.

Craig and de Búrca 2015: Craig and de Búrca, *EU Law: Text, Cases, and Materials* (6th edn, OUP 2015).

Weber, Edwards and Huber 2017: Weber, Edwards and Huber, 'EU Review Clauses in Need of Review? An Analysis of Review Clauses in EU Legislation in the Context of Better Lawmaking', 8(1) *European Journal of Risk Regulation* (2017), 121.

Papers of data protection authorities

EDPS 2011: European Data Protection Supervisor, 'Opinion of the European Data Protection Supervisor on the Communication from the Commission to the European Parliament, the Council, the Economic and Social Committee and the Committee of the Regions—A Comprehensive Approach on Personal Data Protection in the European Union' (14 January 2011).

EDPS 2012: European Data Protection Supervisor, 'Opinion of the European Data Protection Supervisor on The Data Protection Reform Package' (7 March 2012).

EDPS 2017: European Data Protection Supervisor, 'Opinion 5/2017. Upgrading Data Protection Rules for EU Institutions and Bodies: EDPS Opinion on the Proposal for a Regulation on the Protection of Individuals with Regard to the Processing of Personal Data by the Union Institutions, Bodies, Offices and Agencies and on the Free Movement of Such Data, and Repealing Regulation (EC) No. 45/2001 and Decision No. 1247/2002/EC' (15 March 2017).

WP29 2009: Article 29 Working Party, 'The Future of Privacy: Joint Contribution to the Consultation of the European Commission on the Legal Framework for the Fundamental Right to Protection of Personal Data' (WP 168, 1 December 2009).

Reports and recommendations

EP GDPR Draft Report: Draft Report on the proposal for a regulation of the European Parliament and of the Council on the protection of individual with regard to the processing of personal data and on the free movement of such data (General Data Protection Regulation), 2012/0011(COD), 17 December 2012.

Others

EC GDPR Impact Assessment: Commission Staff Working Paper 'Impact Assessment Accompanying the document Regulation of the European Parliament and of the Council on the protection of individuals with regard to the processing of personal data and on the free movement of such data (General Data Protection Regulation) and Directive of the European Parliament and of the Council on the protection of individuals with regard to the processing of personal data by competent authorities for the purposes of prevention, investigation, detection or prosecution of criminal offences or the execution of criminal penalties, and the free movement of such data', SEC(2012) 72 final, 25 January 2012.

Kiendl Krišto and Poutouroudi 2018: Kiendl Krišto and Poutouroudi, *Review Clauses in EU Legislation: A Rolling Checklist* (2018), available at http://www.europarl.europa.eu/RegData/etudes/STUD/2018/621821/EPRS_STU(2018)621821_EN.pdf.

Article 99. Entry into force and application

DOMINIQUE MOORE*

1. This Regulation shall enter into force on the twentieth day following that of its publication in the *Official Journal of the European Union*.
2. It shall apply from 25 May 2018.

Closely Related Provisions

Article 94 (Repeal of Directive 95/46/EC)

Related Provisions in LED [Directive (EU) 2016/680]

Article 63 (Transposition) (see too recital 96); Article 64 (Entry into force)

Related Provisions in EPD [Directive 2002/58/EC]

Article 17 (Transposition); Article 20 (Entry into force)

A. Analysis

The entry into force of the GDPR follows a standard pattern for EU legislation.

The GDPR was published in the EU Official Journal on 4 May 2016. The two-year period from the entry into force of the GDPR on 24 May 2016 (as provided by Article 99(1)) until its application starting on 25 May 2018 (as provided by Article 99(2)), and the concomitant repeal of the DPD under Article 94, was intended to allow sufficient time for all concerned to prepare sufficiently for the important changes to be brought about by the new legal regime of the GDPR. This two-year period is longer than the norm for EU legislation.[1]

Under its Article 63, the LED requires Member States to apply their national measures transposing that Directive 'from 6 May 2018', with Framework Decision 2008/977/JHA[2] being repealed with effect from that same date, thereby giving them a similar two-year period to adjust to these changes in the new legal regime in the police sector also. The slight difference in dates, between 6 May 2018 for the LED and 25 May 2018 for the GDPR, is simply the result of the LED entering into force earlier than the GDPR, in accordance with its Article 64.

---

* The views expressed are solely those of the author and do not necessarily reflect those of the European Parliament.

[1] See Art. 297(1) Treaty on the Functioning of the European Union ('TFEU'), under which legislative acts 'shall enter into force on the date specified in them or, in the absence thereof, on the twentieth day following that of their publication'.

[2] Framework Decision 2008/977/JHA.

The statement that the Regulation is binding in its entirety and directly applicable in all Member States appears after the last article of a regulation and before the closing formula setting out the place and date of adoption of the measure.

Select Bibliography

EU legislation

Framework Decision 2008/977/JHA: Council Framework Decision 2008/977/JHA of 27 November 2008 on the protection of personal data processed in the framework of police and judicial cooperation in criminal matters, OJ 2008 L 350/60.

Index

Note: *For the benefit of digital users, indexed terms that span two pages (e.g., 52–53) may, on occasion, appear on only one of those pages.*

academic, artistic and literary expression 478, 853–54
access, right of data subject
   additional information 460
   against whom right can be exercised 461–62
   algorithms and AI 462–63
   analysis 460–67
   archiving purposes in the public interest, scientific or historical research purposes or statistical purposes 1247, 1249–50
   automated individual decision-making, including profiling 449, 450, 453–54, 456, 462–63, 464–65, 523, 524
   available information as to source 449
   case law 451, 456–60
   categories of data 449
   closely related provisions 450
   compensation, right to and liability 1167
   components of access rights 462–67
   confirmation of processing 453, 460, 462, 464–65
   conformity issues 454
   consequences 450
   consistency mechanism 1001
   control 452–53
   copies 449
   Court of Justice of the European Union (CJEU) 457–58
   data portability 500, 504
   data protection by design and by default 576
   details about processing 462–63
   erasure ('right to be forgotten') 449, 452, 458
   EU legislation 453–54
   European Court of Human Rights (ECtHR) 458–59
   European Data Protection Board (EDPB) 1046–47
   exceptions 459–60
   fees, excessive 458
   health data 450
   improper purpose of request 459–60
   information provision where personal data collected from data subject 413, 418, 419–20, 428–29
   information provision where personal data not collected from data subject 434
   international instruments 455
   law enforcement 453–54
   legal background 453–60
   logic 450
   manifestly unfounded or excessive requests 466
   material scope 66–67
   meaningful information 449, 462–63
   modalities of access 465–67
   national courts 459–60
   national developments 455–56
   object, right to 449
   origin of data 455
   procedure 1093
   provision of access to data 464–65
   public information 452
   purposes of processing 449, 450
   rationale and policy underpinnings 451–53
   reasonable doubts about identity 460
   recipients 449, 450
   rectification 449, 452, 458, 471
   related Articles in EPD 450
   related Articles in EUDPR 451
   related Articles in LED 450
   relevant recitals 449–50
   restrictions 543–44, 546, 550–51
   subject access request (SAR) 459–60
   subject-matter and objectives 57
   time limits 450, 453, 465–66
   transfers on basis of adequacy decision 787–88
   video surveillance 467
   who can exercise access 460–61
   written form 453
   see also access to public documents; transparent information and access rights
access to public documents 1112, 1114–15
accountability
   access, right of data subject 460–61
   activity reports 951–52
   automated individual decision-making, including profiling 538
   certification 733, 734–35, 736
   codes of conduct 719, 720
   compensation, right to and liability 1176
   consent 352
   controller and processor 25–26
   data protection by design and by default 576
   data protection impact assessment (DPIA) 668–69, 671–72, 675
   data protection officer (DPO) designation 694, 696
   establishment rules of supervisory authority 899
   European Data Protection Board (EDPB) 1046–47, 1051
   fines 567
   information provision where personal data collected from data subject 431

Index

accountability *(cont.)*
  information provision where personal data not collected from data subject 440, 446–47
  joint controllership 566
  lawfulness of processing 338
  monitoring approved codes of conduct 727
  object, right to 513
  personal data breach notification to supervisory authority 641, 649–50
  personal data processing 309, 311, 312, 318–19
  position of data protection officer (DPO) 701
  prior consultation 682
  records of processing activities 618, 620
  reports 1086, 1087, 1088
  risk-based approach 26
  security of processing 631–32, 636
  supervisory authority role 8
  supervisory authority tasks 933–34, 936
  transfers: general principles 757
  see also responsibility of controller
accreditation
  monitoring approved codes of conduct 725, 729–30
  opinion of the Board 1005
  reports 1088
  tasks of the Board 1070
  tasks of supervisory authority 928
  see also certification
accreditation bodies 733
accuracy principle
  personal data processing 309, 311, 312, 317
  restriction of processing 485, 487, 489
activity reports
  accountability 950, 951–52
  analysis 951–52
  case law 949
  closely related provisions 949
  EU legislation 950
  infringements 951–52
  international instruments 950
  legal background 950
  national developments 950
  rationale and policy underpinnings 950
  related Articles in LED 949
ad hoc contract/contractual clauses 33, 38–39
additional safeguards 338, 546
adequacy decision *see* transfers on basis of adequacy decision
adequate safeguards *see* appropriate safeguards
administrative fines
  absorption principle 1189
  accountability 567
  action taken to mitigate damage 1180, 1181–82
  additional penalties 1188
  aggravating or mitigating factors 1180, 1181–82
  amount of fine payable 1180, 1190–91
  analysis 1187–91
  appeals 1184–85
  appropriate safeguards 1181–82

approved codes of conduct, adherence to 1180, 1181–82
archiving purposes in the public interest, scientific or historical research purposes or statistical purposes: safeguards and derogations 1250
basic principles for processing 1180
case law 1183, 1187
categories of data affected 1180
certification 736–37, 1180
children and consent 362, 1190
closely related provisions 1182
codes of conduct 718–19
communication of personal data breach to data subject 662
compliance with measures ordered against controller or processor 1180, 1181–82
consent 353, 1180
cooperation 954, 960, 961, 962, 1180, 1181, 1189
corrective powers 1187
criminal convictions and offences 390, 1182, 1184–85, 1188
data protection by design and by default 578, 579
data protection impact assessment (DPIA) 676
data subjects, representation of 1148–49
data subject rights 1181
degree of responsibility of controller or processor 1180, 1181–82, 1189
deprivation of profits 1182
derogation for fewer than 250 employees for record-keeping 1181
derogations for specific situations 855
disproportionate burden on natural person 1189
effective, proportionate and dissuasive 1181, 1182, 1183, 1187, 1188–89
as enforcement power for supervisory authorities 1187–88
Engel criteria 1184–85
enterprise 249
EU legislation 1185–86
fair trial, right to 1184–85, 1187, 1188–89
fine initiated by competent supervisory authority 1181
group of undertakings 254–55
identification, non-requirement of 397
income, general level of and economic situation 1182, 1189
individual persons 1187
infringement of duties of monitoring bodies to take appropriate action for non-compliance with code of conduct 1190
infringements of certification body 1190
infringements of obligations of controller and processors 1190
intentional or negligent character of infringement 1180, 1181–82, 1189
international instruments 1186
international organisations 307

Index

judicial remedy 1181–82, 1185, 1188
legal background 1185–87
legal certainty 1181
limitation on processing, temporary or definitive 1181, 1187, 1191
manner in which infringement became known to supervisory authority 1180, 1181–82
monitoring approved codes of conduct 730
monitoring body obligations 1180
national developments 1186
nature, gravity and duration of infringement 1180, 1181–82, 1189
ne bis idem 1187, 1188
neglect of general obligations 567–1190
non-compliance with an order or decision 1181, 1191
not correctly answering a controller 1191
obligations of controller and processor 1180, 1181
orders 1187
personal data breach notification to supervisory authority 650–51
position of data protection officer (DPO) 702, 707
powers of supervisory authority 939, 941, 943, 944, 945, 946–47
prevention or mitigation of consequences of infringement 1182
previous infringements, relevant 1180, 1181–82, 1189
procedural autonomy 1188
processing contrary to basic principles for lawful processing 1191
processor 604, 610
punishable infringements 1189–91
rationale and policy underpinnings 1184–85
related Articles in EPD 1183
related Articles in EUDPR 1183
related Articles in LED 1183
relevant recitals 1181–82
representative 239
representatives of controllers or processors not established in the Union 592, 597
reprimands for minor infringements 1181–82, 1187, 1189
responsibility of controller 567
right to be heard in court 1184–85
security of processing 636–37
severity of the (highest) punishment foreseen 1184–85
single economic entity 1187–88
special categories of personal data 382
supervisory authority, cooperation with 627–28
tasks of the European Data Protection Board (EDPB) 1069, 1077–78, 1079, 1080
tasks of supervisory authority 934
transfers: general principles 766
transfers on basis of adequacy decision 792
transfers subject to appropriate safeguards 809
transparency 1181

trilogue 7
undertakings 1182, 1187–88
unjustified denial of compliance and non-identification of data subject 1190
upper limit and criteria for setting fines 1182
violations of Member State law 1191
warnings 1182, 1187
whether and to what extent fines may be imposed 1181
administrative penalties 1194–96, 1197, 1198, 1199–201
see also administrative fines
advertising (online)
access, right of data subject 449
automated individual decision-making, including profiling 534–35
joint controllers 587
representatives of controllers or processors not established in the Union 595
territorial scope 91
transparent information and access rights 399
AI *see* **artificial intelligence (AI)**
Aland Islands 83
Albrecht Report 5, 6
Andorra 776
anonymisation
archiving purposes in the public interest, scientific or historical research purposes or statistical purposes 1244, 1246–47, 1250
codes of conduct 719
data protection by design and by default 575, 577
derogations for specific situations 851
identification, non-requirement of 395
lawfulness of processing 342–43
personal data 103, 105–6, 107
processing 121
pseudonymisation 132, 135–36
anti-competitive conduct 628
anti-money laundering
criminal convictions and offences 389–90
information provision where personal data not collected from data subject 440
lawfulness of processing 332
material scope 61
national identification number 1227
prior consultation 684
review of other Union legal acts on data protection 1315
APEC *see* **Asia-Pacific Economic Cooperation (APEC) Cross-Border Privacy Rules (CBPR); Asia-Pacific Economic Cooperation (APEC) Privacy Framework**
API *see* **Application Programme Interface (API)**
Appeal Committee 1282, 1284–86
appeals
administrative fines, general conditions for imposing 1184–85
certification bodies 751–52

appeals *(cont.)*
  complaint, right to lodge with supervisory authority 1119–20
  effective judicial remedy against controller or processor 1136
Application Programme Interface (API) 505
appropriate safeguards
  access, right of data subject 449, 462
  automated individual decision-making, including profiling 522, 539–40
  binding corporate rules (BCRs) 33, 257, 258–60, 815
  codes of conduct 717
  criminal convictions, offences and penalties 387, 389–90
  data protection by design and by default 576, 578
  data transfer to third countries or international organisations 33–34
  derogations for specific situations 35, 846
  information provision where personal data collected from data subject 414, 424, 428
  information provision where personal data not collected from data subject 435–36, 440
  lawfulness of processing 322
  national identification number 1224, 1226–27
  powers of supervisory authority 940–41, 943, 944, 947
  records of processing activities 616
  restrictions of processing 488, 543
  special categories of personal data 365, 367, 381–82
  third countries or international organisations 32
  transfers: general principles 764–65, 766
  transfers on basis of adequacy decision 774, 777, 785
  see also transfers subject to appropriate safeguards
approved codes of conduct
  administrative fines 1180, 1181–82
  controller or processor, processing under authority of 612
  data protection impact assessment (DPIA) 665–66, 671
  processor 600, 607–8
  responsibility of controller 556, 562
  security of processing 630, 636
  tasks of data protection officer (DPO) 709
  transfers subject to appropriate safeguards 797, 804, 806
  see also monitoring approved codes of conduct
aptitude tests 41
archiving purposes in the public interest, scientific or historical research purposes or statistical purposes
  access, right of data subject 456, 1247, 1249–50
  analysis 1244–50
  anonymisation 1244, 1246–47, 1250
  archiving in public interest 1247–48
  case law 1242, 1244

  clinical trials 1240–41, 1249
  closely related provisions 1242
  confidentiality 1241–42, 1249
  consent 1241, 1244–45, 1249
  data minimisation 1240–41, 1246–47
  data portability 497–98, 1240–41, 1247
  data protection by design and by default 578
  deceased persons 1241, 1247–48
  derogations for specific situations 842
  Directive 2002/58/EC 1300
  dissemination to public via publication 1248–49
  enforcement 1250
  erasure ('right to be forgotten') 475–76, 482, 1240–41, 1244, 1247
  EU legislation 1243
  genocide and crimes against humanity 1241, 1247–48
  health data and public health 1241, 1248–49
  human rights 1247–48
  information provision where personal data collected from data subject 414
  information provision where personal data not collected from data subject 435–36, 446–47
  information requirements 1240–41
  international instruments 1243–44
  lawfulness of processing 323–24, 328, 341–42, 343
  legal background 1243–44
  medical research 1244, 1247, 1248
  national developments 1244
  notification obligation regarding rectification, erasure or restriction of processing 493, 495
  object, right to 508, 519, 1247, 1249–50
  personal data 1241
  personal data processing 316–17, 318
  political behaviour under former totalitarian regimes 1241, 1247–48
  pseudonymisation 132–33, 136, 1240–41, 1246–47
  rationale and policy underpinnings 1242–43
  rectification 469–70, 1240–41, 1247, 1249–50
  registries 1241, 1248
  related Articles in LED 1242
  relevant recitals 1240–42
  research results enhancement 1241
  restriction of processing 485–86, 488, 1240–41, 1247, 1249–50
  restrictions 547
  safeguards and purposes of processing 1246–47
  scientific or historical research purposes 174, 853–54, 1248–49
  social science, social conditions and social services 1241
  special categories of personal data 365–66, 367, 376f, 379, 380–81, 1243, 1245
  specific data processing situations 40–41
  statistical purposes 1249–50
  technical and organisational measures 1240–41

Index

area of freedom, security and justice 48, 50, 869, 917, 1080
Argentina 776
armed conflicts 850, 852
Article 93 Committee (Comitology Committee) 1282, 1285, 1286
artificial intelligence (AI) 112, 416, 568
artistic and literary expression *see* journalistic purposes or for artistic and literary expression
Asia-Pacific Economic Cooperation (APEC) Cross-Border Privacy Rules (CBPR)
   Accountability Agent 558
   binding corporate rules (BCRs) 816
   compliance review 558
   dispute resolution and enforcement 558
   recognition/acceptance 558
   self-assessment of data privacy 558
Asia-Pacific Economic Cooperation (APEC) Privacy Framework
   accountability/responsibility of controller 558
   automated individual decision-making, including profiling 528
   binding corporate rules (BCRs) 260
   controller 147
   international cooperation 858–59, 860–61
   main establishment 228
   personal data 106
   processor 158
   profiling 129
   pseudonymisation 134
   representative 240
   third parties 171
auditing
   accountability/responsibility of controller 25, 562, 564
   binding corporate rules (BCRs) 813
   certification, 741
   joint operations of supervisory authorities 990
   monitoring approved codes of conduct 728, 729–30
   powers of supervisory authority 939, 946
   processor 599, 607–8
   tasks of data protection officer (DPO) 712–13
   transfers or disclosures not authorised by Union law 826
Australia
   accountability/responsibility of controller 560
   data protection impact assessment (DPIA) 668
   transfers: general principles 759–60
   transfers or disclosures not authorised by Union law 834
Austria
   access rights of data subject 453
   administrative fines 1185n15
   binding corporate rules (BCRs) 815
   communication of personal data breach to data subject 658
   compensation, right to and liability 1165

Directive 2002/58/EC 1300
   independence 877, 878, 1064–65
   national identification number 1225
   penalties 1200–1
   personal data breach notification to supervisory authority 644
   powers of supervisory authority 945, 947
   pseudonymisation 135
   supervisory authority 268–69, 867
   transfers: general principles 758
   transparent information and access rights 404
automated individual decision-making, including profiling
   analysis 530–40
   automatic refusal of online credit application 523
   banning decisional system 531–32
   Big Data 528n13
   binding corporate rules (BCRs) 539, 813
   case law 525–26, 529
   closely related provisions 525, 526–27
   conditions for application of the right 532–36
   conduct 527
   consent 24, 176–77, 349, 536, 537–38
   consequences 523
   data protection impact assessment (DPIA) 524–25, 531–32, 540, 674
   data subject rights 24
   decision has either legal effects or similarly significant effects 532, 534–36
   decision made based solely on automated processing 532–34
   economic or financial interest 523, 524, 534–35
   EU legislation 527–28
   ex post explanation 538
   health data 523
   hybrid approach 529
   information provision where personal data collected from data subject 413, 429–30
   information rights 524
   international instruments 528
   legal background 527–29
   legal effects 523, 539–40
   linkage factor 534–35
   location or movements 523
   logic involved 523
   mathematical or statistical procedures 524
   national developments 529
   nature of the right 530–32
   personal preferences or interests 523
   profiling 128
   qualifications in Article 22(2) 536–38
   qualifications in Article 22(3) 538
   rationale and policy underpinnings 526–27
   recipients 523
   regional, national or supranational level 524–25
   related Articles in EUDPR 525, 540
   related Articles in LED 525, 539–40
   relevant recitals 522–25

Index

automated individual decision-making, including profiling *(cont.)*
  reliability 523, 527
  restrictions 524
  review of other Union legal acts on data protection 1316
  scope of application 530
  significant effect 539–40
  special categories of personal data 382, 539–40
  statutory authority 536, 537
  suitable measures 536, 537, 538, 539
  take-it-or-leave-it situations 537
  targeted decision-making 529
  technical and organisational measures 524
  transfers on basis of adequacy decision 788–89
automated processing
  biometric data 208–9
  data portability 501, 502, 504
  filing system 138, 140–41
  independence 876
  lawfulness of processing 329
  profiling 127, 128–29, 130
  recipient 163–64
  security of processing 633
Azores 83, 786

B2B *see* **business-to-business (B2B)**
B2C *see* **business-to-consumer (B2C)**
balancing of interests tests 17
Bavaria 360, 705
BCRs *see* **binding corporate rules (BCRs)**
Belgium
  children's consent and information society services 361
  communication of personal data breach to data subject 658
  establishment rules of supervisory authority 898
  filing system 141
  joint operations of supervisory authorities 988–89
  national identification number 1225, 1227
  penalties 1196
  personal data breach notification to supervisory authority 644
  processor 603
  subject-matter and objectives 58
  supervisory authority 870
  supervisory authority members, general conditions for 886
BEREC *see* **Body of European Regulators for Electronic Communications (BEREC)**
Big Data 112, 568
Big Data Analytics 113–14
binding corporate rules (BCRs)
  accountability/responsibility of controller 557, 562, 565
  administrative or judicial redress 257
  analysis 261–63, 816–23
  annulment action 822
  applicant 821*f*
  approval process 821–22
  business partnership 262
  case law 258, 260–61, 814
  closely related provisions 258, 814
  codes of conduct 718
  Committee procedure 1278, 1281
  complaint, right to lodge 813
  compliance verification 813, 814, 817*f*
  conflicting legislation 817*f*
  controllers 814–15, 816
  cooperation between lead supervisory authority and other authorities concerned 961
  corrective actions 813
  data protection principles 817*f*
  data subject 257
  data transfers or set of transfers 813
  definition 101
  delegated acts and implementing acts 42
  derogations 815, 853
  duty to respect 817*f*
  economic activity, engaged in 820
  enforceable rights of data subjects 816
  enterprise 246, 247–48
  establishment 261
  EU legislation 259–60, 815–16
  format of information provided to data subject 813
  fulfilment of requirements 816
  general data protection principles 813
  group of undertakings 820
  individual rights 817*f*
  information exchange 1032
  international cooperation 860–61
  international instruments 260, 816
  joint economic activity 257, 258–59, 262
  legal background 259–61, 815–16
  legally binding nature 813, 816
  liability for breach 813
  monitoring approved codes of conduct 726
  national developments 260
  national transfer authorisations 821*f*
  notice 817*f*
  opinion of the European Data Protection Board (EDPB) 1005
  personnel training 814
  powers of supervisory authority 940, 947
  processors 607, 814–15, 816
  rationale and policy underpinnings 258–59, 814–15
  redress and compensation 813
  relevant recitals 257, 814
  remedies 817*f*, 822–23
  reporting and recording changes to rules 814
  security of processing 637
  structure and contact details of group of undertakings 813, 817*f*
  substantive requirements and scope 816–20

supervisory authorities 8, 257, 259, 814–15, 816, 821*f*, 821
tasks of the European Data Protection Board (EDPB) 1069, 1076, 1080
tasks of supervisory authority 928, 936
transfers: general principles 765
transfers on basis of adequacy decision 773
transfers or disclosures not authorised by Union law 831–33
transfers subject to appropriate safeguards 797–98, 799, 801, 804–5
United Kingdom Withdrawal Agreement and Brexit 822
biological material 107–8n15, 112
biometric data
 analysis 211–15
 Article 29 Working Party (WP29) guidance, relevance of 211–12
 authentication schemes 209
 automated individual decision-making, including profiling 524–25
 automation 208–9
 biometric reference measures 212–13
 case law 208, 211
 closely related provisions 207
 consent 176
 data protection impact assessment (DPIA) 30, 667
 definition and definitional overlap 101, 213
 DNA 211, 212–13
 EU legislation 210
 facial imaging 210
 false positives or false negatives 209
 fingerprinting (dactyloscopic) data 210, 211, 212
 function-creep 209
 genetic data 202–3, 213
 health data 213
 identification and authentication/verification distinction 207, 213–14
 international instruments 210
 legal background 210–11
 national developments 210
 personal data 112, 214–15
 rationale and policy underpinnings 208–9
 related Articles in EUDPR 208
 related Articles in LED 207–8
 relevant recitals 207
 security feature standards in passports and travel documents 210
 special categories of personal data 365, 366, 367, 369–70, 371–72, 374
 specific technical processing (definition) 212
 supervisory authority consultation 30
blocking
 erasure ('right to be forgotten') 493, 494
 identification, non-requirement of 394
 rectification 471, 493, 494
 restriction of processing 124–25, 487, 489, 493, 494

transfers or disclosures not authorised by Union law 827, 828
transparent information and access rights 399, 402
Board, *see* European Data Protection Board (EDPB)
Body of European Regulators for Electronic Communications (BEREC) 916, 997, 1007, 1046, 1057, 1059
breach *see* personal data breach
Budapest Convention on Cybercrime 828, 834–35
business-to-business (B2B) 91, 297
business-to-consumer (B2C) 91, 297

C-ITS *see* Cooperative Intelligent Transport Systems (C-ITS)
Cambridge Analytica scandal 373–74
Canada
 accountability/responsibility of controller 559–60
 codes of conduct 720
 data protection impact assessment (DPIA) 668
 Privacy Commissioner 1051
 transfers: general principles 759–60
 transfers on basis of adequacy decision 786
 see also European Union-Canada Passenger Name Record (PNR) agreement
Canary Islands 83, 786
CCTV 41, 91
CEDPO *see* Confederation of European Data Protection Organisations (CEDPO)
CEEDPA *see* Central Eastern European Data Protection Authorities (CEEDPA)
CEN *see* European Committee for Standardization (CEN)
censorship 480
central administration 225, 228–29, 230–31, 232, 234–35
Central Eastern European Data Protection Authorities (CEEDPA) 976
Centre for Information Policy Leadership (CIPL) 921, 933
certification
 access rights 400
 accountability/responsibility of controller 25–26, 555, 556, 562, 565, 566, 733, 734, 736
 actors and roles 739–40
 aims 736–37
 analysis 736–41
 appropriate safeguards 34
 auditors/assessors 741
 case law 736
 closely related provisions 733
 codes of conduct 717, 718
 Committee procedure 1278, 1281, 1288
 competitive advantage 733–34
 compliance 733, 736, 738–39
 concept 737–38
 conformity 733, 738
 consistency mechanism 38–39
 consumer choice facilitation 733–34

1330 Index

certification (*cont.*)
  controller or processor, processing under authority of 612
  corrective measures 736
  criteria 740–41
  data protection by design and by default 571, 577
  data protection officer (DPO) designation 695–96
  delegated acts 1268, 1269, 1270–71, 1272–73, 1275
  EU legislation 734–35
  evaluation report 741
  information exchange 1032
  issued to controller or processor 738
  language 739
  legal background 734–36
  monitoring approved codes of conduct 725–26
  national development 735–36
  oversight 733
  periodic reviews 739–40
  powers of supervisory authority 939, 940, 946–47
  privacy seals 735–36
  process 741
  processor 600, 605–6, 607–8
  rationale and policy underpinnings 733–34
  relevant recitals 732
  renewal 732, 739–40
  reports 1088
  scope 738–39
  security of processing 630, 636
  single-issue schemes 738–39
  subject-matter 738
  supervisory authorities, role of 8
  tasks of the European Data Protection Board (EDPB) 1070, 1075, 1078, 1080
  tasks of data protection officer (DPO) 709
  tasks of supervisory authority 927, 932, 935, 936
  transfers subject to appropriate safeguards 797, 804, 806, 807–8
  transparency 400, 732, 733–34, 735, 736, 741
  validity periods 735
  withdrawal 732, 735, 736, 739–40
  see also certification bodies; seals and marks
certification bodies
  accreditation 744, 745–46, 747, 749
  accreditation bodies 744, 748–49, 751
  accreditation certification 744, 750, 752
  accreditation models 747–49
  accreditation requirements 750–51
  adherence to criteria 750
  analysis 747–53
  applicant 747
  approval of criteria 748–49
  case law 747
  closely related provisions 745
  compliance 745
  conflicts of interest 744, 748–49, 750, 751
  conformity assessment 746, 747, 748–49, 752
  consumer choice 746
  EU legislation 746
  examination procedure 745
  expertise 744, 748, 750–51
  impartiality 750–51
  implementing and delegated acts 745, 752–53
  independence 744, 748–49, 750–51
  international instruments 746
  joint accreditation 752
  knowledge 750
  legal background 746–47
  legal effects 751–52
  legal, organisational and procedural requirements 750
  mutual recognition 750
  mutual trust and confidence 745–46, 750–51
  national developments 746–47
  non-discrimination 751
  periodic review 744, 748–49, 750
  quality of assessment 750
  rationale and policy underpinnings 745–46
  relevant recitals 745
  renewal 744
  revocation 745
  roles and tasks 749–50
  seals and marks 745–46, 752
  technical standards 752
  transparency 744, 745, 746, 748, 749, 750, 751
  withdrawal of certification 744, 750
CERTs *see* **Computer Emergency Response Teams (CERTs)**
Chair of the European Data Protection Board (EDPB)
  analysis 1096–97
  appointment, renewable 1095
  closely related provisions 1095
  confidentiality 1115
  deputy chairs 1096, 1115
  effective consistency 1096–97
  election procedure 1096
  end of term and dismissal 1096
  EU legislation 1095
  European Free Trade Area (EFTA) States 1095–96
  international instruments 1095–96
  legal background 1095–96
  rationale and policy underpinnings 1095
  related Articles in EUDPR 1095
  simple majority vote 1096
  status 1096–97
  term of office 1095
  Vice-Chairs 1095
  see also tasks of the Chair
charities 250, 255
Chief Information Security Officer (CISO) 672
children's consent and information society services
  age limit and verification 360–61
  analysis 359–62
  at a distance 359
  case law 356, 358–59
  closely related provisions 355

electronic means 359
element of chance 360
enforcement 362
erasure ('right to be forgotten') 481–82
EU legislation 356–57
individual request of recipient of services 359
international instruments 357–58
legal background 356–59
legal competence 359
national developments 358
offering directly to children 360
parental consent and responsibility 355, 358, 361–62
recreational or sporting nature of service 360
related Articles in EUDPR 355–56
related Articles in LED 355
relevant recitals 355
sliding scale approach 360
valid consent 358
vulnerable individuals 357, 358–59
children's personal data
  access, right of data subject 449, 461
  accountability/responsibility of controller 555
  administrative fines 1190
  automated individual decision-making, including profiling 522–23, 527, 534, 535–36
  consent 181, 348
  consent, *see also* consent and information society services
  data protection impact assessment (DPIA) 666, 674
  definitions 14
  free flow of personal data 57–58
  Industry, Research and Energy Committee (ITRE) 5
  information society service 294
  lawfulness of processing 321, 337, 338
  parental responsibility 355, 461
  profiling 128
  review of other Union legal acts on data protection 1316
  transparent information and access rights 398, 399, 407, 410–11
China 757
churches and religious associations
  analysis 1262–66
  case law 1257–58, 1261–62
  Catholic Church 1260–61, 1263–64, 1266
  closely related provisions 1257
  concepts 1262–63
  constitutional law 1258
  cultural, religious and linguistic diversity 1257
  derogations 1258–60, 1262–65
    consequences of 1265–66
  EU legislation 1259–60
  foreseeability criterion 1264
  freedom of thought, conscience and religion 1257, 1262

international instruments 1260
legal background 1259–62
national developments 1260–61
personal data protection 1257
philosophical and non-confessional organisations 1263
pre-existing comprehensive protection rules 1257, 1262, 1263–64
  continuation of 1265
  revision of 1262, 1264–65
privacy 1257, 1260–61
rationale and policy underpinnings 1258–59
relevant recitals 1257
specific data processing situations 40–41
supervision of independent supervisory authority 1257, 1265–66
supervisory authority 870
CIPL *see* Centre for Information Policy Leadership (CIPL)
CIRCABC *see* Communication and Information Resource Centre for Administrations, Businesses and Citizens (CIRCABC)
circumvention of the law, prevention against 757–58
CISO *see* Chief Information Security Officer (CISO)
CJEU *see* Court of Justice of the European Union (CJEU)
clear and plain language
  access, right of data subject 449, 453, 461, 463
  Albrecht Report 21
  communication of data breach to data subject 654
  consent 19, 174, 345, 350
  information provision where personal data collected from data subject 418, 419, 427
  information provision where personal data not collected from data subject 440
  notice obligations and privacy policies 22
  personal data processing 309–10, 314–15
  personal data transfer to third countries or international organisations 32
  rectification 469
  territorial scope 77, 81, 90
  transparent information and access rights 398, 399, 406–7, 410–11
clinical trials/medical research
  archiving purposes in the public interest, scientific or historical research purposes or statistical purposes 1240–41, 1244, 1247, 1248, 1249
  consent 182
  data portability 498
  information provision where personal data collected from data subject 419
  pseudonymisation 132–33, 135
  restriction of processing 485–86
cloud computing
  accountability/responsibility of controller 568
  certification 734–35, 739
  codes of conduct 721
  joint controllers 584, 587

cloud computing (*cont.*)
  processor 157–58, 608–10
  representatives of controllers or processors not established in the Union 593–94
  small and medium-sized enterprises (SMEs) 20
codes of conduct
  accountability/responsibility of controller 25–26, 555, 565
  analysis 721–23
  appropriate safeguards 34
  approval 722
  associations 716, 717–18
  binding corporate rules (BCRs) 259, 260
  binding and enforceable effect 721–22
  case law 720–21
  certification 733–34
  checks and balances 721, 722–23
  children's consent and information society services 361
  closely related provisions 718
  collection of personal data 722
  Committee procedure 1278, 1281
  communication of personal data breach to data subject 660
  compliance with controller obligations 722
  consistency mechanism 38–39, 717, 722
  controller and processor 31
  data protection by design and by default 577
  data subject rights 722
  delegated acts and implementing acts 42
  designation of data protection officer (DPO) 696
  draft code, amendment or extension 716
  drafting 722
  enterprise 246
  EU legislation 719–20
  expert knowledge, reliability and resources 717
  general validity 717, 721, 722, 723
  individual contract or standard contractual clauses 717, 718
  information exchange 1032
  information provided to public and data subjects 722
  international instruments 720
  legal background 719–21
  mitigation best practices 717
  national developments 720
  personal data breach notification to supervisory authority 647
  powers of supervisory authority 940, 947
  publicity measures 723
  purpose and content 721
  rationale and policy underpinnings 718–19
  registration and publication 717
  relevant recitals 717–18
  representation element 721–22
  risk identification and assessment 717
  small and medium-sized enterprises (SMEs) 716, 717–18, 721
  standard protection clauses 718
  status and target group 721–22
  subject-matter and governance 722
  target group expansion 721
  tasks of the Board 1070, 1078, 1080
  tasks of supervisory authority 927, 928, 935, 936
  transfers subject to appropriate safeguards 807
  voluntary adherence to codes 718–19
  see also approved codes of conduct
codes of ethics 898
collective agreements (employment) 1229, 1230
collective redress 1144, 1150
College of Commissioners 1286, 1287*f*
Colombia 559–60
Comitology Register 1283
Committee on Budgetary Control (CONT) 1046–47
Committee procedure
  adoption of implementing acts 1282–87, 1287*f*, 1288
  analysis 1281–89
  Appeal Committee 1282, 1284–86
  Article 93 Committee (Comitology Committee) 1282, 1285, 1286
  blocking minority 1284
  case law 1279, 1280
  certification mechanisms 1278, 1281, 1288
  closely related provisions 1278
  codes of conduct 1278, 1281
  College of Commissioners 1286, 1287*f*
  Comitology Register 1283
  Commission's use of implementing powers under GDPR 1288–89
  control mechanism 1279–80
  delegated act 1288
  delivery of opinion by Appeal Committee 1287*f*
  delivery of opinion by Article 93 Committee 1287*f*
  delivery of opinion by European Data Protection Board (EDPB) and/or European Data Protection Supervisor (EDPS) 1287*f*
  Directorate-General for Justice and Consumers (DG JUST) 1283
  draft—maintain, amend, repeal or withdraw 1283, 1284–85, 1286
  draft adoption 1285
  draft preparation of implementing act and review by Article 93 Committee 1283–85, 1287*f*
  entry into force 1286, 1287*f*
  essential procedural requirements 1280
  EU legislation 1280
  examination procedure 1278, 1282, 1285–86
  implementing acts 1279, 1280, 1287, 1288*f*
  implementing powers 1280, 1281–82
  information exchange 1278, 1281
  international transfer 1280
  legal background 1280
  negative opinion 1284–86
  no opinion/failure to adopt opinion 1285–86
  positive opinion 1284–86

publication in Official Journal 1286, 1287f
qualified majority 1284–85
rationale and policy underpinnings 1279
referral to Appeal Committee 1287f
related Articles in EPD 1279
related Articles in EUDPR 1279
related Articles in LED 1278
relevant recitals 1278
simple majority 1285
submission to Article 93 Committee and publication of draft 1287f
technical standards 1278, 1281, 1288
third countries and international organisations 1278, 1281, 1286
time limits 1285–86
urgency procedure 1286
voting 1284–85
common foreign and security policy 63–64, 70
Communication and Information Resource Centre for Administrations, Businesses and Citizens (CIRCABC) 1035, 1036, 1037
communications sector 1059
compensation
 binding corporate rules (BCRs) 257, 813
 criminal convictions and offences 390
 data subjects, representation of 1142, 1143, 1148–49
 Directive 2002/58/EC 1299
 effective judicial remedy against controller or processor 1133, 1135, 1139
 effective judicial remedy against supervisory authority 1126
 employment context 1231–32
 joint controllers 583
 processor 602, 605
 security of processing 636–37
 transfers subject to appropriate safeguards 797–98
 see also compensation, right to and liability
compensation, right to and liability
 analysis 1174–77
 anxiety and distress, damages for 1173
 case law 1161–62, 1170–74
 choice of where to bring action 1160
 civil, administrative or criminal nature of judicial or non-judicial sanctions 1167
 clear and cumulative rules 1175–76
 closely related provisions 1161
 Court of Justice of the European Union (CJEU) 1170–71
 court proceedings 1160
 deletion 1171
 direct effect 1163, 1168–69, 1175
 disclosure 1170, 1171
 erasure, rectification, completion or amendment of data 1168
 EU legislation 1164–67
 European Court of Human Rights (ECtHR) 1171–73

exemption from liability 1176
 fault, existence of 1176
 general liability clauses 1174–75
 health data 1170–72
 individual control 1164
 information, access, erasure and objection 1167
 insufficient legal means 1172–73
 international instruments 1167–68
 joined to same judicial proceedings 1160
 joint and several liability 1169, 1176–77
 judicial remedy 1163, 1164, 1165–66
 jurisdiction 1161, 1177
 legal background 1164–74
 liability, exemption from 1160, 1176
 moral damages 1174
 more than one controller or processor 1160
 national courts 1173–74
 national developments 1168–69
 non-contractual liability 1166–67, 1168–69, 1171–72, 1173, 1174–75, 1176
 preliminary ruling procedure 1170
 privacy 1165, 1167–68, 1172, 1173
 psychological or social terms 1165
 rationale and policy underpinnings 1162–64
 recourse proceedings 1160
 related Articles in EPD 1161, 1166
 related Articles in EUDPR 1166–67
 related Articles in LED 1161, 1165–66
 relevant recitals 1160–61
 same processing 1160
 strict liability 1176
 ubi jus, ibi remedium (where there is right, there is remedy) 1162–63
 unlawful processing of personal data 1174, 1176
competence
 case law 903, 905–6
 certification bodies 748, 750
 closely related provisions 903
 competence of supervisory authority 906–10
 consent 178
 courts and judicial capacity 902
 derogations 908
 establishment of controller 903–4, 906, 907
 EU legislation 904–5
 exclusive competence only in relation to public tasks 909
 international instruments 905
 investigations 902
 judicial activities and the court 904, 909–10
 legal background 904–6
 material scope 70
 national developments 905
 no rules for applicable law 908
 obligation/competence distinction 907–8
 private bodies 902, 904, 909
 public authorities 902, 904
 public awareness-raising 902
 public interest 902, 904, 909

Index

competence (*cont.*)
  rationale and policy underpinnings 903–4
  related Articles in LED 903
  relevant recitals 902
  territorial competence 906–7
  territorial scope 903–4
  territorial sovereignty 903–4
  see also competence of lead supervisory authority
competence of lead supervisory authority
  analysis 917–24
  binding decisions 914
  Brexit 861, 961, 983, 990, 999
  case law 915
  change to 920
  closely related provisions 914
  complaints-handling 913–14, 915
  compliance 914
  primus inter pares 917–18
  consistency mechanism 917, 922, 924
  contacts, exclusive 923–24
  cross-border processing 913
  data subjects substantially affected 913–14
  draft submission 913, 914
  effectiveness 915
  electronic communications 916
  establishment 918–19, 922
  EU legislation 915–16
  exclusive competence 917, 918
  identification of supervisory authority 919–21
  implementation of decision 914
  Internal Market Information System (IMI) 921, 962, 983
  international instruments 916
  joint decisions 914
  legal background 915–17
  main establishment 913–14, 920
  national developments 917
  one-stop-shop 914, 915, 917, 920–21
  procedural matters 923
  proximity of decision-making to citizen 915, 921
  rationale and policy underpinnings 915
  relevant and reasoned objection 913–14
  relevant recitals 913–14
  scope of application 918–19
  single interlocutor concept 913, 923–24
  subject-matter of local nature 921–23
competition authorities 842, 850
competition law
  administrative fines 1187–88
  consistency mechanism 997
  data portability 499–500, 502
  establishment rules of supervisory authority 899
  independence 1065–66
  penalties 1199
  supervisory authority, cooperation with 628
complaint, right to lodge with supervisory authority
  access, right of data subject 449, 451, 462
  analysis 1121–23

appeal, right of 1119–20
authority does not act on complaint 1117
binding corporate rules (BCRs) 813
case law 1118, 1121
certification bodies 744, 750
closely related provisions 1118
competence 902, 913–14, 915
complaint handling system 1119
complaint submission form 1117
cooperation between lead supervisory authority and other authorities concerned 953–54, 958–59, 962–63, 965, 966–68, 969
cross-border processing 279, 286
dispute resolution by the Board 1014–15, 1024
does not act where such action is necessary to protect rights of data subject 1128
effective judicial remedy 1117, 1119, 1135, 1136, 1138
EU legislation 1119–20
fair trial, right to 1119, 1120, 1121–22
identification, non-requirement of 397
information provision where personal data collected from data subject 413, 418, 429
information provision where personal data not collected from data subject 434
infringements 1117, 1119
intermediate information 1117
international cooperation 860
international instruments 1120
legal background 1119–21
minimum standard 1122–23
monitoring approved codes of conduct 725, 729–30
mutual assistance 978–79
national developments 1120
object, right to 511
obligations to provide information to complainant 1117, 1123
power to issue decisions and impose fines 1120
powers of supervisory authority 940–41, 945
procedural rules 1123
rationale and policy underpinnings 1118–19
rejection or dismissal of complaint 1117
related Articles in EPD 1118
related Articles in EUDPR 1118
related Articles in LED 1118
relevant and reasoned objection 288
relevant recitals 1117
representation of data subjects 1142, 1143, 1147, 1148
responsibility of controller 563
special categories of personal data 382
supervisory authority 863–64, 865–66
supervisory authority concerned 272–73, 278
task of hearing complaints 1121–22
tasks of the European Data Protection Board (EDPB) 1070–71, 1076, 1080
tasks of data protection officer (DPO) 714

Index

tasks of supervisory authority 927, 928–29, 933–34, 935–36
territorial competence to handle complaints 1122–23
transfers on basis of adequacy decision 786, 791
transfers subject to appropriate safeguards 809
transparent information and access rights 398
Computer Emergency Response Teams (CERTs) 323
Computer Security Incident Response Teams (CSIRTs) 323, 656–57
Confederation of European Data Protection Organisations (CEDPO)
  data protection officer (DPO) designation 691, 693, 694, 696, 697
  position of data protection officer (DPO) 702
  tasks of data protection officer (DPO) 712
Conference of Balkan Data Protection Authorities 976
confidentiality
  access, right of data subject 459, 460–61
  analysis 1113–16
  archiving purposes in the public interest, scientific or historical research purposes or statistical purposes 1241–42, 1249
  case law 1111, 1113
  certification bodies 751
  Chair 1115
  closely related provisions 1111
  consent 348
  consistency mechanism 1114
  controller or processor, processing under authority of 613–15
  cooperation 1113
  data breach notification 29
  data protection by design and by default 575–76, 577
  data protection officer (DPO) 31
  decision-making process undermined 1114
  deputy chairs 1115
  Directive 2002/58/EC 1295–96, 1297, 1299–300
  doctor/patient 1255
  establishment rules of supervisory authority 893, 896, 899
  EU legislation 1112–13
  European Data Protection Board (EDPB) discussions 1113–14
  health data 218, 221
  identification, non-requirement of 395–96
  information exchange 1034
  information provision where personal data collected from data subject 421
  information provision where personal data not collected from data subject 438
  international relations 1114
  lawyer/client 1255–56
  legal background 1112–13
  limitations to public access based on grounds of public or private interest 1115

mutual assistance 982
national identification number 1226
observers, external experts and guests 1114
openness 1113
penalties 1196
personal data breach notification to supervisory authority 640, 641, 645, 646
personal data processing 309–10, 311, 312, 318
position of data protection officer (DPO) 700, 704
private interest 1112
procedure 1092, 1093
processor 599, 607
public access to documents 1112, 1114–15
public interest 1112, 1114
rationale and policy underpinnings 1111–12
rectification 469
related Articles in EUDPR 1111
related Articles in LED 1111
restricted documents 1112
restrictions 546, 551–52, 553
secrecy obligations 1253–54
security of processing 630, 631–32, 636
special categories of personal data 373, 381–82
specific individuals 1114
transfers on basis of adequacy decision 788
transparency 1112, 1113
see also professional secrecy; secrecy
conflict rule 1219
conflicts of interest
  certification bodies 744, 748–49, 750, 751
  establishment rules of supervisory authority 898
  independence 1066
  representative 243–44
consent
  administrative fines 1180
  analysis 181–86, 349–53
  archiving purposes in the public interest, scientific or historical research purposes or statistical purposes 1241, 1244–45, 1249
  automated individual decision-making, including profiling 24, 176–77, 349, 522–23, 530–31, 536, 537–38
  autonomy 176
  being informed criterion 183–84
  bundled or tied consent 182–83, 352–53
  case law 176, 179–80, 346, 349
  children 19, 57–58
  children, *see also* children's consent and information society services
  churches and religious associations 1259
  closely related provisions 175, 345–46
  coercion 351–52
  data portability 22, 497
  data subject influence 176
  definition 101
  demonstrating consent 349–50
  derogations for specific situations 35, 176, 844, 845, 847–48

consent *(cont.)*
  Directive 95/46/EC repeal 1291, 1292
  Directive 2002/58/EC 1299
  DNA tests in criminal investigations 178
  electronic means 174, 178, 184–85
  electronic tagging and criminal penalties 178
  employer/employee power imbalance 182
  employment context 1229, 1230, 1235–36
  enforcement 353
  EU legislation 176–78, 347–48
  exceptional circumstances 182
  explicit consent 176, 179, 185–86, 348
    automated individual decision-making, including profiling 523, 537, 539
    biometric data 207
    derogations for specific situations 841, 842, 845, 847
    information provision where personal data collected from data subject 429
    special categories of personal data 365, 366, 371, 376f, 377
    transfers or disclosures not authorised by Union law 831–32
  express consent 347–48
  free services 350
  freely given consent 179, 181, 182–83, 345, 348, 351–52, 537, 845
  general interpretation 181
  genuine or free choice 351
  given as child but now wants removal 475–76, 481–82
  identification or authentication 176
  information provision where personal data collected from data subject 428–29
  information society service 292
  informed consent 174, 177, 181, 183, 345, 348, 352, 419, 439
  international instruments 178–79, 348
  lawfulness of processing 321, 322, 327, 329–34, 343
  legal background 176–80, 347–49
  minimum content requirements 183–84
  national developments 179, 349
  non-ambiguity criterion 184–86
  object, right to 351, 518
  obtaining consent 350
  opt-in 16, 18
  oral statement 174, 178, 184–85
  parental 19, 358, 361–62
  physically or legally incapable of giving 365, 377–78, 831–32, 841, 842, 852
  pre-ticked checkbox 180, 184–85
  presumed consent (passive consent) 177
  principles 18–19
  rationale and policy underpinnings 176–77, 347
  related Articles in EPD 175, 346
  related Articles in EUDPR 176, 346
  related Articles in LED 175, 346
  relevant recitals 174–75, 345

  restriction of processing 485, 490, 545
  special categories of personal data 382
  specific consent 179, 181, 183, 348, 352
  specific data processing situations 41
  supervisory authorities, role of 8
  third parties 179–80
  trans-border transfer of data 348
  transfers: general principles 765
  unambiguous consent 181, 347–48, 352, 847
  unsolicited communications 348
  valid consent 185, 351, 415
  valid contract formation 350
  withdrawal of consent 345, 347, 351
    automated individual decision-making, including profiling 538
    erasure ('right to be forgotten') 23, 475–76, 481
    information provision where personal data collected from data subject 413, 419, 429
    information provision where personal data not collected from data subject 434
    lawfulness of processing 339
    notice obligations and privacy policies 22
    object, right to 509, 511–12, 516, 517
    rectification 469–70
    special categories of personal data 379–80
    written declaration 350
consistency mechanism 37–39, 995, 996–97, 999
  administrative fines 1182, 1189
  analysis 998–1002
  annulment based on non-compliance 1000
  binding corporate rules (BCRs) 38–39, 813, 821
  case law 996, 998
  certification bodies 750
  closely related provisions 995
  Commission reports 1308, 1309–10
  competence 907, 917, 922, 924
  complaint, right to lodge with supervisory authority 1122
  confidentiality 1114
  conflict with DPA independence 1000–01
  controller or processor, processing under authority of 612
  cooperation 995, 996–97, 999
  cooperation with lead supervisory authority and other lead supervisory authorities concerned 953, 964–65, 966
  cross-border processing 284
  data protection impact assessment (DPIA) 665, 676
  dispute resolution 996–97, 1000, 1001, 1015, 1016–17, 1018, 1019, 1021–22
  effective judicial remedy against supervisory authority 1125, 1130–31
  EU legislation 997
  European Data Protection Board (EDPB) 39, 1042, 1044, 1045
  freedom of expression and information 1001, 1202–3
  general application, matters of 38

independence 1057, 1060, 1062, 1063, 1064–66
information exchange 1032–33, 1039
infringement proceedings 1000
international instruments 998
joint operations 992, 995, 999
legal background 997–98
limited scope 1001
monitoring approved codes of conduct 729
mutual assistance 981
national developments 998
one-stop-shop mechanism 996–97, 999, 1000
opinion of the European Data Protection Board (EDPB) 1006, 1007, 1008–09, 1010, 1011–12
penalties 1194
powers of supervisory authority 941, 942–43, 947
procedure 1091–92, 1093
processor 600
rationale and policy underpinnings 996–97
related Articles in EPD 996
related Articles in LED 996
relevant recitals 995
reports 1088
review of other Union legal acts on data protection 1317
risk of lowering standards to accommodate consistency 1001–02
risks and downsides 1000–02
role and scope 998–99
Secretariat 1103
supervisory authority 273–74, 863, 866, 869–71
tasks of the European Data Protection Board (EDPB) 1070, 1071, 1074, 1076, 1077–79, 1080, 1081
tasks of the Chair 1098, 1099
tasks of supervisory authority 930–31, 937
transfers subject to appropriate safeguards 797, 801
triggering of mechanism and European Data Protection Board (EDPB)'s role and powers 999–1000
urgency procedure 996–97, 1028, 1029
consumer protection law 402–3, 1150
CONT *see* **Committee on Budgetary Control (CONT)**
contracts and standard contractual clauses
ad hoc contract/contractual clauses 33, 38–39
adequacy 33
appropriate safeguards 33
automated individual decision-making, including profiling 536
binding corporate rules (BCRs) 257, 815
codes of conduct 716
Committee procedure 1278, 1281
communication of personal data breach to data subject 660
consistency mechanism 38–39
controller or processor, processing under authority of 612, 613, 614
cooperation between lead supervisory authority and other authorities concerned 961

derogations for specific situations 842, 845
information exchange 1032
monitoring approved codes of conduct 726
personal data breach notification to supervisory authority 647
powers of supervisory authority 940, 947
processor 599, 600, 601–3, 605–6, 608–9
security of processing 632, 633, 634, 635
termination of contract 331
transfers: general principles 763, 765
transfers or disclosures not authorised by Union law 831–33
transfers subject to appropriate safeguards 797–98, 799–800, 801–2, 804–6
see also performance of contract
controller
analysis 148–55
automated data 146–47
binding corporate rules (BCRs) 814–15, 816
case law 105, 117, 139, 145
closely related provisions 145
co-controllers *see* joint controllers
cross-border processing 279, 280, 281–82, 283
data subject as controller 154
definition 100
definition in LED and EUDPR 154–55
dependent users 147
derogations for specific situations 846
enterprise 246, 248
EU legislation 146
general approach 148–50
individual natural/physical person acting alone 149
international instruments 146–47
joint controllership 151–53
legal background 148
legal competence 146–47
legally separate from processor 159
liability 153
licensing authorities 147
main establishment 225–26, 227, 228, 229, 230, 232–34
multiple controllers 147, 149–50
national developments 148
processor, relationship between 146–47
purposes and means, determination of 150–51
rationale and policy underpinnings 146
recipient 163–64, 165, 166–67
related Articles in EUDPR 145
related Articles in LED 145
representative 238, 239–41, 242–44
responsibility/control 148
supervisory authority 265, 272–74, 275–76
third parties 170
see also controller, processing under authority of; controller and processor; effective judicial remedy against controller or processor; joint controllers; responsibility of controller

Index

controller, processing under authority of
  analysis 614–15
  case law 613, 614
  categories of data subjects 612
  closely related provisions 612
  contract and standard contractual clauses 612, 613, 614
  EU legislation 613
  international instruments 613–14
  legal background 613–14
  national developments 614
  nature and purposes of processing 612
  rationale and policy underpinnings 613
  related Articles in EPD 612
  related Articles in LED 612
  relevant recitals 612
  return or deletion of data 612
  subject-matter and duration of processing 612
  type of personal data 612
controller and processor 25–32
  certification, seals and marks 31–32
  codes of conduct 31
  data breach notification 29
  data protection by design and default 26
  data protection impact assessment (DPIA) and consultation of supervisory authority 29–30
  data protection officers (DPOs) 30–31
  joint controllers 27
  not established in the Union 88–91
  processing and sub-processing 27–28
  records of processing activities 28
  risk-based approach 26
  security of processing 28
  territorial scope 81–82, 83
  see also controller and processor, processing under authority of
cookies 13, 14, 91, 103, 127, 129, 180
cooperation 37–39
  administrative fines 1180, 1181, 1189
  binding corporate rules (BCRs) 814
  Commission reports 1308, 1309–10
  competence 907, 909, 913–14, 922
  complaint, right to lodge with supervisory authority 1122
  confidentiality 1113
  consistency mechanism 37–39, 995, 996–97, 999
  dispute resolution by the European Data Protection Board (EDPB) 1015, 1016–17, 1018
  European Data Protection Board (EDPB) 39, 1041, 1043, 1044–45
  independence 873, 1055, 1062–63
  independent supervisory authorities 36
  information exchange 1032–34, 1035, 1036, 1037, 1039
  international agreements concerning third countries or international organisations 1302, 1306
  joint operations of supervisory authorities 986–87, 988, 989, 990–91, 992, 993

  opinion of the European Data Protection Board (EDPB) 1006, 1007, 1010
  powers of supervisory authority 942–43, 945, 946, 947
  representatives of controllers or processors not established in the Union 596
  Secretariat 1103, 1108
  supervisory authority 863, 864, 865, 867, 869, 870, 871
  tasks of supervisory authority 927, 928, 930–31, 932–33, 937
  transfers on basis of adequacy decision 772
  urgency procedure 1027, 1028, 1029
  see also cooperation between lead supervisory authority and other authorities concerned; cooperation with supervisory authority; international cooperation; mutual assistance; judicial cooperation in criminal matters and police cooperation
cooperation between lead supervisory authority and other authorities concerned
  additional safeguards 965–66
  administrative fines and sanctions 954–60, 961, 962
  adoption and notification of decision of establishment 953
  advisory measures 961
  agreement with draft decision 953
  amicable settlement 954
  analysis 960–70
  appeal against decision 966–67
  authorisation measures 961
  ban on processing 961
  bilateral agreements 958
  case law 955, 958–59
  closely related provisions 954–55
  co-decision making process 960
  communication of relevant information 953
  complaint, dismissal or rejection of 953–54, 966–67, 969
  complaint upheld 969
  complaints-handling 958–59, 962–63, 965, 967–68
  compliance with decision 954
  consensus 953
  cooperation 954, 969–70
  corrective measures 961–62, 967, 968–69
  draft decision 953, 964
  electronic means using standardised format 963
  EU legislation 956–57
  exchange of all relevant information 953
  final adoption of a decision 965, 966–67
  interim measures 969
  international instruments 957–58
  joint enforcement operations 960, 963
  legal background 956–59
  legal obligations 954
  legally binding decisions 961
  main establishment 959–61, 968–69
  minimum safeguard 965–66

Index

mutual assistance 953, 957, 960, 963
national developments 958
offer of goods or services 954
one-stop-shop mechanism 956–57, 960, 961, 962, 967, 969
  decision-making process 958, 962–67
  notification and enforcement of decision adopted in accordance with 967–69
penalties 958–59
rationale and policy underpinnings 956
referral to the European Data Protection Board (EDPB) 964–66
related Articles in EPD 969, 970
related Articles in EUDPR 955, 969, 970
related Articles in LED 955, 969–70
relevant and reasoned objection 953, 964
relevant recitals 954
revised draft decision 953, 964
specific processing 954
subject-matter and scope of application 960–62
summary of relevant facts and grounds 953
supervision and proximity balance 956
supply of information required 954
urgency procedure 954, 969

cooperation with supervisory authority
analysis 627–28
case law 625–26, 627
closely related provisions 625
cooperation obligation, infringement of 627
EU legislation 626–27
fines, conditions for imposing 625
international instruments 627
legal background 626–27
national developments 627
powers 625
rationale and policy underpinnings 626
related Articles in EUDPR 625
related Articles in LED 625
relevant recitals 625
self-incrimination, right against 628
tasks 625

Cooperative Intelligent Transport Systems (C-ITS) 393
coordinated supervision bodies 1060
copyright protecting software
access, right of data subject 450, 464
automated individual decision-making, including profiling 523
recipient 163–64
transparent information and access rights 399–400, 407

Coreper *see* **Permanent Representatives Committee ('Coreper')**
corporate veil 111
Council of Europe (CoE) Consultative Committee on Protection of Personal Data 976, 989
Council of Europe (CoE) Recommendation on the Protection of Medical Data 200, 203

Council of Europe (CoE) Strategy of the Rights of the Child 357
Council of the European Union
first reading (Common Position) 6
first reading procedure 6
General Approach 6, 7
second reading procedure 6
Court of Auditors 1046–47
Court of Justice of the European Union (CJEU)
access, right of data subject 457–58
compensation, right of 1170–71
competence 904–5
dispute resolution by the European Data Protection Board (EDPB) 1015
effective judicial remedy against supervisory authority 1126, 1130–31
employment context 1232–33
erasure ('right to be forgotten') 9
EU-US Safe Harbour framework 9
European Union-United States Privacy Shield 791
freedom of expression and information 1206–9
independence 1061
information provision where personal data collected from data subject 422–24
legislative procedure 8–10
online identifiers/tracking 8
public access to official documents 1219–20
third countries and international organisations 9
transparency 404–5
court, right to be heard in 1023, 1025, 1184–85
see also fair trial, right to
courts and judicial authorities, data processing by 70–71
covert investigations or video surveillance 418–19, 425
credit applications (online) 534
credit scoring agencies 389–90
creditworthiness 331, 527, 535
criminal convictions and offences
access, right of data subject 453–54
accountability/responsibility of controller 555
administrative fines 1182, 1184–85, 1188
analysis 388–90
automated individual decision-making, including profiling 524–25
business screening of prospective employees 389–90
case law 386, 388
certain rights and obligations 389–90
closely related provisions 386
competence 909–10
data portability 497–98
data protection impact assessment (DPIA) 30, 665, 667, 673, 674
data protection officer (DPO) designation 688–89
early disclosure hampering law enforcement 659, 662
enforcement 390

criminal convictions and offences (*cont.*)
  EU legislation 387
  forensic laboratories 389–90
  genetic data 201
  information provision where personal data not collected from data subject 440, 443
  international instruments 387
  law enforcement 11–12
  lawfulness of processing 321, 322, 328
  legal background 387–88
  legal classification of offence 388
  legitimate interest 17–18
  material scope 60, 61, 65–66, 70
  national developments 387–88
  nature and degree of severity of penalty 388
  nature of offence 388
  penalties 1197, 1200–1
  personal data breach notification to supervisory authority 188, 650
  personal data processing 316, 317
  principles of processing personal data 386–87
  rationale and policy underpinnings 386–87
  records of processing activities 616, 623
  related Articles in EPD 386
  related Articles in LED 386–87
  relevant recitals 385
  restrictions 543–44, 548–50
  scope 388–89
  special categories of personal data 371, 375
  stigmatisation and ability to find employment 388
  supervisory authority consultation 30
  transfers on basis of adequacy decision 777–78
criminal justice cooperation 1303
criminal law 33
  administrative fines 1188
  churches and religious associations 1261
  material scope 64, 65–66
  transfers on basis of adequacy decision 772
CRM *see* **customer relationship management (CRM)**
cross-border processing
  analysis 281–86
  case law 280, 281
  closely related provisions 279
  controller 279, 280, 281–82, 283
  data subjects 279
  establishment 267–83
  establishment in more than one EU country 281–82
  EU legislation 281
  inextricable link 283, 285
  international instruments 281
  legal background 281
  main establishment 279
  one-stop-shop mechanism 280, 281, 285–86
  processor 279, 280, 281–82, 283
  proximity 280–81
  rationale and policy underpinnings 280–81
  relevant recitals 279
  single establishment 279, 281–82, 285–86
  stable arrangement 282–83
  substantially affects or is likely to substantially affect data subjects 279, 280, 282, 284–85, 286
  supervisory authority and lead supervisory authority 279, 280–81, 285–86
  taking place within context of establishments in multiple EU countries 285–86
CSIRTs *see* **Computer Security Incident Response Teams (CSIRTs)**
cultural, religious and linguistic diversity 48, 57
customer relationship management (CRM) 341–42
Cybersecurity Act 579, 643, 657
Cybersecurity Strategy (2013) 734–35
Cyprus 6–7

DAPIX *see* **European Union Council Working Party on Information Exchange and Data Protection (DAPIX)**
data breach *see* **personal data breach**
data controller *see* **controller**
data minimisation *see* **minimisation of data**
data portability *see* **portability of data**
data processing *see* **processing**
data processing agreement 86, 608–9
data processing service bureaux 147
data processor *see* **processor**
data protection authorities (DPAs) *see* **supervisory authorities**
data protection by design and by default
  accreditation and seal programmes 574–75
  actors 578
  amount of personal data collected 571
  analysis 576–79
  automated periodic reminders 577
  basic thrust 576
  best practices 574–75
  case law 572, 575–76
  certification 738–39
  closely related provisions 571–72
  codes of conduct 722
  contextual factors 576
  controller and processor 26
  Cybersecurity Act 579
  differentiation between by design and by default requirements 577
  electronic communications service 574
  employment context 1237–38
  EU legislation 573–74
  extent of processing 571
  homogeneity clause 576
  identification, non-requirement of 394
  internal policies 571
  international instruments 574–75
  international standardisation initiatives 574–75
  legal background 573–76
  measures, types of 577
  monitoring 571

Index 1341

national developments 575
processor 603
pseudonymisation 136, 571, 575, 577, 578–79
public procurement tenders 578
qualifications 576
radio equipment 574
rationale and policy underpinnings 573
regulatory guidance 574–75
related Articles in EPD 572
related Articles in EUDPR 572, 579
related Articles in LED 572, 579
relevant recitals 571
research and development (R&D) 574–75
responsibility of controller 565, 568
responsibility, degree of 578
review of other Union legal acts on data protection 1316
role of Article 25 with respect to other GDPR provisions 578–79
sanctions 579
state of the art 571
technical and organisational measures 574–76, 578
transfers subject to appropriate safeguards 803
Data Protection Coordinator or Contact Person 690–91
data protection impact assessment (DPIA)
access, right of data subject 463
accountability 26
analysis 671–77
automated individual decision-making, including profiling 524–25, 531–32, 540, 674
case law 668, 671
certification 733, 738
children 666, 674
closely related provisions 667
codes of conduct 718
commercial or public interests 672
common application or processing environment 667
consistency mechanism 38–39
content 677
controller and processor 29–30
criminal convictions and offences 388, 665, 673, 674
data portability 500
data protection by design and by default 576
designation of data protection officer (DPO) 693
dispute resolution by the Board 1022
draft lists 676–77
duration or permanence of data 674
early warning systems 668–69
employment context 1237
EU legislation 669–70
evaluation of personal aspects including profiling 665, 673
evaluation or scoring 673
exclusion or discrimination 673
exclusion list 676
exemptions 675

geographical extent of processing activity 674
high risk cases 673–74
inclusion list 676
information provision where personal data not collected from data subject 446–47
international instruments 670
large-scale processing 667, 674
legal background 669–71
list requirements for supervisory authorities 676
matching or combining datasets 674
measures envisaged to address risks 665
mitigating measures, safeguards and mechanisms 667
monitoring of publicly accessible area 665
national developments 670, 1009
nature, scope, context and purpose of processing 667, 669, 677
new technologies or organisational solutions 674
notification 670
number of subjects 674
obligations under LED 677
opinion of the Board 1011
origin, nature, particularity and severity of risk 666
personal data 667
personal data breach notification to supervisory authority 641–42
physical, material and non-material damage 666
prevention of data subjects from exercising right to use service or contract 674
prior checking 669, 670
prior consultation 676, 680–81, 682–84, 685
processor 603, 607
profiling 524–25, 531–32, 540, 665, 667, 673–74
publicly accessible area on a large scale 673
rationale and policy underpinnings 668–69
reassessment 675
records of processing activities 624
related Articles in EPD 668
related Articles in EUDPR 668
related Articles in LED 667
relevant recitals 666–67
representatives of controllers or processors not established in the Union 595
residual risk 676
responsibility of controller 564, 565, 566, 568
review 675
review of other Union legal acts on data protection 1316
risk assessment 672, 673
risk-based approach 26
roles 671–73
sanctions 677
scope of application 671
security of processing 631–32, 636
sources of risk 667
special categories of personal data 382, 665, 673
supervisory authority 665, 666–67, 669, 671–72, 676

data protection impact assessment (DPIA) *(cont.)*
   systematic description of envisaged processing operations 665
   systematic monitoring 674
   tasks of the European Data Protection Board (EDPB) 1076
   tasks of supervisory authority 935
   technology assessments 668
   timing 675
   volume of data 674

data protection notice 415, 519

data protection officer (DPO)
   accountability/responsibility of controller 25, 26, 556, 562–63, 565, 566
   appointment 1093
   binding corporate rules (BCRs) 813
   controller and processor 30–31
   criminal convictions and offences 388
   data protection impact assessment (DPIA) 30, 665, 676, 677
   group of undertakings 254
   independence 30
   personal data breach notification to supervisory authority 650
   prior consultation 682–83
   records of processing activities 618, 620
   representative 243–44
   representatives of controllers or processors not established in the Union 594–95
   review of other Union legal acts on data protection 1316
   special categories of personal data 382
   supervisory authorities, role of 8
   supervisory authority consultation 30
   territorial scope 86, 95–96
   trilogue 7
   see also data protection officer (DPO) Network; designation of data protection officer (DPO); position of data protection officer (DPO); tasks of data protection officer (DPO)

Data Protection Officer (DPO) Network 703–4, 705

data subject rights 20–25
   automated decision-making, including profiling 24
   binding corporate rules (BCRs) 257
   certification 738
   controller, data subject as 154
   cross-border processing 279
   data portability 22
   erasure ('right to be forgotten') 22–23
   joint controllers 587
   lawfulness of processing 321, 322, 338
   notice obligations and privacy policies 21–22
   notification obligation regarding rectification, erasure or restriction of processing 496
   object, right to 23–24
   personal data 13, 106–7
   processing not requiring identification 21
   recipient 163–64, 166–67
   representative 239, 241, 243, 244
   restrictions 24–25
   supervisory authority 265, 272–73, 275, 276–77
   territorial scope 88–89
   third parties 170
   see also access, right of data subject; data subjects, representation of; rectification

data subjects, representation of *see* representation of data subjects

Data Transfer Agreement 605–6

data transfers *see* derogations for data transfers; transfers of data

deceased persons 103, 107, 112, 1241, 1247–48

dedicated addresses or phone numbers 90

defamation 85

definitions 13–16
   child 14
   main establishment 14–15
   personal data 13–14
   principles 16–20
   'producer' of data filing system 15
   pseudonymous data and anonymous data 15–16

delegated acts 41–43
   ad hoc meetings 1272
   adoption and notification to Parliament and Council 1268, 1274*f*
   analysis 1270–75
   appropriate consultations during preparatory work 1268
   case law 1269, 1270
   certification mechanisms 1268, 1269, 1270–71, 1272–73, 1275
   closely related provisions 1268
   Commission's use of power to adopt acts under GDPR 1275
   consultations with experts 1274*f*
   democratic legitimacy 1269
   drafting 1272, 1274*f*
   empowerments, number of 1270–71
   EU legislation 1270
   external experts 1272, 1273, 1275
   legal background 1270
   objections 1271, 1273
   power conferred on Commission 1268
   power conferred for indeterminate period of time 1268
   preparation and adoption of 1272–73
   procedure 1271, 1272–73
   publication in Official Journal and entry into force 1268, 1273, 1274*f*
   quasi-legislative powers 1269, 1270, 1271
   rationale and policy underpinnings 1269
   register of delegated acts 1272, 1273
   related Articles in EUDPR 1269
   relevant recitals 1268
   revocation by Parliament or Council 1268, 1271–72

Index

scrutiny by Parliament and Council 1273, 1274f
standardised icons 1268, 1269, 1270–71, 1272–73
under GDPR 1270–72
veto powers 1273
deletion of data
  codes of conduct 717
  data protection by design and by default 577
  identification, non-requirement of 395
  monitoring approved codes of conduct 726
  processor 599, 600, 607
  specific data processing situations 41
  see also erasure ('right to be forgotten')
democracy principle 950, 1087
denial of service attacks 323
Denmark
  administrative fines 1182
  archiving purposes in the public interest, scientific or historical research purposes or statistical purposes: safeguards and derogation 1244
  contractual clauses 606
  cooperation between lead supervisory authority and other authorities concerned 968
  data portability 499
  deceased persons 112
  enterprise 249n7
  GDPR Proposal 6–7
  joint operations of supervisory authorities 989
  penalties 1194, 1198
  transfers on basis of adequacy decision 786
derogations
  binding corporate rules (BCRs) 257
  biometric data 207
  consent 176
  criminal convictions and offences 389–90
  lawfulness of processing 340
  for less than 250 employees 616, 617–18, 623–24
  personal data transfer to third countries or international organisations 32
  special categories of personal data 366–67
  transfers: general principles 766
  transparent information and access rights 403
  see also derogations for data transfers
derogations for data transfers
  access by foreign authorities 831–32
  analysis 846–55
  assessment by data controller 853
  case law 843, 846
  closely related provisions 843
  conclusion or performance of contract conclusion in interest of data subject 841, 844, 849
  consent 35, 176, 844, 847–48
    explicit 841, 842, 845, 847
    freely given 845
    physical or legal incapability of giving 841, 842, 852
    specific 845
    unambiguous 847
  controllers 846

data subjects, duty to inform 853
data subjects, limited number of 853
data transfer must not be repetitive 853
domestic law 845
enforcement 855
EU legislation 844
international instruments 845
legal background 844–46
legal claims, establishment, exercise or defence of 831–32, 841, 842, 844, 851
legitimate interests of controller 831–32, 841, 842, 845, 853–54
national developments 846
necessity test 848, 851, 853
performance of contract between data subject and controller 841, 844, 848
pre-trial discovery procedures 851
precontractual measures taken at data subject's request 841, 848
processors 846
public interest, important reasons of 831–32, 841–42, 843–44, 845, 846, 849–51,
public interest, limitation of transfers based on 854–55
public register, transfers made from 841, 844, 852–53
rationale and policy underpinnings 843–44
related Articles in LED 843
relevant recitals 842–43
specific interests 845
supervisory authority, duty to inform 853
third countries or international organisations 35, 841, 842, 844, 846, 847, 848, 849–50, 851, 854–55
transfers on basis of adequacy decision 773, 774, 781
vital interests 831–32, 841, 842, 844, 850, 852
designation of data protection officer (DPO)
analysis 692–98
appointment 689–90
assistant data protection officer (DPO) 690–91
case law 689, 691–92
closely related provisions 689
communication skills 694
contact details 697
deontology 696
duration or permanence of activity 693
easy accessibility from each establishment 692
ethical codes 696
EU legislation 690–91
exclusion of judicial authorities 692
experience/maturity 696
expertise and legal knowledge 688, 692, 696
external data protection officer (DPO) 696
failure to notify 691
geographical extent of activity 693
greenwashing strategy 694–95
integrity or ethics 696

designation of data protection officer (DPO) (cont.)
  internal data protection officer (DPO) 696
  international instruments 691
  interpersonal skills 696
  language requirement/translations 694
  legal background 690–92
  location and visibility of data protection
      officer 697
  mandatory designation 692–94
    for public authorities excluding judicial
        authorities 692
    and special categories of data or criminal
        conviction and offences data 693–94
    and systematic monitoring on large-scale 693
  maximum term 690
  minimum term 690
  multiple appointments 690–91
  multiple cross-border notification 698
  national developments 691
  notification to lead supervisory authority under
      one-stop-shop 697–98
  number of data subjects 693
  professional and personal qualities and relevant
      expertise 688, 689–90, 692, 695–96
  publication of contact details 688
  rationale and policy underpinnings 689–90
  reappointment 690
  registration 690
  related Articles in EUDPR 689
  related Articles in LED 689
  relevant recitals 688–89
  self-establishment of informal network 691
  systematic monitoring on large-scale 688–89, 693
  undertakings and several public authorities 694
  volume of data and/or range of specific
      items 693
  voluntary data protection officer (DPO) 694–95
  see also data protection officer (DPO)
DG JUST see Directorate General for Justice (DG
    JUST) interservice draft (2011)
DG MARKT see Directorate General of the
    Commission for the Internal Market (DG
    MARKT) First Report (2003)
Digital Agenda for Europe 734–35, 998
Digital Single Market Strategy for Europe
    (2015) 499
diplomatic mission or consular post 92–93, 94
direct effect 1163, 1168–69, 1175
direct marketing
  automated individual decision-making, including
      profiling 522–23
  consent, conditions for 351
  erasure ('right to be forgotten') 481–82
  lawfulness of processing 337
  marketing 351
  object, right to 508, 509, 510–12, 516–17,
      518, 519
  transfers on basis of adequacy decision 788–89

Directive 95/46/EC
  delegated acts and implementing acts 42
  information provision where personal data collected
      from data subject 417
  see also Directive 95/46/EC repeal
Directive 95/46/EC repeal
  adequacy decisions 1292
  analysis 1292
  authorisations 1292
  closely related provisions 1291
  consent 1291, 1292
  rationale and policy underpinnings 1291–92
  related Articles in EPD 1291
  related Articles in LED 1291
  relevant recitals 1291
Directive 2002/58/EC (ePrivacy Directive)
  access limited to authorised personnel for legally
      authorised purposes 1298
  analysis 1297–300
  case law 1294–95, 1296–97
  closely related provisions 1294
  confidentiality 1295–96, 1297, 1299–300
  cookies 13, 14, 91, 103, 127, 129, 180
  data breach notifications 1298, 1299
  electronic communications sector 1296–97
  EPD 1295, 1296–300
  EPR proposal 1299–300
  EU legislation 1296
  grounds for processing 1298
  implementation of security policy with respect to
      processing 1298
  legal background 1296–97
  lex specialis 1297–98
  machine-to-machine communications 1299
  national developments 1296
  Over-the-Top Communications Services
      (OTTs) 1299
  permitted processing 1300
  privacy, fundamental right of 1296, 1297, 1299
  protection against accidental or unlawful
      destruction, accidental loss or alteration 1298
  protection of end-users' terminal equipment 1300
  publicly available electronic communications
      services in public communication
      networks 1294, 1295
  purposes of processing 1298
  rationale and policy underpinnings 1295–96
  related Articles in EPD 1294
  relevant recitals 1294
  remedies 1299
  restrictions 549–50
  statistical or scientific research purposes 1300
  Voice over IP, messaging services and web-based
      email services 1299
Directorate General of the Commission for the
    Internal Market (DG MARKT) First Report
    (2003) 3
disaster recovery plan 636

Index

disclosure
- access, right of data subject 452, 457, 460–61
- compensation, right to and liability 1170, 1171
- controller or processor, processing under authority of 613, 615
- establishment rules of supervisory authority 899
- filing system 138
- genetic data 198
- health data 218
- information provision where personal data collected from data subject 414
- information provision where personal data not collected from data subject 434, 435–36, 437–38, 440, 444, 445, 447
- international cooperation 857
- lawfulness of processing 321, 322, 323, 335
- notification obligation regarding rectification, erasure or restriction of processing 492, 494
- personal data breach notification 189, 192, 193, 650
- processor 602, 605
- public access to official documents 1213, 1216, 1217
- recipient 163, 165, 167
- records of processing activities 620, 621
- security of processing 631
- *see also* transfers or disclosures not authorised by Union law

discrimination
- automated individual decision-making, including profiling 524, 526, 534–35, 539–40
- communication of personal data breach to data subject 659
- criminal convictions and offences 388
- data breach notification 29
- genetic data 198, 199–200
- health data 218
- information provision where personal data collected from data subject 429–30
- lawfulness of processing 328
- responsibility of controller 555, 565
- special categories of personal data 369–70
- subject-matter and objectives 50–51, 57

dispute resolution
- codes of conduct 722
- competence of lead supervisory authority 918
- consistency mechanism 996–97, 1000, 1001
- opinion of the Board 1006, 1011
- procedure 1091
- reports 1088
- Secretariat 1102
- supervisory authority 274, 871
- tasks of the European Data Protection Board (EDPB) 1071, 1074, 1078
- *see also* dispute resolution by the European Data Protection Board (EDPB)

dispute resolution by the European Data Protection Board (EDPB)
- analysis 1019–25
- annulment action 1015
- binding decision 1016–17
- case law 1016, 1018
- closely related provisions 1016
- competence 1014, 1017, 1019
- complaints, dismissal or rejection of 1015, 1024
- complaints-handling 1014–15
- consensus 1016–17
- consistency mechanism 1015, 1016–17, 1018, 1019, 1021–22
- cooperation 1015, 1016–17, 1018
- corrective measures or actions 1020
- Court of Justice of the European Union (CJEU) 1015
- decision, adoption of without undue delay 1014–15
- decision, overruling of 1017
- decision publication on European Data Protection Board (EDPB) website 1023
- decision-making 1017
- effectiveness 1016–17
- efficiency 1016–17
- EU legislation 1018
- European Data Protection Board (EDPB) decision and lead supervisory authority decision, interaction between 1017–18, 1023–24
- exceptional cases 1017
- infringement 1014
- internal workings of European Data Protection Board (EDPB) 1022–23
- international instruments 1018
- investigative, corrective and authorisation powers 1015
- judicial remedies 1015
- judicial review mechanisms 1024–25
- last resort 1016
- lead supervisory authority, identification of 1017
- legal background 1018
- legal certainty 1017
- legally binding decisions 1015
- limitation in scope 1019
- merits of the case 1015
- national developments 1018
- notification without undue delay 1014, 1023
- one-stop-shop mechanism 1016–17, 1019, 1020
- opinion issued 1015
- overall thrust of Article 1019
- procedural provisions 1017
- rationale and policy underpinnings 1016–18
- relevant and reasoned objection 1014, 1017, 1019, 1020, 1022–23
- relevant recitals 1015
- supervisory authority 1014
  - competence 1020–12
  - does not request European Data Protection Board (EDPB) opinion or does not follow opinion 1014
  - independence 1022
  - powers 1024

dispute resolution by the European Data Protection Board (EDPB) (*cont.*)
   suspension of parallel proceedings 1024
   unsatisfactory outcome 1016
   validity/invalidity 1015, 1025
distance consumer agreement 402
DNA testing 178, 211, 212–13
DPIA *see* **data protection impact assessment (DPIA)**
DPO *see* **data protection officer (DPO)**
due diligence
   competence 907
   complaint, right to lodge with supervisory authority 1121
   effective judicial remedy against supervisory authority 1128
   mutual assistance 978–79
   supervisory authority 867
   tasks of supervisory authority 932, 933, 936
due process 940, 1181–82, 1188, 1255–56

e-evidence package 828
e-recruiting practices 523, 534
ECN *see* **European Competition Network (ECN)**
ECtHR *see* **European Court of Human Rights (ECtHR)**
EDPB *see* **European Data Protection Board (EDPB)**
EDPS *see* **European Data Protection Supervisor (EDPS)**
effective judicial remedy
   administrative fines 1181–82, 1185, 1188
   churches and religious associations 1257
   complaint, right to lodge with supervisory authority 1117, 1119
   Court of Justice of the European Union (CJEU) 1138–39
   data subjects, representation of 1142, 1143–44, 1147, 1148, 1150
   identification, non-requirement of 397
   secrecy obligations 1255–56
   special categories of personal data 382
   subject-matter and objectives 48, 53, 57
   transparent information and access rights 398
   see also effective judicial remedy against controller or processor; effective judicial remedy against supervisory authority
effective judicial remedy against controller or processor
   analysis 1138–40
   appeals 1136
   case law 1134, 1137–38
   closely related provisions 1133
   compensation 1133, 1135, 1139
   complaint, right to lodge 1135, 1136, 1138
   corrective powers 1135
   effective judicial remedy 1138–39
   effectiveness criteria 1135, 1136
   EU legislation 1136–37
   international instruments 1137
   jurisdiction/territorial aspects 1133, 1137, 1139–40

   legal background 1136–38
   legally binding decisions 1136–37
   lex specialis 1137
   national developments 1137
   ombudsman-like role 1136
   personality rights, violation of 1139
   prior exhaustion of administrative remedies 1137–38
   procedural autonomy 1135, 1136
   procedural and organisational law 1138–39
   proceedings against supervisory authority and proceedings against controller or processor, distinction between 1139–40
   rationale and policy underpinnings 1134–36
   related Articles in EPD 1133
   related Articles in EUDPR 1134
   related Articles in LED 1133
   relationship to recast Brussels I Regulation 1140
   relevant recitals 1133
   same subject-matter 1140
effective judicial remedy against supervisory authority
   analysis 1129–32
   annulment action 1125–26, 1131–32
   appeals 1128, 1130
   authority does not inform complainant about progress 1130
   case law 1127, 1129
   closely related provisions 1126
   complaint submission form 1125
   Court of Justice of the European Union (CJEU) 1126, 1130–31
   decision challenged before national court 1126
   does not act on or handle a complaint 1125, 1128
   does not inform data subject 1125
   EU legislation 1128
   fair trial, right to 1127
   fines, issuing 1127
   hearing complaints 1127
   inaction of supervisory authority 1125, 1130
   informing data subject of progress and outcome of complaint 1125
   intermediate information 1125
   international instruments 1128
   investigative, corrective and authorisation powers 1125–26, 1129–30
   judicial review 1130
   jurisdiction 1125–26, 1128, 1130
   legal background 1128–29
   lodge a complaint, right to 1125
   national developments 1129
   opinion or decision forwarded to relevant court 1125
   preliminary ruling procedure 1126, 1130–31
   proceedings brought before court where supervisory authority is established 1125
   rationale and policy underpinnings 1127–28
   rejection or dismissal of complaint 1125–26, 1129–30

related Articles in EPD 1126
related Articles in EUDPR 1127
related Articles in LED 1126
relevant recitals 1125–26
validity of decision 1126, 1130–31
effects doctrine 93–94
EFTA *see* European Free Trade Association (EFTA) States
electoral activities and voter data 367, 379
electronic communications sector 402–3, 656–57, 1296–97
electronic patient dossiers 854–55
electronic tagging and criminal penalties 178
EMA *see* European Medicines Agency (EMA)
EMPL *see* Employment and Social Affairs Committee (EMPL)
employment context of data processing
   analysis 1234–38
   appropriate legal grounds for data processing 1235–36
   case law 1229–30, 1232–34
   closely related provisions 1229
   collective agreements 1229, 1230
   compensation for data breaches 1231–32
   competence of lead supervisory authority 914
   consent 353, 1229, 1230, 1235–36
   consistency mechanism 1001
   contracts 332
   Court of Justice of the European Union (CJEU) 1232–33
   documenting employee data processing 1231–32
   employee information for social insurance purposes 332, 365, 367, 369, 377
   employment relationship 330
   EU legislation 1230
   European Court of Human Rights (ECtHR) 1233–34
   general notice of monitoring measures 1237
   globalisation of employment and services 1231
   human dignity, protection of 1229
   information and communication technology 1231
   international instruments 1231
   legal background 1230–34
   legitimate interest 1236, 1237
   management, planning and organisation of work, equality and diversity, health and safety at work, protection of customer's property and termination of employment 1229
   medical data 1233
   minimum standards 1234–35
   monitoring and accessing personal files and personal emails 1231, 1233
   national developments 1231–32
   notification of adopted specific rules to Commission 1235
   privacy, fundamental right of 1230, 1231, 1232, 1233–34, 1236
   property rights of employer 1234

   rationale and policy underpinnings 1230
   recruitment and performance of employment contract including discharge of obligations 1229
   relevant recitals 1229
   salaries, information on 1232
   sensitive data 1230, 1233, 1235
   specific data processing situations 40–41
   transparency 1229, 1230, 1232, 1234, 1237
   video surveillance, secret 1231–32, 1233–34, 1236, 1237
   working times records 1232
   works agreements 1229
Employment and Social Affairs Committee (EMPL) 5
encryption
   data breach notification 29, 646–47, 654, 659–60, 661
   data protection by design and by default 578
   derogations for specific situations 853
   identification, non-requirement of 395–96
   lawfulness of processing 322, 342–43
   notice obligations and privacy policies 22
   processor 607
   purpose limitation 17
   security of processing 630, 636
   special categories of personal data 371, 381–82
   see also anonymisation; pseudonymisation
energy sector 1059
ENISA *see* European Union Agency for Network and Information Security (ENISA)
ENN-Net *see* European Consumer Centres Network (ECC-Net)
enterprise
   analysis 249–52
   binding corporate rules (BCRs) 246, 247–48
   case law 247, 249
   closely related provisions 246–47
   controllers 246, 248
   definition 101
   economic activity/economic unit 250
   EU legislation 248–49
   joint economic activity 246, 247–48
   legal background 248, 249
   private sector *see* private sector
   processors 246, 248
   public authorities *see* public authorities
   rationale and policy underpinnings 247–48
   relevant recitals 246
   SMEs *see* small and medium-sized enterprises (SMES)
   structure and organisation 250
   supervisory authorities 246
   temporal criterion 250–51
   undertakings *see* group of undertakings
entry into force and application
   analysis 1320–21
   closely related provisions 1320
   related Articles in EPD 1320
   related Articles in LED 1320

environmental data 403, 668, 1214
EPO *see* European Patent Office (EPO)
EPPO *see* European Public Prosecutor's Office (EPPO)
ePrivacy *see* Directive 2002/58/EC (ePrivacy Directive)
equality and diversity 230n18, 241n12, 1229, 1264
erasure ('right to be forgotten')
  active memory of internet, removal from 479
  analysis 479–83
  archiving purposes in the public interest, scientific or historical research purposes or statistical purposes 1240–41, 1244, 1247
  automated individual decision-making, including profiling 524
  blocking 477
  burden of proof following objection 481–82
  case law 476–75, 478–79
  closely related provisions 476
  compensation, right to and liability 1167, 1168
  consent given as child but now wants removal 475–76, 481–82
  consent withdrawal 475–76, 481
  Court of Justice of the European Union (CJEU) 9
  data no longer necessary 475–76, 481
  economic interest 480
  EU legislation 477
  exemptions 482–83
  free of charge and without undue delay 478
  freedom of expression and information 475–76, 477, 478, 479, 480, 481, 482
  freedom of the press 478–80
  grounds for exercising right 481–82
  identification, non-requirement of 394
  implementation and territorial scope of right 481
  impossibility or disproportionate effort exception 477
  information provision where personal data collected from data subject 413, 418, 419, 428–29
  information provision where personal data not collected from data subject 434
  information society services, collection in relation to offer of 475
  international instruments 478
  journalistic purposes 478
  legal background 477–79
  legal claims, establishment, exercise or defence of 475–76, 477
  legal obligation, compliance with 475–76, 482
  national developments 478
  non-compliance 475–76
  notification 483
  object, right to 475–76, 481–82, 511, 512–13, 515, 516–17, 518
  personal data are public 475
  powers of supervisory authority 939
  processor 603
  pseudonymisation 132–33
  public domain, removal from 482–83
  public impact of publication 479
  rationale and policy underpinnings 477
  rectification 469–70, 471, 473, 477–78
  related Articles in EPD 476
  related Articles in LED 476
  relevant recitals 475–76
  restriction of processing 485–87, 488–89, 543–44, 546, 550–51, 553
  tasks of the European Data Protection Board (EDPB) 1076, 1077–78
  transfers on basis of adequacy decision 788
  transparent information and access rights 399, 402
  video surveillance 482
  see also notification obligation regarding rectification, erasure or restriction of processing
essential equivalence 774–75, 777, 781, 782, 1134–35
establishment
  binding corporate rules (BCRs) 261
  competence of lead supervisory authority 918–19, 922
  cross-border processing 267–83, 285–86
  relevant and reasoned objection 288
  representative 241–42
  tasks of the European Data Protection Board (EDPB) 1070–71
  see also establishment rules of supervisory authority; main establishment
establishment rules of supervisory authority
  analysis 896–900
  appointment, rules and procedures for 897
  case law 894, 896
  closely related provisions 894
  confidentiality 893, 896, 899
  enforcement procedures 899
  EU legislation 895
  incompatibilities 895, 897
  independence 893–94, 895–97, 898–99
  influence, direct or indirect 898
  integrity 893–94, 897–99
  international instruments 895–96
  legal background 895–96
  minimum period of appointment 897
  more than one supervisory authority 893
  national developments 896
  obligations for national legislator 893, 897
  prior compliance 897
  professional secrecy for members and staff 893, 895, 897, 899–900
  protection of individual's rights 899
  qualifications and eligibility conditions 893, 897
  rationale and policy underpinnings 895
  related Articles in EPD 894
  related Articles in EUDPR 894
  related Articles in LED 894
  relevant recitals 893–94

revolving door situations 898
rules and procedures 893
staff chosen by supervisory authority 893–94
term of office and reappointment 893, 895–96, 897
Estonia
administrative fines 1182
data protection impact assessment (DPIA) 676
penalties 1194, 1196, 1198
ethical codes 898
ethical standards 568
ethics breaches in regulated professions 497–98, 524, 543–44
ethnicity *see* special categories of personal data
Eurojust
European Data Protection Board (EDPB) 1048–49
independence 1057, 1061–62
Joint Supervisory Body 904–5
material scope 71
penalties 1200
tasks of the European Data Protection Board (EDPB) 1080–81
Europe 2020 998
European Commission (Commission)
Action Plan implementing Stockholm Programme 998
'Comprehensive Approach on Personal Data Protection in the European Union, A' communication 1042
GDPR proposal 3–4
representative 244
see also European Commission (Commission) reports
European Commission (Commission) reports
adequacy decisions 1309–10
analysis 1309–10
binding decisions 1310
case law 1308
closely related provisions 1308
evaluations and reviews 1310
findings of Parliament and Council 1308
guidelines, recommendations and best practices 1310
legal background 1309
periodic review 1310
Publication Service 1309
rationale and policy underpinnings 1309
related Articles in EPD 949
related Articles in LED 1308
submission of amendments 1308
submission to Parliament and Council 1308, 1309–10
European Committee for Standardization (CEN) 602–3
European Competition Network (ECN) 997
European Conference of Data Protection Authorities ('Spring Conference') 976, 989, 1035

European Consumer Centres Network (ECC-Net) 1150
European Court of Human Rights (ECtHR)
access, right of data subject 459
compensation, right to 1171–73
employment context 1233–34
freedom of expression and information 1209–10
information provision where personal data collected from data subject 424–25
public access to official documents 1217–19
transparency and access rights 405–6
European Data Protection Board (EDPB)
accountability 1046–47, 1051
adjudication 1044
administrative behaviour 1044
analysis 1044–52
authorisation 1044
budgetary and administrative activity 1046–47
case law 1042, 1044
chair 1041, 1047
closely related provisions 1041
collegiality and inclusiveness 1044
consistency mechanism 39, 1042, 1044, 1045
cooperation 39, 1041, 1043, 1044–45
decision-making powers 1047
decisions appealed to General Court 1046–47
efficiency and modernisation 1044
EU legislation 1043
European Commission 1041, 1049–50
European Data Protection Supervisor (EDPS) 1041, 1048–49
European Free Trade Association (EFTA) supervisory authorities 1049
Europeanisation 1045
governance 1044–45
head of supervisory authority 1041
independence 876, 1041, 1044, 1047, 1051
international instruments 1043–44
interpretation 1044
joint representatives 1041, 1047–48
legal background 1043–44
legal nature 1046
legal personality 1041, 1045–47
national supervisory authorities 1047–48
nature, characteristics and powers 1044, 1047
observers, external experts, guests or other external parties 1050–52
prerogatives 1045
presentation 1044
proactivity 1044
rationale and policy underpinnings 1042–43
related Articles in EUDPR 1042
related Articles in LED 1041
relevant recitals 1041
replacement of Article 29 Working Party (WP29) 1045
Secretariat 1109
social responsiveness 1046–47

European Data Protection Board (EDPB) (*cont.*)
  supervisory authority 8, 1041
  transparency 1042, 1044
  see also opinion of the European Data Protection Board (EDPB); tasks of the European Data Protection Board (EDPB)
European Data Protection Seal 732, 740, 749, 807–8
European Data Protection Supervisor (EDPS) 1041, 1048–49
  confidentiality 1113
  European Data Protection Board (EDPB) 1041, 1048–49
  independence 1055, 1057
  Parliament 5
  tasks of the European Data Protection Board (EDPB) 1071
  trilogue 7
European Economic Area (EEA) Joint Committee 778, 801, 803
European Electronic Communications Market Authority 1046
European Free Trade Association (EFTA) States
  competence of lead supervisory authority 916
  European Data Protection Board (EDPB) 1043–44, 1048
  information provision where personal data collected from data subject 421
  information provision where personal data not collected from data subject 439–40
  procedure 1091
  transfers on basis of adequacy decision 778
  transfers subject to appropriate safeguards 800–1, 803
European Free Trade Association Surveillance Authority (ESA)
  activity reports 950
  consistency mechanism 998
  dispute resolution by the European Data Protection Board (EDPB) 1017, 1018
  European Data Protection Board (EDPB) 1043–44, 1049, 1050
  independence 1058, 1064
  opinion of the European Data Protection Board (EDPB) 1007–09
  reports 1087
  Secretariat 1104
  tasks of the European Data Protection Board (EDPB) 1073–74, 1076
  transfers on basis of adequacy decision 778
  transfers subject to appropriate safeguards 800–1
European Medicines Agency (EMA) 289
European Network of Competition Authorities 916
European Ombudsman 898, 1046–47, 1216, 1219
European Parliament 5–6, 1046–47
European Patent Office (EPO) 307n31
European Public Prosecutor's Office (EPPO) 71, 1049

European Union Agency for Fundamental Rights (FRA) 314, 875, 886, 1137, 1143–44, 1165, 1195–96
European Union Agency for Network and Information Security (ENISA) 579, 643, 649, 657
European Union Council Working Party on Information Exchange and Data Protection (DAPIX) 6–7, 1035
European Union-Canada Passenger Name Record (PNR) agreement 372, 423–24, 548, 553, 775–76, 782–84
European Union-United States Privacy Shield
  challenge before Court of Justice of the European Union (CJEU) 791
  Committee procedure 1280
  complaint, right to lodge with supervisory authority 1120
  transfers on basis of adequacy decision 786, 790, 791
  transfers or disclosures not authorised by Union law 832–33, 834
European Union-United States Safe Harbour framework
  adequacy 33
  Committee procedure 1280
  Court of Justice of the European Union (CJEU) 9
  rectification 473
  responsibility of controller 566
  transfers: general principles 763
  transfers on basis of adequacy decision 775–76, 779, 780–81, 782
  transfers or disclosures not authorised by Union law 829
European Union-United States Umbrella Agreement 403, 759–60, 777–78, 832–33
Europeanisation 867, 869, 1045
Europol
  European Data Protection Board (EDPB) 1048–49
  genetic data 199
  health data 219
  independence 1057
  international organisations 306–7
  material scope 71
Europol Cooperation Board 1057, 1060, 1080–81
EuroPriSe privacy seal 734, 737
evaluation report 43
examination procedure
  binding corporate rules (BCRs) 814, 817*f*
  certification bodies 745
  codes of conduct 717, 718
  Committee procedure 1278, 1281n10, 1282, 1285–86
  delegated acts and implementing acts 42
  information exchange 1032
  monitoring of approved codes of conduct 726
  mutual assistance 973

object, right to 514
processor 600
transfers on basis of adequacy decision 771–72, 784–85, 789
transfers subject to appropriate safeguards 797, 800–2, 804–5, 808
exceptional circumstances
  cooperation between lead supervisory authority and other authorities concerned 954
  legitimate interest 17
  mutual assistance 973
  urgency procedure 1027, 1028, 1030
exceptions and restrictions clause 65
executive federalism 865, 895, 903, 915
exemptions *see* **derogations**

face recognition 674
Facebook 424, 585–86, 988–89, 1186
fair trial, right to
  administrative fines 1184–85, 1187, 1188–89
  churches and religious associations 1257
  complaint, right to lodge with supervisory authority 1119, 1120, 1121–22
  effective judicial remedy against supervisory authority 1127, 1129
  freedom of expression and information 1202
  secrecy obligations 1255–56
  subject-matter and objectives 48, 53, 57
  supervisory authority, cooperation with 628
  transparent information and access rights 405
fairness and transparency
  automated individual decision-making, including profiling 523, 524, 534, 538
  codes of conduct 722
  compatibility 326–27
  information provision where personal data collected from data subject 413, 414, 415–16, 418–19, 420–24, 427–28
  information provision where personal data not collected from data subject 434, 435, 436–37, 438–39, 440–41, 442, 443, 444, 445–46, 447
  personal data processing 309–10, 311, 312, 313, 314–15
  records of processing activities 621
  tasks of supervisory authority 928–29
  transfers on basis of adequacy decision 788
  see also transparency
Faroe Islands 776
Federation of European Direct and Interactive Marketing (FEDMA) Community Code of Conduct on direct marketing 719
filing system
  alphabetical, geographical or chronological criteria 143
  analysis 142–43
  automated processing 138, 140–41
  case law 139, 142

  closely related provisions 138
  definition 100
  employment records 143
  EU legislation 140
  international instruments 140–41
  lawfulness of processing 329
  legal background 140–42
  manual processing 138, 140–41, 142, 143
  national developments 141–42
  producer 15
  rationale and policy underpinnings 139–40
  recipient 163, 165
  related Articles in EUDPR 139
  related Articles in LED 138
  relevant recitals 138
financial loss 29, 555
financial markets supervision 899, 916
financial messaging data 759–60
financial services sector 670, 786
financial supervisory authorities 842, 850
fines 36, 40
  see also administrative fines
fingerprinting (dactyloscopic) data 210, 211, 212, 372, 674
Finland
  compensation, right to and liability 1165
  filing system 141–42
  joint operations of supervisory authorities 989
  processor 158
forensic laboratories 61, 389–90
forum shopping 921, 930–31, 943, 1197
fragmentation 141–42, 603–4, 943, 996, 999, 1080, 1081, 1317
Framework Service Agreement 605–6
France
  access, right of data subject 456, 462–63
  accountability/responsibility of controller 560
  administrative fines 1186
  automated individual decision-making, including profiling 529, 529n18
  certification 735–36, 746–47
  controller or processor, processing under authority of 614–15
  data portability 499
  data protection impact assessment (DPIA) 670
  designation of data protection officer (DPO) 691, 696
  draft lists 676–77
  enterprise 249
  establishment rules of supervisory authority 898
  genetic data 201
  independence 877
  information provision where personal data collected from data subject 416
  information provision where personal data not collected from data subject 437
  joint controllers 584
  joint operations of supervisory authorities 988–89

France *(cont.)*
  object, right to 510
  personal data breach communication to data subject 658
  personal data breach notification to supervisory authority 644
  powers of supervisory authority 945
  processor 158
  recipient 166, 167
  rectification 472
  special categories of personal data 376–77
  subject-matter and objectives 52, 58
  supervisory authority 866
  supervisory authority members, general conditions for 886, 888
  tasks of data protection officer (DPO) 710–11
  transfers on basis of adequacy decision 786
  transfers or disclosures not authorised by Union law 826, 829
fraud
  automated individual decision-making, including profiling 523
  data breach notification 29
  data portability 505
  lawfulness of processing 323, 337
  legitimate interest 17–18
  personal data breach 189
  responsibility of controller 555, 565
  third parties 170
  see also identity theft
Free Flow of Non-Personal Data Regulation 112, 759
free movement of personal data
  data protection impact assessment (DPIA) 671
  subject-matter and objectives 48, 49, 52–53, 54–55, 56, 57–58
  supervisory authority 868
  tasks of supervisory authority 932
freedom of establishment 230
freedom of expression and information
  access, right of data subject 456
  analysis 1206–11
  audio-visual field and news archives and press libraries 1202–3
  case law 1203, 1205
  churches and religious associations 1257
  closely related provisions 1203
  content, form and consequences of publication 1209
  controller and processor 1202
  Court of Justice of the European Union (CJEU) 1206–9
  cultural, religious and linguistic diversity 1202
  data protection impact assessment (DPIA) 671
  data subject rights 1202–3
  derogations for specific situations 845
  disclosure of information, opinion or ideas to the public 1206–7

  effective remedy, right to 1202
  erasure ('right to be forgotten') 22–23, 475–76, 477, 478, 479, 480, 481, 482
  EU legislation 1204
  European Court of Human Rights (ECtHR) 1209–10
  exemptions or derogations 1202–3, 1204–5, 1207, 1210–11
  general principles 1202–3
  independent supervisory authorities 1202–3
  international instruments 1205
  journalistic, academic, artistic and/or literary expression 1202–3, 1204, 1206, 1207, 1208, 1209, 1210
  legal background 1204–5
  method of obtaining information and its veracity 1209
  national developments 1205
  notification to Commission 1202, 1210–11
  notoriety of person affected 1209
  object, right to 516
  personal data protection 1202–3
  principles 1202
  prior conduct 1209
  privacy, fundamental right of 1202, 1204, 1205, 1208, 1209–10
  public access to official documents 1216–18, 1220
  rationale and policy underpinnings 1204
  rectification 469–70
  relevant recitals 1202–3
  rights and freedoms of others 1205
  specific processing situations 1202–3
  standard set of criteria 1209
  subject of news report 1209
  subject-matter and objectives 48, 50–51, 52, 57
  transparent information and access rights 405
freedom from being monitored 57
freedom of the press 478–80, 1205, 1207–8
freedom of thought, conscience and religion 48, 57, 68–69, 1202, 1257, 1262
freedom to conduct a business 48, 57, 337, 1202, 1257
French Guiana 83, 786

GDPR Interservice Draft 4, 827
general provisions 11–16
  definitions 13–16
  material scope 11–12
  territorial scope 12–13
genetic data
  analysis 201–3
  biological kin 203
  biometric data 202–3, 213
  case law 197, 201
  cellular samples and fingerprints 201
  closely related provisions 196
  Clustered Regularly Interspaced Short Palindromic Repeats (CRISPR) 198

criminal conviction 201
definition 101, 201, 203
direct-to-consumer testing 197
disclosure 198
discrimination and stigma 198, 199–200
DNA analysis 196, 197, 198, 199, 201, 202–3
EU legislation 199
exceptional cases 202
genetic counselling 199–200
health data 202–3, 217, 219, 220–21, 222
international instruments 199–200
legal background 199–201
national developments 200
personal data 103, 108, 112
privacy, fundamental right of 201
rationale and policy underpinnings 197–99
related Articles in EUDPR 196–97
related Articles in LED 196
relevant recitals 196
responsibility of controller 555
RNA analysis 196, 198, 199
special categories of personal data 19–20, 365, 366, 367, 369–70, 371–72, 374
specific data processing situations 41
genocide and crimes against humanity 1241, 1247–48
geo-localisation activities 91
Germany
access, right of data subject 455, 456
administrative fines 1186
automated individual decision-making, including profiling 529
binding corporate rules (BCRs) 815
certification 735–36, 746–47
children's consent and information society services 358
compensation, right to and liability 1169, 1175
competence of lead supervisory authority 917
consent, conditions for 349, 350
consistency mechanism 1001–02
cooperation between lead supervisory authority and other authorities concerned 958
criminal convictions and offences 387–88, 389
data portability 499
data protection by design and by default 575
data protection impact assessment (DPIA) 676
data protection officer (DPO) 31
designation of data protection officer (DPO) 691
dispute resolution by the European Data Protection Board (EDPB) 1018
employment context 1231–32, 1235
enterprise 249
European Data Protection Board (EDPB) 1047–48
GDPR Proposal 4, 7
independence 877–78, 879
information provision where personal data collected from data subject 421

information provision where personal data not collected from data subject 440
joint operations of supervisory authorities 988–89
main establishment 228
object, right to 513
personal data breach notification to supervisory authority 643
position of data protection officer (DPO) 704
powers of supervisory authority 945, 947
processor 603
pseudonymisation 134, 136
restriction of processing 124–25
security of processing 633
subject-matter and objectives 52
supervisory authority 268–69, 865, 866, 867, 870–71
tasks of data protection officer (DPO) 710–11
Global Accountability Dialogue (*Galway Project*) 563
Global Cross Border Enforcement Cooperation Arrangement 859, 977–78, 982, 989–90
Global Privacy Enforcement Network (GPEN) 859, 957–58, 977–78, 989–90, 1034, 1035, 1037
Google privacy policy 989
GPEN *see* **Global Privacy Enforcement Network (GPEN)**
Greece 7, 148, 676
group of undertakings
analysis 255–56
binding corporate rules (BCRs) 254, 257, 258–59, 262–63
case law 253–55
charities 255
closely related provisions 253
controlling undertaking 255–56
data protection officer (DPO) 254
definition 101
economic activity 255
enterprise 246, 247–48
EU legislation 254
international instruments 254
international organisations 307
legal background 254–55
main establishment 235
private entities 255
public bodies 255
rationale and policy underpinnings 246
relevant recitals 253
state-controlled enterprises 255
supervisory authority concerned 272
under 250 employees 30
Guadeloupe 83, 786
Guernsey 776

Hague Convention on the Taking of Evidence Abroad 834
Harvard Draft (1935) 93–94
health data
access, right of data subject 450

health data *(cont.)*
   analysis 222–23
   automated individual decision-making, including profiling 523
   biological samples 217
   biometric data 213, 220–21, 222–23
   case law 218, 221–22
   closely related provisions 217
   compensation, right to and liability 1170–72
   confidentiality 218, 221
   consent 178
   definition 101
   disclosure 218
   discrimination and stigma 218
   employment context 1233
   EU legislation 219
   genetic data 202–3, 217, 219, 220–21, 222
   information security standards 220
   international instruments 219–20
   lawfulness of processing 322
   legal background 219–22
   medical examinations 41
   medical records 163–64
   medical treatment contracts 332
   national developments 220–21
   personal data 103–4, 112
   preventive or occupational medicine 365
   privacy, fundamental right of 220, 222
   rationale and policy underpinnings 218–19
   related Articles in EUDPR 217–18
   related Articles in LED 217
   relevant recitals 217
   responsibility of controller 555
   secrecy obligations of healthcare professionals 1253–54, 1256
   security management practices 220
   special categories of personal data 218–20, 365, 366, 367, 371–72, 373, 374
   specific data processing situations 40–41
   territorial scope 91
   transparent information and access rights 399–400, 406
   see also clinical trials/medical research
heard, right to be 1023, 1024
historical research *see* **archiving purposes in the public interest, scientific or historical research purposes or statistical purposes**
Hong Kong 559–60
human dignity 526
human life, protection of 188
human rights
   archiving purposes in the public interest, scientific or historical research purposes or statistical purposes 1247–48
   data portability 500
   national identification number 1225–26
   personal data 106
   special categories of personal data 369–70
   territorial scope 78, 85
   transfers on basis of adequacy decision 771
humanitarian purposes/humanitarian emergencies
   automated individual decision-making, including profiling 524
   data portability 497–98
   derogations for specific situations 842, 850, 852
   lawfulness of processing 323, 333, 335
   personal data breach 188
   restrictions 543–44
   special categories of personal data 379
Hungary
   binding corporate rules (BCRs) 260
   competence 905, 906, 907
   independence 877, 878
   powers of supervisory authority 947
   processing 118
   supervisory authority 268–69, 867
   supervisory authority members, general conditions for 891

ICDPPC *see* **International Conference of Data Protection and Privacy Commissioners (ICDPPC)**
Iceland 989, 1051
ICRC *see* **International Committee of the Red Cross (ICRC)**
identifiability criterion
   access, right of data subject 450
   consent 176
   identification, non-requirement of 395
   personal data 103, 106, 108–9, 110–11
   pseudonymisation 132
identification, non-requirement of
   additional information 391, 396–97
   analysis 394–97
   authentication mechanism 391
   case law 392, 393–94
   closely related provisions 391–92
   data subject rights 21
   de facto impact 395
   de jure potential impact 395
   enforcement 397
   EU legislation 393
   exemptions 392, 394, 396–97
   fair balance requirement 394
   focus 394–95
   identifiability 395
   integrity 395–96
   international instruments 393
   legal background 393–94
   legal certainty 394
   national developments 393
   objective factors 391
   privilege 395–96
   purpose compatibility test 394
   purpose limitation 392, 393, 395
   rationale and policy underpinnings 392–93
   re-identification 393, 396

refusal, right of 393
related Articles in EUDPR 392
relevant recitals 391
responsibility of controller 394
identity theft 29, 555, 565, 640, 641–42, 659
IETF *see* Internet Engineering Task Force (IETF)
ILO *see* International Labour Organisation (ILO) Code of Conduct
IMCO *see* Internal Market and Consumer Protection Committee (IMCO)
IMI *see* Internal Market Information (IMI) systems
impartiality
　establishment rules of supervisory authority 898
　European Data Protection Board (EDPB) 1044
　independence 1057
　supervisory authority members, general conditions for 885–86, 891
　tasks of supervisory authority 928–29
　see also independence
implementing acts 41–43
impossibility or disproportionate effort exception 22–23, 110–11
　communication of data breach to data subject 654, 660
　erasure ('right to be forgotten') 477
　information to be provided where personal data has been collected from data subject 414
　information to be provided where personal data has not been obtained from data subject 435–36, 438, 439, 443, 446–47
　notification obligation regarding rectification or erasure of data or restriction of processing 492, 493, 494, 495, 496
　rectification 471, 472
　transparency 402
income *see* remuneration
incomplete, false, erroneous or inaccurate data 471–73, 474, 526
independence
　adjudicative role in ensuring consistency of enforcement 1060–61
　advisory tasks 1060–61
　analysis 1059–66
　authoritative advice 1060–61
　case law 1055–56, 1058–59
　certification bodies 744, 748–49, 750–51
　chair representation 1055
　closely related provisions 1055
　Commission's role on the Board 1055, 1064–66
　competence 910
　'complete' independence 1061–62
　consistency mechanism 1001, 1057, 1060, 1062, 1063, 1064–66
　consistent application of Regulation 1055
　cooperation 1055, 1062–63
　data protection 1059
　designation of data protection officer (DPO) 688–89, 691

dispute resolution by the European Data Protection Board (EDPB) 1022
distinct role and specific decision-making powers in dispute resolution 1060
effective supervision 1063–64, 1065
establishment rules of supervisory authority 893–94, 895–97, 898–99
EU legislation 1057
European Data Protection Board (EDPB) 1041, 1044, 1047, 1051
financial support from EU funds 1065–66
guidelines, recommendations and best practice 1060–61
head of supervisory authority 1055
interference by European Data Protection Board (EDPB) and effective supervision 1062–64
international instruments 1058
legal background 1057–59
legal nature and regulatory tasks of the European Data Protection Board (EDPB) 1060–61
level of independence enjoyed by the European Data Protection Board (EDPB) 1059–62
monitoring approved codes of conduct 725, 728
nature and structure of the European Data Protection Board (EDPB) and its advisory role 1060
opinion of the European Data Protection Board (EDPB) 1008, 1012
opinions, issuing 1061
position of data protection officer (DPO) 702–5, 706
procedure 1092
rationale and policy underpinnings 1056
related Articles in EUDPR 874
relevant recitals 1055
reliability of supervision 1063, 1064, 1065
reports 1086
Secretariat 1102, 1104, 1106, 1107, 1108
standard of independence of supervisory authorities 1059–60
supervisory authority 863, 866, 867, 870
supervisory authority members, general conditions for 884, 885–86, 887, 890, 891
tasks of data protection officer (DPO) 714
tasks of supervisory authority 932, 933
third parties 1057
voting rights 1055
see also independence of supervisory authorities
independence of supervisory authorities
　analysis 878–82
　career prospects, effect on 880
　case law 874, 877–78
　closely related provisions 874
　control and monitoring 873, 951
　disciplinary actions 880
　establishment of more than one supervisory authority 873
　EU legislation 876

independence of supervisory authorities (*cont.*)
　external influence, freedom from 880–81
　financial control and budgetary status 873, 882
　functional independence 879
　general conditions for members 873–74
　incompatible actions, prohibition against 881
　influence, direct 880
　influence, indirect 880–81
　international instruments 876–77
　judicial review 873, 879
　legal background 876–78
　legality issues 880
　mutual assistance, cooperation and participation 873
　national developments 877
　organisational independence 879
　prior compliance 880–81
　rationale and policy underpinnings 875–76
　related Articles in LED 874
　relevant recitals 873–74
　service or performance-related aspects 880
　staff exclusive to supervisory authority 873–74
　sufficient resources 881–82
independent supervisory authorities 35–37
　one-stop shop mechanism 36–37
　overview 35–36
　see also independence of supervisory authorities
India 776
individual cases 38, 324, 567–68, 834–35, 1014, 1022, 1065–66
individual rights
　access, right by data subject 453
　automated decision-making, including profiling 528n12, 535n54
　binding corporate rules (BCRs) 817*f*
　compensation, right to and liability 1166
　competence of lead supervisory authority 921
　independence 875, 1064
　representation of data subjects 1145
　supervisory authority role 8
individual self-determination 504–5
individuation requirement 107
Industry, Research and Energy Committee (ITRE) 5
Information Accountability Foundation 318–19
information exchange
　agreements between supervisory authorities under Data Protection Directive (DPD) 1035
　analysis 1035–39
　arrangements not only for one-stop-shop and consistency mechanism 1036–37
　challenges in creating one-size-fits-all system 1037
　closely related provisions 1032
　consistency mechanism 1032–33, 1039
　cooperation 1032–34, 1035, 1036, 1037, 1039
　current arrangements 1038
　EU legislation 1033–34
　formats and procedures by electronic means 1032
　informal ad hoc arrangements 1035

　international cooperation 860
　international instruments 1034
　legal background 1033–34
　mutual assistance 1032, 1034
　national developments 1034
　one-stop-shop 1032–33, 1039
　rationale and policy underpinnings 1032–33
　related Articles in LED 1032
　relevant recitals 1032
　time limits/without undue delay 1033
　tracking mechanism 1038
　translation services and language diversity 1036–37, 1038
information provision
　compensation, right to and liability 1167
　erasure ('right to be forgotten') 479
　international organisation 117
　joint controllers 584–85
　restrictions 543–44, 546, 548
　see also information exchange; information provision where personal data collected from data subject; information provision where personal data not collected from data subject
information provision where personal data collected from data subject
　age of data 414
　algorithmic decision-making 416
　analysis 425–31
　appropriate means 419
　archiving periods 428
　automated individual decision-making, including profiling 413, 429–30
　basic information 421–22
　black box society 416
　case law 415, 422–25
　closely related provisions 414
　completeness and accuracy of information 415, 431
　compulsory provision of data 429
　consent 428–29
　　explicit 429
　　informed 419
　　valid 415
　controller-processor agreement 426–27
　Court of Justice of the European Union (CJEU) 422–24
　details of data protection officer (DPO) 413, 418
　different purposes, processing for 430–31
　EU legislation 417–19
　European Court of Human Rights (ECtHR) 424–25
　exemptions 431
　general information 414
　identity and contact details of controller 413, 418
　information requirements 427–30
　international instruments 420–21
　law enforcement authorities, covert investigations or video surveillance 418–19, 425

lawfulness 415–16
layered notices 427
legal background 417–25
legal basis for processing 413
legal claims, establishment, exercise or defence of 421
legitimate interests 413, 415, 418–19, 421, 428
logic involved in processing 429–30
national developments 421–22
purposes of processing 413, 418
rationale and policy underpinnings 415–16
reasonable period 414
related Articles in EPD 414, 417–18
related Articles in LED 414, 418–19
relevant recitals 414
restriction of processing 418, 428–29
significance and envisaged consequences of processing 413, 430
specific cases 418, 419
statutory or contractual requirement 413
technical storage 417
time-stamped email or web page 431
timing 427
transparency and fairness 413, 414, 415–16, 418–19, 420–24, 427–28, 429–30
value added service 418
video surveillance 426
withdrawal of consent 413, 419, 429
information provision where personal data not collected from data subject
  adequacy decision 434
  age of data 435–36
  analysis 443–47
  case law 436, 441–43
  categories of personal data concerned 434, 444
  closely related provisions 436
  communication channel 445–46
  complex data flows 439
  confidentiality subject to professional secrecy obligation 435, 440, 447
  consent, informed 439
  contact details of data protection officer (DPO) 434
  copies 434
  data subject already has information 446
  delivery modality 445–46
  direct collection 441–42
  disclosure 434, 435–36, 437–38, 440, 444, 445, 447
  embedded control options 445–46
  EU legislation 437–38
  exemptions 446–47
  fairness and transparency 434, 435, 436–37, 438–39, 440–41, 442, 443, 444, 445–46, 447
  household exemption 442–43
  identity and contact details of controller 434
  impossibility or disproportionate effort exception 435–36, 438, 439, 443, 446–47
  indirect collection 441–42, 443, 444, 445, 446–47
  information list 445
  international instruments 438–40
  legal background 437–43
  legal basis for processing 434
  national developments 440–41
  number of data subjects 435–36
  obtaining laid down by Union law 447
  profiling 434, 435
  purposes of processing 434
  rationale and policy underpinnings 436–37
  reasonable period 434, 435
  recipients or categories of recipients 434
  related Articles in EPD 436
  related Articles in LED 436
  relevant recitals 435–36
  source from which data originates 434, 444
  timing 445
Information Security Management Systems 382
information society service
  AIRBNB 299
  analysis 296–301
  at a distance 294, 296, 297–98
  business-to-business service (B2B) 297
  business-to-consumer service (B2C) 297
  case law 293–94, 296
  children 294
  closely related provisions 292
  composite services 298–99
  consent 292
  data portability 504
  definition 102
  educational, charitable or recreational purposes 296–97
  electronic means 292, 294, 296, 298–99
  EU legislation 295
  individual request of recipient of services 294, 296, 299–300
  intermediary service 299
  international instruments 295
  legal background 295–96
  liability rules of intermediary service 292
  national developments 295
  object, right to 508
  oral statement 292
  rationale and policy underpinnings 294
  related Articles in EPD 292
  related Articles in EUDPR 292–93
  relevant recitals 292
  remuneration 296–97
  written statement 292
  see also children's consent and information society services
informational self-determination 52, 176, 347, 401–2
insurance companies and insurance data 371, 389–90, 429–30, 670

integrity
  establishment rules of supervisory authority 893–94, 897–99
  European Data Protection Board (EDPB) 1044
  personal data processing 309, 311, 312, 318
  security of processing 631–32, 636

intellectual property
  access, right of data subject 450, 464
  automated individual decision-making, including profiling 523
  data portability 503
  national identification number 1225–26
  recipient 163–64
  restrictions 548
  transparent information and access rights 399–400, 407

Interinstitutional Agreement on Better Law-Making 1272

Internal Market and Consumer Protection Committee (IMCO) 5

Internal Market Information (IMI) systems 962, 1036, 1038–39, 1157–58

international agreements concerning third countries or international organisations
  amendment, replacement or revocation 1305–6
  analysis 1304–6
  case law 1302
  closed list 1304–5
  closely related provisions 1302
  cooperation 1302, 1306
  criminal justice cooperation 1303
  information exchange 1302
  law enforcement, tax and competition 1302
  legal background 1304
  police and judicial cooperation 1304
  rationale and policy underpinnings 1302–4
  related Articles in LED 1302
  review procedure 1306
  transfers or disclosures not authorised by Union law 827, 829, 830, 834

International Committee of the Red Cross (ICRC) 306, 850, 852

International Complaints Handling Workshop 1034, 1035

International Conference of Data Protection and Privacy Commissioners (ICDPPC) 559, 573, 859, 977–78, 989, 1099

international cooperation
  addressees 859–60
  analysis 859–61
  Brexit 861
  closely related provisions 857–58
  engagement of relevant stakeholders 857
  EU legislation 859
  forms of cooperation 860–61
  international agreements 857
  international instruments 859
  jurisdictional conflicts 857
  legal background 859
  mutual assistance 857, 860
  national developments 859
  rationale and policy underpinnings 858–59
  related Articles in LED 858
  relevant recitals 857
  territorial scope 858
  transfer of data 858
  transfers: general principles 766
  unlawful use or disclosure 857

International Criminal Police Organisation (Interpol) 306–7, 764

International Labour Organisation (ILO) Code of Conduct 1231

International Organisation for Standardisation (ISO)
  conformity assessment framework 737
  data breach definition 191
  health data 220
  ISO 27018 on cloud computing 559
  ISO 29190 Privacy Capability Assessment Model 559
  ISO/IEC 17000:2004 737, 739
  ISO/IEC 17065/2012 741, 744, 746, 747, 748, 749, 750, 751
  ISO/IEC standards 382, 740–41
  ISO/IEC/27001 Auditor/Lead Auditor certification 692

international organisations
  analysis 305–7
  attributes 305
  bilateral or multilateral agreements 305–6
  case law 303, 305
  closely related provisions 303
  data transfers 764
  definition 102
  EU legislation 304
  international instruments 304–5
  legal background 304–5
  non-governmental organisations (NGOs) 307
  public authorities 307
  public international law governance 305–6
  rationale and policy underpinnings 304
  related Articles in EUDPR 303
  related Articles in LED 303
  territorial scope 95
  undertakings 307
  see also international agreements concerning third countries or international organisations; transfer of data to third countries or international organisations

International Standards on the Protection of Personal Data and Privacy 977–78, 989–90

International Telecommunications Union 306

Internet Engineering Task Force (IETF) 151

internet protocol (IP) addresses 8, 13, 14, 103, 127

internet service provider (ISP) 604, 614

internet of things 112, 674

interoperable formats 497, 499, 504–5, 574–75

Index

Interpol *see* **International Criminal Police Organisation (Interpol)**
IP *see* **internet protocol (IP) addresses**
Ireland
  access, right of data subject 404, 451
  codes of conduct 719–20
  communication of personal data breach to data subject 658
  data portability 499
  data protection impact assessment (DPIA) 670
  designation of data protection officer (DPO) 696
  GDPR Proposal 5, 7
  object, right to 513
  penalties 1196
  personal data breach notification to supervisory authority 644
  transparent information 404
Isle of Man 776
ISO *see* **International Organisation for Standardisation**
ISP *see* **internet service provider (ISP)**
Israel 776
Italy
  access, right of data subject 453
  automated individual decision-making, including profiling 537n61
  churches and religious associations 1258, 1260–61, 1263–65
  deceased persons 112
  designation of data protection officer (DPO) 692, 693–94
  enterprise 249n7
  filing system 141–42
  GDPR Proposal 7
  joint operations of supervisory authorities 989
  penalties 1200
  restriction of processing 124–25
  security of processing 637
  third parties 172
  transfers: general principles 758
ITRE *see* **Industry, Research and Energy Committee (ITRE)**

Japan 776, 777, 786
Jersey 776
joint controllers
  analysis 586–87
  arrangements between 583–87
  case law 583, 584–85
  closely related provisions 582
  communication of personal data breach to data subject 660
  controller and processor 27
  controller responsibility 566
  controllers in common 584
  EU legislation 583–84
  Facebook 585–86
  information to be provided where personal data collected from data subject 424
  international instruments 584
  lawfulness of processing 328
  legal background 583–85
  liability 582, 583
  national developments 584
  personal data breach notification to supervisory authority 647
  processor 602
  rationale and policy underpinnings 583
  records of processing activities 620
  related Articles in EPD 582
  related Articles in LED 582
  relevant recitals 582
  responsibility 582
  roles, relationship and responsibilities 583
  written summary of arrangement 587
joint economic activity
  binding corporate rules (BCRs) 34, 257, 258–59, 262
  enterprise 246, 247–48
joint enforcement actions 37
joint operations
  consistency mechanism 995, 999
  opinion of the European Data Protection Board (EDPB) 1005, 1006, 1008–09, 1012
  urgency procedure 1027, 1030
  see also joint operations of supervisory authorities
joint operations of supervisory authorities
  actual operation 991–92
  analysis 990–93
  best practices 992
  closely related provisions 987
  communications 992
  cooperation 986–87, 988, 989, 990–91, 992
  damages and reimbursement 992
  EU legislation 988–89
  geographical proximity 988
  informal cooperation 993
  international instruments 989–90
  investigations or monitoring 988
  investigative powers 986, 991
  legal background 986–90
  making good damage and reimbursement 986
  mutual assistance 987, 989, 990, 993
  obligation to respond to request without undue delay 987
  one-stop-shop mechanism 988, 990, 991, 992, 993
  provisional measures and enforcement 986, 992–93
  rationale and policy underpinnings 987–88
  related Articles in EPD 987
  related Articles in EUDPR 987
  related Articles in LED 987
  relevant recitals 986–87
  response to request to cooperation made without delay 986
  scope and participants 991

Index

joint operations of supervisory authorities (*cont.*)
   senior management support 992
   staff assuming responsibility for actions 986
   urgency procedure 992–93
Joint Supervisory Bodies (JSB) 1048, 1057
journalistic purposes or for artistic and literary expression
   erasure ('right to be forgotten') 478
   freedom of expression and information 1202–3, 1204, 1206, 1207, 1208, 1209, 1210
   specific data processing situations 40–41
JSB *see* **Joint Supervisory Bodies (JSB)**
judicial cooperation in criminal matters and police cooperation 71, 540
judicial review 38, 1130
JURI *see* **Legal Affairs Committee (JURI)**
jurisdiction *see* **compensation, right to and liability; effective judicial remedy against controller or processor; effective judicial remedy against supervisory authority; representation of data subjects; territorial scope; transfer of data to third countries or international organisations**

Korea 776

language *see* **clear and plain language**
Latin America 776
Latvia 7
law enforcement
   information provision where personal data collected from data subject 418–19, 425
   international agreements concerning third countries or international organisations 1302
   material scope 11–12, 64, 65–66, 70, 71
   object, right to 511
   review of other Union legal acts on data protection 1314
   security of processing 633
   transfers: general principles 759–60
   transfers on basis of adequacy decision 776, 780–81, 789
   transfers or disclosures not authorised by Union law 826–27
lawfulness of processing
   analysis 329–43
   balancing test 338, 339
   bases for 322–38
   biometric data 207
   case law 325, 328
   certification 738
   closely related provisions 324
   compatibility 326–27
   compatible further processing 327, 341–43
   compliance with legal obligation to which controller is subject 332–33
   consent 321, 322, 327, 329–34, 343
      withdrawal of 339
   context of contract 322
   context of processing 338

   context in which data has been collected 322
   contract and precontractual relationship 330–32
   criminal offences and criminal penalties 322, 324, 328, 386–87
   data subjects concerned 321, 322, 338
   data use limitations 342–43
   employee information for social insurance purposes 332
   employment contracts 332
   employment relationship 330
   EU legislation 327
   exemptions 340
   fair processing 334
   filing systems 329
   freedom to conduct a business 337
   harmonisation 326
   incompatible further processing 343
   initial and further purpose, relationship between 341–42
   intended further processing, consequences of 322
   intention to enter into contract 322
   international instruments 327
   legal background 327–28
   legal grounds list 329
   legal obligation 321, 322, 330–31, 334, 336, 831–32
   legal provisions 326
   legitimate interests 321, 323, 324, 329, 330–32, 334, 337–39, 343, 831–32
   link between purposes for which data have been collected 321
   malicious code distribution 323
   medical treatment contracts 332
   missing legal bases 330
   money laundering 332
   nature of personal data 322
   network and information security 323
   object, right to 339
   obligations or tasks based exclusively on foreign law 333–36, 339, 340–41
   official authority 321, 322–23, 335–36
   performance of contract 321, 322, 331, 333
   performance of a task carried out in the public interest 831–32
   personal data processing 309–10, 311, 312, 313, 314–15
   precontractual situations 331–32
   private interference 325–26n1
   processing operations and procedures 321
   provisional balance 338
   purpose limitation 321, 322, 326–27, 343
   rationale and policy underpinnings 325–27
   related Articles in EPD 324
   related Articles in LED 324
   relevant recitals 322–24
   risk containment 342–43
   safeguards, special 342–43
   secrecy 324

statistical purposes 328
time of processing 338
transfers on basis of adequacy decision 788
type of personal data subject to
    processing 321, 322
various grounds of lawful processing, relationship
    between 339–40
vital interests, protection of 321, 323, 333–34,
    337–38, 831–32
see also fairness and transparency
Legal Affairs Committee (JURI) 5
**legal claims, establishment, exercise or defence
    of** 841, 842, 844, 851
legal guardian authorisation 19
legal personality
automated individual decision-making, including
    profiling 522–23, 527
binding corporate rules (BCRs) 261
children's consent and information society
    services 355, 359
compensation, right to and liability 1174–75
effective judicial remedy against controller or
    processor 1139
European Data Protection Board (EDPB) 1041,
    1045–47
independence 1055, 1060
tasks of the European Data Protection Board
    (EDPB) 1071
territorial scope 85, 87
Legislative Financial Statement 42–43
legislative history 3–10
Commission's GDPR proposal 3–4
see also legislative procedure
legislative procedure
Court of Justice of the European Union
    (CJEU) 8–10
European Parliament 5–6
supervisory authorities 8
trilogue (Council, Commission and
    Parliament) 7–8
legitimate interests
archiving purposes in the public interest, scientific
    or historical research purposes or statistical
    purposes 1245
automated individual decision-making, including
    profiling 522, 528, 536, 538, 539–40
codes of conduct 722
consent, conditions for 352
data breach notification 29
data protection impact assessment (DPIA) 673
derogations for specific situations 841, 842,
    845, 853–54
Directive 2002/58/EC 1295
employment context 1236, 1237
erasure ('right to be forgotten') 478–79, 480
identification, non-requirement of 395
information provision where personal data collected
    from data subject 413, 415, 418–19, 421, 428

information provision where personal data not
    collected from data subject 434, 435, 440,
    441, 447
lawfulness of processing 321, 323, 324, 328, 329,
    330–32, 334, 337–39, 343
notice obligations and privacy policies 22
object, right to 508, 509, 510, 512, 514, 516, 517–18
principles 17–18
public access to official documents 1219–20
restriction of processing 490
security of processing 637
third parties 170
transfers or disclosures not authorised by Union
    law 831–32
Letters Rogatory 834
liability
accountability/responsibility of controller 555, 561
binding corporate rules (BCRs) 813
certification bodies 751
controller 153, 614–15
joint controllers 582, 583
processor 600, 601–2, 603, 604, 605–7,
    608, 614–15
representative 239
representatives of controllers or processors not
    established in the Union 592, 597
security of processing 636–37
tasks of data protection officer (DPO) 714
see also compensation, right to and liability
licensing authorities 147
Liechtenstein 1051
Lithuania 7
location data
consent 178
controller or processor, processing under authority
    of 613
information provision where personal data collected
    from data subject 418
personal data 14, 103, 108
restrictions 546, 548–49
Luxembourg 644, 658, 691

Macedonia 1196
machine determinism 526
machine-learning 416
machine-readability 504–5, 523
Madeira 83, 786
Madrid Resolution 559, 563
main establishment
analysis 229–36
branch or subsidiary with legal personality 225
case law 226, 228
central administration 225, 228–29, 230–31,
    232, 234–35
change of 236
closely related provisions 226
competence of lead supervisory authority 913–14, 920
concept of 229–30

main establishment *(cont.)*
  of controller 225–26, 227, 228, 229, 230, 232–34
  cross-border processing 279
  definitions 14–15, 101
  designation of data protection officer (DPO) 697–98
  EU legislation 228
  freedom of establishment 230
  of group of undertakings 235
  international instruments 228
  joint controllers 234
  legal background 228
  national developments 228
  one-stop-shop mechanism 227, 228, 234, 236
  of processor 225–26, 227, 228, 229, 230, 233, 234–35
  rationale and policy underpinnings 227
  relevant recitals 225–26
  supervisory authority concerned 272
  supervisory authority/lead supervisory authority 225–26, 227–28, 233–34, 236
malicious code distribution 323
manifestly unfounded or excessive requests
  access, right of data subject 466
  object, right to 520
  tasks 928, 936
  transparency 398, 408–9
manual processing 138, 140–41, 142, 143
market surveys 91
marketing activities 17–18, 348, 355
Martinique 83, 786
material scope 11–12
  activities outside scope of Union law 69
  analysis 66–72
  case law 62–63, 65–66
  closely related provisions 62
  competent authority 70
  courts and judicial authorities, data processing by 70–71
  criminal offences, criminal penalties and public security 60, 61, 64, 65–66, 70
  defence 65–66
  e-Commerce Directive 72
  EPD 71
  EU legislation 64
  Eurojust 71
  European Public Prosecutor's Office (EPPO) 71
  Europol 71
  exceptions and restrictions clause 65
  free movement 61, 62, 67
  intermediaries and liability 72
  international instruments 65
  key terms 66–67
  legal background 64–66
  national development 65
  natural or legal persons 60, 61, 67–69, 71
  processing by EU institutions 12, 71
  purely personal activity 11

  rationale and policy underpinnings 63–64
  related Articles in EPD 62
  related Articles in EUDPR 62
  related Articles in LED 492
  relevant recitals 60–62
  video surveillance 69
meaningful information
  access, right of data subject 449, 462–63
  automated individual decision-making, including profiling 538
  information provision where personal data collected from data subject 413, 429–30
  information provision where personal data not collected from data subject 434, 439
media sector 1059
medical research *see* **clinical trials/medical research**
Mercosur 776
Meroni **doctrine** 1045
minimisation of data
  archiving purposes in the public interest, scientific or historical research purposes or statistical purposes 1240–41, 1246–47
  data portability 498
  data protection by design and by default 571, 574, 578–79
  identification, non-requirement of 392, 393, 395–96
  information provision where personal data not collected from data subject 446–47
  lawfulness of processing 342–43
  national identification number 1227
  personal data processing 309, 311, 312, 317
  pseudonymisation 132–33, 136
  restriction of processing 485–86
  special categories of personal data 381–82
misconduct 192–93
misuse of personal data *see* **fraud; identity theft; personal data breach**
mixed datasets 112
MLATs *see* **mutual legal assistance treaties (MLATs)**
MNCs *see* **multinational corporations (MNCs)**
money laundering *see* **anti-money laundering**
monitoring approved codes of conduct
  accreditation 725, 729–30
  analysis 728–30
  auditing 728, 729–30
  case law 727
  characteristics and qualities of monitoring bodies 728–29
  checks and balances 729
  closely related provisions 726
  conflicts of interests, absence of 725, 728
  conformity assessment bodies 728
  contract or standard contractual clauses 726
  eligibility to apply code 725, 729
  equal treatment of candidate bodies 728
  EU legislation 727
  expertise and prior experience 725, 726, 728

Index

incomplete documentation 730
international instruments 727
legal background 727
monitoring bodies 728
national development 727
oversight and enforcement 727
post-approval period 727
preventive organisational measures 728
rationale and policy underpinnings 727
relevant recitals 725–26
reliability and resources 726
sanctioning of infringing controllers and processors 730
standard protection clauses 726
suspension or exclusion of controller or processor 725
technical standards 726
validity of codes 727, 729
multinational corporations (MNCs) 14, 259, 593–94, 919
multiple data processing operations 352, 602
mutual assistance
analysis 979–83
case law 975, 978–79
closely related provisions 974
codes of conduct 718
Committee procedure 1278, 1281
competence 909
confidential information and personal data 982
consistency mechanism 995, 999
controller or processor, processing under authority of 613–14
cooperation 973–74, 975–77, 978, 979–80, 981, 982
cooperation between lead supervisory authority and other authorities concerned 953, 957, 960, 963
electronic means using standardised format 973, 980
EU legislation 975–77
examination procedure 973
experience 983
free of charge 973, 980
geographical proximity 976
independence 873
independent supervisory authorities 36
informal cooperation 983
information exchange 1032, 1034
and languages 975, 979, 980, 981–82
information requests 979
informing requesting DPA of results 973, 980
international instruments 977–78
investigative powers 978–79
joint operations on bilateral or multilateral basis 974, 979, 983
joint operations of supervisory authorities 987, 989, 990, 993
legal background 975–79

monitoring approved codes of conduct 726
notification 979
one-stop-shop mechanism 975, 979, 983
opinion of the European Data Protection Board (EDPB) 1005, 1006, 1008–09, 1012
penalties 978
powers of supervisory authority 946
prior authorisations and consultations, inspections and investigations 973, 979, 980
provisional measures and enforcement 973, 974, 981
rationale and policy underpinnings 975
refusal to comply with request 973
rejection of request 980
related Articles in EPD 974, 976
related Articles in EUDPR 974, 976, 977
related Articles in LED 974, 976
relevant information 981
relevant recitals 973–74
reply to request from another DPA without undue delay 973, 980
requests for assistance to contain all necessary information 973, 980
task force 976
tasks of supervisory authority 927, 928, 929, 937
transfers or disclosures not authorised by Union law 825, 834–35
translation 982
urgency procedure and urgent binding decision 973, 981, 1027, 1028–29, 1030
mutual legal assistance treaties (MLATs) 829, 834
mutual recognition 815–16, 917

NAB *see* National Accreditation Body (NAB)
National Accreditation Body (NAB) 32, 746, 747–48, 749, 750, 751–52
national competition authorities 916
national identification number
analysis 1225–27
anti-money laundering 1227
appropriate safeguards 1224, 1226–27
case law 1223, 1225
closely related provisions 1223
confidentiality 1226
consistency mechanism 1001
data minimisation 1227
EU legislation 1224
general purpose identifiers 1226
human rights abuses 1225–26
international instruments 1224
legal background 1224–25
Member State protections 1227
minimum standards 1224
national developments 1224–25
personal data 14
privacy, fundamental right of 1225–26
pseudonym, NI number as 1226
rationale and policy underpinnings 1223–24

national identification number (*cont.*)
  re-evaluation or modification of schemes 1227
  restrictions on processing 1225
  risks and uses 1226–27
  special categories of personal data 375, 1224, 1227
  specific sector or purpose identifiers 1226
  types of identifiers 1225–26
national regulatory authorities (NRAs) 916, 1007
natural or legal persons 60, 61, 67–69, 71
NDPOs *see* Network of Data Protection Officers (NDPOs)
ne bis in idem (right not to be tried or punished twice) 1194, 1198, 1199–201
necessity
  archiving purposes in the public interest, scientific or historical research purposes or statistical purposes 1240–41
  biometric data 210
  data portability 498
  data protection impact assessment (DPIA) 665
  derogations for specific situations 848, 851, 853
  information provision where personal data collected from data subject 428–29
  joint operations of supervisory authorities 992
  lawfulness of processing 328, 336
  personal data processing 317
  powers of supervisory authority 943
  prior consultation 686
  pseudonymisation 132–33
  restriction of processing 485–86
  secrecy obligations 1252
negligence 192–93, 1165–66, 1174, 1176
Netherlands
  children's consent and information society services 358
  cooperation between lead supervisory authority and other authorities concerned 958
  data portability 499
  designation of data protection officer (DPO) 691
  enterprise 249n7
  establishment rules of supervisory authority 898
  joint operations of supervisory authorities 988–89
  personal data breach notification to supervisory authority 643, 644, 650–51
  subject-matter and objectives 58
  supervisory authority members, general conditions for 888
  transfers on basis of adequacy decision 786
Network of Data Protection Officers (NDPOs) 696
New Zealand 668, 776
non-governmental organisations (NGOs)
  binding corporate rules (BCRs) 262–63
  data subjects, representation of 1143–44, 1146
  international cooperation 860–61
  international organisations 307
  special categories of personal data 378, 380
Nordic supervisory authorities 976, 989

Norway 670, 989, 1051
not-for-profit organisations
  binding corporate rules (BCRs) 262–63
  certification bodies 751–52
  children's consent in relation to information society services 360
  churches and religious associations 1259
  competence of lead supervisory authority 919
  data subjects, representation of 1142, 1147
  dispute resolution by the European Data Protection Board (EDPB) 1024
  enterprise 250
  group of undertakings 255
  representation of data subjects 1145
  special categories of personal data 365, 376*f*, 378
notice requirements
  binding corporate rules (BCRs) 817*f*
  data subject rights 21–22
  information provision where personal data collected from data subject 426–27
  information provision where personal data not collected from data subject 439, 443, 445
notification obligation regarding rectification or erasure of personal data or restriction of processing
  analysis 494–96
  case law 492, 494
  categories of recipients 495
  closely related provisions 492
  copies or replication 495
  corrective powers of supervisory authority 496
  derogations 493
  EU legislation 493
  impossibility or disproportionate effort exception 492, 494, 495, 496
  international cooperation 860
  international instruments 493
  legal background 493–94
  national developments 493
  number of recipients 494
  personal data processing 318
  rationale and policy underpinnings 492–93
  records of processing activities 617, 618, 619
  related Articles in LED 492
  scope of obligations 495
  time limits for bringing actions 494
  unlawful or incorrect 494
NRAs *see* national regulatory authorities (NRAs)

object, right to
  amendment 512–13
  analysis 516–20
  automated individual decision-making, including profiling 524
  case law 509, 513–16
  closely related provisions 508–9
  compensation, right to and liability 1167
  dedicated Wi-Fi network for mobile phone users 519

direct marketing 508, 509, 510–12, 516–17, 518, 519
  effect of objection right 518
  erasure ('right to be forgotten') 475–76, 481–82, 511, 512–13, 515, 516–17, 518
  EU legislation 510–12
  general right to object 509, 510, 511–12, 515
  identification, non-requirement of 394
  individual participation principle 512–13
  information provision where personal data not collected from data subject 434
  international instruments 512–13
  judicial remedy 511
  legal background 510–16
  legal claims 512, 518
  modalities for exercising right 519–20
  opt-out possibility 519
  public safety grounds 512
  rationale and policy underpinnings 509–10
  reasonable fee if manifestly unfounded or excessive 520
  rejection of request 520
  related Articles in EPD 509
  related Articles in LED 509
  relevant recitals 508
  restriction of processing 485–86, 487, 490, 543–44
  third parties 508, 509, 510–11, 512, 514, 515–16, 517
  time limits on action taken 520
  unsolicited communications 511
  without undue delay 511, 518
OCTs *see* Overseas Countries and Territories (OCTs)
OECD *see* Organisation for Economic Cooperation and Development (OECD) entries
official authority
  biometric data 207
  data protection impact assessment (DPIA) 675
  erasure ('right to be forgotten') 475–76, 482
  lawfulness of processing 321, 322–23, 335–36
  object, right to 508, 509, 511–12
  rectification 469–70
  restriction of processing 490
  special categories of personal data 366
  transfers or disclosures not authorised by Union law 827
Official Journal of the European Union (EU) 7, 772, 785
one-stop-shop mechanism
  competence 902
  competence of lead supervisory authority 914, 915, 917, 920–21
  consistency mechanism 38, 996–97, 999, 1000
  cooperation between lead supervisory authority and other authorities concerned 961
  cross-border processing 280, 281, 285–86
  dispute resolution by the European Data Protection Board (EDPB) 1016–17, 1019, 1020

  independent supervisory authorities 36–37
  information exchange 1032–33, 1039
  joint operations of supervisory authorities 988, 990, 991, 992, 993
  main establishment 14, 227, 228, 234, 236
  mutual assistance 975, 979, 983
  opinion of the European Data Protection Board (EDPB) 1012
  relevant and reasoned objection 289–90
  representative 242
  supervisory authority concerned 273–74, 276
  urgency procedure 1028
  see also cooperation between lead supervisory authority and other authorities concerned
online identifiers/tracking
  Court of Justice of the European Union (CJEU) 8
  personal data 13, 14, 103, 108
  profiling 127, 128
  territorial scope 91
  see also cookies
opinion of the European Data Protection Board (EDPB)
  amendment of draft decision 1006
  analysis 1008–12
  case law 1007, 1008
  closely related provisions 1006
  consistency mechanism 1006, 1007, 1009, 1010, 1011
    risk of overextending 1011–12
    triggering scenarios 1008–09
  contractual clauses 1005
  cooperation 1006, 1007, 1010
  cross-border element 1012
  draft code of conduct or amendment or extension to code of conduct 1005
  draft decision 1005, 1008, 1010
  draft decision amendment 1011
  draft opinion 1009
  effects and consequences of procedure 1011
  electronic means using standardised format 1005, 1006, 1010
  EU legislation 1007
  general applicability 1012
  good administration 1011
  information sharing 1010
  international instruments 1007–08
  joint operations 1005, 1006, 1008–09, 1012
  legal background 1007–08
  legal effects 1011
  legally binding decisions 1006
  list of processing operations 1005
  maintaining draft decision 1006, 1011
  mutual assistance 1005, 1006, 1008–09, 1012
  national developments 1008
  procedure for issuing opinion 1009–10
  rationale and policy underpinnings 1007
  relevant recitals 1006
  simple majority vote 1005

opinion of the European Data Protection
    Board (EDPB) (cont.)
  standard data protection clauses 1005
  translations 1005
  two-thirds majority 1006
  urgent cases 1012
  utmost account of opinion 1006
  without undue delay/time limits 1005,
    1008–10, 1012
optic-electronic devices 524–25, 667, 673
Organisation for Economic Cooperation
    and Development (OECD)
    countries 866, 957–58
Organisation for Economic Cooperation and
    Development (OECD) Recommendation
    on Cross-Border Co-operation in
    the Enforcement of Laws Protecting
    Privacy 1034
Organisation for Economic Cooperation and
    Development (OECD) report 2004 212–13
Organization for Economic Cooperation and
    Development (OECD) Privacy Guidelines
  access, right of data subject 455
  automated individual decision-making, including
    profiling 528
  codes of conduct 720
  compensation, right to and liability 1168
  controller 147
  data protection by design and by default 574
  information provision where personal data collected
    from data subject 420–21
  information provision where personal data not
    collected from data subject 439
  international cooperation 858–59, 860
  main establishment 228
  monitoring approved codes of conduct 727
  object, right to 512–13
  personal data 106, 107
  processor 158
  profiling 129
  pseudonymisation 134
  representative 240
  responsibility of controller 557, 558
  tasks of data protection officer (DPO) 711–12
  third parties 171
  transfers: general principles 760
OTTs see Over-the-Top Communications
    Services (OTTs)
outsourcing 157–58
  see also third parties
Over-the-Top Communications Services
    (OTTs) 1299
Overseas Countries and Territories (OCTs) 786

Passenger Name Record (PNR) data
  analysis 834
  automated individual decision-making, including
    profiling 540

competence 909
competence of lead supervisory authority 918
material scope 64
transfers: general principles 759–60
transfers on basis of adequacy decision 775–76
  see also European Union-Canada Passenger Name
    Record (PNR) agreement
passport databases 854–55
payment service providers 656–57
PbD see Privacy by Design (PbD)
penalties
  administrative penalties 1194–96, 1197, 1198,
    1199–201
  analysis 1198–201
  case law 1195
  circumvention of existing criminal disclosure
    rules 1196
  closely related provisions 1195
  comparator infringements 1198–99
  compulsory community service 1196
  confidentiality, violation of 1196
  coordination 1200–1
  criminal offences 1197, 1200–1
  criminal penalties 1194–97, 1199–200
  custodial sentences 1196
  deprivation of profits 1194
  double text practice 1196–97
  effective, proportionate and dissuasive 1194–95,
    1196–97, 1198–99, 1200, 1201
  enforcement practice 1196–97
  Engel criteria 1199
  EU legislation 1197–98
  failure to notify processing activities 1196
  forum shopping 1197
  imprisonment 1195–96
  income, general level of 1194
  infringements of national rules 1194
  insider dealing 1200
  international instruments 1198
  legal background 1197–98
  legal certainty, detrimental to 1197
  limitation periods 1198–99
  misdemeanour fines 1194, 1196, 1198
  nature, gravity and duration of infringement 1194
  ne bis in idem (right not to be tried or punished
    twice) 1194, 1198, 1199–201
  outcome of criminal proceedings 1196
  personal data breach 192–93
  prevention or mitigation of consequences of
    infringement 1194
  procedural and substantive conditions 1198
  prohibition of specified individuals from managing
    future operations 1196
  rationale and policy underpinnings 1195–97
  related Articles in EPD 1195
  related Articles in LED 1195
  relevant recitals 1194–95
  res judicata effect 1200

security obligations, failure to fulfil 1196
suitable measures 1195–96
undertaking 1194
violations, types of subject to further
    penalties 1199
warnings 1194, 1196
without undue delay 1194
see also administrative fines
performance of contract 321, 322, 331, 333, 497, 522
Permanent Representatives Committee ('Coreper') 7
personal data
    analysis 108–14
    anonymisation 103, 105–6, 107
    'any information' 109
    biological material 107–8n15, 112
    biometric data 112
    breach *see* personal data breach
    case law 104–5, 107–8
    closely related provisions 104
    cookie identifiers 103
    costs of expansive definition 113–14
    data breach notification 29
    data subject 106–7
    deceased persons 103, 107, 112
    definitions 13–14, 103
    differences to DPD 108–9
    EU legislation 106
    genetic data 103, 108, 112
    health data 103–4, 112
    identifiability criterion 103, 106, 108–9, 110–11
    individuation requirement 107
    information provision *see* information provision where personal data collected from data subject; information provision where personal data not collected from data subject
    international instruments 106–7
    internet protocol (IP) address 103
    key constituents of definition 109–11
    legal background 106–8
    legal persons (corporate entities) 107
    location data 103, 108
    'means reasonably likely to be used' 109, 110–11
    mixed datasets (personal and non-personal data) 112
    national developments 107
    natural person 109, 111
    notification obligation *see* notification obligation regarding rectification or erasure of personal data or restriction of processing
    objective factors 108
    online identifiers 103, 108
    particular person 110
    privacy, fundamental right of 106, 107–8n15
    pseudonymisation 103, 112
    radio frequency identification tags 103
    rationale and policy underpinnings 105–6
    re-use 1213
    related Articles in EUDPR 104
    related provisions in LED 104
    'relating to' 109, 110
    relating to criminal convictions and offences *see* criminal convictions and offences
    relevant recitals 103–4
    sensitive data *see* special categories of personal data
    singling out and treating differently 108–9, 110–11
    special categories *see* special categories of personal data
personal data breach
    access, unauthorised 188, 192
    accidental breaches 192–93
    analysis 191–93
    availability of data 192
    circumstances of breach 189
    closely related provisions 189
    confidentiality breach 192
    data protection by design and by default 578
    definition 101
    destruction, accidental or unlawful 192
    disclosure, unauthorised 189, 192, 193
    discrimination, identity theft or fraud, financial loss, damage to reputation, sensitive data, criminal convictions and offences related to security measures 647
    erasure ('right to be forgotten') 188
    EU legislation 190
    human life, protection of 188
    humanitarian purposes 188
    identity fraud 189
    information provision where personal data collected from data subject 418
    information rights 188
    integrity of data 192
    international instruments 190–91
    law enforcement 189
    legal background 189–91
    loss of data 192, 193
    misconduct 192–93
    misuse of personal data 189, 191
    national developments 191
    negligence 192–93
    notification requirements 188, 190, 191
    object, right to 188
    personal data 192
    personal data breach communication to data subject *see* personal data breach communication to data subject
    processor 607, 608, 609
    profiling 188
    public health 188
    rationale and policy underpinnings 190
    rectification 188
    related Articles in EPD 189
    related Articles in EUDPR 189, 193
    related Articles in LED 189, 193

personal data breach (*cont.*)
  relevant recitals 188–89
  risk-based approach 26
  sanctions 192–93
  security breach 191–92
  security of processing 631, 632
  social protection 188
  tasks of the European Data Protection Board (EDPB) 1076
  types of security incidents covered 192
  unauthorised 188, 192
  see also communication of personal data breach to data subject; personal data breach notification requirements
personal data breach communication to data subject
  accidental or unlawful destruction, loss, alteration, unauthorised disclosure or access 659
  analysis 658–62
  application of communication obligation 659–60
  breaches covered 659
  case law 657
  clear and plain language 654, 661
  closely related provisions 655
  code of practice 658
  consequences and adverse effects 654–55, 661
  consequences, severity of 659
  content of communication 661
  contractual arrangements 660
  criminal offences and early disclosure hampering law enforcement 659, 662
  Cybersecurity Act 657
  dedicated messages 661
  disproportionate effort 654, 660
  enforcement 662
  EU legislation 656–57
  financial compensation 655
  financial loss 659
  free of charge 661
  high risk 654, 659
  identification of individuals 659
  identity theft or fraud 659
  impossibility or disproportionate effort exception 654, 660
  information notes 658
  international instruments 657
  law enforcement authorities and early disclosure hampering investigation 655
  legal background 656–57
  measures taken 661
  Member State law and practice 658
  method of communication 661
  mitigation measures 654, 655, 661, 662
  multiple breaches 657
  multiple communication channels 661
  name and contact details 661
  national developments 657
  national laws 658
  nature and gravity of breach 654–55, 661

  nature, sensitivity and volume of data 659
  number of affected individuals 659, 661
  password resetting 661
  physical, material or non-material damage 659
  processor's role 661–62
  rationale and policy underpinnings 655–56
  related Articles in EPD 655
  related Articles in LED 655
  relevant recitals 654–55
  risk no longer likely to materialise 654, 660
  special characteristics of controller 659
  special characteristics of individual 659
  subsequent measures 660
  supervisory authority 654–55, 656, 658, 659, 661, 662
  technical and organisational protection measures 655, 659–60
  territorial scope 658
  third country legal requirements, conflict with 662
  timing of communication 660
  type of breach 659
  unnecessary notification fatigue 659
  without undue delay 654–55, 656–57, 659, 660, 661–62
personal data breach notification requirements
  certification 738
  codes of conduct 722
  controller and processor 29
  data portability 497–98
  Directive 2002/58/EC 1298, 1299
  personal data processing 312
  responsibility of controller 564, 566
  review of other Union legal acts on data protection 1316
  tasks of supervisory authority 933–34
  trilogue 7
  see also personal data breach notification to supervisory authority
personal data breach notification to supervisory authority
  accidental or unlawful destruction, loss, alteration, unauthorised disclosure or access 645
  accountability and documentation of breaches 641, 649–50
  analysis 644–51
  availability breaches 645
  breach response plan 642
  breaches subject to notification 645
  case law 644
  categories and number of records concerned 640, 648
  closely related provisions 641
  code of practice 644
  confidentiality breaches 640, 641, 645, 646
  consequences and adverse effects 640, 641–42, 648
  contractual arrangements 647
  controller obligations 645–47

criminal activity 650
cross-border processing 648–49
Cybersecurity Act 643
digital service providers 642–43
discrimination 640, 641–42
economic or social disadvantage 640
essential services operators 642–43
EU legislation 642–43
financial loss 640
identification of individuals, ease of 647
identity theft or fraud 640, 641–42
information notes 644, 648
integrity breaches 641, 645
internal processes for detection 649
internal register 649
international instruments 643
legal background 642–44
limitation of rights 640, 641–42
loss of control over personal data 640, 641–42
measures taken or proposed 640, 648
Member State law and practice 644
mitigation of adverse effects 640, 648
multiple breaches 646, 648
name and contact details 640, 648
national developments 643
national laws 644
nature and gravity of breach 641, 648
nature, sensitivity and volume of data 647
number of affected individuals 647, 648
online forms 644, 648
payment services providers 642–43
penalties 650–51
physical, material or non-material
    damage 640, 646–47
processor obligations 647–48
public electronic communications networks
    providers 642–43
rationale and policy underpinnings 641–42
related Articles in EPD 641
related Articles in LED 641
relevant recitals 640–41
reputational, psychological or financial
    harm 640, 641–42
risks 646–47
security incidents 645
security measures 641
severity of consequences 647
special characteristics of individual 647
supervisory authority 640, 644–45, 646, 647,
    649, 650–51
territorial scope of notification
    requirement 644–45
trust and confidence, loss of 641–42
trust service providers 642–43
type of breach 647
whom to notify 648–49
without undue delay 640–41, 644,
    645–46, 647–48

personal data processing principles
    analysis 314–19
    case law 310–11, 313–14
    closely related provisions 310
    compatible use dimension 315
    confidentiality 309–10
    data breach notification duty 312
    disproportionate interference in data subject's rights
        and interests 317
    duty to inform data subjects 311
    EU legislation 312
    inaccurate, rectified or deleted data 309–10
    integrity and confidentiality principle 309, 311,
        312, 318
    international instruments 312
    lawfulness, fairness and transparency
        principle 309–10, 311, 312, 313, 314–15
    legal background 312–14
    notification of data breaches 318
    police activity 317
    privacy, fundamental right of 313, 314
    purpose limitation principle 309, 311,
        312, 315–17
    rationale and policy underpinnings 311
    related Articles in LED 310
    relevant recitals 309–10
    security requirement 309–10, 311, 312
    specific purposes 309–10
    storage limitation principle 309, 311, 312, 318
    telephone, email and internet usage 313
    time limits for retention or erasure 309–10,
        313–14, 318
personal profiles 555
PETs *see* **Privacy-Enhancing Technologies (PETs)**
PHAEDRA project 1036–37
Philippines 501
photograph processing 175, 207, 366, 374
    see also biometric data
PIAs *see* **Privacy Impact Assessments (PIAs)**
Platform as a Service (PaaS) 584
PNR *see* **Passenger Name Record (PNR) data**
POA *see* **power of attorney (POA)**
Poland
    churches and religious associations 1258, 1260–
        61, 1264–65, 1266
    compensation, right to and liability 1165
    data portability 499
    joint controllers 584
**police and judicial cooperation in criminal
    matters** 55, 58, 317, 552, 782–83,
    1304, 1320
police records 406
**political behaviour under former totalitarian
    regimes** 497–98, 524, 543–44, 1241,
    1247–48
political factors 776, 785
portability of data
    analysis 502–6

portability of data (*cont.*)
  Application Programme Interface (API) 505
  archiving purposes in the public interest, scientific or historical research purposes or statistical purposes 1240–41, 1247
  automated individual decision-making, including profiling 524
  breach 188, 505
  case law 499, 502
  challenges 505–6
  closely related provisions 498
  commercial purpose 501
  consent 22, 497
  controller responsibilities 504–5
  data subject rights 22
  delay feature enabling identity verification 505–6
  delete, right to 504
  economic rationale 497–98, 499, 500
  erasure ('right to be forgotten') 497–98
  EU legislation 500
  export-import model 505
  identity confirmation 505
  indirect identifiers 505
  information provision where personal data collected from data subject 413, 428–29
  information provision where personal data not collected from data subject 434
  international instruments 501
  legal background 500–2
  limitations 502–4
  lock-in risk 499
  national developments 502
  number portability 500
  object, right to 497–98, 504
  observed data 503
  personal data breach 188
  processed pursuant to consent or contract 501, 502, 504
  provided by data subject 502
  quantified self-application 503
  rationale and policy underpinnings 499–500
  rectification 498
  rejection of internet services 504
  related Articles in LED 498–99
  relevant recitals 497–98
  restriction of processing 485–86, 498, 543–44, 550–51
  review of other Union legal acts on data protection 1316
  rights-based rationale 499
  suspension or freezing of portability mechanisms 505–6
  switching services 499–500
  transfers on basis of adequacy decision 788–89
  wearable devices 503
Portugal 676, 886, 1225
position of data protection officer (DPO)
  age and work experience 704
  analysis 703–7
  authority and expertise 701
  case law 701, 702–3
  closely related provisions 700–1
  conflicts of interests 705–6
  contact by data subjects 700
  direct reporting 700
  EU legislation 702
  expert knowledge 700
  external data protection officer (DPO) 705–6
  independence 702–5, 706
  internal data protection officer (DPO) 705–6
  international instruments 702
  involvement 700
  legal background 702–3
  national developments 702
  nature and stability of job 704
  obligations of appointing organisations 706–7
  other tasks and duties 700
  part-time work 705
  participation in court proceedings as expert or witness 705–6
  position 701
  rationale and policy underpinnings 701–2
  related Articles in EUDPR 701
  related Articles in LED 701
  relevant recitals 700
  resources 706–7
  status and power 704
  support by top management 700, 706
  tasks 701
  team 701
  time 707
  training, continuous 707
  see also data protection officer (DPO)
power of attorney (POA) 805
powers of supervisory authority
  access to all data and information from controller and processor 939
  access to any premises 939, 944–45, 946
  additional powers 940–41, 944, 946–47
  administrative fines and penalties 939, 940, 941, 943, 944, 945, 946–47
  advice to controller 947
  analysis 946–47
  appropriate safeguards 940–41, 943, 944, 947
  audits 939, 946
  authorisation and advisory powers 939–41, 943, 947
  bans on processing 940–41, 946–47
  case law 942, 945
  certification 939, 940, 947
    review 946
    withdrawal 939, 946–47
  closely related provisions 941
  communication requirement of data breach 939
  complaints-handling 940–41, 945
  compliance 939, 946–47

Index

contractual clauses authorisation 940
cooperation 942–43, 945, 946, 947
corrective powers 939, 940–41, 943, 946–47
criminal penalty 945
EU legislation 943–44
information for performance of tasks provided by controller or processor 939, 946
infringements 939, 940–41, 946, 947
international instruments 944
intervention powers 943, 944
investigative powers 940–41, 943, 944, 946
joint operations 947
judicial review/remedy 940–41, 947
legal background 943–45
legal proceedings, power to engage in 943, 944, 947
limitation, temporary or definitive 939, 940–41, 946–47
monitoring and enforcement 940–41
national developments 944–45
negative powers 947
opinions to national parliament 940
prior authorisation 940–41, 944–45
prior consultation procedure 939, 947
rationale and policy underpinnings 942–43
related Articles in EPD 942
related Articles in LED 942
relevant recitals 940–41
reprimands and warnings 939, 946–47
standard data protection clauses 940
suspension of data flows 939, 946–47
precontractual relationship 330–32
preliminary ruling procedure 1126, 1130–31, 1170
principles 16–20
certification 738
consent 18–19
from children 19
legitimate interest 17–18
purpose limitation 16–17
sensitive data 19–20
small and medium-sized enterprises (SMEs) 20
prior consultation
absence of measures by controller 684
analysis 683–87
blockchain 684
case law 682
closely related provisions 681
data protection impact assessment (DPIA) 680–81, 682–84, 685
data protection officer (DPO) 682–83
deadlines 685–86
EU legislation 682–83
international instruments 683
legal background 682–83
national developments 683
necessary documents and information for submission 686
primary or secondary legislation 686

prior checking 682–83
procedural aspects 685–86
related Articles in EUDPR 682
related Articles in LED 681
relevant recitals 680–81
risk-based approach 26
role of supervisory authorities 686–87
size of harm and frequency of occurrence 685
stop the clock suspensions 685–86
time of consultation 683–84
Privacy Bridges Report (2015) 563
Privacy by Design (PbD) 8, 573, 575–76, 577, 578, 607–8
privacy enforcement authorities 267–68
privacy, fundamental right of
access, right of data subject 401–2, 403, 405, 458–59, 460–61
accountability/responsibility of controller 557, 560, 563, 564, 568
automated individual decision-making, including profiling 522, 530–31
biometric data 211
certification 734–35, 737
children's consent and information society services 357, 360–61
churches and religious associations 1257, 1260–61
compensation, right to and liability 1165, 1167–68, 1172, 1173
consent 176, 352
controller 151
cooperation between lead supervisory authority and other authorities concerned 957–58
criminal convictions and offences 388
data breach notification 29
data controller 151
data portability 499, 504–5
data protection by design and by default 573, 574, 578
data protection impact assessment (DPIA) 670, 671, 673
data subject rights 21–22
derogations for specific situations 843–44
designation of data protection officer (DPO) 693–94
Directive 2002/58/EC 1296, 1297, 1299
employment context 1230, 1231, 1232, 1233–34, 1236
erasure ('right to be forgotten') 478–79, 480
filing system 141
freedom of expression and information 1202, 1204, 1205, 1208, 1209–10
genetic data 201
identification, non-requirement of 394
information exchange 1034
information provision where personal data collected from data subject 420, 424–25
information provision where personal data not collected from data subject 439
international cooperation 859

1372 Index

privacy, fundamental right of (*cont.*)
 joint controllers 27, 584–85
 joint operations of supervisory authorities 989
 mutual assistance 977
 national identification number 1225–26
 object, right to 516
 personal data 106, 107–8n15, 313, 314
 public access to official documents 1215–16, 1217–19
 recipient 165
 rectification 472–73
 restrictions 546, 547–48, 551–52, 553
 secrecy obligations 1253–54
 security of processing 634
 special categories of personal data 373
 subject-matter and objectives 48, 50–51, 52, 53, 57
 supervisory authority 270, 866, 868
 tasks of data protection officer (DPO) 711, 714
 tasks of supervisory authority 931, 932, 933
 territorial scope 76, 78, 82, 85, 87, 89
 transfers: general principles 757
 transfers on basis of adequacy decision 776, 779–80, 783, 786
 transparent information 401–2, 403, 405
Privacy Impact Assessments (PIAs) 563, 668, 670
privacy management programme 691, 702
privacy notice 352, 415, 428, 443, 445–46
privacy officers 691, 702, 711–12
privacy professionals 707
privacy seals 735–36
privacy statements 714
Privacy-Enhancing Technologies (PETs) 573, 574–75
private sector
 archiving purposes in the public interest, scientific or historical research purposes or statistical purposes 1241
 competence 902, 904, 909
 competence of lead supervisory authority 914
 criminal offences and criminal penalties 389–90
 designation of data protection officer (DPO) 688–89
 independence 1065–66
 information provision where personal data not collected from data subject 440
 lawfulness of processing 333, 334, 336, 337, 340
 position of data protection officer (DPO) 700
 powers of supervisory authority 943
 supervisory authority 265
 suspension of proceedings 1157
 tasks of data protection officer (DPO) 709–10
 tasks of supervisory authority 928
procedural law 928–29, 943, 944, 945, 947
procedure of European Data Protection Board (EDPB)
 adoption of documents and procedures 1093
 advisory opinions 1093

 agenda preparation 1093
 amendments of rules 1093
 analysis 1091–93
 binding decisions 1091, 1093
 chair and deputy chairs 1092–93
 closely related provisions 1090
 collegiality and inclusiveness 1090
 composition 1092–93
 confidentiality 1092, 1093
 consistency mechanism 1091–92, 1093
 consultations 1092, 1093
 convening of meetings 1092
 dispute resolution procedure 1091
 entry into force of Rules 1093
 establishment and functioning of secretariat 1092
 EU legislation 1090–91
 European Data Protection Board (EDPB) 1092
 final provisions 1093
 financial reports 1093
 general provisions 1093
 information and communication system 1093
 international instruments 1091
 language and translation 1093
 legal background 1090–91
 majority voting (two-thirds majority) 1091
 periodic review 1093
 plenary meetings 1093
 public access to official documents 1093
 publication of annual report 1093
 publication of final documents 1093
 rationale and policy underpinnings 1090
 representation of European Data Protection Board (EDPB) 1093
 restricted access to meetings 1093
 rules of procedure 1092–93
 secretariat and organisation 1093
 simple majority voting 1091
 single voting rule 1090–91
 submission of documents and minutes 1093
 term of office expiry or resignation 1092
 tie-break vote 1091
 time limits 1091–92
 travel cost reimbursement 1093
 videoconferencing 1093
 voting 1091–92, 1093
 work programme 1093
 working methods 1093
 see also European Data Protection Board (EDPB)
processing
 analysis 119–21
 anonymisation 121
 automated means 116, 119
 case law 116–17, 118–19
 closely related provisions 116
 definition 100
 EU legislation 118
 filing system 116, 119
 international instruments 118

legal background 118–19
manual system 116, 118, 119
national developments 118
rationale and policy underpinnings 117
related Articles in EPD 116
related Articles in EUDPR 116
related Articles in LED 116
relevant recitals 116
restriction 118
structuring 118
sub-processing 27–28
third parties 120
processor
ability to restore access to data 607
analysis 159–61, 605–10
assistance to controller 607
audits 599, 607–8
availability of data 607
binding corporate rules (BCRs) 607, 814–15, 816
case law 157, 601, 604–5
categories of data subjects 605–6
closely related provisions 157, 601
competent authorities 603–4
context, specific 605
contract and standard contractual clauses 599, 600, 601–3, 605–6, 608–9
and controller, contract between 605–8
and controller, relationship between 159–60
criminal record data, retention and deletion of 605
cross-border processing 279, 280, 281–82, 283
definition 100
derogations for specific situations 846
enforcement 610
enterprise 246, 248
EU legislation 158, 602–3
informing controller of addition or replacement of other processors 599
infringements 599, 600, 607–8, 610
inspections 599, 607–8
instructions 605–6
integrity 607
international instruments 158, 603
international transfers 602, 607
lawful processing 605
legal background 158, 602–5
legally separate from controller 159
liability 600, 601–2, 603, 604, 605–7, 608
main establishment 225–26, 227, 228, 229, 230, 233, 234–35
multiple controllers 602
national developments 158, 603–4
nature, scope, purpose and context of processing 603, 605–6
non-EU controllers and processors, relationship between 608–9
obligations 603
obligations and rights of controller 605–6
outsourcing 157–58

parties that may be processors 160
rationale and policy underpinnings 157–58, 601–2
recipient 165, 166–67
related Articles in EPD 601
related Articles in EUDPR 157, 161
related Articles in LED 157, 161, 601
relevant recitals 600
as representatives 238, 239–41, 242–44
responsibilities 608
risk assessment 607–8
separate controllers 602
size of controller or processor 603
sub-contracting 158
sub-processors 605
subject-matter and duration of processing 603, 605–6
supervisory authority 265, 600, 603, 607, 609–10
supervisory authority concerned 272–74, 275–76
technical and organisational measures 608
testing, regular 607
to controller status change 609–10
type of data 605–6
volume of data 603
see also controller and processor; effective judicial remedy against controller or processor
professional secrecy
confidentiality 1112–13, 1115–16
controller responsibility 555
establishment rules of supervisory authority 893, 895, 897, 899–900
information provision where personal data have not been obtained from data subject 435, 440, 447
mutual assistance 982
special categories of personal data 365–66, 371, 379–80
specific data processing situations 40–41
profiling
access, right of data subject 399–400
analysis 130–31
automated processing 127, 128–29, 130
case law 128, 130
children 128
closely related provisions 127
consent 176–77
consultation of supervisory authority 30
cookie identifiers 127, 129
data portability 497–98
data protection impact assessment (DPIA) 30, 524–25, 531–32, 540, 665, 667, 673–74
definition 100
EU legislation 129
health, personal preferences, interests, behaviour, location or movements 130
information provision where personal data collected from data subject 413, 414, 420, 429–30
international instruments 129
internet protocol (IP) address 127

profiling (*cont.*)
  legal background 129
  national developments 129
  object, right to 508, 510
  online identifiers/tracking 127, 128
  performance at work, creditworthiness, reliability and conduct 129, 130
  personal data breach 188
  radio frequency identification tags 127
  rationale and policy underpinnings 128
  recipient 163–64
  related Articles in EPD 128
  related Articles in EUDPR 128
  related Articles in LED 128
  relevant recitals 127
  restrictions 543–44
  special categories of personal data 382
  specific data processing situations 41
  supervisory authorities, role of 8
  tasks of the European Data Protection Board (EDPB) 1069, 1076–77
  territorial scope 74–75, 90–91
  transparent information 399–400
  see also automated individual decision-making, including profiling

proportionality
  access, right of data subject 406, 459–60
  administrative fines 1189
  archiving purposes in the public interest, scientific or historical research purposes or statistical purposes 1240–41
  automated individual decision-making, including profiling 522
  biometric data 210, 211
  children's consent and information society services 361
  churches and religious associations 1257
  data portability 498
  data protection by design and by default 576
  data protection impact assessment (DPIA) 665
  employment context 1237
  freedom of expression and information 1202
  lawfulness of processing 334, 336, 338, 339–40
  penalties 1198–99, 1200
  personal data processing 313
  powers of supervisory authority 943
  prior consultation 684–85, 686
  pseudonymisation 132–33
  restriction of processing 485–86, 545, 548
  restrictions 549–50
  secrecy obligations 1252, 1253
  security of processing 635–36
  special categories of personal data 380–82
  specific data processing situations 41
  subject-matter and objectives 48
  territorial scope 95–96
  transfers on basis of adequacy decision 787–88
  transparent information 406

provisional enforcement or compliance actions 37
pseudonymisation 15, 135
  analysis 135–36
  anonymous information/anonymity 132, 135–36
  archiving purposes in the public interest, scientific or historical research purposes or statistical purposes 132–33, 136, 1240–41, 1246–47
  automated decision-making, including profiling 24
  case law 133, 135
  clinical trials/medical research 132–33, 135
  closely related provisions 133
  codes of conduct 722
  data minimisation 132–33, 136
  data portability 132–33, 498, 502–3
  data protection by design and by default 136, 571, 575, 577, 578–79
  definitions 15–16, 100
  derogations for specific situations 851, 853
  encryption 135
  erasure ('right to be forgotten') 132–33
  EU legislation 134
  hash function 135
  identifiability 132
  identification, non-requirement of 391, 392–93, 394, 395–96
  information provision where personal data not collected from data subject 446–47
  international instruments 134
  key-coded data 135
  legal background 133–35
  legitimate interest 17
  national developments 134–35
  personal data 103, 112
  personal data breach notification to supervisory authority 640
  processor 607
  purpose limitation 17
  randomly assigned code 133–34, 135
  rationale and policy underpinnings 133–34
  re-identification 135–36
  rectification 132–33
  related Articles in EPD 133
  related Articles in EUDPR 133
  related Articles in LED 133
  relevant recitals 132–33
  responsibility of controller 555
  restriction of processing 132–33, 485–86
  security of processing 630, 636
  stored key 135
  tokenisation 135
  unauthorised reversal of 29
public access to official documents
  administrative documents 1218
  analysis 1216–21
  case law 1214, 1216
  closely related provisions 1213
  conflict rule 1219

Court of Justice of the European Union (CJEU) 1219–20
disclosure 1213, 1217
 active 1216
 passive 1216
effects of Article 1220
EU legislation 1215
European Court of Human Rights (ECtHR) 1217–19
exemptions and derogations 1216–17
freedom of expression and information 1216–18, 1220
international instruments 1215
legal background 1215–16
legitimate interest 1219–20
national developments 1215
privacy, fundamental right of 1215–16, 1217–19
public interest 1213, 1217, 1218, 1220
rationale and policy underpinnings 1214
re-use of public sector information 1213, 1220–21
related Articles in LED 1213
relation of Article to Directive 2003/98/EC 1220–21
relevant recitals 1213
renvoi interpretation 1219
threshold interpretation 1219
transparency 1214, 1215–16, 1220
validity 1216
public authorities
 administrative fines 1182, 1188
 archiving purposes in the public interest, scientific or historical research purposes or statistical purposes 1241
 binding corporate rules (BCRs) 257, 262–63
 competence 902, 904
 competence of lead supervisory authority 914
 consent 182, 353
 criminal convictions and offences 389
 data protection impact assessment (DPIA) 667, 671
 derogations for specific situations 841
 designation of data protection officer (DPO) 688
 filing system 138
 group of undertakings 255
 independence 1065–66
 information provision where personal data collected from data subject 421
 information provision where personal data not collected from data subject 440
 international organisations 307
 law enforcement 11–12
 lawfulness of processing 323, 325–26n1, 330, 333, 334, 335, 336
 notification obligation regarding rectification, erasure or restriction of processing 495
 object, right to 510
 penalties 1194
 position of data protection officer (DPO) 700
 powers of supervisory authority 941, 943
 public access to official documents 1213
 recipient 163, 165
 representatives of controllers or processors not established in the Union 595
 review of other Union legal acts on data protection 1316
 supervisory authority 265, 267–68, 269–70, 863–64, 870
 tasks of data protection officer (DPO) 709–10
 tasks of supervisory authority 928
 transfers on basis of adequacy decision 781
 transfers subject to appropriate safeguards 797–98, 804
public health
 automated individual decision-making, including profiling 524
 data portability 497–98
 derogations for specific situations 842, 850
 erasure ('right to be forgotten') 22–23, 475
 personal data breach 188
 rectification 469–70
 restrictions 543–44
 special categories of personal data 365, 366, 369, 376f, 379–80
 subject-matter and objectives 58
 see also health data
public interest
 access, right of data subject 452
 activity reports 951–52
 automated individual decision-making, including profiling 539
 biometric data 207
 communication of personal data breach to data subject 656–57
 competence 902, 904, 909
 competence of lead supervisory authority 914
 consent 176
 criminal convictions and offences 389–90
 data portability 497–98, 504
 data protection impact assessment (DPIA) 666, 675
 data subjects, representation of 1149
 derogations for specific situations 35, 841–42, 843–44, 845, 846, 849–50, 854–55
 employment context 1232
 erasure ('right to be forgotten') 22–23, 475, 482
 freedom of expression and information 1205, 1208, 1209
 group of undertakings 255
 information provision where personal data collected from data subject 421
 lawfulness of processing 321, 322, 323–24, 325–27, 328, 335–36, 341, 343
 material scope 67
 object, right to 508, 509, 510, 511–12, 513, 516, 517, 518, 519
 personal data breach 188
 prior consultation 684–85, 687
 processor 599, 602

public interest (*cont.*)
  public access to official documents 1213, 1217, 1218, 1220
  recipient 164
  restriction of processing 485, 490
  restrictions 543–44
  special categories of personal data 365, 366, 367, 369, 376f, 379, 380, 382
  subject-matter and objectives 58
  supervisory authority 265, 863–64
  tasks of supervisory authority 928, 936
  third parties 170
  transfers: general principles 764
  transfers on basis of adequacy decision 776, 780–81
  transfers or disclosures not authorised by Union law 825, 827, 831–32
  see also archiving purposes in the public interest, scientific or historical research purposes or statistical purposes
public international law 92–95
public registers
  automated individual decision-making, including profiling 524
  codes of conduct 723
  data portability 497–98
  derogations for specific situations 841, 844, 852–53
  erasure ('right to be forgotten') 482–83
  personal data breach 188
  records of processing activities 619
  restrictions 543–44
public sector information, reuse of 403, 411
publishers (online) 587
purpose limitation principle
  encryption 17
  identification, non-requirement of 392, 393, 395
  lawfulness of processing 321, 322, 326–27, 343
  personal data processing 309, 311, 312, 315–17
  principles 16–17
  processor 605–6
  pseudonymisation 17
  restrictions 551
  transfers on basis of adequacy decision 787–88

quality of data
  automated individual decision-making, including profiling 526
  information provision where personal data collected from data subject 415–16
  personal data processing 312, 313–15
  responsibility of controller 557, 561
  restrictions 546, 547, 551
  transfers on basis of adequacy decision 787–88

racial or ethnic origin, political opinions, religious or philosophical beliefs, trade union membership and sex life or sexual orientation
  special categories of personal data 365, 366, 369–70, 371, 374–75

radio frequency identification tags (RFIDs) 8, 14, 103, 127
recipient
  analysis 166–68
  automated processing 163–64
  closely related provisions 164
  consent 164
  controller 163–64, 165, 166–67
  copyright protecting software 163–64
  data subject 163–64, 166–67
  definition 100
  disclosure 163, 165, 167
  EU legislation 165
  filing system 163, 165
  intellectual property 163–64
  international instruments 165
  legal background 165–66
  medical records 163–64
  national developments 166
  privacy, fundamental right of 165
  processor 165, 166–67
  profiling 163–64
  public authorities 163, 165
  public authorities, exclusion of 167
  public interest 164
  rationale and policy underpinnings 165
  related Articles in EUDPR 164, 168
  related Articles in LED 164, 168
  relevant recitals 163–64
  third countries and international organisations 164
  third parties 163, 165, 166–67, 171
  trade secrets 163–64
records of processing activities
  analysis 619–24
  binding corporate rules (BCRs) 814
  categories of data 616, 620, 623
  categories of recipients 616, 620, 621
  closely related provisions 617
  controller and processor 28
  criminal convictions and offences 388, 389, 616, 623
  derogations for less than 250 employees 616, 617–18, 623–24
  description of categories of data subjects 616
  EU legislation 618–19
  exemptions from duty to notify 618
  information to be recorded by controllers 620–22
  information to be recorded by processors 622–23
  international instruments 619
  joint controllers 587
  legal background 618–19
  legal basis 620
  logging protocols 621
  name and contact details 616, 620, 622–23
  naming categories of recipients 621
  national developments 619
  prior checking procedure 619
  prior consultation 682

processor 608
purposes of processing 616, 620
rationale and policy underpinnings 617–18
related Articles in EUDPR 617
related Articles in LED 617
relevant recitals 616–17
representative 620
representatives of controllers or processors not established in the Union 596
responsibility of controller 560, 565
review of other Union legal acts on data protection 1316
security of processing 637
special categories of data 623
supervisory authority, cooperation with 625
tasks of supervisory authority 928, 934
technical services 623
time limits for erasure 616, 620
transfers: general principles 757
transfers subject to appropriate safeguards 804

rectification
accuracy 471
analysis 473–74
archiving purposes in the public interest, scientific or historical research purposes or statistical purposes 1240–41, 1247, 1249–50
automated individual decision-making, including profiling 524
case law 470, 472–73
clear and plain language 469
closely related provisions 470
compensation, right to and liability 1168
erasure ('right to be forgotten) 469–70, 471, 473, 477–78
EU legislation 471–72
forwarded rectifications or complementing to previous recipients 471, 474
free of charge 472, 473–74
identification, non-requirement of 394
impossibility or disproportionate effort 471, 472
incomplete, false, erroneous or inaccurate data 471–73, 474
information provision where personal data collected from data subject 413, 418, 419, 428–29
information provision where personal data not collected from data subject 434
international instruments 472
judicial protection 473
lawfulness and fairness 469
legal background 471–73
legal claims, establishment, exercise or defence of 469–70
national developments 472
notification obligation 471
object, right to 512–13
powers of supervisory authority 939
pseudonymisation 132–33
rationale and policy underpinnings 471

related Articles in EUDPR 470
related Articles in LED 470
relevant recitals 469–70
restriction of processing 485–86, 487, 488, 543–44, 550–51, 553
supplementary statement 473
time limits 469
transfers on basis of adequacy decision 787–88
transparent information and access rights 399, 402, 403
without undue delay 472, 473–74
see also notification obligation regarding rectification or erasure of personal data or restriction of processing

registers
certification register 732, 735
see also public registers

relevant and reasoned objection
analysis 290–91
case law 290
closely related provisions 288
definition 102
EU legislation 289
follow the objection 289
international instruments 289–90
legal background 289–90
mutual recognition or decentralised procedure for medicine approval 289
one-stop-shop mechanism 289–90
petty objection 291
rationale and policy underpinnings 288–89
referral procedures 289
relevant recitals 288
submission of matter to European Data Protection Board (EDPB) 289
supervisory authority and lead supervisory authority 288–89, 290–91

religious associations *see* churches and religious associations
remedies, liability and sanctions 39–40
remuneration
children's consent and information society services 359–60
information society service 296–97
lawfulness of processing 337–38

reports of the European Data Protection Board (EDPB)
accountability 1086, 1087, 1088
accredited certification 1088
analysis 1087–88
annual budgetary request 1088
binding decisions 1087–88
case law 1085, 1087
certification mechanisms 1088
closely related provisions 1085
consistency mechanism 1088
EU legislation 1086
governance 1086

reports of the European Data Protection Board (EDPB) (*cont.*)
  guidelines, recommendations and best practices 1085, 1087
  international instruments 1086–87
  language 1087
  legal background 1086–87
  made public 1085
  press conferences 1088
  rationale and policy underpinnings 1085–86
  related Articles in EUDPR 949
  related Articles in LED 1085
  transmission to Parliament, Council and Commission 1085, 1086, 1087
  transparency 1086, 1087, 1088
  see also activity reports; Commission reports
representation of data subjects
  active in field of data protection 1148
  analysis 1147–50
  associations, right to bring complaints and proceedings on their own initiative 1149, 1151
  case law 1143, 1144–46
  closely related provisions 1142
  collective consumer application 1145
  collective redress 1144, 1150
  compensation, right to representation for 1142, 1143, 1148–49
  complaint, right to lodge 1142, 1143, 1147, 1148–,
  'consumer' concept strictly construed 1146
  content of mandate 1148
  EU legislation 1144
  infringement of rights 1142
  international instruments 1144
  judgments in civil and commercial matters 1145
  judicial remedy 1142, 1143–44, 1147, 1148, 1150
  jurisdiction 1145, 1146, 1148
  legal background 1144–46
  national developments 1144
  not-for profit organisations/associations 1142, 1147
  preliminary rulings 1145
  properly constituted 1147
  rationale and policy underpinnings 1143–44
  related Articles in LED 1142
  relevant recitals 1142
  retention of data relating to electronic communications 1145
  specialised non-governmental organisations (NGOs) 1143–44, 1146
  statutory objectives in public interest 1142, 1143–44, 1148
  who can be mandated 1147–48
  who can mandate 1148
representative
  analysis 240–44
  appointment formalities 242–43
  case law 238–39, 240
  closely related provisions 238
  Commission 244
  conflict of interests 243–44
  controllers 238, 239–41, 242–44
  data protection officers (DPOs) 243–44
  data subjects 239, 241, 243, 244
  de facto representative 242
  definition 101
  enforcement proceedings 244
  establishment conditions 241–42
  EU legislation 239–40
  individual representative 240–41
  international instruments 240
  lead contact 241
  legal background 239–40
  legal entity (company) 240–41
  national developments 240
  processors 238, 239–41, 242–44
  rationale and policy underpinnings 239
  relevant recitals 238
  supervisory authorities 238, 239, 242–43, 244
  third parties 244
  written designation 242–43
  see also representatives of controllers or processors not established in the Union
representatives of controllers or processors not established in the Union
  analysis 593–97
  case law 590, 592–93
  closely related provisions 590
  conformity declaration 591
  criminal convictions 589
  designation of representative 595–96
  enforcement 597
  establishment 592–93
  EU legislation 591–92
  exemptions 595
  failure to designate representative 597
  infringement of provisions 597
  international instruments 592
  legal background 591–63
  medical devices 592
  national developments 592
  national market surveillance authorities 591
  no one-stop-shop 594
  obligations of representative 596
  radio equipment 591
  rationale and policy underpinnings 590–91
  related Articles in EPD 590
  relevant recitals 589
  risk assessment 595
  service contract 595–96
  subsidiary or agent 591, 593
  technical documentation 591
  written designation 593–94, 595–96
reprimands for minor infringements 650–51, 659, 1187, 1189

reputation
   children's consent and information society services 357, 358
   communication of personal data breach to data subject 655, 659
   data portability 503
   responsibility of controller 555
   unauthorised reversal of 29

Research Network on European Union Administrative Law 1080

responsibility of controller (accountability)
   accountability and the law 566–68
   accountability-related measures 565–66
   analysis 560–68
   approval and oversight 564
   assessment purpose specification 564
   assignment of responsibility 564
   auditing 562, 564
   binding corporate rules (BCRs) 557, 562, 565
   case law 556
   certification mechanisms 555, 556, 565, 566
   closely related provisions 556
   codes of conduct 555, 565
   codes of practice 566
   common elements of accountability in practice 563–64
   compliance policies 561–62, 566
   controllability 561
   data breach notification 564, 566
   data protection by design and default 565, 568
   data protection impact assessments (DPIAs) 564, 565, 566, 568
   data protection officer (DPO) 562–63, 565, 566
   data protection professionals 563
   development of accountability 568
   documentation 565
   economic and reputational risks 564
   EU legislation 558
   evidential burden of proof 567–68
   implementation of data principles 558
   internal policies and processes 564
   international instruments 558–59
   legal background 558–60
   liability 555, 561
   mapping of process activities 564
   multiple accountabilities disorder 561
   national developments 559–60
   organisational commitment 563
   oversight, review and updating 564
   physical, material or non-material damage 565
   prior authorisation or consultation 565
   rationale and policy underpinnings 557–58
   related Articles in EPD 556
   related Articles in EUDPR 556
   related Articles in LED 556
   relevant recitals 555–56
   remediation and external enforcement 564
   responsibility 561
   responsiveness 561
   risk and objective assessment 555
   risk to rights and freedoms of natural persons 555
   sanctions 566–67
   scalability - nature of processing and level and likelihood of risk 564–65
   statutory elements of accountability 561–63
   supervisory authority 560, 565–66
   terminology 561
   transparency 561, 563, 564
   see also accountability

restriction of processing, right to
   accuracy, contested/inaccuracy 485, 487, 489
   analysis 125, 488–91
   automated filing systems 123, 125, 485
   blocking 124–25, 487, 489
   case law 125, 486, 488
   circumstances allowing restriction 489–90
   closely related provisions 123, 486
   data no longer necessary but required for legal claims 485, 487, 490
   definition 100
   erasure ('right to be forgotten') 485–87, 488–89
   EU legislation 124, 487
   guarantee of right of access 489
   international instruments 124, 487
   legal background 124–25, 487–88
   lifting restriction 491
   marking 125
   modalities and implications 490–91
   national developments 124–25, 488
   no longer available to general public 488
   object, right to 485–86, 487, 490
   rationale and policy underpinnings 124, 486–87
   related Articles in LED 123, 486
   related provisions in EUDPR 123
   relevant recitals 123, 485–86
   storage of information 488
   temporary removal 485, 488
   time limits for deletion 489
   unavailability to users 485
   unlawful processing but opposition to erasure 485, 487, 489–90
   without undue delay 489

restrictions
   access, right of data subject 449, 452, 458
   analysis 550–53
   application to Union law 552–53
   archiving purposes in the public interest, scientific or historical research purposes or statistical purposes 1240–41, 1247, 1249–50
   border checks, asylum and immigration 552
   breach 543–44
   case law 544–45, 547–50
   categories of data 543
   changes in GDPR 550–52
   civil law claims 543
   closely related provisions 544

1380 Index

restrictions (*cont.*)
  criminal convictions and offences 549–50
  data subject rights 24–25
  defence 543
  Directive 2002/58/EC 549–50
  economic or financial interest 543–44
  effective remedy 548
  EU legislation 546
  fundamental rights and freedoms 553
  integrity of data 553
  international instruments 546–47
  judicial independence and judicial proceedings 543
  legal background 546–50
  legislative competence 552
  legislative measures 546, 552–53
  legitimacy 547
  legitimate interest 17–18
  monitoring, inspection or regulatory function 543
  national developments 547
  notification of data breach 547
  obligation of controllers to inform of habitual residence 547
  powers of supervisory authority 939
  privacy, fundamental right of 546, 547–48, 551–52, 553
  publicising of processing operations 546
  purpose limitation principle 551
  purposes or categories of processing 543
  rationale and policy underpinnings 545
  related Articles in EPD 544
  related Articles in LED 544
  relevant recitals 543–44
  risks to rights and freedoms 543
  scope 543
  special categories of personal data 546
  specific provisions 543
  specification of controller 543
  specified purposes 545
  storage periods 543
  surveillance measures 550
  see also notification obligation regarding rectification or erasure of personal data or restriction of processing; restriction of processing, right to
retention of data and retention periods
  access, right of data subject 449, 450, 455, 457, 459
  automated individual decision-making, including profiling 523
  data subjects, representation of 1145
  Directive 2002/58/EC 1298
  information provision where personal data collected from data subject 419, 428
  notification obligation regarding rectification, erasure or restriction of processing 494
  object, right to 514
  restrictions 546
  transfers on basis of adequacy decision 784, 788
retrieval of data 117
return of data 599, 600, 607, 726

Réunion 83, 786
review of other Union legal acts on data protection
  amendment proposals 1315–16
  analysis 1315–17
  application: ePrivacy Regulation and EUDPR 1316–17
  case law 1313, 1314–15
  closely related provisions 1312
  divergences 1317
  EU legislation 1314
  fragmentation 1317
  law enforcement 1314
  legal background 1314–15
  legislative proposals 1315–16
  rationale and policy underpinnings 1313–14
  related Articles in EPD 1312
  related Articles in EUDPR 1312
  related Articles in LED 1312
  related provisions 1317
  relevant recitals 1312
  requirements of Article 98 1315–16
  updates of existing acts 1316
RFIDs *see* radio frequency identification tags (RFIDs)
risks and security of processing 630, 631–33, 635, 636

SaaS *see* Software as a Service (SaaS)
safeguards *see* additional safeguards; adequate safeguards
Safer Internet programme 356
Saint-Barthélemy 83, 786
Saint-Martin 83, 786
salaries, information on 1232
Schrems ruling 53, 779–82
scientific and historic research *see* archiving purposes in the public interest, scientific or historical research purposes or statistical purposes
seals and marks
  accountability/responsibility of controller 562
  certification 732
  certification bodies 745–46, 752
  Committee procedure 1281
  controller and processor 31–32
  reports 1088
  tasks of the European Data Protection Board (EDPB) 1070
  tasks of supervisory authority 927, 935
search-engine providers 90, 480
secrecy obligations
  analysis 1254–56
  case law 1252–53, 1254
  closely related provisions 1252
  competences of supervisory authorities 1255–56
  controller or processor, processing under authority of 613–14
  derogation 1253–54
  doctor/patient confidentiality 1255
  EU legislation 1253–54
  exemptions 1256

health care professionals 1253–54, 1256
independent supervision 1254–55
international instruments 1254
lawfulness of processing 324
lawyer/client confidentiality 1255–56
legal background 1253–54
legitimate interest 17–18
medical data 1256
national competent bodies 1256
national developments 1254
position of data protection officer (DPO) 700
privacy, fundamental right of 1253–54
procedural elements 1254
rationale and policy underpinnings 1253
relevant recitals 1252
self-incrimination, privilege against 1255–56
special categories of data 1253–54
state secrets 1034
substantive elements 1254–55
telecommunications data 1254
see also confidentiality; professional secrecy; trade secrets

Secretariat of the European Data Protection Board (EDPB)
public access to official documents 1109
analysis 1104–9
analytical, administrative and logistical support 1102, 1108–9
budget and financial support 1105, 1106, 1108
case law 1103, 1104
Chair of the European Data Protection Board (EDPB), instructions from 1102
closely related provisions 1102
common approach on decentralised agencies 1105–6
communications 1102, 1109
compliance 1104
control or monitoring mechanisms 1102
cooperation 1103, 1108
data protection expertise 1105
day-to-day business 1102, 1109
dispute settlement opinions and decisions 1102
drafting and publication of opinions 1109
due and timely performance of tasks 1107
efficiency and modernisation 1103
EU legislation 1104
financial administration 1102, 1105
human resources 1105
independence 1102, 1104, 1106, 1107, 1108
information and communication tasks 1109
international instruments 1104
IT infrastructure 1108
judicial review 1102
legal background 1104
liaison coordinator 1107
meetings: preparation and follow-up 1102
Memorandum of Understanding 1102, 1103, 1107–8, 1109

offices 1108
organisation of meetings 1109
preparation and follow-up of meetings 1109
preparation of Secretariat 1106–7
provision of European Data Protection Supervisor (EDPS) 1102, 1104–6
rationale and policy underpinnings 1103
record management 1109
related Articles in EUDPR 1103
relations with other institutions 1109
relevant recitals 1102
representation of the board before courts 1109
security of information 1108, 1109
service level agreements 1106
staff and expertise 1102, 1107–8
staff and separate reporting lines 1102
supervisory authority activities 1109
synergies and effectiveness enhancement 1105–6
translations 1102, 1106, 1109

security of processing
access, right of data subject 406, 456
accidental or unlawful destruction, accidental loss, alteration, unauthorised disclosure or access 630, 631, 632, 633, 634, 635, 636
accountability/responsibility of controller 557, 560, 565
adequacy 33
administrative fines 636–37
analysis 634–37
automated individual decision-making, including profiling 524
availability and resilience of systems 636
case law 631, 634
certification 734–35, 737, 738–39
churches and religious associations 1261
closely related provisions 630–31
codes of conduct 722
compliance with security obligation 635–36
contract and standard contractual clauses 632, 633, 634, 635
controller and processor 28
processing under authority of 612, 614–15
criminal convictions and offences 385, 386–87, 388–89
Cybersecurity Act 643, 657
data portability 497–98, 505–6
data protection by design and by default 571, 573–74, 576
data protection impact assessment (DPIA) 631–32, 636
Directive 2002/58/EC 1298, 1299
disaster recovery plan 636
electronic communications 632–33
encryption 630, 636
EU legislation 632–33
identification, non-requirement of 394
information provision where personal data collected from data subject 421

1382　Index

security of processing (*cont.*)
　information provision where personal data not collected from data subject　440
　international instruments　633
　law enforcement cooperation　633
　lawfulness of processing　324, 342–43
　legal background　632–34
　legality principle　637
　legitimate interest　17–18
　material scope　60, 61, 63, 65–66, 69, 70
　monitoring approved codes of conduct　726
　national developments　633
　personal data breach　188
　personal data breach notification to supervisory authority　641, 645
　personal data processing　309–10, 311, 312
　processor　600, 602–3, 604, 607
　pseudonymisation　630, 636
　rationale and policy underpinnings　631–32
　records of processing activities　616, 620, 622, 623
　rectification　469
　related Articles in EPD　631
　related Articles in LED　631
　relevant recitals　630
　restoring availability and access in timely manner　630, 636
　restrictions　543–44, 553
　risks　26, 630, 631–33, 635, 636
　scope of security obligation　634–35
　Secretariat　1108, 1109
　special categories of personal data　19, 381–82
　subject-matter and objectives　55–56
　testing, assessment and evaluation　630, 636
　transfers: general principles　765
　transfers on basis of adequacy decision　772, 776, 780–81, 783, 787–88, 789
　transfers or disclosures not authorised by Union law　826–27
　transparent information　406
　see also personal data breach
security services　623
self-certification　781
self-incrimination, right against　628
sensitive data *see* special categories of personal data
service contract　241, 696
Service Level Agreement　605–6
singling out and treating differently　108–9, 110–11
Slovakia　676, 905, 968
Slovenia　614–15, 670
small and medium-sized enterprises (SMEs)
　administrative fines　1181
　certification　732, 735
　codes of conduct　716, 717–18, 721
　Committee procedure　1278
　derogations for specific situations　853–54
　enterprise　246, 247–48, 249, 251–52
　joint controllers　587
　monitoring approved codes of conduct　726, 728

　principles　20
　records of processing activities　624
　tasks of supervisory authority　929
　territorial scope　91
　see also multinational corporations (MNCs)
Snowden revelations (United States)　5, 34–35, 826–27, 834
SNS *see* social networks and social networking sites (SNS)
social networks and social networking sites (SNS)　360, 465, 499, 585, 586
　see also Facebook
social protection/social insurance　188, 332, 365, 367, 369, 524, 543–44, 842, 850
Software as a Service (SaaS)　584
Spain
　administrative fines　1186
　children's consent and information society services　358
　compensation, right to and liability　1169
　controller or processor, processing under authority of　614–15
　cooperation between lead supervisory authority and other authorities concerned　958
　designation of data protection officer (DPO)　695–96
　draft lists　676–77
　European Data Protection Board (EDPB)　1047–48
　information provision where personal data collected from data subject　421–22
　information provision where personal data not collected from data subject　441
　joint operations of supervisory authorities　988–89
　personal data breach　192–93
　personal data breach notification to supervisory authority　643
　representatives of controllers or processors not established in the Union　597
　supervisory authority　865, 870
　supervisory authority members, general conditions for　886, 891
　tasks of data protection officer (DPO)　710–11
　tasks of supervisory authority　933–34
special categories of personal data
　access, right of data subject　463
　accountability/responsibility of controller　555, 565
　analysis　373–82
　archiving purposes in the public interest, scientific or historical research purposes or statistical purposes　1243, 1245
　automated individual decision-making, including profiling　524–25, 527, 530, 537, 539–40
　biometric data　19, 20, 207, 214
　case law　368–69, 372–73
　churches and religious associations　1258, 1259
　closely related provisions　368
　communication of personal data breach to data subject　659

consent 175, 176–77, 178, 347–48, 349–50
 explicit 365, 366, 371, 376f, 377
 withdrawal 379–80
consultation of supervisory authority 30
courts acting in judicial capacity 365, 369
criminal convictions and offences 19, 20, 371, 375, 387, 388
data manifestly made public 378
data protection impact assessment (DPIA) 30, 667, 670, 674
defining special categories of personal data 373–74
derogations 366–67, 847
electoral activities and voter data 367, 379
employment, social security and social protection law 365, 367, 369, 377, 1230, 1233, 1235
encryption 371, 381–82
enforcement 382
EU legislation 370–71
exceptional cases 371
fingerprints 372
further rules affecting processing of special categories of personal data 382
genetic data and biometric data 19–20, 365, 366, 367, 369–70, 371–72, 374
health data and medical data 218–20, 365, 366, 367, 371–72, 373, 374
humanitarian purposes and humanitarian emergencies 379
international instruments 371
interpretation 374
lawfulness of processing 332
legal background 370–73
legal claims and judicial activities 365, 376f, 379
legal obligation of controller 376f
manifestly made public by data subject 365, 376f
national developments 372
national identification number 1224, 1227
not-for-profit organisation 365, 376f, 378
notification obligation regarding rectification, erasure or restriction of processing 494
opening clauses 369, 372
penalties 1196
photographs 366, 374
physically or legally incapable of giving consent 365, 377–78
preventive or occupational medicine 365
principles 19–20
processor 605
professional secrecy 365–66, 371, 379–80
public health 365, 366, 369, 376f, 379–80
public interest, substantial 365, 366, 367, 369, 376f, 379, 380, 382
rationale and policy underpinnings 369–70
rectification 472–73
related Articles in EPD 368
related Articles in EUDPR 368
related Articles in LED 368
relevant recitals 366–67

risk analysis 371
secrecy obligations 1253–54
specific data processing situations 41
training personnel 381–82
transfers on basis of adequacy decision 783, 788–89
vital interests 365, 376f, 377–78
specific data processing situations 40–41
standard contractual clauses *see* **contracts and standard contractual clauses**
standardised icons
 access, right of data subject 399, 400, 410–11
 automated individual decision-making, including profiling 523
 delegated acts 1268, 1269, 1270–71, 1272–73
 information provision where personal data collected from data subject 414
 information provision where personal data not collected from data subject 435
 tasks of the European Data Protection Board (EDPB) 1075, 1080
 transparent information 399, 400, 410–11
statistical purposes *see* **archiving purposes in the public interest, scientific or historical research purposes or statistical purposes**
stigma
 criminal convictions and offences 388
 genetic data 198, 199–200
 health data 218
 see also discrimination
storage of data
 codes of conduct 717
 data protection by design and by default 571, 577
 duration 413, 434
 identification, non-requirement of 392, 393
 information provision where personal data not collected from data subject 446–47
 lawfulness of processing 321, 322
 processing 117, 309, 311, 312, 318
 processor 599, 600, 603
 restrictions 551
 transfers on basis of adequacy decision 782
 see also retention of data and retention periods
sub-contracting 158
 see also third parties
sub-processors 623, 635
subject-matter and objectives of the GDPR
 analysis 53–58
 Article 1(1) in light of Article 16(2) TFEU 54–56
 Article 1(2) 56
 case law 50, 52–53
 closely related provisions 49
 consent of minors and minimum age 57–58
 cultural, religious and linguistic diversity 48, 57
 data protection and other fundamental rights 57
 effective remedy 48, 53, 57
 EU legislation 51
 fair trial, right to 48, 53, 57

subject-matter and objectives of the GDPR (*cont.*)
  free movement of personal data 48, 49, 52–53, 54–55, 56, 57–58
  freedom of expression and information 48, 50–51, 52, 57
  freedom from being monitored 57
  freedom of thought, conscience and religion 48, 57
  freedom to conduct a business 48, 57
  fundamental rights and freedoms 48, 50–51, 52, 53, 54, 55, 56–57
  GDPR as continuation of DPD 53–54
  international instruments 52
  legal background 51–53
  national developments 52
  police and judicial cooperation in criminal matters 55, 58
  privacy, fundamental right of 48, 50–51, 52, 53, 57
  protection of natural persons 48, 49
  protection of personal data 48
  public health 58
  rationale and policy underpinnings 51
  related Articles in LED 49
  relevant recitals 48–49
  territorial scope 58
subsequent incompatible processing 17
substantial effect test 277
sunset clause 33
supervisory authorities
  adequacy 33
  analysis 269–70, 867–71
  appropriate safeguards 33
  binding corporate rules (BCRs) 8, 34, 257, 259, 814–15, 816, 817*f*, 821
  case law 266, 268–69, 864, 867
  certification bodies 744, 747–48
  certification, seals and marks 31–32
  churches and religious associations 270
  closely related provisions 265, 864
  codes of conduct 31
  Commission notification 863
  communication of personal data breach to data subject 654–55, 656, 658, 659, 661, 662
  competence, tasks and roles 267, 863–64, 902
  complaints handling 270, 863–64, 865–66
    see also complaint, right to lodge with supervisory authority
  consent, conditions for 348
  consistency mechanism 37–39, 863, 866, 869–71
  control 864–65, 868
  controller and processor 29–30, 265
    processing under authority of 612
  cooperation 37, 863, 864, 865, 867, 869, 870, 871
    see also cooperation between lead supervisory authority and other authorities concerned; cooperation with supervisory authority
  cross-border processing 279, 280–81, 285–86
  data protection by design and by default 573, 577
  data protection impact assessment (DPIA) 665, 666–67, 669, 671–72, 676
  data subject 265
  definition 101
  derogations for specific situations 35, 853
  dual objectives, confirmation of 868
  effective judicial remedy *see* effective judicial remedy against supervisory authority
  enterprise 246
  equality 870, 922
  EU legislation 267, 865–66
  Europeanisation and strengthening role 867, 869
  federal states with more than one data protection authority (DPA) 863–70–
  free movement 270
  independence 267, 269, 863, 866, 867, 870
    see also independence; independence of supervisory authorities
  international cooperation 859–60
  international instruments 267–68, 866
  investigations 863–64
  joint controllers 582, 584
  joint operations *see* joint operations of supervisory authorities
  legal background 267–69, 865–67
  legislative procedure 8
  main establishment 225–26, 227–28, 233–34, 236
  monitoring 863, 864, 868
  national developments 268, 866
  national data protection authorities (DPAs) contributing to EU-wide protection 868–70
  one-stop shop mechanism 36–37
  powers *see* powers of supervisory authority
  prior consultation *see* prior consultation
  private bodies 265
  processor 265, 600, 603, 607, 609–10
  public authorities 265, 267–68, 269–70
  public awareness promotion 863–64
  rationale and policy underpinnings 266, 864–65
  records of processing activities 616–18, 624
  related Articles in EUDPR 266
  related Articles in LED 265, 864
  relevant and reasoned objection 288–89, 290
  relevant recitals 265, 863–64
  remedies, liability and sanctions 40
  representatives 238, 239, 242–43, 244
  representatives of controllers or processors not established in the Union 589, 594–96, 597
  responsibility of controller 560, 565–66
  risk-based approach 26
  taking action on request of another data protection authority (DPA) 37
  tasks *see* tasks of supervisory authority
  tasks of the European Data Protection Board (EDPB) 1080–81
  tasks of data protection officer (DPO) 714
  territorial scope 81–82, 86
  transfers on basis of adequacy decision 771, 785, 792

transfers or disclosures not authorised by Union
    law 34–35, 827
transfers subject to appropriate safeguards 797,
    808, 809
see also supervisory authority concerned;
    supervisory authority members, general
    conditions for
supervisory authority concerned
    analysis 275–78
    case law 273, 274–75
    closely related provisions 273
    complaint submission 272–73, 278
    controller 272–74, 275–76
    data subjects 272–73, 275, 276–77
    definition 101–2
    dispute resolution system 274
    EU legislation 274
    group of undertakings 272
    habitual residence 277
    international instruments 274
    legal background 274–75
    main establishment 272
    one-stop-shop mechanism 273–74, 276
    processor 272–74, 275–76
    rationale and policy underpinnings 273–74
    reference to in Article 52(5) 278
    relevant recitals 272–73
    single establishment 272–73
    stable arrangements 272
    substantial effect test 277
supervisory authority members, general conditions for
    analysis 887–91
    appointment of members 886, 888–89
    candidature, open call for 888
    case law 885, 887
    checks and balances 888
    closely related provisions 884
    dismissal and serious misconduct 884, 886,
        887, 890–91
    ending of duties, expiry of term of office,
        resignation, and compulsory retirement 884,
        886, 887, 890
    EU legislation 886
    expertise 887
    further safeguarding for independent, effective
        and accountable data protection authorities
        (DPAs) 887
    impartiality 885–86, 891
    independence 884, 885–86, 887, 890, 891
    integrity 884
    international instruments 886
    legal background 886–87
    national developments 886–87
    prior compliance 891
    public short list 888
    qualifications, experiences and skills 884, 886, 889
    rationale and policy underpinnings 885–86
    related Articles in EPD 885
    related Articles in EUDPR 885
    related Articles in LED 884–85
    relevant recitals 884
    staff chosen by supervisory authority 884
    transparency 884, 885–86, 888
suspension of proceedings
    administrative fines 1181
    analysis 1155–59
    approach to supervisory authority and directly to
        court 1157
    case law 1153, 1155
    closely related provisions 1153
    consolidation of proceedings 1157
    eligibility of cases for suspension or
        consolidation 1156–57
    EU legislation 1154
    identical cases (same subject matter) 1156
    international instruments 1154
    legal background 1154–55
    multiple procedures in several Member States 1157
    national developments 1155
    parallel appeals 1157
    powers of supervisory authority 939, 946–47
    preliminary ruling 1158
    proceedings in jurisdiction of court or habitual
        residence of data subject 1157
    rationale and policy underpinnings 1153–54
    relevant recitals 1153
    same subject-matter 1155–56
    similar or related cases 1156, 1157–58
    transfers on basis of adequacy decision 791
Sweden
    analysis 866
    compensation, right to and liability 1165
    data portability 499
    designation of data protection officer (DPO) 691
    enterprise 249
    health data 220
    independence 877
    joint operations of supervisory authorities 989
    national identification number 1225
    subject-matter and objectives 52
    supervisory authority 268, 866
    territorial scope 79
    transfers: general principles 758
Switzerland 129, 776, 1051

targeting 82–83, 88, 89–90
tasks of the European Data Protection Board (EDPB)
    accreditation of certification bodies 1070
    administrative fines 1069, 1077–78, 1079, 1080
    advice 1074–78
    advice and opinions on codes of conduct and
        certification 1078
    advice provided in writing 1076
    advice to Commission 1074–76
    advice to Commission on data protection
        issues 1069

1386　Index

tasks of the European Data Protection
　　Board (EDPB) (cont.)
　advice to Commission on formats and procedures
　　　for information exchange 1069
　advice to Commission on proposed
　　　amendments 1073
　advice to stakeholders, including guidelines,
　　　recommendations and best practice 1076–77
　advice to supervisory authorities 1077–78
　amendments 1078
　analysis 1074–81
　answering questions covering application of
　　　Regulation 1069
　assessment of adequacy of level of protection 1070
　best practices 1070
　binding corporate rules (BCRs) 1069, 1076, 1080
　binding decisions 1070
　case law 1072
　certification procedure 1070, 1075, 1080
　Chair 1071
　closely related provisions 1071
　codes of conduct 1070, 1080
　Commission 1071
　complaints-handling 1070–71, 1076, 1080
　consistency of interpretation and application of
　　　GDPR 1072
　consistency mechanism 1070, 1071, 1074, 1076,
　　　1080, 1081
　　opinions and binding decisions 1077–79
　consultation procedure 1070, 1075
　cooperation 1070, 1071, 1073, 1079
　data breaches and high risk 1076
　data transfers 1080
　decisions challenged before General Court 1079
　disagreement on draft decision 1078
　dispute resolution procedure 1071, 1074, 1078
　erasure of links, copies or replications 1069
　EU legislation 1073
　exchange of knowledge and documentation 1070
　extensions 1078
　future coordination tasks 1080–81
　guidelines, recommendations and best
　　　practices 1069, 1070–71, 1074
　head of supervisory authority 1071
　information exchange 1070
　informing Working Party of action taken 1073
　infringement 1071
　international data transfers 1075
　international instruments 1073–74
　joint opinion 1075–76
　legal background 1073–74
　legally binding decisions 1071, 1079
　links 1080
　maintenance of publicly accessible electronic
　　　register of decisions 1070
　monitoring and ensuring correct application of
　　　GDPR 1069, 1080
　opinion 1070, 1071, 1074, 1075
　opinion on certification requirements 1070
　opinion on codes of conduct 1073
　opinion on draft decisions of supervisory
　　　authorities 1070
　opinion on standardised icons 1070
　opinion to Commission 1073
　personal data breaches 1069
　personal data transfers 1069, 1076
　personnel exchanges 1070
　profiling 1069, 1076–77
　proposals or recommendations 1075
　protection, level of 1071
　public availability of consultation procedure 1077
　public register of certification mechanisms 1070
　questions covering application of national measures
　　　adopted 1073
　rationale and policy underpinnings 1072
　related Articles in EPD 1072
　related Articles in EUDPR 1072, 1081
　related Articles in LED 1072, 1080, 1081
　relevant recitals 1070–71
　reporting by natural persons of infringements 1069
　reviewing practical application of guidelines,
　　　recommendation and best practices 1069
　standardised icons 1075, 1080
　supervisory authority failure to follow
　　　procedure 1078
　third countries and international organisations 1074
　time limits and urgency of matters 1070, 1076
　training programmes 1070
　urgency procedure 1078
　without undue delay 1069
　Working Party opinions and
　　　recommendations 1073
tasks of the Chair of the European Data Protection
　　Board (EDPB)
　access to documents procedure 1100
　administrative and procedural tasks 1099
　agenda setting 1099
　analysis 1099–100
　closely related provisions 1098
　confirmatory application 1100
　consistency mechanism 1098, 1099
　convening meetings of the European Data
　　　Protection Board (EDPB) 1099
　deputy chairs 1099–100
　determination of reasonable period in which
　　　members may object to draft decisions 1099
　directing work of Secretariat 1099
　EU legislation 1098
　European Data Protection Board (EDPB),
　　　organisation of work of 1099
　initial application 1100
　international instruments 1098–99
　legal background 1098–99
　non-availability or incapacity 1100

notification of decisions adopted by the European
 Data Protection Board (EDPB) 1099
obligation to communicate activities of the
 European Data Protection Board (EDPB) to
 Commission 1099
organisation of Article 29 Working Party (WP29)
 meetings 1099
part-time capacity 1099–100
power to sign documents 1100
procedural tasks 1099
rationale and policy underpinnings 1098
representation of the European Data Protection
 Board (EDPB) 1099
right to request opinion of the European Data
 Protection Board (EDPB) 1099
role 1098
sending or receiving communications or
 information without undue delay by electronic
 means using standardised format 1099
substantive tasks 1099
tie-breaking power 1099
timely performance of tasks 1099
tasks of data protection officer (DPO)
 advice, provision of 709, 713*f*
 analysis 712–14
 appointing organisation tasks 712–14
 best practice for risk mitigation 709
 case law 710, 712
 closely related provisions 710
 compliance monitoring 709, 713*f*
 contact by data subject 714
 contact point for supervisory authority 709
 cooperation with supervisory authority 709
 data subject tasks 714
 EU legislation 711
 expert knowledge 709–10
 informing, advising and
  awareness-raising 709, 713*f*
 international instruments 711–12
 legal background 711–12
 national developments 712
 nature, scope, context and purpose of
  processing 709
 prior consultation 709
 rationale and policy underpinnings 710–11
 related Articles in EUDPR 710
 related Articles in LED 710
 relevant recitals 709–10
 risk assessment and identification 709
 tasks of supervisory authority 714
 see also data protection officer (DPO)
tasks of supervisory authority
 accountability 933–34, 936
 accreditation 928
 activity reports 932
 advisory powers 927, 928–29, 934–35
 analysis 932–37

authorisations 928–29, 936
awareness-raising 927, 929, 931, 933, 935
binding corporate rules (BCRs) 928, 936
case law 930, 932
certification 927, 932, 935, 936
characterisation of tasks 932–33
closely related provisions 929
codes of conduct 927, 928, 935, 936
complaints handling 927, 928–29,
 933–34, 935–36
consultation and engagement approach 934
control 933, 934
cooperation 927, 928, 930–31, 932–33, 937
corrective powers and sanctions 928–29
democracy, principle of 933
due diligence 932, 933, 936
duty to perform tasks 933–34
effectiveness principle 933–34
empowerment and Europeanisation 930–31
enforcement-related tasks 927, 928–29, 933,
 934, 937
EU legislation 931
free of charge 928, 936
independence 932, 933
information provision and sharing 927, 935, 937
international instruments 931
investigations, conducting 927, 928–29, 933, 934
investigative and corrective powers 934
judicial review 928–29
legal background 931–32
limitation, including a ban on processing 928–29
lists, maintenance of 927, 935
monitoring 927, 928–29, 933, 935
mutual assistance 927, 928, 929, 937
national developments 931
periodic review 927
pivotal provision 932
policy or leadership-oriented tasks 933, 934–35
prior judicial authorisation 928–29, 936
prioritisation 933, 934
privacy, fundamental right of 931, 932, 933
public awareness-raising 927, 928
public interest 928, 936
quasi-judicial functions 933, 935
rationale and policy underpinnings 930–31
reasonable fee 928
related Articles in EPD 930
related Articles in LED 929–30
relevant recitals 928–29
requests manifestly unfounded or
 excessive 928, 936
standard contractual clauses 927, 928, 936
strategic choices 934
tax or customs administrations 523, 548, 842,
 850, 1302
technical and organisational measures/standards 29,
 738, 1032, 1278, 1281, 1288

telecommunications sector
  competence of lead supervisory authority 918
  controller 146, 147
  data protection impact assessment (DPIA) 670
  Directive 2002/58/EC 1295–96
  European Data Protection Board (EDPB) 1046
  independence 1057, 1058–59
  material scope 69
  opinion of the European Data Protection Board (EDPB) 1007
  secrecy obligations 1254
  supervisory authority 870
Terms and Conditions of a service 350
territorial scope 12–13
  analysis 81–96
  applicable law 84–85
  application of GDPR outside EU 83–84
  Asia-Pacific privacy authorities 81, 82
  behavioural advertisement 91
  business-to-business (B2B) 91
  business-to-consumer (B2C) 91
  case law 75–76, 79–81
  CCTV 91
  citizenship, residence or other types of legal status of data subject 88
  closely related provisions 75
  controllers and processors 81–82, 83
    not established in the Union 88–91
  data processing agreement 86
  data protection officer (DPO) 86, 95–96
  data subjects in the Union 88–89
  dedicated addresses or phone numbers 90
  diplomatic mission or consular post 92–93, 94
  effects doctrine 93–94
  enforcement 95–96
  establishment 80
  EU legislation 77
  extraterritoriality 78
  geo-localisation activities 91
  Harvard Draft (1935) 93–94
  international clientele 90
  international instruments 78–79
  language or currency 81, 90
  layered approach 95–96
  legal background 77–81
  legal personality 85, 87
  lex causae 84–85
  mandatory nature of Article 3 and relation to other jurisdictional rules 82
  market surveys 91
  monitoring 90–91
  national developments 79
  national law applicability 77
  online tracking (cookies) 91
  prescriptive (legislative) jurisdiction 93
  privacy, fundamental right of 76, 78, 82, 85, 87, 89
  processing in context of activities of an establishment of controller or processor in EU 85–88

  public international law 92–95
  rationale and policy underpinnings 76–77
  related Articles in EPD 75
  relevant recitals 74–75
  scope 78–79
  search engine operator for internet referencing service 90
  small and medium-sized enterprises (SMEs) 91
  supervisory authority 81–82, 86
  targeting 82–83, 88, 89–90
  top-level domain name 90
  tourist activities 90
  travel instructions 90
  see also see jurisdiction; transfer of data to third countries or international organisations
terrorism and transnational crime 540, 783, 784, 826–27, 850–51
third countries or international organisations
  see **transfer of data to third countries or international organisations**
third parties
  access, right of data subject 409–10, 456, 457, 460–61, 462
  analysis 172
  certification 733, 737, 739
  certification bodies 745–46
  closely related provisions 170
  controllers 170
  data portability 505
  data subjects 170
  definition 100
  derogations for specific situations 849
  erasure ('right to be forgotten') 23, 477, 482–83
  EU legislation 171
  genetic data 198
  information provision where personal data collected from data subject 415, 417, 418, 423, 428
  information provision where personal data not collected from data subject 434, 436–37, 438–39, 440, 445–47
  international instruments 171
  joint controllers 584–85
  lawfulness of processing 323, 329, 334
  legal background 171
  legitimate interest 17–18, 170
  monitoring approved codes of conduct 730
  national developments 171
  notice obligations and privacy policies 22
  notification obligation regarding rectification, erasure or restriction of processing 493, 494
  object, right to 508, 509, 510–11, 512, 514, 515–16, 517
  official authority 170
  personal data breach 193
  personal data breach notification to supervisory authority 650
  processing 120
  processor 158, 159

Index

public interest 170
rationale and policy underpinnings 171
recipient 100, 163, 165, 166–67, 171
rectification 471
related Articles in EPD 171
related Articles in EUDPR 171
related Articles in LED 170
relevant recitals 170
representative 244
restriction of processing 490
restrictions 548
special categories of personal data 367, 380
transparent information and access rights 409–10
top-level domain name 90
tourist activities 90
trade secrets
    access, right of data subject 407, 450, 464
    automated individual decision-making, including profiling 523
    recipient 163–64
    transparent information 399–400, 407
trade sector 402–3, 807
traffic data 90, 418, 546, 548–49, 613
transfer of data to third countries or international organisations 32–35
    access, right of data subject 449, 462
    adequacy 32–33
    administrative fines 1181, 1191
    appropriate safeguards 33–34
    automated individual decision-making, including profiling 528
    binding corporate rules (BCRs) 32, 34, 257, 258–61
    certification 732, 739
    codes of conduct 716, 718, 721
    Commission reports 1308, 1309–10
    Committee procedure 1278, 1281, 1286
    communication of personal data breach to data subject 662
    competence of lead supervisory authority 919
    consent 176–77, 184, 347
    Court of Justice of the European Union (CJEU) 9
    derogations for specific situations 35,
    derogations for specific situations 841, 842, 844, 846, 847, 848, 849–50, 851, 854–55
    European Data Protection Board (EDPB) 1041
    freedom of expression and information 1202–3
    independence 876, 1055
    information exchange 1032
    information provision where personal data collected from data subject 413
    information provision where personal data not collected from data subject 434
    lawfulness of processing 323
    monitoring approved codes of conduct 726
    powers of supervisory authority 945
    processor 599, 607
    recipient 164

records of processing activities 616, 621–22, 623
reports 1085, 1087, 1088
specific data processing situations 41
territorial scope 79, 86
transfers: general principles 755, 759
transfers on basis of adequacy decision 771, 773
transfers or disclosures not authorised by Union law 34–35
see also international agreements concerning third countries or international organisations; international cooperation
transfers: general principles
    adequacy conditions/decisions 757–58, 759, 761–62, 764–66
    analysis 761–66
    case law 756, 761
    circumvention of the law, prevention against 757–58
    closely related provisions 756
    conflicts between data transfer mechanisms 764–65
    contracts and standard contractual clauses 763, 765
    derogations 766
    duties of processors 757
    enforcement 766
    essential equivalence 760
    EU legislation 758–59
    general principles 757
    international agreements/instruments 759–60
    international cooperation 766
    international data transfer (definition) 762–63
    international organisations 763–64
    legal background 758–61
    multilateral agreements 760
    national developments 760–61
    obligation to inform data subjects 757
    onward transfer 763–64, 765
    rationale and policy underpinnings 756–58
    related Articles in LED 756, 766
    relevant recitals 755
    two-step test 831–32
transfers on basis of adequacy decision
    academic expert reports 785
    analysis 784–92
    basic data protection concepts or principles 788
    binding corporate rules (BCRs) 815
    case law 774, 779–84
    closely related provisions 773
    commercial relations 776
    content and procedural principles 788
    cooperation mechanisms 772
    criteria for adequacy 787–89
    data transfer to third countries or international organisations 32–33
    defence 33
    delegated acts and implementing acts 42
    derogations for specific situations 773, 774, 781, 846

transfers on basis of adequacy decision (*cont.*)
  effective administrative and judicial redress 772
  effective and enforceable rights 772
  enforcement 788, 791–92
  essential equivalence 774–75, 777, 781, 782
  EU-Canada Passenger Name Records (PNR) agreement 782–84
  examination procedure 771–72
  international agreements 777–78
  international commitments and obligations 771
  international instruments 777–78
  international organisation 786–87
  issuance and negotiation of decision 784–85
  law enforcement 776, 780–81, 789
  legal background 775–84
  level of protection 773
  monitoring developments 771
  multilateral or regional systems 772–73
  national developments 779
  onward transfer 771, 787–88
  opposition 787–88
  periodic review 771, 773, 775, 781, 785, 790–91
  personal data flows 776
  police cooperation for criminal matters 782–83
  political factors 776, 785
  procedural and enforcement mechanisms 789
  procedures for adequacy decisions 784–86
  public order 772
  rationale and policy underpinnings 774–75
  related Articles in EPD 775–77
  related Articles in LED 773, 792
  relevant recitals 772–73
  repeal, amendment or suspension of decisions 771–72, 789–90
  revocation of decision 772
  rule of law 771
  Schrems ruling 779–82
  scope of adequacy decisions 786–87
  security 772, 776, 780–81, 783, 787–88, 789
  self-certification 781
  status of past decisions 791
  suspension of data flows 791
  territorial and sectoral application of decision 785
  terrorism and transnational crime 783, 784
  third countries and international organisations 771, 773
  transfers or disclosures not authorised by Union law 832–33
transfers of data
  codes of conduct 722
  processor 608, 610
  safeguards *see* transfers subject to appropriate safeguards
  tasks of the European Data Protection Board (EDPB) 1080
  to third countries *see* transfer of data to third countries or international organisations

unauthorised *see* transfers or disclosures not authorised by Union law
see also derogations for data transfers; transfers: general principles; transfers on basis of adequacy decision
transfers or disclosures not authorised by Union law
  analysis 830–36
  binding corporate rules (BCRs) 831–33
  blocking statutes 827–28, 830
  case law 825–26, 829–30
  closely related provisions 825
  consent, explicit 831–32
  consent, physical or legal incapability of giving 831–32
  controllers and processors not based in EU 832
  effects of Article 48 834
  enforcement 837
  EU legislation 828
  EU-US Privacy Shield 832–33
  EU-US Umbrella Agreement 832–33
  GDPR Interservice Draft 827
  international agreements 827, 829, 830, 834, 835
  judgment or decision 832
  legal background 828–30
  legal basis 831–32
  legal claims 831–32
  mutual legal assistance 825, 834–35
  mutual legal assistance treaties (MLATs) 829, 834
  national developments 829
  nature and purpose of Article 48 830–31
  protection, appropriate level of 834–35
  purpose 830–27
  rationale and policy underpinnings 826–27
  recognition and enforcement 833–34
  relationship to other grounds for transfer 835–33
  relevant recitals 825
  transfer of data to third countries or international organisations 34–35
  United Kingdom, application to 836
transfers subject to appropriate safeguards
  ad hoc contractual clauses 799, 801, 804–6
  adequacy decision 799, 802
  administrative arrangements, approval of 809
  administrative arrangements, provisions inserted into 808
  analysis 802–9
  appropriate safeguards, new forms of 806–8
  approved certification mechanisms 797, 804, 806, 807–8
  approved code of conduct 797, 804, 806
  binding corporate rules (BCRs) 797–98, 799, 801, 804–5
  case law 798, 802
  closely related provisions 798
  codes of conduct 807
  contractual clauses and standard data protection clauses 797–98, 799–800, 801–2, 804–6
  duties of processors 804

effective administrative or judicial redress 797–98, 809
enforcement 809
EU legislation 799–800
exceptional circumstances 803
general validity of codes of conduct 807
harmonisation 804
international instruments 800–1
legal background 799–802
legally binding and enforceable instruments 806
national developments 801
obligation to inform data subjects 804
other requirements 804
prior authorisations under DPD 804–5
provisions to be inserted into administrative arrangements 806
rationale and policy underpinnings 799
related Articles in LED 798, 809
relevant recitals 797–98
signature of clauses 805
status 802–3

translation services and language diversity 1036–37, 1038

transparency
access, right of data subject 449, 452–54, 455, 466
activity reports 950, 951–52
archiving purposes in the public interest, scientific or historical research purposes or statistical purposes 1243–44
certification 732, 733–34, 735, 736, 741
certification bodies 744, 745, 746, 748, 749, 750, 751
codes of conduct 723
communication of personal data breach to data subject 660, 661
confidentiality 1112, 1113
consent 183–84
consistency mechanism 996
data protection by design and by default 571
data protection impact assessment (DPIA) 669, 675
data subject rights 20–21
dispute resolution by the European Data Protection Board (EDPB) 1024
employment context 1229, 1230, 1232, 1234, 1237
establishment rules of supervisory authority 893–94, 899
European Data Protection Board (EDPB) 1042, 1044
impossibility or disproportionate effort exception 402
independence 873–74
lawfulness of processing 337–38
monitoring approved codes of conduct 727
notice obligations and privacy policies 22
notification obligation regarding rectification, erasure or restriction of processing 496
object, right to 399, 519

prior consultation 685
procedure 1092
processor 602
public access to official documents 1214, 1215–16, 1220
records of processing activities 618
rectification 469
reports 1086, 1087, 1088
responsibility of controller 561, 563, 564
restrictions 547
supervisory authority 870
supervisory authority members, general conditions for 884, 885–86, 888
transfers on basis of adequacy decision 785, 787–88
see also fairness and transparency; transparent information and access rights

transparent information and access rights
additional information to confirm identity 398, 399, 410
analysis 406–11
blocking 399, 402
case law 401, 404–6
certification mechanisms 400
children 398, 399, 407, 410–11
clear and plain language 398, 399, 406–7, 410–11
closely related provisions 400
confirmation obligations 402, 403
Court of Justice of the European Union (CJEU) 404–5
criminal offences and criminal penalties 403
erasure ('right to be forgotten') 399, 402
EU legislation 402–3
European Court of Human Rights (ECtHR) 405–6
exercise of information 401
facilitation of data subject rights 410
fair balance 404–5
fees 398, 403, 404, 408–9
form of information (writing, electronic means) 408
free of charge 398, 399, 408–9
international instruments 403
legal background 402–6
logic of processing 407
manifestly unfounded or excessive character of request 398, 408–9
national developments 404
official action and declared rule, congruence between 405
rationale and policy underpinnings 401–2
reasonable doubts concerning identity 398
rectification 399, 402, 403
related Articles in EPD 400
related Articles in LED 400
relevant recitals 399–400
retention duties 404–5
standardised icons and symbols 399, 400, 410–11

transparent information and access rights (*cont.*)
   time limits 403, 405, 406, 408, 409
   unidentified parties 409–10
   without constraint at reasonable intervals 402, 403
   without excessive delay or expense 402, 403, 404
   see also access to public documents; access, right of data subject

trilogue (Council, Commission and Parliament) 6, 7–8

trust
   certification bodies 745–46, 750–51
   data subjects, representation of 1150
   joint operations of supervisory authorities 988
   mutual assistance 976
   supervisory authority 870
   supervisory authority members, general conditions for 887

trust service providers 656–57

ubi lex non distinguit, nec nos distinguere debemus 438

UNCRC *see* United Nations Convention on the Rights of the Child (UNCRC)

undertakings *see* group of undertakings

UNESCO *see* United Nations Educational, Scientific and Cultural Organization (UNESCO)—International Declaration on Human Genetic Data

UNICEF *see* United Nations International Children's Emergency Fund (UNICEF)

United Kingdom (UK)
   access, right of data subject 456, 459–60, 461
   activity reports 951
   administrative fines 1186
   children's consent and information society services 358
   churches and religious associations 1264
   codes of conduct 718
   communication of personal data breach to data subject 658
   compensation, right to and liability 1169, 1173
   consent, conditions for 352
   controller 148
   controller or processor, processing under authority of 614–15
   data portability 499, 502
   data protection impact assessment (DPIA) 670
   genetic data 201
   information provision where personal data not collected from data subject 440–41, 443
   joint controllers 584
   joint operations of supervisory authorities 989
   object, right to 513
   penalties 1196
   personal data breach notification to supervisory authority 644
   processing 121
   representatives of controllers or processors not established in the Union 592
   transfers on basis of adequacy decision 786
   transfers or disclosures not authorised by Union law 836
   transfers subject to appropriate safeguards 803
   see also United Kingdom Withdrawal Agreement and Brexit

United Kingdom (UK) Withdrawal Agreement and Brexit
   binding corporate rules (BCRs) 822
   derogations for specific situations 847
   European Data Protection Board (EDPB) 1051
   Information Commissioner (ICO) 861, 961, 983, 990, 999
   lead supervisory authority 861, 961, 983, 990, 999
   opinion of the European Data Protection Board (EDPB) 1009
   territorial scope 83–84
   transfers: general principles 762
   transfers on basis of adequacy decision 787
   transfers subject to appropriate safeguards 803

United Nations Convention on the Rights of the Child (UNCRC) 357

United Nations Educational, Scientific and Cultural Organization (UNESCO)—International Declaration on Human Genetic Data 200

United Nations Guidelines for the Regulation of Computerized Personal Data Files 268

United Nations International Children's Emergency Fund (UNICEF) 358

United Nations Principles relating to the Status of National Institutions for the Promotion and Protection of Human Rights (1993) 881

United States (US)
   children's consent and information society services 360–61
   compensation, right to and liability 1164
   cross-border access to electronic evidence for judicial cooperation in criminal matters 828
   data portability 501
   GDPR Proposal 6–7
   information exchange 1037
   responsibility of controller/accountability 560, 563
   Snowden revelations 5, 34–35, 826–27
   supervisory authority 866
   tasks of data protection officer (DPO) 710–11
   territorial scope 76–77
   transfers: general principles 757, 759–60
   transfers on basis of adequacy decision 775–76
   transfers or disclosures not authorised by Union law 826, 828, 829–30, 835
   see also European Union-United States Privacy Shield; European Union-United States Safe Harbour Framework; European Union-United States Umbrella Agreement

unlawful processing
   compensation, right to and liability 1174, 1176
   erasure ('right to be forgotten') 475, 481
   processor 602

unsolicited communications 348

urgency procedure
  analysis 1029–31
  closely related provisions 1027–28
  consistency mechanism 1028, 1029
  consistency mechanism, derogation from 1027
  cooperation 1027, 1028, 1029
  EU legislation 1028–29
  exceptional circumstances 1027, 1028, 1030
  final measures 1027
  immediate and direct protection 1030
  international instruments 1029
  joint operations 1027, 1030
  legal background 1028–29
  legal effects 1027
  mutual assistance 1027, 1028–29, 1030
  national developments 1029
  procedure for adoption of decision by European Data Protection Board (EDPB) 1031
  protection of rights and freedoms 1027, 1030
  provisional, final or replacement measures 1027, 1030
  rationale and policy underpinnings 1028
  relevant recitals 1027
  simple majority vote 1027
  urgent need to act 1030
  validity period, specified 1027
  what to do, and against whom 1030
  when to act 1030
  who may act 1029
  whom to inform and how to request opinion 1030–31
Uruguay 776
US CLOUD Act 334–36, 339, 831–32, 850–51, 854
user profiles, creation of 355, 359, 522–23, 527

video surveillance 69, 339, 467
  employment context (processing) 1231–32, 1233–34, 1236, 1237

  erasure ('right to be forgotten') 482
  information to be provided where personal data collected from data subject 418–19, 425, 426
vital interests
  derogations for specific situations 841, 842, 844, 850, 852
  lawfulness of processing 334
  special categories of personal data 365, 376f, 377–78
  transfers: general principles 764
  transfers or disclosures not authorised by Union law 831–32
vulnerable individuals
  automated individual decision-making, including profiling 534–36
  competence 906
  data protection impact assessment (DPIA) 674, 676
  responsibility of controller 555
  see also children

W3C *see* World Wide Web Consortium (W3C)
warnings
  administrative fines 1182, 1187
  communication of personal data breach to data subject 662
  penalties 1194, 1196
  personal data breach notification to supervisory authority 650–51
whistleblowing 705, 826
work performance 522, 523, 555
Working Party *see* Article 29 Working Party (WP29)
working times records 1232
work agreements 1229
World Trade Organisation 306, 858
World Wide Web Consortium (W3C) 151

YouTube Kids 360